BASIC STANDARD DEDUCTION AMOUNTS

Filing Status	Standard Deduction Amount	
	1997	1998
Single	$4,150	$4,250
Married, filing jointly	6,900	7,100
Surviving spouse	6,900	7,100
Head of household	6,050	6,250
Married, filing separately	3,450	3,550

AMOUNT OF EACH ADDITIONAL STANDARD DEDUCTION

Filing Status	1997	1998
Single	$1,000	$1,050
Married, filing jointly	800	850
Surviving spouse	800	850
Head of household	1,000	1,050
Married, filing separately	800	850

PERSONAL AND DEPENDENCY EXEMPTION

1997	1998
$2,650	$2,700

INCOME TAX RATES—CORPORATIONS

Taxable Income	Tax Rate
Not over $50,000	15%
Over $50,000 but not over $75,000	25%
Over $75,000 but not over $100,000	34%
Over $100,000 but not over $335,000	39%*
Over $335,000 but not over $10,000,000	34%
Over $10,000,000 but not over $15,000,000	35%
Over $15,000,000 but not over $18,333,333	38%**
Over $18,333,333	35%

*Five percent of this rate represents a phase-out of the benefits of the lower tax rates on the first $75,000 of taxable income.

**Three percent of this rate represents a phase-out of the benefits of the lower tax rate (34% rather than 35%) on the first $10 million of taxable income.

Accounting Team Director: Richard Lindgren
Acquisitions Editor: Alex von Rosenberg
Developmental Editor: Esther Craig
Production Editor: Rebecca Glaab
Copyediting: Patricia A. Lewis
Production House: Peggy Williams with Texterity
Index: Catalyst Communication Arts
Cover Design: Matulionis Design
Internal Design: LightSource Images
Marketing Manager: Maureen L. Riopelle

TurboTax is a registered trademark of Intuit Inc.
Thomson World Class Learning is a trademark used hein under license.

Copyright © 1999
By West/South-Western College Publishing
Cincinnati, Ohio

ISBN: 0-538-88584-X

2 3 4 5 6 7 8 9 C5 6 5 4 3 2 1 0 9 8

Printed in the United States of America

Library of Congress Cataloging-in-Publication Data

Main entry under title:
West's Federal Taxation.
Includes index.
1. Income tax—United States—Law
I. Hoffman, William H.   III.   Willis, Eugene

ISBN 0-538-88584-X, 0-538-88925-X   77-54355

KF6335.H63   343'.73'04

5184

West's Federal Taxo

COMP
VO

1999 Ed

General Editors

Eugene Willis, Ph.D., C.P.A.   William H. Hoffman,

Dad M. Maloney, Ph.D., C.P.A.   William A. Raabe,

Contributing Authors

James H. Boyd
Ph.D., C.P.A.
Arizona State University

D. Larry Crumley
Ph.D., C.P.A.
Louisiana State University

Steven C. Dey
J.D., Ph.D., P.A.
Michigan State University

Mary Sueately
Ph.D., C.P.
Texas Tech University

William H. Hoffman, Jr.
J.D., Ph.D., C.P.A.
University of Houston

David M. Maloney
Ph.D., C.P.A.
University of Virginia

William A. Raabe
Ph.D., C.P.A.
Samford University

Boyd C. Randall
J.D., Ph.D.
Brigham Young University

W. Eugene Seago
J.D., Ph.D., C.P.A.
*Virginia Polytechnic Institute
and State University*

James E. Smith
Ph.D., C.P.A.
College of William and Mary

Eugene Willis
Ph.D., C.P.A.
*University of Illinois
at Urbana*

WEST/SOUTH-WESTERN College Publishing

An International Thomson Publishing Company

PREFACE

The publication of the 1999 Edition marks the twenty-second year of West's Federal Taxation (WFT). From a single text on Corporations, Partnerships, Estates and Trusts with accompanying solutions manual, the WFT series has grown to five major texts and a package of over 50 ancillaries. During this period, WFT has made every effort to improve the quality of the materials and has consistently added attractive innovations. With sales surpassing the one million level, WFT looks forward to continued success in the future.

The *Comprehensive Volume* is designed to provide flexibility for those who offer only one course in Federal taxation or for a two-course sequence. In cases where the *Comprehensive Volume* is used for only one course, a broad scope of coverage could be the ultimate objective. Although the income taxation of individuals may be stressed, it is conceivable that some may wish to devote significant classroom time to other areas of Federal taxation. For example, the allocation of course coverage might be structured as follows: 60 percent to the individual income tax (Chapters 1-15) and 40 percent to the tax treatment of corporations, partnerships, etc. (Chapters 16-28).

For those who encounter time constraints and/or want to emphasize some areas and not others, the last segment of the text (Chapters 16-28) possesses potential for selectivity. For example, an instructor who wants to cover corporations (Chapters 16-21) and tax practice (Chapter 25), but not the other subjects (Chapters 22-24 and 26-28), can proceed accordingly without disrupting the flow of the material. In this regard, the last segment of the text offers the flexibility for partial coverage through a number of different combinations (e.g., for a "light" coverage of corporations, select Chapters 16 through 18, but for a "heavy" concentration, assign Chapters 16-21).

RIA ONPOINT SYSTEM 4, STUDENT VERSION, CD-ROM

As a result of a partnership with RIA and West/South-Western College Publishing, this ultimate tax research tool is now available for student use. RIA OnPoint System 4, Student Version, offers an abbreviated version of this extensive and respected tax database. The OnPoint System 4, Student Version, offers detailed analysis and coherent explanation of the tax law by RIA's in-house experts, treatises written by renowned outside authors, primary source materials, practice aids and more!

RIA OnPoint lets you access a complete and fully integrated tax law database with accuracy, precision, and ease. This database includes:

- Over 600 watershed court cases and private letter rulings.
- The Federal Tax Coordinator.
- In-depth analysis, expert commentary and practical guidance for income, estate and gift tax, excises taxes, employment taxes, and U.S. taxation of foreign income.
- Internal Revenue Code, including complete legislative history since 1954.
- Treasury Regulations, including proposed regulations.
- Code arranged Committee Reports.
- Revenue Rulings, Procedures and Notices from 1954 to present, with he notes and Internal Revenue Code classifications.

- Full text of current year American Federal Tax Reports (AFTR) cases.
- Over 230 of the most frequently requested IRS publications.

This item can be shrinkwrapped with the text and used by students to conduct computerized tax research.

SPECIAL FEATURES

A variety of pedagogical devices is used to assist the student in the learning process. Each chapter begins with a statement of the learning objectives for the chapter. The learning objectives are followed by a topical outline of the material in the chapter. Page references appear in the outline to provide easy access to each topic. The readability of the material in the text is enhanced by the following.

- Including three levels of headings that aid in organization and presentation.
- Using bold print in the text to identify key terms the first time each term is used. Key terms are defined in the Glossary (Appendix C).
- Italicizing key words to emphasize their importance.
- Avoiding legal terminology except where it is beneficial.
- Using Concept Summaries to synthesize important concepts in chart or tabular form.
- Using Exhibits, Figures, and Tables to enhance presentations.
- Organizing material in lists with bullets rather than presenting it in lengthy sentences.
- Using examples frequently to help the student understand the tax concept being discussed.

When the *Comprehensive Volume* is used in whole (or in part) for a one-course tax offering, the pace of coverage of the subject matter may have to be accelerated. In recognition of this fact, we have followed certain guidelines.

- For those users who feel the need for some material on research methodology, the last chapter in the text, "Working with the Tax Law," is available. Along with the usual problem materials, this chapter also includes numerous research problems, arranged by chapter, dealing with the subject matter treated in the text. Instructors who emphasize research can assign Chapter 28 early in the course and then select from these problems as other chapters are covered. The Research Problems section heading includes a CD-ROM icon to emphasize that solutions to all the research problems can be prepared using the RIA OnPoint System 4 Student Version CD-Rom available with this text.
- Once knowledge of the tax law has been acquired, it needs to be used. The tax minimization process normally requires careful planning. Because we recognize the importance of planning procedures, most chapters include a separate section (called *Tax Planning Considerations*) illustrating the applications of such procedures to specific areas.
- The appendixes to the text contain a great deal of useful material. In addition to the usual Subject Index, the following items are included: Tax Rates and Tables (Appendix A); Tax Forms (Appendix B); Glossary of Tax Terms (Appendix C); Table of Code Sections Cited (Appendix D); and Comprehensive Tax Return Problems for 1997 (Appendix E).

ENHANCED PEDAGOGICAL PLAN

In the 1999 edition, we have continued to enhance the pedagogy to assist the student in the learning process and to address the recommendations of the Accounting Education Change Commission (AECC).

- *Learning Objectives*. Each chapter begins with student learning objectives for the chapter. These behavioral objectives provide the students with guidance in learning the key concepts and principles.
- *Chapter Outline*. The learning objectives are followed by a topical outline of the material in the chapter. Page references appear in the outline to provide the student with ready access to each topic.
- *Chapter Introductions*. The introductions link the material in the current chapter to previous chapters and demonstrate its relevance. Frequently, the chapter introduction includes a "real world" illustration to help convey the relevance of the material.
- *Margin Notes*. Each of the learning objectives appears in the margin where the related material is introduced and helps to guide the student through the chapter.
- *Tax in the News*. Tax in the News items appear in each chapter as a boxed feature to enliven the text discussion. These items are drawn from today's business and popular press and present current issues that are relevant to the chapter material.
- *Ethical Considerations*. Ethical Considerations features appear in each chapter, presenting thought-provoking issues related to the chapter topics. They also demonstrate that many issues do not have a single correct answer. The questions raised in the Ethical Considerations were selected to provoke discussion and provide opportunities for debate (oral communication) based on the student's value system. To assist the professor in providing guidance for discussion, material on the Ethical Considerations is included in the *Instructor's Guide with Lecture Notes*. This material identifies the issues raised in the Ethical Consideration, and where appropriate, recommends a solution or alternate solutions.
- *Key Terms*. Before the Problem Materials in each chapter is a list of key terms to assist student learning. When the key term is introduced in the chapter, it appears in bold print. The list of key terms includes page references to the chapter coverage. In addition, each key term is defined in the Glossary (Appendix C).
- *Communication Assignments*. In recognition of the increasing emphasis in accounting and tax education on communication, the Problem Materials include a written communication component. Selected Problems, Cumulative Problems, and Research Problems are identified as communication assignments with a "scroll" icon. These problems ask the student to prepare a tax client letter, a memorandum for the tax files, or other written materials. The discussion of the tax research process in Chapter 28 includes an illustration of a client letter and memo.
- *Issue Recognition Questions*. These problems are unstructured and open-ended. There is not enough information given in the problem to enable the student to develop a definitive answer. However, students are given enough information to identify the important tax questions. These problems, identified by a "lightbulb" icon, are designed to help students develop their *critical thinking skills*.
- *Decision-Making Problems*. The Problem Materials include decision-making problems that are designed to enhance the student's analytical skills. These problems are identified with a "balance" icon.
- *Internet Problems*. These problems are designed to acquaint students with the vast tax resources available on the World Wide Web. Internet problems are found in Chapter 28.

- *Team Projects: Arthur Andersen Tax Challenge Cases*. We indicate at the end of appropriate chapters which parts of selected Tax Challenge cases are related to material covered in the chapter. This will enable students to work on the cases throughout the semester rather than waiting until the end of the semester to prepare solutions.

SUPPLEMENTS

The WFT instructional package includes a wide variety of resources to enhance the educational experience.

- The Arthur Andersen Tax Challenge Cases, a set of four capstone cases and their solutions, are provided to the instructor for classroom use. These cases encompass both tax compliance and tax planning, and provide an opportunity for a team approach in solving tax issues and recommending tax strategies.
- The *Instructor's Guide with Lecture Notes* contains chapter outlines that can be used as lecture notes, as well as teaching aids and information not contained in the text. It also includes solutions to the research problems (Chapter 28 in the text) and the comprehensive tax return problems (Appendix E in the text). We also include additional synopses of many interesting and unusual court cases that can be used to illustrate technical points in the tax law. The lecture notes are also available on disk and on our Web site.
- A *Solutions Manual* that has been checked carefully to ensure accuracy. A matrix is included indicating topic coverage for each problem, which problems are new, modified, or unchanged in the current edition and the problem number for the unchanged and modified problems in the prior edition. The solutions are referenced to pages in the text. The *Solutions Manual* is also available on disk and on our Web site.
- A *Test Bank* provides a comprehensive set of examination questions and solutions. The answers to these are referenced to pages in the text. The questions are arranged in accordance with the sequence of the material in the chapter. To assist the professor in selecting questions for an examination, all questions are labeled by topical coverage in a matrix that also indicates which questions are new, modified, or unchanged in the new edition and the question number for the unchanged and modified questions in the prior edition. Approximately 20 percent of the questions in the 1999 edition are new or modified.
- ITP World Class Test™, a microcomputer test generation program for IBM PCs and compatibles and the Macintosh family of computers.
- Limited free use to qualified adopters of WESTLAW, a computer-assisted tax and legal research service that provides access to hundreds of valuable information sources.
- A *Student Study Guide* prepared by David M. Maloney, University of Virginia, and William A. Raabe, Samford University. This *Study Guide* includes a chapter review of key concepts and self-evaluation test questions with solutions that are referenced to the text.
- *Solutions Transparency Masters* for selected complex and cumulative problems, with a larger typeface for greater readability.
- *PowerPoint Presentation Software* allows qualified adopters to create interactive lectures and manipulate graphs, charts, and figures during in-class lectures. The package contains numerous slides per chapter consisting of alternate figures, outlines, and key points.
- *Teaching Transparency Acetates* contain the key charts and tables from the PowerPoint package for instructors who may wish to use traditional transparencies.

- *Arthur Andersen Tax Challenge: Cases and Solutions* is a separate manual that includes four of the Arthur Andersen Tax Challenge cases and their solutions. This manual is available to adopters with permission to copy the case for classroom use as Team Projects (found at the end of Problem Materials).
- *WFT Individual Practice Sets* prepared by Mark Nixon, Bentley College, and *WFT Corporation, S Corporation, and Partnership Practice Sets* 1998–99 edition, prepared by Donald Trippeer, Lehigh University. They are designed to cover most of the common forms that would be used by a tax practitioner for the average client.
- *West's Internal Revenue Code of 1986 and Treasury Regulations: Annotated and Selected: 1999 Edition* by James E. Smith, College of William and Mary. This provides the opportunity for the student to be exposed to the Code and the Regulations in a single-volume book, that also contains useful annotations.
- The WFT WEB SITE puts the most current information and supplements in the user's hands as soon as it is available. Adopters can log onto the web site (swcollege.com or wft.swcollege.com) and gain access to key information and supplements before they are available in print. The web site also includes extra problem material and quizzes, topical news items, the latest news of West's Federal Tax supplements and publications, and more.

TAX PREPARATION SOFTWARE

The trend toward increased use of the computer as an essential tool in tax practice continues to accelerate. To ensure that the *West's Federal Taxation* instructional package continues to set the pace in this important area, the following tax software product is available to be used with the 1999 edition:

- *TurboTax®* for Windows 97.01 by Intuit is a commercial tax preparation package. It enables students to prepare over 80 forms, schedules, and worksheets and automatically performs all mathematical calculations and data transfers. The *TurboTax* package, available for student purchase, includes the software bound with a workbook containing exercises and problems. The software runs on IBM PCs and compatibles.

This software product is powerful, easy to learn, and easy to use. We believe that tax education can be raised to a higher level through the use of computers and well-designed software. This software package takes the drudgery out of performing the complex computations involved in solving difficult tax problems. This allows students to concentrate on applying concepts and interpreting results.

To enable students to take advantage of this software product, the text contains numerous tax return problems. Problems that lend themselves to computerized solutions are identified by a computer symbol to the left of the problem number.

TAX FORMS COVERAGE

Although it is not our purpose to approach the presentation and discussion of taxation from the standpoint of preparation of tax returns, some orientation to forms is necessary. Because 1998 forms will not be available until later in the year, most tax return problems in this edition are written for tax year 1997. The 1997 problems may be solved manually, or many may be solved using the tax return preparation software (*TurboTax*) that may be purchased by students who use this text.

Appendix E contains comprehensive tax return problems written for tax year 1997. Each of these problems lends itself for use as a term project because of the sophistication required for satisfactory completion. Solutions to the problems in Appendix E are contained in the *Instructor's Guide with Lecture Notes*. For the reader's convenience, Appendix B contains a full reproduction of many of the 1997 tax forms frequently encountered in actual practice.

Most tax textbooks are published in the spring, long before tax forms for the year of publication are available from the government. We believe that students should be exposed to the most current tax forms. As a result, we write several new forms problems and provide adopters with reproducible copies of these problems, along with blank tax forms and solutions on the new forms. Shortly after the beginning of 1999, adopters will receive a *Forms Problems Supplement* containing these tax return problems, updated and solved on 1998 forms.

TAX LAW UPDATES

Since the original edition was issued in 1983, we have followed a policy of annually revising the text material to reflect statutory, judicial, and administrative changes in the Federal tax law and to correct any errors or other shortcomings.

We expect tax legislation to be enacted in 1998. In the event of *significant* tax law changes, we will provide a timely, complete, and easy-to-use supplement.

ACKNOWLEDGMENTS

As is the case with any literary undertaking, we welcome user comments. Please rest assured that any such comments will not be taken lightly and, we hope, will lead to improvements in later editions of *West's Federal Taxation: Comprehensive Volume*.

We are most appreciative of the many suggestions that we have received for revising the text, many of which have been incorporated in past editions and in the 1999 edition. We would especially like to thank Ellen Cook, University of Southwestern Louisiana, and Edsel Grams, University of Wisconsin–Eau Claire, for their detailed comments and suggestions. We would also like to thank those people who have painstakingly worked through all the problems and test questions and acted as problem checkers to ensure the accuracy of the book and ancillary package. They are Tracey A. Anderson, Indiana University at South Bend; Caroline K. Craig, Illinois State University; Frank Linton, University of Scranton; Mark B. Persellin, St. Mary's University; Debra L. Sanders, Washington State University; Randall K. Serrett, Fort Lewis College; Thomas Sternburg, University of Illinois; Donald Trippeer, Lehigh University, and Raymond F. Wacker, Southern Illinois University at Carbondale.

Finally, this 1999 Edition would not have been possible without the technical assistance of and the manuscript review by Bonnie Hoffman, CPA, and Freda Mulhall, CPA. We are indebted to them for their efforts.

Eugene Willis
William H. Hoffman, Jr.
David M. Maloney
William A. Raabe

April 1, 1998

About the Editors

Eugene Willis is the Arthur Andersen Alumni Professor of Accountancy at the University of Illinois (Urbana-Champaign). He joined the Illinois faculty in 1975 after receiving his Ph.D. from the University of Cincinnati. He serves as Head of the department. His articles have appeared in leading academic and professional journals, including the *Accounting Review, Journal of the American Taxation Association, The Journal of Accountancy,* and *The Journal of Taxation.* Professor Willis is co-director of the National Tax Education Program, a continuing education program co-sponsored by the American Institute of CPAs and the University of Illinois.

William H. Hoffman, Jr., earned B.A. and J.D. degrees from the University of Michigan and M.B.A. and Ph.D. degrees from The University of Texas. He is a licensed CPA and attorney in Texas. His teaching experience includes: The University of Texas (1957-1961), Louisiana State University (1961–1967), and the University of Houston (1967 to present). Professor Hoffman has addressed many tax institutes and conferences and has published extensively in academic and professional journals. His articles appear in *The Journal of Taxation, The Tax Adviser, Taxes—The Tax Magazine, The Journal of Accountancy, The Accounting Review,* and *Taxation for Accountants.*

David M. Maloney, Ph.D., CPA, completed his graduate work at the University of Illinois at Urbana-Champaign. He teaches courses in Federal taxation in the graduate and undergraduate programs at the University of Virginia's McIntire School of Commerce. Since joining the Virginia faculty in January 1984, Professor Maloney has been a recipient of major research grants from the Ernst & Young and Peat Marwick Foundations. In addition his work has been published in numerous professional journals, including *The Tax Adviser, Tax Notes, The Journal of Corporate Taxation, Accounting Horizons,* and *The Journal of Accountancy.* He is a member of several professional organizations, including the AICPA, the American Accounting Association, and the American Taxation Association.

William A. Raabe is a Professor in the Samford University School of Business. A graduate of Carroll College and the University of Illinois, Dr. Raabe's teaching and research interests include international and multistate taxation, technology in tax education, personal financial planning, and the economic impact of sports teams and fine arts groups. Dr. Raabe also is the author of *West's Federal Tax Research* and the *Multistate Corporate Tax Guide.* He coordinates the *West's Federal Taxation* material on West Publishing's Internet page, and he has written estate planning software used widely by tax professionals. Professor Raabe has been a visiting tax faculty member for a number of public accounting firms, bar associations, and CPA societies. He has received numerous teaching awards, including the Accounting Educator of the Year award from the Wisconsin Institute of CPAs.

CONTENTS IN BRIEF

CONTENTS

Contents

1

AN INTRODUCTION TO TAXATION AND UNDERSTANDING THE FEDERAL TAX LAW

LEARNING OBJECTIVES

After completing Chapter 1, you should be able to:

1. Understand some of the history, including trends, of the Federal income tax.

2. Explain some of the criteria for selecting a tax structure and understand the components of a tax structure.

3. Identify the different taxes imposed in the United States at the Federal, state, and local levels.

4. Understand the administration of the tax law including the audit process utilized by the IRS.

5. Appreciate some of the ethical guidelines involved in tax practice.

6. Recognize the economic, social, equity, and political considerations that justify various aspects of the tax law.

7. Describe the role played by the IRS and the courts in the evolution of the Federal tax system.

The primary objective of this chapter is to provide an overview of the Federal tax system. Among the topics discussed are the following:

- A brief history of the Federal income tax.
- The different types of taxes imposed at the Federal, state, and local levels.
- Some highlights of tax law administration.
- Tax concepts that help explain the reasons for various tax provisions.
- The influence that the Internal Revenue Service (IRS) and the courts have had in the evolution of current tax law.

Why does a text devoted primarily to the Federal individual income tax discuss state and local taxes? A simple illustration shows the importance of non-Federal taxes.

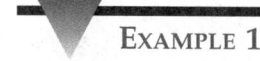

EXAMPLE 1

Rick is employed by Flamingo Corporation in San Antonio, Texas, at a salary of $54,000. Rick's employer offers him a chance to transfer to its New York City office at a salary of $60,000. Neither Texas nor San Antonio imposes an income tax, but New York State and New York City do. A quick computation indicates that the additional income taxes (Federal, state, and local) involved approximately $5,000. ▼

Although Rick must consider many nontax factors before he decides on a job change, he should also evaluate the tax climate. How do state and local taxes compare? In this case, what appears to be a $6,000 pay increase is only $1,000 when the additional income taxes of $5,000 are taken into account.

HISTORY OF U.S. TAXATION

EARLY PERIODS

1 LEARNING OBJECTIVE
Understand some of the history, including trends, of the Federal income tax.

The concept of an income tax can hardly be regarded as a newcomer to the Western Hemisphere. An income tax was first enacted in 1634 by the English colonists in the Massachusetts Bay Colony, but the Federal government did not adopt this form of taxation until 1861. In fact, both the Federal Union and the Confederate States of America used the income tax to raise funds to finance the Civil War. Although modest in its reach and characterized by broad exemptions and low rates, the income tax generated $376 million of revenue for the Federal government during the Civil War.

When the Civil War ended, the need for additional revenue disappeared, and the income tax was repealed. As was true before the war, the Federal government was able to finance its operations almost exclusively from customs duties (tariffs). It is interesting to note that the courts held that the Civil War income tax was not contrary to the Constitution.

When a new Federal income tax on individuals was enacted in 1894, its opponents were prepared to and did again challenge its constitutionality. The U.S. Constitution provided that "... No Capitation, or other direct, Tax shall be laid, unless in Proportion to the Census or Enumeration herein before directed to be taken." In *Pollock v. Farmers' Loan and Trust Co.*,[1] the U.S. Supreme Court found that the income tax was a direct tax that was unconstitutional because it was not apportioned among the states in proportion to their populations.

A Federal corporate income tax, enacted by Congress in 1909, fared better in the judicial system. The U.S. Supreme Court found this tax to be constitutional because it was treated as an excise tax.[2] In essence, it was a tax on the right to do business in the corporate form. As such, it was likened to a form of the franchise tax.[3] The corporate form of doing business had been developed in the late nineteenth century and was an unfamiliar concept to the framers of the U.S. Constitution. Since a corporation is an entity created under law, jurisdictions possess the right to tax its creation and operation. Using this rationale, many states still impose franchise taxes on corporations.

The ratification of the Sixteenth Amendment to the U.S. Constitution in 1913 sanctioned both the Federal individual and corporate income taxes and, as a consequence, neutralized the continuing effect of the *Pollock* decision.

REVENUE ACTS

Following ratification of the Sixteenth Amendment, Congress enacted the Revenue Act of 1913. Under this Act, the first Form 1040 was due on March 1, 1914. The law allowed various deductions and personal exemptions of $3,000 for a single individual and $4,000 for married taxpayers. Rates ranged from a low of 2 percent to a high of 6 percent. The 6 percent rate applied only to taxable income in excess of $500,000![4]

Various revenue acts were passed between 1913 and 1939. In 1939, all of these revenue laws were codified into the Internal Revenue Code of 1939. In 1954, a similar codification of the revenue law took place. The current law is entitled the Internal Revenue Code of 1986, which largely carries over the provisions of the 1954 Code. To date, the Code has been amended several times since 1986. This matter is discussed further in Chapter 28 under Origin of the Internal Revenue Code.

HISTORICAL TRENDS

The income tax has proved to be a major source of revenue for the Federal government. Figure 1–1, which contains a breakdown of the major revenue

---

[1]3 AFTR 2602, 15 S.Ct. 912 (USSC, 1895). See Chapter 28 for an explanation of the citations of judicial decisions.

[2]*Flint v. Stone Tracy Co.*, 3 AFTR 2834, 31 S.Ct. 342 (USSC, 1911).

[3]See the discussion of state franchise taxes later in the chapter.

[4]This should be contrasted with the highest current tax rate of 39.6%, which applies once taxable income exceeds $278,450.

▼ **FIGURE 1–1**
Federal Budget Receipts—1998

Individual income taxes	41%
Corporation income taxes	11
Social insurance taxes and contributions	33
Excise taxes	4
Borrowing	7
Other	4
	100%

sources,[5] demonstrates the importance of the income tax. *Estimated* income tax collections from individuals and corporations amount to 52 percent of the total receipts.

The need for revenues to finance the war effort during World War II converted the income tax into a *mass tax*. For example, in 1939, less than 6 percent of the U.S. population was subject to the Federal income tax. In 1945, over 74 percent of the population was subject to the Federal income tax.[6]

Certain changes in the income tax law are of particular significance in understanding the Federal income tax. In 1943, Congress passed the Current Tax Payment Act, which provided for the first pay-as-you-go tax system. A pay-as-you-go income tax system requires employers to withhold for taxes a specified portion of an employee's wages. Persons with income from other than wages must make periodic (e.g., quarterly) payments to the taxing authority (the Internal Revenue Service) for estimated taxes due for the year.

One trend that has caused considerable concern has been the increasing complexity of the Federal income tax laws. Often, under the name of tax reform, Congress has added to this complexity by frequently changing the tax laws. The recent enactment of the Taxpayer Relief Act (TRA) of 1997 continues this trend. Increasingly, this complexity forces many taxpayers to seek the assistance of tax professionals. At this time, therefore, substantial support exists for tax law simplification.

CRITERIA USED IN THE SELECTION OF A TAX STRUCTURE

2 ▼ **LEARNING OBJECTIVE**
Explain some of the criteria for selecting a tax structure and understand the components of a tax structure.

In the eighteenth century, Adam Smith identified the following *canons of taxation*, which are still considered when evaluating a particular tax structure:[7]

- *Equality*. Each taxpayer enjoys fair or equitable treatment by paying taxes in proportion to his or her income level. Ability to pay a tax is the measure of how equitably a tax is distributed among taxpayers.
- *Convenience*. Administrative simplicity has long been valued in formulating tax policy. If a tax is easily assessed and collected and its administrative

---

[5]Budget of the United States Government for Fiscal Year 1998, Office of Management and Budget (Washington, D.C.: U.S. Government Printing Office, 1997).

[6]Richard Goode, *The Individual Income Tax* (Washington, D.C.: The Brookings Institution, 1964), pp. 2–4.

[7]*The Wealth of Nations*, Book V, Chapter II, Part II (New York: Dutton, 1910).

costs are low, it should be favored. An advantage of the withholding (pay-as-you-go) system is its convenience for taxpayers.

- *Certainty.* A tax structure is *good* if the taxpayer can readily predict when, where, and how a tax will be levied. Individuals and businesses need to know the likely tax consequences of a particular type of transaction.
- *Economy.* A *good* tax system involves only nominal collection costs by the government and minimal compliance costs on the part of the taxpayer. Although the government's cost of collecting Federal taxes amounts to less than one-half of 1 percent of the revenue collected, the complexity of our current tax structure imposes substantial taxpayer compliance costs.

By these canons, the Federal income tax is a contentious product. *Equality* is present as long as one accepts ability to pay as an ingredient of this component. *Convenience* exists due to a heavy reliance on pay-as-you-go procedures. *Certainty* probably generates the greatest controversy. In one sense, certainty is present since a mass of administrative and judicial guidelines exists to aid in interpreting the tax law. In another sense, however, certainty does not exist since many questions remain unanswered and frequent changes in the tax law by Congress lessen stability. *Economy* is present if only the collection procedure of the IRS is considered. Economy is not present, however, if one focuses instead on taxpayer compliance efforts and costs.

THE TAX STRUCTURE

TAX BASE

A tax base is the amount to which the tax rate is applied. In the case of the Federal income tax, the tax base is *taxable income.* As noted later in the chapter (Figure 1–2), taxable income is gross income reduced by certain deductions (both business and personal).

TAX RATES

Tax rates are applied to the tax base to determine a taxpayer's liability. The tax rates may be proportional or progressive. A tax is *proportional* if the rate of tax remains constant for any given income level.

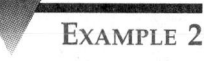
EXAMPLE 2

Bill has $10,000 of taxable income and pays a tax of $3,000, or 30%. Bob's taxable income is $50,000, and the tax on this amount is $15,000, or 30%. If this constant rate is applied throughout the rate structure, the tax is proportional. ▼

A tax is *progressive* if a higher rate of tax applies as the tax base increases. The Federal income tax, Federal gift and estate taxes, and most state income tax rate structures are progressive.

EXAMPLE 3

If Cora, a married individual filing jointly, has taxable income of $10,000, her tax for 1998 is $1,500 for an average tax rate of 15%. If, however, Cora's taxable income is $50,000, her tax will be $8,495 for an average tax rate of 16.99%. The tax is progressive since higher rates are applied to greater amounts of taxable income. ▼

INCIDENCE OF TAXATION

The degree to which various segments of society share the total tax burden is difficult to assess. Assumptions must be made concerning who absorbs the burden for paying the tax. For example, since dividend payments to shareholders are not deductible by a corporation and are generally taxable to shareholders, the same income is subject to a form of double taxation. Concern over double taxation is valid to the extent that corporations are *not* able to shift the corporate tax to the consumer through higher commodity prices. Many research studies have shown a high degree of shifting of the corporate income tax. When the corporate tax can be shifted, it becomes merely a consumption tax that is borne by the ultimate purchasers of goods.

The progressiveness of the U.S. Federal income tax rate structure for individuals has varied over the years. As late as 1986, for example, there were 15 rates, ranging from 0 to 50 percent. These later were reduced to two rates of 15 and 28 percent. Currently, there are five rates, ranging from 15 to 39.6 percent.

MAJOR TYPES OF TAXES

PROPERTY TAXES

3 LEARNING OBJECTIVE
Identify the different taxes imposed in the United States at the Federal, state, and local levels.

Normally referred to as **ad valorem taxes** because they are based on value, property taxes are a tax on wealth, or capital. In this regard, they have much in common with death taxes and gift taxes discussed later in the chapter. Although property taxes do not tax income, the income actually derived (or the potential for any income) may be relevant insofar as it affects the value of the property being taxed.

Property taxes fall into *two* categories: those imposed on realty and those imposed on personalty. Both have added importance since they usually generate a deduction for Federal income tax purposes (see Chapter 9).

Ad Valorem Taxes on Realty. Property taxes on realty are exclusively within the province of the states and their local political subdivisions (e.g., cities, counties, school districts). They represent a major source of revenue for *local* governments, but their importance at the *state* level has waned over the past few years. Some states, for example, have imposed freezes on the upper revaluations of residential housing.

How realty is defined can have an important bearing on which assets are subject to tax. This is especially true in jurisdictions that do not impose ad valorem taxes on personalty. Primarily a question of state property law, **realty** generally includes real estate and any capital improvements that are classified as fixtures. Simply stated, a *fixture* is something so permanently attached to the real estate that its removal will cause irreparable damage. A built-in bookcase might well be a fixture, whereas a movable bookcase would not be a fixture. Certain items such as electrical wiring and plumbing cease to be personalty when installed in a building and become realty.

The following are some of the characteristics of ad valorem taxes on realty:

- Property owned by the Federal government is exempt from tax. Similar immunity usually is extended to property owned by state and local governments and by certain charitable organizations.
- Some states provide for lower valuations on property dedicated to agricultural use or other special uses (e.g., wildlife sanctuaries).

- Some states partially exempt the homestead portion of property from taxation. Modern homestead laws normally protect some or all of a personal residence (including a farm or ranch) from the actions of creditors pursuing claims against the owner.
- Lower taxes may apply to a residence owned by an elderly taxpayer (e.g., age 65 and older).
- When non-income-producing property (e.g., a personal residence) is converted to income-producing property (e.g., a rental house), typically the appraised value increases.
- Some jurisdictions extend immunity from tax for a specified period of time (a *tax holiday*) to new or relocated businesses.

ETHICAL CONSIDERATIONS

Is Ownership Important?

Cynthia, a widow, dies at the age of 70. Andy, her son and sole heir, takes possession of the few assets she owned. He converts Cynthia's personal residence to a rental house and immediately leases it to an elderly couple.

The city and county are not aware of the ownership change and continue to send all tax notices to Cynthia. Since Andy pays these taxes, he sees no reason to have himself listed as the owner of the property. As long as the taxes are paid, what difference does it make who owns the property?

Comment on Andy's actions. Are his perceptions correct?

Unlike the ad valorem tax on personalty (see below), the tax on realty is difficult to avoid. Since real estate is impossible to hide, a high degree of taxpayer compliance is not surprising. The only avoidance possibility that is generally available is associated with the assessed value of the property. For this reason, the assessed value of the property—particularly, a value that is reassessed upward—may be subject to controversy and litigation.

Four methods are currently in use for assessing the value of real estate:

1. Actual purchase or construction price.
2. Contemporaneous sales prices or construction costs of comparable properties.
3. Cost of reproducing a building, less allowance for depreciation and obsolescence from the time of actual construction.
4. Capitalization of income from rental property.

Because all of these methods suffer faults and lead to inequities, a combination of two or more is not uncommon. For example, when real estate values and construction costs are rising, the use of actual purchase or construction price (method 1) places the purchaser of a new home at a definite disadvantage compared with an owner who acquired similar property years before. As another illustration, if the capitalization of income (method 4) is used for property subject to rent controls (e.g., New York City), the property may be undervalued.

The history of the ad valorem tax on realty has been marked by inconsistent application due to a lack of competent tax administration and definitive guidelines for assessment procedures. In recent years, however, some significant improvements have occurred. Some jurisdictions, for example, have computerized their

TAX IN THE NEWS

DOES BILL GATES HAVE A FANCY PAD, OR WHAT?

The county where Bill Gates built his new house assessed the value of the house at approximately $53 million, the cost of its construction. With this assessment, Gates pays annual ad valorem taxes of $600,000. Gates considered disputing the use of construction cost as the measure of value. He feels that because the house is unique, it would be difficult to sell. Consequently, he thinks the assessed value should be discounted for lack of marketability.

Incidentally, the residence is situated on a five-acre wooded lakefront tract near Seattle. The main manor has 40,000 square feet (with a separate, 1,700-square-foot guest house), a 60-foot pool, a sauna, two spas, a 20-seat theater, a reception hall for 100 people, an arcade, a boat dock for water skiing, and a library. Surely, Bill would have no difficulty finding a buyer for this property!

reassessment procedures so they will have an immediate effect on all property located within the jurisdiction. Nevertheless, the property tax area continues to be controversial.

Ad Valorem Taxes on Personalty.   **Personalty** can be defined as all assets that are not realty. It may be helpful to distinguish between the *classification* of an asset (realty or personalty) and the *use* to which it is put. Both realty and personalty can be either business use or personal use property. Examples include a residence (realty that is personal use), an office building (realty that is business use), surgical instruments (personalty that is business use), and regular wearing apparel (personalty that is personal use).[8]

Personalty can also be classified as tangible property or intangible property. For ad valorem tax purposes, intangible personalty includes stocks, bonds, and various other securities (e.g., bank shares).

The following generalizations may be made concerning the ad valorem taxes on personalty:

- Particularly with personalty devoted to personal use (e.g., jewelry, household furnishings), taxpayer compliance ranges from poor to zero. Some jurisdictions do not even attempt to enforce the tax on these items. For automobiles devoted to personal use, many jurisdictions have converted from value as the tax base to arbitrary license fees based on the weight of the vehicle. Some jurisdictions also consider the vehicle's age (e.g., automobiles six years or older are not subject to the ad valorem tax because they are presumed to have little, if any, value).
- For personalty devoted to business use (e.g., inventories, trucks, machinery, equipment), taxpayer compliance and enforcement procedures are measurably better.
- Which jurisdiction possesses the authority to tax movable personalty (e.g., railroad rolling stock) always has been and continues to be a troublesome issue.

---

[8]The distinction, important for ad valorem and for Federal income tax purposes, often becomes confused when personalty is referred to as "personal" property to distinguish it from "real" property. This designation does not give a complete picture of what is involved. The description "personal" residence, however, is clearer, since a residence can be identified as being realty. What is meant, in this case, is realty that is personal use property.

- A few states levy an ad valorem tax on intangibles such as stocks and bonds. Taxpayer compliance may be negligible if the state lacks means of verifying security transactions and ownership.

TRANSACTION TAXES

Transaction taxes, which characteristically are imposed at the manufacturer's, wholesaler's, or retailer's level, cover a wide range of transfers. Like many other types of taxes (e.g., income taxes, death taxes, and gift taxes), transaction taxes usually are not within the exclusive province of any level of taxing authority (Federal, state, local government). As the description implies, these levies place a tax on transfers of property and normally are determined by multiplying the value involved by a percentage rate.

Federal Excise Taxes. Long one of the mainstays of the Federal tax system, Federal **excise taxes** had declined in relative importance until recently. In recent years, Congress substantially increased the Federal excise taxes on such items as tobacco products, fuel and gasoline sales, telephone usage, and air travel. Other Federal excise taxes include the following:

- Manufacturers' excise taxes on trucks, trailers, tires, firearms, sporting equipment, coal, and the gas guzzler tax on automobiles.[9]
- Alcohol taxes.
- Luxury tax on automobiles. For 1998, the tax is 7 percent of the retail price in excess of $36,000 (adjusted each year for inflation). The tax originally was 10 percent and is scheduled to be phased out in yearly increments by year 2003.
- Miscellaneous taxes (e.g., the tax on wagering).

The list of transactions covered, although seemingly impressive, has diminished over the years. At one time, for example, there was a Federal excise tax on admission to amusement facilities (e.g., theaters) and on the sale of such items as leather goods, jewelry, furs, and cosmetics.

When reviewing the list of both Federal and state excise taxes, one should recognize the possibility that the tax laws may be trying to influence social behavior. For example, the gas guzzler tax is intended as an incentive for the automobile companies to build cars that are fuel efficient. Since many consider alcohol and tobacco to be harmful to a person's health, why not increase their cost by imposing excise taxes and thereby discourage their use? Unfortunately, the evidence of the level of correlation between the imposition of an excise tax and consumer behavior is mixed.

State Excise Taxes. Many state and local excise taxes parallel the Federal version. Thus, all states tax the sale of gasoline, liquor, and tobacco products; however, the rates vary significantly. For gasoline products, for example, compare the 39 cents per gallon imposed by the state of Connecticut with the 8 cents per gallon levied by the state of New York. For tobacco sales, contrast the 2.5 cents per pack of cigarettes in effect in Virginia with the $1.00 per pack applicable in Alaska. Given the latter situation, is it surprising that the smuggling of cigarettes for resale elsewhere is so widespread?

---

[9]The gas guzzler tax is imposed on the manufacturers of automobiles and progresses in amount as the mileage ratings per gallon of gas decrease.

Other excise taxes found at some state and local levels include those on admission to amusement facilities; hotel occupancy and the rental of various other facilities; and the sale of playing cards, oleomargarine products, and prepared foods. Most states impose a transaction tax on the transfer of property that requires the recording of documents (e.g., real estate sales).[10] Some extend the tax to the transfer of stocks and other securities.

General Sales Taxes. The distinction between an excise tax and a general **sales tax** is easy to make. One is restricted to a particular transaction (e.g., the 18.4 cents per gallon Federal excise tax on the sale of gasoline), while the other covers a multitude of transactions (e.g., a 5 percent tax on *all* retail sales). In actual practice, however, the distinction is not always that clear. Some state statutes exempt certain transactions from the application of the general sales taxes (e.g., sales of food to be consumed off the premises, sales of certain medicines and drugs). Also, it is not uncommon to find that rates vary depending on the commodity involved. Many states, for example, allow preferential rates for the sale of agricultural equipment or apply different rates (either higher or lower than the general rate) to the sale of automobiles. With many of these special exceptions and classifications of rates, a general sales tax can take on the appearance of a collection of individual excise taxes.

A **use tax** is an ad valorem tax, usually at the same rate as the sales tax, on the use, consumption, or storage of tangible property. The purpose of a use tax is to prevent the avoidance of a sales tax. Every state that imposes a general sales tax levied on the consumer also has a use tax. Alaska, Delaware, Montana, New Hampshire, and Oregon have neither tax.

EXAMPLE 4

Susan resides in a jurisdiction that imposes a 5% general sales tax but lives near a state that has no sales or use tax at all. Susan purchases an automobile for $10,000 from a dealer located in the neighboring state. Has she saved $500 in sales taxes? The state use tax is designed to pick up the difference between the tax paid in another jurisdiction and what would have been paid in the state in which Susan resides. ▼

The use tax is difficult to enforce for many purchases and is therefore often avoided. In some cases, for example, it may be worthwhile to make purchases through an out-of-state mail-order business. In spite of shipping costs, the avoidance of the local sales tax that otherwise might be incurred could make the price of such products as computer components cheaper. Some states are taking steps to curtail this loss of revenue. For items such as automobiles (refer to Example 4), the use tax probably will be collected when the purchaser registers the item in his or her home state.

Local general sales taxes, over and above those levied by the state, are common. It is not unusual to find taxpayers living in the same state but paying different general sales taxes due to the location of their residence.

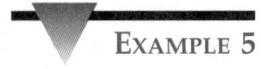
EXAMPLE 5

Pete and Sam both live in a state that has a general sales tax of 3%. Sam, however, resides in a city that imposes an additional general sales tax of 2%. Even though Pete and Sam live in the same state, one is subject to a rate of 3%, while the other pays a tax of 5%. ▼

---

[10]This type of tax has much in common with the stamp tax levied by Great Britain on the American colonies during the pre–Revolutionary War period in U.S. history.

Severance Taxes. **Severance taxes** are an important source of revenue for many states. These transaction taxes are based on the notion that the state has an interest in its natural resources (e.g., oil, gas, iron ore, coal). Therefore, a tax is imposed when the natural resources are extracted.

DEATH TAXES

A **death tax** is a tax on the right to transfer property or to receive property upon the death of the owner. Consequently, a death tax falls into the category of an excise tax. If the death tax is imposed on the right to pass property at death, it is classified as an **estate tax.** If it taxes the right to receive property from a decedent, it is termed an **inheritance tax.** As is typical of other types of excise taxes, the value of the property transferred provides the base for determining the amount of the death tax.

The Federal government imposes only an estate tax. State governments, however, levy inheritance taxes, estate taxes, or both.

EXAMPLE 6

At the time of her death, Wilma lived in a state that imposes an inheritance tax but not an estate tax. Mary, one of Wilma's heirs, lives in the same state. Wilma's estate is subject to the Federal estate tax, and Mary is subject to the state inheritance tax. ▼

The Federal Estate Tax. The Revenue Act of 1916 incorporated the estate tax into the tax law. Never designed to generate a large amount of revenue, the tax was originally intended to prevent large concentrations of wealth from being kept within a family for many generations. Whether this objective has been accomplished is debatable. Like the income tax, estate taxes can be reduced through various planning procedures.

The gross estate includes property the decedent owned at the time of death. It also includes life insurance proceeds when paid to the estate or when paid to a beneficiary other than the estate if the deceased-insured had any ownership rights in the policy. Quite simply, the gross estate represents property interests subject to Federal estate taxation.[11] All property included in the gross estate is valued as of the date of death or, if the alternate valuation date is elected, six months later.[12]

Deductions from the gross estate in arriving at the taxable estate include funeral and administration expenses, certain taxes, debts of the decedent, casualty losses[13] incurred during the administration of the estate, transfers to charitable organizations, and, in some cases, the marital deduction. The *marital deduction* is available for amounts actually passing to a surviving spouse (a widow or widower).

Once the taxable estate has been determined and certain taxable gifts have been added to it, the estate tax can be computed. From the amount derived from the appropriate tax rate schedules, various credits should be subtracted to arrive at the tax, if any, that is due.[14] Although many other credits are also available, probably the most significant is the *unified transfer tax credit*. The main reason for this credit is to eliminate or reduce the estate tax liability for modest estates. For 1998, the amount of the credit is $202,050. Based on the estate tax rates, the credit covers a tax base of $625,000.

---

[11]For further information on these matters, see Chapter 26.

[12]See the discussion of the alternate valuation date in Chapter 12.

[13]For a definition of casualty losses, see the Glossary of Tax Terms in Appendix C.

[14]For tax purposes, it is always crucial to appreciate the difference between a deduction and a credit. A *credit* is a dollar-for-dollar reduction of tax liability. A *deduction*, however, only benefits the taxpayer to the extent of his or her tax bracket. An estate in a 50% tax bracket, for example, would need $2 of deductions to prevent $1 of tax liability from developing. In contrast, $1 of credit neutralizes $1 of tax liability.

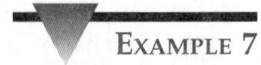

EXAMPLE 7

Ned made no taxable gifts before his death in 1998. If Ned's taxable estate amounts to $625,000 or less, no Federal estate tax is due because of the application of the unified transfer tax credit. Under the tax law, the estate tax on a taxable estate of $625,000 is $202,050. ▼

Because the effect of inflation was causing an increasing number of decedents to incur a Federal estate tax, the TRA of 1997 has scheduled further increases in the unified transfer tax credit. These are to be phased in over a period of years until the credit reaches $345,800 in 2006. This amount covers a taxable estate (or taxable gift) of $1 million.

State Death Taxes.   As noted earlier, states usually levy an inheritance tax, an estate tax, or both. The two forms of death taxes differ according to whether the tax is imposed on the heirs or on the estate.

Characteristically, an inheritance tax divides the heirs into classes based on their relationship to the decedent. The more closely related the heir, the lower the rates imposed and the greater the exemption allowed. Some states completely exempt from taxation amounts passing to a surviving spouse.

GIFT TAXES

Like a death tax, a **gift tax** is an excise tax levied on the right to transfer property. In this case, however, the tax is imposed on transfers made during the owner's life and not at death. Also, a gift tax applies only to transfers that are not supported by full and adequate consideration.

EXAMPLE 8

Carl sells property worth $20,000 to his daughter for $1,000. Although property worth $20,000 has been transferred, only $19,000 represents a gift, since this is the portion not supported by full and adequate consideration. ▼

The Federal Gift Tax.   First enacted in 1932, the Federal gift tax was intended to complement the estate tax. In the absence of a tax applicable to lifetime transfers by gift, it would be possible to avoid the estate tax and escape taxation entirely.

Only taxable gifts are subject to the gift tax. For this purpose, a taxable gift is measured by the fair market value of the property on the date of transfer less the *annual exclusion of $10,000 per donee* and, in some cases, less the *marital deduction*, which allows tax-free transfers between spouses. Each donor is allowed an annual exclusion of $10,000 for each donee.[15]

EXAMPLE 9

On December 31, 1997, Vera (a widow) gives $10,000 to each of her four married children, their spouses, and her eight grandchildren. On January 3, 1998, she repeats the same procedure. Due to the annual exclusion, Vera has not made a taxable gift, although she transferred $160,000 [$10,000 × 16 (number of donees)] in 1997 and $160,000 [$10,000 × 16 (number of donees)] in 1998 for a total of $320,000 ($160,000 + $160,000). ▼

---

[15]The purpose of the annual exclusion is to avoid the need to report and pay a tax on *modest* gifts. Without the exclusion, the IRS could face a real problem of taxpayer noncompliance. After 1998, the annual exclusion of $10,000 will be indexed for inflation.

ETHICAL
CONSIDERATIONS

The Annual Exclusion for Gifts

Arlene, a wealthy widow, would like to transfer $20,000 of cash to her son, Wilbur, in 1998 without exceeding the $10,000 per donee annual exclusion. To achieve this result, Arlene devises the following scheme: she gives $10,000 to Wilbur and $10,000 to her brother, George, who gives $10,000 to Wilbur.

Will Arlene's scheme succeed? What could go wrong?

A special election applicable to married persons allows one-half of the gift made by the donor-spouse to be treated as being made by the nondonor-spouse (*gift splitting*). This election to split the gifts of property made to third persons has the effect of increasing the number of annual exclusions available. Also, it allows the use of the nondonor-spouse's unified transfer tax credit and may lower the tax brackets that will apply.

The gift tax rate schedule is the same as that applicable to the estate tax. The schedule is commonly referred to as the *unified transfer tax schedule*.

The Federal gift tax is *cumulative* in effect. What this means is that the tax base for current taxable gifts includes past taxable gifts. Although a credit is allowed for prior gift taxes, the result of adding past taxable gifts to current taxable gifts is to force the donor into a higher tax bracket.[16] Like the Federal estate tax rates, the Federal gift tax rates are progressive (see Example 3 earlier in this chapter).

The unified transfer tax credit is available for all taxable gifts, and as with the Federal estate tax, the amount of this credit for 1998 is $202,050. There is, however, only one unified transfer tax credit, and it applies both to taxable gifts and to the Federal estate tax. In a manner of speaking, therefore, once the unified transfer tax credit has been exhausted for Federal gift tax purposes, it is no longer available to insulate a decedent from the Federal estate tax.

In summary, transfers by gift and transfers by death are subject to the unified transfer tax. The same rates and credits apply. Further, taxable gifts are added to the taxable estate in arriving at the tax base for applying the unified transfer tax at death.

State Gift Taxes.   The states currently imposing a state gift tax are Connecticut, Delaware, Louisiana, New York, North Carolina, and Tennessee. Most of the laws provide for lifetime exemptions and annual exclusions. Like the Federal gift tax, the state taxes are cumulative in effect. But unlike the Federal version, the amount of tax depends on the relationship between the donor and the donee. Like state inheritance taxes, larger exemptions and lower rates apply when the donor and donee are closely related to each other.

INCOME TAXES

Income taxes are levied by the Federal government, most states, and some local governments. The trend in recent years has been to place greater reliance on this method of taxation. This trend is not consistent with what is happening in other countries, and in this sense, our system of taxation is somewhat different.

---

[16]For further information on the Federal gift tax, see Chapter 26.

Income (broadly conceived)	$ xx,xxx
Less: Exclusions (income that is not subject to tax)	(x,xxx)
Gross income (income that is subject to tax)	$ xx,xxx
Less: Certain business deductions (usually referred to as deductions *for* adjusted gross income)	(x,xxx)
Adjusted gross income	$ xx,xxx
Less: The greater of certain personal and employee deductions (usually referred to as *itemized deductions*) or The standard deduction (including any additional standard deduction) and	(x,xxx)
Less: Personal and dependency exemptions	(x,xxx)
Taxable income	$ xx,xxx
Tax on taxable income (see Tax Rate Schedules in Appendix A)	$ x,xxx
Less: Tax credits (including Federal income tax withheld and other prepayments of Federal income taxes)	(xxx)
Tax due (or refund)	$ xxx

Income taxes generally are imposed on individuals, corporations, and certain fiduciaries (estates and trusts). Most jurisdictions attempt to assure the collection of income taxes by requiring certain pay-as-you-go procedures (e.g., withholding requirements for employees and estimated tax prepayments for other taxpayers).

Federal Income Taxes.   Chapters 2 through 14 deal with the application of the Federal income tax to individuals. The procedure for determining the Federal income tax applicable to individuals is summarized in Figure 1–2.

The application of the Federal corporate income tax does not require the computation of adjusted gross income (AGI) and does not provide for the standard deduction and personal and dependency exemptions. All allowable deductions of a corporation fall into the business-expense category. In effect, therefore, the taxable income of a corporation is the difference between gross income (net of exclusions) and deductions. Chapters 16 through 20 cover the rules relating to corporations.

State Income Taxes.   All but the following states impose an income tax on individuals: Alaska, Florida, Nevada, South Dakota, Texas, Washington, and Wyoming.

Some of the characteristics of state income taxes are summarized as follows:

- With few exceptions, all states require some form of withholding procedures.
- Most states use as the tax base the income determination made for Federal income tax purposes.
- A minority of states go even further and impose a flat rate upon AGI as computed for Federal income tax purposes. Several apply a rate to the Federal income tax liability. This is often referred to as the piggyback approach to state income taxation. Although the term *piggyback* does not lend itself to precise definition, in this context, it means making use, for state income tax purposes, of what was done for Federal income tax purposes.

TAX IN THE NEWS

VISITORS BEWARE! THE CITY AND STATE YOU VISIT MAY NOT BE ALL THAT FRIENDLY

Even if you are not a resident, you may be subject to local and state income taxes if you earn money in that jurisdiction. Besides the nonresident who commutes (e.g., a taxpayer who lives in Connecticut but works full-time in New York City), taxpayers who perform services on an itinerant basis may be vulnerable. For example, the Dallas Cowboys are subject to the city of Philadelphia income tax every time they are hosted by the Eagles. This must be particularly distressing to Troy Aikman, who lives in a city (Dallas) and a state (Texas) that do not have an income tax.

Although these situations are commonly referred to as the application of the "jock tax," other persons besides professional athletes get hit. Particularly susceptible are entertainers, doctors, lawyers, lecturers, and anyone who generates large fees and has a high profile. Ordinary professionals are not targeted because the amount of taxes involved would not justify the collection effort.

Is it any wonder that Las Vegas, which has no city or state income tax, is such a popular place to perform highly paid services (e.g., entertainment, prize fighting)?

- Because of the tie-in to the Federal return, the state may be notified of any changes made by the IRS upon audit of a Federal return.
- Most states allow a deduction for personal and dependency exemptions. Some states substitute a tax credit for a deduction.
- A diminishing minority of states allow a deduction for Federal income taxes.
- Most states allow their residents some form of tax credit for income taxes paid to other states.
- The due date for filing generally is the same as for the Federal income tax (the fifteenth day of the fourth month following the close of the tax year).

Nearly all states have an income tax applicable to corporations. It is difficult to determine those that do not because a state franchise tax sometimes is based in part on the income earned by the corporation.[17]

Local Income Taxes.   Cities imposing an income tax include, but are not limited to, Baltimore, Cincinnati, Cleveland, Detroit, Kansas City (Mo.), New York, Philadelphia, and St. Louis. The application of a city income tax is not limited to local residents.

EMPLOYMENT TAXES

Classification as an employee usually leads to the imposition of **employment taxes** and to the requirement that the employer withhold specified amounts for income taxes. The material that follows concentrates on the two major employment taxes: FICA (Federal Insurance Contributions Act—commonly referred to as the Social Security tax)—and FUTA (Federal Unemployment Tax Act). Both taxes can be justified by social and public welfare considerations: FICA offers some

---

[17]See the discussion of franchise taxes later in the chapter.

measure of retirement security, and FUTA provides a modest source of income in the event of loss of employment.

Employment taxes come into play only if two conditions are satisfied. First, is the individual involved an *employee* (as opposed to *self-employed*)? The differences between an employee and a self-employed person are discussed in Chapter 8.[18] Second, if the individual involved is an employee, is he or she covered under FICA or FUTA or both?

FICA Taxes.   The **FICA tax** rates and wage base have steadily increased over the years. It is difficult to imagine that the initial rate in 1937 was only 1 percent of the first $3,000 of covered wages. Thus, the maximum tax due was only $30!

Currently, the FICA tax has two components: Social Security tax (old age, survivors, and disability insurance) *and* Medicare tax (hospital insurance). The Social Security tax rate is 6.2 percent for 1997 and 1998, and the Medicare tax rate is 1.45 percent for these years. The base amount for Social Security is $65,400 for 1997 and $68,400 for 1998.[19] There is no limit on the base amount for the Medicare tax. The employer must match the employee's portion for both the Social Security tax and the Medicare tax.

A spouse employed by another spouse is subject to FICA. However, children under the age of 18 who are employed in a parent's trade or business are exempted.

FUTA Taxes.   The purpose of the **FUTA tax** is to provide funds that the states can use to administer unemployment benefits. This leads to the somewhat unusual situation of one tax being handled by both Federal and state governments. The end result of such joint administration is to compel the employer to observe a double set of rules. Thus, state and Federal returns must be filed and payments made to both governmental units.

In 1998, FUTA applies at a rate of 6.2 percent on the first $7,000 of covered wages paid during the year to each employee. The Federal government allows a credit for FUTA paid (or allowed under a merit rating system) to the state. The credit cannot exceed 5.4 percent of the covered wages. Thus, the amount required to be paid to the IRS could be as low as 0.8 percent (6.2% − 5.4%).

States follow a policy of reducing the unemployment tax on employers who experience stable employment. Thus, an employer with little or no employee turnover might find that the state rate drops to as low as 0.1 percent or, in some states, even to zero. The reason for the merit rating credit is that the state has to pay fewer unemployment benefits when employment is steady.

FUTA differs from FICA in the sense that the incidence of taxation falls entirely upon the employer. A few states, however, levy a special tax on employees to provide either disability benefits or supplemental unemployment compensation, or both.

OTHER U.S. TAXES

To complete the overview of the U.S. tax system, some missing links need to be covered that do not fit into the classifications discussed elsewhere in this chapter.

---

[18]See also Circular E, Employer's Tax Guide, issued by the IRS as Publication 15.

[19]The base amount is adjusted annually.

Federal Customs Duties.   One tax that has not yet been mentioned is the tariff on certain imported goods.[20] Generally referred to as customs duties or levies, this tax, together with selective excise taxes, provided most of the revenues needed by the Federal government during the nineteenth century. In view of present times, it is remarkable to note that tariffs and excise taxes alone paid off the national debt in 1835 and enabled the U.S. Treasury to pay a surplus of $28 million to the states.

In recent years, tariffs have served the nation more as an instrument for carrying out protectionist policies than as a means of generating revenue. Thus, a particular U.S. industry might be saved from economic disaster, so the argument goes, by placing customs duties on the importation of foreign goods that can be sold at lower prices. Protectionists contend that the tariff therefore neutralizes the competitive edge held by the producer of the foreign goods.[21]

Protectionist policies seem more appropriate for less-developed countries whose industrial capacity has not yet matured. In a world where a developed country should have everything to gain by encouraging international free trade, such policies may be of dubious value. History shows that tariffs often lead to retaliatory action on the part of the nation or nations affected.

Miscellaneous State and Local Taxes.   Most states impose a franchise tax on corporations. Basically, a **franchise tax** is levied on the right to do business in the state. The base used for the determination of the tax varies from state to state. Although corporate income considerations may come into play, this tax most often is based on the capitalization of the corporation (either with or without certain long-term indebtedness).

Closely akin to the franchise tax are **occupational taxes** applicable to various trades or businesses, such as a liquor store license, a taxicab permit, or a fee to practice a profession such as law, medicine, or accounting. Most of these are not significant revenue producers and fall more into the category of licenses than taxes. The revenue derived is used to defray the cost incurred by the jurisdiction in regulating the business or profession in the interest of the public good.

PROPOSED U.S. TAXES

Considerable dissatisfaction with the U.S. Federal income tax has led to several recent proposals that, to say the least, are rather drastic in nature. One proposal would retain the income tax but with substantial change. Two other proposals would replace the Federal income tax with an entirely different system of taxation.

The Flat Tax.   Representative Dick Armey (R, Texas) has proposed a **flat tax** that would replace the current graduated income tax with one rate, 17 percent. Large personal exemptions (e.g., approximately $30,000 for a family of four) would allow many low- and middle-income taxpayers to pay no tax. All other deductions would be eliminated, and no tax would be imposed on income from investments.

Various other versions of the flat tax have been suggested that would retain selected deductions (e.g., interest on home mortgages and charitable contributions) and not exclude all investment income from taxation.

---

[20]Less-developed countries that rely principally on one or more major commodities (e.g., oil, coffee) are prone to favor *export* duties as well.

[21]The North American Free Trade Agreement (NAFTA), enacted in 1993, substantially reduced the tariffs on trade between Canada, Mexico, and the United States. The General Agreement on Tariffs and Trade (GATT) legislation enacted in 1994 also reduced tariffs on selected commodities among 124 signatory nations.

The major advantage of the flat tax is its simplicity. Everyone agrees that the current Federal income tax is unnecessarily complex. Consequently, compliance costs are disproportionately high.

Value Added Tax.   The **value added tax (VAT)** is one of two proposals that would replace the Federal income tax. Under the VAT, a business would pay the tax (approximately 17 percent) on all of the materials and services required to manufacture its product. In effect, the VAT taxes the increment in value as goods move through production and manufacturing stages to the marketplace. Moreover, the VAT paid by the producer will be reflected in the selling price of the goods. Thus, the VAT is a tax on consumption.

Several other countries (e.g., European Union countries) use the VAT either as a supplement to or a replacement for an income tax.

Sales Tax.   A **national sales tax** is favored by Representative Bill Archer (R, Texas), who is the current chairman of the House Ways and Means Committee. This tax differs from a VAT in that it would be collected on the final sale of goods and services. Consequently, it is collected from the consumer and not from businesses that add value to the product. Like the VAT, the national sales tax is intended to replace the Federal income tax.

Critics contend that consumption taxes (both a VAT and a national sales tax) impose more of a burden on low-income taxpayers because they must spend larger proportions of their incomes on essential purchases. Representative Archer's proposal would attempt to remedy this inequity by granting some sort of credit or exemption to low-income taxpayers.

Tax Administration

INTERNAL REVENUE SERVICE

4   Learning Objective
Understand the administration of the tax law including the audit process utilized by the IRS.

The responsibility for administering the Federal tax laws rests with the Treasury Department. Administratively, the IRS is part of the Department of the Treasury and is responsible for enforcing the tax laws. The Commissioner of Internal Revenue is appointed by the President and is responsible for establishing policy and supervising the activities of the entire IRS organization.

The field organization of the IRS includes the following:

- Service Centers (10) that are primarily responsible for processing tax returns, including the selection of returns for audit. The Service Center having proper jurisdiction is where taxpayers must file their Federal tax returns.
- District Directors (33) who are responsible for audits and for the collection of delinquent taxes. Some states have no District Director (e.g., Idaho, Wyoming) while others have more than one (e.g., California, New York).

THE AUDIT PROCESS

Selection of Returns for Audit.   Due to budgetary limitations, only a small minority of returns are audited. For the fiscal year ending September 30, 1996, for example, the IRS audited only 1.63 percent of the total returns.

The IRS utilizes mathematical formulas and statistical sampling techniques to select tax returns that are most likely to contain errors and to yield substantial amounts of additional tax revenues upon audit.

Though the IRS does not openly disclose all of its audit selection techniques, the following observations may be made concerning the probability of selection for audit:

- Certain groups of taxpayers are subject to audit much more frequently than others. These groups include individuals with gross income in excess of $50,000, self-employed individuals with substantial business income and deductions, and taxpayers with prior tax deficiencies. Also vulnerable are cash businesses (e.g., cafes and small service businesses) where the potential for tax avoidance is high.

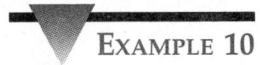

EXAMPLE 10

Jack owns and operates a liquor store on a cash-and-carry basis. Since all of Jack's sales are for cash, he might well be a prime candidate for an audit by the IRS. Cash transactions are easier to conceal than those made on credit. ▼

- If information returns (e.g., Form 1099, Form W–2) are not in substantial agreement with reported income, an audit can be anticipated.
- If an individual's itemized deductions are in excess of norms established for various income levels, the probability of an audit is increased.
- Filing of a refund claim by the taxpayer may prompt an audit of the return.
- Certain returns are selected on a random sampling basis under the Taxpayer Compliance Measurement Program (TCMP). The TCMP is used to develop, update, and improve the mathematical formulas and statistical sampling techniques used by the IRS. For the present, the TCMP has been suspended due to a lack of congressional funding.
- Information obtained from other sources (e.g., informants, news items) may lead to an audit. The tax law permits the IRS to pay rewards to persons who provide information that leads to the detection and punishment of those who violate the tax laws. The rewards may not exceed 15 percent (formerly 10 percent) of the taxes, fines, and penalties recovered as a result of such information.

EXAMPLE 11

After 15 years of service, Rita is discharged by her employer, Dr. Smith. Shortly thereafter, the IRS receives an anonymous letter informing it that Dr. Smith keeps two separate sets of books, one of which substantially understates his cash receipts. ▼

EXAMPLE 12

During a divorce proceeding, it is revealed that Leo, a public official, kept large amounts of cash in a shoe box at home. This information is widely disseminated by the news media and comes to the attention of the IRS. Needless to say, the IRS would be interested in knowing whether these funds originated from a taxable source and, if so, whether they were reported on Leo's income tax returns. ▼

Types of Audits.   Once a return is selected for audit, the taxpayer is notified accordingly. If the issue involved is minor, the matter often can be resolved simply by correspondence (a **correspondence audit**) between the IRS and the taxpayer.

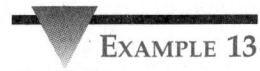

EXAMPLE 13

During 1996, Janet received dividend income from Green Corporation. In early 1997, Green Corporation reported the payment on Form 1099–DIV (an information return for reporting dividend payments), the original being sent to the IRS and a copy to Janet. When preparing her income tax return for 1996, Janet apparently overlooked this particular Form 1099–DIV and failed to include the dividend on Schedule B, Interest and Dividend Income, of Form 1040. In 1998, the IRS sends a notice to Janet calling her attention to the omission and requesting a remittance for additional tax, interest, and penalty. Janet promptly mails a check to the IRS for the requested amount, and the matter is closed. ▼

TAX IN THE NEWS

THE "SNITCH FEE": SOME MISCONCEPTIONS AND PITFALLS

Although the IRS does pay a 10 percent informant fee, this fee is not awarded automatically. To be eligible, the snitcher must furnish evidence that actually leads to the collection of delinquent taxes. Even if this occurs, moreover, the reward need not be a full 10 percent of the amount collected. After the first $75,000 collected, the 10 percent rate is reduced to 5 percent for the next $25,000 and 1 percent for further amounts. In no event, may the reward paid exceed $100,000. Most tips are not specific enough to generate a reward. In 1996, for example, only 650 of the 9,350 informants qualified, and the average payout was just $5,431.

On occasion, a tip can hurt the tipster. This result is particularly likely when a tipster seeks revenge on an ex-spouse. Suppose, for example, an ex-wife tells the IRS about an income tax return filed by her ex-husband. Were they married during the period involved? If so, did they file a joint return that the informant signed? In this case and by virtue of the joint and several liability, the informant could also be vulnerable for any taxes evaded.

Equally adverse, a conviction of the ex-spouse for tax fraud could lead to loss of earning power and cut off (or reduce) future alimony and child support payments.

[Note: A recent change has increased the maximum rate to 15 percent.]

SOURCE: Adapted from J. Novack, "Boomerang!" *Forbes*, July 7, 1997, pp. 42, 43.

Other examinations are generally classified as either office audits or field audits. An **office audit** usually is restricted in scope and is conducted in the facilities of the IRS. In contrast, a **field audit** involves an examination of numerous items reported on the return and is conducted on the premises of the taxpayer or the taxpayer's representative.

Upon the conclusion of the audit, the examining agent issues a Revenue Agent's Report (RAR) that summarizes the findings. The RAR will result in a refund (the tax was overpaid), a deficiency (the tax was underpaid), or a *no change* (the tax was correct) finding.

Settlement Procedures.　If an audit results in an assessment of additional tax and no settlement is reached with the IRS agent, the taxpayer may attempt to negotiate a settlement with the IRS. If an appeal is desired, an appropriate request must be made to the Appeals Division of the IRS. In some cases, a taxpayer may be able to obtain a percentage settlement or a favorable settlement of one or more disputed issues. The Appeals Division is authorized to settle all disputes based on the *hazard of litigation* (the probability of favorable resolution of the disputed issue or issues if litigated).

If a satisfactory settlement is not reached within the administrative appeal process, the taxpayer may wish to litigate the case in the Tax Court, a Federal District Court, or the Court of Federal Claims. However, litigation is recommended only as a last resort because of the legal costs involved and the uncertainty of the final outcome. Tax litigation considerations are discussed more fully in Chapter 28.

STATUTE OF LIMITATIONS

A **statute of limitations** is a provision in the law that offers a party a defense against a suit brought by another party after the expiration of a specified period of time. The purpose of a statute of limitations is to preclude parties from prosecuting stale claims. The passage of time makes the defense of such claims difficult since witnesses may no longer be available or evidence may have been lost or destroyed. Found at the state and Federal levels, such statutes cover a multitude of suits, both civil and criminal.

For our purposes, the relevant statutes deal with the Federal income tax. The two categories involved cover both the period of limitations applicable to the assessment of additional tax deficiencies by the IRS and the period that deals with claims for refunds by taxpayers.

Assessment by the IRS.   Under the general rule, the IRS may assess (impose) an additional tax liability against a taxpayer within *three years* of the filing of the income tax return. If the return is filed early, the three-year period begins to run from the due date of the return (usually April 15 for a calendar year individual taxpayer).

If a taxpayer omits an amount of gross income in excess of 25 percent of the gross income reported on the return, the statute of limitations is increased to six years.

EXAMPLE 14

For 1993, Mark, a calendar year taxpayer, reported gross income of $400,000 on a timely filed income tax return. If Mark omitted more than $100,000 (25% × $400,000), the six-year statute of limitations would apply to the 1993 tax year. ▼

The six-year provision on assessments by the IRS applies only to the omission of income and does not cover other factors that might lead to an understatement of tax liability (e.g., overstatement of deductions and credits).

There is *no* statute of limitations on assessments of tax if *no return* is filed or if a *fraudulent* return is filed.

Limitations on Refunds.   If a taxpayer believes that an overpayment of Federal income tax was made, a claim for refund should be filed with the IRS. A *claim for refund*, therefore, is a request to the IRS that it return to the taxpayer the excessive income taxes paid.[22]

A claim for refund generally must be filed within *three years* from the date the return was filed *or* within *two years* from the date the tax was paid, whichever is later. Income tax returns that are filed early are deemed to have been filed on the date the return was due.

INTEREST AND PENALTIES

Interest rates are determined quarterly by the IRS based on the existing Federal short-term rate. The rates for tax refunds (overpayments) are 1 percent below those applicable to assessments (underpayments). For the first quarter (January 1–March 31) of 1998, the rates were 8 percent for refunds and 9 percent for assessments.[23]

For assessments of additional taxes, the interest begins running on the unextended due date of the return. With refunds, however, no interest is allowed if the overpayment is refunded to the taxpayer within 45 days of the date the return is

---

[22]Generally, an individual filing a claim for refund should use Form 1040X.

[23]The rates applicable after March 31, 1998, were not available when this text went to press.

filed. For this purpose, returns filed early are deemed to have been filed on the due date.

The tax law provides various penalties for lack of compliance by taxpayers. Some of these penalties are summarized as follows:

- For a *failure to file* a tax return by the due date (including extension—see Chapter 2), a penalty of 5 percent per month (up to a maximum of 25 percent) is imposed on the amount of tax shown as due on the return. Any fraction of a month counts as a full month.
- A penalty for a *failure to pay* the tax due (as shown on the return) is imposed in the amount of 0.5 percent per month (up to a maximum of 25 percent). Again, any fraction of a month counts as a full month. During any month in which both the failure to file penalty and the failure to pay penalty apply, the failure to file penalty is reduced by the amount of the failure to pay penalty.

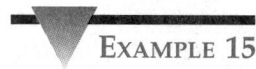

EXAMPLE 15

Adam files his tax return 18 days after the due date of the return. Along with the return, he remits a check for $1,000, which is the balance of the tax he owed. Disregarding the interest element, Adam's total penalties are as follows:

Failure to pay penalty (0.5% × $1,000)		$ 5
Plus:		
Failure to file penalty (5% × $1,000)	$50	
Less failure to pay penalty for the same period	(5)	
Failure to file penalty		45
Total penalties		$50

Note that the penalties for one full month are imposed even though Adam was delinquent by only 18 days. Unlike the method used to compute interest, any part of a month is treated as a whole month. ▼

- A *negligence* penalty of 20 percent is imposed if any of the underpayment was for intentional disregard of rules and regulations without intent to defraud. The penalty applies to just that portion attributable to the negligence.

EXAMPLE 16

Cindy underpaid her taxes for 1997 in the amount of $20,000, of which $15,000 is attributable to negligence. Cindy's negligence penalty is $3,000 (20% × $15,000). ▼

- Various fraud penalties may be imposed. *Fraud* is a deliberate action on the part of the taxpayer evidenced by deceit, misrepresentation, concealment, etc. For possible fraud situations, refer to Examples 11 and 12. The burden of proving fraud is on the IRS. This is in contrast to the usual deficiency assessment made by the IRS, where the burden is on the taxpayer to show that he or she does not owe any additional tax.

TAX PRACTICE

The area of tax practice is largely unregulated. Virtually anyone can aid another in complying with the various tax laws. If a practitioner is a member of a profession, such as law or public accounting, he or she must abide by certain ethical standards. Furthermore, the Internal Revenue Code imposes penalties upon the preparers of Federal tax returns who violate proscribed acts and procedures.

Ethical Guidelines.   The American Institute of CPAs has issued numerous guides for CPAs engaged in tax practice. Called "Statements on Responsibilities in Tax Practice," some of these are summarized below.

- Do not take questionable positions on a client's tax return in the hope that the return will not be selected for audit by the IRS. Any positions taken should be supported by a good-faith belief that they have a realistic chance of being sustained if challenged. The client should be fully advised of the risks involved and of the penalties that would result if the position taken is not successful.
- A practitioner can use a client's estimates if they are reasonable under the circumstances. If the tax law requires verification (e.g., receipts), the client should be so advised. In no event should an estimate be given the appearance of greater accuracy than is the case. For example, an estimate of $1,000 should not be deducted on a return as $999.
- Every effort should be made to answer questions appearing on tax returns. A question need not be answered if the information requested is not readily available, the answer is voluminous, or the question's meaning is uncertain. The failure to answer a question on a return cannot be justified on the grounds that the answer could prove disadvantageous to the taxpayer.
- Upon learning of an error on a past tax return, advise the client to correct it. Do not, however, inform the IRS of the error. If the error is material and the client refuses to correct it, consider withdrawing from the engagement. This will be necessary if the error has a carryover effect and prevents the current year's tax liability from being determined correctly.

Statutory Penalties Imposed on Tax Return Preparers.   In addition to ethical constraints, a tax return preparer may be subject to certain statutorily sanctioned penalties, including the following:

- Various penalties involving procedural matters. Examples include failing to furnish the taxpayer with a copy of the return; endorsing a taxpayer's refund check; failing to sign the return as a preparer; failing to furnish one's identification number; and failing to keep copies of returns or maintain a client list.
- Understatement of a tax liability based on a position that lacks any realistic possibility of being sustained. If the position is not frivolous, the penalty can be avoided by disclosing it on the return.
- Any willful attempt to understate taxes. This usually results when a preparer disregards or makes no effort to obtain pertinent information from a client.
- Failure to exercise due diligence in determining eligibility for, or the amount of, an earned income tax credit.

UNDERSTANDING THE FEDERAL TAX LAW

The Federal tax law is a mosaic of statutory provisions, administrative pronouncements, and court decisions. Anyone who has attempted to work with this body of knowledge would have to admit to its complexity. For the person who has to trudge through a mass of rules to find the solution to a tax problem, it may be of some consolation to know that the law's complexity can generally be explained. Whether sound or not, there is a reason for the formulation of every rule. Knowing these reasons, therefore, is a considerable step toward understanding the Federal tax law.

The Federal tax law has as its *major objective* the raising of revenue. But although the fiscal needs of the government are important, other considerations explain certain portions of the law. Economic, social, equity, and political factors also play a significant role. Added to these factors is the marked impact the IRS and the courts have had and will continue to have on the evolution of Federal tax law. These matters are treated in the remainder of the chapter, and, wherever appropriate, the discussion is referenced to subjects covered later in the text.

REVENUE NEEDS

The foundation of any tax system has to be the raising of revenue to cover the cost of government operations. Ideally, annual outlays should not exceed anticipated revenues, thereby leading to a balanced budget with no resulting deficit. Many states have achieved this objective by passing laws or constitutional amendments precluding deficit spending. Unfortunately, the Federal government has no such conclusive prohibition, and annual deficits have become an increasing concern for many. Legislation enacted in 1997 is supposed to alleviate this problem.

When enacting tax legislation, a deficit-conscious Congress often has been guided by the concept of **revenue neutrality.** The concept means that the changes made will neither increase nor decrease the net result reached under the prior rules. Revenue neutrality does not mean that any one taxpayer's tax liability will remain the same. Since the circumstances involved will differ, one taxpayer's increased tax liability could be another's tax savings. Although revenue-neutral tax reform does not reduce deficits, at least it does not aggravate the problem.

In addition to making changes in the tax law revenue neutral, several other procedures can be taken to reduce the revenue loss. When tax reductions are involved, the full impact of the legislation can be phased in over a period of years. Or, as an alternative, the tax reduction can be limited to a period of years. When the period expires, Congress can then renew or not renew the provision in light of budget considerations.[24]

ECONOMIC CONSIDERATIONS

Using the tax system in an effort to accomplish economic objectives has become increasingly popular in recent years. Generally, proponents of this goal use tax legislation to amend the Internal Revenue Code and promote measures designed to help control the economy or encourage certain activities and businesses.

Control of the Economy. Congress has used depreciation write-offs as a means of controlling the economy. Theoretically, shorter asset lives and accelerated methods should encourage additional investment in depreciable property acquired for business use. Conversely, longer asset lives and the required use of the straight-line method of depreciation dampen the tax incentive for capital outlays.

A change in the tax rate structure has a more immediate impact on the economy. With lower tax rates, taxpayers are able to retain additional spendable funds. If lower tax rates are accompanied by the elimination of certain deductions, exclusions, and credits, however, the overall result may not be lower tax liabilities.

---

[24]An example of a gradual phase-in is the increase in the unified transfer tax credit (discussed earlier in this chapter), which does not become fully implemented at $1 million until year 2006. An example of a temporary tax reduction is the exclusion from gross income of employer-provided educational assistance benefits (discussed in Chapter 4), which are scheduled to expire during year 2000.

Encouragement of Certain Activities. Without passing judgment on the wisdom of any such choices, it is quite clear that the tax law does encourage certain types of economic activity or segments of the economy. For example, the favorable treatment allowed research and development expenditures can be explained by the desire to foster technological progress. Under the tax law, such expenditures can be either deducted in the year incurred or capitalized and amortized over a period of 60 months or more. In terms of the timing of the tax savings, these options usually are preferable to capitalizing the cost with a write-off over the estimated useful life of the asset created. If the asset developed has an indefinite useful life, no write-off would be available without the two options allowed by the tax law.

Is it desirable to encourage the conservation of energy resources? Considering the world energy situation and our own reliance on foreign oil, the answer to this question has to be yes. The concern over energy usage was a prime consideration in the enactment of legislation to make various tax savings for energy conservation expenditures available to taxpayers.

Is preserving the environment a desirable objective? Ecological considerations explain why the tax law permits a 60-month amortization period for costs incurred in the installation of pollution control facilities.

Is it wise to stimulate U.S. exports of goods and services? Considering the pressing and continuing problem of a deficit in the U.S. balance of payments, the answer should be clear. Along this line, Congress has created Foreign Sales Corporations (FSCs), which are designed to encourage domestic exports of goods. The FSC provisions exempt a percentage of profits from export sales from the Federal income tax. Also in an international setting, Congress has deemed it advisable to establish incentives for U.S. citizens who accept employment overseas. Such persons receive generous tax breaks through special treatment of their foreign-source income and certain housing costs.

Is saving desirable for the economy? Saving leads to capital formation and thereby makes funds available to finance home construction and industrial expansion. The tax law encourages saving by according preferential treatment to private retirement plans. Not only are contributions to Keogh (H.R. 10) plans and certain Individual Retirement Accounts (IRAs) deductible, but income from the contributions accumulates free of tax. As noted below, the encouragement of private-sector pension plans can also be justified under social considerations.

Encouragement of Certain Industries. No one can question the proposition that a sound agricultural base is necessary for a well-balanced national economy. Undoubtedly, this can explain why farmers are accorded special treatment under the Federal tax system. Among the benefits are the election to expense rather than capitalize certain soil and water conservation expenditures and fertilizers and the election to defer the recognition of gain on the receipt of crop insurance proceeds.

Encouragement of Small Business. At least in the United States, a consensus exists that what is good for small business is good for the economy as a whole. Whether valid or not, this assumption has led to a definite bias in the tax law favoring small business.

In the corporate tax area, several provisions can be explained by the desire to benefit small business. One provision permits the shareholders of a small business corporation to make a special election that generally will avoid the imposition of the corporate income tax.[25] Furthermore, such an election enables the corporation to pass through its operating losses to its shareholders.

---

[25]Known as the S election, it is discussed in Chapter 21.

SOCIAL CONSIDERATIONS

Some provisions of the Federal tax law, particularly those dealing with the income tax of individuals, can be explained by social considerations. Some notable examples and their rationales include the following:

- Certain benefits provided to employees through accident and health plans financed by employers are nontaxable to employees. Encouraging such plans is considered socially desirable since they provide medical benefits in the event of an employee's illness or injury.
- Most premiums paid by an employer for group term insurance covering the life of the employee are nontaxable to the employee. These arrangements can be justified on social grounds in that they provide funds for the family unit to help it adjust to the loss of wages caused by the employee's death.
- A contribution made by an employer to a qualified pension or profit sharing plan for an employee receives special treatment. The contribution and any income it generates are not taxed to the employee until the funds are distributed. Such an arrangement also benefits the employer by allowing a tax deduction when the contribution is made to the qualified plan. Private retirement plans are encouraged to supplement the subsistence income level the employee otherwise would have under the Social Security system.[26]
- A deduction is allowed for contributions to qualified charitable organizations. The deduction attempts to shift some of the financial and administrative burden of socially desirable programs from the public (the government) to the private (the citizens) sector.
- A tax credit is allowed for amounts spent to furnish care for certain minor or disabled dependents to enable the taxpayer to seek or maintain gainful employment. Who could deny the social desirability of encouraging taxpayers to provide care for their children while they work?
- Various tax credits, deductions, and exclusions that are designed to encourage taxpayers to obtain additional education.[27]
- A tax deduction is not allowed for certain expenditures deemed to be contrary to public policy. This disallowance extends to such items as fines, penalties, illegal kickbacks, bribes to government officials, and gambling losses in excess of gains. Social considerations dictate that the tax law should not encourage these activities by permitting a deduction.

Many other examples could be cited, but the conclusion would be unchanged. Social considerations do explain a significant part of the Federal tax law.

EQUITY CONSIDERATIONS

The concept of equity is relative. Reasonable persons can, and often do, disagree about what is fair or unfair. In the tax area, moreover, equity is most often tied to a particular taxpayer's personal situation. To illustrate, compare the tax positions of those who rent their personal residences with those who own their homes. Renters receive no Federal income tax benefit from the rent they pay. For homeowners, however, a large portion of the house payments they make may qualify for the Federal interest and property tax deductions. Although renters may have difficulty understanding this difference in tax treatment, the

---

[26]The same rationale explains the availability of similar arrangements for self-employed persons (the H.R. 10, or Keogh, plan).

[27]These provisions can also be justified under the category of economic considerations. No one can take issue with the conclusion that a better educated workforce carries a positive economic impact.

encouragement of home ownership can be justified on both economic and social grounds.

In the same vein, compare the tax treatment of a corporation with that of a partnership. Although the two businesses may be of equal size, similarly situated, and competitors in the production of goods or services, they are not treated comparably under the tax law. The corporation is subject to a separate Federal income tax; the partnership is not. Whether the differences in tax treatment can be justified logically in terms of equity is beside the point. The point is that the tax law can and does make a distinction between these business forms.

Equity, then, is not what appears fair or unfair to any one taxpayer or group of taxpayers. It is, instead, what the tax law recognizes. Some recognition of equity does exist, however, and explains part of the law. The concept of equity appears in tax provisions that alleviate the effect of multiple taxation and postpone the recognition of gain when the taxpayer lacks the ability or wherewithal to pay the tax. Provisions that mitigate the effect of the application of the annual accounting period concept and help taxpayers cope with the eroding results of inflation also reflect equity considerations.

Alleviating the Effect of Multiple Taxation.

The income earned by a taxpayer may be subject to taxes imposed by different taxing authorities. If, for example, the taxpayer is a resident of New York City, income might generate Federal, state of New York, and city of New York income taxes. To compensate for this apparent inequity, the Federal tax law allows a taxpayer to claim a deduction for state and local income taxes. The deduction does not, however, neutralize the effect of multiple taxation, since the benefit derived depends on the taxpayer's Federal income tax rate. Only a tax credit, rather than a deduction, would eliminate the effects of multiple taxation on the same income.

Equity considerations can explain the Federal tax treatment of certain income from foreign sources. Since double taxation results when the same income is subject to both foreign and U.S. income taxes, the tax law permits the taxpayer to choose between a credit and a deduction for the foreign taxes paid.

The Wherewithal to Pay Concept.

The **wherewithal to pay** concept recognizes the inequity of taxing a transaction when the taxpayer lacks the means with which to pay the tax. It is particularly suited to situations in which the taxpayer's economic position has not changed significantly as a result of the transaction.

An illustration of the wherewithal to pay concept is the provision of the tax law dealing with the treatment of gain resulting from an involuntary conversion. An involuntary conversion occurs when property is destroyed by casualty or taken by a public authority through condemnation. If gain results from the conversion, it need not be recognized if the taxpayer replaces the property within a specified period of time. The replacement property must be similar or related in service or use to that involuntarily converted.

EXAMPLE 17

Ron, a rancher, has some of his pasture land condemned by the state for use as a game preserve. The condemned pasture land cost Ron $120,000, but the state pays him $150,000 (its fair market value). Shortly thereafter, Ron buys more pasture land for $150,000. ▼

In Example 17, Ron has a realized gain of $30,000 [$150,000 (condemnation award) – $120,000 (cost of land)]. It would be inequitable to force Ron to pay a tax on this gain for two reasons. First, without disposing of the property acquired (the new land), Ron would be hard-pressed to pay the tax. Second, his economic position has not changed.

A warning is in order regarding the application of the wherewithal to pay concept. If the taxpayer's economic position changes in any way, tax consequences may result.

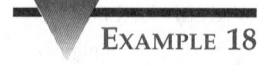

EXAMPLE 18

Assume the same facts as in Example 17, except that Ron reinvests only $140,000 of the award in new pasture land. Now, Ron has a taxable gain of $10,000. Instead of ending up with only replacement property, Ron now has $10,000 in cash. ▼

Mitigating the Effect of the Annual Accounting Period Concept. For purposes of effective administration of the tax law, all taxpayers must report to and settle with the Federal government at periodic intervals. Otherwise, taxpayers would remain uncertain as to their tax liabilities, and the government would have difficulty judging revenues and budgeting expenditures. The period selected for final settlement of most tax liabilities, in any event an arbitrary determination, is one year. At the close of each year, therefore, a taxpayer's position becomes complete for that particular year. Referred to as the annual accounting period concept, its effect is to divide each taxpayer's life, for tax purposes, into equal annual intervals.

The finality of the annual accounting period concept could lead to dissimilar tax treatment for taxpayers who are, from a long-range standpoint, in the same economic position.

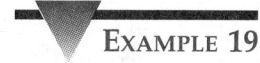

EXAMPLE 19

José and Alicia, both sole proprietors, have experienced the following results during the past four years:

Profit (or Loss)		
Year	José	Alicia
1996	$50,000	$150,000
1997	60,000	60,000
1998	60,000	(40,000)

Although José and Alicia have the same profit of $170,000 over the period from 1996 to 1998, the finality of the annual accounting period concept places Alicia at a definite disadvantage for tax purposes. The net operating loss procedure offers Alicia some relief by allowing her to apply some or all of her 1998 loss to the earlier profitable years (in this case, 1996). Thus, with a net operating loss carryback, Alicia is in a position to obtain a refund for some of the taxes she paid on the $150,000 profit reported for 1996. ▼

The same reasoning used to support the deduction of net operating losses can explain the special treatment the tax law accords to excess capital losses and excess charitable contributions.[28] Carryback and carryover procedures help mitigate the effect of limiting a loss or a deduction to the accounting period in which it was realized. With such procedures, a taxpayer may be able to salvage a loss or a deduction that might otherwise be wasted.

The installment method of recognizing gain on the sale of property allows a taxpayer to spread tax consequences over the payout period.[29] The harsh effect of taxing all the gain in the year of sale is thereby avoided. The installment method

---

[28]The tax treatment of these items is discussed in Chapters 6, 9, and 13.

[29]Under the installment method, each payment received by the seller represents both a recovery of capital (the nontaxable portion) and profit from the sale (the taxable portion). The tax rules governing the installment method are discussed in Chapter 15.

can also be explained by the wherewithal to pay concept since recognition of gain is tied to the collection of the installment notes received from the sale of the property. Tax consequences, then, tend to correspond to the seller's ability to pay the tax.

Coping with Inflation.   Because of the progressive nature of the income tax, a wage adjustment to compensate for inflation can increase the income tax bracket of the recipient. Known as *bracket creep,* its overall impact is an erosion of purchasing power. Congress recognized this problem and began to adjust various income tax components, such as tax brackets, standard deduction amounts, and personal and dependency exemptions, through an indexation procedure. Indexation is based upon the rise in the consumer price index over the prior year.

POLITICAL CONSIDERATIONS

A large segment of the Federal tax law is made up of statutory provisions. Since these statutes are enacted by Congress, is it any surprise that political considerations influence tax law? For purposes of discussion, the effect of political considerations on the tax law is divided into the following topics: special interest legislation, political expediency situations, and state and local government influences.

Special Interest Legislation.   There is no doubt that certain provisions of the tax law can largely be explained by the political influence some pressure groups have had on Congress. Is there any other realistic reason that, for example, prepaid subscription and dues income are not taxed until earned while prepaid rents are taxed to the landlord in the year received?

A recent example of special interest legislation was a provision attached to the House of Representatives's version of the TRA of 1997. The provision would have exempted "bakery drivers" from being classified as employees. Since the drivers would have become self-employed independent contractors, the baking companies would no longer have needed to cover them under Social Security, Medicare, and FUTA. The representative who originated the provision is from Nebraska and represents the district that is the home of Pepperidge Farm and Interstate Bakeries (maker of Wonder bread).

Special interest legislation is not necessarily to be condemned if it can be justified on economic, social, or some other utilitarian grounds. At any rate, it is an inevitable product of our political system.

Political Expediency Situations.   Various tax reform proposals rise and fall in favor with the shifting moods of the American public. That Congress is sensitive to popular feeling is an accepted fact. Therefore, certain provisions of the tax law can be explained by the political climate at the time they were enacted.

Measures that deter more affluent taxpayers from obtaining so-called preferential tax treatment have always had popular appeal and, consequently, the support of Congress. Provisions such as the alternative minimum tax, the imputed interest rules, and the limitation on the deductibility of interest on investment indebtedness can be explained on this basis.[30]

Other changes explained at least partially by political expediency include the lowering of individual income tax rates, the increase in the personal and dependency exemptions, and the increase in the amount of the earned income credit.

---

[30]See Chapters 3, 9, and 14.

One of the expressed objectives of legislation enacted in 1993 was to increase taxes levied on wealthy individuals by instituting new 36 and 39.6 percent rates on higher-income brackets.

State and Local Government Influences. Political considerations have played a major role in the nontaxability of interest received on state and local obligations. In view of the furor that has been raised by state and local political figures every time any modification of this tax provision has been proposed, one might well regard it as next to sacred.

Somewhat less apparent has been the influence state law has had in shaping our present Federal tax law. Such was the case with community property systems. The nine states with community property systems are Louisiana, Texas, New Mexico, Arizona, California, Washington, Idaho, Nevada, and Wisconsin. The rest of the states are classified as common law jurisdictions. The difference between common law and community property systems centers around the property rights possessed by married persons. In a common law system, each spouse owns whatever he or she earns. Under a community property system, one-half of the earnings of each spouse is considered owned by the other spouse.

EXAMPLE 20

Al and Fran are husband and wife, and their only income is the $60,000 annual salary Al receives. If they live in New Jersey (a common law state), the $60,000 salary belongs to Al. If, however, they live in Arizona (a community property state), the $60,000 is divided equally, in terms of ownership, between Al and Fran. ▼

At one time, the tax position of the residents of community property states was so advantageous that many common law states actually adopted community property systems. Needless to say, the political pressure placed on Congress to correct the disparity in tax treatment was considerable. To a large extent this was accomplished in the Revenue Act of 1948, which extended many of the community property tax advantages to residents of common law jurisdictions.

The major advantage extended was the provision allowing married taxpayers to file joint returns and compute the tax liability as if the income had been earned one-half by each spouse. This result is automatic in a community property state, since half of the income earned by one spouse belongs to the other spouse. The income-splitting benefits of a joint return are now incorporated as part of the tax rates applicable to married taxpayers. See Chapter 2.

INFLUENCE OF THE INTERNAL REVENUE SERVICE

7 LEARNING OBJECTIVE
Describe the role played by the IRS and the courts in the evolution of the Federal tax system.

The influence of the IRS is apparent in many areas beyond its role in issuing the administrative pronouncements that make up a considerable portion of our tax law. In its capacity as the protector of the national revenue, the IRS has been instrumental in securing the passage of much legislation designed to curtail the most flagrant tax avoidance practices (to close *tax loopholes*). In its capacity as the administrator of the tax law, the IRS has sought and obtained legislation to make its job easier (to attain administrative feasibility).

The IRS as Protector of the Revenue. Innumerable examples can be given of provisions in the tax law that stem from the direct influence of the IRS. Usually, such provisions are intended to prevent a loophole from being used to avoid the tax consequences intended by Congress. Working within the letter of existing law, ingenious taxpayers and their advisers devise techniques that accomplish indirectly what cannot be accomplished directly. As a consequence, legislation is enacted to close the loopholes that taxpayers have located and exploited. Some tax law can be explained in this fashion and is discussed in the chapters to follow.

In addition, the IRS has secured from Congress legislation of a more general nature that enables it to make adjustments based on the substance, rather than the formal construction, of what a taxpayer has done. One such provision permits the IRS to make adjustments to a taxpayer's method of accounting when the method used by the taxpayer does not clearly reflect income.[31]

EXAMPLE 21

Tina, a cash basis taxpayer, owns and operates a pharmacy. All drugs and other items acquired for resale (e.g., cosmetics) are charged to the purchases account and written off (expensed) for tax purposes in the year of acquisition. As this procedure does not clearly reflect income, it would be appropriate for the IRS to require that Tina establish and maintain an ending inventory account. ▼

Administrative Feasibility.   Some of the tax law is justified on the grounds that it simplifies the task of the IRS in collecting the revenue and administering the law. With regard to collecting the revenue, the IRS long ago realized the importance of placing taxpayers on a pay-as-you-go basis. Elaborate withholding procedures apply to wages, while the tax on other types of income may be paid at periodic intervals throughout the year. The IRS has been instrumental in convincing the courts that accrual basis taxpayers should pay taxes on prepaid income in the year received and not when earned. The approach may be contrary to generally accepted accounting principles, but it is consistent with the wherewithal to pay concept.

Of considerable aid to the IRS in collecting revenue are the numerous provisions that impose interest and penalties on taxpayers for noncompliance with the tax law. Provisions such as the penalties for failure to pay a tax or to file a return that is due, the negligence penalty for intentional disregard of rules and regulations, and various penalties for civil and criminal fraud serve as deterrents to taxpayer noncompliance.

One of the keys to an effective administration of our tax system is the audit process conducted by the IRS. To carry out this function, the IRS is aided by provisions that reduce the chance of taxpayer error or manipulation and therefore simplify the audit effort that is necessary. An increase in the amount of the standard deduction, for example, reduces the number of individual taxpayers who will choose the alternative of itemizing their personal deductions.[32] With fewer deductions to check, the audit function is simplified.[33]

The audit function of the IRS has also been simplified by provisions of the tax law dealing with the burden of proof. Suppose, for example, the IRS audits a taxpayer and questions a particular deduction. Who has the burden of proving the propriety of the deduction? The so-called presumption of correctness that attaches in favor of any deficiency assessed by the IRS can be explained by the nature of our tax system. The Federal income tax is a *self-assessed tax*, which means that each taxpayer is responsible for rendering an accounting to the IRS of all of his or her transactions during the year. A failure to do so means that any doubts will be resolved in favor of the IRS. Only in the case of fraud (which could involve fines and penal sanctions) does the IRS carry the burden of proof.

---

[31]See Chapter 15.
[32]For a discussion of the standard deduction, see Chapter 2.
[33]The same justification was given by the IRS when it proposed to Congress the $100 limitation on personal casualty and theft losses. Imposition of the limitation eliminated many casualty and theft loss deductions and, as a consequence, saved the IRS considerable audit time. Later legislation, in addition to retaining the $100 feature, limits deductible losses to those in excess of 10% of a taxpayer's adjusted gross income. See Chapter 6.

INFLUENCE OF THE COURTS

In addition to interpreting statutory provisions and the administrative pronouncements issued by the IRS, the Federal courts have influenced tax law in two other respects.[34] First, the courts have formulated certain judicial concepts that serve as guides in the application of various tax provisions. Second, certain key decisions have led to changes in the Internal Revenue Code.

Judicial Concepts Relating to Tax.   A leading tax concept developed by the courts deals with the interpretation of statutory tax provisions that operate to benefit taxpayers. The courts have established the rule that these relief provisions are to be narrowly construed against taxpayers if there is any doubt about their application.

Important in this area is the *arm's length* concept. Particularly in dealings between related parties, transactions may be tested by looking to whether the taxpayers acted in an arm's length manner. The question to be asked is: Would unrelated parties have handled the transaction in the same way?

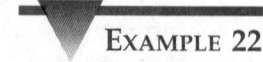
EXAMPLE 22

Rex, the sole shareholder of Silver Corporation, leases property to the corporation for a yearly rent of $6,000. To test whether the corporation should be allowed a rent deduction for this amount, the IRS and the courts will apply the arm's length concept. Would Silver Corporation have paid $6,000 a year in rent if it had leased the same property from an unrelated party (rather than from Rex)? Suppose it is determined that an unrelated third party would have paid an annual rent for the property of only $5,000. Under these circumstances, Silver Corporation will be allowed a deduction of only $5,000. The other $1,000 it paid for the use of the property represents a nondeductible dividend. Accordingly, Rex will be treated as having received rent income of $5,000 and dividend income of $1,000. ▼

Judicial Influence on Statutory Provisions.   Some court decisions have been of such consequence that Congress has incorporated them into statutory tax law. For example, many years ago the courts found that stock dividends distributed to the shareholders of a corporation were not taxable as income. This result was largely accepted by Congress, and a provision in the tax statutes now covers the issue.

On occasion, however, Congress has reacted negatively to judicial interpretations of the tax law.

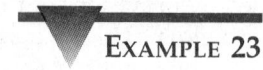
EXAMPLE 23

Nora leases unimproved real estate to Wade for 40 years. At a cost of $200,000, Wade erects a building on the land. The building is worth $100,000 when the lease terminates and Nora takes possession of the property. Does Nora have any income either when the improvements are made or when the lease terminates? In a landmark decision, a court held that Nora must recognize income of $100,000 upon the termination of the lease. ▼

Congress felt that the result reached in Example 23 was inequitable in that it was not consistent with the wherewithal to pay concept. Consequently, the tax law was amended to provide that a landlord does not recognize any income either when the improvements are made (unless made in lieu of rent) or when the lease terminates.

---

[34]A great deal of case law is devoted to ascertaining congressional intent. The courts, in effect, ask: What did Congress have in mind when it enacted a particular tax provision?

SUMMARY

In addition to its necessary revenue-raising objective, the Federal tax law has developed in response to several other factors:

- *Economic considerations.* The emphasis here is on tax provisions that help regulate the economy and encourage certain activities and types of businesses.
- *Social considerations.* Some tax provisions are designed to encourage (or discourage) certain socially desirable (or undesirable) practices.
- *Equity considerations.* Of principal concern in this area are tax provisions that alleviate the effect of multiple taxation, recognize the wherewithal to pay concept, mitigate the effect of the annual accounting period concept, and recognize the eroding effect of inflation.
- *Political considerations.* Of significance in this regard are tax provisions that represent special interest legislation, reflect political expediency, and exhibit the effect of state and local law.
- *Influence of the IRS.* Many tax provisions are intended to aid the IRS in the collection of revenue and the administration of the tax law.
- *Influence of the courts.* Court decisions have established a body of judicial concepts relating to tax law and have, on occasion, led Congress to enact statutory provisions to either clarify or negate their effect.

These factors explain various tax provisions and thereby help in understanding why the tax law developed to its present state. The next step involves learning to work with the tax law, which is the subject of Chapter 28.

KEY TERMS

Ad valorem tax, 1–6

Correspondence audit, 1–19

Death tax, 1–11

Employment taxes, 1–15

Estate tax, 1–11

Excise tax, 1–9

FICA tax, 1–16

Field audit, 1–20

Flat tax, 1–17

Franchise tax, 1–17

FUTA tax, 1–16

Gift tax, 1–12

Inheritance tax, 1–11

National sales tax, 1–18

Occupational tax, 1–17

Office audit, 1–20

Personalty, 1–8

Realty, 1–6

Revenue neutrality, 1–24

Sales tax, 1–10

Severance tax, 1–11

Statute of limitations, 1–21

Use tax, 1–10

Value added tax (VAT), 1–18

Wherewithal to pay, 1–27

PROBLEM MATERIALS

DISCUSSION QUESTIONS

1. Irene, a middle management employee, is offered a pay increase by her employer. As a condition of the offer, Irene must move to another state. What tax considerations should Irene weigh before making a decision on whether to accept the offer?

2. Before the passage of the Sixteenth Amendment to the Constitution, there was no income tax in the United States. Please comment.

3. Did the passage of the Sixteenth Amendment to the U.S. Constitution have any effect on the income tax imposed on corporations? Explain.

4. A tax law that was enacted in 1953 would be part of which Internal Revenue Code (i.e., 1939, 1954, or 1986)? Explain.

5. How does the pay-as-you-go procedure apply to wage earners? To persons who have income from other than wages?

6. Analyze the Federal income tax in light of Adam Smith's canons of taxation.

7. Is the Medicare tax component of FICA a *proportional* or a *progressive* tax? Explain.

8. When Gull Company constructs a climate-controlled warehouse, it is very careful to keep many of the components portable. Thus, the sprinkler system is detachable, air conditioning and heating are provided by window units, and the interior walls can be removed. What is Gull trying to accomplish?

9. Several years ago, Jim and Martha purchased their personal residence from St. Andrew's Methodist Church. The property had previously been used by the church as a parsonage for its minister. Since the purchase, Jim and Martha have received no property tax bills from either the city or the county where the residence is located. Is there a plausible explanation?

10. Al is considering starting a new business that will require the construction of a manufacturing facility. Jefferson County, one of the geographic locations Al is considering, has proposed a tax holiday. What does this mean?

11. Matt buys a new home for $150,000, its cost of construction plus the usual profit margin for the builder. The new home is located in a neighborhood largely developed 10 years ago when the homes sold for approximately $50,000 each. Assuming the homes of his neighbors are worth (in current values) in the vicinity of $150,000, could Matt be at a disadvantage with regard to the ad valorem tax on realty?

12. Recently, one of your friends successfully challenged a reappraisal of his personal residence by the county board of real estate tax assessors. He remarks to you that this should put him "in good shape for the next five years." What does he mean?

13. A taxpayer owns an apartment building in a community where rent controls exist. If these controls are lifted (i.e., rescinded), could this change the amount of the ad valorem tax on the property? Why or why not?

14. The tax on tobacco products and the gas guzzler tax have a common objective. Elaborate.

15. While out of town on business, Paul stays at a motel with an advertised room rate of $80 per night. When checking out, Paul is charged $88. What would be a plausible reason for the extra $8 Paul had to pay?

16. Julia lives in a jurisdiction that imposes a 5% general sales tax. On a recent trip to the supermarket, she spent $100 but paid only $4 in sales tax. The store where Julia shops is a full-line market and sells prepared foods and drugs in addition to groceries. What is a possible explanation as to why Julia paid only $4 in sales tax and not $5 (5% × $100)?

17. At a recent social gathering, Carrie and Daryl were discussing some recent catalog purchases from out-of-state firms. Carrie was surprised to learn that her purchase was subject to use tax while Daryl's was not. Is there a realistic explanation for the difference?

18. Jean lives in Smithville (the major city in Smith County). She does all of her shopping in Madisonville (the major city in Madison County). If the cities' retail outlets are comparable, why does Jean go out of her way to shop?

19. Alaska has no general sales tax and no income tax. Further, Alaska is a large oil producer. What, if any, is the connection between these factors?

20. What was the original justification for the Federal estate tax?

21. Explain the difference between an inheritance tax and an estate tax.

22. A decedent who leaves all of his property to his surviving spouse and to qualified charitable organizations is not subject to a Federal estate tax. Explain.

23. Why was the Federal gift tax enacted?

24. In 1996, Horace makes a taxable gift of $250,000 upon which he pays a Federal gift tax of $70,800. In 1998, Horace makes another taxable gift of $250,000. Will the 1998 taxable gift result in the same gift tax as the 1996 gift? Why or why not?

25. How much property can Herman, a widower, give to his four married children, their spouses, and eight grandchildren over a period of 10 years without making a taxable gift?

26. When married persons elect to split a gift, what tax advantages do they enjoy?

27. Contrast the major differences between the Federal income tax schemes applicable to individuals and to corporations.

28. John, a nationally known vocalist, lives in Nevada. John's agent has been trying to convince him to go on tour to increase his record sales. John, however, refuses to perform anywhere but in Las Vegas clubs. What might explain John's attitude?

29. When a state uses a "piggyback" approach for its state income tax, what is the state doing?

30. Chee lives in a state that imposes an income tax. His Federal income tax return for 1996 is audited in 1998, and, as a result of several adjustments made by the IRS, Chee has to pay additional Federal income tax. Several months later, Chee is notified that his 1996 state income tax return is to be audited. Are these two incidents a coincidence or does a reasonable explanation exist?

31. As to those states that impose an income tax on individuals, comment on the following:
    a. Use of withholding procedures.
    b. Treatment of Federal income taxes paid.
    c. Due date for filing.
    d. Handling of personal and dependency exemptions.

32. Each year, the base amount for the FICA tax is changed. Comment on the validity of this statement.

33. Keith, a sole proprietor, owns and operates a grocery store. Keith's wife and his 17-year-old son work in the business and are paid wages. Will the wife and son be subject to FICA? Explain.

34. Dan, the owner and operator of a construction company that builds outdoor swimming pools, releases most of his construction personnel during the winter months. Should this hurt Dan's FUTA situation? Why or why not?

35. Compare FICA and FUTA in connection with each of the following:
    a. Incidence of taxation.
    b. Justification for taxation.
    c. Rates and base involved.

36. What is a "flat tax"? What is its major advantage?

37. One of your friends contends that a value added tax (VAT) is the same as a national sales tax. Do you agree or disagree and why?

38. Hollis is married and is the sole proprietor of a dry-cleaning business. His sister, Phoebe, is single and is a management-level employee at IBM. Although both earn about the same income each year, Hollis has been audited by the IRS on three different occasions, while Phoebe has never been audited. Is there a rational explanation for the difference in treatment?

39. Elsie notifies the IRS that her ex-husband cheats on his income tax. Elsie is motivated by spite and also hopes to collect an informant's reward. Has Elsie acted wisely?

40. What is the difference between an "office" audit and a "field" audit?

41. As a result of an audit by the IRS of her Federal income tax return, Sophy receives an RAR. What does this mean?

42. On a Federal income tax return filed five years ago, Andy inadvertently omitted a large amount of gross income.
    a. Andy seeks your advice as to whether the IRS is barred from assessing additional income tax in the event he is audited. What is your advice?
    b. Would your advice differ if you are the person who prepared the return in question? Explain.
    c. Suppose Andy asks you to prepare his current year's return. Would you do so? Explain.

43. Jill files her income tax return 45 days after the due date of the return without obtaining an extension from the IRS. Along with the return, she remits a check for $4,000, which is the balance of the tax she owes. Disregarding the interest element, what are Jill's penalties for failure to file and for failure to pay?

44. Ed overstated deductions on his Federal income tax return for 1997. Upon audit by the IRS, it is determined that the overstatement was partially the result of negligence. As a result, Ed owes additional income taxes of $10,000 ($8,000 attributable to the negligence). What is Ed's penalty?

45. In March 1998, Jim asks you to prepare his Federal income tax returns for tax years 1995, 1996, and 1997. In discussing this matter with him, you discover that he also has not filed for tax year 1994. When you mention this fact, Jim tells you that the statute of limitations precludes the IRS from taking any action as to this year.
    a. Is Jim correct about the application of the statute of limitations? Why?
    b. If Jim refuses to file for 1994, should you prepare returns for 1995 through 1997?

46. You are preparing Ellen's Federal income tax return for 1997. Although she has no records, she estimates that she has given cash of about $500 to various charities during the year. She suggests that it would "look better" if you listed $501 as charitable contributions. What should you do?

47. What is meant by revenue-neutral tax reform?

48. How does the tax law foster technological progress?

49. Discuss the probable justification for the following provisions of the tax law:
    a. The election permitting certain corporations to avoid the corporate income tax.
    b. A provision that excludes from gross income certain benefits furnished to employees through accident and health plans financed by employers.
    c. Nontaxable treatment for an employee for premiums paid by an employer for group term insurance covering the life of the employee.

50. The tax law encourages private retirement plans and contributions to charitable organizations. In terms of nonrevenue objectives, what is the common justification for this special tax treatment?

51. What purpose is served by allowing a deduction for home mortgage interest and property taxes?

52. Allowing a taxpayer a deduction for Federal income tax purposes for state income taxes paid eliminates the double taxation of the same income. Do you agree? Why or why not?

53. Wilma, a cattle rancher, has a pasture condemned by the State Parks Commission for use as a recreational facility. The pasture cost Wilma $30,000, and the state paid her its appraised value of $100,000. Shortly thereafter, Wilma purchases additional pasture land for $80,000. Can Wilma avoid the tax on any of the gain under the wherewithal to pay concept? Explain.

54. In what manner does the tax law mitigate the effect of the annual accounting period concept for a net operating loss?

55. How does the tax law cope with the impact of inflation?

56. Forcing accrual basis taxpayers to recognize prepaid income when received (as opposed to when earned) accomplishes what objective?

57. On his income tax return for the year, Henry claims as a deduction certain charitable contributions that he did not make. When you question him about this, he responds:
   a. "How is the IRS going to prove that I did not make these contributions?"
   b. "Even if the IRS disallows the deductions, the worst that can happen is that I will owe the same amount of tax I would have paid anyway."

   Comment on Henry's misconceptions about the tax law.

58. Edward leases real estate to Janet for a period of 20 years. Janet makes capital improvements to the property. When the lease expires, Edward reclaims the property, including the improvements made by Janet.
   a. Under current law, at what point does Edward recognize income as a result of Janet's improvements?
   b. Has the law in (a) always been the rule?
   c. What is the justification, if any, for the current rule?

TEAM PROJECT: ARTHUR ANDERSEN TAX CHALLENGE CASES

Arthur Andersen & Co. has provided two of the cases that have been used in the Arthur Andersen Tax Challenge for use in *West's Federal Taxation: Individual Income Taxes* (or *West's Federal Taxation: Comprehensive Volume*). The Tax Challenge is a nationwide university competition to stimulate student interest in tax careers. The case studies are based on Federal tax issues confronting an individual or family with their own business, with investments made by the individual, compensation matters, itemized deductions, and related issues that affect the taxpayer's filing status and tax profile.

The Tax Challenge is a team competition with four members on each team. Thus, the cases are excellent materials for team projects in tax classes. We suggest that team members read assigned cases in their entirety at this point in the course. Because the cases require the application of knowledge gained throughout the course, it is not possible to prepare a solution early in the course. However, the length and complexity of the cases dictate that students must spend some time working on them during the entire course. To facilitate this course-long effort, we have identified topics related to each chapter and placed instructions regarding these topics in the end-of-chapter problem materials as appropriate.

Information related to tax issues and problems that are discussed in this chapter may be found in the

Day and Ball case on pages 11, 12, 25, and 26
Fence case on pages 39, 40, 52, and 55

Read and analyze the case you have been assigned and *identify* any issues and problems that are related to material covered in this chapter. If the information provided in the case is complete, prepare answers for this part of the case at this time. If you need information that is contained in later parts of the case, write a memo summarizing the questions or problems so you can prepare a complete answer at a later date.

2

TAX DETERMINATION; PERSONAL AND DEPENDENCY EXEMPTIONS; AN OVERVIEW OF PROPERTY TRANSACTIONS

LEARNING OBJECTIVES

After completing Chapter 2, you should be able to:

1. Understand and apply the components of the Federal income tax formula.

2. Apply the rules for arriving at personal and dependency exemptions.

3. Use the proper method for determining the tax liability.

4. Identify and work with kiddie tax situations.

5. Recognize the filing requirements and the proper filing status.

6. Possess an overview of property transactions.

7. Identify tax planning opportunities associated with the individual tax formula.

Individuals are subject to Federal income tax based on taxable income. This chapter explains how taxable income and the income tax of an individual taxpayer are determined.

To compute taxable income, it is necessary to understand the tax formula in Figure 2–1. Although the tax formula is rather simple, determining an individual's taxable income can be quite complex. The complexity stems from the numerous provisions that govern the determination of gross income and allowable deductions.

After computing taxable income, the appropriate rates must be applied. This requires a determination of the individual's filing status, since different rates apply for single taxpayers, married taxpayers, and heads of household. The basic tax rate structure is progressive, with rates ranging from 15 percent to 39.6 percent.[1] For comparison, the lowest rate structure, which was in effect in 1913–1915, ranged

▼ FIGURE 2–1
Tax Formula

Income (broadly conceived)	$xx,xxx
Less: Exclusions	(x,xxx)
Gross income	$xx,xxx
Less: Deductions *for* adjusted gross income	(x,xxx)
Adjusted gross income	$xx,xxx
Less: The greater of—	
Total itemized deductions *or* the standard deduction	(x,xxx)
Personal and dependency exemptions	(x,xxx)
Taxable income	$xx,xxx

[1]The 1998 Tax Table was not available from the IRS at the date of publication of this text. The Tax Table for 1997 and the Tax Rate Schedules for 1997 and 1998 are reproduced in Appendix A. For quick reference, the 1997 and 1998 Tax Rate Schedules are also reproduced inside the front cover of this text.

from 1 to 7 percent, and the highest, in effect during 1944–1945, ranged from 23 to 94 percent.

Once the individual's tax has been computed, prepayments and credits are subtracted to determine whether the taxpayer owes additional tax or is entitled to a refund.

When property is sold or otherwise disposed of, a gain or loss may result, which can affect the determination of taxable income. Although property transactions are covered in detail in Chapters 12 and 13, an understanding of certain basic concepts helps in working with some of the materials to follow. The concluding portion of this chapter furnishes an overview of property transactions, including the distinction between realized and recognized gain or loss, the classification of such gain or loss (ordinary or capital), and treatment for income tax purposes.

TAX FORMULA

1 LEARNING OBJECTIVE
Understand and apply the components of the Federal income tax formula.

Most individuals compute taxable income using the tax formula shown in Figure 2–1. Special provisions govern the computation of taxable income and the tax liability for certain minor children who have unearned income in excess of specified amounts. These provisions are discussed later in the chapter.

Before illustrating the application of the tax formula, a brief discussion of its components is helpful.

COMPONENTS OF THE TAX FORMULA

Income (Broadly Conceived).   This includes all the taxpayer's income, both taxable and nontaxable. Although it is essentially equivalent to gross receipts, it does not include a return of capital or receipt of borrowed funds.

EXAMPLE 1

Dave needed money to purchase a house. He sold 5,000 shares of stock for $100,000. He had paid $40,000 for the stock. In addition, he borrowed $75,000 from a bank. Dave has income that is taxable of $60,000 from the sale of the stock ($100,000 selling price – $40,000 return of capital). He has no income from the $75,000 borrowed from the bank because he has an obligation to repay that amount. ▼

Exclusions.   For various reasons, Congress has chosen to exclude certain types of income from the income tax base. The principal income exclusions are discussed in Chapter 4. A partial list of these exclusions is shown in Exhibit 2–1.

Gross Income.   The Internal Revenue Code defines gross income broadly as "except as otherwise provided . . ., all income from whatever source derived."[2] The "except as otherwise provided" refers to exclusions. Gross income includes, but is not limited to, the items in the partial list in Exhibit 2–2. It does not include unrealized gains. Gross income is discussed in Chapters 3 and 4.

---

[2] § 61(a).

▼ **EXHIBIT 2–1**
Partial List of Exclusions from
Gross Income

Accident insurance proceeds	Meals and lodging (if furnished for employer's convenience)
Annuities (cost element)	Military allowances
Bequests	Minister's dwelling rental value allowance
Child support payments	
Cost-of-living allowance (for military)	Railroad retirement benefits (to a limited extent)
Damages for personal injury or sickness	
Gifts received	Scholarship grants (to a limited extent)
Group term life insurance, premium paid by employer (for coverage up to $50,000)	Social Security benefits (to a limited extent)
	Veterans' benefits
Inheritances	Welfare payments
Interest from state and local (i.e., municipal) bonds	Workers' compensation benefits
Life insurance paid on death	

▼ **EXHIBIT 2–2**
Partial List of Gross Income
Items

Alimony	Group term life insurance, premium paid by employer (for coverage over $50,000)
Annuities (income element)	
Awards	Hobby income
Back pay	Interest
Bargain purchase from employer	Jury duty fees
Bonuses	Living quarters, meals (unless furnished for employer's convenience)
Breach of contract damages	
Business income	
Clergy fees	Mileage allowance
Commissions	Military pay (unless combat pay)
Compensation for services	Notary fees
Death benefits	Partnership income
Debts forgiven	Pensions
Director's fees	Prizes
Dividends	Professional fees
Embezzled funds	Punitive damages
Employee awards (in certain cases)	Rents
Employee benefits (except certain fringe benefits)	Rewards
	Royalties
Estate and trust income	Salaries
Farm income	Severance pay
Fees	Strike and lockout benefits
Gains from illegal activities	Supplemental unemployment benefits
Gains from sale of property	Tips and gratuities
Gambling winnings	Travel allowance (in certain cases)
	Wages

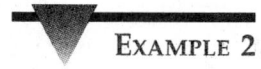

EXAMPLE 2

Beth received the following amounts during the year:

Salary	$30,000
Interest on savings account	900
Gift from her aunt	10,000
Prize won in state lottery	1,000
Alimony from ex-husband	12,000
Child support from ex-husband	6,000
Damages for injury in auto accident	25,000
Increase in the value of stock held for investment	5,000

Review Exhibits 2–1 and 2–2 to determine the amount Beth must include in the computation of taxable income and the amount she may exclude. Then check your answer in footnote 3.[3] ▼

Deductions for Adjusted Gross Income.   Individual taxpayers have two categories of deductions: (1) deductions *for* adjusted gross income (deductions to arrive at adjusted gross income) and (2) deductions *from* adjusted gross income.

Deductions *for* adjusted gross income (AGI) include ordinary and necessary expenses incurred in a trade or business, one-half of self-employment tax paid, alimony paid, certain payments to an Individual Retirement Account and Medical Savings Accounts, moving expenses, forfeited interest penalty for premature withdrawal of time deposits, the capital loss deduction, and others.[4] The principal deductions *for* AGI are discussed in Chapters 5, 6, 7, 8, and 10.

Adjusted Gross Income (AGI).   AGI is an important subtotal that serves as the basis for computing percentage limitations on certain itemized deductions, such as medical expenses and charitable contributions. For example, medical expenses are deductible only to the extent they exceed 7.5 percent of AGI, and charitable contribution deductions may not exceed 50 percent of AGI. These limitations might be described as a 7.5 percent *floor* under the medical expense deduction and a 50 percent *ceiling* on the charitable contribution deduction.

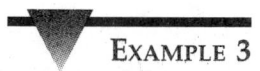

EXAMPLE 3

Keith earned a salary of $23,000 in the current tax year. He contributed $2,000 to his Individual Retirement Account (IRA) and sustained a $1,000 capital loss on the sale of Wren Corporation stock. His AGI is computed as follows:

Gross income		
Salary		$23,000
Less: Deductions *for* AGI		
IRA contribution	$2,000	
Capital loss	1,000	(3,000)
AGI		$20,000

▼

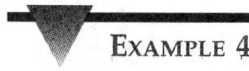

EXAMPLE 4

Assume the same facts as in Example 3, and that Keith also had medical expenses of $1,800. Medical expenses may be included in itemized deductions to the extent they exceed 7.5% of AGI. In computing his itemized deductions, Keith may include medical expenses of $300 [$1,800 medical expenses − $1,500 (7.5% × $20,000 AGI)]. ▼

---

[3]Beth must include $43,900 in computing taxable income ($30,000 salary + $900 interest + $1,000 lottery prize + $12,000 alimony). She can exclude $41,000 ($10,000 gift from aunt + $6,000 child support + $25,000 damages). The unrealized gain on the stock held for investment also is not included in gross income. Such

gain will be included in gross income only when it is realized upon disposition of the stock.
[4]§ 62.

Itemized Deductions.   As a general rule, personal expenditures are disallowed as deductions in arriving at taxable income. However, Congress has chosen to allow specified personal expenses as **itemized deductions.** Such expenditures include medical expenses, certain taxes and interest, and charitable contributions.

In addition to these personal expenses, taxpayers are allowed itemized deductions for expenses related to (1) the production or collection of income and (2) the management of property held for the production of income.[5] These expenses, sometimes referred to as *nonbusiness expenses,* differ from trade or business expenses (discussed previously). Trade or business expenses, which are deductions *for* AGI, must be incurred in connection with a trade or business. Nonbusiness expenses, on the other hand, are expenses incurred in connection with an income-producing activity that does not qualify as a trade or business. Such expenses are itemized deductions.

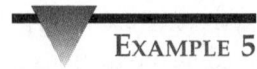

EXAMPLE 5

Leo is the owner and operator of a video game arcade. All allowable expenses he incurs in connection with the arcade business are deductions *for* AGI. In addition, Leo has an extensive portfolio of stocks and bonds. Leo's investment activity is not treated as a trade or business. All allowable expenses that Leo incurs in connection with these investments are itemized deductions. ▼

Itemized deductions include, but are not limited to, the expenses listed in Exhibit 2–3. See Chapter 9 for a detailed discussion of itemized deductions.

Standard Deduction.   The **standard deduction,** which is set by Congress, is a specified amount that depends on the filing status of the taxpayer. The effect of the standard deduction is to exempt a taxpayer's income, up to the specified amount, from Federal income tax liability. In the past, Congress has attempted to

▼ **EXHIBIT 2–3**
Partial List of Itemized
Deductions

Medical expenses in excess of 7.5% of AGI
State and local income taxes
Real estate taxes
Personal property taxes
Interest on home mortgage
Investment interest (to a limited extent)
Charitable contributions (within specified percentage limitations)
Casualty and theft losses in excess of 10% of AGI
Miscellaneous expenses (to the extent such expenses exceed 2% of AGI)
Union dues
Professional dues and subscriptions
Certain educational expenses
Tax return preparation fee
Investment counsel fees
Unreimbursed employee business expenses (after a percentage reduction for meals and entertainment)

[5]§ 212.

set the tax-free amount represented by the standard deduction approximately equal to an estimated poverty level,[6] but it has not always been consistent in doing so.

The standard deduction is the sum of two components: the *basic* standard deduction and the *additional* standard deduction.[7] Table 2–1 lists the basic standard deduction allowed for taxpayers in each filing status. All taxpayers allowed a *full* standard deduction are entitled to the applicable amount listed in Table 2–1. The standard deduction amounts are subject to adjustment for inflation each year.

Certain taxpayers are not allowed to claim *any* standard deduction, and the standard deduction is *limited* for others. These provisions are discussed later in the chapter.

A taxpayer who is age 65 or over *or* blind qualifies for an *additional standard deduction* of $850 or $1,050, depending on filing status (see amounts in Table 2–2). Two additional standard deductions are allowed for a taxpayer who is age 65 or over *and* blind. The additional standard deduction provisions also apply for a qualifying spouse who is age 65 or over or blind, but a taxpayer may not claim an additional standard deduction for a dependent.

To determine whether to itemize, the taxpayer compares the *total* standard deduction (the sum of the basic standard deduction and any additional standard deductions) with total itemized deductions. Taxpayers are allowed to deduct the *greater* of itemized deductions or the standard deduction. Taxpayers whose itemized deductions are less than the standard deduction compute their taxable income using the standard deduction rather than itemizing.

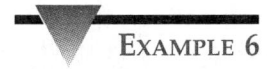

EXAMPLE 6

Sara, who is single, is 66 years old. She had total itemized deductions of $5,100 during 1998. Her total standard deduction is $5,300 ($4,250 basic standard deduction plus $1,050 additional standard deduction). Sara should compute her taxable income for 1998 using the standard deduction ($5,300), since it exceeds her itemized deductions ($5,100). ▼

▼ **TABLE 2–1**
Basic Standard Deduction Amounts

	Standard Deduction Amount	
Filing Status	**1997**	**1998**
Single	$4,150	$4,250
Married, filing jointly	6,900	7,100
Surviving spouse	6,900	7,100
Head of household	6,050	6,250
Married, filing separately	3,450	3,550

▼ **TABLE 2–2**
Amount of Each Additional Standard Deduction

Filing Status	**1997**	**1998**
Single	$1,000	$1,050
Married, filing jointly	800	850
Surviving spouse	800	850
Head of household	1,000	1,050
Married, filing separately	800	850

[6]S.Rep. No. 92–437, 92nd Cong., 1st Sess., 1971, p. 54. Another purpose of the standard deduction was discussed in Chapter 1 under Influence of the Internal Revenue Service—Administrative Feasibility. The size of the standard deduction has a direct bearing on the number of taxpayers who are in a position to itemize deductions.

Reducing the number of taxpayers who itemize also reduces the audit effort required from the IRS. Currently, about 70% of all individual taxpayers choose to use the standard deduction.
[7]§ 63(c)(1).

Personal and Dependency Exemptions. Exemptions are allowed for the taxpayer, for the taxpayer's spouse, and for each dependent of the taxpayer. The exemption amount is $2,650 in 1997 and $2,700 in 1998.

APPLICATION OF THE TAX FORMULA

The tax formula shown in Figure 2–1 is illustrated in Example 7.

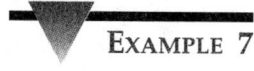

EXAMPLE 7

Grace, age 25, is single and has no dependents. She is a high school teacher and earned a $20,000 salary in 1998. Her other income consisted of a $1,000 prize won in a sweepstakes contest and $500 interest on municipal bonds received as a graduation gift in 1995. During 1998, she sustained a deductible capital loss of $1,000. Her itemized deductions are $4,400. Grace's taxable income for the year is computed as follows:

Income (broadly conceived)		
Salary		$20,000
Prize		1,000
Interest on municipal bonds		500
		$21,500
Less: Exclusion—		
Interest on municipal bonds		(500)
Gross income		$21,000
Less: Deduction *for* adjusted gross income—		
Capital loss		(1,000)
Adjusted gross income		$20,000
Less: The greater of—		
Total itemized deductions	$4,400	
or the standard deduction	$4,250	(4,400)
Personal and dependency exemptions		
(1 × $2,700)		(2,700)
Taxable income		$12,900

The structure of the individual income tax return (Form 1040, 1040A, or 1040EZ) differs somewhat from the tax formula in Figure 2–1. On the tax return, gross income generally is the starting point in computing taxable income. With few exceptions, exclusions are not reported on the tax return.

INDIVIDUALS NOT ELIGIBLE FOR THE STANDARD DEDUCTION

The following individual taxpayers are ineligible to use the standard deduction and must therefore itemize:[8]

- A married individual filing a separate return where either spouse itemizes deductions.
- A nonresident alien.
- An individual filing a return for a period of less than 12 months because of a change in the annual accounting period.

---

[8]§ 63(c)(6).

SPECIAL LIMITATIONS FOR INDIVIDUALS WHO CAN BE CLAIMED AS DEPENDENTS

Special rules apply to the standard deduction and personal exemption of an individual who can be claimed as a dependent on another person's tax return.

When filing his or her own tax return, a *dependent's* basic standard deduction in 1998 is limited to the greater of $700 or the sum of the individual's earned income for the year plus $250.[9] However, if the sum of the individual's earned income plus $250 exceeds the normal standard deduction, the standard deduction is limited to the appropriate amount shown in Table 2–1. These limitations apply only to the basic standard deduction. A dependent who is 65 or over or blind or both is also allowed the additional standard deduction amount on his or her own return (refer to Table 2–2). These provisions are illustrated in Examples 8 through 11.

EXAMPLE 8

Susan, who is 17 years old and single, is claimed as a dependent on her parents' tax return. During 1998, she received $1,200 interest (unearned income) on a savings account. She also earned $300 from a part-time job. When Susan files her own tax return, her standard deduction is $700 (the greater of $700 or the sum of earned income of $300 plus $250). ▼

EXAMPLE 9

Assume the same facts as in Example 8, except that Susan is 67 years old and is claimed as a dependent on her son's tax return. In this case, when Susan files her own tax return, her standard deduction is $1,750 [$700 (the greater of $700 or the sum of earned income of $300 plus $250) + $1,050 (the additional standard deduction allowed because Susan is 65 or over)]. ▼

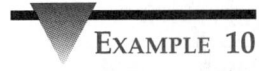

EXAMPLE 10

Peggy, who is 16 years old and single, earned $600 from a summer job and had no unearned income during 1998. She is claimed as a dependent on her parents' tax return. Her standard deduction is $850 (the greater of $700 or the sum of $600 earned income plus $250). ▼

EXAMPLE 11

Jack, who is a 20-year-old, single, full-time college student, is claimed as a dependent on his parents' tax return. He worked as a musician during the summer of 1998, earning $4,300. Jack's standard deduction is $4,250 (the greater of $700 or the sum of $4,300 earned income plus $250, but limited to the $4,250 standard deduction for a single taxpayer). ▼

A taxpayer who claims an individual as a dependent is allowed to claim an exemption for the dependent. The dependent cannot claim a personal exemption on his or her own return. Based on the tax formula, Jack in Example 11 would have taxable income of $50, determined as follows:

Gross income	$ 4,300
Less: Standard deduction	(4,250)
Personal exemption	(–0–)
Taxable income	$ 50

---

[9]§ 63(c)(5). The $700 amount is subject to adjustment for inflation each year. The amount was $650 for 1997. The $250 amount is adjusted for inflation beginning in 1999. The $250 amount is newly created by the Taxpayer Relief Act of 1997.

PERSONAL AND DEPENDENCY EXEMPTIONS

2 **LEARNING OBJECTIVE**
Apply the rules for arriving at personal and dependency exemptions.

The use of exemptions in the tax system is based in part on the idea that a taxpayer with a small amount of income should be exempt from income taxation. An exemption frees a specified amount of income from tax ($2,650 in 1997 and $2,700 in 1998). The exemption amount is indexed (adjusted) annually for inflation. An individual who is not claimed as a dependent by another taxpayer is allowed to claim his or her own personal exemption. In addition, a taxpayer may claim an exemption for each dependent.

▼ EXAMPLE 12

Bonnie, who is single, supports her mother and father, who have no income of their own, and claims them as dependents on her tax return. Bonnie may claim a personal exemption for herself plus an exemption for each dependent. On her 1998 tax return, Bonnie may deduct $8,100 for exemptions ($2,700 per exemption × 3 exemptions). ▼

PERSONAL EXEMPTIONS

The Code provides a **personal exemption** for the taxpayer and an exemption for the spouse if a joint return is filed. However, when separate returns are filed, a married taxpayer cannot claim an exemption for his or her spouse *unless* the spouse has no gross income and is not claimed as the dependent of another taxpayer.

The determination of marital status generally is made at the end of the taxable year, except when a spouse dies during the year. Spouses who enter into a legal separation under a decree of divorce or separate maintenance before the end of the year are considered to be unmarried at the end of the taxable year. The following table illustrates the effect of death or divorce upon marital status:

	Marital Status for 1998
• Walt is the widower of Helen who died on January 3, 1998.	Walt and Helen are considered to be married for purposes of filing the 1998 return.
• Bill and Jane entered into a divorce decree that is effective on December 31, 1998.	Bill and Jane are considered to be unmarried for purposes of filing the 1998 return.

DEPENDENCY EXEMPTIONS

As indicated in Example 12, the Code allows a taxpayer to claim a dependency exemption for each eligible individual. A **dependency exemption** may be claimed for each individual for whom the following five tests are met:

- Support.
- Relationship or member of the household.
- Gross income.
- Joint return.
- Citizenship or residency.

A person who dies during the year can still be claimed as a dependent if all of the tests are met. In such a case, no proration is necessary, and the full amount of the exemption is allowed.

Support Test. Over one-half of the support of the individual must be furnished by the taxpayer. Support includes food, shelter, clothing, medical and dental care, education, etc. However, a scholarship received by a student is not included for purposes of computing whether the taxpayer furnished more than half of the child's support.[10]

EXAMPLE 13

Hal contributed $3,400 (consisting of food, clothing, and medical care) toward the support of his son, Sam, who earned $1,500 from a part-time job and received a $2,000 scholarship to attend a local university. Assuming that the other dependency tests are met, Hal can claim Sam as a dependent since he has contributed more than half of Sam's support. The $2,000 scholarship is not included as support for purposes of this test. ▼

If the individual does not spend funds that have been received from any source, the unexpended amounts are not counted for purposes of the support test.

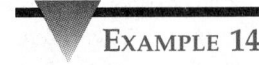

EXAMPLE 14

Emily contributed $3,000 to her father's support during the year. In addition, her father received $2,400 in Social Security benefits, $200 of interest, and wages of $600. Her father deposited the Social Security benefits, interest, and wages in his own savings account and did not use any of the funds for his support. Thus, the Social Security benefits, interest, and wages are not considered as support provided by Emily's father. Emily may claim her father as a dependent if the other tests are met. ▼

Capital expenditures for items such as furniture, appliances, and automobiles are included in total support if the item does, in fact, constitute support.[11]

EXAMPLE 15

Norm purchased a television set costing $150 and gave it to his minor daughter. The television set was placed in the child's bedroom and was used exclusively by her. Norm should include the cost of the television set in determining the support of his daughter. ▼

EXAMPLE 16

Mark paid $6,000 for an automobile that was titled and registered in his name. Mark's minor son is permitted to use the automobile equally with Mark. Since Mark did not give the automobile to his son, the $6,000 cost is not includible as a support item. However, out-of-pocket operating expenses incurred by Mark for the benefit of his son are includible as support. ▼

One exception to the support test involves a **multiple support agreement.** A multiple support agreement permits one of a group of taxpayers who furnish more than half of the support of an individual to claim a dependency exemption for that individual even if no one person provides more than 50 percent of the support.[12] Any person who contributed *more than 10 percent* of the support is entitled to claim the exemption if each person in the group who contributed more than 10 percent files a written consent. This provision frequently enables one of the children of aged dependent parents to claim an exemption when none of the children meets the 50 percent support test. Each person who is a party to the multiple support agreement must meet all other requirements (except the support requirement) for claiming the exemption. A person who does not meet the relationship or member-of-household requirement, for instance, cannot claim the dependency exemption under a multiple support agreement. It does not matter if he or she contributes more than 10 percent of the individual's support.

---

[10]Reg. § 1.152–1(c).
[11]Rev.Rul. 57–344, 1957–2 C.B. 112; Rev.Rul. 58–419, 1958–2 C.B. 57.
[12]§ 152(c).

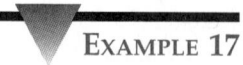

EXAMPLE 17

Wanda, who resides with her son, Adam, received $6,000 from various sources during 1998. This constituted her entire support for the year. She received support from the following:

	Amount	Percentage of Total
Adam, a son	$2,880	48
Bob, a son	600	10
Carol, a daughter	1,800	30
Diane, a friend	720	12
	$6,000	100

If Adam and Carol file a multiple support agreement, either may claim the dependency exemption for Wanda. Bob may not claim Wanda because he did not contribute more than 10% of her support. Bob's consent is not required in order for Adam and Carol to file a multiple support agreement. Diane does not meet the relationship or member-of-household test and cannot be a party to the agreement. The decision as to who claims Wanda rests with Adam and Carol. It is possible for Carol to claim Wanda, even though Adam furnished more of Wanda's support. ▼

Each person who qualifies under the more-than-10 percent rule (except for the person claiming the exemption) must complete Form 2120 (Multiple Support Declaration) waiving the exemption. The person claiming the exemption must attach all Forms 2120 to his or her own return.

A second exception to the 50 percent support requirement can occur for a child of parents who are divorced or separated under a decree of separate maintenance. For decrees executed after 1984, the custodial parent is allowed to claim the exemption unless that parent agrees in writing not to claim a dependency exemption for the child.[13] Thus, claiming the exemption is dependent on whether or not a written agreement exists, *not* on meeting the support test.

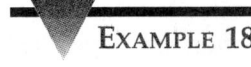

EXAMPLE 18   Ira and Rita obtain a divorce decree in 1990. In 1998, their two children are in Rita's custody. Ira contributed over half of the support for each child. In the absence of a written agreement on the dependency exemptions, Rita (the custodial parent) is entitled to the exemptions in 1998. However, Ira may claim the exemptions if Rita agrees in writing. ▼

For the noncustodial parent to claim the exemption, the custodial parent must complete Form 8332 (Release of Claim to Exemption for Child of Divorced or Separated Parents). The release can apply to a single year, a number of specified years, or all future years. The noncustodial parent must attach a copy of Form 8332 to his or her return.

Relationship or Member-of-the-Household Test.   To be claimed as a dependent, an individual must be either a relative of the taxpayer or a member of the taxpayer's household. The Code contains a detailed listing of the various blood and marriage relationships that qualify. Note, however, that the relationship test is met if the individual is a relative of either spouse. Once established by marriage, a relationship continues regardless of subsequent changes in marital status.

The following individuals may be claimed as dependents of the taxpayer if the other tests for dependency are met:[14]

- A son or daughter of the taxpayer or a descendant of either, such as a grandchild.
- A stepson or stepdaughter of the taxpayer.
- A brother, sister, stepbrother, or stepsister of the taxpayer.
- The father or mother of the taxpayer or an ancestor of either, such as a grandparent.
- A stepfather or stepmother of the taxpayer.
- A nephew or niece of the taxpayer.
- An uncle or aunt of the taxpayer.
- A son-in-law, daughter-in-law, father-in-law, mother-in-law, brother-in-law, or sister-in-law of the taxpayer.
- An individual who, for the entire taxable year of the taxpayer, has as his or her principal place of abode the home of the taxpayer and is a member of the taxpayer's household. This does not include an individual who, at any time during the taxable year, was the spouse of the taxpayer.

The following rules are also prescribed in the Code:[15]

- A legally adopted child is treated as a natural child.
- A foster child qualifies if the child's principal place of abode is the taxpayer's household.

---

[13]§ 152(e).

[14]§ 152(a). However, under § 152(b)(5), a taxpayer may not claim someone who is a member of his or her household as a dependent if their relationship is in violation of local law. For example, the dependency exemption was denied because the taxpayer's relation-

ship to the person claimed as a dependent constituted *cohabitation*, a crime under applicable state law. *Cassius L. Peacock, III*, 37 TCM 177, T.C.Memo. 1978–30.

[15]§ 152(b)(2).

Gross Income Test.   The dependent's gross income must be less than the exemption amount ($2,700 in 1998).[16] The gross income test is measured by income that is taxable. In the case of scholarships, for example, it excludes the nontaxable portion (e.g., amounts received for books and tuition) but includes the taxable portion (e.g., amounts received for room and board).

A parent may claim a dependency exemption for his or her child, even when the child's gross income exceeds $2,700, if the parent provided over half of the child's support and the child, at year-end, is under age 19 or is a full-time student under age 24. If the parent claims a dependency exemption, the dependent child may not claim a personal exemption on his or her own income tax return.

A child is defined as a son, stepson, daughter, stepdaughter, adopted son, or adopted daughter and may include a foster child.[17] For the child to qualify as a student for purposes of the dependency exemption, he or she must be a full-time student at an educational institution during some part of five calendar months of the year.[18] This exception to the gross income test for dependent children who are under age 19 or full-time students under age 24 permits a child or college student to earn money from part-time or summer jobs without penalizing the parent with the loss of the dependency exemption.

Joint Return Test.   If a dependent is married, the supporting taxpayer (e.g., the parent of a married child) generally is not permitted a dependency exemption if the married individual files a joint return with his or her spouse.[19] The joint return rule does not apply, however, if the following conditions are met:

- The reason for filing is to claim a refund for tax withheld.
- No tax liability would exist for either spouse on separate returns.
- Neither spouse is required to file a return.

See Table 2–4 later in the chapter and the related discussion concerning income level requirements for filing a return.

EXAMPLE 19   Paul provides over half of the support of his son Quinn. He also provides over half of the support of Vera, who is Quinn's wife. During the year, both Quinn and Vera had part-time jobs. In order to recover the taxes withheld, they file a joint return. If Quinn and Vera are not required to file a return, Paul is allowed to claim both as dependents. ▼

Citizenship or Residency Test.   To be a dependent, the individual must be either a U.S. citizen, a U.S. resident, or a resident of Canada or Mexico for some part of the calendar year in which the taxpayer's tax year begins.

ETHICAL CONSIDERATIONS

How to Generate More Dependency Exemptions

Raul is a citizen of Honduras but a resident of California. He furnishes most of the support for his family (i.e., parents and grandparents) who are citizens and residents of Honduras. In December 1998, Raul has his family move to Mexico and establish legal residence there. On his income tax return for calendar year 1998, Raul claims four dependency exemptions for his family. Has Raul acted properly? Why?

---

[16]§ 151(c)(1).
[17]Reg. § 1.151–3(a).

[18]Reg. §§ 1.151–3(b) and (c).
[19]§ 151(c)(2).

Phase-out of Exemptions.   Several provisions of the tax law are intended to increase the tax liability of more affluent taxpayers who might otherwise enjoy some benefit from having some of their taxable income subject to the lower income tax brackets (e.g., 15 percent, 28 percent). One such provision phases out personal and dependency exemptions as AGI exceeds specified threshold amounts. For 1997 and 1998, the phase-out *begins* at the following threshold amounts:

	1997	**1998**
Joint returns/surviving spouse	$181,800	$186,800
Head of household	151,500	155,650
Single	121,200	124,500
Married, filing separately	90,900	93,400

These threshold amounts are indexed for inflation each year.

Exemptions are phased out by 2 percent for each $2,500 (or fraction thereof) by which the taxpayer's AGI exceeds the threshold amounts. For a married taxpayer filing separately, the phase-out is 2 percent for each $1,250 or fraction thereof.

The allowable exemption amount can be determined with the following steps:

1. AGI – threshold amount = excess amount
2. Excess amount ÷ $2,500 = reduction factor [rounded up to the next whole increment (e.g., 18.1 = 19)] × 2 = phase-out percentage
3. Phase-out percentage (from step 2) × exemption amount = amount of exemptions phased out
4. Exemption amounts – phase-out amount = allowable exemption deduction

EXAMPLE 20

Frederico is married but files a separate return. His AGI is $113,400. He is entitled to one personal exemption.

1. $113,400 – $93,400 = $20,000 excess amount
2. [($20,000 ÷ $1,250) × 2] = 32% (phase-out percentage)
3. 32% × $2,700 = $864 amount of exemption phased out
4. $2,700 – $864 = $1,836 allowable exemption deduction ▼

Note that the exemption amount is completely phased out when the taxpayer's AGI exceeds the threshold amount by more than $122,500 ($61,250 for a married taxpayer filing a separate return), calculated as follows:

$122,501 ÷ $2,500 = 49.0004, rounded to 50 and multiplied by 2 = 100% (phase-out percentage)

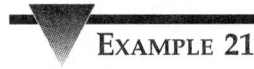

EXAMPLE 21

Bill and Isabella file a joint return claiming two personal exemptions and one dependency exemption for their child. Their AGI equals $310,800.

$310,800 – $186,800 = $124,000 excess amount

Since the excess amount exceeds $122,500, the exemptions are completely phased out. ▼

TAX DETERMINATION

TAX TABLE METHOD

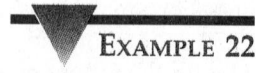

3 **LEARNING OBJECTIVE**
Use the proper method for
determining the tax liability.

Most taxpayers compute their tax using the **Tax Table.** Eligible taxpayers compute taxable income (as shown in Figure 2–1) and *must* determine their tax by reference to the Tax Table. The following taxpayers, however, may not use the Tax Table method:

- An individual who files a short period return (see Chapter 15).
- Individuals whose taxable income exceeds the maximum (ceiling) amount in the Tax Table. The 1997 Tax Table applies to taxable income below $100,000 for Form 1040.
- An estate or trust.

The 1998 Tax Table was not available at the date of publication of this text. Therefore, the 1997 Tax Table will be used to illustrate the tax computation using the Tax Table method.

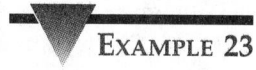

EXAMPLE 22

Pedro, a single taxpayer, is eligible to use the Tax Table. For 1997, he had taxable income of $25,025. To determine Pedro's tax using the Tax Table (see Appendix A), find the $25,000 to $25,050 income line. The first column to the right of the taxable income column is for single taxpayers. Pedro's tax for 1997 is $3,803. ▼

TAX RATE SCHEDULE METHOD

The **Tax Rate Schedules** contain rates of 15, 28, 31, 36, and 39.6 percent. Separate schedules are provided for the following filing statuses: single, married filing jointly, married filing separately, and head of household. The rate schedules for 1997 and 1998 are reproduced inside the front cover of this text and also in Appendix A.

The rate schedules are adjusted for inflation each year. Comparison of the 1997 and 1998 schedules for single taxpayers shows that the top amount to which the 15 percent bracket applies rose from $24,650 in 1997 to $25,350 in 1998. Thus, inflation allowed $700 ($25,350 – $24,650) more taxable income to be subject to the lowest 15 percent rate. The 1998 rate schedule for single taxpayers is reproduced in Table 2–3. This schedule is used to illustrate the tax computations in Examples 23, 24, and 25.

EXAMPLE 23

Pat is single and had $18,000 of taxable income in 1998. His tax is $2,700 ($18,000 × 15%). ▼

▼ **TABLE 2–3**
1998 Tax Rate Schedule for
Single Taxpayers

If Taxable Income Is			Of the Amount
Over	But Not Over	The Tax Is:	Over
$ –0–	$ 25,350	15%	$ –0–
25,350	61,400	$ 3,802.50 + 28%	25,350
61,400	128,100	13,896.50 + 31%	61,400
128,100	278,450	34,573.50 + 36%	128,100
278,450		88,699.50 + 39.6%	278,450

Several terms are used to describe tax rates. The rates in the Tax Rate Schedules are often referred to as *statutory* (or nominal) rates. The *marginal* rate is the highest rate that is applied in the tax computation for a particular taxpayer. In Example 23, the statutory rate and the marginal rate are both 15 percent.

EXAMPLE 24

Chris is single and had taxable income of $41,450 in 1998. Her tax is $8,310.50 [$3,802.50 + 28%($41,450 – $25,350)]. ▼

The *average* rate is equal to the tax liability divided by taxable income. In Example 24, Chris has statutory rates of 15 percent and 28 percent, and a marginal rate of 28 percent. Chris's average rate is 20.05 percent ($8,310.50 tax liability ÷ $41,450 taxable income).

Note that $3,802.50, which is the starting point in the tax computation in Example 24, is 15 percent of the $25,350 taxable income in the first bracket. Income in excess of $25,350 is taxed at a 28 percent rate. This reflects the *progressive* (or graduated) rate structure on which the U.S. income tax system is based. A tax is progressive if a higher rate of tax applies as the tax base increases.

EXAMPLE 25

Carl is single and had taxable income of $81,900 in 1998. His tax is $20,251.50 [$13,896.50 + 31%($81,900 – $61,400)]. Note that the effect of this computation is to tax part of Carl's income at 15%, part at 28%, and part at 31%. An alternative computational method provides a clearer illustration of the progressive rate structure:

Tax on $25,350 at 15%	$ 3,802.50
Tax on $61,400 – $25,350 at 28%	10,094.00
Tax on $81,900 – $61,400 at 31%	6,355.00
Total	$20,251.50

▼

A special computation limits the effective tax rate on mid-term capital gain and long-term capital gain. The beneficial tax treatment of mid-term capital gain and long-term capital gain is discussed in detail in Chapter 13.

COMPUTATION OF NET TAXES PAYABLE OR REFUND DUE

The pay-as-you-go feature of the Federal income tax system requires payment of all or part of the taxpayer's income tax liability during the year. These payments take the form of Federal income tax withheld by employers or estimated tax paid by the taxpayer or both.[20] The payments are applied against the tax from the Tax Table or Tax Rate Schedules to determine whether the taxpayer will get a refund or pay additional tax.

Employers are required to withhold income tax on compensation paid to their employees and to pay this tax over to the government. The employer notifies the employee of the amount of income tax withheld on Form W–2 (Wage and Tax Statement). The employee should receive this form by January 31 after the year in which the income tax is withheld.

If taxpayers receive income that is not subject to withholding or income from which not enough tax is withheld, they must pay estimated tax. These individuals must file Form 1040–ES (Estimated Tax for Individuals) and pay in quarterly installments the income tax and self-employment tax estimated to be due.

---

[20]§ 3402 for withholding; § 6654 for estimated payments.

The income tax from the Tax Table or the Tax Rate Schedules is reduced first by the individual's tax credits. There is an important distinction between tax credits and tax deductions. Tax credits reduce the tax liability dollar-for-dollar. Tax deductions reduce taxable income on which the tax liability is based.

EXAMPLE 26

Gail is a taxpayer in the 28% tax bracket. As a result of incurring $1,000 in child care expenses (see Chapter 11 for details), she is entitled to a $200 child care credit ($1,000 child care expenses × 20% credit rate). She also contributed $1,000 to the American Cancer Society and included this amount in her itemized deductions. The child care credit results in a $200 reduction of Gail's tax liability for the year. The contribution to the American Cancer Society reduces taxable income by $1,000 and results in a $280 reduction in Gail's tax liability ($1,000 reduction in taxable income × 28% tax rate). ▼

Tax credits are discussed in Chapter 11. The following are several of the more common credits:

- Earned income credit.
- Credit for child and dependent care expenses.
- Credit for the elderly.
- Foreign tax credit.
- Child tax credit.

EXAMPLE 27

Kelly, age 30, is a head of household with a disabled dependent mother living with him. During 1998, Kelly had the following: taxable income, $30,000; income tax withheld, $3,950; estimated tax payments, $600; and credit for dependent care expenses, $200. Kelly's net tax payable is computed as follows:

Income tax (from 1998 Tax Rate Schedule, Appendix A)		$ 4,500
Less: Tax credits and prepayments—		
Credit for dependent care expenses	$ 200	
Income tax withheld	3,950	
Estimated tax payments	600	(4,750)
Net taxes payable or (refund due if negative)		$ (250)

▼

UNEARNED INCOME OF CHILDREN UNDER AGE 14 TAXED AT PARENTS' RATE

4 ▼ **LEARNING OBJECTIVE**
Identify and work with kiddie tax situations.

At one time, a dependent child could claim an exemption on his or her own return even if claimed as a dependent by the parents. This enabled a parent to shift investment income (such as interest and dividends) to a child by transferring ownership of the assets producing the income. The child would pay no tax on the income to the extent that it was sheltered by the child's exemption.

Also, an additional tax motivation existed for shifting income from parents to children. Although a child's unearned income in excess of the exemption amount was subject to tax, it was taxed at the child's rate, rather than the parents' rate.

To reduce the tax savings that result from shifting income from parents to children, the net **unearned income** (commonly called investment income) of certain minor children is taxed as if it were the parents' income.[21] Unearned income includes such income as taxable interest, dividends, capital gains, rents,

---

[21]§ 1(g).

royalties, pension and annuity income, and income (other than earned income) received as the beneficiary of a trust. This provision, commonly referred to as the **kiddie tax,** applies to any child for any taxable year if the child has not reached age 14 by the close of the taxable year, has at least one living parent, and has unearned income of more than $1,400. The *kiddie tax* provision does not apply to a child age 14 or older. However, the limitation on the use of the standard deduction and the unavailability of the personal exemption do apply to such a child as long as he or she is eligible to be claimed as a dependent by a parent.

Net Unearned Income.   Net unearned income of a dependent child is computed as follows:

Unearned income
Less: $700
Less: The greater of
   • $700 of the standard deduction *or*
   • The amount of allowable itemized deductions directly connected with the production of the unearned income
Equals: Net unearned income

If net unearned income is zero (or negative), the child's tax is computed without using the parent's rate. If the amount of net unearned income (regardless of source) is positive, the net unearned income is taxed at the parent's rate. The $700 amounts in the preceding formula are subject to adjustment for inflation each year (refer to footnote 9).

Tax Determination.   If a child under age 14 has net unearned income, there are two options for computing the tax on the income. A separate return may be filed for the child, or the parents may elect to report the child's income on their own return. If a separate return is filed for the child, the tax on net unearned income (referred to as the *allocable parental tax*) is computed as though the income had been included on the parents' return. Form 8615 (reproduced in Appendix B) is used to compute the tax. The steps required in this computation are illustrated below.

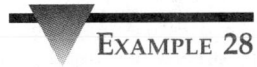

EXAMPLE 28   Olaf and Olga have a child, Hans (age 10). In 1998, Hans received $2,900 of interest and dividend income and paid investment-related fees of $200. Olaf and Olga had $70,000 of taxable income, not including their child's investment income. Olaf and Olga do not make the parental election.

1. Determine Hans's net unearned income

Gross income (unearned)	$2,900
Less: $700	(700)
Less: The greater of	
• $700 or	
• Investment expense ($200)	(700)
Equals: Net unearned income	$1,500

2. Determine allocable parental tax

Parents' taxable income	$ 70,000
Plus: Hans's net unearned income	1,500
Equals: Revised taxable income	$ 71,500
Tax on revised taxable income	$ 14,515
Less: Tax on parents' taxable income	(14,095)
Allocable parental tax	$ 420

3. Determine Hans's nonparental source tax

Hans's AGI	$ 2,900
Less: Standard deduction	(700)
Less: Personal exemption	(–0–)
Equals: Taxable income	$ 2,200
Less: Net unearned income	(1,500)
Nonparental source taxable income	$ 700
Equals: Tax ($700 × 15% rate)	$ 105

4. Determine Hans's total tax liability

Nonparental source tax (step 3)	$ 105
Allocable parental tax (step 2)	420
Total tax	$ 525

▼

Election to Claim Certain Unearned Income on Parent's Return. If a child under age 14 is required to file a tax return and meets all of the following requirements, the parent may elect to report the child's unearned income that exceeds $1,400 on the parent's own tax return:

- Gross income is from interest and dividends only.
- Gross income is more than $700 but less than $7,000.
- No estimated tax has been paid in the name and Social Security number of the child, and the child is not subject to backup withholding.

If the parental election is made, the child is treated as having no gross income and then is not required to file a tax return.

The parent(s) must also pay an additional tax equal to the smaller of $105 or 15 percent of the child's gross income over $700. Parents who have substantial itemized deductions based on AGI (see Chapter 9) may find that making the parental election increases total taxes for the family unit. Taxes should be calculated both with the parental election and without it to determine the appropriate choice.

Other Provisions.   If parents have more than one child subject to the tax on net unearned income, the tax for the children is computed as shown in Example 28 and then allocated to the children based on their relative amounts of income. For children of divorced parents, the taxable income of the custodial parent is used to determine the allocable parental tax. This parent is the one who may elect to report the child's unearned income. For married individuals filing separate returns, the individual with the greater taxable income is the applicable parent.

FILING CONSIDERATIONS

5   LEARNING OBJECTIVE
Recognize the filing
requirements and the proper
filing status.

Under the category of filing considerations, the following questions need to be resolved:

- Is the taxpayer required to file an income tax return?
- If so, which form should be used?
- When and how should the return be filed?
- In computing the tax liability, which column of the Tax Table or which Tax Rate Schedule should be used?

The first three questions are discussed under Filing Requirements, and the last is treated under Filing Status.

FILING REQUIREMENTS

General Rules.   An individual must file a tax return if certain minimum amounts of gross income have been received. The general rule is that a tax return is required for every individual who has gross income that equals or exceeds the sum of the exemption amount plus the applicable standard deduction.[22] For example, a single taxpayer under age 65 must file a tax return in 1998 if gross income equals or exceeds $6,950 ($2,700 exemption plus $4,250 standard deduction). Table 2–4 lists the income levels[23] that require tax returns under the general rule and under certain special rules.

The additional standard deduction for being age 65 or older is considered in determining the gross income filing requirements. For example, note in Table 2–4 that the 1998 filing requirement for a single taxpayer age 65 or older is $8,000 ($4,250 basic standard deduction + $1,050 additional standard deduction + $2,700 exemption). However, the additional standard deduction for blindness is not taken into account. The 1998 filing requirement for a single taxpayer under age 65 and blind is $6,950 ($4,250 basic standard deduction + $2,700 exemption).

A self-employed individual with net earnings of $400 or more from a business or profession must file a tax return regardless of the amount of gross income.

Even though an individual has gross income below the filing level amounts and therefore does not owe any tax, he or she must file a return to obtain a tax refund of amounts withheld. A return is also necessary to obtain the benefits of the earned income credit allowed to taxpayers with little or no tax liability. Chapter 11 discusses the earned income credit.

Filing Requirements for Dependents.   Computation of the gross income filing requirement for an individual who can be claimed as a dependent on another person's tax return is subject to more complex rules. Such an individual must file a return if he or she has *either* of the following:

- Earned income only and gross income that is more than the total standard deduction (including any additional standard deduction) that the individual is allowed for the year.
- Unearned income only and gross income of more than $700 plus any additional standard deduction that the individual is allowed for the year.

---

[22]The gross income amounts for determining whether a tax return must be filed are adjusted for inflation each year.   [23]§ 6012(a)(1).

▼ **TABLE 2–4**
Filing Levels

Filing Status	1997 Gross Income	1998 Gross Income
Single		
Under 65 and not blind	$ 6,800	$ 6,950
Under 65 and blind	6,800	6,950
65 or older	7,800	8,000
Married, filing joint return		
Both spouses under 65 and neither blind	$12,200	$12,500
Both spouses under 65 and one or both spouses blind	12,200	12,500
One spouse 65 or older	13,000	13,350
Both spouses 65 or older	13,800	14,200
Married, filing separate return		
All—whether 65 or older or blind	$ 2,650	$ 2,700
Head of household		
Under 65 and not blind	$ 8,700	$ 8,950
Under 65 and blind	8,700	8,950
65 or older	9,700	10,000
Qualifying widow(er)		
Under 65 and not blind	$ 9,550	$ 9,800
Under 65 and blind	9,550	9,800
65 or older	10,350	10,650

- Both earned and unearned income and gross income of more than the larger of $700 or the sum of earned income plus $250 (but limited to the applicable basic standard deduction), plus any additional standard deduction that the individual is allowed for the year.

Thus, the filing requirement for a dependent who has no unearned income is the total of the *basic* standard deduction plus any *additional* standard deduction, which includes both the additional deduction for blindness and the deduction for being age 65 or older. For example, the 1998 filing requirement for a single dependent who is under 65 and not blind is $4,250, the amount of the basic standard deduction for 1998. The filing requirement for a single dependent under 65 and blind is $5,300 ($4,250 basic standard deduction + $1,050 additional standard deduction).

Selecting the Proper Form.   Individual taxpayers file a return on either Form 1040 (the long form), Form 1040A (the short form), or Form 1040EZ. Taxpayers who cannot use either Form 1040EZ or Form 1040A must use Form 1040. These forms are reproduced in Appendix B. Examine the forms to determine which form is appropriate for a particular taxpayer.

When and Where to File.   Tax returns of individuals are due on or before the fifteenth day of the fourth month following the close of the tax year. For the calendar year taxpayer, the usual filing date is on or before April 15 of the following year.[24] When the due date falls on a Saturday, Sunday, or legal holiday, the last day for

---

[24]§ 6072(a).

TAX IN THE NEWS

IS ALLOWING THE USE OF PLASTIC TO PAY TAXES A GOOD IDEA?

A provision in the Taxpayer Relief Act of 1997 permits the IRS to accept credit, debit, or charge cards for the payment of Federal income taxes. Although the provision is intended to benefit taxpayers, one can argue that it may cause more harm than good. Some feel that the easy accessibility of credit sources has resulted in many Americans becoming overburdened with credit card debt. Allowing the cards to be used for paying taxes will certainly further worsen the situation.

Other potential problems come to mind. What happens if the taxpayer charges the taxes and later refuses to pay the bill? Who gets stuck—the IRS or the credit card company? If the latter, is it desirable to have as a tax collector someone other than the IRS? A further problem is who absorbs the discount rate that merchants pay banks to process credit card transactions? Also, will credit card companies extend current incentives (e.g., cash rebates, frequent flyer miles) to holders who use the cards to pay Federal income taxes?

---

filing falls on the next business day. If the return is mailed to the proper address with sufficient postage and is postmarked on or before the due date, it is deemed timely filed. The Code enables the IRS to prescribe rules governing the filing of returns using various private parcel delivery services (e.g., Airborne Express, DHL, FedEx, UPS).[25]

If a taxpayer is unable to file the return by the specified due date, a four-month extension of time can be obtained by filing Form 4868 (Application for Automatic Extension of Time to File U.S. Individual Income Tax Return).[26] Further extensions may be granted by the IRS upon a showing of good cause by the taxpayer. For this purpose, Form 2688 (Application for Extension of Time to File U.S. Individual Income Tax Return) should be used. An extension of more than six months will not be granted if the taxpayer is in the United States.

Although obtaining an extension excuses a taxpayer from a penalty for failure to file, it does not insulate against the penalty for failure to pay. If more tax is owed, the filing of Form 4868 should be accompanied by an additional remittance to cover the balance due. The failure to file and failure to pay penalties are discussed in Chapter 1.

The return should be sent or delivered to the Regional Service Center of the IRS for the area where the taxpayer lives.[27]

If an individual taxpayer needs to file an amended return (e.g., because of a failure to report income or to claim a deduction or tax credit), Form 1040X is filed. The form generally must be filed within three years of the filing date of the original return or within two years from the time the tax was paid, whichever is later.

---

[25]§ 7502(f). See, for example, Notice 97–50, I.R.B. No. 37, 21.
[26]Reg. § 1.6081–4.
[27]The Regional Service Centers and the geographical area each covers can be found in *Your Federal Income Tax*, IRS Publication 17 for 1997 or at http://www.irs.ustreas.gov.

FILING STATUS

The amount of tax will vary considerably depending on which Tax Rate Schedule is used. This is illustrated in the following example.

EXAMPLE 29

The following amounts of tax are computed using the 1998 Tax Rate Schedules for a taxpayer (or taxpayers in the case of a joint return) with $40,000 of taxable income (see Appendix A).

Filing Status	Amount of Tax
Single	$7,904.50
Married, filing joint return	6,000.00
Married, filing separate return	8,447.25
Head of household	6,786.50

Rates for Single Taxpayers. A taxpayer who is unmarried or separated from his or her spouse by a decree of divorce or separate maintenance and does not qualify for another filing status must use the rates for single taxpayers. Marital status is determined as of the last day of the tax year, except when a spouse dies during the year. In that case, marital status is determined as of the date of death. State law governs whether a taxpayer is considered married, divorced, or legally separated.

Under a special relief provision, however, married persons who live apart may be able to qualify as single. Married taxpayers who are considered single under the *abandoned spouse rules* are allowed to use the head-of-household rates. See the discussion of this filing status under Abandoned Spouse Rules later in the chapter.

Rates for Married Individuals. The joint return (Tax Rate Schedule Y, Code § 1(a)) was originally enacted in 1948 to establish equity between married taxpayers in common law states and those in community property states. Before the joint return rates were enacted, taxpayers in community property states were in an advantageous position relative to taxpayers in common law states because they could split their income. For instance, if one spouse earned $100,000 and the other spouse was not employed, each spouse could report $50,000 of income. Splitting the income in this manner caused the total income to be subject to lower marginal tax rates. Each spouse would start at the bottom of the rate structure.

Taxpayers in common law states did not have this income-splitting option, so their taxable income was subject to higher marginal rates. This inconsistency in treatment was remedied by the joint return provisions. The progressive rates in the joint return Tax Rate Schedule are constructed based on the assumption that income is earned equally by the two spouses.

If married individuals elect to file separate returns, each reports only his or her own income, exemptions, deductions, and credits, and each must use the Tax Rate Schedule applicable to married taxpayers filing separately. It is generally advantageous for married individuals to file a joint return, since the combined amount of tax is lower. However, special circumstances (e.g., significant medical expenses incurred by one spouse subject to the 7.5 percent limitation) may warrant the election to file separate returns. It may be necessary to compute the tax under both assumptions to determine the most advantageous filing status.

When Congress enacted the rate structure available to those filing joint returns, it intended to favor married taxpayers. In certain situations, however,

TAX IN THE NEWS

LOW-INCOME TAXPAYERS ALSO SUFFER FROM THE MARRIAGE PENALTY

The inequity of the marriage penalty is not limited to taxpayers with high incomes (see Example 30).

Consider, for example, Albert and June, each of whom has one dependent child. During 1998, Albert and June both earn wages of $10,000. Neither has any deductions *for* AGI.

Situation A shows the income tax result if Albert and June are married and file a joint return. Situation B assumes Albert and June are not married, qualify for head-of-household status, and file accordingly, with each claiming one child as a dependent. Because the Tax Tables for 1998 were not yet available, the Tax Rate Schedules were used to compute the tax.

The harsh effect of the marriage penalty is apparent. Albert and June are $2,416 better off (refunds totaling $4,542 versus $2,126) by not being married. This result is remarkable when one considers that AGI of only $20,000 is involved!

| | Situation A | Situation B | | |
| | | If They Are Not Married | | |
Their Taxes:	If They Are Married	Albert	June	Total
Adjusted gross income	$20,000	$10,000 +	$10,000 =	$20,000
Personal and dependency exemptions	10,800	5,400 +	5,400 =	10,800
Standard deduction	7,100	6,250 +	6,250 =	12,500
Taxable income	2,100	–0– +	–0– =	–0–
Taxes owed	315	–0– +	–0– =	–0–
Earned income tax credit*	2,126	2,271 +	2,271 =	4,542
Child tax credit*	315	–0– +	–0– =	–0–
Refund	$ 2,126	$ 2,271 +	$ 2,271 =	$ 4,542

*See Chapter 11 for a discussion of the earned income tax credit and the child tax credit. The credits above were calculated following the procedure utilized in Chapter 11.

the parties would incur less tax if they were not married and filed separate returns. The additional tax that a joint return can cause, commonly called the **marriage penalty,** can develop when *both* spouses have larger taxable incomes.

EXAMPLE 30   John and Betty are employed, and each earns taxable income of $55,000. If they *are not married* and file separate returns, each has a tax liability of $12,105, or a total of $24,210 ($12,105 × 2). If they are married to each other, the filing of a joint return produces a tax of $25,526 on taxable income of $110,000 ($55,000 + $55,000). Thus, being married results in $1,316 ($25,526 – $24,210) more tax! ▼

Although some have suggested changes to lessen the impact of the marriage penalty, any remedy is apt to make the tax law more complex.

The Code places some limitations on deductions, credits, etc., when married individuals file separately. If either spouse itemizes deductions, the other spouse must also itemize. Married taxpayers who file separately cannot take either of the following:

- The credit for child and dependent care expenses (in most instances).
- The earned income credit.

The joint return rates also apply for two years following the death of one spouse, if the surviving spouse maintains a household for a dependent child.[28] This is referred to as **surviving spouse** status.

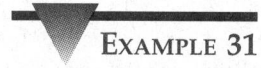

EXAMPLE 31

Fred dies in 1997 leaving Ethel with a dependent child. For the year of Fred's death (1997), Ethel files a joint return with Fred (presuming the consent of Fred's executor is obtained). For the next two years (1998 and 1999), Ethel, as a surviving spouse, may use the joint return rates. In subsequent years, Ethel may use the head-of-household rates if she continues to maintain a household as her home that is the domicile of the child. ▼

Rates for Heads of Household.   Unmarried individuals who maintain a household for a dependent (or dependents) are entitled to use the **head-of-household** rates.[29] The tax liability using the head-of-household rates falls between the liability using the joint return Tax Rate Schedule and the liability using the Tax Rate Schedule for single taxpayers.

To qualify for head-of-household rates, a taxpayer must pay more than half the cost of maintaining a household as his or her home. The household must also be the principal home of a dependent relative.[30] As a general rule, the dependent must live in the taxpayer's household for over half the year.

There are two exceptions to these requirements. One exception is that an *unmarried child* (child also means grandchild, stepchild, or adopted child) need not be a dependent in order for the taxpayer to qualify as a head of household.

EXAMPLE 32

Nancy maintains a household where she and Dan, her nondependent unmarried son, reside. Since Dan is not married, Nancy qualifies for the head-of-household rates. ▼

Another exception to the general rule is that head-of-household status still may be claimed if the taxpayer maintains a *separate home* for his or her *parent or parents* if at least one parent qualifies as a dependent of the taxpayer.[31]

EXAMPLE 33

Rick, an unmarried individual, lives in New York City and maintains a household in Detroit for his dependent parents. Rick may use the head-of-household rates even though his parents do not reside in his New York home. ▼

Head-of-household status is not changed during the year by the death of the dependent. As long as the taxpayer provided more than half of the cost of maintaining the household prior to the dependent's death, head-of-household status is preserved.

---

[28]§ 2(a).
[29]§ 2(b).

[30]As defined in § 152(a). See § 2(b)(1)(A).
[31]§ 2(b)(1)(B).

Abandoned Spouse Rules.   When married persons file separate returns, several unfavorable tax consequences result. For example, the taxpayer must use the Tax Rate Schedule for married taxpayers filing separately. To mitigate such harsh treatment, Congress enacted provisions commonly referred to as the **abandoned spouse** rules. These rules allow a married taxpayer to file as a head of household if all of the following conditions are satisfied:

- The taxpayer does not file a joint return.
- The taxpayer paid more than one-half the cost of maintaining his or her home for the tax year.
- The taxpayer's spouse did not live in the home during the last six months of the tax year.
- The home was the principal residence of the taxpayer's child, stepchild, or adopted child for more than half the year.
- The taxpayer could claim the child, stepchild, or adopted child as a dependent.[32]

GAINS AND LOSSES FROM PROPERTY TRANSACTIONS—IN GENERAL

6   **LEARNING OBJECTIVE**
Possess an overview of property transactions.

Gains and losses from property transactions are discussed in detail in Chapters 12 and 13. Because of their importance in the tax system, however, they are introduced briefly at this point.

When property is sold or otherwise disposed of, gain or loss may result. Such gain or loss has an effect on the income tax position of the party making the sale or other disposition when the *realized* gain or loss is *recognized* for tax purposes. Without realized gain or loss, generally, there can be no recognized gain or loss. The concept of realized gain or loss is expressed as follows:

$$\begin{array}{c} \text{Amount realized} \\ \text{from the sale} \end{array} - \begin{array}{c} \text{Adjusted basis of} \\ \text{the property} \end{array} = \begin{array}{c} \text{Realized gain} \\ \text{(or loss)} \end{array}$$

The amount realized is the selling price of the property less any costs of disposition (e.g., brokerage commissions) incurred by the seller. The adjusted basis of the property is determined as follows:

Cost (or other original basis) at date of acquisition[33]

Add:	Capital additions
Subtract:	Depreciation (if appropriate) and other capital recoveries (see Chapter 7)
Equals:	Adjusted basis at date of sale or other disposition

All realized gains are recognized (taxable) unless some specific part of the tax law provides otherwise (see Chapter 12 dealing with certain nontaxable exchanges).

---

[32]The dependency requirement does not apply, however, if the taxpayer could have claimed a dependency exemption except for the fact that the exemption was claimed by the noncustodial parent under a written agreement. Refer to Example 18 and the related discussion.

[33]Cost usually means purchase price plus expenses related to the acquisition of the property and incurred by the purchaser (e.g., brokerage commissions). For the basis of property acquired by gift or inheritance and other basis rules, see Chapter 12.

Realized losses may or may not be recognized (deductible) for tax purposes, depending on the circumstances involved. Generally, losses realized from the disposition of personal use property (property neither held for investment nor used in a trade or business) are not recognized.

EXAMPLE 34

During the current year, Ted sells his sailboat (adjusted basis of $4,000) for $5,500. Ted also sells one of his personal automobiles (adjusted basis of $8,000) for $5,000. Ted's realized gain of $1,500 from the sale of the sailboat is recognized. On the other hand, the $3,000 realized loss on the sale of the automobile is not recognized and will not provide Ted with any deductible tax benefit. ▼

Once it has been determined that the disposition of property results in a recognized gain or loss, the next step is to classify the gain or loss as capital or ordinary. Although ordinary gain is fully taxable and ordinary loss is fully deductible, the same may not hold true for capital gains and capital losses.

GAINS AND LOSSES FROM PROPERTY TRANSACTIONS—CAPITAL GAINS AND LOSSES

The Taxpayer Relief Act of 1997 (TRA of 1997) made significant changes in the tax treatment of capital gains. Although highly beneficial for the taxpayers affected, the price paid was to add further complexity to the Code. Some of these changes, for example, do not become effective until after the year 2000. Since this chapter is intended to present only an overview of capital gains and losses, refer to Chapter 13 for an in-depth treatment.

DEFINITION OF A CAPITAL ASSET

Capital assets are defined in the Code as any property held by the taxpayer *other than* property listed in § 1221. The list in § 1221 includes inventory, accounts receivable, and depreciable property or real estate used in a business. Thus, the sale or exchange of assets in these categories usually results in ordinary income or loss treatment (see Chapter 13).

EXAMPLE 35

Kelly owns a pizza parlor. During the current year, he sells two automobiles. The first automobile, which had been used as a pizza delivery car for three years, was sold at a loss of $1,000. Because this automobile is an asset used in his business, Kelly has an ordinary loss deduction of $1,000, rather than a capital loss deduction. The second automobile, which Kelly had owned for two years, was his personal use car. It was sold for a gain of $800. The personal use car is a capital asset. Therefore, Kelly has a capital gain of $800. ▼

The principal capital assets held by an individual taxpayer include assets held for personal (rather than business) use, such as a personal residence or an automobile, and assets held for investment purposes (e.g., corporate securities and land). Capital assets generally include collectibles, which are subject to somewhat unique tax treatment. **Collectibles** include art, antiques, gems, metals, stamps, some coins and bullion, and alcoholic beverages that are held as investments.

TAXATION OF NET CAPITAL GAIN

Currently, *net capital gain* (as defined below) is subject to the following *maximum* rates:

	Maximum Rate
Short-term gains (held for 12 months or less)	39.6%
Mid-term gains (held for more than 12 and not more than 18 months)	28%
Long-term gains (held for more than 18 months)	20%

Collectibles, if the holding period requirement is satisfied, are always included in the mid-term category. In no event will a capital gain be taxed at a rate higher than the taxpayer's regular bracket for the year. Further, if a taxpayer has a long-term gain and his or her regular tax bracket for the year is 15 percent, the usual 20 percent rate is reduced to 10 percent.

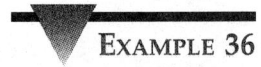

EXAMPLE 36

In 1998, Polly is in the 15% tax bracket and has the following capital gains for the year:

Robin Corporation stock (held for 6 months)	$1,000
Crow Corporation stock (held for 19 months)	1,000

Polly's tax on these transactions is $150 ($1,000 × 15%) as to Robin and $100 ($1,000 × 10%) as to Crow. ▼

DETERMINATION OF NET CAPITAL GAIN

In order to arrive at a net capital gain, capital losses must be taken into account. The capital losses are aggregated by holding period (short-term, mid-term, and long-term) and applied against the gains in that category. If excess losses result, they are then shifted to the category carrying the *highest* tax rate.

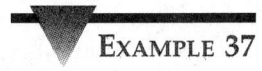

EXAMPLE 37

In 1998, Colin is in the 31% tax bracket and has the following capital transactions for the year:

Penguin Corporation stock (held for 7 months)	$1,000
Owl Corporation stock (held for 9 months)	(3,000)
Stamp collection (held for 4 years)	2,000
Land (held for 3 years)	4,000

The Penguin Corporation gain of $1,000 is offset by the Owl Corporation loss of $3,000. The net short-term capital loss of $2,000 is then applied against the stamp collection gain of $2,000. The end result is a net long-term capital gain of $4,000 from the land sale taxed at a 20% rate. Note that the stamp collection gain would have been taxed at a higher 28% rate had it not been offset by the excess short-term capital loss. ▼

TREATMENT OF NET CAPITAL LOSS

For individual taxpayers, net capital loss can be used to offset ordinary income of up to $3,000. Any remaining net capital loss is carried over indefinitely until exhausted. When carried over, the excess capital loss retains its classification (i.e., short-, mid- or long-term), except that both mid-term and long-term are treated as mid-term.

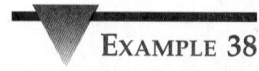

EXAMPLE 38

Tina has a short-term capital loss of $5,000 during the current year and no capital gains. She can deduct $3,000 of this amount as an ordinary loss. The remaining $2,000 is carried over to the next year as a short-term capital loss. ▼

TAX PLANNING CONSIDERATIONS

7 LEARNING OBJECTIVE
Identify tax planning opportunities associated with the individual tax formula.

TAKING ADVANTAGE OF TAX RATE DIFFERENTIALS

It is natural for taxpayers to be concerned about the tax rates they are paying. How does a tax practitioner communicate information about rates to clients? There are several possibilities.

The marginal rate (refer to Examples 23 through 25) provides information that can help a taxpayer evaluate a particular course of action or structure a transaction in the most advantageous manner. For example, a taxpayer who is in the 15 percent bracket this year and expects to be in the 31 percent bracket next year should, if possible, defer payment of deductible expenses until next year to maximize the tax benefit of the deduction.

A note of caution is in order with respect to shifting income and expenses between years. Congress has recognized the tax planning possibilities of such shifting and has enacted many provisions to limit a taxpayer's ability to do so. Some of these limitations on the shifting of income are discussed in Chapters 3, 4, and 15. Limitations that affect a taxpayer's ability to shift deductions are discussed in Chapters 5 through 10 and in Chapter 15.

A taxpayer's *effective rate* can be an informative measure of the effectiveness of tax planning. The effective rate is computed by dividing the taxpayer's tax liability by the total amount of income. A low effective rate can be considered an indication of effective tax planning.

One way of lowering the effective rate is to exclude income from the tax base. For example, a taxpayer might consider investing in tax-free municipal bonds rather than taxable corporate bonds. Although pre-tax income from corporate bonds is usually higher, after-tax income may be higher if the taxpayer invests in tax-free municipals.

Another way of lowering the effective rate is to make sure that the taxpayer's expenses and losses are deductible. For example, losses on investments in passive activities may not be deductible (see Chapter 10). Therefore, a taxpayer who plans to invest in an activity that will produce a loss in the early years should take steps to ensure that the business is treated as active rather than passive. Active losses are deductible while passive losses are not.

INCOME OF MINOR CHILDREN

Taxpayers can use several strategies to avoid or minimize the effect of the rules that tax the unearned income of certain minor children at the parents' rate. The kiddie tax rules do not apply once a child reaches age 14. Parents should consider giving a younger child assets that defer taxable income until the child reaches age 14. For example, U.S. government Series EE savings bonds can be used to defer income until the bonds are cashed in (see Chapter 3).

Growth stocks typically pay little in the way of dividends. However, the profit on an astute investment may more than offset the lack of dividends. The child can hold the stock until he or she reaches age 14. If the stock is sold then at a profit, the profit is taxed at the child's low rates.

Taxpayers in a position to do so can employ their children in their business and pay them a reasonable wage for the work they actually perform (e.g., light office help, such as filing). The child's earned income is sheltered by the standard deduction, and the parents' business is allowed a deduction for the wages. The kiddie tax rules have no effect on earned income, even if it is earned from the parents' business.

DEPENDENCY EXEMPTIONS

The Joint Return Test.   A married person can be claimed as a dependent only if that individual does not file a joint return with his or her spouse. If a joint return has been filed, the damage may be undone if separate returns are substituted on a timely basis (on or before the due date of the return).

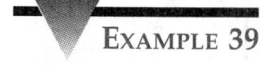

EXAMPLE 39

While preparing a client's 1997 income tax return on April 8, 1998, the tax practitioner discovered that the client's daughter filed a joint return with her husband in late January of 1998. Presuming the daughter otherwise qualifies as the client's dependent, the exemption is not lost if she and her husband file separate returns on or before April 15, 1998. ▼

An initial election to file a joint return must be considered carefully in any situation in which the taxpayers might later decide to amend their return and file separately. As indicated above, separate returns may be substituted for a joint return only if the amended returns are filed on or before the normal due date of the return. If the taxpayers in Example 39 attempt to file separate returns after April 15, 1998, the returns will not be accepted, and the joint return election is binding.[34]

Keep in mind that the filing of a joint return is not fatal to the dependency exemption if the parties are filing solely to recover all income tax withholdings, they are not required to file a return, and no tax liability would exist on separate returns.

The Gross Income Test.   The exception to the gross income test for a person under the age of 19 or a full-time student under the age of 24 applies only to a child of the taxpayer. The term *child* is limited to a son, stepson, daughter, stepdaughter, adopted son, or adopted daughter and may include a foster child.

EXAMPLE 40

Austin provides more than 50% of the support of his son, Irvin, and his daughter-in-law, Donna, who live with him. Donna, age 22, is a full-time student and earns $3,000 from a part-time job. Irvin and Donna do not file a joint return. Austin may claim Irvin as a dependent but not Donna. Although students under the age of 24 are excepted from the gross income test, this applies only to a "child" of the taxpayer. Donna does not come within the exception because she is not Austin's child. ▼

Can the fact that the parties live in a community property state make a difference?

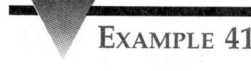

EXAMPLE 41

Assume the same facts as in Example 40 except that all parties live in Nevada, a community property jurisdiction. Now Austin can claim both Irvin and Donna as his dependents. Since Donna's income is only $1,500 (her half of the community), she now satisfies the gross income test (less than $2,700 for 1998). ▼

The Support Test.   Adequate records of expenditures for support should be maintained in the event a dependency exemption is questioned on audit by the IRS. The maintenance of adequate records is particularly important for exemptions arising from multiple support agreements.

---

[34]Reg. § 1.6013–1(a)(1).

Relationship to the Deduction for Medical Expenses. Generally, medical expenses are deductible only if they are paid on behalf of the taxpayer, his or her spouse, and their dependents. Since deductibility may rest on dependency status, planning is important in arranging multiple support agreements.

EXAMPLE 42

During the year, Zelda will be supported by her two sons (Vern and Vito) and her daughter (Maria). Each will furnish approximately one-third of the required support. If the parties decide that the dependency exemption should be claimed by the daughter under a multiple support agreement, any medical expenses incurred by Zelda should be paid by Maria. ▼

In planning a multiple support agreement, take into account which of the parties is most likely to exceed the 7.5 percent limitation (see Chapter 9). In Example 42, for instance, Maria might be a poor choice if she and her family do not expect to incur many medical and drug expenses of their own.

ETHICAL CONSIDERATIONS

Manipulating Deductions

J ason and his two sisters furnish more than 50 percent of the support of their widowed mother. Their mother lives with Jason, and his sisters sign Form 2120 enabling him to claim her as a dependent. During the year, the mother incurred medical expenses that were paid by one of Jason's sisters.

In completing his income tax return for the tax year, Jason claims his mother's medical expenses along with his own. Although he did not pay the expenses, Jason reasons that he could have done so from the funds he furnished for his mother's support.

Comment on the propriety of what Jason has done.

One exception permits the deduction of medical expenses paid on behalf of someone who is not a spouse or a dependent. If the person could be claimed as a dependent *except* for the gross income or joint return test, the medical expenses are, nevertheless, deductible. For additional discussion, see Chapter 9.

KEY TERMS

Abandoned spouse, 2–27

Collectibles, 2–28

Dependency exemption, 2–10

Head of household, 2–26

Itemized deductions, 2–6

Kiddie tax, 2–19

Marriage penalty, 2–25

Multiple support agreement, 2–11

Personal exemption, 2–10

Standard deduction, 2–6

Surviving spouse, 2–26

Tax Rate Schedules, 2–16

Tax Table, 2–16

Unearned income, 2–18

**PROBLEM
MATERIALS**

DISCUSSION QUESTIONS

1. A friend of yours remarks that the current top rate of 39.6% is the highest the Federal income tax has ever been. Please comment.

2. Rearrange the following components to show the formula for arriving at the amount of Federal taxable income:
   a. Deductions *for* AGI.
   b. The greater of the standard deduction or itemized deductions.
   c. Income (broadly conceived).
   d. Adjusted gross income.
   e. Exclusions.
   f. Personal and dependency exemptions.
   g. Gross income.

3. During the year, Ned inherits $5,000 from a great uncle. To help Ned come up with a $15,000 down payment on a condominium, Ned's mother lends him an additional $10,000. How do these transactions affect Ned's gross income for the year?

4. During the year, Mildred's stock investment increased in value by $13,000. She also sold some stock for $4,500; the stock had cost $4,000. How do these facts affect Mildred's gross income?

5. Jason and Kara (both age 64) will itemize their deductions on a joint return for 1998. Since they will not have certain itemized deductions next year, they expect their income tax liability to increase. Comment on their expectation.

6. Al and Melissa are husband and wife, and both are employed. They do not live in a community property state. Since Melissa incurred most of their itemized deductions (e.g., medical, charitable), Al feels that they would save taxes if they filed separate returns. On such returns, Al would claim the standard deduction, and Melissa would itemize her deductions *from* AGI. Comment on this proposed course of action.

7. Discuss the marital status of the parties under the following circumstances:
   a. One spouse dies during the year.
   b. The spouses are divorced during the year.

8. If an individual who may qualify as a dependent does not spend funds that he or she has received (e.g., wages or Social Security benefits), are these unexpended amounts considered in applying the support test?

9. Freda purchased a stereo system for her son Wes, age 16. The stereo was placed in Wes's room and used exclusively by him. Freda also purchased a new sports car, titled and registered in her own name, that was used 90% of the time by Wes. Should the cost of these items be considered as support in determining whether Freda may claim Wes as a dependent?

10. Carol provided 75% of the support of Debra, her niece. Debra was a full-time student during the year and earned $3,800 from a part-time job. Can Carol claim Debra as a dependent?

11. Besides what he furnishes on his own, Walter receives support from his daughter (20%) and his son (25%). Can either the daughter or the son claim Walter as a dependent under a multiple support agreement? Why or why not?

12. After Hugh and Ashley were divorced, Ashley disappeared with their two children. Under the divorce decree (issued in 1997), Ashley is awarded custody, and Hugh is awarded the dependency exemptions for the two children. Does Hugh have a problem? Explain.

13. A taxpayer who is divorced continues to support his former mother-in-law. May he claim her as a dependent? Suppose she does not live with him. Does this make any difference?

14. Roberto, who is single, is a U.S. citizen and resident. He provides almost all of the support of his parents and two aunts, who are citizens and residents of Guatemala.

Roberto's parents and aunts are seriously considering moving to and becoming residents of Mexico. Would such a move have any impact on Roberto? Why or why not?

15. What perceived abuse is the kiddie tax designed to correct?

16. A single individual age 65 or over and blind is required to file a Federal income tax return in 1998 if he or she has gross income of $8,000 or more (refer to Table 2–4).
    a. Explain how the $8,000 filing requirement was computed.
    b. In general, explain the effect of the additional standard deduction on the determination of the gross income requirement for filing.

17. Comment on the so-called marriage penalty in connection with the following:
    a. What it is.
    b. When it is likely to occur.
    c. What income level (i.e., low, modest, high) could be vulnerable.

18. Baron and Cheryl are both professionals who have held jobs since they graduated from college five years ago. For several years, they have been engaged to be married. Both would like to tie the knot, but Cheryl is hesitant because of a "marriage penalty" she has heard about. Baron feels Cheryl's fears are unfounded and says they should be able to avoid any such penalty by filing separate returns as married persons. Comment on Baron and Cheryl's situation.

19. In 1998, Ginger's husband dies. Ginger plans to file as a surviving spouse for tax years 1998 through 2000. Ginger's only dependent is her mother, who lives with her. Comment on any misconceptions Ginger may have regarding the tax law.

20. Jacob is single and lives alone in an apartment. He maintains the home where his parents live, but only his mother qualifies as Jacob's dependent. When Jacob files his own return, he chooses single status since *both* of his parents do not qualify as dependents. Comment on Jacob's filing status.

21. Several years ago, after a particularly fierce argument, Fran's husband moved out and has not been heard from or seen since. Because Fran cannot locate her husband, she has been using "married, filing separate" status when filing her income tax return. Comment on Fran's status.

22. During 1998, Andre had a short-term capital loss, a mid-term capital gain, and a long-term capital gain.
    a. To which category of capital gain (i.e., mid- or long-term) is the capital loss first applied?
    b. Is the approach taken in part (a) favorable or unfavorable to the taxpayer?

23. Are net long-term capital assets (i.e., those held for more than 18 months) always taxed at a rate of 20%? Explain.

24. For 1998, Ann's only capital transaction is a short-term loss of $4,000. How is this loss handled for tax purposes?

25. What are collectibles?
    a. How is the sale of collectibles handled for tax purposes?
    b. In connection with part (a), would it matter if the collectible had been held for more than 18 months? For one year or less?

26. Perry is divorced and has living with him his married daughter, Celia, and her husband, Clark. During the year, Celia earned $3,100 from a part-time job and filed a separate return to recover her withholdings. Clark has no income. Perry can prove that he provided more than 50% of Celia and Clark's support. Perry did not claim Celia as his dependent because he believed she failed the gross income test. Perry filed his return using single taxpayer status. All parties reside in California. Comment on Perry's tax position.

27. Erica and her two brothers equally furnish all of the support of their mother. Erica is married and has four children. Her brothers are single and claim the standard

deduction. Erica's mother is not in good health. What suggestions can you make regarding the tax position of the parties?

PROBLEMS

28. Compute the taxpayer's taxable income for 1998 in each of the following cases:
    a. Jack is married and files a joint return with his wife Alice. Jack and Alice have two dependent children. They have AGI of $50,000 and $8,300 of itemized deductions.
    b. Pete is an unmarried head of household with two dependents. He has AGI of $45,000 and itemized deductions of $5,200.
    c. Iris, age 22, is a full-time college student who is claimed as a dependent by her parents. She earns $4,200 from a part-time job and has interest income of $1,500.
    d. Matt, age 20, is a full-time college student who is claimed as a dependent by his parents. He earns $2,500 from a part-time job and has interest income of $4,100. His itemized deductions related to the investment income are $800.

    Note: Problems 29 and 30 can be solved by referring to Figure 2–1, Exhibits 2–1 through 2–3, Tables 2–1 and 2–2, and the discussion under Deductions for Adjusted Gross Income in this chapter.

29. Compute taxable income for 1998 for Blake on the basis of the following information. His filing status is head of household.

Salary	$60,000
Alimony paid	1,200
Casualty loss (deductible portion)	7,500
Interest on home mortgage	4,200
Property taxes on home	2,200
State and local income taxes	1,500
Number of dependents (two children and both of Blake's parents)	4
Age	46

30. Compute taxable income for 1998 for Amber on the basis of the following information. Her filing status is single.

Inheritance received from mother	$29,000
Gift received from aunt	14,000
Cash dividends from stock investments	15,000
Interest income from savings accounts and money market deposits	11,000
Interest on state and local bonds	11,000
Lottery winnings	3,600
Cash charitable contributions	4,000
Age	66

31. Determine the amount of the standard deduction allowed for 1998 in the following independent situations. In each case, assume the taxpayer is claimed as another person's dependent.
    a. Mona, age 16, has income as follows: $710 interest from a savings account and $800 from a part-time job.
    b. Aaron, age 18, earns $4,300 from a part-time job.
    c. Irving, age 71 and single, has income as follows: $3,100 nontaxable Social Security benefits and $1,050 from a part-time job.
    d. Maureen, age 67, is single and blind and has cash dividends of $1,300 from a stock investment.

32. Determine the number of personal and dependency exemptions in the following independent situations:

a. Wesley, age 45, provides all of the support of Doreen (age 70) who does not live with him. Doreen was Wesley's mother-in-law before his divorce.

b. Carol, age 50, provides all of the support of two cousins, Rick and Jane. Jane lives with Carol but Rick does not.

c. Ron, age 66, provides all of the support of Cynthia and Leona who live with him. Cynthia is Ron's wife, and Leona is unrelated but is a close friend of the family and a member of their church. Ron files a separate return. Neither Cynthia nor Leona has any income, and neither files a return.

d. Nicole, age 60, provides all of the support of Alan, age 66 and blind, and Grace, age 89. Alan, Nicole's husband, died in February of the current year. Grace is Alan's mother and lives in a nursing home. Nicole files a separate return.

33. Compute the number of personal and dependency exemptions in the following independent situations:

a. Roberto, a U.S. citizen and resident, contributes 100% of the support of his parents who are citizens of Mexico and live there.

b. Pablo, a U.S. citizen and resident, contributes 100% of the support of his parents who are citizens of Guatemala. Pablo's father is a resident of Guatemala, and his mother is a legal resident of the United States.

c. Marlena, a U.S. citizen and resident, contributes 100% of the support of her parents who are also U.S. citizens but are residents of Germany.

34. Determine the number of personal and dependency exemptions in each of the following independent situations:

a. Warren and Terri provide more than half of the support of their children, Demi and Paul. Demi, age 19, earns $3,200 from a part-time job. Paul, age 21, earns $2,800 from a part-time job.

b. Hortense, age 64 and widowed, furnishes more than half of the support of her father, age 88 and blind. The father receives Social Security benefits of $4,300, interest on a savings account of $2,400, and interest on tax-exempt bonds of $10,000.

c. Dennis and Ava provide more than half of the support of their son, Henry. Henry, age 25, is a full-time student in medical school. During the year, Henry receives $2,500 in dividends from stock investments.

d. Earl provides more than half of the support of his nephew, Brad, who lives with him. Brad, age 17 and a full-time student, earns $2,500 from a part-time job.

35. Caleb and Carrie are married and file a joint return. Their four children and Carrie's parents qualify as their dependents. If Caleb and Carrie's AGI is $210,000, what is their allowable exemption deduction for 1998?

36. Melvin and Sarah Turner are married and file a joint return. Transactions for 1998 are as follows:

Salaries ($42,000 for Melvin and $39,000 for Sarah)	$81,000
Lottery winnings	1,200
Inheritance from Melvin's father	30,000
Gift from Sarah's mother	10,000
Short-term capital loss from sale of stock held as an investment	3,000

The Turners provided all of the support of their 20-year-old married daughter, Maryanne, and her husband, Boyd. Maryanne and Boyd live with the Turners, and neither has any gross income. The Turners also furnish over half of the support of Sarah's aunt who lives in a nursing home. The aunt, age 76, has interest of $2,700 from State of Alabama bonds. Melvin is age 65, while Sarah is age 45. If the Turners have itemized deductions of $7,000, what is their taxable income for 1998?

37. Bob, age 13, is a full-time student supported by his parents who claim him on their tax return for 1998. Bob's parents present you with the following information and ask that you prepare Bob's Federal income tax return for the year:

Wages from summer job	$2,100
Interest on savings account at First National Bank	950
Interest on City of Chicago bonds Bob received as a gift from his grandfather two years ago	750
Dividend from Owl Corporation	200

   a. What is Bob's taxable income for 1998?

   b. Bob's parents file a joint return for 1998 on which they report taxable income of $66,000. Compute Bob's 1998 tax liability.

38. Walter and Nancy provide 70% of the support of their daughter (age 21) and son-in-law (age 22). The son-in-law (John) is a full-time student at a local university, while the daughter (Irene) holds various part-time jobs from which she earns $3,000. Walter and Nancy engage you to prepare their tax return for 1998. During a meeting with them in late March of 1999, you learn that John and Irene do not file a joint return. What tax advice would you give based on the following assumptions:

   a. All parties live in Louisiana (a community property state).

   b. All parties live in New Jersey (a common law state).

39. Don is a wealthy executive who had taxable income of $200,000 in 1998. He is considering transferring title in a duplex he owns to his son Sam, age 16. Sam has no other income and is claimed as a dependent by Don. Net rent income from the duplex is $10,000 a year, which Sam will be encouraged to place in a savings account. Will the family save income taxes in 1998 if Don transfers title in the duplex to Sam? Explain.

40. Compute the 1998 tax liability for each of the following taxpayers:

   a. Norm and Nancy, both age 46, are married, have two dependent children, and file a joint return. Their combined salaries totaled $66,000. They had deductions *for* AGI of $7,000 and total itemized deductions of $7,400.

   b. Clark, age 45, is single and has no dependents. He had a salary of $52,000, deductions *for* AGI of $3,000, and total itemized deductions of $4,200.

   c. David and Susan, both age 65, are married, have no dependents, and file a joint return. Their combined salaries were $92,000. They had deductions *for* AGI of $2,000 and itemized deductions of $8,500.

41. Dustin and Vicki are married and file a joint return. Dustin is age 70, and Vicki is age 65. Their income is as follows: $32,000 (cash dividends from stock investments); $12,000 (interest income on certificates of deposits); and $18,000 (interest income on City of Detroit bonds). In addition, they incur a long-term capital loss of $2,500 on the sale of stock held as an investment. They furnish more than half of the support of Vicki's cousin who does not live with them. If they have itemized deductions of $8,000, determine their taxable income for 1998.

42. Peter, age 12, is claimed as a dependent on his parents' 1998 Federal income tax return, on which they reported taxable income of $95,000. During the summer, Peter earned $2,500 from a job as a model. His only other income consisted of $1,700 in interest on a savings account. Compute Peter's taxable income and tax liability.

43. Carmen, who is 12 years old, is claimed as a dependent on her parents' tax return. During 1998, she received $12,200 in dividends and interest and had no investment expenses related to this income. She also earned $2,000 wages from a part-time job. Compute the amount of income that is taxed at Carmen's parents' rate.

44. Bruce Smith and Wanda Brown are young professionals who are employed in well-paying jobs. They have been dating each other for several years and are considering getting married in December 1998 or January 1999. For 1998, their respective AGIs are $65,000 and $68,000. They anticipate earning the same income in 1999. In both years, they will claim the standard deduction.

   Bruce and Wanda solicit your tax advice. Specifically, they wish to know what Federal income tax results from their getting married in 1998 or in 1999. Prepare a letter to Wanda (4339 Elm St., Apt. 39A, Cincinnati, OH 45221) setting forth the tax determination under each choice.

45. Which of the following individuals are required to file a tax return for 1998? Should any of these individuals file a return even if filing is not required? Why?
    a. Sam is married and files a joint return with his spouse, Lana. Both Sam and Lana are 67 years old. Their combined gross income was $14,000.
    b. Bobby is a dependent child under age 19 who received $4,000 in wages from a part-time job.
    c. Mike is single and is 67 years old. His gross income from wages was $6,700.
    d. Marge is a self-employed single individual with gross income of $4,500 from an unincorporated business. Business expenses amounted to $4,000.

46. Which of the following taxpayers must file a Federal income tax return for 1998?
    a. Bob, age 19, is a full-time college student. He is claimed as a dependent by his parents. He earned $4,100 wages during the year.
    b. Anita, age 12, is claimed as a dependent by her parents. She earned interest income of $1,200 during the year.
    c. Earl, age 16, is claimed as a dependent by his parents. He earned wages of $2,700 and interest of $1,100 during the year.
    d. Karen, age 16 and blind, is claimed as a dependent by her parents. She earned wages of $2,600 and interest of $1,200 during the year.
    e. Pat, age 17, is claimed as a dependent by her parents. She earned interest of $300 during the year. In addition, she earned $550 during the summer operating her own business at the beach, where she painted caricatures of her customers.

47. In each of the following situations, determine Darlene's filing status for tax year 1998:
    a. Darlene is a widow and maintains a household in which her two dependent children live. Darlene's husband died in 1996.
    b. Same as (a) except that Darlene's husband died in 1994 (not 1996).
    c. Darlene is single and lives alone. She maintains the household of her parents, only one of whom qualifies as her dependent.
    d. Darlene is married, but her husband disappeared for parts unknown in 1997. Darlene maintains the household in which she and her dependent children live.

48. In each of the following situations, determine Isaac's filing status for tax year 1998:
    a. Isaac lives alone. He has not seen or heard from his wife since 1997.
    b. Isaac's wife died in January 1998. He maintains the home in which he and his dependent child live.
    c. Isaac's wife died in 1994. He maintains the home in which he and his unmarried child live. The child does not qualify as Isaac's dependent.
    d. Isaac is divorced and lives alone. He also maintains a home in which his dependent child lives.

49. Henry died on January 1, 1996. He was survived by his wife, Sue, and their 19-year-old son, Mike, who was a college sophomore. Mike was a full-time student in 1997 and earned $3,000 for the year. In 1998, Mike reduced his school load and became a part-time student. He earned $5,200 in 1998. Mike continues to live with his mother, who provides over half of his support. What is Sue's filing status in 1996, 1997, and 1998?

50. Tracy, age 66, is a widow. Her husband died in 1996. Tracy maintains a home in which she and her 28-year-old son reside. Her son Gary is a piano player at a local nightclub, where he earned $12,000 during 1998. Gary contributed $3,000 of his income toward household expenses and put the remainder in a savings account that he used to return to college full-time to pursue a master's degree in music starting in August 1998. Tracy contributed $12,000 toward household expenses. What is the most favorable filing status available to Tracy for 1998, and how many exemptions may she claim?

51. During 1998, Hazel had the following gains from sales of capital assets:

Short-term (held one year or less)	$4,000
Mid-term (held more than one year but not more than 18 months)	2,000
Long-term (held more than 18 months)	5,000

   a. If Hazel is in the 31% tax bracket, how much income tax do these transactions generate?

   b. What if Hazel is in the 15% tax bracket?

52. During 1998, Cole had the following gains and losses from the sale of capital assets:

Loss on Pidgeon Corporation stock (held 9 months)	($4,000)
Gain on a painting (held for 3 years as an investment)	5,000
Gain on unimproved land (held for 3 years as an investment)	3,000

   a. If Cole is in the 36% tax bracket, how much income tax do these transactions generate?

   b. What if Cole is in the 15% tax bracket?

53. Gina, a cash basis taxpayer, is single and has no dependents. She provides you with the following estimates for 1997 and 1998:

	1997	1998
Adjusted gross income	$56,000	$60,000
Charitable contributions	2,200	2,400
Interest on home mortgage	1,000	850
Property taxes	700	700

Can Gina decrease taxable income over the two-year period by prepaying her 1998 charitable contributions in 1997?

CUMULATIVE PROBLEMS

54. Matt and Anita Huerta are married and live at 3486 International Blvd., El Paso, TX 79968. Both have full-time jobs. Matt's Social Security number is 432–23–1111, and Anita's is 437–00–1112. The Huertas have four children who live with them. Three of the children are their own, while the oldest is Anita's child from a prior marriage.

   During 1998, the Huertas had the following receipts:

Salaries (Matt and Anita combined)	$71,000
Child support payments received by Anita from her former husband	3,600
Fees earned by Matt for jury duty service	90
Proceeds from garage sale	1,180
Gift of cash received from Matt's mother	4,000
Cash prize won for being the ninth caller on a radio talk show	1,000

Matt's employer withheld Federal income taxes of $2,600, and Anita's employer withheld $3,400. The garage sale involved used clothing, toys, appliances, furniture and other personal effects, and household goods. The Huertas estimate that the cost of the items was in excess of $4,000.

   Expenses for 1998 are summarized below:

Interest on home mortgage	$5,600
Property taxes on home	3,400
Charitable contributions	4,200

The Huertas furnish all of the support of Anita's widowed mother, who lives with them. The mother, although a U.S. resident, is still a citizen of Mexico. The mother helps with the household chores and takes care of the children while Anita and Matt are at work. The Huertas also furnish all of the support of Anita's grandparents, who are over age 65. The grandparents live in Mexico and are citizens of Mexico.

Compute the Huertas' tax liability for 1998. Suggested software (if available): *TurboTax*.

55. Horace Fern, age 43, lives at 321 Grant Avenue, Cheyenne, WY 82002. Horace's mother Kate (age 65) lived with him until her death in August 1997. Up to the time of her death, Kate qualified as Horace's dependent. Horace maintained the household where he and his mother lived.

Horace is a manager for Bison Lumber Company at a yearly salary of $62,000. Because his job duties will be expanded, Bison plans to increase Horace's salary by 10% starting in 1998.

During 1997, Horace paid $3,300 ($300 each month) in alimony to Janet, his ex-wife. As Janet was remarried in late November, Horace's alimony obligation has terminated.

Besides his salary, Horace received interest income of $5,700 from Western Bank and $6,300 from First Savings Bank on $200,000 in certificates of deposit (CDs) he owns. Horace received the CDs as a gift from his mother several years ago.

Except as otherwise noted, Horace's expenditures for 1997 are summarized below:

Interest on home mortgage	$3,300
Property taxes on home	1,300
Charitable contributions	1,800

Relevant Social Security numbers are as follows:

Horace Fern	520–31–4596
Kate Fern	520–32–3214
Janet Fern	520–33–4432

Federal income taxes withheld from Horace's salary amounted to $10,900. He also paid estimated tax of $300 each quarter.

Part 1—Tax Computation
Compute Horace's net tax payable or refund due for 1997. Horace does not wish to contribute to the Presidential Election Campaign Fund. If he has overpaid, he wants the amount refunded. If you use tax forms for your computations, you will need Form 1040 and Schedules A and B. Suggested software (if available): *TurboTax*.

Part 2—Tax Planning
In addition to preparing the return for 1997, Horace has asked you to advise him regarding his tax situation for 1998. He is particularly concerned about the tax effects of the following:

- The death of Kate.

- The cessation of alimony payments due to Janet's remarriage.

- The salary increase.

- Interest income on the CDs.

Write a letter to Horace in which you summarize (in approximate amounts) how much more (or less) he will owe in income taxes for 1998. Also include recommendations on what can be done to mitigate the tax consequences resulting from the investment in CDs. Assume that Horace's itemized deductions will remain constant in 1998.

Research Problems for this chapter appear at the end of Chapter 28.

TEAM PROJECT: ARTHUR ANDERSEN TAX CHALLENGE CASES

For more information on the Arthur Andersen Tax Challenge Cases, refer to Chapter 1, page 1–37.

Information related to tax issues and problems that are discussed in this chapter may be found in the

Day and Ball case on pages 2, 3, 4, and 7
Fence case on pages 43, 47, and 61

Read and analyze the case you have been assigned and *identify* any issues and problems that are related to material covered in this chapter. If the information provided in the case is complete, prepare answers for this part of the case at this time. If you need information that is contained in the later parts of the case, write a memo summarizing the questions or problems so you can prepare a complete answer at a later date.

GROSS INCOME: CONCEPTS AND INCLUSIONS

LEARNING OBJECTIVES

After completing Chapter 3, you should be able to:

1. Explain the concepts of gross income and realization and distinguish between the economic, accounting, and tax concepts of gross income.

2. Describe the cash and accrual methods of accounting and the related effects of the choice of taxable year.

3. Identify who should pay the tax on a particular item of income in various situations.

4. Apply the Internal Revenue Code provisions on alimony, loans made at below-market interest rates, annuities, prizes and awards, group term life insurance, unemployment compensation, and Social Security benefits.

5. Utilize tax planning strategies for minimizing gross income.

Mr. Zarin lost over $2,500,000 of his own money gambling. The casino then allowed him to gamble on credit. After several months, his liability to the casino totaled more than $3,400,000. Following protracted negotiations, the casino agreed to settle its claim against Mr. Zarin for a mere $500,000. Although Mr. Zarin had paid for gambling losses of $3,000,000, the IRS had the audacity to ask him to pay tax on $2,900,000, that is, the amount the casino marked down his account.[1] Mr. Zarin undoubtedly had difficulty understanding how he could be deemed to have income in this situation.

Given an understanding of the income tax formula, though, one can see how the "free" gambling Mr. Zarin enjoyed could constitute income. The starting point in the formula is the determination of gross income rather than "net income." Once gross income is determined, the next step is to determine the allowable deductions. In Mr. Zarin's way of thinking, these steps were collapsed.

This chapter is concerned with the first step in the computation of taxable income—the determination of gross income. Questions that are addressed include the following:

- What: What is income?
- When: In which tax period is the income recognized?
- Who: Who must include the item of income in gross income?

The Code provides an all-inclusive definition of gross income in § 61. Chapter 4 presents items of income that are specifically excluded from gross income (exclusions).

---

[1]*Zarin v. Comm.,* 90–2 USTC ¶50,530, 66 AFTR2d 90–5679, 916 F.2d 110 (CA–3, 1990).

GROSS INCOME—WHAT IS IT?

DEFINITION

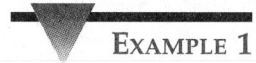

1 **LEARNING OBJECTIVE**
Explain the concepts of gross income and realization and distinguish between the economic, accounting, and tax concepts of gross income.

Section 61(a) of the Internal Revenue Code defines the term **gross income** as follows:

> Except as otherwise provided in this subtitle, gross income means all income from whatever source derived.

This definition is derived from the language of the Sixteenth Amendment to the Constitution.

Supreme Court decisions have made it clear that all sources of income are subject to tax unless Congress specifically excludes the type of income received:

> The starting point in all cases dealing with the question of the scope of what is included in "gross income" begins with the basic premise that the purpose of Congress was to use the full measure of its taxing power.[2]

Although at this point we know that *income* is to be broadly construed, we still do not have a satisfactory definition of the term *income*. Congress left it to the judicial and administrative branches to thrash out the meaning of income. Early in the development of the income tax law, a choice was made between two competing models: economic income and accounting income.

ECONOMIC AND ACCOUNTING CONCEPTS

The term **income** is used in the Code but is not separately defined. Thus, early in the history of our tax laws, the courts were required to interpret "the commonly understood meaning of the term which must have been in the minds of the people when they adopted the Sixteenth Amendment to the Constitution."[3] In determining the definition of income, the Supreme Court rejected the economic concept of income.

Economists measure income (**economic income**) by first determining the fair market value of the individual's net assets at the beginning and end of the year (change in net worth). Then, to arrive at economic income, this change in net worth is added to the goods and services that person actually consumed during the period. Economic income also includes imputed values for such items as the rental value of an owner-occupied home and the value of food a taxpayer might grow for personal consumption.[4]

EXAMPLE 1

Helen's economic income is calculated as follows:

Fair market value of Helen's assets on December 31, 1998	$220,000	
Less liabilities on December 31, 1998	(40,000)	
Net worth on December 31, 1998		$180,000
Fair market value of Helen's assets on January 1, 1998	$200,000	
Less liabilities on January 1, 1998	(80,000)	
Net worth on January 1, 1998		(120,000)

---

[2] *James v. U.S.*, 61–1 USTC ¶9449, 7 AFTR2d 1361, 81 S.Ct. 1052 (USSC, 1961).

[3] *Merchants Loan and Trust Co. v. Smietanka*, 1 USTC ¶42, 3 AFTR 3102, 41 S.Ct. 386 (USSC, 1921).

[4] See Henry C. Simons, *Personal Income Taxation* (Chicago: University of Chicago Press, 1933), Ch. 2–3.

Increase in net worth	$ 60,000
Consumption	
Food, clothing, and other personal expenditures	25,000
Imputed rental value of the home Helen owns and occupies	12,000
Economic income	$ 97,000

The need to value assets annually would make compliance with the tax law burdensome and would cause numerous controversies between the taxpayer and the IRS over valuation. In addition, using market values to determine income for tax purposes could result in liquidity problems. That is, the taxpayer's assets may increase in value even though they are not readily convertible into the cash needed to pay the tax (e.g., commercial real estate). Thus, the IRS, Congress, and the courts have rejected the economic concept of income as impractical.

In contrast, the accounting concept of income is founded on the realization principle.[5] According to this principle, income (**accounting income**) is not recognized until it is realized. For realization to occur, (1) an exchange of goods or services must take place between the accounting entity and some independent, external group, and (2) in the exchange the accounting entity must receive assets that are capable of being objectively valued. Thus, the mere appreciation in the market value of assets before a sale or other disposition is not sufficient to warrant income recognition. In addition, the imputed savings that arise when an individual creates assets for her own use (e.g., feed grown for a farmer's own livestock) are not income because no exchange has occurred. The courts and the IRS have ruled, however, that embezzlement proceeds and buried treasures found satisfy the realization requirement and, therefore, must be recognized as income.[6]

The Supreme Court expressed an inclination toward the accounting concept of income when it adopted the realization requirement in *Eisner v. Macomber*:

> Income may be defined as the gain derived from capital, from labor, or from both combined, provided it is understood to include profit gained through a sale or conversion of capital assets. . . . Here we have the essential matter: not a gain accruing to capital; not a *growth* or *increment* of value *in* investment; but a gain, a profit, something of exchangeable value, *proceeding from* the property, *severed from* the capital however invested or employed, and *coming in*, being *"derived"*—that is, *received* or *drawn by* the recipient for his separate use, benefit and disposal—*that is*, income derived from the property.[7]

In summary, *income* represents an increase in wealth recognized for tax purposes only upon realization.

COMPARISON OF THE ACCOUNTING AND TAX CONCEPTS OF INCOME

Although income tax rules frequently parallel financial accounting measurement concepts, differences do exist. Of major significance, for example, is the fact that unearned (prepaid) income received by an accrual basis taxpayer often is taxed in the year of receipt. For financial accounting purposes, such prepayments are not

---

[5] See the American Accounting Association Committee Report on the "Realization Concept," *The Accounting Review* (April 1965): 312–322.
[6] *Rutkin v. U.S.*, 52–1 USTC ¶9260, 41 AFTR2d 596, 72 S.Ct. 571 (USSC, 1952); Rev.Rul. 61, 1953–1 C.B. 17.

[7] 1 USTC ¶32, 3 AFTR 3020, 40 S.Ct. 189 (USSC, 1920).

TAX IN THE NEWS

IRS CALLS FOUL ON NBA REFEREES

Four NBA referees have been called for "tax fouls" and ejected from the game for not reporting income. The rules of the game were as follows:

- Through a travel agent, the referees would purchase first-class airline tickets to cities where they were officiating.
- The referees would then turn the tickets in to the travel agent in exchange for coach tickets and cash.
- The referees were reimbursed for the first-class tickets by the NBA.
- The referees chose not to include the cash differential received in their gross income.

The IRS filed criminal charges against the four referees (i.e., filing false Federal income tax returns). Three of the four have pleaded guilty.

treated as income until earned.[8] Because of this and other differences, many corporations report financial accounting income that is substantially different from the amounts reported for tax purposes (see Chapter 16, Reconciliation of Taxable Income and Accounting Income).

The Supreme Court provided an explanation for some of the variations between accounting and taxable income in a decision involving inventory and bad debt adjustments:

> The primary goal of financial accounting is to provide useful information to management, shareholders, creditors, and others properly interested; the major responsibility of the accountant is to protect these parties from being misled. The primary goal of the income tax system, in contrast, is the equitable collection of revenue. . . . Consistently with its goals and responsibilities, financial accounting has as its foundation the principle of conservatism, with its corollary that 'possible errors in measurement [should] be in the direction of understatement rather than overstatement of net income and net assets.' In view of the Treasury's markedly different goals and responsibilities, understatement of income is not destined to be its guiding light.
>
> . . . Financial accounting, in short, is hospitable to estimates, probabilities, and reasonable certainties; the tax law, with its mandate to preserve the revenue, can give no quarter to uncertainty.[9]

FORM OF RECEIPT

Gross income is not limited to cash received. "It includes income realized in any form, whether in money, property, or services. Income may be realized [and recognized], therefore, in the form of services, meals, accommodations, stock or other property, as well as in cash."[10]

---

[8]Similar differences exist in the deduction area.

[9]*Thor Power Tool Co. v. Comm.*, 79–1 USTC ¶9139, 43 AFTR2d 79–362, 99 S.Ct. 773 (USSC, 1979).

[10]Reg. § 1.61–1(a).

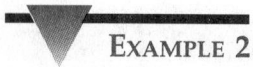

EXAMPLE 2
Ostrich Corporation allowed Bill, an employee, to use a company car for his vacation. Bill realized income equal to the rental value of the car for the time and mileage. ▼

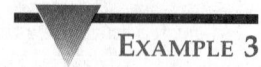

EXAMPLE 3
Terry owed $10,000 on a mortgage. The creditor accepted $8,000 in full satisfaction of the debt. Terry realized income of $2,000 from retiring the debt.[11] ▼

ETHICAL CONSIDERATIONS

Unreported Income

The roof of your office building recently experienced some damage as the result of a storm. You are negotiating with a carpenter who has quoted two prices for the repair work: $600 if you pay in cash ("folding money") and $700 if you pay by check. The carpenter observes that the IRS can more readily discover his receipt of a check. Thus, he hints that he will report the receipt of the check (but not the cash). The carpenter has a full-time job and will do the work after hours and on the weekend. He comments that he should be allowed to keep all he earns after regular working hours. Evaluate what you should do including whether you have an ethical obligation to pay the higher price.

RECOVERY OF CAPITAL DOCTRINE

The Constitution grants Congress the power to tax income but does not define the term. Because the Constitution does not define income, it would seem that Congress could simply tax gross receipts. Although Congress does allow certain deductions, none are constitutionally required. However, the Supreme Court has held that there is no income subject to tax until the taxpayer has recovered the capital invested.[12] This concept is known as the **recovery of capital doctrine.**

In its simplest application, this doctrine means that sellers can reduce their gross receipts (selling price) by the adjusted basis of the property sold.[13] This net amount, in the language of the Code, is gross income.

EXAMPLE 4
Dave sold common stock for $15,000. He had purchased the stock for $12,000. Dave's gross receipts are $15,000. This amount consists of a $12,000 recovery of capital and $3,000 of gross income. ▼

Collections on annuity contracts and installment payments received from sales of property must be allocated between recovery of capital and income. Annuities are discussed in this chapter, and installment sales are discussed in Chapter 15.

---

[11]Reg. § 1.61–12. See *U.S. v. Kirby Lumber Co.,* 2 USTC ¶814, 10 AFTR 458, 52 S.Ct. 4 (USSC, 1931). Exceptions to this general rule are discussed in Chapter 4.

[12]*Doyle v. Mitchell Bros. Co.,* 1 USTC ¶17, 3 AFTR 2979, 38 S.Ct. 467 (USSC, 1916).

[13]For a definition of adjusted basis, see the Glossary of Tax Terms in Appendix C.

YEAR OF INCLUSION

TAXABLE YEAR

2 **LEARNING OBJECTIVE**
Describe the cash and accrual methods of accounting and the related effects of the choice of taxable year.

The annual accounting period or **taxable year** is a basic component of our tax system.[14] Generally, an entity must use the *calendar year* to report its income. However, a *fiscal year* (a period of 12 months ending on the last day of any month other than December) can be elected if the taxpayer maintains adequate books and records. This fiscal year option generally is not available to partnerships, S corporations, and personal service corporations, as discussed in Chapter 15.[15]

Determining the particular year in which the income will be taxed is important for determining when the tax must be paid. But the year each item of income is subject to tax can also affect the total tax liability over the entity's lifetime. This is true for the following reasons:

- With a progressive rate system, a taxpayer's marginal tax rate can change from year to year.
- Congress may change the tax rates.
- The relevant rates may change because of a change in the entity's status (e.g., a person may marry or a business may be incorporated).
- Several provisions in the Code are dependent on the taxpayer's gross income for the year (e.g., whether the person can be claimed as a dependent, as discussed in Chapter 2).

ACCOUNTING METHODS

The year an item of income is subject to tax often depends upon which acceptable **accounting method** the taxpayer regularly employs.[16] The three primary methods of accounting are (1) the cash receipts and disbursements method, (2) the accrual method, and (3) the hybrid method. Most individuals use the cash receipts and disbursements method of accounting, whereas most corporations use the accrual method. The Regulations require the accrual method for determining purchases and sales when inventory is an income-producing factor.[17] Some businesses employ a hybrid method that is a combination of the cash and accrual methods of accounting.

In addition to these overall accounting methods, a taxpayer may choose to spread the gain from the sale of property over the collection periods by using the installment method of income recognition. Contractors may either spread profits from contracts over the periods in which the work is done (the percentage of completion method) or defer all profit until the year in which the project is completed (the completed contract method, which can be used only in limited circumstances).[18]

The IRS has the power to prescribe the accounting method to be used by the taxpayer. Section 446(b) grants the IRS broad powers to determine if the accounting method used *clearly reflects income*:

---

[14]See Accounting Periods in Chapter 15.
[15]§§ 441(a) and (d).
[16]See Accounting Methods in Chapter 15.
[17]Reg. § 1.446–1(c)(2)(i). Other circumstances in which the accrual method must be used are presented in Chapter 15.

[18]§§ 453 and 460. See Chapter 15 for limitations on the use of the installment method and the completed contract method.

Exceptions—If no method of accounting has been regularly used by the taxpayer, or *if the method used does not clearly reflect income, the computation of taxable income shall be made under such method as, in the opinion of the Secretary. . . does clearly reflect income.*

A change in the method of accounting requires the consent of the IRS.[19]

Cash Receipts Method.   Under the **cash receipts method,** property or services received are included in the taxpayer's gross income in the year of actual or constructive receipt by the taxpayer or agent, regardless of whether the income was earned in that year.[20] The income received need not be reduced to cash in the same year. All that is necessary for income recognition is that property or services received have a fair market value—a cash equivalent.[21] Thus, if a cash basis taxpayer receives a note in payment for services, he has income in the year of receipt equal to the fair market value of the note. However, a creditor's mere promise to pay (e.g., an account receivable), with no supporting note, is not usually considered to have a fair market value.[22] Thus, the cash basis taxpayer defers income recognition until the account receivable is collected.

EXAMPLE 5   Dana, an accountant, reports her income by the cash method. In 1998, she performed an audit for Orange Corporation and billed the client for $5,000, which was collected in 1999. In 1998, Dana also performed an audit for Blue Corporation. Because of Blue's precarious financial position, Dana required Blue to issue an $8,000 secured negotiable note in payment of the fee. The note had a fair market value of $6,000. Dana collected $8,000 on the note in 1999. Dana's gross income for the two years is as follows:

	1998	1999
Fair market value of note received from Blue	$6,000	
Cash received		
From Orange on account receivable		$5,000
From Blue on note receivable		8,000
Less: Recovery of capital		(6,000)
Total gross income	$6,000	$7,000

Generally, a check received is considered a cash equivalent. Thus, a cash basis taxpayer must recognize the income when the check is received. This is true even if the taxpayer receives the check after banking hours.[23]

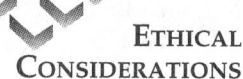

ETHICAL CONSIDERATIONS

Accounting Errors and Omissions

You have prepared Ted and Jane's tax return for the past five years. In the process of preparing the current year's return, you discover that you inadvertently omitted a $10,000 item of income from the previous year's return. Generally, the client does not examine the return in detail before filing it. As a result of your oversight, you are faced

---

[19]§ 446(e). See Chapter 15.
[20]*Julia A. Strauss*, 2 B.T.A. 598 (1925). See the Glossary of Tax Terms in Appendix C for a discussion of the terms "cash equivalent doctrine" and "constructive receipt."

[21]Reg. §§ 1.446–1(a)(3) and (c)(1)(i).
[22]*Bedell v. Comm.*, 1 USTC ¶359, 7 AFTR 8469, 30 F.2d 622 (CA–2, 1929).
[23]*Charles F. Kahler*, 18 T.C. 31 (1952).

with the following choices: (1) ignore the omission; (2) advise Ted and Jane that the previous year's return should be amended; (3) include the $10,000 in the current year's gross income and advise Ted and Jane of the previous omission; or (4) include the $10,000 in the current year's gross income and do not mention the adjustment to Ted and Jane.

Accrual Method.   Under the **accrual method,** an item is generally included in the gross income for the year in which it is earned, regardless of when the income is collected. The income is earned when (1) all the events have occurred that fix the right to receive such income and (2) the amount to be received can be determined with reasonable accuracy.[24]

Generally, the taxpayer's rights to the income accrue when title to property passes to the buyer or the services are performed for the customer or client.[25] If the rights to the income have accrued but are subject to a potential refund claim (e.g., under a product warranty), the income is reported in the year of sale, and a deduction is allowed in subsequent years when actual claims accrue.[26]

Where the taxpayer's rights to the income are being contested (e.g., when a contractor fails to meet specifications), the year in which the income is subject to tax depends upon whether payment has been received. If payment has not been received, no income is recognized until the claim is settled. Only then is the right to the income established.[27] However, if the payment is received before the dispute is settled, the court-made **claim of right doctrine** requires the taxpayer to recognize the income in the year of receipt.[28]

EXAMPLE 6

A contractor completed a building in 1998 and presented a bill to the customer. The customer refused to pay the bill and claimed that the contractor had not met specifications. A settlement with the customer was not reached until 1999. No income would accrue to the contractor until 1999. If the customer paid for the work and then filed suit for damages, the contractor could not defer the income (the income would be taxable in 1998). ▼

The measure of accrual basis income is generally the amount the taxpayer has a right to receive. Unlike the cash basis, the fair market value of the customer's obligation is irrelevant in measuring accrual basis income.

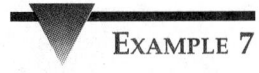

EXAMPLE 7

Assume the same facts as in Example 5, except Dana is an accrual basis taxpayer. Dana must recognize $13,000 ($8,000 + $5,000) income in 1998, the year her rights to the income accrued. ▼

Hybrid Method.   The **hybrid method** is a combination of the accrual method and the cash method. Generally, when the hybrid method is used, inventory is an income-producing factor. Therefore, the Regulations require that the accrual method be used for determining sales and cost of goods sold. In this circumstance, to simplify record keeping, the taxpayer accounts for inventory using the accrual method and uses the cash method for all other income and expense items (e.g., dividend and interest income). The hybrid method is primarily used by small businesses.

[24]Reg. § 1.451–1(a).
[25]*Lucas v. North Texas Lumber Co.*, 2 USTC ¶484, 8 AFTR 10276, 50 S.Ct. 184 (USSC, 1930).
[26]*Brown v. Helvering*, 4 USTC ¶1222, 13 AFTR 851, 54 S.Ct. 356 (USSC, 1933).

[27]*Burnet v. Sanford and Brooks*, 2 USTC ¶636, 9 AFTR 603, 51 S.Ct. 150 (USSC, 1931).
[28]*North American Oil Consolidated Co. v. Burnet*, 3 USTC ¶943, 11 AFTR 16, 52 S.Ct. 613 (USSC, 1932).

A FENDER-BENDER WITH THE IRS

Should used-car dealers be required to include in their gross income amounts they may never receive? They say no—doing so will drive them out of business. The IRS says yes—it is the law.

Creditors such as Credit Acceptance and National Auto Credit provide financing on used-car sales to buyers with poor credit ratings. This enables used-car dealers to sell more cars. But there is a catch. When a sale is financed through such a lender, the used-car dealer receives as little as half of the loan proceeds right away. To reduce their risk, the lenders turn over the rest of the money to the dealer only after they have collected it from the buyer. If the buyer defaults, the used-car dealer may not receive any of the remaining balance.

Dealers complain that having to record all the income at the time of the sale is driving them out of business. The amount involved is huge. For example, at the end of 1997, Credit Acceptance owed $469 million to nearly 5,400 dealers. The National Independent Automobile Dealers Association, which represents used-car dealers, is lobbying Congress for relief.

SOURCE: Adapted from Michael Selz, "Used-Car Dealers Face Fender-Benders with the IRS," *Wall Street Journal*, February 25, 1997, p. B2.

EXCEPTIONS APPLICABLE TO CASH BASIS TAXPAYERS

Constructive Receipt. Income that has not actually been received by the taxpayer is taxed as though it had been received—the income is constructively received—under the following conditions:

- The amount is made readily available to the taxpayer.
- The taxpayer's actual receipt is not subject to substantial limitations or restrictions.[29]

The rationale for the **constructive receipt** doctrine is that if the income is available, the taxpayer should not be allowed to postpone the income recognition. For instance, a taxpayer is not permitted to defer income for December services by refusing to accept payment until January. However, determining whether the income is *readily available* and whether *substantial limitations or restrictions exist* necessitates a factual inquiry that leads to a judgment call.[30] The following are some examples of the application of the constructive receipt doctrine.

EXAMPLE 8   Ted is a member of a barter club. In 1998, Ted performed services for other club members and earned 1,000 points. Each point entitles him to $1 in goods and services sold by other members of the club; the points can be used at any time. In 1999, Ted exchanged his points for a new color TV. Ted must recognize $1,000 income in 1998 when the 1,000 points were credited to his account.[31] ▼

---

[29]Reg. § 1.451–2(a).

[30]*Baxter v. Comm.*, 87–1 USTC ¶9315, 59 AFTR2d 87–1068, 816 F.2d 493 (CA–9, 1987).

[31]Rev.Rul. 80–52, 1980–1 C.B. 100.

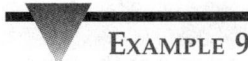
EXAMPLE 9

On December 31, an employer issued a bonus check to an employee but asked her to hold it for a few days until the company could make deposits to cover the check. The income was not constructively received on December 31 since the issuer did not have sufficient funds in its account to pay the debt.[32] ▼

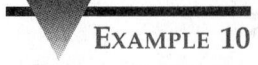
EXAMPLE 10

Rick owned interest coupons that matured on December 31. The coupons could be converted to cash at any bank at maturity. Thus, the income is constructively received on December 31.[33] ▼

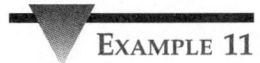
EXAMPLE 11

Dove Company mails dividend checks on December 31, 1998. The checks will not be received by shareholders until January. The shareholders do not realize income until 1999.[34] ▼

The constructive receipt doctrine does not reach income that the taxpayer is not yet entitled to receive even though the taxpayer could have contracted to receive the income at an earlier date.

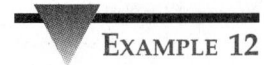
EXAMPLE 12

Sara offered to pay Ivan $100,000 for land in December 1998. Ivan refused but offered to sell the land to Sara on January 1, 1999, when he would be in a lower tax bracket. If Sara accepts Ivan's offer, the gain is taxed to Ivan in 1999 when the sale is completed.[35] ▼

Income set apart or made available is not constructively received if its actual receipt is subject to *substantial restrictions*. The life insurance industry has used substantial restrictions as a cornerstone for designing life insurance contracts with favorable tax features. Ordinary life insurance policies provide (1) current protection—an amount payable in the event of death—and (2) a savings feature—a cash surrender value payable to the policyholder if the policy is terminated during the policyholder's life. The annual increase in cash surrender value is not taxable because the policyholder must cancel the policy to actually receive the increase in value. Because the cancellation requirement is a substantial restriction, the policyholder does not constructively receive the annual increase in cash surrender value.[36] Employees often receive from their employers property subject to substantial restrictions. Generally, no income is recognized until the restrictions lapse.[37]

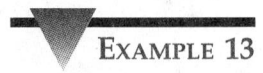
EXAMPLE 13

Carlos is a key employee of Red, Inc. The corporation gave stock with a value of $10,000 to Carlos. The stock could not be sold, however, for five years. Carlos will not be required to recognize income until the restrictions lapse at the end of five years. ▼

Original Issue Discount. Lenders frequently make loans that require a payment at maturity of more than the amount of the original loan. The difference between the amount due at maturity and the amount of the original loan is actually interest but is referred to as **original issue discount.** Under the general rules of tax accounting, the cash basis lender would not report the original issue discount as interest income until the year the amount is collected, although an accrual basis borrower would deduct the interest as it is earned. However, the Code puts the lender and borrower on parity by requiring that the original issue discount be

---

[32]*L. M. Fischer*, 14 T.C. 792 (1950).
[33]Reg. § 1.451–2(b).
[34]Reg. § 1.451–2(b).
[35]*Cowden v. Comm.*, 61–1 USTC ¶9382, 7 AFTR2d 1160, 289 F.2d 20 (CA–5, 1961).

[36]*Theodore H. Cohen*, 39 T.C. 1055 (1963).
[37]§ 83(a).

ORIGINAL ISSUE DISCOUNT RULES MAY DAMPEN ENTHUSIASM FOR INFLATION-ADJUSTED BONDS

The U.S. Treasury Department is now issuing inflation-adjusted bonds. The bonds are aimed at small investors who want to be assured that inflation will not cause their savings to deteriorate. The interest paid each year and the principal are adjusted to reflect the inflation for the year. These bonds present some unique tax accounting issues.

In Temporary Regulation § 1.1275–7T, the Treasury Department concluded that in addition to the interest received each year, the taxpayer is required to include the change in the principal amount as original issue discount amortized during the year. For example, if the bond is issued for $1,000 when the index is 100, and the index at the end of the first year is 102, the bondholder is entitled to $1,020 at maturity assuming no further change in the price level between the end of the first year and the maturity date. The investor is required to include $20 in gross income for the increase in the principal that will not be received until maturity. Thus, inflation adjustments can create gross income before the cash has been received.

reported when it is earned, regardless of the taxpayer's accounting method.[38] The interest "earned" is calculated by the effective interest rate method.

EXAMPLE 14

On January 1, 1998, Mark, a cash basis taxpayer, paid $82,645 for a 24-month certificate. The certificate was priced to yield 10% (the effective interest rate) with interest compounded annually. No interest was paid until maturity, when Mark received $100,000. Thus, Mark's gross income from the certificate is $17,355 ($100,000 – $82,645). Mark's income earned each year is calculated as follows:

1998 (.10 × $82,645) =	$ 8,264
1999 [.10 × ($82,645 + $8,264)] =	9,091
	$17,355

The original issue discount rules do not apply to U.S. savings bonds (discussed in the following paragraphs) or to obligations with a maturity date of one year or less from the date of issue.[39] See Chapter 13 for additional discussion of the tax treatment of original issue discount.

Series E and Series EE Bonds.   Certain U.S. government savings bonds (Series E before 1980 and Series EE after 1979) are issued at a discount and are redeemable for fixed amounts that increase at stated intervals. No interest payments are actually made. The difference between the purchase price and the amount received on redemption is the bondholder's interest income from the investment.

The income from these savings bonds is generally deferred until the bonds are redeemed or mature. Furthermore, Series E bonds can be exchanged within one year of their maturity date for Series HH bonds, and the interest on the Series E

---

[38]§§ 1272(a)(3) and 1273(a).   [39]§ 1272(a)(2).

bonds can be further deferred until maturity of the Series HH bonds.[40] Thus, U.S. savings bonds have attractive income deferral features not available with corporate bonds and certificates of deposit issued by financial institutions.

Of course, the deferral feature of government bonds issued at a discount is not an advantage if the investor has insufficient income to be subject to tax as the income accrues. In fact, the deferral may work to the investor's disadvantage if she has other income in the year the bonds mature or the bunching of the bond interest into one tax year creates a tax liability. Fortunately, U.S. government bonds have a provision for these investors. A cash basis taxpayer can elect to include in gross income the annual increment in redemption value.[41]

EXAMPLE 15

Kate purchases Series EE U.S. savings bonds for $500 (face value of $1,000) on January 2 of the current year. If the bonds are redeemed during the first six months, no interest is paid. At December 31, the redemption value is $519.60.

If Kate elects to report the interest income annually, she must report interest income of $19.60 for the current year. If she does not make the election, she will report no interest income for the current year. ▼

When a taxpayer elects to report the income from the bonds on an annual basis, the election applies to all such bonds the taxpayer owns at the time of the election and to all such securities acquired subsequent to the election. A change in the method of reporting the income from the bonds requires permission from the IRS.

Amounts Received under an Obligation to Repay. The receipt of funds with an obligation to repay that amount in the future is the essence of borrowing. Because the taxpayer's assets and liabilities increase by the same amount, no income is realized when the borrowed funds are received. Because amounts paid to the taxpayer by mistake and customer deposits are often classified as borrowed funds, receipt of these funds is not a taxable event.

EXAMPLE 16

A landlord receives a damage deposit from a tenant. The landlord does not recognize income until the deposit is forfeited because the landlord has an obligation to repay the deposit if no damage occurs.[42] However, if the deposit is in fact a prepayment of rent, it is taxed in the year of receipt. ▼

EXCEPTIONS APPLICABLE TO ACCRUAL BASIS TAXPAYERS

Prepaid Income. For financial reporting purposes, advance payments received from customers are reflected as prepaid income and as a liability of the seller. However, for tax purposes, the prepaid income often is taxed in the year of receipt.

EXAMPLE 17

In December 1998, a tenant paid his January 1999 rent of $1,000. The accrual basis landlord must include the $1,000 in his 1998 income for tax purposes, although the unearned rent income is reported as a liability on the landlord's December 31, 1998, balance sheet. ▼

Taxpayers have repeatedly argued that deferral of income until it is actually earned properly matches revenues and expenses. Moreover, a proper matching of

---

[40]Treas. Dept. Circulars No. 1–80 and No. 2–80, 1980–1 C.B. 714, 715. Note that interest is paid at semiannual intervals on the Series HH bonds and must be included in income as received. Refer to Chapter 4 for a discussion of the savings bond interest exclusion.

[41]§ 454(a).
[42]*John Mantell*, 17 T.C. 1143 (1952).

income with the expenses of earning the income is necessary to clearly reflect income, as required by the Code. The IRS responds that § 446(b) grants it broad powers to determine whether an accounting method clearly reflects income. The IRS further argues that generally accepted financial accounting principles should not dictate tax accounting for prepaid income because of the practical problems of collecting Federal revenues. Collection of the tax is simplest in the year the taxpayer receives the cash from the customer or client.

Over 40 years of litigation, the IRS has been only partially successful in the courts. In cases involving prepaid income from services to be performed at the demand of customers (e.g., dance lessons to be taken at any time in a 24-month period), the IRS's position has been upheld.[43] In such cases, the taxpayer's argument that deferral of the income was necessary to match the income with expenses was not persuasive because the taxpayer did not know precisely when each customer would demand services and, thus, when the expenses would be incurred. However, taxpayers have had some success in the courts when the services were performed on a fixed schedule (e.g., a baseball team's season-ticket sales).[44] In some cases involving the sale of goods, taxpayers have successfully argued that the prepayments were mere deposits[45] or in the nature of loans.[46]

Against this background of mixed results in the courts, congressional intervention, and taxpayers' strong resentment of the IRS's position, in 1971 the IRS modified its prepaid income rules, as explained in the following paragraphs.

Deferral of Advance Payments for Goods. Generally, a taxpayer can elect to defer recognition of income from *advance payments for goods* if the method of accounting for the sale is the same for tax and financial reporting purposes.[47]

EXAMPLE 18

Brown Company will ship goods only after payment for the goods has been received. In December 1998, Brown received $10,000 for goods that were not shipped until January 1999. Brown can elect to report the income for tax purposes in 1999, assuming the company reports the income in 1999 for financial reporting purposes. ▼

Deferral of Advance Payments for Services. Revenue Procedure 71–21[48] permits an accrual basis taxpayer to defer recognition of income for *advance payments for services* to be performed by the end of the tax year following the year of receipt. No deferral is allowed if the taxpayer might be required to perform any services, under the agreement, after the tax year following the year of receipt of the advance payment. In addition, prepaid rent and prepaid interest cannot be deferred under this revenue procedure.

EXAMPLE 19

Yellow Corporation, an accrual basis taxpayer, sells its services under 12-month, 18-month, and 24-month contracts. The corporation provides services to each customer every month. In April of 1998, Yellow Corporation sold the following customer contracts:

[43]*American Automobile Association v. U.S.*, 61–2 USTC ¶9517, 7 AFTR2d 1618, 81 S.Ct. 1727 (USSC, 1961); *Schlude v. Comm.*, 63–1 USTC ¶9284, 11 AFTR2d 751, 83 S.Ct. 601 (USSC, 1963).

[44]*Artnell Company v. Comm.*, 68–2 USTC ¶9593, 22 AFTR2d 5590, 400 F.2d 981 (CA–7, 1968). See also *Boise Cascade Corp. v. U.S.*, 76–1 USTC ¶9203, 37 AFTR2d 76–696, 530 F.2d 1367 (Ct. Cls., 1976).

[45]*Veenstra & DeHavaan Coal Co.*, 11 T.C. 964 (1948).

[46]*Consolidated-Hammer Dry Plate & Film Co. v. Comm.*, 63–1 USTC ¶9494, 11 AFTR2d 1518, 317 F.2d 829 (CA–7, 1963); *Comm. v.*

Indianapolis Power & Light Co., 90–1 USTC ¶50,007, 65 AFTR2d 90–394, 110 S.Ct. 589 (USSC, 1990).

[47]Reg. § 1.451–5(b). See Reg. § 1.451–5(c) for exceptions to this deferral opportunity. The financial accounting conformity requirement is not applicable to contractors who use the completed contract method.

[48]1971–2 C.B. 549.

Length of Contract	Total Proceeds
12 months	$6,000
18 months	3,600
24 months	2,400

Fifteen hundred dollars of the $6,000 may be deferred ($\frac{3}{12} \times \$6,000$), and $1,800 of the $3,600 may be deferred ($\frac{9}{18} \times \$3,600$) because those amounts will not be earned until 1999. However, the entire $2,400 received on the 24-month contracts is taxable in the year of receipt (1998), since a part of the income will still be unearned by the end of the tax year following the year of receipt (part will be earned in 2000). ▼

In summary, Revenue Procedure 71–21 will result in conformity of tax and financial accounting in a very limited number of prepaid income cases. It is not apparent why prepaid rents and interest may not be deferred, why revenues under some service contracts may be spread over two years, and why revenues under longer service contracts must be reported in one year. Although Revenue Procedure 71–21 has reduced the number of controversies involving prepaid income, a consistent policy has not yet evolved.

INCOME SOURCES

PERSONAL SERVICES

3 **LEARNING OBJECTIVE**
Identify who should pay the tax on a particular item of income in various situations.

It is a well-established principle of taxation that income from personal services must be included in the gross income of the person who performs the services. This principle was first established in a Supreme Court decision, *Lucas v. Earl.*[49] Mr. Earl entered into a binding agreement with his wife under which Mrs. Earl was to receive one-half of Mr. Earl's salary. Justice Holmes used the celebrated **fruit and tree metaphor** to explain that the fruit (income) must be attributed to the tree from which it came (Mr. Earl's services). A mere **assignment of income** does not shift the liability for the tax.

Services of an Employee.   Services performed by an employee for the employer's customers are considered performed by the employer. Thus, the employer is taxed on the income from the services provided to the customer, and the employee is taxed on any compensation received from the employer.[50]

EXAMPLE 20

Dr. Shontelle incorporated her medical practice and entered into a contract to work for the corporation for a salary. All patients contracted to receive their services from the corporation, and those services were provided through the corporation's employee, Dr. Shontelle. The corporation must include the patients' fees in its gross income. Dr. Shontelle must include her salary in her gross income. The corporation will be allowed a deduction for the reasonable salary paid to Dr. Shontelle (see the discussion of unreasonable compensation in Chapter 5). ▼

---

[49]2 USTC ¶496, 8 AFTR 10287, 50 S.Ct. 241 (USSC, 1930).
[50]*Sargent v. Comm.*, 91–1 USTC ¶50,168, 67 AFTR2d 91–718, 929 F.2d
1252 (CA–8, 1991).

Services of a Child.   In the case of a child, the Code specifically provides that amounts earned from personal services must be included in the child's gross income. This result applies even though the income is paid to other persons (e.g., the parents).[51]

INCOME FROM PROPERTY

Income from property (interest, dividends, rent) must be included in the gross income of the *owner* of the property. If a father clips interest coupons from bonds shortly before the interest payment date and gives the coupons to his son, the interest will still be taxed to the father. A father who assigns rents from rental property to his daughter will be taxed on the rent since he retains ownership of the property.[52]

Often income-producing property is transferred after income from the property has accrued, but before the income is recognized under the transferor's method of accounting. The IRS and the courts have developed rules to allocate the income between the transferor and the transferee.

Interest.   According to the IRS, interest accrues daily. Therefore, the interest for the period that includes the date of the transfer is allocated between the transferor and transferee based on the number of days during the period that each owned the property.

EXAMPLE 21

Floyd, a cash basis taxpayer, gave his son, Seth, bonds with a face amount of $10,000 and an 8% stated annual interest rate. The gift was made on January 31, 1998, and the interest was paid on December 31, 1998. Floyd must recognize $68 in interest income (8% × $10,000 × $31/365$). Seth will recognize $732 in interest income ($800 – $68). ▼

When the transferor must recognize the income from the property depends upon the method of accounting and the manner in which the property was transferred. In the case of a gift of income-producing property, the donor must recognize his share of the accrued income at the time it would have been recognized had he continued to own the property.[53] However, if the transfer is a sale, the transferor must recognize the accrued income at the time of the sale. This results because the accrued interest will be included in the sales proceeds.

EXAMPLE 22

Assume the same facts as in Example 21, except the interest that was payable as of December 31 was not actually or constructively received by the bondholders until January 3, 1999. As a cash basis taxpayer, Floyd generally does not recognize interest income until it is received. If Floyd had continued to own the bonds, the interest would have been included in his 1999 gross income, the year it would have been received. Therefore, Floyd must include the $68 accrued income in his gross income as of January 3, 1999.

Further assume that Floyd sold identical bonds on the date of the gift. The bonds sold for $9,900, including accrued interest. On January 31, 1998, Floyd must recognize the accrued interest of $68 on the bonds sold. Thus, the selling price of the bonds is $9,832 ($9,900 – $68). ▼

---

[51]§ 73. For circumstances in which the child's unearned income is taxed at the parents' rate, see Unearned Income of Certain Minor Children Taxed at Parents' Rate in Chapter 2.

[52]*Galt v. Comm.*, 54–2 USTC ¶9457, 46 AFTR 633, 216 F.2d 41 (CA–7, 1954); *Helvering v. Horst*, 40–2 USTC ¶9787, 24 AFTR 1058, 61 S.Ct. 144 (USSC, 1940).

[53]Rev.Rul. 72–312, 1972–1 C.B. 22.

Dividends. A corporation is taxed on its earnings, and the shareholders are taxed on the dividends paid to them from the corporation's after-tax earnings. The dividend can take the form of an actual dividend or a constructive dividend (e.g., shareholder use of corporate assets).

Unlike interest, dividends do not accrue on a daily basis because the declaration of a dividend is at the discretion of the corporation's board of directors. Generally, dividends are taxed to the person who is entitled to receive them—the shareholder of record as of the corporation's record date.[54] Thus, if a taxpayer sells stock after a dividend has been declared but before the record date, the dividend generally will be taxed to the purchaser.

If a donor makes a gift of stock to someone (e.g., a family member) after the declaration date but before the record date, the Tax Court has held that the donor does not shift the dividend income to the donee. The *fruit* has sufficiently ripened as of the declaration date to tax the dividend income to the donor of the stock.[55] In a similar set of facts, the Fifth Court of Appeals concluded that the dividend income should be included in the gross income of the donee (the owner at the record date). In this case, the taxpayer gave stock to a qualified charity (a charitable contribution) after the declaration date and before the record date.[56]

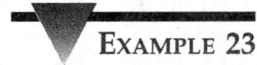

EXAMPLE 23

On June 20, the board of directors of Black Corporation declares a $10 per share dividend. The dividend is payable on June 30, to shareholders of record on June 25. As of June 20, Maria owned 200 shares of Black Corporation's stock. On June 21, Maria sold 100 of the shares to Norm for their fair market value and gave 100 of the shares to Sam (her son). Assume both Norm and Sam are shareholders of record as of June 25. Norm (the purchaser) will be taxed on $1,000 since he is entitled to receive the dividend. However, Maria (the donor) will be taxed on the $1,000 received by Sam (the donee) because the gift was made after the declaration date of the dividend. ▼

INCOME RECEIVED BY AN AGENT

Income received by the taxpayer's agent is considered to be received by the taxpayer. A cash basis principal must recognize the income at the time it is received by the agent.[57]

EXAMPLE 24

Jack, a cash basis taxpayer, delivered cattle to the auction barn in late December. The auctioneer, acting as the farmer's agent, sold the cattle and collected the proceeds in December. The auctioneer did not pay Jack until the following January. Jack must include the sales proceeds in his gross income for the year the auctioneer received the funds. ▼

INCOME FROM PARTNERSHIPS, S CORPORATIONS, TRUSTS, AND ESTATES

A **partnership** is not a separate taxable entity. Rather, the partnership merely files an information return (Form 1065), which serves to provide the data necessary for determining the character and amount of each partner's distributive share of the partnership's income and deductions. Each partner must then report her distributive share of the partnership's income and deductions for the partnership's tax year ending within or with her tax year. The income must be reported by each

---

[54]Reg. § 1.61–9(c). The record date is the cutoff for determining the shareholders who are entitled to receive the dividend.
[55]*M. G. Anton*, 34 T.C. 842 (1960).

[56]*Caruth Corporation v. U.S.*, 89–1 USTC ¶9172, 63 AFTR2d 89–716, 865 F.2d 644 (CA–5, 1989).
[57]Rev.Rul. 79–379, 1979–2 C.B. 204.

partner in the year it is earned, even if such amounts are not actually distributed to the partners. Because a partner pays tax on income as the partnership earns it, a distribution by the partnership to the partner is treated under the recovery of capital rules.[58]

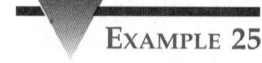

EXAMPLE 25

Tara owned a one-half interest in the capital and profits of T & S Company (a calendar year partnership). For tax year 1998, the partnership earned revenue of $150,000 and had operating expenses of $80,000. During the year, Tara withdrew from her capital account $2,500 per month (for a total of $30,000). For 1998, Tara must report $35,000 as her share of the partnership's profits [½ × ($150,000 − $80,000)] even though she received distributions of only $30,000. ▼

Contrary to the general provision that a corporation must pay tax on its income, a *small business corporation* may elect to be taxed similarly to a partnership. Thus, the shareholders, rather than the corporation, pay the tax on the corporation's income.[59] The electing corporation is referred to as an **S corporation.** Generally, the shareholder reports his proportionate share of the corporation's income and deductions for the year, whether or not the corporation actually makes any distributions to the shareholder.

The *beneficiaries of estates and trusts* generally are taxed on the income earned by the estates or trusts that is actually distributed or required to be distributed to them.[60] Any income not taxed to the beneficiaries is taxable to the estate or trust.

INCOME IN COMMUNITY PROPERTY STATES

General.   State law in Louisiana, Texas, New Mexico, Arizona, California, Washington, Idaho, Nevada, and Wisconsin is based upon a community property system. All other states have a common law property system. The basic difference between common law and community property systems centers around the property rights of married persons. Questions about community property income most frequently arise when the husband and wife file separate returns.

Under a **community property** system, all property is deemed either to be separately owned by the spouse or to belong to the marital community. Property may be held separately by a spouse if it was acquired before marriage or received by gift or inheritance following marriage. Otherwise, any property is deemed to be community property. For Federal tax purposes, each spouse is taxed on one-half of the income from property belonging to the community.

The laws of Texas, Louisiana, Wisconsin, and Idaho distinguish between separate property and the income it produces. In these states, the income from separate property belongs to the community. Accordingly, for Federal income tax purposes, each spouse is taxed on one-half of the income. In the remaining community property states, separate property produces separate income that the owner-spouse must report on his or her Federal income tax return.

What appears to be income, however, may really represent a recovery of capital. A recovery of capital and gain realized on separate property retain their identity as separate property. Items such as nontaxable stock dividends, royalties from mineral interests, and gains and losses from the sale of property take on the same classification as the assets to which they relate.

---

[58]§ 706(a) and Reg. § 1.706–1(a)(1). For further discussion, see Chapter 22.

[59]§§ 1361(a) and 1366. For further discussion, see Chapter 21.

[60]§§ 652(a) and 662(a). For further discussion of the taxation of income from S corporations, partnerships, trusts, and estates, see Chapters 21, 22, and 27.

EXAMPLE 26

Bob and Jane are husband and wife and reside in California. Among other transactions during the year, the following occurred:

- Nontaxable stock dividend received by Jane on stock that was given to her after her marriage by her mother.
- Gain of $10,000 on the sale of unimproved land purchased by Bob before his marriage.
- Oil royalties of $15,000 from a lease Jane acquired after marriage with her separate funds.

Since the stock dividend was distributed on stock held by Jane as separate property, it also is her separate property. The same result occurs for the oil royalties Jane receives. All of the proceeds from the sale of unimproved land (including the gain of $10,000) are Bob's separate property. ▼

In all community property states, income from personal services (e.g., salaries, wages, income from a professional partnership) is generally treated as if one-half is earned by each spouse.

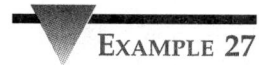

EXAMPLE 27

Fred and Wilma are married but file separate returns. Fred received $25,000 salary and $300 taxable interest on a savings account he established in his name. The deposits to the savings account were made from Fred's salary that he earned since the marriage. Wilma collected $2,000 taxable dividends on stock she inherited from her father. Wilma's gross income is computed as follows under three assumptions as to the state of residency of the couple:

	California	**Texas**	**Common Law States**
Dividends	$ 2,000	$ 1,000	$2,000
Salary	12,500	12,500	–0–
Interest	150	150	–0–
	$14,650	$13,650	$2,000

▼

Community Property Spouses Living Apart. The general rules for taxing the income from services performed by residents of community property states can create complications and even inequities for spouses who are living apart.

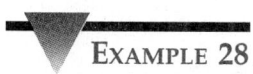

EXAMPLE 28

Cole and Debra were married but living apart for the first nine months of 1998 and were divorced as of October 1, 1998. In December 1998, Cole married Emily, who was married but living apart from Frank before their divorce in June 1998. Cole and Frank had no income from personal services in 1998.

Cole brought into his marriage to Emily a tax liability on one-half of Debra's earnings for the first nine months of the year. However, Emily left with Frank a tax liability on one-half of her earnings for the first six months of 1998. ▼

In circumstances such as those depicted in Example 28, the accrued tax liability could be factored into a property division being negotiated at a time when the parties do not need further complications. In other cases, an abandoned spouse could be saddled with a tax on income earned by a spouse whose whereabouts are unknown.

Congress has developed a simple solution to the many tax problems of community property spouses living apart. A spouse (or former spouse) is taxed only on his or her actual earnings from personal services if the following conditions are met:[61]

- The individuals live apart for the entire year.
- They do not file a joint return with each other.
- No portion of the earned income is transferred between the individuals.

EXAMPLE 29

Jim and Lori reside in a community property state, and both are gainfully employed. On July 1, 1998, they separated, and on June 30, 1999, they were divorced. Assuming their only source of income is wages, one-half of such income for each year is earned by June 30, and they did not file a joint return for 1998, each should report the following gross income:

	Jim's Separate Return	Lori's Separate Return
1998	One-half of Jim's wages	One-half of Jim's wages
	One-half of Lori's wages	One-half of Lori's wages
1999	All of Jim's wages	All of Lori's wages

The results would be the same if Jim or Lori married another person in 1999, except the newlyweds would probably file a joint return. ▼

The IRS may absolve from liability an *innocent spouse* who does not live apart for the entire year and files a separate return but omits his or her share of the community income received by the other spouse. To qualify for the innocent spouse relief, the taxpayer must not know or must have no reason to know of the omitted community income.

ITEMS SPECIFICALLY INCLUDED IN GROSS INCOME

The general principles of gross income determination (discussed in the previous sections) as applied by the IRS and the courts have on occasion yielded results Congress found unacceptable. Consequently, Congress has provided more specific rules for determining the gross income from certain sources. Some of these special rules appear in §§ 71–90 of the Code.

ALIMONY AND SEPARATE MAINTENANCE PAYMENTS

When a married couple divorce or become legally separated, state law generally requires a division of the property accumulated during the marriage. In addition, one spouse may have a legal obligation to support the other spouse. The Code distinguishes between the support payments (alimony or separate maintenance) and the property division in terms of the tax consequences.

Alimony and separate maintenance payments are *deductible* by the party making the payments and are *includible* in the gross income of the party receiving the payments.[62] Thus, income is shifted from the income earner to the income beneficiary, who is the appropriate taxpayer to pay the tax on the amount received.

4 **LEARNING OBJECTIVE**
Apply the Internal Revenue Code provisions on alimony, loans made at below-market interest rates, annuities, prizes and awards, group term life insurance, unemployment compensation, and Social Security benefits.

---

[61]§ 66.   [62]§§ 71 and 215.

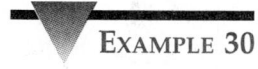
EXAMPLE 30

Pete and Tina were divorced, and Pete was required to pay Tina $15,000 of alimony each year. Pete earns $31,000 a year. The tax law presumes that because Tina received the $15,000, she is better able than Pete to pay the tax on that amount. Therefore, Tina must include the $15,000 in her gross income, and Pete is allowed to deduct $15,000 from his gross income. ▼

A transfer of property *other than cash* to a former spouse under a divorce decree or agreement is not a taxable event. The transferor is not entitled to a deduction and does not recognize gain or loss on the transfer. The transferee does not recognize income and has a cost basis equal to the transferor's basis.[63]

EXAMPLE 31

Paul transfers stock to Rosa as part of a 1998 divorce settlement. The cost of the stock to Paul is $12,000, and the stock's value at the time of the transfer is $15,000. Rosa later sells the stock for $16,000. Paul is not required to recognize gain from the transfer of the stock to Rosa, and Rosa has a realized and recognized gain of $4,000 ($16,000 − $12,000) when she sells the stock. ▼

In the case of *cash payments*, however, it is often difficult to distinguish payments under a support obligation (alimony) and payments for the other spouse's property (property settlement). In 1984, Congress developed objective rules to classify the payments.

Post-1984 Agreements and Decrees. Payments made under post-1984 agreements and decrees are *classified as alimony* only if the following conditions are satisfied:

1. The payments are in cash.
2. The agreement or decree does not specify that the payments are not alimony.
3. The payor and payee are not members of the same household at the time the payments are made.
4. There is no liability to make the payments for any period after the death of the payee.[64]

Requirement 1 simplifies the law by clearly distinguishing alimony from a property division; that is, if the payment is not in cash, it must be a property division. Requirement 2 allows the parties to determine by agreement whether or not the payments will be alimony. The prohibition on cohabitation—requirement 3—is aimed at assuring the alimony payments are associated with duplicative living expenses (maintaining two households).[65] Requirement 4 is an attempt to prevent alimony treatment from being applied to what is, in fact, a payment for property rather than a support obligation. That is, a seller's estate generally will receive payments for property due after the seller's death. Such payments after the death of the payee could not be for the payee's support.

Front-Loading. As a further safeguard against a property settlement being disguised as alimony, special rules apply to post-1986 agreements if payments in the first or second year exceed $15,000. If the change in the amount of the payments exceeds statutory limits, **alimony recapture** results to the extent of the excess alimony payments. In the *third* year, the payor must include the excess alimony

---

[63]§ 1041, added to the Code in 1984 to repeal the rule of *U.S. v. Davis,* 62–2 USTC ¶9509, 9 AFTR2d 1625, 82 S.Ct. 1190 (USSC, 1962). Under the Davis rule, which applied to pre-1985 divorces, a property transfer incident to divorce was a taxable event.

[64]§ 71(b)(1). This set of alimony rules can also apply to pre-1985 agreements and decrees if both parties agree in writing. The rules applicable to pre-1985 agreements and decrees are not discussed in this text.

[65]*Alexander Washington,* 77 T.C. 601 (1981) at 604.

payments for the first and second years in gross income, and the payee is allowed a deduction for these excess alimony payments. The recaptured amount is computed as follows:[66]

$$R = D + E$$

$$D = B - (C + \$15,000)$$

$$E = A - \left(\frac{B - D + C}{2} + \$15,000\right)$$

R = amount recaptured in Year 3 tax return

D = recapture from Year 2

E = recapture from Year 1

A, B, C = payments in the first (A), second (B), and third (C) calendar years of the agreement or decree, where $D \geq 0$, $E \geq 0$

The recapture formula provides an objective technique for determining alimony recapture. Thus, at the time of the divorce, the taxpayers can ascertain the tax consequences. The general concept is that if the alimony payments decrease by more than $15,000 between years in the first three years, there will be alimony recapture with respect to the decrease in excess of $15,000 each year. This rule is applied for the change between Year 2 and Year 3 (D in the above formula). However, rather than making the same calculation for Year 2 payments versus Year 1 payments, the Code requires that the *average* of the payments in Years 2 and 3 be compared with the Year 1 payments (E in the above formula). For this purpose, revised alimony for Year 2 (alimony deducted for Year 2 minus the alimony recapture for Year 2) is used.

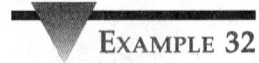

EXAMPLE 32

Wes and Rita were divorced in 1998. Under the agreement, Rita was to receive $50,000 in 1998, $20,000 in 1999, and nothing thereafter. The payments were to cease upon Rita's death or remarriage. In 2000, Wes must include an additional $32,500 in gross income for alimony recapture, and Rita is allowed a deduction for the same amount.

$$D = \$20,000 - (\$0 + \$15,000) = \$5,000$$

$$E = \$50,000 - \left(\frac{\$20,000 - \$5,000 + \$0}{2} + \$15,000\right) = \$27,500$$

$$R = \$5,000 + \$27,500 = \$32,500$$

Note that for 1998 Wes deducts alimony of $50,000 and Rita includes $50,000 in her gross income. For 1999, the amount of the alimony deduction for Wes is $20,000, and Rita's gross income from the alimony is $20,000.

If instead $50,000 were paid in 1998 and nothing is paid for the following years, $35,000 would be recaptured in 2000.

$$D = \$0 - (\$0 + \$15,000) = -\$15,000, \text{ but D must be } \geq \$0$$

$$E = \$50,000 - \left(\frac{\$0 - \$0 + \$0}{2} + \$15,000\right) = \$35,000$$

$$R = \$0 + \$35,000 = \$35,000 \qquad \blacktriangledown$$

Alimony recapture does not apply if the decrease in payments is due to the death of either spouse or the remarriage of the payee.[67] Recapture is not applicable because these events typically terminate alimony under state laws. In addition, the

---

[66]§ 71(f).   [67]§ 71(f)(5)(A).

Y 3-1

f Payments and Transfers Pursuant to Post-1984 Divorce
Decrees

	Payor	Recipient
Alimony	Deduction from gross income.	Included in gross income.
Alimony recapture	Included in gross income of the third year.	Deducted from gross income of the third year.
	Not deductible.	Not includible in gross income.
Property settlement	No income or deduction.	No income or deduction; basis for the property is the same as the transferor's basis.

recapture rules do not apply to payments where the amount is contingent (e.g., a percentage of income from certain property or a percentage of the payor spouse's compensation), the payments are to be made over a period of three years or longer (unless death, remarriage, or other contingency occurs), and the contingencies are beyond the payor's control.[68]

EXAMPLE 33

Under a 1998 divorce agreement, Ed was to receive an amount equal to one-half of Nina's income from certain rental properties for 1998–2001. Payments were to cease upon the death of Ed or Nina or upon the remarriage of Ed. Ed received $50,000 in 1998 and $50,000 in 1999; in 2000, however, the property was vacant, and Ed received nothing. Nina, who deducted alimony in 1998 and 1999, is not required to recapture any alimony in 2000 because the payments were contingent. ▼

Child Support. A taxpayer does not realize income from the receipt of child support payments made by his or her former spouse. This result occurs because the money is received subject to the duty to use the money for the child's benefit. The payor is not allowed to deduct the child support payments because the payments are made to satisfy the payor's legal obligation to support the child.

In many cases, it is difficult to determine whether an amount received is alimony or child support. If the amount of the payments would be reduced upon the happening of a contingency related to a child (e.g., the child attains age 21 or dies), the amount of the future reduction in the payment is deemed child support.[69]

EXAMPLE 34

A divorce agreement provides that Matt is required to make periodic alimony payments of $500 per month to Grace. However, when Matt and Grace's child reaches age 21, marries, or dies (whichever occurs first), the payments will be reduced to $300 per month. Grace has custody of the child. Since the required contingency is the cause for the reduction in the payments, from $500 to $300, child support payments are $200 per month, and alimony is $300 per month. ▼

IMPUTED INTEREST ON BELOW-MARKET LOANS

As discussed earlier in the chapter, generally no income is recognized unless it is realized. Realization generally occurs when the taxpayer performs services or sells

---

[68]§ 71(f)(5)(C).

[69]§ 71(c)(2).

goods and thus becomes entitled to a payment from the other party. It follows that no income is realized if the goods or services are provided at no charge. Under this interpretation of the realization requirement, before 1984, interest-free loans were used to shift income between taxpayers.

EXAMPLE 35

Veneia (daughter) is in the 20% tax bracket and has no investment income. Kareem (father) is in the 50% tax bracket and has $200,000 in a money market account earning 10% interest. Kareem would like Veneia to receive and pay tax on the income earned on the $200,000. Because Kareem would also like to have access to the $200,000 should he need the money, he does not want to make an outright gift of the money, nor does he want to commit the money to a trust.

Before 1984, Kareem could achieve his goals as follows. He could transfer the money market account to Veneia in exchange for her $200,000 non-interest-bearing note, payable on Kareem's demand. As a result, Veneia would receive the income, and the family's taxes would be decreased by $6,000.

Decrease in Kareem's tax—	
(.10 × $200,000).50 =	($10,000)
Increase in Veneia's tax—	
(.10 × $200,000).20 =	4,000
Decrease in the family's taxes	($ 6,000)

Under the 1984 amendments to the Code, Kareem in Example 35 is required to recognize **imputed interest** income.[70] Veneia is deemed to have incurred interest expense equal to Kareem's imputed interest income. Veneia's interest may be deductible on her return as investment interest if she itemizes deductions (see Chapter 9). To complete the fictitious series of transactions, Kareem is then deemed to have given Veneia the amount of the imputed interest she did not pay. The gift received by Veneia is not subject to income tax (see Chapter 4), although Kareem may be subject to the gift tax (unified transfer tax) on the amount deemed given to Veneia (refer to Chapter 1).

Imputed interest is calculated using the rate the Federal government pays on new borrowings and is compounded semiannually. This Federal rate is adjusted monthly and is published by the IRS.[71] Actually, there are three Federal rates: short-term (not over three years and including demand loans), mid-term (over three years but not over nine years), and long-term (over nine years).[72]

EXAMPLE 36

Assume the Federal rate applicable to the loan in Example 35 is 7% through June 30 and 8% from July 1 through December 31. Kareem made the loan on January 1, and the loan is still outstanding on December 31. Kareem must recognize interest income of $15,280, and Veneia has interest expense of $15,280. Kareem is deemed to have made a gift of $15,280 to Veneia.

Interest calculations	
January 1–June 30—	
.07($200,000) (½ year)	$ 7,000
July 1–December 31—	
.08($200,000 + $7,000) (½ year)	8,280
	$15,280

---

[70] § 7872(a)(1).
[71] §§ 7872(b)(2) and (f)(2).

[72] § 1274(d).

CONCEPT SUMMARY 3–2

Effect of Certain Below-Market Loans on the Lender and Borrower

Type of Loan		Lender	Borrower
Gift	Step 1	Interest income	Interest expense
	Step 2	Gift made	Gift received
Compensation-related	Step 1	Interest income	Interest expense
	Step 2	Compensation expense	Compensation income
Corporation to shareholder	Step 1	Interest income	Interest expense
	Step 2	Dividend paid	Dividend income

If interest is charged on the loan but is less than the Federal rate, the imputed interest is the difference between the amount that would have been charged at the Federal rate and the amount actually charged.

EXAMPLE 37

Assume the same facts as in Example 36, except that Kareem charged 6% interest, compounded annually.

Interest at the Federal rate	$15,280
Less interest charged (.06 × $200,000)	(12,000)
Imputed interest	$ 3,280

The imputed interest rules apply to the following *types* of below-market loans:[73]

1. Gift loans (made out of love, affection, or generosity, as in Example 35).
2. Compensation-related loans (employer loans to employees).
3. Corporation-shareholder loans (a corporation's loans to its shareholders).
4. Tax avoidance loans and other loans that significantly affect the borrower's or lender's Federal tax liability (discussed in the following paragraphs).

The effects of the first three types of loans on the borrower and lender are summarized in Concept Summary 3–2.

Tax Avoidance and Other Below-Market Loans.

In addition to the three specific types of loans that are subject to the imputed interest rules, the Code includes a catchall provision for *tax avoidance loans* and other arrangements that have a significant effect on the tax liability of the borrower or lender. The Conference Report provides the following example of an arrangement that might be subject to the imputed interest rules.[74]

EXAMPLE 38

Annual dues for the Good Health Club are $400. In lieu of paying dues, a member can make a $4,000 deposit, refundable at the end of one year. The club can earn $400 interest on the deposit.

---

[73]§ 7872(c).   [74]H. Rep. No. 98–861, 98th Cong., 2d Sess., 1984, p. 1023.

If interest were not imputed, an individual with $4,000 could, in effect, earn tax-exempt income on the deposit. That is, rather than invest the $4,000, earn $400 in interest, pay tax on the interest, and then pay $400 in dues, the individual could avoid tax on the interest by making the deposit. Thus, income and expenses are imputed as follows: interest income and nondeductible health club fees for the club member; income from fees and interest expense for the club. ▼

Many commercially motivated transactions could be swept into this other below-market loans category. However, the temporary Regulations have carved out a frequently encountered exception for customer prepayments. If the prepayments are included in the recipient's income under the recipient's method of accounting, the payments are not considered loans and, thus, are not subject to the imputed interest rules.[75]

EXAMPLE 39

Landlord, a cash basis taxpayer, charges tenants a damage deposit equal to one month's rent on residential apartments. When the tenant enters into the lease, the landlord also collects rent for the last month of the lease.

The prepaid rent for the last month of the lease is taxed in the year received and thus is not considered a loan. The security deposit is not taxed when received and is therefore a candidate for imputed interest. However, no apparent tax benefit is derived by the landlord or the tenant, and thus the security deposit should not be subject to the imputed interest provisions. But if making the deposit would reduce the rent paid by the tenant, the tenant could derive a tax benefit, much the same as the club member in Example 38. ▼

Exceptions and Limitations. No interest is imputed on total outstanding *gift loans* of $10,000 or less between individuals, unless the loan proceeds are used to purchase income-producing property.[76] This exemption eliminates from these complex provisions immaterial amounts that do not result in apparent shifts of income. However, if the proceeds of such a loan are used to purchase income-producing property, the limitations discussed in the following paragraphs apply instead.

On loans of $100,000 or less between individuals, the imputed interest cannot exceed the borrower's net investment income for the year (gross income from all investments less the related expenses).[77] As discussed above, one of the purposes of the imputed interest rules is to prevent high-income taxpayers from shifting income to relatives in a lower marginal bracket. This shifting of investment income is considered to occur only to the extent the borrower has investment income. Thus, the income imputed to the lender is limited to the borrower's net investment income. As a further limitation, or exemption, if the borrower's net investment income for the year does not exceed $1,000, no interest is imputed on loans of $100,000 or less. However, these limitations for loans of $100,000 or less do not apply if a principal purpose of a loan is tax avoidance. In such a case, interest is imputed, and the imputed interest is not limited to the borrower's net investment income.[78]

---

[75]Prop.Reg. § 1.7872–2(b)(1)(i).
[76]§ 7872(c)(2).
[77]§ 7872(d).

[78]*Deficit Reduction Tax Bill of 1984: Explanation of the Senate Finance Committee* (April 2, 1984), p. 484.

EXAMPLE 40

Vicki made interest-free gift loans as follows:

Borrower	Amount	Borrower's Net Investment Income	Purpose
Susan	$ 8,000	$ –0–	Education
Dan	9,000	500	Purchase of stock
Bonnie	25,000	–0–	Purchase of a business
Megan	90,000	15,000	Purchase of a residence
Olaf	120,000	–0–	Purchase of a residence

Assume that tax avoidance is not a principal purpose of any of the loans. The loan to Susan is not subject to the imputed interest rules because the $10,000 exception applies. The $10,000 exception does not apply to the loan to Dan because the proceeds were used to purchase income-producing assets. However, under the $100,000 exception, the imputed interest is limited to Dan's investment income ($500). Since the $1,000 exception also applies to this loan, no interest is imputed.

No interest is imputed on the loan to Bonnie because the $100,000 exception applies. Interest is imputed on the loan to Megan based on the lesser of (1) the borrower's $15,000 net investment income or (2) the interest as calculated by applying the Federal rate to the outstanding loan. None of the exceptions apply to the loan to Olaf because the loan was for more than $100,000.

Assume the relevant Federal rate is 10% and the loans were outstanding for the entire year. Vicki would recognize interest income, compounded semiannually, as follows:

Loan to Megan:	
First 6 months (.10 × $90,000 × ½ year)	$ 4,500
Second 6 months (.10 × $94,500 × ½ year)	4,725
	$ 9,225
Loan to Olaf:	
First 6 months (.10 × $120,000 × ½ year)	$ 6,000
Second 6 months (.10 × $126,000 × ½ year)	6,300
	$12,300
Total imputed interest ($9,225 + $12,300)	$21,525

As with gift loans, there is a $10,000 exemption for *compensation-related loans* and *corporation-shareholder loans*. However, the $10,000 exception does not apply if tax avoidance is one of the principal purposes of a loan.[79] This vague tax avoidance standard makes practically all compensation-related and corporation-shareholder loans suspect. Nevertheless, the $10,000 exception should apply when an employee's borrowing was necessitated by personal needs (e.g., to meet unexpected expenses) rather than tax considerations.

These exceptions to the imputed interest rules are summarized in Concept Summary 3–3.

INCOME FROM ANNUITIES

Annuity contracts generally require the purchaser (the annuitant) to pay a fixed amount for the right to receive a future stream of payments. Typically, the issuer

---

[79]§ 7872(c)(3).

CONCEPT SUMMARY 3–3

Exceptions to the Imputed Interest Rules For Below-Market Loans

Exception	Eligible Loans	Ineligible Loans and Limitations
No interest is imputed (*de minimis*)—aggregate loans of $10,000 or less	Gift loans	Proceeds used to purchase income-producing assets.
	Employer-employee	Principal purpose is tax avoidance.
	Corporation-shareholder	Principal purpose is tax avoidance.
Imputed interest is limited to borrower's net investment income (NII), if NII exceeds $1,000—aggregate loans of $100,000 or less	Between individuals	Principal purpose is tax avoidance.

of the contract is an insurance company and will pay the annuitant a cash value if the annuitant cancels the contract. The insurance company invests the amounts received from the annuitant, and the income earned serves to increase the cash value of the policy. No income is recognized by the annuitant at the time the cash value of the annuity increases because the taxpayer has not actually received any income. The income is not constructively received because, generally, the taxpayer must cancel the policy to receive the increase in value (the increase in value is subject to substantial restrictions).

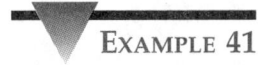

EXAMPLE 41

Jean, age 50, paid $30,000 for an annuity contract that is to pay her $500 per month beginning when she reaches age 65 and continuing until her death. If Jean should cancel the policy after one year, she would receive $30,200. The $200 increase in value is not includible in Jean's gross income as long as she does not actually receive the $200. ▼

The tax accounting problem associated with receiving payments under an annuity contract is one of apportioning the amounts received between recovery of capital and income.

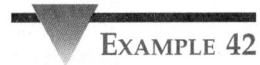

EXAMPLE 42

In 1998, Tom purchased for $15,000 an annuity intended as a source of retirement income. In 2000, when the cash value of the annuity was $17,000, Tom collected $1,000 on the contract. Is the $1,000 gross income, recovery of capital, or a combination of recovery of capital and income? ▼

The statutory solution to this problem depends upon whether the payments began before or after the annuity starting date and upon when the policy was acquired.

Collections before the Annuity Starting Date. Generally, an annuity contract specifies a date on which monthly or annual payments will begin—the annuity starting date. Often the contract will also allow the annuitant to collect a limited amount before the starting date. The amount collected may be characterized as either an actual withdrawal of the increase in cash value or a loan on the policy. In 1982, Congress changed the rules applicable to these withdrawals and loans.

Collections (including loans) equal to or less than the post–August 13, 1982, increases in cash value must be included in gross income. Amounts received in excess of post–August 13, 1982, increases in cash value are treated as a recovery of capital until the taxpayer's cost has been entirely recovered. Additional amounts are included in gross income.[80]

The taxpayer may also be subject to a penalty on early distributions of 10 percent of the income recognized. The penalty generally applies if the amount is received before the taxpayer reaches age 59½ or is disabled.[81] The early distribution penalty is deemed necessary to prevent taxpayers from using annuities as a way of avoiding the original issue discount rules. That is, the investment in the annuity earns a return that is not taxed until it is collected under the annuity rules, whereas the interest on a certificate of deposit is taxed each year as the income accrues. Thus, the annuity offers a tax advantage (deferral of income) that Congress does not want exploited.

EXAMPLE 43

Jack, age 50, purchased an annuity policy for $30,000 in 1997. In 1999, when the cash value of the policy has increased to $33,000, Jack withdraws $4,000. He must recognize $3,000 of income ($33,000 cash value – $30,000 cost) and must pay a penalty of $300 ($3,000 × 10%). The remaining $1,000 is a recovery of capital and reduces Jack's basis in the annuity policy. ▼

Collections on and after the Annuity Starting Date. The annuitant can exclude from income (as a recovery of capital) the proportion of each payment that the investment in the contract bears to the expected return under the contract. The *exclusion amount* is calculated as follows:

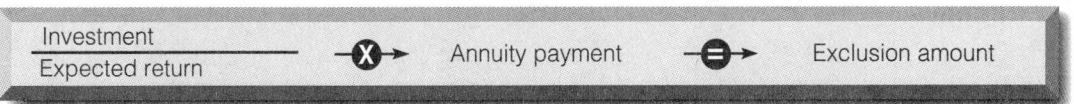

The *expected return* is the annual amount to be paid to the annuitant multiplied by the number of years the payments will be received. The payment period may be fixed (a *term certain*) or for the life of one or more individuals. When payments are for life, the taxpayer generally must use the annuity table published by the IRS to determine the expected return (see Table 3–1). This is an actuarial table that contains life expectancies.[82] The expected return is calculated by multiplying the appropriate multiple (life expectancy) by the annual payment.

EXAMPLE 44

The taxpayer, age 54, purchased an annuity from an insurance company for $90,000. She was to receive $500 per month for life. Her life expectancy (from Table 3–1) is 29.5 years from the annuity starting date. Thus, her expected return is $500 × 12 × 29.5 = $177,000, and the exclusion amount is $3,051 [($90,000 investment/$177,000 expected return) × $6,000 annual payment]. The $3,051 is a nontaxable return of capital, and $2,949 is included in gross income. ▼

The *exclusion ratio* (investment ÷ expected return) applies until the annuitant has recovered her investment in the contract. Once the investment is recovered, the entire amount of subsequent payments is taxable. If the annuitant dies before

---

[80]§ 72(e)(3); Reg. § 1.72–9.
[81]§ 72(q).
[82]The life expectancies in Table 3–1 apply for annuity investments made on or after July 1, 1986. See *Pension and Annuity Income*, IRS

Publication 575 (Rev. Nov. 87), pp. 22–24 for the IRS table to use for investments made before July 1, 1986.

▼ **TABLE 3-1**
Ordinary Life Annuities:
One Life–Expected Return
Multiples

Age	Multiple	Age	Multiple	Age	Multiple
5	76.6	42	40.6	79	10.0
6	75.6	43	39.6	80	9.5
7	74.7	44	38.7	81	8.9
8	73.7	45	37.7	82	8.4
9	72.7	46	36.8	83	7.9
10	71.7	47	35.9	84	7.4
11	70.7	48	34.9	85	6.9
12	69.7	49	34.0	86	6.5
13	68.8	50	33.1	87	6.1
14	67.8	51	32.2	88	5.7
15	66.8	52	31.3	89	5.3
16	65.8	53	30.4	90	5.0
17	64.8	54	29.5	91	4.7
18	63.9	55	28.6	92	4.4
19	62.9	56	27.7	93	4.1
20	61.9	57	26.8	94	3.9
21	60.9	58	25.9	95	3.7
22	59.9	59	25.0	96	3.4
23	59.0	60	24.2	97	3.2
24	58.0	61	23.3	98	3.0
25	57.0	62	22.5	99	2.8
26	56.0	63	21.6	100	2.7
27	55.1	64	20.8	101	2.5
28	54.1	65	20.0	102	2.3
29	53.1	66	19.2	103	2.1
30	52.2	67	18.4	104	1.9
31	51.2	68	17.6	105	1.8
32	50.2	69	16.8	106	1.6
33	49.3	70	16.0	107	1.4
34	48.3	71	15.3	108	1.3
35	47.3	72	14.6	109	1.1
36	46.4	73	13.9	110	1.0
37	45.4	74	13.2	111	.9
38	44.4	75	12.5	112	.8
39	43.5	76	11.9	113	.7
40	42.5	77	11.2	114	.6
41	41.5	78	10.6	115	.5

recovering her investment, the unrecovered cost is deductible in the year the payments cease (usually the year of death).[83]

EXAMPLE 45

Assume the taxpayer in Example 44 received annuity payments for 30.5 years (366 months). For the last 12 months [366 − (12 × 29.5) = 12], the taxpayer would include $500 each month in gross income. If instead the taxpayer died after 36 months, she is eligible for a $80,847 deduction on her final tax return.

[83]§ 72(b).

▼ **TABLE 3–2**
Number of Anticipated
Monthly Annuity Payments
under the Simplified Method

Age	Number of Anticipated Monthly Payments
55 and under	360
56–60	310
61–65	260
66–70	210
71 and over	160

Cost of the contract	$90,000
Cost previously recovered $90,000/$177,000 × 36($500) =	(9,153)
Deduction	$80,847

Simplified Method for Annuity Distributions from Qualified Retirement Plans. A simplified method is available for allocating basis to the annuity payments received under a qualified retirement plan. The portion of each annuity payment that is excluded as a return of capital is the employee's investment in the contract divided by the number of anticipated monthly payments determined in accordance with Table 3–2.[84]

EXAMPLE 46

Andrea, age 62, receives an annuity distribution of $500 per month for life from her qualified retirement plan beginning in January 1998. Her investment in the contract is $100,100. The excludible amount of each payment is $385 ($100,100 investment/260 monthly payments). Thus, $115 ($500 – $385) of each annuity payment is included in Andrea's gross income. ▼

The rules for annuity payments received after the basis has been recovered by the annuitant and for the annuitant who dies before recovering his basis are the same as under the exclusion ratio method discussed earlier.

PRIZES AND AWARDS

The fair market value of prizes and awards (other than scholarships exempted under § 117, to be discussed subsequently) must be included in gross income.[85] Therefore, TV giveaway prizes, magazine publisher prizes, door prizes, and awards from an employer to an employee in recognition of performance are fully taxable to the recipient.

A narrow exception permits a prize or award to be excluded from gross income if *all* of the following requirements are satisfied:

- The prize or award is received in recognition of religious, charitable, scientific, educational, artistic, literary, or civic achievement (e.g., Nobel Prize, Pulitzer Prize).
- The recipient transfers the prize or award to a qualified governmental unit or nonprofit organization.
- The recipient was selected without any action on her part to enter the contest or proceeding.
- The recipient is not required to render substantial future services as a condition for receiving the prize or award.[86]

---

[84]§ 72(d).
[85]§ 74.

[86]§ 74(b).

CONCEPT SUMMARY 3–4

Taxation of Annuities: Exclusion Ratio Method

Term	Description	Formula
A	Amount of each annuity payment under the contract.	
N	Number of expected payments based on the expected life of the annuitant.	
V	Investment in the annuity contract.	
R	Number of annuity payments actually received.	
Expected return	Total amount the annuitant is expected to collect over the life of the contract based on his life expectancy.	$A \times N$
Exclusion percentage	Percentage of each annuity payment that is excluded from gross income.	$\dfrac{V}{A \times N}$
Inclusion percentage	Percentage of each annuity payment that is included in gross income.	$1 - \left(\dfrac{V}{A \times N}\right)$
Post-recovery of capital payments	Once R = N, the total cost has been recovered. The total amount of each subsequent payment is included in gross income.	
Annuitant's deductible loss	If the annuity payments cease before R = N, the annuitant can claim a loss.	$V - \left(\dfrac{V}{A \times N}\right) \times (A \times R)$

Because the transfer of the property to a qualified governmental unit or nonprofit organization ordinarily would be a charitable contribution (an itemized deduction as presented in Chapter 9), the exclusion produces beneficial tax consequences in the following situations:

- The taxpayer does not itemize deductions and thus would receive no tax benefit from the charitable contribution.
- The taxpayer's charitable contributions exceed the annual statutory ceiling on the deduction.
- Including the prize or award in gross income would reduce the amount of deductions the taxpayer otherwise would qualify for because of gross income limitations (e.g., the gross income test for a dependency exemption, the adjusted gross income limitation in calculating the medical expense deduction).

Another exception is provided for certain *employee achievement awards* in the form of tangible personal property (e.g., a gold watch). The awards must be made in recognition of length of service or safety achievement. Generally, the ceiling on the excludible amount for an employee is $400 per taxable year. However, if the award is a qualified plan award, the ceiling on the exclusion is $1,600 per taxable year.[87]

---

[87]§§ 74(c) and 274(j).

▼ TABLE 3–3

Uniform Premiums for $1,000 of Group Term Life Insurance Protection

Attained Age on Last Day of Employee's Tax Year	Cost per $1,000 of Protection for One-Month Period
Under 30	$ .08
30–34	.09
35–39	.11
40–44	.17
45–49	.29
50–54	.48
55–59	.75
60–64	1.17
65–69	2.10
70 and over	3.76

GROUP TERM LIFE INSURANCE

For many years, the IRS did not attempt to tax the value of life insurance protection provided to an employee by the employer. Some companies took undue advantage of the exclusion by providing large amounts of insurance protection for executives. Therefore, Congress enacted § 79, which created a limited exclusion for **group term life insurance.** The premiums on the first $50,000 of group term life insurance protection are excludible from the employee's gross income.

The benefits of this exclusion are available only to employees. Proprietors and partners are not considered employees. Moreover, the Regulations generally require broad-scale coverage of employees to satisfy the *group* requirement (e.g., shareholder-employees would not constitute a qualified group). The exclusion applies only to term insurance (protection for a period of time but with no cash surrender value) and not to ordinary life insurance (lifetime protection plus a cash surrender value that can be drawn upon before death).

As mentioned, the exclusion applies to the first $50,000 of group term life insurance protection. For each $1,000 of coverage in excess of $50,000, the employee must include the amounts indicated in Table 3–3 in gross income.[88]

EXAMPLE 47

Finch Corporation has a group term life insurance policy with coverage equal to the employee's annual salary. Keith, age 52, is president of the corporation and receives an annual salary of $75,000. Keith must include $144 in gross income from the insurance protection for the year.

$$\frac{\$75,000 - \$50,000}{\$1,000} \times .48 \times 12 \text{ months} = \$144$$

▼

Generally, the amount that must be included in gross income, computed from Table 3–3, is much less than the price an individual would pay an insurance company for the same amount of protection. Thus, even the excess coverage provides some tax-favored income for employees when group term life insurance coverage in excess of $50,000 is desirable.

If the plan discriminates in favor of certain key employees (e.g., officers), the key employees are not eligible for the exclusion. In such a case, the key employees must include in gross income the *greater* of actual premiums paid by the employer or the amount calculated from the Uniform Premiums in Table 3–3. The other

[88]Reg. § 1.79–3(d)(2).

employees are still eligible for the $50,000 exclusion and continue to use the Uniform Premiums table to compute the income from excess insurance protection.[89]

UNEMPLOYMENT COMPENSATION

The unemployment compensation program is sponsored and operated by the states and Federal government to provide a source of income for people who have been employed and are temporarily (hopefully) out of work. In a series of rulings over a period of 40 years, the IRS exempted unemployment benefits from tax. These payments were considered social benefit programs for the promotion of the general welfare. After experiencing dissatisfaction with the IRS's treatment of unemployment compensation, Congress amended the Code to provide that the benefits are taxable.[90]

SOCIAL SECURITY BENEFITS

If a taxpayer's income exceeds a specified base amount, as much as 85 percent of Social Security retirement benefits must be included in gross income. The taxable amount of benefits is determined through the application of one of two formulas that utilize a unique measure of income—*modified adjusted gross income (MAGI)*.[91] MAGI is, generally, the taxpayer's adjusted gross income from all sources (other than Social Security) plus the foreign earned income exclusion and any tax-exempt interest income.

In the formulas, two sets of base amounts are established. The first set is as follows:

- $32,000 for married taxpayers who file a joint return.
- $0 for married taxpayers who do not live apart for the entire year but file separate returns.
- $25,000 for all other taxpayers.

The second set of base amounts is as follows:

- $44,000 for married taxpayers who file a joint return.
- $0 for married taxpayers who do not live apart for the entire year but file separate returns.
- $34,000 for all other taxpayers.

If MAGI plus one-half of Social Security benefits exceeds the first set of base amounts, but not the second set, the taxable amount of Social Security benefits is the *lesser* of the following:

- .50(Social Security benefits).
- .50[MAGI + .50(Social Security benefits) − first base amount].

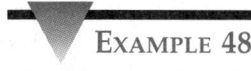

EXAMPLE 48

A married couple with adjusted gross income of $30,000, no tax-exempt interest, and $11,000 of Social Security benefits who file jointly must include $1,750 of the benefits in gross income. This works out as the lesser of the following:

1. .50($11,000) = $5,500.
2. .50[$30,000 + .50($11,000) − $32,000] = .50($3,500) = $1,750.

[89]§ 79(d).
[90]§ 85.

[91]§ 86.

If the couple's adjusted gross income were $15,000 and their Social Security benefits totaled $5,000, none of the benefits would be taxable, since .50[$15,000 + .50($5,000) − $32,000] is not a positive number. ▼

If MAGI plus one-half of Social Security benefits exceeds the second set of base amounts, the taxable amount of Social Security benefits is the *lesser* of 1 or 2 below:

1. .85(Social Security benefits).
2. Sum of:
   a. .85[MAGI + .50(Social Security benefits) − second base amount], and
   b. Lesser of:
      • Amount included through application of the first formula.
      • $4,500 ($6,000 for married filing jointly).

EXAMPLE 49

A married couple who file jointly have adjusted gross income of $72,000, no tax-exempt interest, and $12,000 of Social Security benefits. Their includible Social Security benefits would be $10,200.

Include the lesser of the following:

1. .85($12,000) = $10,200.
2. Sum of:
   a. .85[$72,000 + .50($12,000) − $44,000] = $28,900, and
   b. Lesser of:
      • Amount calculated by the first formula, which is the lesser of:
         • .50($12,000) = $6,000.
         • .50[$72,000 + .50($12,000) − $32,000] = $23,000.
      • $6,000.

The sum equals $34,900 ($28,900 + $6,000). Since 85% of the Social Security benefits received is less than this amount, $10,200 is included in the couples' gross income. ▼

TAX PLANNING CONSIDERATIONS

The materials in this chapter have focused on the following questions:

• What is income?
• When is the income recognized?
• Who is the taxpayer?

5 LEARNING OBJECTIVE
Utilize tax planning strategies for minimizing gross income.

Planning strategies suggested by these materials include the following:

• Maximize economic benefits that are not included in gross income.
• Defer the recognition of income.
• Shift income to taxpayers who are in a lower marginal tax bracket.

Some specific techniques for accomplishing these strategies are discussed in the following paragraphs.

NONTAXABLE ECONOMIC BENEFITS

Home ownership is the prime example of economic income from capital that is not subject to tax. If the taxpayer uses her capital to purchase investments, but pays rent on a personal residence, she would pay the rent from after-tax income. However, if the taxpayer purchases a personal residence instead of the investments, she would give up gross income from the forgone investments in exchange for the rent savings. The savings in rent enjoyed as a result of owning the home are not subject to tax. Thus, the homeowner will have substituted nontaxable for taxable income.

TAX DEFERRAL

General.   Since deferred taxes are tantamount to interest-free loans from the government, the deferral of taxes is a worthy goal of the tax planner. However, the tax planner must also consider the tax rates for the years the income is shifted from and to. For example, a one-year deferral of income from a year in which the taxpayer's tax rate was 28 percent to a year in which the tax rate will be 39.6 percent would not be advisable if the taxpayer expects to earn less than an 11.6 percent after-tax return on the deferred tax dollars.

The taxpayer can often defer the recognition of income from appreciated property by postponing the event triggering realization (the final closing on a sale or exchange of property). If the taxpayer needs cash, obtaining a loan by using the appreciated property as collateral may be the least costly alternative. When the taxpayer anticipates reinvesting the proceeds, a sale may be inadvisable.

EXAMPLE 50

Ira owns 100 shares of Pigeon Company common stock with a cost of $20,000 and a fair market value of $50,000. Although the stock's value has increased substantially in the past three years, Ira thinks the growth days are over. If he sells the Pigeon stock, Ira will invest the proceeds from the sale in other common stock. Assuming Ira's marginal tax rate on the sale is 20%, he will have only $44,000 [$50,000 − .20($50,000 − $20,000)] to reinvest. The alternative investment must substantially outperform Pigeon in the future in order for the sale to be beneficial. ▼

Selection of Investments.   Because no tax is due until a gain has been recognized, the law favors investments that yield appreciation rather than annual income.

EXAMPLE 51

Vera can buy a corporate bond or an acre of land for $10,000. The bond pays $1,000 of interest (10%) each year, and Vera expects the land to increase in value 10% each year for the next 10 years. She is in the 40% (combined Federal and state) tax bracket for ordinary income and 26% for qualifying capital gains. Assuming the bond would mature or the land would be sold in 10 years and Vera would reinvest the interest at a 10% before-tax return, she would accumulate the following amount at the end of 10 years.

		Bond	Land
Original investment		$10,000	$10,000
Annual income	$1,000		
Less tax	(400)		
	$ 600		
Compound amount reinvested for 10 years at 6% after-tax	× 13.18	7,908	
		$17,908	
Compound amount, 10 years at 10%			× 2.59
			$25,900
Less tax on sale: 26%($25,900 − $10,000)			(4,134)
			$21,766

Therefore, the value of the deferral that results from investing in the land rather than in the bond is $3,858 ($21,766 − $17,908). ▼

Series E and EE bonds can also be purchased for long-term deferrals of income. As discussed in the chapter, Series E bonds can be exchanged for new Series HH bonds to further postpone the tax. In situations where the taxpayer's goal is merely to shift income one year into the future, bank certificates of deposit are useful tools. If the maturity period is one year or less, all interest is reported in the year of maturity. Time certificates are especially useful for a taxpayer who realizes an unusually large gain from the sale of property in one year (and thus is in a high tax bracket) but expects his income to be less the following year.

Cash Basis.   The timing of income from services can often be controlled through the use of the cash method of accounting. Although taxpayers are somewhat constrained by the constructive receipt doctrine (they cannot turn their backs on income), seldom will customers and clients offer to pay before they are asked. The usual lag between billings and collections (e.g., December's billings collected in January) will result in a continuous deferring of some income until the last year of operations. A salaried individual approaching retirement may contract with her employer before the services are rendered to receive a portion of compensation in the lower tax bracket retirement years.

Prepaid Income.   For the accrual basis taxpayer who receives advance payments from customers, the transactions should be structured to avoid payment of tax on income before the time the income is actually earned. Revenue Procedure 71–21 provides the guidelines for deferring the tax on prepayments for services, and Regulation § 1.451–5 provides the guidelines for deferrals on sales of goods. In addition, both cash and accrual basis taxpayers can sometimes defer income by stipulating that the payments are deposits rather than prepaid income. For example, a landlord should require an equivalent damage deposit rather than prepayment of the last month's rent under the lease.

SHIFTING INCOME TO RELATIVES

The tax liability of a family can be minimized by shifting income from higher- to lower-bracket family members. This can be accomplished through gifts of income-producing property. Furthermore, in many cases, income can be shifted with no negative effect on the family's investment plans.

▼
EXAMPLE 52

Adam, who is in the 28% tax bracket, would like to save for his children's education. All of the children are under 14 years of age. Adam could transfer income-producing properties to the children, and the children could each receive up to $700 of income each year (refer to Chapter 2) with no tax liability. The next $700 would be taxed at the child's tax rate. After a child has more than $1,400 income, there is no tax advantage to shifting more income to the child (because the income will be taxed at the parents' rate) until the child is 14 years old (when all income will be taxed according to the child's tax rate). ▼

The Uniform Gifts to Minors Act, a model law adopted by all states (but with some variations among the states), facilitates income shifting. Under the Act, a gift of intangibles (e.g., bank accounts, stocks, bonds, life insurance contracts) can be made to a minor but with an adult serving as custodian. Usually, a parent who makes the gift is also named as custodian. The state laws allow the custodian to sell or redeem and reinvest the principal and to accumulate or distribute the income, practically at the custodian's discretion provided there is no commingling of the child's income with the parent's property. Thus, the parent can give appreciated securities to the child, and the donor custodian can then sell the securities and reinvest the proceeds, thereby shifting both the gain and the annual income to the child. Such planning is limited by the tax liability calculation provision for a child under the age of 14 (refer to Chapter 2).

U.S. government bonds (Series E and EE) can be purchased by the parent for his children. When this is done, the children generally should file a return and elect to report the income on the accrual basis.

EXAMPLE 53

Abby pays $7,500 for Series EE bonds in 1998 and immediately gives them to Wade (her son), who will enter college the year of original maturity of the bonds. The bonds have a maturity value of $10,000. Wade elects to report the annual increment in redemption value as income for each year the bonds are held. The first year the increase is $250, and Wade includes that amount in his gross income. If Wade has no other income, no tax will be due on the $250 bond interest, since such an amount will be more than offset by his available standard deduction. The following year, the increment is $260, and Wade includes this amount in income. Thus, over the life of the bonds, Wade will include $2,500 in income ($10,000 − $7,500), none of which will result in a tax liability, assuming he has no other income. However, if the election had not been made, Wade would be required to include $2,500 in income on the bonds in the year of original maturity, if they were redeemed as planned. This amount of income might result in a tax liability. ▼

In some cases, it may be advantageous for the child not to make the accrual election. For example, a child under age 14 with investment income of more than $1,400 each year and parents in the 28, 31, 36, or 39.6 percent tax bracket would probably benefit from deferring the tax on the savings bond interest. The child would also benefit from the use of the usually lower tax rate (rather than subjecting the income to her parents' tax rate) if the bonds mature after the child is age 14 or older.

ACCOUNTING FOR COMMUNITY PROPERTY

The classification of income as community or separate property becomes important when either of two events occurs:

- Husband and wife, married taxpayers, file separate income tax returns for the year.
- Husband and wife obtain a divorce and therefore have to file separate returns for the year (refer to Chapter 2).

For planning purposes, it behooves married persons to keep track of the source of income (community or separate). To be in a position to do this effectively when income-producing assets are involved, it may be necessary to distinguish between separate and community property.[92]

ALIMONY

The person making the alimony payments favors a divorce settlement that includes a provision for deductible alimony payments. On the other hand, the recipient

---

[92]Being able to distinguish between separate and community property is crucial to the determination of a property settlement incident to a divorce. It also is vital in the estate tax area (refer to Chapter 1) since the surviving wife's or husband's share of the community property is not included in the gross estate of the deceased spouse.

prefers that the payments do not qualify as alimony. If the payor is in a higher tax bracket than the recipient, both parties may benefit by increasing the payments and structuring them so that they qualify as alimony.

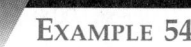

EXAMPLE 54

Carl and Polly are negotiating a divorce settlement. Carl has offered to pay Polly $10,000 each year for 10 years, but payments would cease upon Polly's death. Polly is willing to accept the offer, if the agreement will specify that the cash payments are not alimony. Carl is in the 36% tax bracket, and Polly's marginal rate is 15%.

If Carl and Polly agree that Carl will pay Polly $12,000 of alimony each year, both will have improved after-tax cash flows.

	Annual Cash Flows	
	Carl	**Polly**
Nonalimony payments	($10,000)	$10,000
Alimony payments	($12,000)	$12,000
Tax effects		
.36($12,000)	4,320	
.15($12,000)		(1,800)
After-tax cash flows	($ 7,680)	$10,200
Benefit of alimony option	$ 2,320	$ 200

Both parties benefit at the government's expense if the $12,000 alimony option is used. ▼

KEY TERMS

Accounting income, 3–4

Accounting method, 3–7

Accrual method, 3–9

Alimony and separate maintenance payments, 3–20

Alimony recapture, 3–21

Annuity, 3–27

Assignment of income, 3–15

Cash receipts method, 3–8

Claim of right doctrine, 3–9

Community property, 3–18

Constructive receipt, 3–10

Economic income, 3–3

Fruit and tree metaphor, 3–15

Gross income, 3–3

Group term life insurance, 3–33

Hybrid method, 3–9

Imputed interest, 3–24

Income, 3–3

Original issue discount, 3–11

Partnership, 3–17

Recovery of capital doctrine, 3–6

S corporation, 3–18

Taxable year, 3–7

PROBLEM MATERIALS

DISCUSSION QUESTIONS

1. The Internal Revenue Code contains a broad definition of gross income, but does not provide a listing of all possible types of income subject to tax. Would the tax law be improved if the Code included a complete listing of taxable sources of income?

2. Which of the following would be considered "income" for the current year by an economist but would not be gross income for tax purposes? Explain.

a. Securities acquired two years ago for $10,000 had a value of $12,000 at the beginning of the current year and a value of $13,000 at the end of the year.

b. An individual lives in the home he owns.

c. A shareholder paid a corporation $3,000 for property valued at $5,000.

d. An individual owned property that was stolen. The cost of the property three years ago was $2,000, and an insurance company paid the owner $6,000 (the value of the property on the date of theft).

e. An individual found a box of seventeenth-century Spanish coins while diving off the Virginia coast.

3. Charley visits Reno, Nevada, once each year to gamble. This year his gambling loss was $15,000. He commented to you, "At least I didn't have to pay for my airfare and hotel room. The casino paid that because I am such a good customer. That was worth at least $2,500." What are the relevant tax issues for Charley?

4. Evaluate the following alternative proposals for taxing the income from property:

a. All assets would be valued at the end of the year, any increase in value that occurred during the year would be included in gross income, and any decrease in value would be deductible from gross income.

b. No gain or loss would be recognized until the taxpayer sold or exchanged the property.

c. Increases or decreases in the value of property traded on a national exchange (e.g., the New York Stock Exchange) would be reflected in gross income for the years the changes in value occurred. For all other assets, no gain or loss would be recognized until the property is sold or exchanged.

5. Lief owns 100 acres adjoining a national forest. Lief's cost of the land is $50,000. The park service decided to develop a hiking trail through the forest. To complete the trail, hikers would have to travel approximately 1,000 feet on Lief's property. The park service pays Lief $1,000 for an easement allowing the hikers to walk across his property. Is Lief required to recognize income from the receipt of the $1,000?

6. Sparrow, Inc., receives all of its income from repairing computers. The company reports its income by the cash method. On December 31, an employee went to a customer's office and repaired a computer. The customer gave Sparrow's employee a check for $300, but the employee did not remit the check to Sparrow until January of the following year. When is Sparrow required to recognize the income?

7. Lane is a self-employed consultant who reports his income by the cash method of accounting. In December 1998, Lane received a check for $5,000 from a client. Lane misplaced the check and did not find it until January 1999, when he deposited it in his bank account. Lane uses his deposit records to compute his income. Therefore, he included the $5,000 in his 1999 gross income.

a. In what year should Lane report the income?

b. Why does it matter whether Lane reports the income in 1998 or 1999, so long as he actually reports it?

8. Doug, a cash basis taxpayer, operated Craig's farm under an arrangement whereby Doug would receive one-half of the grain crop, less the cost of seed and fertilizer. The seed and fertilizer cost $8,000, which was paid during the year. In October Doug harvested the crop. A portion of the grain was sold for $28,000 cash in October, and Doug received $10,000 as his share of the $28,000 in November. Also in November, more of the grain was sold for $40,000. The grain was delivered to the purchaser in November, but payment was not to be received until January of the following year. Doug also used a portion of the grain for his personal use. The cost of the personal use grain was $1,200, but it could have been sold for $2,000. In February of the following year, Doug collected the balance Craig owed to him. Identify the relevant tax issues for Doug.

9. Olga, a cash basis taxpayer, sold a bond with accrued interest of $800 for $11,000. Olga's basis in the bond was $10,000. Compute Olga's income from this transaction.

10. Marlene, a cash basis taxpayer, purchased a 10-year zero coupon bond (no interest is paid annually) for $5,083 on January 2, 1998. The maturity value of the bond in 10 years is $10,000, which is the principal plus 7% interest compounded annually.
    a. What is Marlene's interest income from the bond for 1998?
    b. What is her basis for the bond on December 31, 1998?

11. Taupe Car Wash, an accrual basis taxpayer, sells certificates throughout the year that entitle the holder to a free car wash at any time during the next 24 months. At the end of 1998, certificates with a total face amount of $10,000 are outstanding. When is Taupe required to include the $10,000 in gross income?

12. Quinn (father) paid $200 for an automobile that needed repairs. He worked nights and weekends to restore the car. Several individuals offered to purchase the car for $2,800. Quinn gave the car and a list of potential buyers to Ron (son), whose college tuition was due in a few days. Ron sold the car for $2,800 and paid his tuition. Does Quinn have any taxable income from the transaction?

13. Tom Jr., a cash basis minor, performed services and was to be paid $100 in 1998. In 1998, the employer paid the $100 to Tom Sr., who deposited the money in his bank account. The following year, Tom Sr. used the $100 to buy his son a car.
    a. In whose gross income is the $100 included?
    b. When is the $100 included in gross income?

14. Isabella incorporated her law practice. She entered into an employee contract with the corporation, and all contracts with clients are between the client and Isabella's corporation. None of the clients would do business with the corporation if Isabella were not in fact doing all of the work. Who should report the income from the legal services?

15. Who pays the tax on (a) the income of an S corporation and on (b) the income of a partnership?

16. Ted and Alice were residents of a community property state. In 1998, Ted left Alice for parts unknown. Ted and Alice were still married at year-end. How will Ted's absence complicate Alice's 1998 tax return?

17. Hank and Elaine are negotiating their divorce agreement, which requires the division of their jointly owned property. Hank has proposed that he receive the couple's house (basis of $50,000 and fair market value of $75,000) while Elaine would receive (a) securities (basis of $10,000 and fair market value of $75,000) or (b) four annual payments of $22,644 each, which is equivalent to a $75,000 loan at 8% interest. Elaine will probably sell the securities if she receives them. Elaine does not want the house. Which option should she accept?

18. William and Abigail, who live in San Francisco, have been experiencing problems with their marriage. They have a three-year-old daughter, April, who stays with William's parents during the day since both William and Abigail are employed. Abigail worked to support William while he attended medical school, and now she has been accepted into medical school in Mexico. Abigail has decided to divorce William and attend medical school. April will stay in San Francisco because of her strong attachment to her grandparents and because they can provide her with excellent day care. Abigail knows that William will expect her to contribute to the cost of raising April. Abigail also feels that, to finance her education, she must receive cash for her share of the property they accumulated during their marriage. In addition, she feels she should receive some reimbursement for her contribution to William's support while he was in medical school. She expects the divorce proceedings will take several months. Identify the relevant tax issues for Abigail.

19. In the case of below-market loans between relatives, why is the lender deemed to have made a gift?

20. Elisha loaned $11,000 to Andy, her son, who used the money to buy a personal residence. This was the only outstanding loan between them. Elisha did not charge interest on

the loan, although the market rate of interest was 7%. Andy had $600 of net investment income for the year. Do the imputed interest rules apply?

21. In the case of a corporation's interest-free loan to its controlling shareholder who is also an employee of the corporation, why would the corporation prefer that the loan be classified as an employer-employee loan rather than a corporation-shareholder loan?

22. Brad is the president of the Yellow Corporation. He and other members of his family control the corporation. Brad has a temporary need for $50,000, and the corporation has excess cash. He could borrow the money from a bank at 9%, and Yellow is earning 6% on its temporary investments. Yellow has made loans to other employees on several occasions. Therefore, Brad is considering borrowing $50,000 from the corporation. He will repay the loan principal in two years plus interest at 5%. Identify the relevant tax issues for Brad and the Yellow Corporation.

23. Alfred, age 56, is a victim of corporate downsizing. After several months of unsuccessfully searching for a job, Alfred is forced to start drawing upon his annuity contract. The contract is part of a qualified retirement plan to which he contributed $6,200. Under the contract, Alfred is to receive $800 per month for the remainder of his life. How much of each monthly annuity payment is included in his gross income?

24. Gail is a full-time employee of Purple Corporation. One of the fringe benefits the company offers its employees is group term life insurance protection equal to the employee's annual salary. Gail is 45 years old, and her annual salary is $70,000. What is Gail's gross income from the life insurance protection for the year?

25. When a taxpayer is receiving Social Security benefits, could a $1,000 increase in income from services cause the taxpayer's adjusted gross income to increase by more than $1,000?

PROBLEMS

26. Determine the effects of the following on Anne's gross income for the year:
    a. Anne bought a used sofa for $25. After she took the sofa home, she discovered $15,000 in a secret compartment. Anne was unable to determine who placed the money in the sofa. Therefore, she put the money in her bank account.
    b. Anne also discovered oil on her property during the year, and the value of the land increased from $10,000 to $3 million.
    c. One year later, Anne found a diamond in the sofa she had purchased. Apparently, the diamond was in the sofa when Anne purchased it. The value of the diamond was $6,000. Under state law, the diamond became Anne's property when she purchased the sofa.
    d. Anne's bank charges a $3 per month service charge. However, the fee is waived if the customer maintains an average balance for the month of at least $1,000. Anne's account exceeded the minimum deposit requirement, and as a result she was not required to pay any service charges for the year.

27. Compute the taxpayer's (1) economic income and (2) gross income for tax purposes from the following events:
    a. The taxpayer sold securities for $10,000. The securities cost $6,000 in 1994. The fair market value of the securities at the beginning of the year was $9,000.
    b. The taxpayer sold his business and received $15,000 under a covenant not to compete with the new owner.
    c. The taxpayer used her controlled corporation's automobile for her vacation. The rental value of the automobile for the vacation period was $800.
    d. The taxpayer raised vegetables in her garden. The fair market value of the vegetables was $900, and the cost of raising them was $100. She ate some of the vegetables and gave the remainder to neighbors.
    e. The local government changed the zoning ordinances so that some of the taxpayer's residential property was reclassified as commercial. Because of the change, the fair market value of the taxpayer's property increased by $10,000.

f. During the year, the taxpayer borrowed $50,000 for two years at 9% interest. By the end of the year, interest rates had increased to 12%, and the lender accepted $49,000 in full satisfaction of the debt.

28. Kevin, a cash basis taxpayer, received the following from his employer during 1998:

   • Salary of $75,000.

   • Bonus of $10,000. In 1999, the company determined that the bonus had been incorrectly computed and required Kevin to repay $3,000.

   • Use of a company car for his vacation. Rental value for the period would have been $900. Kevin paid for the gas.

   • $4,000 advance for travel expenses. Kevin had spent only $3,400 at the end of the year.

   Determine the effects of these items on Kevin's gross income.

29. Which of the following investments of $10,000 each will yield the greater after-tax value assuming the taxpayer is in the 40% tax bracket (combined Federal and state) for ordinary income and 26% for qualifying capital gains in all years and the investments will be liquidated at the end of five years?
   a. Land that will increase in value by 10% each year.
   b. A taxable bond yielding 10% before tax, and the interest can be reinvested at 10% before tax.

   Prepare a brief speech for your tax class in which you explain why the future value of the land will exceed the future value of the taxable bond.
       Given: Compound amount of $1 and compound value of annuity payments at the end of five years:

Interest Rate	$1 Compounded for 5 Years	$1 Annuity Compounded for 5 Years
6%	$1.33	$5.64
10%	1.61	6.10

30. Determine the taxpayer's income for tax purposes in each of the following cases:
   a. Zelda borrowed $30,000 from the First National Bank. She was required to deliver to the bank stocks with a value of $30,000 and a cost of $10,000. The stocks were to serve as collateral for the loan.
   b. Zelda owned a lot on Sycamore Street that measured 100 feet by 100 feet. The cost of the lot to her is $10,000. The city condemned a 10-foot strip of the land so that it could widen the street. Zelda received a $2,000 condemnation award.
   c. Zelda owned land zoned for residential use only. The land cost $5,000 and had a market value of $7,000. Zelda spent $500 and several hundred hours petitioning the county supervisors to change the zoning to A–1 commercial. When the county approved the zoning change, the value of the property immediately increased to $20,000.

31. Determine Amos Seagull's gross income in each of the following cases:
   a. In the current year, Seagull Corporation purchased an automobile for $25,000. The company was to receive a $1,500 rebate from the manufacturer. However, the corporation directed that the rebate be paid to Amos, the corporation's sole shareholder.
   b. Amos sold his corporation. In addition to the selling price of the stock, he received $50,000 for a covenant not to compete—an agreement that he will not compete with his former business for five years.
   c. Amos and his neighbor got into an argument over Amos's dog. The neighbor built a fence to keep the dog out of his yard. The fence added $1,500 to the value of Amos's property.

32. Al is an attorney who conducts his practice as a sole proprietor. During the year, he received cash of $100,000 for legal services. At the beginning of the year, he had

receivables from clients of $45,000. At the end of the year, his receivables totaled $40,000. Compute Al's gross income from the practice for the year:

a. Using the cash basis of accounting.

b. Using the accrual basis of accounting.

33. The taxpayer began operating a grocery store during the year. Her only books and records are based on cash receipts and disbursements, but she has asked you to compute her gross profit from the business for tax purposes.

Sales of merchandise	$350,000
Purchases of merchandise	220,000

You determine that as of the end of the year the taxpayer has accounts payable for merchandise of $15,000 and accounts receivable from customers totaling $6,000. The cost of merchandise on hand at the end of the year was $9,000. Compute the grocery store's accrual method gross profit for the year.

34. Your client is a new partnership, Aspen Associates, which is an engineering consulting firm. Generally, Aspen bills clients for services at the end of each month. Client billings are about $50,000 each month. On average, it takes 45 days to collect the receivables. Aspen's expenses are primarily for salary and rent. Salaries are paid on the last day of each month, and rent is paid on the first day of each month. The partnership has a line of credit with a bank, which requires monthly financial statements. These must be prepared using the accrual method. Aspen's managing partner, Amanda Sims, has suggested that the firm should also use the accrual method for tax purposes and thus reduce accounting fees by $500. Write a letter to your client explaining why you believe it would be worthwhile for Aspen to file its tax return on the cash basis even though its financial statements are prepared on the accrual basis. Aspen's address is 100 James Tower, Denver, CO 80208.

35. Color Paint Shop, Inc., (459 Ellis Avenue, Harrisburg, PA 17111), is an accrual basis taxpayer that paints automobiles. During the year, the company painted Samuel's car and was to receive a $1,000 payment from his insurance company. Samuel was not satisfied with the work, however, and the insurance company refused to pay. In December 1998, Color and Samuel agreed that Color would receive $600 for the work, subject to final approval by the insurance company. In the past, Color had come to terms with customers only to have the insurance company negotiate an even lesser amount. In May 1999, the insurance company reviewed the claim and paid the $600 to Color. An IRS agent thinks that Color, as an accrual basis taxpayer, should report $1,000 of income in 1998, when the work was done, and then deduct a $400 loss in 1999. Prepare a memo to Susan Apple, a tax partner for whom you are working, with the recommended treatment for the disputed income.

36. Determine the effect of the following on a cash basis taxpayer's gross income for 1998:

a. Received his paycheck for $3,000 from his employer on December 31, 1998. He deposited the paycheck on January 2, 1999.

b. Received a bonus of $5,000 from his employer on January 10, 1999. The bonus was for the outstanding performance of his division during 1998.

c. Received a dividend check from IBM on November 28, 1998. He mailed the check back to IBM in December requesting that additional IBM stock be issued to him under IBM's dividend reinvestment plan.

37. Mohammed owns a life insurance policy. The cash surrender value of the policy increased $800 during the year. He purchased a certificate of deposit on June 30 of the current year for $44,500. The certificate matures in two years when its value will be $50,000 (interest rate of 6%). However, if Mohammed redeems the certificate before the end of the first year, he receives no interest. Mohammed also purchased a Series EE U.S. government savings bond for $7,348. The maturity value of the bond is $10,000 in seven years (yield of 4.5%), and the redemption price of the bond increased by $380 during the year. Mohammed has owned no other savings bonds. What is Mohammed's current-year gross income from the above items?

38. Pelican, Inc., an accrual basis taxpayer, sells and installs consumer appliances. Determine the effects of each of the following transactions on the company's 1998 gross income:
    a. In December 1998, the company received a $1,200 advance payment from a customer. The payment was for an appliance that Pelican specially ordered from the manufacturer. The appliance had not arrived at the end of 1998.
    b. At the end of 1998, the company installed an appliance and collected the full price of $750 for the item. However, the customer claimed the appliance was defective and asked the company for a refund. The company conceded that the appliance was defective, but claimed that the customer should collect from the manufacturer. The dispute had not been settled by the end of 1998. In early 1999, it was determined that Pelican did not install the appliance properly, and the company was required to refund the full sales price.
    c. The company sold an appliance for $1,200 (plus a market rate of interest) and received the customer's note for that amount. However, because of the customer's poor credit rating, the value of the note was only $700.

39. Freda is a cash basis taxpayer. In 1998, she negotiated her salary for 1999. Her employer offered to pay her $20,000 each month—a total of $240,000 for the year. Freda countered that she would accept $20,000 each month for the first nine months of the year and the remaining $60,000 in January 2000. The employer accepted Freda's terms in 1999 and 2000.
    a. Did Freda actually or constructively receive $240,000 in 1999?
    b. What could explain Freda's willingness to spread her salary over a longer period of time?

40. The Heron Apartments requires its new tenants to pay the rent for the first and last months of the annual lease and a $400 damage deposit, all at the time the lease is signed. In December 1998, a tenant paid $800 for January 1999 rent, $800 for December 1999 rent, and $400 for the damage deposit. In January 2000, Heron refunded the tenant's damage deposit. What are the effects of these payments on Heron's taxable income for 1998, 1999, and 2000?
    a. Assume Heron is a cash basis taxpayer.
    b. Assume Heron is an accrual basis taxpayer.

41. Leo has asked you to review portions of his tax return. He provides you with the following information:

Gain on redemption of a 2-year 6% certificate of deposit		
Proceeds received June 30, 1998	$10,000	
Purchase price July 1, 1996	(8,900)	
Gain		$1,100
Gain on redemption of a 6-month 6% certificate of deposit		
Proceeds received March 31, 1998	$ 5,000	
Purchase price October 1, 1997	(4,855)	
Gain		145
Gain from 8% Series E savings bond		
Proceeds received September 30, 1998	$ 2,500	
Purchase price June 30, 1984	(780)	
Gain		1,720
Distributions from a family partnership		1,500

Leo's share of the partnership's earnings were $1,800. Determine Leo's 1998 gross income from the above.

42. a. Gus is a cash basis taxpayer. On September 1, 1998, Gus gave a corporate bond to his son, Hans. The bond had a face amount of $10,000 and paid $900 of interest each January 31. On December 1, 1998, Gus gave common stocks to his daughter, Dena. Dividends totaling $720 had been declared on the stocks on November 30,

1998, and were payable on January 15, 1999. Dena became the shareholder of record in time to collect the dividends. What is Gus's 1999 gross income from the bond and stocks?

b. Gus's mother was unable to pay her bills as they came due. Gus, his employer, and his mother's creditors entered into an arrangement whereby the employer would withhold $500 per month from Gus's salary and pay the $500 to the creditors. Three thousand dollars were withheld from Gus's salary and paid to the creditors. Is Gus required to pay tax on the $3,000?

43. Tracy, a cash basis taxpayer, is employed by Eagle Corporation, also a cash basis taxpayer. Tracy is a full-time employee of the corporation and receives a salary of $60,000 per year. He also receives a bonus equal to 10% of all collections from clients he serviced during the year. Determine the tax consequences of the following events to the corporation and to Tracy:

a. On December 31, 1998, Tracy was visiting a customer. The customer gave Tracy a $3,000 check payable to the corporation for appraisal services Tracy performed during 1998. Tracy did not deliver the check to the corporation until January 1999.

b. The facts are the same as in (a), except that the corporation is an accrual basis taxpayer and Tracy deposited the check on December 31, but the bank did not add the deposit to the corporation's account until January 1999.

c. The facts are the same as in (a), except the customer told Tracy to hold the check until January when the customer could make a bank deposit that would cover the check.

44. Eve, Fran, and Gary each have a one-third interest in the capital and profits of the EFG Partnership. At the beginning of the year, each partner had a $50,000 balance in his or her capital account. The partnership's gross income for the year was $300,000, and its total expenses were $60,000. During the year, Eve contributed an additional $10,000 to the partnership and did not have any withdrawals from her capital account. Fran withdrew $30,000, and Gary withdrew $24,000. Compute each partner's taxable income from the partnership for the year.

45. Diego and Carmen lived together for part of the year but were divorced on December 31, 1998. Diego earned $30,000 salary from his employer during the year. Carmen's salary was $16,000. Carmen also received $8,000 in taxable dividends from stock held as separate property.

a. If Diego and Carmen reside in Texas, how much income should each report on their separate tax returns for 1998?

b. If amounts are withheld from their salaries, how are these amounts reported on Diego and Carmen's separate returns?

c. If Diego and Carmen reside in a common law state, how much income should each report on their separate returns?

46. Liz and Doug were divorced on July 1 of the current year after 10 years of marriage. Their current year's income received before the divorce was as follows:

Doug's salary	$18,000
Liz's salary	25,000
Rent on apartments purchased by Liz 15 years ago	6,000
Dividends on stock Doug inherited from his mother 4 years ago	1,200
Interest on a savings account in Liz's name funded with her salary	1,800

Allocate the income to Liz and Doug assuming they live in:
a. California.
b. Texas.

47. Nell and Kirby are in the process of negotiating their divorce agreement. What would be the tax consequences to Nell and Kirby if the following, considered individually, became part of the agreement:

a. Nell and Kirby will continue as joint owners of the personal residence. Nell can continue to occupy the residence as long as she so desires. If she ever sells the residence, however, Kirby will receive one-half the proceeds. The fair rental value of the residence is $2,000 per month.

 b. Nell will receive $1,000 per month for 100 months, and Kirby will receive the $180,000 in securities (adjusted basis is $100,000) that were formerly owned jointly by the couple. If Nell dies before she receives all of the payments, Kirby is not required to continue the payments.

 c. Nell is to have custody of their 12-year-old son and is to receive $600 per month until (1) the child dies or (2) attains age 21 (whichever occurs first).

48. Under the terms of a post-1986 divorce agreement, Al is to receive payments from Karen as follows: $60,000 in Year 1, $45,000 in Year 2, and $20,000 each year for Years 3 through 10. Al is also to receive custody of their minor son. The payments will decrease by $5,000 per year if the son dies or when he attains age 21 and will cease upon Al's death.

 a. What will be Al's taxable alimony in Year 1?

 b. What will be the effect of the Years 2 and 3 payments on Al's taxable income?

49. Under the terms of their divorce agreement, Barry is to transfer common stock (cost of $25,000, market value of $60,000) to Sandra. Barry and Sandra have a 14-year-old child. Sandra will have custody of the child, and Barry is to pay $300 per month as child support. In addition, Sandra is to receive $1,000 per month for 10 years. However, the payments will be reduced to $750 per month when their child reaches age 21. In the first year under the agreement, Sandra receives the common stock and the correct cash payments for six months. How will the terms of the agreement affect Sandra's gross income?

50. Gus decides to buy a personal residence and goes to the bank for a $50,000 loan. The bank tells him he can borrow the funds at 8% if his father will guarantee the debt. Gus's father, Hal, owns certificates of deposit currently yielding 7%. The Federal rate is 6%. Hal is willing to do either of the following:

• Cash in the certificates and lend Gus the funds at 7% interest.

• Guarantee the loan for Gus.

Hal will consider lending the funds to Gus at an even lower interest rate, depending on the tax consequences. Hal is in the 36% marginal tax bracket. Gus, whose only source of income is his salary, is in the 15% marginal tax bracket. The interest Gus pays on the mortgage will be deductible by him. Considering only the tax consequences, which option will maximize the family's after-tax wealth?

51. On June 30, 1998, Ridge borrowed $52,000 from his employer. On July 1, 1998, Ridge used the money as follows:

Interest-free loan to Ridge's controlled corporation (operated by Ridge on a part-time basis)	$21,000
Interest-free loan to Tab (Ridge's son)	11,000
National Bank of Grundy 6% certificate of deposit ($14,840 due at maturity, June 30, 1999)	14,000
National Bank of Grundy 6.25% certificate of deposit ($6,773 due at maturity, June 30, 2000)	6,000
	$52,000

Ridge's employer did not charge him interest. The applicable Federal rate was 8% throughout the relevant period. Tab had investment income of $800 for the year, and he used the loan proceeds to pay medical school tuition. There were no other outstanding loans between Ridge and Tab. What are the effects of the preceding transactions on Ridge's taxable income for 1998?

52. Indicate whether the imputed interest rules should apply in the following situations:

 a. Mitch is a cash basis attorney who charges his clients based on the number of hours it takes to do the job. The bill is due upon completion of the work. However, for clients who make an initial payment when the work begins, Mitch grants a discount on the final bill. The discount is equal to 10% interest on the deposit.

b. Local Telephone Company requires that customers make a security deposit. The deposit is refunded after the customer has established a good record for paying the telephone bill. The company pays 6% interest on the deposits.

c. Lynn asked Kelly for a $125,000 loan to purchase a new home. Kelly made the loan and did not charge interest. Kelly never intended to collect the loan, and at the end of the year Kelly told Lynn that the debt was forgiven.

53. Vito is the sole shareholder of Vito, Inc. He is also employed by the corporation. On June 30, 1998, Vito borrowed $8,000 from Vito, Inc., and on July 1, 1999, he borrowed an additional $3,000. Both loans were due on demand. No interest was charged on the loans, and the Federal rate was 10% for all relevant dates. Vito used the money to purchase stock, and he had no investment income. Determine the tax consequences to Vito and Vito, Inc., in each of the following situations:
    a. The loans are considered employer-employee loans.
    b. The loans are considered corporation-shareholder loans.

54. Albert purchased an annuity from an insurance company for $100,000 on January 1, 1998. The annuity was to pay him $6,000 per year for life starting in January 1998. At the annuity starting date, Albert was age 65.
    a. Determine Albert's gross income from the annuity in the first year.
    b. Assume Albert lives 25 years after purchasing the contract. What would be his gross income in the twenty-fourth year?
    c. Assume Albert died in 2001, after collecting a total of $20,000. What will be the effect of the annuity on his 2001 adjusted gross income?

55. For each of the following, determine the amount that should be included in gross income:
    a. Joe was selected as the most valuable player in the Super Bowl. In recognition of this, he was awarded a sports car worth $60,000 and $50,000 in cash.
    b. Wanda won the Mrs. America beauty contest. She received various prizes valued at $75,000.
    c. George was awarded the Nobel Peace Prize. He donated the $900,000 check he received to State University, his alma mater.

56. The LMN Partnership has a group term life insurance plan. Each partner has $200,000 protection, and each employee has protection equal to twice his or her annual salary. Employee Alice (age 44) had $110,000 insurance under the plan, and partner Kay (age 56) had $200,000 coverage. The cost of Alice's coverage for the year was $180, and the cost of Kay's protection was $1,500.
    a. Assuming the plan is nondiscriminatory, how much must Alice and Kay include in gross income from the insurance?
    b. Assuming the plan is discriminatory, how much must Kay include in her gross income from the insurance?

57. Herbert was employed for the first six months of the year and earned $60,000 in salary. During the next six months, he collected $7,800 of unemployment compensation, borrowed $6,000 (using his personal residence as collateral), and withdrew $1,000 from his savings account (including $60 interest). His luck was not all bad, for in December he won $800 in the lottery on a $5 ticket. Calculate Herbert's gross income.

58. Linda and Don are married and file a joint return. In 1998, they received $9,000 in Social Security benefits and $28,000 taxable pension benefits, interest, and dividends.
    a. Compute the couple's adjusted gross income on a joint return.
    b. Don would like to know whether they should sell for $100,000 a corporate bond (at no gain or loss) that pays 8% in interest each year and use the proceeds to buy a $100,000 nontaxable State of Virginia bond that will pay $6,000 in interest each year.
    c. If Linda in (a) works part-time and earns $30,000, how much would Linda and Don's adjusted gross income increase?

59. Melissa and James are married and file a joint return. They receive $12,000 in Social Security benefits, $21,000 in pension benefits (all taxable), and $9,000 in taxable

dividends. They are considering selling appreciated stock that they own. They purchased the stock three years ago for $8,000, and it now has a market value of $15,000. Melissa and James have asked you to explain the tax consequences of the sale including the effect on their adjusted gross income.

60. Donna does not think she has an income tax problem but would like to discuss her situation with you just to make sure she will not get hit with an unexpected tax liability. Base your suggestions on the following relevant financial information:
    a. Donna's share of the SAT Partnership income is $70,000, but none of the income can be distributed because the partnership needs the cash for operations.
    b. Donna's Social Security benefits totaled $8,400, but Donna loaned the cash received to her nephew.
    c. Donna assigned to a creditor the right to collect $1,200 interest on some bonds she owned.
    d. Donna and her husband lived together in California until September, when they separated. Donna has heard rumors that her husband had substantial gambling winnings since they separated.

CUMULATIVE PROBLEMS

61. Dan and Freida Butler, husband and wife, file a joint return. The Butlers live at 625 Oak Street, Corbin, KY 27521. Dan's Social Security number is 482–61–1231, and Freida's is 162–79–1245.

    During 1998, Dan and Freida furnished over half of the total support of each of the following individuals:
    a. Gina, their daughter, age 22, a full-time student, who was married on December 21, 1998, has no income of her own, and for 1998 did not file a joint return with her husband, who earned $4,000 during 1998.
    b. Sam, their son, age 20, who had gross income of $2,900 and who dropped out of college in February 1998.
    c. Ben Brow, Freida's brother, age 22, who is a full-time college student with gross income of $4,000.

    Dan, a radio announcer for WJJJ, earned a salary of $60,000 in 1998. Freida was employed part-time as a real estate salesperson by Corbin Realty and was paid commissions of $40,000 in 1998. Freida sold a house on December 30, 1998, and will be paid a commission of $1,500 (not included in the $40,000) on the January 10, 1999, closing date.

    Dan and Freida collected $15,000 on a certificate of deposit that matured on September 30, 1998. The certificate was purchased on October 1, 1996, for $13,102, and the yield to maturity was 7%.

    Other income received consisted of the following:

Dividends on CSX stock	$2,200
Interest on savings account at Second Bank	1,500

    CSX had been instructed by Dan and Freida to pay the dividends directly to Freida's brother, Ben. CSX complied with their instructions.

    Freida is an 8% partner in the Green Partnership. Green reported taxable income of $100,000 for 1998 and made no distributions to any of the partners in 1998.

    Dan and Freida had itemized deductions as follows:

State income tax withheld	$3,600
Personal property taxes paid	300
Real estate taxes paid	2,800
Interest on home mortgage (paid to Corbin Savings and Loan)	5,900
Cash contributions to the Boy Scouts	620

Their employers withheld Federal income tax of $16,500 (Dan $10,400, Freida $6,100), and the Butlers paid estimated tax of $4,000.

Part 1—Tax Computation
Compute Dan and Freida's 1998 Federal income tax payable (or refund due). Suggested software (if available): *TurboTax.*

Part 2—Tax Planning
Dan plans to reduce his work schedule and work only halftime for WJJJ in 1999. He has been writing songs for several years and wants to devote more time to developing a career as a songwriter. Because of the uncertainty in the music business, however, he would like you to make all computations assuming he will have no income from songwriting in 1999. To make up for the loss of income, Freida plans to increase the amount of time she spends selling real estate. She estimates she will be able to earn $65,000 in 1999. Assume all other income and expense items will be approximately the same as they were in 1998. Will the Butlers have more or less disposable income (after Federal income tax) in 1999? Write a letter to the Butlers that contains your advice and prepare a memo for the tax files. Suggested software (if available): *TurboTax.*

62. Cecil C. Seymour is a 66-year-old widower. He had income for 1997 as follows:

Pension from former employer	$23,400
Interest income from Alto National Bank	6,500
Interest income on City of Alto bonds	2,000
Dividends received from AT&T	4,000
Collections on annuity contract he purchased from Great Life Insurance	4,800
Social Security benefits	12,000

The cost of the annuity was $36,000, and Cecil was expected to receive a total of 120 monthly payments of $400. Cecil has received 30 payments through 1997.

Cecil's 40-year-old daughter, Sarah C. Seymour, borrowed $40,000 from Cecil in 1996. She used the money to start a new business. Cecil does not charge her interest because she could not afford to pay it, but he does expect to eventually collect the principal. Sarah is living with Cecil until the business becomes profitable. Except for housing, Sarah provides her own support from her business and $1,500 in dividends on stocks that she inherited from her mother.

Other relevant information is presented below:

- Cecil's Social Security number: 259–83–4444

- Address: 3840 Springfield Blvd., Alto, GA 30754

- Sarah's Social Security number: 257–49–8862

- State income taxes paid: $1,300

- County personal property taxes paid: $1,900

- Payments on estimated 1997 Federal income tax: $6,500

- Charitable contributions of cash to Alto Baptist Church: $4,400

- Federal interest rate: 8%

Compute Cecil's 1997 Federal income tax payable (or refund due). If you use tax forms for your computations, you will need Form 1040 and Schedules A and B. Suggested software (if available): *TurboTax.*

Research Problems for this chapter appear at the end of Chapter 28.

TEAM PROJECT: ARTHUR ANDERSEN TAX CHALLENGE CASES

For more information on the Arthur Andersen Tax Challenge Cases, refer to Chapter 1, page 1–37.

Information related to tax issues and problems that are discussed in this chapter may be found in the

Day and Ball case on pages 1, 2, 4, 11–17, 31, 34, 35, and 37
Fence case on pages 39, 40, 41, 47, 50, 58, 60, and 63

Read and analyze the case you have been assigned and *identify* any issues and problems that are related to material covered in this chapter. If the information provided in the case is complete, prepare answers for this part of the case at this time. If you need information that is contained in the later parts of the case, write a memo summarizing the questions or problems so you can prepare a complete answer at a later date.

4

GROSS INCOME: EXCLUSIONS

LEARNING OBJECTIVES

After completing Chapter 4, you should be able to:

1. Understand that statutory authority is required to exclude an item from gross income.

2. Identify the circumstances under which various items are excludible from gross income.

3. Determine the extent to which receipts can be excluded under the tax benefit rule.

4. Describe the circumstances under which income must be reported from the discharge of indebtedness.

5. Identify tax planning strategies for obtaining the maximum benefit from allowable exclusions.

ITEMS SPECIFICALLY EXCLUDED FROM GROSS INCOME

Chapter 3 discussed the concepts and judicial doctrines that affect the determination of gross income. If an income item is within the all-inclusive definition of gross income, the item can be excluded only if the taxpayer can locate specific authority for doing so. Chapter 4 focuses on the exclusions Congress has authorized. These exclusions are listed in Exhibit 4–1.

Tax advisers spend countless hours trying to develop techniques to achieve tax-exempt status for income. Employee benefits planning is greatly influenced by the availability of certain types of exclusions. Taxes play an important role in employee benefits, as well as in other situations, because attaining an exclusion is another means of enhancing after-tax income. For example, for a person whose combined Federal and state marginal tax rate is 40 percent, $1.00 of tax-exempt income is equivalent to $1.66 in income subject to taxation. The tax adviser's ideal is to attach the right labels or provide the right wording to render income nontaxable without affecting the economics of the transaction.

Consider the case of an employee who is in the 28 percent marginal tax bracket and is paying $3,000 a year for health insurance. If the employer provided this protection in a manner that qualified for exclusion treatment but reduced the employee's salary by $3,000, the employee's after-tax and after-insurance income would increase at no additional cost to the employer.

activities of daily living. These exclusions for the terminally ill and the chronically ill are available only to the insured. Thus, a person who purchases a life insurance policy from the insured does not qualify.

EXAMPLE 3

Tom owned a term life insurance policy at the time he was diagnosed as having a terminal illness. After paying $5,200 in premiums, he sold the policy to Amber Benefits, Inc., a company that is authorized by the State of Virginia to purchase such policies. Amber paid Tom $50,000. When Tom died six months later, Amber collected the face amount of the policy, $75,000. Tom is not required to include the $44,800 gain ($50,000 − $5,200) on the sale of the policy in his gross income. Assume Amber pays additional premiums of $4,000 during the six-month period. When Amber collects the life insurance proceeds of $75,000, it must include the $21,000 gain ($75,000 proceeds − $50,000 cost − $4,000 additional premiums paid) in gross income. ▼

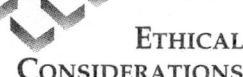
ETHICAL CONSIDERATIONS

Investing in Death

Recent changes in the tax law allow a person with a terminal illness to sell his or her life insurance policy without recognizing gain. Limited partnerships have been formed to purchase the policies insuring AIDS patients. The shorter the patient's life span, the greater the investor's potential profit. When the Food and Drug Administration announces that a potential cure for AIDS cannot be marketed until it has been tested for several years, the market value of these partnership interests increases. Should the tax law be a participant in a system that allows individuals to profit from other people's misfortunes?

TRANSFER FOR VALUABLE CONSIDERATION

A life insurance policy (other than one associated with accelerated death benefits) may be transferred after it is issued by the insurance company. If the policy is *transferred for valuable consideration,* the insurance proceeds are includible in the gross income of the transferee to the extent the proceeds received exceed the amount paid for the policy by the transferee plus any subsequent premiums paid.

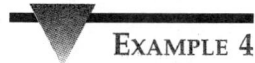
EXAMPLE 4

Adam pays premiums of $500 for an insurance policy in the face amount of $1,000 upon the life of Beth and subsequently transfers the policy to Carol for $600. On Beth's death, Carol receives the proceeds of $1,000. The amount that Carol can exclude from gross income is limited to $600 plus any premiums she paid subsequent to the transfer. ▼

The Code, however, provides four exceptions to the rule illustrated in the preceding example. These exceptions permit exclusion treatment for transfers to the following:

1. A partner of the insured.
2. A partnership in which the insured is a partner.
3. A corporation in which the insured is an officer or shareholder.
4. A transferee whose basis in the policy is determined by reference to the transferor's basis.

The first three exceptions facilitate the use of insurance contracts to fund buy-sell agreements.

EXAMPLE 5 Rick and Sam are equal partners who have an agreement that allows either partner to purchase the interest of a deceased partner for $50,000. Neither partner has sufficient cash to actually buy the other partner's interest, but each has a life insurance policy on his own life in the amount of $50,000. Rick and Sam could exchange their policies (usually at little or no taxable gain), and upon the death of either partner, the surviving partner could collect tax-free insurance proceeds. The proceeds could then be used to purchase the decedent's interest in the partnership. ▼

The fourth exception applies to policies that were transferred pursuant to a tax-free exchange or were received by gift.[13]

Investment earnings arising from the reinvestment of life insurance proceeds are generally subject to income tax. Often the beneficiary will elect to collect the insurance proceeds in installments. The annuity rules (discussed in Chapter 3) are used to apportion the installment payment between the principal element (excludible) and the interest element (includible).[14]

SCHOLARSHIPS

GENERAL INFORMATION

Payments or benefits received by a student at an educational institution may be (1) compensation for services, (2) a gift, or (3) a scholarship. If the payments or benefits are received as compensation for services (past or present), the fact that the recipient is a student generally does not render the amounts received nontaxable.[15]

EXAMPLE 6 State University waives tuition for all graduate teaching assistants. The tuition waived is intended as compensation for services and is therefore included in the graduate assistant's gross income. ▼

As discussed earlier, gifts are not includible in gross income.

The **scholarship** rules are intended to provide exclusion treatment for education-related benefits that cannot qualify as gifts but are not compensation for services. According to the Regulations, "a scholarship is an amount paid or allowed to, or for the benefit of, an individual to aid such individual in the pursuit of study or research."[16] The recipient must be a candidate for a degree (either undergraduate or graduate) at an educational institution.[17]

EXAMPLE 7 Terry enters a contest sponsored by a local newspaper. Each contestant is required to submit an essay on local environmental issues. The prize is one year's tuition at State University. Terry wins the contest. The newspaper has a legal obligation to Terry (as contest winner). Thus, the benefits are not a gift. However, since the tuition payment aids Terry in pursuing her studies, the payment is a scholarship. ▼

A scholarship recipient may exclude from gross income the amount used for tuition and related expenses (fees, books, supplies, and equipment required for courses), provided the conditions of the grant do not require that the funds be

---

[13]See the discussion of gifts and tax-free exchanges in Chapter 12.
[14]Reg. §§ 1.72–7(c)(1) and 1.101–7T.
[15]Reg. § 1.117–2(a). See *C. P. Bhalla*, 35 T.C. 13 (1960), for a discussion of the distinction between a scholarship and compensation. See also *Bingler v. Johnson*, 69–1 USTC ¶9348, 23 AFTR2d 1212, 89

S.Ct. 1439 (USSC, 1969). For potential exclusion treatment, see the subsequent discussion of qualified tuition reductions.
[16]Prop.Reg. § 1.117–6(c)(3)(i).
[17]§ 117(a).

used for other purposes.[18] Amounts received for room and board are *not* excludible and are treated as earned income for purposes of calculating the standard deduction for a taxpayer who is another taxpayer's dependent.[19]

EXAMPLE 8

Kelly received a scholarship of $9,500 from State University to be used to pursue a bachelor's degree. She spent $4,000 on tuition, $3,000 on books and supplies, and $2,500 for room and board. Kelly may exclude $7,000 ($4,000 + $3,000) from gross income. The $2,500 spent for room and board is includible in Kelly's gross income.

    The scholarship was Kelly's only source of income. Her parents provided more than 50% of Kelly's support and claimed her as a dependent. Kelly's standard deduction will equal her $2,500 gross income. Thus, she has no taxable income. ▼

TIMING ISSUES

Frequently, the scholarship recipient is a cash basis taxpayer who receives the money in one tax year but pays the educational expenses in a subsequent year. The amount eligible for exclusion may not be known at the time the money is received. In that case, the transaction is held *open* until the educational expenses are paid.[20]

EXAMPLE 9

In August 1998, Sanjay received $10,000 as a scholarship for the academic year 1998–1999. Sanjay's expenditures for tuition, books, and supplies were as follows:

August–December 1998	$3,000
January–May 1999	4,500
	$7,500

Sanjay's gross income for 1999 includes $2,500 ($10,000 – $7,500) that is not excludible as a scholarship. None of the scholarship is included in his gross income in 1998. ▼

DISGUISED COMPENSATION

Some employers make scholarships available solely to the children of key employees. The tax objective of these plans is to provide a nontaxable fringe benefit to the executives by making the payment to the child in the form of an excludible scholarship. However, the IRS has ruled that the payments are generally includible in the gross income of the parent-employee.[21]

QUALIFIED TUITION REDUCTION PLANS

Employees (including retired and disabled former employees) of nonprofit educational institutions are allowed to exclude a tuition waiver from gross income, if the waiver is pursuant to a **qualified tuition reduction plan**.[22] The plan may not discriminate in favor of highly compensated employees. The exclusion applies to the employee, the employee's spouse, and the employee's dependent children. The exclusion also extends to tuition reductions granted by any nonprofit educational institution to employees of any other nonprofit educational institution (reciprocal agreements).

---

[18]§ 117(b).
[19]Prop.Reg. § 1.117–6(h).
[20]Prop.Reg. § 1.117–6(b)(2).

[21]Rev.Rul. 75–448, 1975–2 C.B. 55. *Richard T. Armantrout*, 67 T.C. 996 (1977).
[22]§ 117(d).

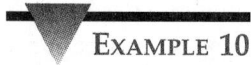

EXAMPLE 10

ABC University allows the dependent children of XYZ University employees to attend ABC University with no tuition charge. XYZ University grants reciprocal benefits to the children of ABC University employees. The dependent children can also attend tuition-free the university where their parents are employed. Employees who take advantage of these benefits are not required to recognize gross income. ▼

Generally, the exclusion is limited to *undergraduate* tuition waivers. However, in the case of teaching or research assistants, graduate tuition waivers may also qualify for exclusion treatment. According to the Proposed Regulations, the exclusion is limited to the value of the benefit in excess of the employee's reasonable compensation.[23] Thus, a tuition reduction that is a substitute for cash compensation cannot be excluded.

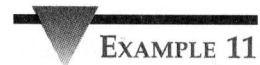

EXAMPLE 11

Susan is a graduate research assistant. She receives a $5,000 salary for 500 hours of service over a nine-month period. This pay, $10 per hour, is reasonable compensation for Susan's services. In addition, Susan receives a waiver of $6,000 for tuition. Susan may exclude the tuition waiver from gross income. ▼

COMPENSATION FOR INJURIES AND SICKNESS

DAMAGES

A person who suffers harm caused by another is often entitled to compensatory damages. The tax consequences of the receipt of damages depend on the type of harm the taxpayer has experienced. The taxpayer may seek recovery for (1) a loss of income, (2) expenses incurred, (3) property destroyed, or (4) personal injury.

Generally, reimbursement for a loss of income is taxed the same as the income replaced. The recovery of an expense is not income, unless the expense was deducted. Damages that are a recovery of the taxpayer's previously deducted expenses are generally taxable under the tax benefit rule, discussed later in this chapter.

A payment for damaged or destroyed property is treated as an amount received in a sale or exchange of the property. Thus, the taxpayer has a realized gain if the damage payments received exceed the property's basis. Damages for personal injuries receive special treatment under the Code.

Personal Injury.   The legal theory of personal injury damages is that the amount received is intended "to make the plaintiff [the injured party] whole as before the injury."[24] It follows that if the damage payments received were subject to tax, the after-tax amount received would be less than the actual damages incurred and the injured party would not be "whole as before the injury."

In terms of personal injury damages, a distinction is made between compensatory damages and punitive damages. Under specified circumstances, compensatory damages may be excluded from gross income. Under no circumstances may punitive damages be excluded from gross income.

Compensatory damages are intended to compensate the taxpayer for the damages incurred. Only those compensatory damages received on account of *physical personal injury or physical sickness* can be excluded from gross income.[25] Compensatory damages awarded on account of emotional distress are not received on account

---

[23]Prop.Reg. § 1.117–6(d).
[24]*C. A. Hawkins*, 6 B.T.A. 1023 (1928).

[25]§ 104(a)(2).

CONCEPT SUMMARY 4-1

Taxation of Damages

Type of Claim	Taxation of Award or Settlement
Breach of contract (generally loss of income)	Taxable.
Property damages	Recovery of cost, gain to the extent of the excess over basis. A loss is deductible for business property and investment property to the extent of basis over the amount realized. A loss may be deductible for personal use property (see discussion of casualty losses in Chapter 6).
Personal injury	
Physical	All compensatory amounts are excluded unless previously deducted (e.g., medical expenses). Amounts received as punitive damages are included in gross income.
Nonphysical	Compensatory damages and punitive damages are included in gross income.

of physical injury or physical sickness and thus cannot be excluded (except to the extent of any amount received for medical care) from gross income. Likewise, any amounts received for age discrimination or injury to one's reputation cannot be excluded.

Punitive damages are amounts the person who caused the harm must pay to the victim as punishment for outrageous conduct. Punitive damages are not intended to compensate the victim, but rather to punish the party who caused the harm. Thus, it follows that amounts received as punitive damages may actually place the victim in a better economic position than before the harm was experienced. Logically, punitive damages are thus included in gross income.

 **EXAMPLE 12**

Tom, a television announcer, was dissatisfied with the manner in which Ron, an attorney, was defending the television station in a libel case. Tom stated on the air that Ron was botching the case. Ron sued Tom for slander, claiming damages for loss of income from clients and potential clients who heard Tom's statement. Ron's claim is for damages to his business reputation, and the amounts received are taxable.

Ron collected on the suit against Tom and was on his way to a party to celebrate his victory when a negligent driver, Norm, drove a truck into Ron's automobile, injuring Ron. Ron filed suit for the physical personal injuries and claimed as damages the loss of income for the period he was unable to work as a result of the injuries. Ron also collected punitive damages that were awarded because of Norm's extremely negligent behavior. Ron's wife also collected damages for the emotional distress she experienced as a result of the accident. Ron may exclude the amounts he received for damages, except the punitive damages. Ron's wife must include the amounts she received for damages in gross income because the amounts were not received because of physical personal injuries or sickness. ▼

WORKERS' COMPENSATION

State workers' compensation laws require the employer to pay fixed amounts for specific job-related injuries. The state laws were enacted so that the employee will not have to go through the ordeal of a lawsuit (and possibly not collect damages because of some defense available to the employer) to recover the damages. Although the payments are intended, in part, to compensate for a loss of future income, Congress has specifically exempted workers' compensation benefits from inclusion in gross income.[26]

ACCIDENT AND HEALTH INSURANCE BENEFITS

The income tax treatment of accident and health insurance benefits depends on whether the policy providing the benefits was purchased by the taxpayer or the taxpayer's employer. Benefits collected under an accident and health insurance policy *purchased by the taxpayer* are excludible. In this case, benefits collected under the taxpayer's insurance policy are excluded even though the payments are a substitute for income.[27]

EXAMPLE 13

Bonnie purchased a medical and disability insurance policy. The insurance company paid Bonnie $200 per week to replace wages she lost while in the hospital. Although the payments serve as a substitute for income, the amounts received are tax-exempt benefits collected under Bonnie's insurance policy. ▼

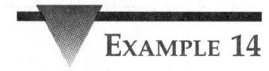

EXAMPLE 14

Joe's injury results in a partial paralysis of his left foot. He receives $5,000 for the injury from his accident insurance company under a policy he had purchased. The $5,000 accident insurance proceeds are tax-exempt. ▼

A different set of rules applies if the accident and health insurance protection was *purchased by the individual's employer*, as discussed in the following section.

EMPLOYER-SPONSORED ACCIDENT AND HEALTH PLANS

Congress encourages employers to provide employees, retired former employees, and their dependents with **accident and health benefits,** disability insurance, and long-term care plans. The *premiums* are deductible by the employer and excluded from the employee's income.[28] Although § 105(a) provides the general rule that the employee has includible income when he or she collects the insurance *benefits*, two exceptions are provided.

Section 105(b) generally excludes payments received for medical care of the employee, spouse, and dependents. However, if the payments are for expenses that do not meet the Code's definition of medical care,[29] the amount received must be included in gross income. In addition, the taxpayer must include in gross income any amounts received for medical expenses that were deducted by the taxpayer on a prior return.

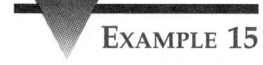

EXAMPLE 15

In 1998, Tab's employer-sponsored health insurance plan paid $4,000 for hair transplants that did not meet the Code's definition of medical care. Tab must include the $4,000 in his gross income for 1998. ▼

---

[26]§ 104(a)(1).
[27]§ 104(a)(3).

[28]§ 106, Reg. § 1.106–1, and Rev.Rul. 82–196, 1982–1 C.B. 106.
[29]See the discussion of medical care in Chapter 9.

Section 105(c) excludes payments for the permanent loss or the loss of the use of a member or function of the body or the permanent disfigurement of the employee, spouse, or a dependent. Payments that are a substitute for salary (e.g., related to the period of time absent) are includible.

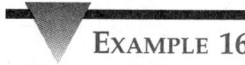

EXAMPLE 16

Jill lost an eye in an automobile accident unrelated to her work. As a result of the accident, Jill incurred $2,000 of medical expenses, which she deducted on her return. She collected $10,000 from an accident insurance policy carried by her employer. The benefits were paid according to a schedule of amounts that varied with the part of the body injured (e.g., $10,000 for loss of an eye, $20,000 for loss of a hand). Because the payment was for loss of a *member or function of the body*, the $10,000 is excluded from income. Jill was absent from work for a week as a result of the accident. Her employer provided her with insurance for the loss of income due to illness or injury. Jill collected $500, which is includible in gross income. ▼

MEDICAL REIMBURSEMENT PLANS

In lieu of providing the employee with insurance coverage for hospital and medical expenses, the employer may agree to reimburse the employee for these expenses. The amounts received through the insurance coverage (insured plan benefits) are excluded from income under § 105 (as previously discussed). Unfortunately in terms of cost considerations, the insurance companies that issue this type of policy usually require a broad coverage of employees. An alternative is to have a plan that is not funded with insurance (a self-insured arrangement). The benefits received under a self-insured plan can be excluded from the employee's income, if the plan does not discriminate in favor of highly compensated employees.[30]

Small employers (50 or fewer employees) have an alternative means of accomplishing a medical reimbursement plan. The employer can purchase a medical insurance plan with a high deductible (e.g., the employee is responsible for the first $2,000 of medical expenses) and then make contributions to the employee's **medical savings account (MSA)**.[31] The employer can make contributions each year up to the maximum contribution of 65 percent of the deductible amount for an individual or 75 percent of the deductible amount in the case of family coverage. Withdrawals from the MSA must be used to reimburse the employee for the medical expenses paid by the employee that are not covered under the high-deductible plan. The employee is not taxed on the employer's contributions to the MSA, the earnings on the funds in the account, or the withdrawals made for medical expenses.[32]

LONG-TERM CARE INSURANCE BENEFITS

Generally, **long-term care insurance,** which covers expenses such as the cost of care in a nursing home, is treated the same as accident and health insurance benefits. Thus, the employee does not recognize income when the employer pays the premiums. When benefits are received from the policy, whether the employer or the individual purchased the policy, the exclusion from gross income is limited to the greater of the following amounts:

---

[30]§ 105(h).

[31]These MSAs are part of a pilot program. They are available only to the first 750,000 participants each year from 1997 through 2000. See additional coverage in Chapter 9.

[32]§§ 106(b) and 220.

- $175 (to be indexed) for each day the patient receives the long-term care.
- The actual cost of the care.

The above amount is reduced by any amounts received from other third parties (e.g., damages received).[33]

EXAMPLE 17

Hazel, who suffers from Alzheimer's disease, was a patient in a nursing home for the last 30 days of the year. While in the nursing home, she incurred total costs of $6,000. Medicare paid $3,200 of the costs. Hazel received $3,600 from her long-term care insurance policy (which paid $120 per day while she was in the facility).

The amount that Hazel may exclude is calculated as follows:

Greater of:		
Daily statutory amount of $175 ($175 × 30 days)	$5,250	
Actual cost of the care	6,000	$ 6,000
Less: Amount received from Medicare		(3,200)
Amount of exclusion		$ 2,800

Therefore, Hazel must include $800 ($3,600 − $2,800) of the long-term care benefits received in her gross income. ▼

The exclusion for long-term care insurance is not available if it is provided as part of a cafeteria plan or a flexible spending plan.

MEALS AND LODGING

FURNISHED FOR THE CONVENIENCE OF THE EMPLOYER

As discussed in Chapter 3, income can take any form, including meals and lodging. However, § 119 excludes from income the value of meals and lodging provided to the employee and the employee's spouse and dependents under the following conditions:[34]

- The meals and/or lodging are *furnished* by the employer, on the employer's *business premises*, for the *convenience of the employer*.
- In the case of lodging, the *employee is required* to accept the lodging as a condition of employment.

The courts have construed both of these requirements strictly.

Furnished by the Employer.   The following two questions have been raised with regard to the *furnished by the employer* requirement:

- Who is considered an *employee*?
- What is meant by *furnished*?

The IRS and some courts have reasoned that because a partner is not an employee, the exclusion does not apply to a partner. However, the Tax Court and the Fifth Court of Appeals have ruled in favor of the taxpayer on this issue.[35]

---

[33]§ 7702B.

[34]§ 119(a). The meals and lodging are also excluded from FICA and FUTA tax. *Rowan Companies, Inc. v. U.S.*, 81–1 USTC ¶9479, 48 AFTR2d 81–5115, 101 S.Ct. 2288 (USSC, 1981).

[35]Rev.Rul. 80, 1953–1 C.B. 62; *Comm. v. Doak*, 56–2 USTC ¶9708, 49 AFTR 1491, 234 F.2d 704 (CA–4, 1956); but see *G. A. Papineau*, 16 T.C. 130 (1951); *Armstrong v. Phinney*, 68–1 USTC ¶9355, 21 AFTR2d 1260, 394 F.2d 661 (CA–5, 1968).

The Supreme Court held that a cash meal allowance was ineligible for the exclusion because the employer did not actually furnish the meals.[36] Similarly, one court denied the exclusion where the employer paid for the food and supplied the cooking facilities but the employee prepared the meal.[37]

On the Employer's Business Premises. The *on the employer's business premises* requirement, applicable to both meals and lodging, has resulted in much litigation. The Regulations define business premises as simply "the place of employment of the employee."[38] Thus, the Sixth Court of Appeals held that a residence, owned by the employer and occupied by an employee, two blocks from the motel that the employee managed was not part of the business premises.[39] However, the Tax Court considered an employer-owned house across the street from the hotel that was managed by the taxpayer to be on the business premises of the employer.[40] Perhaps these two cases can be reconciled by comparing the distance from the lodging facilities to the place where the employer's business was conducted. The closer the lodging to the business operations, the more likely the convenience of the employer is served.

For the Convenience of the Employer. The *convenience of the employer* test is intended to focus on the employer's motivation for furnishing the meals and lodging rather than on the benefits received by the employee. If the employer furnishes the meals and lodging primarily to enable the employee to perform his or her duties properly, it does not matter that the employee considers these benefits to be a part of his or her compensation.

The Regulations give the following examples in which the tests for excluding meals are satisfied:[41]

- A waitress is required to eat her meals on the premises during the busy lunch and breakfast hours.
- A bank furnishes a teller meals on the premises to limit the time the employee is away from his or her booth during the busy hours.
- A worker is employed at a construction site in a remote part of Alaska. The employer must furnish meals and lodging due to the inaccessibility of other facilities.

Required as a Condition of Employment. The *employee is required to accept* test applies only to lodging. If the employee's use of the housing would serve the convenience of the employer, but the employee is not required to use the housing, the exclusion is not available.

EXAMPLE 18

VEP, a utilities company, has all of its service personnel on 24-hour call for emergencies. The company encourages its employees to live near the plant so that the employees can respond quickly to emergency calls. Company-owned housing is available rent-free. Only 10 of the employees live in the company housing because it is not suitable for families.

Although the company-provided housing serves the convenience of the employer, it is not required. Therefore, the employees who live in the company housing cannot exclude its value from gross income. ▼

[36]*Comm. v. Kowalski*, 77–2 USTC ¶9748, 40 AFTR2d 6128, 98 S.Ct. 315 (USSC, 1977).
[37]*Tougher v. Comm.*, 71–1 USTC ¶9398, 27 AFTR2d 1301, 441 F.2d 1148 (CA–9, 1971).
[38]Reg. § 1.119–1(c)(1).

[39]*Comm. v. Anderson*, 67–1 USTC ¶9136, 19 AFTR2d 318, 371 F.2d 59 (CA–6, 1966).
[40]*J. B. Lindeman*, 60 T.C. 609 (1973).
[41]Reg. § 1.119–1(f).

In addition, if the employee has the *option* of cash or lodging, the *required* test is not satisfied.

EXAMPLE 19

Khalid is the manager of a large apartment complex. The employer gives Khalid the option of rent-free housing (value of $6,000 per year) or an additional $5,000 per year. Khalid selects the housing option. Therefore, he must include $6,000 in gross income. ▼

OTHER HOUSING EXCLUSIONS

Employees of Educational Institutions. An employee of an educational institution may be able to exclude the value of campus housing provided by the employer. Generally, the employee does not recognize income if he or she pays annual rents equal to or greater than 5 percent of the appraised value of the facility. If the rent payments are less than 5 percent of the value of the facility, the deficiency must be included in gross income.[42]

EXAMPLE 20

Swan University provides on-campus housing for its full-time faculty during the first three years of employment. The housing is not provided for the convenience of the employer. Professor Edith pays $3,000 annual rent for the use of a residence with an appraised value of $100,000 and an annual rental value of $12,000. Edith must recognize $2,000 gross income [.05($100,000) – $3,000 = $2,000] for the value of the housing provided to her. ▼

Ministers of the Gospel. Ministers of the gospel can exclude (1) the rental value of a home furnished as compensation or (2) a rental allowance paid to them as compensation, to the extent the allowance is used to rent or provide a home.[43] The housing or housing allowance must be provided as compensation for the conduct of religious worship, the administration and maintenance of religious organizations, or the performance of teaching and administrative duties at theological seminaries.

EXAMPLE 21

Pastor Bill is allowed to live rent-free in a house owned by the congregation. The annual rental value of the house is $6,000 and is provided as part of the pastor's compensation for ministerial services. Assistant Pastor Olga is paid a $4,500 cash housing allowance. She uses

---

[42]§ 119(d).   [43]§ 107 and Reg. § 1.107–1.

the $4,500 to pay rent and utilities on a home she and her family occupy. Neither Pastor Bill nor Assistant Pastor Olga is required to recognize gross income associated with the housing or housing allowance. ▼

Military Personnel. Military personnel are allowed housing exclusions under various circumstances. Authority for these exclusions generally is found in Federal laws that are not part of the Internal Revenue Code.[44]

OTHER EMPLOYEE FRINGE BENEFITS

SPECIFIC BENEFITS

Congress has enacted exclusions to encourage employers to (1) finance and make available child care facilities, (2) provide athletic facilities for employees, (3) finance certain employees' education, and (4) pay or reimburse child adoption expenses. These provisions are summarized as follows:

- The employee does not have to include in gross income the value of child and dependent care services paid for by the employer and incurred to enable the employee to work. The exclusion cannot exceed $5,000 per year ($2,500 if married and filing separately). For a married couple, the annual exclusion cannot exceed the earned income of the spouse who has the lesser amount of earned income. For an unmarried taxpayer, the exclusion cannot exceed the taxpayer's earned income.[45]
- The value of the use of a gymnasium or other athletic facilities by employees, their spouses, and their dependent children may be excluded from an employee's gross income. The facilities must be on the employer's premises, and substantially all of the use of the facilities must be by employees and their family members.[46]
- Qualified employer-provided educational assistance (tuition, fees, books, and supplies) at the undergraduate level is excludible from gross income. The exclusion is subject to an annual employee statutory ceiling of $5,250.[47]
- The employee can exclude from gross income up to $5,000 of expenses incurred to adopt a child where the adoption expenses are paid or reimbursed by the employer under a qualified adoption assistance program.[48] The limit on the exclusion is increased to $6,000 if the child has special needs (is not physically or mentally capable of caring for himself or herself). The exclusion is phased out as adjusted gross income increases from $75,000 to $115,000.

CAFETERIA PLANS

Generally, if an employee is offered a choice between cash and some other form of compensation, the employee is deemed to have constructively received the cash even when the noncash option is elected. Thus, the employee has gross income regardless of the option chosen.

---

[44]H. Rep. No. 99–841, 99th Cong., 2d Sess., p. 548 (1986). See also § 134.

[45]§ 129. The exclusion applies to the same types of expenses that, if they were paid by the employee (and not reimbursed by the employer), would be eligible for the Credit for Child and Dependent Care Expense discussed in Chapter 11.

[46]§ 132(j)(4).

[47]§ 127. Exclusion treatment applies for courses that begin before June 1, 2000.

[48]§ 137.

An exception to this constructive receipt treatment is provided under the **cafeteria plan** rules. Under such a plan, the employee is permitted to choose between cash and nontaxable benefits (e.g., group term life insurance, health and accident protection, and child care). If the employee chooses the otherwise nontaxable benefits, the cafeteria plan rules enable the benefits to remain nontaxable.[49] Cafeteria plans provide tremendous flexibility in tailoring the employee pay package to fit individual needs. Some employees (usually the younger group) prefer cash, while others (usually the older group) will opt for the fringe benefit program. However, Congress excluded long-term care insurance from the excludible benefits that can be provided under a cafeteria plan.[50] Thus, the employer must provide these benefits separate from the cafeteria plan.

EXAMPLE 22

Hawk Corporation offers its employees (on a nondiscriminatory basis) a choice of any one or all of the following benefits:

Benefit	Cost
Group term life insurance	$ 200
Hospitalization insurance for family members	2,400
Child care payments	1,800
	$4,400

If a benefit is not selected, the employee receives cash equal to the cost of the benefit. Kay, an employee, has a spouse who works for another employer that provides hospitalization insurance but no child care payments. Kay elects to receive the group term life insurance, the child care payments, and $2,400 of cash. Only the $2,400 must be included in Kay's gross income. ▼

FLEXIBLE SPENDING PLANS

Flexible spending plans (often referred to as flexible benefit plans) operate much like cafeteria plans. Under these plans, the employee accepts lower cash compensation in return for the employer agreeing to pay certain costs that the employer can pay without the employee recognizing gross income. For example, assume the employer's health insurance policy does not cover dental expenses. The employee could estimate his or her dental expenses for the upcoming year and agree to a salary reduction equal to the estimated dental expenses. The employer then pays or reimburses the employee for the actual dental expenses incurred, with a ceiling of the amount of the salary reduction. If the employee's actual dental expenses are less than the reduction in cash compensation, the employee cannot recover the difference. Hence, these plans are often referred to as *use or lose* plans. As is the case for cafeteria plans, flexible spending plans cannot be used to pay long-term care insurance premiums.

GENERAL CLASSES OF EXCLUDED BENEFITS

An employer can confer numerous forms and types of economic benefits on employees. Under the all-inclusive concept of income, the benefits are taxable unless one of the provisions previously discussed specifically excludes the item from gross income. The amount of the income is the fair market value of the

---

[49]§ 125.

[50]§ 125(f).

benefit. This reasoning can lead to results that Congress considers unacceptable, as illustrated in the following example.

EXAMPLE 23

Vern is employed in New York as a ticket clerk for Trans National Airlines. He has a sick mother in Miami, Florida, but has no money for plane tickets. Trans National has daily flights from New York to Miami that often leave with empty seats. The cost of a round-trip ticket is $400, and Vern is in the 28% tax bracket. If Trans National allows Vern to fly without charge to Miami, under the general gross income rules, Vern has income equal to the value of a ticket. Therefore, Vern must pay $112 tax (.28 × $400) on a trip to Miami. Because Vern does not have $112, he cannot visit his mother, and the airplane flies with another empty seat. ▼

If Trans National in Example 23 will allow employees to use resources that would otherwise be wasted, why should the tax laws interfere with the employee's decision to take advantage of the available benefit? Thus, to avoid the undesirable results that occur in Example 23 and in similar situations, as well as to create uniform rules for fringe benefits, Congress established six broad classes of nontaxable employee benefits:[51]

- No-additional-cost services.
- Qualified employee discounts.
- Working condition fringes.
- *De minimis* fringes.
- Qualified transportation fringes.
- Qualified moving expense reimbursements.

No-Additional-Cost Services.   Example 23 illustrates the **no-additional-cost service** type of fringe benefit. The services will be nontaxable if all of the following conditions are satisfied:

- The employee receives services, as opposed to property.
- The employer does not incur substantial additional cost, including forgone revenue, in providing the services to the employee.
- The services are offered to customers in the ordinary course of the business in which the employee works.[52]

EXAMPLE 24

Assume that Vern in Example 23 can fly without charge only if the airline cannot fill the seats with paying customers. That is, Vern must fly on standby. Although the airplane may burn slightly more fuel because Vern is on the airplane and Vern may receive the same meal as paying customers, the additional costs would not be substantial. Thus, the trip could qualify as a no-additional-cost service.

On the other hand, assume that Vern is given a reserved seat on a flight that is frequently full. The employer would be forgoing revenue to allow Vern to fly. This forgone revenue would be a substantial additional cost, and thus the benefit would be taxable. ▼

Note that if Vern were employed in a hotel owned by Trans National, the receipt of the airline ticket would be taxable because Vern did not work in that line of business. However, the Code allows the exclusion for reciprocal benefits offered by employers in the same line of business.

---

[51]See, generally, § 132.   [52]Reg. § 1.132–2.

EXAMPLE 25

Grace is employed as a desk clerk for Plush Hotels, Inc. The company and Chain Hotels, Inc., have an agreement that allows any of their employees to stay without charge in either company's resort hotels during the off-season. Grace would not be required to recognize income from taking advantage of the plan by staying in a Chain Hotel. ▼

The no-additional-cost exclusion extends to the employee's spouse and dependent children and to retired and disabled former employees. In the Regulations, the IRS has conceded that partners who perform services for the partnership are employees for purposes of the exclusion.[53] (As discussed earlier in the chapter, the IRS's position is that partners are not employees for purposes of the § 119 meals and lodging exclusion.) However, the exclusion is not allowed to highly compensated employees unless the benefit is available on a nondiscriminatory basis.

Qualified Employee Discounts.   When the employer sells goods or services (other than no-additional-cost benefits just discussed) to the employee for a price that is less than the price charged regular customers, the employee realizes income equal to the discount. However, the discount, referred to as a **qualified employee discount,** can be excluded from the gross income of the employee, subject to the following conditions and limitations:

- The exclusion is not available for real property (e.g., a house) or for personal property of the type commonly held for investment (e.g., common stocks).
- The property or services must be from the same line of business in which the employee works.
- In the case of *property*, the exclusion is limited to the *gross profit component* of the price to customers.
- In the case of *services*, the exclusion is limited to 20 percent of the customer price.[54]

EXAMPLE 26

Silver Corporation, which operates a department store, sells a television set to a store employee for $300. The regular customer price is $500, and the gross profit rate is 25%. The corporation also sells the employee a service contract for $120. The regular customer price for the contract is $150. The employee must recognize $75 income.

Customer price for property	$ 500
Less: Gross profit (25%)	(125)
	$ 375
Employee price	(300)
Income	$ 75
Customer price for service	$ 150
Less: 20 percent	(30)
	$ 120
Employee price	(120)
Income	$ –0–

▼

EXAMPLE 27

Assume the same facts as in Example 26, except the employee is a clerk in a hotel operated by Silver Corporation. Because the line of business requirement is not met, the employee must recognize $200 income ($500 – $300) from the purchase of the television and $30 income ($150 – $120) from the service contract. ▼

---

[53]Reg. § 1.132–1(b).   [54]§ 132(c).

As in the case of no-additional-cost benefits, the exclusion applies to employees (including service partners), employees' spouses and dependent children, and retired and disabled former employees. However, the exclusion does not apply to highly compensated individuals unless the discount is available on a nondiscriminatory basis.

Working Condition Fringes. Generally, an employee is not required to include in gross income the cost of property or services provided by the employer if the employee could deduct the cost of those items if he or she had actually paid for them.[55] These benefits are called **working condition fringes.**

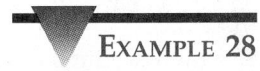

EXAMPLE 28

Mitch is a certified public accountant employed by an accounting firm. The employer pays Mitch's annual dues to professional organizations. Mitch is not required to include the payment of the dues in gross income because if he had paid the dues, he would have been allowed to deduct the amount as an employee business expense (as discussed in Chapter 8). ▼

In many cases, this exclusion merely avoids reporting income and an offsetting deduction. However, in two specific situations, the working condition fringe benefit rules allow an exclusion where the expense would not be deductible if paid by the employee:

- Automobile salespeople are allowed to exclude the value of certain personal use of company demonstrators (e.g., commuting to and from work).[56]
- The employee business expense would be eliminated by the 2 percent floor on miscellaneous deductions under § 67 (see Chapter 9).

Unlike the other fringe benefits discussed previously, working condition fringes can be made available on a discriminatory basis and still qualify for the exclusion.

De Minimis **Fringes.** As the term suggests, *de minimis* **fringe** benefits are so small that accounting for them is impractical. The House Report contains the following examples of *de minimis* fringes:

- The typing of a personal letter by a company secretary, occasional personal use of a company copying machine, occasional company cocktail parties or picnics for employees, occasional supper money or taxi fare for employees because of overtime work, and certain holiday gifts of property with a low fair market value are excluded.
- Subsidized eating facilities (e.g., an employees' cafeteria) operated by the employer are excluded if located on or near the employer's business premises, if revenue equals or exceeds direct operating costs, and if nondiscrimination requirements are met.

When taxpayers venture beyond the specific examples contained in the House Report and the Regulations, there is obviously much room for disagreement as to what is *de minimis*. However, note that except in the case of subsidized eating facilities, the *de minimis* fringe benefits can be granted in a manner that favors highly compensated employees.

---

[55]§ 132(d). [56]§ 132(j)(3).

Qualified Transportation Fringes. The intent of the exclusion for **qualified transportation fringes** is to encourage the use of mass transit for commuting to and from work. Qualified transportation fringes encompass the following transportation benefits provided by the employer to the employee:[57]

1. Transportation in a commuter highway vehicle between the employee's residence and the place of employment.
2. A transit pass.
3. Qualified parking.

Statutory dollar limits are placed on the amount of the exclusion. Categories (1) and (2) above are combined for purposes of applying the limit. In this case, the limit on the exclusion for 1998 is $65 per month. Category (3) has a separate limit. For qualified parking, the limit on the exclusion for 1998 is $175 per month. Both of these dollar limits are indexed annually for inflation.

A *commuter highway vehicle* is any highway vehicle with a seating capacity of at least 6 adults (excluding the driver). In addition, at least 80 percent of the vehicle's use must be for transporting employees between their residences and place of employment.

Qualified parking includes the following:

- Parking provided to an employee on or near the employer's business premises.
- Parking provided to an employee on or near a location from which the employee commutes to work via mass transit, in a commuter highway vehicle, or in a carpool.

Qualified transportation fringes may be provided directly by the employer or may be in the form of cash reimbursements.

EXAMPLE 29   Gray Corporation's offices are located in the center of a large city. The company pays for parking spaces to be used by the company officers. Steve, a vice president, receives $250 of such benefits each month. The parking space rental qualifies as a qualified transportation fringe. Of the $250 benefit received each month by Steve, $175 is excludible from gross income. The balance of $75 is included in his gross income. The same result would occur if Steve paid for the parking and was reimbursed by his employer. ▼

Qualified Moving Expense Reimbursements. Qualified moving expenses that are reimbursed or paid by the employer are excludible from gross income. A qualified moving expense is one that would be deductible under § 217. See the discussion of moving expenses in Chapter 8.

Nondiscrimination Provisions. For no-additional-cost services and qualified employee discounts, if the plan is discriminatory in favor of highly compensated employees, these key employees are denied exclusion treatment. However, the non-highly compensated employees who receive benefits from the plan can still enjoy exclusion treatment for the no-additional-cost services and qualified employee discounts.[58]

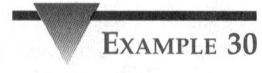

EXAMPLE 30   Dove Company's officers are allowed to purchase goods from the company at a 25% discount. Other employees are allowed only a 15% discount. The company's gross profit margin on these goods is 30%.

---

[57]§ 132(f).   [58]§ 132(j)(1).

Foreign earned income consists of the earnings from the individual's personal services rendered in a foreign country (other than as an employee of the U.S. government). To qualify for the exclusion, the taxpayer must be either of the following:

- A bona fide resident of the foreign country (or countries).
- Present in a foreign country (or countries) for at least 330 days during any 12 consecutive months.[62]

EXAMPLE 32

Sandra's trips to and from a foreign country in connection with her work were as follows:

Arrived in Foreign Country	Arrived in United States
March 10, 1997	February 1, 1998
March 7, 1998	June 1, 1998

During the 12 consecutive months ending on March 10, 1998, Sandra was present in the foreign country for at least 330 days (365 days less 28 days in February and 7 days in March 1998). Therefore, all income earned in the foreign country through March 10, 1998, is eligible for the exclusion. The income earned from March 11, 1998, through May 31, 1998, is also eligible for the exclusion because Sandra was present in the foreign country for 330 days during the 12 consecutive months ending on May 31, 1998. ▼

The exclusion is *limited* to $72,000 in 1998. For married persons, both of whom have foreign earned income, the exclusion is computed separately for each spouse. Community property rules do not apply (the community property spouse is not deemed to have earned one-half of the other spouse's foreign earned income). If all the days in the tax year are not qualifying days, then the taxpayer must compute the maximum exclusion on a daily basis ($72,000 divided by the number of days in the entire year and multiplied by the number of qualifying days).

EXAMPLE 33

Keith qualifies for the foreign earned income exclusion. He was present in France for all of 1998. Keith's salary for 1998 is $90,000. Since all of the days in 1998 are qualifying days, Keith can exclude $72,000 of his $90,000 salary.

Assume instead that only 335 days were qualifying days. Then, Keith's exclusion is limited to $66,082, computed as follows:

$$\$72{,}000 \times \frac{335 \text{ days in foreign country}}{365 \text{ days in the year}} = \$66{,}082$$ ▼

In addition to the exclusion for foreign earnings, the *reasonable housing costs* incurred by the taxpayer and the taxpayer's family in a foreign country in excess of a base amount may be excluded from gross income. The base amount is 16 percent of the U.S. government pay scale for a GS–14 (Step 1) employee, which varies from year to year.[63]

As previously mentioned, the taxpayer may elect to include the foreign earned income in gross income and claim a credit (an offset against U.S. tax) for the foreign tax paid. The credit alternative may be advantageous if the individual's foreign earned income far exceeds the excludible amount so that the foreign taxes paid exceed the U.S. tax on the amount excluded. However, once an election is made,

---

[62]§ 911(d). For the definition of resident, see Reg. § 1.871–2(b). Under the Regulations, a taxpayer is not a resident if he or she is there for a definite period (e.g., until completion of a construction contract).

[63]§ 911(c).

it applies to all subsequent years unless affirmatively revoked. A revocation is effective for the year of the change and the four subsequent years.

INTEREST ON CERTAIN STATE AND LOCAL GOVERNMENT OBLIGATIONS

At the time the Sixteenth Amendment was ratified by the states, there was some question as to whether the Federal government possessed the constitutional authority to tax interest on state and local government obligations. Taxing such interest was thought to violate the doctrine of intergovernmental immunity in that the tax would impair the state and local governments' ability to finance their operations.[64] Thus, interest on state and local government obligations was specifically exempted from Federal income taxation.[65] However, the Supreme Court recently concluded that there is no constitutional prohibition against levying a nondiscriminatory Federal income tax on state and local government obligations.[66] Nevertheless, currently the statutory exclusion still exists.

Obviously, the exclusion of the interest reduces the cost of borrowing for state and local governments. A taxpayer in the 36 percent tax bracket requires only a 5.12 percent yield on a tax-exempt bond to obtain the same after-tax income as a taxable bond paying 8 percent interest [$5.12\% \div (1 - .36) = 8\%$].

ETHICAL CONSIDERATIONS

Tax-Exempt Bonds: Any Redeeming Value?

The exclusion from Federal income tax of state and local bond interest is often criticized as creating a tax haven for the wealthy. These critics, however, often fail to take into account the effect of market forces. In recent months, the long-term tax-exempt rate has been 5.45 percent while the long-term taxable rate for bonds of comparable risk was approximately 6.4 percent.

On the other hand, the state or local governments enjoy a savings in interest costs. To date, Congress has concluded that the benefits gained by the states and municipalities and their residents outweigh any damage to our system of progressive taxation. Do you agree with the proponents or the opponents of the exclusion?

The lower cost for the state and local governments is more than offset by the revenue loss of the Federal government. Also, tax-exempt interest is considered to be a substantial loophole for the very wealthy. For these reasons, bills have been introduced in Congress calling for Federal government subsidies to state and local governments that voluntarily choose to issue taxable bonds. Under the proposals, the tax-exempt status of existing bonds would not be eliminated.

The current exempt status applies solely to state and local government bonds. Thus, income received from the accrual of interest on a condemnation award or

---

[64]*Pollock v. Farmer's Loan & Trust Co.*, 3 AFTR 2602, 15 S.Ct. 912 (USSC, 1895).

[65]§ 103(a).

[66]*South Carolina v. Baker III*, 88–1 USTC ¶9284, 61 AFTR2d 88–995, 108 S.Ct. 1355 (USSC, 1988).

phase-out of the exclusion begins. *Modified adjusted gross income (MAGI)* is adjusted gross income prior to the § 911 foreign earned income exclusion and the educational savings bond exclusion. The threshold amounts are adjusted for inflation each year. For 1998, the phase-out begins at $52,250 ($78,350 on a joint return).[76] The phase-out is completed when MAGI exceeds the threshold amount by more than $15,000 ($30,000 on a joint return). The otherwise excludible interest is reduced by the amount calculated as follows:

$$\frac{MAGI - \$52,250}{\$15,000} \times \frac{\text{Excludible interest}}{\text{before phase-out}} = \frac{\text{Reduction in}}{\text{excludible interest}}$$

On a joint return, $78,350 is substituted for $52,250 (in 1998), and $30,000 is substituted for $15,000.

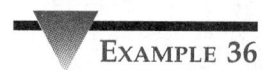

EXAMPLE 36

Assume the same facts as in Example 35, except that Tracy's MAGI for 1998 is $60,000. The phase-out will result in Tracy's interest exclusion being reduced by $861 [($60,000 − $52,250)/ $15,000 × $1,667]. Therefore, Tracy's exclusion is $806 ($1,667 − $861). ▼

QUALIFIED STATE TUITION PROGRAMS

Several states have created programs whereby parents can in effect prepay their child's college tuition. The prepayment serves as a hedge against future increases in tuition. Generally, if the child does not attend college, the parents are refunded their payments plus interest. Upon first impression, these prepaid tuition programs resemble the below-market loans discussed in Chapter 3. That is, assuming the tuition increases, the parent receives a reduction in the child's tuition in exchange for the use of the funds. However, Congress has created an exclusion provision for these programs.[77]

Under a **qualified state tuition program,** the amounts contributed must be used for qualified higher education expenses. These expenses include tuition, fees, books, supplies, room and board, and equipment required for enrollment or attendance at a college, university, or certain vocational schools.

The difference between the amount contributed to the fund and the amount used to pay qualified higher education expenses is included in the gross income of the student (not the parent) using an annuity-type calculation to distinguish between contributions and income.

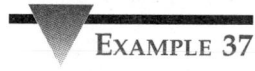

EXAMPLE 37

Agnes paid $15,000 into a qualified state tuition program associated with the future education of her son, Andrew. This amount prepaid four years of tuition ($3,750 per year). By the time Andrew attended college, the annual tuition had increased to $5,000. As Andrew utilizes the tuition prepayment, he must include $1,250 ($5,000 − $3,750) in his gross income each year. ▼

There are no tax consequences to the parent if the amount contributed is used for qualified higher education expenses of the child. If the parent receives a refund (e.g., child does not attend college), however, the excess of the amount refunded over the amount contributed by the parent is included in the parent's gross income.

---

[76]The indexed amounts for 1997 are $50,850 and $76,250.   [77]§ 529.

TAX BENEFIT RULE

3 LEARNING OBJECTIVE
Determine the extent to which receipts can be excluded under the tax benefit rule.

Generally, if a taxpayer obtains a deduction for an item in one year and in a later year recovers all or a portion of the prior deduction, the recovery is included in gross income in the year received.[78]

EXAMPLE 38

A taxpayer deducted as a loss a $1,000 receivable from a customer when it appeared the amount would never be collected. The following year, the customer paid $800 on the receivable. The taxpayer must report the $800 as income in the year it is received. ▼

However, the § 111 **tax benefit rule** provides that no income is recognized upon the recovery of a deduction, or the portion of a deduction, that did not yield a tax benefit in the year it was taken. If the taxpayer in Example 38 had no tax liability in the year of the deduction (e.g., itemized deductions and personal exemptions exceeded adjusted gross income), the recovery would be partially or totally excluded from income in the year of the recovery.[79]

EXAMPLE 39

Before deducting a $1,000 loss from an uncollectible business receivable, Ali had taxable income of $200, computed as follows:

Adjusted gross income	$ 13,300
Itemized deductions and personal exemptions	(13,100)
Taxable income	$ 200

The business bad debt deduction yields only a $200 tax benefit. That is, taxable income is reduced by only $200 (to zero) as a result of the bad debt deduction. Therefore, if the customer

---

[78]§ 111(a).

[79]Itemized deductions are discussed in Chapter 9.

makes a payment on the previously deducted receivable in a subsequent year, only the first $200 is a recovery of a prior deduction and thus is taxable. Any additional amount collected is nontaxable because only $200 of the loss yielded a reduction in taxable income. ▼

INCOME FROM DISCHARGE OF INDEBTEDNESS

4 **LEARNING OBJECTIVE**
Describe the circumstances under which income must be reported from the discharge of indebtedness.

A transfer of appreciated property (fair market value is greater than adjusted basis) in satisfaction of a debt is an event that triggers the realization of income. The transaction is treated as a sale of the appreciated property followed by payment of the debt.[80] Foreclosure by a creditor is also treated as a sale or exchange of the property.[81]

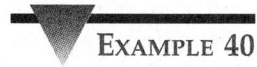
EXAMPLE 40

Juan owed the State Bank $100,000 on an unsecured note. Juan satisfied the note by transferring to the bank common stock with a basis of $60,000 and a fair market value of $100,000. Juan must recognize a $40,000 gain on the transfer. Juan also owed the bank $50,000 on a note secured by land. When Juan's basis in the land was $20,000 and the land's fair market value was $50,000, the bank foreclosed on the loan and took title to the land. Juan must recognize a $30,000 gain on the foreclosure. ▼

In some cases, a creditor will not exercise his or her right of foreclosure and will even forgive a portion of the debt to assure the vitality of the debtor. In such cases, the debtor realizes income from discharge of indebtedness.

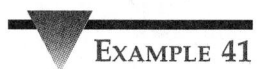
EXAMPLE 41

Brown Corporation is unable to meet the mortgage payments on its factory building. Both the corporation and the mortgage holder are aware of the depressed market for industrial property in the area. Foreclosure would only result in the creditor's obtaining unsalable property. To improve Brown Corporation's financial position and thus improve Brown's chances of obtaining the additional credit from other lenders necessary for survival, the creditor agrees to forgive all amounts past due and to reduce the principal amount of the mortgage. ▼

Generally, the income realized by the debtor from the forgiveness of a debt is taxable.[82] A similar debt discharge (produced by a different creditor motivation) associated with personal use property is illustrated in Example 42.

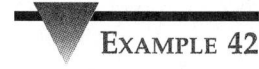
EXAMPLE 42

In 1993, Joyce borrowed $60,000 from National Bank to purchase her personal residence. Joyce agreed to make monthly principal and interest payments for 15 years. The interest rate on the note was 7%. In 1998, when the balance on the note had been reduced through monthly payments to $48,000, the bank offered to accept $45,000 in full settlement of the note. The bank made the offer because interest rates had increased to 11%. Joyce accepted the bank's offer. As a result, Joyce must recognize $3,000 ($48,000 − $45,000) income.[83] ▼

The following discharge of indebtedness situations are subject to special treatment:[84]

---

[80]Reg. § 1.1001–2(a).
[81]*Estate of Delman v. Comm.*, 73 T.C. 15 (1979).
[82]*U.S. v. Kirby Lumber Co.*, 2 USTC ¶814, 10 AFTR 458, 52 S.Ct. 4 (USSC, 1931), codified in § 61(a)(12).

[83]Rev.Rul. 82–202, 1982–1 C.B. 35.
[84]§§ 108 and 1017.

1. Creditors' gifts.
2. Discharges under Federal bankruptcy law.
3. Discharges that occur when the debtor is insolvent.
4. Discharge of the farm debt of a solvent taxpayer.
5. Discharge of **qualified real property business indebtedness.**
6. A seller's cancellation of the buyer's indebtedness.
7. A shareholder's cancellation of the corporation's indebtedness.
8. Forgiveness of loans to students.

If the creditor reduces the debt as an act of *love, affection or generosity*, the debtor has simply received a nontaxable gift (situation 1). Rarely will a gift be found to have occurred in a business context. A businessperson may settle a debt for less than the amount due, but as a matter of business expediency (e.g., high collection costs or disputes as to contract terms) rather than generosity.[85]

In situations 2, 3, 4, and 5, the Code allows the debtor to reduce his or her basis in the assets by the realized gain from the discharge.[86] Thus, the realized gain is merely deferred until the assets are sold (or depreciated). Similarly, in situation 6 (a price reduction), the debtor reduces the basis in the specific assets financed by the seller.[87]

A shareholder's cancellation of the corporation's indebtedness to him or her (situation 7) usually is considered a contribution of capital to the corporation. Thus, the corporation's paid-in capital is increased, and its liabilities are decreased by the same amount.[88]

Many states make loans to students on the condition that the loan will be forgiven if the student practices a profession in the state upon completing his or her studies. The amount of the loan that is forgiven (situation 8) is excluded from gross income.[89]

TAX PLANNING CONSIDERATIONS

5 LEARNING OBJECTIVE
Identify tax planning strategies for obtaining the maximum benefit from allowable exclusions.

The present law excludes certain types of economic gains from taxation. Therefore, taxpayers may find tax planning techniques helpful in obtaining the maximum benefits from the exclusion of such gains. Following are some of the tax planning opportunities made available by the exclusions described in this chapter.

LIFE INSURANCE

Life insurance offers several favorable tax attributes. As discussed in Chapter 3, the annual increase in the cash surrender value of the policy is not taxable (because no income has been actually or constructively received). By borrowing on the policy's cash surrender value, the owner can actually receive the policy's increase in value in cash but without recognizing income.

EMPLOYEE BENEFITS

Generally, employees view accident and health insurance, as well as life insurance, as necessities. Employees can obtain group coverage at much lower rates than individuals would have to pay for the same protection. Premiums paid by the

---

[85]*Comm. v. Jacobson*, 49–1 USTC ¶9133, 37 AFTR 516, 69 S.Ct. 358 (USSC, 1949).
[86]§§ 108(a), (c), (e), and (g). Note that § 108(b) provides that other tax attributes (e.g., net operating loss) will be reduced by the realized gain from the debt discharge prior to the basis adjustment unless the taxpayer elects to apply the basis adjustment first.

[87]§ 108(e)(5).
[88]§ 108(e)(6).
[89]§ 108(f).

TAX IN THE NEWS

WHEN PUBLIC HOUSING AND TAX POLICIES COLLIDE

In testimony before the House Banking Subcommittee on September 17, 1997, Kenneth Kies, chief of staff of the Joint Committee on Taxation, explained how efforts to rescue government-subsidized housing might be thwarted by the tax laws. The Department of Housing and Urban Development wanted to reduce the rent subsidy payments to landlords. However, many of the housing projects eligible for the payments were subject to large amounts of debt. The reduced payments would cause the project owners to default on their mortgages, which were guaranteed by the Federal government. The government did not want to become the landlord. Therefore, the House Banking Subcommittee was considering proposals to restructure the debt by reducing the principal.

Kies explained that altering the mortgages could create income from discharge of indebtedness to the landlord. This would be taxed as ordinary income in the year the debt was restructured. Thus, to prevent the Federal government from becoming a major landlord, a scheme that took into account the tax consequences would have to be developed.

employer can be excluded from the employees' gross income. Because of the exclusion, employees will have a greater after-tax and after-insurance income if the employer pays a lower salary but also pays the insurance premiums.

EXAMPLE 43

Pat receives a salary of $30,000. The company has group insurance benefits, but Pat was required to pay his own premiums as follows:

Hospitalization and medical insurance	$1,400
Term life insurance ($30,000 coverage)	200
Disability insurance	400
	$2,000

To simplify the analysis, assume Pat's tax rate on income is 28%. After paying taxes of $8,400 (.28 × $30,000) and $2,000 for insurance, Pat has $19,600 ($30,000 − $8,400 − $2,000) for his other living needs.

If Pat's employer reduced Pat's salary by $2,000 (to $28,000) but paid his insurance premiums, Pat's tax liability would be only $7,840 ($28,000 × .28). Thus, Pat would have $20,160 ($28,000 − $7,840) to meet his other living needs. The change in the compensation plan would save Pat $560 ($20,160 − $19,600). ▼

Similarly, employees must often incur expenses for child care and parking. The employee can have more income for other uses if the employer pays these costs for the employee but reduces the employee's salary by the cost of the benefits.

The use of cafeteria plans has increased dramatically in recent years. These plans allow employees to tailor their benefits to meet their individual situations. Thus, where both spouses in a married couple are working, duplications of benefits can be avoided and other needed benefits can often be added. If less than all of the employee's allowance is spent, the employee can receive cash.

The meals and lodging exclusion enables employees to receive from their employer what they ordinarily must purchase with after-tax dollars. Although the requirements that the employee live and take his or her meals on the employer's premises limit the tax planning opportunities, the exclusion is an important factor in the employee's compensation in certain situations, (e.g., hotels, motels, restaurants, farms, and ranches).

The employees' discount provision is especially important for manufacturers and wholesalers. Employees of manufacturers can avoid tax on the manufacturer's, wholesaler's, and retailer's markups. The wholesaler's employees can avoid tax on an amount equal to the wholesale and retail markups.

It should be recognized that the exclusion of benefits is generally available only to employees. Proprietors and partners must pay tax on the same benefits their employees receive tax-free. By incorporating and becoming an employee of the corporation, the former proprietor or partner can also receive these tax-exempt benefits. Thus, the availability of employee benefits is a consideration in the decision to incorporate.

INVESTMENT INCOME

Tax-exempt state and local government bonds are almost irresistible investments for many high-income taxpayers. To realize the maximum benefit from the exemption, the investor can purchase zero coupon bonds. Like Series EE U.S. government savings bonds, these investments pay interest only at maturity. The advantage of the zero coupon feature for a tax-exempt bond is that the investor can earn tax-exempt interest on the accumulated principal and interest. If the investor purchases a bond that pays the interest each year, the interest received may be such a small amount that an additional tax-exempt investment cannot be made. In addition, reinvesting the interest may entail transaction costs (broker's fees). The zero coupon feature avoids these problems.

Series EE U.S. government savings bonds can earn tax-exempt interest if the bond proceeds are used for qualified higher education expenses. Many taxpayers can foresee these expenditures being made for their children's educations. In deciding whether to invest in the bonds, however, the investor must take into account the income limitations for excluding the interest from gross income.

KEY TERMS

Accelerated death benefits, 4–6

Accident and health benefits, 4–12

Cafeteria plan, 4–18

Compensatory damages, 4–10

De minimis fringes, 4–21

Death benefits, 4–5

Educational savings bonds, 4–28

Flexible spending plan, 4–18

Foreign earned income exclusion, 4–24

Gift, 4–4

Life insurance proceeds, 4–6

Long-term care insurance, 4–13

Medical savings account (MSA), 4–13

No-additional-cost service, 4–19

Punitive damages, 4–11

Qualified employee discount, 4–20

Qualified real property business indebtedness, 4–32

Qualified state tuition program, 4–29

Qualified transportation fringes, 4–22

Qualified tuition reduction plan, 4–9

Scholarship, 4–8

Tax benefit rule, 4–30

Working condition fringes, 4–21

PROBLEM
MATERIALS

DISCUSSION QUESTIONS

1. In 1995, Grape Corporation constructed a building on property it leased on a long-term basis. In 1997, Grape went bankrupt and forfeited the improvements to the owner of the land. In 1998, the owner sold the land and building. When does the landlord realize income from the improvements made by Grape?

2. Hazel made gifts to her three nephews. The first nephew, Al, received $10,000 cash during Hazel's lifetime. The second nephew, Bob, received $10,000 as a bequest when Hazel died. The third nephew, Carl, was the beneficiary of a $10,000 life insurance policy that Hazel purchased for $4,000. Are Al, Bob, and Carl required to include the amounts they received in gross income?

3. Violet Company gave $500 to each household in the community that had suffered a flood loss. The purpose of the payments was to help the flood victims. If some of the recipients are employees of Violet Company, can the employees exclude the payments from gross income?

4. Hannah, a cash basis taxpayer, died while employed by Purple Corporation. Purple paid Hannah's husband, Wade, $4,600 in sales commissions that Hannah had earned. The company also gave him an additional $3,000 to help with the expenses he had accumulated while caring for his wife in her final days. Are any of the amounts received by Wade includible in his gross income?

5. Matt's truck was stalled on the side of the road. Abby stopped to help and called Al, who agreed to repair the truck for $75. Matt paid Al $75 and Abby $25. The payment to Al was made because of a contractual obligation and therefore is not a gift. The payment to Abby was not made because of a contractual obligation. Does this mean that the payment Abby received is a gift?

6. Ted is diagnosed as having a terminal illness and has substantial liabilities he wants to pay prior to his death. Ted sells his guaranteed renewable term life insurance policy to Purple, Inc., a company that is a state-authorized dealer in such contracts. Ted receives $40,000, and he has paid $16,000 in premiums. Purple pays $3,000 in premiums before Ted dies. Purple collects the $60,000 face value of the policy. How much income are Ted and Purple required to recognize from these transactions?

7. Ed purchased a new tractor for his unincorporated trucking business. The seller, an accrual basis tractor dealer, financed the transaction. Under the financing terms, Ed is required to purchase a term life insurance policy. Ed is the owner of the policy, but he must name the seller as the beneficiary for the amount due on the note at the time of Ed's death. What are the tax consequences to Ed and to the seller if Ed dies and the seller collects from the insurance company an amount equal to the balance due on the note?

8. Black Corporation purchased a $1 million insurance policy on the life of the company's president. The company paid $100,000 of premiums, the president died, and the company collected the face amount of the policy. How much must Black Corporation include in gross income?

9. José is a graduate assistant at State University. He receives $7,000 a year in salary. In addition, tuition of $4,000 is waived. The tuition waiver is available to all full- and part-time employees. The fair market value of José's services is $11,000. How much is José required to include in his gross income?

10. Nancy was injured in an automobile accident caused by a drunk driver. Nancy suffered a broken arm and injuries to her spinal cord. She received damage awards as follows:

Medical expenses	$15,000
Loss of income	4,000
Punitive damages	40,000

None of the medical expenses has been deducted on her tax return. What is Nancy's gross income from the damage awards?

11. Sara was the victim of sexual harassment and collected the following from her employer: $15,000 for lost wages and $50,000 in punitive damages. How much of the damage award of $65,000 must Sara include in her gross income?

12. Holly works in a factory and earns $400 per week. Jill usually works in an office, but she was unable to work for one week because of an infected paper cut sustained at work. Jill collected $400 in workers' compensation as a result of her injury. Is the $400 Holly and Jill each received treated the same for income tax purposes?

13. Pam was hit by an automobile driven by a person under the influence of alcohol. Although Pam's injuries were minor (she did not go to the hospital or visit a doctor), she has recurring nightmares about the accident. Over the past 12 months, she has spent more than $6,000 for psychological therapy. Although she had problems before the accident, the recurring nightmares brought her to the realization that she needed professional help. Pam has not filed a lawsuit, but the driver of the automobile, who is very wealthy, "wants to do the right thing." The driver has offered Pam $30,000 as a settlement. He believes that this is more than she is entitled to under the law, but feels a great deal of remorse about all of the grief he has caused her. Pam is concerned about the tax consequences of the settlement offer. What are the relevant tax issues raised by these facts?

14. Wes purchases an accident and health insurance plan that was advertised in the Sunday newspaper. The annual premiums are $400. During the year, Wes received payments of $1,200 under the plan.
    a. How much of the $1,200 must Wes include in his gross income?
    b. Would the tax consequences differ if the $1,200 represented amounts paid by the insurance company to replace lost wages while Wes was hospitalized?

15. What nontaxable fringe benefits are available to employees that are not available to partners and proprietors?

16. Paula is employed by a telemarketing firm that pays a fixed amount for unlimited long-distance telephone calls. Employees are allowed to use the toll-free line for 5 minutes each month at no charge to the employee. The normal charge for the calls Paula made during the year was $75. How much is Paula required to include in gross income?

17. Gary is employed by Pelican, Inc., an automobile manufacturing company. Pelican sells Gary a new automobile at company cost of $12,000. A dealer would have been charged $14,000, and the retail price of the automobile is $17,000. What is Gary's gross income from the purchase of the automobile?

18. Eagle Life Insurance Company pays its employees $.25 per mile for driving their personal automobiles to and from work. The company reimburses each employee who rides the bus $45 a month for the cost of a pass. Tom collected $60 for his automobile mileage, and Ted received $45 as reimbursement for the cost of a bus pass.
    a. What are the effects of the above on Tom and Ted's gross income?
    b. Assume that Tom and Ted are in the 28% marginal tax bracket, and the actual before-tax cost for Tom to drive to and from work is $.25 per mile. What are Tom and Ted's after-tax costs of commuting to and from work?

19. Zack works for Blue Pest Control, which offers a discount on its extermination services to its employees: officers receive a 50% discount, and all other employees receive a 30% discount. Zack, who is not an officer, had the company treat his home for termites and paid $280 for the service that is normally priced at $400. Zack's supervisor, an officer, had her home treated for carpenter ants and paid $500 for the service that is normally priced at $1,000. How much, if any, will Zack and his supervisor have to include in gross income for the services they received?

20. Several of Egret Company's employees have asked the company to create a hiking trail that employees could use during their lunch hours. The company owns vacant land that is being held for future expansion, but would have to spend approximately $50,000 if it were to make a trail. Nonemployees would be allowed to use the facility as part

of the company's effort to build strong community support. What are the relevant tax issues for the employees?

21. Marla worked for Robin Industries, Inc., and earned $80,000 in 1998. She spent 365 days out of the United States during 1998 working in a foreign country. Marla wants to exclude her foreign-earned income from U.S. taxation if possible. Does Marla qualify for doing so? If she does, how much of her income will be taxable in the United States?

22. Donna and George are married, file a joint return, and are in the 28% marginal tax bracket. They would like to save for their child's education. Currently, Amber, Inc. bonds are yielding 6%. Comparable Series EE U.S. government bonds are yielding 5%. Which investment would be preferable considering Donna and George's objective?

23. Maria, a cash method farmer, owns stock in a farmers' cooperative. During 1997, she purchased from the cooperative $80,000 of feed and fertilizer, which she expensed. This was a very good year for Maria's farm, which produced a $100,000 net profit. The farm was Maria's only source of income. The cooperative also had a very good year in 1997 and declared a patronage dividend that was distributed in early 1998. Maria's dividend was $5,000. What effect does the patronage dividend have on her gross income?

24. Arthur paid $20,000 to the Virginia State Tuition Program. Under the program, if Rachel, his daughter, enrolls in a state college or university, her tuition will be paid by the program. What are the tax consequences to Arthur and to Rachel of the program paying her tuition of $7,500 each year for four years?

25. In 1998, Mary received a $2,000 sales commission. However, in 1999, her employer discovered that Mary should have received only a $1,500 commission in 1998. Therefore, the employer withheld $500 from Mary's 1999 commission. Mary's standard deduction and personal exemption for 1998 exceeded her gross income. What effect would the tax benefit rule have on Mary's gross income for 1999?

26. Ida purchased a ranch. She gave the seller $50,000 cash and a 7% note for $200,000. When the principal on the note had been reduced to $180,000, the seller agreed to accept $165,000 in retirement of the debt. The creditor made the offer because interest rates had increased substantially. Ida was not undergoing bankruptcy and was not insolvent. Did Ida realize income from retiring the debt and, if so, is she required to include the amount in her gross income?

 27. Harry has experienced financial difficulties as a result of his struggling business. He has been behind on his mortgage payments for the last six months. The mortgage holder, who is a friend of Harry's, has offered to accept $80,000 in full payment of the $100,000 owed on the mortgage and payable over the next 10 years. The interest rate of the mortgage is 7%, and the market rate is now 8%. What tax issues are raised by the creditor's offer?

PROBLEMS

28. During the year, Wally received the following:

    • Gift of a car worth $32,000 from his fiancée.

    • Inheritance of stock worth $25,000 from his Aunt Jane's estate. Aunt Jane's basis for the stock was $10,000.

    • Proceeds (cash surrender value) of $20,000 from a life insurance policy he canceled to pay off credit-card debts. Wally had paid total premiums of $17,000.

    Determine the effect on Wally's gross income.

29. Determine the taxable life insurance proceeds in the following cases:
    a. When José died, his wife collected $50,000 on a group term insurance policy purchased by José's employer. José had never included the premiums in gross income.

b. The Cardinal Software Company purchased an insurance policy on the life of a key employee. The company paid $50,000 in premiums and collected $500,000 of insurance proceeds.

c. When Barbara died, she and her husband owed $15,000 on a loan. Under the terms of the loan, Barbara was required to purchase life insurance to pay the creditor the amount due at the date of Barbara's death. The creditor collected from the life insurance company the amount due at the time of Barbara's death. Is the creditor required to recognize income from the collection of the life insurance proceeds?

30. Laura was recently diagnosed as having a terminal case of cancer and has started chemotherapy treatments. She would like to pay all of her debts and make some charitable contributions prior to her death. This will require approximately $50,000. She is considering selling some stock she owns with a cost of $10,000 and a fair market value of $50,000. She also owns a term life insurance policy with a face amount of $100,000. The Viatical Benefits Company has announced that it will purchase any policy from a terminally ill patient for $.50 on the dollar. The company will then pay the premiums until death and will receive the face amount of the policy upon Laura's death. Laura is in the 28% marginal tax bracket. Laura has consulted you regarding the alternatives. What do you recommend?

31. Determine whether the taxpayer has gross income in each of the following situations:

a. Jim is a waiter in a restaurant. The rule of thumb is that a customer should leave the waiter a tip equal to 15% of the customer's bill for food and beverages. Jim collected $6,000 in tips during the year.

b. Tara works at a grocery store, bagging groceries and carrying them to the customers' automobiles. Her employer posts a sign saying that the employees are paid by the hour and the customer is not expected to tip them. Tara received $1,800 in tips from customers.

c. Sheila worked at a hotel. Her home was damaged by a fire. Sheila's employer allowed her to stay at the hotel for no charge until she could return to her home. The normal charge for the room Sheila occupied during this period was $500, and the hotel had several vacant rooms.

32. Donald died at age 35. He was married and had four minor children. Donald's employer, Lark Painting Company, made payments to his wife as follows:

Donald's accrued salary at date of death	$4,000
A payment authorized by the board of directors to help his wife pay debts accumulated by Donald	7,000

In addition, Donald's wife was the beneficiary of her husband's life insurance policy of $50,000. Lark Painting Company had paid for the policy. Donald had excluded all of the premiums paid by the employer from gross income as group term life insurance. His wife left the insurance proceeds with the insurance company and elected to receive an annuity of $4,000 each year for life. Her life expectancy is 40 years. She collected one $4,000 payment at the end of the current year. A joint return was filed in the year of Donald's death. Which of the above amounts must be included in gross income?

33. The Swan Partnership, a financial consulting company, has a cross-purchase agreement that requires the partnership to purchase a deceased partner's interest. The partner's interest is to be purchased from the deceased partner's estate with the price being 150% of the book value at the time of the partner's death. To finance the cross-purchase agreement, the partnership carries an insurance policy on the life of each of its partners. During the year, a partner died. The partnership collected the $250,000 face amount of the life insurance policy on the deceased partner and purchased her interest for $225,000. Swan had paid $100,000 in premiums on the policy. What are the tax consequences of these transactions for the deceased partner and for the partnership?

34. Walt made the all-state football team during his junior and senior years in high school. He accepted an athletic scholarship from State University. The scholarship provided the following:

Tuition and fees	$8,000
Room and board	7,500
Books and supplies	1,000

Determine the effect of the scholarship on Walt's gross income.

35. Alejandro was awarded an academic scholarship to State University. He received $5,000 in August and $6,000 in December 1998. Alejandro had enough personal savings to pay all expenses as they came due. Alejandro's expenditures for the relevant period were as follows:

Tuition, August 1998	$2,900
Tuition, December 1998	3,200
Room and board	
August–December 1998	3,000
January–May 1999	2,400
Books and educational supplies	
August–December 1998	800
January–May 1999	950

Determine the effect on Alejandro's gross income for 1998 and 1999.

36. Liz sued an overzealous bill collector and received the following settlement:

Damage to her automobile the collector attempted to repossess	$ 1,000
Physical damage to her arm caused by the collector	8,000
Loss of income while her arm was healing	6,000
Punitive damages	30,000

    a. What effect does the settlement have on Liz's gross income?

    b. Assume Liz also collected $40,000 of damages for slander to her personal reputation caused by the bill collector misrepresenting the facts to Liz's employer and other creditors. Is this $40,000 included in Liz's gross income?

37. Determine the taxpayer's taxable damages in each of the following cases:

    a. Orange Corporation collected $500,000 for damages to its business reputation.

    b. Don collected $100,000 in lost wages caused by age discrimination by his employer. Under the relevant law, a successful plaintiff can recover only lost wages.

    c. Kirby was injured in an automobile accident and collected $10,000 for loss of the use of his left arm, $15,000 for pain and suffering, $9,000 in lost wages, $5,000 for medical expenses, and $10,000 of punitive damages. Kirby had deducted none of the medical expenses.

    d. Nell received $10,000 of damages for invasion of her privacy by a photographer and $5,000 of punitive damages.

    e. Joanne received compensatory damages of $50,000 and punitive damages of $200,000 from a cosmetic surgeon who botched her nose job.

38. Rex, age 45, is an officer of Blue Company, which provided him with the following nondiscriminatory fringe benefits in 1998:

    a. Hospitalization insurance for Rex and his dependents. The cost of coverage for Rex was $450, and the additional cost for Rex's dependents was $400.

    b. Reimbursement of $700 from an uninsured medical reimbursement plan available to all employees.

    c. Group term life insurance protection of $120,000. (Each employee received coverage equal to twice his or her annual salary.)

    d. Salary continuation payments of $2,600 while Rex was hospitalized for an illness.

While Rex was ill, he collected $1,600 on a salary continuation insurance policy he had purchased. Determine the amounts Rex must include in gross income.

39. The UVW Union and HON Corporation are negotiating contract terms. Assume the union members are in the 28% marginal tax bracket and all benefits are provided on a nondiscriminatory basis. Write a letter to the UVW Union members explaining the tax consequences of the options discussed below. The union's address is 905 Spruce Street, Washington, D.C. 20227.
    a. The company would impose a $100 deductible on medical insurance benefits. Most employees incur more than $100 each year in medical expenses.
    b. Employees would get an additional paid holiday with the same annual income (the same pay but less work).
    c. An employee who did not need health insurance (because the employee's spouse works and receives family coverage) would be allowed to receive the cash value of the coverage.

40. Sally and Bill are married and file a joint return. In 1998, Bill, an accountant, has a salary of $75,000, and Sally receives a salary of $25,000 as an apartment manager. What are the tax consequences of the following benefits that Bill and Sally's employers provide?
    a. Bill receives a reimbursement of $5,000 for child care expenses. Sally and Bill have three children who are not yet school age.
    b. Bill and Sally are provided a free membership at a local fitness and exercise club that allows them to attend three aerobic exercise sessions per week. The value of this type of membership is $1,600 per year.
    c. Bill is provided free parking at work. The value of the parking is $1,800 per year.
    d. Sally is provided with a free apartment. Living in this apartment is a condition of her employment. Similar apartments rent for $1,200 per month.

41. Determine the taxpayer's gross income for each of the following:
    a. Alice is the manager of a plant. The company owns a house one mile from the plant (rental value of $6,000) that Alice is allowed to occupy.
    b. Pam works for an insurance company that allows employees to eat in the cafeteria for $.50 a meal. Generally, the cost to the insurance company of producing a meal is $5.00, and a comparable meal could be purchased for $4.00. Pam ate 150 meals in the cafeteria during the year.
    c. Wade is a Methodist minister and receives a housing allowance of $600 per month from his church. Wade is buying his home and uses the $600 to make house payments ($450) and to pay utilities ($150).
    d. Floyd is a college professor and lives in campus housing. He is not charged rent. The fair market value of the house is $100,000, and the annual rental value is $7,200.

42. Does the taxpayer recognize gross income in the following situations?
    a. Ann is a registered nurse working in a community hospital. She is not required to take her lunch on the hospital premises, but she can eat in the cafeteria at no charge. The hospital adopted this policy to encourage employees to stay on the premises and be available in case of emergencies. During the year, Ann ate most of her meals on the premises. The total value of those meals was $750.
    b. Ira is the manager of a hotel. His employer will allow him to live in one of the rooms rent-free or to receive a $600 per month cash allowance for rent. Ira elected to live in the hotel.
    c. Seth is a forest ranger and lives in his employer's cabin in the forest. He is required to live there, and because there are no restaurants nearby, the employer supplies Seth with groceries that he cooks and eats on the premises.
    d. Rocky is a partner in the BAR Ranch (a partnership). He is the full-time manager of the ranch. BAR has a business purpose for Rocky's living on the ranch.

43. Betty is considering taking an early retirement offered by her employer. She would receive $2,000 per month, indexed for inflation. However, she would no longer be able to use the company's health facilities, and she would be required to pay her hospitalization insurance of $7,800 each year. Betty and her husband will file a joint return and take the standard deduction. She currently receives a salary of $40,000 a year, and her employer pays for all of her hospitalization insurance. If she retires, Betty would not be able to use her former employer's exercise facilities because of the commuting

distance. She would like to continue to exercise, however, and will therefore join a health club at a cost of $50 per month. Betty and her husband have other sources of income and are in and will remain in the 28% marginal tax bracket. She currently pays Social Security taxes of 7.65% on her salary, but her retirement pay would not be subject to this tax. She will earn about $11,000 a year from a part-time job. Betty would like to know whether she should accept the early retirement offer.

44. Sparrow, Inc., has a wide variety of fringe benefits available to its employees. However, not all of the employees actually need the benefits. For example, some employees have working spouses whose employers provide health insurance benefits for the employee's families. In addition, Sparrow reimburses up to $5,000 for child care costs, but not all of the employees have children. Some employees have expressed a strong interest in long-term care insurance. Sparrow's management has asked you to write a memo explaining how the company can accommodate the varying needs of its employees at the lowest after-tax cost to the employee. Sparrow's address is 300 Harbor Drive, Vermillion, SD 57069.

45. Thrush Corporation has 10 employees, three of whom are shareholders in the corporation. The company is considering adopting a group health insurance plan. Some of the employees have even expressed a willingness to take a cut in pay in order to obtain health insurance. Three of the employees are interested in long-term care insurance. Fred Thrush, the majority shareholder, has asked your advice about structuring insurance benefits in a favorable tax manner. He is vaguely familiar with flexible benefit plans and has read some articles on medical savings accounts. Write a letter to Mr. Thrush, explaining the possible tax features of a plan to suit the company's and employees' needs. Thrush's address is 500 Fern Avenue, Scranton, PA 18509.

46. Tara's employer provides a flexible benefits plan. Under the plan, medical and dental expenses incurred during the year that are not covered by the company's group health insurance plan will be paid by the flexible benefits plan. At the first of each year, the employee must set the amount to be covered by the plan. The employee's monthly salary is reduced by one-twelfth of the identified flexible benefit amount for the year. Tara thinks it is highly unlikely that she can accurately estimate her medical and dental expenses not covered by the company's group health insurance plan, but she feels these costs will probably be in the range of $1,500 to $2,500. She expects to be in the 28% marginal tax bracket. Tara would like your advice regarding how much she should reduce her salary in exchange for the expanded dental and medical benefits.

47. Snowbird Corporation would like you to review its employee fringe benefits program with regard to the effects of the plan on the company's president (Polly), who is also the majority shareholder:
   a. All employees receive free tickets to State University football games. Polly is seldom able to attend the games and usually gives her tickets to her nephew. The cost of Polly's tickets for the year was $75.
   b. The company pays all parking fees for its officers but not for other employees. The company paid $1,200 for Polly's parking for the year.
   c. Employees are allowed to use the copy machine for personal purposes as long as the privilege is not abused. Polly is president of a trade association and made extensive use of the copy machine to prepare mailings to members of the association. The cost of the copies was $900.
   d. The company is in the household moving business. Employees are allowed to ship goods without charge whenever there is excess space on a truck. Polly purchased a dining room suite for her daughter. Company trucks delivered the furniture to the daughter. Normal freight charges would have been $600.
   e. The company has a storage facility for household goods. Officers are allowed a 20% discount on charges for storing their goods. All other employees are allowed a 10% discount. Polly's discounts for the year totaled $400.

48. George, a U.S. citizen, is employed by Pelican, Inc., a global company. His salary for 1998 is $66,000 and his 1999 salary is $85,000. George's first foreign assignment is to St. Petersburg, Russia, and began on July 1, 1998. He works in St. Petersburg until

December 31, 1999. Being a workaholic, George did not take any vacation during this period.

a. Compute George's 1998 salary that is includible in his gross income.

b. Compute George's 1999 salary that is includible in his gross income.

49. Determine Hazel's gross income from the following receipts for the year:

Gain on sale of Augusta County bonds	$ 300
Interest on U.S. government savings bonds	700
Interest on state income tax refund	225
Interest on Augusta County bonds	800
Patronage dividend from Potato Growers Cooperative	1,200

The patronage dividend was received in March of the current year for amounts paid and deducted in the previous year as expenses of Hazel's profitable cash basis farming business.

50. Determine Jack's gross income from the following items:

a. Jack owns 100 shares of Roadrunner Company common stock. The company has a dividend reinvestment plan. Under the plan, Jack can receive an $18 cash dividend or an additional share of stock with a fair market of $18. Jack elected to take the stock.

b. Jack owns 100 shares of Bat Corporation. The company declared a dividend, and Jack was to receive an additional share of the company's common stock with a fair market value of $18. Jack did not have the option to receive cash. However, a management group announced a plan to repurchase all available shares for $18 each. The offer was part of a takeover defense.

c. Jack also collected $125 on a corporate debenture. The corporation had been in bankruptcy for several years. Jack had correctly deducted the cost of the bond in a prior year because the bankruptcy judge had informed the bondholders they would not receive anything in the final liquidation. Later the company collected on an unanticipated claim and had the funds to make partial payment on the bonds.

51. Lynn Schwartz recently inherited $25,000. She is considering using the money to finance a college education for her 5-year-old son. She currently earns $45,000 a year. She asks your advice about tax-favored programs for college savings. Write a letter to Lynn advising her as to her options. Lynn's address is 100 Myrtle Cove, Fairfield, CT 06432.

52. Starting in 1990, Chuck and Luane have been purchasing Series EE bonds in their name to use for the higher education of their daughter (Susie who currently is age 18). During the year, they cash in $12,000 of the bonds to use for freshman year tuition, fees, and room and board. Of this amount, $5,000 represents interest. Of the $12,000, $8,000 is used for tuition and fees, and $4,000 is used for room and board. Their AGI, before the educational savings bond exclusion, is $85,000.

a. Determine the tax consequences for Chuck and Luane, who will file a joint return, and for Susie.

b. Assume that Chuck and Luane purchased the bonds in Susie's name. Determine the tax consequences for Chuck and Luane and for Susie.

c. How would your answer for (a) change if Chuck and Luane file separate returns?

53. Carlos made payments to the Qualified State Tuition Program for the benefit of his son, Ramon. Carlos contributed $4,000 each year for a four-year period. This will satisfy Ramon's tuition and fees for four years of college. At the time of Ramon's freshman year, the tuition and fees have increased to $6,000 per year. Determine the effect on Carlos and Ramon's gross income for Ramon's freshman year.

54. How does the tax benefit rule apply in the following cases?

a. In 1998, Wilma paid Vera $5,000 for locating a potential client. The deal fell through, and in 1999, Vera refunded the $5,000 to Wilma.

b. In 1998, Wilma paid an attorney $300 for services in connection with a title search. Because the attorney was negligent, Wilma incurred some additional costs in acquiring the land. In 1999, the attorney refunded his $300 fee to Wilma.

c. In 1998, Wilma received a $90 dividend with respect to 1998 premiums on her life insurance policy.

d. In 1999, Wilma, a cash basis farmer, received a $400 patronage dividend with respect to 1998 purchases of cattle feed.

55. Mary and her two sisters, Cary and Gladys, were injured in a car accident in 1998, and each sustained injuries requiring $1,200 in medical expenses. Because the claim was not settled until 1999, each sister had completed her 1998 income tax return before the settlement. Mary does not itemize deductions. Cary does itemize deductions, but the $1,200 medical expense did not exceed the 7.5%-of-AGI threshold; consequently, the deduction did not result in a reduction of her tax liability. Gladys also itemizes deductions. Because of other medical expenses, the $1,200 expense pushed her $800 over the 7.5%-of-AGI threshold. Therefore, Gladys benefited from the deduction by having her taxes reduced. In 1999, each sister received a $1,200 insurance settlement for her injuries. How much of the $1,200 settlement received does each sister need to include in gross income?

56. Fran, who is in the 36% tax bracket, recently collected $100,000 on a life insurance policy she carried on her father. She currently owes $120,000 on her personal residence and $120,000 on business property. National Bank holds the mortgage on both pieces of property and has agreed to accept $100,000 in complete satisfaction of either mortgage. The interest rate on the mortgages is 8%, and both mortgages are payable over 10 years. What would be the tax consequences of each of the following alternatives, assuming Fran currently deducts the mortgage interest on her tax return?
    a. Retire the mortgage on the residence.
    b. Retire the mortgage on the business property.

    Which alternative should Fran select?

57. Robin Company is experiencing financial troubles and is considering negotiating the following with its creditors. Determine the tax consequences to Robin of the following plan:
    a. The Motor Finance Company will cancel $1,500 in accrued interest. Robin had deducted the interest in the prior year. Motor Finance Company will also reduce the principal on the note by $1,000. The note financed the purchase of equipment from a local dealer.
    b. The Trust Land Company, which sold Robin land and buildings, will reduce the mortgage on the building by $15,000.
    c. Ridge, the sole shareholder in the corporation, will cancel a $50,000 receivable from the corporation in exchange for additional stock.

CUMULATIVE PROBLEMS

58. Albert S. Moore (Social Security number 363–22–1141) is 35 years old and is married to Bonnie B. Moore (Social Security number 259–50–4284). The Moores live at 215 Harper's Road, Newport News, VA 23100. They file a joint return and have two dependent children (Bobby and Cindy). In 1998, Albert and Bonnie had the following transactions:
    a. Albert received $90,000 in salary from Plum Steel Company. He worked on a construction project in Mexico from July 1, 1997, through December 31, 1998. Withholding for Federal income tax was $11,000. The proper amount of FICA taxes was withheld.
    b. Albert and Bonnie received $1,200 of interest on U.S. government bonds and $600 of interest on Montgomery County School bonds.
    c. Bonnie was involved in an automobile accident in 1997 and incurred $12,000 of medical expenses. Insurance paid $8,000 of the expenses, and Albert and Bonnie deducted the remaining $4,000 on their 1997 return. During 1998, Bonnie received a settlement from the other driver's insurance company. She received $12,000 for her medical expenses, $65,000 as compensatory damages for the physical injury, and $35,000 of punitive damages.

    d. Bonnie received 10 shares of Cherry, Inc., as a stock dividend. The shares received had a fair market value of $360. Bonnie had the option of receiving cash equal to the value of the shares, but chose not to do so.

    e. Albert paid $9,000 of alimony to his first wife, Rosa T. Monroe (Social Security number 800–60–2580).

    f. Albert and Bonnie's itemized deductions were as follows:

- State income taxes paid and withheld totaled $2,400. In addition, a $600 overpayment for their 1997 state taxes (deducted on the 1997 Federal return) was applied to their 1998 liability.

- Real estate taxes on their principal residence were $1,500.

- Interest on their principal residence was $3,600.

- Cash contributions to the church were $2,200.

Part 1—Tax Computation
Compute the Moores' net tax payable (or refund due) for 1998. Suggested software (if available): *TurboTax*.

Part 2—Tax Planning
Assume the Moores provided you with the above information late in 1998. They are considering selling Orange, Inc., stock purchased in November 1998 for $6,000. The stock has a present and projected fair market value of $4,000. The sale could occur in late 1998 or early 1999. They do not expect any major changes in their income situation, except Albert's salary will increase to $125,000 and he will be working in the United States for the entire year. Write a letter to the Moores that contains your advice and prepare a memo for the tax files.

59. Alfred E. Old and Beulah Crane, each age 42, married on September 7, 1997. Alfred and Beulah will file a joint return for 1997. Alfred's Social Security number is 262–60–3815. Beulah's Social Security number is 259–68–4285, and she will adopt "Old" as her married name. They live at 211 Brickstone Drive, Atlanta, GA 30304.

Alfred was divorced from Sarah Old in March 1996. Under the divorce agreement, Alfred is to pay Sarah $800 per month for the next 10 years or until Sarah's death, whichever occurs first. Alfred pays Sarah $9,600 in 1997. In addition, in January 1997, Alfred pays Sarah $50,000, which is designated as being for her share of the marital property. Also, Alfred is responsible for all prior years' income taxes and is to receive any refund of overpaid taxes for prior years. Sarah's Social Security number is 444–10–2211.

Alfred's salary for 1997 is $62,000, and his employer, Cherry, Inc., provides him with group term life insurance equal to twice his annual salary. His employer withheld $10,300 for Federal income taxes, $3,000 for state income taxes, and the appropriate amount for FICA.

Beulah recently graduated from law school and is employed by Legal Aid Society, Inc., as a public defender. She receives a salary of $36,000 in 1997. Her employer withheld $5,200 for Federal income taxes, $2,100 for state income taxes, and the appropriate amount for FICA.

Beulah has $1,500 in dividends on Yellow Corporation stock she inherited. Beulah receives a $600 refund of 1996 state income taxes. She used the standard deduction on her 1996 Federal income tax return. Alfred receives a $1,100 refund of his 1996 state income taxes. He itemized deductions on his 1996 Federal income tax return. Alfred and Beulah pay $4,300 interest and $1,200 property taxes on their personal residence in 1997. Their charitable contributions total $800 (all to their church).

Compute the Olds' net tax payable (or refund due) for 1997. If you use tax forms for your solution, you will need Form 1040 and Schedules A and B. Suggested software (if available): *TurboTax*.

Research Problems for this chapter appear at the end of Chapter 28.

TEAM PROJECT: ARTHUR ANDERSEN TAX CHALLENGE CASES

For more information on the Arthur Andersen Tax Challenge Cases, refer to Chapter 1, page 1–37.

Information related to tax issues and problems that are discussed in this chapter may be found in the

Day and Ball case on pages 3, 5, 17, and 30
Fence case on pages: None

Read and analyze the case you have been assigned and *identify* any issues and problems that are related to material covered in this chapter. If the information provided in the case is complete, prepare answers for this part of the case at this time. If you need information that is contained in the later parts of the case, write a memo summarizing the questions or problems so you can prepare a complete answer at a later date.

DEDUCTIONS AND LOSSES: IN GENERAL

LEARNING OBJECTIVES

After completing Chapter 5, you should be able to:

1. Differentiate between deductions *for* and *from* adjusted gross income and understand the relevance of the differentiation.

2. Describe the cash and accrual methods of accounting.

3. Apply the Internal Revenue Code deduction disallowance provisions associated with the following: public policy limitations, political activities, excessive executive compensation, investigation of business opportunities, hobby losses, vacation home rentals, payment of others' expenses, personal expenditures, capital expenditures, related-party transactions, and expenses related to tax-exempt income.

4. Identify tax planning opportunities for maximizing deductions and minimizing the disallowance of deductions.

CLASSIFICATION OF DEDUCTIBLE EXPENSES

1 ▼ LEARNING OBJECTIVE
Differentiate between deductions *for* and *from* adjusted gross income and understand the relevance of the differentiation.

The tax law has an all-inclusive definition of income; that is, income from whatever source derived is includible in gross income. Income cannot be excluded unless there is a specific statement to that effect in the Internal Revenue Code.

Similarly, deductions are disallowed unless a specific provision in the tax law permits them. The inclusive definition of income and the exclusive definition of deductions may not seem fair to taxpayers, but it is the structure of the tax law.

The courts have held that whether and to what extent deductions are allowed depends on legislative grace.[1] In other words, any exclusions from income and all deductions are gifts from Congress!

It is important to classify deductible expenses as **deductions for adjusted gross income** (AGI) or **deductions from adjusted gross income.** Deductions *for* AGI can be claimed whether or not the taxpayer itemizes. Deductions *from* AGI result in a tax benefit only if they exceed the taxpayer's standard deduction. If itemized deductions (*from* AGI) are less than the standard deduction, they provide no tax benefit.

EXAMPLE 1

Steve is a self-employed CPA. Ralph is one of Steve's employees. During the year, Steve and Ralph incur the following expenses:

	Steve	Ralph
Dues to American Institute of CPAs and State Society of CPAs	$ 400	$ 300
Subscriptions to professional journals	500	200
Registration fees for tax conferences	800	800
	$1,700	$1,300

---

[1]*New Colonial Ice Co. v. Helvering,* 4 USTC ¶1292, 13 AFTR 1180, 54 S.Ct. 788 (USSC, 1934).

Steve does not reimburse any of his employees for dues, subscriptions, or educational programs.

Steve's expenses are classified as a deduction *for* AGI. Therefore, he can deduct the $1,700 on his Federal income tax return. Ralph's expenses are classified as deductions *from* AGI. Ralph will be able to benefit from the $1,300 of expenses on his Federal income tax return only if he itemizes deductions. If he takes the standard deduction instead, the $1,300 of expenses will have no effect on the calculation of his taxable income. Even if Ralph does itemize deductions, he must reduce the $1,300 of expenses, which are classified as miscellaneous itemized deductions, by 2% of his AGI. As this example illustrates, whether a deduction is classified as *for* AGI or *from* AGI can affect the benefit the taxpayer receives from the deduction. ▼

Deductions *for* AGI are also important in determining the *amount* of itemized deductions because many itemized deductions are limited to amounts in excess of specified percentages of AGI. Examples of itemized deductions that are limited by AGI are medical expenses and personal casualty losses. Itemized deductions that are deductible only to the extent that they exceed a specified percentage of AGI are increased when AGI is decreased. Likewise, when AGI is increased, these itemized deductions are decreased.

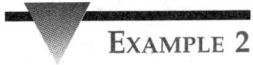

EXAMPLE 2

Tina earns a salary of $20,000 and has no other income. She itemizes deductions during the current year. Medical expenses for the year are $1,800. Since medical expenses are deductible only to the extent they exceed 7.5% of AGI, Tina's medical expense deduction is $300 [$1,800 − (7.5% × $20,000)]. If Tina had a $2,000 deduction *for* AGI, her medical expense deduction would be $450 [$1,800 − (7.5% × $18,000)], or $150 more. If the $2,000 deduction was *from* AGI, her medical expense deduction would remain $300 since AGI is unchanged. ▼

DEDUCTIONS FOR ADJUSTED GROSS INCOME

To understand how deductions of individual taxpayers are classified, it is necessary to examine the role of § 62. The purpose of § 62 is to classify various deductions as deductions *for* AGI. It does not provide the statutory authority for taking the deduction. For example, § 212 allows individuals to deduct expenses attributable to income-producing property. Section 212 expenses that are attributable to rents or royalties are classified as deductions *for* AGI. Likewise, a deduction for trade or business expenses is allowed by § 162. These expenses are classified as deductions *for* AGI.

If a deduction is not listed in § 62, it is an itemized deduction, *not* a deduction *for* AGI. Following is a *partial* list of the items classified as deductions *for* AGI by § 62:

- Expenses attributable to a trade or business carried on by the taxpayer. A trade or business does not include the performance of services by the taxpayer as an employee.
- Expenses incurred by a taxpayer in connection with the performance of services as an employee if the expenses are reimbursed and other conditions are satisfied.
- Deductions that result from losses on the sale or exchange of property by the taxpayer.
- Deductions attributable to property held for the production of rents and royalties.
- The deduction for payment of alimony.
- Certain contributions to pension, profit sharing, and annuity plans of self-employed individuals.
- The deduction for certain retirement savings allowed by § 219 (e.g., IRAs).

TAX IN THE NEWS

MORE OF THE SAME FOR NOW

Prior to the November 1996 elections, the drums were beating in support of simplifying the Federal income tax system. Some advocated "tearing the income tax out by its roots." Others wanted to go even further and repeal the Sixteenth Amendment to the U.S. Constitution.

The first opportunity for meaningful tax reform after the elections occurred in the 1997 tax legislation. Has the tax system been simplified or reformed? Not exactly. The Taxpayer Relief Act of 1997 actually went in the other direction. The TRA of 1997 has created layers of additional complexity in such diverse areas as the earned income credit, IRAs, and capital gains. More than 1,000 changes were made in the tax law. One tax adviser referred to the effect of the legislation as "complexity on stilts." Another quipped that perhaps the layers of additional complexity were added to gain support for future simplification.

- The penalty imposed on premature withdrawal of funds from time savings accounts or deposits.
- The deduction for moving expenses.
- The deduction for interest paid on student loans.

These items are covered in detail in various chapters in the text.

ITEMIZED DEDUCTIONS

The Code defines itemized deductions as the deductions allowed other than "the deductions allowable in arriving at adjusted gross income."[2] Thus, if a deduction is not properly classified as a deduction *for* AGI, then it is classified as an itemized deduction.

Section 212 Expenses.   Section 212 allows deductions for ordinary and necessary expenses paid or incurred for the following:

- The production or collection of income.
- The management, conservation, or maintenance of property held for the production of income.
- Expenses paid in connection with the determination, collection, or refund of any tax.

Section 212 expenses related to rent and royalty income are deductions *for* AGI.[3] Expenses paid in connection with the determination, collection, or refund of taxes related to the income of sole proprietorships, rents and royalties, or farming operations are deductions *for* AGI. All other § 212 expenses are itemized deductions (deductions *from* AGI). For example, investment-related expenses (e.g., safe deposit box rentals) are deductible as itemized deductions attributable to the production of investment income.[4]

---

[2] § 63(d).
[3] § 62(a)(4).

[4] Reg. § 1.212–1(g).

Deductible Personal Expenses. Taxpayers are allowed to deduct certain expenses that are primarily personal in nature. These expenses, which generally are not related to the production of income, are deductions *from* AGI (itemized deductions). Some of the more frequently encountered deductions in this category include the following:

- Contributions to qualified charitable organizations (not to exceed a specified percentage of AGI).
- Medical expenses (in excess of 7.5 percent of AGI).
- Certain state and local taxes (e.g., real estate taxes and state and local income taxes).
- Personal casualty losses (in excess of an aggregate floor of 10 percent of AGI and a $100 floor per casualty).
- Certain personal interest (e.g., mortgage interest on a personal residence).

Itemized deductions are discussed in detail in Chapter 9.

TRADE OR BUSINESS EXPENSES AND PRODUCTION OF INCOME EXPENSES

Section 162(a) permits a deduction for all ordinary and necessary expenses paid or incurred in carrying on a trade or business. These include reasonable salaries paid for services, expenses for the use of business property, and one-half of self-employment taxes paid. Such expenses are deducted *for* AGI.

It is sometimes difficult to determine whether an expenditure is deductible as a trade or business expense. The term "trade or business" is not defined in the Code or Regulations, and the courts have not provided a satisfactory definition. It is usually necessary to ask one or more of the following questions to determine whether an item qualifies as a trade or business expense:

- Was the use of the particular item related to a business activity? For example, if funds are borrowed for use in a business, the interest is deductible as a business expense.
- Was the expenditure incurred with the intent to realize a profit or to produce income? For example, expenses in excess of the income from raising horses are not deductible if the activity is classified as a personal hobby rather than a trade or business.
- Were the taxpayer's operation and management activities extensive enough to indicate the carrying on of a trade or business?

Section 162 *excludes* the following items from classification as trade or business expenses:

- Charitable contributions or gifts.
- Illegal bribes and kickbacks and certain treble damage payments.
- Fines and penalties.

A bribe paid to a domestic official is not deductible if it is illegal under the laws of the United States. Foreign bribes are deductible unless they are unlawful under the Foreign Corrupt Practices Act of 1977.[5]

---

[5]§ 162(c)(1).

TAX IN THE NEWS

PAYING RETAINERS TO KEEP LAWYERS FROM RIVALS

In a recent Claims Court case, the IRS attempted to disallow a deduction for a taxpayer who paid a retainer to a law firm to ensure that the law firm would not do legal work for a hostile suitor. The taxpayer paid a retainer to the law firm for 16 years, even though the firm did little or no legal work for the taxpayer during that time.

The IRS's position was that the payments were not deductible because they were capital expenditures rather than ordinary and necessary business expenses deductible under § 162. The Claims Court concluded that the taxpayer's long history of paying an annual retainer established the payments as an ordinary and necessary business expense and thus they were currently deductible.

SOURCE: Adapted from Tom Herman, "Companies Can Deduct Retainers to Keep Lawyers from Rivals," *Wall Street Journal*, July 28, 1997, p. B8.

Ordinary and Necessary Requirement.   The terms **ordinary and necessary** are found in both §§ 162 and 212. To be deductible, any trade or business expense must be "ordinary and necessary." In addition, compensation for services must be "reasonable" in amount.

Many expenses that are necessary are *not* ordinary. Neither "ordinary" nor "necessary" is defined in the Code or Regulations. The courts have held that an expense is *necessary* if a prudent businessperson would incur the same expense and the expense is expected to be appropriate and helpful in the taxpayer's business.[6]

EXAMPLE 3   Pat purchased a manufacturing concern that had just been adjudged bankrupt. Because the business had a poor financial rating, Pat satisfied some of the obligations to employees and outside salespeople incurred by the former owners. Pat had no legal obligation to pay these debts, but felt this was the only way to keep salespeople and employees. The Second Court of Appeals found that the payments were necessary in that they were both appropriate and helpful.[7] However, the Court held that the payments were *not* ordinary but were in the nature of capital expenditures to build a reputation. Therefore, no deduction was allowed. ▼

An expense is *ordinary* if it is normal, usual, or customary in the type of business conducted by the taxpayer and is not capital in nature.[8] However, an expense need not be recurring to be deductible as ordinary.

EXAMPLE 4   Albert engaged in a mail-order business. The post office judged that his advertisements were false and misleading. Under a fraud order, the post office stamped "fraudulent" on all letters addressed to Albert's business and returned them to the senders. Albert spent $30,000 on legal fees in an unsuccessful attempt to force the post office to stop. The legal fees (though not recurring) were ordinary business expenses because they were normal, usual, or customary in the circumstances.[9] ▼

---

[6]*Welch v. Helvering*, 3 USTC ¶1164, 12 AFTR 1456, 54 S.Ct. 8 (USSC, 1933).

[7]*Dunn and McCarthy, Inc. v. Comm.*, 43–2 USTC ¶9688, 31 AFTR 1043, 139 F.2d 242 (CA–2, 1943).

[8]*Deputy v. DuPont*, 40–1 USTC ¶9161, 23 AFTR 808, 60 S.Ct. 363 (USSC, 1940).

[9]*Comm. v. Heininger*, 44–1 USTC ¶9109, 31 AFTR 783, 64 S.Ct. 249 (USSC, 1943).

For § 212 deductions, the law requires that expenses bear a reasonable and proximate relationship to (1) the production or collection of income or to (2) the management, conservation, or maintenance of property held for the production of income.[10]

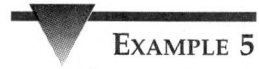

EXAMPLE 5

Wendy owns a small portfolio of investments, including 10 shares of Hawk, Inc., common stock worth $1,000. She incurred $350 in travel expenses to attend the annual shareholders' meeting at which she voted her 10 shares against the current management group. No deduction is permitted because a 10-share investment is insignificant in value in relation to the travel expenses incurred.[11] ▼

Reasonableness Requirement.   The Code refers to **reasonableness** solely with respect to salaries and other compensation for services.[12] But the courts have held that for any business expense to be ordinary and necessary, it must also be reasonable in amount.[13]

What constitutes reasonableness is a question of fact. If an expense is unreasonable, the excess amount is not allowed as a deduction. The question of reasonableness generally arises with respect to closely held corporations where there is no separation of ownership and management.

Transactions between the shareholders and the closely held company may result in the disallowance of deductions for excessive salaries and rent expense paid by the corporation to the shareholders. The courts will view an unusually large salary in light of all relevant circumstances and may find that the salary is reasonable despite its size.[14] If excessive payments for salaries and rents are closely related to the percentage of stock owned by the recipients, the payments are generally treated as dividends.[15] Since dividends are not deductible by the corporation, the disallowance results in an increase in the corporate taxable income. Deductions for reasonable salaries will not be disallowed *solely* because the corporation has paid insubstantial portions of its earnings as dividends to its shareholders.

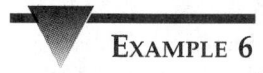

EXAMPLE 6

Sparrow Corporation, a closely held corporation, is owned equally by Lupe, Carlos, and Ramon. The company has been highly profitable for several years and has not paid dividends. Lupe, Carlos, and Ramon are key officers of the company, and each receives a salary of $200,000. Salaries for similar positions in comparable companies average only $100,000. Amounts paid the owners in excess of $100,000 may be deemed unreasonable, and, if so, a total of $300,000 in salary deductions by Sparrow is disallowed. The disallowed amounts are treated as dividends rather than salary income to Lupe, Carlos, and Ramon because the payments are proportional to stock ownership. Salaries are deductible by the corporation, but dividends are not. ▼

BUSINESS AND NONBUSINESS LOSSES

Section 165 provides for a deduction for losses not compensated for by insurance. As a general rule, deductible losses of individual taxpayers are limited to those incurred in a trade or business or in a transaction entered into for profit. Individuals are also allowed to deduct losses that are the result of a casualty. Casualty losses include, but are not limited to, fire, storm, shipwreck, and theft. See Chapter 6 for

---

[10]Reg. § 1.212–1(d).
[11]*J. Raymond Dyer*, 36 T.C. 456 (1961).
[12]§ 162(a)(1).
[13]*Comm. v. Lincoln Electric Co.*, 49–2 USTC ¶9388, 38 AFTR 411, 176 F.2d 815 (CA–6, 1949).

[14]*Kennedy, Jr. v. Comm.*, 82–1 USTC ¶9186, 49 AFTR2d 82–628, 671 F.2d 167 (CA–6, 1982), *rev'g* 72 T.C. 793 (1979).
[15]Reg. § 1.162–8.

a further discussion of this topic. Deductible personal casualty losses are reduced by $100 per casualty, and the aggregate of all personal casualty losses is reduced by 10 percent of AGI. A personal casualty loss is an itemized deduction. See Concept Summary 5–2 near the end of the chapter for the classification of expenses.

REPORTING PROCEDURES

All deductions *for* and *from* AGI wind up on pages 1 and 2 of Form 1040. All deductions *for* AGI are reported on page 1. The last line on page 1 is adjusted gross income.

The first item on page 2 is also adjusted gross income. Itemized deductions are entered next, followed by the deduction for personal and dependency exemptions. The result is taxable income.

Most of the deductions *for* AGI on page 1 originate on supporting schedules. Examples include business expenses (Schedule C) and rent, royalty, partnership, and fiduciary deductions (Schedule E). Other deductions *for* AGI, such as IRAs, Keogh retirement plans, and alimony, are entered directly on page 1 of Form 1040.

All itemized deductions on page 2 are carried over from Schedule A. Some Schedule A deductions originate on other forms. Examples include home mortgage interest, investment interest, noncash charitable contributions in excess of $500, casualty losses, and unreimbursed employee expenses.

Form 1040 becomes a summary of the detailed information entered on the other schedules and forms. See Figure 5–1.

DEDUCTIONS AND LOSSES—TIMING OF EXPENSE RECOGNITION

IMPORTANCE OF TAXPAYER'S METHOD OF ACCOUNTING

2   LEARNING OBJECTIVE
Describe the cash and accrual methods of accounting.

A taxpayer's **accounting method** is a major factor in determining taxable income. The method used determines when an item is includible in income and when an item is deductible on the tax return. Usually, the taxpayer's regular method of record keeping is used for income tax purposes.[16] The taxing authorities do not require uniformity among all taxpayers. They do require that the method used clearly reflect income and that items be handled consistently.[17] The most common methods of accounting are the cash method and the accrual method.

Throughout the portions of the Code dealing with deductions, the phrase "paid or incurred" is used. *Paid* refers to the cash basis taxpayer who gets a deduction only in the year of payment. *Incurred* concerns the accrual basis taxpayer who obtains the deduction in the year in which the liability for the expense becomes certain (refer to Chapter 3).

CASH METHOD REQUIREMENTS

The expenses of cash basis taxpayers are deductible only when they are actually paid with cash or other property. Promising to pay or issuing a note does not satisfy the actually paid requirement.[18] However, the payment can be made with borrowed funds. At the time taxpayers charge expenses on their credit cards, they

---

[16]§ 446(a).
[17]§§ 446(b) and (e); Reg. § 1.446–1(a)(2).

[18]*Page v. Rhode Island Trust Co., Exr.*, 37–1 USTC ¶9138, 19 AFTR 105, 88 F.2d 192 (CA–1, 1937).

▼ **FIGURE 5–1**
Format of Form 1040

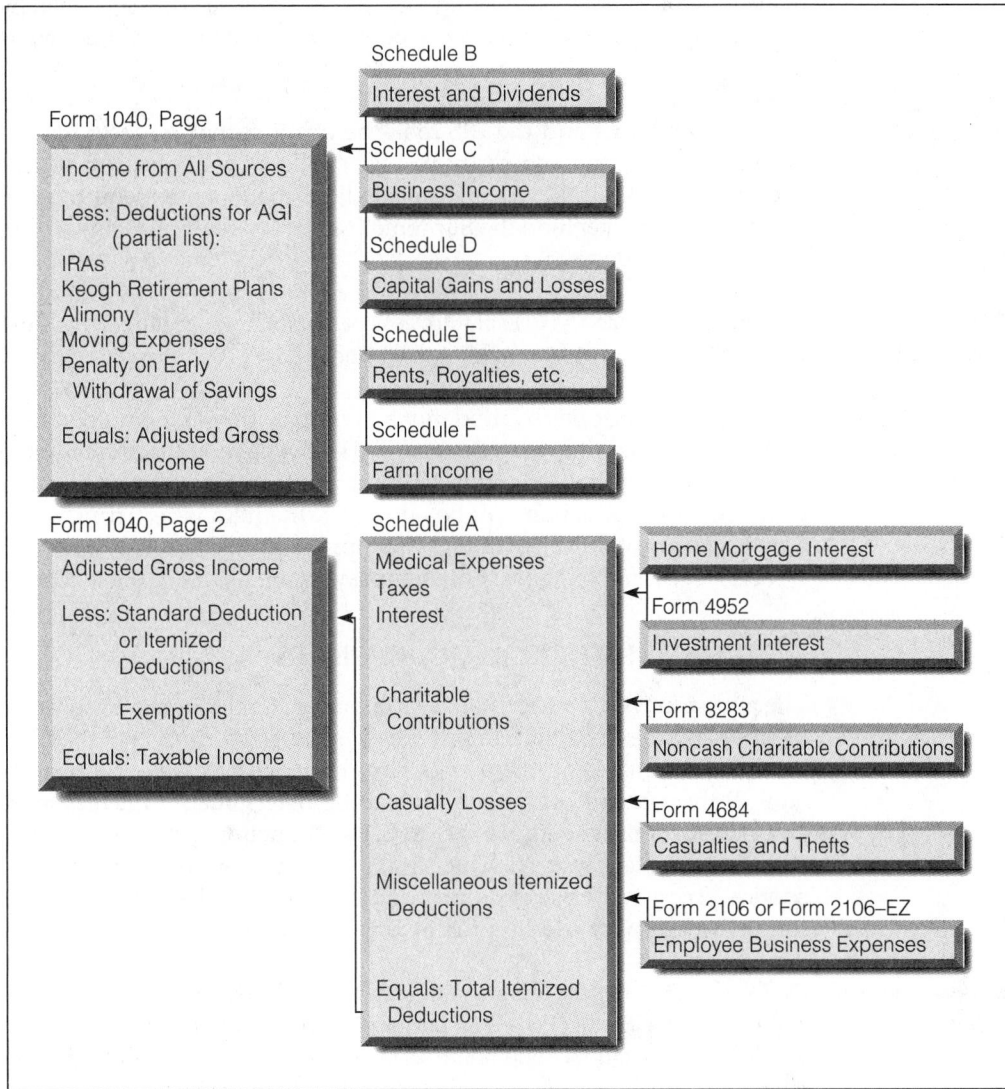

are allowed to claim the deduction. They are deemed to have simultaneously borrowed money from the credit card issuer and constructively paid the expenses.[19]

Although the cash basis taxpayer must have actually or constructively paid the expense, payment does not assure a current deduction. Cash basis and accrual basis taxpayers cannot take a current deduction for capital expenditures except through amortization, depletion, or depreciation over the life (actual or statutory) of the asset. The Regulations set forth the general rule that an expenditure that creates an asset having a useful life that extends substantially beyond the end of the tax year must be capitalized.[20]

[19]Rev.Rul. 78–39, 1978–1 C.B. 73. See also Rev.Rul. 80–335, 1980–2 C.B. 170, which applies to pay-by-phone arrangements.

[20]Reg. § 1.461–1(a).

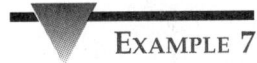

EXAMPLE 7

John, a cash basis taxpayer, rents property from Carl. On July 1, 1998, John paid $2,400 rent for the 24 months ending June 30, 2000. The prepaid rent extends 18 months after the close of the tax year—substantially beyond the year of payment. Therefore, John must capitalize the prepaid rent and amortize the expense on a monthly basis. His deduction for 1998 is $600. ▼

The Tax Court and the IRS took the position that an asset that will expire or be consumed by the end of the tax year following the year of payment must be prorated. The Ninth Court of Appeals held that such expenditures are currently deductible, however, and the Supreme Court apparently concurs (the one-year rule for prepaid expenses).[21]

EXAMPLE 8

Assume the same facts as in Example 7 except that John was required to pay only 12 months' rent in 1998. He paid $1,200 on July 1, 1998. The entire $1,200 would be deductible in 1998. ▼

The payment must be required, not a voluntary prepayment, to obtain the current deduction under the one-year rule.[22] The taxpayer must also demonstrate that allowing the current deduction will not result in a material distortion of income. Generally, the deduction will be allowed if the item is recurring or was made for a business purpose rather than to manipulate income.[23]

As Chapter 15 explains, not all taxpayers are allowed to use the cash method.[24]

ACCRUAL METHOD REQUIREMENTS

The period in which an accrual basis taxpayer can deduct an expense is determined by applying the *all events test* and the *economic performance test*. A deduction cannot be claimed until (1) all the events have occurred to create the taxpayer's liability and (2) the amount of the liability can be determined with reasonable accuracy. Once these requirements are satisfied, the deduction is permitted only if economic performance has occurred. The economic performance test is met only when the service, property, or use of property giving rise to the liability is actually performed for, provided to, or used by the taxpayer.[25]

EXAMPLE 9

On December 22, 1998, Chris's entertainment business sponsored a jazz festival in a rented auditorium at a local college. His business is responsible for cleaning up the auditorium after the festival and for reinstalling seats that were removed so more people could attend the festival. Since the college is closed over the Christmas holidays, the company hired by Chris to perform the work did not begin these activities until January 2, 1999. The cost to Chris is $1,200. Chris cannot deduct the $1,200 until 1999, when the services are performed. ▼

An exception to the economic performance requirements allows certain *recurring items* to be deducted if the following conditions are met:

- The item is recurring in nature and is treated consistently by the taxpayer.
- Either the accrued item is not material, or accruing it results in better matching of income and expenses.

---

[21]*Zaninovich v. Comm.*, 80–1 USTC ¶9342, 45 AFTR2d 80–1442, 616 F.2d 429 (CA–9, 1980), *rev'g* 69 T.C. 605 (1978). Cited by the Supreme Court in *Hillsboro National Bank v. Comm.*, 83–1 USTC ¶9229, 51 AFTR2d 83–874, 103 S.Ct. 1134 (USSC, 1983).

[22]*Bonaire Development Co. v. Comm.*, 82–2 USTC ¶9428, 50 AFTR2d 82–5167, 679 F.2d 159 (CA–9, 1982).

[23]*Keller v. Comm.*, 84–1 USTC ¶9194, 53 AFTR2d 84–663, 725 F.2d 1173 (CA–8, 1984), *aff'g* 79 T.C. 7 (1982).

[24]§ 448.

[25]§ 461(h).

- All the events have occurred that determine the fact of the liability, and the amount of the liability can be determined with reasonable accuracy.
- Economic performance occurs within a reasonable period (but not later than 8½ months after the close of the taxable year).[26]

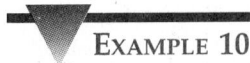

EXAMPLE 10

Rick, an accrual basis, calendar year taxpayer, entered into a monthly maintenance contract during the year. He makes a monthly accrual at the end of every month for this service and pays the fee sometime between the first and fifteenth of the following month when services are performed. The amount involved is immaterial, and all the other tests are met. The December 1998 accrual is deductible even though the service is performed on January 12, 1999. ▼

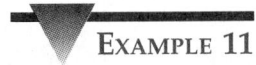

EXAMPLE 11

Rita, an accrual basis, calendar year taxpayer, shipped merchandise sold on December 30, 1998, via Greyhound Van Lines on January 2, 1999, and paid the freight charges at that time. Since Rita reported the sale of the merchandise in 1998, the shipping charge should also be deductible in 1998. This procedure results in a better matching of income and expenses. ▼

Reserves for estimated expenses (frequently employed for financial accounting purposes) generally are not allowed for tax purposes because the economic performance test cannot be satisfied.

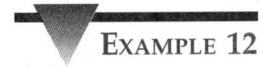

EXAMPLE 12

Blackbird Airlines is required by Federal law to test its engines after 3,000 flying hours. Aircraft cannot return to flight until the tests have been conducted. An unrelated aircraft maintenance company does all of the company's tests for $1,500 per engine. For financial reporting purposes, the company accrues an expense based upon $.50 per hour of flight and credits an allowance account. The actual amounts paid for maintenance are offset against the allowance account. For tax purposes, the economic performance test is not satisfied until the work has been done. Therefore, the reserve method cannot be used for tax purposes. ▼

DISALLOWANCE POSSIBILITIES

3   LEARNING OBJECTIVE
Apply the Internal Revenue Code deduction disallowance provisions associated with the following: public policy limitations, political activities, excessive executive compensation, investigation of business opportunities, hobby losses, vacation home rentals, payment of others' expenses, personal expenditures, capital expenditures, related-party transactions, and expenses related to tax-exempt income.

The tax law provides for the disallowance of certain types of expenses. Without specific restrictions in the tax law, taxpayers might attempt to deduct certain items that in reality are personal expenditures. For example, specific tax rules are provided to determine whether an expenditure is for trade or business purposes or related to a personal hobby.

Certain disallowance provisions are a codification or extension of prior court decisions. After the courts denied deductions for payments considered to be in violation of public policy, the tax law was changed to provide specific authority for the disallowance of these deductions. Discussions of specific disallowance provisions in the tax law follow.

PUBLIC POLICY LIMITATION

Justification for Denying Deductions. The courts developed the principle that a payment that is in violation of public policy is not a necessary expense and is not deductible.[27] Although a bribe or fine may be appropriate, helpful, and even

---

[26]§ 461(h)(3)(A).
[27]*Tank Truck Rentals, Inc. v. Comm.*, 58–1 USTC ¶9366, 1 AFTR2d 1154, 78 S.Ct. 507 (USSC, 1958).

contribute to the profitability of an activity, the courts held that to allow such expenses would frustrate clearly defined public policy. A deduction would dilute the effect of the penalty since the government would be indirectly subsidizing a taxpayer's wrongdoing.

Accordingly, the IRS was free to restrict deductions if, in its view, the expenses were contrary to public policy. But since the law did not explain which actions violated public policy, taxpayers often had to go to court to determine whether or not their expense fell into this category.

Furthermore, the public policy doctrine could be arbitrarily applied in cases where no clear definition had emerged. To solve these problems, Congress enacted legislation that attempts to limit the use of the doctrine. Under the legislation, deductions are disallowed for certain specific types of expenditures that are considered contrary to public policy:

- Bribes and kickbacks including those associated with Medicare or Medicaid (in the case of foreign bribes and kickbacks, only if the payments violate the U.S. Foreign Corrupt Practices Act of 1977).
- Fines and penalties paid to a government for violation of law.

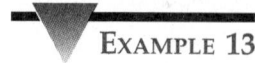

EXAMPLE 13 Brown Corporation, a moving company, consistently loads its trucks with weights in excess of the limits allowed by state law. The additional revenue more than offsets the fines levied. The fines are for a violation of public policy and are not deductible. ▼

- Two-thirds of the treble damage payments made to claimants resulting from violation of the antitrust law.[28]

To be disallowed, the bribe or kickback must be illegal under either Federal or state law and must also subject the payer to a criminal penalty or the loss of license or privilege to engage in a trade or business. For a bribe or kickback that is illegal under state law, a deduction is denied only if the state law is generally enforced.

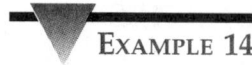

EXAMPLE 14 During the year, Keith, an insurance salesman, paid $5,000 to Karen, a real estate broker. The payment represented 20% of the commissions Keith earned from customers referred by Karen. Under state law, the splitting of commissions by an insurance salesperson is an act of misconduct that could warrant a revocation of the salesperson's license. Keith's $5,000 payments to Karen are not deductible provided the state law is generally enforced. ▼

ETHICAL CONSIDERATIONS

To Obey the Law

Clyde owns a trucking firm that operates in the Mid-Atlantic states. One of his major customers frequently ships goods between Charlotte and Baltimore. Occasionally, the customer sends last-minute shipments that are outbound for Europe on a freighter sailing from Baltimore. To satisfy the delivery schedule in these cases, Clyde's drivers must substantially exceed the speed limit. Clyde's business pays for any related speeding tickets. Twice within the past year, drivers have had their license suspended for 30 days for driving at such excessive speeds. Clyde's firm continues to pay the driver's salary during such suspension periods.

---

[28]§§ 162(c), (f), and (g).

Clyde believes that it is necessary to conduct his business in this manner if it is to be profitable, maintain the support of his drivers, and maintain the goodwill of his customers. Evaluate Clyde's business practices.

Legal Expenses Incurred in Defense of Civil or Criminal Penalties. To deduct legal expenses, the taxpayer must be able to show that the origin and character of the claim are directly related to a trade or business, an income-producing activity, or the determination, collection, or refund of a tax. Personal legal expenses are not deductible. Thus, legal fees incurred in connection with a criminal defense are deductible only if the crime is associated with the taxpayer's trade or business or income-producing activity.[29]

EXAMPLE 15

Debra, a financial officer of Blue Corporation, incurred legal expenses in connection with her defense in a criminal indictment for evasion of Blue's income taxes. Debra may deduct her legal expenses because she is deemed to be in the trade or business of being an executive. The legal action impairs her ability to conduct this business activity.[30] ▼

Deductible legal expenses associated with the following are deductible *for* AGI:

- Ordinary and necessary expenses incurred in connection with a trade or business.
- Ordinary and necessary expenses incurred in conjunction with rental or royalty property held for the production of income.

All other deductible legal expenses are deductible *from* AGI. For example, legal expenses generally are deductible *from* AGI if they are for fees for tax advice relative to the preparation of an individual's income tax return. Contrast this with the deduction *for* classification of legal fees for tax advice relative to the preparation of the portion of the tax return for a sole proprietor's trade or business (Schedule C) or an individual's rental or royalty income (Schedule E).

Expenses Relating to an Illegal Business. The usual expenses of operating an illegal business (e.g., a numbers racket) are deductible.[31] However, § 162 disallows a deduction for fines, bribes to public officials, illegal kickbacks, and other illegal payments.

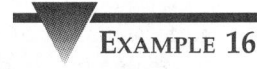

EXAMPLE 16

Sam owns and operates an illegal gambling establishment. In connection with this activity, he had the following expenses during the year:

Rent	$ 60,000
Payoffs to the police	40,000
Depreciation on equipment	100,000
Wages	140,000
Interest	30,000
Criminal fines	50,000
Illegal kickbacks	10,000
Total	$430,000

---

[29]*Comm. v. Tellier,* 66–1 USTC ¶9319, 17 AFTR2d 633, 86 S.Ct. 1118 (USSC, 1966).

[30]Rev.Rul. 68–662, 1968–2 C.B. 69.

[31]*Comm. v. Sullivan,* 58–1 USTC ¶9368, 1 AFTR2d 1158, 78 S.Ct. 512 (USSC, 1958).

All of the usual expenses (rent, depreciation, wages, and interest) are deductible; payoffs, fines, and kickbacks are not deductible. Of the $430,000 spent, $330,000 is deductible and $100,000 is not. ▼

An exception applies to expenses incurred in illegal trafficking in drugs.[32] *Drug dealers* are not allowed a deduction for ordinary and necessary business expenses incurred in their business. In arriving at gross income from the business, however, dealers may reduce total sales by the cost of goods sold.[33] In this regard, no distinction is made between legal and illegal businesses in calculating gross income. Treating cost of goods sold as a negative income item rather than as a deduction item produces the unseemly result that a drug dealer's taxable income is reduced by cost of goods sold.

POLITICAL CONTRIBUTIONS AND LOBBYING ACTIVITIES

Political Contributions.   Generally, no business deduction is permitted for direct or indirect payments for political purposes.[34] Historically, the government has been reluctant to accord favorable tax treatment to business expenditures for political purposes. Allowing deductions might encourage abuses and enable businesses to have undue influence upon the political process.

Lobbying Expenditures.   Lobbying expenses incurred in attempting to influence state or Federal legislation or the actions of certain high-ranking public officials (e.g., the President, Vice President, cabinet-level officials, and the two most senior officials in each agency of the executive branch) are not deductible.[35] The disallowance also applies to a pro rata portion of the membership dues of trade associations and other groups that are used for lobbying activities.

EXAMPLE 17

Egret Company pays a $10,000 annual membership fee to the Free Trade Group, a trade association for plumbing wholesalers. The trade association estimates that 70% of its dues are allocated to lobbying activities. Thus, Egret Company's deduction is limited to $3,000 ($10,000 × 30%). ▼

There are three exceptions to the disallowance of lobbying expenses. An exception is provided for influencing local legislation (e.g., city and county governments). Second, the disallowance provision does not apply to activities devoted solely to monitoring legislation. Third, a *de minimis* exception is provided for annual in-house expenditures (lobbying expenses other than those paid to professional lobbyists or any portion of dues used by associations for lobbying) if such expenditures do not exceed $2,000. If the in-house expenditures exceed $2,000, none of the in-house expenditures can be deducted.

EXCESSIVE EXECUTIVE COMPENSATION

The deduction of executive compensation is subject to two limitations. As discussed earlier in this chapter, the compensation of shareholder-employees of closely held corporations is subject to the reasonableness requirement. The second limitation, the

[32]§ 280E.
[33]Reg. § 1.61–3(a). Gross income is defined as sales minus cost of goods sold. Thus, while § 280E prohibits any deductions for drug dealers, it does not modify the normal definition of gross income.

[34]§ 276.
[35]§ 162(e).

so-called millionaires provision, applies to publicly held corporations (a corporation that has at least one class of stock registered under the Securities Act of 1934).[36]

The millionaires provision does not limit the amount of compensation that can be paid to an employee. Instead, it limits the amount the employer can deduct for the compensation of a covered executive to $1 million annually. Covered employees include the chief executive officer and the four other most highly compensated officers.

Employee compensation *excludes* the following:

- Commissions based on individual performance.
- Certain performance-based compensation based on company performance according to a formula approved by a board of directors compensation committee (comprised solely of two or more outside directors) and by shareholder vote. The performance attainment must be certified by this compensation committee.
- Payments to tax-qualified retirement plans.
- Payments that are excludible from the employees' gross income (e.g., certain fringe benefits).

INVESTIGATION OF A BUSINESS

Investigation expenses are expenses paid or incurred to determine the feasibility of entering a new business or expanding an existing business. They include such costs as travel, engineering and architectural surveys, marketing reports, and various legal and accounting services. How such expenses are treated for tax purposes depends on a number of variables, including the following:

- The current business, if any, of the taxpayer.
- The nature of the business being investigated.
- The extent to which the investigation has proceeded.
- Whether or not the acquisition actually takes place.

If the taxpayer is in a business the *same as or similar to* that being investigated, all investigation expenses are deductible in the year paid or incurred. The tax result is the same whether or not the taxpayer acquires the business being investigated.[37]

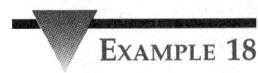

EXAMPLE 18

Terry, an accrual basis sole proprietor, owns and operates three motels in Georgia. In the current year, Terry incurs expenses of $8,500 in investigating the possibility of acquiring several additional motels located in South Carolina. The $8,500 is deductible in the current year whether or not Terry acquires the motels in South Carolina. ▼

When the taxpayer is *not* in a business that is the same as or similar to the one being investigated, the tax result depends on whether the new business is acquired. If the business is not acquired, all investigation expenses generally are nondeductible.[38]

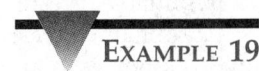

EXAMPLE 19

Lynn, a retired merchant, incurs expenses in traveling from Rochester, New York, to California to investigate the feasibility of acquiring several auto care centers. If no acquisition takes place, none of the expenses are deductible. ▼

---

[36]§ 162(m).
[37]§ 195. *York v. Comm.*, 58–2 USTC ¶9952, 2 AFTR2d 6178, 261 F.2d 421 (CA–4, 1958).

[38]Rev.Rul. 57–418, 1957–2 C.B. 143; *Morton Frank*, 20 T.C. 511 (1953); and *Dwight A. Ward*, 20 T.C. 332 (1953).

If the taxpayer is *not* in a business that is the same as or similar to the one being investigated and actually acquires the new business, the expenses must be capitalized. At the election of the taxpayer, the expenses may be amortized over a period of 60 months or more, beginning with the month in which the business is started.[39]

EXAMPLE 20

Tina owns and operates 10 restaurants located in various cities throughout the Southeast. She travels to Atlanta to discuss the acquisition of an auto dealership. In addition, she incurs legal and accounting costs associated with the potential acquisition. After incurring total investigation costs of $12,000, she acquires the auto dealership on October 1, 1998.

Tina must capitalize the $12,000 of investigation expenses for the auto dealership. If she elects to amortize the expenses over 60 months, she can deduct $600 ($12,000 × 3/60) in 1998. ▼

HOBBY LOSSES

Business or investment expenses are deductible only if the taxpayer can show that the activity was entered into for the purpose of making a profit. Certain activities may have either profit-seeking or personal attributes, depending upon individual circumstances. Examples include raising horses and operating a farm used as a weekend residence. While personal losses are not deductible, losses attributable to profit-seeking activities may be deducted and used to offset a taxpayer's other income. For this reason, the tax law limits the deductibility of **hobby losses.**

General Rules.   If an individual can show that an activity has been conducted with the intent to earn a profit, losses from the activity are fully deductible. The hobby loss rules apply only if the activity is not engaged in for profit. Hobby expenses are deductible only to the extent of hobby income.[40]

The Regulations stipulate that the following nine factors should be considered in determining whether an activity is profit-seeking or a hobby:[41]

- Whether the activity is conducted in a businesslike manner.
- The expertise of the taxpayers or their advisers.
- The time and effort expended.
- The expectation that the assets of the activity will appreciate in value.
- The taxpayer's previous success in conducting similar activities.
- The history of income or losses from the activity.
- The relationship of profits earned to losses incurred.
- The financial status of the taxpayer (e.g., if the taxpayer does not have substantial amounts of other income, this may indicate that the activity is engaged in for profit).
- Elements of personal pleasure or recreation in the activity.

The presence or absence of a factor is not by itself determinative of whether the activity is profit-seeking or a hobby. Rather, the decision is a subjective one that is based on an analysis of the facts and circumstances.

Presumptive Rule of § 183.   The Code provides a rebuttable presumption that an activity is profit-seeking if the activity shows a profit in at least three of any five prior consecutive years.[42] If the activity involves horses, a profit in at least two of seven consecutive years meets the presumptive rule. If these

---

[39]§ 195.
[40]§ 183(b)(2).

[41]Reg. §§ 1.183–2(b)(1) through (9).
[42]§ 183(d).

profitability tests are met, the activity is presumed to be a trade or business rather than a personal hobby. In this situation, the IRS bears the burden of proving that the activity is personal rather than trade or business related.

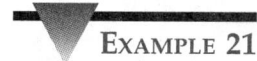

EXAMPLE 21

Camille, an executive for a large corporation, is paid a salary of $200,000. Her husband is a collector of antiques. Several years ago, he opened an antique shop in a local shopping center and spends most of his time buying and selling antiques. He occasionally earns a small profit from this activity but more frequently incurs substantial losses. If the losses are business related, they are fully deductible against Camille's salary income on a joint return. In resolving this issue, consider the following:

- Initially determine whether the antique activity has met the three-out-of-five years profit test.
- If the presumption is not met, the activity may nevertheless qualify as a business if the taxpayer can show that the intent is to engage in a profit-seeking activity. It is not necessary to show actual profits.
- Attempt to fit the operation within the nine criteria prescribed in the Regulations and listed above. These criteria are the factors considered in trying to rebut the § 183 presumption. ▼

Determining the Amount of the Deduction. If an activity is deemed to be a hobby, the expenses are deductible only to the extent of the gross income from the hobby. These expenses must be deducted in the following order:

- Amounts deductible under other Code sections without regard to the nature of the activity, such as property taxes and home mortgage interest.
- Amounts deductible under other Code sections if the activity had been engaged in for profit, but only if those amounts do not affect adjusted basis. Examples include maintenance, utilities, and supplies.
- Amounts that affect adjusted basis and would be deductible under other Code sections if the activity had been engaged in for profit.[43] Examples include depreciation, amortization, and depletion.

These deductions are deductible *from* AGI as itemized deductions to the extent they exceed 2 percent of AGI.[44] If the taxpayer uses the standard deduction rather than itemizing, all hobby loss deductions are wasted.

EXAMPLE 22

Jim, the vice president of an oil company, has AGI of $80,000. He decides to pursue painting in his spare time. He uses a home studio, comprising 10% of the home's square footage. During the current year, Jim incurs the following expenses:

Frames	$ 350
Art supplies	300
Fees paid to models	1,000
Home studio expenses:	
Total property taxes	900
Total home mortgage interest	10,000
Depreciation on 10% of home	500
Total home maintenance and utilities	3,600

---

[43]Reg. § 1.183–1(b)(1).

[44]Reg. § 1.67–1T(a)(1)(iv) and Rev.Rul. 75–14, 1975–1 C.B. 90.

During the year, Jim sold paintings for a total of $3,200. If the activity is held to be a hobby, Jim is allowed deductions as follows:

Gross income		$ 3,200
Deduct: Taxes and interest (10% of $10,900)		(1,090)
Remainder		$ 2,110
Deduct: Frames	$ 350	
Art supplies	300	
Models' fees	1,000	
Maintenance and utilities (10%)	360	(2,010)
Remainder		$ 100
Depreciation ($500, but limited to $100)		(100)
Net income		$ –0–

Jim includes the $3,200 of income in AGI, making his AGI $83,200. The taxes and interest are itemized deductions, deductible in full. The remaining $2,110 of expenses are reduced by 2% of his AGI ($1,664); so the net deduction is $446. Since the property taxes and home mortgage interest are deductible anyway, the net effect is a $2,754 ($3,200 less $446) increase in taxable income. ▼

EXAMPLE 23

Assume that Jim's activity in Example 22 is held to be a business. The business is located in a small office building he owns. Expenses are property taxes of $90, mortgage interest of $1,000, frames of $350, art supplies of $300, models' fees of $1,000, maintenance and utilities of $360, and depreciation of $500. Under these circumstances, Jim could deduct expenses totaling $3,600. All these expenses would be trade or business expenses deductible *for* AGI. His reduction in AGI would be as follows:

Gross income		$ 3,200
Less: Taxes and interest	$ 1,090	
Other business expenses	2,010	
Depreciation	500	(3,600)
Reduction in AGI		($ 400)

▼

RENTAL OF VACATION HOMES

Restrictions on the deductions allowed for part-year rentals of personal **vacation homes** were written into the law to prevent taxpayers from deducting essentially personal expenses as rental losses. Many taxpayers who owned vacation homes had formerly treated the homes as rental property and generated rental losses as deductions *for* AGI. For example, a summer cabin would be rented for 2 months per year, used for vacationing for 1 month, and left vacant the rest of the year. The taxpayer would then deduct 11 months' depreciation, utilities, maintenance, etc., as rental expenses, resulting in a rental loss. Section 280A eliminates this treatment by allowing deductions on residences used primarily for personal purposes only to the extent of the income generated. Only a break-even situation is allowed; no losses can be deducted.

There are three possible tax treatments for residences used for both personal and rental purposes. The treatment depends upon the *relative time* the residence is used for personal purposes versus rental use.

TAX IN THE NEWS

IS A DREAM HOME IN THE MOUNTAINS OR AT THE BEACH FOR YOU?

Most of us have dreamed of having a second home in the mountains or at the beach. The general attitude is that we deserve a second home and that it would be a healthy environment for the kids. Then we encounter the reality of paying for it.

One frequently prescribed technique is to rent a vacation home to others when you are not using it. Supposedly, the second home will generate rent income to use for the mortgage payments and deductions (e.g., mortgage interest and property taxes) on your income tax return, while providing a vacation getaway.

Unfortunately, the dream can become a nightmare. More than likely, the vacation home will be subject to both the § 280A limitation on deducting expenses in excess of rent income and the § 469 passive activity loss provision (see Chapter 10). To make matters worse, the vacation home is unlikely to be self-sustaining (i.e., cash inflows including tax benefits do not at least equal cash outflows). Therefore, those who view the vacation home as a cool investment are likely to be disappointed.

Thomas Ochsenschlanger, a partner in the Washington office of Grant Thornton, recommends discussing the financial aspects of a vacation home with your accountant *before* buying the property.

SOURCE: Adapted from Scott R. Schmedel, "Dream Second Home Can Be a Tax-Return Nightmare," *Wall Street Journal*, March 8, 1996, pp. C1 and C15.

Primarily Personal Use. If the residence is *rented* for *fewer than 15 days* in a year, it is treated as a personal residence. The rent income is excluded from gross income, and mortgage interest and real estate taxes are allowed as itemized deductions, as with any personal residence.[45] No other expenses (e.g., depreciation, utilities, maintenance) are deductible. Although this provision exists primarily for administrative convenience, several bills have been introduced in Congress, including one in 1997, that would have repealed this exclusion from gross income.

EXAMPLE 24

Dixie owns a vacation cottage on the lake. During the current year, she rented it for $1,600 for two weeks, lived in it two months, and left it vacant the remainder of the year. The year's expenses amounted to $6,000 mortgage interest expense, $500 property taxes, $1,500 utilities and maintenance, and $2,400 depreciation. Since the property was not rented for at least 15 days, the income is excluded, the mortgage interest and property tax expenses are itemized deductions, and the remaining expenses are nondeductible personal expenses. ▼

Primarily Rental Use. If the residence is *rented* for 15 days or more in a year and is *not used* for personal purposes for more than the greater of (1) 14 days or (2) 10 percent of the total days rented, the residence is treated as rental property.[46] The expenses must be allocated between personal and rental days if there are any personal use days during the year. The deduction of the expenses allocated to rental days can exceed rent income and result in a rental loss. The loss may be deductible under the passive activity loss rules (discussed in Chapter 10).

---

[45]§ 280A(g).

[46]§ 280A(d) and Prop.Reg. § 1.280A–3(c).

EXAMPLE 25

Assume instead that Dixie in Example 24 used the cottage for 12 days and rented it for 48 days for $4,800. Since she rented the cottage for 15 days or more but did not use it for more than 14 days, the cottage is treated as rental property. The expenses must be allocated between personal and rental days.

| | Percentage of Use | |
	Rental 80%	Personal 20%
Income	$ 4,800	$ –0–
Expenses		
Mortgage interest ($6,000)	($ 4,800)	($1,200)
Property taxes ($500)	(400)	(100)
Utilities and maintenance ($1,500)	(1,200)	(300)
Depreciation ($2,400)	(1,920)	(480)
Total expenses	($ 8,320)	($2,080)
Rental loss	($ 3,520)	$ –0–

Dixie deducts the $3,520 rental loss *for* AGI (assuming she meets the passive activity loss rules, discussed in Chapter 10). She also has an itemized deduction for property taxes of $100 associated with the personal use. The mortgage interest of $1,200 associated with the personal use is not deductible as an itemized deduction because the cottage is not a qualified residence (qualified residence interest) for this purpose (see Chapter 9). The portion of utilities and maintenance and depreciation attributable to personal use is not deductible. ▼

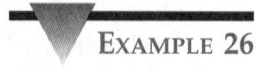

EXAMPLE 26

Assume instead that Dixie in Example 24 rented the cottage for 200 days and lived in it for 19 days. The cottage is primarily rental use since she rented it for 15 days or more and did not use it for personal purposes for more than 20 days (10% of the rental days). The expenses must be allocated between personal and rental days as illustrated in Example 25. ▼

Personal/Rental Use.   If the residence is rented for 15 days or more in a year *and* is used for personal purposes for more than the greater of (1) 14 days or (2) 10 percent of the total days rented, it is treated as a personal/rental use residence. The expenses must be allocated between personal days and rental days. Expenses are allowed only to the extent of rent income.

EXAMPLE 27

Assume instead that Dixie in Example 24 rented the property for 30 days and lived in it for 30 days. The residence is classified as personal/rental use property since she used it more than 14 days and rented it for 15 days or more. The expenses must be allocated between rental use and personal use, and the rental expenses are allowed only to the extent of rent income. ▼

If a residence is classified as personal/rental use property, the expenses that are deductible anyway (e.g., real estate taxes and mortgage interest) must be deducted first. If a positive net income results, otherwise nondeductible expenses that do not affect adjusted basis (e.g., maintenance, utilities, insurance) are allowed next. Finally, if any positive balance remains, depreciation is allowed.

Expenses must be allocated between personal and rental days before the limits are applied. The courts have held that real estate taxes and mortgage interest, which accrue ratably over the year, are allocated on the basis of 365 days.[47] The IRS, however, disagrees and allocates real estate taxes and mortgage interest on the basis of total days of use.[48] Other expenses (utilities, maintenance, depreciation, etc.) are allocated on the basis of total days used.

EXAMPLE 28

Jason rents his vacation home for 60 days and lives in the home for 30 days. The limitations on personal/rental use residences apply. Jason's gross rent income is $10,000. For the entire year (not a leap year), the real estate taxes are $2,190; his mortgage interest expense is $10,220; utilities and maintenance expense equals $2,400; and depreciation is $9,000. Using the IRS approach, these amounts are deductible in this specific order:

Gross income	$ 10,000
Deduct: Taxes and interest ($^{60}/_{90}$ × $12,410)	(8,273)
Remainder to apply to rental operating expenses and depreciation	$ 1,727
Deduct: Utilities and maintenance ($^{60}/_{90}$ × $2,400)	(1,600)
Balance	$ 127
Deduct: Depreciation ($^{60}/_{90}$ × $9,000 = $6,000 but limited to above balance)	(127)
Net rent income	$ –0–

The nonrental use portion of real estate taxes and mortgage interest ($4,137 in this case) is deductible if the taxpayer elects to itemize (see Chapter 9). The personal use portion of utilities, maintenance, and depreciation is not deductible in any case. Also note that the basis of the property is not reduced by the $5,873 depreciation not allowed ($6,000 − $127) because of the above limitation. (See Chapter 12 for a discussion of the reduction in basis for depreciation allowed or allowable.) ▼

EXAMPLE 29

Using the court's approach in allocating real estate taxes and mortgage interest, Jason, in Example 28, would have this result:

Gross income	$ 10,000
Deduct: Taxes and interest ($^{60}/_{365}$ × $12,410)	(2,040)
Remainder to apply to rental operating expenses and depreciation	$ 7,960
Deduct: Utilities and maintenance ($^{60}/_{90}$ × $2,400)	(1,600)
Balance	$ 6,360
Deduct: Depreciation ($^{60}/_{90}$ × $9,000, but limited to $6,360)	(6,000)
Net rent income	$ 360

Jason can deduct $10,370 ($12,410 paid − $2,040 deducted as expense in computing net rent income) of personal use mortgage interest and real estate taxes as itemized deductions. ▼

Note the contrasting results in Examples 28 and 29. The IRS's approach (Example 28) results in no rental gain or loss and an itemized deduction for real estate taxes and mortgage interest of $4,137. In Example 29, Jason has net rent income of $360 and $10,370 of itemized deductions. The court's approach decreases his taxable income by $10,010 ($10,370 itemized deductions less $360 net rent income). The IRS's approach reduces his taxable income by only $4,137.

---

[47]*Bolton v. Comm.,* 82–2 USTC ¶9699, 51 AFTR2d 83–305, 694 F.2d 556 (CA–9, 1982).   [48]Prop.Reg. § 1.280A–3(d)(4).

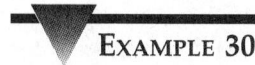

EXAMPLE 30

Assume instead that Jason in Example 28 had not lived in the home at all during the year. The house is rental property. The rental loss is calculated as follows:

Gross income	$ 10,000
Expenses	
Taxes and interest	($ 12,410)
Utilities and maintenance	(2,400)
Depreciation	(9,000)
Total expenses	($ 23,810)
Rental loss	($ 13,810)

Whether any of the rental loss would be deductible depends upon whether Jason actively participated in the rental activity and met the other requirements for passive activity losses (discussed in Chapter 10). ▼

Conversion to Rental Property.   A related issue is whether or not a taxpayer's *primary residence* is subject to the preceding rules if it is converted to rental property. If the vacation home rules apply, a taxpayer who converts a personal residence to rental property during the tax year, without any tax avoidance motive, could have the allowable deductions limited to the rent income. This would occur if the personal use exceeded the greater of 14 days or 10 percent of rental days test (a likely situation). The Code, however, provides that during a *qualified rental period*, any personal use days are not counted as personal use days in terms of classifying the use of the residence as *personal/rental use* rather than as *primarily rental use*.[49] In effect, the deduction for expenses of the property incurred during a qualified rental period is not subject to the personal use test of the vacation home rules. A qualified rental period is a consecutive period of 12 or more months. The period begins or ends in the taxable year in which the residence is rented or held for rental at a fair price. The residence must not be rented to a related party. If the property is sold before the 12-month period expires, the qualified rental period is the actual time rented.

EXAMPLE 31

Rhonda converts her residence to rental property on May 1 and rents it for the remainder of 1998 for $5,600 and for all of 1999 for $8,400. The house would be classified as personal/rental use property (personal use days during 1998 are greater than both 14 days and 10% of rental days) except that this is a qualified rental period. Therefore, Rhonda's deduction for rental expenses is not limited to the gross income of $5,600 in 1998. ▼

See Concept Summary 5–1 for a summary of the vacation home rules.

EXPENDITURES INCURRED FOR TAXPAYER'S BENEFIT OR TAXPAYER'S OBLIGATION

An expense must be incurred for the taxpayer's benefit or arise from the taxpayer's obligation. An individual cannot claim a tax deduction for the payment of the expenses of another individual.

EXAMPLE 32

During the current year, Fred pays the interest on his son, Vern's, home mortgage. Neither Fred nor Vern can take a deduction for the interest paid. Fred is not entitled to a deduction because the mortgage is not his obligation. Vern cannot claim a deduction because he did

---

[49]§ 280A(d).

CONCEPT SUMMARY 5–1

Vacation/Rental Home

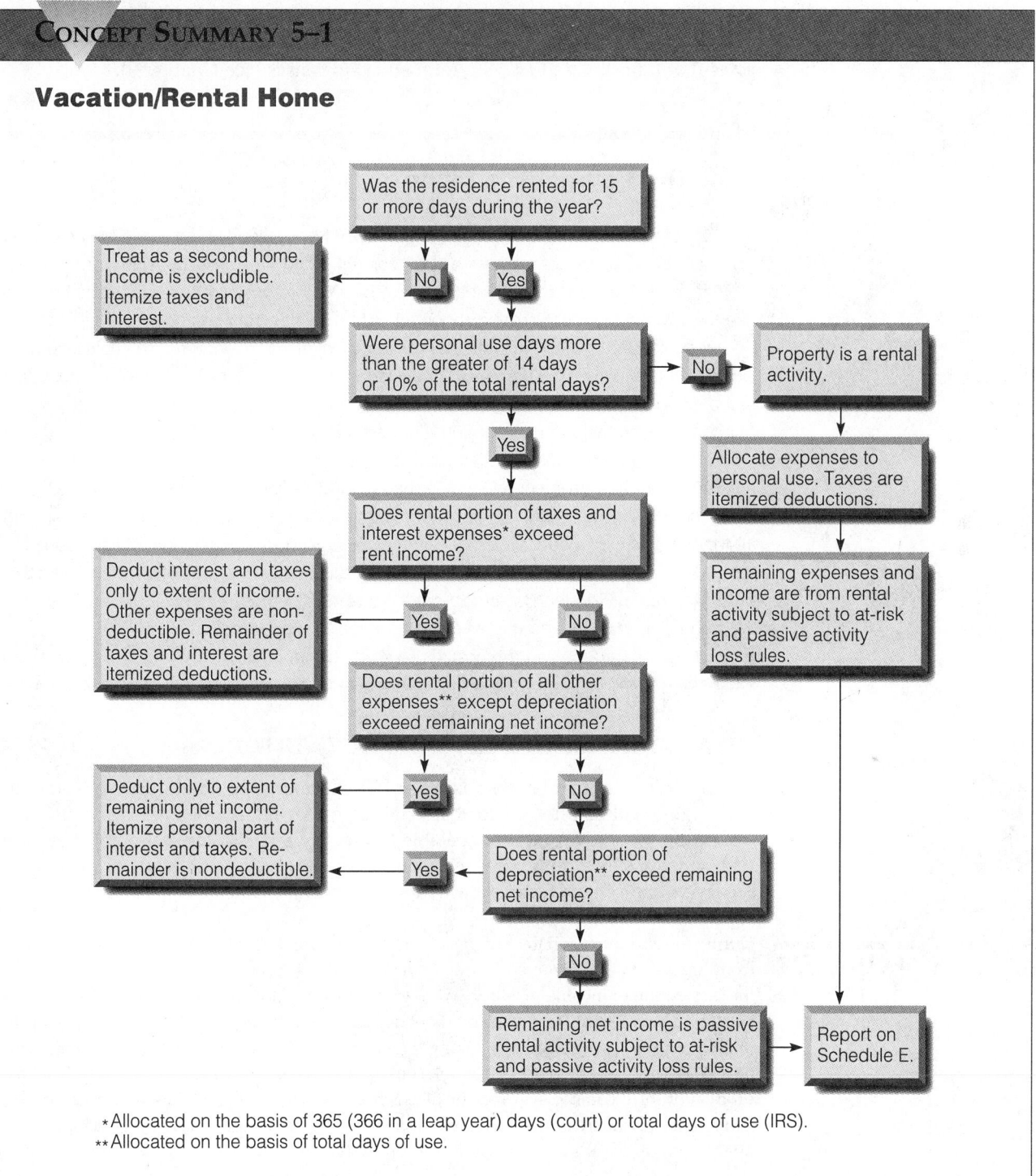

*Allocated on the basis of 365 (366 in a leap year) days (court) or total days of use (IRS).
**Allocated on the basis of total days of use.

not pay the interest. The tax result would have been more favorable had Fred made a cash gift to Vern and let him pay the interest. Then Vern could have deducted the interest, and Fred might not have been liable for any gift taxes depending upon the amount involved. A deduction would have been created with no cash difference to the family. ▼

One exception to this disallowance rule is the payment of medical expenses for a dependent. Such expenses are deductible by the payer subject to the normal rules that limit the deductibility of medical expenses (see Chapter 9).[50]

ETHICAL CONSIDERATIONS

How the Payment Is Made

Dan and Jeff both have sons who graduated from college recently and are employed by the same company in a rural community where rental housing is not readily available. Each father lends his son $10,000; the sons combine their resources and use the $20,000 as a down payment on a house that they buy together.

During 1998, the sons make all the mortgage payments on their house until December when they are furloughed from their jobs. Dan gives his son $900 to use to pay his share of the mortgage payment, and Jeff pays $900 directly to the mortgage company for his son. In each of these $900 amounts, $800 represents interest on the mortgage.

Over lunch recently, Dan and Jeff were discussing their sons' real estate investment and the $900 mortgage payment each father had funded. Jeff indicated that since he had paid the mortgage payment directly, he was going to deduct the $800 of interest on his Form 1040. After this conversation, Dan concludes that, in substance, he and Jeff have done the same thing. Accordingly, Dan calls his son and tells him that he wants to deduct the $800 on his tax return. Though Dan's son is not pleased, he agrees to permit his father to take the deduction and says he will not deduct the mortgage interest on his own return.

Evaluate the propriety of the position taken by Dan.

DISALLOWANCE OF PERSONAL EXPENDITURES

Section 262 states that "except as otherwise expressly provided in this chapter, no deduction shall be allowed for personal, living, or family expenses." To justify a deduction, an individual must be able to identify a particular section of the Code that sanctions the deduction (e.g., charitable contributions, medical expenses). Sometimes the character of a particular expenditure is not easily determined.

EXAMPLE 33

During the current year, Howard pays $1,500 in legal fees and court costs to obtain a divorce from his wife, Vera. Involved in the divorce action is a property settlement that concerns the disposition of income-producing property owned by Howard. In a similar situation, the Tax Court held that the taxpayer could not deduct any such costs.[51] "Although fees primarily related to property division concerning his income-producing property, they weren't ordinary and necessary expenses paid for conservation or maintenance of property held for production of income. Legal fees incurred in defending against claims that arise from a taxpayer's marital relationship aren't deductible expenses regardless of possible consequences on taxpayer's income-producing property." ▼

The IRS has clarified the issue of the deduction of legal fees incurred in connection with a divorce.[52] To be deductible, an expense must relate solely to tax advice in a divorce proceeding. For example, legal fees attributable to the determination of dependency exemptions of children are deductible if the fees are distinguishable

---

[50]§ 213(a).
[51]*Harry H. Goldberg*, 29 TCM 74, T.C.Memo. 1970–27.

[52]Rev.Rul. 72–545, 1972–2 C.B. 179.

from the general legal fees incurred in obtaining a divorce. Other examples are the costs of creating a trust to make periodic alimony payments and the determination of the tax consequences of a property settlement. Therefore, it is advisable to request an itemization of attorney's fees to substantiate a deduction for the tax-related amounts.

DISALLOWANCE OF DEDUCTIONS FOR CAPITAL EXPENDITURES

The Code specifically disallows a deduction for "any amount paid out for new buildings or for permanent improvements or betterments made to increase the value of any property or estate."[53] The Regulations further define capital expenditures to include those expenditures that add to the value or prolong the life of property or adapt the property to a new or different use.[54] Incidental repairs and maintenance of the property are not capital expenditures and can be deducted as ordinary and necessary business expenses. Repairing a roof is a deductible expense, but replacing a roof is a capital expenditure subject to depreciation deductions over its useful life. The tune-up of a delivery truck is an expense; a complete overhaul probably is a capital expenditure.

Capitalization versus Expense.   When an expenditure is capitalized rather than expensed, the deduction is at best deferred and at worst lost forever. Although an immediate tax benefit for a large cash expenditure is lost, the cost may be deductible in increments over a longer period of time.

If the expenditure is for a tangible asset that has an ascertainable life, it is capitalized and may be deducted as depreciation (or cost recovery) over the life of the asset (for depreciation) or over a statutory period (for cost recovery under either ACRS or MACRS).[55] Land is not subject to depreciation (or cost recovery) since it does not have an ascertainable life.

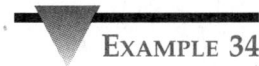
EXAMPLE 34

Stan purchased a prime piece of land located in an apartment-zoned area. Stan paid $500,000 for the property, which had an old but usable apartment building on it. He immediately had the building demolished at a cost of $100,000. The $500,000 purchase price and the $100,000 demolition costs must be capitalized, and the basis of the land is $600,000. Since land is a nondepreciable asset, no deduction is allowed. More favorable tax treatment might result if Stan rented the apartments in the old building for a period of time to attempt to establish that there was no intent to demolish the building. If Stan's attempt is successful, it might be possible to allocate a substantial portion of the original purchase price of the property to the building (a depreciable asset). When the building is later demolished, any remaining adjusted basis can be deducted as an ordinary (§ 1231) loss. (See Chapter 13 for a discussion of the treatment of § 1231 assets.) ▼

If the expenditure is for an intangible asset (e.g., copyright, patent, covenant not to compete, goodwill), the capitalized expenditure can be amortized, regardless of whether or not the intangible asset has an ascertainable life. Intangible assets, referred to as § 197 intangibles, are amortized over a 15-year statutory period using the straight-line method. See Chapter 7 for additional discussion of the amortization of intangibles.

---

[53]§ 263(a)(1).
[54]Reg. § 1.263(a)–1(b).

[55]See Chapter 7 for the discussion of depreciation and cost recovery.

TRANSACTIONS BETWEEN RELATED PARTIES

The Code places restrictions on the recognition of gains and losses from **related-party transactions.** Without these restrictions, relationships created by birth, marriage, and business would provide endless possibilities for engaging in financial transactions that produce tax savings with no real economic substance or change. For example, to create an artificial loss, a wife could sell investment property to her husband at a loss and deduct the loss on their joint return. Her husband could then hold the asset indefinitely, and the family would sustain no real economic loss. A complex set of laws has been designed to eliminate such possibilities.

Losses.   The Code provides for the disallowance of any "losses from sales or exchanges of property . . . directly or indirectly" between related parties.[56] When the property is subsequently sold to a nonrelated party, any gain recognized is reduced by the loss previously disallowed. Any disallowed loss not used by the related-party buyer to offset the recognized gain on a subsequent sale or exchange to an unrelated party is permanently lost.

EXAMPLE 35

Freida sells common stock with a basis of $1,000 to her son, Bill, for $800. Bill sells the stock several years later for $1,100. Freida's $200 loss is disallowed upon the sale to Bill, and only $100 of gain ($1,100 selling price – $800 basis – $200 disallowed loss) is taxable to him upon the subsequent sale. ▼

EXAMPLE 36

George sells common stock with a basis of $1,050 to his son, Ray, for $800. Ray sells the stock eight months later to an unrelated party for $900. Ray's gain of $100 ($900 selling price – $800 basis) is not recognized because of George's previously disallowed loss of $250. Note that the offset may result in only partial tax benefit upon the subsequent sale (as in this case). If the property had not been transferred to Ray, George could have recognized a $150 loss upon the subsequent sale to the unrelated party ($1,050 basis – $900 selling price). ▼

EXAMPLE 37

Pete sells common stock with a basis of $1,000 to an unrelated third party for $800. Pete's son repurchased the same stock in the market on the same day for $800. The $200 loss is not allowed because the transaction is an indirect sale between related parties.[57] ▼

Unpaid Expenses and Interest.   The law prevents related taxpayers from engaging in tax avoidance schemes where one related taxpayer uses the accrual method of accounting and the other uses the cash basis. An accrual basis, closely held corporation, for example, could borrow funds from a cash basis individual shareholder. At the end of the year, the corporation would accrue and deduct the interest, but the cash basis lender would not recognize interest income since no interest had been paid. Section 267 specifically defers the deduction of the accruing taxpayer until the recipient taxpayer must include it in income; that is, when it is actually paid to the cash basis taxpayer. This *matching* provision applies to interest as well as other expenses, such as salaries and bonuses.

This deduction deferral provision does not apply if both of the related taxpayers use the accrual method or both use the cash method. Likewise, it does not apply if the related party reporting income uses the accrual method and the related party taking the deduction uses the cash method.

---

[56]§ 267(a)(1).
[57]*McWilliams v. Comm.*, 47–1 USTC ¶9289, 35 AFTR 1184, 67 S.Ct. 1477 (USSC, 1947).

Relationships and Constructive Ownership. Section 267 operates to disallow losses and defer deductions only between related parties. Losses or deductions generated by similar transactions with an unrelated party are allowed. *Related parties* include the following:

- Brothers and sisters (whether whole, half, or adopted), spouse, ancestors (parents, grandparents), and lineal descendants (children, grandchildren) of the taxpayer.
- A corporation owned more than 50 percent (directly or indirectly) by the taxpayer.
- Two corporations that are members of a controlled group.
- A series of other complex relationships between trusts, corporations, and individual taxpayers.

Constructive ownership provisions are applied to determine whether the taxpayers are related. Under these provisions, stock owned by certain relatives or related entities is *deemed* to be owned by the taxpayer for purposes of applying the loss and expense deduction disallowance provisions. A taxpayer is deemed to own not only his or her stock but the stock owned by lineal descendants, ancestors, brothers and sisters or half-brothers and half-sisters, and spouse. The taxpayer is also deemed to own his or her proportionate share of stock owned by any partnership, corporation, estate, or trust of which he or she is a member. An individual is deemed to own any stock owned, directly or indirectly, by his or her partner. However, constructive ownership by an individual of the partnership's and the other partner's shares does not extend to the individual's spouse or other relatives (no double attribution).

EXAMPLE 38

The stock of Sparrow Corporation is owned 20% by Ted, 30% by Ted's father, 30% by Ted's mother, and 20% by Ted's sister. On July 1 of the current year, Ted loaned $10,000 to Sparrow Corporation at 8% annual interest, principal and interest payable on demand. For tax purposes, Sparrow uses the accrual basis, and Ted uses the cash basis. Both are on a calendar year. Since Ted is deemed to own the 80% owned by his parents and sister, he constructively owns 100% of Sparrow Corporation. If the corporation accrues the interest within the taxable year, no deduction can be taken until payment is made to Ted. ▼

SUBSTANTIATION REQUIREMENTS

The tax law is built on a voluntary system. Taxpayers file their tax returns, report income and take deductions to which they are entitled, and pay their taxes through withholding or estimated tax payments during the year. The taxpayer has the burden of proof for substantiating expenses deducted on the returns and must retain adequate records. Upon audit, the IRS will disallow any undocumented or unsubstantiated deductions. These requirements have resulted in numerous conflicts between taxpayers and the IRS.

Some events throughout the year should be documented as they occur. For example, it is generally advisable to receive a pledge payment statement from one's church, in addition to a canceled check (if available) for proper documentation of a charitable contribution.[58] In addition, for charitable contributions, a donor must obtain a receipt from the donee for contributions of $250 or more. Other types of deductible expenditures may require receipts or some other type of support.

---

[58]Rev.Proc. 92–71, 1992–2 C.B. 437, addresses circumstances where checks are not returned by a financial institution or where electronic transfers are made.

Specific and *more stringent* rules for deducting travel, entertainment, and gift expenses are discussed in Chapter 8. Certain mixed-use (both personal and business use) and listed property are also subject to the adequate records requirement (discussed in Chapter 7).

EXPENSES AND INTEREST RELATING TO TAX-EXEMPT INCOME

Certain income, such as interest on municipal bonds, is tax-exempt.[59] The law also allows the taxpayer to deduct expenses incurred for the production of income.[60] Deduction disallowance provisions, however, make it impossible to make money at the expense of the government by excluding interest income and deducting interest expense.[61]

EXAMPLE 39

Sandy, a taxpayer in the 36% bracket, purchased $100,000 of 6% municipal bonds. At the same time, she used the bonds as collateral on a bank loan of $100,000 at 8% interest. A positive cash flow would result from the tax benefit as follows:

Cash paid out on loan	($8,000)
Cash received from bonds	6,000
Tax savings from deducting interest expense (36% of $8,000 interest expense)	2,880
Net positive cash flow	$ 880

To eliminate the possibility illustrated in Example 39, the Code specifically disallows as a deduction the expenses of producing tax-exempt income. Interest on any indebtedness incurred or continued to purchase or carry tax-exempt obligations also is disallowed.

Judicial Interpretations. It is often difficult to show a direct relationship between borrowings and investment in tax-exempt securities. Suppose, for example, that a taxpayer borrows money, adds it to existing funds, buys inventory and stocks, then later sells the inventory and buys municipal bonds. A series of transactions such as these can completely obscure any connection between the loan and the tax-exempt investment. One solution would be to disallow interest on any debt to the extent that the taxpayer holds any tax-exempt securities. This approach would preclude individuals from deducting part of their home mortgage interest if they owned any municipal bonds. The law was not intended to go to such extremes. As a result, judicial interpretations have tried to be reasonable in disallowing interest deductions.

In one case, a company used municipal bonds as collateral on short-term loans to meet seasonal liquidity needs.[62] The Court disallowed the interest deduction on the grounds that the company could predict its seasonal liquidity needs. The company could anticipate the need to borrow the money to continue to carry the tax-exempt securities. The same company *was* allowed an interest deduction on a building mortgage, even though tax-exempt securities it owned could have been sold to pay off the mortgage. The Court reasoned that short-term liquidity needs would have been impaired if the tax-exempt securities were sold. Furthermore, the Court ruled that carrying the tax-exempt securities bore no relationship to the long-term financing of a construction project.

---

[59]§ 103.
[60]§ 212.
[61]§ 265.

[62]*The Wisconsin Cheeseman, Inc. v. U.S.*, 68–1 USTC ¶9145, 21 AFTR2d 383, 388 F.2d 420 (CA–7, 1968).

EXAMPLE 40

In January of the current year, Alan borrowed $100,000 at 8% interest. He used the loan proceeds to purchase 5,000 shares of stock in White Corporation. In July, he sold the stock for $120,000 and reinvested the proceeds in City of Denver bonds, the income from which is tax-exempt. Assuming the $100,000 loan remained outstanding throughout the entire year, Alan cannot deduct the interest attributable to the period in which he held the bonds. ▼

TAX PLANNING CONSIDERATIONS

TIME VALUE OF TAX DEDUCTIONS

Cash basis taxpayers often have the ability to make early payments for their expenses at the end of the tax year. This permits the payments to be deducted currently instead of in the following tax year. In view of the time value of money, a tax deduction this year may be worth more than the same deduction next year. Before employing this strategy, the taxpayer must consider next year's expected income and tax rates and whether a cash-flow problem may develop from early payments. Thus, the time value of money as well as tax rate changes must be considered when an expense can be paid and deducted in either of two years.

4 **LEARNING OBJECTIVE**
Identify tax planning opportunities for maximizing deductions and minimizing the disallowance of deductions.

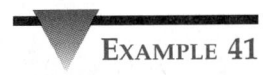

EXAMPLE 41

Jena pledged $5,000 to her church's special building fund. She can make the contribution in December 1998 or January 1999. Jena is in the 36% tax bracket in 1998, and in the 31% bracket in 1999. She itemizes in both years. Assume Jena's discount rate is 8%. If she takes the deduction in 1998, she saves $365 ($1,800 – $1,435), due to the decrease in the tax rates and the time value of money.

	1998	**1999**
Contribution	$5,000	$5,000
Tax bracket	.36	.31
Tax savings	$1,800	$1,550
Discounted @ 8%	1.0	.926
Savings in present value	$1,800	$1,435

▼

EXAMPLE 42

Assume the same facts as in Example 41, except that Jena is in the 31% bracket in both 1998 and 1999. By taking the deduction in 1998, Jena saves $115 ($1,550 – $1,435), due to the time value of money.

	1998	**1999**
Contribution	$5,000	$5,000
Tax bracket	.31	.31
Tax savings	$1,550	$1,550
Discounted @ 8%	1.0	.926
Savings in present value	$1,550	$1,435

▼

UNREASONABLE COMPENSATION

In substantiating the reasonableness of a shareholder-employee's compensation, an internal comparison test is sometimes useful. If it can be shown that nonshareholder-employees and shareholder-employees in comparable positions receive comparable compensation, it is indicative that compensation is not unreasonable.

Classification of Expenses

Expense Item	Deductible For AGI	Deductible From AGI	Not Deductible	Applicable Code §
Investment expenses				
Rent and royalty	X			§ 62(a)(4)
All other investments		X[4]		§ 212
Employee expenses				
Commuting expenses			X	§ 262
Travel and transportation[1]		X[4,5]		§ 162(a)(2)
Reimbursed expenses[1]	X			§ 62(a)(2)(A)
Moving expenses	X			§ 62(a)(15)
Entertainment[1]		X[4,5]		§ 162(a)
All other employee expenses[1]		X[4,5]		§ 162(a)
Certain expenses of performing artists	X			§ 62(a)(2)(B)
Trade or business expenses	X			§§ 162 and 62(a)(1)
Casualty losses				
Business	X			§ 165(c)(1)
Personal		X[6]		§ 165(c)(3)
Tax determination				
Collection or refund expenses	X[8]	X[4]		§§ 212 and 62(a)(1) or (4)
Bad debts	X			§§ 166 and 62(a)(1) or (3)
Medical expenses		X[7]		§ 213
Charitable contributions		X		§ 170
Taxes				
Trade or business	X			§§ 162 and 62(a)(1)
Personal taxes				
Real property		X		§ 164(a)(1)
Personal property		X		§ 164(a)(2)
State and local income		X		§ 164(a)(3)
Investigation of a business[2]	X			§§ 162 and 62(a)(1)
Interest				
Business	X			§§ 162 and 62(a)(1)
Personal		X[3]	X[9]	§§ 163(a), (d), and (h)
All other personal expenses			X	§ 262

1. Deduction *for* AGI if reimbursed, an adequate accounting is made, and employee is required to repay excess reimbursements.
2. Provided certain criteria are met.
3. Subject to the excess investment interest and the qualified residence interest provisions.
4. Subject (in the aggregate) to a 2%-of-AGI floor imposed by § 67.
5. Only 50% of meals and entertainment are deductible.
6. Subject to a $100 floor per event and a 10%-of-AGI floor per tax year.
7. Subject to a 7.5%-of-AGI floor.
8. Only the portion relating to business, rental, or royalty income or losses.
9. Other personal interest is disallowed.

Another possibility is to demonstrate that the shareholder-employee has been underpaid in prior years. For example, the shareholder-employee may have agreed to take a less-than-adequate salary during the unprofitable formative years of the business. The expectation is that the "postponed" compensation would be paid in later, more profitable years. The agreement should be documented, if possible, in the corporate minutes.

Keep in mind that in testing for reasonableness, the *total* pay package must be considered. Look at all fringe benefits or perquisites, such as contributions by the corporation to a qualified pension plan. Even though those amounts are not immediately available to the covered shareholder-employee, they must be taken into account.

EXCESSIVE EXECUTIVE COMPENSATION

With the $1 million limit on the deduction of compensation of covered employees, many corporations and their executives must engage in additional tax planning. Previously, concerns over the deductibility of compensation related primarily to closely held corporations. The $1 million limit applies specifically to publicly held corporations. In many instances, it is now necessary for these corporations to restructure the compensation packages of their top executives in order to deduct payments in excess of $1 million. Opportunities include compensation payable on a commission basis, certain other performance-based compensation, payments to qualified retirement plans, and payments that are excludible fringe benefits.

SHIFTING DEDUCTIONS

Taxpayers should manage their obligations to avoid the loss of a deduction. Deductions can be shifted among family members, depending upon which member makes the payment. For example, a father buys a condo for his daughter and puts the title in both names. The taxpayer who makes the payment gets the deduction for the property taxes. If the condo is owned by the daughter only and her father makes the payment, neither is entitled to a deduction. In this case, the father should make a cash gift to the daughter who then makes the payment to the taxing authority.

HOBBY LOSSES

To demonstrate that an activity has been entered into for the purpose of making a profit, a taxpayer should treat the activity as a business. The business should engage in advertising, use business letterhead stationery, and maintain a business phone.

If a taxpayer's activity earns a profit in three out of five consecutive years, the presumption is that the activity is engaged in for profit. It may be possible for a cash basis taxpayer to meet these requirements by timing the payment of expenses or the receipt of revenues. The payment of certain expenses incurred before the end of the year might be made in the following year. The billing of year-end sales might be delayed so that collections are received in the following year.

Keep in mind that the three-out-of-five-years rule under § 183 is not absolute. All it does is shift the presumption. If a profit is not made in three out of five years, the losses may still be allowed if the taxpayer can show that they are due to the nature of the business. For example, success in artistic or literary endeavors can take a long time. Also, depending on the state of the economy, even full-time farmers and ranchers are often unable to show a profit. How can one expect a part-time farmer or rancher to do so?

Merely satisfying the three-out-of-five-years rule does not guarantee that a taxpayer is automatically home free. If the three years of profits are insignificant relative to the losses of other years, or if the profits are not from the ordinary operation of the business, the taxpayer is vulnerable. The IRS may still be able to establish that the taxpayer is not engaged in an activity for profit.

▼ EXAMPLE 43

Ashley had the following gains and losses in an artistic endeavor:

1994	($50,000)
1995	(65,000)
1996	400
1997	200
1998	125

Under these circumstances, the IRS might try to overcome the presumption. ▼

If Ashley in Example 43 could show conformity with the factors enumerated in the Regulations or could show evidence of business hardships (e.g., injury, death, or illness), the government cannot override the presumption.[63]

CAPITAL EXPENDITURES

On the sale of a sole proprietorship where the sales price exceeds the fair market value of the tangible assets and stated intangible assets, a planning opportunity may exist for both the seller and the buyer. The seller's preference is for the excess amount to be allocated to goodwill. Goodwill is a capital asset whereas a covenant not to compete produces ordinary income treatment (see Chapter 13).

Because both a covenant and goodwill are amortized over a statutory 15-year period, the tax results of a covenant and goodwill are the same for the buyer. However, the buyer should recognize that an allocation to goodwill rather than a covenant may provide a tax benefit to the seller. Therefore, the seller and buyer, in negotiating the sales price, should factor in the tax benefit to the seller of having the excess amount labeled goodwill rather than a covenant not to compete. Of course, if the noncompetition aspects of a covenant are important to the buyer, part of the excess amount can be assigned to a covenant.

KEY TERMS

Accounting method, 5–8	Deductions *from* adjusted gross income, 5–2	Reasonableness, 5–7
Deductions *for* adjusted gross income, 5–2	Hobby losses, 5–16	Related-party transactions, 5–26
	Ordinary and necessary, 5–6	Vacation home, 5–18

---

[63]*Faulconer, Sr. v. Comm.*, 84–2 USTC ¶9955, 55 AFTR2d 85–302, 748 F.2d 890 (CA–4, 1984), *rev'g* 45 TCM 1084, T.C.Memo. 1983–165.

PROBLEM MATERIALS

DISCUSSION QUESTIONS

1. "All income must be reported and all deductions are allowed unless specifically disallowed in the Code." Discuss.

2. Discuss the difference in the tax treatment of deductions *for* and deductions *from* AGI.

3. Does an expenditure that is classified as a deduction *from* AGI produce the same tax benefit as an expenditure that is classified as a deduction *for* AGI?

4. Classify each of the following expenditures as a deduction *for* AGI, a deduction *from* AGI, or not deductible:
   a. Allison pays qualified moving expenses of $3,000.
   b. Emalie gives $1,000 to the Girl Scouts.
   c. Amos pays alimony of $2,500 per month to his former spouse.
   d. Arnold pays $600 for real estate taxes levied by the county on his personal residence.
   e. April gives $1,000 to a family whose house was destroyed by a fire.

5. Classify each of the following expenditures as a deduction *for* AGI, a deduction *from* AGI, or not deductible:
   a. Amos contributes $500 to his H.R. 10 plan (i.e., a retirement plan for a self-employed individual).
   b. Keith pays $500 of child support to his former wife, Renee, for the support of their son, Chris.
   c. Judy pays $500 for professional dues that are reimbursed by her employer.
   d. Ted pays $500 as the monthly mortgage payment on his personal residence. Of this amount, $100 represents a payment on principal, and $400 represents an interest payment.
   e. Lynn pays $500 to a moving company for moving her household goods to Detroit where she is starting a new job.

6. Larry and Susan each invest $10,000 in separate investment activities. They each incur deductible expenses of $800 associated with their respective investments. Explain why Larry's expenses are properly classified as deductions *from* AGI (itemized deductions) and Susan's expenses are appropriately classified as deductions *for* AGI.

7. List the three items that § 162 specifically excludes from classification as a trade or business expense.

8. Wendy, a machinist employed by Silver Airlines, owns 25 shares of Silver Airlines stock. Silver has 900,000 shares of stock outstanding. Wendy spends $800 to travel to Chicago for Silver's annual meeting. Her expenses would have been $500 more, but she was permitted to fly free on Silver. She attended both days of the shareholders' meeting and actively participated. What are the tax consequences of the trip for Wendy?

9. Sam and Vera are the owners of a corporation. To reduce the corporation's taxable income, they pay a $1,000 salary each month to their 7-year-old daughter, Peg. Why is this salary disallowed as a deduction?

10. Which of the following losses are deductible?
    a. Loss on the sale of a factory building used in a trade or business.
    b. Loss on the sale of a truck held for personal use.
    c. Loss from the destruction by a tornado of a warehouse used in a trade or business.
    d. Loss on the destruction by fire of the taxpayer's residence.
    e. Loss on the sale of Lavender Corporation stock held as an investment.

11. Mary Kate owns a building that she leases to an individual who operates a grocery store. Rent income is $10,000 and rental expenses are $6,000. On what Form 1040 schedule or schedules are the income and expenses reported?

12. Distinguish between the timing for the recording of a deduction under the cash method versus the accrual method.

13. Landry, a cash basis taxpayer, decides to reduce his taxable income for 1998 by buying $10,000 worth of supplies on December 28, 1998. The supplies will be used up in 1999.

a. Can Landry deduct this expenditure in 1998?

b. Would your answer differ if Landry bought the supplies because a supplier was going out of business and had given him a significant discount on the supplies?

14. What is the significance of the all events and economic performance tests?

15. James provides a one-year warranty on the vacuum cleaners manufactured by his company. Claims under the warranty typically amount to 2% of sales. Can James use the reserve method to account for the warranty expense?

16. Lemon, Inc., is a soft-drink distributor. Lemon's delivery trucks frequently are required to park in "No Parking" zones in order to make their deliveries. Occasionally, the trucks are ticketed and Lemon pays the parking fine. Can Lemon deduct these fines?

17. Ted is an agent for an airline manufacturer and is negotiating a sale with a representative of the U.S. government and with a representative of a developing country. Ted's company has sufficient capacity to handle only one of the orders. Both orders will have the same contract price. Ted believes that if his employer will authorize a $500,000 payment to the representative of the foreign country, he can guarantee the sale. He is not sure that he can obtain the same result with the U.S. government. Identify the relevant tax issues for Ted.

18. Stuart, an insurance salesman, is arrested for allegedly robbing a convenience store. He hires an attorney who is successful in getting the charges dropped. Is the attorney's fee deductible?

19. Linda operates a drug-running operation. Which of the following expenses she incurs can reduce taxable income?
a. Bribes paid to border guards.
b. Salaries to employees.
c. Price paid for drugs purchased for resale.
d. Kickbacks to police.
e. Rent on an office.

20. Gordon anticipates that being positively perceived by the individual who is elected mayor will be beneficial for his business. Therefore, he contributes to the campaigns of both the Democratic and the Republican candidates. The Republican candidate is elected mayor. Can Gordon deduct any of the political contributions he made?

21. Carmine, Inc., a tobacco manufacturer, incurs certain expenditures associated with political contributions and lobbying activities. Which of these expenditures can be deducted?

Payments to Washington, D.C. law firm to lobby members of Congress	$800,000
Payments to Washington, D.C. law firm to lobby the Vice President	200,000
Payments to Washington, D.C. law firm to lobby the head of the FDA	25,000
Payments to Richmond law firm to lobby members of the state legislature	50,000
Payments to Williamsburg law firm to lobby members of the Williamsburg City Council	5,000
Political contribution to the Democratic National Committee	300,000
Political contribution to the Republican National Committee	350,000
Political contribution to Committee to Re-elect the Mayor of Williamsburg	6,000

22. Agnes, an executive of a large corporation, receives a salary of $1.5 million. Taylor, who is an executive of another large corporation, receives a salary of $1.3 million. Agnes's corporation is permitted to deduct all of her salary while Taylor's corporation is permitted to deduct only part of his. Explain how this could happen. Assume both salaries are reasonable.

23. Ralph owns a restaurant in Baton Rouge. He is considering expanding into New Orleans by purchasing an existing restaurant there. As an alternative, he is considering purchasing an economy motel in New Orleans that does not offer food services. What are the

tax consequences to Ralph of the costs incurred investigating each of these business opportunities?

24. Amanda had been raising quarter horses for three years. Each year, her losses were about $15,000. She projects that her losses for the current year will be about $10,000. However, if she sells a promising mare before the end of the year, the $10,000 projected loss can be converted into a $4,000 projected profit. Without the perceived need to produce a current-year profit, Amanda would prefer to keep the mare for breeding purposes. Identify the relevant tax issues for Amanda.

25. Are there any circumstances under which a taxpayer can rent his or her personal residence and not be required to report the rent income received?

26. Karen and Andy own a beach house. They have an agreement with a rental agent to rent it up to 200 days per year. For the past three years, the agent has been successful in renting it for 200 days. Karen and Andy use the beach house for one week during the summer and one week during Thanksgiving. Their daughter, Sarah, a college student, has asked if she and some friends can use the beach house for the week of spring break. Advise Karen and Andy how they should respond and identify any relevant tax issues.

27. Hank was transferred from Phoenix to North Dakota on March 1 of the current year. He immediately put his home in Phoenix up for rent. The home was rented May 1 to November 30 and was vacant during the month of December. It was rented again on January 1 for six months. What expenses, if any, can Hank deduct on his return? Which deductions are *for* AGI and which ones are *from* AGI?

28. Erika would like to help her daughter Hillary and son-in-law James with what she hopes are short-term financial problems. This assistance will be in the form of paying their monthly mortgage payments for the past six months. If the payments are not made, the mortgage company will foreclose on their residence. Erika's preference is to make the payments directly to the mortgage company. However, she is willing to give the money to Hillary and James who then would pay the arrearages. Advise Erika on which option, if any, offers preferential tax treatment to her.

29. Explain which, if any, legal fees incurred obtaining a divorce are deductible. Are they deductible *for* or *from* AGI?

30. Igor repaired the roof on his factory at a cost of $1,500 in the current year. During the same year, Raisa replaced the roof on her small rental house for $1,500. Both taxpayers are on the cash basis. Are their expenditures treated the same on their tax returns? Why or why not?

31. Ella owns 60% of the stock of Peach. The stock has declined in value since Ella purchased it five years ago. She is going to sell 5% of her stock to a relative to pay her 12-year-old daughter's private school tuition. Ella is also going to make a gift of 10% of her stock to another relative. Identify the relevant tax issues for Ella.

32. Which of the following are related parties under § 267?

- Mother
- Sister
- Nephew
- Aunt
- Cousin
- Granddaughter
- Corporation in which the shareholder owns 45% of the stock

PROBLEMS

33. Sandra is an attorney. She incurs the following expenses when she and her employee, Fred, attend the American Bar Association convention in San Francisco:

Conference registration:	
Sandra	$200
Fred	200
Airline tickets from Pittsburgh to San Francisco:	
Sandra	700
Fred	400
Lodging in San Francisco:	
Sandra	450
Fred	250

Calculate the effect of these expenses on Sandra's AGI.

34. Calvin received the following income and incurred and paid the following expenses during the current tax year:

Salary income	$60,000
Dividend income	4,000
Interest income	3,000
Contributions to First Church	2,500
Real estate taxes on personal residence	1,800
Alimony paid to former spouse	12,000
Retirement plan contribution	2,000
Mortgage interest on personal residence	6,000
State income taxes	3,500
Loss on the sale of stock	900

Calculate Calvin's AGI.

35. Drew and his wife Cassie own all of the stock of Thrush. Cassie is the president and Drew is the vice-president. Cassie and Drew are paid salaries of $400,000 and $300,000, respectively, each year. They consider the salaries to be reasonable based on a comparison with salaries paid for comparable positions in comparable companies. They project Thrush's taxable income for next year, before their salaries, to be $800,000. They decide to place their four teenage children on the payroll and to pay them total salaries of $100,000. The children will each work about five hours per week for Thrush.
    a. What are Drew and Cassie trying to achieve by hiring the children?
    b. Calculate the tax consequences of hiring the children on Thrush, and on Drew and Cassie's family.

36. Amber incurs the following losses during the current tax year:

Loss on the sale of Brown stock	$ 1,100
Theft loss of uninsured car used in Amber's business	1,500
Loss on the sale of Amber's personal use car	3,000
Loss on the sale of Amber's personal residence	12,000
Loss on sale of City of Norfolk bonds	900

Calculate Amber's deductible losses.

37. The income statement for Karl's business reported the following revenues and expenses for 1998, the initial year of operations:

Sales revenue (including $8,000 credit sales uncollected at year-end)	$60,000
Wage expenses ($1,000 unpaid at year-end)	22,000
Office expenses (supplies, copying, etc.)	2,000
Bad debt expense (consists of reserve established for $3,000 with write-offs of $500)	3,000
Utilities and telephone expense*	6,000
Insurance expense*	4,000
Rent expense (January 1, 1998–January 31, 1999)	9,750

*Amount incurred = amount paid.

a. Calculate Karl's AGI using the accrual method.
b. Calculate Karl's AGI using the cash method.

38. Doris is the owner of a sole proprietorship that uses the cash method. She leases an office building for $24,000 for an 18-month period on October 1, 1998. In order to obtain this favorable lease rate, she pays the $24,000 at the inception of the lease. How much rent expense may Doris deduct on her 1998 tax return?

39. Duck, an accrual basis corporation, sponsored a rock concert on December 29, 1998. Gross receipts were $300,000. The following expenses were incurred and paid as indicated:

Expense		**Payment Date**
Rental of coliseum	$ 25,000	December 21, 1998
Cost of goods sold:		
Food	30,000	December 30, 1998
Souvenirs	60,000	December 30, 1998
Performers	100,000	January 5, 1999
Cleaning of coliseum	10,000	February 1, 1999

Since the coliseum was not scheduled to be used again until January 15, the company with which Duck had contracted did not actually perform the cleanup until January 8–10, 1999.

Calculate Duck's net income from the concert for tax purposes for 1998.

40. Doug incurred and paid the following expenses during the year:

- $50 for a ticket for running a red light while he was commuting to work.

- $100 for a ticket for parking in a handicapped parking space.

- $200 to an attorney to represent him for the two above tickets.

- $500 to an attorney to draft a lease agreement with a tenant for a one-year lease on an apartment that Doug owns.

Determine the amount that Doug can deduct for each of these payments.

41. Marcia, an attorney with a leading New York law firm, is convicted of failing to file Federal income tax returns for 1994–1996. Her justification for failing to do so was the pressures of her profession (80–90 hour workweeks). She is assessed taxes, interest, and penalties of $90,000 by the IRS. In addition, she incurs related legal fees of $60,000. Determine the amount that Marcia can deduct, and classify it as a deduction *for* or a deduction *from* AGI.

42. David runs an illegal numbers racket. His gross revenues were $500,000. He incurred the following expenses:

Illegal kickbacks	$20,000
Salaries	80,000
Rent	24,000
Utilities and telephone	9,000
Bribes to police	25,000
Interest	6,000
Depreciation on equipment	12,000

a. What is his net income from this business that is includible in taxable income?

b. If the business was an illegal drug operation and cost of goods sold was $100,000, how would your answer differ?

43. Edward, an attorney, is hired by a major accounting firm to represent it and its clients in dealing with members of the U.S. Congress. The accounting firm is supporting liability reform that would limit the "joint and several" liability of professionals such as attorneys and CPAs. During the year, Edward is paid $10,000 for this representation. The firm also reimburses Edward $2,500 for meal and entertainment expenses incurred in meeting with members of Congress and their staffs. In addition, the firm pays Edward $5,000 for his work in opposing legislation that would adversely affect several of its major clients. What is the amount of these payments that the firm may deduct?

44. Amber, a publicly held corporation, currently pays its president an annual salary of $900,000. In addition, it contributes $20,000 annually to a defined contribution pension plan for him. As a means of increasing company profitability, the board of directors decides to increase the president's compensation. Two proposals are being considered. Under the first proposal, the salary and pension contribution for the president would be increased by 30%. Under the second proposal, Amber would implement a performance-based compensation program that is projected to provide about the same amount of additional compensation and pension contribution for the president.

a. Evaluate the alternatives from the perspective of Amber, Inc.

b. Prepare a letter to Amber's board of directors that contains your recommendations. Address the letter to the board chairperson, Agnes Riddle, whose address is 100 James Tower, Cleveland, OH 44106.

45. Vermillion, Inc., a publicly held corporation, pays the following salaries to its executives:

	Salary	Bonus	Retirement Plan Contribution
CEO	$2,000,000	$100,000	$80,000
Executive vice president	1,800,000	90,000	72,000
Treasurer	1,600,000	–0–	64,000
Marketing vice president	1,500,000	75,000	60,000
Operations vice president	1,400,000	70,000	56,000
Distribution vice president	1,200,000	60,000	48,000
Research vice president	1,100,000	–0–	44,000
Controller	800,000	–0–	32,000

Vermillion normally does not pay bonuses, but after reviewing the results of operations for the year, the board of directors decided to pay a 5% bonus to selected executives. What is the amount of these payments that Vermillion may deduct?

46. Jenny, the owner of a very successful restaurant chain, is exploring the possibility of expanding the chain into a city in the neighboring state. She incurs $20,000 of expenses associated with this investigation. Based on the regulatory environment for restaurants in the city, she decides not to do so. During the year, she also investigates opening a hotel that will be part of a national hotel chain. Her expenses for this are $15,000. The

hotel begins operations on December 1. Determine the amount that Jenny can deduct in the current year for investigating these two businesses.

47. Tim traveled to a neighboring state to investigate the purchase of two restaurants. His expenses included travel, legal, accounting, and miscellaneous expenses. The total was $12,000. He incurred the expenses in March and April 1998.
    a. What can Tim deduct in 1998 if he was in the restaurant business and did not acquire the two restaurants?
    b. What can Tim deduct in 1998 if he was in the restaurant business and acquired the two restaurants and began operating them on July 1, 1998?
    c. What can Tim deduct in 1998 if he did not acquire the two restaurants and was not in the restaurant business?
    d. What can he deduct in 1998 if he acquired the two restaurants, but was not in the restaurant business when he acquired them? Operations began on July 1, 1998.

48. Alfred, who is single, conducts an activity that is appropriately classified as a hobby. The activity produces the following revenues and expenses:

Revenue	$10,000
Property taxes	3,000
Materials and supplies	2,000
Utilities	1,000
Advertising	2,500
Insurance	500
Depreciation	4,000

Without regard to this activity, Alfred's AGI is $40,000. Determine how much income Alfred must report, the amount of the expenses he is permitted to deduct, and his taxable income.

49. Sandra, an orthodontist, is single and has net earnings of $90,000 from her orthodontic practice. In addition, she collects antique books that she buys and sells at antique shows. She participates in six to eight weekend antique shows per year. Her income and expenses for the current year are as follows:

Revenue from sale of antique books	$22,000
Expenses	
Cost of goods sold	12,000
Show registration costs	3,000
Advertising	1,000
Dealer's license—annual fee	500
Insurance	900
Depreciation of display cases	1,200

Sandra has no other items that would affect her AGI. Itemized deductions from taxes, interest, and charitable contributions are $19,000.
    a. Calculate Sandra's taxable income if the antique book activity is classified as a hobby.
    b. Calculate Sandra's taxable income if the antique book activity is classified as a business.

50. Ashley, who lives in a summer resort area, rented her personal residence for two weeks while she was visiting Paris. Rent income was $2,000. Related expenses for the year were as follows:

Real property taxes	$ 3,000
Mortgage interest	6,000
Utilities	2,400
Insurance	1,200
Repairs	600
Depreciation	12,000

Determine the effect on Ashley's AGI.

51. In 1998, Anna rented her vacation home for 60 days, used it personally for 20 days, and left it vacant for 285 days. She had the following income and expenses:

Rent income	$ 6,000
Expenses	
Real estate taxes	2,000
Interest on mortgage	9,000
Utilities	600
Repairs	1,000
Roof replacement	12,000
Depreciation	8,000

 a. Compute Anna's net rent income or loss and the amounts she can itemize on her tax return, using the court's approach in allocating property taxes and interest.
 b. How would your answer in (a) differ using the IRS's method of allocating property taxes and interest?

52. How would your answer in Problem 51 differ if Anna had rented the house for 90 days and had used it personally for 12 days?

53. Chee, single, age 40, had the following income and expenses in 1998:

Income	
Salary	$43,000
Rental of vacation home (rented 60 days, used personally 60 days, vacant 245 days)	4,000
Municipal bond interest	2,000
Dividend from General Motors	400
Expenses	
Interest	
On home mortgage	8,400
On vacation home	4,758
On loan used to buy municipal bonds	3,100
Taxes	
Property tax on home	2,200
Property tax on vacation home	1,098
State income tax	3,300
Charitable contributions	1,100
Tax return preparation fee	300
Utilities and maintenance on vacation home	2,600
Depreciation on rental 50% of vacation home	3,500

Calculate Chee's taxable income for 1998 before personal exemptions.

54. Velma and Clyde operate a retail sports memorabilia shop. For the current year, sales revenue is $50,000 and expenses are as follows:

Cost of goods sold	$19,000
Advertising	1,000
Utilities	2,000
Rent	4,000
Insurance	1,500
Wages to Boyd	7,000

Velma and Clyde pay $7,000 in wages to Boyd, a part-time employee. Since this amount is $1,000 below the minimum wage, Boyd threatens to file a complaint with the appropriate Federal agency. Although Velma and Clyde pay no attention to Boyd's threat, Chelsie (Velma's mother) gives Boyd a check for $1,000 for the disputed wages. Both Velma and Clyde ridicule Chelsie for wasting money when they learn what she has done. The retail shop is the only source of income for Velma and Clyde.
   a. Calculate Velma and Clyde's AGI.
   b. Can Chelsie deduct the $1,000 payment on her tax return?
   c. How could the tax position of the parties be improved?

55. Terry is purchasing a business from the estate of Anne. The amount being paid exceeds the fair market value of the identifiable assets of the business by $150,000. Advise Terry on the tax consequences of the $150,000 being allocated to goodwill versus it being allocated to a 10-year covenant not to compete.

56. Jay's sole proprietorship has the following assets

	Basis	Fair Market Value
Cash	$ 10,000	$ 10,000
Accounts receivable	18,000	18,000
Inventory	25,000	30,000
Patent	22,000	40,000
Land	50,000	75,000
	$125,000	$173,000

The building in which Jay's business is located is leased. The lease expires at the end of the year.

Jay is age 70 and would like to retire. He expects to be in the 36% tax bracket. Jay is negotiating the sale of the business with Lois, a key employee. They have agreed on the fair market value of the assets, as indicated above, and agree the total purchase price should be about $200,000.
   a. Advise Jay regarding how the sale should be structured.
   b. Advise Lois regarding how the purchase should be structured.
   c. What might they do to achieve an acceptable compromise?

57. Janet Saxon sold stock (basis of $40,000) to her brother, Fred, for $32,000.
   a. What are the tax consequences to Janet?
   b. What are the tax consequences to Fred if he later sells the stock for $42,000? For $28,000? For $36,000?
   c. Write a letter to Janet in which you inform her of the tax consequences if she sells the stock to Fred for $32,000 and explain how a sales transaction could be structured that would produce better tax consequences for her. Janet's address is 32 Country Lane, Lawrence, KS 66045.

58. The Robin Corporation is owned as follows:

Irene	20%
Paul, Irene's husband	20%
Sylvia, Irene's mother	15%
Ron, Irene's father	25%
Quinn, an unrelated party	20%

Robin is on the accrual basis, and Irene and Paul are on the cash basis. Irene and Paul each loaned the Robin Corporation $10,000 out of their separate funds. On December 31, 1998, Robin accrued interest at 7% on both loans. The interest was paid on February 4, 1999. What is the tax treatment of this interest expense/income to Irene, Paul, and Robin?

59. What is Kim's constructive ownership of Wren Corporation, given the following information?

Shares owned by Kim	900
Shares owned by Sam, Kim's uncle	600
Shares owned by Barbara, Kim's partner	30
Shares owned by Vera, Kim's granddaughter	670
Shares owned by unrelated parties	800

60. Chris has a brokerage account and buys on the margin, which resulted in an interest expense of $9,000 during the year. Income generated through the brokerage account was as follows:

Municipal interest	$35,000
Taxable dividends and interest	65,000

How much investment interest can Chris deduct?

61. Lee incurred the following expenses in the current tax year. Indicate, in the spaces provided, whether each expenditure is deductible *for AGI*, *from AGI*, or not deductible.

	Expense Item	Deductible For AGI	Deductible From AGI	Not Deductible
a.	Lee's personal medical expenses	————	————	————
b.	Lee's dependent daughter's medical expenses	————	————	————
c.	Real estate taxes on rental property	————	————	————
d.	Real estate taxes on Lee's personal residence	————	————	————
e.	Real estate taxes on daughter's personal residence	————	————	————
f.	Lee's state income taxes	————	————	————
g.	Interest on rental property mortgage	————	————	————
h.	Interest on Lee's personal residence mortgage	————	————	————
i.	Interest on daughter's personal residence mortgage	————	————	————
j.	Interest on business loans	————	————	————
k.	Charitable contributions	————	————	————
l.	Depreciation on rental property	————	————	————
m.	Utilities & maintenance on:			
	(1) Rental property	————	————	————
	(2) Lee's home	————	————	————
	(3) Daughter's home	————	————	————

	Expense Item	Deductible		Not Deductible
		For AGI	From AGI	
n.	Depreciation on auto used in Lee's business	_____	_____	_____
o.	Depreciation on Lee's personal auto	_____	_____	_____
p.	Depreciation on daughter's personal auto	_____	_____	_____

CUMULATIVE PROBLEMS

62. John and Mary Jane Sanders are married, filing jointly. Their address is 204 Shoe Lane, Blacksburg, VA 24061. They are expecting their first two children (twins) in early 1999. John's salary in 1998 was $85,000, from which $11,000 of Federal income tax and $3,600 of state income tax were withheld. Mary Jane made $40,000 and had $4,000 of Federal income tax and $2,000 of state income tax withheld. The appropriate amount of FICA tax was withheld for John and for Mary Jane.

John and Mary Jane are both covered by their employer's medical insurance policies with all of the premiums being paid by the employers. The premiums were $3,600 for John and $3,200 for Mary Jane. Mary Jane received medical benefits of $2,400 under the plan. John was not ill during 1998.

John makes alimony payments of $30,000 per year to June, his former wife. He also makes child support payments of $12,000 for his son, Rod, who lives with June except for two months in the summer when he visits John and Mary Jane.

Mary Jane's father lived with them until his death in October. His only sources of income were salary of $1,600, $500 of unemployment compensation benefits, and Social Security benefits of $3,200. Of this amount, he deposited $3,000 in a savings account. The remainder of his support, including funeral expenses of $5,000, was provided by John and Mary Jane.

Other income received by the Sanders was as follows:

Interest on certificates of deposit	$ 900
Dividend income	600
Share of partnership taxable income (distributions from the partnership to Mary Jane were $200)	300
Award received by Mary Jane from employer for outstanding suggestion for cutting costs	1,000

They made charitable contributions of $3,500 during the year and paid an additional $700 in state income taxes in 1998 upon filing their 1997 state income tax return. Their deductible home mortgage interest was $9,000, and their property taxes came to $2,400. They had no other deductible expenses.

Part 1—Tax Computation
Calculate their tax (or refund) due for 1998. Suggested software (if available): *TurboTax*.

Part 2—Tax Planning
Assume that they come to you for advice in December 1998. John has learned that he will receive a $15,000 bonus. He wants to know if he should take it in December 1998 or in January 1999. Mary Jane will quit work on December 31 to stay home with the twins. Their itemized deductions will decrease by $2,000 because Mary Jane will not have state income taxes withheld. Mary Jane does not expect to receive the employee award in 1999. She expects the medical benefits received to be $4,500.

The Sanders expect all of their other income items to remain the same in 1999. Write a letter to John and Mary Jane that contains your advice and prepare a memo for the tax files. Suggested software (if available): *TurboTax*.

63. Helen Archer, age 30, is single and lives at 120 Sanborne Avenue, Springfield, IL 60740. Her Social Security number is 648–11–9981. Helen has been divorced from her former husband, Albert, for three years. She has a son, Jason, who is age 8. His Social Security number is 648–98–3471. Helen does not wish to contribute $3 to the Presidential Election Campaign Fund.

Helen, an advertising executive, earned a salary of $80,000 in 1997. Her employer withheld $11,000 in Federal income tax, $3,500 in state income tax, and the appropriate amount of FICA tax.

Helen has legal custody of Jason. Jason lives with his father during summer vacation. Albert indicates that his expenses for Jason are $10,000. Helen can document that she spent $4,500 for Jason's support during 1997.

Helen's mother died on January 7, 1997. Helen inherited assets worth $200,000 from her mother. As the sole beneficiary of her mother's life insurance policy, Helen received insurance proceeds of $100,000. Her mother's cost basis for the life insurance policy was $40,000. Helen's favorite aunt gave her $10,000 for her thirtieth birthday in October.

On November 8, 1997, Helen sells for $19,000 Amber stock that she had purchased for $20,000 from her first cousin, Walt, on December 5, 1991. His cost basis for the stock was $12,000, and the stock was worth $20,000 on December 5, 1991. On December 1, 1997, Helen sold Falcon stock for $15,000. She had acquired the stock on July 2, 1997, for $10,000.

An examination of Helen's records reveals the following information:

- Received interest income of $3,500 from First Savings Bank.

- Received groceries valued at $500 from a local grocery store for being the 100,000th customer.

- Received dividend income of $1,500 from Amber.

- Received $2,200 of interest income on City of Springfield school bonds.

- Received alimony of $20,000 from Albert.

- Received a distribution of $2,000 from ST Partnership. Her distributive share of the partnership passive taxable income was $2,800.

From her checkbook records, she determines that she made the following payments during 1997.

- Charitable contributions of $1,500 to First Presbyterian Church and $1,100 to the American Red Cross.

- Mortgage interest on her residence of $6,900.

- Property taxes of $1,900 on her residence and $900 on her car.

- Sales taxes of $1,700.

- Estimated Federal income taxes of $10,300 and estimated state income taxes of $1,000.

- Medical expenses of $4,000 for her and $500 for Jason. Eight hundred dollars of her medical expenses were reimbursed by her medical insurance policy in December.

Calculate Helen's net tax payable or refund due for 1997. If you use tax forms, you will need Form 1040 and Schedules A, B, D, and E. Suggested software (if available): *TurboTax*.

Research Problems for this chapter appear at the end of Chapter 28.

TEAM PROJECT: ARTHUR ANDERSEN TAX CHALLENGE CASES

For more information on the Arthur Andersen Tax Challenge Cases, refer to Chapter 1, page 1–37.

Information related to tax issues and problems that are discussed in this chapter may be found in the

Day and Ball case on pages 2, 3, 5, and 20–24
Fence case on pages 39, 40, 42 and 49

Read and analyze the case you have been assigned and *identify* any issues and problems that are related to material covered in this chapter. If the information provided in the case is complete, prepare answers for this part of the case at this time. If you need information that is contained in the later parts of the case, write a memo summarizing the questions or problems so you can prepare a complete answer at a later date.

DEDUCTIONS AND LOSSES: CERTAIN BUSINESS EXPENSES AND LOSSES

LEARNING OBJECTIVES

After completing Chapter 6 , you should be able to:

1. Determine the amount, classification, and timing of the bad debt deduction.

2. Understand the tax treatment of worthless securities including § 1244 stock.

3. Distinguish between deductible and nondeductible losses of individuals.

4. Identify a casualty and determine the amount, classification, and timing of casualty and theft losses.

5. Recognize and apply the alternative tax treatments for research and experimental expenditures.

6. Understand the nature of the net operating loss and recognize the impact of the carryback and carryover provisions.

7. Identify tax planning opportunities in deducting certain business expenses, business losses, and personal losses.

Working with the tax formula for individuals requires the proper classification of items that are deductible *for* adjusted gross income (AGI) and items that are deductions *from* AGI (itemized deductions). Business expenses and losses, discussed in this chapter, are reductions of gross income to arrive at the taxpayer's AGI. Expenses and losses incurred in connection with a transaction entered into for profit and attributable to rents and royalties are deducted *for* AGI. All other expenses and losses incurred in connection with a transaction entered into for profit are deducted *from* AGI.

The situation of Robert P. Groetzinger provides an interesting insight into the importance of the proper classification for the individual taxpayer. In January 1978, Groetzinger terminated his employment with a private company and devoted virtually all of his working time to pari-mutuel wagering on dog races. He had no other profession or employment, and his only sources of income, apart from his gambling winnings, were interest, dividends, and sales from investments. During the tax year in question, he went to the track six days a week and devoted 60 to 80 hours per week to preparing and making wagers on his own account.

The tax question that this case presents is whether Groetzinger's gambling activities constitute a trade or business. If the gambling is a trade or business, his gambling losses are deductions *for* AGI. If the gambling activity is not a trade or business, the losses are itemized deductions, and Groetzinger's taxes increase by $2,142.[1]

Deductible losses on personal use property are deducted as an itemized deduction. Itemized deductions are deductions *from* AGI. While the general coverage of itemized deductions is in Chapter 9, casualty and theft losses on personal use property are discussed in this chapter.

In determining the amount and timing of the deduction for bad debts, proper classification is again important. A business bad debt is classified as a deduction *for* AGI, and a nonbusiness bad debt is classified as a short-term capital loss.

Other topics discussed in Chapter 6 are research and experimental expenditures and the net operating loss deduction.

---

[1] *Groetzinger v. Comm.*, 85–2 USTC ¶9622, 56 AFTR2d 85–5683, 771 F.2d 269 (CA–7, 1985).

BAD DEBTS

1 LEARNING OBJECTIVE
Determine the amount, classification, and timing of the bad debt deduction.

If a taxpayer sells goods or provides services on credit and the account receivable subsequently becomes worthless, a **bad debt** deduction is permitted only if income arising from the creation of the account receivable was previously included in income.[2] No deduction is allowed, for example, for a bad debt arising from the sale of a product or service when the taxpayer is on the cash basis because no income is reported until the cash has been collected. Permitting a bad debt deduction for a cash basis taxpayer would amount to a double deduction because the expenses of the product or service rendered are deducted when payments are made to suppliers and to employees, or at the time of the sale.

EXAMPLE 1

Tracy, an individual engaged in the practice of accounting, performed accounting services for Pat for which she charged $8,000. Pat never paid the bill, and his whereabouts are unknown.

If Tracy is an accrual basis taxpayer, the $8,000 is included in income when the services are performed. When it is determined that Pat's account will not be collected, the $8,000 is expensed as a bad debt.

If Tracy is a cash basis taxpayer, the $8,000 is not included in income until payment is received. When it is determined that Pat's account will not be collected, the $8,000 is not deducted as a bad debt expense since it was never recognized as income. ▼

A bad debt can also result from the nonrepayment of a loan made by the taxpayer or from purchased debt instruments.

SPECIFIC CHARGE-OFF METHOD

Taxpayers (other than certain financial institutions) may use only the **specific charge-off method** in accounting for bad debts. Certain financial institutions are allowed to use the **reserve method** for computing deductions for bad debts.

A taxpayer using the specific charge-off method may claim a deduction when a specific business debt becomes either partially or wholly worthless or when a

---

[2]Reg. § 1.166–1(e).

specific nonbusiness debt becomes wholly worthless.[3] For the business debt, the taxpayer must satisfy the IRS that the debt is partially worthless and must demonstrate the amount of worthlessness.

If a business debt previously deducted as partially worthless becomes totally worthless in a future year, only the remainder not previously deducted can be deducted in the future year.

In the case of total worthlessness, a deduction is allowed for the entire amount in the year the debt becomes worthless. The amount of the deduction depends on the taxpayer's basis in the bad debt. If the debt arose from the sale of services or products and the face amount was previously included in income, that amount is deductible. If the taxpayer purchased the debt, the deduction is equal to the amount the taxpayer paid for the debt instrument.

One of the more difficult tasks is determining if and when a bad debt is worthless. The loss is deductible only in the year of partial or total worthlessness for business debts and only in the year of total worthlessness for nonbusiness debts. Legal proceedings need not be initiated against the debtor when the surrounding facts indicate that such action will not result in collection.

EXAMPLE 2   In 1996, Ross loaned $1,000 to Kay, who agreed to repay the loan in two years. In 1998, Kay disappeared after the note became delinquent. If a reasonable investigation by Ross indicates that he cannot find Kay or that a suit against Kay would not result in collection, Ross can deduct the $1,000 in 1998. ▼

Bankruptcy is generally an indication of at least partial worthlessness of a debt. Bankruptcy may create worthlessness before the settlement date. If this is the case, the deduction may be taken in the year of worthlessness.

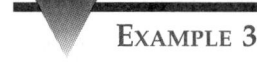

EXAMPLE 3   In Example 2, assume Kay filed for personal bankruptcy in 1997 and that the debt is a business debt. At that time, Ross learned that unsecured creditors (including Ross) were ultimately expected to receive 20¢ on the dollar. In 1998, settlement is made and Ross receives only $150. He should deduct $800 ($1,000 loan – $200 expected settlement) in 1997 and $50 in 1998 ($200 balance – $150 proceeds). ▼

If a receivable has been written off as uncollectible during the current tax year and is subsequently collected during the current tax year, the write-off entry is reversed. If a receivable has been written off as uncollectible, the collection of the receivable in a later tax year may result in income being recognized. Income will

---

[3]§ 166(a) and Reg. § 1.166.

result if the deduction yielded a tax benefit in the year it was taken. See Examples 38 and 39 in Chapter 4.

BUSINESS VERSUS NONBUSINESS BAD DEBTS

A **nonbusiness bad debt** is a debt unrelated to the taxpayer's trade or business either when it was created or when it became worthless. The nature of a debt depends on whether the lender was engaged in the business of lending money or whether there is a proximate relationship between the creation of the debt and the lender's trade or business. The use to which the borrowed funds are put by the debtor is of no consequence. Loans to relatives or friends are the most common type of nonbusiness bad debt.

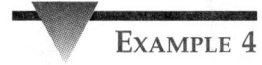

EXAMPLE 4

Jamil loaned his friend, Esther, $1,500. Esther used the money to start a business, which subsequently failed. Even though the proceeds of the loan were used in a business, the loan is a nonbusiness bad debt because the business was Esther's, not Jamil's. ▼

The distinction between a business bad debt and a nonbusiness bad debt is important. A **business bad debt** is deductible as an ordinary loss in the year incurred, whereas a nonbusiness bad debt is always treated as a short-term capital loss. Thus, regardless of the age of a nonbusiness bad debt, the deduction may be of limited benefit due to the capital loss limitations on deductibility in any one year. The maximum amount of a net short-term capital loss that an individual can deduct against ordinary income in any one year is $3,000 (see Chapter 13 for a detailed discussion). Although no deduction is allowed when a nonbusiness bad debt is partially worthless, the taxpayer is entitled to deduct the net amount of the loss upon final settlement.

The following example is an illustration of business bad debts adapted from the Regulations.[4]

EXAMPLE 5

In 1997, Leif sold his business but retained a claim (note or account receivable) against Bob. The claim became worthless in 1998. Leif's loss is treated as a business bad debt because the debt was created in the conduct of his former trade or business. Leif is accorded business bad debt treatment even though he was holding the note as an investor and was no longer in a trade or business when the claim became worthless. ▼

The nonbusiness bad debt provisions are *not* applicable to corporations. It is assumed that any loans made by a corporation are related to its trade or business. Therefore, any bad debts of a corporation are business bad debts.

LOANS BETWEEN RELATED PARTIES

Loans between related parties (especially family members) raise the issue of whether the transaction was a *bona fide* loan or a gift. The Regulations state that a bona fide debt arises from a debtor-creditor relationship based on a valid and enforceable obligation to pay a fixed or determinable sum of money. Thus, individual circumstances must be examined to determine whether advances between related parties are gifts or loans. Some considerations are these:

- Was a note properly executed?
- Was there a reasonable rate of interest?

---

[4]Reg. § 1.166–5(d).

- Was collateral provided?
- What collection efforts were made?
- What was the intent of the parties?

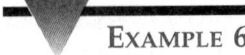

EXAMPLE 6

Lana loans $2,000 to her widowed mother for an operation. Lana's mother owns no property and is not employed, and her only income consists of Social Security benefits. No note is issued for the loan, no provision for interest is made, and no repayment date is mentioned. In the current year, Lana's mother dies leaving no estate. Assuming the loan is not repaid, Lana cannot take a deduction for a nonbusiness bad debt because the facts indicate that no debtor-creditor relationship existed. ▼

ETHICAL
CONSIDERATIONS

Writing Off a Loan to a Friend

Loans to family members and friends raise concerns with respect to whether a deductible bad debt exists. The fact that the debtor is a family member or friend does not preclude a deduction for a bad debt. However, evidence must show that the debt is bona fide and that it is in fact worthless.

Frank, an engineer, loans $8,000 to Chris, a friend from high school who is a musician. Chris uses the money to cut a record. The loan, which is evidenced by a formal written instrument, has a maturity date of three years and an 8 percent interest rate.

The record is unsuccessful, and at the maturity date, Chris does not repay the loan. Frank writes Chris twice requesting repayment. Frank hears from another friend that Chris is now divorced and has a drinking problem.

Frank decides to give up trying to collect the loan. Since Frank's combined Federal and state tax rate is 44 percent, he decides he can live without $4,480 ($8,000 × 56%). He deducts the $8,000 as a nonbusiness bad debt on his Federal and state tax returns.

Evaluate the financial and ethical aspects of what Frank has done.

LOSS ON DEPOSITS IN INSOLVENT FINANCIAL INSTITUTIONS

Qualified individuals can *elect* to deduct losses on deposits in qualified financial institutions as personal casualty losses in the year in which the amount of the loss can be reasonably estimated. If the election is made to treat a loss on a deposit as a personal casualty loss, no bad debt deduction for the loss is allowed.[5] As a personal casualty loss, the loss is subject to the $100 per event floor and the 10 percent-of-AGI aggregate floor. Both floors limiting casualty losses are explained later in the chapter. The amount of loss to be recognized under the election is the difference between (1) the taxpayer's basis in the deposit and (2) a reasonable estimate of the amount to be received.

A *qualified individual* is any individual other than:

- An owner of 1 percent or more of the value of the stock of the institution in which the loss was sustained.
- An officer of the institution.
- Certain relatives and other persons who are tax-related to such owners and officers.

---

[5]§ 165(l).

A *qualified financial institution* is a commercial bank, thrift institution, insured credit union, or any similar institution chartered and supervised under Federal or state law. A *deposit*, for purposes of this provision, is any deposit, withdrawal certificate, or withdrawable or repurchasable share of or in a qualified financial institution. The term *insolvent* generally denotes a situation where the liabilities exceed the fair market value of the assets.

If the individual does not elect to deduct the loss as a casualty loss, it is treated as a nonbusiness bad debt and, hence, as a short-term capital loss. As a short-term capital loss, it is subject to the capital loss limitation rules (see the discussion in Chapter 13).

WORTHLESS SECURITIES

2 **LEARNING OBJECTIVE**
Understand the tax treatment of worthless securities including § 1244 stock.

A loss is allowed for securities that become *completely* worthless during the year (**worthless securities**).[6] Such securities are shares of stock, bonds, notes, or other evidence of indebtedness issued by a corporation or government. The losses generated are treated as capital losses deemed to have occurred on the *last day* of the taxable year. By treating the loss as having occurred on the last day of the taxable year, a loss that would otherwise have been classified as short term (if the date of worthlessness was used) may be classified as a long-term capital loss. Capital losses may be of limited benefit due to the $3,000 capital loss limitation.

EXAMPLE 7

Ali, a calendar year taxpayer, owns stock in Owl Corporation (a publicly held company). The stock was acquired as an investment on May 31, 1997, at a cost of $5,000. On April 1, 1998, the stock became worthless. Since the stock is deemed to have become worthless as of December 31 of 1998, Ali has a capital loss from an asset held for 19 months (a long-term capital loss). ▼

SMALL BUSINESS STOCK

The general rule is that shareholders receive capital gain or loss treatment upon the sale or exchange of stock. However, it is possible to receive an ordinary loss deduction if the loss is sustained on **small business stock (§ 1244 stock).** This loss could arise from a sale of the stock or from the stock becoming worthless. Only *individuals*[7] who acquired the stock *from* the corporation are eligible to receive ordinary loss treatment under § 1244. The ordinary loss treatment is limited to $50,000 ($100,000 for married individuals filing jointly) per year. Losses on § 1244 stock in excess of the statutory limits receive capital loss treatment.

The corporation must meet certain requirements for the loss on § 1244 stock to be treated as an *ordinary*—rather than a capital—loss. The major requirement is that the total amount of money and other property received by the corporation for stock as a contribution to capital (or paid-in surplus) does not exceed $1 million. The $1 million test is made at the time the stock is issued. Section 1244 stock can be common or preferred stock. Section 1244 applies only to

---

[6]§ 165(g).
[7]The term "individuals" for this purpose includes a partnership but not a trust or an estate.

CONCEPT SUMMARY 6–2

Bad Debt Deductions

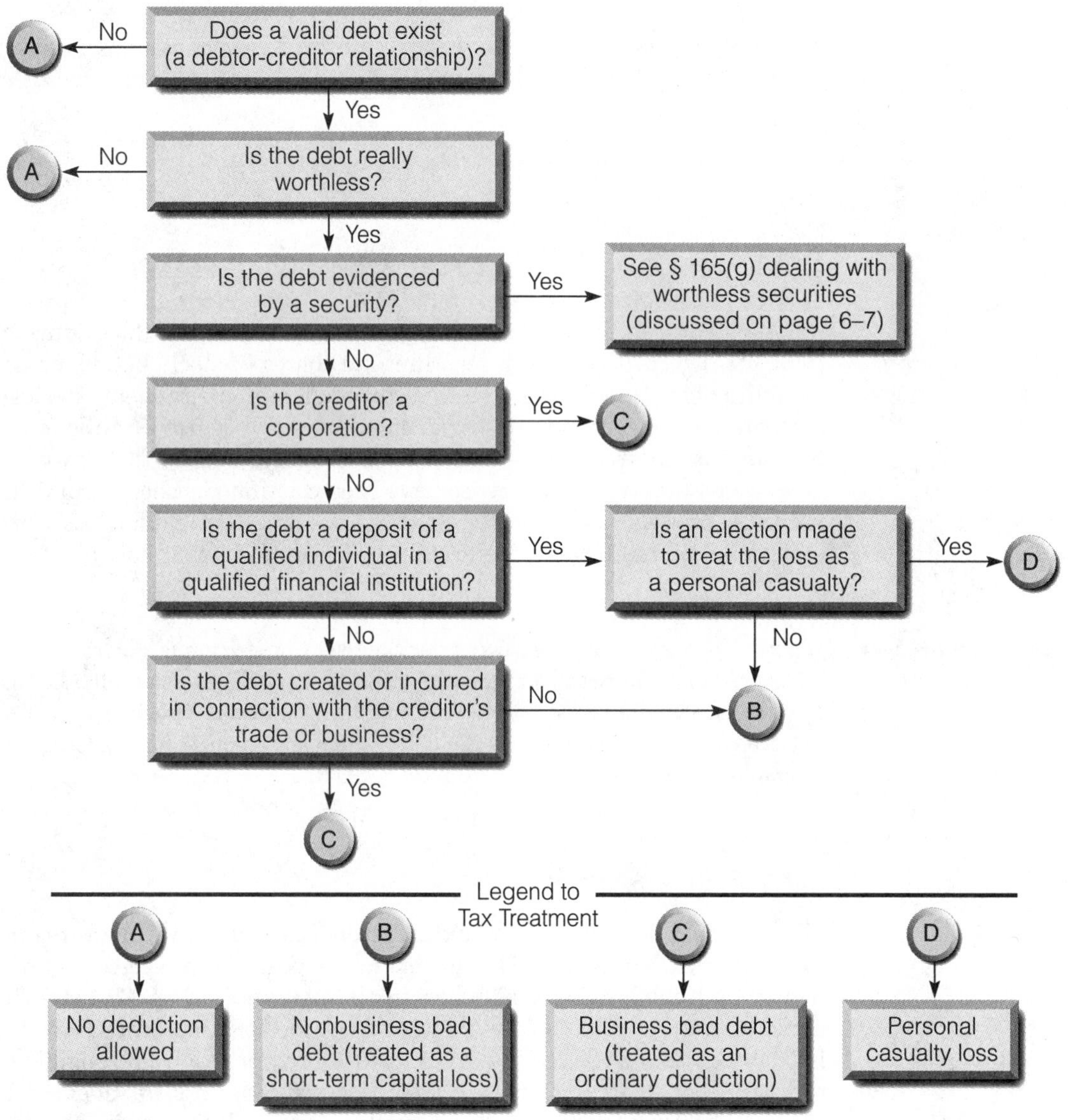

Ⓐ ← No — Does a valid debt exist (a debtor-creditor relationship)?

↓ Yes

Ⓐ ← No — Is the debt really worthless?

↓ Yes

Is the debt evidenced by a security? — Yes → See § 165(g) dealing with worthless securities (discussed on page 6–7)

↓ No

Is the creditor a corporation? — Yes → Ⓒ

↓ No

Is the debt a deposit of a qualified individual in a qualified financial institution? — Yes → Is an election made to treat the loss as a personal casualty? — Yes → Ⓓ

↓ No   ↓ No

Is the debt created or incurred in connection with the creditor's trade or business? — No → Ⓑ

↓ Yes

Ⓒ

―――― Legend to Tax Treatment ――――

Ⓐ	Ⓑ	Ⓒ	Ⓓ
No deduction allowed	Nonbusiness bad debt (treated as a short-term capital loss)	Business bad debt (treated as an ordinary deduction)	Personal casualty loss

losses. If § 1244 stock is sold at a gain, the Section has no application, and the gain is capital gain.

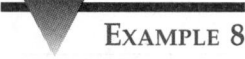

EXAMPLE 8   On July 1, 1996, Iris, a single individual, purchased 100 shares of Eagle Corporation common stock for $100,000. The Eagle stock qualified as § 1244 stock. On June 20, 1998, Iris sold all of the Eagle stock for $20,000. Because the Eagle stock is § 1244 stock, Iris would have $50,000 of ordinary loss and $30,000 of long-term capital loss. ▼

LOSSES OF INDIVIDUALS

3 **LEARNING OBJECTIVE**
Distinguish between deductible and nondeductible losses of individuals.

An individual may deduct the following losses under § 165(c):

- Losses incurred in a trade or business.
- Losses incurred in a transaction entered into for profit.
- Losses caused by fire, storm, shipwreck, or other casualty or by theft.

An individual taxpayer may deduct losses to property used in the taxpayer's trade or business or losses to property used in a transaction entered into for profit. Examples include a loss on property used in a proprietorship, a loss on property held for rent, or a loss on stolen bearer bonds. Note that an individual's losses on property used in a trade or business or on transactions entered into for profit are not limited to losses caused by fire, storm, shipwreck, or other casualty or by theft.

An individual taxpayer suffering losses from damage to nonbusiness property can deduct only those losses attributable to fire, storm, shipwreck, or other casualty or theft. Although the meaning of the terms *fire, storm, shipwreck,* and *theft* is relatively free from dispute, the term *other casualty* needs further clarification. It means casualties analogous to fire, storm, or shipwreck. The term also includes accidental loss of property provided the loss qualifies under the same rules as any other casualty. These rules are that the loss must result from an event that is (1) identifiable; (2) damaging to property; and (3) sudden, unexpected, and unusual in nature.

A *sudden event* is one that is swift and precipitous and not gradual or progressive. An *unexpected event* is an event that is ordinarily unanticipated and occurs without the intent of the individual who suffers the loss. An *unusual event* is one that is extraordinary and nonrecurring and does not commonly occur during the activity in which the taxpayer was engaged when the destruction occurred.[8] Examples include hurricanes, tornadoes, floods, storms, shipwrecks, fires, auto accidents, mine cave-ins, sonic booms, and vandalism. Weather that causes damages (drought, for example) must be unusual and severe for the particular region. Damage must be to the taxpayer's property to qualify as a **casualty loss.**

A taxpayer can take a deduction for a casualty loss from an automobile accident only if the damage was not caused by the taxpayer's willful act or willful negligence.

EXAMPLE 9

Ted parks his car on a hill and fails to set the brake properly and to curb the wheels. As a result of Ted's negligence, the car rolls down the hill and is damaged. The repairs to Ted's car should qualify for casualty loss treatment since Ted's act of negligence appears to be simple rather than willful. ▼

EVENTS THAT ARE NOT CASUALTIES

4 **LEARNING OBJECTIVE**
Identify a casualty and determine the amount, classification, and timing of casualty and theft losses.

Not all acts of God are treated as casualty losses for income tax purposes. Because a casualty must be sudden, unexpected, and unusual, progressive deterioration (such as erosion due to wind or rain) is not a casualty because it does not meet the suddenness test.

Examples of nonsudden events that generally do not qualify as casualties include disease and insect damages. When the damage was caused by termites over

---

[8]Rev.Rul. 72–592, 1972–2 C.B. 101.

a period of several years, some courts have disallowed a casualty loss deduction.[9] On the other hand, some courts have held that termite damage over periods of up to 15 months after infestation constituted a sudden event and was, therefore, deductible as a casualty loss.[10] Despite the existence of some judicial support for the deductibility of termite damage as a casualty loss, the current position of the IRS is that termite damage is not deductible.[11]

Other examples of events that are not casualties are losses resulting from a decline in value rather than an actual loss of the property. No loss was allowed where the taxpayer's home declined in value as a result of a landslide that destroyed neighboring homes but did no actual damage to the taxpayer's home.[12] Similarly, a taxpayer was allowed a loss for the actual flood damage to his property but not for the decline in market value due to the property's being flood-prone.[13]

THEFT LOSSES

Theft includes, but is not necessarily limited to, larceny, embezzlement, and robbery.[14] Theft does not include misplaced items.[15]

Theft losses are computed like other casualty losses (discussed in the following section), but the *timing* for recognition of the loss differs. A theft loss is deducted in the year of discovery, not the year of the theft (unless, of course, the discovery occurs in the same year as the theft). If, in the year of the discovery, a claim exists (e.g., against an insurance company) and there is a reasonable expectation of recovering the adjusted basis of the asset from the insurance company, no deduction is permitted.[16] If, in the year of settlement, the recovery is less than the asset's adjusted basis, a partial deduction may be available. If the recovery is greater than the asset's adjusted basis, gain may be recognized.

EXAMPLE 10

Keith's new sailboat, which he uses for personal purposes, was stolen from the storage marina in December 1996. He discovered the loss on June 3, 1997, and filed a claim with his insurance company that was settled on January 30, 1998. Assuming there is a reasonable expectation of full recovery, no deduction is allowed in 1997. A partial deduction may be available in 1998 if the actual insurance proceeds are less than the lower of the fair market value or the adjusted basis of the asset. (Loss measurement rules are discussed later in this chapter.) ▼

ETHICAL CONSIDERATIONS

Deducting a Theft Loss

Theft losses of personal use assets are itemized deductions in the year of discovery. The taxpayer must show that the property was actually stolen. Losses due to mislaying or losing property cannot be deducted. If there is no positive proof that a theft occurred, all of the details and evidence should be presented. If the reasonable inferences point to a theft, the Tax Court has allowed a deduction. If the inferences point to a mysterious (unexplained) disappearance, however, the deduction will be disallowed.

---

[9]*Fay v. Helvering*, 41–2 USTC ¶9494, 27 AFTR 432, 120 F.2d 253(CA–2, 1941); *U.S. v. Rogers*, 41–1 USTC ¶9442, 27 AFTR 423, 120 F.2d 244 (CA–9, 1941).

[10]*Rosenberg v. Comm.*, 52–2 USTC ¶9377, 42 AFTR 303, 198 F.2d 46 (CA–8, 1952); *Shopmaker v. U.S.*, 54–1 USTC ¶9195, 45 AFTR 758, 119 F.Supp. 705 (D.Ct.Mo., 1953).

[11]Rev.Rul. 63–232, 1963–2 C.B. 97.

[12]*H. Pulvers v. Comm.*, 69–1 USTC ¶9222, 23 AFTR2d 69–678, 407 F.2d 838 (CA–9, 1969).

[13]*S. L. Solomon*, 39 TCM 1282, T.C.Memo. 1980–87.

[14]Reg. § 1.165–8(d).

[15]*Mary Francis Allen*, 16 T.C. 163 (1951).

[16]Reg. §§ 1.165–1(d)(2) and 1.165–8(a)(2).

A taxpayer went shopping in a major city, riding the subway to and from the city. During the day, he purchased items using money from his wallet. When he arrived home, his wallet was missing. He is considering claiming a theft loss deduction for the wallet and the money it contained.

WHEN TO DEDUCT CASUALTY LOSSES

General Rule.   Generally, a casualty loss is deducted in the year the loss occurs. However, no casualty loss is permitted if a reimbursement claim with a *reasonable prospect of full recovery* exists.[17] If the taxpayer has a partial claim, only part of the loss can be claimed in the year of the casualty, and the remainder is deducted in the year the claim is settled.

EXAMPLE 11

Brian's new sailboat was completely destroyed by fire in 1998. Its cost and fair market value were $10,000. Brian's only claim against the insurance company was on a $7,000 policy that was not settled by year-end. The following year, 1999, Brian settled with the insurance company for $6,000. He is entitled to a $3,000 deduction in 1998 and a $1,000 deduction in 1999. If Brian held the sailboat for personal use, the $3,000 deduction in 1998 would be reduced first by $100 and then by 10% of his 1998 AGI. The $1,000 deduction in 1999 would be reduced by 10% of his 1999 AGI (see the following discussion on the $100 and 10% floors). ▼

If a taxpayer receives reimbursement for a casualty loss sustained and deducted in a previous year, an amended return is not filed for that year. Instead, the taxpayer must include the reimbursement in gross income on the return for the year in which it is received to the extent that the previous deduction resulted in a tax benefit.

EXAMPLE 12

Fran had a deductible casualty loss of $5,000 on her 1997 tax return. Fran's taxable income for 1997 was $60,000. In June 1998, Fran was reimbursed $3,000 for the prior year's casualty loss. Fran would include the entire $3,000 in gross income for 1998 because the deduction in 1997 produced a tax benefit. ▼

Disaster Area Losses.   An exception to the general rule for the time of deduction is allowed for **disaster area losses,** which are casualties sustained in an area designated as a disaster area by the President of the United States.[18] In such cases, the taxpayer may *elect* to treat the loss as having occurred in the taxable year immediately *preceding* the taxable year in which the disaster actually occurred. The rationale for this exception is to provide immediate relief to disaster victims in the form of accelerated tax benefits.

If the due date, plus extensions, for the prior year's return has not passed, a taxpayer makes the election to claim the disaster area loss on the prior year's tax return. If the disaster occurs after the prior year's return has been filed, it is necessary to file either an amended return or a refund claim. In any case, the taxpayer must show clearly that such an election is being made.

Disaster loss treatment also applies in the case of a personal residence that has been rendered unsafe for use as a residence because of a disaster. This provision applies when, within 120 days after the President designates the area as a disaster area, the state or local government where the residence is located orders the taxpayer to demolish or relocate the residence.[19]

---

[17]Reg. § 1.165–1(d)(2)(i).
[18]§ 165(h).

[19]§ 165(k).

MEASURING THE AMOUNT OF LOSS

Amount of Loss.   The rules for determining the amount of a loss depend in part on whether business use, income-producing use, or personal use property was involved. Another factor that must be considered is whether the property was partially or completely destroyed.

If business property or property held for the production of income (e.g., rental property) is *completely destroyed*, the loss is equal to the adjusted basis of the property at the time of destruction.

EXAMPLE 13

Vicki's automobile, which was used only for business purposes, was destroyed by fire. Vicki had unintentionally allowed her insurance coverage to expire. The fair market value of the automobile was $9,000 at the time of the fire, and its adjusted basis was $10,000. Vicki is allowed a loss deduction of $10,000 (the basis of the automobile). The $10,000 loss is a deduction *for* AGI. ▼

A different measurement rule applies for *partial destruction* of business property and income-producing property and for *partial* or *complete destruction* of personal use property. In these situations, the loss is the *lesser* of the following:

- The adjusted basis of the property.
- The difference between the fair market value of the property before the event and the fair market value immediately after the event.

EXAMPLE 14

Kelly's uninsured automobile, which was used only for business purposes, was damaged in a wreck. At the date of the wreck, the fair market value of the automobile was $12,000, and its adjusted basis was $9,000. After the wreck, the automobile was appraised at $4,000. Kelly's loss deduction is $8,000 (the lesser of the adjusted basis or the decrease in fair market value). The $8,000 loss is a deduction *for* AGI. ▼

The deduction for the loss of property that is part business and part personal must be computed separately for the business portion and the personal portion.

Any insurance recovery reduces the loss for business, production of income, and personal use losses. In fact, a taxpayer may realize a gain if the insurance proceeds exceed the amount of the loss. Chapter 13 discusses the treatment of net gains and losses on business property and income-producing property.

A taxpayer is not permitted to deduct a casualty loss for damage to insured personal use property unless she files a *timely insurance claim* with respect to the damage to the property. This rule applies to the extent that any insurance policy provides for full or partial reimbursement for the loss.[20]

Generally, an appraisal before and after the casualty is needed to measure the amount of the loss. However, the *cost of repairs* to the damaged property is acceptable as a method of establishing the loss in value provided the following criteria are met:

- The repairs are necessary to restore the property to its condition immediately before the casualty.
- The amount spent for such repairs is not excessive.
- The repairs do not extend beyond the damage suffered.
- The value of the property after the repairs does not, as a result of the repairs, exceed the value of the property immediately before the casualty.[21]

Reduction for $100 and 10 Percent-of-AGI Floors. The amount of the loss for personal use property must be further reduced by a $100 *per event* floor and a 10 percent-of-AGI *aggregate* floor.[22] The $100 floor applies separately to each casualty and applies to the entire loss from each casualty (e.g., if a storm damages both a taxpayer's residence and automobile, only $100 is subtracted from the total amount of the loss). The losses are then added together, and the total is reduced by 10 percent of the taxpayer's AGI. The resulting loss is the taxpayer's itemized deduction for casualty and theft losses.

EXAMPLE 15

Rocky, who had AGI of $30,000, was involved in a motorcycle accident. His motorcycle, which was used only for personal use and had a fair market value of $12,000 and an adjusted basis of $9,000, was completely destroyed. He received $5,000 from his insurance company. Rocky's casualty loss deduction is $900 [$9,000 basis − $5,000 insurance − $100 floor − $3,000 (.10 × $30,000 AGI)]. The $900 casualty loss is an itemized deduction (*from* AGI). ▼

When a nonbusiness casualty loss is spread between two taxable years because of the *reasonable prospect of recovery* doctrine, the loss in the second year is not reduced by the $100 floor. This result occurs because this floor is imposed per event and has already reduced the amount of the loss in the first year. However, the loss in the second year is still subject to the 10 percent floor based on the taxpayer's second-year AGI (refer to Example 11).

Taxpayers who suffer qualified disaster area losses can elect to deduct the losses in the year preceding the year of occurrence. The disaster loss is treated as having occurred in the preceding taxable year. Hence, the 10 percent-of-AGI floor is determined by using the AGI of the year for which the deduction is claimed.[23]

Multiple Losses. The rules for computing loss deductions where multiple losses have occurred are explained in Examples 16 and 17.

EXAMPLE 16

During the year, Tim had the following casualty losses:

| Asset | Adjusted Basis | Fair Market Value of Asset | | Insurance Recovery |
		Before the Casualty	After the Casualty	
A	$900	$600	$–0–	$400
B	300	800	250	100

[20]§ 165(h)(4)(E).
[21]Reg. § 1.165–7(a)(2)(ii).

[22]§ 165(c)(3).
[23]§ 165(i).

Assets A and B were used in Tim's business at the time of the casualty. The following losses are allowed:

Asset A: $500. The complete destruction of a business asset results in a deduction of the adjusted basis of the property (reduced by any insurance recovery) regardless of the asset's fair market value.

Asset B: $200. The partial destruction of a business (or personal use) asset results in a deduction equal to the lesser of the adjusted basis ($300) or the decline in value ($550), reduced by any insurance recovery ($100).

Both Asset A and Asset B losses are deductions *for* AGI. The $100 floor and the 10%-of-AGI floor do not apply because the assets are business assets. ▼

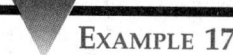

EXAMPLE 17

During the year, Emily had AGI of $20,000 and the following casualty losses:

Asset	Adjusted Basis	Fair Market Value of Asset		Insurance Recovery
		Before the Casualty	After the Casualty	
A	$ 900	$ 600	$ –0–	$200
B	2,500	4,000	1,000	–0–
C	800	400	100	250

Assets A, B, and C were held for personal use, and the losses to these three assets are from three different casualties. The loss for each asset is computed as follows:

Asset A: $300. The lesser of the adjusted basis of $900 or the $600 decline in value, reduced by the insurance recovery of $200, minus the $100 floor.

Asset B: $2,400. The lesser of the adjusted basis of $2,500 or the $3,000 decline in value, minus the $100 floor.

Asset C: $0. The lesser of the adjusted basis of $800 or the $300 decline in value, reduced by the insurance recovery of $250, minus the $100 floor.

Emily's itemized casualty loss deduction for the year is $700:

Asset A loss	$ 300
Asset B loss	2,400
Asset C loss	–0–
Total loss	$ 2,700
Less: 10% of AGI (10% × $20,000)	(2,000)
Itemized casualty loss deduction	$ 700

▼

STATUTORY FRAMEWORK FOR DEDUCTING LOSSES OF INDIVIDUALS

Casualty and theft losses incurred by an individual in connection with a trade or business are deductible *for* AGI.[24] These losses are not subject to the $100 per event and the 10 percent-of-AGI limitations.

[24]§ 62(a)(1).

Casualty and theft losses incurred by an individual in a transaction entered into for profit are not subject to the $100 per event and the 10 percent-of-AGI limitations. If these losses are attributable to rents or royalties, the deduction is *for* AGI.[25] However, if these losses are not connected with property held for the production of rents and royalties, they are deductions *from* AGI. More specifically, these losses are classified as other miscellaneous itemized deductions. An example of this type of loss would be the theft of a security. The aggregate of certain miscellaneous itemized deductions is subject to a 2 percent-of-AGI floor (explained in Chapter 8).

Casualty and theft losses attributable to personal use property are subject to the $100 per event and the 10 percent-of-AGI limitations. These losses are itemized deductions, but they are not subject to the 2 percent-of-AGI floor.[26]

PERSONAL CASUALTY GAINS AND LOSSES

If a taxpayer has personal casualty and theft gains as well as losses, a special set of rules applies for determining the tax consequences. A **personal casualty gain** is the recognized gain from a casualty or theft of personal use property. A **personal casualty loss** for this purpose is a casualty or theft loss of personal use property after the application of the $100 floor. A taxpayer who has both gains and losses for the taxable year must first net (offset) the personal casualty gains and personal casualty losses. If the gains exceed the losses, the gains and losses are treated as gains and losses from the sale of capital assets. The capital gains and losses are short term or long term, depending on the period the taxpayer held each of the assets. In the netting process, personal casualty and theft gains and losses are not netted with the gains and losses on business and income-producing property.

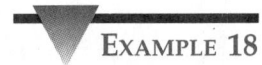

EXAMPLE 18

During the year, Cliff had the following personal casualty gains and losses (after deducting the $100 floor):

Asset	Holding Period	Gain or (Loss)
A	Three months	($ 300)
B	Three years	(2,400)
C	Two years	3,200

Cliff would compute the tax consequences as follows:

Personal casualty gain	$ 3,200
Personal casualty loss ($300 + $2,400)	(2,700)
Net personal casualty gain	$ 500

Cliff would treat all of the gains and losses as capital gains and losses and would have the following:

Short-term capital loss (Asset A)	$ 300
Long-term capital loss (Asset B)	2,400
Long-term capital gain (Asset C)	3,200

If personal casualty losses exceed personal casualty gains, all gains and losses are treated as ordinary items. The gains—and the losses to the extent of gains—are

---

[25]§ 62(a)(4).   [26]§ 67(b)(3).

treated as ordinary income and ordinary loss in computing AGI. Losses in excess of gains are deducted as itemized deductions to the extent the losses exceed 10 percent of AGI.[27]

EXAMPLE 19　During the year, Hazel had AGI of $20,000 and the following personal casualty gain and loss (after deducting the $100 floor):

Asset	Holding Period	Gain or (Loss)
A	Three years	($2,700)
B	Four months	200

Hazel would compute the tax consequences as follows:

Personal casualty loss	($2,700)
Personal casualty gain	200
Net personal casualty loss	($2,500)

Hazel would treat the gain and the loss as ordinary items. The $200 gain and $200 of the loss would be included in computing AGI. Hazel's itemized deduction for casualty losses would be computed as follows:

Casualty loss in excess of gain ($2,700 – $200)	$ 2,500
Less: 10% of AGI (10% × $20,000)	(2,000)
Itemized deduction	$ 500

RESEARCH AND EXPERIMENTAL EXPENDITURES

5 **LEARNING OBJECTIVE**
Recognize and apply the alternative tax treatments for research and experimental expenditures.

Section 174 covers the treatment of research and experimental expenditures. The Regulations define **research and experimental expenditures** as follows:

> . . . all such costs incident to the development of an experimental or pilot model, a plant process, a product, a formula, an invention, or similar property, and the improvement of already existing property of the type mentioned. The term does not include expenditures such as those for the ordinary testing or inspection of materials or products for quality control or those for efficiency surveys, management studies, consumer surveys, advertising, or promotions.[28]

Expenses in connection with the acquisition or improvement of land or depreciable property are not research and experimental expenditures. Rather, they increase the basis of the land or depreciable property. However, depreciation on a building used for research may be a research and experimental expense. Only the depreciation that is a research and experimental expense (not the cost of the asset) is subject to the three alternatives discussed below.

The law permits the following *three alternatives* for the handling of research and experimental expenditures:

- Expensed in the year paid or incurred.
- Deferred and amortized.
- Capitalized.

---

[27]§ 165(h).　　　　　　　　　　　　　　　[28]Reg. § 1.174–2(a)(1).

CONCEPT SUMMARY 6–3

Casualty Gains and Losses

	Business Use or Income-Producing Property	Personal Use Property
Event creating the loss	Any event.	Casualty or theft.
Amount	The lesser of the decline in fair market value or the adjusted basis, but always the adjusted basis if the property is totally destroyed.	The lesser of the decline in fair market value or the adjusted basis.
Insurance	Insurance proceeds received reduce the amount of the loss.	Insurance proceeds received (or for which there is an unfiled claim) reduce the amount of the loss.
$100 floor	Not applicable.	Applicable per event.
Gains and losses	Gains and losses are netted (see detailed discussion in Chapter 13).	Personal casualty and theft gains and losses are netted.
Gains exceeding losses		The gains and losses are treated as gains and losses from the sale of capital assets.
Losses exceeding gains		The gains—and the losses to the extent of gains—are treated as ordinary items in computing AGI. The losses in excess of gains, to the extent they exceed 10% of AGI, are itemized deductions.

If the costs are capitalized, a deduction is not available until the research project is abandoned or is deemed worthless. Since many products resulting from research projects do not have a definite and limited useful life, a taxpayer should ordinarily elect to write off the expenditures immediately or to defer and amortize them. It is generally preferable to elect an immediate write-off of the research expenditures because of the time value of the tax deduction.

The law also provides for a research activities credit. The credit amounts to 20 percent of certain research and experimental expenditures.[29] (The credit is discussed more fully in Chapter 11.)

EXPENSE METHOD

A taxpayer can elect to expense all of the research and experimental expenditures incurred in the current year and all subsequent years. The consent of the IRS is not required if the method is adopted for the first taxable year in which such expenditures were paid or incurred. Once the election is made, the taxpayer must continue to expense all qualifying expenditures unless a request for a change is

---

[29]§ 41. See the information in Chapter 11 on the termination date for the research activities credit.

made to, and approved by, the IRS. In certain instances, a taxpayer may incur research and experimental expenditures before actually engaging in any trade or business activity. In such instances, the Supreme Court has applied a liberal standard of deductibility and permitted a deduction in the year of incurrence.[30]

DEFERRAL AND AMORTIZATION METHOD

Alternatively, research and experimental expenditures may be deferred and amortized if the taxpayer makes an election.[31] Under the election, research and experimental expenditures are amortized ratably over a period of not less than 60 months. A deduction is allowed beginning with the month in which the taxpayer first realizes benefits from the experimental expenditure. The election is binding, and a change requires permission from the IRS.

EXAMPLE 20

Gold Corporation decided to develop a new line of adhesives. The project was begun in 1998. Gold incurred the following expenses in 1998 in connection with the project:

Salaries	$25,000
Materials	8,000
Depreciation on machinery	6,500

Gold incurred the following expenses in 1999 in connection with the project:

Salaries	$18,000
Materials	2,000
Depreciation on machinery	5,700

The benefits from the project will be realized starting in March 2000. If Gold Corporation elects a 60-month deferral and amortization period, there will be no deduction prior to March 2000, the month benefits from the project begin to be realized. The deduction for 2000 would be $10,867, computed as follows:

Salaries ($25,000 + $18,000)	$43,000
Materials ($8,000 + $2,000)	10,000
Depreciation ($6,500 + $5,700)	12,200
Total	$65,200
$65,200 × (10 months/60 months) =	$10,867

The option to treat research and experimental expenditures as deferred expense is usually employed when a company does not have sufficient income to offset the research and experimental expenses. Rather than create net operating loss carryovers that might not be utilized because of the 20-year limitation on such carryovers, the deferral and amortization method may be used. The deferral of research and experimental expenditures should also be considered if the taxpayer expects higher tax rates in the future.

---

[30]*Snow v. Comm.,* 74–1 USTC ¶9432, 33 AFTR2d 74–1251, 94 S.Ct. 1876 (USSC, 1974).

[31]§ 174(b)(2).

Net Operating Losses

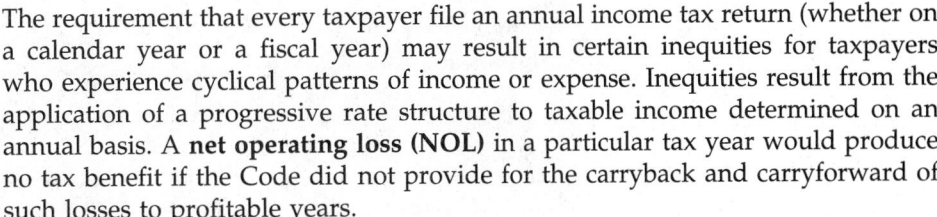

The requirement that every taxpayer file an annual income tax return (whether on a calendar year or a fiscal year) may result in certain inequities for taxpayers who experience cyclical patterns of income or expense. Inequities result from the application of a progressive rate structure to taxable income determined on an annual basis. A **net operating loss (NOL)** in a particular tax year would produce no tax benefit if the Code did not provide for the carryback and carryforward of such losses to profitable years.

EXAMPLE 21

Juanita has a business and realizes the following taxable income or loss over a five-year period: Year 1, $50,000; Year 2, ($30,000); Year 3, $100,000; Year 4, ($200,000); and Year 5, $380,000. She is married and files a joint return. Hubert also has a business and has a taxable income pattern of $60,000 every year. He, too, is married and files a joint return. Note that both Juanita and Hubert have total taxable income of $300,000 over the five-year period. Assume there is no provision for carryback or carryover of NOLs. Juanita and Hubert would have the following five-year tax bills:

Year	Juanita's Tax	Hubert's Tax
1	$ 8,495	$11,295
2	–0–	11,295
3	22,495	11,295
4	–0–	11,295
5	124,084	11,295
	$155,074	$56,475

The computation of tax is made without regard to any NOL benefit.
Rates applicable to 1998 are used to compute the tax.

Even though Juanita and Hubert realized the same total taxable income ($300,000) over the five-year period, Juanita had to pay taxes of $155,074, while Hubert paid taxes of only $56,475. ▼

To provide partial relief from this inequitable tax treatment, a deduction is allowed for NOLs.[32] This provision permits NOLs for any one year to be offset against taxable income of other years. The NOL provision is intended as a form of relief for business income and losses. Thus, only losses from the operation of a trade or business (or profession), casualty and theft losses, or losses from the confiscation of a business by a foreign government can create an NOL. In other words, a salaried individual with itemized deductions and personal exemptions in excess of gross income is not permitted to deduct the excess amounts as an NOL. On the other hand, a personal casualty loss is treated as a business loss and can therefore create (or increase) an NOL for an individual.

CARRYBACK AND CARRYOVER PERIODS

General Rules. An NOL must be applied initially to the two taxable years preceding the year of the loss (unless an election is made not to carry the loss back at all). It is carried first to the second prior year, and then to the immediately preceding tax year (or until used up). If the loss is not fully used in the carryback

---

[32]§ 172.

TAX IN THE NEWS

NET OPERATING LOSSES OF A BIOTECH COMPANY: THE VALUABLE ASSET

Aprogenex, a Houston biotech company, announced that it will reduce its operations to a minimal level. The company spent $29 million trying to develop a new medical testing technology, but the business did not work out to the extent expected. The stock was delisted by the American Stock Exchange, and efforts to raise additional capital were unsuccessful.

Aprogenex does, however, possess substantial NOLs that could be valuable to other biotech companies. In its press release, the company stated that one of its goals was to preserve the loss carryforwards and other items that could benefit shareholders.

SOURCE: Adapted from Bill Mintz, "Aprogenex to Cut Back Operations," *Houston Chronicle*, August 29, 1997, p. 2 of Business section.

period, it must be carried forward to the first year after the loss year, and then forward to the second, third, etc., year after the loss year. The carryover period is 20 years. A loss sustained in 1998 is used in this order: 1996, 1997, 1999 through 2018.

A three-year carryback period is available for any portion of an individual's NOL resulting from a casualty or theft loss. The three-year carryback rule also applies to NOLs that are attributable to presidentially declared disasters and are incurred by a small business or a taxpayer engaged in farming. A small business is one whose average annual gross receipts for a three-year period are $5 million or less.

If the loss is being carried to a preceding year, an amended return is filed on Form 1040X, or a quick refund claim is filed on Form 1045. In any case, a refund of taxes previously paid is requested. When the loss is carried forward, the current return shows an NOL deduction for the prior year's loss.

Sequence of Use of NOLs.   Where there are NOLs in two or more years, the rule is always to use the earliest year's loss first until it is completely absorbed. The later years' losses can then be used until they also are absorbed or lost. Thus, one year's return could show NOL carryovers from two or more years. Each loss is computed and applied separately.

Election to Forgo Carryback.   A taxpayer can *irrevocably elect* not to carry back an NOL to any of the prior years. In that case, the loss is available as a carryover for 20 years. A taxpayer would make the election if it is to his or her tax advantage. For example, a taxpayer might be in a low marginal tax bracket in the carryback years but expect to be in a high marginal tax bracket in future years. Therefore, it would be to the taxpayer's advantage to use the NOL to offset income in years when the tax rate is high rather than use it when the tax rate is relatively low.

7 **LEARNING OBJECTIVE**
Identify tax planning opportunities in deducting certain business expenses, business losses, and personal losses.

TAX CONSEQUENCES OF THE *GROETZINGER* CASE

In the *Groetzinger* case discussed earlier in the chapter, the court established that the appropriate tests for determining if gambling is a trade or business are whether an individual engages in gambling full-time in good faith, with regularity, and for the production of income as a livelihood, and not as a mere hobby. The court held that Robert Groetzinger satisfied the tests because of his constant and large-scale effort. Skill was required and was applied. He did what he did for a livelihood, though with less than successful results. His gambling was not a hobby, a passing fancy, or an occasional bet for amusement. Therefore, his gambling was a trade or business, and hence, he was able to deduct his gambling losses *for* AGI. If the court had ruled that Groetzinger's gambling was not a trade or business, his gambling losses would have been limited to his gambling winnings and would have been classified as itemized deductions.

DOCUMENTATION OF RELATED–TAXPAYER LOANS, CASUALTY LOSSES, AND THEFT LOSSES

Since non-bona fide loans between related taxpayers may be treated as gifts, adequate documentation is needed to substantiate a bad debt deduction if the loan subsequently becomes worthless. Documentation should include proper execution of the note (legal form) and the establishment of a bona fide purpose for the loan. In addition, it is desirable to stipulate a reasonable rate of interest and a fixed maturity date.

Since a theft loss is not permitted for misplaced items, a loss should be documented by a police report and evidence of the value of the property (e.g., appraisals, pictures of the property, newspaper clippings). Similar documentation of the value of property should be provided to support a casualty loss deduction because the amount of loss is measured, in part, by the decline in fair market value of the property.

Casualty loss deductions must be reported on Form 4684 (see Appendix B).

SMALL BUSINESS STOCK

Because § 1244 limits the amount of loss classified as ordinary loss on a yearly basis, a taxpayer might maximize the benefits of § 1244 by selling the stock in more than one taxable year. The result could be that the losses in any one taxable year would not exceed the § 1244 limits on ordinary loss.

EXAMPLE 22

Mitch, a single individual, purchased small business stock in 1996 for $150,000 (150 shares at $1,000 per share). On December 20, 1998, the stock is worth $60,000 (150 shares at $400 per share). Mitch wants to sell the stock at this time. Mitch earns a salary of $80,000 a year, has no other capital transactions, and does not expect any in the future. If Mitch sells all of the small business stock in 1998, his recognized loss will be $90,000 ($60,000 − $150,000). The loss will be characterized as a $50,000 ordinary loss and a $40,000 long-term capital loss. In computing taxable income for 1998, Mitch could deduct the $50,000 ordinary loss but could deduct only $3,000 of the capital loss. The remainder of the capital loss could be carried over and used in future years subject to the $3,000 limitation if Mitch has no capital gains. If Mitch sells 82 shares in 1998, he will recognize an ordinary loss of $49,200 [82 × ($1,000 − $400)]. If Mitch then sells the remainder of the shares in 1999, he will recognize an ordinary loss of $40,800 [68 × ($1,000 − $400)]. Mitch could deduct the $49,200 ordinary loss in computing 1998 taxable income and the $40,800 ordinary loss in computing 1999 taxable income. ▼

CASUALTY LOSSES

A special election is available for taxpayers who sustain casualty losses in an area designated by the President as a disaster area. This election affects only the timing, not the calculation, of the deduction. The deduction can be taken in the year before the year in which the loss occurred. Thus, an individual can take the deduction on the 1997 return for a loss occurring between January 1 and December 31, 1998. The benefit, of course, is a faster refund (or reduction in tax). It will also be advantageous to carry the loss back if the taxpayer's tax rate in the carryback year is higher than the tax rate in the year of the loss.

To find out if an event qualifies as a disaster area loss, one can look in any of the major tax services, the Weekly Compilation of Presidential Documents, or the *Internal Revenue Bulletin*.

NET OPERATING LOSSES

In certain instances, it may be advisable for a taxpayer to elect not to carry back an NOL. For an individual, the benefits from the loss carryback could be scaled down or lost due to the economic adjustments that must be made to taxable income for the year to which the loss is carried. For example, a taxpayer should attempt to minimize the number of taxable years to which an NOL is carried. The more years to which the NOL is applied, the more benefits are lost from adjustments for items such as personal and dependency exemptions.

The election not to carry back the loss might also be advantageous if there is a disparity in marginal tax rates applicable to different tax years.

 **EXAMPLE 23**

Abby sustained an NOL of $10,000 in Year 3. Her marginal tax bracket in Year 1 was 15%. In Year 4, however, she expects her bracket to be 39.6% due to a large profit she will make on a business deal. If Abby carries her loss back, her refund will be $1,500 (15% × $10,000). If she elects not to carry it back to Year 1 but chooses, instead, to carry it forward, her savings will be $3,960 (39.6% × $10,000). Even considering the time value of an immediate tax refund, Abby appears to be better off using the carryover approach. ▼

KEY TERMS

Bad debt, 6–3

Business bad debt, 6–5

Casualty loss, 6–9

Disaster area losses, 6–11

Net operating loss (NOL), 6–19

Nonbusiness bad debt, 6–5

Personal casualty gain, 6–15

Personal casualty loss, 6–15

Research and experimental expenditures, 6–16

Reserve method, 6–3

Section 1244 stock, 6–7

Small business stock, 6–7

Specific charge-off method, 6–3

Theft loss, 6–10

Worthless securities, 6–7

PROBLEM MATERIALS

DISCUSSION QUESTIONS

1. Explain whether a bad debt deduction is allowed for a debt arising from the sale of services by a cash basis taxpayer.

2. Discuss when a deduction may be taken for a business debt.

3. Discuss the tax treatment for the recovery of an account receivable previously written off as uncollectible.

4. Discuss the difference between business and nonbusiness bad debts. How is the distinction determined? How is each treated on the return?

5. What factors are to be considered in determining whether a bad debt arising from a loan between related parties is, in fact, a bad debt?

6. Sam used the cash method of accounting for Federal income tax purposes and filed a joint Federal income tax return for the current year. On February 27 of the current year, Sam instituted a civil lawsuit against Dave, alleging fraud in the handling of a real estate project in which Sam had invested. On June 19 of the current year, a default judgment was entered against Dave and in favor of Sam. Under its terms, Sam was to recover from Dave general damages of $20,000 and punitive damages of $50,000. During the current year, Sam did not recover from Dave any of either the general or the punitive damages. Identify the relevant tax issues for Sam.

7. Discuss a taxpayer's options for the tax treatment of a loss incurred on a deposit in a qualified financial institution. Also note the consequences of each option.

8. John purchased stock six years ago for $10,000. As of the close of the current tax year, John has determined that the stock is worth only $100. Discuss whether John may treat the stock as worthless securities and, hence, claim a capital loss of $9,900 ($100 – $10,000) on his current-year tax return.

9. Discuss the ordinary loss limitations on the sale of § 1244 stock and the advantages of such a characterization.

10. Jim discovers that his sea wall, which protects his personal residence from the ocean, has been extensively damaged by the ocean. Discuss whether he may take a deduction for the damage to the wall.

11. Discuss the provision for determining the year in which a theft loss is deductible.

12. Discuss the tax treatment when a casualty loss is deducted in a prior year and a reimbursement is received in the current year.

13. Discuss the treatment of a disaster area loss.

14. How is a personal casualty loss computed? A business casualty loss? What effect do insurance proceeds have on both types of losses?

15. Discuss the tax consequences of not making an insurance claim when insured business property is subject to a loss.

16. Discuss the circumstances under which the cost of repairs to the damaged property can be used to measure the amount of a casualty loss.

17. During May of the current year, personal use property was stolen from Jim's home. Later in the year, Jim's home and two personal use cars were damaged by a severe storm. Discuss how the $100 floor applies to these casualties.

18. Bonnie sustained a loss on a duplex damaged by fire. She owns the duplex and lives in one unit. She rents out the other unit to a tenant. Discuss the tax treatment of the loss on Bonnie's individual tax return.

19. When casualty losses exceed casualty gains, only the amount of the casualty loss in excess of casualty gains is subject to the 10%-of-AGI floor. Discuss the significance of netting losses against gains in this manner rather than having the entire casualty loss subject to the 10%-of-AGI floor.

20. Monte opened a personal savings account at First National Bank many years ago. Last year, First National's banking license was revoked. In January of this year, Monte was informed that First National had been put into compulsory liquidation. The liquidation was precipitated by the embezzlement of funds by First National's former president. In February Monte submitted a claim for $12,459 to the liquidators of First National. In May of the current year, the liquidators advised Monte that they would keep him informed as to the progress of the liquidation and his prospects of recovery. The letter also stated that claimants would be notified if the liquidators were unable to agree to their claims. In November of the current year, Monte was notified that at the present time the liquidators could not predict with any degree of certainty how much of their funds depositors might eventually recover. Identify the relevant tax issues for Monte.

21. Fred and Diane purchased their home many years ago. The property included a large black oak tree approximately 80 feet in height and about 100 years old. The tree was the dominant feature of the front yard, where it stood alone next to the street. Because of the age and stature of the tree, Fred and Diane had it inspected regularly by a tree expert. In August of the current year, Fred noticed that the entire top or crown of the tree had turned brown. Because none of the leaves on other trees in the area had turned brown, Fred called the tree expert to inspect the tree. The inspection showed that the tree had been attacked by woodborers and was beyond saving and effectively dead. Identify the relevant tax issues for Fred and Diane.

22. What kinds of expenditures qualify as research and experimental expenditures?

23. If a business does not elect to expense or amortize research expenditures, what is the possibility of writing off such expenditures?

24. Power and Light, a public utility company, planned a research and development project. To obtain a construction permit to expand its facilities, the company filed an application with state regulatory agencies and conducted various studies to support its application as required by the agencies. Because the taxpayer's expansion involved both the construction of a nuclear power plant and the installation of an ultrahigh voltage electric transmission line, the agencies required that the company conduct several types of environmental impact studies for site selection. The studies measured specific site conditions and the resulting environmental impact of the construction and operation of the project. The company conducted part of the studies directly and used a research organization to conduct the remainder of the studies on its behalf. Identify the relevant tax issues for Power and Light.

25. Discuss the periods to which an individual's NOL may be carried.

PROBLEMS

26. Several years ago John Johnson loaned his friend Sara $20,000 to help her make a business investment. In May of the current year, Sara filed for bankruptcy, and John was notified that he could expect to receive no more than 60 cents on the dollar. As of the end of the current year, John has not received any payments. John has contacted you about the possibility of taking a bad debt deduction of $8,000 for the current year.

   Write a letter to John that contains your advice as to whether he can claim a bad debt deduction of $8,000 for the current year. Also, prepare a memo for the tax files. John's address is 100 Tyler Lane, Erie, PA 16563.

27. In 1996, Morgan loaned the Peach Company $50,000. In 1997, Morgan was told that he would probably receive $5,000 of the loan. In 1998, Morgan received $3,000 in final settlement on the loan. Determine Morgan's possible deductions with respect to the loan for 1996, 1997, and 1998.

28. In 1997, Wilma deposited $117,500 with a commercial bank. On July 1, 1998, Wilma was notified that the bank was insolvent, and subsequently she received only $100,000 of the deposit. Wilma also has a salary of $40,000, long-term capital gain of $12,000, and itemized deductions (other than casualty and theft) of $7,000. Determine whether Wilma should elect to treat the loss on the deposit as a personal casualty loss or as a bad debt.

29. Zenith, a single taxpayer, had the following items for 1998:

    - Salary of $75,000.

    - Gain of $19,000 on the sale of § 1244 stock acquired three years ago.

    - Loss of $71,000 on the sale of § 1244 stock acquired two years ago.

    - Stock acquired on June 20, 1997, for $2,500 became worthless on April 3, 1998.

    Determine Zenith's AGI for 1998.

30. Mary, a single taxpayer, purchased 10,000 shares of § 1244 stock several years ago at a cost of $20 per share. In November of the current year, Mary received an offer to sell the stock for $12 per share. She has the option of either selling all of the stock now or selling half of the stock now and half of the stock in January of next year. Mary will receive a salary of $80,000 for the current year and $90,000 next year. Mary will have long-term capital gains of $8,000 for the current year and $10,000 next year. If Mary's goal is to minimize her AGI for the two years, determine whether she should sell all of her stock this year or half of her stock this year and half next year.

31. Upon returning from a night out, John, an antique collector, found that a fire had damaged his home and destroyed some of his antiques. John's home was covered by an insurance policy that had a 20% deductible clause. The antiques were insured for their fair market value. Information with respect to the damaged and destroyed assets is as follows:

Asset	Cost	FMV Before	FMV After	Insurance Recovery
Home	$250,000	$300,000	$175,000	$100,000
Antique clock	1,500	2,000	–0–	2,000
Antique table	4,000	3,000	–0–	3,000
Antique organ	15,000	20,000	–0–	20,000

If John's AGI is $80,000 before considering the effects of the fire, determine his deductible loss *from* AGI.

32. Olaf owns a 500-acre farm in Minnesota. A tornado hit the area and destroyed a farm building and some farm equipment and damaged a barn. Fortunately for Olaf, the tornado occurred after he had harvested his corn crop. Applicable information is as follows:

Item	Adjusted Basis	FMV Before	FMV After	Insurance Proceeds
Building	$80,000	$100,000	$ –0–	$60,000
Equipment	40,000	50,000	–0–	25,000
Barn	90,000	120,000	90,000	25,000

Because of the extensive damage caused by the tornado, the President designated the area as a disaster area.

Olaf, who files a joint return with his wife Anna, had $90,000 of taxable income last year. Their taxable income for the current year, excluding the loss from the tornado, is $220,000.

Determine the amount of Olaf and Anna's loss and the year in which they should take the loss.

33. On January 5 of the current year, Janice dropped off to sleep while driving home from a business trip. Luckily, she was only slightly injured in the resulting accident, but her car was completely destroyed.

    Janice had purchased the car new two years ago and had driven it 42,000 miles at the time of the accident. Of these miles, 18,000 were business miles; the remaining miles were personal miles. The car cost $32,000 new. Janice has taken $3,400 of depreciation for the business use of the car. The fair market value at the time of the accident was

$20,000. Janice carried collision insurance with a $5,000 deductible on the car. She made a claim on the policy and received a payment of $15,000.

After Janice was released from the hospital the day after the accident, she could not find her purse (cost $110, fair replacement value $30) or its contents, which included $350 in cash. She also was unable to locate the stone from her diamond ring. The stone cost $4,000 when it was purchased 10 years ago and was worth $7,500 at the time of the accident. If Janice's AGI is $54,000 before considering the effects of the accident, determine her deduction *for* AGI and her deduction *from* AGI as a result of the accident.

34. On November 1 of the current year, Sam Smith was involved in an accident with his personal use automobile. Sam had purchased the car for $25,000. The automobile had a fair market value of $19,000 before the accident and $12,000 after the accident. The car was covered by an insurance policy that had a $1,000 deductible clause. Sam is afraid that the policy will be canceled if he makes a claim for the damages. Therefore, he is considering not filing a claim. Sam believes that the casualty loss deduction will help mitigate the loss of the insurance reimbursement. Sam's AGI for the current year is $25,000.

Write a letter to Sam that contains your advice with respect to the tax consequences of filing versus not filing a claim for the insurance reimbursement for the damages to his car. Also, prepare a memo for the tax files. Sam's address is 450 Colonel's Way, Warrensburg, MO 64093.

35. Green Corporation, a manufacturing company, decided to develop a new line of fireworks. Because of the danger involved, Green purchased an isolated parcel of land for $300,000 and constructed a building for $1,220,000. The building was to be used for research and experimentation in creating the new fireworks. The project was begun in 1998. Green had the following expenses in connection with the project:

	1998	1999
Salaries	$160,000	$200,000
Utilities	20,000	30,000
Materials	40,000	40,000
Insurance	50,000	30,000
Cost of market survey to determine profit potential for new fireworks line	20,000	–0–
Depreciation on the building	30,000	31,000

The benefits from the project will be realized starting in June 2000.
   a. If Green Corporation elects to expense research and experimental expenditures, determine the amount of the deduction for 1998, 1999, and 2000.
   b. If Green Corporation elects a 60-month deferral and amortization period, determine the amount of the deduction for 1998, 1999, and 2000.

36. Nell, single and age 38, had the following income and expense items in 1998:

Nonbusiness bad debt	$ 6,000
Business bad debt	2,000
Nonbusiness long-term capital gain	4,000
Nonbusiness short-term capital loss	3,000
Salary	40,000
Interest income	1,000

Determine Nell's AGI for 1998.

37. Assume that in addition to the information in Problem 36, Nell had the following items in 1998:

Personal casualty gain on an asset held for four months	$10,000
Personal casualty loss on an asset held for two years	1,000

Determine Nell's AGI for 1998.

CUMULATIVE PROBLEMS

38. Alan Rice, age 45 and single, lives at 230 Wood Lane, Salt Lake City, UT 84201. His Social Security number is 885–33–3774. Alan had the following items for the year 1998:

- Salary of $100,000.

- Business bad debt of $8,000.

- Nonbusiness bad debt of $7,000.

- Sale of § 1244 stock resulting in a loss of $80,000. The stock was acquired two years earlier.

- Dividends of $40,000 from domestic corporations.

- Interest income of $10,000 from First Interstate Bank.

- Long-term capital gain of $31,000.

- NOL carryover from 1997 of $12,000.

- On January 1, 1998, a fire severely damaged a two-story building owned by Alan, who occupied the second story of the building as a residence. He had recently opened a flower shop on the ground level. The following information is available with respect to the incident:

Asset	Adjusted Basis	Fair Market Value	
		Before	After
Building	$70,000	$130,000	$50,000
Inventory	35,000	55,000	None
Store equipment	3,000	2,500	None
Home furnishings	12,600	7,000	800
Personal auto	8,900	7,800	7,600

- Alan's fire insurance policy paid the following amounts for damages covered by the policy:

Building	$50,000	(policy maximum)
Inventory	30,000	(policy maximum)
Store equipment	None	
Home furnishings	1,000	(policy maximum)
Personal auto	None	

- Other itemized deductions of $3,500.

- Alan's employer withheld $10,000 of Federal income tax.

Compute Alan's 1998 Federal income tax payable (or refund due). Suggested software (if available): *TurboTax*.

39. Jane Smith, age 40, is single and has no dependents. She is employed as a legal secretary by Legal Services, Inc. She owns and operates Typing Services located near the campus of San Jose State University at 1986 Campus Drive. She is a cash basis taxpayer. Jane lives at 2020 Oakcrest Road, San Jose, CA 95134. Jane's Social Security number is 123-89-6666. Jane indicates that she wishes to designate $3 to the Presidential Election Campaign Fund. During 1997, Jane had the following income and expense items:

a. $50,000 salary from Legal Services, Inc.

b. $20,000 gross receipts from her typing services business.

c. $700 cash dividend from Buffalo Mining Company, a Canadian corporation.

d. $1,000 Christmas bonus from Legal Services, Inc.

e. $60,000 life insurance proceeds on the death of her sister.

f. $5,000 check given to her by her wealthy aunt.

g. $100 won in a bingo game.

h. Expenses connected with the typing service:

Office rent	$7,000
Supplies	4,400
Utilities and telephone	4,680
Wages to part-time typists	5,000
Payroll taxes	500
Equipment rentals	3,000

i. $9,000 interest expense on a home mortgage (paid to San Jose Savings and Loan).
j. $5,000 fair market value of silverware stolen from her home by a burglar on October 12, 1997. Jane had paid $4,000 for the silverware on July 1, 1988. She was reimbursed $1,500 by her insurance company.
k. Jane had loaned $2,100 to a friend, Joan Jensen, on June 3, 1994. Joan declared bankruptcy on August 14, 1997, and was unable to repay the loan.
l. Legal Services, Inc., withheld Federal income tax of $8,500 and the required amount of FICA tax.
m. Alimony of $10,000 received from her former husband, Ted Smith.
n. Interest income of $800 on City of San Jose bonds.
o. Jane made estimated tax payments of $1,000.

Part 1—Tax Computation
Compute Jane Smith's 1997 Federal income tax payable (or refund due). If you use tax forms for your computations, you will need Forms 1040 and 4684 and Schedules A, C, and D. Suggested software (if available): *TurboTax.*

Part 2—Tax Planning
In 1998, Jane plans to continue her job with Legal Services, Inc. Therefore, items a, d, and 1 will recur in 1998. Jane plans to continue her typing services business (refer to item b) and expects gross receipts of $26,000. She projects that all business expenses (refer to item h) will increase by 10%, except for office rent, which, under the terms of her lease, will remain the same as in 1997. Items e, f, g, j, and k will not recur in 1998. Items c, i, m, and n will be approximately the same as in 1997.

   Jane would like you to compute the minimum amount of estimated tax she will have to pay for 1998 so that she will not have to pay any additional tax upon filing her 1998 Federal income tax return. Write a letter to Jane that contains your advice and prepare a memo for the tax files. Suggested software (if available): *TurboTax.*

Research Problems for this chapter appear at the end of Chapter 28.

TEAM PROJECT: ARTHUR ANDERSEN TAX CHALLENGE CASES

For more information on the Arthur Andersen Tax Challenge Cases, refer to Chapter 1, page 1–37.

Information related to tax issues and problems that are discussed in this chapter may be found in the

Day and Ball case on pages: None
Fence case on pages: None

Read and analyze the case you have been assigned and *identify* any issues and problems that are related to material covered in this chapter. If the information provided in the case is complete, prepare answers for this part of the case at this time. If you need information that is contained in the later parts of the case, write a memo summarizing the questions or problems so you can prepare a complete answer at a later date.

DEPRECIATION, COST RECOVERY, AMORTIZATION, AND DEPLETION

LEARNING OBJECTIVES

After completing Chapter 7, you should be able to:

1. Understand the rationale for the cost consumption concept and identify the relevant time periods for depreciation, ACRS, and MACRS.

2. Determine the amount of cost recovery under ACRS and MACRS.

3. Recognize when and how to make the § 179 expensing election, calculate the amount of the deduction, and apply the effect of the election in making the MACRS calculation.

4. Identify listed property and apply the deduction limitations on listed property and on luxury automobiles.

5. Determine when and how to use the alternative depreciation system (ADS).

6. Identify intangible assets that are eligible for amortization and calculate the amount of the deduction.

7. Determine the amount of depletion expense including being able to apply the alternative tax treatments for intangible drilling and development costs.

8. Identify tax planning opportunities for cost recovery, amortization, and depletion.

1 ▼ **LEARNING OBJECTIVE**
Understand the rationale for the cost consumption concept and identify the relevant time periods for depreciation, ACRS, and MACRS.

The Internal Revenue Code provides for a deduction for the consumption of the cost of an asset through depreciation, cost recovery, amortization, or depletion. These deductions are applications of the recovery of capital doctrine (discussed in Chapter 3).

A distinction is made between tangible and intangible property. Tangible property is any property with physical substance (e.g., equipment, buildings), while intangible property lacks such substance (e.g., goodwill, patents).

The **depreciation** rules were completely overhauled by the Economic Recovery Tax Act of 1981 (ERTA). Hence, *most* property placed in service after December 31, 1980, is subject to the accelerated **cost recovery** system (ACRS). However, property placed in service before January 1, 1981, that is still in use, as well as *certain* property placed in service after December 31, 1980, is subject to the pre-ERTA depreciation rules. The Tax Reform Act (TRA) of 1986 completely revised the ACRS rules for property placed in service after December 31, 1986 (MACRS). Therefore, a knowledge of all of the depreciation and cost recovery rules may be needed as Example 1 illustrates.

 **EXAMPLE 1**

The Brown Company owns machinery purchased in 1980. The machinery has a 20-year useful life. The business also owns equipment purchased in 1986 that has a 15-year cost recovery life. In 1998, the business purchased a computer. To compute the depreciation and cost recovery for 1998, Brown will use the pre-ERTA depreciation rules for the machinery, the pre-TRA of 1986 cost recovery rules (ACRS) for the equipment, and the post-TRA of 1986 cost recovery rules (MACRS) for the computer. ▼

This chapter initially focuses on the ACRS and MACRS rules.[1] The chapter then concludes with a discussion of the amortization of intangible property and the depletion of natural resources.

ACRS was one of many provisions in ERTA that were intended to stimulate the economy. The following features of ACRS result in accelerated write-offs:

- Cost recovery periods are shorter than the estimated useful lives required under the pre-1981 depreciation system.
- The use of salvage value, required under the pre-1981 depreciation system, is eliminated under ACRS.

---

[1]§ 168. Refer to IRS Publication 534 for coverage of pre-ERTA rules under § 167.

CONCEPT SUMMARY 7–1

Depreciation and Cost Recovery: Relevant Time Periods

System	Date Property Is Placed in Service
§ 167 depreciation	Before January 1, 1981, and *certain* property placed in service after December 31, 1980.
Original accelerated cost recovery system (ACRS)	After December 31, 1980, and before January 1, 1987.
Modified accelerated cost recovery system (MACRS)	After December 31, 1986.

- For many assets, the methods for computing ACRS deductions are more generous than the allowable methods for computing depreciation.

For assets placed in service after 1986, ACRS is replaced with MACRS. The basic effect of MACRS is to somewhat dampen the economic stimulus effect of ACRS. MACRS cost recovery periods are generally longer than ACRS cost recovery periods. In addition, the cost recovery methods available under MACRS are, in most cases, not as generous as the methods available under ACRS.

OVERVIEW

Taxpayers may write off the cost of certain assets that are used in a trade or business or held for the production of income. A write-off may take the form of depreciation (or cost recovery), depletion, or amortization. Tangible assets, other than natural resources, are *depreciated*. Natural resources, such as oil, gas, coal, and timber, are *depleted*. Intangible assets, such as copyrights and patents, are *amortized*. Generally, no write-off is allowed for an asset that does not have a determinable useful life.

ACRS and MACRS provide separate cost recovery tables for realty (real property) and personalty (personal property). Realty generally includes land and buildings permanently affixed to the land. Write-offs are not available for land because it does not have a determinable useful life. Cost recovery allowances for real property, other than land, are based on recovery lives specified in the law. The IRS provides tables that specify cost recovery allowances for most types of realty.

Personalty is defined as any asset that is not realty.[2] Personalty includes furniture, machinery, equipment, and many other types of assets. Do not confuse personalty (or personal property) with *personal use* property. Personal use property is any property (realty or personalty) that is held for personal use rather than for use in a trade or business or an income-producing activity. Write-offs are not allowed for personal use assets.

In summary, both realty and personalty can be either business use/income-producing property or personal use property. Examples include a residence (realty that is personal use), an office building (realty that is business use), a dump truck (personalty that is business use), and regular wearing apparel (personalty that is personal use). It is imperative that this distinction between the *classification* of an asset (realty or personalty) and the *use* to which the asset is put (business or personal) be understood.

---

[2]Refer to Chapter 1 for a further discussion.

ACCELERATED COST RECOVERY SYSTEM (ACRS AND MACRS)

GENERAL CONSIDERATIONS

2 ▼ LEARNING OBJECTIVE
Determine the amount of cost recovery under ACRS and MACRS.

Under the **accelerated cost recovery system (ACRS),** the cost of an asset is recovered over a predetermined period that is generally shorter than the useful life of the asset or the period the asset is used to produce income. The ACRS system was designed to encourage investment, improve productivity, and simplify the law and its administration. However, the pre-ACRS depreciation rules will continue to apply in the following situations:

- Property placed in service after 1980 whose life is not based on years (e.g., units-of-production method).
- The remaining depreciation on property placed in service by the taxpayer before 1981.
- Personal property acquired after 1980 if the property was owned or used during 1980 by the taxpayer or a related person (antichurning rule).[3]
- Property that is amortized (e.g., leasehold improvements).

The basis for cost recovery generally is the adjusted cost basis used to determine gain if property is sold or otherwise disposed of. The basis is reduced by the amount of the cost recovery deducted.

Cost Recovery Allowed or Allowable. The basis of cost recovery property must be reduced by the cost recovery allowed and by not less than the allowable amount. The *allowed* cost recovery is the cost recovery actually taken, whereas the *allowable* cost recovery is the amount that could have been taken under the applicable cost recovery method. If the taxpayer does not claim any cost recovery on property during a particular year, the basis of the property must still be reduced by the amount of cost recovery that should have been deducted (the allowable cost recovery).

EXAMPLE 2

On March 15, Jack paid $10,000 for a copier to be used in his business. The copier is five-year property. Jack elected to use the straight-line method of cost recovery, but did not take cost recovery in years 3 or 4. Therefore, the allowed cost recovery (cost recovery actually deducted) and the allowable cost recovery are as follows:

	Cost Recovery Allowed	Cost Recovery Allowable
Year 1	$1,000	$1,000
Year 2	2,000	2,000
Year 3	–0–	2,000
Year 4	–0–	2,000
Year 5	2,000	2,000
Year 6	1,000	1,000

If Jack sold the copier for $800 in year 7, he would recognize an $800 gain ($800 amount realized – $0 adjusted basis) because the adjusted basis of the copier is zero. ▼

---

[3] § 168(f). The antichurning rules may also require the use of pre-TRA of 1986 ACRS rules on property placed in service after December 31, 1986 (property that otherwise would be subject to MACRS).

Cost Recovery Basis for Personal Use Assets Converted to Business or Income-Producing Use. If personal use assets are converted to business or income-producing use, the basis for cost recovery and for loss is the *lower* of the adjusted basis or the fair market value at the time the property was converted. As a result of this lower-of-basis rule, losses that occurred while the property was personal use property will not be recognized for tax purposes through the cost recovery of the property.

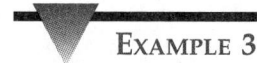

EXAMPLE 3

Hans acquires a personal residence for $120,000. Four years later, when the fair market value is only $100,000, he converts the property to rental use. The basis for cost recovery is $100,000, since the fair market value is less than the adjusted basis. The $20,000 decline in value is deemed to be personal (since it occurred while the property was held for personal use) and therefore nondeductible. ▼

ELIGIBLE PROPERTY UNDER ACRS OR MACRS

Assets used in a trade or business or for the production of income are eligible for cost recovery if they are subject to wear and tear, decay or decline from natural causes, or obsolescence. Assets that do not decline in value on a predictable basis or that do not have a determinable useful life (e.g., land, stock, antiques) are not eligible for cost recovery.

PERSONALTY: RECOVERY PERIODS AND METHODS

Classification of Property: ACRS. ACRS provides that the cost of eligible personalty (and certain realty) is recovered over 3, 5, 10, or 15 years. Property is classified by recovery period as follows:

3 years	Autos, light-duty trucks, R & D equipment, racehorses over 2 years old and other horses over 12 years old, and personalty with an ADR* midpoint life of 4 years or less.[4]
5 years	Most other equipment except long-lived public utility property. Also includes single-purpose agricultural structures and petroleum storage facilities, which are designated as § 1245 property under the law.
10 years	Public utility property with an ADR midpoint life greater than 18 but not greater than 25 years, burners and boilers using coal as a primary fuel if used in a public utility power plant and if replacing or converting oil- or gas-fired burners or boilers, railroad tank cars, mobile homes, and realty with an ADR midpoint life of 12.5 years or less (e.g., theme park structures).
15 years	Public utility property with an ADR midpoint life exceeding 25 years (except certain burners and boilers using coal as a primary fuel).

*ADR refers to the Asset Depreciation Range system.

Taxpayers who own 15-year ACRS property continue to compute cost recovery allowances under the ACRS rules. However, all cost has already been recovered on any 3-year, 5-year, or 10-year ACRS property.

Taxpayers had the choice of using (1) the straight-line method over the regular or optional (see below) recovery period or (2) a prescribed accelerated method over

---

[4]Rev.Proc. 83–35, 1983–1 C.B. 745 is the source for the ADR midpoint lives.

the regular recovery period. These two methods are both part of the ACRS system, but a convenient name is not provided for either method. Hereafter, the straight-line method will be referred to as the *optional* (or *elective*) *straight-line method*. The method using percentages prescribed in the Code will be referred to as the *statutory percentage method*.

The rates to be used in computing the deduction under the statutory percentage method are shown in Table 7–1 (all tables are located at the end of the chapter prior to the Problem Materials) and are based on the 150 percent declining-balance method, using the **half-year convention**[5] and an assumption of zero salvage value. The rates in the cost recovery tables at the end of the chapter reflect the relevant methods, conventions, and assumptions.

EXAMPLE 4

Green Utilities acquired 15-year public utility property in 1985 at a cost of $100,000. The property was placed in service on September 1, 1985. Green's cost recovery allowance for 1998 is determined from Table 7–1. The cost recovery percentage for 1998 (recovery year 14) is 6%, and the cost recovery allowance is $6,000 ($100,000 cost × 6%). ▼

Note that in 1985, Green got a half-year's cost recovery deduction (since the half-year convention is reflected in the percentages in Table 7–1) although it held the property only four months.

In the year that personal property is disposed of, no cost recovery is allowed.

EXAMPLE 5

Assume the same facts as in the previous example and that the property is sold in May 1999. Green is not allowed a cost recovery deduction for the property in 1999. ▼

Reduction of Basis for Investment Tax Credit.   For personalty placed in service after 1982 and before January 1, 1986, taxpayers were required to reduce the basis of the property for the ACRS write-off by one-half the amount of the investment tax credit taken on the property.[6] The investment tax credit was not allowed on realty.

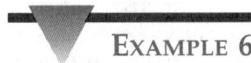

EXAMPLE 6

Beige Electric Company acquired property on September 4, 1985, for $100,000. The property was 15-year ACRS property, and Beige claimed a $10,000 investment tax credit ($100,000 × 10% investment tax credit rate). The basis of the property was reduced by $5,000 (one-half of the $10,000 investment tax credit). Therefore, the basis for cost recovery was $95,000. The cost recovery for 1998 is $5,700 [$95,000 × 6% (Table 7–1)]. ▼

As an alternative to reducing the basis of the property, a taxpayer could elect to take a *reduced* investment tax credit. Under this election, the investment tax credit was 8 percent (rather than 10 percent) for recovery property other than three-year property and 4 percent (instead of 6 percent) for three-year property. In Example 6, if the reduced investment tax credit election were made, Beige's cost recovery basis would be $100,000 rather than $95,000.

TRA of 1986 generally repealed the investment tax credit for property placed in service after December 31, 1985. Therefore, the reduction of basis for the investment tax credit does not apply to such property.

Classification of Property: MACRS.   The general effect of TRA of 1986 was to lengthen asset lives. The **modified accelerated cost recovery system (MACRS)** provides that the cost recovery basis of eligible personalty (and certain realty) is

---

[5]The half-year convention assumes all property is placed in service at mid-year and thus provides for a half-year's cost recovery.

[6]§ 48(q).

recovered over 3, 5, 7, 10, 15, or 20 years. Property is classified by recovery period under MACRS as follows (see Exhibit 7–1 for examples):[7]

3-year 200% class	ADR midpoints of 4 years and less.[8] Excludes automobiles and light trucks. Includes racehorses more than 2 years old and other horses more than 12 years old.
5-year 200% class	ADR midpoints of more than 4 years and less than 10 years, adding automobiles, light trucks, qualified technological equipment, renewable energy and biomass properties that are small power production facilities, research and experimentation property, semiconductor manufacturing equipment, and computer-based central office switching equipment.
7-year 200% class	ADR midpoints of 10 years and more and less than 16 years, adding single-purpose agricultural or horticultural structures and property with no ADR midpoint not classified elsewhere. Includes railroad track and office furniture, fixtures, and equipment.
10-year 200% class	ADR midpoints of 16 years and more and less than 20 years.
15-year 150% class	ADR midpoints of 20 years and more and less than 25 years, including sewage treatment plants, and telephone distribution plants and comparable equipment used for the two-way exchange of voice and data communications.
20-year 150% class	ADR midpoints of 25 years and more, other than real property with an ADR midpoint of 27.5 years and more, and including sewer pipes.

---

[7]§ 168(e).
[8]Rev.Proc. 87–56, 1987–2 C.B. 674 is the source for the ADR midpoint lives.

▼ **EXHIBIT 7–1**

Cost Recovery Periods: MACRS

Class of Property	Examples
3-year	Tractor units for use over-the-road.
	Any horse that is not a racehorse and is more than 12 years old at the time it is placed in service.
	Any racehorse that is more than 2 years old at the time it is placed in service.
	Breeding hogs.
	Special tools used in the manufacturing of motor vehicles such as dies, fixtures, molds, and patterns.
5-year	Automobiles and taxis.
	Light and heavy general-purpose trucks.
	Buses.
	Trailers and trailer-mounted containers.
	Typewriters, calculators, and copiers.
	Computers and peripheral equipment.
	Breeding and dairy cattle.
7-year	Office furniture, fixtures, and equipment.
	Breeding and work horses.
	Agricultural machinery and equipment.
	Single-purpose agricultural or horticultural structures.
	Railroad track.
10-year	Vessels, barges, tugs, and similar water transportation equipment.
	Assets used for petroleum refining or for the manufacture of grain and grain mill products, sugar and sugar products, or vegetable oils and vegetable oil products.
15-year	Land improvements.
	Assets used for industrial steam and electric generation and/or distribution systems.
	Assets used in the manufacture of cement.
	Assets used in pipeline transportation.
	Electric utility nuclear production plant.
	Municipal wastewater treatment plant.
20-year	Farm buildings except single-purpose agricultural and horticultural structures.
	Gas utility distribution facilities.
	Water utilities.
	Municipal sewer.

Accelerated depreciation is allowed for these six MACRS classes of property. Two hundred percent declining-balance is used for the 3-, 5-, 7-, and 10-year classes, with a switchover to straight-line depreciation when it yields a larger amount. One hundred and fifty percent declining-balance is allowed for the 15-and 20-year classes, with an appropriate straight-line switchover.[9]

Taxpayers may *elect* the straight-line method to compute cost recovery allowances for each of these classes of property. Certain property is not eligible for accelerated cost recovery and must be depreciated under an alternative depreciation system (ADS). Both the straight-line election and ADS are discussed later in the chapter.

The original ACRS system gave the taxpayer a half-year of cost recovery for the tax year an asset was placed in service but allowed the taxpayer to recover the

---

[9]§ 168(b).

balance of the cost recovery basis over the years remaining in the property's recovery period. No cost recovery deduction was permitted for the year of disposition or retirement of the property. Thus, conceptually, the taxpayer was considered to have placed property in service at the beginning of the recovery period but was allowed only a half-year's worth of cost recovery for the year it was placed in service.

By contrast, MACRS views property as placed in service in the middle of the first year.[10] Thus, for example, the statutory recovery period for three-year property begins in the middle of the year an asset is placed in service and ends three years later. In practical terms, this means that taxpayers must wait an extra year to recover the cost of depreciable assets. That is, the actual write-off periods are 4, 6, 8, 11, 16, and 21 years. MACRS also allows for a half-year of cost recovery in the year of disposition or retirement.

The procedure for computing the cost recovery allowance under MACRS is the same as under the original ACRS method. The cost recovery basis is multiplied by the percentages that reflect the applicable cost recovery method and the applicable convention. The percentages are shown in Table 7–2.

EXAMPLE 7   Kareem acquires a five-year class asset on April 10, 1998, for $30,000. Kareem's cost recovery deduction for 1998 is $6,000 [$30,000 × .20 (Table 7–2)]. ▼

EXAMPLE 8   Assume the same facts as in Example 7, and that Kareem disposes of the asset on March 5, 2000. Kareem's cost recovery deduction for 2000 is $2,880 [$30,000 × ½ × .192 (Table 7–2)]. ▼

Mid-Quarter Convention.   Under the original ACRS rules for personal property, the half-year convention was used no matter when property was acquired during the year. Thus, if a substantial dollar amount of assets was acquired late in the tax year, the half-year convention still applied. The law now contains a provision to curtail the benefits of such a tax strategy. If more than 40 percent of the value of property other than eligible real estate (see Realty: Recovery Periods and Methods: MACRS for a discussion of eligible real estate) is placed in service during the last quarter of the year, a **mid-quarter convention** applies.[11] Property acquisitions are then grouped by the quarter they were acquired for cost recovery purposes. Acquisitions during the first quarter are allowed 10.5 months of cost recovery; the second quarter, 7.5 months; the third quarter, 4.5 months; and the fourth quarter, 1.5 months. The percentages are shown in Table 7–3.

EXAMPLE 9   Silver Corporation acquires the following five-year class property in 1998:

Property Acquisition Dates	Cost
February 15	$ 200,000
July 10	400,000
December 5	600,000
Total	$1,200,000

If Silver Corporation uses the statutory percentage method, the cost recovery allowances for the first two years are computed as indicated below. Since more than 40% ($600,000/ $1,200,000 = 50%) of the acquisitions are in the last quarter, the mid-quarter convention applies.

---

[10] § 168(d)(4)(A).   [11] § 168(d)(3).

1998

February 15	[$200,000 × .35 (Table 7–3)]	$ 70,000
July 10	($400,000 × .15)	60,000
December 5	($600,000 × .05)	30,000
Total		$160,000

1999

February 15	[$200,000 × .26 (Table 7–3)]	$ 52,000
July 10	($400,000 × .34)	136,000
December 5	($600,000 × .38)	228,000
Total		$416,000

When property to which the mid-quarter convention applies is disposed of, the property is treated as though it were disposed of at the midpoint of the quarter. Hence, in the quarter of disposition, cost recovery is allowed for one-half of the quarter.

EXAMPLE 10 Assume the same facts as in Example 9, except that Silver Corporation sells the $400,000 asset on November 30 of 1999. The cost recovery allowance for 1999 is computed as follows:

February 15	[$200,000 × .26 (Table 7–3)]	$ 52,000
July 10	[$400,000 × .34 × (3.5/4)]	119,000
December 5	($600,000 × .38)	228,000
Total		$399,000

REALTY: RECOVERY PERIODS AND METHODS

ACRS.   Under the original ACRS rules, realty was assigned a 15-year recovery period. Real property other than low-income housing is depreciated using the 175 percent declining-balance method, with a switchover to straight-line depreciation when it yields a larger amount. Low-income housing is depreciated using the 200 percent declining-balance method, with an appropriate straight-line switchover. In either case, zero salvage value is assumed. Statutory percentages for real property are shown in Table 7–4, which contains rates for low-income housing as well as for other 15-year real estate. As explained later in the chapter, taxpayers were allowed to elect the straight-line method for real property.

The half-year convention does not apply to 15-year real property. As a result, Table 7–4 is structured differently from Tables 7–1 and 7–2. The cost recovery deduction for 15-year real property is based on the month the asset is placed in service rather than on the half-year convention. No cost recovery is allowed for the month in which an asset is disposed of if the asset is disposed of before the end of the recovery period.

EXAMPLE 11 Alicia purchased a warehouse for $100,000 on January 1, 1984. The cost recovery allowance for the years 1984 through 1998, using the statutory percentage method, is as follows (see Table 7–4 for percentages).

1984—$12,000 (12% × $100,000)
1985—$10,000 (10% × $100,000)
1986—$9,000 (9% × $100,000)
1987—$8,000 (8% × $100,000)
1988—$7,000 (7% × $100,000)
1989—$6,000 (6% × $100,000)
1990—$6,000 (6% × $100,000)
1991—$6,000 (6% × $100,000)
1992—$6,000 (6% × $100,000)
1993—$5,000 (5% × $100,000)
1994—$5,000 (5% × $100,000)
1995—$5,000 (5% × $100,000)
1996—$5,000 (5% × $100,000)
1997—$5,000 (5% × $100,000)
1998—$5,000 (5% × $100,000)

EXAMPLE 12 Assume the same facts as in Example 11, except the property is low-income housing. Cost recovery deductions using the statutory percentage method for 1984 through 1998 are as follows (see Table 7–4 for percentages):

1984—$13,000 (13% × $100,000)
1985—$12,000 (12% × $100,000)
1986—$10,000 (10% × $100,000)
1987—$9,000 (9% × $100,000)
1988—$8,000 (8% × $100,000)
1989—$7,000 (7% × $100,000)
1990—$6,000 (6% × $100,000)
1991—$5,000 (5% × $100,000)
1992—$5,000 (5% × $100,000)
1993—$5,000 (5% × $100,000)
1994—$4,000 (4% × $100,000)
1995—$4,000 (4% × $100,000)
1996—$4,000 (4% × $100,000)
1997—$4,000 (4% × $100,000)
1998—$4,000 (4% × $100,000)

The Deficit Reduction Act of 1984 changed the recovery period for real property to 18 years. This applies generally to property placed in service after March 15, 1984. However, the 15-year recovery period was retained for low-income housing as well as for other real property placed in service before March 16, 1984.

Eighteen-year real property placed in service after June 22, 1984, is subject to a **mid-month convention.**[12] This means that real property placed in service at any time during a particular month is treated as if it were placed in service in the middle of the month. This allows for one-half month's cost recovery for the month the property is placed in service. If the property is disposed of before the end of the recovery period, one-half month's cost recovery is permitted for the month of disposition regardless of the specific date of disposition. Statutory percentages for 18-year real property with a mid-month convention are shown in Table 7–5.

---

[12]A transitional rule, which provides for a full-month convention, is effective for property placed in service after March 15, 1984, and before June 23, 1984. The cost recovery tables for property placed in service during this period are not included in this chapter.

CONCEPT SUMMARY 7–2

Statutory Percentage Method under ACRS and MACRS

	Personal Property	ACRS		
		Real Property		
		15-Year	18-Year	19-Year
Convention	Half-year	Full-month	Mid-month	Mid-month
Cost recovery deduction in the year of disposition	None	Full-month up to month of disposition	Half-month for month of disposition	Half-month for month of disposition

	MACRS	
	Personal Property	Real Property*
Convention	Half-year or mid-quarter	Mid-month
Cost recovery deduction in the year of disposition	Half-year for year of disposition or half-quarter for quarter of disposition	Half-month for month of disposition

*Straight-line method must be used.

EXAMPLE 13   Rex purchased a building for $300,000 and placed it in service on August 21, 1984. The first year's cost recovery using the statutory percentage method is $12,000 [$300,000 × 4% (Table 7–5)]. ▼

EXAMPLE 14   Assume the same facts as in Example 13 and that Rex disposes of the building on May 3, 1998. The cost recovery in the year of disposition is $4,500 ($300,000 × 4% × 4.5/12). ▼

Public Law 99–121 extended the minimum recovery period for real property (except low-income housing) from 18 years to 19 years. This applies to property placed in service after May 8, 1985, and before January 1, 1987. Statutory percentages for 19-year real property are shown in Table 7–6. Because the percentages are determined using a mid-month convention, the computation of cost recovery is mechanically the same as for 18-year property with the mid-month convention.

MACRS. Under MACRS, the cost recovery period for residential rental real estate is 27.5 years, and the straight-line method is used for computing the cost recovery allowance. **Residential rental real estate** includes property where 80 percent or more of the gross rental revenues are from nontransient dwelling units (e.g., an apartment building). Hotels, motels, and similar establishments are not residential rental property. Low-income housing is classified as residential rental real estate. Nonresidential real estate has a recovery period of 31.5 years (39 years for such property placed in service after May 12, 1993) and is also depreciated using the straight-line method.[13]

[13]§§ 168(b), (c), and (e).

Some items of real property are not treated as real estate for purposes of MACRS. For example, single-purpose agricultural structures are in the 7-year MACRS class. Land improvements are in the 15-year MACRS class.

All eligible real estate is depreciated using the mid-month convention. Regardless of when during the month the property is placed in service, it is deemed to have been placed in service at the middle of the month. In the year of disposition, a mid-month convention is also used.

Cost recovery is computed by multiplying the applicable rate (Table 7–7) by the cost recovery basis.

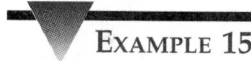

EXAMPLE 15 Alec acquired a building on April 1, 1994, for $800,000. If the building is classified as residential rental real estate, the cost recovery allowance for 1998 is $29,088 (.03636 × $800,000). If the building is classified as nonresidential real estate, the 1998 cost recovery allowance is $25,400 (.03175 × $800,000). (See Table 7–7 for percentages.) ▼

As part of the deficit reduction legislation of the Clinton administration (Revenue Reconciliation Act of 1993), nonresidential real estate placed in service after May 12, 1993, is subject to a 39-year recovery period. Property placed in service before 1994 that was subject to a binding contract to construct or purchase, as of May 12, 1993, may still be treated as 31.5-year property under the prior rules.

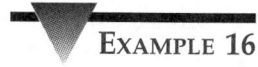

EXAMPLE 16 Assume the same facts as in Example 15, except that Alec acquired the nonresidential building on November 19, 1998. The 1998 cost recovery allowance is $2,568 [$800,000 × .00321 (Table 7–7)]. ▼

STRAIGHT-LINE ELECTION UNDER ACRS AND MACRS

ACRS. Under ACRS, taxpayers could *elect* to write off an asset using the straight-line method rather than the statutory percentage method. The straight-line recovery period could be the same as the prescribed recovery period under the statutory percentage method, or a longer period. The allowable straight-line recovery periods for each class of property are summarized as follows:

3-year property	3, 5, or 12 years
5-year property	5, 12, or 25 years
10-year property	10, 25, or 35 years
15-year property	15, 35, or 45 years
18-year real property and low-income housing (placed in service after March 15, 1984)	18, 35, or 45 years
19-year real property and low-income housing (placed in service after May 8, 1985)	19, 35, or 45 years

If the straight-line option was elected for personal property, the half-year convention applies in computing the cost recovery deduction. The effect of electing the straight-line method for personal property is to extend the statutory recovery period by one year (e.g., three to four and five to six years). There is no cost recovery deduction in the year of the disposition of the property.

EXAMPLE 17 On May 6, 1986, Owl Utilities paid $100,000 for gas-fired boilers to replace coal-fired boilers (10-year property). Owl elected to compute the cost recovery allowance using the optional straight-line method and a 25-year cost recovery period. Owl's cost recovery allowance for 1986 was $2,000 ($100,000 basis × 4% straight-line rate × ½ year), which reflects the effect

of the half-year convention. The cost recovery allowance for 1998 is $4,000 ($100,000 basis × 4% straight-line rate). ▼

For each class of personal property, the straight-line election applied to *all* assets in a *particular class* that were placed in service during the year for which the election was made. The election applies for the entire recovery period of these assets. The election is not binding for personal property of the same class placed in service in another tax year.

Under the straight-line option for 15-year *real* property, the first year's cost recovery deduction and the cost recovery deduction for the year of disposition are computed on the basis of the number of months the property was in service during the year.

EXAMPLE 18   Kate acquired a store building on March 1, 1984, at a cost of $150,000. She elected the straight-line method using a recovery period of 15 years. Kate's cost recovery deduction for 1984 was $8,333 [($150,000 ÷ 15) × 10/12]. ▼

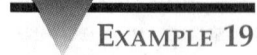

EXAMPLE 19   Assume the same facts as in Example 18 and that Kate disposes of the asset on January 31, 1998. Kate's cost recovery deduction for 1998 is $833 [($150,000 ÷ 15) × 1/12]. ▼

Under the straight-line option for 18-year or 19-year real property, the cost recovery allowances in the year the property is placed in service and in the year of disposition are computed in the same manner (except for the use of different rates) as under the statutory percentage method. Note that 18-year and 19-year real property use a mid-month convention, whereas 15-year real property uses a full-month convention. Table 7–8 contains the applicable percentages to be used under the straight-line option for 19-year real property. (The tables that contain the percentages for 18-year real property using the straight-line method over 18, 35, and 45 years and 19-year real property using the straight-line method over 35 and 45 years are not reproduced in this text.)

EXAMPLE 20   Ned acquired 19-year real property on October 1, 1986, at a cost of $150,000. He elected the straight-line method of cost recovery. Ned's cost recovery deduction for 1986 was $1,650 [$150,000 × 1.1% (Table 7–8)]. ▼

EXAMPLE 21   Assume the same facts as in Example 20 and that Ned disposes of the asset on September 20, 1998. Ned's cost recovery deduction for 1998 is $5,631 {[$150,000 × 5.3% × (8.5/12)] (Table 7–8)}. ▼

The straight-line election for 15-year, 18-year, or 19-year real property may be made on a *property-by-property* basis within the same year.

MACRS. Although MACRS requires straight-line depreciation for all eligible real estate as previously discussed, the taxpayer may *elect* to use the straight-line method for personal property.[14] The property is depreciated using the class life (recovery period) of the asset with a half-year convention or a mid-quarter convention, whichever is applicable. The election is available on a class-by-class and year-by-year basis. The percentages for the straight-line election with a half-year convention appear in Table 7–9.

---

[14]§ 168(b)(5).

CONCEPT SUMMARY 7–3

Straight-Line Election under ACRS and MACRS

ACRS

	Personal Property	Real Property		
		15-Year	18-Year	19-Year
Convention	Half-year	Full-month	Mid-month	Mid-month
Cost recovery deduction in the year of disposition	None	Full-month up to month of disposition	Half-month for month of disposition	Half-month for month of disposition
Elective or mandatory	Elective	Elective	Elective	Elective
Breadth of election	Class by class	Property by property	Property by property	Property by property

MACRS

	Personal Property	Real Property*
Convention	Half-year or mid-quarter	Mid-month
Cost recovery deduction in the year of disposition	Half-year for year of dispositon or half-quarter for quarter of disposition	Half-month for month of disposition
Elective or mandatory	Elective	Mandatory
Breadth of election	Class by class	

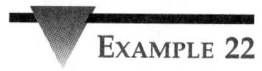

EXAMPLE 22

Terry acquires a 10-year class asset on August 4, 1998, for $100,000. He elects the straight-line method of cost recovery. Terry's cost recovery deduction for 1998 is $5,000 ($100,000 × .050). His cost recovery deduction for 1999 is $10,000 ($100,000 × .100). (See Table 7–9 for percentages.) ▼

ELECTION TO EXPENSE ASSETS

3 ▼ **LEARNING OBJECTIVE**
Recognize when and how to make the § 179 expensing election, calculate the amount of the deduction, and apply the effect of the election in making the MACRS calculation.

Section 179 (Election to Expense Certain Depreciable Business Assets) permits the taxpayer to elect to write off up to $18,500 in 1998[15] of the acquisition cost of *tangible personal property* used in a trade or business. Amounts that are expensed under § 179 may not be capitalized and depreciated. The **§ 179 expensing** election is an annual election and applies to the acquisition cost of property placed in service that year. The immediate expense election is not available for real property or for property used for the production of income.[16]

EXAMPLE 23

Kelly acquires machinery (five-year class) on February 1, 1998, at a cost of $40,000 and elects to expense $18,500 under § 179. Kelly's statutory percentage cost recovery deduction for 1998 is $4,300 [($40,000 cost − $18,500 expensed) × .200]. (See Table 7–2 for percentage.) Kelly's total deduction for 1998 is $22,800 ($18,500 + $4,300). ▼

---

[15]This amount was $10,000 for property placed in service in tax years beginning before January 1, 1993; $17,500 for property placed in service in tax years beginning after December 31, 1992, and before January 1, 1997; and $18,000 for property placed in service in tax years beginning in 1997.

[16]§§ 179(b) and (d). The amount shown is per taxpayer, per year. On a joint return, the statutory amounts apply to the couple. If the taxpayers are married and file separate returns, each spouse is eligible for 50% of the statutory amount.

For tax years beginning in 1997, an increase in the maximum § 179 amount is being phased in as follows:

Tax Year Beginning in	Maximum Expense Deduction
1997	$18,000
1998	18,500
1999	19,000
2000	20,000
2001 or 2002	24,000
2003 and thereafter	25,000

Annual Limitations.   Two additional limitations apply to the amount deductible under § 179. First, the ceiling amount on the deduction is reduced dollar-for-dollar when property (other than eligible real estate) placed in service during the taxable year exceeds $200,000. Second, the amount expensed under § 179 cannot exceed the aggregate amount of taxable income derived from the conduct of any trade or business by the taxpayer. Taxable income of a trade or business is computed without regard to the amount expensed under § 179. Any § 179 expensed amount in excess of taxable income is carried forward to future taxable years and added to other amounts eligible for expensing (and is subject to the ceiling rules for the carryforward years).

EXAMPLE 24

Jill owns a computer service and operates it as a sole proprietorship. In 1998, she will net $11,000 before considering any § 179 deduction. If Jill spends $204,000 on new equipment, her § 179 expense deduction is computed as follows:

§ 179 deduction before adjustment	$18,500
Less: Dollar limitation reduction ($204,000 − $200,000)	(4,000)
Remaining § 179 deduction	$14,500
Business income limitation	$11,000
§ 179 deduction allowed	$11,000
§ 179 deduction carryforward ($14,500 − $11,000)	$ 3,500

▼

Effect on Basis.   The basis of the property for cost recovery purposes is reduced by the § 179 amount after it is adjusted for property placed in service in excess of $200,000. This adjusted amount does not reflect any business income limitation.

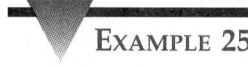

EXAMPLE 25

Assume the same facts as in Example 24 and that the new equipment is five-year class property. Jill's statutory percentage cost recovery deduction for 1998 is $37,900 [($204,000 − $14,500) × .200]. (See Table 7–2 for percentage.) ▼

Conversion to Personal Use.   Conversion of the expensed property to personal use at any time results in recapture income (see Chapter 13). A property is converted to personal use if it is not used predominantly in a trade or business. Regulations provide for the mechanics of the recapture.[17]

---

[17]Reg. § 1.179-1(e).

ETHICAL CONSIDERATIONS

Section 179 and Limited Personal Use

Sam, a salesman, purchased a new computer near the end of last year. He used the computer during the remainder of the year only in connection with his business. On his tax return for last year, Sam expensed the computer under § 179. During the current year, Sam has continued to use the computer in his business. However, he also allows his children to use the computer for their schoolwork. Sam has not maintained a log showing business and personal use of the computer for the current year. He feels that because the computer was expensed last year, no further accounting for it on his tax return is necessary. Do you agree?

BUSINESS AND PERSONAL USE OF AUTOMOBILES AND OTHER LISTED PROPERTY

4 **LEARNING OBJECTIVE**
Identify listed property and apply the deduction limitations on listed property and on luxury automobiles.

Limits exist on ACRS and MACRS deductions for automobiles and other listed property that are used for both personal and business purposes.[18] If the listed property is *predominantly used* for business, the taxpayer is allowed to use the statutory percentage method to recover the cost. In cases where the property is *not predominantly used* for business, the cost is recovered using the straight-line method.

Listed property includes the following:

- Any passenger automobile.
- Any other property used as a means of transportation.
- Any property of a type generally used for purposes of entertainment, recreation, or amusement.
- Any computer or peripheral equipment, with the exception of equipment used exclusively at a regular business establishment, including a qualifying home office.
- Any cellular telephone or other similar telecommunications equipment.
- Any other property specified in the Regulations.[19]

Automobiles and Other Listed Property Used Predominantly in Business. For listed property to be considered as predominantly used in business, its business usage must exceed 50 percent.[20] The use of listed property for production of income does not qualify as business use for purposes of the more-than-50 percent test. However, if the more-than-50 percent test is met, both production of income and business use percentages are used to compute the cost recovery deduction.

EXAMPLE 26

On September 1, 1998, Emma places in service listed five-year recovery property. The property cost $10,000. If Emma uses the property 40% for business and 25% for the production of income, the property is not considered as predominantly used for business. The cost is recovered using straight-line cost recovery. Emma's cost recovery allowance for the year is $650 ($10,000 × 10% × 65%). If, however, Emma uses the property 60% for business and 25% for the production of income, the property is considered as used predominantly for business. Therefore, she may use the statutory percentage method. Emma's cost recovery allowance for the year is $1,700 ($10,000 × .200 × 85%). ▼

---

[18]§ 280F.
[19]§ 280F(d)(4).

[20]§ 280F(b)(4).

The method for determining the percentage of business usage for listed property is specified in the Regulations. The Regulations provide that for automobiles a mileage-based percentage is to be used. Other listed property is to use the most appropriate unit of time (e.g., hours) the property is actually used (rather than available for use).[21]

The law places special limitations on the cost recovery deduction for passenger automobiles. These statutory dollar limits were imposed on passenger automobiles because of the belief that the tax system was being used to underwrite automobiles whose cost and luxury far exceeded what was needed for their business use.

A *passenger automobile* is any four-wheeled vehicle manufactured for use on public streets, roads, and highways with an unloaded gross vehicle weight rating of 6,000 pounds or less.[22] This definition specifically excludes vehicles used directly in the business of transporting people or property for compensation such as taxicabs, ambulances, hearses, and trucks and vans as prescribed by the Regulations.

The following limits apply to the cost recovery deductions for passenger automobiles for 1997:[23]

Year	Recovery Limitation*
1	$3,160
2	5,000
3	3,050
Succeeding years until the cost is recovered	1,775

*The indexed amounts for 1998 were not available at the time of this writing.

These limits are imposed before any percentage reduction for personal use. In addition, the limitation in the first year includes any amount the taxpayer elects to expense under § 179.[24] If the passenger automobile is used partly for personal use, the personal use percentage is ignored for the purpose of determining the unrecovered cost available for deduction in later years.

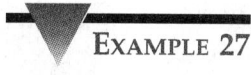

EXAMPLE 27

On July 1, 1998, Dan places in service an automobile that cost $20,000. The car is always used 80% for business and 20% for personal use. The cost recovery for the automobile would be as follows:

1998—$2,528 [$20,000 × 20% (limited to $3,160) × 80%]

1999—$4,000 [$20,000 × 32% (limited to $5,000) × 80%]

2000—$2,440 [$20,000 × 19.2% (limited to $3,050) × 80%]

2001—$1,420 [$20,000 × 11.52% (limited to $1,775) × 80%]

2002—$1,420 [$20,000 × 11.52% (limited to $1,775) × 80%]

2003—$1,420 [$5,240 unrecovered cost ($20,000 – $14,760*) (limited to $1,775) × 80%]

*($3,160 + $5,000 + $3,050 + $1,775 + $1,775). Although the statutory percentage method appears to restrict the deduction to $922 [$20,000 × 5.76% (limited to $1,775) × 80%], the unrecovered cost of $5,240 (limited to $1,775) multiplied by the business usage percentage is deductible. At the start of 2001 (year 4), there is an automatic switch to the straight-line cost recovery method. Under this method, the unrecovered cost up to the maximum allowable limit ($1,775) is deductible in the last year of the recovery period (2003 or year 6). Because the limit may restrict the deduction, any remaining unrecovered cost is deductible in the next or succeeding year(s), subject to the maximum allowable yearly limit ($1,775), multiplied by the business usage percentage.

The total cost recovery for the years 1998–2003 is $13,228. ▼

---

[21]Reg. § 1.280F-6T(e).

[22]§ 280F(d)(5).

[23]§ 280F(a)(2). The 1997 indexed amounts of $3,160, $5,000, $3,050, and $1,775 are used for the 1998 calculations that follow.

[24]§ 280F(d)(1).

The cost recovery limitations are maximum amounts. If the regular calculation produces a lesser amount of cost recovery, the lesser amount is used.

EXAMPLE 28

On April 2, 1998, Gail places in service an automobile that cost $10,000. The car is always used 70% for business and 30% for personal use. The cost recovery allowance for 1998 is $1,400 ($10,000 × 20% × 70%), which is less than $2,212 ($3,160 × 70%). ▼

Note that the cost recovery limitations apply *only* to passenger automobiles and not to other listed property.

Automobiles and Other Listed Property Not Used Predominantly in Business.   The cost of listed property that does not pass the more-than-50 percent business usage test in the year the property is placed in service must be recovered using the straight-line method.[25] The straight-line method to be used is that required under the alternative depreciation system (explained later in the chapter). This system requires a straight-line recovery period of five years for automobiles. However, even though the straight-line method is used, the cost recovery allowance for passenger automobiles cannot exceed the dollar limitations.

EXAMPLE 29

On July 27, 1998, Fred places in service an automobile that cost $20,000. The auto is used 40% for business and 60% for personal use. The cost recovery allowance for 1998 is $800 [$20,000 × 10% (Table 7–11) × 40%]. ▼

EXAMPLE 30

Assume the same facts as in Example 29, except that the auto cost $50,000. The cost recovery allowance for 1998 is $1,264 [$50,000 × 10% (Table 7–11) = $5,000 (limited to $3,160) × 40%]. ▼

If the listed property fails the more-than-50 percent business usage test, the straight-line method must be used for the remainder of the property's life. This applies even if at some later date the business usage of the property increases to more than 50 percent. Even though the straight-line method must continue to be used, however, the amount of cost recovery will reflect the increase in business usage.

EXAMPLE 31

Assume the same facts as in Example 29, except that in 1999, Fred uses the auto 70% for business and 30% for personal use. Fred's cost recovery allowance for 1999 is $2,800 [$20,000 × 20% (Table 7–11) × 70%], which is less than 70% of the second-year limit. ▼

Change from Predominantly Business Use.   If the business use percentage of listed property falls to 50 percent or lower after the year the property is placed in service, the property is subject to *cost recovery recapture*. The amount required to be recaptured and included in the taxpayer's return as ordinary income is the excess cost recovery.

Excess cost recovery is the excess of the cost recovery deduction taken in prior years using the statutory percentage method over the amount that would have been allowed if the straight-line method had been used since the property was placed in service.[26]

EXAMPLE 32

Seth purchased a car on January 22, 1998, at a cost of $20,000. Business usage was 80% in 1998, 70% in 1999, 40% in 2000, and 60% in 2001. Statutory percentage cost recovery deductions in 1998 and 1999 are $2,528 (80% × $3,160) and $3,500 (70% × $5,000), respectively. Seth's excess cost recovery to be recaptured as ordinary income in 2000 is $1,628, calculated as follows:

[25]§ 280F(b)(2).   [26]§ 280F(b)(3).

1998

Statutory percentage allowance	$ 2,528
Straight-line ($20,000 × 10% × 80%)	(1,600)
Excess	$ 928

1999

Statutory percentage allowance	$ 3,500
Straight-line ($20,000 × 20% × 70%)	(2,800)
1999 excess	$ 700
1998 excess	928
Total excess	$ 1,628

After the business usage of the listed property drops below the more-than-50 percent level, the straight-line method must be used for the remaining life of the property.

EXAMPLE 33

Assume the same facts as in Example 32. Seth's cost recovery allowance for the years 2000 and 2001 would be $1,220 and $1,065, computed as follows:

2000—$1,220   [($20,000 × 20%) limited to $3,050 × 40%]
2001—$1,065   [($20,000 × 20%) limited to $1,775 × 60%]

Leased Automobiles.   A taxpayer who leases a passenger automobile must report an *inclusion amount* in gross income. The inclusion amount is computed from an IRS table for each taxable year for which the taxpayer leases the automobile. The purpose of this provision is to prevent taxpayers from circumventing the cost recovery dollar limitations by leasing, instead of purchasing, an automobile.

The dollar amount of the inclusion is based on the fair market value of the automobile and is prorated for the number of days the auto is used during the taxable year. The prorated dollar amount is then multiplied by the business and income-producing usage percentage to determine the amount to be included in gross income.[27] The taxpayer deducts the lease payments, multiplied by the business and income-producing usage percentage. The net effect is that the annual deduction for the lease payment is reduced by the inclusion amount.

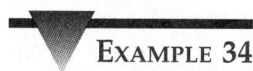

EXAMPLE 34

On April 1, 1998, Jim leases and places in service a passenger automobile worth $40,000. The lease is to be for a period of five years. During the taxable years 1998 and 1999, Jim uses the automobile 70% for business and 30% for personal use. Assuming the dollar amounts from the IRS table for 1998 and 1999 are $188 and $412, Jim must include $99 in gross income for 1998 and $288 for 1999, computed as follows:

1998 $188 × (275/365) × 70% = $99
1999 $412 × (365/365) × 70% = $288

In addition, Jim can deduct 70% of the lease payments each year because this is the business use percentage. ▼

---

[27]Reg. § 1.280F-7T(a).

SUBSTANTIATING A DEPRECIATION DEDUCTION

The IRS disallowed a depreciation deduction of $53,997 on the 1993 income tax return of Daniel Becnel, Jr. Becnel deducted the depreciation on 13 automobiles that he said were used strictly for business. Becnel claimed that the cars, nine of which were Mercedes-Benzes, were used to drive to states where his firm was handling lawsuits. The IRS disallowed the deduction claiming that Becnel didn't establish that the automobiles were used in a trade or business. Becnel has filed a petition with the U.S. Tax Court.

SOURCE: Adapted from Judi Russell and William Ringle, Jr., "Attorney Battles with IRS over Deduction for 13 Cars," *City Business/New Orleans, Inc.*, June 23, 1997.

Substantiation Requirements. Listed property is now subject to the substantiation requirements of § 274. This means that the taxpayer must prove the business usage as to the amount of expense or use, the time and place of use, the business purpose for the use, and the business relationship to the taxpayer of persons using the property. Substantiation requires adequate records or sufficient evidence corroborating the taxpayer's statement. However, these substantiation requirements do not apply to vehicles that, by reason of their nature, are not likely to be used more than a *de minimis* amount for personal purposes.[28]

ALTERNATIVE DEPRECIATION SYSTEM (ADS)

5 **LEARNING OBJECTIVE**
Determine when and how to use the alternative depreciation system (ADS).

The **alternative depreciation system (ADS)** must be used for the following:[29]

- To calculate the portion of depreciation treated as an alternative minimum tax (AMT) adjustment for purposes of the corporate and individual AMT (see Chapter 14).
- To compute depreciation allowances for property for which any of the following is true:
  - Used predominantly outside the United States.
  - Leased or otherwise used by a tax-exempt entity.
  - Financed with the proceeds of tax-exempt bonds.
  - Imported from foreign countries that maintain discriminatory trade practices or otherwise engage in discriminatory acts.
- To compute depreciation allowances for earnings and profits purposes (see Chapter 18).

In general, ADS depreciation is computed using straight-line recovery without regard to salvage value. However, for purposes of the AMT, depreciation of personal property is computed using the 150 percent declining-balance method with an appropriate switch to the straight-line method.

The taxpayer must use the half-year or the mid-quarter convention, whichever is applicable, for all property other than eligible real estate. The mid-month convention is used for eligible real estate. The applicable ADS rates are found in Tables 7–10, 7–11, and 7–12.

---

[28]§§ 274(d) and (i).

[29]§ 168(g).

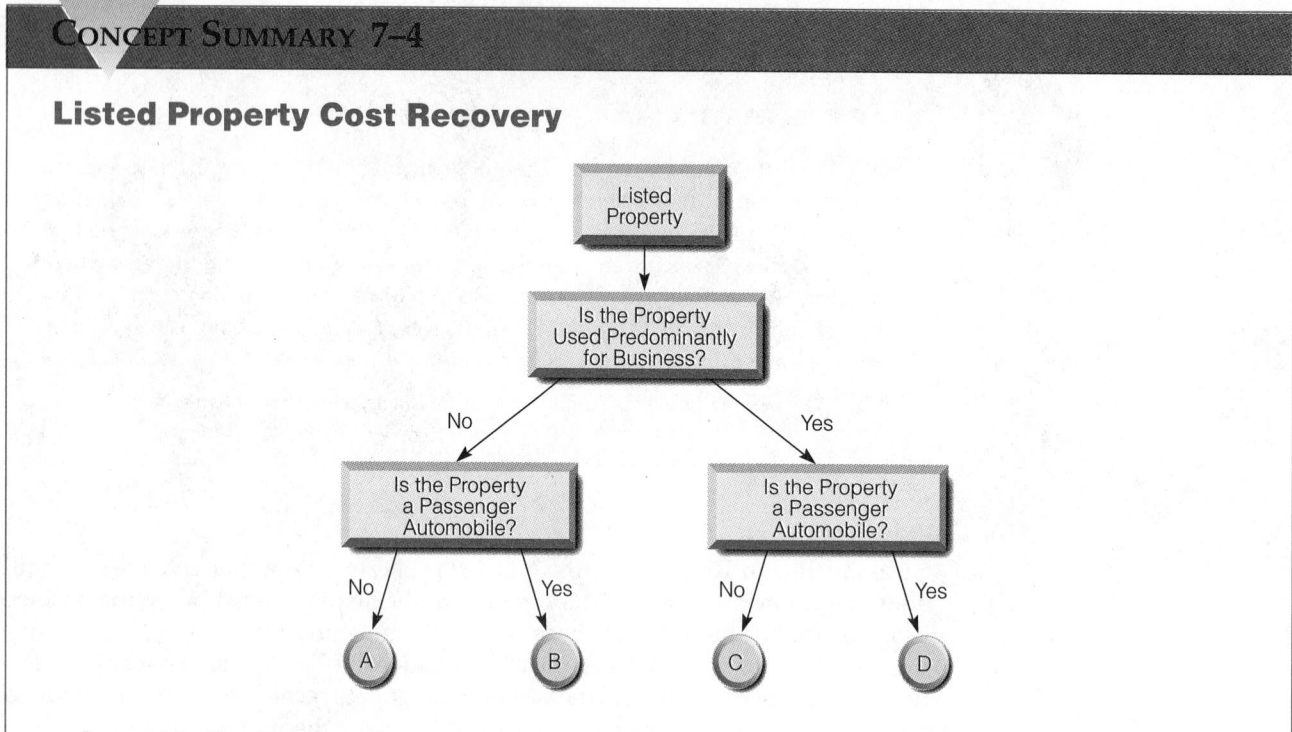

CONCEPT SUMMARY 7–4

Listed Property Cost Recovery

Legend to Tax Treatment

A   Straight-line cost recovery reduced by the personal use percentage.

B   Straight-line cost recovery subject to the recovery limitations ($3,160, $5,000, $3,050, $1,775) and reduced by the personal use percentage.

C   Statutory percentage cost recovery reduced by the personal use percentage.

D   Statutory percentage cost recovery subject to the recovery limitations ($3,160, $5,000, $3,050, $1,775) and reduced by the personal use percentage.

The recovery periods under ADS are as follows:[30]

- The ADR midpoint life for property that does not fall into any of the following listed categories.
- Five years for qualified technological equipment, automobiles, and light-duty trucks.
- Twelve years for personal property with no class life.
- Forty years for all residential rental property and all nonresidential real property.

Taxpayers may *elect* to use the 150 percent declining-balance method to compute the regular income tax rather than the 200 percent declining-balance method that is available for personal property. Hence, if the election is made, there will be no difference between the cost recovery for computing the regular income tax and the AMT. However, taxpayers who make this election must use the ADS recovery periods in computing the cost recovery for the regular income tax, and the ADS recovery periods generally are longer than the regular recovery periods under MACRS. For property placed in service after December 31, 1998, TRA of 1997 provides that the regular income tax MACRS recovery

---

[30]The class life for certain properties described in § 168(e)(3) is specially determined under § 168(g)(3)(B).

periods can be used for both the regular income tax and the AMT rather than the longer ADS recovery periods.

The following are examples of the classification of property by class life for the ADS recovery periods:[31]

3-year . . . . . Special tools used in the manufacture of motor vehicles, breeding hogs.
5-year . . . . . Automobiles, light general-purpose trucks.
7-year . . . . . Breeding and dairy cattle.
9.5-year . . . . Computer-based telephone central office switching equipment.
10-year . . . . Office furniture, fixtures, and equipment, railroad track.
12-year . . . . Racehorses more than 2 years old at the time they are placed in service.

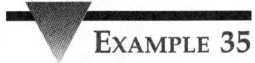

EXAMPLE 35

On March 1, 1998, Abby purchases computer-based telephone central office switching equipment for $80,000. If Abby uses statutory percentage cost recovery (assuming no § 179 election), the cost recovery allowance for 1998 is $16,000 [$80,000 × 20% (Table 7–2, 5-year class property)]. If Abby elects to use ADS 150% declining-balance cost recovery (assuming no § 179 election), the cost recovery allowance for 1998 is $6,312 [$80,000 × 7.89% (Table 7–10, 9.5-year class property)]. Note that if the equipment were placed in service in 1999, the 5-year recovery period could be used with the ADS 150% declining-balance cost recovery. ▼

In lieu of depreciation under the regular MACRS method, taxpayers may *elect* straight-line under ADS for property that qualifies for the regular MACRS method. The election is available on a class-by-class and year-by-year basis for property other than eligible real estate. The election for eligible real estate is on a property-by-property basis. One reason for making this election is to avoid a difference between deductible depreciation and earnings and profits depreciation.

EXAMPLE 36

Polly acquires an apartment building on March 17, 1998, for $700,000. She takes the maximum cost recovery allowance for determining taxable income. Polly's cost recovery allowance for computing 1998 taxable income is $20,153 [$700,000 × .02879 (Table 7–7)]. However, Polly's cost recovery for computing her earnings and profits is only $13,853 [$700,000 × .01979 (Table 7–12)]. ▼

AMORTIZATION

6 **LEARNING OBJECTIVE**
Identify intangible assets that are eligible for amortization and calculate the amount of the deduction.

Taxpayers can claim an **amortization** deduction on intangible assets called "amortizable § 197 intangibles." The amount of the deduction is determined by amortizing the adjusted basis of such intangibles ratably over a 15-year period beginning in the month in which the intangible is acquired.[32]

An *amortizable § 197 intangible* is any § 197 intangible acquired after August 10, 1993, and held in connection with the conduct of a trade or business or for the production of income. Section 197 intangibles include goodwill and going-concern value, franchises (except sports franchises), trademarks, and trade names. Covenants not to compete, copyrights, and patents are also included if they are acquired in connection with the acquisition of a business. Generally, self-created intangibles are not § 197 intangibles. The 15-year amortization period applies regardless of the actual useful life of an amortizable § 197 intangible. No other depreciation or

---

[31]Rev.Proc. 87-56, 1987-2 C.B. 674 is the source for the recovery periods.

[32]§ 197(a).

amortization deduction is permitted with respect to any amortizable § 197 intangible except those permitted under the 15-year amortization rules.

EXAMPLE 37

On June 1, 1998, Neil purchased and began operating the Falcon Cafe. Of the purchase price, $90,000 is correctly allocated to goodwill. The deduction for amortization for 1998 is $3,500 [($90,000/15) × (7/12)]. ▼

ETHICAL CONSIDERATIONS

Allocating Intangible Assets When a Business Is Sold

Marge and Stan are negotiating Stan's purchase of Marge's business. Both are in the 36 percent tax bracket. They have agreed that the tangible assets of the business are worth $100,000. Marge's adjusted basis for these assets is $70,000. The only other asset of the business is the going-concern value. Marge believes that this asset is worth about $50,000. Stan believes that it is worth somewhat less, probably about $40,000.

Marge and Stan are handling their own negotiations since they do not believe in wasting money on attorneys or CPAs when such professional services are not required. Stan knows from an MBA class he took five years ago that goodwill is not deductible, but that a covenant not to compete can be deducted over the covenant period. Stan believes that Marge, who is age 67 and in poor health, is going to retire. In order to maximize the tax benefits to himself, Stan increases his offer from $140,000 to $145,000 (i.e., "we'll split the difference") if Marge will agree to sign a five-year covenant with $45,000 of the $145,000 purchase price allocated to the covenant. Marge, who believes that the tax consequences of the sale ($145,000 amount realized − $70,000 adjusted basis = $75,000 recognized gain) will be the same regardless of whether the $45,000 is for goodwill or for a covenant, accepts the offer. Evaluate the decisions made by Marge and Stan.

DEPLETION

7 LEARNING OBJECTIVE
Determine the amount of depletion expense including being able to apply the alternative tax treatments for intangible drilling and development costs.

Natural resources (e.g., oil, gas, coal, gravel, timber) are subject to **depletion,** which is simply a form of depreciation applicable to natural resources. Land generally cannot be depleted.

The owner of an interest in the natural resource is entitled to deduct depletion. An owner is one who has an economic interest in the property.[33] An economic interest requires the acquisition of an interest in the resource in place and the receipt of income from the extraction or severance of that resource. Like depreciation, depletion is a deduction *for* adjusted gross income.

Although all natural resources are subject to depletion, oil and gas wells are used as an example in the following paragraphs to illustrate the related costs and issues.

In developing an oil or gas well, the producer must make four types of expenditures:

---

[33]Reg. § 1.611-1(b).

- Natural resource costs.
- Intangible drilling and development costs.
- Tangible asset costs.
- Operating costs.

Natural resources are physically limited, and the costs to acquire them (e.g., oil under the ground) are, therefore, recovered through depletion. Costs incurred in making the property ready for drilling such as the cost of labor in clearing the property, erecting derricks, and drilling the hole are **intangible drilling and development costs (IDC).** These costs generally have no salvage value and are a lost cost if the well is dry. Costs for tangible assets such as tools, pipes, and engines are capital in nature. These costs must be capitalized and recovered through depreciation (cost recovery). Costs incurred after the well is producing are operating costs. These costs would include expenditures for such items as labor, fuel, and supplies. Operating costs are deductible when incurred (on the accrual basis) or when paid (on the cash basis).

The expenditures for depreciable assets and operating costs pose no unusual problems for producers of natural resources. The tax treatment of depletable costs and intangible drilling and development costs is quite a different matter.

INTANGIBLE DRILLING AND DEVELOPMENT COSTS (IDC)

Intangible drilling and development costs (IDC) can be handled in one of two ways at the option of the taxpayer. They can be *either* charged off as an expense in the year in which they are incurred *or* capitalized and written off through depletion. The taxpayer makes the election in the first year such expenditures are incurred either by taking a deduction on the return or by adding them to the depletable basis. No formal statement of intent is required. Once made, the election is binding on both the taxpayer and the IRS for all such expenditures in the future. If the taxpayer fails to make the election to expense IDC on the original timely filed return the first year such expenditures are incurred, an automatic election to capitalize them has been made and is irrevocable.

As a general rule, it is more advantageous to expense IDC. The obvious benefit of an immediate write-off (as opposed to a deferred write-off through depletion) is not the only advantage. Since a taxpayer can use percentage depletion, which is calculated without reference to basis (see Example 41), the IDC may be completely lost as a deduction if they are capitalized.

DEPLETION METHODS

There are two methods of calculating depletion: cost and percentage. Cost depletion can be used on any wasting asset (and is the only method allowed for timber). Percentage depletion is subject to a number of limitations, particularly for oil and gas deposits. Depletion should be calculated both ways, and generally the method that results in the *larger* deduction is used. The choice between cost and percentage depletion is an annual election.

Cost Depletion. **Cost depletion** is determined by using the adjusted basis of the asset.[34] The basis is divided by the estimated recoverable units of the asset (e.g., barrels, tons) to arrive at the depletion per unit. The depletion per unit then is multiplied by the number of units sold (*not* the units produced) during the year

---

[34]§ 612.

to arrive at the cost depletion allowed. Cost depletion, therefore, resembles the units-of-production method of calculating depreciation.

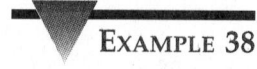

EXAMPLE 38

On January 1, 1998, Pablo purchased the rights to a mineral interest for $1,000,000. At that time, the remaining recoverable units in the mineral interest were estimated to be 200,000. The depletion per unit is $5 [$1,000,000 (adjusted basis) ÷ 200,000 (estimated recoverable units)]. If during the year 60,000 units were mined and 25,000 were sold, the cost depletion would be $125,000 [$5 (depletion per unit) × 25,000 (units sold)]. ▼

If the taxpayer later discovers that the original estimate was incorrect, the depletion per unit for future calculations must be redetermined based on the revised estimate.[35]

EXAMPLE 39

Assume the same facts as in Example 38. In 1999, Pablo realizes that an incorrect estimate was made. The remaining recoverable units now are determined to be 400,000. Based on this new information, the revised depletion per unit is $2.1875 [$875,000 (adjusted basis) ÷ 400,000 (estimated recoverable units)]. Note that the adjusted basis is the original cost ($1,000,000) reduced by the depletion claimed in 1998 ($125,000). If 30,000 units are sold in 1999, the depletion for the year would be $65,625 [$2.1875 (depletion per unit) × 30,000 (units sold)]. ▼

Percentage Depletion. **Percentage depletion** (also referred to as statutory depletion) is a specified percentage provided for in the Code. The percentage varies according to the type of mineral interest involved. A sample of these percentages is shown in Exhibit 7–2. The rate is applied to the gross income from the property, but in no event may percentage depletion exceed 50 percent of the taxable income from the property before the allowance for depletion.[36]

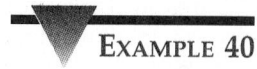

EXAMPLE 40

Assuming gross income of $100,000, a depletion rate of 22%, and other expenses relating to the property of $60,000, the depletion allowance is determined as follows:

Gross income	$100,000
Less: Other expenses	(60,000)
Taxable income before depletion	$ 40,000
Depletion allowance [the lesser of $22,000 (22% × $100,000) or $20,000 (50% × $40,000)]	(20,000)
Taxable income after depletion	$ 20,000

The adjusted basis of the property is reduced by $20,000, the depletion allowed. If the other expenses had been only $55,000, the full $22,000 could have been deducted, and the adjusted basis would have been reduced by $22,000. ▼

Note that percentage depletion is based on a percentage of the gross income from the property and makes no reference to cost. Thus, when percentage depletion is used, it is possible to deduct more than the original cost of the property. If percentage depletion is used, however, the adjusted basis of the property (for computing cost depletion) must be reduced by the amount of percentage depletion taken until the adjusted basis reaches zero.

---

[35] § 611(a).

[36] § 613(a). Special rules apply for certain oil and gas wells under § 613A (e.g., the 50% ceiling is replaced with a 100% ceiling, and the percentage depletion may not exceed 65% of the taxpayer's taxable income from all sources before the allowance for depletion).

▼ **EXHIBIT 7–2**
Sample of Percentage Depletion
Rates

22% Depletion	
Cobalt	Sulfur
Lead	Tin
Nickel	Uranium
Platinum	Zinc
15% Depletion	
Copper	Oil and gas
Gold	Oil shale
Iron	Silver
14% Depletion	
Borax	Magnesium carbonates
Calcium carbonates	Marble
Granite	Potash
Limestone	Slate
10% Depletion	
Coal	Perlite
Lignite	Sodium chloride
5% Depletion	
Gravel	Pumice
Peat	Sand

Effect of Intangible Drilling Costs on Depletion.   The treatment of IDC has an effect on the depletion deduction in two ways. If the costs are capitalized, the basis for cost depletion is increased. As a consequence, the cost depletion is increased. If IDC are expensed, they reduce the taxable income from the property. This reduction may result in application of the provision that limits depletion to 50 percent (100 percent for certain oil and gas wells) of taxable income before deducting depletion.

TAX IN THE NEWS

PERCENTAGE DEPLETION

On March 17, 1997, the U.S. Supreme Court declined to consider the IRS's appeal in a case against Exxon Corporation as to the proper way to calculate a depletion deduction. The disagreement involved the proper sales price of natural gas to be used in computing the percentage depletion deduction. The IRS argued that the depletion deduction for some natural gas sales should not be allowed to exceed the company's total income from those sales. Exxon argued that the law allows the use of a representative market price for natural gas in the field where it was produced, even if that price far exceeds the actual price received. At stake was about $1 billion in tax liability.

SOURCE: Adapted from Bloomberg News, "Supreme Court Declines to Hear IRS Appeal in Exxon Tax Fight," *Fort Worth Star-Telegram*, March 18, 1997, Business, p. 3.

EXAMPLE 41

Iris purchased the rights to an oil interest for $1,000,000. The recoverable barrels were estimated to be 200,000. During the year, 50,000 barrels were sold for $2,000,000. Regular expenses amounted to $800,000, and IDC were $650,000. If the IDC are capitalized, the depletion per unit is $8.25 ($1,000,000 + $650,000 ÷ 200,000 barrels), and the following taxable income results:

Gross income	$2,000,000
Less: Expenses	(800,000)
Taxable income before depletion	$1,200,000
Cost depletion ($8.25 × 50,000) = $412,500	
Percentage depletion (15% × $2,000,000) = $300,000	
Greater of cost or percentage depletion	(412,500)
Taxable income	$ 787,500

If the IDC are expensed, the taxable income is $250,000, calculated as follows:

Gross income	$ 2,000,000
Less: Expenses, including IDC	(1,450,000)
Taxable income before depletion	$ 550,000
Cost depletion [($1,000,000 ÷ 200,000 barrels) × 50,000 barrels] = $250,000	
Percentage depletion (15% of $2,000,000 = $300,000, limited to 100% of $550,000 taxable income before depletion) = $300,000	
Greater of cost or percentage depletion	(300,000)
Taxable income	$ 250,000

For further restrictions on the use or availability of the percentage depletion method, see § 613.

TAX PLANNING CONSIDERATIONS

COST RECOVERY

Cost recovery schedules should be reviewed annually for possible retirements, abandonments, and obsolescence.

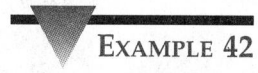

EXAMPLE 42

An examination of the cost recovery schedule of Eagle Company reveals the following:

- Asset A was abandoned when it was discovered that the cost of repairs would be in excess of the cost of replacement. Asset A had an adjusted basis of $3,000.
- Asset J became obsolete this year, at which point, its adjusted basis was $8,000.

Assets A and J should be written off for an additional expense of $11,000 ($3,000 + $8,000). ▼

8 **LEARNING OBJECTIVE**
Identify tax planning opportunities for cost recovery, amortization, and depletion.

Because of the deductions for cost recovery, interest, and ad valorem property taxes, investments in real estate can be highly attractive. In figuring the economics of such investments, one should be sure to take into account any tax savings that result.

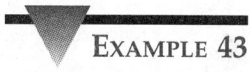

EXAMPLE 43

In early January 1997, Vern purchased residential rental property for $170,000 (of which $20,000 was allocated to the land and $150,000 to the building). Vern made a down payment of $25,000 and assumed the seller's mortgage for the balance. Under the mortgage agreement, monthly payments of $1,000 are required and are applied toward interest, taxes, insurance, and principal. Since the property was already occupied, Vern continued to receive rent of

$1,200 per month from the tenant. Vern actively participates in this activity and hence comes under the special rule for a rental real estate activity with respect to the limitation on passive activity losses (refer to Chapter 10). Vern is in the 31% tax bracket.

During 1998, Vern's expenses were as follows:

Interest	$10,000
Taxes	800
Insurance	1,000
Repairs and maintenance	2,200
Depreciation ($150,000 × .03636)	5,454
Total	$19,454

The deductible loss from the rental property is computed as follows:

Rent income ($1,200 × 12 months)	$ 14,400
Less expenses (see above)	(19,454)
Net loss	($ 5,054)

But what is Vern's overall position for the year when the tax benefit of the loss is taken into account? Considering just the cash intake and outlay, it is summarized as follows:

Intake—		
Rent income	$14,400	
Tax savings [31% (income tax bracket) × $5,054 (loss from the property)]	1,567	$ 15,967
Outlay—		
Mortgage payments ($1,000 × 12 months)	$12,000	
Repairs and maintenance	2,200	(14,200)
Net cash benefit		$ 1,767

It should be noted, however, that should Vern cease being an active participant in the rental activity, the passive activity loss rules would apply, and Vern could lose the current period benefit of the loss.

AMORTIZATION

When a business is purchased, goodwill and covenants not to compete are both subject to a statutory amortization period of 15 years. Therefore, the purchaser does not derive any tax benefits when part of the purchase price is assigned to a covenant rather than to goodwill.

Thus, from the purchaser's perspective, bargaining for a covenant should be based on legal rather than tax reasons. Note, however, that from the seller's perspective, goodwill is a capital asset and the covenant is an ordinary income asset.

Since the amortization period for both goodwill and a covenant is 15 years, the purchaser may want to attempt to minimize these amounts if the purchase price can be assigned to assets with shorter lives (e.g., inventory, receivables, and personalty). Conversely, the purchaser may want to attempt to maximize these amounts if part of the purchase price will otherwise be assigned to assets with longer recovery periods (e.g., realty) or to assets not eligible for cost recovery (e.g., land).

DEPLETION

Since the election to use the cost or percentage depletion method is an annual election, a taxpayer can use cost depletion (if higher) until the basis is exhausted and then switch to percentage depletion in the following years.

EXAMPLE 44

Assume the following facts for Melissa:

Remaining depletable basis	$ 11,000
Gross income (10,000 units)	100,000
Expenses (other than depletion)	30,000

Since cost depletion is limited to the basis of $11,000 and if the percentage depletion is $22,000 (assume a 22% rate), Melissa would choose the latter. Her basis is then reduced to zero. In future years, however, she can continue to take percentage depletion since percentage depletion is taken without reference to the remaining basis. ▼

The election to expense intangible drilling and development costs is a one-time election. Once the election is made to either expense or capitalize the intangible drilling and development costs, it is binding on all future expenditures. The permanent nature of the election makes it extremely important for the taxpayer to determine which treatment will provide the greatest tax advantage. (Refer to Example 41 for an illustration of the effect of using the two different alternatives for a given set of facts.)

TABLES

Summary of Tables

Table 7–5	Original ACRS statutory percentage table for realty.
	Applicable depreciation method: 175 percent declining-balance switching to straight-line.
	Applicable recovery period: 18 years.
	Applicable convention: mid-month.
Table 7–6	Original ACRS statutory percentage table for realty.
	Applicable depreciation method: 175 percent declining-balance switching to straight-line.
	Applicable recovery period: 19 years.
	Applicable convention: mid-month.
Table 7–7	Modified ACRS straight-line table for realty.
	Applicable depreciation method: straight-line.
	Applicable recovery periods: 27.5, 31.5, 39 years.
	Applicable convention: mid-month.
Table 7–8	Original ACRS optional straight-line table for realty.
	Applicable depreciation method: straight-line.
	Applicable recovery period: 19 years.
	Applicable convention: mid-month.
Table 7–9	Modified ACRS optional straight-line table for personalty.
	Applicable depreciation method: straight-line.
	Applicable recovery periods: 3, 5, 7, 10, 15, 20 years.
	Applicable convention: half-year.
Table 7–10	Alternative minimum tax declining-balance table for personalty.
	Applicable depreciation method: 150 percent declining-balance switching to straight-line.
	Applicable recovery periods: 3, 5, 7, 9.5, 10, 12 years.
	Applicable convention: half-year.
Table 7–11	Alternative depreciation system straight-line table for personalty.
	Applicable depreciation method: straight-line.
	Applicable recovery periods: 5, 9.5, 12 years.
	Applicable convention: half-year.
Table 7–12	Alternative depreciation system straight-line table for realty.
	Applicable depreciation method: straight-line.
	Applicable recovery period: 40 years.
	Applicable convention: mid-month.

▼ **TABLE 7–1**

ACRS Statutory Percentages for Property Other Than 15-Year Real Property, 18-Year Real Property, or 19-Year Real Property Assuming Half-Year Convention

For Property Placed in Service after December 31, 1980, and before January 1, 1987

Recovery Year	The Applicable Percentage for the Class of Property Is:			
	3-Year	5-Year	10-Year	15-Year Public Utility
1	25	15	8	5
2	38	22	14	10
3	37	21	12	9
4		21	10	8
5		21	10	7
6			10	6
7			9	6
8			9	6
9			9	6
10			9	6
11				6
12				6
13				6
14				6
15				6

▼ **TABLE 7–2**

MACRS Accelerated Depreciation for Personal Property Assuming Half-Year Convention

For Property Placed in Service after December 31, 1986

Recovery Year	3-Year (200% DB)	5-Year (200% DB)	7-Year (200% DB)	10-Year (200% DB)	15-Year (150% DB)	20-Year (150% DB)
1	33.33	20.00	14.29	10.00	5.00	3.750
2	44.45	32.00	24.49	18.00	9.50	7.219
3	14.81*	19.20	17.49	14.40	8.55	6.677
4	7.41	11.52*	12.49	11.52	7.70	6.177
5		11.52	8.93*	9.22	6.93	5.713
6		5.76	8.92	7.37	6.23	5.285
7			8.93	6.55*	5.90*	4.888
8			4.46	6.55	5.90	4.522
9				6.56	5.91	4.462*
10				6.55	5.90	4.461
11				3.28	5.91	4.462
12					5.90	4.461
13					5.91	4.462
14					5.90	4.461
15					5.91	4.462
16					2.95	4.461
17						4.462
18						4.461
19						4.462
20						4.461
21						2.231

*Switchover to straight-line depreciation.

▼ **TABLE 7–3**
MACRS Accelerated
Depreciation for Personal
Property Assuming Mid-Quarter
Convention

For Property Placed in Service after December 31, 1986 (Partial Table*)

3-Year

Recovery Year	First Quarter	Second Quarter	Third Quarter	Fourth Quarter
1	58.33	41.67	25.00	8.33
2	27.78	38.89	50.00	61.11

5-Year

Recovery Year	First Quarter	Second Quarter	Third Quarter	Fourth Quarter
1	35.00	25.00	15.00	5.00
2	26.00	30.00	34.00	38.00

7-Year

Recovery Year	First Quarter	Second Quarter	Third Quarter	Fourth Quarter
1	25.00	17.85	10.71	3.57
2	21.43	23.47	25.51	27.55

*The figures in this table are taken from the official tables that appear in Rev.Proc.87–57, 1987–2 C.B. 687. Because of their length, the complete tables are not presented.

▼ **TABLE 7–4**
ACRS Statutory Percentages for
15-Year Real Property

For Property Placed in Service after December 31, 1980, and before January 1, 1987: 15-Year Real Property—Low-Income Housing

If the Recovery Year Is:	And the Month in the First Recovery Year the Property Is Placed in Service Is:											
	1	2	3	4	5	6	7	8	9	10	11	12
	The Applicable Percentage Is (Use the Column for the Month in the First Year the Property Is Placed in Service):											
1	13	12	11	10	9	8	7	6	4	3	2	1
2	12	12	12	12	12	12	12	13	13	13	13	13
3	10	10	10	10	11	11	11	11	11	11	11	11
4	9	9	9	9	9	9	9	9	10	10	10	10
5	8	8	8	8	8	8	8	8	8	8	8	9
6	7	7	7	7	7	7	7	7	7	7	7	7
7	6	6	6	6	6	6	6	6	6	6	6	6
8	5	5	5	5	5	5	5	5	5	5	6	6
9	5	5	5	5	5	5	5	5	5	5	5	5
10	5	5	5	5	5	5	5	5	5	5	5	5
11	4	5	5	5	5	5	5	5	5	5	5	5
12	4	4	4	5	4	5	5	5	5	5	5	5
13	4	4	4	4	4	4	5	4	5	5	5	5
14	4	4	4	4	4	4	4	4	4	5	4	4
15	4	4	4	4	4	4	4	4	4	4	4	4
16	—	—	1	1	2	2	2	3	3	3	4	4

▼ **TABLE 7–4 (Continued)**

For Property Placed in Service after December 31, 1980, and before March 16, 1984: 15-Year Real Property—Other Than Low-Income Housing

	12	11	10	9	8	7	6	5	4	3	2	1
1	12	11	10	9	8	7	6	5	4	3	2	1
2	10	10	11	11	11	11	11	11	11	11	11	12
3	9	9	9	9	10	10	10	10	10	10	10	10
4	8	8	8	8	8	8	9	9	9	9	9	9
5	7	7	7	7	7	7	8	8	8	8	8	8
6	6	6	6	6	7	7	7	7	7	7	7	7
7	6	6	6	6	6	6	6	6	6	6	6	6
8	6	6	6	6	6	6	5	6	6	6	6	6
9	6	6	6	6	5	6	5	5	5	6	6	6
10	5	6	5	6	5	5	5	5	5	5	6	5
11	5	5	5	5	5	5	5	5	5	5	5	5
12	5	5	5	5	5	5	5	5	5	5	5	5
13	5	5	5	5	5	5	5	5	5	5	5	5
14	5	5	5	5	5	5	5	5	5	5	5	5
15	5	5	5	5	5	5	5	5	5	5	5	5
16	—	—	1	1	2	2	3	3	4	4	4	5

▼ **TABLE 7–5**
ACRS Cost Recovery Table for
18-Year Real Property

For Property Placed in Service after June 22, 1984, and before May 9, 1985: 18-Year Real Property (18-Year 175% Declining Balance) (Assuming Mid-Month Convention)

	And the Month in the First Recovery Year the Property Is Placed in Service Is:											
If the Recovery Year Is:	1	2	3	4	5	6	7	8	9	10	11	12
	The Applicable Percentage Is (Use the Column for the Month in the First Year the Property Is Placed in Service):											
1	9	9	8	7	6	5	4	4	3	2	1	0.4
2	9	9	9	9	9	9	9	9	9	10	10	10.0
3	8	8	8	8	8	8	8	8	9	9	9	9.0
4	7	7	7	7	7	8	8	8	8	8	8	8.0
5	7	7	7	7	7	7	7	7	7	7	7	7.0
6	6	6	6	6	6	6	6	6	6	6	6	6.0
7	5	5	5	5	6	6	6	6	6	6	6	6.0
8	5	5	5	5	5	5	5	5	5	5	5	5.0
9	5	5	5	5	5	5	5	5	5	5	5	5.0
10	5	5	5	5	5	5	5	5	5	5	5	5.0
11	5	5	5	5	5	5	5	5	5	5	5	5.0
12	5	5	5	5	5	5	5	5	5	5	5	5.0
13	4	4	4	5	4	4	5	4	4	4	5	5.0
14	4	4	4	4	4	4	4	4	4	4	4	4.0
15	4	4	4	4	4	4	4	4	4	4	4	4.0
16	4	4	4	4	4	4	4	4	4	4	4	4.0
17	4	4	4	4	4	4	4	4	4	4	4	4.0
18	4	3	4	4	4	4	4	4	4	4	4	4.0
19		1	1	1	2	2	2	3	3	3	3	3.6

▼ TABLE 7–6
ACRS Cost Recovery Table for
19-Year Real Property

For Property Placed in Service after May 8, 1985, and before January 1, 1987
19-Year Real Property (19-Year 175% Declining Balance)
(Assuming Mid-Month Convention)

	And the Month in the First Recovery Year the Property Is Placed in Service Is:											
If the Recovery Year Is:	1	2	3	4	5	6	7	8	9	10	11	12
	The Applicable Percentage Is (Use the Column for the Month in the First Year the Property Is Placed in Service):											
1	8.8	8.1	7.3	6.5	5.8	5.0	4.2	3.5	2.7	1.9	1.1	0.4
2	8.4	8.5	8.5	8.6	8.7	8.8	8.8	8.9	9.0	9.0	9.1	9.2
3	7.6	7.7	7.7	7.8	7.9	7.9	8.0	8.1	8.1	8.2	8.3	8.3
4	6.9	7.0	7.0	7.1	7.1	7.2	7.3	7.3	7.4	7.4	7.5	7.6
5	6.3	6.3	6.4	6.4	6.5	6.5	6.6	6.6	6.7	6.8	6.8	6.9
6	5.7	5.7	5.8	5.9	5.9	5.9	6.0	6.0	6.1	6.1	6.2	6.2
7	5.2	5.2	5.3	5.3	5.3	5.4	5.4	5.5	5.5	5.6	5.6	5.6
8	4.7	4.7	4.8	4.8	4.8	4.9	4.9	5.0	5.0	5.1	5.1	5.1
9	4.2	4.3	4.3	4.4	4.4	4.5	4.5	4.5	4.5	4.6	4.6	4.7
10	4.2	4.2	4.2	4.2	4.2	4.2	4.2	4.2	4.2	4.2	4.2	4.2
11	4.2	4.2	4.2	4.2	4.2	4.2	4.2	4.2	4.2	4.2	4.2	4.2
12	4.2	4.2	4.2	4.2	4.2	4.2	4.2	4.2	4.2	4.2	4.2	4.2
13	4.2	4.2	4.2	4.2	4.2	4.2	4.2	4.2	4.2	4.2	4.2	4.2
14	4.2	4.2	4.2	4.2	4.2	4.2	4.2	4.2	4.2	4.2	4.2	4.2
15	4.2	4.2	4.2	4.2	4.2	4.2	4.2	4.2	4.2	4.2	4.2	4.2
16	4.2	4.2	4.2	4.2	4.2	4.2	4.2	4.2	4.2	4.2	4.2	4.2
17	4.2	4.2	4.2	4.2	4.2	4.2	4.2	4.2	4.2	4.2	4.2	4.2
18	4.2	4.2	4.2	4.2	4.2	4.2	4.2	4.2	4.2	4.2	4.2	4.2
19	4.2	4.2	4.2	4.2	4.2	4.2	4.2	4.2	4.2	4.2	4.2	4.2
20	0.2	0.5	0.9	1.2	1.6	1.9	2.3	2.6	3.0	3.3	3.7	4.0

▼ **TABLE 7–7**
MACRS Straight-Line
Depreciation for Real Property
Assuming Mid-Month
Convention*

For Property Placed in Service after December 31, 1986: 27.5-Year Residential Real Property

The Applicable Percentage Is (Use the Column for the Month in the First Year the Property Is Placed in Service):

Recovery Year(s)	1	2	3	4	5	6	7	8	9	10	11	12
1	3.485	3.182	2.879	2.576	2.273	1.970	1.667	1.364	1.061	0.758	0.455	0.152
2–18	3.636	3.636	3.636	3.636	3.636	3.636	3.636	3.636	3.636	3.636	3.636	3.636
19–27	3.637	3.637	3.637	3.637	3.637	3.637	3.637	3.637	3.637	3.637	3.637	3.637
28	1.970	2.273	2.576	2.879	3.182	3.485	3.636	3.636	3.636	3.636	3.636	3.636
29	0.000	0.000	0.000	0.000	0.000	0.000	0.152	0.455	0.758	1.061	1.364	1.667

For Property Placed in Service after December 31, 1986, and before May 13, 1993: 31.5-Year Nonresidential Real Property

The Applicable Percentage Is (Use the Column for the Month in the First Year the Property Is Placed in Service):

Recovery Year(s)	1	2	3	4	5	6	7	8	9	10	11	12
1	3.042	2.778	2.513	2.249	1.984	1.720	1.455	1.190	0.926	0.661	0.397	0.132
2–19	3.175	3.175	3.175	3.175	3.175	3.175	3.175	3.175	3.175	3.175	3.175	3.175
20–31	3.174	3.174	3.174	3.174	3.174	3.174	3.174	3.174	3.174	3.174	3.174	3.174
32	1.720	1.984	2.249	2.513	2.778	3.042	3.175	3.175	3.175	3.175	3.175	3.175
33	0.000	0.000	0.000	0.000	0.000	0.000	0.132	0.397	0.661	0.926	1.190	1.455

For Property Placed in Service after May 12, 1993: 39-Year Nonresidential Real Property

The Applicable Percentage Is (Use the Column for the Month in the First Year the Property Is Placed in Service):

Recovery Year(s)	1	2	3	4	5	6	7	8	9	10	11	12
1	2.461	2.247	2.033	1.819	1.605	1.391	1.177	0.963	0.749	0.535	0.321	0.107
2–39	2.564	2.564	2.564	2.564	2.564	2.564	2.564	2.564	2.564	2.564	2.564	2.564
40	0.107	0.321	0.535	0.749	0.963	1.177	1.391	1.605	1.819	2.033	2.247	2.461

*The official tables contain a separate row for each year. For ease of presentation, certain years are grouped in these tables. In some instances, this will produce a difference of .001 for the last digit when compared with the official tables.

▼ **TABLE 7–8**
ACRS Cost Recovery Table for
19-Year Real Property: Optional
Straight-Line

For Property Placed in Service after May 8, 1985, and before January 1, 1987: 19-Year Real Property for Which an Optional 19-Year Straight-Line Method Is Elected (Assuming Mid-Month Convention)

If the Recovery Year Is:	And the Month in the First Recovery Year the Property Is Placed in Service Is:											
	1	2	3	4	5	6	7	8	9	10	11	12
	The Applicable Percentage Is (Use the Column for the Month in the First Year the Property Is Placed in Service):											
1	5.0	4.6	4.2	3.7	3.3	2.9	2.4	2.0	1.5	1.1	.7	.2
2	5.3	5.3	5.3	5.3	5.3	5.3	5.3	5.3	5.3	5.3	5.3	5.3
3	5.3	5.3	5.3	5.3	5.3	5.3	5.3	5.3	5.3	5.3	5.3	5.3
4	5.3	5.3	5.3	5.3	5.3	5.3	5.3	5.3	5.3	5.3	5.3	5.3
5	5.3	5.3	5.3	5.3	5.3	5.3	5.3	5.3	5.3	5.3	5.3	5.3
6	5.3	5.3	5.3	5.3	5.3	5.3	5.3	5.3	5.3	5.3	5.3	5.3
7	5.3	5.3	5.3	5.3	5.3	5.3	5.3	5.3	5.3	5.3	5.3	5.3
8	5.3	5.3	5.3	5.3	5.3	5.3	5.3	5.3	5.3	5.3	5.3	5.3
9	5.3	5.3	5.3	5.3	5.3	5.3	5.3	5.3	5.3	5.3	5.3	5.3
10	5.3	5.3	5.3	5.3	5.3	5.3	5.3	5.3	5.3	5.3	5.3	5.3
11	5.3	5.3	5.3	5.3	5.3	5.3	5.3	5.3	5.3	5.3	5.3	5.3
12	5.3	5.3	5.3	5.3	5.3	5.3	5.3	5.3	5.3	5.3	5.3	5.3
13	5.3	5.3	5.3	5.3	5.3	5.3	5.3	5.3	5.3	5.3	5.3	5.3
14	5.2	5.2	5.2	5.2	5.2	5.2	5.2	5.2	5.2	5.2	5.2	5.2
15	5.2	5.2	5.2	5.2	5.2	5.2	5.2	5.2	5.2	5.2	5.2	5.2
16	5.2	5.2	5.2	5.2	5.2	5.2	5.2	5.2	5.2	5.2	5.2	5.2
17	5.2	5.2	5.2	5.2	5.2	5.2	5.2	5.2	5.2	5.2	5.2	5.2
18	5.2	5.2	5.2	5.2	5.2	5.2	5.2	5.2	5.2	5.2	5.2	5.2
19	5.2	5.2	5.2	5.2	5.2	5.2	5.2	5.2	5.2	5.2	5.2	5.2
20	.2	.6	1.0	1.5	1.9	2.3	2.8	3.2	3.7	4.1	4.5	5.0

▼ **TABLE 7–9**
MACRS Straight-Line
Depreciation for Personal
Property Assuming Half-Year
Convention*

For Property Placed in Service after December 31, 1986

MACRS Class	% First Recovery Year	Other Recovery Years		Last Recovery Year	
		Years	%	Year	%
3-year	16.67	2–3	33.33	4	16.67
5-year	10.00	2–5	20.00	6	10.00
7-year	7.14	2–7	14.29	8	7.14
10-year	5.00	2–10	10.00	11	5.00
15-year	3.33	2–15	6.67	16	3.33
20-year	2.50	2–20	5.00	21	2.50

*The official table contains a separate row for each year. For ease of presentation, certain years are grouped in this table. In some instances, this will produce a difference of .01 for the last digit when compared with the official table.

▼ **TABLE 7–10**
Alternative Minimum Tax: 150%
Declining-Balance Assuming
Half-Year Convention

For Property Placed in Service after December 31, 1986 (Partial Table*)

Recovery Year	3-Year 150%	5-Year 150%	7-Year 150%	9.5-Year 150%	10-Year 150%	12-Year 150%
1	25.00	15.00	10.71	7.89	7.50	6.25
2	37.50	25.50	19.13	14.54	13.88	11.72
3	25.00**	17.85	15.03	12.25	11.79	10.25
4	12.50	16.66**	12.25**	10.31	10.02	8.97
5		16.66	12.25	9.17**	8.74**	7.85
6		8.33	12.25	9.17	8.74	7.33**
7			12.25	9.17	8.74	7.33
8			6.13	9.17	8.74	7.33
9				9.17	8.74	7.33
10				9.16	8.74	7.33
11					4.37	7.32
12						7.33
13						3.66

*The figures in this table are taken from the official table that appears in Rev.Proc. 87–57, 1987–2 C.B. 687. Because of its length, the complete table is not presented.
**Switchover to straight-line depreciation.

▼ **TABLE 7–11**
ADS Straight-Line for Personal
Property Assuming Half-Year
Convention

For Property Placed in Service after December 31, 1986 (Partial Table*)

Recovery Year	5-Year Class	9.5-Year Class	12-Year Class
1	10.00	5.26	4.17
2	20.00	10.53	8.33
3	20.00	10.53	8.33
4	20.00	10.53	8.33
5	20.00	10.52	8.33
6	10.00	10.53	8.33
7		10.52	8.34
8		10.53	8.33
9		10.52	8.34
10		10.53	8.33
11			8.34
12			8.33
13			4.17

*The figures in this table are taken from the official table that appears in Rev.Proc. 87–57, 1987–2 C.B. 687. Because of its length, the complete table is not presented. The tables for the mid-quarter convention also appear in Rev.Proc. 87–57.

▼ **TABLE 7–12**
ADS Straight-Line for Real
Property Assuming Mid-Month
Convention

For Property Placed in Service after December 31, 1986

Recovery Year	Month Placed in Service											
	1	2	3	4	5	6	7	8	9	10	11	12
1	2.396	2.188	1.979	1.771	1.563	1.354	1.146	0.938	0.729	0.521	0.313	0.104
2–40	2.500	2.500	2.500	2.500	2.500	2.500	2.500	2.500	2.500	2.500	2.500	2.500
41	0.104	0.312	0.521	0.729	0.937	1.146	1.354	1.562	1.771	1.979	2.187	2.396

KEY TERMS

Accelerated cost recovery system (ACRS), 7–4

Alternative depreciation system (ADS), 7–21

Amortization, 7–23

Cost depletion, 7–25

Cost recovery, 7–2

Depletion, 7–24

Depreciation, 7–2

Half-year convention, 7–6

Intangible drilling and development costs (IDC), 7–25

Listed property, 7–17

Mid-month convention, 7–11

Mid-quarter convention, 7–9

Modified accelerated cost recovery system (MACRS), 7–6

Percentage depletion, 7–26

Residential rental real estate, 7–12

Section 179 expensing, 7–15

▼
▼
PROBLEM
MATERIALS

DISCUSSION QUESTIONS

1. Discuss whether personal use property is subject to cost recovery.

2. Henry purchased a rental home for $67,000 from Amy. He made a down payment of $17,000 and borrowed $50,000 from James with a mortgage on the home as collateral. The note secured by the mortgage contained an acceleration clause, which provided that the loan would become due if Henry were to sell or convey the property. Several years later, Henry sold the house to John. To avoid triggering the acceleration clause, Henry and John wove a complicated web to deceive James. As part of this plan, the sales agreement provided that Henry would continue to claim the depreciation on his tax return. Henry also owned property where he maintained his office. Last year, because the property generated a loss, Henry did not deduct the depreciation on the property. During the current year, Henry sold this property at a gain. Identify the relevant tax issues for Henry.

3. If a personal use asset is converted to business use, why is it necessary to compute cost recovery on the lower of fair market value or adjusted basis at the date of conversion?

4. Discuss whether a painting is eligible for cost recovery.

5. Pale, an electric utility company, constructed and placed in service during the taxable year a hydroelectric dam. In connection with the dam, Pale was required under a Federal Power Commission license to construct and maintain various facilities for the

preservation of fish and for public recreational purposes. The fish preservation facilities constructed below the dam consisted of an entrance pool, a fish ladder, and a holding pool. The recreational facilities located above the dam included access roads, fixed wharves, landings, and other facilities. All of these facilities are tangible properties, some of which are inextricably associated with the land. Identify the relevant tax issues for Pale.

6. Discuss when the mid-quarter convention must be used.

7. Discuss the computation of cost recovery in the year of sale of an asset when the mid-quarter convention is being used.

8. Discuss the test for determining whether real property is residential rental real estate or nonresidential real estate.

9. Discuss the mid-month convention as it is used in the MACRS rules.

10. Alan is engaged in the sale of rental warehouse space and related services. When he sought a bank loan to expand one of his warehouses, the lender required Alan to abate the problem of exposed and damaged asbestos-containing pipe insulation in the warehouse. Accordingly, Alan incurred costs of $200,000 to employ an asbestos contractor to remedy the problem. The contractor rewrapped and encapsulated the damaged or punctured areas of asbestos-containing pipe insulation and removed insulation that was too damaged to be rewrapped. The pipes requiring encapsulation amounted to less than 25% of the total pipes in the warehouse. Identify the relevant tax issues for Alan.

11. Discuss the applicable conventions if a taxpayer elects to use straight-line cost recovery for property placed in service after December 31, 1986.

12. If a taxpayer makes a straight-line election under MACRS, discuss the possibility of taking a cost recovery deduction, for personal and real property, in the year of disposition.

13. Discuss the type of property that qualifies for limited expensing.

14. Discuss the maximum § 179 expensing amount.

15. Discuss the limitation on the § 179 amount that can be expensed and its impact on the basis of the property.

16. John was employed as a financial officer for an investment bank. By the middle of the year, John realized that he was going to be terminated by the bank. Therefore, he began preparing for a career in financial consulting as a sole practitioner. John became interested in consulting for a marina, but believing that boat owners formed a close fraternity, he decided that he could obtain such work only by acquiring a boat himself. Accordingly, he purchased a 23-foot Sea Ray Boat for $25,000. During the year, John used the boat only once to visit marinas on the lake to discuss potential employment as a consultant. A few days after this one excursion, John injured his back and was unable to use the boat for the remainder of the year. John was unsuccessful in his attempts to obtain a consulting position with any of the marinas.

At the beginning of the year, John also purchased a new car to be used for personal purposes. After John was terminated from the bank in September, he began using the car for business purposes.

Identify the relevant tax issues for John.

17. What are the tax consequences of listed property failing to meet the predominantly business use test?

18. Discuss the limits on cost recovery for a taxicab.

19. Discuss the tax consequences that result when a passenger automobile, which failed the more-than-50% business usage test during the first two years, satisfies the test for the third year.

20. Explain the reason for the inclusion amount with respect to leased passenger automobiles.

21. Explain how an inclusion amount is determined with respect to leased passenger automobiles.

22. Explain the amortization period of a § 197 intangible if the actual useful life is less than 15 years.

23. What is the amortization period for self-created goodwill?

24. Discuss the options for handling intangible drilling and development costs.

25. Briefly discuss the differences between cost depletion and percentage depletion.

PROBLEMS

26. On January 1, 1994, Black Company acquired an asset (three-year property) for $10,000 for use in its business. In the years 1994 and 1995, Black took $3,333 and $4,445 of cost recovery. The allowable cost recovery for the years 1996 and 1997 was $1,481 and $741, but Black did not take the deductions. In those years, Black had net operating losses, and the company wanted to "save" the deductions for later years. On January 1, 1998, the asset was sold for $2,000. Calculate the gain or loss on the sale of the asset in 1998.

27. Eve acquired a personal residence in 1992 for $180,000. In January 1998, when the fair market value was $160,000, she converted the residence to rental property.
    a. Calculate the amount of cost recovery that can be taken in 1998.
    b. What would your answer be if the property were worth $200,000 in 1998?

28. Jane acquired a seven-year class asset on March 1, 1998, for $100,000. She did not elect immediate expensing under § 179.
    a. Determine Jane's cost recovery for 1998.
    b. Determine Jane's cost recovery for 2001.

29. Walt purchased a tugboat for use in his business on March 15, 1998, for $500,000. He does not elect immediate expensing under § 179. On February 16, 2004, Walt sells the tug.
    a. Determine Walt's cost recovery for 1998.
    b. Determine Walt's cost recovery for 2004.

30. Juan acquires a five-year class asset on December 2, 1998, for $150,000. This is the only asset acquired by Juan during the year. He does not elect immediate expensing under § 179. On July 15, 1999, Juan sells the asset.
    a. Determine Juan's cost recovery for 1998.
    b. Determine Juan's cost recovery for 1999.

31. Debra acquired a building for $300,000 (exclusive of land) on January 1, 1984. Calculate the cost recovery using the statutory percentage method for 1984 and 1998 if:
    a. The real property is low-income housing.
    b. The real property is a factory building.

32. On December 2, 1984, Wade purchased and placed in service a warehouse. The warehouse cost $850,000. Wade used the statutory percentage cost recovery method. On July 7, 1998, Wade sold the warehouse.
    a. Determine Wade's cost recovery for 1984.
    b. Determine Wade's cost recovery for 1998.

33. On November 1, 1998, Terry purchases and places in service a building that is used as a warehouse. The cost of the building is $2 million. An appraisal determined that 20% of the total cost was attributed to the value of the land. Determine Terry's cost recovery for 1998.

34. Pat acquires a warehouse on November 1, 1998, at a cost of $4.5 million. On January 30, 2009, Pat sells the warehouse. Calculate Pat's cost recovery for 1998. For 2009.

35. Janice acquired an apartment building on June 4, 1998, for $1.4 million. The value of the land is $200,000. Janice sold the apartment building on November 29, 2004.
    a. Determine Janice's cost recovery for 1998.
    b. Determine Janice's cost recovery for 2004.

36. Lori, who is single, is thinking of acquiring a new copier (five-year class property) for $30,000 in either December of 1998 or January of 1999. Lori expects the taxable income derived from her business (without regard to the amount expensed under § 179) to always be about $100,000. Lori will elect immediate expensing under § 179. Lori acquired three-year property for $140,000 in March 1998 and does not want to elect § 179 for this property.
    a. Determine Lori's total deduction with respect to the copier if she acquires the copier in 1998.
    b. Determine her total deduction with respect to the copier if she acquires the copier in 1999.
    c. What is your advice to Lori?

37. Jack owns a small business that he operates as a sole proprietor. In 1998, Jack will net $10,000 of business income before consideration of any § 179 deduction. Jack spends $207,000 on new equipment in 1998. If Jack also has $3,000 of § 179 deduction carryforwards from 1997, determine his § 179 expense deduction for 1998 and the amount of any carryforward.

38. Olga is the proprietor of a small business. In 1998, her business income, before consideration of any § 179 deduction, is $7,500. Olga spends $202,000 on new equipment and furniture for 1998. If Olga elects to take the § 179 deduction on a desk that cost $20,000 (included in the $202,000), determine her total cost recovery for 1998 with respect to the desk.

39. On March 10, 1998, Yoon purchased three-year class property for $20,000. On December 15, 1998, Yoon purchased five-year class property for $50,000. He has net business income of $19,000 before consideration of any § 179 deduction.
    a. Calculate Yoon's cost recovery for 1998, assuming he does not make the § 179 election or use straight-line cost recovery.
    b. Calculate Yoon's cost recovery for 1998, assuming he does elect to use § 179 and does not elect to use straight-line cost recovery.
    c. Assuming Yoon's marginal tax rate is 36%, determine his tax benefit from electing § 179.

40. On July 1, 1998, Wilma places in service a computer (five-year class property). The computer cost $20,000. Wilma used the computer 65% for business. The remainder of the time she used the computer for personal purposes. If Wilma does not elect § 179, determine her cost recovery deduction for the computer for 1998.

41. John Johnson is considering acquiring an automobile at the beginning of 1998 that he will use 100% of the time as a taxi. The purchase price of the automobile is $25,000. John has heard of cost recovery limits on automobiles and wants to know how much of the $25,000 he can deduct in the first year. Write a letter to John in which you present your calculations. Also, prepare a memo for the tax files. John's address is 100 Morningside, Clinton, MS 39058.

42. On February 16, 1998, Ron purchased and placed into service a new car. The purchase price was $18,000. Ron drove the car 12,000 miles during the remainder of the year, 9,000 miles for business and 3,000 miles for personal use. Ron used the statutory percentage method of cost recovery. Calculate the total deduction Ron may take for 1998 with respect to the car.

43. On June 5, 1998, Leo purchased and placed in service a $19,000 car. The business use percentage for the car is always 100%. Compute Leo's cost recovery deduction in 2004.

44. On June 14, 1998, Helen purchased and placed in service a new car. The purchase price was $16,000. The car was used 75% for business and 25% for personal use in both 1998 and 1999. In 2000, the car was used 40% for business and 60% for personal use. Compute the cost recovery deduction for the car in 2000 and the cost recovery recapture.

45. In 1998, Paul purchased a computer (five-year property) for $120,000. The computer was used 60% for business, 20% for income production, and 20% for personal use. In 1999, the usage changed to 40% for business, 30% for income production, and 30% for

personal use. Compute the cost recovery deduction for 1999 and any cost recovery recapture. Assume Paul did not make a § 179 election on the computer in 1998.

46. Sally purchased a computer (five-year property) for $4,000. Sally could use the computer 100% of the time in her business, or she could allow her family to also use the computer. Sally estimates that if her family uses the computer, the business use will be 45% and the personal use will be 55%. Determine the tax cost to Sally, in the year of acquisition, of allowing her family to use the computer. Assume that Sally would not elect § 179 limited expensing and that her marginal tax rate is 31%.

47. Midway through 1998, Abdel leases and places in service a passenger automobile. The lease will run for five years, and the payments are $430 per month. During 1998, Abdel uses the car 70% for business use and 30% for personal use. Assuming the inclusion dollar amount from the IRS table is $98, determine the tax consequences to Abdel from the lease for the year 1998.

48. Use the information given in Problem 47, but assume the inclusion dollar amount for 1999 is $180. Abdel uses the car 60% for business use and 40% for personal use in 1999. Determine Abdel's tax consequences from the lease in 1999.

49. Dennis Harding is considering acquiring an automobile that he will use 100% for business. The purchase price of the automobile would be $30,500. If Dennis leased the car for five years, the lease payments would be $350 per month. Dennis will acquire the car on January 1, 1998. The inclusion dollar amounts from the IRS table for the next five years are $129, $286, $423, $500, and $590. Dennis desires to know the effect on his adjusted gross income of purchasing versus leasing the car for the next five years. Write a letter to Dennis and present your calculations. Also, prepare a memo for the tax files. His address is 150 Avenue I, Memphis, TN 38112.

50. On March 5, 1998, Nell purchased equipment for $70,000. The equipment has an ADS midpoint of 9.5 years. Determine Nell's cost recovery deduction for computing 1998 taxable income using the straight-line method under ADS and assuming she does not make a § 179 election.

51. In 1998, Muhammad purchased a light-duty truck for $12,000. The truck is used 100% for business. Muhammad did not make a § 179 election with respect to the truck. If Muhammad uses the statutory percentage method, determine his cost recovery deduction for 1998 for computing taxable income and for computing his alternative minimum tax.

52. In June 1998, Cardinal, Inc., purchased and placed in service railroad track costing $600,000.
   a. Calculate Cardinal's cost recovery deduction for 1998 for computing taxable income, assuming Cardinal does not make the § 179 election or use straight-line cost recovery.
   b. Calculate Cardinal's cost recovery deduction for 1998 for computing taxable income, assuming Cardinal does not make the § 179 election but does elect to use ADS 150% declining-balance cost recovery.
   c. Assume that the railroad track was placed in service in June 1999. Calculate Cardinal's cost recovery deduction for 1999 for computing taxable income, assuming Cardinal does not make the § 179 election but does elect to use ADS 150% declining-balance cost recovery.

53. Jamie purchased $60,000 of office furniture for her business in June of the current year. Jamie understands that if she elects to use ADS to compute her regular income tax, there will be no difference between the cost recovery for computing the regular income tax and the AMT. Jamie wants to know the *regular* income tax cost, after three years, of using ADS rather than MACRS. Assume that Jamie does not elect § 179 limited expensing and that her marginal tax rate is 31%.

54. On August 1, 1998, Jake acquired a dental practice from Bob for $250,000. The purchase price was allocated $200,000 to the tangible assets of the practice and $50,000 to the goodwill. Determine Jake's deduction for the amortization of the goodwill for 1998.

55. Mike Saxon is negotiating the purchase of a business. The final purchase price has been agreed upon, but the allocation of the purchase price to the assets is still being discussed. Appraisals on a warehouse range from $1.2 to $1.5 million. If a value of $1.2 million is used for the warehouse, the remainder of the purchase price, $800,000, will be allocated to goodwill. If $1.5 million is allocated to the warehouse, goodwill will be $500,000. Mike wants to know what effect each alternative will have on cost recovery and amortization during the first year. Under the agreement, Mike will take over the business on January 1 of next year. Write a letter to Mike in which you present your calculations and recommendation. Also, prepare a memo for the tax files. Mike's address is 200 Rolling Hills Drive, Shavertown, PA 18708.

56. Wes acquired a mineral interest during the year for $5 million. A geological survey estimated that 250,000 tons of the mineral remained in the deposit. During the year, 80,000 tons were mined, and 45,000 tons were sold for $6 million. Other expenses amounted to $4 million. Assuming the mineral depletion rate is 22%, calculate Wes's lowest taxable income.

57. Chris purchased an oil interest for $2,000,000. Recoverable barrels were estimated to be 500,000. During the year, 120,000 barrels were sold for $3,840,000, regular expenses (including cost recovery) were $1,240,000, and IDC were $1,000,000. Calculate Chris's taxable income under the expensing and capitalization methods of handling IDC.

CUMULATIVE PROBLEMS

58. John Smith, age 31, is single and has no dependents. At the beginning of 1998, John started his own excavation business and named it Earth Movers. John lives at 1045 Center Street, Lindon, UT, and his business is located at 381 State Street, Lindon, UT. The zip code for both addresses is 84059. John's Social Security number is 321–09–6456, and the business identification number is 98–1234567. John is a cash basis taxpayer. During 1998, John had the following items in connection with his business:

Fees for services	$290,000
Building rental expense	36,000
Office furniture and equipment rental expense	6,000
Office supplies	2,500
Utilities	3,000
Salary for secretary	35,000
Salary for equipment operators	78,000
Payroll taxes	9,000
Fuel and oil for the equipment	20,000
Purchase of three front-end loaders on January 15, 1998, for $175,000. John made the election under § 179.	175,000
Purchase of a new dump truck on January 18, 1998	30,000

During 1998, John had the following additional items:

Interest income from First National Bank	$8,000
Dividends from Exxon	2,500
Quarterly estimated tax payments	11,500

On October 8, 1998, John inherited IBM stock from his Aunt Mildred. John had been her favorite nephew. According to the data provided by the executor of Aunt Mildred's estate, the stock had been valued for estate tax purposes at $90,000. John is considering selling the IBM stock for $95,000 on December 29, 1998, and using $60,000 of the proceeds to purchase an Acura NSX. He would use the car 100% for business. John wants to know what effect these transactions would have on his 1998 adjusted gross income.

Write a letter to John in which you present your calculations. Also, prepare a memo for the tax files. Suggested software (if available): *TurboTax*.

59. Janice Morgan, age 32, is single and has no dependents. She is a freelance writer. In January 1997, Janice opened her own office located at 2751 Waldham Road, Pleasantville, NM 17196. She called her business Writers Anonymous. Janice is a cash basis taxpayer. She lives at 132 Stone Avenue, Pleasantville, NM 17196. Her Social Security number is 789–57–6691. Janice desires to contribute to the Presidential Election Campaign Fund.

During 1997, Janice had the following income and expense items connected with her business:

Income from sale of articles	$110,000
Rent	18,000
Utilities	6,900
Supplies	1,300
Travel (including meals of $700)	2,500

Janice purchased and placed in service the following fixed assets for her business:

- Furniture and fixtures costing $15,000 on January 10, 1997.

- Computer equipment costing $20,000 on January 15, 1997.

Janice would like to deduct these costs as soon as possible.

Janice's itemized deductions are as follows:

State income tax	$2,000
Home mortgage interest paid to First Bank	4,800
Property taxes on home	1,100
Property taxes on car	500
Charitable contributions	1,200

Janice has interest income of $3,000 on certificates of deposit at Second Bank. Janice makes estimated tax payments of $19,000 for 1997.

Compute Janice Morgan's 1997 Federal income tax payable (or refund due). If you use tax forms for your computations, you will need Form(s) 1040 and 4562 and Schedules A, B, C, and SE. Suggested software (if available): *TurboTax.*

Research Problems for this chapter appear at the end of Chapter 28.

TEAM PROJECT: ARTHUR ANDERSEN TAX CHALLENGE CASES

For more information on the Arthur Andersen Tax Challenge Cases, refer to Chapter 1, page 1–37.

Information related to tax issues and problems that are discussed in this chapter may be found in the

Day and Ball case on pages 7 and 20
Fence case on pages 40 and 59

Read and analyze the case you have been assigned and *identify* any issues and problems that are related to material covered in this chapter. If the information provided in the case is complete, prepare answers for this part of the case at this time. If you need information that is contained in the later parts of the case, write a memo summarizing the questions or problems so you can prepare a complete answer at a later date.

DEDUCTIONS: EMPLOYEE EXPENSES

LEARNING OBJECTIVES

After completing Chapter 8, you should be able to:

1. Distinguish between employee and self-employed status.

2. Recognize deductible transportation expenses.

3. Know how travel expenses are treated.

4. Determine the moving expense deduction.

5. Differentiate between deductible and nondeductible education expenses.

6. Understand how entertainment expenses are treated.

7. Identify other employee expenses.

8. Appreciate the difference between accountable and nonaccountable employee plans.

9. Work with the limitations on miscellaneous itemized deductions.

10. Develop tax planning ideas related to employee business expenses.

Considering the large number of taxpayers affected, the tax treatment of job-related expenses is unusually complex. To resolve this matter in a systematic fashion, a number of key questions must be asked:

- Is the taxpayer an *employee* or *self-employed?*
- If an employee, what expenses *qualify* as deductions?
- How are the expenses that qualify *classified* for tax purposes?
- To the extent the expenses are classified as deductions *from* AGI, are they subject to any *limitation?*

Once these questions have been posed and answered, the chapter considers various planning procedures available to maximize the deductibility of employee expenses.

EMPLOYEE VERSUS SELF–EMPLOYED

1 LEARNING OBJECTIVE
Distinguish between employee and self-employed status.

When one person performs services for another, the person performing the service is either an employee or self-employed (an **independent contractor**). Failure to recognize employee status can have serious consequences. Not only can interest and penalties result but, in several recent cases, a government career was abruptly squelched. Such was the case with several persons that President Clinton nominated to his cabinet during his first term. Zoe Baird (Attorney General), Kimba Wood (Attorney General), and Retired Admiral Bobby Inman (Secretary of Defense) all

---

TAX IN THE NEWS

ARE GOLF CLUBS IN TROUBLE WITH THE IRS?

For many years, the IRS has not questioned the tax classification of caddies as independent contractors. See, for example, Revenue Ruling 69–26 (1969–1 C.B. 251). This classification is consistent with the manner in which the services are performed. Most caddies work when they want, receive minimum training at their golf courses, and are paid "by the bag" (not by the hour). Further, they are paid by the golfer (not the club).

Recent actions by the IRS, however, indicate that it now regards caddies as employees. If the IRS maintains this position and pursues its enforcement, serious tax consequences could result. Golf clubs could find themselves liable for past Social Security payments and even income tax withholding. Even worse could be the prospect of future record-keeping and reporting requirements. The added compliance costs could convince clubs to ditch the caddie system and replace it with less troublesome electric carts.

SOURCE: Adapted from M. C. Fondo, "IRS Bogey-Man Threatens Caddies," *Wall Street Journal*, June 3, 1997, p. A22.

---

had to withdraw from consideration when it was revealed that they had failed to report and pay payroll taxes on their household employees.

The problem is likely to intensify since businesses are increasingly relying on the services of self-employed persons for numerous reasons. Unlike employees, self-employed persons do not have to be included in various fringe benefit programs (e.g., group term life insurance) and retirement plans. Since they are not covered by FICA and FUTA (see Chapter 1), these payroll costs are avoided.

The IRS is very much aware of the tendency of businesses to wrongly classify workers as self-employed rather than as employees. In terms of tax consequences, employment status also makes a great deal of difference to the persons who perform the services. Expenses of self-employed taxpayers, to the extent allowable, are classified as deductions *for* AGI and are reported on Schedule C (Profit or Loss From Business) of Form 1040.[1] With the exception of reimbursement under an accountable plan (see later in the chapter), expenses of employees are deductions *from* AGI. They are reported on Form 2106 (Employee Business Expenses) and Schedule A (Itemized Deductions) of Form 1040.[2]

But when does an employer-employee relationship exist? Such a relationship exists when the employer has the right to specify the end result and the ways and means by which that result is to be attained.[3] An employee is subject to the will and control of the employer with respect not only to what shall be done but also to how it shall be done. If the individual is subject to the direction or control of another only to the extent of the end result but not as to the means of accomplishment, an employer-employee relationship does not exist. An example is the preparation of a taxpayer's return by an independent CPA.

Certain factors indicate an employer-employee relationship. They include (1) the right to discharge without legal liability the person performing the service, (2) the furnishing of tools or a place to work, and (3) payment based

---

[1] §§ 62(a)(1) and 162(a). See Appendix B for a reproduction of Schedule C.

[2] See Appendix B for a reproduction of Form 2106 and Schedule A.
[3] Reg. § 31.3401(c)–(1)(b).

on time spent rather than the task performed. Each case is tested on its own merits, and the right to control the means and methods of accomplishment is the definitive test. Generally, physicians, lawyers, dentists, contractors, subcontractors, and others who offer services to the public are not classified as employees.

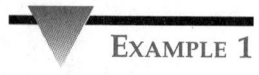

EXAMPLE 1   Arnold is a lawyer whose major client accounts for 60% of his billings. He does the routine legal work and income tax returns at the client's request. He is paid a monthly retainer in addition to amounts charged for extra work. Arnold is a self-employed individual. Even though most of his income comes from one client, he still has the right to determine how the end result of his work is attained. ▼

EXAMPLE 2   Ellen is a lawyer hired by Arnold to assist him in the performance of services for the client mentioned in Example 1. Ellen is under Arnold's supervision; he reviews her work and pays her an hourly fee. Ellen is an employee of Arnold. ▼

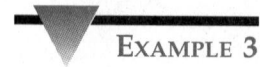

EXAMPLE 3   Frank is a licensed practical nurse who works as a private-duty nurse. He is under the supervision of the patient's doctor and is paid by the patient. Frank is not an employee of either the patient (who pays him) or the doctor (who supervises him). The ways and means of attaining the end result (care of the patient) are under his control. ▼

Employees in a special category are also allowed to file Schedule C to report income and deduct expenses *for* AGI. These employees are called **statutory employees** because they are not common law employees under the rules explained above. The wages or commissions paid to statutory employees are not subject to Federal income tax withholding but are subject to Social Security tax.[4]

EMPLOYEE EXPENSES—IN GENERAL

Once the employment relationship is established, employee expenses fall into one of the following categories:

- Transportation.
- Travel.
- Moving.
- Education.
- Entertainment.
- Other.

These expenses are discussed below in the order presented.

Keep in mind, however, that these expenses are not necessarily limited to employees. A deduction for business transportation, for example, is equally available to taxpayers who are self-employed.

---

[4]See Circular E, *Employer's Tax Guide* (IRS Publication 15), for further discussion of statutory employees.

TRANSPORTATION EXPENSES

QUALIFIED EXPENDITURES

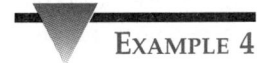

2 LEARNING OBJECTIVE
Recognize deductible
transportation expenses.

An employee may deduct unreimbursed employment-related transportation expenses as an itemized deduction *from* AGI. **Transportation expenses** include only the cost of transporting the employee from one place to another in the course of employment when the employee is *not* away from home *in travel status*. Such costs include taxi fares, automobile expenses, tolls, and parking.

Commuting Expenses.   Commuting between home and one's place of employment is a personal, nondeductible expense. The fact that one employee drives 30 miles to work and another employee walks six blocks is of no significance.[5]

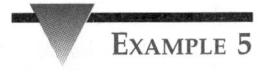

EXAMPLE 4

Geraldo is employed by Sparrow Corporation. He drives 22 miles each way to work. The 44 miles he drives each workday are nondeductible commuting expenses. ▼

The rule that disallows a deduction for commuting expenses has several exceptions. An employee who uses an automobile to transport heavy tools to work and who otherwise would not drive to work is allowed a deduction, but only for the additional costs incurred to transport the work implements. Additional costs are those exceeding the cost of commuting by the same mode of transportation without the tools. For example, the rental of a trailer for transporting tools is deductible, but the expenses of operating the automobile generally are not deductible.[6] The Supreme Court has held that a deduction is permitted only when the taxpayer can show that the automobile would not have been used without the necessity to transport tools or equipment.[7]

Another exception is provided for an employee who has a second job. The expenses of getting from one job to another are deductible. If the employee goes home between jobs, the deduction is based on the distance between jobs.

EXAMPLE 5

In the current year, Cynthia holds two jobs, a full-time job with Blue Corporation and a part-time job with Wren Corporation. During the 250 days that she works (adjusted for weekends, vacation, and holidays), Cynthia customarily leaves home at 7:30 A.M. and drives 30 miles to the Blue Corporation plant, where she works until 5:00 P.M. After dinner at a nearby cafe, Cynthia drives 20 miles to Wren Corporation and works from 7:00 to 11:00 P.M. The distance from the second job to Cynthia's home is 40 miles. Her deduction is based on 20 miles (the distance between jobs). ▼

If the taxpayer is required to incur a transportation expense to travel between work stations, that expense is deductible.

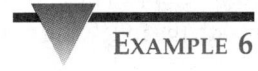

EXAMPLE 6

Thomas, a general contractor, drives from his home to his office, then drives to three building sites to perform his required inspections, and finally drives home. The costs of driving to his office and driving home from the last inspection site are nondeductible commuting expenses. The other transportation costs are deductible. ▼

---

[5]*Tauferner v. U.S.*, 69–1 USTC ¶9241, 23 AFTR2d 69–1025, 407 F.2d 243 (CA–10, 1969).
[6]Rev.Rul. 75–380, 1975–2 C.B. 59.

[7]*Fausner v. Comm.*, 73–2 USTC ¶9515, 32 AFTR2d 73–5202, 93 S.Ct. 2820 (USSC, 1973).

Likewise, the commuting costs from home to a temporary work station and from the temporary work station to home are deductible.[8]

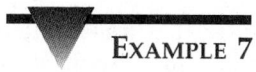

EXAMPLE 7

Vivian works for a firm in downtown Denver and commutes to work. She occasionally works in a customer's office. On one such occasion, Vivian drove directly to the customer's office, a round-trip distance from her home of 40 miles. She did not go into her office, which is a 52-mile round-trip. Her mileage for going to and from the temporary work station is deductible. ▼

Also deductible is the reasonable travel cost between the general working area and a temporary work station outside that area.[9] What constitutes the general working area depends on the facts and circumstances of each situation. Furthermore, if an employee customarily works on several temporary assignments in a localized area, that localized area becomes the regular place of employment. Transportation from home to these locations becomes a personal, nondeductible commuting expense.

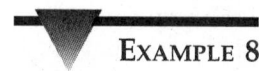

EXAMPLE 8

Sam, a building inspector in Minneapolis, regularly inspects buildings for building code violations for his employer, a general contractor. During one busy season, the St. Paul inspector became ill, and Sam was required to inspect several buildings in St. Paul. The expenses for transportation for the trips to St. Paul are deductible. ▼

COMPUTATION OF AUTOMOBILE EXPENSES

A taxpayer has two choices in computing automobile expenses. The actual operating cost, which includes depreciation (cost recovery), gas, oil, repairs, licenses, and insurance, may be used. Records must be kept that detail the automobile's personal and business use. Only the percentage allocable to business transportation and travel is allowed as a deduction. Complex rules for the computation of depreciation (discussed in Chapter 7) apply if the actual expense method is used.

Use of the **automatic mileage method** (also called the standard mileage method) is the second alternative. For 1998 the deduction is based on 32.5 cents per mile for all business miles.[10] Parking fees and tolls are allowed in addition to expenses computed using the automatic mileage method.

Generally, a taxpayer may elect either method for any particular year. However, the following restrictions apply:

- The vehicle must be owned or leased by the taxpayer.
- If two or more vehicles are in use (for business purposes) at the *same* time (not alternately), a taxpayer may not use the automatic mileage method.
- A basis adjustment is required if the taxpayer changes from the automatic mileage method to the actual operating cost method. Depreciation is considered allowed for the business miles in accordance with the following schedule for the most recent five years:

---

[8]Rev.Rul. 90–23, 1990–1 C.B. 28 as amplified by Rev.Rul. 94–47,1994–2 C.B. 18.

[9]Rev.Rul. 190, 1953–2 C.B. 303 as amplified by Rev.Rul. 94–47,1994–2 C.B. 18.

[10]Rev.Proc. 97–58, I.R.B. No. 52, 24. The rate was 31.5 cents a mile for 1997.

Year	Rate per Mile
1998	12 cents
1997	12 cents
1996	12 cents
1995	12 cents
1994	12 cents

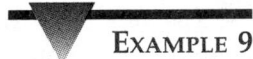

EXAMPLE 9

Tim purchased his automobile in 1995 for $15,000. It is used 90% for business purposes. Tim drove the automobile for 10,000 business miles in 1997; 8,500 miles in 1996; and 6,000 miles in 1995. At the beginning of 1998, the basis of the business portion is $10,560.

Cost ($15,000 × 90%)	$13,500
Less depreciation:	
1997 (10,000 miles × 12 cents)	(1,200)
1996 (8,500 miles × 12 cents)	(1,020)
1995 (6,000 miles × 12 cents)	(720)
Adjusted business basis 1/1/98	$10,560

- Use of the automatic mileage method in the first year the auto is placed in service is considered an election to exclude the auto from the MACRS method of depreciation (discussed in Chapter 7).
- A taxpayer may not switch to the automatic mileage method if the MACRS statutory percentage method or the election to expense under § 179 has been used.

TRAVEL EXPENSES

DEFINITION OF TRAVEL EXPENSES

3   **LEARNING OBJECTIVE**
Know how travel expenses are treated.

An itemized deduction is allowed for unreimbursed travel expenses related to a taxpayer's employment. **Travel expenses** are more broadly defined in the Code than are transportation expenses. Travel expenses include transportation expenses and meals and lodging while away from home in the pursuit of a trade or business. Meals cannot be lavish or extravagant under the circumstances. Transportation expenses (as previously discussed) are deductible even though the taxpayer is not away from home. A deduction for travel expenses is available only if the taxpayer is away from his or her tax home. Travel expenses also include reasonable laundry and incidental expenses.

AWAY-FROM-HOME REQUIREMENT

The crucial test for the deductibility of travel expenses is whether or not the employee is away from home overnight. "Overnight" need not be a 24-hour period, but it must be a period substantially longer than an ordinary day's work and must require rest, sleep, or a relief-from-work period.[11] A one-day business trip is not travel status, and meals and lodging for such a trip are not deductible.

---

[11]*U.S. v. Correll*, 68–1 USTC ¶9101, 20 AFTR2d 5845, 88 S.Ct. 445 (USSC, 1967); Rev.Rul. 75–168, 1975–1 C.B. 58.

Temporary Assignments.   The employee must be away from home for a temporary period. If the taxpayer-employee is reassigned to a new post for an indefinite period of time, that new post becomes his or her tax home. *Temporary* indicates that the assignment's termination is expected within a reasonably short period of time. The position of the IRS is that the tax home is the business location, post, or station of the taxpayer. Thus, travel expenses are not deductible if a taxpayer is reassigned for an indefinite period and does not move his or her place of residence to the new location.

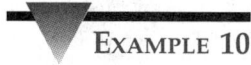
EXAMPLE 10

Malcolm's employer opened a branch office in San Diego. Malcolm was assigned to the new office for three months to train a new manager and to assist in setting up the new office. He tried commuting from his home in Los Angeles for a week and decided that he could not continue driving several hours a day. He rented an apartment in San Diego, where he lived during the week. He spent weekends with his wife and children at their home in Los Angeles. Malcolm's rent, meals, laundry, incidentals, and automobile expenses in San Diego are deductible. To the extent that Malcolm's transportation expense related to his weekend trips home exceeds what his cost of meals and lodging would have been, the excess is personal and nondeductible. ▼

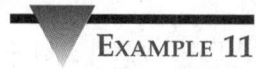
EXAMPLE 11

Assume that Malcolm in Example 10 was transferred to the new location to become the new manager permanently. His wife and children continued to live in Los Angeles until the end of the school year. Malcolm is no longer "away from home" because the assignment is not temporary. His travel expenses are not deductible. ▼

To curtail controversy in this area, the Code specifies that a taxpayer "*shall not* be treated as *temporarily* away from home during any period of employment if such period exceeds 1 year."[12]

Determining the Tax Home.   Under ordinary circumstances, determining the location of a taxpayer's tax home does not present a problem. The tax home is the area in which the taxpayer derives his or her principal source of income. When the taxpayer has more than one place of employment, the tax home is based on the amount of time spent in each area.

It is possible for a taxpayer never to be away from his or her tax home. In other words, the tax home follows the taxpayer.[13] Thus, all meals and lodging remain personal and are not deductible.

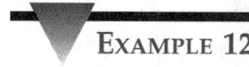
EXAMPLE 12

Bill is employed as a long-haul truck driver. He is single, stores his clothes and other belongings at his parents' home, and stops there for periodic visits. Most of the time, Bill is on the road, sleeping in his truck and in motels. It is likely that Bill is never in travel status, as he is not away from home. Consequently, none of his meals and lodging are deductible. ▼

RESTRICTIONS ON TRAVEL EXPENSES

The possibility always exists that taxpayers will attempt to treat vacation or pleasure travel as deductible business travel. To prevent such practices, the law contains restrictions on certain travel expenses.

---

[12]§ 162(a).

[13]*Moses Mitnick*, 13 T.C. 1 (1949).

Conventions. For travel expenses to be deductible, a convention must be directly related to the taxpayer's trade or business.[14]

EXAMPLE 13

Dr. Hill, a pathologist who works for a hospital in Ohio, travels to Las Vegas to attend a two-day session on recent developments in estate planning. No deduction is allowed for Dr. Hill's travel expenses. ▼

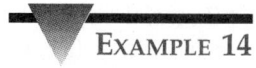

EXAMPLE 14

Assume the same facts as in Example 13 except that the convention deals entirely with recent developments in forensic medicine. Under these circumstances, a travel deduction is allowed. ▼

If the proceedings of the convention are videotaped, the taxpayer must attend convention sessions to view the videotaped materials along with other participants. This requirement does not disallow deductions for costs (other than travel, meals, and entertainment) of renting or using videotaped materials related to business.

EXAMPLE 15

A CPA is unable to attend a convention at which current developments in taxation are discussed. She pays $200 for videotapes of the lectures and views them at home later. The $200 is an itemized deduction if the CPA is an employee. If she is self-employed, the $200 is a deduction *for* AGI. ▼

The Code places stringent restrictions on the deductibility of travel expenses of the taxpayer's spouse or dependent.[15] Generally, the accompaniment by the spouse or dependent must serve a bona fide business purpose, and the expenses must be otherwise deductible.

EXAMPLE 16

Assume the same facts as in Example 14 with the additional fact that Dr. Hill is accompanied by Mrs. Hill. Mrs. Hill is not employed, but possesses secretarial skills and takes notes during the proceedings. No deduction is allowed for Mrs. Hill's travel expenses. ▼

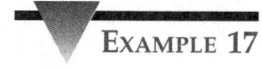

EXAMPLE 17

Modify the facts in Example 16 to make Mrs. Hill a nurse trained in pathology, who is employed by Dr. Hill as his assistant. Now, Mrs. Hill's travel expenses qualify as deductions. ▼

Education. Travel as a form of education is not deductible.[16] If, however, the education qualifies as a deduction, the travel involved is allowed.

EXAMPLE 18

Greta, a German teacher, travels to Germany to maintain general familiarity with the language and culture. No travel expense deduction is allowed. ▼

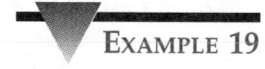

EXAMPLE 19

Jean-Claude, a scholar of French literature, travels to Paris to do specific library research that cannot be done elsewhere and to take courses that are offered only at the Sorbonne. The travel costs are deductible, assuming that the other requirements for deducting education expenses (discussed later in the chapter) are met. ▼

COMBINED BUSINESS AND PLEASURE TRAVEL

To be deductible, travel expenses need not be incurred in the performance of specific job functions. Travel expenses incurred in attending a professional convention are deductible by an employee if attendance is connected with services as an employee.

[14]§ 274(h)(1).
[15]§ 274(m)(3).

[16]§ 274(m)(2).

For example, an employee of a law firm can deduct travel expenses incurred in attending a meeting of the American Bar Association.

Domestic Travel. Travel deductions have been used in the past by persons who claimed a tax deduction for what was essentially a personal vacation. As a result, several provisions have been enacted to govern deductions associated with combined business and pleasure trips. If the business/pleasure trip is from one point in the United States to another point in the United States, the transportation expenses are deductible only if the trip is *primarily for business*.[17] If the trip is primarily for pleasure, no transportation expenses qualify as a deduction. Meals, lodging, and other expenses are allocated between business and personal days.

EXAMPLE 20

In the current year, Hana travels from Seattle to New York primarily for business. She spends five days conducting business and three days sightseeing and attending shows. Her plane and taxi fare amounts to $560. Her meals amount to $100 per day, and lodging and incidental expenses are $150 per day. She can deduct the transportation charges of $560, since the trip is primarily for business (five days of business versus three days of sightseeing). Meals are limited to five days and are subject to the 50% cutback (discussed later in the chapter) for a total of $250 [5 days × ($100 × 50%)], and other expenses are limited to $750 (5 days × $150). If Hana is an employee, the unreimbursed travel expenses are miscellaneous itemized deductions. ▼

EXAMPLE 21

Assume Hana goes to New York for a two-week vacation. While there, she spends several hours renewing acquaintances with people in her company's New York office. Her transportation expenses are not deductible. ▼

Foreign Travel. When the trip is *outside the United States*, special rules apply.[18] Transportation expenses must be allocated between business and personal unless (1) the taxpayer is away from home for seven days or less *or* (2) less than 25 percent of the time was for personal purposes. No allocation is required if the taxpayer has no substantial control over arrangements for the trip or the desire for a vacation is not a major factor in taking the trip. If the trip is primarily for pleasure, no transportation charges are deductible. Days devoted to travel are considered business days. Weekends, legal holidays, and intervening days are considered business days, provided that both the preceding and succeeding days were business days.

EXAMPLE 22

In the current year, Robert takes a trip from New York to Japan primarily for business purposes. He is away from home from June 10 through June 19. He spends three days vacationing and seven days conducting business (including two travel days). His airfare is $2,500, his meals amount to $100 per day, and lodging and incidental expenses are $160 per day. Since Robert is away from home for more than seven days and more than 25% of his time is devoted to personal purposes, only 70% (7 days business/10 days total) of the transportation is deductible. His deductions are as follows:

Transportation (70% × $2,500)		$1,750
Lodging ($160 × 7)		1,120
Meals ($100 × 7)	$ 700	
Less: 50% cutback (discussed later)	(350)	350
Total		$3,220

---

[17]Reg. § 1.162–2(b)(1).   [18]§ 274(c) and Reg. § 1.274–4.

If Robert is gone the same period of time but spends only two days (rather than three) vacationing, no allocation of transportation is required. Since the pleasure portion of the trip is less than 25% of the total, all of the airfare qualifies for the travel deduction. ▼

Certain restrictions are imposed on the deductibility of expenses paid or incurred to attend conventions located outside the North American area. The expenses are disallowed unless it is established that the meeting is directly related to a trade or business of the taxpayer. Disallowance also occurs unless the taxpayer shows that it is as reasonable for the meeting to be held in a foreign location as within the North American area.

The foreign convention rules do not operate to bar a deduction to an employer if the expense is compensatory in nature. For example, a trip to Rome won by a top salesperson is included in the gross income of the employee and is fully deductible by the employer.

MOVING EXPENSES

4 LEARNING OBJECTIVE
Determine the moving expense deduction.

Moving expenses are deductible for moves in connection with the commencement of work at a new principal place of work.[19] Both employees and self-employed individuals can deduct these expenses. To be eligible for a moving expense deduction, a taxpayer must meet two basic tests: distance and time.

DISTANCE TEST

To meet the distance test, the taxpayer's new job location must be at least 50 miles farther from the taxpayer's old residence than the old residence was from the former place of employment. In this regard, the location of the new residence is not relevant. This eliminates a moving deduction for taxpayers who purchase a new home in the same general area without changing their place of employment. Those who accept a new job in the same general area as the old job location are also eliminated.

EXAMPLE 23

Harry is permanently transferred to a new job location. The distance from Harry's former home to his new job (80 miles) exceeds the distance from his former home to his old job (30 miles) by at least 50 miles. Harry has met the distance test for a moving expense deduction. (See the following diagram.)

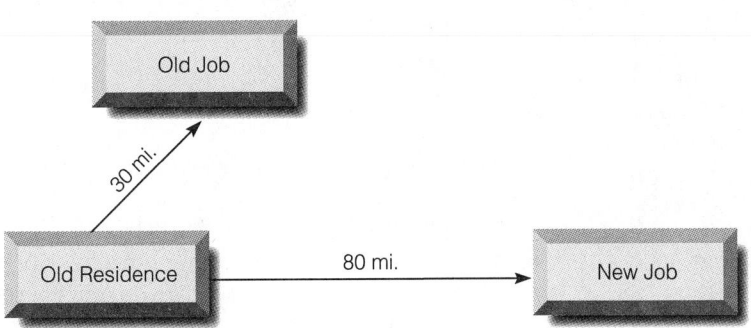

---

[19]§ 217(a).

If Harry is not employed before the move, his new job must be at least 50 miles from his former residence. In this instance, Harry has met the distance test if he was not previously employed. ▼

TIME TEST

To meet the time test, an employee must be employed on a full-time basis at the new location for 39 weeks in the 12-month period following the move. If the taxpayer is a self-employed individual, he or she must work in the new location for 78 weeks during the next two years. The first 39 weeks must be in the first 12 months. The time test is suspended if the taxpayer dies, becomes disabled, or is discharged or transferred by the new employer through no fault of the employee.

A taxpayer might not be able to meet the 39-week test by the due date of the tax return for the year of the move. For this reason, two alternatives are allowed. The taxpayer can take the deduction in the year the expenses are incurred, even though the 39-week test has not been met. If the taxpayer later fails to meet the test, either (1) the income of the following year is increased by an amount equal to the deduction previously claimed for moving expenses, or (2) an amended return is filed for the year of the move. The second alternative is to wait until the test is met and then file an amended tax return for the year of the move.

TREATMENT OF MOVING EXPENSES

What Is Included.   "Qualified" moving expenses include *reasonable* expenses of:

- Moving household goods and personal effects.
- Traveling from the former residence to the new place of residence.

For this purpose, *traveling* includes lodging, but not meals, for the taxpayer and members of the household.[20] It does not include the cost of moving servants or others who are not members of the household. The taxpayer can elect to use actual auto expenses (no depreciation is allowed) or the automatic mileage method. In this case, moving expense mileage is limited in 1998 to 10 cents per mile (10 cents in 1997) for each car. These expenses are also limited by the reasonableness standard. For example, if one moves from Texas to Florida via Maine and takes six weeks to do so, the transportation and lodging must be allocated between personal and moving expenses.

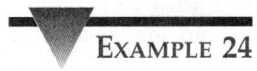

EXAMPLE 24

Jill is transferred by her employer from the Atlanta office to the San Francisco office. In this connection, she spends the following amounts:

Cost of moving furniture	$2,800
Transportation	700
Meals	200
Lodging	300

Jill's total qualified moving expense is $3,800 ($2,800 + $700 + $300). ▼

The moving expense deduction is allowed regardless of whether the employee is transferred by the existing employer or is employed by a new employer. It is allowed if the employee moves to a new area and obtains employment or switches from self-employed status to employee status (and vice versa). The moving expense

---

[20]§ 217(b).

deduction is also allowed if an individual is unemployed before obtaining employment in a new area.

How Treated. Qualified moving expenses that are paid (or reimbursed) by the employer are not reported as part of the gross income of the employee.[21] Moving expenses that are paid (or reimbursed) by the employer and are not qualified moving expenses are included in the employee's gross income and are not deductible. The employer is responsible for allocating the reimbursement between the qualified and nonqualified moving expenses. Reimbursed qualified moving expenses are separately stated on the Form W–2 given to the employee for the year involved. Qualified moving expenses that are not reimbursed and those of self-employed taxpayers are deductions *for* AGI.[22]

Form 3903 is used to report the details of the moving expense deduction if the employee is not reimbursed or a self-employed person is involved.

EDUCATION EXPENSES

GENERAL REQUIREMENTS

5 **LEARNING OBJECTIVE**
Differentiate between deductible and nondeductible education expenses.

An employee can deduct expenses incurred for education (**education expenses**) as ordinary and necessary business expenses provided the expenses are incurred for either of two reasons:

1. To maintain or improve existing skills required in the present job.
2. To meet the express requirements of the employer or the requirements imposed by law to retain his or her employment status.

Education expenses are *not* deductible if the education is for either of the following purposes:

1. To meet the minimum educational standards for qualification in the taxpayer's existing job.
2. To qualify the taxpayer for a new trade or business.[23]

Fees incurred for professional qualification exams (the bar exam, for example) and fees for review courses (such as a CPA review course) are not deductible.[24] If the education incidentally results in a promotion or raise, the deduction still can be taken as long as the education maintained and improved existing skills and did not qualify a person for a new trade or business. A change in duties is not always fatal to the deduction if the new duties involve the same general work. For example, the IRS has ruled that a practicing dentist's education expenses incurred to become an orthodontist are deductible.[25]

REQUIREMENTS IMPOSED BY LAW OR BY THE EMPLOYER FOR RETENTION OF EMPLOYMENT

Teachers are permitted to deduct education expenses if additional courses are required by the employer or are imposed by law. Many states require a minimum of a bachelor's degree and a specified number of additional courses to retain a

---

[21]§§ 132(a)(6) and (g).
[22]§ 62(a)(15).
[23]Reg. §§ 1.162–5(b)(2) and (3).

[24]Reg. § 1.212–1(f) and Rev.Rul. 69–292, 1969–1 C.B. 84.
[25]Rev.Rul. 74–78, 1974–1 C.B. 44.

teaching job. In addition, some public school systems have imposed a master's degree requirement and require teachers to make satisfactory progress toward a master's degree in order to keep their positions. If the required education is the minimum degree required for the job, no deduction is allowed.

A taxpayer classified as an Accountant I who went back to school to obtain a bachelor's degree was not allowed to deduct the expenses. Although some courses tended to maintain and improve his existing skills in his entry-level position, the degree was the minimum requirement for his job.[26]

Expenses incurred for education required by law for various professions will also qualify for deduction.

EXAMPLE 25

In order to satisfy the State Board of Public Accountancy rules for maintaining her CPA license, Nancy takes an auditing course sponsored by a local college. The cost of the education is deductible. ▼

ETHICAL
CONSIDERATIONS

Employer-Imposed Education Requirement

Justin, a CPA, is the owner and operator of Condor Corporation. Condor provides accounting and tax services for a number of regular businesses. These services are provided by Justin and two long-time employees, Martha and Alan. Martha and Alan have expressed a desire to attend a local college part-time and earn bachelor of accounting degrees.

When Justin hears about the college plans that Martha and Alan have made, he adopts the following resolution for Condor Corporation: "Employees performing accounting and tax services for clients must possess or be pursuing a bachelor's degree in accounting."

What is Justin trying to accomplish with the resolution? Will it work? Is this ethical behavior?

MAINTAINING OR IMPROVING EXISTING SKILLS

The "maintaining or improving existing skills" requirement in the Code has been difficult for both taxpayers and the courts to interpret. For example, a business executive is permitted to deduct the costs of obtaining an MBA on the grounds that the advanced management education is undertaken to maintain and improve existing management skills. The executive is eligible to deduct the costs of specialized, nondegree management courses that are taken for continuing education or to maintain or improve existing skills. Expenses incurred by the executive to obtain a law degree are not deductible, however, because the education constitutes training for a new trade or business. The Regulations deny a self-employed accountant a deduction for expenses relating to law school.[27]

CLASSIFICATION OF SPECIFIC ITEMS

Education expenses include books, tuition, typing, and transportation (e.g., from the office to night school) and travel (e.g., meals and lodging while away from home at summer school).

---

[26]Reg. § 1.162–5(b)(2)(iii) Example (2); *Collin J. Davidson*, 43 TCM 743, T.C.Memo. 1982–119.

[27]Reg. § 1.162–5(b)(3)(ii) Example (1).

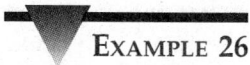

EXAMPLE 26

Bill, who holds a bachelor of education degree, is a secondary education teacher in the Los Angeles school system. The school board recently raised its minimum education requirement for new teachers from four years of college training to five. A grandfather clause allows teachers with only four years of college to continue to qualify if they show satisfactory progress toward a graduate degree. Bill enrolls at the University of California and takes three graduate courses. His unreimbursed expenses for this purpose are as follows:

Books and tuition	$2,600
Lodging while in travel status (June–August)	1,150
Meals while in travel status	800
Laundry while in travel status	220
Transportation	600

Bill has an itemized deduction as follows:

Books and tuition	$2,600
Lodging	1,150
Meals less 50% cutback (see below)	400
Laundry	220
Transportation	600
	$4,970

OTHER PROVISIONS DEALING WITH EDUCATION

The focus of this chapter is on the deduction aspects of certain items. For education, however, two important provisions involve the income aspects. One deals with the exclusion of certain scholarships from gross income.[28] The other deals with the exclusion from gross income of employer amounts provided under certain educational assistance programs.[29] Both of these provisions are discussed in Chapter 4.

ENTERTAINMENT EXPENSES

6   LEARNING OBJECTIVE
Understand how entertainment expenses are treated.

Many taxpayers attempt to deduct personal entertainment expenses as business expenses. For this reason, the tax law restricts the deductibility of entertainment expenses. The Code contains strict record-keeping requirements and provides restrictive tests for the deduction of certain types of **entertainment expenses.**

CUTBACK ADJUSTMENT

During the administration of Jimmy Carter, considerable controversy arose regarding the "three martini" business lunch. By virtue of allowing a tax deduction, should the tax law be subsidizing a practice that contained a significant element of personal pleasure? One possible remedy for the situation was to disallow any deduction for business entertainment, but this option was regarded as being too harsh. Instead the *cutback* rule was instituted. Rather than disallowing *all* of the deduction, allow only a certain percentage, and the rest of the expenditure would

---

[28]§ 117.   [29]§ 127.

be cut back. Currently, only 50 percent of meal and entertainment expenses are allowed as a deduction.[30] The limitation applies in the context of both employment and self-employment status. Although the 50 percent cutback can apply to either the employer or the employee, it will not apply twice. The cutback applies to the one who really pays (economically) for the meals or entertainment.

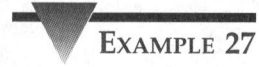
EXAMPLE 27

Jane, an employee of Pelican Corporation, entertains one of her clients. If Pelican Corporation does not reimburse Jane, she is subject to the cutback adjustment. If, however, Pelican Corporation reimburses Jane (or pays for the entertainment directly), Pelican suffers the cutback. ▼

In certain situations, however, a full 50 percent cutback seems unfair. If, for example, the hours of service are regulated (by the U.S. Department of Transportation) and away-from-home meals are frequent and necessary, the "three martini" business lunch type of abuse is unlikely. Consequently, the Taxpayer Relief Act of 1997 (TRA of 1997) eases the cutback rule for the following types of employees:

- Certain air transportation employees, such as flight crews, dispatchers, mechanics, and control tower operators.
- Interstate truck and bus drivers.
- Certain railroad employees, such as train crews and dispatchers.
- Certain merchant mariners.

Starting in 1998, the cutback is reduced by 5 percent at two-year intervals until it reaches 20 percent in year 2008 and thereafter. Thus, 80 percent of the cost of meals will eventually be allowed as a deduction.

What Is Covered. Transportation expenses are not affected by the cutback rule—only meals and entertainment. The cutback also applies to taxes and tips relating to meals and entertainment. Cover charges, parking fees at an entertainment location, and room rental fees for a meal or cocktail party are also subject to the 50 percent rule.

EXAMPLE 28

Joe pays a $30 cab fare to meet his client for dinner. The meal costs $120, and Joe leaves a $20 tip. His deduction is $100 [($120 + $20) × 50% + $30 cab fare]. ▼

What Is Not Covered. The cutback rule has a number of exceptions. One exception covers the case where the full value of the meals or entertainment is included in the compensation of the employee (or independent contractor).[31]

EXAMPLE 29

Myrtle wins an all-expense-paid trip to Europe for selling the most insurance for her company during the year. Her employer treats this trip as additional compensation to Myrtle. The cutback adjustment does not apply to the employer. ▼

Another exception applies to meals and entertainment in a subsidized eating facility or where the *de minimis* fringe benefit rule is met (see Chapter 4).[32]

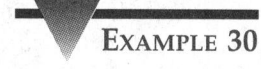
EXAMPLE 30

General Hospital has an employee cafeteria on the premises for its doctors, nurses, and other employees. The cafeteria operates at cost. The cutback rule does not apply to General Hospital. ▼

---

[30] § 274(n).
[31] §§ 274(e)(2) and (9).

[32] § 274(n)(2).

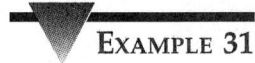

EXAMPLE 31

Canary Corporation gives a ham, a fruitcake, and a bottle of wine to each employee at year-end. Since the *de minimis* fringe benefit exclusion applies to business gifts of packaged foods and beverages, their *full* cost is deductible by Canary. ▼

A similar exception applies to employer-paid recreational activities for employees (e.g., the annual Christmas party or spring picnic).[33]

CLASSIFICATION OF EXPENSES

Entertainment expenses are categorized as follows: those *directly related* to business and those *associated with* business.[34] Directly related expenses are related to an actual business meeting or discussion. These expenses are distinguished from entertainment expenses that are incurred to promote goodwill, such as maintaining existing customer relations. To obtain a deduction for directly related entertainment, it is not necessary to show that actual benefit resulted from the expenditure as long as there was a reasonable expectation of benefit. To qualify as directly related, the expense should be incurred in a clear business setting. If there is little possibility of engaging in the active conduct of a trade or business due to the nature of the social facility, it is difficult to qualify the expenditure as directly related to business.

Expenses associated with, rather than directly related to, business entertainment must serve a specific business purpose, such as obtaining new business or continuing existing business. These expenditures qualify only if the expenses directly precede or follow a bona fide business discussion. Entertainment occurring on the same day as the business discussion meets the test.

RESTRICTIONS UPON DEDUCTIBILITY

Business Meals. Any business meal is deductible only if the following are true:[35]

- The meal is directly related to or associated with the active conduct of a trade or business.
- The expense is not lavish or extravagant under the circumstances.
- The taxpayer (or an employee) is present at the meal.

A business meal with a business associate or customer is not deductible unless business is discussed before, during, or after the meal. This requirement is not intended to disallow the deduction for a meal consumed while away from home on business.

EXAMPLE 32

Lacy travels to San Francisco for a business convention. She pays for dinner with three colleagues and is not reimbursed by her employer. They do not discuss business. She can deduct 50% of the cost of her meal. However, she cannot deduct the cost of her colleagues' meals. ▼

The *clear business purpose* test requires that meals be directly related to or associated with the active conduct of a business. A meal is not deductible if it serves no business purpose.

---

[33]§ 274(e)(4).
[34]§ 274(a)(1)(A).

[35]§ 274(k).

ETHICAL CONSIDERATIONS

Reciprocal Entertaining

Walter (an attorney), Susan (an insurance broker), Richard (a realtor), and Nancy (a banker) are all good friends and do business with each other. Richard's accountant suggests that each might derive a substantial tax benefit if they went to lunch together as often as possible and rotated the tab. Do you believe the procedure suggested by Richard's accountant is proper? Why or why not?

The taxpayer or an employee must be present at the business meal for the meal to be deductible.[36] An independent contractor who renders significant services to the taxpayer is treated as an employee.

EXAMPLE 33   Lance, a party to a contract negotiation, buys dinner for other parties to the negotiation but does not attend the dinner. No deduction is allowed. ▼

Club Dues. The Code provides: "No deduction shall be allowed . . . for amounts paid or incurred for membership in any club organized for business, pleasure, recreation, or other social purpose."[37] Although this prohibition seems quite broad, the IRS does allow a deduction for dues to clubs whose primary purpose is public service and community volunteerism (e.g., Kiwanis, Lions, Rotary).

Even though dues are not deductible, actual entertainment at a club may qualify.

EXAMPLE 34   During the current year, Vincent spent $1,400 on business lunches at the Lakeside Country Club. The annual membership fee was $6,000, and Vincent used the facility 60% of the time for business. Presuming the lunches meet the business meal test, Vincent may claim $700 (50% × $1,400) as a deduction. None of the club dues are deductible. ▼

Ticket Purchases for Entertainment. A deduction for the cost of a ticket for an entertainment activity is limited to the face value of the ticket.[38] This limitation is applied before the 50 percent rule. The face value of a ticket includes any tax. Under this rule, the excess payment to a scalper for a ticket is not deductible. Similarly, the fee to a ticket agency for the purchase of a ticket is not deductible.

Expenditures for the rental or use of a luxury skybox at a sports arena in excess of the face value of regular tickets are disallowed as deductions. If a luxury skybox is used for entertainment that is directly related to or associated with business, the deduction is limited to the face value of nonluxury box seats. All seats in the luxury skybox are counted, even when some seats are unoccupied.

The taxpayer may also deduct stated charges for food and beverages under the general rules for business entertainment. The deduction for skybox seats, food, and beverages is limited to 50 percent of cost.

EXAMPLE 35   In the current year, Pelican Company pays $6,000 to rent a 10-seat skybox at City Stadium for three football games. Nonluxury box seats at each event range in cost from $25 to $35 a seat. In March, a Pelican representative and five clients use the skybox for the first game. The entertainment follows a bona fide business discussion, and Pelican spends $86 for food and beverages during the game. The deduction for the first sports event is as follows:

---

[36]§ 274(k)(1)(B).
[37]§ 274(a)(3).

[38]§ 274(l).

Food and beverages	$ 86
Deduction for seats ($35 × 10 seats)	350
Total entertainment expense	$436
50% limitation	× .50
Deduction	$218

Business Gifts.   Business gifts are deductible to the extent of $25 per donee per year.[39] An exception is made for gifts costing $4 or less (e.g., pens with the employee's or company's name on them) or promotional materials. Such items are not treated as business gifts subject to the $25 limitation. In addition, incidental costs such as engraving of jewelry and nominal charges for gift-wrapping, mailing, and delivery are not included in the cost of the gift in applying the limitation. Gifts to superiors and employers are not deductible.

Records must be maintained to substantiate business gifts.

OTHER EMPLOYEE EXPENSES

OFFICE IN THE HOME

7   LEARNING OBJECTIVE
Identify other employee expenses.

Employees and self-employed individuals are not allowed a deduction for **office in the home expenses** unless a portion of the residence is used *exclusively* on a *regular basis* as either of the following:

- The principal place of business for any trade or business of the taxpayer.
- A place of business used by clients, patients, or customers.

Employees must meet an additional test: The use must be for the *convenience of the employer* rather than merely being "appropriate and helpful."[40]

The precise meaning of "principal place of business" was resolved by the U.S. Supreme Court. In a divided opinion, the Court established a *very restrictive* two-pronged test.[41] First, determine the relative importance of the activities performed at each business location (inside and outside the personal residence). Second, compare the time spent at each business location.

EXAMPLE 36

Dr. Smith is a self-employed anesthesiologist. During the year, he spends 30 to 35 hours per week administering anesthesia and postoperative care to patients in three hospitals, none of which provides him with an office. He also spends two to three hours per day in a room in his home that he uses exclusively as an office. He does not meet patients there, but he performs a variety of tasks related to his medical practice (e.g., contacting surgeons, bookkeeping, reading medical journals). None of Dr. Smith's expenses of the office in the home are deductible because the hospital procedures (administering to patients) are more important than those done at home. Also, more business time is spent outside the home than inside. ▼

---

[39]§ 274(b)(1).
[40]§ 280A(c)(1).
[41]*Comm. v. Soliman*, 93–1 USTC ¶50,014, 71 AFTR2d 93–463, 113 S.Ct. 701 (USSC, 1993) *rev'g.* 91–1 USTC ¶50,291, 67 AFTR2d 91–1112, 935 F.2d 52 (CA–4, 1991) and 94 T.C. 20 (1990).

EXAMPLE 37

Lori is a salesperson. Her only office is a room in her home that she uses regularly and exclusively to set up appointments, store product samples, and write up orders and other reports for the companies whose products she sells. Lori makes most of her sales to customers by telephone or mail from her home office. She spends an average of 30 hours a week working at home and 12 hours a week visiting prospective customers to deliver products and occasionally take orders. Under these circumstances, Lori qualifies for the office in the home deduction. Visiting customers is less important to the business than the activities conducted in Lori's office.[42] ▼

Apparently, Congress was not satisfied with the U.S. Supreme Court's interpretation of the meaning of "principal place of business." In TRA of 1997, the Code was amended to provide that an office in the home qualifies as a principal place of business if both of the following are true:

- The office is used by the taxpayer to conduct administrative or management activities of a trade or business.
- There is no other fixed location of the trade or business where the taxpayer conducts these activities.

Unfortunately, the amendment is not effective until taxable years beginning after December 31, 1998. Once in place, however, the new rule will negate the result reached in Example 36.

The exclusive use requirement means that a specific part of the home must be used *solely* for business purposes. A deduction, if permitted, requires an allocation of total expenses of operating the home between business and personal use based on floor space or number of rooms.

Even if the taxpayer meets the above requirements, the allowable home office expenses cannot exceed the gross income from the business less all other business expenses attributable to the activity. Furthermore, the home office expenses that are allowed as itemized deductions anyway (e.g., mortgage interest and real estate taxes) must be deducted first. All home office expenses of an employee are miscellaneous itemized deductions, except those (such as interest and taxes) that qualify as other personal itemized deductions. Home office expenses of a self-employed individual are trade or business expenses and are deductible *for* AGI.

Any disallowed home office expenses are *carried forward* and used in future years subject to the same limitations.

EXAMPLE 38

Rick is a certified public accountant employed by a regional CPA firm as a tax manager. He operates a separate business in which he refinishes furniture in his home. For this business, he uses two rooms in the basement of his home exclusively and regularly. The floor space of the two rooms constitutes 10% of the floor space of his residence. Gross income from the business totals $8,000. Expenses of the business (other than home office expenses) are $6,500. Rick incurs the following home office expenses:

Real property taxes on residence	$ 4,000
Interest expense on residence	7,500
Operating expenses of residence	2,000
Depreciation on residence (based on 10% business use)	250

Rick's deductions are determined as follows:

---

[42]Notice 93–12, 1993–1 C.B. 298 amplified by Rev.Rul. 94–24,1994–1 C.B. 87.

Business income		$ 8,000
Less: Other business expenses		(6,500)
		$ 1,500
Less: Allocable taxes ($4,000 × 10%)	$400	
Allocable interest ($7,500 × 10%)	750	(1,150)
		$ 350
Allocable operating expenses of the residence ($2,000 × 10%)		(200)
		$ 150
Allocable depreciation ($250, limited to remaining income)		(150)
		$ –0–

Rick has a carryover of $100 (the unused excess depreciation). Because he is self-employed, the allocable taxes and interest ($1,150), the other deductible office expenses ($200 + $150), and $6,500 of other business expenses are deductible *for* AGI. ▼

Form 8829 (Expenses for Business Use of Your Home) is available from the IRS for computation of the office in the home deduction.

The home office limitation cannot be circumvented by leasing part of one's home to an employer, using it as a home office, and deducting the expenses as a rental expense under § 212.

MISCELLANEOUS EMPLOYEE EXPENSES

Deductible miscellaneous employee expenses include special clothing and its upkeep, union dues, and professional expenses. Also deductible are professional dues, professional meetings, and employment agency fees for seeking employment in the same trade or business, whether or not a new job is secured.

To be deductible, *special clothing* must be both specifically required as a condition of employment and not adaptable for regular wear. For example, a police officer's uniform is not suitable for off-duty activities. An exception is clothing used to the extent that it takes the place of regular clothing (e.g., military uniforms).

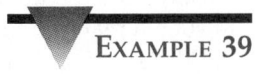

EXAMPLE 39

Captain Roberts is on active duty in the U.S. Army. The cost of his regular uniforms is not deductible since such clothing is suitable for regular wear. Captain Roberts, however, spends over $1,100 purchasing "dress blues." Under military regulations, dress uniforms can only be worn during ceremonial functions (e.g., official events, parades). The $1,100 cost, to the extent it exceeds any clothing allowance, qualifies as a deduction. ▼

The current position of the IRS is that expenses incurred in *seeking employment* are deductible if the taxpayer is seeking employment in the same trade or business. The deduction is allowed whether or not the attempts to secure employment are successful. An unemployed taxpayer can take a deduction providing there has been no substantial lack of continuity between the last job and the search for a new one. No deduction is allowed for persons seeking their first job or seeking employment in a new trade or business.

The basic cost of one *telephone* in the home is not deductible, even if used for business. Any long-distance or toll charges relating to business are deductible.

▼ TABLE 8–1	AGI Filing Status	Phase-Out Begins*	Phase-Out Ends
Phase-Out of IRA Deduction of an Active Participant in 1998	Single and head of household	$30,000	$40,000
	Married, filing joint return	50,000	60,000
	Married, filing separate return	–0–	10,000

*The starting point for the phase-out is increased each year through 2007 for married filing jointly and through 2005 for other filing statuses.

CONTRIBUTIONS TO INDIVIDUAL RETIREMENT ACCOUNTS

An important and popular deduction *for* AGI is the amount contributed to an Individual Retirement Account (IRA). This amount may be as great as $2,000 per year for an individual (or $4,000 for spousal IRAs). Employees not covered by another qualified plan can establish their own tax-deductible Individual Retirement Accounts (IRAs). The contribution ceiling is the smaller of $2,000 (or $4,000 for spousal IRAs) or 100 percent of compensation. If the taxpayer is an active participant in another qualified plan, the traditional IRA deduction limitation is phased out proportionately between certain adjusted gross income (AGI) ranges, as shown in Table 8–1.

AGI is calculated taking into account any § 469 passive losses and § 86 taxable Social Security benefits and ignoring any § 911 foreign income exclusion, § 135 savings bonds interest exclusion, and the IRA deduction. There is a $200 floor on the IRA deduction limitation for individuals whose AGI is not above the phase-out range.

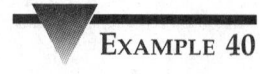

EXAMPLE 40

Daniel, who is single, has compensation income of $37,000 in 1998. He is an active participant in his employer's qualified retirement plan. Dan may contribute $600 to an IRA. The deductible amount is reduced from $2,000 by $1,400 because of the phase-out mechanism [($7,000/$10,000) × $2,000 = $1,400 reduction]. ▼

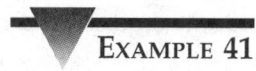

EXAMPLE 41

Ben, an unmarried individual, is an active participant in his employer's qualified retirement plan. With AGI of $39,500, he would normally have an IRA deduction limit of $100 {$2,000 – [($39,500 – $30,000)/$10,000 × $2,000]}. However, because of the special floor provision, Ben is allowed a $200 IRA deduction. ▼

An individual is not considered an active participant in a qualified plan merely because the individual's spouse is an active participant in such a plan for any part of a plan year. Thus, most homemakers may take a full $2,000 deduction regardless of the participation status of their spouse, unless the couple has AGI above $150,000. If their AGI is above $150,000, the phase-out of the deduction begins at $150,000 and ends at $160,000 (phase-out over the $10,000 range).

EXAMPLE 42

Nell is covered by a qualified employer retirement plan at work. Her husband, Nick, is not an active participant in an active qualified plan. If Nell and Nick's combined AGI is $135,000, Nell cannot make a deductible IRA contribution because she exceeds the income threshold for an active participant. However, since Nick is not an active participant, and their combined AGI does not exceed $150,000, he can make a deductible contribution of $2,000 to an IRA. ▼

To the extent that an individual is ineligible to make a deductible contribution to an IRA, nondeductible contributions can be made to separate accounts. The nondeductible contributions are subject to the same dollar limits as deductible contributions ($2,000 of earned income, $4,000 for a spousal IRA). Income in the

---

TAX IN THE NEWS

SOME NBA REFEREES MAY PAY A PRICE FOR A TAXABLE (BUT NOT REPORTED) PAY RAISE

Several NBA referees are the focus of an IRS investigation into a scheme involving millions of dollars in phony travel expenses.

The NBA says it merely reimbursed the referees for travel based on their receipts. But some of the referees say the NBA knowingly paid higher travel reimbursements as a substitute for better pay.

The scheme apparently worked this way: Referees purchased first-class tickets and submitted photocopies of them to the NBA for reimbursement. They then exchanged the tickets for coach seats and pocketed the difference. Needless to say, the referees did not report the difference as income.

As of fall 1997, at least four referees have been indicted by Federal grand juries for income tax fraud with three pleading guilty. Further indictments are expected.

---

account accumulates tax-free until distributed. Only the account earnings are taxed upon distribution because the account basis equals the contributions made by the taxpayer. A taxpayer may elect to treat deductible IRA contributions as nondeductible. If an individual has no taxable income for the year after taking into account other deductions, the election would be beneficial. The election is made on the individual's tax return for the taxable year to which the designation relates.

CLASSIFICATION OF EMPLOYEE EXPENSES

LEARNING OBJECTIVE 8
Appreciate the difference between accountable and nonaccountable employee plans.

The classification of employee expenses depends on whether they are reimbursed by the employer under an accountable plan. If so, then they are not reported by the employee at all. In effect, therefore, this result is equivalent to treating the expenses as deductions *for* AGI.[43] If the expenses are reimbursed under a nonaccountable plan or are not reimbursed at all, then they are classified as deductions *from* AGI and can only be claimed if the employee-taxpayer itemizes. An exception is made for moving expenses and the employment-related expenses of a qualified performing artist.[44] Here, deduction *for* AGI classification is allowed.

For classification purposes, therefore, the difference between accountable and nonaccountable plans is significant.

ACCOUNTABLE PLANS

In General. An **accountable plan** requires the employee to satisfy these two requirements:

- Adequately account for (substantiate) the expenses. An employee renders an *adequate accounting* by submitting a record, with receipts and other substantiation, to the employer.[45]

---

[43]§ 62(a)(2).
[44]As defined in § 62(b).

[45]Reg. § 1.162–17(b)(4).

- Return any excess reimbursement or allowance. An "excess reimbursement or allowance" is any amount that the employee does not adequately account for as an ordinary and necessary business expense.

Substantiation. The law provides that no deduction is allowed for any travel, entertainment, business gift, or listed property (automobiles, computers) expenditure unless properly substantiated by adequate records. The records should contain the following information:[46]

- The amount of the expense.
- The time and place of travel or entertainment (or date of gift).
- The business purpose of the expense.
- The business relationship of the taxpayer to the person entertained (or receiving the gift).

This means the taxpayer must maintain an account book or diary in which the above information is recorded at the time of the expenditure. Documentary evidence, such as itemized receipts, is required to support any expenditure for lodging while traveling away from home and for any other expenditure of $75 or more. If a taxpayer fails to keep adequate records, each expense must be established by a written or oral statement of the exact details of the expense and by other corroborating evidence.[47]

EXAMPLE 43

Bertha has travel expenses substantiated only by canceled checks. The checks establish the date, place, and amount of the expenditure. Because neither the business relationship nor the business purpose is established, the deduction is disallowed.[48] ▼

EXAMPLE 44

Dwight has travel and entertainment expenses substantiated by a diary showing the time, place, and amount of the expenditure. His oral testimony provides the business relationship and business purpose. However, since he has no receipts, any expenditures of $75 or more are disallowed.[49] ▼

Deemed Substantiation. In lieu of reimbursing actual expenses for travel away from home, many employers reduce their paperwork by adopting a policy of reimbursing employees with a *per diem* allowance, a flat dollar amount per day of business travel. Of the substantiation requirements listed above, the *amount* of the expense is proved, or *deemed substantiated*, by using such a per diem allowance or reimbursement procedure. The amount of expenses that is deemed substantiated is equal to the lesser of the per diem allowance or the amount of the Federal per diem rate.

The regular Federal per diem rate is the highest amount that the Federal government will pay to its employees for lodging and meals[50] while in travel status away from home in a particular area. The rates are different for different locations.[51]

The use of the standard Federal per diem for meals constitutes an adequate accounting. Employees and self-employed persons can use the standard meal allowance instead of deducting the actual cost of daily meals, even if not reimbursed. There is no standard lodging allowance, however.

---

[46]§ 274(d).
[47]Reg. § 1.274–5T(c)(3).
[48] *William T. Whitaker*, 56 TCM 47, T.C.Memo. 1988–418.
[49]*W. David Tyler*, 43 TCM 927, T.C.Memo. 1982–160.
[50]The meals per diem rate also covers incidental expenses, including laundry and cleaning of clothing and tips for waiters. Taxi fares and telephone calls are not included.

[51]Each current edition of *Per Diem Rates* (IRS Publication 1542) contains the list and amounts for that year.

Only the amount of the expense is considered substantiated under the deemed substantiated method. The other substantiation requirements must be provided: place, date, business purpose of the expense, and the business relationship of the parties involved.

NONACCOUNTABLE PLANS

A **nonaccountable plan** is one in which an adequate accounting or return of excess amounts, or both, is not required. All reimbursements of expenses are reported in full as wages on the employee's Form W–2. Any allowable expenses are deductible in the same manner as are unreimbursed expenses.

Unreimbursed Employee Expenses.   Unreimbursed employee expenses are treated in a straightforward manner. Meals and entertainment expenses are subject to the 50 percent limit. Total unreimbursed employee business expenses are usually reported as miscellaneous itemized deductions subject to the 2 percent-of-AGI floor (see below). If the employee could have received, but did not seek, reimbursement for whatever reason, none of the employment-related expenses are deductible.

Failure to Comply with Accountable Plan Requirements.   An employer may have an accountable plan and require employees to return excess reimbursements or allowances, but an employee may fail to follow the rules of the plan. In that case, the expenses and reimbursements are subject to nonaccountable plan treatment.

REPORTING PROCEDURES

The reporting requirements range from no reporting at all (accountable plans when all requirements are met) to the use of some or all of the following forms: Form W–2 (Wage and Tax Statement), Form 2106 (Employee Business Expenses) or Form 2106–EZ (Unreimbursed Employee Business Expenses), and Schedule A (Itemized Deductions) for nonaccountable plans and unreimbursed employee expenses.

Reimbursed employee expenses that are adequately accounted for under an accountable plan are deductible *for* AGI on Form 2106. Allowed excess expenses, expenses reimbursed under a nonaccountable plan, and unreimbursed expenses are deductible *from* AGI on Schedule A, subject to the 2 percent-of-AGI floor.

When a reimbursement under an accountable plan is paid in separate amounts relating to designated expenses such as meals or entertainment, no problem arises. The reimbursements and expenses are reported as such on the appropriate forms. If the reimbursement is made in a single amount, an allocation must be made to determine the appropriate portion of the reimbursement that applies to meals and entertainment and to other employee expenses.

EXAMPLE 45

Elizabeth, who is employed by Green Company, had AGI of $42,000. During the year, she incurred $2,000 of transportation and lodging expense and $1,000 of meals and entertainment expense, all fully substantiated. Elizabeth received $1,800 reimbursement under an accountable plan. The reimbursement rate that applies to meals and entertainment is 33.33% ($1,000 meals and entertainment expense/$3,000 total expenses). Thus, $600 ($1,800 × 33.33%) of the reimbursement applies to meals and entertainment, and $1,200 ($1,800 − $600) applies to transportation and lodging. Elizabeth's itemized deduction consists of the $800 ($2,000 total − $1,200 reimbursement) of unreimbursed transportation and lodging expenses and $400 ($1,000 − $600) of unreimbursed meal and entertainment expenses as follows:

Transportation and lodging	$ 800
Meals and entertainment ($400 × 50%)	200
Total (reported on Form 2106)	$1,000
Less: 2% of $42,000 AGI (see limitation discussed below)	(840)
Deduction (reported on Schedule A)	$ 160

In summary, Elizabeth reports $3,000 of expenses and the $1,800 reimbursement on Form 2106 and $160 as a miscellaneous itemized deduction on Schedule A. ▼

LIMITATIONS ON ITEMIZED DEDUCTIONS

9 ▼ **LEARNING OBJECTIVE**
Work with the limitations on miscellaneous itemized deductions.

Many itemized deductions, such as medical expenses and charitable contributions, are subject to limitations expressed as a percentage of AGI. These limitations may be expressed as floors or ceilings. These limitations are discussed in Chapter 9.

MISCELLANEOUS ITEMIZED DEDUCTIONS SUBJECT TO THE 2 PERCENT FLOOR

Certain miscellaneous itemized deductions, including most *unreimbursed employee business expenses*, are aggregated and then reduced by 2 percent of AGI.[52] Expenses subject to the 2 percent floor include the following:

- All § 212 expenses, except expenses of producing rent and royalty income (refer to Chapter 5).
- All unreimbursed employee expenses (after the 50 percent reduction, if applicable) except moving.
- Professional dues and subscriptions.
- Union dues and work uniforms.
- Employment-related education expenses.
- Malpractice insurance premiums.
- Expenses of job hunting (including employment agency fees and resumé-writing expenses).
- Home office expenses of an employee or outside salesperson.
- Legal, accounting, and tax return preparation fees.
- Hobby expenses (up to hobby income).
- Investment expenses, including investment counsel fees, subscriptions, and safe deposit box rental.
- Custodial fees relating to income-producing property or an IRA or a Keogh plan.
- Any fees paid to collect interest or dividends.
- Appraisal fees establishing a casualty loss or charitable contribution.

MISCELLANEOUS ITEMIZED DEDUCTIONS NOT SUBJECT TO THE 2 PERCENT FLOOR

Certain miscellaneous itemized deductions, including the following, are not subject to the 2 percent floor:

---

[52]§ 67.

- Impairment-related work expenses of handicapped individuals.
- Gambling losses to the extent of gambling winnings.
- Certain terminated annuity payments.

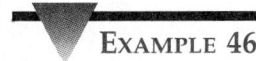

EXAMPLE 46

Ted, who has AGI of $20,000, has the following miscellaneous itemized deductions:

Gambling losses (to extent of gains)	$1,200
Tax return preparation fees	300
Unreimbursed employee transportation	200
Professional dues and subscriptions	260
Safe deposit box rental	30

Ted's itemized deductions are as follows:

Deduction not subject to 2% floor (gambling losses)		$1,200
Deductions subject to 2% floor ($300 + $200 + $260 + $30)	$ 790	
Less 2% of AGI	(400)	390
Total miscellaneous itemized deductions		$1,590

If instead Ted's AGI is $40,000, the floor is $800 (2% of $40,000), and he cannot deduct any expenses subject to the 2% floor. ▼

TAX PLANNING CONSIDERATIONS

10 **LEARNING OBJECTIVE**
Develop tax planning ideas related to employee business expenses.

SELF-EMPLOYED INDIVIDUALS

Some taxpayers have the flexibility to be classified as either employees or self-employed individuals. Examples include real estate agents and direct sellers. These taxpayers should carefully consider all factors and not automatically assume that self-employed status is preferable.

It is advantageous to deduct one's business expenses *for* AGI and avoid the 2 percent floor. However, a self-employed individual may have higher expenses, such as local gross receipts taxes, license fees, franchise fees, personal property taxes, and occupation taxes. In addition, the record-keeping and filing requirements can be quite burdensome.

One of the most expensive considerations is the Social Security tax versus the self-employment tax. For an employee in 1998, for example, the Social Security tax applies at a rate of 6.2 percent on a base amount of wages of $68,400, and the Medicare tax applies at a rate of 1.45 percent with no limit on the base amount. For self-employed persons, the rate, but not the base amount, for each tax doubles. Even though a deduction *for* AGI is allowed for one-half of the self-employment tax paid, an employee and a self-employed individual are not in the same tax position on equal amounts of earnings. For the applicability of these taxes to employees, see Chapter 1.

After analyzing all these factors, a taxpayer may decide that employee status is preferable to self-employed status.

SHIFTING DEDUCTIONS BETWEEN EMPLOYER AND EMPLOYEE

An employee can avoid the 2 percent floor for employee business expenses. Typically, an employee incurs travel and entertainment expenses in the course of employment. The employer gets the deduction if it reimburses the employee, and the employee gets the deduction *for* AGI. An adequate accounting must be made, and excess reimbursements cannot be kept by the employee.

TRANSPORTATION AND TRAVEL EXPENSES

Adequate detailed records of all transportation and travel expenses should be kept. Since the regular mileage allowance is 32.5 cents per mile, a new, expensive automobile used primarily for business may generate a higher expense based on actual cost. The election to expense part of the cost of the automobile under § 179 (although normally not a wise choice), MACRS depreciation, insurance, repairs and maintenance, automobile club dues, and other related costs may result in automobile expenses greater than the automatic mileage allowance.

If a taxpayer wishes to sightsee or vacation on a business trip, it would be beneficial to schedule business on both a Friday and a Monday to turn the weekend into business days for allocation purposes. It is especially crucial to schedule appropriate business days when foreign travel is involved.

MOVING EXPENSES

Persons who retire and move to a new location incur personal nondeductible moving expenses. If the retired person accepts a full-time job in the new location before moving, the moving expenses are deductible.

EXAMPLE 47

At the time of his retirement from the national office of a major accounting firm, Gordon had an annual salary of $220,000. He moves from New York City to Seattle to retire. To qualify for the moving expense deduction, Gordon accepts a full-time teaching position at a Seattle junior college at an annual salary of $15,000. If Gordon satisfies the 39-week test, his moving expenses are deductible. The disparity between the two salaries (previous and current) is of no consequence. ▼

EDUCATION EXPENSES

Education expenses are treated as nondeductible personal items unless the individual is employed or is engaged in a trade or business. A temporary leave of absence for further education is one way to reasonably assure that the taxpayer is still qualified, even if a full-time student. An individual was permitted to deduct education expenses even though he resigned from his job, returned to school full-time for two years, and accepted another job in the same field upon graduation. The Court held that the student had merely suspended active participation in his field.[53]

If the time out of the field is too long, educational expense deductions will be disallowed. For example, a teacher who left the field for four years to raise her child and curtailed her employment searches and writing activities was denied a deduction. She was not actively engaged in the trade or business of being an educator.[54]

To secure the deduction, an individual should arrange his or her work situation to preserve employee or business status.

ENTERTAINMENT EXPENSES

Proper documentation of expenditures is essential because of the strict record-keeping requirements and the restrictive tests that must be met. For example, documentation that consists solely of credit card receipts and canceled checks may be inadequate to substantiate the business purpose and business relationship.[55] Taxpayers should maintain detailed records of amounts, time, place, business purpose, and business relationships. A credit card receipt details the place, date, and amount of the expense. A notation made on the receipt of the names of the person(s) attending, the business relationship, and the topic of discussion should constitute proper documentation.

Associated with or goodwill entertainment is not deductible unless a business discussion is conducted immediately before or after the entertainment. Furthermore, a business purpose must exist for the entertainment. Taxpayers should arrange for a business discussion before or after such entertainment. They must provide documentation of the business purpose, such as obtaining new business from a prospective customer.

Unreimbursed meals and entertainment are subject to the 50 percent cutback rule in addition to the 2 percent floor. Consequently, the procedure of negotiating a salary reduction, as discussed below under Unreimbursed Employee Business Expenses, is even more valuable to the taxpayer.

UNREIMBURSED EMPLOYEE BUSINESS EXPENSES

The 2 percent floor for unreimbursed employee business expenses offers a tax planning opportunity for married couples. If one spouse has high miscellaneous expenses subject to the floor, it may be beneficial for the couple to file separate returns. If they file jointly, the 2 percent floor is based on the incomes of both. Filing separately lowers the reduction to 2 percent of only one spouse's income.

Other provisions of the law should be considered, however. For example, filing separately could cost a couple losses of up to $25,000 from self-managed rental units under the passive activity loss rules (discussed in Chapter 10).

---

[53]*Stephen G. Sherman*, 36 TCM 1191, T.C.Memo. 1977–301.
[54]*Brian C. Mulherin*, 42 TCM 834, T.C.Memo. 1981–454; *George A. Baist*, 56 TCM 778, T.C.Memo. 1988–554.

[55]*Kenneth W. Guenther*, 54 TCM 382, T.C.Memo. 1987–440.

Another possibility is to negotiate a salary reduction with one's employer in exchange for the 100 percent reimbursement of employee expenses. The employee is better off because the 2 percent floor does not apply. The employer is better off because certain expense reimbursements are not subject to Social Security and other payroll taxes.

KEY TERMS

Accountable plan, 8–23

Automatic mileage method, 8–6

Education expenses, 8–13

Entertainment expenses, 8–15

Independent contractor, 8–2

Moving expenses, 8–11

Nonaccountable plan, 8–25

Office in the home expenses, 8–19

Statutory employees, 8–4

Transportation expenses, 8–5

Travel expenses, 8–7

PROBLEM MATERIALS

DISCUSSION QUESTIONS

1. Why might a business prefer to classify a worker as an independent contractor (i.e., self-employed) rather than as an employee?

2. What difference does it make if an individual's expenses are classified as employment-related expenses or as expenses from self-employment?

3. Can a person be both employed and self-employed during the same year? Explain.

4. Joanne is a well-known freelance columnist who works at home. Most of her income comes from this source, but she also receives some income from speaking engagements (both local and out-of-town). Also, she teaches a class in creative writing at a local university. Suggest some of the deductible work-related expenses Joanne might have.

5. Byron is a salesperson with a rather extensive sales territory. He just purchased a new car that will be used in his job. He plans to use the actual operating cost method for the first few years and then switch to the automatic mileage method. What are some of the hurdles Byron may face in carrying out these plans?

6. Distinguish between transportation expenses and travel expenses.

7. Hollis is a key player for the Miami Sharks. During the football season, Hollis lives in a rented apartment near Shark Stadium. For the rest of the year, he stays with his parents in Springfield, Missouri. In the off-season, Hollis is a public relations vice president of a Springfield bank. Presuming no reimbursement, discuss the employment-related expenses Hollis should be able to deduct.

8. Jim works in St. Louis. On Tuesday morning he flies to San Francisco for a business meeting. After the meeting, Jim has lunch by himself and then flies back to St. Louis that same evening. Is the cost of Jim's lunch deductible? Why or why not?

9. Refer to the facts set forth in Example 12 (page 8–8 of the text). What are some of the things Bill might do to avoid the potential tax disaster he faces?

10. Dr. Fuerst, a practicing orthodontist in Buffalo, travels to New York City to attend a two-day convention on experimental orthodontia procedures. Mr. Fuerst accompanies his wife since he prepares their tax return and knows how to properly prepare the required substantiation for the trip. Comment on the deductibility of the trip.

11. Under what circumstances, if any, can travel expenses qualify for the education deduction?

12. Josephine took a combined business and pleasure trip to Europe. She traveled to London from New York on Friday, vacationed on Saturday and Sunday, conducted business on Monday, got snowed in at the airport on Tuesday, traveled to Paris on Wednesday, relaxed on Thursday (a legal holiday), conducted business on Friday, went sightseeing on Saturday and Sunday, picked up business samples and papers on Monday, and flew back to New York on Tuesday. What portion of her airfare can she deduct?

13. Zane is an air-traffic director for Los Angeles International Airport. Since his daily commuting distance of 120 miles (60 miles each way) is exhausting, he sells his residence and moves to Santa Monica. The new home requires a commute of only 6 miles. Are Zane's moving expenses deductible? Why or why not?

14. During 1997, Kelsey incurs qualified moving expenses in changing jobs. By April 1998 when Kelsey files her 1997 income tax return, she has not yet satisfied the 39-week time test.
    a. What are Kelsey's options regarding the handling of the moving expenses?
    b. Suppose Kelsey never meets the time test. Can the moving expenses still be deductible? Explain.

15. What difference does it make whether a taxpayer is improving existing skills or acquiring new ones for the purpose of the education deduction? On what general tax principle is the justification for this rule based?

16. Nancy, a self-employed tax accountant, enrolls in the evening program of a local law school. Although she has no intention of practicing as an attorney, Nancy feels that a legal education would improve the quality of her present work. Comment on the deductibility of Nancy's law school expenses.

17. In each of the following situations, indicate whether there is a cutback adjustment and, if so, to whom it applies (i.e., employer or employee).
    a. The employer expects certain employees to entertain their key customers. The employer does not reimburse the employees for these costs.
    b. Same as (a) except that the employees are reimbursed for these costs.
    c. Each year the employer awards its top salesperson an expense-paid trip to the Cayman Islands.
    d. The employer has a cafeteria for its employees where meals are furnished at cost.
    e. The employer sponsors an annual Fourth of July picnic for its employees.
    f. Every Christmas, the employer gives each employee a turkey.

18. What was the original justification for the cutback adjustment? Has its application been particularly detrimental to certain types of taxpayers? Explain.

19. Discuss the requirements for the deductibility of business meals.

20. Currently, which club dues are deductible? Not deductible?

21. Sandra pays annual dues to belong to the Wichita Country Club. In addition to social and leisure activities, she also utilizes the facilities for business lunches. Presuming adequate substantiation, are any of Sandra's expenses involving the club deductible? Explain.

22. Gull Corporation has purchased several skyboxes at the Superdome for the home games of the New Orleans Saints. It plans to use these facilities to entertain key customers. Discuss the tax treatment of the costs that will be incurred.

23. To what extent may a taxpayer take a deduction for business gifts to a business associate? To an employee? To a superior?

24. Lieutenant Hebert is on active duty with the U.S. Army. To what extent, if any, is the cost of her uniforms deductible?

25. Trent, a resident of Florida, attends Vanderbilt University. After graduation, he moves to New Orleans where he begins a job search. Shortly thereafter, he accepts a position with a local radio station as an announcer. Trent's college degree is in

management. Presuming no reimbursement, what employment-related expenses might Trent be eligible to deduct?

26. Molly is unmarried and is an active participant in a qualified deductible IRA plan. Her modified AGI is $34,000. Calculate the amount that Molly can contribute to the IRA and the amount she can deduct.

27. Answer the following independent questions with respect to IRA contributions:
    a. Juan earns a salary of $25,000 and is not an active participant in any other qualified plan. His wife, Agnes, has no earned income. What is the maximum total deductible contribution to their IRAs? Juan wishes to contribute as much as possible to his own IRA.
    b. Abby has earned income of $23,000 and her husband has earned income of $1,900. They are not active participants in any other qualified plan. What is the maximum contribution to their IRAs?
    c. Leo's employer makes a contribution of $3,500 to Leo's simplified employee pension plan. If Leo is single, has earned income of $32,000, and has AGI of $29,000, what amount, if any, can he contribute to an IRA?

28. What constitutes an adequate accounting to an employer?

29. What tax return reporting procedures must be followed by an employee under the following circumstances?
    a. Expenses and reimbursements are equal under an accountable plan.
    b. Reimbursements at the appropriate Federal per diem rate exceed expenses, and an adequate accounting is made to the employer.
    c. Expenses exceed reimbursements under a nonaccountable plan.

30. Kim has just graduated from college and is interviewing for a position in marketing. Crane Corporation has offered her a job as a sales representative that will require extensive travel and entertainment but provide valuable experience. Under the offer, she has two options: a salary of $48,000 and she absorbs all expenses; a salary of $35,000 and Crane reimburses for all expenses. Crane assures Kim that the $13,000 difference in the two options will be adequate to cover the expenses incurred. What issues should have an impact on Kim's choice?

31. Jeff has been practicing as a physician in Boston. Shortly, he plans to sell his practice to his partners and retire in Taos, New Mexico. Besides the sale of his practice, what should be some of Jeff's concerns?

32. Martha is an associate with a law firm in New York City. Although she already has a J.D. degree, she feels a master of laws from New York University would improve her promotion potential. She can earn the degree on a part-time basis, but Martha is inclined to shorten her career interruption as much as possible. What should be some of Martha's concerns?

PROBLEMS

33. To support his family, Horace holds two jobs during 1998. The relevant distances are as follows:

	Miles
Residence to main job	40
Main job to second job	30
Second job to residence	45

During the 260 days he worked, Horace drove the family car from his residence to the main job. After eight hours, Horace then drove to the second job and worked for four hours. On his way back to the residence, he stopped for dinner. He paid $390 for parking at the second job and $1,100 for dinners. What, if any, is Horace's deduction for the year?

34. Alec has two jobs in 1998. He drives 40 miles to his first job. The distance from the first job to the second is 32 miles. During 1998, Alec worked 200 days at both jobs. On 150 days, he drove from the first job to the second job. On the remaining 50 days, he drove home (40 miles) and then to the second job (42 miles). Presuming the automatic mileage method is used, how much qualifies as a deduction?

35. In 1995, Heidi bought a new automobile for $32,000. The car is used 80% for business. *Total* miles driven are as follows: 11,000 in 1995, 18,000 in 1996, 12,000 in 1997, and 14,000 in 1998. If Heidi uses the automatic mileage method, what is her basis in the car as of January 1, 1999?

36. Louis took a business trip from Chicago to Seattle. He spent two days in travel, conducted business for eight days, and visited friends for five days. He incurred the following expenses:

Airfare	$ 950
Lodging	2,400
Meals	1,200
Entertainment of clients	800

Louis received no reimbursements. What amount can he deduct?

37. Macy is in charge of sales for the Georgia region of a national insurance company and is home-based in Atlanta. The untimely death of the Alabama sales director has created serious transitional problems for Macy's employer. Consequently, Macy spends several consecutive months handling the Alabama business. During this period, Macy flies to Birmingham on Sunday night and returns home to Atlanta on Friday evening. The cost of spending the weekend in Birmingham would have been $310, while the cost of coming home is $320.
   a. Presuming no reimbursement, how much, if any, may Macy deduct for the weekend trips?
   b. Would the answer to part (a) change if the cost of coming home is $200 (not $320)?

38. Chad is a self-employed computer consultant. During the year, he attended a two-day conference on the latest developments in computer technology. His expenses for the conference are as follows:

Airfare	$420
Hotel room	330
Meals	160
Registration fee and course materials	280

How much may Chad deduct for the conference? How is the deduction classified?

39. Odette is a professor of European history at a major midwestern university. In connection with a research paper she is to present at a history symposium, Odette travels to Vienna. While there, she examines archives dealing with the Hapsburg dynasty. During her three-week stay, she goes sightseeing only during nonbusiness hours (e.g., weekends and evenings). Odette's expenses, all carefully documented, are as follows:

Airfare	$1,400
Meals	1,800
Lodging	3,200
Transportation (taxis, airport limos)	210

Presuming no reimbursement, how much, if any, may Odette deduct for the trip?

40. Monica travels from her office in Boston to Lisbon, Portugal, on business. Her absence of 13 days was spent as follows:

Thursday	Depart for and arrive at Lisbon
Friday	Business transacted
Saturday and Sunday	Vacationing
Monday through Friday	Business transacted
Saturday and Sunday	Vacationing
Monday	Business transacted
Tuesday	Depart Lisbon and return to office in Boston

    a. For tax purposes, how many days has Monica spent on business?
    b. What difference does it make?
    c. Could Monica have spent more time than she did vacationing on the trip without loss of existing tax benefits? Explain.

41. Cole is both a CPA and an attorney. For several years, he has practiced law as an employee of a large law firm in Dallas. In 1998, Cole decides to quit his job and move to El Paso, Texas. Four months after arriving in El Paso, Cole establishes a private practice as a CPA. Expenses in moving from Dallas to El Paso are as follows:

Cost of moving household effects	$5,100
Meals	120
Lodging	240

Mileage on two personal autos involved in the move is 1,400.
    a. How much, if any, can be deducted?
    b. How is the deduction, if any, classified?

42. To satisfy a newly imposed school board requirement, Troy spends part of the summer at a college pursuing a master of education degree. Troy, a high school math teacher, spent the following amounts:

Books and tuition	$2,600
Lodging while in travel status	1,800
Meals while in travel status	1,200
Laundry while in travel status	250
Transportation	600

Much to Troy's surprise, after the summer he is promoted to be associate principal of his school.
    a. How much of these amounts may Troy deduct?
    b. How is the deduction classified?

43. After graduating from college with a degree in general business, Shari accepted employment with a bank. Currently, she works in the bank's loan department. During the year, Shari enrolled in an evening MBA program at a local university. In this connection, her expenses are as follows:

Books and tuition	$2,300
Transportation	180
Meals (before or after classes)	310

Shari also takes a correspondence course (cost of $190) entitled "How to Generate Customer Confidence."
    Presuming no reimbursement, what amount of these expenses may Shari deduct?

44. Dudley is a self-employed landscape architect. Since the business is quite competitive, Dudley is compelled to entertain extensively. During 1998, he incurred expenses for business meals as follows:

Taxi fares	$ 380
Meals	4,100
Tips	720
Cover charges	600

Presuming adequate substantiation, what is Dudley's deduction?

45. Swan Corporation spends $25,000 to purchase a 15-seat skybox for eight professional football games. Regular seats at these games normally sell for $40 each. At one game, an employee of Swan entertained 10 clients; Swan furnished food and beverages for the event at a cost of $242. The game was preceded by a bona fide business discussion, and all expenses are adequately substantiated.
    a. How much may Swan Corporation deduct for this event?
    b. Would the answer change if the employee took 14 clients (rather than 10) to the game, and all seats were occupied? Explain.

46. During the current year, Kevin, the assistant manager of a truck leasing firm, made gifts that cost the following amounts:

To Darlene (Kevin's secretary) for Christmas ($2 was for gift wrapping)	$32
To George (Kevin's boss) on his birthday	31
To Susan (a key client) for Christmas	20
To John (a key client) for Christmas	28

Kevin also gave Darlene a box of candy (cost of $18) on her birthday. Presuming Kevin has adequate substantiation and is not reimbursed, how much can he deduct?

47. Ruth is a professor who consults on the side. She uses one-fifth of her home exclusively for her consulting business, and clients regularly meet her there. Ruth is single and under age 65. Her AGI (before considering consulting income) is $50,000. Other relevant data follow:

Income from consulting business	$5,000
Consulting expenses other than home office	2,400
Total costs relating to home	
Interest and taxes	6,000
Utilities	2,000
Maintenance and repairs	600
Depreciation (business part only)	1,500

Calculate Ruth's AGI for 1998.

48. Paige incurred the following expenses related to her employment as a chief executive officer:

Lodging while away from home	$2,800
Meals while away from home	1,200
Entertainment while away from home	2,000
Dues, subscriptions, and books	1,000
Transportation expenses	4,000

Her AGI was $100,000, and she received $6,600 under her employer's accountable plan. What are Paige's deductions *for* and *from* AGI?

49. Kenneth received $4,400 in reimbursements under an accountable plan after he had made an adequate accounting to his employer. His expenses were as follows:

Transportation expenses	$3,200
Meals	1,400
Lodging and incidentals	2,300
Dues and subscriptions	100
Entertainment	1,000

How much can Kenneth deduct *for* and *from* AGI? Assume he had AGI of $50,000 and no other miscellaneous itemized deductions.

50. Thelma, who is age 42 and single, earned a salary of $60,000. She had other income consisting of interest of $2,000, dividends of $1,600, and long-term capital gains of $4,000. Thelma incurred the following expenses during the year:

Transportation	$2,300
Meals	1,600
Dues and subscriptions	800
Entertainment of clients	300
Total	$5,000

Thelma received reimbursements of $3,000 under an accountable plan. Calculate her AGI and itemized employee business expenses.

51. Kyle and Sharon are married, have no dependents, and are full-time employees. Both work for employers who do not reimburse for job-related costs but expect the employee to absorb the expenses. Kyle and Sharon's expenses for 1998 are as follows:

Kyle's union dues	$ 610
Kyle's safety items (e.g., work shoes, glasses, gloves)	340
Kyle's lab clothing	405
Laundry of Kyle's lab clothing	120
Sharon's business lunches with clients	1,340
Sharon's professional dues and journals	610
Sharon's taxi fares to and from work (when personal car was being repaired)	160
Other itemized deductions (e.g., interest on home mortgage, property taxes, charitable contributions)	10,200

If Kyle and Sharon file a joint return and have AGI of $72,000, what is their taxable income?

CUMULATIVE PROBLEMS

52. Debra Bond, age 42 and single, is the personnel manager of the northwest regional office of Olympia Insurance Company. Her Social Security number is 432–60–1000. Debra lives in her own home at 524 Wilcrest Drive, Seattle, WA 98122. Lisa Wall, Debra's 20-year-old niece, lives with her and is a full-time student at a local college. Except for a $3,600 nontaxable scholarship Lisa receives for tuition, Debra provides all of her niece's support. Lisa's Social Security number is 444–11–5555.

Olympia Insurance Company does not reimburse its employees for employment-related expenses. Instead, it estimates the expected expenses of each class of employees and sets their base salary accordingly. During 1998, Debra had the following employment-related expenses:

- Mileage of 5,350 on personal auto (includes 2,200 miles for commuting and 900 for other personal use). Parking and toll charges (not related to commuting or other personal use) are $190.

- Business lunches for potential hires are $1,424. Taxi fares of $132 are not included in this amount.

- Debra attended a three-day seminar on improving managerial skills by using a team approach. The sessions were held at a convention center in Portland, Oregon. Debra's expenses are summarized below.

Transportation	$210
Registration	750
Meals	290
Hotel	375

- Dues to professional organizations of $205 and subscriptions to professional journals of $310.

In 1998, Debra earned wages of $61,200 (not including any bonus). Usually, Olympia Insurance Company follows a policy of issuing a bonus to its employees. The bonus for any one year is determined and paid in January of the following year. Debra's bonus for 1997 (received in January 1998) was $5,900, while her bonus for 1998 (received in January 1999) was $6,100. Debra's employer withheld Federal income taxes of $10,000 and the appropriate amount of FICA.

In 1998, Debra had a certificate of deposit with Bank of the Northwest that earned $1,400 in interest, and she received cash dividends of $1,150 from Mauve, Inc. stock she owns. She also received a check for $120 from Silver Insurance Company as an adjustment on the homeowners insurance premium she paid in 1997. The carrier had mistakenly overcharged Debra by $120.

Expenditures incurred by Debra in 1998 include the following:

Interest on home mortgage	$6,900
Property taxes on personal residence	2,600
Charitable contributions	1,450
Political contribution to reelect representative to Congress	200

Compute Debra's Federal income tax payable or refund due for 1998. Suggested software (if available): *TurboTax*.

53. George M. and Martha J. Jordan have no dependents and are both under age 65. George is a statutory employee of Consolidated Jobbers (business code is 2634), and his Social Security number is 582–99–4444. Martha is an executive with General Corporation, and her Social Security number is 241–88–6642. The Jordans live at 321 Oak Street, Lincoln, NV 89553. They both want to contribute to the Presidential Election Campaign Fund.

In 1997, George earned $49,000 in commissions. His employer withholds FICA but not Federal income taxes. George paid $10,000 in estimated taxes. Martha earned $62,000, from which $8,500 was withheld for Federal income taxes and the appropriate amount was withheld for FICA taxes. Neither George nor Martha received any expense reimbursements.

George uses his two-year-old car (purchased on January 3, 1995) on sales calls and keeps a log of all miles driven. In 1997, he drove 36,000 miles, 24,554 of them for business. He made several out-of-state sales trips, incurring transportation costs of $1,600, meals of $800, and lodging costs of $750. During the year, he also spent $1,400 taking customers to lunch.

Martha incurred the following expenses related to her work: taxi fares of $125, business lunches of $615, and a yearly commuter train ticket of $800. During the year, Martha received $1,200 in interest from the employees' credit union, $100,000 life insurance proceeds upon the death of her mother in December, and $500 in dividends from General Motors. She contributed $2,000 to her Individual Retirement Account. Neither George nor Martha is covered by an employee retirement plan. Martha gave a gift valued at $500 to the president of her firm upon his promotion to that position.

The Jordans had additional expenditures as follows:

Charitable contributions (cash)	$1,200
Medical and dental expenses	1,400
Real property taxes	1,200
Home mortgage interest	9,381
Tax return preparation fee	150

Part 1—Tax Computation

Compute the Jordans' Federal income tax payable or refund due, assuming they file a joint income tax return, for 1997. If they have overpaid, they want the amount refunded. You will need Form 1040, and Schedules A, B, and C. Suggested software (if available): *TurboTax*.

Part 2—Tax Planning

Martha and George ask your help in deciding what to do with the $100,000 of life insurance proceeds Martha received in 1997. They are considering two conservative investment alternatives:

- Invest in 8% long-term U.S. bonds.

- Invest in 6.5% municipal bonds.

    a. Calculate the best alternative for next year. Assume that Martha and George will have the same income and deductions in 1998, except for the income from the investment they choose. In computing the tax, use the tax rate schedules for 1998.

    b. What other factors should the Jordans take into account?

    c. Write a memo to the Jordans, explaining their alternatives.

Suggested software (if available): *TurboTax*.

Research Problems for this chapter appear at the end of Chapter 28.

TEAM PROJECT: ARTHUR ANDERSEN TAX CHALLENGE CASES

For more information on the Arthur Andersen Tax Challenge Cases, refer to Chapter 1, page 1–37.

Information related to tax issues and problems that are discussed in this chapter may be found in the

Day and Ball case on pages 1, 18, and 21
Fence case on pages 39, 41, 57, and 59

Read and analyze the case you have been assigned and *identify* any issues and problems that are related to material covered in this chapter. If the information provided in the case is complete, prepare answers for this part of the case at this time. If you need information that is contained in the later parts of the case, write a memo summarizing the questions or problems so you can prepare a complete answer at a later date.

DEDUCTIONS AND LOSSES: CERTAIN ITEMIZED DEDUCTIONS

LEARNING OBJECTIVES

After completing Chapter 9, you should be able to:

1. Distinguish between deductible and nondeductible personal expenses.

2. Define medical expenses and compute the medical expense deduction.

3. Contrast deductible taxes and nondeductible fees, licenses, etc.

4. Understand the Federal tax treatment of state and local income taxes.

5. Distinguish between deductible and nondeductible interest and apply the appropriate limitations to deductible interest.

6. Understand charitable contributions and their related measurement problems and percentage limitations.

7. List the business and personal expenditures that are deductible either as miscellaneous itemized deductions or as other itemized deductions.

8. Recognize the limitation on certain itemized deductions applicable to high-income taxpayers.

9. Identify tax planning procedures that can maximize the benefit of itemized deductions.

GENERAL CLASSIFICATION OF EXPENSES

1 LEARNING OBJECTIVE
Distinguish between deductible and nondeductible personal expenses.

As a general rule, the deduction of personal expenditures is disallowed by § 262 of the Code. However, Congress has chosen to allow certain personal expenditures to be deducted as itemized deductions. Personal expenditures that are deductible as itemized deductions include medical expenses, certain taxes, mortgage interest, investment interest, and charitable contributions. These expenditures and other personal expenditures that are allowed as itemized deductions are covered in this chapter. Any personal expenditures not specifically allowed as itemized deductions by the tax law are nondeductible.

Allowable itemized deductions are deductible *from* AGI in arriving at taxable income if the taxpayer elects to itemize. The election to itemize is appropriate when total itemized deductions exceed the standard deduction based on the taxpayer's filing status (refer to Chapter 2).[1]

MEDICAL EXPENSES

GENERAL REQUIREMENTS

2 LEARNING OBJECTIVE
Define medical expenses and compute the medical expense deduction.

Medical expenses paid for the care of the taxpayer, spouse, and dependents are allowed as an itemized deduction to the extent the expenses are not reimbursed. The **medical expense** deduction is limited to the amount by which such expenses *exceed* 7.5 percent of the taxpayer's AGI.

---

[1]The total standard deduction is the sum of the basic standard deduction and the additional standard deduction (refer to Chapter 2).

Chapter 2 also describes the situations in which a taxpayer is not eligible for the standard deduction.

AVERAGE ITEMIZED DEDUCTIONS

Are your itemized deductions close to average for your income level? Actually, if you're a typical taxpayer, you take the standard deduction instead of itemizing. Approximately 70 percent of individual taxpayers take the standard deduction each year.

The IRS recently released statistics on the approximately 30 percent of individual taxpayers who did itemize in 1995—a year that saw itemized deductions rise nearly 10 percent over 1994. Statistics for the most popular deductions are listed in the following table. The table omits medical expenses because few taxpayers (approximately 5 percent) have medical expenses in excess of the 7.5 percent floor. Similarly, casualty losses (subject to a 10 percent floor) and miscellaneous itemized deductions (subject to a 2 percent floor) are omitted. For comparison, the standard deduction in 1995 was $3,900 for single taxpayers, $6,550 for married taxpayers filing jointly, and $5,750 for heads of household.

AGI	Taxes	Contributions	Interest	Total
$ 15,000–29,999	$ 2,270	$ 1,338	$ 5,442	$ 9,050
30,000–49,999	3,112	1,465	5,715	10,292
50,000–74,999	4,429	1,768	6,587	12,784
75,000–99,999	6,171	2,286	8,063	16,520
100,000–199,999	9,758	3,433	11,107	24,298
200,000+	36,076	16,882	25,046	78,004

These statistics reveal some interesting aspects of the U.S. lifestyle. For one thing, taxpayers at all income levels—even those with AGI of more than $200,000—owe money. For another, as AGI increases, the percentage given to charity decreases. Those with AGI of $15,000 to $29,999 contribute 5.88 percent of their median income; least generous are taxpayers with AGI of $100,000 to $199,999, who contribute only 2.29 percent of their median income.

Finally, consider what taxpayers have left after meeting the expenses reflected in the table. A single taxpayer with income of $22,500, for example, would have only $13,450 left after paying typical itemized deductions for that income level ($22,500 – $9,050 itemized deductions). After paying $1,646 of this amount as Federal income taxes, the taxpayer would have $11,804 left for other expenses.

SOURCE: Information from "Tax Report: Itemized Deductions Surged on 1995 Returns," *Wall Street Journal*, July 16, 1997, p. A1.

EXAMPLE 1

During the year, Iris had medical expenses of $4,800, of which $1,000 was reimbursed by her insurance company. If her AGI for the year is $40,000, the itemized deduction for medical expenses is limited to $800 [$4,800 – $1,000 = $3,800 – (7.5% × $40,000)]. ▼

MEDICAL EXPENSES DEFINED

The term *medical care* includes expenditures incurred for the "diagnosis, cure, mitigation, treatment, or prevention of disease, or for the purpose of affecting any

▼ **EXHIBIT 9–1**
Examples of Deductible and
Nondeductible Medical
Expenses

Deductible	Nondeductible
Medical (including dental, mental, and hospital) care	Funeral, burial, or cremation expenses
Prescription drugs	Nonprescription drugs (except insulin)
Special equipment	Bottled water
Wheelchairs	Toiletries, cosmetics
Crutches	Diaper service, maternity clothes
Artificial limbs	Programs for the *general* improvement of health
Eyeglasses (including contact lenses)	Weight reduction
Hearing aids	Health spas
Transportation for medical care	Stop-smoking clinic
Medical and hospital insurance premiums	Social activities (e.g., dancing and swimming lessons)
Cost of alcohol and drug rehabilitation	Unnecessary cosmetic surgery

structure or function of the body."[2] A *partial* list of deductible and nondeductible medical items appears in Exhibit 9–1.

A medical expense does not have to relate to a particular ailment to be deductible. Since the definition of medical care is broad enough to cover preventive measures, the cost of periodic physical and dental exams qualifies even for a taxpayer in good health.

Amounts paid for unnecessary *cosmetic surgery* are not deductible medical expenses. However, if cosmetic surgery is deemed necessary, it is deductible as a medical expense. Cosmetic surgery is necessary when it ameliorates (1) a deformity arising from a congenital abnormality, (2) a personal injury, or (3) a disfiguring disease.

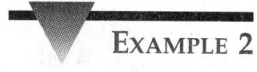

EXAMPLE 2   Art, a calendar year taxpayer, paid $11,000 to a plastic surgeon for a face lift. Art, age 75, merely wanted to improve his appearance. The $11,000 does not qualify as a medical expense since the surgery was unnecessary. ▼

EXAMPLE 3   As a result of a serious automobile accident, Marge's face is disfigured. The cost of restorative cosmetic surgery is deductible as a medical expense. ▼

ETHICAL CONSIDERATIONS

Necessary or Unnecessary Cosmetic Surgery?

Steven, age 37, had his nose broken in a high school football game 20 years ago. As a result, his nose is slightly crooked. In addition, he thinks his nose is too long. In March, he scheduled an appointment with Dr. Keane to discuss surgery to improve his appearance, primarily to shorten his nose. Dr. Keane presented him with computer simulations showing several different possibilities for the size and shape of his nose. Steven selected a nose that was much shorter and completely straight.

---

[2]§ 213(d)(1)(A).

Steven called his CPA to ask if the cost of the surgery would be deductible. His CPA told him that unnecessary cosmetic surgery is not deductible, but hinted that most doctors can come up with a medical reason that would make such surgery deductible.

Steven discussed the tax issue with Dr. Keane on his next visit, and the doctor indicated that the surgery would be necessary to repair Steven's deviated septum, which was caused by his football injury. Dr. Keane said that he would be willing to write a letter for Steven's files, stating that the surgery was medically necessary. Is Steven justified in taking a deduction for the cosmetic surgery?

The cost of care in a *nursing home or home for the aged*, including meals and lodging, can be included in deductible medical expenses if the primary reason for being in the home is to get medical care. If the primary reason for being there is personal, any costs for medical or nursing care can be included in deductible medical expenses, but the cost of meals and lodging must be excluded.[3]

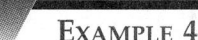

EXAMPLE 4   Norman has a chronic heart ailment. His family decides to place Norman in a nursing home equipped to provide medical and nursing care facilities. Total nursing home expenses amount to $15,000 per year. Of this amount, $4,500 is directly attributable to medical and nursing care. Since Norman is in need of significant medical and nursing care and is placed in the facility primarily for this purpose, all $15,000 of the nursing home costs are deductible (subject to the 7.5% floor). ▼

Tuition expenses of a dependent at a special school may be deductible as a medical expense. The cost of medical care can include the expenses of a special school for a mentally or physically handicapped individual. The deduction is allowed if a principal reason for sending the individual to the school is the school's special resources for alleviating the infirmities. In this case, the cost of meals and lodging, in addition to the tuition, is a proper medical expense deduction.[4]

EXAMPLE 5   Jason's daughter Marcia attended public school through the seventh grade. Because Marcia was a poor student, she was examined by a psychiatrist who diagnosed an organic problem that created a learning disability. Upon the recommendation of the psychiatrist, Marcia is enrolled in a private school so that she can receive individual attention. The school has no special program for students with learning disabilities and does not provide special medical treatment. The expense related to Marcia's attendance is not deductible as a medical expense. The cost of any psychiatric care, however, qualifies as a medical expense. ▼

Example 5 shows that the recommendation of a physician does not automatically make the expenditure deductible.

CAPITAL EXPENDITURES FOR MEDICAL PURPOSES

Some examples of *capital expenditures* for medical purposes are swimming pools if the taxpayer does not have access to a neighborhood pool and air conditioners if they do not become permanent improvements (e.g., window units).[5] Other examples

---

[3]Reg. § 1.213–1(e)(1)(v).
[4]*Donald R. Pfeifer*, 37 TCM 816, T.C.Memo. 1978–189. Also see Rev.Rul. 78–340, 1978–2 C.B. 124.

[5]Rev.Rul. 55–261, 1955–1 C.B. 307, modified by Rev.Rul. 68–212, 1968–1 C.B. 91.

include dust elimination systems,[6] elevators,[7] and a room built to house an iron lung. These expenditures are medical in nature if they are incurred as a medical necessity upon the advice of a physician, the facility is used primarily by the patient alone, and the expense is reasonable.

Capital expenditures normally are adjustments to basis and are not deductible. However, both a capital expenditure for a permanent improvement and expenditures made for the operation or maintenance of the improvement may qualify as medical expenses. If a capital expenditure qualifies as a medical expense, the allowable cost is deductible in the year incurred. Although depreciation is required for most other capital expenditures, it is not required for capital expenditures for medical purposes.

A capital improvement that ordinarily would not have a medical purpose qualifies as a medical expense if it is directly related to prescribed medical care and is deductible to the extent that the expenditure *exceeds* the increase in value of the related property. Appraisal costs related to capital improvements are also deductible, but not as medical expenses. These costs are expenses incurred in the determination of the taxpayer's tax liability.[8]

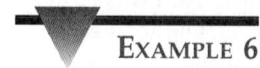

EXAMPLE 6

Fred is afflicted with heart disease. His physician advises him to install an elevator in his residence so he will not be required to climb the stairs. The cost of installing the elevator is $3,000, and the increase in the value of the residence is determined to be only $1,700. Therefore, $1,300 ($3,000 − $1,700) is deductible as a medical expense. Additional utility costs to operate the elevator and maintenance costs are deductible as medical expenses as long as the medical reason for the capital expenditure continues to exist. ▼

The full cost of certain home-related capital expenditures incurred to enable a *physically handicapped* individual to live independently and productively qualifies as a medical expense. Qualifying costs include expenditures for constructing entrance and exit ramps to the residence, widening hallways and doorways to accommodate wheelchairs, installing support bars and railings in bathrooms and other rooms, and adjusting electrical outlets and fixtures.[9] These expenditures are subject to the 7.5 percent floor only, and the increase in the home's value is deemed to be zero.

MEDICAL EXPENSES INCURRED FOR SPOUSE AND DEPENDENTS

In computing the medical expense deduction, a taxpayer may include medical expenses for a spouse and for a person who was a dependent at the time the expenses were paid or incurred. Of the five requirements that normally apply in determining dependency status,[10] neither the gross income nor the joint return test applies in determining dependency status for medical expense deduction purposes.

EXAMPLE 7

Ernie (age 22) is married and a full-time student at a university. During the year, Ernie incurred medical expenses that were paid by Matilda (Ernie's mother). She provided more than half of Ernie's support for the year. Even if Ernie files a joint return with his wife, Matilda may claim the medical expenses she paid for him. Matilda would combine Ernie's expenses with her own before applying the 7.5% floor. ▼

---

[6]*F. S. Delp*, 30 T.C. 1230 (1958).
[7]*Riach v. Frank*, 62–1 USTC ¶9419, 9 AFTR2d 1263, 302 F.2d 374 (CA–9, 1962).
[8]§ 212(3).

[9]For a complete list of the items that qualify, see Rev.Rul. 87–106, 1987–2 C.B. 67.
[10]Refer to Chapter 2 for discussion of these requirements.

For *divorced persons* with children, a special rule applies to the noncustodial parent. The noncustodial parent may claim any medical expenses he or she pays even though the custodial parent claims the children as dependents. This rule applies if the dependency exemptions could have been shifted to the noncustodial parent by the custodial parent's waiver (refer to Chapter 2).

EXAMPLE 8

Irv and Joan are divorced in 1997, and Joan is awarded custody of their child, Keith. During 1998, Irv makes the following payments to Joan: $3,600 for child support and $2,500 for Keith's medical bills. Together, Irv and Joan provide more than half of Keith's support. Even though Joan claims Keith as a dependent, Irv can combine the $2,500 of medical expenses that he pays for Keith with his own. ▼

TRANSPORTATION, MEAL, AND LODGING EXPENSES FOR MEDICAL TREATMENT

Payments for transportation to and from a point of treatment for medical care are deductible as medical expenses (subject to the 7.5 percent floor). Transportation expenses for medical care include bus, taxi, train, or plane fare, charges for ambulance service, and out-of-pocket expenses for the use of an automobile. A mileage allowance of ten cents per mile[11] may be used instead of actual out-of-pocket automobile expenses. Whether the taxpayer chooses to claim out-of-pocket automobile expenses or the ten cents per mile automatic mileage option, related parking fees and tolls can also be deducted. The cost of meals while en route to obtain medical care is not deductible.

A deduction is also allowed for the transportation expenses of a parent who must accompany a child who is receiving medical care or for a nurse or other person giving assistance to a person who is traveling to get medical care and cannot travel alone.

A deduction is allowed for lodging while away from home for medical expenses if the following requirements are met:[12]

- The lodging is primarily for and essential to medical care.
- Medical care is provided by a doctor in a licensed hospital or a similar medical facility (e.g., a clinic).
- The lodging is not lavish or extravagant under the circumstances.
- There is no significant element of personal pleasure, recreation, or vacation in the travel away from home.

The deduction for lodging expenses included as medical expenses cannot exceed $50 *per* night for *each* person. The deduction is allowed not only for the patient but also for a person who must travel with the patient (e.g., a parent traveling with a child who is receiving medical care).

EXAMPLE 9

Herman, a resident of Winchester, Kentucky, is advised by his family physician that Martha, Herman's dependent and disabled mother, needs specialized treatment for her heart condition. Consequently, Herman and Martha fly to Cleveland, Ohio, where Martha receives the therapy at a heart clinic on an out-patient basis. Expenses in connection with the trip are as follows:

Round trip airfare ($250 each)	$500
Lodging in Cleveland for two nights ($60 each per night)	240

---

[11]This amount is adjusted periodically.   [12]§ 213(d)(2).

Herman's medical expense deduction for transportation is $500, and his medical expense deduction for lodging is $200 ($50 per night per person). Because Martha is disabled, it is assumed that his accompanying her is justified. ▼

No deduction is allowed for the cost of meals unless they are part of the medical care and are furnished at a medical facility. When allowable, such meals are not subject to the 50 percent limit.

AMOUNTS PAID FOR MEDICAL INSURANCE PREMIUMS

Medical insurance premiums are included with other medical expenses subject to the 7.5 percent floor. Premiums paid by the taxpayer under a group plan or an individual plan are included as medical expenses. If an employer pays all or part of the taxpayer's medical insurance premiums, the amount paid by the employer is not included in gross income by the employee. Likewise, the premium is not included in the employee's medical expenses.

If a taxpayer is *self-employed*, 45 percent[13] of insurance premiums paid for medical coverage in 1998 is deductible as a *business* expense (*for* AGI). Any excess can be treated as a *medical* expense. The deduction *for* AGI is allowed for premiums paid on behalf of the taxpayer, the taxpayer's spouse, and dependents of the taxpayer. The deduction is not allowed to any taxpayer who is eligible to participate in a subsidized health plan maintained by any employer of the taxpayer or of the taxpayer's spouse. Premiums paid for medical insurance coverage of *employees* are deductible as business expenses.

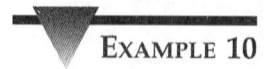

EXAMPLE 10

Ellen, a sole proprietor of a restaurant, has two dependent children. During 1998, she paid health insurance premiums of $1,800 for her own coverage and $1,000 for coverage of her two children. Ellen can deduct $1,260 ($2,800 × 45%) as a business deduction (for AGI) in computing net income from her business. She can include the remaining $1,540 ($2,800 − $1,260) as a medical expense (subject to the 7.5% floor) in computing itemized deductions. ▼

YEAR OF DEDUCTION

Regardless of a taxpayer's method of accounting, medical expenses are deductible only in the year *paid*. In effect, this places all individual taxpayers on a cash basis as far as the medical expense deduction is concerned. One exception, however, is allowed for deceased taxpayers. If the medical expenses are paid within one year from the day following the day of death, they can be treated as being paid at the time they were *incurred*. Thus, such expenses may be reported on the final income tax return of the decedent or on earlier returns if incurred before the year of death.

No current deduction is allowed for payment of medical care to be rendered in the future unless the taxpayer is under an obligation to make the payment.[14] Whether an obligation to make the payment exists depends upon the policy of the physician or the institution furnishing the medical care.

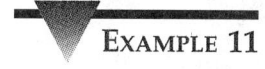

EXAMPLE 11

Upon the recommendation of his regular dentist, in late December 1998 Gary consults Dr. Smith, a prosthodontist, who specializes in crown and bridge work. Dr. Smith tells Gary that he can do the restorative work for $12,000. To cover his lab bill, however, Dr. Smith requires that 40% of this amount be prepaid. Accordingly, Gary pays $4,800 in December

---

[13]§ 162(l). The rate will be 45% in tax years 1998 and 1999, 50% in 2000 and 2001, 60% in 2002, 80% in 2003 through 2005, 90% for 2006, and 100% in 2007 and thereafter. The rate was 40% in 1997.

[14]*Robert S. Basset*, 26 T.C. 619 (1956).

1998. The balance of $7,200 is paid when the work is completed in July 1999. Under these circumstances, the qualifying medical expenses are $4,800 for 1998 and $7,200 in 1999. The result would be the same even if Gary prepaid the full $12,000 in 1998. ▼

REIMBURSEMENTS

If medical expenses are reimbursed in the same year as paid, no problem arises. The reimbursement merely reduces the amount that would otherwise qualify for the medical expense deduction. But what happens if the reimbursement occurs in a later year than the expenditure? In computing casualty losses, any reasonable prospect of recovery must be considered (refer to Chapter 6). For medical expenses, however, any expected reimbursement is disregarded in measuring the amount of the deduction. Instead, the reimbursement is accounted for separately in the year in which it occurs.

Under the *tax benefit rule*, a taxpayer who receives an insurance reimbursement for medical expenses deducted in a previous year might have to include the reimbursement in gross income in the year of receipt. However, a taxpayer who did not itemize deductions in the year the expenses were paid did not receive a tax benefit and is *not* required to include a reimbursement in gross income.

The tax benefit rule applies to reimbursements if the taxpayer itemized deductions in the previous year. In this case, the taxpayer may be required to report some or all of the medical expense reimbursement in income in the year the reimbursement is received. Under the tax benefit rule, the taxpayer must include the reimbursement in income up to the amount of the deductions that decreased taxable income in the earlier year.

EXAMPLE 12

Homer had AGI of $20,000 for 1998. He was injured in a car accident and paid $1,300 for hospital expenses and $700 for doctor bills. Homer also incurred medical expenses of $600 for his dependent child. In 1999, Homer was reimbursed $650 by his insurance company for the medical expenses attributable to the car accident. His deduction for medical expenses in 1998 is computed as follows:

Hospitalization	$ 1,300
Bills for doctor's services	700
Medical expenses for dependent	600
Total	$ 2,600
Less: 7.5% of $20,000	(1,500)
Medical expense deduction (assuming Homer itemizes his deductions)	$ 1,100

Assume that Homer would have elected to itemize his deductions even if he had no medical expenses in 1998. If the reimbursement for medical care had occurred in 1998, the medical expense deduction would have been only $450 [$2,600 (total medical expenses) – $650 (reimbursement) – $1,500 (floor)], and Homer would have paid more income tax.

Since the reimbursement was made in a subsequent year, Homer would include $650 in gross income for 1999. If Homer had not itemized in 1998, he would not include the $650 reimbursement in 1999 gross income because he would have received no tax benefit in 1998. ▼

MEDICAL SAVINGS ACCOUNTS

Certain employees and self-employed taxpayers may deduct contributions to Medical Savings Accounts (MSAs). MSAs, which may be used in connection with *high-deductible* health insurance, can be used to accumulate funds for the payment of health care expenses. Individuals who contribute to MSAs may deduct the contributions as deductions *for* AGI. Individuals whose employers contribute to MSAs may exclude the contributions from gross income. Earnings on MSAs are not included in the gross income of the current year. MSA distributions that are used to pay for amounts not covered by a high-deductible plan are not subject to tax. However, distributions used for purposes other than the payment of medical expenses are taxable and are subject to an additional 15 percent penalty if made before age 65, death, or disability.

MSAs can be established by employers with 50 or fewer employees, self-employed individuals, and individuals without insurance coverage. High-deductible policies are those with deductibles between $1,500 and $2,250 for individuals (between $3,000 and $4,500 for families). The deduction is limited to 65 percent of the policy deductible for individuals (75 percent for families). MSAs are available on a four-year pilot basis, and eligibility is limited to 750,000 MSAs. After the four-year pilot period is over, Congress will decide whether to retain the MSA provisions and extend eligibility.

▼ TAXES

3 ▼ LEARNING OBJECTIVE
Contrast deductible taxes and nondeductible fees, licenses, etc.

A deduction is allowed for certain state and local taxes paid or accrued by a taxpayer.[15] The deduction was created to relieve the burden of multiple taxes upon the same source of revenue.

DEDUCTIBILITY AS A TAX

A distinction must be made between a tax and a fee, since fees are not deductible unless incurred as an ordinary and necessary business expense or as an expense in the production of income. The IRS has defined a tax as follows:

> A tax is an enforced contribution exacted pursuant to legislative authority in the exercise of taxing power, and imposed and collected for the purpose of raising revenue to be used for public or governmental purposes, and not as payment for some special privilege granted or service rendered. Taxes are, therefore, distinguished from various other contributions and charges imposed for particular purposes under particular powers or functions of the government. In view of such distinctions, the question whether a particular contribution or charge is to be regarded as a tax depends upon its real nature.[16]

Accordingly, fees for dog licenses, automobile inspection, automobile titles and registration, hunting and fishing licenses, bridge and highway tolls, drivers' licenses, parking meter deposits, postage, etc., are not deductible if personal in nature. These items, however, could be deductible if incurred as a business expense or for the production of income. Deductible and nondeductible taxes are summarized in Exhibit 9–2.[17]

PROPERTY TAXES

State, local, and foreign taxes on real property are generally deductible only by the person upon whom the tax is imposed. Deductible personal property

---

[15] § 164.
[16] Rev.Rul. 57–345, 1957–2 C.B. 132, and Rev.Rul. 70–622, 1970–2 C.B. 41.

[17] Most deductible taxes are listed in § 164, while the nondeductible items are included in § 275.

▼ **EXHIBIT 9–2**
Deductible and Nondeductible Taxes

Deductible	Nondeductible
State, local, and foreign real property taxes	Federal income taxes
	FICA taxes imposed on employees
State and local personal property taxes	Employer FICA taxes paid on domestic household workers
State, local, and foreign income taxes	Estate, inheritance, and gift taxes
	General sales taxes
The environmental tax	Federal, state, and local excise taxes (e.g., gasoline, tobacco, spirits)
	Foreign income taxes if the taxpayer chooses the foreign tax credit option
	Taxes on real property to the extent such taxes are to be apportioned and treated as imposed on another taxpayer

taxes must be *ad valorem* (assessed in relation to the value of the property). Therefore, a motor vehicle tax based on weight, model, year, and horsepower is not an ad valorem tax. However, a tax based on value and other criteria may qualify in part.

EXAMPLE 13

A state imposes a motor vehicle registration tax on 4% of the value of the vehicle plus 40 cents per hundredweight. Belle, a resident of the state, owns a car having a value of $4,000 and weighing 3,000 pounds. Belle pays an annual registration fee of $172. Of this amount, $160 (4% of $4,000) is deductible as a personal property tax. The remaining $12, based on the weight of the car, is not deductible. ▼

Assessments for Local Benefits.   As a general rule, real property taxes do not include taxes assessed for local benefits since such assessments tend to increase the value of the property (e.g., special assessments for streets, sidewalks, curbing, and other similar improvements). A taxpayer was denied a deduction for the cost of a new sidewalk (relative to a personal residence), even though the construction was required by the city and the sidewalk may have provided an incidental benefit to the public welfare.[18] Such assessments are added to the adjusted basis of the taxpayer's property.

Apportionment of Real Property Taxes between Seller and Purchaser.
Real estate taxes for the entire year are apportioned between the buyer and seller on the basis of the number of days the property was held by each during the real property tax year. This apportionment is required whether the tax is paid by the buyer or the seller or is prorated according to the purchase agreement. It is the apportionment that determines who is entitled to deduct the real estate taxes in the year of sale. In making the apportionment, the assessment date and the lien date are disregarded. The date of sale counts as a day the property is owned by the buyer.

---

[18]*Erie H. Rose,* 31 TCM 142, T.C. Memo. 1972–39; Reg. § 1.164–4(a).

EXAMPLE 14

A county's real property tax year runs from April 1 to March 31. Susan, the owner on April 1, 1998, of real property located in the county, sells the real property to Bob on June 30, 1998. Bob owns the real property from June 30, 1998, through March 31, 1999. The tax for the real property tax year April 1, 1998, through March 31, 1999, is $730. The portion of the real property tax treated as imposed upon Susan, the seller, is $180 [(90/365) × $730, April 1 through June 29, 1998], and $550 [(275/365) × $730, June 30, 1998, through March 31, 1999] of the tax is treated as imposed upon Bob, the purchaser. ▼

If the actual real estate taxes are not prorated between the buyer and seller as part of the purchase agreement, adjustments are required. The adjustments are necessary to determine the amount realized by the seller and the adjusted basis of the property to the buyer. If the buyer pays the entire amount of the tax, he or she has, in effect, paid the seller's portion of the real estate tax and has therefore paid more for the property than the actual purchase price. Thus, the amount of real estate tax that is apportioned to the seller (for Federal income tax purposes) and paid by the buyer is added to the buyer's adjusted basis. The seller must increase the amount realized on the sale by the same amount.

EXAMPLE 15

Seth sells real estate on October 3, 1998, for $50,000. The buyer, Wilma, pays the real estate taxes of $1,095 for the 1998 calendar year, which is the real estate property tax year. Of the real estate taxes, $825 (for 275 days) is apportioned to and is deductible by the seller, Seth, and $270 (for 90 days) of the taxes is deductible by Wilma. The buyer has, in effect, paid Seth's real estate taxes of $825 and has therefore paid $50,825 for the property. Wilma's basis is increased to $50,825, and the amount realized by Seth from the sale is increased to $50,825. ▼

The opposite result occurs if the seller (rather than the buyer) pays the real estate taxes. In this case, the seller reduces the amount realized from the sale by the amount that has been apportioned to the buyer. The buyer is required to reduce his or her adjusted basis by a corresponding amount.

EXAMPLE 16

Ruth sells real estate to Butch for $50,000 on October 3, 1998. While Ruth held the property, she paid the real estate taxes of $1,095 for the calendar year, which is the real estate property tax year. Although Ruth paid the entire $1,095 of real estate taxes, $270 of that amount is apportioned to Butch and is therefore deductible by him. The effect is that the buyer, Butch, has paid only $49,730 for the property. The amount realized by Ruth, the seller, is reduced by $270, and Butch reduces his basis in the property to $49,730. ▼

STATE AND LOCAL INCOME TAXES

4   **LEARNING OBJECTIVE**
Understand the Federal tax treatment of state and local income taxes.

The position of the IRS is that state and local income taxes imposed upon an individual are deductible only as itemized deductions, even if the taxpayer's sole source of income is from a business, rents, or royalties.

Cash basis taxpayers are entitled to deduct state income taxes withheld by the employer in the year the taxes are withheld. In addition, estimated state income tax payments are deductible in the year the payment is made by cash basis taxpayers even if the payments relate to a prior or subsequent year.[19] If the taxpayer overpays state income taxes because of excessive withholdings or estimated tax payments, the refund received is included in gross income of the following year to the extent that the deduction reduced the tax liability in the prior year.

---

[19]Rev.Rul. 71–190, 1971–1 C.B. 70. See also Rev.Rul. 82–208, 1982–2 C.B. 58, where a deduction is not allowed when the taxpayer cannot, in good faith, reasonably determine that there is additional state income tax liability.

TAX IN THE NEWS

WORKING TO PAY TAXES

Although many exclusions, deductions, and other tax breaks are available, Americans still spend a significant part of each working day working to pay Federal, state, and local taxes. According to a Tax Foundation study, the average American worked two hours and 49 minutes of each eight-hour day to pay taxes in 1997. This is a new record, up one minute from 1996. The trend is disturbing. The comparable time in 1930 was 58 minutes.

SOURCE: "Tax Report: Americans Must Work Even Longer This Year to Pay Their Taxes," *Wall Street Journal*, April 4, 1997, p. A1.

EXAMPLE 17

Leona, a cash basis, unmarried taxpayer, had $800 of state income tax withheld during 1998. Additionally in 1998, Leona paid $100 that was due when she filed her 1997 state income tax return and made estimated payments of $300 on her 1998 state income tax. When Leona files her 1998 Federal income tax return in April 1999, she elects to itemize deductions, which amount to $5,500, including the $1,200 of state income tax payments and withholdings, all of which reduce her tax liability.

As a result of overpaying her 1998 state income tax, Leona receives a refund of $200 early in 1999. She will include this amount in her 1999 gross income in computing her Federal income tax. It does not matter whether Leona received a check from the state for $200 or applied the $200 toward her 1999 state income tax. ▼

INTEREST

5 LEARNING OBJECTIVE
Distinguish between deductible and nondeductible interest and apply the appropriate limitations to deductible interest.

A deduction for interest has been allowed since the income tax law was enacted in 1913. Despite its long history of congressional acceptance, the interest deduction has been one of the most controversial areas in the tax law. The controversy centered around the propriety of allowing the deduction of interest charges for the purchase of consumer goods and services and interest on borrowings used to acquire investments (investment interest). Personal (consumer) interest is not deductible. This includes credit card interest, interest on car loans, and any other interest that is not investment interest, home mortgage interest, or business interest. **Investment interest** and **qualified residence** (home mortgage) **interest** continue to be deductible, subject to limits discussed on the following pages.

ALLOWED AND DISALLOWED ITEMS

The Supreme Court has defined *interest* as compensation for the use or forbearance of money.[20] The general rule permits a deduction for interest paid or accrued within the taxable year on indebtedness.[21]

Investment Interest.   Taxpayers frequently borrow funds that they use to acquire investment assets. When the interest expense is large relative to the income from the investments, substantial tax benefits could result. Congress has therefore

---

[20]*Old Colony Railroad Co. v. Comm.*, 3 USTC ¶880, 10 AFTR 786, 52 S.Ct. 211 (USSC, 1932).

[21]§ 163(a).

limited the deductibility of interest on funds borrowed for the purpose of purchasing or continuing to hold investment property. Investment interest expense is *now* limited to net investment income for the year.[22]

Investment income is gross income from interest, dividends, annuities, and royalties not derived in the ordinary course of a trade or business. Income from a passive activity and income from a real estate activity in which the taxpayer actively participates are not included in investment income (see Chapter 10).

Net capital gain attributable to the disposition of property producing the types of income just enumerated or from property held for investment purposes is *not* included in investment income unless the taxpayer elects to do so.

EXAMPLE 18

Terry incurred $13,000 of interest expense related to her investments during the year. Her investment income included $4,000 of interest, $2,000 of dividends, and a $5,000 net capital gain on the sale of securities. Her investment income for purposes of computing the investment income limitation is $6,000 ($4,000 interest + $2,000 dividends). ▼

Taxpayers may *elect* to include the capital gains as investment income, but only if they agree to reduce capital gains qualifying for the alternative tax computation for net capital gain (see Chapter 13) by an equivalent amount.

Net investment income is the excess of investment income over investment expenses. Investment expenses are those deductible expenses directly connected with the production of investment income. Investment expenses *do not* include interest expense. When investment expenses fall into the category of miscellaneous itemized deductions that are subject to the 2 percent-of-AGI floor, some may not enter into the calculation of net investment income because of the floor.

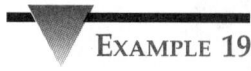

EXAMPLE 19

Gina has AGI of $80,000, which includes dividends and interest income of $18,000. Besides investment interest expense, she paid $3,000 of city ad valorem property tax on stocks and bonds and had the following miscellaneous itemized expenses:

Safe deposit box rental (to hold investment securities)	$ 120
Investment counsel fee	1,200
Unreimbursed business travel	850
Uniforms	600

Before Gina can determine her investment expenses for purposes of calculating net investment income, those miscellaneous expenses that are not investment expenses are disallowed before any investment expenses are disallowed under the 2%-of-AGI floor. This is accomplished by selecting the *lesser* of the following:

1. The amount of investment expenses included in the total of miscellaneous itemized deductions subject to the 2%-of-AGI floor.
2. The amount of miscellaneous expenses deductible after the 2%-of-AGI rule is applied.

The amount under item 1 is $1,320 [$120 (safe deposit box rental) + $1,200 (investment counsel fee)]. The item 2 amount is $1,170 [$2,770 (total of miscellaneous expenses) – $1,600 (2% of $80,000 AGI)].

Then, Gina's investment expenses are calculated as follows:

Deductible miscellaneous deductions investment expense (the lesser of item 1 or item 2)	$1,170
Plus: Ad valorem tax on investment property	3,000
Total investment expenses	$4,170

---

[22]§ 63(d).

Gina's net investment income is $13,830 ($18,000 investment income − $4,170 investment expenses). ▼

After net investment income is determined, deductible investment interest expense can be calculated.

EXAMPLE 20

Adam is a single person employed by a law firm. His investment activities for the year are as follows:

Net investment income	$30,000
Investment interest expense	44,000

Adam's investment interest deduction is $30,000. ▼

The amount of investment interest disallowed is carried over to future years. In Example 20, therefore, the amount that is carried over to the following year is $14,000 ($44,000 investment interest expense − $30,000 allowed). No limit is placed on the length of the carryover period. The investment interest expense deduction is determined by completing Form 4952 (see Appendix B).

Qualified Residence Interest.   *Qualified residence interest* is interest paid or accrued during the taxable year on indebtedness (subject to limitations) *secured* by any property that is a qualified residence of the taxpayer. Qualified residence interest falls into two categories: (1) interest on acquisition indebtedness and (2) interest on home equity loans. Before discussing each of these categories, however, the term qualified residence must be defined.

A *qualified residence* includes the taxpayer's principal residence and one other residence of the taxpayer or spouse. The *principal residence* is one that meets the requirement for nonrecognition of gain upon sale under § 121 (see Chapter 12). The *one other residence,* or second residence, refers to one that is used as a residence if not rented or, if rented, meets the requirements for a personal residence under the rental of vacation home rules (refer to Chapter 5). A taxpayer who has more than one second residence can make the selection each year of which one is the qualified second residence. A residence includes, in addition to a house in the ordinary sense, cooperative apartments, condominiums, and mobile homes and boats that have living quarters (sleeping accommodations and toilet and cooking facilities).

Although in most cases interest paid on a home mortgage would be fully deductible, there are limitations.[23] Interest paid or accrued during the tax year on aggregate **acquisition indebtedness** of $1 million or less ($500,000 for married persons filing separate returns) is deductible as qualified residence interest. Acquisition indebtedness refers to amounts incurred in acquiring, constructing, or substantially improving a qualified residence of the taxpayer.

Qualified residence interest also includes interest on **home equity loans.** These loans utilize the personal residence of the taxpayer as security. Because the funds from home equity loans can be used for personal purposes (e.g., auto purchases, medical expenses), what would otherwise have been nondeductible consumer interest becomes deductible qualified residence interest.

However, interest is deductible only on the portion of a home equity loan that does not exceed the *lesser of*:

---

[23]§ 163(h)(3).

- The fair market value of the residence, reduced by the acquisition indebtedness, *or*
- $100,000 ($50,000 for married persons filing separate returns).

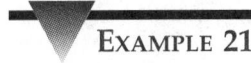

EXAMPLE 21

Larry owns a personal residence with a fair market value of $150,000 and an outstanding first mortgage of $120,000. Therefore, his equity in his home is $30,000 ($150,000 − $120,000). Larry issues a lien on the residence and in return borrows $15,000 to purchase a new family automobile. All interest on the $135,000 of debt is treated as qualified residence interest. ▼

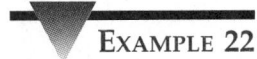

EXAMPLE 22

Leon and Pearl, married taxpayers, took out a mortgage on their home for $200,000 in 1983. In March of the current year, when the home had a fair market value of $400,000 and they owed $195,000 on the mortgage, Leon and Pearl took out a home equity loan for $120,000. They used the funds to purchase a boat to be used for recreational purposes. The boat, which does not have living quarters, does not qualify as a personal residence. On a joint return, Leon and Pearl can deduct all of the interest on the first mortgage since it is acquisition indebtedness. Of the $120,000 home equity loan, only the interest on the first $100,000 is deductible. The interest on the remaining $20,000 is not deductible because it exceeds the statutory ceiling of $100,000. ▼

Interest Paid for Services. Mortgage loan companies commonly charge a fee for finding, placing, or processing a mortgage loan. Such fees are often called **points** and are expressed as a percentage of the loan amount. Borrowers often have to pay points to obtain the necessary financing. To qualify as deductible interest, the points must be considered compensation to a lender solely for the use or forbearance of money. The points cannot be a form of service charge or payment for specific services if they are to qualify as deductible interest.[24]

Points must be capitalized and are amortized and deductible ratably over the life of the loan. A special exception permits the purchaser of a personal residence to deduct qualifying points in the year of payment.[25] The exception also covers points paid to obtain funds for home improvements.

EXAMPLE 23

During 1998, Thelma purchased a new residence for $130,000 and paid points of $2,600 to obtain mortgage financing. At Thelma's election, the $2,600 can be claimed as an interest deduction for tax year 1998. ▼

Points paid to *refinance* an existing home mortgage cannot be immediately expensed, but must be capitalized and amortized as interest expense over the life of the new loan.[26]

EXAMPLE 24

Sandra purchased her residence four years ago, obtaining a 30-year mortgage at an annual interest rate of 12%. In the current year, Sandra refinances the mortgage in order to reduce the interest rate to 9%. To obtain the refinancing, she had to pay points of $2,600. The $2,600 paid comes under the usual rule applicable to points. The $2,600 must be capitalized and amortized over the life of the mortgage. ▼

The rules governing the deductibility of points *paid by a seller* to help a buyer finance the purchase of the residence were changed in 1994.[27] Under prior rules, such points were not deductible by the buyer, but were treated by the seller as a reduction of the selling price of the property.

---

[24]Rev.Rul. 67–297, 1967–2 C.B. 87.
[25]§ 461(g)(2).

[26]Rev.Rul. 87–22, 1987–1 C.B. 146.
[27]Rev.Proc. 94–27, 1994–1 C.B. 613.

The IRS changed its position on this issue, retroactive to tax years beginning after December 31, 1990. In effect, points paid by the seller are treated as an adjustment to the price of the residence, and the buyer is treated as having used cash to pay the points that were paid by the seller. A buyer may deduct seller-paid points in the tax year in which they are paid if several conditions are met. Refer to Revenue Procedure 94–27 for a complete list of these conditions (see footnote 27 for citation).

Prepayment Penalty.   When a mortgage or loan is paid off in full in a lump sum before its term (early), the lending institution may require an additional payment of a certain percentage applied to the unpaid amount at the time of prepayment. This is known as a prepayment penalty and is considered to be interest (e.g., personal, qualified residence, investment) in the year paid. The general rules for deductibility of interest also apply to prepayment penalties.

Interest Paid to Related Parties.   Nothing prevents the deduction of interest paid to a related party as long as the payment actually took place and the interest meets the requirements for deductibility. Recall from Chapter 5 that a special rule for related taxpayers applies when the debtor uses the accrual basis and the related creditor is on the cash basis. If this rule is applicable, interest that has been accrued but not paid at the end of the debtor's tax year is not deductible until payment is made and the income is reportable by the cash basis recipient.

Tax-Exempt Securities.   The tax law provides that no deduction is allowed for interest on debt incurred to purchase or carry tax-exempt securities.[28] A major problem for the courts has been to determine what is meant by the words *to purchase or carry*. Refer to Chapter 5 for a detailed discussion of these issues.

RESTRICTIONS ON DEDUCTIBILITY AND TIMING CONSIDERATIONS

Taxpayer's Obligation.   Allowed interest is deductible if the related debt represents a bona fide obligation for which the taxpayer is liable.[29] Thus, a taxpayer may not deduct interest paid on behalf of another individual. For interest to be deductible, both the debtor and creditor must intend for the loan to be repaid. Intent of the parties can be especially crucial between related parties such as a shareholder and a closely held corporation. A shareholder may not deduct interest paid by the corporation on his or her behalf.[30] Likewise, a husband may not deduct interest paid on his wife's property if he files a separate return, except in the case of qualified residence interest. If both husband and wife consent in writing, either the husband or the wife may deduct the allowed interest on the principal residence and one other residence.

Time of Deduction.   Generally, interest must be paid to secure a deduction unless the taxpayer uses the accrual method of accounting. Under the accrual method, interest is deductible ratably over the life of the loan.

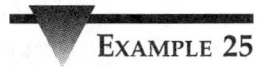
EXAMPLE 25

On November 1, 1998, Ramon borrows $1,000 to purchase appliances for a rental house. The loan is payable in 90 days at 12% interest. On the due date in January 1999, Ramon pays the $1,000 note and interest amounting to $30. Ramon can deduct the accrued portion

---

[28]§ 265(a)(2).
[29]*Arcade Realty Co.*, 35 T.C. 256 (1960).

[30]*Continental Trust Co.*, 7 B.T.A. 539 (1927).

▼

Concept Summary 9–1

Deductibility of Personal, Investment, and Mortgage Interest

Type	Deductible	Comments
Personal (consumer) interest	No	Includes any interest that is not home mortgage interest, investment interest, or business interest. Examples include car loans, credit cards, etc.
Investment interest (*not* related to rental or royalty property)	Yes	Itemized deduction; limited to net investment income for the year; disallowed interest can be carried over to future years.
Investment interest (related to rental or royalty property)	Yes	Deduction *for* AGI; limited to net investment income for the year; disallowed interest can be carried over to future years.
Qualified residence interest on acquisition indebtedness	Yes	Deductible as an itemized deduction; limited to indebtedness of $1 million.
Qualified residence interest on home equity indebtedness	Yes	Deductible as an itemized deduction; limited to indebtedness equal to lesser of $100,000 or FMV of residence minus acquisition indebtedness.

($\frac{2}{3} \times \$30 = \$20$) of the interest in 1998 only if he is an accrual basis taxpayer. Otherwise, the entire amount of interest ($30) is deductible in 1999. ▼

Prepaid Interest.   Accrual method reporting is imposed on cash basis taxpayers for interest prepayments that extend beyond the end of the taxable year.[31] Such payments must be allocated to the tax years to which the interest payments relate. These provisions are intended to prevent cash basis taxpayers from *manufacturing* tax deductions before the end of the year by prepaying interest.

CLASSIFICATION OF INTEREST EXPENSE

Whether interest is deductible *for* AGI or as an itemized deduction (*from*) depends on whether the indebtedness has a business, investment, or personal purpose. If the indebtedness is incurred in relation to a business (other than performing services as an employee) or for the production of rent or royalty income, the interest is deductible *for* AGI. If the indebtedness is incurred for personal use, such as qualified residence interest, any deduction allowed is reported on Schedule A of Form 1040 if the taxpayer elects to itemize. If the taxpayer is an employee who incurs debt in relation to his or her employment, the interest is considered to be personal, or consumer, interest. Business expenses appear on Schedule C of Form 1040, and expenses related to rents or royalties are reported on Schedule E.

If a taxpayer deposits money in a certificate of deposit (CD) that has a term of one year or less and the interest cannot be withdrawn without penalty, the full amount of the interest must still be included in income, even though part of the interest is forfeited due to an early withdrawal. However, the taxpayer will be allowed a deduction *for* AGI as to the forfeited amount.

---

[31]§ 461(g)(1).

CHARITABLE CONTRIBUTIONS

6 **LEARNING OBJECTIVE**
Understand charitable contributions and their related measurement problems and percentage limitations.

Individuals and corporations are allowed to deduct contributions made to qualified *domestic* organizations.[32] Contributions to qualified charitable organizations serve certain social welfare needs and thus relieve the government of the cost of providing these needed services to the community.

The **charitable contribution** provisions are among the most complex in the tax law. To determine the amount deductible as a charitable contribution, several important questions must be answered:

- What constitutes a charitable contribution?
- Was the contribution made to a qualified organization?
- When is the contribution deductible?
- What record-keeping and reporting requirements apply to charitable contributions?
- How is the value of donated property determined?
- What special rules apply to contributions of property that has increased in value?
- What percentage limitations apply to the charitable contribution deduction?

These questions are addressed in the sections that follow.

CRITERIA FOR A GIFT

A *charitable contribution* is defined as a gift made to a qualified organization.[33] The major elements needed to qualify a contribution as a gift are a donative intent, the absence of consideration, and acceptance by the donee. Consequently, the taxpayer has the burden of establishing that the transfer was made from motives of *disinterested generosity* as established by the courts.[34] This test is quite subjective and has led to problems of interpretation (refer to the discussion of gifts in Chapter 4).

Benefit Received Rule. When a donor derives a tangible benefit from a contribution, he or she cannot deduct the value of the benefit.

EXAMPLE 26 Ralph purchases a ticket at $100 for a special performance of the local symphony (a qualified charity). If the price of a ticket to a symphony concert is normally $35, Ralph is allowed only $65 as a charitable contribution. ▼

An exception to this benefit rule provides for the deduction of an automatic percentage of the amount paid for the right to purchase athletic tickets from colleges and universities.[35] Under this exception, 80 percent of the amount paid to or for the benefit of the institution qualifies as a charitable contribution deduction.

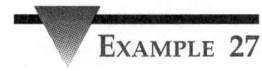
EXAMPLE 27 Janet donates $500 to State University's athletic department. The **payment** guarantees that she will have preferred seating on the 50-yard line. Subsequently, **Janet** buys four $35 game tickets. Under the exception to the benefit rule, she is allowed a $400 (80% of $500) charitable contribution deduction for the taxable year.

---

[32]§ 170.
[33]§ 170(c).
[34]*Comm. v. Duberstein*, 60–2 USTC ¶9515, 5 AFTR2d 1626, 80 S.Ct. 1190 (USSC, 1960).

[35]§ 170(l).

If, however, Janet's $500 donation includes four $35 tickets, that portion [$140 ($35 × 4)] and the remaining portion of $360 ($500 − $140) are treated as separate amounts. Thus, Janet is allowed a charitable contribution deduction of $288 (80% of $360). ▼

Contribution of Services.   No deduction is allowed for a contribution of one's services to a qualified charitable organization. However, unreimbursed expenses related to the services rendered may be deductible. For example, the cost of a uniform (without general utility) that is required to be worn while performing services may be deductible, as are certain out-of-pocket transportation costs incurred for the benefit of the charity. In lieu of these out-of-pocket costs for an automobile, a standard mileage rate of 14 cents per mile is allowed for tax years beginning after December 31, 1997.[36] Deductions are permitted for transportation, reasonable expenses for lodging, and the cost of meals while away from home incurred in performing the donated services. The travel may not involve a significant element of personal pleasure, recreation, or vacation.[37]

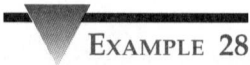

EXAMPLE 28   Grace, a delegate representing her church in Miami, Florida, travels to a two-day national meeting in Denver, Colorado, in February. After the meeting, Grace spends two weeks at a nearby ski resort. Under these circumstances, none of the transportation, meals, or lodging is deductible since the travel involved a significant element of personal pleasure, recreation, or vacation. ▼

Nondeductible Items.   In addition to the benefit received rule and the restrictions placed on contribution of services, the following items may *not* be deducted as charitable contributions:

- Dues, fees, or bills paid to country clubs, lodges, fraternal orders, or similar groups.
- Cost of raffle, bingo, or lottery tickets.
- Cost of tuition.
- Value of blood given to a blood bank.
- Donations to homeowners associations.
- Gifts to individuals.
- Rental value of property used by a qualified charity.

QUALIFIED ORGANIZATIONS

To be deductible, a contribution must be made to one of the following organizations:[38]

- A state or possession of the United States or any subdivisions thereof.
- A corporation, trust, or community chest, fund, or foundation that is situated in the United States and is organized and operated exclusively for religious, charitable, scientific, literary, or educational purposes or for the prevention of cruelty to children or animals.
- A veterans' organization.
- A fraternal organization operating under the lodge system.
- A cemetery company.

---

[36]§ 170(i). The rate was 12 cents per mile for tax year 1997.
[37]§ 170(j).

[38]§ 170(c).

The IRS publishes a list of organizations that have applied for and received tax-exempt status under § 501 of the Code.[39] This publication is updated frequently and may be helpful in determining if a gift has been made to a qualifying charitable organization.

Because gifts made to needy individuals are not deductible, a deduction will not be permitted if a gift is received by a donee in an individual capacity rather than as a representative of a qualifying organization.

ETHICAL CONSIDERATIONS

An Indirect Route to a Contribution Deduction

In July, a devastating tornado touched down in the city of Feldston, causing over $1 million in damage. Arethia's church, a qualified charitable organization, initiated a fund-raising drive to help Feldston citizens whose homes had been damaged. Arethia donated $40,000 to the church and suggested to the pastor that $25,000 of her contribution should be given to her sister, Keisha, whose home had suffered extensive damage. The pastor appointed a committee to award funds to needy citizens. The committee solicited applications from the community and awarded Keisha $18,000. Is Arethia justified in deducting $40,000 as a charitable contribution?

TIME OF DEDUCTION

A charitable contribution generally is deducted in the year the payment is made. This rule applies to both cash and accrual basis individuals. A contribution is ordinarily deemed to have been made on the delivery of the property to the donee. For example, if a gift of securities (properly endorsed) is made to a qualified charitable organization, the gift is considered complete on the day of delivery or mailing. However, if the donor delivers the certificate to his or her bank or broker or to the issuing corporation, the gift is considered complete on the date the stock is transferred on the books of the corporation.

A contribution made by check is considered delivered on the date of mailing. Thus, a check mailed on December 31, 1998, is deductible on the taxpayer's 1998 tax return. If the contribution is charged on a bank credit card, the date the charge is made determines the year of deduction.

RECORD-KEEPING AND VALUATION REQUIREMENTS

Record-Keeping Requirements. No deduction is allowed for contributions of $250 or more unless the taxpayer obtains *written substantiation* of the contribution from the charitable organization. The substantiation must specify the amount of cash and a description (but not value) of any property other than cash contributed. The substantiation must be obtained before the earlier of (1) the due date (including extensions) of the return for the year the contribution is claimed or (2) the date such return is filed.[40]

---

[39]Although this *Cumulative List of Organizations*, IRS Publication 78 (available by purchase from the Superintendent of Documents, U.S. Government Printing Office, Washington, DC 20402), may be helpful, qualified organizations are not required to be listed. Not all organizations that qualify are listed in this publication. The list is also available on the Web at http://www.irs.ustreas.gov.
[40]§ 170(f)(8).

Additional information is required if the value of the donated property is over $500 but not over $5,000. Also, the taxpayer must file Section A of Form 8283 (Noncash Charitable Contributions) for such contributions.

For noncash contributions with a claimed value in excess of $5,000 ($10,000 in the case of nonpublicly traded stock), the taxpayer must obtain a qualified appraisal and must file Section B of Form 8283. This schedule must show a summary of the appraisal and must be attached to the taxpayer's return. Failure to comply with these reporting rules may result in disallowance of the charitable contribution deduction. Additionally, significant overvaluation exposes the taxpayer to rather stringent penalties.

Valuation Requirements. Property donated to a charity is generally valued at fair market value at the time the gift is made. The Code and Regulations give very little guidance on the measurement of the fair market value except to say, "The fair market value is the price at which the property would change hands between a willing buyer and a willing seller, neither being under any compulsion to buy or sell and both having reasonable knowledge of relevant facts."

Generally, charitable organizations do not attest to the fair market value of the donated property. Nevertheless, the taxpayer must maintain reliable written evidence of the following information concerning the donation:

- The fair market value of the property and how that value was determined.
- The amount of the reduction in the value of the property (if required) for certain appreciated property and how that reduction was determined.
- Terms of any agreement with the charitable organization dealing with the use of the property and potential sale or other disposition of the property by the organization.
- A signed copy of the appraisal if the value of the property was determined by appraisal. Only for a contribution of art with an aggregate value of $20,000 or more must the appraisal be attached to the taxpayer's return.

LIMITATIONS ON CHARITABLE CONTRIBUTION DEDUCTION

In General. The potential charitable contribution deduction is the total of all donations, both money and property, that qualify for the deduction. After this determination is made, the actual amount of the charitable contribution deduction that is allowed for individuals for the tax year is limited as follows:

- If the qualifying contributions for the year total 20 percent or less of AGI, they are fully deductible.
- If the qualifying contributions are more than 20 percent of AGI, the deductible amount may be limited to either 20 percent, 30 percent, or 50 percent of AGI, depending on the type of property given and the type of organization to which the donation is made.
- In any case, the maximum charitable contribution deduction may not exceed 50 percent of AGI for the tax year.

To understand the complex rules for computing the amount of a charitable contribution, it is necessary to understand the distinction between capital gain property and ordinary income property. In addition, it is necessary to understand when the 50 percent, 30 percent, and 20 percent limitations apply. If a taxpayer's contributions for the year exceed the applicable percentage limitations, the excess contributions may be carried forward and deducted during a five-year carryover period. These topics are discussed in the sections that follow.

Ordinary Income Property. **Ordinary income property** is any property that, if sold, will result in the recognition of ordinary income. The term includes inventory for sale in the taxpayer's trade or business, a work of art created by the donor, and a manuscript prepared by the donor. It also includes, *for purposes of the charitable contribution calculation*, a capital asset held by the donor for less than the required holding period for long-term capital gain treatment (for charitable contribution purposes, long term is a period longer than one year). To the extent that disposition of property results in the recognition of ordinary income due to the recapture of depreciation, it is ordinary income property.[41]

If ordinary income property is contributed, the deduction is equal to the fair market value of the property less the amount of ordinary income that would have been reported if the property were sold. In most instances, the deduction is limited to the adjusted basis of the property to the donor.

▼
EXAMPLE 29

Tim owned stock in White Corporation that he donated to a university on May 1, 1998. Tim had purchased the stock for $2,500 on March 3, 1998, and the stock had a value of $3,600 when he made the donation. Since he had not held the property long enough to meet the long-term capital gain requirement, Tim would have recognized a short-term capital gain of $1,100 if he had sold the property. Since short-term capital gain property is treated as ordinary income property for charitable contribution purposes, Tim's charitable contribution deduction is limited to the property's adjusted basis of $2,500 ($3,600 − $1,100 = $2,500). ▼

In Example 29, suppose the stock had a fair market value of $2,300 (rather than $3,600) when it was donated to charity. Because the fair market value now is less than the adjusted basis, the charitable contribution deduction is $2,300.

Capital Gain Property. **Capital gain property** is any property that would have resulted in the recognition of long-term capital gain or § 1231 gain if the property had been sold by the donor.[42] As a general rule, the deduction for a contribution of capital gain property is equal to the fair market value of the property.

Two major exceptions disallow the deductibility of the appreciation on long-term capital gain property. One exception concerns certain private foundations. Private foundations are organizations that traditionally do not receive their funding from the general public (e.g., the Ford Foundation). Generally, foundations fall into two categories: operating and nonoperating. A private *operating* foundation is one that spends substantially all of its income in the active conduct of the charitable undertaking for which it was established. Other private foundations are *nonoperating* foundations. However, if a private nonoperating foundation distributes the contributions it receives according to special rules within two and one-half months following the year of the contribution, the organization is treated the same as public charities and private operating foundations. Often, only the private foundation knows its status (operating or nonoperating) for sure, and the status can change from year to year.

If capital gain property is contributed to a private nonoperating foundation, the taxpayer must reduce the contribution by the long-term capital gain that would

---

[41]For a more complete discussion of the difference between ordinary income and capital gain property, see Chapter 13.

[42]For charitable contribution purposes, the term "long term" includes both the mid-term and long-term holding periods. See General Scheme of Taxation in Chapter 13.

have been recognized if the property had been sold at its fair market value. The effect of this provision is to limit the deduction to the property's adjusted basis.[43]

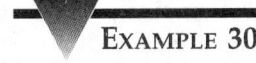

EXAMPLE 30

Walter purchases land for $800 on January 1, 1975, and donates it to a private nonoperating foundation on June 21, 1998, when it is worth $2,000. Walter's charitable contribution is $800 ($2,000 – $1,200), the land's basis. ▼

If, in Example 30, Walter had donated the land to either a public charity or a private operating foundation, his charitable contribution would be $2,000, the fair market value of the land.

A second exception applying to capital gain property relates to *tangible personalty*. Tangible personalty is all property that is not realty (land and buildings) and does not include intangible property such as stock or securities. If tangible personalty is contributed to a public charity such as a museum, church, or university, the charitable deduction may have to be reduced. The amount of the reduction is the long-term capital gain that would have been recognized if the property had been sold for its fair market value. The reduction is required *if* the property is put to an unrelated use. The term *unrelated use* means a use that is unrelated to the exempt purpose or function of the charitable organization.

A taxpayer in this instance must establish that the property is not in fact being put to an unrelated use by the donee. The taxpayer must also establish that at the time of the contribution it was reasonable to anticipate that the property would not be put to an unrelated use. For a contribution of personalty to a museum, if the work of art is the kind of art normally retained by the museum, it is reasonable for a donor to anticipate that the work of art will not be put to an unrelated use. This is the case even if the object is later sold or exchanged by the museum.[44]

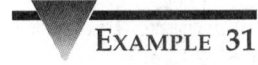

EXAMPLE 31

Myrtle contributes a Picasso painting, for which she paid $20,000, to a local museum. She had owned the painting for four years. It had a value of $30,000 at the time of the donation. The museum displayed the painting for two years and subsequently sold it for $50,000. The charitable contribution is $30,000. It is not reduced by the unrealized appreciation since the painting was put to a related use even though it was later sold by the museum. ▼

Fifty Percent Ceiling.   Contributions made to public charities may not exceed 50 percent of an individual's AGI for the year. Excess contributions may be carried over to the next five years. The 50 percent ceiling on contributions applies to the following types of public charities:

- A church or a convention or association of churches.
- An educational organization that maintains a regular faculty and curriculum.
- A hospital or medical school.
- An organization supported by the government that holds property or investments for the benefit of a college or university.
- A Federal, state, or local governmental unit.
- An organization normally receiving a substantial part of its support from the public or a governmental unit.

---

[43]For a limited period, taxpayers who donate *qualified appreciated stock* to private nonoperating foundations may deduct the fair market value of the stock. Qualified appreciated stock is stock for which market quotations are readily available on an established securities market. This provision applies to stock contributed from July 1, 1996, through May 31, 1998.

[44]Reg. § 1.170A–4(b)(3)(ii)(b).

In the remaining discussion of charitable contributions, public charities and private foundations (both operating and nonoperating) that qualify for the 50 percent ceiling will be referred to as *50 percent organizations.*

The 50 percent ceiling also applies to contributions to the following organizations:

- All private operating foundations.
- Certain private nonoperating foundations that distribute the contributions they receive to public charities and private operating foundations within two and one-half months following the year they receive the contribution.
- Certain private nonoperating foundations in which the contributions are pooled in a common fund and the income and principal sum are paid to public charities.

Thirty Percent Ceiling.   A 30 percent ceiling applies to contributions of cash and ordinary income property to private nonoperating foundations that are not 50 percent organizations. The 30 percent ceiling also applies to contributions of appreciated capital gain property to 50 percent organizations unless the taxpayer makes a special election (see below).

In the event the contributions for any one tax year involve both 50 percent and 30 percent property, the allowable deduction comes first from the 50 percent property.

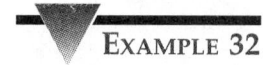

EXAMPLE 32

During the year, Lisa made the following donations to her church: cash of $2,000 and unimproved land worth $30,000. Lisa had purchased the land four years ago for $22,000 and held it as an investment. Therefore, it is long-term capital gain property. Lisa's AGI for the year is $50,000. Disregarding percentage limitations, Lisa's potential deduction is $32,000 [$2,000 (cash) + $30,000 (fair market value of land)].

In applying the percentage limitations, however, the *current* deduction for the land is limited to $15,000 [30% (limitation applicable to long-term capital gain property) × $50,000 (AGI)]. Thus, the total deduction is $17,000 ($2,000 cash + $15,000 land). Note that the total deduction does not exceed $25,000, which is 50% of Lisa's AGI. ▼

Under a special election, a taxpayer may choose to forgo a deduction of the appreciation on capital gain property. Referred to as the *reduced deduction election*, this enables the taxpayer to move from the 30 percent limitation to the 50 percent limitation.

EXAMPLE 33

Assume the same facts as in Example 32, except that Lisa makes the reduced deduction election. Now the deduction becomes $24,000 [$2,000 (cash) + $22,000 (basis in land)] because both donations fall under the 50% limitation. Thus, by making the election, Lisa has increased her charitable contribution deduction by $7,000 [$24,000 – $17,000 (Example 32)]. ▼

Although the reduced deduction election appears attractive, it should be considered carefully. The election sacrifices a deduction for the appreciation on long-term capital gain property that might eventually be allowed. Note that in Example 32, the potential deduction was $32,000, yet in Example 33 only $24,000 is allowed. The reason the potential deduction is decreased by $8,000 ($32,000 – $24,000) is that no carryover is allowed for the amount sacrificed by the election.

CONCEPT SUMMARY 9–2

Determining the Deduction for Contributions of Appreciated Property by Individuals

If the Type of Property Contributed Is:	And the Property Is Contributed to:	The Contribution Is Measured by:	But the Deduction Is Limited to:
1. Capital gain property	A 50% organization	Fair market value of the property	30% of AGI
2. Ordinary income property	A 50% organization	The basis of the property*	50% of AGI
3. Capital gain property (and the property is tangible personal property put to an unrelated use by the donee)	A 50% organization	The basis of the property*	50% of AGI
4. Capital gain property (and the reduced deduction is elected)	A 50% organization	The basis of the property	50% of AGI
5. Capital gain property	A private nonoperating foundation that is not a 50% organization	The basis of the property*	The lesser of: 1. 20% of AGI 2. 50% of AGI minus other contributions to 50% organizations

*If the fair market value of the property is less than the adjusted basis (i.e., the property has declined in value instead of appreciating), the fair market value is used.

Twenty Percent Ceiling. A 20 percent ceiling applies to contributions of appreciated long-term capital gain property to private nonoperating foundations that are not 50 percent organizations.

Contribution Carryovers. Contributions that exceed the percentage limitations for the current year can be carried over for five years. In the carryover process, such contributions do not lose their identity for limitation purposes. Thus, if the contribution originally involved 30 percent property, the carryover will continue to be classified as 30 percent property in the carryover year.

EXAMPLE 34

Assume the same facts as in Example 32. Because only $15,000 of the $30,000 value of the land was deducted in the current year, the balance of $15,000 may be carried over to the following year. But the carryover will still be treated as long-term capital gain property and is subject to the 30%-of-AGI limitation. ▼

In applying the percentage limitations, current charitable contributions must be claimed first before any carryovers can be considered. If carryovers involve more than one year, they are utilized in a first-in, first-out order.

MISCELLANEOUS ITEMIZED DEDUCTIONS

7 **LEARNING OBJECTIVE**
List the business and personal expenditures that are deductible either as miscellaneous itemized deductions or as other itemized deductions.

No deduction is allowed for personal, living, or family expenses.[45] However, a taxpayer may incur a number of expenditures related to employment. If an employee or outside salesperson incurs unreimbursed business expenses or expenses that are reimbursed under a nonaccountable plan, including travel and transportation, the expenses are deductible as **miscellaneous itemized deductions.**[46] Certain other expenses also fall into the special category of miscellaneous itemized deductions. Some are deductible only if, in total, they exceed 2 percent of the taxpayer's AGI. These miscellaneous itemized deductions include (but are not limited to) the following:

- Professional dues to membership organizations.
- Uniforms or other clothing that cannot be used for normal wear.
- Fees incurred for the preparation of one's tax return or fees incurred for tax litigation before the IRS or the courts.
- Job-hunting costs.
- Fee paid for a safe deposit box used to store papers and documents relating to taxable income-producing investments.
- Investment expenses that are deductible under § 212 as discussed in Chapter 5.
- Appraisal fees to determine the amount of a casualty loss or the fair market value of donated property.
- Hobby losses up to the amount of hobby income (see Chapter 5).
- Unreimbursed employee expenses (see Chapter 8).

Certain employee business expenses that are reimbursed are not itemized deductions, but are deducted *for* AGI. Employee business expenses are discussed in depth in Chapter 8.

OTHER MISCELLANEOUS DEDUCTIONS

Certain expenses and losses do not fall into any category of itemized deductions already discussed but are nonetheless deductible. The following expenses and losses are deductible on line 27 of Schedule A as Other Miscellaneous Deductions.

- Gambling losses up to the amount of gambling winnings.
- Impairment-related work expenses of a handicapped person.
- Federal estate tax on income in respect of a decedent.
- Deduction for repayment of amounts under a claim of right if more than $3,000 (discussed in Chapter 15).
- The unrecovered investment in an annuity contract when the annuity ceases by reason of death, discussed in Chapter 3.

Unlike the expenses and losses discussed previously under Miscellaneous Itemized Deductions, the above expenses and losses are not subject to the 2 percent-of-AGI floor.

---

[45]§ 262.
[46]Actors and performing artists who meet certain requirements are not subject to this rule.

COMPREHENSIVE EXAMPLE OF SCHEDULE A

Harry and Jean Brown, married filing jointly, had the following transactions for the current year:

• Medicines that required a prescription	$ 430
• Doctor and dentist bills paid and not reimbursed	2,120
• Medical insurance premium payments	1,200
• Contact lenses	175
• Transportation for medical purposes (380 miles × 10 cents/mile + $5.00 parking)	43
• State income tax withheld	620
• Real estate taxes	1,580
• Interest paid on qualified residence mortgage	2,840
• Charitable contributions in cash	860
• Transportation in performing charitable services (800 miles × 14 cents/mile + $7.00 parking and tolls)	119
• Unreimbursed employee expenses (from a Form 2106)	870
• Tax return preparation	150
• Safe deposit box (used for keeping investment documents and tax records)	170

The Browns' AGI is $40,000. Their completed 1997 Schedule A on the following page reports itemized deductions totaling $7,377.

OVERALL LIMITATION ON CERTAIN ITEMIZED DEDUCTIONS

8 LEARNING OBJECTIVE
Recognize the limitation on certain itemized deductions applicable to high-income taxpayers.

Congress has enacted several provisions limiting tax benefits for high-income taxpayers. These limitations include the exemption phase-out (refer to Chapter 2) and a phase-out of itemized deductions. The phase-out of itemized deductions (also referred to as a cutback adjustment) applies to taxpayers whose AGI exceeds $124,500 ($62,250 for married taxpayers filing separately).[47] The limitation applies to the following frequently encountered itemized deductions:[48]

- Taxes.
- Home mortgage interest, including points.
- Charitable contributions.
- Unreimbursed employee expenses subject to the 2 percent-of-AGI floor.
- All other expenses subject to the 2 percent-of-AGI floor.

The following deductions are *not* subject to the limitation on itemized deductions:

- Medical and dental expenses.
- Investment interest expense.

---

[47]For 1997, the limitation applied if AGI exceeded $121,200 ($60,600 for married taxpayers filing separately).

[48]Other deductions subject to the limitation include Federal estate tax on income in respect of a decedent, certain amortizable bond premiums, the deduction for repayment of certain amounts, certain unrecovered investments in an annuity, and impairment-related work expenses.

SCHEDULES A&B	Schedule A—Itemized Deductions	OMB No. 1545-0074
(Form 1040)	(Schedule B is on back)	1997
Department of the Treasury Internal Revenue Service (99)	▶ **Attach to Form 1040.** ▶ **See Instructions for Schedules A and B (Form 1040).**	Attachment Sequence No. **07**

Name(s) shown on Form 1040

Harry and Jean Brown

Your social security number: 371 30 3987

Medical and Dental Expenses		**Caution:** *Do not include expenses reimbursed or paid by others.*	
	1	Medical and dental expenses (see page A-1)	**1** 3,968
	2	Enter amount from Form 1040, line 33 . **2** 40,000	
	3	Multiply line 2 above by 7.5% (.075)	**3** 3,000
	4	Subtract line 3 from line 1. If line 3 is more than line 1, enter -0-	**4** 968
Taxes You Paid (See page A-2.)	5	State and local income taxes	**5** 620
	6	Real estate taxes (see page A-2)	**6** 1,580
	7	Personal property taxes	**7**
	8	Other taxes. List type and amount ▶ -----------------	**8**
	9	Add lines 5 through 8	**9** 2,200
Interest You Paid (See page A-2.)	10	Home mortgage interest and points reported to you on Form 1098	**10** 2,840
	11	Home mortgage interest not reported to you on Form 1098. If paid to the person from whom you bought the home, see page A-3 and show that person's name, identifying no., and address ▶	**11**
Note: Personal interest is not deductible.	12	Points not reported to you on Form 1098. See page A-3 for special rules	**12**
	13	Investment interest. Attach Form 4952 if required. (See page A-3.)	**13**
	14	Add lines 10 through 13	**14** 2,840
Gifts to Charity If you made a gift and got a benefit for it, see page A-3.	15	Gifts by cash or check. If you made any gift of $250 or more, see page A-3	**15** 860
	16	Other than by cash or check. If any gift of $250 or more, see page A-3. You **MUST** attach Form 8283 if over $500	**16** 119
	17	Carryover from prior year	**17**
	18	Add lines 15 through 17	**18** 979
Casualty and Theft Losses	19	Casualty or theft loss(es). Attach Form 4684. (See page A-4.)	**19**
Job Expenses and Most Other Miscellaneous Deductions (See page A-5 for expenses to deduct here.)	20	Unreimbursed employee expenses—job travel, union dues, job education, etc. You **MUST** attach Form 2106 or 2106-EZ if required. (See page A-4.) ▶ ------------- *Form 2106 $870*	**20** 870
	21	Tax preparation fees	**21** 150
	22	Other expenses—investment, safe deposit box, etc. List type and amount ▶ *Safe deposit box, $170*	**22** 170
	23	Add lines 20 through 22	**23** 1,190
	24	Enter amount from Form 1040, line 33 . **24** 40,000	
	25	Multiply line 24 above by 2% (.02)	**25** 800
	26	Subtract line 25 from line 23. If line 25 is more than line 23, enter -0-	**26** 390
Other Miscellaneous Deductions	27	Other—from list on page A-5. List type and amount ▶ -----------------	**27**
Total Itemized Deductions	28	Is Form 1040, line 33, over $121,200 (over $60,600 if married filing separately)? **NO.** Your deduction is not limited. Add the amounts in the far right column for lines 4 through 27. Also, enter on Form 1040, line 35, the **larger** of this amount or your standard deduction. **YES.** Your deduction may be limited. See page A-5 for the amount to enter.	▶ **28** 7,377

For Paperwork Reduction Act Notice, see Form 1040 instructions. Cat. No. 11330X **Schedule A (Form 1040) 1997**

- Nonbusiness casualty and theft losses.
- Gambling losses.

Taxpayers subject to the limitation must reduce itemized deductions by the lesser of:

- 3 percent of the amount by which AGI exceeds $124,500 ($62,250 if married filing separately).
- 80 percent of itemized deductions that are affected by the limit.

The overall limitation is applied after applying all other limitations to itemized deductions that are affected by the overall limitation. Other limitations apply to charitable contributions, certain meals and entertainment expenses, and certain miscellaneous itemized deductions.

EXAMPLE 35

Herman, who is single, had AGI of $200,000 for 1998. He incurred the following expenses and losses during the year:

Medical expenses before 7.5%-of-AGI limitation	$16,000
State and local income taxes	3,200
Real estate taxes	2,800
Home mortgage interest	7,200
Charitable contributions	2,000
Casualty loss before 10% limitation (after $100 floor)	21,500
Unreimbursed employee expenses subject to 2%-of-AGI limitation	4,300
Gambling losses (Herman had $3,000 gambling income)	7,000

Herman's itemized deductions *before* the overall limitation are computed as follows:

Medical expenses [$16,000 − (7.5% × $200,000)]	$ 1,000
State and local income taxes	3,200
Real estate taxes	2,800
Home mortgage interest	7,200
Charitable contributions	2,000
Casualty loss [$21,500 − (10% × $200,000)]	1,500
Unreimbursed employee expenses ($4,300 − (2% × $200,000)]	300
Gambling losses ($7,000 loss limited to $3,000 of gambling income)	3,000
Total itemized deductions before overall limitation	$21,000

Herman's itemized deductions subject to the overall limitation are as follows:

State and local income taxes	$ 3,200
Real estate taxes	2,800
Home mortgage interest	7,200
Charitable contributions	2,000
Unreimbursed employee expenses	300
Total	$15,500

Herman must reduce this amount by the smaller of the following:

- 3% ($200,000 AGI − $124,500) $ 2,265
- 80% of itemized deductions subject to limitation ($15,500 × .80)   12,400

FEW TAXPAYERS ARE AFFECTED BY THE THREE PERCENT FLOOR

The IRS *Statistics of Income Bulletin* for 1994 (the latest year available) shows that few taxpayers have to be concerned about the 3 percent floor for itemized deductions. In 1994, the AGI threshold for application of this limitation was $111,800 ($55,900 for married taxpayers filing separately). The IRS statistics for 1994 show that taxpayers with AGI of $91,226 or more ranked in the top 5 percent. Obviously, fewer than 5 percent of all taxpayers were subject to the 3 percent floor in 1994.

Therefore, the amount of the reduction is $2,265, and Herman has $18,735 of deductible itemized deductions, computed as follows:

Deductible itemized deductions subject to overall limitation ($15,500 − $2,265)	$13,235
Itemized deductions not subject to overall limitation:	
Medical expenses	1,000
Casualty loss	1,500
Gambling losses	3,000
Deductible itemized deductions	$18,735

TAX PLANNING CONSIDERATIONS

9 **LEARNING OBJECTIVE**
Identify tax planning procedures that can maximize the benefit of itemized deductions.

EFFECTIVE UTILIZATION OF ITEMIZED DEDUCTIONS

Since an individual may use the standard deduction in one year and itemize deductions in another year, it is frequently possible to obtain maximum benefit by shifting itemized deductions from one year to another. For example, if a taxpayer's itemized deductions and the standard deduction are approximately the same for each year of a two-year period, the taxpayer should use the standard deduction in one year and shift itemized deductions (to the extent permitted by law) to the other year. The individual could, for example, prepay a church pledge for a particular year to shift the deduction to the current year or avoid paying end-of-the-year medical expenses to shift the deduction to the following year.

UTILIZATION OF MEDICAL DEDUCTIONS

When a taxpayer anticipates that medical expenses will approximate the percentage floor, much might be done to generate a deductible excess. Any of the following procedures can help build a deduction by the end of the year:

- Incur the obligation for needed dental work or have needed work carried out.[49] Orthodontic treatment, for example, may have been recommended for a member of the taxpayer's family.
- Have elective remedial surgery that may have been postponed from prior years (e.g., tonsillectomies, vasectomies, correction of hernias, hysterectomies).

---

[49]Prepayment of medical expenses does not generate a current deduction unless the taxpayer is under an obligation to make the payment.

- Incur the obligation for capital improvements to the taxpayer's personal residence recommended by a physician (e.g., an air filtration system to alleviate a respiratory disorder).

As an aid to taxpayers who may experience temporary cash-flow problems at the end of the year, the use of bank credit cards is deemed to be payment for purposes of timing the deductibility of charitable and medical expenses.

EXAMPLE 36

On December 13, 1998, Marge (a calendar year taxpayer) purchases two pairs of prescription contact lenses and one pair of prescribed orthopedic shoes for a total of $305. These purchases are separately charged to Marge's credit card. On January 6, 1999, Marge receives her statement containing these charges and makes payment shortly thereafter. The purchases are deductible as medical expenses in the year charged (1998) and not in the year the account is settled (1999). ▼

Recognizing which expenditures qualify for the medical deduction also may be crucial to exceeding the percentage limitations.

EXAMPLE 37

Mortimer employs Lana (an unrelated party) to care for his incapacitated and dependent mother. Lana is not a trained nurse but spends approximately one-half of the time performing nursing duties (e.g., administering injections and providing physical therapy) and the rest of the time doing household chores. An allocable portion of Lana's wages that Mortimer pays (including the employer's portion of FICA taxes) qualifies as a medical expense. ▼

TIMING THE PAYMENT OF DEDUCTIBLE TAXES

It is sometimes possible to defer or accelerate the payment of certain deductible taxes, such as state income tax, real property tax, and personal property tax. For instance, the final installment of estimated state income tax is generally due after the end of a given tax year. Accelerating the payment of the final installment could result in larger itemized deductions for the current year.

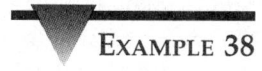

EXAMPLE 38

Jenny, who is single, expects to have itemized deductions of $3,900 in 1998 and $2,500 in 1999. She plans to pay $900 as the final installment on her 1998 estimated state income tax, which is due on January 15, 1999. If Jenny does not pay the final installment until 1999, she will not itemize in either 1998 or 1999. However, if she pays the final installment in December 1998, her itemized deductions will be $4,800 ($3,900 + $900) in 1999, and she will benefit from itemizing. ▼

PROTECTING THE INTEREST DEDUCTION

Although the deductibility of prepaid interest by a cash basis taxpayer has been severely restricted, a notable exception allows a deduction for points paid by the buyer to obtain financing for the purchase or improvement of a principal residence in the year of payment. However, such points must actually be paid by the taxpayer obtaining the loan and must represent a charge for the use of money. It has been held that points paid from the mortgage proceeds do not satisfy the payment requirement.[50] Also, the portion of the points attributable to service charges does not represent deductible interest.[51] Taxpayers financing

---

[50]*Alan A. Rubnitz*, 67 T.C. 621 (1977). Seller-paid points may also be deductible by the buyer under the provisions of Rev.Proc. 94–27, cited in footnote 27.

[51]*Donald L. Wilkerson*, 70 T.C. 240 (1978).

home purchases or improvements usually should direct their planning toward avoiding these two hurdles to immediate deductibility.

In rare instances, a taxpayer may find it desirable to forgo the immediate expensing of points in the year paid. Instead, it could prove beneficial to capitalize the points and write them off as interest expense over the life of the mortgage.

EXAMPLE 39

Gerald purchases a home on December 15, 1998, for $95,000 with $30,000 cash and a 15-year mortgage of $65,000 financed by the Greater Metropolis National Bank. Gerald pays two points in addition to interest allocated to the period from December 15 until December 31, 1998, at an annual rate of 10%. Since Gerald does not have enough itemized deductions to exceed the standard deduction for 1998, he should elect to capitalize the interest expense by amortizing the points over 15 years. In this instance, Gerald would deduct $86.67 for 1999, as part of his qualified residence interest expense [$1,300 (two points) divided by 15 years], if he elects to itemize that year. ▼

Because personal (consumer) interest is not deductible, taxpayers should consider making use of home equity loans. Recall that these loans utilize the personal residence of the taxpayer as security. Since the tracing rules do not apply to home equity loans, the funds from these loans can be used for personal purposes (e.g., auto loans, education). By making use of home equity loans, therefore, what would have been nondeductible consumer interest becomes deductible qualified residence interest.

ASSURING THE CHARITABLE CONTRIBUTION DEDUCTION

For a charitable contribution deduction to be available, the recipient must be a qualified charitable organization. Sometimes the mechanics of how the contribution is carried out can determine whether or not a deduction results.

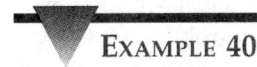
EXAMPLE 40

Fumiko wants to donate $5,000 to her church's mission in Kobe, Japan. In this regard, she considers three alternatives:

1. Send the money directly to the mission.
2. Give the money to her church with the understanding that it is to be passed on to the mission.
3. Give the money directly to the missionary in charge of the mission who is currently in the United States on a fund-raising trip.

If Fumiko wants to obtain a deduction for the contribution, she should choose alternative 2. A direct donation to the mission (alternative 1) is not deductible because the mission is a foreign charity. A direct gift to the missionary (alternative 3) does not comply since an individual cannot be a qualified charity for income tax purposes.[52] ▼

When making noncash donations, the type of property chosen can have decided implications in determining the amount, if any, of the deduction.

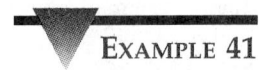
EXAMPLE 41

Sam wants to give $60,000 in value to his church in some form other than cash. In this connection, he considers four alternatives:

1. Stock held for two years as an investment with a basis of $100,000 and a fair market value of $60,000.
2. Stock held for five years as an investment with a basis of $10,000 and a fair market value of $60,000.

---

[52]*Thomas E. Lesslie*, 36 TCM 495, T.C.Memo. 1977–111.

3. The rent-free use for a year of a building that normally leases for $5,000 a month.
4. A valuable stamp collection held as an investment and owned for 10 years with a basis of $10,000 and a fair market value of $60,000. The church plans to sell the collection if and when it is donated.

Alternative 1 is ill-advised as the subject of the gift. Even though Sam would obtain a deduction of $60,000, he would forgo the potential loss of $40,000 that would be recognized if the property were sold.[53] Alternative 2 makes good sense since the deduction still is $60,000 and none of the $50,000 of appreciation that has occurred must be recognized as income. Alternative 3 yields no deduction at all and is not a wise choice. Alternative 4 involves tangible personalty that the recipient does not plan to use. As a result, the amount of the deduction is limited to $10,000, the stamp collection's basis.[54] ▼

For property transfers (particularly real estate), the ceiling limitations on the amount of the deduction allowed in any one year (50 percent, 30 percent, or 20 percent of AGI, as the case may be) could be a factor to take into account. With proper planning, donations can be controlled to stay within the limitations and therefore avoid the need for a carryover of unused charitable contributions.

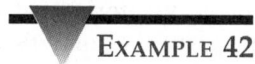

EXAMPLE 42

Andrew wants to donate a tract of unimproved land held as an investment to the University of Maryland (a qualified charitable organization). The land has been held for six years and has a current fair market value of $300,000 and a basis to Andrew of $50,000. Andrew's AGI for the current year is estimated to be $200,000, and he expects much the same for the next few years. In the current year, he deeds (transfers) an undivided one-fifth interest in the real estate to the university. ▼

What has Andrew in Example 42 accomplished for income tax purposes? In the current year, he will be allowed a charitable contribution deduction of $60,000 (⅕ × $300,000), which will be within the applicable limitation of AGI (30% × $200,000). Presuming no other charitable contributions for the year, Andrew has avoided the possibility of a carryover. In future years, Andrew can arrange donations of undivided interests in the real estate to stay within the bounds of the percentage limitations. The only difficulty with this approach is the need to revalue the real estate each year before the donation, since the amount of the deduction is based on the fair market value of the interest contributed at the time of the contribution.

EXAMPLE 43

Tiffany dies in October 1998. In completing her final income tax return for 1998, Tiffany's executor determines the following information: AGI of $104,000 and a donation by Tiffany to her church of stock worth $60,000. Tiffany had purchased the stock two years ago for $50,000 and held it as an investment. Tiffany's executor makes the reduced deduction election and, as a consequence, claims a charitable contribution deduction of $50,000. With the election, the potential charitable contribution deduction of $50,000 ($60,000 − $10,000) is less than the 50% ceiling of $52,000 ($104,000 × 50%). If the executor had not made the election, the potential charitable contribution deduction of $60,000 would have been reduced by the 30% ceiling to $31,200 ($104,000 × 30%). No carryover of the $28,800 ($60,000 − $31,200) would have been available. ▼

---

[53]*LaVar M. Withers*, 69 T.C. 900 (1978).
[54]No reduction of appreciation is necessary in alternative 2 since stock is intangible property and not tangible personalty.

KEY TERMS

Acquisition
indebtedness, 9–15

Capital gain property,
9–23

Charitable contribution,
9–19

Home equity loans,
9–15

Investment income,
9–14

Investment interest,
9–13

Medical expense, 9–2

Miscellaneous itemized
deductions, 9–27

Net investment income,
9–14

Ordinary income
property, 9–23

Points, 9–16

Qualified residence
interest, 9–13

**PROBLEM
MATERIALS**

DISCUSSION QUESTIONS

1. Dan, a self-employed individual taxpayer, prepared his own income tax return for the past year and asked you to check it over for accuracy. Your review indicates that Dan failed to claim certain business entertainment expenses.
   a. Will the correction of this omission affect the amount of medical expenses Dan can deduct? Explain.
   b. Would it matter if Dan were employed rather than self-employed?

2. Pat incurred the following expenses during the year: $450 for an annual physical exam, $80 for a dental checkup, $600 for a weight reduction program, $1,800 for alcohol rehabilitation, and $200 for a stop-smoking clinic. Which of these expenses qualify for the medical deduction? Explain.

3. Juanita, your client, had an accident while competing in a bicycle race. She sustained facial injuries that required cosmetic surgery. While having the surgery done to restore her appearance, she has additional surgery done to reshape her nose, which was not injured in the accident. Under what circumstances, if any, will the cost of Juanita's cosmetic surgery qualify as a deductible medical expense?

4. Don, who lives in a small town in North Dakota, has a back problem that requires regular exercise. He is unable to get outdoor exercise during the cold North Dakota winters. His doctor has recommended that Don go to Arizona and play golf and hike during the winter. He takes his doctor's advice and incurs expenses for transportation, meals, lodging, greens fees, and hiking equipment while in Arizona. Discuss the deductibility of those costs and any limits that will apply to the deduction.

5. Andres was injured in an automobile accident and is confined to a wheelchair. Because he lives alone, he must have extensive modifications made to various rooms in his home, including the kitchen, bathrooms, and hallways. Do the capital expenditures incurred to modify his home constitute a valid medical expense? If so, how much of the expense is deductible?

6. Betty, a sole proprietor of an antique shop, has two dependent children. During the year, she paid health insurance premiums of $1,600 for her own coverage and $2,400 for coverage of her children. How will these premium payments affect Betty's taxable income computation?

7. Rebecca took her daughter, Susan, from Chicago to Rochester, Minnesota, for surgery at the Mayo Clinic. She incurred expenses for gasoline, highway tolls, and meals while traveling. Rebecca stayed in a motel near the clinic for six days while Susan was hospitalized. Discuss the extent to which transportation, meals, and lodging costs incurred by Susan and Rebecca are deductible as medical expenses (ignore the 7.5% floor).

8. Erin incurred medical expenses in 1998 and received a reimbursement from her insurance company in 1999. Under what circumstances must Erin report all or part of the reimbursement in gross income for 1999? Under what circumstances may she exclude the reimbursement from gross income for 1999?

9. By December 1, Ethel had medical expenses of $5,300, of which $1,200 was reimbursed by her insurance company. She expects her AGI for the year to be $60,000 and her other itemized deductions to be $5,600. Can you suggest any tax planning ideas that will enable Ethel to increase her medical expense deduction for the year?

10. A local opthalmologist's advertising campaign included a certificate for a free radial keratotomy for the lucky winner of a drawing. Ahmad held the winning ticket, which was drawn in December 1997. Ahmad had no vision problems and was uncertain what he should do with the prize. In February 1998, Ahmad's daughter, who lives with his former wife, was diagnosed with a vision problem that could be treated either with prescription glasses or a radial keratotomy. The divorce decree requires that Ahmad pay for all medical expenses incurred for his daughter. Identify the relevant tax issues for Ahmad.

11. Julie acquired a personal residence in an older neighborhood that had no sidewalks. The city council passed an ordinance requiring all homeowners to reimburse the city for the cost of installing sidewalks in front of their homes. What is the appropriate tax treatment for the amount Julie is assessed for the sidewalk?

12. Donald owns a principal residence in Chicago, a vacation lodge in New Mexico, and a yacht (with living quarters) on Lake Michigan. All three properties have mortgages on which Donald pays interest. Discuss any limitations that apply to Donald's mortgage interest deduction, and suggest any strategy Donald should consider to maximize his deduction.

13. Ed borrows $20,000 and purchases an automobile. Jack borrows $20,000 to purchase a diamond engagement ring for his fiancée. Ed qualifies for an interest deduction on the amount he borrowed, but Jack does not. Can you offer any explanation for the difference?

14. Jerry purchased a personal residence from Kim. In order to sell the residence, Kim agreed to pay $3,000 in points related to Jerry's mortgage. Discuss the deductibility of the points.

15. Ellen borrows $50,000 from her parents for a down payment on a condominium. She paid interest of $4,200 in 1996, $0 in 1997, and $11,000 in 1998. The IRS disallows the deduction. Can you offer any explanation for the disallowance?

16. The city of Ogden was devastated by a tornado in April 1997, leaving many families in need of food, clothing, shelter, and other necessities. Betty contributed $500 to a family whose home was completely destroyed by the tornado. Jack contributed $700 to the family's church, which gave the money to the family. Discuss the deductibility of these contributions.

17. Sara purchased a ticket to a fund-raising banquet and dance for the Cincinnati Symphony, a public charity. The ticket cost $300, and the normal cost of such an event is $60. How much can Sara deduct as a charitable contribution?

18. Joe, who is in the 39.6% tax bracket in 1998, expects to retire in 1999 and be in the 28% tax bracket. He plans to donate $50,000 to his church. Because he will not have the cash available until 1999, Joe donates land (long-term capital gain property) with a basis of $10,000 and fair market value of $50,000 to the church in December 1998. He reacquires the land for $50,000 in February 1999. Discuss Joe's tax objectives and all tax issues related to his actions.

19. Zina decided to have a garage sale to get rid of a number of items that she no longer needed, including books, old stereo equipment, clothing, bicycles, and furniture. She scheduled the sale for Friday and Saturday, but was forced to close at noon Friday because of a torrential downpour. She had collected $500 for the items she sold before closing. The heavy rains continued through the weekend, and Zina was unable to

continue the sale. She had not enjoyed dealing with the people who came to the sale on Friday morning, so she donated the remaining items to several local organizations. Zina has asked your advice on how she should treat these events on her tax return. List some of the tax issues you would discuss with her.

20. Paula contributed Orange Corporation common stock to the United Way. In addition, she contributed tables and chairs from her proprietorship's inventory to the high school in her city. Should Paula's charitable contribution deduction for these contributions be determined by the basis or fair market value of the contributed items?

21. During the year, Sam donated four suits to Goodwill. He had purchased the suits three years ago at a cost of $1,600 and worn them as personal attire. Because the suits are long-term capital assets, Sam plans to deduct $1,600 on his income tax return. Comment on Sam's understanding of the tax law governing charitable contributions.

 22. The Skins Game, which involves four of the top golfers on the PGA Tour, is held each year on the weekend after Thanksgiving. Total prize money amounts to $510,000, and the leading money winner also receives an automobile as a prize. The announcers point out that 10% of the money won by each player goes to charity. In addition, on some holes, the winner of the hole receives the keys to an automobile, which goes to the player's favorite charity. Identify the relevant tax issues for the players. Consider the following possibilities with respect to the car won by the leading money winner: (1) he might keep the car for his own use and sell his present car; (2) he might sell the new car; (3) he might give the car to a friend or relative; (4) he might donate the car to charity; or (5) he might give the car to his caddy.

 23. Henry is a television evangelist. In August 1997, the IRS ruled that his organization was no longer a qualified charitable organization because of violations of the tax law. Miguel donated $10,000 to Henry's organization in September 1997. At the time, he did not know that Henry's organization had been disqualified as a charitable organization. In 1998, Henry was jailed for mail fraud. Miguel has filed a civil suit demanding return of the $10,000 plus $100,000 in damages. Identify the relevant tax issues for Miguel.

PROBLEMS

24. Ed and Laura are married and together have AGI of $60,000 in 1998. They have no dependents and file a joint return. During the year, they paid $1,600 for medical insurance, $6,000 in doctor bills and hospital expenses, and $900 for prescribed medicine and drugs.
    a. In December 1998, Ed and Laura received an insurance reimbursement of $1,200 for hospitalization expenses. Determine the deduction allowable for medical expenses paid during the year.
    b. Assume instead that Ed and Laura received the $1,200 insurance reimbursement in February 1999. Determine the deduction allowable for medical expenses incurred in 1998.
    c. Assume again that Ed and Laura received the $1,200 insurance reimbursement in February 1999. Discuss whether the reimbursement will be included in their gross income for 1999.

 25. Frank, a widower, had a serious stroke and is no longer capable of caring for himself. He has three sons, all of whom live in different states. Because they are unable to care for Frank in their homes, his sons have placed him in a nursing home equipped to provide medical and nursing care facilities. Total nursing home expenses amount to $45,000 per year. Of this amount, $18,000 is directly attributable to medical and nursing care. Frank's Social Security benefits are used to pay for $12,000 of the nursing home charges. He has no other income. His sons plan to split the remaining medical expenses equally.
    a. What portion of the nursing home charges is potentially deductible as a medical expense?
    b. Can you provide Frank's sons with a tax planning idea for maximizing the deduction for his medical expenses?

26. Ibrahim developed a severe allergy condition, and his physician advised him to install a special air conditioning, heating, and filtration system in his home. The cost of installing the system was $7,200, and the increase in the value of the residence was determined to be $2,300. Ibrahim's AGI for the year was $40,000.
    a. How much of the expenditure can Ibrahim deduct as a medical expense?
    b. Assume the same facts as in (a), except that Ibrahim was paralyzed in a skiing accident and the expenditures were incurred to build entrance and exit ramps and widen the hallways in his home to accommodate his wheelchair. How much of the expenditure can Ibrahim deduct as a medical expense?

27. For calendar year 1998, Julie was a self-employed real estate broker with no employees. She had $80,000 net profit from real estate transactions and paid $5,000 in medical insurance premiums on a policy covering 1998. How much of these premiums may Julie deduct as a deduction *for* AGI and how much may she deduct as an itemized deduction?

28. During the current year, Sara incurred and paid the following expenses for Seth (her son), Emma (her mother), and herself:

Surgery for Seth	$3,800
Trout Valley Academy charges for Seth:	
Tuition	8,000
Room, board, and other expenses	7,600
Psychiatric treatment	6,500
Doctor bills for Emma	2,900
Prescription drugs for Sara, Seth, and Emma	1,100
Insulin for Emma	1,080
Nonprescription drugs for Sara, Seth, and Emma	700
Charges at Riverview Nursing Home for Emma:	
Medical care	6,800
Lodging	7,200
Meals	3,500

Seth qualifies as Sara's dependent, and Emma would also qualify except that she receives $6,100 of taxable retirement benefits from her former employer. Seth's psychiatrist recommended Trout Valley Academy because of its small class sizes and specialized psychiatric treatment program that is needed to treat Seth's illness. Emma is a paraplegic and diabetic, and Riverview offers the type of care that she requires.

Upon the recommendation of a physician, Sara has an air filtration system installed in her personal residence. She suffers from severe allergies. In connection with this equipment, Sara incurs and pays the following amounts during the year:

Filtration system and cost of installation	$6,400
Increase in utility bills due to the system	750
Cost of certified appraisal	320

The system has an estimated useful life of 10 years. The appraisal was to determine the value of Sara's residence with and without the system. The appraisal states that the system increased the value of Sara's residence by $1,200. Ignoring the 7.5% floor, what is the total of Sara's expenses that qualifies for the medical expense deduction?

29. In May, Rebecca's daughter, Susan, sustained a serious injury that made it impossible for her to continue living alone. Susan, who is a novelist, moved back into Rebecca's home after the accident. Susan has begun writing a new novel based on her recent experiences. To accommodate Susan, Rebecca incurred significant remodeling expenses (widening hallways, building a separate bedroom and bathroom, making kitchen appliances accessible to Susan). In addition, Rebecca had an indoor swimming pool constructed so Susan could do rehabilitation exercises prescribed by her physician.

In September, Susan underwent major reconstructive surgery in Denver. The surgery was performed by Dr. Rama Patel, who specializes in treating injuries of the type sustained by Susan. Rebecca drove Susan from Champaign, Illinois, to Denver, a total of 1,100 miles, in Susan's specially equipped van. They left Champaign on Tuesday morning and arrived in Denver on Thursday afternoon. Rebecca incurred expenses for gasoline, highway tolls, meals, and lodging while traveling to Denver. Rebecca stayed in a motel near the clinic for eight days while Susan was hospitalized. Identify the relevant tax issues based on this information and prepare a list of questions that you would need to ask Rebecca and Susan in order to advise them as to the resolution of any issues you have identified.

30. In Meigs County, the real property tax year is the calendar year. The real property tax becomes a personal liability of the owner of real property on January 1 in the current real property tax year, 1998. The tax is payable on June 1, 1998. On May 31, 1998, Geraldo sells his house to Janet for $220,000. On June 1, 1998, Janet pays the entire real estate tax of $8,760 for the year ending December 31, 1998.
    a. How much of the property taxes may Geraldo deduct?
    b. How much of the property taxes may Janet deduct?

31. Assume the same facts as in Problem 30.
    a. What is Janet's basis for the residence?
    b. How much did Geraldo realize from the sale of the residence?

32. Andrea, who uses the cash method of accounting, lives in a state that imposes an income tax. In April 1998, she files her state income tax return for 1997 and pays an additional $1,000 in state income taxes. During 1998, her withholdings for state income tax purposes amount to $7,400, and she pays estimated state income tax of $700. In April 1999, she files her state income tax return for 1998 claiming a refund of $1,800. Andrea receives the refund in August 1999.
    a. Assuming Andrea itemizes deductions in 1998, how much may she claim as a deduction for state income taxes on her Federal return for calendar year 1998 (filed in April 1999)?
    b. Assuming Andrea itemized deductions in 1998, how will the refund of $1,800 that she received in 1999 be treated for Federal income tax purposes?
    c. Assume Andrea itemizes deductions in 1998 and elects to have the $1,800 refund applied toward her 1999 state income tax liability. How will the $1,800 be treated for Federal income tax purposes?
    d. Assuming Andrea did not itemize deductions in 1998, how will the refund of $1,800 received in 1999 be treated for Federal income tax purposes?

33. Irina incurred $39,000 of interest expense related to her investments in 1998. Her investment income included $10,000 of interest, $6,000 of dividends, and a $15,000 net capital gain on the sale of securities.
    a. What is the maximum amount that Irina can treat as investment income for the year?
    b. What other tax factors should Irina consider in deciding whether to elect to include the net capital gain in her investment income?

34. In 1998, Myrna has $8,000 of investment income and the following miscellaneous itemized deductions:

Unreimbursed employee business expenses (meals included at 50%)	$1,400
Tax return preparation fee	440
Investment expenses	500

For purposes of the investment interest expense limitation, what is the total of Myrna's net investment income in each of the following independent situations:
    a. AGI of $20,000.
    b. AGI of $60,000.
    c. AGI of $110,000.

35. Sid and Sara, married taxpayers, took out a mortgage on their home for $100,000 in 1988. In March of the current year, when the home had a fair market value of $200,000 and they owed $85,000 on the mortgage, Sid and Sara took out a home equity loan for

$110,000. They used the funds to purchase an airplane to be used for recreational purposes. What is the maximum amount on which they can deduct home equity interest?

36. Cindy purchased her residence five years ago, obtaining a 20-year mortgage at an annual interest rate of 11%. On January 2, 1998, Cindy refinanced with a 15-year mortgage in order to reduce the interest rate to 7.25%. To obtain the refinancing, she was required to pay points of $3,500. How much, if any, of the $3,500 points can Cindy deduct in 1998?

37. Erin donates $1,000 to State University's athletic department. The payment guarantees that Erin will have preferred seating on the 50-yard line.
    a. Assume Erin subsequently buys four $50 game tickets. How much can she deduct as a charitable contribution to the university's athletic department?
    b. Assume that Erin's $1,000 donation includes four $50 tickets. How much can she deduct as a charitable contribution to the university's athletic department?

38. Diana owned stock in Hippo Corporation with a basis of $7,500. She donated the stock to a qualified charitable organization on June 1, 1998.
    a. What is the amount of Diana's deduction, assuming that she had purchased the stock on February 3, 1998, and the stock had a fair market value of $9,600 when she made the donation?
    b. Assume the same facts as in (a), except that Diana had purchased the stock on June 3, 1995.
    c. Assume the same facts as in (a), except that the stock had a fair market value of $6,900 (rather than $9,600) when Diana donated it to the charity.

39. Darby contributed a painting to an art museum in 1998. She had owned the painting for 20 years, and it had a value of $120,000 at the time of the donation. The museum displayed the painting in its impressionist gallery.
    a. Assume that Darby's AGI is $230,000 and her basis for the painting is $80,000. Would you recommend that she make the reduced deduction election?
    b. Assume that Darby's AGI is $230,000 and her basis for the painting is $115,000. Would you recommend that she make the reduced deduction election?

40. During the year, Al made the following contributions to his church:

Cash	$20,000
Stock in Thrush Corporation (a publicly traded corporation)	30,000

The stock in Thrush Corporation was acquired as an investment three years ago at a cost of $10,000. Al's AGI is $70,000.
    a. What is Al's charitable contribution deduction?
    b. How are excess amounts, if any, treated?

41. Steven, who had AGI of $180,000 in 1998, contributed stock in Azure Corporation (a publicly traded corporation) to State University, a qualified charitable organization. The stock was worth $105,000, and Steven had acquired it as an investment two years ago at a cost of $84,000.
    a. What is the total amount that Steven can deduct as a charitable contribution, assuming he carries over any disallowed contribution from 1998 to future years?
    b. What is the maximum amount that Steven can deduct as a charitable contribution in 1998?
    c. What factors should Steven consider in deciding how to treat the contribution for Federal income tax purposes?
    d. Assume Steven dies in December 1998. What advice would you give the executor of his estate with regard to possible elections that can be made relative to the contribution?

42. On December 30, 1998, Roberta purchased four tickets to a charity ball sponsored by the city of San Diego for the benefit of underprivileged children. Each ticket cost $200 and had a fair market value of $35. On the same day as the purchase, Roberta gave the tickets to the minister of her church for personal use by his family. At the time of the gift of the tickets, Roberta pledged $4,000 to the building fund of her church. The pledge was satisfied by check dated December 31, 1998, but not mailed until January 3, 1999.

a. Presuming Roberta is a cash basis and calendar year taxpayer, how much can she deduct as a charitable contribution for 1998?

b. Would the amount of the deduction be any different if Roberta is an accrual basis taxpayer? Explain.

43. In December each year, Alice Young contributes 10% of her gross income to the United Way (a 50% organization). Alice, who is in the 36% marginal tax bracket, is considering the following alternatives as charitable contributions in December 1998:

	Fair Market Value
(1) Cash donation	$21,000
(2) Unimproved land held for six years ($3,000 basis)	21,000
(3) Blue Corporation stock held for eight months ($3,000 basis)	21,000
(4) Gold Corporation stock held for two years ($26,000 basis)	21,000

Alice has asked you to help her decide which of the potential contributions listed above will be most advantageous taxwise. Evaluate the four alternatives and write a letter to Alice to communicate your advice to her. Her address is 2622 Bayshore Drive, Berkeley, CA 94709.

44. Manuel and Rosa Garcia, both age 45, are married and have no dependents. They have asked you to advise them whether they should file jointly or separately in 1998. They present you with the following information:

	Manuel	Rosa	Joint
Salary	$40,000		
Business net income		$100,000	
Interest income	400	1,200	$2,200
Deductions *for* AGI	2,000	13,000	
Medical expenses	9,500	600	
State income tax	800	2,000	
Real estate tax			3,400
Mortgage interest			5,200
Unreimbursed employee expenses	1,100		

If they file separately, Manuel and Rosa will split the real estate tax and mortgage interest deductions equally. Write Manuel and Rosa a letter in which you make and explain a recommendation on filing status for 1998. Manuel and Rosa reside at 5904 Stevens Avenue, Durham, NC 27707.

45. For calendar year 1998, Joe and Sandra file a joint return reflecting AGI of $180,000. Their itemized deductions are as follows:

Medical expenses	$15,000
Casualty loss (not covered by insurance)	21,000
Interest on home mortgage	11,000
Property taxes on home	12,000
Charitable contributions	13,000
State income tax	17,000

After all necessary adjustments are made, what is the amount of itemized deductions Joe and Sandra may claim?

46. Chris, who is single, had AGI of $220,000 during 1998. He incurred the following expenses and losses during the year:

Medical expenses before 7.5%-of-AGI limitation	$19,000
State and local income taxes	4,100
Real estate taxes	2,200
Home mortgage interest	5,600
Charitable contributions	3,500
Casualty loss before 10% limitation (after $100 floor)	25,000
Unreimbursed employee expenses subject to 2%-of-AGI limitation	5,700
Gambling losses (Chris had $4,200 of gambling income)	8,000

Compute Chris's itemized deductions before and after the overall limitation.

47. Barry and Emily are married, have no dependents, and file a joint return for 1998. Information for the year includes the following:

AGI	$252,500
State and local income taxes	6,000
Real estate taxes	7,800
Home mortgage interest	7,100
Charitable contributions	8,500
Gambling losses (gambling income of $4,500 was included in AGI)	7,000

a. Compute allowable itemized deductions for 1998 for Barry and Emily.
b. Compute taxable income for Barry and Emily for 1998.

48. Andy, who is single, had AGI of $180,000 for 1998. He incurred the following expenses and losses during the year:

Medical expenses before 7.5%-of-AGI limitation	$15,000
State and local income taxes	2,600
Real estate taxes	3,400
Home mortgage interest	6,600
Charitable contribution	3,500
Casualty loss before 10% limitation (after $100 floor)	20,600
Unreimbursed employee expenses subject to 2%-of-AGI limitation	4,100
Gambling losses (Andy had $3,500 of gambling income)	7,000

Calculate Andy's allowable itemized deductions for the year.

CUMULATIVE PROBLEMS

49. Alice and Bruce Byrd are married taxpayers, ages 47 and 45, who file a joint return. Their Social Security numbers are 034–48–4382 and 016–50–9556, respectively. They live at 473 Revere Avenue, Ames, MA 01850. Alice is the office manager for a dental clinic and earns an annual salary of $46,000. Bruce is the manager of a fast-food outlet owned and operated by Plymouth Corporation. His annual salary is $37,000.

The Byrds have two children, Cynthia (age 23 and S.S. no. 017–44–9126) and John (age 22 and S.S. no. 017–27–4148), who live with them. Both children are full-time students at a nearby college. Alice's mother, Myrtle Jones (age 74 and S.S. no. 016–15–8266), also lives with them. Her sole source of income is from Social Security benefits, which she deposits in a savings account.

During 1997, the Byrds furnished one-third of the total support of Bruce's widower father, Sam Byrd (age 70 and S.S. no. 034–82–8583). Sam lives alone and receives the rest of his support from Bruce's sister and brother (one-third each). They have signed a multiple support agreement allowing Bruce to claim Sam as a dependent for 1997. Sam died in November, and Bruce received life insurance proceeds of $270,000 on December 28.

The Byrds had the following expenses relating to their personal residence during 1997:

Property taxes	$2,400
Interest on home mortgage	6,900
Repairs to roof	2,000
Utilities	3,200
Fire and theft insurance	1,300

Medical expenses for 1997 include:

Medical insurance premiums	$4,800
Doctor bill for Sam incurred in 1996 and not paid until 1997	2,600
Operation for Sam	4,900

The operation for Sam represents the one-third Bruce contributed toward his father's support.

Other relevant information follows:

- Alice and Bruce had $2,600 ($1,400 for Alice and $1,200 for Bruce) withheld from their salaries for state income taxes. When they filed their 1996 state return in 1997, they paid additional tax of $480.

- During 1997, Alice and Bruce attended a dinner dance sponsored by the Ames Police Disability Association (a qualified charitable organization). The Byrds paid $100 for the tickets. Cost of comparable entertainment would normally be $40. The Byrds contributed $1,700 to their church and gave used clothing (cost of $800 and fair market value of $200) to the Salvation Army. All donations are supported by receipts.

- In 1997, the Byrds received interest income of $1,950 from a savings account they maintained.

- Alice's employer requires that all employees wear uniforms to work. During 1997, Alice spent $440 on new uniforms and $112 on laundry charges. Bruce paid $120 for an annual subscription to the *Journal of Franchise Management*. Neither Alice's nor Bruce's employers reimburse for employee expenses.

- Alice and Bruce had $6,800 ($3,700 for Alice and $3,100 for Bruce) of Federal income tax withheld in 1997 and paid no estimated Federal income tax. Neither Alice nor Bruce wishes to designate $3 to the Presidential Election Campaign Fund.

Part 1—Tax Computation
Compute net tax payable or refund due for Alice and Bruce Byrd for 1997. If they have overpaid, the amount is to be refunded. If you use tax forms for your computations, you will need Form 1040 and Schedules A and B. Suggested software (if available): *TurboTax.*

Part 2—Tax Planning
Alice and Bruce are planning some significant changes for 1998. They have provided you with the following information and asked you to project their taxable income and tax liability for 1998.

Myrtle became seriously ill in December 1997 and is no longer able to care for herself. As a result, Alice plans to take a one-year leave of absence from work during 1998 to care for her. The Byrds will use $70,000 of the life insurance proceeds they received as a result of Sam's death and pay off their mortgage in early January 1998. They will invest the remaining $200,000 in short-term certificates of deposit (CDs) and use the interest for living expenses during 1998. They expect to earn total interest of $13,500 on the CDs. Bruce has been awarded a 5% raise for 1998, and withholdings on his salary will increase accordingly.

The Byrds will not incur any additional costs related to Sam's medical problem. Alice will not work at all during 1998, so none of her job-related expenses or withholdings will continue. The Byrds do not expect to owe additional state income tax when they file their 1997 return, but they do expect their charitable contributions and medical insurance premiums to continue at the 1997 level. Assume all other income and deduction items will continue at the same level in 1998 unless you have information that indicates otherwise.

50. Paul and Donna Decker are married taxpayers, ages 44 and 42, who file a joint return for 1998. The Deckers live at 1121 College Avenue, Carmel, IN 46032. Paul is an assistant manager at Carmel Motor Inn, and Donna is a teacher at Carmel Elementary School. They present you with W–2 forms that reflect the following information:

	Paul	**Donna**
Salary	$37,000	$41,000
Federal tax withheld	6,992	5,900
State income tax withheld	700	760
FICA (Social Security) withheld	2,831	3,137
Social Security numbers	222–11–4567	333–11–9872

Donna is the custodial parent of two children from a previous marriage who reside with the Deckers through the school year. The children, Larry and Jane Parker, reside with their father, Bob, during the summer. Relevant information for the children follows:

	Larry	**Jane**
Age	11	9
Social Security numbers	305–11–4567	303–11–9872
Months spent with Deckers	9	9

Under the divorce decree, Bob pays child support of $150 per month per child during the nine months the children live with the Deckers. Bob says he spends $200 per month per child during the three summer months they reside with him. Donna and Paul can document that they provide $1,800 support per child per year. The divorce decree is silent as to which parent can claim the exemption for the children.

In August, Paul and Donna added a suite to their home to provide more comfortable accommodations for Hannah Snyder (263–33–4738), Donna's mother, who had moved in with them in February 1997 after the death of Donna's father. Not wanting to borrow money for this addition, Paul sold 300 shares of Acme Corporation stock for $50 per share on May 3, 1998, and used the proceeds of $15,000 to cover construction costs. The Deckers had purchased the stock on April 29, 1995, for $22 per share. They received dividends of $550 on the jointly owned stock a month before the sale.

Hannah, who is 66 years old, received $7,200 in Social Security benefits during the year, of which she gave the Deckers $1,700 to use toward household expenses and deposited the remainder in her personal savings account. The Deckers determine that they have spent $1,500 of their own money for food, clothing, medical expenses, and other items for Hannah. They do not know what the rental value of Hannah's suite would be, but they estimate it would be at least $300 per month.

Interest paid during the year included the following:

Home mortgage interest (paid to Carmel Federal Savings & Loan)	$4,890
Interest on an automobile loan (paid to Carmel National Bank)	920
Interest on Citibank Visa card	855

In July, Paul hit a submerged rock while boating. Fortunately, he was thrown from the boat, landed in deep water, and was uninjured. However, the boat, which was uninsured, was destroyed. Paul had paid $18,000 for the boat in June 1997, and its value was appraised at $14,500 on the date of the accident.

The Deckers paid doctor and hospital bills of $4,100 and were reimbursed $1,600 by their insurance company. They spent $780 for prescription drugs and medicines and

$1,440 for premiums on their health insurance policy. They have filed additional claims of $700 with their insurance company and have been told they will receive payment for that amount in January 1999. Included in the amounts paid for doctor and hospital bills were payments of $360 for Hannah and $750 for the children.

Additional information of potential tax consequence follows:

Real estate taxes paid	$1,900
Cash contributions to church	800
Appraised value of books donated to public library	450
Paul's unreimbursed employee expenses to attend hotel management convention:	
Airfare	340
Hotel	130
Meals	95
Registration fee	100
Refund of state income tax for 1997 (the Deckers itemized on their 1997 return)	910

Compute net tax payable or refund due for the Deckers for 1998. If they have overpaid, the amount is to be credited toward their taxes for 1999. Suggested software (if available): *TurboTax.*

Research Problems for this chapter appear at the end of Chapter 28.

TEAM PROJECT: ARTHUR ANDERSEN TAX CHALLENGE CASES

For more information on the Arthur Andersen Tax Challenge Cases, refer to Chapter 1, page 1–37.

Information related to tax issues and problems that are discussed in this chapter may be found in the

Day and Ball case on pages 3, 4, 5, 7, 11, 12, 25–28, and 33
Fence case on pages 40, 41, 51–55, 58, 62, and 66

Read and analyze the case you have been assigned and *identify* any issues and problems that are related to material covered in this chapter. If the information provided in the case is complete, prepare answers for this part of the case at this time. If you need information that is contained in the later parts of the case, write a memo summarizing the questions or problems so you can prepare a complete answer at a later date.

10

PASSIVE ACTIVITY LOSSES

LEARNING OBJECTIVES

After completing Chapter 10, you should be able to:

1. Discuss tax shelters and the reasons for at-risk and passive loss limitations.

2. Explain the at-risk limitation.

3. Describe how the passive loss rules limit deductions for losses, and identify the taxpayers subject to these restrictions.

4. Discuss the definition of passive activities and the rules for identifying an activity.

5. Analyze and apply the tests for material participation.

6. Understand the nature of rental activities under the passive loss rules.

7. Recognize the relationship between the at-risk and passive activity limitations.

8. Discuss the special treatment available to real estate activities.

9. Determine the proper tax treatment upon the disposition of a passive activity.

10. Suggest tax planning strategies to minimize the effect of the passive loss limitations.

THE TAX SHELTER PROBLEM

1 LEARNING OBJECTIVE
Discuss tax shelters and the reasons for at-risk and passive loss limitations.

Before Congress enacted legislation to reduce or eliminate their effectiveness, **tax shelters** were popular investments for tax avoidance purposes because they could generate deductions and other benefits that could be used to offset income from other sources. Because of the tax avoidance potential of many tax shelters, they were attractive to wealthy taxpayers in high income tax brackets. Many tax shelters merely provided an opportunity for "investors" to buy deductions and credits in ventures that were not expected to generate a profit, even in the long run.

Although it may seem odd that a taxpayer would intentionally invest in an activity that was designed to produce losses, there is a logical explanation. The typical tax shelter operated as a partnership and relied heavily on nonrecourse financing.[1] Accelerated depreciation and interest expense deductions generated large losses in the early years of the activity. At the very least, the tax shelter deductions deferred the recognition of any net income from the venture until the activity was sold. In the best of situations, the investor could realize additional tax savings by offsetting other income (e.g., salary, interest, and dividends) with deductions flowing from the tax shelter. Ultimately, the sale of the investment would result in capital gain. The following examples illustrate what was possible *before* Congress enacted legislation to curb tax shelter abuses.

EXAMPLE 1

Bob, who earned a salary of $300,000 as a business executive and dividend income of $15,000, invested $20,000 for a 10% interest in a cattle-breeding tax shelter. Through the use of $800,000 of nonrecourse financing and available cash of $200,000, the partnership acquired a herd of an exotic breed of cattle costing $1 million. Depreciation, interest, and other deductions related to the activity resulted in a loss of $400,000, of which Bob's share was $40,000. Bob was allowed to deduct the $40,000 loss, even though he had invested and stood to lose only $20,000 if the investment turned sour. The net effect of the $40,000 deduction from the partnership was that a portion of Bob's salary and dividend income was "sheltered," and as a result, he was required to calculate his tax liability on only $275,000 of income [$315,000 (salary and dividends) – $40,000 (deduction)]

---

[1]Nonrecourse debt is an obligation for which the borrower is not personally liable. An example of nonrecourse debt is a liability on real estate acquired by a partnership without the partnership or any of the partners assuming any liability for the mortgage. The acquired property generally is pledged as collateral for the loan.

rather than $315,000. If this deduction were available under current law and if Bob was in the 39.6% income tax bracket, this deduction would generate a tax savings of $15,840 ($40,000 × 39.6%) in the first year alone! ▼

A review of Example 1 shows that the taxpayer took a *two-for-one* write-off ($40,000 deduction, $20,000 investment). In the heyday of tax shelters, promoters often promised *multiple* write-offs for the investor.

The first major provision aimed at tax shelters was the **at-risk limitation.** Its objective is to limit a taxpayer's deductions to the amount at risk, that is, the amount the taxpayer stands to lose if the investment turns out to be a financial disaster.

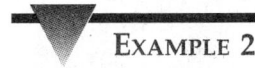

EXAMPLE 2

Returning to the facts of Example 1, under the current at-risk rules Bob would be allowed to deduct $20,000 (i.e., the amount that he could lose if the business failed). This deduction would reduce his other income and as a result, Bob would have to report only $295,000 of income ($315,000 – $20,000). The remaining nondeductible $20,000 loss and any future losses flowing from the partnership would be suspended under the at-risk rules and would be deductible in the future only as his at-risk amount increased. ▼

The second major attack on tax shelters came with the passage of the passive activity loss rules. These rules were intended to halt an investor's ability to benefit from the mismatching of an entity's expenses and income that often occurs in the early years of the business. Congress observed that despite the at-risk limitations, investors could still deduct losses flowing from an entity and thereby defer their tax liability on other income. In effect, passive activity rules have, to a great degree, made the term *tax shelter* obsolete. Now such ventures where investors are not involved in the day-to-day operations of the business are generally referred to as passive investments, or *passive activities*, rather than tax shelters.

The **passive loss** rules require the taxpayer to segregate all income and losses into three categories: active, passive, and portfolio. In general, the passive loss limits disallow the deduction of passive losses against active or portfolio income, even when the taxpayer is at risk to the extent of the loss. Normally, passive losses can only offset passive income.

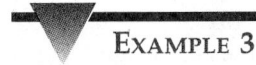

EXAMPLE 3

Returning to the facts of Example 1, the passive activity loss rules further restrict Bob's ability to claim the $20,000 tax deduction shown in Example 2. Because Bob is a passive investor and does not materially participate in any meaningful way in the activities of the cattle-breeding operation, the $20,000 loss allowed under the at-risk rules is disallowed under the passive loss rules. The passive loss is disallowed because Bob does not generate any passive income that could absorb his passive loss. Further, his salary (active income) and dividends (portfolio income) cannot be used to absorb any of the passive loss. Consequently, Bob's-current year taxable income must reflect his nonpassive income of $315,000, and he receives no current benefit from his share of the partnership loss. However, all is not lost because Bob's share of the entity's loss is *suspended*; it is carried forward and can be deducted in the future when he has passive income or sells his interest in the activity. ▼

This chapter explores the nature of the at-risk limits and passive activity loss rules and their impact on investors. An interesting consequence of these rules is that now investors evaluating potential investments must consider mainly the economics of the venture instead of the tax benefits or tax avoidance possibilities that an investment may generate.

THE IMPACT OF RECENT TAX LEGISLATION ON INVESTMENT CHOICES

With the recent reduction in the income tax rates on capital transactions, real estate investments are relatively more attractive than under earlier law. Gains on the sale of capital assets held for more than 18 months are taxed to individuals at no more than 20 percent. Persons contemplating investing in real estate, however, may be better off with stock and securities, which are subject to the same beneficial capital gain rates as real estate, but avoid the difficulties of dealing with the at-risk and passive loss rules. Sorting out the tax differences between the investment choices is not simple, as the tax rate is not the only or most important factor. In arriving at a decision, an investor would need to weigh other factors such as the following:

- Some people don't want the hassle of collecting rents and managing property. Others like the idea of owning physical assets that they can control. Stock investors, unfortunately, are essentially at the mercy of the people who manage the corporation.
- A real estate investor has more leverage than a stockholder. Real estate can be purchased with only a down payment, and the property appreciates while the rental receipts are used to pay off the loan.
- Property owners usually can count on a steady stream of rent income that can be offset for tax purposes by depreciation deductions.

SOURCE: Information from *USA Today*, August 15, 1997, p. 4B.

AT–RISK LIMITS

2   LEARNING OBJECTIVE
Explain the at-risk limitation.

The at-risk provisions limit the deductibility of losses from business and income-producing activities. These provisions, which apply to individuals and closely held corporations, are designed to prevent taxpayers from deducting losses in excess of their actual economic investment in an activity. In the case of an S corporation or a partnership, the at-risk limits apply at the owner level. Under the at-risk rules, a taxpayer's deductible loss from an activity for any taxable year is limited to the amount the taxpayer has at risk at the end of the taxable year (the amount the taxpayer could actually lose in the activity).

While the amount at risk generally vacillates over time, the initial amount considered at risk consists of the following:[2]

- The amount of cash and the adjusted basis of property contributed to the activity by the taxpayer.
- Amounts borrowed for use in the activity for which the taxpayer is personally liable or has pledged as security property not used in the activity.

This amount generally is increased each year by the taxpayer's share of income and is decreased by the taxpayer's share of losses and withdrawals from the activity. In addition, because general partners are jointly and severally liable for recourse

---

[2]§ 465(b)(1).

debts of the partnership, their at-risk amounts are increased when the partnership increases its debt and are decreased when the partnership reduces its debt. However, a taxpayer generally is not considered at risk with respect to borrowed amounts if either of the following is true:

- The taxpayer is not personally liable for repayment of the debt (e.g., nonrecourse debt).
- The lender has an interest (other than as a creditor) in the activity.

An important exception provides that in the case of an activity involving the holding of real property, a taxpayer is considered at risk for his or her share of any *qualified nonrecourse financing* that is secured by real property used in the activity.[3]

Subject to the passive activity rules discussed later in the chapter, a taxpayer may deduct a loss as long as the at-risk amount is positive. However, once the at-risk amount is exhausted, any remaining loss cannot be deducted until a later year. Any losses disallowed for any given taxable year by the at-risk rules may be deducted in the first succeeding year in which the rules do not prevent the deduction—that is, when and to the extent of a positive at-risk amount.

EXAMPLE 4

In 1998, Sue invests $40,000 in an oil partnership that, by the use of nonrecourse loans, spends $60,000 on deductible intangible drilling costs applicable to her interest. Assume Sue's interest in the partnership is subject to the at-risk limits but is not subject to the passive loss limits. Since Sue has only $40,000 of capital at risk, she cannot deduct more than $40,000 against her other income and must reduce her at-risk amount to zero ($40,000 at-risk amount − $40,000 loss deducted). The nondeductible loss of $20,000 ($60,000 loss generated − $40,000 loss allowed) can be carried over to 1999. ▼

EXAMPLE 5

In 1999, Sue has taxable income of $15,000 from the oil partnership and invests an additional $10,000 in the venture. Her at-risk amount is now $25,000 ($0 beginning balance + $15,000 taxable income + $10,000 additional investment). This enables Sue to deduct the carryover loss and requires her to reduce her at-risk amount to $5,000 ($25,000 at-risk amount − $20,000 carryover loss allowed). ▼

An additional complicating factor is that previously allowed losses must be recaptured to the extent the at-risk amount is reduced below zero.[4] That is, previous losses that were allowed must be offset by the recognition of enough income to bring the at-risk amount up to zero. This rule applies in such situations as when the amount at risk is reduced below zero by distributions to the taxpayer or when the status of indebtedness changes from recourse to nonrecourse.

PASSIVE LOSS LIMITS

CLASSIFICATION AND IMPACT OF PASSIVE INCOME AND LOSSES

3 **LEARNING OBJECTIVE**
Describe how the passive loss rules limit deductions for losses, and identify the taxpayers subject to these restrictions.

Classification. The passive loss rules require income and **losses to be** classified into one of three categories: active, passive, or portfolio. **Active income** includes, but is not limited to, the following:

- Wages, salary, commissions, bonuses, and other payments for services rendered by the taxpayer.
- Profit from a trade or business in which the taxpayer is a material participant.

---

[3]§ 465(b)(6).   [4]§ 465(e).

▼ CONCEPT SUMMARY 10–1

Calculation of At-Risk Amount

Increases to a taxpayer's at-risk amount:

- Cash and the adjusted basis of property contributed to the activity.
- Amounts borrowed for use in the activity for which the taxpayer is personally liable or has pledged as security property not used in the activity.
- Taxpayer's share of amounts borrowed for use in the activity that are qualified nonrecourse financing.
- Taxpayer's share of the activity's income.

Decreases to a taxpayer's at-risk amount:

- Withdrawals from the activity.
- Taxpayer's share of the activity's loss.
- Taxpayer's share of any reductions of debt for which recourse against the taxpayer exists or reductions of qualified nonrecourse debt.

- Gain on the sale or other disposition of assets used in an active trade or business.
- Income from intangible property if the taxpayer's personal efforts significantly contributed to the creation of the property.

Portfolio income includes, but is not limited to, the following:

- Interest, dividends, annuities, and royalties not derived in the ordinary course of a trade or business.
- Gain or loss from the disposition of property that produces portfolio income or is held for investment purposes.

Section 469 provides that income or loss from the following activities is treated as *passive:*

- Any trade or business or income-producing activity in which the taxpayer does not materially participate.
- Subject to certain exceptions, all rental activities, whether the taxpayer materially participates or not.

Although the Code defines rental activities as passive activities, several exceptions allow losses from certain real estate rental activities to be offset against nonpassive (active or portfolio) income. The exceptions are discussed under Special Passive Activity Rules for Real Estate Activities later in the chapter.

General Impact.   Deductions or expenses generated by passive activities can be deducted only to the extent of income from all of the taxpayer's passive activities. Any excess may not be used to offset income from active sources or portfolio income. Instead, any unused passive losses are suspended and carried forward to future years to offset passive income generated in those years. Otherwise, suspended losses may be used only when a taxpayer disposes of his or her entire interest in an activity. In that event, all current and suspended losses related to the activity may offset active and portfolio income.

ALL THAT GLITTERS IN TAX REFORM IS NOT GOLD

The topic of major tax reform is arising more frequently as our tax laws have become more complex. Inevitably, various proposals for a "flat tax" are touted as panaceas to these complexity problems. In such discussions, both supporters and opponents of the flat tax may present theoretical, practical, and political arguments, but often the implications of any particular plan are difficult to understand. For example, investors in financial instruments producing interest, dividend, and capital gain income could benefit under some flat tax proposals because they exclude such income from taxation. Individuals who invest in real estate may not be as fortunate, however.

Under certain proposals, the taxpayer could claim a deduction for the full cost of a building and land in the year of purchase, rather than having to capitalize these assets and depreciate only the building over a prolonged period of time. If the entity holding the property is a partnership or S corporation, the deduction would flow through to the entity's owners. The result would be a huge loss at the owner level. For real estate investors, however, the losses may not be deductible in the current year due to the passive activity loss rules. The losses would generate no current benefit unless the investor had a like amount of passive income. Under a flat tax regime, the appeal of real estate investments relative to financial investments could decline.

EXAMPLE 6

Kim, a physician, earns $150,000 from her full-time practice. She also receives $10,000 in dividends and interest from various portfolio investments, and her share of a passive loss from a tax shelter not limited by the at-risk rules is $60,000. Because the loss is a passive loss, it is not deductible against her other income. The loss is suspended and is carried over to the future. If Kim has passive income from this investment or from other passive investments in the future, she can offset the suspended loss against that passive income. If she does not have passive income to offset this suspended loss in the future, she will be allowed to offset the loss against other types of income when she eventually disposes of the passive activity. ▼

Impact of Suspended Losses. When a taxpayer disposes of his or her entire interest in a passive activity, the actual economic gain or loss from the investment, including any suspended losses, can finally be determined. As a result, under the passive loss rules, upon a fully taxable disposition, any overall loss realized from the activity by the taxpayer is recognized and can be offset against any income.

A fully taxable disposition generally involves a sale of the property to a third party at arm's length and thus, presumably, for a price equal to the property's fair market value. Gain recognized upon a transfer of an interest in a passive activity generally is treated as passive and is first offset by the suspended losses from that activity.

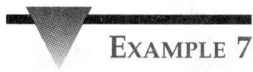

EXAMPLE 7

Rex sells an apartment building, a passive activity, with an adjusted basis of $100,000 for $180,000. In addition, he has suspended losses of $60,000 associated with the building. His total gain, $80,000, and his taxable gain, $20,000, are calculated as follows:

Net sales price	$ 180,000
Less: Adjusted basis	(100,000)
Total gain	$ 80,000
Less: Suspended losses	(60,000)
Taxable gain (passive)	$ 20,000

If current and suspended losses of the passive activity exceed the gain realized or if the sale results in a realized loss, the amount of

- any loss from the activity for the tax year (including losses suspended in the activity disposed of)

in excess of

- net income or gain for the tax year from all passive activities (without regard to the activity disposed of)

is treated as a loss that is not from a passive activity. In computing the loss from the activity for the year of disposition, any gain or loss recognized is included.

EXAMPLE 8   Dean sells an apartment building with an adjusted basis of $100,000 for $150,000. In addition, he has current and suspended losses of $60,000 associated with the building and has no other passive activities. His total gain, $50,000, and his deductible loss, $10,000, are calculated as follows:

Net sales price	$ 150,000
Less: Adjusted basis	(100,000)
Total gain	$ 50,000
Less: Suspended losses	(60,000)
Deductible loss	($ 10,000)

The $10,000 deductible loss is offset against Dean's active income and portfolio income. ▼

Carryovers of Suspended Losses.   In the above examples, it was assumed that the taxpayer had an interest in only one passive activity, and as a result, the suspended loss was related exclusively to the activity that was disposed of. Taxpayers often own interests in more than one activity, however, and in that case, any suspended losses must be allocated among the activities in which the taxpayer has an interest. The allocation to an activity is made by multiplying the disallowed passive activity loss from all activities by the following fraction:

$$\frac{\text{Loss from activity}}{\text{Sum of losses for taxable year from all activities having losses}}$$

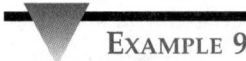

EXAMPLE 9   Diego has investments in three passive activities with the following income and losses for 1997:

Activity A	($30,000)
Activity B	(20,000)
Activity C	25,000
Net passive loss	($25,000)
Net passive loss allocated to:	
Activity A ($25,000 × $30,000/$50,000)	($15,000)
Activity B ($25,000 × $20,000/$50,000)	(10,000)
Total suspended losses	($25,000)

Suspended losses are carried over indefinitely and are offset in the future against any passive income from the activities to which they relate.[5]

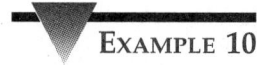

EXAMPLE 10   Assume the same facts as in Example 9 and that Activity A produces $10,000 of income in 1998. Of the suspended loss of $15,000 from 1997 for Activity A, $10,000 is offset against the income from this activity. If Diego sells Activity A in early 1999, then the remaining $5,000 suspended loss is used in determining his taxable gain or loss. ▼

Passive Credits.   Credits arising from passive activities are limited in much the same way as passive losses. Passive credits can be utilized only against regular tax attributable to passive income,[6] which is calculated by comparing the tax on all income (including passive income) with the tax on income excluding passive income.

EXAMPLE 11   Sam owes $50,000 of tax, disregarding net passive income, and $80,000 of tax, considering both net passive and other taxable income (disregarding the credits in both cases). The amount of tax attributable to the passive income is $30,000.

Tax due (before credits) including net passive income	$ 80,000
Less: Tax due (before credits) without including net passive income	(50,000)
Tax attributable to passive income	$ 30,000

Sam in the preceding example can claim a maximum of $30,000 of passive activity credits; the excess credits are carried over. These passive activity credits (such as the low-income housing credit and rehabilitation credit) can only be used against the *regular* tax attributable to passive income. If a taxpayer has a net loss from passive activities during a given year, no credits can be used. Likewise, if a taxpayer has net passive income but the alternative minimum tax applies to that year, no passive activity credits can be used. (The alternative minimum tax is discussed in Chapter 14.)

Carryovers of Passive Credits.   Tax credits attributable to passive activities can be carried forward indefinitely much like suspended passive losses. Unlike passive losses, however, passive credits are lost forever when the activity is disposed of in a taxable transaction where loss is recognized. Credits are allowed on dispositions only when there is sufficient tax on passive income to absorb them.

EXAMPLE 12   Alicia sells a passive activity for a gain of $10,000. The activity had suspended losses of $40,000 and suspended credits of $15,000. The $10,000 gain is offset by $10,000 of the suspended losses, and the remaining $30,000 of suspended losses is deductible against Alicia's active and portfolio income. The suspended credits are lost forever because the sale

[5] § 469(b).   [6] § 469(d)(2).

of the activity did not generate any tax. This is true even if Alicia has positive taxable income or is subject to the alternative minimum tax. ▼

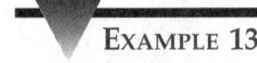

EXAMPLE 13

If Alicia in Example 12 had realized a $100,000 gain on the sale of the passive activity, the suspended credits could have been used to the extent of regular tax attributable to the net passive income.

Gain on sale	$100,000
Less: Suspended losses	(40,000)
Taxable gain	$ 60,000

If the tax attributable to the taxable gain of $60,000 is $15,000 or more, the entire $15,000 of suspended credits can be used. If the tax attributable to the gain is less than $15,000, the excess of the suspended credits over the tax attributable to the gain is lost forever. ▼

When a taxpayer has adequate regular tax liability from passive activities to trigger the use of suspended credits, the credits lose their character as passive credits. They are reclassified as regular tax credits and made subject to the same limits as other credits (discussed in Chapter 11).

TAXPAYERS SUBJECT TO THE PASSIVE LOSS RULES

The passive loss rules apply to individuals, estates, trusts, personal service corporations, and closely held C corporations.[7] Passive income or loss from investments in S corporations or partnerships (see Chapters 21 and 22) flows through to the owners, and the passive loss rules are applied at the owner level.

Personal Service Corporations.   Application of the passive loss limitations to **personal service corporations** is intended to prevent taxpayers from sheltering personal service income by creating personal service corporations and acquiring passive activities at the corporate level.

EXAMPLE 14

Five tax accountants, who earn a total of $1 million a year in their individual practices, form a personal service corporation. Shortly after its formation, the corporation invests in a passive activity that produces a $200,000 loss during the year. Because the passive loss rules apply to personal service corporations, the corporation may not deduct the $200,000 loss against the $1 million of active income. ▼

Determination of whether a corporation is a *personal service corporation* is based on rather broad definitions. A personal service corporation is a corporation that meets *both* of the following conditions:

- The principal activity is the performance of personal services.
- Such services are substantially performed by employee-owners.

Generally, personal service corporations include those in the fields of health, law, engineering, architecture, accounting, actuarial science, performing arts, and consulting.[8] A corporation is treated as a personal service corporation if more than 10 percent of the stock (by value) is held by employee-owners.[9] A shareholder is treated as an employee-owner if he or she is an employee or shareholder on *any*

---

[7] § 469(a).
[8] § 448(d)(2).

[9] § 469(j)(2).

day during the testing period.[10] For these purposes, shareholder status and employee status do not even have to occur on the same day.

Closely Held C Corporations.   Application of the passive loss rules to closely held (non-personal service) corporations is also intended to prevent individuals from incorporating to avoid the passive loss limitations. A corporation is classified as a **closely held corporation** if at any time during the taxable year, more than 50 percent of the value of its outstanding stock is owned, directly or indirectly, by or for not more than five individuals. Closely held C corporations (other than personal service corporations) may offset passive losses against *active* income, but not against portfolio income.

EXAMPLE 15

Silver Corporation, a closely held (non-personal service) C corporation, has $500,000 of passive losses from a rental activity, $400,000 of active income, and $100,000 of portfolio income. The corporation may offset $400,000 of the $500,000 passive loss against the $400,000 of active business income, but may not offset the remainder against the $100,000 of portfolio income. Thus, $100,000 of the passive loss is suspended ($500,000 passive loss − $400,000 offset against active income). ▼

Application of the passive loss limitations to closely held corporations prevents taxpayers from transferring their portfolio investments to such corporations in order to offset passive losses against portfolio income.

PASSIVE ACTIVITIES DEFINED

4 ▼ **LEARNING OBJECTIVE**
Discuss the definition of passive activities and the rules for identifying an activity.

Section 469 specifies that the following types of activities are to be treated as passive:

- Any trade or business or income-producing activity in which the taxpayer does not materially participate.
- Subject to certain exceptions, all rental activities.

To understand the meaning of the term *passive activity* and the impact of the rules, one must address the following issues, each of which is the subject of statutory or administrative guidance:

- What constitutes an activity?
- What is meant by material participation?
- When is an activity a rental activity?

Even though guidance is available to help the taxpayer deal with these issues, their resolution is anything but simple.

Identification of an Activity.   Identifying what constitutes an activity is a necessary first step in applying the passive loss limitations. Taxpayers who are involved in complex business operations need to be able to determine whether a given segment of their overall business operations constitutes a separate activity or is to be treated as part of a single activity. Proper treatment is necessary in order to determine whether income or loss from an activity is active or passive.

EXAMPLE 16

Ben owns a business with two separate departments. Department A generates net income of $120,000, and Department B generates a net loss of $95,000. Ben participates for 700 hours in the operations of Department A and for 100 hours in Department B. If Ben is allowed to

---

[10]§ 269A(b)(2).

treat the departments as components of a single activity, he can offset the $95,000 loss from Department B against the $120,000 income from Department A. ▼

EXAMPLE 17

Assume the same facts as in the previous example. If Ben is required to treat each department as a separate activity, the tax result is not as favorable. Because he is a material participant in Department A (having devoted 700 hours to it), the $120,000 profit is active income. However, he is not considered a material participant in Department B (100 hours), and the $95,000 loss is a passive loss. Therefore, Ben cannot offset the $95,000 passive loss from Department B against the $120,000 of active income from Department A. (A complete discussion of the material participation rules follows.) ▼

Recall that on the disposition of a passive activity, a taxpayer is allowed to offset suspended losses from the activity against other types of income. Therefore, identifying what constitutes an activity is of crucial importance for this purpose too.

EXAMPLE 18

Linda owns a business with two departments. Department A has a net loss of $125,000 in the current year, and Department B has a $70,000 net loss. She disposes of Department B at the end of the year. Assuming Linda is allowed to treat the two departments as separate passive activities, she can offset the passive loss from Department B against other types of income in the following order: gain from disposition of the passive activity, other passive income, and nonpassive income. This treatment leaves her with a suspended loss of $125,000 from Department A. If Departments A and B are treated as components of the same activity, however, on the disposal of Department B, its $70,000 net loss would be suspended along with the other $125,000 of suspended loss of the activity. ▼

The current rules used to delineate what constitutes an activity for purposes of the passive loss limitations are provided in Regulations.[11] These guidelines state that, in general, a taxpayer can treat one or more trade or business activities or rental activities as a single activity if those activities form an *appropriate economic unit* for measuring gain or loss. To determine what ventures form an appropriate economic unit, all of the relevant facts and circumstances must be considered. Taxpayers may use any reasonable method in applying the facts and circumstances. However, the following five factors are given the greatest weight in determining whether activities constitute an appropriate economic unit. It is not necessary to meet all of these conditions in order to treat multiple activities as a single activity.

- Similarities and differences in the types of business conducted in the various trade or business or rental activities.
- The extent of common control over the various activities.
- The extent of common ownership of the activities.
- The geographical location of the different units.
- Interdependencies among the activities.

The following examples, adapted from the Regulations, illustrate the application of the general rules for grouping activities.[12]

EXAMPLE 19

George owns a men's clothing store and a video game parlor in Chicago. He also owns a men's clothing store and a video game parlor in Milwaukee. Reasonable methods of applying the facts and circumstances test may result in any of the following groupings:

---

[11]Reg. § 1.469–4.   [12]Reg. § 1.469–4(c)(3).

- All four activities may be grouped into a single activity.
- The clothing stores may be grouped into an activity, and the video game parlors may be grouped into a separate activity.
- The Chicago activities may be grouped into an activity, and the Milwaukee activities may be grouped into a separate activity.
- Each of the four activities may be treated as a separate activity. ▼

EXAMPLE 20

Sharon is a partner in a business that sells snack items to drugstores. She also is a partner in a partnership that owns and operates a warehouse. Both partnerships, which are under common control, are located in the same industrial park. The predominant part of the warehouse business is warehousing items for the snack business, and it is the only warehousing business in which Sharon is involved. Sharon should treat the snack business and the warehousing business as a single activity. ▼

Regrouping of Activities. Taxpayers should carefully consider all tax factors in deciding how to group their activities. Once activities have been grouped, they cannot be regrouped unless the original grouping was clearly inappropriate or there has been a material change in the facts and circumstances. If a regrouping is necessary for either of these reasons, the taxpayer is required to disclose to the IRS all information relevant to the regrouping.

The Regulations also grant the IRS the right to regroup activities when both of the following conditions exist:[13]

- The taxpayer's grouping fails to reflect one or more appropriate economic units.
- One of the primary purposes of the taxpayer's grouping is to avoid the passive loss limitations.

The following example, adapted from the Regulations, illustrates a situation where the IRS would exercise its prerogative to regroup a taxpayer's activities.

EXAMPLE 21

Baker, Edwards, Andrews, Clark, and Henson are physicians who operate their own separate practices. Each of the physicians owns interests in activities that generate passive losses, so they devise a plan to set up an entity that will generate passive income. They form the BEACH Partnership to acquire and operate X-ray equipment, and each receives a limited partnership interest. They select an unrelated person to operate the X-ray business as a general partner, and none of the limited partners participates in the activity. Substantially all of the services provided by BEACH are provided to the physicians who own limited partnership interests, and fees are set at a level that assures a profit for BEACH. Each physician treats his medical practice and his interest in the partnership as separate activities and offsets losses from passive investments against the passive income from the partnership. The IRS would interpret the physicians' separate groupings as attempts to avoid the passive loss limitations and would regroup each medical practice and the services performed by the partnership as an appropriate economic unit. ▼

Special Grouping Rules for Rental Activities. Two rules deal specifically with the grouping of rental activities. These provisions are designed to prevent taxpayers from grouping rental activities, which are generally passive, with other businesses in a way that would result in a tax advantage.

---

[13]Reg. § 1.469-4(f).

First, a rental activity may be grouped with a trade or business activity only if one activity is insubstantial in relation to the other. That is, the rental activity must be insubstantial in relation to the trade or business activity, or the trade or business activity must be insubstantial in relation to the rental activity. The Regulations provide no clear guidelines as to the meaning of insubstantial.[14]

EXAMPLE 22

Schemers, a firm of CPAs, owns a building in downtown Washington, D.C., in which they conduct their practice of public accounting. The firm also rents space on the street level of the building to several retail establishments. Of the total revenue generated by the firm, 95% is associated with the practice of public accounting, and 5% is related to the rental operation. It is likely that the rental activity would be considered insubstantial relative to the accounting practice and the two ventures could be grouped as one nonrental activity. This grouping could be advantageous to the firm, particularly if the rental operation generates a loss! ▼

Second, taxpayers generally may not treat an activity involving the rental of real property and an activity involving the rental of personal property as a single activity.

5   **LEARNING OBJECTIVE**
Analyze and apply the tests for material participation.

Material Participation.   If an individual taxpayer materially participates in a nonrental trade or business activity, any loss from that activity is treated as an active loss that can be offset against active or portfolio income. If a taxpayer does not materially participate, however, the loss is treated as a passive loss, which can only be offset against passive income. Therefore, controlling whether a particular activity is treated as active or passive is an important part of the tax strategy of a taxpayer who owns an interest in one or more businesses. Consider the following examples.

EXAMPLE 23

Dewayne, a corporate executive, earns a salary of $200,000 per year. In addition, he owns a separate business in which he participates. The business produces a loss of $100,000 during the year. If Dewayne materially participates in the business, the $100,000 loss is an active loss that may be offset against his active income from his corporate employer. If he does not materially participate, the loss is passive and is suspended. Dewayne may use the suspended loss in the future only when he has passive income or disposes of the activity. ▼

EXAMPLE 24

Kay, an attorney, earns $250,000 a year in her law practice. She owns interests in two activities, A and B, in which she participates. Activity A, in which she does *not* materially participate, produces a loss of $50,000. Kay has not yet met the material participation standard for Activity B, which produces income of $80,000. However, she can meet the material participation standard if she spends an additional 50 hours in Activity B during the year. Should Kay attempt to meet the material participation standard for Activity B? If she continues working in Activity B and becomes a material participant, the $80,000 of income from the activity is *active*, and the $50,000 passive loss from Activity A must be suspended. A more favorable tax strategy is for Kay to *not meet* the material participation standard for Activity B, thus making the income from that activity passive. This enables her to offset the $50,000 passive loss from Activity A against the passive income from Activity B. ▼

It is possible to devise numerous scenarios in which the taxpayer could control the tax outcome by increasing or decreasing his or her participation in different activities. Examples 23 and 24 demonstrate some of the possibilities. The conclusion reached in most analyses of this type is that taxpayers will benefit by having

---

[14]Reg. § 1.469-4(d).

profitable activities classified as passive, so that any passive losses can be used to offset passive income. If the activity produces a loss, however, the taxpayer will benefit if it is classified as active so the loss is not subject to the passive loss limitations.

As discussed above, a nonrental trade or business in which a taxpayer owns an interest must be treated as a passive activity unless the taxpayer materially participates. As the Staff of the Joint Committee on Taxation explained, a material participant is one who has "a significant nontax economic profit motive" for taking on activities and selects them for their economic value. In contrast, a passive investor mainly seeks a return from a capital investment (including a possible reduction in taxes) as a supplement to an ongoing source of livelihood.[15] Even if the concept or the implication of being a material participant is clear, the precise meaning of the term **material participation** can be vague. As enacted, § 469 requires a taxpayer to participate on a *regular, continuous, and substantial* basis in order to be a material participant. In many situations, however, it is difficult or impossible to gain any assurance that this nebulous standard is met.

In response to this dilemma, Temporary Regulations[16] provide seven tests that are intended to help taxpayers cope with these issues. Material participation is achieved by meeting any one of the tests. These tests can be divided into three categories:

- Tests based on current participation.
- Tests based on prior participation.
- Test based on facts and circumstances.

Tests Based on Current Participation.   The first four tests are quantitative tests that require measurement, in hours, of the taxpayer's participation in the activity during the year.

1. *Does the individual participate in the activity for more than 500 hours during the year?*

The purpose of the 500-hour requirement is to restrict deductions from the types of trade or business activities Congress intended to treat as passive activities. The 500-hour standard for material participation was adopted for the following reasons:[17]

- Few investors in traditional tax shelters devote more than 500 hours a year to such an investment.
- The IRS believes that income from an activity in which the taxpayer participates for more than 500 hours a year should not be treated as passive.

2. *Does the individual's participation in the activity for the taxable year constitute substantially all of the participation in the activity of all individuals (including nonowner employees) for the year?*

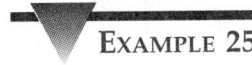

EXAMPLE 25

Ned, a physician, operates a separate business in which he participates for 80 hours during the year. He is the only participant and has no employees in the separate business. Ned meets the material participation standard of Test 2. If he had employees, it would

---

[15]*General Explanation of the Tax Reform Act of 1986 ("Blue Book"),* prepared by The Staff of the Joint Committee on Taxation, May 4, 1987, H.R. 3838, 99th Cong., p. 212.

[16]Temp. and Prop.Reg. § 1.469–5T(a). The Temporary Regulations are also Proposed Regulations. Temporary Regulations have the

same effect as final Regulations. Refer to Chapter 28 for a discussion of the different categories of Regulations.

[17]T.D. 8175, 1988–1 C.B. 191.

be difficult to apply Test 2, because the Temporary Regulations do not define the term *substantially all*. ▼

> 3. *Does the individual participate in the activity for more than 100 hours during the year, and is the individual's participation in the activity for the year not less than the participation of any other individual (including nonowner employees) for the year?*

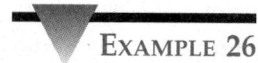
EXAMPLE 26

Adam, a college professor, owns a separate business in which he participates 110 hours during the year. He has an employee who works 90 hours during the year. Adam meets the material participation standard under Test 3, but probably does not meet it under Test 2 because his participation is only 55% of the total participation. It is unlikely that 55% would meet the *substantially all* requirement of Test 2. ▼

Tests 2 and 3 are included because the IRS recognizes that the operation of some activities does not require more than 500 hours of participation during the year.

> 4. *Is the activity a significant participation activity for the taxable year, and does the individual's aggregate participation in all significant participation activities during the year exceed 500 hours?*

A **significant participation activity** is a trade or business in which the individual's participation exceeds 100 hours during the year. This test treats taxpayers as material participants if their aggregate participation in several significant participation activities exceeds 500 hours. Test 4 thus accords the same treatment to an individual who devotes an aggregate of more than 500 hours to several significant participation activities as to an individual who devotes more than 500 hours to a single activity.

EXAMPLE 27

Mike owns five different businesses. He participated in each activity during the year as follows:

Activity	Hours of Participation
A	110
B	140
C	120
D	150
E	100

Activities A, B, C, and D are significant participation activities, and Mike's aggregate participation in those activities is 520 hours. Therefore, Activities A, B, C, and D are not treated as passive activities. Activity E is not a significant participation activity (not more than 100 hours), so it is not included in applying the 500-hour test. Activity E is treated as a passive activity, unless Mike meets one of the other material participation tests for that activity. ▼

EXAMPLE 28

Assume the same facts as in the previous example, except that Activity A does not exist. All of the activities are now treated as passive. Activity E is not counted in applying the more-than-500-hour test, so Mike's aggregate participation in significant participation activities is 410 hours (140 in Activity B + 120 in Activity C + 150 in Activity D). He could meet the significant participation test for Activity E by participating for one more hour in the activity. This would cause Activities B, C, D, and E to be treated as nonpassive activities.

However, before deciding whether to participate for at least one more hour in Activity E, Mike should assess how the participation would affect his overall tax liability. ▼

Tests Based on Prior Participation.   Tests 5 and 6 are based on material participation in prior years. Under these tests, a taxpayer who is no longer a participant in an activity can continue to be *classified* as a material participant. The IRS takes the position that material participation in a trade or business for a long period of time is likely to indicate that the activity represents the individual's principal livelihood, rather than a passive investment. Consequently, withdrawal from the activity, or reduction of participation to the point where it is not material, does not change the classification of the activity from active to passive.

5. *Did the individual materially participate in the activity for any 5 taxable years (whether consecutive or not) during the 10 taxable years that immediately precede the taxable year?*

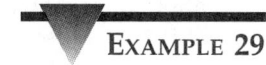

EXAMPLE 29

Dawn, who owns a 50% interest in a restaurant, was a material participant in the operations of the restaurant from 1992 through 1996. She retired at the end of 1996 and is no longer involved in the restaurant except as an investor. Dawn will be treated as a material participant in the restaurant in 1997. Even if she does not become involved in the restaurant as a material participant again, she will continue to be treated as a material participant in 1998, 1999, 2000, and 2001. In 2002 and later years, Dawn's share of income or loss from the restaurant will be classified as passive unless she materially participates in those years. ▼

6. *Is the activity a personal service activity, and did the individual materially participate in the activity for any three preceding taxable years (whether consecutive or not)?*

As indicated above, the material participation standards differ for personal service activities and other businesses. An individual who was a material participant in a personal service activity for *any three years* prior to the taxable year continues to be treated as a material participant after withdrawal from the activity.

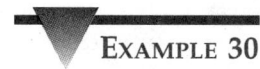

EXAMPLE 30

Evan, a CPA, retires from the EFG Partnership after working full-time in the partnership for 30 years. As a retired partner, he will continue to receive a share of the profits of the firm for the next 10 years, even though he will not participate in the firm's operations. Evan also owns an interest in a passive activity that produces a loss for the year. He continues to be treated as a material participant in the EFG Partnership, and his income from the partnership is active income. Therefore, he is not allowed to offset the loss from his passive investment against the income from the EFG Partnership. ▼

Facts and Circumstances Test.   Test 7 is a facts and circumstances test to determine whether the taxpayer has materially participated.

7. *Based on all the facts and circumstances, did the individual participate in the activity on a regular, continuous, and substantial basis during the year?*

The Temporary Regulations do not define what constitutes regular, continuous, and substantial participation except to say that the taxpayer's activities will *not* be considered material participation under Test 7 in the following three circumstances:[18]

---

[18]Temp. and Prop.Reg. § 1.469–5T(b)(2).

- The taxpayer satisfies the participation standards (whether or not a *material participant*) of any Code section other than § 469.
- The taxpayer manages the activity, unless
  - no other person receives compensation for management services, and
  - no individual spends more hours during the tax year managing the activity than does the taxpayer.
- The taxpayer participates in the activity for 100 hours or less during the tax year.

A part of the Temporary Regulations has been reserved for further development of this test. Presumably, additional guidelines will be issued in the future. For the time being, taxpayers should rely on Tests 1 through 6 in determining whether the material participation standards have been met.

Participation Defined.   Participation generally includes any work done by an individual in an activity that he or she owns. Participation does not include work if it is of a type not customarily done by owners *and* if one of its principal purposes is to avoid the disallowance of passive losses or credits. Also, work done in an individual's capacity as an investor (e.g., reviewing financial reports in a non-managerial capacity) is not counted in applying the material participation tests. However, participation by an owner's spouse counts as participation by the owner.[19]

EXAMPLE 31

Tom, who is a partner in a CPA firm, owns a computer store that has operated at a loss during the year. In order to offset this loss against the income from his CPA practice, Tom would like to avoid having the computer business classified as a passive activity. Through December 15, he has worked 400 hours in the business in management and selling activities. During the last two weeks of December, he works 80 hours in management and selling activities and 30 hours doing janitorial chores. Also during the last two weeks in December, Tom's wife participates 40 hours as a salesperson. She has worked as a salesperson in the computer store in prior years, but has not done so during the current year. If any of Tom's work is of a type not customarily done by owners *and* if one of its principal purposes is to avoid the disallowance of passive losses or credits, it is not counted in applying the material participation tests. It is likely that Tom's 480 hours of participation in management and selling activities will count as participation, but the 30 hours spent doing janitorial chores will not. However, the 40 hours of participation by his wife will count, and Tom will qualify as a material participant under the more-than-500-hour rule (480 + 40 = 520). ▼

Limited Partners.   A *limited* partner is one whose liability to third-party creditors of the partnership is limited to the amount the partner has invested in the partnership. Such a partnership must have at least one *general* partner, who is fully liable in an individual capacity for the debts of the partnership to third parties. Generally, a *limited partner* is not considered a material participant unless he or she qualifies under Test 1, 5, or 6 in the above list. However, a *general partner* may qualify as a material participant by meeting any of the seven tests. If an unlimited, or general, partner also owns a limited interest in the same limited partnership, all interests are treated as a general interest.[20]

---

[19]Temp. and Prop.Reg. § 1.469–5T(f)(3).

[20]Temp. and Prop.Reg. § 1.469–5T(e)(3)(ii).

ETHICAL CONSIDERATIONS

A Lovers' Triangle and the Passive Loss Rules

The troubled marriage of John and Eleanor finally reached an impasse, and they mutually agreed to divorce. Shortly after the divorce was finalized, John married Kristen. The three have known each other for years from working together to harvest the grapes of a vineyard owned by John. Prior to the divorce, each had worked 200 hours in the vineyard in the current year. Because the investment generates a loss for the current year, John wants to classify it as an active rather than a passive loss. In order for the loss to be classified as active, the participation of John and his wife together must exceed 500 hours. John claims that meeting that threshold is no problem. He worked 200 hours and Eleanor, who was his wife when the work was done, worked 200 hours. Kristen, who files a joint return with John, worked 200 hours. "Besides," says John, "there is nothing in the law that says I can't do this." John feels it is proper to aggregate Eleanor's and Kristen's participation with his own. This makes the loss deductible in full. As John's tax return preparer, how do you react?

6 LEARNING OBJECTIVE
Understand the nature of rental activities under the passive loss rules.

Rental Activities Defined. As discussed previously, § 469 specifies that, subject to certain exceptions, all rental activities are to be treated as passive activities.[21] A **rental activity** is defined as any activity where payments are received principally for the use of tangible (real or personal) property.[22] Importantly, an activity that is classified as a rental activity is subject to the passive activity loss rules, even if the taxpayer involved is a material participant.

EXAMPLE 32

Sarah owns an apartment building and spends an average of 60 hours a week in its operation. Assuming that the apartment building operation is classified as a rental activity, it is automatically subject to the passive activity rules, even though Sarah spends more than 500 hours a year in its operation. ▼

As suggested, Temporary Regulations provide that in certain situations activities involving rentals of real and personal property are *not* to be *treated* as rental activities.[23]

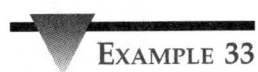

EXAMPLE 33

Dan owns a videocassette rental business. Because the average period of customer use is seven days or less, Dan's videocassette business is not treated as a rental activity. ▼

The fact that Dan's videocassette business in the previous example is not treated as a rental activity does not necessarily mean that it is classified as a nonpassive activity. Instead, the videocassette business is treated as a trade or business activity subject to the material participation standards. If Dan is a material participant, the business is treated as active. If he is not a material participant, it is treated as a passive activity.

Therefore, activities covered by any of the following six exceptions provided by the Temporary Regulations are not *automatically* treated as passive activities because they would not be classified as rental activities. Instead, the activities are subject to the material participation tests.

---

[21]§ 469(c)(2).
[22]§ 469(j)(8).

[23]Temp. and Prop.Reg. § 1.469–1T(e)(3)(ii).

1. *The average period of customer use of the property is seven days or less.*

Under this exception, activities involving the short-term use of tangible property such as automobiles, videocassettes, tuxedos, tools, and other such property are not treated as rental activities. The provision also applies to short-term rentals of hotel or motel rooms.

This exception is based on the presumption that a person who rents property for seven days or less is generally required to provide *significant services* to the customer. Providing such services supports a conclusion that the person is engaged in a service business rather than a rental business.

2. *The average period of customer use of the property is 30 days or less, and the owner of the property provides significant personal services.*

For longer-term rentals, the presumption that significant services are provided is not automatic, as it is in the case of the seven-day exception. Instead, the taxpayer must be able to *prove* that significant personal services are rendered in connection with the activity. Relevant facts and circumstances include the frequency with which such services are provided, the type and amount of labor required to perform the services, and the value of the services relative to the amount charged for the use of the property. Significant personal services include only services provided by *individuals*.[24]

3. *The owner of the property provides extraordinary personal services. The average period of customer use is of no consequence in applying this test.*

Extraordinary personal services are services provided by individuals where the customers' use of the property is incidental to their receipt of the services. For example, a patient's use of a hospital bed is incidental to his or her receipt of medical services. Another example is the use of a boarding school's dormitory, which is incidental to the scholastic services received.

4. *The rental of the property is treated as incidental to a nonrental activity of the taxpayer.*

Rentals of real property incidental to a nonrental activity are not considered a passive activity. The Temporary Regulations provide that the following rentals are not passive activities:[25]

- *Property held primarily for investment.* This occurs where the principal purpose for holding the property is the expectation of gain from the appreciation of the property and the gross rent income is less than 2 percent of the lesser of (1) the unadjusted basis or (2) the fair market value of the property.

EXAMPLE 34

Ramon invests in vacant land for the purpose of realizing a profit on its appreciation. He leases the land during the period it is held. The land's unadjusted basis is $250,000, and the fair market value is $350,000. The lease payments are $4,000 per year. Because gross rent income is less than 2% of $250,000, the activity is not a rental activity. ▼

- *Property used in a trade or business.* This occurs where the property is owned by a taxpayer who is an owner of the trade or business using the rental property. The property must also have been used in the trade or business during the year or during at least two of the five preceding taxable years. The 2 percent test above also applies in this situation.

---

[24]Temp. and Prop.Reg. § 1.469–1T(e)(3)(iv).   [25]Temp. and Prop.Regs. §§ 1.469–1T(e)(3)(vi)(B) through (E).

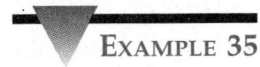

EXAMPLE 35

A farmer owns land with an unadjusted basis of $250,000 and a fair market value of $350,000. He used it for farming purposes in 1996 and 1997. In 1998, he leased the land to another farmer for $4,000. The activity is not a rental activity. ▼

- *Property held for sale to customers.* If property is held for sale to customers and rented during the year, the rental of the property is not a rental activity. If, for instance, an automobile dealer rents automobiles held for sale to customers to persons who are having their own cars repaired, the activity is not a rental activity.
- *Lodging rented for the convenience of an employer.* If an employer provides lodging for an employee incidental to the employee's performance of services in the employer's trade or business, no rental activity exists.
- A partner who rents property to a partnership that is used in the partnership's trade or business does not have a rental activity.

These rules were written to prevent taxpayers from converting active or portfolio income into a passive activity for the purpose of offsetting other passive losses.

5. *The taxpayer customarily makes the property available during defined business hours for nonexclusive use by various customers.*

EXAMPLE 36

Pat is the owner-operator of a public golf course. Some customers pay daily greens fees each time they use the course, while others purchase weekly, monthly, or annual passes. The golf course is open every day from sunrise to sunset, except on certain holidays and on days when the course is closed due to inclement weather conditions. Pat is not engaged in a rental activity, regardless of the average period customers use the course. ▼

6. *The property is provided for use in an activity conducted by a partnership, S corporation, or joint venture in which the taxpayer owns an interest.*

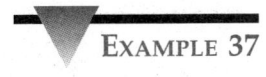

EXAMPLE 37

Joe, a partner in the Skyview Partnership, contributes the use of a building to the partnership. The partnership has net income of $30,000 during the year, of which Joe's share is $10,000. Unless the partnership is engaged in a rental activity, none of Joe's income from the partnership is income from a rental activity. ▼

INTERACTION OF THE AT-RISK AND PASSIVE ACTIVITY LIMITS

7 ▼ LEARNING OBJECTIVE
Recognize the relationship between the at-risk and passive activity limitations.

The determination of whether a loss is suspended under the passive loss rules is made after application of the at-risk rules, as well as other provisions relating to the measurement of taxable income. A loss that is not allowed for the year because the taxpayer is not at risk with respect to it is suspended under the at-risk provision and not under the passive loss rules. Further, a taxpayer's basis is reduced by deductions (e.g., depreciation) even if the deductions are not currently usable because of the passive loss rules.

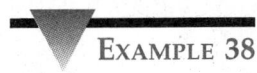

EXAMPLE 38

Jack's adjusted basis in a passive activity is $10,000 at the beginning of 1997. His loss from the activity in 1997 is $4,000. Since Jack had no passive activity income, the $4,000 cannot be deducted. At year-end, Jack has an adjusted basis and an at-risk amount of $6,000 in the activity and a suspended passive loss of $4,000. ▼

EXAMPLE 39

Jack in Example 38 had a loss of $9,000 in the activity in 1998. Since the $9,000 exceeds his at-risk amount ($6,000) by $3,000, that $3,000 loss is disallowed by the at-risk rules. If Jack has no passive activity income, the remaining $6,000 is suspended under the passive activity rules. At year-end, he has a $3,000 loss suspended under the at-risk rules, $10,000 of suspended passive losses, and an adjusted basis and an at-risk amount in the activity of zero. ▼

EXAMPLE 40

Jack in Example 39 realized $1,000 of passive income in 1999. Because the $1,000 increases his at-risk amount, $1,000 of the $3,000 unused loss can be reclassified as a passive loss. If he has no other passive income, the $1,000 income is offset by $1,000 of suspended passive losses. At the end of 1999, Jack has no taxable passive income, $2,000 ($3,000 − $1,000) of unused losses under the at-risk rules, $10,000 of (reclassified) suspended passive losses ($10,000 + $1,000 of reclassified unused at-risk losses − $1,000 of passive losses offset against passive income), and an adjusted basis and an at-risk amount in the activity of zero. ▼

EXAMPLE 41

In 2000, Jack had no gain or loss from the activity in Example 40. He contributed $5,000 more to the passive activity. Because the $5,000 increases his at-risk amount, the $2,000 of losses suspended under the at-risk rules is reclassified as passive. Jack gets no passive loss deduction in 2000. At year-end, he has no suspended losses under the at-risk rules, $12,000 of suspended passive losses ($10,000 + $2,000 of reclassified suspended at-risk losses), and an adjusted basis and an at-risk amount of $3,000 ($5,000 additional investment − $2,000 of reclassified losses). ▼

SPECIAL PASSIVE ACTIVITY RULES FOR REAL ESTATE ACTIVITIES

8 **LEARNING OBJECTIVE**
Discuss the special treatment available to real estate activities.

The passive loss limits contain two exceptions related to real estate activities. These exceptions allow all or part of real estate rental losses to be offset against active or portfolio income, even though the activity is a passive activity.

Material Participation in a Real Property Trade or Business. Losses from real estate rental activities are *not* treated as passive losses for certain real estate professionals.[26] To qualify for nonpassive treatment, a taxpayer must satisfy both of the following requirements:

- More than half of the personal services that the taxpayer performs in trades or businesses are performed in real property trades or businesses in which the taxpayer materially participates.
- The taxpayer performs more than 750 hours of services in these real property trades or businesses as a material participant.

Taxpayers who do not satisfy the above requirements must continue to treat losses from real estate rental activities as passive losses.

EXAMPLE 42

During the current year, Della performed personal service activities as follows: 900 hours as a personal financial planner, 550 hours in a real estate development and leasing business, and 600 hours in real estate rental activities. Any loss Della incurred in either real estate activity will *not* be subject to the passive loss rules, since more than 50% of her personal services were devoted to real property trades or businesses, and her material participation in those real estate activities exceeded 750 hours. Thus, any loss from the real estate rental activity could offset active and portfolio sources of income. ▼

---

[26]§ 469(c)(7).

As discussed earlier, a spouse's work is taken into consideration in satisfying the material participation requirement. However, the hours worked by a spouse are *not* taken into account when ascertaining whether a taxpayer has worked for more than 750 hours in real property trades or businesses during a year.[27] Services performed by an employee are not treated as being related to a real estate trade or business unless the employee performing the services owns more than a 5 percent interest in the employer. Additionally, a closely held C corporation may also qualify for the passive loss relief if more than 50 percent of its gross receipts for the year are derived from real property trades or businesses in which it materially participates.

Real Estate Rental Activities.   The second exception is more significant in that it is not restricted to real estate professionals. This exception allows individuals to deduct up to $25,000 of losses on real estate rental activities against active and portfolio income.[28] The potential annual $25,000 deduction is reduced by 50 percent of the taxpayer's AGI in excess of $100,000. Thus, the entire deduction is phased out at $150,000 of AGI. If married individuals file separately, the $25,000 deduction is reduced to zero unless they lived apart for the entire year. If they lived apart for the entire year, the loss amount is $12,500 each, and the phase-out begins at $50,000. AGI for purposes of the phase-out is calculated without regard to IRA deductions, Social Security benefits, and net losses from passive activities.

To qualify for the $25,000 exception, a taxpayer must meet the following requirements:[29]

- Actively participate in the real estate rental activity.
- Own 10 percent or more (in value) of all interests in the activity during the entire taxable year (or shorter period during which the taxpayer held an interest in the activity).

The difference between *active participation* and *material participation* is that the former can be satisfied without regular, continuous, and substantial involvement in operations as long as the taxpayer participates in making management decisions in a significant and bona fide sense. In this context, relevant management decisions include such decisions as approving new tenants, deciding on rental terms, and approving capital or repair expenditures.

The $25,000 allowance is available after all active participation rental losses and gains are netted and applied to other passive income. If a taxpayer has a real estate rental loss in excess of the amount that can be deducted under the real estate rental exception, that excess is treated as a passive loss.

EXAMPLE 43

Brad, who has $90,000 of AGI before considering rental activities, has $85,000 of losses from a real estate rental activity in which he actively participates. He also actively participates in another real estate rental activity from which he has $25,000 of income. He has other passive income of $36,000. The net rental loss of $60,000 is absorbed by the $36,000 of passive income, leaving $24,000 that can be deducted against other income. ▼

The $25,000 offset allowance is an aggregate of both deductions and credits in deduction equivalents. The deduction equivalent of a passive activity credit is the amount of deductions that reduces the tax liability for the taxable year by an amount equal to the credit.[30] A taxpayer with $5,000 of credits and a tax bracket of 28 percent would have a deduction equivalent of $17,857 ($5,000 ÷ 28%).

---

[27]§ 469(c)(7)(B) and Reg. § 1.469–9.
[28]§ 469(i).

[29]§ 469(i)(6).
[30]§ 469(j)(5).

If the total deduction and deduction equivalent exceed $25,000, the taxpayer must allocate on a pro rata basis, first among the losses (including real estate rental activity losses suspended in prior years) and then to credits in the following order: (1) credits other than rehabilitation and low-income housing credits, (2) rehabilitation credits, and (3) low-income housing credits.

EXAMPLE 44

Kevin is an active participant in a real estate rental activity that produces $8,000 of income, $26,000 of deductions, and $1,500 of credits. Kevin, who is in the 28% tax bracket, may deduct the net passive loss of $18,000 ($8,000 – $26,000). After deducting the loss, he has an available deduction equivalent of $7,000 ($25,000 – $18,000 passive loss). Therefore, the maximum amount of credits that he may claim is $1,960 ($7,000 × 28%). Since the actual credits are less than this amount, Kevin may claim the entire $1,500 credit. ▼

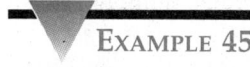

EXAMPLE 45

Kelly, who is in the 28% tax bracket, is an active participant in three separate real estate rental activities. The relevant tax results for each activity are as follows:

- Activity A: $20,000 of losses.
- Activity B: $10,000 of losses.
- Activity C: $4,200 of credits.

Kelly's deduction equivalent from the credits is $15,000 ($4,200 ÷ 28%). Therefore, the total passive deductions and deduction equivalents are $45,000 ($20,000 + $10,000 + $15,000), which exceeds the maximum allowable amount of $25,000. Consequently, Kelly must allocate pro rata first from among losses and then from among credits. Deductions from losses are limited as follows:

- Activity A {$25,000 × [$20,000 ÷ ($20,000 + $10,000)]} = $16,667.
- Activity B {$25,000 × [$10,000 ÷ ($20,000 + $10,000)]} = $8,333.

Since the amount of passive deductions exceeds the $25,000 maximum, the deduction balance of $5,000 and passive credits of $4,200 must be carried forward. Kelly's suspended losses and credits by activity are as follows:

	Total	Activity		
		A	B	C
Allocated losses	$ 30,000	$ 20,000	$10,000	$ –0–
Allocated credits	4,200	–0–	–0–	4,200
Utilized losses	(25,000)	(16,667)	(8,333)	–0–
Suspended losses	5,000	3,333	1,667	–0–
Suspended credits	4,200	–0–	–0–	4,200

ETHICAL CONSIDERATIONS

Applying the Rules on Rental Real Estate

Adam, a management consultant, owns an apartment complex that produces a profit of $60,000 in the current year. He earns $120,000 in his consulting business and has a $40,000 loss on a passive activity (not real estate). Adam works 800 hours at the apartment complex during the year, but characterizes the $60,000 profit as passive income so that he can utilize the $40,000 passive loss. He claims that he is doing nothing wrong because the law is designed only to protect the loss deduction of real estate professionals and is not applicable to profits.

Further, Adam thinks that he is justified in classifying the profit as passive because of the nature of the work he performs during the time he devotes to managing the apartments. Adam feels certain that of the 800 hours, between 300 and 400 hours were spent coaching and supporting about 20 underprivileged children living in the apartment complex as part of a year-round sports program. Adam says that his involvement not only benefits the children, but will make the apartment complex a more desirable place to live. Consequently, his coaching work benefits him economically in the long run. He sees the hours devoted to the sports program as an integral part of his job in managing the apartment complex, but feels that they should not count in determining whether the activity is passive. Adam asks you to prepare his return. What actions should you take?

DISPOSITIONS OF PASSIVE INTERESTS

9 **LEARNING OBJECTIVE**
Determine the proper tax treatment upon the disposition of a passive activity.

Recall from an earlier discussion that if a taxpayer disposes of an entire interest in a passive activity, any suspended losses (and in certain cases, suspended credits) may be utilized when calculating the final economic gain or loss on the investment. In addition, if a loss ultimately results, that loss can be offset against other types of income. However, the consequences may differ if the activity is disposed of in a transaction that is other than a fully taxable transaction. The following discusses the treatment of suspended passive losses in other types of dispositions.

Disposition of a Passive Activity at Death.   A transfer of a taxpayer's interest in an activity by reason of the taxpayer's death results in suspended losses being allowed (to the decedent) to the extent they exceed the amount, if any, of the step-up in basis allowed.[31] Suspended losses are lost to the extent of the amount

---

[31]§ 469(g)(2).

of the basis increase. The losses allowed generally are reported on the final return of the deceased taxpayer.

EXAMPLE 46

A taxpayer dies with passive activity property having an adjusted basis of $40,000, suspended losses of $10,000, and a fair market value at the date of the decedent's death of $75,000. The increase (i.e., step-up) in basis (see Chapter 12) is $35,000 (fair market value at date of death in excess of adjusted basis). None of the $10,000 suspended loss is deductible by either the decedent or the beneficiary. The suspended losses ($10,000) are lost because they do not exceed the step-up in basis ($35,000). ▼

EXAMPLE 47

A taxpayer dies with passive activity property having an adjusted basis of $40,000, suspended losses of $10,000, and a fair market value at the date of the decedent's death of $47,000. Since the step-up in basis is only $7,000 ($47,000 − $40,000), the suspended losses allowed are limited to $3,000 ($10,000 suspended loss at time of death − $7,000 increase in basis). The $3,000 loss available to the decedent is reported on the decedent's final income tax return. ▼

Disposition of a Passive Activity by Gift. In a disposition of a taxpayer's interest in a passive activity by gift, the suspended losses are added to the basis of the property.[32]

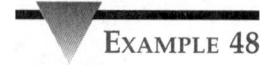

EXAMPLE 48

A taxpayer makes a gift of passive activity property having an adjusted basis of $40,000, suspended losses of $10,000, and a fair market value at the date of the gift of $100,000. The taxpayer cannot deduct the suspended losses in the year of the disposition. However, the suspended losses transfer with the property and are added to the adjusted basis of the property. ▼

Installment Sale of a Passive Activity. An installment sale of a taxpayer's entire interest in a passive activity triggers the recognition of the suspended losses.[33] The losses are allowed in each year of the installment obligation in the ratio that the gain recognized in each year bears to the total gain on the sale.

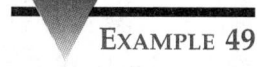

EXAMPLE 49

Stan sold his entire interest in a passive activity for $100,000. His adjusted basis in the property was $60,000. If he uses the installment method, his gross profit ratio is 40% ($40,000/$100,000). If Stan received a $20,000 down payment, he would recognize a gain of $8,000 (40% of $20,000). If the activity had a suspended loss of $25,000, Stan would deduct $5,000 [($8,000 ÷ $40,000) × $25,000] of the suspended loss in the first year. ▼

Passive Activity Changes to Active. If a formerly passive activity becomes an active one, suspended losses are allowed to the extent of income from the now active business.[34] If any of the suspended loss remains, it continues to be treated as a loss from a passive activity. The excess suspended loss can be deducted from passive income or carried over to the next tax year and deducted to the extent of income from the now active business in the succeeding year(s). The activity must continue to be the same activity.

Nontaxable Exchange of a Passive Activity. In a nontaxable exchange of a passive investment, the taxpayer keeps the suspended losses, which generally become deductible when the acquired property is sold. If the activity of the old and new property are the same, suspended losses can be used.

---

[32]§ 469(j)(6).
[33]§ 469(g)(3).

[34]§ 469(f).

CONCEPT SUMMARY 10–2

Passive Activity Loss Rules: General Concepts

What is the fundamental passive activity rule?	Passive activity losses may be deducted only against passive activity income and gains. Losses not allowed are suspended and used in future years.
Who is subject to the passive activity rules?	Individuals. Estates. Trusts. Personal service corporations. Closely held C corporations.
What is a passive activity?	Trade or business or income-producing activity in which the taxpayer does not materially participate during the year, or rental activities, subject to certain exceptions, regardless of the taxpayer's level of participation.
What is an activity?	One or more trade or business or rental activities that comprise an appropriate economic unit.
How is an appropriate economic unit determined?	Based on a reasonable application of the relevant facts and circumstances.
What is material participation?	In general, the taxpayer participates in a regular, continuous, and substantial basis. More specifically, when the taxpayer meets the conditions of one of the seven tests provided in the Regulations.
What is a rental activity?	In general, an activity where payments are received for the use of tangible property. More specifically, a rental activity that does *not* meet one of the six exceptions provided in the Regulations. Special rules apply to rental real estate.

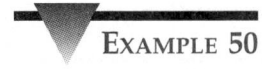

EXAMPLE 50   A taxpayer exchanged a duplex for a limited partnership interest in a § 721 nonrecognition transaction (see Chapter 22 for details). The suspended losses from the duplex are not deductible until the limited partnership interest is sold. Two separate activities exist: a real estate rental activity and a limited partnership activity. If the taxpayer had continued to own the duplex and the duplex had future taxable income, the suspended losses would have become deductible before the time of disposition. ▼

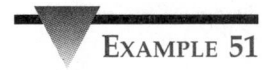

EXAMPLE 51   In a § 1031 nontaxable exchange (see Chapter 12 for details), a taxpayer exchanged a duplex for an apartment building. The suspended losses from the duplex are deductible against future taxable income of the apartment building. The same activity exists. ▼

TAX PLANNING CONSIDERATIONS

10   LEARNING OBJECTIVE
Suggest tax planning strategies to minimize the effect of the passive loss limitations.

UTILIZING PASSIVE LOSSES

Taxpayers who have passive activity losses (PALs) should adopt a strategy of generating passive activity income that can be sheltered by existing passive losses. One approach is to buy an interest in a passive activity that is generating income (referred to as passive income generators, or PIGs). Then the PAL can offset income from the PIG. From a tax perspective, it would be foolish to buy a loss-generating passive activity (PAL) unless one has other passive income (PIG) to shelter or the activity is rental real estate that can qualify for the $25,000 exception or the exception available to real estate professionals.

A taxpayer with existing passive losses might consider buying rental property. If a large down payment is made and the straight-line method of MACRS (discussed in Chapter 7) is elected, a positive net income could be realized. The income would be sheltered by other passive losses, and depreciation expense would be spread out evenly and preserved for future years. Future gain realized upon the sale of the rental property could be sheltered by existing suspended passive losses.

Taxpayers with passive losses should consider all other trades or businesses in which they have an interest. If they show that they do not materially participate in the activity, the activity becomes a passive activity. Any income generated could be sheltered by existing passive losses and suspended losses. Family partnerships in which certain members do not materially participate would qualify. The silent partner in any general partnership engaged in a trade or business would also qualify.

As the chapter has shown, the passive loss rules can have a dramatic effect on a taxpayer's ability to claim passive losses currently. However, several steps can be taken to mitigate their impact:

- Replace passive activity debt with home equity indebtedness.
- Carefully select the year in which a passive activity is to be disposed of at a gain, as it can be to the taxpayer's advantage to wait until sufficient passive losses have been generated to completely offset the gain recognized on the asset's disposition.
- Keep accurate records of all sources of income and losses, particularly any suspended passive losses and credits and the activities to which they relate, so that their potential tax benefit will not be lost.

Finally, because of the restrictive nature of the passive activity loss rules, it may be advantageous for a taxpayer to use a vacation home enough to convert it to a second residence. This would enable all of the qualified interest and real estate taxes to be deducted without limitation. However, this strategy would lead to the loss of other deductions, such as repairs, maintenance, and insurance.

KEY TERMS

Active income, 10–5	Material participation, 10–15	Rental activity, 10–19
At-risk limitation, 10–3		Significant participation activity, 10–16
Closely held corporation, 10–11	Passive loss, 10–3	Tax shelters, 10–2
	Personal service corporation, 10–10	
Extraordinary personal services, 10–20	Portfolio income, 10–6	

PROBLEM MATERIALS

DISCUSSION QUESTIONS

1. Describe the general purpose and effect of the two major provisions discussed in this chapter: the at-risk rules and the passive activity loss rules.

2. Alice invested $50,000 for a 25% interest in a partnership in which she is not a material participant. The partnership borrowed $100,000 from a bank and used the proceeds to

acquire a building. What is Alice's at-risk amount if the $100,000 was borrowed on a recourse loan?

3. List some events that increase and decrease an investor's at-risk amount. What are some strategies that a taxpayer can employ to increase the at-risk amount in order to claim a higher deduction for losses?

4. Roy invested $15,000 in a cattle-feeding operation that used nonrecourse notes to purchase $150,000 in feed, which was fed to the cattle and expensed. His share of the expense was $27,000. How much can Roy deduct?

5. Explain the meaning of the terms *active income*, *portfolio income*, and *passive income*.

6. Manuel owns an interest in an activity that produces a $100,000 loss during the year. Would he generally prefer to have the activity classified as active or passive? Discuss.

7. Kim owns an interest in an activity that produces $100,000 of income during the year. Would Kim prefer to have the activity classified as active or passive? Discuss.

8. Felicia owns a passive activity that she acquired several years ago. She has incurred losses on the activity since its acquisition. This is the only passive activity she has ever owned. How will these passive losses affect Felicia's taxable income when she disposes of the activity?

9. On the taxable disposition of a passive activity, what happens to the suspended losses? The suspended credits?

10. Discuss whether the passive loss rules apply to the following: individuals, closely held C corporations, S corporations, partnerships, and personal service corporations.

11. Gray Corporation has $100,000 of active income and a $55,000 passive loss for the year. Under what circumstances is the corporation prohibited from deducting the loss? Under what circumstances is the corporation allowed to deduct the loss?

12. What factors are given the greatest weight in determining whether activities constitute an appropriate economic unit?

13. Discuss what constitutes a passive activity.

14. Under what circumstances may the IRS regroup activities in a different way than the taxpayer has grouped them? Give an example of a situation to which the regrouping rule would be applied.

15. What is the significance of the term *material participation*? Why is the extent of a taxpayer's participation in an activity important in determining whether a loss from the activity is deductible or nondeductible?

16. Why did the IRS adopt the more-than-500-hour standard for material participation?

17. Keith, a physician, operates a separate business that he acquired nine years ago. During the current year, he participates for 90 hours in the business, which incurs a loss of $20,000. Under what circumstances will the loss be deductible as an active loss?

18. Rene retired from public accounting after a long and successful career of 45 years. As part of her retirement package, she continues to share in the profits and losses of the firm, albeit at a lower rate than when she was working full-time. Because Rene wants to stay busy during her retirement years, she has invested and works in a local hardware business, operated as a partnership. Unfortunately, the business has recently gone through a slump and has not been generating profits. Identify relevant tax issues for Rene.

19. Some types of work are counted in applying the material participation standards, and some types are not counted. Discuss and give examples of each type.

20. During the current year, Alan is determined to make better use of the tax losses that tend to flow from the various businesses that he owns. He is particularly sensitive to the limitations that the passive loss rules place on the deductibility of losses because of the disaster that occurred last year: his accountant informed him that he would not

be able to claim any of the losses on his income tax return because of his lack of material participation. He has even suggested to his wife that she may have to put in some time at the businesses if his goals are to be accomplished. Identify the tax issues that Alan faces.

21. What are *significant personal services,* and what role do they play in determining whether a rental activity is treated as a passive activity?

22. What are *extraordinary personal services,* and what is their importance in determining whether a rental activity is treated as a passive activity?

23. How is passive activity defined in the Code, and what aspects of the definition have been clarified by final or Temporary Regulations?

24. Laura owns an apartment building and a videocassette rental business. She participates for more than 500 hours in the operations of each activity. Are the businesses active or passive?

25. Hilda incurred a loss of $60,000 on a real estate rental activity during the current year. Under what circumstances can Hilda treat the entire loss as nonpassive?

26. In the current year, George and Susie White, both successful CPAs, made a cash investment for a limited partnership interest in a California avocado grove. In addition to the cash generated from the investors, the grove's management borrowed a substantial sum to purchase assets necessary for its operation. The Whites' investment adviser told them that their share of the tax loss in the first year alone would be in excess of their initial cash investment, followed by several more years of losses. They feel confident that their interest in the avocado grove is a sound investment. Identify the tax issues facing the Whites.

27. Rick, a full-time real estate professional, earns $5,000 for development services rendered to an S corporation that owns and manages apartment units. He also owns an interest in the entity. His share of the S corporation's losses for the year totals $5,000. Identify the issues that are relevant in determining how the items of income and loss are treated for tax purposes.

28. Matt owns a small apartment building that generated a loss during the year. Under what circumstances can Matt deduct a loss from the rental activity, and what limitations apply?

29. In connection with passive activities, what is a *deduction equivalent*? How is a deduction equivalent computed?

30. What are the differences between material participation and active participation under the passive loss rules?

31. Betty and Steve received a substantial windfall due to a recent inheritance. Because they have always loved spending time at the beach, they plan to devote some of the newly available cash to a beach-related investment. Their analysis identifies two possibilities that seem to be logical given their particular situation. They could purchase a beach cottage and use it for both personal and rental purposes; or they could pool their money with Steve's brother and purchase several cottages, one of which would be held strictly for personal use, while the others would be held solely for rental use. Identify the tax issues facing Betty and Steve.

PROBLEMS

32. In 1997, Fred invested $50,000 in a partnership. Fred's interest is not considered to be a passive activity. In 1997, his share of the partnership loss was $35,000 and in 1998, his share of the loss is $25,000. How much can Fred deduct in 1997 and 1998?

33. In the current year, Bill Parker (54 Oak Drive, St. Paul, MN 55162) is considering making an investment of $60,000 in Best Choice Partnership. The prospectus provided by Bill's broker indicates that the partnership investment is not a passive activity and that Bill's share of the entity's loss in the current year will likely be $40,000, while his share of

the partnership loss next year will probably be $25,000. Write a letter to Bill in which you indicate how the losses would be treated for tax purposes in the current and next years.

34. Carmen wishes to invest $25,000 in a relatively safe venture and has discovered two alternatives that would produce the following reportable income and loss over the next three years:

Year	Alternative 1 Income (Loss)	Alternative 2 Income (Loss)
1	($15,000)	($30,000)
2	(15,000)	20,000
3	45,000	25,000

She is interested in the after-tax effects of these alternatives over a three-year horizon. Assume that Carmen's investment portfolio produces sufficient passive income to offset any potential passive loss that may arise from these alternatives, that her cost of capital is 8% (the present value factors are 0.92593, 0.85734, and 0.79383), that she is in the 28% tax bracket, that each investment alternative possesses equal growth potential, and that each alternative exposes her to comparable financial risk. In addition, assume that in the loss years for each alternative, there is no cash flow from or to the investment (i.e., the loss is due to depreciation), while in those years when the income is positive, cash flows to Carmen equal the amount of the income. Based on these facts, compute the present value of these two investment alternatives and determine which option Carmen should choose.

35. Tina acquired passive Activity A in January 1993 and Activity B in September 1994. Until 1997, Activity A was profitable. Activity A produced a loss of $200,000 in 1997 and a loss of $100,000 in 1998. Tina has passive income from Activity B of $20,000 in 1997 and $40,000 in 1998. After offsetting passive income, how much of the net losses may she deduct?

36. In 1993, Kay acquired an interest in a partnership in which she is not a material participant. The partnership was profitable until 1997. Kay's basis in her partnership interest at the beginning of 1997 was $40,000. In 1997, Kay's share of the partnership loss was $35,000. In 1998, her share of the partnership income was $15,000. How much can Kay deduct in 1997 and 1998?

37. Bob, an attorney, earns $200,000 from his law practice in the current year. He receives $45,000 in dividends and interest during the year. In addition, he incurs a loss of $50,000 from an investment in a passive activity acquired three years ago. What is Bob's net income for the current year after considering the passive investment?

38. Sarah has $100,000 that she wishes to invest, and she is considering the following two options:

- Option A—Investment in Bluebird Equity Mutual fund, which would be expected to produce dividends of $8,000 per year.

- Option B—Investment in Redbird Limited Partnership (buys, sells, and operates avocado groves). Sarah's share of the partnership's income and loss over the next three years is expected to be:

Year	Income (Loss)
1	($ 8,000)
2	(2,000)
3	34,000

Sarah is interested in the after-tax effects of these alternatives over a three-year horizon. Assume that Sarah's investment portfolio produces no passive income, that her cost of capital is 8% (the present value factors are 0.92593, 0.85734, and 0.79383), that she is in the 31% tax bracket, that each investment alternative possesses equal growth potential, and that each alternative exposes her to comparable financial risk. Based on these facts, compute the present value of these two investment alternatives and determine which option Sarah should choose.

39. Hazel has two investments in nonrental passive activities. Activity A, which was acquired seven years ago, was profitable until the current year. Activity B was acquired this year. Currently, Hazel's share of the loss from Activity A is $10,000, and her share of the loss from Activity B is $6,000. What is the total of Hazel's suspended losses from these activities as of the end of the current year?

40. Leanne has investments in four passive activity partnerships purchased several years ago. Last year, the income and losses were as follows:

Activity	Income (Loss)
A	$ 60,000
B	(30,000)
C	(30,000)
D	(40,000)

In the current year, she sold her interest in Activity D for a $20,000 gain. Activity D, which had been profitable until last year, had a current loss of $1,000. How will the sale of Activity D affect Leanne's taxable income in the current year?

41. Leon sells his interest in a passive activity for $100,000 during the year. Determine the tax effect based on each of the following sets of independent facts:
   a. His adjusted basis in this investment is $35,000. Losses from prior years that were not deductible due to the passive loss restrictions total $40,000.
   b. His adjusted basis in this investment is $75,000. Losses from prior years that were not deductible due to the passive loss restrictions total $40,000.
   c. His adjusted basis in this investment is $75,000. Losses from prior years that were not deductible due to the passive loss restrictions total $40,000. In addition, suspended credits total $10,000.

42. Brown Corporation, a personal service corporation, earns active income of $500,000 in the current year. The corporation receives $60,000 in dividends during the year. In addition, Brown incurs a loss of $80,000 from an investment in a passive activity acquired three years ago. What is Brown's income for the current year after considering the passive investment?

43. White, Inc., earns $400,000 from operations in the current year. White also receives $36,000 in dividends and interest on various portfolio investments. During the year, White pays $150,000 to acquire a 20% interest in a passive activity that produces a $200,000 loss.
   a. How will these facts affect White's taxable income, assuming the corporation is a personal service corporation?
   b. How will these facts affect White's taxable income, assuming the corporation is a closely held, non-personal service corporation?

44. Green Corporation, a closely held, non-personal service corporation, earns active income of $50,000 in the current year. Green receives $60,000 in dividends during the year. In addition, Green incurs a loss of $80,000 from an investment in a passive activity acquired last year. What is Green's net income for the current year after considering the passive investment?

45. Eleanor owns interests in a hardware store, bowling alley, and grocery store. Several full-time employees work at each of the enterprises. As of the end of November of

the current year, Eleanor has worked 150 hours in the hardware store, 250 hours at the bowling alley, and 80 hours at the grocery store. In reviewing her financial records, you learn that she has no passive investments that are generating income and that she expects these three ventures collectively to produce a loss. What recommendation would you offer Eleanor as she plans her activities for the remainder of the year?

46. Ann acquired an activity four years ago. The loss from the activity is $50,000 in the current year. She has AGI of $140,000 before considering the loss from the activity. The activity is a service station, and Ann is a material participant. What is her AGI after considering this activity?

47. Lee acquired a 20% interest in the ABC Partnership for $60,000 in 1993. The partnership was profitable until 1998, and Lee's amount at risk in the partnership interest was $120,000 at the end of 1997. ABC incurs a loss of $400,000 in 1998 and reports income of $200,000 in 1999. Assuming Lee is not a material participant in ABC, how much of his loss from ABC Partnership is deductible in 1998 and 1999, respectively?

48. Ken has a $40,000 loss from an investment in a partnership in which he does not participate. He paid $30,000 for his interest in the partnership. How much of the loss is disallowed by the at-risk rules? How much is disallowed by the passive loss rules?

49. Last year, Fran invested $40,000 for an interest in a partnership in which she is a material participant. Her share of the partnership's loss for the year was $50,000. In the current year, Fran's share of the partnership's income is $30,000. What is the effect on her taxable income for the current year?

50. Soong, a physician, earns $200,000 from his practice. He also receives $18,000 in dividends and interest on various portfolio investments. During the year, he pays $45,000 to acquire a 20% interest in a partnership that produces a $300,000 loss.
    a. Compute Soong's AGI assuming he does not participate in the operations of the partnership.
    b. Compute Soong's AGI assuming he is a material participant in the operations of the partnership.

51. Sam invested $150,000 in a passive activity five years ago. On January 1, 1997, his amount at risk in the activity was $30,000. His shares of the income and losses in the activity were as follows:

Year	Income (Loss)
1997	($40,000)
1998	(30,000)
1999	50,000

    How much can Sam deduct in 1997 and 1998? What is his taxable income from the activity in 1999? Keep in mind the at-risk rules as well as the passive loss rules.

52. Joe Cook (125 Hill Street, Charleston, WV 25311) acquired an activity four years ago. The loss from the activity is $50,000 in the current year. He has AGI of $140,000 before considering the loss from the activity. The activity is an apartment building in an exclusive part of the city, and Joe is an active participant. Write a letter to Joe in which you explain what his AGI is after the loss is considered.

53. Beth acquired an activity four years ago. The loss from the activity is $50,000 in the current year. She has AGI of $140,000 before considering the loss from the activity. The activity is an apartment building, and Beth is not an active participant. What is her AGI after considering the activity?

54. During the current year, Donald works 1,200 hours as a computer consultant, 600 hours in a real estate development business, and 500 hours in real estate rental activities. He earns $60,000 as a computer consultant, but loses $18,000 in the development business

and $26,000 in the real estate rental business. How should Donald treat the losses on his current Federal income tax return?

55. During the current year, Roger performs the following personal services in three separate activities: 800 hours as a CPA in his tax practice, 400 hours in a real estate development business (i.e., not a material participant), and 600 hours in an apartment leasing operation. He expects that losses will be realized from the two real estate ventures while his tax practice will show a profit. Roger files a joint return with his wife whose salary is $200,000. What is the character of the income and losses generated by these activities?

56. Hal and Wanda are married with no dependents and live together in Ohio, which is not a community property state. Since Wanda has large medical expenses, they seek your advice about filing separately to save taxes. Their income and expenses for 1998 are as follows:

Hal's salary	$ 30,000
Wanda's salary	50,000
Dividends and interest (joint)	1,800
Rental loss from actively managed apartments (joint)	(20,000)
Wanda's unreimbursed medical expenses	6,500
All other itemized deductions:*	
Hal	8,000
Wanda	2,000

*None subject to limitations.

Determine whether Hal and Wanda should file jointly or separately for 1998.

57. Lucy and Leon have owned a beach cottage on the New Jersey shore for several years and have always used it as a family retreat. When they acquired the property, they had no intentions of renting it, but because their family circumstances have changed, they are considering using the cottage for only two weeks a year and renting it for the remainder of the year. Their AGI is currently approximately $80,000 per year, and they are in the 33% tax bracket (combined Federal and state). Their financial records indicate that interest and real estate taxes have totaled $8,000 per year, and Lucy and Leon expect these expenditures to continue at this level into the foreseeable future. In addition, if they rent the property, their *incremental* revenue and expenses are projected to be:

Rent income	$ 20,000
Rental commissions	(3,000)
Maintenance expenses	(12,000)
Depreciation expense	(10,000)
	($ 5,000)

If they do convert the cottage to rental property, they insist that they will be actively involved in key rental and maintenance decisions. Given the tax effects of converting the property to rental use, would the cash flow resulting from renting the property be enough to meet the $12,000 annual mortgage payment? This is an important factor in Lucy and Leon's decision.

58. During the current year, Gene performs services as follows: 1,800 hours as a CPA in his tax practice and 50 hours in an apartment leasing operation in which he has a 15% interest. Because of his oversight duties, Gene is considered to be an active participant. He expects that his share of the loss realized from the apartment leasing operation will be $30,000 while his tax practice will show a profit of approximately $80,000. Gene is single and has no other income besides that stated above. Discuss the character of the income and losses generated by these activities.

59. Ella has $105,000 of losses from a real estate rental activity in which she actively participates. She has other rental income of $25,000 and other passive income of $32,000.

How much rental loss can Ella deduct against active and portfolio income (ignoring the at-risk rules)? Does she have any suspended losses to carry over?

60. Faye dies owning an interest in a passive activity property with an adjusted basis of $160,000, suspended losses of $16,000, and a fair market value of $170,000. What can be deducted on her final income tax return?

61. In the current year, Leon gives an interest in a passive activity to his daughter, Lucy. The value of the interest at the date of the gift is $25,000. The adjusted basis of the property to Leon is $13,000. During the time that Leon owned the investment, losses that were not deductible due to the passive loss limitations totaled $3,000. What treatment is given to the suspended passive activity losses?

62. Tonya sells a passive activity in the current year for $150,000. Her adjusted basis in the activity is $50,000, and she uses the installment method of reporting the gain. The activity has suspended losses of $12,000. Tonya receives $60,000 in the year of sale. What is her gain? How much of the suspended losses can she deduct?

Research Problems for this chapter appear at the end of Chapter 28.

TEAM PROJECT: ARTHUR ANDERSEN TAX CHALLENGE CASES

For more information on the Arthur Andersen Tax Challenge Cases, refer to Chapter 1, page 1–37.

Information related to tax issues and problems that are discussed in this chapter may be found in the

Day and Ball case on pages: None
Fence case on pages: 40, 50, 64, 65, 67, and 68

Read and analyze the case you have been assigned and *identify* any issues and problems that are related to material covered in this chapter. If the information provided in the case is complete, prepare answers for this part of the case at this time. If you need information that is contained in the later parts of the case, write a memo summarizing the questions or problems so you can prepare a complete answer at a later date.

TAX CREDITS

LEARNING OBJECTIVES

After completing Chapter 11, you should be able to:

1. Explain how tax credits are used as a tool of Federal tax policy.

2. Distinguish between refundable and nonrefundable credits and understand the order in which they can be used by taxpayers.

3. Describe various business-related tax credits.

4. Describe several other tax credits that are available primarily to individual taxpayers.

5. Identify tax planning opportunities related to tax credits.

As explained in Chapter 1, Federal tax law often serves other purposes besides merely raising revenue for the government. Evidence of equity, social, and economic considerations, among others, is found throughout the tax law. These considerations also bear heavily in the area of **tax credits.** Consider the following examples:

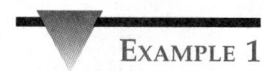

EXAMPLE 1

Paul and Peggy, husband and wife, are both employed outside the home. Their combined salaries are $50,000. However, after paying for child care expenses of $2,000 on behalf of their daughter, Polly, the net economic benefit from both spouses working is $48,000. The child care expenses are, in a sense, business related since they would not have been incurred if both spouses did not work outside the home. If no tax benefits are associated with the child care expenditures, $50,000 is subject to tax.

Another couple, Alicia and Diego, also have a child, John. Diego stays at home to care for John (the value of those services is $2,000) while Alicia earns a $48,000 salary. Because the value of Diego's services rendered is not subject to tax, only Alicia's earnings of $48,000 are subject to tax. ▼

The credit for child and dependent care expenses mitigates the inequity felt by working taxpayers who must pay for child care services in order to work outside the home.

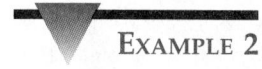

EXAMPLE 2

Olaf is a retired taxpayer who received $10,000 of Social Security benefits as his only source of income in 1998. His Social Security benefits are excluded from gross income. Therefore, Olaf's income tax is $0. In 1998, Olga, a single taxpayer 66 years of age, has, as her sole source of income, $10,000 from a pension plan funded by her former employer. Assuming Olga has no itemized deductions or deductions *for* AGI, her income tax for 1998 (before credits) is $300, based on the following computation:

Pension plan benefits	$ 10,000
Less: Basic standard deduction	(4,250)
Additional standard deduction	(1,050)
Personal exemption	(2,700)
Taxable income	$ 2,000
Income tax (at 15%)	$ 300

▼

The tax credit for elderly or disabled taxpayers was enacted to mitigate this inequity.

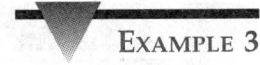

EXAMPLE 3

Jane is a single parent who depends on the government's "safety net" for survival—she receives Aid for Dependent Children in the amount of $10,000 per year. However, she very much wishes to work. Jane has located a job that will pay $10,500 per year and has found an individual to care for her child at no cost. But, with the $803.25 ($10,500 × 7.65%) payroll deduction for Social Security and Medicare taxes, the economic benefit from working is less than remaining reliant on the government ($9,696.75 as compared to $10,000). ▼

To help offset the effect of Social Security and Medicare taxes on wages of the working poor and to provide an incentive to work, the earned income credit is used to increase the after-tax earnings of qualified individuals. In addition, the earned income credit helps offset the regressive nature of certain taxes, such as the Social Security and Medicare taxes, which impose a relatively larger burden on low-income taxpayers than on more affluent taxpayers.

These three tax credits and many of the other important tax credits available to individuals and other types of taxpayers are a major focus of this chapter. The chapter begins by discussing important tax policy considerations relevant to tax credits. Tax credits are categorized as being either refundable or nonrefundable. The distinction between refundable and nonrefundable credits is important because it may affect the taxpayer's ability to enjoy a tax benefit from a particular credit.

Next an overview of the priority of tax credits is presented. The credit portion of the chapter continues with a discussion of the credits available to businesses and to individual taxpayers and the ways in which credits enter into the calculation of the tax liability.

TAX POLICY CONSIDERATIONS

1 LEARNING OBJECTIVE
Explain how tax credits are used as a tool of Federal tax policy.

Congress has generally used tax credits to achieve social or economic objectives or to promote equity among different types of taxpayers. For example, the disabled access credit was enacted to accomplish a social objective: to encourage taxpayers to renovate older buildings so they would be in compliance with the Americans with Disabilities Act. This Act requires businesses and institutions to make their facilities more accessible to persons with various types of disabilities. As another example, the foreign tax credit, which has been a part of the law for decades, has as its purpose the economic and equity objectives of mitigating the burden of multiple taxation on a single stream of income.

A tax credit should not be confused with an income tax deduction. Certain expenditures of individuals (e.g., business expenses) are permitted as deductions from gross income in arriving at adjusted gross income (AGI). Additionally, individuals are allowed to deduct certain nonbusiness and investment-related expenses *from* AGI. While the tax benefit received from a tax deduction depends on the tax rate, a tax credit is not affected by the tax rate of the taxpayer.

EXAMPLE 4

Assume Congress wishes to encourage a certain type of expenditure. One way to accomplish this objective is to allow a tax credit of 25% for such expenditures. Another way is to allow an itemized deduction for the expenditures. Assume Abby's tax rate is 15%, while Bill's tax rate is 39.6%. In addition, assume that Carmen does not incur enough qualifying expenditures to itemize deductions. The following tax benefits are available to each taxpayer for a $1,000 expenditure:

> ## TAX IN THE NEWS
>
> ### A CREDIT THAT WENT UP IN SMOKE
>
> As part of the Taxpayer Relief Act of 1997 (TRA of 1997), Congress passed a special $50 billion tax credit for the tobacco industry to subsidize the cost of a proposed multibillion dollar national settlement between tobacco companies and the 50 states. Several state attorneys general had previously sued tobacco companies in an attempt to recover billions of state Medicaid dollars spent on tobacco-related health problems. Once tobacco industry foes became aware of the significant savings that would accrue to tobacco companies from the tobacco tax credit, Congress was under considerable pressure to repeal the tax break. Less than a month after the credit's passage, legislation was introduced to repeal the controversial credit. As a result, the tobacco credit goes on record as one of the shortest-lived credits in tax history. As several news reports suggested, repeal of the tobacco tax credit may have signaled a change in congressional sentiment concerning special interest legislation for the tobacco industry.

	Abby	Bill	Carmen
Tax benefit if a 25% credit is allowed	$250	$250	$250
Tax benefit if an itemized deduction is allowed	150	396	–0–

As these results indicate, tax credits provide benefits on a more equitable basis than do tax deductions. Equally apparent is that the deduction approach in this case benefits only taxpayers who itemize deductions, while the credit approach benefits all taxpayers who make the specified expenditure. ▼

For many years, Congress has used the tax credit provisions of the Code liberally in implementing tax policy. Although budget constraints and economic considerations often have dictated the repeal of some credits, other credits, such as those applicable to expenses incurred for child and dependent care, have been kept to respond to important social policy considerations. Still other credits, such as the one available to low-income workers, have been retained based on economic and equity considerations. Finally, as the myriad of tax proposals so frequently pending before Congress makes clear, the use of tax credits as a tax policy tool continues to evolve as economic and political circumstances change.

OVERVIEW AND PRIORITY OF CREDITS

2 LEARNING OBJECTIVE
Distinguish between refundable and nonrefundable credits and understand the order in which they can be used by taxpayers.

REFUNDABLE VERSUS NONREFUNDABLE CREDITS

As illustrated in Exhibit 11–1, certain credits are refundable while others are nonrefundable. **Refundable credits** are paid to the taxpayer even if the amount of the credit (or credits) exceeds the taxpayer's tax liability.

▼ **EXHIBIT 11–1**
Partial Listing of Refundable and
Nonrefundable Credits

Refundable Credits
_____

Taxes withheld on wages
Earned income credit

Nonrefundable Credits
_____

Credit for child and dependent care expenses
Credit for the elderly or disabled
Adoption expenses credit
Child tax credit
Education tax credits
Foreign tax credit
General business credit, which is the sum of the following:
• Tax credit for rehabilitation expenditures
• Business energy credits
• Work opportunity tax credit*
• Welfare-to-work credit**
• Research activities credit***
• Low-income housing credit
• Disabled access credit
_____

*Not available for employees hired after June 30, 1998.
**Not available for employees hired after April 30, 1999.
***Scheduled to expire after June 30, 1998.

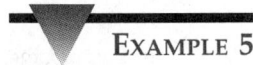

EXAMPLE 5

Ted, who is single, had taxable income of $21,000 in 1998. His income tax from the 1998 Tax Rate Schedule is $3,150. During 1998, Ted's employer withheld income tax of $3,500. Ted is entitled to a refund of $350 because the credit for tax withheld on wages is a refundable credit. ▼

Nonrefundable credits are not paid if they exceed the taxpayer's tax liability.

EXAMPLE 6

Tina is single, age 67, and retired. Her taxable income for 1998 is $1,320, and the tax on this amount is $198. Tina's tax credit for the elderly is $225. This credit can be used to reduce her net tax liability to zero, but it will not result in a refund, even though the credit ($225) exceeds Tina's tax liability ($198). This result occurs because the tax credit for the elderly is a nonrefundable credit. ▼

Some nonrefundable credits, such as the foreign tax credit, are subject to carryover provisions if they exceed the amount allowable as a credit in a given year. Other nonrefundable credits, such as the tax credit for the elderly (refer to Example 6), are not subject to carryover provisions and are lost if they exceed the limitations. Because some credits are subject to carryover provisions while others are not, the order in which credits are offset against the tax liability is important. The Code provides that nonrefundable credits are to be offset against a taxpayer's income tax liability in the order shown in Exhibit 11–1.

GENERAL BUSINESS CREDIT

As shown in Exhibit 11–1, the **general business credit** is comprised of a number of other credits, each of which is computed separately under its own set of rules. The general business credit combines these credits into one amount to limit the amount of business credits that can be used to offset a taxpayer's income tax liability. The idea behind combining the credits is to prevent a taxpayer from completely avoiding an income tax liability in any one year by offsetting it with business credits that would otherwise be available.

Two special rules apply to the general business credit. First, any unused credit must be carried back 1 year, then forward 20 years. Second, for any tax year, the general business credit is limited to the taxpayer's *net income tax* reduced by the greater of:[1]

- The *tentative minimum tax*.
- 25 percent of *net regular tax liability* that exceeds $25,000.[2]

In order to understand the general business credit limitation, several terms need defining:

- *Net income tax* is the sum of the regular tax liability and the alternative minimum tax reduced by certain nonrefundable tax credits.
- *Tentative minimum tax* for this purpose is reduced by the foreign tax credit allowed.
- *Regular tax liability* is determined from the appropriate tax table or tax rate schedule, based on taxable income. However, the regular tax liability does not include certain taxes (e.g., alternative minimum tax).
- *Net regular tax liability* is the regular tax liability reduced by certain nonrefundable credits (e.g., credit for child and dependent care expenses, foreign tax credit).

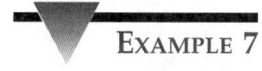 **EXAMPLE 7**

Floyd's general business credit for the current year is $70,000. His net income tax is $150,000, tentative minimum tax is $130,000, and net regular tax liability is $150,000. He has no other tax credits. Floyd's general business credit allowed for the tax year is computed as follows:

Net income tax	$ 150,000
Less: The greater of	
• $130,000 (tentative minimum tax)	
• $31,250 [25% × ($150,000 – $25,000)]	(130,000)
Amount of general business credit allowed for tax year	$ 20,000

Floyd then has $50,000 ($70,000 – $20,000) of unused general business credits that may be carried back or forward as discussed below. ▼

TREATMENT OF UNUSED GENERAL BUSINESS CREDITS

Effective for tax years beginning after December 31, 1997, unused general business credits are initially carried back one year and are applied to reduce the tax liability

---

[1]§ 38(c).
[2]This amount is $12,500 for married taxpayers filing separately unless one of the spouses is not entitled to the general business credit.

during that year. Thus, the taxpayer may receive a tax refund as a result of the carryback. Any remaining unused credits are then carried forward 20 years.[3] For unused general business credits arising in tax years beginning before January 1, 1998, the carryback period is 3 years and the carryforward period is 15 years.

A FIFO method is applied to the carryovers, carrybacks, and utilization of credits earned during a particular year. The oldest credits are used first in determining the amount of the general business credit. The FIFO method minimizes the potential for loss of a general business credit benefit due to the expiration of credit carryovers, since the earliest credits are used before the current credit for the taxable year.

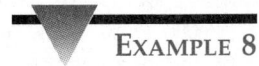

EXAMPLE 8

This example illustrates the use of general business credit carryovers.

General business credit carryovers		
1995	$ 4,000	
1996	6,000	
1997	2,000	
Total carryovers	$ 12,000	
1998 general business credit		$ 40,000
Total credit allowed in 1998 (based on tax liability)	$ 50,000	
Less: Utilization of carryovers		
1995	(4,000)	
1996	(6,000)	
1997	(2,000)	
Remaining credit allowed	$ 38,000	
Applied against		
1998 general business credit		(38,000)
1998 unused amount carried forward to 1999		$ 2,000

BUSINESS-RELATED TAX CREDIT PROVISIONS

3 **LEARNING OBJECTIVE**
Describe various business-related tax credits.

Each component of the general business credit is determined separately under its own set of rules. The components are explained here in the order listed in Exhibit 11–1.

TAX CREDIT FOR REHABILITATION EXPENDITURES

Taxpayers are allowed a tax credit for expenditures incurred to rehabilitate industrial and commercial buildings and certified historic structures. The **rehabilitation expenditures credit** is intended to discourage businesses from moving from older, economically distressed areas (e.g., inner city) to newer locations and to encourage the preservation of historic structures. The current operating features of this credit follow:[4]

---

[3]§ 39(a)(1).   [4]§ 47.

Rate of the Credit for Rehabilitation Expenses	Nature of the Property
10%	Nonresidential buildings and residential rental property, other than certified historic structures, originally placed in service before 1936
20%	Nonresidential and residential certified historic structures

When taking the credit, the basis of a rehabilitated building must be reduced by the full rehabilitation credit allowed.[5]

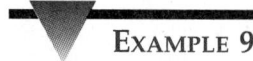

EXAMPLE 9

Juan spent $60,000 to rehabilitate a building (adjusted basis of $40,000) that had originally been placed in service in 1932. He is allowed a credit of $6,000 (10% × $60,000) for rehabilitation expenditures. Juan then increases the basis of the building by $54,000 [$60,000 (rehabilitation expenditures) – $6,000 (credit allowed)]. If the building were a historic structure, the credit allowed would be $12,000 (20% × $60,000), and the building's depreciable basis would increase by $48,000 [$60,000 (rehabilitation expenditures) – $12,000 (credit allowed)]. ▼

To qualify for the credit, buildings must be substantially rehabilitated. A building has been *substantially rehabilitated* if qualified rehabilitation expenditures exceed the greater of:

- The adjusted basis of the property before the rehabilitation expenditures, or
- $5,000.

Qualified rehabilitation expenditures do not include the cost of acquiring a building, the cost of facilities related to a building (such as a parking lot), and the cost of enlarging an existing building. Stringent rules apply concerning the retention of internal and external walls.

Recapture of Tax Credit for Rehabilitation Expenditures. The rehabilitation credit taken must be recaptured if the rehabilitated property is disposed of prematurely or if it ceases to be qualifying property. The **rehabilitation expenditures credit recapture** is based on a holding period requirement of five years and is added to the taxpayer's regular tax liability in the recapture year. In addition, the recapture amount is *added* to the adjusted basis of the rehabilitation expenditures for purposes of determining the amount of gain or loss realized on the property's disposition.

The portion of the credit recaptured is a specified percentage of the credit that was taken by the taxpayer. This percentage is based on the period the property was held by the taxpayer, as shown in Table 11–1.

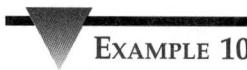

EXAMPLE 10

On March 15, 1995, Rashad placed in service $30,000 of rehabilitation expenditures on a building qualifying for the 10% credit. A credit of $3,000 ($30,000 × 10%) was allowed, and the basis of the building was increased by $27,000 ($30,000 – $3,000). The building was sold on December 15, 1998. Rashad must recapture a portion of the rehabilitation credit based on the schedule in Table 11–1. Because he held the rehabilitated property for more than three years but less than four, 40% of the credit, or $1,200, must be added to his 1998 tax liability. Also, the adjusted basis of the rehabilitation expenditures is increased by the $1,200 recapture amount. ▼

---

[5]§ 50(c).

▼ TABLE 11–1
Recapture Calculation for
Rehabilitation Expenditures
Credit

If the Property Is Held for	The Recapture Percentage Is
Less than 1 year	100
One year or more but less than 2 years	80
Two years or more but less than 3 years	60
Three years or more but less than 4 years	40
Four years or more but less than 5 years	20
Five years or more	0

BUSINESS ENERGY CREDITS

For many years, **business energy credits** have been allowed to encourage the conservation of natural resources and the development of alternative energy sources. Over the years, some of these credits have expired while new ones have been added. The most important business energy credits that remain are the 10 percent credits for solar energy property and geothermal property.

WORK OPPORTUNITY TAX CREDIT

The **work opportunity tax credit** was enacted to encourage employers to hire individuals from one or more of a number of targeted and economically disadvantaged groups who start work before June 30, 1998. Examples of such targeted persons include qualified ex-felons, high-risk youths, food stamp recipients, veterans, summer youth employees, and persons receiving certain welfare benefits.[6]

Computation of the Work Opportunity Tax Credit: General.   The credit generally is equal to 40 percent of the first $6,000 of wages (per eligible employee) for the first 12 months of employment. Thus, the credit is not available for any wages paid to an employee after the first year of employment. If the employee's first year overlaps two of the employer's tax years, however, the employer may take the credit over two tax years. If the credit is elected, the employer's tax deduction for wages is reduced by the amount of the credit. For an employer to qualify for the 40 percent credit, the employee must (1) be certified by a designated local agency as being a member of one of the targeted groups and (2) have completed at least 400 hours of service to the employer. If an employee meets the first condition but not the second, the credit rate is reduced to 25 percent provided the employee has completed a minimum of 120 hours of service to the employer.

EXAMPLE 11

In January 1998, Green Company hires four individuals who are certified to be members of a qualifying targeted group. Each employee is paid wages of $8,000 during the year. Green Company's work opportunity credit is $9,600 [($6,000 × 40%) × 4 employees]. If the tax credit is taken, Green must reduce its deduction for wages paid by $9,600. No credit is available for wages paid to these employees after their first year of employment. ▼

EXAMPLE 12

On June 1, 1998, Maria, a calendar year taxpayer, hired Joe, a member of a targeted group, and obtained the required certification. During the last seven months of 1998, Joe is paid $3,500 for more than 400 hours of work. Maria is allowed a credit of $1,400 ($3,500 × 40%) for 1998. Joe continues to work for Maria in 1999 and is paid $7,000 through May 31, 1999. Because up to $6,000 of first-year wages are eligible for the credit, Maria is allowed a 40% credit on $2,500 [$6,000 − $3,500 (wages paid in 1998)] of wages paid in 1999, or $1,000

($2,500 × 40%). None of Joe's wages paid after May 31, the end of the first year of employment, is eligible for the credit. Likewise, under current law, no credit is allowed for wages paid to persons newly hired after June 30, 1998. ▼

Computation of the Work Opportunity Tax Credit: Qualified Summer Youth Employees. The credit for qualified summer youth employees is allowed on wages for services during any 90-day period between May 1 and September 15. The maximum wages eligible for the credit are $3,000 per summer youth employee. The credit rate is the same as that under the general provision for the work opportunity tax credit. If the employee continues employment after the 90-day period as a member of another targeted group, the amount of the wages eligible for the general work opportunity tax credit as a member of the new target group is reduced by the wages paid to the employee as a qualified summer youth employee.

A *qualified summer youth employee* must be age 16 or 17 on the hiring date. An additional requirement for qualifying is that the individual's principal place of abode must be within an empowerment zone or an enterprise community.

WELFARE-TO-WORK CREDIT

Beginning in 1998, a **welfare-to-work credit**[7] is available to employers hiring individuals who have been long-term recipients of family assistance welfare benefits. In general, long-term recipients are those individuals who are certified by a designated local agency as being a member of a family receiving assistance under a public aid program for at least an 18-month period ending on the hiring date. Unlike the work opportunity credit, which applies only to first-year wages paid to qualified individuals, the welfare-to-work credit is available for qualified wages paid in the first two years of employment. If an employee's first and second work years overlap two or more of the employer's tax years, the employer may take the credit during the applicable tax years. If the welfare-to-work credit is taken, the employer's tax deduction for wages is reduced by the amount of the credit.

An employer is prohibited from taking both the work opportunity credit and the welfare-to-work credit for wages paid to a qualified employee in a given tax year. The welfare-to-work credit is not available for employees hired after April 30, 1999.

Maximum Credit. The credit is equal to 35 percent of the first $10,000 of qualified wages paid to an employee in the first year of employment, plus 50 percent of the first $10,000 of qualified wages paid in the second year of employment, resulting in a maximum credit per qualified employee of $8,500 [$3,500 (year 1) + $5,000 (year 2)]. The credit rate is higher for second-year wages to encourage employers to retain qualified individuals, thereby promoting the overall welfare-to-work goal.

EXAMPLE 13

In April 1998, Blue Company hired three individuals who are certified as long-term family assistance recipients. Each employee is paid $12,000 during 1998. Two of the three individuals continue to work for Blue Company in 1999, earning $9,000 each during the year. No additional qualified employees are hired in 1999. Blue Company's welfare-to-work credit is $10,500 [(35% × $10,000) × 3 employees] for 1998 and $9,000 [(50% × $9,000) × 2 employees] for 1999. ▼

---

[7]§ 51A.

RESEARCH ACTIVITIES CREDIT

To encourage research and experimentation, usually described as research and development (R & D), a credit is allowed for certain qualifying expenditures paid or incurred from July 1, 1996 through June 30, 1998. The **research activities credit** is the *sum* of two components: an incremental research activities credit and a basic research credit.[8]

Incremental Research Activities Credit. The incremental research activities credit applies at a 20 percent rate to the *excess* of qualified research expenses for the taxable year (the credit year) over the base amount.

In general, *research expenditures* qualify if the research relates to discovering technological information that is intended for use in the development of a new or improved business component of the taxpayer. Such expenses qualify fully if the research is performed in-house (by the taxpayer or employees). If the research is conducted by persons outside the taxpayer's business (under contract), only 65 percent of the amount paid qualifies for the credit.[9]

EXAMPLE 14

George incurs the following research expenditures for the tax year.

In-house wages, supplies, computer time	$50,000
Paid to Cutting Edge Scientific Foundation for research	30,000

George's qualified research expenditures are $69,500 [$50,000 + ($30,000 × 65%)]. ▼

Beyond the general guidelines described above, the Code does not give specific examples of qualifying research. However, the credit is *not* allowed for research that falls into certain categories, including the following:[10]

- Research conducted after the beginning of commercial production of the business component.
- Surveys and studies such as market research, testing, and routine data collection.
- Research conducted *outside* the United States.
- Research in the social sciences, arts, or humanities.

Determining the *base amount* involves a relatively complex series of computations. In addition, when the research credit is available for less than a full tax year, as is the case under current law, the base amount is adjusted further. A discussion of these computations is beyond the scope of this presentation.

EXAMPLE 15

Jack, a calendar year taxpayer, incurs qualifying research expenditures of $200,000 during 1998. Assuming the base amount is $100,000, the incremental research activities credit is $20,000 [($200,000 − $100,000) × 20%]. ▼

Qualified research and experimentation expenditures are not only eligible for the 20 percent credit, but can also be *expensed* in the year incurred.[11] In this regard, a taxpayer has two choices:[12]

---

[8]§ 41.
[9]§ 41(b)(3)(A). In the case of payments to a qualified research consortium, 75% of the amount paid qualifies for the credit.
[10]§ 41(d).

[11]§ 174. Also refer to the discussion of rules for deducting research and experimental expenditures in Chapter 6.
[12]§ 280C(c).

- Use the full credit and reduce the expense deduction for research expenses by 100 percent of the credit.
- Retain the full expense deduction and reduce the credit by the product of 100 percent of the credit times the maximum corporate tax rate.

As an alternative to the expense deduction, the taxpayer may *capitalize* the research expenses and *amortize* them over 60 months or more. In this case, the amount capitalized and subject to amortization is reduced by the full amount of the credit *only* if the credit exceeds the amount allowable as a deduction.

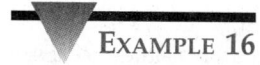 **EXAMPLE 16**

Assume the same facts as in Example 15, which shows that the potential incremental research activities credit is $20,000. The expense that the taxpayer can deduct and the credit amount are as follows:

	Credit Amount	Deduction Amount
• Full credit and reduced deduction		
$20,000 – $0	$20,000	
$200,000 – $20,000		$180,000
• Reduced credit and full deduction		
$20,000 – [(1.00 × $20,000) × .35]	13,000	
$200,000 – $0		200,000
• Full credit and capitalize and elect to amortize costs over 60 months		
$20,000 – $0	20,000	
($200,000/60) × 12		40,000

▼

Basic Research Credit. Corporations (other than S corporations or personal service corporations) are allowed an additional 20 percent credit for basic research payments from July 1, 1996 through June 30, 1998, in *excess* of a base amount. This credit is not available to individual taxpayers. *Basic research payments* are defined as amounts paid in cash to a qualified basic research organization, such as a college or university or a tax-exempt organization operated primarily to conduct scientific research.

Basic research is defined generally as any original investigation for the advancement of scientific knowledge not having a specific commercial objective. The definition excludes basic research conducted outside the United States and basic research in the social sciences, arts, or humanities. This reflects the intent of Congress to encourage high-tech research in the United States.

The calculation of this additional credit for basic research expenditures is complex and is based on expenditures in excess of a specially defined base amount.[13] The portion of the basic research expenditures not in excess of the base amount is treated as a part of the qualifying expenditures for purposes of the regular credit for incremental research activities.

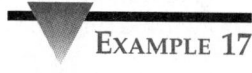 **EXAMPLE 17**

Orange Corporation, a qualifying corporation, pays $75,000 to a university for basic research. Assume that Orange's base amount for the basic research credit is $50,000. The basic research activities credit allowed is $5,000 [($75,000 – $50,000) × 20%]. The $50,000 of basic research expenditures that equal the base amount are treated as research expenses for purposes of the regular incremental research activities credit. ▼

---

[13] § 41(e).

**ETHICAL
CONSIDERATIONS**

When Does "Research" Qualify as R & D?

The research activities credit is designed to encourage taxpayers to engage in research relating to the discovery of technological information that is intended for use in the development of a new or improved business component of the taxpayer.

You are employed as a staff accountant for a privately held corporation that manufactures medical equipment. During the current year, the corporation purchases new communication software and related document-management systems with the goal of enhancing employee efficiency and productivity. To familiarize employees with these new systems, an outside firm is hired to conduct numerous software training seminars during the first six months the new systems are in place. Substantial costs are incurred in connection with these training seminars. Not surprisingly, various inefficiencies are also encountered until the employees have had sufficient training and time to use the new systems.

The corporation's new president, ever mindful of the company's profitability and tax position, urges you to claim the research activities credit with respect to the software training costs. The president justifies this position on the grounds that the employees were "researching" the new software and its use. How do you respond?

LOW-INCOME HOUSING CREDIT

To encourage building owners to make affordable housing available for low-income individuals, Congress has made a credit available to owners of qualified low-income housing projects.[14]

More than any other, the **low-income housing credit** is influenced by nontax factors. For example, certification of the property by the appropriate state or local agency authorized to provide low-income housing credits is required. These credits are issued based on a nationwide allocation.

The amount of the credit is based on the qualified basis of the property. The qualified basis depends on the number of units rented to low-income tenants. Tenants are low-income tenants if their income does not exceed a specified percentage of the area median gross income. The amount of the credit is determined by multiplying the qualified basis by the applicable percentage; the credit is allowed over a 10-year period if the property continues to meet the required conditions.

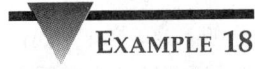

EXAMPLE 18

Sarah spends $100,000 to build a qualified low-income housing project completed January 1, 1998. The entire project is rented to low-income families. The credit rate for property placed in service during January 1998 is 8.41%.[15] Sarah may claim a credit of $8,410 ($100,000 × 8.41%) in 1998 and in each of the following nine years. Generally, first-year credits are prorated based on the date the project is placed in service. A full year's credit is taken in each of the next nine years, and any remaining first-year credit is claimed in the eleventh year. ▼

Recapture of a portion of the credit may be required if the number of units set aside for low-income tenants falls below a minimum threshold, if the taxpayer disposes of the property or the interest in it, or if the taxpayer's amount at risk decreases.

---

[14]§ 42.
[15]Rev.Rul. 98–4, I.R.B. No. 2, 18. The rate is subject to adjustment every month by the IRS.

DISABLED ACCESS CREDIT

The **disabled access credit** is designed to encourage small businesses to make their businesses more accessible to disabled individuals. The credit is available for any eligible access expenditures paid or incurred by an eligible small business. The credit is calculated at the rate of 50 percent of the eligible expenditures that exceed $250 but do not exceed $10,250. Thus, the maximum amount for the credit is $5,000 ($10,000 × 50%).[16]

An *eligible small business* is one that during the previous year either had gross receipts of $1 million or less or had no more than 30 full-time employees. An eligible business can include a sole proprietorship, partnership, regular corporation, or S corporation.

Eligible access expenditures are generally any reasonable and necessary amounts that are paid or incurred to make certain changes to facilities. These changes must involve the removal of architectural, communication, physical, or transportation barriers that would otherwise make a business inaccessible to disabled and handicapped individuals. Examples of qualifying projects include installing ramps, widening doorways, and adding raised markings on elevator control buttons. However, eligible expenditures do *not* include amounts that are paid or incurred in connection with any facility that has been placed into service after the enactment (November 5, 1990) of the provision.

To the extent a disabled access credit is available, no deduction or credit is allowed under any other provision of the tax law. The adjusted basis for depreciation is reduced by the amount of the credit.

EXAMPLE 19

This year Red, Inc., an eligible business, made $11,000 of capital improvements to business realty that had been placed in service in June 1990. The expenditures were intended to make Red's business more accessible to the disabled and were considered eligible expenditures for purposes of the disabled access credit. The amount of the credit is $5,000 [($10,250 – $250) × 50%]. Although $11,000 of eligible expenditures were incurred, only the excess of $10,250 over $250 qualifies for the credit. Further, the depreciable basis of the capital improvement is $6,000 because the basis must be reduced by the amount of the credit [$11,000 (cost) – $5,000 (amount of the credit)]. ▼

OTHER TAX CREDITS

EARNED INCOME CREDIT

LEARNING OBJECTIVE 4
Describe several other tax credits that are available primarily to individual taxpayers.

The **earned income credit,** which has been a part of the law for many years, consistently has been justified as a means of providing tax equity to the working poor. More recently, the credit has also been designed to help offset regressive taxes that are a part of our tax system, such as the gasoline and Social Security taxes. In addition, the credit has been intended to encourage economically disadvantaged individuals to become contributing members of the workforce.[17]

In 1998, the earned income credit is determined by multiplying a maximum amount of earned income by the appropriate credit percentage (see Table 11–2). Generally, earned income includes employee compensation and net earnings from self-employment but excludes items such as interest, dividends, pension benefits, and alimony. If a taxpayer has children, the credit percentage used in the calculation depends on the number of qualifying children. Thus, in 1998, the maximum earned

[16]§ 44.

[17]§ 32.

▼ **TABLE 11–2**
Earned Income Credit and
Phase-out Percentages

Tax Year	Number of Qualifying Children	Maximum Earned Income	Credit Percentage	Phase-out Begins	Phase-out Percentage	Phase-out Ends
1998	One child	$6,680	34.00	$12,260	15.98	$26,473
	Two or more children	9,390	40.00	12,260	21.06	30,095
	No qualifying children	4,460	7.65	5,570	7.65	10,030
1997	One child	6,500	34.00	11,930	15.98	25,760
	Two or more children	9,140	40.00	11,930	21.06	29,290
	No qualifying children	4,340	7.65	5,430	7.65	9,770

income credit for a taxpayer with one qualifying child is $2,271 ($6,680 × 34%) and $3,756 ($9,390 × 40%) for a taxpayer with two or more qualifying children. However, the maximum earned income credit is phased out completely if the taxpayer's earned income or AGI exceeds certain thresholds as shown in Table 11–2.[18] To the extent that the greater of earned income or AGI exceeds $12,260 in 1998, the difference, multiplied by the appropriate phase-out percentage, is subtracted from the maximum earned income credit.

EXAMPLE 20

In 1998, Grace, who otherwise qualifies for the earned income credit, receives wages of $14,000 and has no other income. She has one qualifying child. Grace's earned income credit is $2,271 ($6,680 × 34%) reduced by $278 [($14,000 − $12,260) × 15.98%]. Thus, Grace's earned income credit is $1,993. If Grace has two or more qualifying children, the calculation would produce a credit of $3,756 ($9,390 × 40%) reduced by $366 [($14,000 − $12,260) × 21.06%]. Thus, Grace's earned income credit would be $3,390. ▼

Earned Income Credit Table.   It is not necessary to compute the credit as was done in Example 20. As part of the tax simplification process, the IRS issues an Earned Income Credit Table for the determination of the appropriate amount of the earned income credit. This table and a worksheet are included in the instructions to both Form 1040 and Form 1040A.

Eligibility Requirements.   *Eligibility* for the credit may depend not only on the taxpayer meeting the earned income and AGI thresholds, but also on whether he or she has a qualifying child. A *qualifying child* must meet the following tests:

- *Relationship test.* The individual must be a son, daughter, descendant of the taxpayer's son or daughter, stepson, stepdaughter, or an eligible foster child of the taxpayer. A legally adopted child of the taxpayer is considered the same as a child by blood.
- *Residency test.* The qualifying child must share the taxpayer's principal place of abode, which must be located within the United States, for more than one-half of the tax year of the taxpayer. Temporary absences (e.g., due to illness or education) are disregarded for purposes of this test. For foster children, however, the child must share the taxpayer's home for the entire year.

[18]§ 32(a)(2)(B). AGI is modified for the purpose of this calculation.
See § 32(c)(5).

- *Age test.* The child must not have reached the age of 19 (24 in the case of a full-time student) as of the end of the tax year. In addition, a child who is permanently and totally disabled at any time during the year is considered to meet the age test.

In addition to being available for taxpayers with qualifying children, the earned income credit is also available to certain *workers without children*. However, this provision is available only to taxpayers aged 25 through 64 who cannot be claimed as a dependent on another taxpayer's return. As shown in Table 11–2, the credit for 1998 is calculated on a maximum earned income of $4,460 times 7.65 percent and reduced by 7.65 percent of earned income over $5,570. This credit is phased out completely at $10,030.

EXAMPLE 21

Walt, who is single, 28 years of age, and is not claimed as a dependent on anyone else's return, earns $6,500 during 1998. Even though he does not have any qualifying children, he qualifies for the earned income credit. His credit is $341 ($4,460 × 7.65%) reduced by $71 [($6,500 − $5,570) × 7.65%]. Thus, Walt's earned income credit is $270. If, instead, Walt's earned income is $4,900, his earned income credit is $341. In this situation, there is no phase-out of the maximum credit because his earned income is not in excess of $5,570. ▼

Advance Payment. The earned income credit is a form of negative income tax (a refundable credit for taxpayers who do not have a tax liability). An eligible individual may elect to receive advance payments of the earned income credit from his or her employer (rather than receiving the credit from the IRS upon filing the tax return). The amount that can be received in advance is limited to 60 percent of the credit that is available to a taxpayer with only one qualifying child. If this election is made, the taxpayer must file a certificate of eligibility (Form W–5) with his or her employer and *must* file a tax return for the year the income is earned.

TAX CREDIT FOR ELDERLY OR DISABLED TAXPAYERS

The credit for the elderly was originally enacted in 1954 as the retirement income credit to provide tax relief on retirement income for individuals who were not receiving substantial benefits from tax-free Social Security payments.[19]

Currently, the **tax credit for the elderly or disabled** applies to the following:

- Taxpayers age 65 or older.
- Taxpayers under age 65 who are retired with a permanent and total disability and who have disability income from a public or private employer on account of the disability.

The *maximum* allowable credit is $1,125 (15% × $7,500 of qualifying income), but the credit will be less for a taxpayer who receives Social Security benefits or has AGI exceeding specified amounts. Under these circumstances, the base used in the credit computation is reduced. Many taxpayers receive Social Security benefits or have AGI high enough to reduce the base for the credit to zero.

The eligibility requirements and the tax computation are somewhat complicated. Consequently, an individual may elect to have the IRS compute his or her tax and the amount of the tax credit.

---

[19]§ 22. This credit is not subject to indexation.

TAX IN THE NEWS

"EARNED INCOME CREDIT" OR "EASY INCOME FOR CHEATS"?

The earned income credit was designed to mitigate the effects of the tax system on low-income taxpayers and to encourage individuals to seek work rather than welfare. Recently, however, the benefits the credit provides are being underused and abused.

To be considered a success, the earned income credit would have to be used by those persons it is intended to help. For example, workers who have a qualifying child and income below a certain amount are allowed to receive advance payment of the credit. However, less than 1 percent of qualifying Americans take advantage of this advance payment opportunity. Some commentators contend that the provisions, which have been changed more than 10 times since 1976, have become overly complex, difficult to comply with, and almost unusable by the low-income workers the credit is intended to aid. Estimates show that 14 percent of persons qualifying for the credit fail to claim it.

On the other hand, others who don't qualify have found the lure of the credit too good to pass up. In a recent IRS study, one-half of the electronically filed returns that claimed the earned income credit contained errors suspected to be intentional. In fact, some of the tax fraud schemes involving the credit have been initiated by persons in prison. One IRS investigation uncovered a scam operating out of the Maine Correctional Center. A dozen current and former inmates were indicted for improperly seeking refunds for earned income credit claims. Another taxpayer convicted of cheating the government by improperly using the credit testified before Congress that the earned income tax credit could stand for "easy income for cheats!" In an attempt to curb such abuses, Congress recently enacted several compliance provisions aimed at denying the credit to persons who negligently or fraudulently claimed the earned income credit in prior years.

▼ **TABLE 11–3**
Base Amounts for Tax Credit for Elderly or Disabled Taxpayers

Status	Base Amount
Single, head of household, or surviving spouse	$5,000
Married, joint return, only one spouse qualified	5,000
Married, joint return, both spouses qualified	7,500
Married, separate returns, spouses live apart the entire year	3,750 each

The credit generally is based on an initial amount (referred to as the *base amount*) and the filing status of the taxpayer in accordance with Table 11–3. To qualify for the credit, married taxpayers who live together must file a joint return. For taxpayers under age 65 who are retired on permanent and total disability, the base amounts could be less than those shown in Table 11–3 because these amounts are limited to taxable disability income.

This initial base amount is *reduced* by (1) Social Security, Railroad Retirement, and certain excluded pension benefits and (2) one-half of the taxpayer's AGI in excess of a threshold amount, which is a function of the taxpayer's filing status. The credit may be calculated using the procedure presented in the following template:

Base amount ($3,750, $5,000, or $7,500—see Table 11–3)		____
Less: Qualifying nontaxable benefits	____	
One-half of excess of AGI over: $7,500 for single, head of household, or surviving spouse taxpayers $10,000 for married taxpayers $5,000 for married taxpayers filing separately		
Total reductions	____	
Balance subject to credit		____
Multiply balance subject to credit by 15%—this is the tax credit allowed		====

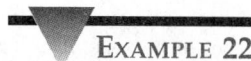

EXAMPLE 22   Paul and Peggy, husband and wife, are both over age 65 and received Social Security benefits of $2,400 in the current year. On a joint return, they reported AGI of $14,000.

Base amount ($3,750, $5,000, or $7,500—see Table 11–3)		$ 7,500
Less: Qualifying nontaxable benefits	$ 2,400	
One-half of excess of AGI over: $7,500 for single, head of household, or surviving spouse taxpayers $10,000 for married taxpayers $5,000 for married taxpayers filing separately	2,000	
Total reductions		(4,400)
Balance subject to credit		$ 3,100
Multiply balance subject to credit by 15%—this is the tax credit allowed		$ 465

Schedule R of Form 1040 (see Appendix B) is used to calculate and report the credit.

FOREIGN TAX CREDIT

Both individual taxpayers and corporations may claim a tax credit for foreign income tax paid on income earned and subject to tax in another country or a U.S. possession.[20] As an alternative, a taxpayer may claim a deduction instead of a credit.[21] In most instances, the **foreign tax credit (FTC)** is advantageous since it provides a direct offset against the tax liability.

The purpose of the FTC is to mitigate double taxation since income earned in a foreign country is subject to both U.S. and foreign taxes. However, the ceiling limitation formula may result in some form of double taxation or taxation at rates in excess of U.S. rates when the foreign tax rates are higher than the U.S. rates. This is a distinct possibility because U.S. tax rates are lower than those of many foreign countries.

Other special tax treatments applicable to taxpayers working outside the United States include the foreign earned income exclusion (refer to Chapter 4) and

---

[20]Section 27 provides for the credit, but the qualifications and calculation procedure for the credit are contained in §§ 901–908.   [21]§ 164.

limitations on deducting expenses of employees working outside the United States (refer to Chapter 8). Recall from the earlier discussion that a taxpayer may not take advantage of *both* the FTC and the foreign earned income exclusion.

Computation. Taxpayers are required to compute the FTC based upon an overall limitation.[22] The FTC allowed is the *lesser* of the foreign taxes imposed or the *overall limitation* determined according to the following formula:

$$\frac{\text{Foreign-source taxable income}}{\text{Worldwide taxable income}} \times \frac{\text{U.S. tax}}{\text{before FTC}}$$

For individual taxpayers, worldwide taxable income in the overall limitation formula is determined *before* personal and dependency exemptions are deducted.

EXAMPLE 23

In 1998, Carlos, a calendar year taxpayer, has $10,000 of income from Country Y, which imposes a 15% tax, and $20,000 from Country Z, which imposes a 50% tax. He has taxable income of $59,200 from within the United States, is married filing a joint return, and claims two dependency exemptions. Thus, although Carlos's taxable income for purposes of determining U.S. tax is $89,200, taxable income amounts used in the limitation formula are not reduced by personal and dependency exemptions. Thus, for this purpose, taxable income is $100,000 [$89,200 + (4 × $2,700)]. Assume that Carlos's U.S. tax before the credit is $19,471. Overall limitation:

$$\frac{\text{Foreign-source taxable income}}{\text{Worldwide taxable income}} = \frac{\$30,000}{\$100,000} \times \$19,471 = \$5,841$$

In this case, $5,841 is allowed as the FTC because this amount is less than the $11,500 of foreign taxes imposed [$1,500 (Country Y) + $10,000 (Country Z)]. ▼

Thus, the overall limitation may result in some of the foreign income being subjected to double taxation. Unused FTCs [e.g., the $5,659 ($11,500 − $5,841) from Example 23] can be carried back two years and forward five years.[23]

Only foreign income taxes, war profits taxes, and excess profits taxes (or taxes paid in lieu of such taxes) qualify for the credit. In determining whether or not a tax is an income tax, U.S. criteria are applied. Thus, value added taxes (VAT), severance taxes, property taxes, and sales taxes do not qualify because they are not regarded as taxes on income. Such taxes may be deductible, however.

ADOPTION EXPENSES CREDIT

Beginning in 1997, qualifying adoption expenses paid or incurred by a taxpayer may give rise to the **adoption expenses credit**.[24] The provision is intended to assist taxpayers who incur nonrecurring costs directly associated with the adoption process, such as adoption fees, attorney fees, court costs, social service review costs, and transportation costs.

Up to $5,000 of costs incurred to adopt an eligible child qualify for the credit.[25] An eligible child is one who is:

- under 18 years of age at the time of the adoption or
- physically or mentally incapable of taking care of himself or herself.

[22]§ 904.
[23]§ 904(c) and Reg. § 1.904–2(g), Example 1.
[24]§ 23.

[25]§ 23(b)(1). The maximum amount of qualifying expenses increases to $6,000 for a "child with special needs." See § 23(d)(3).

A taxpayer may claim the credit in the year qualifying expenses were paid or incurred if the expenses were paid or incurred *during or after* the year in which the adoption was finalized. For qualifying expenses paid or incurred in a tax year *prior* to the year when the adoption was finalized, the credit must be claimed in the year the adoption was finalized. A married couple must file a joint return.

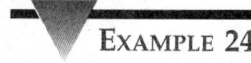

EXAMPLE 24

In late 1998, Sam and Martha pay $2,500 in legal fees, adoption fees, and other expenses directly related to the adoption of an infant daughter, Susan. In 1999, they pay an additional $1,000, and in 2000, the year in which the adoption becomes final, they pay $3,000. Sam and Martha are eligible for a $5,000 credit in 2000. ▼

The amount of the credit that is otherwise available is phased out for taxpayers whose AGI (modified for this purpose) exceeds $75,000, and the credit is completely eliminated when the AGI reaches $115,000. The resulting credit is calculated by reducing the allowable credit (determined without this reduction) by the allowable credit multiplied by the ratio of the excess of the taxpayer's AGI over $75,000 to $40,000.

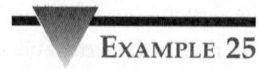

EXAMPLE 25

Assume the same facts as in the previous example, except that Sam and Martha's AGI is $100,000 in each of the relevant years. As a result, their available credit in 2000 is reduced from $5,000 to $1,875 {$5,000 − [$5,000($25,000/$40,000)]}. ▼

The credit is nonrefundable and is available to taxpayers only in a year in which this credit and the other nonrefundable credits do not exceed the taxpayer's tax liability. However, any unused adoption expenses credit may be carried over for up to five years, being utilized on a first-in, first-out basis.

CHILD TAX CREDIT

For the first time, beginning in 1998, individual taxpayers are permitted to take a tax credit based solely on the *number* of their dependent children under age 17. This **child tax credit**[26] is one of several "family-friendly" provisions enacted as part of the Taxpayer Relief Act of 1997 (TRA of 1997). To be eligible for the credit, the child must be under age 17, a U.S. citizen, and claimed as a dependent on the taxpayer's return.

Maximum Credit and Phase-outs.   The maximum credit available is $400 per child beginning in 1998, rising to $500 per child in 1999 and years thereafter. The available credit is phased out for higher-income taxpayers beginning when AGI[27] reaches $110,000 for joint filers ($55,000 for married taxpayers filing separately) and $75,000 for single taxpayers. The credit is phased out by $50 for each $1,000 (or part thereof) of AGI above the threshold amounts. Since the maximum credit amount available to taxpayers depends on the number of qualifying children, the income level at which the credit is phased out completely also depends on the number of children qualifying for the credit.

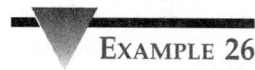

EXAMPLE 26

Juanita and Alberto are married and file a joint tax return claiming their two children, ages six and eight, as dependents. Their AGI for 1998 is $122,400. Juanita and Alberto's available child tax credit for 1998 is $150, computed as their maximum credit of $800 ($400 × 2 children) reduced by a $650 phase-out. Since Juanita and Alberto's AGI is in excess of the $110,000 threshold, the maximum credit must be reduced by $50 for every $1,000 (or part thereof)

---

[26] § 24.

[27] AGI is modified for purposes of this calculation. See § 24(b)(1).

above the threshold amount {$50 × [($122,400 – $110,000)/$1,000]}. Thus, the credit reduction equals $650 [$50 × 13 (rounded from 12.4)]. Therefore, Juanita and Alberto's child tax credit is $150 for 1998. ▼

CREDIT FOR CHILD AND DEPENDENT CARE EXPENSES

A credit is allowed to taxpayers who incur employment-related expenses for child or dependent care.[28] The **credit for child and dependent care expenses** is a specified percentage of expenses incurred to enable the taxpayer to work or to seek employment. Expenses on which the credit for child and dependent care expenses is based are subject to limitations.

Eligibility. To be eligible for the credit, an individual must maintain a household for either of the following:

- A dependent under age 13.
- A dependent or spouse who is physically or mentally incapacitated.

Generally, married taxpayers must file a joint return to obtain the credit. The credit may also be claimed by the custodial parent for a nondependent child under age 13 if the noncustodial parent is allowed to claim the child as a dependent under a pre-1985 divorce agreement or under a waiver in the case of a post-1984 agreement.

Eligible Employment-Related Expenses. Eligible expenses include amounts paid for household services and care of a qualifying individual that are incurred to enable the taxpayer to be employed. Child and dependent care expenses include expenses incurred in the home, such as payments for a housekeeper. Out-of-the-home expenses incurred for the care of a dependent under the age of 13 also qualify for the credit. In addition, out-of-the-home expenses incurred for an older dependent or spouse who is physically or mentally incapacitated qualify for the credit if that person regularly spends at least eight hours each day in the taxpayer's household. This makes the credit available to taxpayers who keep handicapped older children and elderly relatives in the home instead of institutionalizing them. Out-of-the-home expenses incurred for services provided by a dependent care center will qualify only if the center complies with all applicable laws and regulations of a state or unit of local government.

Child care payments to a relative are eligible for the credit unless the relative is a dependent of the taxpayer or the taxpayer's spouse or is a child (under age 19) of the taxpayer.

EXAMPLE 27

Wilma is an employed mother of an eight-year-old child. She pays her mother, Rita, $1,500 per year to care for the child after school. Wilma does not claim Rita as a dependent. Wilma pays her daughter Eleanor, age 17, $900 for the child's care during the summer. Of these amounts, only the $1,500 paid to Rita qualifies as employment-related child care expenses. ▼

Earned Income Ceiling. The total for qualifying employment-related expenses is limited to an individual's earned income. For married taxpayers, this limitation applies to the spouse with the *lesser* amount of earned income. Special rules are provided for taxpayers with nonworking spouses who are disabled or are full-time students. If a nonworking spouse is physically or mentally disabled or is a full-time student, he or she is *deemed* to have earned income for purposes of this limitation. The deemed amount is $200 per month if there is one qualifying individual in the

---

[28]§ 21.

household or $400 per month if there are two or more qualifying individuals in the household. In the case of a student-spouse, the student's income is *deemed* to be earned only for the months that the student is enrolled on a full-time basis at an educational institution.

Calculation of the Credit.   In general, the credit is equal to a percentage of *unreimbursed* employment-related expenses up to $2,400 for one qualifying individual and $4,800 for two or more individuals. The credit rate varies between 20 percent and 30 percent, depending on the taxpayer's AGI. The following chart shows the applicable percentage for taxpayers as AGI increases:

| Adjusted Gross Income | | Applicable Rate of Credit |
Over	But Not Over	
$ 0	$10,000	30%
10,000	12,000	29%
12,000	14,000	28%
14,000	16,000	27%
16,000	18,000	26%
18,000	20,000	25%
20,000	22,000	24%
22,000	24,000	23%
24,000	26,000	22%
26,000	28,000	21%
28,000	No limit	20%

EXAMPLE 28

Nancy, who has two children under age 13, worked full-time while her spouse, Ron, was attending college for 10 months during the year. Nancy earned $21,000 and incurred $5,000 of child care expenses. Ron is *deemed* to be fully employed and to have earned $400 for each of the 10 months (or a total of $4,000). Since Nancy and Ron have AGI of $21,000, they are allowed a credit rate of 24%. Nancy and Ron are limited to $4,000 in qualified child care expenses (the lesser of $4,800 or $4,000). Therefore, they are entitled to a tax credit of $960 (24% × $4,000) for the year. ▼

Dependent Care Assistance Program.   Recall from Chapter 4 that a taxpayer is allowed an exclusion from gross income for a limited amount reimbursed for child or dependent care expenses. However, the taxpayer is not allowed both an exclusion from gross income and a child and dependent care credit on the same amount. The $2,400 and $4,800 ceilings for allowable child and dependent care expenses are reduced dollar for dollar by the amount of reimbursement.[29]

EXAMPLE 29

Assume the same facts as in Example 28, except that of the $5,000 paid for child care, Nancy was reimbursed $2,500 by her employer under a qualified dependent care assistance program. Under the employer's plan, the reimbursement reduces Nancy's taxable wages. Thus, Nancy and Ron have AGI of $18,500 ($21,000 – $2,500). The maximum amount of child care expenses for two or more dependents of $4,800 is reduced by the $2,500 reimbursement, resulting in a tax credit of $575 [25% × ($4,800 – $2,500)]. ▼

[29]§ 21(c).

Reporting Requirements.   The credit is claimed by completing and filing Form 2441, Credit for Child and Dependent Care Expenses (see Appendix B).

EDUCATION TAX CREDITS

Beginning in 1998, two new credits, the **HOPE scholarship credit** and **lifetime learning credit,**[30] are available to help qualifying low- and middle-income individuals defray the cost of higher education. The credits, both of which are nonrefundable, are available for qualifying tuition and related expenses incurred by students pursuing undergraduate or graduate degrees or vocational training. Room, board, and book costs are ineligible for the credits.

Maximum Credit.   The HOPE scholarship credit permits a maximum credit of $1,500 per year (100 percent of first $1,000 of tuition expenses plus 50 percent of the next $1,000 of tuition expenses) for the *first two years* of postsecondary education. The lifetime learning credit permits a maximum credit of 20 percent of tuition expenses (up to $5,000 per year) incurred after June 30, 1998, and in a year in which the HOPE scholarship credit is not claimed with respect to a given student's tuition and related expenses. The lifetime learning credit is intended for individuals who are beyond the first two years of postsecondary education. Beginning in 2003, the lifetime learning credit will be available on the first $10,000 of qualifying costs incurred per year.

Eligible Individuals.   Both education credits are available for qualified tuition and related expenses incurred by a taxpayer, taxpayer's spouse, or taxpayer's dependent. The HOPE scholarship credit is available per eligible student, while the lifetime learning credit is calculated per taxpayer. To be eligible for the HOPE credit, students must take at least one-half the full-time course load for at least one academic term at a qualifying educational institution. No comparable requirement exists for the lifetime learning credit. Therefore, taxpayers who are seeking new job skills or maintaining existing skills through graduate training or continuing education are eligible for the lifetime learning credit. Taxpayers who are married must file joint returns in order to claim either education credit.

Timing of Expenses.   Qualifying tuition expenses must be *paid* during the tax year for education furnished by a qualifying institution during an academic year *beginning* during the tax year in question. If tuition expenses are paid during the tax year for an academic period beginning during the first three months of the following tax year, the expenses may be claimed during the payment year for purposes of the credit computation. This aspect of the credit computation permits taxpayers to prepay tuition expenses in order to maximize the available education credit. As a related item, qualifying tuition expenses paid with student loans are eligible for the education credits during the tax year when the costs are incurred and paid, not the tax year in which the loan is repaid.

Income Limitations.   Both education credits are subject to income limitations and are combined for purposes of the limitation calculation. The allowable credit amount is phased out, beginning when the taxpayer's AGI[31] reaches $40,000 ($80,000 for married taxpayers filing jointly). The credits are completely eliminated when AGI reaches $50,000 ($100,000 for married filing jointly). The calculated credit amount is reduced by the extent to which AGI exceeds $40,000 ($80,000 for married

---

[30]§ 25A.

[31]AGI is modified for purposes of this calculation. See § 25A(d)(3).

filing jointly) as a percentage of the $10,000 ($20,000 for married filing jointly) phase-out range.

Restrictions on Double Tax Benefit.   Taxpayers are prohibited from receiving a double tax benefit associated with qualifying educational expenses. Therefore, taxpayers who claim an education credit may not deduct the expenses, nor may they claim the credit for amounts that are otherwise excluded from income (e.g., scholarships and employer-paid educational assistance).

EXAMPLE 30

Dean and Audry are married, file a joint tax return, have modified AGI under $80,000, and have two children. During fall 1998, Raymond is beginning his freshman year at State University, and Kelsey is beginning her senior year. Both Raymond and Kelsey are full-time students and may be claimed as dependents on their parents' tax return. Raymond's qualifying tuition expenses and fees total $4,600 for the academic year ($2,300 per semester) while Kelsey's qualifying expenses total $5,200 for the academic year ($2,600 per semester). Dean and Audry pay the tuition and related expenses in full at the beginning of each semester. For 1998, Dean and Audry may claim a $1,500 HOPE scholarship credit [(100% × $1,000) + (50% × $1,000)] relating to Raymond's expenses and a $520 lifetime learning credit (20% × $2,600) relating to Kelsey's expenses. Kelsey's tuition expenses are ineligible for the HOPE credit because she is beyond the first two years of postsecondary education. Finally, Dean and Audry could have increased their available lifetime learning credit for 1998 by prepaying some of Kelsey's tuition expenses. ▼

EXAMPLE 31

Assume the same facts as in Example 30, except that Dean and Audry's AGI for 1998 is $92,000. Dean and Audry are eligible to claim $808 in total education credits for 1998. Their available credits totaling $2,020 ($1,500 HOPE credit + $520 lifetime learning credit) must be reduced because their AGI exceeds the $80,000 limit for married taxpayers. The percentage reduction is computed as the amount by which AGI exceeds the limit, expressed as a percentage of the phase-out range, or [($92,000 − $80,000)/$20,000)], resulting in a 60% reduction. Therefore, the maximum available credit for 1998 is $808 ($2,020 × 40% allowable portion). ▼

**TAX PLANNING
CONSIDERATIONS**

5 **LEARNING OBJECTIVE**
Identify tax planning opportunities related to tax credits.

FOREIGN TAX CREDIT

A U.S. citizen or resident working abroad (commonly referred to as an *expatriate*) may elect to take either a foreign tax credit or the foreign earned income exclusion. In cases where the income tax of a foreign country is higher than the U.S. income tax, the credit choice usually is preferable. If the reverse is true, electing the foreign earned income exclusion probably reduces the overall tax burden.

   Unfortunately, the choice between the credit and the earned income exclusion is not without some limitations. The election of the foreign earned income exclusion, once made, can be revoked for a later year. However, once revoked, the earned income exclusion will not be available for a period of five years unless the IRS consents to an earlier date. This will create a dilemma for expatriates whose job assignments over several years shift between low- and high-bracket countries.

EXAMPLE 32

In 1997, Ira, a calendar year taxpayer, is sent by his employer to Saudi Arabia (a low-tax country). For 1997, therefore, Ira elects the foreign earned income exclusion. In 1998, Ira's employer transfers him to France (a high-tax country). Accordingly, he revokes the foreign earned income exclusion election for 1998 and chooses instead to use the foreign tax credit. If Ira is transferred back to Saudi Arabia (or any other low-tax country) within five years, he may not utilize the foreign earned income exclusion. ▼

PAYING FOR COLLEGE—UNDERSTANDING THE TAX LAW MAY BE HALF THE BATTLE

Taxpayers with college-bound children are the beneficiaries of several new tax breaks courtesy of the Taxpayer Relief Act of 1997. Although these new provisions will cut the cost of a college education, many people will likely need help from their friendly neighborhood tax adviser to understand the law and take advantage of these new provisions.

In particular, the 1997 tax bill created five new ways to help pay for college. Beginning in 1998, parents can contribute $500 per year to an education individual retirement account for any child under age 18. No tax is due on the account earnings as long as the money is used for education expenses. Taxpayers will also be able to make penalty-free withdrawals from two other IRAs—a regular IRA or the new Roth IRA. The tax bill also expanded prepaid tuition plans to cover room and board costs in addition to tuition expenses and reinstated the deductibility of interest on student loans. Beginning in 1998, taxpayers can take an "above-the-line" deduction for up to $1,000 in student-loan interest, with the deduction rising to $2,500 in 2001.

Probably, the most significant tax breaks in the 1997 bill were the creation of two new education credits—the HOPE scholarship credit and the lifetime learning credit. The HOPE scholarship credit permits a maximum credit of $1,500 per year for the first two years of college tuition expenses. The lifetime learning credit can be used in subsequent years to save up to $1,000 per year in taxes if tuition expenses equal at least $5,000.

Although these tax law changes seem appealing, consider some of the intricacies involved in their use. To begin with, many of the benefits are phased out for higher-income taxpayers. For married taxpayers filing a joint return, the ability to contribute to an education IRA starts phasing out at $150,000, the student-loan interest deduction starts disappearing at $60,000, and the education credits begin phasing out at $80,000. Unfortunately, the complexity doesn't stop there.

Many of the new provisions are mutually exclusive to prevent taxpayers from receiving a double benefit. For example, taxpayers are prevented from contributing to both an education IRA and a state-sponsored prepaid tuition plan in the same year. Likewise, if money is withdrawn from an education IRA to pay for college, the taxpayer is prohibited from taking either education credit with respect to those expenditures. The new education credits can also create problems for taxpayers with Series EE savings bonds. If a taxpayer cashes in the bonds to pay for college and elects to exclude the bond interest from income, the credits are also unavailable.

Perhaps most subtle of all is the impact of the new education credits on a student's ability to receive financial aid. If the credits are used, the family's disposable income will rise, potentially reducing the amount of financial aid available in future years.

In sum, given the changes made by the 1997 bill, understanding the tax law may indeed be half the battle when paying for college.

SOURCE: Adapted from Jonathan Clements, "Tax Law Leads to Confusion about How to Pay for College," *Wall Street Journal*, August 26, 1997, p. C1.

CONCEPT SUMMARY 11–1

Tax Credits

Credit	Computation	Comments
Tax withheld on wages (§ 31)	Amount is reported to employee on W–2 form.	Refundable credit.
Earned income (§ 32)	Amount is determined by reference to Earned Income Credit Table published by IRS. Computations of underlying amounts in Earned Income Credit Table are illustrated in Example 20.	Refundable credit. A form of negative income tax to assist low-income taxpayers. Earned income and AGI must be less than certain threshold amounts. Generally, one or more qualifying children must reside with the taxpayer.
Child and dependent care (§ 21)	Rate ranges from 20% to 30% depending on AGI. Maximum base for credit is $2,400 for one qualifying individual, $4,800 for two or more.	Nonrefundable personal credit. No carryback or carryforward. Benefits taxpayers who incur employment-related child or dependent care expenses in order to work or seek employment. Eligible dependents include children under age 13 or dependent (any age) or spouse who is physically or mentally incapacitated.
Elderly or disabled (§ 22)	15% of sum of base amount minus reductions for (a) Social Security and other nontaxable benefits and (b) excess AGI. Base amount is fixed by law (e.g., $5,000 for a single taxpayer).	Nonrefundable personal credit. No carryback or carryforward. Provides relief for taxpayers not receiving substantial tax-free retirement benefits.
Adoption expenses (§ 23)	Up to $5,000 of costs incurred to adopt an eligible child qualify for the credit. Taxpayer claims the credit in the year qualified expenses were paid or incurred if expenses were paid during or after year in which adoption was finalized. For expenses paid or incurred in a year prior to when adoption was finalized, credit must be claimed in year adoption was finalized.	Nonrefundable credit. Unused credit may be carried forward 5 years. Purpose is to assist taxpayers who incur nonrecurring costs associated with the adoption process.
Child (§ 24)	Credit is based on *number* of qualifying dependent children under age 17. Maximum credit is $400 per child in 1998 ($500 per child in 1999 and thereafter). Credit is phased out for higher-income taxpayers.	Nonrefundable credit. Purpose is to provide tax relief for low- to moderate-income families with children.
Education (§ 25A)	HOPE scholarship credit is available for qualifying tuition expenses of students in first two years of post-secondary education. Maximum credit is $1,500 per year per eligible student. Credit is phased out for higher-income taxpayers.	Nonrefundable credit. Credit is designed to help defray costs of first two years of higher education for low- to middle-income families.
	Lifetime learning credit permits a maximum credit of 20% of qualifying tuition expenses (up to $5,000 per year) for costs incurred after June 30, 1998, provided HOPE scholarship is not claimed with respect to those expenses. Credit is calculated per taxpayer, not per student, and is phased out for higher-income taxpayers.	Nonrefundable credit. Credit is designed to help defray costs of higher education beyond first two years, and for costs incurred in maintaining or improving existing job skills, for low- to middle-income taxpayers.

Concept Summary 11–1

Tax Credits—Continued

Credit	Computation	Comments
Foreign tax (§ 27)	Foreign income/total worldwide taxable income × U.S. tax = overall limitation. Lesser of foreign taxes imposed or overall limitation.	Nonrefundable credit. Unused credits may be carried back two years and forward five years. Purpose is to prevent double taxation of foreign income.
General business (§ 38)	May not exceed net income tax minus the greater of tentative minimum tax or 25% of net regular tax liability that exceeds $25,000.	Nonrefundable credit. Components include tax credit for rehabilitation expenditures, business energy credits, work opportunity tax credit, welfare-to-work credit, research activities credit, low-income housing credit, and disabled access credit. Unused credit may be carried back 1 year and forward 20 years. FIFO method applies to carryovers, carrybacks, and credits earned during current year.
Investment (§ 46)	Qualifying investment times energy percentage or rehabilitation percentage, depending on type of property. Part of general business credit and subject to its limitations.	Nonrefundable credit. Part of general business credit and therefore subject to same carryback, carryover, and FIFO rules. Energy percentage is 10%. Regular rehabilitation rate is 10%; rate for certified historic structures is 20%.
Research activities (§ 41)	Incremental credit is 20% of excess of computation year expenditures minus the base amount. Basic research credit is allowed to certain corporations for 20% of cash payments to qualified organizations that exceed a specially calculated base amount. To qualify for the credit, research expenditures must be made from July 1, 1996 through June 30, 1998.	Nonrefundable credit. Part of general business credit and therefore subject to same carryback, carryover, and FIFO rules. Purpose is to encourage high-tech research in the United States.
Low-income housing (§ 42)	Appropriate rate times eligible basis (portion of project attributable to low-income units).	Nonrefundable credit. Part of general business credit and therefore subject to same carryback, carryover, and FIFO rules. Credit is available each year for 10 years. Recapture may apply. Purpose is to encourage construction of housing for low-income individuals.
Disabled access (§ 44)	Credit is 50% of eligible access expenditures that exceed $250, but do not exceed $10,250. Maximum credit is $5,000.	Nonrefundable credit. Part of general business credit and therefore subject to same carryback, carryover, and FIFO rules. Available only to eligible small businesses. Purpose is to encourage small businesses to become more accessible to disabled individuals.

CONCEPT SUMMARY 11–1

Tax Credits—Continued

Credit	Computation	Comments
Work opportunity (§ 51)	Credit is limited to 40% of the first $6,000 of wages paid to each eligible employee. The employee must begin work before June 30, 1998.	Nonrefundable credit. Part of the general business credit and therefore subject to the same carryback, carryover, and FIFO rules. Purpose is to encourage employment of individuals in specified groups.
Welfare-to-work (§ 51A)	Credit is limited to 35% of first $10,000 of wages paid to eligible employee in first year of employment, plus 50% of first $10,000 of wages paid to eligible employee in second year of employment.	Nonrefundable credit. Part of general business credit and therefore subject to same carryback, carryover, and FIFO rules. Purpose is to encourage employment of long-term recipients of family assistance welfare benefits.

CREDIT FOR CHILD AND DEPENDENT CARE EXPENSES

A taxpayer may incur employment-related expenses that also qualify as medical expenses (e.g., a nurse is hired to provide in-the-home care for an ill and incapacitated dependent parent). Such expenses may be either deducted as medical expenses (subject to the 7.5 percent limitation) or utilized in determining the credit for child and dependent care expenses. If the credit for child and dependent care expenses is chosen and the employment-related expenses exceed the limitation ($2,400, $4,800, or earned income, as the case may be), the excess may be considered a medical expense. If, however, the taxpayer chooses to deduct qualified employment-related expenses as medical expenses, any portion that is not deductible because of the 7.5 percent limitation may not be used in computing the credit for child and dependent care expenses.

EXAMPLE 33

Alicia, a single taxpayer, has the following tax position for the current tax year.

Adjusted gross income		$30,000
Potential itemized deductions *from* AGI—		
Other than medical expenses	$3,500	
Medical expenses	6,000	$ 9,500

All of Alicia's medical expenses were incurred to provide nursing care for her disabled father while she was working. The father lives with Alicia and qualifies as her dependent. ▼

What should Alicia do in this situation? One approach would be to use $2,400 of the nursing care expenses to obtain the maximum credit for child and dependent care expenses allowed of $480 (20% × $2,400). The balance of these expenses should be claimed as medical expenses. After a reduction of 7.5 percent of AGI, this would produce a medical expense deduction of $1,350 [$3,600 (remaining medical expenses) − (7.5% × $30,000)].

Another approach would be to claim the full $6,000 as a medical expense and forgo the credit for child and dependent care expenses. After the 7.5 percent adjustment of $2,250 (7.5% × $30,000), a deduction of $3,750 remains.

The choice, then, is between a credit of $480 plus a deduction of $1,350 or a credit of $0 plus a deduction of $3,750. Which is better, of course, depends on the relative tax savings involved.

One of the traditional goals of *family tax planning* is to minimize the total tax burden within the family unit. With proper planning and implementation, the credit for child and dependent care expenses can be used to help achieve this goal. For example, payments to certain relatives for the care of qualifying dependents and children qualify for the credit if the care provider is *not* a dependent of the taxpayer or the taxpayer's spouse or is *not* a child (under age 19) of the taxpayer. Thus, if the care provider is in a lower tax bracket than the taxpayer, the following benefits result:

- Income is shifted to a lower-bracket family member.
- The taxpayer qualifies for the credit for child and dependent care expenses.

In addition, the goal of minimizing the family income tax liability can be enhanced in some other situations, but only if the credit's limitations are recognized and avoided. For example, tax savings may still be enjoyed even if the qualifying expenditures incurred by a cash basis taxpayer have already reached the annual ceiling ($2,400 or $4,800). To the extent that any additional payments can be shifted into future tax years, the benefit from the credit may be preserved on these excess expenditures.

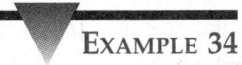

EXAMPLE 34

Andre, a calendar year and cash basis taxpayer, has spent $2,400 by December 1 on qualifying child care expenditures for his dependent 11-year-old son. The $200 that is due the care provider for child care services rendered in December does not generate a tax credit benefit if the amount is paid in the current year because the $2,400 ceiling has been reached. However, if the payment can be delayed until the next year, the total credit over the two-year period for which Andre is eligible may be increased. ▼

A similar shifting of expenditures to a subsequent year may be wise if the potential credit otherwise generated would exceed the tax liability available to absorb the credit.

KEY TERMS

Tax credit for the
elderly or disabled,
11–16

Welfare-to-work credit,
11–10

Work opportunity tax
credit, 11–9

PROBLEM MATERIALS

DISCUSSION QUESTIONS

1. Would an individual taxpayer receive greater benefit from deducting an expenditure or from taking a credit equal to 25% of the expenditure?

2. What is a refundable credit? Give examples. What is a nonrefundable credit? Give examples.

3. Discuss the order in which credits are offset against the tax liability. Why is the order in which credits are utilized important?

4. Discuss the treatment of unused general business credits.

5. John graduated from college several years ago with high hopes and expectations of enjoying a very successful business career. Almost as soon as he completed his final exams, he borrowed over $250,000 from a local bank (the loan was guaranteed by his parents) in order to make several "hot" investments. The investments, as expected, spun off huge tax losses and tax credits in their early years. More recently, however, John has begun to have doubts as to the wisdom of these investments as they have not begun to generate profits as promised. As a result, he is contemplating selling the investments, at yet another loss. Because his investments have not as yet produced any profits to support his lifestyle, he has been forced to live at home with his parents. Identify the relevant tax issues.

6. Clint is a self-employed engineering consultant. He is contemplating purchasing an old building for renovation. After the work is completed, Clint plans to rent out two-thirds of the floor space to businesses and live and work in the remaining portion. Identify the relevant tax issues for Clint.

7. If property on which the tax credit for rehabilitation expenditures was claimed is prematurely disposed of or ceases to be qualified property, how is the tax liability affected in the year of the disposition or disqualification?

8. Discuss the purpose of the work opportunity tax credit. Who receives the tax benefits from the credit? Give examples of the types of individuals who, if hired, give rise to the credit.

9. Explain the purpose and calculation procedure of the welfare-to-work credit.

10. Explain the alternatives a taxpayer has in claiming the deduction and credit for research and experimentation expenditures incurred.

11. Explain the purpose of the disabled access credit and describe the general characteristics of its computation.

12. What three tests must be met for a child to be considered a qualifying child for purposes of the earned income credit? Describe.

13. Briefly discuss the requirements that must be satisfied for a taxpayer to qualify for the earned income tax credit.

14. Individuals who receive substantial Social Security benefits are usually not eligible for the tax credit for the elderly or disabled because these benefits effectively eliminate the base upon which the credit is computed. Explain.

15. What purpose is served by the overall limitation to the foreign tax credit?

16. In general, when would an individual taxpayer find it more beneficial to take advantage of the foreign earned income exclusion rather than the foreign tax credit in computing his or her income tax liability?

17. Sally was recently called into the partner's office and offered a one-year assignment in her public accounting firm's Prague office. Realizing Sally will face incremental expenses while in Prague, such as for foreign income taxes and rent, the firm will try to make her "whole" from a financial perspective by increasing her salary to help offset the expenses she will incur while living overseas. If Sally takes the assignment, she will likely rent her personal residence and sell several major tangible assets such as her personal automobile. Identify the relevant tax issues.

18. Discuss, in general, the calculation of the adoption expenses credit.

19. Distinguish between the child tax credit and the credit for child and dependent care expenses.

20. Pete is not concerned about the credit for child and dependent care expenses because his AGI is considerably in excess of $20,000. Is Pete under a misconception regarding the tax law? Explain.

21. Polly and her spouse, Leo, file a joint return and expect to report AGI of $45,000 in the current year. Polly's employer offers a child and dependent care reimbursement plan that allows up to $2,500 of qualifying expenses to be reimbursed in exchange for a $2,500 reduction in the employee's salary. Because Polly and Leo have one minor child requiring child care that costs $2,500 each year, she is wondering if she should sign up for the program instead of taking advantage of the credit for child and dependent care expenses. Assuming Polly and Leo are in the 28% tax bracket, analyze the effect of the two alternatives. How would your answer differ if Polly and Leo's AGI was $20,000 instead of $45,000?

22. Camilla, a college freshman, was pleased to read of recent tax law changes permitting education tax credits. However, she is confused as to the applicability of the different credits. Briefly explain (1) who is eligible and (2) what the maximum credit amount is for the HOPE scholarship credit and the lifetime learning credit.

23. Discuss the rationale underlying the enactment of the following tax credits:
    a. Tax credit for rehabilitation expenditures.
    b. Low-income housing credit.
    c. Research activities credit.
    d. Earned income credit.
    e. Foreign tax credit.
    f. Business energy credits.

24. Sam and Martha have two preschool-age children. On several occasions during the current year, Sam and Martha took out-of-town trips due to Sam's business. While Sam and Martha were out of town, a 14-year-old neighbor cared for the children during the day; at night, they stayed with their grandparents. Sam and Martha had a neighborhood teenager mow their lawn, but only once, because of the damage he did to Martha's flower garden. On a later out-of-town trip, they hired a professional lawn service to mow the lawn. Identify the relevant tax issues.

PROBLEMS

25. Carol has a tentative general business credit of $110,000 for 1998. Her net regular tax liability before the general business credit is $125,000, and her tentative minimum tax is $100,000. Compute Carol's allowable general business credit for the year.

26. Tan Corporation has the following general business credit carryovers:

1994	$10,000
1995	30,000
1996	10,000
1997	40,000
Total carryovers	$90,000

If the general business credit generated by activities during 1998 equals $90,000 and the total credit allowed during the current year is $160,000 (based on tax liability), what amounts of the current general business credit and carryovers are utilized against the 1998 income tax liability? What is the amount of unused credit carried forward to 1999?

27. In January 1996, William purchased and placed into service a pre-1936 building that houses retail businesses. The cost was $200,000, of which $25,000 applied to the land. In modernizing the facility, William incurred $250,000 of renovation costs of the type that qualify for the rehabilitation credit. These improvements were placed into service in October 1998.
    a. Compute William's rehabilitation tax credit for 1998.
    b. Calculate the cost recovery deductions for the building and the renovation costs for 1998.

28. Red Company hires six individuals on January 15, 1998, qualifying Red for the work opportunity tax credit. Three of these individuals receive wages of $7,000 each during 1998 with each working more than 400 hours during the year. The other three receive wages of $4,000 each in 1998 with each working 300 hours during the year.
    a. Calculate the amount of Red's work opportunity tax credit for 1998.
    b. Assume Red pays total wages of $120,000 to its employees during the year. How much of this amount is deductible in 1998 if the work opportunity tax credit is taken?

29. In March 1998, Wren Corporation hired three individuals, Trent, Bernice, and Benita, all of whom are certified as long-term family assistance recipients. Each employee is paid $11,000 during 1998. Only Bernice continued to work for Wren in 1999, earning $13,500. In February 1999, Wren hired Cassie, who was also certified as a long-term family assistance recipient. During 1999, Cassie earned $12,000. Wren does not claim the work opportunity credit with respect to any of the employees hired in 1998 or 1999.
    a. Compute Wren Corporation's welfare-to-work credit for 1998 and 1999.
    b. Assume Wren Corporation pays total wages of $325,000 to its employees during 1998 and $342,000 during 1999. How much may Wren claim as a wage deduction for 1998 and 1999 if the welfare-to-work credit is claimed in both years?

30. Matt, a calendar year taxpayer, informs you that during the year he incurs expenditures of $30,000 that qualify for the incremental research activities credit. In addition, it is determined that his base amount for the year is $22,800.
    a. Determine Matt's incremental research activities credit for the year.
    b. Matt is in the 28% tax bracket. Determine which approach to the research expenditures and the research activities credit (other than capitalization and subsequent amortization) would provide the greater tax benefit to Matt.

31. Ahmed Zinna (16 Southside Drive, Charlotte, NC 28204), one of your clients, owns two retail establishments in downtown Charlotte, North Carolina, and has come to you seeking advice concerning the tax consequences of complying with the Americans with Disabilities Act. He understands that he needs to install various features at his stores (e.g., ramps, doorways, and restrooms that are handicapped accessible) to make them more accessible to disabled individuals. He inquires whether any tax credits will be available to help offset the cost of the necessary changes. He estimates the cost of the planned changes to his facilities as follows:

Location	Projected Cost
Oak Street	$20,000
Maple Avenue	9,000

He reminds you that the Oak Street store was constructed in 1995 while the Maple Avenue store is in a building that was constructed in 1902. Ahmed operates his business as a sole proprietorship and has approximately eight employees at each location. Write a letter to Ahmed in which you summarize your conclusions concerning the tax consequences of his proposed capital improvements.

32. Which of the following individuals qualify for the earned income credit for 1999?
    a. Eduardo is single, 19 years of age, and has no dependents. His income consists of $8,000 of wages.
    b. Kate maintains a household for a dependent 12-year-old son and is eligible for head-of-household tax rates. Her income consists of $10,500 of salary and $300 of taxable interest.
    c. Keith and Susan are married and file a joint return. Keith and Susan have no dependents. Their combined income consists of $18,500 of salary and $100 of taxable interest. Adjusted gross income is $18,600.
    d. George is a 26-year-old single taxpayer. He has no dependents and generates earnings of $9,000.

33. Vern, a widower, lives in an apartment with his three minor children (ages 3, 4, and 5) whom he supports. Vern earned $19,500 during 1998. He contributed $500 to a deductible IRA and uses the standard deduction. Calculate the amount, if any, of Vern's earned income credit.

34. Joyce, a widow, lives in an apartment with her two minor children (ages 8 and 10) whom she supports. Joyce earns $28,000 during 1998. She uses the standard deduction.
    a. Calculate the amount, if any, of Joyce's earned income credit.
    b. During the year, Joyce is offered a new job that has greater future potential than her current job. If she accepts the job offer, her earnings for the year would be $31,000; however, she will not qualify for the earned income credit. Using after-tax cash-flow calculations, determine whether Joyce should accept the new job offer.

35. Joe, age 68, and Emily, age 69, are married retirees who receive the following income and retirement benefits during the current year:

Fully taxable pension from Joe's former employer	$ 5,000
Dividends and interest	8,000
Social Security benefits	1,750
Total	$14,750

Assume Joe and Emily file a joint return, have no deductions *for* AGI, and do not itemize. Are they eligible for the tax credit for the elderly? If so, calculate the amount of the credit assuming their tax liability (before credits) is $150.

36. Kim, a U.S. citizen and resident, owns and operates a novelty goods business. During 1998, Kim has taxable income of $100,000, made up as follows: $50,000 from foreign sources and $50,000 from U.S. sources. In calculating taxable income, the standard deduction is used. The income from foreign sources is subject to foreign income taxes of $26,000. For 1998, Kim files a joint return claiming his three children as dependents.
    a. Assuming Kim chooses to claim the foreign taxes as an income tax credit, what is his income tax liability for 1998?
    b. Recently, Kim has become disenchanted with the location of his business and is considering moving his foreign operation to a different country. Based on his research, if he moves his business to his country of choice, all relevant revenues and costs would remain approximately the same except that the income taxes payable to that country would be only $10,000. Given that all of the foreign income taxes paid are available to offset the U.S. tax liability (whether he operates in a high-tax or a low-tax foreign jurisdiction), what impact will this have on his decision regarding the potential move?

37. Purple Corporation is an international wholesaler headquartered in the United States. Of its worldwide taxable income of $3 billion, $1.25 billion is foreign-sourced. Before any credits, Purple's U.S. income tax liability is $1.05 billion. If income taxes paid to foreign countries totaled $600 million, what is Purple's U.S. income tax liability after benefiting from the foreign tax credit?

38. Ann and Bill had been on the list of a local adoption agency for several years seeking to adopt a child. Finally, in 1998, good news came their way and an adoption seemed imminent. They paid qualified adoption expenses of $2,000 in 1998 and $4,000 in 1999.

Assume the adoption becomes final in 1999. Ann and Bill always file a joint income tax return.

a. Determine the amount of the adoption expenses credit available to Ann and Bill assuming their combined annual income is $50,000. What year(s) will they benefit from the credit?

b. Assuming Ann and Bill's modified AGI in 1998 and 1999 is $100,000, calculate the amount of the adoption expense credit.

39. Durell and Earline are married, file a joint return, and claim dependency exemptions for their two children, ages 5 years and 6 months. They also claim Earline's son from a previous marriage, age 18, as a dependent. Durell and Earline's combined AGI for 1998 is $56,000.

a. Compute Durell and Earline's child tax credit for 1998.

b. Assume the same facts, except that Durell and Earline's combined AGI for 1998 is $119,000. Compute their child tax credit for 1998.

40. Jim and Jill are husband and wife and have two dependent children under the age of 13. They both are gainfully employed and during the current year earned salaries as follows: $12,000 (Jim) and $4,500 (Jill). To care for their children while they work, they pay Megan (Jim's mother) $5,600. Megan does not qualify as a dependent of Jim and Jill. Assuming Jim and Jill file a joint return, what, if any, is their credit for child and dependent care expenses?

41. Kevin and Jane are husband and wife and have one dependent child, age 9. Kevin is a full-time student for all of the current year, while Jane earns $20,000 as a nurse's aid. In order to provide care for their child while Kevin attends classes and Jane works, they pay Sara (Jane's 17-year-old sister) $2,100. Sara is not a dependent of Kevin and Jane. Assuming Kevin and Jane file a joint return, what, if any, is their credit for child and dependent care expenses?

42. Colin has requested information concerning the availability of the HOPE scholarship credit and lifetime learning credit. Colin has two college-age children, Eliza, a freshman at State University, and Rhett, a senior at Out-of-State University. Both Eliza and Rhett are full-time students. Eliza's expenses for the 1998–1999 academic year are as follows: $4,500 for tuition ($2,250 per semester), $800 for books and supplies, and $3,000 for room and board. Rhett's expenses for the 1998–1999 academic year are as follows: $8,000 for tuition ($4,000 per semester), $900 for books and supplies, and $3,500 for room and board. Tuition and the applicable room and board costs are paid at the beginning of each semester. Colin is married, files a joint tax return, claims both children as dependents, and has a combined AGI with his wife of $95,000 for 1998.

a. Determine Colin's available education tax credit for 1998.

b. What tax planning alternative would you suggest to Colin to increase his education tax credit for 1998?

43. Bernadette, a long-time client of yours, is an architect and president of the local Rotary chapter. To keep up-to-date with the latest developments in her profession, she attends continuing education seminars offered by the national association of architects. During 1998, Bernadette spent $2,000 on course tuition to attend such seminars. She also spent another $400 on architecture books during the year. Bernadette's son is a senior majoring in engineering at the University of the Midwest. During the 1998–1998 academic year, Bernadette's son incurred the following expenses: $4,200 for tuition ($2,100 per semester) and $750 for books and supplies. Bernadette has the option of paying her son's tuition in advance or in installments throughout the academic year. Bernadette's son, whom she claims as a dependent, lives at home while attending school full-time. Bernadette is married, files a joint return, and has a combined AGI with her husband of $88,000.

a. Calculate Bernadette's education tax credit for 1998 assuming her son's tuition expenses are paid in a manner to maximize the available credit in 1998.

b. In her capacity as a president of the local Rotary chapter, Bernadette has asked you to make a 30–45 minute speech outlining the different ways the tax law helps defray (1) the cost of higher education and (2) the cost of continuing education once someone is in the workforce. Prepare an outline of possible topics for presentation. A tentative title for your presentation is "How the Tax Law Can Help Pay for College and Continuing Professional Education."

CUMULATIVE PROBLEMS

44. Wade and Jane London are married and file a joint return. His Social Security number is 222–33–1111 and her Social Security number is 111–22–5555. They reside at 100 Olive Lane, Covington, LA 70400. They have two dependent children, Sean and Debra, ages 12 and 16, respectively. Wade is a self-employed businessman (sole proprietor of an unincorporated business), and Jane is a corporate executive. Wade has the following income and expenses from his business:

Gross income	$280,000
Business expenses	166,000

Records related to Jane's employment provide the following information:

Salary	$130,000
Unreimbursed travel expenses (including $200 of meals)	1,000
Unreimbursed entertainment expenses	600

Other pertinent information relating to 1998 follows:

Proceeds from sale of stock acquired on July 15, 1998 (cost of $10,000) and sold on August 1	$ 8,000
Proceeds from sale of stock acquired on September 18, 1995 (cost of $6,000) and sold on October 5	4,800
Wages paid to full-time domestic worker for housekeeping and child supervision	10,000
Dividends ($6,000) and interest ($2,000) received	8,000
Total itemized deductions (not including any potential deductions above)	26,900
Federal income tax withheld	29,000
Estimated payments on Federal income tax	43,000

Part 1—Tax Computation
Compute the net tax payable or refund due for Wade and Jane London for 1998. Suggested software (if available): *TurboTax.*

Part 2—Tax Planning
Provide tax planning suggestions to Wade and Jane concerning how they might reduce their tax liability for 1999.

45. Beth R. Jordan lives at 2322 Skyview Road, Mesa, AZ 85202. She is a tax accountant with Mesa Manufacturing Company. She also writes computer software programs for tax practitioners and has a part-time tax practice. Beth, age 35, is single and has no dependents. Her Social Security number is 111–35–2222. She wants to contribute $3 to the Presidential Election Campaign Fund.

During 1997, Beth earned a salary of $50,000 from her employer. She received interest of $290 from Home Federal Savings and Loan and $335 from Home State Bank. She received dividends of $500 from Gray Corporation, $400 from Blue Corporation, and $300 from Orange Corporation.

Beth received a $1,200 income tax refund from the state of Arizona on May 12, 1997. On her 1996 Federal income tax return, she reported total itemized deductions of $6,700, which included $2,000 of state income tax withheld by her employer.

Fees earned from her part-time tax practice in 1997 totaled $3,800. She paid $400 to have the tax returns processed by a computerized tax return service.

On February 1, 1997, Beth bought 500 shares of Gray Corporation common stock for $17.60 a share. On July 16, Beth sold the stock for $15 a share.

Beth bought a used sports utility vehicle for $3,000 on June 5, 1997. She purchased the vehicle from her brother-in-law, who was unemployed and was in need of cash. On November 2, 1997, she sold the vehicle to a friend for $3,400.

On January 2, 1997, Beth acquired 100 shares of Blue Corporation common stock for $30 a share. She sold the stock on December 19, 1997, for $75 a share.

During 1997, Beth received royalties of $14,000 on a software program she had written. Beth incurred the following expenditures in connection with her software-writing activities:

Cost of personal computer (100% business use)	$7,000
Cost of printer (100% business use)	2,000
Furniture	3,000
Supplies	650
Fee paid to computer consultant	3,500

Beth elected to expense the maximum portion of the cost of the computer, printer, and furniture allowed under the provisions of § 179. This equipment and furniture were placed in service on January 15, 1997.

Although her employer suggested that Beth attend a convention on current developments in corporate taxation, Beth was not reimbursed for the travel expenses of $1,420 she incurred in attending the convention. The $1,420 included $200 for the cost of meals.

During 1997, Beth paid $300 for prescription medicines and $2,875 in doctor bills, hospital bills, and medical insurance premiums. Her employer withheld state income tax of $1,954. Beth paid real property taxes of $1,766 on her home. Interest on her home mortgage was $3,845, and interest to credit-card companies was $320. Beth contributed $20 each week to her church and $10 each week to the United Way. Professional dues and subscriptions totaled $350.

Beth's employer withheld Federal income taxes of $9,500 during 1997. Beth paid estimated taxes of $1,600. What is the amount of Beth's net tax payable or refund due for 1997? If Beth has a tax refund due, she wants to have it credited toward her 1998 income tax. If you use tax forms for your solution, you will need Forms 1040, 2106, and 4562 and Schedules A, B, C, D, and SE. Suggested software (if available): *TurboTax*.

Research Problems for this chapter appear at the end of Chapter 28.

TEAM PROJECT: ARTHUR ANDERSEN TAX CHALLENGE CASES

For more information on the Arthur Andersen Tax Challenge Cases, refer to Chapter 1, page 1–37.

Information related to tax issues and problems that are discussed in this chapter may be found in the

Day and Ball case on pages 2, 4, 5, 7, 11–13, 15
Fence case on pages 44, 55, 58, 59, and 61

Read and analyze the case you have been assigned and *identify* any issues and problems that are related to material covered in this chapter. If the information provided in the case is complete, prepare answers for this part of the case at this time. If you need information that is contained in the later parts of the case, write a memo summarizing the questions or problems so you can prepare a complete answer at a later date.

CHAPTER

12

PROPERTY TRANSACTIONS: DETERMINATION OF GAIN OR LOSS, BASIS CONSIDERATIONS, AND NONTAXABLE EXCHANGES

LEARNING OBJECTIVES

After completing Chapter 12, you should be able to:

1. Understand the computation of realized gain or loss on property dispositions, and distinguish between realized and recognized gain or loss.

2. Explain how basis is determined for various methods of asset acquisition.

3. Understand and apply the nonrecognition (postponement) of gain or loss provisions in certain property transactions.

4. Describe the provision for the permanent exclusion of gain on the sale of a personal residence.

5. Identify tax planning opportunities related to selected property transactions.

OUTLINE

This chapter and Chapter 13 are concerned with the income tax consequences of property transactions (the sale or other disposition of property). The following questions are considered with respect to the sale or other disposition of property:

- Is there a realized gain or loss?
- If so, is the gain or loss recognized?
- If the gain or loss is recognized, is it ordinary or capital?
- What is the basis of any replacement property that is acquired?

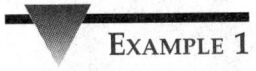

EXAMPLE 1

Alice owns a house that she received from her mother seven months ago. Her mother's cost for the house was $75,000. Alice is considering selling the house to her favorite nephew, Dan, for $75,000. Alice anticipates she will have no gain or loss on the transaction. She comes to you for advice.

As Alice's tax adviser, you need answers to the following questions:

- You are aware that Alice's mother died around the time Alice indicates she received the house from her mother. Did Alice receive the house by gift prior to her mother's

death? If so, what was the mother's adjusted basis? If instead Alice inherited the house from her mother, what was the fair market value of the house on the date of her mother's death?
- Was the house Alice's principal residence during the period she owned it and was it her principal residence prior to receiving it from her mother?
- How long did Alice's mother own the house?
- What is the fair market value of the house?
- Does Alice intend for the transaction with Dan to be a sale or part sale and part gift?
- What does Alice intend to do with the sale proceeds?

Once you have the answers to these questions, you can advise Alice on the tax consequences of the proposed transaction. ▼

This chapter discusses the determination of realized and recognized gain or loss and the basis of property. Chapter 13 covers the classification of the recognized gain or loss as ordinary or capital.

DETERMINATION OF GAIN OR LOSS

REALIZED GAIN OR LOSS

1 LEARNING OBJECTIVE
Understand the computation of realized gain or loss on property dispositions, and distinguish between realized and recognized gain and loss.

Realized gain or loss is measured by the difference between the amount realized from the sale or other disposition of property and the property's adjusted basis on the date of disposition. If the amount realized exceeds the property's adjusted basis, the result is a **realized gain.** Conversely, if the property's adjusted basis exceeds the amount realized, the result is a **realized loss.**[1]

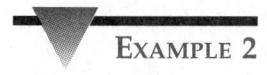

EXAMPLE 2

Tab sells Swan Corporation stock with an adjusted basis of $3,000 for $5,000. Tab's realized gain is $2,000. If Tab had sold the stock for $2,000, he would have had a $1,000 realized loss. ▼

Sale or Other Disposition. The term *sale or other disposition* is defined broadly in the tax law and includes virtually any disposition of property. Thus, transactions such as trade-ins, casualties, condemnations, thefts, and bond retirements are treated as dispositions of property. The most common disposition of property is through a sale or exchange. The key factor in determining whether a disposition has taken place usually is whether an identifiable event has occurred[2] as opposed to a mere fluctuation in the value of the property.[3]

EXAMPLE 3

Lori owns Tan Corporation stock that cost $3,000. The stock has appreciated in value by $2,000 since Lori purchased it. Lori has no realized gain since mere fluctuation in value is not a disposition or identifiable event for tax purposes. Nor would Lori have a realized loss had the stock declined in value by $2,000. ▼

Amount Realized. The **amount realized** from a sale or other disposition of property is the sum of any money received plus the fair market value of other property received. The amount realized also includes any real property taxes treated as imposed on the seller that are actually paid by the buyer.[4] The reason for including

---

[1]§ 1001(a) and Reg. § 1.1001–1(a).
[2]Reg. § 1.1001–1(c)(1).
[3]*Lynch v. Turrish*, 1 USTC ¶18, 3 AFTR 2986, 38 S.Ct. 537 (USSC, 1918).

[4]§ 1001(b) and Reg. § 1.1001–1(b). Refer to Chapter 9 for a discussion of this subject.

these taxes in the amount realized is that by paying the taxes, the purchaser is, in effect, paying an additional amount to the seller of the property.

The amount realized also includes any liability on the property disposed of, such as a mortgage debt, if the buyer assumes the mortgage or the property is sold subject to the mortgage.[5] The amount of the liability is included in the amount realized even if the debt is nonrecourse and the amount of the debt is greater than the fair market value of the mortgaged property.[6]

EXAMPLE 4

Barry sells property on which there is a mortgage of $20,000 to Cole for $50,000 cash. Barry's amount realized from the sale is $70,000 if Cole assumes the mortgage or takes the property subject to the mortgage. ▼

The **fair market value** of property received in a sale or other disposition has been defined by the courts as the price at which property will change hands between a willing seller and a willing buyer when neither is compelled to sell or buy.[7] Fair market value is determined by considering the relevant factors in each case.[8] An expert appraiser is often required to evaluate these factors in arriving at fair market value. When the fair market value of the property received cannot be determined, the value of the property surrendered may be used.[9]

---

[5]*Crane v. Comm.*, 47–1 USTC ¶9217, 35 AFTR 776, 67 S.Ct. 1047 (USSC, 1947). Although a legal distinction exists between the direct assumption of a mortgage and taking property subject to a mortgage, the tax consequences in calculating the amount realized are the same.

[6]*Comm. v. Tufts*, 83–1 USTC ¶9328, 51 AFTR2d 83–1132, 103 S.Ct. 1826 (USSC, 1983).

[7]*Comm. v. Marshman*, 60–2 USTC ¶9484, 5 AFTR2d 1528, 279 F.2d 27 (CA–6, 1960).

[8]*O'Malley v. Ames*, 52–1 USTC ¶9361, 42 AFTR 19, 197 F.2d 256 (CA–8, 1952).

[9]*U.S. v. Davis*, 62–2 USTC ¶9509, 9 AFTR2d 1625, 82 S.Ct. 1190 (USSC, 1962).

In calculating the amount realized, selling expenses such as advertising, commissions, and legal fees relating to the disposition are deducted. The amount realized is the net amount received directly or indirectly by the taxpayer from the disposition of property in the form of cash or anything else of value.

Adjusted Basis.   The **adjusted basis** of property disposed of is the property's original basis adjusted to the date of disposition.[10] Original basis is the cost or other basis of the property on the date the property is acquired by the taxpayer. *Capital additions* increase and *recoveries of capital* decrease the original basis so that on the date of disposition the adjusted basis reflects the unrecovered cost or other basis of the property.[11] Adjusted basis is determined as follows:

> Cost (or other adjusted basis) on date of acquisition
>
> + Capital additions
>
> – Capital recoveries
>
> = Adjusted basis on date of disposition

Capital Additions.   Capital additions include the cost of capital improvements and betterments made to the property by the taxpayer. These expenditures are distinguishable from expenditures for the ordinary repair and maintenance of the property that are neither capitalized nor added to the original basis (refer to Chapter 5). The latter expenditures are deductible in the current taxable year if they are related to business or income-producing property. Amounts representing real property taxes treated as imposed on the seller but paid or assumed by the buyer are part of the cost of the property.[12] Any liability on property that is assumed by the buyer is also included in the buyer's original basis of the property. The same rule applies if property is acquired subject to a liability. Amortization of the discount on bonds increases the adjusted basis of the bonds.[13]

Capital Recoveries.   The following are examples of capital recoveries:

1. *Depreciation and cost recovery allowances.* The original basis of depreciable property is reduced by the annual depreciation charges (or cost recovery allowances) while the property is held by the taxpayer. The amount of depreciation that is subtracted from the original basis is the greater of the *allowed* or *allowable* depreciation on an annual basis.[14] In most circumstances, the allowed and allowable depreciation amounts are the same (refer to Chapter 7).
2. *Casualties and thefts.* A casualty or theft may result in the reduction of the adjusted basis of property.[15] The adjusted basis is reduced by the amount of the deductible loss. In addition, the adjusted basis is reduced by the amount of insurance proceeds received. However, the receipt of insurance proceeds may result in a recognized gain rather than a deductible loss. The gain increases the adjusted basis of the property.[16]

---

[10]§ 1011(a) and Reg. § 1.1011–1.

[11]§ 1016(a) and Reg. § 1.1016–1.

[12]Reg. §§ 1.1001–1(b)(2) and 1.1012–1(b). Refer to Chapter 9 for a discussion of this subject.

[13]See Chapter 13 for a discussion of bond discount and the related amortization.

[14]§ 1016(a)(2) and Reg. § 1.1016–3(a)(1)(i).

[15]Refer to Chapter 6 for the discussion of casualties and thefts.

[16]Reg. § 1.1016–6(a).

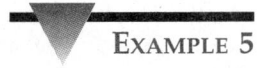

EXAMPLE 5

An insured truck used in a trade or business is destroyed in an accident. The adjusted basis is $8,000, and the fair market value is $6,500. Insurance proceeds of $6,500 are received. The amount of the casualty loss is $1,500 ($6,500 insurance proceeds − $8,000 adjusted basis). The adjusted basis is reduced by the $1,500 casualty loss and the $6,500 of insurance proceeds received. ▼

EXAMPLE 6

An insured truck used in a trade or business is destroyed in an accident. The adjusted basis is $6,500, and the fair market value is $8,000. Insurance proceeds of $8,000 are received. The amount of the casualty gain is $1,500 ($8,000 insurance proceeds − $6,500 adjusted basis). The adjusted basis is increased by the $1,500 casualty gain and is reduced by the $8,000 of insurance proceeds received ($6,500 basis before casualty + $1,500 casualty gain − $8,000 insurance proceeds = $0 basis). ▼

3. *Certain corporate distributions.* A corporate distribution to a shareholder that is not taxable is treated as a return of capital, and it reduces the basis of the shareholder's stock in the corporation.[17] For example, if a corporation makes a cash distribution to its shareholders and has no earnings and profits, the distributions are treated as a return of capital. Once the basis of the stock is reduced to zero, the amount of any subsequent distributions is a capital gain if the stock is a capital asset. These rules are illustrated in Example 1 of Chapter 18.

ETHICAL CONSIDERATIONS

Reporting of a Distribution: Dividend versus Return of Capital

Rebecca purchased 100 shares of stock in Bluebird, Inc., on December 24, 1998, for $50,000. In January 1999, Rebecca receives a Form 1099 for 1998 from the corporation indicating that she should report dividend income of $2,000 on her tax return. While she did receive a check from Bluebird on January 4, 1999 (postmarked December 31), she believes that it is a return of capital. Therefore, she reduces her adjusted basis for the stock to $48,000 and reports no dividend income for 1998. Her justification is that the corporation reported a loss in its fourth quarter financial statements. Evaluate Rebecca's reporting of the $2,000 distribution.

4. *Amortizable bond premium.* The basis in a bond purchased at a premium is reduced by the amortizable portion of the bond premium.[18] Investors in taxable bonds may *elect* to amortize the bond premium, but the premium on tax-exempt bonds *must be* amortized.[19] The amount of the amortized premium on taxable bonds is permitted as an interest deduction. Therefore, the election produces the opportunity for an annual interest deduction to offset ordinary income in exchange for a larger capital gain or smaller capital loss on the disposition of the bond. No such interest deduction is permitted for tax-exempt bonds.

---

[17]§ 1016(a)(4) and Reg. § 1.1016–5(a).

[18]§ 1016(a)(5) and Reg. § 1.1016–5(b). The accounting treatment of bond premium amortization is the same as for tax purposes. The amortization results in a decrease in the bond investment account.

[19]§ 171(c).

CONCEPT SUMMARY 12–1

Recognized Gain or Loss

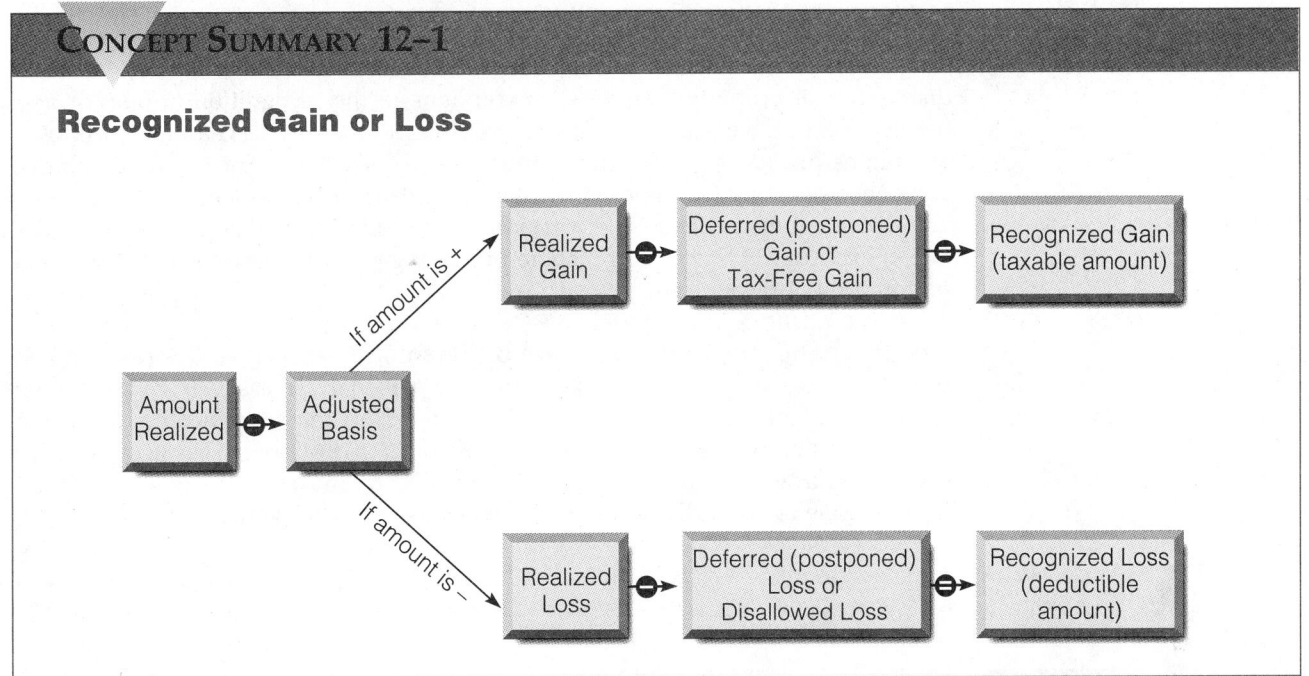

The amortization deduction is allowed for taxable bonds because the premium is viewed as a cost of earning the taxable interest from the bonds. The reason the basis of taxable bonds is reduced is that the amortization deduction is a recovery of the cost or basis of the bonds. The basis of tax-exempt bonds is reduced even though the amortization is not allowed as a deduction. No amortization deduction is permitted on tax-exempt bonds since the interest income is exempt from tax and the amortization of the bond premium merely represents an adjustment of the effective amount of such income.

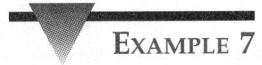

EXAMPLE 7

Antonio purchases Eagle Corporation taxable bonds with a face value of $100,000 for $110,000, thus paying a premium of $10,000. The annual interest rate is 7%, and the bonds mature 10 years from the date of purchase. The annual interest income is $7,000 (7% × $100,000). If Antonio elects to amortize the bond premium, the $10,000 premium is deducted over the 10-year period. Antonio's basis for the bonds is reduced each year by the amount of the amortization deduction. Note that if the bonds were tax-exempt, amortization of the bond premium and the basis adjustment would be mandatory. However, no deduction would be allowed for the amortization. ▼

RECOGNIZED GAIN OR LOSS

Recognized gain is the amount of the realized gain included in the taxpayer's gross income.[20] A **recognized loss,** on the other hand, is the amount of a realized loss that is deductible for tax purposes.[21] As a general rule, the entire amount of a realized gain or loss is recognized.[22]

Concept Summary 12–1 summarizes the realized gain or loss and recognized gain or loss concepts.

---

[20]§ 61(a)(3) and Reg. § 1.61–6(a).   [22]§ 1001(c) and Reg. § 1.1002–1(a).
[21]§ 165(a) and Reg. § 1.165–1(a).

NONRECOGNITION OF GAIN OR LOSS

In certain cases, a realized gain or loss is not recognized upon the sale or other disposition of property. One of the exceptions to the recognition of gain or loss involves nontaxable exchanges, which are covered later in this chapter. Additional exceptions include losses realized upon the sale, exchange, or condemnation of personal use assets (as opposed to business or income-producing property) and gains realized upon the sale of a residence. In addition, realized losses from the sale or exchange of business or income-producing property between certain related parties are not recognized.[23]

Sale, Exchange, or Condemnation of Personal Use Assets.   A realized loss from the sale, exchange, or condemnation of personal use assets (e.g., a personal residence or an automobile not used at all for business or income-producing purposes) is not recognized for tax purposes. An exception exists for casualty or theft losses from personal use assets (see Chapter 6). In contrast, any gain realized from the sale or other disposition of personal use assets is, generally, fully taxable.

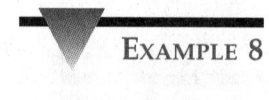

EXAMPLE 8

Freda sells an automobile, which is held exclusively for personal use, for $6,000. The adjusted basis of the automobile is $5,000. Freda has a realized and recognized gain of $1,000. ▼

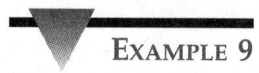

EXAMPLE 9

Freda sells the automobile in Example 8 for $4,000. She has a realized loss of $1,000, but the loss is not recognized. ▼

RECOVERY OF CAPITAL DOCTRINE

Doctrine Defined.   The **recovery of capital doctrine** is very significant and pervades all the tax rules relating to property transactions. The doctrine derives its roots from the very essence of the income tax—a tax on income. Therefore, as a general rule, a taxpayer is entitled to recover the cost or other original basis of property acquired and is not taxed on that amount.

The cost or other original basis of depreciable property is recovered through annual depreciation deductions. The basis is reduced as the cost is recovered over the period the property is held. Therefore, when property is sold or otherwise disposed of, it is the adjusted basis (unrecovered cost or other basis) that is compared to the amount realized from the disposition to determine realized gain or loss.

Relationship of the Recovery of Capital Doctrine to the Concepts of Realization and Recognition.   If a sale or other disposition results in a realized gain, the taxpayer has recovered more than the adjusted basis of the property. Conversely, if a sale or other disposition results in a realized loss, the taxpayer has recovered less than the adjusted basis.

The general rules for the relationship between the recovery of capital doctrine and the realized and recognized gain and loss concepts are summarized as follows:

Rule 1.   A realized gain that is *never recognized* results in the *permanent recovery* of more than the taxpayer's cost or other basis for tax purposes. For example, all or a portion of the realized gain on the sale of a personal residence can be excluded from gross income under § 121.

Rule 2.   A realized gain on which *recognition is postponed* results in the *temporary recovery* of more than the taxpayer's cost or other basis for tax purposes. For example, an exchange of like-kind property under § 1031 and an

---

[23]§ 267(a)(1).

involuntary conversion under § 1033 are both eligible for postponement treatment.

Rule 3. A realized loss that is *never recognized* results in the *permanent recovery*
of less than the taxpayer's cost or other basis for tax purposes. For
example, a loss on the sale of an automobile held for personal use is
not deductible.

Rule 4. A realized loss on which *recognition is postponed* results in the *temporary
recovery* of less than the taxpayer's cost or other basis for tax purposes.
For example, the realized loss on the exchange of like-kind property
under § 1031 is postponed.

These rules are illustrated in discussions to follow in this and the next chapter.

BASIS CONSIDERATIONS

DETERMINATION OF COST BASIS

2 **LEARNING OBJECTIVE**
Explain how basis is determined
for various methods of asset
acquisition.

The basis of property is generally the property's cost. Cost is the amount paid for
the property in cash or other property.[24] This general rule follows logically from
the recovery of capital doctrine; that is, the cost or other basis of property is to be
recovered tax-free by the taxpayer.

A *bargain purchase* of property is an exception to the general rule for determining
basis. A bargain purchase may result when an employer transfers property to an
employee at less than the property's fair market value (as compensation for services)
or when a corporation transfers property to a shareholder at less than the property's
fair market value (a dividend). The basis of property acquired in a bargain purchase
is the property's fair market value.[25] If the basis of the property were not increased
by the bargain amount, the taxpayer would be taxed on this amount again at
disposition.

EXAMPLE 10

Wade buys a machine from his employer for $10,000 on December 30. The fair market value
of the machine is $15,000. Wade must include the $5,000 difference between cost and the
fair market value of the machine in gross income for the taxable year. The bargain element
represents additional compensation to Wade. His basis for the machine is $15,000, the
machine's fair market value. ▼

Identification Problems.   Cost identification problems are frequently encountered in securities transactions. For example, the Regulations require that the taxpayer adequately identify the particular stock that has been sold.[26] A problem arises
when the taxpayer has purchased separate lots of stock on different dates or at
different prices and cannot adequately identify the lot from which a particular sale
takes place. In this case, the stock is presumed to come from the first lot or lots
purchased (a FIFO presumption).[27] When securities are left in the custody of a
broker, it may be necessary to provide specific instructions and receive written
confirmation as to which securities are being sold.

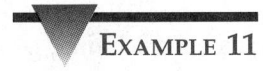
EXAMPLE 11

Polly purchases 100 shares of Olive Corporation stock on July 1, 1996, for $5,000 ($50 a
share) and another 100 shares of Olive stock on July 1, 1997, for $6,000 ($60 a share). She
sells 50 shares of the stock on January 2, 1998. The cost of the stock sold, assuming Polly

---

[24]§ 1012 and Reg. § 1.1012–1(a).
[25]Reg. §§ 1.61–2(d)(2)(i) and 1.301–1(j).

[26]Reg. § 1.1012–1(c)(1).
[27]*Kluger Associates, Inc.,* 69 T.C. 925 (1978).

cannot adequately identify the shares, is $50 a share, or $2,500. This is the cost Polly will compare to the amount realized in determining the gain or loss from the sale. ▼

Allocation Problems.   When a taxpayer acquires *multiple assets in a lump-sum purchase*, the total cost must be allocated among the individual assets.[28] Allocation is necessary because some of the assets acquired may be depreciable (e.g., buildings) and others not (e.g., land). In addition, only a portion of the assets acquired may be sold, or some of the assets may be capital or § 1231 assets that receive special tax treatment upon subsequent sale or other disposition. The lump-sum cost is allocated on the basis of the fair market values of the individual assets acquired.

EXAMPLE 12   Harry purchases a building and land for $800,000. Because of the depressed nature of the industry in which the seller was operating, Harry was able to negotiate a very favorable purchase price. Appraisals of the individual assets indicate that the fair market value of the building is $600,000 and that of the land is $400,000. Harry's basis for the building is $480,000 [($600,000/$1,000,000) × $800,000], and his basis for the land is $320,000 [($400,000/$1,000,000) × $800,000]. ▼

If a business is purchased and **goodwill** is involved, a special allocation rule applies. Initially, the purchase price is assigned to the assets, excluding goodwill, to the extent of their total fair market value. This assigned amount is allocated among the assets on the basis of the fair market value of the individual assets

---

[28]Reg. § 1.61–6(a).

acquired. Goodwill is then assigned the residual amount of the purchase price. The resultant allocation is applicable to both the buyer and the seller.[29]

EXAMPLE 13

Rocky sells his business to Paul. They agree that the values of the individual assets are as follows:

Inventory	$ 50,000
Building	500,000
Land	200,000
Goodwill	150,000

After negotiations, Rocky and Paul agree on a sales price of $1 million. Applying the residual method with respect to goodwill results in the following allocation of the $1 million purchase price:

Inventory	$ 50,000
Building	500,000
Land	200,000
Goodwill	250,000

The residual method requires that all of the excess of the purchase price over the fair market value of the assets ($1,000,000 − $900,000 = $100,000) be allocated to goodwill. Without this requirement, the purchaser could allocate the excess pro rata to all of the assets, including goodwill, based on their respective fair market values. This would have resulted in only $166,667 [$150,000 + ($150,000 ÷ $900,000 × $100,000)] being assigned to goodwill. ▼

In the case of *nontaxable stock dividends*, the allocation depends upon whether the dividend is a common stock dividend on common stock or a preferred stock dividend on common stock. If the dividend is common on common, the cost of the original common shares is allocated to the total shares owned after the dividend.[30]

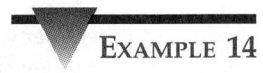

EXAMPLE 14

Susan owns 100 shares of Sparrow Corporation common stock for which she paid $1,100. She receives a 10% common stock dividend, giving her a new total of 110 shares. Before the stock dividend, Susan's basis was $11 per share ($1,100 ÷ 100 shares). The basis of each share after the stock dividend is $10 ($1,100 ÷ 110 shares). ▼

If the dividend is preferred stock on common, the cost of the original common shares is allocated between the common and preferred shares on the basis of their relative fair market values on the date of distribution.[31]

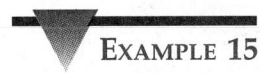

EXAMPLE 15

Fran owns 100 shares of Cardinal Corporation common stock for which she paid $1,000. She receives a stock dividend of 50 shares of preferred stock on her common stock. The fair market values on the date of distribution of the preferred stock dividend are $30 a share for common stock and $40 a share for preferred stock. Thus, the total fair market value is $3,000 ($30 × 100) for common stock and $2,000 ($40 × 50) for preferred stock. The basis of Fran's common stock after the dividend is $600, or $6 a share [($3,000/$5,000) × $1,000], and the basis of the preferred stock is $400, or $8 a share [($2,000/$5,000) × $1,000]. ▼

---

[29]§ 1060.

[30]§§ 305(a) and 307(a). The holding period of the new shares includes the holding period of the old shares. § 1223(5) and Reg.

§ 1.1223–1(e). See Chapter 13 for a discussion of the importance of the holding period.

[31]Reg. § 1.307–1(a).

In the case of *nontaxable stock rights*, the basis of the rights is zero unless the taxpayer elects or is required to allocate a portion of the cost of the stock to the rights. If the fair market value of the rights is 15 percent or more of the fair market value of the stock, the taxpayer is required to allocate. If the value of the rights is less than 15 percent of the fair market value of the stock, the taxpayer may elect to allocate.[32] The result is that either the rights will have no basis or the cost of the stock on which the rights are received will be allocated between the stock and rights on the basis of their relative fair market values.

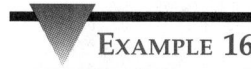

EXAMPLE 16

Donald receives nontaxable stock rights with a fair market value of $1,000. The fair market value of the stock on which the rights were received is $8,000 (cost $10,000). Donald does not elect to allocate. The basis of the rights is zero. If he exercises the rights, the basis of the new stock is the exercise (subscription) price. ▼

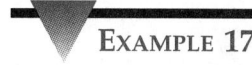

EXAMPLE 17

Assume the same facts as in Example 16, except the fair market value of the rights is $3,000. Donald must allocate because the value of the rights is 15% or more of the value of the stock ($3,000/$8,000 = 37.5%). The basis of the rights is $2,727 [($3,000/$11,000) × $10,000], and the basis of the stock is $7,273 [($8,000/$11,000) × $10,000]. If Donald exercises the rights, the basis of the new stock is the exercise (subscription) price plus the basis of the rights. If he sells the rights, he recognizes gain or loss to the extent of the difference between the amount realized and the basis of the rights. This allocation rule applies only when the rights are exercised or sold. Therefore, if the rights are allowed to lapse (expire), they have no basis, and the basis of the original stock is the stock's cost, $10,000. ▼

The holding period of nontaxable stock rights includes the holding period of the stock on which the rights were distributed. However, if the rights are exercised, the holding period of the newly acquired stock begins with the date the rights are exercised.[33] The significance of the holding period for capital assets is discussed in Chapter 13.

GIFT BASIS

When a taxpayer receives property as a gift, there is no cost to the recipient. Thus, under the cost basis provision, the donee's basis would be zero. However, this would violate the statutory intent that gifts are not subject to the income tax. With a zero basis, a sale by the donee would result in all of the amount realized being treated as realized gain. Therefore, a basis is assigned to the property received depending on the following:[34]

- The date of the gift.
- The basis of the property to the donor.
- The amount of the gift tax paid.
- The fair market value of the property.

Gift Basis Rules if No Gift Tax Is Paid.   Property received by gift can be referred to as *dual basis* property; that is, the basis for gain and the basis for loss might not be the same amount. The present basis rules for gifts of property are as follows:

- If the donee subsequently disposes of gift property in a transaction that results in a gain, the basis to the donee is the same as the donor's adjusted

[32]§ 307(b).
[33]§ 1223(5) and Reg. §§ 1.1223–1(e) and (f).

[34]§ 102(a).

TAX IN THE NEWS

YEAR–END TAX PLANNING AND PROPERTY TRANSACTIONS

As the end of the year approaches, taxpayers should evaluate their investment assets as a way to minimize Federal income tax liability. Underperforming investments whose disposition would produce a loss can be sold before year-end to offset recognized gains.

One procedure that will not work is to sell a security where there is a realized loss before the end of the year to offset recognized gains and then repurchase the same security shortly after the beginning of the year. Section 1091 classifies such a sale and repurchase as a "wash sale" and disallows the recognition of the loss on the sale. From a planning perspective, § 1091 disallowance treatment can be avoided by not repurchasing the security within 30 days before or after the sale date. Thus, a little planning can produce much better tax results.

SOURCE: Adapted from Tom Herman, "Late Moves to Pare Taxes: Now's the Time," *Wall Street Journal*, December 4, 1996, p. C1.

Wash Sales. Section 1091 stipulates that in certain cases, a realized loss on the sale or exchange of stock or securities is not recognized. Specifically, if a taxpayer sells or exchanges stock or securities and within 30 days before *or* after the date of the sale or exchange acquires substantially identical stock or securities, any loss realized from the sale or exchange is not recognized because the transaction is a **wash sale.**[49] The term *acquire* means acquire by purchase or in a taxable exchange and includes an option to purchase substantially identical securities. *Substantially identical* means the same in all important particulars. Corporate bonds and preferred stock are normally not considered substantially identical to the corporation's common stock. However, if the bonds and preferred stock are convertible into common stock, they may be considered substantially identical under certain circumstances.[50] Attempts to avoid the application of the wash sales rules by having a related taxpayer repurchase the securities have been unsuccessful.[51] The wash sales provisions do *not* apply to gains.

Recognition of the loss is disallowed because the taxpayer is considered to be in substantially the same economic position after the sale and repurchase as before the sale and repurchase. This disallowance rule does not apply to taxpayers engaged in the business of buying and selling securities.[52] Investors, however, are not allowed to create losses through wash sales to offset income for tax purposes.

Realized loss that is not recognized is added to the *basis* of the substantially identical stock or securities whose acquisition resulted in the nonrecognition of loss.[53] In other words, the basis of the replacement stock or securities is increased by the amount of the unrecognized loss. If the loss were not added to the basis of the newly acquired stock or securities, the taxpayer would never recover the entire basis of the old stock or securities.

The basis of the new stock or securities includes the unrecovered portion of the basis of the formerly held stock or securities. Therefore, the *holding period* of

---

[49]§ 1091(a) and Reg. §§ 1.1091–1(a) and (f).
[50]Rev.Rul. 56–406, 1956–2 C.B. 523.
[51]*McWilliams v. Comm.*, 47–1 USTC ¶9289, 35 AFTR 1184, 67 S.Ct. 1477 (USSC, 1947).

[52]Reg. § 1.1091–1(a).
[53]§ 1091(d) and Reg. § 1.1091–2(a).

the new stock or securities begins on the date of acquisition of the old stock or securities.[54]

EXAMPLE 34

Bhaskar owns 100 shares of Green Corporation stock (adjusted basis of $20,000), 50 shares of which he sells for $8,000. Ten days later, he purchases 50 shares of the same stock for $7,000. Bhaskar's realized loss of $2,000 ($8,000 amount realized – $10,000 adjusted basis of 50 shares) is not recognized because it resulted from a wash sale. Bhaskar's basis in the newly acquired stock is $9,000 ($7,000 purchase price + $2,000 unrecognized loss from the wash sale). ▼

The taxpayer may acquire less than the number of shares sold in a wash sale. In this case, the loss from the sale is prorated between recognized and unrecognized loss on the basis of the ratio of the number of shares acquired to the number of shares sold.[55]

CONVERSION OF PROPERTY FROM PERSONAL USE TO BUSINESS OR INCOME-PRODUCING USE

As discussed previously, losses from the sale of personal use assets are not recognized for tax purposes, but losses from the sale of business and income-producing assets are deductible. Can a taxpayer convert a personal use asset that has declined in value to business (or income-producing) use and then sell the asset to recognize a business (or income-producing) loss? The tax law prevents this by specifying that the *original basis for loss* on personal use assets converted to business or income-producing use is the *lower* of the property's adjusted basis or fair market value on the date of conversion.[56] The *gain basis* for converted property is the property's adjusted basis on the date of conversion. The tax law is not concerned with gains on converted property because gains are recognized regardless of whether property is business, income producing, or personal use.

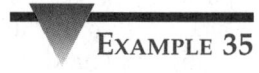

EXAMPLE 35

Diane's personal residence has an adjusted basis of $75,000 and a fair market value of $60,000. Diane converts the personal residence to rental property. Her basis for loss is $60,000 (lower of $75,000 adjusted basis and fair market value of $60,000). The $15,000 decline in value is a personal loss and can never be recognized for tax purposes. Diane's basis for gain is $75,000. ▼

The basis for loss is also the *basis for depreciating* the converted property.[57] This is an exception to the general rule that provides that the basis for depreciation is the gain basis (e.g., property received by gift). This exception prevents the taxpayer from recovering a personal loss indirectly through depreciation of the higher original basis. After the property is converted, both its basis for loss and its basis for gain are adjusted for depreciation deductions from the date of conversion to the date of disposition. These rules apply only if a conversion from personal to business or income-producing use has actually occurred.

EXAMPLE 36

At a time when his personal residence (adjusted basis of $40,000) is worth $50,000, Keith converts one-half of it to rental use. Assume the property is not MACRS recovery property. At this point, the estimated useful life of the residence is 20 years, and there is no estimated salvage value. After renting the converted portion for five years, Keith sells the property for $44,000. All amounts relate only to the building; the land has been accounted for separately. Keith has a $2,000 realized gain from the sale of the personal use portion of the residence and a $7,000 realized gain from the sale of the rental portion. These gains are computed as follows:

---

[54]§ 1223(4) and Reg. § 1.1223–1(d).
[55]§ 1091(b) and Reg. § 1.1091–1(c).

[56]Reg. § 1.165–9(b)(2).
[57]Reg. § 1.167(g)–1.

	Personal Use	Rental
Original basis for gain and loss—adjusted basis on date of conversion (fair market value is greater than the adjusted basis)	$20,000	$20,000
Depreciation—five years	None	5,000
Adjusted basis—date of sale	$20,000	$15,000
Amount realized	22,000	22,000
Realized gain	$ 2,000	$ 7,000

As discussed later in this chapter, Keith may be able to exclude the $2,000 gain realized from the sale of the personal use portion of the residence under § 121. The $7,000 gain from the rental portion is recognized.

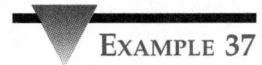

EXAMPLE 37

Assume the same facts as in the previous example, except that the fair market value on the date of conversion is $30,000 and the sales proceeds are $16,000. Keith has a $12,000 realized loss from the sale of the personal use portion of the residence and a $3,250 realized loss from the sale of the rental portion. These losses are computed as follows:

	Personal Use	Rental
Original basis for loss—fair market value on date of conversion (fair market value is less than the adjusted basis)	*	$15,000
Depreciation—five years	None	3,750
Adjusted basis—date of sale	$ 20,000	$11,250
Amount realized	8,000	8,000
Realized loss	$(12,000)	$ (3,250)

*Not applicable.

The $12,000 loss from the sale of the personal use portion of the residence is not recognized. The $3,250 loss from the rental portion is recognized. ▼

ADDITIONAL COMPLEXITIES IN DETERMINING REALIZED GAIN OR LOSS

Amount Realized. The calculation of the amount realized may appear to be one of the least complex areas associated with property transactions. However, because numerous positive and negative adjustments may be required, the calculation of this amount can be complex and confusing. In addition, the determination of the fair market value of the items received by the taxpayer can be difficult. The following example provides insight into various items that can have an impact on the amount realized.

EXAMPLE 38

Ridge sells an office building and the associated land on October 1, 1998. Under the terms of the sales contract, Ridge is to receive $600,000 in cash. The purchaser is to assume Ridge's mortgage of $300,000 on the property. To enable the purchaser to obtain adequate financing to pay the $600,000, Ridge is to pay the $15,000 in points charged by the lender. The broker's commission on the sale is $45,000. The purchaser agrees to pay the $12,000 in property taxes for the entire year. The amount realized by Ridge is calculated as follows:

Selling price		
Cash	$600,000	
Mortgage assumed by purchaser	300,000	
Seller's property taxes paid by purchaser ($12,000 × 9/12)	9,000	$909,000
Less		
Broker's commission	$ 45,000	
Points paid by seller	15,000	(60,000)
Amount realized		$849,000

▼

Adjusted Basis. Three types of items tend to complicate the determination of adjusted basis. First, the applicable tax provisions for calculating the adjusted basis are dependent on how the property was acquired (e.g., purchase, taxable exchange, nontaxable exchange, gift, inheritance). Second, if the asset is subject to depreciation, cost recovery, amortization, or depletion, adjustments must be made to the basis during the time period the asset is held by the taxpayer. Upon disposition of the asset, the taxpayer's records for both of these items may be deficient. For example, the donee does not know the amount of the donor's basis or the amount of gift tax paid by the donor, or the taxpayer does not know how much depreciation he or she has deducted. Third, the complex positive and negative adjustments encountered in calculating the amount realized are also involved in calculating the adjusted basis.

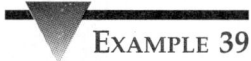

EXAMPLE 39

Jane purchased a personal residence in 1991. The purchase price and the related closing costs were as follows:

Purchase price	$125,000
Recording costs	140
Title fees and title insurance	815
Survey costs	115
Attorney's fees	750
Appraisal fee	60

Other relevant tax information for the house during the time Jane owned it is as follows:

- Constructed a swimming pool for medical reasons. The cost was $10,000, of which $3,000 was deducted as a medical expense.
- Added a solar heating system. The cost was $15,000.
- Deducted home office expenses of $6,000. Of this amount, $3,200 was for depreciation.

The adjusted basis for the house is calculated as follows:

Purchase price	$125,000
Recording costs	140
Title fees and title insurance	815
Survey costs	115
Attorney's fees	750
Appraisal fee	60
Swimming pool ($10,000 − $3,000)	7,000
Solar heating system	15,000
	$148,880
Less: Depreciation deducted on home office	(3,200)
Adjusted basis	$145,680

▼

SUMMARY OF BASIS ADJUSTMENTS

Some of the more common items that either increase or decrease the basis of an asset appear in Concept Summary 12–2.

In discussing the topic of basis, a number of specific techniques for determining basis have been presented. Although the various techniques are responsive to and mandated by transactions occurring in the marketplace, they do possess enough common characteristics to be categorized as follows:

- The basis of the asset may be determined by reference to the asset's cost.
- The basis of the asset may be determined by reference to the basis of another asset.
- The basis of the asset may be determined by reference to the asset's fair market value.
- The basis of the asset may be determined by reference to the basis of the asset to another taxpayer.

GENERAL CONCEPT OF A NONTAXABLE EXCHANGE

3 LEARNING OBJECTIVE
Understand and apply the nonrecognition (postponement) of gain or loss provisions in certain property transactions.

A taxpayer who is going to replace a productive asset (e.g., machinery) used in a trade or business may structure the transactions as a sale of the old asset and the purchase of a new asset. Using this approach, any realized gain or loss on the asset sale is recognized. The basis of the new asset is its cost. Conversely, the taxpayer may be able to trade the old asset for the new asset. This exchange of assets may produce beneficial tax consequences by qualifying for nontaxable exchange treatment.

The tax law recognizes that nontaxable exchanges result in a change in the *form* but not in the *substance* of the taxpayer's relative economic position. The replacement property received in the exchange is viewed as substantially a continuation of the old investment.[58] Additional justification for nontaxable exchange treatment is that this type of transaction does not provide the taxpayer with the wherewithal to pay the tax on any realized gain.

The nonrecognition provisions for nontaxable exchanges do not apply to realized losses from the sale or exchange of personal use assets. Such losses are not recognized (are disallowed) because they are personal in nature and not because of any nonrecognition provision.

In a **nontaxable exchange,** realized gains or losses are not recognized. However, the nonrecognition is usually temporary. The recognition of gain or loss is *postponed* (deferred) until the property received in the nontaxable exchange is subsequently disposed of in a taxable transaction. This is accomplished by assigning a carryover basis to the replacement property.

EXAMPLE 40

Debra exchanges property with an adjusted basis of $10,000 and a fair market value of $12,000 for property with a fair market value of $12,000. The transaction qualifies for nontaxable exchange treatment. Debra has a realized gain of $2,000 ($12,000 amount

---

[58]Reg. § 1.1002–1(c).

CONCEPT SUMMARY 12–2

Adjustments to Basis

Item	Effect	Refer to Chapter	Explanation
Amortization of bond discount.	Increase	13	Amortization is mandatory for certain taxable bonds and elective for tax-exempt bonds.
Amortization of bond premium.	Decrease	12	Amortization is mandatory for tax-exempt bonds and elective for taxable bonds.
Amortization of covenant not to compete.	Decrease	13	Covenant must be for a definite and limited time period. The amortization period is a statutory period of 15 years.
Amortization of intangibles.	Decrease	7	Even goodwill is now subject to amortization.
Assessment for local benefits.	Increase	9	To the extent not deductible as taxes (e.g., assessment for streets and sidewalks that increase the value of the property versus one for maintenance or repair or for meeting interest charges).
Bad debts.	Decrease	6	Only the specific charge-off method is permitted.
Capital additions.	Increase	12	Certain items, at the taxpayer's election, can be capitalized or deducted (e.g., selected medical expenses).
Casualty.	Decrease	6	For a casualty loss, the amount of the adjustment is the summation of the deductible loss and the insurance proceeds received. For a casualty gain, the amount of the adjustment is the insurance proceeds received reduced by the recognized gain.
Condemnation.	Decrease	12	See casualty explanation.
Cost recovery.	Decrease	7	§ 168 is applicable to tangible assets placed in service after 1980 whose useful life is expressed in terms of years.
Depletion.	Decrease	7	Use the greater of cost or percentage depletion. Percentage depletion can still be deducted when the basis is zero.
Depreciation.	Decrease	7	§ 167 is applicable to tangible assets placed in service before 1981 and to tangible assets not depreciated in terms of years.
Easement.	Decrease	12	If the taxpayer does not retain any use of the land, all of the basis is allocable to the easement transaction. However, if only part of the land is affected by the easement, only part of the basis is allocable to the easement transaction.
Improvements by lessee to lessor's property.	Increase	4	Adjustment occurs only if the lessor is required to include the fair market value of the improvements in gross income under § 109.
Imputed interest.	Decrease	15	Amount deducted is not part of the cost of the asset.
Inventory: lower of cost or market.	Decrease	15	Not available if the LIFO method is used.
Limited expensing under § 179.	Decrease	7	Occurs only if the taxpayer elects § 179 treatment.

Item	Effect	Refer to Chapter	Explanation
Medical capital expenditure permitted as a medical expense.	Decrease	9	Adjustment is the amount of the deduction (the effect on basis is to increase it by the amount of the capital expenditure net of the deduction).
Real estate taxes: apportionment between the buyer and seller.	Increase or decrease	9	To the extent the buyer pays the seller's pro rata share, the buyer's basis is increased. To the extent the seller pays the buyer's pro rata share, the buyer's basis is decreased.
Rebate from manufacturer.	Decrease		Since the rebate is treated as an adjustment to the purchase price, it is not included in the buyer's gross income.
Stock dividend.	Decrease	4	Adjustment occurs only if the stock dividend is nontaxable. While the basis per share decreases, the total stock basis does not change.
Stock rights.	Decrease	12	Adjustment to stock basis occurs only for nontaxable stock rights and only if the fair market value of the rights is at least 15% of the fair market value of the stock or, if less than 15%, the taxpayer elects to allocate the basis between the stock and the rights.
Theft.	Decrease	6	See casualty explanation.

realized – $10,000 adjusted basis). Her recognized gain is $0. Her basis in the replacement property is a carryover basis of $10,000. Assume the replacement property is nondepreciable. If Debra subsequently sells the replacement property for $12,000, her realized and recognized gain will be the $2,000 gain that was postponed (deferred) in the nontaxable transaction. If the replacement property is depreciable, the carryover basis of $10,000 is used in calculating depreciation. ▼

In some nontaxable exchanges, only part of the property involved in the transaction qualifies for nonrecognition treatment. If the taxpayer receives cash or other nonqualifying property, part or all of the realized gain from the exchange is recognized. In these instances, gain is recognized because the taxpayer has changed or improved his or her relative economic position and has the wherewithal to pay income tax to the extent of cash or other property received.

It is important to distinguish between a nontaxable disposition, as the term is used in the statute, and a tax-free transaction. First, a direct exchange is not required in all circumstances (e.g., replacement of involuntarily converted property). Second, as previously mentioned, the term *nontaxable* refers to postponement of recognition via a carryover basis. In a *tax-free* transaction, the nonrecognition is permanent (e.g., see the discussion later in the chapter of the § 121 exclusion of realized gain on the sale of a personal residence). Therefore, the basis of any property acquired in a tax-free transaction does not depend on the basis of the property disposed of by the taxpayer.

LIKE–KIND EXCHANGES—§ 1031

Section 1031 provides for nontaxable exchange treatment if the following requirements are satisfied:[59]

- The form of the transaction is an exchange.
- Both the property transferred and the property received are held either for productive use in a trade or business or for investment.
- The property is like-kind property.

Like-kind exchanges include business for business, business for investment, investment for business, or investment for investment property. Property held for personal use, inventory, and partnership interests (both limited and general) do not qualify under the like-kind exchange provisions. Securities, even though held for investment, do not qualify for like-kind exchange treatment.

The nonrecognition provision for like-kind exchanges is *mandatory* rather than elective. A taxpayer who wants to recognize a realized gain or loss will have to structure the transaction in a form that does not satisfy the statutory requirements for a like-kind exchange. This topic is discussed further under Tax Planning Considerations.

LIKE–KIND PROPERTY

"The words 'like-kind' refer to the nature or character of the property and not to its grade or quality. One kind or class of property may not . . . be exchanged for property of a different kind or class."[60]

Although the term *like-kind* is intended to be interpreted very broadly, three categories of exchanges are not included. First, livestock of different sexes do not qualify as like-kind property. Second, real estate can be exchanged only for other real estate, and personalty can be exchanged only for other personalty. For example, the exchange of a machine (personalty) for an office building (realty) is not a like-kind exchange. *Real estate* (or realty) includes principally rental buildings, office and store buildings, manufacturing plants, warehouses, and land. It is immaterial whether real estate is improved or unimproved. Thus, unimproved land can be exchanged for an apartment house. Personalty includes principally machines, equipment, trucks, automobiles, furniture, and fixtures. Third, real property located in the United States exchanged for foreign real property (and vice versa) does not qualify as like-kind property.

EXAMPLE 41

Wade made the following exchanges during the taxable year:

  a. Inventory for a machine used in business.
  b. Land held for investment for a building used in business.
  c. Stock held for investment for equipment used in business.
  d. A business truck for a business truck.
  e. An automobile used for personal transportation for an automobile used in business.
  f. Livestock for livestock of a different sex.
  g. Land held for investment in New York for land held for investment in London.

Exchanges (b), investment real property for business real property, and (d), business personalty for business personalty, qualify as exchanges of like-kind property. Exchanges (a), inventory; (c), stock; (e), personal use automobile (not held for business or investment

---

[59]§ 1031(a) and Reg. § 1.1031(a)–1(a).   [60]Reg. § 1.1031(a)–1(b).

purposes); (f), livestock of different sexes; and (g), U.S. and foreign real estate do not qualify. ▼

A special provision applies for personal property with respect to the location of its use. Personal property used predominantly within the United States and personal property used predominantly outside the United States are not like-kind property. The location of use for the personal property given up is its location during the two-year period ending on the date of disposition of the property. The location of use for the personal property received is its location during the two-year period beginning on the date of the acquisition.

EXAMPLE 42

In October 1997, Walter exchanges a machine used in his factory in Denver for a machine that qualifies as like-kind property. In January 1998, the factory, including the machine, is moved to Berlin. As of January 1998, the exchange is not an exchange of like-kind property. The predominant use of the original machine was in the United States, whereas the predominant use of the new machine is foreign. ▼

Another special provision applies if the taxpayers involved in the exchange are *related parties* under § 267(b). To qualify for like-kind exchange treatment, the taxpayer and the related party must not dispose of the like-kind property received in the exchange within the two-year period following the date of the exchange. If such an early disposition does occur, the postponed gain is recognized as of the date of the early disposition. Dispositions due to death, involuntary conversions, and certain non-tax avoidance transactions are not treated as early dispositions.

Regulations dealing with § 1031 like-kind exchange treatment provide that if the exchange transaction involves multiple assets of a business (e.g., a television station for another television station), the determination of whether the assets qualify as like-kind property will not be made at the business level.[61] Instead, the underlying assets must be evaluated.

The Regulations also provide for greater specificity in determining whether depreciable tangible personal property is of a like kind or class. Such property held for productive use in a business is of a like class only if the exchanged property is within the same *general business asset class* (as specified by the IRS in Revenue Procedure 87–57 or as subsequently modified) or the same *product class* (as specified by the Department of Commerce). Property included in a general business asset class is evaluated under this system rather than under the product class system.

The following are examples of general business asset classes:

- Office furniture, fixtures, and equipment.
- Information systems (computers and peripheral equipment).
- Airplanes.
- Automobiles and taxis.
- Buses.
- Light general-purpose trucks.
- Heavy general-purpose trucks.

These Regulations have made it more difficult for depreciable tangible personal property to qualify for § 1031 like-kind exchange treatment. For example, the exchange of office equipment for a computer does not qualify as an exchange of like-kind property. Even though both assets are depreciable tangible personal property, they are not like-kind property because they are in different general business asset classes.

---

[61]Reg. § 1.1031(j)–1.

ARE THE CLEVELAND INDIANS STILL THE CLEVELAND INDIANS (OR DOES HART HAVE A HEART)?

The Cleveland Indians were in the World Series in 1995 (losing to the Atlanta Braves) and made it to the American League playoffs (losing to the Baltimore Orioles) in 1996. Two key players were Albert Belle and Kenny Lofton. Belle was a free agent at the end of the 1996 season and signed with the Indians' chief competitor in the American League Central, the Chicago White Sox, for a reported $55 million.

But the Indians still had center fielder and leadoff hitter Kenny Lofton. In late March 1997, however, Kenny and left-handed reliever Alan Embree were traded to Atlanta for outfielders David Justice and Marquis Grissom. Cleveland fans wondered whether the trade would help the Indians continue to win.

General Manager John Hart had an additional question when he made the deal: Does the trade qualify for § 1031 like-kind exchange treatment? Since he made the trade, Hart must believe that the answer to both questions is yes. Cleveland's performance in the 1997 postseason indicates that Hart knew what he was doing. The Indians came within two outs of winning game 7 of the World Series.

For the 1998 season, the Indians have signed free agent Kenny Lofton who will be their center fielder and leadoff hitter. Marquis Grissom has been traded.

SOURCE: Adapted from *ESPN Sportszone*, March 26, 1997.

EXCHANGE REQUIREMENT

The transaction must actually involve a direct exchange of property to qualify as a like-kind exchange. The sale of old property and the purchase of new property, even though like kind, is generally not an exchange. However, if the two transactions are mutually dependent, the IRS may treat them as a like-kind exchange. For example, if the taxpayer sells an old business machine to a dealer and purchases a new one from the same dealer, like-kind exchange treatment could result.[62]

The taxpayer may want to avoid nontaxable exchange treatment. Recognition of gain gives the taxpayer a higher basis for depreciation (see Example 72). To the extent that such gains would, if recognized, either receive favorable capital gain treatment or be passive activity income that could offset passive activity losses, it may be preferable to avoid the nonrecognition provisions through an indirect exchange transaction. For example, a taxpayer may sell property to one individual and subsequently purchase similar property from another individual. The taxpayer may also want to avoid nontaxable exchange treatment so that a realized loss can be recognized.

BOOT

If the taxpayer in a like-kind exchange gives or receives some property that is not like-kind property, recognition may occur. Property that is not like-kind property, including cash, is referred to as **boot.** Although the term *boot* does not appear in the Code, tax practitioners commonly use it rather than saying "property that is not like-kind property."

---

[62]Rev.Rul. 61–119, 1961–1 C.B. 395.

The *receipt* of boot will trigger recognition of gain if there is realized gain. The amount of the recognized gain is the *lesser* of the boot received or the realized gain (realized gain serves as the ceiling on recognition).

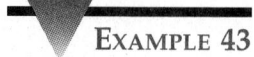
EXAMPLE 43

Emily and Fran exchange machinery, and the exchange qualifies as like-kind under § 1031. Since Emily's machinery (adjusted basis of $20,000) is worth $24,000 and Fran's machine has a fair market value of $19,000, Fran also gives Emily cash of $5,000. Emily's recognized gain is $4,000, the lesser of the realized gain ($24,000 amount realized − $20,000 adjusted basis = $4,000) or the fair market value of the boot received ($5,000). ▼

EXAMPLE 44

Assume the same facts as in the previous example, except that Fran's machine is worth $21,000 (not $19,000). Under these circumstances, Fran gives Emily cash of $3,000 to make up the difference. Emily's recognized gain is $3,000, the lesser of the realized gain ($24,000 amount realized − $20,000 adjusted basis = $4,000) or the fair market value of the boot received ($3,000). ▼

The receipt of boot does not result in recognition if there is realized loss.

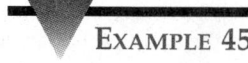
EXAMPLE 45

Assume the same facts as in Example 44, except that the adjusted basis of Emily's machine is $30,000. Emily's realized loss is $6,000 ($24,000 amount realized − $30,000 adjusted basis = $6,000 realized loss). The receipt of the boot of $5,000 does not trigger recognition. Therefore, the recognized loss is $0. ▼

The *giving* of boot usually does not trigger recognition. If the boot given is cash, any realized gain or loss is not recognized.

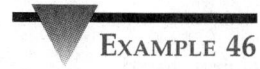
EXAMPLE 46

Fred and Gary exchange equipment in a like-kind exchange. Fred receives equipment with a fair market value of $25,000 and transfers equipment worth $21,000 (adjusted basis of $15,000) and cash of $4,000. Fred's realized gain is $6,000 ($25,000 amount realized − $15,000 adjusted basis − $4,000 cash). However, none of the realized gain is recognized. ▼

If, however, the boot given is appreciated or depreciated property, gain or loss is recognized to the extent of the differential between the adjusted basis and the fair market value of the boot. For this purpose, *appreciated or depreciated property* is defined as property whose adjusted basis is not equal to the fair market value.

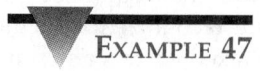
EXAMPLE 47

Assume the same facts as in the previous example, except that Fred transfers equipment worth $10,000 (adjusted basis of $12,000) and boot worth $15,000 (adjusted basis of $9,000). Fred's realized gain appears to be $4,000 ($25,000 amount realized − $21,000 adjusted basis). Since realization previously has served as a ceiling on recognition, it appears that the recognized gain is $4,000 (lower of realized gain of $4,000 or amount of appreciation on boot of $6,000). However, the recognized gain actually is $6,000 (full amount of the appreciation on the boot). In effect, Fred must calculate the like-kind and boot parts of the transaction separately. That is, the realized loss of $2,000 on the like-kind property is not recognized ($10,000 fair market value − $12,000 adjusted basis), and the $6,000 realized gain on the boot is recognized ($15,000 fair market value − $9,000 adjusted basis). ▼

BASIS AND HOLDING PERIOD OF PROPERTY RECEIVED

If an exchange does not qualify as nontaxable under § 1031, gain or loss is recognized, and the basis of property received in the exchange is the property's fair market value. If the exchange qualifies for nonrecognition, the basis of property received must be adjusted to reflect any postponed (deferred) gain or loss. The *basis of like-kind property* received in the exchange is the property's fair market value less postponed gain or plus postponed loss. If the exchange partially qualifies for nonrecognition (if recognition is associated with boot), the basis of like-kind property received in the exchange is the property's fair market value less postponed gain or plus postponed loss. The *basis* of any *boot* received is the boot's fair market value.

If there is a postponed loss, nonrecognition creates a situation in which the taxpayer has recovered *less* than the cost or other basis of the property exchanged in an amount equal to the unrecognized loss. If there is a postponed gain, the taxpayer has recovered *more* than the cost or other basis of the property exchanged in an amount equal to the unrecognized gain.

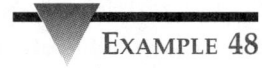

EXAMPLE 48

Jaime exchanges a building (used in his business) with an adjusted basis of $30,000 and fair market value of $38,000 for land with a fair market value of $38,000. The land is to be held as an investment. The exchange qualifies as like kind (an exchange of business real property for investment real property). Thus, the basis of the land is $30,000 (the land's fair market value of $38,000 less the $8,000 postponed gain on the building). If the land is later sold for its fair market value of $38,000, the $8,000 postponed gain is recognized. ▼

EXAMPLE 49

Assume the same facts as in the previous example, except that the building has an adjusted basis of $48,000 and fair market value of only $38,000. The basis in the newly acquired land is $48,000 (fair market value of $38,000 plus the $10,000 postponed loss on the building). If the land is later sold for its fair market value of $38,000, the $10,000 postponed loss is recognized. ▼

The Code provides an alternative approach for determining the basis of like-kind property received:

> Adjusted basis of like-kind property surrendered
> + Adjusted basis of boot given
> + Gain recognized
> – Fair market value of boot received
> – Loss recognized
> = *Basis of like-kind property received*

This approach is logical in terms of the recovery of capital doctrine. That is, the unrecovered cost or other basis is increased by additional cost (boot given) or decreased by cost recovered (boot received). Any gain recognized is included in the basis of the new property. The taxpayer has been taxed on this amount and is now entitled to recover it tax-free. Any loss recognized is deducted from the basis of the new property. The taxpayer has received a tax benefit on that amount.

The holding period of the property surrendered in the exchange carries over and *tacks on* to the holding period of the like-kind property received.[63] The logic of this rule is derived from the basic concept of the new property as a continuation of the old investment. The boot received has a new holding period (from the date of exchange) rather than a carryover holding period.

Depreciation recapture potential carries over to the property received in a like-kind exchange.[64] See Chapter 13 for a discussion of this topic.

The following comprehensive example illustrates the like-kind exchange rules.

---

[63]§ 1223(1) and Reg. § 1.1223–1(a). For this carryover holding period rule to apply to like-kind exchanges after March 1, 1954, the like-kind property surrendered must have been either a capital asset or § 1231 property. See Chapter 13 for the discussion of capital assets and § 1231 property.

[64]Reg. §§ 1.1245–2(a)(4) and 1.1250–2(d)(1).

EXAMPLE 50

Vicki exchanged the following old machines for new machines in five independent like-kind exchanges:

Exchange	Adjusted Basis of Old Machine	Fair Market Value of New Machine	Adjusted Basis of Boot Given	Fair Market Value of Boot Received
1	$4,000	$9,000	$ –0–	$ –0–
2	4,000	9,000	3,000	–0–
3	4,000	9,000	6,000	–0–
4	4,000	9,000	–0–	3,000
5	4,000	3,500	–0–	300

Vicki's realized and recognized gains and losses and the basis of each of the like-kind properties received are as follows:

Exchange	Realized Gain (Loss)	Recognized Gain (Loss)	New Basis Calculation							
			Old Adj. Basis	+	Boot Given	+	Gain Recognized	–	Boot Received	= New Basis
1	$ 5,000	$ –(0)–	$4,000	+	$ –0–	+	$ –0–	–	$ –0–	= $ 4,000*
2	2,000	–(0)–	4,000	+	3,000	+	–0–	–	–0–	= 7,000*
3	(1,000)	–(0)–	4,000	+	6,000	+	–0–	–	–0–	= 10,000**
4	8,000	3,000	4,000	+	–0–	+	3,000	–	3,000	= 4,000*
5	(200)	–(0)–	4,000	+	–0–	+	–0–	–	300	= 3,700**

*Basis may be determined in gain situations under the alternative method by subtracting the gain not recognized from the fair market value of the new property:
$9,000 – $5,000 = $4,000 for exchange 1.
$9,000 – $2,000 = $7,000 for exchange 2.
$9,000 – $5,000 = $4,000 for exchange 4.

**In loss situations, basis may be determined by adding the loss not recognized to the fair market value of the new property:
$9,000 + $1,000 = $10,000 for exchange 3.
$3,500 + $200 = $3,700 for exchange 5.
The basis of the boot received is the boot's fair market value. ▼

If the taxpayer either assumes a liability or takes property subject to a liability, the amount of the liability is treated as boot given. For the taxpayer whose liability is assumed or whose property is taken subject to the liability, the amount of the liability is treated as boot received. Example 51 illustrates the effect of such a liability. In addition, the example illustrates the tax consequences for both parties involved in the like-kind exchange.

EXAMPLE 51

Jane and Leo exchange real estate investments. Jane gives up property with an adjusted basis of $250,000 (fair market value $400,000) that is subject to a mortgage of $75,000 (assumed by Leo). In return for this property, Jane receives property with a fair market value of $300,000 (adjusted basis $200,000) and cash of $25,000.

- Jane's realized gain is $150,000. She gave up property with an adjusted basis of $250,000. Jane received $400,000 from the exchange ($300,000 fair market value of like-kind property plus $100,000 boot received). The boot received consists of the $25,000 cash received from Leo and Jane's mortgage of $75,000 that Leo assumes.
- Jane's recognized gain is $100,000. The realized gain of $150,000 is recognized to the extent of boot received.

TRUMP TRIUMPHS FOR CASINO

"The Donald" owns Trump Plaza Hotel & Casino in Atlantic City. When Trump Plaza decided to expand, it found that a three-story rooming house owned by Vera Colsing was in the way. After she declined to sell, the property was condemned by the New Jersey Casino Development Authority.

Recently, the New Jersey Supreme Court decided not to hear Colsing's appeal of the condemnation ruling. Glenn Zeitz, an attorney for the plaintiff, commented as to the finality of the Supreme Court's announcement: "This is just one round of a 15-round fight. It's not even close to being the final chapter."

SOURCE: Adapted from a wire service report "Trump Triumph," *Newport News Daily Press*, May 14, 1997, p. A2.

- Jane's basis in the real estate received from Leo is $250,000. This basis can be computed by subtracting the postponed gain ($50,000) from the fair market value of the real estate received ($300,000). It can also be computed by adding the recognized gain ($100,000) to the adjusted basis of the real estate given up ($250,000) and subtracting the boot received ($100,000).
- Leo's realized gain is $100,000. Leo gave up property with an adjusted basis of $200,000 plus boot of $100,000 ($75,000 mortgage assumed + $25,000 cash) or a total of $300,000. Leo received $400,000 from the exchange (fair market value of like-kind property received).
- Leo has no recognized gain because he did not receive any boot. The entire realized gain of $100,000 is postponed.
- Leo's basis in the real estate received from Jane is $300,000. This basis can be computed by subtracting the postponed gain ($100,000) from the fair market value of the real estate received ($400,000). It can also be computed by adding the boot given ($75,000 mortgage assumed by Leo + $25,000 cash) to the adjusted basis of the real estate given up ($200,000).[65] ▼

INVOLUNTARY CONVERSIONS—§ 1033

Section 1033 provides that a taxpayer who suffers an involuntary conversion of property may postpone recognition of *gain* realized from the conversion. The objective of this provision is to provide relief to the taxpayer who has suffered hardship and does not have the wherewithal to pay the tax on any gain realized from the conversion. Postponement of realized gain is permitted to the extent that the taxpayer *reinvests* the amount realized from the conversion in replacement property. The rules for nonrecognition of gain are as follows:

- If the amount reinvested in replacement property *equals or exceeds* the amount realized, realized gain is *not recognized*.
- If the amount reinvested in replacement property is *less than* the amount realized, realized gain *is recognized* to the extent of the deficiency.

---

[65]Example (2) of Reg. § 1.1031(d)–2 illustrates a special situation where both the buyer and the seller transfer liabilities that are assumed or property is acquired subject to a liability by the other party.

If a *loss* occurs on an involuntary conversion, § 1033 does not modify the normal rules for loss recognition. That is, if a realized loss would otherwise be recognized, § 1033 does not change the result.

INVOLUNTARY CONVERSION DEFINED

An **involuntary conversion** results from the destruction (complete or partial), theft, seizure, requisition or condemnation, or the sale or exchange under threat or imminence of requisition or condemnation of the taxpayer's property.[66] To prove the existence of a threat or imminence of condemnation, the taxpayer must obtain confirmation that there has been a decision to acquire the property for public use. In addition, the taxpayer must have reasonable grounds to believe the property will be taken.[67] The property does not have to be sold to the authority threatening to condemn it to qualify for § 1033 postponement. If the taxpayer satisfies the confirmation and reasonable grounds requirements, he or she can sell the property to another party.[68] Likewise, the sale of property to a condemning authority by a taxpayer who acquired the property from its former owner with the knowledge that the property was under threat of condemnation also qualifies as an involuntary conversion under § 1033.[69] A voluntary act, such as a taxpayer destroying his or her own property by arson, is not an involuntary conversion.[70]

COMPUTING THE AMOUNT REALIZED

The amount realized from the condemnation of property usually includes only the amount received as compensation for the property.[71] Any amount received that is designated as severance damages by both the government and the taxpayer is not included in the amount realized. *Severance awards* usually occur when only a portion of the entire property is condemned (e.g., a strip of land is taken to build a highway). Severance damages are awarded because the value of the taxpayer's remaining property has declined as a result of the condemnation. Such damages reduce the basis of the property. However, if either of the following requirements is satisfied, the nonrecognition provision of § 1033 applies to the severance damages.

- Severance damages are used to restore the usability of the remaining property.
- The usefulness of the remaining property is destroyed by the condemnation, and the property is sold and replaced at a cost equal to or exceeding the sum of the condemnation award, severance damages, and sales proceeds.

 **EXAMPLE 52**   The government condemns a portion of Ron's farmland to build part of an interstate highway. Because the highway denies his cattle access to a pond and some grazing land, Ron receives severance damages in addition to the condemnation proceeds for the land taken. Ron must reduce the basis of the property by the amount of the severance damages. If the amount of the severance damages received exceeds the adjusted basis, Ron recognizes gain. ▼

 **EXAMPLE 53**   Assume the same facts as in the previous example, except that Ron used the proceeds from the condemnation and the severance damages to build another pond and to clear woodland for grazing. Therefore, all the proceeds are eligible for § 1033 treatment. Thus, there is no

[66]§ 1033(a) and Reg. §§ 1.1033(a)–1(a) and –2(a).
[67]Rev.Rul. 63–221, 1963–2 C.B. 332, and *Joseph P. Balistrieri*, 38 TCM 526, T.C.Memo. 1979–115.
[68]Rev.Rul. 81–180, 1981–2 C.B. 161.
[69]Rev.Rul. 81–181, 1981–2 C.B. 162.
[70]Rev.Rul. 82–74, 1982–1 C.B. 110.
[71]*Pioneer Real Estate Co.*, 47 B.T.A. 886 (1942), *acq.* 1943 C.B. 18.

possibility of gain recognition as the result of the amount of the severance damages received exceeding the adjusted basis. ▼

REPLACEMENT PROPERTY

The requirements for replacement property generally are more restrictive than those for like-kind property under § 1031. The basic requirement is that the replacement property be similar or related in service or use to the involuntarily converted property.[72]

Different interpretations of the phrase *similar or related in service or use* apply depending on whether the involuntarily converted property is held by an *owner-user* or by an *owner-investor* (e.g., lessor). A taxpayer who uses the property in his or her trade or business is subject to a more restrictive test in terms of acquiring replacement property. For an owner-user, the *functional use test* applies, and for an owner-investor, the *taxpayer use test* applies.

Taxpayer Use Test.   The taxpayer use test for owner-investors provides the taxpayer with more flexibility in terms of what qualifies as replacement property than does the functional use test for owner-users. Essentially, the properties must be used by the taxpayer (the owner-investor) in similar endeavors. For example, rental property held by an owner-investor qualifies if replaced by other rental property, regardless of the type of rental property involved. The test is met when an investor replaces a manufacturing plant with a wholesale grocery warehouse if both properties are held for the production of rent income.[73] The replacement of a rental residence with a personal residence does not meet the test.[74]

Functional Use Test.   Under this test, the taxpayer's use of the replacement property and of the involuntarily converted property must be the same. Replacing a manufacturing plant with a wholesale grocery warehouse, whether rented or not, does not meet this test. As indicated above, the IRS applies the taxpayer use test to owner-investors. However, the functional use test still applies to owner-users (e.g., a manufacturer whose manufacturing plant is destroyed by fire is required to replace the plant with another facility of similar functional use). Replacing a rental residence with a personal residence does not meet this test.

Special Rules.   Under one set of circumstances, the broader replacement rules for like-kind exchanges are substituted for the narrow replacement rules normally used for involuntary conversions. This beneficial provision applies if business real property or investment real property is condemned. Therefore, the taxpayer has substantially more flexibility in selecting replacement property. For example, improved real property can be replaced with unimproved real property.

The rules concerning the nature of replacement property are illustrated in Concept Summary 12–3.

TIME LIMITATION ON REPLACEMENT

The taxpayer normally has a two-year period after the close of the taxable year in which any gain is realized from the involuntary conversion to replace the property (*the latest date*).[75] This rule affords as much as three years from the date of realization

---

[72]§ 1033(a) and Reg. § 1.1033(a)–1.

[73]*Loco Realty Co. v. Comm.*, 62–2 USTC ¶9657, 10 AFTR2d 5359, 306 F.2d 207 (CA–8, 1962).

[74]Rev.Rul. 70–466, 1970–2 C.B. 165.

[75]§§ 1033(a)(2)(B) and (g)(4) and Reg. § 1.1033(a)–2(c)(3).

CONCEPT SUMMARY 12–3

Replacement Property Tests

Type of Property and User	Like-Kind Test	Taxpayer Use Test	Functional Use Test
Land used by a manufacturing company is condemned by a local government authority.	X		
Apartment and land held by an investor are sold due to the threat or imminence of condemnation.	X		
An investor's rented shopping mall is destroyed by fire; the mall may be replaced by other rental properties (e.g., an apartment building).		X	
A manufacturing plant is destroyed by fire; replacement property must consist of another manufacturing plant that is functionally the same as the property converted.			X
Personal residence of taxpayer is condemned by a local government authority; replacement property must consist of another personal residence.			X

---

of gain to replace the property if the realization of gain took place on the first day of the taxable year.[76] If the involuntary conversion involved the condemnation of real property used in a trade or business or held for investment, a three-year period is substituted for the normal two-year period. In this case, the taxpayer can actually have as much as four years from the date of realization of gain to replace the property.

EXAMPLE 54

Megan's warehouse is destroyed by fire on December 16, 1997. The adjusted basis is $325,000. Megan receives $400,000 from the insurance company on January 10, 1998. She is a calendar year taxpayer. The latest date for replacement is December 31, 2000 (the end of the taxable year in which realized gain occurred plus two years). The critical date is not the date the involuntary conversion occurred, but rather the date of gain realization. ▼

EXAMPLE 55

Assume the same facts as in the previous example, except that Megan's warehouse is condemned. The latest date for replacement is December 31, 2001 (the end of the taxable year in which realized gain occurred plus three years). ▼

The *earliest date* for replacement typically is the date the involuntary conversion occurs. However, if the property is condemned, it is possible to replace the condemned property before this date. In this case, the earliest date is the date of the threat or imminence of requisition or condemnation of the property. The purpose of this provision is to enable the taxpayer to make an orderly replacement of the condemned property.

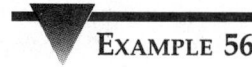

EXAMPLE 56

Assume the same facts as in Example 55. Megan can replace the warehouse before December 16, 1997 (the condemnation date). The earliest date for replacement is the date of the threat or imminence of requisition or condemnation of the warehouse. ▼

---

[76]The taxpayer can apply for an extension of this time period anytime before its expiration [Reg. § 1.1033(a)–2(c)(3)]. Also, the period for filing the application for extension can be extended if the taxpayer shows reasonable cause.

ETHICAL CONSIDERATIONS

Postponing Realized Gain from an Involuntary Conversion

Peggy, age 63 and in frail health, owns a furniture store in Petersburg. Because of competition from two large furniture retailers who opened stores in the Petersburg area during the past three years, Peggy's furniture store has been unprofitable.

Due to this lack of profitability as well as her advancing age, Peggy would like to retire. Unfortunately, she has been unable to locate a purchaser for her store. Her prayers seem to be answered when a tornado destroys her building and its contents. Fortunately, no one is injured or killed by the tornado.

Peggy anticipates that she can live on the insurance proceeds of $800,000 for the rest of her life. However, her realized gain on the involuntary conversion would produce a combined state and Federal tax liability of approximately $175,000. In order to forgo paying this amount associated with her 1998 income tax returns, Peggy elects postponement treatment under § 1033, indicating that she intends to replace the involuntarily converted property with similar property even though she does not intend to do so. Her justification, based on her participation in a 12-step program, is that she lives "one day at a time."

Evaluate Peggy's election of § 1033 postponement under these circumstances.

NONRECOGNITION OF GAIN

Nonrecognition of gain can be either mandatory or elective, depending upon whether the conversion is direct (into replacement property) or into money (indirect).

Direct Conversion.   If the conversion is directly into replacement property rather than into money, nonrecognition of realized gain is *mandatory*. In this case, the basis of the replacement property is the same as the adjusted basis of the converted property. Direct conversion is rare in practice and usually involves condemnations. The following example illustrates the application of the rules for direct conversions.

EXAMPLE 57

Lupe's property with an adjusted basis of $20,000 is condemned by the state. Lupe receives property with a fair market value of $50,000 as compensation for the property taken. Since the nonrecognition of realized gain is mandatory for direct conversions, Lupe's realized gain of $30,000 is not recognized, and the basis of the replacement property is $20,000 (adjusted basis of the condemned property). ▼

Conversion into Money.   If the conversion is into money, at the election of the taxpayer, the realized gain is recognized only to the extent the amount realized from the involuntary conversion exceeds the cost of the qualifying replacement property.[77] This is the usual case, and nonrecognition (postponement) is *elective*. If the election is not made, the realized gain is recognized.

---

[77]§ 1033(a)(2)(A) and Reg. § 1.1033(a)–2(c)(1).

The basis of the replacement property is the property's cost less postponed (deferred) gain.[78] If the election to postpone gain is made, the holding period of the replacement property includes the holding period of the converted property.

Section 1033 applies *only to gains* and *not to losses*. Losses from involuntary conversions are recognized if the property is held for business or income-producing purposes. Personal casualty losses are recognized, but condemnation losses related to personal use assets (e.g., a personal residence) are neither recognized nor postponed.

Examples 58 and 59 illustrate the application of the involuntary conversion provisions.

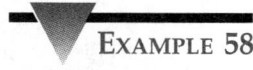
EXAMPLE 58

Walt's building (used in his trade or business), with an adjusted basis of $50,000, is destroyed by fire in 1998. Walt is a calendar year taxpayer. In 1998, he receives an insurance reimbursement of $100,000 for the loss. Walt invests $80,000 in a new building.

- Walt has until December 31, 2000, to make the new investment and qualify for the nonrecognition election.
- Walt's realized gain is $50,000 ($100,000 insurance proceeds received − $50,000 adjusted basis of old building).
- Assuming the replacement property qualifies as similar or related in service or use, Walt's recognized gain is $20,000. He reinvested $20,000 less than the insurance proceeds received ($100,000 proceeds − $80,000 reinvested). Therefore, his realized gain is recognized to that extent.
- Walt's basis in the new building is $50,000. This is the building's cost of $80,000 less the postponed gain of $30,000 (realized gain of $50,000 − recognized gain of $20,000).
- The computation of realization, recognition, and basis would apply even if Walt was a real estate dealer and the building destroyed by fire was part of his inventory. Unlike § 1031, § 1033 generally does not exclude inventory. ▼

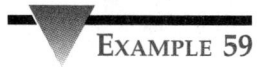
EXAMPLE 59

Assume the same facts as in the previous example, except that Walt receives only $45,000 (instead of $100,000) of insurance proceeds. He has a realized and recognized loss of $5,000. The basis of the new building is the building's cost of $80,000. If the destroyed building was held for personal use, the recognized loss is subject to the following additional limitations.[79] The loss of $5,000 is limited to the decline in fair market value of the property, and the amount of the loss is reduced first by $100 and then by 10% of adjusted gross income (refer to Chapter 6). ▼

INVOLUNTARY CONVERSION OF A PERSONAL RESIDENCE

The tax consequences of the involuntary conversion of a personal residence depend upon whether the conversion is a casualty or condemnation and whether a realized loss or gain results.

Loss Situations.   If the conversion is a condemnation, the realized loss is not recognized. Loss from the condemnation of a personal use asset is never recognized. If the conversion is a casualty (a loss from fire, storm, etc.), the loss is recognized subject to the personal casualty loss limitations (refer to Chapter 6).

---

[78]§ 1033(b).   [79]§ 165(c)(3) and Reg. § 1.165–7.

WHAT GOES DOWN MAY GO UP

Many of us are either not investors or not good investors. Nevertheless, most of us view our home as an asset that we can eventually sell for a higher price than we paid.

Yet what does one do if the home does not turn out to be a good investment? In some areas of the country, housing prices still have not regained their former levels. So, if taxpayers sell, they have a realized loss that is disallowed for tax purposes. To make matters worse, the disallowed loss cannot be added to the basis of the replacement residence.

In this situation, what can the taxpayer who buys a new residence do? Among the options are the following:

- Convert the old residence to rental property until its price increases.
- If the new residence is in the same area as the old residence and is more suitable for renting, convert it to rental property until the price of the old residence increases.
- Sell the house, deduct the loss, and hope your tax return is not audited.
- Sell the house knowing that the loss cannot be deducted on your tax return.

The first two options require careful planning in order to avoid certain tax pitfalls (e.g., satisfying the two-year ownership and use requirement within the five-year window). They also are based on the assumption that the real estate market for housing in the particular area will rebound. The third option should be avoided. With the fourth option, the taxpayer's ego suffers because this is an admission that he or she is not a good investor.

SOURCE: Adapted from Scott R. Schmedel, "Housing and the Tax Man: When Selling at a Loss, the Consequences Are Tricky," *Wall Street Journal*, February 28, 1997, p. C1.

Gain Situations. If the conversion is a casualty, theft, or condemnation, the gain may be postponed under § 1033 or excluded under § 121. That is, the taxpayer may treat the involuntary conversion as a sale under the exclusion of gain rules relating to the sale of a personal residence under § 121 (presented subsequently).

REPORTING CONSIDERATIONS

Involuntary conversions from casualty and theft are reported first on Form 4684, Casualties and Thefts. Casualty and theft losses on personal use property for the individual taxpayer are carried from Form 4684 to Schedule A of Form 1040. For other casualty and theft items, the Form 4684 amounts are generally reported on Form 4797, Sales of Business Property, unless Form 4797 is not required. In the latter case, the amounts are reported directly on the tax return involved.

Except for personal use property, recognized gains and losses from involuntary conversions other than by casualty and theft are reported on Form 4797. As stated previously, if the property involved in the involuntary conversion (other than by casualty and theft) is personal use property, any realized loss is not recognized. Any realized gain is treated as gain on a voluntary sale.

SALE OF A RESIDENCE—§ 121

4 LEARNING OBJECTIVE
Describe the provision for the
permanent exclusion of gain on
the sale of a personal
residence.

A taxpayer's **personal residence** is a personal use asset. Therefore, a realized loss from the sale of a personal residence is not recognized.[80]

A realized gain from the sale of a personal residence is subject to taxation. Limited relief from recognition of gain is provided in the form of the **§ 121 exclusion.** Under this provision, a taxpayer can exclude up to $250,000 of realized gain on the sale.[81]

REQUIREMENTS FOR EXCLUSION TREATMENT

At the date of the sale, the residence must have been *owned* and *used* by the taxpayer as the principal residence for at least two years during the five-year period ending on the date of the sale.[82]

EXAMPLE 60   Alice sells her principal residence on September 18, 1998. She had purchased it on July 5, 1996, and lived in it since then. The sale of Alice's residence qualifies for the § 121 exclusion. ▼

The five-year window enables the taxpayer to qualify for the § 121 exclusion even though the property is not his or her principal residence at the date of the sale.

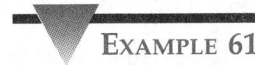

EXAMPLE 61   Benjamin sells his principal residence on August 16, 1998. He had purchased it on April 1, 1990, and lived in it until July 1, 1997, when he converted it to rental property. Even though the property is rental property on August 16, 1998, rather than Benjamin's principal residence, the sale qualifies for the § 121 exclusion. During the five-year period from August 16, 1993, to August 16, 1998, Benjamin owned and used the property as his principal residence for at least two years. ▼

Taxpayers might be tempted to make liberal use of the § 121 exclusion as a means of speculating when the price of residential housing is rising. Without any time restriction on its use, § 121 would permit the exclusion of realized gain on multiple sales of principal residences. The Code curbs this approach by denying the application of the § 121 exclusion to sales occurring within two years of its last use.[83]

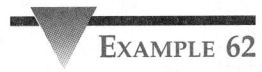

EXAMPLE 62   After Seth sells his principal residence (the first residence) in June 1997 for $150,000 (realized gain of $60,000), he buys and sells the following (all of which qualify as principal residences):

	Date of Purchase	Date of Sale	Amount Involved
Second residence	July 1997		$160,000
Second residence		April 1998	180,000
Third residence	May 1998		200,000

Because multiple sales have taken place within a period of two years, § 121 does not apply to the sale of the second residence. Thus, the realized gain of $20,000 [$180,000 (selling price) − $160,000 (purchase price)] must be recognized. ▼

---

[80]§ 165(c).
[81]§ 121(b).

[82]§ 121(a).
[83]§ 121(b)(3).

The two-year ownership and use requirement and the "only once every two years" provision could create a hardship for taxpayers in certain situations that are beyond their control. Thus, under the following special circumstances, the requirements are waived:[84]

- Change in place of employment.
- Health.
- To the extent provided in the Regulations, other unforeseen circumstances.

EXAMPLE 63

Assume the same facts as in the previous example, except that in March 1998, Seth's employer transfers him to a job in another state. Thus, the sale of the second residence and the purchase of the third residence were due to the relocation of employment. Consequently, the § 121 exclusion is partially available on the sale of the second residence. ▼

The full amount of the § 121 exclusion is not available under this relief provision, however.[85] See the discussion under Relief Provision later in this chapter for the amount of the exclusion.

CALCULATION OF THE AMOUNT OF THE EXCLUSION

General Provisions. The amount of the available § 121 exclusion on the sale of a principal residence is $250,000.[86] If the realized gain does not exceed $250,000, there is no recognized gain.

Realized gain is calculated in the normal manner. The *amount realized* is the selling price less the selling expenses, which include items such as the cost of advertising the property for sale, real estate broker commissions, legal fees in connection with the sale, and loan placement fees paid by the taxpayer as a condition of arranging financing for the buyer. Repairs and maintenance made by the seller to aid in selling the property are treated neither as selling expenses nor as adjustments to the taxpayer's adjusted basis for the residence.

EXAMPLE 64

Mandy, who is single, sells her personal residence (adjusted basis of $130,000) for $290,000. She has owned and lived in the residence for three years. Her selling expenses are $18,000. Three weeks prior to the sale, Mandy paid a carpenter and a painter $1,000 to make some repairs and paint the two bathrooms. Her recognized gain is calculated as follows:

Amount realized ($290,000 − $18,000)	$ 272,000
Adjusted basis	(130,000)
Realized gain	$ 142,000
§ 121 exclusion	(142,000)
Recognized gain	$ –0–

Since the available § 121 exclusion of $250,000 exceeds Mandy's realized gain of $142,000, her recognized gain is $0. ▼

---

[84] § 121(c).
[85] § 121(c)(1).

[86] § 121(b)(1).

EXAMPLE 65

Assume the same facts as in the previous example, except that the selling price is $490,000.

Amount realized ($490,000 – $18,000)	$ 472,000
Adjusted basis	(130,000)
Realized gain	$ 342,000
§ 121 exclusion	(250,000)
Recognized gain	$ 92,000

Since the realized gain of $342,000 exceeds the § 121 exclusion amount of $250,000, Mandy's recognized gain is $92,000 ($342,000 – $250,000). ▼

Effect on Married Couples. If a married couple files a joint return, the $250,000 amount is increased to $500,000 if the following requirements are satisfied:[87]

- Either spouse meets the at-least-two-years *ownership* requirement.
- Both spouses meet the at-least-two-years *use* requirement.
- Neither spouse is ineligible for the § 121 exclusion on the sale of the current principal residence because of the sale of another principal residence within the prior two years.

EXAMPLE 66

Margaret sells her personal residence (adjusted basis of $150,000) for $650,000. She has owned and lived in the residence for six years. Her selling expenses are $40,000. Margaret is married to Ted, and they file a joint return. Ted has lived in the residence since they were married two and one-half years ago.

Amount realized ($650,000 – $40,000)	$ 610,000
Adjusted basis	(150,000)
Realized gain	$ 460,000
§ 121 exclusion	(460,000)
Recognized gain	$ –0–

Since the realized gain of $460,000 is less than the available § 121 exclusion amount of $500,000, no gain is recognized. ▼

If the taxpayer and spouse each own a qualified principal residence, they can separately qualify for the $250,000 exclusion on the sale of their own residences even if they file a joint return.[88]

EXAMPLE 67

Anne and Samuel are married on August 1, 1998. They each own a residence that is eligible for the § 121 exclusion. Anne sells her residence on September 7, 1998, and Samuel sells his residence on October 9, 1998. Relevant data on the sales are as follows:

	Anne	Samuel
Selling price	$320,000	$425,000
Selling expenses	20,000	25,000
Adjusted basis	190,000	110,000

Anne and Samuel intend to rent a condo in Florida or Arizona and to travel. The recognized gain of each is calculated as follows:

---

[87]§ 121(b)(2).

[88]§ 121(b)(1).

	Anne	Samuel
Amount realized	$ 300,000	$ 400,000
Adjusted basis	(190,000)	(110,000)
Realized gain	$ 110,000	$ 290,000
§ 121 exclusion	(110,000)	(250,000)
Recognized gain	$ –0–	$ 40,000

Anne has no recognized gain because the available $250,000 exclusion amount exceeds her realized gain of $110,000. Samuel's recognized gain is $40,000 as his realized gain of $290,000 exceeds the $250,000 exclusion amount. The recognized gains calculated above result regardless of whether Anne and Samuel file a joint return or separate returns. ▼

Relief Provision.   As discussed earlier in Requirements for Exclusion Treatment, partial § 121 exclusion treatment may be available when all the statutory requirements are not satisfied. Under the relief provision, the realized gain (limited to the § 121 exclusion amount) is multiplied by a fraction, the numerator of which is the number of qualifying months and the denominator of which is 24 months. The resulting amount is the excluded gain.[89]

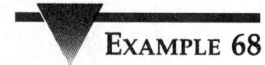

EXAMPLE 68

Rich and Audrey live in Chicago and sell their personal residence on October 1, 1997. The realized gain of $225,000 is excluded under § 121. They purchase another personal residence for $300,000 on October 2, 1997. Audrey's employer transfers her to the Denver office in August 1998. Rich and Audrey sell their Chicago residence on August 2, 1998, and purchase a residence in Denver shortly thereafter. The realized gain on the sale is $120,000.

The $225,000 gain on the first Chicago residence is excluded under § 121. The sale of the second Chicago residence is within the two-year window of the prior sale, but because it resulted from a change in employment, Rich and Audrey can qualify for partial § 121 exclusion treatment as follows:

Realized gain	$120,000
§ 121 exclusion: $\dfrac{10\ \text{months}}{24\ \text{months}} \times \$120{,}000 = \$50{,}000$	(50,000)
Recognized gain	$ 70,000

▼

Basis of New Residence.   As § 121 is an exclusion provision rather than a postponement of gain provision, the basis of a new residence is its cost.[90]

PRINCIPAL RESIDENCE

To be eligible for the § 121 exclusion, the residence must have been owned and used by the taxpayer as the principal residence at least two years during the five-year window (subject to partial exclusion treatment under the relief provision). Whether property is the taxpayer's principal residence ". . . depends upon all of the facts and circumstances in each case."[91]

---

[89]§ 121(c)(1).
[90]§ 1012.

[91]Reg. § 1.1034–1(c)(3).

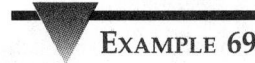

EXAMPLE 69

Mitch graduates from college and moves to Boston, where he is employed. He decides to rent an apartment in Boston because of its proximity to his place of employment. He purchases a beach condo in the Cape Cod area that he occupies most weekends. Mitch does not intend to live at the beach condo except on weekends. The apartment in Boston is his principal residence. ▼

A residence does not have to be a house. For example, a houseboat or a house trailer can qualify.[92]

OTHER NONRECOGNITION PROVISIONS

The typical taxpayer experiences the sale of a personal residence or an involuntary conversion more frequently than the other types of nontaxable exchanges. Several additional nonrecognition provisions that are not as common are treated briefly in the remainder of this chapter.

EXCHANGE OF STOCK FOR PROPERTY—§ 1032

Under § 1032, a corporation does not recognize gain or loss on the receipt of money or other property in exchange for its stock (including treasury stock). In other words, a corporation does not recognize gain or loss when it deals in its own stock. This provision is consistent with the accounting treatment of such transactions.

CERTAIN EXCHANGES OF INSURANCE POLICIES—§ 1035

Under this provision, no gain or loss is recognized from the exchange of certain insurance contracts or policies. The rules relating to exchanges not solely in kind and the basis of the property acquired are the same as under § 1031. Exchanges qualifying for nonrecognition include the following:

- The exchange of life insurance contracts.
- The exchange of a life insurance contract for an endowment or annuity contract.
- The exchange of an endowment contract for another endowment contract that provides for regular payments beginning at a date not later than the date payments would have begun under the contract exchanged.
- The exchange of an endowment contract for an annuity contract.
- The exchange of annuity contracts.

EXCHANGE OF STOCK FOR STOCK OF THE SAME CORPORATION—§ 1036

A shareholder does not recognize gain or loss on the exchange of common stock solely for common stock in the same corporation or from the exchange of preferred stock for preferred stock in the same corporation. Exchanges between individual shareholders as well as between a shareholder and the corporation are included. The rules relating to exchanges not solely in kind and the basis of the property acquired are the same as under § 1031. For example, a nonrecognition exchange occurs when common stock with different rights, such as voting for nonvoting, is

---

[92]Reg. § 1.1034–1(c)(3)(i).

exchanged. A shareholder usually recognizes gain or loss from the exchange of common for preferred or preferred for common even though the stock exchanged is in the same corporation.

CERTAIN REACQUISITIONS OF REAL PROPERTY—§ 1038

Under this provision, no loss is recognized from the repossession of real property sold on an installment basis. Gain is recognized to a limited extent.

TRANSFERS OF PROPERTY BETWEEN SPOUSES OR INCIDENT TO DIVORCE—§ 1041

Section 1041 provides that transfers of property *between spouses or former spouses incident to divorce* are nontaxable transactions. Therefore, the basis to the recipient is a carryover basis. To be treated as incident to the divorce, the transfer must be related to the cessation of marriage or occur within one year after the date on which the marriage ceases.

Section 1041 also provides for nontaxable exchange treatment on property transfers *between spouses during marriage*. The basis to the recipient spouse is a carryover basis.

ETHICAL CONSIDERATIONS

Incident to Divorce or Not?

Randy and Judy are divorced in late 1997 after being married for 10 years. Several years ago they purchased a beach lot for $80,000. They planned to construct a beach house where they "could get away from it all" on weekends and holidays.

Eleven months after the divorce, Randy transfers his interest in the beach lot to Judy for $60,000 (i.e., 50 percent of the fair market value of $120,000). Since Randy is in a lower tax bracket than Judy (15 percent for Randy and 36 percent for Judy), they treat the sales transaction as not incident to the divorce. Randy recognizes a gain of $20,000 ($60,000 – $40,000), and Judy's adjusted basis is $100,000 ($40,000 + $60,000).

Evaluate Randy and Judy's treatment of the sales transaction.

ROLLOVERS INTO SPECIALIZED SMALL BUSINESS INVESTMENT COMPANIES—§ 1044

A postponement opportunity is available for some sellers of publicly traded securities. If the amount realized is reinvested in the common stock or partnership interest of a specialized small business investment company (SSBIC), the realized gain is not recognized. Any amount not reinvested will trigger the recognition of the realized gain on the sale to the extent of the deficiency. The taxpayer must reinvest the proceeds within 60 days of the date of sale in order to qualify. In calculating the basis of the SSBIC stock, the amount of the purchase price is reduced by the amount of the postponed gain.

Statutory ceilings are imposed on the amount of realized gain that can be postponed for any taxable year as follows:

- Individual taxpayer: Lesser of:
  - $50,000 ($25,000 for married filing separately).
  - $500,000 ($250,000 for married filing separately) reduced by the amount of such nonrecognized gain in prior taxable years.
- Corporate taxpayer: Lesser of:
  - $250,000.
  - $1,000,000 reduced by the amount of such nonrecognized gain in prior taxable years.

Investors *ineligible* for this postponement treatment include partnerships, S corporations, estates, and trusts.

ROLLOVER OF GAIN FROM QUALIFIED SMALL BUSINESS STOCK INTO ANOTHER QUALIFIED SMALL BUSINESS STOCK—§ 1045

Realized gain from the sale of qualified small business stock held for more than six months may be postponed if the taxpayer acquires other qualified small business stock within 60 days. Any amount not reinvested will trigger the recognition of the realized gain on the sale to the extent of the deficiency. In calculating the basis of the acquired qualified small business stock, the amount of the purchase price is reduced by the amount of the postponed gain.

Qualified small business stock is stock of a qualified small business that is acquired by the taxpayer at its original issue in exchange for money or other property (excluding stock) or as compensation for services. A qualified small business is a domestic corporation that satisfies the following requirements:

- The aggregate gross assets prior to the issuance of the small business stock do not exceed $50 million.
- The aggregate gross assets immediately after the issuance of the small business stock do not exceed $50 million.

TAX PLANNING CONSIDERATIONS

5 LEARNING OBJECTIVE
Identify tax planning opportunities related to selected property transactions.

TAX CONSEQUENCES OF ALICE'S PROPOSED TRANSACTION

In Example 1 earlier in the chapter, Alice's tax adviser asked a number of questions in order to advise her on a proposed transaction. Alice provided the following answers:

- Alice inherited the house from her mother. The fair market value of the house at the date of her mother's death, based on the estate tax return, was $200,000. Based on an appraisal, the house is worth $230,000. Alice's mother lived in the house for 48 years. According to the mother's attorney, her adjusted basis for the house was $75,000.
- As a child, Alice lived in the house for 10 years. She has not lived there during the 35 years she has been married.
- The house has been vacant during the seven months that Alice has owned it. She has been trying to decide whether she should sell it for its fair market value or sell it to her nephew for $75,000. Alice has suggested a $75,000 price for the sale to Dan because she believes this is the amount at which she will have no gain or loss.
- Alice intends to invest the $75,000 in stock.

You advise Alice that her adjusted basis for the house is the $200,000 fair market value on the date of her mother's death. If Alice sells the house for $230,000 (assuming no selling expenses), she would have a recognized gain of $30,000 ($230,000 amount realized – $200,000 adjusted basis). The house is a capital asset, and her holding period is long term since she inherited the house. Thus, the gain would be classified as a long-term capital gain. If, instead, Alice sells the house to her nephew for $75,000, she will have a part sale and part gift. The realized gain on the sale of $9,783 is recognized.

Amount realized	$ 75,000
Less: Adjusted basis	(65,217)*
Realized gain	$ 9,783
Recognized gain	$ 9,783

*[($75,000/$230,000) × $200,000] = $65,217.

The gain is classified as a long-term capital gain. Alice is then deemed to have made a gift to Dan of $155,000 ($230,000 − $75,000).

With this information, Alice can make an informed selection between the two options.

COST IDENTIFICATION AND DOCUMENTATION CONSIDERATIONS

When multiple assets are acquired in a single transaction, the contract price must be allocated for several reasons. First, some of the assets may be depreciable while others are not. From the different viewpoints of the buyer and the seller, this may produce a tax conflict that needs to be resolved. That is, the seller prefers a high allocation for nondepreciable assets, whereas the purchaser prefers a high allocation for depreciable assets (see Chapter 13). Second, the seller needs to know the amount realized on the sale of the capital assets and the ordinary income assets so that the recognized gains and losses can be classified as capital or ordinary. For example, an allocation to goodwill or to a covenant not to compete (see Chapters 7 and 13) produces different tax consequences to the seller. Third, the buyer needs the adjusted basis of each asset to calculate the realized gain or loss on a subsequent sale or other disposition of each asset.

SELECTION OF PROPERTY FOR MAKING GIFTS

A donor can achieve several tax advantages by making gifts of appreciated property. Income tax on the unrealized gain that would have occurred had the donor sold the property is avoided by the donor. A portion of this amount can be permanently avoided because the donee's adjusted basis is increased by part or all of any gift tax paid by the donor. Even without this increase in basis, the income tax liability on the sale of the property by the donee can be less than the income tax liability that would have resulted from the donor's sale of the property, if the donee is in a lower tax bracket than the donor. In addition, any subsequent appreciation during the time the property is held by the lower tax bracket donee results in a tax savings on the sale or other disposition of the property. Such gifts of appreciated property can be an effective tool in family tax planning.

Taxpayers should generally not make gifts of depreciated property (property that, if sold, would produce a realized loss) because the donor does not receive an income tax deduction for the unrealized loss element. In addition, the donee receives no benefit from this unrealized loss upon the subsequent sale of the property because of the loss basis rule. The loss basis rule provides that the donee's basis is the lower of the donor's basis or fair market value at the date of the gift. If the donor anticipates that the donee will sell the property upon receiving it, the donor should sell the property and take the loss deduction, assuming the loss is deductible. The donor can then give the proceeds from the sale to the donee.

SELECTION OF PROPERTY FOR MAKING BEQUESTS

A decedent's will should generally make bequests of appreciated property. Doing so enables both the decedent and the heir to avoid income tax on the unrealized gain because the recipient takes the fair market value as his or her basis.

Taxpayers generally should not make bequests of depreciated property (property that, if sold, would produce a realized loss) because the decedent does not receive an income tax deduction for the unrealized loss element. In addition, the heir will receive no benefit from this unrealized loss upon the subsequent sale of the property.

EXAMPLE 70

On the date of her death, Marta owned land held for investment purposes. The land had an adjusted basis of $600,000 and a fair market value of $100,000. If Marta had sold the property before her death, the recognized loss would have been $500,000. If Roger inherits the property and later sells it for $60,000, the recognized loss is $40,000 (the decline in value since Marta's death). In addition, regardless of the period of time Roger holds the property, the holding period is long term (see Chapter 13). ▼

From an income tax perspective, it is preferable to transfer appreciated property as a bequest rather than as a gift. This results because inherited property receives a step-up in basis, whereas property received by gift has a carryover basis to the donee. However, in making this decision, the estate tax consequences of the bequest should also be weighed against the gift tax consequences of the gift.

DISALLOWED LOSSES

Section 267 Disallowed Losses.   Taxpayers should be aware of the desirability of avoiding transactions that activate the loss disallowance provisions for related parties. This is so even in light of the provision that permits the related-party buyer to offset his or her realized gain by the related-party seller's disallowed loss. Even with this offset, several inequities exist. First, the tax benefit associated with the disallowed loss ultimately is realized by the wrong party (the related-party buyer rather than the related-party seller). Second, the tax benefit of this offset to the related-party buyer does not occur until the buyer disposes of the property. Therefore, the longer the time period between the purchase and disposition of the property by the related-party buyer, the less the economic benefit. Third, if the property does not appreciate to at least its adjusted basis to the related-party seller during the time period the related-party buyer holds it, part or all of the disallowed loss is permanently lost. Fourth, since the right of offset is available only to the original transferee (the related-party buyer), all of the disallowed loss is permanently lost if the original transferee subsequently transfers the property by gift or bequest.

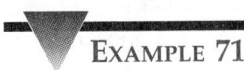

EXAMPLE 71

Tim sells property with an adjusted basis of $35,000 to Wes, his brother, for $25,000, the fair market value of the property. The $10,000 realized loss to Tim is disallowed by § 267. If Wes subsequently sells the property to an unrelated party for $37,000, he has a recognized gain of $2,000 (realized gain of $12,000 reduced by disallowed loss of $10,000). Therefore, from the perspective of the family unit, the original $10,000 realized loss ultimately is recognized. However, if Wes sells the property for $29,000, he has a recognized gain of $0 (realized gain of $4,000 reduced by disallowed loss of $4,000 necessary to offset the realized gain). From the perspective of the family unit, $6,000 of the realized loss of $10,000 is permanently wasted ($10,000 realized loss – $4,000 offset permitted). ▼

Wash Sales.   The wash sales provisions can be avoided if the security is replaced within the statutory time period with a similar rather than a substantially identical security. For example, the sale of Bethlehem Steel common stock and a purchase of Inland Steel common stock is not treated as a wash sale. Such a procedure can enable the taxpayer to use an unrealized capital loss to offset a recognized capital gain. The taxpayer can sell the security before the end of the taxable year, offset the recognized capital loss against the capital gain, and invest the sales proceeds in a similar security.

Because the wash sales provisions do not apply to gains, it may be desirable to engage in a wash sale before the end of the taxable year. This recognized capital gain may be used to offset capital losses or capital loss carryovers from prior years. Since the basis of the replacement stock or securities will be the purchase price, the taxpayer in effect has exchanged a capital gain for an increased basis for the stock or securities.

LIKE–KIND EXCHANGES

Since application of the like-kind exchange provisions is mandatory rather than elective, in certain instances it may be preferable to avoid qualifying for § 1031 nonrecognition. If the like-kind exchange provisions do not apply, the end result may be the recognition of capital gain in exchange for a higher basis in the newly acquired asset. Also, the immediate recognition of gain may be preferable in certain situations. Examples where immediate recognition is beneficial include the following:

- Taxpayer has unused net operating loss carryovers.
- Taxpayer has unused general business credit carryovers.
- Taxpayer has suspended or current passive activity losses.
- Taxpayer expects his or her effective tax rate to increase in the future.

EXAMPLE 72

Alicia disposes of a machine (used in her business) with an adjusted basis of $3,000 for $4,000. She also acquires a new business machine for $9,000. If § 1031 applies, the $1,000 realized gain is not recognized, and the basis of the new machine is reduced by $1,000 (from $9,000 to $8,000). If § 1031 does not apply, a $1,000 gain is recognized and may receive favorable capital gain treatment to the extent that the gain is not recognized as ordinary income due to the depreciation recapture provisions (see Chapter 13). In addition, the basis for depreciation on the new machine is $9,000 rather than $8,000 since there is no unrecognized gain. ▼

The application of § 1031 nonrecognition treatment should also be avoided when the adjusted basis of the property being disposed of exceeds the fair market value.

EXAMPLE 73

Assume the same facts as in the previous example, except that the fair market value of the machine is $2,500. If § 1031 applies, the $500 realized loss is not recognized. To recognize the loss, Alicia should sell the old machine and purchase the new one. The purchase and sale transactions should be with different taxpayers. ▼

On the other hand, the like-kind exchange procedure can be utilized to control the amount of recognized gain.

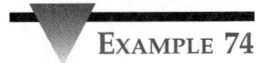

EXAMPLE 74

Rex has property with an adjusted basis of $40,000 and a fair market value of $100,000. Sandra wants to buy Rex's property, but Rex wants to limit the amount of recognized gain on the proposed transaction. Sandra acquires other like-kind property (from an outside party) for $80,000. She then exchanges this property and $20,000 cash for Rex's property. Rex has a realized gain of $60,000 ($100,000 amount realized – $40,000 adjusted basis). His recognized gain is only $20,000, the lower of the $20,000 boot received or the $60,000 realized gain. Rex's basis for the like-kind property is $40,000 ($40,000 adjusted basis + $20,000 gain recognized – $20,000 boot received). If Rex had sold the property to Sandra for its fair market value of $100,000, the result would have been a $60,000 recognized gain ($100,000 amount realized – $40,000 adjusted basis) to him. It is permissible for Rex to identify the like-kind property that he wants Sandra to purchase.[93] ▼

INVOLUNTARY CONVERSIONS

In certain cases, a taxpayer may prefer to recognize gain from an involuntary conversion. Keep in mind that § 1033, unlike § 1031 (dealing with like-kind exchanges), generally is an elective provision.

EXAMPLE 75

Ahmad has a $40,000 realized gain from the involuntary conversion of an office building. He reinvests the entire proceeds of $450,000 in a new office building. He does not elect to postpone gain under § 1033, however, because of an expiring net operating loss carryover that is offset against the gain. Therefore, none of the realized gain of $40,000 is postponed. By not electing § 1033 postponement, Ahmad's basis in the replacement property is the property's cost of $450,000 rather than $410,000 ($450,000 reduced by the $40,000 realized gain). ▼

SALE OF A PRINCIPAL RESIDENCE

Election. The § 121 exclusion automatically applies if the taxpayer is eligible. That is, the taxpayer does not have to make an election. However, if § 121 exclusion treatment is not wanted on an otherwise eligible sale, the taxpayer may elect to avoid the § 121 exclusion.[94]

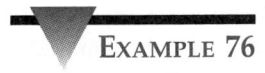

EXAMPLE 76

George owns two personal residences that satisfy the two-year ownership and use test with respect to the five-year window. The Elm Street residence has appreciated by $25,000, and the Maple Street residence has appreciated by $230,000. He intends to sell both of them and move into rental property. He sells the Elm Street residence in December 1998 and expects to sell the Maple Street residence early next year.

Unless George elects not to apply the § 121 exclusion to the sale of the Elm Street residence, he will exclude the $25,000 realized gain on that residence in 1998. In 1999, however, he will have a recognized gain of $230,000 on the sale of the Maple Street residence.

By making the election, George will report a recognized gain of $25,000 on the sale of the Elm Street residence in 1998. But by using the § 121 exclusion in 1999, he will eliminate the recognized gain of $230,000 on the sale of the Maple Street residence. ▼

Negative Effect of Renting or Using as a Home Office. The residence does not have to be the taxpayer's principal residence at the date of sale. During part of the five-year window, it could have been rental property (e.g., either a vacation

---

[93]*Franklin B. Biggs*, 69 T.C. 905 (1978); Rev.Rul. 57–244, 1957–1 C.B. 247; Rev.Rul. 73–476, 1973–2 C.B. 300; *Starker v. U.S.*, 79–2 USTC ¶9541, 44 AFTR2d 79–5525, 602 F.2d 1341 (CA–9, 1979); and *Baird Publishing Co.*, 39 T.C. 608 (1962).

[94]§ 121(f).

home or entirely rental property). In addition, the taxpayer may have used part of the principal residence as a qualifying office in the home.

In either the rental or the home office setting, the taxpayer will have deducted depreciation. Any realized gain on the sale that is attributable to depreciation is not eligible for the § 121 exclusion.[95]

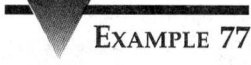

EXAMPLE 77

On December 5, 1998, Amanda sells her principal residence, which qualifies for the § 121 exclusion. Her realized gain is $190,000. From January through November 1998, she rented the residence to a college student. For this period, she deducted MACRS cost recovery of $7,000. Without the depreciation provision, Amanda could exclude the $190,000 realized gain. However, the depreciation taken requires her to recognize $7,000 of the realized gain. ▼

Qualification for § 121 Exclusion.   The key requirement is for the taxpayer to have *owned* and *used* the property as a principal residence for at least two years during the five-year window. As taxpayers advance in age, they quite frequently make decisions such as the following:

- Sell the principal residence and buy a smaller residence or rent the principal residence.
- Sell vacation homes they own.
- Sell homes they are holding as rental property.

There could be substantial appreciation on each of the above. Clearly, the sale of the principal residence is eligible for the § 121 exclusion. Less clear, however, is that proper planning may make it possible to qualify for the exclusion as to the vacation home or the rental property. Although this strategy may require taxpayers to be flexible about where they live, it can result in substantial tax savings.

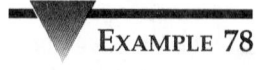

EXAMPLE 78

Thelma and David are approaching retirement. They have substantial appreciation on their principal residence and on a house they own at the beach (about two hours away). After retirement, they plan to move to Florida. They have owned and lived in the principal residence for 28 years and have owned the beach house for 9 years. If they sell their principal residence, it qualifies for the § 121 exclusion. At retirement, they could move into their beach house for two years and make it eligible for the exclusion. If the beach house were not so far away, they could sell the principal residence now and move into the beach house to start the running of the two-year use period. Note that any realized gain on the beach house attributable to depreciation is not eligible for the § 121 exclusion. ▼

Record Keeping.   The taxpayer is required to report the details of the sale of the residence on the tax return (Form 2119, Sale of Your Home) for the taxable year in which the gain is realized. This is the case even if the entire amount of the gain is excluded under § 121. Most, if not all, of the data required should be available on the closing statement associated with the sale.

The taxpayer needs to maintain records on the adjusted basis of the residence including the original cost, any capital improvements, and any deductions that decrease basis (e.g., depreciation on a home office or rental use).

This chapter has covered certain situations in which realized gains or losses are not recognized (nontaxable exchanges). Chapter 13 is concerned with the *classification* of recognized gains and losses. That is, if a gain or loss is recognized, is it an ordinary or capital gain or loss? Chapter 13 discusses the tax consequences of capital gains and losses.

---

[95]§ 121(d)(6).

KEY TERMS

Adjusted basis, 12–5

Amount realized, 12–3

Boot, 12–28

Fair market value, 12–4

Goodwill, 12–10

Holding period, 12–14

Involuntary conversion, 12–33

Like-kind exchange, 12–26

Nontaxable exchange, 12–23

Personal residence, 12–39

Realized gain, 12–3

Realized loss, 12–3

Recognized gain, 12–7

Recognized loss, 12–7

Recovery of capital doctrine, 12–8

Section 121 exclusion, 12–39

Wash sale, 12–19

PROBLEM MATERIALS

DISCUSSION QUESTIONS

1. Ivan invests in land and Grace invests in taxable bonds. The land appreciates by $5,000 each year, and the bonds earn interest of $5,000 each year. After holding the land and bonds for five years, Ivan and Grace sell them. There is a $25,000 realized gain on the sale of the land and no realized gain or loss on the sale of the bonds. Are the tax consequences to Ivan and Grace the same for each of the five years? Explain.

2. Carol and Dave each purchase 100 shares of stock of Burgundy, Inc., a publicly owned corporation, in July for $10,000 each. Carol sells her stock on December 31 for $14,000. Since Burgundy's stock is listed on a national exchange, Dave is able to ascertain that his shares are worth $14,000 on December 31. Does the tax law treat the appreciation in value of the stock differently for Carol and Dave? Explain.

3. Tom is negotiating to buy some land. Under the first option, Tom will give Sandra $70,000 and assume her mortgage on the land for $30,000. Under the second option, Tom will give Sandra $100,000, and she will immediately pay off the mortgage. Tom would like for his basis for the land to be as high as possible. Given this objective, which option should Tom select?

4. The taxpayer owns land and a building with an adjusted basis of $75,000 and a fair market value of $240,000. The property is subject to a mortgage of $360,000. Since the taxpayer is in arrears on the mortgage payments, the creditor is willing to accept the property in return for canceling the amount of the mortgage.
   a. How can the adjusted basis of the property be less than the amount of the mortgage?
   b. If the creditor's offer is accepted, what are the effects on the amount realized, the adjusted basis, and the realized gain or loss?
   c. Does it matter in (b) if the mortgage is recourse or nonrecourse?

5. On August 16, 1998, Todd acquires land and a building for $300,000 to use in his sole proprietorship. Of the purchase price, $200,000 is allocated to the building, and $100,000 is allocated to the land. Cost recovery of $1,926 is deducted in 1998 for the building.
   a. What is the adjusted basis for the land and the building at the acquisition date?
   b. What is the adjusted basis for the land and the building at the end of 1998?

6. Abby owns stock in Orange Corporation and Blue Corporation. She receives a $1,000 distribution from both corporations. The instructions from Orange state that the $1,000 is a dividend. The instructions from Blue state that the $1,000 is not a dividend. What could cause the instructions to differ as to the tax consequences?

7. Kara owns two assets that she is considering selling. One has appreciated in value by $3,000, and the other has declined in value by $3,000. Both assets are held for personal use. Kara believes that she should sell both assets in the same taxable year so that the loss of $3,000 can offset the gain of $3,000. Advise Kara regarding the tax consequences.

8. Ron sold a sailboat for a $5,000 loss in the current year because he was diagnosed as having skin cancer. His spouse wants him to sell his Harley Davidson motorcycle because her brother broke his leg while riding his motorcycle. Since Ron no longer has anyone to ride with, he is seriously considering accepting his wife's advice. Because the motorcycle is a classic, Ron has received two offers. Each offer would result in a $5,000 gain. Joe would like to purchase the motorcycle before Christmas, and Jeff would like to purchase it after New Year's. Identify the relevant tax issues Ron faces in making his decision.

9. Lee owns a life insurance policy that will pay $100,000 to Rita, his spouse, on his death. At the date of Lee's death, he had paid total premiums on the policy of $65,000. In accordance with §101(a)(1), Rita excludes the $100,000 of insurance proceeds. Discuss the relationship, if any, between the §101 exclusion and the recovery of capital doctrine.

10. Simon, who is retired, owns Teal, Inc., stock that has declined in value since he purchased it. He has decided to give the stock to his nephew, Fred, who is a high school teacher, or to sell the stock and give the proceeds to Fred. Because nearly all of his wealth is invested in tax-exempt bonds, Simon is in the 15% tax bracket. Fred will use the cash or the proceeds from his sale of the stock to make the down payment on the purchase of a house. Based on a recent conversation, Simon is aware that Fred is in the 28% bracket. Identify the tax issues relevant to Simon in deciding whether to give the stock or the sale proceeds to Fred.

11. Agnes has been diagnosed with a terminal disease. Her nephew, Stan, will graduate from college in May. She has stock worth $50,000 that she intends to give him as a graduation present. Since she may not be alive then, Agnes is considering giving the stock to him now (i.e., four months prior to graduation). If Agnes should die before making the gift, her will stipulates that Stan will receive the stock. Identify the relevant tax issues that Agnes should consider in making her decision.

12. Gary makes a gift of an appreciated building to Carmen. She dies three months later, and Gary inherits the building from her. During the period that Carmen held the building, she deducted depreciation and made a capital expenditure. What effect might these items have on Gary's basis for the inherited building?

13. Immediately before his death in 1998, Kirby sells securities (adjusted basis of $100,000) for their fair market value of $20,000. The sale was not to a related party. The securities were community property, and Kirby is survived by his wife, Zina, who inherits all of his property.
    a. Did Kirby act wisely? Why or why not?
    b. Suppose the figures are reversed (sale for $100,000 of property with an adjusted basis of $20,000). Would the sale be wise? Why or why not?

14. Amos owns a lathe that he uses in his trade or business. The adjusted basis is $40,000. Although the lathe is only two years old, Amos needs to replace it due to advances in technology. He exchanges the lathe and $20,000 in cash for a new lathe worth $50,000. May Amos elect not to treat the transaction as a like-kind exchange so that the realized loss of $10,000 can be recognized?

15. Which of the following qualify as like-kind exchanges under §1031?
    a. Improved for unimproved real estate.
    b. Vending machine (used in business) for inventory.
    c. Rental house for personal residence.
    d. Business equipment for securities.
    e. Warehouse for office building (both used for business).
    f. Truck for computer (both used in business).
    g. Rental house for land (both held for investment).
    h. Ten shares of stock in Blue Corporation for 10 shares of stock in Red Corporation.
    i. Office furniture for office equipment (both used in business).
    j. General partnership interest in Green Partnership for general partnership interest in Brown Partnership.

16. Melissa owns a residential lot held for investment in Spring Creek that has appreciated substantially in value. She is considering exchanging the lot with her father for a residential lot in McComb that she also will hold for investment. Identify the relevant tax issues for Melissa.

17. Ross would like to dispose of some land that he acquired five years ago because he believes that it will not continue to appreciate. Its value has increased by $50,000 during the five-year period. He also intends to sell stock that has declined in value by $50,000 during the eight-month period he has owned it. Ross has four offers to acquire the stock and land:

Buyer number 1:	Exchange land.
Buyer number 2:	Purchase land for cash.
Buyer number 3:	Exchange stock.
Buyer number 4:	Purchase stock for cash.

Identify the tax issues relevant to Ross in disposing of this land and stock.

18. In connection with like-kind exchanges, discuss each of the following:
    a. Realized gain.
    b. Realized loss.
    c. Recognized gain.
    d. Recognized loss.
    e. Postponed gain.
    f. Postponed loss.
    g. Basis of like-kind property received.
    h. Basis of boot received.

19. Beth's retail store building is destroyed by a tornado. She receives insurance proceeds of $200,000, which is the appraised value of the building prior to its destruction. Her adjusted basis in the building is $225,000. What is the maximum amount that Beth can reinvest in another retail store building and still recognize the $25,000 loss?

20. Ed receives severance damages from the state government for a public road built across his property. Under what circumstances can the § 1033 involuntary conversion provision apply to prevent the recognition of gain?

21. Julia owns a shopping mall that she leases to tenants. The shopping mall is destroyed by a tornado. Is the functional use test or the taxpayer use test applied in terms of appropriate replacement property? Explain the differences between the two tests.

22. Rebecca, a calendar year taxpayer, owns an office building that she uses in her business. The building is involuntarily converted on June 15, 1998. On October 5, 1998, Rebecca receives proceeds large enough to produce a realized gain. What is the latest date she can replace the building if the form of the conversion is:
    a. A flood?
    b. A condemnation?
    c. A tornado?

23. Bob is notified by the city public housing authority on October 5, 1998, that his apartment building is going to be condemned as part of an urban renewal project. On October 12, 1998, Carol offers to buy the building from Bob. Bob sells the building to Carol on October 30, 1998. Condemnation occurs on February 1, 1999, and Carol receives the condemnation proceeds from the city. Assume both Bob and Carol are calendar year taxpayers.
    a. What is the earliest date that Bob can dispose of the building and qualify for § 1033 postponement treatment?
    b. Does the sale to Carol qualify as a § 1033 involuntary conversion?
    c. What is the latest date that Carol can acquire qualifying replacement property and qualify for postponement of the realized gain?
    d. What type of property will be qualifying replacement property?

24. A warehouse owned by Martha and used in her business (i.e., to store inventory) is being condemned by the city to provide a right of way for a highway. The warehouse has appreciated by $100,000 based on Martha's estimate of fair market value. In the negotiations, the city is offering $40,000 less than what Martha believes the property is worth. Alan, a real estate broker, has offered to purchase Martha's property for $25,000 more than the city's offer. Martha plans to invest the proceeds she will receive in an office building that she will lease to various tenants. Identify the relevant tax issues for Martha.

25. Samantha, who is age 39, would like to quit her job, sell her house, buy a sailboat, and sail the seven seas. The projected realized loss on the sale of her personal residence is $50,000. Is it possible for Samantha to recognize the loss or to elect to defer the loss?

26. Sandy owns a personal residence that she has lived in since its acquisition. It has appreciated by $90,000 during this period. Now, however, the school board has redrawn the boundaries for the school districts, and her son will have to transfer to a different high school for his senior year. Sandy is considering selling her residence and buying another one that will enable her son to remain in the same high school. Without this reason, she would not sell the house. Identify the relevant tax issues for Sandy.

27. Mort owns a beach house and a cabin in the mountains. He stays in each during different parts of the year. Mort also rents a townhouse in the city where he is employed. If Mort sells both the beach house and the cabin at a gain, how does he decide which of these properties is his principal residence?

PROBLEMS

28. Anne sold her home for $260,000 in 1998. Selling expenses were $15,000. She had purchased it in 1990 for $190,000. During the period of ownership, Anne had:

   • Deducted $50,500 office-in-home expenses, which included $14,500 in depreciation. (Refer to Chapter 8.)

   • Deducted a casualty loss of residential trees destroyed by a hurricane. The total loss was $19,000 (after the $100 floor and the 10%-of-AGI floor), and Anne's insurance company reimbursed her for $13,500. (Refer to Chapter 6.)

   • Paid street paving assessment of $7,000 and added sidewalks for $11,000.

   • Installed an elevator for medical reasons. The total cost was $20,000, and Anne deducted $12,000 as medical expenses. (Refer to Chapter 9.)

   • Received $7,500 from a utility company for an easement to install underground utility lines across the property.

   What is Anne's realized gain?

29. Kareem bought a rental house at the beginning of 1993 for $80,000, of which $10,000 is allocated to the land and $70,000 to the building. Early in 1995, he had a tennis court built in the backyard at a cost of $5,000. Kareem has deducted $32,200 for depreciation on the house and $1,300 for depreciation on the court. At the beginning of 1998, he sells the house and tennis court for $125,000 cash.
   a. What is Kareem's realized gain or loss?
   b. If an original mortgage of $20,000 is still outstanding and the buyer assumes the mortgage in addition to the cash payment, what is Kareem's realized gain or loss?
   c. If the buyer takes the property subject to the mortgage, what is Kareem's realized gain or loss?

30. Gayla owns a building (adjusted basis of $366,500 on January 1, 1998) that she rents to Len who operates a restaurant in the building. The municipal health department closed the restaurant for two months during 1998 because of health code violations. Under MACRS, the cost recovery deduction for 1998 would be $12,000. However, Gayla deducted cost recovery only for the 10 months the restaurant was open since she waived the rent income during the two-month period the restaurant was closed.

    a. What is the amount of the cost recovery deduction that Gayla should report on her 1998 income tax return?

    b. Calculate the adjusted basis of the building at the end of 1998.

31. Mitch's automobile, which is used exclusively in his business, is stolen. The adjusted basis is $30,000, and the fair market value is $33,000. Mitch's AGI is $50,000.

    a. If Mitch receives insurance proceeds of $33,000, what effect do the theft and the receipt of the insurance proceeds have on the adjusted basis of the automobile?

    b. If the automobile is not insured, what effect do the theft and the absence of insurance have on the adjusted basis of the automobile?

32. Aaron owns stock in Dove Corporation. His adjusted basis for the stock is $57,000. During the year, he receives a distribution from the corporation of $51,000 that is labeled a return of capital (i.e., Dove has no earnings and profits).

    a. Determine the tax consequences to Aaron.

    b. Assume instead that the amount of the distribution is $60,000. Determine the tax consequences to Aaron.

    c. Assume instead in (a) that the $51,000 distribution is labeled a taxable dividend (i.e., Dove has earnings and profits of at least $51,000).

33. Chee purchases Tan, Inc., bonds for $110,000 on January 2, 1998. The face value of the bonds is $100,000, the maturity date is December 31, 2002, and the annual interest rate is 8%. Chee will amortize the premium only if he is required to do so. Chee sells the bonds on July 1, 2000, for $109,000.

    a. Determine the interest income Chee should report for 1998.

    b. Calculate Chee's recognized gain or loss on the sale of the bonds in 2000.

34. Which of the following would definitely result in a recognized gain or loss?

    a. Kay sells her lakeside cabin, which has an adjusted basis of $100,000, for $150,000.

    b. Adam sells his personal residence, which has an adjusted basis of $150,000, for $100,000.

    c. Carl's personal residence is on the site of a proposed airport and is condemned by the city. Carl receives $55,000 for the house, which has an adjusted basis of $65,000.

    d. Olga's land is worth $40,000 at the end of the year. Olga had purchased the land six months earlier for $25,000.

    e. Vera's personal use vehicle is stolen. Her adjusted basis is $22,000. She receives a check from the insurance company for $23,000. Vera has decided that in the future she will use mass transit rather than owning an automobile.

    f. Jerry sells used clothing, adjusted basis of $500, to a thrift store for $50.

35. Hubert's personal residence is condemned as part of an urban renewal project. His adjusted basis for the residence is $200,000. He receives condemnation proceeds of $180,000 and invests the proceeds in stock.

    a. Calculate Hubert's realized and recognized gain or loss.

    b. If the condemnation proceeds are $225,000, what are Hubert's realized and recognized gain or loss?

    c. What are Hubert's realized and recognized gain or loss in (a) if the house was rental property?

36. Walt Barnes is a real estate agent for Governor's Farms, a residential real estate development. Because of his outstanding sales performance, Walt is permitted to buy a lot that normally would sell for $125,000 for $100,000. Walt is the only real estate agent for Governor's Farms who is permitted to do so.

    a. Does Walt have gross income from the transaction?

    b. What is Walt's adjusted basis for the land?

    c. Write a letter to Walt informing him of the tax consequences of his acquisition of the lot. His address is 100 Tower Road, San Diego, CA 92182.

37. Frank purchases 100 shares of Bluebird Corporation stock on June 3, 1998, for $150,000. On August 25, 1998, Frank purchases an additional 50 shares of Bluebird stock for $60,000. According to market quotations, Bluebird stock is selling for $1,100 per share on December 31, 1998. Frank sells 60 shares of Bluebird stock on March 1, 1999, for $51,000.

a. What is the adjusted basis of Frank's Bluebird stock on December 31, 1997?
b. What is Frank's recognized gain or loss from the sale of Bluebird stock on March 1, 1999, assuming the shares sold are from the shares purchased on June 3, 1998?
c. What is Frank's recognized gain or loss from the sale of Bluebird stock on March 1, 1999, assuming Frank cannot adequately identify the shares sold?

38. Randy Morgan purchases Agnes's sole proprietorship for $900,000. The assets of the business are as follows:

Asset	Agnes's Adjusted Basis	FMV
Accounts receivable	$ 70,000	$ 70,000
Inventory	90,000	100,000
Equipment	150,000	160,000
Furniture and fixtures	95,000	130,000
Building	190,000	250,000
Land	25,000	75,000

Randy and Agnes agree that $50,000 of the purchase price is for Agnes's five-year covenant not to compete.
a. Calculate Agnes's realized and recognized gain.
b. Determine Randy's basis for each of the assets.
c. Write a letter to Randy informing him of the tax consequences of the purchase. His address is 300 Riverside Drive, Cincinnati, OH 45207.

39. Diane owns 1,000 shares of Robin, Inc., common stock with an adjusted basis of $100,000. During the year she receives the following distributions associated with the stock:

- $3,000 taxable cash dividend.

- 2% stock dividend in the form of 20 shares of preferred stock. The fair market value of the common stock was $110,000, and the fair market value of the preferred stock was $2,000.

- 5% stock dividend in the form of 50 shares of common stock. The fair market value of the 1,000 shares of common stock was $115,000.

Determine the tax consequences to Diane.

40. Shontelle owns 1,000 shares of Gray Corporation stock with a basis of $15,000 and a fair market value of $20,000. She receives nontaxable stock rights to purchase additional shares. The rights have a fair market value of $2,000.
a. What is the basis of the stock and the basis of the stock rights?
b. What is the holding period for the stock rights?
c. What is the recognized gain or loss if the stock rights are sold for $2,000?
d. What is the recognized gain or loss if the stock rights are allowed to lapse?

41. Rick received various gifts over the years. He has decided to dispose of the following assets that he received as gifts:
a. In 1949, he received land worth $25,000. The donor's adjusted basis was $30,000. Rick sells the land for $87,000 in 1998.
b. In 1955, he received stock in Gold Company. The donor's adjusted basis was $10,000. The fair market value on the date of the gift was $28,000. Rick sells the stock for $40,000 in 1998.
c. In 1961, he received land worth $12,000. The donor's adjusted basis was $25,000. Rick sells the land for $8,000 in 1998.
d. In 1994, he received stock worth $30,000. The donor's adjusted basis was $45,000. Rick sells the stock in 1998 for $39,000.

What is the realized gain or loss from each of the preceding transactions? Assume in each of the gift transactions that no gift tax was paid.

42. Beth received a car from Sam as a gift. Sam paid $18,000 for the car. He had used it for business purposes and had deducted $8,000 for depreciation up to the time he gave the car to Beth. The fair market value of the car is $6,000.
    a. Assuming Beth uses the car for business purposes, what is her basis for depreciation?
    b. If the estimated useful life is two years (from the date of the gift), what is her depreciation deduction for each year? Assume Beth elects the straight-line method.
    c. If Beth sells the car for $900 one year after receiving it, what is her gain or loss?
    d. If Beth sells the car for $6,000 one year after receiving it, what is her gain or loss?

43. On September 18, 1998, Jerry received land and a building from his Uncle Ted as a gift. Uncle Ted's adjusted basis and the fair market value at the date of the gift were as follows:

Asset	Adjusted Basis	FMV
Land	$100,000	$200,000
Building	80,000	100,000

Uncle Ted paid gift tax of $45,000.
    a. Determine Jerry's adjusted basis for the land and building.
    b. Assume instead that the FMV of the land was $90,000 and the FMV of the building was $60,000. Determine Jerry's adjusted basis for the land and building.

44. Ira Cook is planning to make a charitable contribution of Crystal, Inc., stock worth $20,000 to the Boy Scouts. The stock Ira is considering contributing has an adjusted basis of $15,000. A friend has suggested that Ira sell the stock and contribute the $20,000 in proceeds rather than contribute the stock.
    a. Should Ira follow the friend's advice? Why?
    b. Assume the fair market value is only $13,000. In this case, should Ira follow the friend's advice? Why?
    c. Rather than make a charitable contribution to the Boy Scouts, Ira is going to make a gift to Nancy, his niece. Advise Ira regarding (a) and (b).
    d. Write a letter to Ira regarding whether in (a) he should sell the stock and contribute the cash or contribute the stock. He has informed you that he purchased the stock six years ago. Ira's address is 500 Ireland Avenue, De Kalb, IL 60115.

45. Dena inherits property from Mary, her mother. Mary's adjusted basis for the property is $100,000, and the fair market value is $725,000. Six months after Mary's death, the fair market value is $740,000. Dena is the sole beneficiary of Mary's estate.
    a. Can the executor of Mary's estate elect the alternate valuation date?
    b. What is Dena's basis for the property?

46. Earl's estate includes, among other assets, the following available for distribution to Robert, one of Earl's beneficiaries:

Asset	Earl's Adjusted Basis	FMV at Date of Death	FMV at Alternate Valuation Date
Cash	$10,000	$ 10,000	$ 10,000
Stock	40,000	125,000	60,000
Apartment building	60,000	300,000	325,000
Land	75,000	100,000	110,000

The fair market value of the stock six months after Earl's death was $60,000. However, believing that the stock would continue to decline in value, the executor of the estate distributed the stock to Robert one month after Earl's death. Robert immediately sold the stock for $85,000.
    a. Determine Robert's basis for the assets if the primary valuation date and amount apply.
    b. Determine Robert's basis for the assets if the executor elects the alternate valuation date and amount.

47. Larry and Grace live in Arizona, a community property state. They own land (community property) that has an adjusted basis to them of $150,000. When Grace dies, Larry inherits her share of the land. At the date of Grace's death, the fair market value of the land is $200,000. Six months after Grace's death, the land is worth $220,000.
    a. What is Larry's basis for the land?
    b. What would Larry's basis for the land be if he and Grace lived in Virginia, a common law state, and Larry inherited Grace's share?

48. Sheila sells land to Elane, her sister, for $40,000. Six months later Elane gives the land to Jacob, her son. No gift taxes are paid. At the date of the gift, the land is worth $42,000. Jacob sells the land one month later for $43,000.
    a. Assuming Sheila's adjusted basis for the land is $25,000, what are Sheila and Jacob's recognized gain or loss on their respective sales?
    b. Assuming Sheila's adjusted basis for the land is $50,000, what are Sheila and Jacob's recognized gain or loss on their respective sales?

49. Susan owns 100 shares of Drake, Inc., stock with an adjusted basis of $50,000. On December 12, 1998, she sells the 100 shares for their fair market value of $45,000. On January 4, 1999, she purchases 125 shares of Drake stock for $57,500.
    a. What is Susan's realized and recognized gain or loss on the sale of the 100 shares sold on December 12, 1998?
    b. What is Susan's adjusted basis for the 125 shares purchased on January 4, 1999?
    c. How would your answers in (a) and (b) change if Susan purchased only 75 shares for $34,500 on January 4, 1999?
    d. How would your answers in (a) and (b) change if Susan purchased 125 shares on January 15, 1999, instead of January 4, 1999?

50. Kramer sells 150 shares of Lavender, Inc. stock on December 28, 1998, for $75,000. On January 10, 1999, he purchases 100 shares of Lavender, Inc. stock for $80,000.
    a. Assuming Kramer's adjusted basis for the stock sold is $60,000, what is his recognized gain or loss, and what is his basis for the new shares?
    b. Assuming Kramer's adjusted basis for the stock sold is $90,000, what is his recognized gain or loss, and what is his basis for the new shares?
    c. Advise Kramer on how he can avoid any negative tax consequences encountered in (b).

51. James retires from a public accounting firm to enter private practice. He had bought a home two years earlier for $40,000. Upon opening his business, he converts one-fourth of his home into an office. The fair market value of the home on the date of conversion (January 1, 1993) is $75,000. The adjusted basis is $56,000 (ignore land). James lives and works in the home for six years (after converting it to business use) and sells it at the end of the sixth year. He deducted $2,630 of cost recovery using the statutory percentage method.
    a. How much gain or loss is recognized if James sells the property for $44,000?
    b. If he sells the property for $70,000?

52. Surendra's personal residence originally cost $180,000 (ignore land). After living in the house for five years, he converts it to rental property. At the date of conversion, the fair market value of the house is $150,000.
    a. Calculate Surendra's basis for loss for the rental property.
    b. Calculate Surendra's basis for depreciation for the rental property.
    c. Calculate Surendra's basis for gain for the rental property.

53. Kay owns undeveloped land with an adjusted basis of $180,000. She exchanges it for other undeveloped land worth $250,000.
    a. What are Kay's realized and recognized gain or loss?
    b. What is Kay's basis in the undeveloped land she receives?

54. Kareem owns an automobile that he uses exclusively in his business. The adjusted basis is $19,000, and the fair market value is $16,000. Kareem exchanges the car for a car that he will use exclusively in his business.

  a. What are Kareem's realized and recognized gain or loss?
  b. What is his basis in the new car?
  c. What are the tax consequences to Kareem in (a) and (b) if he used the old car and will use the new car exclusively for personal purposes?

55. Tex Wall owns undeveloped land that he is holding for investment. His adjusted basis is $175,000. On October 7, 1998, he exchanges the land with his 23-year-old daughter, Paige, for other undeveloped land that he will hold for investment. The appraised value of Paige's land is $250,000.
  a. Calculate Tex's realized and recognized gain or loss from the exchange with Paige and on a subsequent sale of the land by Tex to Baxter, a real estate broker, for $300,000 on February 15, 1999.
  b. Calculate Tex's realized and recognized gain or loss on the exchange with Paige if Tex does not sell the land received from Paige, but Paige sells the land received from Tex on February 15, 1999. Calculate Tex's basis for the land on October 7, 1998, and on February 15, 1999.
  c. Write a letter to Tex advising him on how he could avoid any recognition of gain associated with the October 7, 1998, exchange prior to his actual sale of the land. His address is The Corral, El Paso, TX 79968.

56. Bonnie owns a personal computer that she uses exclusively in her business. The adjusted basis is $5,000. Bonnie transfers the personal computer and cash of $7,000 to Don for a laser printer worth $16,000 that she will use in her business.
  a. Calculate Bonnie's recognized gain or loss on the exchange.
  b. Calculate Bonnie's basis for the printer.

57. Chee exchanges a light-duty truck used exclusively in his business for a light-duty truck that will be used in his business. The adjusted basis for the old truck is $12,000, and the fair market value of the old truck is $10,000.
  a. Calculate Chee's recognized gain or loss on the exchange.
  b. Calculate Chee's basis for the truck he receives.
  c. How could Chee structure the transaction to produce better tax consequences?

58. Olga owns a machine that she uses in her business. The adjusted basis is $60,000, and the fair market value is $95,000. She exchanges it for another machine worth $70,000. Olga also receives stock worth $25,000.
  a. Calculate Olga's realized and recognized gain or loss on the exchange.
  b. Calculate Olga's basis for the new machine.
  c. Calculate Olga's basis for the stock she received.

59. Ed owns investment land with an adjusted basis of $35,000. Polly has offered to purchase the land from Ed for $175,000 for use in a real estate development. The amount offered by Polly is $10,000 in excess of what Ed perceives as the fair market value of the land. Ed would like to dispose of the land to Polly but does not want to incur the tax liability that would result. He identifies an office building with a fair market value of $175,000 that he would like to acquire. Polly purchases the office building and then exchanges the office building for Ed's land.
  a. Calculate Ed's realized and recognized gain on the exchange and his basis for the office building.
  b. Calculate Polly's realized and recognized gain on the exchange and her basis in the land.

60. What is the basis of the new property in each of the following exchanges?
  a. Apartment building held for investment (adjusted basis $150,000) for office building to be held for investment (fair market value $200,000).
  b. Land and building used as a barber shop (adjusted basis $30,000) for land and building used as a grocery store (fair market value $350,000).
  c. Office building (adjusted basis $30,000) for bulldozer (fair market value $42,000), both held for business use.
  d. IBM common stock (adjusted basis $14,000) for Exxon common stock (fair market value $18,000).

e. Rental house (adjusted basis $90,000) for mountain cabin to be held for personal use (fair market value $115,000).

61. Norm owns Machine A, which he uses in his business. The adjusted basis of Machine A is $12,000, and the fair market value is $18,000. Norm is considering two options for the disposal of Machine A. Under the first option, Norm will transfer Machine A and $3,000 cash to Joan, a dealer, in exchange for Machine B, which has a fair market value of $21,000. Under the second option, Norm will sell Machine A for $18,000 to Tim, who is a dealer. Norm will then purchase Machine B from Joan for $21,000. Machine A and Machine B qualify as like-kind property.
   a. Calculate Norm's recognized gain or loss and the basis for Machine B under the first option.
   b. Calculate Norm's recognized gain or loss and the basis for Machine B under the second option.
   c. Advise Norm on which option he should select.

62. Gus exchanges real estate held for investment plus stock for real estate to be held for investment. The stock transferred has an adjusted basis of $15,000 and a fair market value of $10,000. The real estate transferred has an adjusted basis of $15,000 and a fair market value of $45,000. The real estate acquired has a fair market value of $55,000.
   a. What is Gus's realized gain or loss?
   b. His recognized gain or loss?
   c. The basis of the newly acquired real estate?

63. Agnes exchanges a warehouse and the related land with Damon for an office building and the related land. Agnes's adjusted basis for her warehouse and land is $420,000. The fair market value of Damon's office building and land is $410,000. Agnes's property has a $90,000 mortgage that Damon assumes.
   a. Calculate Agnes's realized and recognized gain or loss.
   b. Calculate Agnes's adjusted basis for the office building and land received.
   c. As an alternative, Damon has proposed that rather than assuming the mortgage, he will transfer cash of $90,000 to Agnes. Agnes would use the cash to pay off the mortgage. Advise Agnes on whether this alternative would be beneficial to her from a tax perspective.

64. Determine the realized, recognized, and postponed gain or loss and the new basis for each of the following like-kind exchanges:

	Adjusted Basis of Old Asset	Boot Given	Fair Market Value of New Asset	Boot Received
a.	$ 7,000	$ –0–	$12,000	$4,000
b.	14,000	2,000	15,000	–0–
c.	3,000	7,000	8,000	500
d.	22,000	–0–	32,000	–0–
e.	10,000	–0–	11,000	1,000
f.	10,000	–0–	8,000	–0–

65. Shontelle owns an apartment house that has an adjusted basis of $1,100,000 but is subject to a mortgage of $250,000. She transfers the apartment house to Dave and receives from him $125,000 in cash and an office building with a fair market value of $1,125,000 at the time of the exchange. Dave assumes the $250,000 mortgage on the apartment house.
   a. What is Shontelle's realized gain or loss?
   b. Her recognized gain or loss?
   c. The basis of the newly acquired office building?

66. Carmen's office building, which has an adjusted basis of $200,000, is destroyed by a tornado. Since Carmen's business has excess office space, she decides not to replace the office building, but instead to contribute the proceeds to the working capital of her business.

a. If the insurance proceeds are $225,000, what is Carmen's recognized gain or loss?

b. If the insurance proceeds are $180,000, what is Carmen's recognized gain or loss?

67. Albert owns 100 acres of land on which he grows spruce Christmas trees. His adjusted basis for the land is $100,000. He receives condemnation proceeds of $10,000 when the city's new beltway takes 5 acres along the eastern boundary of his property. He also receives a severance award of $6,000 associated with the possible harmful effects of exhaust fumes on his Christmas trees. Albert invests the $16,000 in a growth mutual fund.

a. Determine the tax consequences to Albert of the condemnation proceeds.

b. Determine the tax consequences to Albert of the severance award.

68. For each of the following involuntary conversions, indicate whether the property acquired qualifies as replacement property:

a. Frank owns a shopping mall that is destroyed by a tornado. The space in the mall was rented to various tenants. Frank uses the insurance proceeds to build a shopping mall in a neighboring community where no property has been damaged by tornadoes.

b. Ivan owns a warehouse that he uses in his business. The warehouse is destroyed by fire. Due to economic conditions in the area, Ivan decides not to rebuild the warehouse. Instead, he uses the insurance proceeds to build a warehouse to be used in his business in another state.

c. Ridge's personal residence is condemned as part of a local government project to widen the highway from two lanes to four lanes. He uses the condemnation proceeds to purchase another personal residence.

d. Juanita owns a building that she uses in her retail business. The building is destroyed by a hurricane. Due to an economic downturn in the area caused by the closing of a military base, she decides to rent space for her retail outlet rather than to replace the building. She uses the insurance proceeds to buy a four-unit apartment building in another city. A realtor in that city will handle the rental of the apartments for her.

e. Susan and Rick's personal residence is destroyed by a tornado. Since they would like to travel, they decide not to acquire a replacement residence. Instead, they invest the insurance proceeds in a duplex that they rent to tenants.

69. The building that houses LaToya's designer clothing store is destroyed in a mud slide associated with a flood on June 27, 1998. LaToya had anticipated the flood and moved her inventory, furniture, and fixtures to a warehouse outside the floodplain on June 20, 1998. Her adjusted basis for the building is $150,000, and she receives insurance proceeds of $160,000 on July 15, 1998. LaToya intends to purchase another building for her store, but would like to have time to locate one in a safer location. Her taxable year ends on June 30.

a. What are the earliest and latest dates that LaToya can make a qualified replacement?

b. Assuming LaToya makes a qualified replacement costing $160,000, what are her realized gain, recognized gain, and basis for the replacement property?

c. What are the earliest and latest dates that LaToya can make a qualified replacement if the form of the involuntary conversion is a condemnation by a governmental authority? She was officially notified of the pending condemnation on June 1, 1998.

70. Carlos's warehouse, which has an adjusted basis of $325,000 and a fair market value of $490,000, is condemned by an agency of the Federal government to make way for a highway interchange. The initial condemnation offer is $450,000. After substantial negotiations, the agency agrees to transfer to Carlos a surplus warehouse that he believes is worth $490,000.

a. What are the recognized gain or loss and the basis of the replacement warehouse if Carlos's objective is to recognize as much gain as possible?

b. Advise Carlos regarding what he needs to do by what date in order to achieve his objective.

71. What are the *maximum* postponed gain or loss and the basis for the replacement property for the following involuntary conversions?

	Property	Type of Conversion	Amount Realized	Adjusted Basis	Amount Reinvested
a.	Drugstore (business)	Casualty	$160,000	$130,000	$110,000
b.	Apartments (investment)	Condemned	100,000	125,000	175,000
c.	Grocery store (business)	Casualty	400,000	300,000	450,000
d.	Residence (personal)	Casualty	16,000	18,000	17,000
e.	Vacant lot (investment)	Condemned	240,000	160,000	220,000
f.	Residence (personal)	Casualty	20,000	18,000	19,000
g.	Residence (personal)	Condemned	18,000	20,000	26,000
h.	Apartments (investment)	Condemned	150,000	100,000	200,000

72. Rental property owned by Freda, a calendar year taxpayer, is destroyed by a tornado on January 1, 1998. Freda had originally paid $150,000 for the property, of which $125,000 was allocated to the building and $25,000 was allocated to the land. During the time Freda owned the property, MACRS deductions of $46,250 were taken. MACRS deductions of $57,500 would have been taken, except that Freda chose to forgo deductions of $11,250 one year when her tax return showed a net operating loss. Freda receives insurance proceeds of $60,000 in November 1998. As a result of continuing negotiations with the insurance company, Freda receives additional proceeds of $35,000 in August 1999.
    a. What is Freda's adjusted basis for the property?
    b. What is Freda's realized gain or loss on the involuntary conversion in 1998? In 1999?
    c. What is the latest date that Freda can replace the involuntarily converted property to qualify for § 1033 postponement?
    d. What is the latest date that Freda can replace the involuntarily converted property to qualify for § 1033 postponement if the form of the involuntary conversion is a condemnation?

73. On May 1, 1998, Kay sells her principal residence for $225,000. Kay had purchased the residence on January 2, 1997, for $180,000. During 1996, she had lived in it as a tenant under a lease with an option to buy clause. On May 2, 1998, Kay purchases a new residence for $200,000.
    a. What is Kay's recognized gain? Her basis for the new residence?
    b. Assume instead that Kay purchased her original residence on January 2, 1996, rather than on January 2, 1997. What is Kay's recognized gain? Her basis for the new residence?
    c. What could you recommend to Kay to minimize her recognized gain in (a)?

74. Tina has owned and occupied her personal residence for three years, and it has an adjusted basis of $150,000. In April 1998, she sells the residence for $310,000 (selling expenses are $20,000). On the same day as the sale, Tina purchases another house for $350,000. Because of noisy neighbors, she sells the new house after just nine months. The selling price is $385,000 (selling expenses are $18,000).
    a. What is Tina's recognized gain on the sale of the first residence?
    b. What is Tina's basis for her second residence?
    c. What is Tina's recognized gain on the sale of the second residence?
    d. Assume instead that the sale of the second residence was due to Tina's job transfer to another state. What is her recognized gain on the sale of the second residence?

75. Milton, who is single, listed his personal residence with a realtor on March 3, 1998, at a listed price of $250,000. He rejected several offers in the $200,000 range during the summer. Finally, on August 16, 1998, he and the purchaser signed a contract to sell for $245,000. The sale (i.e., closing) took place on September 7, 1998. The closing statement showed the following disbursements being made:

Realtor's commission	$ 14,000
Appraisal fee	500

Exterminator's certificate	300
Recording fees	400
Mortgage to First Bank	180,000
Cash to seller	49,800

Milton's adjusted basis for the house is $150,000. He had owned and occupied the house for eight years. On October 1, Milton purchases another residence for $210,000.
a. Calculate Milton's recognized gain on the sale.
b. What is Milton's adjusted basis for the new residence?
c. Assume instead that the selling price is $735,000. What is Milton's recognized gain? His adjusted basis for the new residence?

76. What are the realized, recognized, and excluded gain or loss and the new basis in each of the following cases?
a. Susan sells her residence for $390,000. The adjusted basis was $55,000. The selling expenses were $15,000. Repair expenses incurred to get the house ready to sell were $3,000. She did not reinvest in a new residence.
b. Rocky sells his residence for $270,000. The adjusted basis was $120,000. The selling expenses were $9,000. Repair expenses incurred to get the house ready to sell were $6,000. Rocky reinvested $260,000 in a new residence.
c. Veneia sells her residence for $465,000. The adjusted basis was $35,000. The selling expenses were $17,000. Repair expenses incurred to get the house ready to sell were $2,000. She reinvested $400,000 in a new residence.
d. Barry sells his residence for $70,000. The adjusted basis was $65,000. The selling expenses were $6,000. He reinvested $80,000 in a new residence.
e. Carl sells his residence for $100,000 in cash, and his mortgage is assumed by the buyer. The adjusted basis was $80,000; the mortgage, $50,000. The selling expenses were $4,000. Repair expenses incurred to get the house ready to sell were $2,000. He reinvested $120,000 in a new residence.

77. Pedro, age 57, is the sole owner of his principal residence. He has owned and occupied it for 10 years. Maria, his spouse, has also lived there for 10 years. He sells the house for a realized gain of $240,000. Pedro does not intend to acquire a replacement residence.
a. Can Pedro use the § 121 exclusion if he and Maria file a joint return? If so, what are the available amount of the exclusion and the recognized gain?
b. Can Pedro use the § 121 exclusion if he files a separate return? If so, what are the available amount of the exclusion and the recognized gain?
c. Assume instead that the realized gain is $340,000 and a joint return is filed.
d. Assume instead that the realized gain is $340,000 and separate returns are filed.

78. Meg and Walt are going to be married in three months. Meg has owned and lived in her home for 42 years, and Walt has owned and occupied his home for 35 years. They both have listed their homes for sale. They anticipate the sales results will be as follows:

	Meg	Walt
Selling price	$450,000	$190,000
Selling expenses	40,000	19,000
Adjusted basis	75,000	60,000

They intend to purchase a residence in an extended care facility for $400,000. They have come to you for advice regarding the following:
a. What is their recognized gain if they marry before they sell their residences?
b. What is their recognized gain if they marry after they sell their residences?
c. Does it matter whether the new residence is jointly owned or owned only by Meg as Walt would prefer to invest his sales proceeds in the stock market?
d. Should Meg and Walt delay their marriage if they have not yet sold their residences?

79. Nell, Nina, and Nora Sanders, who are sisters, sell their principal residence in which they have lived for the past 20 years. The youngest of the sisters is age 58. The selling

price is $750,000, selling expenses and legal fees are $75,000, and the adjusted basis is $60,000 (the fair market value of the residence when inherited from their parents 20 years ago). Since the sisters are going to live in rental housing, they do not plan to acquire another residence. Nell has contacted you on behalf of the three sisters regarding the tax consequences of the sale.

    a. Write a letter to Nell advising her of the tax consequences and how taxes can be minimized. Nell's address is 100 Oak Avenue, Billings, MT 59101.

    b. Prepare a memo for the tax files.

80. Jeff and Jill are divorced on August 1, 1998. According to the terms of the divorce decree, Jeff's ownership interest in the house is to be transferred to Jill in exchange for the release from marital rights. Before the divorce, the house was separately owned by Jeff. The adjusted basis and the fair market value at the date of the transfer are $175,000 and $200,000, respectively.

    a. Does the transfer of the house produce recognized gain to either Jeff or Jill?

    b. What is the basis of the house to Jill?

    c. If the same transfer was made by Jeff to Jill for $200,000 and was not associated with a divorce, would either Jeff or Jill have recognized gain?

81. Sam, age 63, owns a residence in which he has lived for 20 years. The residence is destroyed by fire on August 8, 1998. The adjusted basis is $170,000, and the fair market value is $350,000. Sam receives insurance proceeds of $350,000 for the residence. He is trying to decide whether to purchase a comparable house. He anticipates that he will retire in two years and will move to a warmer climate where he will rent in case he decides to live in different places.

    a. Advise Sam of the tax consequences of replacing versus not replacing the residence.

    b. Which do you recommend to him?

CUMULATIVE PROBLEMS

82. Lori Ann (age 27) and Albert Welch (age 28) are married and file a joint return. They have one child, Margaret (age 3). Lori Ann's Social Security number is 366–55–2222, Albert's is 555–66–4300, and Margaret's is 555–77–7333. They reside at 400 Aspen Drive, Williamsburg, VA 23185.

Lori Ann is employed as an accountant at the College of William and Mary at an annual salary of $48,000. Albert is an executive with Historic Williamsburg and receives a salary of $40,000 annually. The appropriate amounts for FICA taxes were withheld. For Federal income taxes, $10,250 was withheld by Lori Ann's employer, and $7,000 was withheld by Albert's employer. For state income tax purposes, $1,800 was withheld by Lori Ann's employer, and $1,600 was withheld by Albert's employer.

Items of potential tax significance include the following:

- Albert received $1,900 of interest income on certificates of deposit and $900 of interest income on bonds issued by the City of Norfolk.

- Lori Ann received dividend income of $2,750 on Green, Inc., stock. She received the stock as a gift from her Aunt Jane on January 10, 1997, when it was worth $9,500. Aunt Jane's adjusted basis was $2,000 and she had owned the stock for two months.

- On May 10, 1997, Albert sold land for $22,000 that he had inherited from his father in December 1993. His father's adjusted basis for the land was $12,000, and the fair market value on the date of the father's death was $26,000. Albert sold the land to his sister, Marge.

- On August 5, 1997, Lori Ann sold the Green, Inc., stock for $25,000.

- Lori Ann and Albert received rent income of $1,500 for their mountain getaway, which they rented for one week in December. During the year, they spent 80 days at their mountain home. Expenses associated with the mountain home for the year were as follows:

Property taxes	$1,500
Mortgage interest	1,200
Repairs, maintenance, and insurance	1,400
Utilities	600

They purchased the house in January 1994 for $100,000 with $20,000 being allocable to land.

- Potential itemized deductions, in addition to items already mentioned, were:

Charitable contributions	$1,600
Mortgage interest on residence	3,600
Real property taxes	1,700
Personal property taxes	300
State and local sales taxes	3,000
Medical expenses (less reimbursements)	350

- Albert receives a bonus of $5,000 in January 1998 associated with the outstanding performance of his unit in 1997.

- Lori Ann and Albert made estimated tax payments of $4,000.

Compute their net tax payable or refund due for 1997. If you use tax forms for your computations, you will need Form 1040 and Schedules A, B, and D. Suggested software (if available): *TurboTax*.

 83. Arnold Young, age 39, is single. He lives at 1507 Iris Lane, Tucson, AZ 85721. His Social Security number is 999–55–2000. Arnold does not wish to have $3 go to the Presidential Election Campaign Fund.

Arnold was divorced in 1993 after 15 years of marriage. He pays alimony of $36,000 a year to his former spouse, Carol. Carol's Social Security number is 999–33–3000. Arnold's son, Tom, who is age 13, resides with Carol. Arnold pays child support of $6,000 per year.

Arnold owns a sole proprietorship that is on the accrual method of accounting. His revenues and expenses for 1997 are as follows:

Sales revenue	$688,000
Cost of goods sold	430,000
Salary expense	90,000
Rent expense	24,000
Utilities	12,000
Telephone	3,000
Advertising	4,000
Bad debts	6,000
Depreciation	15,000
Insurance	7,000
Accounting and legal fees	4,000
Supplies	1,000

Other income received by Arnold includes the following:

Dividend income:	
Swan, Inc.	$8,000
Wren, Inc.	3,000
Interest income:	
First Bank	5,000
Second Bank	1,000
Lottery winnings (tickets purchased cost $700)	6,000

During the year, Arnold and his sole proprietorship had the following property transactions:

a. Sold Blue, Inc., stock for $27,000 on March 12, 1997. He had purchased the stock on September 5, 1994, for $30,000.

b. Received an inheritance of $50,000 from his Uncle Steve. Arnold used the $50,000 to purchase Green, Inc., stock on May 15, 1997.

c. Received Orange, Inc., stock worth $7,500 as a gift from his Aunt Jane on June 17, 1997. Her adjusted basis for the stock was $5,000. No gift taxes were paid on the transfer. Aunt Jane had purchased the stock on April 1, 1991. Arnold sold the stock on July 1, 1997, for $8,000.

d. On July 15, 1997, Arnold sold one-half of the Green, Inc., stock for $29,000.

e. Arnold is notified on August 1, 1997, that Yellow, Inc., stock he purchased from a colleague on September 1, 1996, for $20,000 is worthless. While he perceived the investment was risky, he did not anticipate that the corporation would declare bankruptcy.

f. On August 15, 1997, Arnold received a parcel of land in Phoenix worth $160,000 in exchange for a parcel of land he owned in Tucson. Since the Tucson parcel was worth $200,000, he also received $40,000 cash. Arnold's adjusted basis for the Tucson parcel was $190,000. He originally purchased it on September 18, 1994.

g. Sold the condominium in which he had been living for the past 10 years on December 1, 1997. He and Carol had purchased the condominium as joint owners for $120,000. Arnold had received Carol's ownership interest as part of the divorce proceedings. The fair market value at that time was $150,000. The sales price is $250,000, selling expenses are $15,000, and repair expenses related to the sale are $5,000. Although he has not yet purchased a replacement residence, negotiations are under way and are likely to be concluded during the first half of 1998. Arnold estimates that the purchase price will be about $235,000.

Arnold's itemized deductions are as follows:

Medical expenses (before the 7.5% floor)	$ 7,000
Property taxes on residence	5,000
State income taxes	6,000
Charitable contributions	10,000
Mortgage interest on residence	8,500

During the year, Arnold makes estimated Federal income tax payments of $20,000.

Compute Arnold's lowest net tax payable or refund due for 1997, assuming he makes any available elections that will reduce the tax. If you use tax forms for your computations, you will need Forms 1040, 2119, and 8824, and Schedules A, B, C, D, and SE. Suggested software (if available): *TurboTax*.

Research Problems for this chapter appear at the end of Chapter 28.

TEAM PROJECT: ARTHUR ANDERSEN TAX CHALLENGE CASES

For more information on the Arthur Andersen Tax Challenge Cases, refer to Chapter 1, page 1–37.

Information related to tax issues and problems that are discussed in this chapter may be found in the

Day and Ball case on page 5
Fence case on pages 40, 41, 47, 51, 53, 56, 59, and 69

Read and analyze the case you have been assigned and *identify* any issues and problems that are related to material covered in this chapter. If the information provided in the case is complete, prepare answers for this part of the case at this time. If you need information that is contained in the later parts of the case, write a memo summarizing the questions or problems so you can prepare a complete answer at a later date.

PROPERTY TRANSACTIONS: CAPITAL GAINS AND LOSSES, SECTION 1231, AND RECAPTURE PROVISIONS

LEARNING OBJECTIVES

After completing Chapter 13, you should be able to:

1. Understand the rationale for separate reporting of capital gains and losses.

2. Distinguish capital assets from ordinary assets.

3. Understand the relevance of a sale or exchange to classification as a capital gain or loss and apply the special rules for the capital gain or loss treatment of the retirement of corporate obligations, options, patents, franchises, and lease cancellation payments.

4. Determine whether the holding period for a capital asset is long term, mid-term, or short term.

5. Describe the beneficial tax treatment for capital gains and the detrimental tax treatment for capital losses for noncorporate taxpayers.

6. Describe the tax treatment for capital gains and the detrimental tax treatment for capital losses for corporate taxpayers.

7. Understand the rationale for and the nature and treatment of gains and losses from the disposition of business assets.

8. Distinguish §1231 assets from ordinary assets and capital assets and calculate the § 1231 gain or loss.

9. Determine when § 1245 recapture applies and how it is computed.

10. Determine when § 1250 recapture applies and how it is computed.

11. Understand considerations common to §§ 1245 and 1250.

12. Apply the special recapture provisions for related parties and IDC and be aware of the special recapture provision for corporations.

13. Describe and apply the reporting procedures for §§ 1231, 1245, and 1250.

14. Identify tax planning opportunities arising from the sale or exchange of capital assets and avoid pitfalls associated with the recapture provisions.

▼ OUTLINE

▼ GENERAL CONSIDERATIONS

RATIONALE FOR SEPARATE REPORTING OF CAPITAL GAINS AND LOSSES

1   LEARNING OBJECTIVE
Understand the rationale for separate reporting of capital gains and losses.

Fourteen years ago, a taxpayer purchased 100 shares of IBM stock for $17 a share. This year the taxpayer sells the shares for $97 a share. Should the $80 per share gain receive any special tax treatment? The $80 gain has built up over 14 years, so it may not be fair to tax it the same as income that was all earned this year.

What if the stock had been purchased for $97 per share and sold for $17 a share? Should the loss be fully deductible? The tax law has an intricate approach to answering these investment activity-related questions.

CAMPAIGNING ON CAPITAL GAINS TAX CUTS

In the 1996 presidential election campaign, both candidates proposed changes in the taxation of capital gains. Candidate Bob Dole proposed reducing the tax rate on capital gains from a maximum of 28 percent to a maximum of 15 percent. President Bill Clinton did not propose any change in the capital gains rate, but wanted to exclude all capital gains from the sale of a principal residence.

The Taxpayer Relief Act of 1997 (TRA of 1997) reduced the maximum capital gains rate to as low as 10 percent in some circumstances and generally made up to $250,000 ($500,000 for a married couple) of capital gains from the sale of a principal residence excludible from gross income.

As you study this chapter, keep in mind that how investment-related gains and losses are taxed can dramatically affect whether taxpayers make investments and which investments are made. Except for a brief discussion in Chapter 2, earlier chapters dwelt on how to determine the amount of gain or loss from a property disposition, but did not discuss the classification of gains and losses. This chapter will focus on that topic.

The tax law requires **capital gains** and **capital losses** to be separated from other types of gains and losses. There are two reasons for this treatment. First, long-term capital gains may be taxed at a lower rate than ordinary gains. An *alternative tax computation* is used to determine the tax when taxable income includes net long-term capital gain. Capital gains and losses must therefore be matched with one another to see if a net long-term capital gain exists. The alternative tax computation is discussed later in the chapter under Tax Treatment of Capital Gains and Losses of Noncorporate Taxpayers.

The second reason the Code requires separate reporting of gains and losses and a determination of their tax character is that a net capital loss is only deductible up to $3,000 per year. Excess loss over the annual limit carries over and may be deductible in a future tax year. Capital gains and losses must be matched with one another to see if a net capital loss exists.

For these reasons, capital gains and losses must be distinguished from other types of gains and losses. Most of this chapter describes the intricate rules for determining what type of gains and losses the taxpayer has.

As a result of the need to distinguish and separately match capital gains and losses, the individual tax forms include very extensive reporting requirements for capital gains and losses. This chapter explains the principles underlying the forms. The forms are illustrated with examples at the end of the chapter.

GENERAL SCHEME OF TAXATION

Recognized gains and losses must be properly classified. Proper classification depends upon three characteristics:

- The tax status of the property.
- The manner of the property's disposition.
- The holding period of the property.

The three possible tax statuses are capital asset, § 1231 asset, or ordinary asset. Property disposition may be by sale, exchange, casualty, theft, or condemnation.

There are three holding periods: short term, mid-term, and long term. The short-term holding period is one year or less. The mid-term holding period is more than one year, but less than or equal to 18 months. The long-term holding period is more than 18 months. For most purposes, however, both the long-term and the mid-term holding period are categorized as "long term." Hence, in this chapter, when the phrases "long-term capital gain," "long-term capital loss," and "long term" are used, *both* the mid-term and the long-term holding period are being referred to unless otherwise specified. When the *alternative tax on net capital gain* is discussed later in this chapter, the difference in the tax on mid-term and long-term capital gains will be illustrated (this is the case where the distinction between mid-term and long term is relevant).

The major focus of this chapter is capital gains and losses. Capital gains and losses usually result from the disposition of a capital asset. The most common disposition is a sale of the asset. Capital gains and losses can also result from the disposition of § 1231 assets, which is discussed later in this chapter.

CAPITAL ASSETS

DEFINITION OF A CAPITAL ASSET

2 LEARNING OBJECTIVE
Distinguish capital assets from ordinary assets.

Personal use assets and investment assets are the most common capital assets owned by individual taxpayers. Personal use assets usually include items such as clothing, recreation equipment, a residence, and automobiles. Investment assets usually include corporate stocks and bonds, government bonds, and vacant land. Remember, however, that losses from the sale or exchange of personal use assets are not recognized. Therefore, the classification of such losses as capital losses can be ignored.

Due to the historical preferential treatment of capital gains, taxpayers have preferred that gains be capital gains rather than ordinary gains. As a result, a great many statutes, cases, and rulings have accumulated in the attempt to define what is and what is not a capital asset.

Capital assets are not directly defined in the Code. Instead, § 1221 defines what is *not* a capital asset. A **capital asset** is property held by the taxpayer (whether or not it is connected with the taxpayer's business) that is *not* any of the following:

- Inventory or property held primarily for sale to customers in the ordinary course of a business. The Supreme Court, in *Malat v. Riddell*, defined *primarily* as meaning *of first importance* or *principally*.[1]
- Accounts and notes receivable acquired from the sale of inventory or acquired for services rendered in the ordinary course of business.
- Depreciable property or real estate used in a business.
- Certain copyrights; literary, musical, or artistic compositions; or letters, memoranda, or similar property held by (1) a taxpayer whose efforts created the property; (2) in the case of a letter, memorandum, or similar property, a taxpayer for whom it was produced; or (3) a taxpayer in whose hands the basis of the property is determined, for purposes of determining gain from a sale or exchange, in whole or in part by reference to the basis of such property in the hands of a taxpayer described in (1) or (2).
- U.S. government publications that are (1) received by a taxpayer from the U.S. government other than by purchase at the price at which they are offered

---

[1] 66–1 USTC ¶9317, 17 AFTR2d 604, 86 S.Ct. 1030 (USSC, 1966).

for sale to the public or (2) held by a taxpayer whose basis, for purposes of determining gain from a sale or exchange, is determined by reference to a taxpayer described in (1).

The Code defines what is not a capital asset. From the preceding list, it is apparent that inventory, accounts and notes receivable, and most fixed assets of a business are not capital assets. The following discussion provides further detail on each part of the capital asset definition.

Inventory. What constitutes inventory is determined by the taxpayer's business.

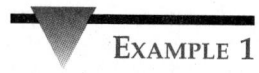
EXAMPLE 1

Green Company buys and sells used cars. Its cars are inventory. Its gains from the sale of the cars are ordinary income. ▼

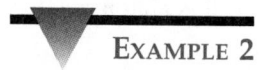
EXAMPLE 2

Soong sells her personal use automobile at a $500 gain. The automobile is a personal use asset and, therefore, a capital asset. The gain is a capital gain. ▼

Accounts and Notes Receivable. Collection of an accrual basis account receivable usually does not result in a gain or loss because the amount collected equals the receivable's basis. The sale of an account or note receivable may generate a gain or loss, and the gain or loss is ordinary because the receivable is not a capital asset. The sale of an accrual basis receivable may result in a gain or loss because it will probably be sold for more or less than its basis. A cash basis account receivable has no basis. Sale of such a receivable generates a gain. Collection of a cash basis receivable generates ordinary income rather than a gain. A gain usually requires a sale of the receivable. See the discussion of Sale or Exchange later in this chapter.

EXAMPLE 3

Oriole Company has accounts receivable of $100,000. Because it needs working capital, it sells the receivables for $83,000 to a financial institution. If Oriole is an accrual basis taxpayer, it has a $17,000 ordinary loss. Revenue of $100,000 would have been recorded and a $100,000 basis would have been established when the receivable was created. If Oriole is a cash basis taxpayer, it has $83,000 of ordinary income because it would not have recorded any revenue earlier; thus, the receivable has no tax basis. ▼

Business Fixed Assets. Depreciable personal property and real estate (both depreciable and nondepreciable) used by a business are not capital assets. Thus, *business fixed assets* are generally not capital assets.

The Code has a very complex set of rules pertaining to such property. One of these rules is discussed under Real Property Subdivided for Sale; the remainder of the rules are discussed later in this chapter. Although business fixed assets are not capital assets, a long-term capital gain can sometimes result from their sale. The potential capital gain treatment for business fixed assets under § 1231 is discussed later in this chapter.

Copyrights and Creative Works. Generally, the person whose efforts led to the copyright or creative work has an ordinary asset, not a capital asset. *Creative works* include the works of authors, composers, and artists. Also, the person for whom a letter, memorandum, or other similar property was created has an ordinary asset. Finally, a person receiving a copyright, creative work, letter, memorandum, or similar property by gift from the creator or the person for whom the work was created has an ordinary asset.

AN ARTIST'S DILEMMA

Artist Peter Max was the creator of valuable paintings that had no tax basis. If he sold the paintings, the gain from the sale would be ordinary income. Instead, Max *exchanged* the paintings for valuable real estate in the United States and in several other countries. The IRS contended that the exchange of the paintings was taxable and charged Max with failing to report more than $1 million of ordinary income.

EXAMPLE 4

Wanda is a part-time music composer. A music publisher purchases one of her songs for $5,000. Wanda has a $5,000 ordinary gain from the sale of an ordinary asset. ▼

EXAMPLE 5

Ed received a letter from the President of the United States in 1962. In the current year, Ed sells the letter to a collector for $300. Ed has a $300 ordinary gain from the sale of an ordinary asset (because the letter was created for Ed). ▼

EXAMPLE 6

Isabella gives a song she composed to her son. The son sells the song to a music publisher for $5,000. The son has a $5,000 ordinary gain from the sale of an ordinary asset. If the son inherits the song from Isabella, his basis for the song is its fair market value at Isabella's death. The song is a capital asset because the son's basis is not related to Isabella's basis for the song. ▼

(Patents are subject to special statutory rules discussed later in the chapter.)

U.S. Government Publications.   U.S. government publications received from the U.S. government (or its agencies) for a reduced price are not capital assets. This prevents a taxpayer from later donating the publications to charity and claiming a charitable contribution equal to the fair market value of the publications. A charitable contribution of a capital asset generally yields a deduction equal to the fair market value. A charitable contribution of an ordinary asset generally yields a deduction equal to less than the fair market value. If such property is received by gift from the original purchaser, the property is not a capital asset to the donee. (For a more comprehensive explanation of charitable contributions of property, refer to Chapter 9.)

EFFECT OF JUDICIAL ACTION

Court decisions play an important role in the definition of capital assets. Because the Code only lists categories of what are *not* capital assets, judicial interpretation is sometimes required to determine whether a specific item fits into one of those categories. The Supreme Court follows a literal interpretation of the categories. For instance, corporate stock is not mentioned in § 1221. Thus, corporate stock is *usually* a capital asset. However, what if corporate stock is purchased for resale to customers? Then it is *inventory* and not a capital asset because inventory is one of the categories in § 1221. (See the discussion of Dealers in Securities below.)

A Supreme Court decision was required to distinguish between capital asset and non-capital asset status when a taxpayer who did not normally acquire stock for resale to customers acquired stock with the intention of resale.[2] The Court decided that since the stock was not acquired primarily for sale to customers (the taxpayer did not sell the stock to its regular customers), the stock was a capital asset.

Often the crux of the capital asset determination hinges on whether the asset is held for investment purposes (capital asset) or business purposes (ordinary asset). The taxpayer's *use* of the property often provides objective evidence.

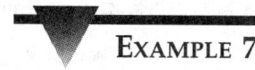
EXAMPLE 7

David's business buys an expensive painting. If the painting is used to decorate David's office and is not of investment quality, the painting is depreciable and, therefore, not a capital asset. If David's business is buying and selling paintings, the painting is inventory and, therefore, an ordinary asset. If the painting is of investment quality and the business purchased it for investment, the painting is a capital asset, even though it serves a decorative purpose in David's office. *Investment quality* generally means that the painting is expected to appreciate in value. ▼

Because of the uncertainty associated with capital asset status, Congress has enacted several Code Sections to clarify the definition. These statutory expansions of the capital asset definition are discussed in the following section.

STATUTORY EXPANSIONS

Congress has often expanded the § 1221 general definition of what is *not* a capital asset.

Dealers in Securities.   As a general rule, securities (stocks, bonds, and other financial instruments) held by a dealer are considered to be inventory and are not, therefore, subject to capital gain or loss treatment. A *dealer in securities* is a merchant (e.g., a brokerage firm) that regularly engages in the purchase and resale of securities to customers. The dealer must identify any securities being held for investment. Generally, if a dealer clearly identifies certain securities as held for investment purposes by the close of business on the acquisition date, gain from the securities' sale will be capital gain. However, the gain will not be capital gain if the dealer ceases to hold the securities for investment prior to the sale. Losses are capital losses if at any time the securities have been clearly identified by the dealer as held for investment.[3]

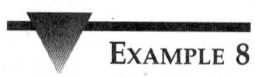
EXAMPLE 8

Tracy is a securities dealer. She purchases 100 shares of Swan stock. If Tracy takes no further action, the stock is inventory and an ordinary asset. If she designates in her records that the stock is held for investment, the stock is a capital asset. Tracy must designate the investment purpose by the close of business on the acquisition date. If Tracy maintains her investment purpose and later sells the stock, the gain or loss is capital gain or loss. If Tracy redesignates the stock as held for resale (inventory) and then sells it, any gain is ordinary, but any loss is capital loss. Stock designated as held for investment and then sold at a loss always yields a capital loss. ▼

---

[2]*Arkansas Best v. Comm.*, 88–1 USTC ¶9210, 61 AFTR2d 88–655, 108 S.Ct. 971 (USSC, 1988).

[3]§§ 1236(a) and (b) and Reg. § 1.1236–1(a).

Capital Asset Status for Stock Held by Securities Dealers

A securities dealer purchases stock for her own account at 10:00 A.M. At the close of business that day, the stock has dropped slightly in price, so the dealer does not designate it as held for investment. By 10:30 A.M. the next morning, however, the value of the stock has risen substantially above the dealer's purchase price. Using her knowledge of computer programming, the dealer could manipulate the firm's computer records so that the stock will appear to have been designated as held for investment at the end of the previous day. She is absolutely certain that neither the firm nor the IRS will ever discover what she has done. Comment on the securities dealer's potential behavior and the motivation for it.

Real Property Subdivided for Sale. Substantial real property development activities may result in the owner being considered a dealer for tax purposes. Income from the sale of real estate property lots is treated as the sale of inventory (ordinary income) if the owner is considered to be a dealer. However, § 1237 allows real estate investors capital gain treatment if they engage *only* in *limited* development activities. To be eligible for § 1237 treatment, the following requirements must be met:

- The taxpayer may not be a corporation.
- The taxpayer may not be a real estate dealer.
- No substantial improvements may be made to the lots sold. *Substantial* generally means more than a 10 percent increase in the value of a lot. Shopping centers and other commercial or residential buildings are considered substantial, while filling, draining, leveling, and clearing operations are not.
- The taxpayer must have held the lots sold for at least 5 years, except for inherited property. The substantial improvements test is less stringent if the property is held at least 10 years.

If the preceding requirements are met, all gain is capital gain until the tax year in which the *sixth* lot is sold. Sales of contiguous lots to a single buyer in the same transaction count as the sale of one lot. Beginning with the tax year the *sixth* lot is sold, some of the gain may be ordinary income. Five percent of the revenue from lot sales is potential ordinary income. That potential ordinary income is offset by any selling expenses from the lot sales. Practically, sales commissions often are at least 5 percent of the sales price, so none of the gain is treated as ordinary income.

Section 1237 does not apply to losses. A loss from the sale of subdivided real property is an ordinary loss unless the property qualifies as a capital asset under § 1221. The following example illustrates the application of § 1237.

EXAMPLE 9

Jack owns a large tract of land and subdivides it for sale. Assume Jack meets all the requirements of § 1237 and during the tax year sells the first 10 lots to 10 different buyers for $10,000 each. Jack's basis in each lot sold is $3,000, and he incurs total selling expenses of $4,000 on the sales. Jack's gain is computed as follows:

Selling price (10 × $10,000)		$100,000	
Basis (10 × $3,000)		(30,000)	
Excess over basis		$ 70,000	
Five percent of selling price	$5,000		
Selling expenses	(4,000)		
Amount of ordinary income			$ 1,000
Five percent of selling price	$5,000		
Excess of expenses over 5% of selling price	–0–	(5,000)	
Capital gain			65,000
Total gain ($70,000 – $4,000 selling expenses)			$66,000

SALE OR EXCHANGE

3 **LEARNING OBJECTIVE**
Understand the relevance of a sale or exchange to classification as a capital gain or loss and apply the special rules for the capital gain or loss treatment of the retirement of corporate obligations, options, patents, franchises, and lease cancellation payments.

Recognition of capital gain or loss usually requires a sale or exchange of a capital asset. The Code uses the term **sale or exchange,** but does not define it. Generally, a property sale involves the receipt of money by the seller and/or the assumption by the purchaser of the seller's liabilities. An exchange involves the transfer of property for other property. Thus, an involuntary conversion (casualty, theft, or condemnation) is not a sale or exchange. In several situations, the determination of whether a sale or exchange has taken place has been clarified by the enactment of Code Sections that specifically provide for sale or exchange treatment.

Recognized gains or losses from the cancellation, lapse, expiration, or any other termination of a right or obligation with respect to personal property (other than stock) that is or would be a capital asset in the hands of the taxpayer are capital gains or losses.[4] See the discussion under Options later in the chapter for more details.

WORTHLESS SECURITIES AND § 1244 STOCK

Occasionally, securities such as stock and, especially, bonds may become worthless due to the insolvency of their issuer. If such a security is a capital asset, the loss is deemed to have occurred as the result of a sale or exchange on the *last day* of the tax year.[5] This last-day rule may have the effect of converting what otherwise would have been a short-term capital loss into a long-term capital loss. See Treatment of Capital Losses later in this chapter.

Section 1244 allows an ordinary deduction on disposition of stock at a loss. The stock must be that of a small business company, and the ordinary deduction is limited to $50,000 ($100,000 for married individuals filing jointly) per year. For a more detailed discussion, refer to Chapter 6.

SPECIAL RULE—RETIREMENT OF CORPORATE OBLIGATIONS

A debt obligation (e.g., a bond or note payable) may have a tax basis in excess of or less than its redemption value because it may have been acquired at a premium or discount. Consequently, the collection of the redemption value may result in a

---

[4]§ 1234A.   [5]§ 165(g)(1).

loss or gain. Generally, the collection of a debt obligation is *treated* as a sale or exchange.[6] Therefore, any loss or gain can be a capital loss or capital gain because a sale or exchange has taken place. However, if the debt obligation was issued by a human being prior to June 9, 1997, and/or purchased by the taxpayer prior to June 9, 1997, the collection of the debt obligation is not a sale or exchange.

EXAMPLE 10

Fran acquires $1,000 of Osprey Corporation bonds for $980 in the open market. If the bonds are held to maturity, the $20 difference between Fran's collection of the $1,000 redemption value and her cost of $980 is treated as capital gain. If the obligation had been issued to Fran by an individual prior to June 9, 1997, her $20 gain would be ordinary, since she did not sell or exchange the debt. ▼

OPTIONS

Frequently, a potential buyer of property wants some time to make the purchase decision, but wants to control the sale and/or the sale price in the meantime. **Options** are used to achieve these objectives. The potential purchaser (grantee) pays the property owner (grantor) for an option on the property. The grantee then becomes the option holder. The option usually sets a price at which the grantee can buy the property and expires after a specified period of time.

Sale of an Option. A grantee may sell or exchange the option rather than exercising it or letting it expire. Generally, the grantee's sale or exchange of the option results in capital gain or loss if the option property is (or would be) a capital asset to the grantee.[7]

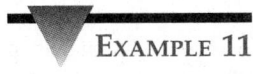

EXAMPLE 11

Rosa wants to buy some vacant land for investment purposes. She cannot afford the full purchase price. Instead, she convinces the landowner (grantor) to sell her the right to purchase the land for $100,000 anytime in the next two years. Rosa (grantee) pays $3,000 to obtain this option to buy the land. The option is a capital asset for Rosa because if she actually purchased the land, the land would be a capital asset. Three months after purchasing the option, Rosa sells it for $7,000. She has a $4,000 ($7,000 − $3,000) short-term capital gain on this sale since she held the option for one year or less. ▼

Failure to Exercise Options. If an option holder (grantee) fails to exercise the option, the lapse of the option is considered a sale or exchange on the option expiration date. Thus, the loss is a capital loss if the property subject to the option is (or would be) a capital asset in the hands of the grantee.

The grantor of an option on *stocks, securities, commodities, or commodity futures* receives short-term capital gain treatment upon the expiration of the option. Options on property other than stocks, securities, commodities, or commodity futures result in ordinary income to the grantor when the option expires. For example, an individual investor who owns certain stock (a capital asset) may sell a call option, entitling the buyer of the option to acquire the stock at a specified price higher than the value at the date the option is granted. The writer of the call receives a premium (e.g., 10 percent) for writing the option. If the price of the stock does not increase during the option period, the option will expire unexercised. Upon the expiration of the option, the grantor must recognize short-term capital gain. These provisions do not apply to options held for sale to customers (the inventory of a securities dealer).

---

[6]§ 1271.

[7]§ 1234(a) and Reg. § 1.1234–1(a)(1).

CONCEPT SUMMARY 13–1

Options

| | Effect on | |
Event	Grantor	Grantee
Option is granted.	Receives value and has a contract obligation (a liability).	Pays value and has a contract right (an asset).
Option expires.	Has a short-term capital gain if the option property is stocks, securities, commodities, or commodity futures. Otherwise, gain is ordinary income.	Has a loss (capital loss if option property would have been a capital asset for the grantee).
Option is exercised.	Amount received for option increases proceeds from sale of the option property.	Amount paid for option becomes part of the basis of the option property purchased.
Option is sold or exchanged by grantee.	Result depends upon whether option later expires or is exercised (see above).	Could have gain or loss (capital gain or loss if option property would have been a capital asset for the grantee).

Exercise of Options by Grantee.   If the option is exercised, the amount paid for the option is added to the optioned property's selling price. This increases the gain (or reduces the loss) to the grantor resulting from the sale of the property. The grantor's gain or loss is capital or ordinary depending on the tax status of the property. The grantee adds the cost of the option to the basis of the property purchased.

EXAMPLE 12

On September 1, 1990, Wes purchases 100 shares of Eagle Company stock for $5,000. On April 1, 1998, he writes a call option on the stock, giving the grantee the right to buy the stock for $6,000 during the following six-month period. Wes (the grantor) receives a call premium of $500 for writing the call.

- If the call is exercised by the grantee on August 1, 1998, Wes has $1,500 ($6,000 + $500 – $5,000) of long-term capital gain from the sale of the stock. The grantee has a $6,500 ($500 option premium + $6,000 purchase price) basis for the stock.
- Assume that Wes decides to sell his stock prior to exercise for $6,000 and enters into a closing transaction by purchasing a call on 100 shares of Eagle Company stock for $5,000. Since the Eagle stock is selling for $6,000, Wes must pay a call premium of $1,000. He recognizes a $500 short-term capital loss [$1,000 (call premium paid) – $500 (call premium received)] on the closing transaction. On the actual sale of the Eagle stock, Wes has a long-term capital gain of $1,000 [$6,000 (selling price) – $5,000 (cost)]. The grantee is not affected by Wes's closing transaction. The original option is still in existence, and the grantee's tax consequences will depend on what action the grantee takes—exercising the option, letting the option expire, or selling the option.
- Assume that the original option expired unexercised. Wes has a $500 short-term capital gain equal to the call premium received for writing the option. This gain is not recognized until the option expires. The grantee has a loss from expiration of the option. The nature of the loss will depend upon whether the option was a capital asset or an ordinary asset. ▼

Concept Summary 13–1 summarizes the rules for options.

PATENTS

Transfer of a **patent** is treated as the sale or exchange of a long-term capital asset when all substantial rights to the patent (or an undivided interest that includes all such rights) are transferred by a holder.[8] The transferor/holder may receive payment in virtually any form. Lump-sum or periodic payments are most common. The amount of the payments may also be contingent on the transferee/purchaser's productivity, use, or disposition of the patent. If the transfer meets these requirements, any gain or loss is *automatically a long-term* capital gain or loss from property held more than 18 months. Whether the asset was a capital asset for the transferor, whether a sale or exchange occurred, and how long the transferor held the patent are not relevant.

This special long-term capital gain or loss treatment for patents is intended to encourage technological progress. Ironically, authors, composers, and artists are not eligible for capital gain treatment when their creations are transferred. Books, songs, and artists' works may be copyrighted, but copyrights and the assets they represent are not capital assets. Thus, the disposition of those assets by their creators usually results in ordinary gain or loss. The following example illustrates the special treatment for patents.

EXAMPLE 13   Diana, a druggist, invents a pill-counting machine, which she patents. In consideration of a lump-sum payment of $200,000 plus $10 per machine sold, Diana assigns the patent to Drug Products, Inc. Assuming Diana has transferred all substantial rights, the question of whether the transfer is a sale or exchange of a capital asset is not relevant. Diana automatically has a long-term capital gain from both the lump-sum payment and the $10 per machine royalty to the extent these proceeds exceed her basis for the patent. ▼

Substantial Rights.   To receive favorable capital gain treatment, all *substantial rights* to the patent (or an undivided interest in it) must be transferred. All substantial rights to a patent means all rights (whether or not then held by the grantor) that are valuable at the time the patent rights (or an undivided interest in the patent) are transferred. All substantial rights have not been transferred when the transfer is limited geographically within the issuing country or when the transfer is for a period less than the remaining life of the patent. The circumstances of the entire transaction, rather than merely the language used in the transfer instrument, are to be considered in deciding whether all substantial rights have been transferred.[9]

EXAMPLE 14   Assume Diana, the druggist in Example 13, only licensed Drug Products, Inc., to manufacture and sell the invention in Michigan. She retained the right to license the machine elsewhere in the United States. Diana has retained a substantial right and is not eligible for automatic long-term capital gain treatment. ▼

Holder Defined.   The *holder* of a patent must be an *individual* and is usually the invention's creator. A holder may also be an individual who purchases the patent rights from the creator before the patented invention is reduced to practice. However, the creator's employer and certain parties related to the creator do not qualify as holders. Thus, in the common situation where an employer has all rights to an employee's inventions, the employer is not eligible for long-term capital gain treatment. More than likely, the employer will have an ordinary asset because the patent was developed as part of its business.

---

[8]§ 1235.   [9]Reg. § 1.1235–2(b)(1).

FRANCHISES, TRADEMARKS, AND TRADE NAMES

A mode of operation, a widely recognized brand name (trade name), and a widely known business symbol (trademark) are all valuable assets. These assets may be licensed (commonly known as franchising) by their owner for use by other businesses. Many fast-food restaurants (such as McDonald's and Taco Bell) are franchises. The franchisee usually pays the owner (franchisor) an initial fee plus a contingent fee. The contingent fee is often based upon the franchisee's sales volume.

For Federal income tax purposes, a **franchise** is an agreement that gives the franchisee the right to distribute, sell, or provide goods, services, or facilities within a specified area.[10] A franchise transfer includes the grant of a franchise, a transfer by one franchisee to another person, or the renewal of a franchise.

A franchise transfer is generally not a sale or exchange of a capital asset. Section 1253 provides that a transfer of a franchise, trademark, or trade name is not a transfer of a capital asset when the transferor retains any significant power, right, or continuing interest in the property transferred.

Significant Power, Right, or Continuing Interest. *Significant powers, rights, or continuing interests* include control over assignment, quality of products and services, sale or advertising of other products or services, and the right to require that substantially all supplies and equipment be purchased from the transferor. Also included are the right to terminate the franchise at will and the right to substantial contingent payments. Most modern franchising operations involve some or all of these powers, rights, or continuing interests.

In the unusual case where no significant power, right, or continuing interest is retained by the transferor, a sale or exchange may occur, and capital gain or loss treatment may be available. For capital gain or loss treatment to be available, the asset transferred must qualify as a capital asset.

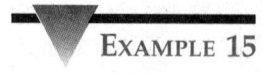

EXAMPLE 15

Orange, Inc., a franchisee, sells the franchise to a third party. Payments to Orange are not contingent, and all significant powers, rights, and continuing interests are transferred. The gain (payments − adjusted basis) on the sale is a capital gain to Orange. ▼

Noncontingent Payments. When the transferor retains a significant power, right, or continuing interest, the transferee's noncontingent payments to the transferor are ordinary income to the transferor. The franchisee capitalizes the payments and amortizes them over 15 years. The amortization is subject to recapture under § 1245.[11]

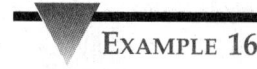

EXAMPLE 16

Grey Company signs a 10-year franchise agreement with DOH Donuts. Grey (the franchisee) makes payments of $3,000 per year for the first 8 years of the franchise agreement—a total of $24,000. Grey cannot deduct $3,000 per year as the payments are made. Instead, Grey may amortize the $24,000 total over 15 years. Thus, Grey may deduct $1,600 per year for each of the 15 years of the amortization period. The same result would occur if Grey made a $24,000 lump-sum payment at the beginning of the franchise period. Assuming DOH Donuts (the franchisor) retains significant powers, rights, or a continuing interest, it will have ordinary income when it receives the payments from Grey. ▼

Contingent Payments. Whether or not the transferor retains a significant power, right, or continuing interest, contingent franchise payments are ordinary income for the franchisor and an ordinary deduction for the franchisee. For this

---

[10]§ 1253(b)(1).

[11]See the discussion of recapture provisions later in this chapter.

CONCEPT SUMMARY 13–2

Franchises

Event	Effect on	
	Franchisor	**Franchisee**
Franchisor Retains Significant Powers and Rights		
Noncontingent payment	Ordinary income.	Capitalized and amortized over 15 years as an ordinary deduction; if franchise is sold, amortization is subject to recapture under § 1245.
Contingent payment	Ordinary income.	Ordinary deduction.
Franchisor Does *Not* Retain Significant Powers and Rights		
Noncontingent payment	Ordinary income if franchise rights are an ordinary asset; capital gain if franchise rights are a capital asset (unlikely).	Capitalized and amortized over 15 years as an ordinary deduction; if the franchise is sold, amortization is subject to recapture under § 1245.
Contingent payment	Ordinary income.	Ordinary deduction.

purpose, a payment qualifies as a contingent payment only if the following requirements are met:

- The contingent amounts are part of a series of payments that are paid at least annually throughout the term of the transfer agreement.
- The payments are substantially equal in amount or are payable under a fixed formula.

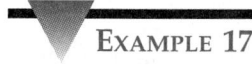

EXAMPLE 17   TAK, a spicy chicken franchisor, transfers an eight-year franchise to Otis. TAK retains a significant power, right, or continuing interest. Otis, the franchisee, agrees to pay TAK 15% of sales. This contingent payment is ordinary income to TAK and a business deduction for Otis as the payments are made. ▼

Sports Franchises.   Professional sports franchises (e.g., the Detroit Tigers) are not covered by § 1253.[12] However, § 1056 restricts the allocation of sports franchise acquisition costs to player contracts. Player contracts are usually one of the major assets acquired with a sports franchise. These contracts last only for the time stated in the contract. Therefore, owners of sports franchises would like to allocate franchise acquisition costs disproportionately to the contracts so that the acquisition costs will be amortizable over the contracts' lives. Section 1056 prevents this by generally limiting the amount that can be allocated to player contracts to no more than 50 percent of the franchise acquisition cost. In addition, the seller of the sports franchise has ordinary income under § 1245 for the portion of the gain allocable to the disposition of player contracts.[13]

Concept Summary 13–2 summarizes the rules for franchises.

---

[12]§ 1253(e).

[13]See the discussion of recapture provisions later in this chapter.

LEASE CANCELLATION PAYMENTS

The tax treatment of payments received for canceling a lease depends on whether the recipient is the **lessor** or the **lessee** and whether the lease is a capital asset or not.

Lessee Treatment.   Lease cancellation payments received by a lessee are treated as an exchange.[14] Thus, these payments are capital gains if the lease is a capital asset. Generally, a lessee's lease is a capital asset if the property (either personalty or realty) is used for the lessee's personal use (e.g., his or her residence). A lessee's lease is an ordinary asset if the property is used in the lessee's trade or business.[15]

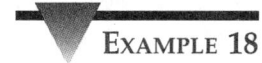

EXAMPLE 18   Mark owns an apartment building that he is going to convert into an office building. Vicki is one of the apartment tenants and receives $1,000 from Mark to cancel the lease. Vicki has a capital gain of $1,000 (which is long term or short term depending upon how long she has held the lease). Mark has an ordinary deduction of $1,000. ▼

Lessor Treatment.   Payments received by a lessor for a lease cancellation are always ordinary income because they are considered to be in lieu of rental payments.[16]

EXAMPLE 19   Floyd owns an apartment building near a university campus. Hui-Fen is one of the tenants. Hui-Fen is graduating early and offers Floyd $800 to cancel the apartment lease. Floyd accepts the offer. Floyd has ordinary income of $800. Hui-Fen has a nondeductible payment since the apartment was personal use property. ▼

HOLDING PERIOD

4   LEARNING OBJECTIVE
Determine whether the holding period for a capital asset is long term, mid-term, or short term.

Property must be held more than one year to qualify for long-term capital gain or loss treatment.[17] Property not held for the required long-term period results in short-term capital gain or loss. To compute the **holding period,** start counting on the day after the property was acquired and include the day of disposition.

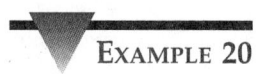

EXAMPLE 20   Marge purchases a capital asset on January 15, 1997, and sells it on January 16, 1998. Marge's holding period is more than one year. If Marge had sold the asset on January 15, 1998, the holding period would have been exactly one year, and the gain or loss would have been short term. ▼

To be held for more than one year, a capital asset acquired on the last day of any month must not be disposed of until on or after the first day of the thirteenth succeeding month.[18]

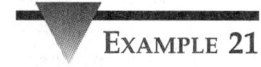

EXAMPLE 21   Leo purchases a capital asset on February 28, 1997. If Leo sells the asset on February 28, 1998, the holding period is one year, and Leo will have a short-term capital gain or loss. If Leo sells the asset on March 1, 1998, the holding period is more than one year, and he will have a long-term capital gain or loss. ▼

---

[14]§ 1241 and Reg. § 1.1241–1(a).
[15]Reg. § 1.1221–1(b).
[16]*Hort v. Comm.*, 41–1 USTC ¶9354, 25 AFTR 1207, 61 S.Ct. 757 (USSC, 1941).

[17]§ 1222.
[18]Rev.Rul. 66–7, 1966–1 C.B. 188.

REVIEW OF SPECIAL HOLDING PERIOD RULES

There are several special holding period rules.[19] The application of these rules depends on the type of asset and how it was acquired.

Nontaxable Exchanges. The holding period of property received in a like-kind exchange includes the holding period of the former asset if the property that has been exchanged is a capital asset or a § 1231 asset. In certain nontaxable transactions involving a substituted basis, the holding period of the former property is *tacked on* to the holding period of the newly acquired property.

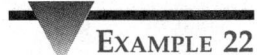

EXAMPLE 22

Vern exchanges a business truck for another truck in a like-kind exchange. The holding period of the exchanged truck tacks on to the holding period of the new truck. ▼

Certain Nontaxable Transactions Involving a Carryover of Another Taxpayer's Basis. A former owner's holding period is tacked on to the present owner's holding period if the transaction is nontaxable and the former owner's basis carries over to the present owner.

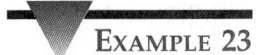

EXAMPLE 23

Kareem acquires 100 shares of Robin Corporation stock for $1,000 on December 31, 1989. He transfers the shares by gift to Megan on December 31, 1997, when the stock is worth $2,000. Kareem's basis of $1,000 becomes the basis for determining gain or loss on a subsequent sale by Megan. Megan's holding period begins with the date the stock was acquired by Kareem. ▼

EXAMPLE 24

Assume the same facts as in Example 23, except that the fair market value of the shares is only $800 on the date of the gift. The holding period begins on the date of the gift if Megan sells the stock for a loss. The value of the shares at the date of the gift is used in the determination of her basis for loss. If she sells the shares for $500 on April 1, 1998, Megan has a $300 recognized capital loss, and the holding period is from December 31, 1997, to April 1, 1998 (thus, the loss is short term). ▼

Certain Disallowed Loss Transactions. Under several Code provisions, realized losses are disallowed. When a loss is disallowed, there is no carryover of holding period. Losses can be disallowed under § 267 (sale or exchange between related taxpayers) and § 262 (sale or exchange of personal use assets) as well as other Code Sections. Taxpayers who acquire property in a disallowed loss transaction will have a new holding period begin and will have a basis equal to the purchase price.

EXAMPLE 25

Janet sells her personal automobile at a loss. She may not deduct the loss because it arises from the sale of personal use property. Janet purchases a replacement automobile for more than the selling price of her former automobile. Janet has a basis equal to the cost of the replacement automobile, and her holding period begins when she acquires the replacement automobile. ▼

Inherited Property. The holding period for inherited property is treated as being *more than 18 months* and thus is long term, no matter how long the property is actually held by the heir. The holding period of the decedent or the decedent's estate is not relevant for the heir's holding period.

---

[19]§ 1223.

EXAMPLE 26

Shonda inherits Blue Company stock from her father. She receives the stock on April 1, 1998, and sells it on November 1, 1998. Even though the stock was not held more than one year by Shonda, she receives long-term capital gain or loss treatment on the sale. ▼

SPECIAL RULES FOR SHORT SALES

General.   The Code provides special rules for determining the holding period of property sold short.[20] A **short sale** occurs when a taxpayer sells borrowed property and repays the lender with substantially identical property either held on the date of the sale or purchased after the sale. Short sales usually involve corporate stock. The seller's objective is to make a profit in anticipation of a decline in the stock's price. If the price declines, the seller in a short sale recognizes a profit equal to the difference between the sales price of the borrowed stock and the price paid for the replacement stock.

A *short sale against the box* occurs when the stock is borrowed from a broker by a seller who already owns the same stock. The box is the safe deposit box where stock owners routinely used to keep stock certificates. Although today stockbrokers generally keep stock certificates for their customers, the terminology short sale against the box is still used.

EXAMPLE 27

Chris does not own any shares of Brown Corporation. However, Chris sells 30 shares of Brown. The shares are borrowed from Chris's broker and must be replaced within 45 days. Chris has a short sale because he was short the shares he sold. He will *close* the short sale by purchasing Brown shares and delivering them to his broker. If the original 30 shares were sold for $10,000 and Chris later purchases 30 shares for $8,000, he has a gain of $2,000. Chris's hunch that the price of Brown stock would decline was correct. Chris was able to profit from selling high and buying low. If Chris had to purchase Brown shares for $13,000 to close the short sale, he would have a loss of $3,000. In this case, Chris has sold low and bought high—not the result he wanted! Chris would be making a short sale against the box if he borrowed shares from his broker to sell and then closed the short sale by delivering other Brown shares he owned at the time he made the short sale. ▼

A short sale gain or loss is a capital gain or loss to the extent that the short sale property constitutes a capital asset of the taxpayer. The gain or loss is not

---

[20]§ 1233.

recognized until the short sale is closed. Generally, the holding period of the short sale property is determined by how long the property used to close the short sale was held. However, if *substantially identical property* (e.g., other shares of the same stock) is held by the taxpayer, the short-term or long-term character of the short sale gain or loss may be affected:

- If substantially identical property has *not* been held for the long-term holding period on the short sale date, the short sale *gain or loss* is short term.
- If substantially identical property has *been* held for the long-term holding period on the short sale date, the short sale *gain* is long term if the substantially identical property is used to close the short sale and short term if it is not used to close the short sale.
- If substantially identical property has *been* held for the long-term holding period on the short sale date, the short sale *loss* is long term whether or not the substantially identical property is used to close the short sale.
- If substantially identical property is acquired *after* the short sale date and on or before the closing date, the short sale *gain or loss* is short term.

Concept Summary 13–3 summarizes the short sale rules. These rules are intended to prevent the conversion of short-term capital gains into long-term capital gains and long-term capital losses into short-term capital losses.

Disposition Rules for Short Sales against the Box.   In a short sale against the box, the taxpayer either owns securities that are substantially identical to the securities sold short at the short sale date or acquires such securities before the closing date. TRA of 1997 contains provisions designed to remove some of the taxpayer's flexibility as to when the short sale gain must be reported (a constructive sale approach). If the taxpayer has not closed the short sale by delivering the short sale securities to the broker *before* January 31 of the year following the short sale, the short sale is deemed to have been closed on the *earlier* of two events:

- On the short sale date if the taxpayer owned substantially identical securities at that time.
- On the date during the year of the short sale that the taxpayer acquired substantially identical securities.[21]

The basis of the shares in the deemed transfer of shares is used to compute the gain or loss on the short sale. Later, when shares are *actually* transferred to the broker to close the short sale, there may be a gain or loss because the shares transferred will have a basis equal to the short sale date price and the value at the *actual* short sale closing date may be different from the short sale date price.

Illustrations.   The following examples illustrate the treatment of short sales against the box.

EXAMPLE 28

On January 4, 1998, Donald purchases five shares of Osprey Corporation common stock for $100. On April 14, 1998, he engages in a short sale of five shares of the same stock for $150. On August 15, Donald closes the short sale by repaying the borrowed stock with the five shares purchased on January 4. Donald has a $50 short-term capital gain from the short sale because he had not held substantially identical shares for the long-term holding period on the short sale date. ▼

---

[21]§ 1259.

CONCEPT SUMMARY 13–3

Short Sales of Securities

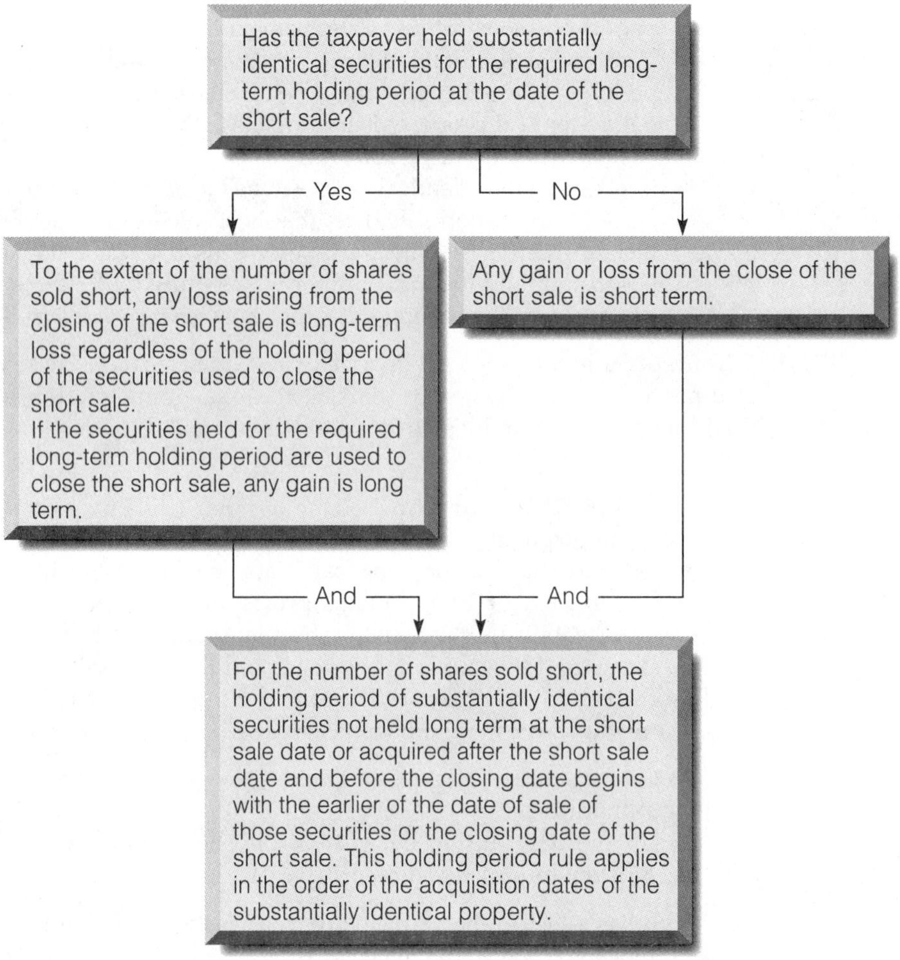

Has the taxpayer held substantially identical securities for the required long-term holding period at the date of the short sale?

— Yes —   — No —

To the extent of the number of shares sold short, any loss arising from the closing of the short sale is long-term loss regardless of the holding period of the securities used to close the short sale.

If the securities held for the required long-term holding period are used to close the short sale, any gain is long term.

Any gain or loss from the close of the short sale is short term.

— And —   — And —

For the number of shares sold short, the holding period of substantially identical securities not held long term at the short sale date or acquired after the short sale date and before the closing date begins with the earlier of the date of sale of those securities or the closing date of the short sale. This holding period rule applies in the order of the acquisition dates of the substantially identical property.

EXAMPLE 29   Assume the same facts as in the previous example, except that Donald closes the short sale on January 28, 1999, by repaying the borrowed stock with five shares purchased on January 27, 1999, for $200. The stock used to close the short sale was not the property purchased on January 4, 1998, but since Donald held short-term property at the April 14, 1998, short sale date, the gain or loss from closing the short sale is short term. Donald has a $50 short-term capital loss ($200 cost of stock purchased January 27, 1999, and a short sale selling price of $150). ▼

EXAMPLE 30   Assume the same facts as in Example 29. On January 31, 1999, Donald sells for $200 the stock purchased January 4, 1998. Donald's holding period for that stock begins January 28, 1999, because the holding period portion of the short sale rules applies to the substantially identical property in order of acquisition. Donald has a short-term capital gain of $100 ($100 cost of stock purchased January 4, 1998, and a selling price of $200). ▼

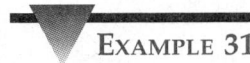

EXAMPLE 31

On January 18, 1997, Rita purchases 200 shares of Owl Corporation stock for $1,000. On November 11, 1998, she sells short for $1,300 200 shares of Owl Corporation stock that she borrows from her broker. On February 10, 1999, Rita closes the short sale by delivering the 200 shares of Owl Corporation stock that she had acquired in 1997. On that date, Owl Corporation stock had a market price of $3 per share. Since Rita owned substantially identical stock on the date of the short sale and did not close the short sale before January 31, 1999, she is *deemed* to have closed the short sale on November 11, 1998 (the date of the short sale). On her 1998 tax return, she reports a $300 long-term capital gain ($1,300 short sale price – $1,000 basis). On February 10, 1999, Rita has a $700 short-term capital loss [$600 short sale closing date price (200 shares × $3 per share) – $1,300 basis] because the holding period of the shares used to close the short sale commences with the date of the short sale. ▼

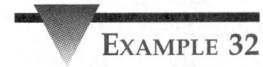

EXAMPLE 32

Assume the same facts as in Example 31, except that Rita did not own any Owl Corporation stock on the short sale date and acquired the 200 shares of Owl Corporation stock for $1,000 on December 12, 1998 (after the November 11, 1998 short sale date). The *deemed* closing of the short sale is December 12, 1998, because Rita held substantially identical shares at the end of 1998 and did not close the short sale before January 31, 1999. Her 1998 short sale gain is a *short-term* gain of $300 ($1,300 short sale price – $1,000 basis), and she still has a short-term capital loss of $700 on February 10, 1999. ▼

TAX TREATMENT OF CAPITAL GAINS AND LOSSES OF NONCORPORATE TAXPAYERS

5 **LEARNING OBJECTIVE**
Describe the beneficial tax treatment for capital gains and the detrimental tax treatment for capital losses for noncorporate taxpayers.

All taxpayers net their capital gains and losses. Short-term gains and losses (if any) are netted against one another, and long-term gains and losses (if any) are netted against one another. The results will be net short-term gain or loss and net long-term gain or loss. If these two net positions are of opposite sign (one is a gain and one is a loss), they are netted against one another.

Six possibilities exist for the result after all possible netting has been completed. Three of these final results are gains, and three are losses. One possible result is a net long-term capital gain (NLTCG). Net long-term capital gains of noncorporate taxpayers are subject to beneficial treatment. A second possibility is a net short-term capital gain (NSTCG). Third, the netting may result in both NLTCG and NSTCG.

The NLTCG portion of these results is eligible for an alternative tax calculation. As many as four different tax rates may be used in the calculation—10, 20, 25, and 28 percent. The tax savings from the alternative tax calculation range from a low of 5 percentage points (15 percent regular tax rate – 10 percent alternative tax rate) to a high of 19.6 percentage points (39.6 percent regular tax rate – 20 percent alternative tax rate). The alternative tax computation is discussed later in the chapter under Alternative Tax on Net Capital Gain.

The last three results of the capital gain and loss netting process are losses. Thus, a fourth possibility is a net long-term capital loss (NLTCL). A fifth result is a net short-term capital loss (NSTCL). Finally, a sixth possibility includes both an NLTCL and an NSTCL. Neither NLTCLs nor NSTCLs are treated as ordinary losses. Treatment as an ordinary loss generally is preferable to capital loss treatment since ordinary losses are deductible in full while the deductibility of capital losses is subject to certain limitations. An individual taxpayer may deduct a maximum of $3,000 of net capital losses for a taxable year.[22]

---

[22]§ 1211(b).

CAPITAL GAIN AND LOSS NETTING PROCESS

Holding Periods for Capital Gain and Loss Netting Purposes.
As mentioned earlier in this chapter, there are two types of long-term capital gain and loss—mid-term and long term. Thus, there are three holding periods for purposes of the capital gain and loss netting process:

- *Short term*—Assets held 12 months or less.
- *Mid-term*—Assets held more than 12 months and less than or equal to 18 months; *collectibles* held more than 12 months.
- *Long term*—Assets held more than 18 months.

Net short-term capital gain is not eligible for any special tax rate. It is taxed at the same rate as the taxpayer's other taxable income. *Net mid-term capital gain* is eligible for an alternative tax rate of 28 percent if that rate is lower than the regular tax rate on such income. *Net long-term capital gain* is generally eligible for one or more of *three* alternative tax rates: 10 percent, 20 percent, and 25 percent.[23] For simplicity, the net **mid-term capital gain** is referred to as the *28% gain*. The net long-term capital gain components are referred to as the *10%/20% gain* and the *25% gain*. The *25% gain* is technically called the **unrecaptured § 1250 gain** and is related to gain from disposition of § 1231 assets. Gains and losses from disposition of § 1231 assets are discussed later in this chapter. The discussion will focus only on how the *25% gain* is taxed and not on how it is determined.

When the combination of mid-term and long-term capital gain exceeds net short-term capital loss, a **net capital gain (NCG)** exists. Net capital gain qualifies for beneficial alternative tax treatment (see the coverage later in the chapter).[24]

Because of the three holding periods, there are three types of capital gain or loss. Thus, an *ordering procedure* is required to net them against each other.

Step 1. Group all gains and losses into short term, mid-term (including collectibles), 25% long term, and 10%/20% long term.

Step 2. Net the gains and losses within each group to obtain net short-term, mid-term, 25% long term, and 10%/20% long-term gain or loss.

Step 3. Offset the net mid-term and net long-term (25% long-term gain first) amounts if they are of opposite sign. Add them if they have the same sign.

Step 4. Offset the result of step 3 with the net short-term gain or loss from step 2 if they are of opposite sign. The netting rules offset net capital losses against the *highest taxed gain first*. Consequently, if there is a net short-term capital loss, it first offsets any net mid-term gain, any remaining loss offsets 25% long-term *gain*, and then any remaining loss offsets *10%/20% gain*.

If the result of step 4 is *only* a short-term capital gain, the taxpayer is not eligible for a reduced tax rate. If the result of step 4 is a loss, the taxpayer may be eligible for a *capital loss deduction* (discussed later in this chapter). If there was no offsetting in step 4 because the short-term and step 3 results were both gains *or* if the result of the offsetting is either a mid-term and/or a long-term gain, a net capital gain exists, and the taxpayer may be eligible for a reduced tax rate. The net capital gain may consist of *10%/20% gain*, *25% gain*, and/or *28% gain*.

The four steps outlined above can have as many as 14 unique final results. See Concept Summary 13–5 later in the chapter for a partial list and the tax effect of each result. The following series of examples illustrates the capital gain and loss netting process.

---

[23]In addition, an 8% or 18% rate can apply for capital assets purchased after 2000 and held for more than 5 years.

[24]§ 1222(11).

EXAMPLE 33

This example shows how a net short-term capital gain may result from the netting process.

Step	Short Term	Mid-Term	Long Term 25% Gain	Long Term 10%/20%	Comment
1	$13,000	$ 12,000		$ 3,000	
	(2,000)	(20,000)			
2	$11,000	($ 8,000)		$ 3,000	
3		8,000	→	(8,000)	Netted because of
		$ –0–		($ 5,000)	opposite sign.
4	(5,000)	←	←	5,000	
	$ 6,000			$ –0–	The net short-term capital gain is taxed as ordinary income.

EXAMPLE 34

This example shows how a net mid-term capital gain may result from the netting process.

Step	Short Term	Mid-Term	Long Term 25% Gain	Long Term 10%/20%	Comment
1	$ 3,000	$ 15,000	$ 4,000	$ 3,000	
	(5,000)	(7,000)		(8,000)	
2	($ 2,000)	$ 8,000	$ 4,000	($ 5,000)	
3		(5,000)	←	5,000	Net 10%/20% loss is netted against 28% gain first.
		$ 3,000		$ –0–	
4	2,000	→ (2,000)			STCL is netted against 28% gain first.
	$ –0–	$ 1,000	$ 4,000		
		Net 28% gain	Net 25% gain		

This example shows how a net long-term capital loss may result from the netting process.

EXAMPLE 35

Step	Short Term	Mid-Term	Long Term 25% Gain	Long Term 10%/20%	Comment
1	$ 3,000	$ 1,000		$ 3,000	
				(8,000)	
2	$ 3,000	$ 1,000		($ 5,000)	
3		(1,000)	→	1,000	Netted because of opposite sign.
		$ –0–		($ 4,000)	
4	(3,000)	→	→	3,000	The net short-term gain is netted against the net long-term loss, and the remaining loss is eligible for the capital loss deduction.
	$ –0–			($ 1,000)	

Use of Capital Loss Carryovers. A short-term capital loss carryover to the current year retains its character as short term and is combined with the short-term items of the current year. A mid-term and/or long-term net capital loss carries over as a mid-term capital loss and is combined with the current-year mid-term items.

SHOULD YOU INVEST IN STOCKS OR STOCK FUNDS?

TRA of 1997 establishes two holding periods that enable the taxpayer to qualify for beneficial tax treatment: mid-term (longer than 12 months) and long term (longer than 18 months). If you invest directly in stocks, you decide how long the stock is held. If you invest in a mutual fund, however, someone else makes that decision.

Some people speculate that the changes in the holding period and tax rates for beneficially taxed capital gains may motivate investors to do more direct investing. It seems that many stock fund managers are a bit like children—they can't sit still. On average, stock fund portfolios experience about a 90 percent turnover annually, which means that managers are hanging on to their stocks for just over 13 months. This would not satisfy the 18-month holding period, but would at least satisfy the 12-month holding period. But considering that 29 percent of the capital gains distributed by diversified U.S. stock funds in 1996 were short-term gains, perhaps the investors should take control.

Ross Levin, a financial planner in Minneapolis, does not believe the mutual funds will change their investment strategies. He reckons that TRA of 1997 "won't make a big difference in the way funds are managed. Mutual fund managers will still focus on getting the highest total return. Taxes are a secondary consideration."

SOURCE: Adapted from Jonathon Clements, "Stock or Stock Funds? The Tax-Cut Plan Could Tip the Balance for Some Investors," *Wall Street Journal*, August 5, 1997, p. C1.

EXAMPLE 36

In 1998, Abigail has a $4,000 short-term capital gain, a $36,000 mid-term capital gain, and a $13,000 long-term capital gain. She also has a $3,000 short-term capital loss carryover and a $2,000 long-term capital loss carryover from 1997. This produces a $1,000 short-term capital gain ($4,000 − $3,000), a $34,000 mid-term capital gain ($36,000 − $2,000), and a $13,000 long-term capital gain for 1998. ▼

Definition of Collectibles.   Collectibles held more than 12 months are classified as mid-term capital assets. Even if the collectibles are held more than 18 months, they are not eligible for the *10%/20%* alternative tax.

For capital gain or loss purposes, **collectibles** include:[25]

- Any work of art.
- Any rug or antique.
- Any metal or gem.
- Any stamp.
- Any alcoholic beverage.
- Most coins.

ALTERNATIVE TAX ON NET CAPITAL GAIN

Section 1 contains the statutory provisions that enable the *net capital gain* to be taxed at special rates (10, 20, 25, and 28 percent). This calculation is referred to as the **alternative tax** on net capital gain.[26] The alternative tax applies only if taxable income includes some mid-term and/or long-term capital gain (there is net capital

---

[25]§ 408(m).   [26]§ 1(h).

gain). Taxable income includes *all* of the net capital gain unless taxable income is less than the net capital gain. In addition, the net capital gain is taxed *last*, after other taxable income (including any short-term capital gain).

EXAMPLE 37

Joan, an unmarried taxpayer, has 1998 taxable income of $78,000, including a $12,000 net capital gain. The last $12,000 of her $78,000 taxable income is the layer related to the net capital gain. The first $66,000 ($78,000 − $12,000) of her taxable income is not subject to any special tax rate, so it is taxed using the regular tax rates. ▼

Since the net capital gain may be made up of various *rate layers*, it is important to know in what order those layers will be taxed. For *each* of the layers, the taxpayer compares the regular tax rate on that layer of income and the alternative tax rate on that portion of the capital gain. The layers are taxed in the following order: *25% gain, 28% gain*, the 10 percent portion of the *10%/20% gain*, and then the 20 percent portion of the *10%/20% gain*. As a result of this layering, a taxpayer will benefit from the 10 percent alternative tax rate only when the total of other taxable income plus the 25 percent and 28 percent capital gain layers does not put the taxpayer above the 15 percent regular tax bracket.

EXAMPLE 38

Assume that Joan's $12,000 net capital gain in Example 37 is made up of $10,000 *28% gain* and $2,000 *10%/20% gain*. Examination of the 1998 tax rates reveals that $66,000 of taxable income for a single individual puts Joan at a marginal tax rate of 31%. Consequently, she will use the alternative tax on both the $10,000 gain and the $2,000 gain. Her alternative tax liability for 1998 is $18,523 [$15,323 (tax on $66,000 of taxable income) + $2,800 ($10,000 × .28) + $400 ($2,000 × .20)]. Since the combination of her $66,000 other taxable income and her 28% gain put her above the 15% regular tax bracket, none of the $2,000 *10%/20% gain* is taxed at 10%. Her regular tax liability for 1998 on $78,000 would be $19,043. Thus, Joan saves $520 ($19,043 − $18,523) by using the alternative tax computation. ▼

EXAMPLE 39

Assume the same facts as in Example 38 except that Joan's taxable income is $23,000. Of this amount, $12,000 is net capital gain, and $11,000 is other taxable income. Her tax liability using the alternative tax computation is $3,350 [$1,650 ($11,000 other taxable income × .15) + $1,500 ($10,000 × .15) + $200 ($2,000 × .10)]. Since her marginal rate after the other taxable income of $11,000 is taxed is still 15%, she uses the 15% regular rate rather than the 28% alternative rate on the $10,000 mid-term capital gain. At that point, $21,000 of the $23,000 taxable income has been taxed, but Joan is still in the 15% regular rate bracket. Consequently, she gets a 10% rate on her *10%/20% gain until the total of that gain plus the earlier taxed gains puts her above the 15% regular rate bracket*. Her total taxable income including the last $2,000 of gain still leaves her in the 15% regular rate bracket, so all of the $2,000 *10%/20% gain* is taxed at 10%. Joan's regular tax liability on $23,000 would be $3,450. Thus, she saves $100 ($3,450 − $3,350) by using the alternative tax computation. ▼

The alternative tax computation allows the taxpayer to receive the *lower of* the regular tax or the alternative tax on *each layer* of net capital gain or *portion of each layer* of net capital gain.

EXAMPLE 40

Assume the same facts as in Example 39, except that Joan's taxable income is $28,000. Of this amount, $12,000 is net capital gain, and $16,000 is other taxable income. Her tax liability using the alternative tax computation is $4,385 [$2,400 ($16,000 other taxable income × 15%) + $1,403 ($9,350 × .15) + $182 ($650 × .28) + $400 ($2,000 × .20)]. Since her marginal rate after the other taxable income of $16,000 is taxed is still 15%, she uses the 15% regular rate rather than the 28% on $9,350 ($25,350 − $16,000) of the $10,000 mid-term capital gain. At that point, $25,350 of the $28,000 taxable income has been taxed, and Joan is at the end of the

CONCEPT SUMMARY 13-4

Income Layers for Alternative Tax on Capital Gain Computation

Compute tax on:　　Ordinary taxable income (including net short-term capital gain) using the regular tax rates.

Compute tax on:　　Each of the layers below using the *lower* of the alternative tax rate or the regular tax rate for that layer (or portion of a layer) of taxable income.

+　25% gain (unrecaptured § 1250 gain) portion of taxable income

+　28% mid-term capital gain

+　10% capital gain (portion of 10%/20% capital gain that is taxed at 10%; available only if ordinary taxable income plus 25% and 28% capital gain layers do not put taxpayer above the 15% bracket; 10% rate is no longer available once income including the portion of the gain taxed at 10% puts taxpayer out of the 15% rate bracket)

+　20% capital gain (remaining portion of 10%/20% capital gain)

=　Alternative tax on taxable income

15% regular rate bracket. Consequently, she gets a 20% rate on her *10%/20% gain*. Joan's regular tax liability on $28,000 would be $4,545. Thus, she saves $160 ($4,545 − $4,385) by using the alternative tax computation. ▼

Concept Summary 13–4 summarizes the alternative tax computation.

ETHICAL CONSIDERATIONS

Failure to Report a Taxable Capital Gain

Jennifer and Fred have been married for three years. Because they worked in different cities 200 miles apart, they each maintained a separate principal residence until six months ago, when Jennifer moved to Fred's house and took a job nearby. She had not owned a house in the city where she had been living. Fred had owned and lived in his house for 10 years. He made a gift of a 50 percent interest in the house to Jennifer when she moved in.

This year they sell the house and have a $350,000 gain. At the closing for the sale of the house, the title transfer agent gave Jennifer and Fred a form to sign indicating that they were eligible to exclude up to $500,000 gain on the sale since they jointly owned the home being sold. Jennifer and Fred signed the form, and as a consequence, the IRS received no notification that the sale had occurred. Jennifer thinks they should report $100,000 of capital gain (the excess over the $250,000 limit on the exclusion of gain for a single person), because she lived in the house for only six months. Fred thinks that reporting the gain would only lead to more problems because the IRS does not even know about the sale. What do you advise?

TREATMENT OF CAPITAL LOSSES

Computation of Net Capital Loss. A **net capital loss (NCL)** results if capital losses exceed capital gains for the year. An NCL may be all long term, all short term, or part long and part short term.[27] As used here, *long term* means mid-term net capital loss and/or long-term net capital loss. The characterization of an NCL as long or short term is important in determining the capital loss deduction (discussed later in this chapter).

EXAMPLE 41

Three different individual taxpayers have the following capital gains and losses during the year:

Taxpayer	LTCG	LTCL	STCG	STCL	Result of Netting	Description of Result
Robert	$1,000	($2,800)	$1,000	($ 500)	($1,300)	NLTCL
Carlos	1,000	(500)	1,000	(2,800)	(1,300)	NSTCL
Troy	400	(1,200)	500	(1,200)	(1,500)	NLTCL ($800)
						NSTCL ($700)

Robert's NCL of $1,300 is all long term. Carlos's NCL of $1,300 is all short term. Troy's NCL is $1,500, $800 of which is long term and $700 of which is short term. ▼

Treatment of Net Capital Loss. An NCL is deductible from gross income to the extent of $3,000 per tax year.[28] Capital losses exceeding the loss deduction limits carry forward indefinitely. Thus, although there may or may not be beneficial treatment for capital gains, there is *unfavorable* treatment for capital losses in terms of the $3,000 annual limitation on deducting NCL against ordinary income. If the NCL includes both long-term and short-term capital loss, the short-term capital loss is counted first toward the $3,000 annual limitation.

EXAMPLE 42

Burt has an NCL of $5,500, of which $2,000 is STCL and $3,500 is LTCL. Burt has a capital loss deduction of $3,000 ($2,000 of STCL and $1,000 of LTCL). He has an LTCL carryforward of $2,500 ($3,500 − $1,000). ▼

Carryovers. Taxpayers are allowed to carry over unused capital losses indefinitely. The short-term capital loss (STCL) retains its character as STCL, but the long-term capital loss (LTCL), whether it is made up of mid-term capital loss (MTCL) and/or LTCL, becomes MTCL in the year to which it is carried.

EXAMPLE 43

In 1998, Mark incurred $1,000 of STCL and $11,000 of LTCL. In 1999, Mark has a $400 LTCG.

- Mark's NCL for 1998 is $12,000. Mark deducts $3,000 ($1,000 STCL and $2,000 LTCL). He has $9,000 of MTCL carried forward to 1999.
- Mark combines the $9,000 MTCL carryforward with the $400 **LTCG for 1999**. He has an $8,600 NMTCL for 1999. Mark deducts $3,000 of MTCL in 1999 **and carries forward** $5,600 of MTCL to 2000. ▼

---

[27]Section 1222(10) defines a net capital loss as the net loss after the capital loss deduction. However, that definition confuses the discussion of net capital loss. Therefore, net capital loss is used here to mean the result after netting capital gains and losses and before considering the capital loss deduction. The capital loss de-

duction is discussed under Treatment of Net Capital Loss in this chapter.

[28]§ 1211(b)(1). Married persons filing separate returns are limited to a $1,500 deduction per tax year.

When a taxpayer has both a capital loss deduction and negative taxable income, a special computation of the capital loss carryover is required.[29] Specifically, the capital loss carryover is the NCL minus the lesser of:

- The capital loss deduction claimed on the return.
- The negative taxable income increased by the capital loss deduction claimed on the return and the personal and dependency exemption deduction.

Without this provision, some of the tax benefit of the capital loss deduction would be wasted when the deduction drives taxable income below zero.

EXAMPLE 44

In 1998, Joanne has a $13,000 NCL (all long term), a $2,700 personal exemption deduction, and $4,000 negative taxable income. The negative taxable income includes a $3,000 capital loss deduction. The capital loss carryover to 1999 is $11,300 computed as follows:

- The $4,000 negative taxable income is treated as a negative number, but the capital loss deduction and personal exemption deduction are treated as positive numbers.
- The normal ceiling on the capital loss deduction is $3,000.
- However, if the $3,000 capital loss deduction and the $2,700 exemption deduction are added back to the $4,000 negative taxable income, only $1,700 of the $3,000 capital loss deduction is needed to make taxable income equal to zero.
- Therefore, this special computation results in only $1,700 of the $13,000 NCL being consumed. The MTCL carryforward is $11,300 ($13,000 – $1,700). ▼

Concept Summary 13–5 summarizes the rules for noncorporate taxpayers' treatment of capital gains and losses.

TAX TREATMENT OF CAPITAL GAINS AND LOSSES OF CORPORATE TAXPAYERS

6   LEARNING OBJECTIVE
Describe the tax treatment for capital gains and the detrimental tax treatment for capital losses for corporate taxpayers.

The treatment of a corporation's net capital gain or loss differs from the rules for individuals. Briefly, the differences are as follows:

- There is an NCG alternative tax rate of 35 percent.[30] However, since the maximum corporate tax rate is 35 percent, the alternative tax is not beneficial.
- Capital losses offset only capital gains. No deduction of capital losses is permitted against ordinary taxable income (whereas a $3,000 deduction is allowed to individuals).[31]
- There is a three-year carryback and a five-year carryover period for net capital losses.[32] Corporate carryovers and carrybacks are always treated as short term, regardless of their original nature.
- There are no mid-term capital gains and losses. There are only long-term capital gains and losses for capital assets held more than 12 months.

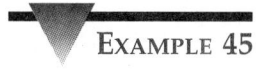

EXAMPLE 45

Sparrow Corporation has a $15,000 NLTCL for the current year and $57,000 of ordinary taxable income. Sparrow may not offset the $15,000 NLTCL against its ordinary income by taking a capital loss deduction. The $15,000 NLTCL becomes a $15,000 STCL for

---

[29]§ 1212(b).
[30]§ 1201.

[31]§ 1211(a).
[32]§ 1212(a)(1).

CONCEPT SUMMARY 13–5

Some Possible Final Results of the Capital Gain and Loss Netting Process

Result	Maximum Tax Rate	Comments
Net short-term capital loss	—	Eligible for capital loss deduction ($3,000 maximum per year).
Net long-term capital loss (includes MTCL and/or LTCL)	—	Eligible for capital loss deduction ($3,000 maximum per year).
Net short-term capital loss *and* net long-term capital loss (includes MTCL and/or LTCL)	—	Eligible for capital loss deduction ($3,000 maximum per year). Short-term capital losses are counted first toward the deduction.
Net short-term capital gain	15–39.6%	Taxed as ordinary income.
Net long-term capital gain without 25% unrecaptured § 1250 gain	20%	Some or all of 20% gain may be taxed at 10% if other taxable income does not put taxpayer out of 15% rate bracket.
Net long-term capital gain with 25% unrecaptured § 1250 gain	20% generally; but 25% on unrecaptured § 1250 gain	Some or all of 20% gain may be taxed at 10% if other taxable income (including 25% gain) does not put taxpayer out of the 15% rate bracket; unrecaptured § 1250 gain is taxed at 25%.
Net mid-term capital gain	28%	This gain is eligible for the alternative tax calculation at a 28% rate.
Net long-term capital gain (without 25% unrecaptured § 1250 gain) *and* net mid-term capital gain	28% on net MTCG; 10%/20% on net LTCG	The portion of taxable income taxed below 28% is absorbed first by ordinary taxable income and then by 28% MTCG.
Net long-term capital gain (with 25% unrecaptured § 1250 gain) *and* net mid-term capital gain	28% on net MTCG; 25% on unrecaptured § 1250 gain; 10%/20% on remainder of net LTCG (if any)	The portion of taxable income taxed below 28% is absorbed first by ordinary taxable income and then by 28% MTCG and 25% gain; then 10%/20% eligible gain is taxed.
Net long-term capital gain (without 25% unrecaptured § 1250 gain) *and* net mid-term capital gain *and* net short-term capital gain	Ordinary tax rate on net STCG; 28% on net MTCG; 10%/20% on net LTCG	The portion of taxable income taxed below 28% is absorbed first by ordinary taxable income (including the net STCG), and then by 28% MTCG.
Net long-term capital gain (with 25% unrecaptured § 1250 gain) *and* net mid-term capital gain *and* net short-term capital gain	Ordinary tax rate on net STCG; 28% on net MTCG; 25% on unrecaptured § 1250 gain; 10%/20% on remainder of net LTCG	The portion of taxable income taxed below 28% is absorbed first by ordinary taxable income (including the net STCG) and then by 28% MTCG and 25% gain; then 10%/20% gain is taxed.

carryback and carryover purposes. This amount may be offset by capital gains in the three-year carryback period or, if not absorbed there, offset by capital gains in the five-year carryforward period. ▼

The rules applicable to corporations are discussed in greater detail in Chapter 16.

OVERVIEW OF § 1231
AND RECAPTURE PROVISIONS

Generic Motors Corporation sold machinery, office furniture, and unneeded production plants for $100 million last year. The corporation's disposition of these assets resulted in $60 million of gains and $13 million of losses. How are these gains and losses treated for tax purposes? Do any special tax rules apply? Could any of the gains and losses receive capital gain or loss treatment? This chapter answers these questions by explaining how to *classify* gains and losses from the disposition of assets that are used in the business rather than held for resale. Chapter 7 discussed how to *depreciate* such assets. Chapter 12 discussed how to determine the *adjusted basis* and the *amount* of gain or loss from their disposition.

A long-term capital gain was defined earlier in this chapter as the recognized gain from the sale or exchange of a capital asset held for the required long-term holding period.[33] As discussed earlier in this chapter, there actually are two "long-term" categories—(1) mid-term and (2) long term. Mid-term capital assets are capital assets held more than 12 months but not more than 18 months and collectibles held more than 12 months. Long-term capital assets are capital assets held more than 18 months. Unless otherwise indicated, the discussion in this chapter will refer to both mid-term and long-term assets as long term. Only if the tax treatment of the mid-term and the long-term categories differs will a distinction be made.

The remainder of this chapter is concerned with classification under § 1231, which applies to the sale or exchange of business properties and to certain involuntary conversions. The business properties are not capital assets because they are depreciable and/or are real property used in business or for the production of income. Section 1221(2) provides that such assets are not capital assets. Nonetheless, these business properties may be held for long periods of time and may be sold at a gain. Congress decided many years ago that such assets deserved *limited* capital gain–type treatment. Unfortunately, this limited capital gain–type treatment is very complex and difficult to understand.

Because the limited capital gain–type treatment sometimes gives too much tax advantage if assets are eligible for depreciation (or cost recovery), certain recapture rules may remove the capital gain treatment when depreciation is taken. Thus, this chapter also covers the recapture provisions that tax as ordinary income certain gains that might otherwise qualify for long-term capital gain treatment.

SECTION 1231 ASSETS

RELATIONSHIP TO CAPITAL ASSETS

7   LEARNING OBJECTIVE
Understand the rationale for and the nature and treatment of gains and losses from the disposition of business assets.

Depreciable property and real property used in business are not capital assets.[34] Thus, the recognized gains from the disposition of such property (principally machinery, equipment, buildings, and land) would appear to be ordinary income rather than capital gain. Due to § 1231, however, *net gain* from the disposition of such property is sometimes *treated* as *long-term capital gain*. A long-term holding period requirement must be met; the disposition must generally be from a sale, exchange, or involuntary conversion; and certain recapture provisions must be

---

[33]§ 1222(3). To be eligible for any beneficial tax treatment, the holding period must be more than one year.

[34]§ 1221(2).

TAX IN THE NEWS

A DEFINITION FOR UNRECAPTURED § 1250 GAIN

The Taxpayer Relief Act of 1997 (TRA of 1997) significantly changed the taxation of long-term capital gains for individuals. Long-term capital gains may now be taxed at 10, 20, 25, or 28 percent depending on the circumstances of the taxpayer. Only a very careful reading of the legislation reveals that § 1231 assets were also involved in the change because § 1231 gains may be taxed as capital gains. On July 28, 1997, the congressional committee shaping the final legislation unexpectedly and with little forethought created the capital gain category that is taxed at 25 percent. This gain is called the "unrecaptured § 1250 gain." Congress failed to specifically define this gain and left it to the IRS to define it in the tax forms and the instructions to those forms. The unrecaptured § 1250 gain is initially a § 1231 gain. Determining *which* of the § 1231 gain is this 25% gain is quite complex, but also very important. Many real estate sales involve § 1231 gain that is ultimately reported as capital gain. Whether that gain is taxed at 10, 20, 25 or 28 percent can make a difference of millions of dollars in tax.

---

satisfied for this result to occur. Section 1231 may also apply to involuntary conversions of capital assets. Since an involuntary conversion is not a sale or exchange, such a disposition would not normally result in a capital gain.

If the disposition of depreciable property and real property used in business results in a *net loss*, § 1231 *treats* the *loss* as an *ordinary loss* rather than as a capital loss. Ordinary losses are fully deductible *for* adjusted gross income (AGI). Capital losses are offset by capital gains, and, if any loss remains, the loss is deductible to the extent of $3,000 per year for individuals and currently is not deductible at all by regular corporations. It seems, therefore, that § 1231 provides the *best* of both potential results: net gain may be treated as long-term capital gain, and net loss is treated as ordinary loss.

EXAMPLE 46

Roberto sells business land and building at a $5,000 gain and business equipment at a $3,000 loss. Both properties were held for the long-term holding period. Roberto's net gain is $2,000, and that net gain may (depending on various recapture rules discussed later in this chapter) be treated as a long-term capital gain under § 1231. ▼

EXAMPLE 47

Samantha sells business equipment at a $10,000 loss and business land at a $2,000 gain. Both properties were held for the long-term holding period. Samantha's net loss is $8,000, and that net loss is an ordinary loss. ▼

The rules regarding § 1231 treatment do *not* apply to *all* business property. Important in this regard are the holding period requirements and the fact that the property must be either depreciable property or real estate used in business. Nor is § 1231 necessarily limited to business property. Transactions involving certain capital assets may fall into the § 1231 category. Thus, § 1231 singles out only some types of business property.

As discussed earlier in this chapter, long-term capital gains receive beneficial tax treatment. Section 1231 requires netting of **§ 1231 gains and losses.** If the result is a gain, it may be treated as a long-term capital gain. The net gain is added to the "real" long-term capital gains (if any) and netted with capital losses (if any). Thus, the net § 1231 gain may eventually be eligible for beneficial capital gain treatment or help avoid the unfavorable net capital loss result. The § 1231 gain and loss netting may result in a loss. In this case, the loss is an ordinary loss and is deductible *for* AGI. Finally, § 1231 assets are treated the same as capital assets for purposes of the appreciated property charitable contribution provisions (refer to Chapter 9).

JUSTIFICATION FOR FAVORABLE TAX TREATMENT

The favorable capital gain/ordinary loss treatment sanctioned by § 1231 can be explained by examining several historical developments. Before 1938, business property had been included in the definition of capital assets. Thus, if such property was sold for a loss (not an unlikely possibility during the depression years), a capital loss resulted. If, however, the property was depreciable and could be retained for its estimated useful life, much (if not all) of its costs could be recovered in the form of depreciation. Because the allowance for depreciation was fully deductible whereas capital losses were not, the tax law favored those who did not dispose of an asset. Congress recognized this inequity when it removed business property from the capital asset classification. During the period 1938–1942, therefore, all such gains and losses were ordinary gains and losses.

With the advent of World War II, two developments in particular forced Congress to reexamine the situation regarding business assets. First, the sale of business assets at a gain was discouraged because the gain would be ordinary income. Gains were common because the war effort had inflated prices. Second, taxpayers who did not want to sell their assets often were required to because the government acquired them through condemnation. Often, as a result of the condemnation awards, taxpayers who were forced to part with their property experienced large gains and were deprived of the benefits of future depreciation deductions. Of course, the condemnations constituted involuntary conversions, so taxpayers could defer the gain by timely reinvestment in property that was "similar or related in service or use." But where was such property to be found in view of wartime restrictions and other governmental condemnations? The end result did not seem equitable: a large ordinary gain due to government action and no possibility of deferral due to government restrictions.

In recognition of these conditions, in 1942, Congress eased the tax bite on the disposition of some business property by allowing preferential capital gain treatment. Thus, the present scheme of § 1231 and the dichotomy of capital gain/ordinary loss treatment evolved from a combination of economic considerations existing in 1938 and 1942.

PROPERTY INCLUDED

LEARNING OBJECTIVE 8
Distinguish § 1231 assets from ordinary assets and capital assets and calculate the § 1231 gain or loss.

Section 1231 property includes the following:

- Depreciable or real property used in business or for the production of income (principally machinery and equipment, buildings, and land).
- Timber, coal, or domestic iron ore.[35]
- Livestock held for draft, breeding, dairy, or sporting purposes.
- Unharvested crops on land used in business.
- Certain *purchased* intangible assets (such as patents and goodwill) that are eligible for amortization.

---

[35]§ 631(a) and Reg. § 1.631–1.

PROPERTY EXCLUDED

Section 1231 property does *not* include the following:

- Property not held for the long-term holding period. Since the benefit of § 1231 is long-term capital gain treatment, the holding period must correspond to the more-than-one-year holding period that applies to capital assets. Livestock must be held at least 12 months (24 months in some cases). Unharvested crops do not have to be held for the required long-term holding period, but the land must be held for the long-term holding period.
- Property where casualty losses exceed casualty gains for the taxable year. If a taxpayer has a net casualty loss, the individual casualty gains and losses are treated as ordinary gains and losses.
- Inventory and property held primarily for sale to customers.
- Copyrights; literary, musical, or artistic compositions, etc.; and certain U.S. government publications.
- Accounts receivable and notes receivable arising in the ordinary course of the trade or business.

SPECIAL RULES FOR ASSETS DISPOSED OF BY CASUALTY OR THEFT

When § 1231 assets are disposed of by casualty or theft, a special netting rule is applied. For simplicity, the term *casualty* is used to mean both casualty and theft dispositions. First, the casualty gains and losses from § 1231 assets *and* the casualty gains and losses from **long-term nonpersonal use capital assets** are determined. A nonpersonal use capital asset might be an investment painting or a baseball card collection held by a nondealer in baseball cards.

Next, the § 1231 asset casualty gains and losses and the nonpersonal use capital asset casualty gains and losses are netted together (see Concept Summary 13–6). If the result is a *net loss*, the § 1231 casualty gains and the nonpersonal use capital asset casualty gains are treated as ordinary gains, the § 1231 casualty losses are deductible *for* AGI, and the nonpersonal use capital asset casualty losses are deductible *from* AGI subject to the 2 percent-of-AGI limitation.

If the result of the netting is a *net gain*, the net gain is treated as a § 1231 gain. Thus, a § 1231 asset disposed of by casualty may or may not get § 1231 treatment, depending on whether the netting process results in a gain or a loss. Also, a nonpersonal use capital asset disposed of by casualty may get § 1231 treatment or ordinary treatment, but will not get capital gain or loss treatment!

Personal use property casualty gains and losses are not subject to the § 1231 rules. If the result of netting these gains and losses is a gain, the net gain is a capital gain. If the netting results in a loss, the net loss is a deduction *from* AGI to the extent it exceeds 10 percent of AGI.

Casualties, thefts, and condemnations are *involuntary conversions*. Involuntary conversion gains may be deferred if conversion proceeds are reinvested; involuntary conversion losses are recognized currently (refer to Chapter 12) regardless of whether the conversion proceeds are reinvested. Thus, the special netting process discussed above for casualties and thefts would not include gains that are not currently recognizable because the insurance proceeds are reinvested.

The special netting process for casualties and thefts also does not include condemnation gains and losses. Consequently, a § 1231 asset disposed of by condemnation will receive § 1231 treatment. This variation between recognized casualty and condemnation gains and losses sheds considerable light on what § 1231 is all about. Section 1231 has no effect on whether or not *realized* gain or loss is

CONCEPT SUMMARY 13–6

Section 1231 Netting Procedure

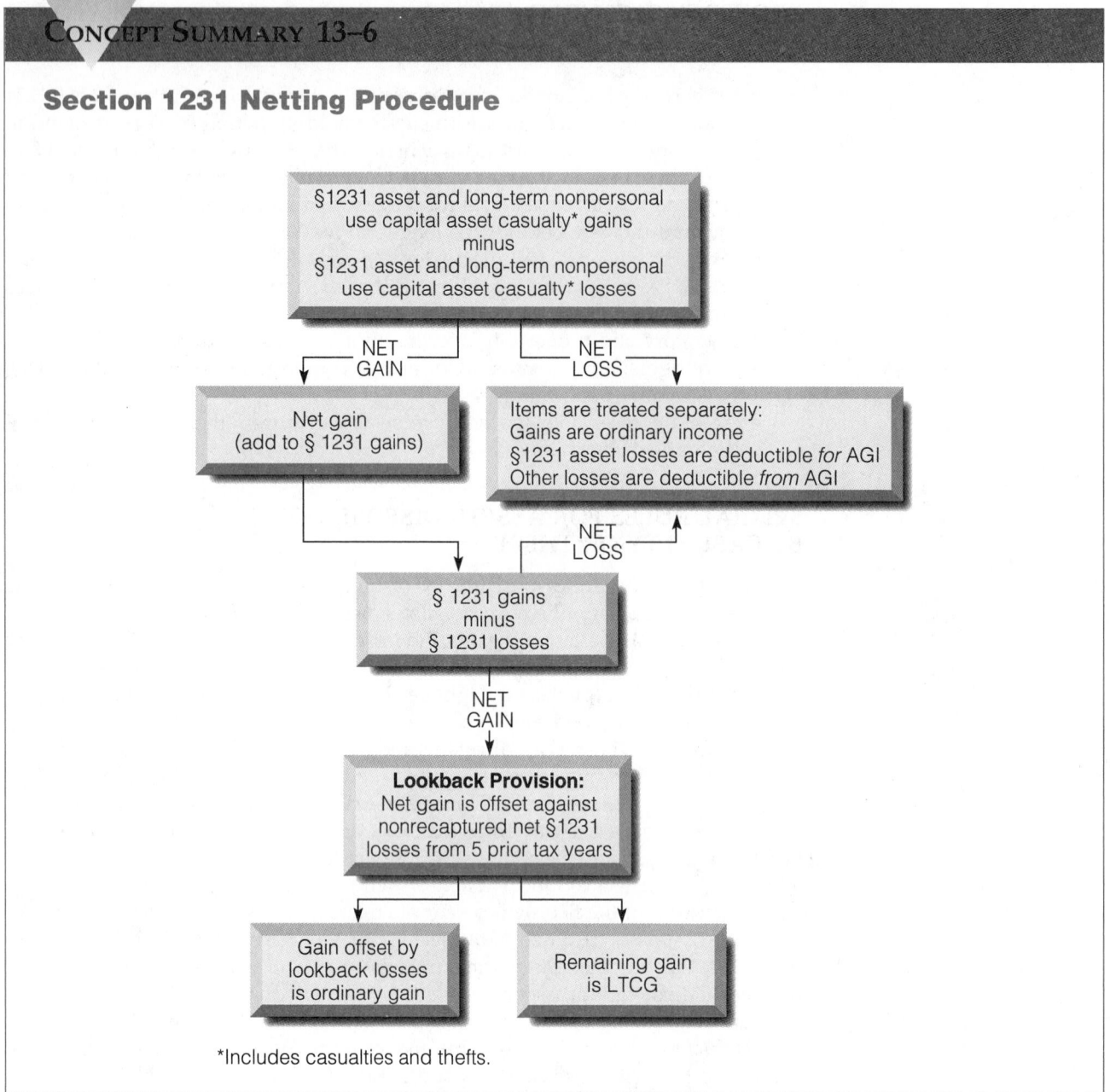

*Includes casualties and thefts.

TAX IN THE NEWS

§ 1231 AND THE SEARS TOWER

Recently, the Sears Tower in Chicago was sold. The property had been owned for more than 12 months by a partnership that held the building as a rental property and depreciated it. Consequently, the building was a § 1231 asset. The partnership sold the building at a loss of approximately $20 million. The loss was a § 1231 loss.

recognized. Instead, § 1231 merely dictates how such *recognized* gain or loss is *classified* (ordinary, capital, or § 1231) under certain conditions.

Personal use property condemnation gains and losses are not subject to the § 1231 rules. The gains are capital gains (because personal use property is a capital asset), and the losses are nondeductible because they arise from the disposition of personal use property.

GENERAL PROCEDURE FOR § 1231 COMPUTATION

The tax treatment of § 1231 gains and losses depends on the results of a rather complex *netting* procedure. The steps in this netting procedure are as follows.

Step 1: Casualty Netting. Net all recognized long-term gains and losses from casualties of § 1231 assets and nonpersonal use capital assets. Casualty gains result when insurance proceeds exceed the adjusted basis of the property. This casualty netting is beneficial because if there is a net gain, the gain may receive long-term capital gain treatment. If there is a net loss, it receives ordinary loss treatment.

    a. If the casualty gains exceed the casualty losses, add the excess to the other § 1231 gains for the taxable year.

    b. If the casualty losses exceed the casualty gains, exclude all casualty losses and gains from further § 1231 computation. If this is the case, all casualty gains are ordinary income. Section 1231 asset casualty losses are deductible *for* AGI. Other casualty losses are deductible *from* AGI.

Step 2: § 1231 Netting. After adding any net casualty gain from Step 1a to the other § 1231 gains and losses (including recognized § 1231 asset condemnation gains and losses), net all § 1231 gains and losses.

    a. If the gains exceed the losses, the net gain is offset by the "lookback" nonrecaptured § 1231 losses (see below) from the five prior tax years. To the extent of this offset, the net § 1231 gain is classified as ordinary gain. Any remaining gain is long-term capital gain.

    b. If the losses exceed the gains, all gains are ordinary income. Section 1231 asset losses are deductible *for* AGI. Other casualty losses are deductible *from* AGI.

Step 3: § 1231 Lookback Provision. The net § 1231 gain from Step 2a is offset by the nonrecaptured net § 1231 losses for the five preceding taxable years. For 1998, the lookback years are 1993, 1994, 1995, 1996, and 1997. To the extent of the nonrecaptured net § 1231 loss, the current-year net § 1231 gain is ordinary income. The *nonrecaptured* net § 1231 losses are those that have not already been used to offset net § 1231 gains. Only the net § 1231 gain exceeding this net § 1231 loss carryforward is given long-term capital gain treatment. Concept Summary 13–6 summarizes the § 1231 computational procedure. Examples 50 and 51 illustrate the **§ 1231 lookback** provision.

Examples 48 through 51 illustrate the application of the § 1231 computation procedure.

EXAMPLE 48

During 1998, Ross had $125,000 of AGI before considering the following recognized gains and losses:

Capital Gains and Losses	
Long-term capital gain	$3,000
Long-term capital loss	(400)
Short-term capital gain	1,000
Short-term capital loss	(200)

Casualties	
Theft of diamond ring (owned four months)	($800)*
Fire damage to personal residence (owned 10 years)	(400)*
Gain from insurance recovery on fire loss to business building (owned two years)	200

§ 1231 Gains and Losses from Depreciable Business Assets Held Long Term	
Asset A	$ 300
Asset B	1,100
Asset C	(500)

Gains and Losses from Sale of Depreciable Business Assets Held Short Term	
Asset D	$ 200
Asset E	(300)

*As adjusted for the $100 floor on personal casualty losses.

Ross had no net § 1231 losses in tax years before 1998.

Disregarding the recapture of depreciation (discussed later in the chapter), Ross's gains and losses receive the following tax treatment:

- The diamond ring and the residence are personal use assets. Therefore, these casualties are not § 1231 transactions. The $800 (ring) plus $400 (residence) losses are potentially deductible *from* AGI. However, the total loss of $1,200 does not exceed 10% of AGI. Thus, only the business building (a § 1231 asset) casualty gain remains. The netting of the § 1231 asset and nonpersonal use capital asset casualty gains and losses contains only one item—the $200 gain from the business building. Consequently, there is a net gain and that gain is treated as a § 1231 gain (added to the § 1231 gains).
- The gains from § 1231 transactions (Assets A, B, and the § 1231 asset casualty gain) exceed the losses by $1,100 ($1,600 – $500). This excess is a long-term capital gain and is added to Ross's other long-term capital gains.
- Ross's net long-term capital gain is $3,700 ($3,000 + $1,100 from § 1231 transactions – $400 long-term capital loss). Ross's net short-term capital gain is $800 ($1,000 – $200). The result is capital gain net income of $4,500. The $3,700 net long-term capital gain portion is eligible for beneficial capital gain treatment, and the $800 net short-term capital gain is subject to tax as ordinary income.[36]
- Ross treats the gain and loss from Assets D and E (depreciable business assets held for less than the long-term holding period) as ordinary gain and loss.

---

[36]Ross's taxable income (unless the itemized deductions and the personal exemption and dependency deductions are extremely large) will put him in at least the 31% bracket. Thus, the alternative tax computation will yield a lower tax. Refer to Example 38.

Results of the Gains and Losses on Ross's Tax Computation

NLTCG	$ 3,700
NSTCG	800
Ordinary gain from sale of Asset D	200
Ordinary loss from sale of Asset E	(300)
AGI from other sources	125,000
AGI	$129,400

- Ross will have personal use property casualty losses of $1,200 [$800 (diamond ring) + $400 (personal residence)]. A personal use property casualty loss is deductible only to the extent it exceeds 10% of AGI. Thus, none of the $1,200 is deductible ($129,400 × 10% = $12,940). ▼

EXAMPLE 49

Assume the same facts as in Example 48, except the loss from Asset C was $1,700 instead of $500.

- The treatment of the casualty losses is the same as in Example 48.
- The losses from § 1231 transactions now exceed the gains by $100 ($1,700 – $1,600). As a result, the gains from Assets A and B and the § 1231 asset casualty gain are ordinary income, and the loss from Asset C is a deduction *for* AGI (a business loss). The same result can be achieved by simply treating the $100 net loss as a deduction *for* AGI.
- Capital gain net income is $3,400 ($2,600 long-term + $800 short-term). The $2,600 net long-term capital gain portion is eligible for beneficial capital gain treatment, and the $800 net short-term capital gain is subject to tax as ordinary income.

Results of the Gains and Losses on Ross's Tax Computation

NLTCG	$ 2,600
NSTCG	800
Net ordinary loss on Assets A, B, and C and § 1231 casualty gain	(100)
Ordinary gain from sale of Asset D	200
Ordinary loss from sale of Asset E	(300)
AGI from other sources	125,000
AGI	$128,200

- None of the personal use property casualty losses will be deductible since $1,200 does not exceed 10% of $128,200. ▼

EXAMPLE 50

Assume the same facts as in Example 48, except that Ross has a $700 nonrecaptured net § 1231 loss from 1997.

- The treatment of the casualty losses is the same as in Example 48.
- The 1998 net § 1231 gain of $1,100 is treated as ordinary income to the extent of the 1997 nonrecaptured § 1231 loss of $700. The remaining $400 net § 1231 gain is a long-term capital gain and is added to Ross's other long-term capital gains.
- Ross's net long-term capital gain is $3,000 ($3,000 + $400 from § 1231 transactions – $400 long-term capital loss). Ross's net short-term capital gain is still $800 ($1,000 – $200). The result is capital gain net income of $3,800. The $3,000 net long-term capital gain portion is eligible for beneficial capital gain treatment, and the $800 net short-term capital gain is subject to tax as ordinary income.

Results of the Gains and Losses on Ross's Tax Computation	
NLTCG	$ 3,000
NSTCG	800
Ordinary gain from recapture of § 1231 losses	700
Ordinary gain from sale of Asset D	200
Ordinary loss from sale of Asset E	(300)
AGI from other sources	125,000
AGI	$129,400

- None of the personal use property casualty losses will be deductible since $1,200 does not exceed 10% of $129,400. ▼

EXAMPLE 51

Assume the same facts as in Example 48, except that Ross had a net § 1231 loss of $2,700 in 1996 and a net § 1231 gain of $300 in 1997.

- The treatment of the casualty losses is the same as in Example 48.
- The 1996 net § 1231 loss of $2,700 will have carried over to 1997 and been offset against the 1997 net § 1231 gain of $300. Thus, the $300 gain will have been classified as ordinary income, and $2,400 of nonrecaptured 1996 net § 1231 loss will carry over to 1998. The 1998 net § 1231 gain of $1,100 will be offset against this loss, resulting in $1,100 of ordinary income. The nonrecaptured net § 1231 loss of $1,300 ($2,400 – $1,100) carries over to 1999.
- Capital gain net income is $3,400 ($2,600 net long-term capital gain + $800 net short-term capital gain). The $2,600 net long-term capital gain portion is eligible for beneficial capital gain treatment, and the $800 net short-term capital gain is subject to tax as ordinary income.

Results of the Gains and Losses on Ross's Tax Computation	
NLTCG	$ 2,600
NSTCG	800
Ordinary gain from recapture of § 1231 losses	1,100
Ordinary gain from sale of Asset D	200
Ordinary loss from sale of Asset E	(300)
AGI from other sources	125,000
AGI	$129,400

- None of the personal use property casualty losses will be deductible since $1,200 does not exceed 10% of $129,400. ▼

SECTION 1245 RECAPTURE

9   LEARNING OBJECTIVE
Determine when § 1245 recapture applies and how it is computed.

Now that the basic rules of § 1231 have been introduced, it is time to add some complications. The Code contains two major *recapture* provisions—§§ 1245 and 1250. These provisions cause *gain* to be treated *initially* as ordinary gain. Thus, what may appear to be a § 1231 gain is ordinary gain instead. These recapture provisions may also cause a gain in a nonpersonal use casualty to be *initially* ordinary gain rather than casualty gain. Classifying gains (and losses) properly initially is important because improper initial classification may lead to incorrect

TAX IN THE NEWS

HARRIED CPA EXPLAINS THE UNEXPLAINABLE

During the spring of 1998, Judy Warren spent a very long day answering taxpayer questions on a radio call-in show. One caller had recently sold business equipment that had been held for more than one year. The caller thought there was a gain on the property disposition and simply wanted to know whether the gain would be taxed at ordinary income rates or capital gain rates. After the first four minutes of Judy's (necessarily) complex explanation, the show's moderator interjected, "I'm sure the rest of Judy's answer will be fascinating to our caller, but enough is enough for the rest of us. It's time for a commercial break."

mixing and matching of gains and losses. This section discusses the § 1245 recapture rules, and the next section discusses the § 1250 recapture rules.

ETHICAL CONSIDERATIONS

"Lost" Depreciation Recapture Potential

Macklin, the owner of a sole proprietorship, has used a drafting table in his business and fully depreciated its $3,700 cost. He bought a new drafting table for the business and took the old drafting table home for use as a workbench. Purchasing a similar workbench for use at home would have cost Macklin $450. Macklin does not report anything about the conversion of the old drafting table on his tax return.

Section 1245 requires taxpayers to treat all gain as ordinary gain unless the property is disposed of for more than was paid for it. This result is accomplished by requiring that all gain be treated as ordinary gain to the extent of the depreciation taken on the property disposed of. Section 1231 gain results only when the property is disposed of for more than its original cost. The excess of the sales price over the original cost is § 1231 gain. Section 1245 applies primarily to non-real estate property such as machinery, trucks, and office furniture. Section 1245 does not apply if property is disposed of at a loss. Generally, the loss will be a § 1231 loss unless the form of the disposition is a casualty.

EXAMPLE 52

Alice purchased a $100,000 business machine and deducted $70,000 depreciation before selling it for $80,000. If it were not for § 1245, the $50,000 gain would be § 1231 gain ($80,000 amount realized − $30,000 adjusted basis). Section 1245 prevents this potentially favorable result by treating as ordinary income (not as § 1231 gain) any gain to the extent of depreciation taken. In this example, the entire $50,000 gain would be ordinary income. If Alice had sold the machine for $120,000, she would have a gain of $90,000 ($120,000 amount realized − $30,000 adjusted basis). The § 1245 gain would be $70,000 (equal to the depreciation taken), and the § 1231 gain would be $20,000 (equal to the excess of the sales price over the original cost). ▼

Section 1245 recapture provides, in general, that the portion of recognized gain from the sale or other disposition of § 1245 property that represents depreciation (including § 167 depreciation, § 168 cost recovery, § 179 immediate expensing, and § 197 amortization) is *recaptured* as ordinary income. Thus, in Example 52, $50,000 of the $70,000 depreciation taken is recaptured as ordinary income when the business machine is sold for $80,000. Only $50,000 is recaptured rather than $70,000 because Alice is only required to recognize § 1245 recapture ordinary gain equal to the lower of the depreciation taken or the gain recognized.

The method of depreciation (e.g., accelerated or straight-line) does not matter. All depreciation taken is potentially subject to recapture. Thus, § 1245 recapture is often referred to as *full recapture*. Any remaining gain after subtracting the amount recaptured as ordinary income will usually be § 1231 gain. The remaining gain would be casualty gain if it were disposed of in a casualty event. If the business machine in Example 52 had been disposed of by casualty and the $80,000 received had been an insurance recovery, Alice would still have a gain of $50,000, and the gain would still be recaptured by § 1245 as ordinary gain. The § 1245 recapture rules apply before there is any casualty gain. Since all the $50,000 gain is recaptured, no casualty gain arises from the casualty.

Although § 1245 applies primarily to non-real estate property, it does apply to certain real estate. Nonresidential real estate acquired after 1980 and before 1987 and for which accelerated depreciation (the statutory percentage method of the accelerated cost recovery system) is used is subject to the § 1245 recapture rules. Such property includes 15-year, 18-year, and 19-year nonresidential real estate.

The following examples illustrate the general application of § 1245.

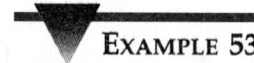

EXAMPLE 53

On January 1, 1998, Gary sold for $13,000 a machine acquired several years ago for $12,000. He had taken $10,000 of depreciation on the machine.

- The recognized gain from the sale is $11,000. This is the amount realized of $13,000 less the adjusted basis of $2,000 ($12,000 cost − $10,000 depreciation taken).
- Depreciation taken is $10,000. Therefore, since § 1245 recapture gain is the lower of depreciation taken or gain recognized, $10,000 of the $11,000 recognized gain is ordinary income, and the remaining $1,000 gain is § 1231 gain.
- The § 1231 gain of $1,000 is also equal to the excess of the sales price over the original cost of the property ($13,000 − $12,000 = $1,000 § 1231 gain). ▼

EXAMPLE 54

Assume the same facts as in the previous example, except the asset is sold for $9,000 instead of $13,000.

- The recognized gain from the sale is $7,000. This is the amount realized of $9,000 less the adjusted basis of $2,000.
- Depreciation taken is $10,000. Therefore, since the $10,000 depreciation taken exceeds the recognized gain of $7,000, the entire $7,000 recognized gain is ordinary income.
- The § 1231 gain is zero. There is no § 1231 gain because the selling price ($9,000) does not exceed the original purchase price ($12,000). ▼

EXAMPLE 55

Assume the same facts as in Example 53, except the asset is sold for $1,500 instead of $13,000.

- The recognized loss from the sale is $500. This is the amount realized of $1,500 less the adjusted basis of $2,000.
- Since there is a loss, there is no depreciation recapture. All of the loss is § 1231 loss. ▼

If § 1245 property is disposed of in a transaction other than a sale, exchange, or involuntary conversion, the maximum amount recaptured is the excess of the property's fair market value over its adjusted basis. See the discussion under Considerations Common to §§ 1245 and 1250 later in the chapter.

SECTION 1245 PROPERTY

Generally, **§ 1245 property** includes all depreciable personal property (e.g., machinery and equipment), including livestock. Buildings and their structural components generally are not § 1245 property. The following property is *also* subject to § 1245 treatment:

- Amortizable personal property such as goodwill, patents, copyrights, and leaseholds of § 1245 property. Professional baseball and football player contracts are § 1245 property.
- Amortization of reforestation expenditures.
- Expensing of costs to remove architectural and transportation barriers that restrict the handicapped and/or elderly.
- Section 179 immediate expensing of depreciable tangible personal property costs.
- Elevators and escalators acquired before January 1, 1987.
- Certain depreciable tangible real property (other than buildings and their structural components) employed as an integral part of certain activities such as manufacturing and production. For example, a natural gas storage tank where the gas is used in the manufacturing process is § 1245 property.
- Pollution control facilities, railroad grading and tunnel bores, on-the-job training, and child care facilities on which amortization is taken.
- Single-purpose agricultural and horticultural structures and petroleum storage facilities (e.g., a greenhouse or silo).
- As noted above, 15-year, 18-year, and 19-year nonresidential real estate for which accelerated cost recovery is used is subject to the § 1245 recapture rules, although it is technically not § 1245 property. Such property would have been placed in service after 1980 and before 1987.

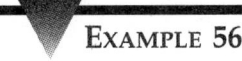

EXAMPLE 56

James acquired nonresidential real property on January 1, 1986, for $100,000. He used the statutory percentage method to compute the ACRS cost recovery. He sells the asset on January 15, 1998, for $120,000. The amount and nature of James's gain are computed as follows:

Amount realized		$120,000
Adjusted basis		
Cost	$100,000	
Less cost recovery: 1986–1997	(70,400)	
1998	(175)	
January 15, 1998, adjusted basis		(29,425)
Gain realized and recognized		$ 90,575

The gain of $90,575 is treated as ordinary income to the extent of *all* depreciation taken because the property is 19-year nonresidential real estate for which accelerated depreciation was used. Thus, James reports ordinary income of $70,575 ($70,400 + $175) and § 1231 gain of $20,000 ($90,575 – $70,575). ▼

OBSERVATIONS ON § 1245

- In most instances, the total depreciation taken will exceed the recognized gain. Therefore, the disposition of § 1245 property usually results in ordinary income rather than § 1231 gain. Thus, generally, no § 1231 gain will occur unless the § 1245 property is disposed of for more than its original cost. Refer to Examples 53 and 54.

- Recapture applies to the total amount of depreciation allowed or allowable regardless of the depreciation method used.
- Recapture applies regardless of the holding period of the property. Of course, the entire recognized gain would be ordinary income if the property were held for less than the long-term holding period because § 1231 would not apply.
- Section 1245 does not apply to losses, which receive § 1231 treatment.
- Gains from the disposition of § 1245 assets may also be treated as passive activity gains (see Chapter 10).

SECTION 1250 RECAPTURE

10 LEARNING OBJECTIVE
Determine when § 1250 recapture applies and how it is computed.

Generally, **§ 1250 property** is depreciable real property (principally buildings and their structural components) that is not subject to § 1245.[37] Intangible real property, such as leaseholds of § 1250 property, is also included.

Section 1250 recapture is substantially less punitive than § 1245 recapture since only the amount of additional depreciation is subject to recapture. To have additional depreciation, accelerated depreciation must have been taken on the asset. Straight-line depreciation (except for property held one year or less) is not recaptured. Since real property placed in service after 1986 can only be depreciated using the straight-line method, there will be *no § 1250 depreciation recapture* on such property.

Section 1250 was enacted in 1964 for depreciable real property and has been revised many times. If straight-line depreciation is taken on the property, § 1250 does not apply. Nor does § 1250 apply if the real property is sold at a loss. The loss will generally be a § 1231 loss unless the property is disposed of by casualty.

Section 1250 as originally enacted required recapture of a percentage of the additional depreciation deducted by the taxpayer. **Additional depreciation** is the excess of accelerated depreciation actually deducted over depreciation that would have been deductible if the straight-line method had been used. Since only the additional depreciation is subject to recapture, § 1250 recapture is often referred to as *partial recapture*.

Post-1969 additional depreciation on nonresidential real property is subject to 100 percent recapture (see Example 57). Post-1969 additional depreciation on residential real property may be subject to less than 100 percent recapture (see Example 58).

If § 1250 property is disposed of in a transaction other than a sale, exchange, or involuntary conversion, the maximum amount recaptured is the excess of the property's fair market value over the adjusted basis. For example, if a corporation distributes property to its shareholders as a dividend, the property will have been disposed of at a gain if the fair market value is greater than the adjusted basis. The maximum amount of § 1250 recapture will be the amount of the gain.

The following discussion describes the computational steps prescribed in § 1250 and reflected on Form 4797 (Sales of Business Property).

---

[37]As previously discussed, in one limited circumstance, § 1245 does apply to nonresidential real estate. If the nonresidential real estate was placed in service after 1980 and before 1987 and accelerated depreciation was used, the § 1245 recapture rules rather than the § 1250 recapture rules apply.

COMPUTING RECAPTURE ON NONRESIDENTIAL REAL PROPERTY

For § 1250 property other than residential rental property, the potential recapture is equal to the amount of additional depreciation taken since December 31, 1969. This nonresidential real property includes buildings such as offices, warehouses, factories, and stores. (The definition of and rules for residential rental housing are discussed later in the chapter.) The lower of the potential § 1250 recapture amount or the recognized gain is ordinary income. The following general rules apply:

- Post-1969 additional depreciation is depreciation taken in excess of straight-line after December 31, 1969.
- If the property is held for one year or less (usually not the case), all depreciation taken, even under the straight-line method, is additional depreciation.

The following procedure is used to compute recapture on nonresidential real property under § 1250:

- Determine the recognized gain from the sale or other disposition of the property.
- Determine post-1969 additional depreciation.
- The lower of the recognized gain or the post-1969 additional depreciation is ordinary income.
- If any recognized gain remains (total recognized gain less recapture), it is § 1231 gain. However, it would be casualty gain if the disposition was by casualty.

The following example shows the application of the § 1250 computational procedure.

EXAMPLE 57

On January 3, 1980, Larry acquired a new building at a cost of $200,000 for use in his business. The building had an estimated useful life of 50 years and no estimated salvage value. Depreciation has been taken under the 150% declining-balance method through December 31, 1997. Pertinent information with respect to depreciation taken follows:

Year	Undepreciated Balance (Beginning of the Year)	Current Depreciation Provision	Straight-Line Depreciation	Additional Depreciation
1980–1996	$200,000	$80,835	$68,000	$12,835
1997	119,165	3,575	4,000	(425)
Total 1980–1997		$84,410	$72,000	$12,410

On January 2, 1998, Larry sold the building for $180,000. Compute the amount of his § 1250 ordinary income and § 1231 gain.

- Larry's recognized gain from the sale is $64,410. This is the difference between the $180,000 amount realized and the $115,590 adjusted basis ($200,000 cost − $84,410 depreciation taken).
- Post-1969 additional depreciation is $12,410.

- The amount of post-1969 ordinary income is $12,410. Since the post-1969 additional depreciation of $12,410 is less than the recognized gain of $64,410, the entire gain is not recaptured.
- The remaining $52,000 ($64,410 − $12,410) gain is § 1231 gain. ▼

COMPUTING RECAPTURE ON RESIDENTIAL RENTAL HOUSING

Section 1250 recapture applies to the sale or other disposition of residential rental housing. Property qualifies as *residential rental housing* only if at least 80 percent of gross rent income is rent income from dwelling units.[38] The rules are the same as for other § 1250 property, except that only the post-1975 additional depreciation may be recaptured. The post-1969 through 1975 recapture percentage is 100 percent less one percentage point for each full month the property is held over 100 months.[39] Therefore, the additional depreciation for periods after 1975 is initially applied against the recognized gain, and such amounts may be recaptured in full as ordinary income. If any of the recognized gain is not absorbed by the recapture rules pertaining to the post-1975 period, the remaining gain is § 1231 gain.

EXAMPLE 58

Assume the same facts as in the previous example, except the building is residential rental housing.

- Post-1975 ordinary income is $12,410 (post-1975 additional depreciation of $12,410).
- The remaining $52,000 ($64,410 − $12,410) gain is § 1231 gain. ▼

Under § 1250, when straight-line depreciation is used, there is no § 1250 recapture potential unless the property is disposed of in the first year of use. Before 1987, accelerated depreciation on real estate generally was available. For real property placed in service after 1986, however, only straight-line depreciation is allowed. Therefore, the § 1250 recapture rules do not apply to such property unless the property is disposed of in the first year of use.

EXAMPLE 59

Sanjay acquires a residential rental building on January 1, 1997, for $300,000. He receives an offer of $450,000 for the building in 1998 and sells it on December 23, 1998.

- Sanjay takes $20,909 {($300,000 × .03485) + [$300,000 × .03636 × (11.5/12)] = $20,909} of total depreciation for 1997 and 1998, and the adjusted basis of the property is $279,091 ($300,000 − $20,909).
- Sanjay's recognized gain is $170,909 ($450,000 − $279,091).
- All of the gain is § 1231 gain. ▼

SECTION 1250 RECAPTURE SITUATIONS

The § 1250 recapture rules apply to the following property for which accelerated depreciation was used:

- Residential rental real estate acquired before 1987.
- Nonresidential real estate acquired before 1981.

---

[38] § 168(e)(2)(A). Note that there may be residential, nonrental housing (e.g., a bunkhouse on a cattle ranch). Such property is commonly regarded as "nonresidential real estate." The rules for such property were discussed in the previous section.

[39] §§ 1250(a)(1) and (2) and Reg. § 1.1250–1(d)(1)(i)(c). Since the post-1969 through 1975 recapture percentage is 100% less one percentage point for each full month the property is held over 100 months, this approach now yields a zero percentage no matter when the property was acquired in the 1969–1975 period. For instance, if a building was acquired on January 3, 1975, and sold on January 3, 1998, it would have been held 276 months. The recapture percentage is zero because 100% − (276% − 100%) is less than zero.

CONCEPT SUMMARY 13–7

Comparison of § 1245 and § 1250 Depreciation Recapture

	§ 1245	§ 1250
Property affected	All depreciable personal property, but also nonresidential real property acquired after December 31, 1980, and before January 1, 1987, for which accelerated cost recovery was used. Also includes miscellaneous items such as § 179 expense and § 197 amortization of intangibles such as goodwill, patents, and copyrights.	Residential rental real property acquired after December 31, 1980, and before January 1, 1987, on which accelerated cost recovery was taken. Nonresidential real property acquired after December 31, 1969, and before January 1, 1976, on which accelerated depreciation was taken. Residential real and nonresidential real property acquired after December 31, 1975, and before January 1, 1981, on which accelerated depreciation was taken.
Depreciation recaptured	Potentially all depreciation taken. If the selling price is greater than or equal to the original cost, all depreciation is recaptured. If the selling price is between the adjusted basis and the original cost, only some depreciation is recaptured.	Additional depreciation (the excess of accelerated cost recovery over straight-line cost recovery or the excess of accelerated depreciation over straight-line depreciation).
Limit on recapture	Lower of depreciation taken or gain recognized.	Lower of additional depreciation or gain recognized.
Treatment of gain exceeding recapture gain	Usually § 1231 gain.	Usually § 1231 gain.
Treatment of loss	No depreciation recapture; loss is usually § 1231 loss.	No depreciation recapture; loss is usually § 1231 loss.

- Real property used predominantly outside the United States.
- Certain government-financed or low-income housing.[40]

Concept Summary 13–7 compares and contrasts the § 1245 and § 1250 depreciation recapture rules.

UNRECAPTURED § 1250 GAIN (REAL ESTATE 25% GAIN)

This section will explain what gain is eligible for the 25 percent tax rate on unrecaptured § 1250 gain. This gain is used in the alternative tax computation for net capital gain discussed earlier in this chapter. Unrecaptured § 1250 gain (25% gain) is some or all of the § 1231 gain that is treated as long-term capital gain and relates to a sale of depreciable real estate.

The maximum amount of this 25% gain is the depreciation taken on real property sold at a recognized gain. That maximum amount is reduced in one or more of the following ways:

- The recognized gain from disposition is less than the depreciation taken. The 25% gain is reduced to the recognized gain amount. Refer to Example

[40]Described in § 1250(a)(1)(B).

57. The depreciation taken was $84,410, but the recognized gain was only $64,410. Consequently, *all* of the recognized gain is potential 25% § 1231 gain.

- There is § 1250 depreciation recapture because the property is residential real estate acquired in 1981–1986 on which accelerated depreciation was taken. The § 1250 recapture reduces the 25% gain. Refer to Example 57 again. Of the $64,410 recognized gain, $12,410 was recaptured by § 1250 as ordinary income, leaving $52,000 of the potential 25% § 1231 gain.

- There is § 1245 depreciation recapture because the property is nonresidential real estate acquired in 1981–1986 on which accelerated depreciation was taken. No 25% § 1231 gain will be left because § 1245 will recapture all of the depreciation or the recognized gain, whichever is less. Refer to Example 56. Depreciation of $70,575 was taken, but all of it was recaptured as ordinary income by § 1245. Thus, there is no remaining potential 25% § 1231 gain. The entire $20,000 § 1231 gain in Example 56 is potential 10%/20% gain.

- § 1231 loss from disposition of other § 1231 assets held long term reduces the gain from real estate.

- § 1231 lookback losses convert some or all of the potential 25% § 1231 gain to ordinary income. According to the IRS, § 1231 lookback losses first absorb 28% § 1231 gain, then 25% § 1231 gain, and then 10%/20% § 1231 gain.

Prior to the enactment of TRA of 1997, gain surviving the § 1231 netting process could receive long-term capital gain treatment and potentially be taxed at a maximum rate of 28 percent. Now real estate gain surviving the § 1231 netting process can receive long-term capital gain treatment and potentially be taxed at a maximum rate of 28, 25, or 10/20 percent.

If the § 1231 gain arises from real property held mid-term (more than 12 months but not more than 18 months) there is no potential 25% gain. If the disposition occurs after July 28, 1997, the 25% gain can only arise from assets held for more than 18 months.

Net § 1231 Gain Limitation.   The amount of unrecaptured § 1250 gain may not exceed the net § 1231 gain that is eligible to be treated as long-term capital gain. The unrecaptured § 1250 gain is the *lesser of* the unrecaptured § 1250 gain or the net § 1231 gain that is treated as capital gain. Thus, if there is a net § 1231 gain, but it is all recaptured by the five-year § 1231 lookback loss provision, there is no surviving § 1231 gain or unrecaptured § 1250 gain. Refer to Example 50. There was $200 of § 1231 gain from the building fire that would also be potential 25% gain if at least $200 of depreciation was taken. The net § 1231 gain was $1,100 including the $200 building gain. Assume all the § 1231 assets were held more than 18 months. The $700 of § 1231 lookback losses would *first* absorb the $200 building gain, so the $400 of § 1231 gain that is treated as long-term capital gain includes no 25% gain.

Section 1250 Property for Purposes of the Unrecaptured § 1250 Gain.   TRA of 1997 did not change the definition of § 1250 property. Such property includes any real property (other than § 1245 property) that is or has been depreciable. Land is *not* § 1250 property because it is not depreciable.

EXAMPLE 60

Bill is a single taxpayer with taxable income of $84,000 comprised of:

- $64,000 ordinary taxable income,
- $3,000 short-term capital loss,

- $15,000 long-term capital gain from sale of stock, and
- $8,000 § 1231 gain that is all unrecaptured § 1250 gain (the actual unrecaptured gain was $11,000, but net § 1231 gain is only $8,000).

Bill's net capital gain is $20,000 ($15,000 long-term capital gain + $8,000 unrecaptured § 1250 gain/net § 1231 gain − $3,000 short-term capital loss). The $3,000 short term capital loss is offset against the $8,000 unrecaptured § 1250 gain, reducing that gain to $5,000 (refer to the earlier discussion concerning netting of capital losses). Bill's adjusted net capital gain is $15,000 ($20,000 net capital gain − $5,000 unrecaptured § 1250 gain). Bill's total tax (using the alternative tax calculation discussed earlier in this chapter) is $18,953 [$14,703 (tax on ordinary taxable income) + $1,250 ($5,000 unrecaptured § 1250 gain × 25%) + $3,000 ($15,000 adjusted net capital gain × 20%)]. ▼

CONSIDERATIONS COMMON TO §§ 1245 AND 1250

EXCEPTIONS

11 **LEARNING OBJECTIVE**
Understand considerations common to §§ 1245 and 1250.

Recapture under §§ 1245 and 1250 does not apply to the following transactions.

Gifts. The recapture potential carries over to the donee.[41]

EXAMPLE 61

Wade gives his daughter, Helen, § 1245 property with an adjusted basis of $1,000. The amount of recapture potential is $700. Helen uses the property in her business and claims further depreciation of $100 before selling it for $1,900. Helen's recognized gain is $1,000 ($1,900 amount realized − $900 adjusted basis), of which $800 is recaptured as ordinary income ($100 depreciation taken by Helen + $700 recapture potential carried over from Wade). The remaining gain of $200 is § 1231 gain. Even if Helen used the property for personal purposes, the $700 recapture potential would still be carried over. ▼

Death. Although not a very attractive tax planning approach, death eliminates all recapture potential.[42] In other words, any recapture potential does not carry over from a decedent to an estate or heir.

EXAMPLE 62

Assume the same facts as in Example 61, except Helen receives the property as a result of Wade's death. The $700 recapture potential from Wade is extinguished. Helen has a basis for the property equal to the property's fair market value (assume $1,700) at Wade's death. She will have a $300 gain when the property is sold because the selling price ($1,900) exceeds the property's adjusted basis of $1,600 ($1,700 original basis to Helen − $1,000 depreciation) by $300. Because of § 1245, $100 is ordinary income. The remaining gain of $200 is § 1231 gain. ▼

Charitable Transfers. The recapture potential reduces the amount of the charitable contribution deduction under § 170.[43]

---

[41]§§ 1245(b)(1) and 1250(d)(1) and Reg. §§ 1.1245–4(a)(1) and 1.1250–3(a)(1).
[42]§§ 1245(b)(2) and 1250(d)(2).

[43]§ 170(e)(1)(A) and Reg. § 1.170A–4(b)(1). In certain circumstances, § 1231 gain also reduces the amount of the charitable contribution. See § 170(e)(1)(B).

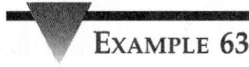

EXAMPLE 63

Kanisha donates to her church § 1245 property with a fair market value of $10,000 and an adjusted basis of $7,000. Assume that the amount of recapture potential is $2,000 (the amount of recapture that would occur if the property were sold). Her charitable contribution deduction (subject to the limitations discussed in Chapter 9) is $8,000 ($10,000 fair market value – $2,000 recapture potential). ▼

Certain Nontaxable Transactions.   These are transactions in which the transferor's adjusted basis of property carries over to the transferee.[44] The recapture potential also carries over to the transferee.[45] Included in this category are transfers of property pursuant to the following:

- Nontaxable incorporations under § 351.
- Certain liquidations of subsidiary companies under § 332.
- Nontaxable contributions to a partnership under § 721.
- Nontaxable reorganizations.

Gain may be recognized in these transactions if boot is received. If gain is recognized, it is treated as ordinary income to the extent of the recapture potential or recognized gain, whichever is lower.[46]

Like-Kind Exchanges (§ 1031) and Involuntary Conversions (§ 1033).
Realized gain will be recognized to the extent of boot received under § 1031. Realized gain also will be recognized to the extent the proceeds from an involuntary conversion are not reinvested in similar property under § 1033. Such recognized gain is subject to recapture as ordinary income under §§ 1245 and 1250. The remaining recapture potential, if any, carries over to the property received in the exchange. Realized losses are not recognized in like-kind exchanges, but are recognized in involuntary conversions (see Chapter 12).

EXAMPLE 64

Anita exchanges § 1245 property with an adjusted basis of $300 for § 1245 property with a fair market value of $6,000. The exchange qualifies as a like-kind exchange under § 1031. Anita also receives $1,000 cash (boot). Her realized gain is $6,700 ($7,000 amount realized – $300 adjusted basis of property). Assuming the recapture potential is $7,500, Anita recognizes § 1245 gain of $1,000 because she received boot of $1,000. The remaining recapture potential of $6,500 carries over to the like-kind property received. ▼

OTHER APPLICATIONS

Sections 1245 and 1250 apply notwithstanding any other provisions in the Code.[47] That is, the recapture rules under these Sections *override* all other Sections. Special applications include installment sales and property dividends.

Installment Sales.   Recapture gain is recognized in the year of the sale regardless of whether gain is otherwise recognized under the installment method.[48] All gain is ordinary income until the recapture potential is fully absorbed. Nonrecapture (§ 1231) gain is recognized under the installment method as cash is received.

---

[44]§§ 1245(b)(3) and 1250(d)(3) and Reg. §§ 1.1245–4(c) and 1.1250–3(c).

[45]Reg. §§ 1.1245–2(a)(4) and –2(c)(2) and 1.1250–2(d)(1) and (3) and –3(c)(3).

[46]§§ 1245(b)(3) and 1250(d)(3) and Reg. §§ 1.1245–4(c) and 1.1250–3(c). Some of these special corporate problems are discussed in Chapter 16. Partnership contributions are also discussed in Chapter 22.

[47]§§ 1245(d) and 1250(i).

[48]§ 453(i). The installment method of reporting gains on the sale of property is discussed in Chapter 15.

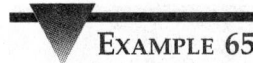
EXAMPLE 65

Seth sells § 1245 property for $20,000, to be paid in 10 annual installments of $2,000 each plus interest at 10%. Seth realizes a $6,000 gain from the sale, of which $4,000 is attributable to depreciation taken. If Seth uses the installment method, he recognizes the entire $4,000 of recapture gain as ordinary income in the year of the sale. The $2,000 of nonrecapture (§ 1231) gain will be recognized at the rate of $200 per year for 10 years. ▼

Gain is also recognized on installment sales in the year of sale in an amount equal to the § 179 (immediate expensing) deductions taken with respect to the property sold.

Property Dividends. A corporation generally recognizes gain if it distributes appreciated property as a dividend. Recapture under §§ 1245 and 1250 applies to the extent of the lower of the recapture potential or the excess of the property's fair market value over the adjusted basis.[49]

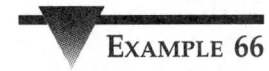
EXAMPLE 66

Emerald Corporation distributes § 1245 property as a dividend to its shareholders. The amount of the recapture potential is $300, and the excess of the property's fair market value over the adjusted basis is $800. Emerald recognizes $300 of ordinary income and $500 of § 1231 gain. ▼

Concept Summary 13–8 integrates the depreciation recapture rules with the § 1231 netting process. It is an expanded version of Concept Summary 13–6.

SPECIAL RECAPTURE PROVISIONS

SPECIAL RECAPTURE FOR CORPORATIONS

Corporations selling depreciable real estate may have ordinary income in addition to that required by § 1250.[50] See the discussion of this topic in Chapter 16.

GAIN FROM SALE OF DEPRECIABLE PROPERTY BETWEEN CERTAIN RELATED PARTIES

12 **LEARNING OBJECTIVE** Apply the special recapture provisions for related parties and IDC and be aware of the special recapture provision for corporations.

When the sale or exchange of property, which in the hands of the *transferee* is depreciable property (principally machinery, equipment, and buildings, but not land), is between certain related parties, any gain recognized is ordinary income.[51] This provision applies to both direct and indirect sales or exchanges. A **related party** is defined as an individual and his or her controlled corporation or partnership or a taxpayer and any trust in which the taxpayer (or the taxpayer's spouse) is a beneficiary.

EXAMPLE 67

Isabella sells a personal use automobile (therefore nondepreciable) to her controlled corporation. The automobile, which was purchased two years ago, originally cost $5,000 and is sold for $7,000. The automobile is to be used in the corporation's business. If the related-party provision did not exist, Isabella would realize a $2,000 long-term capital gain. The income tax consequences would be favorable because Isabella's controlled corporation is entitled to depreciate the automobile based upon the purchase price of $7,000. Under the related-party provision, Isabella's $2,000 gain is ordinary income. ▼

---

[49]§ 311(b) and Reg. §§ 1.1245–1(c) and –6(b) and 1.1250–1(a)(4), –1(b)(4), and –1(c)(2).

[50]§ 291(a)(1).
[51]§ 1239.

CONCEPT SUMMARY 13–8

Depreciation Recapture and § 1231 Netting Procedure

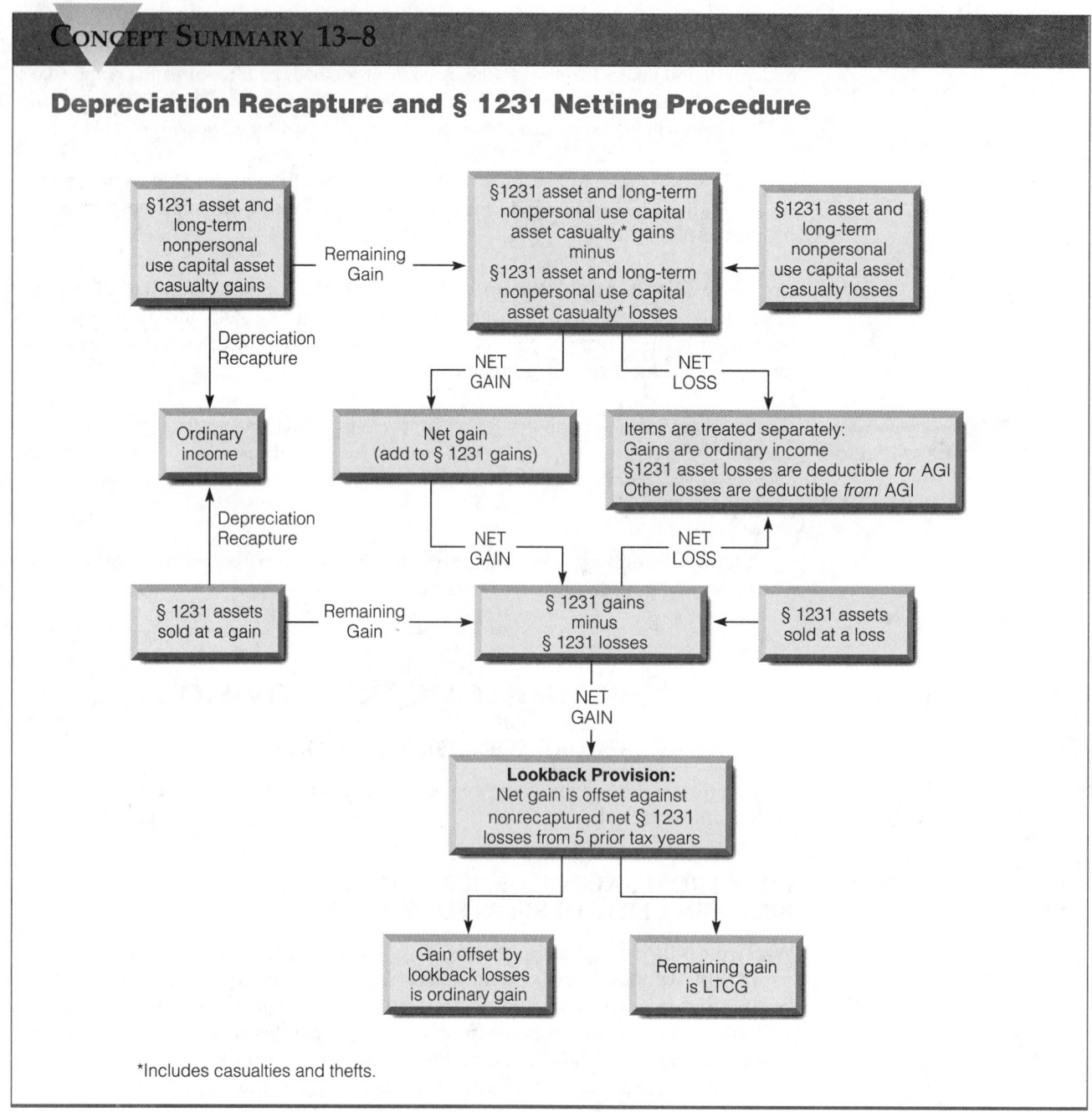

*Includes casualties and thefts.

INTANGIBLE DRILLING COSTS

Taxpayers may elect to either *expense or capitalize* intangible drilling and development costs for oil, gas, or geothermal properties.[52] **Intangible drilling and development costs (IDC)** include operator (one who holds a working or operating interest in any tract or parcel of land) expenditures for wages, fuel, repairs, hauling, and supplies. These expenditures must be incident to and necessary

---

[52]§ 263(c).

for the drilling of wells and preparation of wells for production. In most instances, taxpayers elect to expense IDC to maximize tax deductions during drilling.

Intangible drilling and development costs are subject to § 1254 recapture when the property is disposed of. The gain on the disposition of the property is subject to recapture as ordinary income.

REPORTING PROCEDURES

13 LEARNING OBJECTIVE
Describe and apply the reporting procedures for §§ 1231, 1245, and 1250.

Noncapital gains and losses are reported on Form 4797, Sales of Business Property. Before filling out Form 4797, however, Form 4684, Casualties and Thefts, Part B, must be completed to determine whether or not any casualties will enter into the § 1231 computation procedure. Recall that gains from § 1231 asset casualties may be recaptured by § 1245 or § 1250. These gains will not appear on Form 4684. The § 1231 gains and nonpersonal use long-term capital gains are netted against § 1231 losses and nonpersonal use long-term capital losses on Form 4684 to determine if there is a net gain to transfer to Form 4797, Part I.

TAX PLANNING
CONSIDERATIONS

14 LEARNING OBJECTIVE
Identify tax planning opportunities arising from the sale or exchange of capital assets and avoid pitfalls associated with the recapture provisions.

IMPORTANCE OF CAPITAL ASSET STATUS

Why is capital asset status important? Capital asset status enables the taxpayer to be eligible for the alternative tax on net capital gain. For a taxpayer in the 28, 31, 36, or 39.6 percent regular tax bracket, a 20 percent rate is available on capital assets held longer than 18 months, and a 28 percent rate is available for capital assets held longer than 12 months. For a taxpayer in the 15 percent regular tax bracket, a 10 percent rate is available on capital assets held longer than 18 months. Thus, individuals who can receive income in the form of long-term capital gains have an advantage over taxpayers who cannot receive income in this form.

Capital asset status is also important because capital gains must be offset by capital losses. If a net capital loss results, the maximum deduction is $3,000 per year.

Consequently, capital gains and losses must be segregated from other types of gains and losses and must be reported separately on Schedule D of Form 1040.

PLANNING FOR CAPITAL ASSET STATUS

It is important to keep in mind that capital asset status often is a question of objective evidence. Thus, property that is not a capital asset to one party may qualify as a capital asset to another party.

EXAMPLE 68

Diane, a real estate dealer, transfers by gift a tract of land to Jeff, her son. The land was recorded as part of Diane's inventory (it was held for resale) and was therefore not a capital asset to her. Jeff, however, treats the land as an investment. The land is a capital asset in Jeff's hands, and any later taxable disposition of the property by him will yield a capital gain or loss. ▼

If proper planning is carried out, even a dealer may obtain long-term capital gain treatment on the sale of the type of property normally held for resale.

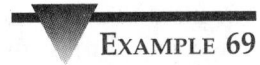

EXAMPLE 69

Jim, a real estate dealer, segregates tract A from the real estate he regularly holds for resale and designates the property as being held for investment purposes. The property is not advertised for sale and is disposed of several years later. The negotiations for the subsequent sale were initiated by the purchaser and not by Jim. Under these circumstances, it would appear that any gain or loss from the sale of tract A should be a capital gain or loss.[53] ▼

When a business is being sold, one of the major decisions usually concerns whether a portion of the sales price is for goodwill. For the seller, goodwill generally represents the disposition of a capital asset. Goodwill has no basis and represents a residual portion of the selling price that cannot be allocated reasonably to the known assets. The amount of goodwill thus represents capital gain.

From a legal perspective, the buyer may prefer that the residual portion of the purchase price be allocated to a covenant not to compete (a promise that the seller will not compete against the buyer by conducting a business similar to the one that the buyer has purchased). Both purchased goodwill and a covenant not to compete are § 197 intangibles. Thus, both must be capitalized and can be amortized over a 15-year statutory period.

To the seller, a covenant produces ordinary income. Thus, the seller would prefer that the residual portion of the selling price be allocated to goodwill—a capital asset. If the buyer does not need the legal protection provided by a covenant, the buyer is neutral regarding whether the residual amount be allocated to a covenant or to goodwill. Since the seller would receive a tax advantage from labeling the residual amount as goodwill, the buyer should factor this into the negotiation of the purchase price.

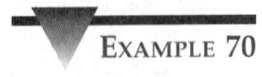

EXAMPLE 70

Marcia is buying Jack's dry cleaning proprietorship. An appraisal of the assets indicates that a reasonable purchase price would exceed the value of the known assets by $30,000. If the purchase contract does not specify the nature of the $30,000, the amount will be for goodwill, and Jack will have a long-term capital gain of $30,000. Marcia will have a 15-year amortizable $30,000 asset. If Marcia is paying the extra $30,000 to prevent Jack from conducting another dry cleaning business in the area (a covenant not to compete), Jack will have $30,000 of ordinary income. Marcia will have a $30,000 deduction over the statutory 15-year amortization period rather than over the actual life of the covenant (e.g., 5 years). ▼

EFFECT OF CAPITAL ASSET STATUS IN TRANSACTIONS OTHER THAN SALES

The nature of an asset (capital or ordinary) is important in determining the tax consequences that result when a sale or exchange occurs. It may, however, be just as significant in circumstances other than a taxable sale or exchange. When a capital asset is disposed of, the result is not always a capital gain or loss. Rather, in general, the disposition must be a sale or exchange. Collection of a debt instrument having a basis less than the face value results in a capital gain if the debt instrument is a capital asset. The collection is a sale or exchange. Sale of the debt shortly before the due date for collection will produce a capital gain.[54] If selling the debt in such circumstances could produce a capital gain but collecting could not, the consistency of what constitutes a capital gain or loss would be frustrated. Another illustration of the sale or exchange principle involves a donation of certain appreciated property to a qualified charity. Recall that in certain circumstances, the measure of the

---

[53]*Toledo, Peoria & Western Railroad Co.*, 35 TCM 1663, T.C.Memo. 1976–366.

[54]§ 1271(b).

charitable contribution is fair market value when the property, if sold, would have yielded a long-term capital gain (refer to Chapter 9 and the discussion of § 170(e)).

EXAMPLE 71

Sharon wants to donate a tract of unimproved land (basis of $40,000 and fair market value of $200,000) held for the required long-term holding period to State University (a qualified charitable organization). However, Sharon currently is under audit by the IRS for capital gains she reported on certain real estate transactions during an earlier tax year. Although Sharon is not a licensed real estate broker, the IRS agent conducting the audit is contending that she has achieved dealer status by virtue of the number and frequency of the real estate transactions she has conducted. Under these circumstances, Sharon would be well-advised to postpone the donation to State University until her status is clarified. If she has achieved dealer status, the unimproved land may be inventory (refer to Example 69 for another possible result), and Sharon's charitable contribution deduction would be limited to $40,000. If not, and if the land is held as an investment, Sharon's deduction is $200,000 (the fair market value of the property). ▼

STOCK SALES

The following rules apply in determining the date of a stock sale:

- The date the sale is executed is the date of the sale. The execution date is the date the broker completes the transaction on the stock exchange.
- The settlement date is the date the cash or other property is paid to the seller of the stock. This date is *not* relevant in determining the date of sale.

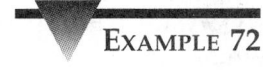

EXAMPLE 72

Lupe, a cash basis taxpayer, sells stock that results in a gain. The sale was executed on December 30, 1997. The settlement date is January 2, 1998. The date of sale is December 30, 1997 (the execution date). The holding period for the stock sold ends with the execution date. ▼

MAXIMIZING BENEFITS

Ordinary losses generally are preferable to capital losses because of the limitations imposed on the deductibility of net capital losses and the requirement that capital losses be used to offset capital gains. The taxpayer may be able to convert what would otherwise have been capital loss to ordinary loss. For example, business (but not nonbusiness) bad debts, losses from the sale or exchange of small business investment company stock, and losses from the sale or exchange of small business company stock all result in ordinary losses.[55]

Although capital losses can be carried over indefinitely, *indefinite* becomes definite when a taxpayer dies. Any loss carryovers not used by the taxpayer are permanently lost. That is, no tax benefit can be derived from the carryovers subsequent to death.[56] Therefore, the potential benefit of carrying over capital losses diminishes when dealing with older taxpayers.

It is usually beneficial to spread gains over more than one taxable year. In some cases, this can be accomplished through the installment sales method of accounting.

YEAR-END PLANNING

The following general rules can be applied for timing the recognition of capital gains and losses near the end of a taxable year:

---

[55]§§ 166(d), 1242, and 1244. Refer to the discussion in Chapter 6.   [56]Rev.Rul. 74–175, 1974–1 C.B. 52.

- If the taxpayer already has recognized more than $3,000 of capital loss, sell assets to generate capital gain equal to the excess of the capital loss over $3,000.

EXAMPLE 73   Kevin has already incurred a $7,000 STCL. Kevin should generate $4,000 of capital gain. The gain will offset $4,000 of the loss. The remaining loss of $3,000 can be deducted against ordinary income. ▼

- If the taxpayer already has recognized capital gain, sell assets to generate capital loss equal to the capital gain. The gain will not be taxed, and the loss will be fully *deductible* against the gain.
- Generally, if the taxpayer has a choice between recognizing short-term capital gain, mid-term capital gain, or long-term capital gain, long-term capital gain should be recognized because it has the lowest tax rate.

TIMING OF § 1231 GAIN

Although §§ 1245 and 1250 recapture much of the gain from the disposition of business property, sometimes § 1231 gain is still substantial. For instance, land held as a business asset will generate either § 1231 gain or § 1231 loss. If the taxpayer already has a capital loss for the year, the sale of land at a gain should be postponed so that the net § 1231 gain is not netted against the capital loss. The capital loss deduction will therefore be maximized for the current tax year, and the capital loss carryforward (if any) may be offset against the gain when the land is sold. If the taxpayer already has a § 1231 loss, § 1231 gains might be postponed to maximize the ordinary loss deduction this year. However, the carryforward of nonrecaptured § 1231 losses will make the § 1231 gain next year an ordinary gain.

EXAMPLE 74   Mark has a $2,000 net STCL for 1998. He could sell business land held 27 months for a $3,000 § 1231 gain. He will have no other capital gains and losses or § 1231 gains and losses in 1998 or 1999. He has no nonrecaptured § 1231 losses from prior years. Mark is in the 28% tax bracket in 1998 and 1999. If he sells the land in 1998, he will have a $1,000 net LTCG ($3,000 § 1231 gain – $2,000 STCL) and will pay a tax of $200 ($1,000 × 20%). If Mark sells the land in 1999, he will have a 1998 tax savings of $560 ($2,000 capital loss deduction × 28% tax rate on ordinary income). In 1999, he will pay tax of $600 ($3,000 × 20%). By postponing the sale for a year, Mark will have the use of $760 ($560 + $200). ▼

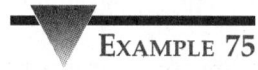

EXAMPLE 75   Beth has a $15,000 § 1231 loss in 1998. She could sell business equipment held 30 months for a $20,000 § 1231 gain and a $12,000 § 1245 gain. Beth is in the 28% tax bracket in 1998 and 1999. She has no nonrecaptured § 1231 losses from prior years. If she sells the equipment in 1998, she will have a $5,000 net § 1231 gain and $12,000 of ordinary gain. Her tax would be $4,360 [($5,000 § 1231 gain × 20%) + ($12,000 ordinary gain × 28%)].

　　If Beth postpones the equipment sale until 1999, she would have a 1998 ordinary loss of $15,000 and tax savings of $4,200 ($15,000 × 28%). In 1999, she would have $5,000 of § 1231 gain (the 1998 § 1231 loss carries over and recaptures $15,000 of the 1999 § 1231 gain as ordinary income) and $27,000 of ordinary gain. Her tax would be $8,560 [($5,000 § 1231 gain × 20%) + ($27,000 ordinary gain × 28%)]. By postponing the equipment sale, Beth has the use of $8,560 ($4,200 + $4,360). ▼

TIMING OF RECAPTURE

Since recapture is usually not triggered until the property is sold or disposed of, it may be possible to plan for recapture in low-bracket or loss years. If a taxpayer has net operating loss carryovers that are about to expire, the recognition of ordinary income from recapture may be advisable to absorb the loss carryovers.

EXAMPLE 76

Ahmad has a $15,000 net operating loss carryover that will expire this year. He owns a machine that he plans to sell in the early part of next year. The expected gain of $17,000 from the sale of the machine will be recaptured as ordinary income under § 1245. Ahmad sells the machine before the end of this year and offsets $15,000 of the ordinary income against the net operating loss carryover. ▼

POSTPONING AND SHIFTING RECAPTURE

It is also possible to postpone recapture or to shift the burden of recapture to others. For example, recapture is avoided upon the disposition of a § 1231 asset if the taxpayer replaces the property by entering into a like-kind exchange. In this instance, recapture potential is merely carried over to the newly acquired property (refer to Example 64).

Recapture can be shifted to others through the gratuitous transfer of § 1245 or § 1250 property to family members. A subsequent sale of such property by the donee will trigger recapture to the donee rather than the donor (refer to Example 61). This procedure would be advisable only if the donee is in a lower income tax bracket than the donor.

AVOIDING RECAPTURE

The immediate expensing election (§ 179) is subject to § 1245 recapture. If the election is not made, the § 1245 recapture potential will accumulate more slowly (refer to Chapter 7). Since using the immediate expense deduction complicates depreciation and book accounting for the affected asset, not taking the deduction may make sense even though the time value of money might indicate it should be taken.

KEY TERMS

Additional depreciation, 13–42

Alternative tax, 13–24

Capital asset, 13–5

Capital gains, 13–4

Capital losses, 13–4

Collectibles, 13–24

Franchise, 13–14

Holding period, 13–16

Intangible drilling and development costs, 13–50

Lessee, 13–16

Lessor, 13–16

Long-term nonpersonal use capital assets, 13–33

Mid-term capital gain, 13–22

Net capital gain (NCG), 13–22

Net capital loss (NCL), 13–27

Options, 13–11

Patent, 13–13

Related party, 13–49

Sale or exchange, 13–10

Section 1231 gains and losses, 13–31

Section 1231 lookback, 13–35

Section 1231 property, 13–32

Section 1245 property, 13–41

Section 1245 recapture, 13–39

Section 1250 property, 13–42

Section 1250 recapture, 13–42

Short sale, 13–18

Unrecaptured § 1250 gain, 13–22

PROBLEM
MATERIALS

DISCUSSION QUESTIONS

1. Todd owns the following assets. Which of them are capital assets?
   a. Ten shares of Standard Motors common stock.
   b. A copyright on a song Todd wrote.
   c. A U.S. government savings bond.
   d. A note Todd received when he loaned $100 to a friend.
   e. A very rare copy of "Your Federal Income Tax" (a U.S. government publication that Todd purchased many years ago from the U.S. Government Printing Office).
   f. Todd's personal use automobile.
   g. A letter Todd received from a former U.S. President. Todd received the letter because he had complained to the President about the President's foreign policy.

2. Joanne purchases song copyrights from composers. What tax issues does Joanne face in determining whether the copyrights are capital assets for her?

3. Jonathan lent $2,000 to a friend who became unemployed unexpectedly. Shortly thereafter, the friend took a new job in another state. After very diligent efforts to locate the friend, Jonathan was unable to find him, and payment of the loan is now 14 months overdue. Assuming the loan is fully noncollectible, what tax issues does Jonathan face?

4. Helen exchanges a computer used in her business for another computer that she will use in her business. The transaction qualifies as a like-kind exchange. Helen had held the computer given up in the exchange for four years. The computers are § 1231 assets. What is the holding period of the computer received in the exchange on the day of its acquisition?

5. Juan purchased corporate stock for $10,000 on April 10, 1996. On July 14, 1998, when the stock was worth $7,000, he gave it to his son, Miguel. What has to happen to the value of the property while Miguel holds it if Miguel is to tack Juan's holding period on to his own holding period?

6. John inherits stock on July 17, 1998. John's father had purchased the stock on April 10, 1997, for $12,000. The stock was worth $15,000 when the father died on December 20, 1997. The stock was worth $18,000 when John received it on July 17, 1998. When does John's holding period for the stock begin?

7. Sue has taxable income of $44,000 including $40,000 of net capital gain. Sue is single, and all of the net capital gain is *10%/20% gain*. What factors will determine whether all of Sue's net capital gain is taxed at 10%?

8. Near the end of 1998, Byron realizes that he has a net short-term capital loss of $13,000 for the year. Byron has taxable income (not including the loss) of $123,000 and is single. He owns numerous stocks that could be sold for a mid-term or long-term capital gain. What should he do before the end of 1998?

9. Ahmad is a farmer who is thinking about raising ostriches. Ostrich meat is very high in protein, low in calories, and low in fat. Ahmad would like to know what tax issues he would face if he decides to raise ostriches in addition to the cattle he is currently raising.

10. Aretha's 100% business use 1996 automobile was destroyed when a tree fell on it. She had a loss of $4,000 after her insurance recovery. She also sold some business land held 10 years for a gain of $3,000. What factors would influence how the automobile loss interacts with the land gain?

11. Sally lives in an area that was hit hard by a hurricane. She has correctly determined that she has a $15,000 business property long-term casualty loss and a $11,000 business property long-term casualty gain. What tax issues must Sally deal with?

12. Phil has nearly completed the tax return for a new client. The client has a net § 1231 gain. Phil had not done tax returns for the client in previous years and does not have the client's returns for prior years. What tax issues do these circumstances present for Phil?

13. Some of Max's business equipment that had been held long term was stolen in a burglary. The property had been purchased for $80,000, and the insurance company paid Max $33,000. What tax issues do these circumstances present for Max?

14. Residential rental real estate is acquired and disposed of in 1998. There is a small gain on the disposition of the property. The gain is less than the depreciation taken on the property. What is the nature of that gain?

15. Abigail sells one § 1231 asset during the year at a gain of $45,000. The asset was depreciable real estate she had held for seven years. She wants to know what her maximum unrecaptured § 1250 gain might be.

PROBLEMS

16. Nancy had three property transactions during the year. She sold a vacation home used for personal purposes at a $21,000 loss. The home had been held for five years and had never been rented. Nancy also sold an antique clock for $3,500 that she had inherited from her grandmother. The clock was valued in Nancy's grandmother's estate at $2,000. Nancy owned the clock for only four months. Nancy sold these assets to finance her full-time occupation as a songwriter. Near the end of the year, Nancy sold one of the songs she had written two years earlier. She received cash of $38,000 and a royalty interest in revenues derived from the merchandising of the song. Nancy had no tax basis for the song. Nancy had no other income and $18,000 in deductible songwriting expenses. Assuming the year is 1998, what is Nancy's adjusted gross income?

17. Revez owns an antique shop. He buys property from estates, often at much less than the retail value of the property. Recently, Revez sold for $4,000 an antique desk for which he had paid $125. Revez had held the desk in his shop for 25 months before selling it. Revez would like the gain on the sale of the desk to be a long-term capital gain. How can he achieve that objective?

18. Gary makes a gift to Barbara of the copyright on his song, "I Love the Spartans." The song has a basis of $20,000 to Gary. Gary had owned the copyright for two years. The copyright has a fair market value of $25,000 at the date of the gift. Three years after receiving the copyright, Barbara sells it to Jim for $30,000.
    a. What is Barbara's recognized gain on the sale?
    b. What is the nature of Barbara's gain?

19. Brenda Reynolds is a dealer in securities. She has spotted a fast-rising company and would like to buy and hold its stock for investment. The stock is currently selling for $45 per share, and Brenda thinks it will climb to $93 a share within two years. Brenda's co-workers have told her that there is "no way" she can get long-term capital gain treatment when she purchases stock because she is a securities dealer. Brenda has asked you to calculate her potential gain and tell her whether her co-workers are right. Draft a letter to Brenda responding to her request. Her address is 200 Morningside Drive, Hattiesburg, MS 39406.

20. Gordon has owned a large tract of land for 15 years and subdivides it for sale. Assume Gordon meets all the requirements of § 1237. During the first year of sales, Gordon sells 20 lots for $20,000 each. His selling expenses are 7% of the sales price of each lot. Gordon has a basis of $11,000 in each lot. Compute Gordon's total gain from the sale of these lots and indicate the nature of the gain.

21. Sue has had a bad year with her investments. She lent a friend $3,700; the friend did not repay the loan when it was due, and then declared bankruptcy. The loan is totally uncollectible. Sue also was notified by her broker that the Willow corporate bonds she owned became worthless on October 13, 1998. She had purchased the bonds for $10,000 on November 10, 1997. Sue also had a $20,000 loss on the disposition of § 1244 corporate stock that she purchased several years ago. Sue is single.

a. What are the nature and amount of Sue's losses?

b. What is Sue's AGI for 1998 assuming she has $65,000 of ordinary gross income from sources other than those discussed above?

c. What are the nature and amount of Sue's loss carryforwards?

22. Samantha is in the business of buying song copyrights from struggling songwriters, holding those copyrights, and then reselling the songs to major record companies and singers. Samantha has a four-month option to purchase a song copyright. She paid $2,000 for this option. A famous singer has heard the song and is willing to buy the option from Samantha for $10,000. Samantha thinks the song may be worth $35,000 in six months. If Samantha exercises the option, she will have to pay $20,000 for the song. Assuming Samantha is in the 36% tax bracket, which of these alternatives will give her a better after-tax cash flow?

23. Marta is looking for vacant land to buy. She would hold the land as an investment. For $10,000, she is granted an 11-month option on January 1, 1998, to buy 10 acres of vacant land for $300,000. The owner (who is holding the land for investment) paid $12,000 for the land several years ago.

a. Does the landowner have gross income when $10,000 is received for granting the option?

b. Does Marta have an asset when the option is granted?

c. If the option lapses, does the landowner have a recognized gain? If so, what type of gain? Does Marta have a recognized loss? If so, what type of loss?

d. If the option is exercised and an additional $300,000 is paid for the land, how much recognized gain does the seller have? What type of gain? What is Marta's tax basis for the property?

24. Frank owns a patent on a part that Teal Corporation wishes to use as a component in a product it manufactures. Frank had purchased the patent from the inventor before the inventor reduced the patent to practice. Frank had intended to use the patented part in his business, but found that it was not suitable. Teal is willing to pay Frank $5,000 per month plus 1% of the manufactured cost of the part. How should Frank construct the contract with Teal so that the $5,000 per month and 1% of manufactured cost are long-term capital gain?

25. Freys, Inc., sells a 12-year franchise to Reynaldo. The franchise contains many restrictions on how Reynaldo may operate his store. For instance, Reynaldo cannot use less than Grade 10 Idaho potatoes, must fry the potatoes at a constant 410 degrees, dress store personnel in Freys-approved uniforms, and have a Freys sign that meets detailed specifications on size, color, and construction. When the franchise contract is signed, Reynaldo makes a noncontingent $40,000 payment to Freys. During the same year, Reynaldo pays Freys $25,000—14% of Reynaldo's sales. How does Freys treat each of these payments? How does Reynaldo treat each of the payments?

26. Irene lives in an apartment near her college campus. Her lease runs out in July 1999, but her landlord could sell the building if he can convince all the tenants to cancel their leases and move out by the end of 1998. The landlord has offered Irene $1,000 to cancel her lease. Irene's lease began on August 1, 1998. What tax factors should Irene consider in deciding whether to take the landlord's offer?

27. On August 10, 1998, Peter received 100 shares of Brown Corporation stock as a gift from his father, John. On that date, the stock was worth $18 per share. John had paid $23 per share for the stock on July 11, 1987. On December 20, 1998, Peter sold all of the shares for $16 per share. What are the amount and the nature of Peter's gain or loss from disposition of the Brown shares?

28. Dennis sells short 100 shares of ARC stock at $20 per share on January 15, 1998. He buys 200 shares of ARC stock on April 1, 1998, at $25 per share. On May 2, 1998, he closes the short sale by delivering 100 of the shares purchased on April 1.

a. What are the amount and nature of Dennis's loss upon closing the short sale?

b. When does the holding period for the remaining 100 shares begin?

c. If Dennis sells (at $27 per share) the remaining 100 shares on January 20, 1999, what will be the nature of his gain or loss?

29. Elaine Case (single with no dependents) has the following transactions in 1998:

Adjusted gross income (exclusive of capital gains and losses)	$240,000
Long-term capital gain	12,000
Mid-term capital loss	(5,000)
Short-term capital gain	19,000
Short-term capital loss	(23,000)

What is Elaine's net capital gain or loss? Draft a letter to Elaine describing how the net capital gain or loss will be treated on her tax return. Assume Elaine's income from other sources puts her in the 36% bracket. Elaine's address is 300 Ireland Avenue, Shepherdstown, WV 25443.

30. In 1998, Betty (head of household with three dependents) had an $18,000 loss from the sale of a personal residence. She also purchased from an individual inventor for $8,000 (and resold in two months for $7,000) a patent on a rubber bonding process. The patent had not yet been reduced to practice. Betty purchased the patent as an investment. Additionally, she had the following capital gains and losses from stock transactions:

Long-term capital loss	($ 3,000)
Mid-term capital loss carryover from 1997	(12,000)
Short-term capital gain	21,000
Short-term capital loss	(6,000)

What is Betty's net capital gain or loss? Draft a letter to Betty explaining the tax treatment of the sale of her personal residence. Assume Betty's income from other sources puts her in the 36% bracket. Betty's address is 1120 West Street, Ashland, OR 97520.

31. For 1998, Ahmad completes the following stock transactions:

	Date Acquired	Cost	Date Sold	Selling Price
1,000 shares ABC	1/6/98	$4,000	8/2/98	$12,000
200 shares DEF	7/1/82	8,800	9/18/98	19,400
3,500 shares GHI	5/2/98	7,000	11/2/98	8,900
5,000 shares JKL	7/15/97	9,700	12/15/98	5,000

a. What is Ahmad's includible gain or deductible loss resulting from these stock sales?
b. Assuming Ahmad's taxable income from sources other than those detailed above is $13,200, what is Ahmad's tax liability?

32. Consuela, a head of household with two dependents, has the following 1998 transactions:

Adjusted gross income (exclusive of capital gains and losses)	$125,250
Long-term capital loss	(5,000)
Mid-term capital gain	20,000
Short-term capital loss carryover	(2,000)

a. What is Consuela's net capital gain or loss?
b. What is Consuela's taxable income assuming she does not itemize?
c. What is Consuela's tax on taxable income?

33. Gold, Inc., has determined its 1998 taxable income as $45,000 before considering the results of its capital gain or loss transactions. Gold has a short-term capital loss of $4,000, a long-term capital loss of $18,000, and a short-term capital gain of $19,000. What is Gold's 1998 taxable income, and what (if any) are the amount and nature of its capital loss carryover?

34. Doria is going to purchase a sole proprietorship that June has owned for five years. They have agreed on a price for all the assets except goodwill and June's covenant not to compete against Doria. June is willing to give Doria a two-year covenant not to compete for only $1 of compensation, but would like $25,000 for the business goodwill. Doria would like to pay June $25,000 for the covenant not to compete and only $1 for the business goodwill. June is in the 36% tax bracket, and Doria is in the 31% tax bracket. Which of these approaches is better for June? For Doria?

35. A painting that Kwan Lee held for investment was destroyed in a flood. The painting was insured, and Kwan had a $10,000 gain from this casualty. He also had a $7,000 loss from an uninsured antique vase that was destroyed by the flood. The vase was also held for investment. Kwan had no other property transactions during the year and has no nonrecaptured § 1231 losses from prior years. Both the painting and the vase had been held more than 18 months when the flood occurred. Compute Kwan's net gain or loss and identify how it would be treated. Also, write a letter to Kwan explaining the nature of the gain or loss. Kwan's address is 2367 Meridian Road, Hannibal Point, MO 34901.

36. Vicki has the following net § 1231 results for each of the years shown. What would be the nature of the net gains in 1997 and 1998?

Tax Year	Net § 1231 Loss	Net § 1231 Gain
1993	$16,000	
1994	13,000	
1995	22,000	
1996		$10,000
1997		20,000
1998		29,000

37. Yoshida owns two parcels of business land (§ 1231 assets). One parcel can be sold at a loss of $30,000, and the other parcel can be sold at a gain of $40,000. Yoshida has no nonrecaptured § 1231 losses from prior years. The parcels could be sold at any time because potential purchasers are abundant. Yoshida has a $25,000 short-term capital loss carryover from a prior tax year and no capital assets that could be sold to generate long-term capital gains. Both the land parcels have been held more than 18 months. What should Yoshida do based upon these facts? (Assume tax rates are constant and ignore the present value of future cash flow.)

38. Gray Industries (a sole proprietorship) sold three § 1231 assets during 1998. Data on these property dispositions are as follows:

Asset	Cost	Acquired	Depreciation	Sold for	Sold on
Rack	$100,000	10/10/94	$60,000	$55,000	10/10/98
Forklift	35,000	10/16/95	23,000	5,000	10/10/98
Bin	87,000	03/12/97	34,000	60,000	10/10/98

a. Determine the amount and the character of the recognized gain or loss from the disposition of each asset.
b. Assuming Gray has no nonrecaptured net § 1231 losses from prior years, how much of the 1998 recognized gains are treated as capital gains?

39. Green Industries (a sole proprietorship) sold three § 1231 assets during 1998. Data on these property dispositions are as follows:

Asset	Cost	Acquired	Depreciation	Sold for	Sold on
Rack	$100,000	10/10/94	$60,000	$155,000	10/10/98
Forklift	35,000	10/16/95	23,000	5,000	10/10/98
Bin	87,000	03/12/97	34,000	60,000	10/10/98

a. Determine the amount and the character of the recognized gain or loss from the disposition of each asset.

b. Assuming Green has $5,000 nonrecaptured net § 1231 losses from the five prior years, how much of the 1998 recognized gains are treated as capital gains?

40. Magenta Industries (a sole proprietorship) sold three § 1231 assets during the year. Data on these property dispositions are as follows:

Asset	Cost	Acquired	Depreciation	Sold for	Sold on
Rack	$110,000	10/10/95	$60,000	$55,000	10/10/98
Forklift	45,000	10/16/94	23,000	5,000	10/10/98
Bin	97,000	03/12/97	34,000	60,000	10/10/98

a. Determine the amount and the character of the recognized gain or loss from the disposition of each asset.

b. Assuming Magenta has $2,000 nonrecaptured net § 1231 losses from prior years, how much of the 1998 recognized gains are treated as capital gains?

41. On December 1, 1996, Gray Manufacturing Company (a corporation) purchased another company's assets, including a patent. The patent was used in Gray's manufacturing operations; $40,500 was allocated to the patent, and it was amortized at the rate of $225 per month. On June 30, 1998, Gray sold the patent for $60,000. Nineteen months of amortization had been taken on the patent. What are the amount and nature of the gain Gray recognizes on the disposition of the patent? Write a letter to Gray discussing the treatment of the gain. Gray's address is 6734 Grover Street, Back Bay Harbor, ME 23890. The letter should be addressed to Siddim Sadatha, Controller.

42. On June 1, 1994, Sparrow Enterprises (not a corporation) acquired a retail store for $400,000. The store was 39-year real property, and the straight-line cost recovery method was used. The store was sold on June 21, 1998, for $370,000.

a. Compute the cost recovery and adjusted basis for the store using Table 7–7 from Chapter 7.

b. What are the amount and nature of Sparrow's gain or loss from disposition of the store? What amount, if any, of the gain is unrecaptured § 1250 gain?

43. On January 1, 1986, Esteban acquired a $600,000 residential building for use in his rental activity. He took $450,000 of cost recovery on the building before disposing of it for $800,000 on January 1, 1998. For the period Esteban held the building, straight-line cost recovery would have been $400,000. What are the amount and nature of Esteban's gain from the disposition of the property? What amount, if any, of the gain is unrecaptured § 1250 gain?

44. Dave is the sole proprietor of a trampoline shop. During 1998, the following transactions occurred:

- Unimproved land adjacent to the store was condemned by the city on February 1. The condemnation proceeds were $25,000. The land, acquired in 1982, had an allocable basis of $40,000. Dave has additional parking across the street and plans to use the condemnation proceeds to build his inventory.

- A truck used to deliver trampolines was sold on January 2 for $3,500. The truck was purchased on January 2, 1994, for $6,000. On the date of sale, the adjusted basis was $2,509.

- Dave sold an antique rowing machine at an auction. Net proceeds were $3,900. The rowing machine was purchased as used equipment 17 years ago for $5,200 and is fully depreciated.

- Dave sold an apartment building for $200,000 on September 1. The rental property was purchased on September 1, 1995, for $150,000 and was being depreciated over a 27.5-year life using the straight-line method. At the date of sale, the adjusted basis was $124,783.

- Dave's personal yacht was stolen September 5. The yacht had been purchased in August at a cost of $25,000. The fair market value immediately preceding the theft was $20,000. Dave was insured for 50% of the original cost, and he received $12,500 on December 1.

- Dave sold a Buick on May 1 for $9,600. The vehicle had been used exclusively for personal purposes. It was purchased on September 1, 1994, for $20,800.

- An adding machine used by Dave's bookkeeper was sold on June 1. Net proceeds of the sale were $135. The machine was purchased on June 2, 1994, for $350. It was being depreciated over a five-year life employing the straight-line method. The adjusted basis on the date of sale was $95.

- Dave's trampoline stretching machine (owned two years) was stolen on May 5, but the business's insurance company will not pay any of the machine's value because Dave failed to pay the insurance premium. The machine had a fair market value of $8,000 and an adjusted basis of $6,000 at the time of theft.

- Dave had AGI of $4,000 from sources other than those described above.

- Dave has no nonrecaptured § 1231 lookback losses.

a. For each transaction, what are the amount and nature of recognized gain or loss?
b. What is Dave's 1998 AGI?

45. On January 1, 1986, Cora Hassant acquired depreciable real property for $100,000. She used accelerated depreciation to compute the asset's cost recovery. The asset was sold for $89,000 on January 3, 1998, when its adjusted basis was $38,000. Straight-line cost recovery for the period of time the asset was held would have been $52,700.
    a. What are the amount and nature of the gain if the real property was residential?
    b. What are the amount and nature of the gain if the real property was nonresidential?
    c. Cora is curious about how the recapture rules differ for residential rental real estate acquired in 1986 and for residential rental real estate acquired in 1987 and thereafter. Write a letter to Cora explaining the differences. Her address is 2345 Westridge Street #23, Homer, MT 67342.

46. Joanne is in the 39.6% tax bracket and owns depreciable business equipment that she purchased several years ago for $135,000. She has taken $100,000 of depreciation on the equipment, and it is worth $85,000. Joanne's niece, Susan, is starting a new business and is short of cash. Susan has asked Joanne to gift the equipment to her so that Susan can use it in her business. Joanne no longer needs the equipment. Identify the alternatives available to Joanne if she wishes to help Susan and the tax effects of those alternatives. (Assume all alternatives involve the business equipment in one way or another, and ignore the gift tax.)

47. Gregor owns business equipment with a $55,000 adjusted basis. He paid $100,000 for the equipment, and it is currently worth $73,000. Gregor dies suddenly, and his son Adrian inherits the property. What is Adrian's basis for the property, and what happens to the § 1245 depreciation recapture potential?

48. Cathy sells § 1245 property for $35,000, to be paid in 10 annual installments of $3,500 each plus interest at 8%. Cathy realizes a $12,000 gain from the sale, of which $12,000 is attributable to depreciation taken. Cathy would like to use the installment method to recognize the gain on the sale. May she do so?

49. Ray owns an unimproved parking lot that was used in his parking lot business for 10 years. A real estate developer purchases the lot from Ray for a total of $300,000. Ray receives $50,000 in 1998 and will receive $50,000 (plus 10% interest) each year for the next five years. Ray has a $120,000 adjusted basis for the lot. What are the nature and amount of the gain recognized in 1998?

50. Orange Corporation sells depreciable equipment for $59,000 to its sole shareholder, Jane. Orange had a $45,000 adjusted basis for the equipment and had originally paid $85,000 for it. Jane will use the equipment in her sole proprietorship business. The $59,000 sale price is the property's fair market value at the time of the sale. What are the consequences of this sale for Orange? For Jane?

51. Jay sold three items of business equipment for a total of $300,000. None of the equipment was appraised to determine its value. Jay's cost and adjusted basis for the assets are as follows:

Asset	Cost	Adjusted Basis
Skidder	$230,000	$ 40,000
Driller	120,000	60,000
Platform	620,000	–0–
Total	$970,000	$100,000

Jay has been unable to establish the fair market values of the three assets. All he can determine is that combined they were worth $300,000 to the buyer in this arm's length transaction. How should Jay allocate the sales price and figure the gain or loss on the sale of the three assets?

CUMULATIVE PROBLEMS

52. Sue Lowe lives at 1310 Meadow Lane, Lima, OH 23412 and her Social Security number is 312–55–8000. Sue is single and has a 10-year-old son, Kania. His Social Security number is 480–01–9030. Kania lives with Sue and she fully supports him. During 1997, Sue spent $2,700 on qualifying support for Kania at the Happy Daze Child Care Center, 18 Oak Lane, Lima, OH 23410. The center's identifying number is 38–6933367.

Sue owns the Lowe Enterprises sole proprietorship (38–1234567) which is located at 456 Hill Street, Lima, OH 23401. Her 1997 Form 1040 Schedule C for Lowe Enterprises shows net income of $30,000. Sue personally purchases health insurance on herself and Kania. The premiums are $3,000 per year.

Sue has an extensive stock portfolio and has prepared the following analysis:

Stock	Number of Shares	Date Purchased	Date Sold	Per Share Cost	Per Share Selling Price	Per Share Dividends
Blue	10	10/18/96	10/11/97	$80	$72	$3
Green	30	10/11/92	10/11/97	33	47	1
Purple	15	3/10/96	3/02/97	62	33	2
Yellow	100	4/11/89	8/02/97	18	46	1
Gold	35	7/12/96	10/11/97	7	12	0
White	100	10/11/96		82		1
Tan	20	4/02/96		15		0
Beige	17	4/11/89		11		0
Amber	75	3/10/94		43		2

Note: The per share cost includes commissions, and the per share selling price is net of commissions. Also, the per share dividends are the actual dividends received in 1997.

Sue had $800 of interest income from State of Ohio bonds and $600 of interest income on her Lima Savings Bank account. She also received $5,000 of alimony payments.

Sue itemizes her deductions and had the following items, which may be relevant to her return:

Item	Amount	Comment
Unreimbursed medical expenses for Sue and Kania (all for visits to doctors)	$1,786	Does not include health insurance premiums.
State income taxes paid	1,830	
Real property taxes on personal residence	3,230	
Interest paid on loans used to purchase stock held for investment	830	
Interest paid on home mortgage (Form 1098)	8,137	The loan is secured by the residence and was incurred when the home was purchased.
Charitable contributions	940	Cash paid to Sue's church.

Sue made a $6,000 Federal estimated income tax payment, does not wish any of her taxes to finance Presidential elections, has no foreign bank accounts or trusts, and wishes any refund to be applied against her 1998 taxes.

Compute Sue's net tax payable or refund due for 1997. If you use tax forms for your computations, you will need Form 1040 and Schedules A, B, C, D, and SE and Forms 2441 and 4952. Suggested software (if available): *TurboTax*.

53. Felix Montoya (Social Security number 390–88–3912) owns Montoya Enterprises, a computer retail sole proprietorship. Felix lives at 112 Green Road, Encidio, CA 45678. The store is located at 3456 Purple Road, Encidio, CA 45679. The following summary reflects the store's results of operations for 1997:

Item	Amount
Sales	$1,875,000
Sales returns and allowances	(5,000)
Beginning inventory (FIFO)	187,000
Purchases	573,000
Ending inventory (FIFO)	129,000
Expenses:	
Advertising	18,000
Employee wages	233,000
Employer FICA	23,000
Depreciation	25,000
Charitable contributions	3,000
Utilities	12,000
Store property taxes	17,000
Lodging and transportation expenses while away from home overnight on store business (no meals)	3,000
Meals and entertainment expense in connection with store business	2,000
Store insurance	15,000
Interest on store mortgage	35,000
Professional service fees	4,000

Other information is as follows:

- In connection with the business, the following information may be relevant: The principal business code is 3747, and the employer ID number is 382345678. The business uses the accrual method of accounting. Felix materially participated in the business, which was started in 1988. The lower of cost or market was used to cost inventory; no store labor was added to inventory; and there was no change from prior years in the method of determining inventories. No vehicles were used in connection with the business.

- Montoya Enterprises has no fringe benefits for its employees. However, Felix paid $5,600 in health insurance premiums for coverage on himself.

- On December 8, 1997, Montoya Enterprises sold office equipment used in its business for $33,000. The equipment had been purchased for $83,000 on January 20, 1994, and $62,000 of depreciation (including 1997) had been taken on it.

- On December 9, 1997, Montoya Enterprises sold for $80,000 a storage building it had used to store excess inventory. The building cost $80,000 on June 10, 1989, and $12,000 of straight-line depreciation (including 1997) had been taken on it.

- Felix has $3,000 (total) of nonrecaptured net § 1231 losses from the prior five years.

- Felix is age 38, single, and has no dependents. He does not wish to contribute to the Presidential Election Campaign Fund. Felix made $150,000 of timely Federal estimated income tax payments. During 1997, he made $67,000 of timely state estimated income tax payments. He wants any Federal tax refund to be applied to his 1998 estimated tax.

- Felix made deductible alimony payments of $350,000 during the year. His former spouse's Social Security number is 309–67–2345.

- Felix had $45,000 of interest income from the Diversified Corporate Bond Fund. He also received a $13,000 mid-term capital gain distribution from the Green High Growth Stock Fund. Felix does not have an interest in any foreign bank accounts or trusts.

- Felix had the following itemized deductions (all with proper documentation):

Unreimbursed medical expenses	$ 3,000
Real estate taxes on his home	45,000
Home mortgage interest	67,000
Charitable contributions	56,000

Compute Felix Montoya's net tax payable or refund due for 1997. If you use tax forms for your computations, you will need Form 1040 and Schedules A, B, C, D, and SE and Form 4797. Suggested software (if available): *TurboTax.*

Research Problems for this chapter appear at the end of Chapter 28.

TEAM PROJECT: ARTHUR ANDERSEN TAX CHALLENGE CASES

For more information on the Arthur Andersen Tax Challenge Cases, refer to Chapter 1, page 1–37.

Information related to tax issues and problems that are discussed in this chapter may be found in the

Day and Ball case on pages 19 and 22
Fence case on pages 39, 40, 50, and 56

Read and analyze the case you have been assigned and *identify* any issues and problems that are related to material covered in this chapter. If the information provided in the case is complete, prepare answers for this part of the case at this time. If you need information that is contained in the later parts of the case, write a memo summarizing the questions or problems so you can prepare a complete answer at a later date.

14

ALTERNATIVE MINIMUM TAX

LEARNING OBJECTIVES

After completing Chapter 14, you should be able to:

1. Explain the rationale for the alternative minimum tax (AMT).

2. Understand the formula for computing the AMT for individuals.

3. Identify the adjustments made in calculating the AMT.

4. Identify the tax preferences that are included in calculating the AMT.

5. Apply the formula for computing the AMT and illustrate Form 6251.

6. Describe the role of the AMT credit in the alternative minimum tax structure.

7. Understand the basic features of the corporate AMT.

8. Identify tax planning opportunities to minimize the AMT.

1 LEARNING OBJECTIVE
Explain the rationale for the alternative minimum tax (AMT).

Bob and Carol are unmarried individuals who work for the same employer and have the same amount of gross income and the same amount of deductions. Bob's tax return is prepared by Adam, and Carol's tax return is prepared by Eve. While discussing their tax liability one day at lunch, Carol is dismayed to learn that she paid $15,000 more in Federal income taxes than Bob did for the tax year. Carol meets with Eve that evening. Eve reviews Carol's tax return and assures her that her tax liability was properly calculated.

The above events raise a number of interesting questions for Bob and Carol that can be answered after completing this chapter. Why didn't Bob and Carol have the same tax liability? Were both tax returns properly prepared? Should Carol consider replacing her tax return preparer Eve with Adam? Is it possible and/or desirable for Carol to file an amended return? Should Bob do anything?

The tax law contains many incentives that are intended to influence the economic and social behavior of taxpayers (refer to Chapter 1). Some taxpayers have been able to take advantage of enough of these incentives to avoid or minimize any liability for Federal income tax. Although these taxpayers were reducing taxes legally, Congress became concerned about the inequity that results when taxpayers with substantial economic incomes can avoid paying any income tax. The **alternative minimum tax (AMT)** was enacted as a backup to the regular income tax. The rationale for the AMT was expressed as follows:

> [T]he minimum tax should serve one overriding objective: to ensure that no taxpayer with substantial economic income can avoid significant tax liability by using exclusions, deductions, and credits. Although these provisions may provide incentives for worthy goals, they become counterproductive when taxpayers are allowed to use them to avoid virtually all tax liability. The ability of high-income taxpayers to pay little or no tax undermines respect for the entire tax system and, thus, for the incentive provisions themselves. In addition, even aside from public perceptions ... it is inherently unfair for high-income taxpayers to pay little or no tax due to their ability to utilize tax preferences.[1]

---

[1] *General Explanation of the Tax Reform Act of 1986 ("Blue Book")*, prepared by The Staff of the Joint Committee on Taxation, May 4, 1987, H.R. 3838, 99th Cong., pp. 432–433.

The individual AMT is discussed in the first part of this chapter. The corporate AMT is similar to the individual AMT, but differs in several important ways. Details of the corporate AMT are presented in the last part of the chapter.

INDIVIDUAL ALTERNATIVE MINIMUM TAX

AMT FORMULA FOR ALTERNATIVE MINIMUM TAXABLE INCOME (AMTI)

2 ▼ **LEARNING OBJECTIVE**
Understand the formula for computing the AMT for individuals.

The AMT is separate from, but parallel to, the regular income tax system.[2] Most income and expense items are treated the same way for both regular income tax and AMT purposes. For example, a taxpayer's salary is included in computing taxable income and is also included in alternative minimum taxable income (AMTI). Alimony paid is allowed as a deduction *for* AGI for both regular income tax and AMT purposes. Certain itemized deductions, such as charitable contributions and gambling losses, are allowed for both regular income tax and AMT purposes.

On the other hand, some income and expense items are treated differently for regular income tax and AMT purposes. For example, interest income on bonds issued by state, county, or local governments is *excluded* in computing taxable income. However, interest on such bonds is *included* in computing AMTI if the bonds are private activity bonds. The deduction for personal and dependency exemptions is *allowed* for regular income tax purposes, but is *disallowed* for AMT purposes.

In other cases, certain items are considered in both the regular income tax and AMT computations, but the amounts are different. For example, the completed contract method can be used to report income from some long-term contracts for regular income tax purposes, but the percentage of completion method is required for AMT purposes. Thus, the amount of income included in taxable income will differ from the amount included in AMTI. Depreciation is allowed as a deduction for both regular income tax and AMT purposes, but the *amount* of the regular income tax deduction may be different from the amount of the AMT deduction. Medical expenses are deductible in calculating both taxable income and AMTI, but the floor on the deduction is different.

The parallel but separate nature of the AMT means that AMTI will differ from taxable income. It is possible to compute AMTI by direct application of the AMT provisions, using the following formula:

> Gross income computed by applying the AMT rules
>
> **Minus:** Deductions computed by applying the AMT rules
>
> **Equals:** AMTI before tax preferences
>
> **Plus:** Tax preferences
>
> **Equals:** Alternative minimum taxable income

While the direct approach for computing AMTI appears quite logical, both the tax law and the tax forms provide a very different approach. Both of these use taxable income (for Form 6251, taxable income *before* the deduction for personal exemptions and dependency deductions) as the starting point for computing AMTI, as shown in Figure 14–1. This indirect approach for computing AMTI is analogous to the indirect approach used in calculating a net operating loss.

---

[2] § 55.

▼ **FIGURE 14–1**
Alternative Minimum Taxable
Income (AMTI) Formula

Taxable income

Plus: Positive AMT adjustments

Minus: Negative AMT adjustments

Equals: Taxable income after AMT adjustments

Plus: Tax preferences

Equals: Alternative minimum taxable income

The purpose of the AMT formula is to *reconcile* taxable income to AMTI. This reconciliation is similar to a bank reconciliation, which reconciles a checkbook balance to a bank balance by considering differences between the depositor's records and the bank's records. The reconciliation of taxable income to AMTI is accomplished by entering reconciling items to account for differences between regular income tax provisions and AMT provisions. These reconciling items are referred to as **AMT adjustments** or **tax preferences**. *Adjustments* can be either positive or negative, as shown in the formula in Figure 14–1. Tax preferences are always positive.

Adjustments.   Most adjustments relate to *timing differences* that arise because of *separate* regular income tax and AMT treatments. Adjustments that are caused by timing differences will eventually *reverse*; that is, positive adjustments will be offset by negative adjustments in the future, and vice versa.[3]

For example, **circulation expenditures** can give rise to a timing difference that requires an AMT adjustment. For regular income tax purposes, circulation expenditures can be deducted in the year incurred. For AMT purposes, however, circulation expenditures must be deducted over a three-year period. This difference

TAX IN THE NEWS

MAKING OUR TAX SYSTEM MORE FRIENDLY

When the National Commission on Restructuring the IRS heard testimony on the current tax system, a frequent complaint was the complexity of the system. Representative of such testimony was that of Michael E. Mares, head of the tax executive committee of the American Institute of CPAs. According to Mares, needless complexity is undermining the system. Although a truly simple system may be impossible, a simpler system is an achievable goal.

Contributing to the complexity is the AMT. Opponents argue that it is a remarkably complex system. Though the AMT was intended to assure that most wealthy taxpayers pay at least some Federal income taxes, its impact is growing and extending beyond the wealthy. In addition, many taxpayers not subject to the AMT must deal with its complexity in ascertaining that it does not apply to them.

SOURCE: Adapted from Tom Herman, "Tax Complexity Draws Growing Fire, Even from Experts," *Wall Street Journal*, November 13, 1996, p. A1.

---

[3]§ 56.

in treatment will be used to illustrate the role of adjustments in the formula for computing AMTI.

EXAMPLE 1

Bob had taxable income of $100,000 in 1997. In computing taxable income, he deducted $30,000 of circulation expenditures incurred in 1997. Bob's allowable deduction for AMT purposes was only $10,000. Therefore, an AMT adjustment was required in 1997 as follows:

Taxable income		$100,000
+AMT adjustment:		
Circulation expenditures deducted for regular income tax purposes	$ 30,000	
Circulation expenditures allowed for AMT purposes	(10,000)	
Positive adjustment		20,000
=AMTI before tax preferences		$120,000
+Tax preferences		–0–
AMTI		$120,000

Analysis of this computation shows that the allowable AMT deduction is $20,000 less than the allowable regular income tax deduction. Therefore, AMTI is $20,000 greater than taxable income. This is accomplished by entering a positive AMT adjustment of $20,000. ▼

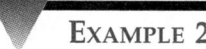

EXAMPLE 2

Assume that Bob from Example 1 has taxable income of $95,000 in 1998. He is allowed to deduct $10,000 of circulation expenditures for AMT purposes, but is not allowed a deduction for regular income tax purposes because all $30,000 was deducted in 1997. Therefore, a *negative* AMT adjustment is required.

Taxable income		$ 95,000
–AMT adjustment:		
Circulation expenditures deducted for regular income tax purposes	$ –0–	
Circulation expenditures allowed for AMT purposes	(10,000)	
Negative adjustment		(10,000)
=AMTI before tax preferences		$ 85,000
+Tax preferences		–0–
AMTI		$ 85,000

Analysis of this computation shows that the allowable AMT deduction is $10,000 more than the allowable regular income tax deduction. Therefore, AMTI is $10,000 less than taxable income. This is accomplished by entering a negative AMT adjustment of $10,000. ▼

As noted previously, timing differences eventually reverse. Therefore, total positive adjustments will be offset by total negative adjustments with respect to a particular item.

EXAMPLE 3

Refer to Examples 1 and 2. The difference in regular income tax and AMT treatments of circulation expenditures will result in AMT adjustments over a three-year period.

Year	Income Tax Deduction	AMT Deduction	AMT Adjustment
1997	$30,000	$10,000	+$ 20,000
1998	–0–	10,000	–10,000
1999	–0–	10,000	–10,000
Total	$30,000	$30,000	$ –0–

As the last column illustrates, if positive and negative AMT adjustments with respect to a particular item are caused by a timing difference, they will eventually net to zero. ▼

The adjustments for circulation expenditures and other items are discussed in detail under AMT Adjustments.

Although most adjustments relate to timing differences, there are exceptions. See the subsequent discussion of such items under Itemized Deductions. Adjustments that do not relate to timing differences result in a permanent difference between taxable income and AMTI.

Tax Preferences. Some deductions and exclusions allowed to taxpayers for regular income tax purposes provide extraordinary tax savings. Congress has chosen to single out these items, which are referred to as tax preferences.[4] The AMT is designed to take back all or part of the tax benefits derived through the use of preferences in the computation of taxable income for regular income tax purposes. This is why taxable income, which is the starting point in computing AMTI, is increased by tax preference items. The effect of adding these preference items is to disallow for *AMT purposes* those preferences that were allowed in the regular income tax computation. Tax preferences include the following items, which are discussed in detail under AMT Preferences:

- Percentage depletion in excess of the property's adjusted basis.
- Excess intangible drilling costs reduced by 65 percent of the net income from oil, gas, and geothermal properties.
- Interest on certain private activity bonds.
- Excess of accelerated over straight-line depreciation on real property placed in service before 1987.
- Excess of accelerated over straight-line depreciation on *leased* personal property placed in service before 1987.
- Excess of amortization allowance over depreciation on pre-1987 certified pollution control facilities.
- Forty-two percent of the exclusion from gross income associated with gains on the sale of certain small business stock.

AMT FORMULA: OTHER COMPONENTS

To convert AMTI to AMT, other formula components including the exemption, rates, credit, and regular tax liability must be considered. The impact of each of these components is depicted in the AMT formula in Figure 14–2.

The relationship between the regular tax liability and the tentative AMT is key to the AMT formula. If the regular tax liability exceeds tentative AMT, then the AMT is zero. If the tentative AMT exceeds the regular tax liability, the amount of the excess is the AMT. In essence, the taxpayer will pay whichever tax liability is greater—that calculated using the regular income tax rules or that calculated using the AMT rules. However, both the tax law and Form 6251 adopt this excess approach with the taxpayer paying the regular tax liability plus any AMT.

EXAMPLE 4

Anna, an unmarried individual, has regular taxable income of $100,000. She has positive adjustments of $40,000 and tax preferences of $25,000. Calculate her AMT for 1998. Anna's regular tax liability is $25,863. Her AMT is calculated as follows:

[4]§ 57.

▼ **FIGURE 14–2**

Alternative Minimum Tax Formula

Regular taxable income

Plus or minus: Adjustments

Equals: Taxable income after AMT adjustments

Plus: Tax preferences

Equals: Alternative minimum taxable income

Minus: Exemption

Equals: Alternative minimum tax base

Times: 26% or 28% rate

Equals: Tentative minimum tax before foreign tax credit

Minus: Alternative minimum tax foreign tax credit

Equals: Tentative minimum tax

Minus: Regular tax liability*

Equals: Alternative minimum tax (if amount is positive)

*This is the regular tax liability for the year reduced by any allowable foreign tax credit.

Taxable income (TI)	$100,000
Plus: Adjustments	40,000
Equals: TI after AMT adjustments	$140,000
Plus: Tax preferences	25,000
Equals: AMTI	$165,000
Minus: AMT exemption ($33,750 – $13,125)	(20,625)*
Equals: AMT base	$144,375
Times: AMT rate	× 26%
Equals: Tentative AMT	$ 37,538
Minus: Regular tax liability	(25,863)
Equals: AMT	$ 11,675

*Discussed below under Exemption Amount.

Anna will pay the IRS a total of $37,538, consisting of her regular tax liability of $25,863 plus her AMT of $11,675. ▼

Exemption Amount. The exemption amount can be thought of as a materiality provision. As such, it enables a taxpayer with a small amount of positive adjustments and tax preferences to avoid being subject to the burden of the AMT.

The *initial* exemption amount is $45,000 for married taxpayers filing joint returns, $33,750 for single taxpayers, and $22,500 for married taxpayers filing separate returns.[5] However, the exemption is *phased out* at a rate of 25 cents on the dollar when AMTI exceeds these levels:

- $112,500 for single taxpayers.
- $150,000 for married taxpayers filing jointly.
- $75,000 for married taxpayers filing separately.

The phase-out of the exemption amount is an application of the wherewithal to pay concept. As a taxpayer's income level increases, so does his or her ability to pay income taxes.

---

[5]§ 55(d).

TAX IN THE NEWS

THE AMT AND INFLATION

The AMT contains exemption amounts for the different taxpayer filing statuses. When the taxpayer's income reaches a certain amount, the exemption is subject to phase-out.

Neither the AMT exemption nor the AMT rates are subject to indexing. Currently, only about 600,000 (0.5 percent) individual income tax returns must pay the AMT. Kenneth Kies, chief of staff of Congress's Joint Tax Committee, estimates that by 2006, the absence of indexing and the increase in AMT rates contained in the Revenue Reconciliation Act of 1993 (RRA of 1993) will cause about 6.2 million (4.5 percent) individual income tax returns to be subject to the AMT.

Several proposals were made to include an indexing provision for the AMT in the Taxpayer Relief Act of 1997 (TRA of 1997), but none of them was included in the AMT legislation that was enacted.

SOURCE: Adapted from Tom Herman, "Chances Improve for Important Changes in the Alternative Minimum Tax," *Wall Street Journal*, May 21, 1997, p. A1.

The following example explains the calculation of the phase-out of the AMT exemption.

EXAMPLE 5

Hugh, who is single, has AMTI of $192,500 for the year. His $33,750 initial exemption amount is reduced by $20,000 [($192,500 – $112,500) × 25% phase-out rate]. Hugh's AMT exemption is $13,750 ($33,750 exemption – $20,000 reduction). ▼

The following table shows the beginning and end of the AMT exemption phase-out range for each filing status.

Status	Exemption	Phase-out Begins at	Phase-out Ends at
Married, joint	$45,000	$150,000	$330,000
Single or head of household	33,750	112,500	247,500
Married, separate	22,500	75,000	165,000

AMT Rate Schedule. A graduated, two-tier AMT rate schedule applies to noncorporate taxpayers. A 26 percent rate applies to the first $175,000 of the AMT base ($87,500 for married, filing separately), and a 28 percent rate applies to the AMT base in excess of $175,000 ($87,500 for married, filing separately).[6] The Taxpayer Relief Act of 1997 (TRA of 1997) provides that the net capital gain included in the AMT base is taxed at the favorable alternative tax rates for capital gains (20 percent or 10 percent) rather than at the AMT statutory rates. This provision applies to gains occurring after May 6, 1997, in tax years ending after May 6, 1997. See the discussion of the alternative tax on capital gains in Chapter 13.

Regular Tax Liability. The AMT is equal to the tentative minimum tax minus the *regular tax liability*. In most cases, the regular tax liability is equal to the amount of tax from the Tax Table or Tax Rate Schedules decreased by any foreign tax credit

---

[6] § 55(b)(1).

allowable for regular income tax purposes. Only the foreign tax credit is allowed as a reduction of the tentative minimum tax. Therefore, taxpayers who pay AMT lose the benefit of all other nonrefundable credits. Furthermore, the foreign tax credit cannot offset more than 90 percent of the tentative minimum tax.

In an AMT year, the taxpayer's total tax liability is equal to the tentative minimum tax (refer to Figure 14–2). The tentative minimum tax consists of two potential components: the regular tax liability and the AMT. The disallowance of credits does not affect a taxpayer's total liability in an AMT year. However, it does decrease the amount of the AMT and, as a consequence, reduces the minimum tax credit (discussed subsequently) available to be carried forward. Thus, for AMT purposes, the government denies all the credits (except the foreign tax credit) that apply in computing the regular income tax liability.

It is also possible that taxpayers who have adjustments and preferences but *do not pay* AMT will lose the benefit of some or all of their nonrefundable credits. This result occurs because a taxpayer may claim nonrefundable credits only to the extent that his or her regular tax liability exceeds the tentative minimum tax.[7]

EXAMPLE 6

Vern has total nonrefundable credits of $10,000, regular tax liability of $33,000, and tentative minimum tax of $25,000. He can claim only $8,000 of the nonrefundable credits in the current year ($33,000 − $8,000 = $25,000). The disallowed $2,000 credit is lost unless a carryover provision applies. ▼

ETHICAL CONSIDERATIONS

Minimizing the Tax Liability

Billy, a single individual, projects his taxable income for 1998 to be approximately $300,000. He also has positive adjustments and tax preferences of $200,000. Billy anticipates taxable income for 1999 to be about the same with no adjustments or tax preferences for AMT purposes. He is evaluating several proposed transactions that would have the effect of reducing his 1998 tax liability.

One such transaction involves an office building for which he is currently negotiating a lease. The starting date for the lease will be July 1, 1998. The annual rent is going to be around $20,000 with an 18-month prepayment clause. Though Billy favors a five-year lease, a real estate agent has suggested that he lease the office building for an 18-month period with a 42-month renewal option. The real estate agent indicates that there are tax advantages (i.e., Billy can deduct the $30,000 of rent paid at the inception of the lease) as well as business reasons for structuring the transaction this way.

Billy takes the agent's advice and calculates his projected tax liability for 1998 with the 18-month lease with the renewal option and with the five-year lease. Based on his calculations, his regular income tax liability and AMT under each option would be as follows:

	18-Month Lease	**5-Year Lease**
Regular income tax liability	$ 85,658	$ 93,273
AMT	42,442	40,427
Total	$128,100	$133,700

---

[7]§ 26(a).

Is it appropriate for Billy to avoid taxes in this manner? Is it wise? Would you be willing to prepare and sign Billy's tax return showing the lease transaction as proposed by the real estate agent?

AMT ADJUSTMENTS

3 LEARNING OBJECTIVE
Identify the adjustments made in calculating the AMT.

Direction of Adjustments. It is necessary to determine not only the amount of an adjustment, but also whether the adjustment is positive or negative. Careful study of Example 3 reveals the following pattern with regard to *deductions*:

- If the deduction allowed for regular income tax purposes exceeds the deduction allowed for AMT purposes, the difference is a positive adjustment.
- If the deduction allowed for AMT purposes exceeds the deduction allowed for regular income tax purposes, the difference is a negative adjustment.

Conversely, the direction of an adjustment attributable to an *income* item can be determined as follows:

- If the income reported for regular income tax purposes exceeds the income reported for AMT purposes, the difference is a negative adjustment.
- If the income reported for AMT purposes exceeds the income reported for regular income tax purposes, the difference is a positive adjustment.

Circulation Expenditures. For regular income tax purposes, circulation expenditures, other than those the taxpayer elects to charge to a capital account, may be expensed in the year incurred.[8] These expenditures include expenses incurred to establish, maintain, or increase the circulation of a newspaper, magazine, or other periodical.

Circulation expenditures are not deductible in the year incurred for AMT purposes. In computing AMTI, these expenditures must be capitalized and amortized ratably over the three-year period beginning with the year in which the expenditures were made.[9]

The AMT adjustment for circulation expenditures is the amount expensed for regular income tax purposes minus the amount that can be amortized for AMT purposes. The adjustment can be either positive or negative (refer to Examples 1, 2, and 3). A taxpayer can avoid the AMT adjustments for circulation expenditures by electing to write off the expenditures over a three-year period for regular income tax purposes.[10]

Depreciation of Post-1986 Real Property. For real property placed in service after 1986 (MACRS property), AMT depreciation is computed under the alternative depreciation system (ADS), which uses the straight-line method over a 40-year life. The depreciation lives for regular tax purposes are 27.5 years for residential rental property and 39 years for all other real property.[11] The difference between AMT depreciation and regular income tax depreciation is treated as an adjustment in computing the AMT. The differences will be positive during the regular income tax life of the asset because the cost is written off over a shorter period for regular income tax purposes. For example, during the 27.5-year income tax life of residential real property, the regular income tax depreciation

---

[8] § 173(a).
[9] § 56(b)(2)(A)(i).
[10] § 59(e)(2)(A).

[11] The 39-year life generally applies to nonresidential real property placed in service on or after May 13, 1993.

will exceed the AMT depreciation because AMT depreciation is computed over a 40-year period.

Table 7–7 is used to compute regular income tax depreciation on real property placed in service after 1986. For AMT purposes, depreciation on real property placed in service after 1986 is computed under the ADS (refer to Table 7–12).

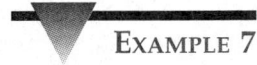

EXAMPLE 7

In January 1998, Sara placed in service a residential building that cost $100,000. Depreciation for 1998 for regular income tax purposes is $3,485 ($100,000 cost × 3.485% from Table 7–7). For AMT purposes, depreciation is $2,396 ($100,000 cost × 2.396% from Table 7–12). In computing AMTI for 1998, Sara has a positive adjustment of $1,089 ($3,485 regular income tax depreciation − $2,396 AMT depreciation). ▼

After real property has been held for the entire depreciation period for regular income tax purposes, the asset will be fully depreciated. However, the depreciation period under the ADS is 41 years due to application of the half-year convention, so depreciation will continue for AMT purposes. This causes negative adjustments after the property has been fully depreciated for regular income tax purposes.

EXAMPLE 8

Assume the same facts as in the previous example, and compute the AMT adjustment for 2026 (the twenty-ninth year of the asset's life). Regular income tax depreciation is zero (refer to Table 7–7). AMT depreciation is $2,500 ($100,000 cost × 2.500% from Table 7–12). Therefore, Sara has a negative AMT adjustment of $2,500 ($0 regular income tax depreciation − $2,500 AMT depreciation). ▼

After real property is fully depreciated for both regular income tax and AMT purposes, the positive and negative adjustments that have been made for AMT purposes will net to zero.

TRA of 1997 eliminated the AMT adjustment for real property by providing that the MACRS recovery periods used in calculating the regular income tax apply in calculating the AMT. Note, however, that this AMT recovery period conformity provision applies only to property placed in service after December 31, 1998. Thus, the adjustment continues to apply for real property placed in service before January 1, 1999.

Depreciation of Post-1986 Personal Property. For most personal property placed in service after 1986 (MACRS property), the modified ACRS (MACRS) deduction for regular income tax purposes is based on the 200 percent declining-balance method with a switch to straight-line when that method produces a larger depreciation deduction for the asset. Refer to Table 7–2 for computing regular income tax depreciation.

For AMT purposes, the taxpayer must use the ADS. This method is based on the 150 percent declining-balance method with a similar switch to straight-line for all personal property.[12] Refer to Table 7–10 for percentages to be used in computing AMT depreciation.

All personal property placed in service after 1986 may be taken into consideration in computing one net adjustment. Using this netting process, the AMT adjustment for a tax year is the difference between the total MACRS depreciation for all personal property computed for regular income tax purposes and the total ADS depreciation computed for AMT purposes. When the total of MACRS deductions

[12]§ 56(a)(1).

exceeds the total of ADS deductions, the amount of the adjustment is positive. When the total of ADS deductions exceeds the total of MACRS deductions, the adjustment for AMTI is negative.

The MACRS deduction for personal property is larger than the ADS deduction in the early years of an asset's life. However, the ADS deduction is larger in the later years. This is so because ADS lives (based on class life) are longer than MACRS lives (based on recovery period).[13] Over the ADS life of the asset, the same amount of depreciation is deducted for both regular income tax and AMT purposes. In the same manner as other timing adjustments, the AMT adjustments for depreciation will net to zero over the ADS life of the asset.

The taxpayer may elect to use the ADS for regular income tax purposes. If this election is made, no AMT adjustment is required because the depreciation deduction is the same for regular income tax and for the AMT. The election eliminates the burden of maintaining two sets of tax depreciation records.

TRA of 1997 either reduces or eliminates the AMT adjustment for the depreciation of personal property. Prior to the effective date of this provision, the difference between regular income tax depreciation and AMT depreciation was caused by longer recovery periods for the AMT (class life versus MACRS recovery periods) and more accelerated depreciation methods for the regular income tax (200 percent declining balance rather than 150 percent declining balance). TRA of 1997 provides that the MACRS recovery periods are to be used in calculating AMT depreciation. Thus, if the taxpayer elects to use the 150 percent declining-balance method for regular income tax purposes, there are no AMT adjustments. Conversely, if the taxpayer uses the 200 percent declining-balance method for regular income tax purposes, there is an AMT adjustment for depreciation. Note, however, that this AMT recovery period conformity provision applies only to property placed in service after December 31, 1998. Thus, the adjustment continues to apply for personal property placed in service before January 1, 1999.

Pollution Control Facilities. For regular income tax purposes, the cost of certified pollution control facilities may be amortized over a period of 60 months. For AMT purposes, the cost of these facilities placed in service after 1986 must be depreciated under the ADS over the appropriate class life, determined as explained above for depreciation of post-1986 property.[14] The required adjustment for AMTI is equal to the difference between the amortization deduction allowed for regular income tax purposes and the depreciation deduction computed under the ADS. The adjustment may be positive or negative.

TRA of 1997 reduces the AMT adjustment for pollution control facilities for property placed in service after December 31, 1998. This reduction is achieved by providing conformity in the recovery periods used for regular income tax purposes and AMT purposes (MACRS recovery periods).

Expenditures Requiring 10-Year Write-off for AMT Purposes. Certain expenditures that may be deducted in the year incurred for regular income tax purposes must be written off over a 10-year period for AMT purposes. These rules apply to (1) mining exploration and development costs and (2) research and experimental expenditures.

---

[13]Class lives and recovery periods are established for all assets in Rev.Proc. 87–56, 1987–2 C.B. 674.

[14]§ 56(a)(5).

In computing taxable income, taxpayers are allowed to deduct certain mining exploration and development expenditures. The deduction is allowed for expenditures paid or incurred during the taxable year for exploration (ascertaining the existence, location, extent, or quality of a deposit or mineral) and for development of a mine or other natural deposit, other than an oil or gas well.[15] Mining development expenditures are expenses paid or incurred after the existence of ores and minerals in commercially marketable quantities has been disclosed.

For AMT purposes, however, mining exploration and development costs must be capitalized and amortized ratably over a 10-year period.[16] The AMT adjustment for mining exploration and development costs that are expensed is equal to the amount expensed minus the allowable expense if the costs had been capitalized and amortized ratably over a 10-year period. This provision does not apply to costs relating to an oil or gas well.

EXAMPLE 9

In 1998, Eve incurs $150,000 of mining exploration expenditures and deducts this amount for regular income tax purposes. For AMT purposes, these mining exploration expenditures must be amortized over a 10-year period. Eve must make a positive adjustment for AMTI of $135,000 ($150,000 allowed for regular income tax – $15,000 for AMT) for 1998, the first year. In each of the next nine years for AMT purposes, Eve is required to make a negative adjustment of $15,000 ($0 allowed for regular income tax – $15,000 for AMT). ▼

To avoid the AMT adjustments for mining exploration and development costs, a taxpayer may elect to write off the expenditures over a 10-year period for regular income tax purposes.[17]

Similar rules apply to computation of the adjustment for research and experimental expenditures.

Use of Completed Contract Method of Accounting. For a long-term contract, taxpayers are required to use the percentage of completion method for AMT purposes.[18] However, in limited circumstances, taxpayers can use the completed contract method for regular income tax purposes.[19] Thus, a taxpayer recognizes a different amount of income for regular income tax purposes than for AMT purposes. The resulting AMT adjustment is equal to the difference between income reported under the percentage of completion method and the amount reported using the completed contract method. The adjustment can be either positive or negative, depending on the amount of income recognized under the different methods.

A taxpayer can avoid an AMT adjustment on long-term contracts by using the percentage of completion method for regular income tax purposes rather than the completed contract method.

Incentive Stock Options. **Incentive stock options (ISOs)** are granted by employers to help attract new personnel and retain those already employed. At the time an ISO is granted, the employer corporation sets an option price for the corporate stock. If the value of the stock increases during the option period, the employee can obtain stock at a favorable price by exercising the option. Employees are generally restricted as to when they can dispose of stock acquired under an ISO (e.g., a certain length of employment may be required). Therefore, the stock may not be freely transferable until some specified period has passed.

---

[15]§§ 617(a) and 616(a).
[16]§ 56(a)(2).
[17]§§ 59(e)(2)(D) and (E).

[18]§ 56(a)(3).
[19]See Chapter 15 for a detailed discussion of the completed contract and percentage of completion methods of accounting.

The exercise of an ISO does not increase regular taxable income.[20] However, for AMT purposes, the excess of the fair market value of the stock over the exercise price (the *spread*) is treated as an adjustment in the first taxable year in which the rights in the stock are freely transferable or are not subject to a substantial risk of forfeiture.[21]

EXAMPLE 10

In 1996, Manuel exercised an ISO that had been granted by his employer, Gold Corporation. Manuel acquired 1,000 shares of Gold stock for the option price of $20 per share. The stock became freely transferable in 1998. The fair market value of the stock at the date of exercise was $50 per share. For AMT purposes, Manuel has a positive adjustment of $30,000 ($50,000 fair market value – $20,000 option price) for 1998. The transaction does not affect regular taxable income in 1996 or 1998. ▼

No adjustment is required if the taxpayer exercises the option and disposes of the stock in the same tax year because the bargain element gain is reported for both regular income tax and AMT purposes in the same tax year.

The regular income tax basis of stock acquired through exercise of ISOs is different from the AMT basis. The regular income tax basis of the stock is equal to its cost, whereas the AMT basis is equal to the fair market value on the date the options are exercised. Consequently, the gain or loss upon disposition of the stock is different for regular income tax purposes and AMT purposes.

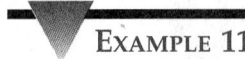

EXAMPLE 11

Assume the same facts as in the previous example and that Manuel sells the stock for $60,000 in 2000. His gain for regular income tax purposes is $40,000 ($60,000 amount realized – $20,000 regular income tax basis). For AMT purposes, the gain is $10,000 ($60,000 amount realized – $50,000 AMT basis). Therefore, Manuel has a $30,000 negative adjustment in computing AMT in 2000 ($40,000 regular income tax gain – $10,000 AMT gain). Note that the $30,000 negative adjustment upon disposition in 2000 offsets the $30,000 positive adjustment when the stock became freely transferable in 1998. ▼

Adjusted Gain or Loss. When property is sold during the year or a casualty occurs to business or income-producing property, gain or loss reported for regular income tax may be different than gain or loss determined for the AMT. This difference occurs because the adjusted basis of the property for AMT purposes must reflect any current and prior AMT adjustments for the following:[22]

- Depreciation.
- Circulation expenditures.
- Research and experimental expenditures.
- Mining exploration and development costs.
- Amortization of certified pollution control facilities.

A negative gain or loss adjustment is required if:

- the gain for AMT purposes is less than the gain for regular income tax purposes;
- the loss for AMT purposes is more than the loss for regular income tax purposes; or
- a loss is computed for AMT purposes and a gain is computed for regular income tax purposes.

Otherwise, the AMT gain or loss adjustment is positive.

[20]§ 421(a).
[21]§ 56(b)(3).

[22]§ 56(a)(7).

EXAMPLE 12

In January 1998, Kate paid $100,000 for a duplex acquired for rental purposes. Regular income tax depreciation in 1998 was $3,485 ($100,000 cost × 3.485% from Table 7–7). AMT depreciation was $2,396 ($100,000 cost × 2.396% from Table 7–12). For AMT purposes, Kate made a positive adjustment of $1,089 ($3,485 regular income tax depreciation − $2,396 AMT depreciation). ▼

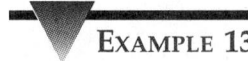

EXAMPLE 13

Kate sold the duplex on December 20, 1999, for $105,000. Regular income tax depreciation for 1999 is $3,485 [($100,000 cost × 3.636% from Table 7–7) × (11.5/12)]. AMT depreciation for 1999 is $2,396 [($100,000 cost × 2.500% from Table 7–12) × (11.5/12)]. Kate's positive AMT adjustment for 1999 is $1,089 ($3,485 regular income tax depreciation − $2,396 AMT depreciation). ▼

Because depreciation on the duplex differs for regular income tax and AMT purposes, the adjusted basis is different for regular income tax and AMT purposes. Consequently, the gain or loss on disposition of the duplex is different for regular income tax and AMT purposes.

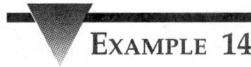

EXAMPLE 14

The adjusted basis of Kate's duplex for regular income tax purposes is $93,030 ($100,000 cost − $3,485 depreciation for 1998 − $3,485 depreciation for 1999). For AMT purposes, the adjusted basis is $95,208 ($100,000 cost − $2,396 depreciation for 1998 − $2,396 depreciation for 1999). The regular income tax gain is $11,970 ($105,000 amount realized − $93,030 regular income tax basis). The AMT gain is $9,792 ($105,000 amount realized − $95,208 AMT basis). Because the regular income tax and AMT gain on the sale of the duplex differ, Kate must make a negative AMT adjustment of $2,178 ($11,970 regular income tax gain − $9,792 AMT gain). Note that this negative adjustment offsets the $2,178 total of the two positive adjustments for depreciation ($1,089 in 1998 + $1,089 in 1999). ▼

Passive Activity Losses. Losses on passive activities are not deductible in computing either the regular income tax or the AMT. This does not, however, eliminate the possibility of adjustments attributable to passive activities.

The rules for computing taxable income differ from the rules for computing AMTI. It follows, then, that the rules for computing a loss for regular income tax purposes differ from the AMT rules for computing a loss. Therefore, any *passive loss* computed for regular income tax purposes may differ from the passive loss computed for AMT purposes.[23]

EXAMPLE 15

Soong acquired two passive activities in 1998. He received net passive income of $10,000 from Activity A and had no AMT adjustments or preferences in connection with the activity. Activity B had gross income of $27,000 and operating expenses (not affected by AMT adjustments or preferences) of $19,000. Soong claimed MACRS depreciation of $20,000 for Activity B; depreciation under the ADS would have been $15,000. In addition, Soong deducted $10,000 of percentage depletion in excess of basis. The following comparison illustrates the differences in the computation of the passive loss for regular income tax and AMT purposes for Activity B.

---

[23]See Chapter 11.

	Regular Income Tax	AMT
Gross income	$ 27,000	$ 27,000
Deductions:		
Operating expenses	($ 19,000)	($ 19,000)
Depreciation	(20,000)	(15,000)
Depletion	(10,000)	–0–
Total deductions	($ 49,000)	($ 34,000)
Passive loss	($ 22,000)	($ 7,000)

Because the adjustment for depreciation ($5,000) applies and the preference for depletion ($10,000) is not taken into account in computing AMTI, the regular income tax passive activity loss of $22,000 for Activity B is reduced by these amounts, resulting in a passive activity loss of $7,000 for AMT purposes. ▼

For regular income tax purposes, Soong would offset the $10,000 of net passive income from Activity A with $10,000 of the passive loss from Activity B. For AMT purposes, he would offset the $10,000 of net passive income from Activity A with the $7,000 passive activity loss allowed from Activity B, resulting in passive activity income of $3,000. Thus, in computing AMTI, Soong makes a positive passive loss adjustment of $3,000 [$10,000 (passive activity loss allowed for regular income tax) – $7,000 (passive activity loss allowed for the AMT)]. To avoid duplication, the AMT adjustment for depreciation and the preference for depletion are *not* reported separately. They are accounted for in determining the AMT passive loss adjustment.

EXAMPLE 16

Assume the same facts as in the previous example. For regular income tax purposes, Soong has a suspended passive loss of $12,000 [$22,000 (amount of loss) – $10,000 (used in 1998)]. This suspended passive loss can offset passive income in the future or can offset active or portfolio income when Soong disposes of the loss activity (refer to Chapter 10). For AMT purposes, Soong's suspended passive loss is $0 [$7,000 (amount of loss) – $7,000 (amount used in 1998)]. ▼

Alternative Tax Net Operating Loss Deduction.   In computing taxable income, taxpayers are allowed to deduct net operating loss (NOL) carryovers and carrybacks (refer to Chapter 6). The regular income tax NOL must be modified, however, in computing AMTI. The starting point in computing the **alternative tax NOL deduction (ATNOLD)** is the NOL computed for regular income tax purposes. The regular income tax NOL is then modified for AMT adjustments and tax preferences with the result being the ATNOLD. Thus, preferences and adjustment items that have benefited the taxpayer in computing the regular income tax NOL are added back, thereby reducing or eliminating the ATNOLD.[24]

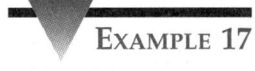

EXAMPLE 17

In 1998, Adam incurred an NOL of $100,000. Adam had no AMT adjustments, but his deductions included tax preferences of $18,000. His ATNOLD carryback to 1996 is $82,000 ($100,000 regular income tax NOL – $18,000 tax preferences deducted in computing the NOL). ▼

In Example 17, if the adjustment was not made to the regular income tax NOL, the $18,000 in tax preference items deducted in 1998 would have the effect of

---

[24]§ 56(a)(4).

reducing AMTI in the year (or years) the 1998 NOL is utilized. This would weaken the entire concept of the AMT.

A ceiling exists on the amount of the ATNOLD that can be deducted in the carryback or carryforward year. The deduction is limited to 90 percent of AMTI (before the ATNOLD) for the carryback or carryforward year.

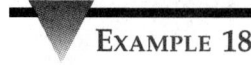

EXAMPLE 18

Assume the same facts as in the previous example. Adam's AMTI (before the ATNOLD) in 1996 is $90,000. Therefore, of the $82,000 ATNOLD carried back to 1996 from 1998, only $81,000 ($90,000 × 90%) can be used in recalculating the 1996 AMT. The unused $1,000 of 1998 ATNOLD is now carried to 1997 for use in recalculating the 1997 AMT. ▼

A taxpayer who has an ATNOLD that is carried back or over to another year must use the ATNOLD against AMTI in the carryback or carryforward year even if the regular income tax, rather than the AMT, applies.

EXAMPLE 19

Matt's ATNOLD for 1999 (carried over from 1998) is $10,000. AMTI before considering the ATNOLD is $25,000. If Matt's regular income tax exceeds the AMT, the AMT does not apply. Nevertheless, Matt's ATNOLD of $10,000 is "used up" in 1999 and is not available for carryover to a later year. ▼

For regular income tax purposes, the NOL can be carried back 2 years and forward 20 years. However, the taxpayer may elect to forgo the 2-year carryback. These rules generally apply to the ATNOLD as well, except that the election to forgo the 2-year carryback is available for the ATNOLD only if the taxpayer elected it for the regular income tax NOL.

Itemized Deductions.   Most of the itemized deductions that are allowed for regular income tax purposes are allowed for AMT purposes. Itemized deductions that are allowed for AMT purposes include the following:

- Casualty losses.
- Gambling losses.
- Charitable contributions.
- Medical expenses in excess of 10 percent of AGI.
- Estate tax on income in respect of a decedent.
- Qualified interest.

Taxes (state, local, foreign income, and property taxes) and miscellaneous itemized deductions that are subject to the 2 percent-of-AGI floor are not allowed in computing AMT.[25] A positive AMT adjustment in the total amount of the regular income tax deduction for each is required.

If the taxpayer's gross income includes the recovery of any tax deducted as an itemized deduction for regular income tax purposes, a negative AMT adjustment in the amount of the recovery is allowed for AMTI purposes.[26] For example, state, local, and foreign income taxes can be deducted for regular income tax purposes, but cannot be deducted in computing AMT. Because of this, any refund of such taxes from a prior year is not included in AMTI. Therefore, in calculating AMTI, the taxpayer must make a negative adjustment for an income tax refund that has been included in computing regular taxable income. Under the tax benefit rule, a tax refund is included in regular taxable income to the extent that the taxpayer obtained a tax benefit by deducting the tax in a prior year.

[25]§ 56(b)(1)(A).   [26]§ 56(b)(1)(D).

Cutback Adjustment.   The 3 percent cutback adjustment that applies to regular income tax itemized deductions of certain high-income taxpayers (refer to Chapter 9) does not apply in computing AMT.[27] The effect of the 3 percent cutback adjustment is to disallow a portion of the taxpayer's itemized deductions for regular income tax purposes. Because this cutback adjustment does not apply for AMT purposes, taxable income, which is the starting point for computing AMTI, must be reduced by the amount of the disallowed deductions. Although this reduction has the same effect on AMTI as a negative adjustment, it is not shown on Form 6251 as such. Instead, it is shown on a separate line (line 18) as a subtraction from taxable income.

Medical Expenses.   The rules for determining the AMT deductions for medical expenses are sufficiently complex to require further explanation. For regular income tax purposes, medical expenses are deductible to the extent they exceed 7.5 percent of AGI. However, for AMT purposes, medical expenses are deductible only to the extent they exceed 10 percent of AGI.[28]

EXAMPLE 20   Joann incurred medical expenses of $16,000 in 1998. She had AGI of $100,000 for the year. Her AMT adjustment for medical expenses is computed as follows:

	Regular Income Tax	AMT
Medical expenses incurred	$ 16,000	$ 16,000
Less reduction:		
$100,000 AGI × 7.5%	(7,500)	
$100,000 AGI × 10%		(10,000)
Medical expense deduction	$ 8,500	$ 6,000

Joann's AMT adjustment for medical expenses is $2,500 ($8,500 regular income tax deduction – $6,000 AMT deduction). ▼

Interest in General.   The AMT itemized deduction allowed for interest expense includes only qualified housing interest and investment interest to the extent of net investment income that is included in the determination of AMTI.[29] Any interest that is deducted in calculating the regular income tax that is not permitted in calculating the AMT is treated as a positive adjustment.

In computing regular taxable income, taxpayers who itemize can deduct the following types of interest (refer to Chapter 9):

- Qualified residence interest.
- Investment interest, subject to the investment interest limitations (discussed under Investment Interest below).
- Qualified interest on student loans.

Housing Interest.   Under current regular income tax rules, taxpayers who itemize can deduct *qualified residence interest* on up to two residences. The deduction is limited to interest on acquisition indebtedness up to $1 million and home equity indebtedness up to $100,000. Acquisition indebtedness is debt that is incurred in acquiring, constructing, or substantially improving a qualified residence of the

---

[27]§ 56(b)(1)(F).
[28]§ 56(b)(1)(B).

[29]§ 56(b)(1)(C).

taxpayer and is secured by the residence. Home equity indebtedness is indebtedness secured by a qualified residence of the taxpayer, but does not include acquisition indebtedness.

EXAMPLE 21

Gail, who used the proceeds of a mortgage to acquire a personal residence, paid mortgage interest of $112,000 in 1998. Of this amount, $14,000 is attributable to acquisition indebtedness in excess of $1 million. For regular income tax purposes, Gail may deduct mortgage interest of $98,000 ($112,000 total − $14,000 disallowed). ▼

The mortgage interest deduction for AMT purposes is limited to *qualified housing interest*, rather than *qualified residence interest*. Qualified housing interest includes only interest incurred to acquire, construct, or substantially improve the taxpayer's principal residence and such interest on one other qualified dwelling used for personal purposes. A home equity loan qualifies only if it meets the definition of qualified housing interest, which frequently is not the case. When additional mortgage interest is incurred (e.g., a mortgage refinancing), interest paid is deductible as qualified housing interest for AMT purposes only if:

- The proceeds are used to acquire or substantially improve a qualified residence.
- Interest on the prior loan was qualified housing interest.
- The amount of the loan was not increased.

A positive AMT adjustment is required in the amount of the difference between qualified *residence* interest allowed as an itemized deduction for regular income tax purposes and qualified *housing* interest allowed in the determination of AMTI.

Investment Interest. Investment interest is deductible for regular income tax purposes and for AMT purposes to the extent of qualified net investment income.

EXAMPLE 22

For the year, Dan had net investment income of $16,000 before deducting investment interest. He incurred investment interest expense of $30,000 during the year. His investment interest deduction is $16,000. ▼

Even though investment interest is deductible for both regular income tax and AMT purposes, an adjustment is required if the amount of investment interest deductible for regular income tax purposes differs from the amount deductible for AMT purposes. For example, an adjustment will arise if proceeds from a home equity loan are used to purchase investments. Interest on a home equity loan is deductible as qualified residence interest for regular income tax purposes, but is not deductible for AMT purposes unless the proceeds are used to acquire or substantially improve a qualified residence. For AMT purposes, however, interest on a home equity loan is deductible as investment interest expense if proceeds from the loan are used for investment purposes.

To determine the AMT adjustment for investment interest expense, it is necessary to compute the investment interest deduction for both regular income tax and AMT purposes. This computation is illustrated in the following example.

EXAMPLE 23

Tom had $20,000 interest income from corporate bonds and $5,000 dividends from preferred stock. He reported the following amounts of investment income for regular income tax and AMT purposes:

	Regular Income Tax	AMT
Corporate bond interest	$20,000	$20,000
Preferred stock dividends	5,000	5,000
Net investment income	$25,000	$25,000

Tom incurred investment interest expense of $10,000 related to the corporate bonds. He also incurred $4,000 interest on a home equity loan and used the proceeds of the loan to purchase preferred stock. For regular income tax purposes, this $4,000 is deductible as qualified residence interest. His *investment* interest expense for regular income tax and AMT purposes is computed below:

	Regular Income Tax	AMT
To carry corporate bonds	$10,000	$10,000
On home equity loan to carry preferred stock	–0–	4,000
Total investment interest expense	$10,000	$14,000

Investment interest expense is deductible to the extent of net investment income. Because the amount deductible for regular income tax purposes ($10,000) differs from the amount deductible for AMT purposes ($14,000), an AMT adjustment is required. The adjustment is computed as follows:

AMT deduction for investment interest expense	$ 14,000
Regular income tax deduction for investment interest expense	(10,000)
Negative AMT adjustment	$ 4,000

As discussed subsequently under AMT Preferences, the interest on private activity bonds is a tax preference for AMT purposes. Such interest can also affect the calculation of the AMT investment interest deduction in that it is included in the calculation of net investment income.

Other Adjustments.   The standard deduction is not allowed as a deduction in computing AMTI.[30] Although a person who does not itemize is rarely subject to the AMT, it is possible. In such a case, the taxpayer is required to enter a positive adjustment for the standard deduction in computing the AMT.

The personal and dependency exemption amount deducted for regular income tax purposes is not allowed in computing AMT.[31] Therefore, taxpayers must enter a positive AMT adjustment for the personal and dependency exemption amount claimed in computing the regular income tax. A separate exemption (see Exemption Amount) is allowed for AMT purposes. To allow both the regular income tax exemption amount and the AMT exemption amount would result in extra benefits for taxpayers.

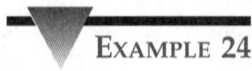

EXAMPLE 24   Eli, who is single, has no dependents and does not itemize deductions. He earned a salary of $106,950 in 1998. Based on this information, Eli's taxable income for 1998 is $100,000 ($106,950 – $4,250 standard deduction – $2,700 exemption). ▼

[30]§ 56(b)(1)(E).   [31]§ 56(b)(1)(E).

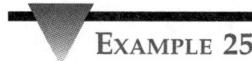

EXAMPLE 25

Assume the same facts as in Example 24. In addition, assume Eli's tax preferences for the year totaled $150,000. Eli's AMTI is $256,950 ($100,000 taxable income + $4,250 adjustment for standard deduction + $2,700 adjustment for exemption + $150,000 tax preferences). ▼

AMT PREFERENCES

4 **LEARNING OBJECTIVE**
Identify the tax preferences that are included in calculating the AMT.

Percentage Depletion. Congress originally enacted the percentage depletion rules to provide taxpayers with incentives to invest in the development of specified natural resources. Percentage depletion is computed by multiplying a rate specified in the Code times the gross income from the property (refer to Chapter 7). The percentage rate is based on the type of mineral involved. The basis of the property is reduced by the amount of depletion taken until the basis reaches zero. However, once the basis of the property reaches zero, taxpayers are allowed to continue taking percentage depletion deductions. Thus, over the life of the property, depletion deductions may greatly exceed the cost of the property.

The percentage depletion preference is equal to the excess of the regular income tax deduction for percentage depletion over the adjusted basis of the property at the end of the taxable year.[32] Basis is determined without regard to the depletion deduction for the taxable year. This preference item is figured separately for each piece of property for which the taxpayer is claiming depletion.

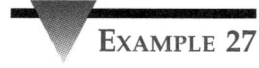

EXAMPLE 26

Kim owns a mineral property that qualifies for a 22% depletion rate. The basis of the property at the beginning of the year is $10,000. Gross income from the property for the year is $100,000. For regular income tax purposes, Kim's percentage depletion deduction (assume it is not limited by taxable income from the property) is $22,000. For AMT purposes, Kim has a tax preference of $12,000 ($22,000 – $10,000). ▼

Intangible Drilling Costs. In computing the regular income tax, taxpayers are allowed to deduct certain intangible drilling and development costs in the year incurred, although such costs are normally capital in nature (refer to Chapter 7). The deduction is allowed for costs incurred in connection with oil and gas wells and geothermal wells.

For AMT purposes, excess intangible drilling costs (IDC) for the year are treated as a preference.[33] The preference for excess IDC is computed as follows:

IDC expensed in the year incurred

Minus: Deduction if IDC were capitalized and amortized over 10 years

Equals: Excess of IDC expense over amortization

Minus: 65% of net oil and gas and geothermal income

Equals: Tax preference item

EXAMPLE 27

Ben, who incurred IDC of $50,000 during the year, elected to expense that amount. His net oil and gas income for the year was $60,000. Ben's tax preference for IDC is $6,000 [($50,000 IDC – $5,000 amortization) – (65% × $60,000 income)]. ▼

A taxpayer can avoid the preference for IDC by electing to write off the expenditures over a 10-year period for regular income tax purposes.

---

[32] § 57(a)(1). Note that the preference label does not apply to percentage depletion on oil and gas wells for independent producers and royalty owners as defined in § 613A(c).

[33] § 57(a)(2).

Interest on Private Activity Bonds. Income from private activity bonds is not included in taxable income, and expenses related to carrying such bonds are not deductible for regular income tax purposes. However, interest on private activity bonds is included as a preference in computing AMTI. Therefore, expenses incurred in carrying the bonds are offset against the interest income in computing the tax preference.[34]

The Code contains a lengthy, complex definition of private activity bonds.[35] In general, **private activity bonds** are bonds issued by states or municipalities with more than 10 percent of the proceeds being used for private business use. For example, a bond issued by a city whose proceeds are used to construct a factory that is leased to a private business at a favorable rate is a private activity bond.

Depreciation. For real property and leased personal property placed in service before 1987, there is an AMT preference for the excess of accelerated depreciation over straight-line depreciation.[36] However, examination of the cost recovery tables for pre-1987 real property (refer to Chapter 7) reveals that from the eighth year on, accelerated depreciation will not exceed straight-line depreciation. Consequently, taxpayers no longer have preferences attributable to pre-1987 real property.

Accelerated depreciation on pre-1987 leased personal property was computed using specified ACRS percentages (refer to Table 7–1, Chapter 7). AMT depreciation was based on the straight-line method, which was computed using the half-year convention, no salvage value, and a longer recovery period.[37] As a result, in the early years of the life of the asset, the cost recovery allowance used in computing the regular income tax was greater than the straight-line depreciation deduction allowed in computing AMT. The excess depreciation was treated as a tax preference item. For all leased personal property placed in service before 1987 (3-year, 5-year, and 10-year), except for 15-year public utility property, the cost recovery period has expired. Since there is no excess depreciation, there is no tax preference for AMT purposes.

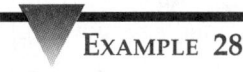

EXAMPLE 28

Paul acquired personal property on January 1, 1986, at a cost of $30,000. The property, which was placed in service as leased personal property on January 1, was 10-year ACRS property. Paul's 1986 depreciation deduction for regular income tax purposes was $2,400 ($30,000 cost × 8% rate from Table 7–1). For AMT purposes, the asset was depreciated over the AMT life of 15 years using the straight-line method with the half-year convention. Thus, AMT depreciation for 1986 was $1,000 [($30,000 ÷ 15) × ½ year convention]. Paul's tax preference for 1986 was $1,400 ($2,400 − $1,000). ACRS depreciation for 1998 is $0 ($30,000 × 0% ACRS rate), and straight-line depreciation is $2,000 ($30,000 ÷ 15). Thus, Paul's tax preference for 1998 is $0 since there is no excess depreciation. ▼

The preference item for excess depreciation on leased personal property is figured separately for each piece of property. No preference is reported in the year the taxpayer disposes of the property.

---

[34]§ 57(a)(5).
[35]§ 141.
[36]§ 57(a)(6).

[37]The specified lives for AMT purposes are 5 years for 3-year property, 8 years for 5-year property, 15 years for 10-year property, and 22 years for 15-year property.

Fifty Percent Exclusion for Certain Small Business Stock. Fifty percent of the gain on the sale of certain small business stock is excludible from gross income for regular income tax purposes. Forty-two percent of the excluded amount is a tax preference for AMT purposes.[38]

5 LEARNING OBJECTIVE
Apply the formula for computing the AMT and illustrate Form 6251.

ILLUSTRATION OF THE AMT COMPUTATION

The computation of the AMT is illustrated in the following example.

EXAMPLE 29

Hans Sims, who is single, had taxable income for 1998 as follows:

Salary		$ 92,000
Interest		8,000
Adjusted gross income		$100,000
Less itemized deductions:		
Medical expenses ($17,500 – 7.5% of $100,000 AGI)[a]	$10,000	
State income taxes	4,000	
Interest[b]		
Home mortgage (for qualified housing)	20,000*	
Investment interest	3,300*	
Contributions (cash)	5,000*	
Casualty losses ($14,000 – 10% of $100,000 AGI)	4,000*	(46,300)
		$ 53,700
Less exemption		(2,700)
Taxable income		$ 51,000

[a]Total medical expenses were $17,500, reduced by 7.5% of AGI, resulting in an itemized deduction of $10,000. However, for AMT purposes, the reduction is 10%, which leaves an AMT itemized deduction of $7,500 ($17,500 – 10% of $100,000 AGI). Therefore, an adjustment of $2,500 ($10,000 – $7,500) is required for medical expenses disallowed for AMT purposes.

[b]In this illustration, all interest is deductible in computing AMTI. Qualified housing interest is deductible. Investment interest ($3,300) is deductible to the extent of net investment income included in the minimum tax base. For this purpose, the $8,000 of interest income is treated as net investment income.

Deductions marked by an asterisk are allowed as *alternative minimum tax itemized deductions*, and AMT adjustments are required for the other itemized deductions. Thus, adjustments are required for state income taxes and for medical expenses to the extent the medical expenses deductible for regular income tax purposes are not deductible in computing AMT (see note (a) above). In addition to the items that affected taxable income, Hans had $35,000 interest on private activity bonds (an exclusion tax preference). AMTI is computed as follows:

---

[38]§ 57(a)(7). Prior to the effective date of TRA of 1997 for this provision (tax years ending after May 6, 1997), the preference was 50% of the excluded amount.

Taxable income	$ 51,000
Plus: Adjustments	
State income taxes	4,000
Medical expenses (see note (a) above)	2,500
Personal exemption	2,700
Plus: Tax preference (interest on private activity bonds)	35,000
Equals: AMTI	$ 95,200
Minus: AMT exemption	(33,750)
Equals: Minimum tax base	$ 61,450
Times: AMT rate	× 26%
Equals: Tentative AMT	$ 15,977
Minus: Regular income tax on taxable income	(10,985)
Equals: AMT	$ 4,992

The solution to Example 29 is also presented on Form 6251. Though this example is for 1998, 1997 tax forms are used because the 1998 tax forms were not available at the time of this writing.

Note that the $2,700 personal exemption amount is a positive adjustment in the Example 29 solution, but does not appear as an adjustment in Form 6251. This difference occurs because line 16 of Form 6251 includes the amount from line 36 of Form 1040. Line 36 of Form 1040 is taxable income before the deduction for personal and dependency exemptions.

ETHICAL CONSIDERATIONS

Effect of the Absence of Inflation Adjustments

Many areas of the regular income tax (e.g., rates, standard deductions, personal and dependency exemptions) are indexed annually for the effect of inflation. The alternative minimum tax system, the AMT, is not subject to indexing.

The AMT is defined as the excess of the tentative AMT over the regular income tax liability. Thus, the AMT calculation results in an AMT tax liability only if there is such an excess. Due to the absence of indexing for the AMT, this AMT tax liability can increase even though no other changes occur in the taxpayer's tax position.

Suppose that for 1997 a taxpayer's regular income tax liability is $110,000 and the tentative AMT is $120,000. The AMT is therefore $10,000. For 1998 all of the taxpayer's tax information is identical to that for 1997. Because of indexing, however, the regular income tax liability is only $107,000. Therefore, the AMT for 1998 is $13,000 ($120,000 − $107,000).

Evaluate the propriety of only the regular income tax being subject to indexing.

AMT CREDIT

6 **LEARNING OBJECTIVE**
Describe the role of the AMT credit in the alternative minimum tax structure.

As discussed previously, timing differences give rise to adjustments to the minimum tax base. In later years, the timing differences reverse, as was illustrated in several of the preceding examples. To provide equity for the taxpayer when timing differences reverse, the regular income tax liability may be reduced by a tax credit for prior years' minimum tax liability attributable to timing differences. The **alternative**

Form **6251**	**Alternative Minimum Tax—Individuals**	OMB No. 1545-0227
Department of the Treasury Internal Revenue Service (99)	► See separate instructions. ► Attach to Form 1040 or Form 1040NR.	**1997** Attachment Sequence No. **32**

Name(s) shown on Form 1040   *Hans Sims* | Your social security number

Part I   Adjustments and Preferences

1	If you itemized deductions on Schedule A (Form 1040), go to line 2. Otherwise, enter your standard deduction from Form 1040, line 35, here and go to line 6	1	
2	Medical and dental. Enter the smaller of Schedule A (Form 1040), line 4 **or** 2½% of Form 1040, line 33	2	*2,500*
3	Taxes. Enter the amount from Schedule A (Form 1040), line 9	3	*4,000*
4	Certain interest on a home mortgage not used to buy, build, or improve your home	4	
5	Miscellaneous itemized deductions. Enter the amount from Schedule A (Form 1040), line 26 . . .	5	
6	Refund of taxes. Enter any tax refund from Form 1040, line 10 or line 21	6	( )
7	Investment interest. Enter difference between regular tax and AMT deduction	7	
8	Post-1986 depreciation. Enter difference between regular tax and AMT depreciation	8	
9	Adjusted gain or loss. Enter difference between AMT and regular tax gain or loss	9	
10	Incentive stock options. Enter excess of AMT income over regular tax income	10	
11	Passive activities. Enter difference between AMT and regular tax income or loss	11	
12	Beneficiaries of estates and trusts. Enter the amount from Schedule K-1 (Form 1041), line 9 . .	12	
13	Tax-exempt interest from private activity bonds issued after 8/7/86	13	*35,000*

14   Other. Enter the amount, if any, for each item below and enter the total on line 14.

a Charitable contributions .		h Loss limitations	
b Circulation expenditures .		i Mining costs	
c Depletion		j Patron's adjustment . .	
d Depreciation (pre-1987) .		k Pollution control facilities .	
e Installment sales . . .		l Research and experimental	
f Intangible drilling costs .		m Tax shelter farm activities .	
g Long-term contracts . .		n Related adjustments . .	14

15	**Total Adjustments and Preferences.** Combine lines 1 through 14 . . . . ►	15	*41,500*

Part II   Alternative Minimum Taxable Income

16	Enter the amount from **Form 1040, line 36.** If less than zero, enter as a (loss) . . . . . ►	16	*53,700*
17	Net operating loss deduction, if any, from Form 1040, line 21. Enter as a positive amount . . .	17	
18	If Form 1040, line 33, is over $121,200 (over $60,600 if married filing separately), and you itemized deductions, enter the amount, if any, from line 9 of the worksheet for Schedule A (Form 1040), line 28	18	( )
19	Combine lines 15 through 18 . . . . ►	19	*95,200*
20	Alternative tax net operating loss deduction. See page 5 of the instructions	20	
21	**Alternative Minimum Taxable Income.** Subtract line 20 from line 19. (If married filing separately and line 21 is more than $165,000, see page 5 of the instructions.) . . . . ►	21	*95,200*

Part III   Exemption Amount and Alternative Minimum Tax

22   **Exemption Amount.** (If this form is for a child under age 14, see page 6 of the instructions.)

IF your filing status is . . .	AND line 21 is not over . . .	THEN enter on line 22 . . .		
Single or head of household	$112,500	$33,750		
Married filing jointly or qualifying widow(er) .	150,000	45,000	22	*33,750*
Married filing separately.	75,000	22,500		

If line 21 is **over** the amount shown above for your filing status, see page 6 of the instructions.

23	Subtract line 22 from line 21. If zero or less, enter -0- here and on lines 26 and 28 . . . . . ►	23	*61,450*
24	If you completed Schedule D (Form 1040), and had an amount on line 25 or line 27 (as refigured for the AMT, if necessary), go to Part IV of Form 6251 to figure line 24. **All others:** If line 23 is $175,000 or less ($87,500 or less if married filing separately), multiply line 23 by 26% (.26). Otherwise, multiply line 23 by 28% (.28) and subtract $3,500 ($1,750 if married filing separately) from the result . . . . . ►	24	*15,977*
25	Alternative minimum tax foreign tax credit. See page 7 of the instructions	25	
26	Tentative minimum tax. Subtract line 25 from line 24 . . . . ►	26	*15,977*
27	Enter your tax from Form 1040, line 39 (minus any tax from Form 4972 and any foreign tax credit from Form 1040, line 43) . . .	27	*10,985*
28	**Alternative Minimum Tax.** (If this form is for a child under age 14, see page 7 of the instructions.) Subtract line 27 from line 26. If zero or less, enter -0-. Enter here and on Form 1040, line 48 . . ►	28	*4,992*

For Paperwork Reduction Act Notice, see separate instructions.   Cat. No. 13600G   Form **6251** (1997)

minimum tax credit may be carried over indefinitely. Therefore, there is no need to keep track of when the minimum tax credit arose.[39]

EXAMPLE 30

Assume the same facts as in Example 3. Also assume that in 1997, Bob paid AMT as a result of the $20,000 positive adjustment arising from the circulation expenditures. In 1998, $10,000 of the timing difference reverses, resulting in regular taxable income that is $10,000 greater than AMTI. Because Bob has already paid AMT as a result of the write-off of circulation expenditures, he is allowed an AMT credit in 1998. The AMT credit can offset Bob's regular income tax liability in 1998 to the extent that his regular income tax liability exceeds his tentative AMT. ▼

The AMT credit is applicable only for the AMT that results from timing differences. It is not available in connection with **AMT exclusions,** which represent permanent differences rather than timing differences between the regular income tax liability and the AMT. These AMT exclusions include the following:

- The standard deduction.
- Personal exemptions.
- Medical expenses, to the extent deductible for regular income tax purposes but not deductible in computing AMT.
- Other itemized deductions not allowable for AMT purposes, including miscellaneous itemized deductions, taxes, and interest expense.
- Excess percentage depletion.
- Tax-exempt interest on specified private activity bonds.

EXAMPLE 31

Don, who is single, has zero taxable income for 1998. He also has positive timing adjustments of $300,000 and AMT exclusions of $100,000. His AMT base is $400,000 because his AMT exemption is phased out completely due to the level of AMTI. Don's tentative AMT is $108,500 [($175,000 × 26% AMT rate) + ($225,000 × 28% AMT rate)]. ▼

To determine the amount of AMT credit to carry over, the AMT must be recomputed reflecting only the AMT exclusions and the AMT exemption amount.

EXAMPLE 32

Assume the same facts as in the previous example. If there had been no positive timing adjustments for the year, Don's tentative AMT would have been $17,225 [($100,000 AMT exclusions − $33,750 exemption) × 26% AMT rate]. Don may carry over an AMT credit of $91,275 ($108,500 AMT − $17,225 related to AMT exclusions) to 1999 and subsequent years. ▼

CORPORATE ALTERNATIVE MINIMUM TAX

7 **LEARNING OBJECTIVE**
Understand the basic features of the corporate AMT.

The AMT applicable to corporations is similar to that applicable to noncorporate taxpayers. However, there are several important differences:

- The corporate AMT rate is 20 percent versus a top rate of 28 percent for noncorporate taxpayers.[40]
- The AMT exemption for corporations is $40,000 reduced by 25 percent of the amount by which AMTI exceeds $150,000.[41]

---

[39]§ 53.
[40]§ 55(b)(1)(B).

[41]§§ 55(d)(2) and (3).

CONCEPT SUMMARY 14–1

AMT Adjustments and Preferences for Individuals

Adjustments	Positive	Negative	Both*
Circulation expenditures			X
Depreciation of post-1986 real property			X
Depreciation of post-1986 personal property			X
Pollution control facilities			X
Mining exploration and development costs			X
Research and experimental expenditures			X
Completed contract method			X
Incentive stock options	X**		
Adjusted gain or loss			X
Passive activity losses			X
Alternative tax NOLD			X
Itemized deductions:			
Medical expenses	X		
State income tax	X		
Property tax on realty	X		
Property tax on personalty	X		
Miscellaneous itemized deductions	X		
Tax benefit rule for state income tax refund		X	
Cutback adjustment		X	
Qualified interest on student loans	X		
Qualified residence interest that is not qualified housing interest	X		
Qualified residence interest that is AMT investment interest	X	X	
Private activity bond interest that is AMT investment interest		X	
Standard deduction	X		
Personal exemptions and dependency deductions	X		

Preferences			
Percentage depletion in excess of adjusted basis	X		
Intangible drilling costs	X		
Private activity bond interest income	X		
Depreciation on pre-1987 leased personal property	X		
§ 1202 exclusion for certain small business stock	X		

*Timing differences.

**While the adjustment is a positive adjustment, the AMT basis for the stock is increased by the amount of the positive adjustment.

- Tax preferences applicable to noncorporate taxpayers are also applicable to corporate taxpayers, but some adjustments differ (see below).

Although there are computational differences, the corporate AMT and the noncorporate AMT have the identical objective: to force taxpayers who are more

▼ **FIGURE 14–3**
AMT Formula for Corporations

Taxable income

Plus: Income tax NOL deduction

Plus or minus: AMT adjustments

Plus: Tax preferences

Equals: AMTI before ATNOLD

Minus: ATNOLD (limited to 90% of AMTI before ATNOLD)

Equals: AMTI

Minus: Exemption

Equals: AMT base

Times: 20% rate

Equals: Tentative minimum tax before AMT foreign tax credit

Minus: AMT foreign tax credit (limited to 90% of AMT before AMT foreign tax credit)

Equals: Tentative minimum tax

Minus: Regular tax liability before credits minus regular foreign tax credit

Equals: AMT if positive

profitable than their taxable income reflects to pay additional tax. The formula for determining the corporate AMT appears in Figure 14–3.

REPEAL OF AMT FOR SMALL CORPORATIONS

TRA of 1997 has repealed the AMT for small corporations for tax years beginning after December 31, 1997. For this purpose, a corporation is classified as a small corporation if it had average annual gross receipts of less than $5 million for the three-year period beginning after December 1994. A corporation will continue to be classified as a small corporation if its average annual gross receipts for the three-year period preceding the current tax year do not exceed $7.5 million.

AMT ADJUSTMENTS

Adjustments Applicable to Individuals and Corporations.   The following adjustments that were discussed in connection with the individual AMT also apply to the corporate AMT:

- Excess of MACRS over ADS depreciation on real and personal property placed in service after 1986.
- Pollution control facilities placed in service after 1986 (AMT requires ADS depreciation over the asset's ADR life; 60-month amortization is allowed for regular income tax purposes).
- Mining and exploration expenditures (AMT requires amortization over 10 years versus immediate expensing allowed for regular income tax purposes).
- Income on long-term contracts (AMT requires percentage of completion method; completed contract method is allowed in limited circumstances for regular income tax purposes).
- Dispositions of assets (if gain or loss for AMT purposes differs from gain or loss for regular income tax purposes).
- Allowable ATNOLD (which cannot exceed 90 percent of AMTI before deduction for ATNOLD).

Adjustments Applicable Only to Corporations. Three AMT adjustments are applicable only to corporations:[42]

- The adjusted current earnings (ACE) adjustment.
- The Merchant Marine capital construction fund adjustment.
- The adjustment for special deductions allowed to Blue Cross/Blue Shield organizations.

The latter two adjustments apply to specific types of corporations and are not discussed in the chapter. On the other hand, the **ACE adjustment** generally applies to all corporations[43] and has a significant impact on both tax and financial accounting.

Corporations are subject to an AMT adjustment equal to 75 percent of the excess of ACE over AMTI before the ACE adjustment.[44] Historically, the government has not required conformity between tax accounting and financial accounting. For many years, the only *direct* conformity requirement was that a corporation that used the LIFO method for tax accounting also had to use LIFO for financial accounting.[45] Through the ACE adjustment, Congress is *indirectly* imposing a conformity requirement on corporations. While a corporation may still choose to use different methods for tax and financial accounting purposes, it may no longer be able to do so without incurring AMT as a result of the ACE adjustment. Thus, a corporation may incur AMT not only because of specifically targeted adjustments and preferences, but also as a result of any methods that cause ACE to exceed AMTI before the ACE adjustment.

The ACE adjustment can be either a positive or a negative amount. AMTI is increased by 75 percent of the excess of ACE over unadjusted AMTI. Or AMTI is reduced by 75 percent of the excess of unadjusted AMTI over ACE. The negative adjustment is limited to the aggregate of the positive adjustments under ACE for prior years, reduced by the previously claimed negative adjustments. See Concept Summary 14–2. Thus, the ordering of the timing differences is crucial because any lost negative adjustment is permanent. Unadjusted AMTI is AMTI without the ACE adjustment or the ATNOLD.[46]

---

[42]§ 56(c).
[43]The ACE adjustment does not apply to S corporations. § 56(g)(6).
[44]§ 56(g).

[45]§ 472(c).
[46]§§ 56(g)(1) and (2).

CONCEPT SUMMARY 14–2

Determining the ACE Adjustment*

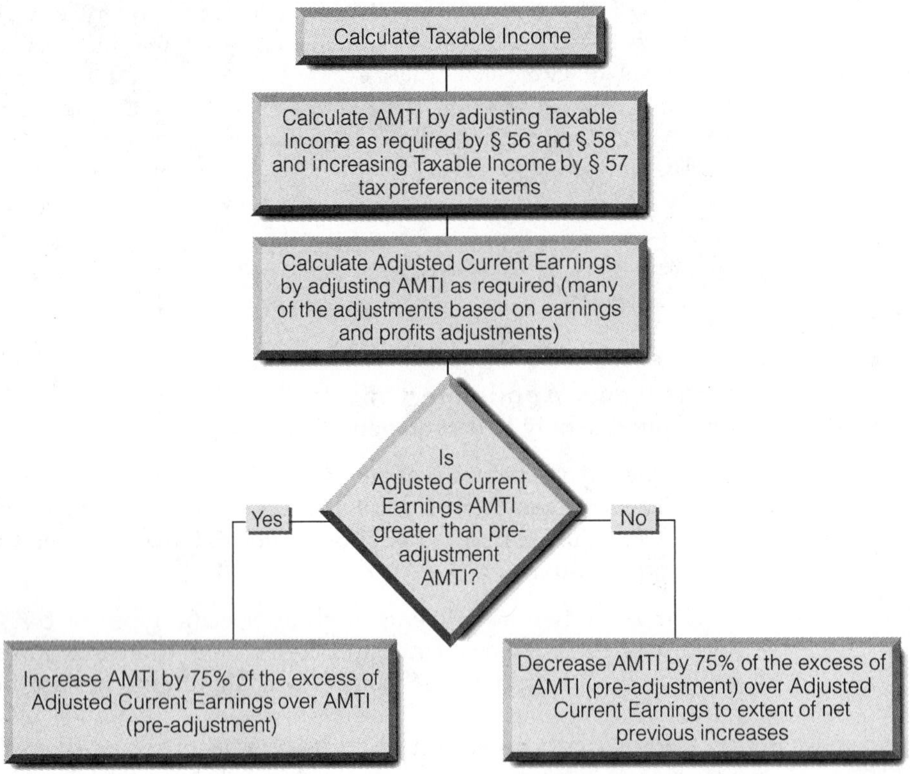

Calculate Taxable Income

Calculate AMTI by adjusting Taxable
Income as required by § 56 and § 58
and increasing Taxable Income by § 57
tax preference items

Calculate Adjusted Current Earnings
by adjusting AMTI as required (many
of the adjustments based on earnings
and profits adjustments)

Is
Adjusted Current
Earnings AMTI
greater than pre-
adjustment
AMTI?

Yes | No

Increase AMTI by 75% of the excess of
Adjusted Current Earnings over AMTI
(pre-adjustment)

Decrease AMTI by 75% of the excess of
AMTI (pre-adjustment) over Adjusted
Current Earnings to extent of net
previous increases

*Adapted from "Corporate Alternative Minimum Tax: The Impact of Current Earnings Adjustment on Oil and Gas Companies"
by Gallun and Zachry, which appeared in the September 1989 issue of the *Oil and Gas Tax Quarterly*, published and
copyrighted 1989 by Matthew Bender & Co., and appears here with their permission.

EXAMPLE 33

A calendar year corporation has the following data:

	1997	1998	1999
Pre-adjusted AMTI	$3,000	$3,000	$3,100
Adjusted current earnings	4,000	3,000	2,000

In 1997, because ACE exceeds unadjusted AMTI by $1,000, $750 (75% × $1,000) is included
as a positive adjustment to AMTI. No adjustment is necessary for 1998. As unadjusted AMTI
exceeds ACE by $1,100 in 1999, there is a potential negative adjustment to AMTI of $825
($1,100 × 75%). Since the total increases to AMTI for prior years equal $750 and there are
no previously claimed negative adjustments, only $750 of the potential negative adjustment
reduces AMTI for 1999. Further, $75 of the negative amount is lost forever. ▼

ACE should not be confused with current earnings and profits. Although many
items are treated in the same manner, certain variations exist. For example, Federal
income taxes, deductible in computing earnings and profits, are not deductible in
determining ACE.

The starting point for computing ACE is AMTI, which is defined as regular taxable income after AMT adjustments (other than the ATNOLD and ACE adjustments) and tax preferences. The resulting figure is adjusted for several items in order to arrive at ACE.

TAX PREFERENCES

AMTI includes designated tax preference items. In some cases, this has the effect of subjecting nontaxable income to the AMT. Tax preference items that apply to individuals also apply to corporations.

EXAMPLE 34

The following information applies to Brown Corporation (a calendar year taxpayer) for 1998:

Taxable income	$200,000
Mining exploration costs	50,000
Percentage depletion claimed (the property has a zero adjusted basis)	70,000
Interest on City of Elmira (Michigan) private activity bonds	30,000

Brown Corporation's AMTI for 1998 is determined as follows:

Taxable income		$200,000
Adjustments:		
Excess mining exploration costs [$50,000 (amount expensed) – $5,000 (amount allowed over a 10-year amortization period)]		45,000
Tax preferences:		
Excess depletion	$70,000	
Interest on private activity bonds	30,000	100,000
AMTI		$345,000

EXEMPTION

The tentative AMT is 20 percent of AMTI that exceeds the corporation's exemption amount. The exemption amount for a corporation is $40,000 reduced by 25 percent of the amount by which AMTI exceeds $150,000.

EXAMPLE 35

Blue Corporation has AMTI of $180,000. The exemption amount is reduced by $7,500 [25% × ($180,000 – $150,000)], and the amount remaining is $32,500 ($40,000 – $7,500). Thus, Blue Corporation's AMT base (refer to Figure 14–3) is $147,500 ($180,000 – $32,500). ▼

Note that the exemption phases out entirely when AMTI reaches $310,000.

OTHER ASPECTS OF THE AMT

Foreign tax credits can be applied against only 90 percent of tentative AMT liability. The 90 percent limit does not apply to certain corporations meeting specified requirements.

All of a corporation's AMT is available for carryover as a minimum tax credit. This is so regardless of whether the adjustments and preferences originate from timing differences or AMT exclusions.

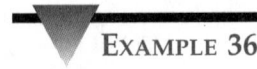

EXAMPLE 36

In Example 34, the AMTI exceeds $310,000, so no exemption is allowed. The tentative minimum tax is $69,000 (20% of $345,000). The regular income tax liability is $61,250, and the AMT liability is $7,750 ($69,000 − $61,250). The amount of the minimum tax credit carryover is $7,750, which is all of the current year's AMT. ▼

**TAX PLANNING
CONSIDERATIONS**

8 **LEARNING OBJECTIVE**
Identify tax planning
opportunities to minimize the
AMT.

RESPONDING TO BOB AND CAROL

The chapter began with a set of circumstances involving Bob and Carol that raised a number of interesting questions. By now, the student should have arrived at a logical reason for the difference in Bob and Carol's tax liabilities and expect the following to happen to Bob.

Bob contacts Adam, his tax return preparer, and explains in an excited voice that he has received a bill from the IRS for $15,000 plus interest associated with the underpayment of his tax liability. Adam has Bob fax him a copy of the IRS deficiency notice. He checks Bob's tax file and then calls Bob to explain that Bob does owe the IRS the $15,000 plus interest. Somehow Bob's tax return was prepared without including a Form 6251 (the alternative minimum tax). Adam suggests that Bob stop by his office later that afternoon to discuss the disposition of the matter further.

AVOIDING PREFERENCES AND ADJUSTMENTS

Several strategies and elections are available to help taxpayers avoid having preferences and adjustments.

- A taxpayer who is in danger of incurring AMT liability should not invest in tax-exempt private activity bonds unless doing so makes good investment sense. Any AMT triggered by interest on private activity bonds reduces the yield on an investment in the bonds. Other tax-exempt bonds or taxable corporate bonds might yield a better after-tax return.
- A taxpayer may elect to expense certain costs in the year incurred or to capitalize and amortize the costs over some specified period. The decision should be based on the present discounted value of after-tax cash flows under the available alternatives. Costs subject to elective treatment include circulation expenditures, mining exploration and development costs, and research and experimental expenditures.

CONTROLLING THE TIMING OF PREFERENCES AND ADJUSTMENTS

The AMT exemption often keeps items of tax preference from being subject to the AMT. To use the AMT exemption effectively, taxpayers should avoid bunching preferences and positive adjustments in any one year. To avoid this bunching, taxpayers should attempt to control the timing of such items when possible.

TAKING ADVANTAGE OF THE AMT/REGULAR TAX RATE DIFFERENTIAL

A taxpayer who cannot avoid triggering the AMT in a given year can usually save taxes by taking advantage of the rate differential between the AMT and the regular income tax.

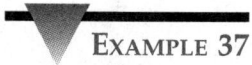

EXAMPLE 37

Peter, a real estate dealer who expects to be in the 31% tax bracket in 1999, is subject to the AMT in 1998. He is considering the sale of a parcel of land (inventory) at a gain of $100,000. If he sells the land in 1999, he will have to pay tax of $31,000 ($100,000 gain × 31% regular income tax rate). However, if he sells the land in 1998, he will pay tax of $26,000 ($100,000 gain × 26% AMT rate). Thus, accelerating the sale into 1998 will save Peter $5,000 in tax. ▼

EXAMPLE 38

Cora, who expects to be in the 39.6% tax bracket in 1999, is subject to the AMT in 1998. She is going to contribute $10,000 in cash to her alma mater, State University. If Cora makes the contribution in 1999, she will save tax of $3,960 ($10,000 contribution × 39.6% regular income tax rate). However, if she makes the contribution in 1998, she will save tax of $2,600 ($10,000 contribution × 26% AMT rate). Thus, deferring the contribution until 1999 will save Cora $1,360 in tax. ▼

This deferral/acceleration strategy should be considered for any income or expenses where the taxpayer can control the timing. This strategy applies to corporations as well as to individuals.

KEY TERMS

ACE adjustment, 14–29

Alternative minimum tax (AMT), 14–2

Alternative minimum tax credit, 14–24

Alternative tax NOL deduction (ATNOLD), 14–16

AMT adjustments, 14–4

AMT exclusions, 14–26

Circulation expenditures, 14–4

Incentive stock options (ISOs), 14–13

Private activity bonds, 14–22

Tax preferences, 14–4

PROBLEM MATERIALS

DISCUSSION QUESTIONS

1. Since there is a regular income tax, why is there a need for an AMT?

2. Distinguish between the direct method of calculating the AMT and the indirect method.

3. What is the difference between AMT adjustments and tax preferences?

4. Identify which of the following are tax preferences:
   a. Forty-two percent exclusion associated with gains on the sale of certain small business stock.
   b. Exclusion on the receipt of property by gift.
   c. Exclusion associated with payment of premiums by the employer on group term life insurance for coverage not in excess of $50,000.
   d. Percentage depletion in excess of the property's adjusted basis.
   e. Tax-exempt interest on certain private activity bonds.

5. Identify which of the following are tax preferences:
   a. Exclusion on the receipt of property by inheritance.
   b. Exclusion to employee on the employer's contribution to the employee's pension plan.
   c. Excess of deduction for circulation expenditures for regular income tax purposes over the deduction for AMT purposes.

d. Excess of amortization allowance over depreciation on pre-1987 certified pollution control facilities.

e. Excess of accelerated over straight-line depreciation on real property placed in service before 1987.

6. Describe the tax formula for the AMT.

7. If the regular income tax liability exceeds the tentative AMT, there is no AMT liability, and the total income tax liability is equal to the regular income tax liability. Evaluate the correctness of this statement.

8. For the exemption amount, indicate the following:
   a. Purpose for the exemption.
   b. Amount of the exemption.
   c. Reason for the phase-out of the exemption.

9. What are the AMT rates for an individual taxpayer? To what levels of income do the rates apply?

10. How do nonrefundable tax credits affect the calculation of the AMT?

11. How can an individual taxpayer avoid having an AMT adjustment for circulation expenditures?

12. Tom, who owns and operates a sole proprietorship, acquired machinery and placed it in service in February 1998. If Tom has to pay AMT in 1998, will he be required to make an AMT adjustment for depreciation on the machinery? Explain.

13. Rick, who is single, incurs mining exploration and development costs associated with his energy company. He would expense the costs in the current year in order to reduce his regular income tax, but is aware that this would create a positive adjustment for AMT purposes. His AGI is large enough to reduce the AMT exemption amount to zero. Therefore, he is considering electing to amortize the mining exploration and development costs over 10 years to avoid having to pay any AMT. Advise Rick.

14. Janice owns a construction company and uses the completed contract method for all of her contracts. April owns a construction company and uses the percentage of completion method for all of her construction contracts. Why does Janice have to be concerned with the AMT associated with her construction company whereas April does not?

15. If the stock received under an incentive stock option (ISO) is sold in the year of exercise, there is no AMT adjustment. If the stock is sold in a later year, there will be an AMT adjustment. Evaluate the validity of these statements.

16. Lucy acquired a machine for $30,000 for use in her business two years ago and depreciated it using an accelerated method under MACRS. When she sold the machine at a gain this year, should her recognized gain for regular income tax purposes be the same as her recognized gain for AMT purposes?

17. Carol is going to be subject to the AMT in 1998. She owns an investment building and is considering disposing of it and investing in other realty. Based on an appraisal of the building's value, the realized gain would be $20,000. Ed has offered to purchase the building from Carol with the closing date being December 29, 1998. Ed wants to close the transaction in 1998 because certain beneficial tax consequences will result only if the transaction is closed prior to the beginning of 1999. Abby has offered to purchase the building with the closing date being January 2, 1999. The building has a $25,000 greater AMT adjusted basis. For regular income tax purposes, Carol expects to be in the 28% tax bracket. What are the relevant tax issues that Carol faces in making her decision?

18. Passive activity losses are not deductible in computing either taxable income or AMTI. Explain why an adjustment for passive activity losses may be required for AMT purposes.

19. What effect do adjustments and preferences have on the calculation of the ATNOLD?

20. The following itemized deductions are allowed for regular income tax purposes: medical expenses, state and local income taxes, real estate taxes, personal property taxes, home mortgage interest, investment interest, charitable contributions of cash, charitable contributions of long-term capital gain property, casualty losses, unreimbursed employee business expenses, and gambling losses. Which of these itemized deductions can result in an AMT adjustment?

21. Matt, who is single, has always elected to itemize deductions rather than take the standard deduction. In prior years, his itemized deductions always exceeded the standard deduction by a substantial amount. As a result of paying off the mortgage on his residence, he projects that his itemized deductions for 1998 will exceed the standard deduction by only $500. Matt anticipates that the amount of his itemized deductions will remain about the same in the foreseeable future. Matt's AGI is $150,000. He is investing the amount of his former mortgage payment each month in tax-exempt bonds. A friend recommends that Matt buy a beach house in order to increase his itemized deductions. What are the relevant tax issues for Matt?

22. Wally's 3% cutback adjustment for regular income tax purposes reduces his itemized deductions from $25,000 to $21,000. What effect will this have in calculating Wally's AMTI?

23. Could computation of the AMT ever require an adjustment for the standard deduction or personal and dependency exemptions? Explain.

24. Alvin owns a mineral deposit that qualifies for the 15% percentage depletion rate. Under what circumstances will the depletion deduction for regular income tax purposes and AMT purposes not be the same?

25. Ira received a gift of $100,000 from his Aunt Lillian. He is going to invest the proceeds in either taxable bonds earning interest at an 8% rate or tax-exempt bonds earning interest at a 6% rate. What are the relevant tax issues for Ira?

26. What is the purpose of the AMT credit? Briefly describe how the credit is computed.

27. What requirements must be satisfied for a corporation to be exempt from the AMT?

28. Some observers believe the ACE adjustment causes corporations to change some of the methods they use for financial accounting and tax accounting purposes. Comment.

29. What is the ACE adjustment, and does it apply to both the individual taxpayer and the corporate taxpayer?

30. Is it ever advisable for a taxpayer to defer deductions from an AMT year into a non-AMT year where the regular income tax applies? Explain and give an example of how such a deferral might be accomplished.

PROBLEMS

31. Use the following data to calculate Rachel's AMT base:

Taxable income	$130,000
Positive AMT adjustments	50,000
Negative AMT adjustments	20,000
AMT preferences	25,000

Rachel is not married.

32. Arthur East, an unmarried individual who is age 66, has taxable income of $100,000. He has AMT positive adjustments of $70,000 and tax preferences of $45,000.
    a. What is Arthur's AMT?
    b. What is the total amount of Arthur's tax liability?
    c. Draft a letter to Arthur explaining why he must pay more than the regular income tax liability. Arthur's address is 100 Colonel's Way, Conway, SC 29526.

33. Calculate the AMT for the following cases. The taxpayer has regular taxable income of $500,000 and does not have any credits.

Filing Status	Tentative AMT	
	Case 1	Case 2
Single	$190,000	$175,000
Married, filing jointly	190,000	175,000

34. Calculate the exemption amount for the following cases for a single taxpayer, a married taxpayer filing jointly, and a married taxpayer filing separately.

Case	AMTI
1	$100,000
2	200,000
3	400,000

35. Leona has nonrefundable credits of $30,000 for 1998. Her regular income tax liability before credits is $42,000, and her tentative AMT is $25,000.
    a. What is the amount of Leona's AMT?
    b. What is the amount of Leona's regular income tax liability after credits?

36. Angela, who is single, incurs circulation expenditures of $123,000 during 1998. She is in the process of deciding whether to expense the $123,000 or to capitalize it and elect to deduct it over a three-year period. Angela already knows that she will be subject to the AMT for 1998 at the 28% rate. Angela is in the 31% bracket for regular income tax purposes this year and expects to remain in that bracket in the future. Advise Angela on whether she should elect the three-year write-off rather than expensing the $123,000 in 1998.

37. Vito owns and operates a news agency (as a sole proprietorship). During 1998, he incurred expenses of $60,000 to increase circulation of newspapers and magazines that his agency distributes. For regular income tax purposes, he elected to expense the $60,000 in 1998. In addition, he incurred $30,000 in circulation expenditures in 1999 and again elected expense treatment. What AMT adjustments will be required in 1998 and 1999 as a result of the circulation expenditures?

38. Lance is a landlord who owns two apartment buildings. He acquired Longwood Acres on February 21, 1986, for $300,000, with $90,000 of the cost allocated to the land. He acquired Colony Square on March 5, 1994, for $800,000, and $175,000 of the cost was allocated to land. Neither apartment complex is low-income housing. Lance elected to write off the cost of each building as fast as possible. What is the effect of depreciation (cost recovery) on Lance's AMTI for 1998?

39. In March 1998, Helen Carlon acquired equipment for her business at a cost of $250,000. The equipment is 5-year class property for regular income tax purposes and 9.5-year class property for AMT purposes.
    a. If Helen depreciates the equipment using the method that will produce the greatest deduction for 1998, what is the amount of the AMT adjustment?
    b. How can Helen reduce the AMT adjustment to $0? What circumstances would motivate her to do so?
    c. Draft a letter to Helen regarding the choice of depreciation methods. Helen's address is 500 Monticello Avenue, Glendale, AZ 85306.

40. In 1998, Gary incurred $180,000 of mining and exploration expenditures. He elects to deduct the expenditures as quickly as the tax law allows for regular income tax purposes.
    a. How will Gary's treatment of mining and exploration expenditures affect his regular income tax and AMT computations for 1998?

    b. How can Gary avoid having AMT adjustments related to the mining and exploration expenditures?

    c. What factors should Gary consider in deciding whether to deduct the expenditures in the year incurred?

41. Josepi's construction company builds personal residences that qualify for the use of the completed contract method. During the three-year period 1998–2000, Josepi recognized the following income on his two construction contracts:

Year	Contract 1	Contract 2
1998	$600,000*	$ –0–
1999	–0–	–0–
2000	–0–	700,000**

  *Construction completed in 1998.

  **Construction completed in 2000.

If Josepi had used the percentage of completion method, he would have recognized the following income:

Year	Contract 1	Contract 2
1998	$40,000	$175,000
1999	–0–	225,000
2000	–0–	300,000

Calculate the amount of the AMT adjustment for 1998, 1999, and 2000.

42. Burt, the CFO of Amber, Inc., is granted stock options in 1998 that qualify as incentive stock options (ISOs). In 2003, the rights in the stock become freely transferable and not subject to a substantial risk of forfeiture. Burt exercises the stock options in 2002 when the option price is $70,000 and the fair market value of the stock is $100,000. He sells the stock in 2006 for $150,000. What are the regular income tax consequences and the AMT consequences for Burt in:

    a. 1998?

    b. 2002?

    c. 2003?

    d. 2006?

43. In 1998, Lori exercised an incentive stock option that had been granted by her employer, Black Corporation. Lori acquired 100 shares of Black stock for the option price of $175 per share. The rights in the stock become freely transferable and not subject to a substantial risk of forfeiture in 1998. The fair market value of the stock at the date of exercise was $210 per share. Lori sells the stock for $320 per share in 1998. What is the amount of her AMT adjustment in 1998, and what is her recognized gain on the sale for regular income tax purposes and AMT purposes?

44. Bobby sells an apartment building for $500,000. His adjusted basis is $300,000 for regular income tax purposes and $330,000 for AMT purposes.

    a. Calculate Bobby's gain for regular income tax purposes.

    b. Calculate Bobby's gain for AMT purposes.

    c. Calculate Bobby's AMT adjustment, if any.

45. Freda acquired a passive activity in 1998. Gross income from operations of the activity was $150,000. Operating expenses, not including depreciation, were $135,000. Regular income tax depreciation of $37,500 was computed under MACRS. AMT depreciation, computed under ADS, was $24,000. Compute Freda's passive loss deduction and passive loss suspended for regular income tax purposes and for AMT purposes.

46. Wally and Gloria incur and pay medical expenses in excess of insurance reimbursements during the year as follows:

For Wally	$8,000
For Gloria (spouse)	3,000
For Chuck (son)	1,000
For Carter (Gloria's father)	9,000

    Wally and Gloria's AGI is $200,000. They file a joint return. Chuck and Carter are Wally and Gloria's dependents.
    a. What is Wally and Gloria's medical expense deduction for regular income tax purposes?
    b. What is Wally and Gloria's medical expense deduction for AMT purposes?
    c. What is the amount of the AMT adjustment for medical expenses?

47. Wolfgang had the following itemized deductions for 1998:

Medical expenses [$5,000 – (7.5% × $50,000)]	$ 1,250
State income taxes	3,000
Charitable contributions	5,000
Home mortgage interest on his personal residence	6,000
Casualty loss	1,500
Miscellaneous itemized deductions [$3,500 – 2%($50,000)]	2,500
	$19,250

    a. Calculate Wolfgang's itemized deductions for AMT purposes.
    b. What is the amount of the AMT adjustment?

48. Tom, who is single, owns a personal residence in the city. He also owns a cabin near a ski resort in the mountains. He uses the cabin as a vacation home. In February 1998, he borrowed $60,000 on a home equity loan and used the proceeds to pay off credit card obligations and other debt. During 1998, he paid the following amounts of interest:

On his personal residence	$12,000
On the cabin	4,800
On the home equity loan	5,000
On credit card obligations	1,200

    What amount, if any, must Tom recognize as an AMT adjustment in 1998?

49. Gail pays investment interest of $45,000. She has interest income of $12,000 on taxable bonds, $6,000 on tax-exempt bonds that are private activity bonds, and $5,000 on tax-exempt bonds that are not private activity bonds. Her other investment expenses are $3,000, none of which relates to the tax-exempt bonds.
    a. What is Gail's deduction for investment interest for regular income tax purposes?
    b. What is the amount of her investment interest carryover for regular income tax purposes?
    c. What is the amount of the adjustment for AMT purposes?

50. Bill, who is single with no dependents, had AGI of $100,000 in 1998. His AGI included net investment income of $15,000 and gambling income of $1,100. Bill incurred the following expenses during the year, all of which resulted in itemized deductions for income tax purposes:

Medical expenses (before 7.5%-of-AGI floor)	$11,000
State income taxes	3,200
Personal property tax	2,000
Real estate tax	8,400
Interest on personal residence	12,200
Interest on vacation home (never rented to others)	3,800
Interest on home equity loan (proceeds were used to buy a new automobile)	2,700
Investment interest expense	3,300
Charitable contribution	5,000
Casualty loss (after $100 floor, before 10%-of-AGI floor)	13,000
Unreimbursed employee expenses (before 2%-of-AGI floor)	2,400
Gambling losses	900

What is the amount of Bill's AMT adjustment for itemized deductions in 1998, and is it positive or negative?

51. Peggy, who is single and has no dependents, had taxable income of $148,000 and tax preferences of $57,500 in 1998. She did not itemize deductions for regular income tax purposes. Compute Peggy's AMT exemption and AMTI for 1998.

52. Hector owns a silver mine that he purchased several years ago for $800,000. His adjusted basis at the beginning of the year is $300,000. For the year, he deducts depletion of $450,000 (greater of cost depletion of $230,000 or percentage depletion of $450,000) for regular income tax purposes.
    a. Calculate Hector's AMT adjustment.
    b. Calculate Hector's adjusted basis for regular income tax purposes.
    c. Calculate Hector's adjusted basis for AMT purposes.

53. Amos incurred and expensed intangible drilling costs (IDC) of $70,000. His net oil and gas income was $60,000. What is the amount of Amos's tax preference item for IDC?

54. Jack, who is single with no dependents and does not itemize, provides you with the following information for 1998:

Short-term capital loss	$ 5,000
Long-term capital gain	25,000
Municipal bond interest received on private activity bonds acquired in 1990	9,000
Dividends from General Motors	1,500
Excess of FMV over cost of incentive stock options (the rights became freely transferable and not subject to a substantial risk of forfeiture in 1998)	35,000

What is the total amount of Jack's tax preference items and AMT adjustments for 1998?

55. Jason receives $10,000 of interest on bonds issued by the State of Iowa that are appropriately classified as private activity bonds. Related carrying costs are $1,000.
    a. Determine the effect on Jason's regular taxable income.
    b. Determine the effect on AMTI.
    c. Calculate the amount of Jason's AMT adjustment.

56. Rosa and Steve, who are married, had taxable income of $150,000 for 1998. They had positive AMT adjustments of $40,000, negative AMT adjustments of $10,000, and tax preference items of $67,500.
    a. Compute their AMTI.
    b. Compute their tentative minimum tax.

57. Tara, who is single, has no dependents and does not itemize. She has the following items relative to her tax return for 1998:

Bargain element from the exercise of an incentive stock option (no restrictions apply to the stock)	$ 45,000
Accelerated depreciation on leased equipment acquired before 1987 (straight-line depreciation would have yielded $26,000)	41,000
Percentage depletion in excess of property's adjusted basis	50,000
Taxable income for regular income tax purposes	121,000

a. Determine Tara's AMT adjustments and preferences for 1998.

b. Calculate the AMT (if any) for 1998.

58. Lynn is single and has no dependents. Based on the financial information presented below, compute Lynn's AMT for 1998.

Income:

Salary	$33,000
Taxable interest on corporate bonds	1,800
Dividend income	1,900
Business income	64,000

Expenditures:

Medical expenses	12,000
State income taxes	6,000
Real estate taxes	8,500
Mortgage (qualified housing) interest	9,200
Investment interest	5,500
Cash contributions to various charities	2,900

Additional information:

a. The $64,000 business income is from Acme Office Supplies Company, a sole proprietorship Lynn owns and operates. Acme claimed MACRS depreciation of $3,175 on real property used in the business. ADS depreciation on the property would have been $2,500.

b. Lynn received interest of $30,000 on City of Columbus private activity bonds.

59. Bonnie, who is single, had taxable income of $0 in 1998. She has positive timing adjustments of $200,000 and AMT exclusion items of $100,000 for the year. What is the amount of Bonnie's AMT credit for carryover to 1999?

60. Aqua, Inc., a calendar year corporation, has the following gross receipts and taxable income for 1994–1998:

Year	Gross Receipts	Taxable Income
1994	$11,000,000	$3,000,000
1995	4,800,000	900,000
1996	5,300,000	1,500,000
1997	4,600,000	700,000
1998	8,500,000	1,900,000

a. Is Aqua subject to the AMT for 1998?

b. Is Aqua subject to the AMT for 1999?

61. Gray Corporation (a calendar year corporation) reports the following information for the years listed below:

	1997	1998	1999
Unadjusted AMTI	$3,000	$2,000	$5,000
Adjusted current earnings	4,000	3,000	2,000

Compute the ACE adjustment for each year.

62. In each of the following independent situations, determine the tentative AMT:

	AMTI (Before the Exemption Amount)
Quincy Corporation	$150,000
Redland Corporation	160,000
Tanzen Corporation	320,000

63. Amber, Inc., has taxable income of $200,000. During the year, Amber paid dividends of $30,000. The corporation had $20,000 of positive AMT adjustments and $25,000 of tax preferences.
   a. Calculate Amber's regular income tax liability.
   b. Calculate Amber's AMTI and AMT.

CUMULATIVE PROBLEMS

64. Ron T. Freeman, age 38, is divorced and has no dependents. He pays alimony of $24,000 per year to his former wife, Kate. Kate's husband was killed in a hunting accident in 1998. At the time of the accident, their baby was only six weeks old. Ron decided to invest $5,000 each year in a mutual fund in Kate's baby's name to be used as a college fund. He made the initial $5,000 investment in 1998. Ron's Social Security number is 444–11–2222, and Kate's is 555–67–2222. Ron's address is 201 Front Street, Missoula, MT 59812. He is independently wealthy as a result of having inherited sizable holdings in real estate and corporate stocks and bonds. Ron is a minister at First Methodist Church, but he accepts no salary from the church. However, he does reside in the church's parsonage free of charge. The rental value of the parsonage is $600 a month. The church also provides him a cash grocery allowance of $150 a week. Examination of Ron's financial records provides the following information for 1998:
   a. On January 16, 1998, Ron sold 2,000 shares of stock for a gain of $30,000. The stock was acquired four years ago.
   b. He received $40,000 of interest on private activity bonds.
   c. He received gross rent income of $145,000 from an apartment complex he owns and manages.
   d. Expenses related to the apartment complex, which he acquired in 1983, were $190,000.
   e. Ron's dividend and interest income (on a savings account) totaled $26,000.
   f. On October 9, 1996, Ron exercised his rights under Egret Corporation's incentive stock option plan. For an option price of $20,000, he acquired stock worth $55,000. The stock became freely transferable in 1998.
   g. Ron had the following potential itemized deductions *from* AGI:

   • $3,000 fair market value of stock contributed to Methodist Church (basis of stock was $2,000). He owned the stock for five years.

   • $2,000 interest on consumer purchases.

   • $2,900 state and local taxes.

   • $7,000 medical expenses (before 7.5% floor) for himself and $4,000 of hospital expenses associated with Kate's deceased husband.

   • $100 for a safe deposit box that is used to store investments and related legal documents.

   • $10,000 of losses associated with playing the state lottery. Ron had no winnings during 1998. Any net winnings would be contributed to the church.

   Compute Ron's tax liability, including AMT if applicable, before prepayments or credits, for 1998. Suggested software (if available): *TurboTax.*

65. Robert M. and Jane R. Armstrong live at 1802 College Avenue, Carmel, IN 46302. They are married and file a joint return for 1997. The Armstrongs have two dependent children, Ellen J. and Sean M., who are 10-year-old twins. Ellen's Social Security number is 333–42–3368, and Sean's is 333–42–3369. Robert pays child support of $3,000 for Amy, his 17-year-old daughter from his previous marriage. Amy's Social Security number is 111–22–4300. According to the divorce decree, Margaret, Robert's former wife, has legal custody of Amy. Margaret provides the balance of Amy's support (about $7,000).

Robert (224–36–9987) is a factory foreman, and Jane (443–56–3421) is a computer systems analyst. The Armstrongs' W-2 forms for 1997 reflect the following information:

	Robert	Jane
Salary (Indiana Foundry, Inc.)	$56,000	
Salary (Carmel Computer Associates)		$80,000
Federal income tax withheld	7,170	15,200
Social Security wages	56,000	65,400
Social Security withheld	3,472	4,055
Medicare wages	56,000	80,000
Medicare tax withheld	812	1,160
State wages	56,000	80,000
State income tax withheld	1,650	2,400

In addition to their salaries, the Armstrongs had the following income items in 1997:

Interest income (Carmel Sanitation District Bonds)	$14,800
Interest income (Carmel National Bank)	2,100
Dividend income (Able Computer Corporation)	2,900
Gambling income	3,000

Jane inherited $200,000 from her grandfather in January and invested the money in the Carmel Sanitation District Bonds, which are private activity bonds.

The Armstrongs incurred the following expenses during 1997:

Medical expenses (doctor and hospital bills)	$16,725
Real property tax on personal residence	4,200
Mortgage interest on personal residence (reported on Form 1098)	5,000
Investment interest expense	1,900
Contributions to Salvation Army	18,000
Gambling losses	3,750

On March 1, Robert and Jane contributed Ace stock to the Carmel Salvation Army, a public charity. They had acquired the stock on February 9, 1979, for $1,500. The stock was listed on the New York Stock Exchange at a value of $18,000 on the date of the contribution.

Robert received a gift of 25 acres of land from his Uncle Ted on May 15. The appraised value of the land at the date of the gift was $63,000, and Uncle Ted's adjusted basis was $10,000. Uncle Ted was not required to pay any gift tax.

Use Forms 1040, 4952, 6251, and 8283 and Schedules A and B to compute the tax liability (including AMT) for Robert and Jane Armstrong for 1997. Suggested software (if available): *TurboTax*. Write a letter to the Armstrongs indicating whether they have a refund or balance due for 1997, and suggest possible tax planning strategies for 1998.

Research Problems for this chapter appear at the end of Chapter 28.

TEAM PROJECT: ARTHUR ANDERSEN TAX CHALLENGE CASES

For more information on the Arthur Andersen Tax Challenge Cases, refer to Chapter 1, page 1–37.

Information related to tax issues and problems that are discussed in this chapter may be found in the

Day and Ball case on pages: None
Fence case on pages 44, 56, and 64

Read and analyze the case you have been assigned and *identify* any issues and problems that are related to material covered in this chapter. If the information provided in the case is complete, prepare answers for this part of the case at this time. If you need information that is contained in the later parts of the case, write a memo summarizing the questions or problems so you can prepare a complete answer at a later date.

15

ACCOUNTING PERIODS AND METHODS

LEARNING OBJECTIVES

After completing Chapter 15, you should be able to:

1. Understand the relevance of the accounting period concept, the different types of accounting periods, and the limitations on their use.

2. Apply the cash method, accrual method, and hybrid method of accounting.

3. Utilize the procedure for changing accounting methods.

4. Determine when the installment method of accounting can be utilized and apply the related calculation techniques.

5. Understand the alternative methods of accounting for long-term contracts (the completed contract method and the percentage of completion method) including the limitations on the use of the completed contract method.

6. Identify tax planning opportunities related to accounting periods and accounting methods.

Tax practitioners must deal with the issue of *when* particular items of income and expense are recognized as well as the basic issue of *whether* the items are includible in taxable income. Earlier chapters discussed the types of income subject to tax (gross income and exclusions) and allowable deductions (the *whether* issue).[1] This chapter focuses on the related issue of the periods in which income and deductions are reported (the *when* issue). Generally, a taxpayer's income and deductions must be assigned to particular 12-month periods—calendar years or fiscal years.

Income and deductions are placed within particular years through the use of tax accounting methods. The basic accounting methods are the cash method, accrual method, and hybrid method. Other special purpose methods, such as the installment method and the methods used for long-term construction contracts, are available for specific circumstances or types of transactions.

Over the long run, the accounting period used by a taxpayer will not affect the aggregate amount of reported taxable income. However, taxable income for any particular year may vary significantly due to the use of a particular reporting period. Also, through the choice of accounting methods or accounting periods, it is possible to postpone the recognition of taxable income and to enjoy the benefits from deferring the related tax. This chapter discusses the taxpayer's alternatives for accounting periods and accounting methods.

ACCOUNTING PERIODS

IN GENERAL

1 ▼ LEARNING OBJECTIVE
Understand the relevance of the accounting period concept, the different types of accounting periods, and the limitations on their use.

A taxpayer who keeps adequate books and records may be permitted to elect to use a **fiscal year,** a 12-month period ending on the *last day* of a month other than December, for the **accounting period.** Otherwise, a *calendar year* must be used.[2] Frequently, corporations can satisfy the record-keeping requirements and elect to use a fiscal year.[3] Often the fiscal year conforms to a natural business year (e.g., a

---

[1]See Chapters 3, 4, and 5.
[2]§ 441(c) and Reg. § 1.441–1(b)(1)(ii).

[3]Reg. § 1.441–1(e)(2).

TAX IN THE NEWS

ACCELERATION OF INCOME

In 1993, the *Wall Street Journal* and various other print and broadcast news sources reported that Hillary Rodham Clinton had the opportunity to receive compensation income in 1992 or 1993. She chose to accelerate the income into 1992. This appears to be at variance with the normal tax planning mode of deferring the reporting of income and accelerating the reporting of deductions.

One possible explanation for reporting the income in 1992 rather than in 1993 is that the family's taxable income was expected to be greater in 1993 than in 1992. However, while the President earns substantially more as President of the United States than as Governor of Arkansas, the First Lady earns substantially less than she did as a partner in an Arkansas law firm.

Another possible explanation is the expectation that the Revenue Reconciliation Act of 1993 with its retroactive increase in tax rates would be passed by Congress. In any event, the First Lady followed sound tax advice in accelerating the income into 1992.

---

summer resort's fiscal year may end on September 30, after the close of the season). Individuals seldom use a fiscal year because they do not maintain the necessary books and records and because complications can arise as a result of changes in the tax law (e.g., often the transition rules and effective dates differ for fiscal year taxpayers).

Generally, a taxable year may not exceed 12 calendar months. However, if certain requirements are met, a taxpayer may elect to use an annual period that varies from 52 to 53 weeks.[4] In that case, the year-end must be on the same day of the week (e.g., the Tuesday falling closest to October 31 or the last Tuesday in October). The day of the week selected for ending the year will depend upon business considerations. For example, a retail business that is not open on Sundays may end its tax year on a Sunday so that it can take an inventory without interrupting business operations.

EXAMPLE 1

Wade is in the business of selling farm supplies. His natural business year terminates at the end of October with the completion of harvesting. At the end of the fiscal year, Wade must take an inventory, which is most easily accomplished on a Tuesday. Therefore, Wade could adopt a 52–53 week tax year ending on the Tuesday closest to October 31. If Wade selects this method, the year-end date may fall in the following month if that Tuesday is closer to October 31. The tax year ending in 1998 will contain 53 weeks beginning on Wednesday, October 29, 1997, and ending on Tuesday, November 3, 1998. The tax year ending in 1999 will have 52 weeks beginning on Wednesday, November 4, 1998, and ending on Tuesday, November 2, 1999. ▼

SPECIFIC PROVISIONS FOR PARTNERSHIPS, S CORPORATIONS, AND PERSONAL SERVICE CORPORATIONS

Partnerships and S Corporations.   When a partner's tax year and the partnership's tax year differ, the partner will enjoy a deferral of income. This results because the partner reports his or her share of the partnership's income and deductions for

---

[4]§ 441(f).

the partnership's tax year ending within or with the partner's tax year.[5] For example, if the tax year of the partnership ends on January 31, a calendar year partner will not report partnership profits for the first 11 months of the partnership tax year until the following year. Therefore, partnerships are subject to special tax year requirements.

In general, the partnership tax year must be the same as the tax year of the majority interest partners. The **majority interest partners** are the partners who own a greater-than-50 percent interest in the partnership capital and profits. If the majority owners do not have the same tax year, the partnership must adopt the same tax year as its principal partners. A **principal partner** is a partner with a 5 percent or more interest in the partnership capital or profits.[6]

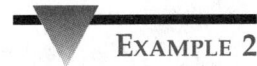

EXAMPLE 2

The RST Partnership is owned equally by Rose Corporation, Silver Corporation, and Tom. The partners have the following tax years.

Partner	Tax Year Ending
Rose	June 30
Silver	June 30
Tom	December 31

The partnership's tax year must end on June 30. If Silver Corporation's as well as Tom's year ended on December 31, the partnership would be required to adopt a calendar year. ▼

If the principal partners do not all have the same tax year and no majority of partners have the same tax year, the partnership must use a year that results in the *least aggregate deferral* of income.[7] Under the **least aggregate deferral method**, the different tax years of the principal partners are tested to determine which produces the least aggregate deferral. This is calculated by first multiplying the combined percentages of the principal partners with the same tax year by the months of deferral for the test year. Once this is done for each set of principal partners with the same tax year, the resulting products are summed to produce the aggregate deferral. After calculating the aggregate deferral for each of the test years, the test year with the smallest summation (the least aggregate deferral) is the tax year for the partnership.

EXAMPLE 3

The DE Partnership is owned equally by Diane and Emily. Diane's fiscal year ends on March 31, and Emily's fiscal year ends on August 31. The partnership must use the partner's fiscal year that will result in the least aggregate deferral of income. Therefore, the fiscal years ending March 31 and August 31 must both be tested.

	Test for Fiscal Year Ending March 31			
Partner	**Year Ends**	**Profit %**	**Months of Deferral**	**Product**
Diane	3–31	50	0	0
Emily	8–31	50	5	2.5
Aggregate deferral months				2.5

---

[5]Reg. § 1.706–1(a).
[6]§§ 706(b)(1)(B) and 706(b)(3).

[7]Temp.Reg. § 1.706–IT(a)(2).

Thus, with a year ending March 31, Emily would be able to defer her half of the income for five months. That is, Emily's share of the partnership income for the fiscal year ending March 31, 1999, would not be included in her income until August 31, 1999.

Test for Fiscal Year Ending August 31

Partner	Year Ends	Profit %	Months of Deferral	Product
Diane	3–31	50	7	3.5
Emily	8–31	50	0	0
Aggregate deferral months				3.5

Thus, with a year ending August 31, Diane would be able to defer her half of the income for seven months. That is, Diane's share of the partnership income for the fiscal year ending August 31, 1999, would not be included in her income until March 31, 2000.

The year ending March 31 must be used because it results in the least aggregate deferral of income. ▼

Generally, S corporations must adopt a calendar year.[8] However, partnerships and S corporations may *elect* an otherwise *impermissible year* under any of the following conditions:

- A business purpose for the year can be demonstrated.[9]
- The partnership's or S corporation's year results in a deferral of not more than three months' income, and the entity agrees to make required tax payments.[10]
- The entity retains the same year as was used for the fiscal year ending in 1987, provided the entity agrees to make required tax payments.

Business Purpose.   The only business purpose for a fiscal year that the IRS has acknowledged is the need to conform the tax year to the natural business year of a business.[11] Generally, only seasonal businesses have a natural business year. For example, the natural business year for a department store may end on January 31, after Christmas returns have been processed and clearance sales have been completed.

Required Tax Payments.   Under the required payments system, tax payments are due from a fiscal year partnership or S corporation by April 15 of each tax year.[12] The amount due is computed by applying the highest individual tax rate plus 1 percent to an estimate of the deferral period income. The deferral period runs from the close of the fiscal year to the end of the calendar year. Estimated income for this period is based on the average monthly earnings for the previous fiscal year. The amount due is reduced by the amount of required tax payments for the previous year.[13]

EXAMPLE 4

Brown, Inc., an S corporation, elected a fiscal year ending September 30. Bob is the only shareholder. For the fiscal year ending September 30, 1998, Brown earned $100,000. The required tax payment for the previous year was $5,000. The corporation must pay $5,150 by April 15, 1999, calculated as follows:

---

[8]§§ 1378(a) and (b).
[9]§§ 706(b)(1)(C) and 1378(b)(2).
[10]§ 444.
[11]Rev.Rul. 87–57, 1987–2 C.B. 117.

[12]§§ 444(c) and 7519. No payment is required if the calculated amount is $500 or less.
[13]§ 7519(b).

$$(\$100{,}000 \times \tfrac{3}{12} \times 40.6\%^*) - \$5{,}000 = \$5{,}150$$

*Maximum § 1 rate of 39.6% + 1%.   ▼

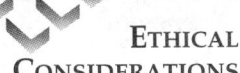

Ethical Considerations

Required Tax Years

Before 1987, partnerships could generally use a fiscal year ending September 30, and S corporations could use any fiscal year. With this latitude, accountants often recommended that their partnership and S corporation clients not use a calendar year. This enabled the accountants to spread their work throughout the year and created a tax deferral for the clients.

Members of the accounting profession argued vociferously against the calendar year requirement that was included in the Tax Reform Act of 1986. The choice Congress had to make was whether some groups should be allowed to benefit (i.e., the accountants and their clients) at the expense of the rest of the general public. Of course, the accounting profession viewed the choices differently: Should some groups be burdened (i.e., the accounting profession) for little benefit to the remaining taxpayers?

The compromise reached was the required payments scheme, whereby the burden was lifted from the accounting profession without the clients enjoying tax deferrals. Was this an acceptable compromise?

Personal Service Corporations (PSCs). A **personal service corporation (PSC)** is a corporation whose shareholder-employees provide personal services (e.g., medical, dental, legal, accounting, engineering, actuarial, consulting, or performing arts). Generally, a PSC must use a calendar year.[14] However, a PSC can *elect* a fiscal year under any of the following conditions:

- A business purpose for the year can be demonstrated.
- The PSC year results in a deferral of not more than three months' income; the corporation pays the shareholder-employee's salary during the portion of the calendar year after the close of the fiscal year; and the salary for that period is at least proportionate to the shareholder-employee's salary received for the preceding fiscal year.[15]
- The PSC retains the same year it used for the fiscal year ending in 1987, provided it satisfies the latter two requirements in the preceding option.

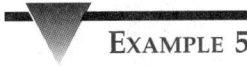

Example 5

Nancy's corporation paid her a salary of $120,000 during its fiscal year ending September 30, 1998. The corporation cannot satisfy the business purpose test for a fiscal year. The corporation can continue to use its fiscal year without any negative tax effects, provided Nancy receives at least $30,000 [(3 months/12 months) × $120,000] of her salary during the period October 1 through December 31, 1998. ▼

If the salary test is not satisfied, the PSC can retain the fiscal year, but the corporation's deduction for salary for the fiscal year is limited to the following:

---

[14]§ 441(i).

[15]§§ 444 and 280H.

$$A + A(F/N)$$

Where A = Amount paid after the close of the fiscal year.
   F = Number of months in fiscal year minus number of months from the end of the fiscal year to the end of the ongoing calendar year.
   N = Number of months from the end of the fiscal year to the end of the ongoing calendar year.

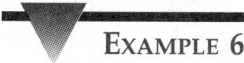

EXAMPLE 6

Assume the corporation in the previous example paid Nancy $10,000 of salary during the period October 1 through December 31, 1998. The deduction for Nancy's salary for the corporation's fiscal year ending September 30, 1999, is thus limited to $40,000 calculated as follows:

$$\$10,000 + \left[\$10,000 \left(\frac{12-3}{3}\right)\right] = \$10,000 + \$30,000 = \$40,000$$

MAKING THE ELECTION

A taxpayer elects to use a calendar or fiscal year by the timely filing of his or her initial tax return. For all subsequent years, the taxpayer must use this same period unless approval for change is obtained from the IRS.[16]

CHANGES IN THE ACCOUNTING PERIOD

A taxpayer must obtain consent from the IRS before changing the tax year.[17] This power to approve or not to approve a change is significant in that it permits the IRS to issue authoritative administrative guidelines that must be met by taxpayers who wish to change their accounting period. An application for permission to change tax years must be made on Form 1128, Application for Change in Accounting Period. The application must be filed on or before the fifteenth day of the second calendar month following the close of the short period that results from the change in accounting period.[18]

EXAMPLE 7

Beginning in 1998, Gold Corporation, a calendar year taxpayer, would like to switch to a fiscal year ending March 31. The corporation must file Form 1128 by May 15, 1998. ▼

IRS Requirements.   The IRS will not grant permission for the change unless the taxpayer can establish a substantial business purpose for the request. One substantial business purpose is to change to a tax year that coincides with the *natural business year* (the completion of an annual business cycle). The IRS applies an objective gross receipts test to determine if the entity has a natural business year. At least 25 percent of the entity's gross receipts for the 12-month period must be realized in the final 2 months of the 12-month period for three consecutive years.[19]

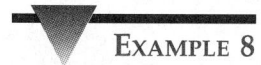

EXAMPLE 8

A Virginia Beach motel had gross receipts as follows:

---

[16]Reg. §§ 1.441–1(b)(3) and 1.441–1(b)(4).

[17]§ 442. Under certain conditions, corporations are allowed to change tax years without obtaining IRS approval. See Reg. § 1.442–1(c)(1).

[18]Reg. § 1.442–1(b)(1). In Example 7, the first period after the change in accounting period (January 1, 1998 through March 31, 1998) is less than a 12-month period and is referred to as a *short period*.

[19]Rev.Proc. 87–32, 1987–1 C.B. 131, and Rev.Rul. 87–57, 1987–2 C.B. 117.

	1996	1997	1998
July–August receipts	$ 300,000	$250,000	$ 325,000
September 1–August 31 receipts	1,000,000	900,000	1,250,000
Receipts for 2 months divided by receipts for 12 months	30.0%	27.8%	26.0%

Since it satisfies the natural business year test, the motel will be allowed to use a fiscal year ending August 31. ▼

The IRS usually establishes certain conditions that the taxpayer must accept if the approval for change is to be granted. In particular, if the taxpayer has a net operating loss for the short period, the IRS may require that the loss be carried forward and allocated equally over the 6 following years.[20] As you may recall (refer to Chapter 6), net operating losses are ordinarily carried back for 2 years and forward for 20 years.

EXAMPLE 9

Parrot Corporation changed from a calendar year to a fiscal year ending September 30. The short-period return for the nine months ending September 30, 1998, reflected a $60,000 net operating loss. The corporation had taxable income for 1996 and 1997. As a condition for granting approval, the IRS requires Parrot to allocate the $60,000 loss over the next six years, rather than carrying the loss back to the two preceding years (the usual order for applying a net operating loss). Thus, Parrot will reduce its taxable income by $10,000 each year ending September 30, 1999, through September 30, 2004. ▼

TAXABLE PERIODS OF LESS THAN ONE YEAR

A **short taxable year** (or **short period**) is a period of less than 12 calendar months. A taxpayer may have a short year for (1) the first income tax return, (2) the final income tax return, or (3) a change in the tax year. If the short period results from a change in the taxpayer's annual accounting period, the taxable income for the period must be *annualized*. Due to the progressive tax rate structure, taxpayers could reap benefits from a short-period return if some adjustments were not required. Thus, the taxpayer is required to do the following:

1. Annualize the short-period income.

$$\text{Annualized income} = \text{Short-period income} \times \frac{12}{\text{Number of months in the short period}}$$

2. Compute the tax on the annualized income.
3. Convert the tax on the annualized income to a short-period tax.

$$\text{Short-period tax} = \text{Tax on annualized income} \times \frac{\text{Number of months in the short period}}{12}$$

EXAMPLE 10

Gray Corporation obtained permission to change from a calendar year to a fiscal year ending September 30, beginning in 1998. For the short period January 1 through September 30, 1998, the corporation's taxable income was $48,000. The relevant tax rates and the resultant short-period tax are as follows:

[20]Rev.Proc. 85–16, 1985–1 C.B. 517.

Amount of Taxable Income	Tax Rates
Not over $50,000	15% of taxable income
Over $50,000 but not over $75,000	$7,500 plus 25% of taxable income in excess of $50,000

Calculation of Short-Period Tax

Annualized income ($48,000 × ¹²⁄₉) = $64,000

Tax on annualized income
  [$7,500 + .25($64,000 − $50,000)] = $7,500 + $3,500 = $11,000

Short-period tax = ($11,000 × ⁹⁄₁₂) = $8,250

Annualizing the income increases the tax by $1,050:

Tax with annualizing	$8,250
Tax without annualizing ($48,000 × .15)	(7,200)
Increase in tax from annualizing	$1,050

Rather than annualize the short-period income, the taxpayer can elect to (1) calculate the tax for a 12-month period beginning on the first day of the short period and (2) convert the tax in (1) to a short-period tax as follows:[21]

$$\frac{\text{Taxable income for short period}}{\text{Taxable income for the 12-month period}} \times \text{Tax on the 12 months of income}$$

EXAMPLE 11

Assume Gray Corporation's taxable income for the calendar year 1998 was $60,000. The tax on the full 12 months of income would have been $10,000 [$7,500 + .25($60,000 − $50,000)]. The short-period tax would be $8,000 [($48,000/$60,000) × $10,000)]. Thus, if the corporation utilized this option, the tax for the short period would be $8,000 (rather than $8,250, as calculated in Example 10). ▼

For individuals, annualizing requires some special adjustments:[22]

- Deductions must be *itemized* for the short period (the standard deduction is not allowed).
- Personal and dependency exemptions must be prorated.

Fortunately, individuals rarely change tax years.

MITIGATION OF THE ANNUAL ACCOUNTING PERIOD CONCEPT

Several provisions in the Code are designed to give the taxpayer relief from the seemingly harsh results that may be produced by the combined effects of an arbitrary accounting period and a progressive rate structure. For example, under the net operating loss carryback and carryover rules, a loss in one year can be carried back and offset against taxable income for the preceding 2 years. Unused net operating losses are then carried over for 20 years.[23] In addition, the Code provides special relief provisions for casualty losses stemming from a disaster and for the reporting of insurance proceeds from destruction of crops.[24]

---

[21]§ 443(b)(1).

[22]§ 443(b)(2) and Reg. § 1.443–1(a)(2).

[23]§ 172. Refer to Chapter 6.

[24]§§ 165(i) and 451(d). Refer to Chapter 6.

Restoration of Amounts Received under a Claim of Right. The court-made **claim of right doctrine** applies when the taxpayer receives property as income and treats it as his or her own but a dispute arises over the taxpayer's rights to the income.[25] According to the doctrine, the taxpayer must include the amount as income in the year of receipt. The rationale for the doctrine is that the Federal government cannot await the resolution of all disputes before exacting a tax. As a corollary to the doctrine, if the taxpayer is later required to repay the funds, generally a deduction is allowed in the year of repayment.[26]

EXAMPLE 12

In 1998, Pedro received a $5,000 bonus computed as a percentage of profits. In 1999, Pedro's employer determined that the 1998 profits had been incorrectly computed, and Pedro had to refund the $5,000 in 1999. Pedro was required to include the $5,000 in his 1998 income, but he can claim a $5,000 deduction in 1999. ▼

In Example 12 the transactions were a wash; that is, the income and deduction were the same ($5,000). Suppose, however, Pedro was in the 36 percent tax bracket in 1998 but in the 15 percent bracket in 1999. Without some relief provision, the mistake would be costly to Pedro. He paid $1,800 tax in 1998 (.36 × $5,000), but the deduction reduced his tax liability in 1999 by only $750 (.15 × $5,000). The Code does provide the needed relief in such cases. Under § 1341, when income that has been taxed under the claim of right doctrine must later be repaid, in effect, the taxpayer gets to apply to the deduction the tax rate of the year that will produce the greater tax benefit. Thus, in Example 12, the repayment in 1999 would reduce Pedro's 1999 tax liability by the greater 1998 rate (.36) applied to the $5,000. However, relief is provided only in cases where the tax is significantly different; that is, when the deduction for the amount previously included in income exceeds $3,000.

ACCOUNTING METHODS

PERMISSIBLE METHODS

2 **LEARNING OBJECTIVE**
Apply the cash method, accrual method, and hybrid method of accounting.

Section 446 requires the taxpayer to compute taxable income using the method of accounting regularly employed in keeping his or her books, provided the method clearly reflects income. The Code recognizes the following as generally permissible **accounting methods:**

- The cash receipts and disbursements method.
- The accrual method.
- A hybrid method (a combination of cash and accrual).

The Regulations under § 446 refer to these alternatives as *overall methods* and add that the term *method of accounting* includes not only the overall method of accounting of the taxpayer but also the accounting treatment of any item.[27]

Generally, any of the three methods of accounting may be used if the method is consistently employed and clearly reflects income. However, the taxpayer is required to use the accrual method for sales and cost of goods sold if inventories are an income-producing factor to the business.[28] Other situations in which the

---

[25]*North American Oil Consolidated v. Burnet*, 3 USTC ¶943, 11 AFTR 16, 52 S.Ct. 613 (USSC, 1932).

[26]*U.S. v. Lewis*, 51–1 USTC ¶9211, 40 AFTR 258, 71 S.Ct. 522 (USSC, 1951).

[27]Reg. § 1.446–1(a)(1).

[28]Reg. § 1.446–1(a)(4)(i).

accrual method is required are discussed later. Special methods are also permitted for installment sales, long-term construction contracts, and farmers.

A taxpayer who has more than one trade or business may use a different method of accounting for each trade or business activity.[29] Furthermore, a different method of accounting may be used to determine income from a trade or business than is used to compute nonbusiness items of income and deductions.[30]

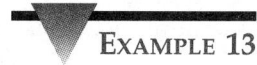

EXAMPLE 13

Linda operates a grocery store and owns stocks and bonds. The sales and cost of goods sold from the grocery store must be computed by the accrual method because inventories are material. However, Linda can report her dividends and interest under the cash method. ▼

The Code grants the IRS broad powers to determine whether the taxpayer's accounting method *clearly reflects income*. Thus, if the method employed does not clearly reflect income, the IRS has the power to prescribe the method to be used by the taxpayer.[31]

CASH RECEIPTS AND DISBURSEMENTS METHOD— CASH BASIS

Most individuals and many businesses use the cash basis to report income and deductions. The popularity of this method can largely be attributed to its simplicity and flexibility.

Under the **cash method,** income is not recognized until the taxpayer actually receives, or constructively receives, cash or its equivalent. Cash is constructively received if it is available to the taxpayer.[32] Deductions are generally permitted in the year of payment. Thus, year-end accounts receivable, accounts payable, and accrued income and deductions are not included in the determination of taxable income.

In many cases, a taxpayer using the cash method can choose the year in which a deduction is claimed simply by postponing or accelerating the payment of expenses. For fixed assets, however, the cash basis taxpayer claims deductions through depreciation or amortization, the same as an accrual basis taxpayer does. In addition, prepaid expenses must be capitalized and amortized if the life of the asset extends substantially beyond the end of the tax year.[33] Most courts have applied the one-year rule (**one-year rule for prepaid expenses**) to determine whether capitalization and amortization are required. According to this rule, capitalization is required only if the asset has a life that extends beyond the tax year following the year of payment.[34]

Restrictions on Use of the Cash Method. Using the cash method to measure income from a merchandising or manufacturing operation would often yield a distorted picture of the results of operations. Income for the period would largely be a function of when payments were made for goods or materials. Thus, the Regulations prohibit the use of the cash method (and require the accrual method) to measure sales and cost of goods sold if inventories are material to the business.[35]

The prohibition on the use of the cash method if inventories are material and the rules regarding prepaid expenses (discussed above) are intended to assure that

[29]§ 446(d).
[30]Reg. § 1.446–1(c)(1)(iv)(b).
[31]§ 446(b).
[32]Reg. § 1.451–1(a). Refer to Chapter 3 for a discussion of constructive receipt.

[33]Reg. § 1.461–1(a)(1).
[34]*Zaninovich v. Comm.,* 80–1 USTC ¶9342, 45 AFTR2d 80–1442, 616 F.2d 429 (CA–9, 1980), *rev'g* 69 T.C. 605 (1978). Refer to Chapter 5 for further discussion of the one-year rule.
[35]Reg. § 1.446–1(a)(4)(i).

annual income is clearly reflected. However, certain taxpayers may not use the cash method of accounting for Federal income tax purposes regardless of whether inventories are material. The accrual basis must be used to report the income earned by (1) a corporation (other than an S corporation), (2) a partnership with a corporate partner, and (3) a tax shelter.[36] This accrual basis requirement has three exceptions:[37]

- A farming business.
- A qualified personal service corporation (e.g., a corporation performing services in health, law, engineering, architecture, accounting, actuarial science, performing arts, or consulting).
- An entity that is not a tax shelter whose average annual gross receipts for the most recent three-year period are $5 million or less.

Farming.   Although inventories are material to farming operations, the IRS long ago created an exception to the general rule that allows farmers to use the cash method of accounting.[38] The purpose of the exception is to relieve the small farmer from the bookkeeping burden of accrual accounting. However, tax shelter promoters recognized, for example, that by deducting the costs of a crop in one tax year and harvesting the crop in a later year, income could be deferred from tax. Thus, §§ 447 and 464 were enacted to prevent certain farming corporations and limited partnerships (farming syndicates) from using the cash method.[39]

Farmers who are allowed to use the cash method of accounting must nevertheless capitalize their costs of raising trees when the preproduction period is longer than two years.[40] Thus, a cash basis apple farmer must capitalize the cost of raising trees until the trees produce in merchantable quantities. Cash basis farmers can elect not to capitalize these costs, but if the election is made, the alternative depreciation system (refer to Chapter 7) must be used for all farming property.

Generally, the cost of purchasing an animal must be capitalized. However, the cash basis farmer's cost of raising the animal can be expensed.[41]

ACCRUAL METHOD

All Events Test for Income.   Under the **accrual method,** an item is generally included in gross income for the year in which it is earned, regardless of when the income is collected. An item of income is earned when (1) all the events have occurred to fix the taxpayer's right to receive the income and (2) the amount of income (the amount the taxpayer has a right to receive) can be determined with reasonable accuracy.[42]

EXAMPLE 14

Andre, a calendar year taxpayer who uses the accrual method of accounting, was to receive a bonus equal to 6% of Blue Corporation's net income for its fiscal year ending each June 30. For the fiscal year ending June 30, 1998, Blue had net income of $240,000, and for the six months ending December 31, 1998, the corporation's net income was $150,000. Andre will report $14,400 (.06 × $240,000) for 1998 because his right to the amount became fixed when Blue's year closed. However, Andre would not accrue income based on the corporation's profits for the last six months of 1998 since his right to the income does not accrue until the close of the corporation's tax year. ▼

---

[36]§ 448(a). For this purpose, the hybrid method of accounting is considered the same as the cash method.

[37]§ 448(b).

[38]Reg. § 1.471–6(a).

[39]Section 447(c) contains counterexceptions that allow certain closely held corporations to use the cash method. See also § 464(c).

[40]§ 263A(d).

[41]Reg. § 1.162–12(a).

[42]Reg. § 1.451–1(a). Refer to Chapter 3 for further discussion of the accrual method.

TAXPAYER AWARDED ATTORNEY FEES IN THE IRS'S FAILED ATTEMPT TO IMPOSE THE ACCRUAL METHOD

In a 1997 Tax Court case, the IRS contended that a corporation that provided nursing services was required to use the accrual method of accounting. The corporation generally paid its employees before the customers paid for the nursing services. At the end of the year, the company had almost $250,000 in accounts receivable that were not included in its cash basis income although all of the related employee expense had been deducted. The IRS argued that the accrual method was required because of the mismatching of revenues and expenses that occurred under the taxpayer's method of accounting. Furthermore, argued the IRS, the substantial difference in taxable income as computed by the cash and accrual methods was evidence that the cash method did not clearly reflect income.

The Tax Court concluded that the cash method had been consistently applied, that the taxpayer was not deliberately prepaying expenses nor deferring income, and that the mismatching was the usual result of applying the cash method of accounting. Furthermore, Congress is well aware that the cash method results in some mismatching but has specifically authorized its use. In short, the Tax Court concluded that the IRS had subjected the taxpayer to a lot of expense when the IRS's position was not substantially supported by the law. Therefore, the IRS was required to pay the taxpayer's attorney fees.

SOURCE: *Laura E. Austin*, T.C.Memo. 1997–157, 73 TCM 2470.

In a situation where the accrual basis taxpayer's right to income is being contested and the income has not yet been collected, generally no income is recognized until the dispute has been settled.[43] Before the settlement, "all of the events have not occurred that fix the right to receive the income."

All Events and Economic Performance Tests for Deductions. An **all events test** applies to accrual basis deductions. A deduction cannot be claimed until (1) all the events have occurred to create the taxpayer's liability and (2) the amount of the liability can be determined with reasonable accuracy.[44] Once these requirements are satisfied, the deduction will be permitted only if economic performance has occurred.[45]

The **economic performance test** addresses situations in which the taxpayer has either of the following obligations:

1. To pay for services or property to be provided in the future.
2. To provide services or property (other than money) in the future.

When services or property are to be provided to the taxpayer in the future (situation 1), economic performance occurs when the property or services are actually provided by the other party.

EXAMPLE 15

An accrual basis, calendar year taxpayer, JAB, Inc., promoted a boxing match held in the company's arena on December 31, 1998. CLN, Inc., had contracted to clean the arena for

---

[43]*Burnet v. Sanford & Brooks Co.*, 2 USTC ¶636, 9 AFTR 603, 51 S.Ct. 150 (USSC, 1931).

[44]§ 461(h)(4).
[45]§ 461(h).

$5,000, but did not actually perform the work until January 1, 1999. JAB, Inc., did not pay the $5,000 until 2000. Although financial accounting would require JAB, Inc., to accrue the $5,000 cleaning expense in 1998 to match the revenues from the fight, the economic performance test was not satisfied until 1999, when CLN, Inc., performed the service. Thus, JAB, Inc., must deduct the expense in 1999. ▼

If the taxpayer is obligated to provide property or services (situation 2), economic performance occurs (and thus the deduction is allowed) in the year the taxpayer provides the property or services.

EXAMPLE 16

Copper Corporation, an accrual basis taxpayer, is in the strip mining business. According to the contract with the landowner, the company must reclaim the land. The estimated cost of reclaiming land mined in 1998 was $500,000, but the land was not actually reclaimed until 2000. The all events test was satisfied in 1998. The obligation existed, and the amount of the liability could be determined with reasonable accuracy. However, the economic performance test was not satisfied until 2000. Therefore, the deduction is not allowed until 2000.[46] ▼

The economic performance test is waived if the *recurring item exception* applies. Year-end accruals can be deducted if all the following conditions are met:

- The obligation exists and the amount of the liability can be reasonably estimated.
- Economic performance occurs within a reasonable period (but not later than 8½ months after the close of the taxable year).
- The item is recurring in nature and is treated consistently by the taxpayer.
- Either the accrued item is not material, or accruing it results in a better matching of revenues and expenses.

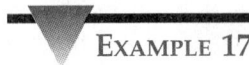
EXAMPLE 17

Green Corporation often sells goods that are on hand but cannot be shipped for another week. Thus, the sales account usually includes revenues for some items that have not been shipped at year-end. Green Corporation is obligated to pay shipping costs. Although the company's obligation for shipping costs can be determined with reasonable accuracy, economic performance is not satisfied until Green (or its agent) actually delivers the goods. However, accruing shipping costs on sold items will better match expenses with revenues for the period. Therefore, the company should be allowed to accrue the shipping costs on items sold but not shipped at year-end. ▼

The economic performance test as set forth in the Code does not address all possible accrued expenses. That is, in some cases the taxpayer incurs costs even though no property or services were received. In these instances, according to Regulations, economic performance generally is not satisfied until the liability is paid. The following liabilities are cases in which payment is generally the only means of satisfying economic performance:[47]

1. Workers' compensation.
2. Torts.
3. Breach of contract.
4. Violation of law.
5. Rebates and refunds.
6. Awards, prizes, and jackpots.

---

[46]See § 468 for an elective method for reporting reclamation costs.   [47]Reg. §§ 1.461–4(g)(2)–(6) and 1.461–5(c).

7. Insurance, warranty, and service contracts.[48]
8. Taxes.

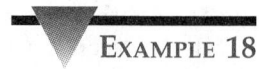

EXAMPLE 18

Yellow Corporation sold defective merchandise that injured a customer. Yellow admitted liability in 1998, but did not pay the claim until January 1999. The customer's tort claim cannot be deducted until it is paid. ▼

However, items (5) through (8) above are eligible for the aforementioned recurring item exception.

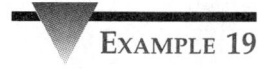

EXAMPLE 19

Pelican Corporation filed its 1998 state income tax return in March 1999. At the time the return was filed, Pelican was required to pay an additional $5,000. The state taxes are eligible for the recurring item exception. Thus, the $5,000 of state income taxes can be deducted on the corporation's 1998 Federal tax return. The deduction is allowed because all the events had occurred to fix the liability as of the end of 1998, the payment was made within 8½ months after the end of the tax year, the item is recurring in nature, and allowing the deduction in 1998 produces a good matching of revenues and expenses. ▼

Reserves. Generally, the all events and economic performance tests will prevent the use of reserves (e.g., for product warranty expense) frequently used in financial accounting to match expenses with revenues. However, small banks are allowed to use a bad debt reserve.[49] Furthermore, an accrual basis taxpayer in a service business is permitted to not accrue revenue that appears uncollectible based on experience. In effect, this approach indirectly allows a reserve.[50]

HYBRID METHOD

A **hybrid method** of accounting involves the use of more than one method. For example, a taxpayer who uses the accrual basis to report sales and cost of goods sold but uses the cash basis to report other items of income and expense is employing a hybrid method. The Code permits the use of a hybrid method provided the taxpayer's income is clearly reflected.[51] A taxpayer who uses the accrual method for business expenses must also use the accrual method for business income (a cash method may not be used for income items if the taxpayer's expenses are accounted for under the accrual method).

It may be preferable for a business that is required to report sales and cost of goods sold on the accrual method to report other items of income and expense under the cash method. The cash method permits greater flexibility in the timing of income and expense recognition.

CHANGE OF METHOD

3 **LEARNING OBJECTIVE**
Utilize the procedure for changing accounting methods.

The taxpayer, in effect, makes an election to use a particular accounting method when an initial tax return is filed using that method. If a subsequent change in method is desired, the taxpayer must obtain the permission of the IRS. The request for change is made on Form 3115, Application for Change in Accounting Method. Generally, the form must be filed within the taxable year of the desired change.[52]

---

[48]This item applies to contracts the taxpayer enters into for his or her own protection, rather than the taxpayer's liability as insurer, warrantor, or service provider.
[49]§ 585.

[50]§ 448(d)(5).
[51]§ 446(c).
[52]Rev.Proc. 97–27, I.R.B. No. 21, 10.

As previously mentioned, the term *accounting method* encompasses not only the overall accounting method used by the taxpayer (the cash or accrual method) but also the treatment of any material item of income or deduction.[53] Thus, a change in the method of deducting property taxes from a cash basis to an accrual basis that results in a deduction for taxes in a different year constitutes a change in an accounting method. Another example of accounting method change is a change involving the method or basis used in the valuation of inventories. However, a change in treatment resulting from a change in underlying facts does not constitute a change in the taxpayer's method of accounting.[54] For example, a change in employment contracts so that an employee accrues one day of vacation pay for each month of service rather than 12 days of vacation pay for a full year of service is a change in the underlying facts and, thus, is not an accounting method change.

Correction of an Error.   A change in accounting method should be distinguished from the *correction of an error*. The taxpayer can correct an error (by filing amended returns) without permission, and the IRS can simply adjust the taxpayer's liability if an error is discovered on audit of the return. Some examples of errors are incorrect postings, errors in the calculation of tax liability or tax credits, deductions of business expense items that are actually personal, and omissions of income and deductions.[55] Unless the taxpayer or the IRS corrects the error within the statute of limitations, the taxpayer's total lifetime taxable income will be overstated or understated by the amount of the error.

Change from an Incorrect Method.   An *incorrect accounting method* is the consistent (year-after-year) use of an incorrect rule to report an item of income or expense. The incorrect accounting method generally will not affect the taxpayer's total lifetime income (unlike the error). That is, an incorrect method has a self-balancing mechanism. For example, deducting freight on inventory in the year the goods are purchased, rather than when the inventory is sold, is an incorrect accounting method. The total cost of goods sold over the life of the business is not affected, but the year-to-year income is incorrect.[56]

If a taxpayer is employing an incorrect method of accounting, permission must be obtained from the IRS to change to a correct method. An incorrect method is not treated as a mechanical error that can be corrected by merely filing an amended tax return.

The tax return preparer as well as the taxpayer will be subject to penalties if the tax return is prepared using an incorrect method of accounting and permission for a change to a correct method has not been requested.[57]

Net Adjustments Due to Change in Accounting Method.   In the year of a change in accounting method, some items of income and expense may have to be adjusted to prevent the change from distorting taxable income.

EXAMPLE 20

In 1998, White Corporation, with consent from the IRS, switched from the cash to the accrual basis for reporting sales and cost of goods sold. The corporation's accrual basis gross profit for the year was computed as follows:

---

[53]Reg. § 1.446–1(a)(1).
[54]Reg. § 1.446–1(e)(2)(ii).
[55]Reg. § 1.446–1(e)(2)(ii)(b).

[56]But see *Korn Industries v. U.S.*, 76–1 USTC ¶9354, 37 AFTR2d 76–1228, 532 F.2d 1352 (Ct.Cls., 1976).
[57]§ 446(f). See Chapter 25.

Sales		$100,000
Beginning inventory	$15,000	
Plus: Purchases	60,000	
Less: Ending inventory	(10,000)	
Cost of goods sold		(65,000)
Gross profit		$ 35,000

At the end of the previous year, White Corporation had accounts receivable of $25,000 and accounts payable for merchandise of $34,000. The accounts receivable from the previous year in the amount of $25,000 were never included in gross income since White was on the cash basis and did not recognize the uncollected receivables. In the current year, the $25,000 was not included in the accrual basis sales since the sales were made in a prior year. Therefore, a $25,000 adjustment to income is required to prevent the receivables from being omitted from income.

The corollary of the failure to recognize a prior year's receivables is the failure to recognize a prior year's accounts payable. The beginning of the year's accounts payable was not included in the current or prior year's purchases. Thus, a deduction for the $34,000 was not taken in either year and is therefore included as an adjustment to income for the period of change.

An adjustment is also required to reflect the $15,000 beginning inventory that White deducted (due to the use of a cash method of accounting) in the previous year. In this instance, the cost of goods sold during the year of change was increased by the beginning inventory and resulted in a double deduction.

The net adjustment due to the change in accounting method is computed as follows:

Beginning inventory (deducted in prior and current year)	$15,000
Beginning accounts receivable (omitted from income)	25,000
Beginning accounts payable (omitted from deductions)	(34,000)
Net increase in taxable income	$ 6,000

▼

Disposition of the Net Adjustment.   Generally, if the IRS *requires* the taxpayer to change an accounting method, the net adjustment is added to or subtracted from the income for the year of the change. In cases of positive (an increase in income) adjustments in excess of $3,000, the taxpayer is allowed to calculate the tax by spreading the adjustment over one or more previous years.[58]

To encourage taxpayers to *voluntarily* change from incorrect methods and to facilitate changes from one correct method to another, the IRS generally allows the taxpayer to spread the adjustment into future years. One-fourth of the adjustment is applied to the year of the change, and one-fourth of the adjustment is applied to each of the next three taxable years.[59]

SPECIAL ACCOUNTING METHODS

4 LEARNING OBJECTIVE
Determine when the installment method of accounting can be utilized and apply the related calculation techniques.

Generally, accrual basis taxpayers recognize income when goods are sold and shipped to the customer. Cash basis taxpayers generally recognize income from a sale on the collection of cash from the customer. The tax law provides special accounting methods for certain installment sales and long-term contracts. These special methods were enacted, in part, to assure that the tax will be due when the taxpayer is best able to pay the tax.

---

[58]§ 481(b).

[59]Rev.Proc. 97–27, I.R.B. No. 21, 10.

INSTALLMENT METHOD

Under the general rule for computing the gain or loss from the sale of property, the taxpayer recognizes the entire amount of gain or loss upon the sale or other disposition of the property.

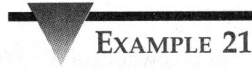

EXAMPLE 21

Mark sells property to Fran for $10,000 cash plus Fran's note (fair market value and face amount of $90,000). Mark's basis for the property was $15,000. Gain or loss is computed under either the cash or accrual basis as follows:

Amount realized:	
Cash down payment	$ 10,000
Note receivable	90,000
	$100,000
Less: Basis in the property	(15,000)
Realized gain	$ 85,000

In Example 21, the general rule for recognizing gain or loss requires Mark to pay a substantial amount of tax on the gain in the year of sale even though he receives only $10,000 cash. Congress enacted the installment sales provisions to prevent this sort of hardship by allowing the taxpayer to spread the gain from installment sales over the collection period. The *installment method* is a very important planning tool because of the tax deferral possibilities.

Eligibility and Calculations.   The **installment method** applies to *gains* (but not losses) from the sale of property where the seller will receive at least one payment *after* the year of sale. For many years, practically all gains from the sale of property were eligible for the installment method. However, over the years, the Code has been amended to *deny* the use of the installment method for the following:[60]

- Gains on property held for sale in the ordinary course of business.
- Depreciation recapture under § 1245 or § 1250.
- Gains on stocks or securities traded on an established market.

As an exception to the first item, the installment method may be used to report gains from sales of the following:[61]

- Time-share units (e.g., the right to use real property for two weeks each year).
- Residential lots (if the seller is not to make any improvements).
- Any property used or produced in the trade or business of farming.

The Nonelective Aspect.   Regardless of the taxpayer's method of accounting, as a general rule, eligible sales *must* be reported by the installment method.[62] A special election is required to report the gain by any other method of accounting (see the discussion in a subsequent section of this chapter).

Computing the Gain for the Period.   The gain reported on each sale is computed by the following formula:

$$\frac{\text{Total gain}}{\text{Contract price}} \times \text{Payments received} = \text{Recognized gain}$$

---

[60]§§ 453(b), (i), and (1).
[61]§ 453(1)(2).

[62]§ 453(a).

TAX IN THE NEWS

ART GALLERY WAS NOT A DEALER WHILE ITS PRINCIPAL EMPLOYEE WAS IN JAIL

After four trips to the courthouse, Andrew Crispo Gallery, Inc., was allowed to use the installment method to report gains from the sales of paintings seized by creditors. Generally, a dealer in personal property cannot use the installment method to report gains from the sale of inventory. In *Andrew Crispo Gallery, Inc. v. Comm.*, 96–1 USTC ¶50,313, 77 AFTR2d 96–2517, 86 F.3d 42 (CA–2, 1996), however, the character of the property changed while the owner of the gallery, who was also its principal salesperson, was in prison for tax fraud. The property was seized and sold to satisfy creditors 21 months after the gallery had been closed. In the first trial, the Tax Court held the property was inventory because it was purchased for resale. In the second trip to the courthouse, the appellate court held that the character of the property had to be determined at the time it was sold (not when it was acquired), and remanded the case to the Tax Court. But the Tax Court reached the same result the third time the gallery was in court on tax matters. Finally, the appellate court held that the paintings were not inventory because they were not held for sale to customers in the ordinary course of business.

Installment sales treatment was especially beneficial to the gallery because if the profits from the sales could be deferred, the company could increase its net operating loss carryback. This would generate additional cash to pay creditors.

The taxpayer must compute each variable as follows:

1. *Total gain* is the selling price reduced by selling expenses and the adjusted basis of the property. The selling price is the total consideration received by the seller, including notes receivable from the buyer, and the seller's liabilities assumed by the buyer.
2. *Contract price* is the selling price less the seller's liabilities that are assumed by the buyer. Generally, the contract price is the amount, other than interest, the seller will receive from the purchaser.
3. *Payments received* are the collections on the contract price received in the tax year. This generally is equal to the cash received less the interest income collected for the period. If the buyer pays any of the seller's expenses, the seller regards the amount paid as a payment received.

EXAMPLE 22

The seller is not a dealer, and the facts are as follows:

Sales price (amount realized):		
Cash down payment	$ 1,000	
Seller's mortgage assumed	3,000	
Notes payable to the seller	13,000	$17,000
Less: Selling expenses		(500)
Less: Seller's basis		(10,000)
Total gain		$ 6,500

The contract price is $14,000 ($17,000 – $3,000). Assuming the $1,000 is the only payment in the year of sale, the recognized gain in that year is computed as follows:

$$\frac{\$6,500 \text{ (total gain)}}{\$14,000 \text{ (contract price)}} \times \$1,000 = \$464 \text{ (gain recognized in year of sale)}$$

If the sum of the seller's basis and selling expenses is less than the liabilities assumed by the buyer, the difference must be added to the contract price and to the payments (treated as *deemed payments*) received in the year of sale.[63] This adjustment to the contract price is required so that the ratio of total gain to contract price will not be greater than one. The adjustment also accelerates the reporting of income from the deemed payments.

EXAMPLE 23   Assume the same facts as in Example 22, except that the seller's basis in the property is only $2,000. The total gain, therefore, is $14,500 [$17,000 − ($2,000 + $500)]. Payments in the year of sale are $1,500 and are calculated as follows:

Down payment	$1,000
Excess of mortgage assumed over seller's basis and expenses ($3,000 − $2,000 − $500)	500
	$1,500

The contract price is $14,500 [$17,000 (sales price) − $3,000 (seller's mortgage assumed) + $500 (excess of mortgage assumed over seller's basis and selling expenses)]. The gain recognized in the year of sale is computed as follows:

$$\frac{\$14,500 \text{ (total gain)}}{\$14,500 \text{ (contract price)}} \times \$1,500 = \$1,500$$

In subsequent years, all amounts the seller collects on the note principal ($13,000) will be recognized gain ($13,000 × 100%). ▼

As previously discussed, gains attributable to ordinary income recapture under §§ 1245 and 1250 are *ineligible* for installment reporting. Therefore, the § 1245 or § 1250 gain realized must be recognized in the year of sale, and the installment sale gain is the remaining gain.

EXAMPLE 24   Olaf sold an apartment building for $50,000 cash and a $75,000 note due in two years. Olaf's basis in the property was $25,000, and he recaptured $40,000 ordinary income under § 1250.
     Olaf's realized gain is $100,000 ($125,000 − $25,000), and the $40,000 recapture must be recognized in the year of sale. Of the $60,000 remaining § 1231 gain, $24,000 must be recognized in the year of sale:

$$\frac{\S 1231 \text{ gain}}{\text{Contract price}} \times \text{Payments received} = \frac{\$125,000 - \$25,000 - \$40,000}{\$125,000} \times \$50,000$$

$$= \frac{\$60,000}{\$125,000} \times \$50,000 = \$24,000$$

The remaining realized gain of $36,000 ($60,000 − $24,000) will be recognized as the $75,000 note is collected. ▼

Imputed Interest.   If a deferred payment contract for the sale of property with a selling price greater than $3,000 does not contain a reasonable interest rate, a reasonable rate is imputed.[64] The imputing of interest effectively restates the selling price of the property to equal the sum of the payments at the date of the sale and the discounted present value of the future payments. The difference between the

---

[63] Temp.Reg. § 15a.453–1(b)(2)(iii).   [64] §§ 483 and 1274.

present value of a future payment and the payment's face amount is taxed as interest income, as discussed in the following paragraphs. Thus, the **imputed interest** rules prevent sellers of capital assets from increasing the selling price to reflect the equivalent of unstated interest on deferred payments and thereby converting ordinary (interest) income into long-term capital gains. In addition, the imputed interest rules are important because they affect the timing of income recognition.

Generally, if the contract does not charge at least the Federal rate, interest will be imputed at the Federal rate. The Federal rate is the interest rate the Federal government pays on new borrowing and is published monthly by the IRS.[65]

As a general rule, the buyer and seller must account for interest on the accrual basis with semiannual compounding.[66] Requiring the use of the accrual basis assures that the seller's interest income and the buyer's interest expense are reported in the same tax year. The following example illustrates the calculation and amortization of imputed interest.

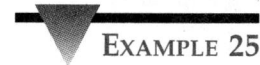

EXAMPLE 25

Peggy, a cash basis taxpayer, sold land on January 1, 1998, for $200,000 cash and $6 million due on December 31, 1999, with 5% interest payable December 31, 1998, and December 31, 1999. At the time of the sale, the Federal rate was 8% (compounded semiannually). Because Peggy did not charge at least the Federal rate, interest will be imputed at 8% (compounded semiannually).

Date	Payment	Present Value (at 8%) on 1/1/1998	Imputed Interest
12/31/1998	$ 300,000	$ 277,500	$ 22,500
12/31/1999	6,300,000	5,386,500	913,500
	$6,600,000	$5,664,000	$936,000

Thus, the selling price will be restated to $5,864,000 ($200,000 + $5,664,000) rather than $6,200,000 ($200,000 + $6,000,000), and Peggy will recognize interest income in accordance with the following amortization schedule:

Year	Beginning Balance	Interest Income (at 8%)*	Received	Ending Balance
1998	$5,664,000	$462,182	$ 300,000	$5,826,182
1999	5,826,182	473,818	6,300,000	–0–

*Compounded semiannually.

Congress has created several exceptions regarding the rate at which interest is imputed and the method of accounting for the interest income and expense. The general rules and exceptions are summarized in Concept Summary 15–1.

Related-Party Sales of Nondepreciable Property. If the Code did not contain special rules, a taxpayer could make an installment sale of property to a related party (e.g., a family member) who would obtain a basis in the property equal to the purchase price (the fair market value of the property). Then, the purchasing family member could immediately sell the property to an unrelated

---

[65]§ 1274(d)(1). There are three Federal rates: short-term (not over three years), mid-term (over three years but not over nine years), and long-term (over nine years).

[66]§§ 1274(a), 1273(a), and 1272(a).

▼ **CONCEPT SUMMARY 15–1**

Interest on Installment Sales

	Imputed Interest Rate
General rule	Federal rate
Exceptions:	
• Principal amount not over $2.8 million.[1]	Lesser of Federal rate or 9%
• Sale of land (with a calendar year ceiling of $500,000) between family members (the seller's spouse, brothers, sisters, ancestors, or lineal descendants).[2]	Lesser of Federal rate or 6%

	Method of Accounting for Interest	
	Seller's Interest Income	Buyer's Interest Expense
General rule[3]	Accrual	Accrual
Exceptions:		
• Total payments under the contract are $250,000 or less.[4]	Taxpayer's overall method	Taxpayer's overall method
• Sale of a farm (sales price of $1 million or less).[5]	Taxpayer's overall method	Taxpayer's overall method
• Sale of a principal residence.[6]	Taxpayer's overall method	Taxpayer's overall method
• Sale for a note with a principal amount of not over $2 million, the seller is on the cash basis, the property sold is not inventory, and the buyer agrees to report expenses by the cash method.[7]	Cash	Cash

[1]§ 1274A. This amount is adjusted annually for inflation. For 1998, the amount is $3,823,100.
[2]§§ 1274(c)(3)(F) and 483(e).
[3]§§ 1274(a) and 1272(a)(3).
[4]§§ 1274(c)(3)(C) and 483.
[5]§§ 1274(c)(3)(A) and 483.
[6]§§ 1274(c)(3)(B) and 483.
[7]§ 1274A(c). This amount is adjusted annually for inflation. For 1998, the amount is $2,730,800.

party for cash with no recognized gain or loss (the amount realized would equal the basis). The related-party purchaser would not pay the installment note to the selling family member until a later year or years. The net result would be that the family has the cash, but no taxable gain is recognized until the intrafamily transfer of the cash (the purchasing family member makes payments on the installment note).

Under special rules designed to combat this scheme, the proceeds from the subsequent sale (the second sale) by the purchasing family member are treated as though they were used to pay the installment note due the selling family member (the first sale). As a result, the recognition of gain from the original sale between the related parties is accelerated.[67]

However, even with these special rules, Congress did not eliminate the benefits of all related-party installment sales.

---

[67]§ 453(e).

- Related parties include the first seller's brothers, sisters, ancestors, lineal descendants, controlled corporations, and partnerships, trusts, and estates in which the seller has an interest.[68]
- There is no acceleration if the second disposition occurs more than two years after the first sale.[69]

Thus, if the taxpayer can sell the property to a relative who is not a "related party" or to a patient family member, the intrafamily installment sale is still a powerful tax planning tool. Other exceptions also can be applied in some circumstances.[70]

ETHICAL CONSIDERATIONS

A Related-Party Installment Sale Has Unexpected Results

Amos has been in the farming business for over 40 years. Since he is nearing retirement age—although he will never retire—he would like to slow down. He decides to sell 300 acres of his land to his 26-year-old son, Chuck, for $465,000 so Chuck can go into the farming business. Amos's basis for the land is $50,000. Since Chuck does not have much equity and Amos would like to keep the financing of the land in the family, the sales contract calls for a $15,000 down payment and annual payments of $30,000 for 15 years plus interest at 8 percent. Amos anticipates Chuck's profits from the farm will be adequate to cover these payments and provide Chuck with a decent living.

Chuck makes the payment for the first year. Unfortunately, he then gets involved with some young people from a nearby city and develops a drug problem. To finance his drug dependency, 14 months after acquiring the farm, he sells it for $500,000 cash to a real estate developer who intends to build 1,000 tract houses on the land.

When Amos learns of this, he is furious. He disowns Chuck and vows never to speak to him again.

Now Amos's CPA tells him that he has another problem. The sale of the land by Chuck should be treated as if Chuck had paid Amos the remaining balance on the installment sale. The CPA explains to Amos that this result occurs because his original sale to Chuck was a related-party transaction. Amos finds this ridiculous and says he no longer has a son.

Who is correct, Amos or the CPA? Evaluate the equity of the related-party provision.

Related-Party Sales of Depreciable Property. The installment method cannot be used to report a gain on the sale of depreciable property to a controlled entity. The purpose of this rule is to prevent the seller from deferring gain (until collections are received) while the related purchaser is enjoying a stepped-up basis for depreciation purposes.[71]

The prohibition on the use of the installment method applies to sales between the taxpayer and a partnership or corporation in which the taxpayer holds a more-than-50 percent interest. Constructive ownership rules are used in applying the ownership test (i.e., the taxpayer is considered to own stock owned by a spouse

---

[68]§ 453(f)(1), cross-referencing §§ 267(b) and 318(a). Although spouses are related parties, the exemption of gain between spouses (§ 1041) makes the second-disposition rules inapplicable when the first sale was between spouses.

[69]§ 453(e)(2). But see § 453(e)(2)(B) for extensions of the two-year period.
[70]See §§ 453(e)(6) and (7).
[71]§ 453(g).

and certain other family members).[72] However, if the taxpayer can establish that tax avoidance was not a principal purpose of the transaction, the installment method can be used to report the gain.

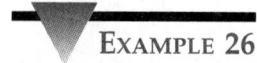

EXAMPLE 26

Alan purchased an apartment building from his controlled corporation, Emerald Corporation. Alan was short of cash at the time of the purchase (December 1998), but was to collect a large cash payment in January 1999. The agreement required Alan to pay the entire arm's length price in January 1999. Alan had good business reasons for acquiring the building. Emerald Corporation should be able to convince the IRS that tax avoidance was not a principal purpose for the installment sale because the tax benefits are not overwhelming. The corporation will report all of the gain in the year following the year of sale, and the building must be depreciated over 27.5 years (the cost recovery period). ▼

DISPOSITION OF INSTALLMENT OBLIGATIONS

Generally, a taxpayer must recognize the deferred profit from an installment sale when the obligation is transferred to another party or otherwise relinquished. The rationale for accelerating the gain is that the deferral should continue for no longer than the taxpayer owns the installment obligation.[73]

The gift or cancellation of an installment note is treated as a taxable disposition by the donor. The amount realized from the cancellation is the face amount of the note if the parties (obligor and obligee) are related to each other.[74]

EXAMPLE 27

Liz cancels a note issued by Tina (Liz's daughter) that arose in connection with the sale of property. At the time of the cancellation, the note had a basis to Liz of $10,000, a face amount of $25,000, and a fair market value of $20,000. Presuming the initial sale by Liz qualified as an installment sale, the cancellation results in gain of $15,000 ($25,000 − $10,000) to Liz. ▼

Certain exceptions to the recognition of gain provisions are provided for transfers of installment obligations pursuant to tax-free incorporations under § 351, contributions of capital to a partnership, certain corporate liquidations, transfers due to the taxpayer's death, and transfers between spouses or incident to divorce.[75] In such instances, the deferred profit is merely shifted to the transferee, who is responsible for the payment of tax on the subsequent collections of the installment obligations.

INTEREST ON DEFERRED TAXES

With the installment method, the seller earns interest on the receivable. The receivable includes the deferred gain. Thus, one could argue that the seller is earning interest on the deferred taxes. Some commentators reason that the government is, in effect, making interest-free loans to taxpayers who report gains by the installment method. Following the argument that the amount of the deferred taxes is a loan, in some situations, the taxpayer is required to pay interest on the deferred taxes.[76]

ELECTING OUT OF THE INSTALLMENT METHOD

A taxpayer can *elect not to use* the installment method. The election is made by reporting on a timely filed return the gain computed by the taxpayer's usual method

---

[72]§§ 1239(b) and (c).
[73]§ 453B(a).
[74]§ 453B(f)(2).

[75]§§ 453B(c), (d), and (g).
[76]See § 453A for details.

of accounting (cash or accrual).[77] However, the Regulations provide that the amount realized by a cash basis taxpayer cannot be less than the value of the property sold. This rule differs from the usual cash basis accounting rules (discussed earlier),[78] which measure the amount realized in terms of the fair market value of the property received. The net effect of the Regulations is to allow the cash basis taxpayer to report his or her gain as an accrual basis taxpayer. The election is frequently applied to year-end sales by taxpayers who expect to be in a higher tax bracket in the following year.

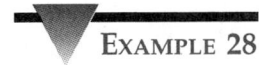

EXAMPLE 28

On December 31, 1998, Kurt sold land to Jodie for $20,000 (fair market value). The cash was to be paid on January 4, 1999. Kurt is a cash basis taxpayer, and his basis in the land is $8,000. Kurt has a large casualty loss and very little other income in 1998. Thus, his marginal tax rate in 1998 is 15%. He expects his rate to increase to 36% in 1999.

The transaction constitutes an installment sale because a payment will be received in a tax year after the tax year of disposition. Jodie's promise to pay Kurt is an installment obligation, and under the Regulations, the value of the installment obligation is equal to the value of the property sold ($20,000). If Kurt elects out of the installment method, he would shift $12,000 of gain ($20,000 – $8,000) from the expected higher rate in 1999 to the 15% rate in 1998. The expected tax savings based on the rate differentials may exceed the benefit of the tax deferral available with the installment method. ▼

Permission of the IRS is required to revoke an election not to use the installment method.[79]

LONG-TERM CONTRACTS

5 **LEARNING OBJECTIVE**
Understand the alternative methods of accounting for long-term contracts (the completed contract method and the percentage of completion method) including the limitations on the use of the completed contract method.

A **long-term contract** is a building, installation, construction, or manufacturing contract that is entered into but not completed within the same tax year. However, a *manufacturing* contract is long term *only* if the contract is to manufacture (1) a unique item not normally carried in finished goods inventory or (2) items that normally require more than 12 calendar months to complete.[80] An item is *unique* if it is designed to meet the customer's particular needs and is not suitable for use by others. A contract to perform services (e.g., auditing or legal services) is not considered a contract for this purpose and thus cannot qualify as a long-term contract.

EXAMPLE 29

Rocky, a calendar year taxpayer, entered into two contracts during the year. One contract was to construct a building foundation. Work was to begin in October 1998 and was to be completed by June 1999. The contract is long term because it will not be entered into and completed in the same tax year. The fact that the contract requires less than 12 calendar months to complete is not relevant because the contract is not for manufacturing. The second contract was for architectural services to be performed over two years. These services will not qualify for long-term contract treatment because the taxpayer will not build, install, construct, or manufacture a product. ▼

Generally, the taxpayer must accumulate all of the direct and indirect costs incurred under a contract. This means the production costs must be accumulated and allocated to individual contracts. Furthermore, mixed services costs, costs that benefit contracts as well as the general administrative operations of the business,

---

[77]§ 453(d) and Temp.Reg. § 15a.453–1(d). See also Rev. Rul. 82–227, 1982–2 C.B. 89.
[78]Refer to Chapter 3.

[79]§ 453(d)(3) and Temp.Reg. § 15a.453–1(d)(4).
[80]§ 460(f) and Reg. § 1.451–3(b).

must be allocated to production. Exhibit 15–1 lists the types of costs that must be accumulated and allocated to contracts. The taxpayer must develop reasonable bases for cost allocations.[81]

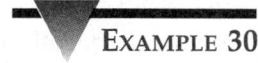

EXAMPLE 30 Falcon, Inc., uses detailed cost accumulation records to assign labor and materials to its contracts in progress. The total cost of fringe benefits is allocated to a contract on the following basis:

$$\frac{\text{Labor on the contract}}{\text{Total salaries and labor}} \times \text{Total cost of fringe benefits}$$

Similarly, storage and handling costs for materials are allocated to contracts on the following basis:

$$\frac{\text{Contract materials}}{\text{Materials purchases}} \times \text{Storage and handling costs}$$

The cost of the personnel operations, a mixed services cost, is allocated between production and general administration based on the number of employees in each function. The personnel cost allocated to production is allocated to individual contracts on the basis of the formula used to allocate fringe benefits. ▼

The accumulated costs are deducted when the revenue from the contract is recognized. Generally, two methods of accounting are used in varying circumstances to determine when the revenue from a contract is recognized:[82]

- The completed contract method.
- The percentage of completion method.

The *completed contract method may be used* for (1) home construction contracts (contracts in which at least 80 percent of the estimated costs are for dwelling units in buildings with four or fewer units) and (2) certain other real estate construction contracts. Other real estate contracts can qualify for the completed contract method if the following requirements are satisfied:

- The contract is expected to be completed within the two-year period beginning on the commencement date of the contract.
- The contract is performed by a taxpayer whose average annual gross receipts for the three taxable years preceding the taxable year in which the contract is entered into do not exceed $10 million.

All other contractors must use the percentage of completion method.

Completed Contract Method.   Under the **completed contract method,** no revenue from the contract is recognized until the contract is completed and accepted. However, a taxpayer may not delay completion of a contract for the principal purpose of deferring tax.[83]

In some instances, the original contract price may be disputed, or the buyer may want additional work to be done on a long-term contract. If the disputed amount is substantial (it is not possible to determine whether a profit or loss will ultimately be realized on the contract), the Regulations provide that no amount of income or loss is recognized until the dispute is resolved. In all other cases, the profit or loss (reduced by the amount in dispute) is recognized in the current period on completion of the contract. However, additional work

---

[81]Reg. §§ 1.263A–1T(b)(3)(iii)(A)(1) and 1.451–3(d)(9).   [83]Reg. § 1.451–3(b)(2).
[82]§ 460.

▼ **EXHIBIT 15–1**
Contract Costs, Mixed Services
Costs, and Current Expense
Items for Contracts

	Contracts Eligible for the Completed Contract Method	Other Contracts
Contract costs:		
Direct materials (a part of the finished product).	Capital	Capital
Indirect materials (consumed in production but not in the finished product, e.g., grease and oil for equipment).	Capital	Capital
Storage, handling, and insurance on materials.	Expense	Capital
Direct labor (worked on the product).	Capital	Capital
Indirect labor (worked in the production process but not directly on the product, e.g., a construction supervisor).	Capital	Capital
Fringe benefits for direct and indirect labor (e.g., vacation, sick pay, unemployment, and other insurance).	Capital	Capital
Pension costs for direct and indirect labor:		
• Current cost.	Expense	Capital
• Past service costs.	Expense	Capital
Depreciation on production facilities:		
• For financial statements.	Capital	Capital
• Tax depreciation in excess of financial statements.	Expense	Capital
Depreciation on idle facilities.	Expense	Expense
Property taxes, insurance, rent, and maintenance on production facilities.	Capital	Capital
Bidding expenses—successful.	Expense	Capital
Bidding expenses—unsuccessful.	Expense	Expense
Interest to finance real estate construction.	Capital	Capital
Interest to finance personal property:		
• Production period of one year or less.	Expense	Expense
• Production period exceeds one year and costs exceed $1 million.	Capital	Capital
• Production period exceeds two years.	Capital	Capital
Mixed services costs:		
• Personnel operations.	Expense	Allocate
• Data processing.	Expense	Allocate
• Purchasing.	Expense	Allocate
Selling, general, and administrative expenses (including an allocated share of mixed services).	Expense	Expense
Losses.	Expense	Expense

may need to be performed with respect to the disputed contract. In this case, the difference between the amount in dispute and the actual cost of the additional work is recognized in the year the work is completed rather than in the year in which the dispute is resolved.[84]

---

[84]Reg. § 1.451–3(d)(2)(ii)–(vii), Example (2).

EXAMPLE 31

Ted, a calendar year taxpayer utilizing the completed contract method of accounting, constructed a building for Brad under a long-term contract. The gross contract price was $500,000. Ted finished construction in 1998 at a cost of $475,000. When Brad examined the building, he insisted that it be repainted or the contract price be reduced. The estimated cost of repainting is $10,000. Since under the terms of the contract, Ted is assured of a profit of at least $15,000 ($500,000 − $475,000 − $10,000) even if the dispute is ultimately resolved in Brad's favor, Ted must include $490,000 ($500,000 − $10,000) in gross income and is allowed deductions of $475,000 for 1998.

In 1999, Ted and Brad resolve the dispute, and Ted repaints certain portions of the building at a cost of $6,000. Ted must include $10,000 in 1999 gross income and may deduct the $6,000 expense in that year. ▼

EXAMPLE 32

Assume the same facts as in the previous example, except the estimated cost of repainting the building is $50,000. Since the resolution of the dispute completely in Brad's favor would mean a net loss on the contract for Ted ($500,000 − $475,000 − $50,000 = $25,000 loss), he does not recognize any income or loss until the year the dispute is resolved. ▼

Frequently, a contractor receives payment at various stages of completion. For example, when the contract is 50 percent complete, the contractor may receive 50 percent of the contract price less a retainage. The taxation of these payments is generally governed by Regulation § 1.451–5 "advance payments for goods and long-term contracts" (discussed in Chapter 3). Generally, contractors are permitted to defer the advance payments until the payments are recognized as income under the taxpayer's method of accounting.

Percentage of Completion Method. The percentage of completion method must be used to account for long-term contracts unless the taxpayer qualifies for one of the two exceptions that permit the completed contract method to be used (home construction contracts and certain other real estate construction contracts).[85] Under the **percentage of completion method,** a portion of the gross contract price is included in income during each period as the work progresses. The revenue accrued each period (except for the final period) is computed as follows:[86]

$$\frac{C}{T} \times P$$

Where C = Contract costs incurred during the period.
T = Estimated total cost of the contract.
P = Contract price.

All of the costs allocated to the contract during the period are deductible from the accrued revenue.[87] The revenue reported in the final period is simply the unreported revenue from the contract. Because T in this formula is an estimate that frequently differs from total actual costs, which are not known until the contract has been completed, the profit on a contract for a particular period may be overstated or understated.

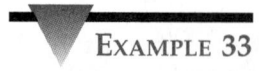

EXAMPLE 33

Tan, Inc., entered into a contract that was to take two years to complete, with an estimated cost of $2,250,000. The contract price was $3,000,000. Costs of the contract for 1998, the first year, totaled $1,350,000. The gross profit reported by the percentage of completion method

---

[85]Certain residential construction contracts that do not qualify for the completed contract method may nevertheless use that method to account for 30% of the profit from the contract, with the remaining 70% reported by the percentage of completion method.

[86]§ 460(b)(1)(A).
[87]Reg. § 1.451–3(c)(3).

for 1998 was $450,000 [($1,350,000/$2,250,000 × $3,000,000) – $1,350,000]. The contract was completed at the end of 1999 at a total cost of $2,700,000. In retrospect, 1998 profit should have been $150,000 [($1,350,000/$2,700,000 × $3,000,000) – $1,350,000]. Thus, taxes were overpaid for 1998. ▼

A *de minimis* rule enables the contractor to delay the recognition of income for a particular contract under the percentage of completion method. If less than 10 percent of the estimated contract costs have been incurred by the end of the taxable year, the taxpayer can elect to defer the recognition of income and the related costs until the taxable year in which cumulative contract costs are at least 10 percent of the estimated contract costs.[88]

Lookback Provisions. In the year a contract is completed, a *lookback* provision requires the recalculation of annual profits reported on the contract under the percentage of completion method. Interest is paid to the taxpayer if taxes were overpaid, and interest is payable by the taxpayer if there was an underpayment.[89] For a corporate taxpayer, the lookback interest paid by the taxpayer is deductible, but for an individual taxpayer, it is nondeductible personal interest associated with a tax liability.

EXAMPLE 34

Assume Tan, Inc., in Example 33, was in the 34% tax bracket in both years and the relevant interest rate was 10%. For 1998, the company paid excess taxes of $102,000 [($450,000 – $150,000) × .34]. When the contract is completed at the end of 1999, Tan, Inc., should receive interest of $10,200 for one year on the tax overpayment ($102,000 × .10). ▼

TAX PLANNING
CONSIDERATIONS

6 LEARNING OBJECTIVE
Identify tax planning opportunities related to accounting periods and accounting methods.

TAXABLE YEAR

Under the general rules for tax years, partnerships and S corporations frequently will be required to use a calendar year. However, if the partnership or S corporation can demonstrate a business purpose for a fiscal year, the IRS will allow the entity to use the requested year. The advantage to a fiscal year is that the calendar year partners and S corporation shareholders may be able to defer from tax the income earned from the close of the fiscal year until the end of the calendar year. Tax advisers for these entities should apply the IRS's gross receipts test described in Revenue Procedure 87–32 to determine if permission for the fiscal year will be granted.

CASH METHOD OF ACCOUNTING

The cash method of accounting gives the taxpayer considerable control over the recognition of expenses and some control over the recognition of income. This method can be used by proprietorships, partnerships, and small corporations (gross receipts of $5 million or less) that provide services (inventories are not material to the service business). Farmers (except certain farming corporations) can also use the cash method.

---

[88]§ 460(b)(5).
[89]§§ 460(b)(2) and (b)(6). The taxpayer can elect to not apply the lookback method in situations where the cumulative taxable income

as of the close of each prior year is within 10% of the correct income for each prior year.

INSTALLMENT METHOD

Unlike the cash and accrual methods, the installment method often results in an interest-free loan (of deferred taxes) from the government. The installment method is not available for the sale of inventory. Nevertheless, the installment method is an important tax planning technique and should be considered when a sale of eligible property is being planned. That is, if the taxpayer can benefit from deferring the tax, the terms of sale can be arranged so that the installment method rules apply. If, on the other hand, the taxpayer expects to be in a higher tax bracket when the payments will be received, he or she can elect to not use the installment method.

Related Parties.   Intrafamily installment sales can still be a useful family tax planning tool. If the related party holds the property more than two years, a subsequent sale will not accelerate the gain from the first disposition. Patience and forethought are rewarded.

The 6 percent limitation on imputed interest on sales of land between family members enables the seller to convert ordinary income into capital gain or make what is, in effect, a nontaxable gift. If the selling price is raised to adjust for the low interest rate charges on an installment sale, the seller has more capital gain but less ordinary income than would be realized from a sale to an unrelated party. If the selling price is not raised and the specified interest of 6 percent is charged, the seller enables the relative to have the use of the property without having to pay for its full market value. As an additional benefit, the bargain sale is not a taxable gift.

Disposition of Installment Obligations.   A disposition of an installment obligation is also a serious matter. Gifts of the obligations will accelerate income to the seller. The list of taxable and nontaxable dispositions of installment obligations should not be trusted to memory. In each instance where transfers of installment obligations are contemplated, the practitioner should conduct research to be sure he or she knows the consequences.

COMPLETED CONTRACT METHOD

Generally, large contractors must use the percentage of completion method of accounting for reporting the income from long-term contracts. Under the percentage of completion method, the taxpayer must recognize profit in each period costs are incurred. Profit is reported in proportion to the cost incurred for the period as a proportion of the total contract cost. However, small contractors (average annual gross receipts do not exceed $10 million) working on contracts that are completed within a two-year period can elect to use the completed contract method and defer profit until the year in which the contract is completed.

KEY TERMS

Accounting methods, 15–10	All events test, 15–13	Completed contract method, 15–26
Accounting period, 15–2	Cash method, 15–11	Economic performance test, 15–13
Accrual method, 15–12	Claim of right doctrine, 15–10	Fiscal year, 15–2

PROBLEM MATERIALS

DISCUSSION QUESTIONS

1. Why would a department store often use a tax year ending the last day of January or February instead of December 31?

2. Megan recently began conducting an office supply business as a corporation. Vito began conducting his law practice through a corporation. Neither corporation has made an S election. What tax year alternatives are available to Megan's business that are not available to Vito's business?

3. Dan, a calendar year taxpayer, recently became a licensed orthopedic surgeon. He has incorporated his practice. Dan's brother suggests that the corporation's tax year should end on September 30 and thus avoid the end-of-the-calendar-year rush. What complications could result from the corporation filing its return on the basis of a fiscal year ending September 30?

4. Freda is a cash basis taxpayer. In 1998, she overcharged a customer $5,000. In 1999, Freda discovered the overcharge and refunded $5,000 to the customer. In 1998, she paid $3,000 on her estimated state income taxes. In 1999, she filed her state tax return and received a $1,000 refund of her 1998 taxes paid. Freda was in the 36% marginal tax bracket in 1998 and in the 15% marginal tax bracket in 1999. Is Freda treated fairly under the system of an annual accounting period?

5. Albert is a cash basis taxpayer and reports his income on a calendar year. Recently, Albert became a partner in a company that imports flowers. If the partnership uses the accrual method of accounting, must Albert change to the accrual method as well?

6. The Cardinal Insurance Agency is a newly formed corporation, and its gross receipts will probably never exceed $2 million in a year. Generally, it takes approximately two months to collect accounts receivable. Accounts payable generally equal expenses for one month. Cardinal does not expect accounts payable and accounts receivable to increase significantly. It prepares monthly financial statements using the accrual method of accounting. Given that the accounts receivable and accounts payable will not significantly change, would Cardinal derive any benefit from filing its tax return using the cash method of accounting?

7. Earl, a certified public accountant, recently obtained a new client. The client is a retail grocery store that has used the cash method to report its income since it began doing business. Will Earl incur any liability if he prepares the tax return in accordance with the cash method and does not advise the client of the necessity of seeking the IRS's permission to change to the accrual method?

8. In December 1998, a cash basis taxpayer paid January through June 1999 management fees in connection with his rental properties. The fees were $4,000 per month. Compute the 1998 expense under the following assumptions:
   a. The fees were paid by an individual who derived substantially all of his income from the properties.
   b. The fees were paid by a tax-shelter partnership.

9. Compare the cash basis and accrual basis of accounting as applied to the following:
   a. Fixed assets.
   b. Prepaid rent income.
   c. Prepaid interest expense.
   d. A note received for services performed if the market value and face amount of the note differ.

10. Salmon Corporation and Betty have formed a partnership to rent real estate and operate a grocery store. Salmon uses the accrual method of accounting, and the company's tax year ends March 31. Betty is a cash basis, calendar year taxpayer. What are the tax accounting issues that the partnership must address?

11. In financial accounting, reserves (or allowances) are frequently used. For example, reserves are created for bad debts and product warranties. Why are reserves generally not allowed for tax purposes?

12. What difference does it make whether the taxpayer or the IRS initiates the change in accounting method?

13. Generally, what incentives are provided to encourage a taxpayer to change voluntarily from an incorrect method of accounting?

14. Irene has made Sara an offer on the purchase of a capital asset. Irene will pay (1) $200,000 cash or (2) $50,000 cash and a 9% installment note for $150,000 guaranteed by City Bank of New York. If Sara sells for $200,000 cash, she will invest the after-tax proceeds in certificates of deposit yielding 9% interest. Sara's cost of the asset is $25,000. Why would Sara prefer the installment sale?

15. On June 1, 1996, Father sold land to Son for $100,000. Father reported the gain by the installment method, with the gain to be spread over five years. In May 1998, Son received an offer of $150,000 for the land, to be paid over three years. What would be the tax consequences of Son's sale? How could the tax consequences be improved?

16. In 1998, Bhaskar sold a building to his 100%-controlled corporation. The entire purchase price is to be paid in 1999. When should Bhaskar report the gain on the sale of the building?

17. Juan, a cash basis taxpayer, sold land in December 1998. At the time of the sale, he received $10,000 cash and a note for $90,000 due in 90 days. Juan expects to be in a much higher tax bracket in 1999. Should Juan report the sale in 1998 or 1999?

18. What is the advantage to using the completed contract method as compared to the percentage of completion method?

19. The Eagle Corporation builds yachts. All vessels are practically identical and sell for more than $2 million. Production does not begin until the company has a contract to sell the vessel. The company has recently changed its production techniques to reduce the time for producing a yacht from 15 months to 9 months. What are the accounting method implications of the change?

PROBLEMS

20. Red, White, and Blue are unrelated corporations engaged in real estate development. The three corporations formed a joint venture (treated as a partnership) to develop a tract of land. Assuming the venture does not have a natural business year, what tax year must the joint venture adopt under the following circumstances?

		Tax Year Ending	Interest in Joint Venture
a.	Red	September 30	60%
	Blue	March 31	20%
	White	May 31	20%

		Tax Year Ending	Interest in Joint Venture
b.	Red	September 30	30%
	White	June 30	40%
	Blue	January 31	30%

21. Zack conducted his professional practice through Zack, Inc. The corporation uses a fiscal year ending September 30 even though the business purpose test for a fiscal year cannot be satisfied. For the year ending September 30, 1998, the corporation paid Zack a salary of $180,000, and during the period January through September 1998, the corporation paid him a salary of $150,000.
    a. How much salary should Zack receive during the period October 1 through December 31, 1998?
    b. Assume Zack received only $30,000 salary during the period October 1 through December 31, 1998. What would be the consequences to Zack, Inc.?

22. Brown Maintenance Corporation has consistently used a fiscal year ending September 30 and generally earns $100,000 per year. Brown's business is seasonal, and the company earns approximately three-fourths of its annual profits during the quarter beginning October 1 and ending December 31. Assume the applicable corporate tax rates are 15% on taxable income of $50,000 or less, 25% on taxable income over $50,000 but not over $75,000, 34% on taxable income over $75,000 but not over $100,000, and 39% on taxable income in excess of $100,000 through $335,000. Brown changes to a calendar year.
    a. Compute Brown's tax liability on taxable income of $75,000 earned during the short period October 1 through December 31.
    b. Why could changing to the calendar year prove costly to Brown?

23. Gold, Inc., is an accrual basis taxpayer. In 1998, an employee accidentally spilled hazardous chemicals on leased property. The chemicals destroyed trees on neighboring property, resulting in $30,000 damages. In 1998, the owner of the property sued Gold, Inc., for the $30,000. Gold's attorney feels that it is liable and the only issue is whether the neighbor will also seek punitive damages that could be as much as three times the actual damages. In addition, as a result of the spill, Gold was in violation of its lease and was therefore required to pay the landlord $15,000. However, the amount due for the lease violation was not payable until the termination of the lease in 2001. None of these costs were covered by insurance. Jeff Stuart, the president of Gold, Inc., is generally familiar with the accrual basis tax accounting rules and is concerned about when the company will be allowed to deduct the amounts the company is required to pay as a result of this environmental disaster. Write Mr. Stuart a letter explaining these issues. Gold's address is 200 Elm Avenue, San Jose, CA 95192.

24. Compute the taxpayer's income or deductions for 1998 using (1) the cash basis and (2) the accrual basis for each of the following:
    a. In 1998, the taxpayer purchased new equipment for $100,000. The taxpayer paid $25,000 in cash and gave a $75,000 interest-bearing note for the balance. The equipment has a MACRS life of five years, the mid-year convention applies, and the § 179 election was not made.
    b. In December 1998, the taxpayer collected $10,000 for January rents. In January 1999, the taxpayer collected $2,000 for December 1998 rents.
    c. In December 1998, the taxpayer paid office equipment insurance premiums of $30,000 for January–June 1999.

25. Which of the following businesses must use the accrual method of accounting?
    a. A corporation with annual gross receipts of $12 million from equipment rentals.
    b. A partnership (not a tax shelter) engaged in farming and with annual gross receipts of $8 million.
    c. A corporation that acts as an insurance agent with annual gross receipts of $1 million.
    d. A manufacturer with annual gross receipts of $600,000.
    e. A retailer with annual gross receipts of $250,000.

26. The Beige Products Manufacturing Company offers a $50 rebate to purchasers of its new appliances. The customer purchases the appliance from a dealer and then must apply to Beige Products for the rebate. The rebate opportunity expires 90 days after the date of sale. According to Beige's accounting records, 50,000 products subject to rebate were sold during 1998. As of the end of 1998, 44,000 rebate requests had been received, and 43,000 had been paid. In January 1999, Beige received an additional 5,000 requests for rebates from the 1998 sales. All unpaid requests were paid in January. No additional rebate requests were received by the company before the expiration date. Beige has had the program in effect for several years. Write a letter to Gerald Fine, Beige's president, explaining the tax consequences of the rebate program. The company's address is 905 Mason Drive, Floyd, VA 24030.

27. In 1998, the taxpayer changed from the cash to the accrual basis of accounting for sales, cost of goods sold, and accrued expenses. Taxable income for 1998 computed under the cash method was $45,000. Relevant account balances are as follows:

	Beginning of the Year	End of the Year
Accounts receivable	$ 6,000	$13,000
Accounts payable	–0–	–0–
Accrued expenses	4,000	6,000
Inventory	10,000	9,000

a. Compute the accrual basis taxable income for 1998 and the adjustment due to the change in accounting method.
b. Assuming the change was voluntary, how will the adjustment due to the change be treated?

28. Floyd, a cash basis taxpayer, has agreed to sell land to Beige, Inc., a well-established and highly profitable company. Beige is willing to (1) pay $100,000 cash or (2) pay $25,000 cash and the balance ($75,000) plus interest at 10% (the Federal rate) in two years. Floyd is in the 35% marginal tax bracket (combined Federal and state) for all years and believes he can reinvest the sales proceeds and earn a 12% before-tax rate of return.
a. Should Floyd accept the deferred payments option if his basis in the land is $10,000?
b. Do you think your results would change if Floyd's basis in the land is $90,000?

29. Kay, who is not a dealer, sold an apartment house to Polly during 1998. The closing statement for the sale is as follows:

Total selling price		$100,000
Add: Polly's share of property taxes (6 months) paid by Kay		2,500
Less: Kay's 11% mortgage assumed by Polly	$55,000	
Polly's refundable binder ("earnest money") paid in 1997	1,000	
Polly's 11% installment note given to Kay	30,000	
Kay's real estate commissions and attorney's fees	7,500	(93,500)
Cash paid to Kay at closing		$ 9,000
Cash due from Polly = $9,000 + $7,500 expenses		$ 16,500

During 1998, Kay collected $4,000 in principal on the installment note and $2,000 interest. Her basis in the property was $70,000 [$85,000 – $15,000 (depreciation)], and there was $9,000 in potential depreciation recapture under § 1250. The Federal rate is 9%.
a. Compute the following:
   1. Total gain.
   2. Contract price.
   3. Payments received in the year of sale.
   4. Recognized gain in the year of sale and the character of such gain.
   (*Hint:* Think carefully about the manner in which the property taxes are handled before you begin your computations.)
b. Same as (a)(2) and (3), except Kay's basis in the property was $45,000.

30. On June 30, 1998, Kelly sold property for $250,000 cash on the date of sale and a $750,000 note due on September 30, 1999. No interest was stated in the contract. The present value of the note (using 13.2%, which was the Federal rate) was $640,000. Kelly's basis in the property was $400,000, and $40,000 of the gain was subject to depreciation recapture under § 1245. Expenses of the sale totaled $10,000, and Kelly was not a dealer in the property sold.
    a. Compute Kelly's gain to be reported in 1998.
    b. Compute Kelly's interest income for 1999.

31. On July 1, 1997, a cash basis taxpayer sold land for $800,000 due on the date of the sale and $6 million principal and $741,600 interest (6%) due on June 30, 1999. The seller's basis in the land was $1 million. The Federal short-term rate was 8%, compounded semiannually.
    a. Compute the seller's interest income and gain in 1997, 1998, and 1999.
    b. Same as (a), except that the amount due in two years was $2 million principal and $508,800 interest and the purchaser will use the cash method to account for interest.

32. On December 30, 1998, Father sold land to Son for $10,000 cash and a 7% installment note with a face amount of $190,000. In 1999, after paying $30,000 on the principal of the note, Son sold the land. In 2000, Son paid Father $25,000 on the note principal. Father's basis in the land was $50,000. Assuming Son sold the land for $250,000, compute Father's taxable gain in 1999.

33. George sold land to an unrelated party in 1997. His basis in the land was $40,000, and the selling price was $100,000: $25,000 payable at closing and $25,000 (plus 10% interest) due January 1, 1998, 1999, and 2000. What would be the tax consequences of the following? [Treat each part independently and assume (1) George did not elect out of the installment method and (2) the installment obligations have values equal to their face amounts.]
    a. In 1998, George gave to his daughter the right to collect all future payments on the installment obligations.
    b. In 1998, after collecting the payment due on January 1, George transferred the installment obligation to his 100%-controlled corporation in exchange for additional shares of stock.
    c. On December 31, 1998, George received the payment due on January 1, 1999. On December 15, 1999, George died, and the remaining installment obligation was transferred to his estate. The estate collected the amount due on January 1, 2000.

34. The Dove Construction Company reports its income by the completed contract method. At the end of 1998, the company completed a contract to construct a building at a total cost of $980,000. The contract price was $1,200,000. However, the customer refused to accept the work and would not pay anything on the contract because he claimed the roof did not meet specifications. Dove's engineers estimated it would cost $140,000 to bring the roof up to the customer's standards. In 1999, the dispute was settled in the customer's favor; the roof was improved at a cost of $170,000, and the customer accepted the building and paid the $1,200,000.
    a. What would be the effects of the above on Dove's taxable income for 1998 and 1999?
    b. Same as (a), except Dove had $1,100,000 of accumulated costs under the contract at the end of 1998.

35. Rust Company is a real estate construction company with average annual gross receipts of $4 million. Rust uses the completed contract method, and the contracts require 18 months to complete.
    a. Which of the following costs would be allocated to construction in progress by Rust?
        1. The payroll taxes on direct labor.
        2. The current services pension costs for employees whose wages are included in direct labor.
        3. Accelerated depreciation on equipment used on contracts.
        4. Sales tax on materials assigned to contracts.
        5. The past service costs for employees whose wages are included in direct labor.
        6. Bidding expenses for contracts awarded.

b. Assume that Rust generally builds commercial buildings under contracts with the owners and reports the income by the completed contract method. The company is considering building a series of similar stores for a retail chain. The gross profit margin would be a low percentage, but the company's gross receipts would triple. Write a letter to your client, Rust Company, explaining the tax accounting implications of entering into these contracts. Rust's mailing address is P.O. Box 1000, Harrisonburg, VA 22807.

36. Indicate the accounting method that should be used to compute the income from the following contracts:
   a. A contract to build six jet aircraft.
   b. A contract to build a new home. The contractor's average annual gross receipts are $15 million.
   c. A contract to manufacture 3,000 pairs of boots for a large retail chain. The manufacturer has several contracts to produce the same boot for other retailers.
   d. A contract to pave a parking lot. The contractor's average annual gross receipts are $2 million.

37. Ostrich Company makes gasoline storage tanks. Everything produced is under contract (that is, the company does not produce until it gets a contract for a product). Ostrich makes three basic models. However, the tanks must be adapted to each individual customer's location and needs (e.g., the location of the valves, the quality of the materials and insulation). Discuss the following issues relative to Ostrich's operations:
   a. An examining IRS agent contends that each of the company's contracts is to produce a "unique product." What difference does it make whether the product is unique or a "shelf item"?
   b. Producing one of the tanks takes over one year from start to completion, and the total price is in excess of $1 million. What costs must be capitalized for this contract that are not subject to capitalization for a contract with a shorter duration and lower cost?
   c. What must Ostrich do with the costs of bidding on contracts?
   d. Ostrich frequently makes several cost estimates for a contract, using various estimates of materials costs. These costs fluctuate almost daily. Assuming Ostrich must use the percentage of completion method to report the income from the contract, what will be the consequence if the company uses the highest estimate of a contract's costs and the actual cost is closer to the lowest estimated cost?

38. Swallow Company is a large real estate construction company that reports its income by the percentage of completion method. In 1999, the company completed a contract at a total cost of $1,960,000. The contract price was $2,400,000. At the end of 1998, the year the contract was begun, Swallow estimated the total cost of the contract would be $2,100,000, and total accumulated costs on the contract at the end of 1998 were $1,400,000. The relevant tax rate is 34%, and the relevant Federal interest rate is 7%. Assume that all returns were filed and taxes were paid on March 15 following the close of the calendar tax year.
   a. Compute the gross profit on the contract for 1998 and 1999.
   b. Compute the lookback interest due with the 1999 return.
   c. Before bidding on a contract, Swallow generally makes three estimates of total contract costs: (1) optimistic, (2) pessimistic, and (3) most likely (based on a blending of optimistic and pessimistic assumptions). The company has asked you to write a letter explaining which of these estimates should be used for percentage of completion purposes. In writing your letter, you should consider the fact that Swallow is incorporated and has made an S corporation election; therefore, the income and deductions flow through to the shareholders who are all individuals in the 36% marginal tax bracket. The relevant Federal interest rate is 8%. Swallow's mailing address is 400 Front Avenue, Ashland, OR 97520.

Research Problems for this chapter appear at the end of Chapter 28.

TEAM PROJECT: ARTHUR ANDERSEN TAX CHALLENGE CASES

For more information on the Arthur Andersen Tax Challenge Cases, refer to Chapter 1, page 1–37.

Information related to tax issues and problems that are discussed in this chapter may be found in the

Day and Ball case on pages 20 and 22
Fence case on pages: None

Read and analyze the case you have been assigned and *identify* any issues and problems that are related to material covered in this chapter. If the information provided in the case is complete, prepare answers for this part of the case at this time. If you need information that is contained in the later parts of the case, write a memo summarizing the questions or problems so you can prepare a complete answer at a later date.

16

CORPORATIONS: INTRODUCTION, OPERATING RULES, AND RELATED CORPORATIONS

LEARNING OBJECTIVES

After completing Chapter 16, you should be able to:

1. Summarize the various forms of conducting a business.

2. Compare the taxation of individuals and corporations.

3. Discuss the tax rules unique to corporations.

4. Compute the corporate income tax.

5. Explain the tax rules unique to multiple corporations.

6. Describe the reporting process for corporations.

7. Evaluate corporations for conducting a business.

TAX TREATMENT OF VARIOUS BUSINESS FORMS

1 **LEARNING OBJECTIVE**
Summarize the various forms of conducting a business.

Business operations can be conducted in a number of different forms. Among the various possibilities are the following:

- Sole proprietorships.
- Partnerships.
- Trusts and estates.
- S corporations (also known as Subchapter S corporations).
- Regular corporations (also called Subchapter C or C corporations).

For Federal income tax purposes, the distinctions among these forms of business organization are very important. The following discussion of the tax treatment of sole proprietorships, partnerships, and regular corporations highlights these distinctions. Trusts and estates are covered in Chapter 27, and S corporations are discussed in Chapter 21.

SOLE PROPRIETORSHIPS

A sole proprietorship is not a taxable entity separate from the individual who owns the proprietorship. The owner of a sole proprietorship reports all business transactions of the proprietorship on Schedule C of Form 1040. The net profit or loss from the proprietorship is then transferred from Schedule C to Form 1040, which is used by the taxpayer to report taxable income. The proprietor reports all of the net profit from the business, regardless of the amount actually withdrawn during the year.

Income and expenses of the proprietorship retain their character when reported by the proprietor. For example, ordinary income of the proprietorship is treated as ordinary income when reported by the proprietor, and capital gain is treated as capital gain.

EXAMPLE 1

George is the sole proprietor of George's Record Shop. Gross income of the business in 1998 is $200,000, and operating expenses are $110,000. George also sells a capital asset held by the business for a $10,000 long-term capital gain. During 1998, he withdraws $60,000 from the business for living expenses. George reports the income and expenses of the business on Schedule C, resulting in net profit (ordinary income) of $90,000. Even though he withdrew only $60,000, George reports all of the $90,000 net profit from the business on Form 1040, where he computes taxable income for the year. He also reports a $10,000 long-term capital gain. ▼

PARTNERSHIPS

Partnerships are not subject to the income tax. However, a partnership is required to file Form 1065, which reports the results of the partnership's business activities. Most income and expense items are aggregated in computing the net profit of the partnership on Form 1065. Any income and expense items that are not aggregated in computing the partnership's net income are reported separately to the partners. Some examples of separately reported income items are interest income, dividend income, and long-term capital gain. Examples of separately reported expenses include charitable contributions and expenses related to interest and dividend income. Partnership reporting is discussed in detail in Chapter 22.

The partnership net profit (loss) and the separately reported items are allocated to each partner according to the partnership's profit sharing agreement, and the partners receive separate K–1 schedules from the partnership. Schedule K–1 reports each partner's share of the partnership net profit (loss) and separately reported income and expense items. Each partner reports these items on his or her own tax return.

EXAMPLE 2

Jim and Bob are equal partners in Canary Enterprises, a calendar year partnership. During the year, Canary Enterprises had $500,000 of gross income and $350,000 of operating expenses. In addition, the partnership sold land that had been held for investment purposes for a long-term capital gain of $60,000. During the year, Jim withdrew $40,000 from the partnership and Bob withdrew $45,000. The partnership's Form 1065 reports net profit of $150,000 ($500,000 income − $350,000 expenses). The partnership also reports the $60,000 long-term capital gain as a separately stated item on Form 1065. Jim and Bob both receive a Schedule K–1 reporting net profit of $75,000 and separately stated long-term capital gain of $30,000. Each partner reports net profit of $75,000 and long-term capital gain of $30,000 on his own return. ▼

REGULAR CORPORATIONS

Corporations are governed by Subchapter C or Subchapter S of the Internal Revenue Code. Those governed by Subchapter C are referred to as **C corporations** or **regular corporations.** Corporations governed by Subchapter S are referred to as **S corporations.**

S corporations, which generally do not pay Federal income tax, are similar to partnerships in that net profit or loss flows through to the shareholders to be reported on their separate returns. Also like partnerships, S corporations do not aggregate all income and expense items in computing net profit or loss. Certain items flow through to the shareholders and retain their separate character when reported on the shareholders' returns. See Chapter 21 for detailed coverage of S corporations.

Unlike proprietorships, partnerships, and S corporations, C corporations are taxpaying entities. This results in what is known as a *double tax effect*. A C corporation reports its income and expenses on Form 1120 (or Form 1120–A, the corporate short form). The corporation computes tax on the net income reported on the corporate tax return using the rate schedule applicable to corporations (the rate schedule is shown on the inside front cover of this text and on the next page). When a corporation distributes its income, the corporation's shareholders report dividend income on their own tax returns. Thus, income that has already been taxed at the corporate level is also taxed at the shareholder level.

EXAMPLE 3

Tan Corporation files Form 1120, which reports net profit of $100,000. The corporation pays tax of $22,250. This leaves $77,750, all of which is distributed as a dividend to Carla, the sole shareholder of the corporation. Carla, who has income from other sources and is in the 39.6% tax bracket, pays income tax of $30,789 ($77,750 × 39.6%) on the distribution. The combined tax on the corporation's net profit is $53,039 ($22,250 + $30,789). ▼

EXAMPLE 4

Assume the same facts as in Example 3, except that the business is organized as a sole proprietorship. Carla reports the $100,000 net profit from the business on her tax return and pays tax of $39,600 ($100,000 net profit × 39.6% marginal rate). Therefore, operating the business as a sole proprietorship results in tax savings of $13,439 ($53,039 tax from Example 3 – $39,600). ▼

Shareholders in closely held corporations frequently attempt to avoid double taxation by paying out all the profit of the corporation as salary to themselves.

EXAMPLE 5

Orange Corporation has net income of $180,000 during the year ($300,000 revenue – $120,000 operating expenses). Emilio is the sole shareholder of Orange Corporation. In an effort to avoid tax at the corporate level, Emilio has Orange pay him a salary of $180,000, which results in zero taxable income for the corporation. ▼

Will the strategy described in Example 5 effectively avoid double taxation? The answer depends on whether the compensation paid to the shareholder is *reasonable*. Section 162 provides that compensation is deductible only to the extent that it is reasonable in amount. The IRS is aware that many taxpayers use this strategy to bail out corporate profits and, in an audit, looks closely at compensation expense. If the IRS believes that compensation is too high based on the amount and quality of services performed by the shareholder, the compensation deduction of the corporation is reduced to a reasonable amount. Compensation that is determined to be unreasonable is usually treated as a constructive dividend to the shareholder and is not deductible by the corporation.

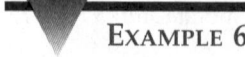

EXAMPLE 6

Assume the same facts as in Example 5, and that the IRS determines that $80,000 of the amount paid to Emilio is unreasonable compensation. As a result, $80,000 of the corporation's compensation deduction is disallowed and treated as a constructive dividend to Emilio. Orange has taxable income of $80,000. Emilio would report salary of $100,000 and a taxable dividend of $80,000. The net effect is that $80,000 is subject to double taxation. ▼

The unreasonable compensation issue is discussed in more detail in Chapter 18.

Comparison of Corporations and Other Forms of Doing Business. Comparison of the tax results in Examples 3 and 4 might lead to the conclusion that incorporation is not a wise tax strategy. In some cases that would be a correct conclusion, but in others it would not. In many situations, tax and nontax factors combine to make the corporate form of doing business the only reasonable choice.

While a detailed comparison of sole proprietorships, partnerships, S corporations, and C corporations as forms of doing business must be made, it is appropriate at this point to consider some of the tax and nontax factors that favor corporations over proprietorships.

Consideration of tax factors requires an examination of the corporate rate structure. The income tax rate schedule applicable to corporations is reproduced below.

Taxable Income		Tax Is:	Of the Amount
Over—	But Not Over—		Over—
$ –0–	$ 50,000	15%	$ –0–
50,000	75,000	$ 7,500 + 25%	50,000
75,000	100,000	13,750 + 34%	75,000
100,000	335,000	22,250 + 39%	100,000
335,000	10,000,000	113,900 + 34%	335,000
10,000,000	15,000,000	3,400,000 + 35%	10,000,000
15,000,000	18,333,333	5,150,000 + 38%	15,000,000
18,333,333	—	35%	–0–

As this schedule shows, corporate rates on taxable income up to $75,000 are lower than individual rates for persons in the 28 percent and higher brackets. Therefore, corporate tax will be lower than individual tax. Furthermore, there is no corporate marginal rate that is higher than the 39.6 percent top bracket for individuals. When dividends are paid, however, the double taxation problem occurs. This leads to an important question: Will incorporation ever result in Federal income tax savings? The following example illustrates a situation where this occurs.

EXAMPLE 7

Ned, an individual in the 39.6% tax bracket, owns a business that produces net profit of $50,000 each year. Ned has significant income from other sources, so he does not withdraw any of the profit from the business. If the business is operated as a proprietorship, Ned's Federal income tax on the net profit of the business is $19,800 ($50,000 × 39.6%). However, if the business is operated as a corporation and pays no dividends, the tax will be $7,500 ($50,000 × 15%). Operating as a corporation saves $12,300 of Federal income tax each year. If Ned invests the $12,300 tax savings each year for several years, it is possible that a positive cash flow will result, even though Ned will be required to pay tax on dividends distributed by the corporation some time in the future. ▼

The preceding example deals with a specific set of facts. The conclusions reached in this situation cannot be extended to all decisions about a form of business organization. Each specific set of facts and circumstances requires a thorough analysis of the tax factors.

Another tax consideration involves the nature of dividend income. All income and expense items of a proprietorship retain their character when reported on the proprietor's tax return. In the case of a partnership, several separately reported items (e.g., charitable contributions and long-term capital gains) retain their character when passed through to the partners. However, the tax attributes of income and expense items of a corporation are lost as they pass through the corporate entity to the shareholders.

EXAMPLE 8   During the current year, Waxwing Company receives tax-exempt interest, which is distributed to its owners. If Waxwing Company is a regular corporation, the distribution to the shareholders constitutes a dividend. The fact that it originated from tax-exempt interest is of no consequence.[1] On the other hand, if Waxwing is a partnership or an S corporation, the tax-exempt interest retains its identity and passes through to the individual owners. ▼

Losses of a C corporation are treated differently than losses of a proprietorship, partnership, or S corporation. A loss incurred by a proprietorship may be deductible by the owner, because all income and expense items are reported by the proprietor. Partnership losses are passed through the partnership entity and may be deductible by the partners, and S corporation losses are passed through to the shareholders. C corporation losses, however, have no effect on the taxable income of the shareholders. Income from a C corporation is reported when the shareholders receive dividends. C corporation losses are not reported by the shareholders.

Nontax Considerations.   Nontax considerations will sometimes override tax considerations and lead to the conclusion that a business should be operated as a corporation. The following are some of the more important nontax considerations:

- Sole proprietors and *general* partners in partnerships face the danger of *unlimited liability*. That is, creditors of the business may file claims not only against the assets of the business but also against the personal assets of proprietors or general partners. Shareholders are protected from claims against their personal assets by state corporate law.
- The corporate form of business organization can provide a vehicle for raising large amounts of capital through widespread stock ownership. Most major businesses in the United States are operated as corporations.
- Shares of stock in a corporation are freely transferable, whereas a partner's sale of his or her partnership interest is subject to approval by the other partners.
- Shareholders may come and go, but a corporation can continue to exist. Death or withdrawal of a partner, on the other hand, may terminate the existing partnership and cause financial difficulties that result in dissolution of the entity. This *continuity of life* is a distinct advantage of the corporate form of doing business.
- Corporations have *centralized management*. All management responsibility is assigned to a board of directors, who appoint officers to carry out the corporation's business. Partnerships, by contrast, may have decentralized management, in which every owner has a right to participate in the organization's business decisions; **limited partnerships,** though, may have centralized management. Centralized management is essential for the smooth operation of a widely held business.

---

[1]As noted in Chapter 18, such items will, however, affect the distributing corporation's earnings and profits.

LIMITED LIABILITY COMPANIES

The **limited liability company (LLC)** has proliferated greatly in recent years, particularly since 1988 when the IRS first ruled that it would treat qualifying LLCs as partnerships for tax purposes. All 50 states and the District of Columbia have passed laws that allow LLCs, and thousands of companies have chosen LLC status. As with a corporation, operating as an LLC allows an entity to avoid unlimited liability, which is a primary *nontax* consideration in choosing the form of business organization. The tax advantage of LLCs is that qualifying businesses may be treated as partnerships for tax purposes, thereby avoiding the problem of double taxation associated with regular corporations.

Some states allow an LLC to have centralized management, but not continuity of life or free transferability of interests. Other states allow LLCs to adopt any or all of the corporate characteristics of centralized management, continuity of life, and free transferability of interests.

ENTITY CLASSIFICATION PRIOR TO 1997

Can an organization not qualifying as a corporation under state law still be treated as such for Federal income tax purposes? Unfortunately, the tax law defines a corporation as including "… associations, joint stock companies, and insurance companies."[2] As the Code contains no definition of what constitutes an "association," the issue became the subject of frequent litigation.

It was finally determined that an entity would be treated as a corporation if it had a majority of characteristics common to corporations. For this purpose, relevant characteristics are:

- Continuity of life.
- Centralized management.
- Limited liability.
- Free transferability of interests.

These criteria did not resolve all of the problems that continued to arise over corporate classification. When a new type of business entity was developed, the limited liability company, the IRS was deluged with inquiries regarding its tax status. As the limited liability company became increasingly popular with professional groups, all states enacted statutes allowing some form of this entity. Invariably the statutes permitted the corporate characteristic of limited liability and, often, that of centralized management. Because continuity of life and free transferability of interests are absent, partnership classification was hoped for. This treatment would avoid the double tax result inherent in the corporate form.

ENTITY CLASSIFICATION AFTER 1996

In late 1996, the IRS issued its so-called **check-the-box Regulations.**[3] Effective beginning in 1997, the Regulations enable taxpayers to choose the tax status of a business entity without regard to its corporate (or noncorporate) characteristics. These new rules should simplify tax administration considerably and should eliminate the type of litigation that arose with regard to the association (i.e., corporation) status.

Under the new rules, entities with more than one owner can elect to be classified as either a partnership or as a corporation. An entity with only one owner can

---

[2]§ 7701(a)(3).

[3]Reg. §§ 301.7701–1 through –4, and –7.

elect to be classified as a corporation or as a sole proprietorship. In the event of default (i.e., no election is made), multi-owned entities will be classified as partnerships and single-person businesses as sole proprietorships.

The election is not available to entities that are actually incorporated under state law or to entities that are required to be corporations under Federal law (e.g., certain publicly traded partnerships). For purposes of these prohibitions, limited liability companies are not treated as being incorporated under state law. Consequently, they can elect either corporation or partnership status.

Eligible entities make the election as to tax status by filing Form 8832 (Entity classification election). New elections are permitted but only after a 60-month waiting period.

An Introduction to the Income Taxation of Corporations

AN OVERVIEW OF CORPORATE VERSUS INDIVIDUAL INCOME TAX TREATMENT

2   LEARNING OBJECTIVE
Compare the taxation of individuals and corporations.

In a discussion of how corporations are treated under the Federal income tax law, a useful approach is to compare their treatment with that applicable to individual taxpayers.

Similarities.   Gross income of a corporation is determined in much the same manner as it is for individuals. Thus, gross income includes compensation for services rendered, income derived from a business, gains from dealings in property, interest, rents, royalties, and dividends—to name only a few items. Both individuals and corporations are entitled to exclusions from gross income. However, corporate taxpayers are allowed fewer exclusions. Interest on municipal bonds is excluded from gross income whether the bondholder is an individual or a corporate taxpayer.

Gains and losses from property transactions are handled similarly. For example, whether a gain or loss is capital or ordinary depends upon the nature of the asset in the hands of the taxpayer making the taxable disposition. In defining what is not a capital asset, § 1221 makes no distinction between corporate and noncorporate taxpayers.

In the area of nontaxable exchanges, corporations are like individuals in that they do not recognize gain or loss on a like-kind exchange and may defer realized gain on an involuntary conversion of property. The nonrecognition of gain provisions dealing with the sale of a personal residence do not apply to corporations. Both corporations and individuals are vulnerable to the disallowance of losses on sales of property to related parties or on wash sales of securities. The wash sales rules do not apply to individuals who are traders or dealers in securities or to corporations that are dealers if the securities are sold in the ordinary course of the corporation's business.

Upon the sale or other taxable disposition of depreciable property, the recapture rules generally make no distinction between corporate and noncorporate taxpayers.[4] However, § 291(a) does cause a corporation to have more recapture on § 1250 property. This difference is discussed later in the chapter.

---

[4]§§ 1245 and 1250.

The business deductions of corporations also parallel those available to individuals. Deductions are allowed for all ordinary and necessary expenses paid or incurred in carrying on a trade or business. Specific provision is made for the deductibility of interest, certain taxes, losses, bad debts, accelerated cost recovery, charitable contributions, net operating losses, research and experimental expenditures, and other less common deductions. A corporation does not distinguish between business and nonbusiness interest or business and nonbusiness bad debts. Thus, these amounts are deductible in full as ordinary deductions by corporations. No deduction is permitted for interest paid or incurred on amounts borrowed to purchase or carry tax-exempt securities. The same holds true for expenses contrary to public policy and certain unpaid expenses and interest between related parties.

Some of the tax credits available to individuals can also be claimed by corporations. This is the case with the foreign tax credit. Not available to corporations are certain credits that are personal in nature, such as the credit for child and dependent care expenses, the credit for elderly or disabled taxpayers, and the earned income credit.

Dissimilarities. The income taxation of corporations and individuals also differs significantly. As noted earlier, different tax rates apply to corporations and to individuals. Corporate tax rates are discussed in more detail later in the chapter (see Examples 26 and 27).

All allowable corporate deductions are treated as business deductions. Thus, the determination of adjusted gross income (AGI), so essential for individual taxpayers, has no relevance to corporations. Taxable income is computed simply by subtracting from gross income all allowable deductions and losses. Corporations thus need not be concerned with itemized deductions or the standard deduction. Likewise, the deduction for personal and dependency exemptions is not available to corporations.

Unlike individuals, corporations are not subject to the $100 floor on the deductible portion of casualty and theft losses. Also inapplicable is the provision limiting the deductibility of nonbusiness casualty losses to the amount in excess of 10 percent of AGI.

SPECIFIC PROVISIONS COMPARED

In comparing the tax treatment of individuals and corporations, the following areas warrant special discussion:

- Accounting periods and methods.
- Capital gains and losses.
- Recapture of depreciation.
- Passive losses.
- Charitable contributions.
- Net operating losses.
- Special deductions available only to corporations.

ACCOUNTING PERIODS AND METHODS

Accounting Periods. Corporations generally have the same choices of accounting periods as do individual taxpayers. Like an individual, a corporation may choose a calendar year or a fiscal year for reporting purposes. Corporations, however, enjoy greater flexibility in the selection of a tax year. For example, corporations usually can have different tax years from those of their shareholders. Also, newly formed corporations (as new taxpayers) usually may choose any approved accounting period without having to obtain the consent of the IRS. **Personal service corporations (PSCs)** and S corporations, however, are subject to severe restrictions in the use of fiscal years. The rules applicable to S corporations are discussed in Chapter 21.

A PSC has as its principal activity the performance of personal services. Such services must be substantially performed by owner-employees and must be in the fields of health, law, engineering, architecture, accounting, actuarial science, performing arts, or consulting.[5] Barring certain exceptions, PSCs must adopt a calendar year for tax purposes.[6] The exceptions that permit the use of a fiscal year are discussed in Chapter 15.[7]

Accounting Methods.   As a general rule, the cash method of accounting is unavailable to *regular* corporations.[8] Exceptions apply to the following types of corporations:

- S corporations.
- Corporations engaged in the trade or business of farming and timber.
- Qualified PSCs.
- Corporations with average annual gross receipts of $5 million-or-less. (In applying the $5 million-or-less test, the corporation uses the average of the three prior taxable years.)

Both individuals and corporations that maintain inventory for sale to customers are required to use the accrual method of accounting for determining sales and cost of goods sold.

A corporation that uses the accrual method of accounting must observe a special rule in dealing with related parties. If the corporation has an accrual outstanding at the end of any taxable year, it cannot claim a deduction until the recipient reports the amount as income.[9] This rule is most often encountered when a corporation deals with a person who owns more than 50 percent of the corporation's stock.

EXAMPLE 9   Teal, an accrual method corporation, uses the calendar year for tax purposes. Bob, a cash method taxpayer, owns more than 50% of the corporation's stock at the end of 1998. On December 31, 1998, Teal has accrued $25,000 of salary to Bob. Bob receives the salary in 1999 and reports it on his 1999 tax return. Teal cannot claim a deduction for the $25,000 until 1999. ▼

CAPITAL GAINS AND LOSSES

Capital gains and losses result from taxable sales or exchanges of capital assets. The holding period of the assets determines the maximum rate at which capital gain will be taxed. Applicable capital gains tax rates are 28 percent, 25 percent, and 20 percent. Gains and losses in the 28 percent category are combined, as are gains and losses in the 20 percent category, resulting in a net gain or loss in each category. There are only gains and no losses in the 25 percent category.[10]

Noncorporate Taxpayers.   The rules applicable to capital gains and losses differ for corporate and noncorporate taxpayers. Short-term capital gains of noncorporate taxpayers are subject to regular income tax rates, while capital gains that are not

---

[5] § 448(d)(2)(A).
[6] § 441(i).
[7] §§ 444 and 280H.
[8] § 448(a).

[9] § 267(a)(2).
[10] The 25% rate applies to unrecaptured gain on § 1250 property. Section 1250 recapture applies only to gains; therefore, there will be no losses in the 25% category.

short term are subject to more favorable tax rates. The alternative rates applicable to post-1997[11] noncorporate capital gains are summarized below:

Rate	Applies to
28% (mid-term)	• Net gain on property (other than collectibles) held for more than 12 months but not more than 18 months. • Net gain on collectibles held for more than 12 months (even if they are held for more than 18 months).
25% (unrecaptured § 1250 gain)	• Unrecaptured § 1250 gain on real property held for more than 18 months (i.e., gain attributable to depreciation that does not have to be recaptured as ordinary income).
20% (long-term)	• Net gain on property held for more than 18 months (other than collectibles gain or unrecaptured § 1250 gain).[12]

The rules applicable to capital losses of noncorporate taxpayers became much more complex under the Taxpayer Relief Act of 1997. After gains and losses are combined, a taxpayer could have net losses in the short-term category, the 28 percent category, or the 20 percent category, or some combination of the categories. Net losses in each category are used to offset net gains in other categories in a specified order, which is summarized below.

Net Loss on	Offsets This Category of Net Gain
Short-term property	28%, then 25%, then 20%
28% property	25%, then 20%
20% property	28%, then 25%

If there is *net gain* in a particular category after the rules for offsetting losses are applied, the net gain is taxed at the rate applicable to that category. If a *net loss* remains after application of the offsetting rules, a noncorporate taxpayer can deduct up to $3,000 against ordinary income. A taxpayer who has total net capital losses in excess of $3,000 must use losses in the following order: short-term, mid-term, and long-term. Capital losses that cannot be deducted in the year incurred can be carried forward to future years until absorbed by capital gains or by the $3,000 deduction. Carryovers of short-term capital losses retain their identity as short-term. However, long-term and mid-term losses are carried over as mid-term capital losses.

EXAMPLE 10

Robin, an individual, incurs a net long-term capital loss of $7,500 for calendar year 1998. Assuming adequate taxable income, Robin may deduct $3,000 of this loss on his 1998 return. The remaining $4,500 ($7,500 − $3,000) of the loss is carried to 1999 and years thereafter until it is offset against future capital gains or deducted against ordinary income (subject to the $3,000 maximum per year). The $4,500 is carried forward as a mid-term capital loss. ▼

Corporate Taxpayers. Corporations do not benefit from special tax rates on capital gains. Corporations must include the entire net capital gain in income and pay tax on the gain at normal corporate rates.

---

[11]The complex transition rules for 1997 capital gains and losses are covered in Chapter 13.

[12]A rate of 10% applies to gain in this category that would otherwise be taxed at the regular income tax rate of 15%. This provision benefits low-income taxpayers who are in the 15% bracket.

Unlike individuals, corporate taxpayers are not permitted to claim any net capital losses as a deduction against ordinary income. Capital losses, therefore, can be used only to offset capital gains. Corporations may, however, carry back net capital losses to three preceding years, applying them first to the earliest year in point of time. Carryforwards are allowed for a period of five years from the year of the loss. When carried back or forward, all corporate capital losses are treated as short-term capital losses, regardless of their initial classification.

EXAMPLE 11

Assume the same facts as in Example 10, except that Robin is a corporation. None of the $7,500 long-term capital loss incurred in 1998 can be deducted in that year. Robin Corporation may, however, carry back the loss to years 1995, 1996, and 1997 (in this order) and offset it against any capital gains recognized in these years. If the carryback does not exhaust the loss, the loss may be carried forward to calendar years 1999, 2000, 2001, 2002, and 2003 (in this order). Either a carryback or a carryforward of the long-term capital loss converts it to a short-term capital loss. Carryback of a capital loss generates a refund of taxes previously paid on the capital gain against which the carryback is offset. ▼

RECAPTURE OF DEPRECIATION

Depreciation recapture for § 1245 property is computed in the same manner for individuals and for corporations. However, corporations may have more depreciation recapture than individuals. Corporations that sell *depreciable real estate* that is § 1250 property are subject to additional recapture of depreciation under § 291(a)(1). This provision requires recapture of 20 percent of the excess of any amount that would be treated as ordinary income under § 1245 over the amount treated as ordinary income under § 1250. The amount of ordinary income under § 291 is computed as shown in Figure 16–1.

▼ **FIGURE 16–1**
Computation of Depreciation
Recapture under § 291

Ordinary income under § 1245	$xx,xxx
Less: Ordinary income under § 1250	(x,xxx)
Equals: Excess ordinary income under § 1245 as compared to ordinary income under § 1250	$ x,xxx
Apply § 291 percentage	× 20%
Equals: Amount of ordinary income under § 291	$ xxx

EXAMPLE 12

Amber Corporation purchased an office building on January 3, 1984, for $300,000. Accelerated depreciation was taken in the amount of $285,000 before the building was sold on January 5, 1998, for $350,000. Straight-line depreciation would have been $280,000 (using a 15-year recovery period under ACRS). The corporation's depreciation recapture and § 1231 gain are computed as follows:

Determine realized gain:	
Sales price	$350,000
Less: Adjusted basis [$300,000 (cost of building) – $285,000 (ACRS depreciation)]	(15,000)
Realized gain	$335,000

Because the building is 15-year real estate, it is treated as § 1245 recovery property. The gain of $335,000 is recaptured to the extent of all depreciation taken. Thus, $285,000 of the gain is ordinary income under § 1245, and there is $50,000 of § 1231 gain. ▼

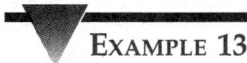

EXAMPLE 13

Assume the building in Example 12 is residential rental property, making it § 1250 property. Gain recaptured under § 1250 is $5,000 ($285,000 depreciation taken – $280,000 straight-line depreciation). However, for a corporate taxpayer, § 291(a)(1) causes additional § 1250 ordinary income of $56,000, computed as follows:

Ordinary income if property were § 1245 property	$285,000
Less: Ordinary income under § 1250	(5,000)
Excess ordinary income under § 1245	$280,000
Apply § 291 percentage	× 20%
Ordinary income under § 291	$ 56,000
Ordinary income ($5,000 + $56,000)	$ 61,000
Section 1231 gain ($335,000 – $5,000 – $56,000)	274,000
Total Gain	$335,000

▼

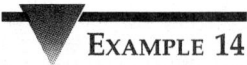

EXAMPLE 14

Assume the building in Example 13 is commercial property and straight-line depreciation was used. An individual would report all of the gain as § 1231 gain. However, under § 291 a corporate taxpayer would recapture as ordinary income 20% of the depreciation that would be ordinary income if the property were § 1245 property.

First, determine realized gain:	
Sales price	$350,000
Less: Adjusted basis [$300,000 (cost of building) – $280,000 (straight-line depreciation)]	(20,000)
Realized gain	$330,000

Second, determine § 291 gain:

Ordinary income if property were § 1245 property	$280,000
Less: Ordinary income under § 1250	(–0–)
Excess ordinary income under § 1245	$280,000
Apply § 291 percentage	× 20%
Ordinary income under § 291	$ 56,000

For a corporate taxpayer, $56,000 of the $330,000 gain would be ordinary, and $274,000 would be § 1231 gain. ▼

PASSIVE LOSSES

The **passive loss** rules apply to noncorporate taxpayers and to closely held C corporations and personal service corporations (PSCs).[13] For S corporations and partnerships, passive income or loss flows through to the owners, and the passive loss rules are applied at the owner level. The passive loss rules are applied to closely held corporations and to PSCs to prevent taxpayers from incorporating to avoid the passive loss limitations (refer to Chapter 10).

A corporation is closely held if, at any time during the taxable year, more than 50 percent of the value of the corporation's outstanding stock is owned, directly or indirectly, by or for not more than five individuals. A corporation is classified as a PSC if it meets the following requirements:

- The principal activity of the corporation is the performance of personal services.
- Such services are substantially performed by owner-employees.
- More than 10 percent of the stock (in value) is held by owner-employees. *Any* stock held by an employee on *any* one day causes the employee to be an owner-employee.

The general passive activity loss rules apply to PSCs. Passive activity losses cannot be offset against either active income or portfolio income. The application of the passive activity rules is not as harsh for closely held corporations. They may offset passive losses against active income, but not against portfolio income.

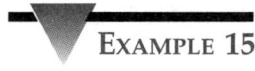
EXAMPLE 15

Brown, a closely held corporation, has $300,000 of passive losses from a rental activity, $200,000 of active business income, and $100,000 of portfolio income. The corporation may offset $200,000 of the $300,000 passive loss against the $200,000 active business income, but may not offset the remainder against the $100,000 of portfolio income. ▼

Individual taxpayers are not allowed to offset passive losses against *either* active or portfolio income.

CHARITABLE CONTRIBUTIONS

Both corporate and noncorporate taxpayers may deduct charitable contributions if the recipient is a qualified charitable organization. Generally, a deduction will be allowed only for the year in which the payment is made. However, an important exception is made for *accrual basis corporations*. They may claim the deduction in the year *preceding* payment if two requirements are met. First, the contribution

---

[13] § 469(a).

must be authorized by the board of directors by the end of that year. Second, it must be paid on or before the fifteenth day of the third month of the next year.

EXAMPLE 16

On December 28, 1998, Blue Company, a calendar year, accrual basis partnership, authorizes a $5,000 donation to the Atlanta Symphony Association (a qualified charitable organization). The donation is made on March 14, 1999. Because Blue Company is a partnership, the contribution cannot be deducted until 1999.[14] However, if Blue Company is a corporation and the December 28, 1998 authorization was made by its board of directors, Blue may claim the $5,000 donation as a deduction for calendar year 1998. ▼

Property Contributions.   The amount that can be deducted for a noncash chari-table contribution depends on the type of property contributed. Property must be identified as long-term capital gain property or ordinary income property. *Long-term capital gain property* is property that, if sold, would result in long-term capital gain for the taxpayer. Such property generally must be a capital asset and must be held for the long-term holding period (more than 12 months for charitable contributions). *Ordinary income property* is property that, if sold, would result in ordinary income for the taxpayer.

The deduction for a charitable contribution of long-term capital property is generally measured by its fair market value.

EXAMPLE 17

In 1998, Mallard Corporation donated a parcel of land (a capital asset) to Oakland Community College. Mallard acquired the land in 1988 for $60,000, and the fair market value on the date of the contribution was $100,000. The corporation's charitable contribution deduction (subject to a percentage limitation discussed later) is measured by the asset's fair market value of $100,000, even though the $40,000 appreciation on the land has never been included in Mallard's income. ▼

In two situations, a charitable contribution of long-term capital gain property is measured by the basis of the property, rather than fair market value. If the corporation contributes *tangible personal property* and the charitable organization puts the property to an unrelated use, the appreciation on the property is not deductible. Unrelated use is defined as use that is not related to the purpose or function that qualifies the organization for exempt status.

EXAMPLE 18

White Corporation donates a painting worth $200,000 to Western States Art Museum (a qualified organization), which exhibits the painting. White had acquired the painting in 1980 for $90,000. Because the museum put the painting to a related use, White is allowed to deduct $200,000, the fair market value of the painting. ▼

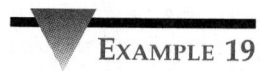
EXAMPLE 19

Assume the same facts as in the previous example, except that White Corporation donates the painting to the American Cancer Society, which sells the painting and deposits the $200,000 proceeds in the organization's general fund. White's deduction is limited to the $90,000 basis because it contributed tangible personal property that was put to an unrelated use by the charitable organization. ▼

---

[14]Each calendar year partner will report an allocable portion of the
charitable contribution deduction as of December 31, 1999 (the end
of the partnership's tax year). See Chapter 22.

ETHICAL CONSIDERATIONS

Is It Better Not to Know?

Puffin Corporation, your client, donated a painting to Tri-City Art Museum. The painting, which has been displayed in the corporate offices for several years, had a basis of $20,000 and a fair market value of $100,000. Puffin deducted a charitable contribution of $100,000 on its tax return.

You have learned that Tri-City Museum, also a client of yours, did not display the painting because it did not fit well with the museum's collection. Instead, Tri-City sold the painting for $100,000 and placed the funds in its operating budget. What action, if any, should you take?

The deduction for charitable contributions of long-term capital gain property to certain *private nonoperating foundations* is also limited to the basis of the property.

Ordinary income property is property that, if sold, would result in ordinary income. Examples of ordinary income property include inventory and capital assets that have not been held long term. In addition, § 1231 property (depreciable property used in a trade or business) is treated as ordinary income property to the extent of any ordinary income recaptured under § 1245 or § 1250. As a general rule, the deduction for a contribution of ordinary income property is limited to the basis of the property. However, *corporations* enjoy two special exceptions where 50 percent of the appreciation (but not to exceed twice the basis) on property is allowed on certain contributions. The first exception concerns inventory if the property is used in a manner related to the exempt purpose of the donee. Also, the charity must use the property solely for the care of the ill, the needy, or infants.

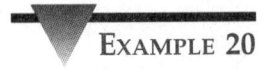

EXAMPLE 20

Lark Corporation, a grocery chain, donates canned goods to the Salvation Army to be used to feed the needy. Lark's basis in the canned goods was $2,000, and the fair market value was $3,000. Lark's deduction is $2,500 [$2,000 basis + 50%($3,000 − $2,000)]. ▼

The second exception involves gifts of scientific property to colleges and certain scientific research organizations for use in research, provided certain conditions are met.[15] As was true of the inventory exception, 50 percent of the appreciation on such property is allowed as an additional deduction.

Limitations Imposed on Charitable Contribution Deductions. Like individuals, corporations are subject to percentage limits on the charitable contribution deduction.[16] For any one year, a corporate taxpayer's contribution deduction is limited to 10 percent of taxable income. For this purpose, taxable income is computed without regard to the charitable contribution deduction, any net operating loss carryback or capital loss carryback, and the dividends received deduction. Any contributions in excess of the 10 percent limitation may be carried forward to the five succeeding tax years. Any carryforward must be added to subsequent contributions and will be subject to the 10 percent limitation. In applying this limitation, the current year's contributions must be deducted first, with excess deductions from previous years deducted in order of time.[17]

---

[15]These conditions are set forth in § 170(e)(4). For the inventory exception, see § 170(e)(3).

[16]The percentage limitations applicable to individuals and corporations are set forth in § 170(b).

[17]The carryover rules relating to all taxpayers are in § 170(d).

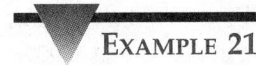

EXAMPLE 21

During 1998, Orange Corporation (a calendar year taxpayer) had the following income and expenses:

Income from operations	$140,000
Expenses from operations	110,000
Dividends received	10,000
Charitable contributions made in May 1998	5,000

For purposes of the 10% limitation *only*, Orange Corporation's taxable income is $40,000 ($140,000 – $110,000 + $10,000). Consequently, the allowable charitable contribution deduction for 1998 is $4,000 (10% × $40,000). The $1,000 unused portion of the contribution can be carried forward to 1999, 2000, 2001, 2002, and 2003 (in that order) until exhausted. ▼

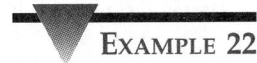

EXAMPLE 22

Assume the same facts as in Example 21. In 1999, Orange Corporation has taxable income (for purposes of the 10% limitation) of $50,000 and makes a charitable contribution of $4,500. The maximum deduction allowed for 1999 would be $5,000 (10% × $50,000). The first $4,500 of the allowed deduction must be allocated to the contribution made in 1999, and $500 of the $1,000 unused contribution is carried over from 1998. The remaining $500 of the 1998 contribution may be carried over to 2000 (and later years, if necessary). ▼

NET OPERATING LOSSES

As for individuals, the net operating loss (NOL) of a corporation may be carried back 2 years and forward 20 to offset taxable income for those years. However, a corporation does not adjust its tax loss for the year for capital losses as do individual taxpayers, because a corporation is not permitted a deduction for net capital losses. Nor does a corporation make adjustments for nonbusiness deductions as do individual taxpayers. Further, a corporation is allowed to include the dividends received deduction (discussed below) in computing its NOL.[18]

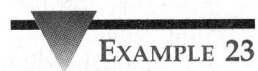

EXAMPLE 23

In 1998, Green Corporation has gross income (including dividends) of $200,000 and deductions of $300,000 excluding the dividends received deduction. Green Corporation had received taxable dividends of $100,000 from Exxon stock. Green has an NOL computed as follows:

Gross income (including dividends)		$ 200,000
Less: Business deductions	$300,000	
Dividends received deduction (70% × $100,000)*	70,000	(370,000)
Taxable income (or loss)		($ 170,000)

*See the discussion of the dividends received deduction in the next section of this chapter.

The NOL is carried back two years to 1996. (Green Corporation may *elect* to forgo the carryback option and instead carry the loss forward.) Assume Green had taxable income of $40,000 in 1996. The carryover to 1997 is computed as follows:

---

[18]The modifications required to arrive at the amount of NOL that can be carried back or forward are in § 172(d).

Taxable income for 1996	$ 40,000
Less: NOL carryback	(170,000)
Taxable income for 1996 after NOL carryback (carryover to 1997)	($ 130,000) ▼

DEDUCTIONS AVAILABLE ONLY TO CORPORATIONS

3 ▼ **LEARNING OBJECTIVE**
Discuss the tax rules unique to corporations.

Dividends Received Deduction. The purpose of the **dividends received deduction** is to mitigate triple taxation. Without the deduction, income paid to a corporation in the form of a dividend would be taxed to the recipient corporation with no corresponding deduction to the distributing corporation. Later, when the recipient corporation paid the income to its individual shareholders, the income would again be subject to taxation with no corresponding deduction to the corporation. The dividends received deduction alleviates this inequity by causing only some or none of the dividend income to be taxable to the recipient corporation.

As the following table illustrates, the amount of the dividends received deduction depends upon the percentage of ownership the recipient corporate shareholder holds in a domestic corporation making the dividend distribution.[19]

Percentage of Ownership by Corporate Shareholder	Deduction Percentage
Less than 20%	70%
20% or more (but less than 80%)	80%
80% or more*	100%

*The payor corporation must be a member of an affiliated group with the recipient corporation.

The dividends received deduction is limited to a percentage of the taxable income of a corporation. For this purpose, taxable income is computed without regard to the NOL, the dividends received deduction, and any capital loss carryback to the current tax year. The percentage of taxable income limitation corresponds to the deduction percentage. Thus, if a corporate shareholder owns less than 20 percent of the stock in the distributing corporation, the dividends received deduction is limited to 70 percent of taxable income. However, the taxable income limitation does not apply if the corporation has an NOL for the current taxable year.[20]

In working with these myriad rules, the following steps are useful:

1. Multiply the dividends received by the deduction percentage.
2. Multiply the taxable income by the deduction percentage.
3. Limit the deduction to the lesser of step 1 or step 2, unless subtracting the amount derived in step 1 from 100 percent of taxable income *generates* an NOL. If so, use the amount derived in step 1. This is referred to as the NOL rule.

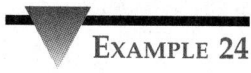
EXAMPLE 24

Red, White, and Blue Corporations are three unrelated calendar year corporations. During the year, they have the following transactions:

---

[19]§ 243(a).   [20]§ 246(b).

	Red Corporation	White Corporation	Blue Corporation
Gross income from operations	$ 400,000	$ 320,000	$ 260,000
Expenses from operations	(340,000)	(340,000)	(340,000)
Dividends received from domestic corporations (less than 20% ownership)	200,000	200,000	200,000
Taxable income before the dividends received deduction	$ 260,000	$ 180,000	$ 120,000

In determining the dividends received deduction, use the three-step procedure described above:

	Red Corporation	White Corporation	Blue Corporation
Step 1 (70% × $200,000)	$140,000	$140,000	$140,000
Step 2			
70% × $260,000 (taxable income)	$182,000		
70% × $180,000 (taxable income)		$126,000	
70% × $120,000 (taxable income)			$ 84,000
Step 3			
Lesser of step 1 or step 2	$140,000	$126,000	
Deduction generates an NOL			$140,000

White Corporation is subject to the 70% of taxable income limitation. It does not qualify for NOL rule treatment since subtracting $140,000 (step 1) from $180,000 (100% of taxable income) does not yield a negative figure. Blue Corporation qualifies for NOL rule treatment because subtracting $140,000 (step 1) from $120,000 (100% of taxable income) yields a negative figure. In summary, each corporation has a dividends received deduction for the year: $140,000 for Red Corporation, $126,000 for White Corporation, and $140,000 for Blue Corporation. ▼

Deduction of Organizational Expenditures.   Expenses incurred in connection with the organization of a corporation normally are chargeable to a capital account. That they benefit the corporation during its existence seems clear. But how can they be amortized when most corporations possess unlimited life? The lack of a determinable and limited estimated useful life would therefore preclude any tax write-off. Section 248 was enacted to solve this problem.

Under § 248, a corporation may elect to amortize **organizational expenditures** over a period of 60 months or more. The period begins with the month in which the corporation begins business.[21] Organizational expenditures *subject to the election* include the following:

- Legal services incident to organization (e.g., drafting the corporate charter, bylaws, minutes of organizational meetings, terms of original stock certificates).
- Necessary accounting services.
- Expenses of temporary directors and of organizational meetings of directors or shareholders, and fees paid to the state of incorporation.

---

[21]The month in which a corporation begins business may not be immediately apparent. See Reg. § 1.248–1(a)(3). For a similar problem in the Subchapter S area, see Chapter 21.

Expenditures that *do not qualify* include those connected with issuing or selling shares of stock or other securities (e.g., commissions, professional fees, and printing costs) or with the transfer of assets to a corporation. Such expenditures reduce the amount of capital raised and are not deductible at all.

To qualify for the election, the expenditures must be *incurred* before the end of the taxable year in which the corporation begins business. In this regard, the corporation's method of accounting is of no consequence. Thus, an expense incurred by a cash basis corporation in its first tax year qualifies even though it is not paid until a subsequent year.

The election is made in a statement attached to the corporation's return for its first taxable year. The return and statement must be filed no later than the due date of the return (including any extensions).

If the election is not made on a timely basis, organizational expenditures cannot be deducted until the corporation ceases to do business and liquidates. These expenditures will be deductible if the corporate charter limits the life of the corporation.

EXAMPLE 25

Black Corporation, an accrual basis taxpayer, was formed and began operations on May 1, 1998. The following expenses were incurred during its first year of operations (May 1 through December 31, 1998):

Expenses of temporary directors and of organizational meetings	$500
Fee paid to the state of incorporation	100
Accounting services incident to organization	200
Legal services for drafting the corporate charter and bylaws	400
Expenses incident to the printing and sale of stock certificates	300

Assume Black Corporation makes a timely election under § 248 to amortize qualifying organizational expenses over a period of 60 months. The monthly amortization is $20 [($500 + $100 + $200 + $400) ÷ 60 months], and $160 ($20 × 8 months) is deductible for tax year 1998. Note that the $300 of expenses incident to the printing and sale of stock certificates does not qualify for the election. These expenses cannot be deducted at all but reduce the amount of the capital realized from the sale of stock. ▼

DETERMINING THE CORPORATE INCOME TAX LIABILITY

CORPORATE INCOME TAX RATES

4 **LEARNING OBJECTIVE**
Compute the corporate income tax.

Corporate income tax rates have fluctuated widely over past years. Refer to the inside front cover of the text for a schedule of the current corporate income tax rates.

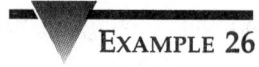

EXAMPLE 26

Gold Corporation, a calendar year taxpayer, has taxable income of $90,000 for 1998. Its income tax liability is $18,850, determined as follows:

Tax on $75,000	$13,750
Tax on $15,000 × 34%	5,100
Tax liability	$18,850

▼

For a corporation that has taxable income in excess of $100,000 for any tax year, the amount of the tax is increased by the lesser of (1) 5 percent of the excess or (2) $11,750. In effect, the additional tax means a 39 percent rate for every dollar of taxable income from $100,000 to $335,000.[22]

EXAMPLE 27

Silver Corporation, a calendar year taxpayer, has taxable income of $335,000 for 1998. Its income tax liability is $113,900, determined as follows:

Tax on $100,000	$ 22,250
Tax on $235,000 × 39%	91,650
Tax liability	$113,900

Note that the tax liability of $113,900 is 34% of $335,000. Thus, due to the 39% rate (34% normal rate + 5% additional tax on taxable income between $100,000 and $335,000), the benefit of the lower rates on the first $75,000 of taxable income completely phases out at $335,000. Note that the normal rate drops back to 34% on taxable income between $335,000 and $10 million. ▼

Qualified PSCs are taxed at a flat 35 percent rate on all taxable income. Thus, they do not enjoy the tax savings of the 15 percent to 34 percent brackets applicable to other corporations. For this purpose, a PSC is a corporation that is substantially employee owned. Also, it must engage in one of the following activities: health, law, engineering, architecture, accounting, actuarial science performing arts, or consulting.

ALTERNATIVE MINIMUM TAX

Corporations are subject to an alternative minimum tax (AMT) that is structured similarly to the AMT applicable to individuals.[23] The AMT for corporations, as for individuals, involves a broader tax base than does the regular tax. Like an individual, a corporation is required to apply a minimum tax rate to the expanded base and to pay the difference between the tentative AMT liability and the regular tax. Many of the adjustments and tax preference items necessary to arrive at alternative minimum taxable income (AMTI) are the same for individuals and corporations. Although the objective of the AMT is the same for individual and corporate taxpayers, the rate and exemptions are different. Refer to Chapter 14 for a detailed discussion of the corporate AMT.

TAX LIABILITY OF RELATED CORPORATIONS

5 ▼ **LEARNING OBJECTIVE**
Explain the tax rules unique to multiple corporations.

Related corporations are subject to special rules for computing the income tax, the accumulated earnings credit, the AMT exemption, and the prior environmental tax exemption.[24] If these restrictions did not exist, the shareholders of a corporation could gain significant tax advantages by splitting a single corporation into *multiple* corporations. The next two examples illustrate the potential *income tax* advantage of multiple corporations.

---

[22]§ 11(b).
[23]Small corporations are not subject to the alternative minimum tax for tax years after 1997. See Chapter 14 for details.

[24]§ 1561(a).

EXAMPLE 28

Gray Corporation annually yields taxable income of $300,000. The corporate tax on $300,000 is $100,250, computed as follows:

Tax on $100,000	$ 22,250
Tax on $200,000 × 39%	78,000
Tax liability	$100,250

▼

EXAMPLE 29

Assume that Gray Corporation in the previous example is divided equally into four corporations. Each corporation would have taxable income of $75,000, and the tax for each (absent the special provisions for related corporations) would be computed as follows:

Tax on $50,000	$ 7,500
Tax on $25,000 × 25%	6,250
Tax liability	$13,750

The total liability for the four corporations would be $55,000 ($13,750 × 4). The savings would be $45,250 ($100,250 − $55,000). ▼

To preclude the advantages that could be gained by using multiple corporations, the tax law requires special treatment for *controlled groups* of corporations. A comparison of Examples 28 and 29 reveals that the income tax savings that could be achieved by using multiple corporations result from having more of the total income taxed at lower rates. To close this potential loophole, the law limits a controlled group's taxable income in the tax brackets below 35 percent to the amount the corporations in the group would have if they were one corporation. Thus, in Example 29, under the controlled corporation rules, only $12,500 (one-fourth of the first $50,000 of taxable income) for each of the four related corporations would be taxed at the 15 percent rate. The 25 percent rate would apply to the next $6,250 (one-fourth of the next $25,000) of taxable income of each corporation. This equal allocation of the $50,000 and $25,000 amounts is required unless all members of the controlled group consent to an apportionment plan providing for an unequal allocation.

Similar limitations apply to the election to expense certain depreciable assets under § 179 (see Chapter 7), to the $250,000 (or $150,000) accumulated earnings credit (see Chapter 20) for controlled groups, and to the $40,000 exemption amount for purposes of computing the AMT (see Chapter 14).

CONTROLLED GROUPS

A **controlled group** of corporations includes parent-subsidiary groups, brother-sister groups, combined groups, and certain insurance companies. Groups of the first three types are discussed in the following sections. Insurance groups are not discussed in this text.

Parent-Subsidiary Controlled Group.   A **parent-subsidiary controlled group** consists of one or more *chains* of corporations connected through stock ownership with a common parent corporation. The ownership connection can be established through either a *voting power test* or a *value test*. The voting power test requires ownership of stock possessing at least 80 percent of the total voting power of all classes of stock entitled to vote.[25]

---

[25]§ 1563(a)(1).

▼ **FIGURE 16–2**
Controlled Groups—
Parent-Subsidiary Corporations

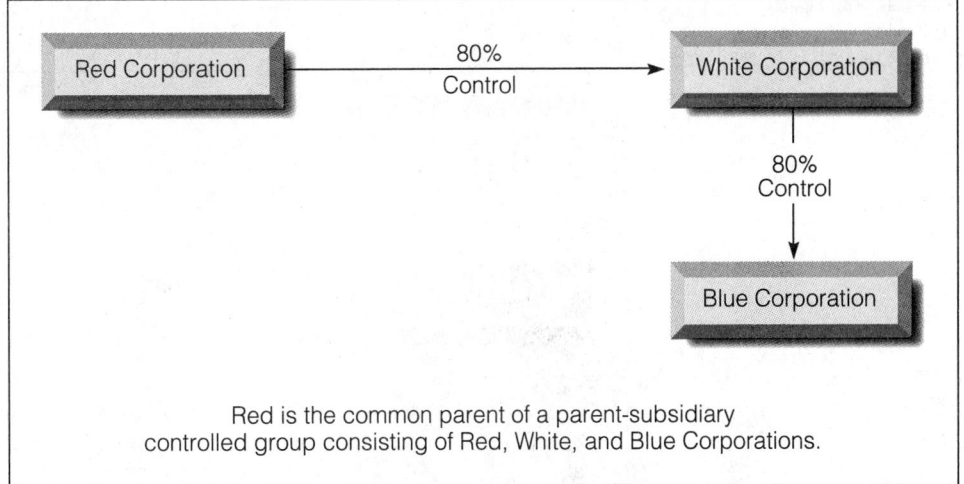

Red is the common parent of a parent-subsidiary
controlled group consisting of Red, White, and Blue Corporations.

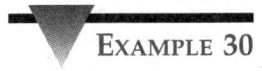

EXAMPLE 30

Acqua Corporation owns 80% of White Corporation. Acqua and White Corporations are members of a parent-subsidiary controlled group. Acqua is the parent corporation, and White is the subsidiary. ▼

The parent-subsidiary relationship illustrated in Example 30 is easy to recognize because Acqua Corporation is the direct owner of White Corporation. Real-world business organizations are often much more complex, sometimes including numerous corporations with chains of ownership connecting them. In these complex corporate structures, determining whether the controlled group classification is appropriate becomes more difficult. The ownership requirements can be met through direct ownership (refer to Example 30) or through indirect ownership, as illustrated in the two following examples.

EXAMPLE 31

Red Corporation owns 80% of the voting stock of White Corporation, and White Corporation owns 80% of the voting stock of Blue Corporation. Red, White, and Blue Corporations constitute a controlled group in which Red is the common parent and White and Blue are subsidiaries. The same result would occur if Red Corporation, rather than White Corporation, owned the Blue Corporation stock. This parent-subsidiary relationship is diagrammed in Figure 16–2. ▼

EXAMPLE 32

Brown Corporation owns 80% of the stock of Green Corporation, which owns 30% of Blue Corporation. Brown also owns 80% of White Corporation, which owns 50% of Blue Corporation. Brown, Green, Blue, and White Corporations constitute a parent-subsidiary controlled group in which Brown is the common parent and Green, Blue, and White are subsidiaries. This parent-subsidiary relationship is diagrammed in Figure 16–3. ▼

The value test requires ownership of at least 80 percent of the total value of all shares of all classes of stock of each of the corporations, except the parent corporation, by one or more of the other corporations.

Brother-Sister Corporations.   A **brother-sister controlled group** *may* exist if two or more corporations are owned by five or fewer *persons* (individuals, estates, or trusts). Brother-sister status will apply if such a shareholder group meets an 80 percent total ownership test *and* a 50 percent common ownership test.[26]

---

[26]§ 1563(a)(2).

▼ FIGURE 16–3
Controlled Groups—
Parent-Subsidiary Corporations

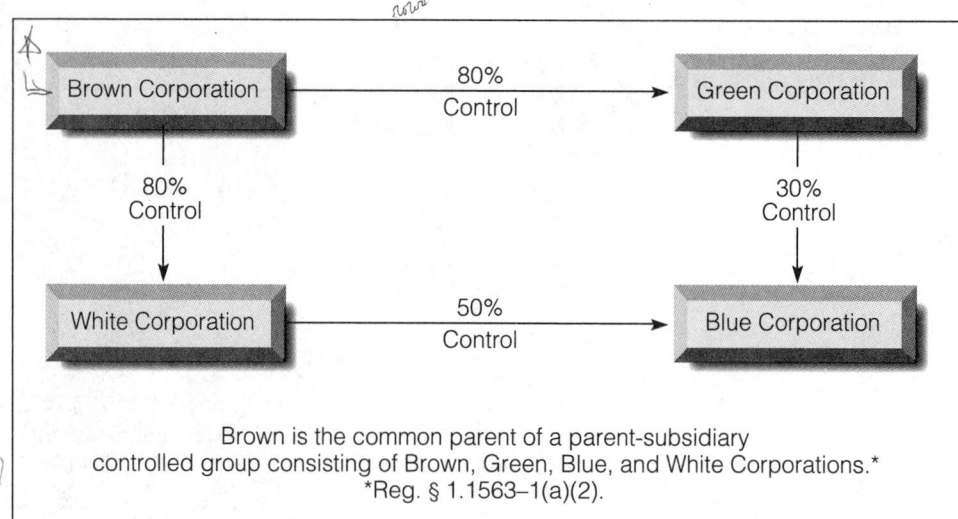

Brown is the common parent of a parent-subsidiary
controlled group consisting of Brown, Green, Blue, and White Corporations.*
*Reg. § 1.1563–1(a)(2).

- The *total* ownership test is met if the shareholder group possesses stock representing at least 80 percent of the total combined voting power of all classes of stock entitled to vote, *or* at least 80 percent of the total value of shares of all classes of stock of each corporation.
- The *common* ownership test is met if the shareholder group owns more than 50 percent of the total combined voting power of all classes of stock entitled to vote, *or* more than 50 percent of the total value of shares of all classes of stock of each corporation.

In applying the common ownership test, the stock held by each person is considered only to the extent that the stock ownership is *identical* for each corporation. That is, if a shareholder owns 30 percent of Silver Corporation and 20 percent of Gold Corporation, such shareholder has identical ownership of 20 percent of each corporation.

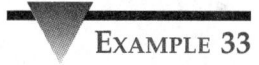

EXAMPLE 33   The outstanding stock of Hawk, Eagle, Crane, and Dove Corporations, each of which has only one class of stock outstanding, is owned by the following unrelated individuals:

	Corporations				Identical
Individuals	**Hawk**	**Eagle**	**Crane**	**Dove**	**Ownership**
Allen	40%	30%	60%	60%	30%
Barton	50%	20%	30%	20%	20%
Carter	10%	30%	10%	10%	10%
Dixon		20%		10%	
Total	100%	100%	100%	100%	60%

Five or fewer individuals (Allen, Barton, and Carter) with more than a 50% common ownership own at least 80% of all classes of stock in Hawk, Eagle, Crane, and Dove. They own 100% of Hawk, 80% of Eagle, 100% of Crane, and 90% of Dove. Consequently, Hawk, Eagle, Crane, and Dove are regarded as members of a brother-sister controlled group. ▼

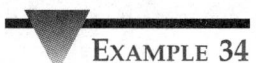

EXAMPLE 34

Changing the facts in Example 33, assume the ownership is as follows:

| | Corporations | | | | Identical Ownership |
Individuals	Hawk	Eagle	Crane	Dove	
Allen	20%	10%	5%	60%	5%
Barton	10%	20%	60%	5%	5%
Carter	10%	70%	35%	25%	10%
Dixon	60%			10%	
Total	100%	100%	100%	100%	20%

In this situation, the identical ownership is only 20%. Consequently, the four corporations are not members of a brother-sister controlled group. However, Eagle and Crane would be brother-sister corporations because both the total ownership and the common ownership tests are met. Allen, Barton, and Carter own 100% of each corporation, and common ownership exceeds 50% (5% by Allen, 20% by Barton, and 35% by Carter). ▼

EXAMPLE 35

The outstanding stock of Black Corporation and Brown Corporation, each of which has only one class of stock outstanding, is owned as follows:

| | Corporations | | Identical Ownership |
Individuals	Black	Brown	
Rossi	55%	100%	55%
Smith	45%		
Total	100%	100%	55%

Although the 50% common ownership test is met, the 80% test is not since there is no common ownership in Brown Corporation. Are Black and Brown brother-sister corporations? No, according to the U.S. Supreme Court.[27] ▼

ETHICAL CONSIDERATIONS

A Bookkeeper's Mistake

You recently agreed to prepare a tax return for Fox Corporation. Fox's bookkeeper, who has little tax experience, has filed a tax return for Fox each year during the corporation's existence. In your discussions with Maria Fox, president and majority shareholder of Fox Corporation, you find that she also owns substantial interests in Wolf Corporation and Coyote Corporation. You also find that two other individuals own stock in each of the three corporations, and that, along with Maria, the group owns 100 percent of all three corporations. Both Wolf and Coyote Corporations have always filed separate returns. What are the tax issues, and what action, if any, should you take?

---

[27]*U.S. v. Vogel Fertilizer Co.*, 82–1 USTC ¶9134, 49 AFTR2d 82–491, 102 S.Ct. 821 (USSC, 1982). See also Reg. § 1.1563–1(a)(3), which was amended to comply with the conclusions reached in *Vogel*.

Combined Groups.   A **combined controlled group** exists if all of the following conditions are met:

- Each corporation is a member of either a parent-subsidiary controlled group or a brother-sister controlled group.
- At least one of the corporations is a parent of a parent-subsidiary controlled group.
- The parent corporation is also a member of a brother-sister controlled group.

EXAMPLE 36

Robert owns 80% of all classes of stock of Red and Orange Corporations. Red Corporation, in turn, owns 80% of all classes of stock of Blue Corporation. Orange owns all the stock of Green Corporation. Red, Blue, Orange, and Green are members of the same combined group. As a result, Red, Blue, Orange, and Green are limited to taxable income in the tax brackets below 35% and the $250,000 (or $150,000) accumulated earnings credit as though they were one corporation. This is also the case for the election to expense certain depreciable business assets under § 179 and the $40,000 exemption for purposes of computing the AMT. ▼

PROCEDURAL MATTERS

FILING REQUIREMENTS FOR CORPORATIONS

6 **LEARNING OBJECTIVE**
Describe the reporting process for corporations.

A corporation must file a Federal income tax return whether it has taxable income or not.[28] A corporation that was not in existence throughout an entire annual accounting period is required to file a return for the fraction of the year during which it was in existence. In addition, a corporation must file a return even though it has ceased to do business if it has valuable claims for which it will bring suit. A corporation is relieved of filing income tax returns only when it ceases to do business and retains no assets.

The corporate return is filed on Form 1120 unless the corporation is a small corporation entitled to file the shorter Form 1120–A. A corporation may file Form 1120–A if it meets all the following requirements:

- Gross receipts or sales are under $500,000.
- Total income (gross profit plus other income including gains on sales of property) is under $500,000.
- Total assets are under $500,000.
- The corporation is not involved in a dissolution or liquidation.
- The corporation is not a member of a controlled group under §§ 1561 and 1563.
- The corporation does not file a consolidated return.
- The corporation does not have ownership in a foreign corporation.
- The corporation does not have foreign shareholders who directly or indirectly own 50 percent or more of its stock.

Corporations electing under Subchapter S (see Chapter 21) file on Form 1120S. Forms 1120, 1120–A, and 1120S are reproduced in Appendix B.

The return must be filed on or before the fifteenth day of the third month following the close of a corporation's tax year. Corporations can receive an automatic extension of six months for filing the corporate return by filing Form 7004

---

[28]§ 6012(a)(2).

by the due date for the return.[29] However, the IRS may terminate the extension by mailing a 10-day notice to the corporation.

ESTIMATED TAX PAYMENTS

A corporation must make payments of estimated tax unless its tax liability can reasonably be expected to be less than $500. The required annual payment (which includes any estimated AMT liability) is the lesser of (1) 100 percent of the corporation's final tax or (2) 100 percent of the tax for the preceding year (if that was a 12-month tax year and the return filed showed a tax liability).[30] Estimated payments can be made in four installments due on or before the fifteenth day of the fourth month, the sixth month, the ninth month, and the twelfth month of the corporate taxable year. The full amount of the unpaid tax is due on the due date of the return.

Failure to make the required estimated tax prepayments results in a nondeductible penalty being imposed on the corporation. The penalty is avoided, however, if any of various exceptions apply.[31]

RECONCILIATION OF TAXABLE INCOME AND FINANCIAL NET INCOME

Schedule M–1 on the last page of Form 1120 is used to reconcile net income as computed for financial accounting purposes with taxable income reported on the corporation's income tax return. The starting point on Schedule M–1 is net income per books (financial accounting net income). Additions and subtractions are entered for items that affect net income per books and taxable income differently. The following items are entered as additions (see lines 2 through 5 of Schedule M–1):

- Federal income tax liability (deducted in computing net income per books but not deductible in computing taxable income).
- The excess of capital losses over capital gains (deducted for financial accounting purposes but not deductible by corporations for income tax purposes).
- Income that is reported in the current year for tax purposes that is not reported in computing net income per books (e.g., prepaid income).
- Various expenses that are deducted in computing net income per books but are not allowed in computing taxable income (e.g., charitable contributions in excess of the 10 percent ceiling applicable to corporations).

The following subtractions are entered on lines 7 and 8 of Schedule M–1:

- Income reported for financial accounting purposes but not included in taxable income (e.g., tax-exempt interest).
- Expenses deducted on the tax return but not deducted in computing net income per books (e.g., a charitable contributions carryover deducted in a prior year for financial accounting purposes but deductible in the current year for tax purposes).

The result is taxable income (before the NOL deduction and the dividends received deduction).

EXAMPLE 37

During the current year, Tern Corporation had the following transactions:

---

[29]§ 6081.
[30]§§ 6655(d) and (e).

[31]See § 6655 for the penalty involved and the various exceptions to it.

Net income per books (after tax)	$92,400
Taxable income	50,000
Federal income tax liability (15% × $50,000)	7,500
Interest income from tax-exempt bonds	5,000
Interest paid on a loan, the proceeds of which were used to purchase the tax-exempt bonds	500
Life insurance proceeds received as a result of the death of a key employee	50,000
Premiums paid on the key employee life insurance policy	2,600
Excess of capital losses over capital gains	2,000

For book and tax purposes, Tern determines depreciation under the straight-line method. Tern's Schedule M–1 for the current year follows.

Schedule M-1 Reconciliation of Income (Loss) per Books With Income per Return (See page 15 of instructions.)

1	Net income (loss) per books	92,400	7	Income recorded on books this year not included on this return (itemize):	
2	Federal income tax	7,500			
3	Excess of capital losses over capital gains	2,000		Tax-exempt interest $ 5,000, Life insurance proceeds on key employee $50,000	55,000
4	Income subject to tax not recorded on books this year (itemize):				
			8	Deductions on this return not charged against book income this year (itemize):	
5	Expenses recorded on books this year not deducted on this return (itemize):			a Depreciation . . . $	
a	Depreciation . . . . $			b Contributions carryover $	
b	Contributions carryover $				
c	Travel and entertainment $ Int. on tax-exempt bonds $500, Prem. on key employee ins. $2,600	3,100	9	Add lines 7 and 8	55,000
6	Add lines 1 through 5	105,000	10	Income (line 28, page 1)—line 6 less line 9	50,000

Schedule M–2 reconciles unappropriated retained earnings at the beginning of the year with unappropriated retained earnings at year-end. Beginning balance plus net income per books, as entered on line 1 of Schedule M–1, less dividend distributions during the year equals ending retained earnings. Other sources of increases or decreases in retained earnings are also listed on Schedule M–2.

EXAMPLE 38 Assume the same facts as in Example 37. Tern Corporation's beginning balance in unappropriated retained earnings is $125,000. During the year, Tern distributed a cash dividend of $30,000 to its shareholders. Based on these further assumptions, Tern's Schedule M–2 for the current year is as follows:

Schedule M-2 Analysis of Unappropriated Retained Earnings per Books (Line 25, Schedule L)

1	Balance at beginning of year	125,000	5 Distributions: a Cash	30,000
2	Net income (loss) per books	92,400	b Stock	
3	Other increases (itemize):		c Property	
			6 Other decreases (itemize):	
			7 Add lines 5 and 6	30,000
4	Add lines 1, 2, and 3	217,400	8 Balance at end of year (line 4 less line 7)	187,400

TAX PLANNING CONSIDERATIONS

7 LEARNING OBJECTIVE
Evaluate corporations for conducting a business.

CORPORATE VERSUS NONCORPORATE FORMS OF BUSINESS ORGANIZATION

The decision to use the corporate form in conducting a trade or business must be weighed carefully. Besides the nontax considerations associated with the corporate form (limited liability, continuity of life, free transferability of interests, centralized management), tax ramifications will play an important role in any such decision. Close attention should be paid to the following:

1. Operating as a regular corporate entity (C corporation) results in the imposition of the corporate income tax. Corporate taxable income will be taxed twice—once as earned by the corporation and again when distributed to the shareholders. Since dividends are not deductible, a closely held corporation has a strong incentive to structure corporate distributions in a deductible form. Thus, profits can be bailed out by the shareholders in the form of salaries, interest, or rents. Such procedures lead to a multitude of problems, one of which, the reclassification of debt as equity, is discussed in Chapter 17. The problems of unreasonable salaries and rents are covered in Chapter 18 in the discussion of constructive dividends.

2. The current tax rates appear to favor corporations over individuals, since corporations have a maximum tax rate of 35 percent and individuals may be subject to a 39.6 percent top rate. Relatively few individuals or corporations are in the top rate brackets, however. For moderate-income taxpayers, the differences in Federal tax brackets between an individual and a corporation may not be substantial. Several state and local governments impose higher taxes on corporations than on individuals. In these jurisdictions, the combined Federal, state, and local tax rates on the two types of taxpayers are practically identical. If a corporation's taxable income does not exceed $100,000, a substantial tax savings may be achieved by accumulating income inside the corporation. Refer to Example 7.

3. Corporate-source income loses its identity as it passes through the corporation to the shareholders. Thus, preferential tax treatment of certain items by the corporation (e.g., interest on municipal bonds) does not carry over to the shareholders.

4. As noted in Chapter 18, it may be difficult for shareholders to recover some or all of their investment in the corporation without an ordinary income result. Most corporate distributions are treated as dividends to the extent of the corporation's earnings and profits.

5. Corporate losses cannot be passed through to the shareholders.[32]

6. The liquidation of a corporation will normally generate tax consequences to both the corporation and its shareholders (see Chapter 19).

7. The corporate form provides shareholders with the opportunity to be treated as employees for tax purposes if the shareholders render services to the corporation. Such status makes a number of attractive tax-sheltered fringe benefits available. They include, but are not limited to, group term life insurance, and excludible meals and lodging. One of the most attractive benefits of incorporation is the ability of the business to provide accident and health insurance to its employees, including shareholders. Such benefits are not included in the employee's gross income. Similar rules apply to other medical costs paid by the employer. These benefits are not available to partners and sole proprietors.

OPERATING THE CORPORATION

Tax planning to reduce corporate income taxes should occur before the end of the tax year. Effective planning can cause income to be shifted to the next tax year and can produce large deductions by incurring expenses before year-end. Particular attention should be focused on the following.

---

[32]Points 1, 2, and 5 could be resolved by making a Subchapter S election (see Chapter 21), assuming the corporation qualifies for the election. In part, the same can be said for point 3.

Charitable Contributions.   Recall that accrual basis corporations may claim a deduction for charitable contributions in the year preceding payment. The contribution must be authorized by the board of directors by the end of the tax year and paid on or before the fifteenth day of the third month of the following year. Even though the contribution may not ultimately be made, it might well be authorized. A deduction cannot be thrown back to the previous year (even if paid within the two and a half months) if it has not been authorized.

Timing of Capital Gains and Losses.   A corporation should consider offsetting profits on the sale of capital assets by selling some of the depreciated securities in the corporate portfolio. In addition, any already realized capital losses should be carefully monitored. Recall that corporate taxpayers are not permitted to claim any net capital losses as deductions against ordinary income. Capital losses can be used only as an offset against capital gains. Further, net capital losses can only be carried back three years and forward five. Gains from the sales of capital assets should be timed to offset any capital losses. The expiration of the carryover period for any net capital losses should be watched carefully so that sales of appreciated capital assets occur before that date.

Net Operating Losses.   In some situations, electing to forgo an NOL carryback and utilizing the carryforward option may generate greater tax savings. When deciding whether to forgo the carryback option, take into account three considerations. First, the time value of the tax refund that is lost by not using the carryback procedure should be calculated. Second, the election to forgo an NOL carryback is irrevocable. Thus, one cannot later choose to change if the predicted high profits do not materialize. Third, consider the future increases (or decreases) in corporate income tax rates that can reasonably be anticipated. This last consideration is the most difficult to work with. Although corporate tax rates have remained relatively stable in recent years, taxpayers have little assurance that future rates will remain constant.

Dividends Received Deduction.   The dividends received deduction is normally limited to the lesser of 70 percent of the qualifying dividends or 70 percent of taxable income. The deduction limits are raised to 80 percent for a dividend received from a corporation in which the recipient owns 20 percent or more but less than 80 percent of the stock. An exception is made when the full deduction yields an NOL. In close situations, therefore, the proper timing of income or deductions to generate an NOL may yield a larger dividends received deduction.

Organizational Expenditures.   To qualify for the 60-month amortization procedure of § 248, only organizational expenditures incurred in the first taxable year of the corporation can be considered. This rule could prove to be an unfortunate trap for corporations formed late in the year.

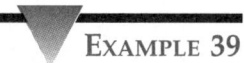

EXAMPLE 39   Thrush Corporation is formed in December 1998. Qualified organizational expenditures are incurred as follows: $2,000 in December 1998 and $3,000 in January 1999. If Thrush uses the calendar year for tax purposes, only $2,000 of the organizational expenditures can be written off over a period of 60 months. ▼

The solution to the problem posed by Example 39 is for Thrush Corporation to adopt a fiscal year that ends at or beyond January 31. All organizational expenditures will then have been incurred before the close of the first taxable year.

CONCEPT SUMMARY 16–1

Income Taxation of Individuals and Corporations Compared

	Individuals	Corporations
Computation of gross income	§ 61.	§ 61.
Computation of taxable income	§ 62 and §§ 63(b) through (h).	§ 63(a). Concept of AGI has no relevance.
Deductions	Trade or business (§ 162); nonbusiness (§ 212); some personal and employee expenses (generally deductible as itemized deductions).	Trade or business (§ 162).
Charitable contributions	Limited in any tax year to 50% of AGI; 30% for long-term capital gain property unless election is made to reduce fair market value of gift.	Limited in any tax year to 10% of taxable income computed without regard to the charitable contribution deduction, NOL carryback, capital loss carryback, and dividends received deduction.
	Excess charitable contributions carried over for five years.	Same as for individuals.
	Amount of contribution is the fair market value of the property; if lower, ordinary income property is limited to adjusted basis; capital gain property is treated as ordinary income property if certain tangible personalty is donated to a nonuse charity or a private nonoperating foundation is the donee.	Same as individuals, but exceptions allowed for certain inventory and for scientific property where one-half of the appreciation also is allowed as a deduction.
	Time of deduction is the year in which payment is made.	Time of deduction is the year in which payment is made unless accrual basis taxpayer. Accrual basis corporation can take deduction in year preceding payment if contribution was authorized by board of directors by end of year and contribution is paid by fifteenth day of third month of following year.
Casualty losses	$100 floor on personal casualty and theft losses; personal casualty losses deductible only to extent losses exceed 10% of AGI.	Deductible in full.
Depreciation recapture under § 1250	Recaptured to extent accelerated depreciation exceeds straight-line.	20% of excess of amount that would be recaptured under § 1245 over amount recaptured under § 1250 is additional ordinary income under § 291.
Net operating loss	Adjusted for several items, including nonbusiness deductions over nonbusiness income and personal exemptions.	Generally no adjustments.
	Carryback period is 2 years and carryforward period is 20 years.	Same as for individuals.

	Individuals	Corporations
Dividends received deduction	None.	70%, 80%, or 100% of dividends received depending on percentage of ownership by corporate shareholder.
Net capital gains	Taxed in full. Tax rate cannot exceed 20% on net long-term capital gains.	Taxed in full.
Capital losses	Only $3,000 of capital loss per year can offset ordinary income; loss is carried forward indefinitely to offset capital gains or ordinary income up to $3,000; short-term carryovers retain their character as short-term; long-term and mid-term losses carry over as mid-term capital losses.	Can offset only capital gains; carried back three years and forward five; carryovers and carrybacks are short-term losses.
Passive losses	Passive activity losses cannot offset either active income or portfolio income.	Passive loss rules apply to closely held C corporations and personal service corporations. For personal service corporations, the rule is the same as for individuals. For closely held C corporations, passive losses may offset active income but not portfolio income.
Tax rates	Progressive with five rates (15%, 28%, 31%, 36%, 39.6%).	Progressive with four rates (15%, 25%, 34%, 35%). Two lowest brackets phased out between $100,000 and $335,000 of taxable income, and additional tax imposed between $15,000,000 and $18,333,333 of taxable income.
Alternative minimum tax	Applied at a graduated rate schedule of 26% and 28%. Exemption allowed depending on filing status (e.g., $45,000 for married filing jointly); phase-out begins when AMTI reaches a certain amount (e.g., $150,000 for married filing jointly).	Applied at a 20% rate on AMTI less exemption; $40,000 exemption allowed but phase-out begins when AMTI reaches $150,000; adjustments and tax preference items are similar to those applicable to individuals, but also include 75% adjusted current earnings adjustment. Small corporations (gross receipts of $5 million or less) are not subject to AMT.

Shareholder-Employee Payment of Corporate Expenses.   In a closely held corporate setting, shareholder-employees often pay corporate expenses (e.g., travel and entertainment) for which they are not reimbursed by the corporation. The IRS often disallows the deduction of these expenses by the shareholder-employee since the payments are voluntary on his or her part. If the deduction is more beneficial at the shareholder-employee level, a corporate policy against reimbursement of such expenses should be established. Proper planning in this regard would be to decide before the beginning of each tax year where the deduction would do the most good. Corporate policy on reimbursement of such expenses could be modified on a year-to-year basis depending upon the circumstances.

In deciding whether corporate expenses should be kept at the corporate level or shifted to the shareholder-employee, the treatment of unreimbursed employee expenses must be considered. First, since employee expenses are itemized deductions, they will be of no benefit to the taxpayer who chooses the standard deduction option. Second, these expenses will be subject to the 2 percent-of-AGI floor. No such limitation will be imposed if the corporation claims the expenses.

RELATED CORPORATIONS

Recall that § 1561 was designed to prevent shareholders from operating a business as multiple corporations to obtain lower tax brackets and multiple accumulated earnings tax credits or AMT exemptions. Corporations in which substantially all the stock is held by five or fewer persons are subject to the provisions of § 1561. Dividing ownership so that control of each corporation does not lie with individuals having common control of all corporations avoids the prohibitions of § 1561.

KEY TERMS

Brother-sister controlled group, 16–23

C corporation, 16–3

Check-the-box Regulations, 16–7

Combined controlled group, 16–26

Controlled group, 16–22

Dividends received deduction, 16–18

Limited liability company (LLC), 16–7

Limited partnerships, 16–6

Organizational expenditures, 16–19

Parent-subsidiary controlled group, 16–22

Passive loss, 16–14

Personal service corporation (PSC), 16–10

Regular corporation, 16–3

Related corporations, 16–21

S corporation, 16–3

Schedule M–1, 16–27

PROBLEM MATERIALS

DISCUSSION QUESTIONS

1. Robin, who owns and operates a sole proprietorship, is considering incorporating her business as a regular corporation. She has asked you to explain how a corporate tax return differs from the return for a sole proprietorship.

2. Edgar owns a sole proprietorship, and Frank is the sole shareholder of a corporation. Both businesses make a profit of $50,000 in 1998. Neither owner withdraws any funds from his business during the year. Discuss the tax treatment of each owner.

3. Art, an executive with Azure Corporation, plans to start a part-time business selling products on the Internet. He will devote about 15 hours each week to running the business. Art's salary from Azure places him in the 39.6% tax bracket. He projects substantial losses from the new business in each of the first three years and expects sizable profits thereafter. Art plans to leave the profits in the business for several years, sell the business, and retire. Would you advise Art to incorporate the business or operate it as a sole proprietorship?

4. Abdul owns 25% of the stock in a C corporation, which earned $100,000 during 1998. He also owns a 25% interest in a partnership, which earned $100,000 during the year. The corporation did not pay any dividends, and the partnership did not make any distributions. Contrast Abdul's tax treatment as a shareholder with his tax treatment as a partner.

5. Rosita, who owns a proprietorship, has scheduled an appointment to talk with you about the advisability of incorporating. At this time, you know nothing about Rosita's business or her existing tax situation. List the questions you will need to ask during the appointment so you can help her make an informed decision.

6. Yolanda is the president and sole shareholder of Canary Corporation. She also lends money and rents a building to the corporation. Discuss how these business relationships between Yolanda and the corporation can help her avoid double taxation.

7. Shareholders in closely held corporations frequently pay themselves large salaries in order to avoid double taxation on corporate income. Explain how this strategy avoids double taxation, but also entails possible pitfalls.

8. Ed and Barbara have formed a new business entity as a limited liability company (LLC). They plan to elect partnership treatment for the LLC. How is this election made?

9. Wren Corporation, a calendar year, cash basis taxpayer, accrues a performance bonus of $50,000 to Brad, a cash basis taxpayer who is the sole shareholder of the corporation. When can Wren deduct the bonus?

10. A taxpayer realized a net long-term capital gain of $10,000 during the year. How is the gain treated if the taxpayer is a corporation? An individual?

11. A taxpayer incurred a net long-term capital loss of $5,000 during the year. How is the loss treated if the taxpayer is a corporation? An individual?

12. John, a sole proprietor, incurs a $5,000 capital loss from the sale of an asset used in his business. Fox Corporation incurs a $5,000 capital loss on the sale of an asset used in its business. How do John and Fox Corporation treat these losses in computing taxable income?

13. A taxpayer sells a warehouse for a gain of $50,000. The warehouse has been depreciated as 15-year property under ACRS. If the straight-line method was used, depreciation recapture will be higher if the taxpayer is a corporation than if the taxpayer is an individual. Explain.

14. On December 30, 1998, Bonnie, a sole proprietor, pledged to make a $10,000 charitable contribution on or before January 15, 1999. Hunter Corporation made a similar pledge on the same date, and the contribution was authorized by Hunter's board of directors. Assuming both Bonnie and Hunter Corporation are calendar year taxpayers, discuss when these contributions will be deductible.

15. Red Corporation owns 78% of the stock of Blue Corporation, which pays Red a substantial dividend each year. Red Corporation plans to acquire an additional 2% of Blue's stock. After acquiring this additional stock, Red Corporation will qualify as Blue Corporation's parent. How will this stock acquisition affect the amount of dividend income that Red Corporation will report for the year?

16. In connection with organizational expenditures, comment on the following:
    a. Those that qualify for amortization.
    b. Those that do not qualify for amortization.
    c. The period over which amortization can take place.
    d. Expenses incurred but not paid by a cash basis corporation.
    e. Expenses incurred by a corporation in its second year of operation.
    f. The alternative if no election to amortize is made.
    g. The timing of the election to amortize.

17. Silver Corporation, which owns stock in Gold Corporation, had net operating income of $150,000 for the year. Gold pays Silver a dividend of $30,000. Under what

circumstances can Silver take a dividends received deduction of $21,000? A dividends received deduction of $30,000?

18. At what level of taxable income does a corporation reach a marginal income tax rate of 35% if it is a PSC? If it is not a PSC? At what level of taxable income does a corporation reach an average income tax rate of 35% if it is not a PSC?

19. Taxable income and financial accounting income for a corporation are seldom the same amount. Discuss some common reasons for differences and how these differences affect the reconciliation of taxable income and financial accounting income on Schedule M–1 of Form 1120.

20. Martin Corporation was organized in 1997 and had profits in 1997 and 1998. The corporation had an NOL in 1999. Under what circumstances should the corporation elect to forgo carrying the NOL back to the two prior years?

PROBLEMS

21. Eagle Company, which was formed in 1998, had operating income of $120,000 and operating expenses of $100,000 in 1998. In addition, Eagle had a long-term capital loss of $3,000. Based on this information, how does Andy, the owner of Eagle Company, report this information on his individual tax return under the following assumptions?
    a. Eagle Company is a corporation and pays no dividends during the year.
    b. Eagle Company is a proprietorship, and Andy does not withdraw any funds from Eagle during the year.

22. Osprey Company had a net loss of $80,000 from merchandising operations in 1998. Mary owns Osprey and works 20 hours a week in the business. She has a large amount of income from other sources and is in the 39.6% marginal tax bracket. Would Mary's tax situation be better if Osprey Company were a proprietorship or a C corporation?

23. Indigo Company has approximately $200,000 in net income in 1998 before deducting any compensation or other payment to its sole owner, Kim. Kim is single. Her income aside from the company's profits is low and would offset her personal exemption and standard deduction. Discuss the tax aspects of each of the following arrangements:
    a. Kim operates Indigo Company as a proprietorship.
    b. Kim incorporates Indigo Company and pays herself a salary of $50,000 and no dividend.
    c. Kim incorporates the company and pays herself a $50,000 salary and a dividend of $108,250 ($150,000 – $41,750 corporate income tax).
    d. Kim incorporates the company and pays herself a salary of $200,000.

24. Mike owns 100% of White Company, which had net operating income of $60,000 in 1998 ($100,000 operating income – $40,000 operating expenses). In addition, White Company had a long-term capital gain of $10,000. Mike has sufficient income from other activities to place him in the 39.6% marginal tax bracket before considering results from White Company. Using this information, explain the tax treatment under the following circumstances:
    a. White Company is a corporation and pays no dividends during the year.
    b. White Company is a corporation and pays Mike $70,000 of dividends during the year.
    c. White Company is a corporation and pays Mike a $70,000 salary during the year.
    d. White Company is a proprietorship, and Mike withdraws $0 during the year.
    e. White Company is a proprietorship, and Mike withdraws $70,000 during the year.

25. In the current year, Hicks, a calendar year taxpayer, suffers a casualty loss of $31,000. How much of the casualty loss will be a tax deduction to Hicks under the following circumstances?

a. Hicks is an individual and has AGI of $80,000. The casualty loss was a personal loss. Hicks recovered insurance of $12,000.

b. Hicks is a corporation. Hicks recovered insurance of $12,000.

26. Benton Company has one owner, who is in the 39.6% Federal income tax bracket. Benton's gross income is $180,000, and its ordinary trade or business deductions are $65,000. It also pays accident and health insurance premiums for the benefit of its owner, in the amount of $3,000 for the current year. Compute the tax liability on Benton's income for 1998 under the following assumptions:

a. Benton Company is operated as a proprietorship, and the owner withdraws $75,000 for personal use.

b. Benton is operated as a corporation, pays out $75,000 as salary, and pays no dividends.

c. Benton is operated as a corporation and pays out no salary or dividends.

d. Benton is operated as a corporation, pays out $75,000 as salary, and pays out the remainder of its earnings as dividends.

e. Assume Robert Benton of 1121 Monroe Street, Ironton, OH 45638 is the owner of Benton Company, which was operated as a proprietorship in 1998. Robert is thinking about incorporating the business in 1999 and asks your advice. He expects about the same amounts of income and expenses in 1999 and plans to take $75,000 per year out of the company whether he incorporates or not. Write a letter to Robert (based on your analysis in [a] and [b] above) containing your recommendations.

27. Tanager Corporation had $400,000 of operating income and $350,000 of operating expenses during the year. In addition, Tanager had a $30,000 long-term capital gain and a $52,000 short-term capital loss.

a. Compute Tanager's taxable income for the year.

b. Assume the same facts as above except that Tanager's long-term capital gain was $64,000. Compute Tanager's taxable income for the year.

28. In 1998, a business sells a capital asset, which it had held for two years, at a loss of $15,000. How much of the capital loss may be deducted in 1998, and how much is carried back or forward under the following circumstances?

a. The business was a sole proprietorship owned by Kim. Kim had a short-term capital gain of $3,000 and a long-term capital gain of $2,000 in 1998. Kim had ordinary net income from the proprietorship of $60,000.

b. The business is incorporated. The corporation had a short-term capital gain of $3,000 and a long-term capital gain of $2,000. Its ordinary net income from the business was $60,000.

29. White Corporation realized net short-term capital gains of $15,000 and net long-term capital losses of $105,000 during 1998. Taxable income from other sources was $400,000. Prior years' transactions included the following:

1994	Net long-term capital gains	$40,000
1995	Net short-term capital gains	18,000
1996	Net long-term capital gains	25,000
1997	Net long-term capital gains	20,000

a. How are the capital gains and losses treated on the 1998 tax return?

b. Compute the capital loss carryback to the carryback years.

c. Compute the amount of capital loss carryover, if any, and designate the years to which the loss may be carried.

30. Falcon (a corporation) purchased residential rental property at a cost of $300,000. Accumulated depreciation in the amount of $174,000 had been correctly claimed on the property when the property was sold for $400,000. Straight-line depreciation would have been $140,000 (using a 15-year recovery period under ACRS). What is the amount of the gain, and how much of it must be reported as ordinary income? As § 1231 gain?

31. Joseph Thompson is president and sole shareholder of Jay Corporation. In December 1998, Joe asks your advice regarding a charitable contribution he plans to have the corporation make to the University of Maine, a qualified public charity. Joe is considering the following alternatives as charitable contributions in December 1998:

	Fair Market Value
(1) Cash donation	$120,000
(2) Unimproved land held for six years ($20,000 basis)	120,000
(3) Maize Corporation stock held for eight months ($20,000 basis)	120,000
(4) Brown Corporation stock held for two years ($170,000 basis)	120,000

Joe has asked you to help him decide which of these potential contributions will be most advantageous taxwise. Jay's taxable income is $3,500,000 before considering the contribution. Rank the four alternatives and write a letter to Joe communicating your advice. The corporation's address is 1442 Main Street, Freeport, ME 04032.

32. Lark Corporation (a calendar year corporation) had the following income and expenses in 1999:

Income from operations	$100,000
Expenses from operations	50,000
Dividends received (less than 20% ownership)	10,000
Charitable contribution	7,000

How much is Lark Corporation's charitable contribution deduction for 1999?

33. Dan Simms is the president and sole shareholder of Simms Corporation, 1121 Madison Street, Seattle, WA 98121. Dan plans for the corporation to make a charitable contribution to the University of Washington, a qualified public charity. He will have the corporation donate Jaybird Corporation stock, held for five years, with a basis of $8,000 and a fair market value of $20,000. Dan projects a $200,000 net profit for Simms Corporation in 1998 and a $100,000 net profit in 1999. Dan calls you on December 5, 1998, and asks whether he should make the contribution in 1998 or 1999. Write a letter advising Dan about the timing of the contribution.

34. During the year, Ruby Corporation (a calendar year taxpayer) has the following transactions:

Income from operations	$300,000
Expenses from operations	375,000
Dividends received from Exxon Corporation	150,000

How much is Ruby Corporation's NOL for the year?

35. In each of the following independent situations, determine the dividends received deduction. Assume that none of the corporate shareholders owns 20% or more of the stock in the corporations paying the dividends.

	Red Corporation	White Corporation	Blue Corporation
Income from operations	$ 700,000	$ 800,000	$ 700,000
Expenses from operations	(600,000)	(900,000)	(740,000)
Qualifying dividends	100,000	200,000	200,000

36. Snipe Corporation was formed on December 1, 1998. Qualifying organizational expenses were incurred and paid as follows:

Incurred and paid in December 1998	$12,000
Incurred in December 1998 but paid in January 1999	6,000
Incurred and paid in February 1999	3,600

Assume Snipe Corporation makes a timely election under § 248 to amortize organizational expenditures over a period of 60 months. What amount may be amortized in the corporation's first tax year under each of the following assumptions?
   a. Snipe Corporation adopts a calendar year and the cash basis of accounting for tax purposes.
   b. Same as (a), except that Snipe Corporation chooses a fiscal year of December 1 through November 30.
   c. Snipe Corporation adopts a calendar year and the accrual basis of accounting for tax purposes.
   d. Same as (c), except that Snipe Corporation chooses a fiscal year of December 1 through November 30.

37. Swallow Corporation, a cash basis and calendar year taxpayer, was formed and began operations on July 1, 1998. Swallow incurred the following expenses during the first tax year of operations (July 1–December 31, 1998):

Expenses of temporary directors and organizational meetings	$2,400
Fee paid to the state of incorporation	1,200
Expenses in printing and sale of stock certificates	900
Legal services for drafting the corporate charter and bylaws (not paid until January of 1999)	3,600
Total	$8,100

If Swallow Corporation makes a timely election under § 248 to amortize qualifying organizational expenses, how much may the corporation deduct for tax year 1998?

38. In each of the following independent situations, determine the corporation's income tax liability. Assume that all corporations use a calendar year for tax purposes and that the tax year involved is 1998.

	Taxable Income
Moose Corporation	$ 44,000
Elk Corporation	246,000
Deer Corporation	1,420,000
Antelope Corporation	22,000,000

39. The outstanding stock in Black and White Corporations, each of which has only one class of stock, is owned by the following unrelated individuals:

	Corporations	
Shareholders	Black	White
Ahmad	20	16
Luis	5	54
Sara	75	30
Total	100	100

a. Determine if a brother-sister controlled group exists.

b. Assume that Luis owns no stock in Black Corporation and Sara owns 80 shares. Would a brother-sister controlled group exist? Why or why not?

40. The outstanding stock of Wren, Robin, Finch, and Jay Corporations is owned by the following unrelated individual and corporate shareholders as follows:

	Corporations			
Shareholders	Wren	Robin	Finch	Jay
Ann	30%	20%	30%	10%
Bob	50%		50%	5%
Carl	20%		20%	
Wren Corporation		80%		

Which corporations, if any, are members of a controlled group?

41. Eagle and Cardinal Corporations both have 100 shares of stock outstanding. Each shareholder paid $500 for his stock in each corporation, and the fair market value of the stock of each corporation is $800 per share. The stock is owned by the following unrelated individuals:

Shareholders	Eagle Shares	Cardinal Shares
George	30	15
Sam	5	50
Tom	65	35
Total	100	100

a. Does a brother-sister controlled group exist?

b. Will a brother-sister controlled group exist if Tom sells 10 of his shares in Cardinal Corporation to Sam?

c. Discuss any tax advantages that will result if Tom sells 10 of his Cardinal shares to Sam.

d. Sam has suggested to Tom that they complete the transaction in (c). Tom asks your advice and says that he is in the 31% marginal bracket. Write a letter to Tom Roland at 3435 Grand Avenue, South Point, OH 45680, explaining the tax advantages that will result if he sells 10 of his Cardinal shares to Sam. Also, identify any problems, both tax and nontax, that the sale could cause for Tom.

42. For 1997, Rose Corporation, an accrual basis, calendar year taxpayer, had net income per books of $172,750 and the following special transactions:

Life insurance proceeds received upon the death of the corporation president	$100,000
Premiums paid on the life insurance policy on the president	10,000
Prepaid rent received and properly taxed in 1996 but credited as rent income in 1997	15,000
Rent income received in 1997 ($10,000 is prepaid and relates to 1998)	25,000
Interest income on tax-exempt bonds	5,000
Interest on loan to carry tax-exempt bonds	3,000
MACRS depreciation in excess of straight-line (straight-line was used for book purposes)	4,000
Capital loss in excess of capital gains	6,000
Federal income tax liability and accrued tax provision for 1997	22,250

Using Schedule M–1 of Form 1120 (the most recent version available), compute Rose Corporation's taxable income for 1997.

43. In January, Don and Steve each invested $100,000 cash to form a corporation to conduct business as a retail golf equipment store. On January 5, they paid Bill, an attorney, to draft the corporate charter, file the necessary forms with the state, and write the bylaws. They leased a building and began to acquire inventory, furniture, display equipment, and office equipment in February. They hired a sales staff and clerical personnel in March and conducted training sessions during the month. They had a successful opening on April 1, and sales increased steadily throughout the summer. The weather turned cold in October, and all local golf courses closed by October 15, which resulted in a drastic decline in sales. Don and Steve expect business to be very good during the Christmas season and then to taper off significantly from January 1 through February 28. The corporation accrued bonuses to Don and Steve on December 31, payable on April 15 of the following year. The corporation made timely estimated tax payments throughout the year. The corporation hired a bookkeeper in February, but he does not know much about taxation. Don and Steve have hired you as a tax consultant and have asked you to identify the tax issues that they should consider.

Research Problems for this chapter appear at the end of Chapter 28.

17

CORPORATIONS: ORGANIZATION AND CAPITAL STRUCTURE

LEARNING OBJECTIVES

After completing Chapter 17, you should be able to:

1. Identify the tax consequences of incorporating a business.

2. Understand the special rules that apply when liabilities are assumed by a corporation.

3. Recognize the basis issues relevant to the shareholder and the corporation.

4. Appreciate the tax aspects of the capital structure of a corporation.

5. Recognize the tax differences between debt and equity investments.

6. Handle the tax treatment of shareholder debt and stock losses.

7. Identify tax planning opportunities associated with organizing and financing a corporation.

Chapter 16 dealt with three principal areas fundamental to working with corporations: (1) determination of whether an entity is a corporation for Federal income tax purposes, (2) tax rules applicable to the day-to-day operation of a corporation, and (3) filing and reporting procedures governing corporations.

Chapter 17 addresses more sophisticated problems in dealing with corporations:

- The tax consequences to the shareholders and the corporation upon the organization of and original transfer of property to the corporation.
- The tax result that ensues when shareholders make transfers of property to a corporation after organization.
- The capital structure of a corporation, including equity and debt financing.
- The tax treatment of investor losses.

ORGANIZATION OF AND TRANSFERS TO CONTROLLED CORPORATIONS

IN GENERAL

1 LEARNING OBJECTIVE
Identify the tax consequences of incorporating a business.

Because gain or loss is realized, property transactions normally have tax consequences. Thus, unless an exception in the Code applies, a transfer of property to a corporation in exchange for stock constitutes a taxable sale or exchange of property. The amount of gain or loss is measured by the difference between the value of the stock received and the tax basis of the property transferred.

The Code, however, does provide special exceptions to the requirement that gain or loss be recognized when a taxpayer's economic status has not changed and the wherewithal to pay is lacking. One such exception is a like-kind exchange. When a taxpayer exchanges property for other property of a like kind, § 1031 provides that gain (or loss) on the exchange is postponed because there has not been a substantive change in the taxpayer's investment. Section 1031 is a deferral mechanism and does not authorize the permanent nonrecognition of gain or loss. The deferral mechanism is accomplished by a carryover of basis. With this carryover of basis, the potential gain or loss on the property given up is recognized when the property received in the exchange is sold.

Another exception to the general rule deals with transfers to controlled corporations. Section 351 provides for the nonrecognition of gain or loss upon the transfer of property to a corporation when certain conditions are met. Section 351 also reflects the principle that gain should not be recognized when a taxpayer's investment has not substantively changed. When a business is incorporated, the owner's economic status remains the same; only the *form* of the investment has changed. The investment in the business assets carries over to the investment in corporate stock. Further, if only stock in the corporation is received, the taxpayer is hardly in a position to pay a tax on any realized gain. As noted later, however, if the taxpayer receives property other than stock (i.e., boot) from the corporation, realized gain may be recognized.

Therefore, the same principles govern the nonrecognition of gain or loss under § 1031 and § 351. With both provisions, gain or loss is postponed until a substantive change in the taxpayer's investment occurs (e.g., a sale to or a taxable exchange with outsiders). In addition, this approach is justified under the wherewithal to pay concept discussed in Chapter 1. Finally, § 351 exists because tax rules should not impede the exercise of sound business judgment (e.g., choice of corporate form of doing business). For example, a taxpayer would think twice about forming a corporation if gain recognition (and the payment of a tax) would always be a consequence.

EXAMPLE 1

Ron is considering incorporating his donut shop in order to obtain the limited liability of the corporate form. Ron realizes that if he incorporates the shop, he will be personally liable only for the debts of the business that he has guaranteed.

If Ron incorporates, the following assets will be transferred to the corporation:

	Tax Basis	Fair Market Value
Cash	$10,000	$ 10,000
Furniture and fixtures	20,000	60,000
Land and building	40,000	100,000
	$70,000	$170,000

If Ron incorporates his business, he will receive the corporation's stock worth $170,000 in exchange for the assets he transfers. Without the nonrecognition provisions of § 351, Ron would recognize a taxable gain of $100,000 on the transfer ($170,000 value of the stock received – $70,000 basis of the assets transferred). Under § 351, however, Ron does not recognize any gain because his economic status has not really changed. Ron's investment in the assets of his unincorporated donut shop is now represented by his ownership of stock in the incorporated donut shop. Thus, § 351 provides for tax neutrality on the incorporation decision. ▼

In a like-kind exchange, the recognition of gain is avoided only to the extent that the taxpayer receives like-kind property. However, the taxpayer must recognize any realized gain when receiving "boot" (i.e., property of an unlike kind, such as cash). For example, if a taxpayer exchanges a truck used in a business for another truck to be used in the business and also receives cash, the taxpayer has the wherewithal to pay an income tax on the cash involved. Further, the taxpayer's economic status has changed to the extent that cash is received. Thus, any realized gain on the exchange is recognized to the extent of the cash received. In like manner, if a taxpayer transfers property to a corporation and receives cash or property other than stock, gain (but not loss) is recognized to the extent of the lesser of the gain realized or the boot received (i.e., the amount of cash and the fair market value of other property received). Any gain recognized is classified (e.g., ordinary, capital) according to the type of assets transferred.[1] As discussed later, the nonrecognition of gain or loss is accompanied by a substituted basis in the shareholder's stock.[2]

EXAMPLE 2

Amanda and Calvin form Quail Corporation. Amanda transfers property with an adjusted basis of $30,000, fair market value of $60,000, for 50% of the stock, worth $60,000. Calvin transfers property with an adjusted basis of $70,000, fair market value of $60,000, for the remaining 50% of the stock. The transfer qualifies under § 351. Amanda has an unrecognized gain of $30,000, and Calvin has an unrecognized loss of $10,000. Both have a substituted basis in the stock in Quail Corporation. Amanda has a basis of $30,000 in her stock, and Calvin has a basis of $70,000 in his stock. Therefore, if either Amanda or Calvin later disposes of the Quail stock in a taxable transaction (e.g., a sale), this deferred gain/loss will then be fully recognized—a $30,000 gain to Amanda and a $10,000 loss to Calvin. ▼

Section 351 is mandatory if a transaction satisfies the provision's requirements. The three requirements for nonrecognition of gain or loss under § 351 are that: (1) *property* is transferred (2) in exchange for *stock* and (3) the property transferors are in *control* of the corporation after the exchange. Therefore, if recognition of gain or loss is *desired*, the taxpayer must plan to fail to meet at least one of these requirements.

PROPERTY DEFINED

Questions have arisen concerning what constitutes **property** for purposes of § 351. In general, the definition of property is comprehensive. For example, unrealized receivables of a cash basis taxpayer and installment obligations are considered property.[3] Although the disposition of an installment note receivable normally triggers deferred gain, its transfer under § 351 is not treated as a disposition. Thus, gain is not recognized to the transferor. Secret processes and formulas, as well as secret information in the general nature of a patentable inventory, also qualify as property under § 351.[4]

However, the Code specifically excludes services rendered from the definition of property. Services are not considered to be property under § 351 for a critical reason. A taxpayer must report as income the fair market value of any consideration received as compensation for services rendered.[5] Consequently, when a taxpayer receives stock in a corporation as consideration for rendering services to the corporation, taxable income results. In this case, the amount of income recognized is equal to the fair market value of the stock received. The taxpayer's basis in the stock received is its fair market value.

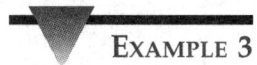
EXAMPLE 3

Ann and Bob form Olive Corporation with the transfer of the following property:

---

[1]§ 351(b) and Rev.Rul. 68–55, 1968–1 C.B. 140.
[2]§ 358(a). See the discussion preceding Example 18.
[3]*Hempt Brothers, Inc. v. U.S.*, 74–1 USTC ¶9188, 33 AFTR2d 74–570, 490 F.2d 1172 (CA–3, 1974), and Reg. § 1.453–9(c)(2).

[4]Rev.Rul. 64–56, 1964–1 C.B. 133.
[5]§§ 61 and 83.

TAX IN THE NEWS

MAKING THE MOST OUT OF STOCK OPTIONS

In certain industries, businesses can enjoy spectacular success. Many high-tech ventures located in the Silicon Valley of California, for example, have achieved amazing growth.

When starting a business in this type of industry, stock options can be included as part of the compensation package to attract promising employees. The prospects of large profits from the exercise of these options can motivate the employees to forgo the larger cash salaries they could obtain elsewhere. Thus, the use of options saves the company much needed start-up capital and allows the recipient employees to share in its equity growth.

The classic example of this type of scenario is Microsoft, whose stock has risen an average 60 percent a year since its founding in 1986.

| | **Property Transferred** | | |
	Basis to Transferor	Fair Market Value	Number of Shares Issued
From Ann:			
Personal services rendered to Olive Corporation	$ –0–	$20,000	200
From Bob:			
Installment obligation	5,000	40,000	
Inventory	10,000	30,000	800
Secret process	–0–	10,000	

The value of each share in Olive Corporation is $100.[6] Ann has income of $20,000 on the transfer because services do not qualify as "property." She has a basis of $20,000 in her 200 shares of Olive. Bob has no recognized gain on the receipt of stock because all of the consideration he transfers to Olive qualifies as "property" and he has "control" of Olive after the transfer (see the discussion below). Bob has a substituted basis of $15,000 in the Olive stock. ▼

STOCK TRANSFERRED

Nonrecognition of gain occurs only when the shareholder receives stock. Stock for this purpose includes both common and most preferred. It does not include "nonqualified preferred stock," which possesses many of the attributes of debt.[7] The Regulations state that the term "stock" does not include stock rights and stock warrants. Otherwise, however, the term "stock" generally needs no clarification.

Thus, under current law, any corporate debt or **securities** (e.g., long-term debt such as bonds) received are treated as boot because they are not an equity interest or stock. Therefore, the receipt of debt in exchange for the transfer of appreciated property to a controlled corporation causes recognition of gain.

---

[6]The value of closely held stock normally is presumed to be equal to the value of the property transferred.

[7]§ 351(g). Examples include stock redeemable within 20 years and whose dividend rate is based on other than corporate performance.

Therefore, gain is recognized up to the fair market value of the nonqualified preferred stock received. See also Reg. § 1.351–1(a)(1)(ii).

CONTROL OF THE CORPORATION

To qualify as a nontaxable transaction under § 351, the property transferors must be in **control** of the corporation immediately after the exchange. Control means that the person or persons transferring the property must have an 80 percent stock ownership in the transferee corporation. More specifically, the transferor shareholders must own stock possessing at least 80 percent of the total combined *voting power* of all classes of stock entitled to vote *and* at least 80 percent of the total *number of shares* of all other classes of stock.[8]

Control Immediately after the Transfer.   Immediately after the exchange, the property transferors must control the corporation. Control can apply to a single person or to several taxpayers if they are all parties to an integrated transaction. When more than one person is involved, the exchange does not necessarily require simultaneous exchanges by those persons. However, the rights of those transferring property to the corporation must be previously set out and determined. Also, the agreement to transfer property should be executed ". . . with an expedition consistent with orderly procedure."[9] Therefore, if two or more persons transfer property to a corporation for stock and want to defer gain, it is helpful if the transfers occur close together in time and are made in accordance with an agreement among the parties.

EXAMPLE 4   Jack exchanges property, basis of $60,000 and fair market value of $100,000, for 70% of the stock of Gray Corporation. The other 30% of the stock is owned by Jane, who acquired it several years ago. The fair market value of Jack's stock is $100,000. Jack recognizes a taxable gain of $40,000 on the transfer because he does not have control of the corporation after his transfer and his transaction cannot be integrated with Jane's for purposes of the control requirement. ▼

EXAMPLE 5   Rebecca, Daryl, and Paige incorporate their businesses by forming Green Corporation. Rebecca exchanges her property for 300 shares in Green on January 5, 1998. Daryl exchanges his property for 400 shares of Green Corporation stock on January 10, 1998, and Paige exchanges her property for 300 shares in Green on March 5, 1998. Because the three exchanges are part of a prearranged plan and the control test is met, the nonrecognition provisions of § 351 apply to all of the exchanges. ▼

Once control has been achieved, it is not necessarily lost if stock received by shareholders is sold or given to persons who are not parties to the exchange shortly after the transaction. However, a different result might materialize if a *plan* for the ultimate disposition of the stock existed *before* the exchange.[10]

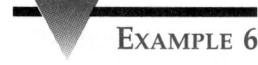

EXAMPLE 6   Naomi and Eric form Eagle Corporation. They transfer appreciated property to the corporation with each receiving 50 shares of the stock. Shortly after the formation, Naomi gives 25 shares to her son. Because Naomi was not committed to make the gift, she is considered to own her original shares of Eagle Corporation stock and, along with Eric, to control Eagle "immediately after the exchange." Therefore, the requirements of § 351 are met, and neither Naomi nor Eric is taxed on the exchange. ▼

---

[8]§ 368(c).
[9]Reg. § 1.351–1(a)(1).

[10]*Wilgard Realty Co. v. Comm.*, 42–1 USTC ¶9452, 29 AFTR 325, 127 F.2d 514 (CA–2, 1942).

ETHICAL CONSIDERATIONS

Intrafamily Transfer Designed to Meet College Costs

Jessie tells you that she has decided to incorporate her extremely successful sole proprietorship, "Tennis and Such," for what she calls "legitimate business reasons." Her plan is to transfer all of her business assets to the new entity in exchange for 85 percent of the corporation's stock. The remaining 15 percent of the stock is to be transferred to her son, Jamal, who will be entering college at the beginning of the next term. Jamal will hold his shares for a short time and then sell them to an independent third party for their fair market value. The sale likely will produce a taxable gain, and the after-tax proceeds will then be available to pay his college tuition. What is Jessie trying to accomplish and is it proper?

Transfers for Property and Services. Nonrecognition treatment for the property transferors may be lost if "too much" stock is transferred to persons who did not contribute property.

EXAMPLE 7

Kate transfers property with a value of $60,000 and a basis of $5,000 for 60% of the stock in newly formed Wren Corporation. Kevin receives 40% of the stock in Wren for services worth $40,000 rendered to the corporation. Both Kate and Kevin have taxable gain on the transaction. Kevin has taxable income of $40,000 because he did not transfer property in exchange for stock. Kate has a taxable gain of $55,000 [$60,000 (fair market value of the stock in Wren Corporation) − $5,000 (basis in the transferred property)] because she, as the sole property transferor, received only 60% of the stock in Wren Corporation. ▼

A person who receives stock both in exchange for services and for property transferred may be treated as a member of the transferring group for purposes of the control test. When this is the case, the person is taxed on the value of the stock issued for services but not on the stock issued for property, assuming the property transferors control the corporation. In this case, all the stock received by the person transferring both property and services is counted in determining whether the transferors acquired control of the corporation.[11]

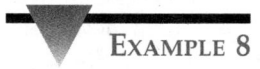

EXAMPLE 8

Assume the same facts as in Example 7 except that Kevin transfers property worth $30,000 (basis of $3,000) in addition to services rendered to the corporation (valued at $10,000). Now Kevin becomes a part of the control group. Kate and Kevin, as property transferors, together received 100% of the stock in Wren Corporation. Consequently, § 351 is applicable to the exchanges. As a result, Kate has no recognized gain. In Kevin's case, he does not recognize gain on the transfer of the property but has taxable income to the extent of the value of the shares issued for services rendered. Kevin has current taxable income of $10,000. ▼

Transfers for Services and Nominal Property. To be a member of the group and aid in qualifying all transferors under the 80 percent control test, the person contributing services must transfer property having more than a "relatively small value" compared to the services performed. The Regulations provide that stock issued for property whose value is relatively small compared to the value of the stock already owned (or to be received for services rendered) will not be treated as issued in return for property. This will be the result

---

[11]Reg. § 1.351–1(a)(2), Ex. 3.

when the primary purpose of the transfer is to qualify the transaction under § 351 for concurrent transferors.[12]

EXAMPLE 9

Rosalyn and Otis transfer property to Redbird Corporation, each in exchange for one-third of the stock. Reed receives the other one-third of the stock for services rendered. The transaction does not qualify under § 351 because Reed is not a member of the group transferring property and Rosalyn and Otis, as the sole property tranferors, together receive only 66⅔% of the stock. As a result, the post-transfer control requirement is not met.

Assume instead that Reed also transfers a substantial amount of property. Then he is a member of the group, and the transaction qualifies under § 351. Reed is taxed on the value of the stock issued for services, but the remainder of the transaction does not trigger gain or loss recognition. However, if the property transferred by Reed is of a relatively small value in comparison to the stock he receives for his services, and the primary purpose for including the property is to cause the transaction to be tax-free for Rosalyn and Otis, the exchange does not qualify under § 351 for any of the taxpayers. ▼

Exactly when a taxpayer who renders services and transfers property is included in the control group is often subject to question. However, the IRS has stated that such a transferor can be included in the control group if the value of the property transferred is at least 10 percent of the value of the services provided.[13] If the value of the property transferred is less than this amount, the IRS will not issue an advance ruling that the exchange meets the requirements of § 351.

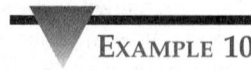

EXAMPLE 10

Sara and Rick form Grouse Corporation. Sara transfers land (worth $100,000, basis of $20,000) for 50% of the stock in Grouse. Rick transfers equipment (worth $50,000, adjusted basis of $10,000) and provides services worth $50,000 for 50% of the stock. Because the relative amount of property transferred is not small compared to the value of the services rendered, Rick's stock in Grouse Corporation is counted in determining control for purposes of § 351; thus, the transferors own 100% of the stock in Grouse. In addition, all of Rick's stock, not just the shares received for the equipment, is counted in determining control. As a result, Sara does not recognize gain on the transfer of the land. Rick, however, must recognize income of $50,000 on the transfer. Even though the transfer of the equipment qualifies under § 351, his transfer of services for stock does not. ▼

Transfers to Existing Corporations.   Once a corporation is in operation, § 351 also applies to any later transfers of property for stock by either new or existing shareholders.

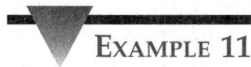

EXAMPLE 11

Tyrone and Seth formed Blue Corporation three years ago. Both Tyrone and Seth transferred appreciated property to Blue in exchange for 50 shares each in the corporation. The original transfers qualified under § 351, and neither Tyrone nor Seth was taxed on the exchange. In the current year, Tyrone transfers property (worth $90,000, adjusted basis of $5,000) for 50 additional Blue shares. Tyrone has a taxable gain of $85,000 on the transfer. The exchange does not qualify under § 351 because Tyrone does not have 80% control of Blue Corporation. (Tyrone has 100 shares of the 150 shares outstanding, or a 66⅔% ownership.) ▼

See the Tax Planning Considerations portion of this chapter for a further discussion of this problem.

---

[12]Reg. § 1.351–1(a)(1)(ii).   [13]Rev.Proc. 77–37, 1977–2 C.B. 568; § 3.07.

ASSUMPTION OF LIABILITIES—§ 357

2 **LEARNING OBJECTIVE**
Understand the special rules that apply when liabilities are assumed by a corporation.

Without special provision, the transfer of mortgaged property to a controlled corporation could trigger gain to the property transferor whether the corporation assumed the mortgage or took property subject to it. This would be consistent with the rule dealing with nontaxable like-kind exchanges under § 1031. Generally, when liabilities are assumed by another party, the party no longer responsible for the debt is treated as having received cash or boot. Section 357(a) provides, however, that when the acquiring corporation **assumes a liability** or takes property subject to a liability in a § 351 transaction, the transfer does *not* result in boot to the transferor shareholder for gain recognition purposes. Nevertheless, liabilities assumed by the transferee corporation are treated as boot in determining the basis of the stock received by the shareholder. The basis of the stock received is reduced by the amount of the liabilities assumed by the corporation. See the more complete discussion of basis computations later.

EXAMPLE 12

Vera transfers property with an adjusted basis of $60,000, fair market value of $100,000, to Oriole Corporation for 100% of the stock in Oriole. The property is subject to a liability of $25,000 that Oriole Corporation assumes. The exchange is tax-free under §§ 351 and 357. However, the basis to Vera of the Oriole stock is $35,000 [$60,000 (basis of property transferred) – $25,000 (amount of mortgage)]. ▼

The general rule of § 357(a) has two exceptions: (1) Section 357(b) provides that if the principal purpose of the assumption of the liabilities is to avoid tax *or* if there is no bona fide business purpose behind the exchange, the liabilities are treated as boot; and (2) Section 357(c) provides that if the sum of the liabilities exceeds the adjusted basis of the properties transferred, the excess is taxable gain.

Exception (1): Tax Avoidance or No Bona Fide Business Purpose.

Unless liabilities are incurred shortly before incorporation, § 357(b) generally poses few problems. A tax avoidance purpose for transferring liabilities to a controlled corporation normally is not a concern in view of the basis adjustment as noted above. Since the liabilities transferred reduce the basis of the stock received, any realized gain merely is deferred and not completely eliminated. Any postponed gain is recognized when and if the stock is disposed of in a taxable sale or exchange.

Satisfying the bona fide business purpose requirement is not difficult if the liabilities were incurred in connection with the transferor's normal course of conducting a trade or business. But this requirement can cause difficulty if the liability is taken out shortly before the property is transferred and the proceeds are utilized for personal purposes.[14] This type of situation is analogous to a cash distribution by the corporation to the shareholder, which is taxed as boot.

EXAMPLE 13

Dan transfers real estate (basis of $40,000 and fair market value of $90,000) to a controlled corporation in return for stock in the corporation. However, shortly before the transfer, Dan mortgages the real estate and uses the $20,000 proceeds to meet personal obligations. Thus, along with the real estate, the mortgage is transferred to the corporation. In this case, the assumption of the mortgage appears to lack a bona fide business purpose. Consequently, the amount of the liability is treated as boot, and Dan has a taxable gain on the transfer of $20,000.[15]

---

[14]See, for example, *Campbell, Jr. v. Wheeler*, 65–1 USTC ¶9294, 15 AFTR2d 578, 342 F.2d 837 (CA–5, 1965).

[15]§ 351(b).

Amount realized:	
Stock	$ 70,000
Release of liability—treated as boot	20,000
Total amount realized	$ 90,000
Less: Basis of real estate	(40,000)
Realized gain	$ 50,000
Recognized gain	$ 20,000

The effect of the application of § 357(b) is to taint *all* liabilities transferred even if some are supported by a bona fide business purpose.

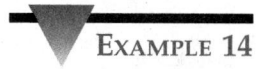

EXAMPLE 14   Tim, an accrual basis taxpayer, incorporates his sole proprietorship. Among the liabilities transferred to the new corporation are trade accounts payable of $100,000 and a MasterCard bill of $5,000. Tim had used the MasterCard to purchase a wedding anniversary gift for his wife. Under these circumstances, all of the $105,000 liabilities are boot and trigger the recognition of gain to the extent gain is realized. ▼

ETHICAL
CONSIDERATIONS

Rectifying a Mistake?

Jean incorporates her sole proprietorship. Inadvertently, she transfers to the new corporation a credit charge for a family dinner she hosted. After the corporation pays the bill, she realizes her mistake and issues a note payable to the corporation in the amount of the charge. Has Jean satisfactorily reconciled her error?

Exception (2): Liabilities in Excess of Basis.   The second exception, § 357(c), provides that if the sum of **liabilities** assumed and the liabilities to which transferred property is subject **exceeds** the total of the adjusted **bases** of the properties transferred, the excess is taxable gain. Without this provision, when liabilities exceed basis in property exchanged, a taxpayer would have a negative basis in the stock received in the controlled corporation.[16] Section 357(c) precludes the negative basis possibility by treating the excess over basis as gain to the transferor.

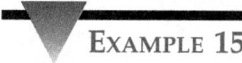

EXAMPLE 15   Andre transfers land and equipment with adjusted tax bases of $35,000 and $5,000, respectively, to a newly formed corporation in exchange for 100% of the stock. The corporation assumes the liability on the transferred properties in the amount of $50,000. Without § 357(c), Andre's basis in the stock of the new corporation would be a negative $10,000 [$40,000 (bases of properties transferred) + $0 (gain recognized) – $0 (boot received) – $50,000 (liability assumed)]. Section 357(c), however, requires Andre to recognize a gain of $10,000 ($50,000 liability assumed – $40,000 bases of assets transferred). As a result, the stock has a zero basis in Andre's hands, determined as follows:

---

[16]*Easson v. Comm.*, 33 T.C. 963 (1960), *rev'd.* in 61–2 USTC ¶9654, 8
AFTR2d 5448, 294 F.2d 653 (CA–9, 1961).

Bases in the properties transferred ($35,000 + $5,000)	$40,000
Add: Gain recognized	10,000
Less: Boot received	–0–
Less: Liability assumed	(50,000)
Basis in the stock received	$ –0–

Thus, Andre recognizes $10,000 of gain, and no negative basis results. ▼

The definition of liabilities under § 357(c) excludes obligations that would have been deductible to the transferor had those obligations been paid before the transfer. Therefore, accounts payable of a cash basis taxpayer are not considered to be liabilities for purposes of § 357(c).

EXAMPLE 16

Tina, a cash basis taxpayer, incorporates her sole proprietorship. In return for all of the stock of the new corporation, she transfers the following items:

	Adjusted Basis	Fair Market Value
Cash	$10,000	$10,000
Unrealized accounts receivable (amounts due to Tina but not yet paid to her)	–0–	40,000
Trade accounts payable	–0–	30,000
Note payable	5,000	5,000

Because the unrealized accounts receivable and trade accounts payable have a zero basis under the cash method of accounting, no income is recognized until the receivables are collected, and no deduction materializes until the payables are satisfied. The note payable has a basis because it was issued for consideration received.

The accounts receivable and the trade accounts payable are disregarded for gain recognition purposes. Thus, for purposes of § 357(c) Tina transfers only cash ($10,000) and a note payable ($5,000) and does not have a problem of liabilities in excess of basis (i.e., liabilities of $5,000 do not exceed the basis in the cash of $10,000). ▼

Conceivably, a situation could arise where both §§ 357(b) and (c) apply in the same transfer. In such a situation, § 357(b) predominates.[17] This could be significant because § 357(b) does not create gain on the transfer, as does § 357(c), but merely converts the liability to boot. Thus, the realized gain limitation continues to apply to § 357(b) transactions.

EXAMPLE 17

Chris forms Robin Corporation by transferring land with a basis of $100,000, fair market value of $1,000,000. The land is subject to a mortgage of $300,000. One month prior to incorporating Robin, Chris borrows $200,000 for personal purposes and gives the lender a second mortgage on the land. Therefore, on the incorporation, Robin issues stock worth $500,000 to Chris and assumes the two mortgages on the land. Section 357(c) seems to apply to the transfer, given that the mortgages on the property ($500,000) exceed the basis of the property ($100,000). Thus, Chris would have a gain of $400,000 under § 357(c). Section 357(b), however, also applies to the transfer because Chris borrowed $200,000 just prior to the transfer and used the $200,000 for personal purposes. Thus, under § 357(b), Chris has boot of $500,000 in the amount of the liabilities (*all* of which are treated as boot). Consequently,

---

[17]§ 357(c)(2)(A).

▼ FIGURE 17–1
Shareholder's Basis in
Stock Received

Adjusted basis of property transferred	$xx,xxx
Plus: Gain recognized	x,xxx
Minus: Boot received (including any liabilities transferred)	(x,xxx)
Equals: Basis of stock received	$xx,xxx

▼ FIGURE 17–2
Corporation's Basis in
Property Received

Adjusted basis of property transferred	$xx,xxx
Plus: Gain recognized by transferor shareholder	xxx
Equals: Basis of property to corporation	$xx,xxx

he has realized gain of $900,000 [$1,000,000 (stock of $500,000 and assumption of liabilities of $500,000) − $100,000 (basis in the land)], and gain is recognized to the extent of the boot of $500,000. Unfortunately for Chris, the relatively more onerous rule of § 357(b) predominates over § 357(c). ▼

BASIS DETERMINATION AND RELATED ISSUES

3 ▲ LEARNING OBJECTIVE
Recognize the basis issues relevant to the shareholder and the corporation.

Recall that § 351(a) postpones gain or loss until the shareholder-transferor disposes of the stock. The postponement of shareholder gain or loss has a corollary effect on the basis of the stock received by the shareholder and the basis of the property received by the corporation. This procedure ensures that any gain or loss postponed under § 351 ultimately will be recognized when the affected asset is disposed of in a taxable transaction.

Basis of Stock to Shareholder. For a taxpayer transferring property to a corporation in a § 351 transaction, the *stock* received in the transfer is given a substituted basis and is the same as the basis the taxpayer had in the property transferred, increased by any gain recognized on the exchange and decreased by boot received. Recall that for basis purposes, boot received includes any liabilities transferred by the shareholder to the corporation. Also note that if the shareholder receives any *other property* (i.e., boot) along with the stock, it takes a basis equal to its fair market value.[18]

Basis of Property to Corporation. The basis of *property* received by the corporation is determined under the carryover basis rules of § 362(a). The basis to the corporation is equal to the basis in the hands of the transferor increased by the amount of any gain recognized to the transferor shareholder.[19]

The basis rules are summarized in Figures 17–1 and 17–2 and illustrated in Examples 18 and 19.

EXAMPLE 18

Kesha and Ned form Brown Corporation. Kesha transfers land (basis of $30,000 and fair market value of $70,000); Ned invests cash ($60,000). They each receive 50 shares in Brown Corporation, worth $60,000, but Kesha also receives $10,000 in cash from Brown. The trans-

---

[18]§ 358(a).   [19]§ 362(a).

fers of property, the realized and recognized gain on the transfers, and the basis of the stock in Brown Corporation to Kesha and Ned are as follows:

	A	B	C	D	E	F
	Basis of Property Transferred	FMV of Stock Received	Boot Received	Realized Gain (B + C − A)	Recognized Gain (Lesser of C or D)	Basis of Stock in Brown (A − C + E)
From Kesha:						
Land	$30,000	$60,000	$10,000	$40,000	$10,000	$30,000
From Ned:						
Cash	60,000	60,000	–0–	–0–	–0–	60,000

Brown Corporation has a basis of $40,000 in the land. The basis to Brown is Kesha's basis of $30,000 plus her recognized gain of $10,000. ▼

EXAMPLE 19

Assume the same facts as in Example 18 except that Kesha's basis in the land is $68,000 (instead of $30,000). Because recognized gain cannot exceed realized gain, the transfer generates only $2,000 of gain to Kesha. The realized and recognized gain and the basis of the stock in Brown Corporation to Kesha are as follows:

	A	B	C	D	E	F
	Basis of Property Transferred	FMV of Stock Received	Boot Received	Realized Gain (B + C − A)	Recognized Gain (Lesser of C or D)	Basis of Stock in Brown (A − C + E)
Land	$68,000	$60,000	$10,000	$2,000	$2,000	$60,000

Brown's basis in the land is $70,000 ($68,000 basis to Kesha + $2,000 gain recognized by Kesha). ▼

Stock Issued for Services Rendered. A transfer of shares for services is not a taxable transaction to a corporation.[20] But another issue arises: Can a corporation deduct the fair market value of the stock it issues in consideration of services as a business expense? Yes, unless the services are such that the payment is characterized as a capital expenditure.[21]

EXAMPLE 20

Esther and Carl form White Corporation. Esther transfers cash of $500,000 for 100 shares of White Corporation stock. Carl transfers property worth $480,000 (basis of $90,000) and agrees to serve as manager of the corporation for one year; in return, Carl receives 100 shares of stock in White. The value of Carl's services to White Corporation is $20,000. Esther's and Carl's transfers qualify under § 351. Neither Esther nor Carl is taxed on the transfer of their property. However, Carl has income of $20,000, the value of the stock received for the services he will render to White Corporation. White has a basis of $90,000 in the property it acquired from Carl, and it may claim a deduction under § 162 for the $20,000 of services Carl will render. ▼

---

[20]Reg. § 1.1032–1(a).
[21]Rev.Rul. 62–217, 1962–2 C.B. 59, modified by Rev.Rul. 74–503, 1974–2 C.B. 117.

EXAMPLE 21

Assume the same facts as in Example 20 except that Carl provides legal services (instead of management services) in organizing the corporation. The value of Carl's legal services is $20,000. Carl has no gain on the transfer of the property but has income of $20,000 for the value of the stock received for the services rendered. White Corporation has a basis of $90,000 in the property it acquired from Carl and must capitalize the $20,000 as an organizational expense. ▼

Holding Period for Shareholder and Transferee Corporation.　In a § 351 transfer, the shareholder's holding period for stock received in exchange for a capital asset or § 1231 property includes the holding period of the property transferred to the corporation. That is, the holding period of the property is "tacked on" to the holding period of the stock. The holding period for stock received for any other property (e.g., inventory or property held primarily for sale) begins on the day after the exchange. The corporation's holding period for property acquired in a § 351 transfer is the holding period of the transferor shareholder, regardless of the character of the property in the transferor's hands.[22]

Recapture Considerations.　In a pure § 351(a) transfer where no gain is recognized, the recapture of accelerated cost recovery rules do not apply.[23] Moreover, any recapture potential associated with the property carries over to the corporation as it steps into the shoes of the transferor-shareholder for purposes of basis determination.

EXAMPLE 22

Paul transfers equipment (adjusted basis of $30,000, original cost of $120,000, and fair market value of $100,000) to a controlled corporation in return for stock. If Paul had sold the equipment, it would have yielded a gain of $70,000, all of which would be recaptured as ordinary income under § 1245. Because the transfer comes within § 351(a), Paul has no recognized gain and no accelerated cost recovery to recapture. However, if the corporation later disposes of the equipment in a taxable transaction, it must take into account the § 1245 recapture potential originating with Paul. ▼

CAPITAL STRUCTURE OF A CORPORATION

CAPITAL CONTRIBUTIONS

4　**LEARNING OBJECTIVE**
Appreciate the tax aspects of the capital structure of a corporation.

When a corporation receives money or property in exchange for capital stock (including treasury stock), neither gain nor loss is recognized by the corporation.[24] Nor does a corporation's gross income include shareholders' contributions of money or property to the capital of the corporation. Moreover, additional money or property received from shareholders through voluntary pro rata transfers also is not income to the corporation. This is the case even though there is no increase in the number of outstanding shares of stock of the corporation. The contributions represent an additional price paid for the shares held by the shareholders and are treated as additions to the operating capital of the corporation.[25]

Contributions by nonshareholders, such as land contributed to a corporation by a civic group or a governmental group to induce the corporation to locate in a

---

[22]§§ 1223(1) and (2).
[23]§§ 1245(b)(3) and 1250(d)(3).

[24]§ 1032.
[25]§ 118 and Reg. § 1.118–1.

particular community, are also excluded from the gross income of a corporation.[26] However, if the property is transferred to a corporation by a nonshareholder in exchange for services or merchandise, then the corporation must recognize income.[27]

EXAMPLE 23

A cable television company charges its customers an initial fee to hook up to a new cable system installed in the area. These payments are used to finance the total cost of constructing the cable facilities. In addition, the customers will make monthly payments for the cable service. The initial payments are used for capital expenditures, but they represent payments for services to be rendered by the cable company. As such, they are taxable income to the cable company and not contributions to capital by nonshareholders. ▼

The basis of property received by a corporation from a shareholder as a **capital contribution** is equal to the basis of the property in the hands of the shareholder increased by any gain recognized to the shareholder on the transfer. The basis of property transferred to a corporation by a nonshareholder as a contribution to capital is zero.

If a corporation receives *money* as a contribution to capital from a nonshareholder, a special rule applies. The basis of any property acquired with the money during a 12-month period beginning on the day the contribution was received is reduced by the amount of the contribution. The excess of money received over the cost of new property reduces the basis of other property held by the corporation and is applied in the following order:

- Depreciable property.
- Property subject to amortization.
- Property subject to depletion.
- All other remaining properties.

The basis of property within each category is reduced in proportion to the relative bases of the properties.[28]

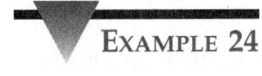

EXAMPLE 24

A city donates land to Teal Corporation as an inducement for Teal to locate in the city. The receipt of the land does not produce taxable income to Teal; however, the land's basis to the corporation is zero. If, in addition, the city pays the corporation $10,000 in cash, the money is not taxable income to the corporation. However, if the corporation purchases property with the $10,000 within the next 12 months, the basis of the acquired property is reduced by $10,000. ▼

DEBT IN THE CAPITAL STRUCTURE

5 **LEARNING OBJECTIVE**
Recognize the tax differences between debt and equity investments.

Advantages of Debt. Significant tax differences exist between debt and equity in the capital structure. The advantages of issuing long-term debt instead of stock are numerous. Interest on debt is deductible by the corporation, while dividend payments are not. Further, loan repayments are not taxable to investors unless the repayments exceed basis. An investment in stock, however, cannot be withdrawn tax-free as long as a corporation has earnings and profits (see Chapter 18). Withdrawals will be deemed to be taxable dividends to the extent of earnings and profits of the distributing corporation.

---

[26]See *Edwards v. Cuba Railroad Co.*, 1 USTC ¶139, 5 AFTR 5398, 45 S.Ct. 614 (USSC, 1925).

[27]Reg. § 1.118–1. See also *Teleservice Co. of Wyoming Valley v. Comm.*, 27 T.C. 722 (1957), *aff'd.* in 58–1 USTC ¶9383, 1 AFTR2d 1249, 254 F.2d 105 (CA–3, 1958), *cert. den.* 78 S.Ct. 1360 (USSC, 1958).

[28]§ 362(a) and Reg. § 1.362–2(b).

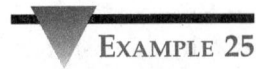

EXAMPLE 25

Wade transfers cash of $100,000 to a newly formed corporation for 100% of the stock. In its initial year, the corporation has net income of $40,000. The income is credited to the earnings and profits account of the corporation. If the corporation distributes $9,500 to Wade, the distribution is a taxable dividend to Wade with no corresponding deduction to the corporation. Assume, instead, that Wade transfers cash of $50,000 for stock. In addition, he transfers cash of $50,000 to the corporation in exchange for a note of the same amount. The note is payable in equal annual installments of $5,000 and bears interest at the rate of 9%. At the end of the year, the corporation pays Wade interest of $4,500 ($50,000 × 9%) and a note repayment of $5,000. The interest payment is deductible to the corporation and taxable to Wade. The $5,000 principal repayment on the note is neither deducted by the corporation nor taxed to Wade. ▼

Reclassification of Debt as Equity (Thin Capitalization Problem). In situations where the corporation is said to be thinly capitalized, the IRS contends that debt is really an equity interest and denies shareholders the tax advantages of debt financing. If the debt instrument has too many features of stock, it may be treated for tax purposes as stock. In that case, the principal and interest payments are considered dividends.

Section 385 lists several factors that *may* be used to determine whether a debtor-creditor relationship or a shareholder-corporation relationship exists. The section authorizes the Treasury to prescribe Regulations that provide more definitive guidelines. To date, the Treasury has not drafted acceptable Regulations. Consequently, taxpayers must rely on judicial decisions to determine whether a true debtor-creditor relationship exists.

For the most part, the principles used to classify debt as equity developed in connection with closely held corporations. Here, the holders of the debt are also shareholders. Consequently, the rules have often proved inadequate for dealing with such problems in large, publicly traded corporations.

Together, Congress, through § 385, and the courts have identified the following factors to be considered in resolving the **thin capitalization** issue:

- Whether the debt instrument is in proper form. An open account advance is more easily characterized as a contribution to capital than a loan evidenced by a properly written note.[29]
- Whether the debt instrument bears a reasonable rate of interest and has a definite maturity date. When a shareholder advance does not provide for interest, the return expected may appear to be a share of the profits or an increase in the value of the shares.[30] Likewise, a lender unrelated to the corporation will usually be unwilling to commit funds to the corporation without a definite due date.
- Whether the debt is paid on a timely basis. A lender's failure to insist upon timely repayment or satisfactory renegotiation indicates that the return sought does not depend upon interest income and the repayment of principal.
- Whether payment is contingent upon earnings. A lender ordinarily will not advance funds that are likely to be repaid only if the venture is successful.
- Whether the debt is subordinated to other liabilities. Subordination tends to eliminate a significant characteristic of the creditor-debtor relationship. Creditors should have the right to share with other general creditors in the event of the corporation's dissolution or liquidation. Subordination also

[29]*Estate of Mixon v. U.S.*, 72–2 USTC ¶9537, 30 AFTR2d 72–5094, 464 F.2d 394 (CA–5, 1972).

[30]*Slappey Drive Industrial Park v. U.S.*, 77–2 USTC ¶9696, 40 AFTR2d 77–5940, 561 F.2d 572 (CA–5, 1977).

destroys another basic attribute of creditor status—the power to demand payment at a fixed maturity date.[31]

- Whether holdings of debt and stock are proportionate. For example, each shareholder owns the same percentage of debt as stock. When debt and equity obligations are held in the same proportion, shareholders are, apart from tax considerations, indifferent as to whether corporate distributions are in the form of interest or dividends.
- Whether funds loaned to the corporation are used to finance initial operations or capital asset acquisitions. Funds used to finance initial operations or to acquire assets the corporation needs in the business are generally obtained through equity investments.
- Whether the corporation has a high ratio of shareholder debt to shareholder equity. Thin capitalization occurs when shareholder debt is high relative to shareholder equity. This indicates the corporation lacks reserves to pay interest and principal on debt when corporate income is insufficient to meet current needs.[32] In determining a corporation's debt-equity ratio, courts look at the relation of the debt both to the book value of the corporation's assets and to their actual fair market value.[33]

Under § 385, the IRS also has the authority to classify an instrument either as *wholly* debt or equity or as *part* debt and *part* equity. This flexible approach is important because some instruments cannot readily be classified either wholly as stock or wholly as debt. It may also provide an avenue for the IRS to address problems in publicly traded corporations.

INVESTOR LOSSES

6 **LEARNING OBJECTIVE**
Handle the tax treatment of shareholder debt and stock losses.

The difference between equity and debt financing involves a consideration of the tax treatment of worthless stock and securities versus that applicable to bad debts.

STOCK AND SECURITY LOSSES

If stocks and bonds are capital assets in the hands of the holder, losses from their worthlessness are governed by § 165(g)(1). Under this provision, a capital loss materializes as of the last day of the taxable year in which the stocks or bonds become worthless. No deduction is allowed for a mere decline in value. The burden of proving complete worthlessness is on the taxpayer claiming the loss. One way to recognize partial worthlessness is to dispose of the stocks or bonds in a taxable sale or exchange.[34] But even then, the **investor loss** is disallowed if the sale or exchange is to a related party.

When the stocks or bonds are not capital assets, worthlessness yields an ordinary loss.[35] For example, if the stocks or bonds are held by a broker for resale to customers in the normal course of business, they are not capital assets. Usually, however, stocks and bonds are held as investments and are capital assets.

---

[31]*Fin Hay Realty Co. v. U.S.*, 68–2 USTC ¶9438, 22 AFTR2d 5004, 398 F.2d 694 (CA–3, 1968).

[32]A court held that a debt-equity ratio of approximately 14.6:1 was not excessive. See *Tomlinson v. 1661 Corp.*, 67–1 USTC ¶9438, 19 AFTR2d 1413, 377 F.2d 291 (CA–5, 1967).

[33]In *Bauer v. Comm.*, 84–2 USTC ¶9996, 55 AFTR2d 84–433, 748 F.2d 1365 (CA–9, 1984), a debt-equity ratio of 92:1 resulted when book

value was used. But the ratio ranged from 2:1 to 8:1 when equity included both paid-in capital and accumulated earnings.

[34]Reg. § 1.165–4(a).

[35]§ 165(a) and Reg. § 1.165–5(b).

Under certain circumstances involving stocks and bonds of affiliated corporations, an ordinary loss is allowed upon worthlessness.[36] A corporation is an affiliate of another corporation if the corporate shareholder owns at least 80 percent of the voting power of all classes of stock entitled to vote and 80 percent of each class of nonvoting stock. Further, to be considered affiliated, the corporation must have derived more than 90 percent of its aggregate gross receipts for all taxable years from sources other than passive income. Passive income for this purpose includes such items as rents, royalties, dividends, and interest.

BUSINESS VERSUS NONBUSINESS BAD DEBTS

In addition to worthlessness of stocks and bonds, the financial demise of a corporation can result in bad debt deductions. These deductions can be either business bad debts or **nonbusiness bad debts.** The distinction between the two types of deductions is important for tax purposes in the following respects:

- Business bad debts are deducted as ordinary losses while nonbusiness bad debts are treated as short-term capital losses.[37] A business bad debt can generate a net operating loss while a nonbusiness bad debt cannot.[38]
- A deduction is allowed for the partial worthlessness of a business debt while nonbusiness debts can be written off only when they become entirely worthless.[39]
- Nonbusiness bad debt treatment is limited to noncorporate taxpayers. However, all of the bad debts of a corporation qualify as business bad debts.[40]

---

[36]§ 165(g)(3).
[37]Compare § 166(a) with § 166(d)(1)(B).
[38]Note the modification required by § 172(d)(2).
[39]Compare § 166(a)(2) with § 166(d)(1)(A).
[40]§ 166(d)(1).

When is a debt business or nonbusiness? Unfortunately, since the Code sheds little light on the matter, the distinction has been left to the courts.[41] In a leading decision, the Supreme Court somewhat clarified the picture when it held that if individual shareholders lend money to a corporation in their capacity as investors, any resulting bad debt is classified as nonbusiness.[42] Nevertheless, the Court did not preclude the possibility of a shareholder-creditor incurring a business bad debt.

If a loan is made in some capacity that qualifies as a trade or business, nonbusiness bad debt treatment is avoided. For example, if an employee, who is also a shareholder, makes a loan to preserve employment status, the loan qualifies for business bad debt treatment.[43] Shareholders also receive business bad debt treatment if they are in the trade or business of lending money or of buying, promoting, and selling corporations.

If the shareholder has multiple motives for making the loan, according to the Supreme Court, the "dominant" or "primary" motive for making the loan controls the classification of the loss.[44]

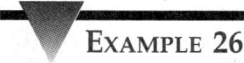

EXAMPLE 26

Norman owns 48% of the stock of Lark Corporation, which he acquired several years ago at a cost of $200,000. Norman is also employed by the corporation at an annual salary of $80,000. At a time when Lark Corporation is experiencing financial problems, Norman lends it $100,000. Subsequently, the corporation becomes bankrupt, and both Norman's stock investment and his loan become worthless. ▼

The loss from Norman's stock investment is treated as a long-term capital loss (assuming § 1244 does not apply, as discussed below). But how is the bad debt classified? If Norman can prove that his dominant or primary reason for making the loan was to protect his salary, a business bad debt deduction results. If not, it is assumed that Norman was trying to protect his stock investment, and nonbusiness bad debt treatment results. Factors to be considered in resolving this matter include the following:

- A comparison of the amount of the stock investment with the trade or business benefit derived. In Example 26, the stock investment of $200,000 is compared with the annual salary of $80,000. In this regard, the salary should be considered as a recurring item and not viewed in isolation. A salary of $80,000 each year means a great deal to a person who has no other means of support and may have difficulty obtaining similar employment elsewhere.
- A comparison of the amount of the loan with the stock investment and the trade or business benefit derived.
- The percentage of ownership held by the shareholder. A minority shareholder, for example, is under more compulsion to lend the corporation money to protect a job than one who is in control of corporate policy.

In summary, it is impossible to conclude whether Norman in Example 26 suffered a business or nonbusiness bad debt without additional facts. Even with such facts, the guidelines are vague. Recall that a taxpayer's intent or motivation is at issue. For this reason, the problem is the subject of frequent litigation.[45]

---

[41]For definitional purposes, § 166(d)(2) is almost as worthless as the debt it purports to describe.

[42]*Whipple v. Comm.*, 63–1 USTC ¶9466, 11 AFTR2d 1454, 83 S.Ct. 1168 (USSC, 1963).

[43]*Trent v. Comm.*, 61–2 USTC ¶9506, 7 AFTR2d 1599, 291 F.2d 669 (CA–2, 1961).

[44]*U.S. v. Generes*, 72–1 USTC ¶9259, 29 AFTR2d 72–609, 92 S.Ct. 827 (USSC, 1972).

[45]See, for example, *Kelson v. U.S.*, 74–2 USTC ¶9714, 34 AFTR2d 74–6007, 503 F.2d 1291 (CA–10, 1974).

SECTION 1244 STOCK

In an exception to the capital treatment that generally results, § 1244 permits ordinary loss treatment for losses on the sale or worthlessness of stock of so-called small business corporations. By placing shareholders on a more nearly equal basis with proprietors and partners in terms of the tax treatment of losses, the provision encourages investment of capital in small corporations. Gain on the sale of § 1244 stock remains capital. Consequently, the shareholder has nothing to lose and everything to gain by complying with § 1244.

Qualification for § 1244.

Only a *small business corporation* can issue qualifying **§ 1244 stock**. To be a small business corporation, the total amount of stock that can be offered under the plan to issue § 1244 stock cannot exceed $1 million. For these purposes, property received in exchange for stock is valued at its adjusted basis, reduced by any liabilities assumed by the corporation or to which the property is subject. The fair market value of the property is not considered. The $1 million limitation is determined by property and money received for the stock as a contribution to capital and as paid-in capital on the date the stock is issued. Consequently, even though a corporation fails to meet these requirements when the stock later is disposed of by the shareholder, the stock can still qualify as § 1244 stock if the requirements were met on the date the stock was issued.

Mechanics of the Loss Deduction.

The amount of ordinary loss deductible in any one year from the disposition of § 1244 stock is limited to $50,000 (or $100,000 for taxpayers filing a joint return with a spouse). If the amount of the loss sustained in the taxable year exceeds these amounts, the remainder is considered a capital loss.

EXAMPLE 27

Harvey acquires § 1244 stock at a cost of $100,000. He sells the stock for $10,000 in the current year. He has an ordinary loss of $50,000 and a capital loss of $40,000. On a joint return, the entire $90,000 loss is ordinary. ▼

Only the original holder of § 1244 stock, whether an individual or a partnership, qualifies for ordinary loss treatment. If the stock is sold or donated, it loses its § 1244 status.

Special treatment applies if § 1244 stock is issued by a corporation in exchange for property that has an adjusted basis above its fair market value immediately before the exchange. For purposes of determining ordinary loss upon a subsequent sale, the stock basis is reduced to the fair market value of the property on the date of the exchange.

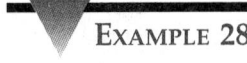

EXAMPLE 28

Dana transfers property with a basis of $10,000 and a fair market value of $5,000 to a corporation in exchange for shares of § 1244 stock. Assuming the transfer qualifies under § 351, the basis of the stock is $10,000, the same as Dana's basis in the property. However, for purposes of § 1244, the stock basis is only $5,000. If the stock is later sold for $3,000, the total loss sustained is $7,000 ($3,000 – $10,000); however, only $2,000 of the loss is ordinary ($3,000 – $5,000). The remaining portion, $5,000, is a capital loss. ▼

Recall the advantages of issuing some debt to shareholders in exchange for cash contributions to a corporation. A disadvantage of issuing debt is that it does not qualify under § 1244. Should the debt become worthless, the taxpayer generally has a short-term capital loss rather than the ordinary loss for § 1244 stock.

GAIN FROM QUALIFIED SMALL BUSINESS STOCK

Shareholders are given special tax relief for gains recognized on the sale or exchange of stock acquired in a **qualified small business corporation.** The holder of **qualified small business stock** may exclude 50 percent of any gain from the sale or exchange of such stock.[46] To qualify for the exclusion, the taxpayer must have held the stock for more than five years and must have acquired the stock as part of an original issue.[47] Only noncorporate shareholders qualify for the exclusion.

A qualified small business corporation is a C corporation whose aggregate gross assets did not exceed $50 million on the date the stock was issued.[48] The corporation must be actively involved in a trade or business. This means that at least 80 percent of the corporation's assets must be used in the active conduct of one or more qualified trades or businesses.

A shareholder can apply the 50 percent exclusion to the greater of (1) $10 million or (2) 10 times the shareholder's aggregate adjusted basis in the qualified stock disposed of during a taxable year.[49]

TAX PLANNING CONSIDERATIONS

7 **LEARNING OBJECTIVE**
Identify tax planning opportunities associated with organizing and financing a corporation.

WORKING WITH § 351

Effective tax planning with transfers of property to corporations requires a clear understanding of § 351 and its related Code provisions. The most important question in planning is simply: Does the desired tax result come from complying with § 351 or from avoiding it?

Utilizing § 351. If the tax-free treatment of § 351 is desired, ensure that the parties transferring property (which includes cash) receive control of the corporation. Simultaneous transfers are not necessary, but a long period of time between transfers could be disastrous if the transfers are not properly documented as part of a single plan. The parties should document and preserve evidence of their intentions. Also, it is helpful to have some reasonable explanation for any delay in the transfers.

To meet the requirements of § 351, mere momentary control on the part of the transferor may not suffice if loss of control is compelled by a prearranged agreement.[50]

EXAMPLE 29

For many years, Paula operated a business as a sole proprietor employing Brooke as manager. To dissuade Brooke from quitting and going out on her own, Paula promised her a 30% interest in the business. To fulfill this promise, Paula transfers the business to newly formed Green Corporation in return for all its stock. Immediately thereafter, Paula transfers 30% of the stock to Brooke. Section 351 probably does not apply to Paula's transfer to Green Corporation because it appears that Paula was under an obligation to relinquish control. However, if this is not the case and the loss of control was voluntary on Paula's part, momentary control would suffice.[51] ▼

---

[46]§ 1202. The 10% and 20% capital gains rates do not apply. Thus, the maximum effective tax rate on the sale of qualified small business stock will be 14% (28% × 50%).

[47]The stock must have been issued after August 10, 1993, which is the effective date of § 1202.

[48]§ 1202(d). Its aggregate assets may not exceed this amount at any time between August 10, 1993, and the date the stock was issued.

[49]§ 1202(b). The amount is $5 million for married taxpayers filing separately.

[50]Rev.Rul. 54–96, 1954–1 C.B. 111.

[51]Compare *Fahs v. Florida Machine and Foundry Co.*, 48–2 USTC ¶9329, 36 AFTR 1161, 168 F.2d 957 (CA–5, 1948), with *John C. O'Connor*, 16 TCM 213, T.C.Memo. 1957–50, *aff'd.* in 58–2 USTC ¶9913, 2 AFTR2d 6011, 260 F.2d 358 (CA–6, 1958).

TAX IN THE NEWS

FINDING BARGAINS IN THE STOCK MARKET

Warren Buffett has amassed a fortune of more than $12 billion from an initial investment of $10,000 in 1956. Buffett has learned to figure a corporation's "intrinsic value"—what the company is worth independent of its market price—and to comb financial statements for firms selling at a huge discount to this value. Buffett likens the value of stock to bonds. A bond's value is the cash flow from future interest payments, discounted back to the present. A stock's worth can be determined in the same manner: it is the discounted value of expected cash flow per share. However, the investor must calculate a stock's "coupon." Buffett tries to find stock whose value is greater than its price. His rules are summarized as follows: pay no attention to the macroeconomic trends or forecasts nor to people's predictions about the future course of stock prices. Focus on long-term business value—on the size of the "coupons" down the road. Stick to stocks within your "circle of competence." Look for managers who treat shareholders' capital with ownerlike care. Study prospects—and their competitors—in great detail. Look at raw data, not analysts' summaries. Trust your own eyes. If you know what a stock is worth—what a corporation is worth—then a falling price quote is no cause for alarm. If you have a conviction about a stock, show courage and buy several shares.

Be sure that later transfers of property to an existing corporation satisfy the control requirement if recognition of gain is to be avoided. In this connection, another transferor's interest cannot be counted if the value of stock received is relatively small compared with the value of stock already owned and the primary purpose of the transfer is to qualify other transferors for § 351 treatment.[52]

Avoiding § 351.   Because § 351 provides for the nonrecognition of gain on transfers to controlled corporations, it is often regarded as a favorable relief provision. In some situations, however, avoiding § 351 may produce a more advantageous tax result. The transferors might prefer to recognize gain on the transfer of property if they cannot be particularly harmed by the gain. For example, they may be in low tax brackets, or the gain may be a capital gain from which substantial capital losses can be offset. The corporation will then have a stepped-up basis in the transferred property.

A transferor might also prefer to avoid § 351 to allow for immediate recognition of a loss. Recall that § 351 provides for the nonrecognition of both gains and losses. A transferor who wishes to recognize loss has several alternatives:

- Sell the property to the corporation for its stock. The IRS could attempt to collapse the "sale," however, by taking the approach that the transfer really falls under § 351.[53] If the sale is disregarded, the transferor ends up with a realized, but unrecognized, loss.
- Sell the property to the corporation for other property or boot. Because the transferor receives no stock, § 351 is inapplicable.

---

[52]Reg. § 1.351–1(a)(1)(ii).
[53]*U.S. v. Hertwig*, 68–2 USTC ¶9495, 22 AFTR2d 5249, 398 F.2d 452
  (CA–5, 1968).

- Transfer the property to the corporation in return for securities. Recall that § 351 does not apply to a transferor who receives securities. In both this and the previous alternatives, watch for the possible disallowance of the loss under the related-party rules.

Suppose the loss property is to be transferred to the corporation and no loss is recognized by the transferor due to § 351. This could present an interesting problem in terms of assessing the economic realities involved.

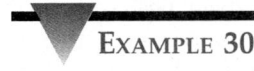

EXAMPLE 30   Iris and Lamont form Wren Corporation with the following investment: property by Iris (basis of $40,000 and fair market value of $50,000) and property by Lamont (basis of $60,000 and fair market value of $50,000). Each receives 50% of the Wren stock. Has Lamont acted wisely in settling for only 50% of the stock? At first, it would appear so, since Iris and Lamont each invested property of the same value ($50,000). But what about tax considerations? Due to the basis carryover rules, the corporation now has a basis of $40,000 in Iris's property and $60,000 in Lamont's property. In essence, Iris has shifted a possible $10,000 gain to the corporation while Lamont has transferred a $10,000 potential loss. With this in mind, an equitable allocation of the Wren stock would call for Lamont to receive a greater percentage interest than Iris. ▼

SELECTING ASSETS TO TRANSFER

When a business is incorporated, the organizers must determine which assets and liabilities should be transferred to the corporation. A transfer of assets that produce passive income (rents, royalties, dividends, and interest) can cause the corporation to be a personal holding company in a tax year when operating income is low. Thus, the corporation could be subject to the personal holding company penalty tax (see the discussion in Chapter 20).

Leasing property to the corporation may be a more attractive alternative than transferring ownership. Leasing provides the taxpayer with the opportunity to withdraw money from the corporation without the payment being characterized as a dividend. If the property is given to a family member in a lower tax bracket, the lease income can be shifted as well. If the depreciation and other deductions available in connection with the property are larger than the lease income, the taxpayer would retain the property until the income exceeds the deductions.

A transfer of the accounts payable of a cash basis taxpayer may prevent the taxpayer from taking a tax deduction when the accounts are paid. These payables should generally be retained. Shareholder debt in a corporation can be given to family members in a lower tax bracket. This technique also causes income to be shifted without a loss of control of the corporation.

DEBT IN THE CAPITAL STRUCTURE

The advantages of debt as opposed to equity have previously been emphasized. To increase debt without incurring the thin capitalization problem, consider the following:

- Preserve the formalities of the debt. This includes providing for written instruments, realistic interest rates, and specified due dates.
- If possible, have the corporation repay the debt when it becomes due. If this is not possible, have the parties renegotiate the arrangement. Try to proceed as a nonshareholder creditor would. It is not unusual, for example, for bondholders of publicly held corporations to extend due dates when default occurs. The alternative is to foreclose and perhaps seriously impair the amount the creditors will recover.

- Avoid provisions in the debt instrument that make the debt convertible to equity in the event of default. These provisions are standard practice when nonshareholder creditors are involved. They serve no purpose if the shareholders are also the creditors and hold debt in proportion to ownership shares.

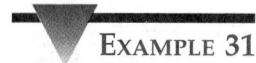

EXAMPLE 31

Gail, Gary, and Grace are equal shareholders in Magenta Corporation. Each transfers cash of $100,000 to Magenta in return for its bonds. The bond agreement provides that the holders will receive additional voting rights in the event Magenta Corporation defaults on its bonds. The voting rights provision is worthless and merely raises the issue of thin capitalization. Gail, Gary, and Grace already control Magenta Corporation, so what purpose is served by increasing their voting rights? The parties probably used a "boilerplate" bond agreement that was designed for third-party lenders (e.g., banks and financial institutions). ▼

- Pro rata holding of debt is difficult to avoid. For example, if each of the shareholders owns one-third of the stock, then each will want one-third of the debt. Nevertheless, some variation is advisable.

EXAMPLE 32

Assume the same facts as Example 31 except that only Gail and Gary acquire the bonds. Grace leases property to Magenta Corporation at an annual rent that approximates the yield on the bonds. Presuming the rent passes the arm's length test (i.e., what unrelated parties would charge), all parties reach the desired result. Gail and Gary withdraw corporate profits in the form of interest income, and Grace is provided for with rent income. Magenta Corporation can deduct both the interest and the rent payments. ▼

- Try to keep the debt-equity ratio within reasonable proportions. A problem frequently arises when the parties form the corporation. Often the amount invested in capital stock is the minimum required by state law. For example, if the state of incorporation permits a minimum of $1,000, limiting the investment to this amount does not provide much safety for later debt financing by the shareholders.
- Stressing the fair market value of the assets rather than their tax basis to the corporation can be helpful in preparing to defend debt-equity ratios.

EXAMPLE 33

Emily, Josh, and Miles form Black Corporation with the following capital investments: cash of $200,000 from Emily; land worth $200,000 (basis of $20,000) from Josh; and a patent worth $200,000 (basis of $0) from Miles. To state that the equity of Black Corporation is $220,000 (the tax basis to the corporation) does not reflect reality. The equity account is more properly stated at $600,000 ($200,000 + $200,000 + $200,000). ▼

- The nature of the business can have an effect on what is an acceptable debt-equity ratio. Capital-intensive industries (e.g., manufacturing, transportation) characteristically rely heavily on debt financing. Consequently, larger debt should be tolerated.

INVESTOR LOSSES

Be aware of the danger of losing § 1244 attributes. Only the original holder of § 1244 stock is entitled to ordinary loss treatment. If, after a corporation is formed, the owner transfers shares of stock to family members to shift income within the family group, the benefits of § 1244 are lost.

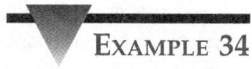

EXAMPLE 34

Norm incorporates his business by transferring property with a basis of $100,000 for 100 shares of stock. The stock qualifies as § 1244 stock. Norm later gives 50 shares each to his children, Susan and Paul. Eventually, the business fails, and the shares of stock become worthless. If Norm had retained the stock, he would have had an ordinary loss deduction of $100,000 (assuming he filed a joint return). Susan and Paul, however, have a capital loss of $50,000 each because the § 1244 attributes were lost (i.e., neither Susan nor Paul was an original holder of the stock). ▼

KEY TERMS

Assumption of liabilities, 17–9

Capital contribution, 17–15

Control, 17–6

Investor losses, 17–17

Liabilities in excess of basis, 17–10

Nonbusiness bad debt, 17–18

Property, 17–4

Qualified small business corporation, 17–21

Qualified small business stock, 17–21

Section 1244 stock, 17–20

Securities, 17–5

Thin capitalization, 17–16

PROBLEM MATERIALS

DISCUSSION QUESTIONS

1. Although the tax consequences of § 351 and § 1031 (like-kind exchange) generally parallel each other, they differ in one major respect. What is this difference?

2. Under what circumstances will gain and/or loss be recognized on a § 351 transfer?

3. Why are services not treated as property under § 351?

4. George agrees to serve as the tax accountant for newly formed Blue Corporation. In compensation for the services rendered, Blue will issue 25 shares of stock to George. What is the tax effect to George from this transaction?

5. Several entrepreneurs plan to form a corporation to construct a housing project. Travis, the party who will be contributing the land for the project, wants more security than shareholder status provides. He is contemplating two possibilities: receive corporate bonds for his land, or take out a mortgage on the land before transferring it to the corporation for stock. Comment on the tax effects of the choices Travis is considering. What other alternatives can you suggest?

6. What is the control requirement of § 351? Describe the effect of the following in satisfying this requirement:
   a. A shareholder renders services to the corporation for stock.
   b. A shareholder both renders services and transfers property to the corporation for stock.
   c. A shareholder has only momentary control after the transfer.
   d. A long period of time elapses between the transfers of property by different shareholders.

7. Marvin and June form Warbler Corporation. They transfer appreciated property to the corporation with each receiving 50 shares of the Warbler stock. If Marvin gives his shares to his daughter immediately after the exchange, is the exchange taxable?

8. Paul and Mary transfer property to Falcon Corporation, each in exchange for one-third of Falcon's stock. Matt receives the other one-third of Falcon's stock for services rendered. Will the exchanges be taxable?

9. May a transferor who receives stock for both property and services be included in the control group in determining whether an exchange meets the requirements of § 351? Explain.

10. At a point when Robin Corporation has been in existence for six years, shareholder Ted transfers real estate (adjusted basis of $20,000 and fair market value of $100,000) to the corporation for additional stock. At the same time, Peggy, the other shareholder, acquires one share of stock for cash. After the two transfers, the percentages of stock ownership are as follows: 79% by Ted and 21% by Peggy.
    a. What were the parties trying to accomplish?
    b. Will it work? Explain.

11. A taxpayer transfers mortgaged property to a controlled corporation and recognizes gain. How does the mortgage affect the transferor shareholder's basis in stock received?

12. Does the transfer of mortgaged property to a controlled corporation trigger gain to the extent of the mortgage? Explain.

13. Keith's sole proprietorship includes assets that, if sold, would yield a gain of $100,000. It also includes assets that would yield a loss of $30,000. Keith incorporates his business using only the gain assets. Two days later, Keith sells the loss assets to the newly formed corporation. What is Keith trying to accomplish, and will his effort be successful? Explain.

14. Why does the application of § 357(c) cause gain to be recognized? Why is this not the case with § 357(b)?

15. In arriving at the basis of stock received by a shareholder in a § 351 transfer, discuss how each of the following affects the calculation:
    a. The receipt of "other property" (i.e., boot) by the shareholder in addition to stock.
    b. The shareholder transferring a liability to the corporation along with property.
    c. The shareholder's basis in the property transferred to the corporation.

16. When, if ever, can a corporation deduct the value of the stock it issues for the rendition of services?

17. A corporation acquires property as a contribution to capital from a shareholder and from a nonshareholder. Are the basis rules the same? Explain.

18. In structuring the capitalization of a corporation, what are the advantages of utilizing debt rather than equity?

19. In determining whether the debt of a corporation should be reclassified as stock, comment on the relevance of the following:
    a. The loan is on open account.
    b. The loan is a demand loan.
    c. Although the loan has a definite maturity date, the corporation has not made payments on a timely basis.
    d. Payments on the loan are contingent upon corporate earnings.
    e. The corporation's shareholders lent funds to the corporation in the same proportion as their shareholdings, and the debt was used to purchase a new building.
    f. The corporation has a debt-equity ratio of 5:1.

20. Assuming § 1244 does not apply, what is the tax treatment of stock that has become worthless?

21. Emily incorporates her sole proprietorship, but does not transfer the building the business uses to the corporation. Subsequently, the building is leased to the corporation for an annual rental. What tax reasons might Emily have for not transferring the building to the corporation when the business was incorporated?

PROBLEMS

22. Cecil and Edie form Heron Corporation with the following investment:

| | Property Transferred | | |
	Basis to Transferor	Fair Market Value	Number of Shares Issued
From Cecil—			
Cash	$ 40,000	$ 40,000	
Installment obligation	140,000	360,000	40
From Edie—			
Cash	140,000	140,000	
Equipment	120,000	180,000	60
Patent	4,000	280,000	

The installment obligation has a face amount of $360,000 and was acquired last year from the sale of land held for investment purposes (adjusted basis of $140,000).

a. How much gain, if any, must Cecil recognize?
b. What is Cecil's basis in the Heron Corporation stock?
c. What is Heron Corporation's basis in the installment obligation?
d. How much gain, if any, must Edie recognize?
e. What is Edie's basis in the Heron Corporation stock?
f. What is Heron Corporation's basis in the equipment and the patent?
g. How would your answer change if Cecil received common stock and Edie received preferred stock?
h. How would your answer change if Edie were a partnership?

23. Brad, Otis, Wade, and Andrea form Teal Corporation with the following investment:

| | Property Transferred | | |
	Basis to Transferor	Fair Market Value	Number of Shares Issued
From Brad—			
Personal services rendered to Teal Corporation	$ –0–	$ 30,000	30
From Otis—			
Equipment	345,000	300,000	270*
From Wade—			
Cash	60,000	60,000	
Unrealized accounts receivable	–0–	90,000	150
From Andrea—			
Land & building	210,000	450,000	
Mortgage on land & building	300,000	300,000	150

*Otis receives $30,000 in cash in addition to the 270 shares.

The mortgage transferred by Andrea is assumed by Teal Corporation. The value of each share of Teal Corporation stock is $1,000.

a. What, if any, is Brad's recognized gain or loss?
b. What is Brad's basis in the Teal Corporation stock?
c. How much gain or loss must Otis recognize?
d. What is Otis's basis in the Teal Corporation stock?
e. What is Teal Corporation's basis in the equipment?
f. What, if any, is Wade's recognized gain or loss?
g. What is Wade's basis in the Teal Corporation stock?
h. What is Teal Corporation's basis in the unrealized accounts receivable?
i. How much gain or loss must Andrea recognize?

j. What is Andrea's basis in the Teal stock?

k. What is Teal Corporation's basis in the land and building?

24. Sam, Seth, Pat, and Kelly form Lark Corporation with the following investment:

| | Property Transferred | | |
	Basis to Transferor	Fair Market Value	Number of Shares Issued
From Sam—			
Inventory	$30,000	$96,000	30*
From Seth—			
Equipment ($30,000 of depreciation taken by Seth in prior years)	45,000	99,000	30**
From Pat—			
Secret process	15,000	90,000	30
From Kelly—			
Cash	30,000	30,000	10

*Sam receives $6,000 in cash in addition to the 30 shares.
**Seth receives $9,000 in cash in addition to the 30 shares.

Assume the value of each share of Lark Corporation stock is $3,000.

a. What, if any, is Sam's recognized gain or loss? How is any such gain or loss treated?

b. What is Sam's basis in the Lark Corporation stock?

c. What is Lark Corporation's basis in the inventory?

d. How much gain or loss must Seth recognize? How is the gain or loss treated?

e. What is Seth's basis in the Lark Corporation stock?

f. What is Lark Corporation's basis in the equipment?

g. What, if any, is Pat's recognized gain or loss?

h. What is Pat's basis in the Lark Corporation stock?

i. What is Lark Corporation's basis in the secret process?

j. How much income, if any, must Kelly recognize?

k. What is Kelly's basis in the Lark Corporation stock?

25. Jane, Jon, and Clyde incorporate their respective businesses and form Starling Corporation. Jane exchanges her property, basis of $50,000 and value of $200,000, for 200 shares in Starling Corporation on March 1 of the current year. Jon exchanges his property, basis of $70,000 and value of $300,000, for 300 shares in Starling a month and a half later on April 15. Clyde transfers his property, basis of $90,000 and value of $500,000, for 500 shares in Starling on May 10 of the current year.

a. If the three exchanges are part of a prearranged plan, what gain will each of the parties recognize on the exchanges?

b. Assume Jane and Jon exchanged their property for stock four years ago while Clyde transfers his property for 500 shares in the current year. The transfer is not part of a prearranged plan with Jane and Jon to incorporate their businesses. What gain will Clyde recognize on the transfer?

c. If the property that Clyde contributes has a basis of $590,000 instead of $90,000, how would you advise the parties to structure the transaction?

26. Lee exchanges property, basis of $20,000 and fair market value of $500,000, for 65% of the stock of Pelican Corporation. The other 35% is owned by Abby, Lee's daughter, who acquired her stock last year. What are the tax issues?

27. Kate transfers property worth $400,000 (basis of $50,000) to Crow Corporation in exchange for 50% of Crow's stock. Kevin transfers a secret process worth $300,000 (zero basis) and services for 50% of Crow's stock. Kevin's services relate to his acquisition of the process and a letter of credit. The letter of credit (worth $100,000 according to

Kevin) states that the newly formed Crow Corporation could obtain a loan to develop the process. What are the tax issues?

28. Perry organized Cardinal Corporation 10 years ago by contributing property worth $1 million, basis of $200,000, for 2,000 shares of stock in Cardinal, representing 100% of the stock in the corporation. Perry later gave each of his children, Brittany and Julie, 500 shares of stock in Cardinal Corporation. In the current year, Perry transfers property worth $320,000, basis of $100,000, to Cardinal for 500 shares in the corporation. What gain, if any, will Perry recognize on this transfer?

29. Ann and Bob form Robin Corporation. Ann transfers property worth $420,000 (basis of $150,000) for 70 shares in Robin Corporation. Bob receives 30 shares for property worth $165,000 (basis of $30,000) and for legal services in organizing the corporation; the services are worth $15,000.
    a. What gain, if any, will the parties recognize on the transfer?
    b. What basis do Ann and Bob have in the stock in Robin Corporation?
    c. What is Robin Corporation's basis in the property and services it received from Ann and Bob?

30. Assume in Problem 29 that the property Bob transfers to Robin Corporation is worth $15,000 (basis of $3,000) and his services in organizing the corporation are worth $165,000. What are the tax consequences to Ann, Bob, and Robin Corporation?

31. Brady transfers property with an adjusted basis of $150,000, fair market value of $1,200,000, to Swift Corporation for 100% of the stock. The property is subject to a liability of $180,000, which Swift assumes. What is the basis of the Swift stock to Brady? What is the basis of the property to Swift Corporation?

32. Three years ago, Chris exchanged an apartment worth $1,500,000 (basis of $300,000), which was subject to a mortgage of $200,000, for land worth $1,150,000, subject to a mortgage of $150,000, and cash of $300,000. In the current year, Chris transfers the land that he received in the exchange to newly formed Amber Corporation for all the stock in Amber. Amber Corporation assumes the original mortgage on the land, currently in the amount of $100,000, and another mortgage in the amount of $20,000 that Chris later places on the land to secure his purchase of some equipment that he uses in his business. What are the tax issues?

33. Sara and Jane form Wren Corporation. Sara transfers property, basis of $25,000 and value of $200,000, for 50 shares in Wren Corporation. Jane transfers property, basis of $10,000 and value of $185,000, and agrees to serve as manager of Wren for one year; in return Jane receives 50 shares in Wren. The value of Jane's services to Wren is $15,000.
    a. What gain do Sara and Jane recognize on the exchange?
    b. What is Wren Corporation's basis in the property transferred by Sara and Jane? How does Wren treat the value of the services Jane renders?

34. Assume in Problem 33, that Jane receives the 50 shares of Wren Corporation stock in consideration for the appreciated property and for providing legal services in organizing the corporation. The value of Jane's services is $15,000.
    a. What gain does Jane recognize?
    b. What is Wren Corporation's basis in the property transferred by Jane? How does Wren treat the value of the services Jane renders?

35. The city of Tucson donates land to Rose Corporation as an inducement for Rose to locate there. The land is worth $100,000. The city also donates $50,000 in cash to Rose.
    a. What income, if any, must Rose recognize as a result of the transfer of land and cash to it by Tucson?
    b. What is Rose's basis in the land?
    c. If Rose purchases property six months later with the $50,000 cash, what basis will it have in the property? If Rose uses $25,000 of its funds along with the $50,000 provided by the city to purchase property costing $75,000, what basis will it have in the property?

36. Emily Patrick (2624 Holkham Drive, Ivy, VA 22945) formed Teal Corporation a number of years ago with an investment of $200,000 cash, for which she received $20,000 in stock and $180,000 in bonds bearing interest of 8% and maturing in nine years. Several years later, Emily lent the corporation an additional $50,000 on open account. In the current year, Teal Corporation becomes insolvent and is declared bankrupt. During the corporation's existence, Emily was paid an annual salary of $60,000. Write a letter to Emily in which you explain how she would treat her losses for tax purposes.

37. Sam, a single taxpayer, acquired stock in a corporation that qualified as a small business corporation under § 1244, at a cost of $100,000 three years ago. He sells the stock for $10,000 in the current tax year. How will the loss be treated for tax purposes?

38. Ann formed Dove Corporation four years ago with an investment of $200,000 for which she received 100% of the stock in Dove. Two years later when Dove was experiencing financial difficulty, Ann loaned Dove $50,000 and received in exchange bonds bearing 9% interest and maturing in five years. Last year she loaned Dove an additional $20,000 on open account. In the current year, Dove is insolvent and is adjudged bankrupt. As president of Dove Corporation, Ann has received an annual salary of $40,000. What are the tax issues in determining the tax treatment of Ann's loss in her investment in Dove and in the amounts she has loaned to Dove?

39. Sam Sanders, a married taxpayer who files a joint return with his wife, acquired stock in a corporation that qualified as a small business corporation under § 1244. The stock cost $100,000 and was acquired three years ago. A few months after he acquired the stock he gave it to his brother, Mike Sanders. The stock was worth $100,000 on the date of the gift. Mike, who is married and files a joint return with his wife, sells the stock for $10,000 in the current tax year. You represent Mike who asks you whether he can take a loss deduction on the sale of the stock. If so, how will the loss be treated for tax purposes? Prepare a letter to your client and a memo to the file. Mike's address is 2600 Riverview Drive, Plank, MO 63701.

40. Troy transfers property with a basis of $40,000 and a fair market value of $20,000 to Thrush Corporation in exchange for shares of § 1244 stock. (Assume the transfer qualifies under § 351.)
    a. What is the basis of the stock to Troy?
    b. What is the basis of the stock for purposes of § 1244 to Troy?
    c. If Troy sells the stock for $10,000 two years later, how will the loss be treated for tax purposes?

41. Frank, Cora, and Mitch are equal shareholders in Blue Corporation. The corporation's assets have a tax basis of $50,000 and a fair market value of $600,000. In the current year, Frank and Cora each loan Blue Corporation $150,000. The notes to Frank and Cora bear interest of 8% per annum. Mitch leases equipment to Blue Corporation for an annual rental of $12,000. Discuss whether the shareholder loans from Frank and Cora might be reclassified as equity. Consider in your discussion whether Blue Corporation has an acceptable debt-equity ratio.

Research Problems for this chapter appear at the end of Chapter 28.

CORPORATIONS: DISTRIBUTIONS NOT IN COMPLETE LIQUIDATION

LEARNING OBJECTIVES

After completing Chapter 18, you should be able to:

1. Identify and understand the concept of earnings and profits.

2. Recognize the importance of earnings and profits in measuring the recipient shareholder's dividend income.

3. Understand the tax impact of property dividends on the recipient shareholder and the corporation making the distribution.

4. Understand the nature and treatment of constructive dividends.

5. Distinguish between taxable and nontaxable stock dividends and stock rights.

6. Identify various stock redemptions that are treated as sales or exchanges of stock rather than as dividend income.

7. Identify tax planning opportunities available to minimize the tax impact in corporate distributions, constructive dividends, and stock redemptions.

Chapter 17 examined the tax consequences of corporate formation. In this chapter and Chapter 19, the focus shifts to the tax treatment of corporate distributions. As will become apparent in the subsequent discussion, the tax treatment of corporate distributions varies, depending on a variety of considerations such as the following:

- The availability of earnings to be distributed.
- The basis of the stock in the hands of the shareholder.
- The character of the property being distributed.
- Whether the shareholder gives up ownership in return for the distribution.
- Whether the distribution is liquidating or nonliquidating in character.

Generally, the corporation cannot deduct distributions made to shareholders, but it may recognize gain on distributions of appreciated property. Losses may also be recognized if a liquidating property distribution is made (see Chapter 19). In contrast, shareholders may be required to treat distributions as ordinary income, capital gain, or a nontaxable recovery of capital.

Since distributions provide no deduction to the paying corporation and often trigger income to shareholders, a double tax results. The possibility of a double tax often raises the tax treatment of distributions to an issue of prime importance when dealing with corporations.

This chapter discusses the tax rules related to nonliquidating distributions (in the form of cash and property). Distributions of stock and stock rights are also addressed. Finally, the discussion concludes with a review of the tax treatment of stock redemptions. Chapter 19 continues the discussion with coverage of corporate liquidations.

TAXABLE DIVIDENDS—IN GENERAL

To the extent that a distribution is made from corporate earnings and profits (E & P), the shareholder is deemed to receive a dividend, taxed as ordinary income. E & P (defined later in this chapter) is allocated to distributions on a pro rata basis, using both the E & P of the corporation accumulated since February 28, 1913, and the current-year E & P.[1] Generally, corporate distributions are presumed to be dividends, taxed as ordinary income, unless the parties to the transaction can show otherwise.

The portion of a corporate distribution that is not taxed as a dividend (because of insufficient E & P) is nontaxable to the extent of the shareholder's basis in the stock. The stock basis is reduced accordingly. The excess of the distribution over the shareholder's basis is treated as a capital gain if the stock is a capital asset.[2]

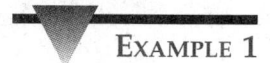

EXAMPLE 1

At the end of the year, Amber Corporation has E & P of $30,000. On this date, the corporation distributes cash of $40,000 to its two *equal* shareholders, Bob and Bonnie. The adjusted basis of the shareholders' stock investment is $8,000 for Bob and $4,000 for Bonnie. The $40,000 distribution should be accounted for as follows:

	Bob	**Bonnie**
Amount distributed	$ 20,000	$ 20,000
Portion from E & P (taxed as a dividend)	(15,000)	(15,000)
	$ 5,000	$ 5,000
Return of capital (reduction of basis)	(5,000)	(4,000)
	$ –0–	$ 1,000
Capital gain	(–0–)	(1,000)
	$ –0–	$ –0–

Thus, of the $20,000 Bob receives, $15,000 is dividend income and $5,000 is a nontaxable return of capital. After the distribution, Bob has a basis in the Amber Corporation stock of $3,000 ($8,000 original adjusted basis – $5,000 return of capital). As to Bonnie, the result is $15,000 of dividend income, $4,000 of nontaxable return of capital, and $1,000 of capital gain. After the distribution, Bonnie has a basis in the Amber stock of $0 ($4,000 original adjusted basis – $4,000 return of capital). ▼

EARNINGS AND PROFITS (E & P)

1   LEARNING OBJECTIVE
Identify and understand the concept of earnings and profits.

The Code does not define the term **earnings and profits.** Although E & P is similar in some respects to the accounting concept of retained earnings, E & P and retained earnings are often not the same.

E & P fixes the upper limit on the amount of dividend income that shareholders must recognize as a result of a distribution by the corporation. In this sense, E & P represents the corporation's economic ability to pay a dividend without impairing its capital. Thus, the effect of a specific transaction on the E & P account may be determined by considering whether or not the transaction increases or decreases the corporation's capacity to pay a dividend.

---

[1]§ 316.   [2]§ 301(c).

COMPUTATION OF E & P

To compute E & P in any year, certain adjustments are made to taxable income
with the aim of making it conform more closely to the corporation's economic
income. Both cash basis and accrual basis corporations use the same approach
when determining E & P.[3]

Additions to Taxable Income.   It is necessary to add all previously excluded
income items back to taxable income to determine current E & P. Included among
these positive adjustments are interest on municipal bonds, excluded life insurance
proceeds (in excess of cash surrender value), Federal income tax refunds from tax
paid in prior years, and the dividends received deduction.

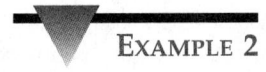

EXAMPLE 2

A corporation collects $100,000 on a key employee life insurance policy (the corporation is
the owner and beneficiary of the policy). At the time the policy matured on the death of
the insured employee, it possessed a cash surrender value of $30,000. None of the $100,000
is included in the corporation's taxable income, but $70,000 is added to taxable income when
computing current E & P (i.e., amount collected on the policy net of its cash surrender
value). ▼

Subtractions from Taxable Income.   Some of the corporation's nondeductible
expenditures are subtracted from taxable income to arrive at E & P. These negative
adjustments include related-party losses, excess capital losses, expenses incurred
to produce tax-exempt income, Federal income taxes paid, nondeductible key employee life insurance premiums (net of increases in cash surrender value), and
nondeductible fines and penalties.

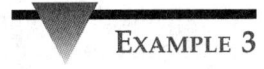

EXAMPLE 3

A corporation sells property (basis of $10,000) to its sole shareholder for $8,000. Because of
§ 267 (disallowance of losses on sales between related parties), the $2,000 loss cannot be
deducted in arriving at the corporation's taxable income. But since the overall economic
effect of the transaction is a decrease in the corporation's assets by $2,000, the loss reduces
the current E & P for the year of sale. ▼

---

[3]Section 312 contains most of the adjustments necessary to determine
E & P. It accomplishes this by setting out the effect of a number
of transactions on E & P. Regulations relating to E & P begin at
Reg. § 1.312–6.

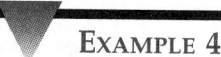

EXAMPLE 4   A corporation pays a $10,000 premium on a key employee life insurance policy covering the life of its president. As a result of the payment, the cash surrender value of the policy is increased by $7,000. Although none of the $10,000 premium is deductible for tax purposes, current E & P is reduced by $3,000 (i.e., amount of the premium payment net of the increase in the cash surrender value). ▼

Some E & P adjustments shift the effect of a transaction from the year of its inclusion in taxable income to the year in which it has an economic effect on the corporation. Charitable contribution carryovers, net operating loss carryovers, and capital loss carryovers all serve as examples of this kind of adjustment.

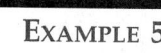

EXAMPLE 5   During 1998, a corporation makes charitable contributions, $12,000 of which cannot be deducted in arriving at the taxable income for the year because of the 10% taxable income limitation. However, the $12,000 is carried forward to 1999 and fully deducted in that year. The excess charitable contribution reduces the corporation's current E & P for 1998 by $12,000 and increases its current E & P for 1999, when the deduction is allowed, by a like amount. The increase in E & P in 1999 is necessary because the charitable contribution carryover reduces the taxable income for that year (the starting point for computing E & P) and already has been taken into account in determining the E & P for 1998. ▼

Other Adjustments.   In addition to the above adjustments, accounting methods used for determining E & P are generally more conservative than those allowed under the income tax. For example, the installment method is not permitted for E & P purposes. Thus, an adjustment is required for the deferred gain attributable to sales of property made during the year under the installment method. In particular, all principal payments are treated as having been received in the year of sale.[4]

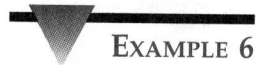

EXAMPLE 6   In 1998, Cardinal Corporation, a calendar year taxpayer, sells unimproved real estate (basis of $20,000) for $100,000. Under the terms of the sale, beginning in 1999, Cardinal will receive two annual payments of $50,000 each with interest of 9%. Cardinal Corporation does not elect out of the installment method. Since Cardinal's taxable income for 1998 will not reflect any of the gain from the sale, the corporation must make an $80,000 positive adjustment for 1998 (the deferred profit component). Similarly, negative adjustments will be required in 1999 and 2000 (when the deferred profit is recognized under the installment method). ▼

The alternative depreciation system (ADS) must be used for purposes of computing E & P.[5] This method requires straight-line depreciation over a recovery period equal to the Asset Depreciation Range (ADR) midpoint life.[6] Thus, if MACRS cost recovery is used for income tax purposes, a positive or negative adjustment equal to the difference between MACRS and ADS must be made each year. Likewise, when assets are disposed of, an additional adjustment to taxable income is required to allow for the difference in gain or loss resulting from the difference in income tax basis and E & P basis.[7] The adjustments arising from depreciation are illustrated in the following example.

---

[4]§ 312(n)(5).

[5]§ 312(k)(3)(A).

[6]See § 168(g)(2). The ADR midpoint life for most assets is set out in Rev.Proc. 87–56, 1987–2 C.B. 674. The recovery period is 5 years for automobiles and light-duty trucks and 40 years for real property.

For assets with no class life, the recovery period is 12 years. Any amount expensed under § 179 is deducted over a period of 5 years in computing E & P. See § 312(k)(3)(B).

[7]§ 312(f)(1).

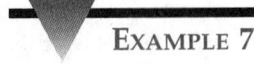

EXAMPLE 7

On January 2, 1996, White Corporation purchased for $30,000 equipment with an ADR midpoint life of 10 years that was then depreciated under MACRS. The asset was sold on July 2, 1998, for $27,000. For purposes of determining taxable income and E & P, cost recovery claimed on the equipment is summarized as follows:

Year	Cost Recovery Computation	MACRS	ADS	Adjustment Amount
1996	$30,000 × 14.29%	$ 4,287		
	$30,000 ÷ 10-year ADR recovery period × ½ (half-year for first year of service)		$1,500	$2,787
1997	$30,000 × 24.49%	7,347		
	$30,000 ÷ 10-year ADR recovery period		3,000	4,347
1998	$30,000 × 17.49% × ½ (half-year for year of disposal)	2,624		
	$30,000 ÷ 10-year ADR recovery period × ½ (half-year for year of disposal)		1,500	1,124
	Total cost recovery	$14,258	$6,000	$8,258

Each year White Corporation will increase taxable income by the adjustment amount indicated above to determine E & P. In addition, when computing E & P for 1998, White will also reduce taxable income by $8,258 to account for the excess gain recognized for income tax purposes, as shown below.

	Income Tax	E & P
Amount realized	$ 27,000	$ 27,000
Adjusted basis for income tax ($30,000 cost – $14,258 MACRS)	(15,742)	
Adjusted basis for E & P ($30,000 cost – $6,000 ADS)		(24,000)
Gain on sale	$ 11,258	$ 3,000
Adjustment amount ($3,000 – $11,258)	($ 8,258)	

Gains and losses from property transactions generally affect the determination of E & P only to the extent that they are recognized for tax purposes. Thus, gains and losses deferred under the like-kind exchange provision and deferred involuntary conversion gains do not affect E & P until recognized. Accordingly, no adjustment is required for these items.

A variety of other adjustments are also required to determine current E & P. For example, cost depletion is required for E & P purposes, so an adjustment must be made to taxable income in cases where percentage depletion is used. Similarly, the percentage of completion method is required for E & P purposes when accounting for long-term contracts, so an adjustment is required when the completed contract method is employed. Intangible drilling costs and mine exploration and development costs may be deducted currently for income tax purposes, but must be capitalized for E & P. Once capitalized, these expenditures

CONCEPT SUMMARY 18–1

E & P Adjustments

Nature of the Transaction	Effect on Taxable Income in Arriving at Current E & P	
	Addition	Subtraction
Tax-exempt income	X	
Collection of proceeds from insurance policy on life of corporate officer	X	
Deferred gain on installment sale (all gain is added to E & P in year of sale)	X	
Future recognition of installment sale gross profit		X
Excess capital loss and excess charitable contribution (over 10% limitation) in year incurred		X
Deduction of charitable contribution, NOL, or capital loss carryovers in succeeding taxable year (increases E & P because deduction reduces taxable income while E & P was reduced in a prior year)	X	
Federal income taxes paid		X
Federal income tax refund	X	
Loss on sale between related parties		X
Nondeductible fines and penalties		X
Payment of premiums on insurance policy on life of corporate officer (in excess of increase in cash surrender value of policy)		X
Realized gain (not recognized) on an involuntary conversion	No effect	
Realized gain or loss (not recognized) on a like-kind exchange	No effect	
Percentage depletion (only cost depletion can reduce E & P)	X	
Accelerated depreciation (E & P is reduced only by straight-line, units-of-production, or machine hours depreciation)	X	
Intangible drilling costs deducted currently (reduce E & P in future years by amortizing costs over 60 months)	X	
Mine exploration and development costs (reduce E & P in future years by amortizing costs over 120 months)	X	

can be amortized under the E & P rules over 60 months for intangible drilling costs and over 120 months for mining exploration and development costs.[8]

SUMMARY OF E & P ADJUSTMENTS

Recall that E & P serves as a measure of the earnings of the corporation that are available for distribution as taxable dividends to the shareholders. Current E & P is determined by making a series of adjustments to the corporation's taxable income. These adjustments are reviewed in Concept Summary 18–1. Other items that affect

---

[8]§ 312(n)(2).

E & P, such as property dividends and stock redemptions, are covered later in the chapter and are not included in Concept Summary 18–1.

CURRENT VERSUS ACCUMULATED E & P

Accumulated E & P is the total of all previous years' current E & P (since February 28, 1913) as computed on the first day of each tax year, reduced by distributions made from E & P. It is important to distinguish between **current E & P** and **accumulated E & P,** since the taxability of corporate distributions depends upon how these two accounts are allocated to each distribution made during the year. A complex set of rules governs the allocation process.[9] These rules are described in the following section and summarized in Concept Summary 18–2.

ALLOCATING E & P TO DISTRIBUTIONS

2   LEARNING OBJECTIVE
Recognize the importance of earnings and profits in measuring the recipient shareholder's dividend income.

When a positive balance exists in both the current and accumulated E & P accounts, corporate distributions are deemed to be made first from current E & P and then from accumulated E & P. When distributions exceed the amount of current E & P, it becomes necessary to allocate current and accumulated E & P to each distribution made during the year. Current E & P is allocated on a pro rata basis to each distribution. Accumulated E & P is applied in chronological order, beginning with the earliest distribution. As can be seen in the following example, this allocation is important if any shareholder sells stock during the year.

EXAMPLE 8

As of January 1 of the current year, Black Corporation has accumulated E & P of $10,000. Current E & P for the year amounts to $30,000. Megan and Matt are sole *equal* shareholders of Black from January 1 to July 31. On August 1, Megan sells all of her stock to Helen. Black makes two distributions to shareholders during the year: $40,000 to Megan and Matt ($20,000 each) on July 1, and $40,000 to Matt and Helen ($20,000 each) on December 1. Current and accumulated E & P are allocated to the two distributions as follows:

	Source of Distribution		
	Current E & P	Accumulated E & P	Return of Capital
July 1 distribution ($40,000)	$15,000	$10,000	$15,000
December 1 distribution ($40,000)	15,000	—	25,000

Thus, since 50% of the total distributions are made on July 1 and December 1, respectively, one-half of current E & P is allocated to each of the two distributions. Accumulated E & P is applied in chronological order, so the entire amount is attributed to the July 1 distribution. The tax consequences to the shareholders are presented below:

---

[9]Regulations relating to the source of a distribution are at Reg. § 1.316–2.

		Shareholder	
	Megan	Matt	Helen
July distribution ($40,000)			
Dividend income—			
From current E & P ($15,000)	$ 7,500	$ 7,500	$ –0–
From accumulated E & P ($10,000)	5,000	5,000	–0–
Return of capital ($15,000)	7,500	7,500	–0–
December distribution ($40,000)			
Dividend income—			
From current E & P ($15,000)	–0–	7,500	7,500
From accumulated E & P ($0)	–0–	–0–	–0–
Return of capital ($25,000)	–0–	12,500	12,500
Total dividend income	$12,500	$20,000	$ 7,500
Nontaxable return of capital (presuming sufficient basis in the stock investment)	$ 7,500	$20,000	$12,500

Because the balance in the accumulated E & P account is exhausted when it is applied to the July 1 distribution, Megan has more dividend income than Helen, even though both receive equal distributions during the year. In addition, each shareholder's basis is reduced by the nontaxable return of capital; any excess over basis results in capital gain. ▼

When the tax years of the corporation and its shareholders are not the same, it may be impossible to determine the amount of current E & P on a timely basis. For example, if shareholders use a calendar year and the corporation uses a fiscal year, then current E & P may not be ascertainable until after the shareholders' returns have been filed. To address this timing problem, the allocation rules presume that current E & P is sufficient to cover every distribution made during the year unless or until the parties can show otherwise.

EXAMPLE 9

Green Corporation uses a fiscal year of July 1 through June 30 for tax purposes. Carol, Green's only shareholder, uses a calendar year. As of July 1, 1998, Green Corporation has a zero balance in its accumulated E & P account. For fiscal year 1998–1999, the corporation suffers a $5,000 operating loss. On August 1, 1998, Green distributes $10,000 to Carol. The distribution is dividend income to Carol and is reported when she files her income tax return for the 1998 calendar year, on or before April 15, 1999. Because Carol cannot prove until June 30, 1999 that the corporation has a deficit for the 1998–1999 fiscal year, she must assume the $10,000 distribution is fully covered by current E & P. When Carol learns of the deficit, she can file an amended return for 1998 showing the $10,000 as a return of capital. ▼

Additional difficulties arise when either the current or the accumulated E & P account has a deficit balance. In particular, when current E & P is positive and accumulated E & P has a deficit balance, accumulated E & P is *not* netted against current E & P. Instead, the distribution is deemed to be a taxable dividend to the extent of the positive current E & P balance.

EXAMPLE 10

At the beginning of the current year, Brown Corporation has a deficit of $30,000 in accumulated E & P. For the year, it has current E & P of $10,000 and distributes $5,000 to its shareholders. The $5,000 distribution is treated as a taxable dividend since it is deemed to have been made from current E & P. This is the case even though Brown Corporation still has a deficit in accumulated E & P at the end of the year. ▼

Allocating E & P to Distributions

1. Current E & P is allocated first to distributions on a pro rata basis; then, accumulated E & P is applied (to the extent necessary) in chronological order beginning with the earliest distribution.
2. Unless and until the parties can show otherwise, it is presumed that current E & P covers all distributions.
3. When a deficit exists in accumulated E & P and a positive balance exists in current E & P, distributions are regarded as dividends to the extent of current E & P.
4. When a deficit exists in current E & P and a positive balance exists in accumulated E & P, the two accounts are netted at the date of distribution. If the resulting balance is zero or a deficit, the distribution is treated as a return of capital, first reducing the basis of the stock to zero, then generating capital gain. If a positive balance results, the distribution is a dividend to the extent of the balance. Any loss is allocated ratably during the year unless the parties can show otherwise.

In contrast to the above rule, when a deficit exists in current E & P and a positive balance exists in accumulated E & P, the accounts are netted at the date of distribution. If the resulting balance is zero or a deficit, the distribution is a return of capital. If a positive balance results, the distribution is a dividend to the extent of the balance. Any loss is allocated ratably during the year unless the parties can show otherwise.

EXAMPLE 11

At the beginning of the current year, Gray Corporation (a calendar year taxpayer) has accumulated E & P of $10,000. During the year, the corporation incurs a $15,000 net loss from operations that accrues ratably. On July 1, Gray distributes $6,000 in cash to Hal, its sole shareholder. To determine how much of the $6,000 cash distribution represents dividend income to Hal, the balances of both accumulated and current E & P as of July 1 are determined and netted. This is necessary because of the deficit in current E & P.

	Source of Distribution	
	Current E & P	**Accumulated E & P**
January 1		$10,000
July 1 (½ of $15,000 net loss)	($7,500)	2,500
July 1 distribution—$6,000:		
. Dividend income: $2,500		
Return of capital: $3,500		

The balance in E & P on July 1 is $2,500. Thus, of the $6,000 distribution, $2,500 is taxed as a dividend, and $3,500 represents a return of capital. ▼

PROPERTY DIVIDENDS—IN GENERAL

3   LEARNING OBJECTIVE
Understand the tax impact of property dividends on the recipient shareholder and the corporation making the distribution.

The previous discussion assumed that all distributions by a corporation to its shareholders are in the form of cash. Although most corporate distributions are cash, a corporation may distribute a **property dividend** for various reasons. The shareholders could want a particular property that is held by the corporation. Or, a corporation that is strapped for cash may want to distribute a dividend to its shareholders.

STOCK BUYBACKS CONTINUE TO GROW

Publicly held companies are finding that buying back their own stock is a good way to reward their shareholders. According to the Securities Data Company of Newark, New Jersey, 1995 yielded a record 1,108 stock buyback announcements. Not only did the number of stock buybacks increase, but the dollar value of the buybacks exploded from $20 billion in 1991 to $99 billion in 1995. The recent increase in stock buybacks can be attributed to a number of factors, including the long-standing double tax on dividends.

Many think excess corporate cash earning the market rate of return is better off in shareholders' pockets. The return earned by the shareholders is only taxed once, at the shareholder level. In many cases, shareholders receive the benefit of offsetting their basis in the purchased shares against the proceeds received, as opposed to a dividend, where the proceeds are fully taxable.

SOURCE: Information from "Corporate Stock Buybacks Are Soaring," *Treasury Manager's Report*, February 16, 1996.

Property distributions have the same impact as distributions of cash except for effects attributable to any difference between the basis and fair market value of the distributed property. In most situations, distributed property is appreciated, so its sale would result in a gain to the corporation. Distributions of property with a basis that differs from fair market value raise several tax questions.

- For the shareholder:

    1. What is the amount of the distribution?
    2. What is the basis of the property in the shareholder's hands?

- For the corporation:

    1. Is a gain or loss recognized as a result of the distribution?
    2. What is the effect of the distribution on E & P?

PROPERTY DIVIDENDS—EFFECT ON THE SHAREHOLDER

When a corporation distributes property rather than cash to a shareholder, the amount distributed is measured by the fair market value of the property on the date of distribution.[10] As with a cash distribution, the portion of a property distribution covered by existing E & P is a dividend, and any excess is treated as a return of capital until basis is recovered. If the fair market value of the property distributed exceeds the corporation's E & P and the shareholder's basis in the stock investment, a capital gain results.

The amount distributed is reduced by any liabilities to which the distributed property is subject immediately before and immediately after the distribution and by any liabilities of the corporation assumed by the shareholder. The basis in the distributed property to the shareholder is the fair market value of the property on the date of the distribution.

---

[10]Section 301 describes the tax treatment of corporate distributions to shareholders.

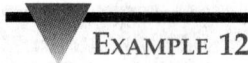

EXAMPLE 12

Robin Corporation has E & P of $60,000. It distributes land with a fair market value of $50,000 (adjusted basis of $30,000) to its sole shareholder, Charles. The land is subject to a liability of $10,000, which Charles assumes. Charles has a taxable dividend of $40,000 ($50,000 fair market value – $10,000 liability). The basis of the land to Charles is $50,000. ▼

EXAMPLE 13

Red Corporation owns 10% of Tan Corporation. Tan has ample E & P to cover any distributions made during the year. One distribution made to Red Corporation consists of a vacant lot with an adjusted basis of $5,000 and a fair market value of $3,000. Red has a taxable dividend of $3,000, and its basis in the lot is $3,000. ▼

Distributing property that has depreciated in value as a property dividend may suggest poor planning. Note what happens in Example 13. The loss of $2,000 (adjusted basis $5,000, fair market value $3,000) disappears. As an alternative, if Tan Corporation sells the lot, it could use the loss to reduce its taxes. Then Tan could distribute the $3,000 of proceeds to shareholders.

PROPERTY DIVIDENDS—EFFECT ON THE CORPORATION

As noted earlier, the distribution of a property dividend raises two questions related to the corporation's tax position: Is a gain or loss recognized? What is the effect on E & P?

Recognition of Gain or Loss. All distributions of appreciated property generate gain recognition to the distributing corporation.[11] In effect, a corporation that distributes property is treated as if it had sold the property to the shareholder for its fair market value. However, the distributing corporation does not recognize loss on distributions of property.

EXAMPLE 14

A corporation distributes land (basis of $10,000 and fair market value of $30,000) to a shareholder. The corporation recognizes a gain of $20,000. ▼

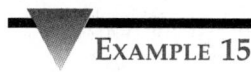

EXAMPLE 15

Assume the property in Example 14 has a fair market value of $10,000 and a basis of $30,000. The corporation does not recognize a loss on the distribution. ▼

If the distributed property is subject to a liability in excess of its basis or the shareholder assumes such a liability, a special rule applies. The fair market value of the property for purposes of determining gain on the distribution is treated as not being less than the amount of the liability.[12]

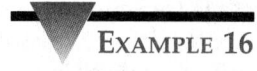

EXAMPLE 16

Assume the land in Example 14 is subject to a liability of $35,000. The corporation recognizes a gain of $25,000 on the distribution ($35,000 – $10,000). ▼

Effect of Corporate Distributions on E & P. Corporate distributions reduce E & P by the amount of money distributed or by the *greater* of the fair market value or the adjusted basis of property distributed, less the amount of any liability on the property.[13] E & P is increased by gain recognized on appreciated property distributed as a property dividend.

---

[11]Section 311 describes how corporations are taxed on distributions.   [13]§§ 312(a), (b), and (c).
[12]§ 311(b)(2).

EXAMPLE 17

Crimson Corporation distributes property (basis of $10,000 and fair market value of $20,000) to Brenda, its shareholder. Crimson recognizes a gain of $10,000, which is added to its E & P, and which is reduced by $20,000, the fair market value of the property. Brenda has dividend income of $20,000. ▼

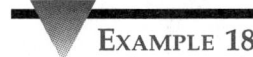

EXAMPLE 18

Assume the same facts as in Example 17, except that the adjusted basis in the hands of Crimson Corporation is $25,000. Because the loss is not recognized and the adjusted basis is greater than fair market value, E & P is reduced by $25,000. Brenda reports dividend income of $20,000. ▼

EXAMPLE 19

Assume the same facts as in Example 18, except that the property is subject to a liability of $6,000. E & P is now reduced by $19,000 ($25,000 adjusted basis – $6,000 liability). Brenda has a dividend of $14,000 ($20,000 amount of the distribution – $6,000 liability), and her basis in the property is $20,000. ▼

Under no circumstances can a distribution, whether cash or property, either generate a deficit in E & P or add to a deficit in E & P. Deficits can arise only through corporate losses.

EXAMPLE 20

Teal Corporation has accumulated E & P of $10,000 at the beginning of the current tax year. During the year, it has current E & P of $15,000. At the end of the year, it distributes cash of $30,000 to its sole shareholder, Walter. Teal's E & P at the end of the year is zero. The beginning E & P of $10,000 is increased by current E & P of $15,000 and reduced by $25,000 because of the dividend distribution. The remaining $5,000 of the distribution to Walter does not reduce E & P because a distribution cannot generate a deficit in E & P. Instead, the remaining $5,000 reduces Walter's stock basis and/or produces a capital gain to Walter. ▼

CONSTRUCTIVE DIVIDENDS

4 **LEARNING OBJECTIVE**
Understand the nature and treatment of constructive dividends.

Any measurable economic benefit conveyed by a corporation to its shareholders can be treated as a dividend for Federal income tax purposes even though it is not formally declared or designated as a dividend. Also, it need not be issued pro rata to all shareholders.[14] Nor must the distribution satisfy the legal requirements of a dividend as set forth by applicable state law. This benefit, often described as a **constructive dividend,** is distinguishable from actual corporate distributions of cash and property in form only.

Constructive dividend situations usually arise in closely held corporations. Here, the dealings between the parties are less structured, and, frequently, formalities are not preserved. The constructive dividend serves as a substitute for actual distributions. Usually, it is intended to accomplish some tax objective not available through the use of direct dividends. The shareholders may be attempting to bail out corporate profits in a form deductible to the corporation.[15] Alternatively, the shareholders may be seeking benefits for themselves while avoiding the recognition of income. Some constructive dividends are, in reality, disguised dividends. But not all constructive dividends are deliberate attempts to avoid actual and formal dividends; many are inadvertent. Thus, an awareness of the various constructive

---

[14]See *Lengsfield v. Comm.,* 57–1 USTC ¶9437, 50 AFTR 1683, 241 F.2d 508 (CA–5, 1957).

[15]Recall that dividend distributions do not provide the distributing corporation with an income tax deduction, although they do reduce E & P.

dividend situations is essential to protect the parties from unanticipated, undesirable tax consequences.

TYPES OF CONSTRUCTIVE DIVIDENDS

The most frequently encountered types of constructive dividends are summarized below.

Shareholder Use of Corporate-Owned Property.   A constructive dividend can occur when a shareholder uses a corporation's property for personal purposes at no cost. Personal use of corporate-owned automobiles, airplanes, yachts, fishing camps, hunting lodges, and other entertainment facilities is commonplace in some closely held corporations. The shareholder has dividend income to the extent of the fair rental value of the property for the period of its personal use.

Bargain Sale of Corporate Property to a Shareholder.   Shareholders often purchase property from a corporation at a cost below the fair market value of the property. These bargain sales produce dividend income to the extent of the difference between the property's fair market value on the date of sale and the amount the shareholder paid for the property.[16] These situations might be avoided by appraising the property on or about the date of the sale. The appraised value should become the price to be paid by the shareholder.

Bargain Rental of Corporate Property.   A bargain rental of corporate property by a shareholder also produces dividend income. Here the measure of the constructive dividend is the excess of the property's fair rental value over the rent actually paid. Again, appraisal data should be used to avoid any questionable situations.

Payments for the Benefit of a Shareholder.   If a corporation pays an obligation of a shareholder, the payment is treated as a constructive dividend. The obligation involved need not be legally binding on the shareholder; it may, in fact, be a moral obligation.[17] Forgiveness of shareholder indebtedness by the corporation creates an identical problem.[18] Excessive rentals paid by a corporation for the use of shareholder property also are treated as constructive dividends.

Unreasonable Compensation.   A salary payment to a shareholder-employee that is deemed to be **unreasonable compensation** is frequently treated as a constructive dividend and therefore is not deductible by the corporation. In determining the reasonableness of salary payments, the following factors are considered:

- The employee's qualifications.
- A comparison of salaries with dividend distributions.
- The prevailing rates of compensation for comparable positions in comparable business concerns.
- The nature and scope of the employee's work.
- The size and complexity of the business.
- A comparison of salaries paid with both gross and net income.
- The taxpayer's salary policy toward all employees.

---

[16]Reg. § 1.301–1(j).

[17]*Montgomery Engineering Co. v. U.S.*, 64–2 USTC ¶9618, 13 AFTR2d 1747, 230 F.Supp. 838 (D.Ct.N.J., 1964); *aff'd.* in 65–1 USTC ¶9368, 15 AFTR2d 746, 344 F.2d 996 (CA–3, 1965).

[18]Reg. § 1.301–1(m).

WHEN IS COMPENSATION UNREASONABLE?

What is reasonable compensation for the head of the Chicago Stadium Corporation, which manages the arena where the Chicago Blackhawks hockey team and the Chicago Bulls basketball team play? For the fiscal year ending on July 31, 1977, the corporation paid its chairman and CEO, Arthur Wirtz, $335,750, but the IRS insisted reasonable compensation would be only $138,000 and disallowed the company's deduction for the remainder.

A long legal battle ensued, but the Federal District Court in Chicago finally upheld the IRS [*Chicago Stadium Corporation v. U.S.*, 91–2 USTC ¶50,352 (D. Ct. Ill., 1991)]. Among other things, the court said that Wirtz was paid considerably more than the executives of similar arenas, yet he did not even work full-time for the corporation. Besides, much of his pay consisted of "commissions" for arranging to lease the arena to the Bulls, which he also controlled. Under the circumstances, said the court, the $138,000 allowed by the IRS was generous.

- For small corporations with a limited number of officers, the amount of compensation paid the employee in question in previous years.[19]

Loans to Shareholders. Advances to shareholders that are not bona fide loans are constructive dividends. Whether an advance qualifies as a bona fide loan is a question of fact to be determined in light of the particular circumstances. Factors considered in determining whether the advance is a bona fide loan include the following:[20]

- Whether the advance is on open account or is evidenced by a written instrument.
- Whether the shareholder furnished collateral or other security for the advance.
- How long the advance has been outstanding.
- Whether any repayments have been made, excluding dividend sources.
- The shareholder's ability to repay the advance.
- The shareholder's use of the funds (e.g., payment of routine bills versus nonrecurring, extraordinary expenses).
- The regularity of the advances.
- The dividend-paying history of the corporation.

If a corporation succeeds in proving that an advance to a shareholder is a bona fide loan, the advance is not a constructive dividend. But the shareholder may still have a constructive dividend equal to any imputed (forgone) interest.[21] Imputed interest is the difference between interest the Federal government pays on new borrowings, compounded semiannually, and the interest charged on the loan. When the imputed interest provision applies, the shareholder is deemed to have made an interest payment to the corporation equal to the amount of imputed interest, and the corporation is deemed to have repaid the imputed

---

[19]*Mayson Manufacturing Co. v. Comm.*, 49–2 USTC ¶9467, 38 AFTR 1028, 178 F.2d 115 (CA–6, 1949).

[20]*Fin Hay Realty Co. v. U.S.*, 68–2 USTC ¶9438, 22 AFTR2d 5004, 398 F.2d 694 (CA–3, 1968).

[21]See § 7872.

interest to the shareholder through a constructive dividend. Consequently, the corporation receives interest income and makes a nondeductible dividend payment, and the shareholder has taxable dividend income that may be offset with an interest deduction.

EXAMPLE 21

Mallard Corporation lends its principal shareholder, Henry, $100,000 on January 2 of the current year. The loan is interest-free. On December 31, the imputed interest rules are applied. Assuming the Federal rate is 6%, compounded semiannually, the amount of imputed interest is $6,180. This amount is deemed paid by Henry to Mallard in the form of interest. Mallard is then deemed to return the amount to Henry as a constructive dividend. Thus, Henry has dividend income of $6,180, which may be offset with a deduction for the interest paid to Mallard. Mallard has interest income of $6,180 for the interest received, with no offsetting deduction for the dividend payment. ▼

Loans to a Corporation by Shareholders.   Shareholder loans to a corporation may be reclassified as equity because the debt has too many features of stock. Any interest and principal payments made by the corporation to the shareholder are then treated as constructive dividends. This topic was covered more thoroughly in the discussion of "thin capitalization" in Chapter 17.

TAX TREATMENT OF CONSTRUCTIVE DIVIDENDS

Constructive distributions are treated the same for tax purposes as actual distributions.[22] Thus, a corporate shareholder is entitled to the dividends received deduction (see Chapter 16). The constructive distribution is taxable as a dividend only to the extent of the corporation's current and accumulated E & P. The burden of proving that the distribution constitutes a return of capital because of inadequate E & P rests with the taxpayer.[23]

STOCK DIVIDENDS AND STOCK RIGHTS

STOCK DIVIDENDS

5   LEARNING OBJECTIVE
Distinguish between taxable and nontaxable stock dividends and stock rights.

Historically, **stock dividends** were excluded from income on the theory that the ownership interest of the shareholder was unchanged as a result of the distribution.[24] The 1954 Code expanded upon this treatment by taxing stock dividends where (1) the stockholder could elect to receive either stock or property or (2) the stock dividends were in discharge of preference dividends. Because of the narrow scope of these provisions, corporations devised an assortment of methods to distribute stock dividends that qualified for tax-free treatment yet still affected shareholders' proportionate interests in the corporation.[25] Section 305 was amended to curtail the use of these methods.

The provisions of § 305 are based on the proportionate interest concept. As a general rule, stock dividends are excluded from income if they are pro rata distributions of stock or stock rights, paid on common stock. Five exceptions to this general rule exist. These exceptions deal with various disproportionate

[22]*Simon v. Comm.*, 57–2 USTC ¶9989, 52 AFTR 698, 248 F.2d 869 (CA–8, 1957).

[23]*DiZenzo v. Comm.*, 65–2 USTC ¶9518, 16 AFTR2d 5107, 348 F.2d 122 (CA–2, 1965).

[24]See *Eisner v. Macomber*, 1 USTC ¶32, 3 AFTR 3020, 40 S.Ct. 189 (USSC, 1920).

[25]See "Stock Dividends," S.Rept. 91–552, 1969–3 C.B. 519.

distribution situations. If stock dividends are not taxable, the corporation's E & P is not reduced.[26] If the stock dividends are taxable, the distributing corporation treats the distribution in the same manner as any other taxable property dividend.

If a stock dividend is taxable, the basis of the newly received shares to the shareholder-distributee is fair market value, and the holding period starts on the date of receipt. If a stock dividend is not taxable, the basis of the stock on which the dividend is distributed is reallocated.[27] If the dividend shares are identical to these formerly held shares, basis in the old stock is reallocated by dividing the taxpayer's basis in the old stock by the total number of shares. If the dividend stock is not identical to the underlying shares (e.g., a stock dividend of preferred on common), basis is determined by allocating the basis of the formerly held shares between the old and new stock according to the fair market value of each. The holding period includes the holding period of the formerly held stock.[28]

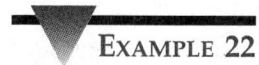

EXAMPLE 22

Gail bought 1,000 shares of stock two years ago for $10,000. In the current tax year, she receives 10 shares of common stock as a nontaxable stock dividend. Gail's basis of $10,000 is divided by 1,010. Each share of stock has a basis of $9.90 instead of the pre-dividend $10 basis. ▼

EXAMPLE 23

Assume Gail received, instead, a nontaxable preferred stock dividend of 100 shares. The preferred stock has a fair market value of $1,000, and the common stock, on which the preferred is distributed, has a fair market value of $19,000. After the receipt of the stock dividend, the basis of the common stock is $9,500, and the basis of the preferred is $500, computed as follows:

Fair market value of common	$19,000
Fair market value of preferred	1,000
	$20,000
Basis of common: 19/20 × $10,000	$ 9,500
Basis of preferred: 1/20 × $10,000	$ 500

▼

STOCK RIGHTS

The rules for determining taxability of **stock rights** are identical to those for determining taxability of stock dividends. If the rights are taxable, the recipient has income to the extent of the fair market value of the rights. The fair market value then becomes the shareholder-distributee's basis in the rights.[29] If the rights are exercised, the holding period for the new stock is the date the rights (whether taxable or nontaxable) are exercised. The basis of the new stock is the basis of the rights plus the amount of any other consideration given.

If stock rights are not taxable and the value of the rights is less than 15 percent of the value of the old stock, the basis of the rights is zero. However, the shareholder may elect to have some of the basis in the formerly held stock allocated to the rights.[30] The election is made by attaching a statement to the shareholder's return for the year in which the rights are received.[31] If the fair market value of the rights is 15 percent or more of the value of the old stock and the rights are exercised or sold, the shareholder *must* allocate some of the basis in the formerly held stock to the rights.

[26]§ 312(d)(1).
[27]§ 307(a).
[28]§ 1223(5).

[29]Reg. § 1.305–1(b).
[30]§ 307(b)(1).
[31]Reg. § 1.307–2.

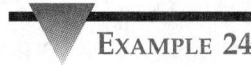

EXAMPLE 24

A corporation with common stock outstanding declares a nontaxable dividend payable in rights to subscribe to common stock. Each right entitles the holder to purchase one share of stock for $90. One right is issued for every two shares of stock owned. Fred owns 400 shares of stock purchased two years ago for $15,000. At the time of the distribution of the rights, the market value of the common stock is $100 per share, and the market value of the rights is $8 per right. Fred receives 200 rights. He exercises 100 rights and sells the remaining 100 rights three months later for $9 per right.

Fred need not allocate the cost of the original stock to the rights because the value of the rights is less than 15% of the value of the stock ($1,600 ÷ $40,000 = 4%). If Fred does not allocate his original stock basis to the rights, the tax consequences are as follows:

- Basis in the new stock is $9,000 ($90 × 100). The holding period of the new stock begins on the date the stock was purchased.
- Sale of the rights produces long-term capital gain of $900 ($9 × 100). The holding period of the rights starts with the date the original 400 shares of stock were acquired.

If Fred elects to allocate basis to the rights, the tax consequences are as follows:

- Basis in the stock is $14,423 [$40,000 ÷ $41,600 (value of rights and stock) × $15,000 (cost of stock)].
- Basis in the rights is $577 [$1,600 (value of rights) ÷ $41,600 (value of rights and stock) × $15,000 (cost of stock)].
- When Fred exercises the rights, his basis in the new stock will be $9,288.50 [$9,000 (cost) + $288.50 (basis in 100 rights)].
- Sale of the rights would produce a long-term capital gain of $611.50 [$900 (selling price) − $288.50 (basis in the remaining 100 rights)]. ▼

STOCK REDEMPTIONS

OVERVIEW

6   LEARNING OBJECTIVE
Identify various stock redemptions that are treated as sales or exchanges of stock rather than as dividend income.

In a **stock redemption,** a corporation purchases its stock from a shareholder. A stock redemption involves an exchange of a shareholder's stock in the corporation for property of the corporation. Except for the fact that the shareholder is selling the stock back to the corporation, the sale resembles a sale of the stock to an outsider, or third party. While a sale of stock to an outsider is invariably given sale or exchange treatment, only a *qualifying* stock redemption will be treated as a sale for tax purposes.

A stock redemption may have the same effect as a dividend. For example, if a shareholder owns all the stock of a corporation and sells a portion of that stock to the corporation, the shareholder's ownership percentage in the corporation will not change. After the redemption, the shareholder still owns all the outstanding stock of the corporation. In this situation, the stock redemption resembles a dividend distribution and is taxed as such.

Stock redemptions occur for numerous reasons. A shareholder may want to retire. Rather than the other shareholders purchasing the retiree's stock, the corporation simply redeems all of the shareholder's stock. Similarly, when a shareholder dies, the corporation may purchase the shareholder's stock from the estate. In both cases, having the corporation provide the funds to purchase the stock relieves the remaining shareholders of the need to use their own money. In addition, stock redemptions often occur with respect to property settlements in divorce actions. For example, in a divorce action involving joint ownership of corporate shares, one spouse will usually wind up owning all the stock. By having the corporation redeem the other spouse's shares, the spouse who remains as a shareholder is relieved of the need to obtain funds for the buyout. As a result, the departing spouse receives a part of the property settlement from the corporation.

As mentioned, a qualifying stock redemption provides *sale or exchange* treatment for the shareholder. Sale or exchange treatment permits a shareholder to recover his or her capital investment tax-free and permits the noncorporate shareholder to avoid dividend consequences. Generally, such treatment results in capital gain or loss to the shareholder, which is calculated by subtracting the redeemed stock's adjusted basis from the sum of any money received plus the fair market value of any property received. However, § 267 disallows loss recognition when the shareholder and the corporation are related under the attribution rules of that provision. The shareholder's basis in any property received in exchange for his or her stock in the corporation is equal to the fair market value of the property.

A capital gain is beneficial for a noncorporate shareholder who is in the highest tax brackets as the tax is limited to 20 percent of the gain recognized, assuming the stock meets the long-term holding requirement. The capital gain also provides a benefit to a shareholder who has substantial capital losses.

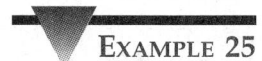

EXAMPLE 25

Abby, a corporate executive, is in the 39.6% tax bracket. She acquired stock in Bluejay Corporation five years ago for $100,000. In the current year, Bluejay Corporation redeems her shares for $200,000. If the redemption qualifies for sale or exchange treatment, Abby has a long-term capital gain of $100,000 [$200,000 (redemption amount) − $100,000 (cost of the shares)]. Her income tax liability on the $100,000 capital gain is $20,000 ($100,000 × 20%). If the $200,000 stock redemption does not qualify as a sale or exchange, it is treated as dividend income, and Abby's tax liability is $79,200 ($200,000 × 39.6%). Thus, Abby saves $59,200 ($79,200 − $20,000) in income taxes if the corporate payment is a qualifying stock redemption. ▼

EXAMPLE 26

Assume Abby, in Example 25, has a capital loss carryover of $80,000 in the current tax year. If the corporate payment is a qualifying stock redemption, Abby can offset the entire $80,000 capital loss against her $100,000 capital gain. As a result, only $20,000 of the gain is taxed, and her tax liability is only $4,000 ($20,000 × 20%). On the other hand, if the corporate payment does not qualify for sale or exchange treatment, the entire $200,000 is taxed at 39.6%. In addition, assuming no other capital gains in the current year, Abby is able to deduct only $3,000 of the $80,000 capital loss carryover to offset her other (ordinary) income. ▼

EXAMPLE 27

Assume Abby, in Example 25, is a corporation, that the stock represents a 40% ownership in Bluejay Corporation, and that Abby has corporate taxable income of $350,000 before the payment from Bluejay. If the corporate payment is a qualifying stock redemption for tax purposes, Abby has a capital gain of $100,000 that is subject to tax at 34%, or $34,000. On the other hand, if the $200,000 payment is a dividend, Abby has a dividends received deduction of $160,000 ($200,000 × 80%), so only $40,000 of the payment is taxed. Consequently, Abby's tax liability on the payment is only $13,600 ($40,000 × 34%). ▼

To determine whether a redemption exists for tax purposes, a taxpayer must look to the Code. The label given to the transaction by the parties *or* by state law is not controlling. One Code section provides that if a corporation redeems its stock pursuant to one of four special rules, the redemption is treated as a sale or exchange of a shareholder's stock.[32] Another section provides that certain distributions of property to a shareholder in exchange for stock included in a decedent's estate are treated as qualifying stock redemptions.[33]

---

[32] § 302(a).

[33] § 303.

HISTORICAL BACKGROUND

Under earlier law, stock redemptions that constituted ordinary taxable dividends were distinguished from those qualifying for capital gain by the so-called *dividend equivalency rule*. When a redemption was essentially equivalent to a dividend, it did not qualify for sale or exchange treatment. The entire amount received by the shareholder was subject to taxation as ordinary income to the extent of the corporation's E & P.

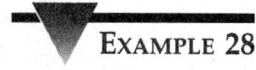

EXAMPLE 28

Adam owns 100% of the stock of White Corporation. White has E & P of $50,000. Adam sells one-half of his shares to the corporation for $50,000. His basis in the stock he sells is $10,000, and he has held the stock for five years. If the sale of the stock to White Corporation were treated as a qualifying stock redemption, Adam would have a long-term capital gain of $40,000. However, in reality, the distribution is essentially equivalent to a dividend because Adam's percentage of ownership in the corporation has not changed. Therefore, he is deemed to have received a taxable dividend of $50,000. ▼

Current Code provisions are designed to eliminate the uncertainty and subjectivity that resulted from reliance on the dividend equivalency rule. Under the Code, the following major types of stock redemptions qualify for sale or exchange treatment and therefore avoid dividend income consequences:

- Distributions not essentially equivalent to a dividend (subsequently referred to as not essentially equivalent redemptions).
- Distributions substantially disproportionate in terms of shareholder effect (subsequently referred to as disproportionate redemptions).
- Distributions in complete termination of a shareholder's interest (subsequently referred to as complete termination redemptions).
- Distributions to pay a shareholder's death taxes (subsequently referred to as redemptions to pay death taxes).

STOCK ATTRIBUTION RULES

A stock redemption that qualifies for sale or exchange treatment generally must result in a substantial reduction in a shareholder's ownership in the corporation. If this does not occur, proceeds received for a redemption of the shareholder's stock are taxed as ordinary dividend income. In determining whether a shareholder's interest has substantially decreased, the stock ownership of certain related parties is attributed to the shareholder whose stock is redeemed. Thus, one must consider the stock **attribution** rules along with the stock redemption provisions.[34] Under these stock attribution rules, related parties are defined to include immediate family, specifically spouses, children, grandchildren, and parents. Attribution also takes place *from* and *to* partnerships, estates, trusts, and corporations (50 percent or more ownership required in the case of regular corporations). Exhibit 18–1 summarizes the relevant stock attribution rules.

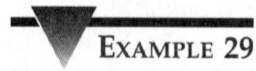

EXAMPLE 29

Larry owns 30% of the stock in Blue Corporation, the other 70% being held by his children. For purposes of the stock attribution rules, Larry is treated as owning 100% of the stock in Blue Corporation. He owns 30% directly and, because of the family attribution rules, 70% indirectly. ▼

---

[34]§ 318.

▼ **EXHIBIT 18–1**
Stock Attribution Rules

Deemed or Constructive Ownership	
• Individual/family	Stock owned by the spouse, children, grandchildren, and parents (not siblings or grandparents) is considered to be owned by the individual.
• Partnership	Partner is deemed to be the owner of shares owned by a partnership to the extent of the partner's proportionate share in the partnership.
	Stock of a partner is deemed to be owned in full by a partnership.
• Estate or trust	Beneficiary or heir is deemed to be the owner of shares owned by an estate or trust to the extent of the beneficiary's or heir's proportionate interest in the estate or trust.
	Stock of a beneficiary or heir is deemed to be owned in full by an estate or trust.
• Corporation	Stock owned by a corporation is considered to be owned proportionately by any shareholder owning 50% or more of the corporation's stock.
	All stock owned by a shareholder who owns 50% or more of a corporation is considered to be owned by the corporation.

EXAMPLE 30

Chris owns 50% of the stock in Gray Corporation. The other 50% is owned by a partnership in which Chris has a 20% interest. Chris is deemed to own 60% of Gray Corporation: 50% directly and, because of the partnership interest, 10% indirectly. ▼

As discussed later, the *family* attribution rules (refer to Example 29) *may* not apply to stock redemptions in *complete termination* of a shareholder's interest. In addition, these stock attribution rules do not apply to stock redemptions to pay death taxes.

NOT ESSENTIALLY EQUIVALENT REDEMPTIONS

Section 302(b)(1) provides that a redemption qualifies for sale or exchange treatment if it is "not essentially equivalent to a dividend." There are few objective tests to determine when a redemption is or is not essentially equivalent to a dividend. This provision was added to provide specifically for redemptions of preferred stock because shareholders often have no control over when corporations call in such stock.[35] Some courts concluded that such a redemption would receive sale or exchange treatment if there was a **business purpose** for the redemption and there was no tax avoidance scheme to bail out dividends at favorable tax rates.[36] However, an unresolved question was whether the stock attribution rules applied to this provision.

The interpretation of the statutory language on this point was settled by the Supreme Court in *U.S. v. Davis.*[37] The Court agreed with the IRS that the redemption of preferred stock in *Davis* was essentially equivalent to a dividend and was taxable as ordinary income because the attribution rules *should* apply. The Court reasoned that the business purpose of the transaction was not

---

[35]See S.Rept. No. 1622, 83d Cong., 2d Sess., at 44.

[36]See, for example, *Kerr v. Comm.*, 64–1 USTC ¶9186, 13 AFTR2d 386, 326 F.2d 225 (CA–9, 1964).

[37]70–1 USTC ¶9289, 25 AFTR2d 70–827, 90 S.Ct. 1041 (USSC, 1970).

controlling in determining whether a stock redemption was "not essentially equivalent to a dividend." It ruled that a redemption would not qualify under this provision unless there was a "meaningful reduction" in the shareholder's ownership in the redeeming corporation.

Based upon this Supreme Court decision, a redemption will qualify as a **not essentially equivalent redemption** only when the shareholder's interest in the redeeming corporation has been meaningfully reduced. As a result, the facts and circumstances of each case must be assessed.[38] A decrease in the redeeming shareholder's voting control appears to be the most significant indicator of a meaningful reduction,[39] but reductions in the rights of redeeming shareholders to share in corporate earnings or to receive corporate assets upon liquidation are also considered.[40] The **meaningful reduction test** is applied whether common stock or preferred stock is being redeemed.

EXAMPLE 31   Pat owns 58% of the common stock of Green Corporation. After a redemption of part of Pat's stock, he owns 51% of the Green stock. Pat continues to have dominant voting rights in Green; thus, the redemption is treated as essentially equivalent to a dividend, and Pat has ordinary income equal to the entire amount of the distribution assuming adequate E & P. ▼

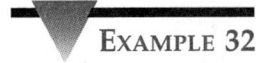

EXAMPLE 32   Brown Corporation redeems 2% of its stock from Maria. Before the redemption, Maria owned 10% of Brown Corporation. In this case, the redemption will likely qualify as "not essentially equivalent to a dividend." Maria experiences a reduction in her voting rights, her right to participate in current earnings and accumulated surplus, and her right to share in net assets upon liquidation. ▼

If a redemption is treated as an ordinary dividend, the shareholder's basis in the stock redeemed attaches to the remaining stock (or to stock the shareholder owns constructively).[41]

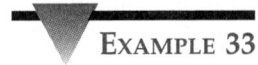

EXAMPLE 33   Fran and Floyd, wife and husband, each own 50 shares in Gray Corporation, representing 100% of the stock of Gray. All the stock was purchased for $50,000. Both Fran and Floyd serve as directors of the corporation. The corporation redeems Floyd's 50 shares. Floyd continues to serve as director of the corporation. The redemption will be treated as a taxable dividend because he constructively owns Fran's stock. Floyd's basis in the stock, $25,000, will attach to Fran's stock. She then will have a basis of $50,000 in the 50 shares she owns in Gray. ▼

DISPROPORTIONATE REDEMPTIONS

A redemption of stock qualifies for capital gain treatment under § 302(b)(2) as a **disproportionate redemption** if two conditions are met:

- The distribution must be substantially disproportionate. To be substantially disproportionate, the shareholder must own, after the distribution, *less than* 80 percent of the interest owned in the corporation before the redemption. For example, if a shareholder owns a 60 percent interest in a corporation that redeems part of the stock, the redemption is substantially disproportionate only if the percentage of ownership after the redemption is less than 48 percent (80 percent of 60 percent).

---

[38]Reg. § 1.302–2(b). See *Mary G. Roebling*, 77 T.C. 30 (1981).

[39]See, for example, *Jack Paparo*, 71 T.C. 692 (1979), and *Blanche S. Benjamin*, 66 T.C. 1084 (1976).

[40]See *Grabowski Trust*, 58 T.C. 650 (1972).

[41]Reg. § 1.302–2(c).

- The shareholder must own, after the distribution, *less than* 50 percent of the total combined voting power of all classes of stock entitled to vote.

Figure 18–1 provides a graphic presentation of qualifying disproportionate redemptions. In determining a shareholder's percentage of ownership, the attribution rules discussed earlier apply.

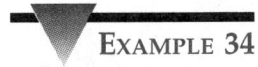

EXAMPLE 34

Bob, Carl, and Dan, unrelated individuals, own 30 shares, 30 shares, and 40 shares, respectively, in Wren Corporation. Wren has E & P of $200,000. The corporation redeems 20 shares of Dan's stock for $30,000. Dan paid $200 a share for the stock two years ago. Dan's ownership in Wren Corporation before and after the redemption is as follows:

	Total Shares	Dan's Ownership	Ownership Percentage	80% of Original Ownership
Before redemption	100	40	40% (40 ÷ 100)	32% (80% × 40%)
After redemption	80	20	25% (20 ÷ 80)*	

*Note that the denominator of the fraction is reduced after the redemption (from 100 to 80).

Dan's 25% ownership after the redemption meets both tests of § 302(b)(2). It is less than 80% of his original ownership and less than 50% of the total voting power. The distribution qualifies as a stock redemption that receives sale or exchange treatment. Therefore, Dan has a long-term capital gain of $26,000 [$30,000 – $4,000 (20 shares × $200)]. ▼

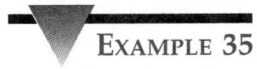

EXAMPLE 35

Given the situation in Example 34, assume instead that Carl and Dan are father and son. The redemption described previously would not qualify for sale or exchange treatment because of the effect of the attribution rules. Dan is deemed to own Carl's stock before and after the redemption. Dan's ownership in Wren Corporation before and after the redemption is as follows:

	Total Shares	Dan's Direct Ownership	Carl's Ownership	Dan's Direct and Indirect Ownership	Ownership Percentage	80% of Original Ownership
Before redemption	100	40	30	70	70% (70 ÷ 100)	56% (80% × 70%)
After redemption	80	20	30	50	62.5% (50 ÷ 80)	

Dan's direct and indirect ownership of 62.5% fails to meet either of the tests of § 302(b)(2). Dan owns more than 80% of his original ownership and more than 50% of the voting stock. Thus, the redemption does not qualify for sale or exchange treatment and results in a taxable dividend of $30,000 to Dan. ▼

Even if a redemption is not substantially disproportionate, it may still qualify as a not essentially equivalent redemption if it meets the "meaningful reduction" test. Refer to Example 32. A reduction in voting control when the shareholder does not have a majority controlling interest will generally qualify as a not essentially equivalent redemption. However, the stock attribution rules apply in determining whether there has been a reduction in voting control.

▼ **FIGURE 18–1**
Qualifying Disproportionate
Redemptions

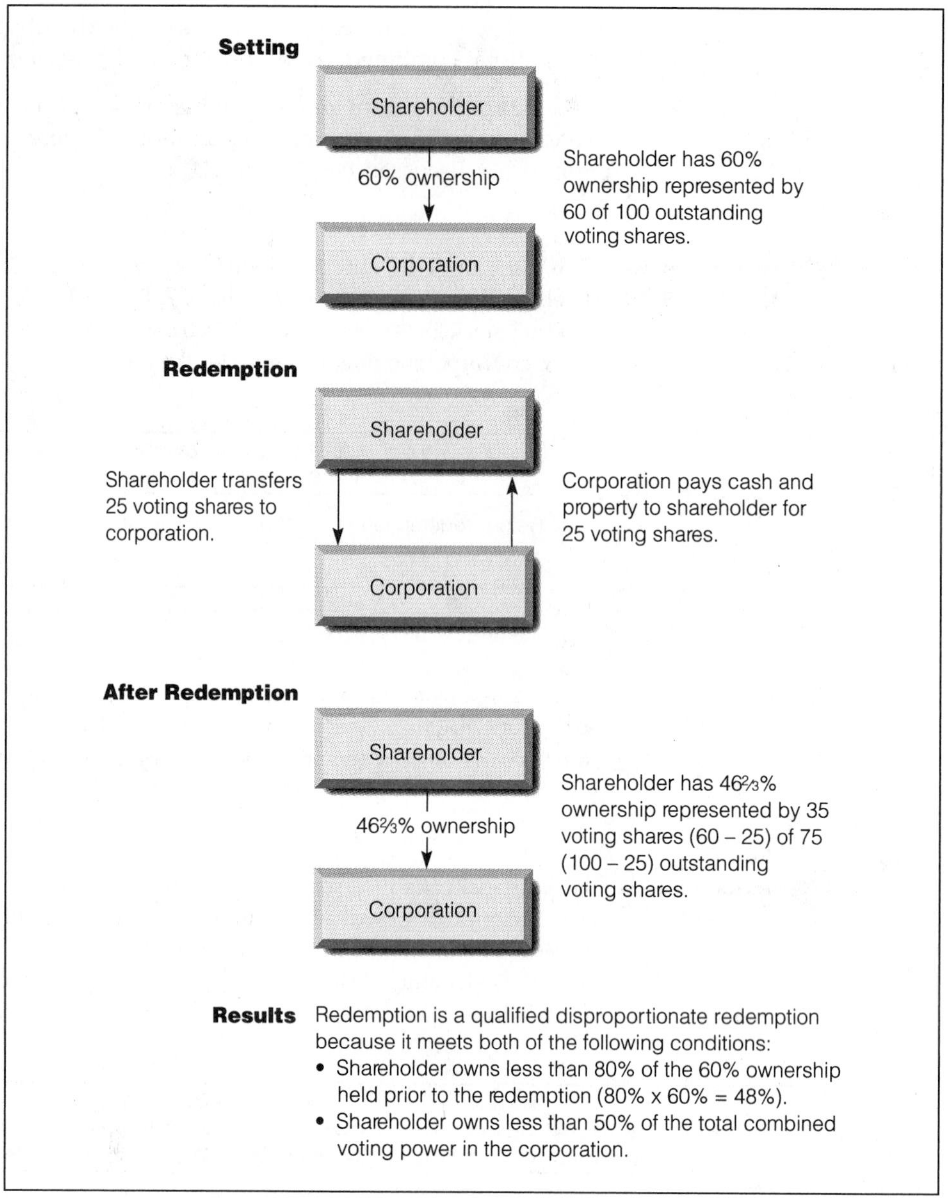

Setting

Shareholder

60% ownership

Corporation

Shareholder has 60%
ownership represented by
60 of 100 outstanding
voting shares.

Redemption

Shareholder transfers
25 voting shares to
corporation.

Shareholder

Corporation

Corporation pays cash and
property to shareholder for
25 voting shares.

After Redemption

Shareholder

46⅔% ownership

Corporation

Shareholder has 46⅔%
ownership represented by 35
voting shares (60 – 25) of 75
(100 – 25) outstanding
voting shares.

Results   Redemption is a qualified disproportionate redemption
because it meets both of the following conditions:
- Shareholder owns less than 80% of the 60% ownership
held prior to the redemption (80% x 60% = 48%).
- Shareholder owns less than 50% of the total combined
voting power in the corporation.

ETHICAL
CONSIDERATIONS

Convertible Preferred Stock—Conversion versus Redemption

A corporation that does not sell its stock publicly sold some convertible preferred stock a few years ago to a small group of passive investors. The holders of the preferred stock have the option of converting the preferred stock into common stock anytime they desire. Because the corporation has developed a successful new invention that has not become known outside the company, the board of directors expects the corporation's earnings will grow substantially in the future. The directors, all of whom own common stock in the corporation, would like to redeem the preferred stock so they can stop paying dividends to the preferred shareholders and prevent the preferred shareholders from sharing in the corporation's future earnings. The board of directors votes to pay the preferred shareholders a premium for redeeming their stock and notifies them that the corporation will redeem their stock unless they instruct otherwise. Did the board of directors act in an ethical manner?

COMPLETE TERMINATION REDEMPTIONS

If a shareholder terminates his or her *entire* stock ownership in a corporation through a stock redemption, the redemption may qualify for sale or exchange treatment. Often a complete termination will not qualify as a disproportionate redemption because the constructive ownership rules are applied. The difference between the two provisions is that the *family* attribution rules *may* not apply to a **complete termination redemption.** This favorable treatment occurs only if *both* of the following conditions are met:

- The former shareholder has no interest, other than that of a creditor, in the corporation after the redemption (including an interest as an officer, director, or employee) for at least 10 years.
- The former shareholder files an agreement to notify the IRS of any disallowed interest within the 10-year period and to retain all necessary records pertaining to the redemption during this time period.

A shareholder can reacquire an interest in the corporation by bequest or inheritance, but in no other manner. The required agreement should be in the form of a separate statement signed by the shareholder and attached to the return for the year in which the redemption occurs. The agreement should state that the shareholder agrees to notify the appropriate District Director within 30 days of reacquiring an interest in the corporation within the 10-year period following the redemption.

EXAMPLE 36

The stock of Green Corporation is held as follows: 40 shares by Kevin (basis of $30,000), 30 shares by Keith (Kevin's son), and 30 shares by Helen (Kevin's wife). At a time when each share is worth $2,000, Green Corporation redeems Kevin's 40 shares for $80,000. Although Kevin filed the necessary agreement with the IRS, he remains an employee of Green at a salary of $12,000. This redemption does not qualify as a complete termination redemption because of Kevin's continued employment status. Consequently, and to the extent of Green Corporation's E & P, the distribution proceeds are a dividend to Kevin.

However, had Kevin not remained as an employee, he would have recognized $50,000 of capital gain because the family attribution rules may be waived. If this waiver were not allowed, Kevin would have been deemed the owner of Helen's and Keith's stock, and the distribution would have been treated as a dividend to the extent of Green's E & P. ▼

REDEMPTIONS TO PAY DEATH TAXES

Section 303 provides sale or exchange treatment when an executor sells stock that represents a substantial amount of the estate of a shareholder-decedent back to a corporation. The purpose of such a redemption is to provide the estate with liquidity. A redemption is often necessary because stock in a closely held corporation is generally not marketable. Although it could be redeemed under the other redemption rules, the transaction would run the risk of being treated as a dividend because of the attribution rules. The special rule under § 303, allowing sale or exchange treatment in a **redemption to pay death taxes** alleviates this problem.

If a stock redemption qualifies as a redemption to pay death taxes, the redemption provisions under § 302(b) do not apply. However, this special treatment is limited to the sum of the death taxes and funeral and administration expenses. The redemption must be of stock held by the estate or by heirs who are liable for the death taxes and other administration expenses.

In a redemption to pay death taxes, the redemption price generally equals the basis of the stock. Under the step-up in basis rules, the income tax basis of property owned by a decedent's estate becomes the property's fair market value on the date of death (or alternate valuation date if available and if elected).[42] When this so-called step-up or step-down in basis that occurs at death (refer to Chapter 12) equals the redemption price, the exchange is free of any income tax consequences to the shareholder's estate.

Section 303 applies to a distribution made with respect to stock of a corporation when the value of the stock in the gross estate of a decedent exceeds 35 percent of the value of the adjusted gross estate. (For a definition of "gross estate" and "adjusted gross estate," see the Glossary of Tax Terms in Appendix C.)

EXAMPLE 37

Juan's adjusted gross estate is $900,000. The death taxes and funeral and administration expenses of the estate total $200,000. Included in the estate is stock in Yellow Corporation, valued at $340,000. Juan had acquired the stock years ago at a cost of $60,000. Yellow redeems $200,000 of the stock from Juan's estate. Because the value of the Yellow stock in Juan's estate exceeds the 35% threshold ($340,000 ÷ $900,000 = 37.8%), the redemption qualifies under § 303 as a sale or exchange instead of being treated as a dividend to Juan's estate. The basis rules apply to give the stock a step-up in basis. Consequently, there is no recognized gain on the redemption [$200,000 (amount realized) – $200,000 (stock basis)]. ▼

In determining whether the value of stock in a corporation exceeds 35 percent of the value of the adjusted gross estate of a decedent, the stock of two or more corporations may be treated as the stock of a single corporation. Stock in corporations in which the decedent held a 20 percent or more interest is treated as stock in a single corporation for this purpose.[43]

EXAMPLE 38

The adjusted gross estate of a decedent is $300,000. The gross estate includes stock in Orange and Red Corporations valued at $100,000 and $80,000, respectively. Unless the two corporations are treated as a single corporation, § 303 does not apply to a redemption of the stock of either corporation. Assuming the decedent owned all the stock of Orange Corporation and 80% of the stock of Red, § 303 applies because the decedent's estate includes a 20% or more interest in stock of both corporations. The 35% test is met when the Orange and Red stock are treated as that of a single corporation [($100,000 + $80,000) ÷ $300,000 = 60%]. ▼

Qualifying redemptions to pay death taxes are also subject to time limitations. For example, sale or exchange treatment under this rule applies only to redemptions made within 90 days after the expiration of the period of limitations for the assessment of the Federal estate tax. If a timely petition for a redetermination of an estate tax deficiency is filed with the U.S. Tax Court, the applicable period for a § 303 redemption is extended to 60 days after the court's decision becomes final.[44]

EFFECT ON THE CORPORATION REDEEMING ITS STOCK

Having considered some of the different types of stock redemptions that will produce sale or exchange treatment for a shareholder, what is the tax effect to the corporation redeeming its stock? If the corporation uses property to carry out the

---

[42]§ 1014.
[43]§ 303(b)(2)(B).

[44]§ 303(b)(1).

STOCK REDEMPTION PROCEEDS TREATED AS COMPENSATION INCOME

In *Estate of Robert E. Cartwright* (71 TCM 3200, T.C.Memo. 1996–286), the decedent was an attorney and shareholder in an incorporated law firm. Upon his death, the corporation made a $5,062,029 distribution to the decedent's estate. On the estate return, the taxpayer treated the entire distribution as proceeds from the redemption of the decedent's stock in the law firm. Unfortunately for the estate, the law firm issued a Form 1099–MISC indicating that $4,080,256 was instead nonemployee compensation. The IRS subsequently assessed the estate a deficiency based on the Form 1099–MISC classification. The Tax Court agreed in part with the IRS, basing its decision on two shareholder agreements that indicated that an estate would be paid for claims for cases or work in process of a decedent attorney/shareholder. The court held that the distribution was a payment for such work to the extent of $3,956,267. This case illustrates an interesting attempt by a taxpayer to disguise compensation as a qualifying stock redemption.

redemption, is gain or loss recognized on the distribution? Furthermore, what effect does the redemption have on the corporation's E & P? These matters are discussed in the following paragraphs.

Recognition of Gain or Loss by the Corporation.   Section 311 provides that corporations are taxed on all distributions of appreciated property whether in the form of a property dividend or a stock redemption. Losses, however, are not recognized.[45] When distributed property is subject to a corporate liability, the fair market value of that property is treated as not being less than the amount of the liability.

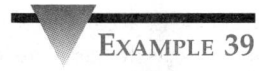

EXAMPLE 39

To carry out a redemption, Bluebird Corporation transfers land (basis of $80,000, fair market value of $300,000) to a shareholder's estate. Bluebird has a recognized gain of $220,000 ($300,000 – $80,000). If the value of the property distributed was less than its adjusted basis, the realized loss would not be recognized. ▼

Because a corporation cannot recognize a loss on a stock redemption, a corporation should not use property that has declined in value as consideration in the redemption of a shareholder's stock. Instead, the corporation should sell the property in a taxable transaction in which it can recognize a loss.

Effect on Earnings and Profits.   A qualified stock redemption reduces the E & P account of a corporation in an amount not in excess of the ratable share of the distributing corporation's E & P that is attributable to the stock redeemed.[46]

EXAMPLE 40

Green Corporation has 100 shares of stock outstanding. It redeems 30 shares for $100,000 at a time when it has paid-in capital of $120,000 and E & P of $150,000. The charge to E & P is 30% of the amount in the E & P account ($45,000), and the remainder of the redemption price ($55,000) is a reduction of the capital account. If, instead, the 30 shares

---

[45]§ 311(a).   [46]§ 312(n)(7).

were redeemed for $40,000, the charge to E & P would be limited to $40,000, the amount Green paid for the stock. ▼

OTHER CORPORATE DISTRIBUTIONS

Partial liquidations of a corporation, if in compliance with the statutory requirements of § 302(e), will result in sale or exchange treatment to noncorporate shareholders. Distributions of stock and securities of a controlled corporation to the shareholders of the parent corporation will be free of any tax consequences if they fall under § 355. Both of these types of corporate distributions are similar to stock redemptions and dividend distributions in some respects but are not discussed here because of their limited applicability.

TAX PLANNING CONSIDERATIONS

7 LEARNING OBJECTIVE
Identify tax planning opportunities available to minimize the tax impact in corporate distributions, constructive dividends, and stock redemptions.

CORPORATE DISTRIBUTIONS

In connection with the discussion of corporate distributions, the following points need reinforcement:

- Because E & P is the measure of dividend income, its periodic determination is essential to corporate planning. Thus, an E & P account should be established and maintained, particularly if the possibility exists that a corporate distribution might be a return of capital.
- Accumulated E & P is the sum of all past years' current E & P. There is no statute of limitations on the computation of E & P. The IRS can, for example, redetermine a corporation's current E & P for a tax year long since passed. Such a change affects accumulated E & P and has a direct impact on the taxability of current distributions to shareholders.
- Distributions can be planned to avoid or minimize dividend exposure.

EXAMPLE 41

After several unprofitable years, Darter Corporation has a deficit in accumulated E & P of $100,000 as of January 1, 1998. Starting in 1998, Darter expects to generate annual E & P of $50,000 for the next four years and would like to distribute this amount to its shareholders. The corporation's cash position (for dividend purposes) will correspond to the current E & P generated. Compare the following possibilities:

1. On December 31 of 1998, 1999, 2000, and 2001, Darter Corporation distributes a cash dividend of $50,000.
2. On December 31 of 1999 and 2001, Darter Corporation distributes a cash dividend of $100,000.

The two alternatives are illustrated as follows:

Year	Accumulated E & P (First of Year)	Current E & P	Distribution	Amount of Dividend
Alternative 1				
1998	($100,000)	$50,000	$50,000	$50,000
1999	(100,000)	50,000	50,000	50,000
2000	(100,000)	50,000	50,000	50,000
2001	(100,000)	50,000	50,000	50,000

CONCEPT SUMMARY 18–3

Corporate Distributions

1. Without a special provision, corporate distributions are taxed as dividend income to the recipient shareholders to the extent of the distributing corporation's E & P accumulated since February 28, 1913, or to the extent of current E & P. Any excess is treated as a return of capital to the extent of the shareholder's basis in the stock and, thereafter, as capital gain.

2. Property distributions are considered dividends (taxed as noted in item 1) in the amount of their fair market value. The amount deemed distributed is reduced by any liabilities on the property distributed. The shareholder's basis in the property is its fair market value.

3. Earnings and profits of a corporation are increased by corporate earnings for the taxable year computed in the same manner as the corporation computes its taxable income. As a general rule, the account is increased for all items of income, whether taxed or not, and reduced by all items of expense, whether deductible or not. Refer to Concept Summary 18–1 for a summary of the effect of certain transactions on taxable income in arriving at current E & P.

4. A corporation recognizes gain, but not loss, on distributions of property to its shareholders. E & P of the distributing corporation is reduced by the amount of money distributed or by the greater of the fair market value or the adjusted basis of property distributed less the amount of any liability applicable to the distributed property.

5. As a general rule, stock dividends or stock rights (representing stock in the distributing corporation) are not taxed, with certain exceptions.

6. Stock redemptions that qualify under § 302(b) are given sale or exchange treatment. This provision requires that such distributions be either substantially disproportionate, complete terminations, or not essentially equivalent to a dividend. In determining whether a transaction is a not essentially equivalent redemption or a disproportionate redemption, the attribution rules apply. However, in a complete termination redemption, the family attribution rules may be waived if certain conditions are met.

7. If stock included in a decedent's estate represents more than 35% of the adjusted gross estate, § 303 provides automatic sale or exchange treatment on its redemption.

8. A corporation is taxed on the appreciation of property distributed in redemption of its stock.

9. In a stock redemption, the E & P account of the distributing corporation generally is reduced in proportion to the amount of the corporation's outstanding stock that is redeemed.

		Alternative 2		
1998	($100,000)	$50,000	$ –0–	$ –0–
1999	(50,000)	50,000	100,000	50,000
2000	(50,000)	50,000	–0–	–0–
2001	–0–	50,000	100,000	50,000

Alternative 1 leads to an overall result of $200,000 in dividend income since each $50,000 distribution is fully covered by current E & P. Alternative 2, however, results in only $100,000 of dividend income to the shareholders. The remaining $100,000 is a return of capital. Why? At the time Darter Corporation made its first distribution of $100,000 on December 31, 1999, it had a deficit of $50,000 in accumulated E & P (the original deficit of $100,000 is reduced by the $50,000 of current E & P from 1998). Consequently, the $100,000 distribution yields a $50,000 dividend (the current E & P for 1999) and $50,000 as a return of capital. As of January 1, 2000, Darter's accumulated E & P has a deficit balance of $50,000, since a distribution cannot increase a deficit in E & P. Add in $50,000 of current E & P from 2000, and the balance as of January 1, 2001, is zero. Thus, the second distribution of $100,000 made on December 31, 2001, also yields $50,000 of dividends (the current E & P for 2001) and $50,000 as a return of capital. ▼

ETHICAL
CONSIDERATIONS

Playing Games with the Statute of Limitations

n 1991, Beige Corporation made a cash distribution to its shareholders, one of whom was Steve Jordan. At that time, the parties involved believed that the distribution was a return of capital because Beige had no E & P. Accordingly, none of the shareholders reported dividend income. In Steve's case, he reduced the $200,000 original basis of his stock investment by $40,000, his share of the distribution. In 1998, it is discovered that E & P had been incorrectly computed. The 1991 distribution was fully covered by E & P and *should not have been treated as a return of capital.*

In 1999, Steve sells his stock in Beige Corporation for $350,000. He plans to report a gain of $150,000 [$350,000 (selling price) – $200,000 (original basis)] on the sale. Although Steve realizes that he should have recognized dividend income of $40,000 for 1991, the statute of limitations has made this a closed year.

Comment on Steve's situation.

CONSTRUCTIVE DIVIDENDS

Tax planning can be particularly effective in avoiding constructive dividend situations. Shareholders should try to structure their dealings with the corporation on an arm's length basis. For example, reasonable rent should be paid for the use of corporate property, and a fair price should be paid for its purchase. The parties should make every effort to support the amount involved with appraisal data or market information obtained from reliable sources at or near the time of the transaction. Dealings between shareholders and a closely held corporation should be as formal as possible. In the case of loans to shareholders, for example, the parties should provide for an adequate rate of interest and written evidence of the debt. Shareholders should also establish and follow a realistic repayment schedule.

If shareholders wish to bail out corporate profits in a form deductible to the corporation, a balanced mix of the possible alternatives lessens the risk of constructive dividend treatment. Rent for the use of shareholder property, interest on amounts borrowed from shareholders, or salaries for services rendered by shareholders are all feasible substitutes for dividend distributions. But overdoing any one approach may attract the attention of the IRS. Too much interest, for example, may mean the corporation is thinly capitalized, and some of the debt may be reclassified as equity investment.

Much can be done to protect against the disallowance of unreasonable compensation. Example 42 is an illustration, all too common in a family corporation, of what *not* to do.

EXAMPLE 42

Bob Cole wholly owns Eagle Corporation. Corporate employees and annual salaries include Mrs. Cole ($30,000), Cole, Jr. ($20,000), Bob Cole ($160,000), and Ed ($80,000). The operation of Eagle Corporation is shared about equally between Bob Cole and Ed, who is an unrelated party. Mrs. Cole performed significant services for Eagle during its formative years but now merely attends the annual meeting of the board of directors. Cole, Jr., Bob Cole's son, is a full-time student and occasionally signs papers for the corporation in his capacity as treasurer. Eagle Corporation has not distributed a dividend for 10 years, although it has accumulated substantial E & P. Mrs. Cole, Cole, Jr., and Bob Cole run the risk of a finding of unreasonable compensation, based on the following factors:

- Mrs. Cole's salary is vulnerable unless proof is available that some or all of her $30,000 annual salary is payment for services rendered to the corporation in prior years, if she was underpaid for those years.[47]
- Cole, Jr.'s salary is also vulnerable; he does not appear to earn the $20,000 paid to him by the corporation. True, neither Cole, Jr., nor Mrs. Cole is a shareholder, but each one's relationship to Bob Cole is enough of a tie-in to raise the unreasonable compensation issue.
- Bob Cole's salary appears susceptible to challenge. Why is he receiving $80,000 more than Ed when it appears they share equally in the operation of the corporation?
- The fact that Eagle Corporation has not distributed dividends over the past 10 years, even though it is capable of doing so, increases the likelihood of a constructive dividend. ▼

ETHICAL
CONSIDERATIONS

Disallowed Deductions

Upon audit of Crow Corporation's income tax return for tax year 1997, the IRS disallowed as a deduction $250,000 of the $600,000 salary paid to Ron, Crow's president and principal shareholder. The disallowed salary was deemed to be unreasonable. In 1998, Crow Corporation again pays Ron a salary of $600,000. Can Crow Corporation deduct this salary on its 1998 tax return or is it bound by the audit conducted by the IRS for the prior year?

STOCK REDEMPTIONS

Stock redemptions offer several possibilities for tax planning:

- A not essentially equivalent redemption provides minimal utility and generally should be relied upon only as a last resort. Instead, the redemption should be structured to fit one of the safe harbors. These include disproportionate redemptions, complete termination redemptions, and redemptions to pay death taxes.
- For a family corporation in which all of the shareholders are related to each other, the only hope of achieving sale or exchange treatment may lie in the use of a redemption that completely terminates a shareholder's interest or one that follows a shareholder's death. In a complete termination redemption, be careful that the family stock attribution rules are avoided. Here, strict compliance with the requirements (e.g., the withdrawing shareholder does not continue as an employee of the corporation and does not reacquire an interest in the corporation within 10 years) is crucial.
- The alternative to a qualifying stock redemption is dividend treatment of the distribution. But do not conclude that a dividend is always undesirable from a tax standpoint. Suppose the distributing corporation has little, if any, E & P. Or the distributee-shareholder is another corporation. In the latter situation, dividend treatment may be preferred because of the availability of the dividends received deduction.
- When using the special redemption rules following a shareholder's death, the amount to be sheltered from dividend treatment is limited to the sum

---

[47]See, for example, *R. J. Nicoll Co.*, 59 T.C. 37 (1972).

of death taxes and certain estate administration expenses. However, a redemption in excess of the limitation does not destroy the applicability of this provision.

- The timing and sequence of a redemption should be handled carefully.

EXAMPLE 43

Bluejay Corporation's stock is held as follows: Abby (60 shares), Antonio (20 shares), and Ali (20 shares). Abby, Antonio, and Ali are not related to each other. The corporation redeems 24 of Abby's shares. Shortly thereafter, it redeems 5 of Antonio's shares. Does Abby's redemption qualify as a disproportionate redemption? Taken in isolation, it would appear to meet the 80% and 50% tests. Yet, if the IRS takes into account the later redemption of Antonio's shares, Abby has not satisfied the 50% test; she still owns $^{36}/_{71}$ of the corporation after both redemptions. A greater time lag between the two redemptions places Abby in a better position to argue against collapsing the series of redemptions into one. ▼

KEY TERMS

Accumulated earnings and profits, 18–8

Attribution, 18–20

Business purpose, 18–21

Complete termination redemption, 18–25

Constructive dividend, 18–13

Current earnings and profits, 18–8

Disproportionate redemption, 18–22

Earnings and profits (E & P), 18–3

Meaningful reduction test, 18–22

Not essentially equivalent redemption, 18–22

Property dividend, 18–10

Redemption to pay death taxes, 18–25

Stock dividend, 18–16

Stock redemption, 18–18

Stock rights, 18–17

Unreasonable compensation, 18–14

PROBLEM MATERIALS

DISCUSSION QUESTIONS

1. How are regular distributions of a corporation's earnings taxed to a shareholder?

2. What is meant by the term *earnings and profits*?

3. Describe the effect of a distribution in a year when the distributing corporation has any of the following:
   a. A deficit in accumulated E & P and a positive amount in current E & P.
   b. A positive amount in accumulated E & P and a deficit in current E & P.
   c. A deficit in both current and accumulated E & P.
   d. A positive amount in both current and accumulated E & P.

4. How do gains and losses from property transactions affect the determination of E & P?

5. Five years ago, a corporation determined its current E & P to be $100,000. In the current year, it makes a distribution of $200,000 to its shareholders. The IRS contends that the current E & P of the corporation five years ago was really $150,000.
   a. In view of the statute of limitations, can the IRS successfully make this contention?
   b. What difference would the additional $50,000 in E & P make?

6. A calendar year corporation has no accumulated E & P but expects to earn current E & P for the year. A cash distribution to its shareholders on January 1 should result in a return of capital. Comment on the validity of this assumption.

7. Why would a corporation distribute a property dividend?

8. Warbler Corporation has an excess of unimproved real estate. It desires to distribute $200,000 in value to its shareholders as a property dividend. Available choices are as follows: parcel A (basis of $150,000); parcel B (basis of $200,000); and parcel C (basis of $250,000). If all parcels have a value of $200,000, what do you suggest? Why?

9. A corporation is considering making a property distribution to its shareholders. If appreciated property is to be used, does it matter to the distributing corporation whether the property distributed is a long-term capital asset or depreciable property subject to recapture?

10. Yellow Corporation distributes $50,000 to each of its three shareholders, Ted, Tiffany, and Maize Corporation. Discuss the issues involved in determining how the distribution is treated for tax purposes both to the shareholders and to Yellow Corporation.

11. Tina is the president and sole shareholder of Buff Corporation. She is paid a salary of $250,000 in the current year. Buff Corporation also advances her $50,000 as an interest-free loan. What are the tax issues?

12. Under what conditions are stock dividends taxable?

13. How are nontaxable stock rights handled for tax purposes? Taxable stock rights?

14. Whether compensation paid to a corporate employee is reasonable is a question of fact to be determined from the surrounding circumstances. How would the resolution of this problem be affected by each of the following factors?
    a. The employee is not a shareholder but is related to the sole owner of the corporate employer.
    b. The shareholder-employee never completed high school.
    c. The shareholder-employee is a full-time college student.
    d. The shareholder-employee was underpaid for her services during the formative period of the corporate employer.
    e. The corporate employer pays only a nominal dividend each year.
    f. Year-end bonuses are paid to all shareholder-employees, but not to nonshareholder-employees.

15. Falcon Corporation is wholly owned by Sharon. Corporate employees and their annual salaries include Sharon, $150,000; Dawn, Sharon's daughter, $60,000; Rick, Sharon's son, $50,000; and Troy, $30,000. Falcon's operation is shared about equally between Sharon and Troy (an unrelated party). Dawn and Rick are full-time college students at a university about 200 miles away. Falcon Corporation has substantial E & P but has not distributed a dividend in the past six years. Discuss problems related to Falcon's salary arrangement.

16. Lana wants to retire and sell her shares in Brown Corporation either to Brown's remaining shareholders, Jack and Ivan, or to a third party. What issues may support a preference for Brown Corporation to redeem Lana's shares rather than for Jack and Ivan or a third party to purchase them?

17. What effect does state law have on the determination of whether a corporate distribution qualifies as a stock redemption for tax purposes?

18. Under the attribution rules, a shareholder is deemed to own the stock of certain "related parties." Under what circumstances is stock attributed from and to an entity?

19. Do the stock attribution rules apply to stock redemptions in complete termination of a shareholder's interest? Explain.

20. Wilma owns 200 shares in Cardinal Corporation, which represents a 60% interest in Cardinal. Wilma also owns 100 shares in Wren Corporation. Cardinal Corporation owns 100 shares in Wren Corporation. Compare Wilma's deemed stock ownership in Wren Corporation with Cardinal's deemed ownership in Wren.

21. When is a redemption considered to be a "not essentially equivalent to a dividend" redemption?

22. Two years ago José transferred property he had used in his sole proprietorship to Cardinal Corporation, a newly formed corporation, for 50 shares of Cardinal stock. The property had an adjusted basis of $300,000 and a fair market value of $800,000. Six months later José's friend, Peggy, transferred property she had used in her sole proprietorship to Cardinal Corporation for 50 shares of Cardinal stock and cash of $100,000. Her property had an adjusted basis of $150,000 and a value of $900,000. Both José and Peggy serve on Cardinal's board of directors. In addition, Peggy has a contract with Cardinal to perform services to the corporation. In the current year, Cardinal Corporation redeems all of Peggy's Cardinal stock for property with a probable value of $1,400,000. What issues must you consider?

23. Under what circumstances is a redemption to pay death taxes available? What is the tax effect of such a transaction?

24. Abby and her daughter, Ann, who are the only shareholders of Bluebird Corporation, each paid $100,000 four years ago for their shares in Bluebird. Abby also owns 20% of the stock in Redbird Corporation. The Redbird stock is worth $500,000, and Abby's basis in the stock is $50,000. Abby died in the current year leaving all her property to her husband, Gary, but Ann wants to be the sole shareholder of Bluebird Corporation. Bluebird has assets worth $2 million (basis of $700,000) and E & P of $1 million. Abby's estate is worth approximately $4 million. Abby had made gifts during her lifetime to Ann. Identify the relevant tax issues.

25. Cardinal Corporation desires to transfer cash of $10,000 or property worth $10,000 to its sole shareholder, Linda, in a transaction that will be treated as a dividend to Linda. Explain the general consequences to Cardinal if it distributes either cash, property whose fair market value exceeds its adjusted basis, or property whose adjusted basis exceeds its fair market value.

PROBLEMS

26. At the beginning of the year, Crane Corporation (a calendar year taxpayer) has accumulated E & P of $75,000. Its current E & P is $45,000. During the year, Crane distributes $135,000 ($67,500 each) to its equal shareholders, Pat and Chris. Pat has a basis of $12,000 in her stock, and Chris has a basis of $3,000 in his stock. How will the $135,000 distribution be treated for tax purposes?

27. In 1998, Gull Corporation received dividend income of $200,000 from a corporation in which it holds a 5% interest. Gull also received interest income of $40,000 from municipal bonds. The municipality used the proceeds from the sale of the bonds to construct a needed facility to house city documents and to provide office space for several city officials. Gull borrowed funds to purchase the municipal bonds and paid $20,000 in interest on the loan in 1998. Gull's taxable income exclusive of the items noted above was $150,000.
    a. What is Gull Corporation's taxable income for 1998 after considering the dividend income, the interest from the municipal bonds, and the interest paid on the indebtedness to purchase the municipals?
    b. What is Gull Corporation's E & P as of December 31, 1998, if its E & P account balance was $90,000 as of January 1, 1998?

28. Orange Corporation has a deficit in E & P of $90,000 on January 1, 1998. For 1998, Orange has a tax loss of $180,000 that increases the deficit in E & P by that amount.

    Orange's 1998 tax loss does not include any effect from a sale of land. The land, which had a basis of $450,000, was sold on November 15, 1998. In exchange, Orange received a $1,800,000 note. The note is to be paid in five installments, the first of which is payable on December 15, 1999. Because Orange did not elect out of the installment method, none of the $1,350,000 gain is taxable income for 1998.

    All of Orange's stock is owned by Nick, who has a basis of $150,000 in the stock. If Orange distributes $200,000 to Nick on December 31, 1998, how must Nick report the distribution for tax purposes?

29. Complete the following schedule for each case. Assume the shareholder has an ample basis in the stock investment.

Accumulated E & P Beginning of Year	Current E & P	Cash Distributions (All on Last Day of Year)	Amount Taxable	Return of Capital
a. $ 80,000	($ 20,000)	$100,000	$ _____	$ _____
b. (100,000)	60,000	80,000	_____	_____
c. 60,000	100,000	140,000	_____	_____
d. 120,000	(40,000)	90,000	_____	_____
e. Same as (d), except the distribution of $90,000 is made on June 30 and the corporation uses the calendar year for tax purposes.			_____	_____

30. Complete the following schedule. For each case, assume that there is one shareholder, whose basis in the corporate stock is $20,000. Also assume that current losses accrue ratably throughout the year.

Accumulated E & P Beginning of Year	Current E & P	Cash Distributions (All on Last Day of Year)	Amount Taxable	Capital Gain
a. ($140,000)	$160,000	$170,000	$ _____	$ _____
b. 80,000	20,000	110,000	_____	_____
c. (100,000)	70,000	50,000	_____	_____
d. 200,000	(170,000)	90,000	_____	_____
e. Same as (d), except the distribution of $90,000 is made on June 30 and the corporation uses the calendar year for tax purposes.			_____	_____

31. Dana, the sole shareholder of Tern Corporation, had a basis of $30,000 in the stock in Tern that he sold to Eli on July 30, 1998, for $180,000. Tern had accumulated E & P of $75,000 on January 1, 1998, and current E & P (for 1998) of $60,000. During 1998, Tern made the following distributions: $120,000 cash to Dana on July 1, and $120,000 cash to Eli on December 30. How will the distributions be taxed to Dana and to Eli? What gain will Dana recognize on the sale of his stock to Eli?

32. In each of the following *independent* situations, indicate the effect on taxable income and E & P, stating the amount of any increase (or decrease) as a result of the transaction. Assume E & P has already been increased by current taxable income.

Transaction	Taxable Income Increase (Decrease)	E & P Increase (Decrease)
a. Receipt of $15,000 tax-exempt income	_____	_____
b. Payment of $15,150 Federal income taxes	_____	_____
c. Collection of $100,000 on life insurance policy on corporate president (assume no cash surrender value)	_____	_____
d. Charitable contribution, $30,000, with $20,000 allowable as a deduction in the current tax year	_____	_____
e. Deduction of remaining $10,000 charitable contribution in succeeding year	_____	_____
f. Realized gain on involuntary conversion of $200,000 ($30,000 of gain is recognized)	_____	_____

33. In each of the following *independent* situations, indicate the effect on taxable income and E & P, stating the amount of any increase (or decrease) as a result of the transaction. Assume E & P has already been increased by current taxable income.

Transaction	Taxable Income Increase (Decrease)	E & P Increase (Decrease)
a. Mine exploration and development costs incurred on July 1 of the current tax year and deductible from current taxable income in the amount of $60,000.	_____	_____
b. A $120,000 refund of Federal income taxes paid in previous year.	_____	_____
c. Payment of key employee life insurance premium. The premium paid was $18,000. As a result of the premium, the cash surrender value of the policy increased by $11,000.	_____	_____
d. MACRS depreciation of $150,000. ADS depreciation would have been $90,000.	_____	_____
e. Interest expense of $30,000 on loan used to purchase municipal bonds.	_____	_____
f. Capital losses incurred during the year of $30,000. Assume capital gains incurred during the year are $18,000.	_____	_____
g. Net operating loss carryforward of $11,000 deducted in the current year.	_____	_____
h. Sale of unimproved real estate, basis of $300,000, fair market value of $900,000 (no election out of installment method; payments in year of sale total $100,000).	_____	_____

34. Penguin Corporation, with E & P of $500,000, distributes land worth $110,000, adjusted basis of $150,000, to Orca, a corporate shareholder. The land is subject to a liability of $30,000, which Orca assumes.
    a. What is the amount of dividend income to Orca?
    b. What is Orca's basis in the land it received?
    c. How does the distribution affect Penguin Corporation's E & P account?

35. At the beginning of the current year, Dove Corporation (a calendar year taxpayer) has accumulated E & P of $40,000. During the year, Dove incurs a $30,000 loss from operations that accrued ratably. On July 1, Dove distributes $35,000 in cash to Mary, its sole shareholder. How will the $35,000 be taxed to Mary?

36. Snipe Corporation has E & P of $100,000. It distributes equipment with a fair market value of $90,000 (adjusted basis of $20,000) to its sole shareholder, Mary. The land is subject to a liability of $15,000, which Mary assumes. What are the tax consequences to Snipe Corporation and to Mary?

37. Copper Corporation has two equal shareholders, Cybil and Sally. Cybil acquired her Copper stock three years ago by transferring property worth $600,000, basis of $200,000, for 60 shares of the stock. Sally acquired 60 shares in Copper Corporation two years ago by transferring property worth $620,000, basis of $70,000. Copper Corporation's accumulated E & P as of January 1 of the current year is $300,000. On March 1 of the current year, the corporation distributed to Cybil property worth $100,000, basis to Copper of $30,000. It distributed cash of $200,000 to Sally. On July 1 of the current year,

Sally sold her stock to Dana for $800,000. On December 1 of the current year, Copper distributed cash of $80,000 each to Dana and to Cybil. What are the tax issues?

38. Emu Corporation is a closely held company with accumulated E & P of $710,000 and current E & P of $175,000. Connor and Cameron equally own Emu. On a day-to-day basis, Connor and Cameron share management responsibilities equally, with Cameron focusing on operations and Connor focusing on sales. What are the tax consequences of the following transactions between Emu, Connor, and Cameron? How does each transaction affect Emu's E & P? Assume each transaction is independent.

   a. Emu sells a vacant lot (adjusted basis of $30,000, fair market value of $23,000) to Connor for $15,000.

   b. Emu lends Cameron $110,000 on January 1 of this year. The loan, evidenced by a note, is due on demand. No interest is charged on the loan. The current applicable Federal interest rate is 10%.

   c. Emu owns a cottage in Aspen, Colorado. It rents the cottage to tourists throughout the year. During the current year, Connor and Cameron each use the cottage for two weeks and pay no rent to Emu. The rental value of the cottage is $3,500 per week. Cameron has indicated that the average maintenance cost per week for the rental is $600.

   d. Cameron leases a truck to Emu for $12,000 for the year. If the corporation were to lease the same truck from a car dealer, the cost of the lease would be $7,000.

39. Verdigris Corporation owns 25% of the stock of Rust Corporation. Rust Corporation, with E & P of $150,000 on December 20, distributes land with a fair market value of $60,000 and a basis of $90,000 to Verdigris. The land is subject to a liability of $50,000, which Verdigris assumes.

   a. How is Verdigris Corporation taxed on the distribution?

   b. What is Rust Corporation's E & P after the distribution?

40. At the beginning of its taxable year, Green Corporation had E & P of $200,000. Green sold an asset at a loss of $200,000 on June 30. It incurred a deficit in current E & P of $220,000, which includes the $200,000 loss on the sale of the asset, for the calendar year. Assume Green made a distribution of $60,000 to its sole individual shareholder on July 1. How will the shareholder be taxed on the $60,000?

41. The stock in White Corporation is owned equally by Fred and Red Corporation. On January 1, White had a deficit in accumulated E & P of $150,000. Its current E & P was $105,000. During the year, White distributed cash of $45,000 to both Fred and Red Corporation. How will Fred and Red Corporation be taxed on the distribution? What will be the accumulated E & P of White Corporation at the end of the year?

42. Myrtle Adams paid $180,000 for 15 shares of stock in Petrel Corporation five years ago. In November 1997, she received a nontaxable stock dividend of 5 additional shares in Petrel Corporation. She sells the 5 shares in March 1998 for $60,000. What is her gain, and how is it taxed? Prepare a letter to your client and a memo for the file. Myrtle's address is 14009 Pine Street, Dover, DE 19901.

43. Lark Corporation declares a nontaxable dividend payable in rights to subscribe to common stock. One right and $60 entitle the holder to subscribe to one share of stock. One right is issued for each share of stock owned. At the date of distribution of the rights, the market value of the stock was $80 per share, and the market value of the rights was $20 per right. Karen, a shareholder, owns 100 shares of stock that she purchased two years ago for $3,000. Karen received 100 rights, of which she exercises 60 to purchase 60 additional shares. She sells the remaining 40 rights for $750. What are the tax consequences of these transactions to Karen?

44. Black Corporation has 200 shares of common stock outstanding, owned as follows: Peggy, 100 shares; Carlos (unrelated to Peggy), 50 shares; estate of Vern (Peggy's father), 50 shares. Peggy is the beneficiary of Vern's estate. Determine whether the following redemptions of Black Corporation receive sale or exchange treatment:

   a. Black Corporation redeems the stock of Vern's estate. Assume that § 303 (redemptions to pay death taxes) is not available.

   b. Black Corporation redeems all of Peggy's 100 shares.

   c. Black Corporation redeems all of Peggy's 100 shares and all of the 50 shares of Vern's estate. Assume that § 303 (redemptions to pay death taxes) is not available.

45. Rosa owns 110 shares of the 200 shares of Bluebird Corporation. Rosa paid $1,000 per share for the stock five years ago. The remaining stock in Bluebird Corporation is owned by several unrelated individuals. In the current year, Bluebird redeems 20 of Rosa's shares for $60,000 ($3,000 per share). Bluebird has E & P of $200,000.

   a. How must Rosa report the $60,000?

   b. What is Rosa's basis in her remaining shares?

46. Robin Corporation has 1,000 shares of common stock outstanding. The shares are owned by unrelated shareholders as follows: Leo Jones, 400 shares; Lori Johnson, 400 shares; and Lana Pierce, 200 shares. The corporation redeems 100 shares of the stock owned by Lana for $45,000. Lana paid $100 per share for her stock two years ago. Robin's E & P was $400,000 on the date of redemption. What is the tax effect to Lana of the redemption? Prepare a letter to Lana (1000 Main Street, Oldtown, MN 55166) and a memo for the file in which you explain your conclusions.

47. In Problem 46, assume Leo is Lana's father. How would this affect the tax status of the redemption? What if Leo were Lana's brother instead of her father?

48. Hal and Hans own all the stock in Green Corporation. Each has a basis of $15,000 in his 50 shares. Green Corporation has accumulated E & P of $550,000. Hal wishes to retire in the current year and wants to sell his stock for $300,000, the fair market value. Hans would like to purchase Hal's shares and, thus, become the sole shareholder in Green Corporation, but Hans is short of funds. What are the tax consequences to Hal, to Hans, and to Green Corporation under the following circumstances?

   a. Green Corporation distributes cash of $300,000 to Hans, and he uses the cash to purchase Hal's shares.

   b. Green Corporation redeems all of Hal's shares for $300,000.

49. In the current year, Red Corporation transfers land to a shareholder's estate to carry out a § 303 redemption (redemption to pay death taxes). The land is worth $1 million and has a tax basis to Red Corporation of $400,000. The estate sells the land nine months later for $1,100,000. What are the tax results to Red Corporation and to the estate as a result of the transfer? The death taxes and funeral and administration costs for the estate total $2 million.

50. White Corporation has 100 shares of common stock outstanding owned as follows: Ann, 50 shares, and Bonnie (an unrelated party), 50 shares. Ann and Bonnie each paid $1,000 per share for the White Corporation stock 10 years ago. White has $100,000 of accumulated E & P and $20,000 of current E & P. White distributes land held as an investment (fair market value of $80,000, adjusted basis of $30,000) to Ann in redemption of 25 of her shares.

   a. What are the tax results to Ann on the redemption of her stock in White Corporation?

   b. What gain or loss results to White Corporation on the redemption?

   c. What is White's E & P after the redemption?

51. Wren Corporation has 500 shares of stock outstanding. It redeems 50 shares for $90,000 when it has paid-in capital of $300,000 and E & P of $400,000. What is the reduction in Wren's E & P as a result of the redemption? Prepare a letter to Wren Corporation (506 Wall Street, Winona, MN 55987) and a memo for the file in which you explain your conclusions.

Research Problems for this chapter appear at the end of Chapter 28.

Corporations: Distributions in Complete Liquidation and an Overview of Reorganizations

LEARNING OBJECTIVES

After completing Chapter 19, you should be able to:

1. Understand the tax consequences of complete liquidations for both the corporation and its shareholders.

2. Understand the general form and tax consequences of corporate reorganizations.

3. Identify tax planning opportunities available to minimize the tax impact in complete liquidations.

LIQUIDATIONS—IN GENERAL

1 LEARNING OBJECTIVE
Understand the tax consequences of complete liquidations for both the corporation and its shareholders.

When a stock redemption occurs or a dividend is distributed, the assumption usually is that the corporation will continue as a going-concern. However, with a complete liquidation, corporate existence terminates. A complete liquidation, like a qualified stock redemption, produces sale or exchange treatment to the shareholder. However, the tax effects of a liquidation to the corporation vary somewhat from those of a stock redemption.

THE LIQUIDATION PROCESS

A **corporate liquidation** exists for tax purposes when a corporation ceases to be a going-concern. The corporation continues solely to wind up affairs, pay debts, and distribute any remaining assets to its shareholders.[1] Legal dissolution under state law is not required for the liquidation to be complete for tax purposes. A transaction will be treated as a liquidation even if the corporation retains a nominal amount of assets to pay remaining debts and preserve its legal status.[2]

A liquidation may occur for one or more of several reasons. The corporate business may have been unsuccessful. But even when a business has been profitable, the shareholders may nonetheless decide to terminate the corporation to acquire its assets. A liquidation often occurs when another person or corporation wants to purchase the assets of the corporation. The purchaser may buy the stock of the shareholders and then liquidate the corporation to acquire the assets. On the other hand, the purchaser may buy the assets directly from the corporation. After the assets are sold, the corporation distributes the sales proceeds to its shareholders and liquidates. As one might expect, the different means used to liquidate a corporation produce varying tax results.

---

[1] Reg. § 1.332–2(c).

[2] Rev.Rul. 54–518, 1954–2 C.B. 142.

LIQUIDATIONS AND OTHER DISTRIBUTIONS COMPARED

A nonliquidating property distribution, whether in the form of a dividend or a stock redemption, produces gain (but not loss) to the distributing corporation. For the shareholder, the receipt of cash or other property produces dividend income to the extent of the corporation's E & P. On the other hand, a qualifying stock redemption results in sale or exchange treatment.

The tax effects to the shareholder in a complete liquidation are similar to those in a qualifying stock redemption in that a liquidation also yields sale or exchange treatment. Still, a complete liquidation produces somewhat different tax consequences to the liquidating corporation. With certain exceptions, a liquidating corporation recognizes gain *and* loss upon the distribution of its assets.

As in the case of a stock redemption, E & P has no tax impact on the gain or loss to be recognized by the shareholders of the corporation undergoing liquidation. The provision governing dividend distributions does not apply to complete liquidations.[3]

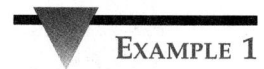

EXAMPLE 1

Green Corporation, with E & P of $40,000, makes a cash distribution of $50,000 to its sole shareholder. Assume the shareholder's basis in the Green stock is $20,000 and the stock is held as an investment. If the distribution is not in complete liquidation or is not a qualifying stock redemption, the shareholder recognizes dividend income of $40,000 (the amount of Green's E & P) and treats the remaining $10,000 of the distribution as a return of capital. If the distribution is pursuant to a complete liquidation or is a qualifying stock redemption, the shareholder has a capital gain of $30,000 [$50,000 (the amount of the distribution) – $20,000 (the basis in the stock)]. In the latter case, Green's E & P is of no consequence to the tax result to the shareholder. ▼

In the event the distribution results in a *loss* to the shareholder, an important distinction can exist between stock redemptions and liquidations. The distinction arises because losses between related parties in a redemption transaction are not allowed whereas losses may be recognized by shareholders in a complete liquidation.[4]

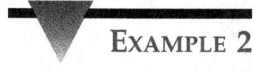

EXAMPLE 2

The stock of Robin Corporation is owned equally by three brothers, Rex, Sam, and Ted. When Ted's basis in his stock investment is $40,000, the corporation distributes $30,000 to him in cancellation of all his shares. If the distribution is a qualifying stock redemption, the $10,000 realized loss is not recognized.[5] Ted and Robin Corporation are related parties because Ted is deemed to own more than 50% in value of the corporation's outstanding stock. Ted's direct ownership is limited to 33⅓%, but through his brothers, he owns indirectly another 66⅔% for a total of 100%. On the other hand, if the distribution qualifies as a complete liquidation, Ted's $10,000 realized loss is recognized. ▼

As to the basis of noncash property received from the corporation, the rules governing liquidations and stock redemptions are identical. Section 334(a) specifies that the basis of property distributed in a taxable complete liquidation is its fair market value on the date of distribution.

In the following pages, the tax consequences of a complete liquidation of a corporation are examined first from the standpoint of the effect on the distributing corporation and then in terms of the effect on the shareholder. Because the tax

---

[3]§ 331(b).
[4]§ 267(a).

[5]*McCarthy v. Conley, Jr.*, 65–1 USTC ¶9262, 15 AFTR2d 447, 341 F.2d 948 (CA–2, 1965).

rules differ when a controlled subsidiary is liquidated, the rules relating to the liquidation of a controlled subsidiary receive separate treatment.

LIQUIDATIONS—EFFECT ON THE DISTRIBUTING CORPORATION

A corporation in the process of complete liquidation may or may not be required to recognize gain or loss, depending on the nature of the transaction. The general rules relating to complete liquidations require the distributing corporation to recognize gain or loss. Loss is not recognized, however, for certain distributions of property to related shareholders and in the case of distributions or sales of built-in loss property. Under § 337, a subsidiary corporation does not recognize gain or loss for distributions to a parent corporation that owns 80 percent or more of the subsidiary's stock.

THE GENERAL RULE

Section 336 provides that a liquidating corporation recognizes gain or loss on the distribution of property in complete liquidation. The property is treated as if it were sold at its fair market value. This requirement is consistent with the notion of double taxation that is inherent in operating a business as a C corporation. As a result, liquidating distributions are subject to tax at both the corporate level and the shareholder level. As in a stock redemption, when property distributed in a complete liquidation is subject to a liability of the liquidating corporation, the deemed fair market value of that property is treated as not being less than the amount of the liability.

EXAMPLE 3

As part of a complete liquidation, Warbler Corporation distributes to its shareholders land held as an investment (basis of $200,000, fair market value of $300,000). The land is subject to a liability of $250,000. Warbler Corporation has a gain of $100,000 on the distribution ($300,000 – $200,000). If, instead, the liability were $350,000, Warbler's gain on the distribution would be $150,000 ($350,000 – $200,000). ▼

ETHICAL CONSIDERATIONS

Reporting Business Activities—Liquidation Consequences?

Ten years ago, Thomas incorporated his laundry service and became the sole shareholder of Tom's Laundry, Inc. Until 1997, Tom's Laundry Inc., filed and paid taxes as a corporate taxpayer (Form 1120). In early 1997, Thomas read about the "check-the-box" Regulations that allow a taxpayer to choose the entity form of doing business for tax purposes. Having tired of the additional requirements and complexities of the corporate entity form, Thomas took advantage of the "check-the-box" Regulations and reported all of the 1997 business activity for Tom's Laundry, Inc., on his 1997 personal income tax return (Form 1040) as a sole proprietorship (Schedule C). Thomas did the same for 1998. Since he continued to report all of the business activity, albeit on his personal return, Thomas did not formally liquidate Tom's Laundry, Inc. You are preparing Thomas's 1999 personal income tax return and become aware of these facts. How should you proceed?

Limitation on Losses.   As a general rule, losses on the distribution of property in a complete liquidation are recognized. There are two exceptions, however. The first exception applies to certain distributions to related parties. The second exception prevents a loss deduction on certain sales and distributions of property that was contributed to the corporation with a built-in loss shortly before the adoption of a plan of liquidation. In this instance, the built-in loss may be disallowed as a deduction upon liquidation even if the distribution is to an unrelated party.

These two exceptions prohibiting loss recognition exist because Congress was concerned that taxpayers might attempt to create artificial losses at the corporate level. Taxpayers could otherwise have accomplished this by contributing property with built-in losses to the corporation before a liquidation. Recall from Chapter 17 that in § 351 transfers (nontaxable transfers to a corporation in exchange for stock when the transferor is in control of the corporation) and contributions to capital, the transferor's tax basis carries over to the transferee corporation. Thus, a taxpayer might transfer high-basis, low-fair market value property to a corporation contemplating liquidation in the hope that the built-in losses would neutralize expected gains from appreciated property distributed or sold in the liquidation process. Consequently, to prevent abuse, the deductibility of losses is limited by these "anti-stuffing" rules in certain related-party situations and in certain sales and distributions of built-in loss property.[6] A corporation and a shareholder are considered related if the shareholder owns (directly or indirectly) more than 50 percent in value of the corporation's outstanding stock.

Related-Party Situations.   Losses are disallowed on distributions to *related parties* in either of the following cases:

- The distribution is *not* pro rata.
- The property distributed is *disqualified property*.

A *pro rata distribution* is one where each shareholder receives his or her share of *each* corporate asset. *Disqualified property* is property acquired by the liquidating corporation in a § 351 transaction or as a contribution to capital during the five-year period ending on the date of the distribution.

EXAMPLE 4

Bluebird Corporation's stock is held equally by three brothers. One year before Bluebird's liquidation, the shareholders transfer property (basis of $150,000, fair market value of $100,000) to the corporation in return for stock (a § 351 transaction). In liquidation, the corporation transfers the property (still worth $100,000) back to the brothers. Because each brother owns directly and indirectly more than 50% (i.e., 100% in this situation) of the stock and disqualified property is involved, Bluebird recognizes none of the $50,000 realized loss. ▼

EXAMPLE 5

Assume that Bluebird Corporation stock is owned by Lee and Terry, who are unrelated. Lee owns 80% and Terry owns 20% of the stock in the corporation. Bluebird has the following assets (none of which was acquired in a § 351 transaction or as a contribution to capital) that are distributed in complete liquidation of the corporation:

---

[6]§ 336(d). Section 267 provides the definition of related party for purposes of this provision.

	Adjusted Basis	Fair Market Value
Cash	$600,000	$600,000
Equipment	150,000	200,000
Building	400,000	200,000

Assume Bluebird Corporation distributes the equipment to Terry and the cash and the building to Lee. Bluebird recognizes a gain of $50,000 on the distribution of the equipment. The loss of $200,000 on the building will be disallowed because the distribution is not pro rata and the loss property is distributed to a related party. ▼

EXAMPLE 6

Assume that Bluebird Corporation in Example 5 distributed the cash and equipment to Lee and the building to Terry. Again, Bluebird recognizes the $50,000 gain on the equipment. However, it can now recognize the $200,000 loss on the building because the loss property is not distributed to a related party (i.e., Terry does not own more than 50% of the stock in Bluebird Corporation). ▼

Built-in Loss Situations.   The loss limitation provisions are extended to distributions to *unrelated parties* when loss property is transferred to a corporation shortly before the corporation is liquidated. This second exception to the general rule likewise is imposed to prevent the doubling of losses.

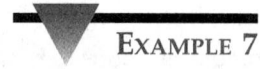

EXAMPLE 7

Nora, a shareholder in White Corporation, transfers property with a basis of $10,000, fair market value of $3,000, to the corporation in a transaction that qualifies under § 351. Nora's basis in the additional White stock acquired in exchange for the property is $10,000. White's basis in the property also is $10,000. A few months after the transfer, White Corporation adopts a plan of complete liquidation. Upon liquidation, White distributes the property to Nora. If White were permitted a loss deduction of $7,000, there would be a double loss because Nora would also recognize a loss of $7,000 upon receipt of the property [$3,000 (fair market value of the property) – $10,000 (basis in Nora's stock)]. To prevent the doubling of losses, the law prohibits White Corporation from taking a loss on the distribution even if Nora is an unrelated party. ▼

Losses are disallowed on distributions to shareholders who are not related parties when the property distributed was acquired in a § 351 transaction or as a contribution to capital. Furthermore, the property must have been contributed as part of a plan whose principal purpose was to cause the corporation to recognize a loss in connection with the liquidation. Such a purpose will be presumed if the transfer occurs within two years of the adoption of the liquidation plan. However, losses can be recognized if a business purpose was associated with the contribution of the property. Further, any *subsequent* decline in value after the property's contribution and prior to the distribution results in a deductible loss (subject to the related-party loss disallowance rule).[7]

The prohibition against a loss deduction on distributions of built-in loss property is broader than the related-party exception, which disallows losses only on certain distributions to related parties. The prohibition applies regardless of whether the shareholder is considered a related party. At the same time, however, the prohibition is narrower than the first exception since it applies only to property that had a built-in loss upon its acquisition by the corporation and only as to the amount of the built-in loss.

---

[7]§ 336(d)(2).

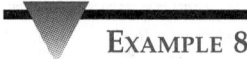

EXAMPLE 8

On January 2, 1998, in a transaction that qualifies under § 351, Brown Corporation acquires property with a basis of $10,000 and fair market value of $3,000. Brown adopts a plan of liquidation on July 1, 1998, and distributes the property to Rick, an unrelated party, on November 10, 1998, when the property is worth $1,000. Brown Corporation can recognize a loss of $2,000, the difference between the value of the property on the date of acquisition and the fair market value of the property on the date of distribution. Only the built-in loss of $7,000 [$3,000 (fair market value on date of acquisition) – $10,000 (basis)] is disallowed. ▼

EXAMPLE 9

Assume the property in Example 8 had a fair market value of $12,000 on the date Brown Corporation acquired it. However, the property has a fair market value of only $2,000 when Brown distributes the property upon the complete liquidation of the corporation. If the distribution is to an unrelated shareholder, Brown will recognize the entire $8,000 loss [$2,000 (fair market value on date of distribution) – $10,000 (basis)]. However, if the distribution is to a related party, Brown cannot recognize any of the loss because the property is disqualified property. When the distribution is to a related party, the loss is disallowed even though the entire decline in value occurred during the period the corporation held the property. ▼

The loss limitation can apply regardless of how long the corporation has held the property prior to liquidation. If the property is held for two years or less, a tax avoidance purpose is presumed. Still, if there is a clear and substantial relationship between the contributed property and the business of the corporation, a loss will be permitted on the *distribution* of the property to an unrelated party. When there was a business reason for transferring the loss property to the liquidating corporation, a loss will also be permitted on the *sale* of the property.

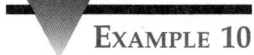

EXAMPLE 10

Cardinal Corporation's stock is held 60% by Manuel and 40% by Jack. One year before Cardinal's liquidation, property (basis of $150,000, fair market value of $100,000) is transferred to the corporation as a contribution to capital. There is no business reason for the transfer. In liquidation, Cardinal transfers the property (now with a fair market value of $90,000) to Jack. Even though the distribution is to an unrelated party, the built-in loss of $50,000 is not recognized. However, Cardinal can recognize the loss of $10,000 ($90,000 – $100,000) that occurred while it held the property. If the property is distributed to Manuel, a related party, even the $10,000 loss is disallowed. ▼

EXAMPLE 11

Assume in Example 10, that the property is transferred to Cardinal Corporation because a bank required the additional capital investment as a condition to making a loan to the corporation. Because there is a business purpose for the transfer, presumably all of the $60,000 loss is recognized if the property is distributed to Jack in liquidation. If the property is distributed to Manuel, a related party, the loss is disallowed. ▼

Rules governing distributions of loss property by a liquidating corporation are summarized in Figure 19–1.

Tax Paid on Net Gain.   To the extent that a corporation pays tax on the net amount of gain recognized at the corporate level, the proceeds available to be distributed to the shareholder are likewise reduced. This reduction for the payment of taxes will reduce the amount realized by the shareholder, which will then reduce the gain or increase the loss recognized.

EXAMPLE 12

Blue Corporation's assets are valued at $2,000,000 after payment of all corporate debts except for $300,000 of taxes payable on net gains it recognized on the liquidation. Therefore, the amount realized by the shareholders is $1,700,000 ($2,000,000 – $300,000). As described

▼ **FIGURE 19–1**
Distributions of Loss Property
by a Liquidating Corporation

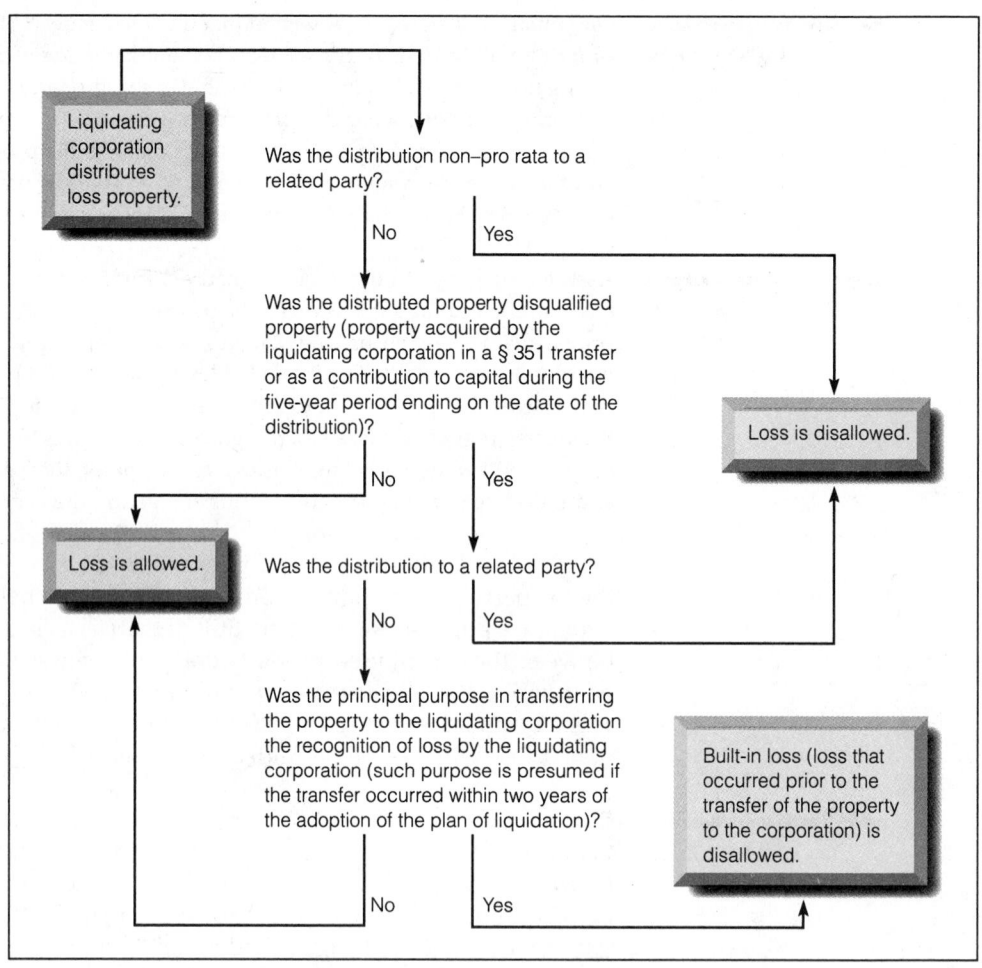

below, in determining the gain or loss recognized by a shareholder, the amount realized is offset by the stock's adjusted basis. ▼

Liquidations—Effect on the Shareholder

The tax consequences to the shareholders of a corporation in the process of liquidation are governed either by the general rule of § 331 or by one of two exceptions relating to the liquidation of a subsidiary.

THE GENERAL RULE

In the case of a complete liquidation, the general rule of § 331 provides for sale or exchange treatment.[8] Since gain or loss must be recognized on the sale or exchange of property unless an exception applies, the shareholder is treated as having sold

---

[8]§ 331(a)(1).

DE FACTO LIQUIDATION REDUCES TAX DEFICIENCY

It is not uncommon for shareholders of a closely held corporation to treat the entity's property as their own without regard to possible tax ramifications. Cases involving constructive corporate distributions are heard frequently by the courts. *Paul A. Rendina* (72 TCM 474, T.C.Memo. 1996–392) is a particularly interesting example of such a case.

The taxpayer, a certified public accountant, received title to two condominium units from a corporation in which he was a 50 percent shareholder. After the distribution, the corporation had no assets or business operations, but it never formally liquidated. The taxpayer did not report the receipt of the condos on his personal return. (The corporation also failed to file a corporate return to report the sale of 16 other condo units or the two distributed units.) The IRS argued that the taxpayer received an ordinary dividend distribution in the form of two condo units. The Tax Court, however, accepted the taxpayer's argument that he received the condo units as a de facto liquidation of his shares in the corporation. Although the taxpayer was still assessed the deficiency and associated penalties, the resulting sale or exchange treatment significantly reduced his total liability to the IRS.

his or her stock to the liquidating corporation. The difference between the fair market value of the assets received from the corporation and the adjusted basis of the stock surrendered is the gain or loss recognized by the shareholder. If the stock is a capital asset in the hands of the shareholder, capital gain or loss results. The burden of proof is on the taxpayer to furnish evidence as to the adjusted basis of the stock. In the absence of such evidence, the stock is deemed to have a zero basis, and the full amount of the liquidation proceeds becomes the amount of the gain recognized.[9]

Under the general liquidation provision, the shareholder's tax basis for property received in a liquidation is the property's fair market value on the date of distribution.[10]

SPECIAL RULE FOR CERTAIN INSTALLMENT OBLIGATIONS

The installment sale rules provide some relief from the bunching of gain that occurs when a liquidating corporation sells its assets on the installment basis. The liquidating corporation must recognize all gain on the distribution of the installment notes. However, the *shareholders'* gain on the receipt of the installment notes may be deferred to the point of collection.[11] This treatment requires the shareholders to allocate their bases in the stock among the various assets received from the corporation.

EXAMPLE 13

After adopting a plan of complete liquidation, Black Corporation sells its only asset, unimproved land held as an investment. The land has appreciated in value and is sold to Jane (an unrelated party) for $100,000. Under the terms of the sale, Black Corporation receives

---

[9]*John Calderazzo*, 34 TCM 1, T.C.Memo. 1975–1.
[10]§ 334(a).
[11]§ 453(h). This provision does not apply to the sale of inventory and other property held by the corporation primarily for sale to

customers in the ordinary course of its trade or business unless such property is sold in bulk to one person.

cash of $25,000 and Jane's notes for the balance of $75,000. The notes are payable over 10 years ($7,500 per year) and carry an appropriate rate of interest. Immediately after the sale, Black Corporation distributes the cash and notes to Earl, the sole shareholder. Earl has an adjusted basis of $20,000 in the Black stock, and the installment notes have a value equal to the face amount ($75,000). These transactions have the following tax result:

- Black Corporation recognizes gain on the distribution of the installment notes, measured by the difference between the $75,000 fair market value and the basis Black had in the notes.
- Earl may defer the gain on the receipt of the notes to the point of collection.
- Earl must allocate the adjusted basis in the stock ($20,000) between the cash and the installment notes as follows:

$$\frac{\text{Cash}}{\text{Total receipts}} = \frac{\$25,000}{\$100,000} \times \$20,000 = \$5,000 \text{ basis allocated to the cash}$$

$$\frac{\text{Notes}}{\text{Total receipts}} = \frac{\$75,000}{\$100,000} \times \$20,000 = \$15,000 \text{ basis allocated to the notes}$$

- Earl must recognize $20,000 of gain [$25,000 (cash received) – $5,000 basis (allocated to the cash)] in the year of liquidation.
- Earl must recognize gain on the notes, computed as follows:

$$\$75,000 \text{ (contract price)} - \$15,000 \text{ (basis allocated to the notes)} =$$
$$\$60,000 \text{ (gross profit)}$$

- The gross profit percentage is 80%:

$$\frac{\$60,000 \text{ (gross profit)}}{\$75,000 \text{ (contract price)}} = 80\%$$

- Thus, Earl must report a gain of $6,000 [$7,500 (amount of note) × 80% (gross profit percentage)] on the collection of each note over the next 10 years (i.e., $60,000 of gain in total).
- The interest element is accounted for separately. ▼

LIQUIDATIONS—PARENT-SUBSIDIARY SITUATIONS

Section 332, an exception to the general rule, provides that a parent corporation does *not* recognize gain or loss on a liquidation of its subsidiary. In addition, the subsidiary corporation recognizes neither gain nor loss on distributions of property to its parent.[12]

The requirements for applying § 332 are as follows:

- The parent must own at least 80 percent of the voting stock of the subsidiary and at least 80 percent of the total value of the subsidiary's stock.
- The subsidiary must distribute all of its property in complete cancellation of all of its stock within the taxable year or within three years from the close of the tax year in which the first distribution occurred.
- The subsidiary must be solvent.[13]

If these requirements are met, nonrecognition of gains and losses becomes mandatory.

---

[12]§ 337.

[13]Reg. §§ 1.332–2(a) and (b).

When a series of distributions occurs in the liquidation of a subsidiary corporation, the parent corporation must own the required amount of stock (at least 80 percent) on the date the plan of liquidation is adopted and at all times until all property has been distributed.[14] If the parent fails to qualify at any time, the provisions for nonrecognition of gain or loss do not apply to any distribution.[15]

TAX TREATMENT WHEN A MINORITY INTEREST EXISTS

A liquidating distribution to a minority shareholder in a parent-subsidiary situation is treated in the same manner as one made pursuant to a *nonliquidating* redemption. That is, the distributing corporation recognizes gain (but not loss) on the property distributed to the minority shareholder.

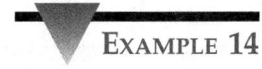

EXAMPLE 14

The stock of Red Corporation is held as follows: 80% by Yellow Corporation and 20% by Dan. Red Corporation is liquidated on December 10, 1998, pursuant to a plan adopted on January 10, 1998. At the time of its liquidation, Red has assets with a basis of $100,000 and fair market value of $500,000. Red Corporation distributes the property pro rata to Yellow Corporation and to Dan. Red must recognize gain of $80,000 [($500,000 fair market value – $100,000 basis) × 20% minority interest]. The corporate tax due on this gain will most likely be deducted from the $100,000 distribution ($500,000 × 20%) going to the minority interest. The remaining gain of $320,000 is sheltered because it is related to property being distributed to Yellow, the parent corporation. ▼

The minority shareholder is subject to the general rule requiring the recognition of gain or loss. Accordingly, the difference between the fair market value of the assets received and the basis of the minority shareholder's stock is the amount of gain or loss recognized. The tax basis of property received by the minority shareholder is the property's fair market value on the date of distribution.[16]

INDEBTEDNESS OF THE SUBSIDIARY TO THE PARENT

If a subsidiary transfers appreciated property to the parent to satisfy a debt, it must recognize gain on the transaction unless § 332 applies. When § 332 applies, the subsidiary does not recognize gain or loss upon the transfer of properties to the parent.[17]

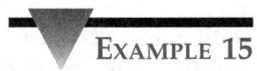

EXAMPLE 15

Green Corporation owes $20,000 to its parent, Gray Corporation. It satisfies the obligation by transferring land worth $20,000 with a tax basis of $8,000. Normally, Green would recognize a gain of $12,000 on the transaction. However, if the transfer is made pursuant to a liquidation under § 332, Green does not recognize a gain. ▼

The special provision noted above will not apply to the parent corporation. The parent corporation recognizes realized gain or loss on the satisfaction of indebtedness, even if property is received during liquidation of the subsidiary.

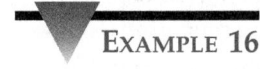

EXAMPLE 16

Redbird Corporation purchased bonds of its subsidiary Bluebird at a discount for $95,000. Upon liquidation of the subsidiary pursuant to § 332, Redbird receives payment of $100,000, the face amount of the bonds. The transaction has no tax effect on Bluebird. However,

---

[14]Establishing the date of the adoption of a plan of complete liquidation could be crucial in determining whether § 332 applies. See, for example, *George L. Riggs, Inc.*, 64 T.C. 474 (1975).

[15]Reg. § 1.332–2(a).
[16]§ 334(a).
[17]§ 337(b).

Redbird Corporation recognizes gain of $5,000—the difference between its basis in the bonds and the amount received in payment. ▼

BASIS OF PROPERTY RECEIVED BY THE PARENT CORPORATION—THE GENERAL RULE

Property received in the complete liquidation of a subsidiary has the same basis it had in the hands of the subsidiary unless the parent corporation makes an election under the exception discussed below.[18] Further, the parent's basis in the stock of the liquidated subsidiary disappears, even if some of the property is transferred to the parent to satisfy a debt owed to the parent by the subsidiary.

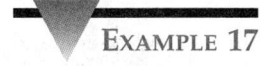

EXAMPLE 17

Wren, the parent corporation, has a basis of $20,000 in stock in Robin Corporation, a subsidiary in which it owns 85% of all classes of stock. Wren purchased the Robin stock 10 years ago. In the current year, Wren liquidates Robin Corporation and acquires assets with a fair market value of $50,000 and a tax basis to Robin of $40,000. Wren Corporation takes a basis of $40,000 in the assets, with a potential gain upon their sale of $10,000. Wren's $20,000 basis in Robin's stock disappears. ▼

EXAMPLE 18

White Corporation has a basis of $60,000 in the stock of Gray Corporation, a subsidiary acquired 10 years ago. It liquidates Gray Corporation and receives assets with a fair market value of $50,000 and a tax basis to Gray of $40,000. White Corporation takes a basis of $40,000 in the assets it acquired from Gray. If it sells the assets for $50,000, it has a gain of $10,000 in spite of the fact that its basis in the Gray stock was $60,000. White's loss will never be recognized. ▼

Because the parent corporation takes the subsidiary's basis in its assets, the carryover rules of § 381 apply. The parent acquires any net operating loss of the subsidiary, any investment credit carryover, any capital loss carryover, and a carryover of the subsidiary's E & P.

BASIS OF PROPERTY RECEIVED BY THE PARENT CORPORATION—THE EXCEPTION

Background.   Under the general rule described above, problems can develop when a subsidiary is liquidated shortly after acquisition by a parent corporation.

- When the basis of the subsidiary's assets is more than the purchase price of the stock, the parent receives a step-up in basis in the assets at no tax cost. If, for example, the parent pays $100,000 for the subsidiary's stock and the basis of the assets transferred to the parent is $150,000, the parent enjoys a $50,000 benefit without any gain recognition. The $50,000 increase in basis of the subsidiary's assets can lead to additional depreciation deductions and either more loss or less gain upon the later disposition of the assets by the parent.

- If the basis of the subsidiary's assets is below the purchase price of the stock, the parent suffers a step-down in basis in the assets with no attendant tax benefit. Return to Example 18, but change the situation slightly so that the subsidiary is liquidated shortly after acquisition. The basic inequity of the "no loss" situation now develops. But why would a corporation pay more for the stock in another corporation than the latter's basis in the assets? One

---

[18]§ 334(b)(1) and Reg. § 1.334–1(b).

reason is that the basis of the assets is not necessarily related to the fair market value. The acquiring corporation may not have the option of purchasing the assets of the acquired corporation instead of its stock. Further, the shareholders in the acquired corporation may prefer to sell their stock rather than the assets of the corporation.

In the landmark decision of *Kimbell-Diamond Milling Co.*,[19] the courts considered these problems. The courts concluded that when a parent corporation liquidates a subsidiary shortly after acquiring its stock, the parent is really purchasing the assets of the subsidiary. Consequently, the basis of the assets should be the same as the cost of the stock. After this decision, § 338 was enacted to provide for certain situations where the basis determination is made under the special rule of § 338 rather than the general rule.

Requirements for Application. Section 338 provides that an acquiring corporation may *elect* to treat the acquisition of stock in an acquired corporation as a purchase of the acquired corporation's assets. The **§ 338 election** must be made by the fifteenth day of the ninth month beginning after the month in which a *qualified stock purchase* occurs. If made, the election is irrevocable.

A purchasing corporation makes a *qualified stock purchase* if it acquires at least 80 percent of the voting power and at least 80 percent of the value of the acquired corporation within a 12-month period beginning with the first purchase of stock. The stock must be acquired in a taxable transaction (i.e., § 351 and other nonrecognition provisions do not apply). An acquisition of stock by any member of an affiliated group that includes the purchasing corporation is considered to be an acquisition by the purchasing corporation.

Tax Consequences. If the parent makes a qualified election under the special rule of § 338, the purchasing corporation has a basis in the subsidiary's assets equal to its basis in the subsidiary's stock. The subsidiary may, but need not, be liquidated.

Under § 338, the acquired corporation is *deemed* to have sold its assets for an amount equal to the purchasing corporation's grossed-up basis in the subsidiary's stock. This amount must be adjusted for liabilities of the subsidiary corporation. The grossed-up basis is the basis in the subsidiary stock multiplied by a fraction. The numerator of the fraction is 100 percent. The denominator is the percentage of value of the subsidiary's stock held by the purchasing corporation on the acquisition date.[20] The amount is allocated among the subsidiary's assets using the residual method described below.

The § 338 election produces gain or loss to the subsidiary. The subsidiary is treated as having sold all of its assets at the close of the acquisition date in a single transaction at the fair market value.[21] The subsidiary is then treated as a new corporation that purchased all of the assets as of the beginning of the day after the acquisition date.

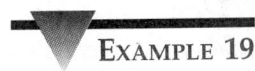

EXAMPLE 19

White Corporation has an $800,000 basis in its assets and $500,000 of liabilities. It has E & P of $200,000, and the assets have a fair market value of $2,000,000. Black Corporation purchases 80% of the White stock on March 10, 1998, for $1,200,000 [(assets worth $2,000,000 – liabilities of $500,000) × 80%]. Because the purchase price of the White stock exceeds White's basis in its assets, and to eliminate White's E & P, Black may choose

---

[19]14 T.C. 74 (1950), *aff'd.* in 51–1 USTC ¶9201, 40 AFTR 328, 187 F.2d 718 (CA–5, 1951), *cert. den.* 72 S.Ct. 50 (USSC, 1951).

[20]§ 338(b)(4).
[21]§ 338(a).

to elect §338 treatment by December 15, 1998. White need not be liquidated for the provision to apply. If Black elects §338, the tax consequences are as follows:

- White is deemed to have sold its assets for an amount equal to Black's grossed-up basis in the White stock.
- Black's grossed-up basis in the White stock is computed as follows: The basis of the White stock is multiplied by a fraction, with 100% the numerator and 80% the denominator. The basis of the White stock, $1,200,000, is multiplied by 100/80. The result is $1,500,000, which is adjusted for White's liabilities of $500,000 for a deemed selling price of $2,000,000.
- The $2,000,000 selling price less $800,000, the basis of White's assets, produces a recognized gain to White Corporation of $1,200,000. ▼

Because Black did not purchase 100 percent of the White stock, different results occur depending on whether White is liquidated. If White is not liquidated, it is treated as a new corporation as of March 11, 1998. The basis of White's assets is $2,000,000, and the E & P is eliminated. If White Corporation is liquidated, Black Corporation has a basis of $1,600,000 in White's assets, representing 80 percent of White's assets. White's E & P does not carry over to Black.

Note the results of the §338 election. White Corporation's assets receive a stepped-up basis but at a substantial tax cost. White must recognize all of its realized gain. Any tax liability White incurs on its recognized gain causes Black Corporation to reduce the amount paid for White's assets.

Allocation of Purchase Price. The new stepped-up basis of the assets of a subsidiary when a §338 election is in effect is allocated among the assets by the **residual method.**[22] The amount of the purchase price that exceeds the aggregate fair market values of the tangible and identifiable intangible assets must be allocated to goodwill or going-concern value. Goodwill and going-concern value are referred to as "§197 intangibles." Costs allocated to acquired §197 intangibles are amortized over a 15-year period.

EXAMPLE 20

For $4,000,000, Red Corporation acquires all of the stock of Orange Corporation and elects the treatment under §338. If the fair market value of Orange's physical assets is $3,500,000, Red must allocate $500,000 of the purchase price either to goodwill or to going-concern value, which may be amortized over a 15-year period. ▼

In Example 20, none of the purchase price would have to be allocated to goodwill or going-concern value if the physical assets were worth $4 million. However, the burden of proof of showing no residual amount is on the taxpayer, not on the IRS.

A Comparison of the General Rule and the §338 Exception. Under the general rule, a subsidiary's basis in its assets carries over to the parent corporation upon liquidation. In addition, the subsidiary liquidation is completely tax-free (except for any minority interest). A liquidation under §338, while tax-free to the parent, is taxable to the subsidiary. The subsidiary assets will have a stepped-up basis.

If the subsidiary is liquidated and a timely election is made under §338, the holding period of the property received by the parent corporation begins on the date the parent acquired the subsidiary's stock. If the corporation is not

---

[22]§1060.

liquidated, the holding period of the assets to the subsidiary starts anew on the day after the acquisition date.[23] In a liquidation under the general rule of § 332, the holding period of the subsidiary carries over to the parent. The rules for an election under § 338 as compared to other liquidation rules appear in Concept Summary 19–1.

CORPORATE REORGANIZATIONS

2 **LEARNING OBJECTIVE**
Understand the general form and tax consequences of corporate reorganizations.

A corporate combination or realignment, usually referred to as a reorganization, can be either a taxable or a nontaxable transaction. Assuming a business combination is taxable, the Code provides that the seller's gain or loss is measured by the difference between the amount realized and the basis of property surrendered. The purchaser's basis in the property received is the amount paid for the property, and the holding period begins on the date of purchase.

Certain exchanges are specifically excepted from tax recognition by the Code. For example, § 1031 provides that no gain or loss shall be recognized if property held for productive use or for investment is exchanged solely for ". . . property of a like kind. . . ." Section 1033, if elected by the taxpayer, provides for partial or complete nonrecognition of gain if property destroyed, seized, or stolen is compulsorily or involuntarily converted into similar property. Further, § 351 provides for nonrecognition of gain upon the transfer of property to a controlled corporation. Finally, §§ 354 and 361 provide for nonrecognition of gain for the participants in certain corporate reorganizations. The Regulations state the underlying assumption behind the nonrecognition of gain or loss.

> . . . the new property is substantially a continuation of the old investment . . .; and, in the case of reorganizations, the new enterprise, the new corporate structure, and the new property are substantially continuations of the old. . . .[24]

SUMMARY OF THE DIFFERENT TYPES OF REORGANIZATIONS

Section 368(a) of the Code specifies seven corporate restructurings or reorganizations that will qualify as nontaxable exchanges. If the transaction fails to qualify, it will not be granted special treatment. Therefore, the planner of a nontaxable business realignment must determine in advance that the proposed transaction falls specifically within one of these seven types.

Section 368(a)(1) states that the term **reorganization** applies to any of the following:

A. A statutory merger or consolidation.
B. The acquisition by one corporation of another when the transaction involves solely the exchange of voting stock of each corporation (stock-for-stock exchange).
C. The acquisition by one corporation of substantially all of the property of another corporation in exchange for voting stock (assets-for-stock exchange).
D. The transfer of all or part of a corporation's assets to another corporation, if the original corporation or any of its shareholders is in control of the new corporation immediately after the transfer (divisive exchange, also known as a spin-off, split-off, or split-up).
E. A recapitalization.

---

[23]§ 338(a).   [24]Reg. § 1.1002–1(c).

CONCEPT SUMMARY 19–1

Summary of Liquidation Rules

Effect on the Shareholder	Basis of Property Received	Effect on the Corporation
§ 331—The general rule provides for capital gain treatment on the difference between the FMV of property received and the basis of the stock in the corporation.	§ 334(a)—Basis of assets received by the shareholder will be the FMV on the date of distribution (except for installment obligations in which gain is deferred to the point of collection).	§ 336—Gain or loss is recognized for distributions in kind and for sales by the liquidating corporation. Losses are not recognized for distributions to related parties if the distribution is not pro rata or if disqualified property is distributed. Losses may be disallowed on sales and distributions of certain other property even if made to unrelated parties.
§ 332—In liquidation of a controlled subsidiary, no gain or loss is recognized to the parent corporation. Subsidiary must distribute all of its property within the taxable year or within three years from the close of the taxable year in which the first distribution occurs.	§ 334(b)(1)—Property has the same basis as it had in the hands of the subsidiary. Parent's basis in the stock disappears. Carryover rules of § 381 apply.	§ 337—No gain or loss is recognized by the subsidiary on distributions to an 80% or more parent. Gain (but not loss) is recognized on distributions to minority shareholders.
	§ 338—Basis of assets is the basis that the parent held in the stock in the subsidiary. Basis is allocated to assets using the residual method. Carryover rules of § 381 do not apply. Subsidiary need not be liquidated.	

F. A mere change in identity, form, or place of organization.

G. A transfer by a corporation of all or a part of its assets to another corporation in a bankruptcy or receivership proceeding.

These seven types of tax-free reorganizations typically are designated by their identifying letters: "Type A," "Type B," "Type C," and so on. For the most part, excepting the recapitalization (E), the change in form (F), and the insolvent corporation (G) provisions, a tax-free reorganization is (1) a statutory merger or consolidation, (2) an exchange of stock for voting stock, (3) an exchange of assets for voting stock, or (4) a divisive reorganization (the so-called spin-off, split-off, or split-up).

SUMMARY OF THE TAX CONSEQUENCES IN A TAX-FREE REORGANIZATION

The tax treatment of the parties to a tax-free reorganization almost exactly parallels the treatment under the like-kind exchange provisions of § 1031. In the simplest like-kind exchange, neither gain nor loss is recognized on the exchange of "like-kind" property. When "boot" (defined as nonlike-kind property) is involved, gain may be recognized. The four-column template of Concept Summary 19–2 can be

HOW TO CHECK OUT A TAKEOVER RUMOR

Is it possible for an investor to predict a takeover? Financial analysts tell investors to look at the trading activity of corporate insiders. Insiders will not buy stock in anticipation of a merger because that is illegal insider trading, but they will halt the sale of their stock. Insiders who know a bid is "percolating" will hold on to their shares in anticipation of a "premium offer price from the prospective bidder." Analysts point to an announcement that Grand Metropolitan would acquire Pet, Inc., for $2.6 billion in a friendly takeover. A review of SEC data on insider trading revealed that insider selling at Pet had "all but dried up" in the months prior to the announcement. When ITT announced that it would buy gambling giant Caesar's World, Inc., in a friendly tender offer, SEC data indicated that insider selling at Caesar's fell off as its stock price rose.

Insider activity can also squelch a takeover rumor. If there are takeover rumors but senior insiders continue to sell their shares, the likelihood of a bid is "fairly slim," according to analysts. Studies reveal that insider selling typically drops off some three months ahead of any announcement of either a takeover or talks about a takeover.

used to compute the amount of gain recognized and the adjusted basis in the new asset.

Unfortunately, the like-kind provisions do not apply to the exchange of stock or securities.[25] Therefore, when an investor exchanges stock in one corporation for stock in another, the exchange is a taxable transaction. If the transaction can qualify as a reorganization under § 368, however, the exchange will be nontaxable. Thus, a § 368 reorganization, in substance, is the nontaxable exchange of like-kind property, and the four-column template of Concept Summary 19–2 is useful for reorganizations as well.

EXAMPLE 21

Ram holds 1,000 shares of Lotus stock that he purchased for $10,000 several years ago. In a merger of Lotus into Iris, Ram exchanges his 1,000 shares of Lotus for 1,000 shares of Iris. Both investments are valued at $18 per share. Ram's realized gain on the exchange is $8,000 [($18 per share × 1,000 shares) – $10,000 basis]. Assuming this exchange qualifies for tax-free treatment under § 368, Ram's recognized gain is zero. Since his postponed gain is $8,000, Ram's basis in his new stock is $10,000 [$18,000 (FMV of new stock) – $8,000 postponed gain]. Lotus and Iris are not taxed on the transaction either. ▼

Gain or Loss.   The general rule is that corporations that are parties to a § 368 reorganization do not recognize gain or loss on the restructuring. There are exceptions to the nonrecognition rule, however. If the acquiring corporation transfers property along with its stock and securities to the target corporation, gain, but not loss, can be recognized. The target may also recognize gain, but not loss, when it fails to distribute the *other property* it receives in the restructuring or distributes its own property to its shareholders.[26] *Other property* in this case is defined as anything received other than stock or securities.

---

[25]§ 1031.

[26]§§ 361(a) and (b).

CONCEPT SUMMARY 19-2

Gain and Basis Rules for Nontaxable Exchanges

(1) Realized Gain/Loss	(2) Recognized Gain (Not Loss)	(3) Postponed Gain/Loss	(4) Basis of New Asset
FMV of asset (stock) surrendered	Lesser of boot or gain realized	Gain/loss realized (column 1)	FMV of asset (stock) received
– Adjusted basis of asset surrendered		– Gain/loss recognized (column 2)	– Postponed gain or + Postponed loss (column 3)
			Adjusted basis in new asset (stock)
Gain/loss realized	Gain recognized	Gain/loss postponed	

Generally, the stock and security holders of the corporations involved in a tax-free reorganization do not recognize gain or loss on the exchange of their stock and securities unless they receive cash or other property in addition to stock and securities.[27] The cash or other property is considered boot, and the gain recognized by the stock or security holder is the lesser of the boot received or the realized gain. This is analogous to the treatment of boot in a like-kind exchange.

Once the amount of the gain is computed, the character of the gain must be determined. Any gain then is treated as a dividend to the extent of the shareholder's proportionate share of the corporation's accumulated earnings and profits (E & P).[28] The remainder is generally treated as capital gain.

EXAMPLE 22

Sarah exchanges her 2% interest in Target stock with a basis of $8,000 for stock in Acquiring with a fair market value of $12,000 and $3,000 cash. The distribution has the effect of a dividend. Target's accumulated earnings and profits are $25,000. Sarah has $3,000 of recognized gain (the boot received), of which $500 ($25,000 × 2%) is taxable as a dividend. The remaining $2,500 is treated as a capital gain. ▼

Security holders recognize gain when the principal amount of the debt securities received is greater than the debt securities given up. If debt securities are received and no securities are surrendered, the security holders also recognize gain.

EXAMPLE 23

Alejandra was a security holder in Hibiscus. She owned bonds with a principal value of $10,000. As part of the merger of Hibiscus with Carnation, Alejandra surrenders her Hibiscus bonds and receives long-term Carnation debt with a principal value of $15,000. Alejandra recognizes a $5,000 gain on the exchange. ▼

---

[27]§ 356(a).

[28]§ 356. Compare *Shimberg v. U.S.*, 78–2 USTC ¶9607, 42 AFTR2d 78–5575, 577 F.2d 283 (CA–5, 1978), with *Comm. v. Clark*, 89–1 USTC ¶9230, 63 AFTR2d 89–860, 109 S.Ct. 1455 (USSC, 1989). In *Comm. v. Clark*, the Supreme Court ruled that the question of whether the payment of boot in a shareholder exchange pursuant to a tax-free reorganization has the effect of a dividend

distribution is answered by examining the effect of the exchange as a whole. Boot can be characterized as capital gain if the requirements relating to qualified redemptions (see Chapter 18) are met. In applying the qualified redemption rules, the Court held that stock ownership reduction is determined by reference to ownership in the acquiring corporation.

CONCEPT SUMMARY 19–3

Basis Rules for a Tax-Free Reorganization

Basis to Acquiring Corporation of Property Received	
Target's basis in property transferred	$xx,xxx
Plus: Gain recognized by Target on the transaction	x,xxx
Equals: Basis of property to Acquiring Corporation	$xx,xxx

Basis to Target Shareholders of Stock and Securities Received	
Basis of stock and securities transferred	$xx,xxx
Plus: Gain and dividend income recognized	x,xxx
Less: Money and fair market value of other property received	(x,xxx)
Equals: Basis of stock and securities received	$xx,xxx

Basis. Property received by the acquiring corporation from the target corporation retains the basis it had in the hands of the target, increased by the amount of gain recognized to the target on the transfer.[29] The tax basis of stock and securities received by a shareholder pursuant to a tax-free reorganization is the same as the basis of those surrendered. This amount is decreased by the amount of boot received and increased by the amount of gain and dividend income, if any, recognized on the transaction.[30] Another way to compute the basis in the stock and securities, using the template of Concept Summary 19–2, is to subtract the gain (or add the loss) postponed from the fair market value of the stock and securities received. Because of the basis computation, the gain or loss effectively is deferred until the new stock or securities are disposed of in a taxable transaction.

EXAMPLE 24

Quinn exchanges all of his stock in Target Corporation for stock in Acquiring plus $3,000 cash. The exchange is pursuant to a tax-free reorganization of both corporations. Quinn paid $10,000 for the stock in Target two years ago. The stock in Acquiring has a fair market value of $12,000. Quinn has a realized gain of $5,000 ($12,000 + $3,000 − $10,000), which is recognized to the extent of the boot received, $3,000. Quinn's basis in the Acquiring stock is $10,000 [$12,000 (value of Acquiring stock) − $2,000 (postponed gain)].

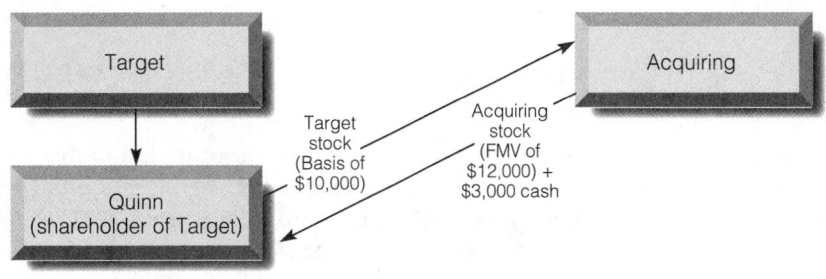

---

[29]§ 362(b).   [30]§ 358.

EXAMPLE 25

Assume the same facts as in Example 24 except that Quinn's basis in the Target stock was $16,000. Quinn realizes a loss of $1,000 on the exchange, none of which is recognized. His basis in the Acquiring stock is $13,000 [$12,000 (value of stock received) + $1,000 (loss postponed)]. ▼

The assets received by the acquiring corporation from the target corporation retain their basis. This carryover basis from the target corporation to the acquiring corporation is increased by any gain recognized by the target on the restructuring. Concept Summary 19–3 summarizes the basis rules for the acquiring corporation.

EXAMPLE 26

Target exchanges its assets with a fair market value of $50,000 and a basis of $30,000 for $45,000 of Acquiring stock and $5,000 of land. Target does not distribute the land to its shareholders. Target recognizes a $5,000 gain on the restructuring. Acquiring's basis in the assets received from Target is $35,000 [$30,000 (Target's basis) + $5,000 (Target's gain recognized)]. ▼

ETHICAL CONSIDERATIONS

Who Benefits from a Corporate Merger?

Mega Bank merges with National Bank in a $70 million stock swap. The new surviving bank, Mega National, will virtually control the banking industry in the states where it does business. Ralph, the CEO of Mega Bank who will receive a bonus of $100 million for his part in structuring the merger, has cited the enormous cost reductions accruing from the merger. Part of the cost savings will result from the ability of the new bank to cut 12,000 jobs. In addition, by controlling the banking market, Mega National will be able to raise its fees for providing banking services to its customers. The shareholders of the merged banks reaped a substantial profit from later sales of their stock. Does the merger present any ethical problems?

TAX PLANNING CONSIDERATIONS

3 **LEARNING OBJECTIVE**
Identify tax planning opportunities available to minimize the tax impact in complete liquidations.

EFFECT OF A LIQUIDATING DISTRIBUTION ON THE CORPORATION

Liquidating distributions are taxed at both the corporate level and the shareholder level. When a corporation liquidates, it can, as a general rule, claim losses on assets that have declined in value. These assets should not be distributed in the form of a property dividend before liquidation because losses are not deductible on nonliquidating distributions of depreciated property. Thus, if such assets are distributed as property dividends, the corporation receives no tax benefit from the potential loss.

EFFECT OF A LIQUIDATING DISTRIBUTION ON THE SHAREHOLDER

Under the general rule for corporate liquidations, shareholders recognize gain or loss equal to the difference between the liquidation proceeds and the basis of the stock given up. In cases of a large gain, a shareholder may consider shifting the gain to others. One approach is to give the stock to family members or donate it to charity. Whether this procedure will be successful depends on the timing of the transfer. If the donee of the stock is not in a position to prevent the liquidation of the corporation, the donor is deemed to have made an anticipatory assignment of income. As a result, the gain is still taxed to the donor. In addition, the gift tax must be considered (see Chapter 26). Hence, advance planning is crucial in arriving at the desired tax result.

Recall that the installment sale provisions provide some relief from the general corporate liquidation rule that the shareholder recognizes all gain upon receiving the liquidation proceeds. Assume that after a plan of liquidation has been adopted, corporate assets are sold in exchange for installment notes. The shareholders receiving the notes as liquidation distributions may be able to report the gain on the installment method. In that case, some gain can be deferred until the notes are collected.

The provision applicable to the liquidation of a subsidiary, § 332, is not elective. Nevertheless, some flexibility may be available:

- Whether § 332 applies depends on the 80 percent stock ownership test. Assuming the transaction has some substance, it may be avoided if a parent corporation reduces its stock ownership in the subsidiary below this percentage. On the other hand, the opposite approach may be desirable. A parent can make the provision applicable by acquiring enough additional stock in the subsidiary to meet the 80 percent test.

- Once § 332 becomes effective, less latitude is allowed in determining the parent's basis in the subsidiary's assets. If the general rule applies, the subsidiary's basis carries over to the parent. If the exception to the general rule is available and a timely § 338 election is made, the parent's basis equals the cost of the stock. If the subsidiary is not liquidated, the basis of the assets to the subsidiary is the parent's cost of the stock. Presumably, the exception of § 338 can be avoided by failing to make a timely election.

- If a timely § 338 election is made, the parent corporation's basis in the stock of the subsidiary is allocated among the assets of the subsidiary.

KEY TERMS

Corporate liquidation, 19–2	Residual method, 19–14	Section 338 election, 19–13
Reorganization, 19–15		

PROBLEM MATERIALS

DISCUSSION QUESTIONS

1. Compare stock redemptions and liquidations with other corporate distributions in terms of the following:
   a. Recognition of gain or loss to the shareholder.
   b. Basis of property received by the shareholder.
   c. Recognition of gain or loss by the distributing corporation.
   d. Effect on the distributing corporation's E & P.

2. Can losses ever be recognized in a complete liquidation if disqualified property is involved? Explain.

3. Explain the tax consequences to a shareholder of a corporation in the process of liquidation under the general rule of § 331.

4. May a shareholder use the installment method to report gain on a complete liquidation? Explain.

5. In terms of the rules applying to the liquidation of a subsidiary by its parent, describe the effect of each of the following:
   a. The adoption of a plan of complete liquidation.
   b. The period of time in which the corporation must liquidate.
   c. The amount of stock held by the parent corporation.
   d. The solvency of the subsidiary being liquidated.

6. What are the tax consequences of a liquidation of a subsidiary by its corporate parent when a minority interest is involved?

7. Does the nonrecognition rule of § 332 apply to a transfer of property by a subsidiary to a parent in satisfaction of indebtedness? Explain.

8. Bluebird Corporation pays $1 million for 100% of the stock in Redbird Corporation. Redbird has a basis of $500,000 in its assets. If Bluebird liquidates Redbird and makes no special election, what basis will it have in Redbird's assets?

9. What are the requirements for the application of § 338?

10. Under what circumstances could the application of § 338 be beneficial to the parent corporation? Detrimental?

11. What is the tax treatment of goodwill and going-concern value when stock of a corporation is purchased and an election is made under § 338?

12. Compare the sale of a corporation's assets with a sale of its stock in terms of problems to the seller.

13. What is the theory underlying nonrecognition of gain or loss in a corporate reorganization?

14. Briefly explain the seven forms of corporate reorganizations that qualify for nonrecognition treatment.

15. Is the gain that shareholders do not recognize on the exchange of their stock in a target corporation for the stock in the acquiring corporation forgiven or merely postponed? Explain.

16. In what situations will the acquiring or the target corporation recognize gain in a § 368 reorganization?

17. Ann purchased 200 shares of stock in Gray Corporation five years ago for $50 per share. Two years ago, Gray redeemed 50 of Ann's shares for $100 per share. In the current year, all of Gray's shareholders exchanged their shares in Gray for voting stock in Blue Corporation. The agreement provided that a sufficient number of shares in Blue, valued at $95 per share, would be issued to the Gray shareholders to equal the value of their Gray shares. In the event the purchase price was not evenly divisible by shares at $95 per share, the difference would be paid in cash. Ann was paid $15 cash and one share of Blue stock for each of her remaining shares in Gray. What are the tax issues to be considered in this situation?

PROBLEMS

18. Robin Corporation distributes to its shareholders land held as an investment (basis of $100,000, fair market value of $600,000) pursuant to a complete liquidation. The land is subject to a liability of $700,000. How much gain does Robin Corporation recognize on a distribution of the land?

19. Gray Corporation acquired land in a § 351 exchange in 1997. At that time, the land had a basis of $500,000 and a fair market value of $550,000. Gray has two equal shareholders, Arnold and Beatrice, who are father and daughter. Gray adopts a plan of liquidation in 1998. During that year and pursuant to the liquidation, the corporation sells the land

(to an unrelated buyer) for its current market value of $400,000 and distributes the
proceeds to Arnold and Beatrice. What amount of loss may Gray recognize on the sale
of the land?

20. Assume in Problem 19 that the land had a fair market value of $460,000 when it was
acquired in the § 351 exchange. What amount of loss may Gray recognize on the 1998
sale of the land for $400,000?

21. Assume in Problem 19 that the land was distributed (instead of sold) proportionately
to Arnold and Beatrice in a liquidating distribution. (The fair market value of the land
at the time of distribution is $400,000). What amount of loss may Gray Corporation
recognize on the 1998 distribution of the land?

22. Blue Corporation acquired land in a § 351 exchange in 1996. The land had a basis of
$1,800,000 and a fair market value of $1,950,000 on the date of the transfer. Blue Corporation has two shareholders, Ann and Paul, who are unrelated. Ann owns 80% of the
stock in the corporation, and Paul owns 20%. Blue adopts a plan of liquidation in 1998.
On this date, the value of the land has decreased to $600,000. In distributing the land
either to Ann or to Paul, or to both, as part of the liquidating distributions from Blue
Corporation, should Blue:
   a. Distribute all the land to Ann?
   b. Distribute all the land to Paul?
   c. Distribute 80% of the land to Ann and 20% to Paul?
   d. Distribute 50% of the land to Ann and 50% to Paul?
   e. Sell the land and distribute the proceeds of $600,000 proportionately to Ann and
      to Paul?

23. Assume in Problem 22 that the plan of liquidation is not adopted until 1999. In addition,
assume the land had a fair market value of $1.5 million on the date of its transfer to
the corporation. On the date of the liquidation, the land's fair market value has decreased
to $600,000. How would your answer to Problem 22 change if:
   a. All the land is distributed to Ann?
   b. All the land is distributed to Paul?
   c. The land is distributed 80% to Ann and 20% to Paul?
   d. The land is distributed 50% to Ann and 50% to Paul?
   e. The land is sold and the proceeds of $600,000 are distributed proportionately to
      Ann and to Paul?

24. Wren Corporation is owned equally by José and Jill, who are not related. Each has a
stock basis of $600,000. Wren Corporation has the following assets and no liabilities:

	Basis to Wren Corporation	Fair Market Value
Cash	$ 200,000	$ 200,000
Inventory	800,000	1,200,000
Equipment ($400,000 depreciation has been taken)	200,000	1,000,000
Building	800,000	2,400,000
Land	200,000	400,000
Stock in Gray Corporation (10% interest)	1,600,000	4,000,000
Total	$3,800,000	$9,200,000

Compute the tax liability to Wren Corporation and the taxable gain to José and Jill if
Wren is liquidated in the current year after the corporation sells each asset for its
fair market value and distributes the after-tax proceeds to José and Jill. Straight-line
depreciation of $1,200,000 had been claimed on the building. The land was used in
Wren Corporation's business.

25. After a plan of complete liquidation has been adopted, Green Corporation sells its only asset, land, to Rex (an unrelated party) for $400,000. Under the terms of the sale, Green receives cash of $100,000 and Rex's note in the amount of $300,000. The note is payable over five years ($60,000 per year) and carries an appropriate rate of interest. Immediately after the sale, Green distributes the cash and notes to Helen, the sole shareholder of Green Corporation. Helen has a basis of $100,000 in the Green stock. What are the tax results to Helen if she wishes to defer as much gain as possible on the transaction? Assume the installment notes possess a value equal to the face amount.

26. The stock of Yellow Corporation is held as follows: 85% by Red Corporation and 15% by Fred. Yellow Corporation is liquidated on October 1, 1998, pursuant to a plan of liquidation adopted on January 15, 1998. At the time of its liquidation, Yellow's assets had a basis of $2 million and a fair market value of $18 million. Red Corporation has a basis of $800,000 in its Yellow Corporation stock. The basis of the Yellow stock to Fred is $80,000.
    a. How much gain, if any, must Yellow Corporation recognize on the liquidation?
    b. How much gain, if any, is recognized on the receipt of property from Yellow Corporation by Red Corporation? By Fred?

27. At the time of its liquidation under § 332, Cardinal Corporation had the following assets and liabilities:

	Basis to Cardinal Corporation	Fair Market Value
Cash	$120,000	$120,000
Marketable securities	90,000	240,000
Unimproved land	150,000	300,000
Unsecured bank loan	(30,000)	(30,000)
Mortgage on land	(90,000)	(90,000)

Wren Corporation, the sole shareholder of Cardinal Corporation, has a basis in its stock investment of $360,000. At the time of its liquidation, Cardinal's E & P was $200,000.
    a. How much gain (or loss) will Cardinal Corporation recognize if it distributes all of its assets and liabilities to Wren Corporation?
    b. How much gain (or loss) will Wren Corporation recognize?
    c. If the general rule of § 334(b)(1) applies, what will be Wren's basis in the marketable securities it receives from Cardinal Corporation?
    d. What will be Wren's basis in the unimproved land?

28. Orange Corporation, owned by two individual shareholders, has a basis of $450,000 (fair market value of $1 million) in its assets and E & P of $80,000. Its liabilities total $100,000. If the assets were sold, all gain would be long-term capital gain or § 1231 gain. Green Corporation purchases 20% of all the stock of Orange Corporation for $180,000 on March 1, 1998; 15% for $135,000 on September 20, 1998; and 60% for $540,000 on December 1, 1998, for a total consideration of $855,000. Assume Orange's marginal tax rate is 34%.
    a. Is Green Corporation entitled to make an election under § 338?
    b. Assume Green Corporation may make an election under § 338. Should Green do so? When must Green make the election?
    c. What are the tax consequences to Orange Corporation and to Green Corporation if Green makes a valid election under § 338 but does not liquidate Orange?
    d. What is the tax result if Orange Corporation is liquidated four months after a valid § 338 election? Eve, who holds the 5% minority interest in Orange Corporation, has a $10,000 basis in her stock in Orange. What is the tax result to Eve upon the liquidation?

29. Green Corporation paid $5,400,000 for all the stock of Gray Corporation 10 years ago. Gray Corporation's balance sheet reflects the following values:

Assets	
Cash	$ 135,000
Inventory	405,000
Machinery	270,000
Equipment	1,080,000
Land	1,350,000
	$3,240,000

Liabilities and Shareholders' Equity	
Accounts payable	$ 5,400,000
Common stock	5,400,000
Deficit	(7,560,000)
	$ 3,240,000

What are the tax consequences to Green Corporation if it liquidates Gray Corporation? Prepare a letter to your client, Green Corporation (1010 Cypress Lane, Community, MN 55166), and a memo for the file in which you explain your conclusions.

30. a. José, a shareholder of White Corporation, exchanges his White Corporation stock for stock in Green Corporation. The exchange is pursuant to a tax-free reorganization of White and Green. José paid $150,000 for his stock in White Corporation three years ago. He receives stock in Green worth $140,000. What is José's basis in the Green Corporation stock?

    b. Assume José receives $60,000 cash in addition to the Green stock worth $140,000. What are the tax consequences to José, and what basis does he have in the Green Corporation stock?

31. Quinn exchanges stock he owns in Redbird Corporation for stock in Bluebird Corporation and additionally receives $80,000 cash. The exchange is pursuant to a tax-free reorganization of both corporations. Quinn paid $40,000 five years ago for the stock in Redbird Corporation. The stock in Bluebird Corporation has a fair market value of $240,000. Quinn's share of Redbird's E & P is $70,000. How will Quinn treat this transaction for tax purposes?

32. Assume the same facts as in Problem 31, except that Quinn paid $360,000 (instead of $40,000) for his stock in Redbird Corporation. How would Quinn treat the transaction for tax purposes?

Research Problems for this chapter appear at the end of Chapter 28.

CORPORATE ACCUMULATIONS

LEARNING OBJECTIVES

After completing Chapter 20, you should be able to:

1. Appreciate the purpose of the accumulated earnings tax.

2. Determine the reasonable needs of the business.

3. Compute the accumulated earnings tax.

4. Discuss the reason for the personal holding company tax.

5. Recognize the requirements for personal holding company status.

6. Compute the personal holding company tax.

7. Compare the accumulated earnings and personal holding company taxes.

8. Plan to minimize (or avoid) the accumulated earnings tax.

9. Plan to minimize (or avoid) the personal holding company tax.

In the eyes of the public, corporations do not always bear their fair share of taxation through the regular corporate income tax. This chapter deals with two taxes imposed by Congress in an attempt to tax these corporations at a more equitable rate:

- The penalty tax on unreasonable accumulations, imposed when a corporation seems to be holding an unreasonable amount of income within the corporation instead of distributing it to shareholders as dividends.
- Personal holding company (PHC) status and the resulting increase in tax rates, also designed to discourage use of the corporate form to shelter shareholder income from the individual income tax.

Another special tax which attempts to address a similar issue is the alternative minimum tax (refer to Chapter 14). The alternative minimum tax is paid by corporations that appear to be earning substantial economic income but otherwise would pay little income tax. The accumulated earnings penalty and PHC status most often apply to small, closely held coporations that are attempting to minimize the total of the corporate tax and the individual tax paid by shareholders. In contrast, after 1998, the AMT applies only to large corporations.

This chapter both describes the accumulated earnings tax and the personal holding company tax and explains some ways tax planning can be used to avoid them.

PENALTY TAX ON UNREASONABLE ACCUMULATIONS

1 ▼ **LEARNING OBJECTIVE**
Appreciate the purpose of the accumulated earnings tax.

One major advantage to the corporate form is the opportunity to control the income tax burden of the owner(s). One way this control can be accomplished is by accumulating the earnings of the business at the corporate level, and thereby deferring the second tax at the shareholder level.

If the board of directors is aware of the shareholders' tax problems, it can then channel earnings into the shareholders' pockets with a minimum of tax cost by using several mechanisms. The corporation might distribute dividends only in years when the major shareholders are in lower tax brackets. Alternatively, dividend distributions might be curtailed, causing the value of the stock to increase in a manner similar to a savings account. Later, the shareholders can sell their stock in the year of their choice at an amount that reflects the increased retained earnings and receive capital gain treatment. In this manner, the capital gain could be postponed to years when the shareholders have capital losses to offset the gains. At most, long-term capital gains (i.e., from capital assets held for more than 18 months) are taxed at 20 percent. Dividend income is ordinary income and can be taxed at a rate as high as 39.6 percent.

Alternatively, the shareholders can retain their shares. Upon death, the estate or heirs will receive a step-up in basis equal to the fair market value of the stock on the date of death or, if elected, on the alternate valuation date. The increment in value represented by the step-up in basis will be largely attributable to the earnings retained by the corporation and will not be subject to income taxation.

Accumulating corporate earnings always entails problems, however. Congress took steps to stem corporate accumulations as early as the first income tax law enacted under the Sixteenth Amendment. Today, in addition to the usual corporate income tax, an extra tax is imposed on earnings accumulated beyond the reasonable needs of the business. Another problem is that a personal holding company tax may be levied on certain accumulated passive income. Consider first the 39.6 percent **accumulated earnings tax (AET).** The tax law is framed to discourage the retention of earnings that are unrelated to the business needs of the company. Earnings retained in the business to avoid the imposition of the tax that would have been imposed on distributions to the shareholders are subject to a 39.6 percent penalty tax.

EXAMPLE 1

Janet operated a consulting business as a sole proprietor in 1997. Assume she is in the 39.6% tax bracket in 1998, and she incorporates her business at the beginning of the year. Her business earns $120,000 in 1998, before her salary of $60,000. Since $60,000 of the income is accumulated, $13,760 of taxes are "saved" ($23,760 individual tax versus $10,000 corporate tax on the $60,000 accumulated). This accumulated savings could occur each year with the corporation reinvesting the saved taxes. Thus, without an accumulated earnings tax or personal holding company tax, Janet could use her corporation like a savings account. For example, the corporation could take advantage of the dividends received deduction for dividend-paying stocks. With the top individual tax rate (39.6% for 1998) above the top corporate tax rate (35% for 1998), it is more attractive to hold investment property in a C corporation than in a flow-through entity (partnership, S corporation, or sole proprietorship). However, the earnings are still at the corporate level, and Janet might be in a higher individual rate bracket when the accumulated earnings are distributed. ▼

THE ELEMENT OF INTENT

Although the penalty tax is normally applied against closely held corporations, a corporation is not exempt from the tax merely because its stock is widely held.[1] For example, a Second Court of Appeals decision[2] imposed the tax upon a widely held corporation with over 1,500 shareholders. However, a much smaller group of shareholders actually controlled the corporation. As a practical matter, a widely held corporation that is not under the legal or effective control of a small group is unlikely to be suspected of accumulating earnings for the purpose of tax avoidance.

The key to imposition of the tax is not the number of the shareholders in the corporation but whether a shareholder group controls corporate policy. If such a group does exist and withholds dividends to protect its own tax position, an AET (§ 531) problem might materialize.

---

[1]§ 532(c).
[2]*Trico Products v. Comm.*, 43–2 USTC ¶9540, 31 AFTR 394, 137 F.2d 424 (CA–2, 1943).

When a corporation is formed or used to shield its shareholders from individual taxes by accumulating rather than distributing earnings and profits, the "bad" purpose for accumulating earnings is considered to exist under § 532(a). This subjective test, in effect, asks, Did the corporation and/or shareholder(s) *intend* to retain the earnings in order to avoid the tax on dividends? According to the Supreme Court, the tax avoidance motive need *not* be the dominant or controlling purpose to trigger application of the penalty tax; it need only be a contributing factor to the retention of earnings.[3] The accumulation of funds beyond the corporation's reasonable needs is determinative of the existence of a "bad" purpose, unless the contrary can be proven by the preponderance of the evidence. The fact that a business is a mere holding or investment company is *prima facie* evidence of this tax avoidance purpose.[4]

IMPOSITION OF THE TAX AND THE ACCUMULATED EARNINGS CREDIT

Contrary to its name, the penalty tax is not levied on the corporate accumulated earnings balance. Instead, the tax is imposed on the current year's *addition* to this balance not needed for a reasonable business purpose. The penalty tax is not imposed upon S corporations, personal holding companies, foreign personal holding companies, tax-exempt organizations, or passive foreign investment companies. The tax is in addition to the regular corporate tax and the 20 percent alternative minimum tax. Currently, the tax rate is 39.6 percent.

The **accumulated earnings credit** is the greater of the following:

1. The current earnings and profits (E & P) for the tax year that are needed to meet the reasonable needs of the business (see the subsequent discussion) *less* the net long-term capital gain for the year (net of any tax). In determining the reasonable needs for any one year, the accumulated E & P of past years must be taken into account.

2. The amount by which the **minimum credit** allowable to the corporation exceeds the accumulated E & P of the corporation at the close of the preceding tax year. Most corporations are allowed a minimum credit of $250,000 against accumulated taxable income, even when earnings are accumulated beyond reasonable business needs. However, certain personal service corporations in health, law, engineering, architecture, accounting, actuarial science, performing arts, and consulting are limited to a $150,000 minimum credit. Moreover, a nonservice corporation (other than a holding or investment company) may retain more than $250,000 (and a service organization may retain more than $150,000) of accumulated earnings if the company can justify that the accumulation is necessary to meet the *reasonable needs of the business.*[5]

EXAMPLE 2

Yellow Corporation, a calendar year manufacturing concern, has accumulated E & P of $120,000 as of December 31, 1997. For 1998, it has no capital gains and has current E & P of $140,000. A realistic estimate places Yellow's reasonable needs of the business for 1998 at $200,000. The allowable credit is the *greater* of (1) or (2).

---

[3] *U.S. v. The Donruss Co.*, 69–1 USTC ¶9167, 23 AFTR2d 69–418, 89 S.Ct. 501 (USSC, 1969).

[4] § 533. See, for example, *H. C. Cockrell Warehouse Corp.*, 71 T.C. 1036 (1979).

[5] §§ 535(c) and 537 and Reg. § 1.537–1.

	(1)	(2)
Reasonable needs	$ 200,000	
Minimum credit		$ 250,000
Accumulated E & P	(120,000)	(120,000)
Potential credit	$ 80,000	$ 130,000

Thus, the credit becomes $130,000 (the *greater* of $80,000 or $130,000). ▼

Several observations can be made about the accumulated earnings credit. First, the minimum credit is of no consequence as long as the prior year's ending balance in accumulated E & P equals or exceeds the allowed threshold ($250,000 or $150,000). Second, when the credit is based on reasonable needs, the credit is the amount by which those needs exceed accumulated E & P. Third, a taxpayer must choose between the reasonable needs credit (item 1) or the minimum credit (item 2). Combining the two in the same year is not permissible. Fourth, although the § 531 tax is not imposed on accumulated E & P, the amount of the credit depends upon the balance of this account as of the end of the preceding year.

REASONABLE NEEDS OF THE BUSINESS

2 **LEARNING OBJECTIVE**
Determine the reasonable needs of the business.

If a corporation's funds are invested in assets essential to the needs of the business, the IRS will have a difficult time imposing the AET. "Thus, the size of the accumulated earnings and profits or surplus is not the crucial factor; rather it is the reasonableness and nature of the surplus."[6] What are the reasonable business needs of a corporation? This question is difficult to answer and can lead to disputes with the IRS.

Justifiable Needs—In General.   The **reasonable needs of a business** include the business's reasonably anticipated needs.[7] These anticipated needs must be specific, definite, and feasible. A number of court decisions illustrate that indefinite plans referred to only briefly in corporate minutes merely give the taxpayer a false feeling of security.[8]

The Regulations list some legitimate reasons that could indicate that a corporation is accumulating earnings to meet the reasonable needs of the business. Earnings may be allowed to accumulate to provide for bona fide expansion of the business enterprise or replacement of plant and facilities as well as to acquire a business enterprise through the purchase of stock or assets. Provision for the retirement of bona fide indebtedness created in connection with the trade or business (e.g., the establishment of a sinking fund for the retirement of bonds issued by the corporation) is a legitimate reason for accumulating earnings under ordinary circumstances. Providing necessary working capital for the business (e.g., to acquire inventories) and providing for investment or loans to suppliers or customers (if necessary to maintain the business of the corporation) are valid grounds for accumulating earnings.[9] Funds may be retained for self-insurance[10] and realistic business contingencies (e.g., lawsuits, patent infringements).[11] Accumulations to avoid an

---

[6]*Smoot Sand & Gravel Corp. v. Comm.*, 60–1 USTC ¶9241, 5 AFTR2d 626, 274 F.2d 495 (CA–4, 1960).
[7]§ 537(a)(1).
[8]See, for example, *Fine Realty, Inc. v. U.S.*, 62–2 USTC ¶9758, 10 AFTR2d 5751, 209 F.Supp. 286 (D.Ct. Minn., 1962).

[9]Reg. § 1.537–2(b).
[10]*Halby Chemical Co., Inc. v. U.S.*, 67–2 USTC ¶9500, 19 AFTR2d 1589, 180 Ct.Cls. 584 (Ct.Cls., 1967).
[11]*Dielectric Materials Co.*, 57 T.C. 587 (1972).

unfavorable competitive position[12] and to carry key employee life insurance policies[13] are justifiable. Accumulation to provide for the loss of a key customer or client is a reasonable need of the business.[14]

The reasonable business needs of a company also include the post-death § 303 redemption requirements of a corporation.[15] Accumulations for such purposes are limited to the amount needed (or reasonably anticipated to be needed) to redeem stock included in the gross estate of the decedent-shareholder.[16] This amount may not exceed the sum of the death taxes and funeral and administration expenses allowable under § 2053 or § 2106.[17]

Section 537(b) provides that reasonable accumulations to pay future product liability losses represent a reasonable anticipated need of the business. Guidelines for the application of this allowance are prescribed in Proposed Regulations.

Justifiable Needs—Working Capital Requirements for Inventory Situations. For many years, the penalty tax on accumulated earnings was based upon the concept of retained earnings. The courts generally looked at retained earnings alone to determine whether there was an unreasonable accumulation. However, a corporation may have a large retained earnings balance and yet possess no liquid assets with which to pay dividends. Therefore, the emphasis should more appropriately be placed upon the liquidity of a corporation. Does the business have liquid assets *not* needed that could be used to pay dividends? The courts, however, did not begin to use this liquidity approach until 1960.

Looking for an objective approach to determine a corporation's need for liquid assets, the courts seized upon the operating cycle. The operating cycle of a business is the average time interval between the acquisition of materials (or services) entering the business and the final realization of cash. A normal business has two distinct cycles:

1. Purchase of inventory → the production process → finished goods inventory.
2. Sale of merchandise → accounts receivable → cash collection.

A systematic operating cycle formula was developed in *Bardahl Manufacturing Co.* and *Bardahl International Corp.*[18] The technique became known as the *Bardahl* formula. This formula is not a precise tool and is subject to various interpretations.

The following is the standard formula used to determine the reasonable working capital needs for a corporation:

$$\text{Inventory cycle} = \frac{\text{Average inventory}}{\text{Cost of goods sold}}$$

Plus

$$\text{Accounts receivable cycle} = \frac{\text{Average accounts receivable}}{\text{Net sales}}$$

---

[12]*North Valley Metabolic Laboratories*, 34 TCM 400, T.C.Memo. 1975–79.

[13]*Emeloid Co. v. Comm.*, 51–1 USTC ¶66,013, 40 AFTR 674, 189 F.2d 230 (CA–3, 1951). Key employee life insurance is a policy on the life of a key employee that is owned by and made payable to the employer. Such insurance enables the employer to recoup some of the economic loss that could materialize upon the untimely death of the key employee.

[14]*EMI Corporation*, 50 TCM 569, T.C.Memo. 1985–386, and *James H. Rutter*, 52 TCM 326, T.C.Memo. 1986–407.

[15]The § 303 redemption to pay death taxes and administration expenses of a deceased shareholder is discussed in Chapter 18. See § 537(a).

[16]§§ 537(a)(2) and (b)(1).

[17]§ 303(a).

[18]*Bardahl Manufacturing Co.*, 24 TCM 1030, T.C.Memo. 1965–200; *Bardahl International Corp.*, 25 TCM 935, T.C.Memo. 1966–182. See also *Apollo Industries, Inc. v. Comm.*, 66–1 USTC ¶9294, 17 AFTR2d 518, 358 F.2d 867 (CA–1, 1966).

Minus

$$\text{Accounts payable cycle} = \frac{\text{Average accounts payable}^{19}}{\text{Purchases} + \text{cash operating expenses}}$$

Equals

A decimal percentage

This imprecise formula assumes that working capital needs are computed on a yearly basis. However, this may not provide the most favorable result. A business that experiences seasonally based high and low cycles illustrates this point. For example, a construction company can justify a greater working capital need if computations are based on a cycle that includes the winter months only and not on an annual average.[20] In the same vein, an incorporated CPA firm would choose a cycle during the slow season.

The decimal percentage derived above, when multiplied by the cost of goods sold plus general, administrative, and selling expenses (not including unpaid Federal income taxes and depreciation),[21] equals the working capital needs of the business. Working capital is the excess of current assets over current liabilities. This amount is the relatively liquid portion of the total business capital that is a buffer for meeting obligations within the normal operating cycle of the business. Paid estimated Federal income taxes are treated as operating expenses, but profit sharing contributions and charitable contributions are not operating expenses.

If the statistically computed working capital needs plus any extraordinary expenses are more than the current year's net working capital, no penalty tax is imposed. However, if working capital needs plus any extraordinary expenses are less than the current year's net working capital, the possibility of the imposition of a penalty tax does exist.[22]

The IRS normally takes the position that the operating cycle should be reduced by the accounts payable cycle. The IRS maintains that the payment of these expenses may be postponed by various credit arrangements that will reduce the operating capital requirements. However, a number of court decisions have omitted such a reduction. Some courts use all payables, while other courts use only material and trade payables. In any case, a corporate tax planner should not have to rely on creditors to avoid the accumulated earnings tax. The corporation with the most acute working capital problem will probably have a large accounts payable balance. If the formula for determining reasonable working capital needs is used, a large accounts payable balance will result in a sizable reduction in the maximum working capital allowable before the tax is imposed. For tax planning purposes, a corporation should hold accounts payable at a reduced level.

Justifiable Needs—Working Capital Requirements for Noninventory Situations. A service business does not purchase inventories, so part of the operating cycle in the *Bardahl* formula is missing. However, a service business incurs certain costs such as salaries and overhead for a period of time before billing customers for services. Some courts have used a rough rule of thumb

---

[19]The accounts payable cycle was developed in *Kingsbury Investments, Inc.*, 28 TCM 1082, T.C.Memo. 1969–205. Some courts have used only purchases and not total operating expenses: *Suwannee Lumber Mfg. Co., Inc.*, 39 TCM 572, T.C.Memo. 1979–477. But see *Snow Manufacturing*, 86 T.C. 260 (1986).

[20]See *Audits of Construction Contracts*, AICPA, 1965, p. 25.

[21]In *W. L. Mead, Inc.*, 34 TCM 924, T.C.Memo. 1975–215, the Tax Court allowed depreciation to be included in the expenses of a

service firm with no inventory. Likewise, in *Doug Long, Inc.*, 72 T.C. 158 (1979), the Tax Court allowed a truckstop to include quarterly estimated tax payments in operating expenses.

[22]*Electric Regulator Corp. v. Comm.*, 64–2 USTC ¶9705, 14 AFTR2d 5447, 336 F.2d 339 (CA–2, 1964) used "quick assets" (current assets less inventory).

TAX IN THE NEWS

APPLYING THE *BARDAHL* FORMULA COULD BE MISLEADING

Experience in tax audits has shown that the *Bardahl* formula is a double-edged sword. The problem is that it measures working capital, not cash. In reality, the payment of dividends—which is the whole purpose of the AET provisions—can be made only in cash. When the *Bardahl* formula works to a corporation's disadvantage, it is important to determine how much cash, on average, is available for distribution. Case law has held that a corporation should not be forced to incur debt or sell off business assets merely to pay dividends so as to avoid the AET. The statement of cash flows may be useful in defending against an AET attack, because it highlights fixed assets acquired and other business investments made. Cash on hand at the end of the year may not be a fair reflection of the average of cash available during the year. In addition, bank covenants, which prevent the payment of dividends or require certain levels of working capital, should be taken into account since they evidence a nonprohibited purpose for accumulating earnings. However, lack of cash due to nonbusiness related activities, such as loans to shareholders, will not help avoid AET exposure.

On the other hand, when the *Bardahl* formula indicates that the working capital needs are greater than the working capital available, weary IRS agents are sometimes willing to accept this as dispositive that no AET should be assessed, rather than investigating the other aspects of potential AET exposure.

SOURCE: Excerpted by permission from Michael J. Goldberg, "The Accumulated Earnings Tax: A Practical Approach to a Subjective Assessment," *The Tax Adviser*, March 1993, p. 146.

---

to determine an inventory equivalent cycle. Under certain circumstances, a human resource accounting (HRA) approach may be used to determine the working capital needs of a noninventory corporation. The use of an HRA approach is based on the contention that the strength of a service business—and its major asset—is its highly educated, skilled technicians. Such individuals must be available both to attract clients and to execute projects efficiently. In the event of a business downturn, it would be foolish to discharge highly paid specialists, recruited and trained at considerable expense. The business decline might prove to be of brief duration.

One court[23] allowed an engineering firm to add to the IRS's *Bardahl*-calculated operating reserve the reasonable professional and technical payroll for an additional period of 60 days. The Court felt that this extra amount would ". . . allow sufficient reserve for one cycle of full operation plus a reasonable period of curtailed operation to recapture business or, in the alternative, to face up to hard decisions on reducing the scope of the entire operation or abandoning it." Further, the Court expressed its opinion that a multiple of reasonable professional and technical salaries is a useful method for determining the amount to be included in an operating reserve. However, the Court did not indicate why it selected two months as the magic number. It can be anticipated that the courts will continue to evolve a *Bardahl*-like formula for noninventory corporations.

---

[23]*Simons-Eastern Co. v. U.S.*, 73–1 USTC ¶9279, 31 AFTR2d 73–640, 354 F.Supp. 1003 (D.Ct. Ga., 1972). See also *Delaware Trucking Co., Inc.*, 32 TCM 105, T.C.Memo. 1973–29; *Magic Mart, Inc.*, 51 T.C. 775 (1969); and *Technalysis*, 101 T.C. 397 (1993), a three-month period.

CONCEPT SUMMARY 20–1

Reasonable Business Needs

Legitimate Reasons	Invalid Reasons
Expansion of a business.	Loans to shareholders.
Replacement of capital assets.	Loans to brother-sister corporations.
Replacement of plant.	Future depression.
Acquisition of a business.	Unrealistic contingencies.
Working capital needs.	Investment in assets unrelated to the business.
Product liability loss.	Retirement of stock without a curtailment of the business.*
Loans to suppliers or customers.	
Redemption under § 303 to pay death taxes and administration expenses of a shareholder.	
Realistic business hazards.	
Loss of a major customer or client.	
Reserve for actual lawsuit.	
Protection of a family business from takeover by outsiders.	
Debt retirement.	
Self-insurance.	

*But see *Technalysis*, 101 T.C. 397 (1993).

No Justifiable Needs.   Certain situations do *not* call for the accumulation of earnings. For example, accumulating earnings to make loans to shareholders[24] or brother-sister corporations is not considered within the reasonable needs of the business.[25] Accumulations to retire stock without curtailment of the business and for unrealistic business hazards (e.g., depression of the U.S. economy) are invalid reasons for accumulating funds.[26] The same holds true for accumulations made to carry out investments in properties or securities unrelated to the corporation's activity.[27]

Concept Summary 20–1 reviews the previous discussion regarding what does and does not constitute a reasonable need of the business.

Measuring the Accumulation.   Should the cost or the fair market value of assets be used to determine whether a corporation has accumulated E & P beyond its reasonable needs? This issue remains unclear. The Supreme Court has indicated that fair market value is to be used when dealing with marketable securities.[28] Although the Court admitted that the concept of E & P does not include unrealized appreciation, it asserted that the current asset ratio must be considered in determining if accumulated earnings are reasonable. Thus, the Court looked to the economic realities of the situation and held that fair market value is to be used with respect to readily marketable securities. The Court's opinion did not address the proper basis for valuation of assets other than marketable securities. However, the IRS

---

[24]Reg. §§ 1.537–2(c)(1), (2) and (3).
[25]See *Young's Rubber Corp.*, 21 TCM 1593, T.C.Memo. 1962–300.
[26]*Turnbull, Inc. v. Comm.*, 67–1 USTC ¶9221, 19 AFTR2d 609, 373 F.2d 91 (CA–5, 1967), and Reg. § 1.537–2(c)(5).

[27]Reg. § 1.537–2(c)(4).
[28]*Ivan Allen Co. v. U.S.*, 75–2 USTC ¶9557, 36 AFTR2d 75–5200, 95 S.Ct. 2501 (USSC, 1975).

may assert that this rule should be extended to include other assets. Therefore, tax advisers and corporate personnel should regularly check all security holdings to guard against accumulations caused by the appreciation of investments.

EXAMPLE 3

Two of Robin Company's shareholders, father and son, own 75% of the stock. Robin had accumulated E & P of approximately $2,000,000. Five years ago, the company invested $150,000 in various stocks and bonds. At the end of the current tax year, the fair market value of these securities approximates $2,500,000. If these securities are valued at cost, current assets minus current liabilities are deemed to be equal to the reasonable needs of the business. However, if the marketable securities are valued at their $2,500,000 fair market value, the value of the liquid assets greatly exceeds the corporation's reasonable needs. Under the Supreme Court's economic reality test, the fair market value is used. Consequently, the corporation is subject to the § 531 penalty tax. ▼

MECHANICS OF THE PENALTY TAX

3 **LEARNING OBJECTIVE**
Compute the accumulated earnings tax.

The taxable base for the AET is a company's *accumulated taxable income (ATI)*. Taxable income of the corporation is modified as follows:[29]

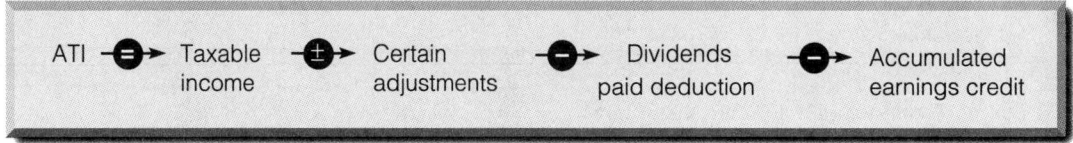

For a corporation that is not a mere holding or investment company, the "certain adjustments" include the following items as deductions:

1. Corporate income tax for the year.
2. Charitable contributions in excess of 10 percent of adjusted taxable income.
3. Capital loss adjustment.[30]
4. Excess of net long-term capital gain over net short-term capital loss, diminished by the capital gain tax and reduced by net capital losses from earlier years.

and the following items as additions:

5. Capital loss carryovers and carrybacks.
6. Net operating loss deduction.
7. Dividends received deduction.

The purpose of each of these adjustments is to produce an amount that more closely represents the dividend-paying capacity of the corporation. For example, the corporate income tax is deducted from taxable income since the corporation does not have this money to pay dividends. Conversely, the dividends received deduction is added to taxable income since the deduction has no impact upon the ability to pay a dividend. Note that item 4, in effect, allows a corporation to accumulate any capital gains without a penalty tax.

---

[29]§ 535(a).
[30]This deduction (item 3) and item 4 are either/or deductions since a corporation will not have both in the same year. For the capital loss adjustment, see § 535(b)(5).

Payment of dividends reduces the amount of ATI subject to the penalty tax. The dividends paid deduction includes any dividends paid during the tax year that the shareholders must report as ordinary income *and* any dividends paid within 2½ months after the close of the tax year.[31] However, a nontaxable stock dividend does not affect the dividends paid deduction.

A shareholder may file a consent statement to treat as a dividend the amount specified in the statement. A *consent dividend* is taxed to the shareholder even though it is not actually distributed. The shareholder treats the consent dividend as a contribution to the capital of the corporation (paid-in capital).[32]

EXAMPLE 4

A nonservice closely held corporation that had no capital gains or losses in prior years has the following financial transactions for calendar year 1998:

Taxable income	$300,000
Tax liability	100,250
Excess charitable contributions	22,000
Short-term capital loss	(40,000)
Dividends received (less than 20% owned)	100,000
Research and development expenses	46,000
Dividends paid in 1998	40,000
Accumulated E & P (1/1/98)	220,000

Presuming the corporation is subject to the § 531 tax and has *no* reasonable business needs that justify its accumulations, ATI is calculated as follows:

Taxable income		$ 300,000
Plus: 70% dividends received deduction		70,000
		$ 370,000
Less: Tax liability	$100,250	
Excess charitable contributions	22,000	
Net short-term capital loss adjustment	40,000	
Dividends paid	40,000	
Accumulated earnings minimum credit ($250,000 – $220,000)	30,000	(232,250)
Accumulated taxable income (ATI)		$ 137,750

Thus, the accumulated earnings penalty tax for 1998 is $54,549 ($137,750 × 39.6%). ▼

EXAMPLE 5

In Example 4, assume that the reasonable needs of the business of § 535(c) amount to $270,000 in 1998. The current year's accumulated earnings are now reduced by $50,000 ($270,000 – $220,000), rather than the $30,000 minimum credit. ATI is $117,750, and the penalty tax is $46,629 ($117,750 × 39.6%). Note that the $220,000 of beginning accumulated earnings *cannot* be omitted in determining whether taxable income for the current year is reasonably needed by the enterprise. ▼

---

[31]§§ 535(a), 561(a), and 563(a).
[32]§§ 565(a) and (c)(2). The consent dividend procedure is appropriate if the corporation is not in a position to make a cash or property distribution to its shareholders. The dividends paid deduction is discussed more fully later in the chapter.

PERSONAL HOLDING COMPANY PENALTY TAX

4 LEARNING OBJECTIVE
Discuss the reason for the personal holding company tax.

The personal holding company (PHC) tax, § 541, was enacted to discourage the sheltering of certain types of passive income in corporations owned by high tax bracket individuals. These "incorporated pocketbooks" were frequently found in the entertainment and construction industries. For example, a taxpayer could shelter the income from securities in a corporation, which would pay no dividends, and allow the corporation's stock to increase in value. Like the accumulated earnings tax, the purpose of the 39.6 percent PHC tax is to force the distribution of corporate earnings to the shareholders. However, in any one year, the IRS cannot impose both the PHC tax and the accumulated earnings tax.[33]

EXAMPLE 6

Considerable tax savings could be achieved by incorporating a "pocketbook" if § 541 did not exist. Assume that investments that yield $50,000 a year are transferred to a corporation by a 39.6% income tax bracket shareholder. A tax savings of $12,300 will occur each year if no dividends are paid to the shareholder. With no corporation, there would be a total tax liability of $19,800 (39.6% × $50,000), but with a corporation the tax liability is only $7,500 (15% × $50,000). Further, if the yield of $50,000 is in the form of dividends, the corporate tax will be even less because of the dividends received deduction. ▼

Whether a corporation will be included within the statutory definition of a PHC for any particular year depends upon the facts and circumstances during that year.[34] Therefore, PHC status may be conferred even in the absence of any avoidance intent on the part of the corporation. In one situation,[35] a manufacturing operation adopted a plan of complete liquidation, sold its business, and invested the proceeds of the sale in U.S. Treasury bills and certificates of deposit. During the liquidating corporation's last tax year, 100 percent of the corporation's adjusted ordinary gross income was interest income. Since the corporation was owned by one shareholder, the corporation was a PHC, even though in the process of liquidation.

Certain types of corporations are expressly excluded from PHC status in § 542(c):

- Tax-exempt organizations under § 501(a).
- Banks and domestic building and loan associations.
- Life insurance companies.
- Surety companies.
- Foreign personal holding companies.
- Lending or finance companies.
- Foreign corporations.
- Small business investment companies.

These exceptions allow the business world to perform necessary activities without a high rate of taxation. For example, a legitimate finance company should not be burdened by the PHC tax because it is performing a valuable business function of lending money. In contrast, in the case of a classic incorporated pocketbook, the major purpose is to shelter the investment income from possible higher individual tax rates.

---

[33]§ 532(b)(1) and Reg. § 1.541–1(a).
[34]*Affiliated Enterprises, Inc. v. Comm.*, 44–1 USTC ¶9178, 32 AFTR 153, 140 F.2d 647 (CA–10, 1944).

[35]*Weiss v. U.S.*, 75–2 USTC ¶9538, 36 AFTR2d 75–5186 (D.Ct. Ohio, 1975). See also *O'Sullivan Rubber Co. v. Comm.*, 41–2 USTC ¶9521, 27 AFTR 529, 120 F.2d 845 (CA–2, 1941).

DEFINITION OF A PERSONAL HOLDING COMPANY

5 **LEARNING OBJECTIVE**
Recognize the requirements for personal holding company status.

The PHC provisions include two tests:

- Was more than 50 percent of the *value* of the outstanding stock owned by five or fewer individuals at any time during the *last half* of the taxable year?
- Is a substantial portion (60 percent or more) of the corporate income (adjusted ordinary gross income) composed of passive types of income such as dividends, interest, rents, royalties, or certain personal service income?

If the answer to *both* of these questions is yes, the corporation is classified as a **personal holding company (PHC).** Once classified as a PHC, the corporation could be required to pay a 39.6 percent penalty tax in addition to the regular corporate income tax.

Stock Ownership Test.   To meet the stock ownership test, more than 50 percent *in value* of the outstanding stock must be owned, directly or indirectly, by or for not more than five individuals sometime during the last half of the tax year. Thus, if the corporation has 9 or fewer shareholders, it automatically meets this test. If 10 unrelated individuals own *equal* portions of the value of the outstanding stock, the stock ownership requirement is not met. However, if these 10 individuals do not hold equal value, the test is met.

The ownership test is based on fair market value and not on the number of shares outstanding. Fair market value is determined in light of all the circumstances and is based on the company's net worth, earning and dividend-paying capacity, appreciation of assets, and other relevant factors. If there are two or more classes of stock outstanding, the total value of all the stock is allocated among the various classes according to the relative value of each class.[36]

In determining the stock ownership of an individual, broad constructive ownership rules apply. Under § 544, the following attribution rules determine indirect ownership:

1. Any stock owned by a corporation, partnership, trust, or estate is considered to be owned proportionately by the shareholders, partners, or beneficiaries.
2. The stock owned by the members of an individual's family (brothers, sisters, spouse, ancestors, and lineal descendants) or by the individual's partner is considered to be owned by the individual.
3. If an individual has an option to purchase stock, the stock is regarded as owned by that person.[37]
4. Convertible securities are treated as outstanding stock.

EXAMPLE 7

During the last half of the tax year, Azure Corporation has 1,000 shares of outstanding stock, 499 of which are held by various individuals having no relationship to one another and none of whom are partners. The remaining 501 shares are held by seven shareholders as follows:

---

[36]Reg. § 1.542–3(c).

[37]For examples of how these constructive ownership rules operate, see Reg. §§ 1.544–2, –3(a), and –4.

Dana	100
Dana's spouse	50
Dana's brother	20
Dana's sister	70
Dana's father	120
Dana's son	80
Dana's daughter	61

Under the family attribution rules of § 544(a)(2), Dana owns 501 shares of Azure for purposes of determining stock ownership in a PHC. ▼

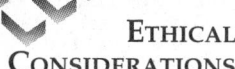

ETHICAL CONSIDERATIONS

Staying Single for the Sake of the Company

Falcon Corporation is a closely held corporation, and for many years it has satisfied the gross income test. The company has avoided PHC status, however, by not meeting the stock ownership test.

Beth James and Harvey Mason, both shareholders in Falcon, have fallen in love and are considering marriage. When the other shareholders learn about the possible marriage and realize that it would cause Falcon to become a PHC, they suggest that Beth and Harvey live together and remain single.

Do you have any comment and advice regarding this moral and legal dilemma?

Basically, the broad constructive ownership rules make it difficult for a closely held corporation to avoid application of the stock ownership test. Attribution rules 2, 3, and 4 are applicable only for the purpose of classifying a corporation as a PHC and cannot be used to avoid the application of the PHC provisions.

Gross Income Test. The gross income test is met if 60 percent or more of the corporation's **adjusted ordinary gross income (AOGI)** consists of certain passive income items (PHC income). AOGI is calculated by subtracting certain items from gross income (as defined by § 61).[38] The adjustments required to arrive at AOGI appear in Figure 20–1.

In Figure 20–1, the deductions from gross income result in the intermediate concept, **ordinary gross income (OGI),** whose use is noted subsequently. The starting point, gross income, is not necessarily synonymous with gross receipts. In fact, for transactions in stocks, securities, and commodities, the term "gross income" includes only the excess of gains over any losses.[39]

PHC income includes income from dividends; interest; royalties; annuities;[40] rents; mineral, oil, and gas royalties; copyright royalties; produced film rents; computer software royalties; and amounts from certain personal service contracts.

EXAMPLE 8

Crow Corporation has four shareholders, and its AOGI is $95,000, consisting of gross income of $40,000 from a merchandising operation, interest income of $15,000, dividend income of $25,000, and adjusted income of $15,000 from rents. Total passive income is

---

[38]§§ 543(b)(1) and (2).
[39]Reg. § 1.542–2.

[40]§ 543(a)(1).

▼ **FIGURE 20–1**
Adjusted Ordinary Gross
Income Determination

Gross income (defined in § 61)

Less: • Capital gains.

• Section 1231 gains.

Equals: Ordinary gross income (OGI).

Less: • Depreciation, property taxes, interest expense, and rental expenses directly related to gross income from rents (not to exceed the income from rents).

• Depreciation, property and severance taxes, interest expense, and rental expenses directly related to gross income from mineral, oil, and gas royalties (not to exceed gross income from the royalties).

• Interest on a condemnation award, a judgment, a tax refund, and an obligation of the United States held by a dealer.

Equals: Adjusted ordinary gross income (AOGI).

$55,000 ($15,000 + $25,000 + $15,000). Since 60% of AOGI (60% × $95,000 = $57,000) is greater than the passive income ($55,000), the corporation is not a PHC. ▼

EXAMPLE 9   Assume in Example 8 that the corporation received $21,000 in interest income rather than $15,000. Total passive income is now $61,000 ($21,000 + $25,000 + $15,000). Since 60% of AOGI (60% × $101,000 = $60,600) is less than the passive income of $61,000, the corporation is a PHC. ▼

Most passive types of income such as dividends, interest, royalties, and annuities cause few classification problems. Certain income items, however, may or may not be classified as PHC income. Special rules apply to rent income, mineral, oil, and gas royalties, and personal service contracts.

Rent Income.   Although rent income is normally classified as PHC income, such income can be excluded from that category if two tests are met. The *first test* is met if a corporation's adjusted income from rents is 50 percent or more of the corporation's AOGI. The *second test* is satisfied if the total dividends for the tax year are equal to or greater than the amount by which the *nonrent* PHC income *exceeds* 10 percent of OGI.[41] Dividends for this purpose include those actually paid, those considered as paid on the last day of the tax year, and consent dividends (see the later discussion of the dividends paid deduction). The taxpayer must meet *both* tests for the rent income to be excluded from PHC income (see Figure 20–4 later in the chapter).

With respect to the 50 percent test, *adjusted income from rents* is defined as gross income from rents reduced by certain deductions. The deductions are depreciation, property taxes, interest, and rent. Generally, compensation is not included in the term "rents" and is not an allowable deduction. The final amount included in AOGI as adjusted income from rents cannot be less than zero.

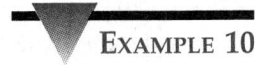

EXAMPLE 10   Assume that a corporation has rent income of $10,000 and the following business deductions:

[41]§ 543(a)(2).

Depreciation on rental property	$1,000
Interest on mortgage	2,500
Real property taxes	1,500
Salaries and other business expenses	3,000

The adjusted income from rents included in AOGI is $5,000 ($10,000 − $1,000 − $2,500 − $1,500). Salaries and other business expenses do not affect the calculation of AOGI. ▼

A company deriving its income primarily from rental activities can avoid PHC status by merely distributing as dividends the amount of nonrent PHC income that exceeds 10 percent of its OGI.

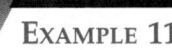

EXAMPLE 11

During the tax year, Amber Corporation receives $15,000 in rent income, $4,000 in dividends, and a $1,000 long-term capital gain. Corporate deductions for depreciation, interest, and real estate taxes allocable to the rent income are $10,000. The company pays a total of $2,500 in dividends to its eight shareholders. To determine whether the rent income is PHC income, OGI, AOGI, and adjusted income from rents must be calculated.

Rent income	$ 15,000
Dividends	4,000
Long-term capital gain	1,000
Gross income	$ 20,000
Deduct: Gains from sale or disposition of capital assets	(1,000)
OGI	$ 19,000
Deduct: Depreciation, interest, and real estate taxes	(10,000)
AOGI	$ 9,000

First, adjusted income from rents must be 50% or more of AOGI.

Rent income	$ 15,000
Deduct: Depreciation, interest, and real estate taxes	(10,000)
Adjusted income from rents	$ 5,000
50% of AOGI	$ 4,500

Amber Corporation has satisfied the first test (adjusted income from rents is equal to or greater than 50% of AOGI).

Second, total dividends paid for the year are $2,500. This figure must be *equal to or greater than* the amount by which nonrent PHC income exceeds 10% of OGI.

Nonrent PHC income	$ 4,000
Less: 10% of OGI	(1,900)
Excess	$ 2,100

Because Amber Corporation meets *both* tests, the adjusted income from rents is *not* PHC income. ▼

Mineral, Oil, and Gas Royalties. As with rent income, adjusted income from mineral, oil, and gas royalties can be excluded from PHC income if certain tests are met.[42] *First*, adjusted income from the royalties must constitute 50 percent or more of AOGI. *Second*, nonroyalty PHC income may not exceed 10 percent of OGI. Note that this 10 percent test is not accompanied by the dividend escape clause

---

[42]§ 543(a)(3).

previously described in relation to rent income. Therefore, corporations receiving income from mineral, oil, or gas royalties must be careful to minimize nonroyalty PHC income. Furthermore, adjusted income from rents and copyright royalties are considered to be nonroyalty PHC income whether or not treated as such by §§ 543(a)(2) and (4). *Third,* the company's business expenses under § 162 (other than compensation paid to shareholders) must be at least 15 percent of AOGI.

EXAMPLE 12

Lark Corporation has gross income of $4,000, which consists of gross income of $2,500 from oil royalties, $400 of dividends, and $1,100 from the sale of merchandise. The total deductions for depletion, interest, and property and severance taxes allocable to the gross income from oil royalties equal $1,000. Ordinary and necessary business expenses allowable under § 162 are $450. Lark Corporation's adjusted income from oil royalties will not be PHC income if the three tests are met. Therefore, OGI, AOGI, and adjusted income from oil royalties must be determined:

Oil royalties income	$ 2,500
Dividends	400
Sale of merchandise	1,100
Gross income (*and* OGI)	$ 4,000
Deduct: Depletion, interest, and property and severance taxes	(1,000)
AOGI	$ 3,000

Adjusted income from oil royalties must be 50% or more of AOGI.

Oil royalties income	$ 2,500
Deduct: Depletion, interest, and property and severance taxes	(1,000)
Adjusted income from oil royalties	$ 1,500
50% of AOGI	$ 1,500

The first test is met (oil royalties are equal to or greater than 50% of AOGI). Since nonroyalty PHC income is $400 (composed solely of the $400 of dividends) and this amount is not more than 10% of OGI, the second test is also satisfied. The third requirement is satisfied if deductible expenses under § 162 amount to at least 15% of AOGI.

§ 162 expenses	$450
15% of $3,000 (AOGI)	$450

Therefore, Lark Corporation's adjusted income from oil royalties is *not* PHC income. ▼

Personal Service Contracts. Any amount from personal service contracts is classified as PHC income only if (1) some person other than the corporation has the right to designate, by name or by description, the individual who is to perform the services and (2) the person so designated owns, directly or indirectly, 25 percent or more in value of the outstanding stock of the corporation at some time during the taxable year.[43]

EXAMPLE 13

Blair, Cody, and Dana (all attorneys) are equal shareholders in Canary Company, a professional association engaged in the practice of law. Irene, a new client, retains Canary Company to pursue a legal claim. Under the terms of the retainer agreement, Irene

---

[43]§ 543(a)(7). For an application of the "right to designate," see *Thomas P. Byrnes, Inc.,* 73 T.C. 416 (1979).

▼ **FIGURE 20–2**
Undistributed PHC Income
Determination

	Taxable income
Plus:	• Dividends received deduction.
	• Net operating loss (NOL), other than the NOL from the preceding year (computed without the dividends received deduction).
	• Certain business expenses and depreciation attributable to nonbusiness property owned by the corporation that exceed the income derived from such property (unless the taxpayer proves that the rent was the highest obtainable and the rental business was a bona fide business activity).*
Less:	• Federal income tax accrual (other than the PHC tax and the accumulated earnings tax).
	• Excess charitable contributions beyond the 10% corporate limitation (with a maximum of the 20%, 30%, or 50% limitation imposed on individuals).**
	• Excess of long-term capital gain over short-term capital loss (net of tax).
Equals:	Adjusted taxable income.
Less:	Dividends paid deduction.
Equals:	Undistributed PHC (UPHC) income.

*§ 545(b).
**Reg. § 1.545–2.

designates Blair as the attorney who will perform the legal services. The suit is successful, and 30% of the judgment Irene recovers is paid to Canary as a fee. Since the parties have met all of the requirements of § 543(a)(7), the fee received by Canary is PHC income.[44] ▼

The result reached in Example 13 could have been avoided if the retainer agreement had not specifically named Blair as the party to perform the services.

CALCULATION OF THE PHC TAX

6 ▼ **LEARNING OBJECTIVE**
Compute the personal holding company tax.

To this point, the discussion has focused on the determination of PHC status. Once a corporation is classified as a PHC, the amount upon which the 39.6 percent penalty tax is imposed must be computed. The tax base is called undistributed PHC income (UPHC income). Basically, this amount is taxable income, subject to certain adjustments, minus the dividends paid deduction. After the adjustments, UPHC income more clearly represents the corporation's dividend-paying capacity. Figure 20–2 shows how this amount is determined.

Dividends Paid Deduction. Since the purpose of the PHC penalty tax is to force a corporation to pay dividends, *five* types of **dividends paid deductions** reduce the amount subject to the penalty tax (see Table 20–1). First, dividends actually paid during the tax year ordinarily reduce UPHC income.[45] However, such distributions must be pro rata. They must exhibit no preference to any shares of stock over shares of the same class or to any class of stock over other classes outstanding.[46] The prohibition is especially harsh when portions of an employee-shareholder's salary are declared unreasonable and classified as a disguised or constructive dividend.[47] In the case of a dividend of appreciated property, the dividends paid deduction is the fair market value of the property (not the adjusted basis to the distributing corporation).

---

[44]The example presumes Canary Company will be treated as a corporation for Federal tax purposes.
[45]§§ 561(a)(1) and 562.

[46]§ 562(c).
[47]Refer to Chapter 18 and *Henry Schwartz Corp.*, 60 T.C. 728 (1973).

▼ **TABLE 20–1**
Dividends Paid Deductions

Type of Dividend	Availability	Timing	Statutory Location	Effect on Shareholders
Current year	Both § 531 and § 541	By end of year.	§ 561(a)(1)	Reduction in ATI and UPHC income.
2½-month grace period	Both § 531 and § 541*	On or before the 15th day of the 3rd month after end of year.	§§ 563(a) and (b)	Reduction in ATI and UPHC income.
Consent dividend	Both § 531 and § 541	Not later than due date of the corporate tax return.	§ 565(a)	Treated as a dividend as of end of tax year and given back as a contribution to capital.
Dividend carryover	§ 541	Not later than due date of the corporate tax return.	§ 564	Reduction in UPHC income.
Deficiency dividend	§ 541	Within 90 days after determination of PHC tax deficiency.	§ 547	Treated as if dividend paid in offending year. No impact on interest and penalties.

*Limited to 20% of current-year dividends paid for a PHC.

EXAMPLE 14

Three individuals are equal shareholders in a PHC. A property dividend with an adjusted basis of $20,000 (FMV of $30,000) is paid to the three shareholders in the following proportion: 25%, 35%, and 40%. This distribution is not pro rata, so the dividend is not deductible from UPHC income. ▼

A 2½-month grace period exists following the close of the tax year. Dividends paid during this period may be treated as paid during the tax year just closed. However, the amount allowed as a deduction from UPHC income cannot exceed either (1) the UPHC income for the tax year or (2) 20 percent of the total dividends distributed during the tax year.[48] Reasonable cause may not be used to overcome the 20 percent limitation, even if the taxpayer relied upon incorrect advice given by an accountant.[49]

The **consent dividend** procedure[50] involves a hypothetical distribution of the corporate income to be taxed to the shareholders. Since the consent dividend is taxable, a dividends paid deduction is allowed. The shareholder's basis in his or her stock is increased by the consent dividend (a contribution to capital). The consent election is filed by the shareholders at any time not later than the due date of the corporate tax return. The consent dividend is considered distributed by the corporation on the last day of the tax year and is included in the gross income of the shareholder in the tax year in which or with which the tax year of the corporation ends. The disadvantage of this special election is that the shareholders must pay taxes on dividends they do not actually receive. However, if cash is not available for dividend distributions, the consent dividend route is a logical alternative.

EXAMPLE 15

Snipe Corporation, a calendar year taxpayer solely owned by Tracy, is a PHC. Dividends of $30,000 must be paid to avoid the PHC tax, but the company has a poor cash position. Tracy elects the consent dividend treatment under § 565 and is taxed on $30,000 of dividends.

---

[48]§§ 563(b) and 543(a)(2)(B)(ii).
[49]*Kenneth Farmer Darrow*, 64 T.C. 217 (1975).

[50]Reg. § 1.565–1.

Her basis in Snipe stock is increased by $30,000 as a result of this special election. Thus, Snipe does not incur the PHC tax, but Tracy is taxed even though she receives no cash from the corporation with which to pay the tax. ▼

Even after a corporation has been classified as a PHC, a delayed dividend distribution made in a subsequent tax year can avoid the PHC penalty tax. This **deficiency dividend** provision allows a dividend to be paid within 90 days after the determination of the PHC tax deficiency for a prior tax year.[51] A determination occurs when a decision of a court is final, a closing agreement (see Chapter 25) is signed, or a written agreement is signed between the taxpayer and a District Director. The dividend distribution *cannot be made* before the determination or after the running of the 90-day time period. Furthermore, the deficiency dividend procedure does not relieve the taxpayer of interest, additional amounts, or assessable penalties computed with respect to the PHC tax.

A dividend carryover from two prior years may be available to reduce the UPHC income. When the dividends paid by a company in its prior years exceed the company's UPHC income for those years, the excess may be deducted in the current year. Table 20–1 summarizes these dividend paid deductions.

Personal Holding Company Planning Model.   Some of the complex PHC provisions may be developed into a flow chart format. Figures 20–3 and 20–4 provide a PHC planning model and the rules for the rent exclusion test.

Computations Illustrated.   After the appropriate adjustments are made to corporate taxable income and the sum of the dividends paid is subtracted, the resulting figure is UPHC income. This amount is multiplied by the 39.6 percent penalty tax rate to obtain the PHC tax.

The consequences of this confiscatory tax can be severe. Taxpayers should monitor their corporations and take the necessary steps to avoid the tax. Because most corporations use planning procedures to avoid PHC status, revenues from the tax are small.

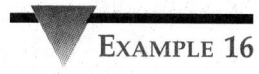
EXAMPLE 16

Bluebird Corporation had the following items of income and expense in the current year:

Dividend income (less than 20% owned)	$ 40,000
Rent income	150,000
Depreciation expense	40,000
Mortgage interest	30,000
Real estate taxes	30,000
Salaries	20,000
Dividends paid (three shareholders)	20,000
Corporate income tax	6,300

OGI is $190,000 ($40,000 + $150,000), and AOGI is $90,000 ($190,000 − $40,000 − $30,000 − $30,000). Taxable income is $42,000, computed as follows:

---

[51] § 547.

▼ **FIGURE 20–3**
Personal Holding Company
Planning Model

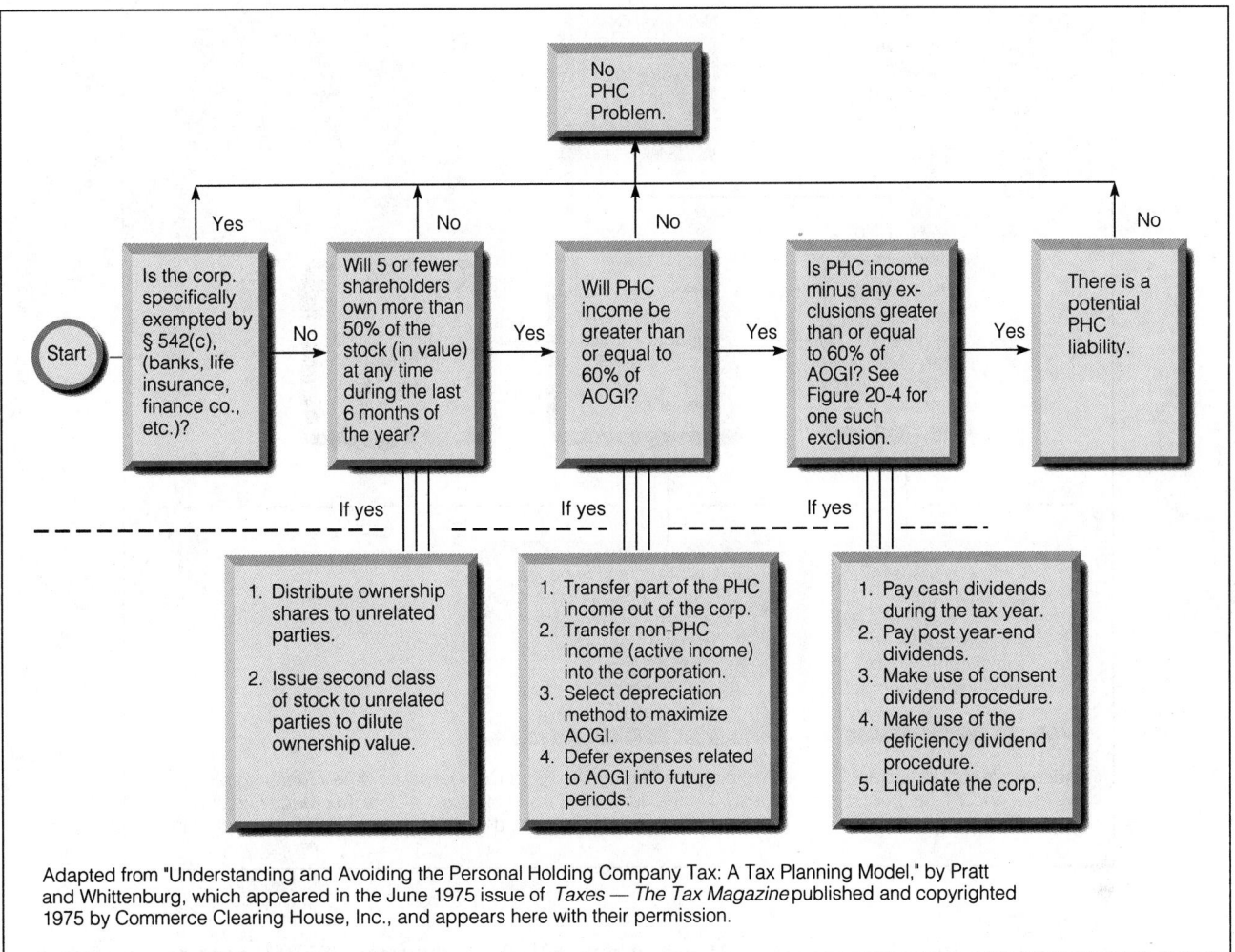

Adapted from "Understanding and Avoiding the Personal Holding Company Tax: A Tax Planning Model," by Pratt and Whittenburg, which appeared in the June 1975 issue of *Taxes — The Tax Magazine* published and copyrighted 1975 by Commerce Clearing House, Inc., and appears here with their permission.

Rent income		$ 150,000
Dividend income		40,000
		$ 190,000
Less: Depreciation expense	$40,000	
Mortgage interest	30,000	
Real estate taxes	30,000	
Salaries	20,000	(120,000)
		$ 70,000
Less: Dividends received deduction		
($40,000 × 70%)		(28,000)
Taxable income		$ 42,000

The adjusted income from rents is $50,000 ($150,000 − $100,000). Bluebird meets the 50% rent income test since $50,000 is greater than 50% of AOGI ($90,000 × 50% = $45,000). But the corporation did not meet the second test for excluding rent income from PHC

▼ **FIGURE 20–4**
Rent Exclusion Test

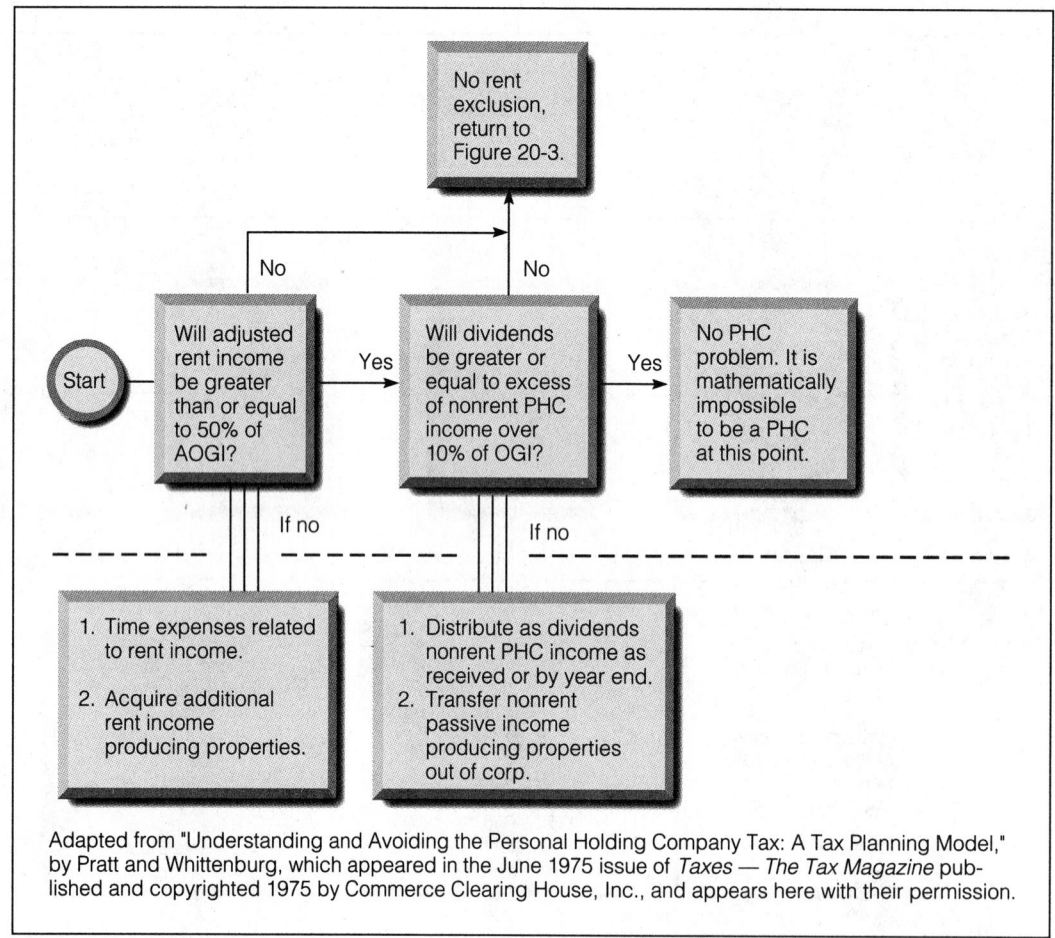

Adapted from "Understanding and Avoiding the Personal Holding Company Tax: A Tax Planning Model," by Pratt and Whittenburg, which appeared in the June 1975 issue of *Taxes — The Tax Magazine* published and copyrighted 1975 by Commerce Clearing House, Inc., and appears here with their permission.

income. It did not pay at least $21,000 of dividends ($40,000 nonrent PHC income − $19,000 = $21,000). Therefore, the 10% test is not met, and the rent income is classified as PHC income. Since all income is passive, Bluebird Corporation is a PHC. The PHC tax of $17,305 is calculated as follows:

Taxable income	$ 42,000
Plus: Dividends received deduction ($40,000 × 70%)	28,000
	$ 70,000
Less: Corporate income tax	(6,300)
	$ 63,700
Less: Dividends paid	(20,000)
UPHC income	$ 43,700
	× .396
PHC tax liability	$ 17,305

▼

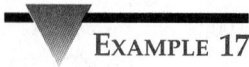

EXAMPLE 17   Assume that in Example 16, dividends of $22,000 (instead of $20,000) are paid to the shareholders. In this case, the rent income is not PHC income because the 10% test is met ($22,000 is equal to or greater than the nonrent PHC income in excess of 10% of OGI).

Thus, an increase of $2,000 in the dividends paid in Example 16 avoids the $17,305 PHC tax liability. ▼

COMPARISON OF THE ACCUMULATED EARNINGS AND PHC TAXES

7 **LEARNING OBJECTIVE**
Compare the accumulated earnings and personal holding company taxes.

A review of several important distinctions between the penalty tax on the unreasonable accumulation of earnings (§ 531) and the tax on PHCs (§ 541) sets the stage for the presentation of tax planning considerations applicable to both taxes.

- Unlike § 531, no element of intent is necessary for the imposition of the § 541 (PHC) tax.[52] Consequently, § 541 can be a real trap for the unwary.
- The imposition of the § 541 tax is not affected by the past history of the corporation. Thus, the tax could be just as applicable to a newly formed corporation as to one that has been in existence for many years. This is not the case with the § 531 tax. Past accumulations have a direct bearing on the determination of the accumulated earnings credit. In this sense, younger corporations are less vulnerable to the § 531 tax since complete insulation generally is guaranteed until accumulations exceed $250,000 (or $150,000).
- Although both taxes pose threats for closely held corporations, the § 541 tax presents the more explicit threat due to the constructive stock ownership rules. However, publicly held corporations can be subject to the § 531 tax if corporate policy is dominated by certain shareholders who are using the corporate form to avoid income taxes on dividends through the accumulation of corporate profits.
- Sufficient dividend distributions can eliminate both taxes. In the case of § 531, however, such dividends must be distributed on a timely basis. Both taxes allow a 2½-month grace period and provide for the consent dividend procedure.[53] Only the § 541 tax allows the deficiency dividend procedure.
- Differences in reporting procedures arise because the § 541 tax is a self-assessed tax while the § 531 tax is not. For example, if a corporation is a PHC, the company must file a Schedule PH along with its Form 1120 (the corporate income tax return) for the year involved. Failure to file the Schedule PH can result in the imposition of interest and penalties and also brings into play a special six-year statute of limitations for the assessment of the § 541 tax.[54] On the other hand, the § 531 tax is assessed by the IRS and consequently requires no reporting procedures on the part of the corporate taxpayer.

TAX PLANNING CONSIDERATIONS

Even in particular situations when corporate rates are higher than individual rates, a corporation can invest accumulated funds in tax-free vehicles or purchase high-yield corporate stocks to take advantage of the dividends received deduction. Thus, the threat of the accumulated earnings tax and the PHC tax can be a prime concern to many corporations.

---

[52]In light of the Supreme Court decision in *Donruss* (refer to Footnote 3 and the related text), what role, if any, will intent play in the future in helping taxpayers avoid the § 531 tax? In this connection, see the dissenting opinion issued by Justice Harlan.

[53]Under the § 531 tax, dividends paid within the first 2½ months of the succeeding year *must* be carried back to the preceding year. In

the case of the § 541 tax, the carryback is optional—some or all of the dividends can be deducted in the year paid. The 20% limit on carrybacks applicable to § 541 [see § 563(a)] does not cover § 531 situations.

[54]§ 6501(f). See also Chapter 25.

THE PENALTY TAX ON UNREASONABLE ACCUMULATIONS

8 **LEARNING OBJECTIVE**
Plan to minimize (or avoid) the accumulated earnings tax.

Justifying the Accumulations. The key defense against imposition of the § 531 tax is to show that the accumulations are necessary to meet the reasonable needs of the business. Several points should be kept in mind:

- To the extent possible, the justification for the accumulation should be documented. If, for example, the corporation plans to acquire additional physical facilities for use in its trade or business, the minutes of the board of directors' meetings should reflect the decision. Furthermore, the documentation should take place during the period of accumulation. This planning may require some foresight on the part of the taxpayer. Meaningful planning to avoid a tax problem should not be based on what happens after the issue has been raised by an agent as the result of an audit. In the case of a profitable closely held corporation that accumulates some or all of its profits, the parties should operate under the assumption that § 531 is always a potential issue. Recognizing a tax problem at an early stage is the first step in a satisfactory resolution.
- Multiple reasons for making an accumulation are not only permissible but invariably advisable. Suppose, for example, a manufacturing corporation plans to expand its plant. It would not be wise to stop with the cost of the expansion as the only justification for all accumulations. What about further justification based on the corporation's working capital requirements as determined under the *Bardahl* formula or some variation? Other reasons for making the accumulation may be present and should be recognized.
- The reasons for the accumulation should be sincere and, once established, pursued to the extent feasible.

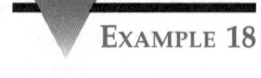

EXAMPLE 18   In 1993, the directors of Gull Corporation decide to accumulate $1 million to fund the replacement of Gull's plant. Five years pass, and no steps are taken to begin construction. ▼

EXAMPLE 19   In 1993, the directors of Grouse Corporation decide to accumulate $1 million to fund the replacement of Grouse's plant. In the ensuing five-year period, the following steps are taken: a site selection committee is appointed (1993); a site is chosen (1994); the site (land) is purchased (1995); an architect is retained, and plans are drawn up for the new plant (1997); bids are requested and submitted for the construction of the new plant (1998). ▼

- Compare Examples 18 and 19. Grouse Corporation is in a much better position to justify the accumulation. Even though the plant has not yet been replaced some five years after the accumulations began, the progress toward its ultimate construction speaks for itself. Gull Corporation may be hard-pressed to prove the sincerity of its objective for the accumulations in light of its failure to follow through on the projected replacement.
- The amount of the accumulation should be realistic under the circumstances.

EXAMPLE 20   Bunting Corporation plans to replace certain machinery at an estimated cost of $500,000. The original machinery was purchased for $300,000 and, because of $200,000 in depreciation deducted for tax purposes, has a present book value of $100,000. How much of an accumulation can be justified for the replacement to avoid the § 531 tax? Initially, $500,000 seems to be the appropriate amount since this is the estimated replacement cost of the machinery. But what about the $200,000 in depreciation that Bunting already deducted? If it is counted again as part of a reasonable accumulation, a double tax benefit results. Only $300,000

($100,000 unrecovered cost of the old machinery + $200,000 additional outlay necessary) can be justified as the amount for an accumulation.[55] ▼

EXAMPLE 21

During the current year, a competitor files a $2 million patent infringement suit against Egret Corporation. Competent legal counsel advises Egret that the suit is groundless. Under such conditions, the corporation can hardly justify accumulating $2 million because of the pending lawsuit. ▼

- Since the § 531 tax is imposed on an annual basis, justification for accumulations may vary from year to year.[56]

EXAMPLE 22

For calendar years 1997 and 1998, Red Corporation was able to justify large accumulations owing to a pending additional income tax assessment. In early 1999, the assessment is settled and paid. After the settlement, Red Corporation can no longer consider the assessment as a reasonably anticipated need of the business. ▼

Danger of Loans to Shareholders. The presence of loans made by a corporation to its shareholders often raises the § 531 issue. If this same corporation has a poor dividend-paying record, the company becomes particularly vulnerable. The avowed goal of the § 531 tax is to force certain corporations to distribute dividends. If a corporation can spare funds for loans to shareholders, the company certainly has the capacity to pay dividends. Unfortunately, the presence of such loans can also cause other tax problems for the parties.

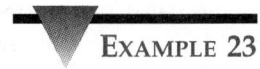

EXAMPLE 23

During the year in question, Quail Corporation made advances of $120,000 to its sole shareholder, Tom. Although prosperous and maintaining substantial accumulations, Quail has never paid a dividend. Under these circumstances, the IRS could move in either of two directions. It could assess the § 531 tax against Quail for its unreasonable accumulation of earnings. Alternatively, the IRS could argue that the advances were not bona fide loans but, instead, taxable dividends. The dual approach places the taxpayers in a difficult position. If, for example, they contend that the advance was a bona fide loan, Tom avoids dividend income, but Quail becomes vulnerable to the imposition of the § 531 tax.[57] On the other hand, a concession that the advance was not a loan hurts Tom but helps Quail avoid the penalty tax. ▼

Role of Dividends. The relationship between dividend distributions and the § 531 tax can be further clarified. The payment of enough dividends can completely avoid the § 531 tax due to the operation of § 535. This provision defines accumulated taxable income as *taxable income* (adjusted by certain items) *minus the sum of the dividends paid deduction and the accumulated earnings credit.* Since the § 531 tax is imposed on accumulated taxable income, no tax is due if the taxable dividends paid and the accumulated earnings credit are large enough to offset taxable income.

But can the payment of a smaller dividend completely avoid the § 531 tax? Theoretically, even significant dividend distributions will not insulate a corporation from the tax. From a practical standpoint, however, the payment of dividends indicates that the corporation is not being used exclusively to shield its shareholders from tax consequences. In applying § 531, the IRS will consider such payments

[55]*Battelstein Investment Co. v. U.S.,* 71–1 USTC ¶9227, 27 AFTR2d 71–713, 442 F.2d 87 (CA–5, 1971).

[56]Compare *Hardin's Bakeries, Inc. v. Martin, Jr.,* 67–1 USTC ¶9253, 19 AFTR2d 647, 293 F.Supp. 1129 (D.Ct. Miss., 1967), with *Hardin v. U.S.,* 70–2 USTC ¶9676, 26 AFTR2d 70–5852 (D.Ct. Miss., 1970),

aff'd., rev'd., rem'd. by 72–1 USTC ¶9464, 29 AFTR2d 72–1446, 461 F.2d 865 (CA–5, 1972).

[57]*Ray v. U.S.,* 69–1 USTC ¶9334, 23 AFTR2d 69–1141, 409 F.2d 1322 (CA–6, 1969).

to the extent that they reflect the good faith of the parties and the lack of tax avoidance motivation.

AVOIDING THE PHC TAX

9 ▼ **LEARNING OBJECTIVE**
Plan to minimize (or avoid) the personal holding company tax.

The classification of a corporation as a PHC requires the satisfaction of *both* the stock ownership and the gross income tests. Failure to meet either of these tests avoids PHC status and the § 541 tax. The following planning suggestions may help in avoiding the PHC tax:

- The stock ownership test can be handled through a dispersion of stock ownership. In this regard, however, watch the application of the stock attribution rules.
- Remember the following relationship when working with the gross income test:

$$\frac{\text{PHC income}}{\text{AOGI}} = 60\% \text{ or more}$$

Decreasing the numerator (PHC income) or increasing the denominator (AOGI) of the fraction reduces the resulting percentage. Keeping the percentage below 60 percent precludes classification as a PHC. To control PHC income, investments in low-yield growth securities are preferable to those that generate heavy interest or dividend income. Capital gains from the sale of such securities will not affect PHC status since they are not included in either the numerator or the denominator of the fraction. Investments in tax-exempt securities are attractive because the interest income, like capital gains, has no effect in applying the gross income test.

- Income from personal service contracts may, under certain conditions, be PHC income. Where a 25 percent or more owner of a PHC is specifically designated in a retainer agreement as the party to perform the services, the personal service contract income will be PHC income. See Example 13 earlier in this chapter.
- Rent income may or may not be PHC income. The relative amount of rent income is the key consideration. If

$$\frac{\text{Adjusted income from rents}}{\text{AOGI}} = 50\% \text{ or more}$$

and nonrent PHC income less 10 percent of OGI is distributed as a dividend, rent income is not PHC income. Maximizing adjusted income from rents clearly improves the situation for taxpayers. Since adjusted income from rents represents gross rents less attributable expenses, a conservative approach in determining such expenses is helpful. The taxpayer should minimize depreciation (e.g., choose straight-line over the modified accelerated cost recovery method). This approach to handling expenses attributable to rental property is confusing to many taxpayers because it contradicts what is normally done to reduce income tax consequences.

PHC status need not carry tragic tax consequences if the parties are aware of the issue and take appropriate steps. Since the tax is imposed on undistributed PHC income, properly timed dividend distributions neutralize the tax and avoid interest and penalties. Also, as long as a corporation holds PHC status, the § 531 tax cannot be imposed.

KEY TERMS

Accumulated earnings credit, 20–4

Accumulated earnings tax (AET), 20–3

Adjusted ordinary gross income (AOGI), 20–14

Consent dividend, 20–19

Deficiency dividend, 20–20

Dividends paid deductions, 20–18

Minimum credit, 20–4

Ordinary gross income (OGI), 20–14

Personal holding company (PHC), 20–13

Reasonable needs of a business, 20–5

PROBLEM MATERIALS

DISCUSSION QUESTIONS

1. Charlene creates a corporation in order to obtain limited liability. She would prefer to avoid the second tax at the shareholder level. Suggest some techniques that would help Charlene avoid double taxation.

2. Explain the purpose(s) underlying the enactment of the accumulated earnings penalty tax and the PHC tax.

3. Omar is considering merging two of his brother-sister corporations. Outline any relevant tax issues facing this merger.

4. How can human resource accounting be used in an accumulated earnings situation?

5. Cecil McDowell is preparing *Bardahl* calculations for his closely held corporation. Should he include other operating expenses in the calculation of the accounts payable cycle?

6. Determine whether the following factors or events will increase (+), decrease (–), or have no effect (NE) on the working capital needs of a corporation when calculating the *Bardahl* formula:
   a. An increase in depreciation deduction.
   b. Use of a peak inventory figure rather than average inventory.
   c. A decrease in the annual cost of goods sold.
   d. Purchase of a tract of land for a future parking lot.
   e. Use of average receivables rather than peak receivables.
   f. An increase in annual net sales.
   g. A decrease in accounts payable.
   h. An increase in the annual expenses.
   i. A loss on the sale of treasury stock.

7. ATI = Taxable income – Certain adjustments + Dividends paid deduction – Accumulated earnings credit. Please comment.

8. In making the "certain adjustments" (refer to Question 7) necessary in arriving at ATI, which of the following items should be added (+), should be subtracted (–), or will have no effect (NE) on taxable income?
   a. A nontaxable stock dividend distributed by the corporation to its shareholders.
   b. Corporate income tax incurred and paid.
   c. Charitable contributions paid in the amount of 10% of taxable income.
   d. Deduction of an NOL carried over from a prior year.
   e. The dividends received deduction.

9. Ms. Janson (a widow) and Mr. Kimbell (a bachelor) are both shareholder-employees in Tern Corporation (closely held). If they elope during the year, what are the relevant tax issues with respect to Tern Corporation's vulnerability to the accumulated earnings tax or the PHC tax?

10. Jay Corporation is a consulting firm. Its entire outstanding stock is owned by three individuals. Jay enters into a contract with Warbler Corporation to perform certain consulting services in consideration of which Warbler is to pay Jay $40,000. The individual who is to perform the services is not designated by name or description in the contract, and no one but Jay has the right to designate such person. Does the $40,000 constitute PHC income?

11. Which of the following income items *could* be PHC income?
    a. Annuities.
    b. Interest.
    c. Rent income.
    d. Sales of inventory.
    e. Dividends.
    f. Coal royalties.
    g. Copyright royalties.
    h. Produced film rents.
    i. Gain from sale of a parking lot.
    j. Oil royalties.

12. The election to capitalize (rather than to depreciate) certain expenses for rental property could make a difference in determining whether or not the corporate lessor is a PHC. How could this be so?

13. Explain the deficiency dividend procedure for purposes of the accumulated earnings tax and the PHC tax.

14. If a corporation has an effective Federal income tax rate of 34% and also incurs a PHC tax, what is the company's aggregate tax rate in 1998?

15. The payment of enough dividends can avoid *either* the accumulated earnings tax or the PHC tax. Explain.

16. General Motors Corporation has no difficulty avoiding *both* the accumulated earnings tax and the PHC tax. Explain.

17. Which of the following purposes can be used to justify accumulations to meet the reasonable needs of the business?
    a. A corporation creates a reserve for a depression that might occur in 2000.
    b. A corporation has an extraordinarily high working capital need.
    c. A manufacturing corporation invests in several oil and gas drilling funds.
    d. A hotel corporation is being sued because of a structural accident that injured 27 people.
    e. A corporation is considering establishing a sinking fund to retire some bonds.
    f. A corporation carries seven key employee life insurance policies.
    g. Robin Corporation makes loans to Crane Corporation, an unrelated party that is having financial problems and is a key customer.
    h. A corporation agrees to retire 15% of its outstanding stock without curtailing its business.

18. Explain how each of the following points is related to the avoidance of the PHC tax:
    a. Sale of stock to outsiders.
    b. An increase in AOGI.
    c. A decrease in PHC income.
    d. Section 1231 gains recognized by the corporation.
    e. Corporate investment in tax-exempt bonds.
    f. Income from personal service contracts.
    g. The choice of straight-line depreciation for rental property owned by the corporation.

19. Compare the accumulated earnings tax to the PHC tax with respect to the following items:
    a. The element of intent.
    b. Applicability of the tax to a newly created corporation.
    c. Applicability of the tax to a publicly held corporation.
    d. The 2½-month rule with respect to the dividends paid deduction.
    e. The availability of the deficiency dividend procedure.
    f. Procedures for reporting and paying the tax.

PROBLEMS

20. Diver, Inc., a calendar year consulting corporation, has accumulated E & P of $90,000 on January 1, 1998. For the calendar year 1998, the corporation has taxable income of $100,000. Diver has no reasonable needs that justify an accumulation of its E & P. Calculate the amount vulnerable to the accumulated earnings tax.

21. In 1998, Finch Corporation, a manufacturing company, retained $60,000 for its reasonable business needs. The company had a long-term capital gain of $20,000 and a short-term capital loss of $15,000, with a resulting capital gains tax of $1,250. The accumulated E & P at the end of 1997 was $260,000. On January 25, 1998, Finch paid a taxable dividend of $90,000. Calculate the accumulated earnings credit for 1998.

22. A retail corporation had accumulated E & P of $250,000 on January 1, 1998. Its taxable income for 1998 was $75,000. The corporation paid no dividends during the year. There were no other adjustments to determine accumulated taxable income. Assume a court determined that the corporation is subject to the accumulated earnings tax and that the reasonable needs of the business required E & P in the total amount of $270,500. Determine the accumulated earnings tax and explain your calculations.

23. A manufacturing corporation in Oxford, Mississippi, is accumulating a significant amount of E & P. Although the corporation is closely held, it is not a PHC. The following facts relate to 1998:

Taxable income	$450,000
Federal income tax	153,000
Dividend income from a qualified domestic corporation (less than 20% owned)	40,000
Dividends paid in 1998	70,000
Consent dividends	35,000
Dividends paid on February 1, 1999	5,000
Accumulated earnings credit	10,000
Excess charitable contributions (the portion in excess of the amount allowed as a deduction in computing the corporate income tax)	12,000
Net capital loss adjustment	6,000

Compute the accumulated earnings tax, if any.

24. The following data relate to a closely held manufacturing corporation's 1998 tax year:

Net taxable income	$500,000
Federal income taxes	170,000
Excess charitable contributions	30,000
Capital loss adjustment	20,000
Dividends received (14% owned)	140,000
Dividends paid	60,000
Accumulated earnings, 1/1/98	130,000

a. Assume that the corporation is not a PHC. Calculate any accumulated earnings tax and total tax payable in 1998.

b. Can the deficiency dividend procedure be used to avoid this accumulated earnings tax?

25. Garcia Pullig, CEO for a local company, asks you to calculate his company's operating cycle needs without considering accrued Federal income taxes as an operating expense. March is the longest operating cycle for the company, which has reasonable business needs of $40,000 in addition to the working capital required for one operating cycle. Additional information is provided as follows:

Accounts receivable—March	$ 120,000
Inventory—March	160,000
Accounts payable—March	101,000
Cost of goods sold	1,000,000
Other expenses (less depreciation)	100,000
Depreciation	90,000
Sales	2,000,000
Dividends paid	7,000
Accumulated earnings (beginning)	180,000
Accrued Federal income taxes	220,000

Respond to Mr. Pullig in a letter dated June 2, 1998. Mr. Pullig's address is 451 Maple St., Athens, OH 45701.

26. A wholly owned motor freight corporation has permitted its earnings to accumulate. The company has no inventory but wishes to use the *Bardahl* formula to determine the amount of operating capital required for a business cycle. The following facts are relevant:

Yearly revenues	$3,300,000
Average accounts receivable	300,000
Yearly expenses	3,500,000
Average accounts payable	213,000

  a. Determine the turnover rate of average accounts receivable.
  b. Determine the number of days in the accounts receivable cycle.
  c. Determine the expenses for one accounts receivable cycle.
  d. Determine the number of days in the accounts payable cycle.
  e. Determine the operating capital needed for one business cycle.
  f. Explain why the time allowed a taxpayer for the payment of accounts payable should be taken into consideration in applying the *Bardahl* formula.

27. The stock of Dove Corporation is owned as follows:

Sand Corporation (wholly owned by Karl)	100 shares
Karl's wife	100 shares
Karl's partner	100 shares
Karl's wife's sister	100 shares
Abe	50 shares
Betty	30 shares
Charles	20 shares
Unrelated individuals with 10 or fewer shares	500 shares
Total	1,000 shares

Do five or fewer individuals own more than 50% of Dove Corporation?

28. Teal Corporation has gross income of $200,000, which consists of $110,000 of rent income and $90,000 of interest income. The corporation has $30,000 of rent income adjustments and pays $80,000 to its nine shareholders.
  a. Calculate adjusted income from rents.
  b. Calculate AOGI.
  c. Is the 50% test met? Show calculations.
  d. Is the 10% rent income test met? Show calculations.
  e. Is the corporation a PHC?

29. Assume the same facts as in Problem 28, except that rent income adjustments decrease from $30,000 to $20,000. Answer the same questions as in Problem 28.

30. Harrier Corporation has gross income of $165,000, which consists of gross income from rent of $100,000, $40,000 from the sale of merchandise, interest of $15,000, and income from annuities of $10,000. Deductions directly related to the rent income total $28,000.
    a. Calculate OGI.
    b. Calculate AOGI.
    c. Calculate adjusted income from rent.
    d. Does the rent income constitute PHC income? Explain.
    e. Is this corporation a PHC (assuming there are seven shareholders)?
    f. Should the company pay $9,000 of dividends?

31. Daryl is the sole owner of a corporation in Raleigh, North Carolina. The following information is relevant to the corporation's tax year just ended:

Capital gain	$ 20,000
Dividend income	30,000
Rent income	130,000
Rent expenses	40,000
Section 162 business expenses	15,000
Dividends paid	12,000

    a. Calculate OGI.
    b. Calculate AOGI.
    c. Calculate adjusted income from rents.
    d. Calculate nonrent PHC income.
    e. Does this corporation meet the 50% rent income test? Explain.
    f. Does this corporation meet the 10% rent income test? Explain.
    g. Is this company a PHC?
    h. Would payment of $15,000 in dividends avoid any PHC tax?

32. Blue Corporation has the following financial data for the tax year 1998:

Rent income	$430,000
Dividend income	2,900
Interest income	50,000
Operating income	9,000
Depreciation (rental warehouses)	100,000
Mortgage interest (rental warehouses)	125,000
Real estate taxes (rental warehouses)	35,000
Officers' salaries	85,000
Dividends paid	2,000

    a. Calculate OGI.
    b. Calculate AOGI.
    c. Does Blue's adjusted income from rents meet the 50%-or-more-of-AOGI test?
    d. Does Blue Corporation meet the 10% dividend test?
    e. How much in dividends could Blue pay within the 2½-month grace period during 1999?
    f. If the 1998 corporate income tax return has not been filed, what would you suggest for Blue Corporation?

33. Using the legend provided, classify each of the following statements accordingly:

Legend

A	=	Relates only to the tax on unreasonable accumulation of earnings (the § 531 tax)
P	=	Relates only to the PHC tax (the § 541 tax)
B	=	Relates to both the § 531 tax and the § 541 tax
N	=	Relates to neither the § 531 tax nor the § 541 tax

a. The tax is applied to taxable income of the corporation after adjustments are made.
b. The tax is a self-assessed tax.
c. Showing that an accumulation of funds is for reasonable business purposes will help avoid the tax.
d. A consent dividend mechanism can be used to avoid the tax.
e. If the stock of the corporation is equally held by 10 unrelated individuals, the tax cannot be imposed.
f. Any charitable deduction in excess of the 10% limitation is allowed as a deduction before the tax is imposed.
g. Gains from the sale or disposition of capital assets are *not* subject to the tax.
h. A sufficient amount of rent income will cause the tax *not* to be imposed.
i. A life insurance company would *not* be subject to the tax.
j. A corporation with only dividend income would avoid the tax.

34. In each of the following independent situations, indicate whether the corporation involved is a PHC (assume the stock ownership test is met):

	Whistler Corporation	Wren Corporation	Stork Corporation	Swallow Corporation
Sales of merchandise	$ 8,000	$ –0–	$ –0–	$ 2,500
Capital gains	–0–	–0–	–0–	1,000
Dividend income	15,000	5,000	1,000	2,500
Gross rent income	10,000	5,000	9,000	15,000
Expenses related to rents	8,000	2,500	8,000	10,000
Dividends paid	–0–	–0–	–0–	500
Personal holding company? (Circle Y for yes or N for no.)	Y N	Y N	Y N	Y N

35. In each of the following independent situations, indicate whether the corporation involved is a PHC (assume the stock ownership test is met):

	White Corporation	Red Corporation	Lavender Corporation	Aqua Corporation
Sales of merchandise	$ –0–	$3,000	$ –0–	$ –0–
Capital gains	–0–	–0–	1,000	–0–
Interest income	20,000	4,800	2,000	60,000
Gross rent income	80,000	1,200	20,000	50,000
Expenses related to rents	60,000	1,000	10,000	–0–
Dividends paid	12,000	–0–	–0–	20,000
Personal holding company? (Circle Y for yes or N for no.)	Y N	Y N	Y N	Y N

36. In each of the following independent situations, calculate the PHC tax liability in 1998:

	Flamingo Corporation	Pidgeon Corporation
Taxable income	$140,000	$580,000
Dividends received deduction	37,000	90,000
Contributions in excess of 10%	3,000	10,000
Federal income taxes	37,850	197,200
Net capital gain	70,000	40,000
Capital gain tax	25,350	13,600
NOL under § 172		12,000
Current-year dividends paid	14,000	120,000
Consent dividends		40,000
Two and one-half month dividends	4,000	

Research Problems for this chapter appear at the end of Chapter 28.

S CORPORATIONS

LEARNING OBJECTIVES

After completing Chapter 21, you should be able to:

1. Explain the tax effects associated with S corporation status.

2. Identify corporations that qualify for the S election.

3. Understand how to make an S election.

4. Explain how an S election can be terminated.

5. Compute nonseparately stated income and identify separately stated items.

6. Allocate income, deductions, and credits to shareholders.

7. Understand how distributions to S corporation shareholders are taxed.

8. Calculate a shareholder's basis in S corporation stock.

9. Explain how losses in an S corporation are treated.

10. Compute the built-in gains tax.

11. Compute the passive investment income penalty tax.

INTRODUCTION

1 LEARNING OBJECTIVE
Explain the tax effects associated with S corporation status.

The **S corporation** rules were enacted to minimize the role of tax considerations in the entity choice that many small businesses face. S corporation status provides a compromise for small businesses: they can avoid the double taxation and loss limitations inherent in the regular corporate form while still enjoying many of the nontax benefits extended to C corporations.

S corporations are treated as corporations under state law. They are recognized as separate legal entities and generally provide shareholders with the same liability protection afforded by C corporations. Some states (such as Michigan) treat S corporations as C corporations for tax purposes, resulting in a state corporate income or franchise tax liability. For Federal income tax purposes, taxation of S corporations resembles that of partnerships. As with partnerships, the income, deductions, and tax credits of an S corporation flow through to shareholders annually, regardless of whether dividends are paid. Thus, income is taxed at the shareholder level and not at the corporate level. Dividends paid by the corporation are distributed tax-free to shareholders to the extent that the distributed earnings were previously taxed to the shareholders.

Although the tax treatment of S corporations and partnerships is similar, it is not identical. For instance, liabilities affect owners' basis differently and S corporations may incur a tax liability at the corporate level. In addition, a variety of C corporation provisions apply to S corporations. For example, the liquidation of C and S corporations is taxed in the same way. As a rule, where the S corporation provisions are silent, C corporation rules apply.

S corporation status must be elected by a *qualifying* corporation and consented to by its shareholders. Rules related to the S election and the tax treatment of S corporations are addressed in **Subchapter S** of the Internal Revenue Code (§§ 1361–1379). These rules are introduced in this chapter.

AN OVERVIEW OF S CORPORATIONS

Since the inception of S corporations in 1958, their popularity has waxed and waned with changes in the tax law. Before the Tax Reform Act of 1986, their ranks grew slowly. In contrast, in the two years following the 1986 law, the population of S corporations exploded, as their numbers increased by 52 percent. By 1993, more than 1.9 million businesses were filing S corporation returns—48 percent of all corporate returns filed in that year. This rapid growth was driven by a change in the relationship of individual and corporate tax rates. Prior to 1986, maximum individual rates were higher than maximum corporate rates. Following the 1986 tax act, the relationship reversed. After 1993, maximum individual income tax rates were increased to 39.6 percent, again exceeding the maximum corporate rate (by 4.6 percent). Consequently, S corporations declined in popularity, although they remained the preferred business form of a wide range of enterprises. As the following examples illustrate, S corporations can be advantageous even when the top individual tax rate exceeds the top corporate tax rate.

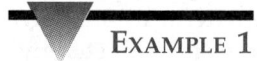

EXAMPLE 1

Assume that an S corporation earns $300,000 in 1998, the marginal individual tax rate applicable to shareholders is 39.6%, the applicable marginal corporate tax rate is 34%, and all after-tax income is distributed currently. The entity's available after-tax earnings, compared with those of a similar C corporation, are as follows:

	C Corporation	**S Corporation**
Earnings	$ 300,000	$ 300,000
Less: Corporate tax	(102,000)	–0–
Available for distribution	$ 198,000	$ 300,000
Less: Tax at owner level	(78,408)	(118,800)
Available after-tax earnings	$ 119,592	$ 181,200

The S corporation generates an extra $61,608 of after-tax earnings ($181,200 – $119,592), when compared with a similar C corporation. The C corporation might be able to reduce this disadvantage, however, by paying out its earnings as compensation, rents, or interest expense. Tax at the owner level can also be deferred or avoided by not distributing after-tax earnings. ▼

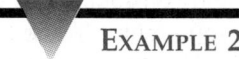

EXAMPLE 2

Assume that a new corporation elects S status and incurs a net operating loss (NOL) of $300,000. The shareholders of the corporation may use their proportionate shares of the NOL to offset other taxable income in the current year, providing an immediate tax savings. In contrast, a newly formed C corporation is required to carry the NOL forward for up to 20 years and does not receive any tax benefit in the current year. Hence, an S corporation can accelerate NOL deductions and thereby provide greater present value for tax savings generated by the loss. ▼

Two recent developments have affected the popularity of S corporation status. First, a new form of business entity recently emerged that offers many of the advantages of S corporations. These new entities, called limited liability companies (LLCs), avoid restrictions that are imposed on S corporations. Second, the Small Business Protection Act of 1996 liberalized a number of the S corporation rules. These changes, which provide greater flexibility in forming, operating, and restructuring S corporations, promise to reinvigorate their status as a viable alternative to LLCs.

WHEN TO ELECT S CORPORATION STATUS

Effective planning with S corporations begins with determining the appropriateness of an S election. The following factors should be considered:

- If shareholders have high marginal rates relative to C corporation rates, it may be desirable to avoid S corporation status. Although a C corporation will be subject to double taxation, the effect of the tax can be minimized with careful planning. For example, profits of the corporation may be taken out by the shareholders as capital gain income through stock redemptions, liquidations, or sales of stock to others. Alternatively, profits may be paid out as dividends in low tax years. Any distribution of profits or sale of stock can be deferred to a later year, thereby reducing the present value of shareholder taxes. Finally, shareholder-level tax on corporate profits can be eliminated by a step-up in basis of the stock upon the shareholder's death.

- S corporation status allows shareholders to realize tax benefits from corporate losses immediately—an important consideration in new business enterprises where losses are common. Thus, if corporate NOLs are anticipated and there is unlikely to be corporate income over the near term to offset with the NOLs, S corporation status is advisable. However, the deductibility of the losses to shareholders must also be considered. The at-risk and passive loss limitations apply to losses generated by an S corporation (see Chapter 10). In addition, as discussed later in this chapter, shareholders may not deduct losses in excess of the basis in their stock. Together these limits may significantly reduce the benefits of an S election in a loss setting.

- If the entity electing S corporation status is currently a C corporation, any NOL carryovers from prior years cannot be used in an S corporation year. Even worse, S corporation years reduce the 20-year carryover period. Also, the corporation may be subject to some corporate-level taxes if it elects S status (see the discussion of the built-in gains tax later in this chapter).

- Distributions of earnings from C corporations are usually taxed as ordinary income. In contrast, because S corporations are flow-through entities, all deduction and income items retain any special tax characteristics when they are reported on shareholders' returns. Whether this consideration favors S status depends upon the character of income and deductions of the S corporation.

- The S corporation rules impose significant requirements for qualifying as an S corporation. When electing S status, one should consider whether any of these requirements are likely to be violated at some point in the future.

- State and local tax laws should also be considered when making the S election. Although an S corporation usually escapes Federal income tax, it may not be immune from state and local taxes.

- The choice of S corporation status is affected by a variety of other factors. For example, the corporate alternative minimum tax (see Chapter 14) may be avoided in an S corporation setting.

QUALIFYING FOR S CORPORATION STATUS

DEFINITION OF A SMALL BUSINESS CORPORATION

2 **LEARNING OBJECTIVE**
Identify corporations that qualify for the S election.

To achieve S corporation status, a corporation *first* must qualify as a **small business corporation.** A small business corporation has the following characteristics:

- Is a domestic corporation (incorporated and organized in the United States).
- Is an eligible corporation (e.g., *not* an insurance company or a nonqualifying bank).
- Issues only one class of stock.

- Is limited to a maximum of 75 shareholders (35 shareholders before 1997).
- Has only individuals, estates, and certain trusts as shareholders.
- Has no nonresident alien shareholder.

Unlike other provisions in the tax law (e.g., § 1244), no maximum or minimum dollar sales or capitalization restrictions apply to small business corporations.

If each of the above requirements is met, then the entity can elect S corporation status. The small business corporation definition is discussed in detail in the following paragraphs.

Ineligible Corporations.   Foreign corporations, certain banks, insurance companies, and Puerto Rico or possessions corporations do not qualify as small business corporations. Prior to 1997, small business corporations were prohibited from being members of affiliated groups. Now, ownership of up to 100 percent of a C corporation is permitted. In addition, small business corporations are permitted (after 1996) to have wholly owned S corporation subsidiaries.[1]

One Class of Stock.   A small business corporation may have only one class of stock issued and outstanding.[2] This restriction permits differences in voting rights, but not differences in distribution or liquidation rights.[3] Thus, two classes of common stock that are identical except that one class is voting and the other is nonvoting would be treated as a single class of stock for small business corporation purposes. In contrast, voting common stock and voting preferred stock (with a preference on dividends) would be treated as two classes of stock. Authorized and unissued stock or treasury stock of another class does not disqualify the corporation. Likewise, unexercised stock options, phantom stock, stock appreciation rights, warrants, and convertible debentures usually do not constitute a second class of stock.

The determination of whether stock provides identical rights to distributions and liquidation proceeds is made based on the provisions governing the operation of the corporation. These *governing provisions* include the corporate charter, articles of incorporation, bylaws, applicable state law, and binding agreements relating to distribution and liquidation proceeds. Employment contracts, loan agreements, and other commercial contracts are *not* considered governing provisions.[4] Such contracts will not violate the one-class-of-stock requirement unless their principal purpose is to circumvent the requirement.

EXAMPLE 3

Blue, a small business corporation, has two equal shareholders, Smith and Jones. Both shareholders are employed by Blue and have binding employment contracts with the corporation. The compensation paid by Blue to Jones under her employment contract is reasonable. The compensation paid to Smith under his employment contract, however, is excessive (a constructive dividend results). Smith's employment contract was not prepared to circumvent the one-class-of-stock requirement. Because employment contracts are not considered governing provisions, Blue has only one class of stock. ▼

Similarly, constructive dividends paid to shareholders as a result of the application of the imputed interest rules under § 7872 generally do not violate the one-class-of-stock requirement, because debt instruments are not governing provisions.

Although the one-class-of-stock requirement seems straightforward, it is possible for debt to be reclassified as stock, resulting in unexpected loss of S corporation

---

[1]§ 1361(b)(2).

[2]§ 1361(b)(1)(D).

[3]§ 1361(c)(4).

[4]Reg. §§ 1.1361–1(l)(2).

status.[5] To mitigate concern over possible reclassification of debt as a second class of stock, the law provides a set of *safe harbor* provisions.

First, straight debt *issued in an S corporation year* will not be treated as a second class of stock and will not disqualify the S election.[6] The characteristics of straight debt include the following:

- The debtor is subject to a written, unconditional promise to pay on demand or on a specified date a sum certain in money.
- The interest rate and payment date are not contingent on corporate profit, management discretion, or similar factors.
- The debt is not convertible into stock.
- The creditor is an individual (other than a nonresident alien), an estate, or qualified trust.
- Straight debt can be held by creditors actively and regularly engaged in the business of lending money.

In addition to the straight debt safe harbor, short-term unwritten advances from a shareholder that do not exceed $10,000 in the aggregate at any time during the corporation's taxable year generally are not treated as a second class of stock. Likewise, debt that is held by stockholders in the same proportion as their stock is not treated as a second class of stock, even if it would be reclassified as equity otherwise.[7] If safe-harbor debt is transferred to a nonqualifying creditor or if the debt instrument is modified significantly after its issue, the safe harbors may no longer apply.

Number of Shareholders.   A small business corporation is limited to 75 shareholders (35 before 1997). If shares of stock are owned jointly by two individuals, they will generally be treated as separate shareholders. However, a husband and wife are considered one shareholder. Similarly, a widower or widow and his or her spouse's estate are treated as a single shareholder.[8] The treatment of a husband and wife as a single shareholder can have unexpected consequences in a divorce, as illustrated in the following example.

EXAMPLE 4

Fred and Wilma (husband and wife) jointly own 10 shares in Marlins, Inc., an S corporation, with the remaining 90 shares outstanding owned by 74 other shareholders. Fred and Wilma get divorced; pursuant to the property settlement approved by the court, the 10 shares held by Fred and Wilma are divided between them (5 to each). Before the divorce settlement, Marlins had 75 shareholders under the small business corporation rules. After the settlement, it has 76 shareholders and no longer qualifies as a small business corporation. ▼

Type of Shareholder Limitation.   Small business corporation shareholders may be individuals, estates, or certain trusts.[9] This limitation prevents partnerships and corporations from owning stock. Partnership and corporate shareholders could easily circumvent the 75-shareholder limitation as illustrated in the following example.

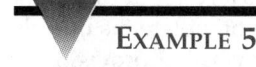

EXAMPLE 5

Saul and 80 of his close friends wish to form an S corporation. Saul reasons that if he and his friends form a partnership, the partnership can then form an S corporation and act as a single shareholder, thereby avoiding the 75-shareholder rule. Saul's plan will not work because partnerships cannot own stock in a small business corporation. ▼

---

[5]Refer to the discussion of debt-versus-equity classification in Chapter 17.
[6]§ 1361(c)(5)(A).

[7]Reg. § 1.1361–1(l)(4).
[8]§ 1361(c)(1).
[9]§ 1361(b)(1)(B).

Although partnerships and corporations cannot own small business corporation stock, small business corporations can be partners in a partnership or shareholders in a corporation. This ability allows the 75-shareholder requirement to be bypassed in a limited sense. For example, if two small business corporations, each with 75 shareholders, form a partnership, then the shareholders of both corporations can enjoy the limited liability conferred by S corporation status and a single level of tax on partnership profits.

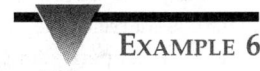

ETHICAL CONSIDERATIONS

Extortion Payments

Burt is the custodian at Quaker Inn, an S corporation in Grand Isle, Louisiana. Over the years, he has received a total of 276 shares of stock in the corporation through bonus payments.

While listening to a debate on television about a national health care plan, Burt decides that the company's health coverage is unfair. He is concerned about this because his wife is seriously ill.

During the second week in December, Burt informs the president of Quaker that he would like a Christmas bonus of $75,000, or else he will sell 10 shares of his stock to one of his relatives who is a nonresident alien. Burt calculates that the resulting corporate tax on the approximately $400,000 of corporate income would amount to about $136,000.

How do you react to Burt's actions?

Nonresident Aliens. Nonresident aliens cannot own stock in a small business corporation.[10] That is, individuals who are not U.S. citizens *must live in the United States* to own S corporation stock. Shareholders with nonresident alien spouses in community property states[11] therefore cannot own S corporation stock because the nonresident alien spouse would be treated as owning half of the community property.[12] Similarly, if a resident alien shareholder moves outside the United States, the S election will be terminated.

MAKING THE ELECTION

3 ▼ LEARNING OBJECTIVE
Understand how to make an S election.

To become an S corporation, a *small business corporation* (defined above) must file a valid election with the IRS. The election is made on Form 2553. For the election to be valid, it must be filed on a timely basis and all shareholders must consent. For S corporation status to apply in the current tax year, the election must be filed either in the previous year or on or before the fifteenth day of the third month of the current year.[13]

▼ EXAMPLE 6

In 1998, a calendar year C corporation in Auburn, Alabama, decides to become an S corporation beginning January 1, 1999. The S corporation election can be made at any time in 1998 or by March 15, 1999. An election after March 15, 1999, will not be effective until the 2000 tax year. ▼

---

[10]§ 1362(b)(1)(C).

[11]Assets acquired by a married couple are generally considered community property in nine states: Louisiana, Texas, New Mexico, Arizona, California, Washington, Idaho, Nevada, and Wisconsin.

[12]See *Ward v. U.S.*, 81–2 USTC ¶9674, 48 AFTR2d 81–5942, 661 F.2d 226 (Ct.Cls., 1981), where the court found that the stock was owned

as community property. Since the taxpayer-shareholder (a U.S. citizen) was married to a citizen and resident of Mexico, the nonresident alien prohibition was violated. If the taxpayer-shareholder had held the stock as separate property, the S election would have been valid.

[13]§ 1362(b).

Even if the 2½-month deadline is met, a current election is not valid unless the corporation qualifies as a small business corporation for the *entire* tax year. Otherwise, the election will be effective for the following tax year. Late current-year elections, after the 2½-month deadline, may be considered timely if there is reasonable cause for the late filing.

A corporation that does not yet exist cannot make an S corporation election.[14] Thus, for new corporations, a premature election may not be effective. A new corporation's 2½-month election period begins at the earliest occurrence of any of the following events: (1) when the corporation has shareholders, (2) when it acquires assets, or (3) when it begins doing business.[15]

EXAMPLE 7   Several individuals acquire assets on behalf of Rock Corporation on June 29, 1998, and begin doing business on July 3, 1998. They subscribe to shares of stock, file articles of incorporation for Rock, and become shareholders on July 7, 1998. The S election must be filed no later than 2½ months after June 29, 1998 (on or before September 12) to be effective for 1998. ▼

SHAREHOLDER CONSENT

A qualifying election requires the consent of all of the corporation's shareholders.[16] Consent must be in writing, and it must generally be filed by the election deadline. However, while no statutory authority exists for obtaining an extension of time for filing an S election (Form 2553), a shareholder may receive an extension of time to file consent. A consent extension is available only if Form 2553 is filed on a timely basis, reasonable cause is given, and the interests of the government are not jeopardized.[17]

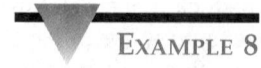

EXAMPLE 8   Vern and Yvonne decide to convert their C corporation into a calendar year S corporation for 1999. At the end of February 1999 (before the election is filed), Yvonne travels to Ukraine and forgets to sign a consent to the election. Yvonne will not return to the United States until June and cannot be reached by fax. Vern files the S election on Form 2553 and also requests an extension of time to file Yvonne's consent to the election. Vern indicates that there is a reasonable cause for the extension: a shareholder is out of the country. Since the government's interest is not jeopardized, the IRS probably will grant Yvonne an extension of time to file the consent. Vern must file the election on Form 2553 on or before March 15, 1999, for the election to be effective for the 1999 calendar year. ▼

Both husband and wife must consent if they own their stock jointly (as joint tenants, tenants in common, tenants in the entirety, or community property). This requirement has led to considerable taxpayer grief—particularly in community property states where the spouses may not realize that their stock is jointly owned as a community asset.

EXAMPLE 9   Three shareholders, Monty, Dianne, and Amy, incorporate in January and file Form 2553. Amy is married and lives in California. Monty is single and Dianne is married; they live in South Carolina. Because Amy is married and lives in a community property state, her husband must also consent to the S election. Since South Carolina is not a community property state, Dianne's husband does not need to consent. ▼

---

[14]See, for example, *T.H. Campbell & Bros., Inc.,* 34 TCM 695, T.C.Memo. 1975–149; Ltr.Rul. 8807070.

[15]Reg. § 1.1372–2(b)(1). Also see, for example, *Nick A. Artukovich,* 61 T.C. 100 (1973).

[16]§ 1362(a)(2).

[17]Rev.Rul. 60–183, 1960–1 C.B. 625; *William Pestcoe,* 40 T.C. 195 (1963); Temp.Reg. § 18.1362–2(e).

Finally, for current-year S elections, persons who were shareholders during any part of the taxable year before the election date, but were not shareholders when the election was made, must also consent to the election.[18]

EXAMPLE 10 On January 15, 1998, the stock of Columbus Corporation (a calendar year C corporation) was held equally by three individual shareholders: Jim, Sally and LuEllen. On that date, LuEllen sells her interest to Jim and Sally. On March 14, 1998, Columbus Corporation files Form 2553. Jim and Sally indicate their consent by signing the form. Columbus cannot become an S corporation until 1999 because LuEllen did not indicate consent. Had all three shareholders consented by signing Form 2553, S status would have taken effect as of January 1, 1998. ▼

ETHICAL CONSIDERATIONS

A Missing S Election Form

Eel Corporation, in Spivey Corners, North Carolina, has filed a Form 1120S for six years, and the local IRS office has sent the company a letter requesting an audit next month. Carrie, who is in charge of tax matters at Eel, cannot find a copy of the original S election, Form 2553.

The original shareholders and officers all agree that a local accountant filed the form, but he passed away last year. Several of the shareholders instruct Carrie to prepare a backdated Form 2553, which they will sign. Carrie could then copy the form and tell the agent that this was a copy of the original Form 2553. What should Carrie do? She estimates that any proposed deficiency would be in the range of $625,000.

LOSS OF THE ELECTION

4 **LEARNING OBJECTIVE**
Explain how an S election can be terminated.

An S election can be lost if any of the following occurs:

- Shareholders owning a majority of shares (voting and nonvoting) voluntarily revoke the election.
- A new shareholder owning more than one-half of the stock affirmatively refuses to consent to the election.
- The corporation no longer qualifies as a small business corporation.
- The corporation does not meet the passive investment income limitation.

Each of these conditions is discussed in detail in this section.

Voluntary Revocation. A voluntary revocation of the S election requires the consent of shareholders owning a majority of shares on the day that the revocation is to be made.[19] A revocation filed up to and including the fifteenth day of the third month of the tax year is effective for the entire tax year, unless a later date is specified. Similarly, unless an effective date is specified, revocation made after the first 2½ months of the current tax year is effective for the following tax year.

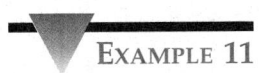

EXAMPLE 11 The shareholders of Petunia Corporation, a calendar year S corporation, voluntarily revoke the S election on January 5, 1998. They do not specify a future effective date in the revocation. Assuming the revocation is properly executed and timely filed, Petunia will be a C corporation for the entire 1998 calendar year. If the election is not made until June 1998, Petunia

---

[18]§ 1362(b)(2)(B)(ii).

[19]§ 1362(d)(1).

will remain an S corporation in 1998 and will become a C corporation at the beginning of 1999. ▼

A corporation can revoke its S status *prospectively* by specifying a future date when the revocation is to be effective. A revocation that designates a future effective date splits the corporation's tax year into a short S corporation year and a short C corporation year. The day on which the revocation occurs is treated as the first day of the C corporation year. The corporation allocates income or loss for the entire year on a pro rata basis (based on the number of days in each short year).

EXAMPLE 12
Assume the same facts as in the preceding example, except that Petunia designates July 1, 1998, as the revocation date. Accordingly, June 30, 1998, is the last day of the S corporation's tax year. The C corporation's tax year runs from July 1, 1998 to December 31, 1998. Any income or loss for the 12-month period is allocated evenly between the two short years, because the two short years lasted an equal number of days. ▼

Rather than using pro rata allocation, the corporation can elect to compute actual income or loss attributable to the two short years. This election requires the consent of everyone who was a shareholder at any time during the S corporation's short year and everyone who owns stock on the first day of the C corporation's year.[20]

Loss of Small Business Corporation Status. If an S corporation fails to qualify as a small business corporation at any time after the election has become effective, its status as an S corporation ends. The termination occurs on the day that the corporation ceases to be a small business corporation.[21] Thus, if the corporation ever has more than 75 shareholders, a second class of stock, or a nonqualifying shareholder, or otherwise fails to meet the definition of a small business corporation, the S election is immediately terminated.

EXAMPLE 13
Peony Corporation has been a calendar year S corporation for three years. On August 13, 1998, one of its 75 shareholders sells *some* of her stock to an outsider. Peony now has 76 shareholders, and it ceases to be a small business corporation. For 1998, Peony is an S corporation through August 12, 1998, and a C corporation from August 13 to December 31, 1998. ▼

Passive Investment Income Limitation. The Code provides a **passive investment income (PII)** limitation for S corporations that were previously C corporations or for S corporations that have merged with C corporations. If an S corporation has C corporation E & P and passive income in excess of 25 percent of its gross receipts for three consecutive taxable years, the S election is terminated as of the beginning of the fourth year.[22]

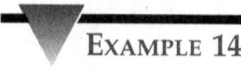

EXAMPLE 14
For 1995, 1996, and 1997, Diapason Corporation, a calendar year S corporation, derived passive income in excess of 25% of its gross receipts. If Diapason holds accumulated E & P from years in which it was a C corporation, its S election is terminated as of January 1, 1998. ▼

---

[20] § 1362(e)(3).
[21] § 1362(d)(2)(B).

[22] § 1362(d)(3)(A)(ii).

PII includes dividends, interest, rents, gains and losses from sales of securities, and royalties net of investment deductions. Rents are not considered PII if the corporation renders significant personal services to the occupant.

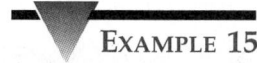

EXAMPLE 15

Violet Corporation owns and operates an apartment building. The corporation provides utilities for the building, maintains the lobby, and furnishes trash collection for tenants. These activities are not considered significant personal services, so any rent income earned by the corporation will be considered PII.

Alternatively, if Violet also furnishes maid services to its tenants (personal services beyond what normally would be expected from a landlord in an apartment building), the rent income would no longer be PII. ▼

Reelection after Termination. After an S election has been terminated, the corporation must wait five years before reelecting S corporation status. The five-year waiting period is waived if

- there is a more-than-50-percent change in ownership of the corporation after the first year for which the termination is applicable, or
- the event causing the termination was not reasonably within the control of the S corporation or its majority shareholders.

OPERATIONAL RULES

S corporations are treated much like partnerships for tax purposes. With a few exceptions,[23] S corporations generally make tax accounting and other elections at the corporate level. Each year, the S corporation determines nonseparately stated income or loss and separately stated income, deductions, and credits. These items are taxed only once, at the shareholder level. All items are allocated to each shareholder based on average ownership of stock throughout the year. The *flow-through* of each item of income, deduction, and credit from the corporation to the shareholder is illustrated in Figure 21–1.

COMPUTATION OF TAXABLE INCOME

5 **LEARNING OBJECTIVE**
Compute nonseparately stated income and identify separately stated items.

Subchapter S taxable income or loss is determined in a manner similar to the tax rules that apply to partnerships, except that S corporations can amortize organizational expenditures[24] and must recognize gains (but not losses) on distributions of appreciated property to shareholders.[25] Other special provisions affecting only the computation of C corporation income, such as the dividends received deduction, do not extend to S corporations.[26] Finally, as with partnerships, certain deductions of individuals are not permitted, including alimony payments, personal moving expenses, certain dependent care expenses, the personal exemption, and the standard deduction.

---

[23]A few elections can be made at the shareholder level (e.g., the choice between a foreign tax deduction or credit).
[24]§§ 248 and 1363(b).

[25]§ 1363(d).
[26]§ 703(a)(2).

▼ **FIGURE 21–1**
Flow-Through of Separate Items
of Income and Loss to S
Corporation Shareholders

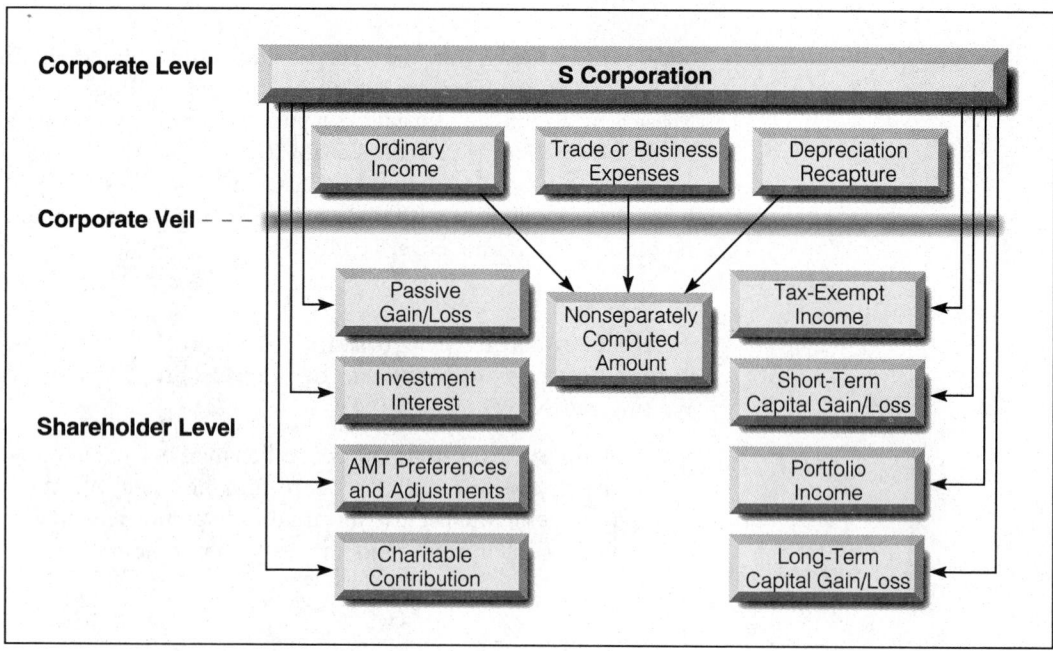

In general, S corporation items are divided into (1) nonseparately stated income or loss and (2) separately stated income, losses, deductions, and credits that could uniquely affect the tax liability of a shareholder. In essence, nonseparate items are aggregated into an undifferentiated amount that constitutes Subchapter S taxable income or loss. An S corporation's separately stated items are identical to those separately stated by partnerships. These items retain their tax attributes on the shareholder's return. Separately stated items are listed on Schedule K of the 1120S. They include the following:

- Tax-exempt income.
- Long-term and short-term capital gains and losses.
- Section 1231 gains and losses.
- Charitable contributions.
- Passive gains, losses, and credits.
- Certain portfolio income.
- Section 179 expense deduction.
- Tax preferences for the alternative minimum tax.
- Depletion.
- Foreign income or loss.
- Wagering gains or losses.
- Recoveries of tax benefit items.
- Intangible drilling costs.
- Investment interest, income, and expenses.

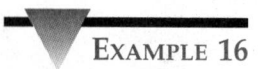

EXAMPLE 16

The following is the income statement for Jersey, Inc., an S corporation:

Sales		$ 40,000
Less: Cost of sales		(23,000)
Gross profit on sales		$ 17,000
Less: Interest expense	$1,200	
Charitable contributions	400	
Advertising expenses	1,500	
Other operating expenses	2,000	(5,100)
		$ 11,900
Add: Tax-exempt interest	$ 300	
Dividend income	200	
Long-term capital gain	500	1,000
Less: Short-term capital loss		(150)
Net income per books		$ 12,750

Subchapter S taxable income for Jersey is calculated as follows, using net income for book purposes as a starting point.

Net income per books		$12,750
Separately stated items		
Deduct: Tax-exempt interest	$300	
Dividend income	200	
Long-term capital gain	500	(1,000)
Subtotal		$11,750
Add: Charitable contributions	$400	
Short-term capital loss	150	550
Subchapter S taxable income		$12,300

The $12,300 of Subchapter S taxable income, as well as each of the separately stated items, are divided among the shareholders based upon their stock ownership. ▼

ALLOCATION OF INCOME AND LOSS

6 ▼ **LEARNING OBJECTIVE**
Allocate income, deductions, and credits to shareholders.

Each shareholder is allocated a pro rata portion of nonseparately stated income or loss and all separately stated items. The pro rata allocation method assigns an equal amount of each of the S items to each day of the year. If a shareholder's stock holding changes during the year, this allocation assigns the shareholder a pro rata share of each item for *each* day the stock is owned. On the date of transfer, the transferee (and not the transferor) is considered to own the stock.[27]

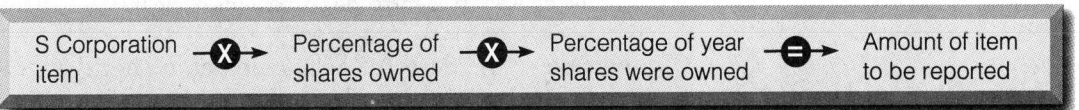

The per-day allocation must be used, unless the shareholder disposes of his or her entire interest in the entity.[28] In case of a complete termination, a short year may result, as discussed below. If a shareholder dies during the year, his or her share of the pro rata items up to the date of death is reported on the final individual income tax return.

---

[27]Reg. § 1374–1(b)(3).   [28]§§ 1366(a)(1) and 1377(a)(1).

EXAMPLE 17

Assume in Example 16 that Pat, a shareholder, owned 10% of Jersey's stock for 100 days and 12% for the remaining 265 days. Using the required per-day allocation method, Pat's share of the S corporation items is as follows:

	Schedule K Totals	Pat's Share		Pat's Schedule K–1 Totals
		10%	12%	
Subchapter S taxable income	$12,300	$337	$1,072	$1,409
Tax-exempt interest	300	8	26	34
Dividend income	200	5	17	22
Long-term capital gain	500	14	44	58
Charitable contributions	400	11	35	46
Short-term capital loss	150	4	13	17

Pat's share of the Subchapter S taxable income is the total of $12,300 \times [0.10 \times (100/365)]$ plus $12,300 \times [0.12 \times (265/365)]$, or $1,409. Pat's Schedule K–1 totals flow through to his individual income tax return (Form 1040). ▼

EXAMPLE 18

If Pat in Example 17 dies after owning the stock 100 days, his share of the S corporation items is reported on his final individual income tax return (Form 1040). Thus, only the items in the column labeled 10% in Example 17 are reported on Pat's final tax return. S corporation items that occur after Pat's death most likely would flow through to the income tax return of Pat's estate (Form 1041). ▼

The Short-Year Election. If a shareholder's interest is completely terminated during the tax year (by disposition or death), all shareholders holding stock during the year and the corporation may elect to treat the S taxable year as two taxable years. The first year ends on the date of the termination. Under this election, an interim closing of the books is undertaken, and the shareholders report their shares of the S corporation items as they occurred during the short tax year.[29]

The short-year election provides an opportunity to shift income, losses, and credits between shareholders. The election is desirable in circumstances where more loss can be allocated to taxpayers with higher marginal rates.

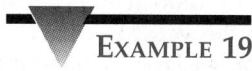

EXAMPLE 19

Alicia, the owner of all of the shares of an S corporation, transfers her stock to Cindy halfway through the tax year. There is a $100,000 NOL for the entire tax year, but $30,000 of the loss occurs during the first half of the year. Without a short-year election, $50,000 of the loss is allocated to Alicia, and $50,000 is allocated to Cindy. If the corporation makes the short-year election, Cindy is allocated $70,000 of the loss. Of course, the sales price of the stock would probably be increased to recognize the tax benefits being transferred from Alicia to Cindy. ▼

In the case of the death of a shareholder, a short-year election prevents the income and loss allocation to a deceased shareholder from being affected by post-death events.

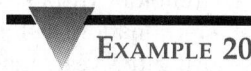

EXAMPLE 20

Joey and Karl equally own Rose, Inc., a calendar year S corporation. Joey dies on June 29 (not a leap year). Rose has income of $250,000 for January 1 through June 29 and $750,000 for the remainder of the year. Without a short-year election, the income is allocated by assigning an equal portion of the annual income of $1 million to each day (or $2,739.73 per day) and allocating the daily portion between the shareholders. Joey is allocated 50% of the

---

[29]§ 1377(a)(2).

daily income for the 180 days from January 1 to June 29, or $246,575.70 [($2,739.73/2) × 180]. Joey's *estate* is allocated 50% of the income for the 185 days from June 30 to December 31, or $253,425.02 [($2,739.73/2) × 185].

If the short-year election is made, the income of $250,000 from January 1 to June 29 is divided equally between Joey and Karl, so that each is taxed on $125,000. The income of $750,000 from June 30 to December 31 is divided equally between Joey's estate and Karl, or $375,000 to each. ▼

TAX TREATMENT OF DISTRIBUTIONS TO SHAREHOLDERS

The amount of any distribution to an S corporation shareholder is equal to the cash plus the fair market value of any other property distributed. How the distribution is taxed depends upon whether the S corporation has accumulated earnings and profits (AEP) from Subchapter C years.

If the S corporation has never been a C corporation or if it has no AEP from C corporation years, the distribution is a tax-free recovery of capital to the extent that it does not exceed the shareholder's adjusted basis in the stock of the S corporation. When the amount of the distribution exceeds the adjusted basis of the stock, the excess is treated as a gain from the sale or exchange of property (capital gain in most cases).

EXAMPLE 21

Twirl, Inc., a calendar year S corporation, has no AEP. During the year, Juan, an individual shareholder of the corporation, receives a cash dividend of $12,200 from Twirl. Juan's basis in his stock is $9,700. Juan recognizes a capital gain of $2,500, the excess of the distribution over the stock basis ($12,200 − $9,700). The remaining $9,700 is tax-free, but it reduces Juan's basis in his stock to zero. ▼

For S corporations with AEP from C corporation years, a more complex set of rules applies. These rules blend the entity and conduit approaches to taxation. This blending treats distributions of preelection (C corporation) and postelection (S corporation) earnings differently. Distributions of C corporation AEP are taxed as dividends, while distributions of previously taxed S corporation earnings are tax-free to the extent of the shareholder's adjusted basis in the stock. A special account is used to track undistributed earnings of an S corporation that have been taxed to shareholders previously. Distributions from this account, known as the **accumulated adjustments account (AAA)** are tax-free.

The Accumulated Adjustments Account.   Essentially, the AAA is a cumulative total of undistributed nonseparately and separately stated items for S corporation taxable years beginning after 1982. It provides a mechanism to ensure that the earnings of an S corporation are taxed to shareholders only once.

The AAA is adjusted in a similar fashion to the shareholder's stock basis (discussed later in this chapter), except there is no adjustment for tax-exempt income and related expenses or for Federal taxes attributable to a C corporation tax year. Further, any decreases in stock basis have no impact on the AAA when the AAA balance is negative.

The AAA balance is determined at the end of each year rather than at the time distributions are made. When more than one distribution occurs in the same year, a pro rata portion of each distribution is treated as having been made out of the AAA. The AAA is computed by making the adjustments in the order specified in Exhibit 21–1.

In calculating the amount in the AAA for purposes of determining the tax treatment of distributions during a tax year by an S corporation with AEP, the net

▼ **EXHIBIT 21–1**
Adjustments to the Corporate
AAA

Increase by:
1. Schedule K items other than tax-exempt income.
2. Nonseparately computed income.
3. Depletion in excess of basis in the property.

Decrease by:
4. Adjustments other than distributions (e.g., losses, deductions).
5. Any portion of a distribution that is considered to be tax-free from AAA (but not below zero).

NOTE: When the combination of items 1 through 4 results in a negative number, the AAA is adjusted first for the distribution and then for the adjustments in items 1 through 4.

negative adjustments (e.g., the excess of losses and deductions over income) for that tax year are ignored.

A shareholder has a proportionate interest in the AAA, regardless of the size of his or her stock basis.[30] However, since the AAA is a corporate account, no connection exists between the prior accumulated S corporation income and any specific shareholder.[31] Thus, the benefits of the AAA can be shifted from one shareholder to another shareholder. For example, when one S shareholder transfers stock to another shareholder, any AAA on the purchase date may be distributed tax-free to the purchaser. Similarly, issuing additional stock to a new shareholder in an S corporation having AAA dilutes the account relative to the existing shareholders.

The AAA (unlike the stock basis) can have a negative balance. All losses decrease the AAA balance, even those in excess of the shareholder's stock basis. However, *distributions* may not make the AAA negative or increase a negative balance.

Distribution Ordering Rules.   A cash distribution from an S corporation with AEP comes first from the AAA (limited to stock basis). The distribution is then deemed to be made from previously taxed income[32] (PTI) generated under old S corporation rules (pre-1983). Distributions from the AAA and PTI are tax-free. The remaining distribution is taxed as a dividend to the extent of AEP. After AEP is fully distributed, any residual amount is applied against the shareholder's remaining stock basis. This amount is a tax-free recovery of capital.[33] Any distributions in excess of stock basis are taxed as capital gains.

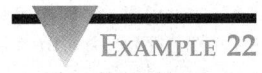
EXAMPLE 22

Salvia, a calendar year S corporation, distributes $1,300 cash to its only shareholder, Otis, on December 31, 1998. Otis's basis in his stock is $1,400, his AAA is $500, and the corporation has AEP of $750 on December 31, 1998.

According to the distribution ordering rules, the first $500 is a tax-free recovery of basis from the AAA. The next $750 is a taxable dividend distribution from AEP. Finally, the remaining $50 of cash is a tax-free recovery of basis. Immediately after the distribution, Salvia has no AAA or AEP, and Otis's stock basis equals $850.

---

[30]§ 1368(c).
[31]§ 1368(e)(1)(A).
[32]§§ 1368(c)(1) and (e)(1). Before 1983, an account similar to the AAA was in place, namely, previously taxed income (PTI). Any S corpo-

rations in existence before 1983 may have PTI, which currently may be distributed tax-free.
[33]§ 1368(c).

CONCEPT SUMMARY 21–1

Classification Procedures for Distributions from an S Corporation*

Where Earnings and Profits Exist	Where No Earnings and Profits Exist
1. Distributions are tax-free to the extent of the AAA.**	
2. Any PTI from pre-1983 tax years can be distributed tax-free.	
3. The remaining distribution constitutes ordinary dividend from AEP.†	
4. Any residual amount is applied as a tax-free reduction in basis of stock.	1. Distributions are nontaxable to the extent of adjusted basis in stock.
5. Excess is treated as gain from a sale or exchange of stock (capital gain in most cases).	2. Excess is treated as gain from a sale or exchange of stock (capital gain in most cases).

*A distribution of appreciated property by an electing corporation results in a gain that is first allocated to and reported by the shareholders.

**Once stock basis reaches zero, any distribution from the AAA is treated as a gain from the sale or exchange of stock. Thus, basis is an upper limit on what a shareholder may receive tax-free.

†The AAA bypass election is available to pay out AEP before reducing the AAA [§ 1368(e)(3)]. For its first taxable year beginning after December 31, 1996, an S corporation may reduce the total AEP by any pre-1983 AEP from an S tax year.

	Corporate AAA	Corporate AEP	Otis's Stock Basis
Balance, 12/31/98	$ 500	$ 750	$1,400
Distribution ($1,300)	(500)	(750)	(550)*
Balance, 12/31/98	$ –0–	$ –0–	$ 850

*The reduction in basis includes the decrease in the AAA. It is the excess of the total distribution ($1,300) over the distribution of AEP ($750). ▼

EXAMPLE 23

Assume the same facts as in the preceding example. During 1999, Salvia has no earnings and distributes $1,000 to Otis. Of the distribution, $850 is a tax-free recovery of basis, and $150 is taxed to Otis as a capital gain. ▼

With the consent of all of its shareholders, an S corporation can elect to have a distribution treated as if it were made from AEP rather than from the AAA. This mechanism is known as an *AAA bypass election*. This election may be desirable for distributions in years when S corporation shareholders have low marginal tax rates.

Where an S corporation has both pre-1983 and post-1982 AEP, for its first tax year beginning after December 31, 1996, the total AEP is reduced by the pre-1983 S corporation AEP, possibly eliminating either or both.

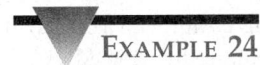
EXAMPLE 24

Collett, a calendar year S corporation, has pre-1983 S corporation AEP of $12,000 and total AEP of $20,000 in 1996. Collett Corporation may offset the $12,000 of pre-1983 S corporation AEP against the $20,000 of AEP, leaving a balance of $8,000 in AEP. ▼

Schedule M–2. Schedule M–2 on page 4 of Form 1120S (reproduced on page 21–18) contains a column labeled *Other adjustments account (OAA)*. This account includes items that affect basis but not the AAA, such as tax-exempt income and any related nondeductible expenses. Distributions are made from the OAA after AEP and the AAA are reduced to zero. Since the OAA represents adjustments to stock basis, distributions from this account are tax-free recoveries of capital.

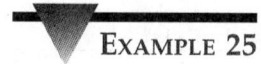

EXAMPLE 25

During 1998, Sparrow, an S corporation, records the following items:

AAA, beginning of the year	$ 8,500
Previously taxed income, beginning of the year	6,250
Ordinary income	25,000
Tax-exempt interest	4,000
Key employee life insurance proceeds received	5,000
Payroll penalty expense	2,000
Charitable contributions	3,000
Unreasonable compensation	5,000
Premiums on key employee life insurance	2,100
Distributions to shareholders	16,000

Sparrow's Schedule M–2 for the current year appears as follows:

Schedule M-2	**Analysis of Accumulated Adjustments Account, Other Adjustments Account, and Shareholders' Undistributed Taxable Income Previously Taxed** (see page 21 of the instructions)		
	(a) Accumulated adjustments account	**(b)** Other adjustments account	**(c)** Shareholders' undistributed taxable income previously taxed
1 Balance at beginning of tax year . . .	8,500		6,250
2 Ordinary income from page 1, line 21 . .	25,000		
3 Other additions		9,000**	
4 Loss from page 1, line 21.	( )	( )	
5 Other reductions	(10,000*)	(2,100)	
6 Combine lines 1 through 5	23,500	6,900	
7 Distributions other than dividend distributions .	16,000		
8 Balance at end of tax year. Subtract line 7 from line 6	7,500	6,900	6,250

* $2,000 (payroll penalty) + $3,000 (charitable contributions) + $5,000 (unreasonable compensation).
** $4,000 (tax-exempt interest) + $5,000 (life insurance proceeds).

Effect of Terminating the S Election. Normally, distributions to shareholders from a C corporation are taxed as dividends to the extent of E & P. However, any distribution of *cash* by a corporation to shareholders during a one-year period[34] following S election termination receives special treatment. Such a distribution is treated as a tax-free recovery of stock basis to the extent that it does not exceed the AAA.[35] Since *only* cash distributions reduce the AAA during this *postelection termination period*, a corporation should not make property distributions during this time. Instead, the entity should sell property and distribute the proceeds to shareholders.

EXAMPLE 26

Quinn, the sole shareholder of Roman, Inc., a calendar year S corporation, elects during 1998 to terminate the S election, effective January 1, 1999. As of the end of 1998, Roman has an AAA of $1,300. Quinn can receive a nontaxable distribution of cash during a post-termination period of approximately one year to the extent of Roman's AAA. Although a cash distribution of $1,300 during 1999 would be nontaxable to Quinn, it would reduce the adjusted basis of his stock. ▼

---

[34] The period is *approximately* one year in length.   [35] §§ 1371(e) and 1377(b).

▼
CONCEPT SUMMARY 21–2
▼

Distribution of Property

	Appreciated Property	**Depreciated Property**
S corporation	Realized gain is recognized by the corporation, which passes it through to the shareholders. Such gain increases a shareholder's stock basis, generating a basis in the property equal to FMV. On the distribution, the shareholder's stock basis is reduced by the FMV of the property (but not below zero).	Realized loss is not recognized. The shareholder assumes a FMV basis in the property. Loss is postponed indefinitely.
C corporation	Realized gain is recognized under § 311(b) and increases E & P (net of tax). The shareholder assumes a FMV basis and has a FMV taxable dividend.	Realized loss is not recognized.
Partnership	No gain to the partnership or partner. Basis to the partner is limited to the partner's basis in the partnership.	Realized loss is not recognized.

TAX TREATMENT OF PROPERTY DISTRIBUTIONS BY THE CORPORATION

7   **LEARNING OBJECTIVE**
Understand how distributions to S corporation shareholders are taxed.

An S corporation recognizes a gain on any distribution of appreciated property (other than in a reorganization) in the same manner as if the asset had been sold to the shareholder at its fair market value.[36] The corporate gain is passed through to the shareholders. There is an important reason for this rule. Without it, property might be distributed tax-free (other than for certain recapture items) and later sold without income recognition to the shareholder because the shareholder's basis equals the asset's fair market value. The character of the gain—capital gain or ordinary income—depends upon the type of asset being distributed.

The S corporation does not recognize a loss for assets that are worth less than their basis. As with gain property, the shareholder's basis is equal to the asset's fair market value. Thus, the potential loss is postponed until the shareholder sells the stock of the S corporation. Since loss property receives a step-down in basis without any loss recognition by the S corporation, distributions of loss property should be avoided. See Concept Summary 21–2.

EXAMPLE 27

Turnip, Inc., an S corporation for 10 years, distributes a tract of land held as an investment to its majority shareholder. The land was purchased for $22,000 many years ago and is currently worth $82,000. Turnip recognizes a capital gain of $60,000, which increases the AAA by $60,000. Then the property dividend reduces AAA by $82,000 (the fair market value). The tax consequences are the same for appreciated property, whether it is distributed to the shareholders and they dispose of it, or the corporation sells the property and distributes the proceeds to the shareholders.

---

[36]§ 311(b).

If the land had been purchased for $80,000 many years ago and was currently worth $30,000, the $50,000 realized loss would not be recognized at the corporate level, and the shareholder would receive a $30,000 basis in the land. The $50,000 realized loss disappears from the corporate level. Since loss is not recognized on the distribution of property that has declined in value, the AAA is not reduced by the unrecognized loss. For the loss on the property to be recognized, the S corporation must sell the property. ▼

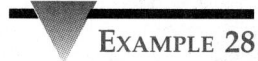

EXAMPLE 28

Assume the same facts as in Example 27, except that Turnip is a C corporation or a partnership. The partner's basis in the partnership is $25,000.

	Appreciated Property		
	S Corporation	**C Corporation**	**Partnership**
Entity gain/loss	$60,000	$60,000	$ –0–
Owner's gain/loss/dividend	60,000	82,000*	–0–
Owner's basis	82,000	82,000	22,000

	Property That Has Declined in Value		
	S Corporation	**C Corporation**	**Partnership**
Entity gain/loss	$ –0–	$ –0–	$ –0–
Owner's gain/loss/dividend	–0–	30,000*	–0–
Owner's basis	30,000	30,000	25,000

*Assume sufficient E & P. ▼

SHAREHOLDER'S BASIS

8 LEARNING OBJECTIVE
Calculate a shareholder's basis in S corporation stock.

The calculation of the initial tax basis of stock in an S corporation is similar to that for the basis of stock in a C corporation and depends upon the manner in which the shares are acquired (e.g., gift, inheritance, purchase, exchange under § 351). Once the initial tax basis is determined, various transactions during the life of the corporation affect the shareholder's basis in the stock. Although each shareholder is required to compute his or her own basis in the S shares, neither Form 1120S nor Schedule K–1 provides a place for deriving this amount.

A shareholder's basis is increased by stock purchases and capital contributions. Operations during the year cause the following upward adjustments to basis.[37]

- Nonseparately computed income.
- Separately stated income items (e.g., nontaxable income).
- Depletion in excess of basis in the property.

Basis then is reduced by distributions not reported as income by the shareholder (e.g., an AAA or PTI distribution). Next, the following items reduce basis (but not below zero).

- Nondeductible expenses of the corporation (e.g., fines, penalties, illegal kickbacks).
- Nonseparately computed loss.
- Separately stated loss and deduction items.

As under the partnership rule, basis is first increased by income items; then it is decreased by distributions and finally by losses. Pass-through items (other than

---

[37]§ 1367(a).

distributions) that reduce stock basis are governed by special ordering rules. Non-capital, nondeductible expenditures reduce stock basis before losses or deductible items. A taxpayer may irrevocably elect under Regulation § 1.1367–1(f) to have deductible items pass through before any noncapital, nondeductible items. In most cases, this election is advantageous.

EXAMPLE 29

In its first year of operations, Iris, Inc., a calendar year S corporation in Clemson, South Carolina, earns income of $2,000. On February 2 in its second year of operations, Iris distributes $2,000 to Marty, its sole shareholder. During the remainder of the second year, the corporation incurs a $2,000 loss.

Under the S corporation ordering rules, the $2,000 distribution is tax-free AAA to Marty, and the $2,000 loss is *not* passed through because the stock basis cannot be reduced below zero. ▼

A shareholder's basis in the stock can never be reduced below zero. Once stock basis is zero, any additional basis reductions (losses or deductions, but *not* distributions) decrease (but not below zero) the shareholder's basis in loans made to the S corporation. Any excess of losses or deductions over both bases is *suspended* until there are subsequent bases. Once the basis of any debt is reduced, it is later increased (only up to the original amount) by the subsequent *net* increase resulting from *all* positive and negative basis adjustments. The debt basis is adjusted before any increase is made in the stock basis.[38] A distribution below stock basis does not reduce any debt basis. If a loss and a distribution occur in the same year, the loss reduces the basis before the distribution.[39]

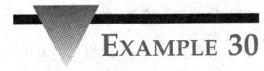

EXAMPLE 30

Stacey, a sole shareholder, has a $7,000 stock basis and a $2,000 basis in a loan that she made to a calendar year S corporation at the beginning of 1998. Subchapter S net income during 1998 is $8,200. The corporation received $2,000 of tax-exempt interest income. Cash of $17,300 is distributed to Stacey on November 15, 1998. As a result, Stacey's basis in her stock is zero, and her loan basis is still $2,000 at the end of 1998, because only losses and deductions (and not distributions) reduce the debt basis. Stacey recognizes a $100 gain ($17,300 – $17,200).

	Corporate AAA	Stacey's Stock Basis	Stacey's Loan Basis
Beginning balance	$ –0–	$ 7,000	$2,000
S net income	8,200	8,200	–0–
Tax-exempt income	–0–	2,000	–0–
Subtotal	$ 8,200	$ 17,200	$2,000
Distribution ($17,300)	(8,200)	(17,200)	–0–
Ending balance	$ –0–	$ –0–	$2,000

Although stock basis cannot be reduced below zero, the $100 excess distribution does not reduce Stacey's loan basis. ▼

The basis rules for an S corporation are similar to the rules for determining a partner's interest basis in a partnership. However, a partner's basis in the partnership interest includes the partner's direct investment plus a *ratable share* of any partnership liabilities.[40] If a partnership borrows from a partner, the partner receives

---

[38]§ 1367(b)(2).
[39]§§ 1366(d)(1)(A) and 1368(d)(1).

[40]§ 752(a).

a basis increase as if the partnership had borrowed from an unrelated third party.[41] In contrast, except for loans from the shareholder to the corporation, corporate borrowing has no effect on S corporation shareholder basis. Loans from a shareholder to the S corporation have a tax basis only for the shareholder making the loan.

Except in the Eleventh Circuit, the fact that a shareholder has guaranteed a loan made to the corporation by a third party has no effect upon the shareholder's loan basis, unless payments actually have been made as a result of that guarantee.[42] If the corporation defaults on indebtedness and the shareholder makes good on the guarantee, the shareholder's indebtedness basis is increased to that extent.[43]

If a loan's basis has been reduced and is not restored, income is recognized when the loan is repaid. If the corporation issued a note as evidence of the debt, repayment constitutes an amount received in exchange for a capital asset, and the amount that exceeds the shareholder's basis is entitled to capital gain treatment.[44] However, if the loan is made on open account, the repayment constitutes ordinary income to the extent that it exceeds the shareholder's basis in the loan. Each repayment is prorated between the gain portion and the repayment of the debt.[45] Thus, a note should be given to ensure capital gain treatment for the income that results from a loan's repayment.

Since the basis rule requires that corporate income be used to restore debt basis before it can be used to restore stock basis, a double tax on current income can result. Any current income distributed, after both debt and stock basis have been reduced to zero, is taxed as capital gain because it is considered a return of capital, but only to the extent of stock basis. To avoid this double tax, shareholders should consider forgiving debt that a solvent S corporation owes them. Such forgiveness is considered a contribution of capital, with a resulting increase in the shareholder's stock basis. For an insolvent S corporation, discharge-of-indebtedness income is tax-deferred (not tax-exempt) and does not increase the shareholder's basis.

TREATMENT OF LOSSES

9 ▼ **LEARNING OBJECTIVE**
Explain how losses in an S corporation are treated.

Net Operating Loss.   One major advantage of an S election is the ability to pass through any net operating loss (NOL) of the corporation directly to the shareholders. A shareholder can deduct an NOL for the year in which the S corporation's tax year ends. The corporation is not entitled to any deduction for the NOL. A shareholder's basis in the stock is reduced to the extent of any pass-through of the NOL, and the shareholder's AAA is reduced by the same deductible amount.[46]

 **EXAMPLE 31**

An S corporation in Chapel Hill, North Carolina, incurs a $20,000 NOL for the current year. At all times during the tax year, the stock was owned equally by the same 10 shareholders. Each shareholder is entitled to deduct $2,000 for the tax year in which the corporate tax year ends. ▼

Deductions for an S corporation's NOL pass-through cannot exceed a shareholder's adjusted basis in the stock *plus* the basis of any loans made by the shareholder to the corporation. If a taxpayer is unable to prove the tax basis, the NOL pass-through can be denied.[47] As noted previously, once a shareholder's adjusted stock basis has been eliminated by an NOL, any excess NOL is used to reduce the

[41]Reg. § 1.752–1(e).

[42]See, for example, *Estate of Leavitt*, 90 T.C. 206 (1988), *aff'd.* 89–1 USTC ¶9332, 63 AFTR2d 89–1437, 875 F.2d 420 (CA–4, 1989); *Selfe v. U.S.*, 86–1 USTC ¶9115, 57 AFTR2d 86–464, 778 F.2d 769 (CA–11, 1985); *James K. Calcutt*, 91 T.C. 14 (1988).

[43]Rev.Rul. 70–50, 1970–1 C.B. 178.

[44]*Joe M. Smith*, 48 T.C. 872 (1967), *aff'd.* and *rev'd.* in 70–1 USTC ¶9327, 25 AFTR2d 70–936, 424 F.2d 219 (CA–9, 1970), and Rev.Rul. 64–162, 1964–1 C.B. 304.

[45]Rev.Rul. 68–537, 1968–2 C.B. 372.

[46]§§ 1368(a)(1)(A) and (e)(1)(A).

[47]See *Donald J. Sauvigne*, 30 TCM 123, T.C.Memo. 1971–30.

shareholder's basis for any loans made to the corporation (but never below zero). The basis for loans is established by the actual advances made to the corporation, and not by indirect loans.[48] If the shareholder's basis is insufficient to allow a full flow-through and there is more than one type of loss (e.g., in the same year the taxpayer incurs both a passive loss and a net capital loss), the flow-through amounts are determined on a pro rata basis.

EXAMPLE 32

Ralph is a 50% owner of an S corporation for the entire year. His stock basis is $10,000, and his shares of the various corporate losses are as follows:

Ordinary loss from operations	$8,000
Capital loss	5,000
Section 1231 loss	3,000
Passive loss	2,000

Based upon a pro rata approach, the total $10,000 allocable flow-through would be split among the various losses as follows:

$$\text{Ordinary loss} = \frac{\$8,000}{\$18,000} \times \$10,000 = \$\ 4,444.44$$

$$\text{Capital loss} = \frac{\$5,000}{\$18,000} \times \$10,000 = \$\ 2,777.78$$

$$\S\ 1231\ \text{loss} = \frac{\$3,000}{\$18,000} \times \$10,000 = \$\ 1,666.67$$

$$\text{Passive loss} = \frac{\$2,000}{\$18,000} \times \$10,000 = \underline{\$\ 1,111.11}$$

Total allocated loss	$10,000.00

When a shareholder has acquired stock at different times and for varying amounts, losses are applied against stock basis using a separate-share method.[49] Under the separate-share method, the basis of each share of stock is increased or decreased by an amount equal to the owner's pro rata portion of an income or loss item, determined on a per-share, per-day basis. Thus, an S corporation maintains a separate basis account for each block of stock. A *spillover rule* allows a shareholder to apply losses or distributions attributable to one share of stock that are in excess of its basis against the basis of all other stock owned by the shareholder. Where a net basis reduction exceeds a shareholder's total available stock basis for a tax year, any excess (other than distributions) reduces the shareholder's debt basis (but not below zero).

EXAMPLE 33

On December 31, 1998, Erica owns one share of an S corporation's 10 outstanding shares of stock. The basis of Erica's share is $300. On July 3, 1999, Erica purchases two shares from another shareholder for $250 each. During 1999, the S corporation has no income or deductions, but incurs a loss of $3,650. Under the separate-share approach, the amount of the loss assigned to each day of the S corporation's tax year is $10 ($3,650 ÷ 365 days). For each day, $1 is allocated to each outstanding share ($10 ÷ 10 shares).

Since Erica owned one share for 365 days, a $365 loss is attributable to that share ($1 × 365 days). Since she owned the other two shares for 182 days, the basis of each of these shares is reduced by $182 ($1 × 182 days), resulting in a basis of $68 for each share ($250 –

[48]*Ruth M. Prashker*, 59 T.C. 172 (1972); *Frederick G. Brown v. U.S.*, 83–1   [49]Reg. §§ 1.1367–1(b)(2) and (c)(3).
USTC ¶9364, 52 AFTR2d 82–5080, 706 F.2d 755 (CA–6, 1983).

$182). Because the decrease in basis attributable to the first share exceeds its basis by $65 ($365 − $300), the excess is applied proportionately to reduce the remaining bases of the other two shares; thus, each is reduced by $32.50 [$65 × ($68/$136)]. After this reduction, each of the two shares has a $35.50 basis ($68 − $32.50). ▼

The distribution adjustments made by an S corporation during a tax year are taken into account *before* applying the loss limitation for the year. Thus, distributions during a year reduce the adjusted basis for determining the allowable loss for the year, but the loss for the year does *not* reduce the adjusted basis for purposes of determining the tax status of the distributions made during the year.

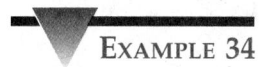

EXAMPLE 34

Pylon, Inc., a calendar year S corporation is partly owned by Doris, who has a beginning stock basis of $10,000. During the year, Doris's share of a long-term capital gain is $2,000, and her share of an ordinary loss is $9,000. If Doris receives a $6,000 distribution, her deductible loss is calculated as follows.

Beginning stock basis	$10,000
Add: LTCG	2,000
Subtotal	$12,000
Less: Distribution	(6,000)
Basis for loss limitation	$ 6,000
Deductible loss	($ 6,000)
Unused loss	($ 3,000)

▼

EXAMPLE 35

Marjorie is a shareholder in a calendar year S corporation in 1998. At the beginning of the year, her stock basis is $10,000, her share of AAA is $2,000, and her share of corporate AEP is $5,000. She receives a $6,000 distribution, and her share of S items includes a $2,000 long-term capital gain and a $9,000 ordinary loss. The effects of these events on AAA, stock basis, and AEP are as follows.

	AAA	Stock Basis	AEP
Beginning balance	$ 2,000	$10,000	$5,000
Distribution ($6,000)	(2,000)	(2,000)	(4,000)
Balance	$ –0–	$ 8,000	$1,000
LTCG	2,000	2,000	No effect
Balance	$ 2,000	$10,000	$1,000
Loss ($9,000)	(9,000)	(9,000)	No effect
Ending balances	($ 7,000)	$ 1,000	$1,000

▼

A shareholder's share of an NOL may be greater than both stock basis and loan basis. A shareholder is entitled to carry forward a loss to the extent that the loss for the year exceeds basis. Any loss carried forward may be deducted *only* by the *same* shareholder if and when the basis in the stock of or loans to the corporation is restored.[50]

Any loss carryover (due to insufficient basis) remaining at the end of an approximately one-year post-termination transition period is lost forever. The post-termination period includes the 120-day period beginning on the date of any determination pursuant to an audit of a taxpayer that follows the termination of

---

[50]§ 1366(d).

the S corporation's election and that adjusts a Subchapter S item. Thus, if a shareholder has a loss carryover, he or she should increase the stock or loan basis and flow through the loss before disposing of the stock.

EXAMPLE 36

Dana has a stock basis of $4,000 in an S corporation. He has loaned $2,000 to the corporation and has guaranteed another $4,000 loan made to the corporation by a local bank. Although his share of the S corporation's NOL for the current year is $9,500, Dana may deduct only $6,000 of the NOL on his individual tax return. Dana may carry forward $3,500 of the NOL, to be deducted when the basis in his stock or loan to the corporation is restored. Dana has a zero basis in both the stock and the loan after the flow-through of the $6,000 NOL. ▼

Net operating losses from C corporation years cannot be utilized at the corporate level (except with respect to built-in gain, discussed later in this chapter), nor can they be passed through to the shareholders. Further, the carryforward period continues to run during S status.[51] Consequently, the S election may not be appropriate for a corporation with NOL carryforwards. When a corporation is expecting losses in the future, an S election should be made *before* the loss years.

Passive Losses and Credits.   Section 469 provides that net passive losses and credits are not deductible when incurred and must be carried over to a year when there is passive income. Thus, one must be aware of three major classes of income, losses, and credits—active, portfolio, and passive. S corporations are not directly subject to the limits of § 469, but corporate rental activities are inherently passive, and other activities of an S corporation may be passive unless the shareholder(s) materially participate(s) in operating the business. An S corporation may engage in more than one such activity. If the corporate activity is rental or the shareholders do not materially participate, any passive losses or credits flow through. The shareholders are able to apply the losses or credits only against their income from other passive activities. A shareholder's stock basis is reduced by passive losses that flow through to the shareholder, even though the shareholder may not be entitled to a current deduction due to the passive loss limitations. In general, elections involving the aggregation of amounts are made at the entity level, but they affect individual shareholders. The existence of material participation is determined at the shareholder level. There are seven tests for material participation, including a need to participate in the activity for more than 500 hours during the taxable year.[52]

EXAMPLE 37

Heather is a 50% owner of an S corporation engaged in a passive activity. A nonparticipating shareholder, she receives a salary of $6,000 for services as a result of the passive activity. This deduction creates a $6,000 passive loss at the corporate level. Heather has $6,000 of earned income as a result of the salary. The $6,000 salary creates a $6,000 deduction/passive loss, which flows through to the shareholders. Heather's $3,000 share of the loss may not be deducted against the $6,000 earned income. Under § 469(e)(3), earned income is not taken into account in computing the income or loss from a passive activity. ▼

At-Risk Rules.   The at-risk rules generally apply to S corporation shareholders. Essentially, an amount at risk is determined separately for each shareholder. The amount of the corporate losses that are passed through and deductible by the shareholders is not affected by the amount the corporation has at risk. A shareholder usually is considered at risk with respect to an activity to the extent of cash and the adjusted basis of other property contributed to the electing corporation, any amount borrowed for use in the activity for which the taxpayer has personal liability

---

[51]§ 1377(b).   [52]Reg. § 1.469–5T(a).

for payment from personal assets, and the net fair market value of personal assets that secure nonrecourse borrowing. Any losses that are suspended under the at-risk rules are carried forward and are available during the post-termination transition period. The S stock basis limitations and at-risk limitations are applied before the passive activity limitations.[53]

EXAMPLE 38

Shareholder Ricketts has a basis of $35,000 in his S corporation stock. He takes a $15,000 nonrecourse loan from a local bank and lends the proceeds to the S corporation. Ricketts now has a stock basis of $35,000 and a debt basis of $15,000. However, due to the at-risk limitation, he can deduct only $35,000 of losses from the S corporation. ▼

TAX ON PRE-ELECTION BUILT-IN GAIN

10   LEARNING OBJECTIVE
Compute the built-in gains tax.

Without the **built-in gains (§ 1374) tax,** it would be possible to avoid the corporate double tax on disposition of appreciated property by electing S corporation status.

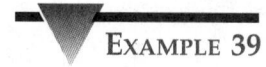

EXAMPLE 39

Zinnia, Inc., a C corporation, owns a single asset with a basis of $100,000 and a fair market value of $500,000. If Zinnia sells this asset and distributes the cash to shareholders, there will be two levels of tax, one at the corporate level and one at the shareholder level. Alternatively, if Zinnia distributes the asset to shareholders, a double tax will still result. In an attempt to avoid the double tax, Zinnia elects S corporation status. It then sells the asset and distributes the proceeds to shareholders. Without the § 1374 tax, the gain would be taxed only once, at the shareholder level. The distribution of sales proceeds would be a tax-free reduction of the AAA. ▼

The § 1374 tax generally applies to C corporations converting to S status after 1986. It is a *corporate-level* tax on any built-in gain recognized when the S corporation disposes of an asset in a taxable disposition within 10 calendar years after the date on which the S election took effect.

General Rules. The base for the § 1374 tax includes any unrealized gain (appreciation) on assets (e.g., real estate, cash basis receivables, and goodwill) held by a corporation on the day it elects S status. The highest corporate tax rate (currently 35 percent) is applied to the unrealized gain when it is recognized by the corporation (e.g., when the asset is sold). Furthermore, the gain from the sale (net of the § 1374 tax)[54] passes through as a taxable gain to shareholders.

EXAMPLE 40

Assume the same facts as in the preceding example. Section 1374 imposes a corporate-level tax that must be paid by Zinnia after it has elected S status. Upon sale of the asset, the corporation owes a tax of $140,000 (0.35 × $400,000). The shareholders have a $260,000 taxable gain ($400,000 – $140,000). Hence, the built-in gains tax effectively imposes a double tax on Zinnia and its shareholders. ▼

The maximum amount of gain that is recognized over the 10-year period is limited to the *aggregate net* built-in gain of the corporation at the time it converted to S status. Thus, at the time of the S election, unrealized gains of the corporation are offset against unrealized losses. The net amount of gains and losses sets an upper limit on the tax base for the built-in gains tax. Any appreciation after the conversion to S status is subject to the regular S corporation pass-through rules.

---

[53]Reg. § 1.469–2T(d)(6).   [54]§ 1366(f)(2).

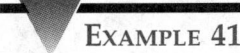

EXAMPLE 41

Quadrant, Inc., is a former C corporation whose first S corporation year began on January 1, 1998. At that time, Quadrant had two assets: X, with a value of $1,000 and a basis of $400, and Y, with a value of $400 and a basis of $600. The net unrealized built-in gain as of January 1, 1998, is $400. If asset X is sold for $1,200 during 1998, and asset Y is retained, the recognized built-in gain is limited to $400. The additional $200 of appreciation after electing S status is not part of the built-in gain. ▼

Loss assets on the date of conversion reduce the maximum built-in gain and any potential tax under § 1374.[55] In addition, built-in losses and built-in gains are netted each year to determine the annual § 1374 tax base. Thus, an incentive exists to contribute loss assets to a corporation before electing S status. However, the IRS indicates that contributions of loss property within two years before the earlier of the date of conversion or the date of filing an S election are presumed to have a tax avoidance motive and will not reduce the corporation's net unrealized built-in gain.

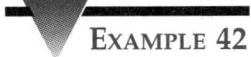

EXAMPLE 42

Donna owns all the stock of an S corporation, which in turn owns two assets on the S conversion date: asset 1 (basis of $5,000 and fair market value of $2,500) and asset 2 (basis of $1,000 and fair market value of $5,000). The S corporation has a potential net realized built-in gain of $1,500 (i.e., the built-in gain of $4,000 in asset 2 reduced by the built-in loss of $2,500 in asset 1). However, if Donna contributed the loss asset to the corporation within two years before the S election, built-in gain potential becomes $4,000 (the loss asset cannot be used to reduce built-in gain). ▼

The amount of built-in gain recognized in any year is limited to an "as if" taxable income for the year, computed as if the corporation were a C corporation. Any built-in gain that escapes taxation due to the taxable income limitation is carried forward and recognized in future tax years. Thus, a corporation can defer § 1374 tax liability whenever it has a low or negative taxable income.

EXAMPLE 43

Assume the same facts as in Example 41, except that if Quadrant were a C corporation, its taxable income in 1998 would be $300. The amount of built-in gain subject to tax in 1998 is $300. The excess built-in gain of $100 is carried forward and taxed in 1999 (assuming adequate C corporation taxable income). There is no statutory limit on the carryforward period, but the gain would effectively expire at the end of the 10-year recognition period applicable to all built-in gains (except for installment sales after March 25, 1990).[56] ▼

ETHICAL CONSIDERATIONS

A Helpful Appraisal

Scuba Unlimited, a diving center in Miami, Florida, is in the process of converting to S corporation status. Some of the assets of the company are highly appreciated.

Jason, the company's accountant, is familiar with the problems of the § 1374 built-in gains tax. His cousin, a qualified appraiser, has agreed to "lowball" the appraisal of the S corporation's assets. How would you react in Jason's situation?

---

[55]§§ 1374(c)(2) and (d)(1).

[56]§ 1374(d)(7); Notice 90–27, 1990–1 C.B. 336.

CONCEPT SUMMARY 21–3

Calculation of the Built-in Gains Tax Liability

Step 1. Select the smaller of built-in gain or taxable income.*

Step 2. Deduct unexpired NOLs and capital losses from C corporation tax years.

Step 3. Multiply the tax base obtained in step 2 by the top corporate tax rate.

Step 4. Deduct any business credit carryforwards and AMT credit carryovers arising in a C corporation tax year from the amount obtained in step 3.

Step 5. The corporation pays any tax resulting in step 4.

*Any net recognized built-in gain in excess of taxable income may be carried forward to the next year, as long as the next year is within the 10-year recognition period.

Gains on sales or distributions of all assets by an S corporation are presumed to be built-in gains unless the taxpayer can establish that the appreciation accrued after the conversion to S status. Thus, it may be advisable to obtain an independent appraisal when converting a C corporation to an S corporation. Certainly, a memorandum should be prepared listing the fair market values of all assets, along with the methods used to arrive at the values.

Normally, tax attributes of a C corporation do not carry over to a converted S corporation. For purposes of the tax on built-in gain, however, certain carryovers are allowed. In particular, an S corporation can offset built-in gains with unexpired NOLs or capital losses from C corporation years.

 **EXAMPLE 44**   Maple Corporation elects S status, effective for calendar year 1998. Maple has a $10,000 NOL carryover when it elects S status. As of January 1, 1998, one of Maple's capital assets has a basis of $50,000 and a fair market value of $110,000. Early in 1999, the asset is sold for $110,000. Maple recognizes a $60,000 built-in gain when the asset is sold. Maple's NOL reduces its built-in gain from $60,000 to $50,000. Thus, only $50,000 is subject to the built-in gains tax. ▼

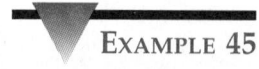 **EXAMPLE 45**   An S corporation has a built-in gain of $100,000 and taxable income of $90,000. The built-in gain tax liability is calculated as follows:

Lesser of taxable income or built-in gain	$ 90,000
Less: NOL carryforward from C year	(12,000)
Capital loss carryforward from C year	(8,000)
Tax base	$ 70,000
Highest corporate tax rate	× 0.35
Tentative tax	$ 24,500
Less: Business credit carryforward from C year	(4,000)
Built-in gains tax liability	$ 20,500

The $10,000 realized (but not taxed) built-in gain in excess of taxable income may be carried forward to the next year, as long as the next year is within the 10-year recognition period. ▼

Concept Summary 21–3 summarizes the calculation of the built-in gains tax.

LIFO Recapture Tax.   When a corporation uses the FIFO method for its last year before making the S election, any built-in gain is recognized and taxed as the inventory is sold. A LIFO-basis corporation does not recognize this gain unless the corporation invades the LIFO layer during the 10-year recognition period. To preclude deferral of gain recognition under LIFO, any LIFO recapture amount at the time of the S election is subject to a corporate-level tax.

The taxable LIFO recapture amount equals the excess of the inventory's value under FIFO over the LIFO value. No negative adjustment is allowed if the LIFO value is higher than the FIFO value. The resulting tax is payable in four equal installments, with the first payment due on or before the due date for the corporate return for the last C corporation year (without regard to any extensions). The remaining three installments must be paid on or before the due dates of the succeeding corporate returns. No interest is due if payments are made by the due dates, and no estimated taxes are due on the four tax installments. The basis of the LIFO inventory is adjusted to account for this LIFO recapture amount, but the AAA is not decreased by payment of the tax.

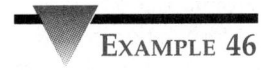

EXAMPLE 46

Engelage Corporation converts from a C corporation to an S corporation at the beginning of 1999. Engelage used the LIFO inventory method in 1998 and had an ending LIFO inventory of $110,000 (FIFO value of $190,000). Engelage must add $80,000 of LIFO recapture amount to its 1998 taxable income, resulting in an increased tax liability of $28,000 ($80,000 × 35%). Thus, Engelage must pay one-fourth of the tax (or $7,000) with its 1998 corporate tax return. The three succeeding installments of $7,000 each are paid with Engelage's next three tax returns. ▼

PASSIVE INVESTMENT INCOME PENALTY TAX

11   LEARNING OBJECTIVE
Compute the passive investment income penalty tax.

A tax is imposed on the excess passive income of S corporations that possess AEP from C corporation years. The tax rate is the highest corporate rate for the year. The rate is applied to excess net passive income (ENPI), which is determined using the following formula:

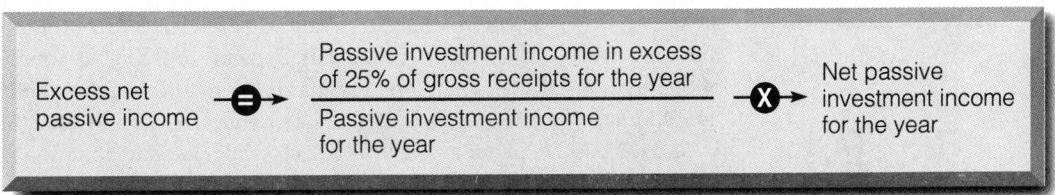

Passive investment income (PII) includes gross receipts derived from royalties, rents, dividends, interest, annuities, and sales and exchanges of stocks and securities.[57] Only the net gain from the disposition of capital assets (other than stocks and securities) is taken into account in computing gross receipts. Net passive income is passive income reduced by any deductions directly connected with the production of that income. Any passive income tax reduces the amount the shareholders must take into income.

The excess net passive income cannot exceed the corporate taxable income for the year before considering any NOL deduction or the special deductions allowed by §§ 241–250 (except the organizational expense deduction of § 248).[58]

---

[57]§ 1362(d)(3)(D)(i).

[58]§§ 1374(d)(4), and 1375(a) and (b).

No Avoidance of LIFO Recapture on S Conversion

When a C corporation elects S corporation status, the tax law requires that it recapture any LIFO reserve it has accumulated to date. The recapture must be included in the income of the corporation's final C corporation return. The additional tax resulting from the LIFO recapture is payable in four equal annual installments, beginning with the tax payment for the final C corporation year.

A LIFO reserve is essentially the amount by which LIFO has reduced taxable income during the years of its use. When a company has used LIFO for many years and there has been a fair amount of cost inflation during that time, the LIFO reserve can be quite a substantial number.

This LIFO recapture provision was Congress's way of making sure that corporations with LIFO inventories did not avoid the tax that FIFO (first-in, first-out) corporations have to pay on the built-in gains in their inventories.

A consolidated group thought it had found a way around the LIFO reserve recapture. Before collapsing the subsidiaries into the parent corporation in anticipation of the parent corporation electing S status (this transaction occurred before S corporations could have subsidiaries), the subsidiaries transferred their operating assets, including inventories, to partnerships.

An IRS agent examining the final return of the consolidated group proposed to include in the income of that return the LIFO reserves associated with the inventories the subsidiaries had transferred to the partnerships. The IRS National Office in a Technical Advice Memorandum agreed that permitting a corporation to avoid LIFO recapture by holding LIFO inventory in a partnership would circumvent the purpose of the LIFO recapture rule.

SOURCE: Adapted from "Partnership Technique Did Not Avoid LIFO Recapture on S Conversion," by Eileen J. O'Connor, *Grant Thornton's Tax & Business Adviser*, May/June 1997.

EXAMPLE 47

At the end of 1998, Barnhardt Corporation, an electing S corporation, has gross receipts totaling $264,000 (of which $110,000 is PII). Expenditures directly connected to the production of the PII total $30,000. Therefore, Barnhardt has net PII of $80,000 ($110,000 − $30,000), and its PII for tax year 1998 exceeds 25% of its gross receipts by $44,000 ($110,000 PII − $66,000). Excess net passive income (ENPI) is $32,000, calculated as follows:

$$\text{ENPI} = \frac{\$44,000}{\$110,000} \times \$80,000 = \$32,000$$

Barnhardt's PII tax for 1998 is $11,200 ($32,000 × 35%). ▼

OTHER OPERATIONAL RULES

Several other points may be made about the possible effects of various Code provisions on S corporations:

- An S corporation is required to make estimated tax payments with respect to tax exposure because of any recognized built-in gain and excess passive investment income.
- An S corporation may own stock in another corporation, but an S corporation may not have a C corporation shareholder. An S corporation is *not* eligible for a dividends received deduction.

- An S corporation is *not* subject to the 10 percent of taxable income limitation applicable to charitable contributions made by a C corporation.
- Any family member who renders services or furnishes capital to an electing corporation must be paid reasonable compensation. Otherwise, the IRS can make adjustments to reflect the value of the services or capital.[59] This rule may make it more difficult for related parties to shift Subchapter S taxable income to children or other family members.
- Although § 1366(a)(1) provides for a flow-through of S items to a shareholder, it does not apply to self-employment income.[60] Thus, a shareholder's portion of S income is not self-employment income and is not subject to the self-employment tax. Compensation for services rendered to an S corporation is, however, subject to FICA taxes.

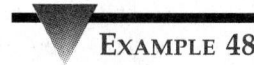

EXAMPLE 48

Cody and Dana each own one-third of a fast-food restaurant, and their 14-year-old son owns the other shares. Both parents work full-time in the restaurant operations, but the son works infrequently. Neither parent receives a salary this year, when the taxable income of the S corporation is $160,000. The IRS can require that reasonable compensation be paid to the parents to prevent the full one-third of the $160,000 from being taxed to the son. Otherwise, this would be an effective technique to shift earned income to a family member to reduce the total family tax burden. Furthermore, low or zero salaries can reduce FICA taxes due to the Federal government. ▼

- An S corporation is placed on the cash method of accounting for purposes of deducting business expenses and interest owed to a cash basis related party.[61] Thus, the timing of the shareholder's income and the corporate deduction must match.
- The S election is not recognized by the District of Columbia and several states, including Connecticut, Michigan, New Hampshire, and Tennessee. Thus, some or all of the entity's income may be subject to a state-level income tax.
- If § 1244 stock is issued to an S corporation, the S corporation and its shareholders may not treat losses on such stock as ordinary losses, notwithstanding § 1363, which provides that the taxable income of an S corporation must be computed in the same manner as that of an individual. However, an S corporation may issue § 1244 stock to its shareholders to obtain ordinary loss treatment.
- Losses may be disallowed due to a lack of a profit motive. If the activities at the corporate level are not profit motivated, the losses may be disallowed under the hobby loss rule of § 183.[62]

TAX PLANNING CONSIDERATIONS

WHEN THE ELECTION IS ADVISABLE

Effective tax planning with S corporations begins with the determination of whether the election is appropriate. In light of many changes made by the Small Business Job Protection Act of 1996 and the Taxpayer **Relief Act** of 1997, the taxpayer may wish to reevaluate the desirability of using a C corporation as a means of conducting a trade or business. In this context, one should consider the following factors:

---

[59]§ 1366(e). In addition, beware of an IRS search for the "real owner" of the stock under Reg. § 1.1373–1(a)(2).

[60]Rev.Rul. 59–221, 1959–1 C.B. 225.

[61]§ 267(b).

[62]*Michael J. Houston*, T.C.Memo. 1995–159; *Mario G. De Mendoza, III*, T.C.Memo. 1994–314.

- Are losses from the business anticipated? If so, the S election may be highly attractive because these losses pass through to the shareholders.
- What are the tax brackets of the shareholders? If the shareholders are in high individual income tax brackets, it may be desirable to avoid S corporation status and have profits taxed to the corporation at lower C rates (e.g., 15 percent or 25 percent).
- When the immediate pass-through of Subchapter S taxable income is avoided, profits of the corporation may later be taken out by the shareholders as capital gain income through stock redemptions, liquidating distributions, or sales of stock to others; received as dividend distributions in low tax bracket years; or negated by a partial or complete step-up in basis upon the death of the shareholder.[63] On the other hand, if the shareholders are in low individual income tax brackets, the pass-through of corporate profits has less effect, and the avoidance of the corporate income tax becomes the paramount consideration. Under these circumstances, the S election could be highly attractive. Although an S corporation usually escapes Federal taxes, it may not be immune from state and local taxes imposed on corporations or from several Federal penalty taxes.
- Does a C corporation have an NOL carryover from a prior year? Such a loss cannot be used in an S year (except for purposes of the built-in gains tax). Even worse, S years count in the 20-year carryover limitation. Thus, even if the S election is made, one might consider terminating the election before the carryover limitation expires. Such a termination would permit the loss to be utilized by what is now a C corporation.
- Both individuals and C corporations are subject to the alternative minimum tax. Many of the tax preference and adjustment items are the same, but some apply only to corporate taxpayers while others are limited to individuals. The alternative minimum tax adjustment relating to accumulated current earnings could create havoc with some C corporations (refer to Chapter 14). S corporations themselves are not subject to this tax.
- Some C corporations must convert from the cash method to the accrual method of accounting (refer to Chapter 16).
- S corporations and partnerships have lost some of the flexibility in the choice of their accounting period (see also Chapter 22).
- By taxing C corporations on nonliquidating and liquidating distributions of appreciated property (refer to Chapters 18 and 19), the effect of double taxation is reinforced.
- Since the S election may or may not provide the shareholders with tax advantages, one must consider all of the provisions that affect the owners.

EXAMPLE 49

Tracey has a basis of $500,000 in his business assets, including some land, which is subject to a liability of $700,000. Tracey transfers all of the assets of the business to a newly formed corporation, Red, Inc., in exchange for all of the stock in Red. Red elects to be taxed as an S corporation. Red incurs ordinary losses as follows: Year 1, $50,000; Year 2, $80,000; Year 3, $90,000. Tracey deducts the losses to offset income from other sources. Red is audited in Year 3.

- The IRS asserts that Tracey must recognize a $200,000 gain upon the incorporation of Red under § 357(c), because the liabilities exceed his basis in the assets. Tracey's basis in the Red stock is zero: $500,000 (basis of Tracey's assets) – $700,000 (liabilities assumed by Red) + $200,000 (gain recognized to Tracey).

---

[63]See the discussion of § 1014 in Chapter 26.

- Because Tracey's basis in the Red stock is zero, he is not entitled to deduct any of the losses for Year 1, Year 2, or Year 3.
- Because Tracey was actively involved in his business, had he not incorporated, he could have offset total losses of $220,000 against other ordinary income. He would also have eliminated the $200,000 gain upon the incorporation of his business. Thus, the incorporation and S election caused Tracey to generate additional income for tax purposes of $420,000. ▼

The choice of the form of doing business often is dictated by other factors. For example, many businesses cannot qualify for the S election—due to the possibility of a public offering or a need for substantial capital inflow—or would find the partnership or limited liability company forms more practical. Therefore, freedom of action based on tax considerations may not be an attainable goal. Comparative tax attributes of partnerships, S corporations, and C corporations are summarized in Concept Summary 22–6 in Chapter 22.

MAKING A PROPER ELECTION

Once the parties have decided the election is appropriate, it becomes essential to ensure that the election is made properly.

- Make sure all shareholders consent. If any doubt exists concerning the shareholder status of an individual, it would be wise to have that party issue a consent anyway.[64] Too few consents are fatal to the election; the same cannot be said for too many consents.
- Be sure that the election is timely and properly filed. Either hand carry the election to an IRS office or send it by certified or registered mail. The date used to determine timeliness is the postmark date, not the date the IRS receives the election. A copy of the election should become part of the corporation's permanent files.
- Be careful to ascertain when the timely election period begins to run for a newly formed corporation. An election made too soon (before the corporation is in existence) is worse than one made too late. If serious doubts exist as to when this period begins, filing more than one election might be considered a practical means of guaranteeing the desired result.
- It still is beneficial for an S corporation to issue § 1244 stock (refer to Chapter 17). This type of stock allows the original shareholder to obtain an ordinary deduction for a loss on the sale or worthlessness of the stock, rather than long-term capital loss treatment. Shareholders have nothing to lose by complying with § 1244.

ETHICAL CONSIDERATIONS

A Divorce Threatens S Status

Golden Cowrie, Inc., has operated successfully as an S corporation for eight years in Greer, South Carolina. In July 1998, the company had 75 shareholders, but one of the shareholders, Morrie Williams, is considering obtaining a divorce. Both Morrie and his wife Kristy own shares in the corporation.

[64]See *William B. Wilson*, 34 TCM 463, T.C.Memo. 1975–92.

Morrie discusses the situation with the board of directors, who offer several suggestions:

- Morrie should postpone the divorce until 1999, while the company tries to purchase all of the stock from one of the smaller owners.
- Morrie and Kristy should remain married indefinitely for the good of the S election.
- Two of the unmarried shareholders will be encouraged to marry for the "benefit of the company."
- The company will continue to list Morrie and Kristy as married on Form 1120S after they divorce.

The S election saves the group about $280,000 each year. How would you counsel Morrie to respond to the board's proposals?

PRESERVING THE ELECTION

Recall how an election can be lost and that a five-year waiting period generally is imposed before another S election is available. To preserve an S election, the following points should be kept in mind:

- As a starting point, all parties concerned should be made aware of the various transactions that lead to the loss of an election.
- Watch for possible disqualification of a small business corporation. For example, the divorce of a shareholder, accompanied by a property settlement, could violate the 75-shareholder limitation (35 before 1997). The death of a shareholder could result in a nonqualifying trust becoming a shareholder. The latter circumstance might be avoided by utilizing a buy-sell agreement or binding the deceased shareholder's estate to turn in the stock to the corporation for redemption or, as an alternative, to sell it to the surviving shareholders.[65]
- Make sure a new majority shareholder (including the estate of a deceased shareholder) does not file a refusal to continue the election.
- Watch for the passive investment income limitation. Avoid a consecutive third year with excess passive income if a corporation has Subchapter C accumulated earnings and profits. In this connection, assets that produce passive investment income (e.g., stocks and bonds, certain rental assets) might be retained by the shareholders in their individual capacities and thereby kept out of the corporation.
- Do not transfer stock to a nonresident alien.
- Do not issue a second class of stock.

PLANNING FOR THE OPERATION OF THE CORPORATION

Operating an S corporation to achieve optimum tax savings for all parties involved requires a great deal of care and, most important, an understanding of the applicable tax rules.

Accumulated Adjustment Account.   Although the corporate-level accumulated adjustments account (AAA) is used primarily by an S corporation with accumulated earnings and profits (AEP) from a Subchapter C year, all S corporations

---

[65]Most such agreements do not create a second class of S stock. Rev.Rul. 85–161, 1985–2 C.B. 191; *Portage Plastics Co. v. U.S.,* 72–2 USTC ¶9567, 30 AFTR2d 72–5229, 470 F.2d 308 (CA–7, 1973).

should maintain an accurate record of the AAA. Because there is a grace period for distributing the AAA after termination of the S election, the parties must be in a position to determine the balance of the account.

EXAMPLE 50

Nobles, Inc., an S corporation during 1997, has no AEP from a Subchapter C year. Over the years, Nobles made no attempt to maintain an accurate accounting for the AAA. In 1998, the S election is terminated, and Nobles has a grace period for distributing the AAA tax-free to its shareholders. A great deal of time and expense may be necessary to reconstruct the AAA balance in 1998. ▼

Tax-exempt income is not included in gross income and does not increase AAA. For an S corporation with AEP, tax-exempt income usually is a bad investment. Any subsequent distribution of tax-exempt income that exceeds the AAA balance is treated as dividend income to the extent of any AEP.

When AEP is present, a negative AAA may cause double taxation of S corporation income. With a negative AAA, a distribution of current income restores the negative AAA balance to zero, but is considered to be a distribution in excess of AAA and is taxable as a dividend to the extent of AEP. For tax years beginning after 1996, distributions during the year reduce the stock basis for determining the allowable loss for the year, but the loss does *not* reduce the stock basis for determining the tax status of distributions made during the year. In determining the tax treatment of distributions by an S corporation having AEP, any net adjustments (e.g., excess of losses and deductions over income) for the tax year are ignored.

The AAA bypass election may be used to avoid the accumulated earnings tax or personal holding company tax in the year preceding the first tax year under Subchapter S. This bypass election allows the AEP to be distributed instead.

EXAMPLE 51

Zebra, Inc., an S corporation during 1997, has a significant amount in its AEP account. The shareholders expect to terminate the election in 1998, when they will be subject to low income tax rates. Since the new C corporation may be subject to the accumulated earnings penalty tax in 1998, the shareholders may wish to use the AAA bypass election to distribute some or all of the AEP. Of course, any distributions of the AEP account in 1997 would be taxable to the shareholders. ▼

A net loss allocated to a shareholder reduces the AAA. This required adjustment should encourage an electing corporation to make annual distributions of net income to avoid the reduction of an AAA by a future net loss.

Salary Structure. The amount of salary paid to a shareholder-employee of an S corporation can have varying tax consequences and should be considered carefully. Larger amounts might be advantageous if the maximum contribution allowed under the retirement plan has not been reached. Smaller amounts may be beneficial if the parties are trying to shift taxable income to lower-bracket shareholders, reduce payroll taxes, curtail a reduction of Social Security benefits, or restrict losses that do not pass through because of the basis limitation.

A strategy of decreasing compensation and correspondingly increasing distributions to shareholder-employees often results in substantial savings in employment taxes. However, a shareholder of an S corporation cannot always perform substantial services and arrange to receive distributions rather than compensation so that the corporation may avoid paying employment taxes. The shareholder may be deemed an employee, with any distributions recharacterized as wages subject to FICA and FUTA taxes.[66] For planning purposes, some level of compensation should be paid to all shareholder-employees to avoid any recharacterization of distributions as deductible salaries—especially in personal service corporations.

The IRS can require that reasonable compensation be paid to family members who render services or provide capital to the S corporation. The IRS, though, can adjust the items taken into account by family-member shareholders to reflect the value of services or capital they provided. Refer to Example 48.

Unreasonable compensation traditionally has not been a problem for S corporations, but deductible compensation under § 162 reduces an S corporation's taxable income, which is relevant to the built-in gains tax. Compensation may be one of the larger items that an electing corporation can use to reduce taxable income to minimize any built-in gains penalty tax. Thus, IRS agents may attempt to classify compensation as unreasonable to increase the § 1374 tax.

Loss Considerations.　A net loss in excess of tax basis may be carried forward and deducted only by the same shareholder in succeeding years. Thus, before disposing of the stock, a shareholder should increase the basis of such stock/loan to flow through the loss. The next shareholder does not obtain the carryover loss.

Any unused carryover loss in existence upon the termination of the S election may be deducted only in the next tax year and is limited to the individual's *stock* basis (not loan basis) in the post-termination year.[67] The shareholder may wish to purchase more stock to increase the tax basis in order to absorb the loss.

The NOL provisions create a need for sound tax planning during the last election year and the post-termination transition period. If it appears that the S corporation is going to sustain an NOL or use up any loss carryover, each shareholder's basis should be analyzed to determine if it can absorb the share of the loss. If basis is insufficient to absorb the loss, further investments should be considered before the end of the post-termination transition year. Such investments can be accomplished through additional stock purchases from the corporation, or from other shareholders, to increase basis. This action ensures the full benefit from the NOL carryover.

EXAMPLE 52　A calendar year C corporation has an NOL of $20,000 in 1997. The corporation makes a valid S election in 1998 and has another $20,000 NOL in that year. At all times during 1998, the stock of the corporation was owned by the same 10 shareholders, each of whom owned 10% of the stock. Tim, one of the 10 shareholders, has an adjusted basis of $1,800 at the beginning of 1998. None of the 1997 NOL may be carried forward into the S year. Although Tim's share of the 1998 NOL is $2,000, the deduction for the loss is limited to $1,800 in 1998 with a $200 carryover. ▼

Avoiding the Passive Investment Income Tax.　Too much passive investment income (PII) may cause an S corporation to incur a § 1375 penalty tax and/or terminate the S election. Several planning techniques can be used to avoid both of these unfavorable events. Where a small amount of AEP exists, an AAA bypass election may be appropriate to purge the AEP, thereby avoiding the passive income tax altogether. Alternatively, the corporation might reduce taxable income below the excess net passive income; similarly, PII might be accelerated into years in which there is an (offsetting) NOL. In addition, the tax can be avoided if the

[66]Rev.Rul. 74–44, 1974–1 C.B. 287; *Spicer Accounting, Inc. v. U.S.*, 91–1 USTC ¶50,103, 66 AFTR 2d, 90–5806, 918 F.2d 90 (CA–9, 1990); *Radtke v. U.S.*, 90–1 USTC ¶50,113, 65 AFTR 2d, 90–1155, 895 F.2d 1196 (CA–7, 1990).

[67]§ 1366(d)(3).

corporation manufactures needed gross receipts. By increasing gross receipts without increasing PII, the amount of PII in excess of 25 percent of gross receipts is reduced.

EXAMPLE 53

An S corporation has paid a passive income penalty tax for two consecutive years. In the next year, the corporation has a large amount of AAA. If the AEP account is small, a bypass election may be appropriate to purge the corporation of the AEP. Without any AEP, no passive income tax applies, and the S election is not terminated. Any distribution of AEP to the shareholders constitutes taxable dividends, however.

Another alternative is to manufacture a large amount of gross receipts without increasing PII (merge with a grocery store). If the gross receipts from the grocery store are substantial, the amount of the PII in excess of 25% of gross receipts is reduced. ▼

Managing the Built-in Gains Tax.   The taxable income limitation encourages an S corporation to create deductions or accelerate deductions in the years that built-in gains are recognized. Although the postponed built-in gain is carried forward to future years, the time value of money makes the postponement beneficial. For example, payment of compensation, rather than a distribution, creates a deduction that reduces taxable income and postpones the built-in gains tax.

EXAMPLE 54

Mundy, Inc., an S corporation, has built-in gain of $110,000 and taxable income of $120,000 before payment of salaries to its two shareholders. If Mundy pays at least $120,000 in salaries to the shareholders (rather than a distribution), taxable income will drop to zero, and the built-in gain will be postponed. Thus, Mundy needs to keep the salaries as high as possible to postpone the built-in gains tax in future years and reap a benefit from the time value of money. Of course, paying the salaries may increase the payroll tax burden if the salaries are below FICA and FUTA limits. ▼

Giving built-in gain property to a charitable organization does not trigger the built-in gains tax. However, the built-in gain may be a preference item at the shareholder level for purposes of the alternative minimum tax. Built-in *loss* property may be sold in the same year that built-in gain property is sold, to reduce or eliminate the built-in gains tax. Generally, the taxpayer should sell built-in loss property in a year when an equivalent amount of built-in gain property is sold. Otherwise, the built-in loss could be wasted.

EXAMPLE 55

Green Corporation elects S status effective for calendar year 1997. As of January 1, 1997, Green's only asset has a basis of $40,000 and a fair market value of $100,000. If this asset is sold for $120,000 in 1998, Green recognizes an $80,000 gain, of which $60,000 is subject to the corporate built-in gains tax. The other $20,000 of gain is subject to the S corporation pass-through rules and bypasses the corporate income tax.

Unless the taxpayer can show otherwise, any appreciation existing at the sale or exchange is presumed to be preconversion built-in gain. Therefore, Green incurs a built-in gain of $80,000 unless it can prove that the $20,000 gain developed after the effective date of the election. ▼

Controlling Adjustments and Preference Items.   The individual alternative minimum tax (AMT) affects more taxpayers than ever before, because the tax base has expanded and the difference between regular tax rates and the individual AMT rate has been narrowed. In an S corporation setting, tax preferences flow through proportionately to the shareholders, who, in computing the individual AMT, treat the preferences as if they were directly realized. Thus, the S corporation may not take advantage of the $5 and $7.5 million average gross receipts exemptions for a small corporation.

A flow-through of tax preferences can be a tax disaster for a shareholder who is an "almost-AMT taxpayer." Certain steps can be taken to protect such a shareholder from being pushed into the AMT. For example, a large S corporation preference from tax-exempt interest on private activity bonds could adversely affect an "almost-AMT taxpayer." Certain adjustment and preference items are subject to elections that can remove them from a shareholder's AMT computation. Certain positive adjustments can be removed from a shareholder's AMTI base if the S corporation elects to capitalize and amortize certain expenditures over a prescribed period of time. These expenditures include excess intangible drilling and development expenditures, research and experimental costs, mining exploration and development expenditures, and circulation expenses.

Other corporate choices can protect an "almost-AMT shareholder." Using a straight-line method of cost recovery (rather than an accelerated method) can be beneficial to certain shareholders. Many of these decisions and elections may generate conflicts of interest, however, when some shareholders are not so precariously situated and would not suffer from the flow-through of adjustments and tax preference items.

Allocation of Tax Items.   If a shareholder dies or stock is transferred during the taxable year, tax items may be allocated under the pro rata approach or the per-books method. Absent the per-books election, a shareholder's pro rata share of tax items is determined by assigning an equal portion of each item to each day of the tax year and then dividing that portion pro rata among the shares outstanding on the transfer day. With the consent of all affected shareholders and the corporation, an S corporation can elect to allocate tax items according to the permanent records using normal tax accounting rules.

The allocation is made as if the taxable year consists of two taxable years. The first portion ends on the date of termination. On the day the shares are transferred, the shares are considered owned by the acquiring shareholder. The selected method may be beneficial to the terminating shareholder and harmful to the acquiring shareholder. An election might result in a higher allocation of losses to a taxpayer who is better able to utilize the losses. In the case of the death of a shareholder, a per-books election prevents the income and loss allocation to a deceased shareholder from being affected by postdeath events.

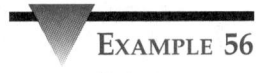

EXAMPLE 56   Alicia, the owner of all of the shares of an S corporation, transfers all of the stock to Bhaskar at the middle of the tax year. There is a $100,000 NOL for the entire tax year, but $30,000 of the loss occurs during the first half of the year. Without a per-books election, $50,000 of the loss is allocated to Alicia, with $50,000 allocated to Bhaskar. If the corporation makes the per-books election, Bhaskar receives $70,000 of the loss. Of course, Bhaskar may have a difficult time convincing Alicia to consent to the election. ▼

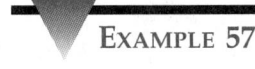

EXAMPLE 57   Mountain, a calendar year S corporation, is equally owned by Joey and Karl. Joey dies on June 29 (not a leap year). Mountain has income of $250,000 for January 1 through June 29 and $750,000 for the remainder of the year. Without the per-books election, the income is allocated by assigning an equal portion of the annual income of $1 million to each day (or $2,739.73 per day) and allocating the daily portion between the shareholders. Joey is allocated 50% of the daily income for the 180 days from January 1 to June 29, or $246,575.70 ($2,739.73/2 × 180). Joey's estate is allocated 50% of the income for the 185 days from June 30 to December 31, or $253,425.02 [($2,739.73/2) × 185].

If the per-books election is made, the income of $250,000 from January 1 to June 29 is divided equally between Joey and Karl, so that each is allocated $125,000. The income of $750,000 from June 30 to December 31 is divided equally between Joey's estate and Karl, or $375,000 to each. ▼

Termination Aspects. It is always advisable to avoid accumulated earnings and profits (AEP) in an S corporation. There is the ever-present danger of terminating the election because of excess passive investment income in three consecutive years. Further, the § 1375 penalty tax is imposed on excess passive net income. Thus, one should try to eliminate such AEP through a dividend distribution or liquidation of the corporation with a subsequent reincorporation. If the AEP account is small, to eliminate the problem, all the shareholders may consent under § 1368(e)(3) to have distributions treated as made first from AEP rather than from the AAA (the AAA bypass election).

One should issue straight debt to avoid creating a second class of stock and establish an instrument with a written unconditional promise to pay on demand or on a specific date a sum certain in money with a fixed interest rate and payment date.

If the shareholders of an S corporation decide to terminate the election other than through voluntary revocation, they should make sure that the disqualifying act possesses substance. When the intent of the parties is obvious and the act represents a technical noncompliance rather than a real change, the IRS may be able to disregard it and keep the parties in S status.[68]

If a trust or estate terminates before the end of an S corporation's tax year, the estate or trust takes in consideration its pro rata share of S corporation items in its final year.

Liquidation of an S Corporation. S corporations are subject to many of the same liquidation rules applicable to C corporations (refer to Chapter 19). In general, the distribution of appreciated property to S shareholders in complete liquidation is treated as if the property were sold to the shareholders in a taxable transaction. Unlike a C corporation, however, the S corporation incurs no incremental tax on the liquidation gains, because such gains flow through to the shareholders subject only to the built-in gains tax of § 1374. Any corporate gain increases the shareholder's stock basis by a like amount and reduces any gain realized by the shareholder when he or she receives the liquidation proceeds. Thus, an S corporation usually avoids the double tax that is imposed on C corporations.

With respect to loss property, a liquidation is more favorable than a nonliquidating distribution. Recall that a loss is not recognized for nonliquidating property distributions. With certain exceptions, an S corporation does recognize a loss on the liquidating distribution of depreciated property.

Until it was changed in 1996, the law itself appeared to preclude an S corporation from making an election under § 338 to have a stock purchase treated as an asset acquisition or from taking advantage of a § 332 liquidation. Section 1371(a)(2) provides that an S corporation in its capacity as a shareholder of another corporation shall be treated as an individual. Since only a corporation can make an election under § 338, before 1997 an S corporation appeared to be unable to make such an election.[69] In one letter ruling, however, the IRS allowed an S corporation to take advantage of §§ 338 and 332.[70]

For tax years beginning after 1996, liquidations of S corporations are governed by the applicable C corporation rules (e.g., §§ 332 and 337), allowing a tax-free

---

[68]See *Clarence L. Hook*, 58 T.C. 267 (1972).
[69]Doc. 8818049; GCM 39768.

[70]Doc. 9245004. The Regulations are silent on this matter.

liquidation of a corporation into its parent corporation. Any built-in gains of the liquidating corporation may later be subject to the § 1374 penalty tax on disposition. An S corporation is also eligible to make a § 338 election, resulting in the immediate recognition of all of the acquired C corporation's income and losses plus the resulting tax.

KEY TERMS

Accumulated adjustments account (AAA), 21–15

Built-in gains (§ 1374) tax, 21–26

Passive investment income (PII), 21–10

S corporation, 21–2

Small business corporation, 21–4

Subchapter S, 21–2

PROBLEM MATERIALS

DISCUSSION QUESTIONS

1. Victoria must decide which type of flow-through entity she will choose for her new service business. Help Victoria decide between a limited liability company and an S corporation vehicle by listing the advantages and disadvantages of an S election.

2. May an S corporation own a subsidiary and obtain a dividends received deduction for any dividends? May an S corporation own an S corporation subsidiary? May an S corporation be a member of a consolidated tax return?

3. On March 2, 1998, the two 50% shareholders of a calendar year corporation decide to elect S status. One of the shareholders, Terry, had purchased her stock from a previous shareholder (a nonresident alien) on January 18, 1998. Identify any potential problems for Terry or the corporation.

4. Elvis Stojko calls you and says that his two-person S corporation was involuntarily terminated in February 1998. He asks you if they can make a new election because of the law changes in 1997. Draft a memo for the file dated September 8, 1998, outlining what you told Elvis.

5. How can an S corporation meet the natural business year exception to qualify for a fiscal year?

6. How are nonseparately computed income or losses and Schedule K items allocated to a shareholder?

7. Collett's S corporation has a small amount of accumulated earnings and profits (AEP), requiring the use of the more complex distribution rules. His accountant tells him that this AEP forces the maintenance of the AAA figure each year. Identify relevant tax issues facing Collett.

8. Caleb Hudson owns 10% of an S corporation. He is confused with respect to his AAA and stock basis. Write a brief memo dated November 1, 1998, to Caleb identifying the key differences between AAA and his stock basis.

9. How do the at-risk rules affect an S corporation?

10. Lynch's share of her S corporation's net operating loss is $41,000, but her stock basis is only $29,000. Point out any tax consequences to Lynch.

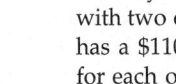

11. One of your clients is considering electing S status. Texas, Inc., is a six-year-old company with two equal shareholders, both of whom paid $30,000 for their stock. In 1998, Texas has a $110,000 NOL carryforward. Estimated income is $40,000 for 1999 and $25,000 for each of the next three years. Should Texas make an S election for 1998?

PROBLEMS

12. An S corporation's profit and loss statement for 1998 shows net profits of $99,000 (book income). The corporation has four equal shareholders. From supplemental data, you obtain the following information about the corporation for 1998.

Administrative expenses	$21,200
Tax-exempt interest	2,000
Dividends received	9,000
Section 1231 gain	6,000
Section 1245 gain	10,000
Recovery of state income taxes	3,400
Short-term capital loss	6,000
Salary to owners (each)	10,000
Cost of goods sold	95,000

   a. Compute Subchapter S taxable income or loss for 1998.
   b. What would be the portion of taxable income or loss for Chang, one of the shareholders?

13. Noon, Inc., a calendar year S corporation in Ruston, Louisiana, is equally owned by Ralph and Thomas. Thomas dies on April 1 (not a leap year), and his estate selects a March 31 fiscal year. Noon has $400,000 of income for January 1 through March 31 and $600,000 for the remainder of the year.
   a. Determine how income is allocated to Ralph and Thomas under the pro rata approach.
   b. Determine how income is allocated to Ralph and Thomas under the per-books method.

14. Polly has been the sole shareholder of a calendar year S corporation since 1981. Polly's stock basis is $15,500, and she receives a distribution of $17,000 in 1997. Corporate-level accounts are as follows (including $100 of pre-1983 AEP).

AAA	$6,000
PTI*	9,000
AEP	500

*PTI = previously taxed income, under old-law provisions.

How is Polly taxed on the distribution?

15. On January 1, 1998, Kinney, Inc., an electing S corporation, has $4,000 of AEP and a balance of $10,000 in AAA. Kinney has two shareholders, Erin and Frank, each of whom owns 500 shares of Kinney's stock. Kinney's 1998 taxable income is $5,000. Kinney distributes $6,000 to each shareholder on February 1, 1998, and distributes another $3,000 to each shareholder on September 1. Assuming that Erin and Frank have sufficient stock basis, how are they taxed on the distributions?

16. Goblins, Inc., a calendar year S corporation, has $90,000 of AEP. Tobias, the sole shareholder, has an adjusted basis of $80,000 in his stock with a zero balance in the AAA. Determine the tax aspects if a $90,000 salary is paid to Tobias.

17. Assume the same facts as in Problem 16, except that Tobias receives a dividend of $90,000.

18. Using the categories in the following legend, classify each transaction as a plus (+) or minus (−) on Schedule M–2 of Form 1120S.

Legend

PTI = Shareholders' undistributed taxable income previously taxed

AAA = Accumulated adjustments account

OAA = Other adjustments account

NA = No direct effect on Schedule M

---

a. Receipt of tax-exempt interest income.
b. Unreasonable compensation determined.
c. Section 1245 recapture income.
d. Distribution of nontaxable income (PTI) from 1981.
e. Nontaxable life insurance proceeds.
f. Expenses related to tax-exempt securities.
g. Charitable contributions.
h. Business gifts in excess of $25.
i. Nondeductible fines and penalties.
j. Organization expenses.

19. Individuals Adam and Bonnie form an S corporation, with Adam contributing cash of $100,000 for a 50% interest and Bonnie contributing appreciated ordinary income property with an adjusted basis of $20,000 and a FMV of $100,000.
    a. Determine Bonnie's initial basis in her stock, assuming that she receives a 50% interest.
    b. The S corporation sells the property for $120,000. Determine Adam's and Bonnie's stock basis after the sale.
    c. Determine Adam's and Bonnie's gain or loss if the company is liquidated.

20. In 1998, Ourso, Inc., an S corporation with one shareholder, has a loss of $55,000 and makes a distribution of $70,000 to the shareholder, Bip Wallace. Bip's stock basis at the beginning of the year is $100,000. Write a memo dated October 21, 1998, to your manager discussing the solution.

21. Fabrizius, Inc., an S corporation in Saint Cloud, Minnesota, had a balance in AAA of $100,000 and AEP of $55,000 on December 31, 1998. During 1999, Fabrizius distributes $70,000 to its shareholders, while sustaining a loss of $60,000. Determine any balance in the AAA and the AEP account.

22. An S corporation's Form 1120S shows taxable income of $88,000 for the year. Matthew owns 40% of the stock throughout the year. The following information is obtained from the corporate records.

Salary paid to Matthew	$52,000
Tax-exempt interest income	3,000
Charitable contributions	6,000
Dividends received from a foreign corporation	5,000
Long-term capital loss	6,000
§ 1245 gain	11,000
Refund of prior state income taxes	5,000
Cost of goods sold	72,000
Short-term capital loss	7,000
Administrative expenses	18,000
Long-term capital gains	14,000
Selling expenses	11,000
Matthew's beginning stock basis	22,000
Matthew's additional stock purchases	9,000

Matthew's beginning AAA	21,000
Matthew's loan to corporation	20,000

   a. Compute book income or loss.
   b. Compute Matthew's ending stock basis.
   c. Calculate ending corporate AAA.

23. At the beginning of the year, Malcolm, a 50% shareholder of a calendar year S corporation, has a stock basis of $22,000. During the year, the corporation has taxable income of $32,000. The following data are obtained from supplemental sources.

Dividends received	$12,000
Tax-exempt interest	18,000
Short-term capital gain	6,000
§ 1245 gain	10,000
§ 1231 gain	7,000
Charitable contributions	5,000
Political contributions	8,000
Short-term capital loss	12,000
Dividends to Malcolm	6,000
Selling expense	14,000
Beginning AAA	40,000

   a. Compute Malcolm's ending stock basis.
   b. Compute ending AAA.

24. For each of the following independent statements, indicate whether the transaction will increase (+), decrease (−), or have no effect (NE) on the adjusted basis of a shareholder's stock in an S corporation.
   a. Expenses related to tax-exempt income.
   b. Long-term capital gain.
   c. Nonseparately computed loss.
   d. Section 1231 gain.
   e. Depletion *not* in excess of basis.
   f. Separately computed income.
   g. Nontaxable return-of-capital distribution by the corporation.
   h. Selling expenses.
   i. Business gifts in excess of $25.
   j. Section 1250 gain.
   k. Dividends received by the S corporation.
   l. LIFO recapture tax at S election.
   m. Recovery of a bad debt.
   n. Short-term capital loss.
   o. Corporate dividends out of AAA.

25. McHugh, Inc., a calendar year corporation in Grand Isle, Louisiana, has a tax loss of $90,000 and a long-term capital loss of $20,000. Ieyoub, an individual, owns 30% of the corporate stock and has a $25,000 basis in the stock. Calculate the amount of the tax loss and capital loss, if any, that flows through to Ieyoub.

26. Cangelosh owns 40% of the stock of an S corporation in University Park, Pennsylvania, throughout 1998 and lends the corporation $8,000 during the year. Her stock basis in the corporation at the end of the year is $25,000. If the corporation sustains a $110,000 operating loss during the year, what amount, if any, can Cangelosh deduct with respect to the operating loss? Prepare a tax memo for the files dated December 3, 1998.

27. Crew Corporation elects S status effective for tax year 1997. As of January 1, 1997, Crew's assets were appraised as follows.

	Adjusted Basis	Fair Market Value
Cash	$ 16,010	$ 16,010
Accounts receivable	–0–	55,400
Inventory (FIFO)	70,000	90,000
Investment in land	110,000	195,000
Building	220,000	275,000
Goodwill	–0–	93,000

In each of the following situations, calculate any § 1374 tax, assuming that the highest corporate rate is 35%.

a. During 1997, Crew collects $40,000 of the accounts receivable and sells 80% of the inventory for $99,000.

b. In 1998, Crew sells the land held for investment for $203,000.

c. In 1999, the building is sold for $270,000.

28. Alomar, Inc., a cash basis S corporation in Orlando, Florida, has the following assets and liabilities on January 1, 1998, the date the S election is made.

	Adjusted Basis	Fair Market Value
Cash	$ 200,000	$ 200,000
Accounts receivable	–0–	105,000
Equipment	110,000	100,000
Land	1,800,000	2,500,000
Accounts payable	–0–	110,000

During 1998, Alomar collects the accounts receivable and pays the accounts payable. The land is sold for $3 million, and the taxable income for the year is $590,000. Calculate any § 1374 penalty tax.

29. Lejeune, Inc., an S corporation in Boone, North Carolina, has operating revenues of $400,000, taxable interest of $380,000, operating expenses of $250,000, and deductions attributable to the interest income of $140,000. Calculate any § 1375 penalty tax payable by this S corporation or its shareholders.

30. At the end of 1998, Brew, an S corporation, has gross receipts of $190,000 and gross income of $170,000. Brew has AEP of $22,000 and taxable income of $30,000. It has passive investment income of $100,000, with $40,000 of expenses directly related to the production of passive investment income. Calculate Brew's excess net passive income and any § 1375 penalty tax.

31. At the end of the year, a calendar year S corporation has rent income of $400,000 (significant services are rendered), interest income of $200,000, and royalty income of $150,000 (the trademark was purchased). It incurred operating expenses of $250,000 and deductions attributable to the interest income and trademark of $80,000. Calculate any passive income penalty tax.

32. Savoy, Inc., in Auburn, Alabama, is an accrual basis S corporation with three equal shareholders. The three cash basis shareholders have the following stock basis at the beginning of 1998: Andre, $18,000; Crum, $22,000; and Barbara, $30,000. Savoy has the following income and expense items during 1998.

Net tax operating loss	$30,000
Short-term capital gain	37,500
Long-term capital loss	6,000
Nondeductible fees and penalties	3,000

The electing corporation distributes $5,000 cash to each of the shareholders during the tax year. Calculate the shareholders' stock bases at the end of 1998.

33. Bonnie and Clyde each own one-third of a fast-food restaurant, and their 13-year-old daughter owns the other shares. Both parents work full-time in the restaurant, but the daughter works infrequently. Neither Bonnie nor Clyde receives a salary during the year, when the taxable income of the S corporation is $180,000. An IRS agent estimates that reasonable salaries for Bonnie, Clyde, and the daughter are $30,000, $35,000, and $10,000, respectively. What adjustments would you expect the IRS to impose upon these taxpayers?

34. Friedman, Inc., an S corporation, pays for the medical care of two shareholder-employees during the current year. Yvette, owning 2% of the stock, receives $1,900 for this purpose. Jack, owning 21% of the stock, receives $3,300. Arnold Schwartz, the CFO, calls you, asking how to treat these transactions. Prepare a tax memo dated June 18, 1998, indicating what you told Arnold over the phone.

35. One of your clients is considering electing S status. Dickens, Inc., is a seven-year-old company with two equal shareholders who are in the 39.6% tax bracket. In 1997, Dickens will have an NOL carryforward of approximately $310,000. The difference between LIFO and FIFO inventory is $200,000, and the company will distribute about 50% of taxable income (before any NOL). The company's estimated income, built-in gain recognition, and 8% present value of $1 are as follows.

	Taxable Income	Built-in Gain	Present Value of $1
1998	$210,000	$50,000	0.926
1999	250,000	40,000	0.857
2000	300,000	50,000	0.794
2001	400,000	40,000	0.735
2002	600,000	30,000	0.681

a. Should the corporation elect S corporation status?
b. Would your answer change if most of the taxable income is distributed?

Research Problems for this chapter appear at the end of Chapter 28.

22

PARTNERSHIPS

LEARNING OBJECTIVES

After completing Chapter 22, you should be able to:

1. Discuss governing principles and theories of partnership taxation.

2. Describe the tax effects of forming a partnership with cash and property contributions.

3. Examine the tax treatment of expenditures of a newly formed partnership and identify elections the partnership should make.

4. Specify the methods of determining a partnership's tax year.

5. Calculate partnership taxable income and describe how partnership items affect a partner's income tax return.

6. Determine a partner's basis in the partnership interest.

7. Explain how liabilities affect a partner's basis.

8. Describe the limitations on deducting partnership losses.

9. Review the treatment of transactions between a partner and the partnership.

10. Determine the tax treatment of proportionate nonliquidating distributions from a partnership to a partner.

11. Determine the tax treatment of proportionate distributions that liquidate a partnership.

12. Calculate the selling partner's amount and character of gain or loss on the sale or exchange of a partnership interest.

13. Provide insights regarding advantageous use of a partnership.

OVERVIEW OF PARTNERSHIP TAXATION

▼

This chapter and the previous chapter analyze two types of entities that offer certain advantages over regular corporations. These entities are partnerships and S corporations, which are called *flow-through* or *pass-through* entities because the owners of the trade or business choose to avoid treating the enterprise as a separate taxable entity. Instead, the owners are taxed on a proportionate share of the entity's taxable income at the end of each of its taxable years.

A partnership may be an especially advantageous entity form in many cases. A partnership is subject to only a single level of taxation, whereas C corporation income is subject to *double taxation*. Corporate income is taxed at the entity level, currently at rates up to 35 percent. Any after-tax income that is distributed to corporate owners is taxed again as a dividend at the owner level. Though partnership income may be subject to high individual rates (currently up to 39.6 percent), the resulting tax will likely be lower than a combined corporate-level tax and a second tax on a dividend distribution.

In addition, administrative and filing requirements are relatively simple for a partnership, and it offers certain planning opportunities not available to other entity forms. Both C and S corporations are subject to rigorous allocation and distribution requirements (generally, each allocation or distribution is proportionate to the ownership interest of the shareholder). A partnership, though, may adjust its allocations of income and cash flow among the partners each year according to their needs, as long as certain standards (discussed later in this chapter) are met. Also, any previously unrealized income (such as appreciation of corporate assets) of an

---

TAX IN THE NEWS

PARTNERSHIPS IN THE MOVIES

As movies have become more expensive to produce, many production studios have turned to limited partnerships as a lucrative source of investment capital. For example, the Walt Disney Company has sold limited partnership interests in Silver Screen Partnerships I, II, III, and IV and in Touchwood Pacific Partners I, L.P. Other studios have formed similar production partnerships.

In most cases, the sponsoring studio injects capital for a small (1–5 percent) general partnership interest, and the investors contribute the remaining capital—hundreds of millions of dollars or more. The partnership agreement spells out the number and types of films the partnership intends to produce and provides a formula for allocating cash flows to the partners. Often the partnership agreement includes various benefits for the general partner (studio), such as a preferred allocation of cash flows (the first $1 million per year, for example), distribution fees for marketing the movies, and/or reimbursement of specified amounts of corporate overhead. Any cash remaining after these expenses is allocated under a fixed formula between the general and limited partners (for example, the limited partners may receive 90 percent of remaining cash flows).

Think about bank financing in comparison, and you will see why the studio finds partnerships so appealing: How many banks would allow the general partner to receive reimbursements and allocations before debt principal and interest are paid?

This capital-raising technique has proved so advantageous to the studios that some related industries, such as movie lighting contractors and special effects companies, have also used limited partnerships to raise capital. The next time you go to a movie, watch the credits at the end and think about the tremendous number of people who invested cash in the movie hoping for a blockbuster!

S or C corporation is taxed at the entity level when the corporation liquidates, but a partnership generally may liquidate tax-free. Finally, many states impose reporting and licensing requirements on corporate entities, including S corporations. These include franchise or capital stock tax returns that may require annual assessments and costly professional preparation assistance. Partnerships, on the other hand, often have no reporting requirements beyond Federal and state informational tax returns.

For smaller business operations, a partnership enables several owners to combine their resources at low cost. It also offers simple filing requirements, the taxation of income only once, and the ability to discontinue operations relatively inexpensively.

For larger business operations, a partnership offers a unique ability to raise capital with low filing and reporting costs (compared to corporate bond issuances, for example). Special allocations of income and cash-flow items are available in all partnerships to meet the objectives of the owners.

Since partnerships and S corporations are so widespread, a study of related tax problems will prove useful to students, business owners, and consultants. This chapter addresses partnership formations, operations, and nonliquidating distributions, and, in addition, sales of partnership interests and partnership liquidating distributions. Concept Summary 22–6 (beginning on page 22–52) provides a comparative analysis of the forms through which a business can be conducted.

WHAT IS A PARTNERSHIP?

A partnership is an association of two or more persons to carry on a trade or business, with each contributing money, property, labor, or skill, and with all expecting to share in profits and losses.[1] For Federal income tax purposes, a partnership includes a syndicate, group, pool, joint venture, or other unincorporated organization through which any business, financial operation, or venture is carried on. The entity must not be otherwise classified as a corporation, trust, or estate.

The four types of entities that are taxed as partnerships are general partnerships, limited liability partnerships, limited partnerships, and limited liability companies. A partnership that conducts a service business, such as accounting, law, or medicine, is usually established as either a **general partnership** or a **limited liability partnership (LLP).** A general partnership consists of one or more general partners. Creditors of a general partnership can collect amounts owed them from both the partnership assets and the personal assets of the owner-partners. A general partner can be bankrupted by a malpractice judgment brought against the partnership, even though the partner was not personally involved in the malpractice.

An LLP is a recently created form of entity. Owners of an LLP are also general partners. The primary difference between an LLP and a general partnership is that an LLP partner is not liable for any malpractice committed by the other partners. The LLP is currently the operational form of choice for the large accounting firms.

A **limited partnership** is often used for acquiring capital in activities such as real estate development. A limited partnership is comprised of at least one general partner and often many limited partners. Typically, only the general partners are liable to creditors; each limited partner's risk of loss is restricted to his or her equity investment in the entity.

An alternative entity form, the **limited liability company (LLC),** is now permitted to operate in all states and the District of Columbia. An LLC combines the corporate benefit of limited liability of owners with the benefits of partnership taxation, including the single level of tax and special allocations of income, losses, and cash flows. Owners are technically considered to be "members" rather than partners, but a properly structured LLC is treated as a partnership for all tax purposes. Almost all states permit capital-intensive companies as well as nonprofessional service-oriented businesses and some professional service-providing companies to operate as LLCs. This is highly advantageous to a business entity since the LLC can protect each member's personal assets from being exposed to the entity's debts.

ELECTIONS RELATED TO PARTNERSHIP STATUS

The IRS's "check-the-box" Regulations allow most unincorporated business entities—such as general partnerships, limited partnerships, LLPs, and LLCs—to select their Federal tax status.[2] If an entity has two or more owners, it can choose to be taxed as either a partnership or as a C corporation. This provides the entity with flexibility regarding its Federal tax classification. The Regulations, however, do not permit all unincorporated business or investment entities to choose their tax status. Newly formed publicly traded partnerships, for example, must be taxed as corporations.

A few entities that would otherwise be classified as partnerships may be excluded from the partnership taxation rules if used for the following purposes:

- Investment (rather than the active conduct of a trade or business).

---

[1] § 7701(a)(2).

[2] Reg. §§ 301.7701–1 to 301.7701–3.

- Joint production, extraction, or use of property.
- Underwriting, selling, or distributing a specific security issue.[3]

Such entities are simply disregarded for Federal tax purposes, and their operations must be reported directly on the owners' tax returns.

PARTNERSHIP TAXATION

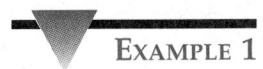
LEARNING OBJECTIVE
Discuss governing principles and theories of partnership taxation.

A partnership is not a taxable entity.[4] Rather, the taxable income or loss of the partnership flows through to the partners at the end of the entity's tax year.[5] Partners report their allocable share of the partnership's income or loss for the year on their tax returns. As a result, the partnership itself pays no Federal income tax on its income; instead, the partners' individual tax liabilities are affected by the activities of the entity.

EXAMPLE 1

Adam is a 40% partner in the ABC Partnership. Both Adam's and the partnership's tax years end on December 31. In 1998, the partnership generates $200,000 of ordinary taxable income. However, because the partnership needs capital for expansion and debt reduction, Adam makes no cash withdrawals during 1998. He meets his living expenses by reducing his investment portfolio. Adam is taxed on his $80,000 allocable share of the partnership's 1998 income, even though he receives no distributions from the entity during 1998. This allocated income is included in Adam's gross income. ▼

EXAMPLE 2

Assume the same facts as in Example 1, except the partnership recognizes a 1998 taxable loss of $100,000. Adam's 1998 AGI is reduced by $40,000 because his proportionate share of the loss flows through to him from the partnership. He claims a $40,000 partnership loss for the year. (Note: Loss limitation rules discussed later in the chapter may result in some or all of this loss being deferred to a later year.) ▼

Many items of partnership income, expense, gain, or loss retain their identity as they flow through to the partners. Each **separately stated item** is an item that *might* affect any two partners' tax liabilities in different ways. When preparing a personal tax return, a partner takes each of these items into account separately.[6] Charitable contributions are separately stated because partners need to compute their own personal limitation on charitable contributions. Some partners are able to deduct the entire amount they are allocated. Others are limited in what they can deduct by the amount of their adjusted gross income.

EXAMPLE 3

Beth is a 25% partner in the BR Partnership. The cash basis entity collected sales income of $60,000 during 1998 and incurred $15,000 in business expenses. In addition, it sold a corporate bond for a $9,000 long-term capital gain. Finally, the partnership made a $1,000 contribution to the local Performing Arts Fund drive. The fund is a qualifying charity. BR and all of its partners use a calendar tax year.

For 1998, Beth is allocated ordinary taxable income of $11,250 [($60,000 − $15,000) × 25%] from the partnership. She also is allocated a flow-through of a $2,250 long-term capital gain and a $250 charitable contribution deduction. The ordinary income increases Beth's gross income, and the capital gain and charitable contribution are combined with her other similar activities for the year as though she had incurred them herself. The capital gain and charitable contribution could be treated differently on the tax returns of the various partners (e.g., because a partner may be subject to a percentage limitation

---

[3]§ 761(a).
[4]§ 701.

[5]§ 702.
[6]§ 703(a)(1).

on charitable contribution deductions for 1998), so they are not included in the computation of ordinary partnership income. Instead, the items flow through to the partners separately. ▼

The number of items that are separately reported to the partners varies and depends upon whether the partnership is an **electing large partnership.** A partnership qualifies as a large partnership if it had at least 100 partners during its immediately preceding taxable year and elects simplified reporting of its taxable items. Such partnerships separately report no more than 11 different categories of items to their partners. This means that many items are netted at the partnership level. An example of one of these items is capital gain or loss. An electing large partnership nets all long-term, mid-term, and short-term capital gains and losses at the partnership level and reports to each partner only that partner's share of the partnership's net capital gain (loss). The netting of items at the partnership level makes each partner's tax return easier to complete. Unless otherwise indicated, in this chapter assume that the partnership is *not* an electing large partnership.

As most partnerships are not electing large partnerships, they separately report more than 11 categories of items. The only pass-through items that are netted at the partnership level are the ordinary income and expenses related to the partnership's trade or business activities. These ordinary income and expense items are netted to produce a single income or loss amount that is passed through to the partners. All other partnership items are separately stated. For example, net long-term, mid-term, and short-term capital gains (losses) are determined at the partnership level and reported separately to the partners.

Other items that are allocated separately to the partners include recognized gains and losses from property transactions; dividend income; tax preferences and adjustments for the alternative minimum tax; expenditures that qualify for the foreign tax credit; and expenditures the partners would treat as itemized deductions.[7]

PARTNERSHIP REPORTING

Even though it is not a taxpaying entity, a partnership must file an information tax return, Form 1065. Look at Form 1065 in Appendix B, and refer to it during the following discussion. The partnership reports the results of its trade or business activities (ordinary income or loss) on Form 1065, page 1. Schedule K (page 3 of Form 1065) accumulates all items that must be separately reported to the partners, including net trade or business income or loss (from page 1). The amounts on Schedule K are allocated to all the partners. Each partner receives a Schedule K–1, which shows that partner's share of partnership items.

EXAMPLE 4

The BR Partnership in Example 3 reports its $60,000 sales income on Form 1065, page 1, line 1. The $15,000 of business expenses are reported in the appropriate amounts on page 1, line 2 or lines 9–20. Partnership ordinary income of $45,000 is shown on page 1, line 22, and on Schedule K, line 1. The $9,000 net long-term capital gain and the $1,000 charitable contribution are reported only on Schedule K, on lines 4e and 8, respectively.

Beth receives a Schedule K–1 from the partnership that shows her shares of partnership ordinary income of $11,250, long-term capital gain of $2,250, and charitable contributions of $250 on lines 1, 4e, and 8, respectively. She then combines these amounts with similar items from sources other than BR on her personal tax return. For example, if she has a $5,000 long-term capital loss from a stock transaction in 1998, her overall net capital loss is

---

[7] § 702(a).

$2,750 ($2,250 – $5,000). She evaluates this net amount to determine the amount she may deduct on her Form 1040. ▼

As this example shows, one must look at both page 1 and Schedule K to get complete information regarding a partnership's operations for the year. Schedule K accumulates all partnership tax items and arrives at a total amount on line 25a. Schedule M–1, page 4, reconciles accounting income with this total of partnership tax items on Schedule K (line 25a). Schedule L generally shows an accounting-basis balance sheet, and Schedule M–2 reconciles beginning and ending partners' capital accounts.

PARTNER'S OWNERSHIP INTEREST IN A PARTNERSHIP

Each partner typically owns both a **capital interest** and a **profits (loss) interest** in the partnership. A capital interest is measured by a partner's **capital sharing ratio,** which is the partner's percentage ownership of the capital of the partnership. A partner's capital interest can be determined in several ways. The most widely accepted method measures the capital interest as the percentage of net assets (assets remaining after payment of all partnership liabilities) a partner would receive on immediate liquidation of the partnership.

A profits (loss) interest is simply the partner's percentage allocation of current partnership operating results. **Profit and loss sharing ratios** are usually specified in the partnership agreement and are used to determine each partner's allocation of partnership ordinary taxable income and separately stated items.[8] The partnership can change its profit and loss allocations at any time simply by amending the partnership agreement.

Each partner's profit, loss, and capital sharing ratios may appear on the partner's Schedule K–1. In many cases, the three ratios are the same. A partner's capital sharing ratio generally equals the profit and loss sharing ratios if all profit and loss allocations, for each year of the partnership's existence, are in the same proportion as the partner's initial contributions to the partnership.

The partnership agreement may, in some cases, provide for a **special allocation** of certain items to specified partners, or it may allocate items in a different proportion from general profit and loss sharing ratios. These items are separately reported to the partner receiving the allocation. To be recognized for tax purposes, a special allocation must produce nontax economic consequences for the partners receiving it.[9]

EXAMPLE 5

When the George-Helen Partnership was formed, George contributed cash, and Helen contributed some City of Iuka bonds that she had held for investment purposes. The partnership agreement allocates all of the tax-exempt interest income from the bonds to Helen as an inducement for her to remain a partner. This is an acceptable special allocation for income tax purposes; it reflects the differing economic circumstances that underlie the partners' contributions to the capital of the entity. Since Helen would have received the exempt income if she had not joined the partnership, she can retain the tax-favored treatment via the special allocation. ▼

EXAMPLE 6

Assume the same facts as in Example 5. Three years after it was formed, the George-Helen Partnership purchased some City of Butte bonds. The municipal bond interest income of $15,000 flows through to the partners as a separately stated item, so that it retains its tax-exempt status. The partnership agreement allocates all of this income to George because

---

[8] § 704(a).   [9] § 704(b).

he is subject to a higher marginal income tax bracket than is Helen. The partnership also allocates $15,000 more of the partnership taxable income to Helen than to George. These allocations are not effective for income tax purposes because they have no purpose other than the reduction of the partners' combined income tax liability. ▼

A partner has a **basis in the partnership interest.** When income flows through to a partner from the partnership, the partner's basis in the partnership interest increases accordingly. When a loss flows through to a partner, basis is reduced.

EXAMPLE 7

Paul contributes $20,000 cash to acquire a 30% capital and profits interest in the Red Robin Partnership. In its first year of operations, the partnership earns ordinary income of $40,000 and makes no distributions to Paul. Paul's initial basis is the $20,000 he paid for the interest. He reports ordinary income of $12,000 (30% × $40,000 partnership income) on his individual return and increases his basis by the same amount, to $32,000. ▼

In allowing increases and decreases in a partner's basis in a partnership interest, the Code ensures that only one level of tax arises on the income or loss from partnership operations. In Example 7, if Paul sold his interest at the end of the first year for $32,000, he would have no gain or loss. If the Code did not provide for an adjustment of a partner's basis, Paul's basis would be $20,000, and he would be taxed on the gain of $12,000 in addition to being taxed on his $12,000 share of income. In other words, without the basis adjustment, partnership income would be subject to double taxation.

As the following sections discuss in detail, a partner's basis is important for determining the treatment of distributions from the partnership to the partner, establishing the deductibility of partnership losses, and calculating gain or loss on the partner's disposition of the partnership interest.

A partner's basis is not reflected anywhere on the Schedule K–1. Instead, each partner should maintain a personal record of adjustments to basis. Schedule K–1 does reconcile a partner's **capital account,** but the ending capital account balance is rarely the same amount as the partner's basis. Just as the tax and accounting bases of a specific asset may differ, a partner's capital account and basis in the partnership interest may not be equal for a variety of reasons. For example, a partner's basis also includes the partner's share of partnership liabilities. These liabilities are not reported as part of the partner's capital account but are included in question F at the top of the partner's Schedule K–1.

CONCEPTUAL BASIS FOR PARTNERSHIP TAXATION

The unique tax treatment of partners and partnerships can be traced to two legal concepts that evolved long ago: the **aggregate** (or conduit) **concept** and the **entity concept.** These concepts influence practically every partnership tax rule.

Aggregate (or Conduit) Concept. The aggregate (or conduit) concept treats the partnership as a channel through which income, credits, deductions, and the like flow to the partners. Under this concept, the partnership is regarded as a collection of taxpayers joined in an agency relationship with one another. The imposition of the income tax on individual partners reflects the influence of this doctrine. The aggregate concept has influenced the tax treatment of other pass-through entities, such as S corporations (Chapter 21) and trusts and estates (Chapter 27).

Entity Concept. The entity concept treats partners and partnerships as separate units and gives the partnership its own tax "personality" by (1) requiring a partnership to file an information tax return and (2) treating partners as separate and distinct from the partnership in certain transactions between a partner and the entity. A partner's recognition of capital gain or loss on the sale of the partnership interest further illustrates this doctrine.

Combined Concepts. Some rules such as the various provisions governing the formation, operation, and liquidation of a partnership contain a blend of both the entity and aggregate concepts.

ANTI–ABUSE PROVISIONS

As described in this chapter, partnership taxation is often flexible. For example, partnership operating income or losses can sometimes be shifted among partners, and partnership property gains and losses can sometimes be shifted from one partner to another. The Code contains many provisions designed to thwart unwarranted allocations, but the IRS believes opportunities for tax avoidance still abound. The IRS has adopted Regulations that will allow it to recharacterize transactions that it considers to be "abusive."[10]

FORMATION OF A PARTNERSHIP: TAX EFFECTS

GAIN OR LOSS ON CONTRIBUTIONS TO THE PARTNERSHIP

2 LEARNING OBJECTIVE
Describe the tax effects of forming a partnership with cash and property contributions.

When a taxpayer transfers property to an entity in exchange for valuable consideration, a taxable exchange normally results. Typically, both the taxpayer and the entity realize and recognize gain or loss on the exchange.[11] The gain or loss recognized by the transferor is the difference between the fair market value of the consideration received and the adjusted basis of the property transferred.[12]

In most situations, however, neither the partner nor the partnership recognizes the realized gain or loss when a partner contributes property to a partnership in exchange for a partnership interest. Instead, the realized gain or loss is deferred.[13]

There are two reasons for this nonrecognition treatment. First, forming a partnership allows investors to combine their assets toward greater economic goals than could be achieved separately. Only the form of ownership, rather than the amount owned by each investor, has changed. Requiring that gain be recognized on such transfers would make the formation of some partnerships economically unfeasible (e.g., two existing proprietorships are combined to form one larger business). Congress does not want to hinder the creation of valid economic partnerships by requiring gain recognition when a partnership is created. Second, because the partnership interest received is typically not a liquid asset, the partner may not be able to find the cash to pay the tax. Thus, deferral of the gain recognizes the economic realities of the business world and follows the wherewithal to pay principle of taxation.

EXAMPLE 8

Alicia transfers two assets to the Wren Partnership on the day the entity is created, in exchange for a 60% profit and loss interest (worth $60,000). She contributes cash of $40,000 and retail display equipment (basis to her as a sole proprietor, $8,000; fair market value,

---

[10]Reg. § 1.701–2.
[11]§ 1001(c).

[12]§ 1001(a).
[13]§ 721.

$20,000). Since an exchange has occurred between two parties, Alicia *realizes* a $12,000 gain on this transaction. The gain realized is the fair market value of the partnership interest of $60,000 less the basis of the assets that she surrendered to the partnership [$40,000 (cash) + $8,000 (equipment)].

Under § 721, Alicia *does not recognize* the $12,000 realized gain in the year of contribution. Alicia might not have sufficient cash to pay tax on the $12,000 gain. All that she received from the partnership was an illiquid partnership interest; she received no cash with which to pay any resulting tax liability. ▼

EXAMPLE 9

Assume the same facts as in Example 8, except that the equipment Alicia contributes to the partnership has an adjusted basis of $25,000. She has a $5,000 *realized* loss [$60,000 – ($40,000 + $25,000)], but she cannot deduct the loss. Realized losses, as well as realized gains, are deferred by § 721.

Unless it is essential that the partnership receive Alicia's display equipment rather than similar equipment purchased from an outside supplier, Alicia should have considered selling the equipment to a third party. This would allow her to deduct a $5,000 loss in the year of the sale. Alicia could then contribute $60,000 cash (including the proceeds from the sale) for her interest in the partnership, and the partnership would have funds to purchase similar equipment. ▼

EXAMPLE 10

Five years after the Wren Partnership (Examples 8 and 9) was created, Alicia contributes another piece of equipment to the entity from her sole proprietorship. This property has a basis of $35,000 and a fair market value of $50,000. Alicia can defer the recognition of the $15,000 realized gain. Section 721 is effective whenever a partner makes a contribution to the capital of the partnership. ▼

If a partner contributes only capital and § 1231 assets, the partner's holding period in the partnership interest is the same as that partner's holding period for these assets. If assets that are not capital or § 1231 assets (including cash) are contributed, the holding period in the partnership interest begins on the date the partnership interest is acquired. If multiple assets are contributed, the partnership interest is apportioned, and a separate holding period applies to each portion.

EXCEPTIONS TO § 721

The nonrecognition provisions of § 721 do not apply in the following situations:

- When appreciated stocks and securities are contributed to an investment partnership.
- When the transaction is essentially a taxable exchange of properties.
- When the transaction is a disguised sale of properties.
- When the partnership interest is received in exchange for services rendered to the partnership by the partner.

Investment Partnership. If the transfer consists of appreciated stocks and securities and the partnership is an investment partnership, it is likely that the realized gain on the stocks and securities will be recognized by the contributing partner at the time of contribution.[14] This provision prevents multiple investors from using the partnership form to diversify their investment portfolios on a tax-free basis.

---

[14]§ 721(b).

Exchange. If a transaction is essentially a taxable exchange of properties, the tax is not deferred under the nonrecognition provisions of § 721.[15]

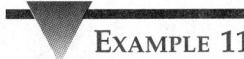

EXAMPLE 11

Sara owns land, and Bob owns stock. Sara would like to have Bob's stock, and Bob wants Sara's land. If Sara and Bob both contribute their property to newly formed SB Partnership in exchange for interests in the partnership, the tax on the transaction appears to be deferred under § 721. If the partnership then distributes the land to Bob and the stock to Sara, the tax on this transaction also appears to be deferred under § 731 (discussed later in the chapter). According to a literal interpretation of the statutes, no taxable exchange has occurred. Sara and Bob will find, however, that this type of tax subterfuge is not permitted. The IRS will disregard the passage of the properties through the partnership and will hold, instead, that Sara and Bob exchanged the land and stock directly. Thus, the transactions will be treated as any other taxable exchange. ▼

Disguised Sale. A similar result occurs in a **disguised sale** of properties. A disguised sale may occur where a partner contributes property to a partnership and soon thereafter receives a distribution from the partnership. This distribution may be viewed as a payment by the partnership for purchase of the property.[16]

EXAMPLE 12

Kim transfers property to the KLM Partnership. The property has an adjusted basis of $10,000 and a fair market value of $30,000. Two weeks later, the partnership makes a distribution of $30,000 cash to Kim. Under the distribution rules of § 731, the distribution would not be taxable to Kim if the basis of her partnership interest prior to the distribution was greater than the $30,000 cash distributed. However, the transaction appears to be a disguised purchase-sale transaction, rather than a contribution and distribution. Therefore, Kim must recognize gain of $20,000 on transfer of the property, and the partnership is deemed to have purchased the property for $30,000. ▼

Services. A final exception to the nonrecognition provision of § 721 occurs when a partner receives an interest in the partnership as compensation for services rendered to the partnership. This is not a tax-deferred transaction because services are not treated as "property" that can be transferred to a partnership on a tax-free basis. Instead, the partner performing the services recognizes ordinary compensation income equal to the fair market value of the partnership interest received.[17]

The partnership may deduct the amount included in the service partner's income if the services are of a deductible nature. If the services are not deductible to the partnership, they must be capitalized to an asset account. For example, architectural plans created by a partner are capitalized to the structure built with those plans. Alternatively, day-to-day management services performed by a partner for the partnership are usually deductible by the partnership.

EXAMPLE 13

Bill, Carl, and Dave form the BCD Partnership, with each receiving a one-third interest in the entity. Dave receives his one-third interest as compensation for the accounting and tax planning services he renders during the formation of the partnership. The value of a one-third interest in the partnership (for each of the parties) is $20,000. Dave recognizes $20,000 of compensation income, and he has a $20,000 basis in his partnership interest. The same result would occur if the partnership had paid Dave $20,000 for his services and he immediately contributed that amount to the entity for a one-third ownership interest. ▼

---

[15]Reg. § 1.731–1(c)(3).
[16]§ 707(a)(2)(B).

[17]§ 83(a).

TAX ISSUES RELATIVE TO CONTRIBUTED PROPERTY

When a partner makes a tax-deferred contribution of an asset to the capital of a partnership, the tax law assigns a carryover basis to the property.[18] The entity's basis in the asset is equal to the basis the partner held in the property prior to its transfer to the partnership. The partner's basis in the new partnership interest equals his prior basis in the contributed asset. The tax term for this basis concept is substituted basis. Thus, two assets are created out of one when a partnership is formed, namely, the property in the hands of the new entity and the new asset (the partnership interest) in the hands of the partner. Both assets are assigned a basis that is derived from the partner's existing basis in the contributed property.

These rules are logical in view of what Congress was attempting to accomplish in this deferral transaction. As noted earlier, gain or loss is deferred when property is contributed to a partnership in exchange for a partnership interest. The deferral is implemented by calculating the partnership's basis in the transferred property and the partner's basis for the partnership interest. The bases are the amounts necessary to allow for recognition of the deferred gain or loss if the property or the partnership interest is subsequently disposed of in a taxable transaction. This treatment is similar to the treatment of assets transferred to a controlled corporation[19] and the treatment of like-kind exchanges.[20]

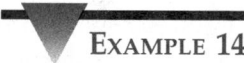

EXAMPLE 14

On June 1, 1998, Luis transfers property to the JKL Partnership in exchange for a one-third interest in the partnership. The property has an adjusted basis to Luis of $10,000 and a fair market value on June 1 of $30,000. Luis's realized gain on the exchange is $20,000 ($30,000 – $10,000), but under § 721, none of the gain is recognized. Luis's basis for his partnership interest is the amount necessary to recognize the $20,000 deferred gain if he subsequently sells the interest for its $30,000 fair market value. This amount, $10,000, is referred to as a substituted basis. The basis of the property contributed to the partnership is the amount necessary to allow for the recognition of the $20,000 deferred gain if the property is subsequently sold for its $30,000 fair market value. This amount, also $10,000, is referred to as a carryover basis. ▼

The holding period for the contributed asset also carries over to the partnership. Thus, the partnership's holding period for the asset includes the period during which the partner owned the asset individually.

Depreciation Method and Period.   If depreciable property is contributed to the partnership, the partnership is usually required to use the same cost recovery method and life used by the partner. The partnership merely "steps into the shoes" of the partner and continues the same cost recovery calculations. If the property is not MACRS or ACRS property, the partnership must treat the property as used property for depreciation purposes. The partnership may not immediately expense any part of the basis of depreciable property it receives from the transferor partner under § 179.

Receivables, Inventory, and Losses.   To prevent the conversion of ordinary income into capital gain, gain or loss is treated as ordinary when the partnership disposes of either of the following:[21]

---

[18]§ 723.
[19]§ 351.
[20]§ 1031.

[21]§ 724. For this purpose, § 724(d)(2) waives the holding period requirement in defining § 1231 property.

- Contributed receivables that were unrealized in the contributing partner's hands at the contribution date. Such receivables include the right to receive payment for goods or services delivered (or to be delivered).
- Contributed property that was inventory in the contributor's hands on the contribution date, if the partnership disposes of the property within *five years of the contribution*. For this purpose inventory includes all property except capital assets and real or depreciable business assets.

EXAMPLE 15

Tyrone operates a cash basis retail electronics and television store as a sole proprietor. Ramon is an enterprising individual who likes to invest in small businesses. On January 2 of the current year, Tyrone and Ramon form the TR Partnership. Their partnership contributions are as follows:

	Adjusted Basis	Fair Market Value
From Tyrone:		
Receivables	$ –0–	$ 2,000
Land used as parking lot*	1,200	5,000
Inventory	2,500	5,000
From Ramon:		
Cash	12,000	12,000

*The parking lot had been held for nine months at the contribution date.

Within 30 days of formation, TR collects the receivables and sells the inventory for $5,000 cash. It uses the land for the next 10 months as a parking lot, then sells it for $3,500 cash. TR realizes the following income in the current year from these transactions:

- Ordinary income of $2,000 from collecting the receivables.
- Ordinary income of $2,500 from the sale of inventory.
- Section 1231 gain of $2,300 from the sale of land.

Since the land takes a carryover holding period, it is treated as having been held 19 months at the sale date. ▼

A similar rule is designed to prevent a capital loss from being converted into an ordinary loss. Under the rule, if contributed property is disposed of at a loss and the property had a "built-in" capital loss to the contributing partner at the contribution date, the loss is treated as a capital loss if the partnership disposes of the property *within five years of the contribution*. The capital loss is limited to the "built-in" loss on the date of contribution.

EXAMPLE 16

Assume the same facts as Example 15, except for the following:

- Tyrone held the land he contributed for investment purposes. It had a fair market value of $800 at the contribution date.
- TR used the land as a parking lot for 10 months and sold it for $650.

TR realizes the following income and loss from these transactions:

- Ordinary income of $2,000 from collecting the receivables.
- Ordinary income of $2,500 from the sale of inventory.
- Capital loss of $400 from the sale of land ($1,200 – $800).
- Section 1231 loss of $150 from the sale of land ($800 – $650).

CONCEPT SUMMARY 22–1

Partnership Formation and Basis Computation

1. The *entity concept* treats partners and partnerships as separate units. The nature and amount of gains and losses are determined at the partnership level.
2. The *aggregate concept* is used to connect partners and partnerships. It allows income, gains, losses, credits, deductions, etc., to flow through to the partners for separate tax reporting.
3. Sometimes both the *aggregate* and the *entity* concepts apply, but one usually dominates.
4. Generally, partners or partnerships do not recognize gain or loss when property is contributed for capital interests.
5. Partners contributing property for partnership interests take the contributed property's adjusted basis for their *outside basis* in their partnership interest. The partners are said to take a substituted basis in their partnership interest.
6. The partnership will continue to use the contributing partner's basis for the *inside basis* in property it receives. The contributed property is said to take a carryover basis.
7. The holding period of a partner's interest includes that of contributed property when the property was a § 1231 asset or capital asset in the partner's hands. Otherwise, the holding period starts on the day the interest is acquired. The holding period of an interest acquired by a cash contribution starts at acquisition.
8. The partnership's holding period for contributed property includes the contributing partner's holding period.

Since the land was sold within five years of the contribution date, the $400 built-in loss is a capital loss. The post-contribution loss of $150 is a § 1231 loss since TR used the property in its business. ▼

INSIDE AND OUTSIDE BASES

Throughout this chapter, reference is made to the partnership's inside basis and a partner's outside basis. **Inside basis** refers to the adjusted basis of each *partnership asset*, as determined from the partnership's tax accounts. **Outside basis** represents each partner's basis in the partnership interest. Each partner "owns" a share of the partnership's inside basis for all its assets and should maintain a record of the outside basis.

In many cases—especially on formation of the partnership—the total of all the partners' outside bases equals the partnership's inside bases for all its assets. Differences between inside and outside basis arise when a partner's interest is sold to another person for more or less than the selling partner's share of the inside basis of partnership assets. The buying partner's outside basis equals the price paid for the interest, but the buyer's share of the partnership's inside basis is the same amount as the seller's share of the inside basis.

Concept Summary 22–1 reviews the rules that apply to partnership asset contributions and basis adjustments.

TAX ACCOUNTING ELECTIONS

A newly formed partnership must make numerous tax accounting elections. These elections are formal decisions on how a particular transaction or tax attribute should be handled. Most of these elections must be made by the partnership rather than by the partners individually.[22] The *partnership* makes the elections for the following items:

---
[22]§ 703(b).

- Inventory method.
- Cost or percentage depletion method, excluding oil and gas wells.
- Accounting method (cash, accrual, or hybrid).
- Cost recovery methods and assumptions.
- Tax year.
- Amortization of organizational costs and amortization period.
- Amortization of start-up expenditures and amortization period.
- Section 179 deductions for certain tangible personal property.
- Nonrecognition treatment for involuntary conversions gains.

Each partner is bound by the decisions made by the partnership relative to the elections. If the partnership fails to make an election, a partner cannot compensate for the error by making the election individually.

Though most elections are made by the partnership, each *partner* individually is required to make a specific election on the following relatively narrow tax issues:

- Whether to reduce the basis of depreciable property when first excluding income from discharge of indebtedness.
- Whether to claim cost or percentage depletion for oil and gas wells.
- Whether to take a deduction or credit for taxes paid to foreign countries and U.S. possessions.

INITIAL COSTS OF A PARTNERSHIP

3 **LEARNING OBJECTIVE**
Examine the tax treatment of expenditures of a newly formed partnership and identify elections the partnership should make.

In its initial stages, a partnership incurs expenses relating to some or all of the following: forming the partnership (organization costs), admitting partners to the partnership, marketing and selling partnership units to prospective partners (syndication costs), acquiring assets, starting business operations (start-up costs), negotiating contracts, and other items. Many of these expenditures are not currently deductible. However, the Code permits a ratable amortization of "organization" and "start-up" costs; acquisition costs for depreciable assets are included in the initial basis of the acquired assets; and costs related to some intangible assets may be amortized. "Syndication costs" may be neither amortized nor deducted.

Organization Costs. The partnership may elect to amortize organization costs ratably over a period of 60 months or more, starting with the month in which it began business.[23] The election must be made by the due date (including extensions) of the partnership return for the year it began business.

Organization costs include expenditures that are (1) incident to the creation of the partnership; (2) chargeable to a capital account; and (3) of a character that, if incident to the creation of a partnership with an ascertainable life, would be amortized over that life. These expenditures include accounting fees and legal fees incident to the partnership's formation. To be amortizable, the expenditures must be incurred within a period that starts a reasonable time before the partnership begins business. The period ends with the due date (without extensions) of the tax return for the initial tax year.

Cash method partnerships are not allowed to deduct *in the year incurred* the portion of organization costs that are paid after the end of the first year. The partnership can deduct, in the year of payment, the portion of the expenditures that would have been deductible in a prior year, if they had been paid before that year's end.

---

[23]§ 709.

EXAMPLE 17

The calendar year Bluejay Partnership is formed on May 1 of the current year and immediately starts business. Bluejay incurs $720 in legal fees for drafting the partnership agreement and $480 in accounting fees for tax advice of an organizational nature. The legal fees are paid in October of the current year. The accounting fees are paid in January of the following year. The partnership selects the cash method of accounting and elects to amortize its organization costs.

On its first tax return, Bluejay deducts $96 of organization costs [($720 legal fees/60 months) × 8 months]. No deduction is taken for the accounting fees since the partnership selected the cash method and the fees were paid the following year. On its tax return for next year, Bluejay deducts organization costs of $304 {[($720 legal fees/60 months) × 12 months] + [($480 accounting fees/60 months) × 20 months]}. Note that the second-year deduction ($304) includes the $64 of accounting fees [($480/60) × 8] that could have been deducted on Bluejay's first tax return if they had been paid by the end of that year. ▼

Costs incurred for the following items are not organization costs:

- Acquiring assets for the partnership.
- Transferring assets to the partnership.
- Admitting partners, other than at formation.
- Removing partners, other than at formation.
- Negotiating operating contracts.
- Syndication costs.

Start-up Costs.   Operating costs that are incurred after the entity is formed but before it begins business may not be deducted. Instead, these costs are capitalized. If so elected, they may be amortized over a period of 60 months or more, starting with the month in which the partnership begins business.[24] Such costs include marketing surveys prior to conducting business, pre-operating advertising expenses, costs of establishing an accounting system, and salaries paid to executives and employees before the start of business.

Acquisition Costs of Depreciable Assets.   Certain expenses may be incurred in changing the legal title in which certain assets are held from that of the contributing partner to the partnership name. These costs include legal fees for transferring assets or transfer taxes imposed by some states. Such costs are added to the basis of the assets in the hands of the partnership and are included in the basis the partnership may depreciate.

Syndication Costs.   **Syndication costs** are capitalized, but no amortization election is available. Syndication costs include the following expenditures incurred for promoting and marketing partnership interests:

- Brokerage fees.
- Registration fees.
- Legal fees paid for security advice or advice on the adequacy of tax disclosures in the prospectus or placement memo for securities law purposes.
- Accounting fees related to offering materials.
- Printing costs of prospectus, placement memos, and other selling materials.

---

[24] § 195.

METHOD OF ACCOUNTING

A newly formed partnership may adopt the cash or accrual method of accounting, or a hybrid of these two methods.

The cash method of accounting may not be adopted, however, by a partnership that

- has one or more C corporation partners or
- is a tax shelter.

A C corporation partner does *not* preclude cash basis treatment if

- the partnership meets the $5 million gross receipts test described below,
- the C corporation partner(s) is a qualified personal service corporation, such as an incorporated attorney, or
- the partnership is engaged in the business of farming.

A partnership meets the $5 million gross receipts test if it has not, during any year after 1985, received average annual gross receipts of more than $5 million. "Average annual gross receipts" is the average of gross receipts for the three tax years ending with the tax period in question. For new partnerships, the period of existence is used. Gross receipts are annualized for short taxable periods. A partnership must change to the accrual method the first year in which its average annual gross receipts exceed $5 million and must use the accrual method thereafter.

A tax shelter is a partnership whose interests have been sold in a registered offering or a partnership in which 35 percent of the losses are allocated to limited partners.

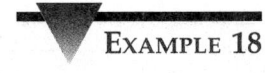

EXAMPLE 18

Jason and Julia are both attorneys. In 1995, each of them formed a professional personal service corporation to operate their separate law practices. In 1998, the two attorneys decided to form the JJ Partnership, which consists of the two professional corporations. In 1998, JJ's gross receipts are $6 million. JJ may adopt the cash method of accounting, since it is a partnership consisting of qualified personal service corporations. Because JJ has no C corporation partners that are not personal service corporations, the cash method is available even though JJ's average annual gross receipts are greater than $5 million. JJ may also adopt the accrual method of accounting or a hybrid of the cash and accrual methods. ▼

TAXABLE YEAR OF THE PARTNERSHIP

4 **LEARNING OBJECTIVE**
Specify the methods of determining a partnership's tax year.

Partnership taxable income (and any separately stated items) flows through to each partner at the end of the *partnership's* taxable year. A *partner's* taxable income, then, includes the distributive share of partnership income for any *partnership* taxable year that ends within the partner's tax year.

When all partners use the calendar year, it would be beneficial in present value terms for a profitable partnership to adopt a fiscal year ending with January 31. Why? As Figure 22–1 illustrates, when the adopted year ends on January 31, the reporting of income from the partnership and payment of related taxes can be deferred for up to 11 months. For instance, income earned by the partnership in September 1997 is not taxable to the partners until January 31, 1998. It is reported in the partner's tax return for the year ended December 31, 1998, which is not due until April 15, 1999. Even though each partner may be required to make quarterly estimated tax payments, some deferral is still possible.

▼ **FIGURE 22-1**
Deferral Benefit When Fiscal
Year Is Used and All Partners
Are on the Calendar Year

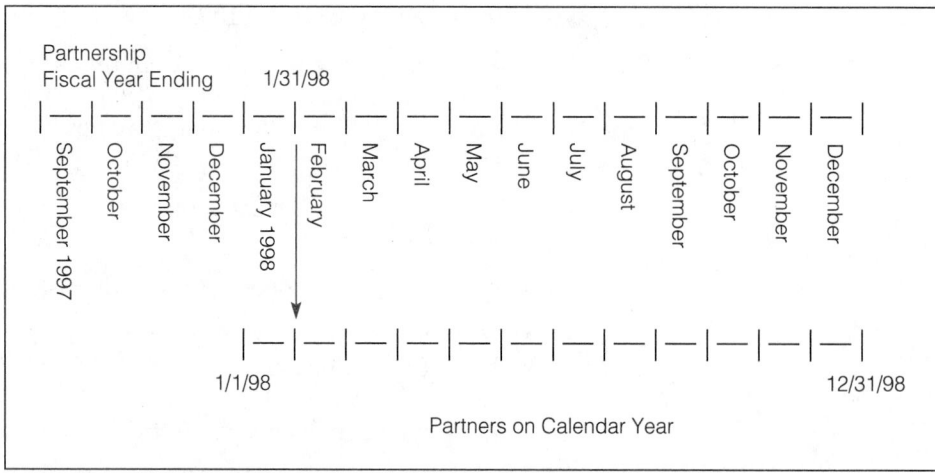

▼ **FIGURE 22-2**
Required Tax Year of
Partnership

In Order, Partnership Must Use	Requirements
Majority partners' tax year	• More than 50% of capital *and* profits is owned by partners who have the same taxable year.
Principal partners' tax year	• All partners who own 5% or more of capital *or* profits are principal partners.
	• All principal partners must have the same tax year.
Year with smallest amount of income deferred	• "Least aggregate deferral" method (Example 19).

Required Taxable Years. To prevent excessive deferral of taxation of partnership income, Congress and the IRS have adopted a series of rules that prescribe the *required* taxable year an entity must adopt if no alternative tax years (discussed below) are available. Three rules are presented in Figure 22-2.[25] The partnership must consider each rule, in order. If a taxable year is available under a given rule, that is the partnership's required taxable year.

The first two rules are relatively self-explanatory. Under the **least aggregate deferral method,** the partnership tests the year-ends that are used by the various partners to determine the weighted-average deferral of partnership income. The year-end that offers the least amount of deferral is the *required tax year* for the partnership.

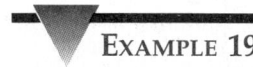

EXAMPLE 19

Anne and Bonnie are equal partners in the AB Partnership. Anne uses the calendar year, and Bonnie uses a fiscal year ending August 31. Neither Anne nor Bonnie is a majority partner since neither owns more than 50%. Although Anne and Bonnie are both principal partners, they do not have the same tax year. Therefore, the general rules indicate that the partnership's required tax year must be determined by the "least aggregate deferral" method. The following computations support August 31 as AB's tax year, since the 2.0 product using that year-end is less than the 4.0 product when December 31 is used. ▼

---

[25]§ 706(b).

Test for 12/31 Year-End						
Partner	**Year Ends**	**Profit Interest**		**Months of Deferral**		**Product**
Anne	12/31	50%	×	–0–	=	0.0
Bonnie	8/31	50%	×	8	=	4.0
Aggregate number of deferral months						4.0

Test for 8/31 Year-End						
Partner	**Year Ends**	**Profit Interest**		**Months of Deferral**		**Product**
Anne	12/31	50%	×	4	=	2.0
Bonnie	8/31	50%	×	–0–	=	0.0
Aggregate number of deferral months						2.0

Alternative Tax Years. If the required tax year is undesirable to the entity, three other alternative tax years may be available:

- Establish to the IRS's satisfaction that a *business purpose* exists for a different tax year (a natural business year at the end of a peak season or shortly thereafter). It is difficult to obtain IRS approval when using the business purpose exception unless the 25 percent, two-month test described next can be satisfied.
- Follow IRS procedures to obtain approval for using a *natural business tax year*. The IRS has stated that a natural business year exists when 25 percent or more of the partnership's gross receipts were recognized during the last 2 months of the same 12-month period for three consecutive years.[26] New partnerships cannot use this natural business year justification because they lack the required three-year history.
- Elect a tax year so that taxes on partnership income are deferred for not more than *three months* from the *required* tax year.[27] Then, have the partnership maintain with the IRS a prepaid, non-interest-bearing deposit of estimated deferred taxes.[28] This alternative may not be desirable since the deposit is based on the highest individual tax rate of 39.6 percent plus 1 percent, or 40.6 percent.

OPERATIONS OF THE PARTNERSHIP

5 LEARNING OBJECTIVE
Calculate partnership taxable income and describe how partnership items affect a partner's income tax return.

An individual, corporation, trust, estate, or another partnership can become a partner in a partnership. Since a partnership is a tax-reporting, rather than a taxpaying, entity for purposes of its Federal (and state) income tax computations, the partnership's income, deductions, credits, and alternative minimum tax (AMT) preferences and adjustments can ultimately be reported and taxed on any of a number of income tax forms [e.g., Forms 1040 (individuals), 1041 (fiduciaries), 1120 (C corporations), and 1120S (S corporations)].

A partnership is subject to all other taxes in the same manner as any other business. Thus, the partnership files returns and pays the outstanding amount of

---

[26]Rev.Proc. 74–33, 1974–2 C.B. 489; Rev.Rul. 87–57, 1987–2 C.B. 117; and Rev.Proc. 87–32, 1987–1 C.B. 396.

[27]§ 444.

[28]§ 7519.

pertinent sales taxes, property taxes, and Social Security, unemployment, and other payroll taxes.

MEASURING AND REPORTING INCOME

The partnership's Form 1065 organizes and reports the transactions of the entity for the tax year, and each of the partnership's tax items is reported on Schedule K of that return. Each partner—and the IRS—receives a Schedule K–1 that reports the partner's allocable share of partnership income, credits, adjustments, and preferences for the year. Form 1065 is due on the fifteenth day of the fourth month following the close of the partnership's tax year; for a calendar year partnership, this is April 15. The partnership must provide a copy of Schedule K–1 to each partner by the same date. However, partners of an electing large partnership must receive their K–1s one month earlier (March 15 for a calendar year partnership).

Income Measurement.   The measurement and reporting of partnership income require a two-step approach. Certain items must be netted at the partnership level, and other items must be segregated and reported separately on the partnership return and each partner's Schedule K–1.

Items passed through separately include the following:

- Short- and long-term capital gains and losses.
- Section 1231 gains and losses.
- Charitable contributions.
- Portfolio income items (dividends, interest, and royalties).
- Immediately expensed tangible personal property (§ 179).
- Items allocated differently from the general profit and loss ratio.
- Recovery of items previously deducted (tax benefit items).
- AMT preference and adjustment items.
- Passive activity items (rental real estate income or loss).
- Expenses related to portfolio income.
- Intangible drilling and development costs.
- Taxes paid to foreign countries and U.S. possessions.
- Nonbusiness and personal items (e.g., alimony, medical, and dental).[29]

The reason for separately reporting the preceding items is rooted in the aggregate or conduit concept. These items affect various exclusions, deductions, and credits at the partner level and must pass through without loss of identity so that the proper tax for each partner may be determined.[30]

A partnership is not allowed the following deductions:

- Net operating losses.
- Depletion of oil and gas interests.
- Dividends received deduction.

In addition, items that are only allowed by legislative grace to individuals, such as standard deductions or personal exemptions, are not allowed to the partnership. Also, if a partnership makes a payment on behalf of a partner, such as for alimony, medical expenses, or other items that constitute itemized deductions to individuals, the partnership treats the payment as a distribution or guaranteed payment (discussed later) to the partner, and the partner determines whether she may claim the deduction.

---

[29]§ 702(a).

[30]§ 702(b).

EXAMPLE 20

Tiwanda is a one-third partner in the TUV Partnership. This year, the partnership entered into the following transactions:

Fees received	$100,000
Salaries paid	30,000
Cost recovery deductions	10,000
Supplies, repairs	3,000
Payroll taxes paid	9,000
Charitable contribution to art museum	6,000
Short-term capital gain	12,000
Passive income (rental operations)	7,500
Portfolio income (dividends received)	1,500
Tax-exempt income (bond interest)	2,100
AMT adjustment (cost recovery)	3,600
Payment of partner Vern's alimony obligations	4,000

The partnership experienced a $20,000 net loss from operations last year, its first year of business.

The two-step computational process that is used to determine partnership income is applied in the following manner:

Nonseparately Stated Items (Ordinary Income)	
Fee income	$100,000
Salaries paid	(30,000)
Cost recovery deductions	(10,000)
Supplies, repairs	(3,000)
Payroll taxes paid	(9,000)
Ordinary income	$ 48,000

Separately Stated Items	
Charitable contribution to art museum	$ 6,000
Short-term capital gain	12,000
Passive income (rental operations)	7,500
Portfolio income (dividends received)	1,500
Tax-exempt income (bond interest)	2,100
AMT adjustment (cost recovery)	3,600

Each of the separately stated items passes through proportionately to each partner and is included on the appropriate schedule or netted with similar items that the partner generated for the year. Thus, in determining what her tax liability will be on her Form 1040, Tiwanda includes a $2,000 charitable contribution, a $4,000 short-term capital gain, $2,500 of passive rent income, $500 of dividend income, and a $1,200 positive adjustment in computing alternative minimum taxable income. Tiwanda treats these items as if she had generated them herself. She must disclose her $700 share of tax-exempt interest on the first page of her Form 1040. In addition, Tiwanda reports $16,000 as her share of the partnership's ordinary income, the net amount of the nonseparately stated items.

The partnership is not allowed a deduction for last year's $20,000 net operating loss—this item was passed through to the partners in the previous year. Moreover, the partnership is not allowed a deduction for personal expenditures (payment of Vern's alimony). ▼

Withdrawals. Capital withdrawals by partners during the year do not affect the partnership's income measuring and reporting process. These items are usually treated as distributions made on the last day of the partnership's tax year. Thus, in Example 20 above, the payment of Vern's alimony by the partnership is probably treated as a distribution from the partnership to Vern. When withdrawals exceed the partners' shares of partnership income, the excess is taxed under the distribution rules (discussed later in the chapter).[31]

Penalties. Each partner's share of partnership items should be reported on the respective tax return in the same manner as presented on the Form 1065. If a partner treats an item differently, the IRS must be notified of the inconsistent treatment.[32] If a partner fails to notify the IRS, a negligence penalty may be added to the tax due.

To encourage the filing of a partnership return, a penalty is imposed on the partnership of $50, per partner, per month (or fraction thereof, but not to exceed five months) for failure to file a complete and timely information return without reasonable cause.[33]

A partnership with 10 or fewer "natural persons" or corporations as partners, where each partner's share of partnership items is the same for all items, is automatically excluded from these penalties.[34]

ETHICAL CONSIDERATIONS

A Preparer's Responsibility for Partners' Tax Returns

A partnership's tax return preparer is responsible for accurately presenting information supplied by the partnership in that return. If a flow-through amount is significant to a certain partner, the preparer of the *partnership* return can be treated as the preparer of a *partner's* tax return with respect to that item.

If a preparer misstates an item on a partnership return, either by taking a position that is not supportable under current law or by willfully misreporting an item on the return, "preparer penalties" can be assessed. While these penalties are relatively small, their imposition may also result in the preparer being suspended from practice before the IRS or by a state accountancy board.

As an example, assume Stan, a CPA, knowingly reported a $20,000 deduction for fines and penalties (nondeductible items) in determining the JB Partnership's $30,000 income from operations. This amount was allocated equally to partners Joe and Barb. Joe has other income of $35,000. Barb has other income of $1 million. Stan is treated as the preparer of Joe's tax return with respect to the improper $10,000 flow-through item, since the fines and penalties are significant relative to Joe's income. Stan is not considered the preparer of Barb's return, since the fines and penalties are not significant to her income.

In a recent case, the court held that the preparer of the partnership return was the preparer of several partners' returns with respect to partnership items flowing through to the partners. The court reached this decision even though the return preparer never met the individual partners, received no direct fees from the partners, and performed no other services for the partners.

---

[31] §§ 731(a)(1) and 733.
[32] § 6222.
[33] § 6698.

[34] §§ 6231(a)(1)(B) and (I). Natural persons for this purpose include individuals who are not nonresident aliens, as well as the estate of a decedent who was not a nonresident alien.

Do you believe this is a reasonable approach for allocating responsibility for accurate preparation of a partner's tax return? Why or why not?

PARTNERSHIP ALLOCATIONS

So far, all examples in this chapter have assumed that the partner has the same percentage interest in capital, profits, and losses. Thus, a partner who owns a 25 percent interest in partnership capital has been assumed to own 25 percent of partnership profits and 25 percent of partnership losses.

Economic Effect. The partnership agreement can provide that any partner may share capital, profits, and losses in different ratios. For example, a partner could have a 25 percent capital sharing ratio, yet be allocated 30 percent of the profits and 20 percent of the losses of the partnership. Such *special* allocations are permissible if they follow certain rules contained in the Regulations under § 704(b).[35] Although these rules are too complex to discuss in detail, the general outline of one of these rules—the **economic effect test**—can be easily understood.

In general, the economic effect test requires the following:

- An allocation of income or gain to a partner must increase the partner's capital account, and an allocation of deduction or loss must decrease the partner's capital account.
- When the partner's interest is liquidated, the partner must receive assets that have a fair market value equal to the positive balance in the capital account.
- A partner with a negative capital account must restore that account upon liquidation of the interest. Restoration of a negative capital account can best be envisioned as a contribution of cash to the partnership equal to the negative balance.

These requirements are designed to ensure that a partner bears the economic burden of a loss or deduction allocation and receives the economic benefit of an income or gain allocation.

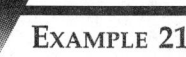

EXAMPLE 21

Eli and Sanjay each contribute $20,000 cash to the newly formed ES Partnership. The partnership uses the cash to acquire a depreciable asset for $40,000. The partnership agreement provides that the depreciation is allocated 90% to Eli and 10% to Sanjay. Other items of partnership income, gain, loss, or deduction are allocated equally between the partners. Upon liquidation of the partnership, property will be distributed to the partners in accordance with their positive capital account balances. Any partner with a negative capital account must restore the capital account upon liquidation. Assume the first-year depreciation on the equipment is $4,000. Also, assume nothing else happens in the first year that affects the partners' capital accounts.

Eli's capital account is $16,400 ($20,000 − $3,600), and Sanjay's capital account has a balance of $19,600 ($20,000 − $400) after the first year of partnership operations. The Regulations require that a hypothetical sale of the asset for its $36,000 of adjusted basis on the last day of the year and an immediate liquidation of the partnership should result in Eli and Sanjay receiving distributions equal to their capital accounts. According to the partnership agreement, Eli would receive $16,400, and Sanjay would receive $19,600 of the cash in a liquidating distribution. Eli, therefore, bears the economic burden of

---

[35]Reg. § 1.704–1(b).

$3,600 of depreciation since he contributed $20,000 to the partnership and would receive only $16,400 upon liquidation. Likewise, Sanjay's economic burden is $400 since he would receive only $19,600 of his original $20,000 investment. The agreement, therefore, has economic effect.

If the partnership agreement had provided that Eli and Sanjay should each receive $18,000 of the liquidation proceeds, the "special" allocation of the depreciation would be defective. The IRS would require that the depreciation be allocated equally ($2,000 each) to the two partners to reflect the $2,000 economic burden borne by each partner. ▼

Precontribution Gain or Loss.   Income, gain, loss, and deductions relative to contributed property may not be allocated under the § 704(b) rules described above. Instead, **precontribution gain or loss** must be allocated among the partners to take into account the variation between the basis of the property and its fair market value on the date of contribution.[36] For nondepreciable property, this means that *built-in* gain or loss on the date of contribution must be allocated to the contributing partner when the property is eventually disposed of by the partnership in a taxable transaction.

EXAMPLE 22

Seth and Tim form the equal profit and loss sharing ST Partnership. Seth contributes cash of $10,000, and Tim contributes land purchased two years ago that was held for investment. The land has an adjusted basis of $6,000 and fair market value of $10,000 at the contribution date. For accounting purposes, the partnership records the land at its fair market value of $10,000. For tax purposes, the partnership takes a carryover basis in the land of $6,000. After using the land as a parking lot for five months, ST sells it for $10,600. No other transactions have taken place.

The accounting and tax gain from the land sale are computed as follows:

	Accounting	**Tax**
Amount realized	$ 10,600	$ 10,600
Less: Adjusted basis	(10,000)	(6,000)
Gain realized	$ 600	$ 4,600
Gain at contribution date to Tim	(–0–)	(4,000)
Remaining gain (split equally)	$ 600	$ 600

Seth recognizes $300 of the gain ($600 remaining gain ÷ 2), and Tim recognizes $4,300 of gain [$4,000 built-in gain + ($600 ÷ 2)]. ▼

Regulations outline specific allocation calculations that may be used and describe allowable methods of allocating depreciation deductions if the property is depreciable.[37]

Concept Summary 22–2 reviews the tax reporting rules for partnership activities.

---

[36]§ 704(c)(1)(A).

[37]Reg. § 1.704–3. The three allowable methods are the "traditional method," the "traditional method with curative allocation," and the "remedial allocation."

CONCEPT SUMMARY 22–2

Tax Reporting of Partnership Activities

Event	Partnership Level	Partner Level
1. Compute partnership ordinary income.	Form 1065, line 22, page 1. Schedule K, Form 1065, line 1, page 3.	Schedule K–1 (Form 1065), line 1, page 1. Each partner's share is passed through for separate reporting. Each partner's basis is increased.
2. Compute partnership ordinary loss.	Form 1065, line 22, page 1. Schedule K, Form 1065, line 1, page 3.	Schedule K–1 (Form 1065), line 1, page 1. Each partner's share is passed through for separate reporting. Each partner's basis is decreased. The amount of a partner's loss deduction may be limited. Losses that may not be deducted are carried forward for use in future years.
3. Separately reported items like portfolio income, capital gain and loss, and § 179 deductions.	Schedule K, Form 1065, various lines, page 3.	Schedule K–1 (Form 1065), various lines, pages 1 and 2. Each partner's share of each item is passed through for separate reporting.
4. Net earnings from self-employment.	Schedule K, Form 1065, line 15, page 3.	Schedule K–1 (Form 1065), line 15, page 2.

BASIS OF A PARTNERSHIP INTEREST

6 LEARNING OBJECTIVE
Determine a partner's basis in the partnership interest.

Previously, this chapter discussed how to compute a partner's adjusted basis when the partnership is formed. It was noted that the partner's adjusted basis in the newly formed partnership usually equals (1) the adjusted basis in any property contributed to the partnership plus (2) the fair market value of any services the partner performed for the partnership (i.e., the amount of ordinary income reported by the partner for services rendered to the partnership).

A partnership interest also can be acquired after the partnership has been formed. The method of acquisition controls how the partner's initial basis is computed. If the partnership interest is purchased from another partner, the purchasing partner's basis is the amount paid (cost basis) for the partnership interest. The basis of a partnership interest acquired by gift is the donor's basis for the interest plus, in certain cases, some or all of the transfer (gift) tax paid by the donor. The basis of a partnership interest acquired through inheritance is the fair market value of the interest on the date the partner dies (or alternate valuation date).

After the partnership begins its activities, or after a transferee partner is admitted to the partnership, the partner's basis is adjusted for numerous items. The following operating results *increase* a partner's adjusted basis:

- The partner's proportionate share of partnership income (including capital gains and tax-exempt income).
- The partner's proportionate share of any increase in partnership liabilities.

The following operating results *decrease* the partner's adjusted basis in the partnership:

- The partner's proportionate share of partnership deductions and losses (including capital losses).
- The partner's proportionate share of nondeductible expenses.
- The partner's proportionate share of any reduction in partnership liabilities.[38]

Under no circumstances can the partner's adjusted basis for the partnership interest be reduced below zero.

Increasing the adjusted basis for the partner's share of partnership taxable income is logical since the partner has already been taxed on the income. By increasing the partner's basis, the Code ensures that the partner is not taxed again on the income when the interest is sold or a distribution is received from the partnership.

It is also logical that the tax-exempt income should increase the partner's basis. If the income is exempt in the current period, it should not contribute to the recognition of gain when the partner either sells the interest or receives a distribution from the partnership.

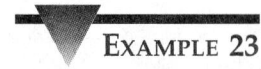

EXAMPLE 23

Yuri is a one-third partner in the XYZ Partnership. His proportionate share of the partnership income during the current year consists of $20,000 of ordinary taxable income and $10,000 of tax-exempt income. None of the income is distributed to Yuri. The adjusted basis of Yuri's partnership interest before adjusting for his share of income is $35,000, and the fair market value of the interest before considering the income items is $50,000.

The unrealized gain inherent in Yuri's investment in the partnership is $15,000 ($50,000 − $35,000). Yuri's proportionate share of the income items should increase the fair market value of the interest to $80,000 ($50,000 + $20,000 + $10,000). By increasing the adjusted basis of Yuri's partnership interest to $65,000 ($35,000 + $20,000 + $10,000), the Code ensures that the unrealized gain inherent in Yuri's partnership investment remains at $15,000. This makes sense because the $20,000 of ordinary taxable income is taxed to Yuri this year and should not be taxed again when he either sells his interest or receives a distribution. Similarly, the exempt income is exempt this year and should not increase Yuri's gain when he either sells his interest or receives a distribution from the partnership. ▼

Decreasing the adjusted basis for the partner's share of deductible losses, deductions, and noncapitalizable, nondeductible expenditures is logical for the same reasons. An item that is deductible currently should not contribute to creating a loss when the partnership interest is sold or a distribution is received from the partnership. Similarly, a noncapitalizable, nondeductible expenditure should never be deductible nor contribute to a loss when a subsequent sale or distribution transaction occurs.

7   LEARNING OBJECTIVE
Explain how liabilities affect a partner's basis.

Liability Sharing.   A partner's adjusted basis is affected by the partner's share of partnership debt.[39] Partnership debt includes any partnership obligation that creates an asset; results in a deductible expense; or results in a nondeductible, noncapitalizable item at the partnership level. The definition of partnership debt includes most debt that is considered a liability under financial accounting rules except for accounts payable of a *cash basis* partnership and certain contingent liabilities.

Under § 752, an increase in a partner's share of partnership debt is treated as a cash contribution by the partner to the partnership. A partner's share of partnership debt increases as a result of increases in the total amount of partnership debt.

---

[38]§§ 705 and 752.   [39]§ 752.

A decrease in a partner's share of partnership debt is treated as a cash distribution from the partnership to the partner. A partner's share of partnership debt decreases as a result of (1) decreases in the total amount of partnership debt and (2) assumption of the partner's debt by the partnership.

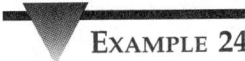

EXAMPLE 24

Jim and Becky contribute property to form the JB Partnership. Jim contributes cash of $30,000. Becky contributes land with an adjusted basis and fair market value of $45,000, subject to a liability of $15,000. The partnership borrows $50,000 to finance construction of a building on the contributed land. At the end of the first year, the accrual basis partnership owes $3,500 in trade accounts payable to various vendors. Assume no other operating activities occurred.

Partnership debt sharing rules are discussed later in this section, but assuming for simplicity that Jim and Becky share equally in liabilities, the partners' bases in their partnership interests are determined as follows:

Jim's Basis		Becky's Basis	
Contributed cash	$ 30,000	Basis in contributed land	$ 45,000
Share of debt on land (assumed by partnership)	7,500	Less: Debt assumed by partnership	(15,000)
Share of construction loan	25,000	Share of debt on land (assumed by partnership)	7,500
Share of trade accounts payable	1,750	Share of construction loan	25,000
		Share of trade accounts payable	1,750
	$ 64,250		$ 64,250

In this case, it is reasonable that the parties have an equal basis after contributing their respective properties, because each is a 50% owner and they contributed property with identical net bases and identical *net* fair market values. ▼

Decreases in a partner's share of partnership liabilities are treated as cash distributions and can result in extremely negative tax consequences. Liability balances should be reviewed carefully near the partnership's year-end to ensure the partners have no unanticipated tax results.

EXAMPLE 25

Assume the same facts as in Example 24, except the partnership reported an ordinary loss of $100,000 in its first year of operations. Ignoring possible loss deduction limitations, Jim and Becky each deduct a $50,000 ordinary loss, and their bases in their respective partnership interests are reduced to $14,250 (including a $34,250 share of liabilities).

In the second year, the partnership generated no taxable income or loss from operations, but repaid the $50,000 construction loan (assume from collection of accounts receivable reported as income in the prior year). The $25,000 reduction of each partner's share of partnership liabilities is treated as a cash distribution by the partnership to each partner. A cash distribution in excess of basis usually results in a capital gain (in this case $10,750) to each partner. The partners must pay tax on $10,750 of capital gain even though the partnership reported no taxable income. This gain can be thought of as a recapture of loss deductions the partners claimed during the first year, but such gains cause cash-flow difficulties to partners who are unaware that such a gain may occur. ▼

Two types of partnership debt exist. **Recourse debt** is partnership debt for which the partnership or at least one of the partners is personally liable. This liability can exist, for example, through the operation of state law or through personal guarantees that a partner makes to the creditor. Personal liability of a party related to a partner (under attribution rules) is treated as the personal liability of the partner. **Nonrecourse debt** is debt for which no partner (or party related to a partner) is personally liable. Lenders of nonrecourse debt generally require that collateral be pledged against the loan. Upon default, the lender can claim only the collateral, not the partners' personal assets.

How liabilities are shared among the partners depends upon whether the debt is recourse or nonrecourse and when the liability was incurred. For most debt *created* before January 29, 1989, the rules are relatively straightforward. Recourse debt is shared among the partners in accordance with their loss sharing ratios while nonrecourse debt is shared among the partners in accordance with the way they share partnership profits. Although questions arise about the calculation of the profit or loss sharing ratios and the treatment of personal guarantees of debt, the rules for sharing this earlier debt are easy to apply.

The rules for sharing partnership debt created after January 29, 1989, are much more complex. A complete analysis of these rules is beyond the scope of this text. The basic principles of these rules can be illustrated, however.

Current Recourse Debt Rules. Recourse debt created after January 29, 1989, is shared in accordance with a **constructive liquidation scenario.**[40] Under this scenario, the following events are *deemed* to occur at the end of each taxable year of the partnership:

1. Most partnership assets (including cash) become worthless.
2. The worthless assets are sold at fair market value ($0), and losses on the deemed sales are determined.
3. These losses are allocated to the partners according to their loss sharing ratios. These losses reduce the partners' capital accounts.
4. Any partner with a (deemed) negative capital account balance is treated as contributing cash to the partnership to restore that negative balance to zero.
5. The cash deemed contributed by the partners with negative capital balances is used to pay the liabilities of the partnership.
6. The partnership is deemed to be liquidated immediately, and any remaining cash is distributed to partners with positive capital account balances.

The amount of a partner's cash contribution that would be used (in step 5 above) in payment of partnership recourse liabilities is that partner's share of these partnership recourse liabilities.

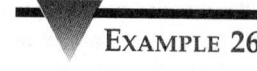

EXAMPLE 26

On January 1 of the current year, Nina and Otis each contribute $20,000 cash to the newly created NO General Partnership. Each partner has a 50% interest in partnership capital, profits, and losses. The first year of partnership operations resulted in the following balance sheet as of December 31:

	Basis	Fair Market Value
Cash	$12,000	$12,000
Receivables	7,000	7,000
Land and buildings	50,000	50,000
	$69,000	$69,000

---

[40]Transition rules (beyond the scope of this text) apply to debt created between January 29, 1989, and December 28, 1991.

	Basis	Fair Market Value
Recourse payables	$30,000	$30,000
Nina, capital	19,500	19,500
Otis, capital	19,500	19,500
	$69,000	$69,000

The recourse debt is shared in accordance with the constructive liquidation scenario. All of the partnership assets (including cash) are deemed to be worthless and sold for $0. This creates a loss of $69,000 ($12,000 + $7,000 + $50,000), which is allocated equally between the two partners. The $34,500 loss allocated to each partner creates negative capital accounts of $15,000 each for Nina and Otis. If the partnership were actually liquidated, each partner would contribute $15,000 cash to the partnership; the cash would be used to pay the partnership recourse payables; and the partnership would be liquidated. Because each partner would be required to contribute $15,000 to pay the liabilities, each shares in $15,000 of the recourse payables. Accordingly, Nina and Otis will each have an adjusted basis for their partnership interests of $34,500 ($19,500 + $15,000) on December 31. ▼

EXAMPLE 27

Assume the same facts as in Example 26, except that the partners allocate partnership losses 60% to Nina and 40% to Otis. The constructive liquidation scenario results in the $69,000 loss being allocated $41,400 to Nina and $27,600 to Otis. As a consequence, Nina's capital account has a negative balance of $21,900, and Otis's account has a negative balance of $8,100. Each partner is deemed to contribute cash equal to these negative capital accounts, and the cash would be used to pay the recourse liabilities under the liquidation scenario. Accordingly, Nina and Otis share $21,900 and $8,100, respectively, in the recourse debt. Note that the debt allocation percentages (73% to Nina and 27% to Otis) bear no relation to the partners' 60%/40% loss sharing ratios. ▼

Current Nonrecourse Debt Rules. Nonrecourse debt is allocated in three stages. First, an amount of debt equal to the amount of *minimum gain* is allocated to partners who share in minimum gain. The calculation of minimum gain is complex, and its details are beyond the scope of this text. In general, minimum gain approximates the amount of nonrecourse (mortgage) liability on a property in excess of the "book" basis of the property. Generally, the "book" basis for a property item is the same as the "tax" basis, although sometimes the amounts are different. For example, the "book" basis for contributed property on the date of contribution is its fair market value at that date, not its "tax" basis.

If a lender forecloses on partnership property, the result is treated as a deemed sale of the property for the mortgage balance. Gain is recognized for at least the amount of the liability in excess of the property's "book" basis—hence, minimum gain. Allocation of minimum gain among the partners should be addressed in the partnership agreement.

Second, the amount of nonrecourse debt equal to a *precontribution gain* under § 704(c) is allocated to the partner who contributed the property and debt to the partnership. For this purpose, the § 704(c) amount is the excess of the nonrecourse debt assumed by the partnership over the tax basis of the property.[41] Note that

---

[41] A more complex calculation applies when the partnership allocates built-in gain under the "remedial allocation" method. (See footnote 37.)

this calculation is only relevant when the "book" and "tax" bases of the contributed property are different.

Third, any remaining nonrecourse debt is allocated to the partners in accordance with either their profit sharing ratios or the manner in which they share in nonrecourse deductions. The partnership agreement should specify which allocation method is chosen. Most often, the profit sharing ratio is used.

EXAMPLE 28

Ted contributes a nondepreciable asset to the TK Partnership in exchange for a one-third interest in the capital, profits, and losses of the partnership. The asset has an adjusted tax basis to Ted and the partnership of $24,000 and a fair market value and "book" basis on the contribution date of $50,000. The asset is encumbered by a nonrecourse note (created January 1, 1995) of $35,000. Because the "book" basis exceeds the nonrecourse debt, there is no minimum gain. Under § 704(c) principles, the Regulations provide that the first $11,000 of the nonrecourse debt ($35,000 debt − $24,000 basis) is allocated to Ted. The remaining $24,000 nonrecourse debt is shared according to the profit sharing ratio, of which Ted's share is $8,000. Therefore, Ted shares in $19,000 ($11,000 + $8,000) of the nonrecourse debt.

Ted's basis in his partnership interest is determined as follows:

Substituted basis of contributed property	$ 24,000
Less: Liability assumed by partnership	(35,000)
Plus: Allocation of § 704(c) debt	11,000
Basis before remaining allocation	$ –0–
Plus: Allocation of remaining nonrecourse debt	8,000
Basis in partnership interest	$ 8,000

The § 704(c) allocation of nonrecourse debt prevents Ted from receiving a deemed distribution ($35,000) in excess of his basis in property he contributed ($24,000). Without this required allocation of nonrecourse debt, in some cases, a contributing partner would be required to recognize gain on a contribution of property encumbered by nonrecourse debt. ▼

Other Factors Affecting Basis Calculations.   The partner's basis is also affected by (1) postacquisition contributions of cash or property to the partnership; (2) postacquisition distributions of cash or property from the partnership; and (3) special calculations that are designed to allow the full deduction of percentage depletion for oil and gas wells. Postacquisition contributions of cash or property affect basis in the same manner as contributions made upon the creation of the partnership. Postacquisition distributions of cash or property reduce basis.

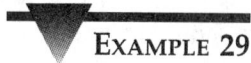

EXAMPLE 29

Ed is a one-third partner in the ERM Partnership. On January 1, 1998, Ed's basis in his partnership interest was $50,000. During 1998, the calendar year, accrual basis partnership generated ordinary taxable income of $210,000. It also received $60,000 of interest income from City of Buffalo bonds. It paid $3,000 in nondeductible bribes to local law enforcement officials, so that the police would not notify the Federal government about the products that the entity had imported without paying the proper tariffs. On July 1, 1998, Ed contributed $20,000 cash and a computer (zero basis to him) to the partnership. Ed's monthly draw from the partnership is $3,000; this is treated as a distribution and not as a guaranteed payment. The only liabilities that the partnership has incurred are trade accounts payable. On January 1, 1998, the trade accounts payable totaled $45,000; this account balance was $21,000 on December 31, 1998. Ed shares in one-third of the partnership liabilities for basis purposes.

Ed's basis in the partnership on December 31, 1998, is $115,000, computed as follows:

Basis is generally adjusted in the following order:

Initial basis. Amount paid for interest, or gift or inherited basis (including share of partnership debt). Amount paid can be amount contributed to partnership or amount paid to another partner or former partner.

+ Partner's contributions

+ Since interest acquired, partner's share of partnership's

- Debt increase
- Taxable income items
- Tax-exempt income items
- Excess of depletion deductions over adjusted basis of property subject to depletion

– Partner's distributions and withdrawals

– Since interest acquired, partner's share of partnership's

- Debt decrease
- Nondeductible items not chargeable to a capital account
- Special depletion deduction for oil and gas wells
- Loss items

The basis of a partner's interest can never be negative.

Beginning balance	$ 50,000
Share of ordinary partnership income	70,000
Share of tax-exempt income	20,000
Share of nondeductible expenditures	(1,000)
Ed's basis in noncash capital contribution	–0–
Additional cash contributions	20,000
Capital withdrawal	(36,000)
Share of net decrease in partnership liabilities [⅓ × ($45,000 – $21,000)]	(8,000)
	$115,000

EXAMPLE 30

Assume the same facts as in Example 29. If Ed withdraws cash of $115,000 from the partnership on January 1, 1999, the withdrawal is tax-free to him and reduces his basis to zero. The distribution is tax-free because he has recognized his share of the partnership's net income throughout his association with the entity, via the annual flow-through of his share of the partnership's income and expense items. Note that the $20,000 cash withdrawal of his share of the municipal bond interest retains its nontaxable character in this distribution. Ed receives the $20,000 tax-free because his basis was increased in 1998 when the partnership received the interest income. ▼

A partner is required to compute the adjusted basis only when necessary and thus can avoid the inconvenience of making day-to-day calculations of basis. When a partnership interest is sold, exchanged, or retired, however, the partner must compute the adjusted basis as of the date the transaction occurs. Computation of gain or loss requires an accurate calculation of the partner's adjusted basis on the transaction date.

Figure 22–3 summarizes the rules for computing a partner's basis in a partnership interest.

LOSS LIMITATIONS

8 ▼ LEARNING OBJECTIVE
Describe the limitations on deducting partnership losses.

Partnership losses flow through to the partners for use on their income tax returns. However, the amount and nature of the losses that may be used in a partner's tax computations may be limited. When limitations apply, all or a portion of the losses are held in suspension until a triggering condition occurs. Only then can the losses be used to determine the partner's tax liability.

Three different limitations may apply to partnership losses that are passed through to a partner. The first is the overall limitation contained in § 704(d). This limitation allows the deduction of losses only to the extent the partner has adjusted basis for the partnership interest. Losses that are deductible under the overall limitation may then be subject to the at-risk limitation of § 465. Losses are deductible under this provision only to the extent the partner is at risk for the partnership interest. Any losses that survive this second limitation may be subject to a third limitation, the passive loss rules of § 469. Only losses that make it through all these applicable limitations are eligible to be deducted on the partner's tax return.

EXAMPLE 31

Meg is a partner in a partnership that does not invest in real estate. On January 1, 1998, Meg's adjusted basis for her partnership interest is $50,000, and her at-risk amount is $35,000. Her share of losses from the partnership for 1998 is $60,000, all of which is passive. She has one other passive income-producing investment that produced $25,000 of passive income during 1998.

Meg will be able to deduct $25,000 of partnership losses on her Form 1040 for 1998. Her deductible loss is calculated as follows:

Applicable Provision	Deductible Loss	Suspended Loss
Overall limitation	$50,000	$10,000
At-risk limitation	35,000	15,000
Passive loss limitation	25,000	10,000

Meg can deduct only $50,000 under the overall limitation. Of this $50,000, only $35,000 is deductible under the at-risk limitation. Under the passive loss limitation, passive losses can be deducted only against passive income. Thus, Meg can deduct only $25,000 on her return in 1998. ▼

Overall Limitation. A partner may only deduct losses flowing through from the partnership to the extent of the partner's adjusted basis in the partnership. A partner's adjusted basis in the partnership is determined at the end of the partnership's taxable year. It is adjusted for distributions and any partnership gains during the year, but it is determined before considering any losses for the year.

Losses that cannot be deducted because of this rule are suspended and carried forward (never back) for use against future increases in the partner's adjusted basis. Such increases might result from additional capital contributions or from sharing in additional partnership debt or future partnership income.

EXAMPLE 32

Carol and Dan do business as the CD Partnership, sharing profits and losses equally. All parties use the calendar year. At the start of the current year, the basis of Carol's partnership interest is $25,000. The partnership sustains an operating loss of $80,000 in the current year. For the current year, only $25,000 of Carol's $40,000 allocable share of the partnership loss (one-half of the $80,000 loss) can be deducted under the overall limitation. As a result, the basis of Carol's partnership interest is zero as of January 1 of the following year, and she must carry forward the remaining $15,000 of partnership losses. ▼

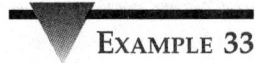

EXAMPLE 33

Assume the same facts as in Example 32, and that the partnership earns a profit of $70,000 for the next calendar year. Carol reports net partnership income of $20,000 ($35,000 distributive share of income – the $15,000 carryforward loss). The basis of Carol's partnership interest becomes $20,000. ▼

In Example 32, Carol's entire $40,000 share of the current-year partnership loss could have been deducted under the overall limitation in the current year if she had contributed an additional $15,000 or more in capital by December 31. Alternatively, if the partnership had incurred additional debt by the end of the current year, Carol's basis might have been increased to permit some or all of the loss to be deducted in that year. Thus, if partnership losses are projected for a given year, careful tax planning can ensure their deductibility under the overall limitation.

Notice that in Figure 22–3, contributions to capital, distributions from the partnership, and partnership income items are taken into account before loss items. This ordering produces some unusual results in taxation of partnership distributions and deductibility of losses.

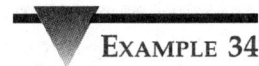

EXAMPLE 34

The Ellen-Glenn Partnership is owned equally by partners Ellen and Glenn. At the beginning of the year, Ellen's basis in her partnership interest is $0. Her share of partnership income is $10,000 for the year, and she receives a $10,000 distribution from the partnership.

Under the basis adjustment ordering rules of Figure 22–3, Ellen's basis is first increased by the $10,000 of partnership income, then is decreased by her $10,000 distribution. She reports her $10,000 share of partnership taxable income on her personal tax return. Her basis at the end of the year is again $0 ($0 + $10,000 income – $10,000 distribution). ▼

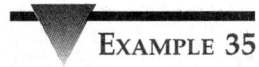

EXAMPLE 35

Assume the same facts as in Example 34, except that Ellen's share of partnership operating results is a $10,000 loss instead of $10,000 income. She again receives a $10,000 distribution.

As mentioned earlier, a distribution of cash in excess of basis in the partnership interest results in a gain to the distributee partner (see Example 25). Under the basis adjustment ordering rules of Figure 22–3, Ellen's distribution is considered before the deductibility of the loss is evaluated under the overall limitation.

Ellen recognizes gain on the $10,000 distribution because she has no basis in her partnership interest. The gain effectively ensures that she still has a $0 basis after the distribution. The loss cannot be deducted under the overall loss limitation rule because Ellen has no basis in her partnership interest. ▼

Given this $20,000 difference in partnership earnings in the two examples ($10,000 income to $10,000 loss), does income taxed to Ellen exhibit a similar change? Actually, Ellen reports $10,000 of income (gain) in each case: ordinary income in Example 34, and (probably) a capital gain from the distribution in Example 35. In Example 35, she also has a $10,000 suspended loss carryforward. These results are due solely to the basis adjustment ordering rules. Remember these rules, and the appropriate results can be determined. Income and contributions are considered first, then distributions—and *last*, loss items.

At-Risk Limitation. Under the at-risk rules, the partnership losses from business and income-producing activities that individual partners and closely held C corporation partners can deduct are limited to amounts that are economically invested in the partnership. Invested amounts include the adjusted basis of cash and property contributed by the partner and the partner's share of partnership earnings that has not been withdrawn.[42] A closely held C corporation exists when five or fewer individuals own more than 50 percent of the entity's stock under appropriate attribution and ownership rules.

When some or all of the partners are personally liable for partnership recourse debt, that debt is included in the adjusted basis of those partners. Usually, those partners also include the debt in their amount at risk.

No partner, however, carries any financial risk on nonrecourse debt. Therefore, as a general rule, partners cannot include nonrecourse debt in their amount at risk even though that debt is included in the adjusted basis of their partnership interest. In many cases, however, an exception to this general rule applies. Real estate nonrecourse financing provided by a bank, retirement plan, or similar party, or by a Federal, state, or local government generally is deemed to be at risk.[43] Such debt is termed **qualified nonrecourse debt.** In summary, although the general rule provides that nonrecourse debt is not at risk, the overriding exception may provide that it is deemed to be at risk.

When determining a partner's loss deduction, the overall limitation rule is invoked first. That is, the deduction is limited to the partner's outside basis at the end of the partnership year. Then, the at-risk provisions are applied to see if the remaining loss is still deductible. Suspended losses are carried forward until a partner has a sufficient amount at risk in the activity to absorb them.[44]

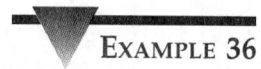

EXAMPLE 36

Kelly invests $5,000 in the Kelly Green Limited Partnership as a 5% general partner. Shortly thereafter, the partnership acquires the master recording of a well-known vocalist for $250,000 ($50,000 from the partnership and $200,000 secured from a local bank via a *recourse* mortgage). Assume Kelly's share of the recourse debt is $10,000, and her basis in her partnership interest is $15,000 ($5,000 cash investment + $10,000 debt share). Since the debt is recourse, Kelly's at-risk amount is also $15,000. Kelly's share of partnership losses in the first year of operations is $11,000. She is entitled to deduct the full $11,000 of partnership losses under both the overall and the at-risk limitations because this amount is less than both her outside basis and at-risk amount. ▼

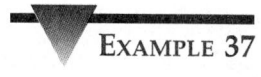

EXAMPLE 37

Assume the same facts as in Example 36, except the bank loan is nonrecourse (the partners have no direct liability under the terms of the loan in the case of a default). Kelly's basis in her partnership interest still is $15,000, but she can deduct only $5,000 of the flow-through loss. The amount she has at risk in the partnership does not include the nonrecourse debt. (The debt does not relate to real estate so it is not qualified nonrecourse debt.) ▼

Passive Activity Rules.   A partnership loss share may be disallowed under the passive activity rules. These rules apply to partners who are individuals, estates, trusts, closely held C corporations, or personal service corporations. The rules require the partners to separate their activities into three groups:

- *Active.* Earned income, such as salary and wages; income or loss from a trade or business in which the partner materially participates; and guaranteed payments received by the partner for services.
- *Portfolio.* Annuity income, interest, dividends, guaranteed payments from a partnership for interest on capital, royalties not derived in the ordinary course of a trade or business, and gains and losses from disposal of investment assets.

---

[42]§ 465(a).
[43]§ 465(b)(6).

[44]§ 465(a)(2).

- *Passive.* Income from a trade or business activity in which the partner does not materially participate on a regular, continuous, and substantial basis, or income from many rental activities.[45]

Material participation in an activity is determined annually. The burden is on the partner to prove material participation. The IRS has provided a number of objective tests for determining material participation. These tests require the partner to have substantial involvement in daily operations of the activity. Thus, a Maine vacation resort operator investing in a California grape farm or an electrical engineer employed in Virginia investing in an Iowa corn and hog farm may have difficulty proving material participation in the activities.

Rent income from real or personal property generally is passive income, regardless of the partner's level of participation. Exceptions are made for rent income from activities where substantial services are provided (e.g., certain developers, resorts); from hotels, motels, and other transient lodging; from short-term equipment rentals; and from certain developed real estate.

Usually, passive activity losses can only offset passive activity income.[46] In determining the net passive activity loss for a year, losses and income from all passive activities are aggregated. The amount of suspended losses carried forward from a particular activity is determined by the ratio of the net loss from that activity to the aggregate net loss from all passive activities for the year. A special rule for rental real estate (discussed in the following section) allows a limited $25,000 offset against nonpassive income.[47]

A partner making a taxable disposition of an entire interest in a passive activity takes a full deduction for suspended passive activity losses from that activity in the year of disposal.[48] Suspended losses are deductible against income in the following order: income or gain from the passive activity, net income or gain from all passive activities, and other income. When a passive activity is transferred in a primarily nontaxable exchange (e.g., a like-kind exchange or contribution to a partnership), suspended losses are deductible only to the extent of gains recognized on the transfer. Remaining losses are deducted on disposal of the activity received in the exchange.

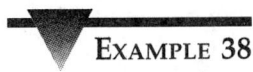

EXAMPLE 38

Debra has several investments in passive activities that generate aggregate losses of $10,000 in the current year. Debra wants to deduct all of these losses on her current-year tax return. To assure a loss deduction, she needs to invest in some passive activities that generate income. One of her long-time friends, an entrepreneur in the women's apparel business, is interested in opening a new apparel store in a nearby community. Debra is willing to finance a substantial part of the expansion but does not want to get involved with day-to-day operations. Debra also wants to limit any possible loss to her initial investment.

After substantial discussions, Debra and her friend decide to form a limited partnership, which will own the new store. Debra's friend will be the general partner, and Debra will be a limited partner. Debra invests $100,000, and her friend invests $50,000 and sweat equity (provides managerial skills and know-how). Each has a 50% interest in profits and losses. In the first year of operations, the store generates a profit of $30,000. Since Debra's share of the profit ($15,000) is passive activity income, it can be fully utilized against any of her passive activity losses on other investments. Thus, via her share of the apparel store profits, Debra assures a full deduction of her $10,000 of passive activity losses. ▼

---

[45]§§ 469(c)(1) and (2).
[46]§ 469(a)(1).

[47]§ 469(i).
[48]§ 469(g).

Rental Real Estate Losses.   Individuals can offset up to $25,000 of passive losses from rental real estate against active and portfolio income in any one year. The $25,000 maximum is reduced by 50 percent of the difference between the taxpayer's modified adjusted gross income (AGI) and $100,000. Thus, when the taxpayer's modified AGI reaches $150,000, the offset is eliminated.

The offset is available to those who actively (rather than materially) participate in rental real estate activities. Active participation is an easier test to meet. Unlike material participation, it does not require regular, continuous, and substantial involvement with the activity. However, the taxpayer must own at least 10 percent of the fair market value of all interests in the rental property and either contribute to the activity's management decisions in a significant and bona fide way or actively participate in arranging for others to make such decisions.

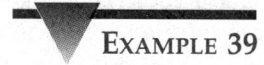

EXAMPLE 39

Raoul invests $10,000 cash in the Sparrow Limited Partnership in the current year for a 10% limited interest in capital and profits. Shortly thereafter, the partnership purchases rental real estate subject to a qualified nonrecourse mortgage of $120,000 obtained from a commercial bank. Raoul has no other passive loss activities during the current year.

Raoul does not participate in any of Sparrow's activities. His share of losses from Sparrow's first year of operations is $27,000. His AGI before considering the loss is $60,000. Before considering the loss, Raoul's basis in the partnership interest is $22,000 [$10,000 cash + (10% × $120,000 debt)], and his loss deduction is limited to this amount under the overall limitation. The debt is included in Raoul's amount at risk because it is qualified nonrecourse financing. It may seem that Raoul should be allowed to deduct the $22,000 loss share from portfolio or active income under the rental real estate exception to the passive loss rules. However, the loss may not be offset against this income because Raoul is not an active participant in the partnership. ▼

TRANSACTIONS BETWEEN PARTNERS AND PARTNERSHIPS

9 ▼ LEARNING OBJECTIVE
Review the treatment of transactions between a partner and the partnership.

Many types of transactions occur between a partnership and one of its partners. The partner may contribute property to the partnership, perform services for the partnership, or receive distributions from the partnership. The partner may borrow money from or lend money to the partnership. Property may be bought and sold between the partner and the partnership. Several of these transactions were discussed earlier in the chapter. The remaining types of partner-partnership transactions are the focus of this section.

GUARANTEED PAYMENTS

If a partnership makes a payment to a partner in his capacity as a partner, the payment may be a draw against the partner's share of partnership income; a return of some or all of the partner's original capital contribution; or a guaranteed payment, among other treatments. A **guaranteed payment** is a payment for services performed by the partner or for the use of the partner's capital. The payment may not be determined by reference to partnership income. Guaranteed payments are usually expressed as a fixed-dollar amount or as a percentage of capital that the partner has invested in the partnership. Whether the partnership deducts or capitalizes the guaranteed payment depends on the nature of the payment.

EXAMPLE 40

David, Donald, and Dale formed the accrual basis DDD Partnership in 1998. According to the partnership agreement, David is to manage the partnership and receive a $21,000 distribution from the entity every year, payable in 12 monthly installments. Donald is to receive an amount that is equal to 18% of his capital account, as it is computed by the firm's accountant at the beginning of the year, payable in 12 monthly installments. Dale is the partnership's advertising specialist. He withdraws 3% of the partnership's net income every month for his personal use. David and Donald receive guaranteed payments from the partnership, but Dale does not. ▼

Guaranteed payments resemble the salary or interest payments of other businesses and receive somewhat similar treatment under partnership tax law.[49] In contrast to the provision that usually applies to withdrawals of assets by partners from their partnerships, guaranteed payments are deductible (or capitalized) by the entity. Deductible guaranteed payments, like other deductible expenses of a partnership, can create an ordinary loss for the entity. A partner who receives guaranteed payments during a partnership year must include the payments in income as if they were received on the last day of the partnership year. Guaranteed payments are always taxable as ordinary income to the recipient partner.

EXAMPLE 41

Continue with the situation introduced in Example 40. For calendar year 1998, David receives the $21,000 as provided by the partnership agreement, Donald's guaranteed payment for 1998 is $17,000, and Dale withdraws $20,000. Before considering these amounts, the partnership's ordinary income for 1998 is $650,000.

The partnership can deduct its payments to David and Donald, so the final amount of its 1998 ordinary income is $612,000 ($650,000 – $21,000 – $17,000). Thus, each of the equal partners is allocated $204,000 of ordinary partnership income for their 1998 individual income tax returns ($612,000 ÷ 3). In addition, David reports the $21,000 of guaranteed payment income on his 1998 tax return, and Donald similarly includes the $17,000 guaranteed payment in his 1998 income. Dale's partnership draw is deemed to have come from his allocated $204,000 (or from the accumulated partnership income that was taxed to him in prior years) and is not taxed separately to him. Dale's basis, though, is reduced by the $20,000 distribution to him. ▼

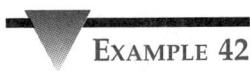

EXAMPLE 42

Assume the same facts as in Example 40, except that the partnership's tax year ends on March 31, 1999. The total amount of the guaranteed payments is taxable to the partners on that date. Thus, even though David receives 9 of his 12 payments for fiscal 1999 in calendar 1998, all of his guaranteed payments are taxable to him in 1999. Similarly, all of Donald's guaranteed payments are taxable to him in 1999 and not when they are received. The deduction for, and the gross income from, guaranteed payments are allowed on the same date that all of the other income and expense items relative to the partnership are allocated to the partners (on the last day of the entity's tax year). ▼

OTHER TRANSACTIONS BETWEEN PARTNERS AND PARTNERSHIPS

Certain transactions between a partner and the partnership are treated as if the partner were an outsider, dealing with the partnership at arm's length.[50] Loan transactions, rental payments, and sales of property between the partner and the partnership are treated in this manner. In addition, payments for services are generally treated this way when the services are short-term technical services that the partner also provides for parties other than the partnership.

---

[49]§ 707(c).   [50]§ 707(a).

EXAMPLE 43

Emilio, a one-third partner in the CDE Partnership, owns a tract of land that the partnership wishes to purchase. The land has a fair market value of $30,000 and an adjusted basis to Emilio of $17,000. If Emilio sells the land to the partnership, he recognizes a $13,000 gain on the sale, and the partnership takes a $30,000 cost basis in the land. If the land has a fair market value of $10,000 on the sale date, Emilio recognizes a $7,000 loss. ▼

The timing of the deduction for a payment by an accrual basis partnership to a cash basis service partner depends upon whether the payment is a guaranteed payment or a payment to a partner who is treated as an outsider. A guaranteed payment is includible in the partner's income on the last day of the partnership year when it is properly accrued by the partnership, even though the payment may not be made to the partner until the next taxable year. Conversely, the *partner's* method of accounting controls the timing of deduction if the payment is treated as made to an outsider. This is because a deduction cannot be claimed for such amounts until the recipient partner is required to include the amount in income under the partner's method of accounting.[51] Thus, a partnership cannot claim a deduction until it actually makes the payment to the cash basis partner, but it could accrue and deduct a payment due to an accrual basis partner even if payment was not yet made.

EXAMPLE 44

Rachel, a cash basis taxpayer, is a partner in the accrual basis RTC Partnership. On December 31, 1998, the partnership accrues but does not pay $10,000 for deductible services that Rachel performed for the partnership during the year. Both Rachel and the partnership are calendar year taxpayers.

If the $10,000 accrual is a guaranteed payment, the partnership deducts the $10,000 in its calendar year ended December 31, 1998, and Rachel includes the $10,000 in her income for the 1998 calendar year. The fact that Rachel is a cash basis taxpayer and does not actually receive the cash in 1998 is irrelevant.

If the payment is classified as a payment to an outsider, the partnership cannot deduct the payment until Rachel actually receives the cash. If, for example, Rachel performs janitorial services (i.e., not in her capacity as a partner) and receives the cash on March 25, 1999, the partnership deducts the payment and Rachel recognizes the income on that date. ▼

Sales of Property. Certain sales of property fall under special rules. No loss is recognized on a sale of property between a person and a partnership when the person owns, directly or indirectly, more than 50 percent of partnership capital or profits.[52] The disallowed loss may not vanish entirely, however. If the transferee eventually sells the property at a gain, the disallowed loss reduces the gain that the transferee would otherwise recognize.

EXAMPLE 45

Barry sells land (adjusted basis to him, $30,000; fair market value, $45,000) to a partnership in which he controls a 60% capital interest. The partnership pays him $20,000 for the land. Barry cannot deduct his $10,000 realized loss. The sale apparently was not at arm's length, but the taxpayer's intentions are irrelevant. Barry and the partnership are related parties, and the loss is disallowed.

When the partnership sells the land to an outsider at a later date, it receives a sales price of $44,000. The partnership can offset the recognition of its $24,000 realized gain on the subsequent sale ($44,000 sales proceeds – $20,000 adjusted basis) by the amount of the $10,000 prior disallowed loss ($20,000 – $30,000). Thus, the partnership recognizes a $14,000 gain on its sale of the land. ▼

---

[51] § 267(a)(2).

[52] § 707(b).

Partner-Partnership Transactions

1. Partners can transact business with their partnerships in a nonpartner capacity. These transactions include such things as the sale and exchange of property, rentals, loans of funds, etc.
2. A payment to a partner may be classified as a guaranteed payment if it is for services or use of the partner's capital and is not based on partnership income. A guaranteed payment may be deductible by the partnership and is included in the partner's income on the last day of the partnership's tax year.
3. A payment to a partner may be treated as being to an outside (though related) party. Such a payment is deductible or capitalizable by the partnership at the time the partner must include the amount in income under his or her method of accounting.
4. Guaranteed payments and payments to a partner that are treated as being to an outside party are only deductible if the underlying reason for the payment constitutes an ordinary and necessary (rather than capitalizable) business expense.
5. Losses are disallowed between a partner or related party and a partnership when the partner or related party owns more than a 50% interest in the partnership's capital or profits.
6. When there is income from a related-party sale, it is treated as ordinary income if the property is not a capital asset to both the transferor and the transferee.

Using a similar rationale, any gain that is realized on a sale or exchange between a partner and a partnership in which the partner controls a capital or profit interest of more than 50 percent must be recognized as ordinary income, unless the asset is a capital asset to both the seller and the purchaser.[53]

EXAMPLE 46

Kristin purchases some land (adjusted basis, $30,000; fair market value, $45,000) for $45,000 from a partnership in which she controls a 90% profit interest. The land was a capital asset to the partnership. If Kristin holds the land as a capital asset, the partnership recognizes a $15,000 capital gain. However, if Kristin is a land developer and the property is not a capital asset to her, the partnership must recognize $15,000 of ordinary income from the sale, even though the property was a capital asset to the partnership. ▼

PARTNERS AS EMPLOYEES

A partner usually does not qualify as an employee for tax purposes. Thus, a partner receiving guaranteed payments is not regarded as an employee of the partnership for purposes of withholding taxes. Moreover, since a partner is not an employee, the partnership cannot deduct its payments for the partner's fringe benefits. A general partner's distributive share of ordinary partnership income and guaranteed payments for services are generally subject to the Federal self-employment tax.[54]

Concept Summary 22–3 reviews partner-partnership transactions.

DISTRIBUTIONS FROM THE PARTNERSHIP

The tax treatment of withdrawals from a partnership to a partner was introduced earlier. This section will expand that discussion by examining in greater detail the

---

[53]§ 707(b)(2).   [54]§ 1402(a).

effect of nonliquidating distributions made during the normal operations of the partnership. In addition, distributions to partners in complete liquidation of their ownership interests and sales of partnership interests are discussed. For a more complete discussion of these topics, see Chapter 11 of *West's Federal Taxation: Corporations, Partnerships, Estates, and Trusts* (1999 edition).

A **nonliquidating distribution** is any distribution from a continuing partnership to a continuing partner—that is, any distribution that is not a liquidating distribution. There are two types of nonliquidating distributions: draws or partial liquidations. A *draw* is a distribution of a partner's share of current or accumulated partnership profits that have been taxed to the partner in current or prior taxable years of the partnership. A *partial liquidation* is a distribution that reduces the partner's interest in partnership capital but does not liquidate the partner's entire interest in the partnership. The distinction between the two types of *nonliquidating* distributions is largely semantic, since the basic tax treatment typically does not differ.

EXAMPLE 47

Kay joins the calendar year KLM Partnership on January 1, 1998, by contributing $40,000 of cash to the partnership in exchange for a one-third interest in partnership capital, profits, and losses. Her distributive share of partnership income for the year is $25,000. If the partnership distributes $65,000 ($25,000 share of partnership profits + $40,000 initial capital contribution) to Kay on December 31, 1998, the distribution is a nonliquidating distribution as long as Kay continues to be a partner in the partnership. This is true even though Kay receives her share of profits plus her entire investment in the partnership. In this case, $25,000 is considered a draw, and the remaining $40,000 is a partial liquidation of Kay's interest. ▼

A payment from a partnership to a partner is not necessarily treated as a distribution. For example, as discussed earlier, a partnership may pay interest or rent to a partner for use of the partner's capital or property, make a guaranteed payment to a partner, or purchase property from a partner. If a payment *is* treated as a distribution, it is not necessarily treated under the general tax deferral rules that apply to most partnership distributions. In certain circumstances, the partner may recognize gain when marketable securities are received from the partnership.

Finally, a distribution may be either proportionate or disproportionate. In a **proportionate distribution,** a partner receives his or her respective share of certain ordinary income-producing assets of the partnership. A **disproportionate distribution** occurs when the distribution increases or decreases the distributee partner's interest in certain ordinary income-producing assets. The tax treatment of disproportionate distributions is very complex and is beyond the scope of this discussion.

PROPORTIONATE NONLIQUIDATING DISTRIBUTIONS

10 **LEARNING OBJECTIVE**
Determine the tax treatment of proportionate nonliquidating distributions from a partnership to a partner.

In general, neither the partner nor the partnership recognizes gain or loss when a nonliquidating distribution occurs.[55] The partner usually takes a carryover basis in the assets distributed.[56] The distributee partner's outside basis is reduced (but not below zero) by the amount of cash and the adjusted basis of property distributed.[57]

Note the difference between the tax theory governing distributions from C corporations and partnerships. In a C corporation, a distribution from current or

---

[55]§ 731(a)(1).
[56]§ 732(a)(1).

[57]§ 733.

accumulated income (earnings and profits) is taxable as a dividend to the share-holder, and the corporation does not receive a deduction for the amount distributed. This is an example of corporate income being subject to double taxation. In a partnership, a distribution from current or accumulated profits is not taxable be-cause Congress has decided that partnership income should be subject to only a single level of taxation. Because a partner pays taxes when the share of income is earned by the partnership, this income is not taxed again when distributed.

These results make sense under the entity and aggregate concepts. The entity concept is applicable to corporate dividends, so any amount paid as a dividend is treated as a transfer by the corporate entity to the shareholder and is taxed accord-ingly. Under the aggregate theory, though, a partner receiving a distribution of partnership income is treated as merely receiving something already owned. Whether the partner chooses to leave the income in the partnership or receive it in a distribution makes no difference. The following examples illustrate that a distribution does not change a partner's economic position.

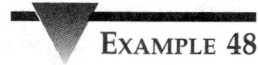

EXAMPLE 48

Jay is a one-fourth partner in the JP Partnership. His basis in his partnership interest is $40,000 on December 31, 1998. The fair market value of the interest is $70,000. The partnership distributes $25,000 of cash to him on that date. The distribution is not taxable to Jay or the partnership. The distribution reduces Jay's adjusted basis in the partnership to $15,000 ($40,000 – $25,000), and the fair market value of his partnership interest is, arguably, reduced to $45,000 ($70,000 – $25,000). ▼

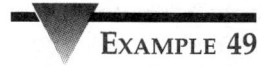

EXAMPLE 49

Assume the same facts as in Example 48, except that the partnership distributes both the $25,000 cash and land with an adjusted basis to the partnership of $13,000 and a fair market value of $30,000 on the date of distribution. The distribution is not taxable to Jay or the partnership. Jay reduces his basis in the partnership to $2,000 [$40,000 – ($25,000 + $13,000)] and takes a carryover basis of $13,000 in the land. The fair market value of Jay's remaining interest in the partnership is, arguably, reduced to $15,000 [$70,000 – ($25,000 + $30,000)].

If Jay had sold his partnership interest for $70,000 rather than receiving the distribution, he would have realized and recognized gain of $30,000 ($70,000 selling price – $40,000 outside basis). Because he has not recognized any gain or loss on the distribution of cash and land, he should still have the $30,000 of deferred gain to recognize at some point in the future. This is exactly what will happen. If Jay sells the cash, land, and remaining partnership interest on January 1, 1999, the day after the distribution, he realizes and recognizes gains of $17,000 ($30,000 – $13,000) on the land and $13,000 ($15,000 – $2,000) on the partnership interest. These gains total $30,000, which is the amount of the original deferred gain. ▼

Gain and Loss Recognition. A partner recognizes gain from a nonliquidating distribution to the extent that the *cash* received exceeds the outside basis of his or her interest in the partnership.[58] In a nonliquidating distribution, losses are not recognized by the partner.

EXAMPLE 50

Samantha is a one-third partner in the SMP Partnership. Her basis in this ownership interest is $50,000 on December 31, 1998, after accounting for the calendar year partnership's 1998 operations and for her 1998 capital contributions. On December 31, 1998, the partnership distributes $60,000 cash to Samantha. She recognizes a $10,000 gain from this distribution ($60,000 cash received – $50,000 basis in her partnership interest). Most likely, this gain is taxed as a capital gain.[59] ▼

---

[58]§ 731(a)(1).

[59]§ 731(a). If the partnership holds any "hot assets," however, Samantha will probably recognize some ordinary income. See § 751(b) and the related discussion of ordinary income ("hot") assets later in this chapter.

While distributions *from* accumulated earnings are taxed differently to shareholders and partners, cash distributions *in excess* of accumulated profits are taxed similarly for corporate shareholders and partners in partnerships. Both shareholders and partners are allowed to recover the cumulative capital invested in the entity tax-free.

Recall from earlier in the chapter that the reduction of a partner's share of partnership debt is treated as a distribution of cash from the partnership to the partner. A reduction of a partner's share of partnership debt, then, first reduces the partner's basis in the partnership. Any reduction of a share of debt in excess of a partner's basis in the partnership is taxable as a gain.

EXAMPLE 51

Returning to the facts of Example 50, assume that Samantha's $50,000 basis in her partnership interest included a $60,000 share of partnership liabilities. If the partnership repays all of its liabilities, Samantha is treated as receiving a $60,000 distribution from the partnership. The first $50,000 of this distribution reduces her basis to $0. The last $10,000 distributed creates a taxable gain to her of $10,000. ▼

A distribution of marketable securities can also be treated as a distribution of cash. Determining treatment of such distributions is complicated though, since several exceptions may apply and the basis in the distributed stock must be calculated. Discussion of such distributions is beyond the scope of this chapter.

Property Distributions.   In general, a distributee partner does not recognize gain from a property distribution. If the basis of property distributed by a partnership exceeds the partner's basis in the partnership interest, the distributed asset takes a substituted basis. This ensures that the partner does not receive asset basis that is not "paid for."

EXAMPLE 52

Mary has a $50,000 basis in her partnership interest. The partnership distributes land it owns with a basis and a fair market value of $60,000. Mary does not recognize any gain on this distribution because it is a distribution of property. However, Mary should not be allowed to take a carryover basis of $60,000 in the land, when her basis in her partnership interest is only $50,000. Therefore, the Code provides that Mary takes a substituted basis of $50,000 in the land. Her basis in her partnership interest is reduced by the basis she takes in the asset received, or $50,000. Therefore, Mary has a $50,000 basis in the land and a $0 basis in her partnership interest, and she recognizes no gain on this distribution. ▼

Ordering Rules.   When the inside basis of the distributed assets exceeds the distributee partner's outside basis, the Code requires that the assets be deemed distributed in the following order:

- Cash is distributed first.
- Unrealized receivables and inventory are distributed second.
- All other assets are distributed last.

Since the partner typically does not recognize a gain from a *property* distribution, the Code provides that the partner's basis for property received cannot exceed the partner's basis in the partnership interest immediately before the distribution. For each level of asset distribution, the relevant adjustments are made to the partner's basis in the interest. In other words, after a cash distribution, the partner's basis in the interest is recomputed before determining the effect of a distribution of unrealized receivables or inventory. The basis is recomputed again before determining the effect of a distribution of other assets. If the remaining outside basis at the end of any step is insufficient to cover the entire inside basis of the assets in the next step, that remaining outside basis is allocated pro rata among the assets within that class.[60]

EXAMPLE 53

Sally has a $48,000 basis in her partnership interest. On September 10, 1998, the partnership distributes to her cash of $12,000, cash basis receivables with an inside basis of $0 and a fair market value of $10,000, and a parcel of land with a basis to the partnership of $60,000 and a fair market value of $100,000. Sally has realized gain on the distribution of $74,000 ($12,000 + $10,000 + $100,000 − $48,000). None of that gain is recognized, however, since the $12,000 cash distribution does not exceed her $48,000 adjusted basis for her partnership interest. In determining the basis effects of the distribution, the cash is treated as being distributed first, reducing Sally's adjusted basis to $36,000 ($48,000 − $12,000). The receivables are distributed next, taking a $0 carryover basis to Sally. Her adjusted basis remains at $36,000. The land is distributed last, taking a substituted basis of $36,000 and reducing her adjusted basis for her partnership interest to $0. ▼

When more than one asset in a particular class is distributed, special rules apply. For most proportionate nonliquidating distributions made after August 5, 1997, if the partner's remaining adjusted basis for the partnership interest is less than the partnership's adjusted basis for the distributed assets in the particular class, the partner's adjusted basis for each distributed asset is computed by following three steps:

Step 1. Each distributed asset within the class initially takes a carryover basis.

Step 2. Then, this carryover basis for each of these assets is reduced in proportion to their respective amounts of unrealized depreciation (amount that carryover basis is greater than fair market value). Under no circumstances, however, can the basis of any asset be reduced below its fair market value in step 2.

Step 3. Any remaining decrease in basis is allocated among all the distributed assets in the class in proportion to their respective adjusted bases (as adjusted in step 2).

EXAMPLE 54

Assume the same facts as in Example 53, except that Sally receives two parcels of land, rather than a single parcel. The partnership's basis for the parcels is $15,000 for Parcel 1 and $45,000 for Parcel 2. Each parcel has a fair market value of $30,000. Sally has a realized gain on the distribution of $34,000 ($12,000 + $10,000 + $60,000 − $48,000). None of that gain is recognized, however, because the $12,000 cash distribution does not exceed her $48,000 adjusted basis.

As in Example 53, Sally takes a $12,000 basis for the cash and a $0 carryover basis for the receivables and has a $36,000 adjusted basis for her partnership interest after these two items are distributed. Because two parcels of land are distributed, and because Sally's remaining $36,000 adjusted basis for her partnership interest is less than the partnership's $60,000 total basis for the two parcels of land, Sally's adjusted basis for each parcel of land is computed by following these steps:

Step 1. She initially takes a carryover basis of $15,000 for Parcel 1 and $45,000 for Parcel 2.

Step 2. She reduces the basis of Parcel 2 to its lower fair market value of $30,000. The basis for Parcel 1 is not adjusted in this step because Parcel 1 has a fair market value greater than its basis.

Step 3. The remaining $9,000 difference between her $36,000 basis for the partnership interest and the $45,000 ($15,000 + $30,000) basis for the land parcels after step 2 is allocated to the two parcels in proportion to their respective bases (as

---

[60]§ 732.

computed in step 2). Therefore, the amount of the step 3 basis reduction allocated to Parcel 1 is:

$$\$9,000 \times \frac{\$15,000}{\$45,000} = \$3,000$$

Sally's basis for Parcel 1 is $12,000 ($15,000 – $3,000). The amount of step 3 basis reduction allocated to Parcel 2 is:

$$\$9,000 \times \frac{\$30,000}{\$45,000} = \$6,000$$

Sally's basis for Parcel 2 is $24,000 ($30,000 – $6,000). ▼

EXAMPLE 55

Assume the same facts as in Example 54, and that Sally sells both parcels of land early in 1999 for their fair market values, receiving proceeds of $60,000 ($30,000 + $30,000). She also collects $10,000 from the cash basis receivables. Now she recognizes all of the $34,000 gain that she deferred upon receiving the property from the partnership [$60,000 amount realized – $36,000 basis for the two parcels ($12,000 + $24,000) + $10,000 received – $0 basis for the receivables]. ▼

Review the tax results of Example 53 and 54. Although Sally does not recognize any of the gain from the distribution, she has a zero outside basis for her partnership interest. If Sally expects the partnership to generate net losses in the near future, she will *not* find this zero basis attractive. She may be unable to deduct her share of these future losses when they flow through to her on the last day of the partnership's subsequent tax year.

The low basis that Sally has assigned to the parcels of land is of no tax detriment to her if she does not intend to sell the land in the near future. Since land does not generate cost recovery deductions, the substituted basis is used only to determine Sally's gain or loss upon her disposition of the parcels in a taxable sale or exchange.

Concept Summary 22–4 summarizes the rules for nonliquidating distributions.

PROPORTIONATE LIQUIDATING DISTRIBUTIONS

11   LEARNING OBJECTIVE
Determine the tax treatment of proportionate distributions that liquidate a partnership.

Proportionate **liquidating distributions** consist of a single distribution or a series of distributions that result in the termination of the partner's entire interest in the partnership. This section examines situations when a partner's interest is liquidated because the partnership is liquidating.

Gain Recognition and Ordering Rules.   When a partnership liquidates, the liquidating distributions to a partner usually consist of an interest in several or all of the partnership assets. The gain recognition and ordering rules parallel those for nonliquidating distributions, except that the partner's *entire* basis in the partnership interest is allocated to the assets received in the liquidating distribution, unless the partner is required to recognize a loss. A loss may be recognized when *only* cash, unrealized receivables, or inventory are received in the distribution. As a result of the ordering rules, the basis of some assets may be adjusted upward or downward to absorb the partner's remaining outside basis. Unrealized receivables or inventory are never "stepped up," although they may be "stepped down." The partnership itself typically does not recognize either gain or loss on a liquidating distribution.

The general ordering and gain recognition rules for a proportionate liquidating distribution are summarized as follows:

CONCEPT SUMMARY 22–4

Proportionate Nonliquidating Distributions (General Rules)

1. In general, neither the distributee partner nor the partnership recognizes any gain or loss on a nonliquidating distribution. If cash distributed exceeds the distributee partner's outside basis, however, gain is recognized. Property distributions generally do not result in gain recognition.
2. The distributee partner usually takes the same basis the distributed property had to the partnership (carryover basis). However, where the inside basis of distributed property exceeds the partner's outside basis, the basis assigned to the distributed property cannot exceed that outside basis (substituted basis).
3. Gain recognized by the distributee partner on a nonliquidating distribution is usually capital in nature.
4. Loss is never recognized on a proportionate nonliquidating distribution.

Calculations

1. Partner's outside basis.   _____
2. Less: Cash distributed to partner.   _____
3. Gain recognized by partner (excess of Line 2 over Line 1).   _____
4. Partner's remaining outside basis (Line 1 – Line 2). If less than $0, enter $0.   _____
5. Partner's basis in unrealized receivables and inventory distributed (enter lesser of Line 4 or
   the partnership's inside basis in the unrealized receivables and inventory).   _____
6. Basis available to allocate to other property distributed (Line 4 – Line 5).   _____
7. Partnership's inside basis of other property distributed.   _____
8. Basis to partner of other property distributed (enter lesser of Line 6 or Line 7).   _____
9. Partner's remaining outside basis (Line 6 – Line 8).   _____

- Cash is distributed first and results in a capital gain to the extent the distribution exceeds the partner's basis in the partnership interest. The amount distributed reduces the liquidated partner's outside basis dollar for dollar. The partner's basis cannot be reduced below zero.
- The partner's remaining outside basis is then allocated to unrealized receivables and inventory up to an amount equal to the partnership's adjusted bases in that property. If the partnership's bases in the unrealized receivables and inventory exceed the partner's remaining outside basis, the remaining outside basis is allocated to the unrealized receivables and inventory.
- Finally, if the liquidating partner has any outside basis left, that basis is allocated to the other assets received.[61]

EXAMPLE 56

When Tara's basis in her partnership interest is $70,000, she receives cash of $15,000, a proportionate share of inventory, and a building in a distribution that liquidates both the partnership and her entire partnership interest. The inventory has a basis to the partnership of $20,000 and a fair market value of $30,000. The building's basis is $8,000, and the fair market value is $12,000. The building is not subject to depreciation recapture. Under these circumstances, Tara recognizes no gain or loss. After reducing Tara's $70,000 basis by the $15,000 cash received, the remaining $55,000 is allocated. The basis of the inventory in Tara's hands is $20,000, and the basis of the building is $35,000. ▼

---

[61]§§ 731 and 732.

When more than one asset in a particular class is distributed, special rules may apply. For most proportionate liquidating distributions made after August 5, 1997, if the partner's remaining basis for the partnership interest is less than the partnership's basis for the distributed assets in the particular class, the partner's basis for each distributed asset is computed in the same manner as illustrated previously in Example 54. If, however, the partner's remaining basis for the partnership interest is greater than the partnership's basis for the distributed assets in the last class (all "other assets"), the partner's basis for each distributed asset is computed by following three steps:

Step 1. Each distributed asset within the class initially takes a carryover basis.

Step 2. Then, this carryover basis for each of these assets is increased in proportion to their respective amounts of unrealized appreciation (amount that fair market value is greater than carryover basis). Under no circumstances, however, can the basis of any asset be increased above its fair market value in step 2.

Step 3. Any remaining increase in basis is allocated among all the distributed assets in the "other assets" class in proportion to their respective fair market values.

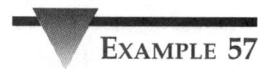

EXAMPLE 57

Assume the same facts as in Example 56, except that Tara receives two parcels of land, rather than a single parcel. The partnership's basis for the parcels is $2,000 for Parcel 1 and $6,000 for Parcel 2. Each parcel has a fair market value of $6,000.

Tara takes a $15,000 basis for the cash and a $20,000 carryover basis for the inventory. She has a $35,000 basis for her partnership interest after these two items are distributed. Because two parcels of land are distributed, and because Tara's remaining $35,000 basis for her partnership interest exceeds the partnership's $8,000 basis for the two parcels of land, Tara's basis for each parcel of land is computed by following these steps:

Step 1. She initially takes a carryover basis of $2,000 for Parcel 1 and $6,000 for Parcel 2.

Step 2. She increases the basis of Parcel 1 by $4,000 to its fair market value of $6,000. The basis for Parcel 2 is not affected in this step because Parcel 2 has a fair market value equal to its basis.

Step 3. Tara's $23,000 ($35,000 − $6,000 − $6,000) remaining basis for her partnership interest is allocated to each land parcel in proportion to each parcel's respective $6,000 fair market value. Therefore, $11,500 [($6,000/$12,000) × $23,000] is allocated to each parcel. Tara's basis in Parcel 1 is $17,500 ($2,000 + $4,000 + $11,500). Her basis in Parcel 2 is $17,500 ($6,000 + $11,500). ▼

Loss Recognition.   The distributee partner may also recognize a *loss* on a liquidating distribution. The partner recognizes a loss if both of the following are true:

- The partner receives *only* money, unrealized receivables, or inventory.
- The partner's outside basis in the partnership interest exceeds the partnership's inside basis for the assets distributed. This excess amount is the loss recognized by the distributee partner.[62]

The word "only" is important. A distribution of any other property postpones recognition of the loss.

EXAMPLE 58

When Ramon's outside basis is $40,000, he receives a liquidating distribution of $7,000 cash and a proportionate share of inventory having a partnership basis of $3,000 and a fair market value of $10,000. Ramon is not allowed to "step up" the basis in the inventory, so it is allocated a $3,000 carryover basis. Ramon's unutilized outside basis is $30,000. Since he

---

[62]§ 731(a)(2).

received a liquidating distribution of *only* cash and inventory, he recognizes a capital loss of $30,000 on the liquidation. ▼

EXAMPLE 59

Assume the same facts as in Example 58, except that in addition to the cash and inventory, Ramon receives the desk he used in the partnership. The desk has an adjusted basis of $100 to the partnership. Applying the rules outlined above to this revised fact situation produces the following results:

Step 1. Cash of $7,000 is distributed to Ramon and reduces his outside basis to $33,000.

Step 2. Inventory is distributed to Ramon. He takes a $3,000 carryover basis in the inventory and reduces his outside basis in the partnership to $30,000.

Step 3. The desk is distributed to Ramon. Since the desk is a § 1231 asset and not cash, an unrealized receivable, or inventory, he cannot recognize a loss. Therefore, Ramon's remaining basis in his partnership interest is allocated to the desk. He takes a $30,000 basis for the desk. ▼

What can Ramon do with a $30,000 desk? If he continues to use it in a trade or business, he can depreciate it. Once he has established his business use of the desk, he could sell it and recognize a large § 1231 loss. If the loss is isolated in the year of the sale, it is an ordinary loss. Thus, with proper planning, no liquidated partner should be forced to recognize a capital loss.

Gain recognized by the withdrawing partner on the subsequent disposition of inventory is always ordinary income, unless the disposition occurs more than five years after the distribution.[63] The withdrawing partner's holding period for all other property received in a liquidating distribution includes the partnership's related holding period.

SALE OF A PARTNERSHIP INTEREST

12 LEARNING OBJECTIVE
Calculate the selling partner's amount and character of gain or loss on the sale or exchange of a partnership interest.

A partner can sell or exchange a partnership interest, in whole or in part. The transaction can be between the partner and a third party; in this case, it is similar (in concept) to a sale of corporate stock. The transfer of a partnership interest produces different results than the transfer of corporate stock, though, because both the entity and aggregate concepts apply to the partnership situation, whereas only the entity concept applies to a sale of stock. The effect of the different rules is that gain or loss resulting from a sale of a partnership interest may be divided into capital gain or loss and ordinary income.

GENERAL RULES

Generally, the sale or exchange of a partnership interest results in gain or loss, measured by the difference between the amount realized and the selling partner's adjusted basis in the partnership interest.[64]

Liabilities. In computing the amount realized and the adjusted basis of the interest sold, the selling partner's share of partnership liabilities must be determined. The purchasing partner includes any assumed indebtedness as a part of the consideration paid for the partnership interest.[65]

---

[63]§ 735(a)(2).
[64]§ 741.

[65]§ 742.

EXAMPLE 60

Cole originally contributed $50,000 in cash for a one-third interest in the CDE Partnership. During the time Cole was a partner, his share of partnership income was $90,000, and he withdrew $60,000 cash. Cole's capital account balance is now $80,000, and partnership liabilities are $45,000, of which Cole's share is $15,000. Cole's outside basis is $95,000 ($80,000 capital account + $15,000 share of partnership debts).

Cole sells his partnership interest to Freda for $110,000 cash, with Freda assuming Cole's share of partnership liabilities. The total amount realized by Cole is $125,000 ($110,000 cash received + $15,000 of partnership debts transferred to Freda). Cole's gain on the sale is $30,000 ($125,000 realized − adjusted basis of $95,000).

Freda's adjusted basis for her partnership interest is the purchase price of $125,000 ($110,000 cash paid + $15,000 assumed partnership debt). ▼

Tax Years That Close.   When a partner disposes of an entire investment in the partnership, the partnership's tax year closes for that partner as of the sale date. When a partnership's tax year closes with respect to a partner, the partner's share of income for the period during which he or she was a partner is calculated. This amount is taxed to the partner and increases the selling partner's basis. There are several acceptable methods of determining the partner's share of income.[66]

EFFECT OF HOT ASSETS

A major exception to capital gain or loss treatment on the sale or exchange of a partnership interest arises when a partnership has **hot assets**. In general, *hot assets* are certain assets that when collected or disposed of by the partnership would cause it to recognize ordinary income. When a partner sells the interest in a partnership, it is as if he or she sold a proportionate interest in the partnership's hot assets. The partner's basis in interest must be allocated between "hot" and "non-hot" assets. The selling price of the interest is similarly allocated. The gain on hot assets is taxed as ordinary income. The sale of the non-hot assets can result in capital gain or loss.

Two types of hot assets must be considered: **unrealized receivables** and **appreciated inventory.** An amount realized from the sale of a partnership interest that is attributable to *unrealized receivables* or *appreciated inventory* is treated as being from the sale of a noncapital asset.[67] The purpose of this rule is to prevent a partner from converting ordinary income into capital gain through the sale of a partnership interest.

Unrealized Receivables.   Unrealized receivables generally include receivables from the sales of ordinary income property and rights to payments for services. They also include the accounts receivable of a cash basis partnership, the ordinary income portion (if any) of a deferred installment gain, and, for sale or exchange purposes, depreciation recapture potential.[68]

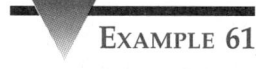

EXAMPLE 61

The cash basis Thrush Partnership owns only a $10,000 receivable for rendering health care advice. Its basis in the receivable is zero because no income has been recognized. This item is a hot asset because ordinary income is generated when Thrush collects on the account.

Harry, a 50% partner, sells his interest to Mark for $5,000. If Harry's basis in his partnership interest is $0, his total gain is $5,000. The entire gain is attributable to the unrealized receivable, so Harry's gain is taxed as ordinary income. ▼

---

[66]§ 706(d)(1) and related Regulations.
[67]§ 751(a).

[68]§ 751(a)(1).

Appreciated Inventory. Inventory items are appreciated if, at the time of their sale or distribution, their aggregate fair market value exceeds their total adjusted basis to the partnership. In applying this test, inventory items are evaluated as a group, rather than individually. If appreciation of the entire inventory has occurred, all of the inventory items are treated as appreciated, even if a specific item has not appreciated.

For this purpose, the term *inventory* includes all partnership property except money, capital assets, and § 1231 assets. Receivables of an accrual partnership are included in the definition of inventory, since they are neither capital assets nor § 1231 assets.[69]

This definition is broad enough to include all items considered to be unrealized receivables. The disadvantage of their inclusion can be seen in the calculation to determine whether the inventory is appreciated. Since unrealized receivables are included at a zero basis in the appreciation tests, they improve the partner's chances of having appreciated inventory.

EXAMPLE 62

Jan sells her interest in the JKL Partnership to Matt for $20,000 cash. The interest has an outside basis of $15,000. On the sale date, the partnership balance sheet reflects the following:

	Adjusted Basis	Fair Market Value
Cash	$10,000	$10,000
Inventory	21,000	30,000
Nonhot assets	14,000	20,000
Total	$45,000	$60,000
Jan, capital	$15,000	$20,000
Kelly, capital	15,000	20,000
Lynn, capital	15,000	20,000
Total	$45,000	$60,000

The inventory is appreciated. Jan's share of the inside basis of the inventory is $7,000 ($21,000 × ⅓). Jan is deemed to have sold this share of inventory for $10,000 ($30,000 × ⅓), thereby creating ordinary income of $3,000 on the sale of the hot asset. Jan recognizes the $3,000 ordinary income and $2,000 of capital gain from the rest of the sale:

Remaining sales price ($20,000 gross sales price – $10,000 allocated to hot asset sale)	$10,000
Remaining outside basis ($15,000 original outside basis – $7,000 allocated to hot asset sale)	(8,000)
Capital gain	$ 2,000

▼

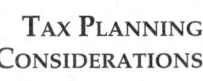

TAX PLANNING CONSIDERATIONS

CHOOSING PARTNERSHIP TAXATION

Concept Summary 22–5 lists various factors that the owners of a business should consider in deciding whether to use a C corporation, S corporation, or partnership as a means of doing business.

[69]§ 751(d).

CONCEPT SUMMARY 22–5

Advantages and Disadvantages of the Partnership Form

The partnership form may be attractive when one or more of the following factors is present:

- The entity is generating net taxable losses and/or valuable tax credits, which will be of use to the owners.
- Other means by which to reduce the effects of the double taxation of business income (e.g., compensation to owners, interest, and rental payments) have been exhausted.
- The entity does not generate material amounts of tax preference and adjustment items, which increase the alternative minimum tax liabilities of its owners.
- The entity is generating net passive income, which its owners can use to claim immediate deductions for net passive losses that they have generated from other sources.
- Given the asset holdings and distribution practices of the entity, the possibility of liability under the accumulated earnings and personal holding company taxes is significant.
- The owners wish to make special allocations of certain income or deduction items that are not possible under the C or S corporation forms.
- The owners anticipate liquidation of the entity within a short period of time. Liquidation of a C or S corporation would generate entity-level recognized gains on appreciated property distributed.
- The owners have adequate bases in their partnership interests to facilitate the deduction of flow-through losses and the assignment of an adequate basis to assets distributed in-kind to the partners.

The partnership form may be less attractive when one or more of the following factors is present:

- The maximum marginal tax rate applicable to the individual owners is above that applicable to C corporations. Currently, marginal tax rates for individuals may exceed rates applicable to corporations.
- The entity is generating net taxable income, which is taxed directly to the owners who do not necessarily receive any funds from the entity with which to pay the tax.
- The type of income that the entity is generating (e.g., business and portfolio income) is not as attractive to its owners as net passive income would be because the owners could use net passive income to offset the net passive losses that they have generated on their own.
- The entity is in a high-exposure business, and the owners desire protection from personal liability. An LLC or LLP structure may be available, however, to limit personal liability.
- The owners want to avoid Federal self-employment tax.

FORMATION AND OPERATION OF A PARTNERSHIP

13 LEARNING OBJECTIVE
Provide insights regarding advantageous use of a partnership.

Potential partners should be cautious in transferring assets to a partnership to ensure that they are not required to recognize any gain upon the creation of the entity. The nonrecognition provisions of § 721 are relatively straightforward and resemble the provisions under § 351. However, any partner can make a tax-deferred contribution of assets to the entity either at the inception of the partnership or later. This possibility is not available to less-than-controlling shareholders in a corporation.

   The partners should anticipate the tax benefits and pitfalls that are presented in Subchapter K and should take appropriate actions to resolve any potential problems before they arise. Typically, all that is needed is an appropriate provision in the partnership agreement (e.g., with respect to differing allocation percentages for gains and losses). Recall, however, that a special allocation of income, expense, or credit items in the partnership agreement must satisfy certain requirements before it is acceptable to the IRS.

PARTNERSHIPS AROUND THE WORLD—AND BEYOND

Technology continues to act as a catalyst—and incentive—for the creation of multinational joint ventures. AT&T, MCI, and Sprint are racing each other to align with partners in foreign telecommunications markets: each wants to have the widest service coverage area so it can offer efficient communications and computer networking to business clients with a global presence.

Pharmaceutical companies find it advantageous to allow foreign partners to promote and distribute such products as imaging agents used in the detection of various cancers. Reciprocal agreements sometimes give each partner exclusive distribution rights for products created in the partners' separate research facilities.

Finally, Primestar is a partnership formed by several media and cable companies to offer digital satellite television services on 85 to 95 channels to customers for a monthly fee.

At least one country, Bermuda, has recognized this trend and is trying to lure multinational joint ventures to its shores. In 1995, it passed the Overseas Partnerships Act and other legislation designed to encourage foreign investment.

TRANSACTIONS BETWEEN PARTNERS AND PARTNERSHIPS

Partners should be careful when engaging in transactions with the partnership to ensure that no negative tax results occur. A partner who owns a majority of the partnership generally should not sell property at a loss to the partnership because the loss is disallowed. Similarly, a majority partner should not sell a capital asset to the partnership at a gain, if the asset is to be used by the partnership as other than a capital asset. The gain on this transaction is taxed as ordinary income to the selling partner rather than as capital gain.

As an alternative to selling property to a partnership, the partner may lease it to the partnership. The partner recognizes rent income, and the partnership has a rent expense. If the partner needs more cash immediately, the partner can sell the property to an outside third party who leases the property to the partnership for a fair rental.

The timing of the deduction for payments by accrual basis partnerships to cash basis partners varies depending on whether the payment is a guaranteed payment or is treated as a payment to an outsider. If the payment is a guaranteed payment, the deduction occurs when the partnership properly accrues the payment. If the payment is treated as a payment to an outsider, the actual date the payment is made controls the timing of the deduction.

DRAFTING THE PARTNERSHIP AGREEMENT

Although a written partnership agreement is not required, many rules governing the tax consequences to partners and their partnership refer to such an agreement. Remember that a partner's distributive share of income, gain, loss, deduction, or credit is determined in accordance with the partnership agreement. Consequently, if taxpayers operating a business in partnership form want a measure of certainty as to the tax consequences of their activities, a carefully drafted partnership agreement is crucial. An agreement that sets forth the obligations, rights, and powers of the partners should prove invaluable in settling controversies among them and provide some degree of certainty as to the tax consequences of the partners' actions.

OVERALL COMPARISON: FORMS OF DOING BUSINESS

See Concept Summary 22–6 for a detailed comparison of the tax consequences of the following forms of doing business: sole proprietorship, partnership, S corporation, and regular corporation.

CONCEPT SUMMARY 22–6

Tax Attributes of Different Forms of Business (Assume Partners and Shareholders Are All Individuals)

	Sole Proprietorship	Partnership	S Corporation*	Regular (C) Corporation**
Restrictions on type or number of owners	One owner. The owner must be an individual.	Must have at least 2 owners.	Only individuals, estates, and certain trusts can be owners. Maximum number of shareholders limited to 75.	None, except some states require a minimum of 2 shareholders.
Incidence of tax	Sole proprietorship's income and deductions are reported on Schedule C of the individual's Form 1040. A separate Schedule C is prepared for each business.	Entity not subject to tax. Partners in their separate capacity subject to tax on their distributive share of income. Partnership files Form 1065.	Except for certain built-in gains and passive investment income when earnings and profits are present from C corporation tax years, entity not subject to Federal income tax. S corporation files Form 1120S. Shareholders are subject to tax on income attributable to their stock ownership.	Income subject to double taxation. Entity subject to tax, and shareholder subject to tax on any corporate dividends received. Corporation files Form 1120.
Highest tax rate	39.6% at individual level.	39.6% at partner level.	39.6% at shareholder level.	35% at corporate level plus 39.6% on any corporate dividends at shareholder level.
Choice of tax year	Same tax year as owner.	Selection generally restricted to coincide with tax year of majority partners or principal partners, or to tax year determined under the least aggregate deferral method.	Restricted to a calendar year unless IRS approves a different year for business purposes or other exceptions apply.	Unrestricted selection allowed at time of filing first tax return.

	Sole Proprietorship	Partnership	S Corporation*	Regular (C) Corporation**
Timing of taxation	Based on owner's tax year.	Partners report their share of income in their tax year with or within which the partnership's tax year ends. Partners in their separate capacities are subject to payment of estimated taxes.	Shareholders report their shares of income in their tax year with or within which the corporation's tax year ends. Generally, the corporation uses a calendar year, but see "Choice of tax year" above. Shareholders may be subject to payment of estimated taxes. Corporation may be subject to payment of estimated taxes for the taxes imposed at the corporate level.	Corporation subject to tax at close of its tax year. May be subject to payment of estimated taxes. Dividends will be subject to tax at the shareholder level in the tax year received.
Basis for allocating income to owners	Not applicable (only one owner).	Profit and loss sharing agreement. Cash basis items of cash basis partnerships are allocated on a daily basis. Other partnership items are allocated after considering varying interests of partners.	Pro rata share based on stock ownership. Shareholder's pro rata share is determined on a daily basis, according to the number of shares of stock held on each day of the corporation's tax year.	Not applicable.
Contribution of property to the entity	Not a taxable transaction.	Generally not a taxable transaction.	Is a taxable transaction unless the § 351 requirements are satisfied.	Is a taxable transaction unless the § 351 requirements are satisfied.
Character of income taxed to owners	Retains source characteristics.	Conduit—retains source characteristics.	Conduit—retains source characteristics.	All source characteristics are lost when income is distributed to owners.
Basis for allocating a net operating loss to owners	Not applicable (only one owner).	Profit and loss sharing agreement. Cash basis items of cash basis partnerships are allocated on a daily basis. Other partnership items are allocated after considering varying interests of partners.	Prorated among shareholders on a daily basis.	Not applicable.
Limitation on losses deductible by owners	Investment plus liabilities.	Partner's investment plus share of liabilities.	Shareholder's investment plus loans made by shareholder to corporation.	Not applicable.
Subject to at-risk rules	Yes, at the owner level. Indefinite carryover of excess loss.	Yes, at the partner level. Indefinite carryover of excess loss.	Yes, at the shareholder level. Indefinite carryover of excess loss.	Yes, for closely held corporations. Indefinite carryover of excess loss.

	Sole Proprietorship	Partnership	S Corporation*	Regular (C) Corporation**
Subject to passive activity loss rules	Yes, at the owner level. Indefinite carryover of excess loss.	Yes, at the partner level. Indefinite carryover of excess loss.	Yes, at the shareholder level. Indefinite carryover of excess loss.	Yes, for closely held corporations and personal service corporations. Indefinite carryover of excess loss.
Tax consequences of earnings retained by entity	Taxed to owner when earned and increases his or her investment in the sole proprietorship.	Taxed to partners when earned and increases their respective interests in the partnership.	Taxed to shareholders when earned and increases their respective bases in stock.	Taxed to corporation as earned and may be subject to penalty tax if accumulated unreasonably.
Nonliquidating distributions to owners	Not taxable.	Not taxable unless money received exceeds recipient partner's basis in partnership interest. Existence of § 751 assets may cause recognition of ordinary income.	Generally not taxable unless the distribution exceeds the shareholder's AAA or stock basis. Existence of accumulated earnings and profits could cause some distributions to be dividends.	Taxable in year of receipt to extent of earnings and profits or if exceeds basis in stock.
Capital gains	Taxed at owner level with opportunity to use alternative tax rate.	Conduit—partners must account for their respective shares.	Conduit, with certain exceptions (a possible penalty tax)—shareholders must account for their respective shares.	Taxed at corporate level with a maximum 35% rate. No other benefits.
Capital losses	Only $3,000 of capital losses can be offset each tax year against ordinary income. Indefinite carryover.	Conduit—partners must account for their respective shares.	Conduit—shareholders must account for their respective shares.	Carried back three years and carried forward five years. Deductible only to the extent of capital gains.
§ 1231 gains and losses	Taxable or deductible at owner level. Five-year lookback rule for § 1231 losses.	Conduit—partners must account for their respective shares.	Conduit—shareholders must account for their respective shares.	Taxable or deductible at corporate level only. Five-year lookback rule for § 1231 losses.
Foreign tax credits	Available at owner level.	Conduit—passed through to partners.	Generally conduit—passed through to shareholders.	Available at corporate level only.
§ 1244 treatment of loss on sale of interest	Not applicable.	Not applicable.	Available.	Available.
Basis treatment of entity liabilities	Includible in interest basis.	Includible in interest basis.	Not includible in stock basis.	Not includible in stock basis.
Built-in gains	Not applicable.	Not applicable.	Possible corporate tax.	Not applicable.

	Sole Proprietorship	Partnership	S Corporation*	Regular (C) Corporation**
Special allocations to owners	Not applicable (only one owner).	Available if supported by substantial economic effect.	Not available.	Not applicable.
Availability of fringe benefits to owners	None.	None.	None unless a 2%-or-less shareholder.	Available within antidiscrimination rules.
Effect of liquidation/ redemption/ reorganization on basis of entity assets	Not applicable.	Usually carried over from entity to partner unless a § 754 election is made, excessive cash is distributed, or more than 50% of the capital interests are transferred within 12 months.	Taxable step-up to fair market value.	Taxable step-up to fair market value.
Sale of ownership interest	Treated as the sale of individual assets. Classification of recognized gain or loss depends on the nature of the individual assets.	Treated as the sale of a partnership interest. Recognized gain or loss is classified as capital under § 741, subject to ordinary income treatment under § 751.	Treated as the sale of corporate stock. Recognized gain is classified as capital gain. Recognized loss is classified as capital loss, subject to ordinary loss treatment under § 1244.	Treated as the sale of corporate stock. Recognized gain is classified as capital gain. Recognized loss is classified as capital loss, subject to ordinary loss treatment under § 1244.
Distribution of appreciated property	Not taxable.	No recognition at the partnership level.	Recognition at the corporate level to the extent of the appreciation. Conduit—amount of recognized gain is passed through to shareholders.	Taxable at the corporate level to the extent of the appreciation.
Splitting of income among family members	Not applicable (only one owner).	Difficult—IRS will not recognize a family member as a partner unless certain requirements are met.	Rather easy—gift of stock will transfer tax on a pro rata share of income to the donee. However, IRS can make adjustments to reflect adequate compensation for services.	Same as an S corporation, except that donees will be subject to tax only on earnings actually or constructively distributed to them. Other than unreasonable compensation, IRS generally cannot make adjustments to reflect adequate compensation for services and capital.
Organizational costs	Start-up expenditures are amortizable over 60 months.	Amortizable over 60 months.	Same as partnership.	Same as partnership.
Charitable contributions	Limitations apply at owner level.	Conduit—partners are subject to deduction limitations in their own capacities.	Conduit—shareholders are subject to deduction limitations in their own capacities.	Limited to 10% of taxable income before certain deductions.

	Sole Proprietorship	Partnership	S Corporation*	Regular (C) Corporation**
Alternative minimum tax	Applies at owner level. AMT rates are 26% and 28%.	Applies at the partner level rather than at the partnership level. AMT preferences and adjustments are passed through from the partnership to the partners.	Applies at the shareholder level rather than at the corporate level. AMT preferences and adjustments are passed through from the S corporation to the shareholders.	Applies at the corporate level. AMT rate is 20%. Exception for small corporations.
ACE adjustment	Does not apply.	Does not apply.	Does not apply.	The adjustment is made in calculating AMTI. The adjustment is 75% of the excess of adjusted current earnings over unadjusted AMTI. If the unadjusted AMTI exceeds adjusted current earnings, the adjustment is negative.
Tax preference items	Apply at owner level in determining AMT.	Conduit—passed through to partners who must account for such items in their separate capacities.	Conduit—passed through to shareholders who must account for such items in their separate capacities.	Subject to AMT at corporate level.

*Refer to Chapter 21 for additional details on S corporations.
**Refer to Chapters 16 through 20 for additional details on regular (C) corporations.

KEY TERMS

Aggregate concept, 22–8

Appreciated inventory, 22–48

Basis in partnership interest, 22–8

Capital account, 22–8

Capital interest, 22–7

Capital sharing ratio, 22–7

Constructive liquidation scenario, 22–28

Disguised sale, 22–11

Disproportionate distribution, 22–40

Economic effect test, 22–23

Electing large partnership, 22–6

Entity concept, 22–8

General partnership, 22–4

Guaranteed payment, 22–36

Hot assets, 22–48

Inside basis, 22–14

Least aggregate deferral method, 22–18

Limited liability company (LLC), 22–4

Limited liability partnership (LLP), 22–4

Limited partnership, 22–4

Liquidating distribution, 22–44

Nonliquidating distribution, 22–40

Nonrecourse debt, 22–28

Outside basis, 22–14

Precontribution gain or loss, 22–24

Profit and loss sharing ratio, 22–7

Profits (loss) interest, 22–7

Proportionate distribution, 22–40

Qualified nonrecourse debt, 22–34

PROBLEM MATERIALS

DISCUSSION QUESTIONS

1. What is a partnership for Federal income tax purposes?

2. Compare the nonrecognition of gain or loss provision on contributions to a partnership with the similar provision with respect to corporate formation. What are the major differences and similarities?

3. Harlen will contribute $50,000 cash to the HJ Partnership. Jane currently operates a sole proprietorship with assets valued at $50,000. Jane's tax basis in these assets is $75,000. Jane will either contribute these assets to the partnership in exchange for a 50% interest, or she will sell the assets to Brady Salvage (a third party) for their $50,000 fair market value and contribute that cash to the partnership. The partnership needs assets similar to those Jane owns, but it can purchase new assets from a third party for $60,000. Describe the tax consequences of each alternative to both Jane and the partnership.

4. Block, Inc., a calendar year general contractor, and Strauss, Inc., a development corporation with a July 31 year-end, formed the equal SB Partnership on January 1 of the current year. Both partners are C corporations. The partnership was formed to construct and lease shopping centers in Wilmington, Delaware. Block contributed equipment (basis of $650,000, fair market value of $650,000), building permits, and architectural designs that had been created by Block's employees (basis of $0, fair market value of $100,000).

   Strauss contributed land (basis of $50,000, fair market value of $250,000) and cash of $500,000. The cash was used as follows:

Legal fees for drafting partnership agreement	$ 10,000
Materials and labor costs for construction in progress on shopping center	400,000
Office expense (utilities, rent, overhead, etc.)	90,000

   What issues must the partnership address in preparing its initial tax return?

5. Browne and Red, both C corporations, formed the BR Partnership on January 1, 1998. Neither Browne nor Red is a personal service corporation, and BR is not a tax shelter. BR's gross receipts were $4.6 million, $5 million, and $6 million, respectively, for the three tax years ending in 1998, 1999, and 2000. Describe the methods of accounting available to BR in each tax year.

6. What effect does the contribution of property subject to a liability have on the basis of the contributing partner's interest? What is the effect on the basis of the other partners' interests?

7. What is the purpose of the three rules that implement the economic effect test?

8. Describe the procedure for allocating a nonrecourse debt related to appreciated property contributed by a partner, where the debt exceeds the partner's basis in the contributed property. What is the purpose of this allocation system?

9. Discuss the adjustments that must be made to a partner's basis in the partnership interest. When are such adjustments made?

10. To what extent can partners deduct their distributive shares of partnership losses? What happens to any unused losses?

11. Discuss the advantages and disadvantages of the partnership entity form.

12. Sam has operated a microbrewery (sole proprietorship) in southern Oregon for the past 15 years. The business has been highly profitable lately, and demand for the product will soon exceed the amount Sam can produce with his present facilities. Marcie, a long-time fan of the brewery, has offered to invest $1.5 million for equipment to expand production. The assets and goodwill of the brewery are currently worth $1 million (tax basis is only $200,000). Sam will continue to manage the business. He is not willing to own less than 50% of whatever arrangement they arrive at. What issues should Sam and Marcie address and document before finalizing their venture?

13. Comment on the validity of the following statements:
    a. Since a partnership is not a taxable entity, it is not required to file any type of tax return.
    b. Each partner can choose a different method of accounting and depreciation computation in determining the gross income from the entity.
    c. Generally, a transfer of appreciated property to a partnership results in recognized gain to the contributing partner at the time of the transfer.
    d. A partner can carry forward, for an unlimited period of time, the share of any partnership operating losses that exceed the partner's basis in the entity, provided the partner retains an ownership interest in the partnership.
    e. When a partner renders services to the entity in exchange for an unrestricted interest, that partner does not recognize any gross income.
    f. Losses on sales between a partner and the partnership always are nondeductible.
    g. A partnership may choose a year that results in the least aggregate deferral of tax to the partners, unless the IRS requires the use of a natural business year.
    h. A partner's basis in a partnership interest includes that partner's share of partnership recourse and nonrecourse liabilities.
    i. Built-in loss related to nondepreciable property contributed to a partnership must be allocated to the contributing partner to the extent the loss is eventually recognized by the partnership.
    j. Property that was held as inventory by a contributing partner, but is a capital asset in the hands of the partnership, results in a capital gain if the partnership immediately sells the property.

PROBLEMS

14. Dan is an attorney who is financially quite successful. Mary is a real estate developer who has little cash for investment. The two decide to buy some real estate. Dan will contribute the money to buy the properties and have veto power over which properties to purchase. Mary will make all other decisions. Profits and losses from the operation will be shared equally.
    a. Is this a partnership for tax purposes? Why or why not?
    b. Would your answer change if Dan had no veto power and was to receive a guaranteed 10% annual return on his money?

15. Larry and Ken form an equal partnership with a cash contribution of $50,000 from Larry and a property contribution (adjusted basis of $30,000 and a fair market value of $50,000) from Ken.
    a. How much gain, if any, must Larry recognize on the transfer? Must Ken recognize any gain?
    b. What is Larry's interest basis in the partnership?
    c. What is Ken's interest basis in the partnership?
    d. What basis does the partnership take in the property transferred by Ken?

16. James and Lynn form an equal partnership with a cash contribution of $40,000 from James and a property contribution (adjusted basis of $60,000 and a fair market value of $40,000) from Lynn.
    a. How much gain or loss, if any, does Lynn realize on the transfer? May Lynn recognize any gain or loss?

b. What is James's basis in his partnership interest?

c. What is Lynn's basis in her partnership interest?

d. What basis does the partnership take in the property transferred by Lynn?

e. Are there more effective ways to structure the formation?

17. Three years after the S&P Partnership is formed, Sylvia, a 25% partner, contributes an additional $25,000 cash and land she has held for investment. Sylvia's basis in the land is $15,000, and its fair market value is $10,000. Her basis in the partnership interest was $50,000 before this contribution. The partnership uses the land as a parking lot for four years and then sells it for $8,000.

a. How much gain or loss does Sylvia recognize on the contribution?

b. What is Sylvia's basis in her partnership interest immediately following this contribution?

c. How much gain or loss does S&P recognize on this contribution?

d. What is S&P's basis in the property it receives from Sylvia?

e. How much gain or loss does the partnership recognize on the later sale of the land, and what is the character of the gain or loss? How much is allocated to Sylvia?

18. Craig and Beth are equal members of the CB Partnership, formed on June 1 of the current year. Craig contributed land that he inherited from his father three years ago. Craig's father purchased the land in 1946 for $6,000. The land was worth $50,000 when the father died. The fair market value of the land was $75,000 at the date it was contributed to the partnership.

Beth has significant experience developing real estate. After the partnership is formed, she will prepare a plan for developing the property and secure zoning approvals for the partnership. She would normally bill a third party $25,000 for these efforts. Beth will also contribute $50,000 cash in exchange for her 50% interest in the partnership. The value of her 50% interest is $75,000.

a. How much gain or income will Craig recognize on his contribution of the land to the partnership? What is the character of any gain or income recognized?

b. What basis will Craig take in his partnership interest?

c. How much gain or income will Beth recognize on the formation of the partnership? What is the character of any gain or income recognized?

d. What basis will Beth take in her partnership interest?

e. Construct an opening balance sheet for the partnership reflecting the partnership's basis in assets and the fair market value of these assets.

f. Outline any planning opportunities that may minimize current taxation to any of the parties.

19. Continue with the facts presented in Problem 18. At the end of the first year, the partnership distributes the $50,000 cash to Craig. No distribution is made to Beth.

a. Under general tax rules, how would the payment to Craig be treated?

b. How much income or gain would Craig recognize as a result of the payment?

c. Under general tax rules, what basis would the partnership take in the land Craig contributed?

d. What alternate treatment might the IRS try to impose?

e. Under the alternate treatment, how much income or gain would Craig recognize?

f. Under the alternate treatment, what basis would the partnership take in the land contributed by Craig?

20. The SAM Partnership was formed to acquire land and subdivide it as residential housing lots. On July 1, 1997, Sue contributed land valued at $100,000 to the partnership, in exchange for a one-third interest in SAM. She had purchased the land in 1991 for $76,000 and held it for investment purposes (capital asset). The partnership holds the land as inventory.

On the same date, Aaron contributed land valued at $100,000 that he had purchased in 1989 for $120,000. He also became a one-third owner. Aaron is a real estate developer, but this land was held personally for investment purposes. The partnership holds this land as inventory.

Margie had sold a parcel of land held for development purposes in 1994 on the installment basis. She, too, is a real estate developer. The installment note has a fair market value and remaining principal balance of $100,000. She contributed this note to the partnership on the same day in exchange for her one-third interest. Margie's basis in the note was $60,000 on the contribution date; the deferred gain on the installment sale is $40,000.

From 1997 to 2001, the partnership collects $20,000 per year on the installment obligation (plus adequate interest on the unpaid balance). In 1998, the partnership sells the land contributed by Sue for $124,000. In 1999, the partnership sells one-half of the subdivided real estate contributed by Aaron for $44,000. The other half is finally sold in 2005 for $54,000.

a. What is each partner's initial basis in his or her partnership interest?
b. What is the amount of gross profit recognized each year on collection of the installment proceeds? What is the character of the gain or loss?
c. What is the amount of gain or loss recognized on the sale of the land contributed by Sue? What is the character of this gain or loss?
d. What is the amount of gain or loss recognized each year on the sale of the land contributed by Aaron? What is the character of this gain or loss?

21. Continuing with Problem 20, the SAM Partnership agreement provides that all gains and losses are allocated equally among the partners, unless otherwise required under the tax law.
a. How will the gains or losses determined in parts (b), (c), and (d) above be allocated to each of the partners?
b. If the partnership earns $24,000 of interest income over the term of the installment note, how will this income be allocated to the partners? Assume no accrued interest existed on the day the note was contributed.
c. Calculate each partner's basis in his or her partnership interest at December 31, 2005. Assume the partnership has no transactions through the end of the year 2005 other than the transactions described in Problem 20 and the collection of $24,000 of interest income per (b) above. Why are these balances the same or different?

22. The cash method Thrush Partnership, which reports on a calendar year basis, incurred the following organization and syndication costs in 1998:

Attorney fees for preparing partnership agreement	$2,100
Printing costs for preparing documents that were used to help sell the partnership interests	4,000
Accounting fees for tax advice of an organizational nature	2,400

The attorney fees and printing costs were incurred and paid in 1998. The accounting fees were incurred in December 1998 and paid in February 1999. If the partnership begins business in July 1998, how much of the organization costs can be amortized in 1998? In 1999?

23. Jim, John, and Judy form the JJJ Partnership on January 1 of the current year. Jim is a 50% partner, and John and Judy are each 25% partners. Each partner and JJJ use the cash method of accounting. For reporting purposes, Jim uses a calendar year, John uses an August 31 fiscal year, and Judy uses a May 31 fiscal year. What is JJJ's required tax year under the least aggregate deferral method?

24. Lisa and Lori are equal members of the Redbird Partnership. They are real estate investors who formed the partnership several years ago with equal cash contributions. Redbird then purchased a piece of land.

On January 1 of the current year, to acquire a one-third interest in the entity, Lana contributed some land she had held for investment to the partnership. Lana purchased the land three years ago for $30,000; its fair market value at the contribution date was $40,000. No special allocation agreements were in effect before or after Lana was admitted to the partnership. The Redbird Partnership holds all land for investment.

Immediately before Lana's property contribution, the balance sheet of the Redbird Partnership was as follows:

	Basis	FMV		Basis	FMV
Land	$5,000	$80,000	Lisa, capital	$2,500	$40,000
			Lori, capital	2,500	40,000
	$5,000	$80,000		$5,000	$80,000

a. At the contribution date, what is Lana's basis in her interest in the Redbird Partnership?
b. When does the partnership's holding period begin for the contributed land?
c. On June 30 of the current year, the partnership sold the land contributed by Lana for $40,000. How much is the recognized gain or loss, and how is it allocated among the partners?
d. Prepare a balance sheet reflecting basis and fair market value for the partnership immediately after the land sale.

25. Assume the same facts as in Problem 24, with the following exceptions.

- Lana purchased the land three years ago for $50,000. Its fair market value was $40,000 when it was contributed to the partnership.

- Redbird sold the land contributed by Lana for $34,000.

a. How much is the recognized gain or loss, and how is it allocated among the partners?
b. Prepare a balance sheet reflecting basis and fair market value for the partnership immediately after the land sale, along with schedules that support the amount in each partner's capital account.

26. Earl and Zelda are equal partners in the accrual basis EZ Partnership. At the beginning of the current year, Earl's capital account has a balance of $10,000, and the partnership has recourse debts of $30,000 payable to unrelated parties. All partnership recourse debt is shared equally between the partners. The following information about EZ's operations for the current year is obtained from the partnership's records.

Taxable income	$ 8,000
Tax-exempt interest income	2,000
§ 1231 gain	6,000
Long-term capital gain	2,000
Long-term capital loss	120
Short-term capital loss	600
IRS penalty	630
Charitable contribution to Girl Scouts	200
Cash distribution to Earl	14,000
Payment of Earl's medical expenses	6,000

Assume that year-end partnership debt payable to unrelated parties is $40,000.
a. If all transactions are reflected in his beginning capital and basis in the same manner, what is Earl's basis in the partnership interest at the beginning of the year?
b. If all transactions are reflected in his beginning capital and basis in the same manner, what is Earl's basis in the partnership interest at the end of the current year?

27. The RUB Partnership reported the following items during the current tax year:

Taxable income	$120,000
Municipal bond interest income	10,000
Gain on sale of real estate	60,000

Taxable income includes $20,000 of income from collection of cash basis accounts receivable contributed by 25% partner Rolfe at the beginning of the year.

The municipal bond income was earned on bonds contributed by 50% partner Una. None of the interest was accrued on the contribution date. The partnership agreement provides that all this income will be specially allocated to Una this year, and no offsetting allocation will be made now or later.

The real estate gain resulted from the sale of a parcel of land contributed by 25% partner Bart. When the property was contributed, it was valued at $100,000 and Bart's basis was $80,000. Assume the real estate is a capital asset to both Bart and the partnership.

Prepare a schedule showing how each item is allocated to each of the three partners. Assume the partnership will maintain capital account balances and perform all other record keeping required to meet the substantial economic effect requirements of § 704(b).

28. The RB Partnership is owned equally by Rob and Bob. Rob's basis is $6,000 at the beginning of the tax year. Bob's basis is $15,000 at the beginning of the year. RB reported the following income and expenses for the current tax year:

Sales revenue	$130,000
Cost of sales	45,000
Guaranteed payment to Rob	24,000
Depreciation expense	12,500
Utilities	15,000
Rent	16,000
Interest income	3,000
Tax-exempt interest income	4,500
Long-term capital loss	3,200
Payment to Mount Vernon Hospital for Bob's medical expenses	10,000

a. Determine the ordinary partnership income and separately stated items for the partnership.
b. Calculate Bob's basis in his partnership interest at the end of the tax year. What items should Bob report on his Federal income tax return?
c. Calculate Rob's basis in his partnership interest at the end of the tax year. What items should Rob report on his Federal income tax return?

29. Assume the same facts as in Problem 28, except for the following:

- Partnership revenues were $90,000 instead of $130,000.

- Rob also received a distribution of $10,000 cash.

a. Redetermine the ordinary income and separately stated items for the partnership.
b. Calculate Bob's basis in his partnership interest at the end of the tax year. How much income or loss should Bob report on his Federal income tax return?
c. Calculate Rob's basis in his partnership interest at the end of the tax year. How much income or loss should Rob report on his Federal income tax return?

30. As of January 1 of last year, Don's outside basis and at-risk basis for his 25% interest in the DEF Partnership were $24,000. Don and the partnership use the calendar year for tax purposes. The partnership incurred an operating loss of $100,000 for the last year and a profit of $12,000 for the current year. Don is a material participant in the partnership.
a. How much loss, if any, may Don recognize for last year?
b. How much net reportable income must Don recognize for the current year?
c. What is Don's basis in the partnership as of December 31 of last year?
d. What is Don's basis in the partnership as of December 31 of the current year?
e. What year-end tax planning would you suggest to ensure that Don can deduct his share of partnership losses?

31. Your client, the Williams Institute of Technology (WIT), is a 60% partner in the Research Industries Partnership (RIP). WIT is located at 76 Bradford Lane, St. Paul, MN 55164. The controller, Jeanine West, has sent you the following note and a copy of WIT's 1998 Schedule K–1 from the partnership.

    Excerpt from client's note:
    "RIP expects its 1999 operations to include the following:

Net loss from operations	$200,000
Capital gain from sale of land	100,000

    The land was contributed by DASH, the other partner, when its value was $260,000. The partnership sold the land for $300,000. The partnership used this cash to repay all the partnership debt and pay for research and development expenditures, which a tax partner in your firm has said RIP can deduct this year.

    We want to be sure we can deduct our full share of this loss, but we do not believe we will have enough basis. We are a material participant in this partnership's activities."

Items Reported on the 1998 Schedule K–1	
WIT's share of partnership recourse liabilities	$90,000
WIT's ending capital account balance	30,000

    Draft a letter to the controller that describes the following:

    - WIT's allocation of partnership items.

    - WIT's basis in the partnership interest following the allocation.

    - Any limitations on loss deductions.

    - Any recommendations you have that would allow WIT to claim the full amount of losses in 1999.

    Assume WIT's 1998 K–1 accurately reflects the information needed to compute the basis in the partnership interest. Also assume the research expenditures are fully deductible this year, as the partner said.

    Your client has experience researching issues in the Internal Revenue Code, so you may use some citations. However, be sure the letter is written in layperson's terms and cites are minimized.

32. Lee, Brad, and Rick form the LBR Partnership on January 1 of the current year. In return for a 25% interest, Lee transfers property (basis of $15,000, fair market value of $17,500) subject to a nonrecourse liability of $10,000. The liability is assumed by the partnership. Brad transfers property (basis of $16,000, fair market value of $7,500) for a 25% interest, and Rick transfers cash of $15,000 for the remaining 50% interest. (See Example 24.)
    a. How much gain must Lee recognize on the transfer?
    b. What is Lee's basis in his interest in the partnership?
    c. How much loss may Brad recognize on the transfer?
    d. What is Brad's basis in his interest in the partnership?
    e. What is Rick's basis in his interest in the partnership?
    f. What basis does the LBR Partnership take in the property transferred by Lee?
    g. What is the partnership's basis in the property transferred by Brad?

33. Assume the same facts as in Problem 32, except that the property contributed by Lee has a fair market value of $27,500 and is subject to a nonrecourse mortgage of $20,000. (See Example 28.)
    a. What is Lee's basis in his partnership interest?
    b. How much gain must Lee recognize on the transfer?
    c. What is Brad's basis in his partnership interest?
    d. What is Rick's basis in his partnership interest?
    e. What basis does the LBR Partnership take in the property transferred by Lee?

34. Jen and Ken establish the JK General Partnership on December 31 of the current year. Each partner contributed $20,000 cash to the partnership in exchange for the partnership interest. The partnership used the $40,000 cash to help purchase a parcel of land for $100,000. The other $60,000 of financing for the land was obtained from a local bank. In addition to using the land as collateral, both partners are also personally liable on the note.

    The capital accounts are properly maintained, and each partner has to restore any deficit in the capital account. The partnership agreement provides that Jen will be allocated 90% of the partnership income, gains, losses, deductions, and credits until she has been allocated income and gains equal to her previous allocations of losses and deductions. Thereafter, all partnership items will be allocated equally.

    Draft a letter to the partnership that describes how the note will be shared between the partners for purposes of computing the adjusted basis of each partnership interest. Address the letter to Ms. Jen Ayers and Mr. Ken Montgomery, 123 Byrd Street, Amarillo, TX 79105.

35. Chris Elton is a 15% partner in the Cardinal Partnership, which is a lessor of residential rental property. Her share of the partnership's losses for the current year is $70,000. Immediately before considering the deductibility of this loss, Chris's capital account (which, in this case, corresponds to her basis excluding liabilities) reflected a balance of $40,000. Her share of partnership recourse liabilities is $10,000, and her share of the nonrecourse liabilities is $6,000. The nonrecourse liability was obtained from an unrelated bank and is secured solely by the real estate. Chris is also a partner in the Bluebird Partnership, which has generated income from long-term (more than 30 days) equipment rental activities. Chris's share of Bluebird's income is $23,000. Chris performs substantial services for Bluebird and spends several hundred hours a year working for the Cardinal Partnership. Chris's modified AGI before considering partnership activities is $100,000. Your manager has asked you to determine how much of the $70,000 loss Chris can deduct on her current calendar year return. Using the format (1) facts, (2) issues, (3) conclusion, and (4) law and analysis, draft a memo to the client's tax file describing the loss limitations. Be sure to identify the Code sections under which the losses are suspended.

36. Fred and Fran are equal partners in the calendar year F & F Partnership. Fred uses a fiscal year ending June 30, and Fran uses a calendar year. Fred receives an annual guaranteed payment of $50,000 from F & F. F & F's taxable income (after deducting Fred's guaranteed payment) was $40,000 for 1998 and $50,000 for 1999.
    a. What is the aggregate amount of income from the partnership that Fred must report for his tax year ending June 30, 1999?
    b. What is the aggregate amount of income from the partnership that Fran must report for her tax year ending December 31, 1999?
    c. If Fred's annual guaranteed payment is increased to $60,000 starting on January 1, 1999, and the partnership's taxable income for 1998 and 1999 is the same (i.e., $40,000 and $50,000, respectively), what is the aggregate amount of income from the partnership that Fred must report for his tax year ending June 30, 1999?

37. Ned, a 50% partner in the MN Partnership, is to receive a payment of $35,000 for services. He will also be allocated 50% of the partnership's profits or losses. After deducting the payment to Ned, the partnership has a loss of $25,000. Ned's basis in his partnership interest was $10,000 before these items.
    a. How much, if any, of the $25,000 partnership loss will be allocated to Ned?
    b. What is the net income from the partnership that Ned must report on his Federal income tax return?
    c. What is Ned's basis in his partnership interest following the guaranteed payment and loss allocation?

38. Four Lakes Partnership is owned by four sisters. Anne holds a 70% interest; each of the others own 10%. Anne sells investment property to the partnership for its fair market value of $100,000 (Anne's basis is $150,000).

a. How much loss, if any, may Anne recognize?

b. If the partnership later sells the property for $160,000, how much gain must it recognize?

c. If Anne's basis in the investment property was $20,000 instead of $150,000, how much, if any, capital gain would she recognize on the sale?

39. When Peggy's outside basis in the PQR Partnership is $25,000, the partnership distributes to her $10,000 cash, an account receivable (fair market value of $70,000, inside basis to the partnership of $0), and a parcel of land (fair market value of $30,000, inside basis to the partnership of $20,000). Peggy remains a partner in the partnership, and the distribution is proportionate to the partners.

a. Determine the recognized gain or loss to the partnership as a result of this distribution.

b. Determine the recognized gain or loss to Peggy as a result of the distribution.

c. Determine Peggy's basis in the land, account receivable, and PQR Partnership after the distribution.

40. In each of the following independent cases in which the partnership owns no hot assets, indicate:

- Whether the partner recognizes gain or loss.

- Whether the partnership recognizes gain or loss.

- The partner's adjusted basis for the property distributed.

- The partner's outside basis in the partnership after the distribution.

a. Mora receives $35,000 of cash in partial liquidation of her interest in the partnership. Mora's outside basis for her partnership interest immediately before the distribution is $30,000.

b. Mark receives $15,000 of cash and land with an inside basis to the partnership of $4,000 (value $6,000) in partial liquidation of his interest. Mark's outside basis for his partnership interest immediately before the distribution is $20,000.

c. Assume the same facts as in (b), except that Mark's outside basis for his partnership interest immediately before the distribution is $15,000.

d. Brad receives $10,000 cash and an account receivable with a basis of $0 and a fair market value of $10,000 in partial liquidation of his partnership interest. His basis was $6,000 before the distribution. All partners received proportionate distributions.

41. Tom's basis in his partnership interest is $41,000. In a proportionate nonliquidating distribution, Tom receives $20,000 cash and two inventory items, each with a basis of $20,000 to the partnership. The values of the inventory items are $30,000 and $10,000, respectively.

a. How much gain or loss, if any, must Tom recognize on the distribution?

b. What basis will Tom take in each inventory item?

42. The basis of Lou's partnership interest is $40,000. Lou receives a pro rata liquidating distribution consisting of $22,500 cash and his proportionate share of inventory with a basis of $24,500 to the partnership and a fair market value of $28,000. Assume the partnership also liquidates.

a. How much gain or loss, if any, must Lou recognize as a result of the distribution?

b. What basis will Lou take in the inventory?

c. If the inventory is sold two years later for $28,000, what are the tax consequences to Lou?

d. What are the tax consequences to the partnership as a result of the liquidating distribution?

e. Would your answer to (b) change if this had been a nonliquidating distribution?

43. In 1998, Gabriella contributed land with a basis of $16,000 and a fair market value of $25,000 to the Meadowlark Partnership in exchange for a 25% interest in capital and profits. In 2000, the partnership distributes this property to Juanita, also a 25% partner, in a nonliquidating distribution. The fair market value has increased to $30,000 at the

time the property is distributed. Juanita's and Gabriella's bases in their partnership interests are each $30,000 at the time of the distribution.

a. How much gain or loss, if any, does Gabriella recognize on the distribution to Juanita? What is Gabriella's basis in her partnership interest following the distribution?

b. What is Juanita's basis in the land she received in the distribution?

c. How much gain or loss, if any, does Juanita recognize on the distribution? What is Juanita's basis in her partnership interest following the distribution?

d. How much gain or loss would Juanita recognize if she later sells the land for its $30,000 fair market value? Is this result equitable?

e. Would your answers to (a) and (b) change if Gabriella originally contributed the property to the partnership in 1990?

44. Donald sells his interest in the equal DDP Partnership to his partner, Paul, for $47,000 cash and the assumption of Donald's share of partnership liabilities. On the sale date, the partnership's cash basis balance sheet reflects the following (assume capital accounts reflect the partners' bases in their partnership interests, excluding liabilities):

	Basis	FMV
Cash	$51,000	$ 51,000
Accounts receivable	–0–	60,000
Capital assets	9,000	39,000
Total	$60,000	$150,000

	Basis	FMV
Note payable	$ 9,000	$ 9,000
Capital accounts		
Dale	17,000	47,000
Donald	17,000	47,000
Paul	17,000	47,000
Total	$60,000	$150,000

a. What is the total amount realized by Donald on the sale?

b. How much, if any, ordinary income must Donald recognize on the sale?

c. How much capital gain must Donald report?

Research Problems for this chapter appear at the end of Chapter 28.

23

EXEMPT ENTITIES

LEARNING OBJECTIVES

After completing Chapter 23, you should be able to:

1. Identify the different types of exempt organizations.

2. Enumerate the requirements for exempt status.

3. Know the tax consequences of exempt status, including the different consequences for public charities and private foundations.

4. Determine which exempt organizations are classified as private foundations.

5. Recognize the taxes imposed on private foundations and calculate the related initial tax and additional tax amounts.

6. Determine when an exempt organization is subject to the unrelated business income tax and calculate the amount of the tax.

7. List the reports exempt organizations must file with the IRS and the related due dates.

8. Identify tax planning opportunities for exempt organizations.

▼ GENERAL CONSIDERATIONS

Ideally, any entity that generates profit would prefer not to be subject to the Federal income tax. All of the types of entities discussed thus far are subject to the Federal income tax at one (e.g., sole proprietorships, partnerships, and S corporations generally are only subject to single taxation) or more (e.g., C corporations are subject to double taxation) levels. However, organizations classified as **exempt organizations** may be able to escape Federal income taxation altogether.

Churches are among the types of organizations that are exempt from Federal income tax. Nevertheless, one must be careful not to conclude that everything labeled a church will qualify for exempt status.

During the 1970s and 1980s, a popular technique for attempting to avoid Federal income tax was the establishment of so-called mail-order churches. For example, in one scheme, a nurse obtained a certificate of ordination and a church charter from an organization that sold such documents.[1] The articles of incorporation stated that the church was organized exclusively for religious and charitable purposes, including a religious mission of healing the spirit, mind, emotions, and body. The nurse was the church's minister, director, and principal officer. Taking a vow of poverty, she transferred all her assets, including a house and car, to the church. The church assumed all of the nurse's liabilities, including the mortgage on her house and her credit card bills. The nurse continued to work at a hospital and deposited her salary in the church's bank account. The church provided her with a living allowance sufficient to maintain or improve her previous standard of living. She was also permitted to use the house and car for personal purposes.

The IRS declared that such organizations were shams and not bona fide churches. For a church to be tax-exempt under § 501(c)(3), none of its net earnings may be used to the benefit of any private shareholder or individual. In essence, the organization should serve a public rather than a private interest. Although the courts have consistently upheld the IRS position, numerous avoidance schemes such as this have been attempted.

---

[1]Rev.Rul. 81–94, 1981–1 C.B. 330.

As discussed in Chapter 1, the major objective of the Federal tax law is to raise revenue. If revenue raising were the only objective, however, the Code would not contain provisions that permit certain organizations to be either partially or completely exempt from Federal income tax. Social considerations may also affect the tax law. This objective bears directly on the decision by Congress to provide for exempt organization tax status. The House Report on the Revenue Act of 1938 provides as follows:

> The exemption from taxation of money or property devoted to charitable and other purposes is based upon the theory that the Government is compensated for the loss of revenue by its relief from the financial burden which would otherwise have to be met by appropriations from public funds, and by the benefits resulting from the promotion of the general welfare.[2]

In recognition of this social consideration objective, Subchapter F (Exempt Organizations) of the Code (§§ 501–529) provides the authority under which certain organizations are exempt from Federal income tax. Exempt status is not open-ended in that two general limitations exist. First, the nature or scope of the organization may result in it being only partially exempt from tax.[3] Second, the organization may engage in activities that are subject to special taxation.[4]

TYPES OF EXEMPT ORGANIZATIONS

1 **LEARNING OBJECTIVE**
Identify the different types of exempt organizations.

An organization qualifies for exempt status *only* if it fits into one of the categories provided in the Code. Examples of qualifying exempt organizations and the specific statutory authority for their exempt status are listed in Exhibit 23–1.[5]

REQUIREMENTS FOR EXEMPT STATUS

2 **LEARNING OBJECTIVE**
Enumerate the requirements for exempt status.

Exempt status frequently requires more than mere classification in one of the categories of exempt organizations. Many of the organizations that qualify for exempt status share the following characteristics.

- The organization serves some type of *common good*.[6]
- The organization is a *not-for-profit* entity.[7]
- *Net earnings* do not benefit the members of the organization.[8]
- The organization does not exert *political influence*.[9]

SERVING THE COMMON GOOD

The underlying rationale for all exempt organizations is that they serve some type of *common good*. However, depending on the type of the exempt organization, the

---

[2]See 1939–1 (Part 2) C.B. 742 for a reprint of H.R. No. 1860, 75th Congress, 3rd Session.
[3]See the subsequent discussion of Unrelated Business Income Tax.
[4]See the subsequent discussions of Prohibited Transactions and Taxes Imposed on Private Foundations.
[5]Section 501(a) provides for exempt status for organizations described in §§ 401 and 501. The orientation of this chapter is toward organizations that conduct business activities. Therefore,

the exempt organizations described in § 401 (qualified pension, profit sharing, and stock bonus trusts) are outside the scope of the chapter and are not discussed.
[6]See, for example, §§ 501(c)(3) and (4).
[7]See, for example, §§ 501(c)(3), (4), (6), (13), and (14).
[8]See, for example, §§ 501(c)(3), (6), (7), (9), (10), (11), and (19).
[9]See, for example, § 501(c)(3).

▼ EXHIBIT 23–1
Types of Exempt Organizations

Statutory Authority	Brief Description	Examples or Comments
§ 501(c)(1)	Federal and related agencies.	Commodity Credit Corporation, Federal Deposit Insurance Corporation, Federal Land Bank.
§ 501(c)(2)	Corporations holding title to property for and paying income to exempt organizations.	Corporation holding title to college fraternity house.
§ 501(c)(3)	Religious, charitable, educational, scientific, literary, etc., organizations.	Boy Scouts of America, Red Cross, Salvation Army, Episcopal Church, United Fund, University of Richmond.
§ 501(c)(4)	Civic leagues and employee unions.	Garden club, tenants' association promoting tenants' legal rights in entire community, League of Women Voters.
§ 501(c)(5)	Labor, agricultural, and horticultural organizations.	Teachers' association, organization formed to promote effective agricultural pest control, organization formed to test soil and to educate community members in soil treatment, garden club.
§ 501(c)(6)	Business leagues, chambers of commerce, real estate boards, etc.	Chambers of Commerce, American Plywood Association, National Football League (NFL), medical association peer review board, organization promoting acceptance of women in business and professions.
§ 501(c)(7)	Social clubs.	Country club, rodeo and riding club, press club, bowling club, college fraternities.
§ 501(c)(8)	Fraternal beneficiary societies.	Lodges. Must provide for the payment of life, sickness, accident, or other benefits to members or their dependents.
§ 501(c)(9)	Voluntary employees' beneficiary associations.	Provide for the payment of life, sickness, accident, or other benefits to members, their dependents, or their designated beneficiaries.
§ 501(c)(10)	Domestic fraternal societies.	Lodges. Must not provide for the payment of life, sickness, accident, or other benefits; and must devote the net earnings exclusively to religious, charitable, scientific, literary, educational, and fraternal purposes.
§ 501(c)(11)	Local teachers' retirement fund associations.	Only permitted sources of income are amounts received from (1) public taxation, (2) assessments on teaching salaries of members, and (3) income from investments.
§ 501(c)(12)	Local benevolent life insurance associations, mutual or cooperative telephone companies, etc.	Local cooperative telephone company, local mutual water company, local mutual electric company.
§ 501(c)(13)	Cemetery companies.	Must be operated exclusively for the benefit of lot owners who hold the lots for burial purposes.
§ 501(c)(14)	Credit unions.	Other than credit unions exempt under § 501(c)(1).
§ 501(c)(15)	Mutual insurance companies.	Mutual fire insurance company, mutual automobile insurance company.
§ 501(c)(16)	Corporations organized by farmers' cooperatives for financing crop operations.	Related farmers' cooperative must be exempt from tax under § 521.
§ 501(c)(19)	Armed forces members' posts or organizations.	Veterans of Foreign Wars (VFW), Reserve Officers Association.
§ 501(c)(20)	Group legal service plans.	Provided by a corporation for its employees.
§ 501(d)	Religious and apostolic organizations.	Communal organization. Members must include pro rata share of the net income of the organization in their gross income as dividends.
§ 501(e)	Cooperative hospital service organizations.	Centralized purchasing organization for exempt hospitals.
§ 501(f)	Cooperative service organization of educational institutions.	Organization formed to manage universities' endowment funds.
§ 529	Qualified state tuition programs.	State-sponsored prepaid tuition and educational savings programs.

term *common good* may be interpreted broadly or narrowly. If the test is interpreted broadly, the group being served is the general public or some large subgroup thereof. If it is interpreted narrowly, the group is the specific group referred to in the statutory language. One of the factors in classifying an exempt organization as a private foundation is the size of the group it serves.

NOT-FOR-PROFIT ENTITY

The organization may not be organized or operated for the purpose of making a profit. For some types of exempt organizations, the *for-profit prohibition* appears in the statutory language. For other types, the prohibition is implied.

NET EARNINGS AND MEMBERS OF THE ORGANIZATION

What uses are appropriate for the net earnings of tax-exempt organizations? The logical answer would seem to be that the earnings should be used for the exempt purpose of the organization. However, where the organization exists for the good of a specific group of members, such an open-ended interpretation could permit net earnings to benefit specific group members. Therefore, the Code specifically prohibits certain types of exempt organizations from using their earnings in this way.

> . . . no part of the net earnings . . . inures to the benefit of any private shareholder or individual . . .[10]

In other instances, a statutory prohibition is unnecessary because the definition of the exempt organization in the Code effectively prevents such use.

> . . . the net earnings of which are devoted exclusively to religious, charitable, scientific, literary, educational, and fraternal purposes . . .[11]

POLITICAL INFLUENCE

Religious, charitable, educational, etc., organizations are generally prohibited from attempting to influence legislation or participate in political campaigns. Participation in political campaigns includes participation both *on behalf of* a candidate and *in opposition to* a candidate.

Only in limited circumstances are such exempt organizations permitted to attempt to influence legislation. See the subsequent discussion under Prohibited Transactions.

ETHICAL CONSIDERATIONS

A Church Attempts to Change Society

Amos Heck is the founder, and the man behind the throne, of the Church of the Future television ministry. Ministry broadcasts originate from church services in California and New York and are broadcast via cable throughout the United States. While the membership of the Church of the Future is small (approximately 1,500 members), the typical member is quite wealthy. In addition to receiving contributions from its members,

---

[10]§ 501(c)(6).   [11]§ 501(c)(10).

the church solicits and receives donations from viewers of the TV broadcasts. The church is tax-exempt under § 501(c)(3).

The stated mission of the church is religious in nature. However, Amos firmly believes, as do the members of the board of deacons of the church, that certain societal goals must be accomplished for the prophecies of the church to come true (i.e., their divine being expects them to be active missionaries). Among its basic beliefs, the church advocates government control and possession of all guns, the legalization of drugs, abortion on demand once approved by the appropriate government agency, the withdrawal of all U.S. troops from foreign soil and the termination of all military alliances, the abolition of capital punishment, and the availability of tuition-free university education to all U.S. citizens.

The ministers of the Church of the Future are expected to include these basic beliefs, at the subliminal level, in their sermons. Some do so more effectively and more frequently than others, but all are required to do so. Amos and the board of deacons are dismayed that more of their beliefs have not been incorporated into American society.

Amos proposes to the board of deacons that the church take a more proactive role. The employment contract of the ministers will now require them to include the basic beliefs in their sermons in an active manner. No longer can the beliefs just be incorporated subliminally. All the beliefs must be covered quarterly, and every sermon must present at least one of the basic beliefs. The ministers will encourage the church members and TV viewers to actively support these positions at both the state and the Federal levels.

As a new member of the board of deacons, you wholeheartedly support Amos's position. However, you are concerned about the effect of this open advocacy of positions on the tax-exempt status of the church. Amos responds that the "church has friends in high places" and assures you that the tax-exempt status will not be endangered.

TAX CONSEQUENCES OF EXEMPT STATUS: GENERAL

3   LEARNING OBJECTIVE
Know the tax consequences of exempt status, including the different consequences for public charities and private foundations.

An organization that is appropriately classified as one of the types of exempt organizations is generally exempt from Federal income tax. Four exceptions to this general statement exist, however. An exempt organization that engages in a *prohibited transaction*, or is a so-called *feeder organization*, is subject to tax. If the organization is classified as a *private foundation*, it may be partially subject to tax. Finally, an exempt organization is subject to tax on its *unrelated business taxable income* (which includes unrelated debt-financed income).

In addition to being exempt from Federal income tax, an exempt organization may be eligible for other benefits, including the following.

- The organization may be exempt from state income tax, state franchise tax, sales tax, or property tax.
- The organization may receive discounts on postage rates.
- Donors of property to the exempt organization may qualify for charitable contribution deductions on their Federal and state income tax returns. However, *not* all exempt organizations are qualified charitable contribution recipients (e.g., gifts to the National Football League, PGA Tour, and Underwriters Laboratories are not deductible).

PROHIBITED TRANSACTIONS

Engaging in a prohibited transaction can produce two negative results. First, part or all of the organization's income may be subject to Federal income tax. Even worse, the organization may forfeit its exempt status.

Failure to Continue to Qualify. Organizations initially qualify for exempt status only if they are organized as indicated in Exhibit 23–1. The initial qualification requirements then effectively become maintenance requirements. Failure to continue to meet the qualification requirements results in the loss of the entity's exempt status.

New Faith, Inc., is an excellent example of an exempt organization that failed to continue to qualify for tax exemption.[12] The stated purposes of the organization were to feed and shelter the poor. In its application for exempt status, New Faith indicated that it would derive its financial support from donations, bingo games, and raffles. The IRS approved the exempt status.

New Faith's only source of income was the operation of several lunch trucks, which provided food to the general public in exchange for scheduled "donations." Evidence provided by the organization to the Tax Court did not show that the food from the lunch trucks was provided free of charge or at reduced prices. In addition, no evidence was presented to show that the people who received food for free or at below-cost prices were impoverished or needy. The court concluded that the primary purpose of the activity was the conduct of a trade or business. It upheld the IRS's revocation of New Faith's exempt status.

Election Not to Forfeit Exempt Status for Lobbying. Organizations exempt under § 501(c)(3) (religious, charitable, educational, etc., organizations) generally are prohibited from attempting to influence legislation (lobbying activities) or from participating in political campaigns.[13] Any violation can result in the forfeiture of exempt status.

Certain § 501(c)(3) exempt organizations are permitted to engage in lobbying activities on a limited basis.[14] Eligible for such treatment are most § 501(c)(3) exempt organizations (educational institutions, hospitals, and medical research organizations; organizations supporting government schools; organizations publicly supported by charitable contributions; certain organizations that are publicly supported by various sources including admissions, sales, gifts, grants, contributions, or membership fees; and certain organizations that support certain types of public charities). Churches, their integrated auxiliaries, and *private foundations* are not permitted to engage in lobbying activities, however.

An eligible § 501(c)(3) organization must make an affirmative election to participate in lobbying activities on a limited basis. The lobbying expenditures of electing § 501(c)(3) organizations are subject to a ceiling. Exceeding the ceiling can lead to the forfeiture of exempt status. Even when the ceiling is not exceeded, a tax may be imposed on some of the lobbying expenditures (discussed subsequently).

Two terms are key to the calculation of the ceiling amount: **lobbying expenditures** and **grass roots expenditures.** Lobbying expenditures are made for the purpose of influencing legislation through either of the following.

---

[12]*New Faith, Inc.,* 64 TCM 1050, T.C.Memo. 1992–601.
[13]§ 501(c)(3).

[14]§ 501(h). An affirmative election to lobby must be made.

MORE AUDITS OF TAX–EXEMPTS

The IRS plans to conduct more audits of tax-exempt organizations. A major concern is the possible participation of tax-exempts in political activities. Asked what "political activity" will trigger an audit, IRS spokesperson Frank Keith said that "it's a facts-and-circumstances issue that's decided on a case by case basis."

Recent media reports have raised the question of whether several high-profile conservative organizations have been targeted in politically motivated audits. In the past, the Oliver North Freedom Alliance has been audited, and organizations currently under audit include the National Rifle Association, the Heritage Foundation, and the Citizens Against Government Waste. The IRS contends that these audits are not politically motivated and that it is merely following leads about noncompliance with the tax law.

For 1995, the IRS audited 10,500 of the 1.2 million tax-exempt organizations and assessed a total of $126.6 million in taxes and penalties.

SOURCE: Adapted from Jacob M. Schlesinger, "IRS Planning More Audits of Nonprofits," *Wall Street Journal*, February 10, 1997, p. A3.

- Attempting to affect the opinions of the general public or any segment thereof.
- Communicating with any legislator or staff member or with any government official or staff member who may participate in the formulation of legislation.

Grass roots expenditures are made for the purpose of influencing legislation by attempting to affect the opinions of the general public or any segment thereof.

The statutory ceiling is imposed on both lobbying expenditures and grass roots expenditures and is computed as follows.

- 150% × lobbying nontaxable amount = lobbying expenditures ceiling.
- 150% × grass roots nontaxable amount = grass roots expenditures ceiling.

The *lobbying nontaxable amount* is the lesser of (1) $1 million or (2) the amount determined in Figure 23–1.[15] The *grass roots nontaxable amount* is 25 percent of the lobbying nontaxable amount.[16]

A tax may be assessed on an electing exempt organization's **excess lobbying expenditures** as follows.[17]

- 25% × excess lobbying expenditures = tax liability.

Excess lobbying expenditures are the greater of the following.[18]

- Excess of the lobbying expenditures for the taxable year over the lobbying nontaxable amount.
- Excess of the grass roots expenditures for the taxable year over the grass roots nontaxable amount.

---

[15] § 4911(c)(2).
[16] § 4911(c)(4).

[17] § 4911(a)(1).
[18] § 4911(b).

▼ **FIGURE 23–1**
Calculation of Lobbying
Nontaxable Amount

Exempt Purpose Expenditures	Lobbying Nontaxable Amount Is
Not over $500,000	20% of exempt purpose expenditures*
Over $500,000 but not over $1 million	$100,000 + 15% of the excess of exempt purpose expenditures over $500,000
Over $1 million but not over $1.5 million	$175,000 + 10% of the excess of exempt purpose expenditures over $1 million
Over $1.5 million	$225,000 + 5% of the excess of exempt purpose expenditures over $1.5 million

*Exempt purpose expenditures generally are the amounts paid or incurred for the taxable year to accomplish the following purposes: religious, charitable, scientific, literary, educational, fostering national or international amateur sports competition, or the prevention of cruelty to children or animals.

EXAMPLE 1

Tan, Inc., a qualifying § 501(c)(3) organization, incurs lobbying expenditures of $500,000 for the taxable year and grass roots expenditures of $0. Exempt purpose expenditures for the taxable year are $5,000,000. Tan elects to be eligible to make lobbying expenditures on a limited basis.

Applying the data in Figure 23–1, the lobbying nontaxable amount is $400,000 [$225,000 + 5%($5,000,000 − $1,500,000)]. The ceiling on lobbying expenditures is $600,000 (150% × $400,000). Therefore, the $500,000 of lobbying expenditures are under the permitted $600,000. However, the election results in the imposition of tax on the excess lobbying expenditures of $100,000 ($500,000 lobbying expenditures − $400,000 lobbying nontaxable amount). The resulting tax liability is $25,000 ($100,000 × 25%). ▼

A § 501(c)(3) organization that makes disqualifying lobbying expenditures is subject to a 5 percent tax on the lobbying expenditures for the taxable year. A 5 percent tax may also be levied on the organization's management. The tax is imposed on management only if the managers knew that making the expenditures was likely to result in the organization no longer qualifying under § 501(c)(3) and if the managers' actions were willful and not due to reasonable cause. The tax does not apply to private foundations (see the subsequent discussion).[19]

Concept Summary 23–1 capsulizes the rules on influencing legislation.

FEEDER ORGANIZATIONS

A **feeder organization** carries on a trade or business for the benefit of an exempt organization (remits its profits to the exempt organization). Such organizations are not exempt from Federal income tax. This provision is intended to prevent an entity whose primary purpose is to conduct a trade or business for profit from escaping taxation merely because all of its profits are payable to one or more exempt organizations.[20]

Some income and activities are *not* subject to the feeder organization rules:[21]

- Rent income that would be excluded from the definition of the term *rent* for purposes of the unrelated business income tax (discussed subsequently).

---

[19]§ 4912.
[20]§ 502(a).

[21]§ 502(b).

CONCEPT SUMMARY 23–1

Exempt Organizations and Influencing Legislation

Factor	Tax Result
Entity subject to rule	§ 501(c)(3) organization.
Effect of influencing legislation	Subject to tax on lobbying expenditures under § 4912.
	Forfeit exempt status under § 501(c)(3).
	Not eligible for exempt status under § 501(c)(4).
Effect of electing to make lobbying expenditures	Permitted to make limited lobbying expenditures.
	Subject to tax under § 4911.

- A trade or business where substantially all the work is performed by volunteers.
- The trade or business of selling merchandise where substantially all the merchandise has been received as contributions or gifts.

Concept Summary 23–2 highlights the consequences of exempt status.

PRIVATE FOUNDATIONS

TAX CONSEQUENCES OF PRIVATE FOUNDATION STATUS

Certain exempt organizations are classified as **private foundations.** This classification produces two negative consequences. First, the classification may have an adverse impact on the contributions received by the donee exempt organization. Contributions may decline because the tax consequences for donors may not be as favorable as if the entity were not a private foundation.[22] Second, the classification may result in taxation at the exempt organization level. The reason for this less

---

CONCEPT SUMMARY 23–2

Consequences of Exempt Status

General	Exempt from Federal income tax.
	Exempt from most state and local income, franchise, sales, and property taxes.
	Qualify for reductions in postage rates.
	Gifts to the organization often can be deducted by donor.
Exceptions	May be subject to Federal income tax associated with the following.
	• Engaging in a prohibited transaction.
	• Being a feeder organization.
	• Being a private foundation.
	• Generating unrelated business taxable income.

---

[22]§ 170(e)(1)(B)(ii).

beneficial tax treatment is that private foundations define common good more narrowly and therefore are seen as not being supported by, and operated for the good of, the public.

Definition of a Private Foundation.   The following § 501(c)(3) organizations are *not* private foundations.[23]

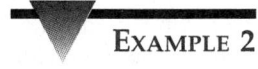

4   LEARNING OBJECTIVE
Determine which exempt organizations are classified as private foundations.

1. Churches; educational institutions; hospitals and medical research organizations; charitable organizations receiving a major portion of their support from the general public or the United States, a state, or a political subdivision thereof that is operated for the benefit of a college or university; and governmental units (favored activities category).
2. Organizations that are broadly supported by the general public (excluding disqualified persons), by governmental units, or by organizations described in (1) above.
3. Entities organized and operated exclusively for the benefit of organizations described in (1) or (2) (a supporting organization).
4. Entities organized and operated exclusively for testing for public safety.

To meet the broadly supported requirement in (2) above, both the following tests must be satisfied.

*   External support test.
*   Internal support test.

Under the *external support test*, more than one-third of the organization's support each taxable year *normally* must come from the three groups listed in (2) above, in the following forms.

*   Gifts, grants, contributions, and membership fees.
*   Gross receipts from admissions, sales of merchandise, performance of services, or the furnishing of facilities in an activity that is not an unrelated trade or business for purposes of the unrelated business income tax (discussed subsequently). However, such gross receipts from any person or governmental agency in excess of the greater of $5,000 or 1 percent of the organization's support for the taxable year are not counted.

The *internal support test* limits the amount of support *normally* received from the following sources to one-third of the organization's support for the taxable year.[24]

*   Gross investment income (gross income from interest, dividends, rents, and royalties).
*   Unrelated business taxable income (discussed subsequently) minus the related tax.

EXAMPLE 2

Lion, Inc., a § 501(c)(3) organization, received the following support during the taxable year.

Governmental unit A for services rendered	$ 30,000
Governmental unit B for services rendered	20,000
General public for services rendered	20,000
Gross investment income	15,000
Contributions from individual substantial contributors (disqualified persons)	15,000
	$100,000

---

[23]§ 509(a).

[24]Reg. § 1.509(a)–3(c) generally requires that the external and internal support tests be met in each of the four preceding tax years.

For purposes of the *external support test*, the support from A is counted only to the extent of $5,000 (greater of $5,000 or 1% of $100,000 support). Likewise, for B, only $5,000 is counted as support. Thus, the total countable support is $30,000 ($20,000 from the general public + $5,000 + $5,000), and Lion fails the test for the taxable year ($30,000/$100,000 = 30%; need > 33.3%). The $15,000 received from disqualified persons is excluded from the numerator but is included in the denominator.

In calculating the *internal support test,* only the gross investment income of $15,000 is included in the numerator. Thus, the test is satisfied ($15,000/$100,000 = 15%; cannot > 33.3%) for the taxable year.

Since Lion did not satisfy both tests, it does not qualify as an organization that is broadly supported. ▼

The intent of the two tests is to exclude from private foundation status those § 501(c)(3) organizations that are responsive to the general public rather than to the private interests of a limited number of donors or other persons.

Examples of § 501(c)(3) organizations that are properly classified as private foundations receiving broad public support include the United Fund, the Boy Scouts, university alumni associations, symphony orchestras, and the PTA.

TAXES IMPOSED ON PRIVATE FOUNDATIONS

▼ **5 LEARNING OBJECTIVE**
Recognize the taxes imposed on private foundations and calculate the related initial tax and additional tax amounts.

In general, a private foundation is exempt from Federal income tax. However, because a private foundation is usually not a broadly, publicly supported organization, it may be subject to the following taxes.[25]

- Tax based on investment income.
- Tax on self-dealing.
- Tax on failure to distribute income.
- Tax on excess business holdings.
- Tax on investments that jeopardize charitable purposes.
- Tax on taxable expenditures.

These taxes serve to restrict the permitted activities of private foundations. Two levels of tax may be imposed on the private foundation and the foundation manager: an initial tax and an additional tax. The initial taxes (first-level), with the exception of the tax based on investment income, are imposed because the private foundation engages in so-called *prohibited transactions*. The additional taxes (second-level) are imposed only if the prohibited transactions are not modified within a statutory time period.[26] See Concept Summary 23–3 for additional details.

The tax on a failure to distribute income will be used to illustrate how expensive these taxes can be and the related importance of avoiding their imposition. For failure to distribute a sufficient portion of a private nonoperating foundation's income, both an initial tax (first-level) and an additional tax (second-level) may be imposed. The initial tax is imposed at a rate of 15 percent on the income for the taxable year that is not distributed during the current or the following taxable year. The initial tax is imposed on the undistributed income for each year until the IRS assesses the tax.

The additional tax is imposed at a rate of 100 percent on the amount of the inadequate distribution that is not distributed by the assessment date. The additional tax is effectively waived if the undistributed income is distributed within 90 days after the mailing of the deficiency notice for the additional tax. Extensions of this period may be obtained.

---

[25]§§ 4940–4945.   [26]§ 4961.

CONCEPT SUMMARY 23–3

Taxes Imposed on Private Foundations

Type of Tax	Code Section	Purpose	Private Foundation		Foundation Manager	
			Initial Tax	Additional Tax	Initial Tax	Additional Tax
On investment income	§ 4940	Audit fee to defray IRS expenses.	2%*			
On self-dealing	§ 4941	Engaging in transactions with disqualified persons.	5%**	200%**	2.5%†	50%†
On failure to distribute income	§ 4942	Failing to distribute adequate amount of income for exempt purposes.	15%	100%		
On excess business holdings	§ 4943	Investments that enable the private foundation to control unrelated businesses.	5%	200%		
On jeopardizing investments	§ 4944	Speculative investments that put the private foundation's assets at risk.	5%	25%	5%††	5%†
On taxable expenditures	§ 4945	Expenditures that should not be made by private foundations.	10%	100%	2.5%††	50%†

*May be possible to reduce the tax rate to 1%. In addition, an exempt operating foundation [see §§ 4940(d)(2) and 4942(j)(3)] is not subject to the tax.
**Imposed on the disqualified person rather than the foundation.
†Subject to a statutory ceiling of $10,000.
††Subject to a statutory ceiling of $5,000.

Undistributed income is the excess of the distributable amount (in effect, the amount that should have been distributed) over qualifying distributions made by the entity. The distributable amount is the excess of the minimum investment return over the sum of the (1) unrelated business income tax and (2) the excise tax based on net investment income.[27] The minimum investment return is 5 percent of the excess of the fair market value of the foundation's assets over the unpaid debt associated with acquiring or improving these assets. Assets of the foundation that are employed directly in carrying on the foundation's exempt purpose are not used in making this calculation.

EXAMPLE 3

Gold, Inc., a private foundation, has undistributed income of $80,000 for its taxable year 1995. It distributes $15,000 of this amount during 1996 and an additional $45,000 during 1997. The IRS deficiency notice is mailed to Gold on August 5, 1998. The initial tax is $12,750 [($65,000 × 15%) + ($20,000 × 15%)].

At the date of the deficiency notice, no additional distributions have been made from the 1995 undistributed income. Therefore, since the remaining undistributed income of $20,000 has not been distributed by August 5, 1998, an additional tax of $20,000 ($20,000 × 100%) is imposed.

---

[27]§ 4940.

If Gold distributes the $20,000 of undistributed income for 1995 within 90 days of the deficiency notice, the additional tax is waived. Without this distribution, however, the foundation will owe $32,750 ($12,750 + $20,000) in taxes. ▼

UNRELATED BUSINESS INCOME TAX

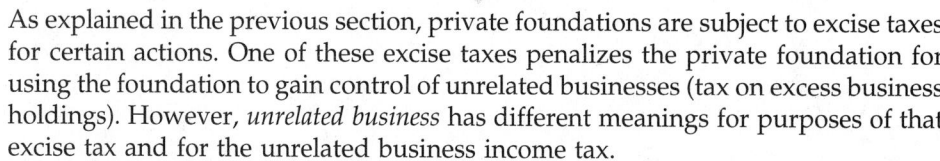

6 LEARNING OBJECTIVE
Determine when an exempt organization is subject to the unrelated business income tax and calculate the amount of the tax.

As explained in the previous section, private foundations are subject to excise taxes for certain actions. One of these excise taxes penalizes the private foundation for using the foundation to gain control of unrelated businesses (tax on excess business holdings). However, *unrelated business* has different meanings for purposes of that excise tax and for the unrelated business income tax.

The **unrelated business income tax (UBIT)** is designed to treat the entity as if it were subject to the corporate income tax. Thus, the rates that are used are those applicable to a corporate taxpayer.[28] In general, **unrelated business income** is derived from activities not related to the exempt purpose of the exempt organization. The tax is levied because the organization is engaging in substantial commercial activities.[29] Without such a tax, nonexempt organizations (regular taxable business entities) would be at a substantial disadvantage when trying to compete with the exempt organization. Thus, the UBIT is intended to neutralize the exempt entity's tax advantage.[30]

EXAMPLE 4

Historic, Inc., is an exempt private foundation. Its exempt activity is to maintain a restoration of eighteenth-century colonial life (houses, public buildings, taverns, businesses, and craft demonstrations) that is visited by more than a million people each year. A fee is charged for admission to the "restored area." In addition to this "museum" activity, Historic operates two hotels and three restaurants that are available to the general public. The earnings from the hotel and restaurant businesses are used to defray the costs of operating the "museum" activity.

The "museum" activity is not subject to the Federal income tax, except to the extent of any tax liability for any of the aforementioned excise taxes that are levied on private foundations. However, even though the income from the hotel and restaurant businesses is used for exempt purposes, that income is unrelated business income and is subject to the UBIT. ▼

The UBIT applies to all organizations that are exempt from Federal income tax under § 501(c), except Federal agencies. In addition, the tax applies to state colleges and universities.[31]

A materiality exception generally exempts an entity from being subject to the UBIT if such income is insignificant. See the later discussion of the $1,000 statutory deduction generally available to all exempt organizations.

UNRELATED TRADE OR BUSINESS

An exempt organization may be subject to the UBIT in the following circumstances.[32]

- The organization conducts a trade or business.
- The trade or business is not substantially related to the exempt purpose of the organization.
- The trade or business is regularly carried on by the organization.

---

[28]§ 511(a)(1).
[29]§ 512(a)(1).
[30]Reg. § 1.513–1(b).

[31]§ 511(a)(2) and Reg. § 1.511–2(a)(2).
[32]§ 513(a) and Reg. § 1.513–2(a).

The Code specifically exempts the following activities from classification as an unrelated trade or business. Thus, even if all of the above factors are present, the activity is not classified as an unrelated trade or business.[33]

- The individuals performing substantially all the work of the trade or business do so without compensation (e.g., an orphanage operates a retail store for sales to the general public, and all the work is done by volunteers).
- The trade or business consists of selling merchandise, and substantially all of the merchandise has been received as gifts or contributions (e.g., thrift shops).
- For § 501(c)(3) organizations and for state colleges or universities, the trade or business is conducted primarily for the convenience of the organization's members, students, patients, officers, or employees (e.g., a laundry operated by the college for laundering dormitory linens and students' clothing, a college bookstore).
- For most employee unions, the trade or business consists of selling to members, at their usual place of employment, work-related clothing and equipment and items normally sold through vending machines, snack bars, or food dispensing facilities.

Definition of Trade or Business.   Trade or business, for this purpose, is broadly defined. It includes any activity conducted for the production of income through the sale of merchandise or the performance of services. An activity need not generate a profit to be treated as a trade or business. The activity may be part of a larger set of activities conducted by the organization, some of which may be related to the exempt purpose. Being included in a larger set does not cause the activity to lose its identity as an unrelated trade or business.[34]

EXAMPLE 5

Health, Inc., is an exempt hospital that operates a pharmacy. The pharmacy provides medicines and supplies to the patients in the hospital (i.e., it contributes to the conduct of the hospital's exempt purpose). In addition, the pharmacy sells medicines and supplies to the

[33]§ 513(a).   [34]Reg. § 1.513–1(b).

general public. The activity of selling to the general public constitutes a trade or business for purposes of the UBIT. ▼

Not Substantially Related to the Exempt Purpose. Exempt organizations frequently conduct unrelated trades or businesses in order to provide income to help defray the costs of conducting the exempt purpose (like the hotel and restaurant businesses in Example 4). Providing financial support for the exempt purpose will not prevent an activity from being classified as an unrelated trade or business and thereby being subject to the UBIT.

To be related to the accomplishment of the exempt purpose, the conduct of the business activities must be causally related and contribute importantly to the exempt purpose. Whether a causal relationship exists and the degree of its importance are determined by examining the facts and circumstances. One must consider the size and extent of the activities in relation to the nature and extent of the exempt function that the activities serve.[35]

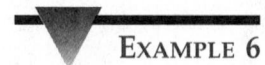

EXAMPLE 6

Art, Inc., an exempt organization, operates a school for training children in the performing arts. As an essential part of that training, the children perform for the general public. The children are paid at the minimum wage for the performances, and Art derives gross income by charging admission to the performances.

The income from admissions is not income from an unrelated trade or business, because the performances by the children contribute importantly to the accomplishment of the exempt purpose of providing training in the performing arts. ▼

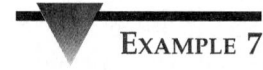

EXAMPLE 7

Assume the same facts as in Example 6, except that four performances are conducted each weekend of the year. Assume that this number of performances far exceeds that required for training the children. Thus, the part of the income derived from admissions for these excess performances is income from an unrelated trade or business. ▼

The trade or business may sell merchandise that has been produced as part of the accomplishment of the exempt purpose. The sale of such merchandise is normally treated as related to the exempt purpose. However, if the merchandise is not sold in substantially the same state it was in at the completion of the exempt purpose, the gross income subsequently derived from the sale of the merchandise is income from an unrelated trade or business.[36]

EXAMPLE 8

Help, Inc., an exempt organization, conducts programs for the rehabilitation of the handicapped. One of the programs includes training in radio and television repair. Help derives gross income by selling the repaired items. The income is substantially related to the accomplishment of the exempt purpose. ▼

An asset or facility used in the exempt purpose may also be used in a nonexempt purpose. Income derived from the use in a nonexempt purpose is income from an unrelated trade or business.[37]

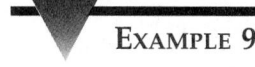

EXAMPLE 9

Civil, Inc., an exempt organization, operates a museum. As part of the exempt purpose of the museum, educational lectures are given in the museum's theater during the operating hours of the museum. In the evening, when the museum is closed, the theater is leased to an individual who operates a movie theater. The lease income received from the individual who operates the movie theater is income from an unrelated trade or business. ▼

---

[35]Reg. § 1.513–1(d).
[36]Reg. § 1.513–1(d)(4)(ii).

[37]Reg. § 1.513–1(d)(4)(iii) addresses the allocation of expenses to exempt and nonexempt activities.

Special Rule for Corporate Sponsorship Payments. The Taxpayer Relief Act of 1997 (TRA of 1997) clarifies the treatment of corporate sponsorship payments. The term *unrelated trade or business* does not include the soliciting and receiving of qualified sponsorship payments.[38]

A payment qualifies as a qualified sponsorship if it meets the following requirements.

- There is no arrangement or expectation that the trade or business making the payment will receive any substantial benefit other than the use or acknowledgment of its name, logo, or product lines in connection with the activities of the exempt organization.
- Such use or acknowledgment does not include advertising the payor's products or services.
- The payment does not include any payment for which the amount is contingent upon the level of attendance at one or more events, broadcast ratings, or other factors indicating the degree of public exposure to one or more events.

EXAMPLE 10

Pets, Inc., a manufacturer of cat food, contributes $25,000 to Feline Care, Inc., an exempt organization that cares for abandoned cats. In return for the contribution, Feline agrees to put Pets' corporate logo in its monthly newsletter to donors. Under these circumstances, the $25,000 payment is a qualified sponsorship payment and is not subject to the UBIT. ▼

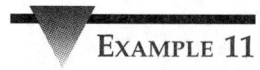

EXAMPLE 11

Assume the same facts as in Example 10, except that Feline agrees to endorse Pets' cat food in its monthly newsletter by stating that it feeds only Pets' cat food to its cats. The $25,000 is not a qualified sponsorship payment and is subject to the UBIT. ▼

Special Rule for Bingo Games. A special provision applies in determining whether income from bingo games is from an unrelated trade or business. Under this provision, a *qualified bingo game* is not an unrelated trade or business if both of the following requirements are satisfied.[39]

- The bingo game is legal under both state and local law.
- Commercial bingo games (conducted for a profit motive) ordinarily are not permitted in the jurisdiction.

EXAMPLE 12

Play, Inc., an exempt organization, conducts weekly bingo games. The laws of the state and municipality in which Play conducts the games expressly provide that exempt organizations may conduct bingo games, but do not permit profit-oriented entities to do so. Since both of the requirements for bingo games are satisfied, the bingo games conducted by Play are not an unrelated trade or business. ▼

EXAMPLE 13

Game, Inc., an exempt organization, conducts weekly bingo games in City X and City Y. State law expressly permits exempt organizations to conduct bingo games. State law also provides that profit-oriented entities may conduct bingo games in X, which is a resort community. Several businesses regularly conduct bingo games there.

The bingo games conducted by Game in Y are not an unrelated trade or business. However, the bingo games that Game conducts in X are an unrelated trade or business, because commercial bingo games are regularly permitted to be conducted there. ▼

---

[38]§ 513(i).   [39]§ 513(f).

Bingo Is Not for Everyone Even Though It's Educational

The Commonwealth of Virginia has certain standards that it feels must be maintained. In recent years, the Commonwealth has expanded permitted forms of gambling from bingo games sponsored by tax-exempt entities to a state-run lottery and a state-approved horse racing track where bets can be placed.

But the Commonwealth is not ready to accept all gambling: it will not permit children to play bingo. The question arose because Virginians spend about $200 million a year on bingo games, which by state law must benefit charities. Unfortunately, after the operations pay prizes and overhead costs, only about $4 million is left for the charities.

In an attempt to aid the charities, the staff of the Charitable Gaming Commission proposed to allow children to play charitable games of chance with parental supervision or to play for noncash prizes without supervision. By doing so, the children could learn math skills, social skills, and participate in family bingo outings. Said one commision member, "I don't think we're teaching kids to gamble, not necessarily." The state rejected the proposal, however. The commission is still looking for ways to enable the charities to receive more, but it will not do so by allowing anyone under the age of 21 to legally participate in games of chance.

SOURCE: Adapted from "State Panel Won't Let Children Play Bingo," *Newport News Daily Press*, November 20, 1996, p. B3.

Special Rule for Distribution of Low-Cost Articles.   If an exempt organization distributes low-cost items as an incidental part of its solicitation for charitable contributions, the distributions may not be considered an unrelated trade or business. A low-cost article is one that costs $7.10 (for 1998—indexed annually) or less. Examples are pens, stamps, stickers, stationery, and address labels. If more than one item is distributed to a person during the calendar year, the costs of the items are combined.[40]

Special Rule for Rental or Exchange of Membership Lists.   If an exempt organization conducts a trade or business that consists of either exchanging with or renting to other exempt organizations the organization's donor or membership list (mailing lists), the activity is not an unrelated trade or business.[41]

Other Special Rules.   Other special rules are used in determining whether each of the following activities is an unrelated trade or business.[42]

- Qualified public entertainment activities (e.g., a state fair).
- Qualified convention and trade show activities.
- Certain services provided at cost or less by a hospital to other small hospitals.
- Certain pole rentals by telephone or electric companies.

Discussion of these special rules is beyond the scope of this text.

---

[40]§ 513(h)(1)(A).
[41]§ 513(h)(1)(B).

[42]§§ 513(d), (e), and (g).

UNRELATED BUSINESS INCOME

Even when an exempt organization conducts an unrelated trade or business, a tax is assessed only if the exempt organization regularly conducts the activity and the business produces unrelated business income.

Regularly Carried on by the Organization. An activity is classified as unrelated business income only if it is regularly carried on by the exempt organization. This provision assures that only activities that are actually competing with taxable organizations are subject to the unrelated business income tax. Accordingly, factors to be considered in assessing *regularly carried on* include the frequency of the activity, the continuity of the activity, and the manner in which the activity is pursued.[43]

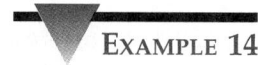

EXAMPLE 14

Silver, Inc., an exempt organization, owns land that is located next to the state fairgrounds. During the 10 days of the state fair, Silver uses the land as a parking lot and charges individuals attending the state fair for parking there. The activity is not regularly carried on. ▼

EXAMPLE 15

Black, Inc., an exempt organization, has its offices in the downtown area. It owns a parking lot adjacent to its offices on which its employees park during the week. On Saturdays, it rents the spaces in the parking lot to individuals shopping or working in the downtown area. Black is conducting a business activity on a year-round basis, even though it is only for one day per week. Thus, an activity is regularly being carried on. ▼

Unrelated Business Income Defined. Unrelated business income is generally that derived from the unrelated trade or business. To convert it from a gross income measure to a net income measure, it must be reduced by the deductions directly connected with the conduct of the unrelated trade or business.[44]

UNRELATED BUSINESS TAXABLE INCOME

General Tax Model. The model for unrelated business taxable income (UBTI) appears in Figure 23–2.

Positive adjustments[45]

1. The charitable contribution deduction is permitted without regard to whether the charitable contributions are associated with the unrelated trade or business. However, to the extent the charitable contributions deducted in calculating net unrelated business income (see Figure 23–2) exceed 10 percent of UBTI (without regard to the charitable contribution deduction), the excess is treated as a positive adjustment.

▼ **FIGURE 23–2**
Tax Formula for Unrelated
Business Taxable Income

Gross unrelated business income

– Deductions

= Net unrelated business income

± Modifications

= Unrelated business taxable income

[43]§ 512(a)(1) and Reg. § 1.513–1(c).
[44]§ 512(a)(1).

[45]§§ 512(a)(1) and (b) and Reg. § 1.512(b)–1.

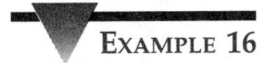

EXAMPLE 16

Brown, Inc., an exempt organization, has UBTI of $100,000 (excluding any modifications associated with charitable contributions). Total charitable contributions (all associated with the unrelated trade or business) are $13,000. Assuming that the $13,000 is deducted in calculating net unrelated business income, the excess of $3,000 [$13,000 – 10%($100,000)] is a positive adjustment in calculating UBTI. ▼

2. Unrelated debt-financed income net of the unrelated debt-financed deductions (see the subsequent discussion of Unrelated Debt-Financed Income).
3. Certain interest, annuity, royalty, and rent income received by the exempt organization from an organization it controls (80 percent test). Note that this provision overrides the modifications for these types of income (negative adjustment 3).

Negative adjustments

1. Income from dividends, interest, and annuities net of all deductions directly related to producing such income.
2. Royalty income, regardless of whether it is measured by production, gross income, or taxable income from the property, net of all deductions directly related to producing such income.
3. Rent income from real property and from certain personal property net of all deductions directly related to producing such income. Personal property rents are included in the negative adjustment only if the personal property is leased with the real property. In addition, the personal property rent income must be incidental (does not exceed 10 percent of the total rent income under the lease) to be used in computing the negative adjustment. In both of the following cases, however, none of the rent income is treated as a negative adjustment.

   - More than 50 percent of the rent income under the lease is from personal property.
   - Rent income is calculated using the tenant's profits.

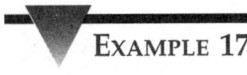

EXAMPLE 17

Beaver, Inc., an exempt organization, leases land and a building (realty) and computers (personalty) housed in the building. Under the lease, $46,000 of the rent is for the land and building, and $4,000 is for the computers. Expenses incurred for the land and building are $10,000. The net rent income from the land and building of $36,000 ($46,000 – $10,000) and the $4,000 from the computers are negative adjustments. ▼

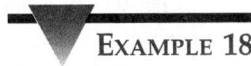

EXAMPLE 18

Assume the same facts as in Example 17, except that the rent income is $35,000 from the land and building and $15,000 from the computers. Since the rent income from the computers exceeds $5,000 (i.e., 10% of the total rent under the lease) and is not incidental, it is not a negative adjustment. ▼

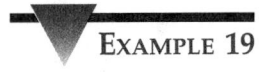

EXAMPLE 19

Assume the same facts as in Example 17, except that the rent income is $20,000 from the land and building and $30,000 from the computers. Since more than 50% of the rent income under the lease is from the computers, neither the rent income from the land and building nor that from the computers is a negative adjustment. ▼

If the lessor of real property provides significant services to the lessee, such income, for this purpose, is not rent income.
4. Gains and losses from the sale, exchange, or other disposition of property *except for* inventory.

EXAMPLE 20

Beaver, the owner of the land, building, and computers in Example 17, sells these assets for $450,000. Their adjusted basis is $300,000. Beaver's recognized gain of $150,000 is a negative adjustment. ▼

5. Certain research income net of all deductions directly related to producing that income.
6. The charitable contribution deduction is permitted without regard to whether the charitable contributions are associated with the unrelated trade or business. Therefore, to the extent that the charitable contributions exceed those deducted in calculating net unrelated business income (see Figure 23–2), the excess is a negative adjustment in calculating UBTI. In making this calculation, be aware that the 10 percent of UBTI (without regard to the charitable contribution deduction) limit still applies (see positive adjustment 1).

EXAMPLE 21

Canine, Inc., an exempt organization, has unrelated business taxable income of $100,000 (excluding any modifications associated with charitable contributions). The total charitable contributions are $9,000, of which $7,000 (those associated with the unrelated trade or business) has been deducted in calculating net unrelated business income. Therefore, the remaining $2,000 of charitable contributions is a negative adjustment in calculating UBTI. ▼

7. A specific deduction of $1,000 is permitted.

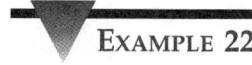

EXAMPLE 22

Petit Care, Inc., an exempt organization, has net unrelated business income of $800. Since Petit will receive a specific deduction of $1,000, its UBTI is $0. Therefore, its income tax liability is $0. ▼

EXAMPLE 23

Patient, Inc., an exempt organization, has UBTI of $500,000. Patient's income tax liability is $170,000 ($500,000 UBTI × 34% corporate tax rate). ▼

UNRELATED DEBT–FINANCED INCOME

In the formula for calculating the tax on unrelated business income (refer to Figure 23–2), unrelated debt-financed income is one of the positive adjustments. Examples of income from debt-financed property include rent income from real estate or tangible personal property, dividends from corporate stock, and gains from the disposition of debt-financed property. Gains from property that is unrelated business income property are also included to the extent the gains are not otherwise treated as unrelated business income. Because of the importance of this item, it is discussed separately here.

In terms of the UBIT, the positive adjustment for unrelated debt-financed income is a significant one. Without this provision, a tax-exempt organization could use borrowed funds to acquire unrelated business or investment property and use the untaxed (i.e., exempt) earnings from the acquisition to pay for the property.

Definition of Debt-Financed Income. **Debt-financed income** is the gross income generated from debt-financed property. *Debt-financed property* is all property of the exempt organization that is held to produce income and on which there is acquisition indebtedness, *except* for the following.[46]

---

[46]§ 514(b).

- Property where substantially all (at least 85 percent) of the use is for the achievement of the exempt purpose of the exempt organization.[47]
- Property whose gross income is otherwise treated as unrelated business income.
- Property whose gross income is from the following sources and is not otherwise treated as unrelated business income.
  - Income from research performed for the United States, a Federal governmental agency, or a state or a political subdivision thereof.
  - For a college, university, or hospital, income from research.
  - For an organization that performs fundamental (i.e., not applied) research for the benefit of the general public, income from research.
- Property used in an activity that is not an unrelated trade or business.

If the 85 percent test is not satisfied, only the portion of the property that is *not* used for the exempt purpose is debt-financed property.

EXAMPLE 24

Deer, Inc., an exempt organization, owns a five-story office building on which there is acquisition indebtedness. Three of the floors are used for Deer's exempt purpose. The two other floors are leased to Purple Corporation. In this case, the *substantially all* test is not satisfied. Therefore, 40% of the office building is debt-financed property, and 60% is not. ▼

Certain land that is acquired by an exempt organization for later exempt use is excluded from debt-financed property if the following requirements are satisfied.[48]

- The principal purpose of acquiring the land is for use (substantially all) in achieving the organization's exempt purpose.
- This use will begin within 10 years of the acquisition date.
- At the date when the land is acquired, it is located in the *neighborhood* of other property of the organization for which substantially all the use is for achieving the organization's exempt purpose.

Even if the third requirement is not satisfied (the property is not located in the neighborhood), the land still is excluded from debt-financed property if it is converted to use for achieving the organization's exempt purpose within the 10-year period. Qualification under this provision will result in a refund of taxes previously paid. If the exempt organization is a church, the 10-year period becomes a 15-year period, and the neighborhood requirement is waived.

Definition of Acquisition Indebtedness. Acquisition indebtedness is debt sustained by the exempt organization in association with the acquisition of property. More precisely, *acquisition indebtedness* consists of the unpaid amounts of the following for debt-financed property.[49]

- Debt incurred in acquiring or improving the property.
- Debt incurred before the property was acquired or improved, but which would not have been incurred without the acquisition or improvement.
- Debt incurred after the property was acquired or improved, but which would not have been incurred without the acquisition or improvement.

---

[47]Reg. § 1.514(b)–1(b)(1)(ii).

[48]§ 514(b)(3).

[49]§ 514(c)(1). Educational organizations in certain limited circumstances can exclude debt incurred for real property acquisitions from classification as acquisition indebtedness.

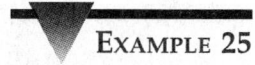

EXAMPLE 25

Red, Inc., an exempt organization, acquires land for $100,000. In order to finance the acquisition, Red mortgages the land with a bank and receives loan proceeds of $80,000. Red leases the land to Duck Corporation. The mortgage is acquisition indebtedness. ▼

EXAMPLE 26

Rose, Inc., an exempt organization, makes improvements to an office building that it rents to Bird Corporation. Excess working capital funds are used to finance the improvements. Rose is later required to mortgage its laboratory building, which it uses for its exempt purpose, to replenish working capital. The mortgage is acquisition indebtedness. ▼

Portion of Debt-Financed Income and Deductions Treated as Unrelated Business Taxable Income.

Once the amount of the debt-financed income and deductions is determined, it is necessary to ascertain what portion is unrelated debt-financed income and deductions. Unrelated debt-financed income increases unrelated business taxable income, and unrelated debt-financed deductions decrease unrelated business taxable income.

The calculation is made for each debt-financed property. The gross income from the property is multiplied by the following percentage.[50]

$$\frac{\text{Average acquisition indebtedness for the property}}{\text{Average adjusted basis of the property}} = \text{Debt/basis percentage}$$

This percentage cannot exceed 100. If debt-financed property is disposed of during the taxable year at a gain, average acquisition indebtedness in the formula is replaced with highest acquisition indebtedness. *Highest acquisition indebtedness* is the largest amount of acquisition indebtedness for the property during the 12-month period preceding the date of disposition.[51]

Deductions are allowed for expenses directly related to the debt-financed property and the income from it. Cost recovery deductions must be calculated using the straight-line method. Once allowable deductions are determined, this amount is multiplied by the debt/basis percentage.[52]

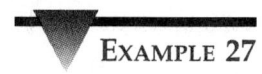

EXAMPLE 27

White, Inc., an exempt organization, owns an office building that it leases to Squirrel Corporation for $120,000 per year. The average acquisition indebtedness is $300,000, and the average adjusted basis is $500,000. Since the office building is debt-financed property, the unrelated debt-financed income is:

$$\frac{\$300,000}{\$500,000} \times \$120,000 = \$72,000.$$ ▼

Average Acquisition Indebtedness.

The *average acquisition indebtedness* for debt-financed property is the average amount of the outstanding debt for the taxable year (ignoring interest) during the portion of the year the property is held by the exempt organization. This amount is calculated by summing the outstanding debt on the first day of each calendar month the property is held by the exempt organization. Then this total is divided by the number of months the property is held by the organization.[53]

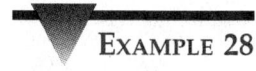

EXAMPLE 28

On August 12, Yellow, Inc., an exempt organization, acquires an office building that is debt-financed property for $500,000. The initial mortgage on the property is $400,000. The principal amount of the debt on August 12 and on the first of each subsequent month is as follows.

---

[50]§ 514(a)(1).
[51]§ 514(c)(7).
[52]§ 514(a)(3).

[53]§ 514(c)(7) and Reg. § 1.514(a)–1(a)(3). A partial month is treated as a full month.

CONCEPT SUMMARY 23–4

Unrelated Business Income Tax

Purpose	To tax the entity on unrelated business income as if it were subject to the corporate income tax.
Applicable tax rates	Corporate tax rates.
Exempt organizations to which applicable	All organizations exempt under § 501(c), except Federal agencies.
Entities subject to the tax	The organization conducts a trade or business; the trade or business is not substantially related to the exempt purpose of the organization; and the trade or business is regularly carried on by the organization.
Exceptions to the tax	• All the work is performed by volunteers. • Substantially all of the merchandise being sold has been received by gift. • For § 501(c)(3) organizations, the business is conducted primarily for the benefit of the organization's members, students, patients, officers, or employees. • For most employee unions, the trade or business consists of selling to members work-related clothing and equipment and items normally sold through vending machines, snack bars, or food-dispensing facilities.
$1,000 provision	If the gross income from an unrelated trade or business is less than $1,000, it is not necessary to file a return associated with the unrelated business income tax.

Month	Principal Amount
August 12	$ 400,000
September 1	380,000
October 1	360,000
November 1	340,000
December 1	320,000
Total	$1,800,000

Average acquisition indebtedness is $360,000 ($1,800,000 ÷ 5 months). Note that even though August is only a partial month, it is treated as a full month. ▼

Average Adjusted Basis.   The *average adjusted basis* of debt-financed property is calculated by summing the adjusted bases of the property on the first and last days during the taxable year the property is held by the exempt organization and then dividing by two.[54]

EXAMPLE 29   Assume the facts are the same as in Example 28. In addition, during the taxable year, depreciation of $5,900 is deducted. The average adjusted basis is $497,050 [($500,000 + $494,100) ÷ 2]. ▼

Concept Summary 23–4 presents the rules concerning the UBIT.

---

[54]§ 514(a)(1) and Reg. § 1.514(a)–1(a)(2).

REPORTING REQUIREMENTS

OBTAINING EXEMPT ORGANIZATION STATUS

7 **LEARNING OBJECTIVE**
List the reports exempt organizations must file with the IRS and the related due dates.

Not all exempt organizations are required to obtain IRS approval for their exempt status. Among those required by statute to do so are organizations exempt under §§ 501(c)(3), 501(c)(9), and 501(c)(20).[55] Even in these cases, exceptions are provided (e.g., churches).

Even when not required to obtain IRS approval, most exempt organizations do apply for exempt status. Typically, an organization does not want to assume that it qualifies for exempt status and describe itself in that way to the public, only to have the IRS rule later that it does not qualify.

If an organization is required to obtain IRS approval for its exempt status and does not do so, it does not qualify as an exempt organization.

ETHICAL CONSIDERATIONS

Filing for Exempt Status: A CPA's Dilemma

Waldo is the treasurer of the Alpine Sky Divers Club. In his opinion, the club satisfies all the requirements for exempt status as a social club under § 501(c)(7). When Annette, the club president and an assistant DA, asks him if he has completed all the paperwork with the IRS relating to the club's tax-exempt status, Waldo assures her that he has taken care of everything.

If this were another client, Waldo would have filed a Form 1024 [Application for Recognition of Exemption under Section 501(a)]. He has not done so for Alpine because he has been very busy at work and feels fairly certain that the IRS will never raise the issue of whether the club qualifies for tax-exempt status. He told Annette he had filed the papers with the IRS because she is a stickler for detail and does everything by the book. He also has had several dates with her and does not want to take a chance on spoiling their relationship.

Evaluate Waldo's behavior.

ANNUAL FILING REQUIREMENTS

Most exempt organizations are required to file an annual information return.[56] The return is filed on Form 990 (Return of Organization Exempt from Income Tax). The following exempt organizations need not file Form 990.[57]

- Federal agencies.
- Churches.
- Organizations whose annual gross receipts do not exceed $25,000.
- Private foundations.

Private foundations are required to file Form 990–PF (Return of Private Foundation).

The due date for Form 990 or Form 990–PF is the fifteenth day of the fifth month after the end of the taxable year. These returns are filed with the appropriate IRS Service Center based on the location of the exempt organization's principal

---

[55]§§ 505(c), 508(a), and 508(c).
[56]§ 6033(a)(1).

[57]§ 6033(a)(2).

office. Requests for extensions on filing are made by filing Form 2758 (Applications for Extension of Time).

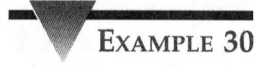

EXAMPLE 30

Green, Inc., a § 501(c)(3) organization, has a fiscal year that ends June 30, 1998. The due date for the annual return is November 15, 1998. If Green were a calendar year entity, the due date for the 1998 annual return would be May 15, 1999. ▼

Exempt organizations that are subject to the UBIT may be required to file Form 990–T (Exempt Organization Business Income Tax Return). The return must be filed if the organization has gross income of at least $1,000 from an unrelated trade or business. The due date for the return is the fifteenth day of the fifth month after the end of the taxable year.

EXAMPLE 31

During the year, the First Church of Kentwood receives parishioner contributions of $450,000. Of this amount, $125,000 is designated for the church building fund. First Church is not required to file an annual return (Form 990) because churches are exempt from doing so. In addition, it is not required to file Form 990–T because it has no unrelated business income.

Colonial, Inc., is an exempt private foundation. Gross receipts for the year total $800,000, of which 60% is from admission fees paid by members of the general public who visit Colonial's museum of eighteenth-century life. The balance is endowment income. Because Colonial is a private foundation, it must file Form 990–PF.

Orange, Inc., is an exempt organization and is not a private foundation. Gross receipts for the year are $20,000. None of this amount is unrelated business income. Orange is not required to file Form 990 because its annual gross receipts do not exceed $25,000.

Restoration, Inc., is an exempt private foundation. Gross receipts for the year are $20,000. None of this amount is unrelated business income. Restoration must file Form 990–PF because private foundations are not eligible for the $25,000 filing exception.

During the year, the Second Church of Port Allen receives parishioner contributions of $300,000. In addition, the church has unrelated business income of $5,000. Second Church is not required to file Form 990 because churches are exempt from doing so. Form 990–T must be filed, however, because churches are not exempt from the UBIT and Second Church has exceeded the $1,000 floor. ▼

TAX PLANNING CONSIDERATIONS

8 **LEARNING OBJECTIVE**
Identify tax planning opportunities for exempt organizations.

GENERAL

Exempt organizations provide at least two potential tax benefits. First, the entity may be exempt from Federal income tax. Second, contributions to the entity may be deductible by the donor.

An organization that qualifies as an exempt organization may still be subject to certain types of Federal income tax, including the following.

- Tax on prohibited transactions.
- Tax on feeder organizations.
- Tax on private foundations.
- Tax on unrelated business income.

Therefore, classification as an exempt organization should not be interpreted to mean that the organization need not be concerned with any Federal income tax. Such a belief can result in the organization engaging in transactions that produce a substantial tax liability.

An organization is exempt from taxation only if it fits into one of the categories enumerated in the Code. Thus, particular attention must be given to the qualification requirements. These requirements must continue to be satisfied to avoid termination of exempt status (in effect, they are now maintenance requirements).

MAINTAINING EXEMPT STATUS

To maintain exempt status, the organization must satisfy both an organizational test and an operational test. The organizational test requires that the entity satisfy the statutory requirements for exempt status on paper. The operational test ensures that the entity does, in fact, satisfy the statutory requirements for exempt status.

King Shipping Consum., Inc. (Zion Coptic Church, Inc.) indicates that it is usually much easier to satisfy the organizational test than the operational test.[58] Zion's stated purpose was to engage in activities usually and normally associated with churches. Based on this, the IRS approved Zion's exempt status as a § 501(c)(3) organization.

Zion's real intent, however, was to smuggle illegal drugs into the country and to distribute them for profit. The church's justification for the drugs was that it used marijuana in its sacrament. During a four-month period, however, the police confiscated 33 tons of marijuana from church members. The IRS calculated that, even assuming the maximum alleged church membership of several thousand, each member would have had to smoke over 33 pounds of marijuana during the four-month confiscation period.

The court concluded that Zion's real purpose was to cloak a large commercial drug smuggling operation. Since this activity was inconsistent with the religious purpose for exempt status, the court upheld the IRS's revocation of Zion's exempt status and the deficiency assessment of approximately $1.6 million.

PRIVATE FOUNDATION STATUS

Exempt organizations that can qualify as public charities receive more beneficial tax treatment than those that qualify as private foundations. Thus, if possible, the organization should be structured to qualify as a public charity. The following can result when an exempt organization is classified as a private foundation.

- Taxes may be imposed on the private foundation.
  - Tax based on investment income.
  - Tax on self-dealing.
  - Tax on failure to distribute income.
  - Tax on excess business holdings.
  - Tax on investments that jeopardize charitable purposes.
  - Tax on taxable expenditures.
- Donors may receive less favorable tax deduction treatment under § 170 than they would if the exempt organization were not a private foundation.

EXAMPLE 32

David has IBM stock ($25,000 adjusted basis, $100,000 fair market value) that he is going to contribute to one of the following exempt organizations: Blue, Inc., a public charity, or Teal, Inc., a private nonoperating foundation. David has owned the stock for five years.

David asks the manager of each organization to describe the tax benefits of contributing to that organization. He tells them he is in the 31% tax bracket and his AGI exceeds $130,000.

---

[58] 58 TCM 574, T.C.Memo. 1989–593.

CONCEPT SUMMARY 23-5

Private Foundation Status

	Exempt Organization Is	
	A Private Foundation	**Not a Private Foundation**
Reason for classification	Does not serve the common good because it lacks an approved exempt purpose or does not receive broad public financial support.	Serves the common good.
Eligible for exempt status?	Yes	Yes
Most beneficial charitable contribution deduction treatment available to donors?	Depends. No, if the private foundation is classified as a private *nonoperating* foundation.	Yes
Subject to excise taxes levied on prohibited transactions?	Yes	No
Subject to tax on unrelated business income?	Yes	Yes

Based on the data provided by the managers, David decides to contribute the stock to Blue, Inc. He calculates the amount of the charitable contribution under each option as follows.[59]

Donee	Contribution Deduction	Tax Rate	Contribution Borne by U.S. Government
Blue	$100,000	31%	$31,000
Teal	25,000 ($100,000 – $75,000)	31%	7,750

One method of avoiding private foundation status is to have a tax-exempt purpose that results in the organization not being classified as a private foundation (the *organization* approach). If this is not feasible, it may be possible to operate the organization so that it receives broad public support and thereby avoids private foundation status (the *operational* approach).

If the organization is a private foundation, care must be exercised to avoid the assessment of tax liability on prohibited transactions. This objective can best be achieved by establishing controls that prevent the private foundation from engaging in transactions that trigger the imposition of the taxes. If an initial tax is assessed, corrective actions should be implemented to avoid the assessment of an additional tax. See Concept Summary 23–5.

UNRELATED BUSINESS INCOME TAX

If the exempt organization conducts an unrelated trade or business, it may be subject to tax on the unrelated business income. Worse yet, the unrelated trade or business could result in the loss of exempt status if the IRS determines that the

---

[59]See Chapter 9.

activity is the primary purpose of the organization. Thus, caution and planning should be used to eliminate the latter possibility and to minimize the former.

KEY TERMS

Debt-financed income,
23–21

Excess lobbying
expenditure, 23–8

Exempt organization,
23–2

Feeder organization,
23–9

Grass roots
expenditure, 23–7

Lobbying expenditure,
23–7

Private foundation,
23–10

Unrelated business
income, 23–14

Unrelated business
income tax (UBIT),
23–14

**PROBLEM
MATERIALS**

DISCUSSION QUESTIONS

1. Are all churches exempt from Federal income tax?

2. Why are certain organizations either partially or completely exempt from Federal income tax?

3. Which of the following organizations qualify for exempt status?
    a. Tulane University.
    b. Virginia Qualified Tuition Program.
    c. Red Cross.
    d. Disneyland.
    e. PTA.
    f. Jacksonville Chamber of Commerce.
    g. Colonial Williamsburg Foundation.
    h. National Football League (NFL).
    i. Green Bay Packers.
    j. Cleveland Indians.

4. Identify the statutory authority under which each of the following is exempt from Federal income tax.
    a. Kingsmill Country Club.
    b. Shady Lawn Cemetery.
    c. Amber Credit Union.
    d. Veterans of Foreign Wars.
    e. Boy Scouts of America.
    f. United Fund.
    g. Federal Deposit Insurance Corporation.
    h. Bruton Parish Episcopal Church.
    i. PTA.
    j. National Press Club.

5. Adrenna is the treasurer for two exempt organizations. One exempt organization pays no Federal income taxes for 1998, and the other pays Federal income taxes of $100,000 for 1998. Discuss potential reasons for this difference in tax results.

6. Roy contributes $1,000 to an exempt organization. Abby contributes $1,000 to a different exempt organization. Why is Abby permitted a $1,000 charitable contribution deduction in calculating her itemized deductions and Roy is not?

7. Can a church make an election that will enable it to engage in lobbying on a limited basis?

8. Cashmier, Inc., a § 501(c)(3) organization, loses its exempt status in 1998 for attempting to influence legislation. Golden, Inc., another § 501(c)(3) organization, also attempts to influence legislation and is in no danger of losing its exempt status. Explain.

9. Rex is the chief executive officer of Helping People, Inc., a § 501(c)(3) exempt organization located in Mobile, Alabama. He and the organization's board of directors are concerned about the effect that proposed legislation would have on the organization's budget and its ability to carry out its mission. They are discussing a proposal to have a law firm in Washington, D.C., aid in opposing the legislation. What tax issues are relevant to Helping People, Inc., as it makes this decision?

10. Service, Inc., an exempt organization, owns all of the stock of Blue, Inc., a retailer of boating supplies. Blue remits all of its profits to Service. According to a policy adopted by Service's board, 60% of the amount received from Blue is to be spent annually in carrying out Service's tax-exempt mission, and 40% is to be invested in Service's endowment fund. What are the tax consequences to Service and to Blue?

11. Which of the following activities are not subject to the tax imposed on feeder organizations?
    a. Substantially all of the work is performed by volunteers.
    b. Substantially all of the services are performed by paid employees of the exempt organization.
    c. Substantially all of the merchandise being sold is used property.
    d. Substantially all of the merchandise being sold was received as contributions or gifts.
    e. Rental of building to a tenant who uses the building as a warehouse for her business.

12. What is a private foundation, and what are the disadvantages of an exempt organization being classified as a private foundation?

13. Describe the external support test and the internal support test for a private foundation.

14. A private foundation generally is exempt from Federal income tax. However, it may be subject to two types of taxes. Identify these taxes and discuss why they are imposed on private foundations.

15. What is the purpose of the tax on the investment income of a private foundation? Discuss the applicable tax rates.

16. A private foundation engages in a transaction with a disqualified person. What are the tax consequences to the private foundation and to the disqualified person?

17. Welcome, Inc., a tax-exempt organization, receives 25% of its support from disqualified persons. Another disqualified person has agreed to match this support if Welcome will appoint him to the organization's board of directors. What tax issues are relevant to Welcome as it makes this decision?

18. An exempt organization has unrelated business taxable income of $400,000 and total earnings of $1 million. Why is only the $400,000 subject to the Federal income tax?

19. First Church has been selling cards and small books in the church tower. A contribution box was provided in which payments were to be deposited. To increase church revenues, a task force is evaluating setting up a gift shop in the church parish house. What tax issues are relevant to the task force as it makes its decision?

20. An exempt hospital operates a pharmacy that is staffed by a pharmacist 24 hours per day. The pharmacy serves only hospital patients. Is the pharmacy an unrelated trade or business?

21. Second Church is going to operate a gift and book shop that will include only religious articles in its inventory. The shop will be staffed by employees who are not church members. Under consideration are two options: (1) organizing the shop as a wholly owned corporate subsidiary and (2) including it within the organizational structure of Second Church. The projected annual profits of $100,000 are to be used in the church's outreach mission. What are the tax consequences of each option? Which should Second Church select?

22. To which of the following tax-exempt organizations may the unrelated business income tax apply?
    a. Red Cross.
    b. Salvation Army.
    c. United Fund.
    d. College of William and Mary.
    e. Rainbow, Inc., a private foundation.
    f. Federal Land Bank.

23. Sight, Inc., a tax-exempt organization that trains the visually impaired to restore and to tune pianos, receives pianos as contributions. When the number of pianos on hand exceeds 15, Sight sells the excess; the pianos used in the training program the longest are sold first. Is the revenue from the sale of excess pianos subject to the unrelated business income tax?

24. An exempt organization is considering conducting bingo games on Thursday nights as a way of generating additional revenue to support its exempt purpose. Before doing so, however, the president of the organization has come to you for advice regarding the effect on the organization's exempt status and whether the net income from the bingo games will be taxable. Identify the relevant tax issues.

25. Define each of the following with respect to unrelated debt-financed property.
    a. Debt-financed income.
    b. Debt-financed property.
    c. Acquisition indebtedness.
    d. Average acquisition indebtedness.
    e. Average adjusted basis.

26. Tom is the treasurer of the City Garden Club, a new garden club. A friend, who is the treasurer of the garden club in a neighboring community, tells Tom that it is not necessary for the garden club to file a request for exempt status with the IRS. Has Tom received correct advice?

PROBLEMS

27. Teach, Inc., a § 501(c)(3) educational institution, makes lobbying expenditures of $320,000. Teach incurs exempt purpose expenditures of $1.7 million in carrying out its educational mission.
    a. Determine the tax consequences to Teach if it does not elect to be eligible to participate in lobbying activities on a limited basis.
    b. Determine the tax consequences to Teach if it does elect to be eligible to participate in lobbying activities on a limited basis.

28. Roadrunner, Inc., is an exempt medical organization. Quail, Inc., a sporting goods retailer, is a wholly owned subsidiary of Roadrunner. Roadrunner inherited the Quail stock last year from a major benefactor of the medical organization. Quail's taxable income is $400,000. Quail will remit all of its earnings, net of any taxes, to Roadrunner to support the exempt purpose of the parent.
    a. Is Quail subject to Federal income tax? If so, calculate the liability.
    b. Arthur Morgan, the treasurer of Roadrunner, has contacted you regarding minimizing or eliminating Quail's tax liability. He would like to know if the tax consequences would be better if Quail were liquidated into Roadrunner. Write a letter to Morgan that contains your advice. Roadrunner's address is 500 Rouse Tower, Rochester, NY 14627.

29. Determine which of the following organizations are *not* private foundations.
    a. Baptist Church.
    b. Girl Scouts.
    c. League of Women Voters.
    d. PGA Tour.
    e. American Institute of CPAs.

f. PTA.
g. American Red Cross.
h. Salvation Army.
i. Veterans of Foreign Wars.

30. Cardinal, Inc., a § 501(c)(3) organization, received support from the following sources.

Governmental unit A for services rendered	$ 6,000
General public for services rendered	80,000
Gross investment income	40,000
Contributions from disqualified persons	20,000
Contributions from other than disqualified persons	95,000

a. Does Cardinal satisfy the test for receiving broad public support?
b. Is Cardinal a private foundation?
c. Arnold Horn, Cardinal's treasurer, has asked you to advise him on whether Cardinal is a private foundation. Write a letter to him in which you address the issue. His address is 250 Bristol Road, Charlottesville, VA 22903.

31. Gray, Inc., a private foundation, has the following items of income and deductions.

Interest income	$18,000
Rent income	60,000
Dividend income	15,000
Royalty income	5,000
Unrelated business income	50,000
Rent expenses	12,000
Unrelated business expenses	10,000

Gray is not an exempt operating foundation and is not eligible for the 1% tax rate.
a. Calculate the net investment income.
b. Calculate the tax on net investment income.
c. What is the purpose of the tax on net investment income?

32. Eagle, Inc., is a private foundation that has been in existence for 10 years. During this period, it has been unable to satisfy the requirements for classification as a private operating foundation. At the end of 1997, it had undistributed income of $100,000. Of this amount, $40,000 was distributed in 1998, and $60,000 was distributed during the first quarter of 1999. The IRS deficiency notice was mailed on August 1, 2000.
a. Calculate the initial tax for 1997, 1998, and 1999.
b. Calculate the additional tax for 2000.

33. Otis is the CEO of Rectify, Inc., a private foundation. Otis invests $500,000 (80%) of the foundation's investment portfolio in derivatives. Previously, the $500,000 had been invested in corporate bonds with an AA rating that earned 7% per annum. If the derivatives investment works as Otis's investment adviser claims, the annual earnings could be as high as 20%.
a. Determine if Rectify is subject to any of the taxes imposed on private foundations.
b. If so, calculate the amount of the initial tax.
c. If so, calculate the amount of the additional tax if the act causing the imposition of the tax is not addressed within the correction period.
d. Are Otis and the foundation better off financially if the prohibited transaction, if any, is addressed within the correction period?

34. The board of directors of Pearl, Inc., a private foundation, consists of Alice, Beth, and Carlos. They vote unanimously to provide a $100,000 grant to Doug, their business associate. The grant is to be used for travel and education and does not qualify as a permitted grant to individuals (i.e., it is a taxable expenditure under § 4945). Each

director knows that Doug was selected for the grant because he is a friend of the organization and that the grant is a taxable expenditure.

a. Calculate the initial tax imposed on the private foundation.

b. Calculate the initial tax imposed on the foundation manager (i.e., board of directors).

35. The Open Museum is an exempt organization that operates a gift shop. The museum's annual operations budget is $2.5 million. Gift shop sales generate a profit of $750,000. Another $500,000 of endowment income is generated. Both the income from the gift shop and the endowment income are used to support the exempt purpose of the museum. The balance of $1.25 million required for annual operations is provided through admission fees. Wayne Davis, a new board member, does not understand why the museum is subject to tax at all, particularly since the profits are used in carrying out the mission of the museum. The museum's address is 250 Oak Avenue, Peoria, IL 61625.

a. Calculate the amount of unrelated business income.

b. Assume that the endowment income is reinvested rather than being used to support annual operations. Calculate the amount of unrelated business income.

c. As the museum treasurer, write a letter to Wayne explaining the reason for the tax consequences. Mr. Davis's address is 45 Pine Avenue, Peoria, IL 61625.

36. Salmon, Inc., an exempt organization, has unrelated business taxable income of $20 million.

a. Calculate Salmon's UBIT.

b. Prepare an outline of a presentation you are going to give to the new members of Salmon's board on why Salmon is subject to the UBIT even though it is an exempt organization.

37. For each of the following organizations, determine the amount of the UBIT.

a. AIDS, Inc., an exempt charitable organization that provides support for individuals with AIDS, operates a retail medical supply store open to the general public. The net income of the store, before any Federal income taxes, is $325,000.

b. The local Episcopal Church operates a retail gift shop. The inventory consists of the typical items sold by commercial gift shops in the city. The director of the gift shop estimates that 80% of the gift shop sales are to tourists and 20% are to church members. The net income of the gift shop, before the salaries of the three gift shop employees and any Federal income taxes, is $300,000. The salaries of the employees total $80,000.

c. Education, Inc., a private university, has vending machines in the student dormitories and academic buildings on campus. In recognition of recent tuition increases, the university has adopted a policy of merely trying to recover its costs associated with the vending machine activity. For the current year, however, the net income of the activity, before any Federal income taxes, is $75,000.

d. Worn, Inc., an exempt organization, provides food for the homeless. It operates a thrift store that sells used clothing to the general public. The thrift shop is staffed by four salaried employees. All of the clothes it sells are received as contributions. The $100,000 profit generated for the year by the thrift shop is used in Worn's mission of providing food to the homeless.

e. Small, Inc., an exempt organization, has unrelated business income of $900 and unrelated business expenses of $400.

38. Kentwood Spring Water, Inc., contributes $5,000 to the Kentwood Krackers Baseball League, an exempt organization that sponsors summer baseball games for children under age 9. In return for the contribution, Kentwood Krackers includes Spring Water's corporate logo on the cover of the program it sells at the baseball games.

a. Determine the effect of the contribution to Kentwood Krackers.

b. Instead of including the logo on the cover of its programs, Kentwood Krackers endorses Spring Water's bottled water by advertising in the program that team players drink only Kentwood Spring Water's bottled water at its games. Determine the effect of the contribution to Kentwood Krackers.

39. Bluebird, Inc., an exempt organization, has unrelated business taxable income (before any modification associated with charitable contributions) of $2,000. Charitable contributions made by Bluebird that are associated with the unrelated trade or business are $15,000, and those made that are not associated with the unrelated trade or business are $10,000. Calculate the effect of the charitable contributions on Bluebird's unrelated business taxable income.

40. Rabbit, Inc., an exempt organization, has net unrelated business income of $75,000 excluding any rent income received. Rabbit owns two buildings that are leased to tenants. The net rent income on the first building is $32,000, and that on the second building is $35,000. The lessee of the first building is unrelated to Rabbit whereas the lessee of the second building is a 100%-owned for-profit subsidiary. Calculate Rabbit's unrelated business taxable income.

41. Assistance, Inc., an exempt organization, sells the following assets during the taxable year:

Asset	Gain (Loss)	Use
Land and building	$ 80,000	In exempt purpose
Land	50,000	Leased to a taxable entity
Equipment	(20,000)	Leased to a taxable entity
Automobile	(5,000)	In exempt purpose

Determine the effect of these transactions on Assistance's unrelated business taxable income.

42. Fix, Inc., an exempt organization, owns a one-story building. Fix's adjusted basis for the building is $900,000. Of the building's total area of 10,000 square feet, the front portion (approximately 3,000 square feet) is used in carrying out Fix's exempt purpose. The remainder of the building is leased for $300,000 each year to Belts, Inc., a taxable entity, to use for storing its inventory. The unamortized balance of a mortgage relating to the original acquisition of the building is $600,000. Determine the portion of the adjusted basis that is treated as debt-financed property and the amount of the mortgage that is acquisition indebtedness.

43. Rodeo, Inc. is a social club that is exempt under § 501(c)(7). Its annual gross receipts are $250,000. Of this amount, $20,000 is from an unrelated trade or business. Rodeo's fiscal year ends on April 30.
    a. Is Rodeo required to file an annual information return? If so, what form should be used?
    b. Is Rodeo subject to the UBIT? If so, what form should be used?
    c. If tax returns must be filed, what are the due dates?

44. Historic Burg is an exempt organization that operates a museum depicting eighteenth-century life. Sally gives the museum an eighteenth-century chest that she has owned for 10 years. Her adjusted basis is $55,000, and the chest's appraised value is $100,000. Sally's adjusted gross income is $300,000.
    a. Calculate Sally's charitable contribution deduction if Historic Burg is a private operating foundation.
    b. Calculate Sally's charitable contribution deduction if Historic Burg is a private nonoperating foundation.

Research Problems for this chapter appear at the end of Chapter 28.

TAXATION OF INTERNATIONAL TRANSACTIONS

LEARNING OBJECTIVES

After completing Chapter 24, you should be able to:

1. Use the foreign tax credit provisions.

2. Apply the rules for sourcing income and allocating deductions into U.S. and foreign categories.

3. Utilize the U.S. tax provisions concerning nonresident alien individuals and foreign corporations.

4. Appreciate the tax benefits available to certain U.S. individuals working abroad.

5. Apply the U.S. tax rules for foreign corporations controlled by U.S. persons.

6. Explain how foreign currency exchange affects the tax consequences of international transactions.

OVERVIEW OF INTERNATIONAL TAXATION

International taxation is an integral part of the U.S. involvement in the world economy. In an age when economic isolation is no longer feasible for most countries, the United States, as a large and influential nation, plays a particularly important role in the global economy. In 1995, cross-border services (exports and imports) totaled almost $196.5 billion. Nonpetroleum imports were $731 billion in 1996, while nonagricultural exports were $550.2 billion for the same period.

The world economy also has implications for the U.S. domestic economy. The global economy influences the interest rate that a small U.S. business pays for new equipment or a U.S. family pays for a new home, automobile, or television set.

More and more U.S. corporations are developing international ties. Even the local oil company and cotton cooperative in a city of less than 200,000 are entering into negotiations with former Soviet bloc nations. For 1996, U.S. direct investment abroad totaled $970.8 billion. Direct investment is defined as at least a 10 percent ownership interest. The United Kingdom attracted the largest percentage of this investment—17.9 percent—while Canada was second at 11.5 percent.

As a result of this growing globalization of business, tax practitioners who are employed by a company with even a small amount of foreign-source income or who have clients generating foreign-source income must deal with, at minimum, the foreign tax credit and U.S. income tax treaties. More complex international transactions require an in-depth knowledge of international taxation.

U.S. persons with international transactions encounter many of the same Federal tax laws as any U.S. taxpayer. Income is subject to U.S. taxation, certain expenses and losses are deductible, and credits are available. Earnings of domestic corporations face double taxation. However, U.S. taxpayers with international transactions face another set of provisions that apply to international business. These laws are meant to prevent double (two-country) taxation, allow the United States to remain competitive internationally, and prevent taxpayers from evading U.S. taxes by moving income-producing activities abroad.

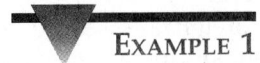

EXAMPLE 1

Jorge Ramirez is a U.S. citizen working as chief accountant for a U.S. corporation's bridge building project in Brazil. His annual salary is $120,000, and the company annually provides $35,000 of living expenses for Jorge and his family. Jorge has U.S. investments that earn about $2,500 a year, and he is a shareholder in a Brazilian corporation that is controlled by U.S. persons.

Without special provisions to deal with Jorge's foreign-earned income, he would be subject to double taxation—once by the United States, which taxes worldwide income on the basis of citizenship or residency, and once by Brazil, which taxes on the basis of residency. Additionally, Jorge's company might be at a competitive disadvantage when bidding on such contracts. If the company compensated its employees for this double taxation, it would incur a greater wage and salary expense than companies from countries where double taxation was not a problem. Further, without special U.S. tax provisions, Jorge and the other U.S. shareholders could invest in the Brazilian corporation, which would not incur any U.S. taxation until distributions were made to shareholders. ▼

THE FOREIGN TAX CREDIT

1 **LEARNING OBJECTIVE**
Use the foreign tax credit provisions.

The United States retains the right to tax its citizens and residents on their worldwide taxable income. This approach can result in double taxation and presents a potential problem to U.S. persons who invest abroad.

To reduce the possibility of double taxation, the U.S. Congress enacted the **foreign tax credit (FTC)** provisions. Under these provisions, a qualified taxpayer is allowed a tax credit for foreign income taxes paid. The credit provides a dollar-for-dollar reduction of the U.S. income tax liability. For 1994, corporations filing U.S. tax returns claimed $25.4 billion in FTCs. For the same period, individuals claimed $2.3 billion in FTCs. In 1996, income receipts on U.S. direct investment abroad were $98.3 billion. Without the benefit of the FTC, much of this income would be subject to double taxation.

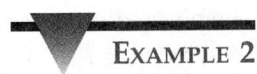

EXAMPLE 2

Ace Tools, Inc., a U.S. corporation, has a branch operation in Mexico, from which it earns taxable income of $750,000 for the current year. Ace pays income tax of $150,000 on these earnings to the Mexican tax authorities. Ace must also include the $750,000 in gross income for U.S. tax purposes. Assume that, before considering the FTC, Ace would owe $255,000 in U.S. income taxes on this foreign-source income. Thus, total taxes on the $750,000 could equal $405,000 ($150,000 + $255,000), a 54% effective rate. But Ace takes the FTC of $150,000 against its U.S. tax liability on the foreign-source income. Ace Tools' total taxes on the $750,000 now are $255,000 ($150,000 + $105,000), a 34% effective rate. ▼

THE CREDIT PROVISIONS

The Direct Credit. Section 901 provides a direct FTC to U.S. taxpayers who pay or incur a foreign income tax. For purposes of the direct credit, only the taxpayer who bears the legal incidence of the foreign tax is eligible for the credit. Ace Tools, in Example 2 above, would be eligible for the direct credit.

The Indirect Credit.   If a U.S. corporation operates in a foreign country through a branch, the direct credit is available for foreign taxes paid. If, however, a U.S. corporation operates in a foreign country through a foreign subsidiary, the direct credit is not available for foreign taxes paid by the foreign corporation. An indirect credit is available to U.S. *corporate* taxpayers who receive actual or constructive dividends from foreign corporations that have paid a foreign tax on earnings. These foreign taxes are deemed paid by the corporate shareholders in the same proportion as the dividends actually or constructively received bear to the foreign corporation's post-1986 undistributed earnings and profits (E & P). A domestic corporation that chooses the FTC for deemed-paid foreign taxes must *gross up* dividend income by the amount of deemed-paid taxes.

EXAMPLE 3

Wren, Inc., a domestic corporation, owns 50% of Finch, Inc., a foreign corporation. Wren receives a dividend of $120,000 from Finch. Finch paid foreign taxes of $500,000 on post-1986 E & P. Finch's post-1986 E & P (after taxes) totals $1,200,000. Wren's deemed-paid foreign taxes for FTC purposes are $50,000.

Cash dividend from Finch	$120,000
Deemed-paid foreign taxes $\left(\$500,000 \times \dfrac{\$120,000}{\$1,200,000}\right)$	50,000
Gross income to Wren	$170,000

Wren must include the $50,000 in gross income due to the gross-up adjustment if the FTC is elected. ▼

Certain ownership requirements must be met before the indirect credit is available to a domestic corporation. The domestic corporation must own 10 percent or more of the voting stock of the foreign corporation. The credit is also available for deemed-paid foreign taxes of second- and third-tier foreign corporations if the 10 percent ownership requirement is met at the second- and third-tier level. A 5 percent indirect ownership requirement must also be met. This indirect credit is also available for foreign taxes paid by fourth-through-sixth-tier foreign corporations, if additional requirements are met, including that these corporations are controlled foreign corporations. The § 902 ownership requirements are summarized in Figure 24–1.

FTC Limitations.   To prevent foreign taxes from being credited against U.S. taxes levied on *U.S.-source taxable income*, the FTC is subject to a limitation. The FTC for any *taxable* year cannot exceed the lesser of the actual foreign taxes paid or accrued, or the U.S. taxes (before the FTC) on foreign-source taxable income (the *general limitation*). The latter limitation formula is derived in the following manner.

$$\text{U.S. tax before FTC} \times \frac{\text{Foreign-source taxable income}}{\text{Worldwide taxable income}^1}$$

EXAMPLE 4

Terry, a U.S. resident, invests in foreign securities. Her worldwide taxable income (before personal exemptions) for the tax year is $120,000, consisting of $100,000 in salary from a U.S. employer and $20,000 of income from foreign sources. Foreign taxes of $6,000 were withheld by foreign tax authorities. Assume that Terry's U.S. tax before the FTC is $33,600.

---

[1]For FTC purposes, the taxable income of an individual, estate, or trust is computed without any deduction for personal exemptions. § 904(b)(1).

▼ **FIGURE 24–1**
Section 902 Ownership
Requirements

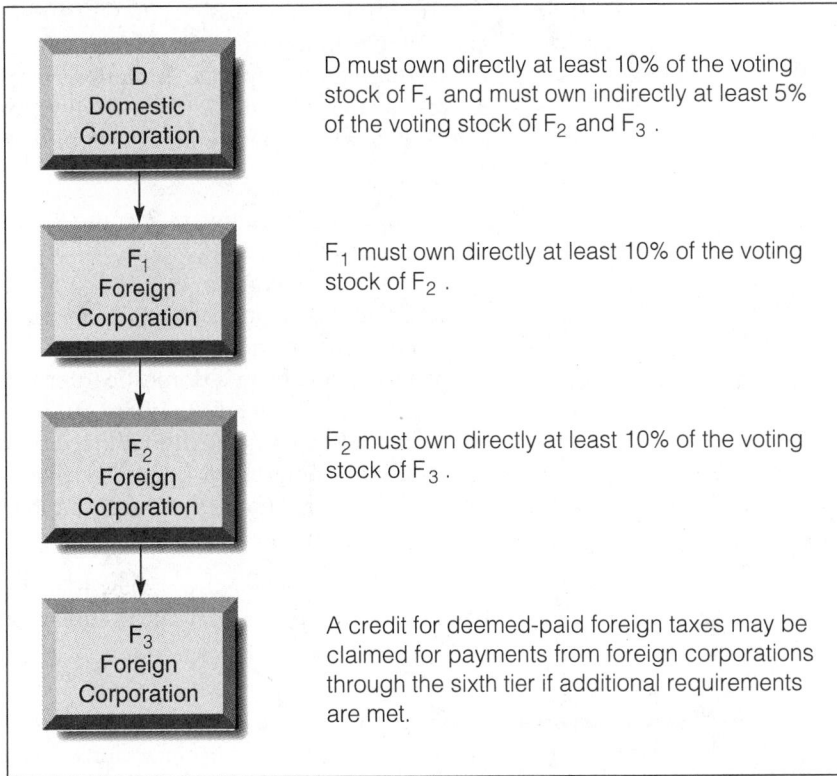

Her FTC is $5,600 [$33,600 × ($20,000/$120,000)]. Her net U.S. tax liability is $28,000 ($33,600 − $5,600). ▼

As Example 4 illustrates, the limitation can prevent some portion of foreign taxes paid in high-tax jurisdictions from being credited. Taxpayers could overcome this problem by generating additional foreign-source income that is subject to no, or low, foreign taxation.

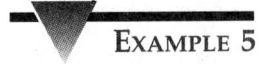

EXAMPLE 5

Compare Domestic Corporation's FTC situation when the corporation has only $500,000 of highly taxed foreign-source income with the situation where Domestic also has $100,000 of low-taxed foreign-source interest income.

	Only Highly Taxed Income	With Low-Taxed Interest
Foreign-source income	$500,000	$600,000
Foreign taxes	275,000	280,000
U.S.-source income	700,000	700,000
U.S. taxes (34%)	408,000	442,000
FTC limitation	170,000*	204,000**

*$408,000 × ($500,000/$1,200,000).
**$442,000 × ($600,000/$1,300,000).

Domestic's foreign taxes increase by only $5,000, while its FTC limitation increases by $34,000. ▼

To prevent the *cross-crediting* of foreign taxes as in Example 5, Congress has enacted legislation providing for several separate limitation *baskets*. These provisions require that a separate limitation be calculated for certain categories of foreign-source taxable income and the foreign taxes attributable to that income. Section 904(d) provides separate limitation baskets for the following.

- Passive income.
- High withholding tax income.
- Financial services income.
- Shipping income.
- Dividends from each § 902 corporation that is not a U.S.-controlled foreign corporation (non-CFC).
- Dividends from a domestic international sales corporation (DISC) or former DISC to the extent they are treated as foreign-source income.
- Taxable income attributable to foreign trade income under § 923(b).
- Distributions from a foreign sales corporation (FSC) or former FSC out of E & P attributable to foreign trade income or qualified interest and carrying charges under § 263(c).

All other *foreign-source income* is included in a general (or overall) limitation basket. These separate limitations are diagrammed in Concept Summary 24–1.

EXAMPLE 6

Wood Products, Inc., a U.S. corporation, has a foreign branch in Canada that earns taxable income of $1,000,000 from manufacturing operations and $500,000 from shipping operations. Wood Products also earns Canada-source high withholding tax interest of $100,000. Wood Products pays foreign taxes of $400,000 (40%), $250,000 (50%), and $15,000 (15%), respectively, on this foreign-source income. The corporation also earns $4,000,000 of U.S.-source taxable income, resulting in worldwide taxable income of $5,600,000. The U.S. taxes before the FTC are $1,904,000 (at 34%). The following tabulation illustrates the effect of the separate limitation baskets on cross-crediting.

Foreign Income Category	Net Taxable Amount	Foreign Taxes	U.S. Tax before FTC at 34%	FTC with Separate Limits
Manufacturing	$1,000,000	$400,000	$340,000	$340,000
Shipping	500,000	250,000	170,000	170,000
High withholding tax interest	100,000	15,000	34,000	15,000
Total	$1,600,000	$665,000	$544,000	$525,000

Without the separate limitation provisions, the FTC would be the lesser of $665,000 foreign taxes paid or accrued, or $544,000 [i.e., $1,904,000 × ($1,600,000/$5,600,000)]. The separate limitation provisions reduce the total FTC by $19,000 ($544,000 – $525,000). The foreign-source income taxed at the foreign tax rates of 40% and 50% cannot be aggregated with foreign-source income taxed at only 15%. ▼

The limitations can result in unused (noncredited) foreign taxes for the tax year. A two-year carryback and a five-year carryover of excess foreign taxes are allowed. The taxes can be credited in years when the formula limitation for that year exceeds the foreign taxes attributable to the same tax year. The carryback and carryover provision is available only within the separate baskets. In other words,

CONCEPT SUMMARY 24–1

Foreign Tax Credit: Separate Income Limitations

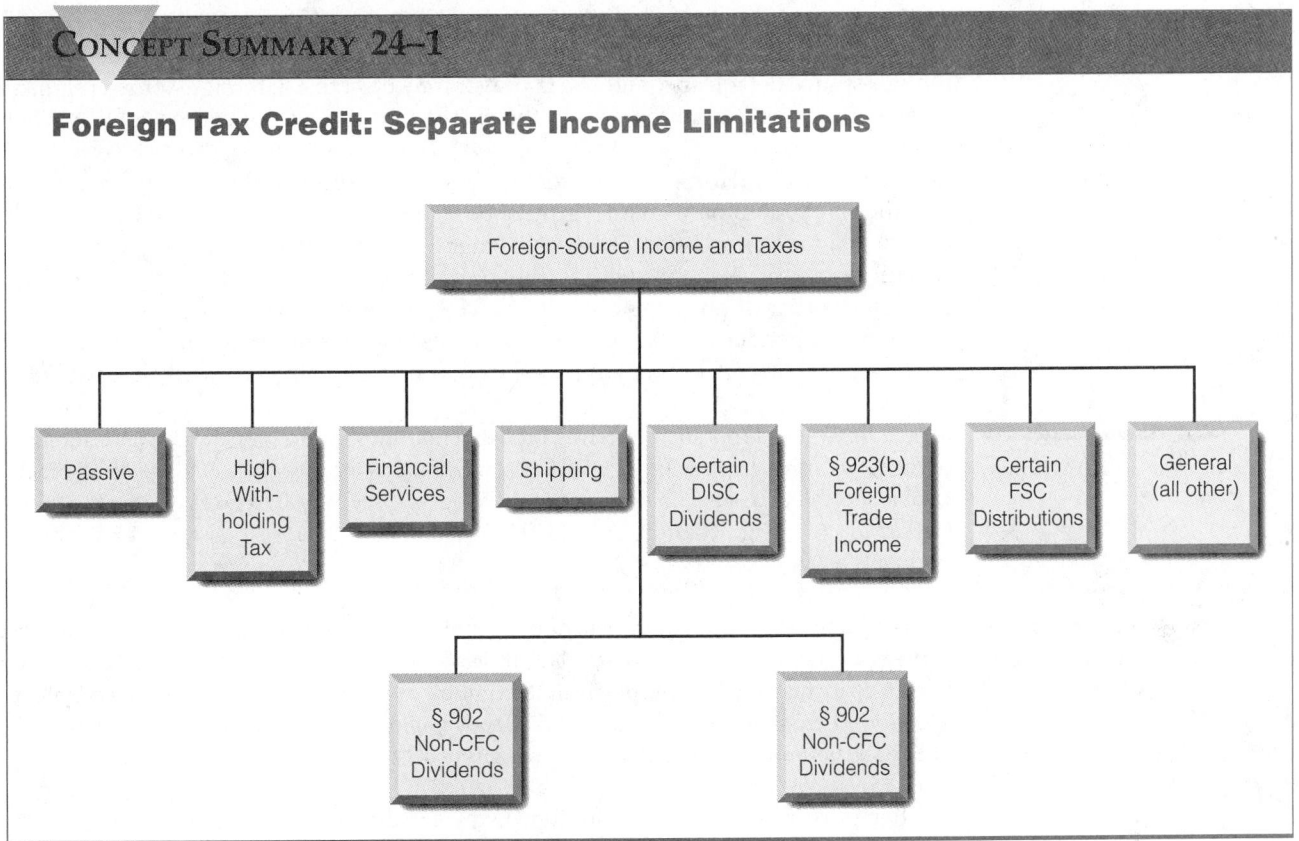

excess foreign taxes in one basket cannot be carried over unless there is an excess limitation in the same basket for the carryover year.

The Alternative Minimum Tax FTC. For purposes of the alternative minimum tax, the FTC is limited to the lesser of the credit for regular tax purposes or 90 percent of the tentative minimum tax before the credit.[2] The 10 percent cutback is calculated on the tentative minimum tax without regard to the alternative tax NOL deduction. The general FTC limitation is calculated by using foreign-source alternative minimum taxable income (AMTI) in the numerator and worldwide

TAX IN THE NEWS

MORE U.S. COMPANIES SET UP FOREIGN OPERATIONS

As international trade continues to expand, more U.S. companies must consider the international tax implications of their operations. U.S. companies with international operations include Original Log Cabin Homes, Ltd., with 70 percent of its sales outside the United States. Mrs. Fields Chocolate Chip Cookies has operations in foreign locations such as Hong Kong, Japan, and Thailand.

SOURCE: Adapted from *Inc.*, May 20, 1997.

---

[2]§ 59. A "small corporation" exception is available.

AMTI in the denominator of the formula and the tentative minimum tax rather than the regular tax. The source of AMTI must be determined for the purpose of foreign-source taxable income. The taxpayer may elect to use foreign-source regular taxable income in the numerator to the extent that it does not exceed total AMTI.

Other Considerations. For a foreign levy to qualify for the FTC, it must be a tax, and its predominant character must be that of an income tax in the U.S. sense.[3] A levy is a tax if it is a compulsory payment, as contrasted with a payment for a specific economic benefit such as the right to extract oil. A tax's predominant character is that of an income tax in the U.S. sense if it reaches realized net gain and is not dependent on being credited against the income tax of another country (not a *soak-up* tax). A tax that is levied in lieu of an income tax is also creditable.[4]

EXAMPLE 7

Rigs, a domestic corporation, receives oil extraction income from operations in a foreign country. The other country levies a 50% tax on extraction income and a 30% tax on all other taxable income derived within the country. If Rigs pays $700,000 in taxes on its extraction income to the foreign country, only $420,000 [$700,000 × (30% ÷ 50%)] of that amount is creditable as an income tax. ▼

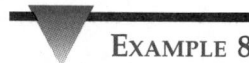

EXAMPLE 8

Hoops, a domestic corporation, generates $2 million of taxable income from operations in Larissa, a foreign country. Larissa's law levies a tax on income generated in Larissa by foreign residents only in cases in which the country of residence (such as the United States) allows a tax credit for foreign taxes paid. Hoops will not be allowed an FTC for taxes paid to Larissa, because the foreign tax is a soak-up tax. ▼

For purposes of the FTC, foreign taxes are attributable to the year in which they are paid or accrued. Taxpayers using the cash method of accounting for tax purposes may elect to take the FTC in the year in which the foreign taxes accrue. The election is binding on the taxpayer for the year in which it is made, and for all subsequent years. Foreign taxes accrued in taxable years beginning after December 31, 1997, generally must be translated to U.S. dollars at the average exchange rate for the tax year to which the taxes relate.[5]

The FTC is elective for any particular tax year. If the taxpayer does not choose to take the FTC, a deduction may be allowed for foreign taxes paid or incurred. However, a taxpayer cannot take a credit and a deduction for the same foreign income taxes.[6] A taxpayer can take a deduction in the same year as an FTC for foreign taxes that are not creditable (e.g., soak-up taxes).

ETHICAL CONSIDERATIONS

Taxes on Foreign Investments and the Public Good

The decision to invest abroad is strongly influenced by the availability of the FTC. Without the FTC, U.S. investors, in many cases, would incur double taxation—once by the United States (based on residency or citizenship), then also by the country in which the investment is made (based on source). The FTC generally allows the U.S. investor, with regard to tax consequences, to be indifferent between investment abroad and in the United States when the tax rates are equal. As a result of the FTC, the investor will receive the same net return (after taxes).

---

[3]Reg. § 1.901–2.
[4]§ 903 and Reg. § 1.903–1.

[5]§§ 986(a).
[6]§ 275.

You are the CEO of a multinational corporation based in Iowa. Your Vice President of Taxation brings you a draft of a position paper prepared by a national tax policy think tank of which she is a member. The paper argues that only a deduction should be allowed for foreign taxes incurred by U.S. taxpayers. The argument is based on "public good" considerations. Even though investors may be indifferent to the location of their investments, the U.S. "public good" is not served when the taxes paid on those investments remain offshore. Do you agree? How would you propose to modify the think tank's position?

POSSESSIONS CORPORATIONS

To encourage the economic development of U.S. possessions, Congress enacted a credit provision for income from operations in U.S. possessions. Domestic corporations could elect to receive a § 936 credit against U.S. taxes. The credit is equal to the portion of the U.S. tax attributable to the sum of possession-source taxable income and qualified investment income, even if no tax is paid or due to the possession. This is referred to as a *tax-sparing* credit. No additional credit or deduction is allowed for income taxes actually paid to the possession. A number of pharmaceutical companies, including Eli Lilly Company, have used subsidiaries with operations in Puerto Rico to take advantage of this and local tax benefits. The pharmaceutical and electrical machinery industries receive more than 60 percent of the total § 936 credits allowed. More than $3.7 billion in U.S. possessions tax credits were claimed for 1994. According to Congressional Budget Office estimates, the § 936 incentive would result in $15 billion of tax revenue being lost between 1993 and 1997. For this reason, in 1996 Congress enacted legislation that repealed the credit except for existing claimants. For § 936 corporations conducting an active trade or business in a possession on October 13, 1995, the credit will be phased out by January 1, 2006. A § 936 corporation that adds a new line of business after October 13, 1995, will cease to be eligible for the credit.

The phase-out period rules apply differently to corporations in different circumstances. For example, credit claimants in Puerto Rico that use the economic activity limitation will calculate the credit under new § 30A, which provides a cap on the credit based on possession income over the five preceding tax years. In some cases, the phase-out period will end before 2006.

The credit is allowed against the U.S. tax attributable to foreign-source taxable income from the active conduct of a trade or business in a U.S. possession. It is also allowed on the sale or exchange of substantially all the assets used by the domestic corporation in that active trade or business. The credit is not allowed against certain taxes, though, such as the accumulated earnings tax under § 531 and the personal holding company tax under § 541. The credit is not available for income received in the United States unless it is possession-source income received from an unrelated person and is attributable to an active trade or business conducted in a possession.

The credit is not available for income from intangible assets, such as formulas and patents. Intangible property income is includible in taxable income by a domestic corporation as U.S.-source income. If a domestic corporation elects the credit, however, all of its shareholders who are U.S. persons include their pro rata share of that item in gross income as U.S.-source income. In this case, the domestic corporation is not taxed on such income.

EXAMPLE 9

A qualified possessions corporation generates the following foreign-source income on which it pays the following foreign taxes.

Taxable Income	Source	Foreign Taxes
$450,000 active trade or business income	Possession	$40,000
10,000 passive investment income	Possession	–0–
40,000 investment income	Nonpossession	16,000

Assume that the corporation's worldwide taxable income is $500,000 and its U.S. tax before the FTC is $170,000. The § 936 possessions corporation credit is $153,000 (34% × $450,000) before consideration of the § 936 limitation, and the direct FTC is $13,600, the lesser of $16,000 or $13,600 [$170,000 × ($40,000/$500,000)]. ▼

SOURCING OF INCOME AND ALLOCATION OF DEDUCTIONS

2 **LEARNING OBJECTIVE**
Apply the rules for sourcing income and allocating deductions into U.S. and foreign categories.

The sourcing of income within or without the United States has a direct bearing on a number of tax provisions. The numerator of the FTC limitation formula is foreign-source taxable income. Generally, **nonresident aliens** and foreign corporations are subject to Federal taxation only on U.S.-source income. The foreign earned income exclusion is available only for foreign-source income.

INCOME SOURCED WITHIN THE UNITED STATES

The determination of the source depends on the type of income realized. This makes the classification of income an important consideration (e.g., income from the sale of property versus income for the use of property). A detailed discussion of the characterization of income, however, is beyond the scope of this chapter. Section 861 contains source rules for most types of income. Other rules pertaining to the source of income are found in §§ 862–865.

Interest.   Interest income received from the U.S. government, from the District of Columbia, and from noncorporate U.S. residents or domestic corporations is sourced within the United States. There are a few exceptions to this rule, most notably, certain interest received from a resident alien individual or domestic corporation. This exception applies if an 80 percent foreign business requirement is met. Interest received on amounts deposited with a foreign branch of a U.S. corporation is also treated as foreign-source income if the branch is engaged in the commercial banking business.

EXAMPLE 10

John holds a bond issued by Delta, a domestic corporation. For the immediately preceding three tax years, 82% of Delta's gross income was active foreign business income. The interest income that John receives for the tax year from Delta is foreign-source income. ▼

Dividends.   Dividends received from domestic corporations (other than certain possessions corporations) are sourced within the United States. For 1994, U.S. corporations reported receiving more than $30.3 billion in dividends from foreign corporations. Generally, dividends paid by a foreign corporation are foreign-source income. However, an exception applies if 25 percent or more of a foreign corporation's gross income for the immediately preceding three tax years was effectively connected with the conduct of a U.S. trade or business. In this case, the dividends received in the taxable year are U.S.-source income to the extent of the proportion of gross **income** that was **effectively connected** with the conduct of a U.S. trade or business for the immediately preceding three-year period. Dividends from **foreign sales corporations (FSCs)** and domestic international sales corporations (DISCs) can be treated as U.S.-source income.

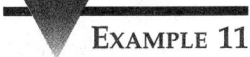
EXAMPLE 11

Ann receives dividend income from the following corporations for the tax year.

Amount	Corporation	Effectively Connected Income for Past 3 Years	Active Foreign Business Income for Past 3 Years	U.S.-Source Income
$500	Green, domestic	85%	15%	$500
600	Brown, domestic	13%	87%	600
300	Orange, foreign	80%	20%	240

The 80% active foreign business requirement affects only interest income received from Green Corporation and Brown Corporation, not dividend income. The dividends received from Green and Brown are U.S.-source income. Because Orange Corporation is a foreign corporation meeting the 25% test, 80% of the dividend from Orange is U.S.-source income. ▼

Personal Services Income. The source of income from personal services is determined by the location in which the services are performed (within or without the United States). A limited *commercial traveler* exception is available. Personal services income must meet the following requirements to avoid U.S.-source treatment.

- The services must be performed by a nonresident alien who is in the United States for 90 days or less during the taxable year.
- The compensation for the services performed in the United States may not exceed $3,000 in total.
- The services must be performed on behalf of
  - a nonresident alien, foreign partnership, or foreign corporation that is not engaged in a U.S. trade or business, or
  - an office or place of business maintained in a foreign country or possession of the United States by an individual who is a citizen or resident of the United States, a domestic partnership, or a domestic corporation.

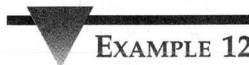
EXAMPLE 12

Mark, a nonresident alien, is an engineer employed by a foreign oil company. He spent four weeks in the United States arranging the purchase of field equipment for his company. His salary for the four weeks was $3,500. Even though the oil company is not engaged in a U.S. trade or business, and Mark was in the United States for less than 90 days during the taxable year, the income is U.S.-source income because it exceeds $3,000. ▼

The issue of whether income is derived from the performance of personal services is important in determining the income's source. The courts have held that a corporation can perform personal services[7] and that, in the absence of capital as an income-producing factor, personal services income can arise even though

---

[7]See *British Timken Limited*, 12 T.C. 880 (1949), and Rev.Rul. 60–55, 1960–1 C.B. 270.

there is no recipient of the services.[8] If payment is received for services performed partly within and partly without the United States, the income must be allocated for source purposes on some reasonable basis, such as days worked.[9]

Rents and Royalties. The source of income received for the use of tangible property is the country in which the property producing the income is located. The source of income received for the use of intangible property (e.g., patents, copyrights, secret processes, and formulas) is the country in which the property producing the income is used.

Sale or Exchange of Property. Income from the disposition of U.S. real property interests is U.S.-source income. The definition of a U.S. real property interest is discussed subsequently under the Foreign Investment in Real Property Tax Act (FIRPTA). Generally, the location of real property determines the source of any income derived from the property.

The source of income from the sale of personal property (assets other than real property) depends on several factors, including whether the property was produced by the seller, the type of property sold (e.g., inventory or a capital asset), and the residence of the seller. Generally, income, gain, or profit from the sale of personal property is sourced according to the residence of the seller. Income from the sale of purchased inventory, however, is sourced in the country in which the sale takes place.[10]

When the seller has produced the property, the income must be apportioned between the country of production and the country of sale. Gross income is sourced under a 50/50 allocation method unless the taxpayer elects to use the independent factory price (IFP) method or the books and records method. The IFP method may only be elected where an IFP exists.[11] If the manufacturer or producer regularly sells to wholly independent distributors, this can establish an *independent* factory or production price.

Under § 865, income from the sale of personal property is sourced at the residence of the seller unless an exception applies, as discussed below. Current Regulations source losses from such sales according to the source of any income that may have been generated by the property prior to its disposition. Recently, the courts have relied on the residence of the seller rule in sourcing losses from the sale of personal property.[12]

The general rule for the sourcing of income from the sale of personal property has several exceptions.

- Gain on the sale of depreciable personal property is sourced according to prior depreciation deductions to the extent of the deductions. Any excess gain is sourced as the sale of inventory.

---

[8]See *Robida v. Comm.*, 72–1 USTC ¶9450, 29 AFTR2d 72–1223, 460 F.2d 1172 (CA–9, 1972). The taxpayer was employed in military PXs around the world. He had large slot machine winnings and claimed the foreign earned income exclusion. The IRS challenged the exclusion on the grounds that the winnings were not earned income because there was no recipient of Robida's services. The Court, however, found that, in the absence of capital, the winnings were earned income.

[9]Reg. § 1.861–4(b).

[10]§§ 861(a)(6) and 865. The sale is deemed to take place where title passes. See Reg. § 1.861–7(c) regarding title passage. There has been

considerable conflict in this area of tax law. See, for example, *Kates Holding Company, Inc.*, 79 T.C. 700 (1982) and *Miami Purchasing Service Corporation*, 76 T.C. 818 (1981).

[11]§ 863(b)(2), Reg. § 1.863–3, and Notice 89–10, 1989–1 C.B. 631.

[12]See Reg. § 1.861–8(e)(7) and (8) and *International Multifoods Corporation*, 108 T.C. No. 26 (1997). The Treasury has issued Prop.Reg. § 1.865–2 dealing with the source of losses on the disposition of stock of a foreign corporation.

- Gain attributable to an office or fixed place of business maintained outside the United States by a U.S. resident is foreign-source income.
- Income or gain attributable to an office or fixed place of business maintained in the United States by a nonresident is U.S.-source income.
- Gain on the sale of intangibles is sourced according to prior amortization deductions to the extent of the deductions. Contingent payments, however, are sourced as royalty income.

The Treasury has issued Proposed Regulations providing rules for determining whether a sale or exchange, or a lease generating rent income, has occurred on the transfer of computer programs.[13]

Transportation and Communication Income. Income from transportation beginning *and* ending in the United States is U.S.-source income. Fifty percent of the income from transportation beginning *or* ending in the United States is U.S.-source income, unless the U.S. point is only an intermediate stop. This rule does not apply to personal services income unless the transportation is between the United States and a possession. Income from space and ocean activities conducted outside the jurisdiction of any country is sourced according to the residence of the person conducting the activity.

International communication income derived by a U.S. person is sourced 50 percent within the United States in cases where transmission is between the United States and a foreign country. International communication income derived by foreign persons is foreign-source income unless it is attributable to an office or other fixed place of business within the United States. In that case, it is U.S.-source income.

INCOME SOURCED WITHOUT THE UNITED STATES

The provisions for sourcing income without the United States are not as detailed and specific as those for determining U.S.-source income. Basically, § 862 provides that if interest, dividends, compensation for personal services, income from the use or sale of property, or other income is not U.S.-source income, then it is foreign-source income.

ALLOCATION AND APPORTIONMENT OF DEDUCTIONS

The United States levies a tax on *taxable income*. The FTC limitation is based on taxable income. Deductions and losses, therefore, must be allocated and apportioned between U.S.- and foreign-source gross income to determine U.S.- and foreign-source taxable income. Deductions directly related to an activity or property are allocated to classes of income. This is followed by apportionment between the statutory and residual groupings on some reasonable basis. **For FTC purposes, U.S.-source income is the residual grouping.**[14]

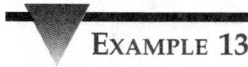

EXAMPLE 13

Ace, Inc., a domestic corporation, has $2 million of gross income and a $50,000 expense, all related to real estate activities. The expense is allocated and apportioned as follows:

---

[13]Prop.Reg. § 1.861–18.

[14]Reg. § 1.861–8.

	Gross Income			Apportionment	
	Foreign	**U.S.**	**Allocation**	**Foreign**	**U.S.**
Sales	$1,000,000	$500,000	$37,500*	$25,000	$12,500**
Rentals	400,000	100,000	12,500	10,000	2,500
			$50,000	$35,000	$15,000

*$50,000 × ($1,500,000/$2,000,000).
**$37,500 × ($500,000/$1,500,000).

If Ace could show that $45,000 of the expense was directly related to sales income, the $45,000 would be allocated to that class of gross income, with the remainder apportioned ratably. ▼

Interest expenses are allocated and apportioned based on the theory that money is fungible. With limited exceptions, interest expense is attributable to all the activities and property of the taxpayer, regardless of the specific purpose for incurring the debt on which interest is paid.[15] Generally, taxpayers must allocate and apportion interest expense on the basis of assets, using either the fair market value or the tax book value of assets.[16] Once the fair market value is used, the taxpayer must continue to use this method. Special rules apply in allocating and apportioning interest expense in an affiliated group of corporations.

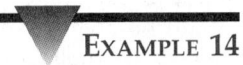

EXAMPLE 14

Black, Inc., a domestic corporation, generates U.S.-source and foreign-source gross income for 1998. Black's assets (tax book value) are as follows:

Generating U.S.-source income	$18,000,000
Generating foreign-source income	5,000,000
	$23,000,000

Black incurs interest expense of $800,000 for 1998. Using the asset method and the tax book value, interest expense is apportioned to foreign-source income as follows:

$$\frac{\$5,000,000 \text{ (foreign assets)}}{\$23,000,000 \text{ (total assets)}} \times \$800,000 = \$173,913$$ ▼

Specific rules also apply to research and development (R & D) expenditures, certain stewardship expenses, legal and accounting fees and expenses, income taxes, and losses. U.S. companies incur about 90 percent of their R & D expenditures at U.S. facilities. Nevertheless, U.S. companies spent $9.8 billion in 1993 on foreign R & D, most of which was performed in Germany, the United Kingdom, Canada, France, and Japan. The Regulations provide that a portion of a U.S. company's R & D expenditures must be apportioned to foreign-source income at least indirectly attributable to that R & D.

A deduction not definitely related to any class of gross income is ratably allocated to all classes of gross income and apportioned between U.S.- and foreign-source income.

---

[15]Reg. § 1.861–10T(b) describes circumstances where interest expense can be directly allocated to specific debt. This exception to the fungibility concept is limited to cases in which specific property is purchased or improved with nonrecourse debt.

[16]Reg. § 1.861–9T.

PARTYING AROUND THE WORLD

The major portion of U.S. companies' business abroad has been in developed countries, but that trend may be changing. For example, Partyland, Inc., a Philadelphia company that is the world's largest international retail franchise for party supplies, has more than 200 stores in 17 countries, including Saudi Arabia. John L. Barry, vice president of Partyland's franchise development, says that Partyland has worldwide prospects for growth because every culture celebrates some events or rites of passage. Barry notes that a Saudi family may spend $5,000 to $10,000 on a young child's birthday party. Before Partyland entered Saudi Arabia, party supplies were available only at the grocery store.

SOURCE: Adapted from *Inc.*, September 1997.

SECTION 482 CONSIDERATIONS

Taxpayers may be tempted to manipulate the source of income and the allocation of deductions arbitrarily to minimize taxation. This manipulation is more easily accomplished between or among related persons. The IRS uses § 482 to counter such actions. The provision gives the IRS the power to reallocate gross income, deductions, credits, or allowances between or among organizations, trades, or businesses owned or controlled directly or indirectly by the same interests. This can be done whenever the IRS determines that reallocation is necessary to prevent the evasion of taxes or to reflect income more clearly. Section 482 is a "one-edged" sword available only to the IRS. The taxpayer cannot invoke it to reallocate income and expenses.[17]

The reach of § 482 is quite broad. The IRS takes the position that a corporation and its sole shareholder who works full-time for the corporation can be treated as two separate trades or businesses for purposes of § 482.[18] Two unrelated shareholders who each owned 50 percent of a corporation were held to be acting in concert for their common good and, thus, together controlled the corporation.[19]

One of six methods can be used in determining an arm's length price on the sale of tangible property: the comparable uncontrolled price method, the resale price method, the cost plus method, the comparable profits method, the profit split method, and other unspecified methods. Methods available for pricing intangible property include the comparable uncontrolled transactions method, the comparable profits method, the profit split method, the cost-sharing method, and other unspecified methods. The major problem with most pricing methods is that uncontrolled comparable transactions are needed as a benchmark.

An accuracy-related penalty of 20 percent is provided by § 6662 for net § 482 transfer price adjustments for a taxable year that exceed the lesser of $5 million or 10 percent of the taxpayer's gross receipts. In addition, there is a 40 percent penalty for "gross misstatements."

As a further aid to reducing pricing disputes, the IRS has initiated an Advanced Pricing Agreement (APA) program whereby the taxpayer can propose a transfer

---

[17]Reg. § 1.482–1(b)(3).

[18]Rev.Rul. 88–38, 1988–1 C.B. 246. But see *Foglesong v. Comm.*, 82–2 USTC ¶9650, 50 AFTR2d 82–6016, 691 F.2d 848 (CA–7, 1982), *rev'g.* 77 T.C. 1102 (1981).

[19]See *B. Forman Company, Inc. v. Comm.*, 72–1 USTC ¶9182, 29 AFTR2d 72–405, 453 F.2d 1144 (CA–2, 1972).

pricing method for certain international transactions.[20] The taxpayer provides relevant data, which is then evaluated by the IRS. If accepted, the APA provides a safe harbor transfer pricing method for the taxpayer. Apple Computer, Inc., accomplished the first successful APA submission.

U.S. TAXATION OF NONRESIDENT ALIENS AND FOREIGN CORPORATIONS

3 **LEARNING OBJECTIVE**
Utilize the U.S. tax provisions concerning nonresident alien individuals and foreign corporations.

Generally, only the U.S.-source income of nonresident aliens (NRAs) and foreign corporations is subject to U.S. taxation. This reflects the reach of U.S. tax jurisdiction. The constraint, however, does not prevent the United States from also taxing the foreign-source income of NRAs and foreign corporations, when that income is effectively connected with the conduct of a U.S. trade or business.[21]

NONRESIDENT ALIEN INDIVIDUALS

An NRA individual is an individual who is not a citizen or resident of the United States. For example, Queen Elizabeth is an NRA since she is not a citizen or resident of the United States.[22] Citizenship is determined under the immigration and naturalization laws of the United States. Basically, the citizenship statutes are broken down into two categories, nationality at birth and nationality through naturalization.

Residency. For many years, the definition of residency for Federal income tax purposes was very subjective, requiring an evaluation of a person's intent and actions with regard to the length and nature of stay in the United States. In 1984, Congress enacted a more objective test of residency. A person is a resident of the United States for income tax purposes if he or she meets either the **green card test** or the substantial presence test. If either of these tests is met for the calendar year, the individual is deemed a U.S. resident for the year.

An alien issued a green card is considered a U.S. resident on the first day he or she is physically present in the United States after issuance. The green card is Immigration Form I–551. Newly issued cards are now rose (off-pink), but the form is still referred to as the "green card." Status as a U.S. resident remains in effect until the green card has been revoked or the individual has abandoned lawful permanent resident status.

The substantial presence test is applied to an alien without a green card. It is a mathematical test involving physical presence in the United States. An individual who is physically present in the United States for at least 183 days during the calendar year is a U.S. resident for income tax purposes. This 183-day requirement can also be met over a three-year period that includes the two immediately preceding years and the current year. For this purpose, each day of the current calendar year is counted as a full day, each day of the first preceding year as one-third day, and each day of the second preceding year as one-sixth day.

---

[20]Rev.Proc. 96–53, 1996–49 I.R.B. 9.
[21]§§ 871, 881, and 882.

[22]Title 8, Aliens and Nationality, *United States Code.*

EXAMPLE 15

Li, an alien, was present in the United States for 90 days in 1996, 180 days in 1997, and 110 days in 1998. For Federal income tax purposes, Li is a U.S. resident for 1998, since she was physically present for 185 days [(90 days × ⅙) + (180 days × ⅓) + (110 days × 1)] during the three-year period. ▼

The substantial presence test allows for several exceptions. Commuters from Mexico and Canada who are employed in the United States, but return home each day, are excepted. Also excepted are individuals who are prevented from leaving the United States due to a medical condition that arose while in the United States. Some individuals are exempt from the substantial presence test, including foreign government-related individuals (e.g., diplomats), qualified teachers, trainees and students, and certain professional athletes.

Residence, under the substantial presence test, begins the first day the individual is physically present in the United States and ends the last day of physical presence for the calendar year. This assumes the substantial presence test is not satisfied for the next calendar year. Nominal presence of 10 days or less can be ignored in determining whether the substantial presence test is met. A 31-day per-year exception and a 183-day current-year exception may apply to prevent residence under this test.[23]

ETHICAL CONSIDERATIONS

Should There Be Some "Heart" In Tax Law?

In determining whether an alien is a U.S. resident for U.S. income tax purposes under the substantial presence test, days on which the person is prevented from leaving the United States due to a medical condition are not counted as days present in the United States. The medical condition (e.g., illness or injury) must arise after the alien has been present in the United States. In other words, it generally must be an unexpected illness or accident. No such exception is available, however, for a family member or other NRA who is significant to the person who becomes ill or injured. Thus, under this rule, the relative or other significant person may have to either risk being classified as a U.S. resident for the tax year or leave the ill person (or accident victim) to remain alone in the United States. Does this limited exception ignore the human element in illness and recovery?

Nonresident Aliens Not Engaged in a U.S. Trade or Business. Certain U.S.-source income that is *not* effectively connected with the conduct of a U.S. trade or business is subject to a flat 30 percent tax. This income includes dividends, interest, rents, royalties, certain compensation, premiums, annuities, and other fixed, determinable, annual or periodic (FDAP) income. This tax generally is levied by a withholding mechanism that requires the payors of the income to withhold 30 percent of gross amounts.[24] This method eliminates the problems of assuring payment by nonresidents, determining allowable deductions, and, in many instances, the filing of tax returns by nonresidents. Residents of countries contiguous to the United States (i.e., Canada and Mexico) are allowed dependency exemptions as well. Interest received from certain portfolio debt investments, even though U.S.-sourced, is exempt from taxation. Interest earned on deposits with banking

---

[23]§ 7701(b)(3).

[24]§§ 873 and 1441.

institutions is also exempt as long as it is not effectively connected with the conduct of a U.S. trade or business.

Capital gains *not* effectively connected with the conduct of a U.S. trade or business are exempt from tax, as long as the NRA individual was not present in the United States for 183 days or more during the taxable year. If an NRA has not established a taxable year, the calendar year is used. NRAs are not permitted to carry forward capital losses.[25]

Nonresident Aliens Engaged in a U.S. Trade or Business.

As long as FDAP income and capital gains are not effectively connected income, the tax treatment of these income items is the same, whether NRAs are engaged in a U.S. trade or business or not. Effectively connected income, however, is taxed at the same rates that apply to U.S. citizens and residents, and deductions for expenses attributable to that income are allowed. NRAs with effectively connected income also are allowed a deduction for casualty and theft losses related to property located within the United States, a deduction for qualified charitable contributions, and one personal exemption. NRAs with income effectively connected with the conduct of a U.S. trade or business may also be subject to the alternative minimum tax.

Two important definitions determine the U.S. tax consequences to NRAs with U.S.-source income: *the conduct of a U.S. trade or business* and *effectively connected income*. General criteria for determining if a U.S. trade or business exists include the location of production activities, management, distribution activities, and other business functions. Trading in commodities and securities ordinarily does not constitute a trade or business. Dealers, however, need to avoid maintaining a U.S. trading office and trading for their own account. Corporations (other than certain personal holding companies) that are not dealers can trade for their own account. There are no restrictions on individuals who are not dealers. An NRA who performs services in the United States for a foreign employer is not engaged in a U.S. trade or business.

A U.S. trade or business is a prerequisite to having effectively connected income. Income is effectively connected with a U.S. trade or business if it is derived from assets used in, or held for use in, the trade or business (asset-use test) or if the activities of the trade or business are a material factor in the production of the income (business-activities test).[26]

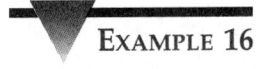

EXAMPLE 16

Ingrid, an NRA, operates a U.S. business. During the year, excess cash funds accumulate. Ingrid invests these funds on a short-term basis so that they remain available to meet her business needs. Any income earned from these investments is effectively connected income under the asset-use test. ▼

Withholding Provisions.

The 30 percent U.S. tax on FDAP is generally administered by requiring the payor of the income to withhold the tax and remit it to the U.S. tax authorities. This assures the government of timely collection and relieves it of jurisdictional problems that could arise if it had to rely on recipients residing outside the United States to pay the tax. As of March 1997, the United States had more than 45 income tax treaties with other countries. Most of these treaties provide for reduced withholding on certain types of income. For example, the income tax

---

[25]§ 871(a)(2).   [26]§ 864(c).

treaty with Austria, signed on May 31, 1996, reduced the withholding tax on dividends to 5 or 15 percent, depending on the circumstances.

FOREIGN CORPORATIONS

Definition. The classification of an entity as a foreign corporation for U.S. tax purposes is an important consideration. Section 7701(a)(5) defines a foreign corporation as one that is not domestic. A domestic corporation is a corporation that is created or organized in the United States. Even though McDonald's is, in reality, a multinational corporation, it is considered a domestic corporation for U.S. tax purposes, solely because it was organized in the United States.

Income Not Effectively Connected with a U.S. Trade or Business. U.S.-source FDAP income of foreign corporations is taxed by the United States in the same manner as that of NRA individuals—at a flat 30 percent rate. Generally, foreign corporations qualify for the same exemptions from U.S. taxation for interest and dividend income as do NRA individuals. The U.S.-source capital gains of foreign corporations are exempt from the Federal income tax if they are not effectively connected with the conduct of a U.S. trade or business.

Effectively Connected Income. Foreign corporations conducting a trade or business within the United States are subject to Federal income taxation on effectively connected income. Additionally, any U.S.-source income attributable to the U.S. office of a foreign corporation is deemed to be effectively connected.[27] For such purposes, foreign corporations are subject to the same tax rates as domestic corporations.

Branch Profits Tax. In addition to the income tax imposed under § 882 on effectively connected income of a foreign corporation, a tax equal to 30 percent of the **dividend equivalent amount (DEA)** for the taxable year is imposed on *any* foreign corporation.[28]

The objective of the **branch profits tax** is to afford equal tax treatment to income generated by a domestic corporation controlled by a foreign corporation and to income generated by other U.S. operations controlled by foreign corporations. If the foreign corporation operates through a U.S. subsidiary (a domestic corporation), the income of the subsidiary is taxable by the United States when derived and is also subject to a withholding tax when repatriated (returned as dividends to the foreign parent). Before the branch profits tax was enacted, a foreign corporation with a branch in the United States paid only the initial tax on its U.S. earnings; remittances were not taxed.

The DEA is the foreign corporation's effectively connected earnings for the taxable year, adjusted for increases and decreases in the corporation's U.S. net equity (investment in the U.S. operations). The DEA is limited to current E & P and post-1986 accumulated E & P that are effectively connected, or treated as effectively connected, with the conduct of a U.S. trade or business. U.S. net equity is the sum of money and the aggregate adjusted basis of assets and liabilities directly connected to U.S. operations that generate effectively connected income.

---

[27]§ 865(e)(2).

[28]§ 884.

CONCEPT SUMMARY 24–2

U.S. Taxation of NRAs and Foreign Corporations (FCs)

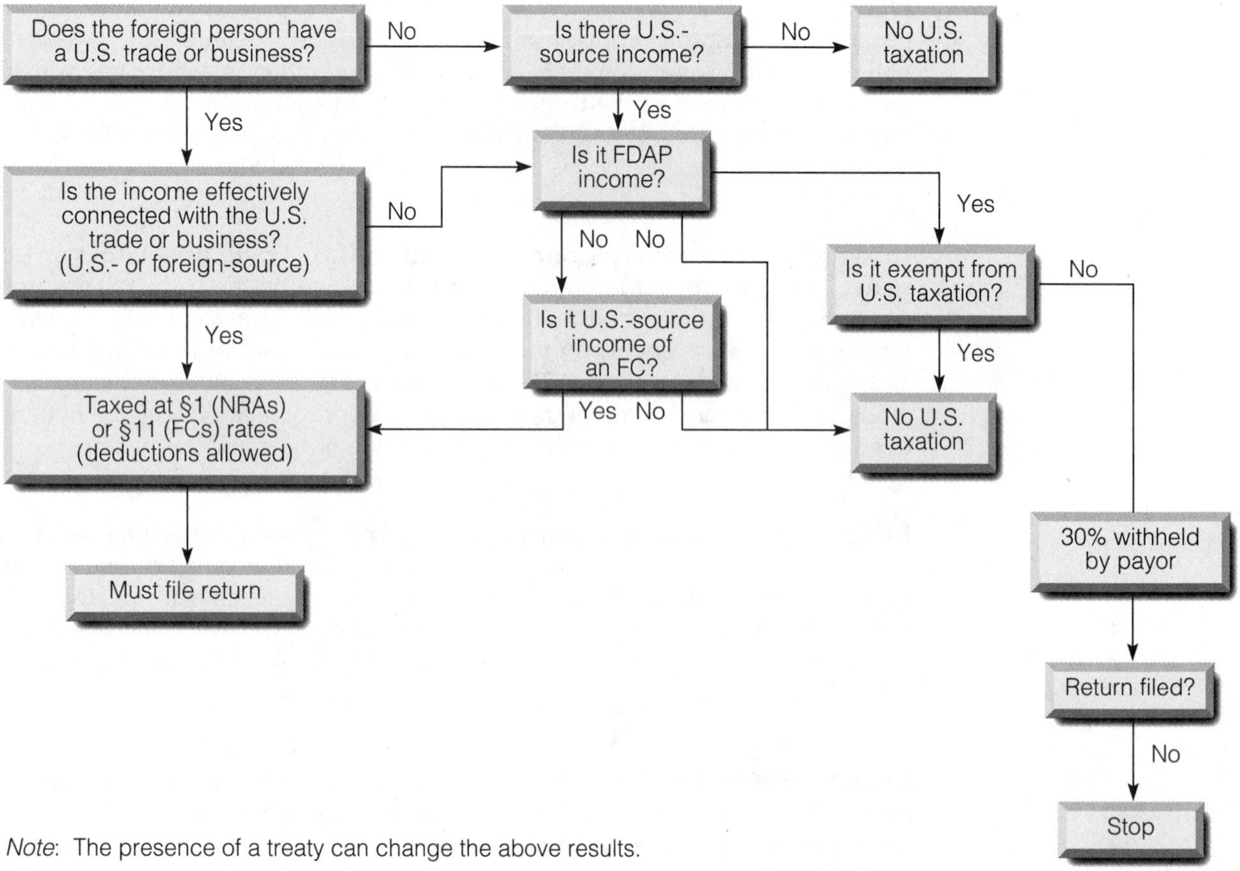

Does the foreign person have a U.S. trade or business? —No→ Is there U.S.-source income? —No→ No U.S. taxation

↓ Yes

Is there U.S.-source income? ↓ Yes

Is the income effectively connected with the U.S. trade or business? (U.S.- or foreign-source) —No→ Is it FDAP income?

Is it FDAP income? —Yes→ Is it exempt from U.S. taxation? —No→

Is it FDAP income? No No → Is it U.S.-source income of an FC?

Is it exempt from U.S. taxation? ↓ Yes → No U.S. taxation

↓ Yes

Taxed at §1 (NRAs) or §11 (FCs) rates (deductions allowed)

Is it U.S.-source income of an FC? Yes No

↓

Must file return

30% withheld by payor

↓

Return filed?

↓ No

Stop

Note: The presence of a treaty can change the above results.

EXAMPLE 17

Robin, Inc., a foreign corporation, has a U.S. branch operation with the following tax results and other information for the year.

E & P effectively connected with a U.S. trade or business	$2,000,000
U.S. corporate tax (at 34%)	680,000
Remittance to home office	1,000,000
Increase in U.S. net equity	320,000

Robin's DEA and branch profits tax are computed as follows.

After-tax E & P effectively connected with a U.S. trade or business	$1,320,000
Less: Increase in U.S. net equity	(320,000)
Dividend equivalent amount	$1,000,000
Branch profits tax rate	× 30%
Branch profits tax	$ 300,000

The 30 percent rate of the branch profits tax may be reduced or eliminated by a treaty provision. If a foreign corporation is subject to the branch profits tax, no other tax is levied on the dividend actually paid by the corporation during the taxable year.

THE FOREIGN INVESTMENT IN REAL PROPERTY TAX ACT

Under prior law, NRAs and foreign corporations could avoid U.S. taxation on gains from the sale of U.S. real estate if the gains were treated as capital gains and were not effectively connected with the conduct of a U.S. trade or business. Furthermore, the United States has a number of income tax treaties that allow for an annual election to treat real estate operations as a trade or business. Persons who were residents of the treaty countries could take advantage of the election for tax years prior to the year of sale and then revoke the election for the year in which the sale took place. In the mid-1970s, midwestern farmers put pressure on Congress to eliminate what they saw as a tax advantage that would allow nonresidents to bid up the price of farmland. This and other concerns regarding the foreign ownership of U.S. real estate led to enactment of the Foreign Investment in Real Property Tax Act (FIRPTA) of 1980.

Under **FIRPTA,** gains and losses realized by NRAs and foreign corporations from the sale or other disposition of U.S. real property interests are treated as effectively connected with the conduct of a U.S. trade or business even where those persons are not actually so engaged. NRA individuals must pay a tax equal to at least 26 (or 28) percent of the lesser of their alternative minimum taxable income or regular U.S. rates on the net U.S. real property gain for the taxable year.[29]

For purposes of this provision, losses of individual taxpayers are taken into account only to the extent they are deductible as business losses, losses on transactions entered into for profit, and losses from casualties and thefts.

U.S. Real Property Interest (USRPI). Any direct interest in real property situated in the United States and any interest in a domestic corporation (other than solely as a creditor) are U.S. real property interests (USRPIs). This definition applies unless the taxpayer can establish that a domestic corporation was not a U.S. real property holding corporation (USRPHC) during the shorter of the period during which the taxpayer held an interest in the corporation or the five-year period ending on the date on which the interest was disposed of (the base period). A domestic corporation is not a USRPHC if it holds no USRPIs on the date of disposition of its stock and if any USRPIs held by the corporation during the base period were disposed of in a transaction in which gain, if any, was fully recognized.

EXAMPLE 18

From January 1, 1993, through January 1, 1998, Francis (a foreign investor) holds shares in Door, Inc., a U.S. corporation. During this period, Door holds two parcels of U.S. real estate and stock of Sash, Inc., another U.S. corporation. Sash also owns U.S. real estate. The two parcels of real estate held directly by Door were disposed of on December 15, 1994, in a nontaxable transaction. Sash disposed of its U.S. real estate in a taxable transaction on January 1, 1998.

An interest in Door is treated as a USRPI because Door did not recognize gain on the December 15, 1994, disposition of the USRPIs. If Door's ownership of U.S. real estate had been limited to its indirect ownership through Sash, as of January 2, 1998, an interest in Door would not constitute a USRPI. This is because Sash disposed of its USRPIs in a taxable transaction in which gain was fully recognized. ▼

---

[29]§ 897.

A USRPHC is any corporation (whether foreign or domestic) where the fair market value of the corporation's USRPIs equals or exceeds 50 percent of the aggregate of fair market value of certain specific assets. These assets are the corporation's USRPIs, its interests in real property located outside the United States, plus any other of its assets that are used or held for use in a trade or business. Stock regularly traded on an established securities market is not treated as a USRPI where a person holds no more than 5 percent of the stock.

Withholding Provisions.   Following the same rationale as the withholding provisions for FDAP, any purchaser or agent acquiring a USRPI from a foreign person must withhold 10 percent of the amount realized on the disposition.[30] The amount withheld must be submitted along with Form 8288 within at least 20 days after the transfer. A domestic partnership, trust, or estate with a foreign partner, foreign grantor treated as owner, or foreign beneficiary must withhold 35 percent (or 20 percent where allowed by the IRS) of the gain allocable to that person on a disposition of a USRPI. Foreign corporations are also subject to withholding provisions on certain distributions. Without this withholding, NRAs could sell USRPIs, receiving the sales proceeds outside the United States, and jurisdictional issues could make it difficult for the U.S. tax authorities to collect any U.S. tax that might be due on gains.

Failure to withhold can subject the purchaser or the purchaser's agent to interest on any unpaid amount.[31] A civil penalty of 100 percent of the amount required to be withheld and a criminal penalty of up to $10,000 or five years in prison can be imposed for willful failure to withhold.[32]

EXPATRIATION TO AVOID U.S. TAXATION

Section 877 provides for U.S. taxation of U.S.-source income earned by persons who relinquished their U.S. citizenship within 10 years of deriving that income if those persons gave up their U.S. citizenship to avoid U.S. taxation. Tax legislation enacted in 1996 expanded these provisions.

NRAs who lost U.S. citizenship within a 10-year period immediately preceding the close of the tax year must pay taxes on their U.S.-source income as though they were still U.S. citizens. This provision applies only if the NRA's expatriation had as one of its principal purposes the avoidance of U.S. taxes. Individuals are presumed to have a tax avoidance purpose if they meet either of the following criteria.

- Average annual net income tax for the five taxable years ending before the date of loss of U.S. citizenship is more than $100,000.
- Net worth as of that date is $500,000 or more.

This provision applies to loss of U.S. citizenship at any time on or after February 6, 1995. The dollar amounts are adjusted for inflation. These provisions also apply to "long-term lawful permanent residents" who cease to be taxed as U.S. residents. A long-term permanent resident is an individual (other than a citizen of the United States) who is a lawful permanent resident of the United States in at least 8 taxable years during the 15-year period ending with the taxable year in which the individual either ceases to be a lawful permanent resident of the United States or begins to be treated as a resident of another country under an income tax treaty between the United States and the other country (and does not waive the benefits of the

---

[30] § 1445.
[31] §§ 6601, 6621, and 6651.

[32] §§ 6672 and 7202.

▼ EXHIBIT 24–1
U.S. Income Tax Treaties in
Force as of March 1997

Australia	Hungary	New Zealand
Austria	Iceland	Norway
Barbados	India	Pakistan
Belgium	Indonesia	Philippines
Canada	Ireland	Poland
China	Israel	Portugal
Commonwealth of	Italy	Romania
Independent States*	Jamaica	Russian Federation
Cyprus	Japan	Slovak Republic
Czech Republic	Kazakhstan	Spain
Denmark	Korea, Republic of	Sweden
Egypt	Luxembourg	Switzerland
Finland	Malta	Trinidad and Tobago
France	Mexico	Tunisia
Germany	Morocco	United Kingdom
Greece	Netherlands	

*The income tax treaty between the United States and the Soviet Union now applies to the
countries of Armenia, Azerbaijan, Belarus, Georgia, Kyrgyzstan, Moldova, Tajikistan,
Turkmenistan, Ukraine, and Uzbekistan. The Commonwealth of Independent States is an
association of many of the former constituent republics of the Soviet Union.

treaty to residents of that country). An exception applies to certain individuals
with dual citizenship. Special source rules also apply for purposes of expatriate
taxation. The expatriate tax will not apply if U.S. taxation of the NRA under the
normal provisions applicable to NRAs results in a greater tax liability. Certain
expatriate provisions also apply for estate and gift tax purposes.

TAX TREATIES

Income Tax. More than 45 income **tax treaties** between the United States and
other countries are in effect (see Exhibit 24–1). These treaties generally provide
taxing rights with regard to the taxable income of residents of one treaty country
who have income sourced in the other treaty country. For the most part, neither
country is prohibited from taxing the income of its residents. The treaties generally
provide for primary taxing rights that require the *other* treaty partner to allow a
credit for the taxes paid on the twice-taxed income.

EXAMPLE 19

Caterina, a resident of a foreign country with which the United States has an income tax
treaty, earns income attributable to a permanent establishment (e.g., place of business) in
the United States. Under the treaty, the United States has primary taxing rights with regard
to this income. The other country can also require that the income be included in gross
income and subject to its income tax, but must allow a credit for the taxes paid to the United
States on the income. ▼

Primary taxing rights usually depend on the residence of the taxpayer or the
presence of a permanent establishment in a treaty country to which the income
is attributable. Generally, a permanent establishment is a branch, office, factory,
workshop, warehouse, or other fixed place of business.

Most U.S. income tax treaties reduce the withholding rate on certain items of
FDAP income, such as interest and dividends. For example, treaties with France
and Sweden reduce the withholding on portfolio dividends to 15 percent and on

TAX IN THE NEWS

WHY THE TREATY PROCESS STALLS

The United States has negotiated several income tax treaties that have never been signed or ratified (e.g., with Argentina, Bangladesh, and Brazil). The treaty process sometimes stalls for several reasons. One is the desire (on the part of some less developed countries) for a tax-sparing provision in the treaty. In other words, the United States would allow an FTC against U.S. taxes even though the treaty partner had a lower tax rate or even gave a tax holiday to U.S. companies operating there.

Another reason is the exchange of information provision. Some countries, for example, have anonymous bank rules that would preclude the exchange of information. In September 1996, the Parliament of Kazakhstan voted on a provision to eliminate anonymous bank accounts so that the United States–Kazakhstan income tax treaty could be ratified.

certain interest income to zero. The United States has developed a Model Income Tax Treaty[33] as the starting point for negotiating income tax treaties with other countries.

U.S. TAXPAYERS ABROAD

4 LEARNING OBJECTIVE
Appreciate the tax benefits available to certain U.S. individuals working abroad.

Citizens and residents of the United States are subject to Federal taxation on their worldwide taxable income. U.S. taxpayers who operate in a foreign country as a sole proprietor, or through a foreign branch or foreign partnership, must include foreign-source income in gross income for U.S. tax purposes. They are allowed a deduction for related expenses and losses.

Income tax treaties can reduce or eliminate the taxation of the income by the foreign country party to the treaty. Since, under the treaty, the United States reserves the right to tax its citizens and residents, relief from double taxation is achieved with the FTC. In addition to the FTC, several other tax provisions involve certain foreign-source income of U.S. citizens and residents.

THE FOREIGN EARNED INCOME EXCLUSION

To help U.S. multinational entities be competitive in the world market, Congress enacted legislation granting an exclusion (from U.S. gross income) for a certain amount of qualified foreign *earned* income. This exclusion allows multinational entities to employ U.S. citizens and residents for foreign operations without having to pay them a wage or salary far in excess of that paid to nationals of the particular foreign country or countries. As Example 1 illustrates, the tax burden on a U.S. taxpayer working abroad could be much greater than that on a native of the foreign country. The **foreign earned income exclusion** reduces this problem.

Currently, § 911 allows a foreign earned income exclusion for (1) a qualified housing cost amount and (2) foreign earned income not in excess of $70,000. The statutory exclusion limit is scheduled to reach $80,000, phased in over a five-year

---

[33]Treasury Department Model Income Tax Treaty (September 20, 1996).

period. The limit is $72,000 for the 1998 calendar year and $74,000 for 1999. Beginning in calendar year 2008, the limitation will be indexed for inflation. The exclusion is elective and is made by filing Form 2555 with the income tax return, or with an amended return, for the first taxable year for which the election is to be effective. An election once made remains in effect for that year and for all subsequent years, unless revoked. If the election is revoked for any taxable year, the taxpayer may not make the election again (without consent of the IRS) until the sixth taxable year following the taxable year for which revocation was first effective.[34]

Qualified Individuals.   The exclusion is available to an individual whose tax home is in a foreign country and who is either (1) a U.S. citizen and bona fide resident of a foreign country or countries or (2) a citizen or resident of the United States who, during any 12 consecutive months, is physically present in a foreign country or countries for at least 330 full days. *Tax home* has the same meaning as for U.S. cases relating to travel expenses while away from home.[35] The issue of whether a stay abroad is temporary can be troublesome. If the stay abroad is deemed to be temporary, the taxpayer's tax home has not shifted to the foreign country. A stay that exceeds one year is not temporary.

Only whole days count for the physical presence test. The taxpayer has some flexibility in choosing the 12-month period.

EXAMPLE 20

Carla, a U.S. citizen, arrived in Ireland from Boston at 3 P.M. on March 28, 1997. She remained in Ireland until 8 A.M. on March 1, 1998, when she departed for the United States. Among other possible 12-month periods, Carla was present in a foreign country an aggregate of 331 full days during each of the following 12-month periods: March 1, 1997, through February 28, 1998, and March 29, 1997, through March 28, 1998.[36] ▼

The General Exclusion.   The foreign earned income (general) exclusion is available for foreign earned income and is limited to the lesser of (1) $72,000 for 1998 or (2) foreign earned income less the housing cost amount exclusion. The exclusion is available for the tax year in which the income would be recognized. The limitation, however, is determined for each tax year in which services were performed. Income received after the close of the taxable year following the taxable year in which the services were performed does not qualify for the exclusion.

EXAMPLE 21

Tom, a U.S. resident, is present in a foreign country for all of 1998. He earns $100,000 from the performance of personal services. On January 1, 1999, he returns to the United States and remains there. Of the $100,000 foreign earned income, Tom receives $60,000 in 1998 and $40,000 in 1999. Tom can take a foreign earned income exclusion of $60,000 for 1998 and $12,000 for 1999 ($72,000 statutory limit for 1998 − $60,000 excluded for 1998). If Tom did not receive the $40,000 until 2000, no exclusion would be allowed for 2000 because he received the $40,000 after the close of the taxable year following the taxable year in which the services were performed. ▼

The statutory amount is prorated on a daily basis where the taxpayer does not qualify for the exclusion for the full tax year. If Tom in Example 21 qualified for only 11 months of the year, the $72,000 statutory amount would be $65,885 [$72,000 × (334 days/365 days)].

---

[34]Reg. § 1.911–7.
[35]§ 162(a)(2).

[36]Reg. § 1.911–2(d).

The Housing Cost Amount.   The housing cost amount is equal to the qualified housing expenses of an individual for the tax year less a base amount. The base amount is 16 percent of the salary of an employee of the United States for Step 1 Grade GS–14. The base amount is determined on a daily basis. The base amount for a full year is $9,426 for 1997 and $9,643 for 1998. For a qualified individual employed overseas for 250 days of the year, the applicable base amount for 1998 would be $6,605 [$9,643 × (250 days/365 days)]. The housing cost amount exclusion is limited to foreign earned income.

EXAMPLE 22

Charles, a U.S. citizen, works as an engineer for a U.S. multinational company in Bahrain. He is a bona fide resident of Bahrain for the entire calendar and tax year (1998) and earns a salary of $80,000. In addition, his employer provides $16,000 in housing costs. If the base amount is $9,643 and Charles elects both exclusions, the housing cost amount exclusion is $6,357 ($16,000 − $9,643), and the foreign earned income exclusion is $72,000 (the lesser of $96,000 foreign earned income − $6,357 housing cost amount exclusion, or the $72,000 statutory limit). Charles's gross income includes $17,643 of foreign earned income ($80,000 + $16,000 − $6,357 − $72,000). ▼

A self-employed individual is not eligible to exclude housing expenses, but can elect to deduct them.

FOREIGN CORPORATIONS CONTROLLED BY U.S. PERSONS

5   **LEARNING OBJECTIVE**
Apply the U.S. tax rules for foreign corporations controlled by U.S. persons.

To minimize current tax liability, taxpayers often attempt to defer the recognition of taxable income. As Example 1 suggests, one way of trying to defer income recognition is to shift the income-generating activity to a foreign entity that is not within the U.S. tax jurisdiction. A foreign corporation is the most suitable entity for such an endeavor since, unlike a partnership, it is not a conduit through which income is taxed directly to the owner.

CONTROLLED FOREIGN CORPORATIONS

Subpart F, §§ 951–964 of the Code, provides that certain types of income generated by **controlled foreign corporations (CFCs)** are currently included in gross income by the *U.S. shareholders.* For Subpart F to apply, the foreign corporation must have been a CFC for an uninterrupted period of 30 days or more during the taxable year. When this is the case, U.S. shareholders must include in gross income their pro rata share of Subpart F income and increase in earnings that the CFC has invested in U.S. property for the tax year. This rule applies to U.S. shareholders who own stock in the corporation on the last day of the tax year in which the corporation is a CFC. The gross income inclusion must be made for the taxable year in which or with which the taxable year of the corporation ends.

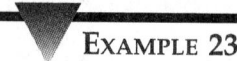

EXAMPLE 23

Gray, Inc., a calendar year corporation, is a CFC for the entire tax year. Chance Company, a U.S. corporation, owns 60% of Gray's one class of stock for the entire year. Subpart F income is $100,000, investment in U.S. property has not increased, and no distributions have been made during the year. Chance, a calendar year taxpayer, includes $60,000 in gross income as a constructive dividend for the tax year. ▼

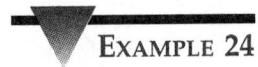

EXAMPLE 24

Gray, Inc., is a CFC until July 1 of the tax year (a calendar year). Terry, a U.S. citizen, owns 30% of its one class of stock for the entire year. Subpart F income is $100,000. He includes $14,877 [$100,000 × 30% × (181 days/365 days)] in gross income as a constructive dividend for the tax year. ▼

A CFC is any foreign corporation in which more than 50 percent of the total combined voting power of all classes of stock entitled to vote or the total value of the stock of the corporation is owned by U.S. shareholders on any day during the taxable year of the foreign corporation. For purposes of determining if a foreign corporation is a CFC, a **U.S. shareholder** is defined as a U.S. person who owns, or is considered to own, 10 percent or more of the total combined voting power of all classes of voting stock of the foreign corporation. Stock owned directly, indirectly, and constructively is counted. The foreign subsidiaries of most multinational U.S. parent corporations are CFCs. Hallmark Cards, Inc., has a Canadian subsidiary that is a CFC.

Indirect ownership involves stock held through a foreign entity, such as a foreign corporation, foreign partnership, or foreign trust. This stock is considered as actually owned proportionately by the shareholders, partners, or beneficiaries. Constructive ownership rules, with certain modifications, apply in determining if a U.S. person is a U.S. shareholder, in determining whether a foreign corporation is a CFC, and for certain related-party provisions of Subpart F.[37] The following are some of the modifications.

- Stock owned by a nonresident alien individual is not considered constructively owned by a U.S. citizen or resident alien individual.
- If a partnership, estate, trust, or corporation owns, directly or indirectly, more than 50 percent of the voting power of a corporation, it is deemed to own all of its stock.
- The threshold for corporate attribution is 10 percent rather than 50 percent.

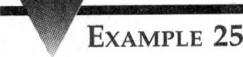

EXAMPLE 25

Shareholders of Foreign Corporation	Voting Power	Classification
Alan	30%	U.S. person
Bill	9%	U.S. person
Carla	41%	Foreign person
Dora	20%	U.S. person

Bill is Alan's son. Alan, Bill, and Dora are *U.S. shareholders*. Alan owns 39%, 30% directly and 9% constructively through Bill. Bill also owns 39%, 9% directly and 30% constructively through Alan. Dora owns 20% directly. The corporation is a CFC because U.S. shareholders own 59% of the voting power. If Bill were not related to Alan or to any other U.S. persons who were shareholders, Bill would not be a U.S. shareholder, and the corporation would not be a CFC. ▼

U.S. shareholders must include their pro rata share of the applicable income in their gross income only to the extent of their actual ownership. Stock held indirectly is considered actually owned for this purpose.

---

[37]§§ 958 and 318(a).

EXAMPLE 26

Bill, in Example 25, would recognize only 9% of the Subpart F income as a constructive dividend. Alan would recognize 30% and Dora would recognize 20%. If Bill were a foreign corporation wholly owned by Alan, Alan would recognize 39% as a constructive dividend. If Carla owned only 40% of the stock and Ed, a U.S. person, owned 1% and was not related to any of the other shareholders, Ed would not be a *U.S. shareholder* and would not have to include any of the Subpart F income in gross income. ▼

Subpart F Income.   Subpart F income consists of the following:

- Insurance income (§ 953).
- Foreign base company income (§ 954).
- International boycott factor income (§ 999).
- Illegal bribes.
- Income derived from a § 901(j) foreign country.

Foreign Base Company Income.   There are five categories of foreign base company income (FBCI).

- Foreign personal holding company income.
- Foreign base company sales income.
- Foreign base company services income.
- Foreign base company shipping income.
- Foreign base company oil-related income.

A *de minimis* rule provides that if the total amount of a foreign corporation's FBCI and gross insurance income for the taxable year is less than the lesser of 5 percent of gross income or $1 million, none of its gross income is treated as FBCI for the tax year. The *de minimis* rule does not apply to other types of income under Subpart F, such as increases in investment in U.S. property. However, if a foreign corporation's FBCI and gross insurance income exceed 70 percent of total gross income, all the corporation's gross income for the tax year is treated as FBCI or insurance income.

FBCI and insurance income subject to high foreign taxes are not included under Subpart F if the taxpayer establishes that the income was subject to an effective rate, imposed by a foreign country, of more than 90 percent of the maximum corporate rate under § 11. For example, this rate must be greater than 31.5 percent (90% × 35%), where 35 percent represents the highest U.S. corporate rate.

Foreign personal holding company (FPHC) income consists of the following:

- Dividends, interest, royalties, rents, and annuities.
- Excess gains over losses from the sale or exchange of property (including any interest in a trust or partnership) that gives rise to FPHC income or that does not give rise to any income.
- Excess of foreign currency gains over foreign currency losses (other than from any transaction directly related to the business needs of the CFC).
- Income from notional principal contracts.
- Certain payments in lieu of dividends.

Foreign base company (FBC) sales income is income derived from the purchase of personal property from or on behalf of a related person, or from the sale of personal property to or on behalf of a related person.

EXAMPLE 27

A CFC owned 100% by Romus, a U.S. corporation, generates FBC sales income in any one of the following situations:

- Purchase of widgets from anyone as commission agent for Romus Corporation.
- Purchase of widgets from Romus and sale to anyone.
- Purchase of widgets from anyone and sale to Romus Corporation.
- Sale of widgets to anyone as commission agent for Romus. ▼

An exception applies to property that is manufactured, produced, grown, or extracted in the country in which the CFC was organized or created and also to property sold for use, consumption, or disposition within that country. Certain income derived by a branch of the CFC in another country can be deemed FBC sales income. This would be the case if the effect of using the branch is the same as if the branch were a wholly owned subsidiary.[38]

FBC services income is income derived from the performance of services for or on behalf of a related person and performed outside the country in which the CFC was created or organized. Income from services performed before and in connection with the sale of property by a CFC that has manufactured, produced, grown, or extracted such property is not FBC services income.

FBC shipping income includes several classifications of income, including dividends and interest received from a foreign corporation, to the extent that income is attributable to, or is derived from or in connection with, the shipping activity. Thus, income attributable to the use of any aircraft or vessel in foreign commerce, performance of services directly related to the use of that aircraft or vessel, or sale or exchange of any such aircraft or vessel is shipping income.

FBC oil-related income is income, other than extraction income, derived in a foreign country in connection with the sale of oil and gas products sold by the CFC or a related person for use or consumption within the country in which the oil or gas was extracted. Only corporations with production of at least 1,000 barrels per day are treated as deriving FBC oil-related income.

U.S. shareholders must include in gross income their pro rata share of the CFC's increase in investment in U.S. property for the taxable year. Subpart F income is considered attributable first to the increase in investment in U.S. property and thus is not taxed twice.

Distributions of Previously Taxed Income.

Distributions from a CFC are treated as being first from E & P attributable to increases in investment in U.S. property previously taxed as a constructive dividend, second from E & P attributable to excess passive assets previously taxed as a constructive dividend, third from E & P attributable to previously taxed Subpart F income other than that described above, and last from other E & P. Thus, distributions of previously taxed income are not taxed as a dividend, but they reduce E & P.

EXAMPLE 28

In 1998, Jet, Inc., a U.S. shareholder, owns 100% of a CFC, from which Jet receives a $100,000 distribution. The CFC's E & P is composed of the following amounts:

- $50,000 attributable to previously taxed increases in investment in U.S. property.
- $30,000 attributable to previously taxed Subpart F income.
- $40,000 attributable to other E & P.

Jet has a taxable dividend of only $20,000, all attributable to other E & P. The remaining $80,000 is previously taxed income. The CFC's E & P is reduced by $100,000. The remaining E & P is attributable to other E & P. ▼

---

[38]§ 954(d)(2).

CONCEPT SUMMARY 24–3

Income of a CFC That Is Included in Gross Income of a U.S. Shareholder

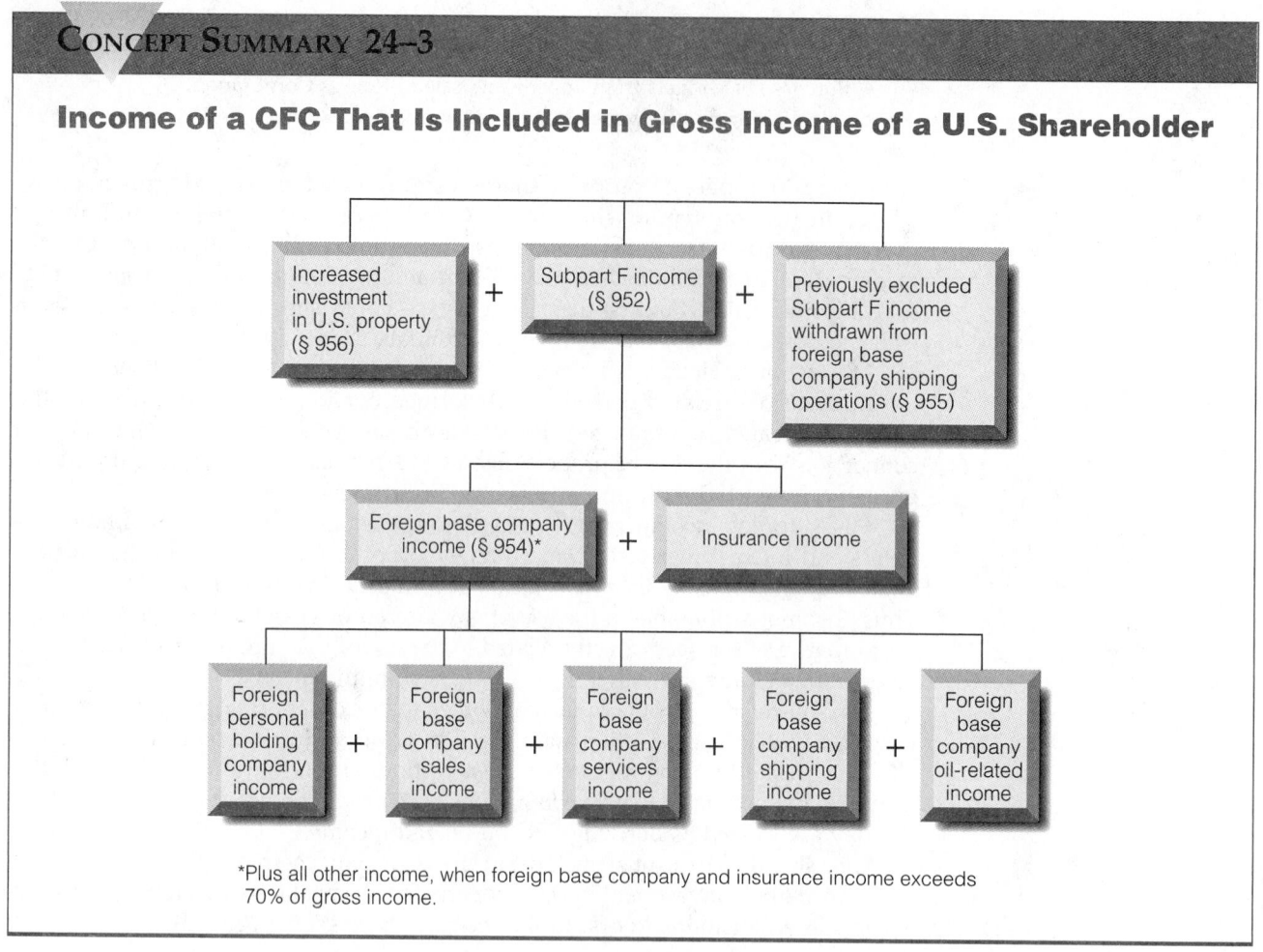

*Plus all other income, when foreign base company and insurance income exceeds 70% of gross income.

A U.S. shareholder's basis in CFC stock is increased by constructive dividends included in income under Subpart F and decreased by subsequent distributions of previously taxed income. U.S. corporate shareholders who own at least 10 percent of the voting stock of a foreign corporation are allowed an indirect FTC for foreign taxes deemed paid on constructive dividends included in gross income under Subpart F. The indirect credit also is available for Subpart F income attributable to second- and third-tier foreign corporations as long as the 10 percent ownership requirement is met from tier to tier.

Income of a CFC that is included in a U.S. shareholder's income is summarized in Concept Summary 24–3.

FOREIGN SALES CORPORATIONS

Prior to 1985, the Domestic International Sales Corporations (DISC) provisions (§§ 991–997) allowed for a deferral of the tax on a portion of the export income of a DISC until actual repatriation of the earnings. Over the years, Congress cut the amount of export income on which deferral was allowed. As the result of charges by the General Agreement on Trade and Tariffs (GATT—whose members include some of the United States' major trading partners)—that the DISC provisions were a prohibited *export subsidy,* the DISC provisions were curtailed. As an alternative, the Foreign Sales Corporation (FSC) provisions (§§ 921–927) were enacted. Most

THE BENEFITS OF LOCATING AN FSC IN GUAM

Since the FSC provisions were enacted in 1984, approximately 500 FSCs have been created in Guam. Companies such as Boeing, Exxon, General Electric, and Computerland have FSCs located there. The tax climate of Guam makes such a location very attractive. For example, there are no registration fees for incorporating in Guam. In contrast, registration fees in Bermuda range from $1,600 to $8,000, and the franchise tax in the Virgin Islands can run as high as $25,000.

Guam recently has enhanced the tax benefits of locating there by extending FSC licenses for an additional 30 years and expanding the tax exemption. FSCs are completely exempt from taxation in Guam. Furthermore, the government of Guam has made it easy for U.S. corporations to form and operate an FSC there. The political climate is stable, and communication with the U.S. mainland is not complicated.

SOURCE: *Tax Notes International* 9, No. 10 (September 5, 1994), p. 719.

remaining DISCs are "interest charge DISCs"—the price of deferral is an annual interest charge on the deferred taxes.[39] Only export sales up to $10 million qualify for deferral. Amounts in excess of $10 million are deemed distributed.

Most large multinational firms prefer CFCs to FSCs because they establish a more permanent active foreign presence, as in manufacturing. Mid-sized companies, such as Convex, often use FSCs, however, as do companies with very high-profit margins (e.g., 50 to 60 percent). In addition, the FSC has been used as a lessor that receives lease income, a portion of which will be exempt from U.S. taxation. Some large airlines, such as KLM, have entered into long-term leasing agreements with FSCs.

FSCs are not allowed a tax deferral on export income. Instead, a certain percentage (about 15 or 16 percent, depending on taxpayer status) of export income is exempt from U.S. taxation (exempt foreign trade income). Pricing methods are provided for determining exempt foreign trade income. FSC tax benefits now available for software companies enable computer software to be treated as export property, even in cases where an agreement provides that the software may be reproduced abroad.

To elect FSC status, a foreign corporation must meet a foreign presence requirement. An exception to this requirement is provided if the foreign corporation's export receipts do not exceed $5 million (the small FSC). The foreign presence requirement includes the following:

- Maintaining a foreign office.
- Operating under foreign management.
- Keeping a permanent set of books at the foreign office.
- Conducting foreign economic processes (e.g., selling activities).
- Being a foreign corporation.[40]

TAX HAVENS

All other considerations being equal, a U.S. corporation generally would prefer to make its foreign investment in (or through) a **tax haven.** A tax haven can be

[39]§ 995(f).   [40]§ 922.

Antigua and Barbuda	Leeward Islands
Aruba	Liberia
Austria	Liechtenstein
Bahamas	Luxembourg
Bahrain	Monaco
Barbados	Netherlands
Belize	Netherlands Antilles
Bermuda	Panama
Cayman Islands	Singapore
Costa Rica	Switzerland
Gibraltar	Turks and Caicos Islands
Hong Kong	Windward Islands

*The United States classifies a country as a tax haven if its income tax rates are lower than U.S. rates.

SOURCE: *SOI Bulletin*, Winter 1995–96, p. 114.

described as a country in which either locally sourced income or residents of the country are subject to no or low internal taxation. One method of avoiding taxation is to invest through a foreign corporation incorporated in a tax haven. Since the foreign corporation is a resident of the tax haven, the income it earns is subject to no or low internal taxes. Tax haven countries may also require the confidentiality of financial and commercial information. Exhibit 24–2 lists countries classified as tax havens.

A tax haven can, in effect, be created by an income tax treaty. For example, under an income tax treaty between Country A and Country B, residents of A are subject to a withholding tax of only 5 percent on dividend and interest income sourced in B. The United States and A have a similar treaty. The United States does not have a treaty with B. The U.S. corporation can create a foreign subsidiary in Country A and use that subsidiary to make investments in Country B. This is referred to as **treaty shopping.** If the Country B investment income had been earned directly by the U.S. corporation, it would be subject to a 30 percent withholding tax. By investing through the foreign subsidiary created in Country A, the U.S. parent corporation pays only 10 percent in foreign taxes on the income earned (i.e., 5 percent to B and 5 percent to A).

In recent years, many countries have enacted "treaty shopping" provisions that provide that treaty benefits for withholding taxes are not available to a resident corporation unless a certain percentage of its beneficial interests are owned, directly or indirectly, by one or more individual residents of the country in which the corporation is resident. The most controversial article in the U.S. Model Treaty is Article 22, Limitation on Benefits, which is meant to prevent treaty shopping. Article 22 disallows treaty benefits to an entity unless more than 50 percent of the beneficial interest in the entity is owned, directly or indirectly, by one or more individual residents of the same treaty country in which the entity is resident.

OTHER CONSIDERATIONS

Interest expense deductions are limited for certain foreign-controlled U.S. corporations. While primarily aimed at these foreign-controlled entities, this provision can also apply to U.S. parent corporations paying interest to their foreign subsidiaries. This rule is referred to as the *earnings stripping* provision, since it applies only if the payer's debt-to-equity ratio exceeds 1.5 to 1, and a high proportion of earnings is paid out as interest expense. Disallowed amounts can be carried over to future years.

The tax years of CFCs must conform to that of a more-than-50 percent U.S. owner. Additionally, a CFC is allowed to use a tax year ending such that no more than one month's deferral of income recognition is provided to the majority U.S. shareholder.

FOREIGN CURRENCY TRANSACTIONS

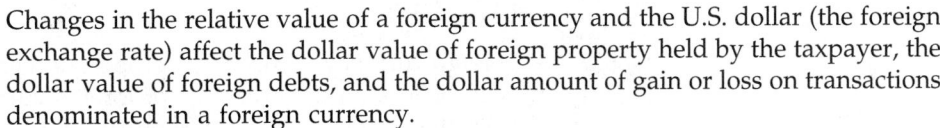

6 LEARNING OBJECTIVE
Explain how foreign currency exchange affects the tax consequences of international transactions.

Changes in the relative value of a foreign currency and the U.S. dollar (the foreign exchange rate) affect the dollar value of foreign property held by the taxpayer, the dollar value of foreign debts, and the dollar amount of gain or loss on transactions denominated in a foreign currency.

EXAMPLE 29

Dress, Inc., a domestic corporation, purchases merchandise for resale from Fiesta, Inc., a foreign corporation, for 50,000K. On the date of purchase, 1K (a foreign currency) is equal to $1 U.S. (1K:$1). At this time, the account payable is $50,000. On the date of payment by Dress (the foreign exchange date), the exchange rate is 1.25K:$1. In other words, the foreign currency has declined in value in relation to the U.S. dollar, and Dress will pay Fiesta 50,000K, which costs Dress $40,000. Dress must record the purchase of the merchandise at $50,000 and recognize a foreign currency gain of $10,000 ($50,000 − $40,000). ▼

By the end of 1996, U.S. currency abroad amounted to $209.6 billion, or 53 percent of the U.S. currency in circulation. Taxpayers may find it necessary to translate amounts denominated in foreign currency into U.S. dollars for any of the following purposes:

- Purchase of goods, services, and property.
- Sale of goods, services, and property.
- Collection of foreign receivables.
- Payment of foreign payables.
- FTC calculations.
- Recognition of income or loss from foreign branch activities.

The foreign currency exchange rates, however, have no effect on the transactions of a U.S. person who arranges all international transactions in U.S. dollars.

EXAMPLE 30

Sellers, Inc., a domestic corporation, purchases goods from Rose, Inc., a foreign corporation, and pays for these goods in U.S. dollars. Rose then exchanges the U.S. dollars for the currency of the country in which it operates. Sellers has no foreign exchange considerations with which to contend. If Sellers purchased goods from Rose and was required to pay Rose in a foreign currency, Sellers would have to exchange U.S. dollars for the foreign currency in order to make payment. If the exchange rate had changed from the date of purchase to the date of payment, Sellers would have a foreign currency gain or loss on the currency exchange. ▼

TAX ISSUES

The following are the major tax issues that must be considered in the taxation of foreign currency exchange.

- The character of the gain or loss (ordinary or capital).
- The date of recognition of any gain or loss.
- The source (U.S. or foreign) of the foreign currency gain or loss.

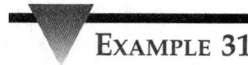

EXAMPLE 31

Batch, Inc., a domestic corporation, purchases computer parts for resale from Chips, a foreign corporation, for 125,000K. On the date of purchase, .75K (a foreign currency) is equal to $1 U.S. (.75K:$1). On the date of payment by Batch (the foreign exchange date), the exchange rate is .8K:$1. In other words, Batch paid 125,000K, which cost Batch $156,250 in U.S. dollars (125,000K/.8K). Batch, however, must record the purchase of the computer parts for inventory purposes at $166,667 (125,000K/.75K) and recognize a foreign currency gain of $10,417 ($166,667 – $156,250). ▼

The following concepts are important when dealing with the tax aspects of foreign exchange.

- Foreign currency is treated as property other than money.
- Gain or loss on the exchange of foreign currency is considered separately from the underlying transaction (e.g., the purchase or sale of goods).
- No gain or loss is recognized until a transaction is closed.

FUNCTIONAL CURRENCY

Prior to 1987, the Code contained no provisions for determining tax results when foreign operations could be recorded in a foreign currency. However, in 1981, the Financial Accounting Standards Board adopted FAS 52 on foreign currency translation. FAS 52 introduced the **functional currency** approach (the currency of the economic environment in which the foreign entity operates generally is to be used as the monetary unit to measure gains and losses). TRA of 1986 adopted this approach for the most part.

Under § 985, all income tax determinations are to be made in the taxpayer's functional currency. Generally, a taxpayer's functional currency is the U.S. dollar. In certain circumstances, a qualified business unit (QBU) may be required to use a foreign currency as its functional currency. A QBU is a separate and clearly identified unit of a taxpayer's trade or business (e.g., a foreign branch). An individual is not a QBU; however, a trade or business conducted by an individual may be a QBU.[41]

SECTION 988 TRANSACTIONS

The disposition of a nonfunctional currency can result in a foreign currency gain or loss under § 988. Section 988 transactions include those in which gain or loss is determined with regard to the value of a nonfunctional currency, such as the following.

- Acquisition of (or becoming obligor under) a debt instrument.
- Accruing (or otherwise taking into account) any item of expense or gross income or receipts that is to be paid or received at a later date.
- Entering into or acquiring nearly any forward contract, futures contract, option, or similar investment position.
- Disposition of nonfunctional currency.

Section 988 generally treats exchange gain or loss falling within its provisions as ordinary income or loss. Certain exchange gain or loss is apportioned in the same manner as interest income or expense.[42] Capital gain or loss treatment may be elected with regard to forward contracts, futures contracts, and options that constitute capital assets in the hands of the taxpayer.

---

[41]Reg. § 1.989(a)–1(b).   [42]Temp.Reg. § 1.861–9T(b).

A closed or completed transaction is required. The residence of the taxpayer generally determines the source of a foreign exchange gain or loss.

BRANCH OPERATIONS

Where a QBU (a foreign branch, in this case) uses a foreign currency as its functional currency, the profit or loss is computed in the foreign currency each year and translated into U.S. dollars for tax purposes. The entire amount of profit or loss, without taking remittances into account, is translated using the average exchange rate for the taxable year. Exchange gain or loss is recognized on remittances from the QBU. One compares the U.S. dollar amount of the remittance at the exchange rate in effect on the date of remittance with the U.S. dollar value (basis pool) of the equity pool of the branch (i.e., initial capitalization plus contributions to the branch plus undistributed profits minus remittances and losses—all measured in the QBU's functional currency).[43] This gain or loss is ordinary, and it is sourced according to the income to which the remittance is attributable.

DISTRIBUTIONS FROM FOREIGN CORPORATIONS

An actual distribution of E & P from a foreign corporation is included in income by the U.S. recipient at the exchange rate in effect on the *date of distribution.* Thus, no exchange gain or loss is recognized. Deemed dividend distributions under Subpart F are translated at the weighted-average exchange rate for the CFC's tax year to which the deemed distribution is attributable. Exchange gain or loss can result when an actual distribution of this previously taxed income is made.

For FTC purposes, foreign taxes accrued in tax years beginning after December 31, 1997, are translated at the average exchange rate for the tax year to which the taxes relate. Under exceptions to this rule, foreign taxes must be translated at the exhange rate when the foreign taxes were paid.[44] If foreign taxes are paid within two years of accrual and differ from the accrued amount merely due to currency exchange fluctuation, no redetermination is required even though the actual dollar value paid may differ from the accrued amount. In other cases, where the taxes paid differ from the amount accrued, a redetermination is required.

EXAMPLE 32

Music, Inc., a domestic corporation, has a foreign branch. Foreign taxes attributable to branch income amount to 5,000K (a foreign currency). The taxes are paid within two years of being accrued. The average foreign exchange rate for the tax year to which the foreign taxes relate is .5K:$1, and on the date the taxes are paid, it is .6K:$1. Music has foreign taxes of $1,000 for purposes of the FTC. ▼

TAX PLANNING CONSIDERATIONS

Tax legislation tends progressively to reduce the ability to plan transactions and operations in a manner that minimizes tax liability. However, taxpayers who are not limited by the constraints of a particular transaction or operation can use the following suggestions to plan for maximum tax benefits.

THE FOREIGN TAX CREDIT LIMITATION AND SOURCING PROVISIONS

The FTC limitation is partially based on the amount of foreign-source taxable income in the numerator of the limitation ratio. Consequently, the sourcing of

---

[43]Prop.Reg. § 1.987–2.   [44]§ 986(a)(1)(B) and (C).

▼

Concept Summary 24–4

Recognition of Foreign Exchange Gain or Loss

Transaction	Date of Recognition
Purchase or sale of inventory or business asset	Date of disposition of foreign currency
Branch profits	Remittance of branch profits
Subpart F income	Receipt of previously taxed income (accumulated E & P)
Dividend from current E & P or untaxed accumulated E & P	No gain or loss to recipient

income is extremely important. Income that is taxed by a foreign tax jurisdiction benefits from the FTC only to the extent that it is classified as foreign-source income under U.S. tax law. Thus, elements that affect the sourcing of income, such as the place of title passage, should be considered carefully before a transaction is undertaken.

After the TRA of 1986, which added several limitation baskets to the FTC calculation, many companies found themselves with excess foreign taxes. Since the condition persists, these companies have not been able to take advantage of the carryback and carryover provision for the FTC. It may be possible for a U.S. corporation to alleviate the problem of excess foreign taxes with some of the following techniques:

- Generate "same basket" foreign-source income that is subject to a tax rate lower than the U.S. tax rate.
- Reduce highly taxed foreign-source income in favor of foreign-source income that is taxed at a lower rate.
- Time the repatriation of foreign-source earnings to coincide with excess limitation years.
- Deduct foreign taxes for years in which the deduction benefit would exceed the FTC benefit.

A taxpayer who can control the timing of income and loss recognition will want to avoid recognizing losses in years in which the loss is apportioned among the FTC limitation baskets. Otherwise, the foreign taxes for which a credit is allowed for the tax year are reduced.

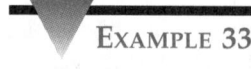 **EXAMPLE 33**

Della, a U.S. citizen, has U.S.-source taxable income of $200,000, worldwide taxable income of $300,000, and a U.S. tax liability (before FTC) of $84,000. She receives foreign-source taxable income, pays foreign income taxes, and has an FTC as shown.

Basket	Amount	Foreign Taxes	FTC Limitation	FTC
Passive	$ 20,000	$ 800	$ 5,600	$ 800
General	50,000	20,500	14,000	14,000
Non-CFC § 902 corporation #1	15,000	3,000	4,200	3,000
Non-CFC § 902 corporation #2	15,000	4,500	4,200	4,200
	$100,000	$28,800		$22,000

If Della had a foreign-source loss of $10,000 in the shipping limitation basket, the FTC is reduced by $1,820. The U.S. tax liability before the FTC is $81,200; 50% of the loss would be apportioned to the general limitation basket, reducing the FTC limitation for this basket to $12,600 [$81,200 × ($45,000/$290,000)]; and 15% is apportioned to the non-CFC § 902 corporation #2 basket, reducing the FTC limitation for this basket to $3,780 [$81,200 × ($13,500/$290,000)]. Della would avoid this result if she could defer recognition of the loss to a tax year in which it would not have a negative effect on the FTC. ▼

THE FOREIGN CORPORATION AS A TAX SHELTER

An NRA who is able to hold U.S. investments through a foreign corporation can accomplish much in the way of avoiding U.S. taxation. Capital gains (other than dispositions of U.S. real property interests) are not subject to U.S. taxation. This assumes that they are not effectively connected with a U.S. trade or business. The NRA can dispose of the stock of a foreign corporation that holds U.S. real property and not be subject to taxation under § 897 (FIRPTA). Furthermore, the stock of a foreign corporation is not included in the U.S. gross estate of a deceased NRA, even if all the assets of the foreign corporation are located in the United States.

Caution is advised where the foreign corporation may generate income effectively connected with the conduct of a U.S. trade or business. The income may be taxed at a higher rate than if the NRA individually generated the income. The trade-off between a higher U.S. tax on this income and protection from the U.S. estate tax and § 897 must be weighed.

PLANNING UNDER SUBPART F

The *de minimis* rule allows a CFC to avoid the classification of income as FBC income or insurance income and prevents the U.S. shareholder from having to include it in gross income as a constructive dividend. Thus, a CFC with total FBC income and insurance income in an amount close to the 5 percent or $1 million level should monitor income realization to assure that the *de minimis* rule applies for the tax year. At least as important is avoiding the classification of all the gross income of the CFC as FBC income or insurance income. This happens when the sum of the FBC income and gross insurance income for the taxable year exceeds 70 percent of total gross income.

Careful timing of increases in investment in U.S. property can reduce the potential for constructive dividend income to U.S. shareholders. The gross income of U.S. shareholders attributable to increases in investment in U.S. property is limited to the E & P of the CFC.[45] E & P that is attributable to amounts that have been included in gross income as Subpart F income either in the current year or a prior tax year is not taxed again when invested in U.S. property.

THE FOREIGN EARNED INCOME EXCLUSION

The tax benefit of the foreign earned income exclusion depends on the tax the income will incur in the country in which earned and the year in which received. If the foreign country levies little or no tax on the income, the U.S. taxpayer can exclude the housing cost amount plus up to $72,000 (for 1998) of foreign earned income and pay little or no tax on the income to the foreign tax jurisdiction. Since

---

[45]§§ 959(a)(1) and (2).

foreign earned income qualifies for the exclusion only if received in the year in which earned or the immediately succeeding tax year, the timely payment of such income is necessary.

In high-tax jurisdictions, the taxpayer may benefit more from taking the FTC than from excluding the earnings from gross income. The taxpayer earning income in a high-tax jurisdiction should compare the tax result of taking the exclusion with the tax result of forgoing either or both exclusions for the FTC. If U.S. taxes on the income are eliminated under all options and the taxpayer has excess foreign taxes to carry back or carry forward, then the FTC generally is more beneficial than the exclusion.

Taxpayers must also carefully monitor trips to the United States when attempting to qualify for the exclusion under the physical presence test. Taxpayers who are attempting to establish a bona fide foreign residence must make sure that their ties to the foreign country predominate over their ties to the United States for the period for which bona fide foreign residence is desired.

KEY TERMS

Branch profits tax, 24–19

Controlled foreign corporation (CFC), 24–26

Dividend equivalent amount (DEA), 24–19

Effectively connected income, 24–11

FIRPTA, 24–21

Foreign earned income exclusion, 24–24

Foreign sales corporation (FSC), 24–11

Foreign tax credit (FTC), 24–3

Functional currency, 24–34

Green card test, 24–16

Nonresident alien, 24–10

Subpart F, 24–26

Tax haven, 24–31

Tax treaty, 24–23

Treaty shopping, 24–32

U.S. shareholder, 24–27

PROBLEM MATERIALS

DISCUSSION QUESTIONS

1. What is meant by "grossing up" dividend income?

2. Anchor, Inc., a domestic corporation, owns 15% of Dorkin, Inc., and 12% of Felton, Inc., both foreign corporations. Anchor is paid gross dividends of $35,000 and $18,000 from Dorkin and Felton, respectively. Dorkin withheld and paid more than $10,500 in foreign taxes on the $35,000 dividend. Dorkin's country of residence levies a 20% tax on dividends paid to nonresident corporations. However, the tax rate is increased to 30% if the recipient is a resident of a country that provides an FTC. Taxes of $3,600 are withheld on the dividend from Felton. What tax issues must be considered in determining the availability and amount of the FTC allowed to Anchor?

3. Explain the difference in the source rules for the use of tangible and intangible assets.

4. Will dividends paid by a foreign corporation be treated as foreign-source in all cases? Explain.

5. Generally, U.S. taxpayers with foreign operations desire to increase foreign-source income and reduce deductions against that foreign-source income in order to increase their FTC limitations. What provision enables the IRS to prevent taxpayers from manipulating the source of income and allocation of deductions? Explain.

6. Trader, Inc., a foreign corporation, sells transistors in several countries, including the United States. In fact, currently 18% of Trader's sales income is sourced in the United States (through branches in New York and Miami). Trader is considering opening additional branches in San Francisco and Houston in order to increase U.S. sales. What tax issues must Trader consider before making this move?

7. Explain why the following statement is false: Income tax treaties between the United States and foreign countries allow only one of the treaty partners (either the United States or the foreign country) to tax income earned in one treaty country by residents of the other treaty country.

8. Write a memorandum to an NRA client explaining why stock of a foreign corporation held by NRA individuals may be considered a tax shelter for U.S. tax purposes.

9. How does the U.S. tax law attempt to assure that the tax will be paid when NRAs and foreign corporations dispose of U.S. real property interests at a gain?

10. How does a person qualify for the foreign earned income exclusion?

11. Joanna owns 5% of Axel, a foreign corporation. Joanna's son, Fred, is considering acquiring 15% of Axel from an NRA. The remainder of Axel is owned 34% by unrelated U.S. persons and 53% by unrelated NRAs. Currently, Fred operates a manufacturing business (as a sole proprietorship) that sells goods to Axel for resale outside the United States and outside Axel's country of residence. Joanna is not concerned about the concentration of investment since she expects to sell her stock in Axel in three years at a significant capital gain. Are there tax issues that Joanna and Fred need to address?

12. Eleven unrelated U.S. persons are considering forming a foreign corporation in which they will own equal interests. Will they have to be concerned with the CFC provisions?

13. What is the maximum profit allowed an FSC?

14. What are the important concepts when dealing with the tax aspects of foreign exchange?

PROBLEMS

15. Ellen, a U.S. resident, operates an import/export company. This year, the business generated taxable income of $120,000 from foreign sources and $90,000 from U.S. sources. All of Ellen's foreign-source income is in the general limitation basket. The remainder of her taxable income is from U.S. investments. Her total worldwide taxable income (before personal exemptions) is $250,000. Ellen pays foreign taxes of $48,000. Her U.S. income taxes (before FTC) are $70,000. What is Ellen's FTC for the tax year?

16. Space, Inc., a domestic corporation, owns 40% of Satellite, Inc., a foreign corporation. Space receives a gross dividend of $42,000 from Satellite. Satellite's after-tax post-1986 E & P is $320,000, and its post-1986 foreign taxes total $96,000. Space's taxable income before consideration of the dividend is $300,000. Assume that Space is subject to a flat U.S. tax rate of 34%.
    a. What are Space's deemed-paid foreign taxes with respect to the dividend from Satellite?
    b. What is Space's FTC?

17. Prepare a flowchart for your colleagues in the Tax Department, illustrating the steps in determining a company's FTC.

18. Parent, Inc., a U.S. corporation, owns an interest in a chain of foreign corporations. Given the following chains of ownership, from which foreign corporation(s) is it possible for Parent to claim the deemed-paid (indirect) FTC?
    a. Parent owns 45% of FC1, FC1 owns 90% of FC2, FC2 owns 25% of FC3, and FC3 owns 50% of FC4.
    b. Parent owns 30% of FC1, FC1 owns 30% of FC2, and FC2 owns 15% of FC3.

19. Jasper, a U.S. resident, received the following income items for the current tax year. What is the source (U.S. or foreign) of each income item?

a. $800 dividend from U.S. Power Company, a U.S. corporation that operates solely in the western United States.

b. $1,200 dividend from Star Trading Corporation, a U.S. corporation that had total gross income of $2,100,000 from the active conduct of a foreign trade or business for the immediately preceding three tax years. Star's worldwide gross income for the same period was $2,600,000.

c. $750 dividend from International Consolidated, Inc., a foreign corporation that had gross income of $800,000 effectively connected with the conduct of a U.S. trade or business for the immediately preceding three tax years. International's worldwide gross income for the same period was $3,000,000.

d. $300 interest from a savings account at a Houston bank.

e. $2,500 interest on Rolan Corporation bonds. Rolan is a U.S. corporation that derived $3,000,000 of its gross income for the immediately preceding three tax years from operation of an active foreign business. Rolan's worldwide gross income for this same period was $3,600,000.

20. Rita, a nonresident alien, is a professional golfer. She played in 7 tournaments in the United States in the current year and earned $50,000 in prizes from these tournaments. She deposited the winnings in a bank account she opened in Mexico City after she won her first tournament money for the year. Rita played a total of 30 tournaments for the year and earned $200,000 in total prize money. She spent 40 days in the United States, 60 days in England, 20 days in Scotland, and the rest of the time in South America. Write a letter to Rita explaining how much U.S.-source income she will generate, if any, from her participation in these tournaments and whether any of her winnings are subject to U.S. taxation. Rita's address is Av. Rio Branco, 149–4#, Rio de Janeiro, RJ 22421, Brazil.

21. Determine the source of income (U.S. or foreign) of the following sales:

a. Robert, a nonresident alien, sells Wal-Mart stock at a gain on the New York Stock Exchange.

b. Jennifer, a resident of El Paso, Texas, sells equipment used in her trade or business, which is operated in Juarez, Mexico. Title passes in El Paso.

c. A U.S. company sells inventory purchased from a New Hampshire manufacturer to a Canadian company, title passing on shipment from Kennedy Airport in New York.

d. A U.S. corporation manufactures inventory in Mexico and sells it to wholesale customers in Australia, title passing on delivery in Sydney.

22. Jeanette, a citizen and resident of France, comes to the United States on March 3, 1998, and remains until July 20 of the same year, at which time she returns to France. Jeanette comes back to the United States on November 15, 1998, and remains until December 20, 1998, when she again returns to France. Jeanette does not possess a green card, but she was a U.S. resident for 1997 under the substantial presence test, spending 210 days in the United States in that year. Jeanette was never physically present in the United States before 1997. Write a memorandum to Jeanette explaining whether she is a U.S. resident for 1998 under the physical presence test and, if so, how she may be able to overcome the presumption of residence.

23. For the current year, Carla, a NRA, has the U.S.-source income shown below. Determine Carla's U.S. tax liability, assuming that she is single and has no allowable itemized deductions. Assume the personal exemption amount is $2,650. Also assume that the 28% bracket for a single taxpayer begins at taxable income of $24,650.

Dividend from U.S. corporation*	$ 1,200
Interest from U.S. bank account**	1,500
Capital gain from sale of U.S. corporate stock†	6,000
Share of partnership taxable income††	20,000

*Carla owns less than 1% of the corporate stock.
**Not effectively connected with a U.S. trade or business.
†Carla was in the United States 25 days during the tax year, and the gain is not effectively connected with a U.S. trade or business.
††Carla is an investor in a U.S. partnership.

24. Toma, a resident of France, is sent to the United States by Felp Corporation, a foreign employer, to arrange the purchase of some machine tools. Toma spends three weeks in the United States. This is her only trip to the United States during the year.

Toma's gross monthly salary is $3,500. Her paycheck is deposited in her French bank account while she is in the United States. The salary is attributable to 15 U.S. and 6 French working days. The foreign employer does not have a U.S. trade or business. What is the amount of Toma's U.S.-source income?

25. Provo Corporation, a pharmaceutical corporation resident in Switzerland, sells certain products through a U.S. office. Current-year taxable income from such sales in the United States is $3,500,000. Provo's U.S. office deposits working capital funds short term in certificates of deposit with U.S. banks. Current-year income from these deposits is $25,000.

Provo also invests in U.S. securities traded on the New York Stock Exchange. This investing is done by the home office. For the current year, Provo has realized capital gains of $35,000 and dividend income of $18,000 from these stock investments. Compute Provo's U.S. tax liability, assuming that the U.S.-Switzerland income tax treaty reduces withholding on dividends to 15% and on interest to 5%.

26. Flipp, a foreign corporation, operates a trade or business in the United States. Flipp's U.S.-source taxable income effectively connected with this trade or business is $300,000 for the current tax year. Flipp's current E & P is $250,000. Net U.S. equity was $1.5 million at the beginning of the year and $1.4 million at the end of the year. Flipp is resident in a country with which the United States does not have an income tax treaty. What is the effect of the branch profits tax on Flipp for the current tax year?

27. Niles, a NRA individual, owns 20% of the stock of Sandstone, a U.S. corporation. Sandstone's balance sheet on the last day of the taxable year is as follows:

		Adjusted Basis	Fair Market Value
Cash (used as working capital)		$ 500,000	$ 500,000
Investment in foreign land		200,000	400,000
Investment in U.S. real estate:			
Land		100,000	150,000
Buildings	$1,400,000		
Less: Depreciation	(300,000)	1,100,000	1,500,000
		$1,900,000	$2,550,000
Accounts payable		$ 300,000	$ 300,000
Notes payable		500,000	500,000
Capital stock		400,000	800,000
Retained earnings		700,000	950,000
		$1,900,000	$2,550,000

Niles was in the United States only 50 days in the tax year. He sold 70% of his stock in Sandstone on the last day of the tax year for $350,000. Niles's adjusted basis in the stock sold was $245,000. He sold the stock for cash. What are the U.S. tax consequences, if any, to Niles?

28. Linda is single, a chemist, and a U.S. citizen. For the past three years, she has worked in the lab of a foreign refinery owned by a U.S. corporation. She is a bona fide resident of a foreign country. For the current year, Linda receives $75,000 of foreign earned income (FEI) and has qualified housing benefits provided by her employer of $35,000. Assuming that the base amount is $9,500, the personal exemption is $2,650, the standard deduction for a single taxpayer is $4,150, the 28% tax bracket for a single taxpayer begins at $24,650, and the 31% bracket begins at $59,750,

compute Linda's U.S. tax liability (a) taking both the FEI exclusion and the housing exclusion, (b) taking only the FEI exclusion, and (c) taking only the housing exclusion. Linda does not pay any foreign taxes. Write a memorandum to Linda explaining the results of your calculations.

29. Dart is a U.S. corporation. Three of the company's engineers have been working in Bahrain for 18 months as of January 1, 1998. They are U.S. citizens who have worked for Dart for 8 to 12 years. The company controller asks you to summarize the tax provisions of the foreign earned income exclusion for these employees. In writing this summary, include Code sections and subsections where appropriate.

30. Profit, Inc., a foreign corporation resident in Ireland, is owned 100% by Balance, Inc., a domestic corporation. Profit is a CFC. Determine Profit's Subpart F income (before expenses and cost of goods sold) for the tax year, given the following items of income:
    a. Income of $120,000 from the sale of merchandise to Balance. The merchandise was purchased from an unrelated manufacturer resident in Italy.
    b. Income of $240,000 from the sale of merchandise (purchased from Balance) to customers in France.
    c. Commissions of $80,000 from the sale of merchandise on behalf of Balance to residents of Ireland, for use within Ireland.
    d. Income of $250,000 from the performance on a construction contract entered into by Balance. The services were performed by Profit's personnel in Italy.

31. Box, Inc., a U.S. corporation, owns 30% of the only class of stock of Jewel, Inc., a CFC. Jewel is a CFC until July 1 of the current tax year. Box has held the stock since Jewel was organized and continues to hold it for the entire year. Box and Jewel are both calendar year taxpayers. If Jewel's Subpart F income for the tax year is $400,000, current E & P is $600,000, and no distributions have been made for the tax year, what is the amount, if any, that Box must include in gross income under Subpart F for the tax year?

32. Health, Inc., a domestic corporation, sells vitamins (inventory) to Svent, a Swiss drugstore chain, for 1,000,000 Swiss francs (Sf). The sale is made on January 15, with payment on the sale due in 180 days. On the date of sale, the exchange rate is .8125Sf:$1. On the date of collection, the exchange rate is .8640Sf:$1. Assuming that Health, Inc., converts the Swiss francs to U.S. dollars on the date of collection, what is the exchange gain or loss, if any?

33. Delane, Inc., a foreign corporation, pays a dividend to its shareholders on June 10. Parkco, a U.S. corporation and 5% shareholder in Delane, receives a dividend of 3,000K (a foreign currency). Pertinent exchange rates are as follows.

June 10	.8K:$1
Average for year	.9K:$1
December 31	1K:$1

What is the dollar amount of the dividend received by Parkco, and does Parkco have a foreign exchange gain or loss on receipt of the dividend?

34. Market, Inc., a foreign subsidiary of Export, Inc., a U.S. corporation, has pretax income of FF75,000 for 1998. Market accrues FF18,750 in foreign taxes on this income. The average exchange rate for the tax year to which the taxes relate is FF.1961:$1. None of the income is Subpart F income. If the net earnings of FF56,250 are distributed when the exchange rate is FF.2152:$1, what are the deemed-paid taxes available to Export? Assume that 1998 is Market's first year of operation.

35. Mega Corporation, a foreign corporation, is owned by Multi Corporation, a domestic corporation. Mega earns income of 3 million K (Mega's functional currency) and accrues foreign taxes of 750,000K. The average exchange rate for the tax year to which the taxes relate is .3K:$1. If none of Mega's income is Subpart F income and Multi receives a dividend of 1.5 million K when the exchange rate is .5K:$1, what is the dollar amount of the dividend and of the deemed-paid foreign taxes to Multi?

36. Money, Inc., a U.S. corporation, has $500,000 to invest overseas for 1997. For U.S. tax purposes, any additional income earned by Money will be taxed at 34%. Two viable possibilities for investment exist.

    a. Invest the $500,000 in Exco (a foreign corporation) common stock. Exco common stock pays a dividend of $3 per share each year. The $500,000 would purchase 10,000 shares (or 10%) of Exco's only class of stock (voting common). Exco expects to earn $10 million before taxes for 1998 and to be taxed at a flat rate of 40%. Its 1998 E & P before taxes is estimated to be $9,400,000. Exco's government does not withhold on dividends paid to foreign investors.

    b. Invest the $500,000 in Exco bonds which pay interest at 7% per year. Assume that the bonds will be acquired at par, or face, value. Exco's government withholds 25% on interest paid to foreign investors.

    Analyze these two investment opportunities and determine which would give Money the best return after taxes. Be sure to consider the effect of the foreign tax credit. Write a memorandum to Money, Inc., advising the corporation of your findings.

37. Georgia Calder is considering two offers that she has received from prospective employers. Overseas Projects, Inc., has offered Calder a position in Istanbul that will last for a minimum of three years. She will earn approximately $130,000 a year, which includes employer-provided housing costs of $28,000. During this period, she is required to return to the United States for two-week executive meetings at least three times a year. She also will receive a three-week vacation that she can spend anywhere she chooses.

    Foreign Lands, Inc., has offered Calder a position in New Delhi that also will last for approximately three years. She will earn $110,000 a year, which does not include housing costs. However, her employer will reimburse her for up to $25,000 of qualified housing expenses. There is no requirement that she return to the United States for meetings. She will receive a four-week vacation that she can spend as she chooses. However, Foreign Lands will provide for her transportation if she wishes to spend her vacation in the United States.

    Write a detailed memo to Ms. Calder explaining the tax consequences that she should consider in making her decision. Be sure to include a discussion of the bona fide residence versus physical presence rules. In your deliberations, use $9,500 as the base amount for the housing exclusion. Be careful not to overwhelm Ms. Calder with tax jargon such as "expatriate" and "outbound." Use plain language that a novice would understand. Do not let your tax knowledge cause you to use a "superior" attitude when addressing Ms. Calder.

Research Problems for this chapter appear at the end of Chapter 28.

Tax Administration
and Practice

LEARNING OBJECTIVES

After completing Chapter 25, you should be able to:

1. Identify the various administrative pronouncements issued by the IRS and explain how they can be used in tax practice.

2. Summarize the administrative powers of the IRS, including the examination of taxpayer records, the assessment and demand process, and collection procedures.

3. Describe the audit process, including how returns are selected for audit and the various types of audits.

4. Explain the taxpayer appeal process, including various settlement options available.

5. Determine the amount of interest on a deficiency or a refund and when it is due.

6. Discuss the various penalties that can be imposed on acts of noncompliance by taxpayers and return preparers.

7. Understand the rules governing the statute of limitations on assessments and on refunds.

8. Summarize the legal and ethical guidelines that apply to those engaged in tax practice.

Few events arouse so much fear in the typical individual or corporation as the receipt of a letter from the Internal Revenue Service (IRS), notifying the taxpayer that prior years' tax returns are to be the subject of an audit. Almost immediately, calls are made to the tax adviser. Advice is sought as to what to reveal (or not reveal) in the course of the audit, how to delay or avoid the audit, and how friendly one should be with the auditor when he or she ultimately does arrive.

Indeed, many tax practitioners' reputations with their clients have been made or broken by the way they are observed to behave under the pressure of an audit situation. The strategy and tactics of audits—including such seemingly unimportant issues as whether the tax adviser brings donuts or other refreshments to the audit session, the color of his or her suit and tie, and the most effective negotiation techniques—are the subject of both cocktail party banter and scholarly review.

In actuality, the practitioner can render valuable services to the taxpayer in an audit context, thereby assuring that tax payments for the disputed years are neither under- nor overreported, as part of an ongoing tax practice. In this regard, the adviser must appreciate the following.

- The elements of the Treasury's tax administration process and opportunities for appeal within the structure of the IRS.
- The extent of the negative sanctions that can be brought to bear against taxpayers whose returns are found to have been inaccurate.
- The ethical and professional constraints on the advice tax advisers can give and the actions they can take on behalf of their clients within the context of an adversarial relationship with the IRS.

▼ TAX ADMINISTRATION

The Treasury has delegated the administration and enforcement of the tax laws to its subsidiary agency, the IRS. In this process, the Service is responsible for providing adequate information, in the form of publications and forms with instructions, to taxpayers so that they can comply with the laws in an appropriate manner. The IRS also identifies delinquent tax payments and carries out assessment and collection procedures under the restrictions of due process and other constitutional guarantees.

In meeting these responsibilities, the Service conducts audits of selected tax returns. Less than 2 percent of all individual tax returns are subjected to audit in

---

TAX IN THE NEWS

SHOULD THE IRS BE LARGER?

What is the optimal size of the IRS? The IRS maintains that it can produce three to four dollars of revenue for every dollar spent on its ongoing operations. Actually, the rate of return might be higher, especially for special projects that the Service itself devises and undertakes. As the agency becomes more proficient with computers and more aggressive in finding and treating nonfilers, the temptation to enlarge the Service increases as well.

Given the Federal budget deficits and an underground economy measured in the hundreds of billions of dollars, one might expect the IRS personnel count to keep increasing, even though it is one of the largest Federal agencies, with a staff averaging between 100,000 and 115,000 throughout the year. Yet, the last few presidents have found that (1) pledges to cut back the size of government also apply to the IRS (i.e., the public does not apply such a rate of return test itself), and (2) the image of the Service as the taxpayer's friend and educator has become seriously tainted as a series of hearings has brought to the public stories of abuses of IRS authority across the country. The public seems to support an IRS that aggressively finds unreported income from foreign corporations or drug dealers, but not from targets closer to home. Some candidates call for a complete shutdown of the agency.

Despite its potential to help balance the Federal budget, the IRS has received only one budget increase in four years. Thus, more than an economic cost/benefit analysis seems to be going on when it comes to the IRS.

---

a given tax year. However, certain types of both taxpayers and income—including, for instance, high-income individuals (5 percent), cash-oriented businesses, real estate transactions, and estate- and gift-taxable transfers (15 percent)—are subject to much higher probabilities of audit. One's residence also affects the chance of audit, which ranges from 1.5 percent in California to 0.37 percent in Cincinnati.

Recently, much of the IRS's effort has been devoted to developing statutory and administrative requirements relative to information reporting and document matching. For instance, when a taxpayer engages in a like-kind exchange or sells a personal residence, various parties to the transaction are required to report the nature and magnitude of the transaction to the IRS. Later the Treasury's computers determine whether the transaction has been reported properly by comparing the information reported by the third parties with the events included on the relevant taxpayers' returns for the year.

In addition, the IRS has been placing increasing pressure on the community of tax advisers. Severe penalties may be assessed on those who have prepared a taxpayer's return when the Service's interpretation of applicable law conflicts with that of the preparer.

The IRS processes more than 110 million tax returns every year, about 15 million of which are filed electronically. It collects about $1.5 trillion in tax revenues and pays refunds to about 90 million taxpayers every year. The Mission Statement of the IRS commits the agency to the following:

> The purpose of the Internal Revenue Service is to collect the proper amount of tax revenue at the least cost; serve the public by continually improving the quality of our products and services; and perform in a manner warranting the highest degree of public confidence in our integrity, efficiency and fairness.

Current operational strategies of the IRS include the following.

- Focusing on taxpayer education.
- Developing a "customer first" orientation in working with individual taxpayers.
- Putting emphasis on dealing with nonfilers.
- Adapting to the changing cultural and linguistic needs of the public.
- Accelerating the modernization of equipment and operating methods.
- Making the Regulations and tax procedures as simple and fair as possible.

The IRS believes that, under these principles, the taxpayer will benefit in a number of ways.

- Taxpayers will spend significantly less time dealing with the IRS.
- Taxpayers will pay less interest.
- Taxpayers will have more filing and payment choices.
- The IRS will issue refunds more rapidly.

IRS PROCEDURE—LETTER RULINGS

1 LEARNING OBJECTIVE
Identify the various administrative pronouncements issued by the IRS and explain how they can be used in tax practice.

When a tax issue is controversial or a transaction involves considerable tax dollars, the taxpayer often wishes to obtain either assurance or direction from the IRS as to the treatment of the event. The **letter ruling** process is an effective means of dealing directly with the IRS while in the planning stages of a large or otherwise important transaction.

Rulings issued by the National Office provide a written statement of the position of the IRS concerning the tax consequences of a course of action contemplated by the taxpayer. Letter rulings do not have the force and effect of law, but they do provide guidance and support for taxpayers in similar transactions. The IRS will issue rulings only on uncompleted, actual (rather than hypothetical) transactions or on transactions completed before the filing of the tax return for the year in question.

The IRS will not issue a ruling in certain circumstances. It ordinarily will not rule in cases that essentially involve a question of fact.[1] For example, no ruling will be issued to determine whether compensation paid to employees is reasonable in amount and therefore allowable as a deduction.[2]

A letter ruling represents the current opinion of the IRS on the tax consequences of a transaction with a given set of facts. IRS rulings are not unchangeable. They are frequently declared obsolete or are superseded by new rulings in response to tax law changes. However, revocation or modification of a ruling is usually not applied retroactively to the taxpayer who received the ruling, if it was relied on in good faith and if the facts in the ruling request were in agreement with the completed transaction. The IRS may revoke any ruling if, upon subsequent audit, the agent finds a misstatement or omission of facts or substantial discrepancies between the facts in the ruling request and the actual situation. A ruling may be relied upon only by the taxpayer who requested and received it.

Letter rulings benefit both the IRS and the taxpayer. Not only do they help promote a uniform application of the tax laws, but they may also reduce the potential for litigation or disputes with revenue agents. In addition, they make the IRS aware of significant transactions being consummated by taxpayers. A fee is charged for processing a ruling request.

---

[1]Rev.Proc. 98–1, I.R.B. No. 1, 7.

[2]Rev.Proc. 98–3, I.R.B. No. 1, 100.

IRS PROCEDURE—OTHER ISSUANCES

In addition to issuing unpublished letter rulings and published rulings and procedures, the IRS issues determination letters and technical advice memoranda.

The District Director orders a **determination letter** for a completed transaction when the issue involved is covered by judicial or statutory authority, Regulations, or rulings. Determination letters are issued for various death, gift, income, excise, and employment tax matters.

EXAMPLE 1

True Corporation recently opened a car clinic and has employed numerous mechanics. The corporation is not certain whether its educational reimbursement plan is nondiscriminatory. True may request a determination letter from the appropriate District Director. ▼

EXAMPLE 2

Assume the same facts as in Example 1. True would like to establish a pension plan that qualifies for the tax advantages of § 401(k). To determine whether the plan qualifies, True should request and obtain a determination letter from the IRS. ▼

EXAMPLE 3

A group of physicians plans to form an association to construct and operate a hospital. The determination letter procedure is appropriate to ascertain whether the group is either subject to the Federal income tax or tax-exempt. ▼

A **technical advice memorandum** is issued by the National Office to the District Director and/or Regional Commissioner in response to a specific request by an agent, Appellate Conferee, or District Director. The taxpayer may request a technical advice memorandum if an issue in dispute is not treated by the law or precedent and/or published rulings or Regulations. Technical advice memoranda also are appropriate when there is reason to believe that the IRS is not administering the tax law consistently. For example, a taxpayer may inquire why an agent proposes to disallow a certain expenditure when agents in other districts permit the deduction. Technical advice requests arise from the audit process, whereas ruling requests are issued before an IRS audit.

ADMINISTRATIVE POWERS OF THE IRS

2 ▼ **LEARNING OBJECTIVE**
Summarize the administrative powers of the IRS, including the examination of taxpayer records, the assessment and demand process, and collection procedures.

Examination of Records. The Code authorizes the IRS to examine the taxpayer's books and records as part of the process of determining the correct amount of tax due. The IRS also can require the persons responsible for the return to appear and to produce any necessary books and records.[3] Taxpayers are required to maintain certain record-keeping procedures and retain the records necessary to facilitate the audit. Therefore, the taxpayer and not the IRS has the burden of substantiating any item on the tax return that is under examination. The files, workpapers, and other memoranda of a tax practitioner may be subpoenaed, since communications between CPAs and their clients generally are not privileged.

Assessment and Demand. The Code permits the IRS to assess a deficiency and to demand payment for the tax.[4] However, no assessment or effort to collect the tax may be made until 90 days after a statutory notice of a deficiency (the *90-day letter*) is issued. The taxpayer therefore has 90 days to file a petition to the U.S. Tax Court, effectively preventing the deficiency from being assessed or collected pending the outcome of the case.[5]

---

[3]§ 7602.
[4]§ 6212.

[5]§ 6213.

Following assessment of the tax, the IRS issues a notice and demand for payment. The taxpayer is usually given 30 days after the notice and demand for payment to pay the tax. This assessment procedure has certain exceptions.

- The IRS may issue a deficiency assessment without waiting 90 days if mathematical errors on the return incorrectly state the tax at less than the true liability.
- If the IRS believes the assessment or collection of a deficiency is in jeopardy, it may assess the deficiency and demand immediate payment.[6] The taxpayer can avoid (*stay*) the collection of the jeopardy assessment by filing a bond for the amount of the tax and interest. This action prevents the IRS from selling any property it has seized.

IRS Collection Procedures. If the taxpayer neglects or refuses to pay the tax after receiving the demand for payment, a lien in favor of the IRS is placed on all property (realty and personalty, tangible and intangible) belonging to the taxpayer.

The levy power of the IRS is very broad. It allows the IRS to garnish (*attach*) wages and salary and to seize and sell all nonexempt property by any means. The IRS can also make successive seizures on any property owned by the taxpayer until the levy is satisfied.[7] In exceptional cases, the IRS grants an extension for payment of a deficiency to prevent "undue hardship."[8]

If property is transferred and any related tax is not paid, the subsequent owners of the property may be liable for the tax. For example, if an estate is insolvent and unable to pay the estate tax, the executor or the beneficiaries may be liable for the payment.[9]

THE AUDIT PROCESS

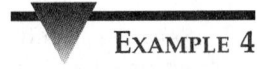

3 LEARNING OBJECTIVE Describe the audit process, including how returns are selected for audit and the various types of audits.

Selection of Returns for Audit. The IRS uses mathematical formulas to select tax returns that are most likely to contain errors and yield substantial amounts of additional tax revenues upon audit. The IRS does not openly disclose all of its audit selection techniques. However, some observations can be made regarding the probability that a return will be selected for audit.

- Certain groups of taxpayers are subject to audit more frequently than others. These groups include individuals with gross income in excess of $100,000, self-employed individuals with substantial business income and deductions, and cash businesses where the potential for tax evasion is high.

EXAMPLE 4   Tracey owns and operates a liquor store. As nearly all of her sales are for cash, Tracey might be a prime candidate for an audit by the IRS. Cash transactions are easier to conceal than those made on credit. ▼

---

[6]§ 6861. A jeopardy assessment is appropriate, for instance, where the IRS fears that the taxpayer will flee the country or destroy valuable property.

[7]The taxpayer can keep certain personal and business property and a minimal amount of his or her income as a subsistence allowance, even if a lien is outstanding. § 6334.

[8]§ 6161(b).
[9]§ 6901.

Do You Live in an Audit-Friendly Part of the Country?

Tax advisers have long suspected that the area of the country in which taxpayers live is one of the most important factors determining their susceptibility to audit. Theoretically, why should taxpayers living in Las Vegas be more likely to be audited than those living in Baltimore? Aren't all tax returns created equal?

Not even close. For the roughly one million individual income tax returns that are audited every year, the taxpayer's zip code partly determines not only the probability of being audited, but also the chances of success in reaching compromises with the IRS as the audit is settled.

The official IRS answer to this problem is that "[a]ny perceived 'geographic' variations result from (other factors, such as) differences in compliance levels, taxpayer behavior, and economic and business trends." But are Phoenix taxpayers more likely to cheat than those in Des Moines?

When a tax return is audited and the tax liability is not changed, has the government's money been wasted? Are auditors in the low-audit-rate areas lazier or less productive than those who produce more dollars for the government?

- If a taxpayer has been audited in a past year and the audit led to the assessment of a substantial deficiency, the IRS often makes a return visit.
- An audit might materialize if information returns (e.g., Form W-2, Form 1099) are not in substantial agreement with the income reported on a taxpayer's return. Obvious discrepancies do not necessitate formal audits and usually can be handled by correspondence with the taxpayer.
- If an individual's itemized deductions are in excess of norms established for various income levels, the probability of an audit increases. Certain deductions (e.g., casualty and theft losses, business use of the home, tax-sheltered investments) are sensitive areas since the IRS realizes that many taxpayers determine the amount of the deduction incorrectly or may not be entitled to the deduction at all.
- The filing of a refund claim by the taxpayer may prompt an audit of the return.
- Certain returns are chosen on a random basis (known as the Taxpayer Compliance Measurement Program [TCMP]) to develop, update, and improve the mathematical formulas used in selecting returns. TCMP is a long-term project designed to measure and evaluate taxpayer compliance characteristics. TCMP audits are tedious and time-consuming, as the taxpayer is generally asked to verify most or all items on the tax return. The last TCMP audits took place nearly two decades ago.
- Information is often obtained from other sources (e.g., other government agencies, news items, informants). The IRS then applies an "economic reality" check and may audit the return to address questions such as, Why did dividend income increase so much this year? Why did mortgage interest payments decrease? How did the taxpayer pay for such a large vacation home, sold this year? Sometimes the IRS sends a questionnaire to the taxpayer on Form 4448, asking how he or she spends income, where the children go to school, and so on. Funding for economic reality audits is under review by Congress.

- The IRS can pay rewards to persons who provide information that leads to the detection and punishment of those who violate the tax laws. The rewards are paid at the discretion of a District Director and cannot exceed 15 percent of the taxes, fines, and penalties recovered as a result of the information.[10]

EXAMPLE 5

Phil reports to the police that burglars broke into his home while he was out of town and took a shoe box containing $25,000 in cash, among other things. A representative of the IRS reading the newspaper account of the burglary might wonder why Phil kept such a large amount of cash in a shoe box at home. ▼

EXAMPLE 6

After 15 years, Betty is discharged by her employer, Dr. Franklin. Shortly thereafter, the IRS receives a letter from Betty informing it that Franklin keeps two sets of books, one of which substantially understates the actual cash receipts. ▼

Many individual taxpayers mistakenly assume that if they do not hear from the IRS within a few weeks after filing their return or if they receive a refund check, no audit will be forthcoming. As a practical matter, most individual returns are examined about two years from the date of filing. If not, they generally remain unaudited. All large corporations, however, are subject to annual audits.

Verification and Audit Procedures.   The tax return is immediately reviewed for mathematical accuracy. A check is also made for deductions, exclusions, etc., that are clearly erroneous. An example of obvious error would be the failure to comply with the 7.5 percent limitation on the deduction for medical expenses. In such cases, the Service Center merely sends the taxpayer revised computations and a bill or refund as appropriate. Taxpayers are usually able to settle such matters through direct correspondence with the IRS without the necessity of a formal audit.

Office audits are conducted by representatives of the District Director's Office, either in the office of the IRS or through correspondence. Individual returns with few or no items of business income are usually handled through an office audit. In most instances, the taxpayer is required merely to substantiate a deduction, credit, or item of income that appears on the return. The taxpayer presents documentation in the form of canceled checks, invoices, etc., for the items in question.

The *field audit* is commonly used for corporate returns and for returns of individuals engaged in business or professional activities. This type of audit generally involves a more complete examination of a taxpayer's transactions.

A field audit is conducted by IRS agents at the office or home of the taxpayer or at the office of the taxpayer's representative. The agent's work may be facilitated by a review of certain tax workpapers and discussions with the taxpayer's representative about items appearing on the tax return.

Prior to or at the initial interview, the IRS must provide the taxpayer with an explanation of the audit process that is the subject of the interview and describe the taxpayer's rights under that process. If the taxpayer clearly states at any time during the interview the desire to consult with an attorney, CPA, enrolled agent, or any other person permitted to represent the taxpayer before the IRS, then the IRS representative must suspend the interview.[11]

Any officer or employee of the IRS must, upon advance request, allow a taxpayer to make an audio recording of any in-person interview with the officer or employee concerning the determination and collection of any tax. The recording of IRS audit conferences may have significant legal implications. For example, if

---

[10]§ 7623 and Reg. § 301.7623–1T.   [11]§ 7521(b).

an IRS employee recklessly or intentionally disregards pertinent rules in the collection of Federal tax, the taxpayer can bring a civil action for damages in a U.S. District Court.[12]

Settlement with the Revenue Agent. Following an audit, the IRS agent may either accept the return as filed or recommend certain adjustments. The **Revenue Agent's Report (RAR)** is reviewed by the agent's group supervisor and the Review Staff within the IRS. In most instances, the agent's proposed adjustments are approved. However, the Review Staff or group supervisor may request additional information or raise new issues.

Agents must adhere strictly to IRS policy as reflected in published rulings, Regulations, and other releases. The agent cannot settle an unresolved issue based upon the probability of winning the case in court. Usually, issues involving factual questions can be settled at the agent level, and it may be advantageous for both the taxpayer and the IRS to reach agreement at the earliest point in the settlement process. For example, it may be to the taxpayer's advantage to reach agreement at the agent level and avoid any further opportunity for the IRS to raise new issues.

A deficiency (an amount in excess of the tax shown on the return or the tax previously assessed) may be proposed at the agent level. The taxpayer may wish to pursue to a higher level the disputed issues upon which this deficiency is based. The taxpayer's progress through the appeal process is discussed in subsequent sections of this chapter.

If agreement is reached upon the proposed deficiency, the taxpayer signs Form 870 (Waiver of Restrictions on Assessment and Collection of Deficiency in Tax). One advantage to the taxpayer of signing Form 870 at this point is that interest stops accumulating on the deficiency 30 days after the form is filed.[13] When this form is signed, the taxpayer effectively waives the right to receive a statutory notice of deficiency (the 90-day letter) and to subsequently petition the Tax Court. In addition, it is no longer possible for the taxpayer to go to the IRS Appeals Division. Signing Form 870 at the agent level generally closes the case. However, the IRS is not restricted by Form 870 and may assess additional deficiencies if deemed necessary.

THE TAXPAYER APPEAL PROCESS

If agreement cannot be reached at the agent level, the taxpayer receives a copy of the Revenue Agent's Report and a **30-day letter.** The taxpayer has 30 days to request an administrative appeal. If an appeal is not requested, a **90-day letter** is issued. Figure 25–1 illustrates the taxpayer's alternatives when a disagreement with the IRS persists.

A taxpayer who wishes to appeal must make an appropriate request to the Appeals Division. The request must be accompanied by a written protest except in the following cases.

- The proposed tax deficiency does not exceed $10,000 for any of the tax periods involved in the audit.
- The deficiency resulted from a correspondence or office audit (i.e., not as a result of a field audit).

The Appeals Division is authorized to settle all tax disputes based on the hazards of litigation (i.e., the chances of winning in court). Since the Appeals Division has final settlement authority until a 90-day letter has been issued, the taxpayer may be able to negotiate a settlement. In addition, an overall favorable

---

[12]§ 7433.

[13]§ 6601(c).

▼ **FIGURE 25–1**
Income Tax Appeal Procedure

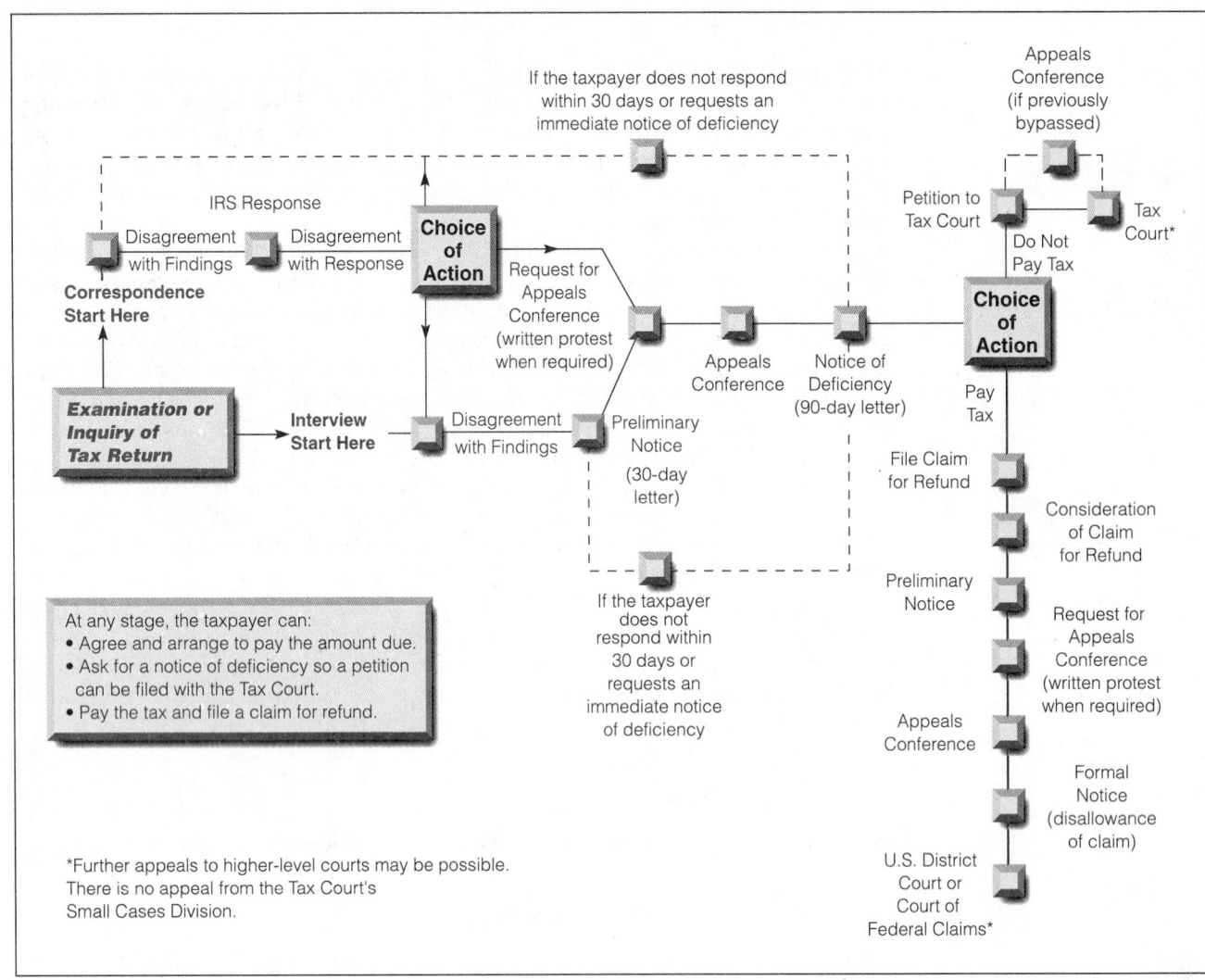

settlement may be reached by "trading" disputed issues. The Appeals Division occasionally may raise new issues if the grounds are substantial and of significant tax impact.

Both the Appeals Division and the taxpayer have the right to request technical advice memoranda from the National Office of the IRS. A technical advice memorandum that is favorable to the taxpayer is binding on the Appeals Division. Even if the technical advice memorandum is favorable to the IRS, however, the Appeals Division may nevertheless settle the case based on other considerations.

A taxpayer who files a petition with the U.S. Tax Court has the option of having the case heard before the more informal Small Cases Division if the amount of tax in dispute does not exceed $10,000.[14] If the Small Cases Division is used, neither

---

[14] § 7463(a).

party may appeal the case. The decisions of the Small Cases Division are not published or otherwise available as precedents for other cases.

The economic costs of a settlement offer from the Appeals Division should be weighed against the costs of litigation and the probability of winning the case. The taxpayer should also consider the impact of the settlement upon the tax liability for future periods, in addition to the years under audit.

If a settlement is reached with the Appeals Division, the taxpayer is required to sign Form 870AD. According to the IRS, this settlement is binding upon both parties unless fraud, malfeasance, concealment, or misrepresentation of material fact has occurred.

OFFERS IN COMPROMISE AND CLOSING AGREEMENTS

The IRS can negotiate a compromise if there is doubt about the taxpayer's ability to pay the tax.[15] If the taxpayer is financially unable to pay the total amount of the tax, a Form 656 (**Offer in Compromise**) can be filed with the District Director or the IRS Service Center.

The IRS investigates the claim by evaluating the taxpayer's financial ability to pay the tax. In some instances, the compromise settlement includes an agreement for final settlement of the tax through payments of a specified percentage of the taxpayer's future earnings. The District Director must obtain approval from the IRS Regional Counsel if the amount involved exceeds $500. This settlement procedure usually entails lengthy periods of negotiation with the IRS.

The IRS has statutory authority to enter into a written agreement allowing taxes to be paid on an installment basis if that arrangement facilitates the tax collection. The agreement may later be modified or terminated because of (1) inadequate information, (2) subsequent change in financial condition, or (3) failure to pay an installment when due or to provide requested information.[16]

A **closing agreement** is binding on both the taxpayer and the IRS except upon a subsequent showing of fraud, malfeasance, or misrepresentation of a material fact.[17] The closing agreement may be used when disputed issues carry over to future years. It may also be employed to dispose of a dispute involving a specific issue for a prior year or a proposed transaction involving future years. If, for example, the IRS is willing to make substantial concessions in the valuation of assets for death tax purposes, it may require a closing agreement from the recipient of the property to establish the income tax basis of the assets.

INTEREST

5 LEARNING OBJECTIVE
Determine the amount of interest on a deficiency or a refund and when it is due.

Determination of the Interest Rate. Congress sets the interest rates applicable to Federal tax underpayments (deficiencies) and overpayments (refunds) close to the rates available in financial markets. The Code provides for rates to be determined quarterly.[18] For example, the rates that are determined during January are effective for the following April through June.

IRS interest rates are based on the Federal short-term rates published periodically by the IRS in Revenue Rulings. The Federal rates are based on the average market yield on outstanding marketable obligations of the United States with remaining maturity of three years or less.

Underpayments are subject to the Federal short-term rates plus three percentage points, and overpayments carry the Federal short-term rates plus two percentage

---

[15]§ 7122.
[16]§ 6159.

[17]§ 7121(b).
[18]§ 6621.

TAX IN THE NEWS

THE IRS STRIVES TO BECOME CONSUMER-FRIENDLY

When country singer Willie Nelson was found guilty of underreporting his Federal income taxes, chiefly due to his involvement in real estate tax shelters, the total deficiency, including taxes, interest, and penalties, came to $16.7 million. The IRS intended to collect the full amount by forcing auctions of Nelson's most valuable possessions, placing claims on royalties from his recordings, encouraging him to make television commercials for fast-food outlets, and prompting him to sue his prior tax advisers for offsetting damages (to be paid directly to the IRS). Three years of such collections totaled only about $4 million.

As part of a nationwide effort to expand the use of the offer in compromise program, the IRS then settled with Nelson for total collections of $9 million, to be paid over a five-year period, with no future liens or collection activities. An IRS spokesperson asserted that the broader use of the compromise powers indicated the agency was "willing to settle for something less than the entire amount . . . to be more reasonable with taxpayers" having difficulty finding the full deficiency amount. As more taxpayers are having such difficulties, the IRS seems willing to collect what it can, rather than haggle in court for years to collect the "last penny" due.

Nelson's new adviser stated that the IRS was "taking a much more pragmatic and realistic approach to tax collection," as indicated by the change in the offer in compromise policy. In previous years, the IRS accepted only 25 percent of taxpayers' offers, covering about $40 million in deficiencies. Acceptance rates now average about 60 percent, for more than $100 million in collections.

In fact, the taxpayer can now initiate an installment payment plan on the original return. Form 9465, Installment Agreement Request, lays out the taxpayer's plan for payment, which incurs only a 0.5 percent penalty in addition to the late-payment interest charge. Where the amount due is less than $10,000, the standard arrangement appears to be a three-year payment plan; subsequent-year tax liabilities must be satisfied in full.

points. Consequently, the rate for tax deficiencies is one percentage point higher than the rate for tax refunds. For the first quarter of 1998, interest on tax deficiencies was set at 9 percent, and interest on refunds was 8 percent. In previous years, interest rates have ranged from 6 percent to 20 percent.

Computation of the Amount of Interest.   Interest is compounded daily.[19] Depending on the applicable interest rate, daily compounding doubles the payable amount over a period of five to eight years.

Tables for determining the daily compounded amount are available from the IRS. The tables ease the burden of those who prepare late returns where additional taxes are due.[20]

IRS Deficiency Assessments.   Interest usually accrues from the unextended due date of the return until 30 days after the taxpayer agrees to the deficiency by signing Form 870. If the taxpayer does not pay the amount shown on the IRS's

---

[19]§ 6622.

[20]Rev.Proc. 95–17, 1995–1 C.B. 556.

"notice and demand" (tax bill) within 30 days, interest again accrues on the deficiency.

Refund of Taxpayer's Overpayments.   If an overpayment is refunded to the taxpayer within 45 days after the date the return is filed or is due, no interest is allowed. When the taxpayer files an amended return or makes a claim for refund of a prior year's tax (e.g., when net operating loss carrybacks result in refunds of a prior year's tax payments), however, interest is authorized from the original due date of the return through the date when the amended return is filed. In general, taxpayers applying for refunds receive interest as follows.

- When a return is filed after the due date, interest on any overpayment accrues from the date of filing. However, no interest is due if the IRS makes the refund within 45 days of the date of filing.

EXAMPLE 7

Naomi, a calendar year taxpayer, files her 1998 return on December 1, 1999. The return reflects an overwithholding of $2,500. On June 8, 2000, Naomi receives a refund of her 1998 overpayment. Interest on the refund began to accrue on December 1, 1999 (not April 15, 1999). ▼

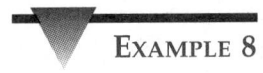

EXAMPLE 8

Assume the same facts as in Example 7, except that the refund is paid to Naomi on January 5, 2000 (rather than June 8, 2000). No interest is payable by the IRS, since the refund was made within 45 days of the filing of the return. ▼

- In no event will interest accrue on an overpayment unless the return that is filed is in "processible form." Generally, this means that the return must contain enough information in a readable format to enable the IRS to identify the taxpayer and to determine the tax (and overpayment) involved.

TAXPAYER PENALTIES

6 **LEARNING OBJECTIVE**
Discuss the various penalties that can be imposed on acts of noncompliance by taxpayers and return preparers.

To promote and enforce taxpayer compliance with the U.S. voluntary self-assessment system of taxation, Congress has enacted a comprehensive array of penalties. Tax penalties may involve both criminal and civil offenses. Criminal tax penalties are imposed only after the usual criminal process, in which the taxpayer is entitled to the same constitutional guarantees as nontax criminal defendants. Normally, a criminal penalty provides for imprisonment. Civil tax penalties are collected in the same manner as other taxes and usually provide only for monetary fines. Criminal and civil penalties are not mutually exclusive; therefore, both types of sanctions may be imposed on a taxpayer.

The Code characterizes tax penalties as additions to tax; thus, they cannot subsequently be deducted by the taxpayer. *Ad valorem penalties* are additions to tax that are based upon a percentage of the owed tax. *Assessable penalties*, on the other hand, typically include a flat dollar amount. Assessable penalties are not subject to review by the Tax Court, but *ad valorem* penalties are subject to the same deficiency procedures that apply to the underlying tax.

Failure to File and Failure to Pay.   For a failure to file a tax return by the due date (including extensions), a penalty of 5 percent per month (up to a maximum of 25 percent) is imposed on the amount of tax shown as due on the return, with a minimum penalty amount of $100. If the failure to file is attributable to fraud, the penalty becomes 15 percent per month, to a maximum of 75 percent of the tax.[21]

---

[21]§§ 6651(a) and (f).

For a failure to pay the tax due as shown on the return, a penalty of 0.5 percent per month (up to a maximum of 25 percent) is imposed on the amount of the tax. The penalty is doubled if the taxpayer fails to pay the tax after receiving a deficiency assessment.

In all of these cases, a fraction of a month counts as a full month. These penalties relate to the net amount of the tax due.

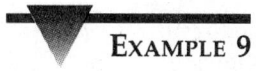

EXAMPLE 9

Conchita, a calendar year self-employed taxpayer, prepays $18,000 for income taxes during 1999. Her total tax liability for 1999 proves to be $20,000. Without obtaining an extension from the IRS, she files her Form 1040 in early August 2000 and encloses a check for the balance due of $2,000. The failure to file and the failure to pay penalties apply to $2,000 (not $20,000). ▼

During any month in which both the failure to file penalty and the failure to pay penalty apply, the failure to file penalty is reduced by the amount of the failure to pay penalty.

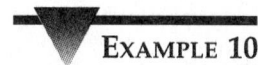

EXAMPLE 10

Jason files his tax return 10 days after the due date. Along with the return, he remits a check for $3,000, which is the balance of the tax owed. Disregarding any interest liabilities, Jason's total penalties are as follows.

Failure to pay penalty (0.5% × $3,000)		$ 15
Plus: Failure to file penalty (5% × $3,000)	$150	
Less: Failure to pay penalty for the same period	(15)	
Failure to file penalty		135
Total penalties		$150

The penalties for one full month are imposed even though Jason was delinquent by only 10 days. Unlike the method used to compute interest, any part of a month is treated as a whole month. ▼

These penalties can be avoided if the taxpayer shows that the failure to file and/or failure to pay was due to reasonable cause and not due to willful neglect. The Code is silent on what constitutes reasonable cause, and the Regulations do little to clarify this important concept.[22] Reasonable cause for failure to pay is presumed under the automatic four-month extension (Form 4868) when the additional tax due is not more than 10 percent of the tax liability shown on the return. In addition, the courts have ruled on some aspects of **reasonable cause.**

- Reasonable cause was found where the taxpayer relied on the advice of a competent tax adviser given in good faith, the facts were fully disclosed to the adviser, and he or she considered that the specific question represented reasonable cause.[23] No reasonable cause was found, however, where the taxpayer delegated the filing task to another, even when that person was an accountant or an attorney.[24]
- Among the reasons not qualifying as reasonable cause were lack of information on the due date of the return,[25] illness that did not incapacitate a taxpayer

---

[22]Reg. § 301.6651–1(c)(1) likens reasonable cause to the exercise of "ordinary business care and prudence" on the part of the taxpayer.

[23]*Estate of Norma S. Bradley*, 33 TCM 70, T.C.Memo. 1974–17.

[24]*U.S. v. Boyle*, 85–1 USTC ¶13,602, 55 AFTR2d 85–1535, 105 S.Ct. 687 (USSC, 1985).

[25]*Beck Chemical Equipment Co.*, 27 T.C. 840 (1957).

from completing a return,[26] refusal of the taxpayer's spouse to cooperate for a joint return,[27] and ignorance or misunderstanding of the tax law.[28]

Accuracy-Related Penalties. Major civil penalties relating to the accuracy of tax return data, including misstatements stemming from taxpayer negligence and improper valuation of income and deductions, are coordinated under the umbrella term **accuracy-related penalties.**[29] This consolidation of related penalties into a single levy eliminates the possibility that multiple penalties will be stacked together (i.e., when more than one type of penalty applies to a single understatement of tax).

The accuracy-related penalties each amount to 20 percent of the portion of the tax underpayment that is attributable to one or more of the following infractions.

- Negligence or disregard of rules and Regulations.
- Substantial understatement of tax liability.
- Substantial valuation overstatement.
- Substantial valuation understatement.

The penalties apply only where the taxpayer fails to show a reasonable basis for the position taken on the return.[30]

Negligence. For purposes of this accuracy-related penalty, **negligence** includes any failure to make a reasonable attempt to comply with the provisions of the tax law. The penalty also applies to any disregard (whether careless, reckless, or intentional) of rules and Regulations.[31] The penalty can be avoided upon a showing of reasonable cause and that the taxpayer acted in good faith.[32] The negligence penalty applies to *all* taxes, except when fraud is involved.

A negligence penalty may be assessed when the taxpayer fails to report gross income, overstates deductions, or fails to keep adequate records. When the taxpayer takes a nonnegligent position on the return that is contrary to a published pronouncement of the IRS, the penalty is waived if the taxpayer has a reasonable basis for the interpretation and has disclosed the disputed position on Form 8275.

Substantial Understatements of Tax Liability. The understatement penalty is designed to strike at middle- and high-income taxpayers who are tempted to play the so-called *audit lottery.*[33] Some taxpayers take questionable and undisclosed positions on their tax returns in the hope that the return will not be selected for audit. Disclosing the positions would have called attention to the return and increased the probability of audit.

A *substantial understatement of a tax liability* transpires when the understatement exceeds the larger of 10 percent of the tax due or $5,000 ($10,000 for a C corporation). The understatement to which the penalty applies is the difference between the amount of tax required to be shown on the return and the amount of tax actually shown on the return.

The penalty is avoided under any of the following circumstances.

- The taxpayer has **substantial authority** for the treatment.
- The relevant facts affecting the treatment are adequately disclosed in the return by attaching Form 8275.

---

[26]*Jacob Gassman*, 26 TCM 213, T.C.Memo. 1967–42, and *Babetta Schmidt*, 28 T.C. 367 (1957). Compare *Estate of Kirchner*, 46 B.T.A. 578 (1942).

[27]*Electric and Neon, Inc.*, 56 T.C. 1324 (1971).

[28]*Stevens Brothers Foundation, Inc.*, 39 T.C. 93 (1965).

[29]§ 6662.

[30]Temporary Regulations issued as TD 8533, 1994–1 C.B. 307. Most tax professionals measure this standard as a one-fourth probability of prevailing in court.

[31]§ 6662(c).

[32]§ 6664(c)(1).

[33]§ 6662(b)(2).

- The taxpayer has a reasonable basis for taking the disputed position.

Penalty for Overvaluation.   The objective of the overvaluation penalty is to deter taxpayers from inflating values (or basis), usually for charitable contributions of property, to reduce income taxes.[34]

- The penalty is 20 percent of the additional tax that would have been paid had the correct valuation (or basis) been used.[35]
- The penalty applies only when the valuation (or basis) used is 200 percent or more of the correct valuation (or basis).
- The penalty applies only to the extent that the resulting income tax underpayment exceeds $5,000 ($10,000 for C corporations).

EXAMPLE 11

Gretchen (a calendar year taxpayer) purchased a painting for $10,000. Years later, when the painting is worth $18,000 (as later determined by the IRS), Gretchen donates the painting to an art museum. Based on the appraisal of a cousin who is an amateur artist, she deducts $40,000 for the donation. Since Gretchen was in a 31% tax bracket, overstating the deduction by $22,000 results in a tax underpayment of $6,820.

Gretchen's penalty for overvaluation is $1,364 [20% × $6,820 (the underpayment that resulted from using $40,000 instead of $18,000)]. ▼

The substantial valuation overstatement penalty is avoided if the taxpayer can show reasonable cause and good faith. However, when the overvaluation involves *charitable deduction property*, the taxpayer must show *two additional* facts.

- The claimed value of the property is based on a qualified appraisal made by a qualified appraiser.
- The taxpayer made a good faith investigation of the value of the contributed property.[36]

Based on these criteria, Gretchen in Example 11 would find it difficult to avoid the penalty. A cousin who is an amateur artist does not meet the definition of a qualified appraiser. Likewise, she apparently has not made a good faith investigation of the value of the contributed property.

Penalty for Undervaluation.   When attempting to minimize the income tax, it is to the benefit of taxpayers to *overvalue* deductions. When attempting to minimize transfer taxes (i.e., estate and gift taxes), however, executors and donors may be inclined to *undervalue* the assets transferred. A lower valuation reduces estate and gift taxes. An accuracy-related penalty is imposed for substantial estate or gift tax valuation understatements.[37] As with other accuracy-related penalties, reasonable cause and good faith on the part of the taxpayer are a defense.

The penalty is 20 percent of the additional transfer tax that would have been due had the correct valuation been used on Form 706 (estate and generation-skipping transfer tax return) or Form 709 (gift and generation-skipping transfer tax return). The penalty only applies if the value of the property claimed on the return is 50 percent or less than the amount determined to be correct. The penalty applies only to an additional transfer tax liability in excess of $5,000. The penalty is doubled if the reported valuation was 25 percent or less than the correct determination.

---

[34]§ 6662(b)(3).
[35]For gross valuation misstatements (i.e., 400% or more), the penalty increases to 40%. § 6662(h).

[36]§ 6664(c)(2).
[37]§ 6662(b)(5).

ETHICAL CONSIDERATIONS

Good Faith Valuations

The undervaluation penalty pushes the tax adviser from a position of adversarial alliance with the taxpayer to one of mediator for the court. Good faith estimates of value, especially for family-owned businesses, can easily vary by as much as the 50 percentage points specified for the penalty. Even a gross undervaluation can occur when someone in the business other than the donor or decedent is a particularly talented entrepreneur, an effective sales representative, and/or the founder of the company; similarly, a business may be substantially undervalued when a minority equity interest is involved, or an intangible asset conveys a sizable nominal amount of goodwill to the valuation.

Because most taxpayers are highly averse to incurring any nondeductible penalties, the client may be tempted to compromise on the business valuation "too soon" (i.e., when the return is filed), eliminating any possibility of a more favorable valuation being presented before the Appeals Division or a court. Keeping in mind all of the potential taxpayer and preparer penalties that might apply, the tax professional should stick with a good faith appraisal of the business value, no matter what its nominal amount.

How would you react if your client, a musical composer, wanted to deduct $100,000 for the contribution of an obscure manuscript to the Symphony Society? What if your (first) appraiser placed the value of the manuscript at $15,000? What course of action would you propose to the client concerning the deduction? Any consequent penalties?

Civil Fraud Penalty. A 75 percent civil penalty is imposed on any underpayment resulting from **fraud** by the taxpayer who has filed a return.[38] For this penalty, the burden of proof is *on the IRS* to show by a preponderance of the evidence that the taxpayer had a specific intent to evade a tax. Once the IRS initially has established that fraud has occurred, the taxpayer then bears the burden of proof to show by a preponderance of the evidence the portion of the underpayment that is not attributable to fraud.

Although the Code and Regulations do not provide any assistance in ascertaining what constitutes civil fraud, it is clear that mere negligence on the part of the taxpayer (however great) will not suffice. Fraud has been found in cases of manipulation of the books,[39] substantial omissions from income,[40] and erroneous deductions.[41]

EXAMPLE 12

Frank underpaid his income tax by $90,000. The IRS can prove that $60,000 of the underpayment was due to fraud. Frank responds by a preponderance of the evidence that $30,000 of the underpayment was not due to fraud. The civil fraud penalty is $45,000 (75% × $60,000). ▼

If the underpayment of tax is partly attributable to negligence and partly attributable to fraud, the fraud penalty is applied first.

Criminal Penalties. In addition to civil fraud penalties, the Code provides numerous criminal sanctions that carry various monetary fines and/or imprisonment. The difference between civil and criminal fraud is often one of degree. A

---

[38]§ 6663. Underpayments traceable to fraudulent acts are not subject to a statute of limitations.

[39]*Dogget v. Comm.*, 60–1 USTC ¶9342, 5 AFTR2d 1034, 275 F.2d 823 (CA–4, 1960).

[40]*Harvey Brodsky*, 21 TCM 578, T.C. Memo. 1962–105.

[41]*Lash v. Comm.*, 57–2 USTC ¶9725, 51 AFTR 492, 245 F.2d 20 (CA–1, 1957).

BLAMING THE TAX PRACTITIONER

In the last few years, some courts have been amenable to taxpayers who defend against criminal charges by asserting that their dependence upon competent tax counsel led to the understatement of tax. Taxpayers who have used this defense successfully have usually shown that they relied on the practitioner's advice because of his or her professional expertise. Other successful defenses have included the argument that it was the practitioner's idea to willfully evade the tax, or that the adviser was not current with the controlling law and therefore issued bad advice that led to the error.

For instance, taxpayers have succeeded with this defense where they could show that the practitioner initiated and implemented the practice of keeping two sets of books or manipulating the cash receipts. Similarly, where the adviser facilitated the underpayment of tax estimates or payroll tax deposits, the IRS's charges against the taxpayer were severely weakened.

Often, taxpayers have submitted videotapes or written materials prepared by the practitioner as evidence in such cases. Severe preparer penalties compound the IRS's retribution against the practitioner when such a defense by the taxpayer prevails in court.

characteristic of criminal fraud is the presence of willfulness on the part of the taxpayer. Thus, § 7201, dealing with attempts to evade or defeat a tax, contains the following language.

> Any person who *willfully* attempts in any manner to evade or defeat any tax imposed by this title or the payment thereof shall, in addition to other penalties provided by law, be guilty of a felony and, upon conviction thereof, shall be fined not more than $100,000 ($500,000 in the case of a corporation), or imprisoned not more than five years, or both, together with the costs of prosecution. (Emphasis added.)

As to the burden of proof, the IRS must show that the taxpayer was guilty of willful evasion "beyond the shadow of any reasonable doubt." Recall that for civil fraud, the standard applied to measure culpability is "by a preponderance of the evidence."

Failure to Pay Estimated Taxes.   A penalty is imposed for a failure to pay estimated income taxes. The penalty applies to individuals and corporations and is based on the rate of interest in effect for deficiency assessments.[42] The penalty also applies to trusts and certain estates that are required to make estimated tax payments.

The penalty is not imposed if the tax due for the year (less amounts withheld and credits) is less than $500 for corporations, $1,000 for all others. For employees, an equal amount of withholding is deemed paid on each due date.

Quarterly payments are to be made on or before the fifteenth day of the fourth month (April 15 for a calendar year taxpayer), sixth month, and ninth month of the current year, and the first month of the following year. Corporations must make the last quarterly payment by the twelfth month of the same year.

---

[42]§§ 6655 (corporations) and 6654 (other taxpayers). Other computations can avoid the penalty. See §§ 6654(d)(2) and (k), 6655(e) and (i).

An individual's underpayment of estimated tax is the difference between the estimates that were paid and the least of (1) 90 percent of the current-year tax, (2) 100 percent of the prior-year tax (the tax year must have been a full 12 months and a return must have been filed), and (3) 90 percent of the tax that would be due on an annualized income computation for the period running through the end of the quarter. When the taxpayer's prior-year adjusted gross income (AGI) exceeds $150,000, the required payment percentage for the prior-year alternative is 105 percent.

A corporation's underpayment of estimated tax is the difference between the estimates that were paid and the least of (1) the current-year tax, (2) the prior-year tax, and (3) the tax on an annualized income computation using one of three methods of computation sanctioned by the Code. For the prior-year alternative, (1) the prior-tax year must have been a full 12 months, (2) a nonzero tax amount must have been generated for that year, and (3) large corporations (taxable income of $1 million or more in any of the three immediately preceding tax years) can use the alternative only for the first installment of a year.

In computing the penalty, Form 2210 (Underpayment of Estimated Tax by Individuals) or Form 2220 (Underpayment of Estimated Tax by Corporations) is used.

False Information with Respect to Withholding.

Withholding from wages is an important element of the Federal income tax system, which is based on a pay-as-you-go approach. One way employees might hope to avoid this withholding would be to falsify the information provided to the employer on Form W–4 (Employee Withholding Allowance Certificate). For example, by overstating the number of exemptions, income tax withholdings could be reduced or completely eliminated.

To encourage compliance, a civil penalty of $500 applies when a taxpayer claims withholding allowances based on false information. The criminal penalty for willfully failing to supply information or for willfully supplying false or fraudulent information in connection with wage withholding is an additional fine of up to $1,000 and/or up to one year of imprisonment.[43]

Failure to Make Deposits of Taxes and Overstatements of Deposits.

When the business is not doing well or cash-flow problems develop, employers have a great temptation to "borrow" from Uncle Sam. One way this can be done is to fail to pay to the IRS the amounts that have been withheld from the wages of employees for FICA and income tax purposes. The IRS does not appreciate being denied the use of these funds and has a number of weapons at its disposal to discourage the practice.

- A penalty of up to 15 percent of any underdeposited amount not paid, unless the employer can show that the failure is due to reasonable cause and not to willful neglect.[44]
- Various criminal penalties.[45]
- A 100 percent penalty if the employer's actions are willful.[46] The penalty is based on the amount of the tax evaded, not collected, or not accounted for or paid over. Since the penalty is assessable against the "responsible person" of the business, more than one party may be vulnerable (e.g., the president *and* treasurer of a corporation). Although the IRS may assess the penalty against several persons, it cannot collect more than the 100 percent due.

---

[43]§§ 6682 and 7205.
[44]§ 6656.

[45]See, for example, § 7202 (willful failure to collect or pay over a tax).
[46]§ 6672.

In addition to these penalties, the actual tax due must be remitted. An employer remains liable for the amount that should have been paid, even if the withholdings have not been taken out of the wages of its employees.[47]

STATUTES OF LIMITATIONS

7   **LEARNING OBJECTIVE**
Understand the rules governing the statute of limitations on assessments and on refunds.

A **statute of limitations** defines the period of time during which one party may pursue against another party a cause of action or other suit allowed under the governing law. Failure to satisfy any requirement provides the other party with an absolute defense should the statute be invoked. Inequity would result if no limits were placed on such suits. Permitting an extended period of time to elapse between the initiation of a claim and its pursuit could place the defense at a serious disadvantage. Witnesses may have died or disappeared; records or other evidence may have been discarded or destroyed.

Assessment and the Statute of Limitations.   In general, any tax that is imposed must be assessed within three years of the filing of the return (or, if later, the due date of the return).[48] Some exceptions to this three-year limitation exist.

- If no return is filed or a fraudulent return is filed, assessments can be made at any time. There is, in effect, no statute of limitations in these cases.
- If a taxpayer omits an amount of gross income in excess of 25 percent of the gross income stated on the return, the statute of limitations is increased to six years. The courts have interpreted this rule as including only items affecting income and not the omission of items affecting cost of sales.[49] In addition, gross income includes capital gains in the *gross* income amount (not reduced by capital losses).

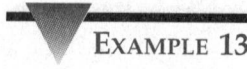
EXAMPLE 13

During 1994, Jerry had the following income transactions (all of which were duly reported on his timely filed return).

Gross receipts		$480,000
Less: Cost of sales		(400,000)
Net business income		$ 80,000
Capital gains and losses		
Capital gain	$ 36,000	
Capital loss	(12,000)	24,000
Total income		$104,000

Jerry retains your services in 1999 as a tax consultant. It seems that he inadvertently omitted some income on his 1994 return and he wishes to know if he is "safe" under the statute of limitations. The six-year statute of limitations would apply, putting Jerry in a vulnerable position, only if he omitted more than $129,000 on his 1994 return [($480,000 + $36,000) × 25%]. ▼

- The statute of limitations may be extended by mutual consent of the District Director and the taxpayer.[50] This extension covers a definite period and is

---

[47]§ 3403.
[48]§§ 6501(a) and (b)(1).
[49]*The Colony, Inc. v. Comm.*, 58–2 USTC ¶9593, 1 AFTR2d 1894, 78 S.Ct. 1033 (USSC, 1958).
[50]§ 6501(c)(4).

made by signing Form 872 (Consent to Extend the Time to Assess Tax). The extension is frequently requested by the IRS when the lapse of the statutory period is imminent and the audit has not been completed. This practice is often applied to audits of corporate taxpayers and explains why many corporations have more than three "open years."

Special rules relating to assessment are applicable in the following situations.

- Taxpayers (corporations, estates, etc.) may request a prompt assessment of the tax.
- The period for assessment of the personal holding company tax is extended to six years after the return is filed only if certain filing requirements are met.
- If a partnership or trust files a tax return (a partnership or trust return) in good faith and a later determination renders the entity taxable as a corporation, the return is deemed to be the corporate return for purposes of the statute of limitations.
- The assessment period for capital loss, net operating loss, and general business credit carrybacks is generally related to the determination of tax in the year of the loss or unused credit rather than in the carryback years.

If the tax is assessed within the period of limitations, the IRS has 10 years from the date of assessment to collect the tax. However, if the IRS issues a statutory notice of deficiency to the taxpayer, who then files a Tax Court petition, the statute is suspended on both the deficiency assessment and the period of collection until 60 days after the decision of the Tax Court becomes final.

Refund Claims and the Statute of Limitations. To receive a tax refund, the taxpayer is required to file a valid refund claim. The official form for filing a claim is Form 1040X for individuals and Form 1120X for corporations. If the refund claim does not meet certain procedural requirements, the IRS may reject the claim with no consideration of its merit.

- A separate claim must be filed for each taxable period.
- The grounds for the claim must be stated in sufficient detail.
- The statement of facts must be sufficient to permit the IRS to evaluate the merits of the claim.

The refund claim must be filed within three years of the filing of the tax return or within two years following the payment of the tax if this period expires on a later date.[51]

EXAMPLE 14

On March 10, 1996, Louise filed her 1995 income tax return reflecting a tax of $10,500. On July 10, 1997, she filed an amended 1995 return showing an additional $3,000 of tax that was then paid. On May 18, 1999, she filed a claim for refund of $4,500.

Assuming Louise is correct in claiming a refund, how much tax can she recover? The answer is only $3,000. Because the claim was not filed within the three-year period, Louise is limited to the amount she actually paid during the last two years. ▼

Special rules are available for claims relating to bad debts and worthless securities. A seven-year period of limitations applies in lieu of the normal three-year rule.[52] The extended period is provided in recognition of the inherent difficulty of identifying the exact year in which a bad debt or security becomes worthless.

---

[51]§§ 6511(a) and 6513(a).   [52]§ 6511(d)(1).

TAX PRACTICE

THE TAX PRACTITIONER

8 LEARNING OBJECTIVE
Summarize the legal and ethical guidelines that apply to those engaged in tax practice.

Definition.   Who is a tax practitioner? What service does the practitioner perform? To begin defining the term *tax practitioner*, one should consider whether the individual is qualified to practice before the IRS. Generally, practice before the IRS is limited to CPAs, attorneys, and persons who have been enrolled to practice before the IRS (called **enrolled agents [EAs]**). In most cases, EAs are admitted to practice only if they pass an examination administered by the IRS. CPAs and attorneys are not required to take this examination and are automatically admitted to practice if they are in good standing with the appropriate licensing board regulating their profession.

Persons other than CPAs, attorneys, and EAs may be allowed to practice before the IRS in limited situations. Circular 230 (entitled "Rules Governing the Practice of Attorneys and Agents Before the Internal Revenue Service") issued by the Treasury Department permits certain notable exceptions.

- A taxpayer may always represent himself or herself. A person may also represent a member of the immediate family if no compensation is received for such services.
- Regular full-time employees may represent their employers.
- Corporations may be represented by any of their bona fide officers.
- Partnerships may be represented by any of the partners.
- Trusts, receiverships, guardianships, or estates may be represented by their trustees, receivers, guardians, or administrators or executors.
- A taxpayer may be represented by whoever prepared the return for the year in question. However, such representation cannot proceed beyond the agent level.

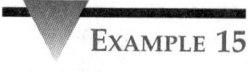

EXAMPLE 15

Joel is currently undergoing audit by the IRS for tax years 1996 and 1997. He prepared the 1996 return but paid AddCo, a bookkeeping service, to prepare the 1997 return. AddCo may represent Joel only in matters concerning 1997. However, even for 1997, AddCo would be unable to represent Joel at an Appeals Division proceeding. Joel could represent himself, or he could retain a CPA, attorney, or EA to represent him in matters concerning both years under examination. ▼

Rules Governing Tax Practice.   Circular 230 further prescribes the rules governing practice before the IRS. The following are some of the most important rules imposed on CPAs, attorneys, and EAs.

- A prohibition against taking a position on a tax return unless there is a *realistic possibility* of the position being sustained on its merits. Generally, the realistic possibility standard is met when a person knowledgeable in the tax law would conclude that the position has at least a one-in-three probability of prevailing in court.
- A prohibition against taking frivolous tax return positions.
- A requirement that nonfrivolous tax return positions that fail the realistic possibility standard be disclosed in the return (i.e., using Form 8275).
- A requirement to inform clients of both penalties likely to apply to return positions and ways such penalties can be avoided.
- A requirement to make known to a client any error or omission the client may have made on any return or other document submitted to the IRS.
- A duty to submit records or information lawfully requested by the IRS.

- An obligation to exercise due diligence in preparing and filing tax returns accurately.
- A restriction against unreasonably delaying the prompt disposition of any matter before the IRS.
- A restriction against charging the client "an unconscionable fee" for representation before the IRS.
- A restriction against representing clients with conflicting interests.

Anyone can prepare a tax return or render tax advice, regardless of his or her educational background or level of competence. Likewise, nothing prevents the "unlicensed" tax practitioner from advertising his or her specialty, directly soliciting clients, or otherwise violating any of the standards of conduct controlling CPAs, attorneys, and EAs. Nevertheless, some restraints do govern all parties engaged in rendering tax advice or preparing tax returns for the general public.

- If the party holds himself or herself out to the general public as possessing tax expertise, he or she could be liable to the client if services are performed in a negligent manner. At a minimum, the practitioner is liable for any interest and penalties the client incurs because of the practitioner's failure to exercise due care.
- If one agrees to perform a service (e.g., prepare a tax return) and subsequently fails to do so, the aggrieved party may be in a position to obtain damages for breach of contract.
- The IRS requires any person who prepares tax returns for a fee to sign as preparer of the return.[53] Failure to comply with this requirement could result in penalty assessment against the preparer.
- The Code prescribes various penalties for the deliberate filing of false or fraudulent returns. These penalties apply to a tax practitioner who either was aware of the situation or actually perpetrated the false filing or the fraud.[54]
- Penalties are prescribed for tax practitioners who disclose to third parties information they have received from clients in connection with the preparation of tax returns or the rendering of tax advice.[55]

EXAMPLE 16

Sarah operates a tax return preparation service. Her brother-in-law, Butch, has just taken a job as a life insurance salesman. To help Butch find contacts, Sarah furnishes him with a list of the names and addresses of all of her clients who report AGI of $10,000 or more. Sarah is subject to penalties. ▼

- All nonattorney tax practitioners should avoid becoming engaged in activities that constitute the unauthorized practice of law. If they engage in this practice (e.g., by drafting legal documents for a third party), action could be instituted against them in the appropriate state court by the local or state bar association. What actions constitute the unauthorized practice of law is largely undefined, though, and such charges are filed only rarely today.

Preparer Penalties. The Code also provides for penalties to discourage improper actions by tax practitioners.

---

[53]Reg. § 1.6065–1(b)(1). Rev.Rul. 84–3, 1984–1 C.B. 264, contains a series of examples illustrating when a person is deemed to be a preparer of the return.

[54]§ 7206.

[55]§ 7216.

1. A $250 penalty for understatements due to taking unrealistic positions.[56] Unless adequate tax return disclosure of the position is made, the penalty is imposed if two conditions are satisfied.

   - Any part of any understatement of tax liability on any return or claim for refund is due to a position that did not have a realistic possibility of being sustained on its merits.
   - Any person who was an income tax return preparer for that return or claim knew (or should have known) of this position.

   The penalty can be avoided by showing reasonable cause and by showing that the preparer acted in good faith.

2. A $1,000 penalty for willful and reckless conduct.[57] The penalty applies if any part of the understatement of a taxpayer's liability on a return or claim for refund is due to:

   - The preparer's willful attempt to understate the taxpayer's tax liability in any manner.
   - Any reckless or intentional disregard of IRS rules or Regulations by the preparer.

   Adequate disclosure can avoid the penalty. If both this penalty and the unrealistic position penalty (see item 1 above) apply to the same return, the total penalty cannot exceed $1,000.

3. A $1,000 ($10,000 for corporations) penalty per return or document is imposed against persons who aid in the preparation of returns or other documents that they know (or have reason to believe) would result in an understatement of the tax liability of another person.[58] Clerical assistance in the preparation process does not incur the penalty.

   If this penalty applies, neither the unrealistic position penalty (item 1) nor the willful and reckless conduct penalty (item 2) is assessed.

4. A $50 penalty is assessed against the preparer for failure to sign a return or furnish the preparer's identifying number.[59]

5. A $50 penalty is assessed if the preparer fails to furnish a copy of the return or claim for refund to the taxpayer.

6. A $500 penalty may be assessed if a preparer endorses or otherwise negotiates a check for refund of tax issued to the taxpayer.

ETHICAL CONSIDERATIONS—"STATEMENTS ON RESPONSIBILITIES IN TAX PRACTICE"

Tax practitioners who are CPAs, attorneys, or EAs must abide by the codes or canons of professional ethics applicable to their respective professions. The various codes and canons have much in common with and parallel the standards of conduct set forth in Circular 230.[60]

In the belief that CPAs engaged in tax practice require further guidance in the resolution of ethical problems, the Tax Committee of the AICPA began issuing periodic statements on selected topics. The first of these Statements on Responsibilities in Tax Practice was released in 1964. All of the Statements were

---

[56]§ 6694(a).
[57]§ 6694(b).
[58]§ 6701.
[59]§ 6695.

[60]For an additional discussion of tax ethics, see Raabe, Whittenburg, and Bost, *West's Federal Tax Research*, 4th ed. (St. Paul: West Publishing Co., 1997), Chapters 1 and 13.

revised in August of 1988. The most important Statements that have been issued to date are discussed below.[61]

The Statements merely represent guides to action and are not part of the AICPA's Code of Professional Ethics. But because the Statements are representative of standards followed by members of the profession, a violation might indicate a deviation from the standard of due care exercised by most CPAs. The standard of due care is usually at the heart of any suit charging negligence that is brought against a CPA.

Statement No. 1: Positions Contrary to IRS Interpretations.

Under certain circumstances, a CPA may take a position that is contrary to that taken by the IRS. In order to do so, however, the CPA must have a good faith belief that the position, if challenged, has a realistic possibility of being sustained administratively or judicially on its merits.

The client should be fully advised of the risks involved and should know that certain penalties may result if the position taken by the CPA is not successful. The client should also be informed that disclosure on the return may avoid some or all of these penalties.

In no case, though, should the CPA exploit the audit lottery; that is, to take a questionable position based on the probabilities that the client's return will not be chosen by the IRS for audit. Furthermore, the CPA should not "load" the return with questionable items in the hope that they might aid the client in a later settlement negotiation with the IRS.

Statement No. 2: Questions on Returns.

A CPA should make a reasonable effort to obtain from the client, and provide to the IRS, appropriate answers to all questions on a tax return before signing as preparer. Reasonable grounds may exist for omitting an answer.

- The information is not readily available, and the answer is not significant in computing the tax.
- The meaning of the question as it applies to a particular situation is genuinely uncertain.
- The answer to the question is voluminous.

The fact that an answer to a question could prove disadvantageous to the client does not justify omitting the answer.

Statement No. 3: Procedural Aspects of Preparing Returns.

In preparing a return, a CPA may in good faith rely without verification on information furnished by the client or by third parties. However, the CPA should make reasonable inquiries if the information appears to be incorrect, incomplete, or inconsistent. In this regard, the CPA should refer to the client's prior returns whenever appropriate.

EXAMPLE 17

A CPA normally can take a client's word for the validity of dependency exemptions. But suppose a recently divorced client wants to claim his three children as dependents (when he does not have custody). A CPA must act in accordance with § 152(e)(2) in preparing the return. Claiming the dependency exemption will require evidence of a waiver by the custodial parent. Without this waiver, the CPA should not claim the dependency exemptions on the client's tax return. ▼

---

[61]Other, less frequently encountered Statements are omitted from this discussion.

EXAMPLE 18

While preparing a client's income tax return for 1999, a CPA reviews her income tax return for 1998. In comparing the dividend income reported on the 1998 Schedule B with that received in 1999, the CPA notes a significant decrease. Further investigation reveals the variation is due to a stock sale in 1999 that, until now, was unknown to the CPA. Thus, the review of the 1998 return has unearthed a transaction that should be reported on the 1999 return. ▼

If the Code or Regulations require certain types of verification (as is the case with travel and entertainment expenditures), the CPA must advise the client of these rules. Further, inquiry must be made to ascertain whether the client has complied with the verification requirements.

Statement No. 4: Estimates.   A CPA may prepare a tax return using estimates received from a taxpayer if it is impracticable to obtain exact data. The estimates must be reasonable under the facts and circumstances known to the CPA. When estimates are used, they should be presented in such a manner as to avoid implying that greater accuracy exists.

Statement No. 5: Recognition of Administrative Proceeding.   As facts may vary from year to year, so may the position taken by a CPA. In these types of situations, the CPA is not bound by an administrative or judicial proceeding involving a prior year.

EXAMPLE 19

Upon audit of Ramon Corporation's income tax return for 1997, the IRS disallowed $180,000 of the $400,000 salary paid to its president and sole shareholder on the grounds that it was unreasonable [§ 162(a)(1)]. A CPA has been engaged to prepare Ramon's income tax return for 1999. Again the corporation paid its president a salary of $400,000 and chose to deduct this amount. Because the CPA is not bound in 1999 by what the IRS deemed reasonable for 1997, the full $400,000 can be claimed as a salary deduction. ▼

Other problems that require a CPA's use of judgment include reclassification of corporate debt as equity (thin capitalization) and corporate accumulations beyond the reasonable needs of the business (for the penalty tax under § 531).

Statement No. 6: Knowledge of Error.   A CPA should promptly advise a client upon learning of an error on a previously filed return or upon learning of a client's failure to file a required return. The advice can be oral or written and should include a recommendation of the corrective measures, if any, to be taken. The error or other omission should not be disclosed to the IRS without the client's consent.

If the past error is material and is not corrected by the client, the CPA may be unable to prepare the current year's tax return. This situation might occur if the error has a carryover effect that prevents the CPA from determining the correct tax liability for the current year.

EXAMPLE 20

In preparing a client's 1999 income tax return, a CPA discovers that final inventory for 1998 was materially understated. First, the CPA should advise the client to file an amended return for 1998 reflecting the correct amount in final inventory. Second, if the client refuses to make this adjustment, the CPA should consider whether the error will preclude preparation of a substantially correct return for 1999. Because this will probably be the case (the final inventory for 1998 becomes the beginning inventory for 1999), the CPA should withdraw from the engagement.

If the client corrects the error, the CPA may proceed with the preparation of the tax return for 1999. However, the CPA must ensure that the error is not repeated. ▼

Statement No. 8: Advice to Clients.   In providing tax advice to a client, the CPA must use judgment to ensure that the advice reflects professional competence and appropriately serves the client's needs. No standard format or guidelines can be established to cover all situations and circumstances involving written or oral advice by the CPA.

The CPA may communicate with the client when subsequent developments affect previous advice on significant matters. However, the CPA cannot be expected to assume responsibility for initiating the communication, unless he or she is assisting a client in implementing procedures or plans associated with the advice. The CPA may undertake this obligation by specific agreement with the client.

TAX PLANNING CONSIDERATIONS

STRATEGIES IN SEEKING AN ADMINISTRATIVE RULING

Determination Letters.   In many instances, the request for an advance ruling or a determination letter from the IRS is a necessary or desirable planning strategy. The receipt of a favorable ruling or determination reduces the risk associated with a transaction when the tax results are in doubt. For example, the initiation or amendment of a qualified pension or profit sharing plan should be accompanied by a determination letter from the District Director. Otherwise, on subsequent IRS review, the plan may not qualify, and the tax deductibility of contributions to the plan will be disallowed. In some instances, the potential tax effects of a transaction are so numerous and of such consequence that proceeding without a ruling is unwise.

Letter Rulings.   In some cases, it may not be necessary or desirable to request an advance ruling. For example, it is generally not desirable to request a ruling if the tax results are doubtful and the company is committed to complete the transaction in any event. If a ruling is requested and negotiations with the IRS indicate that an adverse determination will be forthcoming, it is usually possible to have the ruling request withdrawn. However, the National Office of the IRS may forward its findings, along with a copy of the ruling request, to the District Director. In determining the advisability of a ruling request, the taxpayer should consider the potential exposure of other items in the tax returns of all "open years."

A ruling request may delay the consummation of a transaction if the issues are novel or complex. Frequently, a ruling can be processed within six months, although in some instances a delay of a year or more may be encountered.

Technical Advice Memoranda.   A taxpayer in the process of contesting a proposed deficiency with the Appeals Division should consider requesting a technical advice memorandum from the National Office of the IRS. If such advice is favorable to the taxpayer, it is binding on the Appeals Division. The request may be particularly appropriate when the practitioner feels that the agent or Appeals Division has been too literal in interpreting an IRS ruling.

CONSIDERATIONS IN HANDLING AN IRS AUDIT

As a general rule, a taxpayer should attempt to settle disputes at the earliest possible stage of the administrative appeal process. New issues may be raised by IRS personnel if the case goes beyond the agent level. It is usually possible to limit the scope of the examination by furnishing pertinent information requested by the

CONCEPT SUMMARY 25–1

Tax Administration and Practice

1. The Internal Revenue Service (IRS) enforces the tax laws of the United States.
2. The IRS issues various pronouncements, communicating its position on certain tax issues. These pronouncements promote uniform enforcement of the tax law among taxpayers and among the internal divisions of the IRS. Taxpayers should seek such rulings and memoranda when the nature or magnitude of a pending transaction requires a high degree of certainty in the planning process.
3. IRS audits can take several forms. Taxpayers are selected for audit based on the probable net dollar return to the Treasury from the process. Offers in compromise and closing agreements can be a useful means of completing an audit without resorting to litigation.
4. Certain IRS personnel are empowered to consider the hazards of litigation in developing a settlement with the taxpayer during the audit process.
5. The IRS pays interest to taxpayers on overpaid taxes, starting essentially 45 days after the due date of the return, at two percentage points over the Federal short-term rate. Interest paid to the IRS on underpayments is computed at three points over this Federal rate, starting essentially on the due date of the return. Interest for both purposes is compounded daily.
6. The Treasury assesses penalties when the taxpayer fails to file a required tax return or pay a tax. Penalties also are assessed when an inaccurate return is filed due to negligence or other disregard of IRS rules. Tax preparers are subject to penalties for assisting a taxpayer in filing an inaccurate return, failing to follow IRS rules in an appropriate manner, or mishandling taxpayer data or funds.
7. Statutes of limitations place outer boundaries on the timing and amounts of proposed amendments to completed tax returns that can be made by the taxpayer or the IRS.
8. Tax practitioners must operate under constraints imposed on them by codes of ethics of pertinent professional societies and by Treasury Circular 230. These rules also define the parties who can represent others in an IRS proceeding.

agent. Extraneous information or thoughtless comments may result in the opening of new issues and should be avoided. Agents usually appreciate prompt and efficient responses to inquiries, since their performance may in part be judged by their ability to close or settle assigned cases.

To the extent possible, it is advisable to conduct the investigation of field audits in the practitioner's office, rather than the client's office. This procedure permits greater control over the audit investigation and facilitates the agent's review and prompt closure of the case.

Many practitioners feel that it is generally not advisable to have clients present at the scheduled conferences with the agent, since the client may give emotional or gratuitous comments that impair prompt settlement. If the client is not present, however, he or she should be advised of the status of negotiations. The client makes the final decision on any proposed settlement.

ETHICAL CONSIDERATIONS

Should the Client Attend an Audit?

Whether the client should be present during an audit is a matter of some debate. Certainly, the client's absence tends to slow down the negotiating process because the taxpayer must make all final decisions on settlement terms and is the best source of information for open questions of fact. Nevertheless, most practitioners discourage their clients from attending audits or conferences with the Appeals Division involving an income tax dispute. Ignorance of the law and of the conventions of the audit process can make the taxpayer a "loose cannon" that can do more harm than good if unchecked. All too often, they say, a client will "say too much" in the presence of a government official.

In reality, though, by discouraging clients from attending the audit, practitioners may be interfering with the IRS's function of gathering evidence, depending on what precisely the taxpayer is being prevented from saying. To many practitioners, a "wrong" answer is one that increases taxes, not one that misrepresents the truth. A popular saying among tax advisers is "Don't tell me more than I want to know." Although this philosophy is supportable under various professional codes of conduct, it is hardly defensible in the larger scheme of things.

In your opinion, under what circumstances should the client attend such a session? To what degree should the tax professional "coach" the client as to how to behave in that setting? Or do a taxpayer's rights include the right to increase his or her own tax liability?

Preparing for the Audit. The tax professional must prepare thoroughly for the audit or Appeals proceeding. Practitioners often cite the following steps as critical to such preparations. Carrying out a level of due diligence in preparing for the proceeding is part of the tax professional's responsibility in representing the client.

- Make certain that both sides agree on the issues to be resolved in the audit. The goal here is to limit the agent's list of open issues.
- Identify all of the facts underlying the issues in dispute, including those favorable to the IRS. Gather evidence to support the taxpayer's position, and evaluate the evidence supporting the other side.
- Research current tax law authorities that bear on the facts and open issues. Remember that the IRS agent is bound only by Supreme Court cases and IRS pronouncements. Determine the degree of discretion that the IRS is likely to have in disposing of the case.
- Prepare a list of points supporting and contradicting the taxpayer's case. Include both minor points bearing little weight and core principles. Short research memos will also be useful in the discussion with the agent. Points favoring the taxpayer should be mentioned during the discussion and "entered into the record."
- Prepare tax and interest computations showing the effects of points that are in dispute, so that the consequences of closing or compromising an issue can be readily determined.
- Determine a "litigation point" (i.e., at which the taxpayer will withdraw from further audit negotiation and pursue the case in the courts). This position should be based on the dollars of tax, interest, and penalty involved, the chances of prevailing in various trial-level courts, and other strategies discussed with the taxpayer. One must have an "end game" strategy for the audit, and thorough tax research is critical in developing that position in this context.

Offers in Compromise. The IRS is encouraging the use of offers in compromise to a greater degree than ever before as part of its "consumer-friendly" approach to its enforcement obligations and its efforts to bring more nonfilers into compliance with the tax system.

Both parties to a tax dispute may find a compromise offer useful because it conclusively settles all of the issues covered by the agreement and may include a favorable payment schedule for the taxpayer. On the other hand, several attributes of an offer in compromise may work to the detriment of the taxpayer. Just as the IRS no longer can raise new issues as part of the audit proceedings against the taxpayer, he or she cannot contest or appeal any such agreement. As part of the offer process, the taxpayer must disclose all relevant finances and resources, including details he or she might not want the government to know. Furthermore, both parties are bound to the filing positions established by the compromise for five tax years, a level of inflexibility that may work against a taxpayer whose circumstances change over time.

Documentation Issues.   The tax practitioner's workpapers should include all research memoranda, and a list of resolved and unresolved issues should be continually updated during the course of the IRS audit. Occasionally, agents request access to excessive amounts of accounting data in order to engage in a so-called fishing expedition. Providing blanket access to workpapers should be avoided. Workpapers should be carefully reviewed to minimize opportunities for the agent to raise new issues not otherwise apparent. It is generally advisable to provide the agent with copies of specific workpapers upon request. An accountant's workpapers generally are not privileged and may be subpoenaed by the IRS.

In unusual situations, a Special Agent may appear to gather evidence in the investigation of possible criminal fraud. When this occurs, the taxpayer should be advised to seek legal counsel to determine the extent of his or her cooperation in providing information to the agent. Further, it is frequently desirable for the tax adviser to consult personal legal counsel in such situations. If the taxpayer receives a Revenue Agent's Report (RAR), it generally indicates that the IRS has decided not to initiate criminal prosecution proceedings. The IRS usually does not take any action upon a tax deficiency until the criminal matter has been resolved.

PENALTIES

Penalties are imposed upon a taxpayer's failure to file a return or pay a tax when due. These penalties can be avoided if the failure is due to reasonable cause and not to willful neglect. Reasonable cause, however, has not been liberally interpreted by the courts and should not be relied upon in the routine situation.[62] A safer way to avoid the failure to file penalty is to obtain an extension of time for filing the return from the IRS.

The penalty for failure to pay estimated taxes can become quite severe. Often trapped by the provision are employed taxpayers with outside income. They may forget about their outside income and assume the amount withheld from wages and salaries is adequate to cover their liability. Not only does April 15 provide a real shock (in terms of the additional tax owed) for these persons, but a penalty situation may have evolved. One way for an employee to mitigate this problem (presuming the employer is willing to cooperate) is described in the following example.

EXAMPLE 21   Patty, a calendar year taxpayer, is employed by Finn Corporation and earns (after withholding) a monthly salary of $4,000 payable at the end of each month. Patty also receives income from outside sources (interest, dividends, and consulting fees). After some quick

---

[62]*Dustin v. Comm.*, 72–2 USTC ¶9610, 30 AFTR2d 72–5313, 467 F.2d
47 (CA–9, 1972), *aff'g.* 53 T.C. 491 (1969).

calculations in early October, Patty determines that she has underestimated her tax liability by $7,500 and will be subject to the penalty for the first two quarters of the year and part of the third quarter. Patty, therefore, completes a new Form W–4 in which she arbitrarily raises her income tax withholding by $2,500 a month. Finn accepts the Form W–4, and as a result, an extra $7,500 is paid to the IRS on Patty's account for the payroll period from October through December.

Patty avoids penalties for the underpayment for the first three quarters because withholding of taxes is allocated pro rata over the year involved. Thus, a portion of the additional $7,500 withheld in October–December is assigned to the January 1–April 15 period, the April 16–June 15 period, etc. Had Patty merely paid the IRS an additional $7,500 in October, the penalty would still have been assessed for the earlier quarters. ▼

KEY TERMS

Accuracy-related penalty, 25–15	Letter ruling, 25–4	Revenue Agent's Report (RAR), 25–9
Closing agreement, 25–11	Negligence, 25–15	Statute of limitations, 25–20
Determination letter, 25–5	Ninety-day letter, 25–9	
	Offer in compromise, 25–11	Substantial authority, 25–15
Enrolled agent (EA), 25–22	Reasonable cause, 25–14	Technical advice memorandum, 25–5
Fraud, 25–17		Thirty-day letter, 25–9

PROBLEM MATERIALS

DISCUSSION QUESTIONS

1. What is the role of the IRS in the revenue process?

2. What techniques other than the random selection of returns for audit does the IRS use in its enforcement function?

3. Should the IRS audit more or fewer returns every year? What issues would you consider in this regard if you were a politician? A wealthy individual?

4. Your tax supervisor has informed you that the firm has received an unfavorable answer to a ruling request. In a memo to the supervisor, describe the appropriate weight that she should assign to the holding in the ruling.

5. Who bears the burden of proof when the IRS challenges items reported on a tax return?

6. Sarah tells you, "I was worried about getting audited on the tax return I filed two months ago, but I received my refund check today, so the IRS must agree with my figures." Comment.

7. When should a taxpayer take a matter to the Tax Court's Small Cases Division?

8. On February 9, 1999, Quon, a calendar year taxpayer, files her 1998 income tax return on which she claims a $1,200 refund. If Quon receives her refund check on May 2, 1999, will it include any interest? Explain.

9. Indicate whether each of the following statements is true or false.
   a. The government never pays a taxpayer interest on an overpayment of tax.
   b. Penalties may be included as an itemized deduction on an individual's tax return, but net of the 2%-of-AGI floor.

    c. An extension of time for filing a return results in an automatic extension of the time in which the tax may be paid.

    d. The IRS can compromise on the amount of tax liability if there is doubt as to the taxpayer's ability to pay.

    e. The statute of limitations for assessing a tax never extends beyond three years from the filing of a return.

    f. A taxpayer's claim for a refund is not subject to a statute of limitations.

10. What is the role of the statute of limitations in the Federal income tax system? How do such statutes protect the taxpayer? The government?

11. In each of the following cases, distinguish between the terms.
    a. Offer in compromise and closing agreement.
    b. Failure to file and failure to pay.
    c. Ninety-day letter and thirty-day letter.
    d. Negligence and fraud.
    e. Criminal and civil penalties.

12. Lorraine, a vice president of Scott Corporation, prepared and filed the corporate Form 1120 for 1996. This return is being audited by the IRS in 1998.
    a. May Lorraine represent Scott during the audit?
    b. Can Lorraine's representation continue beyond the agent level (e.g., before the Appeals Division)?

13. Indicate which codes, canons, and other bodies of ethical statements apply to each of the following tax practitioners.
    a. CPAs who are members of the AICPA.
    b. CPAs who are not members of the AICPA.
    c. Attorneys.
    d. Enrolled agents.
    e. Tax preparers who are not CPAs, EAs, or attorneys.

PROBLEMS

14. Compute the failure to pay and failure to file penalties for John, who filed his 1997 income tax return on December 20, 1998, paying the $4,000 amount due. On April 1, 1998, John had received a four-month extension of time in which to file his return. He has no reasonable cause for failing to file his return by August 15 or for failing to pay the tax that was due on April 15, 1998. John's failure to comply with the tax laws was not fraudulent.

15. Rhoda, a calendar year taxpayer, files her 1998 return on March 11, 2000. She did not obtain an extension for filing her return, and the return reflects additional income tax due of $5,000.
    a. What are Rhoda's penalties for failure to file and to pay?
    b. Would your answer change if Rhoda, before the due date of the return, had retained a CPA to prepare the return and the CPA's negligence caused the delay?

16. Kim underpaid her taxes by $15,000. Of this amount, $9,500 was due to negligence on her part, as her record-keeping system is highly inadequate. Determine the amount of any negligence penalty.

17. Dana underpaid his taxes by $250,000. A portion of the underpayment was shown to be attributable to Dana's negligence ($40,000). Another portion of the deficiency was found to constitute civil fraud ($100,000). Compute the total penalties incurred.

18. Olivia, a calendar year taxpayer, does not file her 1997 return until June 4, 1998. At this point, she pays the $3,000 balance due on her 1997 tax liability of $30,000. Olivia did not apply for and obtain any extension of time for filing the 1997 return. When questioned by the IRS on her delinquency, Olivia asserts: "If I was too busy to file my regular tax return, I was too busy to request an extension."

    a. Is Olivia liable for any penalties for failure to file and for failure to pay?

    b. If so, compute the penalty amounts.

19. Compute the overvaluation penalty for each of the following independent cases involving the taxpayer's reporting of the fair market value of charitable contribution property. In each case, assume a marginal income tax rate of 30%.

Taxpayer	Corrected IRS Value	Reported Valuation
a. Individual	$ 40,000	$ 50,000
b. C corporation	40,000	60,000
c. S corporation	40,000	60,000
d. Individual	150,000	200,000
e. Individual	150,000	500,000
f. C corporation	150,000	800,000

20. Compute the undervaluation penalty for each of the following independent cases involving the executor's reporting of the value of a closely held business in the decedent's gross estate. In each case, assume a marginal estate tax rate of 50%.

	Reported Value	Corrected IRS Valuation
a.	$22,000	$ 25,000
b.	80,000	150,000
c.	80,000	200,000
d.	80,000	400,000

21. Arnold made a charitable contribution of property that he valued at $70,000. He deducted this amount as an itemized deduction on his tax return. The IRS can prove that the real value of the property is $55,000. Arnold is in the 36% income tax bracket. Determine Arnold's overvaluation penalty.

22. Marla owns and operates a tavern. Because she had been keeping "two sets of books," one for herself and one for the benefit of the IRS, she has been charged with civil fraud in the District Court. The IRS assesses an additional $75,000 in taxes, but Marla shows by a preponderance of the evidence that half of that amount was due to mere negligence, not to her fraudulent actions. Compute Marla's civil fraud tax penalty in this matter.

23. Moose, a former professional athlete, now supplements his income by signing autographs at collectors' shows. Unfortunately, Moose has not been conscientious about reporting all of this income on his tax return. Now, the IRS has charged him with additional taxes of $50,000 due to negligence in his record-keeping and $80,000 due to an intent to defraud the U.S. government of income taxes. No criminal fraud charges are brought against Moose. The District Court finds a preponderance of the evidence that only half of the $80,000 underpayment was due to Moose's fraudulent action; the remainder was due to mere negligence. Compute the accuracy-related and civil fraud penalties in this matter.

24. Trudy's AGI last year was $170,000. Her Federal income tax came to $50,000, which she paid through a combination of withholding and estimated payments. This year, her AGI will be $270,000, with a projected tax liability of $85,000, all to be paid through estimates. Ignore the annualized income method. Compute Trudy's quarterly estimated payment schedule for this year.

25. Kold Corporation estimates that its 1999 taxable income will be $500,000. Thus, it is subject to a flat 34% income tax rate and incurs a $170,000 liability. For each of the following independent cases, compute Kold's minimum quarterly estimated tax payments that will avoid an underpayment penalty.

    a. For 1998, taxable income was ($100,000). Kold carried back all of this loss to prior years and exhausted the entire net operating loss in creating a zero 1998 liability.

b. For 1998, taxable income was $300,000, and tax liability was $102,000.

c. For 1997, taxable income was $2 million, and tax liability was $680,000. For 1998, taxable income was $300,000, and tax liability was $102,000.

26. The Scooter Company, owned equally by Julie (chair of the board of directors) and Jeff (company president), is in very difficult financial straits. Last month, Jeff used the $100,000 withheld from employee paychecks for Federal payroll and income taxes to pay off a creditor who threatened to cut off all supplies. To keep the company afloat, Jeff used these government funds willfully for the operations of the business, but even that effort was not enough. The company missed the next two payrolls, and today other creditors took action to shut down Scooter altogether. How much will the IRS assess in taxes and penalties in this matter, and from whom? How can you as a tax professional best offer service to Julie, Jeff, and Scooter? Address these matters in a memo for the tax research file.

27. What is the applicable statute of limitations in each of the following independent situations?

a. No return was filed by the taxpayer.

b. In 1992, the taxpayer incurred a bad debt loss that she failed to claim.

c. On his 1992 return, a taxpayer inadvertently omitted a large amount of gross income.

d. Same as (c), except that the omission was deliberate.

e. For 1992, a taxpayer innocently overstated her deductions by a large amount.

28. Suzanne, a calendar year taxpayer, had the following transactions, all of which were properly reported on a timely return.

Gross receipts		$960,000
Less: Cost of sales		(800,000)
Gross profit		$160,000
Capital gain	$72,000	
Less: Capital loss	(24,000)	48,000
Total income		$208,000

a. Presuming the absence of fraud, how much of an omission from gross income is required before the six-year statute of limitations applies?

b. Would it matter if cost of sales had been inadvertently overstated by $100,000?

c. How does the situation change in the context of fraud by Suzanne?

29. On April 2, 1996, Mark filed his 1995 income tax return, which showed a tax due of $40,000. On June 1, 1998, he filed an amended return for 1995 that showed an additional tax of $12,000. Mark paid the additional amount. On May 18, 1999, Mark filed a claim for a refund of $18,000.

a. If Mark's claim for a refund is correct in amount, how much tax will he recover?

b. What is the period that interest runs with respect to Mark's claim for a refund?

c. How would you have advised him differently?

30. Mimi had $40,000 withheld in 1995. Due to a sizable amount of itemized deductions, she figured that she had no further tax to pay for the year. For this reason, and because of personal problems, and without securing an extension, she did not file her 1995 return until July 1, 1996. Actually, the return showed a refund of $2,400, which Mimi ultimately received. On May 10, 1999, Mimi filed a $16,000 claim for refund of her 1995 taxes.

a. How much, if any, of the $16,000 may Mimi recover?

b. Would it have made any difference if Mimi had requested and secured from the IRS an extension of time for filing her 1995 tax return?

31. Rod's Federal income tax returns (Form 1040) for the indicated three years were prepared by the following persons.

Year	Preparer
1997	Rod
1998	Ann
1999	Cheryl

Ann is Rod's next-door neighbor and owns and operates a pharmacy. Cheryl is a licensed CPA and is engaged in private practice. In the event Rod is audited and all three returns are examined, who may represent him before the IRS at the agent level? Who may represent Rod before the Appeals Division?

32. Discuss which penalties, if any, might be imposed on the tax adviser in each of the following independent circumstances. In this regard, assume that the tax adviser:
   a. Suggested to the client various means by which to acquire excludible income.
   b. Suggested to the client various means by which to conceal cash receipts from gross income.
   c. Suggested to the client means by which to improve her cash flow by delaying for six months or more the deposit of the employees' share of Federal employment taxes.
   d. Kept in his own safe deposit box the cash of item (b).
   e. Failed, because of pressing time conflicts, to conduct the usual review of the client's tax return. The IRS later discovered that the return included fraudulent data.
   f. Failed, because of pressing time conflicts, to conduct the usual review of the client's tax return. The IRS later discovered a mathematical error in the computation of the personal exemption.

33. Compute the preparer penalty that the IRS could assess on Gerry in each of the following independent cases.
   a. On March 21, the copy machine was not working, so Gerry gave original returns to her 30 clients that day without providing any duplicates for them. Copies for Gerry's files and for use in preparing state tax returns had been made on March 20.
   b. Because Gerry extended her vacation a few days, she missed the Annual Tax Update seminar that she usually attends. As a result, she was unaware that Congress had changed a law affecting limited partnerships. The change affected the transactions of 20 of Gerry's clients, all of whom understated their tax as a result.
   c. Gerry heard that the IRS was increasing its audits of corporations that hold assets in a foreign trust. As a result, Gerry instructed the intern who prepared the initial drafts of the returns for three corporate clients to leave blank the question about such trusts. Not wanting to lose his position, the intern, a senior accounting major at State University, complied with Gerry's instructions.

34. You are the chair of the Ethics Committee of your state's CPA Licensing Commission. Interpret controlling AICPA authority in addressing the following assertions by your membership.
   a. When a CPA has reasonable grounds for not answering an applicable question on a client's return, a brief explanation of the reason for the omission should not be provided, because it would flag the return for audit by the IRS.
   b. If a CPA discovers during an IRS audit that the client has a material error on the return under examination, he should immediately withdraw from the engagement.
   c. If the client tells you that she had contributions of $500 for unsubstantiated cash donations to her church, you should deduct an odd amount on her return (e.g., $499), because an even amount (i.e., $500) would indicate to the IRS that her deduction was based on an estimate.
   d. Basing an expense deduction on the client's estimates is not acceptable.
   e. If a CPA knows that the client has a material error on a prior year's return, he should not, without the client's consent, disclose the error to the IRS.
   f. If a CPA's client will not correct a material error on a prior year's return, the CPA should not prepare the current year's return for the client.

Research Problems for this chapter appear at the end of Chapter 28.

TEAM PROJECT: ARTHUR ANDERSEN TAX CHALLENGE CASES

For more information on the Arthur Andersen Tax Challenge Cases, please refer to Chapter 1, page 1–37.

Information related to tax issues and problems that are discussed in this chapter may be found in the

Day and Ball case on pages 1 and 4
Fence case on page 42

Read and analyze the case you have been assigned and *identify* any issues and problems that are related to material covered in this chapter. If the information provided in the case is complete, prepare answers for this part of the case at this time. If you need information that is contained in the later parts of the case, please write a memo summarizing the questions or problems so you can prepare a complete answer at a later date.

26

THE FEDERAL GIFT AND ESTATE TAXES

LEARNING OBJECTIVES

After completing Chapter 26, you should be able to:

1. Understand the nature of the Federal gift and estate taxes.

2. Work with the Federal gift tax formula.

3. Work with the Federal estate tax formula.

4. Explain the operation of the Federal gift tax.

5. Illustrate the computation of the Federal gift tax.

6. Review the components of the gross estate.

7. Describe the components of the taxable estate.

8. Determine the Federal estate tax liability.

9. Appreciate the role of the generation-skipping transfer tax.

TRANSFER TAXES—IN GENERAL

Until now, this text has dealt primarily with the various applications of the Federal income tax. Also important in the Federal tax structure are various excise taxes that cover transfers of property. Sometimes called transaction taxes, excise taxes are based on the value of the property transferred and not on the income derived from the property. Two such taxes—the Federal gift tax and the Federal estate tax—are the central focus of this chapter.

The importance of being familiar with rules governing transfer taxes can be shown with a simple illustration.

EXAMPLE 1

After 20 years of marriage to George, Helen decides to elope with Mark, a bachelor and long-time friend. Helen and Mark travel to a country in the Caribbean where Helen obtains a divorce, and she and Mark are married. Fifteen years later, Helen dies. Her will leaves all of her property (estimated value of $2,500,000) to Mark. Under the unlimited marital deduction (discussed later in the chapter), Helen's estate has no tax to pay. ▼

But the marital deduction applies only to transfers between husband and wife. Suppose the jurisdiction where Helen and Mark live does not recognize the validity of divorces granted by the Caribbean country involved. If this is the case, Helen and Mark are not married because Helen was never legally divorced from George. If Mark is not Helen's spouse, no marital deduction is available. Before considering the effect of any potential tax credits, Helen's estate must pay an estate tax of $1,025,800.

NATURE OF THE TAXES

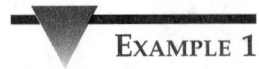
1 LEARNING OBJECTIVE
Understand the nature of the Federal gift and estate taxes.

Before the enactment of the Tax Reform Act of 1976, Federal law imposed a tax on the gratuitous transfer of property in one of two ways. If the transfer was during the owner's life, it was subject to the Federal gift tax. If the property passed by virtue of the death of the owner, the Federal estate tax applied. The two taxes were governed by different rules including a separate set of tax rates. As Congress felt that lifetime transfers of wealth should be encouraged, the gift tax rates were lower than the estate tax rates.

The Tax Reform Act of 1976 significantly changed the approach taken by the Federal gift and estate taxes. Much of the distinction between life and death

TAX IN THE NEWS

DO TRANSFER TAXES ADVERSELY AFFECT THE ECONOMY?

A recent study found that transfer taxes (i.e., estate and gift taxes) impose especially high economic costs in terms of lost savings and capital formation. This burden is particularly high on small family-owned businesses.

As another layer of tax on savings, transfer taxes increase the cost of wealth accumulation as compared to the cost of consumption. According to an econometric simulation of what would have happened to the U.S. economy between 1971 and 1991 without Federal transfer taxes, 262,000 more jobs would have been created, the stock of capital would have been $398.6 billion higher, and the gross domestic product would have been $46.3 billion higher in 1991.

The study concludes that repeal of the Federal estate and gift taxes would strengthen the incentive people have to create capital and would lead to higher wages, greater employment, and larger overall tax collections over the long run.

SOURCE: Richard E. Wagner, *Federal Transfer Taxation: A Study in Social Cost* (Washington, D.C.: Institute for Research on the Economics of Taxation, The Center for the Study of Taxation, 1993).

transfers was eliminated. Instead of subjecting these different types of transfers to two separate tax rate schedules, the Act substituted a **unified transfer tax** to cover all gratuitous transfers. Thus, gifts are subject to tax at the same rates as those applicable to transfers at death. In addition, current law eliminates the prior exemptions allowed under each tax and replaces them with a unified tax credit.

The Federal estate (or death) tax is designed to tax transfers at death. The tax differs, in several respects, from the typical **inheritance tax** imposed by many states and some local jurisdictions. First, the Federal *estate tax* is imposed on the decedent's entire taxable estate. It is a tax on the right to pass property at death. *Inheritance taxes* are taxes on the right to receive property at death and are therefore levied on the heirs. Second, the relationship of the heirs to the decedent usually has a direct bearing on the inheritance tax. In general, the more closely related the parties, the larger the exemption and the lower the applicable rates.[1] Except for transfers to a surviving spouse that may result in a marital deduction, the relationship of the heirs to the decedent has no effect on the Federal estate tax.

The Federal gift tax, enacted several years after the enactment of the Federal estate tax, was designed to make the income and estate taxes more effective. Congress felt that individuals should not be able to give away property—thereby shifting the income tax consequences to others and avoiding estate taxes—without incurring some tax liability. The result is the Federal gift tax, which covers *inter vivos* (lifetime) transfers.

The Federal gift tax is imposed on the right of one person (the donor) to transfer property to another (the donee) for less than full and adequate consideration. The tax is payable by the donor.[2] If the donor fails to pay the tax when

---

[1] For example, one state's inheritance tax provides an exemption of $50,000 for surviving spouses, with rates ranging from 5% to 10% on the taxable portion. This is to be contrasted with an exemption of only $1,000 for strangers (persons unrelated to the deceased), with rates ranging from 14% to 18% on the taxable portion. Other exemptions and rates fall between these extremes to cover beneficiaries variously related to the decedent.

[2] § 2502(c).

due, the donee may be held liable for the tax to the extent of the value of the property received.[3]

Persons Subject to the Tax. To determine whether a transfer is subject to the Federal gift tax, first ascertain if the donor is a citizen or resident of the United States. If the donor is not a citizen or a resident, it is important to determine whether the property involved in the gift was situated within the United States.

The Federal gift tax is applied to all transfers by gift of property wherever located by individuals who, at the time of the gift, were *citizens* or *residents* of the United States. The term "United States" includes only the 50 states and the District of Columbia; it does not include U.S. possessions or territories.[4] For a U.S. citizen, the place of residence at the time of the gift is irrelevant.

For individuals who are neither citizens nor residents of the United States, the Federal gift tax is applied only to gifts of property situated within the United States.[5] A gift of intangible personal property (e.g., stocks and bonds) by a nonresident alien usually is not subject to the Federal gift tax.[6]

A gift by a corporation is considered a gift by the individual shareholders. A gift to a corporation is generally considered a gift to the individual shareholders. In certain cases, however, a gift to a charitable, public, political, or similar organization may be regarded as a gift to the organization as a single entity.[7]

The Federal estate tax is applied to the entire taxable estate of a decedent who, at the time of death, was a resident or citizen of the United States. If the decedent was a U.S. citizen, the residence at death makes no difference.[8]

ETHICAL CONSIDERATIONS

Can You Run Away?

During his lifetime, Willard Heard has accumulated considerable wealth. Upon consulting with a tax planner, Willard is appalled by how much Federal estate tax will be due upon his death.

To avoid the estate tax, Willard proposes to do the following:

- Renounce his U.S. citizenship.
- Abandon U.S. residency.
- Become a resident and citizen of Belize. Belize imposes neither an income tax nor a death tax.

Comment on Willard's proposed planning approach.

If the decedent was neither a resident nor a citizen of the United States at the time of death, the Federal estate tax is imposed on the value of any property located within the United States. In that case, the tax determination is controlled by a

---

[3] § 6324(b). Known as the doctrine of transferee liability, this rule also operates to enable the IRS to enforce the collection of other taxes (e.g., income tax, estate tax).
[4] § 7701(a)(9).
[5] § 2511(a).
[6] §§ 2501(a)(2) and (3). But see § 2511(b) and Reg. §§ 25.2511–3(b)(2), (3), and (4) for exceptions.

[7] Reg. §§ 25.0–1(b) and 25.2511–1(h)(1). But note the exemption from the Federal gift tax for certain transfers to political organizations discussed later.
[8] § 2001(a).

separate subchapter of the Internal Revenue Code.[9] In certain instances, these tax consequences outlined in the Code may have been modified by death tax conventions (treaties) between the United States and various foreign countries.[10] Further coverage of this area is beyond the scope of this text. The following discussion is limited to the tax treatment of decedents who were residents or citizens of the United States at the time of death.[11]

2 LEARNING OBJECTIVE
Work with the Federal gift tax formula.

Formula for the Gift Tax. Like the income tax, which uses taxable income (and not gross income) as a tax base, the gift tax usually does not apply to the full amount of the gift. Deductions and the annual exclusion may be allowed to arrive at an amount called the **taxable gift.** However, unlike the income tax, which does not consider taxable income from prior years, *prior taxable gifts* must be added to arrive at the tax base to which the unified transfer tax rate is applied. Otherwise, the donor could start over again each year with a new set of progressive rates.

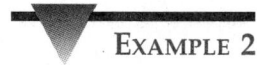

EXAMPLE 2

Don makes taxable gifts of $500,000 in 1985 and $500,000 in 1998. Presuming no other taxable gifts and disregarding the effect of the unified tax credit, Don must pay a tax of $155,800 (see applicable tax rate schedule in Appendix A) on the 1985 transfer and a tax of $345,800 on the 1998 transfer (using a tax base of $1 million). If the 1985 taxable gift had not been included in the tax base for the 1998 gift, the tax would have been $155,800. The correct tax liability of $345,800 is more than twice $155,800! ▼

Because the gift tax is cumulative in effect, a credit is allowed for the gift taxes paid (or deemed paid) on prior taxable gifts included in the tax base. The deemed paid credit is explained later in the chapter.

EXAMPLE 3

Assume the same facts as in Example 2. Don is allowed a credit of $155,800 against the gift tax of $345,800. Thus, his gift tax liability for 1998 becomes $190,000 ($345,800 – $155,800). ▼

In 1982, the annual exclusion was increased from $3,000 to $10,000. By allowing larger amounts to be exempt from the gift tax, taxpayer compliance may improve, as the tax will apply only to larger, planned gifts and not to day-to-day transfers. As noted in Chapter 1, the result is to ease the audit function of the IRS. Effective for years after 1998, the annual exclusion will be indexed to account for inflation.

The formula for the gift tax is summarized in Figure 26–1. [Note: Section (§) references are to the portion of the Internal Revenue Code involved.]

3 LEARNING OBJECTIVE
Work with the Federal estate tax formula.

Formula for the Federal Estate Tax. The Federal unified transfer tax at death, commonly known as the Federal estate tax, is summarized in Figure 26–2.

The gross estate is determined by using the fair market value of the property on the date of the decedent's death (or on the alternate valuation date if applicable).

The reason post-1976 taxable gifts are added to the taxable estate to arrive at the tax base goes back to the scheme of the unified transfer tax. Starting in 1977, all transfers, whether lifetime or by death, are treated the same. Consequently, taxable gifts made after 1976 must be accounted for upon the death

---

[9]Subchapter B (§§ 2101 through 2108) covers the estate tax treatment of decedents who are neither residents nor citizens. Subchapter A (§§ 2001 through 2056A) covers the estate tax treatment of those who are either residents or citizens.

[10]At present, the United States has death tax conventions with the following countries: Australia, Austria, Canada, Denmark, Finland, France, Germany, Greece, Ireland, Italy, Japan, Netherlands, Norway, Republic of South Africa, Sweden, Switzerland, and the

United Kingdom. The United States has gift tax conventions with Australia, Austria, Denmark, France, Germany, Japan, and the United Kingdom.

[11]Further information concerning Subchapter B (§§ 2101 through 2108) can be obtained from the relevant Code sections (and the current Treasury Regulations thereunder). See also the Instructions to Form 706NA (U.S. Estate Tax Return of Nonresident Not a Citizen of the U.S.).

▼ **FIGURE 26–1**
Gift Tax Formula

Determine whether the transfers are considered gifts by referring to §§ 2511 through 2519; list the fair market value of only the covered transfers		$ xxx,xxx
Determine the deductions allowed by §§ 2522 (charitable) and 2523 (marital)	$xx,xxx	
Claim the annual exclusion ($10,000 per donee) under § 2503(b), if available	xx,xxx	(xx,xxx)
Taxable gifts [as defined by § 2503(a)] for the current period		$ xx,xxx
Add: Taxable gifts from prior years		xx,xxx
Total of current and past taxable gifts		$ xx,xxx
Compute the gift tax on the total of current and past taxable gifts by using the rates in Appendix A		$ x,xxx
Subtract: Gift tax paid or deemed paid on past taxable gifts and the unified tax credit		(xxx)
Gift tax due on transfers during the current period		$ xxx

▼ **FIGURE 26–2**
Estate Tax Formula

Gross estate (§§ 2031–2046)		$ xxx,xxx
Subtract:		
Expenses, indebtedness, and taxes (§ 2053)	$xx,xxx	
Losses (§ 2054)	xx,xxx	
Charitable bequests (§ 2055)	xx,xxx	
Marital deduction (§§ 2056 and 2056A)	xx,xxx	(xx,xxx)
Taxable estate (§ 2051)		$ xx,xxx
Add: Post-1976 taxable gifts [§ 2001(b)]		x,xxx
Tax base		$ xxx,xxx
Tentative tax on total transfers [§ 2001(c)]		$ xx,xxx
Subtract:		
Unified transfer tax on post-1976 taxable gifts (gift taxes paid or deemed paid)	$ x,xxx	
Tax credits (including the unified tax credit) (§§ 2010–2016)	x,xxx	(x,xxx)
Estate tax due		$ x,xxx

of the donor. Note that the double tax effect of including these gifts is eliminated by allowing a credit against the estate tax for the gift taxes previously paid or deemed paid.

Role of the Unified Tax Credit.   Before the unified transfer tax, the gift tax allowed a $30,000 specific exemption for the lifetime of the donor. A comparable $60,000 exemption was allowed for estate tax purposes. The purpose of these exemptions was to allow donors and decedents to transfer modest amounts of wealth without being subject to the gift and estate taxes. Unfortunately, inflation took its toll, and more taxpayers became subject to these transfer taxes than Congress

▼ TABLE 26–1
Phase-in of Unified Tax Credit

Year of Death	Amount of Credit	Exemption Equivalent
1977	$ 30,000	$ 120,667
1978	34,000	134,000
1979	38,000	147,333
1980	42,500	161,563
1981	47,000	175,625
1982	62,800	225,000
1983	79,300	275,000
1984	96,300	325,000
1985	121,800	400,000
1986	155,800	500,000
1987 through 1997	192,800	600,000
1998	202,050	625,000
1999	211,300	650,000
2000 and 2001	220,550	675,000
2002 and 2003	229,800	700,000
2004	287,300	850,000
2005	326,300	950,000
2006 and after	345,800	1,000,000

felt was appropriate. The congressional solution, therefore, was to rescind the exemptions and replace them with the **unified tax credit.**[12]

To curtail revenue loss, the credit was phased in as shown in Table 26–1. The **exemption equivalent** is the amount of the transfer that will pass free of the gift or estate tax by virtue of the credit.

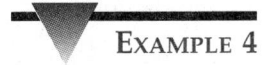

EXAMPLE 4

In 1998, Janet makes a taxable gift of $625,000. Presuming she has made no prior taxable gifts, Janet will not owe any gift tax. Under the applicable tax rate schedule (see Appendix A), the tax on $625,000 is $202,050, which is the exact amount of the credit allowed.[13] ▼

The Tax Reform Act of 1976 allowed donors one last chance to use the $30,000 specific exemption on lifetime gifts. If, however, the exemption was used on gifts made after September 8, 1976 (and before January 1, 1977), the unified tax credit must be reduced by 20 percent of the exemption utilized.[14] The credit must be readjusted whether the gift tax or the estate tax is involved. No adjustment is necessary for post-1976 gifts since the specific exemption is no longer available for such transfers.

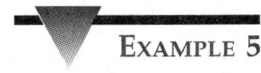

EXAMPLE 5

Net of the annual exclusion, Myrtle, a widow, made gifts of $10,000 in June 1976 and $20,000 in December 1976. Assume Myrtle had never used any of her specific exemption and chose to use the full $30,000 to cover the 1976 gifts. Under these circumstances, the unified tax credit will be reduced by $4,000 (20% × $20,000). The use of the specific exemption on transfers made before September 9, 1976, has no effect on the credit. ▼

---

[12]§§ 2010 and 2505.

[13]The rate schedules are contained in § 2001(c). Neither the credit nor the rate schedule is subject to indexation.

[14]§§ 2010(c) and 2505(c).

VALUATION FOR ESTATE AND GIFT TAX PURPOSES

The value of the property on the date of its transfer generally determines the amount that is subject to the gift tax or the estate tax. Under certain conditions, however, an executor can elect to value estate assets on the **alternate valuation date** (§ 2032).

The alternate valuation date election was designed as a relief provision to ease the economic hardship that could result when estate assets decline in value over the six months after the date of death. If the election is made, all assets of the estate are valued six months after death *or* on the date of disposition if this occurs earlier.[15] The election covers *all* assets in the gross estate and cannot be applied to only a portion of the property.

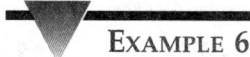

EXAMPLE 6

Robert's gross estate consists of the following property:

	Value on Date of Death	Value Six Months Later
Land	$ 800,000	$ 840,000
Stock in Brown Corporation	900,000	700,000
Stock in Green Corporation	500,000	460,000
Total	$2,200,000	$2,000,000

If Robert's executor elects the alternate valuation date, the estate must be valued at $2,000,000. It is not permissible to value the land at its date of death value ($800,000) and choose the alternate valuation date for the rest of the gross estate. ▼

EXAMPLE 7

Assume the same facts as in Example 6, except that the executor sells the stock in Green Corporation for $480,000 four months after Robert's death. If the alternate valuation date is elected, the estate must be valued at $2,020,000 ($840,000 + $700,000 + $480,000). As to the Green stock, the value on its date of disposition controls because that date occurred prior to the six months' alternate valuation date. ▼

The election of the alternate valuation date must decrease the value of the gross estate *and* decrease the estate tax liability.[16] The reason for this last requirement is that the income tax basis of property acquired from a decedent will be the value used for estate tax purposes.[17] Without a special limitation, the alternate valuation date could be elected solely to add to income tax basis.

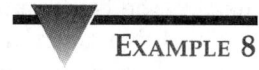

EXAMPLE 8

Al's gross estate is comprised of assets with a date of death value of $1,000,000 and an alternate valuation date value of $1,100,000. Under Al's will, all of his property passes outright to Jean (Al's wife). Because of the marital deduction, no estate tax results regardless of which value is used. But if the alternate valuation date could be elected, Jean would have an income tax basis of $1,100,000 in the property acquired from Al. ▼

The alternate valuation date cannot be elected in Example 8 for two reasons, either of which would suffice. First, the alternate valuation date will not decrease Al's gross estate. Second, the election will not decrease Al's estate tax liability. Thus, his estate must use the date of death valuation of $1,000,000. As a result, Jean's income tax basis in the property received from Al is $1,000,000.

---

[15] § 2032(a).
[16] § 2032(c).

[17] § 1014(a).

KEY PROPERTY CONCEPTS

When property is transferred either by gift or by death, the form of ownership can have a direct bearing on any transfer tax consequences. Understanding the different forms of ownership is necessary for working with Federal gift and estate taxes.

Undivided Ownership. Assume Dan and Vicky own an undivided but equal interest in a tract of land. Such ownership can fall into any of four categories: joint tenancy, tenancy by the entirety, tenancy in common, or community property.

If Dan and Vicky hold ownership as **joint tenants** or **tenants by the entirety,** the right of survivorship exists. This means that the last tenant to survive receives full ownership of the property. Thus, if Dan predeceases Vicky, the land belongs entirely to Vicky. None of the land passes to Dan's heirs or is subject to administration by Dan's executor. A tenancy by the entirety is a joint tenancy between husband and wife.

If Dan and Vicky hold ownership as **tenants in common** or as community property, death does not defeat an owner's interest. Thus, if Dan predeceases Vicky, Dan's half interest in the land passes to his estate or heirs.

Community property interests arise from the marital relationship. Normally, all property acquired after marriage, except by gift or inheritance, by husband and wife residing in a community property state becomes part of the community. The following states have the community property system in effect: Louisiana, Texas, New Mexico, Arizona, California, Washington, Idaho, Nevada, and Wisconsin. All other states follow the common law system of ascertaining a spouse's rights to property acquired after marriage.

Partial Interests. Interests in assets can be divided in terms of rights to income and rights to principal. Particularly when property is placed in trust, it is not uncommon to carve out various income interests that must be accounted for separately from the ultimate disposition of the property itself.

EXAMPLE 9

Under Bill's will, a ranch is to be placed in trust, life estate to Sam, Bill's son, with remainder to Sam's children (Bill's grandchildren). Under this arrangement, Sam is the life tenant and, as such, is entitled to the use of the ranch (including any income) during his life. Upon Sam's death, the trust terminates, and its principal passes to his children. Thus, Sam's children receive outright ownership of the ranch when Sam dies. ▼

THE FEDERAL GIFT TAX

GENERAL CONSIDERATIONS

4 **LEARNING OBJECTIVE**
Explain the operation of the Federal gift tax.

Requirements for a Gift. For a gift to be complete under state law, the following elements must be present:

- A donor competent to make the gift.
- A donee capable of receiving and possessing the property.
- Donative intent on behalf of the donor.
- Actual or constructive delivery of the property to the donee or the donee's representative.
- Acceptance of the gift by the donee.

PAYING OFF THE LONGTIME COMPANION

A wealthy banker entered into a "close and exclusive" relationship with a woman not his wife. To devote more time to the banker, the friend closed an interior decorating business she was operating. After nine years, the banker ended the relationship. To keep the matter from becoming public and to secure his friend's release from any support claim (i.e., palimony), the banker purchased a 20-year annuity for her. The relationship and its settlement remained secret until the banker died a decade later.

The IRS is pursuing the banker's estate for the gift tax that should have been paid as a result of the annuity settlement. The estate maintains that the settlement was not a gift but was in "exchange for a good and valuable consideration." According to the estate, the consideration was the "general release" from any support claim signed by the former companion and her agreement not to disclose the relationship.

At this time, the controversy is still pending before the U.S. Tax Court.

Incomplete Transfers.   The Federal gift tax does not apply to transfers that are incomplete. Thus, if the transferor retains the right to reclaim the property or has not really parted with the possession of the property, a taxable event has not taken place.

EXAMPLE 10

Lesly creates a trust with income payable to Mary for life, remainder to Paul. Under the terms of the trust instrument, Lesly can revoke the trust at any time and repossess the trust principal and income earned. No gift takes place on the creation of the trust; Lesly has not ceased to have dominion and control over the property. ▼

EXAMPLE 11

Assume the same facts as in Example 10, except that one year after the transfer, Lesly relinquishes his right to terminate the trust. At this point, the transfer becomes complete, and the Federal gift tax applies. ▼

Business versus Personal Setting.   In a business setting, full and adequate consideration is apt to exist. Regulation § 25.2512–8 provides that "a sale, exchange, or other transfer of property made in the ordinary course of business (a transaction that is bona fide, at arm's length, and free of any donative intent) will be considered as made for an adequate and full consideration in money or money's worth." If the parties are acting in a personal setting, a gift is usually the result. Regulation § 25.2512–8 also holds that valuable consideration (such as would preclude a gift result) does not include a payment or transfer based on "love and affection . . . promise of marriage, etc." Consequently, property settlements in consideration of marriage (i.e., pre- or antenuptial agreements) are regarded as gifts.

Do not conclude that the presence of *some* consideration is enough to preclude Federal gift tax consequences. Again, the answer may rest on whether the transfer occurred in a business setting.

EXAMPLE 12

Peter sells Bob some real estate for $40,000. Unknown to Peter, the property contains valuable mineral deposits and is really worth $100,000. Peter may have made a bad business deal, but he has not made a gift of $60,000 to Bob. ▼

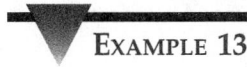

EXAMPLE 13

Assume the same facts as in Example 12, except that Peter and Bob are father and son. In addition, Peter is very much aware that the property is worth $100,000. Peter has made a gift of $60,000 to Bob. ▼

Certain Excluded Transfers. Transfers to political organizations are exempt from the application of the Federal gift tax.[18] This provision in the Code made unnecessary the previous practice whereby candidates for public office established multiple campaign committees to maximize the number of annual exclusions available to their contributors. As noted, an annual exclusion of $10,000 (previously $3,000) for each donee passes free of the Federal gift tax.

The Federal gift tax does not apply to tuition payments made to an educational organization (e.g., a college) on another's behalf. Nor does it apply to amounts paid on another's behalf for medical care.[19] In this regard, the law is realistic since it is unlikely that most donors would recognize these items as being transfers subject to the gift tax.

Satisfying an obligation of support is not subject to the gift tax. Thus, no gift takes place when parents pay for their children's education because one of the obligations of parents is to educate their children. What constitutes an obligation of support is determined by applicable state law.

Lifetime versus Death Transfers. Be careful to distinguish between lifetime (inter vivos) and death (testamentary) transfers.

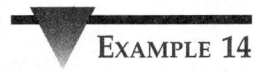

EXAMPLE 14

Wilbur buys a U.S. savings bond, which he registers as follows: "Wilbur, payable to Alice upon Wilbur's death." No gift is made when Wilbur buys the bond; Alice has received only a mere expectancy (right to obtain ownership of the bond at Wilbur's death). Anytime before his death, Wilbur may redeem or otherwise dispose of the bond and cut off Alice's interest. On Wilbur's death, no gift is made because the bond passes to Alice by testamentary disposition. As noted later, the bond will be included in Wilbur's gross estate as property in which the decedent had an interest (§ 2033). ▼

TRANSFERS SUBJECT TO THE GIFT TAX

Whether a transfer is subject to the Federal gift tax depends upon the application of §§ 2511 through 2519 and the applicable Regulations.

Gift Loans. To understand the tax ramifications of gift loans, an illustration is helpful.

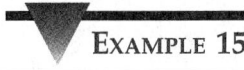

EXAMPLE 15

Before his daughter Denise leaves for college, Victor lends her $300,000. Denise signs a note that provides for repayment in five years. The loan contains no interest element, and neither Victor nor Denise expects any interest to be paid. Following Victor's advice, Denise invests the loan proceeds in income-producing securities. During her five years in college, she uses the income from the investments to pay for college costs and other living expenses. On the maturity date of the note, Denise repays the $300,000 she owes Victor. ▼

In a gift loan arrangement, the following consequences result:

- Victor has made a gift to Denise of the interest element. The amount of the gift is determined by the difference between the amount of interest charged

---

[18]§ 2501(a)(5).

[19]§ 2503(e).

(in this case, none) and the market rate (as determined by the yield on certain U.S. government securities).

- The interest element is included in Victor's gross income and is subject to the Federal income tax.
- Denise may be allowed an income tax deduction for the interest element, but may benefit from this result only if she is in a position to itemize her deductions *from* adjusted gross income.

The Code defines a gift loan as "any below-market loan where the forgoing of interest is in the nature of a gift."[20] Unless tax avoidance was one of the principal purposes of the loan, special limitations apply if the gift loan does not exceed $100,000. In such a case, the interest element may not exceed the borrower's net investment income.[21] Furthermore, if the net investment income does not exceed $1,000, it is treated as zero. Under a $1,000 *de minimis* rule, the interest element is disregarded.

Certain Property Settlements (§ 2516).

Normally, the settlement of certain marital rights is not regarded as being for consideration and is subject to the Federal gift tax.[22] As a special exception to this general approach, Congress enacted § 2516. By this provision, transfers of property interests made under the terms of a written agreement between spouses in settlement of their marital or property rights are deemed to be for adequate consideration. The transfers are exempt from the Federal gift tax if a final decree of divorce is obtained within the three-year period beginning on the date one year before the parties entered into the agreement. Likewise excluded are transfers to provide a reasonable allowance for the support of minor children (including legally adopted children) of a marriage. The agreement need not be approved by the divorce decree.

Disclaimers (§ 2518).

A **disclaimer** is a refusal by a person to accept property that is designated to pass to him or her. The effect of the disclaimer is to pass the property to someone else.

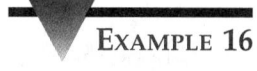

EXAMPLE 16

Earl dies without a will and is survived by a son, Andy, and a grandson, Jay. At the time of his death, Earl owned real estate that, under the applicable state law, passes to the closest lineal descendant, Andy in this case. If, however, Andy disclaims his interest in the real estate, state law provides that the property passes to Jay. At the time of Earl's death, Andy has considerable property of his own, and Jay has none. ▼

Why might Andy want to consider disclaiming his inheritance and have the property pass directly from Earl to Jay? By doing so, an extra transfer tax may be avoided. If the disclaimer does not take place (Andy accepts the inheritance), and the property eventually passes to Jay (either by gift or by death), the later transfer is subject to the application of either the gift tax or the estate tax.

For many years, whether a disclaimer was effective in avoiding a Federal transfer tax depended on the application of state law. To illustrate by using the facts of Example 16, if state law determined that the real estate was deemed to have passed through Andy despite his disclaimer after Earl's death, the Federal gift tax applied. In essence, Andy was treated as if he had inherited the property from Earl and then given it to Jay. As state law was not always

---

[20]§ 7872(f)(3).

[21]Net investment income has the same meaning given to the term by § 163(d). Generally, net investment income is investment income (e.g., interest, dividends) less related expenses.

[22]Reg. § 25.2512–8.

consistent in this regard and sometimes was not even known, the application or nonapplication of Federal transfer taxes depended on where the parties lived. To remedy this situation and provide some measure of uniformity, §§ 2046 (relating to disclaimers for estate tax purposes) and 2518 were added to the Code.

In the case of the gift tax, when the requirements of § 2518 are met and Andy makes a timely lifetime disclaimer (refer to Example 16), the property is treated as if it goes directly from Earl to Jay. Since the property is not treated as passing through Andy (regardless of what state law holds), it is not subject to the Federal gift tax.

The tax law also permits the Federal gift tax to be avoided in cases of a partial disclaimer of an undivided interest.

EXAMPLE 17

Assume the same facts as in Example 16, except that Andy wishes to retain half of the real estate for himself. If Andy makes a timely disclaimer of an undivided one-half interest in the property, the Federal gift tax does not apply to the portion passing to Jay. ▼

Other Transfers Subject to Gift Tax. Other transfers that may carry gift tax consequences (e.g., the creation of joint ownership) are discussed and illustrated in connection with the Federal estate tax.

ANNUAL EXCLUSION

The first $10,000 of gifts made to any one person during any calendar year (except gifts of future interests in property) is excluded in determining the total amount of gifts for the year.[23] The **annual exclusion** applies to all gifts of a present interest made during the calendar year in the order in which they are made until the $10,000 exclusion per donee is exhausted. For a gift in trust, each beneficiary of the trust is treated as a separate person for purposes of the exclusion.

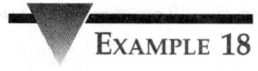

EXAMPLE 18

During the current year, Laura makes the following cash gifts: $8,000 to Rita and $12,000 to Maureen. Laura may claim an annual exclusion of $8,000 with respect to Rita and $10,000 with respect to Maureen. ▼

A **future interest** is defined as one that will come into being (as to use, possession, or enjoyment) at some future date. Examples of future interests include such rights as remainder interests that are commonly encountered when property is transferred to a trust. A *present interest* is an unrestricted right to the immediate use, possession, or enjoyment of property or of the income.

EXAMPLE 19

By a lifetime gift, Ron transfers property to a trust with a life estate (with income payable annually) to June and remainder upon June's death to Albert. Ron has made two gifts: one to June of a life estate and one to Albert of a remainder interest. The life estate is a present interest and qualifies for the annual exclusion. The remainder interest granted to Albert is a future interest and does not qualify for the exclusion. Note that Albert's interest does not come into being until some future date (on the death of June). ▼

Although Example 19 indicates that the gift of an income interest is a present interest, this is not always the case. If a possibility exists that the income beneficiary may not receive the immediate enjoyment of the property, the transfer is of a future interest.

---

[23]§ 2503(b).

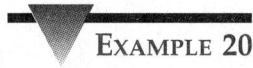
EXAMPLE 20

Assume the same facts as in Example 19, except that the income from the trust need not be payable annually to June. It may, at the trustee's discretion, be accumulated and added to corpus. Since June's right to receive the income from the trust is conditioned on the trustee's discretion, it is not a present interest. No annual exclusion is allowed. The mere possibility of diversion is enough. It would not matter if the trustee never exercised the discretion to accumulate and did, in fact, distribute the trust income to June annually. ▼

Trust for Minors.   Section 2503(c) offers an exception to the future interest rules just discussed. Under this provision, a transfer for the benefit of a person who has not attained the age of 21 years on the date of the gift may be considered a gift of a present interest. This is true even though the minor is not given the unrestricted right to the immediate use, possession, or enjoyment of the property. For the exception to apply, however, certain stringent conditions must be satisfied. One such condition is that all of the property and its income must be made available to the minor upon attaining age 21. Thus, the exception allows a trustee to accumulate income on behalf of a minor beneficiary without converting the income interest to a future interest.

DEDUCTIONS

In arriving at taxable gifts, a deduction is allowed for transfers to certain qualified charitable organizations. On transfers between spouses, a marital deduction may be available. Since both the charitable and marital deductions apply in determining the Federal estate tax, they are discussed later in the chapter.

COMPUTING THE FEDERAL GIFT TAX

5 **LEARNING OBJECTIVE**
Illustrate the computation of the Federal gift tax.

The Unified Transfer Tax Rate Schedule.   The top rates of the unified transfer tax rate schedule originally reached as high as 70 percent. Over the years, these top rates have been reduced to 55 percent. As noted later in the chapter, the benefits of the graduated rates are phased out for larger gifts. Keep in mind that the unified transfer tax rate schedule applies to all transfers (by gift or death) after 1976. Different rate schedules applied for pre-1977 gifts and pre-1977 death transfers.

The Deemed-Paid Adjustment.   Review the formula for the gift tax (refer to Figure 26–1) and note that the tax base for a current gift includes *all* past taxable gifts. The effect of the inclusion is to force the current taxable gift into a higher bracket due to the progressive nature of the unified transfer tax rates (refer to Example 2). To mitigate such double taxation, the donor is allowed a credit for any gift tax previously paid or deemed paid (refer to Example 3).

Limiting the donor to a credit for the gift tax *actually paid* on pre-1977 taxable gifts would be unfair. Pre-1977 taxable gifts were subject to a lower set of rates than those in the unified transfer tax rate schedule. As a consequence, the donor is allowed a *deemed-paid* credit on pre-1977 taxable gifts. This is the amount that would have been due under the unified transfer tax rate schedule had it been applicable. *Post-1976* taxable gifts *also* are subject to the deemed-paid adjustment because the same rate schedule may not be involved in all gifts.

EXAMPLE 21

In early 1976, Lisa made taxable gifts of $500,000, upon which a Federal gift tax of $109,275 was paid. Assume Lisa makes further taxable gifts of $700,000 in 1998. The unified transfer tax on the 1998 gifts is determined as follows:

Taxable gifts made in 1998	$ 700,000
Add: Taxable gifts made in 1976	500,000
Total of current and past taxable gifts	$1,200,000
Unified transfer tax on total taxable gifts per Appendix A [$345,800 + (41% × $200,000)]	$ 427,800
Subtract:	

Deemed-paid tax on pre-1977 taxable gifts per Appendix A [$70,800 + (34% × $250,000)]	$155,800	
Unified tax credit for 1998	202,050	(357,850)
Gift tax due on the 1998 taxable gift		$ 69,950

Note that the gift tax actually paid on the 1976 transfer was $109,275. Nevertheless, Lisa is allowed a deemed-paid credit on the gift of $155,800, considerably different from the amount paid. ▼

The Election to Split Gifts by Married Persons.
To understand the reason for the gift-splitting election of § 2513, consider the following situations:

EXAMPLE 22

Dick and Margaret are husband and wife and reside in Michigan, a common law state. Dick has been the only breadwinner in the family, and Margaret has no significant property of her own. Neither has made any prior taxable gifts or used the $30,000 specific exemption previously available for pre-1977 gifts. In 1998, Dick makes a gift to Leslie of $1,220,000. Presuming the election to split gifts did not exist, Dick's gift tax is as follows:

Amount of gift	$1,220,000
Subtract: Annual exclusion	(10,000)
Taxable gift	$1,210,000
Gift tax on $1,210,000 per Appendix A [$345,800 + (41% × $210,000)]	$ 431,900
Subtract: Unified tax credit for 1998	(202,050)
Gift tax due on the 1998 taxable gift	$ 229,850

▼

EXAMPLE 23

Assume the same facts as in Example 22, except that Dick and Margaret have always resided in California, a community property state. Even though Dick is the sole breadwinner, income from personal services generally is community property. Consequently, the gift to Leslie probably involves community property. If this is the case, the gift tax is as follows:

	Dick	Margaret
Amount of the gift (50% × $1,220,000)	$ 610,000	$ 610,000
Subtract: Annual exclusion	(10,000)	(10,000)
Taxable gifts	$ 600,000	$ 600,000
Gift tax on $600,000 per Appendix A	$ 192,800	$ 192,800
Subtract: Unified tax credit for 1998	(202,050)	(202,050)
Gift tax due on the 1998 taxable gifts	$ –0–	$ –0–

▼

As the results of Examples 22 and 23 indicate, married donors residing in community property jurisdictions possessed a significant gift tax advantage over those residing in common law states. To rectify this inequity, the Revenue Act of 1948 incorporated the predecessor to § 2513 into the Code. Under this provision, a gift made by a person to someone other than his or her spouse may be considered, for Federal gift tax purposes, as having been made one-half by each spouse. Returning to Example 22, Dick and Margaret could treat the gift passing to Leslie as being made one-half by each of them, even though the property belonged to Dick. As a result, the parties are able to achieve the same tax consequence as in Example 23.

To split gifts, the spouses must be legally married to each other at the time of the gift. If they are divorced later in the calendar year, they may still split the gift if neither marries anyone else during that year. They both must indicate on their separate gift tax returns their consent to have all gifts made in that calendar year split between them. In addition, both must be citizens or residents of the United States on the date of the gift. A gift from one spouse to the other spouse cannot be split. Such a gift might, however, be eligible for the marital deduction.

The election to split gifts is not necessary when husband and wife transfer community property to a third party. It is needed if the gift consists of the separate property of one of the spouses. Generally, separate property is property acquired before marriage and property acquired after marriage by gift or inheritance. The election, then, is not limited to residents of common law states.

PROCEDURAL MATTERS

Having determined which transfers are subject to the Federal gift tax and the various deductions and exclusions available to the donor, the procedural aspects of the tax should be considered. The following sections discuss the return itself, the due dates for filing and paying the tax, and other related matters.

The Federal Gift Tax Return.   For transfers by gift, a Form 709 (U.S. Gift Tax Return) must be filed whenever the gifts for any one calendar year exceed the annual exclusion or involve a gift of a future interest. A Form 709 need not be filed, however, for transfers between spouses that are offset by the unlimited marital deduction, regardless of the amount of the transfer.[24]

EXAMPLE 24

In 1998, Larry makes five gifts, each in the amount of $10,000, to his five children. If the gifts do not involve future interests, a Form 709 need not be filed to report the transfers. ▼

EXAMPLE 25

During 1998, Esther makes a gift of $20,000 cash of her separate property to her daughter. To double the amount of the annual exclusion allowed, Jerry (Esther's husband) is willing to split the gift. Since the § 2513 election can be made only on a gift tax return, a form must be filed even though no gift tax will be due as a result of the transfer. Useful for this purpose is Form 709–A (U.S. Short Form Gift Tax Return). This form is available to simplify the gift-splitting procedure. ▼

Presuming a gift tax return is due, it must be filed on or before the fifteenth day of April following the year of the gift.[25] As with other Federal taxes, when the due date falls on Saturday, Sunday, or a legal holiday, the date for filing the return is the next business day. Note that the filing requirements for Form 709 have no correlation to the accounting year used by a donor for Federal income tax purposes. Thus, a fiscal year taxpayer must follow the April 15 rule for any reportable gifts. If sufficient reason is shown, the IRS is authorized to grant reasonable extensions of time for filing the return.[26]

---

[24]§ 6019(a)(2).
[25]§ 6075(b)(1).

[26]§ 6081. Under § 6075(b)(2), an extension of time granted to a calendar year taxpayer for filing an income tax return automatically extends the due date of a gift tax return.

THE FEDERAL ESTATE TAX

The following discussion of the estate tax coincides with the formula that appeared earlier in the chapter in Figure 26–2. The key components in the formula are the gross estate, the taxable estate, the tax base, and the credits allowed against the tentative tax. This formula can be summarized as follows:

GROSS ESTATE

6 LEARNING OBJECTIVE
Review the components of the gross estate.

Simply stated, the **gross estate** includes all property subject to the Federal estate tax. Thus, the gross estate depends on the provisions of the Internal Revenue Code as supplemented by IRS pronouncements and the judicial interpretations of Federal courts.

In contrast to the gross estate, the **probate estate** is controlled by state (rather than Federal) law. The probate estate consists of all of a decedent's property subject

---

CONCEPT SUMMARY 26–1

Federal Gift Tax Provisions

1. The Federal gift tax applies to all gratuitous transfers of property made by U.S. citizens or residents. In this regard, it does not matter where the property is located.

2. In the eyes of the IRS, a gratuitous transfer is one not supported by full and adequate consideration. If the parties are acting in a business setting, such consideration usually exists. If purported sales are between family members, a gift element may be suspected.

3. If a lender loans money to another and intends some or all of the interest element to be a gift, the arrangement is categorized as a gift loan. To the extent that the interest provided for is less than the market rate, three tax consequences result. First, a gift has taken place between the lender and the borrower as to the interest element. Second, income may result to the lender. Third, an income tax deduction may be available to the borrower.

4. Property settlements can escape the gift tax if a divorce occurs within a prescribed period of time.

5. A disclaimer is a refusal by a person to accept property designated to pass to that person. The effect of a disclaimer is to pass the property to someone else. If certain conditions are satisfied, the issuance of a disclaimer will not be subject to the Federal gift tax.

6. Except for gifts of future interests, a donor is allowed an annual exclusion of $10,000. The future interest limitation does not apply to certain trusts created for minors.

7. The election to split a gift enables a married couple to be treated as two donors. The election doubles the annual exclusion and makes the unified tax credit available to the nonowner spouse.

8. The election to split gifts is not necessary if the property is jointly owned by the spouses. That is the case when the property is part of the couple's community.

9. In determining the tax base for computing the gift tax, all prior taxable gifts must be added to current taxable gifts. Thus, the gift tax is cumulative in nature.

10. Gifts are reported on Form 709 or Form 709–A. The return is due on April 15 following the year of the gift.

to administration by the executor or administrator of the estate. The administration is supervised by a local court of appropriate jurisdiction (usually called a probate court). An executor (or executrix) is the decedent's personal representative appointed under the decedent's will. When a decedent dies without a will or fails to name an executor in the will (or that person refuses to serve), the local probate court appoints an administrator (or administratrix).

The probate estate is frequently smaller than the gross estate. It contains only property owned by the decedent at the time of death and passing to heirs under a will or under the law of intestacy (the order of distribution for those dying without a will). As noted later, such items as the proceeds of many life insurance policies become part of the gross estate but are not included in the probate estate.

All states provide for an order of distribution in the event someone dies without a will. After the surviving spouse receives some or all of the estate, the preference is usually in the following order: down to lineal descendants (e.g., children, grandchildren), up to lineal ascendants (e.g., parents, grandparents), and out to collateral relations (e.g., brothers, sisters, aunts, and uncles).

Property Owned by the Decedent (§ 2033).   Property owned by the decedent at the time of death is included in the gross estate. The nature of the property or the use to which it was put during the decedent-owner's lifetime has no significance as far as the estate tax is concerned. Thus, personal effects (such as clothing), stocks, bonds, furniture, jewelry, works of art, bank accounts, and interests in businesses conducted as sole proprietorships and partnerships are all included in the deceased's gross estate. No distinction is made between tangible or intangible, depreciable or nondepreciable, business or personal assets. However, a deceased spouse's gross estate does not include the surviving spouse's share of the community property.

The application of § 2033 is illustrated as follows:

EXAMPLE 26

Irma dies owning some City of Denver bonds. The fair market value of the bonds plus any interest accrued to the date of Irma's death is included in her gross estate. Although interest on municipal bonds is normally not taxable under the Federal income tax, it is property owned by Irma at the time of death. However, any interest accrued after death is not part of Irma's gross estate. ▼

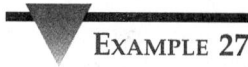

EXAMPLE 27

Sharon dies on April 8, 1998, at a time when she owns stock in Robin Corporation and in Wren Corporation. On March 3 of this year, both corporations had authorized a cash dividend payable on May 2. Robin's dividend is payable to shareholders of record as of April 1. Wren's date of record is April 11. Sharon's gross estate includes the following: the stock in Robin Corporation, the stock in Wren Corporation, and the dividend on the Robin stock. It does not include the dividend on the Wren stock. ▼

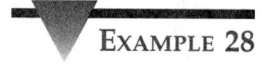

EXAMPLE 28

Ray dies holding some promissory notes issued to him by his son. In his will, Ray forgives these notes, relieving the son of the obligation to make any payments. The fair market value of these notes is included in Ray's gross estate. ▼

Exclusion for Qualified Family-Owned Businesses (§ 2033A).   To provide a form of limited tax relief for small business, Congress has enacted an exclusion from the gross estate. Applicable to estates of U.S. citizens or residents dying after 1997, the provision allows an exclusion of up to $1,300,000 in value. Unfortunately, the amount of the exclusion is tied to the exemption equivalent.

Since the total of the two cannot exceed $1,300,000, as the exemption equivalent increases, the business exclusion decreases.[27]

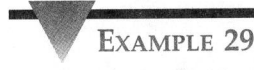

EXAMPLE 29

Mark Collins dies in 2001. At the time of death, one of his assets is the family business, valued at $900,000. Presuming all of the requirements of § 2033A are met, only $625,000 of the value of this business may be excluded from his gross estate. The amount of the exclusion ($625,000) plus the exemption equivalent for 2001 ($675,000—see Table 26–1 earlier in the chapter) cannot exceed $1,300,000. ▼

By the year 2006, when the full exemption equivalent of $1,000,000 is phased in, the business exclusion is a mere $300,000 ($1,300,000 – $1,000,000).

Because the business exclusion is intended to alleviate the need for small businesses to liquidate to pay estate taxes, its provisions are restrictive and very detailed. Although detail leads to complexity, Congress had no intention of allowing this provision to be manipulated so as to permit widespread estate tax avoidance.

The small business exclusion applies only when the value of the business interest exceeds 50 percent of the adjusted gross estate.[28] To meet this requirement, the value of the business interest must be reduced by certain passive assets (e.g., cash, marketable securities) not needed in business operations. It must be increased by certain gifts of the interest made to family members during the decedent's lifetime.[29] The adjusted gross estate is the gross estate less deductible claims and mortgages under §§ 2053(a)(1) and (2).[30]

The interest can be a sole proprietorship or complete or partial ownership in an entity (i.e., partnership, corporation). In the case of an ownership interest in an entity, it must be held 50 percent by one family, 70 percent by two families, or 90 percent by three families (of which the decedent's family owns at least 30 percent).[31]

To ensure that the business is truly operated by the decedent (or family), several tests must be satisfied.

- The decedent (or a family member) must have owned and materially participated in the business for at least five of the eight years prior to death.
- A qualified heir must materially participate in the business for at least five years in an eight-year period during the 10 years following the decedent's death.

For both pre- and post-death purposes, "material participation" is intended to carry the same meaning as it does in satisfying the requirement for electing § 2032A. This provision deals with special use valuation, which is beyond the scope of this chapter. The definition of "family member" is broad and includes the decedent's ancestors (e.g., parents, grandparents), spouse, lineal descendants (e.g., children, grandchildren), spouse's lineal descendants (e.g., stepchildren, stepgrandchildren), the spouses of any lineal descendants (e.g., son-in-law), and any lineal descendants of the decedent's ancestors (e.g., brothers and sisters, nieces and nephews).

"Qualified heir" includes heirs who are family members. The term also includes an active employee of the business if the person held this status for a period of at least 10 years before the decedent's death.[32]

The business exclusion is intended to keep the business intact for the benefit of the deceased owner's family. Consequently, it is not surprising that the tax savings are taken back (i.e., recaptured) when this objective is compromised. The

---

[27]§ 2033A(a)(2). The $1,300,000 amount is *not* subject to indexation.
[28]§ 2033A(b)(1).
[29]§ 2033A(d).

[30]§ 2033A(c).
[31]§ 2033A(e).
[32]§ 2033A(i)(1).

effect of recapture is to yield an additional estate tax equivalent to the tax that would have resulted had the exclusion not been utilized.[33]

Recapture can be triggered by any of the following events:

- The qualified heir ceases to meet the material participation requirements.
- The business is disposed of to outsiders.
- The business is removed from the United States, or the qualified heir loses U.S. citizenship.

Full recapture (100 percent) is required if the disqualifying act occurs during the first six years after the owner's death. Thereafter, the recapture percentage is reduced by 20 percent for each additional year. Thus, the recapture potential disappears if the business continues in the family for 10 years.

The business exclusion is an elective provision. The election is made by the executor of the owner's estate.[34] The election must be accompanied by an agreement executed by the qualifying heirs accepting liability as to recapture consequences, should they take place.[35]

Dower and Curtesy Interests (§ 2034). In its common law (nonstatutory) form, dower generally gave a surviving widow a life estate in a portion of her husband's estate (usually the real estate he owned) with the remainder passing to their children. Most states have modified and codified these common law rules, and the resulting statutes often vary among jurisdictions. In some states, for example, by statute, a widow is entitled to outright ownership of a percentage of her deceased husband's real estate and personal property. Curtesy is a similar right held by the husband in his wife's property, taking effect in the event he survives her. Most states have abolished the common law curtesy concept and have, in some cases, substituted a modified statutory version.

Dower and curtesy rights are incomplete interests and may never materialize. Thus, if a wife predeceases her husband, the dower interest in her husband's property is lost.

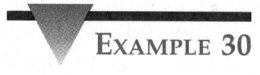

EXAMPLE 30

Martin dies without a will, leaving an estate of $900,000. Under state law, Belinda (Martin's widow) is entitled to one-third of his property. The $300,000 Belinda receives is included in Martin's gross estate. Depending on the nature of the interest Belinda receives in the $300,000, this amount could qualify Martin's estate for a marital deduction. (This possibility is discussed at greater length later in the chapter. For the time being, however, the focus is on what is or is not included as part of the decedent's gross estate.) ▼

Adjustments for Gifts Made within Three Years of Death (§ 2035). At one time, all taxable gifts made within three years of death were included in the donor's gross estate unless it could be shown that the gifts were not made in contemplation of death. The prior rule was intended to preclude tax avoidance since the gift tax and estate tax rates were separate and the former was lower than the latter. When the gift and estate tax rates were combined into the unified transfer tax, the reason for the rule for gifts in contemplation of death largely disappeared. The three-year rule has, however, been retained for the following items:

- Any gift tax paid on gifts made within three years of death. Called the *gross-up* procedure, this prevents the gift tax amount from escaping the estate tax.

---

[33]§ 2033A(f).
[34]§ 2033A(b)(1)(B).

[35]§ 2033A(h).

- Any property interests transferred by gift within three years of death that would have been included in the gross estate by virtue of the application of § 2036 (transfers with a retained life estate), § 2037 (transfers taking effect at death), § 2038 (revocable transfers), and § 2042 (proceeds of life insurance). All except § 2037 transfers are discussed later in the chapter.

EXAMPLE 31

Before her death in 1998, Jennifer made the following taxable gifts:

Year of Gift	Nature of the Asset	Fair Market Value		Gift Tax Paid
		Date of Gift	Date of Death	
1990	Hawk Corporation stock	$100,000	$150,000	$ –0–
1996	Insurance policy on Jennifer's life	40,000 (cash value)	200,000 (face value)	–0–
1997	Land	400,000	410,000	8,200

Jennifer's *gross estate* includes $208,200 ($200,000 life insurance proceeds + $8,200 gross-up for the gift tax on the 1997 taxable gift) as to these transfers. Referring to the formula for the estate tax (Figure 26–2), the other post-1976 taxable gifts are added to the *taxable estate* (at the fair market value on the date of the gift) in arriving at the tax base. Jennifer's estate is allowed a credit for the gift tax paid (or deemed paid) on the 1997 transfer. ▼

Transfers with a Retained Life Estate (§ 2036). Code §§ 2036 through 2038 were enacted on the premise that the estate tax can be avoided on lifetime transfers only if the decedent does not retain control over the property. The logic of this approach is somewhat difficult to dispute. One should not be able to escape the tax consequences of property transfers at death while remaining in a position during life to enjoy some or all of the fruits of ownership.

Under § 2036, the value of any property transferred by the deceased during lifetime for less than adequate consideration must be included if either of the following was retained:

- The possession or enjoyment of, or the right to the income from, the property.
- The right, either alone or in conjunction with any person, to designate the persons who shall possess or enjoy the property or the income.

"The possession or enjoyment of, or the right to the income from, the property," as it appears in § 2036(a)(1), is considered to have been retained by the decedent to the extent that such income, etc., is to be applied toward the discharge of a legal obligation of the decedent. The term "legal obligation" includes a legal obligation of the decedent to support a dependent during the decedent's lifetime.[36]

The following examples illustrate the practical application of § 2036.

EXAMPLE 32

Carl's will passes all of his property to a trust in which income goes to Alan for his life (Alan is given a life estate). Upon Alan's death, the principal goes to Melissa (Melissa is granted a remainder interest). On Alan's death, none of the trust property is included in his gross estate. Although Alan held a life estate, § 2036 is inapplicable because Alan was not the transferor (Carl was) of the property. Section 2033 (property owned by the decedent) causes any income distributions Alan was entitled to receive at the time of his death to be included in his gross estate. ▼

---

[36]Reg. § 20.2036–1(b)(2).

EXAMPLE 33

By deed, Nora transfers the remainder interest in her ranch to Marcia, retaining for herself the right to continue occupying the property until death. Upon Nora's death, the fair market value of the ranch is included in her gross estate. Furthermore, Nora is subject to the gift tax. The amount of the gift is the fair market value of the ranch on the date of the gift less the portion applicable to Nora's retained life estate. ▼

Revocable Transfers (§ 2038). Another type of lifetime transfer that is drawn into a decedent's gross estate is covered by § 2038. The gross estate includes the value of property interests transferred by the decedent (except to the extent that the transfer was made for full consideration) if the enjoyment of the property transferred was subject, at the date of the decedent's death, to any power of the decedent to *alter, amend, revoke, or terminate* the transfer. This includes the power to change beneficiaries or to accelerate or increase any beneficiary's enjoyment of the property.

The capacity in which the decedent could exercise the power is immaterial. If the decedent gave property in trust, making himself or herself the trustee with the power to revoke the trust, the property is included in his or her gross estate. If the decedent named another person as trustee with the power to revoke but reserved the power to later appoint himself or herself trustee, the property is also included in his or her gross estate. If, however, the power to alter, amend, revoke, or terminate was held at all times solely by a person other than the decedent and the decedent did not reserve a right to assume these powers, the property is not included in the decedent's gross estate.

The Code and the Regulations make it clear that one cannot avoid inclusion in the gross estate under § 2038 by relinquishing a power within three years of death.[37] Recall that § 2038 is one of several types of situations listed as exceptions to the usual rule excluding gifts made within three years of death from the gross estate.

In the event § 2038 applies, the amount includible in the gross estate is the portion of the property transferred that is subject, at the decedent's death, to the decedent's power to alter, amend, revoke, or terminate.

The classic § 2038 situation results from the use of a revocable trust.

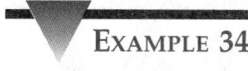

EXAMPLE 34

Maria creates a trust, life estate to her children, remainder to her grandchildren. Under the terms of the trust, Maria reserves the right to revoke the trust and revest the trust principal and income in herself. As noted in Example 10, the creation of the trust does not result in a gift because the transfer is not complete. However, if Maria dies still retaining the power to revoke, the trust is included in her gross estate under § 2038. ▼

In application, the provisions related to incomplete transfers (§§ 2036 and 2038) tend to overlap. It is not unusual to find that either or both sections apply to a particular transfer.

Annuities (§ 2039). Annuities can be divided by their origin into commercial and noncommercial contracts. Noncommercial annuities are issued by private parties and, in some cases, charitable organizations that do not regularly issue annuities. The two varieties have much in common, but noncommercial annuities present special income tax problems and are not treated further in this discussion.

Regulation § 20.2039–1(b)(1) defines an annuity as representing "one or more payments extending over any period of time." According to the Regulation, the payments may be equal or unequal, conditional or unconditional, periodic or

---

[37]§ 2038(a)(1) and Reg. § 20.2038–1(e)(1).

sporadic. Annuity contracts that terminate upon the death of the person covered (i.e., annuitant) are designated as straight-life annuities. Other contracts provide for a survivorship feature (e.g., reduced payments to a surviving spouse).

In the case of a straight-life annuity, nothing is included in the gross estate of the annuitant at death. Section 2033 (property in which the decedent had an interest) does not apply because the annuitant's interest in the contract is terminated by death. Section 2036 (transfers with a retained life estate) does not cover the situation; a transfer made for full consideration is specifically excluded from § 2036 treatment. A commercial annuity is presumed to have been purchased for full consideration unless some evidence exists to indicate that the parties were not acting at arm's length.

 **EXAMPLE 35**
Arnold purchases a straight-life annuity that will pay him $6,000 a month when he reaches age 65. Arnold dies at age 70. Except for the payments he received before his death, nothing relating to this annuity affects Arnold's gross estate. ▼

In the case of a survivorship annuity, the estate tax consequences under § 2039(a) are usually triggered by the death of the first annuitant. The amount included in the gross estate is the cost from the same company of a comparable annuity covering the survivor at his or her attained age on the date of the deceased annuitant's death.

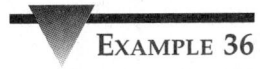 **EXAMPLE 36**
Assume the same facts as in Example 35, except that the annuity contract provides for Veronica to be paid $3,000 a month for life as a survivorship feature. Veronica is 62 years of age when Arnold dies. Under these circumstances, Arnold's gross estate includes the cost of a comparable contract that provides an annuity of $3,000 per month for the life of a female, age 62. ▼

Full inclusion of the survivorship element in the gross estate is subject to an exception under § 2039(b). The amount includible is to be based on the proportion of the deceased annuitant's contribution to the total cost of the contract. This is expressed by the following formula:

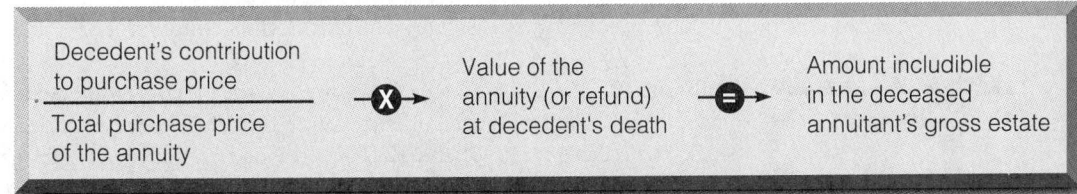

$$\frac{\text{Decedent's contribution to purchase price}}{\text{Total purchase price of the annuity}} \times \text{Value of the annuity (or refund) at decedent's death} = \text{Amount includible in the deceased annuitant's gross estate}$$

 **EXAMPLE 37**
Assume the same facts as in Example 36, except that Arnold and Veronica are husband and wife and have always lived in a community property state. The premiums on the contract were paid with community funds. Since Veronica contributed half of the cost of the contract, only half of the amount determined under Example 36 is included in Arnold's gross estate. ▼

The result reached in Example 37 is not unique to community property jurisdictions. The outcome would have been the same in a noncommunity property state if Veronica had furnished half of the consideration from her own funds.

Joint Interests (§§ 2040 and 2511). Recall that joint tenancies and tenancies by the entirety are characterized by the right of survivorship. Thus, upon the death of a joint tenant, title to the property passes to the surviving tenant. None of the property is included in the *probate* estate of the deceased tenant. In the case of tenancies in common and community property, death does not defeat an ownership interest; rather, the deceased owner's interest is part of the probate estate.

The *Federal estate tax treatment* of tenancies in common or of community property follows the logical approach of taxing only the portion of the property included in the deceased owner's probate estate. Thus, if Homer, Wilma, and Thelma are tenants in common in a tract of land, each owning an equal interest, and Homer dies, only one-third of the value of the property is included in the gross estate. This one-third interest is also the same amount that passes to Homer's heirs.

EXAMPLE 38

Homer, Wilma, and Thelma acquire a tract of land with ownership listed as tenants in common, each party furnishing $20,000 of the $60,000 purchase price. When the property is worth $90,000, Homer dies. If Homer's undivided interest in the property is 33⅓%, the gross estate *and* probate estate each include $30,000. ▼

Unless the parties have provided otherwise, each tenant is deemed to own an interest equal to the portion of the original consideration he or she furnished. The parties in Example 38 could have provided that Homer would receive an undivided half interest in the property although he contributed only one-third of the purchase price. In that case, Wilma and Thelma have made a gift to Homer when the tenancy was created, and Homer's gross estate and probate estate each include $45,000.

For certain joint tenancies, the tax consequences are different. All of the property is included in the deceased co-owner's gross estate unless it can be proven that the surviving co-owners contributed to the cost of the property.[38] If a contribution can be shown, the amount to be *excluded* is calculated by the following formula:

$$\frac{\text{Surviving co-owner's contribution}}{\text{Total cost of the property}} \times \text{Fair market value of the property}$$

In computing a survivor's contribution, any funds received as a gift *from the deceased co-owner* and applied to the cost of the property cannot be counted. However, income or gain from gift assets can be counted.

If the co-owners receive the property as a gift *from another*, each co-owner is deemed to have contributed to the cost of his or her own interest.

The preceding rules can be illustrated as follows:

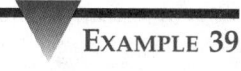

EXAMPLE 39

Keith and Steve (father and son) acquire a tract of land with ownership listed as joint tenancy with right of survivorship. Keith furnished $40,000 and Steve $20,000 of the $60,000 purchase price. Of the $20,000 provided by Steve, $10,000 had previously been received as a gift from Keith. When the property is worth $90,000, Keith dies. Because only $10,000 of Steve's contribution can be counted (the other $10,000 was received as a gift from Keith), Steve has furnished only one-sixth ($10,000/$60,000) of the cost. Thus, Keith's gross estate must include five-sixths of $90,000, or $75,000. This presumes Steve can prove that he did in fact make the $10,000 contribution. In the absence of such proof, the full value of the property is included in Keith's gross estate. Keith's death makes Steve the immediate owner of the property by virtue of the right of survivorship. None of the property is part of Keith's probate estate. ▼

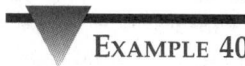

EXAMPLE 40

Francis transfers property to Irene and Martin as a gift, listing ownership as joint tenancy with the right of survivorship. Upon Irene's death, one-half of the value of the property is included in the gross estate. Since the property was received as a gift and the donees are equal owners, each is considered to have furnished half of the consideration. ▼

---

[38]§ 2040(a).

To simplify the joint ownership rules for *married persons*, § 2040(b) provides for an automatic inclusion rule upon the death of the first joint-owner spouse to die. Regardless of the amount contributed by each spouse, one-half of the value of the property is included in the gross estate of the spouse who dies first. The special rule eliminates the need to trace the source of contributions and recognizes that any inclusion in the gross estate is neutralized by the marital deduction.

EXAMPLE 41

In 1986, Hank purchases real estate for $100,000 using his separate funds and lists title as "Hank and Louise, joint tenants with the right of survivorship." Hank predeceases Louise 10 years later when the property is worth $300,000. If Hank and Louise are husband and wife, Hank's gross estate includes $150,000 (½ of $300,000) as to the property. ▼

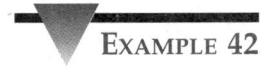

EXAMPLE 42

Assume the same facts as in Example 41, except that Louise (instead of Hank) dies first. Presuming the value at the date of death is $300,000, Louise's gross estate includes $150,000 as to the property. In this regard, it is of no consequence that Louise did not contribute to the cost of the real estate. ▼

In both Examples 41 and 42, inclusion in the gross estate of the first spouse to die is neutralized by the unlimited marital deduction allowed for estate tax purposes (see the discussion of the marital deduction later in the chapter). Under the right of survivorship, the surviving joint tenant obtains full ownership of the property. The marital deduction generally is allowed for property passing from one spouse to another.

Whether or not a *gift* results when property is transferred into some form of joint ownership depends on the consideration furnished by each of the contributing parties for the ownership interest acquired.

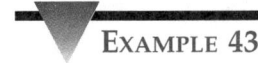

EXAMPLE 43

Brenda and Sarah purchase real estate as tenants in common, each furnishing $40,000 of the $80,000 cost. If each is an equal owner in the property, no gift has occurred. ▼

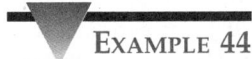

EXAMPLE 44

Assume the same facts as in Example 43, except that of the $80,000 purchase price, Brenda furnishes $60,000 and Sarah furnishes only $20,000. If they are equal owners in the property, Brenda has made a gift to Sarah of $20,000. ▼

EXAMPLE 45

Martha purchases real estate for $240,000, the title to the property being listed as follows: "Martha, Sylvia, and Dan as joint tenants with the right of survivorship." If under state law the mother (Martha), the daughter (Sylvia), and the son (Dan) are deemed to be equal owners in the property, Martha is treated as having made gifts of $80,000 to Sylvia and $80,000 to Dan. ▼

Several important *exceptions* exist to the general rule that the creation of a joint ownership with disproportionate interests resulting from unequal consideration triggers gift treatment. First, if the transfer involves a joint bank account, there is no gift at the time of the contribution.[39] If a gift occurs, it is when the noncontributing party withdraws the funds provided by the other joint tenant. Second, the same rule applies to the purchase of U.S. savings bonds. Again, any gift tax consequences are postponed until the noncontributing party appropriates some or all of the proceeds for his or her individual use.

---

[39]Reg. § 25.2511–1(h)(4).

ETHICAL CONSIDERATIONS

A Joint Bank Account and a Subsequent Marriage

Horace, a well-to-do widower, wants to marry Fran, his much younger secretary. Fran is agreeable to marriage but would like to achieve some degree of financial independence. Upon advice of his attorney, Horace uses $900,000 to establish a bank account listing himself and Fran as joint tenants. Horace and Fran are married, and shortly thereafter she withdraws the $900,000 and places the funds in a new account in her name only.

If the transfer from Horace to Fran took place before their marriage, it generates a Federal gift tax. The position of the IRS is that premarital settlements are gifts because they are not supported by adequate consideration. If the transfer from Horace to Fran took place after marriage, a gift tax is avoided due to the application of the marital deduction.

Has Horace successfully avoided the Federal gift tax?

Life Insurance (§ 2042). Under § 2042, the gross estate includes the proceeds of life insurance on the decedent's life if (1) they are receivable by the estate, (2) they are receivable by another for the benefit of the estate, or (3) the decedent possessed an incident of ownership in the policy.

Life insurance on the life of another owned by a decedent at the time of death is included in the gross estate under § 2033 (property in which the decedent had an interest) and not under § 2042. The amount includible is the replacement value of the policy.[40] Under these circumstances, inclusion of the face amount of the policy is inappropriate as the policy has not yet matured.

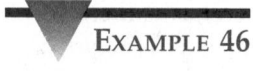

EXAMPLE 46

At the time of his death, Luigi owned a life insurance policy on the life of Benito, face amount of $100,000 and replacement value of $25,000, with Sofia as the designated beneficiary. Since the policy had not matured at Luigi's death, § 2042 would be inapplicable. However, § 2033 (property in which the decedent had an interest) compels the inclusion of $25,000 (the replacement value) in Luigi's gross estate. If Luigi and Sofia owned the policy as community property, only $12,500 is included in Luigi's gross estate. ▼

The term "life insurance" includes whole life policies, term insurance, group life insurance, travel and accident insurance, endowment contracts (before being paid up), and death benefits paid by fraternal societies operating under the lodge system.[41]

As just noted, proceeds of insurance on the life of the decedent receivable by the executor or administrator or payable to the decedent's estate are included in the gross estate. The estate need not be specifically named as the beneficiary. Assume, for example, the proceeds of the policy are receivable by an individual beneficiary and are subject to an obligation, legally binding upon the beneficiary, to pay taxes, debts, and other charges enforceable against the estate. The proceeds are included in the decedent's gross estate to the extent of the beneficiary's obligation. If the proceeds of an insurance policy made payable to a decedent's estate

---

[40]Reg. § 20.2031–8(a)(1).
[41]Reg. § 20.2042–1(a)(1). As to travel and accident insurance, see *Comm. v. Estate of Noel,* 65–1 USTC ¶12,311, 15 AFTR2d 1397, 85 S.Ct. 1238 (USSC, 1965).

are community assets and, under state law, one-half belongs to the surviving spouse, only one-half of the proceeds will be considered as receivable by or for the benefit of the decedent's estate.

Proceeds of insurance on the life of the decedent not receivable by or for the benefit of the estate are includible if the decedent at death possessed any of the incidents of ownership in the policy. In this connection, the term "incidents of ownership" means more than the ownership of the policy in a technical legal sense. Generally speaking, the term refers to the right of the insured or his or her estate to the economic benefits of the policy. Thus, it also includes the power to change beneficiaries, revoke an assignment, pledge the policy for a loan, or surrender or cancel the policy.[42]

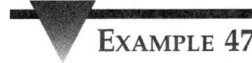

EXAMPLE 47

At the time of death, Broderick was the insured under a policy (face amount of $100,000) owned by Gregory with Demi as the designated beneficiary. Broderick took out the policy five years ago and immediately transferred it as a gift to Gregory. Under the assignment, Broderick transferred all rights in the policy except the right to change beneficiaries. Broderick died without having exercised this right, and the policy proceeds are paid to Demi. Under § 2042(2), Broderick's retention of an incident of ownership in the policy (i.e., the right to change beneficiaries) causes $100,000 to be included in his gross estate. ▼

Assuming that the deceased-insured holds the incidents of ownership in a policy, how much is included in the gross estate if the insurance policy is a community asset? Only one-half of the proceeds becomes part of the deceased spouse's gross estate.

In determining whether or not a policy is *community property* or what portion of it might be so classified, state law controls. The states appear to follow one of two general approaches. Under the inception of title approach, the classification depends on when the policy was originally purchased. If purchased before marriage, the policy is separate property regardless of how many premiums were paid after marriage with community funds. However, if the noninsured spouse is not the beneficiary of the policy, he or she may be entitled to reimbursement from the deceased-insured spouse's estate for half of the premiums paid with community funds. The inception of title approach is followed in at least three states: Louisiana, Texas, and New Mexico.

Some community property jurisdictions classify a policy using the tracing approach: The nature of the funds used to pay the premiums controls. Thus, a policy paid for 20 percent with separate funds and 80 percent with community funds is 20 percent separate property and 80 percent community property. The point in time when the policy was purchased makes no difference. Conceivably, a policy purchased after marriage with the premiums paid exclusively from separate funds is classified entirely as separate property. The tracing approach appears to be the rule in California and Washington.

Merely purchasing a life insurance contract and designating someone else as the beneficiary thereunder does not constitute a *gift*. As long as the purchaser still owns the policy, nothing has really passed to the beneficiary. Even on the death of the insured-owner, no gift takes place. The proceeds paid to the beneficiary constitute a testamentary and not a lifetime transfer. But consider the following possibility:

---

[42]Reg. § 20.2042–1(c)(2).

EXAMPLE 48

Kurt purchases an insurance policy on his own life and transfers the policy to Olga. Kurt retains no interest in the policy (such as the power to change beneficiaries). In these circumstances, Kurt has made a gift to Olga. Furthermore, if Kurt continues to pay the premiums on the transferred policy, each payment constitutes a separate gift. ▼

Under certain conditions, the death of the insured may constitute a gift to the beneficiary of part or all of the proceeds. This occurs when the owner of the policy is not the insured.

EXAMPLE 49

Randolph owns an insurance policy on the life of Frank, with Tracy as the designated beneficiary. Up until the time of Frank's death, Randolph retained the right to change the beneficiary of the policy. The proceeds paid to Tracy by the insurance company by reason of Frank's death constitute a gift from Randolph to Tracy.[43] ▼

TAXABLE ESTATE

7 **LEARNING OBJECTIVE**
Describe the components of the taxable estate.

After the gross estate has been determined, the next step is to determine the taxable estate. By virtue of § 2051, the **taxable estate** is the gross estate less the following: expenses, indebtedness, and taxes (§ 2053); losses (§ 2054); charitable transfers (§§ 2055 and 2522); and the marital deduction (§§ 2056 and 2056A). As previously noted, the charitable and marital deductions also have gift tax ramifications.

Expenses, Indebtedness, and Taxes (§ 2053).   A deduction is allowed for funeral expenses; expenses incurred in administering property; claims against the estate; and unpaid mortgages and other charges against property, whose value is included in the gross estate (without reduction for the mortgage or other indebtedness).

Expenses incurred in administering community property are deductible only in proportion to the deceased spouse's interest in the community.[44]

Administration expenses include commissions of the executor or administrator, attorney's fees of the estate, accountant's fees, court costs, and certain selling expenses for disposition of estate property.

Claims against the estate include property taxes accrued before the decedent's death, unpaid income taxes on income received by the decedent before he or she died, and unpaid gift taxes on gifts made by the decedent before death.

Amounts that may be deducted as claims against the estate are only for enforceable personal obligations of the decedent at the time of death. Deductions for claims founded on promises or agreements are limited to the extent that the liabilities were contracted in good faith and for adequate and full consideration. However, a pledge or subscription in favor of a public, charitable, religious, or educational organization is deductible to the extent that it would have constituted an allowable deduction had it been a bequest.[45]

Deductible funeral expenses include the cost of interment, the burial plot or vault, a gravestone, perpetual care of the grave site, and the transportation expense of the person bringing the body to the place of burial. If the decedent had, before death, acquired cemetery lots for himself or herself and family, no deduction is allowed, but the lots are not included in the decedent's gross estate under § 2033 (property in which the decedent had an interest).

[43]*Goodman v. Comm.*, 46–1 USTC ¶10,275, 34 AFTR 1534, 156 F.2d 218 (CA–2, 1946).

[44]*U.S. v. Stapf*, 63–2 USTC ¶12,192, 12 AFTR2d 6326, 84 S.Ct. 248 (USSC, 1963).

[45]§ 2053(c)(1)(A) and Reg. § 20.2053–5.

Losses (§ 2054). Section 2054 permits an estate tax deduction for losses from casualty or theft incurred during the period when the estate is being settled. As is true with casualty or theft losses for income tax purposes, any anticipated insurance recovery must be taken into account in arriving at the amount of the deductible loss. Unlike the income tax, however, the deduction is not limited by a floor ($100) or a percentage amount (the excess of 10 percent of adjusted gross income). If the casualty occurs to property after it has been distributed to an heir, the loss belongs to the heir and not to the estate. If the casualty occurs before the decedent's death, it should be claimed on the appropriate Form 1040. The fair market value of the property (if any) on the date of death plus any insurance recovery is included in the gross estate.

As is true of certain administration expenses, a casualty or theft loss of estate property can be claimed as an income tax deduction on the fiduciary return of the estate (Form 1041). But a double deduction prohibition applies, and claiming the income tax deduction requires a waiver of the estate tax deduction.[46]

Transfers to Charity (§§ 2055 and 2522). A deduction is allowed for the value of property in the decedent's gross estate that is transferred by the decedent through testamentary disposition to (or for the use of) any of the following:

- The United States or any of its political subdivisions.
- Any corporation or association organized and operated exclusively for religious, charitable, scientific, literary, or educational purposes.
- Various veterans' organizations.

The organizations just described are identical to those that qualify for the Federal gift tax deduction under § 2522. With the following exceptions, they are also the same organizations that qualify a donee for an income tax deduction under § 170:

- Certain nonprofit cemetery associations qualify for income tax but not estate and gift tax purposes.
- Foreign charities may qualify under the estate and gift tax but not under the income tax.

No deduction is allowed unless the charitable bequest is specified by a provision in the decedent's will or the transfer was made before death and the property is subsequently included in the gross estate. Generally speaking, a deduction does not materialize when an individual dies intestate (without a will). The amount of the bequest to charity must be mandatory and cannot be left to someone else's discretion. It is, however, permissible to allow another person, such as the executor of the estate, to choose which charity will receive the specified donation. Likewise, a bequest may be expressed as an alternative and still be effective if the noncharitable beneficiary disclaims (refuses) the intervening interest before the due date for the filing of the estate tax return (nine months after the decedent's death plus any extensions of time granted for filing).

Marital Deduction (§§ 2056, 2056A, and 2523). The **marital deduction** originated with the Revenue Act of 1948 as part of the same legislation that permitted married persons to secure the income-splitting advantages of filing joint income tax returns. The purpose of these statutory changes was to eliminate the major tax variations that existed between taxpayers residing in community property and

---

[46]§ 642(g).

common law states. The marital deduction was designed to provide equity in the estate and gift tax areas.

In a community property state, for example, no marital deduction generally was allowed since the surviving spouse already owned one-half of the community and that portion was not included in the deceased spouse's gross estate. In a common law state, however, most if not all of the assets often belonged to the breadwinner of the family. When that spouse died first, all of these assets were included in the gross estate. Recall that a dower or curtesy interest (regarding a surviving spouse's right to some of the deceased spouse's property) does not reduce the gross estate. To equalize the situation, therefore, a marital deduction, usually equal to one-half of all separate assets, was allowed upon the death of the first spouse.

Ultimately, Congress decided to dispense with these historical justifications and recognize husband and wife as a single economic unit. Consistent with the approach taken under the income tax, spouses are considered as one for transfer tax purposes. By making the marital deduction unlimited in amount, neither the gift tax nor the estate tax is imposed on outright interspousal transfers of property. The unlimited marital deduction even includes one spouse's share of the community property transferred to the other spouse.

Under § 2056, the marital deduction is allowed only for property that is included in the deceased spouse's gross estate and that passes or has passed to the surviving spouse. In determining whether the parties are legally married, look to state law (see Example 1 earlier). Property that passes from the decedent to the surviving spouse includes any interest received as (1) the decedent's heir or donee; (2) the decedent's surviving tenant by the entirety or joint tenant; (3) the appointee under the decedent's exercise (or lapse or release) of a general power of appointment; or (4) the beneficiary of insurance on the life of the decedent.

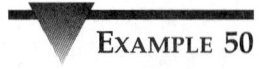

EXAMPLE 50

At the time of his death in the current year, Matthew owned an insurance policy on his own life (face amount of $100,000) with Minerva (his wife) as the designated beneficiary. Matthew and Minerva also owned real estate (worth $250,000) as tenants by the entirety (Matthew had furnished all of the purchase price). As to these transfers, $225,000 ($100,000 + $125,000) is included in Matthew's gross estate, and this amount represents the property that passes to Minerva for purposes of the marital deduction.[47] ▼

Disclaimers can affect the amount passing to the surviving spouse. If, for example, the surviving spouse is the remainderperson under the will of the deceased spouse, a disclaimer by another heir increases the amount passing to the surviving spouse. This, in turn, will increase the amount of the marital deduction allowed to the estate of the deceased spouse.

A problem arises when a property interest passing to the surviving spouse is subject to a mortgage or other encumbrance. In this case, only the net value of the interest after reduction by the amount of the mortgage or other encumbrance qualifies for the marital deduction. To allow otherwise results in a double deduction since a decedent's liabilities are separately deductible under § 2053.

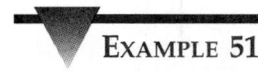

EXAMPLE 51

In his will, Oscar leaves real estate (fair market value of $200,000) to his wife. If the real estate is subject to a mortgage of $40,000 (upon which Oscar was personally liable), the marital deduction is limited to $160,000 ($200,000 − $40,000). The $40,000 mortgage is deductible under § 2053 as an obligation of the decedent (Oscar). ▼

---

[47]Inclusion in the gross estate falls under § 2042 (proceeds of life insurance) and § 2040 (joint interests). Although Matthew provided the full purchase price for the real estate, § 2040(b) requires inclu-sion of only half of the value of the property when one spouse predeceases the other.

However, if the executor is required under the terms of the decedent's will or under local law to discharge the mortgage out of other assets of the estate or to reimburse the surviving spouse, the payment or reimbursement is an additional interest passing to the surviving spouse.

EXAMPLE 52

Assume the same facts as in Example 51, except that Oscar's will directs that the real estate is to pass to his wife free of any liabilities. Accordingly, Oscar's executor pays off the mortgage by using other estate assets and distributes the real estate to Oscar's wife. The marital deduction now becomes $200,000. ▼

Federal estate taxes or other death taxes paid out of the surviving spouse's share of the gross estate are not included in the value of property passing to the surviving spouse. Therefore, it is usually preferable for the deceased spouse's will to provide that death taxes be paid out of the portion of the estate that does not qualify for the marital deduction.

Certain interests in property passing from the deceased spouse to the surviving spouse are referred to as **terminable interests.** Such an interest will terminate or fail after the passage of time, upon the happening of some contingency, or upon the failure of some event to occur. Examples are life estates, annuities, estates for terms of years, and patents. A terminable interest will not qualify for the marital deduction if another interest in the same property passed from the deceased spouse to some other person. By reason of the passing, that other person or his or her heirs may enjoy part of the property after the termination of the surviving spouse's interest.[48]

EXAMPLE 53

Vicky's will places her property in trust with a life estate to her husband, Brett, remainder to Andrew or his heirs. The interest passing from Vicky to Brett does not qualify for the marital deduction. Brett's interest will terminate on his death, and Andrew or his heirs will then possess or enjoy the property. ▼

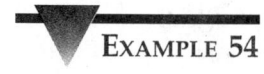

EXAMPLE 54

Assume the same facts as in Example 53, except that Vicky created the trust during her life. No marital deduction is available for gift tax purposes for the same reason as in Example 53.[49] ▼

The justification for the terminable interest rule can be illustrated by examining the possible results of Examples 53 and 54 more closely. Without the rule, Vicky could have passed property to Brett at no cost because of the marital deduction. Yet, on Brett's death, none of the property would have been included in his gross estate. Section 2036 (transfers with a retained life estate) would not apply to Brett since he was not the original transferor of the property. The marital deduction should not be available in situations where the surviving spouse can enjoy the property and still pass it to another without tax consequences. The marital deduction is intended to merely postpone the transfer tax on the death of the first spouse and to shift any such tax to the surviving spouse.

Consistent with the objective of the terminable interest rule, an alternative means for obtaining the marital deduction is available. Under this provision the marital deduction is allowed for transfers of **qualified terminable intere** **property** (commonly referred to as **QTIP**). This is defined as property

---

[48]§§ 2056(b)(1) and 2523(b)(1).

[49]Both Examples 53 and 54 contain the potential for a qualified terminable interest property (QTIP) election discussed later in this section.

passes from one spouse to another by gift or at death and for which the transferee-spouse has a qualifying income interest for life.

For a donee or a surviving spouse, a qualifying income interest for life exists under the following conditions:

- The person is entitled for life to all of the income from the property (or a specific portion of it), payable at annual or more frequent intervals.
- No person (including the spouse) has a power to appoint any part of the property to any person other than the surviving spouse during his or her life.[50]

If these conditions are met, an election can be made to claim a marital deduction as to the QTIP. For estate tax purposes, the executor of the estate makes the election on Form 706 (estate tax return). For gift tax purposes, the donor spouse makes the election on Form 709 (gift tax return). The election is irrevocable.

If the election is made, a transfer tax is imposed upon the QTIP when the transferee-spouse disposes of it by gift or upon death. If the disposition occurs during life, the gift tax applies, measured by the fair market value of the property as of that time.[51] If no lifetime disposition takes place, the fair market value of the property on the date of death (or alternate valuation date if applicable) is included in the gross estate of the transferee-spouse.[52]

EXAMPLE 55

In 1998, Clyde dies and provides in his will that certain assets (fair market value of $400,000) are to be transferred to a trust under which Gertrude (Clyde's wife) is granted a life estate with the remainder passing to their children upon Gertrude's death. Presuming all of the preceding requirements are satisfied and Clyde's executor so elects, his estate receives a marital deduction of $400,000. ▼

EXAMPLE 56

Assume the same facts as in Example 55, with the further stipulation that Gertrude dies in 2000 when the trust assets are worth $900,000. This amount is included in her gross estate. ▼

Because the estate tax is imposed on assets not physically included in the probate estate, the law allows the liability for those assets to be shifted to the heirs. The amount shifted is determined by comparing the estate tax liability both with and without the inclusion of the QTIP. This right of recovery can be canceled by a provision in the deceased spouse's will.[53]

COMPUTING THE FEDERAL ESTATE TAX

8 LEARNING OBJECTIVE
Determine the Federal estate tax liability.

Once the taxable estate has been determined, post-1976 taxable gifts are added to arrive at the tax base. Note that pre-1977 taxable gifts do not enter into the computation of the tax base.

EXAMPLE 57

Joyce dies in 1998, leaving a taxable estate of $800,000. During her life, Joyce made taxable gifts as follows: $50,000 in 1975 and $100,000 in 1982. For estate tax purposes, the Federal estate tax base becomes $900,000, determined as follows: $800,000 taxable estate + $100,000 taxable gift made in 1982. ▼

Next the tentative tax on the tax base is computed using the unified transfer tax rate schedule contained in § 2001(c). Using the facts in Example 57, the tentative tax on $900,000 is $306,800 [$248,300 + (39% × $150,000)]—see Appendix A. (See

---

§§ 2523(f) and 2056(b)(7).
 2519.

[52]§ 2044.
[53]§ 2207A(a).

the discussion below for the phase-out of the unified tax credit and the graduated tax rates for certain large estates.)

All available estate tax credits are subtracted from the tentative estate tax to arrive at the estate tax (if any) that is due.

ESTATE TAX CREDITS

Unified Tax Credit (§ 2010). Recall from previous discussion of this credit that the amount of the credit allowed depends upon the year of the transfer. Returning to Example 57, the credit allowed on the gift in 1982 was $62,800. Since the exemption equivalent of this amount is $225,000 (refer to Table 26–1), no gift tax was due on the transfer. On Joyce's death in 1998, however, the unified tax credit is $202,050, which is less than the tentative tax of $306,800 (refer to the discussion following Example 57). Disregarding the effect of any other estate tax credits, Joyce's estate owes a tax of $104,750 [$306,800 (tentative tax on a tax base of $900,000) – $202,050 (unified tax credit for 1998)].

An adjustment to the unified tax credit is necessary if any portion of the specific exemption was utilized on gifts made after September 8, 1976, and before January 1, 1977. In this regard, refer to Example 5.

Under current law, the benefit of the unified tax credit and the graduated unified tax rates is phased out for taxable transfers exceeding a certain amount. The gift and estate tax liability for taxable transfers in excess of $10 million is increased by 5 percent of the excess until the benefit of the credit and graduated brackets is recaptured.

Credit for State Death Taxes (§ 2011). The Code allows a limited credit for the amount of any death tax actually paid to any state (or to the District of Columbia) attributable to any property included in the gross estate. Like the credit for foreign death taxes paid, this provision mitigates the harshness of subjecting the same property to multiple death taxes.

The credit allowed is limited to the lesser of the amount of tax actually paid or the amount provided for in a table contained in § 2011(b). (See Appendix A.) The table amount is based on the *adjusted taxable estate*, which for this purpose is the taxable estate less $60,000. No credit is allowed if the adjusted taxable estate is $40,000 or less.

EXAMPLE 58   Butch's taxable estate is $98,000, and the state of appropriate jurisdiction imposes a death tax of $1,500 on this amount. Since the adjusted taxable estate is $38,000 ($98,000 – $60,000), none of the $1,500 paid qualifies for the state death tax credit. ▼

EXAMPLE 59   Butch's taxable estate is $200,000, and the state of appropriate jurisdiction imposes a death tax of $3,000 on this amount. Because the adjusted taxable estate is $140,000 ($200,000 – $60,000), the table amount limits the death tax credit to $1,200. (See Appendix A.) ▼

As Examples 58 and 59 illustrate, the credit allowed by § 2011 may be less than the amount of state death taxes paid. The reverse is possible but usually is not the case. Most states make sure that the minimum tax payable to the jurisdiction is at least equal to the credit allowed by the table. Sometimes this result is accomplished by a soak-up or sponge tax superimposed on the regular inheritance tax. Thus, if the regular inheritance tax yielded $2,500, but the maximum credit allowed by the table is $3,200, a soak-up tax would impose an additional $700 in state death taxes. In other states, the state death tax liability depends entirely upon the amount allowed for Federal estate tax purposes under the table. In the previous illustration, the state death tax would be an automatic $1,200.

Credit for Tax on Prior Transfers (§ 2013).   Suppose Floyd owns some property that he passes at death to Sarah. Shortly thereafter, Sarah dies and passes the property to Juan. Assuming both estates are subject to the Federal estate tax, the successive deaths result in a multiple effect. To mitigate the possible multiple taxation that might result, § 2013 provides relief in the form of a credit for a death tax on prior transfers. In the preceding hypothetical case, Sarah's estate may be able to claim as an estate tax credit some of the taxes paid by Floyd's estate.

The credit is limited to the lesser of the following:

1. The amount of the Federal estate tax attributable to the transferred property in the transferor's estate.
2. The amount of the Federal estate tax attributable to the transferred property in the decedent's estate.

To apply the limitations, certain adjustments must be made that are not covered in this text.[54] However, it is not necessary for the transferred property to be identified in the present decedent's estate or for it to be in existence at the time of the present decedent's death. It is sufficient that the transfer of property was subjected to the Federal estate tax in the estate of the transferor and that the transferor died within the prescribed period of time.

If the transferor dies within two years after or before the present decedent's death, the credit is allowed in full (subject to the preceding limitations). If the transferor died more than two years before the decedent, the credit is a certain percentage: 80 percent if the transferor died within the third or fourth year preceding the decedent's death, 60 percent if within the fifth or sixth year, 40 percent if within the seventh or eighth year, and 20 percent if within the ninth or tenth year.

EXAMPLE 60

Under Floyd's will, Sarah inherits property. One year later Sarah dies. Assume the estate tax attributable to the inclusion of the property in Floyd's gross estate was $15,000 and that attributable to the inclusion of the property in Sarah's gross estate is $12,000. Under these circumstances, Sarah's estate claims a credit against the estate tax of $12,000 (refer to limitation 2). ▼

---

[54]See the instructions to Form 706 and Reg. §§ 20.2013–2 and –3.

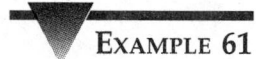
EXAMPLE 61

Assume the same facts as in Example 60, except that Sarah dies three years after Floyd. The applicable credit is now 80% of $12,000, or $9,600. ▼

Credit for Foreign Death Taxes (§ 2014). A credit is allowed against the estate tax for any estate, inheritance, legacy, or succession tax actually paid to a foreign country. For purposes of this provision, the term "foreign country" means not only states in the international sense but also possessions or political subdivisions of foreign states and possessions of the United States.

PROCEDURAL MATTERS

A Federal estate tax return, if required, is due nine months after the date of the decedent's death.[55] The time limit applies to all estates regardless of the nationality or residence of the decedent. Frequently, an executor will request and obtain from the IRS an extension of time for filing Form 706 (estate tax return).[56]

The filing requirements parallel the exemption equivalent amounts of the unified tax credit available for each year (refer to Table 26–1). The filing requirements may be lower when the decedent has made taxable gifts after 1976 or has utilized any of the $30,000 specific gift tax exemption after September 8, 1976.

EXAMPLE 62

Carlos dies in 1998, leaving a gross estate of $620,000. If Carlos did not make any post-1976 taxable gifts or use the specific gift tax exemption after September 8, 1976, his estate need not file Form 706. ▼

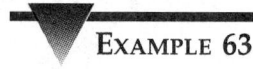
EXAMPLE 63

Assume the same facts as in Example 62, except that Carlos made a taxable gift of $20,000 in 1980. Since the filing requirement now becomes $605,000 ($625,000 regular filing requirement for 1998 – $20,000 post-1976 taxable gift), Carlos's estate must file Form 706. ▼

THE GENERATION–SKIPPING TRANSFER TAX

In order to prevent partial avoidance of Federal gift and estate taxes on large transfers, the tax law imposes an additional generation-skipping transfer tax.

9 ▼ **LEARNING OBJECTIVE**
Appreciate the role of the generation-skipping transfer tax.

THE PROBLEM

Previously, it was possible to bypass a generation of transfer taxes by structuring the transaction carefully.

EXAMPLE 64

Under his will, Edward creates a trust, life estate to Stephen (Edward's son) and remainder to Ava (Edward's granddaughter) upon Stephen's death. Edward is subject to the Federal estate tax, but no tax results on Stephen's death. Stephen held a life estate, but § 2036 does not apply because he was not the grantor of the trust. Nor does § 2033 (property owned by the decedent) come into play because Stephen's interest disappeared upon his death. The ultimate result is that the property in trust skips a generation of transfer taxes. ▼

EXAMPLE 65

Amy gives assets to Eric (her grandson). Called a direct skip, the gift would circumvent any transfer taxes that would have resulted had the assets been channeled through Eric's parents. ▼

---

[55]§ 6075(a).   [56]§ 6081.

THE SOLUTION

The generation-skipping transfer tax (GSTT) is imposed when a younger generation is bypassed in favor of a later generation.[57] The GSTT applies to lifetime transfers by gift and to transfers by death. The tax rate imposed is the highest rate under the gift and estate tax schedule, or 55 percent. Consequently, the GSTT does not permit the use of the graduated rate structure.

The application of the GSTT depends upon the type of arrangement involved. In Example 64, the GSTT would be imposed upon the death of Stephen (the life tenant). The tax, however, is levied against the trust. In effect, it reduces the amount that is distributed to Ava (the remainderperson).

In Example 65, the GSTT is imposed upon Amy when the gift is made to Eric. In this situation, not only will Amy be subject to the GSTT, but the amount of the tax represents an additional gift to Eric.[58] Thus, if a gift is a direct skip (such as Example 65), the total transfer tax (the GSTT plus the gift tax) may exceed what the donee receives.

Though the GSTT may appear to yield a confiscatory result, every grantor is entitled to a $1 million exemption.[59] The exemption can be applied to whichever transfers the grantor (or personal representative of the grantor) chooses. Any appreciation attributable to the exempted portion of the transfer is not subject to the GSTT.

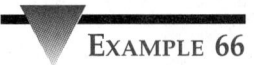

EXAMPLE 66

Assume the same facts as in Example 64, except that the trust created by Edward contained assets valued at $1 million. Ten years later when Stephen dies, the trust is now worth $3 million. If the exemption of $1 million is used upon the creation of the trust, no GSTT results upon Stephen's death. ▼

ETHICAL CONSIDERATIONS

A Gift That Keeps Giving!

Should a tax cheat be treated less harshly than a rich person under the tax system? First, consider Joe, who is in the 39.6 percent income tax bracket. Joe deliberately omits $100,000 of income from his Form 1040. He is caught and forced to pay a tax of $39,600 and a civil fraud penalty of $75,000 (75% × $100,000) for a total outlay of $114,600.

Second, consider Jack, who makes a gift of $100,000 to his grandson. Assuming Jack has exhausted the $1 million generation-skipping transfer tax (GSTT) exemption and is in the top gift tax bracket, his tax is computed as follows.

Gift tax (55% × $100,000)	$ 55,000
GSTT (55% × $100,000)	55,000
Gift tax on GSTT (55% × $55,000)	30,250
Total tax	$140,250

Compare $114,600 (Joe, the tax cheat) with $140,250 (Jack, the rich person), and see who is better off. Keep in mind that in each case the same amount (i.e., $100,000) is involved. Needless to say, the GSTT is a gift that keeps giving!

---

[57]The generation-skipping transfer tax provisions are contained in §§ 2601–2663.

[58]§ 2515.

[59]Beginning in 1999, the $1 million exemption will be indexed for inflation.

TAX PLANNING CONSIDERATIONS

THE FEDERAL GIFT TAX

For gifts that generate a tax, consideration must be given to the time value to the donor of the gift taxes paid. Since the donor loses the use of these funds, the expected interval between a gift (the imposition of the gift tax) and death (the imposition of the death tax) may make the gift less attractive from an economic standpoint. On the plus side, however, are the estate tax savings that result from any gift tax paid. Since these funds are no longer in the gross estate of the donor (except for certain gifts within three years of death), the estate tax thereon is avoided.

Gifts possess distinct advantages. First, and often most important, income from the property is generally shifted to the donee. If the donee is in a lower bracket than the donor, the family unit will save on income taxes. Second, the proper spacing of gifts can further cut down the Federal gift tax by maximizing the number of annual exclusions available. Third, all states impose some type of death tax, but only a minority impose a gift tax. Thus, a gift may completely avoid a state transfer tax.

In minimizing gift tax liability in lifetime giving, the optimum use of the annual exclusion can have significant results. Important in this regard are the following observations:

- Because the annual exclusion is available every year, space the gifts over as many years as possible. To carry out this objective, start the program of lifetime giving as soon as is feasible. As an illustration, a donor could give as much as $100,000 to a donee if equally spaced over a 10-year period without using any of the unified tax credit and incurring any gift tax.
- To the extent consistent with the wishes of the donor, maximize the number of donees. For example, a donor could give $500,000 to five donees over a 10-year period ($100,000 apiece) without using any of the unified tax credit and incurring any gift tax.
- For the married donor, make use of the election to split gifts. As an example, a married couple can give $1 million to five donees over a 10-year period ($20,000 per donee each year) without using any of their unified tax credits and incurring any gift tax.
- Watch out for gifts of future interests. As noted earlier in the chapter, the annual exclusion is available only for gifts of a present interest.

THE FEDERAL ESTATE TAX

Controlling the Amount of the Gross Estate.   Presuming an estate tax problem is anticipated, the starting point for planning purposes is to reduce the size of the potential gross estate. Aside from initiating a program of lifetime giving, several other possibilities exist.

Proper Handling of Estate Tax Deductions.   Estate taxes can be saved either by reducing the size of the gross estate or by increasing the total allowable deductions. Thus, the lower the taxable estate, the less the amount of estate tax generated. Planning in the deduction area generally involves the following considerations:

- Making proper use of the marital deduction.
- Working effectively with the charitable deduction.
- Properly handling other deductions and losses allowed under §§ 2053 and 2054.

CONCEPT SUMMARY 26-2

Federal Estate Tax Provisions

1. The Federal gift and estate taxes are both excise taxes on the transfer of wealth.
2. The starting point for applying the Federal estate tax is to determine which assets are subject to tax. Such assets constitute a decedent's gross estate.
3. The gross estate generally will not include any gifts made by the decedent within three years of death. It does include any gift tax paid on these transfers.
4. Based on the premise that one should not continue to enjoy or control property and not have it subject to the estate tax, certain incomplete transfers are included in the gross estate.
5. Upon the death of a joint tenant, the full value of the property is included in the gross estate unless the survivor(s) made a contribution toward the cost of the property. Spouses are subject to a special rule that calls for automatic inclusion of half of the value of the property in the gross estate of the first tenant to die. The creation of joint ownership is subject to the gift tax when a tenant receives a lesser interest in the property than is warranted by the consideration furnished.
6. If the decedent is the insured, life insurance proceeds are included in the gross estate if either of two conditions is satisfied. First, the proceeds are paid to the estate or for the benefit of the estate. Second, the decedent possessed incidents of ownership (e.g., the right to change beneficiaries) over the policy.
7. In moving from the gross estate to the taxable estate, certain deductions are allowed. Under § 2053, deductions are permitted for various administration expenses (e.g., executor's commissions, funeral costs), debts of the decedent, and certain unpaid taxes. Casualty and theft losses incurred during the administration of an estate can be deducted in arriving at the taxable estate.
8. Charitable transfers are deductible if the designated organization holds qualified status with the IRS at the time of the gift or upon death.
9. Transfers to a spouse qualify for the gift or estate tax marital deduction. Except as noted in (10), such transfers are subject to the terminable interest limitation.
10. The terminable interest limitation will not apply if the QTIP election is made. In the case of a lifetime transfer, the donor spouse makes the QTIP election. In the case of a testamentary transfer, the executor of the estate of the deceased spouse has the election responsibility.
11. The tax base for determining the estate tax is the taxable estate plus post-1976 taxable gifts. All available credits are subtracted from the tax.
12. Of prime importance in the tax credit area is the unified tax credit. Except for large taxable transfers, the unified tax credit varies and depends upon the year of death.
13. Other Federal estate tax credits include credits for state death taxes, tax on prior transfers, and foreign death taxes.
14. If due, a Federal estate tax return (Form 706) must be filed within nine months of the date of the decedent's death.

Approaches to the Marital Deduction. When planning for the estate tax marital deduction, both tax and nontax factors have to be taken into account. In the tax area, planning is guided by two major goals: the *equalization* and *deferral* approaches.

- Attempt to equalize the estates of both spouses. Clearly, for example, the estate tax on $2 million is more than double the estate tax on $1 million [compare $780,800 with $691,600 ($345,800 × 2)].
- Try to postpone estate taxation as long as possible. On a $1 million amount, for example, what is the time value of $345,800 in estate taxes deferred for a period of, say, 10 years?

Barring certain circumstances, the deferral approach generally is preferable. By maximizing the marital deduction on the death of the first spouse to die, not only are taxes saved, but the surviving spouse is enabled to trim his or her future estate by entering into a program of lifetime giving. By making optimum use of the annual exclusion, considerable amounts can be shifted without incurring *any* transfer tax.

Tax planning must remain flexible and be tailored to the individual circumstances of the parties involved. Before the equalization approach is cast aside, therefore, consider the following variables:

- Both spouses are of advanced age and/or in poor health, and neither is expected to survive the other for a prolonged period of time.
- The spouse who is expected to survive has considerable assets of his or her own. To illustrate, a spouse who passes a $250,000 estate to a survivor who already has assets of $1 million is trading a 32 percent bracket for a later 43 percent bracket.
- Because of appreciation, property worth $250,000 when it passes to the surviving spouse today may be worth $1 million five years later when the survivor dies.

The Marital Deduction—Sophistication of the Deferral Approach. When saving estate taxes for the family unit is the sole consideration, the equalization and deferral approaches can be combined with maximum effect.

EXAMPLE 67

At the time of his death in 1998, Vito had never made any taxable gifts. Under Vito's will, his *disposable estate* of $1,100,000 passes to his wife, Zina.[60] ▼

EXAMPLE 68

Assume the same facts as in Example 67, except that Vito's will provides as follows: $625,000 to the children and the remainder ($475,000) to Zina. ▼

From a tax standpoint, which is the better plan? Although no estate tax results from either arrangement, Example 67 represents an overfunding in terms of the marital deduction. Why place an additional $625,000 in Zina's potential estate when it can pass free of tax to the children through the application of the $202,050 unified tax credit available for 1998? (The exemption equivalent of $202,050 is $625,000.) The exemption equivalent is known as the *bypass amount*. The arrangement in Example 68 is preferred, as it avoids unnecessary concentration of wealth in Zina's estate.

On occasion, the disclaimer procedure can be used to maximize the deferral approach.

EXAMPLE 69

At the time of his death in 1998, Pete had never made any taxable gifts. Under Pete's will, his disposable estate of $1,500,000 passes as follows: $700,000 to Jim (Pete's adult son) and the remainder ($800,000) to Clare (Pete's surviving spouse). Shortly after Pete's death, Jim issues a disclaimer as to $75,000 of his $700,000 bequest. This amount, therefore, passes to Clare as the remainderperson under Pete's will. ▼

Because the unified tax credit for 1998 is $202,050 (with an exemption equivalent of $625,000), Jim's disclaimer avoids an estate tax on $75,000. The end result is an increase of $75,000 in the marital deduction and the elimination of *any* estate tax upon Pete's death.

Effectively Working with the Charitable Deduction. As a general guide to obtain overall tax savings, lifetime charitable transfers are preferred over testamentary dispositions. For example, an individual who gave $10,000 to a qualified

---

[60]For this purpose, the *disposable estate* includes the gross estate less all deductions (e.g., debts, administration and funeral expenses) except the marital deduction. The term is not in the Code but is useful in evaluating tax options.

charity during his or her life would secure an income tax deduction, avoid any gift tax, and reduce the gross estate by the amount of the gift. By way of contrast, if the $10,000 had been willed to charity, no income tax deduction would be available, and the amount of the transfer would be includible in the decedent's gross estate (though later deducted for estate tax purposes). In short, the lifetime transfer provides a double tax benefit (income tax deduction plus reduced estate taxes) at no gift tax cost. The testamentary transfer merely neutralizes the effect of the inclusion of the property in the gross estate (inclusion under § 2033 and then deduction under § 2055).

On occasion, a charitable bequest depends on the issuance of a disclaimer by a noncharitable heir. Such a situation frequently arises with special types of property or collections, which the decedent may feel a noncharitable heir should have a choice of receiving.

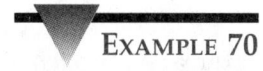

EXAMPLE 70

Megan specified in her will that her valuable art collection is to pass to her son or, if the son refuses, to a designated and qualified art museum. At the time the will was drawn, Megan knew that her son was not interested in owning the collection. If, after Megan's death, the son issues a timely disclaimer, the collection will pass to the designated museum, and Megan's estate is allowed a charitable deduction for its death tax value. ▼

EXAMPLE 71

Dick's will specifies that one-half of his disposable estate is to pass to his wife, and the remainder of his property to a designated and qualified charitable organization. If the wife issues a timely disclaimer after Dick's death, all of the property passes to the charity and qualifies for the § 2055 charitable deduction. ▼

Did the son in Example 70 act wisely if he issued the disclaimer in favor of the museum? Although the disclaimer will provide Megan's estate with a deduction for the value of the art collection, consider the income tax deduction alternative. If the son accepts the bequest, he can still dispose of the collection (and fulfill his mother's philanthropic objectives) through a lifetime donation to the museum. At the same time, he obtains an income tax deduction under § 170. Whether this will save taxes for the family unit depends on a comparison of Megan's estate tax bracket with the estimated income tax bracket of the son. If the value of the collection runs afoul of the percentage limitations of § 170(b)(1), the donations can be spread over more than one year. If this is done, and to protect against the contingency of the son's dying before the entire collection is donated, the son can neutralize any potential death tax consequences by providing in his will for the undonated balance to pass to the museum.

The use of a disclaimer in Example 71 would be sheer folly. It would not reduce Dick's estate tax; it would merely substitute a charitable deduction for the marital deduction. Whether the wife issues a disclaimer or not, no estate taxes will be due. The wife should accept her bequest and, if she is so inclined, make lifetime gifts of it to a qualified charity. In so doing, she generates an income tax deduction for herself.

Proper Handling of Other Deductions and Losses under §§ 2053 and 2054. Many § 2053 and § 2054 deductions and losses may be claimed either as estate tax deductions or as income tax deductions of the estate on the fiduciary return (Form 1041), but a choice must be made.[61] The deduction for income tax purposes is not allowed unless the estate tax deduction is waived. It is possible for these deductions to be apportioned between the two returns.

---

[61]§ 642(g) and Reg. § 20.2053–1(d).

KEY TERMS

Alternate valuation date, 26–8

Annual exclusion, 26–13

Disclaimer, 26–12

Exemption equivalent, 26–7

Future interest, 26–13

Gross estate, 26–17

Inheritance tax, 26–3

Joint tenants, 26–9

Marital deduction, 26–29

Probate estate, 26–17

Qualified terminable interest property (QTIP), 26–31

Taxable estate, 26–28

Taxable gift, 26–5

Tenants by the entirety, 26–9

Tenants in common, 26–9

Terminable interests, 26–31

Unified tax credit, 26–7

Unified transfer tax, 26–3

PROBLEM MATERIALS

DISCUSSION QUESTIONS

1. Why can the unified transfer tax be categorized as an excise tax? In this regard, how does it differ from an income tax?

2. Do Federal transfer taxes carry negative economic implications? Explain.

3. What are the major differences between the Federal estate tax and the typical inheritance tax levied by some states?

4. What was the intended purpose of the Federal gift tax?

5. Omar is a wealthy citizen and resident of Yemen. His family physician has recommended that Omar go to the Mayo Clinic in Minnesota for an operation to remove a malignant growth. Omar is hesitant to do so because he fears the imposition of the U.S. Federal estate tax if the operation is unsuccessful. Does place of death control the application of the Federal estate tax? Explain.

6. Onishi Yamato is a resident and citizen of Japan. Because real estate is so expensive and scarce in Japan, he is intrigued by the investment opportunities in such locales as Arizona and New Mexico. As a result, he has invested heavily in unimproved land that has development potential. Discuss what could happen for estate tax purposes in the event of Onishi's death.

7. Pearl comes to you regarding the making of gifts to family members in the current year. When you ask her about prior gifts, she responds, "What difference does it make what I did in the past?" Please clarify matters for Pearl.

8. In determining the *tax base* for computing the *tentative estate tax*, all prior taxable gifts must be added to the taxable estate. Do you agree or disagree? Why?

9. What is the justification for the alternate valuation date election?

10. What conditions must be satisfied before the alternate valuation date can be used?

11. What are the similarities between each of the following?
    a. Joint tenancy and tenancy by the entirety.
    b. Tenancy in common and community property.
    c. Tenancy by the entirety and community property.

12. Carla purchases a U.S. savings bond and registers ownership as follows: "Carla, payable to George on Carla's death." Four years later, Carla dies and George redeems the bond. When has a gift taken place? Explain.

13. What purpose does § 2516 serve?

14. Under Leon's will, all of his property is to pass to his son, Jody. Jody is a widower, and his only survivor is a daughter, Brenda. Jody has considerable wealth of his own and is in poor health. Do you recognize an attractive estate tax option for the parties?

15. In connection with the gift-splitting provision of § 2513, comment on the following:
    a. What it was designed to accomplish.
    b. How the election is made.
    c. Its utility in a community property jurisdiction.

16. In connection with the filing of a Federal gift tax return, comment on the following:
    a. No Federal gift tax is due.
    b. The § 2513 election to split gifts is to be used.
    c. A gift of a future interest is involved.
    d. The donor uses a fiscal year for Federal income tax purposes.
    e. The donor obtained from the IRS an extension of time for filing his or her Federal income tax return.

17. Distinguish between the following:
    a. The gross estate and the taxable estate.
    b. The gross estate and the probate estate.

18. Jerry, the owner of a prosperous wholesale business, is delighted to learn about the enactment of the $1,300,000 exclusion for small business. He figures that when the exemption equivalent reaches $1,000,000 in 2006, a total of $2,300,000 ($1,300,000 + $1,000,000) can be sheltered from the estate tax. Is Jerry's understanding of the tax law correct? Why or why not?

19. Under the new $1,300,000 exclusion for small business, is it possible for a qualifying heir to not be a member of the deceased owner's family? Explain.

20. What was the original justification for § 2035? Does this justification still exist? Explain.

21. At the time of Emile's death, he was a joint tenant with Colette in a parcel of real estate. With regard to the inclusion in Emile's gross estate under § 2040, comment on the following independent assumptions:
    a. Emile and Colette received the property as a gift from Douglas.
    b. Colette provided all of the purchase price of the property.
    c. Colette's contribution was received as a gift from Emile.
    d. Emile's contribution was derived from income generated by property he received as a gift from Colette.

22. Warren owns an insurance policy on the life of Sylvia with Eric as the designated beneficiary. Of the three persons involved, Sylvia is the eldest and in poor health. What potential tax problems are involved?

23. Zane and Kara are husband and wife when Zane dies. Which of the following *independent* situations satisfies the "passing" requirement for marital deduction purposes?
    a. Kara elects her dower interest. Under state law, this gives her one-third outright ownership in Zane's property.
    b. Zane and Kara held real estate as tenants by the entirety.
    c. Kara owned an insurance policy on Zane's life, with Kim (their son) as the designated beneficiary.

24. In terms of the QTIP (qualified terminable interest property) election, comment on the following:
    a. Who makes the election.
    b. What the election accomplishes.
    c. The tax effect of the election upon the death of the surviving spouse.

25. Does the credit for state death taxes (§ 2011) eliminate the double taxation of an estate? Explain.

26. Would the credit for tax on prior transfers (§ 2013) ever apply in the husband and wife–type of situation? Explain.

27. Which of the following provisions are scheduled to be indexed for inflation?
    a. The annual exclusion.
    b. The unified transfer tax rate schedules.
    c. The unified tax credit.
    d. The $1,300,000 exclusion for small business.
    e. The $1,000,000 generation skipping transfer tax exemption.

PROBLEMS

28. An estate holds the following assets:

	Value on Date of Death	Value Six Months Later
Land	$1,780,000	$1,800,000
Stock in Amber Corporation	1,580,000	1,360,000
Stock in Aqua Corporation	1,400,000	1,420,000

The stock in Amber Corporation is sold by the estate for $1,380,000 eight months after the owner's death, while the stock in Aqua Corporation is sold for $1,410,000 four months after death.
    a. Is the § 2032 election available to the estate?
    b. If so and the election is made, what value results?
    c. What value results if the § 2032 election is not available or is not made?

29. In which, if any, of the following *independent* situations, could the alternate valuation date *not be* elected in 1998? In all cases, Rudy and Ashley are husband and wife, and Rudy dies first.
    a. Rudy's will passes all of his property to Ashley.
    b. Rudy's will passes one-half of his property to Ashley and the other half to the city of Boise, Idaho.
    c. The election would decrease the estate tax liability but increase the value of the gross estate.
    d. Rudy's gross estate is $620,000.
    e. Rudy's gross estate is $595,000. Rudy made a taxable gift of $35,000 four years ago.

30. In each of the following independent situations, indicate whether or not the transfer by Phillip is, or could be, subject to the Federal gift tax:
    a. Phillip makes a contribution to an influential political figure.
    b. Phillip makes a contribution to Crow Corporation, of which he is not a shareholder.
    c. In consideration of his upcoming marriage to Teri, Phillip establishes a savings account in Teri's name.
    d. Same as (c). After their marriage, Phillip establishes a joint checking account in the names of "Phillip and Teri."
    e. Same as (d). One year after the checking account is established, Teri withdraws all of the funds.
    f. Phillip enters into an agreement with Teri where he will transfer property to her in full satisfaction of her marital rights. One month after the agreement, the transfer occurs. Later Phillip and Teri are divorced.
    g. Phillip purchases U.S. savings bonds, listing ownership as "Phillip and Teri." Several years later, and after Phillip's death, Teri redeems the bonds.

31. In each of the following independent situations, indicate whether or not the transfer by Jeff is, or could be, subject to the Federal gift tax:
    a. Jeff purchases real estate and lists title as "Jeff and Chris as joint tenants." Jeff and Chris are brothers.
    b. Same as (a), except that Jeff and Chris are husband and wife.

c. Jeff creates a revocable trust with Chris as the designated beneficiary.

d. Same as (c). One year after creating the trust, Jeff releases all power to revoke the trust.

e. Jeff takes out an insurance policy on his life, designating Chris as the beneficiary.

f. Same as (e). Two years later, Jeff dies and the policy proceeds are paid to Chris.

g. Jeff takes out an insurance policy on the life of Gretchen and designates Chris as the beneficiary. Shortly thereafter, Gretchen dies and the policy proceeds are paid to Chris.

h. Jeff pays for Chris's college tuition.

32. In January 1998, Roger and Jean enter into a property settlement under which Roger agrees to pay $500,000 to Jean in return for the release of her marital rights. At the time the agreement is signed, Roger pays Jean $100,000 as a first installment. Although the parties intended to obtain a divorce, Roger dies in July 1998 before legal proceedings have been instituted. After Roger's death, the executor of his estate pays to Jean the $400,000 remaining balance due under the property settlement.

a. What are the gift tax consequences of the $100,000 payment made upon the signing of the agreement? Why?

b. What are the estate tax consequences of the $400,000 paid to Jean from estate assets after Roger's death? Why?

33. In 1998, Polly made gifts of stock (fair market value of $900,000) to her adult son. Polly has never made any prior taxable gifts. Polly's husband, Ted, previously made a taxable gift of $1,000,000 in early 1976 upon which he paid a gift tax of $244,275. At the time of the gift, Ted was not married to Polly.

a. Determine the amount of the gift tax on the 1998 transfer if the § 2513 election is not made.

b. If the § 2513 election is made.

34. On the date of her death on May 7, 1998, Geraldine owned the following property:

	Fair Market Value
Stock in Falcon Corporation	$300,000
Stock in Harrier Corporation	410,000
City of Richmond bonds	505,000

Falcon Corporation declared a dividend on March 27, 1998, payable on May 15, 1998, to shareholders of record as of April 30, 1998. Harrier Corporation declared a dividend on April 3, 1998, payable on May 22, 1998, to shareholders of record as of May 8, 1998.

In the month of May 1998, Geraldine's executor receives the following amounts: $5,000 dividend from Falcon; $7,000 dividend from Harrier; and $12,500 interest ($12,200 accrued to date of death) from the City of Richmond.

How much of these amounts is included in Geraldine's gross estate?

35. Austin is the sole proprietor of a business that meets the requirements for electing § 2033A. Assume that Austin's business has a constant value of $640,000. What is the amount allowed for the small business exclusion if Austin dies in:

a. 1998?

b. 1999?

c. 2004?

d. 2007?

36. Will, a widower, dies in 1998. Previously, he made the following transfers:

- Land, fair market value of $400,000, given to his son in 1996 . A gift tax of $20,000 was paid as a result of the gift. The land has a date of death value of $450,000.

- Insurance policy on Will's life given to his daughter (the designated beneficiary) in 1996. Because it was term insurance, the policy had a value of less than the annual exclusion. Consequently, no taxable gift resulted. The policy has a maturity value of $70,000.

- Stock worth $80,000 given to Will's grandson in 1981. The transfer resulted in no gift tax and had a date of death value of $200,000.

As to these transfers, how much is included in Will's gross estate?

37. In 1976, Irma created a revocable trust with securities worth $300,000. National Trust Company was designated as the trustee. Under the terms of the trust, Irma retained a life estate with remainder to her children. In 1996, Irma releases her right to revoke the trust. Irma dies in 1998 when the trust assets have a fair market value of $1,200,000.
    a. What, if any, are Irma's gift tax consequences in 1976?
    b. What, if any, is included in Irma's gross estate in 1998?
    c. Would your answer to (b) change if Irma *also* released her life estate in 1996? Explain.

38. In 1980, Jim and Maude purchase a commercial annuity. Jim furnishes 75% of the cost, and Maude provides the balance. Under the terms of the contract, Jim is to receive $48,000 per year for his life. If Jim predeceases Maude, she is to receive $36,000 per year for her life.
    a. If Jim dies first when the value of the survivorship feature is $400,000, how much, if any, is included in his gross estate?
    b. Would anything regarding the annuity be included in Maude's gross estate when she dies five years after Jim? Explain.

39. In 1974, John purchased real estate for $400,000, listing ownership as follows: "John and Mary, equal tenants in common." John predeceases Mary in 1998, when the property is worth $900,000. Before 1974, John had not made any taxable gifts or utilized the $30,000 specific exemption. Assume John and Mary are father and daughter.
    a. Determine John's gift tax consequences, if any, in 1974.
    b. How much, if any, of the property should be included in John's gross estate?

40. In 1966, Myrna transfers by gift a personal residence to Louise and Leon, her daughter and son-in-law. The gift is a wedding present, and title to the property is listed as "Louise and Leon, tenants in common."
    a. Did Myrna have gift tax consequences in 1966? Explain.
    b. If the value of the residence is $400,000 when Louise predeceases Leon in 1998, how much, if any, is included in her gross estate?

41. In 1984, Rusty purchased real estate for $800,000, listing title to the property as follows: "Rusty and Alma, joint tenants with the right of survivorship." Alma predeceases Rusty in 1998, when the real estate is worth $1,000,000. Assume Rusty and Alma are sisters and that neither has made any other taxable gifts or utilized the $30,000 specific exemption.
    a. Determine Rusty's gift tax consequences, if any, in 1984.
    b. How much, if any, of the property should be included in Alma's gross estate?

42. Assume the same facts as in Problem 41, except that Rusty and Alma are husband and wife (rather than sisters).
    a. Determine Rusty's gift tax consequences, if any, in 1984.
    b. How much, if any, of the property should be included in Alma's gross estate? Will any such inclusion generate an estate tax liability? Explain.

43. In each of the following independent situations, determine how much should be included in Burton's gross estate under § 2042 as to the various life insurance policies involved. Assume that none of the policies are community property.
    a. At the time of his death, Burton owned a paid-up policy on the life of Suzanna, with Penny as the designated beneficiary. The policy had a replacement cost of $80,000 and a maturity value of $300,000.
    b. Nancy owns a policy on the life of Burton ($300,000 maturity value) with Burton's estate as the designated beneficiary. Upon Burton's death, the insurance company pays $300,000 to his estate.

   c. Four years before his death, Burton transferred a policy on his life ($300,000 maturity value) to Ann as a gift. Burton retained the power to change beneficiaries. At the time of the transfer, the designated beneficiary was Ann. Because Burton had never exercised his right to change beneficiaries, the insurance company pays Ann $300,000 upon his death.

   d. Same as (c), except that Burton releases the power to change beneficiaries one year before his death.

44. Comment on how each of the following independent situations should be handled for estate tax purposes:

   a. Before her death, Linda issued a note payable to her daughter in the amount of $100,000. Linda never received any consideration for the note. After Linda's death, the daughter files a claim against the estate and collects $100,000 on the note.

   b. At the time of her death, Saleka (a widow) owned 10 cemetery lots (each worth $5,000), which she had purchased many years before for herself and her family.

   c. At the time of his death, Stanley was delinquent in the payment of back Federal income taxes. Stanley's executor pays the taxes from assets of the estate.

45. At the time of his death in the current year, Jerome owned the following real estate:

Tract A	$1,000,000
Mortgage on tract A	(200,000)
Tract B	700,000
Mortgage on tract B	(100,000)

Under Jerome's will, both tracts of land pass to Janice (Jerome's surviving spouse). However, Jerome's will directs the executor to pay off the mortgage on tract B from the remainder interest passing to the children.

   a. How much marital deduction will Jerome's estate be allowed?

   b. What is the deduction for indebtedness under § 2053?

46. Determine the credit for state death taxes in each of the following independent situations:

   a. The adjusted taxable estate is $124,000. The amount of state death tax paid is $1,200.

   b. The adjusted taxable estate is $450,000. The amount of state death tax paid is $9,500.

   c. The adjusted taxable estate is $900,000. The state death tax is a soak-up tax that was paid.

47. Under Ira's will, Jill (Ira's sister) inherits property. Three years later, Jill dies. Determine Jill's credit for tax on prior transfers based on the following assumptions:

   a. The estate tax attributable to the inclusion of the property in Ira's gross estate is $70,000, and the estate tax attributable to the inclusion of the property in Jill's gross estate is $50,000.

   b. The estate tax attributable to the inclusion of the property in Ira's gross estate is $60,000, and the estate tax attributable to the inclusion of the property in Jill's gross estate is $80,000.

48. In each of the following independent situations, determine the decedent's final estate tax liability (net of any unified tax credit):

	Decedent		
	Lucinda	**Roland**	**Warren**
Year of death	1984	1986	1998
Taxable estate	$400,000	$600,000	$900,000
Post-1976 taxable gift			
Made in 1982	300,000	—	—
Made in 1984	—	350,000	
Made in 1989	—	—	500,000

Research Problems for this chapter appear at the end of Chapter 28.

INCOME TAXATION OF TRUSTS AND ESTATES

LEARNING OBJECTIVES

After completing Chapter 27, you should be able to:

1. Use working definitions with respect to trusts, estates, beneficiaries, and other parties.

2. Identify the steps in determining the accounting and taxable income of a trust or estate, and the related taxable income of the beneficiaries.

3. Illustrate the uses and implications of distributable net income.

4. Understand various tax planning procedures that can be used to minimize the tax consequences of trusts and estates and their beneficiaries.

AN OVERVIEW OF SUBCHAPTER J

Taxpayers create trusts for a variety of reasons. Some trusts are established primarily for tax purposes while others are designed to accomplish a specific financial goal or to provide for the orderly management of assets in case of emergency. Table 27–1 lists some of the more common reasons for creating a trust.

Because a trust is a separate tax entity, its gross income and deductions must be measured, and an annual tax return must be filed. Similarly, when an individual dies, a legal entity is created in the form of his or her estate. This chapter examines the rules related to the income taxation of trusts and estates. Figure 27–1 illustrates the structure of a typical estate and trust.

The income taxation of trusts and estates is governed by Subchapter J of the Internal Revenue Code, §§ 641 through 692. Certain similarities are apparent between Subchapter J and the income taxation of individuals (e.g., the definitions of gross income and deductible expenditures), partnerships (e.g., the conduit principle), and S corporations (e.g., the conduit principle and the trust as a separate taxable entity). Trusts also involve several important unique concepts, however, including the determination of distributable net income and the tier system of distributions to beneficiaries.

WHAT IS A TRUST?

1 LEARNING OBJECTIVE
Use working definitions with respect to trusts, estates, beneficiaries, and other parties.

The Code does not contain a definition of a trust. However, the term usually refers to an arrangement created by a will or by an *inter vivos* (lifetime) declaration, through which trustees take title to property for the purpose of protecting or conserving it for the beneficiaries.[1]

Typically, the creation of a trust involves at least three parties: (1) The **grantor** (sometimes referred to as the settler or donor) transfers selected assets to the trust

---

[1] Reg. § 301.7701–4(a).

▼ **TABLE 27–1**
Motivations for Creating a Trust

Type of Trust	Financial and Other Goals
Life insurance trust	Holds life insurance policies on the insured, removes the proceeds of the policies from the gross estate (if an irrevocable trust), and safeguards against a young or inexperienced beneficiary receiving the proceeds.
"Living" (revocable) trust	Manages assets, reduces probate costs, provides privacy for asset disposition, protects against medical or other emergencies, and provides relief from the necessity of day-to-day management of the underlying assets.
Trust for minors	Provides funds for a college education, shifts income to lower-bracket taxpayers, and transfers accumulated income without permanently parting with the underlying assets.
"Blind" trust	Holds and manages the assets of the grantor without his/her input or influence (e.g., while the grantor holds political office or some other sensitive position).
Retirement trust	Manages asset contributions under a qualified retirement plan.
Alimony trust	Manages the assets of an ex-spouse and assures they will be distributed in a timely fashion to specified beneficiaries.
Liquidation trust	Collects and distributes the last assets of a corporation that is undergoing a complete liquidation.

entity. (2) The trustee, who may be either an individual or a corporation, is charged with the fiduciary duties associated with the trust. (3) The beneficiary is designated to receive income or property from the trust; the beneficiary's rights are defined by state law and by the trust document.

In some situations, fewer than three persons may be involved, as specified by the trust agreement. For instance, an elderly individual who can no longer manage his or her own property (e.g., because of ill health) may create a trust under which he or she is both the grantor and the beneficiary. In this case, a corporate trustee is charged with the management of the grantor's assets.

In another situation, the grantor might designate himself or herself as the trustee of the trust assets. For example, a parent who wants to transfer selected assets to a minor child could use a trust entity to ensure that the minor does not waste the property. By naming himself or herself as the trustee, the parent retains virtual control over the property that is transferred.

Under the general rules of Subchapter J, the **grantor trusts** just described are not recognized for income tax purposes. Similarly, when only one party is involved (when the same individual is grantor, trustee, and sole beneficiary of the trust), Subchapter J rules do not apply, and the entity is ignored for income tax purposes.

OTHER DEFINITIONS

When the grantor transfers title of selected assets to a trust, those assets become the **corpus** (body), or principal, of the trust. Trust corpus, in most situations, earns *income*, which may be distributed to the beneficiaries, or accumulated for the future by the trustee, as the trust instrument directs.

In the typical trust, the grantor creates two types of beneficiaries: one who receives the accounting income of the trust and one who receives trust corpus that remains at the termination of the trust entity. Beneficiaries in the first category hold an *income interest* in the trust, and those in the second category hold a *remainder interest* in the trust's assets. If the grantor retains the remainder interest, the interest

▼ **FIGURE 27–1**
Structure of a Typical Trust and
Estate

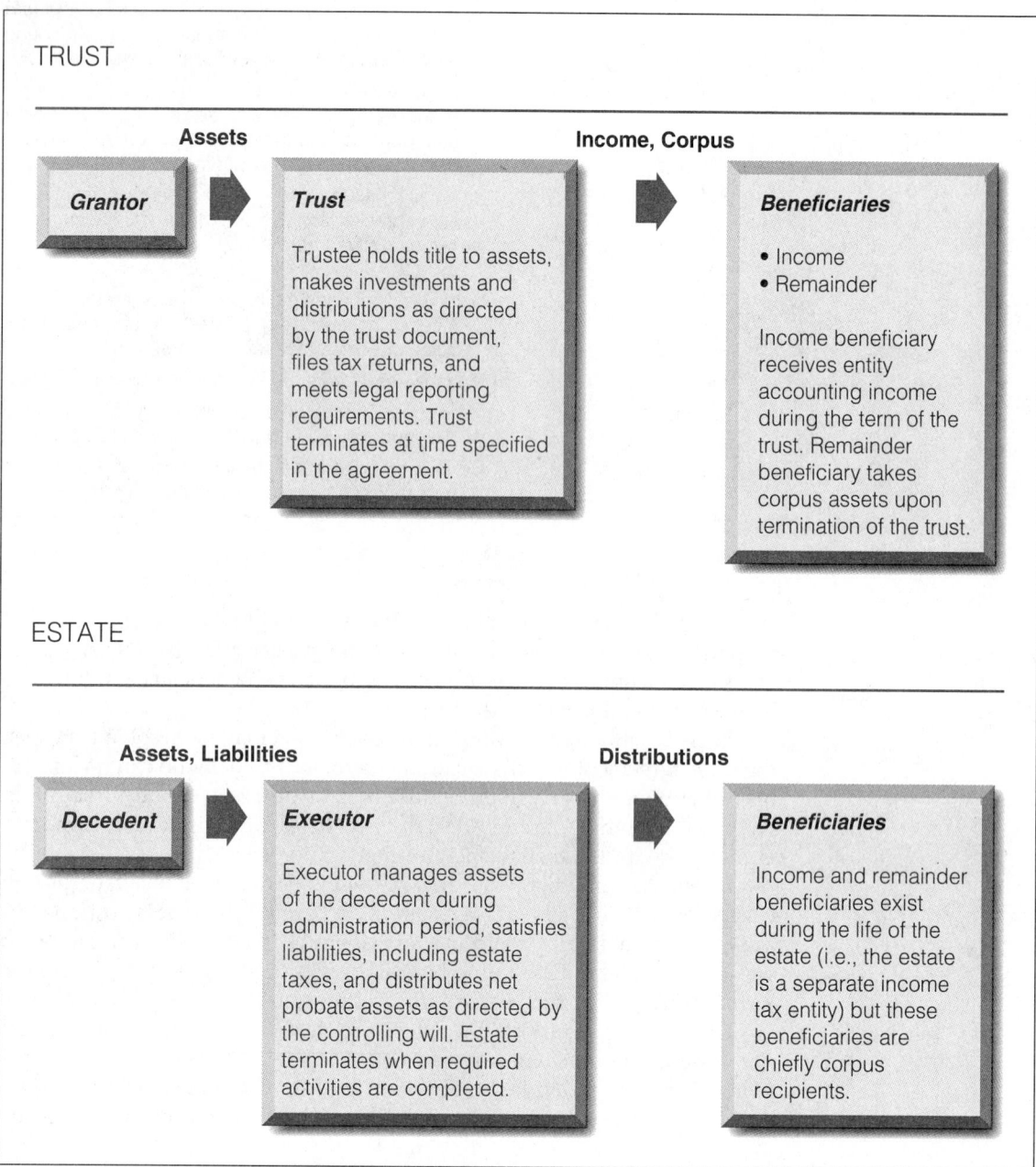

TRUST

Assets   **Income, Corpus**

Grantor   *Trust*   *Beneficiaries*

Trustee holds title to assets,   • Income
makes investments and   • Remainder
distributions as directed
by the trust document,   Income beneficiary
files tax returns, and   receives entity
meets legal reporting   accounting income
requirements. Trust   during the term of the
terminates at time specified   trust. Remainder
in the agreement.   beneficiary takes
                                            corpus assets upon
                                            termination of the trust.

ESTATE

Assets, Liabilities   **Distributions**

Decedent   *Executor*   *Beneficiaries*

Executor manages assets   Income and remainder
of the decedent during   beneficiaries exist
administration period, satisfies   during the life of the
liabilities, including estate   estate (i.e., the estate
taxes, and distributes net   is a separate income
probate assets as directed by   tax entity) but these
the controlling will. Estate   beneficiaries are
terminates when required   chiefly corpus
activities are completed.   recipients.

is known as a **reversionary interest** (corpus reverts to the grantor when the trust entity terminates).

The trust document establishes the term of the trust. The term may be for a specific number of years (a *term certain*) or until the occurrence of a specified event. For instance, a trust might exist (1) for the life of the income beneficiary, in which case the income beneficiary is known as a *life tenant* in trust corpus; (2) for the life of some other individual; (3) until the income or remainder beneficiary reaches the age of majority; or (4) until the beneficiary, or another individual, marries, receives a promotion, or reaches some specified age.

The trustee may be required to distribute the accounting income of the entity according to a distribution schedule specified in the agreement. Sometimes, however, the trustee is given more discretion with respect to the timing and nature of the distributions. If the trustee can determine, within guidelines that may be included in the trust document, either the timing of the income or corpus distributions or the specific beneficiaries who will receive them (from among those identified in the agreement), the trust is called a **sprinkling trust.** Here, the trustee can "sprinkle" the distributions among the various beneficiaries. Family-unit income taxes can be reduced by directing income to those who are subject to lower marginal tax rates. Thus, by giving the trustee a sprinkling power, the income tax liability of the family unit can be manipulated through the trust agreement.

For purposes of certain provisions of Subchapter J, a trust must be classified as either a **simple trust** or a **complex trust.** A simple trust (1) is required to distribute its entire accounting income to designated beneficiaries every year, (2) has no beneficiaries that are qualifying charitable organizations, and (3) makes no distributions of trust corpus during the year. A complex trust is any trust that is not a simple trust.[2] These criteria are applied to the trust every year. Thus, every trust is classified as a complex trust in the year in which it terminates (because it will be distributing all of its corpus during that year).

WHAT IS AN ESTATE?

An estate is created upon the death of every individual. The estate is charged with collecting and conserving all of the individual's assets, satisfying all liabilities, and distributing the remaining assets to the heirs identified by state law or the will.

Typically, the creation of an estate involves at least three parties: the decedent, all of whose probate assets are transferred to the estate for disposition; the executor, who is appointed under the decedent's valid will (or the administrator, if no valid will exists); and the beneficiaries of the estate, who are to receive assets or income from the entity, as the decedent indicated in the will. The executor or administrator holds the fiduciary responsibility to manage the estate as directed by the will, applicable state law, and the probate court.

Recall that the assets that make up the probate estate are not identical to those that constitute the gross estate for transfer tax purposes (refer to Chapter 26). Many gross estate assets are not a part of the probate estate and thus are not subject to disposition by the executor or administrator. For instance, property held by the decedent as a joint tenant passes to the survivor(s) by operation of the applicable state's property law rather than through the probate estate. Proceeds of insurance policies on the life of the decedent, over which the decedent held the incidents of ownership, are not under the control of the executor or administrator. The designated beneficiaries of the policy receive the proceeds outright under the insurance contract.

An estate is a separate taxable entity. Under certain circumstances, taxpayers may find it profitable to prolong an estate's existence. This situation is likely to arise when the heirs are already in a high income tax bracket and would, therefore, prefer to have the income generated by the estate assets taxed at the estate's lower marginal income tax rates. If an estate's existence is unduly prolonged, however, the IRS can terminate it for Federal income tax purposes

---

[2]Reg. § 1.651(a)–1.

DOING ESTATE PLANNING ON TELEVISION

The chief technique offered by those who sell books and seminars on "How to Avoid Probate" is the living or revocable trust. Materials supporting these media productions often consist of no more than "fill-in-the-blank" templates that enable an individual to draft and adopt such a trust document, assuming no special rules apply in the state of residence or asset location.

Revocable trusts are especially attractive where the probate process might be especially long or costly because of the nature of the assets held by the decedent (perhaps a family business or important art collection) or a need for privacy (say, where a celebrity is involved).

Yet executing such an arrangement is costly in itself. Titles to assets must all be recast to show the trustee as owner of the property. An attorney should be consulted, at least to determine the extent to which the standard forms being used will be accepted by local probate courts. And when the grantor dies and the document is used to distribute assets, legal fees often are incurred to address challenges from beneficiaries who feel that they have received too little from the dearly departed.

Moreover, in view of the more competitive legal community and of statutory "simple probate" procedures in many states, many estate planners believe these sales pitches overstate the cost and difficulty associated with probate today.

after the expiration of a reasonable period for the executor to complete the duties of administration.[3]

NATURE OF TRUST AND ESTATE TAXATION

In general, the taxable income of a trust or estate is taxed to the entity or to its beneficiaries to the extent that each has received the accounting income of the entity. Thus, Subchapter J creates a modified conduit principle relative to the income taxation of trusts, estates, and their beneficiaries. Whoever receives the accounting income of the entity, or some portion of it, is liable for the income tax that results.

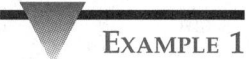

EXAMPLE 1

Adam receives 80% of the accounting income of the Zero Trust. The trustee accumulated the other 20% of the income at her discretion under the trust agreement and added it to trust corpus. Adam is liable for income tax only on the amount of the distribution, and Zero is liable for the income tax on the accumulated portion of the income. ▼

The modified conduit principle of Subchapter J is subject to several exceptions. For instance, some trusts may be treated as associations and therefore will be subject to the corporate income tax.[4] In addition, part or all of the income of certain trusts is taxed to the grantor if too much control over the trust property or income is retained.[5]

---

[3]Reg. § 1.641(b)–3(a).
[4]*Morrissey v. Comm.*, 36–1 USTC ¶9020, 16 AFTR 1274, 56 S.Ct. 289 (USSC, 1936).

[5]§§ 671–679.

FILING REQUIREMENTS

The fiduciary is required to file a Form 1041 (U.S. Fiduciary Income Tax Return) in the following situations.[6]

- For an estate that has gross income of $600 or more for the year.
- For a trust that either has any taxable income or, if there is no taxable income, has gross income of $600 or more.

The fiduciary return (and any related tax liability) is due no later than the fifteenth day of the fourth month following the close of the entity's taxable year. The return is filed with the Internal Revenue Service Center for the region in which the fiduciary resides or has his or her principal place of business.

TAX ACCOUNTING PERIODS, METHODS, AND PAYMENTS

An estate or trust may use any of the tax accounting methods available to individuals. The method of accounting used by the grantor of a trust or the decedent of an estate need not carry over to the entity.

An estate has the same options for choosing a tax year as any new taxpayer. Thus, the estate of a calendar year decedent dying on March 3 can select any fiscal year or report on a calendar year basis. If the calendar year basis is selected, the estate's first taxable year will include the period from March 3 to December 31. If the first or last tax year of an estate is a short year (less than one calendar year), income for that year need not be annualized.

To eliminate the possibility of deferring the taxation of fiduciary-source income simply by using a fiscal tax year, all trusts (other than tax-exempt trusts) are required to use a calendar tax year.[7]

Trusts and estates are required to make estimated Federal income tax payments, using the same quarterly schedule that applies to individual taxpayers. This requirement applies to estates only for tax years that end two or more years after the date of the decedent's death. Charitable trusts and private foundations are exempt from estimated payment requirements altogether.[8]

The two-year estimated tax exception for estates recognizes the liquidity problems that an executor often faces during the early months of administering the estate. The exception does not ensure, however, that an estate in existence less than 24 months will never be required to make an estimated tax payment.

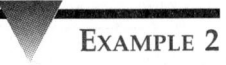

EXAMPLE 2

Juanita died on March 15, 1998. Her executor elected a fiscal year ending on July 31 for the estate. Estimated tax payments will be required from the estate starting with the tax year that begins on August 1, 1999. ▼

TAX RATES AND PERSONAL EXEMPTION

Congress's desire to stop trusts from being used as income-shifting devices has made the fiduciary entity the highest-taxed taxpayer in the Code.[9] The entity reaches a 39.6 percent marginal rate with only $8,100 of taxable income in 1997, so the grantor's ability to shift income in a tax-effective manner is nearly eliminated. The following table, which lists the 1997 taxes paid by various entities on taxable income of $30,000, shows how expensive the accumulation of income within an estate or

---

[6]§ 6012(a).
[7]§ 645.

[8]§ 6654(l).
[9]§ 1(e) (see Appendix A).

TAX IN THE NEWS

EVERYONE GETS WET WHEN YOU SOAK THE RICH

Fiduciary taxation has fallen prey to the "soak the rich" approach to tax reform. In an environment of taxes on millionaires and luxury vehicles, the tax rates that apply to trusts and estates have also increased, and the width of the lower brackets has become so narrow that these entities now are subject to the highest marginal rate structure in U.S. income tax law. Higher tax rates for trusts and estates affect all fiduciary arrangements, however, even those designed for reasons other than tax avoidance.

Perhaps by design, these rate changes have dampened the planning potential of fiduciary entities as a means of shifting income among generations (e.g., from parent to child) or over time (i.e., from the taxpayer's present tax return to a future one). But they have also deepened the tax burden on fixed-income retirees, handicapped individuals, children of divorced parents, and other commonly encountered fiduciary beneficiaries.

Most trust beneficiaries are passive recipients of investment income generated by a stock portfolio managed by a corporate trustee or by the distant managers of the mutual funds in which the funds are invested. In a typical year, a trust enters into very few "new" transactions. For the most part, there is a little portfolio turnover, and periodic interest and dividends are collected. The beneficiaries exercise little decision-making authority over the yield or timing of the entity's distributions, which are fixed by the controlling instrument. Under such circumstances, tax rate increases seem to punish the powerless as well as to soak the rich.

trust can be. Proper income shifting now would move assets *out of* the estate or trust and into the hands of the grantor or beneficiary.

Filing Status/Entity	Taxable Income	1997 Tax Liability
Single	$30,000	$ 5,195*
Married, filing jointly	30,000	4,500*
C corporation	30,000	4,500
Trust or estate	30,000	10,959

*Based on the 1997 Tax Table applicable to individual taxpayers.

A fiduciary's net long-term capital gains can be taxed at a nominal rate of no more than 20 percent. In addition to the regular income tax, an estate or trust may be subject to the alternative minimum tax.[10]

Both trusts and estates are allowed a personal exemption in computing the fiduciary tax liability. All estates are allowed a personal exemption of $600. The exemption available to a trust depends upon the type of trust involved. A trust that is required to distribute all of its income is currently allowed an exemption of $300. All other trusts are allowed an exemption of $100 per year.[11]

The classification of trusts as to the appropriate personal exemption is similar, but not identical, to the distinction between simple and complex trusts. The classification as a simple trust is more stringent.

---

[10]§ 55.   [11]§ 642(b).

EXAMPLE 3

Trust Alpha is required to distribute all of its current accounting income to Susan. Trust Beta is required to distribute all of its current accounting income, one-half to Tyrone and one-half to State University, a qualifying charitable organization. The trustee of Trust Gamma can, at her discretion, distribute the current accounting income or corpus of the trust to Dr. Chapman. None of the trusts makes any corpus distributions during the year. All of the accounting income of Trust Gamma is distributed to Dr. Chapman.

Trust Alpha is a simple trust; it will receive a $300 personal exemption. Trust Beta is a complex trust; it will receive a $300 personal exemption. Trust Gamma is a complex trust; it will receive a $100 personal exemption. ▼

ALTERNATIVE MINIMUM TAX

The alternative minimum tax (AMT) may apply to a trust or estate in any tax year. Given the nature and magnitude of the tax preferences, adjustments, and exemptions that determine alternative minimum taxable income (AMTI), however, most trusts and estates are unlikely to incur the tax. Nevertheless, they could be vulnerable if they are actively engaged in a business that uses the accelerated cost recovery provisions. Similarly, an estate may be liable for the AMT if it receives a sizable portfolio of stock options shortly after the decedent's death under a deferred compensation plan.

In general, derivation of AMTI for the entity follows the rules that apply to individual taxpayers. Thus, the corporate ACE adjustment does not apply to fiduciary entities, but AMTI may be created through the application of most of the other AMT preference and adjustment items discussed in Chapter 14.

The entity has a $22,500 annual exemption, similar to that available to a married individual who files a separate return. The exemption phases out at a rate of one-fourth of the amount by which AMTI exceeds $75,000.

A 26 percent tax rate is applied to AMTI, increasing to 28 percent when AMTI in excess of the exemption reaches $175,000. In addition, estimated tax payments for the entity must include any applicable AMT liability.

TAXABLE INCOME OF TRUSTS AND ESTATES

2 LEARNING OBJECTIVE
Identify the steps in determining the accounting and taxable income of a trust or estate, and the related taxable income of the beneficiaries.

Generally, the taxable income of a trust or estate is computed similarly to that for an individual. Subchapter J does, however, include several important exceptions and provisions that make it necessary to use a systematic approach to calculating the taxable income of these entities. Figure 27–2 illustrates the procedure implied by the Code, and Figure 27–3 presents a systematic computation method to be followed in this chapter.

ENTITY ACCOUNTING INCOME

The first step in determining the taxable income of a trust or estate is to compute the entity's accounting income for the period. Although this prerequisite is not apparent from a cursory reading of Subchapter J, a closer look at the Code reveals a number of references to the *income* of the entity.[12] Wherever the term *income* is used in Subchapter J without some modifier (e.g., *gross* income or *taxable* income), the statute is referring to the accounting income of the trust or estate for the tax year.

---

[12]For example, see §§ 651(a)(1), 652(a), and 661(a)(1).

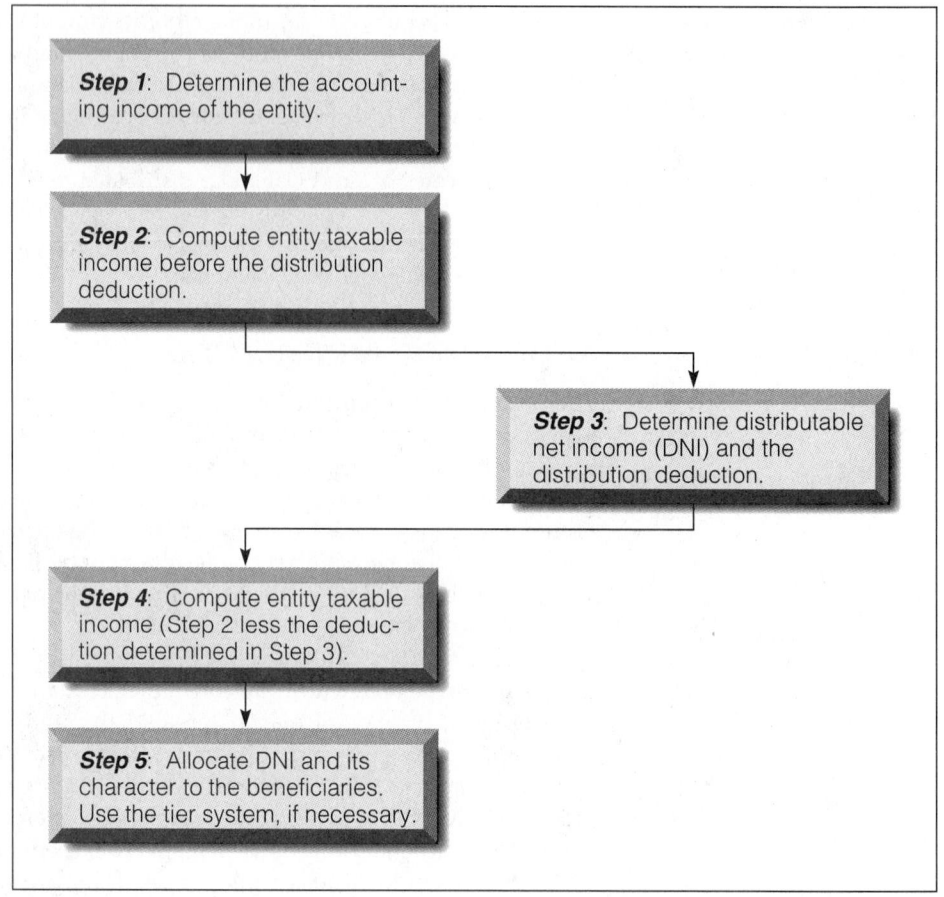

▼ **FIGURE 27–2**
Accounting Income, Distributable Net Income, and Taxable Income of the Entity and Its Beneficiaries (Five Steps)

Step 1: Determine the accounting income of the entity.

Step 2: Compute entity taxable income before the distribution deduction.

Step 3: Determine distributable net income (DNI) and the distribution deduction.

Step 4: Compute entity taxable income (Step 2 less the deduction determined in Step 3).

Step 5: Allocate DNI and its character to the beneficiaries. Use the tier system, if necessary.

A definition of entity accounting income is critical to understanding the Subchapter J computation of fiduciary taxable income. Under state law, entity accounting income is the amount that the income beneficiary of the simple trust or estate is eligible to receive from the entity. More importantly, the calculation of accounting income is virtually under the control of the grantor or decedent (through a properly drafted trust agreement or will). If the document has been drafted at arm's length, a court will enforce a fiduciary's good faith efforts to carry out the specified computation of accounting income.

By allocating specific items of income and expenditure either to the income beneficiaries or to corpus, the desires of the grantor or decedent are put into effect. Table 27–2 shows typical assignments of revenue and expenditure items to fiduciary income or corpus.

Where the controlling document is silent as to whether an item should be assigned to income or corpus, state law prevails. These allocations are an important determinant of the benefits received from the entity by its beneficiaries and the timing of those benefits.

EXAMPLE 4

The Arnold Trust is a simple trust. Mrs. Bennett is its sole beneficiary. In the current year, the trust earns $20,000 in taxable interest and $15,000 in tax-exempt interest. In addition, the trust recognizes an $8,000 long-term capital gain. The trustee assesses a fee of $11,000 for the year. If the trust agreement allocates fees and capital gains to corpus, trust accounting

▼ **FIGURE 27–3**

Computational Template
Applying the Five-Step
Procedure

Item	Totals	Accounting Income	Taxable Income	Distributable Net Income/Distribution Deduction
Income	_____	_____	_____	
Income	_____	_____	_____	
Expense	_____	_____	_____	
Expense	_____	_____	_____	
Personal exemption			_____	
Accounting income/taxable income before the distribution deduction	**Step 1** _____		**Step 2** _____	_____
Personal exemption				_____
Corpus capital gain/loss				_____
Net tax-exempt income				_____
Distributable net income				_____
Distribution deduction			**Step 3** _____	
Entity taxable income			**Step 4** _____	

Note: Beneficiary taxable income is addressed in **Step 5**.

▼ **TABLE 27–2**

Common Allocations of Items to
Income or Corpus

Allocable to Income	Allocable to Corpus
• Ordinary and operating net income from trust assets. • Interest, dividend, rent, and royalty income. • Stock dividends. • One-half of fiduciary fees/ commissions.	• Depreciation on business assets. • Casualty gain/loss on income-producing assets. • Insurance recoveries on income-producing assets. • Capital gain/loss on investment assets. • Stock splits. • One-half of fiduciary fees/ commissions.

income is $35,000, and Mrs. Bennett receives that amount. Thus, the income beneficiary
receives no immediate benefit from the trust's capital gain, and she bears none of the financial
burden of the fiduciary's fees.

Interest income	$35,000
Long-term capital gain—allocable to corpus	–0–
Fiduciary's fees—allocable to corpus	(–0–)
Trust accounting income	$35,000

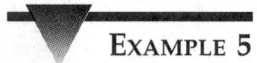

EXAMPLE 5 Assume the same facts as in Example 4, except that the trust agreement allocates the fiduciary's fees to income. The trust accounting income is $24,000, and Mrs. Bennett receives that amount.

Interest income	$35,000
Long-term capital gain—allocable to corpus	–0–
Fiduciary's fees	(11,000)
Trust accounting income	$24,000

EXAMPLE 6 Assume the same facts as in Example 4, except that the trust agreement allocates to income all capital gains and losses and one-half of the trustee's commissions. The trust accounting income is $37,500, and Mrs. Bennett receives that amount.

Interest income	$35,000
Long-term capital gain	8,000
Fiduciary's fees—one-half allocable to corpus	(5,500)
Trust accounting income	$37,500

GROSS INCOME

The gross income of an estate or trust is similar to that of an individual. In determining the gain or loss to be recognized by an estate or trust upon the sale or other taxable disposition of assets, the rules for basis determination are similar to those applicable to other taxpayers. Thus, an estate's basis for property received from a decedent is stepped up or stepped down to gross estate value (refer to Chapter 12 for a more detailed discussion). Property received as a gift (the usual case in most trust arrangements) usually takes the donor's basis. Property purchased by the trust from a third party is assigned a basis equal to the purchase price.

Property Distributions.   In general, the entity does not recognize gain or loss upon its distribution of property to a beneficiary under the provisions of the will or trust document. The distributed property has the same basis to the beneficiary of the distribution as it did to the estate or trust. Moreover, the distribution absorbs distributable net income (DNI) and qualifies for a distribution deduction (both of which are explained later in this chapter) to the extent of the lesser of the distributed asset's basis to the beneficiary or the asset's fair market value as of the distribution date.[13]

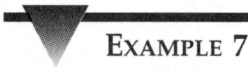

EXAMPLE 7 The Howard Trust distributes a painting, basis of $40,000 and fair market value of $90,000, to beneficiary Kate. Kate's basis in the painting is $40,000. The distribution absorbs $40,000 of the trust's DNI, and Howard claims a $40,000 distribution deduction relative to the transaction. ▼

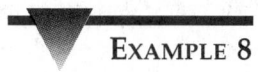

EXAMPLE 8 Assume the same facts as in Example 7, except that Howard's basis in the painting is $100,000. Kate's basis in the painting is also $100,000. The distribution absorbs $90,000 of the trust's DNI, and Howard claims a $90,000 distribution deduction. ▼

---

[13]§ 643(e).

A trustee or executor can *elect* to recognize gain or loss with respect to all of the entity's in-kind property distributions for the year. If the election is made, the beneficiary's basis in the asset is equal to the asset's fair market value as of the distribution date. The distribution absorbs DNI and qualifies for a distribution deduction to the extent of the asset's fair market value. Note, however, that § 267 can restrict an estate or trust's deduction for losses.

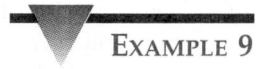

EXAMPLE 9 The Green Estate distributes an antique piano, basis to Green of $10,000 and fair market value of $15,000, to beneficiary Kyle. The executor elects that the estate recognize the related $5,000 gain on the distribution. Accordingly, Kyle's basis in the piano is $15,000 ($10,000 basis to Green + $5,000 gain recognized). Without the election, the estate would not recognize any gain, and Kyle's basis in the piano would be $10,000. ▼

EXAMPLE 10 Assume the same facts as in Example 9, except that Green's basis in the piano is $18,000. The executor elects that the estate recognize the related $3,000 loss on the distribution. Accordingly, Kyle's basis in the piano is $15,000 ($18,000 – $3,000). Without the election, the estate would not recognize any loss, and Kyle's basis in the piano would be $18,000. The estate cannot deduct this loss, however. Because an estate and its beneficiaries are related parties, realized losses cannot be recognized immediately.[14] The loss would be recognized if Kyle later sells the piano to a stranger. ▼

Income in Respect of a Decedent. The gross income of a trust or estate includes **income in respect of a decedent (IRD)** that the entity received.[15] For a cash basis decedent, IRD includes accrued salary, interest, rent, and other income items that were not constructively received before death. For both cash and accrual basis decedents, IRD includes, for instance, death benefits from qualified retirement plans and deferred compensation contracts.

The tax consequences of IRD are as follows.

- The fair market value of the right to IRD on the appropriate valuation date is included in the decedent's gross estate. Thus, it is subject to the Federal estate tax.[16]
- The decedent's basis in the property carries over to the recipient (the estate or heirs). There is no step-up or step-down in the basis of IRD items.
- The recipient of the income recognizes gain or loss, measured by the difference between the amount realized and the adjusted basis of the IRD in the hands of the decedent. The character of the gain or loss depends upon the treatment that it would have received had it been realized by the decedent before death. Thus, if the decedent would have realized capital gain, the recipient must do likewise.[17]
- Expenses related to the IRD (such as interest, taxes, and depletion) that properly were not reported on the final income tax return of the decedent may be claimed by the recipient. These items are known as **expenses in respect of a decedent.** Typically, such expenses also include fiduciary fees, commissions paid to dispose of estate assets, and state gift taxes payable. They are deductible for both Federal estate and income tax purposes, *for* or *from* AGI as would have been the case for the decedent.

---

[14]§ 267(b)(13).

[15]§ 691.

[16]To mitigate the effect of double taxation (imposition of both the estate tax and the income tax), § 691(c) allows the recipient an income tax deduction for the incremental estate tax attributable to the net IRD. For individual recipients, this is an itemized deduction, not subject to the 2%-of-AGI floor.

[17]§ 691(a)(3) and Reg. § 1.691(a)–3.

- If the IRD item would have created an AMT preference or adjustment for the decedent (e.g., with respect to the collection of certain tax-exempt interest by the entity), an identical AMT item is created for the recipient.

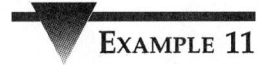

EXAMPLE 11

Amanda died on July 13 of the current year. On August 2, her estate received a check (before deductions) for $1,200 from Amanda's former employer; this was Amanda's compensation for the last pay period of her life. On November 23, Amanda's estate received a $45,000 distribution from her employer's qualified profit sharing plan, the full amount to which she was entitled under the plan. Both Amanda and the estate are calendar year, cash basis taxpayers.

The last salary payment and the profit sharing plan distribution constitute IRD to Amanda's estate. Amanda had earned these items during her lifetime, and the estate had an enforceable right to receive each of them after Amanda's death. Consequently, Amanda's gross estate includes $46,200 with respect to these two items. However, the income tax basis to the estate for these items is not stepped up (from zero to $1,200 and $45,000, respectively) upon distribution to the estate.

The estate must report gross income of $46,200 with respect to the IRD items. The gain recognized upon the receipt of the IRD is $46,200 [($1,200 + $45,000) amounts realized − ($0) adjusted bases]. ▼

Including the IRD in both the taxpayer's gross estate and the gross income of the estate may seem harsh. Nonetheless, the tax consequences of IRD are similar to the treatment that applies to all of a taxpayer's earned income. The item is subject to income tax upon receipt, and to the extent that it is not consumed by the taxpayer before death, it is included in the gross estate.

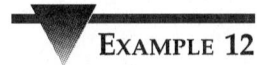

EXAMPLE 12

Assume the same facts as in Example 11, except that Amanda was an accrual basis taxpayer. IRD now includes only the $45,000 distribution from the qualified retirement plan. Amanda's last paycheck is included in the gross income of her own last return (January 1 through date of death). The $1,200 salary is already recognized properly under Amanda's usual method of tax accounting. It does not constitute IRD and is not gross income when received by the executor. ▼

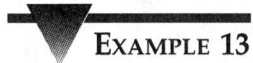

EXAMPLE 13

Assume the same facts as in Example 11. Amanda's last paycheck was reduced by $165 for state income taxes that were withheld by her employer. The $165 tax payment is an expense in respect of a decedent and is allowed as a deduction on *both* Amanda's estate tax return *and* the estate's income tax return. ▼

ORDINARY DEDUCTIONS

As a general rule, the taxable income of an estate or trust is similar to that of an individual. Deductions are allowed for ordinary and necessary expenses paid or incurred in carrying on a trade or business; for the production or collection of income; for the management, conservation, or maintenance of property; and in connection with the determination, collection, or refund of any tax.[18] Reasonable administration expenses, including fiduciary fees and litigation costs in connection with the duties of administration, also are deductible.

The trust or estate must apply the 2 percent-of-AGI floor to many of the § 212 expenses that it incurs. For this purpose, AGI appears to be the greater of (1) the

---

[18]§§ 162 and 212.

pertinent-year AGI of the grantor of the trust or (2) the AGI of the trust or estate, computed as though the entity were an individual. The floor does not apply, however, to items like fiduciary fees or the personal exemption (i.e., items that would not be incurred by an individual).[19]

Expenses attributable to the production or collection of tax-exempt income are not deductible.[20] The amount of the disallowed deduction is found by using a formula based upon the composition of the income elements of entity accounting income for the year of the deduction. The § 212 deduction is apportioned without regard to the accounting income allocation of such expenses to income or to corpus. The deductibility of the fees is determined strictly by the Code (under §§ 212 and 265), and the allocation of expenditures to income and to corpus is controlled by the trust agreement or will or by state law.

Under § 642(g), amounts deductible as administration expenses or losses for estate tax purposes (under §§ 2053 and 2054) cannot be claimed by the estate for income tax purposes, unless the estate files a waiver of the estate tax deduction. Although these expenses cannot be deducted twice, they may be allocated between Forms 706 and 1041 as the fiduciary sees fit; they need not be claimed in their entirety on either return.[21] The prohibition against double deductions does not extend to expenses in respect of a decedent.

Trusts and estates are allowed cost recovery deductions. However, such deductions are assigned proportionately among the recipients of entity accounting income.[22]

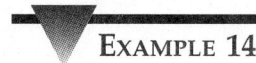

EXAMPLE 14

Lisa and Martin are the equal income beneficiaries of the Needle Trust. Under the terms of the trust agreement, the trustee has complete discretion as to the timing of the distributions from Needle's current accounting income. The trust agreement allocates all depreciation expense to income. In the current year, the trustee distributes 40% of the current trust accounting income to Lisa and 40% to Martin; thus, 20% of the income is accumulated. The depreciation deduction allowable to Needle is $100,000. This deduction is allocated among the trust and its beneficiaries on the basis of the distribution of current accounting income: Lisa and Martin each can claim a $40,000 deduction, and the trust can deduct $20,000. ▼

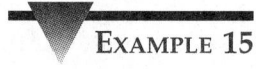

EXAMPLE 15

Assume the same facts as in Example 14, except that the trust agreement allocates all depreciation expense to corpus. Lisa and Martin both still claim a $40,000 depreciation deduction, and Needle retains its $20,000 deduction. The Code assigns the depreciation deduction proportionately to the recipients of current entity accounting income. Allocation of depreciation to income or to corpus is irrelevant in determining which party can properly claim the deduction. ▼

When a trust sells property received by transfer from the grantor, the amount of depreciation subject to recapture includes the depreciation claimed by the grantor before the transfer of the property to the trust. However, depreciation recapture potential disappears at death.

EXAMPLE 16

Jaime transferred an asset to the Shoulder Trust via a lifetime gift. The asset's total depreciation recapture potential was $40,000. If the trust sells the asset at a gain, it will recognize

---

[19]§§ 67(b) and (e). *O'Neill Trust v. Comm.*, 93–1 USTC ¶50,332, 71 AFTR2d 93–2052, 994 F.2d 302 (CA–6, 1993), *rev'g* 98 T.C. 227 (1992).

[20]§ 265.

[21]Reg. § 1.642(g)–2.

[22]§ 167(h) and §§ 611(b)(3) and (4).

ordinary income not to exceed $40,000. Had Jaime transferred the asset after his death to his estate through a bequest, the $40,000 recapture potential would have disappeared. ▼

DEDUCTIONS FOR LOSSES

An estate or trust is allowed a deduction for casualty or theft losses not covered by insurance or other arrangement. Such losses may also be deductible by an estate for Federal estate tax purposes under § 2054. As a result, an estate is not allowed an income tax deduction unless the estate tax deduction is waived.[23]

The net operating loss (NOL) deduction is available for estates and trusts (i.e., where trade or business income is generated). The carryback of an NOL may reduce the distributable net income of the trust or estate for the carryback year and therefore affect the amount taxed to the beneficiaries for that year.

Certain losses realized by an estate or trust may also be disallowed, as they are for all taxpayers. Thus, the wash sales provisions of § 1091 disallow losses on the sale or other disposition of stock or securities when the estate or trust acquires substantially identical stock or securities within the prescribed 30-day period. Likewise, § 267 disallows certain losses, expenses, and interest with respect to transactions between related taxpayers. Generally, related parties include a trust, its trustee, grantor, and beneficiaries, as well as an estate, its executor, and beneficiaries.

Except for the possibility of unused losses in the year of termination, the net capital losses of an estate or trust are used only on the fiduciary income tax return.[24] The tax treatment of these losses is the same as for individual taxpayers.

CHARITABLE CONTRIBUTIONS

An estate or complex trust is allowed a deduction for contributions to charitable organizations under certain conditions.

- The contribution is made pursuant to the will or trust instrument, and its amount is determinable using the language of that document.
- The recipient is a qualified organization. For this purpose, qualified organizations include the same charities for which individual and corporate donors are allowed deductions, except that estates and trusts are permitted a deduction for contributions to certain foreign charitable organizations.
- Generally, the contribution is claimed in the tax year paid, but a fiduciary can treat amounts paid in the year immediately following as a deduction for the preceding year.[25] Under this rule, estates and complex trusts receive more liberal treatment than individuals or corporations.

Unlike the charitable contribution deductions of individuals and corporations, the deductions of estates and complex trusts are not limited (e.g., to a percentage of taxable or adjusted gross income). Nonetheless, an entity's charitable contribution may not be fully deductible.[26] Specifically, the deduction is limited to amounts included in the gross income of the entity in the year of the contribution.

A contribution is deemed to have been made proportionately from each of the income elements of entity accounting income. Thus, in the event that the entity has tax-exempt income, the contribution is deductible only to the extent that the

---

[23]See Reg. § 1.642(g)–1 for the required statement waiving the estate tax deduction. In addition, see Reg. §§ 1.165–7(c) and 1.165–8(b), requiring that a statement be filed to allow an income tax deduction for such losses.

[24]§ 642(h).

[25]§ 642(c)(1) and Reg. § 1.642(c)–1(b).

[26]Reg. §§ 1.642(c)–3(b) and (c).

income elements of entity accounting income for the year of the deduction are included in the entity's gross income.

This rule is similar to that used to limit the § 212 deduction for fiduciary fees and other expenses incurred to generate tax-exempt income. However, if the will or trust agreement requires that the contribution be made from a specific type of income or from the current income from a specified asset, the contribution will not have to be allocated to taxable and tax-exempt income.

EXAMPLE 17

The Capper Trust has 1998 gross rent income of $80,000, expenses attributable to the rents of $60,000, and tax-exempt interest from state bonds of $20,000. Under the trust agreement, the trustee is to pay 30% of the annual trust accounting income to the United Way, a qualifying organization. Accordingly, the trustee pays $12,000 (30% × $40,000) to the charity in 1999. The charitable contribution deduction allowed for 1998 is $9,600 [($80,000/$100,000) × $12,000]. ▼

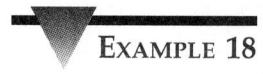

EXAMPLE 18

Assume the same facts as Example 17, except that the trust instrument also requires that the contribution be paid from the net rent income. The agreement controls, and the allocation formula need not be applied. The entire $12,000 is allowed as a charitable contribution deduction. ▼

DEDUCTION FOR DISTRIBUTIONS TO BENEFICIARIES

3 ▼ **LEARNING OBJECTIVE**
Illustrate the uses and implications of distributable net income.

The modified conduit approach of Subchapter J is embodied in the deduction allowed to trusts and estates for the distributions made to beneficiaries during the year. Some portion of any distribution that a beneficiary receives from a trust may be subject to income tax on his or her own return. At the same time, the distributing entity is allowed a deduction for some or all of the distribution. Consequently, the modified conduit principle of Subchapter J is implemented. A good analogy is to the taxability of corporate profits distributed to employees as taxable wages. The corporation is allowed a deduction for the payment, but the employee receives gross income in the form of compensation.

A critical value that is used in computing the amount of the entity's distribution deduction is **distributable net income (DNI).** As it is defined in Subchapter J, DNI serves several functions.

- DNI is the maximum amount of the distribution on which the beneficiaries can be taxed.[27]
- DNI is the maximum amount that the entity can use as a distribution deduction for the year.[28]
- The makeup of DNI carries over to the beneficiaries (the items of income and expenses retain their DNI character in the hands of the distributees).[29]

Subchapter J defines DNI in a circular manner, however. The DNI value is necessary to determine the entity's distribution deduction and therefore its taxable income for the year. Nonetheless, the Code defines DNI as a modification of the entity's taxable income itself. Using the systematic approach to determining the taxable income of the entity and of its beneficiaries, as shown earlier in Figure 27–2, one must first compute *taxable income before the distribution deduction*, modify

---

[27]§§ 652(a) and 662(a).
[28]§§ 651(b) and 661(c).

[29]§§ 652(b) and 662(b).

that amount to determine DNI and the distribution deduction, return to the calculation of *taxable income*, and apply the deduction that has resulted.

Taxable income before the distribution deduction includes all of the entity's items
of gross income, deductions, gains, losses, and exemptions for the year. Therefore,
to compute this amount, (1) determine the appropriate personal exemption for
the year and (2) account for all of the other gross income and deductions of the
entity.

The next step in Figure 27–2 is the determination of *distributable net income*,
computed by making the following adjustments to the entity's *taxable income before
the distribution deduction.*[30]

- Add back the personal exemption.
- Add back *net* tax-exempt interest. To arrive at this amount, reduce the total
  tax-exempt interest by charitable contributions and by related expenses not
  deductible under § 265.
- Add back the entity's *net* capital losses.
- Subtract any net capital gains allocable to corpus. In other words, the only net
  capital gains included in DNI are those attributable to income beneficiaries or
  to charitable contributions.

Since taxable income before the distribution deduction is computed by deducting
all of the expenses of the entity (whether they were allocated to income or to
corpus), DNI is reduced by expenses that are allocated to corpus. The effect is to
reduce the taxable income of the income beneficiaries. The actual distributions to
the beneficiaries exceed DNI because the distributions are not reduced by expenses
allocated to corpus. Aside from this shortcoming of Subchapter J, DNI offers a
good approximation of the current-year economic income available for distribution
to the entity's income beneficiaries.

DNI includes the net tax-exempt interest income of the entity, so that amount
must be removed from DNI in computing the distribution deduction. Moreover,
for estates and complex trusts, the amount actually distributed during the year
may include discretionary distributions of income and distributions of corpus
permissible under the will or trust instrument. Thus, the distribution deduction
for estates and complex trusts is computed as the lesser of (1) the deductible portion
of DNI or (2) the taxable amount actually distributed to the beneficiaries during
the year. For a simple trust, however, full distribution always is assumed, relative
to both the entity and its beneficiaries, in a manner similar to the partnership and
S corporation conduit entities.

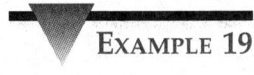

EXAMPLE 19

The Zinc Trust is a simple trust. Because of severe liquidity problems, its 1998 accounting
income is not distributed to its sole beneficiary, Mark, until early in 1999. Zinc is still allowed
a full distribution deduction for, and Mark is still taxed upon, the entity's 1998 income
in 1998. ▼

EXAMPLE 20

The Pork Trust is required to distribute its current accounting income annually to its sole
income beneficiary, Barbara. Capital gains and losses and all other expenses are allocable
to corpus. For the current year, the trust records the following items.

---

[30]These and other (less common) adjustments are detailed in § 643.

Dividend income	$25,000
Taxable interest income	15,000
Tax-exempt interest income	20,000
Net long-term capital gain	10,000
Fiduciary fees	6,000

Item	Totals		Accounting Income		Taxable Income	Distributable Net Income/ Distribution Deduction
Dividend income	$25,000		$25,000		$ 25,000	
Taxable interest income	15,000		15,000		15,000	
Tax-exempt interest income	20,000		20,000			
Net long-term capital gain	10,000				10,000	
Fiduciary fees	6,000				(4,000)	
Personal exemption					(300)	
Accounting income/taxable income before the distribution deduction		*Step 1*	$60,000	*Step 2*	$ 45,700	$ 45,700
Personal exemption						300
Corpus capital gain/loss						(10,000)
Net tax-exempt income						18,000
Distributable net income						$ 54,000
Distribution deduction				*Step 3*	(36,000)	
Entity taxable income				*Step 4*	$ 9,700	

Step 1   Trust accounting income is $60,000; this includes the tax-exempt interest income, but not the fees or the capital gains, pursuant to the trust document. Barbara receives $60,000 from the trust for the current year.

Step 2   Taxable income before the distribution deduction is computed as directed by the Code. The tax-exempt interest is excluded under § 103. Only a portion of the fees is deductible because some of the fees are traceable to the tax-exempt income. The trust receives a $300 personal exemption as it is required to distribute its annual trust accounting income.

Step 3   DNI and the distribution deduction reflect the required adjustments. The distribution deduction is the lesser of the distributed amount ($60,000) or the deductible portion of DNI ($54,000 – $18,000 net tax-exempt income).

Step 4   Finally, return to the computation of the taxable income of the Pork Trust. A simple test should be applied at this point to ensure that the proper figure for the trust's taxable income has been determined. On what is Pork to be taxed? All of the trust's gross income has been distributed to Barbara except the $10,000 net long-term capital gains. The $300 personal exemption reduces the trust's taxable income to $9,700. ▼

EXAMPLE 21

The Quick Trust is required to distribute all of its current accounting income equally to its two beneficiaries, Faith and the First Methodist Church, a qualifying charitable organization. Capital gains and losses and depreciation expenses are allocable to income. Fiduciary fees are allocable to corpus. In the current year, Quick incurs various items as indicated.

Item	Totals	Accounting Income		Taxable Income		Distributable Net Income/ Distribution Deduction
Rent income	$100,000		$ 100,000		$ 100,000	
Expenses—rent income	30,000		(30,000)		(30,000)	
Depreciation—rent income	15,000		(15,000)			
Net long-term capital gain	20,000		20,000		20,000	
Charitable contribution					(37,500)	
Fiduciary fees	18,000				(18,000)	
Personal exemption					(300)	
Accounting income/taxable income before the distribution deduction		Step 1	$ 75,000	Step 2	$ 34,200	$34,200
Personal exemption						300
Corpus capital gain/loss						
Net tax-exempt income						
Distributable net income						$34,500
Distribution deduction				Step 3	(34,500)	
Entity taxable income				Step 4	($ 300)	

Step 1   Trust accounting income of $75,000 reflects the indicated allocations of items to income and to corpus. Each income beneficiary receives $37,500.

Step 2   In the absence of tax-exempt income, a deduction is allowed for the full amount of the fiduciary's fees. Quick is a complex trust, but since it is required to distribute its full accounting income annually, a $300 exemption is allowed. The trust properly does not deduct any depreciation for the rental property. The depreciation deduction is available only to the recipients of the entity's accounting income for the period. Thus, the deduction will be split equally between Faith and the church. The deduction probably is of no direct value to the church, as the church is not subject to the income tax. The trust's charitable contribution deduction is based upon the $37,500 that the charity actually received (one-half of trust accounting income).

Step 3   As there is no tax-exempt income, the only adjustment needed to compute DNI is to add back the trust's personal exemption. Subchapter J requires no adjustment for the charitable contribution. DNI is computed only from the perspective of Faith, who also received $37,500 from the trust.

Step 4   Finally, the trust's taxable income before the distribution deduction is reduced by the distribution deduction to produce the trust's taxable income of ($300). Perform the simple test (referred to above) to ensure that the proper taxable income for the Quick Trust has been computed. All of the trust's gross income has been distributed to Faith and the church. As is the case with most trusts that distribute all of their annual income, the Quick Trust "wastes" the personal exemption. ▼

TAX CREDITS

An estate or trust may claim the foreign tax credit to the extent that it is not passed through to the beneficiaries.[31] Similarly, other credits must be apportioned between

---

[31]§§ 642(a)(1) and 901.

IS IT A CHARITY OR A BENEFICIARY?

The general prohibition against "double deductions" is unclear when the beneficiary of a distribution from the fiduciary is a charity. Does the entity claim a charitable deduction or a distribution deduction for the payment?

Neither the Code nor the Regulations under Subchapter J address this question. Most practitioners apply a "volume" test, as was done in Example 21, using the charitable deduction for small payments from the estate's gross income and the distribution deduction for larger (especially recurring) contributions.

In *U.S. Trust Co. v. Comm.*, 86–2 USTC ¶9777, 58 AFTR2d 86–6152, 803 F.2d 1363 (CA–5, 1986), though, the taxpayer boldly claimed two deductions for a $2.5 million payment by the decedent to a qualifying charity, one as a charitable deduction on the estate tax return and the other as a distribution deduction on the estate's income tax return. The trustee explained that the distribution deduction was used because the will did not specify that the payment be made from the gross income of the estate.

The taxpayer's approach is not strictly prohibited by the Code. In fact, the Federal Appeals Court noted that multiple tax benefits accrue when an estate makes a payment to charity. The double deduction would have survived had the will specified the amount and source of the charitable gift as some type of gross income recognized by the estate.

But that was not the case here, and the distribution deduction was denied. In essence, the Appeals Court viewed the gift as a bequest specified by the will, not a distribution of postdeath income. Bequests are not deductible for income tax purposes, and neither was this payment.

the estate or trust and the beneficiaries on the basis of the entity accounting income allocable to each.

TAXATION OF BENEFICIARIES

The beneficiaries of an estate or trust receive taxable income from the entity under the modified conduit principle of Subchapter J. DNI determines the maximum amount that can be taxed to the beneficiaries for any tax year. The constitution of DNI also carries over to the beneficiaries (e.g., net long-term capital gains retain their character when they are distributed from the entity to the beneficiary).

The timing of any tax consequences to the beneficiary of a trust or estate presents a problem only when the parties involved use different tax years. A beneficiary must include in gross income an amount based upon the DNI of the trust for any taxable year or years of the trust or estate ending with or within his or her taxable year.[32]

EXAMPLE 22

An estate uses a fiscal year ending on March 31 for tax purposes. Its sole income beneficiary is a calendar year taxpayer. For calendar year 1999, the beneficiary reports whatever income was assignable to her for the entity's fiscal year April 1, 1998, to March 31, 1999. If the estate

---

[32]§§ 652(c) and 662(c).

is terminated by December 31, 1999, the beneficiary must also include any income assignable to her for the short year. This could result in a bunching of income in 1999. ▼

DISTRIBUTIONS BY SIMPLE TRUSTS

The amount taxable to the beneficiaries of a simple trust is limited by the trust's DNI. However, since DNI includes net tax-exempt income, the amount included in the gross income of the beneficiaries could be less than DNI. When there is more than one income beneficiary, the elements of DNI must be apportioned ratably according to the amount required to be distributed currently to each.

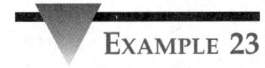

EXAMPLE 23

A simple trust has ordinary income of $40,000, a long-term capital gain of $15,000 (allocable to corpus), and a trustee commission expense of $4,000 (payable from corpus). The two income beneficiaries, Allie and Bart, are entitled to the trust's annual accounting income, based on shares of 75% and 25%, respectively. Although Allie receives $30,000 as her share (75% × $40,000 trust accounting income), she will be allocated DNI of only $27,000 (75% × $36,000). Likewise, Bart is entitled to receive $10,000 (25% × $40,000), but he will be allocated DNI of only $9,000 (25% × $36,000). The $15,000 capital gain is taxed to the trust. ▼

DISTRIBUTIONS BY ESTATES AND COMPLEX TRUSTS

A problem arises with estates and complex trusts when more than one beneficiary receives a distribution from the entity and the controlling document does not require a distribution of the entire accounting income of the entity.

EXAMPLE 24

The trustee of the Wilson Trust has the discretion to distribute the income or corpus of the trust in any proportion between the two beneficiaries of the trust, Wong and Washington. Under the trust instrument, Wong must receive $15,000 from the trust every year. In the current year, the trust's accounting income is $50,000, and its DNI is $40,000. The trustee pays $35,000 to Wong and $25,000 to Washington for the current year. ▼

How is Wilson's DNI to be divided between Wong and Washington? Several arbitrary methods of allocating DNI between the beneficiaries could be devised. Subchapter J resolves the problem by creating a two-tier system to govern the taxation of beneficiaries in such situations.[33] The tier system determines which distributions will be included in the gross income of the beneficiaries in full, which will be included in part, and which will not be included at all.

Income that is required to be distributed currently, whether or not it is distributed, is categorized as a *first-tier distribution*. All other amounts properly paid, credited, or required to be distributed are considered to be *second-tier distributions*.[34] A formula is used to allocate DNI among the appropriate beneficiaries when only first-tier distributions are made and those amounts exceed DNI.

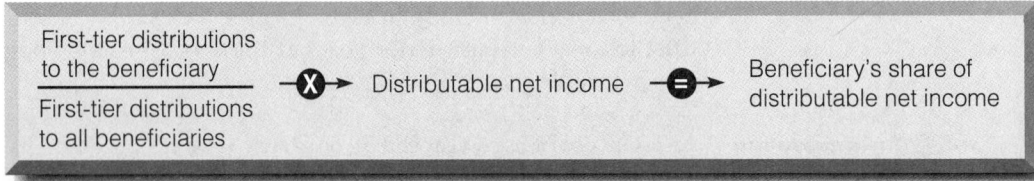

---

[33]§§ 662(a)(1) and (2).   [34]Reg. §§ 1.662(a)–2 and –3.

When both first-tier and second-tier distributions are made and the first-tier distributions exceed DNI, the above formula is applied to the first-tier distributions. In this case, none of the second-tier distributions are taxed because all of the DNI has been allocated to the first-tier beneficiaries.

If both first-tier and second-tier distributions are made and the first-tier distributions do not exceed DNI, but the total of both first-tier and second-tier distributions does exceed DNI, the second-tier beneficiaries must recognize income as shown below.

$$\frac{\text{Second-tier distributions to the beneficiary}}{\text{Second-tier distributions to all beneficiaries}} \; \otimes \; \frac{\text{Remaining distributable net income (after first-tier distributions)}}{} \; \ominus \; \frac{\text{Beneficiary's share of distributable net income}}{}$$

EXAMPLE 25

The trustee of the Gray Trust is required to distribute $10,000 per year to both Harriet and Wally, the two beneficiaries of the entity. In addition, he is empowered to distribute other amounts of trust income or corpus at his sole discretion. In the current year, the trust has accounting income of $60,000 and DNI of $50,000. However, the trustee distributes only the required $10,000 each to Harriet and to Wally. The balance of the income is accumulated and added to trust corpus.

In this case, only first-tier distributions have been made, but the total amount of the distributions does not exceed DNI for the year. Although DNI is the maximum amount that is included by the beneficiaries for the year, they can include no more in gross income than is distributed by the entity. Thus, both Harriet and Wally are subject to tax on $10,000 as their proportionate shares of DNI. ▼

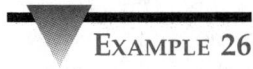
EXAMPLE 26

Assume the same facts as in Example 25, except that DNI is $12,000. Harriet and Wally each receive $10,000, but they cannot be taxed in total on more than DNI. Each is taxed on $6,000 [$12,000 DNI × ($10,000/$20,000 of the first-tier distributions)]. ▼

EXAMPLE 27

Return to the facts in Example 24. Wong receives a first-tier distribution of $15,000. Second-tier distributions include $20,000 to Wong and $25,000 to Washington. Wilson Trust's DNI is $40,000. The DNI is allocated between Wong and Washington as follows.

1. First-tier distributions

To Wong	$15,000 DNI
To Washington	–0–
Remaining DNI = $25,000 ($40,000 DNI – $15,000 distributed)	

2. Second-tier distributions

To Wong [(20/45) × $25,000]	$11,111 DNI
To Washington [(25/45) × $25,000]	13,889 DNI

▼

Separate Share Rule. For the sole purpose of determining the amount of DNI for a complex trust or estate with more than one beneficiary, the substantially separate and independent shares of different beneficiaries in the trust or estate are treated as *separate* trusts or estates.[35] An illustration shows the need for this special rule.

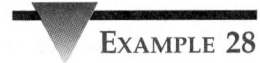

EXAMPLE 28

A trustee has the discretion to distribute or accumulate income on behalf of Greg and Hannah (in equal shares). The trustee also has the power to invade corpus for the benefit of either beneficiary to the extent of that beneficiary's one-half interest in the trust. For the current year, DNI is $10,000. Of this amount, $5,000 is distributed to Greg, and $5,000 is accumulated on behalf of Hannah. In addition, the trustee pays $20,000 from corpus to Greg. Without the separate share rule, Greg is taxed on $10,000 (the full amount of the DNI). With the separate share rule, Greg is taxed on only $5,000 (his share of the DNI) and receives the $20,000 corpus distribution tax-free. The trust will be taxed on Hannah's $5,000 share of the DNI that is accumulated. ▼

The separate share rule is designed to prevent the inequity that results if the corpus payments are treated under the regular rules applicable to second-tier beneficiaries. In Example 28, the effect of the separate share rule is to produce a two-trust result: one trust for Greg and one for Hannah, each with DNI of $5,000. The rule also results in the availability of extra entity personal exemptions and in a greater use of lower entity tax brackets.

CHARACTER OF INCOME

Consistent with the modified conduit principle of Subchapter J, various classes of income (e.g., dividends, passive or portfolio gain and loss, AMT preferences and adjustments, and tax-exempt interest) retain the same character for the beneficiaries that they had when they were received by the entity. If there are multiple beneficiaries *and* if all of the DNI is distributed, a problem arises in allocating the various classes of income among the beneficiaries.

Distributions are treated as consisting of the same proportion as the items that enter into the computation of DNI. This allocation does not apply, however, if the governing instrument specifically allocates different classes of income to different beneficiaries.[36]

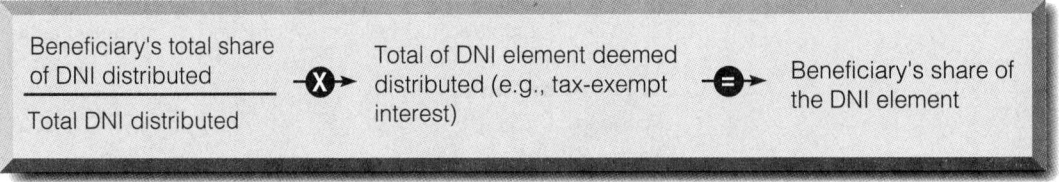

If the entity distributes only a part of its DNI, the amount of a particular class of DNI that is deemed distributed must first be determined.

---

[35]§ 663(c); Reg. § 1.663(c)–1(a).
[36]Reg. § 1.662(b)–1 seems to allow special allocations, but see *Harkness v. U.S.*, 72–2 USTC ¶9740, 30 AFTR2d 72–5754, 469 F.2d 310 (Ct.Cls., 1972).

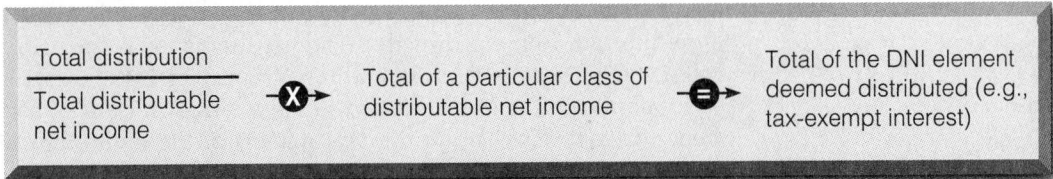

	Total distribution
	───────────────
	Total distributable net income

✕ Total of a particular class of distributable net income **=▶** Total of the DNI element deemed distributed (e.g., tax-exempt interest)

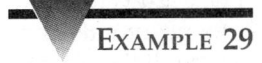

EXAMPLE 29

During the current year, a trust has DNI of $40,000, including the following: $10,000 of taxable interest, $10,000 of tax-exempt interest, and $20,000 of passive activity income. The trustee distributes, at her discretion, $8,000 to Mike and $12,000 to Nancy.

		Income Type		
Beneficiary	**Amount Received**	**Taxable Interest**	**Exempt Interest**	**Passive Income**
Mike	$ 8,000	$2,000*	$2,000	$4,000
Nancy	12,000	3,000	3,000	6,000

*$8,000 distribution/$40,000 total DNI × $10,000 taxable interest in DNI. ▼

Special Allocations.   Under certain circumstances, the parties may modify the character-of-income allocation method set forth above. A modification is permitted only to the extent that the allocation is required in the trust instrument and only to the extent that it has an economic effect independent of the cash-flow and income tax consequences of the allocation.[37]

EXAMPLE 30

Return to the facts in Example 29. Assume that the beneficiaries are elderly individuals who have pooled their investment portfolios to avail themselves of the trustee's professional asset management skills. Suppose the trustee has the discretion to allocate different classes of income to different beneficiaries and that she designates all of Nancy's $12,000 distribution as being from the tax-exempt income. Such a designation *would not be recognized* for tax purposes, and the allocation method of Example 29 must be used.

Suppose, however, that the trust instrument stipulated that Nancy was to receive all of the income from tax-exempt securities because she alone contributed the exempt securities to trust corpus. Under this provision, the $10,000 of the nontaxable interest is paid to Nancy. This allocation *is recognized*, and $10,000 of Nancy's distribution is tax-exempt. ▼

LOSSES IN THE TERMINATION YEAR

The ordinary net operating and capital losses of a trust or estate do not flow through to the entity's beneficiaries, as would such losses from a partnership or an S corporation. However, in the year in which an entity terminates its existence, the beneficiaries do receive a direct benefit from the loss carryovers of the trust or estate.[38]

Net operating losses and net capital losses are subject to the same carryover rules that otherwise apply to an individual. Consequently, NOLs can be carried back 2 years and then carried forward 20 years while net capital losses can be carried forward only, and for an indefinite period of time. However, if the entity incurs a negative taxable income in the last year of its existence, the excess of

---

[37]Reg. § 1.652(b)–2(b). This is similar to the § 704(b) requirement for partnerships.

[38]Reg. §§ 1.642(h)–1 and –2.

deductions over the entity's gross income is allowed to the beneficiaries (it will flow through to them directly). The net loss is available as a deduction *from* AGI in the beneficiary's tax year with or within which the entity's tax year ends. The amount allowed is in proportion to the relative amount of corpus assets that each beneficiary receives upon the termination of the entity, and it is subject to the 2 percent-of-AGI floor.

Any carryovers of the entity's other losses flow through to the beneficiaries in the year of termination in proportion to the relative amount of corpus assets that each beneficiary receives. The character of the loss carryforward is retained by the beneficiary, except that a carryover of a net capital loss to a corporate beneficiary is always treated as short term. Beneficiaries who are individuals use these carryforwards as deductions *for* AGI.

EXAMPLE 31

The Edgar Estate terminates on December 31, 1998. It had used a fiscal year ending July 31. For the termination year, the estate incurred a $15,000 negative taxable income. In addition, the estate had an unused NOL carryforward of $23,000 from the year ending July 31, 1995, and an unused net long-term capital loss carryforward of $10,000 from the year ending July 31, 1997. Upon termination, Dawn receives $60,000 of corpus, and Blue Corporation receives the remaining $40,000. Dawn and Blue are calendar year taxpayers.

Dawn can claim an itemized deduction of $9,000 [($60,000/$100,000) × $15,000] for the entity's negative taxable income in the year of termination. This deduction is subject to the 2%-of-AGI floor on miscellaneous itemized deductions. In addition, she can claim a $13,800 deduction *for* AGI in 1998 (60% × $23,000) for Edgar's NOL carryforward, and she can use $6,000 (60% × $10,000) of the estate's net long-term capital loss carryforward with her other 1998 capital transactions.

Blue Corporation receives ordinary business deductions in 1998 for Edgar's NOLs: $6,000 for the loss in the year of termination and $9,200 for the carryforward from fiscal year 1995. Moreover, Blue can use the $4,000 carryforward of Edgar's net capital losses to offset against its other 1998 capital transactions, although the loss must be treated as short term. ▼

TAX PLANNING CONSIDERATIONS

Many of the tax planning possibilities for estates and trusts were discussed in Chapter 26. However, several specific tax planning possibilities are available to help minimize the income tax effects on estates and trusts and their beneficiaries.

A TRUST OR ESTATE AS AN INCOME-SHIFTING DEVICE

4 LEARNING OBJECTIVE
Understand various tax planning procedures that can be used to minimize the tax consequences of trusts and estates and their beneficiaries.

The compressed tax rate schedule applicable to Subchapter J entities may have reversed the traditional techniques by which families set aside funds for long-term activities, such as business start-ups, college education, and home purchases. When the tax rate schedules for trusts and estates were more accommodating, high-income individuals would shift income-producing assets to trusts to take advantage of the lower tax rate that would fall on the income accumulated within the trust. The target of the plan, usually a child, would receive the accumulated income (and, perhaps, trust corpus) at a designated age, and more funds would be available because a lower tax rate had been applied over the life of the investment in the trust.

Today, such an income shift would *deplete*, rather than shelter, the family's assets, as the rates falling on individuals are much more graduated than are those applicable to fiduciaries, and the kiddie tax also penalizes attempts to shift taxable

---

▼

CONCEPT SUMMARY 27–1

Income Taxation of Trusts and Estates

1. Estates and trusts are temporary entities, created to locate, maintain, and distribute assets and to satisfy liabilities according to the wishes of the decedent or grantor as expressed in the will or trust document.
2. Generally, the estate or trust acts as a conduit of the taxable income that it receives. To the extent that the income is distributed by the entity, it is taxed to the beneficiary. Taxable income retained by the entity is taxed to the entity itself.
3. The entity's accounting income must be determined first. Accounting conventions that are stated in the controlling document or, lacking such provisions, in state law allocate specific items of receipt and expenditure either to income or to corpus. Income beneficiaries typically receive payments from the entity that are equal to the accounting income.
4. The taxable income of the entity is computed using the scheme in Figure 27–3. The entity usually recognizes income in respect of a decedent. Deductions for fiduciary's fees and for charitable contributions may be reduced if the entity received any tax-exempt income during the year. Cost recovery deductions are assigned proportionately to the recipients of accounting income. Upon election, realized gain or loss on assets that properly are distributed in kind can be recognized by the entity.
5. A distribution deduction, computationally derived from distributable net income (DNI), is allowed to the entity. DNI is the maximum amount on which entity beneficiaries can be taxed. Moreover, the constitution of DNI is assigned to the recipients of the distributions.

---

income to children. Assuming that the objectives of the plan remain unchanged, possible strategies in view of these rate changes include the following:

- Trust corpus should be invested in growth assets that are low on yield but high on appreciation, so that the trustee can determine the timing of the gain and somewhat control the effective tax rate that applies.
- Trust corpus should be invested in tax-exempt securities, such as municipal bonds and mutual funds that invest in them, to eliminate the tax costs associated with the investment. If this approach is taken, a trust might be unnecessary—the parent should simply retain full control over the assets and invest in the exempt securities in his or her own account.
- The grantor should retain high-yield assets, so that control over the assets is not surrendered when the tax cost is too high.
- Use of trust vehicles should be reserved for cases where professional management of the assets is necessary for portfolio growth and the additional tax costs can be justified.
- An income-shifting strategy may require several steps to achieve the desired result. For instance, the grantor might increase contributions to his or her own qualified retirement plan, thereby sheltering the funds from all tax liabilities. Then the grantor could use the tax dollars saved from these contributions to purchase tax-deferred annuity contracts, savings bonds, exempt securities, or other assets where the tax liabilities are reduced or deferred. The grantor could then either retain these exempt securities as discussed above or transfer them to the trust at a later date.

INCOME TAX PLANNING FOR ESTATES

As a separate taxable entity, an estate can select its own tax year and accounting methods. The executor of an estate should consider selecting a fiscal year because this will determine when beneficiaries must include income distributions from the estate in their own tax returns. Beneficiaries must include the income for their tax year with or within which the estate's tax year ends. Proper selection of the estate's tax year can result in a smoothing out of income and a reduction of the income taxes for all parties involved.

Caution should be taken in determining when the estate is to be terminated. Selecting a fiscal year for the estate can result in a bunching of income to the beneficiaries in the year in which the estate is closed. Prolonging the termination of an estate can be effective income tax planning, but the IRS carefully examines the purpose of keeping the estate open. Since the unused losses of an estate pass through to the beneficiaries only in the termination year, the estate should be closed when the beneficiaries can enjoy the maximum tax benefit of the losses.

The timing and amounts of income distributions to the beneficiaries also present important tax planning opportunities. If the executor can make discretionary income distributions, he or she should evaluate the relative marginal income tax rates of the estate and its beneficiaries. By timing the distributions properly, the overall income tax liability can be minimized. Care should be taken, however, to time the distributions in light of the estate's DNI.

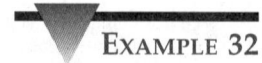

EXAMPLE 32

For several years before his death on March 7, Don had entered into annual deferred compensation agreements with his employer. These agreements collectively called for the payment of $200,000 six months after Don's retirement or death. To provide a maximum 12-month period within which to generate deductions to offset this large item of IRD, the executor or administrator of the estate should elect a fiscal year ending August 31. The election is made simply by filing the estate's first tax return for the short period of March 7 to August 31. ▼

EXAMPLE 33

Carol, the sole beneficiary of an estate, is a calendar year, cash basis taxpayer. If the estate elects a fiscal year ending January 31, all distributions during the period of February 1 to December 31, 1999, will be reported on Carol's tax return for calendar year 2000 (due April 15, 2001). Thus, assuming estimated tax requirements have otherwise been met, any income taxes that result from a $50,000 distribution made by the estate on February 20, 1999, will be deferred until April 15, 2001. ▼

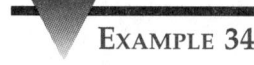

EXAMPLE 34

Assume the same facts as in Example 33. If the estate is closed on December 15, 2000, the DNI for both the fiscal year ending January 31, 2000, and the final tax year ending December 15, 2000, is included in Carol's tax return for the same calendar year. To avoid the effect of this bunching of income, the estate should not be closed until calendar year 2001. ▼

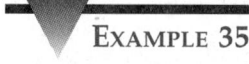

EXAMPLE 35

Assume the same facts as in Example 34, except that the estate has a substantial NOL for the period February 1 to December 15, 2000. If Carol is subject to a high income tax rate for calendar year 2000, the estate should be closed in that year so that the excess deductions are passed through to its beneficiary. However, if Carol anticipates being in a higher tax bracket in 2001, the termination of the estate should be postponed. ▼

In general, beneficiaries who are subject to high tax rates should be made beneficiaries of second-tier (but not IRD) distributions of the estate. Most likely, these individuals will have less need for an additional steady stream of (taxable) income while their income tax savings can be relatively large. Moreover, a special allocation of tax-favored types of income and expenses should be considered. For example, tax-exempt income can be directed more easily to beneficiaries in higher income tax brackets.

ETHICAL CONSIDERATIONS

Should a Tax Adviser Also Be a Trustee?

Tax clients need to be counseled on the best use of the trust entity and the proper choice of beneficiary of the trust income. The objectives of the grantor typically will best be served by transferring more power to the trustee; sprinkling powers, in particular, enable the trustee to be sensitive to the short-term and ongoing needs of the various beneficiaries. The client, however, may not appreciate this suggestion when the trust document is drafted. Especially if the tax adviser is the trustee or a co-trustee, the client may balk at the professional's well-intended suggestion that future developments might favor one beneficiary over another in a manner that cannot be anticipated at the time.

Should the source of the estate plan—the tax adviser—also then be designated as the trustee by the grantor? When the adviser serves in that capacity, who is "the client"? Merely the grantor? How about the beneficiaries? And the trust itself? To avoid any potential for conflict with their clients, some professional firms have adopted a policy of refusing to serve as trustee of a client's trust (or executor of his or her estate). Certainly, surrendering a sprinkling power to a fiduciary who is less sensitive to the tax ramifications of Subchapter J may be costly to all of the parties, but these firms see the preservation of the client relationship as more valuable in the long term.

Recall, also, that although both of her children are attorneys, Jacqueline Kennedy Onassis was careful to make other parties the executor of her estate and the trustees of her fiduciary entities. In more typical estates, though, the grantor must address critical issues: How much power and control over assets and income should be "surrendered to outsiders" through the trust? Which items lend themselves to such transfers of control?

INCOME TAX PLANNING WITH TRUSTS

The great variety of trusts provides the grantor, trustee, and beneficiaries with excellent opportunities for tax planning. Many of the same tax planning opportunities available to the executor of an estate are available to the trustee. For instance, the distributions from a trust are taxable to the trust's beneficiaries to the extent of the trust's DNI. If income distributions are discretionary, the trustee can time the distributions to minimize the income tax consequences to all parties.

DISTRIBUTIONS OF IN-KIND PROPERTY

The ability of the trustee or executor to elect to recognize the realized gain or loss relative to a distributed noncash asset allows the gain or loss to be allocated to the optimal taxpayer.

EXAMPLE 36

The Yorba Linda Estate distributed some stock, basis of $40,000 and fair market value of $41,500, to beneficiary Larry. Yorba Linda is subject to a 15% income tax rate, and Larry is subject to a 31% tax rate. The executor of Yorba Linda should elect that the entity recognize the related $1,500 realized gain, thereby subjecting the gain to the estate's lower tax rate and reducing Larry's future capital gain income (by increasing his basis). ▼

KEY TERMS

Complex trust, 27–5

Corpus, 27–3

Distributable net income (DNI), 27–17

Expenses in respect of a decedent, 27–13

Grantor, 27–2

Grantor trusts, 27–3

Income in respect of a decedent (IRD), 27–13

Reversionary interest, 27–4

Simple trust, 27–5

Sprinkling trust, 27–5

PROBLEM MATERIALS

DISCUSSION QUESTIONS

1. When should a client be counseled to create a trust? What tax motivations might lead to the use of a fiduciary? List important tax and nontax objectives that might be satisfied by the use of a trust created during the taxpayer's lifetime.

2. Identify the parties involved in the creation of a trust. Do the same for an estate.

3. Why has Congress subjected trusts and estates to such a compressed tax rate schedule? Demonstrate this compression numerically.

4. Is the fiduciary entity subject to the alternative minimum tax? What tax rates and exemptions apply?

5. Outline the five-step process of determining the taxable income amounts for the parties to a trust arrangement.

6. What happens when a trust distributes an asset to a beneficiary and the asset's basis is less than its fair market value?

7. How does Subchapter J assign the cost recovery deductions attributable to the operations of a trust?

8. How does a trust or estate treat charitable contribution deductions?

9. The Flan Trust is scheduled to terminate in two years, when Amy Flan reaches age 30. The trust operated a business several years ago, and it generated a sizable NOL carryforward that the trust has not been able to use. In addition, due to poor investment advice, the value of the entity's investment portfolio declined 15% from its purchase price. What issues must you consider in giving Amy and the corporate trustee tax planning advice?

10. Write a memo for the tax research file discussing the tax planning opportunities presented by an estate's ability to select a noncalendar tax year. Your clients seek advice as to the estate of a decedent who died on May 3. Large payments of IRD will be received in the first three months after the date of death.

PROBLEMS

11. Illustrate the nature and operations of each of the following trusts by creating a fact pattern to match each result.
    a. A simple trust.
    b. A complex trust with a $300 personal exemption.
    c. A complex trust with a $100 personal exemption.

12. The Purple Trust incurred the following items this year.

Taxable interest income	$30,000
Tax-exempt interest income, not on private activity bonds	40,000
Tax-exempt interest income, on private activity bonds	50,000

Compute Purple's tentative minimum tax for the year. Purple does not have any credits available to reduce the AMT liability.

13. Complete the following chart, indicating the comparative attributes of the typical trust and estate by answering yes/no or explaining the differences between the entities where appropriate.

Attribute	Estate	Trust
Separate income tax entity	_____	_____
Controlling document	_____	_____
Termination date is determinable from controlling document	_____	_____
Legal owner of assets under fiduciary's control	_____	_____
Document identifies both income and remainder beneficiaries	_____	_____
Separate share rules apply	_____	_____
Generally must use calendar tax year	_____	_____

14. In its first tax year, the Wittmann Estate generated $50,000 of taxable interest income and $25,000 of tax-exempt interest income. It paid fiduciary fees of $4,000. The estate is subject to a 37% marginal estate tax rate and a 31% marginal income tax rate.
    a. How should the executor assign the deductions for the payment of the fees?
    b. How does the 2%-of-AGI floor apply to these fees assigned to the estate's income tax return?

15. Brown incurred the following items in 1999.

Business income	$20,000
Tax-exempt interest income	5,000
Payment to charity from 1999 income, paid 3/1/2000	3,000

Complete the following chart, indicating how the Code treats charitable contributions under the various assumptions.

Assumption	1999 Deduction for Contribution
Brown is a cash basis individual.	_____
Brown is an accrual basis corporation.	_____
Brown is a trust.	_____

16. The Ricardo Trust is a simple trust that correctly uses the calendar year for tax purposes. Its three income beneficiaries (Lucy, Mark, and Ethel) are entitled to the trust's annual accounting income in shares of one-third each. For the current calendar year, the trust generates ordinary income of $75,000, a long-term capital gain of $15,000 (allocable to corpus), and a trustee commission expense of $9,000 (allocable to corpus). Use the format of Figure 27–3 to address the following items.
    a. How much income is each beneficiary entitled to receive?
    b. What is the trust's DNI?
    c. What is the trust's taxable income?
    d. How much is taxed to each of the beneficiaries?

17. Assume the same facts as in Problem 16, except that the trust instrument allocates the capital gain to income.
    a. How much income is each beneficiary entitled to receive?
    b. What is the trust's DNI?
    c. What is the trust's taxable income?
    d. How much is taxed to each of the beneficiaries?

18. Under the terms of the trust instrument, the trustee has discretion to distribute or accumulate income on behalf of Willie, Sylvia, and Drahman in equal shares. The trustee also can invade corpus for the benefit of any of the beneficiaries to the extent of each person's respective one-third interest in the trust. In the current year, the trust has DNI of $48,000. Of this amount, $16,000 is distributed to Willie and $10,000 is distributed to Sylvia. The remaining $6,000 of Sylvia's share of DNI and Drahman's entire $16,000 share are accumulated by the trust. Additionally, the trustee distributes $20,000 from corpus to Willie.
    a. How much income is taxed to Willie?
    b. To Sylvia?
    c. To Drahman?
    d. To the trust?

19. A trust is required to distribute $40,000 annually to its two income beneficiaries, Clare and David, in shares of 75% and 25%, respectively. If trust income is not sufficient to pay these amounts, the trustee can invade corpus to the extent necessary. During the current year, the trust generates only taxable interest income and has DNI of $90,000; the trustee distributes $60,000 to Clare and $40,000 to David.
    a. How much of the $60,000 distributed to Clare must be included in her gross income?
    b. How much of the $40,000 distributed to David must be included in his gross income?
    c. Are these distributions considered to be first-tier or second-tier distributions?

20. An estate has $75,000 of DNI, composed of $30,000 in dividends, $20,000 in taxable interest, $15,000 passive activity income, and $10,000 in tax-exempt interest. The trust's two noncharitable income beneficiaries, Brenda and Del, receive $30,000 each. How much of each class of income is deemed to have been distributed to Brenda? To Del?

21. The trustee of the Purple Trust can distribute any amount of accounting income and corpus to the trust's beneficiaries, Lydia and Kent. This year, the trust incurred the following.

Taxable interest income	$40,000
Tax-exempt interest income	60,000
Long-term capital gains—allocable to corpus	35,000
Fiduciary's fees—allocable to corpus	12,000

The trustee distributed $40,000 to Lydia and $30,000 to Kent.
    a. What is Purple's trust accounting income?
    b. What is Purple's DNI?
    c. What is Purple's taxable income?
    d. How much is taxed to each of the beneficiaries?

22. Each of the following items was incurred by José, the cash basis, calendar year decedent. Applying the rules for income and deductions in respect of a decedent, indicate on which return each item should be reported: the recipient/heir's last Form 1040 income tax (*Form 1040*); José's estate's first Form 1041 income tax (*Form 1041*); or José's estate's Form 706 estate tax (*Form 706*). More than one alternative may apply in some cases.

Item Incurred	Form(s) Reported on
a. Wages, last paycheck	_____
b. State income tax withheld on last paycheck	_____
c. Capital gain portion of installment payment received	_____
d. Ordinary income portion of installment payment received	_____
e. Dividend income, record date was two days prior to José's death	_____
f. Unrealized appreciation on a mutual fund investment	_____
g. Depreciation recapture accrued as of date of death	_____
h. Medical expenses of last illness	_____
i. Apartment building, rents accrued but not collected as of death	_____
j. Apartment building, property tax accrued and assessed but not paid as of death	_____

23. Determine the tax effects of the indicated losses for the Yellow Estate for both tax years. The estate holds a variety of investment assets, which it received from the decedent, Mrs. Yellow. The estate's sole income and remainder beneficiary is Yellow, Jr.

Tax Year	Loss Generated
1999 (first tax year)	Taxable income ($300) Capital loss ($5,000)
2000 (final tax year)	Taxable income ($12,000)

Research Problems for this chapter appear at the end of Chapter 28.

28

WORKING WITH THE TAX LAW

LEARNING OBJECTIVES

After completing Chapter 28, you should be able to:

1. Distinguish between the statutory, administrative, and judicial sources of the tax law and understand the purpose of each source.

2. Locate and work with the appropriate tax law sources.

3. Understand the tax research process.

4. Communicate the results of the tax research process in a client letter and a tax file memorandum.

5. Apply tax research techniques and planning procedures.

6. Have an awareness of electronic tax research.

TAX SOURCES

1 ◤ **LEARNING OBJECTIVE**
Distinguish between the statutory, administrative, and judicial sources of the tax law and understand the purpose of each source.

Understanding taxation requires a mastery of the sources of the *rules of tax law*. These sources include not only legislative provisions in the form of the Internal Revenue Code, but also congressional Committee Reports, Treasury Department Regulations, other Treasury Department pronouncements, and court decisions. Thus, the *primary sources* of tax information include pronouncements from all three branches of government: legislative, executive, and judicial.

In addition to being able to locate and interpret the sources of the tax law, a tax professional must understand the relative weight of authority within these sources. The tax law is of little significance, however, until it is applied to a set of facts and circumstances. This chapter, therefore, both introduces the statutory, administrative, and judicial sources of the tax law *and* explains how the law is applied to individual and business transactions. It also explains how to apply research techniques and use planning procedures effectively.

A large part of tax research focuses on determining the intent of Congress. While Congress often claims simplicity as one of its goals, a cursory examination of the tax law indicates that it has not been very successful. Faced with a 48-page tax return, James Michener, the author, said, "it is unimaginable in that I graduated from one of America's better colleges, yet I am totally incapable of understanding tax returns." David Brinkley, the former television news commentator, observed that "settling a dispute is difficult when our tax regulations are all written in a foreign tongue whose language flows like damp sludge leaking from a sanitary landfill."

Frequently, uncertainty in the tax law causes disputes between the Internal Revenue Service (IRS) and taxpayers. Due to these *gray areas* and the complexity of the tax law, a taxpayer may have more than one alternative for structuring a business transaction. In structuring business transactions and engaging in other tax planning activities, the tax adviser must be cognizant that the objective of tax planning is not necessarily to minimize the tax liability. Instead a taxpayer should maximize his or her after-tax return, which may include maximizing nontax as well as noneconomic benefits.

STATUTORY SOURCES OF THE TAX LAW

Origin of the Internal Revenue Code. Before 1939, the statutory provisions relating to taxation were contained in the individual revenue acts enacted by Congress. The inconvenience and confusion that resulted from dealing with many separate acts led Congress to codify all of the Federal tax laws. Known as the Internal Revenue Code of 1939, the codification arranged all Federal tax provisions in a logical sequence and placed them in a separate part of the Federal statutes. A further rearrangement took place in 1954 and resulted in the Internal Revenue Code of 1954, which continued in effect until it was replaced by the Internal Revenue Code of 1986.

The following observations help clarify the codification procedure:

- Neither the 1939, the 1954, nor the 1986 Code changed all of the tax law existing on the date of enactment. Much of the 1939 Code, for example, was incorporated into the 1954 Code. The same can be said for the transition from the 1954 to the 1986 Code. This point is important in assessing judicial and administrative decisions interpreting provisions under prior codes. For example, a decision interpreting § 121 of the Internal Revenue Code of 1954 will have continuing validity since this provision carried over unchanged to the Internal Revenue Code of 1986.

- Statutory amendments to the tax law are integrated into the existing Code. Thus, subsequent tax legislation, such as the Small Business Job Protection Act of 1996 and the Taxpayer Relief Act of 1997, have become part of the Internal Revenue Code of 1986. In view of the frequency with which tax legislation has been enacted in recent years, it appears that the tax law will continue to be amended frequently.

The Legislative Process. Federal tax legislation generally originates in the House of Representatives, where it is first considered by the House Ways and Means Committee. Tax bills originate in the Senate when they are attached as riders to other legislative proposals.[1] If acceptable to the committee, the proposed bill is referred to the entire House of Representatives for approval or disapproval. Approved bills are sent to the Senate, where they initially are considered by the Senate Finance Committee.

The next step is referral from the Senate Finance Committee to the entire Senate. Assuming no disagreement between the House and Senate, passage by the Senate means referral to the President for approval or veto. If the bill is approved or if the President's veto is overridden, the bill becomes law and part of the Internal Revenue Code of 1986.

When the Senate version of the bill differs from that passed by the House, the Joint Conference Committee, which includes members of both the House Ways and Means Committee and the Senate Finance Committee, is called upon to resolve the differences. Major tax bills frequently have differing versions. One reason bills are often changed in the Senate is that each individual senator has considerable latitude to make amendments when the Senate as a whole is voting on a bill referred to it by the Senate Finance Committee. In contrast, the entire House of Representatives either accepts or rejects what is proposed by the House Ways and Means Committee, and changes from the floor are rare. The deliberations of the Joint Conference Committee usually produce a compromise between the two versions, which is then voted on by both the House and the Senate. If both bodies accept the bill, it is referred to the President for approval or veto.

Effective January 1, 1997, the President has the line-item veto power to delete objectionable clauses in tax and spending laws rather than being required to veto the entire bill. In August 1997, President Clinton used this authority to veto a tax shelter for financial firms, another one for sellers of food-processing plants, and a provision that allowed the state of New York more than its fair share of Federal health subsidies. Congress did not override these line-item vetoes.

Referrals from the House Ways and Means Committee, the Senate Finance Committee, and the Joint Conference Committee are usually accompanied by Committee Reports. These Committee Reports often explain the provisions of the proposed legislation and are therefore a valuable source for ascertaining the *intent of Congress*. What Congress had in mind when it considered and enacted tax legislation is the key to interpreting the legislation. Since Regulations normally are not issued immediately after a statute is enacted, taxpayers and the courts look to legislative history materials to determine congressional intent.

The typical legislative process for dealing with tax bills is summarized as follows:

---

[1]The Tax Equity and Fiscal Responsibility Act of 1982 originated in the Senate, and its constitutionality was unsuccessfully challenged in the courts. The Senate version of the Deficit Reduction Act of 1984 was attached as an amendment to the Federal Boat Safety Act.

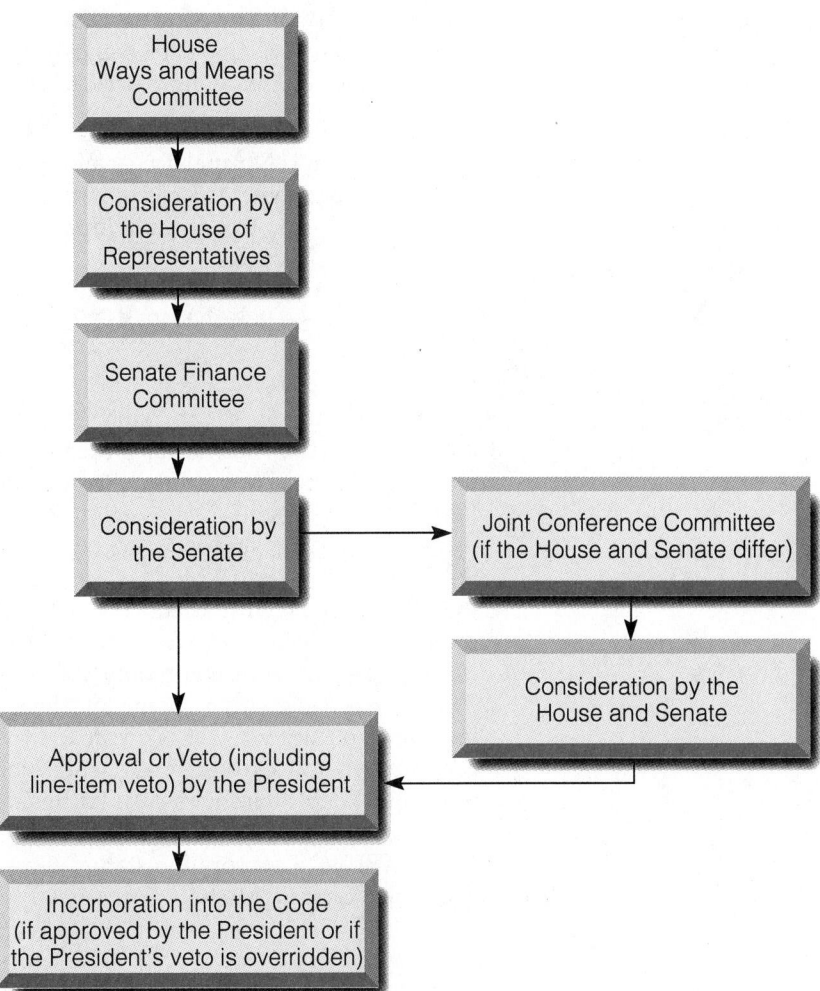

The role of the Joint Conference Committee indicates the importance of compromise in the legislative process. As an example of the practical effect of the compromise process, consider what happened to a limitation on contributions by employees to their education Individual Retirement Accounts in the Taxpayer Relief Act of 1997 (TRA of 1997).

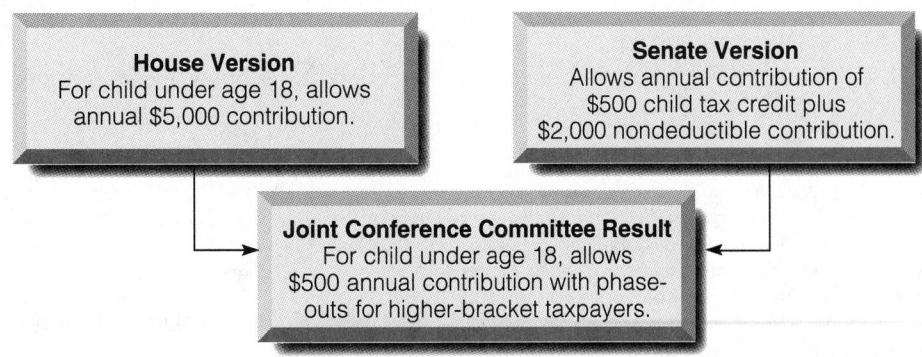

Arrangement of the Code.   The Internal Revenue Code of 1986 is found in Title 26 of the U.S. Code. In working with the Code, it helps to understand the format. Note the following partial table of contents:

Subtitle A. Income Taxes
Chapter 1. Normal Taxes and Surtaxes
Subchapter A. Determination of Tax Liability
Part I. Tax on Individuals
Sections 1–5
Part II. Tax on Corporations
Sections 11–12

* * *

In referring to a provision of the Code, the key is usually the Section number. In citing Section 2(a) (dealing with the status of a surviving spouse), for example, it is unnecessary to include Subtitle A, Chapter 1, Subchapter A, Part I. Merely mentioning Section 2(a) will suffice, since the Section numbers run consecutively and do not begin again with each new Subtitle, Chapter, Subchapter, or Part. Not all Code Section numbers are used, however. Note that Part I ends with Section 5 and Part II starts with Section 11 (at present there are no Sections 6, 7, 8, 9, and 10).[2]

Tax practitioners commonly refer to a specific area of income tax law by Subchapter designation. Some of the more common Subchapter designations include Subchapter C ("Corporate Distributions and Adjustments"), Subchapter K ("Partners and Partnerships"), and Subchapter S ("Tax Treatment of S Corporations and Their Shareholders"). Particularly in the last situation, it is much more convenient to describe the effect of the applicable Code provisions (Sections 1361–1379) as "S corporation status" than as the "Tax Treatment of S Corporations and Their Shareholders."

Citing the Code.   Code Sections are often broken down into subparts.[3] Section 2(a)(1)(A) serves as an example.

Broken down by content, Section 2(a)(1)(A) appears as follows:

---

[2]When the Code was drafted, Section numbers were intentionally omitted so that later changes could be incorporated into the Code without disrupting its organization. When Congress does not leave enough space, subsequent Code Sections are given A, B, C, etc., designations. A good example is the treatment of Sections 280A through 280H.

[3]Some Code Sections do not have subparts. See, for example, §§ 211 and 241.

[4]Some Code Sections omit the subsection designation and use, instead, the paragraph designation as the first subpart. See, for example, §§ 212(1) and 1221(1).

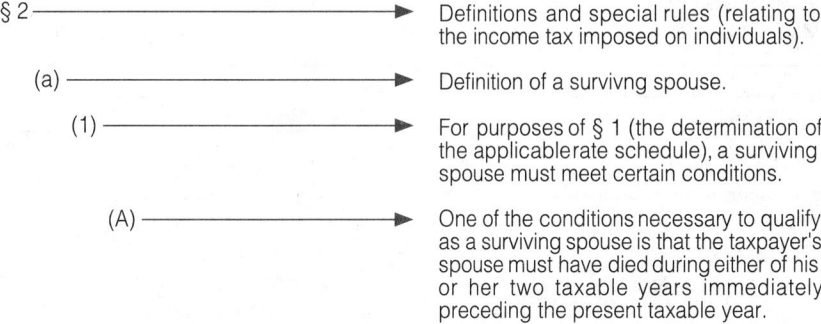

Throughout the text, references to the Code Sections are in the form given above. The symbols "§" and "§§" are used in place of "Section" and "Sections." Unless otherwise stated, all Code references are to the Internal Revenue Code of 1986. The following table summarizes the format used in the text:

Complete Reference	Text Reference
Section 2(a)(1)(A) of the Internal Revenue Code of 1986	§ 2(a)(1)(A)
Sections 1 and 2 of the Internal Revenue Code of 1986	§§ 1 and 2
Section 2 of the Internal Revenue Code of 1954	§ 2 of the Internal Revenue Code of 1954
Section 12(d) of the Internal Revenue Code of 1939[5]	§ 12(d) of the Internal Revenue Code of 1939

Effect of Treaties.   The United States signs certain tax treaties (sometimes called tax conventions) with foreign countries to render mutual assistance in tax enforcement and to avoid double taxation. Neither a tax law nor a tax treaty automatically takes precedence. When there is a direct conflict, the most recent item will take precedence. A taxpayer must disclose on the tax return any position where a treaty overrides a tax law.[6] There is a $1,000 per *failure to disclose* penalty for individuals and a $10,000 per failure to disclose penalty for corporations.[7]

ADMINISTRATIVE SOURCES OF THE TAX LAW

The administrative sources of the Federal tax law can be grouped as follows: Treasury Department Regulations, Revenue Rulings and Revenue Procedures, and various other administrative pronouncements (see Exhibit 28–1). All are issued by either the U.S. Treasury Department or one of its instrumentalities (e.g., the IRS or a District Director).

Treasury Department Regulations.   Regulations are issued by the U.S. Treasury Department under authority granted by Congress.[8] Interpretive by nature, they provide taxpayers with considerable guidance on the meaning and application of the Code. Regulations carry considerable weight. They are an important factor to consider in complying with the tax law.

Since Regulations interpret the Code, they are arranged in the same sequence as the Code. A number is added at the beginning, however, to indicate the type

---

[5]Section 12(d) of the Internal Revenue Code of 1939 is the predecessor to § 2 of the Internal Revenue Code of 1954 and the Internal Revenue Code of 1986.

[6]§ 7852(d).

[7]Reg. §§ 301.6114–1 and 301.6712–1.

[8]§ 7805.

▼ **EXHIBIT 28–1**
Administrative Sources

Source	Location	Authority**
Regulations	*Federal Register**	Force and effect of law.
Temporary Regulations	*Federal Register** *Internal Revenue Bulletin* *Cumulative Bulletin*	May be cited as a precedent.
Proposed Regulations	*Federal Register** *Internal Revenue Bulletin* *Cumulative Bulletin*	Preview of final Regulations.
Revenue Rulings Revenue Procedures Action on Decision	*Internal Revenue Bulletin* *Cumulative Bulletin*	Do not have the force and effect of law.
General Counsel's Memoranda Technical Advice Memoranda	*Tax Analysts' Tax Notes;* RIA's *Internal Memoranda of the IRS;* CCH's *IRS Position Reporter*	May not be cited as a precedent.
Letter Rulings	Research Institute of America and Commerce Clearing House loose-leaf services	Applicable only to taxpayer addressed. No precedential force.

*Finalized, Temporary, and Proposed Regulations are published in soft-cover form by several publishers.
**Each of these sources may be substantial authority for purposes of the accuracy-related penalty in § 6662.
  Notice 90–20, 1990–1 C.B. 328.

of tax or administrative, procedural, or definitional matter to which they relate. For example, the prefix 1 designates the Regulations under the income tax law. Thus, the Regulations under Code § 2 would be cited as Reg. § 1.2, with subparts added for further identification. The numbering pattern of these subparts often has no correlation with the Code subsections. The prefix 20 designates estate tax Regulations, 25 covers gift tax Regulations, 31 relates to employment taxes, and 301 refers to procedure and administration. This list is not all-inclusive.

New Regulations and changes in existing Regulations are usually issued in proposed form before they are finalized. The interval between the proposal of a Regulation and its finalization permits taxpayers and other interested parties to comment on the propriety of the proposal. **Proposed Regulations** under Code § 2, for example, are cited as Prop.Reg. § 1.2. The Tax Court indicates that Proposed Regulations carry no more weight than a position advanced in a written brief prepared by a litigating party before the Tax Court. **Finalized Regulations** have the force and effect of law.[9]

Sometimes the Treasury Department issues **Temporary Regulations** relating to elections and other matters where speed is important. These Regulations are issued without the comment period required for Proposed Regulations. Temporary Regulations have the same authoritative value as final Regulations and may be cited as precedents. Temporary Regulations now must also be issued as Proposed Regulations and automatically expire within three years after the date of issuance.[10]

Proposed, Temporary, and final Regulations are published in the *Federal Register* and are reproduced in major tax services. Final Regulations are issued as Treasury Decisions (TDs).

---

[9]*F. W. Woolworth Co.*, 54 T.C. 1233 (1970); *Harris M. Miller*, 70 T.C. 448 (1978); and *James O. Tomerlin Trust*, 87 T.C. 876 (1986).

[10]§ 7805(e).

A Potpourri of News About the IRS

- The Tax Reform Act of 1997 includes a provision that allows the Federal government to accept credit cards and debit cards for the payment of Federal income taxes. An interesting feature of the legislation is that it prohibits the IRS from paying the discount rate (typically 1 to 2 percent) that merchants normally pay banks to process their credit-card transactions.
- New IRS Regulations will allow more people to qualify for rewards that help the IRS collect taxes people have not paid. The new finders fee can be as large as 15 percent of the amount collected excluding interest.
- Most disputes with the IRS are resolved without litigation. Only about 25,000 to 30,000 Tax Court petitions are filed each year. Most of these are settled, so the Tax Court actually tries and decides only about 1,200 to 1,500 cases each year.
- For 1996, the top 10 percent of taxpayers in terms of adjusted gross income paid 63 percent of the total Federal income tax.

Regulations may also be classified as *legislative, interpretive,* or *procedural.* This classification scheme is discussed under Assessing the Validity of a Treasury Regulation later in the chapter.

Revenue Rulings and Revenue Procedures.   Revenue Rulings are official pronouncements of the National Office of the IRS.[11] Like Regulations, they are designed to provide interpretation of the tax law. However, they do not carry the same legal force and effect as Regulations and usually deal with more restricted problems. In addition, Regulations are approved by the Secretary of the Treasury, whereas Revenue Rulings are not. Both Revenue Rulings and Revenue Procedures serve an important function in that they provide *guidance* to IRS personnel and taxpayers in handling routine tax matters. Revenue Rulings and Revenue Procedures generally apply retroactively and may be revoked or modified by subsequent rulings or procedures, Regulations, legislation, or court decisions.

A Revenue Ruling often results from a specific taxpayer's request for a letter ruling. If the IRS believes that a taxpayer's request for a letter ruling deserves official publication due to its widespread impact, the holding will be converted into a Revenue Ruling and issued for the information and guidance of taxpayers, tax practitioners, and IRS personnel. Names, identifying descriptions, and money amounts are changed to conceal the identity of the requesting taxpayer.

In addition to arising from taxpayer requests, Revenue Rulings may arise from Technical Advice to District Offices of the IRS, court decisions, suggestions from tax practitioner groups, and various tax publications.

Revenue Procedures are issued in the same manner as Revenue Rulings, but deal with the internal management practices and procedures of the IRS. Familiarity with these procedures increases taxpayer compliance and helps make the administration of the tax laws more efficient. The failure of a taxpayer to follow a Revenue Procedure can result in unnecessary delay or, in a discretionary situation, can cause the IRS to decline to act on behalf of the taxpayer.

---

[11] § 7805(a).

Revenue Rulings and Revenue Procedures are published weekly by the U.S. Government in the *Internal Revenue Bulletin* (I.R.B.). Semiannually, the *Bulletins* for a six-month period are gathered together, reorganized by Code Section classification, and published in a bound volume called the *Cumulative Bulletin* (C.B.).[12]

The proper form for citing Rulings and Procedures depends on whether the item has been published in the *Cumulative Bulletin* or is available only in I.R.B. form. Consider, for example, the following transition:

Temporary Citation { Rev.Rul. 97–8, I.R.B. No. 7, 4.
Explanation: Revenue Ruling Number 8, appearing on page 4 of the 7th weekly issue of the *Internal Revenue Bulletin* for 1997.

Permanent Citation { Rev.Rul. 97–8, 1997–1 C.B. 326.
Explanation: Revenue Ruling Number 8, appearing on page 326 of Volume 1 of the *Cumulative Bulletin* for 1997.

Since the first volume of the 1997 *Cumulative Bulletin* was not published until December of 1997, the I.R.B. citation had to be used until that time. After the publication of the *Cumulative Bulletin*, the C.B. citation is proper. The basic portion of both citations (Rev.Rul. 97–8) indicates that this was the 8th Revenue Ruling issued by the IRS during 1997.

Revenue Procedures are cited in the same manner, except that "Rev.Proc." is substituted for "Rev.Rul." Some recent Revenue Procedures had the following effects:

- Specified the procedures for requesting consent to changes in accounting methods.
- Issued guidance on the deadline for amending qualified plans to comply with changes made by the Small Business Job Protection Act of 1996.
- Announced a new procedure for relief for late S corporation elections.

Letter Rulings.   Individual **letter rulings** are issued for a fee upon a taxpayer's request and describe how the IRS will treat a proposed transaction for tax purposes. They apply only to the taxpayer who asks for and obtains the ruling, but post-1984 letter rulings may be substantial authority for purposes of the accuracy-related penalty.[13] The IRS issues about 40 letter rulings each week. This procedure may seem like the only real way to carry out effective tax planning. However, the IRS limits the issuance of individual rulings to restricted, preannounced areas of taxation. The main reason the IRS will not rule in certain areas is that they involve fact-oriented situations. Thus, a ruling may not be obtained on many of the problems that are particularly troublesome to taxpayers.[14]

Although letter rulings once were private and not available to the public, the law now requires the IRS to make such rulings available for public inspection after

---

[12]Usually, only two volumes of the *Cumulative Bulletin* are published each year. However, when Congress has enacted major tax legislation, other volumes may be published containing the Congressional Committee Reports supporting the Revenue Act. See, for example, the two extra volumes for 1984 dealing with the Deficit Reduction Act of 1984. The 1984–3 *Cumulative Bulletin*, Volume 1, contains the text of the law itself; 1984–3, Volume 2, contains the Committee Reports. There are a total of four volumes of the *Cumulative Bulletin* for 1984: 1984–1; 1984–2; 1984–3, Volume 1; and 1984–3, Volume 2.

[13]Notice 90–20, 1990–1 C.B. 328. In this regard, letter rulings differ from Revenue Rulings, which are applicable to *all* taxpayers. Letter rulings may later lead to the issuance of a Revenue Ruling if the holding involved affects many taxpayers. In its Agents' Manual, the IRS indicates that letter rulings may be used as a guide with other research materials in formulating a District Office position on an issue. The IRS is required to charge a taxpayer a fee for letter rulings, determination letters, etc.

[14]Rev.Proc. 98–3, I.R.B. No. 1, 100 contains a list of areas in which the IRS will not issue advance rulings. From time to time, subsequent Revenue Procedures are issued that modify or amplify Rev.Proc. 98–3.

identifying details are deleted.[15] Published digests of private letter rulings can be found in RIA's *Private Letter Rulings*, BNA *Daily Tax Reports*, and Tax Analysts' *Tax Notes. IRS Letter Rulings Reports* (published by Commerce Clearing House) contain both digests and full texts of all letter rulings. *Letter Ruling Review* (published by Tax Analysts), a monthly publication, selects and discusses the more important of the approximately 160 letter rulings issued each month.

Letter rulings are issued multidigit file numbers, which indicate the year and week of issuance as well as the number of the ruling during that week. Consider, for example, Ltr.Rul. 9730032, which deals with unsolicited contributions to a health care charity:

97	30	032
Year 1997	30th week of issuance	Number of the ruling issued during the 30th week

Other Administrative Pronouncements.   *Treasury Decisions* (TDs) are issued by the Treasury Department to promulgate new Regulations, amend or otherwise change existing Regulations, or announce the position of the Government on selected court decisions. Like Revenue Rulings and Revenue Procedures, TDs are published initially in the *Internal Revenue Bulletin* and subsequently transferred to the *Cumulative Bulletin*.

The IRS publishes other administrative communications in the *Internal Revenue Bulletin*, such as Announcements, Notices, LRs (Proposed Regulations), and Prohibited Transaction Exemptions.

Like letter rulings, **determination letters** are issued at the request of taxpayers and provide guidance on the application of the tax law. They differ from letter rulings in that the issuing source is the District Director rather than the National Office of the IRS. Also, determination letters usually involve completed (as opposed to proposed) transactions. Determination letters are not published and are made known only to the party making the request.

EXAMPLE 1   The shareholders of Red Corporation and Green Corporation want assurance that the consolidation of the corporations into Blue Corporation will be a nontaxable reorganization. The proper approach would be to ask the National Office of the IRS to issue a letter ruling concerning the income tax effect of the proposed transaction. ▼

EXAMPLE 2   Chris operates a barber shop in which he employs eight barbers. To comply with the rules governing income tax and payroll tax withholdings, Chris wants to know whether the barbers working for him are employees or independent contractors. The proper procedure would be to request a determination letter on their status from the appropriate District Director. ▼

The National Office of the IRS releases **Technical Advice Memoranda (TAMs)** weekly. TAMs resemble letter rulings in that they give the IRS's determination of an issue. Letter rulings, however, are responses to requests by taxpayers, whereas TAMs are issued by the National Office of the IRS in response to questions raised by IRS field personnel during audits. TAMs deal with completed rather than proposed transactions and are often requested for questions relating to exempt organizations and employee plans. TAMs are not officially published and may not be cited or used as precedent.[16]

---

[15]§ 6110.   [16]§ 6110(j)(3).

TAX IN THE NEWS

TAX FREEDOM DAY SETS A NEW RECORD

According to the Tax Foundation, the average American had to work 128 days in 1997 to pay off his or her total tax bill. In other words, a taxpayer only earned tax freedom on the 129th day, or May 9, 1997. Tax Freedom Day, says the Tax Foundation, is the day that the average American is free to spend his or her income on other goods and services.

The majority of the tax burden—82 days—stems from individual income taxes and social insurance taxes. On average, Americans spent 2 hours and 49 minutes of each working day laboring to pay for the various government services and programs.

The law now requires that several internal memoranda that constitute the working law of the IRS be released. These General Counsel Memoranda (GCMs) and TAMs are not officially published, and the IRS indicates that they may not be cited as precedents by taxpayers.[17] However, these working documents do explain the IRS's position on various issues.

JUDICIAL SOURCES OF THE TAX LAW

The Judicial Process in General.   After a taxpayer has exhausted some or all of the remedies available within the IRS (no satisfactory settlement has been reached at the agent level or at the Appeals Division level), the dispute can be taken to the Federal courts. The dispute is first considered by a **court of original jurisdiction** (known as a trial court), with any appeal (either by the taxpayer or the IRS) taken to the appropriate appellate court. In most situations, the taxpayer has a choice of any of four trial courts: a **Federal District Court,** the **U.S. Court of Federal Claims,** the **U.S. Tax Court,** or the **Small Cases Division** of the U.S. Tax Court. The trial and *appellate court* system for Federal tax litigation is illustrated in Figure 28–1.

The broken line between the U.S. Tax Court and the Small Cases Division indicates that there is no appeal from the Small Cases Division. The jurisdiction of the Small Cases Division is limited to cases involving amounts of $10,000 or less.

American law, following English law, is frequently "made" by judicial decisions. Under the doctrine of *stare decisis,* each case (except in the Small Cases Division) has precedential value for future cases with the same controlling set of facts. Most Federal and state appellate court decisions and some decisions of trial courts are published. More than 4 million judicial opinions have been published in the United States, and over 130,000 cases are published each year. Published court decisions are organized by jurisdiction (Federal or state) and level of court (trial or appellate).

A decision of a particular court is called its *holding.* Sometimes a decision includes dicta or incidental opinions beyond the current facts. Such passing remarks, illustrations, or analogies are not essential to the current holding. Although the holding has precedential value under *stare decisis,* dicta are not binding on a future court.

---

[17]These are unofficially published by the publishers listed in Exhibit 28–1. Such internal memoranda for post-1984 may be substantial authority for purposes of the accuracy-related penalty. Notice 90–20, 1990–1 C.B. 328.

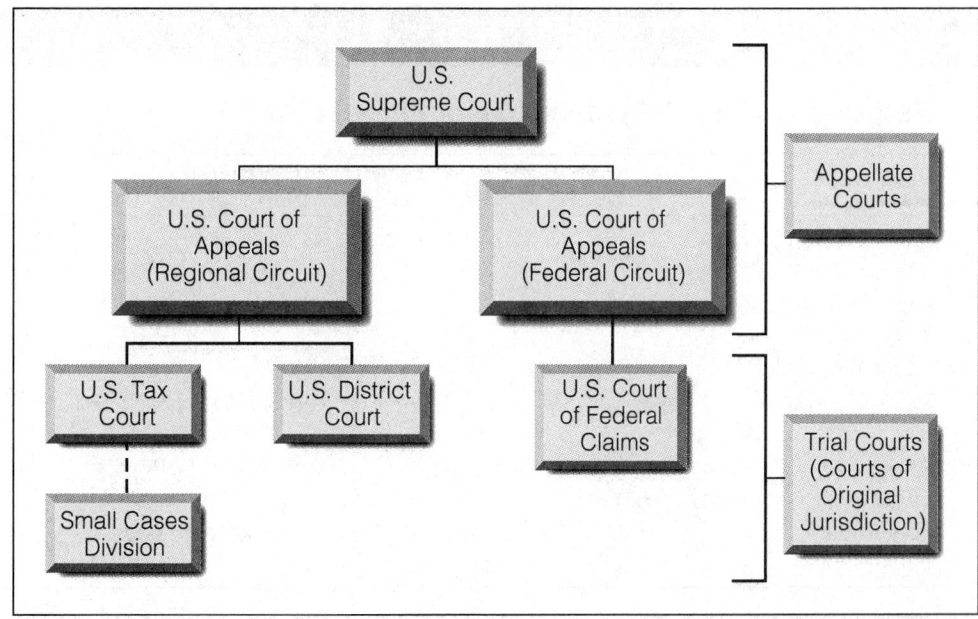

Trial Courts.   The differences between the various trial courts (courts of original jurisdiction) can be summarized as follows:

- *Number of courts.* There is only one U.S. Court of Federal Claims and only one Tax Court, but there are many Federal District Courts. The taxpayer does not select the District Court that will hear the dispute but must sue in the one that has jurisdiction.

- *Number of judges.* Each District Court has only 1 judge, the Court of Federal Claims has 16 judges, and the Tax Court has 19 regular judges. The entire Tax Court, however, will review a case (the case is sent to court conference) only when important or novel tax issues are involved. Most cases will be heard and decided by 1 of the 19 judges.

- *Location.* The Court of Federal Claims meets most often in Washington, D.C., while a District Court meets at a prescribed seat for the particular district. Each state has at least one District Court, and many of the populous states have more than one. Choosing the District Court usually minimizes the inconvenience and expense of traveling for the taxpayer and his or her counsel. The Tax Court is officially based in Washington, D.C., but the various judges travel to different parts of the country and hear cases at predetermined locations and dates. This procedure eases the distance problem for the taxpayer, but it can mean a delay before the case comes to trial and is decided.

- *Jurisdiction of the Court of Federal Claims.* The Court of Federal Claims has jurisdiction over any claim against the United States that is based upon the Constitution, any Act of Congress, or any Regulation of an executive department. Thus, the Court of Federal Claims hears nontax litigation as well as tax cases. This forum appears to be more favorable for issues having an equitable or pro-business orientation (as opposed to purely technical issues) and those requiring extensive discovery.

- *Jurisdiction of the Tax Court and District Courts.* The Tax Court hears only tax cases and is the most popular forum. The District Courts hear nontax litigation as well as tax cases. Many Tax Court justices have been appointed from

▼

CONCEPT SUMMARY 28–1

Federal Judicial System: Trial Courts

Issue	U.S. Tax Court	U.S. District Court	U.S. Court of Federal Claims
Number of judges per court	19*	1	16
Payment of deficiency before trial	No	Yes	Yes
Jury trial available	No	Yes	No
Types of disputes	Tax cases only	Mostly criminal and civil issues	Claims against the United States
Jurisdiction	Nationwide	Location of taxpayer	Nationwide
IRS acquiescence policy	Yes	Yes	Yes
Appeal route	U.S. Court of Appeals	U.S. Court of Appeals	U.S. Court of Appeals for the Federal Circuit

*There are also 14 special trial judges and 9 senior judges.

IRS or Treasury Department positions. For this reason, some people suggest that the Tax Court has more expertise in tax matters.

- *Jury trial.* The only court in which a taxpayer can obtain a jury trial is a District Court. Juries can decide only questions of fact and not questions of law. Therefore, taxpayers who choose the District Court route often do not request a jury trial. If a jury trial is not elected, the judge will decide all issues. Note that a District Court decision is controlling only in the district in which the court has jurisdiction.

- *Payment of deficiency.* Before the Court of Federal Claims or a District Court can have jurisdiction, the taxpayer must pay the tax deficiency assessed by the IRS and then sue for a refund. If the taxpayer wins (assuming no successful appeal by the Government), the tax paid plus appropriate interest will be recovered. Jurisdiction in the Tax Court, however, is usually obtained without first paying the assessed tax deficiency. In the event the taxpayer loses in the Tax Court (and no appeal is taken or an appeal is unsuccessful), the deficiency must be paid with accrued interest. With the elimination of the deduction for personal (consumer) interest, the Tax Court route of delaying payment of the deficiency can become expensive. For example, to earn 11 percent after tax, a taxpayer with a 39.6 percent marginal tax rate will have to earn 18.2 percent. By paying the tax, a taxpayer limits underpayment interest and penalties on the underpayment.

- *Appeals.* Appeals from a District Court or a Tax Court decision are to the appropriate U.S. Court of Appeals. Appeals from the Court of Federal Claims go to the Court of Appeals for the Federal Circuit.

- *Bankruptcy.* When a taxpayer files a bankruptcy petition, the IRS, like other creditors, is prevented from taking action against the taxpayer. Sometimes a bankruptcy court may settle a tax claim.

For a summary of the Federal trial courts, see Concept Summary 28–1.

▼ **FIGURE 28–2**
The Federal Circuit Courts of
Appeals

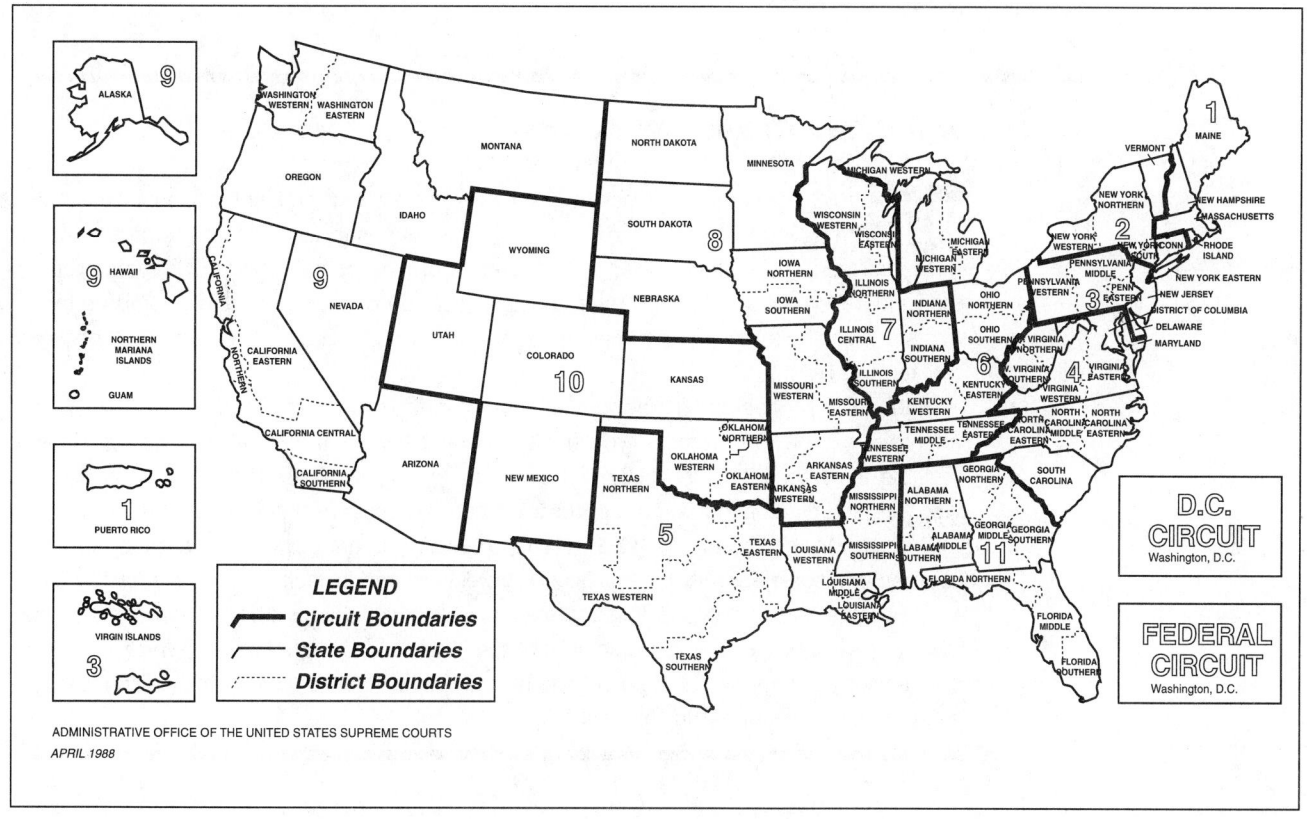

Appellate Courts.   The losing party can appeal a trial court decision to a **Circuit Court of Appeals.** The 11 geographical circuits, the circuit for the District of Columbia, and the Federal Circuit[18] are shown in Figure 28–2. The appropriate circuit for an appeal depends upon where the litigation originated. For example, an appeal from New York goes to the Second Circuit.

If the Government loses at the trial court level (District Court, Tax Court, or Court of Federal Claims), it need not (and frequently does not) appeal. The fact that an appeal is not made, however, does not indicate that the IRS agrees with the result and will not litigate similar issues in the future. The IRS may decide not to appeal for a number of reasons. First, the current litigation load may be heavy. As a consequence, the IRS may decide that available personnel should be assigned to other, more important cases. Second, the IRS may determine that this is not a good case to appeal. For example, the taxpayer may be in a sympathetic position, or the facts may be particularly strong in his or her favor. In that event, the IRS may wait to test the legal issues involved with a taxpayer who has a much weaker case. Third, if the appeal is from a District Court or the Tax Court, the Court of Appeals of jurisdiction could have some bearing on whether the IRS decides to pursue an appeal. Based on past experience and precedent, the IRS may conclude

---

[18]The Court of Appeals for the Federal Circuit was created, effective October 1, 1982, by P.L. 97–164 (4/2/82) to hear decisions appealed from the Claims Court (now the Court of Federal Claims).

that the chance for success on a particular issue might be more promising in another Court of Appeals. If so, the IRS will wait for a similar case to arise in a different jurisdiction.

ETHICAL CONSIDERATIONS

Choosing Cases for Appeal

The U.S. Government loses a tax case against a prominent citizen in the U.S. District Court of Iowa. The taxpayer, a minister, had set up three separate trusts for each of his three children (i.e., a total of nine trusts). The Government argued that under Reg. § 1.641(a)–0(c) these trusts should be consolidated and treated as three trusts to stop the taxpayer from mitigating the progressive tax structure (e.g., 39.6 percent top tax bracket).

The IRS has decided to appeal a case in this multiple trust area. As one of the attorneys for the Government, you must choose between the Iowa case and a similar multiple trust conflict in the U.S. District Court of Virginia. Here the taxpayer is a CPA who has established four separate trusts for her two children (i.e., a total of eight trusts). See *Estelle Morris Trusts*, 51 T.C. 20 (1968). Factors you are considering are the potential sympathy associated with the minister's profession and a lack thereof associated with the CPA, the facts indicating that the attempt at tax avoidance is more egregious in the Iowa case, and a colleague's opinion that the Virginia case is winnable. Which case will you select? Comment on the fairness of the Government's ability and willingness to select a case to appeal in this fashion.

The Federal Circuit at the appellate level provides a taxpayer with an alternative forum to the Court of Appeals of his or her home circuit for the appeal. Appeals from both the Tax Court and the District Court go to a taxpayer's home circuit. Now, when a particular circuit has issued an adverse decision, the taxpayer may wish to select the Court of Federal Claims route since any appeal will be to the Federal Circuit.

District Courts, the Tax Court, and the Court of Federal Claims must abide by the **precedents** set by the Court of Appeals of jurisdiction. A particular Court of Appeals need not follow the decisions of another Court of Appeals. All courts, however, must follow the decisions of the **U.S. Supreme Court.**

The Tax Court is a national court, meaning that it hears and decides cases from all parts of the country. For many years, the Tax Court followed a policy of deciding cases based on what it thought the result should be, even when its decision might be appealed to a Court of Appeals that had previously decided a similar case differently. A number of years ago this policy was changed in the *Golsen*[19] decision. Now the Tax Court will decide a case as it feels the law should be applied *only* if the Court of Appeals of appropriate jurisdiction has not yet passed on the issue or has previously decided a similar case in accord with the Tax Court's decision. If the Court of Appeals of appropriate jurisdiction has previously held otherwise, the Tax Court will conform even though it disagrees with the holding. This policy is known as the *Golsen* rule.

---

[19]*Jack E. Golsen*, 54 T.C. 742 (1970).

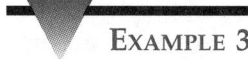

EXAMPLE 3

Emily lives in Texas and sues in the Tax Court on Issue A. The Fifth Court of Appeals is the appellate court of appropriate jurisdiction. The Fifth Court of Appeals has already decided, in a case involving similar facts but a different taxpayer, that Issue A should be resolved against the Government. Although the Tax Court feels that the Fifth Court of Appeals is wrong, under its *Golsen* policy it will render judgment for Emily. Shortly thereafter, Rashad, a resident of New York, in a comparable case, sues in the Tax Court on Issue A. Assume that the Second Court of Appeals, the appellate court of appropriate jurisdiction, has never expressed itself on Issue A. Presuming the Tax Court has not reconsidered its position on Issue A, it will decide against Rashad. Thus, it is entirely possible for two taxpayers suing in the same court to end up with opposite results merely because they live in different parts of the country. ▼

Appeal to the U.S. Supreme Court is by **Writ of Certiorari.** If the Court accepts jurisdiction, it will grant the Writ (*Cert. Granted*). Most often, it will deny jurisdiction (*Cert. Denied*). For whatever reason or reasons, the Supreme Court rarely hears tax cases. The Court usually grants certiorari to resolve a conflict among the Courts of Appeals (e.g., two or more appellate courts have assumed opposing positions on a particular issue) or where the tax issue is extremely important. The granting of a *Writ of Certiorari* indicates that at least four members of the Supreme Court believe that the issue is of sufficient importance to be heard by the full Court.

The *role* of appellate courts is limited to a review of the record of trial compiled by the trial courts. Thus, the appellate process usually involves a determination of whether the trial court applied the proper law in arriving at its decision. Usually, an appellate court will not dispute a lower court's fact-finding determination.

An appeal can have any of a number of possible outcomes. The appellate court may approve (affirm) or disapprove (reverse) the lower court's finding, or it may send the case back for further consideration (remand). When many issues are involved, a mixed result is not unusual. Thus, the lower court may be affirmed (*aff'd.*) on Issue A and reversed (*rev'd.*) on Issue B, while Issue C is remanded (*rem'd.*) for additional fact finding.

When more than one judge is involved in the decision-making process, disagreements are not uncommon. In addition to the majority view, one or more judges may concur (agree with the result reached but not with some or all of the reasoning) or dissent (disagree with the result). In any one case, the majority view controls. But concurring and dissenting views can have influence on other courts or, at some subsequent date when the composition of the court has changed, even on the same court.

Knowledge of several terms is important in understanding court decisions. The term *plaintiff* refers to the party requesting action in a court, and the *defendant* is the party against whom the suit is brought. Sometimes a court uses the terms *petitioner* and *respondent*. In general, "petitioner" is a synonym for "plaintiff," and "respondent" is a synonym for "defendant." At the trial court level, a taxpayer is normally the plaintiff (or petitioner), and the Government is the defendant (or respondent). If the taxpayer wins and the Government appeals as the new petitioner (or appellee), the taxpayer becomes the new respondent.

2 **LEARNING OBJECTIVE**
Locate and work with the appropriate tax law sources.

Judicial Citations—General. Having briefly described the judicial process, it is appropriate to consider the more practical problem of the relationship of case law to tax research. As previously noted, court decisions are an important source of tax law. The ability to locate a case and to cite it is therefore a must in working with the tax law. Judicial citations usually follow a standard pattern:

case name, volume number, reporter series, page or paragraph number, and court (where necessary). Specific citation formats for each court are presented in the following sections.

Judicial Citations—The U.S. Tax Court.   A good starting point is the U.S. Tax Court (formerly the Board of Tax Appeals). The Tax Court issues two types of decisions: Regular and Memorandum. The Chief Judge decides whether the opinion is issued as a Regular or Memorandum decision. The distinction between the two involves both substance and form. In terms of substance, *Memorandum* decisions deal with situations necessitating only the application of already established principles of law. *Regular* decisions involve novel issues not previously resolved by the Court. In actual practice, however, this distinction is not always preserved. Not infrequently, Memorandum decisions will be encountered that appear to warrant Regular status, and vice versa. At any rate, do not conclude that Memorandum decisions possess no value as precedents. Both represent the position of the Tax Court and, as such, can be relied upon.

The Regular and Memorandum decisions issued by the Tax Court also differ in form. Memorandum decisions are not officially published, while regular decisions are published by the U.S. Government in a series called *Tax Court of the United States Reports*. Each volume of these *Reports* covers a six-month period (January 1 through June 30 and July 1 through December 31) and is given a succeeding volume number. But, as was true of the *Cumulative Bulletins*, there is usually a time lag between the date a decision is rendered and the date it appears in bound form. A temporary citation may be necessary to help the researcher locate a recent Regular decision. Consider, for example, the temporary and permanent citations for *Sprint Corporation and Subsidiaries*, a decision filed on April 30, 1997:

Temporary Citation   { *Sprint Corporation and Subsidiaries*, 108 T.C. ___, No. 4 (1997).
                        Explanation: Page number left blank because not yet known.

Permanent Citation   { *Sprint Corporation and Subsidiaries*, 108 T.C. 384 (1997).
                        Explanation: Page number now available.

Both citations tell us that the case will ultimately appear in Volume 108 of the *Tax Court of the United States Reports*. Until this volume is bound and made available to the general public, however, the page number must be left blank. Instead, the temporary citation identifies the case as being the 4th Regular decision issued by the Tax Court since Volume 107 ended. With this information, the decision can easily be located in either of the special Tax Court services published by Commerce Clearing House and Research Institute of America (formerly by Prentice-Hall). Once Volume 108 is released, the permanent citation can be substituted and the number of the case dropped.

Before 1943, the Tax Court was called the Board of Tax Appeals, and its decisions were published as the *United States Board of Tax Appeals Reports* (B.T.A.). These 47 volumes cover the period from 1924 to 1942. For example, the citation *Karl Pauli*, 11 B.T.A. 784 (1928) refers to the 11th volume of the *Board of Tax Appeals Reports*, page 784, issued in 1928.

If the IRS loses in a decision, it may indicate whether it agrees or disagrees with the results reached by the court by publishing an **acquiescence** ("A" or "Acq.") or **nonacquiescence** ("NA" or "Nonacq."), respectively. Until 1991, acquiescences and nonacquiescences were published only for certain Regular decisions of the Tax Court, but the IRS has expanded its acquiescence program to include other civil tax cases where guidance is helpful. The acquiescence or nonacquiescence is published in the *Internal Revenue Bulletin* and the *Cumulative Bulletin* as an *Action on Decision*. The IRS can retroactively revoke an acquiescence.

Although Memorandum decisions are not published by the U.S. Government, they are published by Commerce Clearing House (CCH) and Research Institute of America (RIA [formerly by Prentice-Hall]). Consider, for example, the three different ways that *Jack D. Carr* can be cited:

> *Jack D. Carr*, T.C.Memo. 1985–19
> The 19th Memorandum decision issued by the Tax Court in 1985.
>
> *Jack D. Carr*, 49 TCM 507
> Page 507 of Vol. 49 of the CCH *Tax Court Memorandum Decisions*.
>
> *Jack D. Carr*, RIA T.C.Mem.Dec. ¶85,019
> Paragraph 85,019 of the RIA *T.C. Memorandum Decisions*.

Note that the third citation contains the same information as the first. Thus, ¶85,019 indicates the following information about the case: year 1985, 19th T.C. Memo. decision.[20] Although the RIA citation does not include a specific volume number, the paragraph citation (85,019) indicates that the decision can be found in the 1985 volume of the RIA Memorandum Decision service.

Judicial Citations—The U.S. District Court, Court of Federal Claims, and Courts of Appeals.

District Court, Court of Federal Claims, Court of Appeals, and Supreme Court decisions dealing with Federal tax matters are reported in both the CCH *U.S. Tax Cases* (USTC) and the RIA *American Federal Tax Reports* (AFTR) series.

Federal District Court decisions, dealing with *both* tax and nontax issues, are also published by West Publishing Company in its *Federal Supplement Series*. A District Court case can be cited in three different forms as the following examples illustrate:

> *Simons-Eastern Co. v. U.S.*, 73–1 USTC ¶9279 (D.Ct.Ga., 1972).
>
> *Explanation:* Reported in the first volume of the *U.S. Tax Cases* (USTC) published by Commerce Clearing House for calendar year 1973 (73–1) and located at paragraph 9279 (¶9279).
>
> *Simons-Eastern Co. v. U.S.*, 31 AFTR2d 73–640 (D.Ct.Ga., 1972).
>
> *Explanation:* Reported in the 31st volume of the second series of the *American Federal Tax Reports* (AFTR2d) published by RIA and beginning on page 640. The "73" preceding the page number indicates the year the case was published but is a designation used only in recent decisions.
>
> *Simons-Eastern Co. v. U.S.*, 354 F.Supp. 1003 (D.Ct.Ga., 1972).
>
> *Explanation:* Reported in the 354th volume of the *Federal Supplement Series* (F.Supp.) published by West Publishing Company and beginning on page 1003.

In all of the preceding citations, note that the name of the case is the same (Simons-Eastern Co. being the taxpayer), as are the references to the Federal District Court of Georgia (D.Ct.Ga.) and the year the decision was rendered (1972).[21]

Decisions of the Court of Federal Claims[22] and the Courts of Appeals are published in the USTCs, AFTRs, and a West Publishing Company reporter called the *Federal Second Series* (F.2d). Volume 999, published in 1993, is the last volume of the *Federal Second Series*. It is followed by the *Federal Third Series* (F.3d). Beginning

---

[20]In this text, this Memorandum decision of the U.S. Tax Court would be cited as *Jack D. Carr*, 49 TCM 507, T.C.Memo. 1985–19.

[21]In this text, the case would be cited in the following form: *Simons-Eastern Co. v. U.S.*, 73–1 USTC ¶9279, 31 AFTR2d 73–640, 354 F.Supp. 1003 (D.Ct.Ga., 1972). Prentice-Hall Information Services is now owned by Research Institute of America. Although recent

volumes contain the RIA imprint, many of the older volumes continue to have the P-H imprint.

[22]Before October 29, 1992, the Court of Federal Claims was called the Claims Court. Before October 1, 1982, the Court of Federal Claims was called the Court of Claims.

with October 1982, decisions of the Court of Federal Claims are published in another West Publishing Company reporter entitled the *Claims Court Reporter* (abbreviated as *Cls. Ct.*). Beginning with Volume 27 on October 30, 1992, the name of the reporter changed to the *Federal Claims Reporter* (abbreviated as *Fed.Cl.*). The following examples illustrate the different forms:

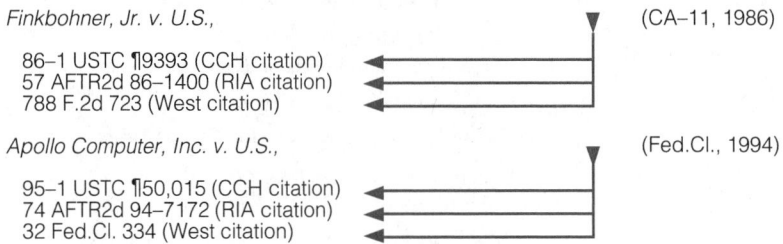

Finkbohner, Jr. v. U.S.,   (CA–11, 1986)

    86–1 USTC ¶9393 (CCH citation)
    57 AFTR2d 86–1400 (RIA citation)
    788 F.2d 723 (West citation)

Apollo Computer, Inc. v. U.S.,   (Fed.Cl., 1994)

    95–1 USTC ¶50,015 (CCH citation)
    74 AFTR2d 94–7172 (RIA citation)
    32 Fed.Cl. 334 (West citation)

Note that *Finkbohner, Jr.* is a decision rendered by the Eleventh Court of Appeals in 1986 (CA–11, 1986), while *Apollo Computer, Inc.* was issued by the Court of Federal Claims in 1994 (Fed.Cl., 1994).

Judicial Citations—The U.S. Supreme Court.   Like all other Federal tax decisions (except those rendered by the U.S. Tax Court), Supreme Court decisions are published by Commerce Clearing House in the USTCs and by RIA (formerly by Prentice-Hall) in the AFTRs. The U.S. Government Printing Office also publishes these decisions in the *United States Supreme Court Reports* (U.S.), as do West Publishing Company in its *Supreme Court Reporter* (S.Ct.) and the Lawyer's Co-operative Publishing Company in its *United States Reports, Lawyer's Edition* (L.Ed.). The following illustrates the different ways the same decision can be cited:

U.S. v. The Donruss Co.,   (USSC, 1969)

    69–1 USTC ¶9167 (CCH citation)
    23 AFTR2d 69–418 (RIA citation)
    89 S.Ct. 501 (West citation)
    393 U.S. 297 (U.S. Government Printing Office citation)
    21 L.Ed.2d 495 (Lawyer's Co-operative Publishing Co. citation)

The parenthetical reference (USSC, 1969) identifies the decision as having been rendered by the U.S. Supreme Court in 1969. In this text, the citations of Supreme Court decisions are limited to the CCH (USTC), RIA (AFTR), and West (S.Ct.) versions. See Concept Summary 28–2.

WORKING WITH THE TAX LAW—
TAX RESEARCH

3 ▼ **LEARNING OBJECTIVE**
Understand the tax research process.

Tax research is the method used to determine the best available solution to a situation that possesses tax consequences. In other words, it is the process of finding a competent and professional conclusion to a tax problem. The problem may originate from completed or proposed transactions. In the case of a completed transaction, the objective of the research is to determine the tax result of what has already taken place. For example, is the expenditure incurred by the taxpayer deductible or not deductible for tax purposes? When dealing with proposed transactions, the tax research process is concerned with the determination of possible tax consequences. To the extent that tax research leads to a choice of alternatives or

CONCEPT SUMMARY 28–2

Judicial Sources

Court	Location	Authority
U.S. Supreme Court	S.Ct. Series (West) U.S. Series (U.S. Gov't.) L.Ed. (Lawyer's Co-op.) AFTR (RIA) USTC (CCH)	Highest authority
U.S. Courts of Appeal	Federal 3d (West) AFTR (RIA) USTC (CCH)	Next highest appellate court
Tax Court (Regular decisions)	U.S. Gov't. Printing Office, RIA/CCH separate services	Highest trial court*
Tax Court (Memorandum decisions)	RIA T.C.Memo. (RIA) TCM (CCH)	Less authority than Regular T.C. decision
U.S. Court of Federal Claims**	Federal Claims Reporter (West) AFTR (RIA) USTC (CCH)	Similar authority as Tax Court
U.S. District Courts	F.Supp. Series (West) AFTR (RIA) USTC (CCH)	Lowest trial court
Small Cases Division of Tax Court	Not published	No precedent value

*Theoretically, the Tax Court, Court of Federal Claims, and District Courts are on the same level of authority. But some people believe that since the Tax Court hears and decides tax cases from all parts of the country (it is a national court), its decisions may be more authoritative than a Court of Federal Claims or District Court decision.

**Before October 29, 1992, the U.S. Claims Court.

otherwise influences the future actions of the taxpayer, it becomes the key to effective tax planning.

Tax research involves the following procedures:

- Identifying and refining the problem.
- Locating the appropriate tax law sources.
- Assessing the validity of the tax law sources.
- Arriving at the solution or at alternative solutions while giving due consideration to nontax factors.
- Effectively communicating the solution to the taxpayer or the taxpayer's representative.
- Following up on the solution (where appropriate) in light of new developments.

This process is depicted schematically in Figure 28–3. The broken lines indicate steps of particular interest when tax research is directed toward proposed, rather than completed, transactions.

IDENTIFYING THE PROBLEM

Problem identification starts with a compilation of the relevant facts involved. In this regard, *all* of the facts that may have a bearing on the problem must be gathered,

▼ FIGURE 28-3
Tax Research Process

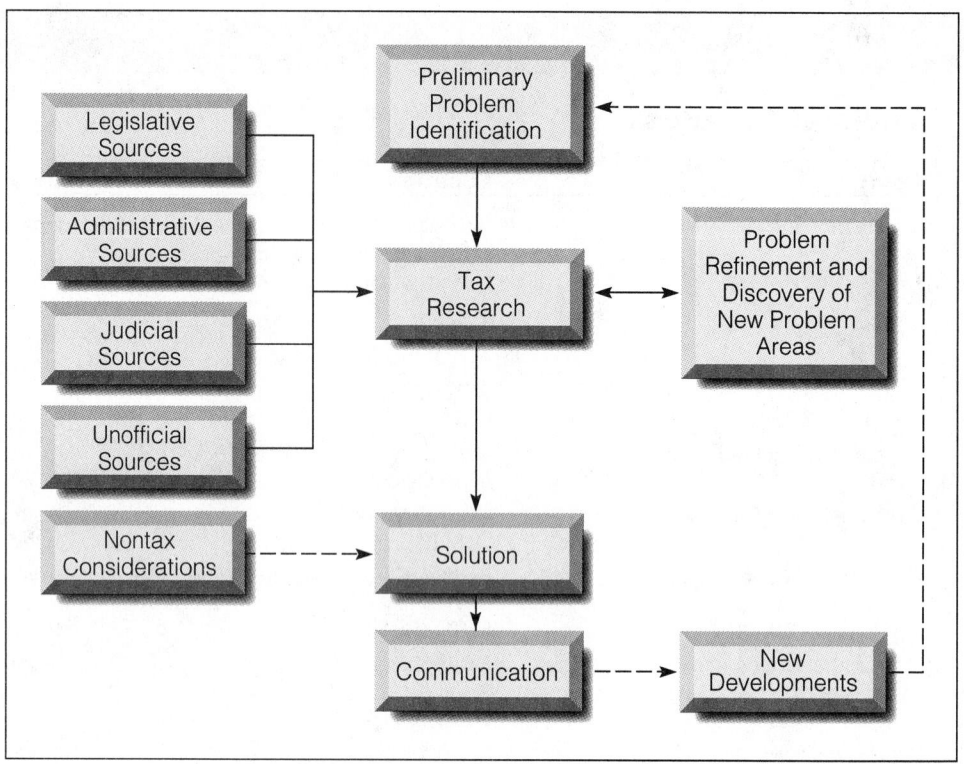

as any omission could modify the solution reached. To illustrate, consider what appears to be a very simple problem.

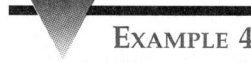

EXAMPLE 4

Early in December, Fred and Megan review their financial and tax situation with their son, Sam, and daughter-in-law, Dana. Fred and Megan are in the 28% tax bracket. Both Sam and Dana are age 21. Sam, a student at a nearby university, owns some publicly traded stock that he inherited from his grandmother. A current sale of the stock would result in approximately $7,000 of gross income. At this point, Fred and Megan provide about 55% of Sam and Dana's support. Although neither is now employed, Sam has earned $960 and Dana has earned $900. The problem: Should the stock be sold, and would the sale prohibit Fred and Megan from claiming Sam and Dana as dependents? ▼

REFINING THE PROBLEM

Initial reaction is that Fred and Megan in Example 4 could not claim Sam and Dana as dependents if the stock is sold, since Sam would then have earned more than the exemption amount under § 151(d). However, Sam is a full-time student, and § 151(c)(1)(B) allows a son or daughter who is a full-time student and is under age 24 to earn more than the exemption amount without penalizing the parents with the loss of the dependency exemption. Thus, Sam could sell the stock without penalizing his parents under the gross income test. However, the $7,000 income from the sale of the stock might lead to the failure of the greater-than-50 percent support test, depending on how much Sam spends for his (or Dana's) support.

Assume, however, that further fact gathering reveals the following additional information:

- Sam does not really need to spend the proceeds from the sale of the stock.
- Sam receives a sizable portion of his own support from a scholarship.

With these new facts, additional research leads to § 152(d) and Regulation § 1.152–1(c), which indicate that a scholarship received by a student is not included for purposes of determining whether the parents furnished more than one-half of the child's support. Further, if Sam does not spend the proceeds from the sale of stock, the unexpended amount is not counted for purposes of the support test. Thus, it appears that the parents would not be denied the dependency exemptions for Sam and Dana.

LOCATING THE APPROPRIATE TAX LAW SOURCES

Once the problem is clearly defined, what is the next step? Although the next step is a matter of individual judgment, most tax research begins with the index volume of the tax service, a keyword search on an on-line tax service, or a CD-ROM search (see the subsequent discussion of Electronic Tax Research). If the problem is not complex, the researcher may bypass the tax service or on-line service and turn directly to the Internal Revenue Code and the Treasury Regulations. For the beginner, the latter procedure saves time and will solve many of the more basic problems. If the researcher does not have a personal copy of the Code or Regulations, resorting to the appropriate volume(s) of a tax service is necessary.[23] The major tax services available are as follows:

Standard Federal Tax Reporter, Commerce Clearing House.

United States Tax Reporter, Research Institute of America (entitled *Federal Taxes* prior to July 1992).

Federal Tax Coordinator 2d, Research Institute of America.

Tax Management Portfolios, Bureau of National Affairs.

Rabkin and Johnson, *Federal Income, Gift and Estate Taxation,* Matthew Bender, Inc.

CCH's Federal Tax Service, Commerce Clearing House.

Mertens Law of Federal Income Taxation, Callaghan and Co.

Working with Tax Services.   In this text, it is not feasible to explain the use of any particular tax service—this ability can be obtained only by practice.[24] However, several important observations about the use of tax services cannot be overemphasized. First, never forget to check for current developments. The main text of any service is revised too infrequently to permit reliance on that portion as the *latest* word on any subject. Where current developments can be found depends on which service is being used. Commerce Clearing House's *Standard Federal Tax Reporter* contains a special volume devoted to current matters. Both RIA's *U.S. Tax Reporter* and *Federal Tax Coordinator 2d* integrate the new developments into the body of the service throughout the year. Second, when dealing with a tax service synopsis of a Treasury Department pronouncement or a judicial decision, remember there is no substitute for the original source.

---

[23]Several of the major tax services publish paperback editions of the Code and Treasury Regulations that can be purchased at modest prices. These editions are usually revised twice each year. For an annotated and abridged version of the Code and Regulations that is published annually, see James E. Smith, *West's Internal Revenue*

Code of 1986 and Treasury Regulations: Annotated and Selected (St. Paul, Minn.: West Publishing Company, 1998).

[24]The representatives of the various tax services are prepared to provide the users of their services with printed booklets and individual instruction on the use of the materials.

To illustrate, do not base a conclusion solely on a tax service's commentary on *Simons-Eastern Co. v. U.S.* If the case is vital to the research, look it up! The facts of the case may be distinguishable from those involved in the problem being researched. This is not to say that the case synopsis contained in the tax service is wrong—it might just be misleading or incomplete.

Tax Periodicals.   The various tax periodicals are another source of information. The easiest way to locate a journal article on a particular tax problem is through Commerce Clearing House's *Federal Tax Articles*. This multivolume service includes a subject index, a Code Section number index, and an author's index. In addition, the RIA tax service has a topical "Index to Tax Articles" section that is organized using the RIA paragraph index system. Also, beginning in 1992, *The Accounting & Tax Index* is available in three quarterly issues plus a cumulative year-end volume covering all four quarters. The original *Accountant's Index* started in 1921 and ended in 1991.

The following are some of the more useful tax periodicals:

The Journal of Taxation
Warren, Gorham and Lamont
31 St. James Avenue
Boston, MA 02116

Tax Law Review
Warren, Gorham and Lamont
31 St. James Avenue
Boston, MA 02116

Trusts and Estates
6151 Powers Ferry Road NW
Atlanta, GA 30339

Oil, Gas, and Energy Quarterly
Matthew Bender & Co.
2 Park Avenue
New York, NY 10016

The Practical Accountant
11 Penn Plaza
New York, NY 10001

Estate Planning
Warren, Gorham and Lamont
31 St. James Avenue
Boston, MA 02116

Taxation for Accountants
Warren, Gorham and Lamont
31 St. James Avenue
Boston, MA 02116

The Tax Executive
1001 Pennsylvania Avenue NW
Suite 320
Washington, D.C. 20004

Tax Notes
6830 Fairfax Drive
Arlington, VA 22213

The International Tax Journal
Panel Publishers
14 Plaza Road
Greenvale, NY 11548

TAXES—The Tax Magazine
Commerce Clearing House, Inc.
2700 Lake Cook Road
Riverwood, IL 60015

National Tax Journal
5310 East Main Street
Columbus, OH 43213

The Tax Adviser
AICPA
1211 Avenue of the Americas
New York, NY 10036

Journal of Taxation for Individuals
Warren, Gorham and Lamont
31 St. James Avenue
Boston, MA 02116

The Tax Lawyer
American Bar Association
750 N. Lake Shore Drive
Chicago, IL 60611

Journal of the American Taxation Association
American Accounting Association
5717 Bessie Drive
Sarasota, FL 34233

Journal of Corporate Taxation
Warren, Gorham and Lamont
31 St. James Avenue
Boston, MA 02116

ASSESSING THE VALIDITY OF THE TAX LAW SOURCES

Once a source has been located, the next step is to assess it in light of the problem at hand. Proper assessment involves careful interpretation of the tax law and consideration of its relevance and validity.

Interpreting the Internal Revenue Code.   The language of the Code can be extremely difficult to comprehend fully. For example, one subsection [§ 341(e)] relating to collapsible corporations contains *one* sentence of more than 450 words (twice as many as in the Gettysburg Address). Within this same subsection is another sentence of 300 words.

Assessing the Validity of a Treasury Regulation.   Treasury Regulations are often said to have the force and effect of law. This is certainly true for most Regulations, but some judicial decisions have held a Regulation or a portion thereof invalid. Usually, this is done on the grounds that the Regulation is contrary to the intent of Congress. Most often the courts do not question the validity of Regulations because of the belief that "the first administrative interpretation of a provision as it appears in a new act often expresses the general understanding of the times or the actual understanding of those who played an important part when the statute was drafted."[25]

Keep in mind the following observations when assessing the validity of a Regulation:

- IRS agents must give the Code and the Regulations issued thereunder equal weight when dealing with taxpayers and their representatives.
- Proposed Regulations provide a preview of future final Regulations, but they are not binding on the IRS or taxpayers.
- In a challenge, the burden of proof is on the taxpayer to show that a Regulation is wrong. However, a court may invalidate a Regulation that varies from the language of the statute and has no support in the Committee Reports.
- If the taxpayer loses the challenge, the negligence penalty may be imposed.[26] This accuracy-related penalty applies to any failure to make a reasonable attempt to comply with the tax law and to any disregard of rules and Regulations.[27]
- Final Regulations tend to be procedural, interpretive, or legislative. **Procedural Regulations** neither establish tax laws nor attempt to explain tax laws. Procedural Regulations are *housekeeping-type* instructions, indicating information that taxpayers should provide the IRS, as well as information about the internal management and conduct of the IRS itself.
- Some **interpretive Regulations** merely reprint or rephrase what Congress stated in the Committee Reports that were issued when the tax legislation was enacted. Such Regulations are *hard and solid* and almost impossible to overturn because they clearly reflect the intent of Congress.
- In some Code Sections, Congress has given the *Secretary or his delegate* the authority to prescribe Regulations to carry out the details of administration or to otherwise complete the operating rules. Under such circumstances, it could almost be said that Congress is delegating its legislative powers to the Treasury Department. Regulations issued pursuant to this type of authority truly possess the force and effect of law and are often called **legislative Regulations** (e.g., consolidated return Regulations).

---

[25]*Augustus v. Comm.*, 41–1 USTC ¶9255, 26 AFTR 612, 118 F.2d 38 (CA–6, 1941).

[26]§§ 6662(a) and (b)(1).
[27]§ 6662(c).

Assessing the Validity of Other Administrative Sources of the Tax Law. Revenue Rulings issued by the IRS carry less weight than Treasury Department Regulations. Revenue Rulings are important, however, in that they reflect the position of the IRS on tax matters. In any dispute with the IRS on the interpretation of tax law, taxpayers should expect agents to follow the results reached in any applicable Revenue Rulings.

Actions on Decisions further tell the taxpayer the IRS's reaction to certain court decisions and Revenue Rulings. Recall that the IRS follows a practice of either acquiescing (agreeing) or nonacquiescing (not agreeing) with selected decisions. A nonacquiescence does not mean that a particular court decision is of no value, but it does indicate that the IRS will continue to litigate the issue involved.

Assessing the Validity of Judicial Sources of the Tax Law. The judicial process as it relates to the formulation of tax law has been described. How much reliance can be placed on a particular decision depends upon the following variables:

- The level of the court. A decision rendered by a trial court (e.g., a Federal District Court) carries less weight than one issued by an appellate court (e.g., the Fifth Court of Appeals). Unless Congress changes the Code, decisions by the U.S. Supreme Court represent the last word on any tax issue.
- The legal residence of the taxpayer. If, for example, a taxpayer lives in Texas, a decision of the Fifth Court of Appeals means more than one rendered by the Second Court of Appeals. This is the case because any appeal from a District Court or the Tax Court would be to the Fifth Court of Appeals and not to the Second Court of Appeals.[28]
- A Tax Court Regular decision carries more weight than a Memorandum decision because the Tax Court does not consider Memorandum decisions to be binding precedents.[29] Furthermore, a Tax Court *reviewed* decision carries even more weight. All of the Tax Court judges participate in a reviewed decision.
- A Circuit Court decision where certiorari has been requested and denied by the Supreme Court carries more weight than a Circuit Court decision that was not appealed. A Circuit Court decision heard *en banc* (all the judges participate) carries more weight than a normal Circuit Court case.
- Whether the decision represents the weight of authority on the issue. In other words, is it supported by the results reached by other courts?
- The outcome or status of the decision on appeal. For example, was the decision appealed and, if so, with what result?

In connection with the last two variables, a citator is helpful to tax research.[30] The use of a citator is not illustrated in this text.

Assessing the Validity of Other Sources. *Primary sources* of tax law include the Constitution, legislative history materials, statutes, treaties, Treasury Regulations, IRS pronouncements, and judicial decisions. In general, the IRS regards only primary sources as substantial authority. However, reference to *secondary materials* such as legal periodicals, treatises, legal opinions, General Counsel Memoranda, and written determinations may be useful. In general, secondary sources are not authority.

---

[28]Before October 1, 1982, an appeal from the then-named U.S. Court of Claims (the other trial court) was directly to the U.S. Supreme Court.
[29]*Severino R. Nico, Jr.,* 67 T.C. 647 (1977).

[30]The major citators are published by Commerce Clearing House, RIA, and Shepard's Citations, Inc.

Although the statement that the IRS regards only primary sources as substantial authority is generally true, there is one exception. In Notice 90–20,[31] the IRS expanded the list of substantial authority *for purposes of* the accuracy-related penalty in § 6662 to include a number of secondary materials (e.g., letter rulings, General Counsel Memoranda, the Bluebook). As under former § 6661, "authority" does not include conclusions reached in treatises, legal periodicals, and opinions rendered by tax professionals.

A letter ruling or determination letter is substantial authority only for the taxpayer to whom it is issued, except as noted above with respect to the accuracy-related penalty.

Upon the completion of major tax legislation, the staff of the Joint Committee on Taxation (in consultation with the staffs of the House Ways and Means and Senate Finance Committees) often will prepare a General Explanation of the Act, commonly known as the Bluebook because of the color of its cover. The IRS will not accept this detailed explanation as having legal effect. The Bluebook does, however, provide valuable guidance to tax advisers and taxpayers until Regulations are issued, and some letter rulings and General Counsel Memoranda of the IRS cite its explanations.

ARRIVING AT THE SOLUTION OR AT ALTERNATIVE SOLUTIONS

Example 4 raised the question of whether a taxpayer would be denied dependency exemptions for a son and a daughter-in-law if the son sold some stock near the end of the year. A refinement of the problem supplies the following additional information:

- Sam was a full-time student during four calendar months of the year.
- Sam and Dana anticipate filing a joint return.

Additional research leads to Regulation § 1.151–3(b), which indicates that to qualify as a student, Sam must be a full-time student during each of *five* calendar months of the year at an educational institution. Thus, proceeds from Sam's sale of the stock would cause his parents to lose at least one dependency exemption because Sam's gross income would exceed the exemption amount. The parents still might be able to claim Dana as an exemption if the support test is met.

Section 151(c)(2) indicates that a supporting taxpayer is not permitted a dependency exemption for a married dependent if the married individual files a joint return. Initial reaction is that a joint return by Sam and Dana would be disastrous to the parents. However, more research uncovers two Revenue Rulings that provide an exception if neither the dependent nor the dependent's spouse is required to file a return but does so solely to claim a refund of tax withheld. The IRS asserts that each spouse must have gross income of less than the exemption amount.[32] Therefore, if Sam sells the stock and he and Dana file a joint return, the parents would lose the dependency exemption for both Sam and Dana.

If the stock is not sold until January, both exemptions may still be available to the parents. However, under § 151(d)(2), a personal exemption is not available to

---

[31]1990–1 C.B. 328; see also Reg. § 1.6661–3(b)(2).   [32]Rev.Rul. 54–567, 1954–2 C.B. 108; Rev.Rul. 65–34, 1965–1 C.B. 86.

▼ **FIGURE 28–4**
Tax File Memorandum

August 16, 1998

TAX FILE MEMORANDUM

FROM: John J. Jones

SUBJECT: Fred and Megan Taxpayer
Engagement: Issues

Today I talked to Fred Taxpayer with respect to his August 14, 1998 letter requesting tax assistance. He wishes to know if his son, Sam, can sell stock worth $19,000 (basis = $12,000) without the parents losing the dependency exemptions for Sam and Sam's wife, Dana.

Fred Taxpayer is married to Megan, and Sam is a full-time student at a local university. Sam inherited the stock from his grandmother about five years ago. If he sells the stock, he will save the proceeds from the sale. Sam does not need to spend the proceeds if he sells the stock because he receives a $3,000 scholarship that he uses for his own support (i.e., to pay for tuition, books, and fees). Fred and Megan are in the 28% tax bracket and furnish approximately 55% of Sam and Dana's support.

ISSUE: If the stock is sold, would the sale prohibit Fred and Megan from claiming Sam and Dana as dependents? I told Fred that we would have an answer for him within two weeks.

a taxpayer who can be claimed as a dependent by another taxpayer (whether actually claimed or not). Thus, if the parents can claim Sam and Dana as dependents, Sam and Dana would lose their personal exemptions on their tax return.

COMMUNICATING TAX RESEARCH

4   LEARNING OBJECTIVE
Communicate the results of the tax research process in a client letter and a tax file memorandum.

Once the problem has been researched adequately, a memo, letter, or oral presentation setting forth the result may need to be prepared. The form such a communication takes could depend on a number of considerations. For example, does an employer or instructor recommend a particular procedure or format for tax research memos? Is the memo to be given directly to the client or will it first go to the preparer's employer? Who is the audience for the oral presentation? How long should you talk?[33] Whatever form it takes, a good tax research communication should contain the following elements.

- A clear statement of the issue.
- In more complex situations, a short review of the fact pattern that raises the issue.
- A review of the controlling tax law sources (e.g., Code, Regulations, Revenue Rulings, judicial authority).
- Any assumptions made in arriving at the solution.
- The solution recommended and the logic or reasoning supporting it.
- The references consulted in the research process.

Illustrations of the memos for the tax file and the client letter associated with Example 4 appear in Figures 28–4, 28–5, and 28–6.

---

[33]For more on crafting oral presentations, see W. A. Raabe and G. E. Whittenburg, "Talking Tax: How to Make a Tax Presentation," *The Tax Adviser,* March 1997, pp. 179–182.

▼ FIGURE 28–5
Tax File Memorandum

August 26, 1998

TAX FILE MEMORANDUM

FROM: John J. Jones

SUBJECT: Fred and Megan Taxpayer
           Engagement: Conclusions

Section 152(a) provides that in order for a taxpayer to take a dependency exemption, the taxpayer must provide over 50% of the support of the potential dependent. Fred and Megan provide about 55% of the support of their son, Sam, and their daughter-in-law, Dana. If Sam should sell the stock in 1998, he would not need to spend the proceeds for support purposes (i.e., would save the proceeds). Thus, the stock sale would not affect his qualifying for the support test. In calculating the percentage of support provided by Fred and Megan, a $3,000 scholarship received by Sam is not counted in determining the amount of support Sam provides for himself [see Reg. § 1.152–1(c)].

Section 151(c)(1) provides that in order to qualify for a dependency exemption, the potential dependent's gross income must be less than the exemption amount (i.e., $2,700 in 1998). Without the stock sale, the gross income of both Sam ($960) and Dana ($900) will be below the exemption amount in 1998. The $3,000 Sam receives as a scholarship is excluded from his gross income under § 117(a) because he uses the entire amount to pay for his tuition, books, and fees at a local university.

The key issue then is whether the stock, which will generate $7,000 gain for Sam, will cause the gross income test to be violated. The gain will increase Sam's gross income to $7,960 ($7,000 + $960). However, § 151(c)(1)(B) permits a child's gross income to exceed the exemption amount if the child is a student under the age of 24. Under Reg. § 1.151–3(b), to qualify as a student, the person must be a full-time student during each of five calendar months. A telephone call to Megan provided the information that Sam was a student for only four months in 1998. Thus, since Sam is not eligible for the student exception, the sale of the stock by Sam in 1998 would result in Fred and Megan losing the dependency exemption for Sam.

The stock sale would also result in the loss of the dependency exemption for Dana if Sam and Dana file a joint return for 1998 [see § 151(c)(2)].

From a tax planning perspective, Sam should not sell the stock until 1999. This will enable Fred and Megan to claim dependency exemptions on their 1998 return for Sam and Dana. Note, however, that neither Sam nor Dana will be permitted to take a personal exemption deduction on their 1998 tax return since they are claimed as dependents on someone else's return [see § 151(d)(2)]. However, this will not produce any negative tax consequences since their tax liability will be zero if the stock is not sold in 1998.

Working with the Tax Law—
Tax Planning

5 Learning Objective
Apply tax research techniques and planning procedures.

Tax research and tax planning are inseparable. The *primary* purpose of effective tax planning is to maximize the taxpayer's after-tax wealth. This statement does not mean that the course of action selected must produce the lowest possible tax under the circumstances. The minimization of tax liability must be considered in the context of the legitimate business goals of the taxpayer.

A *secondary* objective of effective tax planning is to reduce or defer the tax in the current tax year. Specifically, this objective aims to accomplish one or more results. Some possibilities are eradicating the tax entirely, eliminating the tax in the current year, deferring the receipt of income, proliferating taxpayers (i.e., forming partnerships and corporations or making lifetime gifts to family members), eluding double taxation, avoiding ordinary income, or creating, increasing, or accelerating deductions. However, this second objective should be approached with considerable reservation and moderation. For example, a tax election in one year may accomplish a current reduction in taxes, but it could saddle future years with a disadvantageous tax position.

▼ **FIGURE 28–6**
Client Letter

> Willis, Hoffman, Maloney, and Raabe, CPAs
> 5101 Madison Road
> Cincinnati, Ohio 45227
>
> August 30, 1998
>
> Mr. and Ms. Fred Taxpayer
> 111 Boulevard
> Williamsburg, Virginia 23185
>
> Dear Mr. and Ms. Taxpayer:
>
> This letter is in response to your request for us to review your family's financial and tax situation. Our conclusions are based upon the facts as outlined in your August 14th letter. Any change in the facts may affect our conclusions.
>
> You provide over 50% of the support for your son, Sam, and his wife, Dana. The scholarship Sam receives is not included in determining support. If the stock is not sold, you will qualify for a dependency exemption for both Sam and Dana.
>
> However, if the stock is sold, a gain of approximately $7,000 will result. This amount will result in the gross income requirement being violated (i.e., potential dependent's gross income must not exceed $2,700) for Sam. Therefore, you will not qualify to receive a dependency exemption for Sam. In addition, if Sam sells the stock and he and Dana file a joint return, you also will not qualify for a dependency exemption for Dana.
>
> From a tax planning perspective, Sam should not sell the stock in 1998. Delaying the stock sale will enable you to claim dependency exemptions for both Sam and Dana. If the stock is sold, Sam and Dana should not file a joint return. This will still enable you to qualify for a dependency exemption for Dana.
>
> Should you need more information or need to clarify our conclusions, do not hesitate to contact me.
>
> Sincerely yours,
>
> John J. Jones, CPA
> Partner

NONTAX CONSIDERATIONS

There is a danger that tax motivations may take on a significance that does not conform to the true values involved. In other words, tax considerations can operate to impair the exercise of sound business judgment. Thus, the tax planning process can lead to ends that are socially and economically objectionable. Unfortunately, a tendency exists for planning to go toward the opposing extremes of either not enough or too much emphasis on tax considerations. The happy medium is a balance that recognizes the significance of taxes, but not beyond the point at which planning detracts from the exercise of good business judgment.

The remark is often made that a good rule is to refrain from pursuing any course of action that would not be followed were it not for certain tax considerations. This statement is not entirely correct, but it does illustrate the desirability of preventing business logic from being *sacrificed at the altar of tax planning*.

TAX EVASION AND TAX AVOIDANCE

A fine line exists between legal tax planning and illegal tax planning—tax avoidance versus tax evasion. **Tax avoidance** is merely tax minimization through legal techniques. In this sense, tax avoidance is the proper objective of all tax planning. Though eliminating or reducing taxes is also a goal of tax evasion, the term implies the use of subterfuge and fraud as a means to this end. Perhaps because common goals are involved, popular usage has blurred the distinction between the two concepts. Consequently, the association of tax avoidance with tax evasion has kept some taxpayers from properly taking advantage of planning possibilities. The now classic words of Judge Learned Hand in *Commissioner v. Newman* reflect the true values a taxpayer should have:

> Over and over again courts have said that there is nothing sinister in so arranging one's affairs as to keep taxes as low as possible. Everybody does so, rich or poor; and all do right, for nobody owes any public duty to pay more than the law demands: taxes are enforced extractions, not voluntary contributions. To demand more in the name of morals is mere cant.[34]

ETHICAL CONSIDERATIONS

Tax Avoidance

In a speech class, a philosophy student argues that tax advisers are immoral because they help people cheat the government. Each time a tax adviser shows a taxpayer a tax planning idea that reduces the client's liability, all other taxpayers have to pay more taxes. Society would be better off if all tax advisers would work at improving our environment or living conditions in the inner cities.

An accounting student argues that the primary purpose of tax planning is to reduce a taxpayer's overall liability. This advisory process can result in avoiding, deferring, or postponing the tax burden until the future. There is nothing illegal or immoral about tax avoidance. Taxpayers have every legal right to be concerned about tax avoidance and to arrange their affairs so as to pay no more taxes than the law demands. There is no difference between reducing a tax expense through the help of a tax adviser and reducing a cost of operating a business with the aid of a cost accountant.

Comment on each student's position.

FOLLOW-UP PROCEDURES

Because tax planning usually involves a proposed (as opposed to a completed) transaction, it is predicated upon the continuing validity of the advice based upon the tax research. A change in the tax law (either legislative, administrative, or judicial) could alter the original conclusion. Additional research may be necessary to test the solution in light of current developments (refer to the broken lines at the right in Figure 28–3).

TAX PLANNING—A PRACTICAL APPLICATION

Returning to the facts of Example 4, what could be done to protect the dependency exemptions for the parents? If Sam and Dana were to refrain from filing a joint return, both could be claimed by the parents. This result assumes that the stock is not sold.

An obvious tax planning tool is the installment method. Could the securities be sold using the installment method under § 453 so that most of the gain is deferred into the next year? Under the installment method, certain gains may be postponed and recognized as the cash proceeds are received. The problem

---

[34]*Comm. v. Newman*, 47–1 USTC ¶9175, 35 AFTR 857, 159 F.2d 848
  (CA–2, 1947).

is that the installment method is not available for stock traded on an established securities market.[35]

A little more research, however, indicates that Sam may be able to sell the stock and postpone the recognition of gain until the following year by selling short an equal number of substantially identical shares and covering the short sale in the subsequent year with the shares originally held. Selling short means that Sam sells borrowed stock (substantially identical) and repays the lender with the stock held on the date of the short sale. This *short against the box* technique would allow Sam to protect his $7,000 profit and defer the closing of the sale until the following year.[36] However, additional research indicates that TRA of 1997 provides that the short against the box technique will no longer produce the desired postponement of recognized gain. That is, at the time of the short sale, Sam will have a recognized gain of $7,000 from a constructive sale. Note the critical role of obtaining the correct facts in attempting to resolve the proper strategy for the taxpayers.

Throughout this text, most chapters include observations on Tax Planning Considerations. Such observations are not all-inclusive but are intended to illustrate some of the ways in which the material covered can be effectively utilized to minimize taxes.

ELECTRONIC TAX RESEARCH

6 **LEARNING OBJECTIVE**
Have an awareness of electronic tax research.

Computer-based tax research tools now hold a prominent position in tax practice. Electronic tax resources allow the tax library to reflect the tax law itself, including its dynamic and daily changes. Nevertheless, using electronic means to locate tax law sources cannot substitute for developing and maintaining a thorough knowledge of the tax law or for logical and analytical review in addressing open tax research issues.

Accessing tax documents through electronic means offers several important advantages over a strictly paper-based approach:

- Materials generally are available to the practitioner faster through an electronic system, as delays related to typesetting, proofreading, production, and distribution of the new materials are streamlined.
- Some tax documents, such as so-called slip opinions of trial-level court cases and interviews with policymakers, are available only through electronic means.
- Commercial subscriptions to electronic tax services are likely to provide, at little or no cost, additional tax law sources to which the researcher would not have access through stand-alone purchases of traditional material. For example, the full text of private letter rulings are quite costly to acquire in a paper-based format, but electronic publishers may bundle the rulings with other materials for a reasonable cost.

Strict cost comparisons of paper and electronic tax research materials are difficult to construct, especially when the practitioner uses hardware, including workstations and communications equipment, that is already in place and employed elsewhere in the practice. Over time, though, the convenience, cost, and reliability of electronic research tools clearly will make them the dominant means of finding and analyzing the law in tax practice.

---

[35]See Chapter 15 for a discussion of installment sales.

[36]§§ 1233(a) and 1233(b)(2). See Chapter 13 for a discussion of short sales.

▼ **EXHIBIT 28–2**
CD-ROM Tax Services

CD Tax Service	Description
CCH ACCESS	Includes the CCH tax service, primary sources including treatises, and other subscription materials. Ten to twenty disks.
RIA OnPoint	Includes the RIA topical *Coordinator* and the annotated tax service formerly provided by Prentice-Hall. The citator has elaborate document-linking features, and major tax treatises also are provided. One to ten disks.
WESTLAW	Code, Regulations, *Cumulative Bulletins*, cases, citators, and editorial material. About 12 disks.
Kleinrock's	A single disk with all tax statutory, administrative, and judicial law. Another single disk provides tax forms and instructions for Federal and state jurisdictions.

Using Electronic Services.   Tax researchers often use electronic means to find sources of the tax law. Usually, the law is found using one of the following strategies:

- *Search* various databases using keywords that are likely to be found in the underlying documents, as written by Congress, the judiciary, or administrative sources.
- *Link* to tax documents for which all or part of the proper citation is known.
- *Browse* the tax databases, examining various tables of contents and indexes in a traditional manner or using cross-references in the documents to jump from one tax law source to another.

Virtually all of the major commercial tax publishers and some of the primary sources of the law itself, such as the Supreme Court and some of the Courts of Appeals, now provide tax materials in electronic formats. Competitive pressures are forcing computer literacy upon tax practitioners, and the user-friendliness of the best of the tax search software is of great benefit to both the daily and the occasional user.

CD-ROM Services.   The CD has been a major source of electronic tax data for about a decade. Data compression techniques continue to allow more tax materials to fit on a single disk every year. CCH, RIA, WESTLAW, and others offer vast tax libraries to the practitioner, often in conjunction with a subscription to traditional paper-based resources or accompanied by newsletters, training seminars, and ongoing technical support.

At its best, a CD-based tax library provides the archival data that make up a permanent, core library of tax documents. For about $200 a year, the tax CD is updated quarterly, providing more comprehensive tax resources than the researcher is ever likely to need. The CD is comparable in scope to a paper-based library of a decade ago costing perhaps $20,000 to establish and $5,000 per year in perpetuity to maintain. If the library is contained on a small number of disks, it also can offer portability through use on laptop computers. Exhibit 28–2 summarizes the most popular of the CD tax services on the market today.

On-Line Systems.   An on-line research system allows a practitioner to obtain virtually instantaneous use of tax law sources by accessing the computer of the service provider. On-line services generally employ price-per-search cost structures, which can average close to $200 per hour, significantly higher than the cost of CD

On-Line Service	Description
LEXIS/NEXIS	Federal and state statutory, administrative, and judicial material. Extensive libraries of newspapers, magazines, patent records, and medical and economic databases, both U.S. and foreign-based.
RIA	Includes the RIA tax services, major tax treatises, Federal and state statutes, administrative documents, and court opinions. Extensive citator access, editorial material, and practitioner aids.
CCH	Includes the CCH tax service, primary sources including treatises, and other subscription materials. Tax and economic news sources, extensive editorial material, and practitioner support tools.
WESTLAW	Federal and state statutes, administrative documents, and court opinions. Extensive citator access, editorial material, and gateways to third-party publications. Extensive government document databases.

services. Thus, unless a practitioner can pass along related costs to clients or others, on-line searching generally is limited to the most important issues and to the researchers with the most experience and training in search techniques.

Perhaps the best combination of electronic tax resources is to conduct day-to-day work on a CD system, so that the budget for the related work is known in advance, and augment the CD search with on-line access where it is judged to be critical. Exhibit 28–3 lists the most commonly used commercial on-line tax services.

The Internet.   The Internet provides a wealth of tax information in several popular forms, sometimes at no direct cost to the researcher. Using so-called browser software that often is distributed with new computer systems and their communication devices, the tax professional can access information provided around the world that can aid the research process.

- *Home pages (sites) on the World Wide Web (WWW)* are provided by accounting and consulting firms, publishers, tax academics and libraries, and governmental bodies as a means of making information widely available or of soliciting subscriptions or consulting engagements. The best sites offer links to other sites and direct contact to the site providers. One of the best sites available to the tax practitioner is the Internal Revenue Service's *Digital Daily*, as illustrated in Exhibit 28–4. This site offers downloadable forms and instructions, "plain English" versions of Regulations, and news update items. Exhibit 28–5 lists some of the Web sites that may be most useful to tax researchers and their Internet addresses as of press date.

- *Newsgroups* provide a means by which information related to the tax law can be exchanged among taxpayers, tax professionals, and others who subscribe to the group's services. Newsgroup members can read the exchanges among other members and offer replies and suggestions to inquiries as desired. Discussions address the interpretation and application of existing law, analysis of proposals and new pronouncements, and reviews of tax software.

▼ **EXHIBIT 28–4**
The IRS *Digital Daily*

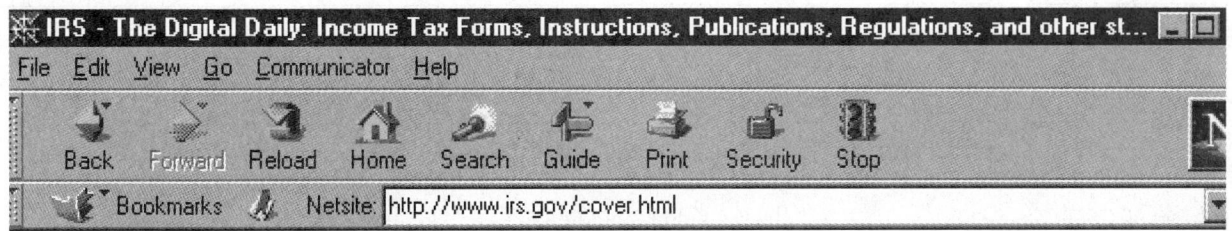

[Text Only Version]

IN TODAY'S ISSUE

Employment Opportunities

Famous Physicist Finds Fabulous Formula For E-File

• *E-mail capabilities* are available to most tax professionals through an employer's equipment or by a subscription providing Internet access at a low and usually fixed cost for the period. E-mail allows for virtually instantaneous sending and receiving of messages, letters, tax returns and supporting data, spreadsheets, and other documents necessary to solve tax problems.

In many situations, solutions to research problems will benefit from, or require, the use of various electronic tax research tools. A competent tax professional must become familiar and proficient with these tools and be able to use them to meet the expectations of clients and the necessities of work in the modern world.[37]

---

[37]For a more detailed discussion of the use of electronic tax research in the modern tax practice, see W. A. Raabe, G. E. Whittenburg, and J. C. Bost, *West's Federal Tax Research*. 4th ed (St. Paul, Minn.: West Publishing Co., 1997).

▼ **EXHIBIT 28–5**
Tax-Related Web Sites

Web Site	WWW Address at Press Date (Usually preceded by http://www.)	Description
Internal Revenue Service	**irs.gov/cover.html**	News releases, downloadable forms and instructions, tables, and E-mail
Court opinions	The site at **law.emory.edu/FEDCTS/** allows the researcher to link to the site of the jurisdiction (other than the Tax Court) that is the subject of the query (see Exhibit 28–6).	
Discussion groups moderated by Tax Analysts	**tax.org/notes**	Policy-oriented discussions of tax laws and proposals to change the law, links to student tax clinics, excerpts from the Tax Notes newsletter, and a tax calendar
Tax Sites Directory	**taxsites.com/**	References and links to tax sites on the Internet, including state and Federal tax sites, academic and professional pages, tax forms, and software
Tax laws on-line	Regulations are at **access.gpo.gov/nara/cfr/cfr-table-search.html**, and the Code is at **fourmilab.ch/ustax/ustax.html**	
Tax World	**omer.actg.uic.edu**	References and links to tax sites on the Internet, including property tax and international tax links
Commercial tax publishers	For instance, **riatax.com** and **cch.com**	Information about products and services available by subscription, and newsletter excerpts
Large accounting firms and professional organizations	For instance, the AICPA's page is at **aicpa.org.** and an Ernst and Young LLP Tax Services page is at **taxcast.com**	Tax planning newsletters, descriptions of services offered and career opportunities, and exchange of data with clients and subscribers
South-Western College Publishing	**swcollege.com/tax/tax.html**	Informational updates, newsletters, support materials for subscribers and adopters, and continuing education

Note: Caution: addresses change frequently

KEY TERMS

Acquiescence, 28–18

Circuit Court of Appeals, 28–15

Court of original jurisdiction, 28–12

Determination letters, 28–11

Federal District Court, 28–12

Finalized Regulations, 28–8

Interpretive Regulations, 28–25

Legislative Regulations, 28–25

Letter rulings, 28–10

Nonacquiescence, 28–18

Precedents, 28–16

▼ **EXHIBIT 28–6**
The Emory *Federal Courts Finder*

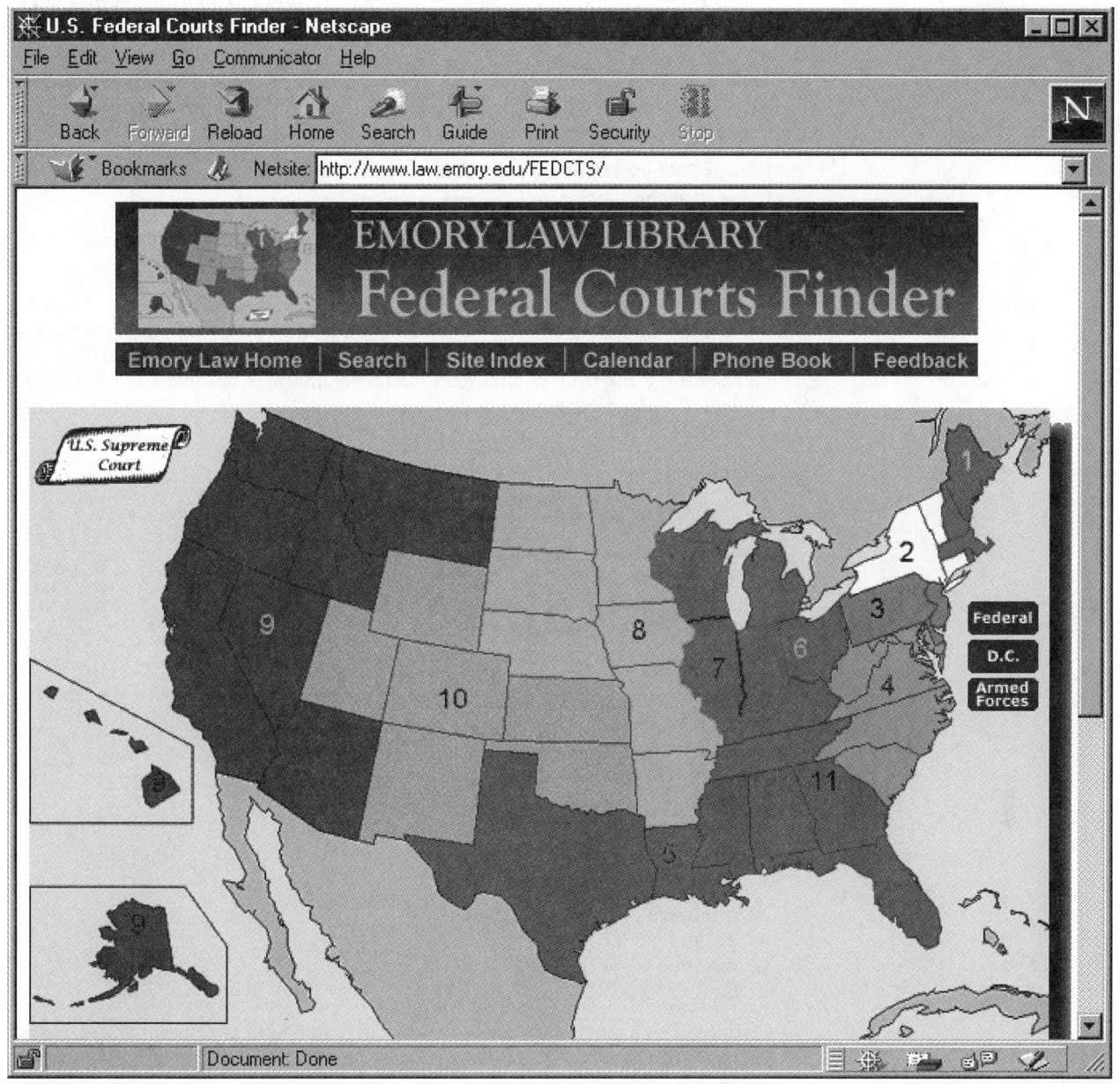

PROBLEM MATERIALS

DISCUSSION QUESTIONS

1. Judicial decisions interpreting a provision of the Internal Revenue Code of 1939 or 1954 are no longer of any value in view of the enactment of the Internal Revenue Code of 1986. Assess the validity of this statement.

2. When was the last time Congress codified the tax laws?

3. Tax legislation normally originates in the House Ways and Means Committee. Assess the validity of this statement.

4. What is the function of the Joint Conference Committee of the House Ways and Means Committee and the Senate Finance Committee?

5. Why are certain Code Section numbers missing from the Internal Revenue Code (e.g., §§ 6, 7, 8, 9, 10)?

6. Paul Jacobs operates a small international firm named Teal, Inc. A new treaty between the United States and Ukraine conflicts with a Section of the Internal Revenue Code. Paul asks you for advice. If he follows the treaty position, does he need to disclose this on his tax return? If he is required to disclose, are there any penalties for failure to disclose? Prepare a letter in which you respond to Paul. Teal's address is 100 International Drive, Tampa, FL 33620.

7. Interpret this Regulation citation: Reg. § 1.274–2(a)(1)(i).

8. Distinguish between legislative, interpretive, and procedural Regulations.

9. Distinguish between the following:
   a. Treasury Regulations and Revenue Rulings.
   b. Revenue Rulings and Revenue Procedures.
   c. Revenue Rulings and letter rulings.
   d. Letter rulings and determination letters.

10. Rank the following items from the highest authority to the lowest in the Federal tax law system:
    a. Interpretive Regulation.
    b. Legislative Regulation.
    c. Letter ruling.
    d. Revenue Procedure.
    e. Internal Revenue Code.
    f. Proposed Regulation.

11. Interpret each of the following citations:
    a. Rev.Rul. 65–235, 1965–2 C.B. 88.
    b. Rev.Proc. 87–56, 1987–2 C.B. 674.
    c. Ltr.Rul. 9046036.

12. Caleb receives a ninety-day letter after his discussion with an appeals officer. He is not satisfied with the $92,000 settlement offer. Identify the relevant tax research issues facing Caleb.

13. Which of the following would be considered advantages of the Small Cases Division of the Tax Court?
    a. Appeal to the U.S. Tax Court is possible.
    b. A hearing of a deficiency of $12,000 is considered on a timely basis.
    c. Taxpayer can handle the litigation without using a lawyer or certified public accountant.
    d. Taxpayer can use Small Cases Division decisions for precedential value.
    e. The actual hearing is conducted informally.
    f. Travel time will probably be reduced.

14. List an advantage and a disadvantage of using a U.S. District Court as the trial court for Federal tax litigation.

15. Sam Brown is considering litigating a tax deficiency of approximately $317,000 in the court system. He asks you to provide him with a short description of his alternatives indicating the advantages and disadvantages of each. Prepare your response to Sam in the form of a letter. His address is 200 Mesa Drive, Tuscon, AZ 85714.

16. List an advantage and a disadvantage of using the U.S. Court of Federal Claims as the trial court for Federal tax litigation.

17. A taxpayer lives in Michigan. In a controversy with the IRS, the taxpayer loses at the trial court level. Describe the appeal procedure for each of the following trial courts:
    a. Small Cases Division of the U.S. Tax Court.
    b. U.S. Tax Court.
    c. U.S. District Court.
    d. U.S. Court of Federal Claims.

18. Suppose the U.S. Government loses a tax case in the U.S. District Court of South Carolina and does not appeal the result. What does the failure to appeal signify?

19. For the U.S. Tax Court, U.S. District Court, and the U.S. Court of Federal Claims, indicate the following:
    a. Number of regular judges per court.
    b. Availability of a jury trial.
    c. Whether the deficiency must be paid before the trial.

20. In which of the following states could a taxpayer appeal the decision of a U.S. District Court to the Ninth Court of Appeals?
    a. Alaska.
    b. Arkansas.
    c. New York.
    d. South Carolina.
    e. Utah.

21. What is the Supreme Court's policy on hearing tax cases?

22. In assessing the validity of a prior court decision, discuss the significance of the following on the taxpayer's issue:
    a. The decision was rendered by the U.S. District Court of Wyoming. Taxpayer lives in Wyoming.
    b. The decision was rendered by the U.S. Court of Federal Claims. Taxpayer lives in Wyoming.
    c. The decision was rendered by the Second Court of Appeals. Taxpayer lives in California.
    d. The decision was rendered by the U.S. Supreme Court.
    e. The decision was rendered by the U.S. Tax Court. The IRS has acquiesced in the result.
    f. Same as (e), except that the IRS has nonacquiesced in the result.

23. The IRS may acquiesce or nonacquiesce to what court decisions? Can an acquiescence be withdrawn retroactively?

24. Interpret each of the following citations:
    a. 54 T.C. 1514 (1970).
    b. 408 F.2d 117 (CA–2, 1969).
    c. 69–1 USTC ¶9319 (CA–2, 1969).
    d. 23 AFTR2d 69–1090 (CA–2, 1969).
    e. 293 F.Supp. 1129 (D.Ct.Miss., 1967).
    f. 67–1 USTC ¶9253 (D.Ct.Miss., 1967).
    g. 19 AFTR2d 647 (D.Ct.Miss., 1967).
    h. 56 S.Ct. 289 (USSC, 1935).
    i. 36–1 USTC ¶9020 (USSC, 1935).
    j. 16 AFTR 1274 (USSC, 1935).
    k. 422 F.2d 1336 (Ct.Cls., 1970).

25. Explain the following abbreviations:

a. CA–2   i. USTC
b. Fed.Cl.   j. AFTR
c. *aff'd.*   k. F.3d
d. *rev'd.*   l. F.Supp.
e. *rem'd.*   m. USSC
f. *Cert. Denied*   n. S.Ct.
g. *acq.*   o. D.Ct.
h. B.T.A.

26. Give the Commerce Clearing House citation for each of the following courts:
    a. Small Cases Division of the Tax Court.
    b. Federal District Court.
    c. U.S. Supreme Court.
    d. U.S. Court of Federal Claims.
    e. Tax Court Memorandum decision.

27. Where can you locate a published decision of the U.S. Court of Federal Claims?

28. Which of the following items can probably be found in the *Cumulative Bulletin*?
    a. Revenue Ruling.
    b. Small Cases Division of the U.S. Tax Court decision.
    c. Letter ruling.
    d. Revenue Procedure.
    e. Proposed Regulation.
    f. District Court decision.
    g. Senate Finance Committee Report.
    h. Acquiescences to Tax Court decisions.
    i. Tax Court Memorandum decision.

29. As part of her coursework for a Masters of Tax degree, Ann is required to prepare a 30-page term paper about limited liability partnerships. Identify some relevant research steps Ann may take.

30. Budgetwise, how can electronic tax resources best be combined for day-to-day tax research?

PROBLEMS

31. Tom has just been audited by the IRS and, as a result, has been assessed a substantial deficiency (which he has not yet paid) in additional income taxes. In preparing his defense, Tom advances the following possibilities:
    a. Although a resident of Kentucky, Tom plans to sue in a U.S. District Court in Oregon that appears to be more favorably inclined toward taxpayers.
    b. If (a) is not possible, Tom plans to take his case to a Kentucky state court where an uncle is the presiding judge.
    c. Since Tom has found a B.T.A. decision that seems to help his case, he plans to rely on it under alternative (a) or (b).
    d. If he loses at the trial court level, Tom plans to appeal to either the U.S. Court of Federal Claims or the U.S. Second Court of Appeals because he has relatives in both Washington, D.C., and New York. Staying with these relatives could save Tom lodging expense while his appeal is being heard by the court selected.
    e. Even if he does not win at the trial court or appeals court level, Tom feels certain of success on an appeal to the U.S. Supreme Court.

    Evaluate Tom's notions concerning the judicial process as it applies to Federal income tax controversies.

32. Using the legend provided, classify each of the following statements (more than one answer per statement may be appropriate):

Legend

D = Applies to the U.S. District Court

T = Applies to the U.S. Tax Court

C = Applies to the U.S. Court of Federal Claims

A = Applies to the U.S. Court of Appeals

U = Applies to the U.S. Supreme Court

N = Applies to none of the above

---

a. Decides only Federal tax matters.
b. Decisions are reported in the F.3d Series.
c. Decisions are reported in the USTCs.
d. Decisions are reported in the AFTRs.
e. Appeal is by *Writ of Certiorari.*
f. Court meets most often in Washington, D.C.
g. Offers the choice of a jury trial.
h. Is a trial court.
i. Is an appellate court.
j. Allows appeal to the Court of Appeals for the Federal Circuit and bypasses the taxpayer's particular Court of Appeals.
k. Has a Small Cases Division.
l. Is the only trial court where the taxpayer does not have to first pay the tax assessed by the IRS.

33. Using the legend provided, classify each of the following citations as to the type of court:

Legend

D = Applies to the U.S. District Court

T = Applies to the U.S. Tax Court

C = Applies to the U.S. Court of Federal Claims

A = Applies to the U.S. Court of Appeals

U = Applies to the U.S. Supreme Court

N = Applies to none of the above

---

a. 241 F.2d 197 (CA–4, 1957).
b. 90 T.C. 1 (1988).
c. 54 S.Ct. 8 (USSC, 1933).
d. 3 B.T.A. 1042 (1926).
e. T.C.Memo. 1954–141.
f. 597 F.2d 760 (Ct.Cls., 1979).
g. Ltr.Rul. 9414051.
h. 354 F.Supp. 1003 (D.Ct.Ga., 1972).
i. Rev.Rul. 74–164.

34. Using the legend provided, classify each of the following citations as to publisher:

Legend

RIA = Research Institute of America

CCH = Commerce Clearing House

W = West Publishing Company

U.S. = U.S. Government

O = Others

---

a. 83–2 USTC ¶9600.
b. 52 AFTR2d 83–5954.
c. 67 T.C. 293 (1976).
d. 39 TCM 32 (1979).
e. 416 U.S. 938.
f. RIA T.C.Memo. ¶80,582.
g. 89 S.Ct. 501.
h. 2 Cl.Ct. 600.
i. 415 F.2d 488.
j. 592 F.Supp. 18.
k. Rev.Proc. 77–37, 1977–2 C.B. 568.
l. 21 L.Ed.2d 495.
m. S. Rep. No. 1622, 83rd Cong., 2d Sess. 42 1954.

35. Using the legend provided, classify each of the following statements:

Legend

A = Tax avoidance
E = Tax evasion
N = Neither

a. Terry writes a $250 check as a charitable contribution on December 28, 1998, but does not mail the check to the charitable organization until January 10, 1999. She takes a deduction in 1998.
b. Robert decides not to report interest income from a bank because the amount is only $11.75.
c. Jim pays property taxes on his home in December 1997 rather than waiting until February 1998.
d. Jane switches her investments from taxable corporate bonds to tax-exempt municipal bonds.
e. Ted encourages his mother to save most of her Social Security benefits so that he will be able to claim her as a dependent.

RESEARCH PROBLEMS

*Note: Use the **RIA OnPoint System 4 Student Version CD-ROM**, which is available to accompany this text, in preparing solutions to the Research Problems. Alternatively, tax research materials found in a standard tax library can be used.*

Use the tax resources of the Internet to address the Research Problems marked with this icon. Do not restrict your search to the World Wide Web, but include a review of newsgroups and general reference materials, practitioner sites and resources, primary sources of the tax law, chat rooms and discussion groups, and other opportunities.

Chapter 2

Research Problem 1. In the state of Texas, a lawsuit was instituted charging that the state schools for the mentally retarded furnished inadequate, unsafe, and improper care, treatment, and education. As part of the settlement of this suit, the Texas Department of Mental Health offered to pay a fixed daily amount to third-party providers of these services. Under this arrangement, the taxpayers received $16,425 during the year for the care of their mentally retarded daughter. This amount covered a daily per diem for food and board, medical expenses, cost of special food, clothing, transportation, special laundry, home repairs, and other living expenses. The daughter lived with the taxpayers and during the year attended classes at a special school operated by the local school district.

  Although the taxpayers did not pay for more than 50% of their daughter's support, they claimed her as a dependent for the year. The taxpayers contend that the amount they received from the state is a scholarship and, therefore, should not be taken into account in applying the support test. The IRS disagrees. What is the appropriate result?

Research aids:
§ 152(d).
Rev.Rul. 61–186, 1961–2 C.B. 30.
Rev.Rul. 64–221, 1964–2 C.B. 46.

Research Problem 2. Judy and Greg married in 1989 and have since resided in California. In October 1995, Judy filed in state court to have her marriage to Greg annulled. The annulment was granted in May 1996. Under California law, an annulment voids the marriage and, in effect, treats it as if it never occurred.

Judy files her Federal income tax return for calendar year 1995 using "single" status. Upon audit of the return, the IRS contends that Judy's correct filing status is "married filing separate." Who is correct and why?

Research aids:
§ 7703(a)(1).
Reg. § 1.6013–4(a)(1).
Harold K. Lee, 64 T.C. 552 (1975).
Betty J. Shackelford, 70 TCM 945, T.C.Memo. 1995–484.

Research Problem 3. Many tax advisers with materials on the Internet propose tax planning techniques for minimizing liabilities under the kiddie tax. Summarize the most effective of these proposals, and cite the providers of the information.

Chapter 3

Research Problem 4. Ted owns a convertible bond issued by Blue Corporation. His original cost is $1,000, and the bond is convertible into 10 shares of Blue common stock. Two years after he purchased the bond, Ted is considering whether to exercise his conversion rights. The value of the Blue common stock is now $130 per share. Ted would like to know whether the conversion will result in a taxable gain.

Research Problem 5. The First Central Bank, an accrual basis taxpayer, has a credit card operation. Customers pay $30 per year for the right to use the card. If the customer decides to cancel the card during the year, the customer receives a refund of a prorated amount. The IRS position is that the amounts received are interest and thus are not eligible for deferral under Revenue Procedure 71–21. The taxpayer argues that the prepaid income is for services that are to be rendered over 12 months and thus the prepaid income can be amortized over the 12-month period. Determine the appropriate tax treatment.

Research Problem 6. Go to the Web page of a consulting firm that offers counseling services to individuals as they negotiate the terms of a divorce. What specific tax-related services do these firms offer? Send an e-mail message to one of these firms suggesting that it add a specific service or revise its Web page to emphasize other tax-related sevices for its clients.

Chapter 4

Research Problem 7. David Hobson is the minister at the First Baptist Church. As part of his compensation, he receives an $800 per month housing allowance. David is purchasing his residence, and he uses the $800 each month to make mortgage and property tax payments. The mortgage interest and property taxes are deducted (as itemized deductions) on David's tax return. The examining IRS agent thinks David would be enjoying a double benefit if the housing allowance is excluded and the itemized deductions are allowed. In addition, the agent contends that the housing allowance exclusion should apply only where the church provides the residence or the minister uses the funds to pay rent. Therefore, the agent maintains that David should include the $800 received each month in gross income. David has asked for your assistance in this matter. Write a letter to David that contains your advice and prepare a memo for the tax files. David's address is 982 Richmond Drive, Hollis, OK 73550.

Research Problem 8. Your client operates a well-known chain of retail stores. A shopping center developer has offered to rent space to your client at a very low price under a 10-year lease. Your client will be an "anchor tenant." While other tenants will lease a mere shell and be responsible for making the improvements necessary to operate their businesses, the developer has offered to make improvements with a maximum cost of $500,000 to meet specific needs of your client. These expenditures will be made as an inducement to your client to locate in the shopping center. Before deciding whether to accept the offer, your client asks your opinion about the tax consequences of receiving the $500,000 in improvements.

Research Problem 9. Go to the IRS site on the Internet and download instructions and Regulations relative to educational savings bonds and qualified state tuition programs. Summarize one of the key provisions in these materials in outline format.

Chapter 5

Research Problem 10. Gray Chemical Company manufactured pesticides that were toxic. Over the course of several years, the toxic waste contaminated the air and water around the company's plant. Several employees suffered toxic poisoning, and the Environmental Protection Agency cited the company for violations. In court, the judge found Gray guilty and imposed fines of $15 million. The company voluntarily set up a charitable fund for the purpose of bettering the environment and funded it with $8 million. The company incurred legal expenses in setting up the foundation and defending itself in court. The court reduced the fine from $15 million to $7 million.

Gray Chemical Company deducted the $8 million paid to the foundation and the legal expenses incurred. The IRS disallowed both deductions on the grounds that the payment was, in fact, a fine and in violation of public policy.

Gray's president, Ted Jones, has contacted you regarding the deductibility of the $7 million fine, the $8 million payment to the foundation, and the legal fees. Write a letter to Mr. Jones that contains your advice and prepare a memo for the tax files. Gray's address is 200 Lincoln Center, Omaha, NE 68182.

Research aids:
§§ 162(a) and (f).
Reg. § 1.162–21(b).

Research Problem 11. Rex and Agnes Harrell purchased a beach house at Duck, North Carolina, in early 1996. Although they intended to use the beach house occasionally for recreational purposes, they also planned to rent it through the realty agency that had handled the purchase in order to help pay the mortgage payments, property taxes, and maintenance costs. Rex is a surgeon, and Agnes is a counselor.

The beach house was in need of substantial repairs. Rather than hiring a contractor, Rex and Agnes decided they would make the repairs themselves. During both high school and college, Rex had worked summers in construction. In addition, he had taken an advanced course in woodworking and related subjects from a local community college several years ago.

During 1996, according to a log maintained by the Harrells, they occupied the beach house on 38 days and rented it on 49 days. The log also indicated that on 24 of the 38 days that they occupied the beach house, one or both of them were engaged in work on the beach house. Their two teenage children were with them on all of these days, but did not help with the work being done. On their 1996 income tax return, Rex and Agnes, who filed a joint return, treated the beach house as a rental property and deducted a pro rata share of the property taxes, mortgage interest, utilities, maintenance and repairs, and depreciation in determining their net loss from the beach home. A Revenue Agent has limited the deductions to the rent income. He contends that the 14-day personal use provision was exceeded and that many of the alleged repairs were capital expenditures. Advise the Harrells on how they should respond to the IRS.

Research Problem 12. Locate and read a recent judicial or administrative ruling regarding the deductibility of hobby losses. Look for rulings that deal with horse breeding, professional sports teams, or art collecting activities. Which criteria did the ruling emphasize in upholding or reversing the taxpayer's deduction for such losses?

Chapter 6

Research Problem 13. While Ralph was in the process of obtaining a divorce, his wife, without Ralph's knowledge, had the furniture removed from his apartment. Discuss whether Ralph is entitled to a tax deduction for the loss of the furniture.

Research aids:
Landis G. Brown, 30 TCM 257, T.C.Memo 1971–60.
Jerry L. Goode, 42 TCM 1209, T.C.Memo 1981–548.

Research Problem 14. George Johnson, a Minnesota resident, parked his car on a lake while he was watching an iceboat race. During the race, the ice beneath his car unexpectedly gave way, and the car sank to the bottom of the lake. Write a letter to George advising him as to whether he can claim a casualty loss for the damage to the car. Also prepare a memo for the tax files. George's address is 100 Apple Lane, St. Paul, MN 55123.

Research Problem 15. Find a newspaper article that discusses tax planning for casualty losses when a disaster area designation is made. Does the article convey the pertinent tax rules correctly? Then list all of the locations identified by the President as Federal disaster areas in the last two years.

Chapter 7

Research Problem 16. Sandra purchased the following personal property during 1998:

Date	Asset	Cost
June 1	Machine A	$20,000
July 10	Machine B	10,000
November 15	Machine C	25,000

Sandra elects to take the § 179 expense on Machine C. Discuss what convention Sandra must use to determine her cost recovery deduction for 1998.

Research Problem 17. Juan owns a business that acquires exotic automobiles that are high-tech, state-of-the-art vehicles with unique design features or equipment. The exotic automobiles are not licensed nor are they set up to be used on the road. Rather, the cars are used exclusively for car shows or related promotional photography. Juan would like to know whether he can take a cost recovery deduction with respect to the exotic automobiles on his Federal income tax return.

Research Problem 18. Changes to depreciation systems often are discussed by policy makers and observers of the tax system. Outline the terms and policy objectives of one of the changes currently proposed by the Treasury, a member of Congress, or a tax policy think tank.

Chapter 8

Research Problem 19. Rick Beam has been an independent sales representative for various textile manufacturers for many years. His products consist of soft goods, such as tablecloths, curtains, and drapes. Rick's customers are clothing store chains, department stores, and smaller specialty stores. The employees of these companies responsible for the purchase of merchandise are known as buyers. These companies generally prohibit their buyers from accepting gifts from manufacturers' sales representatives.

Each year Rick gives cash gifts (never more than $25) to most of the buyers who are his customers. Generally, he cashes a large check in November and gives the money personally to the buyers around Christmas. Rick says, "This is one of the ways that I have maintained my relationship with my buyers." He maintains adequate substantiation of all the gifts.

Rick's deductions for these gifts have been disallowed by the IRS, based on § 162(c)(2). Rick is confused and comes to you, a CPA, for advice.

a. Write a letter to Rick concerning his tax position on this issue. Rick's address is 948 Octavia Street, New Orleans, LA 70113.

b. Prepare a memo for your files supporting the advice you have given.

Research Problem 20.   Lyle has been a schoolteacher since he earned his bachelor of education degree 10 years ago. In 1996, the governing board of his school district passed a resolution requiring all teachers to begin pursuing an advanced degree in education. Because of this new requirement, Lyle spent the summer of 1997 taking graduate courses in education at a major university. For the summer activity, Lyle *estimates* his expenses to be:

Books	$ 220
Tuition	3,200
Room and board	1,800
Transportation	1,500

Lyle kept no receipts and made no record of these expenses. When he files his income tax return for 1997, Lyle claims all of these expenses on Schedule C of Form 1040.

In the event Lyle is audited by the IRS, comment on his vulnerability.

Research aids:
§§ 274(d), 6001, and 6662(b)(1).
Cohan v. Comm., 2 USTC 489, 8 AFTR 10552, 39 F.2d 540 (CA–2, 1930).
William F. Sanford, 50 T.C. 823 (1968).

Research Problem 21.   Determine whether your city qualifies for the "high-cost" travel per diem allowances provided by the IRS.

Chapter 9

Research Problem 22.   In January, Ron, a fireman, was injured in the line of duty as a result of interference by a homeowner. He incurred medical expenses of $6,500 related to his injuries. Ron sued the homeowner and was awarded damages of $26,500 in December. The court indicated that $6,500 of the award was for payment of Ron's medical expenses and $20,000 was for punitive damages. Ron has prepared his return for the year and has asked you to review it. You notice that Ron has not reported any part of the award as income and has included the medical expense in computing his itemized deductions. Write a brief summary of the advice you should give Ron.

Research Problem 23.   Tamika, a shareholder in a corporation with stores in five states, donated stock with a basis of $10,000 to a qualified charitable organization in 1995. Although the stock of the corporation was not traded on a public stock exchange, many shares had been sold over the last three years. Based on the average selling price for the stock in 1995, Tamika deducted $95,000 on her 1995 tax return. Tamika received a notice from the IRS that the $95,000 deduction had been reduced to $10,000 because she had not obtained a qualified appraisal or attached a summary of an appraisal to her tax return. Tamika has asked you to advise her on this matter. Write a letter containing your conclusions to Ms. Tamika Claussen, 2422 Arthur Court, San Bruno, CA 94066.

Research aids:
Reg. § 1.170A–13(c)(2).

Research Problem 24.   Look over the Web pages of several large charities. Print some of the most effective materials by which such organizations solicit charitable contributions over the Internet. Concentrate especially on the solicitation of gifts of appreciated securities and on the use of private foundations as the recipients of large charitable gifts.

Chapter 10

Research Problem 25. Bill owns an interest in a small engine repair shop in which he works 425 hours during the year. He has four full-time employees at the repair shop. Bill also owns an apartment building to which he devotes 1,300 hours during the year. He has no employees for the apartment activity. Are these activities active or passive? In your response, consider the impact of the significant participation activity rules.

Research Problem 26. Over the years, Bill Johnson (30 Brookfield Drive, Hampton, VA 23666) has taken great pride in his ability to spot exceptional rental real estate investments, particularly in terms of their appreciation potential. As a result, he has accumulated several properties. In the early years of his investment activities, he was able to devote only a limited amount of time to these ventures. In the current year, he retires from his full-time job and is able to devote most of his time to the management and operation of the rental activities. Bill summarizes the relevant tax attributes of each of the properties as follows:

Property	Suspended Passive Losses	Expected Current Year's Income (Loss)
A	None	$ 25,000
B	($20,000)	15,000
C	(40,000)	(15,000)

Bill is astute enough to know that he is a qualifying real estate professional for the current year and materially participates in all three properties within the meaning of § 469(c)(7). However, he is uncertain whether he should treat the properties as three separate activities or aggregate them and treat them as one activity.

Write a letter to Bill to assist him in making the decision. Because of Bill's expertise in the tax law, feel free to use technical language in your letter.

Research aid:
Reg. § 1.469–9(e).

Research Problem 27. Scan the materials offered in several newsgroups frequented by tax consultants. In what context are "tax shelters" still discussed by these professionals? Do these advisers adequately take into account the rules of §§ 465 and 469? Post a message to one of these newsgroups explaining the interaction of these two sections in a paragraph or two.

Chapter 11

Research Problem 28. Sandy and John Via (12 Maple Avenue, Albany, NY 12205) are married, file a joint Federal income tax return, and have a 12-year-old son and a 10-year-old daughter. Sandy is currently in the U.S. Air Force and has been stationed in Germany for the entire year. John and their children have remained in the United States where John picks up work only on an irregular basis. In working on their Federal income tax return for 1997, John wonders if they qualify for the earned income credit. Sandy's income consists of salary of $18,000 (taxable) and food and lodging provided by the Air Force, valued at $7,000 (not taxable), while John's earnings for the current year total $5,000. John approaches you and asks your advice. Write a letter to Sandy and John that contains your conclusion and prepare a memo for the tax files.

Research Problem 29. Isabella, a lover of early twentieth-century American history and architecture, discovers a 1920s house in a downtown district of Atlanta during a recent visit. She decides not only to purchase and renovate this particular home, but also to move the structure to her hometown of Little Rock, Arkansas, so her community can enjoy its architectural features. Also, being aware of the availability of the tax credit for rehabilitation expenditures incurred on old structures, she wants to maximize her use of the provision once the renovation work begins in Arkansas. Comment on whether the renovation expenditures incurred will qualify for the tax credit for rehabilitation expenditures.

Research Problem 30.   The foreign tax credit is especially valuable when a U.S. individual works in a country whose marginal income tax rates exceed those of the United States. List five countries whose tax rates on individuals exceed those of the United States, and five where the corresponding U.S. rates are higher.

Chapter 12

Research Problem 31.   As the result of a large inheritance from her grandmother, Beverly has a substantial investment portfolio. The securities are held in street name by her brokerage firm. Beverly's broker, Max, has standing oral instructions from her on sales transactions to sell the shares with the highest cost basis.

In October 1996, Beverly phoned Max and instructed him to sell 6,000 shares of Color, Inc. Her portfolio has 15,000 shares of Color, Inc., which were purchased in several transactions over a three-year period. At the end of each month, the brokerage firm provides Beverly with a monthly statement that includes sales transactions. It does not identify the specific certificates transferred.

In filing her 1996 income tax return, Beverly used the specific identification method to calculate the $90,000 gain on the sale of the Color shares. Now her 1996 return is being audited. The Revenue Agent has taken the position that under Reg. § 1.1012–1(c) Beverly should have used the FIFO method to report the sale of the Color shares. This would result in a recognized gain of $160,000. According to his interpretation of the Regulations, Beverly may not use the specific identification method and must use the FIFO method because the broker did not provide written confirmation of Beverly's sales instructions as required by the Regulations.

Beverly has come to you for tax advice.

Research Problem 32.   You are the new general manager of the Cleveland Indians, Inc. In order for the Indians to become a more serious contender to win the World Series, you believe that player changes are necessary. In particular, you believe that you need to improve your pitching staff. Discussions are in progress with the general manager of the Seattle Mariners. He has offered to trade Randy Johnson (an all-star pitcher) and $5 million to the Indians in exchange for Marquis Grissom (an outfielder) and David Justice (an all-star outfielder). You have countered by expressing interest in receiving Johnson and Edgar Martinez (an all-star third baseman) rather than cash. You believe that if you are going to give up the speed provided by Grissom and the power of Justice, you need more than a starting pitcher in return. In addition, you vaguely remember from your MBA days that a player trade with no cash involved will provide better tax results. Before you finalize a trade, you need to know the tax consequences. Obtain a written opinion from your CPA on the way you should structure the trade. The mailing address is Jacobs Field, Cleveland, OH 44118.

Research Problem 33.   A number of public policy think tanks, taxpayer unions, and other private interest groups have proposed changes to the tax rules that apply to like-kind exchanges of realty. Summarize several of these proposals, including your assessment of the motivations underlying the suggested changes.

Chapter 13

Research Problem 34.   Ali owns 100 shares of Brown Corporation stock. He purchased the stock at five different times and at five different prices per share as indicated:

Share Block	Number of Shares	Per Share Price	Purchase Date
A	10	$60	10/10/93
B	20	20	8/11/94
C	15	15	10/24/94
D	35	30	4/23/96
E	20	25	7/28/96

On April 28, 1998, Ali will sell 40 shares of Brown stock for $40 per share. All of Ali's shares are held by his stockbroker. The broker's records track when the shares were purchased. May Ali designate the shares he sells and, if so, which shares should he sell? Assume Ali wants to maximize his gain because he has a capital loss carryforward.

 Research Problem 35. Sidney owns a professional football franchise. He has received an offer of $80 million for the franchise, all the football equipment, the rights to concession receipts, the rights to a stadium lease, and the rights to all the player contracts he owns. Most of the players have been with the team for quite a long time and have contracts that were signed several years ago. The contracts have been substantially depreciated. Sidney is concerned about potential § 1245 recapture when the contracts are sold. He has heard about "previously unrecaptured depreciation with respect to initial contracts" and would like to know more about it. Find a definition for that phrase and write an explanation of it.

 Research Problem 36. Go to a newsgroup frequented by inventors and patent consultants. Answer one of the queries there relative to the tax effects of buying and selling patents, receiving royalties on patents, or otherwise investing in new technology.

Chapter 14

 Research Problem 37. Tony Bost is a full-time gambler whose only source of income is money that he wins from his gambling activities. The IRS contends that Tony's gambling losses should be treated as itemized deductions for purposes of computing the AMT. Tony argues that the gambling losses should be treated as trade or business expenses. Write a letter to Tony that contains your advice on the classification of the gambling losses. Also prepare a memo for the tax files. Tony's address is 200 Cole Lane, Wichita Falls, TX 76308.

Research Problem 38. Carol owns two warehouses that were placed in service before 1987. Accelerated depreciation for 1998 on Warehouse A was $12,000, and straight-line depreciation would have been $8,000. On Warehouse B, accelerated depreciation was $6,000, and straight-line depreciation would have been $7,500. What is the amount of Carol's tax preference for excess depreciation in 1998?

 Research Problem 39. Locate an outstanding proposal to modify the structure or scope of the AMT for individuals. Describe the proposal, the entity making the proposal, and potential motivations for submitting the modification to Congress.

Chapter 15

Research Problem 40. You recently contracted to perform tax services for a new funeral home. In preparing the initial tax return, you must decide whether the funeral home can use the cash method of accounting. When discussing this issue with the manager, the manager points out that the company is actually a service business and that the only materials involved are caskets, which average only 15% of the price of a funeral. Is the funeral home required to use the accrual method of accounting?

Research Problem 41. In 1998, your client, Clear Corporation, changed from the cash to the accrual method of accounting for its radio station. The company had a positive § 481 adjustment of $2,400,000 as a result of the change and began amortizing the adjustment in 1998. In 1999, Clear received an offer to purchase the assets of the radio station business (this would be considered a sale of a trade or business under § 1060). If the offer is accepted, Clear plans to purchase a satellite television business. Clear has asked you to explain the consequences of the sale of the radio station on the amortization of the § 481 adjustment.

 Research Problem 42. Find a solicitation for a purchase of electronic equipment or furniture advertised as "no payment" or "no interest due" until next year. Analyze the language of the solicitation in light of applicable Federal income tax law.

Chapter 16

Research Problem 43. Joe and Tom Moore are brothers and equal shareholders in Black Corporation, a calendar year taxpayer. In 1997, they incurred certain travel and entertainment expenditures, as employees, on behalf of Black Corporation. Because Black was in a precarious financial condition, Joe and Tom decided not to seek reimbursement for these expenditures. Instead, each brother deducted what he spent on his own individual return (Form 1040). Upon audit of the returns filed by Joe and Tom for 1997, the IRS disallowed these expenditures. Write a letter to Joe at 568 Inwood Avenue, Waynesburg, PA 15370, and indicate whether he should challenge the IRS action. Explain your conclusion to Joe using nontechnical language.

Research Problem 44. Soon-Yi owns all the stock of White Corporation and 90% of the stock of Red Corporation. Red has had profitable years whereas White has suffered losses for several years. Red loaned White Corporation $90,000 in 1997 and did not charge White any interest on the loan. Upon audit of its 1997 return, the IRS determined that Red Corporation had interest income for 1997 in the amount of $9,900, causing Red to have a tax deficiency of $3,366 for 1997. Red is challenging the tax deficiency. It contends that White Corporation produced no taxable income from the use of the $90,000. Is the IRS correct in increasing the taxable income of Red Corporation?

Research aids:
Reg. §§ 1.482–2(a)(1) and 1.482–1(d)(4).
§ 7872.

Research Problem 45. The Code subsidizes charitable contributions by corporations through the income tax deduction for such gifts. How have corporations responded? Find the dollar amount of charitable gifts by corporations for the last two years.

Chapter 17

Research Problem 46. For bona fide business purposes, Salisbury Group, Inc., decides to transfer its chemical manufacturing operation to a newly formed corporation, Concord Corporation, in a transaction that qualifies under § 351. Salisbury transfers all of the assets related to the chemical manufacturing operation in exchange for all of the Concord stock and Concord's assumption of all of the existing and contingent liabilities related to the chemical business. Both Salisbury Group and Concord are accrual basis corporations. Top management is aware that potential soil and groundwater environmental remediation costs may have to be incurred eventually to clean up the land of the chemical operation because of spillage over many years. Nevertheless, no attempts were made prior to the transfer to explore the scope of the potential cleanup or to initiate even a limited cleanup. In addition, Salisbury had not booked an entry reflecting the potential cleanup exposure. Two years later, however, Concord incurs $32 million to clean up the soil and water damages. Concord appropriately deducts a portion of the costs and capitalizes the remaining amount.

In reflecting back on these transactions, Salisbury's tax accountant, Fay Holmes, inquires whether the liability that was believed to exist at the time of Concord's incorporation could have triggered gain to Salisbury if, when aggregated with the other liabilities transferred, the liabilities exceeded the basis of the assets that Salisbury transferred to Concord. Prepare a letter that documents your response. Because Fay's background in tax matters is extensive, you should feel free to use technical language if appropriate. Ms. Holmes's address is Salisbury Group, Inc., P.O. Box 71, Concord, NC 28026.

Research Problem 47. In 1990, Pat and Maria formed Robin Corporation by transferring assets in exchange for stock. Pat and Maria each received 100 shares in Robin Corporation. Robin Corporation filed a proper election to qualify as an S corporation. In 1992, Pat and Maria obtained a $100,000 loan from a bank and transferred the cash to Robin Corporation as a contribution to its capital. Robin used the $100,000 to purchase stock in Bluebird Corporation. Bluebird met the requirements of a small business corporation under § 1244.

Bluebird Corporation ultimately encountered financial problems and filed for bankruptcy in 1996. Robin Corporation sold its Bluebird stock in 1997 for $20,000. On their 1997 tax returns, Pat and Maria each deducted an ordinary loss of $40,000.

Upon audit of Pat's return in 1998, the IRS disallowed the deduction of the entire $40,000 loss as an ordinary loss. The IRS contends the Bluebird stock does not qualify for ordinary loss treatment under § 1244 because the stock was held by an S corporation. According to the IRS, § 1244 treatment is available only where § 1244 stock is issued to an individual or to a partnership and then is sold by that individual or partnership. Pat insists she is entitled to ordinary loss treatment because income of an S corporation flows through to the shareholders of the corporation in the same manner as partnership income. How would you advise Pat?

Research aid:
Virgil Rath, 101 T.C. 196 (1993).

Research Problem 48.   Trace developments in the tax law during the last twelve months with respect to the rules of § 357.

Chapter 18

Research Problem 49.   Aqua Corporation wholly owns Egret Corporation. Aqua formed Egret four years ago with the transfer of several assets to the corporation, together with a substantial amount of cash. Aqua's basis in Egret stock is $5.5 million. Since it was formed, Egret has been a very profitable software company and currently has accumulated E & P of $4 million. The company's principal assets are software patents currently worth $5 million and cash and marketable securities of approximately $4.5 million (a total fair market value of $9.5 million).

Aqua and Egret are members of an affiliated group and have made the election under § 243(b) so that Aqua is entitled to a 100% dividends received deduction. From a strategic perspective, Aqua is no longer interested in the software industry and so is considering a sale of Egret. In anticipation of a sale in the next year or two, the management of Aqua has contacted you for advice. If Egret is sold outright, then Aqua Corporation will have a capital gain of $4 million ($9.5 million fair market value less a basis of $5.5 million). As an alternative, it has been suggested that taxes on a future sale would be minimized if Egret pays Aqua a dividend (using existing cash and securities) equal to its E & P. With the 100% dividends received deduction, this payment would be a tax-free transfer from Egret to Aqua. Subsequent to the dividend payment, Egret could be sold for its remaining value of $5,500,000 ($5 million in software patents plus $500,000 in cash), generating no additional gain or loss to Egret.

a. Prepare a letter to the president of Aqua Corporation describing the results of your research on the proposed plan. The president's name is Bill Gateson, 601 Pittsfield Dr., Champaign, IL 61821.

b. Prepare a memo for your firm's client files.

Research aids:
Waterman Steamship Corporation v. Comm., 70–2 USTC ¶9514, 26 AFTR2d 70–5185, 430 F.2d 1185 (CA–5, 1970).

Research Problem 50.   Dave Smith (1256 Pine Tree Lane, Waverly, MN 55390) owns 40% of Brown Corporation; his father owns the remaining 60%. Dave also owns 70% of White Corporation, with the remaining 30% being owned by his wife. Dave terminates his entire interest in Brown Corporation through a stock redemption that he reports as a long-term capital gain pursuant to § 302(b)(3). Three years later, White Corporation enters into a contract with Brown Corporation whereby White is given exclusive management authority over Brown's operations. Upon audit, the IRS disallowed the long-term capital gain treatment on the stock redemption in Brown Corporation contending that Dave acquired an interest in Brown within 10 years from the date of the redemption because of White's management contract with Brown. What is the result? Prepare a letter to Dave and a memo to the file documenting your conclusions.

Research Problem 51.   Financial planners have begun to tout dividend reinvestment plans (DRIPs) as an effective way to hold down the costs of building a portfolio. Outline the key advantages and disadvantages of DRIPs, by reviewing analyses of them provided by investor organizations, brokerage houses, and corporations providing such plans themselves.

Chapter 19

Research Problem 52. Green Corporation was liquidated two years ago. In the year of liquidation, Green reported taxable gain of $8 million, based upon a value in its assets of $10 million and a basis of $2 million. After paying its tax liability of $2,720,000, Green distributed its remaining assets, valued at $7,280,000 ($10 million – $2,720,000 tax paid), to its 10 shareholders. Shareholder Beth received $728,000 and reported a long-term capital gain of $628,000 ($728,000 distribution – $100,000 stock basis). In the current year, the IRS audited Green Corporation and determined that the corporation had an additional gain of $1 million in the year of liquidation. The IRS assessed additional tax of $340,000 plus penalties and interest against Green Corporation and then against Beth, based on transferee liability. Beth comes to you for advice. She is not certain where the other shareholders are located.

   a. If Beth is required to pay all of the tax liability, will she be entitled to deduct the amount paid as a loss?

   b. What is the nature of the loss—capital or ordinary?

   c. Would § 1341 apply?

   d. How can a shareholder be protected from the problem facing Beth?

Research Problem 53. The stock of Bluebird Corporation is held 15% by Rosa and 85% by Beth. José would like to purchase all the stock but has only enough cash to pay for 70%. Bluebird Corporation has enough cash on hand to redeem 30% of its shares. Consider and evaluate the following alternatives in terms of Bluebird Corporation, Rosa, and Beth.

   a. Bluebird Corporation redeems 30% of the shares from Beth. José purchases the remaining 55% held by Beth and the 15% held by Rosa.

   b. Bluebird distributes 85% of its cash to Beth and 15% to Rosa. This reduces the value of the stock to a level where José's cash is adequate to purchase Rosa's and Beth's shares.

   c. Bluebird Corporation redeems all of Rosa's shares. José purchases 70% of the shares held by Beth. Bluebird Corporation then redeems the remainder of Beth's shares.

   d. José borrows money from a bank to purchase all of Rosa's and Beth's shares. Later, José has Bluebird redeem 30% of the shares he purchased so that he can pay off the bank loan.

Research aids:

Bernard E. Niedermeyer, 62 T.C. 280 (1974).

Television Industries, Inc. v. Comm., 60–2 USTC ¶9795, 6 AFTR2d 5864, 284 F.2d 322 (CA–2, 1960).

Research Problem 54. The repeal of the *General Utilities* doctrine by the 1986 Tax Reform Act has been described as making corporate liquidations more expensive. Make a list of tax advisers on the Internet who discuss this point in their solicitations and newsletters. Do they discuss *General Utilities* for C corporations only or also for S corporations and their shareholders?

Chapter 20

Research Problem 55. Vechnalysis was a computer programming services business listed on the National Market System of the over-the-counter market. Pamela Wilson, the president, and three other members of the company's board of directors each owned about 25% of the company's stock. The company had accumulated earnings and profits of $5.3, $6, and $7 million in 1988, 1989, and 1990, respectively.

   The Tax Court agreed with the IRS that Vechnalysis had unreasonable accumulated earnings and profits to the extent of $1.77 million in 1988 and $600,000 in 1990. The Tax Court applied the *Bardahl* formula using a 22-day business cycle and the succeeding year's operating expenses to compute the company's working capital needs. To reach excess working capital where net liquid assets exceeded accumulated earnings and profits, the Tax Court subtracted the working capital needs from accumulated earnings and profits. The excess working capital was thus computed as follows:

Year	Accumulated E & P Less Working Capital Needs	Excess Working Capital
1988	$5,346,888 – $2,526,695	= $2,820,193
1989	$6,082,042 – $3,179,233	= 2,902,809
1990	$7,062,764 – $3,578,723	= 3,484,041

The company had adopted a stock purchase plan, which the directors believed would arouse interest in Vechnalysis shares and maintain the shareholders' confidence in their investment. Based upon these facts, calculate the Tax Court's eventual accumulated earning tax for this corporation.

Research Problem 56. Dr. Bob owns 90% of the stock of Dental Services, Inc. Dr. Bob performs medical services under an employment contract with the corporation. He is the only dentist employed and is the only officer of the corporation actively engaged in the production of income. Dental Services, Inc., furnishes office space and equipment and employs a dental hygienist and a receptionist to assist Dr. Bob.

a. Various patients receive dental care from Dr. Bob. Does Dental Services have PHC income under § 543(a)(7)?

b. Suppose Jack, a patient, secures an absolute binding promise from Dr. Bob that the dentist will personally perform a root canal operation and that the dentist has no right to substitute another dentist. Would your answer change?

Research Problem 57. Owners of closely held businesses and their tax advisers make available substantial in-depth information about the dangers of the PHC tax and the best means by which to avoid it. Outline the key techniques promoted by these sources as effective in minimizing § 541 exposure.

Chapter 21

Research Problem 58. Mel Bonilla contacts you with respect to the creation of two S corporations, each having approximately 40 shareholders. Most of the assets of the business will be held inside a limited liability company. Both S corporations will be 50% partners in the limited liability company. Draft a letter to Mel dated January 14, 1998, indicating whether this business arrangement is appropriate. Mel's address is 10 Newton Avenue, Ocala, FL 34482.

Research Problem 59. Andy creates an S corporation, Heredia, Inc., with a $100,000 cash investment and a $900,000 loan from a local bank in 1997. During the first year of operation, the company incurs a loss of $150,000. Andy deducts only $100,000 because this is the amount he personally put into the business. Lacking any more stock basis, he now has $50,000 of losses he is unable to claim.

In 1998, the business loses the entire $1 million, and Andy shuts the business down. Since the bank cannot collect from the S corporation or Andy, the bank writes off the debt. What are the tax consequences of this situation?

Research Problem 60. Find a question about S corporation tax planning that has been posted to a newsgroup. Submit to the group your answer to the query. Make a copy of the question and answer.

Chapter 22

Research Problem 61. Your clients, Mark Henderson and John Burton, each contributed $10,000 cash to form the Realty Management Partnership, a limited partnership. Mark is the general partner and John is the limited partner. The partnership used the $20,000 cash to make a down payment on a building. The rest of the building's $200,000 purchase price was financed with an interest-only nonrecourse loan of $180,000, which was obtained from an independent third-party bank. The partnership allocates all partnership items equally except for the MACRS deductions and building maintenance, which are allocated 70% to John and 30% to Mark. The partnership definitely wishes to satisfy the "economic effect" requirements of Reg. §§ 1.704–1 and

1.704–2 and will reallocate MACRS, if necessary, to satisfy the requirements of the Regulations. Under the partnership agreement, liquidation distributions will be paid in proportion to the partners' positive capital account balances. Capital accounts are maintained as required in the Regulations. Mark has an unlimited obligation to restore his capital account while John is subject to a qualified income offset provision. Assume all partnership items, except for MACRS, will net to zero throughout the first three years of the partnership operations. Also, assume that each year's MACRS deduction will be $10,000 (to simplify the calculations).

Draft a letter to the partnership evaluating the allocation of MACRS in each of the three years under Reg. §§ 1.704–1 and 1.704–2. The partnership's address is 53 East Marsh Ave., Smyrna, GA 30082. Do not address the "substantial" test.

Research Problem 62. In 1995, Texas Land, Inc., a development company, had the opportunity to acquire and develop 100 acres of land in west Texas for $10 million. Mortgage Guaranty Company (MGC) agreed to lend $6 million at favorable interest rates toward the purchase if Texas Land put forward capital of the other $4 million.

Texas Land had only $2 million of cash available, so it turned to Gateway Savings & Loan, a struggling S & L with significant tax losses. Gateway agreed to contribute $2 million to a partnership (TG Partners) that would acquire and develop the property. In return, Gateway would receive a guaranteed payment of 10% of its capital each year, plus 50% of any profits on the development and sale of the property. The parties agreed that Texas Land would manage the property and oversee its developement and that Gateway would make additional funds available for the development of the property. No partnership agreement was ever drafted or signed.

Before the closing on the 100-acre purchase, Texas Land located a third party willing to purchase 30 acres of the property for $5 million. As it turned out, the closing on the 100-acre purchase occurred on the same day as the closing on the 30-acre sale to the third party. The $5 million sales proceeds were sufficient to fund both the Texas Land and the Gateway $2 million capital contributions, with adequate funds remaining to begin improvements on the remaining 70-acre parcel. Therefore, neither Texas Land nor Gateway was required to contribute cash to form TG Partners.

TG Partners reflected a gain of $2 million on the 30-acre land sale [$5 million selling price less $3 million basis (30% × $10 million cost of 100-acre parcel)]. The partnership's balance sheet at the close of the day of the land transfers was as follows:

Assets:	
Cash	$1,000,000
Land	7,000,000
Total assets	$8,000,000
Liabilities:	
Note payable to MGC	$6,000,000
Partners' capital:	
Texas Land (½ of gain)	1,000,000
Gateway S & L (½ of gain)	1,000,000
Total liabilities and capital	$8,000,000

The IRS has audited the TG Partners partnership tax return for this initial year and has questioned whether a partnership was actually formed. The IRS claims Gateway merely promised to lend money to an entity and was never required to follow through on the loan. The gain allocation, per the IRS, was simply to shift a tax liability from Texas Land to an entity with no tax liability.

a. TG Partners is your client. Determine whether a valid partnership was formed, even though no cash was contributed to the entity by either party in 1995.

b. Consider the effect of the "check-the-box" Regulations under Reg. § 301.7701. If the transactions had occurred in 1998, would your answer to (a) be different? If so, how?

Research Problem 63. Print an article posted by a law firm that comments on pitfalls to avoid in drafting partnership agreements. Ideally, use the home page of a firm that has offices in your state.

Chapter 23

Research Problem 64. Allied Fund, a charitable organization exempt under § 501(c)(3), has branches located in each of the 50 states. Allied is not a private foundation. Rather than having each of the state units file an annual return with the IRS, Allied would like to file a single return that reports the activities of all of its branches. Is this permissible? What is the due date of the return?

Research aids:
§ 6033.
§ 6072.
Reg. § 1.6033–2(d).

Research Problem 65. Great Outdoors, Inc., is a tax-exempt organization. Its mission is to explore, enjoy, and protect the wild places of the earth; to practice and promote the responsible use of the earth's ecosystems and resources; to educate and enlist humanity to protect and restore the quality of the natural and human environment; and to use all lawful means to carry out these objectives.

William Johnson, the chief financial officer, presents you with the following information. Great Outdoors raises funds to support its mission in a variety of ways including contributions and membership fees. As part of this effort, Great Outdoors develops and maintains mailing lists of its members, donors, catalog purchasers, and other supporters. Great Outdoors has exclusive ownership rights in its mailing lists. To acquire the names of prospective members and supporters, Great Outdoors occasionally exchanges membership lists with other organizations. In addition, Great Outdoors permits other tax-exempt organizations and commercial entities to pay a fee, as set forth in a fee schedule, to use its mailing lists on a one-time basis per transaction.

Johnson is aware of the unrelated business income tax. He also is aware of the § 512(b)(2) provision that excludes royalties from the unrelated business income tax. A Revenue Agent has raised the issue that the revenue from the use of the mailing lists by other entities may be taxable as unrelated business income. Johnson would like for you to research this issue for him.

Write a letter to Johnson that contains your findings, and prepare a memo for the tax files. Great Outdoors's address is 100 Central Avenue, Pocatello, ID 83209.

Research Problem 66. Summarize a recent newspaper or magazine story that relates a perceived abuse of the § 501(c)(3) provisions by a business owner or politician.

Chapter 24

Research Problem 67. A U.S. corporation had the following net taxable income (loss) for the tax year. Its U.S. taxes before the foreign tax credit (FTC) are $6,750. Determine the FTC limitation for each basket of foreign-source income.

Source (Basket)	Income (Loss)	Foreign Taxes
U.S.-source	($54,000)	$ –0–
Foreign-source passive	80,000	24,000
Foreign-source shipping	40,000	14,800
Foreign-source overall	(21,000)	–0–

Research aids:
§ 904(f)(5).
General Explanation of the Tax Reform Act of 1986 (the Bluebook), Joint Committee on Taxation, pp. 909–912.
Instructions accompanying Form 1118, Foreign Tax Credit—Corporations, Dept. of the Treasury, Internal Revenue Service.

Research Problem 68.   Jay, a U.S. citizen, lives in Switzerland. He is an artist who sells his paintings throughout the world. As a U.S. citizen, he is subject to taxation on his worldwide income. Jay seeks to take a foreign earned income exclusion with regard to the income he receives from the sales of the paintings. An IRS agent questions the claim that the income from sale of the paintings is "earned" income for purposes of the exclusion. How would you advise Jay?

Research aids:
Mark Tobey, 60 T.C. 227 (1973), *acq.* 1979–1 C.B. 1.
Robida, 72–1 USTC ¶9450, 29 AFTR2d 72–1223, 460 F.2d 460 (CA–9, 1972).
Ingram v. Bowers, 3 USTC ¶915, 10 AFTR 1513, 57 F.2d 65 (CA–2, 1932).

Research Problem 69.   What is the current exchange rate between the U.S. dollar and the currency of each of the following countries?
  a. Argentina.
  b. Canada.
  c. France.
  d. Malaysia.
  e. Slovak Republic.

Chapter 25

Research Problem 70.   Leigh Van Camp was convicted of underpayment of Federal income tax. He had set up several branches of the "Church of America's Salvation" in Arizona, and he was found to have used church donations to support an extravagant lifestyle for himself and his family, rather than to advance the goals of the church. In the Tax Court proceedings, Leigh bargained down the charges from criminal fraud to mere underpayment of tax. The settlement did not end the bad feelings between Leigh and personnel in the local IRS office, however.

Leigh owed $250,000 in interest, penalty, and tax after the Tax Court issued its verdict. He placed $200,000 in escrow with respect to this tax. IRS agents then received a tip that Leigh had sold his largest remaining asset, the family home, and was "moving to Niagara Falls in two days." Fearing that Leigh would leave the country without paying the tax from the court settlement or the tax on the gain from the sale of the residence, the agents placed a jeopardy assessment on the $500,000 cash proceeds of the sale.

Angry at the way the IRS is intruding into his life, Leigh calls you from New York and hires you to "get the IRS off my back" and obtain the return of his funds in full. Assess the IRS's position in a memo to the research file.

Research aids:
Reg. §§ 1.6851–1(a)(1)(i) through (iii).
Robert Lee McWilliams, 103 T.C. 320 (1994).

Research Problem 71.   Kent Brockmann, president of the struggling Simpson Corporation, is an individual client of your firm. A few months ago, he attended a local CEO-support seminar and learned about the steep penalties that the IRS can assess under § 6672 when payroll taxes are withheld from employee paychecks but not remitted promptly to the government. The seminar presenter characterized this penalty as falling upon the "undercapitalized small business, forced into using the government as the source of a working capital loan," but with severe consequences.

Brockmann knew that Simpson was having cash-flow problems, so he checked with Marge Flanders, the corporate treasurer, about this issue. Brockmann emphasized that these taxes "must be paid," because he did not want the company to get into trouble with the IRS. Flanders said that there was a delinquency in the withholding deposits, but assured him that she was working to solve it and had already made partial payments.

In reality, there was not enough cash to go around, and Flanders had made no deposits for six months running. When the resulting § 6672 penalty was assessed, Simpson halted operations and liquidated its few remaining assets. As the "responsible person" for Simpson tax matters, Brockmann's personal assets were attached by the IRS. In attempting to waive the penalty, Brockmann's position is that he thought he had taken care of the matter in his meeting with Flanders, who was last seen in Mexico. Can Brockmann avoid the penalty? Address this issue on his behalf in a memo to the tax research file.

Research Problem 72.   Who is your IRS District Director? What are his or her address and phone number? Who is your state's Secretary of Revenue? What are his or her address and phone number?

Chapter 26

Research Problem 73.   In 1992, Marge Hurt creates an irrevocable trust using income-producing real estate worth $70,000. The trust arrangement is as follows:

- Frank and Lillian (Marge's adult children) are designated as co-trustees.

- The income from the trust is to be distributed to Frank and Lillian during Marge's life and for 120 days thereafter.

- If Frank and Lillian survive Marge by 120 days, each is to receive an equal share of the corpus.

- If either Frank or Lillian does not survive Marge by 120 days, income from the trust is payable to his or her children. If Marge dies and either Frank or Lillian does not survive her by 120 days, corpus is to pass to his or her children (Marge's grandchildren). Frank has two children; Lillian has three.

- As to every annual gift to the trust by Marge, all present (Frank and Lillian) and potential (the children of Frank and Lillian) beneficiaries have the right to withdraw the amount of the § 2503(b) gift tax exclusion. The right of withdrawal exists for 15 days after the gift in trust.

In 1993, Marge contributes additional real estate (worth $70,000) to the trust. Marge dies in 1994 before any further gifts can be made. One hundred and twenty days after Marge's death, the trust corpus and accumulated income are divided between Frank and Lillian, and the trust is dissolved. Following the gifts made by Marge, none of the beneficiaries (neither Frank nor Lillian nor their children) exercise the right of withdrawal.

No gift tax return is filed reflecting either the 1992 or 1993 gifts by Marge. Nor are these gifts noted on the estate tax return filed by the executors of Marge's estate.

Upon audit of the estate tax return, the IRS determines that Marge made taxable gifts of $50,000 in both 1992 and 1993.

a. Why did the IRS choose $50,000 as the amount of each taxable gift?

b. On an audit of Marge's estate tax return, why should the IRS care about the possibility of prior taxable gifts?

c. Is the IRS correct or not about the existence of prior taxable gifts? Explain.

Research aid:
Crummey v. Comm., 68–1 USTC ¶12,541, 22 AFTR2d 6023, 397 F.2d 82 (CA–9, 1968).

Research Problem 74.   Hector dies on April 24, 1989, and under his will a major portion of the estate passes to a trust. The provisions of the trust grant a life estate to Ellen (Hector's surviving spouse), remainder to their adult children. The income is payable to Ellen quarterly or at more frequent intervals. Income accrued or held undistributed by the trust at the time of Ellen's death shall pass to the remainder interest.

On January 24, 1990, Hector's estate filed a Federal estate tax return and made the QTIP election. On July 3, 1990, Hector's estate filed an amended return based on the premise that the QTIP election was improper. As a result of the loss of the marital deduction, the amended return was accompanied by a payment of additional estate taxes.

On February 11, 1990, Ellen dies. All of her assets, including those in Hector's trust, pass to the children.

a. Why did Hector's estate file an amended return revoking the QTIP election?

b. Is the revocation of the election proper procedure?

c. Did Hector's estate ever qualify for the election?

Research aids:
§§ 2056(b)(7) and 2013.
Estate of Rose D. Howard, 91 T.C. 329 (1988), *rev'd* in 90–2 USTC ¶60,033, 66 AFTR2d 90–5994, 910 F.2d 633 (CA–9, 1990).

Research Problem 75. Find an estate and gift planning article posted by a tax professional. Reply via e-mail to this posting, offering an additional planning suggestion.

Chapter 27

Research Problem 76. Your client, Chuck Konkol, is a self-employed investment adviser who provides services to individuals and small investment clubs for an hourly fee. He is aware of the difficulty that his clients have in deducting payments to him due to the 2%-of-AGI floor on miscellaneous itemized deductions, such as advisory fees.

His new client, the Ferguson Trust, wants to be certain that it can deduct such fees in computing entity taxable income. Konkol asks you to make a presentation to the trust's officers on this subject. Provide a speaker's outline for this purpose, with citations only to the most important statutory and judicial law.

Research Problem 77. Your client, Annie O'Toole, (22 Beneficiary Lane, Bowling Green, KY 42101), has come to you for some advice regarding gifts of property. She has just learned that she must undergo major surgery, and she would like to make certain gifts before entering the hospital. On your earlier advice, she had established a plan of lifetime giving for four prior years.

Build a spreadsheet, supplemented by a list of your assumptions, and write a cover letter to Annie, discussing each of the following assets that she is thinking of using as gifts to family and friends. In doing so, evaluate the income tax consequences of having the property pass through her estate to the designated legatee. *For this purpose, you need consult only the Code and pertinent Regulations.*

a. Annie plans to give a cottage to her son to fulfill a promise made many years ago. She has owned the cottage for the past 15 years and has a basis in it of $30,000 (fair market value of $20,000).

b. Annie has $100,000 of long-term capital losses that she has been carrying forward for the past few years. Now, she is considering making a gift of $200,000 in installment notes to her daughter. Her basis in the notes is $100,000, and the notes' current fair market value is $190,000.

c. Annie has promised to make a special cash bequest of $25,000 to her grandson in her will. However, she does not anticipate having that much cash immediately available after her death. Annie requests your advice concerning the income tax consequences to the estate if the cash bequest is settled with some other property.

Research Problem 78. List some of the most important steps to be followed when an individual selects a trustee to manage his or her assets.

Appendix A

Tax Rate Schedules and Tables

1997 Tax Rate Schedules

Single—Schedule X

If taxable income is: Over—	But not over—	The tax is:	of the amount over—
$0	$ 24,650	. . . . . . .15%	$0
24,650	59,750	$3,697.50 + 28%	24,650
59,750	124,650	13,525.50 + 31%	59,750
124,650	271,050	33,644.50 + 36%	124,650
271,050	. . . . . .	86,348.50 + 39.6%	271,050

Head of household—Schedule Z

If taxable income is: Over—	But not over—	The tax is:	of the amount over—
$0	$ 33,050	. . . . . . .15%	$0
33,050	85,350	$4,957.50 + 28%	33,050
85,350	138,200	19,601.50 + 31%	85,350
138,200	271,050	35,985.00 + 36%	138,200
271,050	. . . . . .	83,811.00 + 39.6%	271,050

Married filing jointly or Qualifying widow(er)—Schedule Y–1

If taxable income is: Over—	But not over—	The tax is:	of the amount over—
$0	$ 41,200	. . . . . . .15%	$0
41,200	99,600	$6,180.00 + 28%	41,200
99,600	151,750	22,532.00 + 31%	99,600
151,750	271,050	38,698.50 + 36%	151,750
271,050	. . . . . .	81,646.50 + 39.6%	271,050

Married filing separately—Schedule Y–2

If taxable income is: Over—	But not over—	The tax is:	of the amount over—
$0	$ 20,600	. . . . . . .15%	$0
20,600	49,800	$3,090.00 + 28%	20,600
49,800	75,875	11,266.00 + 31%	49,800
75,875	135,525	19,349.25 + 36%	75,875
135,525	. . . . . .	40,823.25 + 39.6%	135,525

1998 Tax Rate Schedules

Single—Schedule X

If taxable income is: Over—	But not over—	The tax is:	of the amount over—
$0	$ 25,350	. . . . . . .15%	$0
25,350	61,400	$3,802.50 + 28%	25,350
61,400	128,100	13,896.50 + 31%	61,400
128,100	278,450	34,573.50 + 36%	128,100
278,450	. . . . . .	88,699.50 + 39.6%	278,450

Head of household—Schedule Z

If taxable income is: Over—	But not over—	The tax is:	of the amount over—
$0	$ 33,950	. . . . . . .15%	$0
33,950	87,700	$5,092.50 + 28%	33,950
87,700	142,000	20,142.50 + 31%	87,700
142,000	278,450	36,975.50 + 36%	142,000
278,450	. . . . . .	86,097.50 + 39.6%	278,450

Married filing jointly or Qualifying widow(er)—Schedule Y–1

If taxable income is: Over—	But not over—	The tax is:	of the amount over—
$0	$ 42,350	. . . . . . .15%	$0
42,350	102,300	$6,352.50 + 28%	42,350
102,300	155,950	23,138.50 + 31%	102,300
155,950	278,450	39,770.00 + 36%	155,950
278,450	. . . . . .	83,870.00 + 39.6%	278,450

Married filing separately—Schedule Y–2

If taxable income is: Over—	But not over—	The tax is:	of the amount over—
$0	$ 21,175	. . . . . . .15%	$0
21,175	51,150	$3,176.25 + 28%	21,175
51,150	77,975	11,569.25 + 31%	51,150
77,975	139,225	19,885.00 + 36%	77,975
139,225	. . . . . .	41,935.00 + 39.6%	139,225

1997 Tax Table

Use if your taxable income is less than $100,000. If $100,000 or more, use the Tax Rate Schedules.

Example. Mr. and Mrs. Brown are filing a joint return. Their taxable income on line 38 of Form 1040 is $25,300. First, they find the $25,300–25,350 income line. Next, they find the column for married filing jointly and read down the column. The amount shown where the income line and filing status column meet is $3,799. This is the tax amount they should enter on line 39 of their Form 1040.

Sample Table

At least	But less than	Single	Married filing jointly *	Married filing separately	Head of a household
			Your tax is—		
25,200	25,250	3,859	3,784	4,385	3,784
25,250	25,300	3,873	3,791	4,399	3,791
25,300	25,350	3,887	(3,799)	4,413	3,799
25,350	25,400	3,901	3,806	4,427	3,806

If line 38 (taxable income) is— At least	But less than	Single	Married filing jointly *	Married filing separately	Head of a house-hold
			Your tax is—		
$0	$5	$0	$0	$0	$0
5	15	2	2	2	2
15	25	3	3	3	3
25	50	6	6	6	6
50	75	9	9	9	9
75	100	13	13	13	13
100	125	17	17	17	17
125	150	21	21	21	21
150	175	24	24	24	24
175	200	28	28	28	28
200	225	32	32	32	32
225	250	36	36	36	36
250	275	39	39	39	39
275	300	43	43	43	43
300	325	47	47	47	47
325	350	51	51	51	51
350	375	54	54	54	54
375	400	58	58	58	58
400	425	62	62	62	62
425	450	66	66	66	66
450	475	69	69	69	69
475	500	73	73	73	73
500	525	77	77	77	77
525	550	81	81	81	81
550	575	84	84	84	84
575	600	88	88	88	88
600	625	92	92	92	92
625	650	96	96	96	96
650	675	99	99	99	99
675	700	103	103	103	103
700	725	107	107	107	107
725	750	111	111	111	111
750	775	114	114	114	114
775	800	118	118	118	118
800	825	122	122	122	122
825	850	126	126	126	126
850	875	129	129	129	129
875	900	133	133	133	133
900	925	137	137	137	137
925	950	141	141	141	141
950	975	144	144	144	144
975	1,000	148	148	148	148
1,000					
1,000	1,025	152	152	152	152
1,025	1,050	156	156	156	156
1,050	1,075	159	159	159	159
1,075	1,100	163	163	163	163
1,100	1,125	167	167	167	167
1,125	1,150	171	171	171	171
1,150	1,175	174	174	174	174
1,175	1,200	178	178	178	178
1,200	1,225	182	182	182	182
1,225	1,250	186	186	186	186
1,250	1,275	189	189	189	189
1,275	1,300	193	193	193	193

If line 38 (taxable income) is— At least	But less than	Single	Married filing jointly *	Married filing separately	Head of a house-hold
			Your tax is—		
1,300	1,325	197	197	197	197
1,325	1,350	201	201	201	201
1,350	1,375	204	204	204	204
1,375	1,400	208	208	208	208
1,400	1,425	212	212	212	212
1,425	1,450	216	216	216	216
1,450	1,475	219	219	219	219
1,475	1,500	223	223	223	223
1,500	1,525	227	227	227	227
1,525	1,550	231	231	231	231
1,550	1,575	234	234	234	234
1,575	1,600	238	238	238	238
1,600	1,625	242	242	242	242
1,625	1,650	246	246	246	246
1,650	1,675	249	249	249	249
1,675	1,700	253	253	253	253
1,700	1,725	257	257	257	257
1,725	1,750	261	261	261	261
1,750	1,775	264	264	264	264
1,775	1,800	268	268	268	268
1,800	1,825	272	272	272	272
1,825	1,850	276	276	276	276
1,850	1,875	279	279	279	279
1,875	1,900	283	283	283	283
1,900	1,925	287	287	287	287
1,925	1,950	291	291	291	291
1,950	1,975	294	294	294	294
1,975	2,000	298	298	298	298
2,000					
2,000	2,025	302	302	302	302
2,025	2,050	306	306	306	306
2,050	2,075	309	309	309	309
2,075	2,100	313	313	313	313
2,100	2,125	317	317	317	317
2,125	2,150	321	321	321	321
2,150	2,175	324	324	324	324
2,175	2,200	328	328	328	328
2,200	2,225	332	332	332	332
2,225	2,250	336	336	336	336
2,250	2,275	339	339	339	339
2,275	2,300	343	343	343	343
2,300	2,325	347	347	347	347
2,325	2,350	351	351	351	351
2,350	2,375	354	354	354	354
2,375	2,400	358	358	358	358
2,400	2,425	362	362	362	362
2,425	2,450	366	366	366	366
2,450	2,475	369	369	369	369
2,475	2,500	373	373	373	373
2,500	2,525	377	377	377	377
2,525	2,550	381	381	381	381
2,550	2,575	384	384	384	384
2,575	2,600	388	388	388	388
2,600	2,625	392	392	392	392
2,625	2,650	396	396	396	396
2,650	2,675	399	399	399	399
2,675	2,700	403	403	403	403

If line 38 (taxable income) is— At least	But less than	Single	Married filing jointly *	Married filing separately	Head of a house-hold
			Your tax is—		
2,700	2,725	407	407	407	407
2,725	2,750	411	411	411	411
2,750	2,775	414	414	414	414
2,775	2,800	418	418	418	418
2,800	2,825	422	422	422	422
2,825	2,850	426	426	426	426
2,850	2,875	429	429	429	429
2,875	2,900	433	433	433	433
2,900	2,925	437	437	437	437
2,925	2,950	441	441	441	441
2,950	2,975	444	444	444	444
2,975	3,000	448	448	448	448
3,000					
3,000	3,050	454	454	454	454
3,050	3,100	461	461	461	461
3,100	3,150	469	469	469	469
3,150	3,200	476	476	476	476
3,200	3,250	484	484	484	484
3,250	3,300	491	491	491	491
3,300	3,350	499	499	499	499
3,350	3,400	506	506	506	506
3,400	3,450	514	514	514	514
3,450	3,500	521	521	521	521
3,500	3,550	529	529	529	529
3,550	3,600	536	536	536	536
3,600	3,650	544	544	544	544
3,650	3,700	551	551	551	551
3,700	3,750	559	559	559	559
3,750	3,800	566	566	566	566
3,800	3,850	574	574	574	574
3,850	3,900	581	581	581	581
3,900	3,950	589	589	589	589
3,950	4,000	596	596	596	596
4,000					
4,000	4,050	604	604	604	604
4,050	4,100	611	611	611	611
4,100	4,150	619	619	619	619
4,150	4,200	626	626	626	626
4,200	4,250	634	634	634	634
4,250	4,300	641	641	641	641
4,300	4,350	649	649	649	649
4,350	4,400	656	656	656	656
4,400	4,450	664	664	664	664
4,450	4,500	671	671	671	671
4,500	4,550	679	679	679	679
4,550	4,600	686	686	686	686
4,600	4,650	694	694	694	694
4,650	4,700	701	701	701	701
4,700	4,750	709	709	709	709
4,750	4,800	716	716	716	716
4,800	4,850	724	724	724	724
4,850	4,900	731	731	731	731
4,900	4,950	739	739	739	739
4,950	5,000	746	746	746	746

Continued on next page

* This column must also be used by a qualifying widow(er).

1997 Tax Table—*Continued*

5,000 / 8,000 / 11,000

At least	But less than	Single	Married filing jointly *	Married filing separately	Head of a household	At least	But less than	Single	Married filing jointly *	Married filing separately	Head of a household	At least	But less than	Single	Married filing jointly *	Married filing separately	Head of a household
5,000	5,050	754	754	754	754	8,000	8,050	1,204	1,204	1,204	1,204	11,000	11,050	1,654	1,654	1,654	1,654
5,050	5,100	761	761	761	761	8,050	8,100	1,211	1,211	1,211	1,211	11,050	11,100	1,661	1,661	1,661	1,661
5,100	5,150	769	769	769	769	8,100	8,150	1,219	1,219	1,219	1,219	11,100	11,150	1,669	1,669	1,669	1,669
5,150	5,200	776	776	776	776	8,150	8,200	1,226	1,226	1,226	1,226	11,150	11,200	1,676	1,676	1,676	1,676
5,200	5,250	784	784	784	784	8,200	8,250	1,234	1,234	1,234	1,234	11,200	11,250	1,684	1,684	1,684	1,684
5,250	5,300	791	791	791	791	8,250	8,300	1,241	1,241	1,241	1,241	11,250	11,300	1,691	1,691	1,691	1,691
5,300	5,350	799	799	799	799	8,300	8,350	1,249	1,249	1,249	1,249	11,300	11,350	1,699	1,699	1,699	1,699
5,350	5,400	806	806	806	806	8,350	8,400	1,256	1,256	1,256	1,256	11,350	11,400	1,706	1,706	1,706	1,706
5,400	5,450	814	814	814	814	8,400	8,450	1,264	1,264	1,264	1,264	11,400	11,450	1,714	1,714	1,714	1,714
5,450	5,500	821	821	821	821	8,450	8,500	1,271	1,271	1,271	1,271	11,450	11,500	1,721	1,721	1,721	1,721
5,500	5,550	829	829	829	829	8,500	8,550	1,279	1,279	1,279	1,279	11,500	11,550	1,729	1,729	1,729	1,729
5,550	5,600	836	836	836	836	8,550	8,600	1,286	1,286	1,286	1,286	11,550	11,600	1,736	1,736	1,736	1,736
5,600	5,650	844	844	844	844	8,600	8,650	1,294	1,294	1,294	1,294	11,600	11,650	1,744	1,744	1,744	1,744
5,650	5,700	851	851	851	851	8,650	8,700	1,301	1,301	1,301	1,301	11,650	11,700	1,751	1,751	1,751	1,751
5,700	5,750	859	859	859	859	8,700	8,750	1,309	1,309	1,309	1,309	11,700	11,750	1,759	1,759	1,759	1,759
5,750	5,800	866	866	866	866	8,750	8,800	1,316	1,316	1,316	1,316	11,750	11,800	1,766	1,766	1,766	1,766
5,800	5,850	874	874	874	874	8,800	8,850	1,324	1,324	1,324	1,324	11,800	11,850	1,774	1,774	1,774	1,774
5,850	5,900	881	881	881	881	8,850	8,900	1,331	1,331	1,331	1,331	11,850	11,900	1,781	1,781	1,781	1,781
5,900	5,950	889	889	889	889	8,900	8,950	1,339	1,339	1,339	1,339	11,900	11,950	1,789	1,789	1,789	1,789
5,950	6,000	896	896	896	896	8,950	9,000	1,346	1,346	1,346	1,346	11,950	12,000	1,796	1,796	1,796	1,796

6,000 / 9,000 / 12,000

At least	But less than	Single	Married filing jointly *	Married filing separately	Head of a household	At least	But less than	Single	Married filing jointly *	Married filing separately	Head of a household	At least	But less than	Single	Married filing jointly *	Married filing separately	Head of a household
6,000	6,050	904	904	904	904	9,000	9,050	1,354	1,354	1,354	1,354	12,000	12,050	1,804	1,804	1,804	1,804
6,050	6,100	911	911	911	911	9,050	9,100	1,361	1,361	1,361	1,361	12,050	12,100	1,811	1,811	1,811	1,811
6,100	6,150	919	919	919	919	9,100	9,150	1,369	1,369	1,369	1,369	12,100	12,150	1,819	1,819	1,819	1,819
6,150	6,200	926	926	926	926	9,150	9,200	1,376	1,376	1,376	1,376	12,150	12,200	1,826	1,826	1,826	1,826
6,200	6,250	934	934	934	934	9,200	9,250	1,384	1,384	1,384	1,384	12,200	12,250	1,834	1,834	1,834	1,834
6,250	6,300	941	941	941	941	9,250	9,300	1,391	1,391	1,391	1,391	12,250	12,300	1,841	1,841	1,841	1,841
6,300	6,350	949	949	949	949	9,300	9,350	1,399	1,399	1,399	1,399	12,300	12,350	1,849	1,849	1,849	1,849
6,350	6,400	956	956	956	956	9,350	9,400	1,406	1,406	1,406	1,406	12,350	12,400	1,856	1,856	1,856	1,856
6,400	6,450	964	964	964	964	9,400	9,450	1,414	1,414	1,414	1,414	12,400	12,450	1,864	1,864	1,864	1,864
6,450	6,500	971	971	971	971	9,450	9,500	1,421	1,421	1,421	1,421	12,450	12,500	1,871	1,871	1,871	1,871
6,500	6,550	979	979	979	979	9,500	9,550	1,429	1,429	1,429	1,429	12,500	12,550	1,879	1,879	1,879	1,879
6,550	6,600	986	986	986	986	9,550	9,600	1,436	1,436	1,436	1,436	12,550	12,600	1,886	1,886	1,886	1,886
6,600	6,650	994	994	994	994	9,600	9,650	1,444	1,444	1,444	1,444	12,600	12,650	1,894	1,894	1,894	1,894
6,650	6,700	1,001	1,001	1,001	1,001	9,650	9,700	1,451	1,451	1,451	1,451	12,650	12,700	1,901	1,901	1,901	1,901
6,700	6,750	1,009	1,009	1,009	1,009	9,700	9,750	1,459	1,459	1,459	1,459	12,700	12,750	1,909	1,909	1,909	1,909
6,750	6,800	1,016	1,016	1,016	1,016	9,750	9,800	1,466	1,466	1,466	1,466	12,750	12,800	1,916	1,916	1,916	1,916
6,800	6,850	1,024	1,024	1,024	1,024	9,800	9,850	1,474	1,474	1,474	1,474	12,800	12,850	1,924	1,924	1,924	1,924
6,850	6,900	1,031	1,031	1,031	1,031	9,850	9,900	1,481	1,481	1,481	1,481	12,850	12,900	1,931	1,931	1,931	1,931
6,900	6,950	1,039	1,039	1,039	1,039	9,900	9,950	1,489	1,489	1,489	1,489	12,900	12,950	1,939	1,939	1,939	1,939
6,950	7,000	1,046	1,046	1,046	1,046	9,950	10,000	1,496	1,496	1,496	1,496	12,950	13,000	1,946	1,946	1,946	1,946

7,000 / 10,000 / 13,000

At least	But less than	Single	Married filing jointly *	Married filing separately	Head of a household	At least	But less than	Single	Married filing jointly *	Married filing separately	Head of a household	At least	But less than	Single	Married filing jointly *	Married filing separately	Head of a household
7,000	7,050	1,054	1,054	1,054	1,054	10,000	10,050	1,504	1,504	1,504	1,504	13,000	13,050	1,954	1,954	1,954	1,954
7,050	7,100	1,061	1,061	1,061	1,061	10,050	10,100	1,511	1,511	1,511	1,511	13,050	13,100	1,961	1,961	1,961	1,961
7,100	7,150	1,069	1,069	1,069	1,069	10,100	10,150	1,519	1,519	1,519	1,519	13,100	13,150	1,969	1,969	1,969	1,969
7,150	7,200	1,076	1,076	1,076	1,076	10,150	10,200	1,526	1,526	1,526	1,526	13,150	13,200	1,976	1,976	1,976	1,976
7,200	7,250	1,084	1,084	1,084	1,084	10,200	10,250	1,534	1,534	1,534	1,534	13,200	13,250	1,984	1,984	1,984	1,984
7,250	7,300	1,091	1,091	1,091	1,091	10,250	10,300	1,541	1,541	1,541	1,541	13,250	13,300	1,991	1,991	1,991	1,991
7,300	7,350	1,099	1,099	1,099	1,099	10,300	10,350	1,549	1,549	1,549	1,549	13,300	13,350	1,999	1,999	1,999	1,999
7,350	7,400	1,106	1,106	1,106	1,106	10,350	10,400	1,556	1,556	1,556	1,556	13,350	13,400	2,006	2,006	2,006	2,006
7,400	7,450	1,114	1,114	1,114	1,114	10,400	10,450	1,564	1,564	1,564	1,564	13,400	13,450	2,014	2,014	2,014	2,014
7,450	7,500	1,121	1,121	1,121	1,121	10,450	10,500	1,571	1,571	1,571	1,571	13,450	13,500	2,021	2,021	2,021	2,021
7,500	7,550	1,129	1,129	1,129	1,129	10,500	10,550	1,579	1,579	1,579	1,579	13,500	13,550	2,029	2,029	2,029	2,029
7,550	7,600	1,136	1,136	1,136	1,136	10,550	10,600	1,586	1,586	1,586	1,586	13,550	13,600	2,036	2,036	2,036	2,036
7,600	7,650	1,144	1,144	1,144	1,144	10,600	10,650	1,594	1,594	1,594	1,594	13,600	13,650	2,044	2,044	2,044	2,044
7,650	7,700	1,151	1,151	1,151	1,151	10,650	10,700	1,601	1,601	1,601	1,601	13,650	13,700	2,051	2,051	2,051	2,051
7,700	7,750	1,159	1,159	1,159	1,159	10,700	10,750	1,609	1,609	1,609	1,609	13,700	13,750	2,059	2,059	2,059	2,059
7,750	7,800	1,166	1,166	1,166	1,166	10,750	10,800	1,616	1,616	1,616	1,616	13,750	13,800	2,066	2,066	2,066	2,066
7,800	7,850	1,174	1,174	1,174	1,174	10,800	10,850	1,624	1,624	1,624	1,624	13,800	13,850	2,074	2,074	2,074	2,074
7,850	7,900	1,181	1,181	1,181	1,181	10,850	10,900	1,631	1,631	1,631	1,631	13,850	13,900	2,081	2,081	2,081	2,081
7,900	7,950	1,189	1,189	1,189	1,189	10,900	10,950	1,639	1,639	1,639	1,639	13,900	13,950	2,089	2,089	2,089	2,089
7,950	8,000	1,196	1,196	1,196	1,196	10,950	11,000	1,646	1,646	1,646	1,646	13,950	14,000	2,096	2,096	2,096	2,096

* This column must also be used by a qualifying widow(er).

Continued on next page

1997 Tax Table—*Continued*

14,000

If line 38 (taxable income) is— At least	But less than	Single	Married filing jointly *	Married filing separately	Head of a household
			Your tax is—		
14,000	14,050	2,104	2,104	2,104	2,104
14,050	14,100	2,111	2,111	2,111	2,111
14,100	14,150	2,119	2,119	2,119	2,119
14,150	14,200	2,126	2,126	2,126	2,126
14,200	14,250	2,134	2,134	2,134	2,134
14,250	14,300	2,141	2,141	2,141	2,141
14,300	14,350	2,149	2,149	2,149	2,149
14,350	14,400	2,156	2,156	2,156	2,156
14,400	14,450	2,164	2,164	2,164	2,164
14,450	14,500	2,171	2,171	2,171	2,171
14,500	14,550	2,179	2,179	2,179	2,179
14,550	14,600	2,186	2,186	2,186	2,186
14,600	14,650	2,194	2,194	2,194	2,194
14,650	14,700	2,201	2,201	2,201	2,201
14,700	14,750	2,209	2,209	2,209	2,209
14,750	14,800	2,216	2,216	2,216	2,216
14,800	14,850	2,224	2,224	2,224	2,224
14,850	14,900	2,231	2,231	2,231	2,231
14,900	14,950	2,239	2,239	2,239	2,239
14,950	15,000	2,246	2,246	2,246	2,246

15,000

At least	But less than	Single	Married filing jointly *	Married filing separately	Head of a household
15,000	15,050	2,254	2,254	2,254	2,254
15,050	15,100	2,261	2,261	2,261	2,261
15,100	15,150	2,269	2,269	2,269	2,269
15,150	15,200	2,276	2,276	2,276	2,276
15,200	15,250	2,284	2,284	2,284	2,284
15,250	15,300	2,291	2,291	2,291	2,291
15,300	15,350	2,299	2,299	2,299	2,299
15,350	15,400	2,306	2,306	2,306	2,306
15,400	15,450	2,314	2,314	2,314	2,314
15,450	15,500	2,321	2,321	2,321	2,321
15,500	15,550	2,329	2,329	2,329	2,329
15,550	15,600	2,336	2,336	2,336	2,336
15,600	15,650	2,344	2,344	2,344	2,344
15,650	15,700	2,351	2,351	2,351	2,351
15,700	15,750	2,359	2,359	2,359	2,359
15,750	15,800	2,366	2,366	2,366	2,366
15,800	15,850	2,374	2,374	2,374	2,374
15,850	15,900	2,381	2,381	2,381	2,381
15,900	15,950	2,389	2,389	2,389	2,389
15,950	16,000	2,396	2,396	2,396	2,396

16,000

At least	But less than	Single	Married filing jointly *	Married filing separately	Head of a household
16,000	16,050	2,404	2,404	2,404	2,404
16,050	16,100	2,411	2,411	2,411	2,411
16,100	16,150	2,419	2,419	2,419	2,419
16,150	16,200	2,426	2,426	2,426	2,426
16,200	16,250	2,434	2,434	2,434	2,434
16,250	16,300	2,441	2,441	2,441	2,441
16,300	16,350	2,449	2,449	2,449	2,449
16,350	16,400	2,456	2,456	2,456	2,456
16,400	16,450	2,464	2,464	2,464	2,464
16,450	16,500	2,471	2,471	2,471	2,471
16,500	16,550	2,479	2,479	2,479	2,479
16,550	16,600	2,486	2,486	2,486	2,486
16,600	16,650	2,494	2,494	2,494	2,494
16,650	16,700	2,501	2,501	2,501	2,501
16,700	16,750	2,509	2,509	2,509	2,509
16,750	16,800	2,516	2,516	2,516	2,516
16,800	16,850	2,524	2,524	2,524	2,524
16,850	16,900	2,531	2,531	2,531	2,531
16,900	16,950	2,539	2,539	2,539	2,539
16,950	17,000	2,546	2,546	2,546	2,546

17,000

At least	But less than	Single	Married filing jointly *	Married filing separately	Head of a household
17,000	17,050	2,554	2,554	2,554	2,554
17,050	17,100	2,561	2,561	2,561	2,561
17,100	17,150	2,569	2,569	2,569	2,569
17,150	17,200	2,576	2,576	2,576	2,576
17,200	17,250	2,584	2,584	2,584	2,584
17,250	17,300	2,591	2,591	2,591	2,591
17,300	17,350	2,599	2,599	2,599	2,599
17,350	17,400	2,606	2,606	2,606	2,606
17,400	17,450	2,614	2,614	2,614	2,614
17,450	17,500	2,621	2,621	2,621	2,621
17,500	17,550	2,629	2,629	2,629	2,629
17,550	17,600	2,636	2,636	2,636	2,636
17,600	17,650	2,644	2,644	2,644	2,644
17,650	17,700	2,651	2,651	2,651	2,651
17,700	17,750	2,659	2,659	2,659	2,659
17,750	17,800	2,666	2,666	2,666	2,666
17,800	17,850	2,674	2,674	2,674	2,674
17,850	17,900	2,681	2,681	2,681	2,681
17,900	17,950	2,689	2,689	2,689	2,689
17,950	18,000	2,696	2,696	2,696	2,696

18,000

At least	But less than	Single	Married filing jointly *	Married filing separately	Head of a household
18,000	18,050	2,704	2,704	2,704	2,704
18,050	18,100	2,711	2,711	2,711	2,711
18,100	18,150	2,719	2,719	2,719	2,719
18,150	18,200	2,726	2,726	2,726	2,726
18,200	18,250	2,734	2,734	2,734	2,734
18,250	18,300	2,741	2,741	2,741	2,741
18,300	18,350	2,749	2,749	2,749	2,749
18,350	18,400	2,756	2,756	2,756	2,756
18,400	18,450	2,764	2,764	2,764	2,764
18,450	18,500	2,771	2,771	2,771	2,771
18,500	18,550	2,779	2,779	2,779	2,779
18,550	18,600	2,786	2,786	2,786	2,786
18,600	18,650	2,794	2,794	2,794	2,794
18,650	18,700	2,801	2,801	2,801	2,801
18,700	18,750	2,809	2,809	2,809	2,809
18,750	18,800	2,816	2,816	2,816	2,816
18,800	18,850	2,824	2,824	2,824	2,824
18,850	18,900	2,831	2,831	2,831	2,831
18,900	18,950	2,839	2,839	2,839	2,839
18,950	19,000	2,846	2,846	2,846	2,846

19,000

At least	But less than	Single	Married filing jointly *	Married filing separately	Head of a household
19,000	19,050	2,854	2,854	2,854	2,854
19,050	19,100	2,861	2,861	2,861	2,861
19,100	19,150	2,869	2,869	2,869	2,869
19,150	19,200	2,876	2,876	2,876	2,876
19,200	19,250	2,884	2,884	2,884	2,884
19,250	19,300	2,891	2,891	2,891	2,891
19,300	19,350	2,899	2,899	2,899	2,899
19,350	19,400	2,906	2,906	2,906	2,906
19,400	19,450	2,914	2,914	2,914	2,914
19,450	19,500	2,921	2,921	2,921	2,921
19,500	19,550	2,929	2,929	2,929	2,929
19,550	19,600	2,936	2,936	2,936	2,936
19,600	19,650	2,944	2,944	2,944	2,944
19,650	19,700	2,951	2,951	2,951	2,951
19,700	19,750	2,959	2,959	2,959	2,959
19,750	19,800	2,966	2,966	2,966	2,966
19,800	19,850	2,974	2,974	2,974	2,974
19,850	19,900	2,981	2,981	2,981	2,981
19,900	19,950	2,989	2,989	2,989	2,989
19,950	20,000	2,996	2,996	2,996	2,996

20,000

At least	But less than	Single	Married filing jointly *	Married filing separately	Head of a household
20,000	20,050	3,004	3,004	3,004	3,004
20,050	20,100	3,011	3,011	3,011	3,011
20,100	20,150	3,019	3,019	3,019	3,019
20,150	20,200	3,026	3,026	3,026	3,026
20,200	20,250	3,034	3,034	3,034	3,034
20,250	20,300	3,041	3,041	3,041	3,041
20,300	20,350	3,049	3,049	3,049	3,049
20,350	20,400	3,056	3,056	3,056	3,056
20,400	20,450	3,064	3,064	3,064	3,064
20,450	20,500	3,071	3,071	3,071	3,071
20,500	20,550	3,079	3,079	3,079	3,079
20,550	20,600	3,086	3,086	3,086	3,086
20,600	20,650	3,094	3,094	3,097	3,094
20,650	20,700	3,101	3,101	3,111	3,101
20,700	20,750	3,109	3,109	3,125	3,109
20,750	20,800	3,116	3,116	3,139	3,116
20,800	20,850	3,124	3,124	3,153	3,124
20,850	20,900	3,131	3,131	3,167	3,131
20,900	20,950	3,139	3,139	3,181	3,139
20,950	21,000	3,146	3,146	3,195	3,146

21,000

At least	But less than	Single	Married filing jointly *	Married filing separately	Head of a household
21,000	21,050	3,154	3,154	3,209	3,154
21,050	21,100	3,161	3,161	3,223	3,161
21,100	21,150	3,169	3,169	3,237	3,169
21,150	21,200	3,176	3,176	3,251	3,176
21,200	21,250	3,184	3,184	3,265	3,184
21,250	21,300	3,191	3,191	3,279	3,191
21,300	21,350	3,199	3,199	3,293	3,199
21,350	21,400	3,206	3,206	3,307	3,206
21,400	21,450	3,214	3,214	3,321	3,214
21,450	21,500	3,221	3,221	3,335	3,221
21,500	21,550	3,229	3,229	3,349	3,229
21,550	21,600	3,236	3,236	3,363	3,236
21,600	21,650	3,244	3,244	3,377	3,244
21,650	21,700	3,251	3,251	3,391	3,251
21,700	21,750	3,259	3,259	3,405	3,259
21,750	21,800	3,266	3,266	3,419	3,266
21,800	21,850	3,274	3,274	3,433	3,274
21,850	21,900	3,281	3,281	3,447	3,281
21,900	21,950	3,289	3,289	3,461	3,289
21,950	22,000	3,296	3,296	3,475	3,296

22,000

At least	But less than	Single	Married filing jointly *	Married filing separately	Head of a household
22,000	22,050	3,304	3,304	3,489	3,304
22,050	22,100	3,311	3,311	3,503	3,311
22,100	22,150	3,319	3,319	3,517	3,319
22,150	22,200	3,326	3,326	3,531	3,326
22,200	22,250	3,334	3,334	3,545	3,334
22,250	22,300	3,341	3,341	3,559	3,341
22,300	22,350	3,349	3,349	3,573	3,349
22,350	22,400	3,356	3,356	3,587	3,356
22,400	22,450	3,364	3,364	3,601	3,364
22,450	22,500	3,371	3,371	3,615	3,371
22,500	22,550	3,379	3,379	3,629	3,379
22,550	22,600	3,386	3,386	3,643	3,386
22,600	22,650	3,394	3,394	3,657	3,394
22,650	22,700	3,401	3,401	3,671	3,401
22,700	22,750	3,409	3,409	3,685	3,409
22,750	22,800	3,416	3,416	3,699	3,416
22,800	22,850	3,424	3,424	3,713	3,424
22,850	22,900	3,431	3,431	3,727	3,431
22,900	22,950	3,439	3,439	3,741	3,439
22,950	23,000	3,446	3,446	3,755	3,446

* This column must also be used by a qualifying widow(er).

Continued on next page

1997 Tax Table—*Continued*

23,000 / 24,000 / 25,000

If line 38 (taxable income) is— At least	But less than	Single	Married filing jointly *	Married filing separately	Head of a house-hold
23,000					
23,000	23,050	3,454	3,454	3,769	3,454
23,050	23,100	3,461	3,461	3,783	3,461
23,100	23,150	3,469	3,469	3,797	3,469
23,150	23,200	3,476	3,476	3,811	3,476
23,200	23,250	3,484	3,484	3,825	3,484
23,250	23,300	3,491	3,491	3,839	3,491
23,300	23,350	3,499	3,499	3,853	3,499
23,350	23,400	3,506	3,506	3,867	3,506
23,400	23,450	3,514	3,514	3,881	3,514
23,450	23,500	3,521	3,521	3,895	3,521
23,500	23,550	3,529	3,529	3,909	3,529
23,550	23,600	3,536	3,536	3,923	3,536
23,600	23,650	3,544	3,544	3,937	3,544
23,650	23,700	3,551	3,551	3,951	3,551
23,700	23,750	3,559	3,559	3,965	3,559
23,750	23,800	3,566	3,566	3,979	3,566
23,800	23,850	3,574	3,574	3,993	3,574
23,850	23,900	3,581	3,581	4,007	3,581
23,900	23,950	3,589	3,589	4,021	3,589
23,950	24,000	3,596	3,596	4,035	3,596
24,000					
24,000	24,050	3,604	3,604	4,049	3,604
24,050	24,100	3,611	3,611	4,063	3,611
24,100	24,150	3,619	3,619	4,077	3,619
24,150	24,200	3,626	3,626	4,091	3,626
24,200	24,250	3,634	3,634	4,105	3,634
24,250	24,300	3,641	3,641	4,119	3,641
24,300	24,350	3,649	3,649	4,133	3,649
24,350	24,400	3,656	3,656	4,147	3,656
24,400	24,450	3,664	3,664	4,161	3,664
24,450	24,500	3,671	3,671	4,175	3,671
24,500	24,550	3,679	3,679	4,189	3,679
24,550	24,600	3,686	3,686	4,203	3,686
24,600	24,650	3,694	3,694	4,217	3,694
24,650	24,700	3,705	3,701	4,231	3,701
24,700	24,750	3,719	3,709	4,245	3,709
24,750	24,800	3,733	3,716	4,259	3,716
24,800	24,850	3,747	3,724	4,273	3,724
24,850	24,900	3,761	3,731	4,287	3,731
24,900	24,950	3,775	3,739	4,301	3,739
24,950	25,000	3,789	3,746	4,315	3,746
25,000					
25,000	25,050	3,803	3,754	4,329	3,754
25,050	25,100	3,817	3,761	4,343	3,761
25,100	25,150	3,831	3,769	4,357	3,769
25,150	25,200	3,845	3,776	4,371	3,776
25,200	25,250	3,859	3,784	4,385	3,784
25,250	25,300	3,873	3,791	4,399	3,791
25,300	25,350	3,887	3,799	4,413	3,799
25,350	25,400	3,901	3,806	4,427	3,806
25,400	25,450	3,915	3,814	4,441	3,814
25,450	25,500	3,929	3,821	4,455	3,821
25,500	25,550	3,943	3,829	4,469	3,829
25,550	25,600	3,957	3,836	4,483	3,836
25,600	25,650	3,971	3,844	4,497	3,844
25,650	25,700	3,985	3,851	4,511	3,851
25,700	25,750	3,999	3,859	4,525	3,859
25,750	25,800	4,013	3,866	4,539	3,866
25,800	25,850	4,027	3,874	4,553	3,874
25,850	25,900	4,041	3,881	4,567	3,881
25,900	25,950	4,055	3,889	4,581	3,889
25,950	26,000	4,069	3,896	4,595	3,896

26,000 / 27,000 / 28,000

If line 38 (taxable income) is— At least	But less than	Single	Married filing jointly *	Married filing separately	Head of a house-hold
26,000					
26,000	26,050	4,083	3,904	4,609	3,904
26,050	26,100	4,097	3,911	4,623	3,911
26,100	26,150	4,111	3,919	4,637	3,919
26,150	26,200	4,125	3,926	4,651	3,926
26,200	26,250	4,139	3,934	4,665	3,934
26,250	26,300	4,153	3,941	4,679	3,941
26,300	26,350	4,167	3,949	4,693	3,949
26,350	26,400	4,181	3,956	4,707	3,956
26,400	26,450	4,195	3,964	4,721	3,964
26,450	26,500	4,209	3,971	4,735	3,971
26,500	26,550	4,223	3,979	4,749	3,979
26,550	26,600	4,237	3,986	4,763	3,986
26,600	26,650	4,251	3,994	4,777	3,994
26,650	26,700	4,265	4,001	4,791	4,001
26,700	26,750	4,279	4,009	4,805	4,009
26,750	26,800	4,293	4,016	4,819	4,016
26,800	26,850	4,307	4,024	4,833	4,024
26,850	26,900	4,321	4,031	4,847	4,031
26,900	26,950	4,335	4,039	4,861	4,039
26,950	27,000	4,349	4,046	4,875	4,046
27,000					
27,000	27,050	4,363	4,054	4,889	4,054
27,050	27,100	4,377	4,061	4,903	4,061
27,100	27,150	4,391	4,069	4,917	4,069
27,150	27,200	4,405	4,076	4,931	4,076
27,200	27,250	4,419	4,084	4,945	4,084
27,250	27,300	4,433	4,091	4,959	4,091
27,300	27,350	4,447	4,099	4,973	4,099
27,350	27,400	4,461	4,106	4,987	4,106
27,400	27,450	4,475	4,114	5,001	4,114
27,450	27,500	4,489	4,121	5,015	4,121
27,500	27,550	4,503	4,129	5,029	4,129
27,550	27,600	4,517	4,136	5,043	4,136
27,600	27,650	4,531	4,144	5,057	4,144
27,650	27,700	4,545	4,151	5,071	4,151
27,700	27,750	4,559	4,159	5,085	4,159
27,750	27,800	4,573	4,166	5,099	4,166
27,800	27,850	4,587	4,174	5,113	4,174
27,850	27,900	4,601	4,181	5,127	4,181
27,900	27,950	4,615	4,189	5,141	4,189
27,950	28,000	4,629	4,196	5,155	4,196
28,000					
28,000	28,050	4,643	4,204	5,169	4,204
28,050	28,100	4,657	4,211	5,183	4,211
28,100	28,150	4,671	4,219	5,197	4,219
28,150	28,200	4,685	4,226	5,211	4,226
28,200	28,250	4,699	4,234	5,225	4,234
28,250	28,300	4,713	4,241	5,239	4,241
28,300	28,350	4,727	4,249	5,253	4,249
28,350	28,400	4,741	4,256	5,267	4,256
28,400	28,450	4,755	4,264	5,281	4,264
28,450	28,500	4,769	4,271	5,295	4,271
28,500	28,550	4,783	4,279	5,309	4,279
28,550	28,600	4,797	4,286	5,323	4,286
28,600	28,650	4,811	4,294	5,337	4,294
28,650	28,700	4,825	4,301	5,351	4,301
28,700	28,750	4,839	4,309	5,365	4,309
28,750	28,800	4,853	4,316	5,379	4,316
28,800	28,850	4,867	4,324	5,393	4,324
28,850	28,900	4,881	4,331	5,407	4,331
28,900	28,950	4,895	4,339	5,421	4,339
28,950	29,000	4,909	4,346	5,435	4,346

29,000 / 30,000 / 31,000

If line 38 (taxable income) is— At least	But less than	Single	Married filing jointly *	Married filing separately	Head of a house-hold
29,000					
29,000	29,050	4,923	4,354	5,449	4,354
29,050	29,100	4,937	4,361	5,463	4,361
29,100	29,150	4,951	4,369	5,477	4,369
29,150	29,200	4,965	4,376	5,491	4,376
29,200	29,250	4,979	4,384	5,505	4,384
29,250	29,300	4,993	4,391	5,519	4,391
29,300	29,350	5,007	4,399	5,533	4,399
29,350	29,400	5,021	4,406	5,547	4,406
29,400	29,450	5,035	4,414	5,561	4,414
29,450	29,500	5,049	4,421	5,575	4,421
29,500	29,550	5,063	4,429	5,589	4,429
29,550	29,600	5,077	4,436	5,603	4,436
29,600	29,650	5,091	4,444	5,617	4,444
29,650	29,700	5,105	4,451	5,631	4,451
29,700	29,750	5,119	4,459	5,645	4,459
29,750	29,800	5,133	4,466	5,659	4,466
29,800	29,850	5,147	4,474	5,673	4,474
29,850	29,900	5,161	4,481	5,687	4,481
29,900	29,950	5,175	4,489	5,701	4,489
29,950	30,000	5,189	4,496	5,715	4,496
30,000					
30,000	30,050	5,203	4,504	5,729	4,504
30,050	30,100	5,217	4,511	5,743	4,511
30,100	30,150	5,231	4,519	5,757	4,519
30,150	30,200	5,245	4,526	5,771	4,526
30,200	30,250	5,259	4,534	5,785	4,534
30,250	30,300	5,273	4,541	5,799	4,541
30,300	30,350	5,287	4,549	5,813	4,549
30,350	30,400	5,301	4,556	5,827	4,556
30,400	30,450	5,315	4,564	5,841	4,564
30,450	30,500	5,329	4,571	5,855	4,571
30,500	30,550	5,343	4,579	5,869	4,579
30,550	30,600	5,357	4,586	5,883	4,586
30,600	30,650	5,371	4,594	5,897	4,594
30,650	30,700	5,385	4,601	5,911	4,601
30,700	30,750	5,399	4,609	5,925	4,609
30,750	30,800	5,413	4,616	5,939	4,616
30,800	30,850	5,427	4,624	5,953	4,624
30,850	30,900	5,441	4,631	5,967	4,631
30,900	30,950	5,455	4,639	5,981	4,639
30,950	31,000	5,469	4,646	5,995	4,646
31,000					
31,000	31,050	5,483	4,654	6,009	4,654
31,050	31,100	5,497	4,661	6,023	4,661
31,100	31,150	5,511	4,669	6,037	4,669
31,150	31,200	5,525	4,676	6,051	4,676
31,200	31,250	5,539	4,684	6,065	4,684
31,250	31,300	5,553	4,691	6,079	4,691
31,300	31,350	5,567	4,699	6,093	4,699
31,350	31,400	5,581	4,706	6,107	4,706
31,400	31,450	5,595	4,714	6,121	4,714
31,450	31,500	5,609	4,721	6,135	4,721
31,500	31,550	5,623	4,729	6,149	4,729
31,550	31,600	5,637	4,736	6,163	4,736
31,600	31,650	5,651	4,744	6,177	4,744
31,650	31,700	5,665	4,751	6,191	4,751
31,700	31,750	5,679	4,759	6,205	4,759
31,750	31,800	5,693	4,766	6,219	4,766
31,800	31,850	5,707	4,774	6,233	4,774
31,850	31,900	5,721	4,781	6,247	4,781
31,900	31,950	5,735	4,789	6,261	4,789
31,950	32,000	5,749	4,796	6,275	4,796

* This column must also be used by a qualifying widow(er).

Continued on next page

1997 Tax Table—Continued

If line 38 (taxable income) is—		And you are—			
At least	But less than	Single	Married filing jointly *	Married filing separately	Head of a house-hold
		Your tax is—			

32,000

At least	But less than	Single	Married filing jointly *	Married filing separately	Head of a house-hold
32,000	32,050	5,763	4,804	6,289	4,804
32,050	32,100	5,777	4,811	6,303	4,811
32,100	32,150	5,791	4,819	6,317	4,819
32,150	32,200	5,805	4,826	6,331	4,826
32,200	32,250	5,819	4,834	6,345	4,834
32,250	32,300	5,833	4,841	6,359	4,841
32,300	32,350	5,847	4,849	6,373	4,849
32,350	32,400	5,861	4,856	6,387	4,856
32,400	32,450	5,875	4,864	6,401	4,864
32,450	32,500	5,889	4,871	6,415	4,871
32,500	32,550	5,903	4,879	6,429	4,879
32,550	32,600	5,917	4,886	6,443	4,886
32,600	32,650	5,931	4,894	6,457	4,894
32,650	32,700	5,945	4,901	6,471	4,901
32,700	32,750	5,959	4,909	6,485	4,909
32,750	32,800	5,973	4,916	6,499	4,916
32,800	32,850	5,987	4,924	6,513	4,924
32,850	32,900	6,001	4,931	6,527	4,931
32,900	32,950	6,015	4,939	6,541	4,939
32,950	33,000	6,029	4,946	6,555	4,946

33,000

At least	But less than	Single	Married filing jointly *	Married filing separately	Head of a house-hold
33,000	33,050	6,043	4,954	6,569	4,954
33,050	33,100	6,057	4,961	6,583	4,965
33,100	33,150	6,071	4,969	6,597	4,979
33,150	33,200	6,085	4,976	6,611	4,993
33,200	33,250	6,099	4,984	6,625	5,007
33,250	33,300	6,113	4,991	6,639	5,021
33,300	33,350	6,127	4,999	6,653	5,035
33,350	33,400	6,141	5,006	6,667	5,049
33,400	33,450	6,155	5,014	6,681	5,063
33,450	33,500	6,169	5,021	6,695	5,077
33,500	33,550	6,183	5,029	6,709	5,091
33,550	33,600	6,197	5,036	6,723	5,105
33,600	33,650	6,211	5,044	6,737	5,119
33,650	33,700	6,225	5,051	6,751	5,133
33,700	33,750	6,239	5,059	6,765	5,147
33,750	33,800	6,253	5,066	6,779	5,161
33,800	33,850	6,267	5,074	6,793	5,175
33,850	33,900	6,281	5,081	6,807	5,189
33,900	33,950	6,295	5,089	6,821	5,203
33,950	34,000	6,309	5,096	6,835	5,217

34,000

At least	But less than	Single	Married filing jointly *	Married filing separately	Head of a house-hold
34,000	34,050	6,323	5,104	6,849	5,231
34,050	34,100	6,337	5,111	6,863	5,245
34,100	34,150	6,351	5,119	6,877	5,259
34,150	34,200	6,365	5,126	6,891	5,273
34,200	34,250	6,379	5,134	6,905	5,287
34,250	34,300	6,393	5,141	6,919	5,301
34,300	34,350	6,407	5,149	6,933	5,315
34,350	34,400	6,421	5,156	6,947	5,329
34,400	34,450	6,435	5,164	6,961	5,343
34,450	34,500	6,449	5,171	6,975	5,357
34,500	34,550	6,463	5,179	6,989	5,371
34,550	34,600	6,477	5,186	7,003	5,385
34,600	34,650	6,491	5,194	7,017	5,399
34,650	34,700	6,505	5,201	7,031	5,413
34,700	34,750	6,519	5,209	7,045	5,427
34,750	34,800	6,533	5,216	7,059	5,441
34,800	34,850	6,547	5,224	7,073	5,455
34,850	34,900	6,561	5,231	7,087	5,469
34,900	34,950	6,575	5,239	7,101	5,483
34,950	35,000	6,589	5,246	7,115	5,497

35,000

At least	But less than	Single	Married filing jointly *	Married filing separately	Head of a house-hold
35,000	35,050	6,603	5,254	7,129	5,511
35,050	35,100	6,617	5,261	7,143	5,525
35,100	35,150	6,631	5,269	7,157	5,539
35,150	35,200	6,645	5,276	7,171	5,553
35,200	35,250	6,659	5,284	7,185	5,567
35,250	35,300	6,673	5,291	7,199	5,581
35,300	35,350	6,687	5,299	7,213	5,595
35,350	35,400	6,701	5,306	7,227	5,609
35,400	35,450	6,715	5,314	7,241	5,623
35,450	35,500	6,729	5,321	7,255	5,637
35,500	35,550	6,743	5,329	7,269	5,651
35,550	35,600	6,757	5,336	7,283	5,665
35,600	35,650	6,771	5,344	7,297	5,679
35,650	35,700	6,785	5,351	7,311	5,693
35,700	35,750	6,799	5,359	7,325	5,707
35,750	35,800	6,813	5,366	7,339	5,721
35,800	35,850	6,827	5,374	7,353	5,735
35,850	35,900	6,841	5,381	7,367	5,749
35,900	35,950	6,855	5,389	7,381	5,763
35,950	36,000	6,869	5,396	7,395	5,777

36,000

At least	But less than	Single	Married filing jointly *	Married filing separately	Head of a house-hold
36,000	36,050	6,883	5,404	7,409	5,791
36,050	36,100	6,897	5,411	7,423	5,805
36,100	36,150	6,911	5,419	7,437	5,819
36,150	36,200	6,925	5,426	7,451	5,833
36,200	36,250	6,939	5,434	7,465	5,847
36,250	36,300	6,953	5,441	7,479	5,861
36,300	36,350	6,967	5,449	7,493	5,875
36,350	36,400	6,981	5,456	7,507	5,889
36,400	36,450	6,995	5,464	7,521	5,903
36,450	36,500	7,009	5,471	7,535	5,917
36,500	36,550	7,023	5,479	7,549	5,931
36,550	36,600	7,037	5,486	7,563	5,945
36,600	36,650	7,051	5,494	7,577	5,959
36,650	36,700	7,065	5,501	7,591	5,973
36,700	36,750	7,079	5,509	7,605	5,987
36,750	36,800	7,093	5,516	7,619	6,001
36,800	36,850	7,107	5,524	7,633	6,015
36,850	36,900	7,121	5,531	7,647	6,029
36,900	36,950	7,135	5,539	7,661	6,043
36,950	37,000	7,149	5,546	7,675	6,057

37,000

At least	But less than	Single	Married filing jointly *	Married filing separately	Head of a house-hold
37,000	37,050	7,163	5,554	7,689	6,071
37,050	37,100	7,177	5,561	7,703	6,085
37,100	37,150	7,191	5,569	7,717	6,099
37,150	37,200	7,205	5,576	7,731	6,113
37,200	37,250	7,219	5,584	7,745	6,127
37,250	37,300	7,233	5,591	7,759	6,141
37,300	37,350	7,247	5,599	7,773	6,155
37,350	37,400	7,261	5,606	7,787	6,169
37,400	37,450	7,275	5,614	7,801	6,183
37,450	37,500	7,289	5,621	7,815	6,197
37,500	37,550	7,303	5,629	7,829	6,211
37,550	37,600	7,317	5,636	7,843	6,225
37,600	37,650	7,331	5,644	7,857	6,239
37,650	37,700	7,345	5,651	7,871	6,253
37,700	37,750	7,359	5,659	7,885	6,267
37,750	37,800	7,373	5,666	7,899	6,281
37,800	37,850	7,387	5,674	7,913	6,295
37,850	37,900	7,401	5,681	7,927	6,309
37,900	37,950	7,415	5,689	7,941	6,323
37,950	38,000	7,429	5,696	7,955	6,337

38,000

At least	But less than	Single	Married filing jointly *	Married filing separately	Head of a house-hold
38,000	38,050	7,443	5,704	7,969	6,351
38,050	38,100	7,457	5,711	7,983	6,365
38,100	38,150	7,471	5,719	7,997	6,379
38,150	38,200	7,485	5,726	8,011	6,393
38,200	38,250	7,499	5,734	8,025	6,407
38,250	38,300	7,513	5,741	8,039	6,421
38,300	38,350	7,527	5,749	8,053	6,435
38,350	38,400	7,541	5,756	8,067	6,449
38,400	38,450	7,555	5,764	8,081	6,463
38,450	38,500	7,569	5,771	8,095	6,477
38,500	38,550	7,583	5,779	8,109	6,491
38,550	38,600	7,597	5,786	8,123	6,505
38,600	38,650	7,611	5,794	8,137	6,519
38,650	38,700	7,625	5,801	8,151	6,533
38,700	38,750	7,639	5,809	8,165	6,547
38,750	38,800	7,653	5,816	8,179	6,561
38,800	38,850	7,667	5,824	8,193	6,575
38,850	38,900	7,681	5,831	8,207	6,589
38,900	38,950	7,695	5,839	8,221	6,603
38,950	39,000	7,709	5,846	8,235	6,617

39,000

At least	But less than	Single	Married filing jointly *	Married filing separately	Head of a house-hold
39,000	39,050	7,723	5,854	8,249	6,631
39,050	39,100	7,737	5,861	8,263	6,645
39,100	39,150	7,751	5,869	8,277	6,659
39,150	39,200	7,765	5,876	8,291	6,673
39,200	39,250	7,779	5,884	8,305	6,687
39,250	39,300	7,793	5,891	8,319	6,701
39,300	39,350	7,807	5,899	8,333	6,715
39,350	39,400	7,821	5,906	8,347	6,729
39,400	39,450	7,835	5,914	8,361	6,743
39,450	39,500	7,849	5,921	8,375	6,757
39,500	39,550	7,863	5,929	8,389	6,771
39,550	39,600	7,877	5,936	8,403	6,785
39,600	39,650	7,891	5,944	8,417	6,799
39,650	39,700	7,905	5,951	8,431	6,813
39,700	39,750	7,919	5,959	8,445	6,827
39,750	39,800	7,933	5,966	8,459	6,841
39,800	39,850	7,947	5,974	8,473	6,855
39,850	39,900	7,961	5,981	8,487	6,869
39,900	39,950	7,975	5,989	8,501	6,883
39,950	40,000	7,989	5,996	8,515	6,897

40,000

At least	But less than	Single	Married filing jointly *	Married filing separately	Head of a house-hold
40,000	40,050	8,003	6,004	8,529	6,911
40,050	40,100	8,017	6,011	8,543	6,925
40,100	40,150	8,031	6,019	8,557	6,939
40,150	40,200	8,045	6,026	8,571	6,953
40,200	40,250	8,059	6,034	8,585	6,967
40,250	40,300	8,073	6,041	8,599	6,981
40,300	40,350	8,087	6,049	8,613	6,995
40,350	40,400	8,101	6,056	8,627	7,009
40,400	40,450	8,115	6,064	8,641	7,023
40,450	40,500	8,129	6,071	8,655	7,037
40,500	40,550	8,143	6,079	8,669	7,051
40,550	40,600	8,157	6,086	8,683	7,065
40,600	40,650	8,171	6,094	8,697	7,079
40,650	40,700	8,185	6,101	8,711	7,093
40,700	40,750	8,199	6,109	8,725	7,107
40,750	40,800	8,213	6,116	8,739	7,121
40,800	40,850	8,227	6,124	8,753	7,135
40,850	40,900	8,241	6,131	8,767	7,149
40,900	40,950	8,255	6,139	8,781	7,163
40,950	41,000	8,269	6,146	8,795	7,177

* This column must also be used by a qualifying widow(er).

Continued on next page

1997 Tax Table—Continued

41,000 / 42,000 / 43,000

If line 38 (taxable income) is— At least	But less than	Single	Married filing jointly *	Married filing separately	Head of a household
41,000				Your tax is—	
41,000	41,050	8,283	6,154	8,809	7,191
41,050	41,100	8,297	6,161	8,823	7,205
41,100	41,150	8,311	6,169	8,837	7,219
41,150	41,200	8,325	6,176	8,851	7,233
41,200	41,250	8,339	6,187	8,865	7,247
41,250	41,300	8,353	6,201	8,879	7,261
41,300	41,350	8,367	6,215	8,893	7,275
41,350	41,400	8,381	6,229	8,907	7,289
41,400	41,450	8,395	6,243	8,921	7,303
41,450	41,500	8,409	6,257	8,935	7,317
41,500	41,550	8,423	6,271	8,949	7,331
41,550	41,600	8,437	6,285	8,963	7,345
41,600	41,650	8,451	6,299	8,977	7,359
41,650	41,700	8,465	6,313	8,991	7,373
41,700	41,750	8,479	6,327	9,005	7,387
41,750	41,800	8,493	6,341	9,019	7,401
41,800	41,850	8,507	6,355	9,033	7,415
41,850	41,900	8,521	6,369	9,047	7,429
41,900	41,950	8,535	6,383	9,061	7,443
41,950	42,000	8,549	6,397	9,075	7,457
42,000					
42,000	42,050	8,563	6,411	9,089	7,471
42,050	42,100	8,577	6,425	9,103	7,485
42,100	42,150	8,591	6,439	9,117	7,499
42,150	42,200	8,605	6,453	9,131	7,513
42,200	42,250	8,619	6,467	9,145	7,527
42,250	42,300	8,633	6,481	9,159	7,541
42,300	42,350	8,647	6,495	9,173	7,555
42,350	42,400	8,661	6,509	9,187	7,569
42,400	42,450	8,675	6,523	9,201	7,583
42,450	42,500	8,689	6,537	9,215	7,597
42,500	42,550	8,703	6,551	9,229	7,611
42,550	42,600	8,717	6,565	9,243	7,625
42,600	42,650	8,731	6,579	9,257	7,639
42,650	42,700	8,745	6,593	9,271	7,653
42,700	42,750	8,759	6,607	9,285	7,667
42,750	42,800	8,773	6,621	9,299	7,681
42,800	42,850	8,787	6,635	9,313	7,695
42,850	42,900	8,801	6,649	9,327	7,709
42,900	42,950	8,815	6,663	9,341	7,723
42,950	43,000	8,829	6,677	9,355	7,737
43,000					
43,000	43,050	8,843	6,691	9,369	7,751
43,050	43,100	8,857	6,705	9,383	7,765
43,100	43,150	8,871	6,719	9,397	7,779
43,150	43,200	8,885	6,733	9,411	7,793
43,200	43,250	8,899	6,747	9,425	7,807
43,250	43,300	8,913	6,761	9,439	7,821
43,300	43,350	8,927	6,775	9,453	7,835
43,350	43,400	8,941	6,789	9,467	7,849
43,400	43,450	8,955	6,803	9,481	7,863
43,450	43,500	8,969	6,817	9,495	7,877
43,500	43,550	8,983	6,831	9,509	7,891
43,550	43,600	8,997	6,845	9,523	7,905
43,600	43,650	9,011	6,859	9,537	7,919
43,650	43,700	9,025	6,873	9,551	7,933
43,700	43,750	9,039	6,887	9,565	7,947
43,750	43,800	9,053	6,901	9,579	7,961
43,800	43,850	9,067	6,915	9,593	7,975
43,850	43,900	9,081	6,929	9,607	7,989
43,900	43,950	9,095	6,943	9,621	8,003
43,950	44,000	9,109	6,957	9,635	8,017

44,000 / 45,000 / 46,000

If line 38 (taxable income) is— At least	But less than	Single	Married filing jointly *	Married filing separately	Head of a household
44,000				Your tax is—	
44,000	44,050	9,123	6,971	9,649	8,031
44,050	44,100	9,137	6,985	9,663	8,045
44,100	44,150	9,151	6,999	9,677	8,059
44,150	44,200	9,165	7,013	9,691	8,073
44,200	44,250	9,179	7,027	9,705	8,087
44,250	44,300	9,193	7,041	9,719	8,101
44,300	44,350	9,207	7,055	9,733	8,115
44,350	44,400	9,221	7,069	9,747	8,129
44,400	44,450	9,235	7,083	9,761	8,143
44,450	44,500	9,249	7,097	9,775	8,157
44,500	44,550	9,263	7,111	9,789	8,171
44,550	44,600	9,277	7,125	9,803	8,185
44,600	44,650	9,291	7,139	9,817	8,199
44,650	44,700	9,305	7,153	9,831	8,213
44,700	44,750	9,319	7,167	9,845	8,227
44,750	44,800	9,333	7,181	9,859	8,241
44,800	44,850	9,347	7,195	9,873	8,255
44,850	44,900	9,361	7,209	9,887	8,269
44,900	44,950	9,375	7,223	9,901	8,283
44,950	45,000	9,389	7,237	9,915	8,297
45,000					
45,000	45,050	9,403	7,251	9,929	8,311
45,050	45,100	9,417	7,265	9,943	8,325
45,100	45,150	9,431	7,279	9,957	8,339
45,150	45,200	9,445	7,293	9,971	8,353
45,200	45,250	9,459	7,307	9,985	8,367
45,250	45,300	9,473	7,321	9,999	8,381
45,300	45,350	9,487	7,335	10,013	8,395
45,350	45,400	9,501	7,349	10,027	8,409
45,400	45,450	9,515	7,363	10,041	8,423
45,450	45,500	9,529	7,377	10,055	8,437
45,500	45,550	9,543	7,391	10,069	8,451
45,550	45,600	9,557	7,405	10,083	8,465
45,600	45,650	9,571	7,419	10,097	8,479
45,650	45,700	9,585	7,433	10,111	8,493
45,700	45,750	9,599	7,447	10,125	8,507
45,750	45,800	9,613	7,461	10,139	8,521
45,800	45,850	9,627	7,475	10,153	8,535
45,850	45,900	9,641	7,489	10,167	8,549
45,900	45,950	9,655	7,503	10,181	8,563
45,950	46,000	9,669	7,517	10,195	8,577
46,000					
46,000	46,050	9,683	7,531	10,209	8,591
46,050	46,100	9,697	7,545	10,223	8,605
46,100	46,150	9,711	7,559	10,237	8,619
46,150	46,200	9,725	7,573	10,251	8,633
46,200	46,250	9,739	7,587	10,265	8,647
46,250	46,300	9,753	7,601	10,279	8,661
46,300	46,350	9,767	7,615	10,293	8,675
46,350	46,400	9,781	7,629	10,307	8,689
46,400	46,450	9,795	7,643	10,321	8,703
46,450	46,500	9,809	7,657	10,335	8,717
46,500	46,550	9,823	7,671	10,349	8,731
46,550	46,600	9,837	7,685	10,363	8,745
46,600	46,650	9,851	7,699	10,377	8,759
46,650	46,700	9,865	7,713	10,391	8,773
46,700	46,750	9,879	7,727	10,405	8,787
46,750	46,800	9,893	7,741	10,419	8,801
46,800	46,850	9,907	7,755	10,433	8,815
46,850	46,900	9,921	7,769	10,447	8,829
46,900	46,950	9,935	7,783	10,461	8,843
46,950	47,000	9,949	7,797	10,475	8,857

47,000 / 48,000 / 49,000

If line 38 (taxable income) is— At least	But less than	Single	Married filing jointly *	Married filing separately	Head of a household
47,000				Your tax is—	
47,000	47,050	9,963	7,811	10,489	8,871
47,050	47,100	9,977	7,825	10,503	8,885
47,100	47,150	9,991	7,839	10,517	8,899
47,150	47,200	10,005	7,853	10,531	8,913
47,200	47,250	10,019	7,867	10,545	8,927
47,250	47,300	10,033	7,881	10,559	8,941
47,300	47,350	10,047	7,895	10,573	8,955
47,350	47,400	10,061	7,909	10,587	8,969
47,400	47,450	10,075	7,923	10,601	8,983
47,450	47,500	10,089	7,937	10,615	8,997
47,500	47,550	10,103	7,951	10,629	9,011
47,550	47,600	10,117	7,965	10,643	9,025
47,600	47,650	10,131	7,979	10,657	9,039
47,650	47,700	10,145	7,993	10,671	9,053
47,700	47,750	10,159	8,007	10,685	9,067
47,750	47,800	10,173	8,021	10,699	9,081
47,800	47,850	10,187	8,035	10,713	9,095
47,850	47,900	10,201	8,049	10,727	9,109
47,900	47,950	10,215	8,063	10,741	9,123
47,950	48,000	10,229	8,077	10,755	9,137
48,000					
48,000	48,050	10,243	8,091	10,769	9,151
48,050	48,100	10,257	8,105	10,783	9,165
48,100	48,150	10,271	8,119	10,797	9,179
48,150	48,200	10,285	8,133	10,811	9,193
48,200	48,250	10,299	8,147	10,825	9,207
48,250	48,300	10,313	8,161	10,839	9,221
48,300	48,350	10,327	8,175	10,853	9,235
48,350	48,400	10,341	8,189	10,867	9,249
48,400	48,450	10,355	8,203	10,881	9,263
48,450	48,500	10,369	8,217	10,895	9,277
48,500	48,550	10,383	8,231	10,909	9,291
48,550	48,600	10,397	8,245	10,923	9,305
48,600	48,650	10,411	8,259	10,937	9,319
48,650	48,700	10,425	8,273	10,951	9,333
48,700	48,750	10,439	8,287	10,965	9,347
48,750	48,800	10,453	8,301	10,979	9,361
48,800	48,850	10,467	8,315	10,993	9,375
48,850	48,900	10,481	8,329	11,007	9,389
48,900	48,950	10,495	8,343	11,021	9,403
48,950	49,000	10,509	8,357	11,035	9,417
49,000					
49,000	49,050	10,523	8,371	11,049	9,431
49,050	49,100	10,537	8,385	11,063	9,445
49,100	49,150	10,551	8,399	11,077	9,459
49,150	49,200	10,565	8,413	11,091	9,473
49,200	49,250	10,579	8,427	11,105	9,487
49,250	49,300	10,593	8,441	11,119	9,501
49,300	49,350	10,607	8,455	11,133	9,515
49,350	49,400	10,621	8,469	11,147	9,529
49,400	49,450	10,635	8,483	11,161	9,543
49,450	49,500	10,649	8,497	11,175	9,557
49,500	49,550	10,663	8,511	11,189	9,571
49,550	49,600	10,677	8,525	11,203	9,585
49,600	49,650	10,691	8,539	11,217	9,599
49,650	49,700	10,705	8,553	11,231	9,613
49,700	49,750	10,719	8,567	11,245	9,627
49,750	49,800	10,733	8,581	11,259	9,641
49,800	49,850	10,747	8,595	11,274	9,655
49,850	49,900	10,761	8,609	11,289	9,669
49,900	49,950	10,775	8,623	11,305	9,683
49,950	50,000	10,789	8,637	11,320	9,697

* This column must also be used by a qualifying widow(er).

Continued on next page

1997 Tax Table—Continued

| If line 38 (taxable income) is— | | And you are— | | | | If line 38 (taxable income) is— | | And you are— | | | | If line 38 (taxable income) is— | | And you are— | | | |
At least	But less than	Single	Married filing jointly *	Married filing separately	Head of a household	At least	But less than	Single	Married filing jointly *	Married filing separately	Head of a household	At least	But less than	Single	Married filing jointly *	Married filing separately	Head of a household
					Your tax is—						Your tax is—						Your tax is—
50,000						**53,000**						**56,000**					
50,000	50,050	10,803	8,651	11,336	9,711	53,000	53,050	11,643	9,491	12,266	10,551	56,000	56,050	12,483	10,331	13,196	11,391
50,050	50,100	10,817	8,665	11,351	9,725	53,050	53,100	11,657	9,505	12,281	10,565	56,050	56,100	12,497	10,345	13,211	11,405
50,100	50,150	10,831	8,679	11,367	9,739	53,100	53,150	11,671	9,519	12,297	10,579	56,100	56,150	12,511	10,359	13,227	11,419
50,150	50,200	10,845	8,693	11,382	9,753	53,150	53,200	11,685	9,533	12,312	10,593	56,150	56,200	12,525	10,373	13,242	11,433
50,200	50,250	10,859	8,707	11,398	9,767	53,200	53,250	11,699	9,547	12,328	10,607	56,200	56,250	12,539	10,387	13,258	11,447
50,250	50,300	10,873	8,721	11,413	9,781	53,250	53,300	11,713	9,561	12,343	10,621	56,250	56,300	12,553	10,401	13,273	11,461
50,300	50,350	10,887	8,735	11,429	9,795	53,300	53,350	11,727	9,575	12,359	10,635	56,300	56,350	12,567	10,415	13,289	11,475
50,350	50,400	10,901	8,749	11,444	9,809	53,350	53,400	11,741	9,589	12,374	10,649	56,350	56,400	12,581	10,429	13,304	11,489
50,400	50,450	10,915	8,763	11,460	9,823	53,400	53,450	11,755	9,603	12,390	10,663	56,400	56,450	12,595	10,443	13,320	11,503
50,450	50,500	10,929	8,777	11,475	9,837	53,450	53,500	11,769	9,617	12,405	10,677	56,450	56,500	12,609	10,457	13,335	11,517
50,500	50,550	10,943	8,791	11,491	9,851	53,500	53,550	11,783	9,631	12,421	10,691	56,500	56,550	12,623	10,471	13,351	11,531
50,550	50,600	10,957	8,805	11,506	9,865	53,550	53,600	11,797	9,645	12,436	10,705	56,550	56,600	12,637	10,485	13,366	11,545
50,600	50,650	10,971	8,819	11,522	9,879	53,600	53,650	11,811	9,659	12,452	10,719	56,600	56,650	12,651	10,499	13,382	11,559
50,650	50,700	10,985	8,833	11,537	9,893	53,650	53,700	11,825	9,673	12,467	10,733	56,650	56,700	12,665	10,513	13,397	11,573
50,700	50,750	10,999	8,847	11,553	9,907	53,700	53,750	11,839	9,687	12,483	10,747	56,700	56,750	12,679	10,527	13,413	11,587
50,750	50,800	11,013	8,861	11,568	9,921	53,750	53,800	11,853	9,701	12,498	10,761	56,750	56,800	12,693	10,541	13,428	11,601
50,800	50,850	11,027	8,875	11,584	9,935	53,800	53,850	11,867	9,715	12,514	10,775	56,800	56,850	12,707	10,555	13,444	11,615
50,850	50,900	11,041	8,889	11,599	9,949	53,850	53,900	11,881	9,729	12,529	10,789	56,850	56,900	12,721	10,569	13,459	11,629
50,900	50,950	11,055	8,903	11,615	9,963	53,900	53,950	11,895	9,743	12,545	10,803	56,900	56,950	12,735	10,583	13,475	11,643
50,950	51,000	11,069	8,917	11,630	9,977	53,950	54,000	11,909	9,757	12,560	10,817	56,950	57,000	12,749	10,597	13,490	11,657
51,000						**54,000**						**57,000**					
51,000	51,050	11,083	8,931	11,646	9,991	54,000	54,050	11,923	9,771	12,576	10,831	57,000	57,050	12,763	10,611	13,506	11,671
51,050	51,100	11,097	8,945	11,661	10,005	54,050	54,100	11,937	9,785	12,591	10,845	57,050	57,100	12,777	10,625	13,521	11,685
51,100	51,150	11,111	8,959	11,677	10,019	54,100	54,150	11,951	9,799	12,607	10,859	57,100	57,150	12,791	10,639	13,537	11,699
51,150	51,200	11,125	8,973	11,692	10,033	54,150	54,200	11,965	9,813	12,622	10,873	57,150	57,200	12,805	10,653	13,552	11,713
51,200	51,250	11,139	8,987	11,708	10,047	54,200	54,250	11,979	9,827	12,638	10,887	57,200	57,250	12,819	10,667	13,568	11,727
51,250	51,300	11,153	9,001	11,723	10,061	54,250	54,300	11,993	9,841	12,653	10,901	57,250	57,300	12,833	10,681	13,583	11,741
51,300	51,350	11,167	9,015	11,739	10,075	54,300	54,350	12,007	9,855	12,669	10,915	57,300	57,350	12,847	10,695	13,599	11,755
51,350	51,400	11,181	9,029	11,754	10,089	54,350	54,400	12,021	9,869	12,684	10,929	57,350	57,400	12,861	10,709	13,614	11,769
51,400	51,450	11,195	9,043	11,770	10,103	54,400	54,450	12,035	9,883	12,700	10,943	57,400	57,450	12,875	10,723	13,630	11,783
51,450	51,500	11,209	9,057	11,785	10,117	54,450	54,500	12,049	9,897	12,715	10,957	57,450	57,500	12,889	10,737	13,645	11,797
51,500	51,550	11,223	9,071	11,801	10,131	54,500	54,550	12,063	9,911	12,731	10,971	57,500	57,550	12,903	10,751	13,661	11,811
51,550	51,600	11,237	9,085	11,816	10,145	54,550	54,600	12,077	9,925	12,746	10,985	57,550	57,600	12,917	10,765	13,676	11,825
51,600	51,650	11,251	9,099	11,832	10,159	54,600	54,650	12,091	9,939	12,762	10,999	57,600	57,650	12,931	10,779	13,692	11,839
51,650	51,700	11,265	9,113	11,847	10,173	54,650	54,700	12,105	9,953	12,777	11,013	57,650	57,700	12,945	10,793	13,707	11,853
51,700	51,750	11,279	9,127	11,863	10,187	54,700	54,750	12,119	9,967	12,793	11,027	57,700	57,750	12,959	10,807	13,723	11,867
51,750	51,800	11,293	9,141	11,878	10,201	54,750	54,800	12,133	9,981	12,808	11,041	57,750	57,800	12,973	10,821	13,738	11,881
51,800	51,850	11,307	9,155	11,894	10,215	54,800	54,850	12,147	9,995	12,824	11,055	57,800	57,850	12,987	10,835	13,754	11,895
51,850	51,900	11,321	9,169	11,909	10,229	54,850	54,900	12,161	10,009	12,839	11,069	57,850	57,900	13,001	10,849	13,769	11,909
51,900	51,950	11,335	9,183	11,925	10,243	54,900	54,950	12,175	10,023	12,855	11,083	57,900	57,950	13,015	10,863	13,785	11,923
51,950	52,000	11,349	9,197	11,940	10,257	54,950	55,000	12,189	10,037	12,870	11,097	57,950	58,000	13,029	10,877	13,800	11,937
52,000						**55,000**						**58,000**					
52,000	52,050	11,363	9,211	11,956	10,271	55,000	55,050	12,203	10,051	12,886	11,111	58,000	58,050	13,043	10,891	13,816	11,951
52,050	52,100	11,377	9,225	11,971	10,285	55,050	55,100	12,217	10,065	12,901	11,125	58,050	58,100	13,057	10,905	13,831	11,965
52,100	52,150	11,391	9,239	11,987	10,299	55,100	55,150	12,231	10,079	12,917	11,139	58,100	58,150	13,071	10,919	13,847	11,979
52,150	52,200	11,405	9,253	12,002	10,313	55,150	55,200	12,245	10,093	12,932	11,153	58,150	58,200	13,085	10,933	13,862	11,993
52,200	52,250	11,419	9,267	12,018	10,327	55,200	55,250	12,259	10,107	12,948	11,167	58,200	58,250	13,099	10,947	13,878	12,007
52,250	52,300	11,433	9,281	12,033	10,341	55,250	55,300	12,273	10,121	12,963	11,181	58,250	58,300	13,113	10,961	13,893	12,021
52,300	52,350	11,447	9,295	12,049	10,355	55,300	55,350	12,287	10,135	12,979	11,195	58,300	58,350	13,127	10,975	13,909	12,035
52,350	52,400	11,461	9,309	12,064	10,369	55,350	55,400	12,301	10,149	12,994	11,209	58,350	58,400	13,141	10,989	13,924	12,049
52,400	52,450	11,475	9,323	12,080	10,383	55,400	55,450	12,315	10,163	13,010	11,223	58,400	58,450	13,155	11,003	13,940	12,063
52,450	52,500	11,489	9,337	12,095	10,397	55,450	55,500	12,329	10,177	13,025	11,237	58,450	58,500	13,169	11,017	13,955	12,077
52,500	52,550	11,503	9,351	12,111	10,411	55,500	55,550	12,343	10,191	13,041	11,251	58,500	58,550	13,183	11,031	13,971	12,091
52,550	52,600	11,517	9,365	12,126	10,425	55,550	55,600	12,357	10,205	13,056	11,265	58,550	58,600	13,197	11,045	13,986	12,105
52,600	52,650	11,531	9,379	12,142	10,439	55,600	55,650	12,371	10,219	13,072	11,279	58,600	58,650	13,211	11,059	14,002	12,119
52,650	52,700	11,545	9,393	12,157	10,453	55,650	55,700	12,385	10,233	13,087	11,293	58,650	58,700	13,225	11,073	14,017	12,133
52,700	52,750	11,559	9,407	12,173	10,467	55,700	55,750	12,399	10,247	13,103	11,307	58,700	58,750	13,239	11,087	14,033	12,147
52,750	52,800	11,573	9,421	12,188	10,481	55,750	55,800	12,413	10,261	13,118	11,321	58,750	58,800	13,253	11,101	14,048	12,161
52,800	52,850	11,587	9,435	12,204	10,495	55,800	55,850	12,427	10,275	13,134	11,335	58,800	58,850	13,267	11,115	14,064	12,175
52,850	52,900	11,601	9,449	12,219	10,509	55,850	55,900	12,441	10,289	13,149	11,349	58,850	58,900	13,281	11,129	14,079	12,189
52,900	52,950	11,615	9,463	12,235	10,523	55,900	55,950	12,455	10,303	13,165	11,363	58,900	58,950	13,295	11,143	14,095	12,203
52,950	53,000	11,629	9,477	12,250	10,537	55,950	56,000	12,469	10,317	13,180	11,377	58,950	59,000	13,309	11,157	14,110	12,217

* This column must also be used by a qualifying widow(er).

Continued on next page

1997 Tax Table—Continued

If line 38 (taxable income) is— At least	But less than	Single	Married filing jointly *	Married filing separately	Head of a household
59,000					
59,000	59,050	13,323	11,171	14,126	12,231
59,050	59,100	13,337	11,185	14,141	12,245
59,100	59,150	13,351	11,199	14,157	12,259
59,150	59,200	13,365	11,213	14,172	12,273
59,200	59,250	13,379	11,227	14,188	12,287
59,250	59,300	13,393	11,241	14,203	12,301
59,300	59,350	13,407	11,255	14,219	12,315
59,350	59,400	13,421	11,269	14,234	12,329
59,400	59,450	13,435	11,283	14,250	12,343
59,450	59,500	13,449	11,297	14,265	12,357
59,500	59,550	13,463	11,311	14,281	12,371
59,550	59,600	13,477	11,325	14,296	12,385
59,600	59,650	13,491	11,339	14,312	12,399
59,650	59,700	13,505	11,353	14,327	12,413
59,700	59,750	13,519	11,367	14,343	12,427
59,750	59,800	13,533	11,381	14,358	12,441
59,800	59,850	13,549	11,395	14,374	12,455
59,850	59,900	13,564	11,409	14,389	12,469
59,900	59,950	13,580	11,423	14,405	12,483
59,950	60,000	13,595	11,437	14,420	12,497
60,000					
60,000	60,050	13,611	11,451	14,436	12,511
60,050	60,100	13,626	11,465	14,451	12,525
60,100	60,150	13,642	11,479	14,467	12,539
60,150	60,200	13,657	11,493	14,482	12,553
60,200	60,250	13,673	11,507	14,498	12,567
60,250	60,300	13,688	11,521	14,513	12,581
60,300	60,350	13,704	11,535	14,529	12,595
60,350	60,400	13,719	11,549	14,544	12,609
60,400	60,450	13,735	11,563	14,560	12,623
60,450	60,500	13,750	11,577	14,575	12,637
60,500	60,550	13,766	11,591	14,591	12,651
60,550	60,600	13,781	11,605	14,606	12,665
60,600	60,650	13,797	11,619	14,622	12,679
60,650	60,700	13,812	11,633	14,637	12,693
60,700	60,750	13,828	11,647	14,653	12,707
60,750	60,800	13,843	11,661	14,668	12,721
60,800	60,850	13,859	11,675	14,684	12,735
60,850	60,900	13,874	11,689	14,699	12,749
60,900	60,950	13,890	11,703	14,715	12,763
60,950	61,000	13,905	11,717	14,730	12,777
61,000					
61,000	61,050	13,921	11,731	14,746	12,791
61,050	61,100	13,936	11,745	14,761	12,805
61,100	61,150	13,952	11,759	14,777	12,819
61,150	61,200	13,967	11,773	14,792	12,833
61,200	61,250	13,983	11,787	14,808	12,847
61,250	61,300	13,998	11,801	14,823	12,861
61,300	61,350	14,014	11,815	14,839	12,875
61,350	61,400	14,029	11,829	14,854	12,889
61,400	61,450	14,045	11,843	14,870	12,903
61,450	61,500	14,060	11,857	14,885	12,917
61,500	61,550	14,076	11,871	14,901	12,931
61,550	61,600	14,091	11,885	14,916	12,945
61,600	61,650	14,107	11,899	14,932	12,959
61,650	61,700	14,122	11,913	14,947	12,973
61,700	61,750	14,138	11,927	14,963	12,987
61,750	61,800	14,153	11,941	14,978	13,001
61,800	61,850	14,169	11,955	14,994	13,015
61,850	61,900	14,184	11,969	15,009	13,029
61,900	61,950	14,200	11,983	15,025	13,043
61,950	62,000	14,215	11,997	15,040	13,057

If line 38 (taxable income) is— At least	But less than	Single	Married filing jointly *	Married filing separately	Head of a household
62,000					
62,000	62,050	14,231	12,011	15,056	13,071
62,050	62,100	14,246	12,025	15,071	13,085
62,100	62,150	14,262	12,039	15,087	13,099
62,150	62,200	14,277	12,053	15,102	13,113
62,200	62,250	14,293	12,067	15,118	13,127
62,250	62,300	14,308	12,081	15,133	13,141
62,300	62,350	14,324	12,095	15,149	13,155
62,350	62,400	14,339	12,109	15,164	13,169
62,400	62,450	14,355	12,123	15,180	13,183
62,450	62,500	14,370	12,137	15,195	13,197
62,500	62,550	14,386	12,151	15,211	13,211
62,550	62,600	14,401	12,165	15,226	13,225
62,600	62,650	14,417	12,179	15,242	13,239
62,650	62,700	14,432	12,193	15,257	13,253
62,700	62,750	14,448	12,207	15,273	13,267
62,750	62,800	14,463	12,221	15,288	13,281
62,800	62,850	14,479	12,235	15,304	13,295
62,850	62,900	14,494	12,249	15,319	13,309
62,900	62,950	14,510	12,263	15,335	13,323
62,950	63,000	14,525	12,277	15,350	13,337
63,000					
63,000	63,050	14,541	12,291	15,366	13,351
63,050	63,100	14,556	12,305	15,381	13,365
63,100	63,150	14,572	12,319	15,397	13,379
63,150	63,200	14,587	12,333	15,412	13,393
63,200	63,250	14,603	12,347	15,428	13,407
63,250	63,300	14,618	12,361	15,443	13,421
63,300	63,350	14,634	12,375	15,459	13,435
63,350	63,400	14,649	12,389	15,474	13,449
63,400	63,450	14,665	12,403	15,490	13,463
63,450	63,500	14,680	12,417	15,505	13,477
63,500	63,550	14,696	12,431	15,521	13,491
63,550	63,600	14,711	12,445	15,536	13,505
63,600	63,650	14,727	12,459	15,552	13,519
63,650	63,700	14,742	12,473	15,567	13,533
63,700	63,750	14,758	12,487	15,583	13,547
63,750	63,800	14,773	12,501	15,598	13,561
63,800	63,850	14,789	12,515	15,614	13,575
63,850	63,900	14,804	12,529	15,629	13,589
63,900	63,950	14,820	12,543	15,645	13,603
63,950	64,000	14,835	12,557	15,660	13,617
64,000					
64,000	64,050	14,851	12,571	15,676	13,631
64,050	64,100	14,866	12,585	15,691	13,645
64,100	64,150	14,882	12,599	15,707	13,659
64,150	64,200	14,897	12,613	15,722	13,673
64,200	64,250	14,913	12,627	15,738	13,687
64,250	64,300	14,928	12,641	15,753	13,701
64,300	64,350	14,944	12,655	15,769	13,715
64,350	64,400	14,959	12,669	15,784	13,729
64,400	64,450	14,975	12,683	15,800	13,743
64,450	64,500	14,990	12,697	15,815	13,757
64,500	64,550	15,006	12,711	15,831	13,771
64,550	64,600	15,021	12,725	15,846	13,785
64,600	64,650	15,037	12,739	15,862	13,799
64,650	64,700	15,052	12,753	15,877	13,813
64,700	64,750	15,068	12,767	15,893	13,827
64,750	64,800	15,083	12,781	15,908	13,841
64,800	64,850	15,099	12,795	15,924	13,855
64,850	64,900	15,114	12,809	15,939	13,869
64,900	64,950	15,130	12,823	15,955	13,883
64,950	65,000	15,145	12,837	15,970	13,897

If line 38 (taxable income) is— At least	But less than	Single	Married filing jointly *	Married filing separately	Head of a household
65,000					
65,000	65,050	15,161	12,851	15,986	13,911
65,050	65,100	15,176	12,865	16,001	13,925
65,100	65,150	15,192	12,879	16,017	13,939
65,150	65,200	15,207	12,893	16,032	13,953
65,200	65,250	15,223	12,907	16,048	13,967
65,250	65,300	15,238	12,921	16,063	13,981
65,300	65,350	15,254	12,935	16,079	13,995
65,350	65,400	15,269	12,949	16,094	14,009
65,400	65,450	15,285	12,963	16,110	14,023
65,450	65,500	15,300	12,977	16,125	14,037
65,500	65,550	15,316	12,991	16,141	14,051
65,550	65,600	15,331	13,005	16,156	14,065
65,600	65,650	15,347	13,019	16,172	14,079
65,650	65,700	15,362	13,033	16,187	14,093
65,700	65,750	15,378	13,047	16,203	14,107
65,750	65,800	15,393	13,061	16,218	14,121
65,800	65,850	15,409	13,075	16,234	14,135
65,850	65,900	15,424	13,089	16,249	14,149
65,900	65,950	15,440	13,103	16,265	14,163
65,950	66,000	15,455	13,117	16,280	14,177
66,000					
66,000	66,050	15,471	13,131	16,296	14,191
66,050	66,100	15,486	13,145	16,311	14,205
66,100	66,150	15,502	13,159	16,327	14,219
66,150	66,200	15,517	13,173	16,342	14,233
66,200	66,250	15,533	13,187	16,358	14,247
66,250	66,300	15,548	13,201	16,373	14,261
66,300	66,350	15,564	13,215	16,389	14,275
66,350	66,400	15,579	13,229	16,404	14,289
66,400	66,450	15,595	13,243	16,420	14,303
66,450	66,500	15,610	13,257	16,435	14,317
66,500	66,550	15,626	13,271	16,451	14,331
66,550	66,600	15,641	13,285	16,466	14,345
66,600	66,650	15,657	13,299	16,482	14,359
66,650	66,700	15,672	13,313	16,497	14,373
66,700	66,750	15,688	13,327	16,513	14,387
66,750	66,800	15,703	13,341	16,528	14,401
66,800	66,850	15,719	13,355	16,544	14,415
66,850	66,900	15,734	13,369	16,559	14,429
66,900	66,950	15,750	13,383	16,575	14,443
66,950	67,000	15,765	13,397	16,590	14,457
67,000					
67,000	67,050	15,781	13,411	16,606	14,471
67,050	67,100	15,796	13,425	16,621	14,485
67,100	67,150	15,812	13,439	16,637	14,499
67,150	67,200	15,827	13,453	16,652	14,513
67,200	67,250	15,843	13,467	16,668	14,527
67,250	67,300	15,858	13,481	16,683	14,541
67,300	67,350	15,874	13,495	16,699	14,555
67,350	67,400	15,889	13,509	16,714	14,569
67,400	67,450	15,905	13,523	16,730	14,583
67,450	67,500	15,920	13,537	16,745	14,597
67,500	67,550	15,936	13,551	16,761	14,611
67,550	67,600	15,951	13,565	16,776	14,625
67,600	67,650	15,967	13,579	16,792	14,639
67,650	67,700	15,982	13,593	16,807	14,653
67,700	67,750	15,998	13,607	16,823	14,667
67,750	67,800	16,013	13,621	16,838	14,681
67,800	67,850	16,029	13,635	16,854	14,695
67,850	67,900	16,044	13,649	16,869	14,709
67,900	67,950	16,060	13,663	16,885	14,723
67,950	68,000	16,075	13,677	16,900	14,737

* This column must also be used by a qualifying widow(er).

Continued on next page

1997 Tax Table—_Continued_

If line 38 (taxable income) is— At least	But less than	Single	Married filing jointly *	Married filing separately	Head of a household
68,000					
68,000	68,050	16,091	13,691	16,916	14,751
68,050	68,100	16,106	13,705	16,931	14,765
68,100	68,150	16,122	13,719	16,947	14,779
68,150	68,200	16,137	13,733	16,962	14,793
68,200	68,250	16,153	13,747	16,978	14,807
68,250	68,300	16,168	13,761	16,993	14,821
68,300	68,350	16,184	13,775	17,009	14,835
68,350	68,400	16,199	13,789	17,024	14,849
68,400	68,450	16,215	13,803	17,040	14,863
68,450	68,500	16,230	13,817	17,055	14,877
68,500	68,550	16,246	13,831	17,071	14,891
68,550	68,600	16,261	13,845	17,086	14,905
68,600	68,650	16,277	13,859	17,102	14,919
68,650	68,700	16,292	13,873	17,117	14,933
68,700	68,750	16,308	13,887	17,133	14,947
68,750	68,800	16,323	13,901	17,148	14,961
68,800	68,850	16,339	13,915	17,164	14,975
68,850	68,900	16,354	13,929	17,179	14,989
68,900	68,950	16,370	13,943	17,195	15,003
68,950	69,000	16,385	13,957	17,210	15,017
69,000					
69,000	69,050	16,401	13,971	17,226	15,031
69,050	69,100	16,416	13,985	17,241	15,045
69,100	69,150	16,432	13,999	17,257	15,059
69,150	69,200	16,447	14,013	17,272	15,073
69,200	69,250	16,463	14,027	17,288	15,087
69,250	69,300	16,478	14,041	17,303	15,101
69,300	69,350	16,494	14,055	17,319	15,115
69,350	69,400	16,509	14,069	17,334	15,129
69,400	69,450	16,525	14,083	17,350	15,143
69,450	69,500	16,540	14,097	17,365	15,157
69,500	69,550	16,556	14,111	17,381	15,171
69,550	69,600	16,571	14,125	17,396	15,185
69,600	69,650	16,587	14,139	17,412	15,199
69,650	69,700	16,602	14,153	17,427	15,213
69,700	69,750	16,618	14,167	17,443	15,227
69,750	69,800	16,633	14,181	17,458	15,241
69,800	69,850	16,649	14,195	17,474	15,255
69,850	69,900	16,664	14,209	17,489	15,269
69,900	69,950	16,680	14,223	17,505	15,283
69,950	70,000	16,695	14,237	17,520	15,297
70,000					
70,000	70,050	16,711	14,251	17,536	15,311
70,050	70,100	16,726	14,265	17,551	15,325
70,100	70,150	16,742	14,279	17,567	15,339
70,150	70,200	16,757	14,293	17,582	15,353
70,200	70,250	16,773	14,307	17,598	15,367
70,250	70,300	16,788	14,321	17,613	15,381
70,300	70,350	16,804	14,335	17,629	15,395
70,350	70,400	16,819	14,349	17,644	15,409
70,400	70,450	16,835	14,363	17,660	15,423
70,450	70,500	16,850	14,377	17,675	15,437
70,500	70,550	16,866	14,391	17,691	15,451
70,550	70,600	16,881	14,405	17,706	15,465
70,600	70,650	16,897	14,419	17,722	15,479
70,650	70,700	16,912	14,433	17,737	15,493
70,700	70,750	16,928	14,447	17,753	15,507
70,750	70,800	16,943	14,461	17,768	15,521
70,800	70,850	16,959	14,475	17,784	15,535
70,850	70,900	16,974	14,489	17,799	15,549
70,900	70,950	16,990	14,503	17,815	15,563
70,950	71,000	17,005	14,517	17,830	15,577

If line 38 (taxable income) is— At least	But less than	Single	Married filing jointly *	Married filing separately	Head of a household
71,000					
71,000	71,050	17,021	14,531	17,846	15,591
71,050	71,100	17,036	14,545	17,861	15,605
71,100	71,150	17,052	14,559	17,877	15,619
71,150	71,200	17,067	14,573	17,892	15,633
71,200	71,250	17,083	14,587	17,908	15,647
71,250	71,300	17,098	14,601	17,923	15,661
71,300	71,350	17,114	14,615	17,939	15,675
71,350	71,400	17,129	14,629	17,954	15,689
71,400	71,450	17,145	14,643	17,970	15,703
71,450	71,500	17,160	14,657	17,985	15,717
71,500	71,550	17,176	14,671	18,001	15,731
71,550	71,600	17,191	14,685	18,016	15,745
71,600	71,650	17,207	14,699	18,032	15,759
71,650	71,700	17,222	14,713	18,047	15,773
71,700	71,750	17,238	14,727	18,063	15,787
71,750	71,800	17,253	14,741	18,078	15,801
71,800	71,850	17,269	14,755	18,094	15,815
71,850	71,900	17,284	14,769	18,109	15,829
71,900	71,950	17,300	14,783	18,125	15,843
71,950	72,000	17,315	14,797	18,140	15,857
72,000					
72,000	72,050	17,331	14,811	18,156	15,871
72,050	72,100	17,346	14,825	18,171	15,885
72,100	72,150	17,362	14,839	18,187	15,899
72,150	72,200	17,377	14,853	18,202	15,913
72,200	72,250	17,393	14,867	18,218	15,927
72,250	72,300	17,408	14,881	18,233	15,941
72,300	72,350	17,424	14,895	18,249	15,955
72,350	72,400	17,439	14,909	18,264	15,969
72,400	72,450	17,455	14,923	18,280	15,983
72,450	72,500	17,470	14,937	18,295	15,997
72,500	72,550	17,486	14,951	18,311	16,011
72,550	72,600	17,501	14,965	18,326	16,025
72,600	72,650	17,517	14,979	18,342	16,039
72,650	72,700	17,532	14,993	18,357	16,053
72,700	72,750	17,548	15,007	18,373	16,067
72,750	72,800	17,563	15,021	18,388	16,081
72,800	72,850	17,579	15,035	18,404	16,095
72,850	72,900	17,594	15,049	18,419	16,109
72,900	72,950	17,610	15,063	18,435	16,123
72,950	73,000	17,625	15,077	18,450	16,137
73,000					
73,000	73,050	17,641	15,091	18,466	16,151
73,050	73,100	17,656	15,105	18,481	16,165
73,100	73,150	17,672	15,119	18,497	16,179
73,150	73,200	17,687	15,133	18,512	16,193
73,200	73,250	17,703	15,147	18,528	16,207
73,250	73,300	17,718	15,161	18,543	16,221
73,300	73,350	17,734	15,175	18,559	16,235
73,350	73,400	17,749	15,189	18,574	16,249
73,400	73,450	17,765	15,203	18,590	16,263
73,450	73,500	17,780	15,217	18,605	16,277
73,500	73,550	17,796	15,231	18,621	16,291
73,550	73,600	17,811	15,245	18,636	16,305
73,600	73,650	17,827	15,259	18,652	16,319
73,650	73,700	17,842	15,273	18,667	16,333
73,700	73,750	17,858	15,287	18,683	16,347
73,750	73,800	17,873	15,301	18,698	16,361
73,800	73,850	17,889	15,315	18,714	16,375
73,850	73,900	17,904	15,329	18,729	16,389
73,900	73,950	17,920	15,343	18,745	16,403
73,950	74,000	17,935	15,357	18,760	16,417

If line 38 (taxable income) is— At least	But less than	Single	Married filing jointly *	Married filing separately	Head of a household
74,000					
74,000	74,050	17,951	15,371	18,776	16,431
74,050	74,100	17,966	15,385	18,791	16,445
74,100	74,150	17,982	15,399	18,807	16,459
74,150	74,200	17,997	15,413	18,822	16,473
74,200	74,250	18,013	15,427	18,838	16,487
74,250	74,300	18,028	15,441	18,853	16,501
74,300	74,350	18,044	15,455	18,869	16,515
74,350	74,400	18,059	15,469	18,884	16,529
74,400	74,450	18,075	15,483	18,900	16,543
74,450	74,500	18,090	15,497	18,915	16,557
74,500	74,550	18,106	15,511	18,931	16,571
74,550	74,600	18,121	15,525	18,946	16,585
74,600	74,650	18,137	15,539	18,962	16,599
74,650	74,700	18,152	15,553	18,977	16,613
74,700	74,750	18,168	15,567	18,993	16,627
74,750	74,800	18,183	15,581	19,008	16,641
74,800	74,850	18,199	15,595	19,024	16,655
74,850	74,900	18,214	15,609	19,039	16,669
74,900	74,950	18,230	15,623	19,055	16,683
74,950	75,000	18,245	15,637	19,070	16,697
75,000					
75,000	75,050	18,261	15,651	19,086	16,711
75,050	75,100	18,276	15,665	19,101	16,725
75,100	75,150	18,292	15,679	19,117	16,739
75,150	75,200	18,307	15,693	19,132	16,753
75,200	75,250	18,323	15,707	19,148	16,767
75,250	75,300	18,338	15,721	19,163	16,781
75,300	75,350	18,354	15,735	19,179	16,795
75,350	75,400	18,369	15,749	19,194	16,809
75,400	75,450	18,385	15,763	19,210	16,823
75,450	75,500	18,400	15,777	19,225	16,837
75,500	75,550	18,416	15,791	19,241	16,851
75,550	75,600	18,431	15,805	19,256	16,865
75,600	75,650	18,447	15,819	19,272	16,879
75,650	75,700	18,462	15,833	19,287	16,893
75,700	75,750	18,478	15,847	19,303	16,907
75,750	75,800	18,493	15,861	19,318	16,921
75,800	75,850	18,509	15,875	19,334	16,935
75,850	75,900	18,524	15,889	19,349	16,949
75,900	75,950	18,540	15,903	19,367	16,963
75,950	76,000	18,555	15,917	19,385	16,977
76,000					
76,000	76,050	18,571	15,931	19,403	16,991
76,050	76,100	18,586	15,945	19,421	17,005
76,100	76,150	18,602	15,959	19,439	17,019
76,150	76,200	18,617	15,973	19,457	17,033
76,200	76,250	18,633	15,987	19,475	17,047
76,250	76,300	18,648	16,001	19,493	17,061
76,300	76,350	18,664	16,015	19,511	17,075
76,350	76,400	18,679	16,029	19,529	17,089
76,400	76,450	18,695	16,043	19,547	17,103
76,450	76,500	18,710	16,057	19,565	17,117
76,500	76,550	18,726	16,071	19,583	17,131
76,550	76,600	18,741	16,085	19,601	17,145
76,600	76,650	18,757	16,099	19,619	17,159
76,650	76,700	18,772	16,113	19,637	17,173
76,700	76,750	18,788	16,127	19,655	17,187
76,750	76,800	18,803	16,141	19,673	17,201
76,800	76,850	18,819	16,155	19,691	17,215
76,850	76,900	18,834	16,169	19,709	17,229
76,900	76,950	18,850	16,183	19,727	17,243
76,950	77,000	18,865	16,197	19,745	17,257

* This column must also be used by a qualifying widow(er).

Continued on next page

1997 Tax Table—*Continued*

77,000 / 78,000 / 79,000

If line 38 (taxable income) is— At least	But less than	Single	Married filing jointly *	Married filing separately	Head of a household
77,000					
77,000	77,050	18,881	16,211	19,763	17,271
77,050	77,100	18,896	16,225	19,781	17,285
77,100	77,150	18,912	16,239	19,799	17,299
77,150	77,200	18,927	16,253	19,817	17,313
77,200	77,250	18,943	16,267	19,835	17,327
77,250	77,300	18,958	16,281	19,853	17,341
77,300	77,350	18,974	16,295	19,871	17,355
77,350	77,400	18,989	16,309	19,889	17,369
77,400	77,450	19,005	16,323	19,907	17,383
77,450	77,500	19,020	16,337	19,925	17,397
77,500	77,550	19,036	16,351	19,943	17,411
77,550	77,600	19,051	16,365	19,961	17,425
77,600	77,650	19,067	16,379	19,979	17,439
77,650	77,700	19,082	16,393	19,997	17,453
77,700	77,750	19,098	16,407	20,015	17,467
77,750	77,800	19,113	16,421	20,033	17,481
77,800	77,850	19,129	16,435	20,051	17,495
77,850	77,900	19,144	16,449	20,069	17,509
77,900	77,950	19,160	16,463	20,087	17,523
77,950	78,000	19,175	16,477	20,105	17,537
78,000					
78,000	78,050	19,191	16,491	20,123	17,551
78,050	78,100	19,206	16,505	20,141	17,565
78,100	78,150	19,222	16,519	20,159	17,579
78,150	78,200	19,237	16,533	20,177	17,593
78,200	78,250	19,253	16,547	20,195	17,607
78,250	78,300	19,268	16,561	20,213	17,621
78,300	78,350	19,284	16,575	20,231	17,635
78,350	78,400	19,299	16,589	20,249	17,649
78,400	78,450	19,315	16,603	20,267	17,663
78,450	78,500	19,330	16,617	20,285	17,677
78,500	78,550	19,346	16,631	20,303	17,691
78,550	78,600	19,361	16,645	20,321	17,705
78,600	78,650	19,377	16,659	20,339	17,719
78,650	78,700	19,392	16,673	20,357	17,733
78,700	78,750	19,408	16,687	20,375	17,747
78,750	78,800	19,423	16,701	20,393	17,761
78,800	78,850	19,439	16,715	20,411	17,775
78,850	78,900	19,454	16,729	20,429	17,789
78,900	78,950	19,470	16,743	20,447	17,803
78,950	79,000	19,485	16,757	20,465	17,817
79,000					
79,000	79,050	19,501	16,771	20,483	17,831
79,050	79,100	19,516	16,785	20,501	17,845
79,100	79,150	19,532	16,799	20,519	17,859
79,150	79,200	19,547	16,813	20,537	17,873
79,200	79,250	19,563	16,827	20,555	17,887
79,250	79,300	19,578	16,841	20,573	17,901
79,300	79,350	19,594	16,855	20,591	17,915
79,350	79,400	19,609	16,869	20,609	17,929
79,400	79,450	19,625	16,883	20,627	17,943
79,450	79,500	19,640	16,897	20,645	17,957
79,500	79,550	19,656	16,911	20,663	17,971
79,550	79,600	19,671	16,925	20,681	17,985
79,600	79,650	19,687	16,939	20,699	17,999
79,650	79,700	19,702	16,953	20,717	18,013
79,700	79,750	19,718	16,967	20,735	18,027
79,750	79,800	19,733	16,981	20,753	18,041
79,800	79,850	19,749	16,995	20,771	18,055
79,850	79,900	19,764	17,009	20,789	18,069
79,900	79,950	19,780	17,023	20,807	18,083
79,950	80,000	19,795	17,037	20,825	18,097

80,000 / 81,000 / 82,000

If line 38 (taxable income) is— At least	But less than	Single	Married filing jointly *	Married filing separately	Head of a household
80,000					
80,000	80,050	19,811	17,051	20,843	18,111
80,050	80,100	19,826	17,065	20,861	18,125
80,100	80,150	19,842	17,079	20,879	18,139
80,150	80,200	19,857	17,093	20,897	18,153
80,200	80,250	19,873	17,107	20,915	18,167
80,250	80,300	19,888	17,121	20,933	18,181
80,300	80,350	19,904	17,135	20,951	18,195
80,350	80,400	19,919	17,149	20,969	18,209
80,400	80,450	19,935	17,163	20,987	18,223
80,450	80,500	19,950	17,177	21,005	18,237
80,500	80,550	19,966	17,191	21,023	18,251
80,550	80,600	19,981	17,205	21,041	18,265
80,600	80,650	19,997	17,219	21,059	18,279
80,650	80,700	20,012	17,233	21,077	18,293
80,700	80,750	20,028	17,247	21,095	18,307
80,750	80,800	20,043	17,261	21,113	18,321
80,800	80,850	20,059	17,275	21,131	18,335
80,850	80,900	20,074	17,289	21,149	18,349
80,900	80,950	20,090	17,303	21,167	18,363
80,950	81,000	20,105	17,317	21,185	18,377
81,000					
81,000	81,050	20,121	17,331	21,203	18,391
81,050	81,100	20,136	17,345	21,221	18,405
81,100	81,150	20,152	17,359	21,239	18,419
81,150	81,200	20,167	17,373	21,257	18,433
81,200	81,250	20,183	17,387	21,275	18,447
81,250	81,300	20,198	17,401	21,293	18,461
81,300	81,350	20,214	17,415	21,311	18,475
81,350	81,400	20,229	17,429	21,329	18,489
81,400	81,450	20,245	17,443	21,347	18,503
81,450	81,500	20,260	17,457	21,365	18,517
81,500	81,550	20,276	17,471	21,383	18,531
81,550	81,600	20,291	17,485	21,401	18,545
81,600	81,650	20,307	17,499	21,419	18,559
81,650	81,700	20,322	17,513	21,437	18,573
81,700	81,750	20,338	17,527	21,455	18,587
81,750	81,800	20,353	17,541	21,473	18,601
81,800	81,850	20,369	17,555	21,491	18,615
81,850	81,900	20,384	17,569	21,509	18,629
81,900	81,950	20,400	17,583	21,527	18,643
81,950	82,000	20,415	17,597	21,545	18,657
82,000					
82,000	82,050	20,431	17,611	21,563	18,671
82,050	82,100	20,446	17,625	21,581	18,685
82,100	82,150	20,462	17,639	21,599	18,699
82,150	82,200	20,477	17,653	21,617	18,713
82,200	82,250	20,493	17,667	21,635	18,727
82,250	82,300	20,508	17,681	21,653	18,741
82,300	82,350	20,524	17,695	21,671	18,755
82,350	82,400	20,539	17,709	21,689	18,769
82,400	82,450	20,555	17,723	21,707	18,783
82,450	82,500	20,570	17,737	21,725	18,797
82,500	82,550	20,586	17,751	21,743	18,811
82,550	82,600	20,601	17,765	21,761	18,825
82,600	82,650	20,617	17,779	21,779	18,839
82,650	82,700	20,632	17,793	21,797	18,853
82,700	82,750	20,648	17,807	21,815	18,867
82,750	82,800	20,663	17,821	21,833	18,881
82,800	82,850	20,679	17,835	21,851	18,895
82,850	82,900	20,694	17,849	21,869	18,909
82,900	82,950	20,710	17,863	21,887	18,923
82,950	83,000	20,725	17,877	21,905	18,937

83,000 / 84,000 / 85,000

If line 38 (taxable income) is— At least	But less than	Single	Married filing jointly *	Married filing separately	Head of a household
83,000					
83,000	83,050	20,741	17,891	21,923	18,951
83,050	83,100	20,756	17,905	21,941	18,965
83,100	83,150	20,772	17,919	21,959	18,979
83,150	83,200	20,787	17,933	21,977	18,993
83,200	83,250	20,803	17,947	21,995	19,007
83,250	83,300	20,818	17,961	22,013	19,021
83,300	83,350	20,834	17,975	22,031	19,035
83,350	83,400	20,849	17,989	22,049	19,049
83,400	83,450	20,865	18,003	22,067	19,063
83,450	83,500	20,880	18,017	22,085	19,077
83,500	83,550	20,896	18,031	22,103	19,091
83,550	83,600	20,911	18,045	22,121	19,105
83,600	83,650	20,927	18,059	22,139	19,119
83,650	83,700	20,942	18,073	22,157	19,133
83,700	83,750	20,958	18,087	22,175	19,147
83,750	83,800	20,973	18,101	22,193	19,161
83,800	83,850	20,989	18,115	22,211	19,175
83,850	83,900	21,004	18,129	22,229	19,189
83,900	83,950	21,020	18,143	22,247	19,203
83,950	84,000	21,035	18,157	22,265	19,217
84,000					
84,000	84,050	21,051	18,171	22,283	19,231
84,050	84,100	21,066	18,185	22,301	19,245
84,100	84,150	21,082	18,199	22,319	19,259
84,150	84,200	21,097	18,213	22,337	19,273
84,200	84,250	21,113	18,227	22,355	19,287
84,250	84,300	21,128	18,241	22,373	19,301
84,300	84,350	21,144	18,255	22,391	19,315
84,350	84,400	21,159	18,269	22,409	19,329
84,400	84,450	21,175	18,283	22,427	19,343
84,450	84,500	21,190	18,297	22,445	19,357
84,500	84,550	21,206	18,311	22,463	19,371
84,550	84,600	21,221	18,325	22,481	19,385
84,600	84,650	21,237	18,339	22,499	19,399
84,650	84,700	21,252	18,353	22,517	19,413
84,700	84,750	21,268	18,367	22,535	19,427
84,750	84,800	21,283	18,381	22,553	19,441
84,800	84,850	21,299	18,395	22,571	19,455
84,850	84,900	21,314	18,409	22,589	19,469
84,900	84,950	21,330	18,423	22,607	19,483
84,950	85,000	21,345	18,437	22,625	19,497
85,000					
85,000	85,050	21,361	18,451	22,643	19,511
85,050	85,100	21,376	18,465	22,661	19,525
85,100	85,150	21,392	18,479	22,679	19,539
85,150	85,200	21,407	18,493	22,697	19,553
85,200	85,250	21,423	18,507	22,715	19,567
85,250	85,300	21,438	18,521	22,733	19,581
85,300	85,350	21,454	18,535	22,751	19,595
85,350	85,400	21,469	18,549	22,769	19,609
85,400	85,450	21,485	18,563	22,787	19,625
85,450	85,500	21,500	18,577	22,805	19,640
85,500	85,550	21,516	18,591	22,823	19,656
85,550	85,600	21,531	18,605	22,841	19,671
85,600	85,650	21,547	18,619	22,859	19,687
85,650	85,700	21,562	18,633	22,877	19,702
85,700	85,750	21,578	18,647	22,895	19,718
85,750	85,800	21,593	18,661	22,913	19,733
85,800	85,850	21,609	18,675	22,931	19,749
85,850	85,900	21,624	18,689	22,949	19,764
85,900	85,950	21,640	18,703	22,967	19,780
85,950	86,000	21,655	18,717	22,985	19,795

* This column must also be used by a qualifying widow(er).

Continued on next page

1997 Tax Table—Continued

If line 38 (taxable income) is—		And you are—			
At least	But less than	Single	Married filing jointly *	Married filing separately	Head of a household
		Your tax is—			

86,000

At least	But less than	Single	Married filing jointly *	Married filing separately	Head of a household
86,000	86,050	21,671	18,731	23,003	19,811
86,050	86,100	21,686	18,745	23,021	19,826
86,100	86,150	21,702	18,759	23,039	19,842
86,150	86,200	21,717	18,773	23,057	19,857
86,200	86,250	21,733	18,787	23,075	19,873
86,250	86,300	21,748	18,801	23,093	19,888
86,300	86,350	21,764	18,815	23,111	19,904
86,350	86,400	21,779	18,829	23,129	19,919
86,400	86,450	21,795	18,843	23,147	19,935
86,450	86,500	21,810	18,857	23,165	19,950
86,500	86,550	21,826	18,871	23,183	19,966
86,550	86,600	21,841	18,885	23,201	19,981
86,600	86,650	21,857	18,899	23,219	19,997
86,650	86,700	21,872	18,913	23,237	20,012
86,700	86,750	21,888	18,927	23,255	20,028
86,750	86,800	21,903	18,941	23,273	20,043
86,800	86,850	21,919	18,955	23,291	20,059
86,850	86,900	21,934	18,969	23,309	20,074
86,900	86,950	21,950	18,983	23,327	20,090
86,950	87,000	21,965	18,997	23,345	20,105

87,000

At least	But less than	Single	Married filing jointly *	Married filing separately	Head of a household
87,000	87,050	21,981	19,011	23,363	20,121
87,050	87,100	21,996	19,025	23,381	20,136
87,100	87,150	22,012	19,039	23,399	20,152
87,150	87,200	22,027	19,053	23,417	20,167
87,200	87,250	22,043	19,067	23,435	20,183
87,250	87,300	22,058	19,081	23,453	20,198
87,300	87,350	22,074	19,095	23,471	20,214
87,350	87,400	22,089	19,109	23,489	20,229
87,400	87,450	22,105	19,123	23,507	20,245
87,450	87,500	22,120	19,137	23,525	20,260
87,500	87,550	22,136	19,151	23,543	20,276
87,550	87,600	22,151	19,165	23,561	20,291
87,600	87,650	22,167	19,179	23,579	20,307
87,650	87,700	22,182	19,193	23,597	20,322
87,700	87,750	22,198	19,207	23,615	20,338
87,750	87,800	22,213	19,221	23,633	20,353
87,800	87,850	22,229	19,235	23,651	20,369
87,850	87,900	22,244	19,249	23,669	20,384
87,900	87,950	22,260	19,263	23,687	20,400
87,950	88,000	22,275	19,277	23,705	20,415

88,000

At least	But less than	Single	Married filing jointly *	Married filing separately	Head of a household
88,000	88,050	22,291	19,291	23,723	20,431
88,050	88,100	22,306	19,305	23,741	20,446
88,100	88,150	22,322	19,319	23,759	20,462
88,150	88,200	22,337	19,333	23,777	20,477
88,200	88,250	22,353	19,347	23,795	20,493
88,250	88,300	22,368	19,361	23,813	20,508
88,300	88,350	22,384	19,375	23,831	20,524
88,350	88,400	22,399	19,389	23,849	20,539
88,400	88,450	22,415	19,403	23,867	20,555
88,450	88,500	22,430	19,417	23,885	20,570
88,500	88,550	22,446	19,431	23,903	20,586
88,550	88,600	22,461	19,445	23,921	20,601
88,600	88,650	22,477	19,459	23,939	20,617
88,650	88,700	22,492	19,473	23,957	20,632
88,700	88,750	22,508	19,487	23,975	20,648
88,750	88,800	22,523	19,501	23,993	20,663
88,800	88,850	22,539	19,515	24,011	20,679
88,850	88,900	22,554	19,529	24,029	20,694
88,900	88,950	22,570	19,543	24,047	20,710
88,950	89,000	22,585	19,557	24,065	20,725

89,000

At least	But less than	Single	Married filing jointly *	Married filing separately	Head of a household
89,000	89,050	22,601	19,571	24,083	20,741
89,050	89,100	22,616	19,585	24,101	20,756
89,100	89,150	22,632	19,599	24,119	20,772
89,150	89,200	22,647	19,613	24,137	20,787
89,200	89,250	22,663	19,627	24,155	20,803
89,250	89,300	22,678	19,641	24,173	20,818
89,300	89,350	22,694	19,655	24,191	20,834
89,350	89,400	22,709	19,669	24,209	20,849
89,400	89,450	22,725	19,683	24,227	20,865
89,450	89,500	22,740	19,697	24,245	20,880
89,500	89,550	22,756	19,711	24,263	20,896
89,550	89,600	22,771	19,725	24,281	20,911
89,600	89,650	22,787	19,739	24,299	20,927
89,650	89,700	22,802	19,753	24,317	20,942
89,700	89,750	22,818	19,767	24,335	20,958
89,750	89,800	22,833	19,781	24,353	20,973
89,800	89,850	22,849	19,795	24,371	20,989
89,850	89,900	22,864	19,809	24,389	21,004
89,900	89,950	22,880	19,823	24,407	21,020
89,950	90,000	22,895	19,837	24,425	21,035

90,000

At least	But less than	Single	Married filing jointly *	Married filing separately	Head of a household
90,000	90,050	22,911	19,851	24,443	21,051
90,050	90,100	22,926	19,865	24,461	21,066
90,100	90,150	22,942	19,879	24,479	21,082
90,150	90,200	22,957	19,893	24,497	21,097
90,200	90,250	22,973	19,907	24,515	21,113
90,250	90,300	22,988	19,921	24,533	21,128
90,300	90,350	23,004	19,935	24,551	21,144
90,350	90,400	23,019	19,949	24,569	21,159
90,400	90,450	23,035	19,963	24,587	21,175
90,450	90,500	23,050	19,977	24,605	21,190
90,500	90,550	23,066	19,991	24,623	21,206
90,550	90,600	23,081	20,005	24,641	21,221
90,600	90,650	23,097	20,019	24,659	21,237
90,650	90,700	23,112	20,033	24,677	21,252
90,700	90,750	23,128	20,047	24,695	21,268
90,750	90,800	23,143	20,061	24,713	21,283
90,800	90,850	23,159	20,075	24,731	21,299
90,850	90,900	23,174	20,089	24,749	21,314
90,900	90,950	23,190	20,103	24,767	21,330
90,950	91,000	23,205	20,117	24,785	21,345

91,000

At least	But less than	Single	Married filing jointly *	Married filing separately	Head of a household
91,000	91,050	23,221	20,131	24,803	21,361
91,050	91,100	23,236	20,145	24,821	21,376
91,100	91,150	23,252	20,159	24,839	21,392
91,150	91,200	23,267	20,173	24,857	21,407
91,200	91,250	23,283	20,187	24,875	21,423
91,250	91,300	23,298	20,201	24,893	21,438
91,300	91,350	23,314	20,215	24,911	21,454
91,350	91,400	23,329	20,229	24,929	21,469
91,400	91,450	23,345	20,243	24,947	21,485
91,450	91,500	23,360	20,257	24,965	21,500
91,500	91,550	23,376	20,271	24,983	21,516
91,550	91,600	23,391	20,285	25,001	21,531
91,600	91,650	23,407	20,299	25,019	21,547
91,650	91,700	23,422	20,313	25,037	21,562
91,700	91,750	23,438	20,327	25,055	21,578
91,750	91,800	23,453	20,341	25,073	21,593
91,800	91,850	23,469	20,355	25,091	21,609
91,850	91,900	23,484	20,369	25,109	21,624
91,900	91,950	23,500	20,383	25,127	21,640
91,950	92,000	23,515	20,397	25,145	21,655

92,000

At least	But less than	Single	Married filing jointly *	Married filing separately	Head of a household
92,000	92,050	23,531	20,411	25,163	21,671
92,050	92,100	23,546	20,425	25,181	21,686
92,100	92,150	23,562	20,439	25,199	21,702
92,150	92,200	23,577	20,453	25,217	21,717
92,200	92,250	23,593	20,467	25,235	21,733
92,250	92,300	23,608	20,481	25,253	21,748
92,300	92,350	23,624	20,495	25,271	21,764
92,350	92,400	23,639	20,509	25,289	21,779
92,400	92,450	23,655	20,523	25,307	21,795
92,450	92,500	23,670	20,537	25,325	21,810
92,500	92,550	23,686	20,551	25,343	21,826
92,550	92,600	23,701	20,565	25,361	21,841
92,600	92,650	23,717	20,579	25,379	21,857
92,650	92,700	23,732	20,593	25,397	21,872
92,700	92,750	23,748	20,607	25,415	21,888
92,750	92,800	23,763	20,621	25,433	21,903
92,800	92,850	23,779	20,635	25,451	21,919
92,850	92,900	23,794	20,649	25,469	21,934
92,900	92,950	23,810	20,663	25,487	21,950
92,950	93,000	23,825	20,677	25,505	21,965

93,000

At least	But less than	Single	Married filing jointly *	Married filing separately	Head of a household
93,000	93,050	23,841	20,691	25,523	21,981
93,050	93,100	23,856	20,705	25,541	21,996
93,100	93,150	23,872	20,719	25,559	22,012
93,150	93,200	23,887	20,733	25,577	22,027
93,200	93,250	23,903	20,747	25,595	22,043
93,250	93,300	23,918	20,761	25,613	22,058
93,300	93,350	23,934	20,775	25,631	22,074
93,350	93,400	23,949	20,789	25,649	22,089
93,400	93,450	23,965	20,803	25,667	22,105
93,450	93,500	23,980	20,817	25,685	22,120
93,500	93,550	23,996	20,831	25,703	22,136
93,550	93,600	24,011	20,845	25,721	22,151
93,600	93,650	24,027	20,859	25,739	22,167
93,650	93,700	24,042	20,873	25,757	22,182
93,700	93,750	24,058	20,887	25,775	22,198
93,750	93,800	24,073	20,901	25,793	22,213
93,800	93,850	24,089	20,915	25,811	22,229
93,850	93,900	24,104	20,929	25,829	22,244
93,900	93,950	24,120	20,943	25,847	22,260
93,950	94,000	24,135	20,957	25,865	22,275

94,000

At least	But less than	Single	Married filing jointly *	Married filing separately	Head of a household
94,000	94,050	24,151	20,971	25,883	22,291
94,050	94,100	24,166	20,985	25,901	22,306
94,100	94,150	24,182	20,999	25,919	22,322
94,150	94,200	24,197	21,013	25,937	22,337
94,200	94,250	24,213	21,027	25,955	22,353
94,250	94,300	24,228	21,041	25,973	22,368
94,300	94,350	24,244	21,055	25,991	22,384
94,350	94,400	24,259	21,069	26,009	22,399
94,400	94,450	24,275	21,083	26,027	22,415
94,450	94,500	24,290	21,097	26,045	22,430
94,500	94,550	24,306	21,111	26,063	22,446
94,550	94,600	24,321	21,125	26,081	22,461
94,600	94,650	24,337	21,139	26,099	22,477
94,650	94,700	24,352	21,153	26,117	22,492
94,700	94,750	24,368	21,167	26,135	22,508
94,750	94,800	24,383	21,181	26,153	22,523
94,800	94,850	24,399	21,195	26,171	22,539
94,850	94,900	24,414	21,209	26,189	22,554
94,900	94,950	24,430	21,223	26,207	22,570
94,950	95,000	24,445	21,237	26,225	22,585

* This column must also be used by a qualifying widow(er).

Continued on next page

1997 Tax Table—*Continued*

If line 38 (taxable income) is—		And you are—				If line 38 (taxable income) is—		And you are—			
At least	But less than	Single	Married filing jointly *	Married filing separately	Head of a house-hold	At least	But less than	Single	Married filing jointly *	Married filing separately	Head of a house-hold
		Your tax is—						Your tax is—			
95,000						**98,000**					
95,000	95,050	24,461	21,251	26,243	22,601	98,000	98,050	25,391	22,091	27,323	23,531
95,050	95,100	24,476	21,265	26,261	22,616	98,050	98,100	25,406	22,105	27,341	23,546
95,100	95,150	24,492	21,279	26,279	22,632	98,100	98,150	25,422	22,119	27,359	23,562
95,150	95,200	24,507	21,293	26,297	22,647	98,150	98,200	25,437	22,133	27,377	23,577
95,200	95,250	24,523	21,307	26,315	22,663	98,200	98,250	25,453	22,147	27,395	23,593
95,250	95,300	24,538	21,321	26,333	22,678	98,250	98,300	25,468	22,161	27,413	23,608
95,300	95,350	24,554	21,335	26,351	22,694	98,300	98,350	25,484	22,175	27,431	23,624
95,350	95,400	24,569	21,349	26,369	22,709	98,350	98,400	25,499	22,189	27,449	23,639
95,400	95,450	24,585	21,363	26,387	22,725	98,400	98,450	25,515	22,203	27,467	23,655
95,450	95,500	24,600	21,377	26,405	22,740	98,450	98,500	25,530	22,217	27,485	23,670
95,500	95,550	24,616	21,391	26,423	22,756	98,500	98,550	25,546	22,231	27,503	23,686
95,550	95,600	24,631	21,405	26,441	22,771	98,550	98,600	25,561	22,245	27,521	23,701
95,600	95,650	24,647	21,419	26,459	22,787	98,600	98,650	25,577	22,259	27,539	23,717
95,650	95,700	24,662	21,433	26,477	22,802	98,650	98,700	25,592	22,273	27,557	23,732
95,700	95,750	24,678	21,447	26,495	22,818	98,700	98,750	25,608	22,287	27,575	23,748
95,750	95,800	24,693	21,461	26,513	22,833	98,750	98,800	25,623	22,301	27,593	23,763
95,800	95,850	24,709	21,475	26,531	22,849	98,800	98,850	25,639	22,315	27,611	23,779
95,850	95,900	24,724	21,489	26,549	22,864	98,850	98,900	25,654	22,329	27,629	23,794
95,900	95,950	24,740	21,503	26,567	22,880	98,900	98,950	25,670	22,343	27,647	23,810
95,950	96,000	24,755	21,517	26,585	22,895	98,950	99,000	25,685	22,357	27,665	23,825
96,000						**99,000**					
96,000	96,050	24,771	21,531	26,603	22,911	99,000	99,050	25,701	22,371	27,683	23,841
96,050	96,100	24,786	21,545	26,621	22,926	99,050	99,100	25,716	22,385	27,701	23,856
96,100	96,150	24,802	21,559	26,639	22,942	99,100	99,150	25,732	22,399	27,719	23,872
96,150	96,200	24,817	21,573	26,657	22,957	99,150	99,200	25,747	22,413	27,737	23,887
96,200	96,250	24,833	21,587	26,675	22,973	99,200	99,250	25,763	22,427	27,755	23,903
96,250	96,300	24,848	21,601	26,693	22,988	99,250	99,300	25,778	22,441	27,773	23,918
96,300	96,350	24,864	21,615	26,711	23,004	99,300	99,350	25,794	22,455	27,791	23,934
96,350	96,400	24,879	21,629	26,729	23,019	99,350	99,400	25,809	22,469	27,809	23,949
96,400	96,450	24,895	21,643	26,747	23,035	99,400	99,450	25,825	22,483	27,827	23,965
96,450	96,500	24,910	21,657	26,765	23,050	99,450	99,500	25,840	22,497	27,845	23,980
96,500	96,550	24,926	21,671	26,783	23,066	99,500	99,550	25,856	22,511	27,863	23,996
96,550	96,600	24,941	21,685	26,801	23,081	99,550	99,600	25,871	22,525	27,881	24,011
96,600	96,650	24,957	21,699	26,819	23,097	99,600	99,650	25,887	22,540	27,899	24,027
96,650	96,700	24,972	21,713	26,837	23,112	99,650	99,700	25,902	22,555	27,917	24,042
96,700	96,750	24,988	21,727	26,855	23,128	99,700	99,750	25,918	22,571	27,935	24,058
96,750	96,800	25,003	21,741	26,873	23,143	99,750	99,800	25,933	22,586	27,953	24,073
96,800	96,850	25,019	21,755	26,891	23,159	99,800	99,850	25,949	22,602	27,971	24,089
96,850	96,900	25,034	21,769	26,909	23,174	99,850	99,900	25,964	22,617	27,989	24,104
96,900	96,950	25,050	21,783	26,927	23,190	99,900	99,950	25,980	22,633	28,007	24,120
96,950	97,000	25,065	21,797	26,945	23,205	99,950	100,000	25,995	22,648	28,025	24,135
97,000											
97,000	97,050	25,081	21,811	26,963	23,221						
97,050	97,100	25,096	21,825	26,981	23,236						
97,100	97,150	25,112	21,839	26,999	23,252						
97,150	97,200	25,127	21,853	27,017	23,267						
97,200	97,250	25,143	21,867	27,035	23,283						
97,250	97,300	25,158	21,881	27,053	23,298						
97,300	97,350	25,174	21,895	27,071	23,314						
97,350	97,400	25,189	21,909	27,089	23,329						
97,400	97,450	25,205	21,923	27,107	23,345						
97,450	97,500	25,220	21,937	27,125	23,360						
97,500	97,550	25,236	21,951	27,143	23,376						
97,550	97,600	25,251	21,965	27,161	23,391						
97,600	97,650	25,267	21,979	27,179	23,407						
97,650	97,700	25,282	21,993	27,197	23,422						
97,700	97,750	25,298	22,007	27,215	23,438						
97,750	97,800	25,313	22,021	27,233	23,453						
97,800	97,850	25,329	22,035	27,251	23,469						
97,850	97,900	25,344	22,049	27,269	23,484						
97,900	97,950	25,360	22,063	27,287	23,500						
97,950	98,000	25,375	22,077	27,305	23,515						

$100,000 or over — use the Tax Rate Schedules on page A–2

* This column must also be used by a qualifying widow(er).

INCOME TAX RATES—ESTATES AND TRUSTS

TAX YEAR 1998

Taxable Income		The Tax Is:	Of the Amount Over—
Over—	But not Over—		
$ 0	$1,700	15%	$ 0
1,700	4,000	$ 255 + 28%	1,700
4,000	6,100	899 + 31%	4,000
6,100	8,350	1,550 + 36%	6,100
8,350	—	2,360 + 39.6%	8,350

TAX YEAR 1997

Taxable Income		The Tax Is:	Of the Amount Over—
Over—	But not Over—		
$ 0	$1,650	15%	$ 0
1,650	3,900	$ 247.50 + 28%	1,650
3,900	5,950	877.50 + 31%	3,900
5,950	8,100	1,513.00 + 36%	5,950
8,100	—	2,287.00 + 39.6%	8,100

INCOME TAX RATES—CORPORATIONS

Taxable Income		Tax Is:	Of the Amount Over—
Over—	But not Over—		
$ 0	$ 50,000	15%	$ 0
50,000	75,000	$ 7,500 + 25%	50,000
75,000	100,000	13,750 + 34%	75,000
100,000	335,000	22,250 + 39%	100,000
335,000	10,000,000	113,900 + 34%	335,000
10,000,000	15,000,000	3,400,000 + 35%	10,000,000
15,000,000	18,333,333	5,150,000 + 38%	15,000,000
18,333,333	—	35%	0

Unified Transfer Tax Rates

FOR GIFTS MADE AND FOR DEATHS AFTER 1983

If the Amount with Respect to Which the Tentative Tax to Be Computed Is:	The Tentative Tax Is:
Not over $10,000	18 percent of such amount.
Over $10,000 but not over $20,000	$1,800, plus 20 percent of the excess of such amount over $10,000.
Over $20,000 but not over $40,000	$3,800, plus 22 percent of the excess of such amount over $20,000.
Over $40,000 but not over $60,000	$8,200, plus 24 percent of the excess of such amount over $40,000.
Over $60,000 but not over $80,000	$13,000, plus 26 percent of the excess of such amount over $60,000.
Over $80,000 but not over $100,000	$18,200, plus 28 percent of the excess of such amount over $80,000.
Over $100,000 but not over $150,000	$23,800, plus 30 percent of the excess of such amount over $100,000.
Over $150,000 but not over $250,000	$38,800, plus 32 percent of the excess of such amount over $150,000.
Over $250,000 but not over $500,000	$70,800, plus 34 percent of the excess of such amount over $250,000.
Over $500,000 but not over $750,000	$155,800, plus 37 percent of the excess of such amount over $500,000.
Over $750,000 but not over $1,000,000	$248,300, plus 39 percent of the excess of such amount over $750,000.
Over $1,000,000 but not over $1,250,000	$345,800, plus 41 percent of the excess of such amount over $1,000,000.
Over $1,250,000 but not over $1,500,000	$448,300, plus 43 percent of the excess of such amount over $1,250,000.
Over $1,500,000 but not over $2,000,000	$555,800, plus 45 percent of the excess of such amount over $1,500,000.
Over $2,000,000 but not over $2,500,000	$780,800, plus 49 percent of the excess of such amount over $2,000,000.
Over $2,500,000 but not over $3,000,000	$1,025,800, plus 53 percent of the excess of such amount over $2,500,000.
Over $3,000,000*	$1,290,800, plus 55 percent of the excess of such amount over $3,000,000.

*For large taxable transfers (generally in excess of $10 million) there is a phase-out of the graduated rates and the unified tax credit.

TABLE FOR COMPUTATION OF MAXIMUM CREDIT FOR STATE DEATH TAXES

(A)	(B)	(C)	(D)
Adjusted Taxable Estate* Equal to or More Than	Adjusted Taxable Estate* Less Than	Credit on Amount in Column (A)	Rate of Credit on Excess Over Amount in Column (A) (Percentage)
0	$ 40,000	0	None
$ 40,000	90,000	0	0.8
90,000	140,000	$ 400	1.6
140,000	240,000	1,200	2.4
240,000	440,000	3,600	3.2
440,000	640,000	10,000	4.0
640,000	840,000	18,000	4.8
840,000	1,040,000	27,600	5.6
1,040,000	1,540,000	38,800	6.4
1,540,000	2,040,000	70,800	7.2
2,040,000	2,540,000	106,800	8.0
2,540,000	3,040,000	146,800	8.8
3,040,000	3,540,000	190,800	9.6
3,540,000	4,040,000	238,800	10.4
4,040,000	5,040,000	290,800	11.2
5,040,000	6,040,000	402,800	12.0
6,040,000	7,040,000	522,800	12.8
7,040,000	8,040,000	650,800	13.6
8,040,000	9,040,000	786,800	14.4
9,040,000	10,040,000	930,800	15.2
10,040,000		1,082,800	16.0

*Adjusted Taxable Estate = Taxable Estate − $60,000

APPENDIX B

Tax Forms

Department of Treasury
Internal Revenue Service

Form 656 (Rev. 1-97)
Catalog Number 16728N

Form 656

Offer in Compromise

Item 1

Taxpayer's Name and Home or Business Address

_____

Name

_____

Street Address

_____

City   State   Zip Code

_____

Mailing Address (if different from above)

_____

City   State   Zip Code

Item 2

Social Security Numbers

(a) Primary_____

(b) Secondary_____

Item 3

Employer Identification Number (Included in offer)

_____

Item 4

Other Employer Identification Numbers (Not included in offer)

_____

_____

_____

_____

Item 5

To: Commissioner of Internal Revenue Service

I/we (includes all types of taxpayers) submit this offer to compromise the tax liabilities plus any interest, penalties, additions to tax, and additional amounts required by law (tax liability) for the tax type and period marked below: (Please mark an "X" for the correct description and fill-in the correct tax periods(s), adding additional periods if needed.)

☐ **1040/1120 Income tax** – Year(s)_____

☐ **941 Employer's Quarterly Federal Tax Return** – Quarterly Period(s)_____

☐ **940 Employer's Annual Federal Unemployment (FUTA) Tax Return** – Year(s)_____

☐ **Trust Fund Recovery Penalty** as a responsible person of (enter corporation name)_____

for failure to pay withholding and Federal Insurance Contributions Act Taxes (Social Security taxes) – Period(s)_____

☐ **Other Federal taxes** (specify type and periods(s),_____

Item 6

I/we submit this offer for the reason(s) checked below:

☐ **Doubt as to Liability** – "I do not believe I owe this amount." You *must* include a detailed explanation of the reasons you believe you do not owe the tax.

☐ **Doubt as to Collectibility** – "I have insufficient assets and income to pay the full amount." You *must* include a complete financial statement (Form 433-A and/ or Form 433-B).

Item 7

I/We offer to pay $_____

☐ **Paid in full with this offer.**
☐ **Deposit of $_____ with this offer.**
☐ **No deposit.**
Check one of the following boxes.

☐ Balance to be paid in ☐ 10, ☐ 30, ☐ 60, or ☐ 90 days from notice of acceptance of the offer. If more than one payment will be paid during the time frame checked, provide the amount of the payment and date to be paid on the line below.

_____

☐ Other proposed payment terms. Enter the specific dates (mm/dd/yy format) and dollar amounts of the the payment terms you propose on the lines below.

_____

_____

In addition to the above amount, IRS will add interest from the date IRS accepts the offer until the date you completely pay the amount offered, as required by section 6621 of the Internal Revenue Code, IRS compounds interest daily, as required by section 6622 of the Internal Revenue Code.

Form **870** (Rev. March 1992)	Department of the Treasury — Internal Revenue Service **Waiver of Restrictions on Assessment and Collection of Deficiency in Tax and Acceptance of Overassessment**	Date received by Internal Revenue Service

Names and address of taxpayers *(Number, street, city or town, State, ZIP code)*	Social security or employer identification number

Increase (Decrease) in Tax and Penalties

Tax year ended	Tax	Penalties			
	$	$	$	$	$
	$	$	$	$	$
	$	$	$	$	$
	$	$	$	$	$
	$	$	$	$	$
	$	$	$	$	$
	$	$	$	$	$

(For instructions, see back of form)

Consent to Assessment and Collection

I consent to the immediate assessment and collection of any deficiencies *(increase in tax and penalties)* and accept any overassessment *(decrease in tax and penalties)* shown above, plus any interest provided by law. I understand that by signing this waiver, I will not be able to contest these years in the United States Tax Court, unless additional deficiencies are determined for these years.

YOUR SIGNATURE→ HERE		Date
SPOUSE'S SIGNATURE→		Date
TAXPAYER'S REPRESENTATIVE HERE →		Date
CORPORATE NAME →		
CORPORATE OFFICER(S) SIGN HERE		Title	Date
		Title	Date

Form 1040EZ

Department of the Treasury—Internal Revenue Service

Income Tax Return for Single and Joint Filers With No Dependents (99) 1997

OMB No. 1545-0675

Use the IRS label here

Your first name and initial   Last name

If a joint return, spouse's first name and initial   Last name

Home address (number and street). If you have a P.O. box, see page 7.   Apt. no.

City, town or post office, state, and ZIP code. If you have a foreign address, see page 7.

Your social security number

Spouse's social security number

Presidential Election Campaign (See page 7.)

Note: Checking "Yes" will not change your tax or reduce your refund.

Do you want $3 to go to this fund? ▶   Yes ☐ No ☐

If a joint return, does your spouse want $3 to go to this fund? ▶   Yes ☐ No ☐

Dollars   Cents

Income

Attach Copy B of Form(s) W-2 here. Enclose but do not attach any payment with your return.

1 Total wages, salaries, and tips. This should be shown in box 1 of your W-2 form(s). Attach your W-2 form(s).   1

2 Taxable interest income. If the total is over $400, you cannot use Form 1040EZ.   2

3 Unemployment compensation (see page 9).   3

4 Add lines 1, 2, and 3. This is your **adjusted gross income.** If under $9,770, see page 9 to find out if you can claim the earned income credit on line 8a.   4

Note: You **must** check Yes or No.

5 Can your parents (or someone else) claim you on their return?

Yes. Enter amount from worksheet on back. ☐

No. If **single,** enter 6,800.00. If **married,** enter 12,200.00. See back for explanation.   5

6 Subtract line 5 from line 4. If line 5 is larger than line 4, enter 0. This is your **taxable income.** ▶   6

Payments and tax

7 Enter your Federal income tax withheld from box 2 of your W-2 form(s).   7

8a Earned income credit (see page 9).
b Nontaxable earned income: enter type and amount below.

Type _____ $ _____   8a

9 Add lines 7 and 8a. These are your **total payments.**   9

10 Tax. Use the amount on **line 6** to find your tax in the tax table on pages 20–24 of the booklet. Then, enter the tax from the table on this line.   10

Refund

Have it directly deposited! See page 13 and fill in 11b, 11c, and 11d.

11a If line 9 is larger than line 10, subtract line 10 from line 9. This is your **refund.**   11a

b Routing number

c Type: Checking ☐   Savings ☐

d Account number

Amount you owe

12 If line 10 is larger than line 9, subtract line 9 from line 10. This is the **amount you owe.** See page 13 for details on how to pay.   12

For Official Use Only

1 2 3 4 5
6 7 8 9 10

I have read this return. Under penalties of perjury, I declare that to the best of my knowledge and belief, the return is true, correct, and accurately lists all amounts and sources of income I received during the tax year.

Sign here ▶

Keep copy for your records.

Your signature   Spouse's signature if joint return

Date   Your occupation   Date   Spouse's occupation

For Privacy Act and Paperwork Reduction Act Notice, see page 18.   Cat. No. 11329W   1997 Form 1040EZ

1997 Form 1040EZ page 2

Use this form if

- Your filing status is single or married filing jointly.
- You do not claim any dependents.

- You (and your spouse if married) were under 65 on January 1, 1998, and not blind at the end of 1997.
- Your taxable income (line 6) is less than $50,000.

- You had **only** wages, salaries, tips, taxable scholarship or fellowship grants, unemployment compensation, or Alaska Permanent Fund dividends, and your taxable interest income was not over $400. **But** if you earned tips, including allocated tips, that are not included in box 5 and box 7 of your W-2, you may not be able to use Form 1040EZ. See page 8.

- You did not receive any advance earned income credit payments.

If you are not sure about your filing status, see page 6. If you have questions about dependents, use TeleTax topic 354 (see page 18). If you **cannot use this form,** use TeleTax topic 352 (see page 18).

Filling in your return

For tips on how to avoid common mistakes, see page 3.

Because this form is read by a machine, please print your numbers inside the boxes like this:

9 8 7 6 5 4 3 2 1 0   Do not type your numbers. Do not use dollar signs.

If you received a scholarship or fellowship grant or tax-exempt interest income, such as on municipal bonds, see the booklet before filling in the form. Also, see the booklet if you received a Form 1099-INT showing Federal income tax withheld or if Federal income tax was withheld from your unemployment compensation or Alaska Permanent Fund dividends.

Remember, you must report all wages, salaries, and tips even if you do not get a W-2 form from your employer. You must also report all your taxable interest income, including interest from banks, savings and loans, credit unions, etc., even if you do not get a Form 1099-INT.

Worksheet for dependents who checked "Yes" on line 5

Use this worksheet to figure the amount to enter on line 5 if someone can claim you (or your spouse if married) as a dependent, even if that person chooses not to do so. To find out if someone can claim you as a dependent, use TeleTax topic 354 (see page 18).

A. Enter the amount from line 1 on the front.   **A.** _____

B. Minimum standard deduction.   **B.** _____ 650.00

C. Enter the LARGER of line A or line B here.   **C.** _____

D. Maximum standard deduction. If single, enter 4,150.00; if married, enter 6,900.00.   **D.** _____

E. Enter the SMALLER of line C or line D here. This is your standard deduction.   **E.** _____

F. Exemption amount.
  - If single, enter 0.
  - If married and—
    —both you and your spouse can be claimed as dependents, enter 0.
    —only one of you can be claimed as a dependent, enter 2,650.00.   **F.** _____

G. Add lines E and F. Enter the total here and on line 5 on the front.   **G.** _____

If you checked "No" on line 5 because no one can claim you (or your spouse if married) as a dependent, enter on line 5 the amount shown below that applies to you.

- Single, enter 6,800.00. This is the total of your standard deduction (4,150.00) and your exemption (2,650.00).

- Married, enter 12,200.00. This is the total of your standard deduction (6,900.00), your exemption (2,650.00), and your spouse's exemption (2,650.00).

Mailing your return

Mail your return by **April 15, 1998.** Use the envelope that came with your booklet. If you do not have that envelope, see page 28 for the address to use.

Paid preparer's use only

See page 14.

Under penalties of perjury, I declare that I have examined this return, and to the best of my knowledge and belief, it is true, correct, and accurately lists all amounts and sources of income received during the tax year. This declaration is based on all information of which I have any knowledge.

Preparer's signature ▶		Date	Check if self-employed ☐	Preparer's SSN
Firm's name (or yours if self-employed) and address ▶			EIN	
			ZIP code	

Form **1040A** (99)   Department of the Treasury—Internal Revenue Service
U.S. Individual Income Tax Return   **1997**   IRS Use Only—Do not write or staple in this space.

Label (See page 14.) **Use the IRS label.** Otherwise, please print in **ALL CAPITAL LETTERS.**	OMB No. 1545-0085

L A B E L H E R E

Your first name   Init.   Last name

If a joint return, spouse's first name   Init.   Last name

Home address (number and street). If you have a P.O. box, see page 14.   Apt. no.

City, town or post office. If you have a foreign address, see page 14.   State   ZIP code

Your social security number

Spouse's social security number

For Privacy Act and Paperwork Reduction Act Notice, see page 42.

Presidential Election Campaign Fund (See page 14.)   Yes | No

Do you want $3 to go to this fund? . . . .

If a joint return, does your spouse want $3 to go to this fund? . . . .

Note: *Checking "Yes" will not change your tax or reduce your refund.*

1 ☐ Single

2 ☐ Married filing joint return (even if only one had income)

3 ☐ Married filing separate return. Enter spouse's social security number above and full name here. ▶ _____

4 ☐ Head of household (with qualifying person). (See page 15.) If the qualifying person is a child but not your dependent, enter this child's name here. ▶ _____

5 ☐ Qualifying widow(er) with dependent child (year spouse died ▶ 19____). (See page 16.)

6a ☐ **Yourself.** If your parent (or someone else) can claim you as a dependent on his or her tax return, **do not** check box 6a.

b ☐ **Spouse**

No. of boxes checked on 6a and 6b ☐

c **Dependents.** If more than six dependents, see page 16.

(1) First name Last name	(2) Dependent's social security number	(3) Dependent's relationship to you	(4) No. of months lived in your home in 1997

No. of your children on 6c who:
- **lived with you** ☐
- **did not live with you due to divorce or separation** (see page 17) ☐

Dependents on 6c not entered above ☐

Add numbers entered in boxes above ☐

d Total number of exemptions claimed . . . . ▶

		Dollars	Cents
7	Wages, salaries, tips, etc. Attach Form(s) W-2.	**7**	
8a	**Taxable** interest income. Attach Schedule 1 if required.	**8a**	
b	**Tax-exempt** interest. DO NOT include on line 8a. **8b**		
9	Dividends. Attach Schedule 1 if required.	**9**	
10a	Total IRA distributions. **10a** ____ **10b** Taxable amount (see page 19).	**10b**	
11a	Total pensions and annuities. **11a** ____ **11b** Taxable amount (see page 19).	**11b**	
12	Unemployment compensation.	**12**	
13a	Social security benefits. **13a** ____ **13b** Taxable amount (see page 21).	**13b**	
14	Add lines 7 through 13b (far right column). This is your **total income.** ▶	**14**	
15	IRA deduction (see page 21).	**15**	
16	Subtract line 15 from line 14. This is your **adjusted gross income.** If under $29,290 (under $9,770 if a child did not live with you), see the EIC instructions on page 27. ▶	**16**	

Attach Copy B of W-2 and 1099-R here.   Cat. No. 11327A   **1997 Form 1040A**

1997 Form 1040A page 2

			17	

17 Enter the amount from line 16.

18a Check if:
- ☐ **You** were 65 or older   ☐ Blind
- ☐ **Spouse** was 65 or older   ☐ Blind

Enter number of boxes checked ▶ 18a ☐

b If you are married filing separately and your spouse itemizes deductions, see page 23 and check here . . . . ▶ 18b ☐

19 Enter the **standard deduction** for your filing status. **But** see page 24 if you checked any box on line 18a or 18b **OR** someone can claim you as a dependent.
- Single—4,150   • Married filing jointly or Qualifying widow(er)—6,900
- Head of household—6,050   • Married filing separately—3,450   **19**

20 Subtract line 19 from line 17. If line 19 is more than line 17, enter 0.   **20**

21 Multiply $2,650 by the total number of exemptions claimed on line 6d.   **21**

22 Subtract line 21 from line 20. If line 21 is more than line 20, enter 0. This is your **taxable income. If you want the IRS to figure your tax, see page 24.** ▶ **22**

23 Find the tax on the amount on line 22 (see page 24).   **23**

24a Credit for child and dependent care expenses. Attach Schedule 2.   **24a**

b Credit for the elderly or the disabled. Attach Schedule 3.   **24b**

c Adoption credit. Attach Form 8839.   **24c**

d Add lines 24a, 24b, and 24c. These are your **total credits.**   **24d**

25 Subtract line 24d from line 23. If line 24d is more than line 23, enter 0.   **25**

26 Advance earned income credit payments from Form(s) W-2.   **26**

27 Household employment taxes. Attach Schedule H.   **27**

28 Add lines 25, 26, and 27. This is your **total tax.** ▶ **28**

29a Total Federal income tax withheld from Forms W-2 and 1099.   **29a**

b 1997 estimated tax payments and amount applied from 1996 return.   **29b**

c **Earned income credit.** Attach Schedule EIC if you have a qualifying child.   **29c**

d Nontaxable earned income: amount ▶ [   ] and type ▶

e Add lines 29a, 29b, and 29c. These are your **total payments.** ▶ **29e**

30 If line 29e is more than line 28, subtract line 28 from line 29e. This is the amount you **overpaid.**   **30**

31a Amount of line 30 you want **refunded to you.** If you want it directly deposited, see page 33 and fill in 31b, 31c, and 31d.   **31a**

b Routing number [   ]   **c** Type: ☐ Checking   ☐ Savings

d Account number [   ]

32 Amount of line 30 you want **applied to your 1998 estimated tax. 32**

33 If line 28 is more than line 29e, subtract line 29e from line 28. This is the **amount you owe.** For details on how to pay, see page 34.   **33**

34 Estimated tax penalty (see page 34).   **34**

Sign here

Under penalties of perjury, I declare that I have examined this return and accompanying schedules and statements, and to the best of my knowledge and belief, they are true, correct, and accurately list all amounts and sources of income I received during the tax year. Declaration of preparer (other than the taxpayer) is based on all information of which the preparer has any knowledge.

Keep a copy of this return for your records.

Your signature	Date	Your occupation
Spouse's signature. If joint return, BOTH must sign.	Date	Spouse's occupation

Paid preparer's use only

Preparer's signature ▶	Date	Check if self-employed ☐	Preparer's SSN
Firm's name (or yours if self-employed) and address ▶		EIN	
		ZIP code	

Schedule 1
(Form 1040A)
(99)

Department of the Treasury—Internal Revenue Service

Interest and Dividend Income for Form 1040A Filers

1997

OMB No. 1545-0085

Name(s) shown on Form 1040A: First and initial(s)	Last	Your social security number

Part I   Interest Income   (See pages 18 and 49.)

Note: *If you received a Form 1099±INT, Form 1099±OID, or substitute statement from a brokerage firm, enter the firm's name and the total interest shown on that form.*

1   List name of payer. If any interest is from a seller-financed mortgage and the buyer used the property as a personal residence, see page 49 and list this interest first. Also, show that buyer's social security number and address.

		Dollars	Cents
1			

2	Add the amounts on line 1.	2		
3	Excludable interest on series EE U.S. savings bonds issued after 1989 from Form 8815, line 14. You **must** attach Form 8815 to Form 1040A.	3		
4	Subtract line 3 from line 2. Enter the result here and on Form 1040A, line 8a.	4		

Part II   Dividend Income   (See pages 19 and 49.)

Note: *If you received a Form 1099±DIV or substitute statement from a brokerage firm, enter the firm's name and the total dividends shown on that form.*

5   List name of payer

		Dollars	Cents
5			

| 6 | Add the amounts on line 5. Enter the total here and on Form 1040A, line 9. | 6 | | |

For Paperwork Reduction Act Notice, see Form 1040A instructions.   Cat. No. 12075R   **1997 Schedule 1 (Form 1040A)**

Form **1040**   Department of the Treasury—Internal Revenue Service
U.S. Individual Income Tax Return   **1997**   (99)   IRS Use Only—Do not write or staple in this space.

For the year Jan. 1–Dec. 31, 1997, or other tax year beginning _____, 1997, ending _____, 19____ | OMB No. 1545-0074

Label

(See instructions on page 10.)

Use the IRS label. Otherwise, please print or type.

L A B E L H E R E	Your first name and initial	Last name	Your social security number
	If a joint return, spouse's first name and initial	Last name	Spouse's social security number
	Home address (number and street). If you have a P.O. box, see page 10.	Apt. no.	For help in finding line instructions, see pages 2 and 3 in the booklet.
	City, town or post office, state, and ZIP code. If you have a foreign address, see page 10.		

Presidential Election Campaign
(See page 10.)

Do you want $3 to go to this fund? . . . .
If a joint return, does your spouse want $3 to go to this fund? . . . .

| | Yes | No | Note: Checking "Yes" will not change your tax or reduce your refund. |

Filing Status

Check only one box.

1   ☐ Single
2   ☐ Married filing joint return (even if only one had income)
3   ☐ Married filing separate return. Enter spouse's social security no. above and full name here. ▶ _____
4   ☐ Head of household (with qualifying person). (See page 10.) If the qualifying person is a child but not your dependent, enter this child's name here. ▶ _____
5   ☐ Qualifying widow(er) with dependent child (year spouse died ▶ 19____). (See page 10.)

Exemptions

If more than six dependents, see page 10.

6a ☐ **Yourself.** If your parent (or someone else) can claim you as a dependent on his or her tax return, **do not** check box 6a. . . . .
b   ☐ **Spouse** . . . .
c   **Dependents:**

(1) First name Last name	(2) Dependent's social security number	(3) Dependent's relationship to you	(4) No. of months lived in your home in 1997

No. of boxes checked on 6a and 6b ____

No. of your children on 6c who:
• lived with you
• did not live with you due to divorce or separation (see page 11)

Dependents on 6c not entered above ____

Add numbers entered on lines above ▶ ☐

d   Total number of exemptions claimed . . . .

Income

Attach Copy B of your Forms W-2, W-2G, and 1099-R here.

If you did not get a W-2, see page 12.

Enclose but do not attach any payment. Also, please use Form 1040-V.

7	Wages, salaries, tips, etc. Attach Form(s) W-2	7	
8a	**Taxable** interest. Attach Schedule B if required	8a	
b	**Tax-exempt** interest. DO NOT include on line 8a . . .	8b		
9	Dividends. Attach Schedule B if required	9	
10	Taxable refunds, credits, or offsets of state and local income taxes (see page 12) . .	10	
11	Alimony received	11	
12	Business income or (loss). Attach Schedule C or C-EZ	12	
13	Capital gain or (loss). Attach Schedule D	13	
14	Other gains or (losses). Attach Form 4797	14	
15a	Total IRA distributions .	15a		b Taxable amount (see page 13)	15b	
16a	Total pensions and annuities	16a		b Taxable amount (see page 13)	16b	
17	Rental real estate, royalties, partnerships, S corporations, trusts, etc. Attach Schedule E	17	
18	Farm income or (loss). Attach Schedule F	18	
19	Unemployment compensation	19	
20a	Social security benefits .	20a		b Taxable amount (see page 14)	20b	
21	Other income. List type and amount—see page 15 _____	21	
22	Add the amounts in the far right column for lines 7 through 21. This is your **total income ▶**	22	

Adjusted Gross Income

If line 32 is under $29,290 (under $9,770 if a child did not live with you), see EIC inst. on page 21.

23	IRA deduction (see page 16)	23	
24	Medical savings account deduction. Attach Form 8853 .	24	
25	Moving expenses. Attach Form 3903 or 3903-F . . .	25	
26	One-half of self-employment tax. Attach Schedule SE .	26	
27	Self-employed health insurance deduction (see page 17)	27	
28	Keogh and self-employed SEP and SIMPLE plans . .	28	
29	Penalty on early withdrawal of savings	29	
30a	Alimony paid b Recipient's SSN ▶ _____	30a	
31	Add lines 23 through 30a	31	
32	Subtract line 31 from line 22. This is your **adjusted gross income** . . . . ▶	32	

For Privacy Act and Paperwork Reduction Act Notice, see page 38.   Cat. No. 11320B   Form **1040** (1997)

Form 1040 (1997)   Page **2**

Tax Compu-tation	33	Amount from line 32 (adjusted gross income)	33	
	34a	Check if: ☐ **You** were 65 or older, ☐ Blind; ☐ **Spouse** was 65 or older, ☐ Blind. Add the number of boxes checked above and enter the total here . . . . ▶ **34a**		
	b	If you are married filing separately and your spouse itemizes deductions or you were a dual-status alien, see page 18 and check here . . . . . . ▶ **34b** ☐		
	35	Enter the **larger** of your: { **Itemized deductions** from Schedule A, line 28, **OR** **Standard deduction** shown below for your filing status. **But** see page 18 if you checked any box on line 34a or 34b **or** someone can claim you as a dependent. • Single—$4,150 • Married filing jointly or Qualifying widow(er)—$6,900 • Head of household—$6,050 • Married filing separately—$3,450 }	35	
If you want the IRS to figure your tax, see page 18.	36	Subtract line 35 from line 33	36	
	37	If line 33 is $90,900 or less, multiply $2,650 by the total number of exemptions claimed on line 6d. If line 33 is over $90,900, see the worksheet on page 19 for the amount to enter .	37	
	38	**Taxable income.** Subtract line 37 from line 36. If line 37 is more than line 36, enter -0-	38	
	39	**Tax.** See page 19. Check if any tax from **a** ☐ Form(s) 8814 **b** ☐ Form 4972 . . ▶	39	
Credits	40	Credit for child and dependent care expenses. Attach Form 2441	40	
	41	Credit for the elderly or the disabled. Attach Schedule R .	41	
	42	Adoption credit. Attach Form 8839	42	
	43	Foreign tax credit. Attach Form 1116	43	
	44	Other. Check if from **a** ☐ Form 3800 **b** ☐ Form 8396 **c** ☐ Form 8801 **d** ☐ Form (specify)_____	44	
	45	Add lines 40 through 44	45	
	46	Subtract line 45 from line 39. If line 45 is more than line 39, enter -0- . . . . . . ▶	46	
Other Taxes	47	Self-employment tax. Attach Schedule SE	47	
	48	Alternative minimum tax. Attach Form 6251	48	
	49	Social security and Medicare tax on tip income not reported to employer. Attach Form 4137	49	
	50	Tax on qualified retirement plans (including IRAs) and MSAs. Attach Form 5329 if required	50	
	51	Advance earned income credit payments from Form(s) W-2	51	
	52	Household employment taxes. Attach Schedule H	52	
	53	Add lines 46 through 52. This is your **total tax** . . . . ▶	53	
Payments Attach Forms W-2, W-2G, and 1099-R on the front.	54	Federal income tax withheld from Forms W-2 and 1099 . .	54	
	55	1997 estimated tax payments and amount applied from 1996 return .	55	
	56a	**Earned income credit.** Attach Schedule EIC if you have a qualifying child **b** Nontaxable earned income: amount ▶ [ ] and type ▶ _____	56a	
	57	Amount paid with Form 4868 (request for extension) . . .	57	
	58	Excess social security and RRTA tax withheld (see page 27)	58	
	59	Other payments. Check if from **a** ☐ Form 2439 **b** ☐ Form 4136	59	
	60	Add lines 54, 55, 56a, 57, 58, and 59. These are your **total payments** . . . . . ▶	60	
Refund Have it directly deposited! See page 27 and fill in 62b, 62c, and 62d.	61	If line 60 is more than line 53, subtract line 53 from line 60. This is the amount you **OVERPAID**	61	
	62a	Amount of line 61 you want **REFUNDED TO YOU**. . . . . ▶	62a	
	▶ b	Routing number [ ] ▶ **c** Type: ☐ Checking ☐ Savings		
	▶ d	Account number [ ]		
	63	Amount of line 61 you want **APPLIED TO YOUR 1998 ESTIMATED TAX** ▶	63	
Amount You Owe	64	If line 53 is more than line 60, subtract line 60 from line 53. This is the **AMOUNT YOU OWE.** For details on how to pay, see page 27 . . . . ▶	64	
	65	Estimated tax penalty. Also include on line 64	65	

Sign Here
Keep a copy of this return for your records.

Under penalties of perjury, I declare that I have examined this return and accompanying schedules and statements, and to the best of my knowledge and belief, they are true, correct, and complete. Declaration of preparer (other than taxpayer) is based on all information of which preparer has any knowledge.

▶ Your signature	Date	Your occupation
▶ Spouse's signature. If a joint return, BOTH must sign.	Date	Spouse's occupation

Paid Preparer's Use Only

Preparer's signature ▶	Date	Check if self-employed ☐	Preparer's social security no.
Firm's name (or yours if self-employed) and address ▶			EIN ZIP code

SCHEDULES A&B	Schedule A—Itemized Deductions	OMB No. 1545-0074

(Form 1040)

(Schedule B is on back)

19 97

Department of the Treasury
Internal Revenue Service (99)

► Attach to Form 1040. ► See Instructions for Schedules A and B (Form 1040).

Attachment Sequence No. **07**

Name(s) shown on Form 1040

Your social security number

Medical and Dental Expenses		**Caution:** *Do not include expenses reimbursed or paid by others.*	
	1	Medical and dental expenses (see page A-1)	1
	2	Enter amount from Form 1040, line 33 . [2]	
	3	Multiply line 2 above by 7.5% (.075)	3
	4	Subtract line 3 from line 1. If line 3 is more than line 1, enter -0-	4
Taxes You Paid (See page A-2.)	5	State and local income taxes	5
	6	Real estate taxes (see page A-2)	6
	7	Personal property taxes	7
	8	Other taxes. List type and amount ► -----------------	
			8
	9	Add lines 5 through 8	9
Interest You Paid (See page A-2.)	10	Home mortgage interest and points reported to you on Form 1098	10
	11	Home mortgage interest not reported to you on Form 1098. If paid to the person from whom you bought the home, see page A-3 and show that person's name, identifying no., and address ►	
Note: Personal interest is not deductible.		-------------------------------------	11
	12	Points not reported to you on Form 1098. See page A-3 for special rules	12
	13	Investment interest. Attach Form 4952 if required. (See page A-3.)	13
	14	Add lines 10 through 13	14
Gifts to Charity If you made a gift and got a benefit for it, see page A-3.	15	Gifts by cash or check. If you made any gift of $250 or more, see page A-3	15
	16	Other than by cash or check. If any gift of $250 or more, see page A-3. You **MUST** attach Form 8283 if over $500	16
	17	Carryover from prior year	17
	18	Add lines 15 through 17	18
Casualty and Theft Losses	19	Casualty or theft loss(es). Attach Form 4684. (See page A-4.)	19
Job Expenses and Most Other Miscellaneous Deductions (See page A-5 for expenses to deduct here.)	20	Unreimbursed employee expenses—job travel, union dues, job education, etc. You **MUST** attach Form 2106 or 2106-EZ if required. (See page A-4.) ► -----------	
			20
	21	Tax preparation fees	21
	22	Other expenses—investment, safe deposit box, etc. List type and amount ► -----------------	
			22
	23	Add lines 20 through 22	23
	24	Enter amount from Form 1040, line 33 . [24]	
	25	Multiply line 24 above by 2% (.02)	25
	26	Subtract line 25 from line 23. If line 25 is more than line 23, enter -0- . . .	26
Other Miscellaneous Deductions	27	Other—from list on page A-5. List type and amount ► -----------------	
			27
Total Itemized Deductions	28	Is Form 1040, line 33, over $121,200 (over $60,600 if married filing separately)?	
		NO. Your deduction is not limited. Add the amounts in the far right column for lines 4 through 27. Also, enter on Form 1040, line 35, the **larger** of this amount or your standard deduction.	► 28
		YES. Your deduction may be limited. See page A-5 for the amount to enter.	

For Paperwork Reduction Act Notice, see Form 1040 instructions.   Cat. No. 11330X   Schedule A (Form 1040) 1997

Schedules A&B (Form 1040) 1997   OMB No. 1545-0074   Page **2**

Name(s) shown on Form 1040. Do not enter name and social security number if shown on other side.	Your social security number

Schedule B—Interest and Dividend Income

Attachment Sequence No. **08**

Part I Interest Income

(See pages 12 and B-1.)

Note: If you received a Form 1099-INT, Form 1099-OID, or substitute statement from a brokerage firm, list the firm's name as the payer and enter the total interest shown on that form.

Note: *If you had over $400 in taxable interest income, you must also complete Part III.*

1 List name of payer. If any interest is from a seller-financed mortgage and the buyer used the property as a personal residence, see page B-1 and list this interest first. Also, show that buyer's social security number and address ▶

	Amount
1	

2 Add the amounts on line 1 . . . . **2**

3 Excludable interest on series EE U.S. savings bonds issued after 1989 from Form 8815, line 14. You MUST attach Form 8815 to Form 1040 . . . . **3**

4 Subtract line 3 from line 2. Enter the result here and on Form 1040, line 8a ▶ **4**

Part II Dividend Income

(See pages 12 and B-1.)

Note: If you received a Form 1099-DIV or substitute statement from a brokerage firm, list the firm's name as the payer and enter the total dividends shown on that form.

Note: *If you had over $400 in gross dividends and/or other distributions on stock, you must also complete Part III.*

5 List name of payer. Include gross dividends and/or other distributions on stock here. Any capital gain distributions and nontaxable distributions will be deducted on lines 7 and 8 ▶

	Amount
5	

6 Add the amounts on line 5 . . . . **6**

7 Capital gain distributions. Enter here and on Schedule D   **7**

8 Nontaxable distributions. (See the inst. for Form 1040, line 9.)   **8**

9 Add lines 7 and 8 . . . . **9**

10 Subtract line 9 from line 6. Enter the result here and on Form 1040, line 9 . ▶ **10**

Part III Foreign Accounts and Trusts

(See page B-2.)

You must complete this part if you **(a)** had over $400 of interest or dividends; **(b)** had a foreign account; or **(c)** received a distribution from, or were a grantor of, or a transferor to, a foreign trust.

	Yes	No

11a At any time during 1997, did you have an interest in or a signature or other authority over a financial account in a foreign country, such as a bank account, securities account, or other financial account? See page B-2 for exceptions and filing requirements for Form TD F 90-22.1 . . . .

b If "Yes," enter the name of the foreign country ▶

12 During 1997, did you receive a distribution from, or were you the grantor of, or transferor to, a foreign trust? If "Yes," you may have to file Form 3520 or 926. See page B-2 . . . .

For Paperwork Reduction Act Notice, see Form 1040 instructions.   **Schedule B (Form 1040) 1997**

SCHEDULE C
(Form 1040)

Department of the Treasury
Internal Revenue Service   (99)

Profit or Loss From Business

(Sole Proprietorship)

► **Partnerships, joint ventures, etc., must file Form 1065.**

► **Attach to Form 1040 or Form 1041.**   ► **See Instructions for Schedule C (Form 1040).**

OMB No. 1545-0074

19 97

Attachment
Sequence No. **09**

Name of proprietor

Social security number (SSN)

A Principal business or profession, including product or service (see page C-1)	**B Enter principal business code** (see page C-6) ►
C Business name. If no separate business name, leave blank.	**D Employer ID number (EIN), if any**

E Business address (including suite or room no.) ► ....
City, town or post office, state, and ZIP code

F Accounting method: **(1)** ☐ Cash   **(2)** ☐ Accrual   **(3)** ☐ Other (specify) ► ....

G Did you "materially participate" in the operation of this business during 1997? If "No," see page C-2 for limit on losses .   ☐ Yes   ☐ No

H If you started or acquired this business during 1997, check here . . . . ► ☐

Part I   Income

1	Gross receipts or sales. **Caution:** *If this income was reported to you on Form W-2 and the "Statutory employee" box on that form was checked, see page C-2 and check here* . . . . ► ☐	**1**	
2	Returns and allowances	**2**	
3	Subtract line 2 from line 1	**3**	
4	Cost of goods sold (from line 42 on page 2)	**4**	
5	**Gross profit.** Subtract line 4 from line 3	**5**	
6	Other income, including Federal and state gasoline or fuel tax credit or refund (see page C-2) . . .	**6**	
7	**Gross income.** Add lines 5 and 6 . . . . ►	**7**	

Part II   Expenses. Enter expenses for business use of your home **only** on line 30.

8	Advertising	**8**		**19** Pension and profit-sharing plans	**19**	
9	Bad debts from sales or services (see page C-3) . .	**9**		**20** Rent or lease (see page C-4):		
				a Vehicles, machinery, and equipment .	**20a**	
10	Car and truck expenses (see page C-3)	**10**		**b** Other business property . .	**20b**	
11	Commissions and fees . .	**11**		**21** Repairs and maintenance . .	**21**	
12	Depletion	**12**		**22** Supplies (not included in Part III) .	**22**	
13	Depreciation and section 179 expense deduction (not included in Part III) (see page C-3) . .	**13**		**23** Taxes and licenses	**23**	
				24 Travel, meals, and entertainment:		
				a Travel	**24a**	
14	Employee benefit programs (other than on line 19) . . .	**14**		**b** Meals and entertainment .		
15	Insurance (other than health) .	**15**		**c** Enter 50% of line 24b subject to limitations (see page C-4) .		
16	Interest:					
a	Mortgage (paid to banks, etc.) .	**16a**		**d** Subtract line 24c from line 24b .	**24d**	
b	Other	**16b**		**25** Utilities	**25**	
17	Legal and professional services	**17**		**26** Wages (less employment credits) .	**26**	
18	Office expense	**18**		**27** Other expenses (from line 48 on page 2)	**27**	

28	**Total expenses** before expenses for business use of home. Add lines 8 through 27 in columns . ►	**28**	
29	Tentative profit (loss). Subtract line 28 from line 7	**29**	
30	Expenses for business use of your home. Attach **Form 8829**	**30**	
31	**Net profit or (loss).** Subtract line 30 from line 29.		
	• If a profit, enter on **Form 1040, line 12,** and ALSO on **Schedule SE, line 2** (statutory employees, see page C-5). Estates and trusts, enter on Form 1041, line 3.	**31**	
	• If a loss, you MUST go on to line 32.		
32	If you have a loss, check the box that describes your investment in this activity (see page C-5).		
	• If you checked 32a, enter the loss on **Form 1040, line 12,** and ALSO on **Schedule SE, line 2** (statutory employees, see page C-5). Estates and trusts, enter on Form 1041, line 3.	**32a** ☐ All investment is at risk.	
	• If you checked 32b, you MUST attach **Form 6198.**	**32b** ☐ Some investment is not at risk.	

For Paperwork Reduction Act Notice, see Form 1040 instructions.   Cat. No. 11334P   **Schedule C (Form 1040) 1997**

Schedule C (Form 1040) 1997   Page **2**

| **Part III** | **Cost of Goods Sold** (see page C-5) |

33 Method(s) used to
value closing inventory: **a** ☐ Cost   **b** ☐ Lower of cost or market   **c** ☐ Other (attach explanation)

34 Was there any change in determining quantities, costs, or valuations between opening and closing inventory? If
"Yes," attach explanation . . . . ☐ **Yes**   ☐ **No**

35	Inventory at beginning of year. If different from last year's closing inventory, attach explanation . .	35	
36	Purchases less cost of items withdrawn for personal use	36	
37	Cost of labor. Do not include salary paid to yourself	37	
38	Materials and supplies	38	
39	Other costs	39	
40	Add lines 35 through 39	40	
41	Inventory at end of year	41	
42	**Cost of goods sold.** Subtract line 41 from line 40. Enter the result here and on page 1, line 4 . .	42	

| **Part IV** | **Information on Your Vehicle.** Complete this part **ONLY** if you are claiming car or truck expenses on line 10 and are not required to file Form 4562 for this business. See the instructions for line 13 on page C-3 to find out if you must file. |

43 When did you place your vehicle in service for business purposes? (month, day, year) ▶ .... / .... / ....

44 Of the total number of miles you drove your vehicle during 1997, enter the number of miles you used your vehicle for:

a Business .... **b** Commuting .... **c** Other ....

45 Do you (or your spouse) have another vehicle available for personal use? . . . . ☐ **Yes**   ☐ **No**

46 Was your vehicle available for use during off-duty hours? . . . . ☐ **Yes**   ☐ **No**

47a Do you have evidence to support your deduction? . . . . ☐ **Yes**   ☐ **No**

  b If "Yes," is the evidence written? . . . . ☐ **Yes**   ☐ **No**

| **Part V** | **Other Expenses.** List below business expenses not included on lines 8–26 or line 30. |

--	
--	
--	
--	
--	
--	
--	
--	
48 Total other expenses. Enter here and on page 1, line 27	48	

SCHEDULE D
(Form 1040)

Department of the Treasury
Internal Revenue Service   (99)

Capital Gains and Losses

▶ Attach to Form 1040.   ▶ See Instructions for Schedule D (Form 1040).

▶ Use Schedule D-1 for more space to list transactions for lines 1 and 8.

OMB No. 1545-0074

1997

Attachment
Sequence No. **12**

Name(s) shown on Form 1040

Your social security number

Part I   Short-Term Capital Gains and Losses—Assets Held One Year or Less

(a) Description of property (Example: 100 sh. XYZ Co.)	(b) Date acquired (Mo., day, yr.)	(c) Date sold (Mo., day, yr.)	(d) Sales price (see page D-3)	(e) Cost or other basis (see page D-4)	(f) GAIN or (LOSS) FOR ENTIRE YEAR. Subtract (e) from (d)	
1						

2 Enter your short-term totals, if any, from Schedule D-1, line 2 . . . .   **2**

3 **Total short-term sales price amounts.** Add column (d) of lines 1 and 2 . . .   **3**

4 Short-term gain from Forms 2119 and 6252, and short-term gain or (loss) from Forms 4684, 6781, and 8824 . .   **4**

5 Net short-term gain or (loss) from partnerships, S corporations, estates, and trusts from Schedule(s) K-1 . . . .   **5**

6 Short-term capital loss carryover. Enter the amount, if any, from line 9 of your 1996 Capital Loss Carryover Worksheet . . . .   **6** ( )

7 **Net short-term capital gain or (loss).** Combine lines 1 through 6 in column (f). . . . . ▶   **7**

Part II   Long-Term Capital Gains and Losses—Assets Held More Than One Year

(a) Description of property (Example: 100 sh. XYZ Co.)	(b) Date acquired (Mo., day, yr.)	(c) Date sold (Mo., day, yr.)	(d) Sales price (see page D-3)	(e) Cost or other basis (see page D-4)	(f) GAIN or (LOSS) FOR ENTIRE YEAR. Subtract (e) from (d)	(g) 28% RATE GAIN or (LOSS) * (see instr. below)
8						

9 Enter your long-term totals, if any, from Schedule D-1, line 9 . . . .   **9**

10 **Total long-term sales price amounts.** Add column (d) of lines 8 and 9 . . .   **10**

11 Gain from Form 4797, Part I; long-term gain from Forms 2119, 2439, and 6252; and long-term gain or (loss) from Forms 4684, 6781, and 8824 . .   **11**

12 Net long-term gain or (loss) from partnerships, S corporations, estates, and trusts from Schedule(s) K-1 . . . .   **12**

13 Capital gain distributions **13**

14 Long-term capital loss carryover. Enter in both columns (f) and (g) the amount, if any, from line 14 of your 1996 Capital Loss Carryover Worksheet . . .   **14** ( )( )

15 Combine lines 8 through 14 in column (g) **15**

16 **Net long-term capital gain or (loss).** Combine lines 8 through 14 in column (f). . . . . ▶   **16**

*28% Rate Gain or Loss includes all gains and losses in Part II, column (f) from sales, exchanges, or conversions (including installment payments received) **either:** ● **Before** May 7, 1997, **or**
● **After** July 28, 1997, for assets held more than 1 year but **not** more than 18 months.
It also includes **ALL** "collectibles gains and losses" (as defined on page D-4).

For Paperwork Reduction Act Notice, see Form 1040 instructions.   Cat. No. 11338H   **Schedule D (Form 1040) 1997**

Part III   Summary of Parts I and II

17   Combine lines 7 and 16. If a loss, go to line 18. If a gain, enter the gain on Form 1040, line 13 | **17** |

    Next: Complete Form 1040 through line 38. Then, go to **Part IV** to figure your tax if:
- Both lines 16 and 17 are gains, **and**
- Form 1040, line 38, is more than zero.

18   If line 17 is a loss, enter here and as a (loss) on Form 1040, line 13, the **smaller** of these losses:
- The loss on line 17; **or**
- ($3,000) or, if married filing separately, ($1,500) . . . . | **18** (   )

    Next: Complete Form 1040 through line 36. Then, complete the **Capital Loss Carryover Worksheet** on page D-4 if:
- The loss on line 17 exceeds the loss on line 18, **or**
- Form 1040, line 36, is a loss.

Part IV   Tax Computation Using Maximum Capital Gains Rates

19	Enter your taxable income from Form 1040, line 38		**19**
20	Enter the **smaller** of line 16 or line 17	**20**	
21	If you are filing Form 4952, enter the amount from Form 4952, line 4e	**21**	
22	Subtract line 21 from line 20. If zero or less, enter -0-	**22**	
23	Combine lines 7 and 15. If zero or less, enter -0-	**23**	
24	Enter the **smaller** of line 15 or line 23, but not less than zero . . .	**24**	
25	Enter your unrecaptured section 1250 gain, if any (see page D-4) .	**25**	
26	Add lines 24 and 25	**26**	
27	Subtract line 26 from line 22. If zero or less, enter -0-		**27**
28	Subtract line 27 from line 19. If zero or less, enter -0-		**28**
29	Enter the **smaller** of line 19 or $41,200 ($24,650 if single; $20,600 if married filing separately; $33,050 if head of household)		**29**
30	Enter the **smaller** of line 28 or line 29		**30**
31	Subtract line 22 from line 19. If zero or less, enter -0-		**31**
32	Enter the **larger** of line 30 or line 31		**32**
33	Figure the tax on the amount on line 32. Use the Tax Table or Tax Rate Schedules, whichever applies . . . . ▶		**33**
34	Enter the amount from line 29		**34**
35	Enter the amount from line 28		**35**
36	Subtract line 35 from line 34. If zero or less, enter -0-		**36**
37	Multiply line 36 by 10% (.10) . . . . ▶		**37**
38	Enter the **smaller** of line 19 or line 27		**38**
39	Enter the amount from line 36		**39**
40	Subtract line 39 from line 38. If zero or less, enter -0-		**40**
41	Multiply line 40 by 20% (.20) . . . . ▶		**41**
42	Enter the **smaller** of line 22 or line 25		**42**
43	Add lines 22 and 32	**43**	
44	Enter the amount from line 19	**44**	
45	Subtract line 44 from line 43. If zero or less, enter -0-		**45**
46	Subtract line 45 from line 42. If zero or less, enter -0-		**46**
47	Multiply line 46 by 25% (.25) . . . . ▶		**47**
48	Enter the amount from line 19		**48**
49	Add lines 32, 36, 40, and 46		**49**
50	Subtract line 49 from line 48		**50**
51	Multiply line 50 by 28% (.28) . . . . ▶		**51**
52	Add lines 33, 37, 41, 47, and 51		**52**
53	Figure the tax on the amount on line 19. Use the Tax Table or Tax Rate Schedules, whichever applies		**53**
54	**Tax.** Enter the **smaller** of line 52 or line 53 here and on Form 1040, line 39 . . . . ▶		**54**

SCHEDULE E
(Form 1040)

Department of the Treasury
Internal Revenue Service (99)

Supplemental Income and Loss

(From rental real estate, royalties, partnerships,
S corporations, estates, trusts, REMICs, etc.)

▶ **Attach to Form 1040 or Form 1041.**   ▶ **See Instructions for Schedule E (Form 1040).**

OMB No. 1545-0074

1997

Attachment
Sequence No. **13**

Name(s) shown on return | Your social security number

| **Part I** | **Income or Loss From Rental Real Estate and Royalties** **Note:** *Report income and expenses from your business of renting personal property on **Schedule C** or **C-EZ** (see page E-1). Report farm rental income or loss from **Form 4835** on page 2, line 39.* |

1 Show the kind and location of each **rental real estate property:**	2 For each rental real estate property listed on line 1, did you or your family use it during the tax year for personal purposes for more than the greater of:		Yes	No
A		A		
B	● 14 days, **or**			
	● 10% of the total days rented at fair rental value?	B		
C	(See page E-1.)	C		

		Properties			Totals
Income:		A	B	C	(Add columns A, B, and C.)
3 Rents received	3				3
4 Royalties received	4				4
Expenses:					
5 Advertising	5				
6 Auto and travel (see page E-2) .	6				
7 Cleaning and maintenance . . .	7				
8 Commissions	8				
9 Insurance	9				
10 Legal and other professional fees	10				
11 Management fees	11				
12 Mortgage interest paid to banks, etc. (see page E-2)	12				12
13 Other interest	13				
14 Repairs	14				
15 Supplies	15				
16 Taxes	16				
17 Utilities	17				
18 Other (list) ▶............................	18				
19 Add lines 5 through 18	19				19
20 Depreciation expense or depletion (see page E-2)	20				20
21 Total expenses. Add lines 19 and 20	21				
22 Income or (loss) from rental real estate or royalty properties. Subtract line 21 from line 3 (rents) or line 4 (royalties). If the result is a (loss), see page E-3 to find out if you must file **Form 6198**. . .	22				
23 Deductible rental real estate loss. **Caution:** *Your rental real estate loss on line 22 may be limited. See page E-3 to find out if you must file **Form 8582**. Real estate professionals must complete line 42 on page 2*	23	(	)(	)(	)
24 **Income.** Add positive amounts shown on line 22. **Do not** include any losses				24	
25 **Losses.** Add royalty losses from line 22 and rental real estate losses from line 23. Enter total losses here				25	( )
26 Total rental real estate and royalty income or (loss). Combine lines 24 and 25. Enter the result here. If Parts II, III, IV, and line 39 on page 2 do not apply to you, also enter this amount on Form 1040, line 17. Otherwise, include this amount in the total on line 40 on page 2				26	

For Paperwork Reduction Act Notice, see Form 1040 instructions.   Cat. No. 11344L   **Schedule E (Form 1040) 1997**

Schedule E (Form 1040) 1997 | Attachment Sequence No. **13** | Page **2**

Name(s) shown on return. Do not enter name and social security number if shown on other side.	Your social security number

Note: *If you report amounts from farming or fishing on Schedule E, you must enter your gross income from those activities on line 41 below. Real estate professionals must complete line 42 below.*

Part II   Income or Loss From Partnerships and S Corporations

Note: *If you report a loss from an at-risk activity, you MUST check either column (e) or (f) on line 27 to describe your investment in the activity. See page E-4. If you check column (f), you must attach Form 6198.*

27	(a) Name	(b) Enter **P** for partnership; **S** for S corporation	(c) Check if foreign partnership	(d) Employer identification number	Investment At Risk? (e) All is at risk	(f) Some is not at risk
A						
B						
C						
D						
E						

	Passive Income and Loss		Nonpassive Income and Loss		
	(g) Passive loss allowed (attach **Form 8582** if required)	(h) Passive income from **Schedule K–1**	(i) Nonpassive loss from **Schedule K–1**	(j) Section 179 expense deduction from **Form 4562**	(k) Nonpassive income from **Schedule K–1**
A					
B					
C					
D					
E					
28a Totals					
b Totals					

29	Add columns (h) and (k) of line 28a	29	
30	Add columns (g), (i), and (j) of line 28b	30	( )
31	Total partnership and S corporation income or (loss). Combine lines 29 and 30. Enter the result here and include in the total on line 40 below	31	

Part III   Income or Loss From Estates and Trusts

32	(a) Name	(b) Employer identification number
A		
B		

	Passive Income and Loss		Nonpassive Income and Loss	
	(c) Passive deduction or loss allowed (attach **Form 8582** if required)	(d) Passive income from **Schedule K–1**	(e) Deduction or loss from **Schedule K–1**	(f) Other income from **Schedule K–1**
A				
B				
33a Totals				
b Totals				

34	Add columns (d) and (f) of line 33a	34	
35	Add columns (c) and (e) of line 33b	35	( )
36	Total estate and trust income or (loss). Combine lines 34 and 35. Enter the result here and include in the total on line 40 below	36	

Part IV   Income or Loss From Real Estate Mortgage Investment Conduits (REMICs)—Residual Holder

37	(a) Name	(b) Employer identification number	(c) Excess inclusion from **Schedules Q**, line 2c (see page E-5)	(d) Taxable income (net loss) from **Schedules Q**, line 1b	(e) Income from **Schedules Q**, line 3b

38	Combine columns (d) and (e) only. Enter the result here and include in the total on line 40 below	38	

Part V   Summary

39	Net farm rental income or (loss) from **Form 4835**. Also, complete line 41 below	39	
40	TOTAL income or (loss). Combine lines 26, 31, 36, 38, and 39. Enter the result here and on Form 1040, line 17 ▶	40	

41	**Reconciliation of Farming and Fishing Income.** Enter your **gross** farming and fishing income reported on Form 4835, line 7; Schedule K-1 (Form 1065), line 15b; Schedule K-1 (Form 1120S), line 23; and Schedule K-1 (Form 1041), line 14 (see page E-5)	41	
42	**Reconciliation for Real Estate Professionals.** If you were a real estate professional (see page E-4), enter the net income or (loss) you reported anywhere on Form 1040 from all rental real estate activities in which you materially participated under the passive activity loss rules . . .	42	

Schedule R
(Form 1040)

Department of the Treasury
Internal Revenue Service   (99)

Credit for the Elderly or the Disabled

▶ **Attach to Form 1040.**   ▶ **See separate instructions for Schedule R.**

OMB No. 1545-0074

1997

Attachment
Sequence No. **16**

Name(s) shown on Form 1040

Your social security number

You may be able to take this credit and reduce your tax if by the end of 1997:

- You were age 65 or older, **OR** • You were under age 65, you retired on **permanent and total** disability, and you received taxable disability income.

But you must also meet other tests. See the separate instructions for Schedule R.

TIP: In most cases, the IRS can figure the credit for you. See the instructions.

Part I   **Check the Box for Your Filing Status and Age**

If your filing status is:	And by the end of 1997:	Check only one box:

Single, Head of household, or Qualifying widow(er) with dependent child

1 You were 65 or older . . . . **1** ☐

2 You were under 65 and you retired on permanent and total disability . . . **2** ☐

Married filing a joint return

3 Both spouses were 65 or older . . . . **3** ☐

4 Both spouses were under 65, but only one spouse retired on permanent and total disability . . . . **4** ☐

5 Both spouses were under 65, and both retired on permanent and total disability . . . . **5** ☐

6 One spouse was 65 or older, and the other spouse was under 65 and retired on permanent and total disability . . . . **6** ☐

7 One spouse was 65 or older, and the other spouse was under 65 and **NOT** retired on permanent and total disability . . . . **7** ☐

Married filing a separate return

8 You were 65 or older and you lived apart from your spouse for all of 1997 . . **8** ☐

9 You were under 65, you retired on permanent and total disability, and you lived apart from your spouse for all of 1997 . . . . **9** ☐

Did you check box 1, 3, 7, or 8?

Yes ───▶ Skip Part II and complete Part III on back.

No ───▶ Complete Parts II and III.

Part II   **Statement of Permanent and Total Disability** (Complete **only** if you checked box 2, 4, 5, 6, or 9 above.)

IF: 1 You filed a physician's statement for this disability for 1983 or an earlier year, or you filed a statement for tax years after 1983 and your physician signed line B on the statement, **AND**

2 Due to your continued disabled condition, you were unable to engage in any substantial gainful activity in 1997, check this box . . . . ▶ ☐

- If you checked this box, you do not have to file another statement for 1997.
- If you **did not** check this box, have your physician complete the statement below.

Physician's Statement (See instructions on back.)

I certify that _____
Name of disabled person

was permanently and totally disabled on January 1, 1976, or January 1, 1977, **OR** was permanently and totally disabled on the date he or she retired. If retired after 1976, enter the date retired. ▶ _____

Physician: Sign your name on **either** line A or B below.

A The disability has lasted or can be expected to last continuously for at least a year . . . . _____

Physician's signature   Date

B There is no reasonable probability that the disabled condition will ever improve . . . . _____

Physician's signature   Date

Physician's name   Physician's address

For Paperwork Reduction Act Notice, see Form 1040 instructions.   Cat. No. 11359K   **Schedule R (Form 1040) 1997**

Schedule R (Form 1040) 1997   Page **2**

| **Part III** | **Figure Your Credit** |

10 If you checked (in Part I):   **Enter:**

   Box 1, 2, 4, or 7 . . . . $5,000 ⎫
   Box 3, 5, or 6 . . . . $7,500 ⎬ **10**
   Box 8 or 9 . . . . $3,750 ⎭

   | Did you check box 2, 4, 5, 6, or 9 in Part I? | **Yes** ➤ You **must** complete line 11. |
   | | **No** ➤ Enter the amount from line 10 on line 12 and go to line 13. |

11 If you checked:

   • Box 6 in Part I, add $5,000 to the taxable disability income of the spouse who was under age 65. Enter the total.

   • Box 2, 4, or 9 in Part I, enter your taxable disability income.   ⎫
                                                                        ⎬ **11**
   • Box 5 in Part I, add your taxable disability income to your spouse's taxable disability income. Enter the total. ⎭

   TIP: For more details on what to include on line 11, see the instructions.

12 If you completed line 11, enter the **smaller** of line 10 or line 11; **all others,** enter the amount from line 10 . . . . **12**

13 Enter the following pensions, annuities, or disability income that you (and your spouse if filing a joint return) received in 1997:

   a Nontaxable part of social security benefits, and
      Nontaxable part of railroad retirement benefits treated as   ⎫
      social security. See instructions.   ⎬ . . . **13a**
                                                                    ⎭

   b Nontaxable veterans' pensions, and   ⎫
      Any other pension, annuity, or disability benefit that is   ⎬ . . . **13b**
      excluded from income under any other provision of law.   ⎭
      See instructions.

   c Add lines 13a and 13b. (Even though these income items are not taxable, they **must** be included here to figure your credit.) If you did not receive any of the types of nontaxable income listed on line 13a or 13b, enter -0- on line 13c **13c**

14 Enter the amount from Form 1040, line 33   **14**

15 If you checked (in Part I):   **Enter:**

   Box 1 or 2 . . . . $7,500 ⎫
   Box 3, 4, 5, 6, or 7 . . . . $10,000 ⎬ **15**
   Box 8 or 9 . . . . $5,000 ⎭

16 Subtract line 15 from line 14. If zero or less, enter -0- **16**

17 Enter one-half of line 16 . . . . **17**

18 Add lines 13c and 17 . . . . **18**

19 Subtract line 18 from line 12. If zero or less, **stop;** you **cannot** take the credit. Otherwise, go to line 20 . . . . **19**

20 Multiply line 19 by 15% (.15). Enter the result here and on Form 1040, line 41. **Caution:** *If you file Schedule C, C-EZ, D, E, or F (Form 1040), your credit may be limited. See the instructions for line 20 for the amount of credit you can claim* **20**

Instructions for Physician's Statement

Taxpayer

If you retired after 1976, enter the date you retired in the space provided in Part II.

Physician

A person is permanently and totally disabled if **both** of the following apply:

   1. He or she cannot engage in any substantial gainful activity because of a physical or mental condition, and

   2. A physician determines that the disability has lasted or can be expected to last continuously for at least a year or can lead to death.

SCHEDULE SE
(Form 1040)

Department of the Treasury
Internal Revenue Service   (99)

Self-Employment Tax

▶ See Instructions for Schedule SE (Form 1040).

▶ Attach to Form 1040.

OMB No. 1545-0074

1997

Attachment
Sequence No. **17**

Name of person with **self-employment** income (as shown on Form 1040)	Social security number of person with **self-employment** income ▶

Who Must File Schedule SE

You must file Schedule SE if:

● You had net earnings from self-employment from **other than** church employee income (line 4 of Short Schedule SE or line 4c of Long Schedule SE) of $400 or more, **OR**

● You had church employee income of $108.28 or more. Income from services you performed as a minister or a member of a religious order **is not** church employee income. See page SE-1.

Note: *Even if you had a loss or a small amount of income from self-employment, it may be to your benefit to file Schedule SE and use either "optional method" in Part II of Long Schedule SE. See page SE-3.*

Exception. If your only self-employment income was from earnings as a minister, member of a religious order, or Christian Science practitioner **and** you filed Form 4361 and received IRS approval not to be taxed on those earnings, **do not** file Schedule SE. Instead, write "Exempt–Form 4361" on Form 1040, line 47.

May I Use Short Schedule SE or MUST I Use Long Schedule SE?

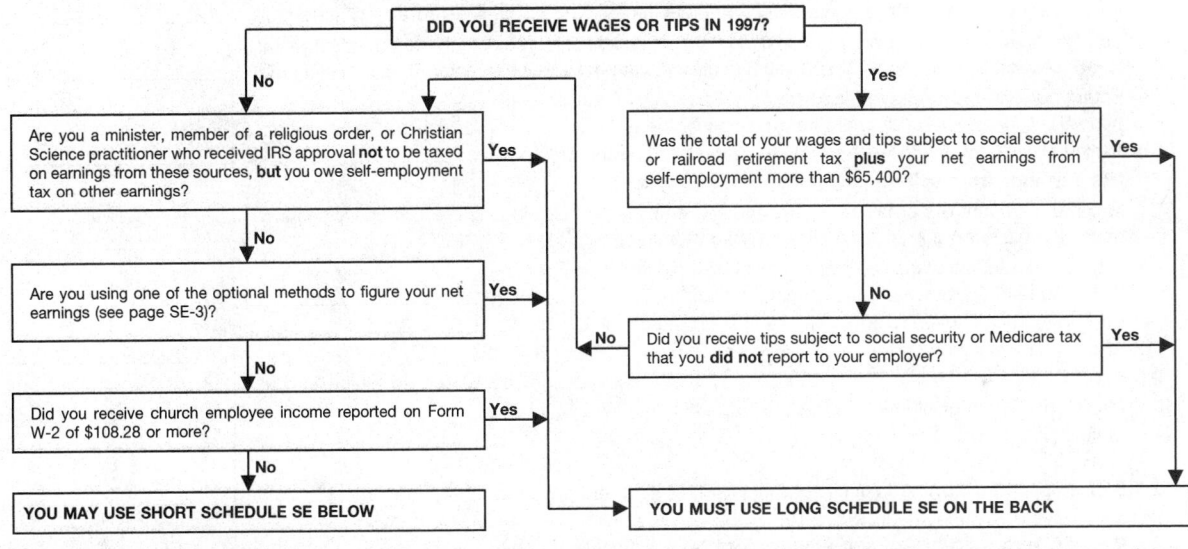

Section A—Short Schedule SE. Caution: *Read above to see if you can use Short Schedule SE.*

1	Net farm profit or (loss) from Schedule F, line 36, and farm partnerships, Schedule K-1 (Form 1065), line 15a	**1**	
2	Net profit or (loss) from Schedule C, line 31; Schedule C-EZ, line 3; and Schedule K-1 (Form 1065), line 15a (other than farming). Ministers and members of religious orders, see page SE-1 for amounts to report on this line. See page SE-2 for other income to report	**2**	
3	Combine lines 1 and 2	**3**	
4	**Net earnings from self-employment.** Multiply line 3 by 92.35% (.9235). If less than $400, **do not** file this schedule; you do not owe self-employment tax . . . . ▶	**4**	
5	**Self-employment tax.** If the amount on line 4 is: ● $65,400 or less, multiply line 4 by 15.3% (.153). Enter the result here and on **Form 1040, line 47.** ● More than $65,400, multiply line 4 by 2.9% (.029). Then, add $8,109.60 to the result. Enter the total here and on **Form 1040, line 47.**	**5**	
6	**Deduction for one-half of self-employment tax.** Multiply line 5 by 50% (.5). Enter the result here and on **Form 1040, line 26**	**6**	

For Paperwork Reduction Act Notice, see Form 1040 instructions.   Cat. No. 11358Z   **Schedule SE (Form 1040) 1997**

Schedule SE (Form 1040) 1997 | Attachment Sequence No. **17** | Page **2**

Name of person with **self-employment** income (as shown on Form 1040)	Social security number of person with **self-employment** income ▶	

Section B—Long Schedule SE

Part I Self-Employment Tax

Note: *If your only income subject to self-employment tax is* **church employee income,** *skip lines 1 through 4b. Enter -0- on line 4c and go to line 5a. Income from services you performed as a minister or a member of a religious order* **is not** *church employee income. See page SE-1.*

A If you are a minister, member of a religious order, or Christian Science practitioner **and** you filed Form 4361, but you had $400 or more of **other** net earnings from self-employment, check here and continue with Part I . . . . . . ▶ ☐

1	Net farm profit or (loss) from Schedule F, line 36, and farm partnerships, Schedule K-1 (Form 1065), line 15a. **Note:** *Skip this line if you use the farm optional method. See page SE-3* . .	**1**		
2	Net profit or (loss) from Schedule C, line 31; Schedule C-EZ, line 3; and Schedule K-1 (Form 1065), line 15a (other than farming). Ministers and members of religious orders, see page SE-1 for amounts to report on this line. See page SE-2 for other income to report. **Note:** *Skip this line if you use the nonfarm optional method. See page SE-3.*	**2**		
3	Combine lines 1 and 2	**3**		
4a	If line 3 is more than zero, multiply line 3 by 92.35% (.9235). Otherwise, enter amount from line 3	**4a**		
b	If you elected one or both of the optional methods, enter the total of lines 15 and 17 here . .	**4b**		
c	Combine lines 4a and 4b. If less than $400, **do not** file this schedule; you do not owe self-employment tax. **Exception.** If less than $400 and you had **church employee income,** enter -0- and continue ▶	**4c**		
5a	Enter your **church employee income** from Form W-2. **Caution:** *See page SE-1 for definition of church employee income* **5a**			
b	Multiply line 5a by 92.35% (.9235). If less than $100, enter -0-	**5b**		
6	**Net earnings from self-employment.** Add lines 4c and 5b	**6**		
7	Maximum amount of combined wages and self-employment earnings subject to social security tax or the 6.2% portion of the 7.65% railroad retirement (tier 1) tax for 1997	**7**	65,400	00
8a	Total social security wages and tips (total of boxes 3 and 7 on Form(s) W-2) and railroad retirement (tier 1) compensation **8a**			
b	Unreported tips subject to social security tax (from Form 4137, line 9) **8b**			
c	Add lines 8a and 8b	**8c**		
9	Subtract line 8c from line 7. If zero or less, enter -0- here and on line 10 and go to line 11 . ▶	**9**		
10	Multiply the **smaller** of line 6 or line 9 by 12.4% (.124)	**10**		
11	Multiply line 6 by 2.9% (.029)	**11**		
12	**Self-employment tax.** Add lines 10 and 11. Enter here and on **Form 1040, line 47**	**12**		
13	**Deduction for one-half of self-employment tax.** Multiply line 12 by 50% (.5). Enter the result here and on **Form 1040, line 26** **13**			

Part II Optional Methods To Figure Net Earnings (See page SE-3.)

Farm Optional Method. You may use this method **only** if:

- Your gross farm income[1] was not more than $2,400, **or**
- Your gross farm income[1] was more than $2,400 and your net farm profits[2] were less than $1,733.

14	Maximum income for optional methods	**14**	1,600	00
15	Enter the **smaller** of: two-thirds (⅔) of gross farm income[1] (not less than zero) or $1,600. Also, include this amount on line 4b above	**15**		

Nonfarm Optional Method. You may use this method **only** if:

- Your net nonfarm profits[3] were less than $1,733 and also less than 72.189% of your gross nonfarm income,[4] **and**
- You had net earnings from self-employment of at least $400 in 2 of the prior 3 years.

Caution: *You may use this method no more than five times.*

16	Subtract line 15 from line 14	**16**		
17	Enter the **smaller** of: two-thirds (⅔) of gross nonfarm income[4] (not less than zero) or the amount on line 16. Also, include this amount on line 4b above	**17**		

[1]From Schedule F, line 11, and Schedule K-1 (Form 1065), line 15b.
[2]From Schedule F, line 36, and Schedule K-1 (Form 1065), line 15a.
[3]From Schedule C, line 31; Schedule C-EZ, line 3; and Schedule K-1 (Form 1065), line 15a.
[4]From Schedule C, line 7; Schedule C-EZ, line 1; and Schedule K-1 (Form 1065), line 15c.

Form **1041**

Department of the Treasury—Internal Revenue Service

U.S. Income Tax Return for Estates and Trusts

1997

For calendar year 1997 or fiscal year beginning _____ , 1997, and ending _____ , 19 ____

OMB No. 1545-0092

A Type of entity:

☐ Decedent's estate
☐ Simple trust
☐ Complex trust
☐ Grantor type trust
☐ Bankruptcy estate–Ch. 7
☐ Bankruptcy estate–Ch. 11
☐ Pooled income fund

B Number of Schedules K-1 attached (see instructions) ▶

Name of estate or trust (If a grantor type trust, see page 8 of the instructions.)

Name and title of fiduciary

Number, street, and room or suite no. (If a P.O. box, see page 8 of the instructions.)

City or town, state, and ZIP code

C Employer identification number

D Date entity created

E Nonexempt charitable and split-interest trusts, check applicable boxes (see page 10 of the instructions):

☐ Described in section 4947(a)(1)
☐ Not a private foundation
☐ Described in section 4947(a)(2)

F Check applicable boxes:
☐ Initial return ☐ Final return ☐ Amended return
☐ Change in fiduciary's name ☐ Change in fiduciary's address

G Pooled mortgage account (see page 10 of the instructions):
☐ Bought ☐ Sold Date:

Income

1	Interest income	1
2	Dividends	2
3	Business income or (loss) (attach Schedule C or C-EZ (Form 1040))	3
4	Capital gain or (loss) (attach Schedule D (Form 1041))	4
5	Rents, royalties, partnerships, other estates and trusts, etc. (attach Schedule E (Form 1040))	5
6	Farm income or (loss) (attach Schedule F (Form 1040))	6
7	Ordinary gain or (loss) (attach Form 4797)	7
8	Other income. List type and amount _____	8
9	**Total income.** Combine lines 1 through 8 ▶	9

Deductions

10	Interest. Check if Form 4952 is attached ▶ ☐	10
11	Taxes	11
12	Fiduciary fees	12
13	Charitable deduction (from Schedule A, line 7)	13
14	Attorney, accountant, and return preparer fees	14
15a	Other deductions NOT subject to the 2% floor (attach schedule)	15a
b	Allowable miscellaneous itemized deductions subject to the 2% floor	15b
16	**Total.** Add lines 10 through 15b	16
17	Adjusted total income or (loss). Subtract line 16 from line 9. Enter here and on Schedule B, line 1 ▶	17
18	Income distribution deduction (from Schedule B, line 15) (attach Schedules K-1 (Form 1041))	18
19	Estate tax deduction (including certain generation-skipping taxes) (attach computation)	19
20	Reserved	20
21	Exemption	21
22	**Total deductions.** Add lines 18, 19, and 21 ▶	22

Tax and Payments

23	Taxable income. Subtract line 22 from line 17. If a loss, see page 14 of the instructions	23
24	**Total tax** (from Schedule G, line 8)	24
25	**Payments: a** 1997 estimated tax payments and amount applied from 1996 return	25a
b	Estimated tax payments allocated to beneficiaries (from Form 1041-T)	25b
c	Subtract line 25b from line 25a	25c
d	Tax paid with extension of time to file: ☐ Form 2758 ☐ Form 8736 ☐ Form 8800	25d
e	Federal income tax withheld. If any is from Form(s) 1099, check ▶ ☐	25e
	Other payments: **f** Form 2439 _____ ; **g** Form 4136 _____ ; Total ▶	25h
26	**Total payments.** Add lines 25c through 25e, and 25h ▶	26
27	Estimated tax penalty (see page 15 of the instructions)	27
28	**Tax due.** If line 26 is smaller than the total of lines 24 and 27, enter amount owed	28
29	**Overpayment.** If line 26 is larger than the total of lines 24 and 27, enter amount overpaid	29
30	Amount of line 29 to be: **a** Credited to 1998 estimated tax ▶ _____ ; **b** Refunded ▶	30

Please Sign Here

Under penalties of perjury, I declare that I have examined this return, including accompanying schedules and statements, and to the best of my knowledge and belief, it is true, correct, and complete. Declaration of preparer (other than fiduciary) is based on all information of which preparer has any knowledge.

▶ Signature of fiduciary or officer representing fiduciary | Date | EIN of fiduciary if a financial institution (see page 5 of the instructions)

Paid Preparer's Use Only

Preparer's signature ▶ | Date | Check if self-employed ▶ ☐ | Preparer's social security no.

Firm's name (or yours if self-employed) and address ▶ | EIN ▶

ZIP code ▶

For Paperwork Reduction Act Notice, see the separate instructions.

Cat. No. 11370H

Form **1041** (1997)

Form 1041 (1997)   Page **2**

Schedule A — Charitable Deduction. Do not complete for a simple trust or a pooled income fund.

1	Amounts paid or permanently set aside for charitable purposes from gross income (see page 15)	**1**		
2	Tax-exempt income allocable to charitable contributions (see page 16 of the instructions) . .	**2**		
3	Subtract line 2 from line 1	**3**		
4	Capital gains for the tax year allocated to corpus and paid or permanently set aside for charitable purposes	**4**		
5	Add lines 3 and 4	**5**		
6	Section 1202 exclusion allocable to capital gains paid or permanently set aside for charitable purposes (see page 16 of the instructions)	**6**		
7	**Charitable deduction.** Subtract line 6 from 5. Enter here and on page 1, line 13	**7**		

Schedule B — Income Distribution Deduction

1	Adjusted total income (from page 1, line 17) (see page 16 of the instructions)	**1**		
2	Adjusted tax-exempt interest	**2**		
3	Total net gain from Schedule D (Form 1041), line 16, column (1) (see page 16 of the instructions)	**3**		
4	Enter amount from Schedule A, line 4 (reduced by any allocable section 1202 exclusion). . .	**4**		
5	Capital gains for the tax year included on Schedule A, line 1 (see page 16 of the instructions)	**5**		
6	Enter any gain from page 1, line 4, as a negative number. If page 1, line 4, is a loss, enter the loss as a positive number	**6**		
7	**Distributable net income (DNI).** Combine lines 1 through 6. If zero or less, enter -0-.	**7**		
8	If a complex trust, enter accounting income for the tax year as determined under the governing instrument and applicable local law **8**			
9	Income required to be distributed currently	**9**		
10	Other amounts paid, credited, or otherwise required to be distributed	**10**		
11	Total distributions. Add lines 9 and 10. If greater than line 8, see page 17 of the instructions	**11**		
12	Enter the amount of tax-exempt income included on line 11	**12**		
13	Tentative income distribution deduction. Subtract line 12 from line 11	**13**		
14	Tentative income distribution deduction. Subtract line 2 from line 7. If zero or less, enter -0-	**14**		
15	**Income distribution deduction.** Enter the smaller of line 13 or line 14 here and on page 1, line 18	**15**		

Schedule G — Tax Computation (see page 17 of the instructions)

1	**Tax: a** ☐ Tax rate schedule or ☐ Schedule D (Form 1041) . .	**1a**		
	b Other taxes	**1b**		
	c Total. Add lines 1a and 1b . . . . ▶	**1c**		
2a	Foreign tax credit (attach Form 1116)	**2a**		
b	Check: ☐ Nonconventional source fuel credit ☐ Form 8834 . . .	**2b**		
c	General business credit. Enter here and check which forms are attached: ☐ Form 3800 or ☐ Forms (specify) ▶ _____	**2c**		
d	Credit for prior year minimum tax (attach Form 8801)	**2d**		
3	**Total credits.** Add lines 2a through 2d . . . . ▶	**3**		
4	Subtract line 3 from line 1c	**4**		
5	Recapture taxes. Check if from: ☐ Form 4255 ☐ Form 8611	**5**		
6	Alternative minimum tax (from Schedule I, line 42)	**6**		
7	Household employment taxes. Attach Schedule H (Form 1040)	**7**		
8	**Total tax.** Add lines 4 through 7. Enter here and on page 1, line 24 . . . . ▶	**8**		

Other Information

		Yes	No
1	Did the estate or trust receive tax-exempt income? If "Yes," attach a computation of the allocation of expenses. Enter the amount of tax-exempt interest income and exempt-interest dividends ▶ $ _____		
2	Did the estate or trust receive all or any part of the earnings (salary, wages, and other compensation) of any individual by reason of a contract assignment or similar arrangement?		
3	At any time during calendar year 1997, did the estate or trust have an interest in or a signature or other authority over a bank, securities, or other financial account in a foreign country? See page 19 of the instructions for exceptions and filing requirements for Form TD F 90-22.1. If "Yes," enter the name of the foreign country ▶ _____		
4	During the tax year, did the estate or trust receive a distribution from, or was it the grantor of, or transferor to, a foreign trust? If "Yes," the estate or trust may have to file Form 3520 or 926. See page 19 of the instructions . . .		
5	Did the estate or trust receive, or pay, any seller-financed mortgage interest? If "Yes," see page 19 for required attachment .		
6	If this is an estate or a complex trust making the section 663(b) election, check here (see page 19) . . ▶ ☐		
7	To make a section 643(e)(3) election, attach Schedule D (Form 1041), and check here (see page 19). . ▶ ☐		
8	If the decedent's estate has been open for more than 2 years, check here . . . . ▶ ☐		
9	Are any trust beneficiaries skip persons? See page 19 of the instructions		

Schedule I Alternative Minimum Tax (see pages 19 through 24 of the instructions)

Part I—Estate's or Trust's Share of Alternative Minimum Taxable Income

1	Adjusted total income or (loss) (from page 1, line 17)	**1**
2	Net operating loss deduction. Enter as a positive amount	**2**
3	Add lines 1 and 2	**3**
4	**Adjustments and tax preference items:**	

a	Interest	**4a**
b	Taxes	**4b**
c	Miscellaneous itemized deductions (from page 1, line 15b)	**4c**
d	Refund of taxes	**4d** ( )
e	Depreciation of property placed in service after 1986	**4e**
f	Circulation and research and experimental expenditures	**4f**
g	Mining exploration and development costs	**4g**
h	Long-term contracts entered into after February 28, 1986	**4h**
i	Amortization of pollution control facilities	**4i**
j	Installment sales of certain property	**4j**
k	Adjusted gain or loss (including incentive stock options)	**4k**
l	Certain loss limitations	**4l**
m	Tax shelter farm activities	**4m**
n	Passive activities	**4n**
o	Beneficiaries of other trusts or decedent's estates	**4o**
p	Tax-exempt interest from specified private activity bonds	**4p**
q	Depletion	**4q**
r	Accelerated depreciation of real property placed in service before 1987	**4r**
s	Accelerated depreciation of leased personal property placed in service before 1987	**4s**
t	Intangible drilling costs	**4t**
u	Other adjustments	**4u**

5	Combine lines 4a through 4u	**5**
6	Add lines 3 and 5	**6**
7	Alternative tax net operating loss deduction (see page 23 of the instructions for limitations) . .	**7**
8	Adjusted alternative minimum taxable income. Subtract line 7 from line 6. Enter here and on line 14	**8**
	Note: *Complete Part II below before going to line 9.*	
9	Income distribution deduction from line 28 below	**9**
10	Estate tax deduction (from page 1, line 19)	**10**
11	Reserved	**11**
12	Add lines 9 and 10	**12**
13	Estate's or trust's share of alternative minimum taxable income. Subtract line 12 from line 8 .	**13**

If line 13 is:

- $22,500 or less, stop here and enter -0- on Schedule G, line 6. The estate or trust is not liable for the alternative minimum tax.
- Over $22,500, but less than $165,000, go to line 29.
- $165,000 or more, enter the amount from line 13 on line 35 and go to line 36.

Part II—Income Distribution Deduction on a Minimum Tax Basis

14	Adjusted alternative minimum taxable income (from line 8)	**14**
15	Adjusted tax-exempt interest (other than amounts included on line 4p)	**15**
16	Total net gain from Schedule D (Form 1041), line 16, column (1). If a loss, enter -0-	**16**
17	Capital gains for the tax year allocated to corpus and paid or permanently set aside for charitable purposes (from Schedule A, line 4)	**17**
18	Capital gains paid or permanently set aside for charitable purposes from gross income (see page 23 of the instructions) .	**18**
19	Capital gains computed on a minimum tax basis included on line 8	**19** ( )
20	Capital losses computed on a minimum tax basis included on line 8. Enter as a positive amount	**20**
21	Distributable net alternative minimum taxable income (DNAMTI). Combine lines 14 through 20. If zero or less, enter -0- .	**21**
22	Income required to be distributed currently (from Schedule B, line 9)	**22**
23	Other amounts paid, credited, or otherwise required to be distributed (from Schedule B, line 10)	**23**
24	Total distributions. Add lines 22 and 23	**24**
25	Tax-exempt income included on line 24 (other than amounts included on line 4p)	**25**
26	Tentative income distribution deduction on a minimum tax basis. Subtract line 25 from line 24 .	**26**
27	Tentative income distribution deduction on a minimum tax basis. Subtract line 15 from line 21. If zero or less, enter -0- .	**27**
28	**Income distribution deduction on a minimum tax basis.** Enter the smaller of line 26 or line 27. Enter here and on line 9	**28**

Form 1041 (1997)   Page **4**

Part III—Alternative Minimum Tax

29	Exemption amount	**29**	$22,500
30	Enter the amount from line 13	**30**	
31	Phase-out of exemption amount	**31** $75,000	
32	Subtract line 31 from line 30. If zero or less, enter -0- . . .	**32**	
33	Multiply line 32 by 25% (.25)		**33**
34	Subtract line 33 from line 29. If zero or less, enter -0-		**34**
35	Subtract line 34 from line 30		**35**
36	If the estate or trust completed Schedule D (Form 1041) and had an amount on line 24 or 27 (as refigured for the AMT, if necessary), go to Part IV to figure line 36. **All others:** If line 35 is— • $175,000 or less, multiply line 35 by 26% (.26). • Over $175,000, multiply line 35 by 28% (.28) and subtract $3,500 from the result		**36**
37	Alternative minimum foreign tax credit (see page 24 of instructions)		**37**
38	Tentative minimum tax. Subtract line 37 from line 36		**38**
39	Regular tax before credits (see page 24 of instructions)	**39**	
40	Section 644 tax included on Schedule G, line 1b	**40**	
41	Add lines 39 and 40.		**41**
42	**Alternative minimum tax.** Subtract line 41 from line 38. If zero or less, enter -0-. Enter here and on Schedule G, line 6		**42**

Part IV—Line 36 Computation Using Maximum Capital Gains Rates

43	Enter the amount from line 35		**43**
44	Enter the amount from Schedule D (Form 1041), line 27 (as refigured for AMT, if necessary)	**44**	
45	Enter the amount from Schedule D (Form 1041), line 24 (as refigured for AMT, if necessary)	**45**	
46	Add lines 44 and 45. If zero or less, enter -0-	**46**	
47	Enter the amount from Schedule D (Form 1041), line 21 (as refigured for AMT, if necessary)	**47**	
48	Enter the **smaller** of line 46 or line 47		**48**
49	Subtract line 48 from line 43. If zero or less, enter -0-		**49**
50	If line 49 is $175,000 or less, multiply line 49 by 26% (.26). Otherwise, multiply line 49 by 28% (.28) and subtract $3,500 from the result . . . . ▶		**50**
51	Enter the amount from Schedule D (Form 1041), line 36 (as figured for the regular tax) . . .		**51**
52	Enter the **smallest** of line 43, line 44, or line 51		**52**
53	Multiply line 52 by 10% (.10) . . . . ▶		**53**
54	Enter the **smaller** of line 43 or line 44		**54**
55	Enter the amount from line 52		**55**
56	Subtract line 55 from line 54. If zero or less, enter -0-		**56**
57	Multiply line 56 by 20% (.20) . . . . ▶		**57**
58	Enter the amount from line 43		**58**
59	Add lines 49, 52, and 56		**59**
60	Subtract line 59 from line 58		**60**
61	Multiply line 60 by 25% (.25) . . . . ▶		**61**
62	Add lines 50, 53, 57, and 61		**62**
63	If line 43 is $175,000 or less, multiply line 43 by 26% (.26). Otherwise, multiply line 43 by 28% (.28) and subtract $3,500 from the result		**63**
64	Enter the **smaller** of line 62 or line 63 here and on line 36 . . . . ▶		**64**

SCHEDULE K-1 (Form 1041)	**Beneficiary's Share of Income, Deductions, Credits, etc.**	OMB No. 1545-0092
Department of the Treasury Internal Revenue Service	for the calendar year 1997, or fiscal year beginning ...., 1997, ending ...., 19 .... ▶ Complete a separate Schedule K-1 for each beneficiary.	**1997**

Name of trust or decedent's estate

☐ Amended K-1
☐ Final K-1

Beneficiary's identifying number ▶   **Estate's or trust's EIN ▶**

Beneficiary's name, address, and ZIP code   Fiduciary's name, address, and ZIP code

(a) Allocable share item		(b) Amount	(c) Calendar year 1997 Form 1040 filers enter the amounts in column (b) on:
1 Interest.	1		Schedule B, Part I, line 1
2 Dividends	2		Schedule B, Part II, line 5
3 Net short-term capital gain	3		Schedule D, line 5
4 Net long-term capital gain: **a** 28% rate gain . .	4a		Schedule D, line 12, column (g)
b Unrecaptured section 1250 gain	4b		See the instructions for Schedule D, line 25
c Total for year	4c		Schedule D, line 12, column (f)
5a Annuities, royalties, and other nonpassive income before directly apportioned deductions	5a		Schedule E, Part III, column (f)
b Depreciation	5b		⎫
c Depletion	5c		Include on the applicable line of the appropriate tax form
d Amortization	5d		⎭
6a Trade or business, rental real estate, and other rental income before directly apportioned deductions (see instructions) .	6a		Schedule E, Part III
b Depreciation	6b		⎫
c Depletion	6c		Include on the applicable line of the appropriate tax form
d Amortization	6d		⎭
7 Income for minimum tax purposes	7		
8 Income for regular tax purposes (add lines 1, 2, 3, 4c, 5a, and 6a)	8		
9 Adjustment for minimum tax purposes (subtract line 8 from line 7)	9		Form 6251, line 12
10 Estate tax deduction (including certain generation-skipping transfer taxes)	10		Schedule A, line 27
11 Foreign taxes	11		Form 1116 or Schedule A (Form 1040), line 8
12 Adjustments and tax preference items (itemize):			
a Accelerated depreciation	12a		⎫ Include on the applicable line of Form 6251
b Depletion	12b		
c Amortization	12c		⎭
d Exclusion items	12d		1998 Form 8801
13 Deductions in the final year of trust or decedent's estate:			
a Excess deductions on termination (see instructions)	13a		Schedule A, line 22
b Short-term capital loss carryover	13b	( )	Schedule D, line 5
c Long-term capital loss carryover	13c	( )	Schedule D, line 12, columns (f) and (g)
d Net operating loss (NOL) carryover for regular tax purposes	13d	( )	Form 1040, line 21
e NOL carryover for minimum tax purposes	13e		See the instructions for Form 6251, line 20
f	13f		⎫ Include on the applicable line of the appropriate tax form
g	13g		⎭
14 Other (itemize):			
a Payments of estimated taxes credited to you . .	14a		Form 1040, line 55
b Tax-exempt interest	14b		Form 1040, line 8b
c	14c		⎫
d	14d		
e	14e		Include on the applicable line of the appropriate tax form
f	14f		
g	14g		
h	14h		⎭

For Paperwork Reduction Act Notice, see the Instructions for Form 1041.   Cat. No. 11380D   **Schedule K-1 (Form 1041) 1997**

Instructions for Beneficiary Filing Form 1040

Note: *The fiduciary's instructions for completing Schedule K-1 are in the Instructions for Form 1041.*

General Instructions

Purpose of Form

The fiduciary of a trust or decedent's estate uses Schedule K-1 to report your share of the trust's or estate's income, credits, deductions, etc. **Keep it for your records. Do not file it with your tax return.** A copy has been filed with the IRS.

Inconsistent Treatment of Items

Generally, you must report items shown on your Schedule K-1 (and any attached schedules) the same way that the estate or trust treated the items on its return.

If the treatment on your original or amended return is inconsistent with the estate's or trust's treatment, or if the estate or trust was required to but has not filed a return, you must file **Form 8082,** Notice of Inconsistent Treatment or Administrative Adjustment Request (AAR), with your original or amended return to identify and explain any inconsistency (or to note that an estate or trust return has not been filed).

If you are required to file Form 8082 but fail to do so, you may be subject to the accuracy-related penalty. This penalty is in addition to any tax that results from making your amount or treatment of the item consistent with that shown on the estate's or trust's return. Any deficiency that results from making the amounts consistent may be assessed immediately.

Errors

If you believe the fiduciary has made an error on your Schedule K-1, notify the fiduciary and ask for an amended or a corrected Schedule K-1. **Do not** change any items on your copy. Be sure that the fiduciary sends a copy of the amended Schedule K-1 to the IRS. **If you are unable to reach agreement with the fiduciary regarding the inconsistency, you must file Form 8082.**

Tax Shelters

If you receive a copy of **Form 8271,** Investor Reporting of Tax Shelter Registration Number, see the instructions for Form 8271 to determine your reporting requirements.

Beneficiaries of Generation-Skipping Trusts

If you received **Form 706-GS(D-1),** Notification of Distribution From a Generation-Skipping Trust, and paid a generation-skipping transfer (GST) tax on **Form 706-GS(D),** Generation-Skipping Transfer Tax Return for Distributions, you can deduct the GST tax paid on income distributions on Schedule A (Form 1040), line 8. To figure the deduction, see the instructions for Form 706-GS(D).

Specific Instructions

Lines 3 and 4

If there is an attachment to this Schedule K-1 reporting a disposition of a passive activity, see the instructions for **Form 8582,** Passive Activity Loss Limitations, for information on the treatment of dispositions of interests in a passive activity.

Lines 6b through 6d

The deductions on lines 6b through 6d may be subject to the passive loss limitations of Internal Revenue Code section 469, which generally limits deductions from passive activities to the income from those activities. The rules for applying these limitations to beneficiaries have not yet been issued. For more details, see **Pub. 925,** Passive Activity and At-Risk Rules.

Line 12d

If you pay alternative minimum tax in 1997, the amount on line 12d will help you figure any minimum tax credit for 1998. See the 1998 **Form 8801,** Credit for Prior Year Minimum Tax—Individuals, Estates, and Trusts, for more information.

Line 14a

To figure any underpayment and penalty on **Form 2210,** Underpayment of Estimated Tax by Individuals, Estates, and Trusts, treat the amount entered on line 14a as an estimated tax payment made on January 15, 1998.

Lines 14c through 14h

The amount of gross farming and fishing income is included on line 6a. This income is also separately stated on line 14 to help you determine if you are subject to a penalty for underpayment of estimated tax. Report the amount of gross farming and fishing income on Schedule E (Form 1040), line 41.

Form **1065**

Department of the Treasury
Internal Revenue Service

U.S. Partnership Return of Income

For calendar year 1997, or tax year beginning .... , 1997, and ending .... , 19 ... .
▶ See separate instructions.

OMB No. 1545-0099

1997

A Principal business activity	Use the IRS label. Other-wise, please print or type.
B Principal product or service	
C Business code number	

Name of partnership

Number, street, and room or suite no. If a P.O. box, see page 10 of the instructions.

City or town, state, and ZIP code

D Employer identification number

E Date business started

F Total assets (see page 10 of the instructions)

$

G Check applicable boxes: **(1)** ☐ Initial return **(2)** ☐ Final return **(3)** ☐ Change in address **(4)** ☐ Amended return

H Check accounting method: **(1)** ☐ Cash **(2)** ☐ Accrual **(3)** ☐ Other (specify) ▶ ....

I Number of Schedules K-1. Attach one for each person who was a partner at any time during the tax year ▶ ....

Caution: *Include **only** trade or business income and expenses on lines 1a through 22 below. See the instructions for more information.*

Income

1a Gross receipts or sales	1a	
b Less returns and allowances	1b	1c
2 Cost of goods sold (Schedule A, line 8)		2
3 Gross profit. Subtract line 2 from line 1c		3
4 Ordinary income (loss) from other partnerships, estates, and trusts *(attach schedule)*		4
5 Net farm profit (loss) *(attach Schedule F (Form 1040))*		5
6 Net gain (loss) from Form 4797, Part II, line 18		6
7 Other income (loss) *(attach schedule)*		7
8 **Total income (loss).** Combine lines 3 through 7		8

Deductions (see page 11 of the instructions for limitations)

9 Salaries and wages (other than to partners) (less employment credits)		9
10 Guaranteed payments to partners		10
11 Repairs and maintenance		11
12 Bad debts		12
13 Rent		13
14 Taxes and licenses		14
15 Interest		15
16a Depreciation (if required, attach Form 4562)	16a	
b Less depreciation reported on Schedule A and elsewhere on return	16b	16c
17 Depletion **(Do not deduct oil and gas depletion.)**		17
18 Retirement plans, etc.		18
19 Employee benefit programs		19
20 Other deductions *(attach schedule)*		20
21 **Total deductions.** Add the amounts shown in the far right column for lines 9 through 20		21
22 **Ordinary income (loss)** from trade or business activities. Subtract line 21 from line 8		22

Please Sign Here

Under penalties of perjury, I declare that I have examined this return, including accompanying schedules and statements, and to the best of my knowledge and belief, it is true, correct, and complete. Declaration of preparer (other than general partner or limited liability company member) is based on all information of which preparer has any knowledge.

▶ Signature of general partner or limited liability company member

▶ Date

Paid Preparer's Use Only

Preparer's signature ▶	Date	Check if self-employed ▶ ☐	Preparer's social security no.
Firm's name (or yours if self-employed) and address ▶		EIN ▶	
		ZIP code ▶	

For Paperwork Reduction Act Notice, see separate instructions.   Cat. No. 11390Z   Form **1065** (1997)

Form 1065 (1997)   Page **2**

Schedule A   Cost of Goods Sold (see page 13 of the instructions)

1	Inventory at beginning of year	1
2	Purchases less cost of items withdrawn for personal use	2
3	Cost of labor	3
4	Additional section 263A costs (attach schedule)	4
5	Other costs (attach schedule)	5
6	**Total.** Add lines 1 through 5	6
7	Inventory at end of year	7
8	**Cost of goods sold.** Subtract line 7 from line 6. Enter here and on page 1, line 2	8

9a   Check all methods used for valuing closing inventory:

     (i) ☐ Cost as described in Regulations section 1.471-3

     (ii) ☐ Lower of cost or market as described in Regulations section 1.471-4

     (iii) ☐ Other (specify method used and attach explanation) ▶ _____

    b   Check this box if there was a writedown of "subnormal" goods as described in Regulations section 1.471-2(c) . . . ▶ ☐

    c   Check this box if the LIFO inventory method was adopted this tax year for any goods (if checked, attach Form 970) . . ▶ ☐

    d   Do the rules of section 263A (for property produced or acquired for resale) apply to the partnership? . . ☐ **Yes** ☐ **No**

    e   Was there any change in determining quantities, cost, or valuations between opening and closing inventory? ☐ **Yes** ☐ **No**
       If "Yes," attach explanation.

Schedule B   Other Information

		Yes	No
1	What type of entity is filing this return? Check the applicable box:		
	a ☐ General partnership **b** ☐ Limited partnership **c** ☐ Limited liability company		
	d ☐ Other (see page 14 of the instructions) ▶ _____		
2	Are any partners in this partnership also partnerships?		
3	Is this partnership a partner in another partnership?		
4	Is this partnership subject to the consolidated audit procedures of sections 6221 through 6233? If "Yes," see **Designation of Tax Matters Partner** below		
5	Does this partnership meet **ALL THREE** of the following requirements?		
	a The partnership's total receipts for the tax year were less than $250,000;		
	b The partnership's total assets at the end of the tax year were less than $600,000; **AND**		
	c Schedules K-1 are filed with the return and furnished to the partners on or before the due date (including extensions) for the partnership return.		
	If "Yes," the partnership is not required to complete Schedules L, M-1, and M-2; Item F on page 1 of Form 1065; or Item J on Schedule K-1		
6	Does this partnership have any foreign partners?		
7	Is this partnership a publicly traded partnership as defined in section 469(k)(2)?		
8	Has this partnership filed, or is it required to file, **Form 8264,** Application for Registration of a Tax Shelter?		
9	At any time during calendar year 1997, did the partnership have an interest in or a signature or other authority over a financial account in a foreign country (such as a bank account, securities account, or other financial account)? See page 14 of the instructions for exceptions and filing requirements for Form TD F 90-22.1. If "Yes," enter the name of the foreign country. ▶ _____		
10	During the tax year, did the partnership receive a distribution from, or was it the grantor of, or transferor to, a foreign trust? If "Yes," the partnership may have to file Form 3520 or 926. See page 14 of the instructions		
11	Was there a distribution of property or a transfer (e.g., by sale or death) of a partnership interest during the tax year? If "Yes," you may elect to adjust the basis of the partnership's assets under section 754 by attaching the statement described under **Elections Made By the Partnership** on page 5 of the instructions		

Designation of Tax Matters Partner (see page 15 of the instructions)

Enter below the general partner designated as the tax matters partner (TMP) for the tax year of this return:

Name of designated TMP ▶	Identifying number of TMP ▶
Address of designated TMP ▶	

Schedule K	Partners' Shares of Income, Credits, Deductions, etc.		
	(a) Distributive share items	**(b) Total amount**	

Income (Loss)	**1** Ordinary income (loss) from trade or business activities (page 1, line 22)	**1**		
	2 Net income (loss) from rental real estate activities *(attach Form 8825)*	**2**		
	3a Gross income from other rental activities			
	b Expenses from other rental activities *(attach schedule)*			
	c Net income (loss) from other rental activities. Subtract line 3b from line 3a	**3c**		
	4 Portfolio income (loss):			
	a Interest income	**4a**		
	b Dividend income	**4b**		
	c Royalty income	**4c**		
	d Net short-term capital gain (loss) *(attach Schedule D (Form 1065))*	**4d**		
	e Net long-term capital gain (loss) *(attach Schedule D (Form 1065))*:			
	(1) 28% rate gain (loss) ▶ .... **(2)** Total for year ▶	**4e(2)**		
	f Other portfolio income (loss) *(attach schedule)*	**4f**		
	5 Guaranteed payments to partners	**5**		
	6 Net section 1231 gain (loss) (other than due to casualty or theft) *(attach Form 4797)*:			
	a 28% rate gain (loss) ▶................................ **b** Total for year ▶	**6b**		
	7 Other income (loss) *(attach schedule)*	**7**		
Deductions	**8** Charitable contributions *(attach schedule)*	**8**		
	9 Section 179 expense deduction *(attach Form 4562)*	**9**		
	10 Deductions related to portfolio income (itemize)	**10**		
	11 Other deductions *(attach schedule)*	**11**		
Credits	**12a** Low-income housing credit:			
	(1) From partnerships to which section 42(j)(5) applies for property placed in service before 1990	**12a(1)**		
	(2) Other than on line 12a(1) for property placed in service before 1990	**12a(2)**		
	(3) From partnerships to which section 42(j)(5) applies for property placed in service after 1989	**12a(3)**		
	(4) Other than on line 12a(3) for property placed in service after 1989	**12a(4)**		
	b Qualified rehabilitation expenditures related to rental real estate activities *(attach Form 3468)*	**12b**		
	c Credits (other than credits shown on lines 12a and 12b) related to rental real estate activities	**12c**		
	d Credits related to other rental activities	**12d**		
	13 Other credits	**13**		
Investment Interest	**14a** Interest expense on investment debts	**14a**		
	b (1) Investment income included on lines 4a, 4b, 4c, and 4f above	**14b(1)**		
	(2) Investment expenses included on line 10 above	**14b(2)**		
Self-Employment	**15a** Net earnings (loss) from self-employment	**15a**		
	b Gross farming or fishing income	**15b**		
	c Gross nonfarm income	**15c**		
Adjustments and Tax Preference Items	**16a** Depreciation adjustment on property placed in service after 1986	**16a**		
	b Adjusted gain or loss	**16b**		
	c Depletion (other than oil and gas)	**16c**		
	d (1) Gross income from oil, gas, and geothermal properties	**16d(1)**		
	(2) Deductions allocable to oil, gas, and geothermal properties	**16d(2)**		
	e Other adjustments and tax preference items *(attach schedule)*	**16e**		
Foreign Taxes	**17a** Type of income ▶			
	b Name of foreign country or U.S. possession ▶			
	c Total gross income from sources outside the United States *(attach schedule)*	**17c**		
	d Total applicable deductions and losses *(attach schedule)*	**17d**		
	e Total foreign taxes (check one): ▶ ☐ Paid ☐ Accrued	**17e**		
	f Reduction in taxes available for credit *(attach schedule)*	**17f**		
	g Other foreign tax information *(attach schedule)*	**17g**		
Other	**18** Section 59(e)(2) expenditures: **a** Type ▶ .... **b** Amount ▶	**18b**		
	19 Tax-exempt interest income	**19**		
	20 Other tax-exempt income	**20**		
	21 Nondeductible expenses	**21**		
	22 Distributions of money (cash and marketable securities)	**22**		
	23 Distributions of property other than money	**23**		
	24 Other items and amounts required to be reported separately to partners *(attach schedule)*			

Form 1065 (1997)   Page **4**

Analysis of Net Income (Loss)

1 Net income (loss). Combine Schedule K, lines 1 through 7 in column (b). From the result, subtract the
sum of Schedule K, lines 8 through 11, 14a, 17e, and 18b **1**

2 Analysis by partner type:	**(i)** Corporate	**(ii)** Individual (active)	**(iii)** Individual (passive)	**(iv)** Partnership	**(v)** Exempt organization	**(vi)** Nominee/Other
a General partners						
b Limited partners						

Schedule L — Balance Sheets per Books (Not required if Question 5 on Schedule B is answered "Yes.")

Assets	Beginning of tax year (a)	(b)	End of tax year (c)	(d)
1 Cash				
2a Trade notes and accounts receivable				
b Less allowance for bad debts				
3 Inventories				
4 U.S. government obligations				
5 Tax-exempt securities				
6 Other current assets (attach schedule)				
7 Mortgage and real estate loans				
8 Other investments (attach schedule)				
9a Buildings and other depreciable assets				
b Less accumulated depreciation				
10a Depletable assets				
b Less accumulated depletion				
11 Land (net of any amortization)				
12a Intangible assets (amortizable only)				
b Less accumulated amortization				
13 Other assets (attach schedule)				
14 **Total** assets				
Liabilities and Capital				
15 Accounts payable				
16 Mortgages, notes, bonds payable in less than 1 year				
17 Other current liabilities (attach schedule)				
18 All nonrecourse loans				
19 Mortgages, notes, bonds payable in 1 year or more				
20 Other liabilities (attach schedule)				
21 Partners' capital accounts				
22 **Total** liabilities and capital				

Schedule M-1 — Reconciliation of Income (Loss) per Books With Income (Loss) per Return
(Not required if Question 5 on Schedule B is answered "Yes." See page 23 of the instructions.)

1 Net income (loss) per books

2 Income included on Schedule K, lines 1 through 4, 6, and 7, not recorded on books this year (itemize): ....

3 Guaranteed payments (other than health insurance) . . . .

4 Expenses recorded on books this year not included on Schedule K, lines 1 through 11, 14a, 17e, and 18b (itemize):
a Depreciation $ ....
b Travel and entertainment $ ....

5 Add lines 1 through 4 . . . . . .

6 Income recorded on books this year not included on Schedule K, lines 1 through 7 (itemize):
a Tax-exempt interest $ ....

7 Deductions included on Schedule K, lines 1 through 11, 14a, 17e, and 18b, not charged against book income this year (itemize):
a Depreciation $ ....

8 Add lines 6 and 7 . . . .

9 Income (loss) (Analysis of Net Income (Loss), line 1). Subtract line 8 from line 5 . . . .

Schedule M-2 — Analysis of Partners' Capital Accounts (Not required if Question 5 on Schedule B is answered "Yes.")

1 Balance at beginning of year . . . .

2 Capital contributed during year . . . .

3 Net income (loss) per books . . . . .

4 Other increases (itemize): ....

5 Add lines 1 through 4 . . . .

6 Distributions: **a** Cash . . . .
            b Property . . . . . .

7 Other decreases (itemize): ....

8 Add lines 6 and 7 . . . .

9 Balance at end of year. Subtract line 8 from line 5

SCHEDULE K-1
(Form 1065)
Department of the Treasury
Internal Revenue Service

Partner's Share of Income, Credits, Deductions, etc.
▶ See separate instructions.

For calendar year 1997 or tax year beginning   , 1997, and ending   , 19

OMB No. 1545-0099

1997

Partner's identifying number ▶

Partnership's identifying number ▶

Partner's name, address, and ZIP code

Partnership's name, address, and ZIP code

A This partner is a ☐ general partner ☐ limited partner
   ☐ limited liability company member
B What type of entity is this partner? ▶ ....
C Is this partner a ☐ domestic or a ☐ foreign partner?
D Enter partner's percentage of:

	(i) Before change or termination	(ii) End of year
Profit sharing	.... %	.... %
Loss sharing	.... %	.... %
Ownership of capital	.... %	.... %

E IRS Center where partnership filed return:

F Partner's share of liabilities (see instructions):
   Nonrecourse . . . . $ ....
   Qualified nonrecourse financing . $ ....
   Other . . . . $ ....
G Tax shelter registration number . ▶ ....
H Check here if this partnership is a publicly traded partnership as defined in section 469(k)(2) . . . . . ☐
I Check applicable boxes: **(1)** ☐ Final K-1 **(2)** ☐ Amended K-1

J **Analysis of partner's capital account:**

(a) Capital account at beginning of year	(b) Capital contributed during year	(c) Partner's share of lines 3, 4, and 7, Form 1065, Schedule M-2	(d) Withdrawals and distributions	(e) Capital account at end of year (combine columns (a) through (d))
			( )	

(a) Distributive share item		(b) Amount	(c) 1040 filers enter the amount in column (b) on:
1 Ordinary income (loss) from trade or business activities . . .	1		See page 6 of Partner's Instructions for Schedule K-1 (Form 1065).
2 Net income (loss) from rental real estate activities	2		
3 Net income (loss) from other rental activities	3		
4 Portfolio income (loss):			
a Interest	4a		Sch. B, Part I, line 1
b Dividends	4b		Sch. B, Part II, line 5
c Royalties	4c		Sch. E, Part I, line 4
d Net short-term capital gain (loss)	4d		Sch. D, line 5, col. (f)
e Net long-term capital gain (loss):			
(1) 28% rate gain (loss)	e(1)		Sch. D, line 12, col. (g)
(2) Total for year	e(2)		Sch. D, line 12, col. (f)
f Other portfolio income (loss) (attach schedule)	4f		Enter on applicable line of your return.
5 Guaranteed payments to partner	5		See page 6 of Partner's Instructions for Schedule K-1 (Form 1065).
6 Net section 1231 gain (loss) (other than due to casualty or theft):			
a 28% rate gain (loss)	6a		
b Total for year	6b		
7 Other income (loss) (attach schedule)	7		Enter on applicable line of your return.
8 Charitable contributions (see instructions) (attach schedule) . .	8		Sch. A, line 15 or 16
9 Section 179 expense deduction	9		See page 7 of Partner's Instructions for Schedule K-1 (Form 1065).
10 Deductions related to portfolio income (attach schedule) . . .	10		
11 Other deductions (attach schedule)	11		
12a Low-income housing credit:			
(1) From section 42(j)(5) partnerships for property placed in service before 1990	a(1)		Form 8586, line 5
(2) Other than on line 12a(1) for property placed in service before 1990	a(2)		
(3) From section 42(j)(5) partnerships for property placed in service after 1989	a(3)		
(4) Other than on line 12a(3) for property placed in service after 1989	a(4)		
b Qualified rehabilitation expenditures related to rental real estate activities	12b		See page 8 of Partner's Instructions for Schedule K-1 (Form 1065).
c Credits (other than credits shown on lines 12a and 12b) related to rental real estate activities	12c		
d Credits related to other rental activities	12d		
13 Other credits	13		

Income (Loss) · *Deductions* · *Credits*

For Paperwork Reduction Act Notice, see Instructions for Form 1065.   Cat. No. 11394R   **Schedule K-1 (Form 1065) 1997**

	(a) Distributive share item		(b) Amount	(c) 1040 filers enter the amount in column (b) on:
Investment Interest	**14a** Interest expense on investment debts	14a		Form 4952, line 1
	b (1) Investment income included on lines 4a, 4b, 4c, and 4f . .	b(1)		See page 8 of Partner's
	(2) Investment expenses included on line 10	b(2)		Instructions for Schedule K-1 (Form 1065).
Self-em- ployment	**15a** Net earnings (loss) from self-employment	15a		Sch. SE, Section A or B
	b Gross farming or fishing income	15b		See page 9 of Partner's
	c Gross nonfarm income	15c		Instructions for Schedule K-1 (Form 1065).
Adjustments and Tax Preference Items	**16a** Depreciation adjustment on property placed in service after 1986	16a		
	b Adjusted gain or loss	16b		See page 9 of Partner's
	c Depletion (other than oil and gas)	16c		Instructions for Schedule K-1
	d (1) Gross income from oil, gas, and geothermal properties . .	d(1)		(Form 1065) and
	(2) Deductions allocable to oil, gas, and geothermal properties	d(2)		Instructions for Form 6251.
	e Other adjustments and tax preference items (attach schedule)	16e		
Foreign Taxes	**17a** Type of income ▶			Form 1116, check boxes
	b Name of foreign country or possession ▶			
	c Total gross income from sources outside the United States (attach schedule)	17c		Form 1116, Part I
	d Total applicable deductions and losses (attach schedule) . . .	17d		
	e Total foreign taxes (check one): ▶ ☐ Paid ☐ Accrued . .	17e		Form 1116, Part II
	f Reduction in taxes available for credit (attach schedule) . . .	17f		Form 1116, Part III
	g Other foreign tax information (attach schedule)	17g		See Instructions for Form 1116.
Other	**18** Section 59(e)(2) expenditures: **a** Type ▶			See page 9 of Partner's Instructions for Schedule K-1 (Form 1065).
	b Amount	18b		
	19 Tax-exempt interest income	19		Form 1040, line 8b
	20 Other tax-exempt income	20		
	21 Nondeductible expenses	21		See page 9 of Partner's Instructions for Schedule K-1 (Form 1065).
	22 Distributions of money (cash and marketable securities) . . .	22		
	23 Distributions of property other than money	23		
	24 Recapture of low-income housing credit:			
	a From section 42(j)(5) partnerships	24a		Form 8611, line 8
	b Other than on line 24a	24b		

25 Supplemental information required to be reported separately to each partner (attach additional schedules if more space is needed):

Form **1120-A**	**U.S. Corporation Short-Form Income Tax Return**	OMB No. 1545-0890
Department of the Treasury Internal Revenue Service	See separate instructions to make sure the corporation qualifies to file Form 1120-A.	**1997**

For calendar year 1997 or tax year beginning ...., 1997, ending ...., 19 ....

A Check this box if the corp. is a personal service corp. (as defined in Temporary Regs. section 1.441-4T—see instructions) ▶ ☐

Use IRS label. Other-wise, print or type.	Name	**B** Employer identification number
	Number, street, and room or suite no. (If a P.O. box, see page 5 of instructions.)	**C** Date incorporated
	City or town, state, and ZIP code	**D** Total assets (see page 5 of instructions) $

E Check applicable boxes: **(1)** ☐ Initial return **(2)** ☐ Change of address

F Check method of accounting: **(1)** ☐ Cash **(2)** ☐ Accrual **(3)** ☐ Other (specify) . . ▶

Income

1a Gross receipts or sales	**b** Less returns and allowances	**c** Balance ▶	**1c**	
2 Cost of goods sold (see page 10 of instructions).	**2**	
3 Gross profit. Subtract line 2 from line 1c	**3**	
4 Domestic corporation dividends subject to the 70% deduction	**4**	
5 Interest	**5**	
6 Gross rents	**6**	
7 Gross royalties	**7**	
8 Capital gain net income (attach Schedule D (Form 1120))	**8**	
9 Net gain or (loss) from Form 4797, Part II, line 18 (attach Form 4797) . . .	**9**	
10 Other income (see page 6 of instructions).	**10**	
11 **Total income.** Add lines 3 through 10 . . . . ▶	**11**	

Deductions

(See instructions for limitations on deductions.)

12 Compensation of officers (see page 7 of instructions)	**12**	
13 Salaries and wages (less employment credits)	**13**	
14 Repairs and maintenance	**14**	
15 Bad debts	**15**	
16 Rents	**16**	
17 Taxes and licenses	**17**	
18 Interest	**18**	
19 Charitable contributions (see page 8 of instructions for 10% limitation) .	**19**	
20 Depreciation (attach Form 4562) **20**		
21 Less depreciation claimed elsewhere on return **21a**	**21b**	
22 Other deductions (attach schedule)	**22**	
23 **Total deductions.** Add lines 12 through 22 . . . . ▶	**23**	
24 Taxable income before net operating loss deduction and special deductions. Subtract line 23 from line 11	**24**	
25 **Less: a** Net operating loss deduction (see page 9 of instructions). **25a**		
b Special deductions (see page 10 of instructions) **25b**	**25c**	

Tax and Payments

26 **Taxable income.** Subtract line 25c from line 24	**26**	
27 **Total tax** (from page 2, Part I, line 7)	**27**	
28 **Payments:**		
a 1996 overpayment credited to 1997 **28a**		
b 1997 estimated tax payments . **28b**		
c Less 1997 refund applied for on Form 4466 **28c** ( ) **Bal** ▶ **28d**		
e Tax deposited with Form 7004 . . . . **28e**		
f Credit for tax paid on undistributed capital gains (attach Form 2439). **28f**		
g Credit for Federal tax on fuels (attach Form 4136). See instructions . **28g**		
h Total payments. Add lines 28d through 28g	**28h**	
29 Estimated tax penalty (see page 10 of instructions). Check if Form 2220 is attached . . . ▶ ☐	**29**	
30 **Tax due.** If line 28h is smaller than the total of lines 27 and 29, enter amount owed . . .	**30**	
31 **Overpayment.** If line 28h is larger than the total of lines 27 and 29, enter amount overpaid . .	**31**	
32 Enter amount of line 31 you want: **Credited to 1998 estimated tax** ▶	**Refunded** ▶ **32**	

Sign Here

Under penalties of perjury, I declare that I have examined this return, including accompanying schedules and statements, and to the best of my knowledge and belief, it is true, correct, and complete. Declaration of preparer (other than taxpayer) is based on all information of which preparer has any knowledge.

▶ Signature of officer	Date	▶ Title

Paid Preparer's Use Only

Preparer's signature ▶	Date	Check if self-employed ▶ ☐	Preparer's social security number
Firm's name (or yours if self-employed) and address ▶		EIN ▶	
		ZIP code ▶	

For Paperwork Reduction Act Notice, see page 1 of the instructions.   Cat. No. 11456E   Form **1120-A** (1997)

Form 1120-A (1997)   Page **2**

Part I   Tax Computation (See page 12 of instructions.)

1	Income tax. If the corporation is a qualified personal service corporation (see page 13), check here ▶ ☐	**1**	
2a	General business credit. Check if from Form(s): ☐ 3800 ☐ 3468		
	☐ 5884 ☐ 6478 ☐ 6765 ☐ 8586 ☐ 8830 ☐ 8826		
	☐ 8835 ☐ 8844 ☐ 8845 ☐ 8846 ☐ 8820 ☐ 8847 ☐ 8861	**2a**	
b	Credit for prior year minimum tax (attach Form 8827)	**2b**	
3	**Total credits.** Add lines 2a and 2b	**3**	
4	Subtract line 3 from line 1	**4**	
5	Recapture taxes. Check if from: ☐ Form 4255 ☐ Form 8611	**5**	
6	Alternative minimum tax (attach Form 4626)	**6**	
7	**Total tax.** Add lines 4 through 6. Enter here and on line 27, page 1	**7**	

Part II   Other Information (See page 14 of instructions.)

1 See page 16 and state the principal: **a.** Business activity code no. ▶ _____

    b Business activity ▶ _____

    c Product or service ▶ _____

2 At the end of the tax year, did any individual, partnership, estate, or trust own, directly or indirectly, 50% or more of the corporation's voting stock? (For rules of attribution, see section 267(c).) . . . . ☐ Yes ☐ No

If "Yes," attach a schedule showing name and identifying number.

3 Enter the amount of tax-exempt interest received or accrued during the tax year . . . . ▶ |$

4 Enter amount of cash distributions and the book value of property (other than cash) distributions made in this tax year . . . . ▶ |$

5a If an amount is entered on line 2, page 1, enter amounts from worksheet on page 10:

  (1) Purchases . . . . . .

  (2) Additional sec. 263A costs (attach schedule) . . . .

  (3) Other costs (attach schedule) .

b If property is produced or acquired for resale, do the rules of section 263A apply to the corporation? . . . . . ☐ Yes ☐ No

6 At any time during the 1997 calendar year, did the corporation have an interest in or a signature or other authority over a financial account (such as a bank account, securities account, or other financial account) in a foreign country? . . . . . ☐ Yes ☐ No
If "Yes," the corporation may have to file Form TD F 90-22.1
If "Yes," enter the name of the foreign country ▶ _____

Part III   Balance Sheets per Books

		(a) Beginning of tax year		(b) End of tax year	
1	Cash				
2a	Trade notes and accounts receivable				
b	Less allowance for bad debts	(	)	(	)
3	Inventories				
4	U.S. government obligations				
5	Tax-exempt securities (see instructions)				
6	Other current assets (attach schedule) . . .				
7	Loans to stockholders				
8	Mortgage and real estate loans				
9a	Depreciable, depletable, and intangible assets . . .				
b	Less accumulated depreciation, depletion, and amortization	(	)	(	)
10	Land (net of any amortization)				
11	Other assets (attach schedule)				
12	Total assets				
13	Accounts payable				
14	Other current liabilities (attach schedule)				
15	Loans from stockholders				
16	Mortgages, notes, bonds payable				
17	Other liabilities (attach schedule)				
18	Capital stock (preferred and common stock) . . .				
19	Additional paid-in capital				
20	Retained earnings				
21	Adjustments to shareholders' equity (attach schedule) .				
22	Less cost of treasury stock	(	)	(	)
23	Total liabilities and stockholders' equity				

Assets (rows 1–12) / *Liabilities and Stockholders' Equity* (rows 13–23)

Part IV   Reconciliation of Income (Loss) per Books With Income per Return *(You are not required to complete Part IV if the total assets on line 12, column (b), Part III are less than $25,000.)*

1 Net income (loss) per books		**6** Income recorded on books this year not included on this return (itemize) _____	
2 Federal income tax			
3 Excess of capital losses over capital gains . .		**7** Deductions on this return not charged against book income this year (itemize) _____	
4 Income subject to tax not recorded on books this year (itemize) _____		_____	
5 Expenses recorded on books this year not deducted on this return (itemize)		**8** Income (line 24, page 1). Enter the sum of lines 1 through 5 less the sum of lines 6 and 7 . .	

U.S. Corporation Income Tax Return

Form **1120**

Department of the Treasury
Internal Revenue Service

For calendar year 1997 or tax year beginning .... , 1997, ending .... , 19 ...
▶ Instructions are separate. See page 1 for Paperwork Reduction Act Notice.

OMB No. 1545-0123

1997

A Check if a:				
1 Consolidated return (attach Form 851) ☐	**Use IRS label. Otherwise, print or type.**	Name		**B** Employer identification number
2 Personal holding co. (attach Sch. PH) ☐		Number, street, and room or suite no. (If a P.O. box, see page 5 of instructions.)		**C** Date incorporated
3 Personal service corp. (as defined in Temporary Regs. sec. 1.441-4T— see instructions) ☐		City or town, state, and ZIP code		**D** Total assets (see page 5 of instructions) $

E Check applicable boxes: (1) ☐ Initial return (2) ☐ Final return (3) ☐ Change of address

Income

1a	Gross receipts or sales	**b** Less returns and allowances	**c** Bal ▶ **1c**
2	Cost of goods sold (Schedule A, line 8)		**2**
3	Gross profit. Subtract line 2 from line 1c		**3**
4	Dividends (Schedule C, line 19)		**4**
5	Interest		**5**
6	Gross rents		**6**
7	Gross royalties		**7**
8	Capital gain net income (attach Schedule D (Form 1120)) . . .		**8**
9	Net gain or (loss) from Form 4797, Part II, line 18 (attach Form 4797) .		**9**
10	Other income (see page 6 of instructions—attach schedule) . . .		**10**
11	**Total income.** Add lines 3 through 10 . . . . ▶		**11**

Deductions (See instructions for limitations on deductions.)

12	Compensation of officers (Schedule E, line 4)		**12**
13	Salaries and wages (less employment credits)		**13**
14	Repairs and maintenance		**14**
15	Bad debts		**15**
16	Rents		**16**
17	Taxes and licenses		**17**
18	Interest		**18**
19	Charitable contributions (see page 8 of instructions for 10% limitation) . .		**19**
20	Depreciation (attach Form 4562)	**20**	
21	Less depreciation claimed on Schedule A and elsewhere on return . . .	**21a**	**21b**
22	Depletion		**22**
23	Advertising		**23**
24	Pension, profit-sharing, etc., plans		**24**
25	Employee benefit programs		**25**
26	Other deductions (attach schedule)		**26**
27	**Total deductions.** Add lines 12 through 26 . . . . ▶		**27**
28	Taxable income before net operating loss deduction and special deductions. Subtract line 27 from line 11		**28**
29	**Less:** **a** Net operating loss deduction (see page 9 of instructions) . .	**29a**	
	b Special deductions (Schedule C, line 20)	**29b**	**29c**

Tax and Payments

30	**Taxable income.** Subtract line 29c from line 28			**30**
31	**Total tax** (Schedule J, line 10)			**31**
32	**Payments: a** 1996 overpayment credited to 1997	**32a**		
b	1997 estimated tax payments . .	**32b**		
c	Less 1997 refund applied for on Form 4466	**32c** ( )	**d** Bal ▶ **32d**	
e	Tax deposited with Form 7004	**32e**		
f	Credit for tax paid on undistributed capital gains (attach Form 2439) . .	**32f**		
g	Credit for Federal tax on fuels (attach Form 4136). See instructions . . .	**32g**	**32h**	
33	Estimated tax penalty (see page 10 of instructions). Check if Form 2220 is attached . . . ▶ ☐			**33**
34	**Tax due.** If line 32h is smaller than the total of lines 31 and 33, enter amount owed . .			**34**
35	**Overpayment.** If line 32h is larger than the total of lines 31 and 33, enter amount overpaid .			**35**
36	Enter amount of line 35 you want: **Credited to 1998 estimated tax** ▶ Refunded ▶			**36**

Sign Here

Under penalties of perjury, I declare that I have examined this return, including accompanying schedules and statements, and to the best of my knowledge and belief, it is true, correct, and complete. Declaration of preparer (other than taxpayer) is based on all information of which preparer has any knowledge.

▶ _____ ▶ _____
Signature of officer   Date   Title

Paid Preparer's Use Only

Preparer's signature ▶	Date	Check if self-employed ☐	Preparer's social security number
Firm's name (or yours if self-employed) and address ▶		EIN ▶	
		ZIP code ▶	

Cat. No. 11450Q

Form 1120 (1997)   Page **2**

Schedule A | Cost of Goods Sold (See page 10 of instructions.)

1	Inventory at beginning of year	1
2	Purchases	2
3	Cost of labor	3
4	Additional section 263A costs (attach schedule)	4
5	Other costs (attach schedule)	5
6	**Total.** Add lines 1 through 5	6
7	Inventory at end of year	7
8	**Cost of goods sold.** Subtract line 7 from line 6. Enter here and on page 1, line 2	8

9a Check all methods used for valuing closing inventory:

    (i) ☐ Cost as described in Regulations section 1.471-3

    (ii) ☐ Lower of cost or market as described in Regulations section 1.471-4

    (iii) ☐ Other (Specify method used and attach explanation.) ▶ ---

  b Check if there was a writedown of subnormal goods as described in Regulations section 1.471-2(c) . . . . ▶ ☐

  c Check if the LIFO inventory method was adopted this tax year for any goods (if checked, attach Form 970) . . . . ▶ ☐

  d If the LIFO inventory method was used for this tax year, enter percentage (or amounts) of closing inventory computed under LIFO . . . . | 9d |

  e If property is produced or acquired for resale, do the rules of section 263A apply to the corporation? . . . . . ☐ Yes ☐ No

  f Was there any change in determining quantities, cost, or valuations between opening and closing inventory? If "Yes," attach explanation . . . . ☐ Yes ☐ No

Schedule C | Dividends and Special Deductions (See page 11 of instructions.)

		(a) Dividends received	(b) %	(c) Special deductions (a) × (b)
1	Dividends from less-than-20%-owned domestic corporations that are subject to the 70% deduction (other than debt-financed stock)		70	
2	Dividends from 20%-or-more-owned domestic corporations that are subject to the 80% deduction (other than debt-financed stock)		80	
3	Dividends on debt-financed stock of domestic and foreign corporations (section 246A)		see instructions	
4	Dividends on certain preferred stock of less-than-20%-owned public utilities . . .		42	
5	Dividends on certain preferred stock of 20%-or-more-owned public utilities . . .		48	
6	Dividends from less-than-20%-owned foreign corporations and certain FSCs that are subject to the 70% deduction		70	
7	Dividends from 20%-or-more-owned foreign corporations and certain FSCs that are subject to the 80% deduction		80	
8	Dividends from wholly owned foreign subsidiaries subject to the 100% deduction (section 245(b))		100	
9	**Total.** Add lines 1 through 8. See page 12 of instructions for limitation			
10	Dividends from domestic corporations received by a small business investment company operating under the Small Business Investment Act of 1958		100	
11	Dividends from certain FSCs that are subject to the 100% deduction (section 245(c)(1))		100	
12	Dividends from affiliated group members subject to the 100% deduction (section 243(a)(3))		100	
13	Other dividends from foreign corporations not included on lines 3, 6, 7, 8, or 11 . .			
14	Income from controlled foreign corporations under subpart F (attach Form(s) 5471) .			
15	Foreign dividend gross-up (section 78)			
16	IC-DISC and former DISC dividends not included on lines 1, 2, or 3 (section 246(d)) .			
17	Other dividends			
18	Deduction for dividends paid on certain preferred stock of public utilities			
19	**Total dividends.** Add lines 1 through 17. Enter here and on line 4, page 1 . . ▶			
20	**Total special deductions.** Add lines 9, 10, 11, 12, and 18. Enter here and on line 29b, page 1 . . . . . . ▶			

Schedule E | Compensation of Officers (See instructions for line 12, page 1.)

Complete Schedule E only if total receipts (line 1a plus lines 4 through 10 on page 1, Form 1120) are $500,000 or more.

	(a) Name of officer	(b) Social security number	(c) Percent of time devoted to business	Percent of corporation stock owned		(f) Amount of compensation
				(d) Common	(e) Preferred	
1			%	%	%	
			%	%	%	
			%	%	%	
			%	%	%	
			%	%	%	

2	Total compensation of officers	
3	Compensation of officers claimed on Schedule A and elsewhere on return	
4	Subtract line 3 from line 2. Enter the result here and on line 12, page 1	

Form 1120 (1997)   Page **3**

Schedule J — Tax Computation (See page 12 of instructions.)

1 Check if the corporation is a member of a controlled group (see sections 1561 and 1563) . . . . ▶ ☐

Important: Members of a controlled group, see instructions on page 12.

2a If the box on line 1 is checked, enter the corporation's share of the $50,000, $25,000, and $9,925,000 taxable income brackets (in that order):

    (1) $ _____ **(2)** $ _____ **(3)** $ _____

b Enter the corporation's share of:

    (1) Additional 5% tax (not more than $11,750) $ _____

    (2) Additional 3% tax (not more than $100,000) $ _____

3 Income tax. Check this box if the corporation is a qualified personal service corporation as defined in section 448(d)(2) (see instructions on page 13) . . . . ▶ ☐ | **3** |

4a Foreign tax credit (attach Form 1118) . . . . | **4a** |

b Possessions tax credit (attach Form 5735) . . . . | **4b** |

c Check: ☐ Nonconventional source fuel credit ☐ QEV credit (attach Form 8834) | **4c** |

d General business credit. Enter here and check which forms are attached: ☐ 3800

    ☐ 3468 ☐ 5884 ☐ 6478 ☐ 6765 ☐ 8586 ☐ 8830 ☐ 8826

    ☐ 8835 ☐ 8844 ☐ 8845 ☐ 8846 ☐ 8820 ☐ 8847 ☐ 8861 | **4d** |

e Credit for prior year minimum tax (attach Form 8827) . . . . | **4e** |

5 **Total credits.** Add lines 4a through 4e . . . . | **5** |

6 Subtract line 5 from line 3 . . . . | **6** |

7 Personal holding company tax (attach Schedule PH (Form 1120)) . . . . | **7** |

8 Recapture taxes. Check if from: ☐ Form 4255 ☐ Form 8611 . . . . . | **8** |

9 Alternative minimum tax (attach Form 4626) . . . . | **9** |

10 **Total tax.** Add lines 6 through 9. Enter here and on line 31, page 1 . . . . . | **10** |

Schedule K — Other Information (See page 14 of instructions.)

	Yes	No

1 Check method of accounting: a ☐ Cash

    b ☐ Accrual c ☐ Other (specify) ▶ _____

2 See page 16 of the instructions and state the principal:

a Business activity code no. ▶ _____

b Business activity ▶ _____

c Product or service ▶ _____

3 At the end of the tax year, did the corporation own, directly or indirectly, 50% or more of the voting stock of a domestic corporation? (For rules of attribution, see section 267(c).) . . . . .

If "Yes," attach a schedule showing: **(a)** name and identifying number, **(b)** percentage owned, and **(c)** taxable income or (loss) before NOL and special deductions of such corporation for the tax year ending with or within your tax year.

4 Is the corporation a subsidiary in an affiliated group or a parent-subsidiary controlled group? . . . . . .

If "Yes," enter employer identification number and name of the parent corporation ▶ _____

5 At the end of the tax year, did any individual, partnership, corporation, estate or trust own, directly or indirectly, 50% or more of the corporation's voting stock? (For rules of attribution, see section 267(c).) . . . . . .

If "Yes," attach a schedule showing name and identifying number. (Do not include any information already entered in **4** above.) Enter percentage owned ▶ _____

6 During this tax year, did the corporation pay dividends (other than stock dividends and distributions in exchange for stock) in excess of the corporation's current and accumulated earnings and profits? (See secs. 301 and 316.) . . . .

If "Yes," file Form 5452. If this is a consolidated return, answer here for the parent corporation and on **Form 851,** Affiliations Schedule, for each subsidiary.

7 Was the corporation a U.S. shareholder of any controlled foreign corporation? (See sections 951 and 957.) . . .

If "Yes," attach Form 5471 for each such corporation. Enter number of Forms 5471 attached ▶ _____

8 At any time during the 1997 calendar year, did the corporation have an interest in or a signature or other authority over a financial account (such as a bank account, securities account, or other financial account) in a foreign country?

If "Yes," the corporation may have to file Form TD F 90-22.1.

If "Yes," enter name of foreign country ▶ _____

9 During the tax year, did the corporation receive a distribution from, or was it the grantor of, or transferor to, a foreign trust? If "Yes," see page 15 of the instructions for other forms the corporation may have to file . . . .

10 At any time during the tax year, did one foreign person own, directly or indirectly, at least 25% of: **(a)** the total voting power of all classes of stock of the corporation entitled to vote, or **(b)** the total value of all classes of stock of the corporation? If "Yes,"

a Enter percentage owned ▶ _____

b Enter owner's country ▶ _____

c The corporation may have to file Form 5472. Enter number of Forms 5472 attached ▶ _____

11 Check this box if the corporation issued publicly offered debt instruments with original issue discount . . ▶ ☐

If so, the corporation may have to file Form 8281.

12 Enter the amount of tax-exempt interest received or accrued during the tax year ▶ $ _____

13 If there were 35 or fewer shareholders at the end of the tax year, enter the number ▶ _____

14 If the corporation has an NOL for the tax year and is electing to forego the carryback period, check here ▶ ☐

15 Enter the available NOL carryover from prior tax years (Do not reduce it by any deduction on line 29a.) ▶ $ _____

Form 1120 (1997) Page **4**

Schedule L — Balance Sheets per Books

	Assets	Beginning of tax year (a)	(b)	End of tax year (c)	(d)
1	Cash				
2a	Trade notes and accounts receivable . . .				
b	Less allowance for bad debts	( )		( )	
3	Inventories				
4	U.S. government obligations . . .				
5	Tax-exempt securities (see instructions) . .				
6	Other current assets (attach schedule) . .				
7	Loans to stockholders				
8	Mortgage and real estate loans . . .				
9	Other investments (attach schedule) . .				
10a	Buildings and other depreciable assets . .				
b	Less accumulated depreciation . . .	( )		( )	
11a	Depletable assets				
b	Less accumulated depletion	( )		( )	
12	Land (net of any amortization)				
13a	Intangible assets (amortizable only) . . .				
b	Less accumulated amortization	( )		( )	
14	Other assets (attach schedule)				
15	Total assets				
	Liabilities and Stockholders' Equity				
16	Accounts payable				
17	Mortgages, notes, bonds payable in less than 1 year				
18	Other current liabilities (attach schedule) . .				
19	Loans from stockholders				
20	Mortgages, notes, bonds payable in 1 year or more				
21	Other liabilities (attach schedule)				
22	Capital stock: **a** Preferred stock . . .				
	b Common stock . . .				
23	Additional paid-in capital				
24	Retained earnings—Appropriated (attach schedule)				
25	Retained earnings—Unappropriated . . .				
26	Adjustments to shareholders' equity (attach schedule)				
27	Less cost of treasury stock	( )		( )	
28	Total liabilities and stockholders' equity . .				

Note: *You are not required to complete Schedules M-1 and M-2 below if the total assets on line 15, column (d) of Schedule L are less than $25,000.*

Schedule M-1 — Reconciliation of Income (Loss) per Books With Income per Return (See page 15 of instructions.)

1	Net income (loss) per books		7 Income recorded on books this year not included on this return (itemize):	
2	Federal income tax		Tax-exempt interest $	
3	Excess of capital losses over capital gains .		....	
4	Income subject to tax not recorded on books this year (itemize):		....	
	....		8 Deductions on this return not charged against book income this year (itemize):	
5	Expenses recorded on books this year not deducted on this return (itemize):		**a** Depreciation . . . . $............	
a	Depreciation . . . . $		**b** Contributions carryover $	
b	Contributions carryover $		....	
c	Travel and entertainment $		....	
	....		9 Add lines 7 and 8	
6	Add lines 1 through 5		10 Income (line 28, page 1)—line 6 less line 9	

Schedule M-2 — Analysis of Unappropriated Retained Earnings per Books (Line 25, Schedule L)

1	Balance at beginning of year		5 Distributions: **a** Cash	
2	Net income (loss) per books		**b** Stock	
3	Other increases (itemize):		**c** Property	
	....		6 Other decreases (itemize):	
	....		7 Add lines 5 and 6	
4	Add lines 1, 2, and 3		8 Balance at end of year (line 4 less line 7)	

✹

Form **1120-F**
Department of the Treasury
Internal Revenue Service

U.S. Income Tax Return of a Foreign Corporation

For calendar year 1997, or tax year beginning ...., 1997, and ending ...., 19 .....
▶ **See separate instructions.**

OMB No. 1545-0126

1997

Please type or print

Name

Number, street, and room or suite no. (see page 6 of instructions)

City or town, state and ZIP code, or country (see page 6 of instructions)

Employer identification number

Check applicable boxes:
☐ Initial return ☐ Amended return
☐ Final return ☐ Change of address

A Country of incorporation ....

B Foreign country under whose laws the income reported on this return is subject to tax ....

C Date incorporated ....

D Location of corporation's primary books and records:

City, state and country ....

Principal location of business ....

E If the corporation had an agent in the United States at any time during the tax year, enter:

Kind of agent ....
Name ....
Address ....

F Refer to the list on page 18 of the instructions and state the corporation's principal:

(1) Business activity code number ▶ ....
(2) Business activity ▶ ....
(3) Product or service ▶ ....

G Check method of accounting: **(1)** ☐ Cash **(2)** ☐ Accrual
(3) ☐ Other (specify) ▶ ....

	Yes	No
H Did the corporation file a U.S. income tax return for the preceding tax year?		
I At any time during the tax year, was the corporation engaged in a trade or business in the United States?		
J At any time during the tax year, did the corporation have a permanent establishment in the United States for purposes of applying section 894(b) and any applicable tax treaty between the United States and a foreign country?		

If "Yes," enter the name of the foreign country:
....

	Yes	No
K Is the corporation a foreign personal holding company? (See section 552 for definition.) . .		

If "Yes," have you filed Form 5471? (Sec. 6035). See page 3 of the instructions . . . . .

	Yes	No
L Did the corporation have any transactions with related parties?		

If "Yes," you may have to file Form 5472 (section 6038A and section 6038C). See page 3 of the instructions.

Enter number of Forms 5472 attached ▶ ......

Note: *Additional information is required at the bottom of pages 2 and 5.*

Computation of Tax Due or Overpayment

1	Tax from Section I, line 11, page 2	**1**	
2	Tax from Section II, Schedule J, line 9, page 4	**2**	
3	Tax from Section III (add lines 6 and 10 on page 5)	**3**	
4	Personal holding company tax (attach Schedule PH (Form 1120))—see page 6 of instructions	**4**	
5	**Total tax.** Add lines 1 through 4	**5**	
6	**Payments:**		
a	1996 overpayment credited to 1997 **6a**		
b	1997 estimated tax payments . . **6b**		
c	Less 1997 refund applied for on Form 4466 **6c** ( ) Bal ▶	**6d**	
e	Tax deposited with Form 7004	**6e**	
f	Credit for tax paid on undistributed captial gains (attach Form 2439) . .	**6f**	
g	Credit for Federal tax on fuels (attach Form 4136). See instructions . .	**6g**	
h	U.S. income tax paid or withheld at source (add line 12, page 2, and amounts from Forms 8288-A and 8805 (attach Forms 8288-A and 8805))	**6h**	
i	Total payments. Add lines 6d through 6h	**6i**	
7	Estimated tax penalty (see page 6 of instructions). Check if Form 2220 is attached . . . . . ▶ ☐	**7**	
8	**Tax due.** If line 6i is smaller than the total of lines 5 and 7, enter amount owed	**8**	
9	**Overpayment.** If line 6i is larger than the total of lines 5 and 7, enter amount overpaid	**9**	
10	Enter amount of line 9 you want: **Credited to 1998 estimated tax** ▶ .... Refunded ▶	**10**	

Please Sign Here

Under penalties of perjury, I declare that I have examined this return, including accompanying schedules and statements, and to the best of my knowledge and belief, it is true, correct, and complete. Declaration of preparer (other than taxpayer) is based on all information of which preparer has any knowledge.

▶ _____ Signature of officer   Date _____   ▶ _____ Title

Paid Preparer's Use Only

Preparer's signature ▶	Date	Check if self-employed ▶ ☐	Preparer's social security number
Firm's name (or yours if self-employed) and address ▶		EIN ▶	
		ZIP code ▶	

For Paperwork Reduction Act Notice, see page 17 of separate instructions.   Cat. No. 11470I   Form **1120-F** (1997)

SECTION I.—Certain Gains, Profits, and Income From U.S. Sources That Are NOT Effectively Connected With the Conduct of a Trade or Business in the United States (See page 6 of instructions.)

If you are required to complete Section II or are using Form 1120-F as a claim for refund of tax withheld at source, include below **ALL** income from U.S. sources that is **NOT** effectively connected with the conduct of a trade or business in the United States. Otherwise, include only those items of income on which the U.S. income tax was not fully paid at the source. The rate of tax on each item of **gross** income listed below is 30% (4% for the gross transportation tax) or such lower rate specified by tax treaty. No deductions are allowed against these types of income. Fill in treaty rates where applicable. **If the corporation claimed a lower treaty rate, also complete Item W, page 5.**

Name of treaty country, if any ▶

(a) Nature of income	(b) Gross income	(c) Rate of tax (%)	(d) Amount of tax	(e) Amount of U.S. income tax paid or withheld at the source
1 Interest				
2 Dividends				
3 Rents				
4 Royalties				
5 Annuities				
6 Gains from disposal of timber, coal, or domestic iron ore with a retained economic interest (attach supporting schedule)				
7 Gains from sale or exchange of patents, copyrights, etc.				
8 Fiduciary distributions (attach supporting schedule)				
9 Gross transportation income (see page 7 of instructions).		4		
10 Other fixed or determinable annual or periodic gains, profits, and income .				
....				
11 Total. Enter here and on line 1, page 1 . . . . ▶				
12 Total. Enter here and include on line 6h, page 1. . . . . ▶				

Additional Information Required *(continued from page 1)*

	Yes	No
M Is the corporation a personal holding company? (See section 542 for definition.).		
N Is the corporation a controlled foreign corporation? (See section 957 for definition.)		
O Is the corporation a personal service corporation? (See page 7 of instructions for definition.).		

P Enter tax-exempt interest received or accrued during the tax year (see instructions) ▶ $ ....

Q At the end of the tax year, did the corporation own, directly or indirectly, 50% or more of the voting stock of a U.S. corporation? (See section 267(c) for rules of attribution.) . . . .

If "Yes," attach a schedule showing (1) name and identifying number of such U.S. corporation; (2) percentage owned; and (3) taxable income or (loss) before NOL and special deductions of such U.S. corporation for the tax year ending with or within your tax year.

R If the corporation has a net operating loss (NOL) for the tax year and is electing to forego the carryback period, check here . . . . ▶ ☐

S Enter the available NOL carryover from prior tax years. (Do not reduce it by any deduction on line 30a, page 3.) ▶ $ ....

	Yes	No
T Is the corporation a subsidiary in a parent-subsidiary controlled group?		

If "Yes," enter the name and employer identification number of the parent corporation ▶ ....

U At the end of the tax year, did any individual, partnership, corporation, estate, or trust own, directly or indirectly, 50% or more of the corporation's voting stock? (See section 267(c) for attribution rules.) . .

If "Yes," attach a schedule showing the name and identifying number. (Do not include any information already entered in **T** above).

Enter percentage owned ▶..................

Note: *Additional information is required at the bottom of page 5.*

SECTION II.—Income Effectively Connected With the Conduct of a Trade or Business in the United States
(See page 7 of instructions.)

IMPORTANT—Fill in all applicable lines and schedules. If you need more space, see **Attachments** on page 3 of instructions.

Income	**1a** Gross receipts or sales _____ **b** Less returns and allowances _____ **c** Bal ▶	**1c**	
	2 Cost of goods sold (Schedule A, line 8)	**2**	
	3 Gross profit (subtract line 2 from line 1c)	**3**	
	4 Dividends (Schedule C, line 14)	**4**	
	5 Interest	**5**	
	6 Gross rents	**6**	
	7 Gross royalties	**7**	
	8 Capital gain net income (attach Schedule D (Form 1120))	**8**	
	9 Net gain or (loss) from Form 4797, Part II, line 18 (attach Form 4797) . . .	**9**	
	10 Other income (see page 8 of instructions—attach schedule).	**10**	
	11 **Total income.** Add lines 3 through 10 . . . . ▶	**11**	

Deductions (See instructions for limitations on deductions.)	**12** Compensation of officers (Schedule E, line 4). Deduct only amounts connected with a U.S. business	**12**	
	13 Salaries and wages (less employment credits)	**13**	
	14 Repairs and maintenance	**14**	
	15 Bad debts	**15**	
	16 Rents	**16**	
	17 Taxes and licenses	**17**	
	18 Interest allowable under Regulations section 1.882-5 (see page 10 of instructions—attach schedule).	**18**	
	19 Charitable contributions (see page 10 of instructions for 10% limitation)	**19**	
	20 Depreciation (attach Form 4562) **20**		
	21 Less depreciation claimed on Schedule A and elsewhere on return **21**		
	22 Balance (subtract line 21 from line 20)	**22**	
	23 Depletion	**23**	
	24 Advertising	**24**	
	25 Pension, profit-sharing, etc., plans	**25**	
	26 Employee benefit programs	**26**	
	27 Other deductions (see page 11 of instructions—attach schedule)	**27**	
	28 **Total deductions.** Add lines 12 through 27 . . . . ▶	**28**	
	29 Taxable income before NOL deduction and special deductions (subtract line 28 from line 11) .	**29**	
	30 **Less:** **a** Net operating loss deduction (see page 12 of instructions) **30a**		
	b Special deductions (Schedule C, line 15) **30b**	**30c**	
	31 Taxable income or (loss). Subtract line 30c from line 29	**31**	

Schedule A   Cost of Goods Sold (See page 12 of instructions.)

1 Inventory at beginning of year	**1**	
2 Purchases	**2**	
3 Cost of labor	**3**	
4 Additional section 263A costs (see instructions—attach schedule)	**4**	
5 Other costs (attach schedule)	**5**	
6 Add lines 1 through 5	**6**	
7 Inventory at end of year	**7**	
8 **Cost of goods sold.** Subtract line 7 from line 6. Enter here and on Section II, line 2	**8**	

9a Check all methods used for valuing closing inventory:

   (1) ☐ Cost as described in Regulations section 1.471-3

   (2) ☐ Lower of cost or market as described in Regulations section 1.471-4

   (3) ☐ Other (Specify method used and attach explanation.) ▶ ---------------------------------

  b Check if there was a writedown of subnormal goods as described in Regulations section 1.471-2(c) . . . . . ▶ ☐

  c Check if the LIFO inventory method was adopted this tax year for any goods . . . . ▶ ☐
    If checked, attach Form 970.

  d If the LIFO inventory method was used for this tax year, enter percentage (or amounts) of closing
    inventory computed under LIFO . . . . **9d** |

  e Do the rules of section 263A (for property produced or acquired for resale) apply to the corporation? . . ☐ **Yes** ☐ **No**

  f Was there any change in determining quantities, cost, or valuations between opening and closing inventory? ☐ **Yes** ☐ **No**
    If "Yes," attach explanation.

Form 1120-F (1997)   Page **4**

Schedule C Dividends and Special Deductions (See instructions.)

	(a) Dividends received	**(b)** %	**(c)** Special deductions: (a) × (b)
1 Dividends from less-than-20%-owned domestic corporations that are subject to the 70% deduction (other than debt-financed stock) . . .		70	
2 Dividends from 20%-or-more-owned domestic corporations that are subject to the 80% deduction (other than debt-financed stock) . . .		80	
3 Dividends on debt-financed stock of domestic and foreign corporations (section 246A)		see instructions	
4 Dividends on certain preferred stock of less-than-20%-owned public utilities		42	
5 Dividends on certain preferred stock of 20%-or-more-owned public utilities		48	
6 Dividends from less-than-20%-owned foreign corporations that are subject to the 70% deduction		70	
7 Dividends from 20%-or-more-owned foreign corporations that are subject to the 80% deduction		80	
8 Total. Add lines 1 through 7. See page 13 of instructions for limitation .			
9 Other dividends from foreign corporations not included on lines 3, 6, and 7			
10 Foreign dividend gross-up (section 78)			
11 IC-DISC and former DISC dividends not included on lines 1, 2, or 3 (section 246(d))			
12 Other dividends			
13 Deduction for dividends paid on certain preferred stock of a public utility			
14 Total dividends. Add lines 1 through 12. Enter here and on line 4, page 3			
15 Total deductions. Add lines 8 and 13. Enter here and on line 30b, page 3			

Schedule E Compensation of Officers (Complete Schedule E only if total receipts (line 1a plus lines 4 through 10 of Section II) are $500,000 or more. See **Line 12. Compensation of officers** on page 9 of instructions.)

(a) Name of officer	**(b)** Social security number	**(c)** Percent of time devoted to business	Percent of corporation stock owned		**(f)** Amount of compensation
			(d) Common	**(e)** Preferred	
1		%	%	%	
		%	%	%	
		%	%	%	
		%	%	%	
		%	%	%	
		%	%	%	
		%	%	%	

2 Total compensation of officers . . . .

3 Compensation of officers claimed on Schedule A and elsewhere on this return . . . . .

4 Subtract line 3 from line 2. Enter the result here and on line 12, page 3 . . . .

Schedule J Tax Computation (See instructions beginning on page 13.)

1 Check if the corporation is a member of a controlled group (see sections 1561 and 1563) ▶ ☐
Important: Members of a controlled group, see page 13 of instructions.

2a If the box on line 1 is checked, enter the corporation's share of the $50,000, $25,000, and $9,925,000 taxable income bracket amounts (in that order):

(1) $ _____ **(2)** $ _____ **(3)** $ _____

b Enter the corporation's share of:

(1) Additional 5% tax (not more than $11,750) $ _____

(2) Additional 3% tax (not more than $100,000) $ _____

3 Income tax. Check this box if the corporation is a qualified personal service corporation (see page 14 of the instructions) ▶ ☐ . . . . | **3** |

4a Foreign tax credit (attach Form 1118) . . . . | **4a** |

b Check: ☐ Nonconventional source fuel credit
☐ QEV credit (attach Form 8834) | **4b** |

c General business credit. Enter here and check which **forms** are attached:
☐ 3800 ☐ 3468 ☐ 5884 ☐ 6478 ☐ 6765
☐ 8586 ☐ 8830 ☐ 8826 ☐ 8835 ☐ 8844
☐ 8845 ☐ 8846 ☐ 8820 ☐ 8847 ☐ 8861 | **4c** |

d Credit for prior year minimum tax (attach Form 8827) . . . . . | **4d** |

5 **Total credits.** Add lines 4a through 4d . . . . | **5** |

6 Subtract line 5 from line 3 . . . . | **6** |

7 Recapture taxes. Check if from: ☐ Form 4255 ☐ Form 8611 . . . . . | **7** |

8 Alternative minimum tax (attach Form 4626) . . . . | **8** |

9 **Total tax under section 882(a).** Add lines 6 through 8. Enter here and on line 2, page 1 . . | **9** |

Form 1120-F (1997)   Page **5**

SECTION III.—Branch Profits Tax and Tax on Excess Interest (See page 15 of the instructions.)

Part I—Branch Profits Tax

1	Enter the amount from Section II, line 29	**1**	
2	Enter total adjustments made to get effectively connected earnings and profits. (Attach a schedule showing the nature and amount of adjustments.) (See instructions.)	**2**	
3	Effectively connected earnings and profits. Combine line 1 and line 2. Enter the result here . .	**3**	
4a	Enter U.S. net equity at the end of the current tax year. (Attach schedule.)	**4a**	
b	Enter U.S. net equity at the end of the prior tax year. (Attach schedule.)	**4b**	
c	Increase in U.S. net equity. If line 4a is greater than or equal to line 4b, subtract line 4b from line 4a. Enter the result here and skip to line 4e	**4c**	
d	Decrease in U.S. net equity. If line 4b is greater than line 4a, subtract line 4a from line 4b. Enter the result here	**4d**	
e	Non-previously taxed accumulated effectively connected earnings and profits. Enter excess, if any, of effectively connected earnings and profits for preceding tax years beginning after 1986 over any dividend equivalent amounts for those tax years	**4e**	
5	Dividend equivalent amount. Subtract line 4c from line 3. Enter the result here. If zero or less, enter -0-. If no amount is entered on line 4c, add the lesser of line 4d or line 4e to line 3 and enter the total here	**5**	
6	**Branch profits tax.** Multiply line 5 by 30% (or lower treaty rate if the corporation is a qualified resident or otherwise qualifies for treaty benefits). Enter here and include on line 3, page 1. (See instructions.) **Also complete Items W and X below**	**6**	

Part II—Tax on Excess Interest

7a	Enter the interest from Section II, line 18	**7a**	
b	Enter the interest apportioned to the effectively connected income of the foreign corporation that is capitalized or otherwise nondeductible.	**7b**	
c	Add lines 7a and 7b	**7c**	
8	Enter the branch interest (including capitalized and other nondeductible interest). (See instructions for definition.) If the interest paid by the foreign corporation's U.S. trade or business was increased because 80% or more of the foreign corporation's assets are U.S. assets, check this box . . . . ▶ ☐	**8**	
9a	Excess interest. Subtract line 8 from line 7c. If zero or less, enter -0-.	**9a**	
b	If the foreign corporation is a bank, enter the excess interest treated as interest on deposits. Otherwise, enter -0-. (See page 16 of instructions.).	**9b**	
c	Subtract line 9b from line 9a	**9c**	
10	**Tax on excess interest.** Multiply line 9c by 30% or lower treaty rate (if the corporation is a qualified resident or otherwise qualifies for treaty benefits). (See page 16 of instructions.) Enter here and include on line 3, page 1. **Also complete Items W and X below**	**10**	

Additional Information Required *(continued from page 2)*

	Yes	No			Yes	No
V Is the corporation claiming a reduction in, or exemption from, the branch profits tax due to:			**W** Is the corporation taking a position on this return that a U.S. tax treaty overrules or modifies an Internal Revenue law of the United States thereby causing a reduction of tax?		
(1) A complete termination of all U.S. trades or businesses?			If "Yes," complete and attach Form 8833.		
(2) The tax-free liquidation or reorganization of a foreign corporation?.			**Note:** *Failure to disclose a treaty-based return position may result in a $10,000 penalty (see section 6712).*		
(3) The tax-free incorporation of a U.S. trade or business?			**X** If the corporation is claiming it is a qualified resident of its country of residence for purposes of computing its branch profits tax and excess interest tax, check the basis for that claim:		

If **(1)** applies or **(2)** applies and the transferee is domestic, attach Form 8848.

If **(3)** applies, attach the statement required by Regulations section 1.884-2T(d)(5).

Stock ownership and base erosion test . . . . ☐
Publicly traded test . . . . ☐
Active trade or business test . . . . ☐
Private letter ruling . . . . ☐

Form 1120-F (1997)   Page **6**

Additional schedules to be completed for Section II or Section III (See page 17 of instructions.)

Schedule L Balance Sheets per Books

ASSETS	Beginning of tax year (a)	(b)	End of tax year (c)	(d)
1 Cash				
2a Trade notes and accounts receivable				
b Less allowance for bad debts	( )		( )	
3 Inventories				
4 U.S. government obligations				
5 Tax-exempt securities (see instructions)				
6 Other current assets (attach schedule)				
7 Loans to stockholders				
8 Mortgage and real estate loans				
9 Other investments (attach schedule)				
10a Buildings and other fixed depreciable assets				
b Less accumulated depreciation	( )		( )	
11a Depletable assets				
b Less accumulated depletion	( )		( )	
12 Land (net of any amortization)				
13a Intangible assets (amortizable only)				
b Less accumulated amortization	( )		( )	
14 Other assets (attach schedule)				
15 Total assets				
LIABILITIES AND STOCKHOLDERS' EQUITY				
16 Accounts payable				
17 Mtges., notes, bonds payable in less than 1 year				
18 Other current liabilities (attach schedule)				
19 Loans from stockholders				
20 Mtges., notes, bonds payable in 1 year or more				
21 Other liabilities (attach schedule)				
22 Capital stock: **a** Preferred stock				
b Common stock				
23 Additional paid-in capital				
24 Retained earnings—Appropriated (attach schedule)				
25 Retained earnings—Unappropriated				
26 Adjustments to shareholders' equity (attach schedule)				
27 Less cost of treasury stock		( )		( )
28 Total liabilities and stockholders' equity				

Note: *The corporation is not required to complete Schedules M-1 and M-2 below if the total assets on Schedule L, line 15, column (d) are less than $25,000.*

Schedule M-1 **Reconciliation of Income (Loss) per Books With Income per Return**

1 Net income (loss) per books		**7** Income recorded on books this year not included on this return (itemize):	
2 Federal income tax		**a** Tax-exempt interest . $ _____	
3 Excess of capital losses over capital gains			
4 Income subject to tax not recorded on books this year (itemize): _____		**8** Deductions on this return not charged against book income this year (itemize):	
		a Depreciation . . . $ _____	
5 Expenses recorded on books this year not deducted on this return (itemize):		**b** Contributions carryover $ _____	
a Depreciation . . . $ _____			
b Contributions carryover $ _____		**9** Add lines 7 and 8	
c Travel and entertainment $ _____		**10** Income (line 29, page 3)—line 6 less line 9	
6 Add lines 1 through 5			

Schedule M-2 **Analysis of Unappropriated Retained Earnings per Books (Schedule L, line 25)**

1 Balance at beginning of year		**5** Distributions: **a** Cash	
2 Net income (loss) per books		**b** Stock	
3 Other increases (itemize): _____		**c** Property	
		6 Other decreases (itemize): _____	
		7 Add lines 5a through 6	
4 Add lines 1, 2, and 3		**8** Balance at end of year (line 4 less line 7)	

✱

Form **1120S**

Department of the Treasury
Internal Revenue Service

U.S. Income Tax Return for an S Corporation

▶ **Do not file this form unless the corporation has timely filed
Form 2553 to elect to be an S corporation.**
▶ See separate instructions.

OMB No. 1545-0130

1997

For calendar year 1997, or tax year beginning _____ , 1997, and ending _____ , 19___

A Date of election as an S corporation	Use IRS label. Other-wise, please print or type.	Name	C Employer identification number
B Business code no. (see Specific Instructions)		Number, street, and room or suite no. (If a P.O. box, see page 9 of the instructions.)	D Date incorporated
		City or town, state, and ZIP code	E Total assets (see Specific Instructions) $

F Check applicable boxes: (1) ☐ Initial return   (2) ☐ Final return   (3) ☐ Change in address   (4) ☐ Amended return
G Enter number of shareholders in the corporation at end of the tax year . . . . ▶

Caution: *Include **only** trade or business income and expenses on lines 1a through 21. See the instructions for more information.*

Income

1a	Gross receipts or sales _____ b Less returns and allowances _____ c Bal ▶	**1c**	
2	Cost of goods sold (Schedule A, line 8)	**2**	
3	Gross profit. Subtract line 2 from line 1c	**3**	
4	Net gain (loss) from Form 4797, Part II, line 18 (attach Form 4797) . . .	**4**	
5	Other income (loss) (attach schedule)	**5**	
6	**Total income (loss).** Combine lines 3 through 5 . . . . ▶	**6**	

Deductions (see page 10 of the instructions for limitations)

7	Compensation of officers	**7**	
8	Salaries and wages (less employment credits)	**8**	
9	Repairs and maintenance.	**9**	
10	Bad debts	**10**	
11	Rents	**11**	
12	Taxes and licenses.	**12**	
13	Interest	**13**	
14a	Depreciation (if required, attach Form 4562) **14a**		
b	Depreciation claimed on Schedule A and elsewhere on return . . **14b**		
c	Subtract line 14b from line 14a	**14c**	
15	Depletion (**Do not deduct oil and gas depletion.**)	**15**	
16	Advertising	**16**	
17	Pension, profit-sharing, etc., plans	**17**	
18	Employee benefit programs	**18**	
19	Other deductions (attach schedule)	**19**	
20	**Total deductions.** Add the amounts shown in the far right column for lines 7 through 19 ▶	**20**	
21	Ordinary income (loss) from trade or business activities. Subtract line 20 from line 6	**21**	

Tax and Payments

22	**Tax: a** Excess net passive income tax (attach schedule). . . . **22a**		
b	Tax from Schedule D (Form 1120S) **22b**		
c	Add lines 22a and 22b (see pages 12 and 13 of the instructions for additional taxes) . . .	**22c**	
23	**Payments: a** 1997 estimated tax payments and amount applied from 1996 return **23a**		
b	Tax deposited with Form 7004 . . . . **23b**		
c	Credit for Federal tax paid on fuels (attach Form 4136) **23c**		
d	Add lines 23a through 23c	**23d**	
24	Estimated tax penalty. Check if Form 2220 is attached . . . . ▶☐	**24**	
25	**Tax due.** If the total of lines 22c and 24 is larger than line 23d, enter amount owed. See page 4 of the instructions for depository method of payment . . . . ▶	**25**	
26	**Overpayment.** If line 23d is larger than the total of lines 22c and 24, enter amount overpaid ▶	**26**	
27	Enter amount of line 26 you want: **Credited to 1998 estimated tax** ▶ _____	Refunded ▶ **27**	

Please Sign Here

Under penalties of perjury, I declare that I have examined this return, including accompanying schedules and statements, and to the best of my knowledge and belief, it is true, correct, and complete. Declaration of preparer (other than taxpayer) is based on all information of which preparer has any knowledge.

▶ _____   _____   ▶ _____
Signature of officer   Date   Title

Paid Preparer's Use Only

Preparer's signature ▶	Date	Check if self-employed ▶ ☐	Preparer's social security number
Firm's name (or yours if self-employed) and address ▶		EIN ▶	
		ZIP code ▶	

For Paperwork Reduction Act Notice, see the separate instructions.   Cat. No. 11510H   Form **1120S** (1997)

Schedule A   **Cost of Goods Sold** (see page 13 of the instructions)

1	Inventory at beginning of year	**1**	
2	Purchases	**2**	
3	Cost of labor	**3**	
4	Additional section 263A costs *(attach schedule)*	**4**	
5	Other costs *(attach schedule)*	**5**	
6	**Total.** Add lines 1 through 5	**6**	
7	Inventory at end of year	**7**	
8	**Cost of goods sold.** Subtract line 7 from line 6. Enter here and on page 1, line 2	**8**	

9a Check all methods used for valuing closing inventory:

    (i) ☐ Cost as described in Regulations section 1.471-3

    (ii) ☐ Lower of cost or market as described in Regulations section 1.471-4

    (iii) ☐ Other (specify method used and attach explanation) ▶ ....

  b Check if there was a writedown of "subnormal" goods as described in Regulations section 1.471-2(c) . . . . ▶ ☐

  c Check if the LIFO inventory method was adopted this tax year for any goods *(if checked, attach Form 970)*. . . . . ▶ ☐

  d If the LIFO inventory method was used for this tax year, enter percentage (or amounts) of closing
inventory computed under LIFO **9d**

  e Do the rules of section 263A (for property produced or acquired for resale) apply to the corporation?. . . . . ☐ Yes ☐ No

  f Was there any change in determining quantities, cost, or valuations between opening and closing inventory? . . ☐ Yes ☐ No
If "Yes," attach explanation.

Schedule B   **Other Information**

		Yes	No
1	Check method of accounting: **(a)** ☐ Cash **(b)** ☐ Accrual **(c)** ☐ Other (specify) ▶		
2	Refer to the list on page 23 of the instructions and state the corporation's principal: **(a)** Business activity ▶ .... **(b)** Product or service ▶		
3	Did the corporation at the end of the tax year own, directly or indirectly, 50% or more of the voting stock of a domestic corporation? (For rules of attribution, see section 267(c).) If "Yes," attach a schedule showing: **(a)** name, address, and employer identification number and **(b)** percentage owned.		
4	Was the corporation a member of a controlled group subject to the provisions of section 1561?		
5	At any time during calendar year 1997, did the corporation have an interest in or a signature or other authority over a financial account in a foreign country (such as a bank account, securities account, or other financial account)? (See page 14 of the instructions for exceptions and filing requirements for Form TD F 90-22.1.) . . . . If "Yes," enter the name of the foreign country ▶		
6	During the tax year, did the corporation receive a distribution from, or was it the grantor of, or transferor to, a foreign trust? If "Yes," the corporation may have to file Form 3520 or 926. See page 14 of the instructions		
7	Check this box if the corporation has filed or is required to file **Form 8264,** Application for Registration of a Tax Shelter . . . . ▶ ☐		
8	Check this box if the corporation issued publicly offered debt instruments with original issue discount . . ▶ ☐ If so, the corporation may have to file **Form 8281,** Information Return for Publicly Offered Original Issue Discount Instruments.		
9	If the corporation: **(a)** filed its election to be an S corporation after 1986, **(b)** was a C corporation before it elected to be an S corporation **or** the corporation acquired an asset with a basis determined by reference to its basis (or the basis of any other property) in the hands of a C corporation, and **(c)** has net unrealized built-in gain (defined in section 1374(d)(1)) in excess of the net recognized built-in gain from prior years, enter the net unrealized built-in gain reduced by net recognized built-in gain from prior years (see page 14 of the instructions) . . . . . ▶ $		
10	Check this box if the corporation had accumulated earnings and profits at the close of the tax year (see page 14 of the instructions) . . . . ▶ ☐		

Schedule K	**Shareholders' Shares of Income, Credits, Deductions, etc.**		
	(a) Pro rata share items		**(b)** Total amount

	(a) Pro rata share items		**(b)** Total amount	
Income (Loss)	**1** Ordinary income (loss) from trade or business activities (page 1, line 21)	**1**		
	2 Net income (loss) from rental real estate activities *(attach Form 8825)*	**2**		
	3a Gross income from other rental activities	**3a**		
	b Expenses from other rental activities *(attach schedule)*. .	**3b**		
	c Net income (loss) from other rental activities. Subtract line 3b from line 3a	**3c**		
	4 Portfolio income (loss):			
	a Interest income	**4a**		
	b Dividend income.	**4b**		
	c Royalty income	**4c**		
	d Net short-term capital gain (loss) *(attach Schedule D (Form 1120S))*	**4d**		
	e Net long-term capital gain (loss) *(attach Schedule D (Form 1120S))*:			
	(1) 28% rate gain (loss) ▶ ------------------------------ **(2)** Total for year ▶	**4e(2)**		
	f Other portfolio income (loss) *(attach schedule)*	**4f**		
	5 Net section 1231 gain (loss) (other than due to casualty or theft) *(attach Form 4797)*:			
	a 28% rate gain (loss) ▶ ------------------------------ **b** Total for year ▶	**5b**		
	6 Other income (loss) *(attach schedule)*	**6**		
Deductions	**7** Charitable contributions *(attach schedule)*	**7**		
	8 Section 179 expense deduction *(attach Form 4562)*.	**8**		
	9 Deductions related to portfolio income (loss) (itemize)	**9**		
	10 Other deductions *(attach schedule)*	**10**		
Investment Interest	**11a** Interest expense on investment debts	**11a**		
	b (1) Investment income included on lines 4a, 4b, 4c, and 4f above	**11b(1)**		
	(2) Investment expenses included on line 9 above	**11b(2)**		
Credits	**12a** Credit for alcohol used as a fuel *(attach Form 6478)*	**12a**		
	b Low-income housing credit:			
	(1) From partnerships to which section 42(j)(5) applies for property placed in service before 1990	**12b(1)**		
	(2) Other than on line 12b(1) for property placed in service before 1990.	**12b(2)**		
	(3) From partnerships to which section 42(j)(5) applies for property placed in service after 1989	**12b(3)**		
	(4) Other than on line 12b(3) for property placed in service after 1989	**12b(4)**		
	c Qualified rehabilitation expenditures related to rental real estate activities *(attach Form 3468)* .	**12c**		
	d Credits (other than credits shown on lines 12b and 12c) related to rental real estate activities	**12d**		
	e Credits related to other rental activities	**12e**		
	13 Other credits	**13**		
Adjustments and Tax Preference Items	**14a** Depreciation adjustment on property placed in service after 1986	**14a**		
	b Adjusted gain or loss	**14b**		
	c Depletion (other than oil and gas)	**14c**		
	d (1) Gross income from oil, gas, or geothermal properties	**14d(1)**		
	(2) Deductions allocable to oil, gas, or geothermal properties	**14d(2)**		
	e Other adjustments and tax preference items *(attach schedule)*	**14e**		
Foreign Taxes	**15a** Type of income ▶ --------------------------------------			
	b Name of foreign country or U.S. possession --------------------------			
	c Total gross income from sources outside the United States *(attach schedule)*	**15c**		
	d Total applicable deductions and losses *(attach schedule)*	**15d**		
	e Total foreign taxes (check one): ▶ ☐ Paid ☐ Accrued	**15e**		
	f Reduction in taxes available for credit *(attach schedule)*	**15f**		
	g Other foreign tax information *(attach schedule)*	**15g**		
Other	**16** Section 59(e)(2) expenditures: **a** Type ▶ --------------------- **b** Amount ▶	**16b**		
	17 Tax-exempt interest income	**17**		
	18 Other tax-exempt income	**18**		
	19 Nondeductible expenses	**19**		
	20 Total property distributions (including cash) other than dividends reported on line 22 below	**20**		
	21 Other items and amounts required to be reported separately to shareholders *(attach schedule)*			
	22 Total dividend distributions paid from accumulated earnings and profits	**22**		
	23 **Income (loss).** (Required only if Schedule M-1 must be completed.) Combine lines 1 through 6 in column (b). From the result, subtract the sum of lines 7 through 11a, 15e, and 16b	**23**		

Form 1120S (1997)   Page **4**

Schedule L — Balance Sheets per Books

		Beginning of tax year		End of tax year	
Assets		(a)	(b)	(c)	(d)
1	Cash				
2a	Trade notes and accounts receivable				
b	Less allowance for bad debts				
3	Inventories				
4	U.S. Government obligations				
5	Tax-exempt securities				
6	Other current assets (attach schedule)				
7	Loans to shareholders				
8	Mortgage and real estate loans				
9	Other investments (attach schedule)				
10a	Buildings and other depreciable assets				
b	Less accumulated depreciation				
11a	Depletable assets				
b	Less accumulated depletion				
12	Land (net of any amortization)				
13a	Intangible assets (amortizable only)				
b	Less accumulated amortization				
14	Other assets (attach schedule)				
15	Total assets				
Liabilities and Shareholders' Equity					
16	Accounts payable				
17	Mortgages, notes, bonds payable in less than 1 year				
18	Other current liabilities (attach schedule)				
19	Loans from shareholders				
20	Mortgages, notes, bonds payable in 1 year or more				
21	Other liabilities (attach schedule)				
22	Capital stock				
23	Additional paid-in capital				
24	Retained earnings				
25	Adjustments to shareholders' equity (attach schedule)				
26	Less cost of treasury stock		( )		( )
27	Total liabilities and shareholders' equity				

Schedule M-1 — Reconciliation of Income (Loss) per Books With Income (Loss) per Return (You are not required to complete this schedule if the total assets on line 15, column (d), of Schedule L are less than $25,000.)

1 Net income (loss) per books

2 Income included on Schedule K, lines 1 through 6, not recorded on books this year (itemize): _____

_____

3 Expenses recorded on books this year not included on Schedule K, lines 1 through 11a, 15e, and 16b (itemize):

a Depreciation $ _____

b Travel and entertainment $ _____

_____

4 Add lines 1 through 3

5 Income recorded on books this year not included on Schedule K, lines 1 through 6 (itemize):

a Tax-exempt interest $ _____

_____

6 Deductions included on Schedule K, lines 1 through 11a, 15e, and 16b, not charged against book income this year (itemize):

a Depreciation $ _____

_____

7 Add lines 5 and 6

8 Income (loss) (Schedule K, line 23). Line 4 less line 7

Schedule M-2 — Analysis of Accumulated Adjustments Account, Other Adjustments Account, and Shareholders' Undistributed Taxable Income Previously Taxed (see page 21 of the instructions)

		(a) Accumulated adjustments account	(b) Other adjustments account	(c) Shareholders' undistributed taxable income previously taxed
1	Balance at beginning of tax year			
2	Ordinary income from page 1, line 21			
3	Other additions			
4	Loss from page 1, line 21	( )		
5	Other reductions	( )	( )	
6	Combine lines 1 through 5			
7	Distributions other than dividend distributions			
8	Balance at end of tax year. Subtract line 7 from line 6			

SCHEDULE K-1
(Form 1120S)

Department of the Treasury
Internal Revenue Service

Shareholder's Share of Income, Credits, Deductions, etc.

▶ **See separate instructions.**

For calendar year 1997 or tax year
beginning   , 1997, and ending   , 19

OMB No. 1545-0130

1997

Shareholder's identifying number ▶

Shareholder's name, address, and ZIP code

Corporation's identifying number ▶

Corporation's name, address, and ZIP code

A Shareholder's percentage of stock ownership for tax year (see instructions for Schedule K-1) . . . . ▶ _____ %

B Internal Revenue Service Center where corporation filed its return ▶ ....

C Tax shelter registration number (see instructions for Schedule K-1) . . . . . ▶ ....

D Check applicable boxes: **(1)** ☐ Final K-1   **(2)** ☐ Amended K-1

	(a) Pro rata share items		(b) Amount	(c) Form 1040 filers enter the amount in column (b) on:
Income (Loss)	**1** Ordinary income (loss) from trade or business activities . . .	**1**		See pages 4 and 5 of the Shareholder's Instructions for Schedule K-1 (Form 1120S).
	2 Net income (loss) from rental real estate activities	**2**		
	3 Net income (loss) from other rental activities	**3**		
	4 Portfolio income (loss):			
	a Interest	**4a**		Sch. B, Part I, line 1
	b Dividends	**4b**		Sch. B, Part II, line 5
	c Royalties	**4c**		Sch. E, Part I, line 4
	d Net short-term capital gain (loss)	**4d**		Sch. D, line 5, col. (f)
	e Net long-term capital gain (loss):			
	(1) 28% rate gain (loss)	**e(1)**		Sch. D, line 12, col. (g)
	(2) Total for year	**e(2)**		Sch. D, line 12, col. (f)
	f Other portfolio income (loss) *(attach schedule)*	**4f**		(Enter on applicable line of your return.)
	5 Net section 1231 gain (loss) (other than due to casualty or theft):			See Shareholder's Instructions for Schedule K-1 (Form 1120S).
	a 28% rate gain (loss)	**5a**		
	b Total for year	**5b**		
	6 Other income (loss) *(attach schedule)*	**6**		(Enter on applicable line of your return.)
Deductions	**7** Charitable contributions *(attach schedule)*	**7**		Sch. A, line 15 or 16
	8 Section 179 expense deduction	**8**		See page 6 of the Shareholder's Instructions for Schedule K-1 (Form 1120S).
	9 Deductions related to portfolio income (loss) *(attach schedule)* .	**9**		
	10 Other deductions *(attach schedule)*	**10**		
Investment Interest	**11a** Interest expense on investment debts	**11a**		Form 4952, line 1
	b (1) Investment income included on lines 4a, 4b, 4c, and 4f above	**b(1)**		See Shareholder's Instructions for Schedule K-1 (Form 1120S).
	(2) Investment expenses included on line 9 above	**b(2)**		
Credits	**12a** Credit for alcohol used as fuel	**12a**		Form 6478, line 10
	b Low-income housing credit:			
	(1) From section 42(j)(5) partnerships for property placed in service before 1990	**b(1)**		Form 8586, line 5
	(2) Other than on line 12b(1) for property placed in service before 1990	**b(2)**		
	(3) From section 42(j)(5) partnerships for property placed in service after 1989	**b(3)**		
	(4) Other than on line 12b(3) for property placed in service after 1989	**b(4)**		
	c Qualified rehabilitation expenditures related to rental real estate activities	**12c**		See pages 6 and 7 of the Shareholder's Instructions for Schedule K-1 (Form 1120S).
	d Credits (other than credits shown on lines 12b and 12c) related to rental real estate activities	**12d**		
	e Credits related to other rental activities	**12e**		
	13 Other credits	**13**		

For Paperwork Reduction Act Notice, see the Instructions for Form 1120S.   Cat. No. 11520D   **Schedule K-1 (Form 1120S) 1997**

	(a) Pro rata share items		(b) Amount	(c) Form 1040 filers enter the amount in column (b) on:
Adjustments and Tax Preference Items	**14a** Depreciation adjustment on property placed in service after 1986	14a		See page 7 of the Shareholder's Instructions for Schedule K-1 (Form 1120S) and Instructions for Form 6251
	b Adjusted gain or loss	14b		
	c Depletion (other than oil and gas)	14c		
	d (1) Gross income from oil, gas, or geothermal properties . . .	d(1)		
	(2) Deductions allocable to oil, gas, or geothermal properties .	d(2)		
	e Other adjustments and tax preference items *(attach schedule)* .	14e		
Foreign Taxes	**15a** Type of income ▶			Form 1116, Check boxes
	b Name of foreign country or U.S. possession ▶			
	c Total gross income from sources outside the United States *(attach schedule)*	15c		Form 1116, Part I
	d Total applicable deductions and losses *(attach schedule)* . . .	15d		
	e Total foreign taxes (check one): ▶ ☐ Paid ☐ Accrued .	15e		Form 1116, Part II
	f Reduction in taxes available for credit *(attach schedule)* . . .	15f		Form 1116, Part III
	g Other foreign tax information *(attach schedule)*	15g		See Instructions for Form 1116
Other	**16** Section 59(e)(2) expenditures: **a** Type ▶			See Shareholder's Instructions for Schedule K-1 (Form 1120S).
	b Amount	16b		
	17 Tax-exempt interest income	17		Form 1040, line 8b
	18 Other tax-exempt income	18		
	19 Nondeductible expenses	19		See page 7 of the Shareholder's Instructions for Schedule K-1 (Form 1120S).
	20 Property distributions (including cash) other than dividend distributions reported to you on Form 1099-DIV	20		
	21 Amount of loan repayments for "Loans From Shareholders" . .	21		
	22 Recapture of low-income housing credit:			
	a From section 42(j)(5) partnerships	22a		Form 8611, line 8
	b Other than on line 22a	22b		

Supplemental Information

23 Supplemental information required to be reported separately to each shareholder *(attach additional schedules if more space is needed)*:

Form **2106**
Department of the Treasury
Internal Revenue Service (99)

Employee Business Expenses

▶ See separate instructions.

▶ Attach to Form 1040.

OMB No. 1545-0139

19 97

Attachment
Sequence No. **54**

Your name	Social security number	Occupation in which you incurred expenses

---

Part I Employee Business Expenses and Reimbursements

STEP 1 Enter Your Expenses

		Column A Other Than Meals and Entertainment		Column B Meals and Entertainment	
1	Vehicle expense from line 22 or line 29	**1**			
2	Parking fees, tolls, and transportation, including train, bus, etc., that **did not** involve overnight travel or commuting to and from work . .	**2**			
3	Travel expense while away from home overnight, including lodging, airplane, car rental, etc. **Do not** include meals and entertainment	**3**			
4	Business expenses not included on lines 1 through 3. **Do not** include meals and entertainment	**4**			
5	Meals and entertainment expenses (see instructions)	**5**			
6	**Total expenses.** In Column A, add lines 1 through 4 and enter the result. In Column B, enter the amount from line 5	**6**			

Note: *If you were not reimbursed for any expenses in Step 1, skip line 7 and enter the amount from line 6 on line 8.*

STEP 2 Enter Reimbursements Received From Your Employer for Expenses Listed in STEP 1

7	Enter reimbursements received from your employer that were **not** reported to you in box 1 of Form W-2. Include any reimbursements reported under code "L" in box 13 of your Form W-2 (see instructions)	**7**			

STEP 3 Figure Expenses To Deduct on Schedule A (Form 1040)

8	Subtract line 7 from line 6	**8**			
	Note: *If **both columns** of line 8 are zero, **stop here.** If Column A is less than zero, report the amount as income on Form 1040, line 7.*				
9	In Column A, enter the amount from line 8. In Column B, multiply the amount on line 8 by 50% (.50). If either column is zero or less, enter -0- in that column	**9**			
10	Add the amounts on line 9 of both columns and enter the total here. **Also, enter the total on Schedule A (Form 1040), line 20.** (Fee-basis state or local government officials, qualified performing artists, and individuals with disabilities: See the instructions for special rules on where to enter the total.) . . . . ▶	**10**			

For Paperwork Reduction Act Notice, see instructions.   Cat. No. 11700N   Form **2106** (1997)

Form 2106 (1997)   Page **2**

Part II	**Vehicle Expenses** (See instructions to find out which sections to complete.)			

Section A—General Information | | **(a)** Vehicle 1 | **(b)** Vehicle 2

			(a) Vehicle 1	(b) Vehicle 2
11	Enter the date vehicle was placed in service	**11**	/ /	/ /
12	Total miles vehicle was driven during 1997	**12**	miles	miles
13	Business miles included on line 12	**13**	miles	miles
14	Percent of business use. Divide line 13 by line 12	**14**	%	%
15	Average daily round trip commuting distance	**15**	miles	miles
16	Commuting miles included on line 12	**16**	miles	miles
17	Other miles. Add lines 13 and 16 and subtract the total from line 12 . . .	**17**	miles	miles

18 Do you (or your spouse) have another vehicle available for personal purposes? . . . . ☐ Yes ☐ No

19 If your employer provided you with a vehicle, is personal use during off-duty hours permitted? ☐ Yes ☐ No ☐ Not applicable

20 Do you have evidence to support your deduction? . . . . ☐ Yes ☐ No

21 If "Yes," is the evidence written? . . . . ☐ Yes ☐ No

Section B—Standard Mileage Rate (Use this section only if you own the vehicle.)

22	Multiply line 13 by 31½¢ (.315). Enter the result here and on line 1. (Rural mail carriers, see instructions.)	**22**		

Section C—Actual Expenses | | **(a)** Vehicle 1 | | **(b)** Vehicle 2 | |

			(a) Vehicle 1		(b) Vehicle 2	
23	Gasoline, oil, repairs, vehicle insurance, etc.	**23**				
24a	Vehicle rentals	**24a**				
b	Inclusion amount (see instructions)	**24b**				
c	Subtract line 24b from line 24a	**24c**				
25	Value of employer-provided vehicle (applies only if 100% of annual lease value was included on Form W-2—see instructions)	**25**				
26	Add lines 23, 24c, and 25 . .	**26**				
27	Multiply line 26 by the percentage on line 14 . . .	**27**				
28	Depreciation. Enter amount from line 38 below	**28**				
29	Add lines 27 and 28. Enter total here and on line 1.	**29**				

Section D—Depreciation of Vehicles (Use this section only if you own the vehicle.)

			(a) Vehicle 1		(b) Vehicle 2	
30	Enter cost or other basis (see instructions)	**30**				
31	Enter amount of section 179 deduction (see instructions) .	**31**				
32	Multiply line 30 by line 14 (see instructions if you elected the section 179 deduction) . . .	**32**				
33	Enter depreciation method and percentage (see instructions) .	**33**				
34	Multiply line 32 by the percentage on line 33 (see instructions) . .	**34**				
35	Add lines 31 and 34	**35**				
36	Enter the limit from the table in the line 36 instructions . . .	**36**				
37	Multiply line 36 by the percentage on line 14 . . .	**37**				
38	Enter the **smaller** of line 35 or line 37. Also, enter this amount on line 28 above	**38**				

Form **2119**	**Sale of Your Home**	OMB No. 1545-0072

Form **2119**

Department of the Treasury
Internal Revenue Service (99)

Sale of Your Home

▶ Attach to Form 1040 for year of sale.

▶ See separate instructions. ▶ Please print or type.

OMB No. 1545-0072

1997

Attachment
Sequence No. **20**

Your first name and initial. If a joint return, also give spouse's name and initial.	Last name	**Your social security number**

If you are filing this form by itself and not with your tax return, see instructions on page 3.	Present address (no., street, and apt. no., rural route, or P.O. box no. if mail is not delivered to street address)	**Spouse's social security number**
	City, town or post office, state, and ZIP code	

Part I   Gain on Sale

1 Date your former main home was sold. If sold after May 6, 1997, see page 3 . . . . . ▶ | **1** | / | / |

mo.   day   yr.

2 Have you bought or built a new main home? . . . . ☐ Yes ☐ No

3 If any part of either main home was ever rented out or used for business, check here ▶ ☐ and see page 3.

4 Selling price of home. Do not include personal property items you sold with your home . . | **4** |

5 Expense of sale (see page 4) . . . . | **5** |

6 Subtract line 5 from line 4 . . . . | **6** |

7 Adjusted basis of home sold (see page 4) . . . . . . | **7** |

8 **Gain on sale.** Subtract line 7 from line 6. **If zero or less, stop** and attach this form to your return | **8** |

• For sales **before May 7, 1997,** you must go to Part II or Part III, whichever applies. **But** if line 2 is "No," go to line 9.

• For sales **after May 6, 1997,** you must go to Part IV on the back to figure any exclusion. **But** if you qualify and elect to use the rules for sales before May 7, 1997, go to Part II or Part III, whichever applies.

9 If you haven't replaced your home, do you plan to do so within the **replacement period** (see page 1)? . ☐ Yes ☐ No

• If line 9 is "Yes," stop here, attach this form to your return, and see **Additional filing requirements** on page 1.

• If line 9 is "No," you **must** go to Part II or Part III, whichever applies.

Part II   One-Time Exclusion of Gain for People Age 55 or Older—By completing this part, you are electing to take the one-time exclusion (see page 2). If you are not electing to take the exclusion, go to Part III now.

10 Who was age 55 or older on the date of sale? . . . . ☐ You ☐ Your spouse ☐ Both of you

11 Did the person who was 55 or older own and use the property as his or her main home for a total of at least 3 years of the 5-year period before the sale? See page 2 for exceptions. If "No," go to Part III now . . . ☐ Yes ☐ No

12 At the time of sale, who owned the home? . . . . ☐ You ☐ Your spouse ☐ Both of you

13 Social security number of spouse at the time of sale if you had a different spouse from the one above. If you were not married at the time of sale, enter "None" . . . . ▶ | **13** |

14 **Exclusion.** Enter the **smaller** of line 8 or $125,000 ($62,500 if married filing separate return). Then, go to line 15 . . . . | **14** |

Part III   Adjusted Sales Price, Taxable Gain, and Adjusted Basis of New Home

15 If line 14 is blank, enter the amount from line 8. Otherwise, subtract line 14 from line 8 . . | **15** |

• If line 15 is zero, stop and attach this form to your return.

• If line 15 is more than zero and line 2 is "Yes," go to line 16 now.

• If you are reporting this sale on the installment method, stop and see page 4.

• All others, stop and **enter the amount from line 15 on Schedule D, line 4 or line 11.**

16 Fixing-up expenses (see page 4 for time limits) . . . . | **16** |

17 If line 14 is blank, enter amount from line 16. Otherwise, add lines 14 and 16 . . . . . | **17** |

18 **Adjusted sales price.** Subtract line 17 from line 6 . . . . | **18** |

19a Date you moved into new home ▶ | / | / | **b** Cost of new home (see page 5) . | **19b** |

20 Subtract line 19b from line 18. If zero or less, enter -0- . . . . | **20** |

21 **Taxable gain.** Enter the **smaller** of line 15 or line 20 . . . . | **21** |

• If line 21 is zero, go to line 22 and attach this form to your return.

• If you are reporting this sale on the installment method, see the line 15 instructions and go to line 22.

• All others, **enter the amount from line 21 on Schedule D, line 4 or line 11,** and go to line 22.

22 Postponed gain. Subtract line 21 from line 15 . . . . | **22** |

23 **Adjusted basis of new home.** Subtract line 22 from line 19b . . . . | **23** |

For Paperwork Reduction Act Notice, see page 6 of instructions.   Cat. No. 11710J   Form **2119** (1997)

Form 2119 (1997)   Page **2**

Part IV	**Exclusion and Taxable Gain for Sales After May 6, 1997**		

24   Did you (or your spouse if filing a joint return) own and use the property as your main home for a total of at least 2 years of the 5-year period before the sale? See page 3 for exceptions   ☐ Yes   ☐ No

25   Maximum exclusion. See page 5 for the amount to enter. **25**

26   Enter the amount from line 8 . . . .   **26**

27   **Exclusion.** Enter the **smaller** of line 25 or line 26. If line 26 is the smaller amount, stop and attach this form to your return. Otherwise, go to line 28 . . . .   **27**

28   **Taxable gain.** Subtract line 27 from line 26 . . . .   **28**

     ● If you are reporting this sale on the installment method, see the line 15 instructions.

     ● All others, enter the amount from line 28 on **Schedule D, line 4 or line 11.**

Sign here only if you are filing this form by itself and not with your tax return.	Under penalties of perjury, I declare that I have examined this form, including attachments, and to the best of my knowledge and belief, it is true, correct, and complete.

    Your signature   Date   Spouse's signature   Date

▶ _____   _____ ▶ _____   _____

    If a joint return, both must sign.

Form **2120**
(Rev. January 1997)

Department of the Treasury
Internal Revenue Service

Multiple Support Declaration

▶ Attach to Form 1040 or Form 1040A of person claiming the dependent.

OMB No. 1545-0071

Attachment
Sequence No. **50**

Name of person claiming the dependent

Social security number

During the calendar year 19 ...., I paid over 10% of the support of

----
Name of person

I could have claimed this person as a dependent except that I did not pay over half of his or her support. I understand that the person named above is being claimed as a dependent on the income tax return of

----
Name

Address

I agree not to claim this person as a dependent on my Federal income tax return for any tax year that began in this calendar year.

Your signature

Your social security number

Address (number, street, apt. no.)

Date

City, state, and ZIP code

Instructions

Paperwork Reduction Act Notice

We ask for the information on this form to carry out the Internal Revenue laws of the United States. You are required to give us the information. We need it to ensure that you are complying with these laws and to allow us to figure and collect the right amount of tax.

You are not required to provide the information requested on a form that is subject to the Paperwork Reduction Act unless the form displays a valid OMB control number. Books or records relating to a form or its instructions must be retained as long as their contents may become material in the administration of any Internal Revenue law. Generally, tax returns and return information are confidential, as required by Internal Revenue Code section 6103.

The time needed to complete and file this form will vary depending on individual circumstances. The estimated average time is: **Recordkeeping,** 7 minutes; **Learning about the law or the form,** 3 minutes; **Preparing the form,** 7 minutes; and **Copying, assembling, and sending the form to the IRS,** 10 minutes.

If you have comments concerning the accuracy of these time estimates or suggestions for making this form simpler, we would be happy to hear from you. See the instructions for the tax return with which this form is filed.

Purpose of Form

When two or more persons together pay over half of another person's support, only one of them can claim the person they support as a dependent for tax purposes.

Each person who does not claim the dependent completes and signs a Form 2120 (or similar statement containing the same information required by the form) and gives the form (or statement) to the person claiming the dependent. That person attaches all the forms or statements to his or her tax return. See **How To File** on this page.

Who Can Claim the Dependent

Generally, to claim someone as a dependent, you must pay over half of that person's living expenses (support). However, even if you did not meet this support test, you might still be able to claim him or her as a dependent if **all five** of the following apply:

1. You and one or more other eligible person(s) (see below) together paid over half of another person's support.

2. You paid over 10% of the support.

3. No one alone paid over half of the person's support.

4. The other four dependency tests are met. See **Dependents** in the Form 1040 or Form 1040A instructions.

5. Each other eligible person who paid over 10% of the support agrees not to claim the dependent by completing a **Form 2120** or similar statement.

An **eligible person** is someone who could have claimed another person as a dependent except that he or she did not pay over half of that person's support.

How To File

The person claiming the dependent must attach all the completed and signed Form(s) 2120 or similar statement(s) to his or her tax return. The name and social security number of the person claiming the dependent must be at the top of each Form 2120 or similar statement.

Additional Information

See **Pub. 501,** Exemptions, Standard Deduction, and Filing Information, for details.

Cat. No. 11712F

Form **2120** (Rev. 1-97)

Form **2210**	**Underpayment of** **Estimated Tax by Individuals, Estates, and Trusts**	OMB No. 1545-0140
Department of the Treasury Internal Revenue Service	▶ See separate instructions. ▶ **Attach to Form 1040, 1040A, 1040NR, 1040NR-EZ, or 1041.**	19**97** Attachment Sequence No. **06**

Name(s) shown on tax return	Identifying number

Note: *In most cases, you **do not** need to file Form 2210. The IRS will figure any penalty you owe and send you a bill. File Form 2210 **only** if one or more boxes in Part I apply to you. If you do not need to file Form 2210, you still may use it to figure your penalty. Enter the amount from line 20 or line 32 on the penalty line of your return, but **do not** attach Form 2210.*

Part I	**Reasons for Filing**—If 1a, b, or c below applies to you, you may be able to lower or eliminate your penalty. But you MUST check the boxes that apply and file Form 2210 with your tax return. If 1d below applies to you, check that box and file Form 2210 with your tax return.

1   Check whichever boxes apply (if none apply, see the **Note** above):

a ☐ You request a **waiver.** In certain circumstances, the IRS will waive all or part of the penalty. See **Waiver of Penalty** on page 1 of the instructions.

b ☐ You use the **annualized income installment method.** If your income varied during the year, this method may reduce the amount of one or more required installments. See page 4 of the instructions.

c ☐ You had Federal income tax withheld from wages and, for estimated tax purposes, you treat the withheld tax as paid on the dates it was actually withheld, instead of in equal amounts on the payment due dates. See the instructions for line 22 on page 3.

d ☐ Your required annual payment (line 13 below) is based on your 1996 tax and you filed or are filing a joint return for either 1996 or 1997 but not for both years.

Part II	**Required Annual Payment**

2	Enter your 1997 tax after credits (see page 2 of the instructions). **Caution:** *Also see page 2 for a special rule if claiming the research credit*	**2**
3	Other taxes (see page 2 of the instructions)	**3**
4	Add lines 2 and 3	**4**
5	Earned income credit **5**	
6	Credit for Federal tax paid on fuels **6**	
7	Add lines 5 and 6	**7**
8	Current year tax. Subtract line 7 from line 4	**8**
9	Multiply line 8 by 90% (.90) **9**	
10	Withholding taxes. **Do not** include any estimated tax payments on this line (see page 2 of the instructions)	**10**
11	Subtract line 10 from line 8. If less than $500, stop here; **do not** complete or file this form. You do not owe the penalty	**11**
12	Enter the tax shown on your 1996 tax return (110% of that amount if the adjusted gross income shown on that return is more than $150,000, or if married filing separately for 1997, more than $75,000). **Caution:** *See page 2 of the instructions*	**12**
13	**Required annual payment.** Enter the **smaller** of line 9 or line 12	**13**
	Note: *If line 10 is equal to or more than line 13, stop here; you do not owe the penalty. Do not file Form 2210 unless you checked box 1d above.*	

Part III	**Short Method (Caution:** *See page 2 of the instructions to find out if you can use the short method. If you checked box **1b** or **c** in Part I, skip this part and go to Part IV.***)**

14	Enter the amount, if any, from line 10 above **14**	
15	Enter the total amount, if any, of estimated tax payments you made **15**	
16	Add lines 14 and 15	**16**
17	**Total underpayment for year.** Subtract line 16 from line 13. If zero or less, stop here; you do not owe the penalty. Do not file Form 2210 unless you checked box 1d above	**17**
18	Multiply line 17 by .05986	**18**
19	● If the amount on line 17 was paid **on or after** 4/15/98, enter -0-.	
	● If the amount on line 17 was paid **before** 4/15/98, make the following computation to find the amount to enter on line 19. Amount on $\times$ Number of days paid $\times$ .00025	
	line 17 before 4/15/98	**19**
20	**PENALTY.** Subtract line 19 from line 18. Enter the result here and on Form 1040, line 65; Form 1040A, line 34; Form 1040NR, line 65; Form 1040NR-EZ, line 26; or Form 1041, line 27 . . ▶	**20**

For Paperwork Reduction Act Notice, see page 1 of separate instructions.	Cat. No. 11744P	Form **2210** (1997)

Form 2210 (1997)   Page **2**

Part IV **Regular Method** (See page 2 of the instructions if you are filing Form 1040NR or 1040NR-EZ.)

		Payment Due Dates			
Section A—Figure Your Underpayment		**(a)** 4/15/97	**(b)** 6/15/97	**(c)** 9/15/97	**(d)** 1/15/98
21	**Required installments.** If box 1b applies, enter the amounts from Schedule AI, line 26. Otherwise, enter ¼ of line 13, Form 2210, in each column **21**				
22	Estimated tax paid and tax withheld (see page 3 of the instructions). For column (a) only, also enter the amount from line 22 on line 26. If line 22 is equal to or more than line 21 for all payment periods, stop here; you do not owe the penalty. Do not file Form 2210 unless you checked a box in Part I **22**				
	Complete lines 23 through 29 of one column before going to the next column.				
23	Enter amount, if any, from line 29 of previous column **23**				
24	Add lines 22 and 23 . . . . **24**				
25	Add amounts on lines 27 and 28 of the previous column **25**				
26	Subtract line 25 from line 24. If zero or less, enter -0-. For column (a) only, enter the amount from line 22 . **26**				
27	If the amount on line 26 is zero, subtract line 24 from line 25. Otherwise, enter -0- **27**				
28	**Underpayment.** If line 21 is equal to or more than line 26, subtract line 26 from line 21. Then go to line 23 of next column. Otherwise, go to line 29 . . ▶ **28**				
29	Overpayment. If line 26 is more than line 21, subtract line 21 from line 26. Then go to line 23 of next column **29**				

Section B—Figure the Penalty (Complete lines 30 and 31 of one column before going to the next column.)

		4/15/97	6/15/97	9/15/97	1/15/98
30	Number of days FROM the date shown above line 30 TO the date the amount on line 28 was paid **or** 4/15/98, whichever is earlier **30**	*Days:*	*Days:*	*Days:*	*Days:*
31	Underpayment on line 28 (see page 3 of the instructions) $\times$ $\dfrac{\text{Number of days on line 30}}{365}$ $\times$ .09 ▶ **31**	$	$	$	$
32	**PENALTY.** Add the amounts in each column of line 31. Enter the total here and on Form 1040, line 65; Form 1040A, line 34; Form 1040NR, line 65; Form 1040NR-EZ, line 26; or Form 1041, line 27 . . . . ▶ **32** $					

Form 2210 (1997)   Page **3**

Schedule AI—Annualized Income Installment Method (see pages 4 and 5 of the instructions)

Estates and trusts, **do not** use the period ending dates shown to the right. Instead, use the following: 2/28/97, 4/30/97, 7/31/97, and 11/30/97.

		(a) 1/1/97–3/31/97	(b) 1/1/97–5/31/97	(c) 1/1/97–8/31/97	(d) 1/1/97–12/31/97

Part I   Annualized Income Installments   Caution: *Complete lines 20–26 of one column **before** going to the next column.*

#	Description	(a)	(b)	(c)	(d)
1	Enter your adjusted gross income for each period (see instructions). (Estates and trusts, enter your taxable income without your exemption for each period.)				
2	Annualization amounts. (Estates and trusts, see instructions.)	4	2.4	1.5	1
3	Annualized income. Multiply line 1 by line 2				
4	Enter your itemized deductions for the period shown in each column. If you do not itemize, enter -0- and skip to line 7. (Estates and trusts, enter -0-, skip to line 9, and enter the amount from line 3 on line 9.)				
5	Annualization amounts	4	2.4	1.5	1
6	Multiply line 4 by line 5 (see instructions if line 3 is more than $60,600)				
7	In each column, enter the full amount of your standard deduction from Form 1040, line 35, or Form 1040A, line 19 (Form 1040NR or 1040NR-EZ filers, enter -0-. **Exception:** Indian students and business apprentices, enter standard deduction from Form 1040NR, line 34 or Form 1040NR-EZ, line 10.)				
8	Enter the **larger** of line 6 or line 7				
9	Subtract line 8 from line 3				
10	In each column, multiply $2,650 by the total number of exemptions claimed (see instructions if line 3 is more than $90,900). (Estates and trusts and Form 1040NR or 1040NR-EZ filers, enter the exemption amount shown on your tax return.)				
11	Subtract line 10 from line 9				
12	Figure your tax on the amount on line 11 (see instructions)				
13	Form 1040 filers only, enter your self-employment tax from line 35 below				
14	Enter other taxes for each payment period (see instructions)				
15	Total tax. Add lines 12, 13, and 14				
16	For each period, enter the same type of credits as allowed on Form 2210, lines 2, 5, and 6 (see instructions)				
17	Subtract line 16 from line 15. If zero or less, enter -0-				
18	Applicable percentage	22.5%	45%	67.5%	90%
19	Multiply line 17 by line 18				
20	Add the amounts in all preceding columns of line 26				
21	Subtract line 20 from line 19. If zero or less, enter -0-				
22	Enter ¼ of line 13 on page 1 of Form 2210 in each column				
23	Enter amount from line 25 of the preceding column of this schedule				
24	Add lines 22 and 23 and enter the total				
25	Subtract line 21 from line 24. If zero or less, enter -0-				
26	Enter the **smaller** of line 21 or line 24 here and on Form 2210, line 21 ▶				

Part II   Annualized Self-Employment Tax

#	Description	(a)	(b)	(c)	(d)
27a	Net earnings from self-employment for the period (see instructions)				
b	Annualization amounts	4	2.4	1.5	1
c	Multiply line 27a by line 27b				
28	Social security tax limit	$65,400	$65,400	$65,400	$65,400
29	Enter actual wages subject to social security tax or the 6.2% portion of the 7.65% railroad retirement (tier 1) tax				
30	Annualization amounts	4	2.4	1.5	1
31	Multiply line 29 by line 30				
32	Subtract line 31 from line 28. If zero or less, enter -0-				
33	Multiply the smaller of line 27c or line 32 by .124				
34	Multiply line 27c by .029				
35	Add lines 33 and 34. Enter the result here and on line 13 above ▶				

Form **2220**	**Underpayment of Estimated Tax by Corporations**	OMB No. 1545-0142
Department of the Treasury Internal Revenue Service	▶ See separate instructions. ▶ Attach to the corporation's tax return.	19**97**

Name	Employer identification number

Note: *In most cases, the corporation **does not** need to file Form 2220. (See Part I below for exceptions.) The IRS will figure any penalty owed and bill the corporation. If the corporation does not need to file Form 2220, it may still use it to figure the penalty. Enter the amount from line 32 on the estimated tax penalty line of the corporation's income tax return, but do not attach Form 2220.*

Part I **Reasons for Filing**—Check the boxes below that apply to the corporation. If any box is checked or the **Note** below applies, the corporation must file Form 2220 with the corporation's tax return, even if it does not owe the penalty. If the box on line 1 or line 2 applies, the corporation may be able to lower or eliminate the penalty. See page 1 of the instructions.

1 ☐ The corporation is using the annualized income installment method.

2 ☐ The corporation is using the adjusted seasonal installment method.

3 ☐ The corporation is a "large corporation" figuring its first required installment based on the prior year's tax.

Note: *The corporation must also file Form 2220 if it is claiming a waiver of the penalty. See **Waiver of penalty** on page 2 of the instructions.*

Part II **Figuring the Underpayment**

4	Total tax. **(Caution:** *See page 2 of the instructions, which includes a special rule if claiming the research credit).*	**4**	
5a	Personal holding company tax included on line 4 (Schedule PH (Form 1120), line 26).	**5a**	
b	Interest due under the look-back method of section 460(b)(2) for completed long-term contracts included on line 4	**5b**	
c	Credit for Federal tax paid on fuels (see page 2 of the instructions)	**5c**	
d	**Total.** Add lines 5a through 5c	**5d**	
6	Subtract line 5d from line 4. If the result is less than $500, **do not** complete or file this form. The corporation does not owe the penalty	**6**	
7	Enter the tax shown on the corporation's 1996 income tax return. (**CAUTION:** *See page 2 of the instructions before completing this line.*)	**7**	
8	Enter the **smaller** of line 6 or line 7. If the corporation must skip line 7, enter the amount from line 6 on line 8 .	**8**	

		(a)	(b)	(c)	(d)
9	**Installment due dates.** Enter in columns (a) through (d) the 15th day of the 4th (5th month of a private foundation's tax year that begins after August 5, 1997), 6th, 9th, and 12th months of the corporation's tax year . . . . . . ▶				
10	**Required installments.** If the box on line 1 and/or line 2 above is checked, enter the amounts from Schedule A, line 41. If the box on line 3 (but not 1 or 2) is checked, see page 2 of the instructions for the amounts to enter. If none of these boxes are checked, enter 25% of line 8 above in each column				
11	Estimated tax paid or credited for each period (see page 2 of the instructions). For column (a) only, enter the amount from line 11 on line 15				
	Complete lines 12 through 18 of one column before going to the next column.				
12	Enter amount, if any, from line 18 of the preceding column				
13	Add lines 11 and 12				
14	Add amounts on lines 16 and 17 of the preceding column.				
15	Subtract line 14 from line 13. If zero or less, enter -0- .				
16	If the amount on line 15 is zero, subtract line 13 from line 14. Otherwise, enter -0-				
17	**Underpayment.** If line 15 is less than or equal to line 10, subtract line 15 from line 10. Then go to line 12 of the next column (see page 2 of the instructions). Otherwise, go to line 18. . . .				
18	**Overpayment.** If line 10 is less than line 15, subtract line 10 from line 15. Then go to line 12 of the next column. . .				

Complete Part III on page 2 to figure the penalty. If there are no entries on line 17, no penalty is owed.

For Paperwork Reduction Act Notice, see page 4 of the instructions.   Cat. No. 11746L   Form **2220** (1997)

Part III Figuring the Penalty

		(a)	(b)	(c)	(d)
19 Enter the date of payment or the 15th day of the 3rd month after the close of the tax year, whichever is earlier (see page 3 of the instructions). *(Form 990-PF and Form 990-T filers:* Use 5th month instead of 3rd month.)	**19**				
20 Number of days from due date of installment on line 9 to the date shown on line 19	**20**				
21 Number of days on line 20 after 4/15/97 and before 4/1/98 .	**21**				
22 Underpayment on line 17 × $\frac{\text{Number of days on line 21}}{365}$ × 9% . .	**22**	$	$	$	$
23 Number of days on line 20 after 3/31/98 and before 7/1/98 .	**23**				
24 Underpayment on line 17 × $\frac{\text{Number of days on line 23}}{365}$ × *% . .	**24**	$	$	$	$
25 Number of days on line 20 after 6/30/98 and before 10/1/98.	**25**				
26 Underpayment on line 17 × $\frac{\text{Number of days on line 25}}{365}$ × *% . .	**26**	$	$	$	$
27 Number of days on line 20 after 9/30/98 and before 1/1/99 .	**27**				
28 Underpayment on line 17 × $\frac{\text{Number of days on line 27}}{365}$ × *% . .	**28**	$	$	$	$
29 Number of days on line 20 after 12/31/98 and before 2/16/99	**29**				
30 Underpayment on line 17 × $\frac{\text{Number of days on line 29}}{365}$ × *% . .	**30**	$	$	$	$
31 Add lines 22, 24, 26, 28, and 30	**31**	$	$	$	$

32 Penalty. Add columns (a) through (d), of line 31. Enter the total here and on Form 1120, line 33; Form 1120-A, line 29; or the comparable line for other income tax returns . . . . **32** $

*For underpayments paid after March 31, 1998, see **Lines 24, 26, 28,** and **30** on page 3 of the instructions.

| Schedule A | Annualized Income Installment Method and/or the Adjusted Seasonal Installment Method Under Section 6655(e) (see pages 3 and 4 of the instructions) |

Form 1120S filers: *For lines 2, 14, 15, and 16, below, "taxable income" refers to excess net passive income or the amount on which tax is imposed under section 1374(a) (or the corresponding provisions of prior law), whichever applies.*

Part I—Annualized Income Installment Method

			(a)	(b)	(c)	(d)
			First ____ months	First ____ months	First ____ months	First ____ months
1	Annualization periods (see page 3 of the instructions).	1				
2	Enter taxable income for each annualization period.	2				
3	Annualization amounts (see page 3 of the instructions).	3				
4	Annualized taxable income. Multiply line 2 by line 3.	4				
5	Figure the tax on the amount in each column on line 4 using the instructions for Form 1120, Schedule J, line 3 (or the comparable line of the tax return).	5				
6	Enter other taxes for each payment period (see page 3 of the instructions).	6				
7	Total tax. Add lines 5 and 6.	7				
8	For each period, enter the same type of credits as allowed on Form 2220, lines 4 and 5c (see page 3 of the instructions).	8				
9	Total tax after credits. Subtract line 8 from line 7. If zero or less, enter -0-.	9				
10	Applicable percentage.	10	25%	50%	75%	100%
11	Multiply line 9 by line 10.	11				
12	Add the amounts in all preceding columns of line 41 (see page 3 of the instructions).	12				
13	**Annualized income installments.** Subtract line 12 from line 11. If zero or less, enter -0-.	13				

Part II—Adjusted Seasonal Installment Method (Caution: *Use this method only if the base period percentage for any 6 consecutive months is at least 70%. See pages 3 and 4 of the instructions for more information.*)

			(a)	(b)	(c)	(d)
			First 3 months	First 5 months	First 8 months	First 11 months
14	Enter taxable income for the following periods:					
a	Tax year beginning in 1994	14a				
b	Tax year beginning in 1995	14b				
c	Tax year beginning in 1996	14c				
15	Enter taxable income for each period for the tax year beginning in 1997.	15				
			First 4 months	First 6 months	First 9 months	Entire year
16	Enter taxable income for the following periods:					
a	Tax year beginning in 1994	16a				
b	Tax year beginning in 1995	16b				
c	Tax year beginning in 1996	16c				
17	Divide the amount in each column on line 14a by the amount in column (d) on line 16a.	17				
18	Divide the amount in each column on line 14b by the amount in column (d) on line 16b.	18				
19	Divide the amount in each column on line 14c by the amount in column (d) on line 16c.	19				

Form 2220 (1997)   Page **4**

		(a)	(b)	(c)	(d)
		First 4 months	First 6 months	First 9 months	Entire year
20	Add lines 17 through 19.	**20**				
21	Divide line 20 by 3.	**21**				
22	Divide line 15 by line 21.	**22**				
23	Figure the tax on the amount on line 22 using the instructions for Form 1120, Schedule J, line 3 (or the comparable line of the return).	**23**				
24	Divide the amount in columns (a) through (c) on line 16a by the amount in column (d) on line 16a.	**24**				
25	Divide the amount in columns (a) through (c) on line 16b by the amount in column (d) on line 16b.	**25**				
26	Divide the amount in columns (a) through (c) on line 16c by the amount in column (d) on line 16c.	**26**				
27	Add lines 24 through 26.	**27**				
28	Divide line 27 by 3.	**28**				
29	Multiply the amount in columns (a) through (c) of line 23 by columns (a) through (c) of line 28. In column (d), enter the amount from line 23, column (d).	**29**				
30	Enter other taxes for each payment period (see page 4 of the instructions).	**30**				
31	Total tax. Add lines 29 and 30.	**31**				
32	For each period, enter the same type of credits as allowed on Form 2220, lines 4 and 5c (see page 4 of the instructions).	**32**				
33	Total tax after credits. Subtract line 32 from line 31. If zero or less, enter -0-.	**33**				
34	Add the amounts in all preceding columns of line 41 (see page 4 of the instructions).	**34**				
35	**Adjusted seasonal installments.** Subtract line 34 from line 33. If zero or less, enter -0-.	**35**				

Part III—Required Installments

		1st installment	2nd installment	3rd installment	4th installment
36	If only one of the above parts is completed, enter the amount in each column from line 13 or line 35. If both parts are completed, enter the **smaller** of the amounts in each column from line 13 or line 35.	**36**				
37	Enter 25% of line 8 on page 1 of Form 2220 in each column. (**Note:** *"Large corporations" see the instructions for line 10, on page 2, for the amounts to enter.*)	**37**				
38	Enter the amount from line 40 of the preceding column.	**38**				
39	Add lines 37 and 38.	**39**				
40	If line 39 is more than line 36, subtract line 36 from line 39. Otherwise, enter -0-.	**40**				
41	**Required installments.** Enter the **smaller** of line 36 or line 39 here and on page 1 of Form 2220, line 10.	**41**				

Form **2441**

Department of the Treasury
Internal Revenue Service   (99)

Child and Dependent Care Expenses

▶ Attach to Form 1040.

▶ See separate instructions.

OMB No. 1545-0068

19**97**

Attachment
Sequence No. **21**

Name(s) shown on Form 1040	Your social security number

Before you begin, you need to understand the following terms. See **Definitions** on page 1 of the instructions.

- **Dependent Care Benefits**
- **Qualifying Person(s)**
- **Qualified Expenses**
- **Earned Income**

Part I **Persons or Organizations Who Provided the Care**—You **must** complete this part.
(If you need more space, use the bottom of page 2.)

1	(a) Care provider's name	(b) Address (number, street, apt. no., city, state, and ZIP code)	(c) Identifying number (SSN or EIN)	(d) Amount paid (see instructions)

Did you receive
dependent care benefits?

— **NO** ————▶ Complete only Part II below.

— **YES** ————▶ Complete Part III on the back next.

Caution: *If the care was provided in your home, you may owe employment taxes. See the instructions for Form 1040, line 52.*

Part II **Credit for Child and Dependent Care Expenses**

2 Information about your **qualifying person(s).** If you have more than two qualifying persons, see the instructions.

(a) Qualifying person's name		(b) Qualifying person's social security number	(c) **Qualified expenses** you incurred and paid in 1997 for the person listed in column (a)
First	Last		

3	Add the amounts in column (c) of line 2. DO NOT enter more than $2,400 for one qualifying person or $4,800 for two or more persons. If you completed Part III, enter the amount from line 24	**3**	
4	Enter YOUR **earned income**	**4**	
5	If married filing a joint return, enter YOUR SPOUSE'S earned income (if student or disabled, see the instructions); **all others,** enter the amount from line 4	**5**	
6	Enter the **smallest** of line 3, 4, or 5	**6**	

7 Enter the amount from Form 1040, line 33 . . . . . | **7** |

8 Enter on line 8 the decimal amount shown below that applies to the amount on line 7

If line 7 is—		Decimal amount is	If line 7 is—		Decimal amount is
Over	But not over		Over	But not over	
$0—10,000		.30	$20,000—22,000		.24
10,000—12,000		.29	22,000—24,000		.23
12,000—14,000		.28	24,000—26,000		.22
14,000—16,000		.27	26,000—28,000		.21
16,000—18,000		.26	28,000—No limit		.20
18,000—20,000		.25			

8 X .

9 Multiply **line 6** by the decimal amount on line 8. Enter the result. Then, see the instructions for the amount of credit to enter on Form 1040, line 40 . . . .   **9**

For Paperwork Reduction Act Notice, see page 3 of the instructions.   Cat. No. 11862M   Form **2441** (1997)

Part III Dependent Care Benefits

10 Enter the total amount of **dependent care benefits** you received for 1997. This amount should be shown in box 10 of your W-2 form(s). DO NOT include amounts that were reported to you as wages in box 1 of Form(s) W-2 . . . . | **10** |

11 Enter the amount forfeited, if any. See the instructions . . . . | **11** |

12 Subtract line 11 from line 10 . . . . | **12** |

13 Enter the total amount of **qualified expenses** incurred in 1997 for the care of the **qualifying person(s)** . . . | **13** |

14 Enter the **smaller** of line 12 or 13 . . . . | **14** |

15 Enter YOUR **earned income** . . . . | **15** |

16 If married filing a joint return, enter YOUR SPOUSE'S earned income (if student or disabled, see the line 5 instructions); if married filing a separate return, see the instructions for the amount to enter; **all others,** enter the amount from line 15 . . . . | **16** |

17 Enter the **smallest** of line 14, 15, or 16 . . . . | **17** |

18 **Excluded benefits.** Enter here the **smaller** of the following:

   • The amount from line 17, or
   • $5,000 ($2,500 if married filing a separate return **and** you were required to enter your spouse's earned income on line 16). . . . . | **18** |

19 **Taxable benefits.** Subtract line 18 from line 12. Also, include this amount on Form 1040, line 7. On the dotted line next to line 7, write "DCB" . . . . | **19** |

To claim the child and dependent care
credit, complete lines 20–24 below.

20 Enter $2,400 ($4,800 if two or more qualifying persons) . . . . | **20** |

21 Enter the amount from line 18 . . . . | **21** |

22 Subtract line 21 from line 20. If zero or less, **STOP.** You cannot take the credit. **Exception.** If you paid 1996 expenses in 1997, see the line 9 instructions . . . . . . | **22** |

23 Complete line 2 on the front of this form. DO NOT include in column (c) any excluded benefits shown on line 18 above. Then, add the amounts in column (c) and enter the total here . . . . | **23** |

24 Enter the **smaller** of line 22 or 23. Also, enter this amount on line 3 on the front of this form and complete lines 4–9 . . . . | **24** |

Form **2688**

Application for Additional Extension of Time To File
U.S. Individual Income Tax Return
► See instructions on back.
► You MUST complete all items that apply to you.

OMB No. 1545-0066

1997

Department of the Treasury
Internal Revenue Service

Please type or print.	Your first name and initial	Last name	Your social security number
File by the due date for filing your return.	If a joint return, spouse's first name and initial	Last name	Spouse's social security number

Home address (number and street)

City, town or post office, state, and ZIP code

Please fill in the Return Label at the bottom of this page.

1 I request an extension of time until .... , 19........... , to file Form 1040EZ, Form 1040A, Form 1040, Form 1040NR-EZ, or Form 1040NR for the calendar year 1997, or other tax year ending .... , 19.... .

2 Explain why you need an extension. You must give an adequate explanation ► ....
....
....
....
....

3 Have you filed Form 4868 to request an automatic extension of time to file for this tax year? . . . . ☐ **Yes** ☐ **No**
If you checked "No," we will grant your extension only for undue hardship. Fully explain the hardship in item 2. Attach any information you have that helps explain the hardship.

If you expect to have to file a gift or generation-skipping transfer (GST) tax return, complete line 4.

4 If you or your spouse plan to file a gift or GST tax return (Form 709 or 709-A) for 1997, generally ⎱ **Yourself** . . ► ☐
due by April 15, 1998, see the instructions and check here . . . . ⎰ **Spouse** . . ► ☐

Signature and Verification

Under penalties of perjury, I declare that I have examined this form, including accompanying schedules and statements, and to the best of my knowledge and belief, it is true, correct, and complete; and, if prepared by someone other than the taxpayer, that I am authorized to prepare this form.

Signature of taxpayer ► _____ Date ► _____

Signature of spouse ► _____ Date ► _____
(If filing jointly, BOTH must sign even if only one had income.)

Signature of preparer
other than taxpayer ► _____ Date ► _____

Please fill in the **Return Label** below with your name, address, and social security number. The IRS will complete the **Notice to Applicant** and return it to you. If you want it sent to another address or to an agent acting for you, enter the other address and add the agent's name.

(Do not detach)

Notice to Applicant

To Be Completed by the IRS

☐ We **HAVE** approved your application.
☐ We **HAVE NOT** approved your application.
However, we have granted a 10-day grace period to .... This grace period is considered a valid extension of time for elections otherwise required to be made on a timely return.
☐ We **HAVE NOT** approved your application. After considering the information you provided in item 2 above, we cannot grant your request for an extension of time to file. We are not granting a 10-day grace period.
☐ We cannot consider your application because it was filed after the due date of your return.
☐ Other ....

Director	Date

Return Label (Please type or print) (Agents: Always include taxpayer's name.)

Taxpayer's name (and agent's name, if applicable). If a joint return, also give spouse's name.	Taxpayer's social security number
Number and street (include suite, room, or apt. no.) or P.O. box number	Spouse's social security number
City, town or post office, state, and ZIP code	

For Paperwork Reduction Act Notice, see back of form.   Cat. No. 11958F   Form **2688** (1997)

General Instructions

Purpose of Form

Use Form 2688 to ask for more time to file **Form 1040EZ, Form 1040A, Form 1040, Form 1040NR-EZ,** or **Form 1040NR.** Generally, use it only if you already asked for more time on **Form 4868** (the "automatic" extension form) and that time was not enough. We will make an exception **only** for undue hardship. The maximum extension of time allowed by law is 6 months.

To get the extra time you **MUST:**

● Complete and file Form 2688 on time, **AND**

● Have a good reason why the first 4 months were not enough. Explain the reason in item 2.

Generally, we will not give you more time to file just for the convenience of your tax return preparer. But if the reasons for being late are beyond his or her control or, despite a good effort, you cannot get professional help in time to file, we will usually give you the extra time.

Caution: *If we give you more time to file and later find that the statements made on this form are false or misleading, the extension is null and void. You will owe the late filing penalty explained on this page.*

You cannot have the IRS figure your tax if you file after the regular due date of your return.

Note: *An extension of time to file your 1997 calendar year income tax return also extends the time to file a gift or generation-skipping transfer (GST) tax return* **(Form 709** or **709-A)** *for 1997.*

If you live abroad. U.S. citizens or resident aliens living abroad may qualify for special tax treatment if they meet the required foreign residence or presence tests. If you do not expect to meet either of those tests by the due date of your return, request an extension to a date after you expect to qualify. Ask for it on **Form 2350,** Application for Extension of Time To File U.S. Income Tax Return. See **Pub. 54,** Tax Guide for U.S. Citizens and Resident Aliens Abroad.

Total Time Allowed

Generally, we cannot extend the due date of your return for more than 6 months. This includes the 4 extra months allowed by Form 4868. There may be an exception if you live abroad. See the previous discussion.

When To File

If you filed Form 4868, file Form 2688 by the extended due date of your return. For most people, this is August 17, 1998. If you did not file Form 4868 first because of undue hardship, file Form 2688 by the due date of your return. The due date is April 15, 1998, for a calendar year return. Be sure to fully explain in item 2 why you are filing Form 2688 first. Also, file Form 2688 early so that if your request is not approved, you can still file your return on time.

Out of the country. If you are a U.S. citizen or resident out of the country on the regular due date of your return, you are allowed 2 extra months to file beyond that date. "Out of the country" means either **(a)** you live outside the United States and Puerto Rico **and** your main place of work is outside the United States and Puerto Rico, **or (b)** you are in military or naval service outside the United States and Puerto Rico. To get an additional extension, first file Form 4868 (for a further 2 months), and then, if necessary, file Form 2688 by the extended due date.

Where To File

Mail **Form 2688** to the Internal Revenue Service Center for the place where you live.

Filing Your Tax Return

You may file your tax return any time before the extension expires. But remember, Form 2688 does not extend the time to pay taxes. If you do not pay the amount due by the regular due date, you will owe interest. You may also be charged penalties.

Interest. You will owe interest on any tax not paid by the regular due date of your return. The interest runs until you pay the tax. Even if you had a good reason for not paying on time, you will still owe interest.

Late payment penalty. The penalty is usually ½ of 1% of any tax (other than estimated tax) not paid by the regular due date. It is charged for each month or part of a month the tax is unpaid. The maximum penalty is 25%. You might not owe this penalty if you have a good reason for not paying on time. Attach a statement to your return, not Form 2688, explaining the reason.

Late filing penalty. A penalty is usually charged if your return is filed after the due date (including extensions). It is usually 5% of the tax not paid by the regular due date for each month or part of a month your return is late. Generally, the maximum penalty is 25%. If your return is more than 60 days late, the minimum penalty is $100 or the balance of tax due on your return, whichever is smaller. You might not owe the penalty if you have a good reason for filing late. Attach a statement to your return, not Form 2688, explaining the reason.

How to claim credit for payment made with this form. Include any payment you sent with Form 2688 on the appropriate line of your tax return. If you file Form 1040EZ, the instructions for line 9 of that form tell you how to report the payment. If you file Form 1040A, see the instructions for line 29e. If you file Form 1040, enter the payment on line 57. If you file Form 1040NR-EZ, see the instructions for line 21; if you file Form 1040NR, enter the payment on line 54.

If you and your spouse each filed a separate Form 2688 but later file a joint return for 1997, enter the total paid with both Forms 2688 on the appropriate line of your joint return.

If you and your spouse jointly filed Form 2688 but later file separate returns for 1997, you may enter the total amount paid with Form 2688 on either of your separate returns. Or you and your spouse may divide the payment in any agreed amounts. Be sure each separate return has the social security numbers of both spouses.

Specific Instructions

Name, Address, and Social Security Number (SSN)

Enter your name, address, and SSN. If you plan to file a joint return, also enter your spouse's name and SSN. If a joint return, be sure the names and SSNs are listed in the same order.

Item 2

Clearly describe the reasons that will delay your return. We cannot accept incomplete reasons, such as "illness" or "practitioner too busy," without adequate explanations. If it is clear that you have no important reason but only want more time, we will deny your request. The 10-day grace period will also be denied.

Line 4

If you or your spouse plan to file Form 709 or 709-A for 1997, check whichever box applies. Also, write "Gift Tax" at the top of the form. But if your spouse files a separate Form 2688, do not check the box for your spouse.

Signature and Verification

This form must be signed. If you plan to file a joint return, both of you should sign. If there is a good reason why one of you cannot, the other spouse may sign for both. Attach a statement explaining why the other spouse cannot sign.

Others who can sign for you. Anyone with a power of attorney can sign. But the following can sign for you without a power of attorney:

● Attorneys, CPAs, and enrolled agents.

● A person in close personal or business relationship to you who is signing because you cannot. There must be a good reason why you cannot sign, such as illness or absence. Attach an explanation.

Return Label

You must complete the **Return Label** to receive the **Notice to Applicant.** We will use it to tell you if your application has been approved. Do not attach it to your return—keep it for your records.

If the post office does not deliver mail to your street address, enter the P.O. box number instead.

Note: *If you changed your mailing address after you filed your last return, you should use* **Form 8822,** *Change of Address, to notify the IRS of the change. Showing a new address on Form 2688 will not update your record. You can get Form 8822 by calling 1-800-829-3676.*

Paperwork Reduction Act Notice. We ask for the information on this form to carry out the Internal Revenue laws of the United States. You are required to give us the information. We need it to ensure that you are complying with these laws and to allow us to figure and collect the right amount of tax.

You are not required to provide the information requested on a form that is subject to the Paperwork Reduction Act unless the form displays a valid OMB control number. Books or records relating to a form or its instructions must be retained as long as their contents may become material in the administration of any Internal Revenue law. Generally, tax returns and return information are confidential, as required by Internal Revenue Code section 6103.

The time needed to complete and file this form will vary depending on individual circumstances. The estimated average time is: **Learning about the law or the form,** 8 min.; **Preparing the form,** 10 min.; and **Copying, assembling, and sending the form to the IRS,** 20 min.

If you have comments concerning the accuracy of these time estimates or suggestions for making this form simpler, we would be happy to hear from you. You can write to the Tax Forms Committee, Western Area Distribution Center, Rancho Cordova, CA 95743-0001. **DO NOT** send the form to this address. Instead, see **Where To File** on this page.

Form 3903

Department of the Treasury
Internal Revenue Service

Moving Expenses

► **Attach to Form 1040.**

OMB No. 1545-0062

1997

Attachment
Sequence No. **62**

Name(s) shown on Form 1040

Your social security number

Caution: *If you are a member of the armed forces, see the instructions before completing this form.*

1   Enter the number of miles from your **old home** to your **new workplace** . .   **1**   miles

2   Enter the number of miles from your **old home** to your **old workplace** . .   **2**   miles

3   Subtract line 2 from line 1. Enter the result but not less than zero . . . .   **3**   miles

Is line 3 at least 50 miles?

Yes.   Go to line 4. Also, see **Time Test** in the instructions.

No.   You **cannot** deduct your moving expenses. Do not complete the rest of this form.

4   Transportation and storage of household goods and personal effects (see instructions) . . .   **4**

5   Travel and lodging expenses of moving from your old home to your new home. **Do not** include meals (see instructions) **5**

6   Add lines 4 and 5 . . . .   **6**

7   Enter the total amount your employer paid for your move (including the value of services furnished in kind) that is **not** included in the wages box (box 1) of your W-2 form. This amount should be identified with code **P** in box 13 of your W-2 form **7**

Is line 6 more than line 7?

Yes.   Go to line 8.

No.   You **cannot** deduct your moving expenses. If line 6 is less than line 7, subtract line 6 from line 7 and include the result in income on Form 1040, line 7.

8   Subtract line 7 from line 6. Enter the result here and on Form 1040, line 25. This is your **moving expense deduction** **8**

General Instructions

Purpose of Form

Use Form 3903 to figure your moving expense deduction if you moved to a new principal place of work (workplace) within the United States or its possessions. If you qualify to deduct expenses for more than one move, use a separate Form 3903 for each move.

For more details, see **Pub. 521,** Moving Expenses.

Note: *Use Form 3903-F, Foreign Moving Expenses, instead of this form if you are a U.S. citizen or resident alien who moved to a new principal workplace outside the United States or its possessions.*

Another Form You May Have To File

If you sold your main home in 1997, you must file **Form 2119,** Sale of Your Home, to report the sale.

Who May Deduct Moving Expenses

If you moved to a different home because of a change in job location, you may be able to deduct your moving expenses. You may be able to take the deduction whether you are self-employed or an employee. But you must meet certain tests explained next.

Distance Test

Your new principal workplace must be at least 50 miles farther from your old home than your old workplace was. For example,

if your old workplace was 3 miles from your old home, your new workplace must be at least 53 miles from that home. If you did not have an old workplace, your new workplace must be at least 50 miles from your old home. The distance between the two points is the shortest of the more commonly traveled routes between them.

Time Test

If you are an employee, you must work full time in the general area of your new workplace for at least 39 weeks during the 12 months right after you move. If you are self-employed, you must work full time in the general area of your new workplace for at least 39 weeks during the first 12 months and a total of at least 78 weeks during the 24 months right after you move.

You may deduct your moving expenses even if you have not met the time test before your return is due. You may do this

For Paperwork Reduction Act Notice, see back of form.   Cat. No. 12490K   Form **3903** (1997)

if you expect to meet the 39-week test by the end of 1998 or the 78-week test by the end of 1999. If you deduct your moving expenses on your 1997 return but do not meet the time test, you will have to either:

● Amend your 1997 tax return by filing **Form 1040X,** Amended U.S. Individual Income Tax Return, or

● Report the amount of your 1997 moving expense deduction that reduced your 1997 income tax as income in the year you cannot meet the test. For more details, see **Time Test** in Pub. 521.

If you do not deduct your moving expenses on your 1997 return and you later meet the time test, you may take the deduction by filing an amended return for 1997. To do this, use Form 1040X.

Exceptions to the Time Test. The time test does not have to be met if any of the following apply:

● Your job ends because of disability.

● You are transferred for your employer's benefit.

● You are laid off or discharged for a reason other than willful misconduct.

● You meet the requirements (explained later) for retirees or survivors living outside the United States.

● You are filing this form for a decedent.

Members of the Armed Forces

If you are in the armed forces, you do not have to meet the **distance and time tests** if the move is due to a permanent change of station. A permanent change of station includes a move in connection with and within 1 year of retirement or other termination of active duty.

How To Complete the Form

First, complete lines 4 through 6 using your actual expenses. **Do not** reduce your expenses by any reimbursements or allowances you received from the government in connection with the move. Also, do not include any expenses for moving services that were provided by the government. If you and your spouse and dependents are moved to or from different locations, treat the moves as a single move.

Next, enter on line 7 the total reimbursements and allowances you received from the government in connection with the expenses you claimed on lines 4 and 5. **Do not** include the value of moving services provided by the government. Then, complete line 8 if applicable.

Retirees or Survivors Living Outside the United States

If you are a retiree or survivor who moved to a home in the United States or its possessions and you meet the following requirements, you are treated as if you moved to a new workplace located in the United States. You are subject to the distance test. Use this form instead of Form 3903-F to figure your moving expense deduction.

Retirees

You may deduct moving expenses for a move to a new home in the United States when you actually retire if both your old principal workplace and your old home were outside the United States.

Survivors

You may deduct moving expenses for a move to a home in the United States if you are the spouse or dependent of a person whose principal workplace at the time of death was outside the United States. In addition, the expenses must be for a move **(1)** that begins within 6 months after the decedent's death, and **(2)** from a former home outside the United States that you lived in with the decedent at the time of death.

Reimbursements

If your employer paid for any part of your move, your employer must give you a statement showing a detailed breakdown of reimbursements or payments for moving expenses. Employers may use **Form 4782,** Employee Moving Expense Information, or their own form.

You may choose to deduct moving expenses in the year you are reimbursed by your employer, even though you paid the expenses in a different year. However, special rules apply. See **How To Report** in Pub. 521.

Specific Instructions

You may deduct the following expenses you incurred in moving your family and dependent household members. Do not deduct expenses for employees such as a maid, nanny, or nurse.

Line 4

Enter the actual cost to pack, crate, and move your household goods and personal effects. You may also include the cost to store and insure household goods and personal effects within any period of 30 days in a row after the items were moved from your old home and before they were delivered to your new home.

Line 5

Enter the costs of travel from your old home to your new home. These include transportation and lodging on the way. Include costs for the day you arrive. Although not all the members of your household have to travel together or at the same time, you may only include expenses for one trip per person.

If you use your own car(s), you may figure the expenses by using either:

● Actual out-of-pocket expenses for gas and oil, or

● Mileage at the rate of 10 cents a mile.

You may add parking fees and tolls to the amount claimed under either method. Keep records to verify your expenses.

Paperwork Reduction Act Notice. We ask for the information on this form to carry out the Internal Revenue laws of the United States. You are required to give us the information. We need it to ensure that you are complying with these laws and to allow us to figure and collect the right amount of tax.

You are not required to provide the information requested on a form that is subject to the Paperwork Reduction Act unless the form displays a valid OMB control number. Books or records relating to a form or its instructions must be retained as long as their contents may become material in the administration of any Internal Revenue law. Generally, tax returns and return information are confidential, as required by Internal Revenue Code section 6103.

The time needed to complete and file this form will vary depending on individual circumstances. The estimated average time is:

Recordkeeping . . . . . . 33 min.

Learning about the law or the form . . . . . . 7 min.

Preparing the form . . . . . 13 min.

Copying, assembling, and sending the form to the IRS . 20 min.

If you have comments concerning the accuracy of these time estimates or suggestions for making this form simpler, we would be happy to hear from you. See the Instructions for Form 1040.

Form **4562**	**Depreciation and Amortization**	OMB No. 1545-0172
Department of the Treasury Internal Revenue Service (99)	**(Including Information on Listed Property)** ▶ See separate instructions. ▶ Attach this form to your return.	**19 97** Attachment Sequence No. **67**

Name(s) shown on return	Business or activity to which this form relates	Identifying number

Part I   **Election To Expense Certain Tangible Property (Section 179)** (**Note:** *If you have any "listed property," complete Part V before you complete Part I.)*

1	Maximum dollar limitation. If an enterprise zone business, see page 2 of the instructions . .	**1**	$18,000
2	Total cost of section 179 property placed in service. See page 2 of the instructions	**2**	
3	Threshold cost of section 179 property before reduction in limitation	**3**	$200,000
4	Reduction in limitation. Subtract line 3 from line 2. If zero or less, enter -0-	**4**	
5	Dollar limitation for tax year. Subtract line 4 from line 1. If zero or less, enter -0-. If married filing separately, see page 2 of the instructions	**5**	

(a) Description of property	(b) Cost (business use only)	(c) Elected cost
6		

7	Listed property. Enter amount from line 27. . . . . **7**		
8	Total elected cost of section 179 property. Add amounts in column (c), lines 6 and 7 . . .	**8**	
9	Tentative deduction. Enter the smaller of line 5 or line 8	**9**	
10	Carryover of disallowed deduction from 1996. See page 3 of the instructions	**10**	
11	Business income limitation. Enter the smaller of business income (not less than zero) or line 5 (see instructions)	**11**	
12	Section 179 expense deduction. Add lines 9 and 10, but do not enter more than line 11 . .	**12**	
13	Carryover of disallowed deduction to 1998. Add lines 9 and 10, less line 12 ▶ **13**		

Note: *Do not use Part II or Part III below for listed property (automobiles, certain other vehicles, cellular telephones, certain computers, or property used for entertainment, recreation, or amusement). Instead, use Part V for listed property.*

Part II   **MACRS Depreciation For Assets Placed in Service ONLY During Your 1997 Tax Year (Do Not Include Listed Property.)**

Section A—General Asset Account Election

14   If you are making the election under section 168(i)(4) to group any assets placed in service during the tax year into one or more general asset accounts, check this box. See page 3 of the instructions . . . . ▶ ☐

Section B—General Depreciation System (GDS) (See page 3 of the instructions.)

(a) Classification of property	(b) Month and year placed in service	(c) Basis for depreciation (business/investment use only—see instructions)	(d) Recovery period	(e) Convention	(f) Method	(g) Depreciation deduction
15a 3-year property						
b 5-year property						
c 7-year property						
d 10-year property						
e 15-year property						
f 20-year property						
g 25-year property			25 yrs.		S/L	
h Residential rental property			27.5 yrs.	MM	S/L	
			27.5 yrs.	MM	S/L	
i Nonresidential real property			39 yrs.	MM	S/L	
				MM	S/L	

Section C—Alternative Depreciation System (ADS) (See page 6 of the instructions.)

16a Class life					S/L	
b 12-year			12 yrs.		S/L	
c 40-year			40 yrs.	MM	S/L	

Part III   **Other Depreciation (Do Not Include Listed Property.)** (See page 6 of the instructions.)

17	GDS and ADS deductions for assets placed in service in tax years beginning before 1997	**17**	
18	Property subject to section 168(f)(1) election	**18**	
19	ACRS and other depreciation	**19**	

Part IV   **Summary** (See page 7 of the instructions.)

20	Listed property. Enter amount from line 26.	**20**	
21	**Total.** Add deductions on line 12, lines 15 and 16 in column (g), and lines 17 through 20. Enter here and on the appropriate lines of your return. Partnerships and S corporations—see instructions . .	**21**	
22	For assets shown above and placed in service during the current year, enter the portion of the basis attributable to section 263A costs **22**		

For Paperwork Reduction Act Notice, see the separate instructions.   Cat. No. 12906N   Form **4562** (1997)

Form 4562 (1997)   Page **2**

Part V Listed Property—Automobiles, Certain Other Vehicles, Cellular Telephones, Certain Computers, and Property Used for Entertainment, Recreation, or Amusement

> **Note:** *For any vehicle for which you are using the standard mileage rate or deducting lease expense, complete **only** 23a, 23b, columns (a) through (c) of Section A, all of Section B, and Section C if applicable.*

Section A—Depreciation and Other Information (Caution: *See page 8 of the instructions for limits for passenger automobiles.*)

23a Do you have evidence to support the business/investment use claimed? ☐ **Yes** ☐ **No** **23b** If "Yes," is the evidence written? ☐ **Yes** ☐ **No**

(a) Type of property (list vehicles first)	(b) Date placed in service	(c) Business/ investment use percentage	(d) Cost or other basis	(e) Basis for depreciation (business/investment use only)	(f) Recovery period	(g) Method/ Convention	(h) Depreciation deduction	(i) Elected section 179 cost
24 Property used more than 50% in a qualified business use (See page 7 of the instructions.):								
		%						
		%						
		%						
25 Property used 50% or less in a qualified business use (See page 7 of the instructions.):								
		%				S/L –		
		%				S/L –		
		%				S/L –		

26 Add amounts in column (h). Enter the total here and on line 20, page 1 . . . . . **26**

27 Add amounts in column (i). Enter the total here and on line 7, page 1 . . . . **27**

Section B—Information on Use of Vehicles

Complete this section for vehicles used by a sole proprietor, partner, or other "more than 5% owner," or related person.

If you provided vehicles to your employees, first answer the questions in Section C to see if you meet an exception to completing this section for those vehicles.

	(a) Vehicle 1		(b) Vehicle 2		(c) Vehicle 3		(d) Vehicle 4		(e) Vehicle 5		(f) Vehicle 6	
28 Total business/investment miles driven during the year (DO NOT include commuting miles)												
29 Total commuting miles driven during the year												
30 Total other personal (noncommuting) miles driven												
31 Total miles driven during the year. Add lines 28 through 30.												
	Yes	No	Yes	No	Yes	No	Yes	No	Yes	No	Yes	No
32 Was the vehicle available for personal use during off-duty hours?												
33 Was the vehicle used primarily by a more than 5% owner or related person?												
34 Is another vehicle available for personal use?												

Section C—Questions for Employers Who Provide Vehicles for Use by Their Employees

*Answer these questions to determine if you meet an exception to completing Section B for vehicles used by employees who **are not** more than 5% owners or related persons.*

	Yes	No
35 Do you maintain a written policy statement that prohibits all personal use of vehicles, including commuting, by your employees?		
36 Do you maintain a written policy statement that prohibits personal use of vehicles, except commuting, by your employees? See page 9 of the instructions for vehicles used by corporate officers, directors, or 1% or more owners		
37 Do you treat all use of vehicles by employees as personal use?		
38 Do you provide more than five vehicles to your employees, obtain information from your employees about the use of the vehicles, and retain the information received?		
39 Do you meet the requirements concerning qualified automobile demonstration use? See page 9 of the instructions . .		

> **Note:** *If your answer to 35, 36, 37, 38, or 39 is "Yes," you need not complete Section B for the covered vehicles.*

Part VI Amortization

(a) Description of costs	(b) Date amortization begins	(c) Amortizable amount	(d) Code section	(e) Amortization period or percentage	(f) Amortization for this year
40 Amortization of costs that begins during your 1997 tax year:					

41 Amortization of costs that began before 1997 . . . . **41**

42 **Total.** Enter here and on "Other Deductions" or "Other Expenses" line of your return . . . **42**

✪

Form **4626** Department of the Treasury Internal Revenue Service	**Alternative Minimum Tax—Corporations** ▶ See separate instructions. ▶ Attach to the corporation's tax return.	OMB No. 1545-0175 19**97**

Name | | Employer identification number

1	Taxable income or (loss) before net operating loss deduction	**1**
2	**Adjustments and preferences:**	
a	Depreciation of post-1986 property	**2a**
b	Amortization of certified pollution control facilities	**2b**
c	Amortization of mining exploration and development costs	**2c**
d	Amortization of circulation expenditures (personal holding companies only) . .	**2d**
e	Adjusted gain or loss	**2e**
f	Long-term contracts	**2f**
g	Installment sales	**2g**
h	Merchant marine capital construction funds	**2h**
i	Section 833(b) deduction (Blue Cross, Blue Shield, and similar type organizations only)	**2i**
j	Tax shelter farm activities (personal service corporations only)	**2j**
k	Passive activities (closely held corporations and personal service corporations only)	**2k**
l	Loss limitations	**2l**
m	Depletion	**2m**
n	Tax-exempt interest from specified private activity bonds	**2n**
o	Charitable contributions	**2o**
p	Intangible drilling costs	**2p**
q	Accelerated depreciation of real property (pre-1987)	**2q**
r	Accelerated depreciation of leased personal property (pre-1987) (personal holding companies only)	**2r**
s	Other adjustments	**2s**
t	Combine lines 2a through 2s	**2t**
3	Preadjustment alternative minimum taxable income (AMTI). Combine lines 1 and 2t	**3**
4	**Adjusted current earnings (ACE) adjustment:**	
a	Enter the corporation's ACE from line 10 of the worksheet on page 8 of the instructions	**4a**
b	Subtract line 3 from line 4a. If line 3 exceeds line 4a, enter the difference as a negative amount (see examples beginning on page 4 of the instructions) . .	**4b**
c	Multiply line 4b by 75% (.75). Enter the result as a positive amount	**4c**
d	Enter the excess, if any, of the corporation's total increases in AMTI from prior year ACE adjustments over its total reductions in AMTI from prior year ACE adjustments (see page 5 of the instructions). **Note:** *You **must** enter an amount on line 4d (even if line 4b is positive)*	**4d**
e	ACE adjustment: • If you entered a positive number or zero on line 4b, enter the amount from line 4c here as a positive amount. • If you entered a negative number on line 4b, enter the smaller of line 4c or line 4d here as a negative amount.	**4e**
5	Combine lines 3 and 4e. If zero or less, stop here; the corporation does not owe alternative minimum tax . . .	**5**
6	Alternative tax net operating loss deduction (see page 5 of the instructions)	**6**
7	**Alternative minimum taxable income.** Subtract line 6 from line 5. If the corporation held a residual interest in a REMIC, see page 5 of the instructions	**7**

For Paperwork Reduction Act Notice, see separate instructions.   Cat. No. 12955I   Form **4626** (1997)

8 Enter the amount from line 7 (alternative minimum taxable income) . . . . | **8** |

9 **Exemption phase-out computation** (if line 8 is $310,000 or more, skip lines 9a and 9b and enter -0- on line 9c):

  a Subtract $150,000 from line 8 (if you are completing this line for a member of a controlled group, see page 5 of the instructions). If zero or less, enter -0- . . | **9a** |

  b Multiply line 9a by 25% (.25). . . . . | **9b** |

  c Exemption. Subtract line 9b from $40,000 (if you are completing this line for a member of a controlled group, see page 5 of the instructions). If zero or less, enter -0- . . . . | **9c** |

10 Subtract line 9c from line 8. If zero or less, enter -0- . . . . | **10** |

11 Multiply line 10 by 20% (.20). . . . . | **11** |

12 Alternative minimum tax foreign tax credit. See page 5 of the instructions . . . . | **12** |

13 Tentative minimum tax. Subtract line 12 from line 11. . . . . | **13** |

14 Regular tax liability before all credits except the foreign tax credit and possessions tax credit . . . | **14** |

15 **Alternative minimum tax.** Subtract line 14 from line 13. Enter the result on the appropriate line of the corporation's income tax return (e.g., Form 1120, Schedule J, line 9). If zero or less, enter -0- . | **15** |

Form 4684

Department of the Treasury
Internal Revenue Service

Casualties and Thefts

▶ See separate instructions.
▶ Attach to your tax return.
▶ Use a separate Form 4684 for each different casualty or theft.

OMB No. 1545-0177

1997

Attachment
Sequence No. **26**

Name(s) shown on tax return

Identifying number

SECTION A—Personal Use Property (Use this section to report casualties and thefts of property **not** used in a trade or business or for income-producing purposes.)

1 Description of properties (show type, location, and date acquired for each):

Property **A** ....
Property **B** ....
Property **C** ....
Property **D** ....

Properties (Use a separate column for each property lost or damaged from one casualty or theft.)

		A	B	C	D
2	Cost or other basis of each property				
3	Insurance or other reimbursement (whether or not you filed a claim). See instructions . . . . . **Note:** If line 2 is **more than** line 3, skip line 4.				
4	Gain from casualty or theft. If line 3 is **more than** line 2, enter the difference here and skip lines 5 through 9 for that column. See instructions if line 3 includes insurance or other reimbursement you did not claim, or you received payment for your loss in a later tax year				
5	Fair market value **before** casualty or theft . . .				
6	Fair market value **after** casualty or theft				
7	Subtract line 6 from line 5				
8	Enter the **smaller** of line 2 or line 7				
9	Subtract line 3 from line 8. If zero or less, enter -0-				

10	Casualty or theft loss. Add the amounts on line 9. Enter the total	10	
11	Enter the amount from line 10 or $100, whichever is **smaller**	11	
12	Subtract line 11 from line 10 . . . . **Caution:** Use only one Form 4684 for lines 13 through 18.	12	
13	Add the amounts on line 12 of all Forms 4684	13	
14	Combine the amounts from line 4 of all Forms 4684	14	
15	• If line 14 is **more than** line 13, enter the difference here and on Schedule D. Do not complete the rest of this section (see instructions). • If line 14 is **less than** line 13, enter -0- here and continue with the form. • If line 14 is **equal to** line 13, enter -0- here. Do not complete the rest of this section.	15	
16	If line 14 is **less than** line 13, enter the difference	16	
17	Enter 10% of your adjusted gross income (Form 1040, line 33). Estates and trusts, see instructions	17	
18	Subtract line 17 from line 16. If zero or less, enter -0-. Also enter result on Schedule A (Form 1040), line 19. Estates and trusts, enter on the "Other deductions" line of your tax return	18	

For Paperwork Reduction Act Notice, see page 4 of separate instructions.   Cat. No. 12997O   Form **4684** (1997)

Form 4684 (1997)   Attachment Sequence No. **26**   Page **2**

Name(s) shown on tax return. Do not enter name and identifying number if shown on other side.	Identifying number

SECTION B—Business and Income-Producing Property (Use this section to report casualties and thefts of property used in a trade or business or for income-producing purposes.)

Part I   **Casualty or Theft Gain or Loss** (Use a separate Part I for each casualty or theft.)

19 Description of properties (show type, location, and date acquired for each):

Property **A** ....

Property **B** ....

Property **C** ....

Property **D** ....

		Properties (Use a separate column for each property lost or damaged from one casualty or theft.)			
		A	**B**	**C**	**D**
20 Cost or adjusted basis of each property	**20**				
21 Insurance or other reimbursement (whether or not you filed a claim). See the instructions for line 3 . **Note:** *If line 20 is more than line 21, skip line 22.*	**21**				
22 Gain from casualty or theft. If line 21 is **more than** line 20, enter the difference here and on line 29 or line 34, column (c), except as provided in the instructions for line 33. Also, skip lines 23 through 27 for that column. See the instructions for line 4 if line 21 includes insurance or other reimbursement you did not claim, or you received payment for your loss in a later tax year	**22**				
23 Fair market value **before** casualty or theft . . .	**23**				
24 Fair market value **after** casualty or theft	**24**				
25 Subtract line 24 from line 23	**25**				
26 Enter the **smaller** of line 20 or line 25	**26**				
Note: *If the property was totally destroyed by casualty or lost from theft, enter on line 26 the amount from line 20.*					
27 Subtract line 21 from line 26. If zero or less, enter -0-	**27**				
28 Casualty or theft loss. Add the amounts on line 27. Enter the total here and on line 29 **or** line 34 (see instructions).			**28**		

Part II   **Summary of Gains and Losses** (from separate Parts I)

(a) Identify casualty or theft	**(b)** Losses from casualties or thefts		**(c)** Gains from casualties or thefts includible in income
	(i) Trade, business, rental or royalty property	*(ii)* Income-producing property	

Casualty or Theft of Property Held One Year or Less

29 _____	( )	( )	
_____	( )	( )	
30 Totals. Add the amounts on line 29 . . . . **30**	( )	( )	

31 Combine line 30, columns (b)(i) and (c). Enter the net gain or (loss) here and on Form 4797, line 14. If Form 4797 is not otherwise required, see instructions **31**

32 Enter the amount from line 30, column (b)(ii) here and on Schedule A (Form 1040), line 22. Partnerships, S corporations, estates and trusts, see instructions **32**

Casualty or Theft of Property Held More Than One Year

33 Casualty or theft gains from Form 4797, line 32			**33**	
34 _____	( )	( )	
_____	( )	( )	
35 Total losses. Add amounts on line 34, columns (b)(i) and (b)(ii) . . . **35**	( )	( )	

36 Total gains. Add lines 33 and 34, column (c) **36**

37 Add amounts on line 35, columns (b)(i) and (b)(ii) **37**

38 If the loss on line 37 is **more than** the gain on line 36:

  a Combine line 35, column (b)(i) and line 36, and enter the net gain or (loss) here. Partnerships and S corporations see the note below. All others enter this amount on Form 4797, line 14. If Form 4797 is not otherwise required, see instructions **38a**

  b Enter the amount from line 35, column (b)(ii) here. Partnerships and S corporations see the note below. Individuals enter this amount on Schedule A (Form 1040), line 22. Estates and trusts, enter on the "Other deductions" line of your tax return   **38b**

39 If the loss on line 37 is **equal to** or **less than** the gain on line 36, combine these lines and enter here. Partnerships, see the note below. All others, enter this amount on Form 4797, line 3, column (g) and the net 28% rate gain or (loss), if applicable, in column (h) **39**

  Note: *Partnerships, enter the amount from line 38a, 38b, or line 39 on Form 1065, Schedule K, line 7. S corporations, enter the amount from line 38a or 38b on Form 1120S, Schedule K, line 6.*

✪

Form **4797**

Department of the Treasury
Internal Revenue Service (99)

Sales of Business Property
(Also Involuntary Conversions and Recapture Amounts
Under Sections 179 and 280F(b)(2))
▶ Attach to your tax return.   ▶ See separate instructions.

OMB No. 1545-0184

19**97**

Attachment
Sequence No. **27**

Name(s) shown on return

Identifying number

1 Enter here the gross proceeds from the sale or exchange of real estate reported to you for 1997 on Form(s) 1099-S (or a substitute statement) that you will be including on line 2, 10, or 20 . . . . | **1** |

Part I Sales or Exchanges of Property Used in a Trade or Business and Involuntary Conversions From Other Than Casualty or Theft—Property Held More Than 1 Year

(a) Description of property	(b) Date acquired (mo., day, yr.)	(c) Date sold (mo., day, yr.)	(d) Gross sales price	(e) Depreciation allowed or allowable since acquisition	(f) Cost or other basis, plus improvements and expense of sale	(g) GAIN or (LOSS) for entire year. Subtract (f) from the sum of (d) and (e)	(h) 28% RATE GAIN or (LOSS) * (see instr. below)
2							

3 Gain, if any, from Form 4684, line 39 . . . . | **3** |

4 Section 1231 gain from installment sales from Form 6252, line 26 or 37 . . . . . . | **4** |

5 Section 1231 gain or (loss) from like-kind exchanges from Form 8824 . . . . | **5** |

6 Gain, if any, from line 32, from other than casualty or theft . . . . | **6** |

7 Combine lines 2 through 6 in columns (g) and (h). Enter gain or (loss) here, and on the appropriate line as follows: | **7** |

Partnerships—Enter the gain or (loss) on Form 1065, Schedule K, lines 6a and 6b. Skip lines 8, 9, 11, and 12 below.

S corporations—Report the gain or (loss) following the instructions for Form 1120S, Schedule K, lines 5 and 6. Skip lines 8, 9, 11, and 12 below, unless line 7, column (g) is a gain and the S corporation is subject to the capital gains tax.

All others—If line 7, column (g) is zero or a loss, enter that amount on line 11 below and skip lines 8 and 9. If line 7, column (g) is a gain and you did not have any prior year section 1231 losses, or they were recaptured in an earlier year, enter the gain or (loss) in each column as a long-term capital gain or (loss) on Schedule D and skip lines 8, 9, and 12 below.

8 Nonrecaptured net section 1231 losses from prior years (see instructions) . . . . | **8** |

9 Subtract line 8 from line 7. If zero or less, enter -0-. Also enter on the appropriate line as follows (see instructions): | **9** |

S corporations—Enter only the gain in column (g) on Schedule D (Form 1120S), line 14, and skip lines 11 and 12 below.

All others—If line 9, column (g) is zero, enter the gain from line 7, column (g) on line 12 below. If line 9, column (g) is more than zero, enter the amount from line 8, column (g) on line 12 below, and enter the gain or (loss) in each column of line 9 as a long-term capital gain or (loss) on Schedule D.

* Corporations (other than S corporations) should not complete column (h). Partnerships and S corporations must complete column (h). All others must complete column (h) only if line 7, column (g), is a gain. 28% rate gain or loss includes all gains and losses in column (g) from sales, exchanges, or conversions (including installment payments received) **either (a) before** 5/7/97 **or (b) after** 7/28/97 for assets held more than 1 year but not more than 18 months.

Part II Ordinary Gains and Losses

10 Ordinary gains and losses not included on lines 11 through 17 (include property held 1 year or less):

11 Loss, if any, from line 7, column (g) . . . . | **11** |

12 Gain, if any, from line 7, column (g) or amount from line 8, column (g) if applicable . . . . | **12** |

13 Gain, if any, from line 31 . . . . | **13** |

14 Net gain or (loss) from Form 4684, lines 31 and 38a . . . . | **14** |

15 Ordinary gain from installment sales from Form 6252, line 25 or 36 . . . . | **15** |

16 Ordinary gain or (loss) from like-kind exchanges from Form 8824 . . . . | **16** |

17 Recapture of section 179 expense deduction for partners and S corporation shareholders from property dispositions by partnerships and S corporations (see instructions) . . . . | **17** |

18 Combine lines 10 through 17 in column (g). Enter gain or (loss) here, and on the appropriate line as follows: | **18** |

a For all except individual returns: Enter the gain or (loss) from line 18 on the return being filed.

b For individual returns:

(1) If the loss on line 11 includes a loss from Form 4684, line 35, column (b)(ii), enter that part of the loss here and on line 22 of Schedule A (Form 1040). Identify as from "Form 4797, line 18b(1)." See instructions . . . . | **18b(1)** |

(2) Redetermine the gain or (loss) on line 18, excluding the loss, if any, on line 18b(1). Enter here and on Form 1040, line 14 . . . . | **18b(2)** |

For Paperwork Reduction Act Notice, see separate instructions.   Cat. No. 13086I   Form **4797** (1997)

Part III Gain From Disposition of Property Under Sections 1245, 1250, 1252, 1254, and 1255

19	(a) Description of section 1245, 1250, 1252, 1254, or 1255 property:	(b) Date acquired (mo., day, yr.)	(c) Date sold (mo., day, yr.)
A			
B			
C			
D			

	These columns relate to the properties on lines 19A through 19D. ▶		Property A	Property B	Property C	Property D
20	Gross sales price (**Note:** See line 1 before completing.)	**20**				
21	Cost or other basis plus expense of sale	**21**				
22	Depreciation (or depletion) allowed or allowable	**22**				
23	Adjusted basis. Subtract line 22 from line 21	**23**				
24	Total gain. Subtract line 23 from line 20	**24**				
25	**If section 1245 property:**					
a	Depreciation allowed or allowable from line 22	**25a**				
b	Enter the **smaller** of line 24 or 25a	**25b**				
26	**If section 1250 property:** If straight line depreciation was used, enter -0- on line 26g, except for a corporation subject to section 291.					
a	Additional depreciation after 1975 (see instructions)	**26a**				
b	Applicable percentage multiplied by the **smaller** of line 24 or line 26a (see instructions)	**26b**				
c	Subtract line 26a from line 24. If residential rental property or line 24 is not more than line 26a, skip lines 26d and 26e	**26c**				
d	Additional depreciation after 1969 and before 1976	**26d**				
e	Enter the **smaller** of line 26c or 26d	**26e**				
f	Section 291 amount (corporations only)	**26f**				
g	Add lines 26b, 26e, and 26f	**26g**				
27	**If section 1252 property:** Skip this section if you did not dispose of farmland or if this form is being completed for a partnership.					
a	Soil, water, and land clearing expenses	**27a**				
b	Line 27a multiplied by applicable percentage (see instructions)	**27b**				
c	Enter the **smaller** of line 24 or 27b	**27c**				
28	**If section 1254 property:**					
a	Intangible drilling and development costs, expenditures for development of mines and other natural deposits, and mining exploration costs (see instructions)	**28a**				
b	Enter the **smaller** of line 24 or 28a	**28b**				
29	**If section 1255 property:**					
a	Applicable percentage of payments excluded from income under section 126 (see instructions)	**29a**				
b	Enter the **smaller** of line 24 or 29a (see instructions)	**29b**				

Summary of Part III Gains. Complete property columns A through D through line 29b before going to line 30.

30	Total gains for all properties. Add property columns A through D, line 24	**30**	
31	Add property columns A through D, lines 25b, 26g, 27c, 28b, and 29b. Enter here and on line 13	**31**	
32	Subtract line 31 from line 30. Enter the portion from casualty or theft on Form 4684, line 33. Enter the portion from other than casualty or theft on Form 4797, line 6, column (g), and if applicable, column (h)	**32**	

Part IV Recapture Amounts Under Sections 179 and 280F(b)(2) When Business Use Drops to 50% or Less
See instructions.

			(a) Section 179	(b) Section 280F(b)(2)
33	Section 179 expense deduction or depreciation allowable in prior years	**33**		
34	Recomputed depreciation. See instructions	**34**		
35	Recapture amount. Subtract line 34 from line 33. See the instructions for where to report	**35**		

Form 4868
Department of the Treasury
Internal Revenue Service

Application for Automatic Extension of Time To File U.S. Individual Income Tax Return

OMB No. 1545-0188

1997

General Instructions

Purpose of Form

Use Form 4868 to apply for 4 more months to file **Form 1040EZ, Form 1040A,** or **Form 1040.**

To get the extra time you **MUST:**

● Properly estimate your 1997 tax liability using the information available to you,

● Enter your tax liability on line 9 of Form 4868, **AND**

● File Form 4868 by the regular due date of your return.

You are not required to send a payment of the tax you estimate as due. However, see **Interest** and **Late Payment Penalty** on page 3. Any remittance you send with your application for extension will be treated as a payment of tax.

You do not have to explain why you are asking for the extension. We will contact you only if your request is denied.

Do not file Form 4868 if you want the IRS to figure your tax or you are under a court order to file your return by the regular due date.

If you need an additional extension, see **If You Need Additional Time** on this page.

Note: *An extension of time to file your 1997 **calendar year** income tax return also extends the time to file a gift or generation-skipping transfer (GST) tax return **(Form 709 or 709-A)** for 1997.*

Out of the Country

If you already had 2 extra months to file because you were a U.S. citizen or resident and were out of the country, use this form to obtain an additional 2 months to file. Write "Taxpayer Abroad" across the top of Form 4868. "Out of the country" means either **(a)** you live outside the United States and Puerto Rico **and** your main place of work is outside the United States and Puerto Rico, **or (b)** you are in military or naval service outside the United States and Puerto Rico.

When To File Form 4868

File Form 4868 by April 15, 1998. Fiscal year taxpayers, file Form 4868 by the regular due date of the return.

If you had 2 extra months to file your return because you were out of the country, file Form 4868 by June 15, 1998, for a 1997 calendar year return.

How To Send In Your Payment

● When sending a payment with Form 4868, use the addresses in the middle column under **Where To File** on page 2.

● Make your check or money order payable to "Internal Revenue Service" (not "IRS"). Do not send cash.

● Write your social security number, daytime phone number, and "1997 Form 4868"on the front of your check or money order.

● Do not staple or attach your payment to the form.

If You Need Additional Time

If the automatic 4-month extension (until August 17, 1998, for most calendar year taxpayers) does not give you enough time, you can ask for additional time later. But you will have to give a good reason, and it must be approved by the IRS. To ask for the additional time, you must **either:**

1. File **Form 2688,** Application for Additional Extension of Time To File U.S. Individual Income Tax Return, or

2. Explain your reason in a letter. Mail it to the address in the right column under **Where To File** on page 2.

File Form 4868 **before** you file Form 2688 or write a letter asking for more time. Only in cases of undue hardship will the IRS approve your request for an additional extension without receiving Form 4868 first. Ask early for this extra time. Then, you can still file your return on time if your request is not approved.

For Paperwork Reduction Act Notice, see page 4.   Cat. No. 13141W   Form **4868** (1997)

▼ DETACH HERE ▼

Form 4868
Department of the Treasury
Internal Revenue Service

Application for Automatic Extension of Time To File U.S. Individual Income Tax Return

For calendar year 1997, or other tax year beginning _____,1997, ending _____,19____ .

OMB No. 1545-0188

1997

Part I	**Identification**

1 Your name(s) (see instructions)

Address (see instructions)

City, town or post office, state, and ZIP code

2 Your social security number   **3** Spouse's social security no.

This form also extends the time for filing a gift or generation-skipping transfer (GST) tax return if you file a calendar (not fiscal) year income tax return. Check below if requesting a gift or GST tax return extension, and enter your tax payment(s) in Part III:

Yourself ▶ ☐   Spouse ▶ ☐

Part II	**Individual Taxes**

4 Total tax liability for 1997 . . . . $ _____

5 Total 1997 payments . . . . . . _____

6 **Balance.** Subtract 5 from 4 . . . . _____

Part III	**Gift/GST Tax**—If you are not filing a gift or GST tax return, go to Part IV now. See the instructions.

7 Your gift or GST tax payment. . . $ _____
8 **Your spouse's** gift/GST tax payment . _____

Part IV	**Total**

9 **Total liability.** Add lines 6, 7, and 8 $ _____

10 Amount you are paying. . . . . ▶ _____

If line 10 is less than line 9, you may be liable for interest and penalties. See page 3.

Where To File

If you live in:	And you are making a payment, send Form 4868 with your payment to IRS:	And you are NOT making a payment, send Form 4868 to Internal Revenue Service Center:
Florida, Georgia, South Carolina	P.O. Box 105073 Atlanta, GA 30348-5073	Atlanta, GA 39901
New Jersey, New York (*New York City and counties of Nassau, Rockland, Suffolk, and Westchester*)	P.O. Box 22423 Newark, NJ 07101-2423	Holtsville, NY 00501
New York (*all other counties*), Connecticut, Maine, Massachusetts, New Hampshire, Rhode Island, Vermont	P.O. Box 371410 Pittsburgh, PA 15250-7410	Andover, MA 05501
Illinois, Iowa, Minnesota, Missouri, Wisconsin	P.O. Box 970028 St. Louis, MO 63197-0028	Kansas City, MO 64999
Delaware, District of Columbia, Maryland, Pennsylvania, Virginia	P.O. Box 7990 Philadelphia, PA 19162-7990	Philadelphia, PA 19255
Indiana, Kentucky, Michigan, Ohio, West Virginia	P.O. Box 6252 Chicago, IL 60680-6252	Cincinnati, OH 45999
Kansas, New Mexico, Oklahoma, Texas	P.O. Box 970027 St. Louis, MO 63197-0027	Austin, TX 73301
Alaska, Arizona, California (*counties of Alpine, Amador, Butte, Calaveras, Colusa, Contra Costa, Del Norte, El Dorado, Glenn, Humboldt, Lake, Lassen, Marin, Mendocino, Modoc, Napa, Nevada, Placer, Plumas, Sacramento, San Joaquin, Shasta, Sierra, Siskiyou, Solano, Sonoma, Sutter, Tehama, Trinity, Yolo, and Yuba*), Colorado, Idaho, Montana, Nebraska, Nevada, North Dakota, Oregon, South Dakota, Utah, Washington, Wyoming	P.O. Box 7122 San Francisco, CA 94120-7122	Ogden, UT 84201
California (*all other counties*), Hawaii	P.O. Box 54916 Los Angeles, CA 90054-0916	Fresno, CA 93888
Alabama, Arkansas, Louisiana, Mississippi, North Carolina, Tennessee	P.O. Box 1236 Charlotte, NC 28201-1236	Memphis, TN 37501
American Samoa or Puerto Rico (*or exclude income under section 933*); are a nonpermanent resident of Guam or the Virgin Islands; have an APO, FPO, or foreign address; are a dual-status alien; or file Form 2555, 2555-EZ, or 4563	P.O. Box 7990 Philadelphia, PA 19162-7990	Philadelphia, PA 19255
Guam: Permanent residents	Send Form 4868 and payments to:	Department of Revenue and Taxation Government of Guam P.O. Box 23607 GMF, GU 96921
Virgin Islands: Permanent residents	Send Form 4868 and payments to:	V.I. Bureau of Internal Revenue 9601 Estate Thomas Charlotte Amalie St. Thomas, VI 00802

Filing Your Tax Return

You may file your tax return any time before the extension expires. But remember, Form 4868 does not extend the time to pay taxes. If you do not pay the amount due by the regular due date, you will owe interest. You may also be charged penalties.

Do not attach a copy of Form 4868 to your return.

For your convenience, we have included an extra copy of Form 4868. However, only file one.

Interest

You will owe interest on any tax not paid by the regular due date of your return. The interest runs until you pay the tax. Even if you had a good reason for not paying on time, you will still owe interest.

Late Payment Penalty

The penalty is usually ½ of 1% of any tax (other than estimated tax) not paid by the regular due date. It is charged for each month or part of a month the tax is unpaid. The maximum penalty is 25%.

The late payment penalty will not be charged if you can show reasonable cause for not paying on time. Attach a statement to your return fully explaining the reason. **Do not** attach the statement to Form 4868.

You are considered to have "reasonable cause" for the period covered by this automatic extension if at least 90% of your actual 1997 tax liability is paid before the regular due date of your return through withholding, estimated tax payments, or with Form 4868.

Late Filing Penalty

A penalty is usually charged if your return is filed after the due date (including extensions). It is usually 5% of the tax not paid by the regular due date for each month or part of a month your return is late. Generally, the maximum penalty is 25%. If your return is more than 60 days late, the minimum penalty is $100 or the balance of the tax due on your return, whichever is smaller. You might not owe the penalty if you have a good reason for filing late. Attach a statement to your return fully explaining the reason. **Do not** attach the statement to Form 4868.

How To Claim Credit for Payment Made With This Form

When you file your return, include the amount of any payment you sent with Form 4868 on the appropriate line of your tax return. If you file Form 1040EZ, the instructions for line 9 of that form will tell you how to report the payment. If you file Form 1040A, see the instructions for line 29e. If you file Form 1040, enter the payment on line 57.

If you and your spouse each filed a separate Form 4868 but later file a joint return for 1997, enter the total paid with both Forms 4868 on the appropriate line of your joint return.

If you and your spouse jointly file Form 4868 but later file separate returns for 1997, you may enter the total amount paid with Form 4868 on either of your separate returns. Or you and your spouse may divide the payment in any agreed amounts. Be sure each separate return has the social security numbers of both spouses.

Specific Instructions
How To Complete Form 4868

Skip Part III unless you are requesting an extension of time to file a gift or GST tax return.

Part I—Identification

Enter your name(s) and address. If you plan to file a joint return, include both spouses' names in the order in which they will appear on the return.

If you want correspondence regarding this extension to be sent to you at an address other than your own or to an agent acting for you, include the agent's name, if any, and enter that address instead.

If you changed your name after you filed your last return because of marriage, divorce, etc., be sure to report this to your local Social Security Administration office before filing Form 4868. This prevents delays in processing your extension request.

If you changed your mailing address after you filed your last return, you should use **Form 8822,** Change of Address, to notify the IRS of the change. Showing a new address on Form 4868 will not update your record. You can get Form 8822 by calling 1-800-TAX-FORM (1-800-829-3676).

▼ DETACH HERE ▼   (This is an extra copy. File only one Form 4868.)

Form **4868**	**Application for Automatic Extension of Time To File U.S. Individual Income Tax Return**	OMB No. 1545-0188
Department of the Treasury Internal Revenue Service	For calendar year 1997, or other tax year beginning ,1997, ending ,19 .	**19**97

Part I Identification	**Part II** Individual Taxes
1 Your name(s) (see instructions)	4 Total tax liability for 1997 . . . . . $ _____
	5 Total 1997 payments . . . . _____
Address (see instructions)	6 **Balance.** Subtract 5 from 4 . . . . . _____
City, town or post office, state, and ZIP code	**Part III** Gift/GST Tax—If you are not filing a gift or GST tax return, go to Part IV now. See the instructions.
2 Your social security number 3 Spouse's social security no.	7 Your gift or GST tax payment. . . $ _____
	8 **Your spouse's** gift/GST tax payment
This form also extends the time for filing a gift or generation-skipping transfer (GST) tax return if you file a calendar (not fiscal) year income tax return. Check below if requesting a gift or GST tax return extension, and enter your tax payment(s) in Part III:	**Part IV** Total
	9 **Total liability.** Add lines 6, 7, and 8 $ _____
	10 Amount you are paying . . . . . ▶ _____
Yourself ▶ ☐ Spouse ▶ ☐	If line 10 is less than line 9, you may be liable for interest and penalties. See page 3.

If you plan to file jointly, enter on line 2 the SSN that you will show first on your return. Enter your spouse's SSN on line 3.

Part II—Individual Taxes

Line 4—Total Tax Liability for 1997

This is the amount you expect to enter on Form 1040EZ, line 10; Form 1040A, line 28; or Form 1040, line 53. If you expect this amount to be zero, enter zero.

Caution: *You can estimate this amount, but be as exact as you can with the information you have. If we later find that your estimate was not reasonable, the extension will be null and void.*

Line 5—Total Payments for 1997

This is the amount you expect to enter on Form 1040EZ, line 9; Form 1040A, line 29e; or Form 1040, line 60 (excluding line 57).

Line 6—Balance

Subtract line 5 from line 4. If line 5 is more than line 4, enter zero.

If you find you cannot pay the amount shown on line 6, you can still get the extension. But you should pay as much as you can to limit the amount of interest you will owe. Also, you may be charged the late payment penalty on the unpaid tax from the regular due date of your return. See **Late Payment Penalty** on page 3.

Part III—Gift/GST Tax

Fill in this part only if you or your spouse plan to file Form 709 or 709-A **and** you are also using Form 4868 to apply for an extension of time to file your 1997 **calendar year** income tax return. **Do not** include income tax on lines 7 and 8.

Enter the amount of gift and GST tax you (or your spouse) are paying on these lines. If your spouse files a **separate** Form 4868, **do not** check the box for your spouse; enter on your form only the total gift and GST tax **you** are paying. Pay in full with this form to avoid interest and penalties.

Part IV—Total

Enter the total of line 6 (and 7 and 8, if applicable) on line 9. If you are paying your entire estimate of tax liability, both lines 9 and 10 should be the same.

Paperwork Reduction Act Notice. We ask for the information on this form to carry out the Internal Revenue laws of the United States. You are required to give us the information. We need it to ensure that you are complying with these laws and to allow us to figure and collect the right amount of tax.

You are not required to provide the information requested on a form that is subject to the Paperwork Reduction Act unless the form displays a valid OMB control number. Books or records relating to a form or its instructions must be retained as long as their contents may become material in the administration of any Internal Revenue law. Generally, tax returns and return information are confidential, as required by Internal Revenue Code section 6103.

The time needed to complete and file this form will vary depending on individual circumstances. The estimated average time is: **Recordkeeping,** 26 min.; **Learning about the law or the form,** 12 min.; **Preparing the form,** 17 min.; and **Copying, assembling, and sending the form to the IRS,** 10 min.

If you have comments concerning the accuracy of these time estimates or suggestions for making this form simpler, we would be happy to hear from you. You can write to the Tax Forms Committee, Western Area Distribution Center, Rancho Cordova, CA 95743-0001. **DO NOT** send the form to this address. Instead, see **Where To File** on page 2.

OMB No. 1545-0191

Form **4952**

Department of the Treasury
Internal Revenue Service (99)

Investment Interest Expense Deduction

► **Attach to your tax return.**

1997

Attachment
Sequence No. **72**

Name(s) shown on return

Identifying number

Part I **Total Investment Interest Expense**

1 Investment interest expense paid or accrued in 1997. See instructions . . . . | **1**

2 Disallowed investment interest expense from 1996 Form 4952, line 7 . . . . | **2**

3 **Total investment interest expense.** Add lines 1 and 2 . . . . | **3**

Part II **Net Investment Income**

4a Gross income from property held for investment (excluding any net gain from the disposition of property held for investment) . . . . | **4a**

b Net gain from the disposition of property held for investment . . . | **4b**

c Net capital gain from the disposition of property held for investment | **4c**

d Subtract line 4c from line 4b. If zero or less, enter -0- . . . . | **4d**

e Enter all or part of the amount on line 4c that you elect to include in investment income. Do not enter more than the amount on line 4b. See instructions . . . . ► | **4e**

f Investment income. Add lines 4a, 4d, and 4e. See instructions . . . . | **4f**

5 Investment expenses. See instructions . . . . | **5**

6 **Net investment income.** Subtract line 5 from line 4f. If zero or less, enter -0- . . . . . . | **6**

Part III **Investment Interest Expense Deduction**

7 Disallowed investment interest expense to be carried forward to 1998. Subtract line 6 from line 3. If zero or less, enter -0- . . . . | **7**

8 **Investment interest expense deduction.** Enter the smaller of line 3 or 6. See instructions . . | **8**

Section references are to the Internal Revenue Code unless otherwise noted.

General Instructions

Purpose of Form

Interest expense paid by an individual, estate, or trust on a loan allocable to property held for investment may not be fully deductible in the current year. Use Form 4952 to figure the amount of investment interest expense deductible for the current year and the amount, if any, to carry forward to future years.

For more details, see **Pub. 550,** Investment Income and Expenses.

Who Must File

If you are an individual, estate, or a trust, and you claim a deduction for investment interest expense, you must complete and attach Form 4952 to your tax return, unless **all** the following apply.

● Your only investment income was from interest or dividends.

● You have no other deductible expenses connected with the production of interest or dividends.

● Your investment interest expense is not more than your investment income.

● You have no disallowed investment interest expense from 1996.

Allocation of Interest Expense Under Temporary Regulations Section 1.163-8T

If you paid or accrued interest on a loan and used the loan proceeds for more than one purpose, you may have to allocate the interest. This is necessary because different rules apply to investment interest, personal interest, trade or business interest, home mortgage interest, and passive activity interest. See **Pub. 535,** Business Expenses.

Specific Instructions

Part I—Total Investment Interest Expense

Line 1

Enter the investment interest paid or accrued during the tax year, regardless of when you incurred the indebtedness. Investment interest is interest paid or accrued on a loan (or part of a loan) that is allocable to property held for investment (as defined later).

Include investment interest expense reported to you on Schedule K-1 from a partnership or an S corporation. Include amortization of bond premium on taxable bonds purchased after October 22, 1986, but before January 1, 1988, unless you elected to offset amortizable bond premium against the interest payments on the bond. A taxable bond is a bond on which the interest is includible in gross income.

Investment interest expense **does not** include the following:

● Home mortgage interest.

● Interest expense that is properly allocable to a passive activity. Generally, a passive activity is any business activity in which you **do not** materially participate and any rental activity. See the separate instructions for **Form 8582,** Passive Activity Loss Limitations, for more details.

● Any interest expense that is capitalized, such as construction interest subject to section 263A.

● Interest expense related to tax-exempt interest income under section 265.

● Interest expense, disallowed under section 264, on indebtedness with respect to life insurance, endowment, or annuity contracts issued after June 8, 1997, even if the proceeds were used to purchase any property held for investment.

Cat. No. 13177Y

Form **4952** (1997)

Property held for investment. Property held for investment includes property that produces income (unless derived in the ordinary course of a trade or business) from interest, dividends, annuities, or royalties; and gains from the disposition of property that produces those types of income or is held for investment. However, it does not include an interest in a passive activity.

Property held for investment also includes an interest in an activity of conducting a trade or business in which you did not materially participate and that is not a passive activity. For example, a working interest in an oil or gas property that you held directly or through an entity that did not limit your liability is property held for investment if you did not materially participate in the activity.

Part II—Net Investment Income

Line 4a

Gross income from property held for investment to enter on line 4a includes income (unless derived in the ordinary course of a trade or business) from:

- Interest,
- Dividends (except Alaska Permanent Fund dividends),
- Annuities, and
- Royalties.

If you are filing **Form 8814,** Parents' Election To Report Child's Interest and Dividends, part or all of your child's income may be included on line 4a. See Form 8814 for details.

Also, include on line 4a net income from the following passive activities:

- Rental of substantially nondepreciable property,
- Equity-financed lending activities, and
- Acquisition of certain interests in a pass-through entity licensing intangible property.

See Regulations section 1.469-2(f)(10) for details.

Also include on line 4a (or 4b, if applicable) net passive income from a passive activity of a publicly traded partnership (as defined in section 469(k)(2)). See Notice 88-75, 1988-2 C.B. 386, for details.

Include investment income reported to you on Schedule K-1 from a partnership or an S corporation. Also include net investment income from an estate or a trust.

Do not include on line 4a any net gain from the disposition of property held for investment. Instead, enter this amount on line 4b.

Line 4b

Net gain from the disposition of property held for investment is the excess, if any, of total gains over total losses from the disposition of property held for investment. When figuring this amount, include capital gain distributions from mutual funds.

Line 4c

Net capital gain from the disposition of property held for investment is the excess, if any, of net long-term capital gain over net short-term capital loss from the disposition of property held for investment. When figuring this amount, include capital gain distributions from mutual funds.

Line 4e

Net capital gain from the disposition of property held for investment is excluded from investment income. However, you may elect to include in investment income all or part of the net capital gain from the disposition of property held for investment. If you make the election, you also must reduce the amount of net capital gain eligible for capital gains tax rates by the amount of net capital gain you included in investment income. Therefore, you should consider the effect on your tax using the capital gains tax rates before making this election. You must make the election no later than the due date (including extensions) of your income tax return. Once made, the election may not be revoked without IRS consent.

To make the election, enter all or part of the amount on line 4c, but not more than the amount on line 4b, that you elect to include in investment income. Also enter this amount on line 21 of Schedule D (Form 1040), or on line 20 of Schedule D (Form 1041), if applicable.

Line 5

Investment expenses are your allowed deductions, other than interest expense, directly connected with the production of investment income. For example, depreciation or depletion allowed on assets that produce investment income is an investment expense.

Include investment expenses reported to you on Schedule K-1 from a partnership or an S corporation.

Investment expenses **do not** include any deductions taken into account in determining your income or loss from a passive activity.

If you have investment expenses that are included as a miscellaneous itemized deduction on Schedule A (Form 1040), line 22, you may not have to use the entire amount for purposes of Form 4952, line 5. The 2% adjusted gross income limitation on Schedule A (Form 1040), line 25, may reduce the amount you must enter on Form 4952, line 5.

To figure the amount to use, compare the amount of the investment expenses included on Schedule A (Form 1040), line 22, with the total miscellaneous expenses on Schedule A (Form 1040), line 26. The smaller of **(a)** the investment expenses included on Schedule A (Form 1040), line 22, or **(b)** the total on Schedule A (Form 1040), line 26, is the amount of investment expenses included as a miscellaneous itemized deduction to use when figuring Form 4952, line 5.

Example. Assume Schedule A, line 22, includes investment expenses of $3,000, and line 26 is $1,300 after the 2% adjusted gross income limitation. Investment expenses from Schedule A of $1,300 are used to figure the amount of investment expenses for line 5. If investment expenses of $800 were included on line 22 and line 26 was $1,300, investment expenses from Schedule A of $800 would be used.

Part III—Investment Interest Expense Deduction

Line 8

This is the amount you may deduct as investment interest expense.

Individuals. Generally, enter the amount from line 8 on Schedule A (Form 1040), line 13, even if all or part of it is attributable to a partnership or an S corporation. If any portion of this amount is attributable to royalties, enter that part of the interest expense on Schedule E (Form 1040). If any portion is attributable to a trade or business in which you did not materially participate and that is not a passive activity, enter that part of the interest expense on the schedule where you report other expenses for that trade or business.

Estates and trusts. Enter the amount from line 8 on Form 1041, line 10.

Form 6198. If any portion of the deductible investment interest expense is attributable to an activity for which you are not at risk, you must also use **Form 6198,** At-Risk Limitations, to figure your deductible investment interest expense. Enter the portion attributable to the at-risk activity on Form 6198, line 4. Reduce Form 4952, line 8, by the amount entered on Form 6198. See Form 6198 and its instructions for more details, especially the instructions for line 4 of that form.

Alternative minimum tax (AMT). Deductible interest expense is an adjustment for the AMT. Get **Form 6251,** Alternative Minimum Tax—Individuals, or Form 1041, Schedule I, for estates and trusts.

Form **6251**

Department of the Treasury
Internal Revenue Service (99)

Alternative Minimum Tax—Individuals

▶ See separate instructions.

▶ Attach to Form 1040 or Form 1040NR.

OMB No. 1545-0227

1997

Attachment Sequence No. **32**

Name(s) shown on Form 1040

Your social security number

Part I — Adjustments and Preferences

1	If you itemized deductions on Schedule A (Form 1040), go to line 2. Otherwise, enter your standard deduction from Form 1040, line 35, here and go to line 6	**1**
2	Medical and dental. Enter the smaller of Schedule A (Form 1040), line 4 **or** 2½% of Form 1040, line 33	**2**
3	Taxes. Enter the amount from Schedule A (Form 1040), line 9	**3**
4	Certain interest on a home mortgage not used to buy, build, or improve your home	**4**
5	Miscellaneous itemized deductions. Enter the amount from Schedule A (Form 1040), line 26 . . .	**5**
6	Refund of taxes. Enter any tax refund from Form 1040, line 10 or line 21	**6** ( )
7	Investment interest. Enter difference between regular tax and AMT deduction	**7**
8	Post-1986 depreciation. Enter difference between regular tax and AMT depreciation	**8**
9	Adjusted gain or loss. Enter difference between AMT and regular tax gain or loss	**9**
10	Incentive stock options. Enter excess of AMT income over regular tax income	**10**
11	Passive activities. Enter difference between AMT and regular tax income or loss	**11**
12	Beneficiaries of estates and trusts. Enter the amount from Schedule K-1 (Form 1041), line 9	**12**
13	Tax-exempt interest from private activity bonds issued after 8/7/86	**13**

14 Other. Enter the amount, if any, for each item below and enter the total on line 14.

- a Charitable contributions .
- b Circulation expenditures .
- c Depletion . . . . .
- d Depreciation (pre-1987) .
- e Installment sales . . .
- f Intangible drilling costs .
- g Long-term contracts . .

- h Loss limitations . . . .
- i Mining costs . . . .
- j Patron's adjustment . .
- k Pollution control facilities .
- l Research and experimental
- m Tax shelter farm activities .
- n Related adjustments . .

14

15	**Total Adjustments and Preferences.** Combine lines 1 through 14 . . . . ▶	**15**

Part II — Alternative Minimum Taxable Income

16	Enter the amount from **Form 1040, line 36.** If less than zero, enter as a (loss) . . . . . ▶	**16**
17	Net operating loss deduction, if any, from Form 1040, line 21. Enter as a positive amount	**17**
18	If Form 1040, line 33, is over $121,200 (over $60,600 if married filing separately), and you itemized deductions, enter the amount, if any, from line 9 of the worksheet for Schedule A (Form 1040), line 28	**18** ( )
19	Combine lines 15 through 18 . . . . ▶	**19**
20	Alternative tax net operating loss deduction. See page 5 of the instructions	**20**
21	**Alternative Minimum Taxable Income.** Subtract line 20 from line 19. (If married filing separately and line 21 is more than $165,000, see page 5 of the instructions.) . . . . ▶	**21**

Part III — Exemption Amount and Alternative Minimum Tax

22 **Exemption Amount.** (If this form is for a child under age 14, see page 6 of the instructions.)

IF your filing status is . . .	AND line 21 is not over . . .	THEN enter on line 22 . . .
Single or head of household	$112,500	$33,750
Married filing jointly or qualifying widow(er) .	150,000	45,000
Married filing separately	75,000	22,500

22

If line 21 is **over** the amount shown above for your filing status, see page 6 of the instructions.

23	Subtract line 22 from line 21. If zero or less, enter -0- here and on lines 26 and 28 . . . . . ▶	**23**
24	If you completed Schedule D (Form 1040), and had an amount on line 25 or line 27 (as refigured for the AMT, if necessary), go to Part IV of Form 6251 to figure line 24. **All others:** If line 23 is $175,000 or less ($87,500 or less if married filing separately), multiply line 23 by 26% (.26). Otherwise, multiply line 23 by 28% (.28) and subtract $3,500 ($1,750 if married filing separately) from the result . . . . . ▶	**24**
25	Alternative minimum tax foreign tax credit. See page 7 of the instructions	**25**
26	Tentative minimum tax. Subtract line 25 from line 24 . . . . ▶	**26**
27	Enter your tax from Form 1040, line 39 (minus any tax from Form 4972 and any foreign tax credit from Form 1040, line 43)	**27**
28	**Alternative Minimum Tax.** (If this form is for a child under age 14, see page 7 of the instructions.) Subtract line 27 from line 26. If zero or less, enter -0-. Enter here and on Form 1040, line 48 . . ▶	**28**

For Paperwork Reduction Act Notice, see separate instructions.   Cat. No. 13600G   Form **6251** (1997)

Part IV   **Line 24 Computation Using Maximum Capital Gains Rates**

29	Enter the amount from line 23	**29**	
30	Enter the amount from Schedule D (Form 1040), line 27 (as refigured for the AMT, if necessary)	**30**	
31	Enter the amount from Schedule D (Form 1040), line 25 (as refigured for the AMT, if necessary)	**31**	
32	Add lines 30 and 31 .	**32**	
33	Enter the amount from Schedule D (Form 1040), line 22 (as refigured for the AMT, if necessary)	**33**	
34	Enter the **smaller** of line 32 or line 33	**34**	
35	Subtract line 34 from line 29. If zero or less, enter -0-	**35**	
36	If line 35 is $175,000 or less ($87,500 or less if married filing separately), multiply line 35 by 26% (.26). Otherwise, multiply line 35 by 28% (.28) and subtract $3,500 ($1,750 if married filing separately) from the result . . . . ▶	**36**	
37	Enter the amount from Schedule D (Form 1040), line 36 (as figured for the regular tax)	**37**	
38	Enter the **smallest** of line 29, line 30, or line 37	**38**	
39	Multiply line 38 by 10% (.10) . . . . ▶	**39**	
40	Enter the **smaller** of line 29 or line 30	**40**	
41	Enter the amount from line 38	**41**	
42	Subtract line 41 from line 40. If zero or less, enter -0-	**42**	
43	Multiply line 42 by 20% (.20) . . . . ▶	**43**	
44	Enter the amount from line 29	**44**	
45	Add lines 35, 38, and 42	**45**	
46	Subtract line 45 from line 44	**46**	
47	Multiply line 46 by 25% (.25) . . . . ▶	**47**	
48	Add lines 36, 39, 43, and 47	**48**	
49	If line 29 is $175,000 or less ($87,500 or less if married filing separately), multiply line 29 by 26% (.26). Otherwise, multiply line 29 by 28% (.28) and subtract $3,500 ($1,750 if married filing separately) from the result	**49**	
50	Enter the **smaller** of line 48 or line 49 here and on line 24 . . . . ▶	**50**	

Form **8283**
(Rev. October 1995)

Department of the Treasury
Internal Revenue Service

Noncash Charitable Contributions

▶ Attach to your tax return if you claimed a total deduction
of over $500 for all contributed property.

▶ See separate instructions.

OMB No. 1545-0908

Attachment
Sequence No. **55**

Name(s) shown on your income tax return | Identifying number

Note: *Figure the amount of your contribution deduction before completing this form. See your tax return instructions.*

Section A—List in this section **only** items (or groups of similar items) for which you claimed a deduction of $5,000 or less. Also, list certain publicly traded securities even if the deduction is over $5,000 (see instructions).

Part I   **Information on Donated Property**—If you need more space, attach a statement.

1	(a) Name and address of the donee organization	(b) Description of donated property
A		
B		
C		
D		
E		

Note: *If the amount you claimed as a deduction for an item is $500 or less, you do not have to complete columns (d), (e), and (f).*

	(c) Date of the contribution	(d) Date acquired by donor (mo., yr.)	(e) How acquired by donor	(f) Donor's cost or adjusted basis	(g) Fair market value	(h) Method used to determine the fair market value
A						
B						
C						
D						
E						

Part II   **Other Information**—Complete line 2 if you gave less than an entire interest in property listed in Part I. Complete line 3 if restrictions were attached to a contribution listed in Part I.

2   If, during the year, you contributed less than the entire interest in the property, complete lines a – e.

  a   Enter the letter from Part I that identifies the property ▶ _____ . If Part II applies to more than one property, attach a separate statement.

  b   Total amount claimed as a deduction for the property listed in Part I: **(1)** For this tax year ▶ _____

      (2) For any prior tax years ▶ _____ .

  c   Name and address of each organization to which any such contribution was made in a prior year (complete only if different than the donee organization above):

Name of charitable organization (donee)

Address (number, street, and room or suite no.)

City or town, state, and ZIP code

  d   For tangible property, enter the place where the property is located or kept ▶ _____

  e   Name of any person, other than the donee organization, having actual possession of the property ▶ _____

3   If conditions were attached to any contribution listed in Part I, answer questions a – c and attach the required statement (see instructions).

		Yes	No
a	Is there a restriction, either temporary or permanent, on the donee's right to use or dispose of the donated property?		
b	Did you give to anyone (other than the donee organization or another organization participating with the donee organization in cooperative fundraising) the right to the income from the donated property or to the possession of the property, including the right to vote donated securities, to acquire the property by purchase or otherwise, or to designate the person having such income, possession, or right to acquire?		
c	Is there a restriction limiting the donated property for a particular use?		

For Paperwork Reduction Act Notice, see separate instructions.   Cat. No. 62299J   Form **8283** (Rev. 10-95)

Form 8283 (Rev. 10-95)   Page **2**

Name(s) shown on your income tax return	Identifying number

Section B—Appraisal Summary—List in this section only items (or groups of similar items) for which you claimed a deduction of more than $5,000 per item or group. **Exception.** Report contributions of certain publicly traded securities only in Section A.

If you donated art, you may have to attach the complete appraisal. See the **Note** in Part I below.

Part I   **Information on Donated Property**—To be completed by the taxpayer and/or appraiser.

4   Check type of property:

☐ Art* (contribution of $20,000 or more)   ☐ Real Estate   ☐ Gems/Jewelry   ☐ Stamp Collections

☐ Art* (contribution of less than $20,000)   ☐ Coin Collections   ☐ Books   ☐ Other

*Art includes paintings, sculptures, watercolors, prints, drawings, ceramics, antique furniture, decorative arts, textiles, carpets, silver, rare manuscripts, historical memorabilia, and other similar objects.

Note: *If your total art contribution deduction was $20,000 or more, you must attach a complete copy of the signed appraisal. See instructions.*

5	(a) Description of donated property (if you need more space, attach a separate statement)	(b) If tangible property was donated, give a brief summary of the overall physical condition at the time of the gift	(c) Appraised fair market value
A			
B			
C			
D			

	(d) Date acquired by donor (mo., yr.)	(e) How acquired by donor	(f) Donor's cost or adjusted basis	(g) For bargain sales, enter amount received	See instructions	
					(h) Amount claimed as a deduction	(i) Average trading price of securities
A						
B						
C						
D						

Part II   **Taxpayer (Donor) Statement**—List each item included in Part I above that is separately identified in the appraisal as having a value of $500 or less. See instructions.

I declare that the following item(s) included in Part I above has to the best of my knowledge and belief an appraised value of not more than $500 (per item). Enter identifying letter from Part I and describe the specific item. See instructions. ▶ _____

Signature of taxpayer (donor) ▶ _____   Date ▶ _____

Part III   **Declaration of Appraiser**

I declare that I am not the donor, the donee, a party to the transaction in which the donor acquired the property, employed by, or related to any of the foregoing persons, or married to any person who is related to any of the foregoing persons. And, if regularly used by the donor, donee, or party to the transaction, I performed the majority of my appraisals during my tax year for other persons.

Also, I declare that I hold myself out to the public as an appraiser or perform appraisals on a regular basis; and that because of my qualifications as described in the appraisal, I am qualified to make appraisals of the type of property being valued. I certify that the appraisal fees were not based on a percentage of the appraised property value. Furthermore, I understand that a false or fraudulent overstatement of the property value as described in the qualified appraisal or this appraisal summary may subject me to the penalty under section 6701(a) (aiding and abetting the understatement of tax liability). I affirm that I have not been barred from presenting evidence or testimony by the Director of Practice.

Sign Here

Signature ▶	Title ▶	Date of appraisal ▶

Business address (including room or suite no.)	Identifying number

City or town, state, and ZIP code

Part IV   **Donee Acknowledgment**—To be completed by the charitable organization.

This charitable organization acknowledges that it is a qualified organization under section 170(c) and that it received the donated property as described in Section B, Part I, above on ▶ _____

(Date)

Furthermore, this organization affirms that in the event it sells, exchanges, or otherwise disposes of the property described in Section B, Part I (or any portion thereof) within 2 years after the date of receipt, it will file **Form 8282,** Donee Information Return, with the IRS and give the donor a copy of that form. This acknowledgment does not represent agreement with the claimed fair market value.

Name of charitable organization (donee)	Employer identification number
Address (number, street, and room or suite no.)	City or town, state, and ZIP code
Authorized signature	Title	Date

✹ *Printed on recycled paper*

Form **8332**

(Rev. June 1996)

Department of the Treasury
Internal Revenue Service

Release of Claim to Exemption
for Child of Divorced or Separated Parents

▶ **ATTACH** to noncustodial parent's return **EACH YEAR** exemption claimed.

OMB No. 1545-0915

Attachment
Sequence No. **51**

Name(s) of parent claiming exemption

Social security number

| **Part I** | **Release of Claim to Exemption for Current Year** |

I agree not to claim an exemption for_____
Name(s) of child (or children)

for the tax year 19_____ .

Signature of parent releasing claim to exemption   Social security number   Date

If you choose not to claim an exemption for this child (or children) for future tax years, complete Part II.

| **Part II** | **Release of Claim to Exemption for Future Years** (If completed, see **Noncustodial Parent** below.) |

I agree not to claim an exemption for_____
Name(s) of child (or children)

for the tax year(s)_____ .
(Specify. See instructions.)

Signature of parent releasing claim to exemption   Social security number   Date

General Instructions

Paperwork Reduction Act Notice.—We ask for the information on this form to carry out the Internal Revenue laws of the United States. You are required to give us the information. We need it to ensure that you are complying with these laws and to allow us to figure and collect the right amount of tax.

You are not required to provide the information requested on a form that is subject to the Paperwork Reduction Act unless the form displays a valid OMB control number. Books or records relating to a form or its instructions must be retained as long as their contents may become material in the administration of any Internal Revenue law. Generally, tax returns and return information are confidential, as required by Internal Revenue Code section 6103.

The time needed to complete and file this form will vary depending on individual circumstances. The estimated average time is: **Recordkeeping,** 7 min.; **Learning about the law or the form,** 5 min.; **Preparing the form,** 7 min.; and **Copying, assembling, and sending the form to the IRS,** 14 min.

If you have comments concerning the accuracy of these time estimates or suggestions for making this form simpler, we would be happy to hear from you. See the instructions for the tax return with which this form is filed.

Purpose of Form.—If you are a **custodial parent,** you may use this form to release your claim to your child's exemption. To do so, complete this form and give it to the **noncustodial parent** who will claim the child's exemption. Then, the noncustodial parent must attach this form or a similar statement to his or her tax return EACH YEAR the exemption is claimed.

You are the **custodial parent** if you had custody of the child for most of the year. You are the **noncustodial parent** if you had custody for a shorter period of time or did not have custody at all.

Instead of using this form, you (the custodial parent) may use a similar statement as long as it contains the same information required by this form.

Children of Divorced or Separated Parents.—Special rules apply to determine if the support test is met for children of parents who are divorced or legally separated under a decree of divorce or separate maintenance or separated under a written separation agreement. The rules also apply to children of parents who did not live together at any time during the last 6 months of the year, even if they do not have a separation agreement.

The general rule is that the custodial parent is treated as having provided over half of the child's support if:

1. The child received over half of his or her total support for the year from both of the parents, **AND**

2. The child was in the custody of one or both of his or her parents for more than half of the year.

Note: *Public assistance payments, such as Aid to Families with Dependent Children, are not support provided by the parents.*

If both **1** and **2** above apply, and the other four dependency tests in your tax return instruction booklet are also met, the custodial parent can claim the child's exemption.

Exception. The general rule does not apply if **any** of the following apply:

● The custodial parent agrees not to claim the child's exemption by signing this form or similar statement. The noncustodial parent **must** attach this form or similar statement to

his or her tax return for the tax year. See **Custodial Parent** later.

● The child is treated as having received over half of his or her total support from a person under a multiple support agreement (**Form 2120,** Multiple Support Declaration).

● A pre-1985 divorce decree or written separation agreement states that the noncustodial parent can claim the child as a dependent. But the noncustodial parent must provide at least $600 for the child's support during the year. This rule does not apply if the decree or agreement was changed after 1984 to say that the noncustodial parent cannot claim the child as a dependent.

Additional Information.—For more details, get **Pub. 504,** Divorced or Separated Individuals.

Specific Instructions

Custodial Parent.—You may agree to release your claim to the child's exemption for the current tax year or for future years, or both.

● Complete **Part I** if you agree to release your claim to the child's exemption for the current tax year.

● Complete **Part II** if you agree to release your claim to the child's exemption for any or all future years. If you do, write the specific future year(s) or "all future years" in the space provided in Part II.

Noncustodial Parent.—Attach Form 8332 or similar statement to your tax return for the tax year in which you claim the child's exemption. You may claim the exemption **only** if the other four dependency tests in your tax return instruction booklet are met.

Note: *If the custodial parent completed Part II, you **must** attach a copy of this form to your tax return for each future year in which you claim the exemption.*

Cat. No. 13910F

Form **8332** (Rev. 6-96)

Form **8582**

Department of the Treasury
Internal Revenue Service   (99)

Passive Activity Loss Limitations

▶ See separate instructions.
▶ Attach to Form 1040 or Form 1041.

OMB No. 1545-1008

1997

Attachment
Sequence No. **88**

Name(s) shown on return

Identifying number

Part I   **1997 Passive Activity Loss**

Caution: *See the instructions for Worksheets 1 and 2 on page 7 before completing Part I.*

Rental Real Estate Activities With Active Participation (For the definition of active participation see **Active Participation in a Rental Real Estate Activity** on page 3 of the instructions.)

1a Activities with net income (enter the amount from Worksheet 1, column (a)).	**1a**	
b Activities with net loss (enter the amount from Worksheet 1, column (b)).	**1b** ( )	
c Prior years unallowed losses (enter the amount from Worksheet 1, column (c)).	**1c** ( )	
d Combine lines 1a, 1b, and 1c	**1d**	

All Other Passive Activities

2a Activities with net income (enter the amount from Worksheet 2, column (a)).	**2a**	
b Activities with net loss (enter the amount from Worksheet 2, column (b)).	**2b** ( )	
c Prior years unallowed losses (enter the amount from Worksheet 2, column (c)).	**2c** ( )	
d Combine lines 2a, 2b, and 2c	**2d**	

3 Combine lines 1d and 2d. If the result is net income or zero, all losses are allowed, including any prior year unallowed losses entered on line 1c or 2c. **Do not** complete Form 8582. Take the losses to the form or schedule you normally report them on.
If this line and line 1d are losses, go to line 4. Otherwise, enter -0- on line 9 and go to line 10 .   **3**

Part II   **Special Allowance for Rental Real Estate With Active Participation**

Note: *Enter all numbers in Part II as positive amounts. See page 7 of the instructions for examples.*

4 Enter the **smaller** of the loss on line 1d or the loss on line 3   **4**

5 Enter $150,000. If married filing separately, see page 7 of the instructions   **5**

6 Enter modified adjusted gross income, but not less than zero (see page 7 of the instructions)   **6**

Note: *If line 6 is equal to or greater than line 5, skip lines 7 and 8, enter -0- on line 9, and then go to line 10. Otherwise, go to line 7.*

7 Subtract line 6 from line 5   **7**

8 Multiply line 7 by 50% (.5). **Do not** enter more than $25,000. If married filing separately, see page 9 of the instructions   **8**

9 Enter the **smaller** of line 4 or line 8   **9**

Part III   **Total Losses Allowed**

10 Add the income, if any, on lines 1a and 2a and enter the total   **10**

11 **Total losses allowed from all passive activities for 1997.** Add lines 9 and 10. See page 9 of the instructions to find out how to report the losses on your tax return   **11**

For Paperwork Reduction Act Notice, see separate instructions.   Cat. No. 63704F   Form **8582** (1997)

Caution: *The worksheets are not required to be filed with your tax return and may be detached before filing Form 8582. Keep a copy of the worksheets for your records.*

Worksheet 1—For Form 8582, Lines 1a, 1b, and 1c (See page 6 of the instructions.)

Name of activity	Current year		Prior years	Overall gain or loss	
	(a) Net income (line 1a)	(b) Net loss (line 1b)	(c) Unallowed loss (line 1c)	(d) Gain	(e) Loss
Total. Enter on Form 8582, lines 1a, 1b, and 1c. . . . . ▶					

Worksheet 2—For Form 8582, Lines 2a, 2b, and 2c (See page 7 of the instructions.)

Name of activity	Current year		Prior years	Overall gain or loss	
	(a) Net income (line 2a)	(b) Net loss (line 2b)	(c) Unallowed loss (line 2c)	(d) Gain	(e) Loss
Total. Enter on Form 8582, lines 2a, 2b, and 2c. . . . . ▶					

Worksheet 3—Use this worksheet if an amount is shown on Form 8582, line 9 (See page 8 of the instructions.)

Name of activity	Form or schedule to be reported on	(a) Loss	(b) Ratio	(c) Special allowance	(d) Subtract column (c) from column (a)
Total . . . . ▶			1.00		

Worksheet 4—Allocation of Unallowed Losses (See page 8 of the instructions.)

Name of activity	Form or schedule to be reported on	(a) Loss	(b) Ratio	(c) Unallowed loss
Total . . . . ▶			1.00	

Worksheet 5—Allowed Losses (See page 8 of the instructions.)

Name of activity	Form or schedule to be reported on	(a) Loss	(b) Unallowed loss	(c) Allowed loss
Total . . . . ▶				

Worksheet 6—Activities With Losses Reported on Two or More Different Forms or Schedules (See page 8 of the instructions.)

Name of Activity:	(a)	(b)	(c) Ratio	(d) Unallowed loss	(e) Allowed loss
Form or Schedule To Be Reported on:					
1a Net loss plus prior year unallowed loss from form or schedule . ▶					
b Net income from form or schedule . . . . ▶					
c Subtract line 1b from line 1a. If zero or less, enter -0- ▶					
Form or Schedule To Be Reported on:					
1a Net loss plus prior year unallowed loss from form or schedule . ▶					
b Net income from form or schedule . . . . ▶					
c Subtract line 1b from line 1a. If zero or less, enter -0- ▶					
Form or Schedule To Be Reported on:					
1a Net loss plus prior year unallowed loss from form or schedule . ▶					
b Net income from form or schedule . . . . ▶					
c Subtract line 1b from line 1a. If zero or less, enter -0- ▶					
Total . . . . ▶			1.00		

Form **8615**	**Tax for Children Under Age 14** **Who Have Investment Income of More Than $1,300**	OMB No. 1545-0998 19**97**
Department of the Treasury Internal Revenue Service (99)	▶ **Attach ONLY to the child's Form 1040, Form 1040A, or Form 1040NR.**	Attachment Sequence No. **33**

Child's name shown on return	Child's social security number

A Parent's name (first, initial, and last). **Caution:** *See instructions on back before completing.* | **B** Parent's social security number

C Parent's filing status (check one):

☐ Single   ☐ Married filing jointly   ☐ Married filing separately   ☐ Head of household   ☐ Qualifying widow(er)

Part I Child's Net Investment Income

1	Enter the child's investment income, such as taxable interest and dividends. See instructions. If this amount is $1,300 or less, **stop;** do not file this form	**1**
2	If the child **did not** itemize deductions on Schedule A (Form 1040 or Form 1040NR), enter $1,300. If the child **did** itemize deductions, see instructions	**2**
3	Subtract line 2 from line 1. If the result is zero or less, **stop;** do not complete the rest of this form but **do** attach it to the child's return	**3**
4	Enter the child's **taxable** income from Form 1040, line 38; Form 1040A, line 22; or Form 1040NR, line 37 . . . . ▶	**4**
5	Enter the **smaller** of line 3 or line 4 . . . . ▶	**5**

Part II Tentative Tax Based on the Tax Rate of the Parent Listed on Line A

6	Enter the parent's **taxable** income from Form 1040, line 38; Form 1040A, line 22; Form 1040EZ, line 6; TeleFile Tax Record, line J; Form 1040NR, line 37; or Form 1040NR-EZ, line 13. If the parent transferred property to a trust, see instructions	**6**
7	Enter the total net investment income, if any, from Forms 8615, line 5, of **all other** children of the parent identified above. **Do not** include the amount from line 5 above	**7**
8	Add lines 5, 6, and 7	**8**
9	Enter the tax on line 8 based on the **parent's** filing status. See instructions. If **Schedule D** (Form 1040) is used to figure the tax, check here . . . . ▶ ☐	**9**
10	Enter the parent's tax from Form 1040, line 39; Form 1040A, line 23; Form 1040EZ, line 10; TeleFile Tax Record, line J; Form 1040NR, line 38; or Form 1040NR-EZ, line 14. If **Schedule D** (Form 1040) was used to figure the tax, check here . . . . ▶ ☐	**10**
11	Subtract line 10 from line 9 and enter the result. If line 7 is blank, enter on line 13 the amount from line 11 and go to **Part III**	**11**
12a	Add lines 5 and 7 . . . . **12a**	
b	Divide line 5 by line 12a. Enter the result as a decimal (rounded to three places)	**12b** × .
13	Multiply line 11 by line 12b . . . . ▶	**13**

Part III Child's Tax—If lines 4 and 5 above are the same, enter -0- on line 15 and go to line 16.

14	Subtract line 5 from line 4 . . . . **14**	
15	Enter the tax on line 14 based on the **child's** filing status. See instructions. If **Schedule D** (Form 1040) is used to figure the tax, check here . . . . ▶ ☐	**15**
16	Add lines 13 and 15	**16**
17	Enter the tax on line 4 based on the **child's** filing status. See instructions. If **Schedule D** (Form 1040) is used to figure the tax, check here . . . . ▶ ☐	**17**
18	Enter the **larger** of line 16 or line 17 here and on Form 1040, line 39; Form 1040A, line 23; or Form 1040NR, line 38 . . . . ▶	**18**

General Instructions

Section references are to the Internal Revenue Code.

Purpose of form. For children under age 14, investment income over $1,300 is taxed at the parent's rate if the parent's rate is higher than the child's rate. If the child's investment income is more than $1,300, use this form to figure the child's tax.

Investment income. As used on this form, "investment income" includes all taxable income other than earned income as

defined on page 2. It includes taxable interest, dividends, capital gains, rents, royalties, etc. It also includes pension and annuity income and income (other than earned income) received as the beneficiary of a trust.

Who must file. Generally, Form 8615 must be filed for any child who was under age 14 on January 1, 1998, had more than $1,300 of investment income, and is required to file a tax return. But if neither parent was alive on December 31, 1997, do not use Form 8615. Instead, figure the child's tax in the normal manner.

Note: *The parent may be able to elect to report the child's interest and dividends on his or her return. If the parent makes this election, the child will not have to file a return or Form 8615. For more details, see* **Form 8814,** *Parents' Election To Report Child's Interest and Dividends.*

Additional information. For more details, see **Pub. 929,** Tax Rules for Children and Dependents.

Incomplete information for parent. If the parent's taxable income or filing status or the net investment income of the parent's other children is not known by the due

---

For Paperwork Reduction Act Notice, see back of form.   Cat. No. 64113U   Form **8615** (1997)

date of the child's return, reasonable estimates may be used. Write "Estimated" on the appropriate line(s) of Form 8615. For more details, see Pub. 929.

Amended return. If after the child's return is filed the parent's taxable income changes or the net investment income of any of the parent's other children changes, the child's tax must be refigured using the adjusted amounts. If the child's tax changes, file **Form 1040X,** Amended U.S. Individual Income Tax Return, to correct the child's tax.

Alternative Minimum Tax. A child whose tax is figured on Form 8615 may owe the alternative minimum tax. For details, see **Form 6251,** Alternative Minimum Tax— Individuals, and its instructions.

Line Instructions

Lines A and B. If the child's parents were married to each other and filed a joint return, enter the name and social security number (SSN) of the parent who is listed first on the joint return.

If the parents were married but filed separate returns, enter the name and SSN of the parent who had the **higher** taxable income. If you do not know which parent had the higher taxable income, see Pub. 929.

If the parents were unmarried, treated as unmarried for Federal income tax purposes, or separated either by a divorce or separate maintenance decree, enter the name and SSN of the parent who had custody of the child for most of the year (the custodial parent).

Exception. If the custodial parent remarried and filed a joint return with his or her new spouse, enter the name and SSN of the person listed first on the joint return, even if that person is not the child's parent. If the custodial parent and his or her new spouse filed separate returns, enter the name and SSN of the person with the **higher** taxable income, even if that person is not the child's parent.

Note: *If the parents were unmarried but lived together during the year with the child, enter the name and SSN of the parent who had the **higher** taxable income.*

Line 1. If the child had no earned income (defined later), enter the child's adjusted gross income from Form 1040, line 33; Form 1040A, line 17; or Form 1040NR, line 33.

Child's Investment Income Worksheet—Line 1 (keep a copy for your records)

1. Enter the amount from the child's Form 1040, line 22; Form 1040A, line 14; or Form 1040NR, line 23, whichever applies . . . . .   **1.** _____

2. Enter the child's **earned income** (defined on this page) plus any deduction the child claims on Form 1040, line 29, or Form 1040NR, line 29, whichever applies . . . .   **2.** _____

3. Subtract line 2 from line 1. Enter the result here and on Form 8615, line 1 . . . .   **3.** _____

If the child had earned income, use the worksheet on this page to figure the amount to enter on line 1. But if the child files **Form 2555** or **2555-EZ** (relating to foreign earned income), has a net loss from self-employment, or claims a net operating loss deduction, you **must** use the worksheet in Pub. 929 instead.

Earned income includes wages, tips, and other payments received for personal services performed. Generally, it is the total of the amounts reported on Form 1040, lines 7, 12, and 18; Form 1040A, line 7; or Form 1040NR, lines 8, 13, and 19.

Line 2. If the child itemized deductions, enter the **greater** of:

- $1,300, **or**

- $650 plus the portion of the amount on **Schedule A** (Form 1040), line 28, or **Schedule A** (Form 1040NR), line 17, that is directly connected with the production of the investment income on Form 8615, line 1.

Line 6. If the parent's taxable income is less than zero, enter zero on line 6. If the parent filed a joint return, enter the taxable income shown on that return even if the parent's spouse is not the child's parent. If the parent transferred property to a trust that sold or exchanged the property in 1997 before August 6, 1997, include any gain that was taxed to the trust under section 644 in the amount entered on line 6. Enter "Sec. 644" and the amount on the dotted line next to line 6. Also, see the instructions for line 10.

Line 9. Figure the tax using the Tax Table, Tax Rate Schedules, or **Schedule D** (Form 1040), whichever applies. If any net capital gain is included on line 5, 6, or 7, Part IV of Schedule D must be used to figure the tax on the amount on line 8. See Pub. 929 for details on how to figure the net capital gain included on line 8.

Line 10. If the parent filed a joint return, enter the tax shown on that return even if the parent's spouse is not the child's parent. If the parent filed Form 8814, enter "Form 8814" and the total tax from line 8 of Form(s) 8814 on the dotted line next to line 10 of Form 8615.

If line 6 includes any gain taxed to a trust under section 644, add the tax imposed under section 644(a)(2)(A) to the tax shown on the parent's return and enter the total on line 10. Also, enter "Sec. 644" on the dotted line next to line 10.

Line 15. Figure the tax using the Tax Table, Tax Rate Schedule X, or Schedule D, whichever applies. If line 14 includes any net capital gain, use Schedule D to figure the tax. See Pub. 929 for details on how to figure the net capital gain included on line 14.

Line 17. Figure the tax as if these rules did not apply. For example, if the child has a net capital gain, use Schedule D to figure his or her tax.

Paperwork Reduction Act Notice. We ask for the information on this form to carry out the Internal Revenue laws of the United States. You are required to give us the information. We need it to ensure that you are complying with these laws and to allow us to figure and collect the right amount of tax.

You are not required to provide the information requested on a form that is subject to the Paperwork Reduction Act unless the form displays a valid OMB control number. Books or records relating to a form or its instructions must be retained as long as their contents may become material in the administration of any Internal Revenue law. Generally, tax returns and return information are confidential, as required by section 6103.

The time needed to complete and file this form will vary depending on individual circumstances. The estimated average time is: **Recordkeeping,** 13 min.; **Learning about the law or the form,** 13 min.; **Preparing the form,** 45 min.; and **Copying, assembling, and sending the form to the IRS,** 17 min.

If you have comments concerning the accuracy of these time estimates or suggestions for making this form simpler, we would be happy to hear from you. See the instructions for the tax return with which this form is filed.

Form **8829**	**Expenses for Business Use of Your Home**	OMB No. 1545-1266
Department of the Treasury Internal Revenue Service (99)	▶ File only with Schedule C (Form 1040). Use a separate Form 8829 for each home you used for business during the year. ▶ See separate instructions.	**19**97 Attachment Sequence No. **66**

Name(s) of proprietor(s) | Your social security number

Part I — Part of Your Home Used for Business

1	Area used regularly and exclusively for business, regularly for day care, or for storage of inventory or product samples. See instructions	**1**	
2	Total area of home	**2**	
3	Divide line 1 by line 2. Enter the result as a percentage	**3**	%

- For day-care facilities not used exclusively for business, also complete lines 4–6.
- All others, skip lines 4–6 and enter the amount from line 3 on line 7.

4	Multiply days used for day care during year by hours used per day	**4**	hr.
5	Total hours available for use during the year (365 days × 24 hours). See instructions	**5**	8,760 hr.
6	Divide line 4 by line 5. Enter the result as a decimal amount	**6**	.
7	Business percentage. For day-care facilities not used exclusively for business, multiply line 6 by line 3 (enter the result as a percentage). All others, enter the amount from line 3 ▶	**7**	%

Part II — Figure Your Allowable Deduction

8	Enter the amount from Schedule C, line 29, **plus** any net gain or (loss) derived from the business use of your home and shown on Schedule D or Form 4797. If more than one place of business, see instructions	**8**		

See instructions for columns (a) and (b) before completing lines 9–20.

			(a) Direct expenses	(b) Indirect expenses
9	Casualty losses. See instructions	**9**		
10	Deductible mortgage interest. See instructions	**10**		
11	Real estate taxes. See instructions	**11**		
12	Add lines 9, 10, and 11	**12**		
13	Multiply line 12, column (b) by line 7	**13**		
14	Add line 12, column (a) and line 13	**14**		
15	Subtract line 14 from line 8. If zero or less, enter -0-	**15**		
16	Excess mortgage interest. See instructions	**16**		
17	Insurance	**17**		
18	Repairs and maintenance	**18**		
19	Utilities	**19**		
20	Other expenses. See instructions	**20**		
21	Add lines 16 through 20	**21**		
22	Multiply line 21, column (b) by line 7	**22**		
23	Carryover of operating expenses from 1996 Form 8829, line 41	**23**		
24	Add line 21 in column (a), line 22, and line 23	**24**		
25	Allowable operating expenses. Enter the **smaller** of line 15 or line 24	**25**		
26	Limit on excess casualty losses and depreciation. Subtract line 25 from line 15	**26**		
27	Excess casualty losses. See instructions	**27**		
28	Depreciation of your home from Part III below	**28**		
29	Carryover of excess casualty losses and depreciation from 1996 Form 8829, line 42	**29**		
30	Add lines 27 through 29	**30**		
31	Allowable excess casualty losses and depreciation. Enter the **smaller** of line 26 or line 30	**31**		
32	Add lines 14, 25, and 31	**32**		
33	Casualty loss portion, if any, from lines 14 and 31. Carry amount to **Form 4684**, Section B	**33**		
34	Allowable expenses for business use of your home. Subtract line 33 from line 32. Enter here and on Schedule C, line 30. If your home was used for more than one business, see instructions ▶	**34**		

Part III — Depreciation of Your Home

35	Enter the **smaller** of your home's adjusted basis or its fair market value. See instructions	**35**		
36	Value of land included on line 35	**36**		
37	Basis of building. Subtract line 36 from line 35	**37**		
38	Business basis of building. Multiply line 37 by line 7	**38**		
39	Depreciation percentage. See instructions	**39**	%
40	Depreciation allowable. Multiply line 38 by line 39. Enter here and on line 28 above. See instructions	**40**		

Part IV — Carryover of Unallowed Expenses to 1998

41	Operating expenses. Subtract line 25 from line 24. If less than zero, enter -0-	**41**		
42	Excess casualty losses and depreciation. Subtract line 31 from line 30. If less than zero, enter -0-	**42**		

For Paperwork Reduction Act Notice, see page 3 of separate instructions. ✪   Cat. No. 13232M   Form **8829** (1997)

Form **8832**
(December 1996)
Department of the Treasury
Internal Revenue Service

Entity Classification Election

OMB No. 1545-1516

Please Type or Print

Name of entity	Employer identification number (EIN)
Number, street, and room or suite no. If a P.O. box, see instructions.	
City or town, state, and ZIP code. If a foreign address, enter city, province or state, postal code and country.	

1   Type of election (see instructions):

a ☐ Initial classification by a newly-formed entity (or change in current classification of an existing entity to take effect on January 1, 1997)

b ☐ Change in current classification (to take effect later than January 1, 1997)

2   Form of entity (see instructions):

a ☐ A domestic eligible entity electing to be classified as an association taxable as a corporation.

b ☐ A domestic eligible entity electing to be classified as a partnership.

c ☐ A domestic eligible entity with a single owner electing to be disregarded as a separate entity.

d ☐ A foreign eligible entity electing to be classified as an association taxable as a corporation.

e ☐ A foreign eligible entity electing to be classified as a partnership.

f ☐ A foreign eligible entity with a single owner electing to be disregarded as a separate entity.

3   Election is to be effective beginning (month, day, year) (see instructions) . . . . ▶ ___ / ___ / ___

4 Name and title of person whom the IRS may call for more information	5 That person's telephone number

Consent Statement and Signature(s) (see instructions)

Under penalties of perjury, I (we) declare that I (we) consent to the election of the above-named entity to be classified as indicated above, and that I (we) have examined this consent statement, and to the best of my (our) knowledge and belief, it is true, correct, and complete. If I am an officer, manager, or member signing for all members of the entity, I further declare that I am authorized to execute this consent statement on their behalf.

Signature(s)	Date	Title

For Paperwork Reduction Act Notice, see page 2.   Cat. No. 22598R   Form **8832** (12-96)

General Instructions

Section references are to the Internal Revenue Code unless otherwise noted.

Paperwork Reduction Act Notice

We ask for the information on this form to carry out the Internal Revenue laws of the United States. You are required to give us the information. We need it to ensure that you are complying with these laws and to allow us to figure and collect the right amount of tax.

You are not required to provide the information requested on a form that is subject to the Paperwork Reduction Act unless the form displays a valid OMB control number. Books or records relating to a form or its instructions must be retained as long as their contents may become material in the administration of any Internal Revenue law. Generally, tax returns and return information are confidential, as required by section 6103.

The time needed to complete and file this form will vary depending on individual circumstances. The estimated average time is:

Recordkeeping . . .1 hr., 20 min.
Learning about the law or the form . . .1 hr., 41 min.
Preparing and sending the form to the IRS . . . .17 min.

If you have comments concerning the accuracy of these time estimates or suggestions for making this form simpler, we would be happy to hear from you. You can write to the Tax Forms Committee, Western Area Distribution Center, Rancho Cordova, CA 95743-0001. **DO NOT** send the form to this address. Instead, see **Where To File** on page 3.

Purpose of Form

For Federal tax purposes, certain business entities automatically are classified as corporations. See items **1** and **3** through **8** under the definition of corporation on this page. Other business entities may choose how they are classified for Federal tax purposes. Except for a business entity automatically classified as a corporation, a business entity with at least two members can choose to be classified as either an association taxable as a corporation or a partnership, and a business entity with a single member can choose to be classified as either an association taxable as a corporation or disregarded as an entity separate from its owner.

Generally, an eligible entity that does not file this form will be classified under the default rules described below. An eligible entity that chooses not to be classified under the default rules or that wishes to change its current classification must file Form 8832 to elect a classification. The IRS will use the information entered on this form to establish the entity's filing and reporting requirements for Federal tax purposes.

Default Rules

Existing entity default rule.— Certain domestic and foreign entities that are already in existence before January 1, 1997, and have an established Federal tax classification, generally do not need to make an election to continue that classification. However, for an eligible entity with a single owner that claimed to be a partnership under the law in effect before January 1, 1997, that entity will now be disregarded as an entity separate from its owner. If an existing entity decides to change its classification, it may do so subject to the rules in Regulations section 301.7701-3(c)(1)(iv). A foreign eligible entity is treated as being in existence prior to the effective date of this section only if the entity's classification is relevant at any time during the 60 months prior to January 1, 1997.

Domestic default rule.—Unless an election is made on Form 8832, a domestic eligible entity is:

1. A partnership if it has two or more members.

2. Disregarded as an entity separate from its owner if it has a single owner.

Foreign default rule.—Unless an election is made on Form 8832, a foreign eligible entity is:

1. A partnership if it has two or more members and at least one member does not have limited liability.

2. An association if all members have limited liability.

3. Disregarded as an entity separate from its owner if it has a single owner that does not have limited liability.

Definitions

Business entity.—A business entity is any entity recognized for Federal tax purposes that is not properly classified as a trust under Regulations section 301.7701-4 or otherwise subject to special treatment under the Code. See Regulations section 301.7701-2(a).

Corporation.—For Federal tax purposes, a corporation is any of the following:

1. A business entity organized under a Federal or state statute, or under a statute of a federally recognized Indian tribe, if the statute describes or refers to the entity as incorporated or as a corporation, body corporate, or body politic.

2. An association (as determined under Regulations section 301.7701-3).

3. A business entity organized under a state statute, if the statute describes or refers to the entity as a joint-stock company or joint-stock association.

4. An insurance company.

5. A state-chartered business entity conducting banking activities, if any of its deposits are insured under the Federal Deposit Insurance Act, as amended, 12 U.S.C. 1811 et seq., or a similar Federal statute.

6. A business entity wholly owned by a state or any political subdivision thereof.

7. A business entity that is taxable as a corporation under a provision of the Code other than section 7701(a)(3).

8. A foreign business entity listed in Regulations section 301.7701-2(b)(8). However, a foreign business entity listed in those regulations generally will not be treated as a corporation if all of the following apply:

a. The entity was in existence on May 8, 1996.

b. The entity's classification was relevant (as defined below) on May 8, 1996.

c. No person (including the entity) for whom the entity's classification was relevant on May 8, 1996, treats the entity as a corporation for purposes of filing that person's Federal income tax returns, information returns, and withholding documents for the tax year including May 8, 1996.

d. Any change in the entity's claimed classification within the 60 months prior to May 8, 1996, was a result of a change in the organizational documents of the entity, and the entity and all members of the entity recognized the Federal tax consequences of any change in the entity's classification within the 60 months prior to May 8, 1996.

e. The entity had a reasonable basis (within the meaning of section 6662) for treating the entity as other than a corporation on May 8, 1996.

f. Neither the entity nor any member was notified in writing on or before May 8, 1996, that the classification of the entity was under examination (in which case the entity's classification will be determined in the examination).

Binding contract rule.—If a foreign business entity described in Regulations section 301.7701-2(b)(8)(i) is formed after May 8, 1996, under a written binding contract (including an accepted bid to develop a project) in effect on May 8, 1996, and all times thereafter, in which the parties agreed to engage (directly or indirectly) in an active and substantial business operation in the jurisdiction in which the entity is formed, **8** on page 2 is applied by substituting the date of the entity's formation for May 8, 1996.

Eligible entity.—An eligible entity is a business entity that is not included in items **1** or **3** through **8** under the definition of corporation on page 2.

Limited liability.—A member of a foreign eligible entity has limited liability if the member has no personal liability for any debts of or claims against the entity by reason of being a member. This determination is based solely on the statute or law under which the entity is organized (and, if relevant, the entity's organizational documents). A member has personal liability if the creditors of the entity may seek satisfaction of all or any part of the debts or claims against the entity from the member as such. A member has personal liability even if the member makes an agreement under which another person (whether or not a member of the entity) assumes that liability or agrees to indemnify that member for that liability.

Partnership.—A partnership is a business entity that has **at least** two members and is not a corporation as defined on page 2.

Relevant.—A foreign eligible entity's classification is relevant when its classification affects the liability of any person for Federal tax or information purposes. The date the classification of a foreign eligible entity is relevant is the date an event occurs that creates an obligation to file a Federal tax return, information return, or statement for which the classification of the entity must be determined.

Effect of Election

The resulting tax consequences of a change in classification remain the same no matter how a change in entity classification is achieved. For example, if an organization classified as an association elects to be classified as a partnership, the organization and its owners must recognize gain, if any, under the rules applicable to liquidations of corporations.

Who Must File

File this form for an **eligible entity** that is one of the following:

● A domestic entity electing to be classified as an association taxable as a corporation.

● A domestic entity electing to change its current classification (even if it is currently classified under the default rule).

● A foreign entity that has more than one owner, all owners have limited liability, and it elects to be classified as a partnership.

● A foreign entity that has at least one owner without limited liability, and it elects to be classified as an association taxable as a corporation.

● A foreign entity with a single owner having limited liability, and it elects to have the entity disregarded as an entity separate from its owner.

● A foreign entity electing to change its current classification (even if it is currently classified under the default rule).

Do not file this form for an eligible entity that is:

● Tax-exempt under section 501(a), or

● A real estate investment trust (REIT), as defined in section 856.

When To File

See the instructions for line 3.

Where To File

File Form 8832 with the Internal Revenue Service Center, Philadelphia, PA 19255. Also attach a copy of Form 8832 to the entity's Federal income tax or information return for the tax year of the election. If the entity is not required to file a return for that year, a copy of its Form 8832 must be attached to the Federal income tax or information returns of all direct or indirect owners of the entity for the tax year of the owner that includes the date on which the election took effect. Although failure to attach a copy will not invalidate an otherwise valid election, each member of the entity is required to file returns that are consistent with the entity's election. In addition, penalties may be assessed against persons who are required to, but who do not, attach Form 8832 to their returns. Other penalties may apply for filing Federal income tax or information returns inconsistent with the entity's election.

Specific Instructions

Employer Identification Number (EIN)

Show the correct EIN on Form 8832. If the entity does not have an EIN, it generally must apply for one on **Form SS-4,** Application for Employer Identification Number. If the filing of Form 8832 is the only reason the entity is applying for an EIN, check the "Other" box on line 9 of Form SS-4 and write "Form 8832" to the right of that box. If the entity has not received an EIN by the time Form 8832 is due, write "Applied for" in the space for the EIN. **Do not** apply for a new EIN for an existing entity that is changing its classification. If you are electing to disregard an entity as separate from its owner, enter the owner's EIN.

Address

Include the suite, room, or other unit number after the street address. If the Post Office does not deliver mail to the street address and the entity has a P.O. box, show the box number instead of the street address.

Line 1

Check box 1a if the entity is choosing a classification for the first time **and** the entity does not want to be classified under the applicable default classification. **Do not** file this form if the entity wants to be classified under the default rules.

Check box 1b if the entity is changing its current classification to take effect later than January 1, 1997, whether or not the entity's current classification is the default classification. However, once an eligible entity makes an election to change its classification (other than an election made by an existing entity to change its classification as of January 1, 1997), the entity cannot change its classification by election again during the 60 months after the effective date of the election. However, the IRS may permit (by private letter ruling) the entity to change its classification by election within the 60-month period if more than 50% of the ownership interests in the entity as of the effective date of the election are owned by persons that did not own any interests in the entity on the effective date of the prior election.

Line 2

Check the appropriate box if you are changing a current classification (no matter how achieved), or are electing out of a default classification. **Do not** file this form if you fall within a default classification that is the desired classification for the new entity.

Line 3

Generally, the election will take effect on the date you enter on line 3 of this form or on the date filed if no date is entered on line 3. However, an election specifying an entity's classification for Federal tax purposes can take effect no more than 75 days prior to the date the election is filed, nor can it take effect later than 12 months after the date on which the election is filed. If line 3 shows a date more than 75 days prior to the date on which the election is filed, the election will take effect 75 days before the date it is filed. If line 3 shows an effective date more than 12 months from the filing date, the election will take effect 12 months after the date the election was filed.

Regardless of the date filed, an election will in no event take effect before January 1, 1997.

Consent Statement and Signatures

Form 8832 must be signed by:

1. Each member of the electing entity who is an owner at the time the election is filed; or

2. Any officer, manager, or member of the electing entity who is authorized (under local law or the organizational documents) to make the election and who represents to having such authorization under penalties of perjury.

If an election is to be effective for any period prior to the time it is filed, each person who was an owner between the date the election is to be effective and the date the election is filed, and who is not an owner at the time the election is filed, must also sign.

If you need a continuation sheet or use a separate consent statement, attach it to Form 8832. The separate consent statement must contain the same information as shown on Form 8832.

APPENDIX C
Glossary of Tax Terms

The words and phrases in this glossary have been defined to reflect their conventional use in the field of taxation. The definitions may therefore be incomplete for other purposes.

A

Abandoned spouse. The abandoned spouse provision enables a married taxpayer with a dependent child whose spouse did not live in the taxpayer's home during the last six months of the tax year to file as a head of household rather than as married filing separately.

Accelerated cost recovery system (ACRS). A method in which the cost of tangible property is recovered over a prescribed period of time. Enacted by the Economic Recovery Tax Act (ERTA) of 1981 and substantially modified by the Tax Reform Act (TRA) of 1986 (the modified system is referred to as MACRS), the approach disregards salvage value, imposes a period of cost recovery that depends upon the classification of the asset into one of various recovery periods, and prescribes the applicable percentage of cost that can be deducted each year. § 168.

Accelerated death benefits. The amount received from a life insurance policy by the insured who is terminally ill or chronically ill. Any realized gain may be excluded from the gross income of the insured if the policy is surrendered to the insurer or is sold to a licensed viatical settlement provider. § 101(g).

Accelerated depreciation. Various methods of depreciation that yield larger deductions in the earlier years of the life of an asset than the straight-line method. Examples include the double declining-balance and the sum-of-the-years' digits methods of depreciation.

Accountable plan. An accountable plan is a type of expense reimbursement plan that requires an employee to render an adequate accounting to the employer and return any excess reimbursement or allowance. If the expense qualifies, it will be treated as a deduction *for* AGI.

Accounting method. The method under which income and expenses are determined for tax purposes. Important accounting methods include the cash basis and the accrual basis. Special methods are available for the reporting of gain on installment sales, recognition of income on construction projects (the completed contract and percentage of completion methods), and the valuation of inventories (last-in, first-out and first-in, first-out). §§ 446–474. See also *accrual method,*

cash receipts method, completed contract method, and *percentage of completion method.*

Accounting period. The period of time, usually a year, used by a taxpayer for the determination of tax liability. Unless a fiscal year is chosen, taxpayers must determine and pay their income tax liability by using the calendar year (January 1 through December 31) as the period of measurement. An example of a fiscal year is July 1 through June 30. A change in accounting period (e.g., from a calendar year to a fiscal year) generally requires the consent of the IRS. Some new taxpayers, such as a newly formed corporation, are free to select either an initial calendar or a fiscal year without the consent of the IRS. §§ 441–444. See also *annual accounting period concept.*

Accrual basis. See *accrual method.*

Accrual method. A method of accounting that reflects expenses incurred and income earned for any one tax year. In contrast to the cash basis of accounting, expenses do not have to be paid to be deductible, nor does income have to be received to be taxable. Unearned income (e.g., prepaid interest and rent) generally is taxed in the year of receipt regardless of the method of accounting used by the taxpayer. § 446(c)(2). See also *accounting method, cash receipts method,* and *unearned income.*

Accumulated adjustments account (AAA). An account that aggregates an S corporation's post-1982 income, loss, and deductions for the tax year (including nontaxable income and nondeductible losses and expenses). After the year-end income and expense adjustments are made, the account is reduced by distributions made during the tax year.

Accumulated earnings and profits. Net undistributed tax-basis earnings of the corporation aggregated from March 1, 1913, to the end of the prior tax year. Used to determine the amount of dividend income associated with a distribution to shareholders. See *current earnings and profits* and *earnings and profits.* § 316 and Reg. § 1.316–2.

Accumulated earnings credit. A reduction allowed in arriving at accumulated taxable income in determining the accumulated earnings tax. See also *accumulated earnings tax* and *accumulated taxable income.*

Accumulated earnings tax (AET). A special tax imposed on corporations that accumulate (rather than distribute) their earnings beyond the reasonable needs of the business. The accumulated earnings tax and related interest are imposed on accumulated taxable income in addition to the corporate income tax. §§ 531–537.

Accumulated taxable income. The base upon which the accumulated earnings tax is imposed. Generally, it is the taxable income of the corporation as adjusted for certain items (e.g., the Federal income tax, excess charitable contributions, the dividends received deduction) less the dividends paid deduction and the accumulated earnings credit. § 535.

Accumulating trust. See *discretionary trust*.

Accuracy-related penalty. Major civil taxpayer penalties relating to the accuracy of tax return data, including misstatements stemming from taxpayer negligence and improper valuation of income and deductions, are coordinated under this umbrella term. The penalty usually equals 20 percent of the understated tax liability.

Acquiescence. Agreement by the IRS on the results reached in certain judicial decisions; sometimes abbreviated *Acq.* or *A*. See also *nonacquiescence*.

Acquisition. See *corporate acquisition*.

Acquisition indebtedness. Debt incurred in acquiring, constructing, or substantially improving a qualified residence of the taxpayer. The interest on such loans is deductible as *qualified residence interest*. However, interest on such debt is deductible only on the portion of the indebtedness that does not exceed $1,000,000 ($500,000 for married persons filing separate returns). § 163(h)(3). See also *home equity loans*.

ACRS. See *accelerated cost recovery system*.

Ad valorem tax. A tax imposed on the value of property. The most common ad valorem tax is that imposed by states, counties, and cities on real estate. Ad valorem taxes can be imposed on personal property as well. See also *personalty*.

Adjusted basis. The cost or other basis of property reduced by depreciation allowed or allowable and increased by capital improvements. Other special adjustments are provided in § 1016 and the related Regulations. See also *basis*.

Adjusted current earnings (ACE) adjustment. An adjustment in computing corporate alternative minimum taxable income (AMTI), computed at 75 percent of the excess of adjusted current earnings and profits over unadjusted AMTI. ACE computations reflect restrictions on the timing of certain recognition events. Exempt interest, life insurance proceeds, and other receipts that are included in earnings and profits but not in taxable income also increase the ACE adjustment. If unadjusted AMTI exceeds adjusted current earnings and profits, the ACE adjustment is negative. The negative adjustment is limited to the aggregate of the positive adjustments under ACE for prior years, reduced by any previously claimed negative adjustments. See also *alternative minimum tax* and *earnings and profits*.

Adjusted gross estate. The gross estate of a *decedent* reduced by § 2053 expenses (e.g., administration, funeral) and § 2054 losses (e.g., casualty). The determination of the adjusted gross estate is necessary in testing for the extension of time for installment payment of estate taxes under § 6166. See also *gross estate*.

Adjusted gross income (AGI). A tax determination unique to individual taxpayers. Generally, it represents the gross income of an individual, less business expenses and less any appropriate capital loss adjustment. See also *gross income*.

Adjusted ordinary gross income. A determination unique to the *personal holding company tax*. In ascertaining whether a corporation is a personal holding company, personal holding company income divided by adjusted ordinary gross income must equal 60 percent or more. Adjusted ordinary gross income is the corporation's gross income less capital gains, § 1231 gains, and certain expenses. §§ 541 and 543(b)(2). See also *personal holding company income*.

Adjusted sales price. The amount realized from the sale of a residence reduced by the fixing-up expenses is the adjusted sales price. An amount equal to the adjusted sales price must be reinvested in a replacement residence to defer the recognition of the realized gain on the sale of a residence. This term is not relevant for the sale of a principal residence after May 6, 1997. The Taxpayer Relief Act of 1997 (TRA of 1997) repealed § 1034. See also *amount realized, fixing-up expenses*, and *realized gain or loss*.

Adjusted taxable estate. The taxable estate reduced by $60,000. The adjusted taxable estate is utilized in applying § 2011 for determining the limit on the credit for state death taxes paid that will be allowed against the Federal estate tax. See also *taxable estate*.

Administration. The supervision and winding up of an estate. The administration of an estate runs from the date of an individual's death until all assets have been distributed and liabilities paid.

Administrator. A person appointed by the court to administer (manage or take charge of) the assets and liabilities of a decedent (the deceased). See also *executor*.

Adoption expenses credit. The provision is intended to assist taxpayers who incur nonrecurring costs directly associated with the adoption process such as legal costs, social service review costs, and transportation costs. Up to $5,000 ($6,000 for a child with special needs) of costs incurred to adopt an eligible child qualify for the credit. A taxpayer may claim the credit in the year qualifying expenses are paid or incurred if the expenses are paid during or after the year in which the adoption is finalized. For qualifying expenses paid or incurred in a tax year prior to the year the adoption is finalized, the credit must be claimed in the year the adoption is finalized. § 23.

Affiliated group. A parent-subsidiary group of corporations that is eligible to elect to file on a consolidated basis. Eighty percent ownership of the voting power and value of all of the corporations must be achieved on every day of the tax year, and an identifiable parent corporation must exist (i.e., it must own at least 80 percent of another group member without applying attribution rules).

AFTR. Published by Research Institute of America (formerly by Prentice-Hall), *American Federal Tax Reports* contain all of the Federal tax decisions issued by the U.S. District Courts, U.S. Court of Federal Claims, U.S. Courts of Appeals, and the U.S. Supreme Court.

AFTR2d. The second series of the *American Federal Tax Reports*, dealing with 1954 and 1986 Code case law.

AFTR3d. The third series of the *American Federal Tax Reports*.

Aggregate concept. The theory of partnership taxation under which, in certain cases, a partnership is treated as a mere extension of each partner.

Alimony and separate maintenance. Alimony deductions result from the payment of a legal obligation arising from the termination of a marital relationship. Payments designated as alimony generally are included in the gross income of the recipient and are deductible *for AGI* by the payer.

Allocable share of income. Certain entities receive conduit treatment under the Federal income tax law. This means the earned income or loss is not taxed to the entity, but is allocated to the owners or beneficiaries, regardless of the magnitude or timing of corresponding distributions. The portion of the entity's income that is taxed to the owner or beneficiary is the allocable share of the entity's income or loss for the period. The allocations are determined by (1) the partnership agreement for partners, (2) a weighted-average stock ownership computation for shareholders of an S corporation, and (3) the controlling will or trust instrument for the beneficiaries of an estate or trust.

Allocate. The assignment of income for various tax purposes. The income and expense items of an estate or trust are allocated between income and corpus components. Specific items of income, expense, gain, loss, and credit can be allocated to specific partners or shareholders in an S corporation, if a substantial economic nontax purpose for the allocation is established. See also *substantial economic effect*.

Alternate valuation date. Property passing from a decedent by death may be valued for estate tax purposes as of the date of death or the alternate valuation date. The alternate valuation date is six months from the date of death or the date the property is disposed of by the estate, whichever comes first. To use the alternate valuation date, the *executor* or *administrator* of the estate must make an affirmative election. Election of the alternate valuation date is not available unless it decreases the amount of the gross estate *and* reduces the estate tax liability.

Alternative minimum tax (AMT). The AMT is a fixed percentage of alternative minimum taxable income (AMTI). AMTI generally starts with the taxpayer's adjusted gross income (for individuals) or taxable income (for other taxpayers). To this amount, the taxpayer (1) adds designated preference items (e.g., tax-exempt interest income on private activity bonds), (2) makes other specified adjustments (e.g., to reflect a longer, straight-line cost recovery deduction), (3) subtracts certain AMT itemized deductions for individuals (e.g., interest incurred on housing but not taxes paid), and (4) subtracts an exemption amount (e.g., $40,000 on an individual joint return). The taxpayer must pay the greater of the resulting AMT (reduced by only the foreign tax credit) or the regular income tax (reduced by all allowable tax credits).

Alternative minimum tax credit. The AMT can result from timing differences that give rise to positive adjustments in calculating the AMT base. To provide equity for the taxpayer when these timing differences reverse, the regular tax liability may be reduced by a tax credit for prior year's minimum tax liability attributable to timing differences. § 53.

Alternative minimum taxable income (AMTI). A major component of the base for computing a taxpayer's *alternative minimum tax* (AMT). Generally, it is the taxable income for the year, modified for AMT adjustments and preferences.

Alternative tax. An option that is allowed in computing the tax on net capital gain. For the corporate taxpayer, the rate is 35 percent (the same as the highest regular corporate tax rate). Thus, for corporate taxpayers, the alternative tax does not produce a beneficial result. For noncorporate taxpayers, the rate is usually either 20 percent (i.e., holding period is longer than 18 months) or 28 percent (i.e., holding period is longer than 12 months but not longer than 18 months). However, if the noncorporate taxpayer is in the 15 percent tax bracket, the alternative tax rate is 10 percent if the holding period is longer than 18 months. §§ 1(h) and 1201. See also *mid-term net capital gain or loss* and *net capital gain*.

Alternative tax NOL deduction (ATNOLD). In calculating the AMT, the taxpayer is allowed to deduct NOL carryovers and carrybacks. However, for this purpose, a special calculation is required that is referred to as the ATNOLD. The regular income tax is modified for AMT adjustments and preferences to produce the ATNOLD. § 56(d).

Amortization. The tax deduction for the cost or other basis of an intangible asset over the asset's estimated useful life. Examples of amortizable intangibles include patents, copyrights, and leasehold interests. The intangible goodwill can be amortized for income tax purposes over a 15-year period. For tangible assets, see *depreciation*. For natural resources, see *depletion*. See also *estimated useful life* and *goodwill*.

Amount realized. The amount received by a taxpayer upon the sale or exchange of property. Amount realized is the sum of the cash and the fair market value of any property or services received by the taxpayer, plus any related debt assumed by the buyer. Determining the amount realized is the starting point for arriving at realized gain or loss. § 1001(b). See also *realized gain or loss* and *recognized gain or loss*.

AMT adjustments. In calculating AMTI, certain adjustments are added to or deducted from taxable income. These adjustments generally reflect timing differences. § 56.

Annual accounting period concept. In determining a taxpayer's income tax liability, only transactions taking place during a specified tax year are taken into consideration. For reporting and payment purposes, therefore, the tax life of taxpayers is divided into equal annual accounting periods. See also *accounting period* and *mitigation of the annual accounting period concept*.

Annual exclusion. In computing the taxable gifts for the year, each donor excludes the first $10,000 of a gift to each donee. Usually, the annual exclusion is not available for gifts of future interests. § 2503(b). See also *future interest* and *gift splitting*.

Annuitant. The party entitled to receive payments from an annuity contract. See also *annuity*.

Annuity. A fixed sum of money payable to a person at specified times for a specified period of time or for life. If the party making the payment (i.e., the obligor) is regularly engaged in this type of business (e.g., an insurance company), the arrangement is classified as a commercial annuity. A so-called private annuity involves an obligor that is not regularly engaged in selling annuities (e.g., a charity or family member).

Anticipatory assignment of income. See *assignment of income*.

Appellate court. For Federal tax purposes, appellate courts include the Courts of Appeals and the Supreme Court. If the party losing in the trial (or lower) court is dissatisfied with the result, the dispute may be carried to the appropriate appellate court. See also *Court of Appeals* and *trial court*.

Appreciated inventory. In partnership taxation, appreciated inventory is a *"hot asset"* for which a partner's share of the ordinary income potential is required to be allocated. If a partner sells an interest in the partnership, ordinary income must be recognized to the extent of the partner's share in the partnership's inventory and *unrealized receivables*. For disproportionate distributions and distributions in liquidation of a partner's interest in the partnership under § 736, the partner (or partnership, in some cases) is only required to recognize ordinary income to the extent of a shift in ownership of "substantially appreciated inventory." Inventory is substantially appreciated if its fair market value exceeds 120 percent of the partnership's basis in the inventory. The definition of "inventory" is broad enough to include any accounts receivable, including unrealized receivables.

Arm's length concept. The standard under which unrelated parties would carry out a transaction. Suppose Cardinal Corporation sells property to its sole shareholder for $10,000. In determining whether $10,000 is an arm's length price, one would ascertain the amount for which the corporation could have sold the property to a disinterested third party.

Articles of incorporation. The legal document specifying a corporation's name, period of existence, purpose and powers, authorized number of shares, classes of stock, and other conditions for operation. The organizers of the corporation file the articles with the state of incorporation. If the articles are satisfactory and other conditions of the law are satisfied, the state will issue a charter recognizing the organization's status as a corporation.

Assessment. The process whereby the IRS imposes an additional tax liability. If, for example, the IRS audits a taxpayer's income tax return and finds gross income understated or deductions overstated, it will assess a deficiency in the amount of the tax that should have been paid in light of the adjustments made. See also *deficiency*.

Assignment of income. A procedure whereby a taxpayer attempts to avoid the recognition of income by assigning to another the property that generates the income. Such a procedure will not avoid the recognition of income by the taxpayer making the assignment if it can be said that the income was earned at the point of the transfer. In this case, usually referred to as an anticipatory assignment of income, the income will be taxed to the person who earns it.

Assumption of liabilities. In a corporate takeover or asset purchase, the buyer often takes assets subject to preexisting debt. Such actions do not create *boot* received on the transaction for the new shareholder, unless there is no *bona fide* business purpose for the exchange, or the principal purpose of the debt assumption is the avoidance of tax liabilities. Gain is recognized to the extent that liabilities assumed exceed the bases of the transferred assets. § 357.

At-risk amount. A taxpayer has an amount at risk in a business or investment venture to the extent that personal assets have been subjected to the risks of the business. Typically, the taxpayer's at-risk amount includes (1) the amount of money or other property that the investor contributed to the venture for the investment, (2) the amount of any of the entity's liabilities for which the taxpayer personally is liable and that relate to the investment, and (3) an allocable share of nonrecourse debts incurred by the venture from third parties in arm's length transactions for real estate investments.

At-risk limitation. Generally, a taxpayer can deduct losses related to a trade or business, S corporation, partnership, or investment asset only to the extent of the at-risk amount.

Attribution. Under certain circumstances, the tax law applies attribution (constructive ownership) rules to assign to one taxpayer the ownership interest of another taxpayer. If, for example, the stock of Gold Corporation is held 60 percent by Marsha and 40 percent by Sidney, Marsha may be deemed to own 100 percent of Gold Corporation if Marsha and Sidney are mother and son. In that case, the stock owned by Sidney is attributed to Marsha. Stated differently, Marsha has a 60 percent direct and a 40 percent indirect interest in Gold Corporation. It can also be said that Marsha is the constructive owner of Sidney's interest.

Audit. Inspection and verification of a taxpayer's return or other transactions possessing tax consequences. See also *correspondence audit*, *field audit*, and *office audit*.

Automobile expenses. Automobile expenses are generally deductible only to the extent the automobile is used in business or for the production of income. Personal commuting expenses are not deductible. The taxpayer may deduct actual expenses (including depreciation and insurance), or the standard (automatic) mileage rate may be used (31.5 cents per mile for 1997 and 32.5 cents per mile for 1998) during any one year. Automobile expenses incurred for medical purposes or in connection with job-related moving expenses are deductible to the extent of actual out-of-pocket expenses or at the rate of 10 cents per mile (14 cents for charitable activities for 1998 and 12 cents for 1997).

B

Bailout. Various procedures whereby the owners of an entity can obtain the entity's profits with favorable tax consequences. With corporations, for example, the bailout of corporate profits without dividend consequences might be the desired objective. The alternative of distributing the profits to the shareholders as dividends generally is less attractive since dividend payments are not deductible. See also *preferred stock bailout*.

Bargain sale or purchase. A sale or purchase of property for less than fair market value. The difference between the sale or purchase price and the fair market value of the property may have tax consequences. If, for example, a corporation sells property worth $1,000 to one of its shareholders for $700, the $300 difference probably represents a constructive dividend to the shareholder. Suppose, instead, the shareholder sells the property (worth $1,000) to his or her corporation for $700. The $300 difference probably represents a contribution by the shareholder to the corporation's capital. Bargain sales and purchases among members of the same family may lead to gift tax consequences. See also *constructive dividend*.

Basis. The acquisition cost assigned to an asset for income tax purposes. For assets acquired by purchase, basis is cost (§ 1012). Special rules govern the basis of property received by virtue of another's death (§ 1014) or by gift (§ 1015), the basis of stock received on a transfer of property to a controlled corporation (§ 358), the basis of the property transferred to the corporation (§ 362), and the basis of property received upon the liquidation of a corporation (§ 334). See also *adjusted basis*.

Basis in partnership interest. The acquisition cost of the partner's ownership interest in the *partnership*. Includes purchase price and associated debt acquired from other partners and in the course of the entity's trade or business.

Beneficiary. A party who will benefit from a transfer of property or other arrangement. Examples include the beneficiary of a trust, the beneficiary of a life insurance policy, and the beneficiary of an estate.

Bequest. A transfer of personal property by will. To bequeath is to leave such property by will. See also *devise* and *personal property*.

Blockage rule. A factor to be considered in valuing a large block of stock. Application of this rule generally justifies a discount in the fair market value since the disposition of a large amount of stock at any one time may depress the value of the shares in the marketplace.

Bona fide. In good faith, or real. In tax law, this term is often used in connection with a business purpose for carrying out a transaction. Thus, was there a bona fide business purpose for a shareholder's transfer of a liability to a controlled corporation? § 357(b)(1)(B). See also *business purposes*.

Book value. The net amount of an asset after reduction by a related reserve. The book value of machinery, for example, is the amount of the machinery less the reserve for depreciation.

Boot. Cash or property of a type not included in the definition of a nontaxable exchange. The receipt of boot will cause an otherwise nontaxable transfer to become taxable to the extent of the lesser of the fair market value of the boot or the realized gain on the transfer. For example, see transfers to controlled corporations under § 351(b) and like-kind exchanges under § 1031(b). See also *like-kind exchange* and *realized gain or loss*.

Branch profits tax. A tax on the effectively connected earnings and profits of the U.S. branch of a foreign corporation. The tax is levied in addition to the usual §11 tax, in an amount equal to 30 percent of the dividend equivalent amount. Treaties can override the tax or reduce the withholding percentage. Earnings reinvested in the U.S. operations of the entity are not subject to the tax until repatriation.

Bribes and illegal payments. Section 162 denies a deduction for bribes or kickbacks, fines, and penalties paid to a government official or employee for violation of law, and two-thirds of the treble damage payments made to claimants for violation of the antitrust law. Denial of a deduction for bribes and illegal payments is based upon the judicially established principle that allowing such payments would be contrary to public policy.

Brother-sister controlled group. More than one corporation owned by the same shareholders. If, for example, Chris and Pat each own one-half of the stock in Wren Corporation and Redbird Corporation, Wren and Redbird form a brother-sister controlled group.

B.T.A. The Board of Tax Appeals was a trial court that considered Federal tax matters. This Court is now the U.S. Tax Court.

Built-in gains tax. A penalty tax designed to discourage a shift of the incidence of taxation on unrealized gains from a C corporation to its shareholders, via an S election. Under this provision, any recognized gain during the first 10 years of S status generates a corporate-level tax on a base not to exceed the aggregate untaxed built-in gains brought into the S corporation upon its election from C corporation taxable years.

Burden of proof. The requirement in a lawsuit to show the weight of evidence and thereby gain a favorable decision. Except in cases of tax fraud, the burden of proof in a tax case generally is on the taxpayer. See also *fraud*.

Business bad debt. A tax deduction allowed for obligations obtained in connection with a trade or business that have become either partially or completely worthless. In contrast to nonbusiness bad debts, business bad debts are deductible as business expenses. § 166. See also *nonbusiness bad debt*.

Business purposes. A justifiable business reason for carrying out a transaction. Mere tax avoidance is not an acceptable business purpose. The presence of a business purpose is crucial in the area of corporate reorganizations and certain liquidations. See also *bona fide*.

Buy-sell agreement. An arrangement, particularly appropriate in the case of a closely held corporation or a partnership, whereby the surviving owners (shareholders or partners) or the entity agrees to purchase the interest of a withdrawing owner. The buy-sell agreement provides for an orderly disposition of an interest in a business and may aid in setting the value of the interest for death tax purposes. See also *cross-purchase buy-sell agreement* and *entity buy-sell agreement*.

By-pass amount. The amount that can be transferred by gift or death free of any unified transfer tax. Currently, the by-pass amount is scheduled to reach $1,000,000. See also *exemption equivalent amount*.

C

Cafeteria benefit plan. An employee benefit plan under which an employee is allowed to select from among a variety of employer-provided fringe benefits. Some of the benefits may be taxable and some may be statutory nontaxable benefits (e.g. health and accident insurance and group term life insurance). The employee is taxed only on the taxable benefits selected. A cafeteria benefit plan is also referred to as a flexible benefit plan. § 125.

Cafeteria plan. See *cafeteria benefit plan*.

Calendar year. See *accounting period*.

Capital account. The financial accounting analog of a partner's tax basis in the entity.

Capital asset. Broadly speaking, all assets are capital except those specifically excluded by the Code. Major categories of noncapital assets include property held for resale in the normal course of business (inventory), trade accounts and notes receivable, and depreciable property and real estate used in a trade or business (§ 1231 assets). § 1221. See also *capital gain* and *capital loss*.

Capital contribution. Various means by which a shareholder makes additional funds available to the corporation (placed at the risk of the business), sometimes without the receipt of additional stock. If no stock is received, the contributions are added to the basis of the shareholder's existing stock investment and do not generate gross income to the corporation. § 118.

Capital expenditure. An expenditure that should be added to the basis of the property improved. For income tax purposes, this generally precludes a full deduction for the expenditure in the year paid or incurred. Any cost recovery in the form of a tax deduction comes in the form of depreciation, depletion, or amortization. § 263.

Capital gain. The gain from the sale or exchange of a capital asset. See also *capital asset, mid-term capital gain or loss* and *net capital gain*.

Capital gain property. Property contributed to a charitable organization that, if sold rather than contributed, would have resulted in long-term capital gain to the donor. See also *ordinary income property*.

Capital interest. Usually, the percentage of the entity's net assets that a partner would receive on liquidation. Typically determined by the partner's capital sharing ratio.

Capital loss. The loss from the sale or exchange of a capital asset. See also *capital asset*.

Capital sharing ratio. A partner's percentage ownership of the entity's capital.

Capital stock tax. A state-level tax, usually imposed on out-of-state corporations for the privilege of doing business in the state. The tax may be based on the entity's apportionable income or payroll, or on its apportioned net worth as of a specified date.

Carryover basis. When a taxpayer exchanges one asset for another, many provisions in the tax law allow the basis assigned to the received asset to be precisely that of the traded asset. Thus, no step-up or -down of basis occurs as a result of the exchange. For instance, when an investor contributes an asset to a corporation or partnership, the entity generally takes a carryover basis in the property.

Cash method. See *cash receipts method*.

Cash receipts method. A method of accounting that reflects deductions as paid and income as received in any one tax year. However, deductions for prepaid expenses that benefit more than one tax year (e.g., prepaid rent and prepaid interest) usually must be spread over the period benefited rather than deducted in the year paid. § 446(c)(1). See also *constructive receipt of income*.

Cash surrender value. The amount of money that an insurance policy would yield if cashed in with the insurance company that issued the policy.

Casualty loss. A casualty is defined as "the complete or partial destruction of property resulting from an identifiable event of a sudden, unexpected or unusual nature" (e.g., floods, storms, fires, auto accidents). Individuals may deduct a casualty loss only if the loss is incurred in a trade or business or in a transaction entered into for profit or arises from fire, storm, shipwreck, or other casualty or from theft. Individuals usually deduct personal casualty losses as itemized deductions subject to a $100 nondeductible amount and to an annual floor equal to 10 percent of adjusted gross income that applies after the $100 per casualty floor has been applied. Special rules are provided for the netting of certain casualty gains and losses. See also *Section 1231 gains and losses.*

CCH. Commerce Clearing House (CCH) is the publisher of a tax service and of Federal tax decisions (USTC series).

C corporation. A separate taxable entity, subject to the rules of Subchapter C of the Code. This business form may create a double taxation effect relative to its shareholders. The entity is subject to the regular corporate tax and a number of penalty taxes at the Federal level.

Cert. den. By denying the Writ of Certiorari, the U.S. Supreme Court refuses to accept an appeal from a U.S. Court of Appeals. The denial of certiorari does not, however, mean that the U.S. Supreme Court agrees with the result reached by the lower court. See also *certiorari.*

Certiorari. Appeal from a U.S. Court of Appeals to the U.S. Supreme Court is by Writ of Certiorari. The Supreme Court need not accept the appeal, and it usually does not (*cert. den.*) unless a conflict exists among the lower courts that must be resolved or a constitutional issue is involved. See also *cert. den.*

Cf. Compare.

Charitable contributions. Contributions are deductible (subject to various restrictions and ceiling limitations) if made to qualified nonprofit charitable organizations. A cash basis taxpayer is entitled to a deduction solely in the year of payment. Accrual basis corporations may accrue contributions at year-end if payment is properly authorized before the end of the year and payment is made within two and one-half months after the end of the year. § 170.

Check the box. Business entities can elect to be taxed as a partnership, S corporation, or C corporation by indicating such preference on the tax return. Legal structure and operations are irrelevant in this regard.

Child tax credit. A tax credit based solely on the number of qualifying children under age 17. The maximum credit available is $400 per child in 1998 ($500 per child in 1999 and after). A qualifying child must be claimed as a dependent on a parent's tax return in order to qualify for the credit. Taxpayers who qualify for the child tax credit may also qualify for a supplemental credit. The supplemental credit is treated as a component of the earned income credit and is therefore refundable. The credit is phased out for higher-income taxpayers. § 24.

Circuit Court of Appeals. See *Court of Appeals.*

Civil fraud. See *fraud.*

Closely held corporation. A corporation where stock ownership is not widely dispersed. Rather, a few shareholders are in control of corporate policy and are in a position to benefit personally from that policy.

Closing agreement. In a tax dispute, the parties sign a closing agreement to spell out the terms under which the matters are settled. The agreement is binding on both the Service and the taxpayer, for the disputed year and for all future years.

Collapsing. To disregard a transaction or one of a series of steps leading to a result. See also *step transaction, substance vs. form concept,* and *telescoping.*

Collectibles. A special type of capital asset, the gain from which is taxed at a maximum rate of 28 percent if the holding period is more than 12 months. Examples include art, rugs, antiques, gems, metals, stamps, some coins and bullion, and alcoholic beverages held for investment.

Commissioner of the IRS. The head of IRS operations, a presidential appointee.

Common law state. See *community property.*

Community property. Louisiana, Texas, New Mexico, Arizona, California, Washington, Idaho, Nevada, and Wisconsin have community property systems. The rest of the states are common law property jurisdictions. The difference between common law and community property systems centers around the property rights possessed by married persons. In a common law system, each spouse owns whatever he or she earns. Under a community property system, one-half of the earnings of each spouse is considered owned by the other spouse. Assume, for example, Jeff and Alice are husband and wife and their only income is the $50,000 annual salary Jeff receives. If they live in New York (a common law state), the $50,000 salary belongs to Jeff. If, however, they live in Texas (a community property state), the $50,000 salary is owned one-half each by Jeff and Alice. See also *separate property.*

Compensatory damages. Damages received or paid by the taxpayer can be classified as compensatory damages or as punitive damages. Compensatory damages are those paid to compensate one for harm caused by another. Compensatory damages are excludible from the recipient's gross income. See also *punitive damages.*

Complete liquidation. See *corporate liquidation.*

Complete termination redemption. See *redemption (complete termination).*

Completed contract method. A method of reporting gain or loss on certain long-term contracts. Under this method of accounting, gross income and expenses are recognized in the tax year in which the contract is completed. Reg. § 1.451–3. See also *percentage of completion method* and *long-term contract.*

Complex trust. Not a *simple trust.* Such trusts may have charitable beneficiaries, accumulate income, and distribute corpus. §§ 661–663. See also *simple trust.*

Concur. To agree with the result reached by another, but not necessarily with the reasoning or the logic used in reaching the result. For example, Judge Ricks agrees with Judges Stone and Talent (all being members of the same court) that the income is taxable but for a different reason. Judge Ricks would issue a concurring opinion to the majority opinion issued by Judges Stone and Talent.

Condemnation. The taking of property by a public authority. The taking is by legal action, and the owner of the property is compensated by the public authority.

Conduit concept. See *aggregate concept*.

Consent dividend. For purposes of avoiding or reducing the penalty tax on the unreasonable accumulation of earnings or the personal holding company tax, a corporation may declare a consent dividend. In a consent dividend, no cash or property is distributed to the shareholders, although the corporation obtains a dividends paid deduction. The consent dividend is taxed to the shareholders and increases the basis in their stock investment. § 565.

Consolidated return. A procedure whereby certain affiliated corporations may file a single return, combine the tax transactions of each corporation, and arrive at a single income tax liability for the group. The election to file a consolidated return is usually binding on future years. See §§ 1501–1505 and related Regulations.

Consolidation. The combination of two or more corporations into a newly created corporation. Thus, White Corporation and Black Corporation combine to form Gray Corporation. A consolidation may qualify as a nontaxable *reorganization* if certain conditions are satisfied. §§ 354 and 368(a)(1)(A).

Constructive dividend. A taxable benefit derived by a shareholder from his or her corporation that is not actually called a dividend. Examples include unreasonable compensation, excessive rent payments, bargain purchases of corporate property, and shareholder use of corporate property. Constructive dividends generally are found in closely held corporations. See also *bargain sale or purchase, closely held corporation*, and *unreasonable compensation*.

Constructive liquidation scenario. The means by which recourse debt is shared among partners in basis determination.

Constructive ownership. See *attribution*.

Constructive receipt of income. If income is unqualifiedly available although not physically in the taxpayer's possession, it is subject to the income tax. An example is accrued interest on a savings account. Under the constructive receipt of income concept, the interest is taxed to a depositor in the year available, rather than the year actually withdrawn. The fact that the depositor uses the cash basis of accounting for tax purposes is irrelevant. See Reg. § 1.451–2. See also *cash receipts method*.

Continuity of business enterprise. In a tax-free reorganization, a shareholder or corporation that has substantially the same investment after an exchange as before should not be taxed on the transaction. Specifically, the transferee corporation must continue the historic business of the transferor, or it must use a significant portion of the transferor's assets in the new business.

Continuity of interest test. In a tax-free reorganization, a shareholder or corporation that has substantially the same investment after an exchange as before should not be taxed on the transaction. Specifically, the seller must acquire an equity interest in the purchasing corporation equal in value to at least 50 percent of all formerly outstanding stock of the acquired entity.

Continuity of life or existence. The death or other withdrawal of an owner of an entity does not terminate the existence of the entity. This is a characteristic of a corporation since the death or withdrawal of a shareholder does not affect the corporation's existence. Reg. § 301.7701–2(b). See also *association*.

Contributions to the capital of a corporation. See *capital contribution*.

Contributory qualified pension or profit sharing plan. A plan funded with both employer and employee contributions. Since the employee's contributions to the plan are subject to income tax, a later distribution of the contributions to the employee generally is tax-free. See also *qualified pension or profit sharing plan*.

Control. Holding a specified level of stock ownership in a corporation. For § 351, the new shareholder(s) must hold at least 80 percent of the total combined voting power of all voting classes of stock, and at least 80 percent of the shares of all nonvoting classes. Other tax provisions require different levels of control to bring about desired effects, such as 50 or 100 percent.

Controlled foreign corporation (CFC). A non-U.S. corporation in which more than 50 percent of the total combined voting power of all classes of stock entitled to vote or the total value of the stock of the corporation is owned by "U.S. shareholders" on any day during the taxable year of the foreign corporation. For purposes of this definition, a U.S. shareholder is any U.S. person who owns, or is considered as owning, 10 percent or more of the total combined voting power of all classes of voting stock of the foreign corporation. Stock owned directly, indirectly, and constructively is used in this measure.

Controlled group. A controlled group of corporations is required to share the lower-level corporate tax rates and various other tax benefits among the members of the group. A controlled group may be either a brother-sister or a parent-subsidiary group.

Corporate acquisition. The takeover of one corporation by another if both parties retain their legal existence after the transaction. An acquisition can be effected via a stock purchase or through a tax-free exchange of stock. See also *corporate reorganization* and *merger*.

Corporate liquidation. Occurs when a corporation distributes its net assets to its shareholders and ceases to be a going concern. Generally, a shareholder recognizes capital gain or loss upon the liquidation of the entity, regardless of the corporation's balance in its earnings and profits account. However, the distributing corporation recognizes gain and loss on assets that it distributes to shareholders in kind.

Corporate reorganization. Occurs, among other instances, when one corporation acquires another in a merger or acquisition, a single corporation divides into two or more entities, a corporation makes a substantial change in its capital structure, or a corporation undertakes a change in its legal name or domicile. The exchange of stock and other securities in a corporate reorganization can be effected favorably for tax purposes if certain statutory requirements are followed strictly. Tax consequences include the nonrecognition of any gain that is realized by the shareholders except to the extent of boot received. See also *corporate acquisition* and *merger*.

Corpus. The body or principal of a trust. Suppose, for example, Grant transfers an apartment building into a trust, income payable to Ruth for life, remainder to Shawn upon Ruth's death. Corpus of the trust is the apartment building.

Correspondence audit. An audit conducted by the IRS by mail. Typically, the IRS writes to the taxpayer requesting the verification of a particular deduction or exemption. The completion of a special form or the remittance of copies of records or other support is all that is requested of the taxpayer. See also *audit, field audit*, and *office audit*.

Cost depletion. Depletion that is calculated based on the adjusted basis of the asset. The adjusted basis is divided by the expected recoverable units to determine the depletion per unit. The depletion per unit is multiplied by the units sold during the tax year to calculate cost depletion. See also *percentage depletion*.

Court of Appeals. Any of 13 Federal courts that consider tax matters appealed from the U.S. Tax Court, a U.S. District Court, or the U.S. Court of Federal Claims. Appeal from a U.S. Court of Appeals is to the U.S. Supreme Court by *Writ of Certiorari*. See also *appellate court* and *trial court*.

Court of Federal Claims. A trial court (court of original jurisdiction) that decides litigation involving Federal tax matters. Appeal from this court is to the Court of Appeals for the Federal Circuit.

Court of original jurisdiction. The Federal courts are divided into courts of original jurisdiction and appellate courts. A dispute between a taxpayer and the IRS is first considered by a court of original jurisdiction (i.e., a trial court). The four Federal courts of original jurisdiction are the U.S. Tax Court, U.S. District Court, the Court of Federal Claims, and the Small Cases Division of the U.S. Tax Court. See *Court of Appeals*.

Credit for prior transfers. The death tax credit for prior transfers applies when property is taxed in the estates of different decedents within a 10-year period. The credit is determined using a decreasing statutory percentage, with the magnitude of the credit decreasing as the length of time between the multiple deaths increases. § 2013.

Criminal fraud. See *fraud*.

Cross-purchase buy-sell agreement. Under this type of arrangement, the surviving owners of the business agree to buy out the withdrawing owner. Assume, for example, Ruth and Sam are equal shareholders in Eagle Corporation. Under a cross-purchase buy-sell agreement, Ruth and Sam would contract to purchase the other's interest should that person decide to withdraw from the business. See also *buy-sell agreement* and *entity buy-sell agreement*.

Current earnings and profits. Net tax-basis earnings of the corporation aggregated during the current tax year. A corporate distribution is deemed to be first from the entity's current earnings and profits and then from accumulated earnings and profits. Shareholders recognize dividend income to the extent of the earnings and profits of the corporation. A dividend results to the extent of current earnings and profits, even if there is a larger negative balance in accumulated earnings and profits.

Current use valuation. See *special use value*.

Curtesy. A husband's right under state law to all or part of his wife's property upon her death. See also *dower*.

D

Death benefit. A payment made by an employer to the beneficiary or beneficiaries of a deceased employee on account of the death of the employee.

Death tax. A tax imposed on property transferred by the death of the owner. See also *credit for prior transfers, estate tax*, and *inheritance tax*.

Debt-financed income. Included in computations of the *unrelated business income* of an *exempt organization*, the gross income generated from debt-financed property.

Decedent. An individual who has died.

Deduction. The Federal income tax is not imposed upon gross income. Rather, it is imposed upon taxable income. Congressionally identified deductions are subtracted from gross income to arrive at the tax base, taxable income.

Deductions in respect of a decedent. Deductions accrued at the moment of death but not recognizable on the final income tax return of a decedent because of the method of accounting used. Such items are allowed as deductions on the estate tax return and on the income tax return of the estate (Form 1041) or the heir (Form 1040). An example of a deduction in respect of a decedent is interest expense accrued to the date of death by a cash basis debtor.

Deferred compensation. Compensation that will be taxed when received and not when earned. An example is contributions by an employer to a qualified pension or profit sharing plan on behalf of an employee. The contributions will not be taxed to the employee until they are distributed (e.g., upon retirement). See also *qualified pension or profit sharing plan*.

Deficiency. Additional tax liability owed by a taxpayer and assessed by the IRS. See also *assessment* and *statutory notice of deficiency*.

Deficiency dividend. Once the IRS has established a corporation's liability for the personal holding company tax in a prior year, the tax may be reduced or avoided by the issuance of a deficiency dividend under § 547. The deficiency dividend procedure is not available in cases where the deficiency was due to fraud with intent to evade tax or to a willful failure to file the appropriate tax return [§ 547(g)]. Nor does the deficiency dividend procedure avoid the usual penalties and interest applicable for failure to file a return or pay a tax.

Deficit.　A negative balance in the earnings and profits account.

Demand loan.　A loan payable upon request by the creditor, rather than on a specific date.

De minimis fringe.　Benefits provided to employees that are too insignificant to warrant the time and effort required to account for the benefits received by each employee and the value of those benefits. Such amounts are excludible from the employee's gross income. § 132.

Dependency exemption. See *personal and dependency exemptions.*

Depletion.　The process by which the cost or other basis of a natural resource (e.g., an oil or gas interest) is recovered upon extraction and sale of the resource. The two ways to determine the depletion allowance are the cost and percentage (or statutory) methods. Under cost depletion, each unit of production sold is assigned a portion of the cost or other basis of the interest. This is determined by dividing the cost or other basis by the total units expected to be recovered. Under percentage (or statutory) depletion, the tax law provides a special percentage factor for different types of minerals and other natural resources. This percentage is multiplied by the gross income from the interest to arrive at the depletion allowance. §§ 613 and 613A.

Depreciation.　The deduction for the cost or other basis of a tangible asset over the asset's estimated useful life. For intangible assets, see *amortization.* For natural resources, see *depletion.* See also *estimated useful life.*

Depreciation recapture.　Upon the disposition of depreciable property used in a trade or business, gain or loss is measured by the difference between the consideration received (the amount realized) and the adjusted basis of the property. The gain recognized could be § 1231 gain and qualify for long-term capital gain treatment. The recapture provisions of the Code (e.g., §§ 291, 1245, and 1250) may operate to convert some or all of the § 1231 gain into ordinary income. The justification for depreciation recapture is that it prevents a taxpayer from converting a dollar of ordinary deduction (in the form of depreciation) into deferred tax-favored income (§ 1231 or long-term capital gain). The depreciation recapture rules do not apply when the property is disposed of at a loss or via a gift. See also *Section 1231 gains and losses.*

Determination letter.　Upon the request of a taxpayer, an IRS District Director will comment on the tax status of a completed transaction. Determination letters frequently are used to clarify employee status, determine whether a retirement or profit sharing plan qualifies under the Code, and

determine the tax-exempt status of certain nonprofit organizations.

Devise.　A transfer of real estate by will. See also *bequest.*

Disabled access credit.　A tax credit designed to encourage small businesses to make their facilities more accessible to disabled individuals. The credit is equal to 50 percent of the eligible expenditures that exceed $250 but do not exceed $10,250. Thus, the maximum amount for the credit is $5,000. The adjusted basis for depreciation is reduced by the amount of the credit. To qualify, the facility must have been placed in service before November 6, 1990. § 44. See also *general business credit.*

Disclaimers.　Rejections, refusals, or renunciations of claims, powers, or property. Section 2518 sets forth the conditions required to avoid gift tax consequences as the result of a disclaimer.

Discretionary trust.　Trusts under which the trustee or another party has the right to accumulate (rather than distribute) the income for each year. Depending on the terms of the trust instrument, the income may be accumulated for future distributions to the income beneficiaries or added to corpus for the benefit of the remainderperson. See also *corpus* and *income beneficiary.*

Disguised sale.　When a partner contributes property to the entity and soon thereafter receives a distribution from the partnership, the transactions are collapsed, and the distribution is seen as a purchase of the asset by the partnership. § 707(a)(2)(B).

Disproportionate.　Not pro rata or ratable. Suppose, for example, Blue Corporation has two shareholders, Chris and Diane, each of whom owns 50 percent of its stock. If Blue Corporation distributes a cash dividend of $2,000 to Chris and only $1,000 to Diane, the distribution is disproportionate. The distribution would have been proportionate if Chris and Diane had received $1,500 each.

Disproportionate distribution.　A distribution from a partnership to one or more of its partners in which at least one partner's interest in partnership hot assets is increased or decreased. For example, a distribution of cash to one partner and hot assets to another changes both partners' interest in hot assets and is disproportionate. The intent of rules for taxation of disproportionate distributions is to ensure each partner eventually recognizes his or her proportionate share of partnership ordinary income.

Disproportionate redemption. See *redemption (disproportionate).*

Dissent.　To disagree with the majority. If, for example, Judge Brown disagrees with the result reached by Judges Charles and Davis (all of whom are members of the same court), Judge Brown could issue a dissenting opinion.

Distributable net income (DNI).　The measure that determines the nature and amount of the distributions from estates and trusts that the beneficiaries must include in income. DNI also limits the amount that estates and trusts can claim as a deduction for such distributions. § 643(a).

Distribution deduction. Used to compute an estate's or trust's taxable income for the year. The lesser of the amount distributed to beneficiaries from income, or the deductible portion of distributable net income for the period.

Distributions in kind. A transfer of property "as is." If, for example, a corporation distributes land to its shareholders, a distribution in kind has taken place. A sale of land followed by a distribution of the cash proceeds would not be a distribution in kind of the land.

District Court. A Federal District Court is a trial court for purposes of litigating Federal tax matters. It is the only trial court in which a jury trial can be obtained. See also *trial court*.

District Director. The head of an IRS district's operations.

Dividend. A nondeductible distribution to the shareholders of a corporation. A dividend constitutes gross income to the recipient if it is from the current or accumulated earnings and profits of the corporation.

Dividend equivalent amount (DEA). The amount subject to the branch profits tax, it is equal to the effectively connected E&P of the U.S. branch of a foreign corporation, reduced/(increased) by an increase/(reduction) in U.S. net equity.

Dividends paid deduction. Relative to the accumulated earnings and personal holding company taxes, reductions in the tax base are allowed to the extent that the corporation made dividend payments during the year. Thus, this adjustment reduces accumulated taxable income and personal holding company income.

Dividends received deduction. A deduction allowed a shareholder that is a corporation for dividends received from a domestic corporation. The deduction usually is 70 percent of the dividends received, but it could be 80 or 100 percent depending upon the ownership percentage held by the recipient corporation. §§ 243–246.

Divisive reorganization. A corporate division: some of the assets of one corporation are transferred to another corporation, in exchange for control of the transferee. Then, in a spin-off, split-off, or split-up, stock of the transferee is distributed to the transferor's shareholders.

Domestic corporation. A corporation created or organized in the United States or under the law of the United States or any state. § 7701(a)(4). Only dividends received from domestic corporations qualify for the dividends received deduction (§ 243). See also *foreign corporation*.

Domicile. A person's legal home.

Donee. The recipient of a gift.

Donor. The maker of a gift.

Dower. A wife's right to all or part of her deceased husband's property, unique to common law states as opposed to community property jurisdictions. See also *curtesy*.

E

Earned income. Income from personal services. Distinguished from passive, portfolio, and other unearned income (sometimes referred to as "active" income). See §§ 469, 911, and the related Regulations.

Earned income credit. A tax credit designed to provide assistance to certain low-income individuals who generally have a qualifying child. This is a refundable credit. To receive the most beneficial treatment, the taxpayer must have qualifying children. However, it is possible to qualify for the credit without having a child. To calculate the credit for a taxpayer with one or more children for 1998, a statutory rate of 34 percent for one child (40 percent for two or more children) is multiplied by the earned income (subject to a statutory maximum of $6,680 with one qualifying child or $9,390 with two or more qualifying children). Once the earned income exceeds $12,260, the credit is phased out using a 15.98 percent rate for one qualifying child and a 21.06 percent rate for two qualifying children. For the qualifying taxpayer without children, the credit is calculated on a maximum earned income of $4,460 applying a 7.65 percent rate with the phase-out beginning at $5,570 applying the same rate.

Earnings and profits (E&P). Measures the economic capacity of a corporation to make a distribution to shareholders that is not a return of capital. Such a distribution results in dividend income to the shareholders to the extent of the corporation's current and accumulated earnings and profits.

Economic effect test. Requirements that must be met before a special allocation may be used by a partnership. The premise behind the test is that each partner who receives an allocation of income or loss from a partnership bears the economic benefit or burden of the allocation.

Economic income. The change in the taxpayer's net worth, as measured in terms of market values, plus the value of the assets the taxpayer consumed during the year. Because of the impracticality of this income model, it is not used for tax purposes.

Economic performance test. One of the requirements that must be satisfied in order for an accrual basis taxpayer to deduct an expense. The accrual basis taxpayer first must satisfy the all events test. That test is not deemed satisfied until economic performance occurs. This occurs, when property or services are provided to the taxpayer, or in the case in which the taxpayer is required to provide property or services, whenever the property or services are actually provided by the taxpayer.

Educational savings bonds. U.S. Series EE bonds whose proceeds are used for qualified higher educational expenses for the taxpayer, the taxpayer's spouse, or a dependent. The interest may be excluded from gross income, provided the taxpayer's adjusted gross income does not exceed certain amounts. § 135.

Effectively connected income. Income of a nonresident alien or foreign corporation that is attributable to the operation of a U.S. trade or business under either the asset-use or business-activities test.

Electing large partnership. A partnership with 100 or more partners may elect to be subject to simplified tax reporting and audit procedures. The election allows the partnership to combine certain income and expense amounts and report net amounts to the partners. The result is fewer "pass-through" items to the partners, which makes the partners' tax returns easier to prepare. As an example, an electing large partnership with a long-term capital gain and a short-term capital loss would offset the two amounts and allocate the net amount among the partners.

Employee stock ownership plan (ESOP). A type of qualified profit sharing plan that invests in securities of the employer. In a noncontributory ESOP, the employer usually contributes its shares to a trust and receives a deduction for the fair market value of the stock. Generally, the employee does not recognize income until the stock is sold after its distribution to him or her upon retirement or other separation from service. See also *qualified pension or profit sharing plan.*

Employment taxes. Employment taxes are those taxes that an employer must pay on account of its employees. Employment taxes include FICA (Federal Insurance Contributions Act) and FUTA (Federal Unemployment Tax Act) taxes. Employment taxes are paid to the IRS in addition to income tax withholdings at specified intervals. Such taxes can be levied on the employees, the employer, or both. See also *FICA tax* and *FUTA tax.*

En banc. The case was considered by the whole court. Typically, for example, only one of the judges of the U.S. Tax Court will hear and decide on a tax controversy. However, when the issues involved are unusually novel or of wide impact, the case will be heard and decided by the full Court sitting *en banc.*

Energy tax credit. A 10 percent tax credit is available to businesses that invest in certain energy property. The purpose of the credit is to create incentives for conservation and to develop alternative energy sources. The credit is available on the acquisition of solar and geothermal property. §§ 46 and 48.

Enrolled agent (EA). A tax practitioner who has gained admission to practice before the IRS by passing an IRS examination.

Entertainment expenses. These expenses are deductible only if they are directly related to or associated with a trade or business. Various restrictions and documentation requirements have been imposed upon the deductibility of entertainment expenses to prevent abuses by taxpayers. See, for example, the provision contained in § 274(n) that disallows 50 percent (20 percent prior to 1994) of entertainment expenses. § 274.

Entity. An organization or being that possesses separate existence for tax purposes. Examples are corporations, partnerships, estates, and trusts. See also *disregard of corporate entity.*

Entity accounting income. Entity accounting income is not identical to the taxable income of a trust or estate, nor is it determined in the same manner as the entity's financial accounting income would be. The trust document or will determines whether certain income, expenses, gains, or losses are allocated to the corpus of the entity or to the entity's income beneficiaries. Only the items that are allocated to the income beneficiaries are included in entity accounting income.

Entity buy-sell agreement. The entity is to purchase a withdrawing owner's interest. When the entity is a corporation, the agreement generally involves a stock redemption on the part of the withdrawing shareholder. See also *buy-sell agreement* and *cross-purchase buy-sell agreement.*

Entity concept. The theory of partnership taxation under which a partnership is treated as a separate and distinct entity from the partners, and has its own tax attributes.

Equity structure shift. A tax-free reorganization other than a *divisive reorganization* or *recapitalization.* If there is a more than 50 percent change in the ownership of a loss corporation in an equity structure shift, § 382 limits the use of NOL carryovers of the loss corporation. Specifically, the annual NOL carryover deduction is limited to the value of the loss corporation immediately before the equity structure shift times the *long-term tax-exempt rate.*

Escrow. Money or other property placed with a third party as security for an existing or proposed obligation. Ramon, for example, agrees to purchase Rashad's stock in Orange Corporation but needs time to raise the necessary funds. Rashad places the stock with Eve (the escrow agent), with instructions to deliver it to Ramon when the purchase price is paid.

Estate. An entity that locates, collects, distributes, and discharges the assets and liabilities of a decedent.

Estate freeze. Procedures directed toward fixing and stabilizing the value of an interest retained in a business while transferring the growth portion to family members. In the case of a closely held corporation, usually the estate freeze involves keeping the preferred stock and giving away the common stock. The ultimate objective is to reduce estate value when the original owner-donor dies.

Estate tax. A tax imposed on the right to transfer property by death. Thus, an estate tax is levied on the decedent's estate and not on the heir receiving the property. See also *death tax* and *inheritance tax.*

Estimated useful life. The period over which an asset will be used by the taxpayer. Some assets do not have an estimated useful life. The estimated useful life of an asset is essential to measuring the annual tax deduction for depreciation and amortization.

Estoppel.   The process of being stopped from proving something (even if true) in court due to a prior inconsistent action. It is usually invoked as a matter of fairness to prevent one party (either the taxpayer or the IRS) from taking advantage of a prior error.

Excess lobbying expenditure.   An excise tax is applied on otherwise tax-exempt organizations with respect to the excess of total lobbying expenditures over *grass roots lobbying expenditures* for the year.

Excess loss account.   When a subsidiary has generated more historical losses than its parent has invested in the entity, the parent's basis in the subsidiary is zero, and the parent records additional losses in an excess loss account. This treatment allows the parent to continue to deduct losses of the subsidiary, even where no basis reduction is possible, while avoiding the need to show a negative stock basis on various financial records. If the subsidiary stock is sold while an excess loss account exists, capital gain income usually is recognized to the extent of the balance in the account.

Excise tax.   A tax on the manufacture, sale, or use of goods; on the carrying on of an occupation or activity; or on the transfer of property. Thus, the Federal estate and gift taxes are, theoretically, excise taxes.

Executor.   A person designated by a will to administer (manage or take charge of) the assets and liabilities of a decedent. See also *administrator*.

Exemption.   An amount by which the tax base is reduced for all qualifying taxpayers. Individuals can receive personal and dependency exemptions, and taxpayers apply an exemption in computing their alternative minimum taxable income. Often, the exemption amount is phased out as the tax base becomes sizable.

Exemption equivalent amount.   The amount of value (scheduled to reach $1,000,000) that is the equivalent of the unified transfer tax credit allowed. See also *by-pass amount*.

Exempt organization.   An organization that is either partially or completely exempt from Federal income taxation. § 501.

Expenses in respect of a decedent.   See *deductions in respect of a decedent*.

F

Fair market value.   The amount at which property would change hands between a willing buyer and a willing seller, neither being under any compulsion to buy or to sell, and both having reasonable knowledge of the relevant facts. Reg. § 20.2031–1(b).

Federal District Court.   See *district court*.

Federal Register.   The first place that the rules and regulations of U.S. administrative agencies (e.g., the U.S. Treasury Department) are published.

Feeder organization.   An entity that carries on a trade or business for the benefit of an *exempt organization*. However, such a relationship does not result in the feeder organization itself being tax-exempt. § 502.

FICA tax.   An abbreviation that stands for Federal Insurance Contributions Act, commonly referred to as the Social Security tax. The FICA tax is comprised of the Social Security tax (old age, survivors, and disability insurance) and the Medicare tax (hospital insurance) and is imposed on both employers and employees. The employer is responsible for withholding from the employee's wages the Social Security tax at a rate of 6.2 percent on a maximum wage base of $68,400 (for 1998) and the Medicare tax at a rate of 1.45 percent (no maximum wage base). The employer is required to match the employee's contribution. See also *employment taxes*.

Fiduciary.   A person who manages money or property for another and who must exercise a standard of care in the management activity imposed by law or contract. A trustee, for example, possesses a fiduciary responsibility to the beneficiaries of the trust to follow the terms of the trust and the requirements of applicable state law. A breach of fiduciary responsibility would make the trustee liable to the beneficiaries for any damage caused by the breach.

Field audit.   An audit conducted by the IRS on the business premises of the taxpayer or in the office of the tax practitioner representing the taxpayer. See also *audit, correspondence audit*, and *office audit*.

Finalized Regulation.   See *regulations*.

FIRPTA.   Under the Foreign Investment in Real Property Tax Act, gains or losses realized by nonresident aliens and non-U.S. corporations on the disposition of U.S. real estate create U.S.-source income and are subject to U.S. income tax.

First-in, first-out (FIFO).   An accounting method for determining the cost of inventories. Under this method, the inventory on hand is deemed to be the sum of the cost of the most recently acquired units. See also *last-in, first-out (LIFO)*.

Fiscal year.   A fiscal year is a 12-month period ending on the last day of a month other than December. In certain circumstances, a taxpayer is permitted to elect a fiscal year instead of being required to use a calendar year. See also *accounting period* and *taxable year*.

Fixing-up expense.   An expense that is incurred to assist in the sale of a residence and is deductible in calculating the adjusted sales price. Fixing-up expenses include such items as ordinary repairs, painting, and wallpapering. To qualify, the expense must (1) be incurred on work performed during the 90-day period ending on the date of the contract of sale, (2) be paid within 30 days after the date of the sale, and (3) not be a capital expenditure. This term is not relevant for the sale of a principal residence after May 6, 1997. The Taxpayer Relief Act of 1997 (TRA of 1997) repealed § 1034. See also *adjusted sales price*.

Flat tax. In its pure form, a flat tax would eliminate all exclusions, deductions, and credits and impose a one-rate tax on gross income.

Flexible spending plan. An employee benefit plan that allows the employee to take a reduction in salary in exchange for the employer paying benefits that can be provided by the employer without the employee being required to recognize income (e.g., medical and child-care benefits).

Foreign corporation. A corporation that is not created in the United States or organized under the laws of one of the states of the United States. § 7701(a)(5). See also *domestic corporation.*

Foreign currency transaction. An exchange that could generate a foreign currency gain or loss for a U.S. taxpayer. For example, if a taxpayer contracts to purchase foreign goods, payable in a currency other than U.S. dollars, at a specified date in the future, any change in the exchange rate between the dollar and that currency will generate a foreign currency gain or loss upon completion of the contract. This gain or loss is treated as separate from the underlying transaction; it may create ordinary or capital gain or loss.

Foreign earned income exclusion. The Code allows exclusions for earned income generated outside the United States to alleviate any tax base and rate disparities among countries. In addition, the exclusion is allowed for housing expenditures incurred by the taxpayer's employer with respect to the non-U.S. assignment, and self-employed individuals can deduct foreign housing expenses incurred in a trade or business.

Foreign personal holding company (FPHC). A foreign corporation in which (1) 60 percent or more of the gross income for the taxable year is FPHC income and (2) more than 50 percent of the total combined voting power or the total value of the stock is owned, directly or indirectly, by five or fewer individuals who are U.S. persons (the U.S. group) at any time during the taxable year. The 60 percent of gross income test drops to 50 percent or more after the 60 percent requirement has been met for one tax year, until the foreign corporation does not meet the 50 percent test for three consecutive years or the stock ownership requirement is not met for an entire tax year.

Foreign sales corporation (FSC). An entity qualifying for a partial exemption of its gross export receipts from U.S. tax. Most FSCs must maintain a presence in a foreign country. In addition, an FSC cannot issue preferred stock, nor can it have more than 25 shareholders.

Foreign-source income. Income that is not sourced within the United States. Examples include earnings from the performance of a personal services contract outside the United States, interest received from a non-U.S. corporation, and income from the use of property outside the United States.

Foreign tax credit or deduction. A U.S. citizen or resident who incurs or pays income taxes to a foreign country on income subject to United States tax may be able to claim some of these taxes as a deduction or a credit against the U.S. income tax. §§ 27, 164, and 901–905.

Form 706. The U.S. Estate Tax Return. In certain cases, this form must be filed for a decedent who was a resident or citizen of the United States.

Form 709. The U.S. Gift Tax Return.

Form 709–A. The U.S. Short Form Gift Tax Return.

Form 870. The signing of Form 870 (Waiver of Restriction on Assessment and Collection of Deficiency in Tax and Acceptance of Overassessments) by a taxpayer permits the IRS to assess a proposed deficiency without issuing a statutory notice of deficiency (90-day letter). This means the taxpayer must pay the deficiency and cannot file a petition to the U.S. Tax Court. § 6213(d).

Form 872. The signing of this form by a taxpayer extends the period during which the IRS can make an assessment or collection of a tax. In other words, Form 872 extends the applicable statute of limitations. § 6501(c)(4).

Form 1041. The U.S. Fiduciary Income Tax Return, required to be filed by estates and trusts. See Appendix B for a specimen form.

Form 1065. The U.S. Partnership Return of Income. See Appendix B for a specimen form.

Form 1120. The U.S. Corporation Income Tax Return. See Appendix B for a specimen form.

Form 1120–A. The U.S. Short-Form Corporation Income Tax Return. See Appendix B for a specimen form.

Form 1120S. The U.S. Small Business Corporation Income Tax Return, required to be filed by S corporations. See Appendix B for a specimen form.

Franchise. An agreement that gives the transferee the right to distribute, sell, or provide goods, services, or facilities within a specified area. The cost of obtaining a franchise may be amortized over a statutory period of 15 years. In general, the franchisor's gain on the sale of franchise rights is an ordinary gain because the franchisor retains a significant power, right, or continuing interest in the subject of the franchise. §§ 197 and 1253.

Franchise tax. A tax levied on the right to do business in a state as a corporation. Although income considerations may come into play, the tax usually is based on the capitalization of the corporation.

Fraud. Tax fraud falls into two categories: civil and criminal. Under civil fraud, the IRS may impose as a penalty an amount equal to as much as 75 percent of the underpayment [§ 6651(f)]. Fines and/or imprisonment are prescribed for conviction of various types of criminal tax fraud (§§ 7201–7207). Both civil and criminal fraud involve a specific intent on the part of the taxpayer to evade the tax; mere negligence is not enough. Criminal fraud requires the additional element of willfulness (i.e., done deliberately and with evil purpose). In practice, it becomes difficult to distinguish between the degree of intent necessary to support criminal, rather than civil, fraud. In either situation, the IRS has the burden of proving fraud. See also *burden of proof.*

Free transferability of interests.   The capability of the owner of an entity to transfer his or her ownership interest to another without the consent of the other owners. It is a characteristic of a corporation since a shareholder usually can freely transfer the stock to others without the approval of the existing shareholders. Reg. § 301.7701–2(e).

Fringe benefits.   Compensation or other benefits received by an employee that are not in the form of cash. Some fringe benefits (e.g., accident and health plans, group term life insurance) may be excluded from the employee's gross income and thus are not subject to the Federal income tax.

Functional currency.   The currency of the economic environment in which the taxpayer carries on most of its activities, and in which the taxpayer transacts most of its business.

F.3d.   An abbreviation for the third series of the *Federal Reporter,* the official series in which decisions of the U.S. Court of Federal Claims and the U.S. Court of Appeals are published. The second series is denoted F.2d.

F.Supp.   The abbreviation for the *Federal Supplement,* the official series in which the reported decisions of the Federal District Courts are published.

FUTA tax.   An employment tax levied on employers. Jointly administered by the Federal and state governments, the tax provides funding for unemployment benefits. FUTA applies at a rate of 6.2 percent in 1998 on the first $7,000 of covered wages paid during the year for each employee. The Federal government allows a credit for FUTA paid (or allowed under a merit rating system) to the state. The credit cannot exceed 5.4 percent of the covered wages. See also *employment taxes.*

Future interest.   An interest that will come into being at some future time. It is distinguished from a present interest, which already exists. Assume that Dan transfers securities to a newly created trust. Under the terms of the trust instrument, income from the securities is to be paid each year to Wilma for her life, with the securities passing to Sam upon Wilma's death. Wilma has a present interest in the trust since she is currently entitled to receive the income from the securities. Sam has a future interest since he must wait for Wilma's death to benefit from the trust. The *annual exclusion* of $10,000 is not allowed for a gift of a future interest. § 2503(b). See also *annual exclusion* and *gift splitting.*

G

General business credit.   The summation of various nonrefundable business credits, including the tax credit for rehabilitation expenditures, welfare-to-work credit, work opportunity credit, research activities credit, low-income housing credit, and disabled access credit. The amount of general business credit that can be used to reduce the tax liability is limited to the taxpayer's net income tax reduced by the greater of (1) the tentative minimum tax or (2) 25 percent of the net regular tax liability that exceeds $25,000. Unused general business credits can be carried back 1 year and forward 20 years (back 3 years and forward 15 years for tax years beginning before January 1, 1998). § 38.

General partner.   A partner who is fully liable in an individual capacity for the debts of the partnership to third parties. A general partner's liability is not limited to the investment in the partnership. See also *limited partner.*

General partnership.   A partnership that is owned by one or more *general partners.* Creditors of a general partnership can collect amounts owed them from both the partnership assets and the assets of the partners individually.

General power of appointment.   See *power of appointment.*

Gift.   A transfer of property for less than adequate consideration. Gifts usually occur in a personal setting (such as between members of the same family). They are excluded from the income tax base but may be subject to a transfer tax.

Gift splitting.   A special election for Federal gift tax purposes under which husband and wife can treat a gift by one of them to a third party as being made one-half by each. If, for example, George (the husband) makes a gift of $20,000 to Shirley, Barbara (the wife) may elect to treat $10,000 of the gift as coming from her. The major advantage of the election is that it enables the parties to take advantage of the nonowner spouse's (Barbara in this case) annual exclusion and unified credit. § 2513. See also *annual exclusion.*

Gift tax.   A tax imposed on the transfer of property by gift. The tax is imposed upon the donor of a gift and is based on the fair market value of the property on the date of the gift.

Gifts within three years of death.   Some taxable gifts automatically are included in the gross estate of the donor if death occurs within three years of the gift. § 2035.

Goodwill.   The reputation and built-up business of a company. For accounting purposes, goodwill has no basis unless it is purchased. In the purchase of a business, goodwill generally is the difference between the purchase price and the fair market value of the assets acquired. The intangible asset goodwill can be amortized for tax purposes over a 15-year period. Reg. § 1.167(a)–3. See also *amortization.*

Grantor.   A transferor of property. The creator of a trust is usually referred to as the grantor of the trust.

Grantor trust.   A trust under which the grantor retains control over the income or corpus (or both) to such an extent that he or she is treated as the owner of the property and its income for income tax purposes. Income from a grantor trust is taxable to the grantor and not to the beneficiary who receives it. §§ 671–679. See also *reversionary interest.*

Grass roots lobbying expenditures.   Exempt organizations are prohibited from engaging in political activities, but spending incurred to influence the opinions of the general public relative to specific legislation is permitted by the law. See also *excess lobbying expenditures.*

Green card test. Form I–551, received from a U.S. consul as a receipt showing that the holder has immigration status in the United States and used to refute alien status for tax purposes.

Gross estate. The property owned or previously transferred by a *decedent* that is subject to the Federal estate tax. The gross estate can be distinguished from the *probate estate*, which is property actually subject to administration by the *administrator* or *executor* of an estate. §§ 2031–2046. See also *adjusted gross estate* and *taxable estate*.

Gross income. Income subject to the Federal income tax. Gross income does not include all economic income. That is, certain exclusions are allowed (e.g., interest on municipal bonds). For a manufacturing or merchandising business, gross income usually means gross profit (gross sales or gross receipts less cost of goods sold). § 61 and Reg. § 1.61–3(a). See also *adjusted gross income* and *taxable income*.

Gross up. To add back to the value of the property or income received the amount of the tax that has been paid. For gifts made within three years of death, any gift tax paid on the transfer is added to the gross estate. § 2035(c).

Group term life insurance. Life insurance coverage provided by an employer for a group of employees. Such insurance is renewable on a year-to-year basis, and typically no cash surrender value is built up. The premiums paid by the employer on the insurance are not taxed to the employees on coverage of up to $50,000 per person. § 79 and Reg. § 1.79–1(b).

Guaranteed payment. Payments made by a partnership to a partner for services rendered or for the use of capital to the extent that the payments are determined without regard to the income of the partnership. The payments are treated as though they were made to a nonpartner and thus are usually deductible by the entity.

Guardianship. A legal arrangement under which one person (a guardian) has the legal right and duty to care for another (the ward) and his or her property. A guardianship is established because the ward is unable to act legally on his or her own behalf [e.g., because of minority (he or she is not of age) or mental or physical incapacity].

H

Half-year convention. The half-year convention is a cost recovery convention that assumes all property is placed in service at mid-year and thus provides for a half-year's cost recovery for that year.

Head of household. An unmarried individual who maintains a household for another and satisfies certain conditions set forth in § 2(b). This status enables the taxpayer to use a set of income tax rates that are lower than those applicable to other unmarried individuals but higher than those applicable to surviving spouses and married persons filing a joint return.

Heir. A person who inherits property from a decedent.

Highly compensated employee. The employee group is generally divided into two categories for fringe benefit (including pension and profit sharing plans) purposes. These are (1) highly compensated employees and (2) nonhighly compensated employees. For most fringe benefits, if the fringe benefit plan discriminates in favor of highly compensated employees, it will not be a qualified plan with respect, at a minimum, to the highly compensated employees.

Hobby. An activity not engaged in for profit. The Code restricts the amount of losses that an individual can deduct for hobby activities so that these transactions cannot be used to offset income from other sources. § 183.

Holding period. The period of time during which property has been held for income tax purposes. The holding period is significant in determining whether gain or loss from the sale or exchange of a capital asset is long-term, mid-term, or short-term. § 1223.

Home equity loans. Loans that utilize the personal residence of the taxpayer as security. The interest on such loans is deductible as *qualified residence interest*. However, interest is deductible only on the portion of the loan that does not exceed the lesser of: (1) the fair market value of the residence, reduced by the *acquisition indebtedness* or (2) $100,000 ($50,000 for married persons filing separate returns. A major benefit of a home equity loan is that there are no tracing rules regarding the use of the loan proceeds. § 163(h)(3).

HOPE scholarship credit. A tax credit for qualifying tuition expenses paid for the first two years of postsecondary education. Room, board, and book costs are ineligible for the credit. The maximum credit available is $1,500 per year per student, computed as 100 percent of the first $1,000 of tuition expenses, plus 50 percent of the second $1,000 of tuition expenses. Eligible students include the taxpayer, taxpayer's spouse, and taxpayer's dependents. To qualify for the credit, a student must take at least one-half the full-time course load for at least one academic term at a qualifying educational institution. The credit is phased out for higher-income taxpayers. § 25A.

Hot assets. Unrealized receivables and substantially appreciated inventory under § 751. When hot assets are present, the sale of a partnership interest or the disproportionate distribution of the assets can cause ordinary income to be recognized.

H.R. 10 plans. See *Keogh plans*.

Hybrid method. A combination of the accrual and cash methods of accounting. That is, the taxpayer may account for some items of income on the accrual method (e.g., sales and cost of goods sold) and other items (e.g., interest income) on the cash method.

I

Imputed interest. For certain long-term sales of property, the IRS can convert some of the gain from the sale into interest income if the contract does not provide for a minimum rate of interest to be paid by the purchaser. The application of this procedure has the effect of forcing the seller to recognize less long-term capital gain and more ordinary income (interest income). § 483 and the related Regulations.

Incident of ownership.   An element of ownership or degree of control over a life insurance policy. The retention by an insured of an incident of ownership in a life insurance policy will cause the policy proceeds to be included in the insured's gross estate upon death. § 2042(2) and Reg. § 20.2042–1(c). See also *gross estate* and *insured*.

Income.   For tax purposes, an increase in wealth that has been realized.

Income beneficiary.   The party entitled to income from property. In a typical trust situation, Alan is to receive the income for life with corpus or principal passing to Gertrude upon Alan's death. In this case, Alan is the income beneficiary of the trust.

Income in respect of a decedent (IRD).   Income earned by a decedent at the time of death but not reportable on the final income tax return because of the method of accounting that appropriately is utilized. Such income is included in the gross estate and is taxed to the eventual recipient (either the estate or heirs). The recipient is, however, allowed an income tax deduction for the estate tax attributable to the income. § 691.

Income interest.   The right of a beneficiary to receive distributions from the fiduciary income of a trust or estate.

Income shifting.   Occurs when an individual transfers some of his or her gross income to a taxpayer who is subject to a lower tax rate, thereby reducing the total income tax liability of the group. Income shifting produces a successful assignment of income. It can be accomplished by transferring income-producing property to the lower-bracket taxpayer or to an effective trust for his or her benefit, or by transferring ownership interests in a family partnership or in a closely held corporation.

Incomplete transfer.   A transfer made by a decedent during lifetime that, because of certain control or enjoyment retained by the transferor, is not considered complete for Federal estate tax purposes. Thus, some or all of the fair market value of the property transferred is included in the transferor's gross estate. §§ 2036–2038. See also *gross estate* and *revocable transfer*.

Independent contractor.   A self-employed person as distinguished from one who is employed as an employee.

Indexation.   Various components of the tax formula are adjusted periodically for the effects of inflation, so that the effects of the formula are not eroded by price level changes. Tax rate schedules, personal and dependency exemption amounts, and the standard deduction, among other items, are indexed in this manner.

Individual retirement account (IRA).   A type of retirement plan to which an individual with earned income can contribute a maximum of $2,000 ($2,000 each in the case of a married couple with a spousal IRA) per tax year. IRAs can be classified as traditional IRAs or Roth IRAs. With a traditional IRA, an individual can contribute and deduct a maximum of $2,000 per tax year. The deduction is a deduction *for* AGI. However, if the individual is an active participant in another qualified retirement plan, the deduction is phased out proportionally between certain AGI ranges (note that the phase-out limits the amount of the deduction and not the amount of the contribution). With a Roth IRA, an individual can contribute a maximum of $2,000 per tax year. No deduction is permitted. However, if a five-year holding period requirement is satisfied and if the distribution is a qualified distribution, the taxpayer can make tax-free withdrawals from a Roth IRA. The maximum annual contribution is phased out proportionally between certain AGI ranges. § 219.

Inheritance tax.   A tax imposed on the right to receive property from a *decedent*. Thus, theoretically, an inheritance tax is imposed on the heir. The Federal estate tax is imposed on the estate. See also *death tax* and *estate tax*.

In kind.   See *distributions in kind*.

Inside basis.   A partnership's basis in the assets it owns.

Installment method.   A method of accounting enabling certain taxpayers to spread the recognition of gain on the sale of property over the collection period. Under this procedure, the seller arrives at the gain to be recognized by computing the gross profit percentage from the sale (the gain divided by the contract price) and applying it to each payment received. § 453.

Insured.   A person whose life is the subject of an insurance policy. Upon the death of the insured, the life insurance policy matures, and the proceeds become payable to the designated beneficiary. See also *life insurance*.

Intangible asset.   Property that is a "right" rather than a physical object. Examples are patents, stocks and bonds, goodwill, trademarks, franchises, and copyrights. See also *amortization* and *tangible property*.

Interest-free loans.   Bona fide loans that carry no interest (or a below-market rate). If made in a nonbusiness setting, the imputed interest element is treated as a gift from the lender to the borrower. If made by a corporation to a shareholder, a constructive dividend could result. In either event, the lender may recognize interest income. § 7872.

Interest on student loans.   The Taxpayer Relief Act of 1997 (TRA of 1997) provides for a limited ability to deduct interest on student loans used to pay qualified higher education expenses (i.e., tuition, fees, books, supplies, room and board). For 1998, the ceiling on the deduction is $1,000. The deduction is allowed only with respect to interest paid on the loan during the first 60 months in which interest payments are required. The deduction is a deduction *for* AGI. § 221.

Internal Revenue Code.   The collected statutes that govern the taxation of income, property transfers, and other transactions in the United States and the enforcement of those provisions. Enacted by Congress, the Code is amended frequently, but it has not been reorganized since 1954. However, because of the extensive revisions to the statutes that occurred with the Tax Reform Act of 1986, Title 26 of the U.S. Code is now known as the Internal Revenue Code of 1986.

Internal Revenue Service.   The Federal agency, a division of the Department of the Treasury, charged with implementing the U.S. revenue enforcement and collection provisions.

Interpolated terminal reserve.   The measure used in valuing insurance policies·for gift and estate tax purposes when the policies are not paid up at the time of their transfer. Reg. § 20.2031–8(a)(3), Ex. (3).

Interpretive Regulation.   A Regulation issued by the Treasury Department that purports to explain the meaning of a particular Code Section. An interpretive Regulation is given less deference than a legislative Regulation. See also *legislative regulation* and *procedural regulation*. § 7805.

Inter vivos transfer.   A transfer of property during the life of the owner. Distinguished from testamentary transfers, where the property passes at death.

Intestate.   No will exists at the time of death. In such cases, state law prescribes who will receive the decedent's property. The laws of intestate succession generally favor the surviving spouse, children, and grandchildren, and then parents and grandparents and brothers and sisters.

Investment income.   Consisting of virtually the same elements as portfolio income, a measure by which to justify a deduction for interest on investment indebtedness. See also *investment indebtedness* and *portfolio income*.

Investment indebtedness.   Debt incurred to carry or incur investments by the taxpayer in assets that will produce portfolio income. Limitations are placed upon interest deductions that are incurred in connection with the debt (generally to the corresponding amount of investment income).

Investment interest.   Payment for the use of funds used to acquire assets that produce investment income. The deduction for investment interest is limited to net investment income for the tax year. See also *investment income*.

Investment tax credit (ITC).   A tax credit that usually was equal to 10 percent (unless a reduced credit was elected) of the qualified investment in tangible personalty used in a trade or business. If the tangible personalty had a recovery period of five years or more, the full cost of the property qualified for the credit. Only 60 percent qualified for property with a recovery period of three years. However, the regular investment tax credit was repealed by TRA of 1986 for property placed in service after December 31, 1985. § 46. See also *general business credit*.

Investor losses.   Losses on stock and securities. If stocks and bonds are capital assets in the hands of the holder, a capital loss materializes as of the last day of the taxable year in which the stocks or bonds become worthless. Under certain circumstances involving stocks and bonds of affiliated corporations, an ordinary loss is permitted upon worthlessness.

Involuntary conversion.   The loss or destruction of property through theft, casualty, or condemnation. Any gain realized on an involuntary conversion can, at the taxpayer's election, be deferred for Federal income tax purposes if the owner reinvests the proceeds within a prescribed period of time in property that is similar or related in service or use. See also *nontaxable exchange*. § 1033.

IRA.   See *individual retirement account*.

Itemized deductions.   Personal and employee expenditures allowed by the Code as deductions from adjusted gross income. Examples include certain medical expenses, interest on home mortgages, state income taxes, and charitable contributions. Itemized deductions are reported on Schedule A of Form 1040. Certain miscellaneous itemized deductions are reduced by 2 percent of the taxpayer's adjusted gross income. In addition, a taxpayer whose adjusted gross income exceeds a certain level (indexed annually) must reduce the itemized deductions by 3 percent of the excess of adjusted gross income over that level. Medical, casualty and theft, and investment interest deductions are not subject to the 3 percent reduction. The 3 percent reduction may not reduce itemized deductions that are subject to the reduction to below 20 percent of their initial amount.

J

Jeopardy assessment.   If the collection of a tax appears in question, the IRS may assess and collect the tax immediately without the usual formalities. The IRS can terminate a taxpayer's taxable year before the usual date if it feels that the collection of the tax may be in peril because the taxpayer plans to leave the country. §§ 6851 and 6861–6864.

Joint and several liability.   Permits the IRS to collect a tax from one or all of several taxpayers. A husband and wife who file a joint income tax return usually are collectively or individually liable for the full amount of the tax liability. § 6013(d)(3).

Joint tenants.   Two or more persons having undivided ownership of property with the right of survivorship. Right of survivorship gives the surviving owner full ownership of the property. Suppose Bob and Tami are joint tenants of a tract of land. Upon Bob's death, Tami becomes the sole owner of the property. For the estate tax consequences upon the death of a joint tenant, see § 2040. See also *tenancy by the entirety* and *tenancy in common*.

Joint venture.   A one-time grouping of two or more persons in a business undertaking. Unlike a partnership, a joint venture does not entail a continuing relationship among the parties. A joint venture is treated like a partnership for Federal income tax purposes. § 7701(a)(2).

K

Keogh plans.   Retirement plans available to self-employed taxpayers. They are also referred to as H.R. 10 plans. Under such plans, a taxpayer may deduct each year up to either 20 percent of net earnings from self-employment or $30,000, whichever is less.

Kiddie tax. See *tax on unearned income of a child under age 14.*

L

Lapse. The expiration of a right either by the death of the holder or upon the expiration of a period of time. Thus, a power of appointment lapses upon the death of the holder if he or she has not exercised the power during life or at death (through a will).

Last-in, first-out (LIFO). An accounting method for valuing inventories for tax purposes. Under this method, it is assumed that the inventory on hand is valued at the cost of the earliest acquired units. § 472. See also *first-in, first-out (FIFO).*

Leaseback. The transferor of property later leases it back. In a sale-leaseback situation, for example, Richard sells property to Sally and subsequently leases the property from Sally. Thus, Richard becomes the lessee and Sally the lessor.

Least aggregate deferral method. An algorithm set forth in the Regulations to determine the tax year for a partnership or S corporation with owners whose tax years differ. The tax year selected is the one that produces the least aggregate deferral of income for the owners.

Legacy. A transfer of cash or other property by will.

Legal age. The age at which a person may enter into binding contracts or commit other legal acts. In most states, a minor reaches legal age or majority (comes of age) at age 18.

Legal representative. A person who oversees the legal affairs of another; for example, the executor or administrator of an estate or a court-appointed guardian of a minor or incompetent person.

Legatee. The recipient of property under a will and transferred by the death of the owner.

Legislative Regulation. Some Code Sections give the Secretary of the Treasury or his delegate the authority to prescribe Regulations to carry out the details of administration or to otherwise complete the operating rules. Regulations issued pursuant to this type of authority truly possess the force and effect of law. In effect, Congress is almost delegating its legislative powers to the Treasury Department. See also *interpretive regulation* and *procedural regulation.*

Lessee. One who rents property from another. In the case of real estate, the lessee is also known as the tenant.

Lessor. One who rents property to another. In the case of real estate, the lessor is also known as the landlord.

Letter ruling. The written response of the IRS to a taxpayer's request for interpretation of the revenue laws, with respect to a proposed transaction (e.g., concerning the tax-free status of a reorganization). Not to be relied on as precedent by other than the party who requested the ruling.

LEXIS. An on-line database system with which the tax researcher can obtain access to the Internal Revenue Code, Regulations, administrative rulings, and court case opinions.

Liabilities in excess of basis. On the contribution of capital to a corporation, an investor recognizes gain on the exchange to the extent that contributed assets carry liabilities with a face amount in excess of the tax basis of the contributed assets. This rule keeps the investor from holding the investment asset received with a negative basis. § 357(c).

Life estate. A legal arrangement under which the beneficiary (the life tenant) is entitled to the income from property for his or her life. Upon the death of the life tenant, the property is transferred to the holder of the remainder interest. See also *income beneficiary* and *remainder interest.*

Life insurance. A contract between the holder of a policy and an insurance company (the carrier) under which the company agrees, in return for premium payments, to pay a specified sum (the face value or maturity value of the policy) to the designated beneficiary upon the death of the insured. See also *insured.*

Lifetime learning credit. A tax credit for qualifying tuition expenses for taxpayers pursuing education beyond the first two years of postsecondary education. Individuals who are completing their last two years of undergraduate studies, pursuing graduate or professional degrees, or otherwise seeking new job skills or maintaining existing job skills are all eligible for the credit. Eligible individuals include the taxpayer, taxpayer's spouse, and taxpayer's dependents. The maximum credit is 20 percent of the first $5,000 ($10,000 beginning in 2003) of qualifying tuition expenses and is computed per taxpayer. The credit is phased out for higher-income taxpayers. § 25A.

Like-kind exchange. An exchange of property held for productive use in a trade or business or for investment (except inventory and stocks and bonds) for other investment or trade or business property. Unless non-like-kind property (boot) is received, the exchange is fully nontaxable. § 1031. See also *boot* and *nontaxable exchange.*

Limited liability. The liability of an entity and its owners to third parties is limited to the investment in the entity. This is a characteristic of a corporation, as shareholders generally are not responsible for the debts of the corporation and, at most, may lose the amount paid in for the stock issued. Reg. § 301.7701–2(d).

Limited liability company (LLC). A form of entity allowed by all of the states. The entity is taxed as a partnership in which all members or owners of the LLC are treated much like limited partners. There are no restrictions on ownership, all members may participate in management, and none has personal liability for the entity's debts.

Limited liability partnership (LLP). A form of entity allowed by many of the states, where a general partnership registers with the state as an LLP. Owners are general partners, but a partner is not liable for any malpractice committed by other partners. The personal assets of the partners are at risk for the entity's contractual liabilities, such as accounts payable. The personal assets of a specific partner are at risk for his or her own professional malpractice and tort liability, and for malpractice and torts committed by those whom he or she supervises.

Limited partner.   A partner whose liability to third-party creditors of the partnership is limited to the amount he or she has invested in the partnership. See also *general partner* and *limited partnership*.

Limited partnership.   A partnership in which some of the partners are limited partners. At least one of the partners in a limited partnership must be a general partner. See also *general partner* and *limited partner*.

Liquidating distribution.   A distribution by a partnership or corporation that is in complete liquidation of the entity's trade or business activities. Typically, such distributions generate capital gain or loss to the investors without regard, for instance, to the earnings and profits of the corporation or to the partnership's basis in the distributed property. They can, however, lead to recognized gain or loss at the corporate level.

Liquidation.   See *corporate liquidation*.

Listed property.   The term listed property includes (1) any passenger automobile, (2) any other property used as a means of transportation, (3) any property of a type generally used for purposes of entertainment, recreation, or amusement, (4) any computer or peripheral equipment (with an exception for exclusive business use), (5) any cellular telephone (or other similar telecommunications equipment), and (6) any other property of a type specified in the Regulations. If listed property is predominantly used for business, the taxpayer is allowed to use the statutory percentage method of cost recovery. Otherwise, the straight-line cost recovery method must be used. § 280F.

Living trust.   A revocable trust. Often touted as a useful means of avoiding some probate costs.

Lobbying expenditure.   An expenditure made for the purpose of influencing legislation. Such payments can result in the loss of the exempt status of, and the imposition of Federal income tax on, an exempt organization.

Long-term capital gain or loss.   Results from the sale or other taxable exchange of a capital asset that had been held by the seller for more than 18 months or from other transactions involving statutorily designated assets, including § 1231 property and patents.

Long-term care insurance.   Insurance that helps pay the cost of care when the insured is unable to care for himself or herself. Such insurance is generally thought of as insurance against the cost of an aged person entering a nursing home. The employer can provide the insurance and the premiums may be excluded from the employee's gross income. § 7702B.

Long-term contract.   A building, installation, construction, or manufacturing contract that is entered into but not completed within the same tax year. A manufacturing contract is a long-term contract only if the contract is to manufacture (1) a unique item not normally carried in finished goods inventory or (2) items that normally require more than 12 calendar months to complete. The two available methods to account for long-term contracts are the percentage of completion method and the completed contract method. The completed contract method can be used only in limited circumstances. § 460. See also *completed contract method* and *percentage of completion method*.

Long-term tax-exempt rate.   Used in the derivation of NOL limitations in the context of an equity structure shift. The highest of the Federal long-term interest rates in effect for any of the last three months.

Low-income housing credit.   Beneficial treatment to owners of low-income housing is provided in the form of a tax credit. The calculated credit is claimed in the year the building is placed in service and in the following nine years. § 42. See also *general business credit*.

Lump-sum distribution.   Payment of the entire amount due at one time rather than in installments. Such distributions often occur from qualified pension or profit sharing plans upon the retirement or death of a covered employee.

M

MACRS.   See *accelerated cost recovery system (ACRS)*.

Majority.   See *legal age*.

Malpractice.   Professional misconduct; an unreasonable lack of skill.

Marital deduction.   A deduction allowed against the taxable estate or taxable gifts upon the transfer of property from one spouse to another.

Market value.   See *fair market value*.

Marriage penalty.   The additional tax liability that results for a married couple when compared with what their tax liability would be if they were not married and filed separate returns.

Meaningful reduction test.   A decrease in the shareholder's voting control. Used to determine whether a redemption qualifies for sale or exchange treatment.

Medical savings account.   A plan available to employees of small firms (50 or fewer employees) with high-deductible health insurance. The employee can place money in the fund and then deduct the contributions (within limits) from gross income. If the employer contributes to the fund, the employee can exclude the contribution from gross income. Income earned from the fund and withdrawals for medical care are not subject to tax. §§ 106(b) and 220.

Merger.   The absorption of one corporation by another with the corporation being absorbed losing its legal identity. Orange Corporation is merged into Blue Corporation, and the shareholders of Orange receive stock in Blue in exchange for their stock in Orange Corporation. After the merger, Orange

Corporation ceases to exist as a separate legal entity. If a merger meets certain conditions, it is nontaxable to the parties involved. § 368(a)(1)(A). See also *corporate acquisition* and *corporate reorganization.*

Mid-month convention.　The mid-month convention is a cost recovery convention that assumes property is placed in service in the middle of the month that it is actually placed in service.

Mid-quarter convention.　The mid-quarter convention is a cost recovery convention that assumes property placed in service during the year is placed in service at the middle of the quarter in which it is actually placed in service. The mid-quarter convention applies if more than 40 percent of the value of property (other than eligible real estate) is placed in service during the last quarter of the year.

Mid-term capital gain or loss.　Gain or loss from the disposition of a capital asset if the holding period is longer than 12 months but not longer than 18 months.

Minimum credit (AET).　A fixed amount, $150,000 for personal service firms and $250,000 for all others, below which the *accumulated earnings credit* cannot be derived. Assures that small and start-up corporations can generate a minimum amount of earnings before being subject to the AET.

Minimum tax.　See *alternative minimum tax (AMT).*

Minimum tax credit (AMT).　When a corporation pays an alternative minimum tax, a minimum tax credit is created on a dollar-for-dollar basis, to be applied against regular tax liabilities incurred in future years. The credit is carried forward indefinitely, but it is not carried back. The effect of the credit for corporate taxpayers alternating between the AMT and regular tax models is to make the AMT liabilities a prepayment of regular taxes. Noncorporate AMT taxpayers are allowed the credit only with respect to the elements of the AMT that reflect timing differences between the two tax models.

Minority.　See *legal age.*

Miscellaneous itemized deductions.　A special category of itemized deductions that includes such expenses as professional dues, tax return preparation fees, job-hunting costs, unreimbursed employee business expenses, and certain investment expenses. Such expenses are deductible only to the extent they exceed 2 percent of adjusted gross income. § 67. See also *itemized deductions.*

Mitigate.　To make less severe. See also *mitigation of the annual accounting period concept.*

Mitigation of the annual accounting period concept. Various tax provisions that provide relief from the effect of the finality of the annual accounting period concept. For example, the net operating loss carryover provisions allow the taxpayer to apply the negative taxable income of one year against a corresponding positive amount in another tax accounting period. See also *annual accounting period concept.*

Modified accelerated cost recovery system (MACRS).　See *accelerated cost recovery system (ACRS).*

Mortgagee.　The party who holds the mortgage; the creditor.

Mortgagor.　The party who mortgages the property; the debtor.

Most suitable use value.　For gift and estate tax purposes, property that is transferred normally is valued in accordance with its most suitable or optimal use. Thus, if a farm is worth more as a potential shopping center, the value as a shopping center is used, even though the transferee (the donee or heir) continues to use the property as a farm. For an exception to this rule concerning the valuation of certain kinds of real estate transferred by death, see *special use value.*

Multitiered partnerships.　See *tiered partnerships.*

N

National sales tax.　Intended as a replacement for the current Federal income tax. Unlike a value added tax (VAT), which is levied on the manufacturer, it would be imposed on the consumer upon the final sale of goods and services. To keep the tax from being regressive, low-income taxpayers would be granted some kind of credit or exemption.

Necessary.　Appropriate and helpful in furthering the taxpayer's business or income-producing activity. §§ 162(a) and 212. See also *ordinary.*

Negligence.　Failure to exercise the reasonable or ordinary degree of care of a prudent person in a situation that results in harm or damage to another. Code § 6651 imposes a penalty on taxpayers who exhibit negligence or intentional disregard of rules and Regulations with respect to the underpayment of certain taxes. See also *accuracy-related penalty.*

Net capital gain.　The excess of the net long-term capital gain for the tax year over the net short-term capital loss. The net capital gain of an individual taxpayer is eligible for the alternative tax. § 1222(11). See also *alternative tax* and *mid-term capital gain or loss.*

Net capital loss.　The excess of the losses from sales or exchanges of capital assets over the gains from sales or exchanges of such assets. Up to $3,000 per year of the net capital loss may be deductible by noncorporate taxpayers against ordinary income. The excess net capital loss carries over to future tax years. For corporate taxpayers, the net capital loss cannot be offset against ordinary income, but it can be carried back 3 years and forward 5 years to offset net capital gains. §§ 1211, 1212 and 1221(10).

Net operating loss.　To mitigate the effect of the annual accounting period concept, § 172 allows taxpayers to use an excess loss of one year as a deduction for certain past or future years. In this regard, a carryback period of 2 years and a carryforward period of 20 years currently are allowed. For NOLs in tax years beginning before August 6, 1997, the carryback period is 3 years and the carryforward period is 15 years. See also *mitigation of the annual accounting period concept.*

Net worth method.   An approach used by the IRS to reconstruct the income of a taxpayer who fails to maintain adequate records. Under this method, the gross income for the year is estimated as the increase in net worth of the taxpayer (assets in excess of liabilities) with appropriate adjustment for nontaxable receipts and nondeductible expenditures. The net worth method often is used when tax fraud is suspected.

Ninety-day letter.   See *statutory notice of deficiency*.

No-additional-cost-services.   Services that the employer may provide the employee at no additional cost to the employer. Generally, the benefit is the ability to utilize employer's excess capacity (vacant seats on an airliner). Such amounts are excludible from the recipient's gross income.

Nonaccountable plan.   An expense reimbursement plan that does not have an accountability feature. The result is that employee expenses must be claimed as deductions *from* AGI. An exception is moving expenses that are deductions *for* AGI. See also *accountable plan*.

Nonacquiescence.   Disagreement by the IRS on the result reached in certain judicial decisions. *Nonacq.* or *NA*. See also *acquiescence*.

Nonbusiness bad debt.   A bad debt loss that is not incurred in connection with a creditor's trade or business. The loss is classified as a short-term capital loss and is allowed only in the year the debt becomes entirely worthless. In addition to family loans, many investor losses are nonbusiness bad debts. § 166(d). See also *business bad debt*.

Nonbusiness income.   Income generated from investment assets or from the taxable disposition thereof.

Noncontributory qualified pension or profit sharing plan.   A plan funded entirely by the employer with no contributions being made by the covered employees. See also *qualified pension or profit sharing plan*.

Nonliquidating distribution.   A payment made by a partnership or corporation to the entity's owner is a nonliquidating distribution when the entity's legal existence does not cease thereafter. If the payor is a corporation, such a distribution can result in dividend income to the shareholders. If the payor is a partnership, the partner usually assigns a basis in the distributed property that is equal to the lesser of the partner's basis in the partnership interest or the basis of the distributed asset to the partnership. In this regard, the partner first assigns basis to any cash that he or she receives in the distribution. The partner's remaining basis, if any, is assigned to the noncash assets according to their relative bases to the partnership.

Nonrecourse debt.   Debt secured by the property that it is used to purchase. The purchaser of the property is not personally liable for the debt upon default. Rather, the creditor's recourse is to repossess the related property. Nonrecourse debt generally does not increase the purchaser's at-risk amount.

Nonrefundable credit.   A nonrefundable credit is a credit that is not paid if it exceeds the taxpayer's tax liability. Some nonrefundable credits qualify for carryback and carryover treatment. See also *refundable credit*.

Nonresident alien.   An individual who is neither a citizen nor a resident of the United States. Citizenship is determined under the immigration and naturalization laws of the United States. Residency is determined under § 7701(b) of the Internal Revenue Code.

Nonseparately stated income.   The net income of an S corporation that is combined and allocated to the shareholders. Other items, such as capital gains and charitable contributions, that could be treated differently on the individual tax returns of the shareholders are not included in this amount but are allocated to the shareholders separately.

Nontaxable exchange.   A transaction in which realized gains or losses are not recognized. The recognition of gain or loss is postponed (deferred) until the property received in the nontaxable exchange is subsequently disposed of in a taxable transaction. Examples are § 1031 like-kind exchanges and § 1033 involuntary conversions. See also *involuntary conversion* and *like-kind exchange*.

Not essentially equivalent redemption.   See *redemption (not equivalent to a dividend)*.

O

Obligee.   The party to whom someone else is obligated under a contract. Thus, if Carol loans money to Dan, Carol is the obligee and Dan is the obligor under the loan.

Obligor.   See *obligee*.

Occupational tax.   A tax imposed on various trades or businesses. A license fee that enables a taxpayer to engage in a particular occupation.

Offer in compromise.   A settlement agreement offered by the IRS in a tax dispute, especially where there is doubt as to the collectibility of the full deficiency. Offers in compromise can include installment payment schedules, as well as reductions in the tax and penalties owed by the taxpayer.

Office audit.   An audit conducted by the IRS in the agent's office. See also *audit*, *correspondence audit*, and *field audit*.

On all fours.   A judicial decision exactly in point with another as to result, facts, or both.

Optimal use value.   Synonym for most suitable use value.

Ordinary.   Common and accepted in the general industry or type of activity in which the taxpayer is engaged. It comprises one of the tests for the deductibility of expenses incurred or paid in connection with a trade or business; for the production or collection of income; for the management, conservation, or maintenance of property held for the production of income; or in connection with the determination, collection, or refund of any tax. §§ 162(a) and 212. See also *necessary*.

Ordinary and necessary.   See *necessary* and *ordinary*.

Ordinary gross income.   A concept unique to personal holding companies and defined in § 543(b)(1). See also *adjusted ordinary gross income.*

Ordinary income property.   Property contributed to a charitable organization that, if sold rather than contributed, would have resulted in other than long-term capital gain to the donor (i.e., ordinary income property and short-term capital gain property). Examples are inventory and capital assets held for less than the long-term holding period.

Organizational expenditures.   Items incurred early in the life of a corporate entity, qualifying for a 60-month amortization under Federal tax law. Amortizable expenditures exclude those incurred to obtain capital (underwriting fees) or assets (subject to cost recovery). Typically, amortizable expenditures include legal and accounting fees, and state incorporation payments. Such items must be incurred by the end of the entity's first tax year. § 248.

Original issue discount.   The difference between the issue price of a debt obligation (e.g., a corporate bond) and the maturity value of the obligation when the issue price is *less than* the maturity value. OID represents interest and must be amortized over the life of the debt obligation using the effective interest method. The difference is not considered to be original issue discount for tax purposes when it is less than one-fourth of 1 percent of the redemption price at maturity multiplied by the number of years to maturity. §§ 1272 and 1273(a)(3).

Outside basis.   A partner's basis in his or her partnership interest.

Owner shift.   Any change in the respective ownership of stock by a 5 percent-or-more shareholder. Change is determined relative to a testing period of the prior three years. If there is a more-than-50 percent change in the ownership of a loss corporation, § 382 limitations apply to the use of NOL carryovers of the loss corporation.

P

Parent-subsidiary controlled group.   A *controlled* or *affiliated group* of corporations, where at least one corporation is at least 80 percent owned by one or more of the others. The affiliated group definition is more difficult to meet.

Partial liquidation.   A stock redemption where noncorporate shareholders are permitted sale or exchange treatment, where an active business has existed for at least five years, and a portion of the outstanding stock in the entity is retired.

Partner.   See *general partner* and *limited partner.*

Partnership.   For income tax purposes, a partnership includes a syndicate, group, pool, or joint venture, as well as ordinary partnerships. In an ordinary partnership, two or more parties combine capital and/or services to carry on a business for profit as co-owners. § 7701(a)(2). See also *limited partnership* and *tiered partnerships.*

Passive foreign investment company (PFIC).   A non-U.S. corporation that generates a substantial amount of personal holding company income. Upon receipt of an excess distribution from the entity or the sale of its shares, its U.S. shareholders are taxable on their pro rata shares of the tax that has been deferred with respect to the corporation's taxable income, plus an applicable interest charge.

Passive investment holding company.   A means by which a multistate corporation can reduce the overall effective tax rate by isolating investment income in a low- or no-tax state.

Passive investment income (PII).   Gross receipts from royalties, certain rents, dividends, interest, annuities, and gains from the sale or exchange of stock and securities. With certain exceptions, if the passive investment income of an S corporation exceeds 25 percent of the corporation's gross receipts for three consecutive years, S status is lost.

Passive loss rules.   Any loss from (1) activities in which the taxpayer does not materially participate or (2) rental activities (subject to certain exceptions). Net passive losses cannot be used to offset income from nonpassive sources. Rather, they are suspended until the taxpayer either generates net passive income (and a deduction of such losses is allowed) or disposes of the underlying property (at which time the loss deductions are allowed in full). One relief provision allows landlords who actively participate in the rental activities to deduct up to $25,000 of passive losses annually. However, a phase-out of the $25,000 amount commences when the landlord's AGI exceeds $100,000. See also *portfolio income.*

Pecuniary bequest.   A bequest of money to an heir by a decedent. See also *bequest.*

Percentage depletion.   Percentage depletion is depletion based on a statutory percentage applied to the gross income from the property. The taxpayer deducts the greater of cost depletion or percentage depletion. § 613. See also *cost depletion.*

Percentage of completion method.   A method of reporting gain or loss on certain long-term contracts. Under this method of accounting, the gross contract price is included in income as the contract is completed. Reg. § 1.451–3. See also *completed contract method* and *long-term contract.*

Personal and dependency exemptions.   The tax law provides an exemption for each individual taxpayer and an additional exemption for the taxpayer's spouse if a joint return is filed. An individual may also claim a dependency exemption for each dependent, provided certain tests are met. The amount of the personal and dependency exemptions is $2,700 in 1998 ($2,650 in 1997). The exemption is subject to phase-out once adjusted gross income exceeds certain statutory threshold amounts.

Personal and household effects.   Items owned by a decedent at the time of death. Examples include clothing, furniture, sporting goods, jewelry, stamp and coin collections, silverware, china, crystal, cooking utensils, books, cars, televisions, radios, stereo equipment, etc.

Personal casualty gain.   The recognized gain from any involuntary conversion of personal use property arising from fire, storm, shipwreck, or other casualty, or from theft. See also *personal casualty loss.*

Personal casualty loss.   The recognized loss from any involuntary conversion of personal use property arising from fire, storm, shipwreck, or other casualty, or from theft. See also *personal casualty gain.*

Personal exemption.   See *personal and dependency exemptions.*

Personal holding company (PHC).   A corporation that satisfies the requirements of § 542. Qualification as a personal holding company means a penalty tax may be imposed on the corporation's undistributed personal holding company income for the year.

Personal holding company income.   Income as defined by § 543. It includes interest, dividends, certain rents and royalties, income from the use of corporate property by certain shareholders, income from certain personal service contracts, and distributions from estates and trusts. Such income is relevant in determining whether a corporation is a personal holding company and is therefore subject to the penalty tax on personal holding companies. See also *adjusted ordinary gross income.*

Personal holding company tax.   A penalty tax imposed on certain closely held corporations with excessive investment income. The tax is assessed at the top individual tax rate on adjusted taxable income reduced by dividends paid. § 541.

Personal property.   Generally, all property other than real estate. It is sometimes referred to as personalty when real estate is termed realty. Personal property can also refer to property not used in a taxpayer's trade or business or held for the production or collection of income. When used in this sense, personal property can include both realty (e.g., a personal residence) and personalty (e.g., personal effects such as clothing and furniture). See also *bequest.*

Personal service corporation (PSC).   A corporation whose principal activity is the performance of personal services (e.g., health, law, engineering, architecture, accounting, actuarial science, performing arts, or consulting) and where such services are substantially performed by the employee-owners.

Personalty.   Personalty is all property that is not attached to real estate (realty) and is movable. Examples of personalty are machinery, automobiles, clothing, household furnishings, inventory, and personal effects. See also *ad valorem tax, realty,* and *personal property.*

Portfolio income.   Income from interest, dividends, rentals, royalties, capital gains, or other investment sources. Net passive losses cannot be used to offset net portfolio income. See also *passive loss rules* and *investment income.*

Power of appointment.   A legal right granted to someone by will or other document that gives the holder the power to dispose of property or the income from property. When the holder may appoint the property to his or her own benefit, the power usually is called a general power of appointment. If the holder cannot benefit himself or herself but may only appoint to certain other persons, the power is a special power of appointment. Assume Gus places $500,000 worth of securities in trust granting Debbie the right to determine each year how the trustee is to divide the income between Ann and Bill. Under these circumstances, Debbie has a special power of appointment. If Debbie had the further right to appoint the income to herself, she probably possesses a general power of appointment. For the estate tax and gift tax effects of powers of appointment, see §§ 2041 and 2514. See also *testamentary power of appointment.*

Precedents.   A previously decided court decision that is recognized as authority for the disposition of future decisions.

Precontribution gain.   Partnerships allow for a variety of *special allocations* of gain or loss among the partners, but gain or loss that is "built-in" on an asset contributed to the partnership is assigned specifically to the contributing partner. § 704(c)(1)(A).

Preferences (AMT).   See *alternative minimum tax (AMT)* and *tax preferences.*

Preferred stock bailout.   A process where a shareholder used the issuance, sale, and later redemption of a preferred stock dividend to obtain long-term capital gains, without any loss of voting control over the corporation. In effect, the shareholder receives corporate profits without suffering the consequences of dividend income treatment. This procedure led Congress to enact § 306, which, if applicable, converts the prior long-term capital gain on the sale of the stock to ordinary income. Under these circumstances, the amount of ordinary income is limited to the shareholder's portion of the corporation's earnings and profits existing when the preferred stock was issued as a stock dividend. See also *bailout.*

Present interest.   See *future interest.*

Presumption.   An inference in favor of a particular fact. If, for example, the IRS issues a notice of deficiency against a taxpayer, a presumption of correctness attaches to the assessment. Thus, the taxpayer has the burden of proof of showing that he or she does not owe the tax listed in the deficiency notice. See also *rebuttable presumption.*

Previously taxed income (PTI).   Before the Subchapter S Revision Act of 1982, the undistributed taxable income of an S corporation was taxed to the shareholders as of the last day of the corporation's tax year and usually could be withdrawn by the shareholders without tax consequences at some later point in time. The role of PTI has been taken over by the accumulated adjustments account. See also *accumulated adjustments account (AAA).*

Principal.   Property as opposed to income. The term is often used as a synonym for the corpus of a trust. If, for example, Gwen places real estate in trust with income payable to Abby for life and the remainder to Karen upon Abby's death, the real estate is the principal, or corpus, of the trust.

Private foundation. An *exempt organization* that is subject to additional statutory restrictions on its activities and on contributions made to it. Excise taxes may be levied on certain prohibited transactions, and the Code places more stringent restrictions on the deductibility of contributions to private foundations. § 509.

Probate. The legal process by which the estate of a decedent is administered. Generally, the probate process involves collecting a decedent's assets, liquidating liabilities, paying necessary taxes, and distributing property to heirs.

Probate costs. The costs incurred in administering a decedent's estate. See also *probate estate.*

Probate court. The usual designation for the state or local court that supervises the administration (probate) of a decedent's estate.

Probate estate. The property of a decedent that is subject to administration by the executor or administrator of an estate. See also *administration.*

Procedural Regulation. A Regulation issued by the Treasury Department that is a housekeeping-type instruction indicating information that taxpayers should provide the IRS as well as information about the internal management and conduct of the IRS itself. See also *interpretive regulation* and *legislative regulation.*

Profit and loss sharing ratios. Specified in the partnership agreement and used to determine each partner's allocation of ordinary taxable income and separately stated items. Profits and losses can be shared in different ratios. The ratios can be changed by amending the partnership agreement. § 704(a).

Profits interest. A partner's percentage allocation of partnership operating results, determined by the *profits and loss sharing ratios.*

Property. Assets defined in the broadest legal sense. Property includes the *unrealized receivables* of a cash basis taxpayer, but not services rendered. § 351.

Proposed Regulation. A Regulation issued by the Treasury Department in proposed, rather than final, form. The interval between the proposal of a Regulation and its finalization permits taxpayers and other interested parties to comment on the propriety of the proposal. See also *regulations.*

Pro rata. Proportionately. Assume, for example, a corporation has 10 shareholders, each of whom owns 10 percent of the stock. A pro rata dividend distribution of $1,000 would mean that each shareholder would receive $100.

Pro se. The taxpayer represents himself or herself before the court without the benefit of counsel.

Property dividend. Generally treated in the same manner as a cash distribution, measured by the FMV of the property on the date of distribution. The portion of the distribution representing E & P is a dividend; any excess is treated as a return of capital. Distribution of appreciated property causes the distributing corporation to recognize gain. The distributing corporation does not recognize loss on property that has depreciated in value.

Property tax. An *ad valorem* tax, usually levied by a city or county government, on the value of real or personal property that the taxpayer owns on a specified date. Most states exclude intangible property and assets owned by exempt organizations from the tax base, and some exclude inventory, pollution control or manufacturing equipment, and other items to provide relocation or retention incentives for the taxpayer.

Proportionate distribution. A distribution in which each partner in a partnership receives a pro rata share of hot assets being distributed. For example, a distribution of $10,000 of hot assets equally to two 50 percent partners is a proportionate distribution.

Prop.Reg. An abbreviation for Proposed Regulation. See *proposed regulation.*

PTI. See *previously taxed income (PTI).*

Public policy limitation. A concept developed by the courts precluding an income tax deduction for certain expenses related to activities deemed to be contrary to the public welfare. In this connection, Congress has incorporated into the Code specific disallowance provisions covering such items as illegal bribes, kickbacks, and fines and penalties. §§ 162(c) and (f).

Punitive damages. Damages received or paid by the taxpayer can be classified as compensatory damages or as punitive damages. Punitive damages are those awarded to punish the defendant for gross negligence or the intentional infliction of harm. Such damages are includible in gross income. § 104. See also *compensatory damages.*

Q

Qualified employee discounts. Discounts offered employees on merchandise or services that the employer ordinarily sells or provides to customers. The discounts must be generally available to all employees. In the case of property, the discount cannot exceed the employer's gross profit (the sales price cannot be less than the employer's cost). In the case of services, the discounts cannot exceed 20 percent of the normal sales price. § 132.

Qualified nonrecourse debt. Issued on realty by a bank, retirement plan, or governmental agency. Included in the *at-risk amount* by the investor. § 465(b)(6).

Qualified pension or profit sharing plan. An employer-sponsored plan that meets the requirements of § 401. If these requirements are met, none of the employer's contributions to the plan will be taxed to the employee until distributed to him or her (§ 402). The employer is allowed a deduction in the year the contributions are made (§ 404). See also *contributory qualified pension or profit sharing plan, deferred compensation,* and *noncontributory pension or profit sharing plan.*

Qualified small business corporation. A C corporation that has aggregate gross assets not exceeding $50 million and that is conducting an active trade or business. § 1202.

Qualified small business stock. Stock in a qualified small business corporation, purchased as part of an original issue after August 10, 1993. The shareholder may exclude from gross income 50 percent of the realized gain on the sale of the stock, if he or she held the stock for more than five years. § 1202.

Qualified terminable interest property (QTIP). Generally, the *marital deduction* (for gift and estate tax purposes) is not available if the interest transferred will terminate upon the death of the transferee spouse and pass to someone else. Thus, if Jim (the husband) places property in trust, life estate to Mary (the wife), and remainder to their children upon Mary's death, this is a terminable interest that will not provide Jim (or Jim's estate) with a marital deduction. If, however, the transfer in trust is treated as qualified terminable interest property (the QTIP election is made), the terminable interest restriction is waived and the marital deduction becomes available. In exchange for this deduction, the surviving spouse's gross estate must include the value of the QTIP election assets, even though he or she has no control over the ultimate disposition of the asset. Terminable interest property qualifies for this election if the donee (or heir) is the only beneficiary of the asset during his or her lifetime and receives income distributions relative to the property at least annually. For gifts, the donor spouse is the one who makes the QTIP election. For property transferred by death, the *executor* of the estate of the deceased spouse has the right to make the election. §§ 2056(b)(7) and 2523(f).

Qualified state tuition program. A program established by the individual states that allows a resident to prepay college tuition for a beneficiary. When the tuition is used, the beneficiary must recognize income equal to the difference between the amount placed in the fund and the charges for tuition at the time it is used using an annuity-type approach. § 529.

Qualified transportation fringes. Transportation benefits provided by the employer to the employee. Such benefits include (1) transportation in a commuter highway vehicle between the employee's residence and the place of employment, (2) a transit pass, and (3) qualified parking. Qualified transportation fringes are excludible from the employee's gross income to the extent categories (1) and (2) above do not exceed $65 per month and category (3) does not exceed $175 per month. These amounts are indexed annually for inflation. § 132.

Qualified tuition reduction plan. A type of fringe benefit plan that is available to employees of nonprofit educational institutions. Such employees (and the spouse and dependent children) are allowed to exclude a tuition waiver pursuant to a qualified tuition reduction plan from gross income. The exclusion applies to undergraduate tuition. In limited circumstances, the exclusion also applies to the graduate tuition of teaching and research assistants. § 117(d).

R

RAR. A *Revenue Agent's Report*, which reflects any adjustments made by the agent as a result of an audit of the taxpayer. The RAR is mailed to the taxpayer along with the *30-day letter*, which outlines the appellate procedures available to the taxpayer.

Realistic possibility. A preparer penalty is assessed where a tax return includes a position that has no realistic possibility of being sustained by a court.

Realized gain or loss. The difference between the amount realized upon the sale or other disposition of property and the adjusted basis of the property. § 1001. See also *adjusted basis*, *amount realized*, *basis*, and *recognized gain or loss*.

Realty. Real estate. See also *personalty*.

Reasonable cause. Relief from taxpayer and preparer penalties often is allowed where a reasonable cause is found for the taxpayer's actions. For example, a reasonable cause for the late filing of a tax return might be the incidence of a flood that damaged taxpayer record-keeping systems and made difficult a timely completion of the return.

Reasonable needs of the business. A means of avoiding the penalty tax on unreasonable accumulation of earnings. In determining the base for this tax (*accumulated taxable income*), § 535 allows a deduction for "such part of earnings and profits for the taxable year as are retained for the reasonable needs of the business." § 537.

Reasonableness. The Code includes a reasonableness requirement with respect to the deduction of salaries and other compensation for services. What constitutes reasonableness is a question of fact. If an expense is unreasonable, the amount that is classified as unreasonable is not allowed as a deduction. The question of reasonableness generally arises with respect to closely held corporations where there is no separation of ownership and management. § 162(a)(1).

Rebuttable presumption. A presumption that can be overturned upon the showing of sufficient proof. See also *presumption*.

Recapitalization. An E reorganization, constituting a major change in the character and amount of outstanding equity of a corporation. For instance, common stock exchanged for preferred stock can qualify for tax-free E reorganization treatment.

Recapture. To recover the tax benefit of a deduction or a credit previously taken. See also *depreciation recapture*.

Recapture potential. A measure with respect to property that, if disposed of in a taxable transaction, would result in the recapture of depreciation (§§ 1245 or 1250), deferred LIFO gain, or deferred installment method gain.

Recognized gain or loss. The portion of realized gain or loss subject to income taxation. See also *realized gain or loss*.

Recourse debt. Debt for which the lender may both foreclose on the property and assess a guarantor for any payments due under the loan. A lender may also make a claim against the assets of any general partner in a partnership to which debt is issued, without regard to whether the partner has guaranteed the debt.

Redemption. See *stock redemption*.

Redemption (complete termination). Sale or exchange treatment is available relative to this type of redemption. The shareholder must retire all of his or her outstanding shares in the corporation (ignoring family attribution rules), and cannot hold an interest, other than that of a creditor, for the 10 years following the redemption. § 302(b)(3).

Redemption (disproportionate). Sale or exchange treatment is available relative to this type of redemption. After the exchange, the shareholder owns less than 80 percent of his or her pre-redemption interest in the corporation, and only a minority interest in the entity. § 302(b)(2).

Redemption (not equivalent to a dividend). Sale or exchange treatment is given to this type of redemption. Although various safe harbor tests are failed, the nature of the redemption is such that dividend treatment is avoided, because it represents a meaningful reduction in the shareholder's interest in the corporation. § 302(b)(1).

Redemption to pay death taxes. Sale or exchange treatment is available relative to this type of redemption, to the extent of the proceeds up to the total amount paid by the estate or heir for death taxes and administration expenses. The stock value must exceed 35 percent of the value of the decedent's adjusted gross estate. In meeting this test, one can combine shareholdings in corporations where the decedent held at least 20 percent of the outstanding shares.

Refundable credit. A refundable credit is a credit that is paid to the taxpayer even if the amount of the credit (or credits) exceeds the taxpayer's tax liability. See also *nonrefundable credit*.

Regular corporation. See *C corporation*.

Regulations. The U.S. Treasury Department Regulations (abbreviated Reg.) represent the position of the IRS as to how the Internal Revenue Code is to be interpreted. Their purpose is to provide taxpayers and IRS personnel with rules of general and specific application to the various provisions of the tax law. Regulations are published in the *Federal Register* and in all tax services. See also *interpretive regulation, legislative regulation, procedural regulation,* and *proposed regulation*.

Rehabilitation expenditures credit. A credit that is based on expenditures incurred to rehabilitate industrial and commercial buildings and certified historic structures. The credit is intended to discourage businesses from moving from older, economically distressed areas to newer locations and to encourage the preservation of historic structures. § 47. See *rehabilitation expenditures credit recapture*.

Rehabilitation expenditures credit recapture. When property that qualifies for the rehabilitation expenditures credit is disposed of or ceases to be used in the trade or business of the taxpayer, some or all of the tax credit claimed on the property may be recaptured as additional tax liability. The amount of the recapture is the difference between the amount of the credit claimed originally and what should have been claimed in light of the length of time the property was actually held or used for qualifying purposes. § 50. See *rehabilitation expenditures credit*.

Related corporation. See *controlled group*.

Related parties. Various Code sections define related parties and often include a variety of persons within this (usually detrimental) category. Generally, related parties are accorded different tax treatment from that applicable to other taxpayers who enter into similar transactions. For instance, realized losses that are generated between related parties are not recognized in the year of the loss. However, these deferred losses can be used to offset recognized gains that occur upon the subsequent sale of the asset to a nonrelated party. Other uses of a related-party definition include the conversion of gain upon the sale of a depreciable asset into all ordinary income (§ 1239) and the identification of constructive ownership of stock relative to corporate distributions, redemptions, liquidations, reorganizations, and compensation.

Remainder interest. The property that passes to a beneficiary after the expiration of an intervening income interest. If, for example, Gail places real estate in trust with income to Tom for life and remainder to Randy upon Tom's death, Randy has a remainder interest. See also *life estate* and *reversionary interest*.

Remand. To send back. An appellate court may remand a case to a lower court, usually for additional fact finding. In other words, the appellate court is not in a position to decide the appeal based on the facts determined by the lower court. Remanding is abbreviated *"rem'g."*

Reorganization. See *corporate reorganization*.

Research activities credit. A tax credit whose purpose is to encourage research and development. It consists of two components: the incremental research activities credit and the basic research credit. The incremental research activities credit is equal to 20 percent of the excess qualified research expenditures over the base amount. The basic research credit is equal to 20 percent of the excess of basic research payments over the base amount. § 41. See also *general business credit*.

Residential rental property. Buildings for which at least 80 percent of the gross rents are from dwelling units (e.g., an apartment building). This type of building is distinguished from nonresidential (commercial or industrial) buildings in applying the recapture of depreciation provisions. The term also is relevant in distinguishing between buildings that are eligible for a 27.5-year life versus a 39-year life for MACRS purposes. Generally, residential buildings receive preferential treatment.

Residual method. The new stepped-up basis of a subsidiary's assets is allocated among its property when a § 338 election is in effect, using this method. The purchase price that exceeds the aggregate fair market values of the tangible and identifiable intangible assets is allocated to goodwill or going-concern value. § 1060.

Restoration event. Sales between members of a *consolidated return*, and other intra-group transactions, are subject to special recognition deferral rules, so that such members cannot artificially create taxable gains or losses solely when tax conditions call for them. Rather, when a restoration event occurs (e.g., when the asset ultimately is sold outside of the group), the recognition of all intra-group gains and losses is restored.

Return of capital. When a taxpayer reacquires financial resources that he or she previously had invested in an entity or venture, the return of his or her capital investment itself does not increase gross income for the recovery year. A return of capital may result from an annuity or insurance contract, the sale or exchange of any asset, or a distribution from a partnership or corporation.

Revenue Agent's Report. See *RAR*.

Revenue neutrality. A description that characterizes tax legislation when it neither increases nor decreases the revenue result. Thus, any tax revenue losses are offset by tax revenue gains.

Revenue Procedure. A matter of procedural importance to both taxpayers and the IRS concerning the administration of the tax laws is issued as a Revenue Procedure (abbreviated Rev.Proc.). A Revenue Procedure is first published in an *Internal Revenue Bulletin* (I.R.B.) and later transferred to the appropriate *Cumulative Bulletin* (C.B.). Both the *Internal Revenue Bulletins* and the *Cumulative Bulletins* are published by the U.S. Government Printing Office.

Revenue Ruling. A Revenue Ruling (abbreviated Rev.Rul.) is issued by the National Office of the IRS to express an official interpretation of the tax law as applied to specific transactions. It is more limited in application than a Regulation. A Revenue Ruling is first published in an *Internal Revenue Bulletin* (I.R.B.) and later transferred to the appropriate *Cumulative Bulletin* (C.B.). Both the *Internal Revenue Bulletins* and the *Cumulative Bulletins* are published by the U.S. Government Printing Office.

Reversed (Rev'd). An indication that a decision of one court has been reversed by a higher court in the same case.

Reversing (Rev'g). An indication that the decision of a higher court is reversing the result reached by a lower court in the same case.

Reversionary interest. The property that reverts to the grantor after the expiration of an intervening income interest. Assume Phil places real estate in trust with income to Junior for 11 years, and upon the expiration of this term, the property returns to Phil. Under these circumstances, Phil holds a reversionary interest in the property. A reversionary interest is the same as a remainder interest, except that, in the latter case, the property passes to someone other than the original owner (e.g., the grantor of a trust) upon the expiration of the intervening interest. See also *grantor trust* and *remainder interest*.

Revocable transfer. A transfer of property where the transferor retains the right to recover the property. The creation of a revocable trust is an example of a revocable transfer. § 2038. See also *incomplete transfer*.

Rev.Proc. Abbreviation for an IRS Revenue Procedure. See *Revenue Procedure*.

Rev.Rul. Abbreviation for an IRS Revenue Ruling. See *Revenue Ruling*.

RIA. Research Institute of America is the publisher of two tax services and of Federal tax decisions (AFTR and AFTR2d series).

Right of survivorship. See *joint tenants*.

S

Sale of principal residence. If a residence has been owned and used by the taxpayer as the principal residence for at least two years during the five-year period ending on the date of sale, up to $250,000 of realized gain is excluded from gross income. For a married couple filing a joint return, the $250,000 is increased to $500,000 if either spouse satisfies the ownership requirement and both spouses satisfy the use requirement. § 121.

Sale or exchange. A requirement for the recognition of capital gain or loss. Generally, the seller of property must receive money or relief from debt in order to have sold the property. An exchange involves the transfer of property for other property. Thus *collection* of a debt is neither a sale nor an exchange. The term *sale or exchange* is not defined by the Code.

Sales tax. A state- or local-level tax on the retail sale of specified property. Generally, the purchaser pays the tax, but the seller collects it, as an agent for the government. Various taxing jurisdictions allow exemptions for purchases of specific items, including certain food, services, and manufacturing equipment. If the purchaser and seller are in different states, a *use tax* usually applies.

Schedule M–1. On the Form 1120, a reconciliation of book net income with Federal taxable income. Accounts for timing and permanent differences in the two computations, such as depreciation differences, exempt income, and nondeductible items.

Schedule PH. A tax form required to be filed by corporations that are personal holding companies. The form must be filed in addition to Form 1120 (U.S. Corporation Income Tax Return).

S corporation. The designation for a small business corporation. See also *Subchapter S*.

Section 121 exclusion. See *sale of principal residence*.

Section 306 stock. Preferred stock issued as a nontaxable stock dividend that, if sold or redeemed, would result in ordinary income recognition. § 306(c). See also *preferred stock bailout*.

Section 306 taint. The ordinary income that would result upon the sale or other taxable disposition of § 306 stock.

Section 338 election. When a corporation acquires at least 80 percent of a subsidiary in a 12-month period, it can elect to treat the acquisition of such stock as an asset purchase. The acquiring corporation's basis in the subsidiary's assets then is the cost of the stock. The subsidiary is deemed to have sold its assets for an amount equal to the grossed-up basis in its stock.

Section 1231 assets. Depreciable assets and real estate used in a trade or business and held for the appropriate holding period. Under certain circumstances, the classification also includes timber, coal, domestic iron ore, livestock (held for draft, breeding, dairy, or sporting purposes), and unharvested crops. § 1231 (b). See also *Section 1231 gains and losses*.

Section 1231 gains and losses. If the combined gains and losses from the taxable dispositions of § 1231 assets plus the net gain from business involuntary conversions (of both § 1231 assets and long-term capital assets) is a gain, the gains and losses are treated as long-term capital gains and losses. In arriving at § 1231 gains, however, the depreciation recapture provisions (e.g., §§ 1245 and 1250) are first applied to produce ordinary income. If the net result of the combination is a loss, the gains and losses from § 1231 assets are treated as ordinary gains and losses. § 1231(a). See also *depreciation recapture* and *Section 1231 assets*.

Section 1244 stock. Stock issued under § 1244 by qualifying small business corporations. If § 1244 stock becomes worthless, the shareholders may claim an ordinary loss rather than the usual capital loss, within statutory limitations.

Section 1245 recapture. Upon a taxable disposition of § 1245 property, all depreciation claimed on the property is recaptured as ordinary income (but not to exceed recognized gain from the disposition).

Section 1250 recapture. Upon a taxable disposition of § 1250 property, some of the depreciation or cost recovery claimed on the property may be recaptured as ordinary income.

Securities. Generally, stock, debt, and other financial assets. To the extent securities other than the stock of the transferee corporation are received in a § 351 exchange, the new shareholder realizes a gain.

Separate property. In a community property jurisdiction, property that belongs entirely to one of the spouses is separate property. Generally, it is property acquired before marriage or acquired after marriage by gift or inheritance. See also *community property*.

Separately stated item. Any item of a partnership or S corporation that might be taxed differently to any two owners of the entity. These amounts are not included in ordinary income of the entity, but are instead reported separately to the owners; tax consequences are determined at the owner level.

Severance tax. A tax imposed upon the extraction of natural resources.

Sham. A transaction without substance that will be disregarded for tax purposes.

Short taxable year (short period). A tax year that is less than 12 months. A short taxable year may occur in the initial reporting period, in the final tax year, or when the taxpayer changes tax years.

Short-term capital gain or loss. Results from the sale or other taxable exchange of a capital asset that had been held by the seller for one year or less or from other transactions involving statutorily designated assets, including nonbusiness bad debts.

Simple trust. Simple trusts are those that are not complex trusts. Such trusts may not have a charitable beneficiary, accumulate income, or distribute corpus. See also *complex trust*.

Small business corporation. A corporation that satisfies the definition of § 1361(b), § 1244(c), or both. Satisfaction of § 1361(b) permits an S election, and satisfaction of § 1244 enables the shareholders of the corporation to claim an ordinary loss on the worthlessness of stock.

Small business stock. See *small business corporation*.

Small Cases Division of the U.S. Tax Court. Jurisdiction is limited to claims of $10,000 or less. There is no appeal from this court.

Special allocation. Any amount for which an agreement exists among the partners of a partnership outlining the method used for spreading the item among the partners.

Special power of appointment. See *power of appointment*.

Special use value. An option that permits the executor of an estate to value, for death tax purposes, real estate used in a farming activity or in connection with a closely held business at its current use value rather than at its most suitable or optimal use value. Under this option, a farm is valued for farming purposes even though, for example, the property might have a higher potential value as a shopping center. For the executor of an estate to elect special use valuation, the conditions of § 2032A must be satisfied. See also *most suitable use value*.

Spin-off. A type of reorganization where, for example, Gold Corporation transfers some assets to Silver Corporation in exchange for enough Silver stock to represent control. Gold then distributes the Silver stock to its shareholders.

Split-off. A type of reorganization where, for example, Gold Corporation transfers some assets to Silver Corporation in exchange for enough Silver stock to represent control. Gold then distributes the Silver stock to its shareholders.

Split-off. A type of reorganization where, for example, Gold Corporation transfers some assets to Silver Corporation in exchange for enough Silver stock to represent control. Gold then distributes the Silver stock to its shareholders in exchange for some of their Gold stock.

Split-up.   A type of reorganization where, for example, Gold Corporation transfers some assets to Silver Corporation and the remainder to Platinum Corporation. In return, Gold receives enough Silver and Platinum stock to represent control of each corporation. Gold then distributes the Silver and Platinum stock to its shareholders in return for all of their Gold stock. The result of the split-up is that Gold is liquidated, and its shareholders now have control of Silver and Platinum.

Sprinkling trust.   When a trustee has the discretion to either distribute or accumulate the entity accounting income of the trust and to distribute it among the trust's income beneficiaries in varying magnitudes, a sprinkling trust exists. The trustee can "sprinkle" the income of the trust.

Standard deduction.   The individual taxpayer can either itemize deductions or take the standard deduction. The amount of the standard deduction depends on the taxpayer's filing status (single, head of household, married filing jointly, surviving spouse, or married filing separately). For 1998, the amount of the standard deduction ranges from $3,550 (for married, filing separately) to $7,100 (for married, filing jointly). Additional standard deductions of either $850 (for married taxpayers) or $1,050 (for single taxpayers) are available if the taxpayer is either blind or age 65 or over. Limitations exist on the amount of the standard deduction of a taxpayer who is another taxpayer's dependent. The standard deduction amounts are adjusted for inflation each year. § 63(c).

Statute of limitations.   Provisions of the law that specify the maximum period of time in which action may be taken on a past event. Code §§ 6501–6504 contain the limitation periods applicable to the IRS for additional assessments, and §§ 6511–6515 relate to refund claims by taxpayers.

Statutory depletion.   See *depletion.*

Statutory notice of deficiency.   Commonly referred to as the *90-day letter,* this notice is sent to a taxpayer upon request, upon the expiration of the *30-day letter,* or upon exhaustion by the taxpayer of his or her administrative remedies before the IRS. The notice gives the taxpayer 90 days in which to file a petition with the U.S. Tax Court. If a petition is not filed, the IRS will demand payment of the assessed deficiency. §§ 6211–6216. See also *deficiency* and *thirty-day letter.*

Step-down in basis.   A reduction in the tax basis of property.

Step transaction.   Disregarding one or more transactions to arrive at the final result. Assume, for example, that the shareholders of Black Corporation liquidate the corporation and receive cash and operating assets. Immediately after the liquidation, the shareholders transfer the operating assets to newly formed Brown Corporation. Under these circumstances, the IRS may contend that the liquidation of Black should be disregarded (thereby depriving the shareholders of capital gain treatment). What may really have happened is a reorganization of Black with a distribution of boot (ordinary income) to Black's shareholders. If so, there will be a carryover of basis in the assets transferred from Black to Brown.

Step-up in basis.   An increase in the tax basis of property. The classic step-up in basis occurs when a decedent dies owning appreciated property. Since the estate or heir acquires a basis in the property equal to the property's fair market value on the date of death (or alternate valuation date if available and elected), any appreciation is not subject to the income tax. Thus, a step-up in basis is the result, with no income tax consequences.

Stock attribution.   See *attribution.*

Stock dividend.   Not taxable if pro rata distributions of stock or stock rights on common stock. Section 305 governs the taxability of stock dividends and sets out five exceptions to the general rule that stock dividends are nontaxable.

Stock redemption.   A corporation buys back its own stock from a specified shareholder. Typically, the corporation recognizes any realized gain on the noncash assets that it uses to effect a redemption, and the shareholder obtains a capital gain or loss upon receipt of the purchase price.

Stock rights.   An asset that conveys to the holder the power to purchase corporate stock at a specified price, often for a limited period of time. Stock rights received may be taxed as a distribution of earnings and profits. After the right is exercised, the basis of the acquired share includes the investor's purchase price or gross income, if any, to obtain the right. Disposition of the right also is a taxable event, with basis often assigned from the shares held prior to the issuance of the right.

Subchapter S.   Sections 1361–1379 of the Internal Revenue Code. An elective provision permitting certain small business corporations (§ 1361) and their shareholders (§ 1362) to elect to be treated for income tax purposes in accordance with the operating rules of §§ 1363–1379. However, some S corporations usually avoid the corporate income tax and corporate losses can be claimed by the shareholders.

Subpart F.   That subpart of the Code that identifies the current tax treatment of income earned by a controlled foreign corporation. Certain types of income are included in U.S. gross income by U.S. shareholders of such an entity as they are generated, not when they are repatriated.

Substance vs. form concept.   A standard used when one must ascertain the true reality of what has occurred. Suppose, for example, a father sells stock to his daughter for $1,000. If the stock is really worth $50,000 at the time of the transfer, the substance of the transaction is probably a gift to her of $49,000.

Substantial authority.   Taxpayer understatement penalties are waived where there existed substantial authority for the disputed position taken on the return.

Substantial economic effect.   Partnerships are allowed to *allocate* items of income, expense, gain, loss, and credit in any manner that is authorized in the partnership agreement, provided that the allocation has an economic effect aside from the corresponding tax results. The necessary substantial economic effect is present, for instance, if the post-contribution appreciation in the value of an asset that was contributed to the partnership by a partner was allocated to that partner for cost recovery purposes.

Substantial risk of forfeiture.   A term that is associated with a restricted property plan. Generally, an employee who receives property (e.g., stock of the employer-corporation) from the employee at a bargain price or at no cost must include the bargain element in gross income. However, the employee does not have to do so presently if there is a substantial risk of forfeiture. A substantial risk of forfeiture exists if a person's rights to full enjoyment of property are conditioned upon the future performance, or the refraining from the performance, of substantial services by the individual. § 83.

Substituted basis.   When a taxpayer exchanges one asset for another, many provisions in the tax law allow an assignment of basis in the received asset to be that of the traded asset(s) in the hands of its former owner. Thus, no step-up or -down of basis occurs as a result of the exchange. For example, when an investor contributes an asset to a corporation or partnership, the partner generally takes a substituted basis in the partnership interest [i.e., the investment asset (partnership interest) has a basis equal to the aggregated bases of the assets contributed by that partner].

Surviving spouse.   When a husband or wife predeceases the other spouse, the survivor is known as a surviving spouse. Under certain conditions, a surviving spouse may be entitled to use the income tax rates in § 1(a) (those applicable to married persons filing a joint return) for the two years after the year of death of his or her spouse. § 2.

Survivorship.   See *joint tenants*.

Syndication costs.   Incurred in promoting and marketing partnership interests for sale to investors. Examples include legal and accounting fees, printing costs for prospectus and placement documents, and state registration fees. These items are capitalized by the partnership as incurred, with no amortization thereof allowed.

T

Tangible property.   All property that has form or substance and is not intangible. See also *intangible asset*.

Taxable estate.   The taxable estate is the *gross estate* of a *decedent* reduced by the deductions allowed by §§ 2053–2057 (e.g., administration expenses, marital, and charitable deductions). The taxable estate is subject to the unified transfer tax at death. See also *adjusted taxable estate* and *gross estate*. § 2051.

Taxable gift.   Amount of a gift that is subject to the unified transfer tax. Thus, a taxable gift has been adjusted by the annual exclusion and other appropriate deductions (e.g., marital and charitable). § 2053.

Taxable income.   The tax base with respect to the prevailing Federal income tax. Taxable income is defined by the Internal Revenue Code, Treasury Regulations, and pertinent court cases. Currently, taxable income includes gross income from all sources except those specifically excluded by statute. In addition, taxable income is reduced for certain allowable deductions. Deductions for business taxpayers must be related to a trade or business. Individuals can also deduct certain personal expenses in determining their taxable incomes. See also *gross income*.

Taxable year.   The annual period over which income is measured for income tax purposes. Most individuals use a calendar year, but many businesses use a fiscal year based on the natural business year. See also *accounting period* and *fiscal year*.

Tax benefit rule.   A provision that limits the recognition of income from the recovery of an expense or loss properly deducted in a prior tax year to the amount of the deduction that generated a tax saving. Assume that last year Gary had medical expenses of $3,000 and adjusted gross income of $30,000. Because of the 7.5 percent limitation, Gary could deduct only $750 of these expenses [$3,000 − (7.5% × $30,000)]. If, this year, Gary is reimbursed by his insurance company for $900 of these expenses, the tax benefit rule limits the amount of income from the reimbursement to $750 (the amount previously deducted with a tax saving).

Tax Court.   The U.S. Tax Court is one of four trial courts of original jurisdiction that decide litigation involving Federal income, death, or gift taxes. It is the only trial court where the taxpayer must not first pay the deficiency assessed by the IRS. The Tax Court will not have jurisdiction over a case unless a statutory notice of deficiency (90-day letter) has been issued by the IRS and the taxpayer files the petition for hearing within the time prescribed.

Tax credits.   Tax credits are amounts that directly reduce a taxpayer's tax liability. The tax benefit received from a tax credit is not dependent on the taxpayer's marginal tax rate, whereas the benefit of a tax deduction or exclusion is dependent on the taxpayer's tax bracket.

Tax-free exchange.   Transfers of property specifically exempted from income tax consequences by the tax law. Examples are a transfer of property to a controlled corporation under § 351(a) and a like-kind exchange under § 1031(a). See also *nontaxable exchange*.

Tax haven.   A country in which either locally sourced income or residents of the country are subject to a low rate of taxation.

Tax on unearned income of a child under age 14.   Passive income, such as interest and dividends, that is recognized by such a child is taxed *to him or her* at the rates that would have applied had the income been incurred by the child's parents, generally to the extent that the income exceeds $1,400. The additional tax is assessed regardless of the source of the income or the income's underlying property. If the child's parents are divorced, the custodial parent's rates are used. The parents' rates reflect any applicable alternative minimum tax and the phase-outs of lower tax brackets and other deductions. § 1(g).

Tax preferences. Various items that may result in the imposition of the alternative minimum tax. §§ 55–58. See also *alternative minimum tax (AMT)*.

Tax research. The method used to determine the best available solution to a situation that possesses tax consequences. Both tax and nontax factors are considered.

TAXRIA. (Formerly called PHINet.) An on-line database system, with which the tax researcher can obtain access to the Internal Revenue Code, Regulations, administrative rulings, and court case opinions.

Tax treaty. An agreement between the U.S. Department of State and another country, designed to alleviate double taxation of income and asset transfers, and to share administrative information useful to tax agencies in both countries. The United States has income tax treaties with over 40 countries, and transfer tax treaties with about 20.

Tax year. See *accounting period*.

T.C. An abbreviation for the U.S. Tax Court used in citing a Regular Decision of the U.S. Tax Court.

T.C.Memo. An abbreviation used to refer to a Memorandum Decision of the U.S. Tax Court.

Technical advice memoranda (TAMs). TAMs are issued by the National Office of the IRS in response to questions raised by IRS field personnel during audits. They deal with completed rather than proposed transactions and are often requested for questions related to exempt organizations and employee plans.

Telescoping. To look through one or more transactions to arrive at the final result. It is also referred to as the *step transaction* approach or the *substance vs. form concept*.

Temporary Regulation. A Regulation issued by the Treasury Department in temporary form. When speed is critical, the Treasury Department issues Temporary Regulations that take effect immediately. These Regulations have the same authoritative value as Final Regulations and may be cited as precedent for three years. Temporary Regulations are also issued as proposed Regulations. See also *proposed regulation* and *regulations*.

Tenancy by the entirety. Essentially, a joint tenancy between husband and wife. See also *joint tenants* and *tenancy in common*.

Tenancy in common. A form of ownership where each tenant (owner) holds an undivided interest in property. Unlike a joint tenancy or a tenancy by the entirety, the interest of a tenant in common does not terminate upon that individual's death (there is no right of survivorship). Assume Tim and Cindy acquire real estate as equal tenants in common, each having furnished one-half of the purchase price. Upon Tim's death, his one-half interest in the property passes to his estate or heirs, not to Cindy. For a comparison of results, see also *joint tenants* and *tenancy by the entirety*.

Term certain. A fixed period of years, used to determine the length of an income interest (i.e., prior to the termination of a trust or estate).

Terminable interest rule. An interest in property that terminates upon the death of the holder or upon the occurrence of some other specified event. The transfer of a terminable interest by one spouse to the other may not qualify for the marital deduction. §§ 2056(b) and 2523(b). See also *marital deduction*.

Testamentary disposition. The passing of property to another upon the death of the owner.

Testamentary power of appointment. A power of appointment that can be exercised only through the will (upon the death) of the holder. See also *power of appointment*.

Theft loss. A loss from larceny, embezzlement and robbery. It does not include misplacement of items. See also *casualty loss*.

Thin capitalization. When debt owed by a corporation to the shareholders becomes too large in relation to the corporation's capital structure (i.e., stock and shareholder equity), the IRS may contend that the corporation is thinly capitalized. In effect, this means that some or all of the debt is reclassified as equity. The immediate result is to disallow any interest deduction to the corporation on the reclassified debt. To the extent of the corporation's earnings and profits, interest payments and loan repayments on the reclassified debt are treated as dividends to the shareholders.

Thirty-day letter. A letter that accompanies a Revenue Agent's Report issued as a result of an IRS audit of a taxpayer (or the rejection of a taxpayer's claim for refund). The letter outlines the taxpayer's appeal procedure before the IRS. If the taxpayer does not request any such procedures within the 30-day period, the IRS will issue a statutory notice of deficiency (the 90-day letter). See also *statutory notice of deficiency*.

Tiered partnerships. An ownership arrangement where one partnership (the parent or first tier) is a partner in one or more partnerships (the subsidiary/subsidiaries or second tier). Frequently, the first tier is a holding partnership, and the second tier is an operating partnership.

Trade or business. Any business or professional activity conducted by a taxpayer. The mere ownership of rental or other investment assets does not constitute a trade or business. Generally, a trade or business generates relatively little passive investment income.

Transfer tax. A tax imposed upon the transfer of property. See also *unified transfer tax*.

Transferee liability. Under certain conditions, if the IRS is unable to collect taxes owed by a transferor of property, it may pursue its claim against the transferee of the property. The transferee's liability for taxes is limited to the extent of the value of the assets transferred. For example, the IRS can force a donee to pay the gift tax when the tax cannot be paid by the donor making the transfer. §§ 6901–6905.

Treasury Regulations.   See *regulations*.

Treaty shopping.   An international investor attempts to use the favorable aspects of a tax treaty to his or her advantage, often elevating the form of the transaction over its substance (e.g., by establishing only a nominal presence in the country offering the favorable treaty terms).

Trial court.   The court of original jurisdiction; the first court to consider litigation. In Federal tax controversies, trial courts include U.S. District Courts, the U.S. Tax Court, the U.S. Court of Federal Claims, and the Small Cases Division of the U.S. Tax Court. See also *appellate court, Court of Federal Claims, District Court, Small Cases Division of the U.S. Tax Court,* and *Tax Court*.

Trust.   A legal entity created by a grantor for the benefit of designated beneficiaries under the laws of the state and the valid trust instrument. The trustee holds a fiduciary responsibility to manage the trust's corpus assets and income for the economic benefit of all of the beneficiaries.

Trustee.   An individual or corporation that takes the fiduciary responsibilities under a trust agreement.

U

Undistributed personal holding company income.   The penalty tax on personal holding companies is imposed on the corporation's undistributed personal holding company income for the year. The adjustments necessary to convert taxable income to undistributed personal holding company income are set forth in § 545.

Unearned income.   Income received but not yet earned. Normally, such income is taxed when received, even for accrual basis taxpayers.

Unified tax credit.   A credit allowed against any unified transfer tax. §§ 2010 and 2505.

Unified transfer tax.   Rates applicable to transfers by gift and death made after 1976. § 2001(c).

Uniform Gift to Minors Act.   A means of transferring property (usually stocks and bonds) to a minor. The designated custodian of the property has the legal right to act on behalf of the minor without requiring a guardianship. Generally, the custodian possesses the right to change investments (e.g., sell one type of stock and buy another), apply the income from the custodial property to the minor's support, and even terminate the custodianship. In this regard, however, the custodian is acting in a fiduciary capacity on behalf of the minor. The custodian could not, for example, appropriate the property for his or her own use because it belongs to the minor. During the period of the custodianship, the income from the property is taxed to the minor. The custodianship terminates when the minor reaches legal age. See also *guardianship* and *legal age*.

Unrealized receivables.   Amounts earned by a cash basis taxpayer but not yet received. Because of the method of accounting used by the taxpayer, these amounts have no income tax basis. When unrealized receivables are distributed to a partner, they generally convert a transaction from nontaxable to taxable or convert otherwise capital gain to ordinary income.

Unreasonable compensation.   A deduction is allowed for "reasonable" salaries or other compensation for personal services actually rendered. To the extent compensation is "excessive" ("unreasonable"), no deduction is allowed. The problem of unreasonable compensation usually is limited to closely held corporations, where the motivation is to pay out profits in some form that is deductible to the corporation. Deductible compensation therefore becomes an attractive substitute for nondeductible dividends when the shareholders also are employed by the corporation.

Unrecaptured § 1250 gain (25 percent gain).   Gain from the sale of depreciable real estate held more than 18 months. The gain is equal to or less than the depreciation taken on such property and is reduced by § 1245 and § 1250 gain.

Unrelated business income.   Income recognized by an exempt organization that is generated from activities not related to the exempt purpose of the entity. For instance, the pharmacy located in a hospital often generates unrelated business income. § 511.

Unrelated business income tax.   Levied on the *unrelated business income* of an *exempt organization*.

U.S. Court of Federal Claims.   See *Court of Federal Claims*.

Use tax.   A sales tax that is collectible by the seller where the purchaser is domiciled in a different state.

U.S.-owned foreign corporation.   A foreign corporation in which 50 percent or more of the total combined voting power or total value of the stock of the corporation is held directly or indirectly by U.S. persons. A U.S. corporation is treated as a U.S.-owned foreign corporation if the dividend or interest income it pays is classified as foreign source under § 861.

U.S. real property interest.   Any direct interest in real property situated in the United States and any interest in a domestic corporation (other than solely as a creditor) unless the taxpayer can establish that a domestic corporation was not a U.S. real property holding corporation during the five-year period ending on the date of disposition of the interest (the base period). See *FIRPTA*.

USSC.   An abbreviation for the U.S. Supreme Court.

U.S. shareholder.   For purposes of classification of an entity as a *controlled foreign corporation,* a U.S. person who owns, or is considered to own, 10 percent or more of the total combined voting power of all classes of voting stock of a foreign corporation. Stock owned directly, indirectly, and constructively is counted for this purpose.

U.S. source income.   Generally, income taxed by the United States, regardless of the citizenship or residence of its creator. Examples include income from sales of U.S. real estate and dividends from U.S. corporations.

U.S. Supreme Court. The highest appellate court or the court of last resort in the Federal court system and in most states. Only a small number of tax decisions of the U.S. Courts of Appeal are reviewed by the U.S. Supreme Court under its certiorari procedure. The Supreme Court usually grants certiorari to resolve a conflict among the Courts of Appeal (e.g., two or more appellate courts have assumed opposing positions on a particular issue) or when the tax issue is extremely important (e.g., size of the revenue loss to the Federal government).

U.S. Tax Court. See *Tax Court.*

USTC. Published by Commerce Clearing House, *U.S. Tax Cases* contain all of the Federal tax decisions issued by the U.S. District Courts, U.S. Court of Federal Claims, U.S. Courts of Appeals, and the U.S. Supreme Court.

V

Value. See *fair market value.*

Value added tax (VAT). A national sales tax that taxes the increment in value as goods move through the production process. A VAT is much used in other countries but has not yet been incorporated as part of the U.S. Federal tax structure.

Vested. Absolute and complete. If, for example, a person holds a vested interest in property, the interest cannot be taken away or otherwise defeated.

Voting trust. A trust that holds the voting rights to stock in a corporation. It is a useful device when a majority of the shareholders in a corporation cannot agree on corporate policy.

W

Wash sale. A loss from the sale of stock or securities that is disallowed because the taxpayer within 30 days before or after the sale, has acquired stock or securities substantially identical to those sold. § 1091.

Welfare-to-work credit. A tax credit available to employers hiring individuals who have been long-term recipients of family assistance welfare benefits. In general, long-term recipients are those individuals who are certified by a designated local agency as being members of a family receiving assistance under a public aid program for at least an 18-month period ending on the hiring date. The welfare-to-work credit is available for qualified wages paid in the first two years of employment. The maximum credit is equal to $8,500 per qualified employee, computed as 35 percent of the first $10,000 of qualified wages paid in the first year of employment, plus 50 percent of the first $10,000 of qualified wages paid in the second year of employment. § 51A. See also *general business credit.*

WESTLAW. An on-line database system, produced by West Publishing Company, that the tax researcher can use to obtain access to the Internal Revenue Code, Regulations, administrative rulings, and court case opinions.

Wherewithal to pay. This concept recognizes the inequity of taxing a transaction when the taxpayer lacks the means with which to pay the tax. Under it, there is a correlation between the imposition of the tax and the ability to pay the tax. It is particularly suited to situations in which the taxpayer's economic position has not changed significantly as a result of the transaction.

Withholding allowances. The number of withholding allowances serves as the basis for determining the amount of income taxes withheld from an employee's salary or wages. The more withholding allowances claimed, the less income tax withheld by an employer. An employee may claim withholding allowances for personal exemptions for self and spouse (unless claimed as a dependent of another person), dependency exemptions, and special withholding allowances.

Working condition fringe. A type of fringe benefit received by the employee that is excludible from the employee's gross income. It consists of property or services provided (paid or reimbursed) by the employer for which the employee could take a tax deduction if the employee had paid for them. § 132.

Work opportunity tax credit. Employers are allowed a tax credit equal to 40 percent of the first $6,000 of wages (per eligible employee) for the first year of employment. Eligible employees include certain hard-to-employ individuals (e.g., qualified ex-felons, high-risk youth, food stamp recipients, and veterans). The employer's deduction for wages is reduced by the amount of the credit taken. For qualified summer youth employees, the 40 percent rate is applied to the first $3,000 of qualified wages. §§ 51 and 52.

Writ of Certiorari. See *certiorari.*

Appendix **D–1**
Table of Code Sections Cited

APPENDIX D–2
Table of Regulations Cited

APPENDIX D–3
Table of Revenue Procedures and Revenue Rulings Cited

APPENDIX E
Comprehensive Tax Return Problems

PROBLEM 1—INDIVIDUALS

1. Dan B. and Marla R. Luce, ages 44 and 46, are married and file a joint income tax return. Dan is a specialist in horticulture and is employed by the Harlan Seed Corporation as director of research activities. Marla is a schoolteacher and is employed by the Methodist Middle School, a private institution owned and operated by a religious group. Salary and tax withholdings for 1997 were:

	Salary	Federal	State
Dan	$72,000	$6,340	$2,580
Marla	33,000	4,300	1,550

   The proper Social Security tax and Medicare tax amounts have been withheld from their salaries.

2. The Luces have always lived and worked in Des Moines, Iowa. They reside at 4010 Green Avenue, Des Moines, IA 50312. Living with them are their three children, Bo (age 13), Julius (age 15), and Mona (age 22). Also living with the Luces is Dan's widower father, Peter (age 70). Mona is a full-time student at Drake University. During the year, she earned $3,000 from a part-time job. Peter received $8,000 in Social Security benefits, which he deposited in his savings account. The Luces contributed more than 50% of the support of their children and of Peter.

3. The Luces contributed 25% of the support of Marla's aunt, Mary Lyons, who lives with Marla's sister. Mary receives the remainder of her support from Marla's sister and two brothers, 25% each. Marla's sister and brothers have each signed a multiple support agreement allowing Marla to claim the dependency exemption for Mary. As noted below, the Luces have provided their share of support by paying Mary's medical expenses.

4. Relevant Social Security numbers are:

Dan	478–12–6024
Marla	477–19–1002
Bo	479–22–6018
Julius	479–29–5025
Mona	479–31–4129
Peter	481–15–6113
Mary	480–42–1266

5. Because Peter is confined to a wheelchair due to a stroke he suffered several years ago, the Luces spent $7,200 during the year adding impairment-related improvements to their personal residence (e.g., wheelchair ramp, widening of hallways, bathtub railings). A friend who is in the real estate business estimates that these changes increased the value of the residence by $3,500.

6. During 1997, the Luces' personal residence suffered water damage. They had purchased this house on June 15, 1973, and paid $55,000 for it. A professional appraisal, for which the Luces paid $500, indicates that the value of the residence decreased by $14,000 ($120,000 before and $106,000 after) due to the water damage caused by the storm. The Luce's homeowner's insurance policy does not cover water damage.

7. On June 1, 1992, as a favor to a former college roommate, Dan loaned $4,200 to Bill Wild. Bill signed a note, maturity date of June 1, 1997, with annual interest of 10%. Dan has never recovered any of the loan or received any interest. Bill was declared bankrupt in April 1997 and is currently under investigation for mail fraud.

8. Marla has a Bachelor of Education degree that she received many years ago. Recently, the directors at her school resolved that all of its teachers must earn a Master of Education degree in order to continue in their present jobs. The teachers are allowed 10 years in which to satisfy this new requirement. During the summer of 1997, Marla enrolled at a local university and took several graduate courses in education. Marla lived at home and commuted to her classes. Her expenses were as follows:

Books and tuition	$2,100
Transportation	
Bus fares	125
Personal auto mileage (170 miles)	?
Meals while on campus (between classes)	105
Parking charges	82

When Marla did not take the bus, usually on rainy days, she drove the family auto (use the automatic mileage method—31.5 cents for 1997). When Marla drove, she had to pay for on-campus parking.

9. During 1997, the Luces sold the following stocks:

Owl Corporation	
(400 shares common) July 5	$34,000
Falcon Corporation	
(300 shares preferred) August 10	18,000

The Owl Corporation stock was received from Marla's mother as a gift on January 2, 1997, when it had a fair market value of $30,000. Her mother had purchased the stock on June 1, 1996, for $30,500. No gift tax was due or paid on the mother's gift.

Dan inherited the Falcon Corporation stock from his mother. She died on December 10, 1996, and her estate was settled on March 3, 1997 (the day Dan received the stock). The stock was worth $15,600 on December 10, 1996, and $14,900 on March 3, 1997. Dan has found a broker's statement that shows his mother purchased the stock on September 9, 1996, for $15,100 (including brokerage fee).

10. Besides any other items mentioned elsewhere, the Luces had the following receipts for 1997:

Interest on CD (Iowa State Bank)		$2,920
Interest on City of Des Moines general purpose bonds		700
Dividends		
Owl Corporation stock	$1,050	
Falcon Corporation stock	820	1,870
Garage sale of old clothes and household goods (reasonable cost estimate of items sold is $8,500)		2,100

11. As to medical expenses, the Luces had the following during 1997:

Hospital and doctor bills for Mary	$3,200
Dan's contribution toward the cost of his employer's medical insurance premiums	2,800
Insurance recovery for 1996 expenses under employment medical policy	880
Orthodontia expenses for children	4,600

Prescription drugs	500
Doctor bills for family	1,100
Tonsillectomy for Bo (surgeon and hospital)	1,700
Wheelchair and hearing aid for Peter	2,250

The $880 insurance recovery for the year 1996 was for medical expenses the Luces deducted on their 1996 Federal income tax return.

The Luces have not yet submitted any claims to the insurance company for their 1997 medical expenses. They estimate that, after the required deductible, the reimbursed amount will be $1,800.

12. Other expenditures for 1997 are summarized below:

Interest on home mortgage	$5,200
Property taxes on home	3,200
Payment of church pledge ($300 was for the 1996 remaining balance)	1,850
Additional state income tax due for 1996	130
School supplies Marla uses for her classes (not provided by her school)	205
Professional dues (Dan and Marla)	310
Professional journals (Dan and Marla)	400
Lab coats (used by Dan at work)	240
Laundry of lab coats	115
Safety goggles and shoes (used by Dan at work)	90
Riverboat casino losses (supported by adequate records)	300

13. On a timely basis, the Luces made four quarterly estimated Federal income tax payments of $300 each.

14. The Luces do not wish to designate a contribution to the Presidential Election Campaign Fund. If they have overpaid, any refund is to be applied toward their 1998 Federal income tax liability.

Requirements

You are to prepare a joint Federal income tax return for the Luces for 1997.

PROBLEM 2—INDIVIDUALS

1. Al P. Hart, age 44, is divorced and lives alone at 426 Latner Lane, Cincinnati, OH 45221. He provides more than half of the cost of maintaining a household for Norma Hart, who lives in an apartment nearby. Norma, age 70, is Al's widowed mother and qualifies as his dependent.

2. Al and Leona were married 18 years ago and were divorced in 1994. Leona was awarded custody of their only child, Peter, now 12 years old. Under the divorce decree, Al must pay Leona $400 each month until Peter reaches age 21 or dies (whichever occurs first). Upon the occurrence of either event, the monthly payment becomes $100. Since Al and Leona have been alternating claiming Peter as a dependent, Leona completed and sent to Al a Form 8332 for 1997. Al sent Leona the required $4,800 ($400 × 12) for 1997. Furthermore, he sent Leona an additional $400 for dental work she had done on her teeth. He also paid an optometrist/optician $300 for Peter's eye exams and prescription glasses.

3. Al is a licensed hair stylist and beautician and operates his own salon under the business name "Al's Creations." Although the number varies, Al's business consists of four to six stations operated by himself and other licensed beauticians. The beauticians who work in the salon are treated as independent contractors. In this regard, each has his or her own telephone line. They maintain their own appointment books, have their own customers, and collect and keep the fees charged. For the use of the work stations

and various facilities (e.g., hair dryers, shampoo sinks, waiting area), each beautician pays Al a monthly rental. Al does not control their work hours, although most choose to follow Al's own work schedule.

4. Al's Creations is well-known for the selection and quality of its men's hairpieces (i.e., toupees) and women's wigs. The business also sells a considerable quantity of beauty products (e.g., conditioners, shampoos, curling irons). Some of these items are sold to other beauticians, but most are sold to regular patrons and walk-in customers.

5. Al's Creations is located at 6194 Taft Street, Cincinnati, OH 45221. The employer identification number is 31–0009521; the professional activity code for beauticians is 8110.

6. The building in which the business is located is rented under a long-term lease for $1,000 each month. Al pays his own utilities. Before Al moved in, the landlord customized the facilities for its intended use. The only employee Al has is a shampoo person, who also performs light janitorial services. Al hires an outside service to do the heavier janitorial duties. Likewise, a local accounting group is on retainer to keep the financial records and prepare the tax returns for the business.

7. Al's Creations had the following receipts for 1997:

Sales of cosmetics	$18,000
Sales of hairpieces, wigs	30,000
Fees received from patrons by Al (including tips received)	35,000
Rent charged other beauticians	25,000

The amounts shown for the retail sales of cosmetics, hairpieces, and wigs include state sales tax.

8. Al's Creations had the following expenses for 1997:

Purchases of cosmetics	$ 7,980
Purchases of hairpieces, wigs	11,800
Operating supplies (shampoo, permanent wave solution, color, etc.)	4,900
Rent for building	12,000
Utilities and telephone	5,800
Payroll expense	5,200
Payroll taxes (FICA, FUTA, state unemployment)	590
Sales taxes remitted to state	2,400
Health insurance coverage for employee	810
City of Cincinnati occupation permit for 1997	400
State beautician license fee	210
Liability insurance premiums (coverage is for calendar years 1997–1999)	4,800
Casualty insurance on business furnishings and equipment for 1997	1,400
Janitorial services	2,400
Accounting services	4,100
Waiting room furniture	3,000
Magazine subscriptions for waiting room	300
Advertising	600
Fine paid to city of Cincinnati	200

9. Al decided to completely renovate the furnishings in his waiting room. Consequently, he spent $3,000 for chairs, sofa, lamps, coffee table, etc., all placed in service on April 20, 1997. The old furnishings were given to patrons or thrown away. The old furniture was completely depreciated and had a zero tax basis. Al has always followed a policy of claiming as much depreciation as soon as possible. All of his other business assets (e.g., hair dryers, work-station chairs) have been fully depreciated by 1997.

Account	Debit	Credit
Salaries—officers	347,000	
Salaries—clerical and sales	402,000	
Taxes (state, local, and payroll)	103,000	
Repairs	61,500	
Interest expense		
Loan to purchase state bonds	$ 7,200	
Other business loans	24,800	32,000
Advertising	75,400	
Rental expense	177,700	
Depreciation	36,000	

A comparative balance sheet for SnowPro Corporation reveals the following information:

Assets	January 1, 1997	December 31, 1997
Cash	$ 409,000	$ 281,194
Trade notes and accounts receivable	750,560	996,140
Inventories	540,000	640,800
Federal bonds	114,000	114,000
State bonds	156,000	156,000
Prepaid Federal tax	—	1,620
Buildings and other depreciable assets	216,000	216,000
Accumulated depreciation	(79,920)	(115,920)
Land	15,500	15,500
Other assets	5,740	4,300
Total assets	$2,126,880	$2,309,634

Liabilities and Equity		
Accounts payable	$ 238,000	$ 220,004
Other current liabilities	104,270	63,600
Mortgages	234,000	225,000
Capital stock	405,000	405,000
Retained earnings	1,145,610	1,396,030
Total liabilities and equity	$2,126,880	$2,309,634

Net income per books (before any income tax accrual) is $454,000. During 1997, SnowPro Corporation made estimated tax payments of $133,200 to the IRS. Prepare a Form 1120 for SnowPro Corporation for tax year 1997.

PROBLEM 4—PARTNERSHIP (Form 1065)

Sarah Henley (246–32–1958) and James Morgan (923–65–4326) are equal partners in the BBB Partnership—for "Bake-a-Better-Bagel"—a general partnership that operates a bakery in an exclusive retail area in Paradise Valley, Arizona. BBB's Federal I.D. number is 23–9676512. The partnership uses the accrual method of accounting and the calendar year for reporting purposes. It began business operations on June 6, 1992. Its current address is 5816 North Valley Boulevard, Paradise Valley, AZ 85023. The 1997 income statement for the partnership reflected net income of $112,010. The following information was taken from the partnership's financial statements for the current year:

Receipts

Sales revenues	$429,900
Taxable interest from investments	3,200
Tax-exempt interest	1,000
Dividend income	1,800
Total receipts	$435,900

Cash payments

Purchases	$175,390
Rent	16,800
Utilities	18,250
Employee salaries	25,400
Contribution to United Fund	600
Meals and entertainment, subject to 50% disallowance	2,080
Guaranteed payment, James Morgan, managing partner	24,000
Office expense	995
Accounting fees	1,225
Payroll taxes	2,790
Sales tax	30,660
Business interest on mortgage on leasehold improvements	6,000
Repairs	1,200
Payment of beginning accounts payable	6,200
Commercial oven (§ 179 deduction)	8,600
Total cash disbursements	$320,190

Noncash expenses

Amortization	$ 600
Depreciation (excluding depreciation on commercial oven)	12,360
Accrual of ending utilities payable	3,000

The beginning and ending tax basis balance sheets for the partnership were as follows for 1997:

	Beginning	Ending
Cash	$ 15,505	$ 59,215
Inventory	36,875	42,935
U.S. Treasury notes	20,000	20,000
Short-term investments	26,000	26,000
Leasehold improvements	65,000	?
Equipment	30,000	?
Accmulated depreciation and § 179 write off	(16,830)	?
Organization fees	3,000	3,000
Accumulated amortization	(950)	(1,550)
Total assets	$ 178,600	$?
Accounts payable	$ 6,200	3,000
Mortgage payable on leasehold improvements and equipment	75,000	75,000
Capital, Henley	48,700	?
Capital, Morgan	48,700	?
Total liabilities and capital	$ 178,600	$?

The partnership uses the lower of cost or market method for valuing inventory. It is not subject to the provisions of § 263A. The partnership will claim a § 179 deduction for the commercial oven acquired during the year. The partnership has a $2,600 tax preference item for depreciation on property placed in service after 1986.

No salaries were paid to partners other than James Morgan. Instead, both partners withdrew $3,000 per month as a distribution (draw) of operating profits. The partners have both guaranteed payment of the mortgage on the improvements and equipment. The partners share equally in all partnership liabilities, since all initial contributions and all ongoing allocations and distributions are pro rata.

Neither of the partners sold any portion of their interests in the partnership during 1997. The partnership's operations are entirely restricted to the Phoenix metropolitan area (which includes Paradise Valley). Both partners are U.S. citizens. The partnership had no foreign operations, no foreign bank accounts, and no interest in any foreign trusts or other partnerships. The partnership is not publicly traded and is not a statutory tax shelter.

The IRS's business code for the partnership operations is 5460. The partnership is not subject to the consolidated audit procedures and does not have a tax matters partner. The partnership files its tax return in Ogden, Utah. Partner James Morgan lives at 297 E. Cactus Road, Tempe, AZ 85287.

a. Prepare Form 1065 and Schedule K for the BBB Partnership, leaving blank any items where insufficient information has been provided. Prepare any supporting schedules necessary. Hint: Prepare Schedule A first to determine cost of goods sold.

b. Prepare Schedule K–1 for James Morgan.

PROBLEM 5—S CORPORATION (Form 1120S)

Jay Mitchell (243–58–8695) and Stan Marshall (221–51–8695) are 70% and 30% owners of Dana, Inc. (73–8264911), a service company located in Dime Box, Texas. The company's S corporation election was on January 15, 1997. The following information was taken from the income statement for 1997.

Tax-exempt interest	$ 10,000	
Gross rents	50,000	
Gross royalties	100,000	
Service income	1,100,000	$1,260,000
Salaries and wages	$ 550,000	
Repairs	20,000	
Officers' compensation	150,000	
Bad debts	50,000	
Rent expense (operating)	50,000	
Taxes	50,000	
Expenses relating to tax-exempt income	5,000	
Charitable contributions	20,000	
Payroll penalties	15,000	
Advertising expenses	50,000	
Other deductions	100,000	1,060,000
Book income		$ 200,000

A partially completed comparative balance sheet appears as follows.

	Beginning of the Year	End of the Year
Cash	$60,000	$ 65,000
Accounts receivable	20,000	40,000
Loan to Jay Mitchell	–0–	20,000
Total	$80,000	$125,000
Accounts payable	$20,000	$ 18,000
Other current liabilities	–0–	12,000
Capital stock	60,000	60,000
Retained earnings	–0–	?
Previously taxed income	–0–	?
Accumulated adjustments account	–0–	?
Other adjustments account	–0–	?
Total liabilities/shareholders' equity	$80,000	$125,000

The corporation distributed $165,000 to the two shareholders during the year. From the available information, prepare Form 1120S and Schedule K–1 for Jay Mitchell. If any information is missing, make realistic assumptions.

PROBLEM 6—GIFT TAX RETURN (Form 709)

During 1997, Robert and Nancy Lang (Social Security numbers 363–06–7912 and 371–42–6891) resided at 421 Elm Court, Custer, MI 48864. In their 25 years of marriage, the Langs have always lived in common law states. Robert is a dermatologist; Nancy is an attorney specializing in labor relations. Both practices have been highly successful. Over the years, the Langs have received gifts and inheritances from various relatives and have invested the funds wisely.

In 1997, the Langs made the following transfers (without adjustment for the annual exclusion or the marital deduction).

	Robert	Nancy
Cash donation to the building fund of the Custer First Methodist Church	$ 4,000	$ 2,000
Donation of unimproved land to the city of Custer for use as a park. Nancy inherited the land from her father.		110,000
Contribution of cash to the campaign fund of Mike Raby, who is running for the State Senate.		1,000
Payment of surgeon's fee and hospital charges for Laura Burke's gallbladder operation. Laura is Robert's aunt and does not qualify as his dependent. Payment is made directly to the care provider.	21,000	
Gift of BMW auto by Robert to Nancy on her birthday	42,000	
Gift to Nicole Lang (16-year old daughter) of stock that the Langs previously acquired as joint tenants at a cost of $60,000	90,000	90,000
Payment of college expenses for Rick Lang (19-year-old son)	15,000	15,000
Gift of Exxon stock to Michelle Lang (14-year-old daughter). Nancy received the stock as a gift from her mother. Nancy designates Robert as the custodian under the Michigan Uniform Gifts to Minors Act.		150,000

In past years, the Langs have made the following *taxable* gifts.

Year	Robert	Nancy
1979	$200,000	$280,000
1985	101,000	200,000
1986	400,000	160,000
1991	110,000	110,000

For all past gifts, the Langs have elected the gift-splitting provisions of § 2513.

a. Determine how much, if any, Federal gift tax had to be paid on the pre-1997 taxable gifts by Robert and Nancy Lang.

b. Complete Form 709 (U.S. Federal Gift Tax Return) for the gifts made in 1997. As in the past, the § 2513 election is made.

PROBLEM 7—TRUST (Form 1041)

Prepare the 1997 fiduciary income tax return (Form 1041) for the Rodriguez Trust. In addition, determine the amount and character of the income and expense items that each beneficiary must report for 1997 and prepare a Schedule K–1 for Maria Lopez.

The 1997 activities of the trust include the following.

Business operating income	$200,000
Dividend income, all U.S. stocks	25,000
Taxable interest income	100,000
Tax-exempt interest income	50,000
Net long-term capital gain	125,000
Fiduciary's fees	20,000

Under the terms of the trust instrument, depreciation, net capital gains and losses, and any fiduciary's fees are allocable to corpus. The trustee is required to distribute $200,000 to Maria every year. For 1997, the trustee distributed $250,000 to Maria and $100,000 to her sister, Elena Rodriguez. No other distributions were made.

In computing DNI, the trustee properly assigned all of the deductible fiduciary fees to the dividend income. Similarly, any income accumulated was assumed to constitute dividend income.

The trustee paid $35,000 in estimated taxes for the year on behalf of the trust. Any 1997 refund is to be credited to 1998 estimates. The exempt income was not derived from private activity bonds.

The trust was created on December 14, 1953. It is not subject to any recapture taxes, nor does it have any tax credits. None of its income was derived under a personal services contract. The trust has no economic interest in any foreign trust. Its Federal identification number is 89–7842067.

The trustee, Wisconsin State National Bank, is located at 3100 East Wisconsin Avenue, Milwaukee, WI 53201. Its employer identification number is 84–7602487.

Maria lives at 9880 East North Avenue, Shorewood, WI 53211. Her identification number is 498–01–8058.

Elena lives at 6772 East Oklahoma Avenue, St. Cecilia, WI 53204. Her identification number is 499–02–6531.

INDEX